WITHDRAWN

AMERICAN NATIONAL BIOGRAPHY
Supplement 1

AMERICAN NATIONAL BIOGRAPHY

GENERAL EDITOR

Mark C. Carnes
Ann Whitney Olin Professor of History, Barnard College

EDITORIAL ADVISORY BOARD

Drew Gilpin Faust

John A. Garraty

Doris Kearns Goodwin

Douglas Greenberg

Ramón Gutiérrez

Joan D. Hedrick

David Levering Lewis

Arthur M. Schlesinger, Jr.

AMERICAN
NATIONAL BIOGRAPHY
Supplement 1

Published under the auspices of the
AMERICAN COUNCIL OF LEARNED SOCIETIES

Editors

Paul Betz

Mark C. Carnes

With a Cumulative Index by Occupations and Realms of Renown

OXFORD UNIVERSITY PRESS
New York   2002   Oxford

OXFORD UNIVERSITY PRESS

Oxford   New York
Auckland   Bangkok   Buenos Aires   Cape Town   Chennai
Dar es Salaam   Delhi   Hong Kong   Istanbul   Karachi   Kolkata
Kuala Lumpur   Madrid   Melbourne   Mexico City   Mumbai   Nairobi
São Paulo   Shanghai   Singapore   Taipei   Tokyo   Toronto
and an associated company in Berlin

Copyright © 2002 by the American Council of Learned Societies

Published by Oxford University Press, Inc.
198 Madison Avenue, New York, New York 10016
www.oup.com

Oxford is a registered trademark of Oxford University Press

All rights reserved. No part of this publication may be reproduced,
stored in a retrieval system, or transmitted, in any form or by any means,
electronic, mechanical, photocopying, recording, or otherwise,
without the prior permission of Oxford University Press.

Funding for this publication was provided in part by the Andrew W. Mellon Foundation, the Rockefeller
Foundation, and the National Endowment for the Humanities, a federal agency.

Library of Congress Cataloging-in-Publication Data

American national biography / general editors, John A. Garraty, Mark C. Carnes
p.   cm.
"Published under the auspices of the American Council of Learned Societies."
Includes bibliographical references and index.
1. United States—Biography—Dictionaries.   I. Garraty, John Arthur,
1920–   .   II. Carnes, Mark C. (Mark Christopher), 1950–   .
III. American Council of Learned Societies.
CT213.A68   1998   98-20826   920.073—dc21   CIP
ISBN 0-19-515063-5 (Suppl. 1)
1 3 5 7 9 8 6 4 2

Printed in the United States of America
on acid-free paper

A

ABZUG, Bella (24 July 1920–31 Mar. 1998), lawyer, feminist leader, and U.S. representative, was born Bella Savitsky in the Bronx, New York, the daughter of Emmanuel Savitsky, butcher, and Ester Tanklefsky Savitsky. She attended local schools before entering Hunter College in Manhattan, where she took part in student government and was active in the Zionist movement. She entered Columbia University Law School following her graduation in 1942 but soon left school and took a wartime job in a shipyard. She married Martin Abzug, a writer who later became a stockbroker, in 1944; the couple had two daughters. Abzug returned to Columbia and served as editor of the *Columbia Law Review* prior to receiving her LL.B. degree in 1947.

As an attorney, Abzug specialized in labor law and also worked for the American Civil Liberties Union and the Civil Rights Congress, often for little or no money. By the 1950s, she was also defending individuals accused of Communist leanings before Senator Joseph McCarthy's committee and had traveled to Mississippi to represent Willie McGee, an African-American man who faced a death sentence for allegedly raping a white woman. Although pregnant at the time, Abzug managed to ignore death threats and obtained two stays of execution for McGee, who was nevertheless put to death in 1951. It was during this time that Abzug also began wearing her trademark wide-brimmed hats, explaining, "When I was a young lawyer . . . working women wore hats. It was the only way they would take you seriously."

Alarmed by the resumption of nuclear testing on the part of both the United States and the Soviet Union, Abzug expanded her horizons to international politics when she joined with a number of women to found Women Strike for Peace in 1961. As the group's legislative director from its inception until 1970, she gained experience in Washington politics, leading mass rallies and lobbying efforts against the arms race and, later, the Vietnam War. Abzug also became active in Democratic party politics: she was deeply involved in the "Dump Johnson" movement (the campaign to keep Lyndon Baines Johnson from running for a second term as president) and rallied support among various peace groups for liberal candidates such as Paul O'Dwyer (for the U.S. Senate from New York) and Eugene McCarthy (for president), neither of whom won. Closer to home, she chaired the Taxpayers' Campaign for Urban Priorities, which assisted in reelecting New York City mayor John Lindsay in 1969.

In 1970 Abzug announced her candidacy for the U.S. House of Representatives. Running from New York's 19th District (which covered most of southeastern Manhattan), she received support from the reform wing of the Democratic party in her primary campaign against long-time incumbent Leonard Farbstein. Abzug insisted that hers would be the stronger voice in Washington and, armed with the slogan "This woman's place is in the House," she scored an upset primary victory and faced Republican-Liberal candidate Barry Farber in the general election. At this point something of a celebrity, Abzug soon gathered citywide support from women (she was an early and vociferous champion of the Equal Rights Amendment) and prominent figures in the arts. Loud and outspoken by nature—author Norman Mailer claimed she had a voice that "could boil the fat off a taxicab driver's neck"—she made enemies nearly as quickly as she made friends. Abzug fought off Farber's spurious claims that she was anti-Israel and won the general election in convincing fashion.

By her own estimation always more of an activist than a politician, Abzug quickly made a name for herself in Congress. Contemptuous of the well-entrenched seniority system, she applied for a seat on the Armed Services Committee, which was unheard of for a freshman member of Congress. She also introduced a resolution seeking the immediate withdrawal of American troops from Vietnam. Among the other causes championed by Abzug were ending the draft, obtaining statehood for New York City, and increased funding for health care and child day-care programs. Although thwarted in most of her grander ambitions, Abzug did obtain additional funding for New York's infrastructure as a member of the Committee on Public Works and Transportation; as a member of the Government Operations Committee, she helped draft the Freedom of Information Act, the Right to Privacy Act, and the so-called "Sunshine Law," which went a long way toward opening government operations to public scrutiny.

In 1972, forced by redistricting to run against a well-regarded incumbent Democrat, William Ryan, Abzug lost in the primary, only to regain her seat in Congress as the replacement candidate following Ryan's death shortly before the election. After three terms in the House, she passed up certain reelection in 1976 in order to make a bid for the U.S. Senate but lost a close primary battle to Daniel Patrick Moynihan. She also lost in a crowded primary for mayor of New York City in 1977 and failed in an attempt to return to the House of Representatives in 1978. That same year President Jimmy Carter appointed her cochairwoman of his National Advisory Committee on Women; he was later to dismiss her when she disagreed with his economic policies.

Despite her electoral setbacks, Abzug remained an influential figure among feminists. She attended a number of international women's conferences (Mexico City in 1975; Copenhagen in 1980; and Nairobi in 1985) and was instrumental in founding both the Women USA Fund (a nonprofit advocacy group) and the Women's Environment and Development Organization (WEDO) in 1990. Back in New York, she chaired Mayor David Dinkins's Commission on the Status of Women, from 1993 to 1995. Her last major appearance was in 1995 at the United Nations' Fourth World Conference on Women held in Beijing, China, where, feisty as ever, she responded to an insult from former President George Bush by saying, "He was addressing a fertilizer group? That's appropriate." By her own admission never quite the same after her husband's death in 1986 and long in failing health, Abzug died in New York City.

Loved by her devoted followers and despised by others, Bella Abzug fell short of realizing many of the goals that drove her public life. Her career, however, did result in a legacy of solid legislative achievements as well as serving as an inspiration to a new generation of women in public life.

• Biographical information can be gleaned from Doris Faber, *Bella Abzug* (1976), and two books by Abzug, *Bella! Ms. Abzug Goes to Washington* (1972) and (with Mim Kelber) *Gender Gap: Bella Abzug's Guide to Political Power for American Women* (1984). An article by Abzug in a 1990 issue of *Ms.* magazine—"Martin, What Should I Do Now?" (reprinted in *Time to Ourselves: A Celebration of Women Making a Difference*, ed. Nancy M. Neuman [1998])—reveals a gentler, even poignant side to her personality. Her career received extensive media coverage; some of the better written sources are T. Hiss, "Dilemma in the New 20th Congressional District," *New York Times Magazine*, 18 June 1972; Mim Kelber, "What Bella Knew," *Ms.*, Apr. 1979; and D. K. Mano, "Abzug," *National Review*, 14 Mar. 1975. Her obituary appeared in the *New York Times*, 1 Apr. 1998.

EDWARD L. LACH, JR.

AGNEW, Spiro T. (9 Nov. 1918–17 Sept. 1996), vice president, was born Spiro Theodore Agnew in Baltimore, Maryland, the son of Margaret Pollard Akers Agnew and Theodore Spiro Agnew, who, after immigrating from Greece in 1897, changed his name from Anagnostopoulos. Agnew's father was a successful restaurateur and a leader in the Greek community until the Great Depression, when he lost his business and turned to selling fruit and vegetables on the street. Agnew supplemented the family income by doing odd jobs while he attended public schools in Baltimore. After graduating from Forest Park High School, he entered Johns Hopkins in 1937, majoring in chemistry, but in 1940 he left and began taking night classes at the University of Baltimore School of Law. During the day he worked alternately as an assistant personnel manager of a grocery-store chain and as an insurance investigator and claims adjuster. In 1942 he married Elinor Isabel Judefind, a coworker at his insurance company; they had four children.

Agnew was drafted into the army in 1941 and served as a tank commander in France and Germany, attaining the rank of captain and winning a Bronze Star. When he was discharged in 1945, he returned to school on the GI Bill of Rights and received an LL.B. from the University of Baltimore in 1947 and an LL.D. two years later from the University of Maryland. Admitted to the bar in 1949, he practiced briefly with a Baltimore firm and then moved to the prosperous white suburb of Towson, the Baltimore County seat, to open his own law practice. Remembering the taunts his first name had brought him when he was a schoolboy, he began calling himself "Ted" and decided never to give any of his children Greek names.

Although he was registered as a Democrat and his father was a Democratic ward leader in Baltimore, Agnew had severed his connection with that party in 1946 with an avowed hope for a political career. In Towson he was a dedicated joiner, active in the Kiwanis Club, the Parent-Teacher Association, and various social groups. In 1956 he formally joined the Republican party. His first government position was with the Baltimore County Zoning Board of Appeals, a one-year appointment that he earned for his help in the reelection campaign of a Republican congressman. In 1957 the still struggling lawyer welcomed the $3,000 yearly salary and the professional benefits of the position. Years later he recalled, "[I]t was good for my law practice to have the prestige connected with this" (quoted in Cohen and Witcover, p. 21). He performed the job diligently and earned a reputation for rigid adherence to the rules and a high moral code, characteristics that were to become his political trademarks. In 1958 he was reappointed for a full three-year term and became chairman.

Agnew's first campaign for elective office was not a promising beginning: he ran for associate circuit judge in 1960 and came in last in a field of five. As a Republican in a predominantly Democratic county, he lost his seat on the zoning board when a new county executive decided to replace him in 1961. He protested vigorously and so effectively that while he didn't get back his seat on the Board he acquired enough public recognition to run successfully for county executive in 1962, becoming the first Republican to win that office since 1895. In his four years as county executive he was responsible for improvements in the state's school system, water supply, and sewer system and earned a reputation as a reformer and a progressive.

In 1966 Agnew ran for governor of Maryland and beat segregationist Walter Mahoney by a wide margin. Charging his opponent with bigotry, he earned an enthusiastic following among liberals of both parties. In his first year in office, much was accomplished: substantial tax reforms, increased aid to antipoverty programs, repeal of the state law against racial intermarriage, support for open housing, a liberalized abortion law, and the strictest state law in the country against water pollution. His second year as governor, how-

ever, saw a marked shift to the right; he drastically cut the state budget for welfare and health and took a strong stand for law and order, ordering the arrest of 227 black protesters at Bowie State College. He responded to riots following the assassination of Martin Luther King, Jr., by summoning eighty moderate leaders of Baltimore's African-American community to his office and chastising them for their failure to denounce the black militants. Half of the leaders walked out of the hall before the end of Agnew's speech. The governor expressed no regrets. "If they had all walked out," he told reporters, "I would simply be faced with a situation where I would have to find other Negro leaders" (quoted in Marsh, p. 104).

Agnew rallied support for New York governor Nelson Rockefeller in the 1968 presidential campaign. When Rockefeller announced his withdrawal from the race, Agnew transferred his allegiance to former vice president Richard Nixon, whom he nominated at the Republican convention. Nixon surprised the nation by selecting the relatively unknown Maryland governor as his running mate. The public response, echoed widely in the press, was "Spiro who?" Historians differ on whether Agnew was an asset or a liability to Nixon's campaign; he appealed to conservative white southerners disturbed by civil rights agitation and race riots, but he antagonized many by such ethnic slurs as referring to Polish Americans as "Polacks" and a Japanese newspaperman as a "fat Jap." The Nixon-Agnew ticket won the 1968 election by a slim margin.

In office as vice president, Agnew spoke dynamically against political dissidents, antiwar protesters, and the liberal press. He became known for his colorful public statements, such as that "some newspapers are fit only to line the bottom of bird cages." He defined opponents of the Vietnam War in May 1970 as "an effete corps of impudent snobs who characterize themselves as intellectuals" and, in a nationally televised address in November 1969, defined the press as "a tiny and closed fraternity of privileged men, elected by no one, and enjoying a monopoly sanctioned and licensed by government." His use of alliteration was widely parodied. He called enemies of Nixon "pusillanimous pussyfooters" and "vicars of vacillation," and, in a speech in San Diego in September 1970, described his critics as "nattering nabobs of negativity" and "hopeless, hysterical hypochondriacs of history." His insensitivity to the disadvantaged was reflected in his widely quoted excuse for declining to make a campaign visit in 1968 to an impoverished urban neighborhood with the words "I've been into many [ghettoes] and . . . to some extent, if you've seen one city slum, you've seen them all." Although his relations with the president were often strained, he was seen as a useful "hatchet man," expressing what Nixon felt but could not say publicly. Many of his addresses are believed to have been composed by White House speechwriters Pat Buchanan and William Safire, but the flair with which Agnew delivered them made him a major speaker for the Republican party. He was returned to office with Nixon in 1972.

Early in his second term as vice president, Agnew learned that a federal grand jury in Maryland was investigating charges that he had accepted bribes from construction firms seeking state contracts, paid while he was county executive and governor, and that payments of kickbacks had continued even after his election as vice-president. He stoutly denied the allegations and assured California audiences, "I won't resign if indicted." The evidence was, however, irrefutable, and he consented to plead no contest to a charge of tax evasion. His official explanation for pleading nolo contendere was that "protracted proceedings before the grand jury, the Congress, and the courts . . . would seriously prejudice the national interest" (quoted in Cohen and Witcover, p. 350). He was sentenced to three years' probation, fined $10,000, and required to resign his office. His resignation took effect on 10 October 1973. The next year he was disbarred in Maryland, and in 1983 a civil court in that state ordered him to repay the amount of the bribes he had received plus interest, totaling $268,000.

Agnew retired to Ocean City, Maryland, and for the rest of his life kept a low profile, never granting interviews or making public appearances. In 1974 he founded Pathlite, Inc., an international consulting firm. Two years later he published a novel, *The Canfield Decision*, about a vice president who becomes involved in international intrigue. Critics received it coolly, dismissing it as a dated Cold War thriller. He also wrote a memoir of his vice presidency and the scandal that brought it to an end, *Go Quietly . . . or Else* (1980), in which he argued that the money he had received consisted of campaign contributions and personal gifts, and that such payments were standard procedure in Maryland politics. He died in a hospital in Berlin, Maryland.

Agnew had had many enthusiastic supporters who honored him as the country's most unflinching and articulate spokesman for the political right and who proudly wore campaign pins reading "Spiro Is My Hero," but his fall from power was swift and permanent. The first American vice president to resign from office in disgrace, ironically after a political career largely based on an image of rectitude and devotion to "law and order," he contributed to the cynicism of a public already profoundly disenchanted with national politics.

• The major collection of Agnew's papers, letters, campaign material, and clippings is in the University of Maryland Archives and Manuscripts Department in College Park. An insightful account of Agnew's career up to his election as vice president is provided by Robert Marsh, *Agnew: The Unexamined Man—A Political Profile* (1971). A detailed and highly critical study of his life to the time of its publication is Joseph Albright, *What Makes Spiro Run* (1972), while more balanced and objective examinations are Theo Lippman, *Spiro Agnew's America* (1972), and Jules Witcover, *White Knight: The Rise of Spiro Agnew* (1972). Agnew's adversarial relationship with the press is well covered in John R. Coyne, *The Impudent Snobs: Agnew vs. the Intellectual Establishment* (1972), and the best and most comprehensive account of the subject's political downfall is Richard M. Co-

hen and Jules Witcover, *A Heartbeat Away: The Investigation and Resignation of Vice President Spiro T. Agnew* (1974). Obituaries are in the *New York Times*, 18 Nov. 1996, and the *Washington Post*, 19 Nov. 1996.

DENNIS WEPMAN

AIN, Gregory (28 Mar. 1908–10 Jan. 1988), architect and educator, was born Gregory Samuel Ain in Pittsburgh, Pennsylvania, the son of Baer Ain, who ran a small business, and Chiah Ain (maiden name unknown); the couple had recently fled Russian Tsarist rule together. In 1911 the family settled in Los Angeles. Ain was raised in Boyle Heights, a dense mixed neighborhood of Eastern European immigrants. His father, a shopkeeper, openly despised capitalism and participated in socialist political groups. In fact, his father's socialist convictions ran so deep that in 1916 he moved the family to Llano del Rio, an experimental collective farming colony in the Antelope Valley of California. The Ains were among the colony's earliest members. Although the family returned to East Los Angeles a year and a half later, the experience contributed decisively to Ain's developing political beliefs and his social conscience. Cooperative housing projects became a consistent area of exploration later, in his architectural practice.

After graduating from Lincoln High School, Ain studied mathematics and physics at the University of California, Southern Branch (now UCLA). During his sophomore year he met architect Rudolph Schindler. Later in life, he recalled that the Schindler house was the "first stimulus" toward his interest in architecture. Against his father's wishes, he left UCLA to study architecture at the University of Southern California. USC's architecture curriculum followed the Beaux-Arts neoclassical method, and Ain soon recoiled from its historicist imitation of established architectural styles. He left USC without a degree in 1927, later declaring that it had been an "utter waste of time."

After a brief apprenticeship with art deco theater designer B. Marcus Priteca, Ain worked for Richard Neutra, who was well on his way to international acclaim as a modern architect. He worked alongside Neutra until 1935, involved in such major works as the VDL Research House, Los Angeles (1933), the Corona Avenue Elementary School, Bell, California (1934–1935), and the all-steel Beard House, Altadena, California (1934). After a series of disputes, both architectural and personal, he left Neutra's office in anger. Although Neutra was certainly the most important figure in Ain's architectural education, the two remained distant. Ain considered Schindler his primary influence.

In the late 1930s, working independently for the first time, Ain designed several residences. The Edwards House, Los Angeles (1936), and the Ernst House, Los Angeles (1937), showed major innovations in functional planning, addressing "the common architectural problems of common people" ("Jury Comments," *Arts & Architecture* 62 [Feb. 1945]: 30.) In these buildings he made strong relationships between the kitchen and the children's indoor and outdoor play spaces so that the mother could keep watch while doing housework. Ain's floor plans consistently exhibited his sensitivity to the demands of domestic labor.

The Dunsmuir Flats, Los Angeles (1937), was Ain's most important commission of this period, an apartment building that gained him national recognition. Four two-bedroom units were set obliquely to the street and staggered back along a narrow site, affording each unit a private entrance on the north and a generous garden on the south. Because of the ingenuity of the site plan and the structural logic of the building itself, some critics have likened it to a mathematical game. The Dunsmuir Flats design was published widely and later included in the Museum of Modern Art exhibition *Built in the U.S.A.: Modern Architecture 1932–1944*.

In 1940, with the sponsorship of Ludwig Mies van der Rohe and Walter Gropius, Ain won a prestigious Guggenheim fellowship that enabled him to study low-cost housing the following year. His first project included moveable interior partition walls, which he frequently employed in his later work. During the war, Ain was chief engineer for the Moulded Plywood Division of the Evans Product Company, where he assisted Charles Eames in the development of the latter's well-known plywood chairs.

After the war Ain formed a partnership with Joseph Johnson and Alfred Day in order to design large tracts of cooperative housing. The first of these, 280 "Community Homes" in Reseda, was conceived as a fully realized social and aesthetic solution to the Los Angeles housing emergency. Ain designed four different floor plans for compact two-bedroom homes. The project was never built, largely because the Federal Housing Administration refused to finance mixed-race projects.

Ain, Johnson, and Day's Mar Vista Housing development, Los Angeles, planned in 1947, stands as a major landmark in postwar housing. As in Reseda, Ain developed a variety of floor plans to give spatial variety to the neighborhood, enhanced again by Garrett Eckbo's landscape design. The units themselves featured plywood built-in furniture and flexible partition walls. In 1947 the firm completed Avenel Homes, Los Angeles, an extraordinarily imaginative ten-unit veterans' cooperative. In Altadena, Ain designed sixty units called the "Park Planned Homes," using many Buckminster Fuller–inspired innovations, such as precut structural members and prefabricated plumbing units, but the building trades resisted these changes and costs skyrocketed. Only twenty-eight of the sixty units were built, and Ain himself was discouraged that his ideas did not discernibly influence the mass housing market.

These projects attracted the attention of Philip Johnson, the curator of architecture at the Museum of Modern Art, who engaged Ain to build a house in the museum's garden in 1950. While this project should have been Ain's crowning achievement and a springboard to greater works, the suburban house looked

conspicuously out of place in Manhattan and it was widely criticized. At the same time, Ain was perceived as a communist, and the growing "Red Scare" caused him to lose several opportunities, including partici-pation in the Case Study Program, which was orga-nized by *Arts & Architecture* editor John Entenza in order to promote modern design for mass-produced housing.

Ain taught architecture at USC from 1949 to 1963, where he was exceptionally well respected and influ-ential. Students remember him for his inquisitive mind and intellectual curiosity and for his ability to inspire them to do their best work. It is a testament to his teaching skills that architects as diverse as Bernard Judge, Frank Gehry, and Jon Jerde cite Ain as a major influence. He was hired as chair of the architecture department at Penn State in 1963, where he success-fully guided the program to professional accreditation.

As an educator, Ain was able to reflect on his earlier career and the state of the profession. In 1965 he wrote, "We must affirm the truism that architecture is a social art, and that its aesthetic power must be de-rived from a social ethos." He retired to Los Angeles in 1967 and was named a fellow of the American In-stitute of Architects (FAIA) in 1971. After a long bout with Alzheimer's disease, he died in Los Angeles in 1988.

• Ain's archives are in the Architectural Drawing Collection at the University of California, Santa Barbara. Valuable in-formation on Ain is in Esther McCoy, *The Second Generation* (1984), and David Gebhard et al., *The Architecture of Gregory Ain* (1980). Ain's essay "Form Follows Faction" was printed in *Architectural Record* 137 (May 1965), and his "In Search of Theory" in *Arts & Architecture* 83 (January 1966).

ANTHONY DENZER

AINSWORTH, Mary (1 Dec. 1913–21 Mar. 1999), developmental psychologist who devised an experi-mental procedure called the Strange Situation to in-vestigate attachment patterns in young children, was born Mary Dinsmore Salter in Glendale, Ohio, the daughter of Charles Salter, a successful businessman, and Mary Dinsmore Salter. She spent most of her childhood in Toronto, Canada, where she attended the University of Toronto, which awarded her a B.A. (1935), an M.A. (1936), and a Ph.D. (1939), the last two for work at the Department of Psychology. She mainly worked with the child psychologist William E. Blatz, whose security theory, research on children's emotional development, and use of naturalistic obser-vation methods inspired her subsequent work on at-tachment. Mary Salter was a lecturer at the Depart-ment of Psychology at the University of Toronto from 1939 until 1942, when she was commissioned in the Canadian Women's Army Corps, attaining the rank of major. In 1946 she returned to the University of Toronto as assistant professor and further developed her psychodiagnostic skills (co-authoring a book on the evaluation of results obtained with the Rorschach inkblot test in the process). In 1950 she married Leon-

ard Ainsworth, a graduate student in psychology, and moved with him to London, England. There, she worked with the psychoanalytically trained child psy-chiatrist John Bowlby at the Tavistock Institute. At that time, Bowlby was investigating the detrimental effects on young children of being placed in institu-tions providing foster care and of prolonged separa-tion from primary caregivers in general. Breaking with then-prevalent psychoanalytic assumptions, Bowlby intended to investigate the effects of actual life events on the course of child development. Ainsworth and Bowlby initiated a lifelong collaborative association; Ainsworth contributed two chapters to Bowlby's sem-inal *Child Care and the Growth of Love* (1965).

In 1954, Ainsworth moved to Kampala, Uganda, where she conducted a year-long longitudinal inves-tigation on individual differences and developmental changes in attachment patterns in young children. This study was based on observations conducted in naturalistic settings of mother-infant interactions dur-ing the weaning period with a specific emphasis on the effect of mother-infant separations. She found that children used their mothers as a secure base from which they explored the world around them and, when they were securely attached, could handle tem-porary separations well. Her observations confirmed aspects of her earlier work at Toronto and Bowlby's theoretical formulations.

In 1955, Ainsworth was appointed lecturer at Johns Hopkins University, where she became an associate professor in 1958 and a full professor in 1963. At Johns Hopkins, she analyzed the data she had col-lected in Uganda. After her divorce in 1960 she un-derwent psychoanalysis and commenced the study on attachment patterns for which she has become most famous. In this study, Ainsworth systematically inves-tigated the formation of attachment patterns in the first year of life. Her research was based on intensive observations in the home environment of twenty-six families collected in four-hour episodes made at three-week intervals commencing shortly after the baby was born. She also tested the attachment patterns of these children in an experimental procedure called the Strange Situation, in which the behavior of one-year-old toddlers is observed in the presence of a stranger, with the mother alternately present and absent. The observational and experimental findings corroborated each other, leading Ainsworth to formulate three dis-tinct attachment patterns.

The first and by far the largest group of toddlers explored the new environment provided in the Strange Situation happily in the presence of their mothers, every once in a while making sure she was still there. They protested when she left but were happy to see her return; after a reunion, they contin-ued exploring. Ainsworth deemed these children se-curely attached; they used the presence of the primary caregiver as a secure base to explore the world around them and acquire new skills. The toddlers in the sec-ond group were clingy and rather hesitant to explore the new situation. They became anxious and agitated

upon separation and were eager to reestablish contact with their mothers when they returned, while simultaneously expressing anger at her. Ainsworth deemed these children to be ambivalently attached. The third group displayed explorative behavior irrespective of the mother's presence. When their mothers returned after a brief absence, they snubbed or avoided them. Ainsworth labeled these children avoidant. Relating the behavior displayed in the Strange Situation to the observations made in the home environment, Ainsworth concluded that caregivers' consistent responsiveness and sensitivity to their children led to secure attachments in children. When parents picked up their children when they cried, they were reassured that they were important. Contrary to the expectations of behaviorist psychologists, this subsequently led to less crying.

In 1975, Ainsworth was appointed Commonwealth professor at the University of Virginia in Charlottesville, where she retired in 1984 at the age of seventy. She remained professionally active until 1992. Ainsworth's work on attachment has been very influential in developmental psychology and provided the basic tools to study attachment patterns in young children. Her students and others have conducted extensive investigations that have mostly corroborated her findings. Ainsworth received a number of prestigious awards for her work on attachment. In 1989 the American Psychological Association awarded her and John Bowlby jointly the Distinguished Scientific Contributions Award. In 1998, she received the American Psychological Foundation's Gold Medal Award for Life Achievement in the Science of Psychology. Ainsworth died in Charlottesville, Virginia.

• Ainsworth's work on the Rorschach test in collaboration with Bruno Klopfer appeared in their co-authored *Developments in the Rorschach Technique* (1954). Her first contributions to attachment theory were published as two chapters in John Bowlby's *Child Care and the Growth of Love* (2d ed., 1965). The results of her work in Uganda were published in *Infancy in Uganda: Infant Care and the Growth of Love* (1967). The results of her influential work at Johns Hopkins were published as *Patterns of Attachment: A Psychological Study of the Strange Situation* (1978). Ainsworth's address, written with John Bowlby, to the American Psychological Association after receiving the Distinguished Scientific Contribution Award was published as "An Ethological Approach to Personality Development," *American Psychologist* 46, 4 (1991): 331–41. She wrote an informative autobiographical account in Agnes N. O'Connell and Nancy Felipe Russo, eds., *Models of Achievement: Reflections of Eminent Women in Psychology* (1983). An obituary can be found in the *American Psychologist* 55, 10 (2000): 1148–49.

HANS POLS

ALIOTO, Joseph L. (12 Feb. 1916–29 Jan. 1998), businessman and mayor, was born Joseph Lawrence Alioto in San Francisco, California, the son of Giuseppe Alioto, a businessman, and Domenica Lazio Alioto. After receiving his early education in local parochial schools, he earned a B.A. from St. Mary's College in Moraga, California, in 1937. An excellent student, he entered the law school at Catholic University on a scholarship and received his J.D. in 1940. Although he gained admittance to the California bar that same year, he remained in Washington and began working at the Antitrust Division of the Department of Justice. He married Angelina Genaro on 2 June 1941; the couple would have six children.

In 1942 Alioto moved to the Board of Economic Warfare, where he calculated the most effective industrial targets for Allied air raids. At war's end he returned to his hometown and opened a legal practice that specialized in price-fixing, antitrust, and restraint-of-trade litigation. The practice thrived, and his client list eventually included such high-profile figures from the entertainment industry as Walter Wanger, Walt Disney, and Samuel Goldwyn. Alioto's efforts for Goldwyn in 1951, in a suit against both Twentieth Century–Fox and a group of movie theaters for collusion, was particularly notable. When the case was finally settled fifteen years later, Goldwyn was awarded $1.9 million in compensation, and an important legal precedent regarding the fair distribution of films was established.

Long interested in politics, Alioto served from 1948 until 1954 on the San Francisco Board of Education (as president in 1953–1954); he sought higher teacher salaries and educational reforms that included allowing teachers to vote for school board members. A moderate Democrat, he also completed a stint as chairman of the city's Redevelopment Agency, where he worked to balance the need for new commercial and residential construction against the legitimate proprietary concerns of local businessmen and homeowners. Alioto also fought against the then-emerging trend toward mass urban renewal, attacking the practice of wholesale demolition of blighted areas as shortsighted.

His experience from boyhood jobs in his father's International Fish Company kept Alioto interested in food distribution. He conducted a survey in the late 1950s of South American agricultural production and marketing practices for the federal government and assisted in the creation of the Food for Peace program. In 1959 he became executive vice president of the Rice Growers Association of California, and during his tenure that group (of which he became president in 1964) experienced a growth in annual sales from $25 million to $70 million; in 1967 he negotiated a sale with the Republic of Korea for $48 million worth of rice—a record at that time. Alioto also oversaw operational improvements in production and transportation methods, which included the use of ships as silos for transporting bulk rice.

Alioto entered the arena of partisan politics almost by accident. When San Francisco's incumbent Democratic mayor John L. Shelley declined to run for reelection because of failing health in 1967, another Democrat, state senator Eugene McAteer, became the front-runner to replace him. McAteer, however, died in September 1967, leaving a vacancy in the race less than two months before the election. With Shelley's

support, Alioto replaced McAteer and won a landslide victory over seventeen other candidates after running a vigorous campaign during which he pledged to support law enforcement as well as combat emerging social and economic problems.

Once in office, Alioto quickly addressed a series of crises. Faced with an ongoing strike by the city's two daily newspapers, he appointed a mediator and on 25 February 1968 announced the end of the 52-day-old strike. Having received substantial support from ghetto areas in his election bid, Alioto immediately sought to increase the city's hiring of minorities. He not only persuaded both the local business community and the labor unions to increase their minority hiring and training opportunities; he even convinced several major airlines to train poor urban youth for jobs at the San Francisco airport. In return for union cooperation in his push for racial equality, Alioto aimed to create new jobs by expanding downtown construction, most notably in the case of the Transamerica Building and the Embarcadero Center. Alioto also faced a delicate situation at San Francisco State College, where the firing of a radical faculty member in the fall of 1968 had resulted in violence. As campus unrest continued, he worked with the college's acting president, S. I. Hayakawa, and dispatched police units to the school when order had to be restored. Much as he had done during his election campaign, Alioto tried to steer a moderate course, in this instance between the demands of militant students and the need to maintain civil authority.

Popular among voters, Alioto became a national spokesman for the concerns of urban America. His star clearly seemed on the rise when he gave the speech nominating Hubert H. Humphrey for president at the 1968 Democratic National Convention in Chicago. He was thought to be on Humphrey's short list for vice-presidential candidates; his prospects for the governorship of California also looked good. His reputation, however, suffered what proved to be irreparable damage when a July 1969 article in *Look* magazine accused him of ties to the Mafia. He withdrew from the governor's race in January 1970 and was narrowly reelected as mayor in 1971. But his troubles were not over: the state of Washington charged him with illegally taking $2.3 million from a $16 million antitrust settlement. Although that case was dismissed before it went to the jury, and he was able to settle with *Look* for $450,000 after four trials and eleven years of wrangling, he had no political future, and he returned to his legal practice in 1976. After divorcing his first wife in 1977, he was married a year later to Kathleen Sullivan, with whom he had two children. After a long battle with prostate cancer, he died at his home in San Francisco.

Joseph Alioto successfully addressed as mayor a host of urban and social problems in the late 1960s, only to see his career in politics derailed by a group of criminal charges that remained unproven. What he achieved in San Francisco stands as a model for communities with finite resources that have to confront complex issues of minority hiring, demands for sweeping growth, and the often conflicting interests of residents and business.

• Alioto's papers are held at the San Francisco Public Library. His career has received attention in Frederick M. Wirt, *Power in the City: Decision Making in San Francisco* (1974), and Charles P. Larrowe, *Harry Bridges: The Rise and Fall of Radical Labor in the United States* (1972). Obituaries are in the *Los Angeles Times*, 30 Jan. 1998, and the *Washington Post*, 31 Jan. 1998.

EDWARD L. LACH, JR.

ALLEN, Mel (14 Feb. 1913–16 June 1996), sportscaster, was born Melvin Allen Israel in Birmingham, Alabama, the eldest child of Julius Israel and Anna Leib Israel. His parents were Russian immigrants who made their home in the small town of Johns, outside Birmingham. Julius Israel ran a general store in Johns and later sold women's apparel to support his family, which included Melvin's younger brother and sister. The elder Israel moved his family to various small towns in Alabama and to Greensboro, North Carolina, while he pursued his selling career; by Melvin's early teens the family had settled in Birmingham.

Melvin Israel showed an early aptitude for sports as well as academic achievement. At Phillips High School in Birmingham he earned letters in basketball and football as well as baseball, which he had played since the age of nine. He graduated from high school at age fifteen, in 1928, and that fall entered the University of Alabama. In college he continued to play all three sports until his junior year, when he began writing a sports column for the school newspaper. Melvin Israel received a B.A. degree in political science in 1932 and went on to the University of Alabama School of Law, from which he graduated four years later. To support himself during his eight years at the university, he worked for a while as a clerk in a shoe store. As a graduate student he received a fellowship to teach speech, a subject in which he showed exceptional aptitude. Because of his skills he was appointed manager of the campus public address system, but at this point he was still intent on becoming a lawyer.

Melvin Israel's future career as a sportscaster was initiated in the fall of 1935, when Alabama's football coach asked him to give play-by-play details of a Crimson Tide game over the stadium loudspeakers. He was soon hired to do the same thing for other Alabama games on a Birmingham radio station. He went on to graduate from law school in 1936 and passed the Alabama bar exam that summer. Meanwhile, his distinctive voice and manner on his football broadcasts had attracted favorable attention from executives of the Columbia Broadcasting System, and in December 1936, during a visit with friends in New York City, he auditioned at CBS. He was immediately offered a job, which he accepted, as an announcer in New York. Although Melvin Israel could probably have earned a more than respectable living as a lawyer, the fact that the country was suffering through the darkest days of

the Great Depression undoubtedly influenced his decision to go into broadcasting. He began work in January 1937, assuming the on-air name of Mel Allen. Six years later he made Mel Allen his legal name when he joined the army.

For more than two and a half years Mel Allen worked as a disk jockey and newscaster for CBS Radio in New York. His debut as a sportscaster for the network occurred in the summer of 1939, when he was asked at the last minute to cover a major boat race, the Vanderbilt Cup, off Long Island, broadcasting from an airplane. Such aerial coverage was then a novelty, initiated days earlier by the major CBS rival, the National Broadcasting Company. Although nervous about plane travel—he remained afraid of flying throughout his life—Allen ad-libbed for more than an hour, reporting on the progress of the yachts as well as tennis matches he could see from the air. The broadcast was a huge success, and Allen was launched on his lifetime career as a sportscaster. He began doing play-by-play broadcasts of major league baseball games that same year, and soon he was also broadcasting basketball games played at Madison Square Garden. By 1941 he had become a regular sportscaster of both Yankee and Giant baseball games on the CBS network, with an annual income of $30,000.

In 1943, as U.S. troops fought overseas in World War II, Allen enlisted in the army as a private. By this time he had broadcast three World Series games for CBS and had earned a national following as a sportscaster. For two years Allen served in the infantry in Europe, achieving the rank of staff sergeant. Toward the end of the war, in early 1945, he was reassigned to the Armed Forces Radio Service, where he worked as an announcer on the program *Army Hour.*

In 1946 Allen left the army and returned to New York, where he was hired by the Yankees as their radio "voice." Under the terms of his contract, he became the game announcer over CBS radio station WINS-AM, and his play-by-play coverage was carried throughout the United States. During the next eighteen years Allen became known as the "Golden Voice of the Yankees." He covered not only all Yankee games but also All-Star games and the World Series. Allen's affable and exuberant personality and his muted southern accent were an irresistible draw for millions of listeners, who heard him open every broadcast with a friendly "Hello, everybody, this is Mel Allen!" His often repeated exclamation, "How about that!," first used after an injured Joe DiMaggio hit a home run in a 1949 game, became a national slogan, and his enthusiastic on-air promotion of Ballantine Ale and White Owl cigars endeared him to his broadcast sponsors. Several famous players earned their nicknames courtesy of Allen, including "Joltin' Joe" DiMaggio and Tommy "Old Reliable" Henrich. Allen was in the radio booth for many memorable moments in Yankee history, including the moving farewells of Lou Gehrig in 1939 and Babe Ruth in 1948, and the celebrated home run streak of DiMaggio in

1941. In the course of his career he trained several other sportscasters who became nationally known and with whom he sometimes shared the microphone, including Red Barber and Phil Rizzuto.

When the Yankees began televised coverage of their games in the 1950s, Allen also appeared on TV broadcasts as a commentator and increasingly as the game announcer. However, in the 1964 World Series between the Yankees and the Cardinals, he was abruptly replaced by Phil Rizzuto, and when the series ended he was fired altogether. Allen was stunned by this action, which has never been fully explained. According to some sources, he was dismissed at the behest of one broadcast sponsor, Ballantine, in an attempt to cut costs; there were also rumors that his garrulous style had worn thin among Ballantine management.

Allen was to spend most of the next thirteen years away from broadcasting, an interval that included only one on-air stint—as an announcer for the Cleveland Indians during the 1968 season. His long absence from the airwaves finally ended nearly a decade later, in 1977, when he became the host of the syndicated TV show "This Week in Baseball." A year later, in 1978, the new Yankees owner, George Steinbrenner, hired Allen as the sportscaster for the team's games on cable TV's SportsChannel, and he remained at that post for eight seasons. Allen's affiliation with "This Week in Baseball" continued until his death.

In 1978 Mel Allen, along with Red Barber, was the first inductee into the newly founded broadcasting wing of the Baseball Hall of Fame. Allen, who never married, lived for many years in Greenwich, Connecticut, and had shared his home with his sister since 1977. He died at his home.

• For biographical information on Mel Allen, see H. Horn, "Baseball's Babbling Brook," *Sports Illustrated,* 9 July 1962, pp. 54–58ff; B. Davidson, "Mel Allen: Baseball's Most Controversial Voice," *Look,* 27 Sept. 1960, pp. 97–98ff; "Allen, Mel," in *Current Biography Yearbook* for 1950 and 1996; and *Who's Who in America,* vol. 32, 1963–1964. For a posthumous assessment of his career, see R. B. Cramer, "Mel Allen," *New York Times Magazine,* 29 Dec. 1996, p. 20. An obituary appears in the *New York Times,* 17 June 1996.

ANN T. KEENE

ALSOP, Richard (23 Jan. 1761–20 Aug. 1815), poet and businessman, was born in Middletown, Connecticut, the son of Richard Alsop, Sr., a merchant, and Mary Wright Alsop. When Alsop was fifteen, his father died, leaving his wife, Mary, a strict Episcopalian, in comfortable circumstances but with eight children. Alsop was a precocious reader and enjoyed impersonating heroes of Homer's *Iliad.* After being tutored, he attended school in Norwich, Connecticut. He demonstrated literary and linguistic abilities, learning Greek and Latin, and eventually mastering French, Italian, Spanish, and Scandinavian languages. In 1777 Alsop was tutored in mathematics at Yale College, did not attend classes, and left without a degree. He developed an interest in the

sciences, including ornithology and taxidermy, and also in field sports.

In 1777 or so, Alsop began lifelong friendships with a number of writers in Hartford. The oldest were John Trumbull, Timothy Dwight, David Humphreys, and Joel Barlow. Others included Dr. Mason F. Cogswell, Theodore Dwight, Lemuel Hopkins, and Elihu Hubbard Smith. Alsop was not the most brilliant man in the group, but none was more gracious. He combined literary pursuits and interest in the family shipping business along the Connecticut River. He became one of the few American millionaires of his day. He and his literary friends became the Connecticut (or Hartford) Wits. They modeled their work after that of witty British authors earlier in the century. Alsop added touches of fashionable primitive, exotic Gothicism, notably in a 1777 unpublished versification of bits of a Saxon poem published in the *Ladies Magazine* six years earlier.

In 1787 Alsop married Mary Wyllys Pomeroy; the couple had three children. While in his mid-twenties, he wrote most of *The Charms of Fancy*, a four-canto poem of a hundred-odd pages, with almost a hundred pages of annotations. Canto I begins by invoking Fancy, with bookish flourishes. Canto II discusses China, Japan, and their customs and leaders. Canto III focuses on India, the Dutch Indies, the Middle East, their varied landscapes, and many of their prominent historical figures. Canto IV is highly didactic: as the persona ages, Fancy yields to Melancholy, cheered, however, for

With joy she [Hope] sees the arts of peace expand,
And willing nations own the mild command.

Alsop never sought publication of *The Charms of Fancy*, in virtually final form by 1788 but published only in 1856. E. H. Smith included in his pioneering *American Poems, Selected and Original* (1793) Alsop's *The Conquest of Scandinavia*, his unfinished epic of Scandinavian mythology. It owed its origin to part of *Temora*, which James Macpherson had published in 1763 and dishonestly attributed to "Ossian." Smith also anthologized Alsop's "Runic Poetry . . . ," his verse redaction of part of the Scandinavian *Edda*.

During this time, Alsop became involved with *The Echo* (8 Aug. 1791 to 20 Aug. 1798), a twenty-number set of satires by several Wits. Its initial aim was to ridicule false taste in American literary efforts. It soon focused its pro-Federalist fire on Samuel Adams, Hugh Henry Brackenridge, John Hancock, Thomas Jefferson, and indeed all Jacobins—American republicans favoring the dangerous political effects of the French Revolution. Alsop is thought to have partly written at least two of the numbers. In one, he and Theodore Dwight spoof the grandiloquent description of a storm published in a Boston newspaper in July 1791; in another, Alsop, Cogswell, and Smith complain about the word "Jacobin" as used in the 5 December 1792 *Virginian Gazette*, and criticize Hancock, Jefferson, and the French Revolution for good measure. Conservative Connecticut citizens so rel-

ished *The Echo* that Alsop and his brother-in-law, Isaac Riley, a New York City bookseller, published eighteen of its numbers, along with ten poems by Alsop, Theodore Dwight, and Hopkins, as *The Echo, with Other Poems* (1807). Included was "The Political Green-house, for the Year 1798" (1799) by Alsop, Dwight, and Hopkins, and lambasting Jefferson, other Jacobins, and even Barlow, who had turned republican, to the Wits' distress. Among Alsop's other poems during this period was "A Poem, Sacred to the Memory of George Washington, late President of the United States and Commander-in-Chief of the Armies of the United States," a eulogy that he read as part of a huge Middletown courthouse ceremony (28 Feb. 1800). At one point he wonders lugubriously

Why o'er those martial bands gay standards wave
In mournful pomp the colors of the grave?

In 1800 Alsop traveled to New York, Philadelphia, and the West Indies, then joined Riley as a partner in his bookselling business. The two also published books in New York and Middletown. Alsop returned to translating. In 1806 Riley published Alsop's translation, with a learned introduction, of a short allegory, rendered in sing-song heroic couplets, from Matteo Maria Boiardo's *Orlando Innamorato*, as rewritten by Francesco Berni. *The Enchanted Lake of the Fairy Morgana* (Alsop's title) summarizes Orlando's adventures, including his frustration while trying "[t]he elusive fairy's lovely form to seize." In 1808 Riley published two more works translated by Alsop. One was *The Lovers of La Vendée, or Revolutionary Tyranny*, a four-volume novel by Etienne Gosse. It is a love story set against the backdrop of civil war between French peasants and their republican foes during the French Revolution. The more significant translation was of *The Geographical, Natural, and Civil History of Chili* [*sic*] by Abbe Don J. Ignatius Molina. Volume I concerns Chile's geography, climate, flora, and fauna; Volume II, its people, customs, and history. Alsop's translations reveal not only his linguistic expertise but also his interest in Renaissance literature, contemporary politics, and South American socio-scientific history.

In 1813 Alsop returned to Middletown, where he met an Englishman named John R. Jewitt, who had been a captive of Indians in Vancouver. He escaped in 1805, published an account of his experiences in 1807, and told Alsop about them. Intrigued, Alsop wrote, as by Jewitt, *A Narrative of the Adventures and Suffering of John R. Jewitt* (1815). Not surprisingly, Alsop stresses the nature, customs, and politics of the Indians, in addition to narrating Jewitt's tribulations at sea and in captivity. Alsop planned to revise his manuscript before it went to press. However, while visiting relatives in Flatbush, Long Island, New York, he suddenly died. Only in 1860 was his authorship of Jewitt's popular story publicly revealed.

Alsop is no longer highly regarded either by contemporary critics or by any general reading public. He is now associated almost exclusively with the Con-

necticut Wits, of whom he was a revered member. His political poetry has a satirical bite too old-fashioned to retain much relish.

• Most of Alsop's manuscripts, letters, and documents are at the New-York Historical Society, the Historical Society of Pennsylvania, and the Yale University Library. Karl P. Harrington, *Richard Alsop: "A Hartford Wit"* (1939), is a thorough, sympathetic biography, with a partial bibliography of his works. Joseph G. Fucilla, "An Early American Translation of the Count Ugolino Episode," *Modern Language Quarterly* 11 (Dec. 1950): 480–85, identifies Alsop's prose translation, in manuscript, of parts of Cantos XXXII and XXXIII of Dante's *Inferno*; Fucilla says the undated fragment may have been prepared as early as 1788 and regards it as competent if slightly flawed. *The George W. and Harriet B. Davison Art Center* (1952) describes the Alsop house, built in Middletown in 1839–1840 by Alsop's son Richard Alsop IV for his widowed mother, who later married Samuel Dana. For a time, the beautiful mansion was called the Dana House. Few critics have been kind to Alsop's poetry. Robert D. Arner, "The Connecticut Wits," in *American Literature 1764–1789: The Revolutionary Years*, ed. Everett Emerson (1977), pp. 233–52, says that Alsop "seem[s] so conservative, so reactionary, as to be an anachronism." Alan Golding, *From Outlaw to Classic: Canons in American Poetry* (1995), suggests that E. H. Smith included selections of Alsop in his *American Poems, Selected and Original* (1793) partly because Alsop had been excluded in an anthology published two years earlier by Matthew Carey. Robert Lawson-Peebles, *Landscape and Written Expression in Revolutionary America, The World Turned Upside Down* (1988), touches on Alsop's descriptions of plague, his dislike of the Jacobins, and his criticism of the supposed fertility of Louisiana soil. Samuel Marion Tucker, "The Beginnings of Verse, 1610–1808," in *The Cambridge History of American Literature*, ed. William Peterfield Trent et al. (vol. 1, 1917), pp. 150–84, says Alsop's *The Charms of Fancy* lacks fresh imagery and original ideas. An obituary is in the Hartford *Connecticut Courant*, 30 Aug. 1815.

ROBERT L. GALE

AMORY, Cleveland (2 Sept. 1917–14 Oct. 1998), writer and animal rights advocate, was born in Nahant, Massachusetts, the son of Robert Amory, a textile manufacturer, and his wife, Leonore Cobb Amory. Both parents were descendants of long-established upper-class families in Boston, where Cleveland grew up in a privileged household. He was educated at private schools, including Milton Academy, and enrolled at Harvard in 1935. After graduating four years later, he worked briefly as a reporter for the *Nashua Telegraph*, a newspaper in Nashua, New Hampshire, before moving to Arizona, where he worked as a reporter for the *Arizona Star* in Tucson and then as managing editor of the *Prescott Evening Courier*. From 1939 to 1941 he was also a roving editor for the *Saturday Evening Post*. During World War II Amory served overseas with U.S. Army Intelligence; at war's end in 1945 he moved back to the East Coast and became a freelance writer and lecturer. By the early 1950s he was also appearing from time to time as a television commentator; he pursued all three careers until his death.

Amory devoted much of his professional life to an exploration, at once caustic and whimsical, of the mores of the upper classes, beginning with his first book, *The Proper Bostonians* (1947), a nonfiction account of Boston's old moneyed families. The book firmly established his reputation as a sardonic chronicler of the rich. While pursuing this subject in essays and broadcasting appearances, he also wrote other books, including his first novel, *Home Town* (1950), a satiric and semiautobiographical account of an Arizona journalist-turned-novelist on a visit to New York City. In 1952 Amory published his second nonfiction work, *The Last Resorts*. This sequel to *The Proper Bostonians* described the vacation locales of the families he had chronicled in his first book. All three works attracted a wide readership as well as plaudits from most critics, who praised his malicious wit and his keen eye for social nuance and absurdity.

By the mid-1950s, when the culture of celebrity was beginning to take hold in the United States, Amory had become recognized as a nonacademic authority on the American upper class, one who could explain its workings and foibles to the general public. In 1959 he joined with Earl Blackwell to edit the *Celebrity Register*, a book that profiled America's rich and famous. A year later, with Frederic Bradlee, he edited a collection of articles and fiction from the old *Vanity Fair*, a leading American magazine of the early twentieth century. Also in 1960, Amory published *Who Killed Society?*, an account of the decline of high society. A dozen years later he wrote another sequel to his first book, titled *The Proper Bostonians Revisited* (1972). But by this time Amory's witty social investigations were beginning to wear a bit thin: to many, in the wake of the revolutionary 1960s, the lives of the rich no longer seemed a subject worthy of such intense scrutiny.

Indeed, Amory's own interests had already shifted dramatically, from the lives of the privileged to the plight of animals at the hands of modern man. Although he continued to offer acerbic commentary on the rich and proper for the remainder of his life, animal welfare became his main passion—the result, he said later, of having witnessed an especially bloody bullfight in Mexico—and he argued on its behalf in magazine and newspaper articles and in television and radio appearances. He also became active in virtually every major animal welfare organization in the United States. In 1967, to further his concern, he founded his own organization, a group called the Fund for Animals, to work for improvements in the welfare of both wild and domesticated animals, and he served as its president until his death. In his book *Man Kind?: Our Incredible War on Wildlife*, published in 1974, he attacked Americans' exploitation of animals for both amusement and economic purposes. In the book Amory often used mordant wit to make his points, but it did not mute his outrage. *Man Kind?* attracted a wide readership and established Amory as the best-known animal welfare spokesman in the United States.

For nearly three decades at the helm of the Fund for Animals, Amory led a nationwide campaign to raise public awareness of the cruelty being inflicted on animals, from research labs to hunting ranges, and to take legal steps to end it. Focusing on what he described as the four cornerstones of the Fund—"litigation, legislation, education, and confrontation"—his efforts resulted in a number of memorable and successful efforts by Fund members, including the saving of baby seals from fur hunters in the Canadian Arctic in 1978 and the rescue two years later of thousands of burros in the Grand Canyon that were slated for slaughter by the U.S. National Park Service. Through his efforts, the Fund established a refuge in Texas for abused and injured horses called Black Beauty Ranch, named after the equine heroine of the famous children's book.

In 1987 Amory published *The Cat Who Came for Christmas*, an engaging account of a scrawny alley cat he had taken into his New York City home one Christmas Eve. The book sold more than a million copies, and Amory donated the proceeds to the Fund for Animals. A sequel about his continuing relationship with the cat, whose name was Polar Bear, was published as *The Cat and the Curmudgeon* in 1990; a third and final book about Polar Bear, *The Best Cat Ever*, appeared in 1993. Four years later he published his last book, *Ranch of Dreams*, an account of Black Beauty Ranch.

In addition to his books, his work with the Fund for Animals, and his articles and public appearances on behalf of animal welfare, Amory wrote a column on various topics for the magazine *Saturday Review* for two decades (1952–1972); was a commentator on NBC-TV's "Today" show (1952–1963); served as a television critic for *TV Guide* (1960–1974); and was a contributing editor to *Parade* magazine from 1983 until his death. In the 1970s he also wrote a syndicated newspaper column called "Animail," and a collection of his columns, titled *Cleveland Amory's Animail*, was published in book form in 1976. Besides heading the Fund for Animals, Amory served as president of the New England Anti-Vivisection Society beginning in 1987.

Amory's last novel, *The Trouble with Nowadays: A Curmudgeon Strikes Back* (1979), was a sardonic attack on modern manners—and the lack thereof. A self-styled curmudgeon, Amory often ridiculed fellow members of the upper class as insistently as he pleaded for the rights of animals, but he did revere tradition and decried the loss of civility in modern life. A lifelong Episcopalian and a self-described social conservative, he maintained an old-fashioned belief, both religious and cultural in origin, that those who are privileged have an obligation to help those—both human and animal—who are not. According to one of his most widely quoted phrases, "The mark of a civilized person is how he treats what's underneath him."

Amory was married twice. His first marriage, to Cora Fields Craddock, in 1941 ended in divorce six years later. He married his second wife, Martha Hodge,

in 1953; the couple separated in the 1980s and she predeceased him. Amory died at his home in New York City. He was buried beside his cat, Polar Bear, at Black Beauty Ranch.

• For biographical information on Cleveland Amory, see "Amory, Cleveland," in *Contemporary Authors: New Revision Series*, vol. 29 (1990), pp. 9–13, which includes a lengthy interview. See also D. Rottenberg, "He Fights for Animals," *Reader's Digest*, Dec. 1981, pp. 59–60ff. An obituary appears in the *New York Times*, 16 Oct. 1998.

ANN T. KEENE

ARBUCKLE, Roscoe "Fatty" (24 Mar. 1887–29 June 1933), actor, was born Roscoe Conkling Arbuckle in Smith Center, Kansas, the son of William Arbuckle, a wheat farmer. His mother's name and occupation are unknown. At birth, he weighed approximately fourteen pounds; his mother almost died during the delivery, and her health remained tenuous throughout his childhood. His father, an alcoholic, blamed him for her condition and routinely beat him and berated him about his weight. Around 1889 his family moved to Santa Ana, California. Shortly thereafter his father moved alone to northern California, where he worked as a crop picker and eventually purchased a small hotel in San Jose.

Arbuckle attended school sporadically after the second grade, instead spending his time at local theaters, where he was fascinated by vaudeville performers. In 1895 he appeared on stage as a "pickanniny" with the Frank Bacon Stock Company. When his mother died in 1899, he was sent to live with his father in San Jose, but upon his arrival he found that his father had sold his hotel three days earlier and abruptly left town. Arbuckle was permitted to perform odd jobs at the hotel in return for room and board. He also began to sing for tips in the hotel's dining room and to appear at a theater on amateur nights. By 1900 he had gained a local reputation as a singer of "illustrated songs," leading audiences in singalongs as the song lyrics were projected on a screen. In 1902 he signed a contract with David Grauman, a prominent impresario, to sing illustrated songs at Grauman's Unique Theater in San Jose.

From 1904 to 1906 Arbuckle sang illustrated songs on the prestigious Pantages vaudeville circuit. But he wanted to perform comedy instead, and around 1907 he took a substantial pay cut to join the burlesque comic team of Leon Errol and Pete Gerald, with whom he juggled and appeared in drag as a sensuous, pudgy diva. In 1908 he joined the Elwood Tabloid Musical Company in San Francisco. That year he married Minta Durfee, an actress; they had no children and would divorce around 1925. In 1909, during a period of financial difficulty, he dabbled in movie acting, making two one-reelers for Selig Studios (*Ben's Kid* and *Mrs. Jones' Birthday*). Because people in the "legitimate" theater viewed the crude movies of the nickelodeon with scorn, however, he told no one—not even his wife—about his screen efforts. With the co-

median Walter Reed, Arbuckle and Durfee formed their own musical-comedy troupe, "The Reed and Arbuckle Show," and for several months they enjoyed vaudeville success. After the troupe disbanded in 1910, the couple appeared in a smash-hit play, *The Campus*, in Los Angeles. In 1911 they starred in a royal command performance in Honolulu of Walter De Leon's *The Girl and the Boy* for the queen of Hawaii, and afterward they spent approximately a year touring Japan, China, and the Philippines in Gilbert and Sullivan's operetta *The Mikado*.

On returning to the United States in February 1913, Arbuckle had trouble finding stage work and again turned to the movies out of financial necessity. According to Mack Sennett, the production head at the Keystone Film Company, the 265-pound actor made a memorable first impression when introducing himself at the studio: "'Name's Arbuckle,' he said. . . . 'I'm a funnyman and an acrobat. Bet I could do good in pictures.' . . . With no warning, he went into a feather-light step, clapped his hands, and did a backward somersault as gracefully as a girl tumbler" (Sennett, *King of Comedy*, p. 195). He was hired by Sennett as a stock player for three dollars a day; within a year he was the studio's biggest star, writing and directing almost all of his own one- and two-reel films. His athletic abilities made him ideal for Keystone's chaotic slapstick comedies, which often endangered actors' lives. For example, in *Fatty's Tintype Tangle* (1915), he was required to scamper frantically back and forth along telephone wires thirty feet above the ground, then drop from the wires over a housetop, crash through a skylight, and land on a bed twenty feet below. In *A Noise from the Deep* (1913), he made screen history when he became the first comedian to be hit in the face by a custard pie. An ambidextrous pie catcher and thrower, he was hailed as "the Hercules of the winged dessert, the Ajax of the hurtling fritter" (quoted in Yallop, *The Day the Laughter Stopped*, p. 45). Between 1913 and 1916 he often teamed with actress Mabel Normand, in such films as *Mabel and Fatty's Wash Day* (1915) and *Mabel and Fatty's Married Life* (1915). In these comedies he typically played a cheerful, mischievous country bumpkin or a love-sick suitor. The films were among the most popular of the period, and they made Arbuckle and Normand into international celebrities.

In August 1916 Arbuckle was lured away from Keystone by Joseph Schenck at Paramount Pictures. The comedian had been making $500 a week with the notoriously cheap Sennett. Schenck offered him $1,000 a day and 25 percent of the profits from his films—a combination that provided him with an annual salary of over one million dollars, the highest in Hollywood. His contract became a *cause célèbre* in newspapers, which reported his lavish expenditures—$15,000 to import a front door from Spain for his mansion, $25,000 for a custom-built Pierce-Arrow automobile that included a cocktail bar and a toilet. Given complete creative control over his films, he formed his own production company, the Comique

Film Corporation. His first Comique film, *The Butcher Boy* (1917), marked the screen debut of Buster Keaton. They appeared together in fifteen films, and Keaton later called Arbuckle his most important film mentor. At Comique, Arbuckle relied less on the broad, knockabout comedy that was typical of his Keystone one-reelers. Instead, in films such as *The Sheriff* (1918), a satire on Douglas Fairbanks action pictures, and *The Round-Up* (1920), a seven-reel western, he carefully built elaborate comic sequences and placed a greater emphasis on characterization. Film historians regard his work at Comique as an important bridge between the slapstick of the Keystone era and the sophistication of the great silent film comedies of the 1920s, the heyday of Keaton, Charles Chaplin, and Harold Lloyd.

In 1921 Arbuckle's screen popularity came to a shocking end when he was involved in one of Hollywood's most famous scandals. Over Labor Day weekend, he threw a bootleg liquor–soaked party in a suite at the St. Francis Hotel in San Francisco. Virginia Rappe, a young actress best known for appearing on the sheet-music cover of the hit song "Let Me Call You Sweetheart," was seized by severe convulsions during the party; a few days later she died of acute peritonitis caused by a ruptured bladder. On 10 September, San Francisco police detectives arrested Arbuckle and charged him with murdering Rappe; the charge was reduced to manslaughter at a subsequent police court hearing. Arbuckle's accuser was another partygoer, Bambina Maude Delmont, who insisted to newspaper reporters that the comedian had grabbed Rappe at the party, cried, "I have been trying to get you for five years and now I've got you!" and dragged her into his bedroom. When he later emerged, grinning and wearing Rappe's Panama hat, the actress was lying semiconscious and nude on his bed, screaming that he had hurt her. Based on Delmont's accusation, investigators believed that Arbuckle had raped the actress and that the force of his weight had caused her fatal internal injury. Although they soon realized that Delmont was an unreliable witness—she had a long police record that included charges of blackmail, bigamy, and racketeering, and none of the other partygoers fully corroborated her story—they nevertheless decided to pursue the high-profile case.

The public reaction to the Arbuckle scandal verged on hysteria. The Hearst newspapers ran inflammatory headlines, such as "ARBUCKLE DANCES WHILE GIRL IS DYING. JOYOUS FROLIC AMID TRAGEDY." Ministers across the nation denounced the "Sodom and Gomorrah" immorality of Hollywood. Arbuckle's films were banned in Los Angeles, Chicago, and Philadelphia, and in Thermopolis, Wyoming, 150 cowboys shot up a screen where an Arbuckle comedy was playing, which later turned out to be a publicity stunt concocted by the theater's owner. When Arbuckle appeared at a hearing, members of the San Francisco Women's Vigilant Committee spat on him. At his first trial in November and December, his attorneys offered evidence that Rappe

AMERICAN NATIONAL BIOGRAPHY
Supplement 1

Updates of the *ANB Online* and further print supplements will be issued at regular intervals. We welcome suggestions of other notable figures of the past who have not yet entered the pages of the *ANB*. Although we have gone to considerable lengths to ensure the accuracy of the articles already published, we also welcome corrections of inadvertent errors, which can be readily rectified in the online edition.

As a collective biography of the American nation in all its diversity, the *ANB* will remain a dynamic resource for historians, students, and the general reader.

Paul Betz
Mark C. Carnes

PREFACE

This is the first supplement to the twenty-four-volume *American National Biography*, which was published in 1999. After the contents of the print edition were issued in an online format (www.anb.org) in the spring of 2000, newly commissioned articles were added to the website. With the publication of the present volume, those new articles are now in print.

Under the general editorship of John A. Garraty and Mark C. Carnes, the *ANB* was designed to provide as broad a coverage as possible of notable figures in American history, from the earliest recorded contact of Europeans in North America to very nearly the present. To be included in the original print edition, a person had to have died before 1996. The reason for having a cut-off date was a matter of both practicality and principle. Without a fixed terminal date, the coverage of recently deceased people of note would probably have been hit or miss, with some articles being completed in time for publication but not others. Of greater concern, however, was the question of retaining historical perspective. The subjects included in the print edition were meant to be people whose significance had not only been well established but about whom definite judgments could also be made. One could not expect that to be necessarily true of celebrities still in the midst of their careers, the forty-second president of the United States being a case in point.

The American Council of Learned Societies and Oxford University Press always meant for the *ANB* to remain an active enterprise, so that people of fame or notoriety who died after 1995 would, at the appropriate time, be incorporated. The first supplement to the print edition spans the period from 1996 through early 2001. Among the subjects of new articles are the notables one would expect to find, such as Joe DiMaggio, Ella Fitzgerald, Allen Ginsberg, Barry Goldwater, Barbara Jordan, Carl Sagan, Frank Sinatra, Benjamin Spock, James Stewart, and Tammy Wynette. As in the base set, a concerted effort has been made to profile individuals from all walks of life—biochemists and religious leaders, economists and business executives, philosophers and political operatives. A few people of admittedly ephemeral significance appear in these pages, too—Sonny Bono, for example—but the aim is to show how they were representative of American popular culture at a given moment in the country's history.

The ACLS and Oxford University Press anticipated that some significant subjects would be missed in the process of compiling the articles for the original print edition, and the present supplement is intended in part to redress those omissions. Among the figures from the more distant past who have now found their place in the *ANB* are Eliot Ness, Roscoe "Fatty" Arbuckle, Dawn Powell, and the members of the Donner Party. In the interest of completeness, several first ladies, signers of the Constitution, and Supreme Court justices who failed to make it into the 1999 edition of the *ANB* are now the subjects of articles.

Following the articles in this volume is an updated Index by Occupations and Realms of Renown, which is in a somewhat different format than the one found in the 1999 edition of the *ANB*. Although the specific occupational categories are largely unchanged, they have been grouped under general headings, such as Art and Architecture, Government and Politics, and Science and Technology. Thus the reader can more easily identify subjects in related fields, as in the case of Nurses, Pharmacists, Physicians, and Surgeons General, who are listed, along with other types of health-care workers, under the rubric of Health and Medicine.

EDITORIAL AND PRODUCTION STAFF

MANAGING EDITOR
Paul Betz

SENIOR PRODUCER, NEW MEDIA
Laura Calderone

SENIOR PROJECT EDITOR
Jonathan Wiener

ASSISTANT PROJECT EDITOR
Mary Bryson

COPYEDITORS
Marion Laird, Anne H. Wimer

GRAPHIC DESIGNER
Joan Greenfield

PROOFREADERS
Elisabeth B. Parker, Alan Richtmyer

FACTCHECKERS
Lisa Chensvold, Kristen Williams

PUBLISHER
Karen Day

NEWARK PUBLIC LIBRARY
NEWARK, OHIO 43055-5087

Ref 920.073 Am Supp.1
American national biography

451 3288

"the winningest jockey of all time": that title still belongs to Willie Shoemaker, whose string of victories totals nearly twice that of Arcaro's and may never be broken. Nor did Arcaro even place or show in the record book of lifetime wins: at present, Johnny Longden and Gordon Richards are also ahead of him. Arcaro's total earnings have been far surpassed by others as well. But total wins and money earned are not the only measures of an outstanding jockey. Arcaro will be remembered as one of the greatest figures in the history of American racing not only for his record-breaking Triple Crown wins but also because he rode some of the greatest horses of the twentieth century, and rode them well. As his longtime friend, the venerable Calumet Farms trainer Jimmy Jones, said, "He was the perfect extension of the trainer on the horse. And nobody had his sense of the way the race was being run."

• For biographical information, see "Arcaro, Eddie," in *Current Biography Yearbook 1958* and an obituary from the *New York Times* in *Current Biography Yearbook 1998*; see also *Who Was Who in America*, vol. 12 (1998) as well as Arcaro's anecdotal memoir, *I Ride to Win!* (1951), written with Jack O'Hara. See also Stanley Frank, "A Visit with Eddie Arcaro," *Saturday Evening Post*, 28 June 1958, pp. 26ff.; W. C. Heinz, "You Have to Ride Rough," *Look*, 17 Apr. 1956, pp. 116–23; and W. C. Heinz, "How to Win the Derby," *Look*, 1 May 1956, pp. 90ff. For a description of Arcaro's riding and racing techniques, see a five-part series, "The Art of Race Riding," written by Arcaro, which appeared in *Sports Illustrated* in the summer of 1957: part 1, in the issue of 17 June 1957, pp. 14ff., includes biographical information; subsequent installments appeared in the issues of 24 June, 1 July, 8 July, and 15 July. For a posthumous assessment of Arcaro's career, see especially William Nack, "The Headiest Horseman," *Sports Illustrated*, 24 Nov. 1997, pp. 21–22. An obituary appears in the *New York Times*, 15 Nov. 1997.

ANN T. KEENE

ARTHUR, Jean (17 Oct. 1900–19 June 1991), actress, was born Gladys Georgianna Greene in Plattsburgh, New York, the daughter of Hubert Greene, a photographer, and Johannah Nelson Greene. Gladys Greene's father led a peripatetic lifestyle: in pursuit of seasonal photography work, he frequently moved his family to locations in New England and Florida, but in 1909 he abandoned them. When he reappeared in 1910, they were living in Rochester, Maine, and thereafter he came and went for months at a time as he pleased. In 1915 the Greene family moved to New York City. Financial difficulties led her to drop out of high school during her junior year. Around 1918 she began to work as a commercial model. She later explained that she had made up her mind not to be like other women who only wanted "husbands and furnished apartments on the installment plan" (quoted in Oller, p. 34). By the early 1920s she had posed for Alfred Cheney Johnston, the photographer for Ziegfeld's Follies, and as a "Christy Girl" for the acclaimed magazine illustrator Howard Chandler Christy. Her modeling success drew the interest of Fox Films. In 1923, with no prior acting experience, she was given a one-year contract and moved with her mother to Hollywood. At this time, Gladys Greene adopted the name Jean Arthur, derived from two of her heroes, Jeanne d'Arc and King Arthur.

Arthur's introduction to filmmaking was a personal disaster. After appearing in a small part in John Ford's *Cameo Kirby* (1923), she was given a starring role in *The Temple of Venus*; but, showing herself to be a novice, she was fired three days into production. Arthur later said that the experience gave her an "inferiority complex" that hindered her career. For the remainder of her Fox contract, she was relegated to two-reel comedies. Between 1924 and 1928 she freelanced for a variety of studios, usually playing ingenues in "quickie" westerns such as *Bringin' Home the Bacon* (1924) and *The Cowboy Cop* (1926). In 1928 her marriage to Julian Ancker, a photographer, was annulled after one day when their parents objected. That year she appeared as a baseball pitcher's girlfriend in *Warming Up* for Paramount. The mediocre silent film became a major hit when the studio added synchronized sound effects to exploit the public craze for talking pictures. Although Paramount rewarded Arthur with a three-year contract, she continued to appear in colorless ingenue roles, and in 1931 the studio dropped her.

Arthur returned to New York City that year, as she later recalled, determined "to learn how to act" (quoted in Kendall, p. 111). She spent the next two years playing a variety of roles on Broadway; none of the plays were popular successes, but critics familiar with her film work were surprised to note her knack for comedy. They also found that, from play to play, she learned to make effective use of her unusual voice, described by the director Frank Capra as "low, husky—at times it breaks pleasingly into the higher octaves like a thousand tinkling bells" (Capra, p. 189). In 1932 she married Frank Ross, a real estate developer who later became a film producer; they had no children and divorced in 1949.

Arthur returned to Hollywood in 1934 under contract to Columbia Pictures. Her breakthrough role came opposite Edward G. Robinson in John Ford's *The Whole Town's Talking* (1935). Audiences delighted at the contrast between Arthur's character, Wilhelmina "Bill" Jones, a bluff, self-reliant stenographer, and Robinson's mousy bookkeeper. Capra's *Mr. Deeds Goes to Town* (1936) offered Arthur a similar role, as a cynical newspaper reporter opposite Gary Cooper's whimsical greeting-card poet, Longfellow Deeds. In one of the film's most famous scenes, Arthur's character, in a moment of relaxed silliness, sings "Swanee River" and drums out the rhythm on a trash can while Deeds tries to sing "Humoresque" in counterpoint. For audiences used to the ditzy heiresses of Hollywood romantic comedy, Arthur in these films offered a new kind of heroine: a smart professional woman, more competent than the male hero, but who also possesses the capacity to have great fun and to fall in love.

Over the next several years Arthur starred in a string of box-office successes. Having been cast by Cecil B. De Mille as Calamity Jane in *The Plainsman* (1937), with Cooper as Wild Bill Hickok, she told an interviewer that she relished the opportunity to play a female character who "wore trousers" (quoted in Oller, p. 96). *Easy Living* (1937), with a screenplay by Preston Sturges, was the first of her major films in which she played the focal character—a working girl who is struck by a fur coat that has been thrown out of a window by a millionaire and then is mistaken for his mistress. Critics today cite the film as a classic of the screwball comedy genre. Capra, who called Arthur his favorite actress, cast her in *You Can't Take It with You* (1938), which won the Academy Award for Best Picture. Their collaboration continued in *Mr. Smith Goes to Washington* (1939), in which she played the crucial role of Saunders, a congressional aide who shows James Stewart's character the ropes in a corrupt Washington, D.C. In 1938 she screen-tested for the role of Scarlett O'Hara in *Gone with the Wind* and was widely reported by the Hollywood press to be producer David O. Selznick's choice, but the rumors were dispelled when Vivien Leigh was picked early the next year. In the early 1940s Arthur appeared in a pair of comedies directed by George Stevens: *The Talk of the Town* (1942), with Cary Grant and Ronald Colman, and *The More the Merrier* (1943), for which she received her sole Academy Award nomination, as best actress. Critics often cite these films as her most fully comic performances: unlike the wise-cracking career women that she played for Capra, her characters in Stevens's pictures are ordinary girls-next-door, with none of "the good lines." Yet she manages to make their very ordinariness interesting, sexy, and funny.

In 1944, at the height of her success, Arthur abruptly retired. Several factors precipitated her decision. She had repeatedly clashed with Columbia Pictures' president Harry Cohn over the quality of her projects; for example, in 1942 she was suspended by the studio after refusing nine scripts in a row assigned to her by Cohn. Also, she had little patience for the responsibilities that came with Hollywood stardom: she rarely promoted her films through interviews or cheesecake photographs and was on chilly terms with the press. In 1942 the gossip columnist Hedda Hopper dubbed her the "Least Popular Woman in Hollywood." Arthur's reputation for being "difficult" had financial repercussions: at a time when top female stars commanded over $100,000 per film, she was paid $50,000 for *The Talk of the Town*. Perhaps most significantly, she continued to feel insecure about her performances—Capra said that she had the worst "chronic case of stage jitters" he had ever seen—and as an aging actress, she was painfully self-conscious about her appearance on screen.

Periodically during her long retirement, Arthur returned to the public eye to act in projects that appealed to her. In 1948 she starred in Billy Wilder's *Foreign Affair*, a satire on American-German relations in postwar Berlin. In 1950 she fulfilled a lifelong am-bition by playing Peter Pan on Broadway. In her final film, she gave a quietly effective performance as a frontier mother in Stevens's classic western *Shane* (1953). She ventured onto television in 1966 with "The Jean Arthur Show," which was canceled after a few episodes. In the early seventies she taught drama at Vassar College. Thereafter, she retreated into the privacy of her home in Carmel, California, gaining a reputation among film buffs for being as reclusive a star of Golden Age Hollywood as Greta Garbo. She died in Carmel.

• The Jean Arthur Collection, including Arthur's small personal collection of mementoes from her film and stage career, is part of the Gish Film Theater Collection at the Popular Culture Library, Bowling Green State University. "Who Wants to Be a Lady?"—an article that Arthur wrote for *Screen and Radio Weekly*, 20 Sept. 1936—expresses her enthusiasm for playing Calamity Jane in *The Plainsman*. She was notoriously tight-lipped about her personal history, not only with Hollywood reporters but also with her closest friends. Rare candid interviews are Martha Kerr, "Jean Explains Miss Arthur," *Modern Screen*, May 1937, and George Pettit, "Now You'll Understand Jean Arthur," *Photoplay*, Feb. 1937. John Oller's biography, *Jean Arthur: The Actress Nobody Knew* (1997), is especially valuable for the light it sheds on her private life; it also clears up previously published misinformation regarding her birth date and her marriage to Julian Ancker. Arthur Pierce and Douglas Swarthout, *Jean Arthur, a Bio-bibliography* (1990), includes a complete filmography. For a sprightly and perceptive appraisal of Arthur's screen career, see Dennis Drabelle, "'What Do You Think I Am, a Goop?': Jean Arthur,"*Film Comment*, Mar./Apr. 1996. Elizabeth Kendall, *The Runaway Bride: Hollywood Romantic Comedy in the 1930s* (1990), analyzes *Mr. Deeds Goes to Town*. James Harvey, *Romantic Comedy in Hollywood* (1987), perhaps the finest critical overview of the genre, devotes an entire chapter to Arthur and also discusses her work with George Stevens. For views of Arthur by her Hollywood peers, see Frank Capra, *The Name above the Title* (1971), and Garson Kanin, *Hollywood* (1974). An obituary is in the *New York Times*, 20 June 1991.

THOMAS W. COLLINS, JR.

ASHBURN, Richie (19 Mar. 1927–9 Sept. 1997), baseball player, was born Don Richie Ashburn in Tilden, Nebraska, the son of Neil Ashburn, a machine-shop owner, and Genevieve Ashburn (maiden name unknown). A natural athlete, he later claimed that as a child he chased rabbits through the cornfields outside his small hometown: "I'd run alongside them and catch the fat ones." While attending high school, he was a star catcher for a local American Legion baseball team and set a Nebraska state sprinting record for the 100-yard dash; his mark of 9.6 seconds stood for 25 years. He attracted the active interest of several major league baseball scouts. In 1944 he signed with the Cleveland Indians, but baseball commissioner Kenesaw Mountain Landis nullified the contract because Ashburn was too young. Later that year, following his seventeenth birthday, he signed with the Chicago Cubs, but again his contract was nullified, this time because of an irregularity. Afterward both the New York Yankees and the Philadelphia Phillies jumped at the chance to sign him. Although the Yankees offered more money, he chose the Phillies, reasoning that he could make the majors more quickly with their less formidable ball club. That winter he studied journalism at Norfolk Junior College.

In 1945 Ashburn batted .312 for Utica, New York, in the Eastern League. During the course of the season manager Eddie Sawyer, who would later also manage him as part of the "Whiz Kid" Phillies, converted him from catcher to center fielder to take advantage of his superior speed. He spent a year and a half in the armed services and then rejoined Utica in 1947, hitting .362 and helping the club win the league championship. Baseball observers touted him as "another Ty Cobb but without Cobb's meanness" (quoted in Westcott and Bilovsky, p. 178). But because the Phillies' starting center fielder, Harry Walker, won the National League batting championship in 1947, Ashburn was expected to spend at least one more season in the minors. But when Walker showed up at spring training in 1948 out of shape and then injured his foot, Ashburn won the starting center fielder job. He batted .333 that year, although some critics maintained that he was "hitting .133 and running .200"; notoriously lacking in power, he relied on his speed to manufacture many of his hits, often beating out bunts or infield ground balls. He started in center field for the National League in the All-Star game, led the league with 32 stolen bases, and put together a blistering 23-game hitting streak—tying a National League record for rookies—during which he had 43 hits in 98 at bats. Although his season was truncated when he suffered a broken finger in August, he was named National League Rookie of the Year by the *Sporting News*.

In 1949 Ashburn married Herberta Cox; they had six children and separated in 1977. In 1950 he and the Phillies enjoyed a memorable season. Composed primarily of young players who had recently come up through the club's farm system, such as pitchers Robin Roberts and Curt Simmons, the "Whiz Kids" led the league for most of the season and seemed guaranteed to win the first Philadelphia pennant in 35 years. A horrible late-season slump, however, left them with a bare one-game lead going into the final game of the season, against the second-place Brooklyn Dodgers at Ebbets Field. In that game Ashburn made the most famous play of his career: with the score tied 1–1 in the bottom of the ninth inning, the Dodgers had runners on first and second and nobody out when Duke Snider lashed a single to center field. Because Ashburn had a weak throwing arm, the Dodgers' third base coach, Milt Stock, chose to send their man on second, Cal Abrams, home for the winning run. But Ashburn threw a perfect strike to the catcher, beating Abrams to the plate by twenty feet; the Phillies went on to win the game—and the championship—on a Dick Sisler home run in the tenth inning. In an anticlimactic World Series against the New York Yankees, Philadelphia was swept in four games and Ashburn batted a disappointing .176.

With his unimpressive build (five feet ten inches, 170 pounds) and his penchant for hitting singles, Ashburn was often overshadowed by the great slugging center fielders of his era, Snider, Willie Mays, and Mickey Mantle. But he was undeniably one of the finest players of the 1950s. He won National League batting titles in 1955, when he hit .338, and in 1958, when he hit .350. Between 1950 and 1958 he batted above .300 seven times. During those years he led the league in hits three times, in triples two times, and in walks three times. He possessed superb bat control and the ability to hit the ball exactly where he wanted it; for example, he grounded into only 101 double plays during his career, and in one plate appearance in 1954 he fouled off 14 consecutive pitches from Cincinnati Reds' pitcher Corky Valentine before drawing a walk. An alert, hustling player, he was nicknamed "Putt-Putt" by Boston Red Sox star Ted Williams, who observed that he seemed to have twin motors in his pants; he was better known to Philadelphia fans by the nickname "Whitey" because of his light blond hair. Thanks to his speed, he was able to cover a large chunk of the outfield. He established a major league record for most seasons with 500 or more outfield putouts (four), and he tied Max Carey for the major league record for most seasons with 400 or more outfield putouts (nine). In addition, he and Carey held major league records for most seasons leading the league in total outfield chances (nine) and most seasons leading the league in outfield putouts (nine). Ashburn also led the National League in outfield assists three times. An extremely durable player, he missed only 22 games between 1949 and 1958, and between June 1950 and September 1954 he played in 730 consecutive games.

In 1959 Ashburn slumped to a .266 batting average; after the season, he was traded to the Chicago Cubs for shortstop Alvin Dark. He batted .291 for the Cubs in 1960 and led the league in walks; the following year, however, he batted a mediocre .257, and the Cubs decided to expose him to the expansion draft that would stock two new clubs, the New York Mets and the Houston Colt 45s. He was chosen by the Mets, who in 1962 proved to be one of the worst teams in major league history, losing 120 games. Ashburn led the team with a .306 average and later recalled the "dubious honor" of being chosen their most valuable player: "I was awarded a 24-foot boat equipped with a galley and sleeping facilities for six. After the season ended, I docked the boat in Ocean City, New Jersey, and it sank" (quoted in the *New York Times*, 10 Sept. 1997). He then had the boat salvaged and sold it, only to discover that the check he received had bounced. After his travails with the Mets, he decided to retire. In his fifteen-season career he batted .308 with 2,574 hits. Among them were 2,119 singles and only 29 home runs. Indicative of his superior knowledge of the strike zone, he drew 1,198 walks while striking out 571 times. Over the course of his career he reached base four times in every ten at bats. He ranks fifth in baseball history for career outfield putouts and total chances. He was named to five National League All-Star teams, batting a remarkable .556. In 1995 he was elected to the National Baseball Hall of Fame by the veterans' committee.

After his retirement, Ashburn toyed with the idea of returning to Nebraska to enter politics as a Republican. But in 1963 the Phillies hired him as a baseball broadcaster, and he would continue in that capacity for the rest of his life. Terry Bitman, a local newspaper reporter, described him as "the Will Rogers of Philadelphia sports broadcasting—droll, homespun, opinionated and self-deprecating" (*Philadelphia Inquirer*, 10 Sept. 1997). He especially enjoyed telling stories about his playing days; one of his favorites, often repeated, involved a game on 17 August 1957, when he hit a fan named Alice Roth with two foul balls in the same at bat: once while she sat in the stands and again while she was being carried out of the stadium on a stretcher. Between 1974 and 1991 he also worked as a newspaper columnist, first for the *Philadelphia Bulletin* and then for the *Philadelphia Daily News*. He was much beloved by Philadelphians; reportedly, 200 busloads of Phillies fans traveled to Cooperstown, New York, for his Hall of Fame induction. In 1987 he experienced a personal tragedy when one of his daughters was killed in an automobile accident. During his later years he suffered from diabetes. He died of a heart attack in New York City, soon after broadcasting a Phillies game.

• A clipping file on Ashburn is at the National Baseball Library, Cooperstown, N.Y. The only biography is Joe Archibald, *The Richie Ashburn Story* (1960). For useful short overviews of his career, see Rich Westcott and Frank Bilovsky, *The New Phillies Encyclopedia* (1993), and Donald Dewey and Nicholas Acocella, *The Biographical History of Baseball* (1995). Richard Orodenker, ed., *The Phillies Reader* (1996), includes an article that describes Ashburn's defensive prowess. Dozens of retrospective articles on Ashburn were published in Philadelphia newspapers at the time of his death; two especially good ones are Jayson Stark, "For a City, a Loss Like No Other," *Philadelphia Inquirer*, 10 Sept. 1997, and Frank Fitzpatrick, "A Phillie for the Ages, Richie Ashburn Dies," *Philadelphia Inquirer*, 10 Sept. 1997. An obituary is in the *New York Times*, 10 Sept. 1997.

THOMAS W. COLLINS, JR.

ATWATER, Lee (27 Feb. 1951–29 Mar. 1991), political strategist, was born Harvey LeRoy Atwater in Atlanta, Georgia, the son of Harvey Dillard Atwater, an insurance claims adjuster, and Sarah Alma "Toddy" Page Atwater. Atwater displayed several trademark characteristics from the time he was a child growing up in South Carolina. The first was a set of fidgety mannerisms, which may have stemmed from hyperactivity. The second was a flamboyant disregard for authority, which prompted his parents to send him briefly to a military school. The third was a love for blues and rock music: he learned to play the guitar and would later befriend famous musicians.

In 1969 Atwater entered Newberry College, a small Lutheran institution in Newberry, South Carolina. A

1971 summer internship with the state's senior senator, Republican Strom Thurmond, ignited his political interest. When school resumed, he joined the College Republicans and soon became the group's state chairman. After graduating in 1973, he managed Karl Rove's successful race for the chairmanship of the College Republican National Committee. (During the presidential campaign of 2000, Rove would serve as a strategist for George W. Bush.) Rove made Atwater the committee's executive director. In that post, Atwater got to know the chairman of the Republican National Committee, George H. W. Bush. This connection not only opened professional doors but also enhanced Atwater's personal life when he was allowed to use Bush's boat to impress his girlfriend. The young woman, Sally Dunbar, married Atwater in 1978. They would have three daughters: Sara Lee, Ashley Page, and Sally Theodosia.

Atwater returned to South Carolina for the 1974 election season, managing campaigns for governor and lieutenant governor. Both candidates lost. "I tried to do too much, too fast," he said. "So I started all over again. First I had to win local. Then state. Then regional. Then . . . more" (quoted in Remnick, p. 286). Atwater subsequently built an impressive record of victories. He also earned a master's degree in journalism from the University of South Carolina in 1977.

The 1980 elections enlarged Atwater's reputation, for both good and ill. As southern regional director for the Republican presidential campaign, Atwater helped the Reagan-Bush ticket carry every southern state except Georgia. Working in the reelection campaign of Representative Floyd Spence (R-S.C.), Atwater openly noted that Democratic opponent Tom Turnipseed had once undergone electroshock therapy or, as Atwater put it, "was hooked up to jumper cables" (quoted in Brady, p. 84). The comment marked him as a practitioner of rough politics. Atwater often quoted Sun Tzu's ancient military text, *The Art of War*, which stressed deception and psychological harassment. "Everything in it you can relate to my profession, you can relate to the campaign," Atwater once said (quoted in Sewell, p. 20).

During the first Ronald Reagan administration, Atwater worked in the White House political office and then served as political director of the Reagan reelection drive. Atwater laid out the campaign's strategy, which included an effort to "drive a wedge between the liberal Democrats who run the national party and the Southern Democrats" (quoted in Goldman and Fuller, p. 386)—a close paraphrase of Sun Tzu's advice on dividing the enemy. After Reagan's landslide victory, Atwater joined a political consulting firm. In December 1985 he rejoined his old friend George H. W. Bush, who was now Reagan's vice president and likely to be the party's presidential candidate in 1988. As head of Bush's political action committee and then as manager of the Bush nomination campaign, Atwater convinced Bush that he should make peace with party conservatives and build a "firewall" of southern support that would sustain him even if he lost early nomination contests. Despite setbacks, Atwater's firewall held and Bush became the nominee.

During the 1988 general election campaign, Atwater was subordinate to former treasury secretary James A. Baker, III. Still, he set the tone of the effort, which included sharp attacks on the Democratic presidential nominee, Governor Michael S. Dukakis of Massachusetts. One such attack would follow Atwater to his grave. Massachusetts had a unique policy of granting furloughs to prisoners serving life sentences without the possibility of parole. A murderer named William R. "Willie" Horton, Jr., escaped while on furlough, later breaking into a Maryland home, where he beat a man and raped the man's fiancée. During the Democratic primary campaign, Senator Al Gore (D-Tenn.) used the issue against Dukakis. Following Gore's lead, Atwater pounded the furlough program, producing a television ad showing a prison with a revolving door. Meanwhile, an independent group made its own ad featuring a photo of Horton, who was African-American. Atwater had no role in the latter ad, and, arguing that the issue was crime and not race, he took pains not to show Horton in any Bush campaign materials. Critics, however, angrily accused him of fanning racial fears, noting that he could rely on the mass media to highlight Horton's background.

After winning the presidency, Bush named Atwater chairman of the Republican National Committee. In an effort to reach out to African-American voters, Atwater joined the board of trustees of Howard University, a historically black institution. But when students criticized his use of the Horton issue, he withdrew from the board.

Atwater sought to make the Republican National Committee a new political powerhouse. But in early 1990 physicians discovered that he had an inoperable brain tumor. As his condition worsened, he apologized for certain incidents, though—contrary to a common belief—he did not voice regret for the content of the 1988 campaign or for his aggressive approach to politics. After thirteen months of illness, Atwater died at George Washington University Hospital in Washington, D.C. The program for his memorial service included an epigraph from Sun Tzu.

As the first chair of a national party committee who had made a full-time career of campaign consulting, Atwater advanced the professionalization of American politics. Although he did not invent any new techniques, he practiced politics with an intensity that made him a role model for some, a cautionary example for others.

• The one full-length biography of Lee Atwater is John Brady, *Bad Boy: The Life and Politics of Lee Atwater* (1997). A particularly useful article, on which Brady and other writers have relied, is David Remnick, "Why Is Lee Atwater So Hungry?" in the Dec. 1986 edition of *Esquire*. For analysis of Atwater's use of Sun Tzu, see Dan Sewell, "'The Art of War': Learning How to Fight, According to the Book," *Los Angeles Times*, 23 Nov. 1989, as well as John J. Pitney, Jr., *The Art of Political Warfare* (2000). For several Atwater documents from the 1984 campaign, consult Peter Goldman and Tony Fuller, *The Quest for the Presidency 1984* (1985). For a transcript of Atwater discussing strategy in the 1988 campaign, see David R. Runkel, ed., *Campaign for President: The Managers Look at '88* (1989).

JOHN J. PITNEY, JR.

AUTRY, Gene (29 Sept. 1908–2 Oct. 1998), country singer, actor, and baseball team owner, was born Orvon Gene Autry in Tioga, Texas, the son of Delbert Autry, a livestock dealer and tenant farmer, and Elnora Ozmont Autry. He later recalled that his family was poor but "never Tobacco Road poor. My father earned good money, when he felt like it, which was some of the time" (Autry, p. 4). They moved frequently during his childhood, to small farms and hamlets in northern Texas and southern Oklahoma, eventually settling outside Ravia, Oklahoma. His grandfather, a Baptist minister, taught him to sing when he was five years old so he could join the church choir; his musically talented mother taught him how to play a mail-order guitar. As a teenager he sang ballads for tips at cafes, and around 1923 he toured for three months with the Fields Brothers Marvelous Medicine Show. During these years he was reportedly fired from a job as a ranch hand because his singing distracted the other hands from their labor.

Following his graduation from high school in 1925, Autry was employed by the St. Louis & Frisco Railroad, eventually rising to the position of telegraph operator. He later described the night in 1927 that would "change my life forever," when he was working the "graveyard shift" in Chelsea, Oklahoma, passing the tedious hours by singing and playing his guitar. "This farmer-looking guy, with glasses on the tip of his nose, came into the office and gave me some pages to send. Then he spotted the guitar. 'You play that?' he asked. 'Like to hear you'" (quoted in the *New York Times*, 3 Oct. 1998). The man was the famous humorist Will Rogers, who encouraged Autry to go to New York City to pursue a professional singing career.

In September 1927 Autry used a free railroad pass to travel to New York City, where he spent a month calling on various record companies. After a failed audition at Victor Records at which he sang an Al Jolson hit, "Climb Upon My Knee, Sonny Boy," he was urged to return home and learn to yodel instead; he was also given a "To Whom It May Concern" letter of recommendation, which noted that he had talent. This letter gained him a regular, unpaid radio spot singing for a station in Tulsa, on which he learned to do the "blue yodels" popularized by country star Jimmie Rodgers. In October 1929 he returned to New York City to record several sides for Victor. The following year he recorded for Victor, the American Record Corporation, Columbia, Grey Gull, and Gennett. His early recordings were heavily influenced by Rodgers, skillful but derivative; indeed, almost half of the approximately forty sides that he recorded between 1929 and early 1931 were Rodgers tunes. In 1931 he signed a contract with the American Record Company, which marketed its records through chain stores such as Sears, Roebuck. That year he enjoyed a major hit with one of his own songs, "That Silver-Haired Daddy of Mine," a plaintive, hillbilly-style ballad recorded in a duet with its coauthor, Jimmy Long. The record sold thirty thousand copies in its first month of release; by 1940 it had sold over five million copies.

As a result of this success, in 1932 Autry was given a prominent spot on the "National Barn Dance," a popular radio program broadcast on Chicago station WLS, which was owned by Sears. On this program he first adopted the persona for which he became famous—the genial singing cowboy. The persona was not Autry's idea but rather that of American Record Company executive Arthur Satherley. Autry recalled his own initial hesitation about the role: "That sort of stuff didn't sound very glamorous to me, as my recollections of ranch life included aching muscles and . . . sun and dust. I wanted to be a dreamy-eyed singer of love songs like Rudy Vallee. . . . [But] Arthur Satherley made me a proposition, and told me that if I'd do exactly as he said, I'd never be sorry" (quoted in Green, p. 15). Proving true to his word, Satherley quickly built Autry into the "Nation's Number One Singing Cowboy." He was given his own radio program on WLS, "Conqueror Record Time," on which he promoted his latest songs for Conqueror Records, an American Record Company label sold exclusively through the Sears mail-order catalogue. This catalogue featured an entire section devoted to Autry's records; it also offered several Gene Autry songbooks (for example, *Rhymes of the Range* and *Cowboy Songs and Mountain Ballads*) and a popular "Gene Autry Roundup Guitar" that sold for $9.95. Thus, through this system of tie-ins between the American Record Company and Sears, Autry became the first mass-marketed, mass-merchandised country music star.

In 1934 Autry was brought to Hollywood to sing in a square-dance sequence in a low-budget western, *In Old Santa Fe*, for Mascot Films. The movie's producer, Nat Levine, realizing that the western film market was becoming glutted, wanted to introduce a fresh element to the genre by having his cowboy stars sing popular songs. Previous efforts in Hollywood to make singing cowboys out of two action-oriented stars, Ken Maynard and John Wayne, had met with limited success. But when the public responded positively to Autry's performance, Mascot cast him as the star of his own serial, *The Phantom Empire* (1935), which proved to be popular. In 1935 Mascot merged with several other small studios to form Republic Pictures. Autry's first feature film for Republic was *Tumbling Tumbleweeds* (1935). Over the next seven years he made approximately fifty "B" westerns for the studio, most of which were shot on six-week schedules and given relatively large budgets, with titles such as *The Sagebrush Troubadour* (1935), *Rootin' Tootin' Rhythm* (1937), *Yodelin' Kid from Pine Ridge* (1937), and *Ridin' on a Rainbow* (1941).

Autry's films for Republic were virtually interchangeable: they all featured his pleasant, rather bland star persona; several lengthy musical sequences; a few scenes of broad comedy performed by his sidekick, Smiley Burnette; and action scenes of Autry on his well-trained horse, Champion. The films were almost devoid of gunplay, which had long been considered the "bread and butter" of the "B" western. They also rarely included a romantic subplot (the studio received thousands of protest letters from small boys after Autry kissed his leading lady, Ann Rutherford, in *Comin' Round the Mountain* [1936]). They were primarily targeted to a young, Saturday matinee audience, and the star followed a strict "Cowboy Code" on-screen, which he encouraged his fans to emulate: "The hero must not take unfair advantage of anyone, including the bad guys. He must not hit anyone smaller than himself. He must always keep his word. He respects womanhood, his parents, and the laws of his country." Curiously, Autry's westerns were not set in the historical West but rather in modern-day America. While they offered many traditional western elements (black-hatted villains, cattle stampedes, stagecoach holdups), they also featured automobiles, airplanes, and tanks, and their plots tended to focus on issues of contemporary concern, such as political corruption, wartime spies, and the Dust Bowl. Some western film historians have speculated that this awkward mixture of the old and the new may have contributed to the films' appeal, reassuring audiences that they might cope with a rapidly changing society through traditional virtues. While Autry's "horse operas" were mocked by critics and ignored in many urban areas, they proved to be enormously popular with rural and small-town audiences. Between 1938 and 1942 he was listed by movie theater owners as among the top ten box-office draws in Hollywood, ranked alongside major-studio stars such as Clark Gable, Spencer Tracy, and Mickey Rooney.

Possessing a gentle, folksy baritone singing voice, Autry was a prolific songwriter, recording more than 150 of his own songs during his career. He frequently collaborated with talented country songwriters such as Fred Rose (whom he brought to Hollywood in the late 1930s), Johnny Marvin, and Ray Whitley. Prominent country musicians who played on his recordings included Johnny Bond, Jimmy Wakely, Merle Travis, and Frankie Marvin. Most of his songs incorporated western themes and were tied in to his movies, although he recorded a number of love songs during World War II. Among his million-selling records were "Tumbling Tumbleweeds" (the best-selling record for 1935), "Back in the Saddle Again" (1939; co-written by Autry and Whitley), "South of the Border" (1939), and "You Are My Sunshine" (1941). In addition to his work on records and in films, he toured relentlessly throughout the late 1930s and early 1940s. His elaborate traveling stage show included American Indian dancers, two or three comedians, male and female singing trios, a full complement of backup musicians, and tricks performed by Champion, who was billed as the "World's Wonder Horse." In addition, he had his own rodeo that played to capacity crowds in

New York City's Madison Square Garden and the Boston Garden. He later recalled that his finest hour in show business occurred in Dublin, Ireland, during a tour in 1939, when a huge crowd gathered in O'Connell Square spontaneously serenaded him with the song "Come Back to Erin." From 1940 to 1956 (with an interruption from 1942 to 1945) he starred on his own radio program for CBS, "Melody Ranch," which featured "Back in the Saddle Again" as its theme song.

In 1942 Autry enlisted in the U.S. Army Air Forces. He spent four years in the service, stationed primarily in the China-Burma-India theater, where he flew cargo planes. During the war he began to shrewdly plan for a post-show business career. He later explained his reasoning: "It was a jolt to the nervous system to find myself staring at an Air Force salary of less than two thousand dollars a *year*, after earning up to ten thousand dollars a *week*. I thought to myself, well, as long as I can work I know I can make money. But what if . . . my voice went haywire. Times change, too. If you don't part your hair right, they, the public, will find someone who does. I knew the time had come to start looking for an interest that did not depend on my being able to perform" (Autry, p. 168). He became further alarmed when he returned to Hollywood in late 1945 to find that he had been supplanted at Republic by Roy Rogers, who was being promoted as "King of the Cowboys." Realizing that there wasn't room at the studio for two singing-cowboy superstars, Autry left Republic to form his own production company, Gene Autry Productions, which released its films through Columbia Studios. He also began to invest aggressively in real estate and oil concerns; by the late 1940s he owned a chain of Texas movie theaters, a flying school, several cattle ranches, two music publishing companies, and three radio stations. In 1949 he enjoyed the biggest hit of his career, the children's Christmas song "Rudolph, the Red-Nosed Reindeer." He readily admitted that the song was a happy fluke: he had initially dismissed it as "silly" and had performed it in a single take, at the very end of a recording session, because he needed to fill ten minutes of booked time; by the 1970s it had become the second-largest-selling single of all time, behind only Bing Crosby's "White Christmas," earning him over a millions dollars in royalties. He had major pop hits with other children's holiday songs, "Here Comes Santa Claus" (1947; written by Autry), "Peter Cottontail" (1950), and "Frosty the Snowman" (1950).

Autry was one of the first Hollywood stars to embrace the medium of television. He purchased a television station, KOOL in Phoenix, in the late 1940s. Although he lost up to $35,000 a month on the station initially, he correctly guessed that television would soon become a profitable outlet for inexpensive westerns. During the early 1950s he began to phase out his film work to concentrate on his own television series, *The Gene Autry Show*, which ran on CBS between 1950 and 1956. His television production company, Flying A Productions, produced his show as well as

several others with western themes: *Annie Oakley*, *Buffalo Bill, Jr.*, and *The Range Rider*. During the 1950s he continued to expand his business interests to include several television stations and luxury hotels. An ardent baseball fan, in December 1960 he became the principal owner of an expansion American League franchise, the Los Angeles Angels (renamed the California Angels in 1965). Engrossed by his career as a businessman, he found that he no longer had the time or the desire to perform. He made his last public appearances as an entertainer around 1964. In 1969 he was elected to the Country Music Hall of Fame.

Over the next two decades Autry spent heavily on the California Angels, particularly after the introduction of free agency in the 1970s. Although at different times the team boasted stars such as pitcher Nolan Ryan, first baseman Rod Carew, and outfielder Reggie Jackson, it usually posted losing records and never won a pennant for Autry, who noted ruefully: "In the movies I never lost a fight. In baseball I have hardly ever won one" (Autry, p. 166). He continued to enjoy extraordinary success as a businessman, however; for example, in 1982 he sold one of his television stations, KTLA in Los Angeles, for $245 million. In 1988 he founded the Autry Museum of Western Heritage in Los Angeles, a $54-million project that housed his extensive collection of western memorabilia and art. Because of infirmities brought on by old age, he sold a part interest in the Angels to the Walt Disney Company in 1995; Disney took over operating control of the club in 1996.

Autry was married twice: to Ina Mae Spivey from 1932 until her death in 1980, and to Jacqueline Ellam, a bank executive, in 1981. He had no children from either marriage. He died in Los Angeles.

Some country music historians have denigrated Autry's contributions to the genre, suggesting that his singing cowboy persona was largely synthetic, the creation of record company executives and Hollywood producers. They find that he was motivated primarily by pecuniary rather than artistic concerns. Nevertheless, as Country Music Foundation director Douglas B. Green has pointed out, Autry's seminal achievement was to bring "hillbilly" music into the mainstream of American popular culture. "No youngster in the thirties and forties ever wanted to grow up to be a hillbilly, but thousands upon thousands wanted to be cowboys." By combining cowboy heroics and rural-oriented songs, Autry succeeded in giving country music "a deserved and long-needed dignity" (Green, p. 154).

• The best source for information on Autry's life is his autobiography, written with Mickey Herskowitz, *Back in the Saddle Again* (1978). Douglas B. Green has written perceptively about his role in country music history; see "Gene Autry" in *Stars of Country Music: Uncle Dave Macon to Johnny Rodriguez*, ed. Bill C. Malone and Judith McCulloh (1975; repr., 1991). For his Hollywood career, see Green, "The Singing Cowboy: An American Dream," *Journal of Country Music* 7 (May 1978): 4–61; Richard Maurice Hurst, *Republic Studios: Between Poverty Row and the Majors* (1979);

William K. Everson, *A Pictorial History of the Western Film* (1969); and Everson and George N. Fenin, *The Western, from Silents to Cinerama* (1962). For an excellent compilation of his early, Jimmie Rodgers–influenced recordings, see *Gene Autry: Blues Singer 1929–1931: "Booger Rooger Saturday Nite!"* (Columbia/Legacy, 1996). The best single-disc compilation of his hits is *The Essential Gene Autry, 1933–1946* (Columbia/Legacy, 1992). An obituary is in the *New York Times*, 3 Oct. 1998.

THOMAS W. COLLINS, JR.

AYRES, Lew (28 Dec. 1908–30 Dec. 1996), actor, was born Lewis Frederick Ayres III in Minneapolis, Minnesota. (No information about his parents could be obtained for this article, although it is assumed that he shared his father's name.) After graduating from high school in San Diego, California, he attended the University of Arizona, planning to earn a medical degree. A talented banjo and guitar player and pianist, he played in a university jazz band and became a musician in Los Angeles. An agent who spotted Ayres performing in a Hollywood nightclub, and dancing with the actress Lily Damita, in 1928, obtained a small part for him in *The Sophomore*, a 1929 silent movie. Handsome and soft-spoken, he was next cast as a boyish fellow asking Greta Garbo for a kiss in *The Kiss* (1929).

Ayres's performance in the Garbo film was deemed so excellent that he was cast as Paul Baumer, the sensitive World War I German soldier in *All Quiet on the Western Front*, the 1930 film based on Erich Maria Remarque's antiwar novel *Im Westen nichts Neues* (1929). In the final scene, the soldier, who has killed one of the enemy and poignantly regrets the act, reaches for a butterfly and is shot dead by a sniper. This heartbreaking scene was a departure from the novel; its impact endures in the history of American movies. Oddly, the comedienne ZaSu Pitts was originally cast as Mrs. Paul Baumer, but laughter at her performance by preview audiences prompted the studio to cut her footage and reshoot it with Beryl Mercer in her role. *All Quiet on the Western Front* received the Academy Award for best film of the year and was immensely popular everywhere, except in the Germany of the early 1930s. In interviews, Ayres voiced sensible comments on the novel and its film adaptation, on patriotism, which he called admirable, but also on "the utter futility of war." No acting role Ayres later played ever quite rose to this career peak. In 1930 he was featured in three more movies, all trivial, including *Doorway to Hell*, in which he was miscast as a gangster too juvenile to be taken seriously.

Between 1931 and the time the United States entered World War II, Ayres appeared in forty-six movies. The best were *The Impatient Maiden* (1932), *Don't Bet on Love* and *My Weakness* (1933), *Holiday* (1938), and *Young Dr. Kildare* (also 1938). Beginning with *The Impatient Maiden*, in which he played a doctor opposite Mae Clarke's lead, Ayres was earning $1,750 a week. *Don't Bet on Love* costarred Ginger Rogers. *My Weakness* was a musical. *Holiday*, based on Philip

Barry's 1928 play and starring Cary Grant and Katharine Hepburn, featured Ayres as a gentle alcoholic; he felt that his work in this role represented his best performance. *Young Dr. Kildare* was the first of nine Dr. Kildare films in which he appeared, opposite Lionel Barrymore. In 1936 Ayres tried his hand at directing, *Hearts in Bondage* being the unimportant result.

In 1931 he had married actress Lola Lane, whose first film role was in *Speakeasy* (1929), the first talkie featuring the prize ring and illegal barrooms. She and Ayres were divorced in 1933. A year later he married Ginger Rogers, whose versatile career as actress and dancer had begun with *Young Man of Manhattan* and three other movies in 1930. Studio conflicts caused Ayres and Rogers to separate in 1936 and obtain a divorce in 1941.

World War II altered Ayres's career dramatically. In 1941 he registered as a conscientious objector, was vilified by Hollywood at once, and suffered the humiliation of seeing movies in which he appeared picketed and banned. He spent two months in a labor camp but thereafter served as a noncombatant in the U.S. Army in the Southwest Pacific theater of operations, both as an assistant chaplain and as a medical corps technician in a mobile evacuation hospital. He distinguished himself under fire during three beachhead landings with invasion forces—including the formidable Leyte landing in October 1944—and won three battle stars. Home again, he picked up the pieces of his private life.

Beginning in 1946, Ayres restabilized his movie career, first with *The Dark Mirror* (1946). *The Unfaithful* (1947) and *Johnny Belinda* (1948) followed. His role as a village doctor in *Johnny Belinda* earned him a nomination for an Oscar as best actor. He also played Dr. Kildare, again with Lionel Barrymore, in a radio drama series (1950–1952). During the early 1950s, Ayres became somewhat less effective on the screen. Early in 1954 he and Robert Duncan, an accomplished photographer and technician, embarked on a year-long, 40,000-mile trip around the world to study the non-Christian religions of the Far East. They went from Japan to Formosa, and Hong Kong, Thailand, Burma, through India and Pakistan, and into the Middle East and Israel. Ayres's motives were threefold: to help, if in only a small way, bring "surcease of international armed conflict . . . and overcome the subhuman environment degrading and demoralizing more than one half of the inhabitants of our shrinking earth"; to reinforce his own deep spiritual convictions; and to enlighten and entertain the public. He accomplished his third goal in two ways: he produced a documentary film titled *Altars of the East* (1955), which recounts his trip throughout Asia; and he published a book with the same title (1956), a narrative of his geographical and spiritual adventures that concludes with an expression of his ecumenical faith in God and the brotherhood of man.

From 1958 to 1961 Ayres hosted summer reruns of western dramas on television. In 1961 he demonstrated a sense of conscience and a concern for human health by declining to reprise Dr. Kildare in a proposed television series on the grounds that children watching the show would be exposed to ads by the tobacco company sponsoring it. Richard Chamberlain accepted the assignment and starred in the successful program for five years.

Otto Preminger, the movie director, persuaded Ayres to return to the screen as a star and directed him in *Advise and Consent* (1962), a pioneering "White House" film. In it, the selfish, obstinate president of the United States dies, and the upright vice president, played by Ayres, takes over. Ayres appeared in *The Carpetbaggers* in 1964, the same year that he married Diana Hall, a young Englishwoman with whom he was to have one child. Ayres appeared in only seven more movies, including the popular *Battle for the Planet of the Apes* (1973) and the intriguing *Damien: Omen II* (1978). In the meantime, in 1972 and again in 1974 he recorded radio dramas for the American Armed Forces Radio and Television Services. Between 1973 and 1989 he appeared in several telefilms, most notably in *Of Mice and Men* (1981). Ayres's last major work was *Altars of the World* (1976), a 150-minute documentary on various religions, which he wrote, directed, photographed, produced, and edited. In the fall of 1985 he ended his acting career as a member of the cast of "Lime Street," a short-lived TV adventure/detective show. He retired in Brentwood, California, made tentative plans to write his autobiography, and died in Los Angeles.

Ayres was a rare Hollywood personality: a gifted, steady actor, a brave noncombatant wartime soldier, a competent writer, and a sincere idealist who did what he could to make the world a better place.

• The following reference books contain basic information about Ayres's movie career: Alan G. Fetrow, *Sound Films, 1927–1939: A United States Filmography* (1992); Ephraim Katz, *The Film Encyclopedia* (3d ed., 1998); Leonard Maltin, *Leonard Maltin's Movie Encyclopedia* (1994); David Ragan, *Who's Who in Hollywood: The Largest Cast of Film Personalities Ever Assembled* (2 vols., 1992); and David Thomson, *A Biographical Dictionary of Film* (3d ed., 1994). Discussions of Ayres and *All Quiet on the Western Front* appear in Larry Langman and Ed Borg, *Encyclopedia of American War Films* (1989), and in Anthony Slide, "All Quiet on the Western Front," in *Magill's American Film Guide*, ed. Frank N. Magill, vol. 1 (1983), pp. 80–82. Jon D. Swartz and Robert C. Reinehr, *Handbook of Old-Time Radio: A Comprehensive Guide to Golden Age Radio Listening and Collecting* (1993), reports on Ayres's "Dr. Kildare" work. Details of Ayres's work in television are in Alex McNeil, *Total Television: The Comprehensive Guide to Programming from 1948 to the Present* (4th ed., 1996), and *Leonard Maltin's TV Movies and Video Guide*, 1989 ed. (1988). In *Ginger: My Story* (1991), Ginger Rogers discusses, with touching sensitivity, her relationship with Ayres. Obituaries are in the *New York Times*, 1 Jan. 1997, and *U.S. News and World Report*, 13 Jan. 1997.

ROBERT L. GALE

B

BAER, Max (11 Feb. 1909–21 Nov. 1959), world heavyweight boxing champion, was born Maximilian Adelbert Baer in Omaha, Nebraska, the oldest son of Jacob Baer and Dora Baer (maiden name unknown). His father, a cattle dealer and buyer for Swift and Company in Omaha, later moved his family to Durango, Colorado, and then to Livermore, California, where he bought a ranch and raised livestock. Max graduated from elementary school in Livermore and attended high school for one year, then quit school and went to work herding cattle and butchering meat for his father. Later Baer worked in an Oakland, California, factory in which diesel engines were manufactured.

It was while employed in Oakland that Baer first became interested in boxing. Although more than one story exists as to how he took up the sport, the stories do agree that Max decided to enter boxing after being involved in an altercation with an older man whom he knocked out. His first manager was J. Hamilton Lorimer, the son of the owner of the factory in which he worked, under whom he became a professional in March 1929.

Baer's rise to prominence as a boxer was rapid. Fighting in California, he won fifteen of sixteen fights in 1929, and in 1930 he won nine of twelve fights, one of his opponents dying of injuries. After this tragedy Lorimer handed over his management to Ancil Hoffman, a San Francisco boxing promoter, who managed Baer until the end of his ring career. In his last 1930 fight, Baer fought for the first time in New York City, losing to contender Ernie Schaaf.

In 1931 Baer won seven fights out of ten, including a knockout of Tom Heeney, who had fought Gene Tunney for the heavyweight championship, but his limitations were demonstrated when he was decisively outboxed by former light-heavyweight champion Tommy Loughran. In 1932 he won all seven of his fights, including victories over heavyweight contenders such as Schaaf, Heeney, King Levinsky, and Tuffy Griffiths.

Baer was then matched with former heavyweight champion Max Schmeling, who was the leading contender for the title. They met at Yankee Stadium on 8 June 1933, with Schmeling the heavy favorite. For seven rounds, Schmeling outboxed Baer, but Baer then unleashed a devastating assault that finally resulted in Schmeling being floored in the tenth round. He arose but Baer resumed the attack and the referee quickly stopped the fight.

The Schmeling fight exemplified Baer's style in the ring. Nat Fleischer described him thus: "Baer is not what is termed a great fighter. He is purely a slugger . . . So far as fighting ability is concerned, he ranks with the greatest of this era, but as far as science goes, he seems to lack that entirely . . . [He has] tremendous power behind his fists [and] utter disregard for personal safety." Baer was also noted for clownish behavior in the ring, displayed even in his most important fights.

Outside the ring, Baer was debonair, smiling, wise-cracking—an incorrigible playboy, always out to have a good time. His handsome features, curly hair, and Adonis-like physique, six feet two and 205 pounds, combined with his friendly and light-hearted disposition, made him popular with everyone, especially his numerous female admirers. He was linked romantically with actresses such as Mae West and Jean Harlow.

On 14 June 1934 Baer fought Primo Carnera for the world heavyweight title at the Garden Bowl on Long Island. The 55,000 spectators saw Baer at his best. While he engaged in antics that puzzled his opponent and amused the audience, he mounted a devastating attack that floored the 263-pound heavyweight champion a dozen times and caused the referee to stop the fight in the eleventh round. A new champion was crowned.

With the title in his hands, Baer for the next year satisfied his inclination for good times and high living, then made his first and only defense of the heavyweight title against Jim Braddock at the Garden Bowl on 13 June 1935. Braddock was not a highly regarded opponent, having emerged as a title challenger because of a few good victories after years of mediocrity. He was a clever boxer, however, and Baer apparently did not take him seriously. The result was the most shocking upset in heavyweight history: Braddock decisively outpointed the champion and took the title.

At this time, Joe Louis, a new and exciting heavyweight challenger, was attracting a great deal of attention. Baer sought to quickly reestablish himself by fighting Louis, and they met at Yankee Stadium, 24 September 1935. Although landing some good punches, enough for Louis to say many years later that Baer was the hardest hitter he ever faced, Baer took a severe beating and was knocked down three times, the last time for the full count in round four.

After the Louis fight, Baer announced his retirement but returned to the ring in 1936 and fought a long series of exhibitions. He resumed serious fighting in 1937 with two fights in London, England, losing to Tommy Farr and knocking out Ben Foord. In 1938 he defeated Farr in a return fight and knocked out Hank Hankinson, thus gaining recognition as the second contender for the heavyweight title. He fought the leading contender, Lou Nova, in June 1939, but Nova outboxed and outslugged him and stopped him in the eleventh round. In 1940 Baer knocked out Tony Galento and Pat Comiskey, thereby reestablishing himself as leading heavyweight contender. He might have gotten another title fight, but the public remembered the ease with which the current champion, Joe Louis, had beaten Baer in 1935. Instead, in 1941, Baer was rematched with Nova, the winner to fight Louis. He nearly knocked out Nova in the fourth round but interrupted his attack to clown and mock his opponent, thus allowing Nova to recover and later stop him in the eighth round. This was Baer's last fight.

Baer married actress Dorothy Dunbar in 1932, but they were divorced in 1933, at about the time he was being romantically linked with other actresses. In 1935 he married Mary Ellen Sullivan of Washington, D.C.; they had three children and remained together until Baer's death. Baer was persuaded by Ancil Hoffman to put a considerable part of his $750,000 ring earnings into an annuity, which enabled him and his family to live comfortably in later years. In 1933 he had a prominent role in a successful movie, *The Prizefighter and the Lady*, and after leaving the ring he appeared in a number of other movies. In the late 1940s he had a successful nightclub act with another ex-boxer, Maxie Rosenbloom.

Baer enlisted in the army in 1942 and served until 1945, mostly at the rank of staff sergeant. Later in his life he supplemented his show business appearances in various ways: as a referee for boxing and wrestling matches; as public relations director for an automobile agency in Sacramento, California, where he lived; and even for a time as a disk jockey for a Sacramento radio station. He died of a heart attack in Los Angeles. In 1995 he was inducted into the International Boxing Hall of Fame.

• Baer's ring record is available in Herbert G. Goldman, ed., *The Ring 1986–87 Record Book and Boxing Encyclopedia*. His only biography is a 42-page booklet by Nat Fleischer, *Max Baer, the Glamour Boy of the Ring* (1941). Several articles in *The Ring* magazine provide information on Baer's ring career and early life, including Eddie Merrill, "Baer's Rapid Rise," July 1934, pp. 14–15, 45; Nat Loubet, "Max Adelbert Baer: the Magnificent One," Feb. 1960, pp. 38–39, 49, 58, 65; "Max Baer: Facts about Max, a Picture Story of Boxing's Merry Madcap," Sept. 1962, pp. 9–15; and John Dimambro, "Max Baer: The Clown Prince of Boxing," Sept. 1982, pp. 68–83. Baer's obituary appears in the *New York Times*, 22 Nov. 1959.

LUCKETT V. DAVIS

BAIRD, Bil (15 Aug. 1904–18 Mar. 1987), master puppeteer, the eldest son of William Hull Baird and Louise Hetzel Baird, was born William Britton Baird in Grand Island, Nebraska. His father, a chemical engineer, was manager of the American Crystal Sugar plant, the first beet sugar plant in the United States. His job required the family to move several times, but in 1915 they settled permanently in Mason City, Iowa. Baird's artistic talents were products of both heredity and environment. When Baird was seven, his father made a puppet for him and he was hooked. As a youth, his father had traveled with Buffalo Bill Cody's Wild West shows; he was also an amateur playwright. Baird's mother was active in community theater, and his younger brother, George, helped him stage puppet shows at home and later, in New York, constructed sets and managed his puppet shop. At the age of seventeen Baird saw Tony Sarg, America's premier puppeteer, perform in Mason City and knew immediately that puppetry was his personal calling. He built a puppet theater in the attic and converted an automobile dashboard into his light board.

Beyond puppeteering, Baird developed other artistic talents. His sketches and cartoons appeared in school publications, and he mastered a number of musical instruments, including accordion, banjo, flugelhorn, bagpipes, and marimba. While attending the University of Iowa, he was active in theater, both on and off stage, was art director for the campus humor magazine, and played with a dance band, staging puppet shows during intermissions. He graduated in 1926 with a double major in art and biology so that he could study anatomy, especially the movement of joints. The following year he attended the Chicago Academy of Fine Arts, where he studied stage design and cartooning. During this time he dropped the terminal *l* from his nickname. Some sources state that he did this in order to join a club whose members were required to have three-letter names, but during various interviews Baird's explanation was that he wanted to save time because no one ever pronounced the last *l*. Either story could be true or false, since Baird had a keen sense of humor and may have just wanted to enjoy a joke.

In 1927 he lived in Paris, studying and playing accordion in nightclubs and movie theaters. The following year he became an assistant to Tony Sarg in New York City, helping to build the huge balloons for Macy's annual Thanksgiving Day Parade. (He described these as upside-down marionettes, whose strings were worked from the bottom instead of the top.) Baird formed his own company in 1934, specializing in commercial trade shows. In a show he developed for Swift and Company at the Chicago World's Fair, his ballet-dancing cow, Brooksie, received thousands of fan letters. He then created puppet characters of the Seven Deadly Sins for Orson Welles's New York production of *The Tragedy of Dr. Faustus*. While working on this project Baird met Cora Eisenberg, an actress who used the stage name Cora Burlar. She was the voice of Sloth, Envy, and Gluttony. Baird recognized her potential as a puppeteer, and soon their association blossomed personally and professionally; they married on 13 January 1937. At least two newspaper sources list her as the third of Baird's four wives, but apparently there are no available records of previous marriages, and all other sources name her as the first of two.

During the 1940s the Bairds toured with their puppets for the Shell Oil Company, the puppets explaining humorously the importance of safety rules, and for furrier I. J. Fox, with the puppets in the roles of villainous moths. They also performed at the New York World's Fair, appeared in the Ziegfeld Follies, and sang with folksinger Burl Ives in one of Baird's movie shorts, which was based on a Scottish folk song. With the onset of World War II, the U.S. government asked the Bairds to produce educational films in which puppets demonstrated desirable dietary and agricultural practices.

Needing more space for living, working, and storing the puppets, the Bairds renovated a fire company coach house and named it "Fire House Manor." They lived here on the second floor, using the first floor as their workshop, until 1959. During this time they adopted two children, Peter and Laura.

The Baird puppets were also semiregulars on CBS's morning show and appeared on most of the popular variety shows. In 1951 they performed on Broadway in a play, *Flahooley*, that received mixed reviews, but the puppets received unqualified praise. Baird's next Broadway production was a full-length marionette musical, *Davy Jones' Locker* (1952). That same year he created a half-hour show, "The Whistling Wizard," for Saturday morning CBS television. Every segment began with Flannel Mouse, who read to Charlemane the Lion, emphasizing the joy of reading and regular visits to the library.

In the summers of 1964 and 1965 Baird spent two six-month seasons at the Chrysler Corporation's pavilion at the New York World's Fair. The puppets were featured in the "Lonely Goatherd" segment of the 1965 film version of *The Sound of Music*. Baird's book, *The Art of the Puppet*, was published in 1965. Many consider it to be the definitive text on puppetry; it includes a comprehensive array of pictures, philosophy, and history. In 1966, *Bil Baird: The World of Puppets*, two marionette ballets, broke attendance records for five months at Lincoln Center, and the puppets appeared on television simulations for six Gemini and four Apollo space flights. His first production for a theme park was *Once upon a Dragon*, which opened on 2 April 1977 at the Old Country Busch Gardens in Williamsburg, Virginia.

When Firehouse Manor was condemned to make way for the Lincoln Square Performing Arts Project in 1959, the Bairds bought a building in Greenwich Village. On 25 December 1966 they opened the 193-seat Bil Baird Theater as a permanent home for their puppet productions. The Outer Circle, an association of theater writers based in places other than New York City, honored the Bairds for establishing and maintaining the theater. A little less than a year after its opening, on 6 December 1967 Cora Baird died at the age of fifty-five. Several years later Bil Baird married Susanna Lloyd.

During their long career, the Baird's puppets appeared in a variety of venues, including five world's fairs, vaudeville, burlesque, night clubs, theater, television and movies, and a theme park. One memorable character was a stripper named Bubbles La Rue who, when asked to "take it off," obliged by removing her head. Another, Snarky Parker, starred in his own daily television show, "Life with Snarky Parker." Baird received many awards. In 1952 he and his wife, Cora, were listed for the first time in *Who's Who in America*. "Art Carney Meets Peter and the Wolf" brought Baird an Emmy nomination in 1958, and in 1974 he received the American Theater Association's Best Children's Theater award.

Baird believed his puppets were excellent educators. Throughout his career, his socially conscious puppets taught the dangers of air pollution, the need for family planning, the effects of cerebral palsy, and the importance of financial responsibility. He presented seminars in colleges and made puppets for an aerospace exhibit at the Smithsonian Institute in Washington, D.C.

In his 1957 television show for middle-school children, "Adventures in Numbers and Space," puppets taught mathematical concepts and history. In 1962, the U.S. government asked the Bairds to participate in a cultural exchange program with India. Baird created an Indian puppet to act as interpreter. The puppet spoke in all fifteen major Indian dialects. The following year, they went on a similar mission to the Soviet Union with a Russian puppet interpreter. In 1970 Baird returned to India for an international family planning conference, then attended a workshop in Izmir, Turkey, for the U.S. Agency for International Development, and in 1972 he traveled to England to appear at an International Planned Parenthood Foundation meeting.

Baird maintained ties to Mason City, Iowa, where his parents lived for many years. He, his wife, and their children were honored guests during the 1959 Mason City band festival. Mason City eventually became home to an extensive collection of Baird's puppets. In 1972 he gave the Kinney Pioneer Museum three puppets representing Edgar Allan Poe, Dickens, and Dostoyevsky. He donated many of his childhood toys to the Children's Room of the Mason City Public Library. In 1980 he began donating puppets, props, costumes, photographs, and posters to the MacNider Art Museum, where they are now on permanent rotating display.

Bil Baird died at the age of eighty-two in New York on 18 March 1987 of complications from bone cancer.

• More information about Baird can be found at the Mason City Public Library in *Mason City Sketches: The Bairds of Mason City*, compiled, edited, and written by Terry Harrison, Katrina Bowen, and Art Fischbeck, with assistance from Margaret Wellen and Bob Bowen. This three-ring binder contains a compilation of news articles, letters, writings, pictures, and other personal documents. *Bil Baird . . . He Pulled Lots of Strings* (1988), a monograph by Richard Leet, is kept at the Charles H. MacNider Museum in Mason City, Iowa. Bil Baird and Woman's Day Workshop, *Making and Staging Marionettes* (1951), is a booklet produced by the editors of *Woman's Day* magazine.

JEAN SANDERS

BALTZELL, E. Digby (14 Nov. 1915–17 Aug. 1996), sociologist and educator, was born Edward

in Chicago, and he rode for that stable until 1936, when he was hired by the famed Greentree Stable owned by Helen Hay Whitney.

Meanwhile, by May 1935 Arcaro was ready to enter his first Kentucky Derby, atop Nellie Flag. Though the horse finished fourth, Arcaro was determined to someday reach the winner's circle at Churchill Downs, the Derby site. That moment came three years later: riding the thoroughbred Lawrin, Arcaro won the 1938 Derby by a length to great acclaim. In seven years he had risen to the top of his profession, and he was only twenty-three years old.

There were other prizes to covet, however, chief among them racing's so-called Triple Crown—the Derby, followed at brief intervals by the Preakness, held at Pimlico in Baltimore, and the Belmont Stakes in New York. Arcaro's opportunity to make that sweep came in 1941 with a mount named Whirlaway, nicknamed "the little horse with steel springs," though at first he was a reluctant rider. Acknowledging later that he found it difficult to warm up to Whirlaway, Arcaro nevertheless brought his unique gifts of instinct and intuition to his handling of the horse, and it responded, winning the Derby in the then-record-breaking time of two minutes, one and two-fifths seconds. Victories at the Preakness and Belmont followed in quick succession, earning Arcaro his first Triple Crown. That same year Whirlaway was named Horse of the Year, an honor that would be bestowed on Arcaro's mounts seven more times in the course of his career.

Even more honors were to come for Arcaro himself. He won the Kentucky Derby three more times: in 1945 on Hoop Jr.; on Citation in 1948; and on Hill Gail in 1952. He also won the Preakness and the Belmont Stakes a total of six times each. But his greatest honor came in 1948 when he won a record-breaking second Triple Crown with Citation. He remains the only jockey to win more than one Triple Crown, and his record of seventeen Triple Crown event wins has not been surpassed.

One of Arcaro's most famous races occurred in the summer of 1955, nine years after he had become a freelance rider. The two celebrity horses of that year were Swaps, ridden by Arcaro, and Nashua, the mount of another celebrated jockey, Willie Shoemaker. Shoemaker on Nashua had narrowly defeated Arcaro at the Derby, but Arcaro and Swaps had gone on to win the Preakness and Belmont. In a special match race at Washington Park that drew the rich and famous from around the world, Arcaro rode Swaps to a third victory—just as he had proclaimed he would prior to the race.

Street-smart and sometimes pugnacious, Arcaro had a colorful personality to complement his jockey silks, and occasionally it got him into trouble—most notably in 1942, when he was suspended for a year from racing after crowding a Cuban jockey at Aqueduct in New York. He might have avoided the penalty had he simply acknowledged to investigators following the race that he had perhaps been a bit out of line.

But when he was asked what he'd been up to, the piqued Arcaro—perhaps unaware that a tape recorder was at hand—screamed, "I was trying to kill the S.O.B.!" He spent the year at a horse farm in South Carolina and later acknowledged that the break had been productive, allowing him "time to think and take stock of myself."

Arcaro needed a certain amount of bravado to carry him through the upsets, literal and figurative, that are standard for jockeys. His most serious spill occurred at the 1959 Belmont Stakes, when his horse went down in the final turn. The throw landed him unconscious and facedown in a six-inch puddle, and he narrowly escaped drowning. After several weeks of recuperation from head, neck, and back injuries, he was ready to return to racing, but the years were taking their toll. Though still a relatively young man—he was only forty-three—he was getting too old to be a jockey. By this time he had already received racing's highest accolades, including election in 1955 to the Jockeys' Hall of Fame—one of the first three jockeys to be named—and induction into the Racing Hall of Fame at Saratoga Springs, New York, three years later. In November 1961 he rode for the last time, but he remained active in the sport for several decades as an occasional commentator for ABC. Though Arcaro's final three years as a jockey produced no more Triple Crown racing victories, he had the distinction of seeing two of his mounts named Horse of the Year during this time: Sword Dancer in 1959, and Kelso in 1960 and 1961. Kelso, he later said, was the best horse he ever rode.

An intense but graceful figure in the saddle, Arcaro was known for being a "smart" dresser off the track—he owned numerous pairs of shoes and custom-tailored suits. He was also an astute businessman, investing his purses in oil wells, drive-in restaurants, and a wholesale saddlery and making himself a multimillionaire in the process. He also cofounded, with fellow jockeys Sam Renick and Johnny Longden, the Jockeys' Guild in the 1940s and served as president of the guild from 1949 until his retirement twelve years later. Under his direction the guild began providing jockeys with life and health insurance as well as old-age pensions.

Arcaro and his wife, Ruth (maiden name unknown), a former model whom he married in 1937, had two children. They lived for many years in Garden City, Long Island, not far from Belmont. After his retirement he began spending more time at the couple's home in Miami, Florida, where he could frequent racetracks and play golf, his longtime hobby, year-round. His friends and frequent golfing partners included not only prominent racing figures but also baseball Hall-of-Famer Joe DiMaggio. Arcaro suffered from liver cancer in the final months of his life. He died at his Miami home.

Arcaro rode in 24,921 races and won 4,779 of them, winning some $30 million along the way. Although he often said he always rode to win, a sentiment echoed in the title of a 1951 memoir, he was not

was in poor health at the time of her death: she had a history of painful seizures; she was suffering from chronic cystitis and syphilis; and she had undergone at least five illegal abortions. They maintained that her bladder had ruptured spontaneously. When Arbuckle took the stand, he offered his own version of events at the party. He claimed that he had gone into his bedroom to change clothes and had found an inebriated Rappe on his bathroom floor. After carrying her to his bed, he proceeded to change clothes in his bathroom; when he came out, he found that she had torn off her dress and was clutching her stomach, moaning that she was sick. But because he assumed that she was merely drunk, he initially made light of the situation. Arbuckle's first trial ended in a hung jury, with ten of the twelve jurors voting for acquittal. A second trial in January 1922 again ended in a hung jury, with nine jurors voting for conviction. At a third trial in March and April 1922, the comedian was acquitted and the jurors released a statement: "Acquittal is not enough for Roscoe Arbuckle. We feel that a great injustice has been done him. . . . Under the evidence . . . there was not the slightest proof adduced to connect him in any way with the commission of a crime" (quoted in Yallop, p. 253). One week after Arbuckle's acquittal, Will Hays, the U.S. postmaster general who was appointed by Hollywood moguls to clean up the image of the industry, banned his films throughout the United States.

Following his trials, Arbuckle suffered through bouts of heavy drinking and depression. He also experienced financial difficulties: he had incurred over $1,000,000 in debt, including approximately $750,000 in legal fees. In 1923 Hays lifted the ban against his films, which led to a public outcry: the New York Times complained that "an odor still clings to him"; the St. Paul Pioneer Press warned that bringing him back to the screen would "jeopardize the morals and mental integrity of millions of impressionable young persons." Between 1923 and 1927, working under the pseudonym William Goodrich, he directed several films for Educational Pictures and Metro-Goldwyn-Mayer. In 1924 Buster Keaton hired him to direct his comedy Sherlock Jr.; but Arbuckle proved to be impatient and ill-tempered on the set, and he was fired early during the production. In 1925 he married Doris Deane, an actress; they had no children and divorced in 1928. During the late 1920s, he successfully operated a nightclub in Culver City, California. In 1932 he married Addie McPhail, an actress; they had no children. That year he finally returned to the screen under his own name, starring in six two-reel comedies for Vitaphone. In the midst of this comeback, he died of a heart attack in New York City.

• In 1995 the U.S. Library of Congress named Fatty's Tintype Tangle (1915) to the National Film Registry of "culturally, historically, or aesthetically important" films; prints and shooting scripts for this picture and other Arbuckle titles can be found at the Library of Congress, the American Film Institute, and the Academy of Motion Picture Arts and Sciences. The best biography of Arbuckle is David Yallop, The Day the Laughter Stopped (1976), which includes a careful analysis of the transcripts from the court proceedings against the comedian. Other biographies are Andy Edmonds, Frame-Up!: The Untold Story of Roscoe "Fatty" Arbuckle (1991), and Stuart Oderman, Roscoe "Fatty" Arbuckle: A Biography of the Silent Film Comedian, 1887–1933 (1994). For Arbuckle's films with Mabel Normand, see Betty Harper Fussell, Mabel (1982). For his relationship with Buster Keaton, see Rudi Blesh's excellent biography, Keaton (1966). For the cultural significance of the Arbuckle scandal and trials, see Robert Sklar, Movie-Made America: A Cultural History of American Movies (1975; rev. ed., 1994). Kenneth Anger, Hollywood Babylon (1965), delights in the lasciviousness of the scandal. For views of Arbuckle by his contemporaries, see Buster Keaton, My Wonderful World of Slapstick (1960); Mack Sennett, King of Comedy (1954); and Adela Rogers St. Johns, Love, Laughter and Tears: My Hollywood Story (1978).

THOMAS W. COLLINS, JR.

ARCARO, Eddie (19 Feb. 1916–14 Nov. 1997), jockey, was born George Edward Arcaro in Cincinnati, Ohio, the son of Pasquale Arcaro and Josephine Giancola Arcaro. (It is not known what his parents did for a living.) At birth he weighed barely three pounds, and though he was not a sickly child he remained small in stature throughout his life, growing to an adult height of only five feet two inches and weighing a maximum 114 pounds. From an early age he loved all sports, especially baseball, but because of his size he was never chosen to play on school teams. To make matters worse, a devastating sledding accident when he was twelve, following a move by the family to Southgate, Kentucky, almost cost him the use of his right leg, but the spunky youth began walking on his own even before the doctors allowed him to.

Still determined to be an athlete, yet realizing by adolescence that he was always going to be small, the teenage Arcaro focused on a career as a jockey and discovered that here at last was a field that welcomed him. He loved horses and began riding at area tracks, and he proved to be a natural in the saddle. In May 1931, at the age of sixteen, he competed in his first race, at Bainbridge near Cleveland. He did not win, but that loss—and forty-four more that followed over the next nine months—did not deter him. Less than a year later, in January 1932, he rode his first winner at Agua Caliente, in Mexico, launching him on a thirty-year career that would see him ultimately hailed as "the king of jockeys."

But there were to be a few pitfalls along the way: the occupational hazard of jockeys is spills, and Arcaro had his share. His first serious throw occurred in 1933 at Washington Park, a major track south of Chicago: unconscious for three days with a fractured skull, a broken nose, and a punctured lung, he remained hospitalized for three months. But by 1934 he was riding again, thanks to the tutelage of trainer Clarence Davison, who had signed him to a contract after his first win at Agua Caliente and given him valuable pointers on handling his mounts. That year his contract was bought by Warren Wright at Calumet Farms

Digby Baltzell on Rittenhouse Street in Philadelphia, the son of Edward Digby Baltzell and Caroline Adelaide Duhring Baltzell. Baltzell's Protestant patrician family, though it had become in his words "impecuniously genteel," was nonetheless able to send him to Chestnut Hill Academy, a private day school, and later to St. Paul's, a select boarding school in New Hampshire. During Baltzell's senior year, his father, an alcoholic, lost his job because of drinking, and the subsequent strain on family finances kept him from going away to college. Instead, he attended the University of Pennsylvania, starting out in the School of Architecture, but financial difficulties forced him to drop out of school after his freshman year. Later, with a loan from a friend, Baltzell resumed his studies at Penn. But he forsook his dream of becoming an architect and enrolled in the Wharton School, where be majored in insurance. A series of odd jobs, including parking lot attendant and chauffeur, enabled him to meet his expenses. He graduated in 1939 and went to work with an insurance company as an underwriter and then at a pharmaceutical company, Smith, Kline, and French Laboratories, where he helped to conduct attitude surveys.

In 1942, after the United States entered World War II, Baltzell abandoned his business career and joined the Navy. He became a pilot and served in the Pacific. Removed from his Main Line family and friends, and exposed to men from different social backgrounds and experiences, he came to question some of his upper-class prejudices. "You couldn't share the hardships, the dangers and boredom with people of all races and backgrounds," he explained once, "and then turn around and exclude them from opportunities to which they were entitled" (*Philadelphia Inquirer*, 19 Aug. 1996). While in the service, Baltzell also began to read extensively, particularly in the field of sociology.

Baltzell had married Jane Piper after his flight training in 1943, and after his discharge from the Navy in 1945 he decided he wanted to write and teach. Taking advantage of the GI Bill's educational benefits, he enrolled in the doctoral program in the sociology department at Columbia University. At the time, the department possessed a broadly talented faculty. Among its members who had an impact on Baltzell's thinking were Robert Lynd, whose research focused on presenting a wide-ranging factual portrait of life in a Midwestern city, and W. Lloyd Warner, whose "Yankee City" series stressed subjective factors in measuring status and class position in a Massachusetts community. Baltzell was also deeply impressed by Robert K. Merton, about whom he once wrote: "I learned everything from Bob Merton." Finally, the classic works of Max Weber and Alexis de Tocqueville were significant in the formation of Baltzell's ideas about social class.

Baltzell left Columbia in 1947 (though he did not receive his doctorate until 1952) and returned to the University of Pennsylvania as an instructor in the sociology department. Possessed of a sharp wit and an equally sharp tongue, he was a popular teacher who relished contact with students. During his tenure at Penn, Baltzell was a Danforth fellow for religion in higher education at Princeton Theological Seminary (1967–1968), a Charles Warren research fellow at Harvard University (1972–1973), and a Guggenheim fellow (1978–1979). After officially retiring as a full professor in 1986, he continued to teach one course each academic year.

Baltzell's first book, *Philadelphia Gentlemen: The Making of a National Upper Class* (1958), dealt with a subject that in one way or another was the consuming focus of all his research. Because his family occupied a position at the margin of the Philadelphia aristocracy, he had an uncommon perspective on the American patriciate. *Philadelphia Gentlemen*, which developed out of his doctoral dissertation, is an examination of the city's upper class from its colonial origins to 1940. The jargon-free narrative is ingeniously supported by the use of the *Social Register* and *Who's Who in America* (1940) to gauge the degree of overlap between, respectively, Philadelphia's old-line families and the city's emerging elite. Baltzell concluded that the proper Philadelphia families had successfully incorporated the newly rich men of power and wealth to form by1940 a stable Protestant business aristocracy. Baltzell closed his book, however, with a question: "What is the future function of a predominantly Anglo-Saxon and Protestant upper class in an ethnically and religiously heterogeneous democracy?"

In his best-known book, *The Protestant Establishment: Aristocracy and Caste in America* (1964), Baltzell left little doubt about his answer to that question. He declared that the WASPs (a term he is credited with coining) had excluded from their ranks the ascending elite of Jews and other minority groups. By cutting themselves off from the rest of American society, so Baltzell contended in his Tocquevillean analysis, the WASPs had ceased to be a true aristocracy and had instead become a caste. Moreover, the decline of the WASPs had created a "paralysis of leadership in modern America." Indeed, in Baltzell's frankly elitist view, no democracy could survive without a stable core of old-line families to provide leadership and to act as a shield against political demagoguery.

In his most ambitious study, *Puritan Boston and Quaker Philadelphia* (1979), a detailed and elegantly written volume that won the Sorokin Award of the American Sociological Association, Baltzell posed the question of why the Boston Brahmins made so many more contributions to American politics, letters, and business than the Philadelphia upper class. He found the explanation in the differing religious traditions of the two cities: the hierarchical ethic of the Puritans encouraged leadership and the assumption of responsibility, while Quakerism fostered an anti-institutional and equalitarian ethic that prized private profit over public commitment. In short, where Philadelphians valued *noblesse*, Bostonians placed greater stress on *oblige*. Needless to say, Baltzell favored the Puritan value system over that of the Quakers.

Baltzell's last book, *Sporting Gentlemen* (1995), followed the history of competitive tennis from the age when it was an upper-class amateur's game to the modern era in which it had become a professional, money-dominated, and, at times, rowdy enterprise. Clearly, Baltzell intended tennis to serve as a metaphor for the decline of the American upper class and its mores.

One might well question Baltzell's insistence that a stable democracy requires a hierarchical social order and upper-class leadership. As Nicholas Lemann has perceptively observed, "Like Henry Adams at the beginning of this century, Baltzell at the end of it is so distressed by the loss of power of the traditional leadership class that he can't see the current situation as being anything but chaotic" (*Washington Monthly*, Jan.–Feb. 1992, "Ruling by Degree: Why the New Meritocracy Is Bad for America," p. 43). Regardless of his social philosophy, though, in tracing the rise and decline of the WASP establishment Baltzell made a lasting contribution to the sociological literature on the American upper class.

Baltzell's first wife, with whom he had two children, died in 1991. He married Jocelyn Carlson in 1993. He died in Boston three years later.

• Howard G. Schneiderman's introductory essay in *The Protestant Establishment Revisited* (1991) is by far the best sketch of Baltzell's life and work. Several of Baltzell's essays in this collection contain autobiographical material. Two worthwhile articles on Baltzell's career and ideas are Don Rottenberg, "E. Digby Baltzell, In Defense of the WASP," *Town and Country*, June 1992, pp. 39–41, and Art Carey, "A Look Back at a Gentleman," *Philadelphia Inquirer*, 5 Jan. 1997. Irving Louis Horowitz has an appreciative assessment in "Losing Giants," *Society*, Apr. 1997, pp. 56–63. An obituary is in the *Philadelphia Inquirer*, 19 Aug. 1996.

RICHARD HARMOND

BANNING, Phineas (19 Aug. 1830–8 Mar. 1885), southern California pioneer, was born at Oak Farm near Wilmington, Delaware, the ninth of the eleven children of John Alford Banning, a Princeton graduate, shipbuilder, and farmer, and his wife, Elizabeth Lower Banning. Phineas is said to have left school at thirteen and walked from Wilmington to Philadelphia, where he worked at first in the law office of one of his brothers and later in the wholesale trade.

In 1851 Banning was accompanying his employer, a merchant, on a trip to Mexico when he was stranded in San Diego, California, the merchant having been arrested for debt and the ship seized. Banning traveled to San Pedro, a seaside town near Los Angeles, itself a small town in a new state, and quickly formed a partnership with David Alexander. Banning and Alexander became the region's first major wagon-train haulers. In subsequent years Banning had many junior partners in many businesses.

Within two years Banning and Alexander had warehouses, fifteen wagons, and seventy-five mules and had established a stagecoach line between San Pedro and Los Angeles. Banning built his own carriages along the lines of the Concord carriage, the era's outstanding design. As early as 1854 there were rumors of San Pedro becoming a designated U.S. port of entry, and Banning moved to exploit the possibility. During the early 1850s he built in San Pedro a wharf on a rock jetty–sheltered harbor whose channel was deep enough to float barges and steam tugs. On disputed land (litigation between 1880 and 1917 was eventually settled in the Banning family's favor) Banning dug the deepest well in Los Angeles county. In 1857 alone he shipped 21,000 crates of wine grapes (forty-five pounds per crate) to San Francisco.

In 1854 Banning married Rebecca Sanford, having first tried to kill the man who had killed her brother. The couple had eight children, of whom only three survived infancy, and remained married until Mrs. Banning's death. In 1857, seeking to monopolize the area, Banning and a group of associates led by Los Angeles County landowner Benjamin "Don Benito" Wilson purchased from the old-line Dominguez family 2,400 acres of the nearby Rancho San Pedro. Here Banning laid out New San Pedro, a town that in 1858 he named Wilmington, after his birthplace. He gave away lots in the new town to his friends, built a new wharf, and had a steamer and "lighters" built in San Francisco in order to carry passengers and baggage from large steamships offshore to his new beach resort. Soon he was running three packets between San Pedro, San Francisco, and San Diego every ten days.

Banning's inland ventures also expanded. In 1858 Banning himself drove a seventeen-mule team 230 miles from San Pedro to Fort Yuma, Arizona, in twelve to thirteen days in order to bring poles for a new telegraph line between Los Angeles and San Pedro for which he became subcontractor. By that year his Wilmington Transportation Company was running stages and freight wagons to Los Angeles and San Bernardino, as well as northward to mining camps in the farthest reaches of the Mojave Desert and points as far east as Santa Fe, New Mexico, and as far inland as Salt Lake City, Utah. Banning's first apparent contact with Santa Catalina Island, twenty-six miles offshore from his ports, was in 1859. His descendants eventually purchased the island and developed it as a transportation port and resort until 1919, when they sold it to William Wrigley, Jr.

Banning, memorably described by one of his contemporaries at first sight in the early 1850s as a "large, powerful man, coatless and vestless, without necktie or collar, pantaloons at least 6 inches too short, brogans and socks with large holes, bright colored suspenders," earned the title "Transportation King." From time to time he dealt in meatpacking, lumbering, and whatever paid. He had already established a reputation for throwing the best parties in provincial Los Angeles, replete with barbecues and sparkling beverages.

The Civil War provided Banning, a Republican and abolitionist, with further opportunities, and he responded in typical "go-ahead" fashion. He became the commander of the first division of the California militia. (After the war he was one of the Rangers who were unofficial dispensers of rough justice.) Banning persuaded General Winfield Hancock to recommend the purchase of two acres from Banning and Wilson, on which were established the Union army's western regional headquarters. This siting of Camp Drum and Drum Barracks further bolstered Wilmington's future claim as the new port for Los Angeles. Banning secured the right to carry government supplies to soldiers inland, and soon soldiers were helping guard Banning's wagon trains to the mining camps in the Owens River Valley. A brief setback to Banning's rise came when one of his boats exploded in 1863, killing twenty-six on board, wounding his wife, and tossing Banning twenty feet into the air.

As early as 1863, when friends in the legislature told him that eastern capitalists were talking of a railroad between San Pedro and Los Angeles, Banning talked the state legislature into giving him the franchise and authorizing a bond issue to underwrite the project; but the railroad could not advance until local voters voted more funds. In 1865 Banning assumed the presidency of the new Pioneer Oil Company, a speculative venture that he eventually abandoned. Also in 1865 he divested himself of some business interests and became a state senator; throughout his two-year term he pushed the railroad project. In 1868 his wife, Rebecca, died, and in 1870 Banning married Mary Hollister. They had three children, two of whom survived infancy, and they remained married until Banning's death.

Banning's struggle for the San Pedro–Los Angeles railroad was primarily against the area's large ranchers, who feared the road's impact on their horse-centered life. A longtime rival of Banning's in the haulage business led the opposition, but he died two weeks before the pivotal 1868 referendum for $125,000 in city and county bonds to supplement the state's funding. It was said that Banning's stages were very active in transporting voters to the polls. The bonds passed by 700 to 672. The railroad, the first in southern California, was completed in 1869, and by 1874 sixty freight cars daily were traveling between Wilmington and Los Angeles.

By this time, Banning, always referred to as "General," was lobbying Washington on behalf of his harbor, and in 1871 the U.S. government agreed to deepen and otherwise improve the harbor of Wilmington–San Pedro. Although Banning did not get as much money for a new breakwater and lighthouse as he had hoped, the project went ahead and San Pedro's lighthouse opened in 1874. Several years of controversial contact between Banning and the "octopus"—the Southern Pacific Railroad—culminated in 1876, when, with the blessing of Governor Leland Stanford, the Southern Pacific took over the Wilmington–Los Angeles line. Banning became a Southern Pacific official and in that year served as chairman of the Los Angeles Centennial Committee.

Thereafter, Banning spent an increasing amount of time at the two-story Delaware-style colonial mansion he had created in Wilmington in 1864. During his years there it was estimated he had spent $250,000 on his fabled dinner parties, or "Regales." After some months of illness that began in 1884, Banning died in San Francisco and was buried in Wilmington. In time a Los Angeles street, a town in the southern California desert foothills, and a high school in Wilmington were named after him. Banning's descendants continued to wield influence in Los Angeles, founding civic enterprises including a children's hospital. In 1930 William and George Banning coauthored a book about stagecoaching called *Six Horses*.

Kevin Starr, the authoritative historian of California, has summed up Banning: "[T]eamster, harbor master, contractor, banker, speculator in oil and land—[he] perhaps best embodies [the] first phase of economic entrepreneurship in Southern California, with its diversity and optimism, its unambiguous satisfaction in fulfilling obvious . . . needs."

• The papers of the Banning Company (1859–1948) are held in the Huntington Library, San Marino, Calif. Marco R. Newmark, "Phineas Banning: Intrepid Pioneer," *Huntington Quarterly* 35, pp. 265–74, is a clear statement of historical fact. An irreplaceable firsthand account of the era that spawned Banning is *Sixty Years in Southern California 1853–1913: Containing the Reminiscences of Harris Newmark*, ed. Maurice H. and Marco R. Newmark (1970). A useful smaller publication by the Security Trust and Savings Bank, Los Angeles, is Laurance L. Hill, *La Reina: Los Angeles, in Three Centuries* (4th ed., 1931). Banning's Wilmington legacy is dealt with by Walter E. Holstein in an unpublished typed pamphlet, "A History of Wilmington from the Spanish Period to 1931" (in the collection of the Banning Museum, Wilmington, California). Most general histories of California—beginning with Hubert Howe Bancroft's—deal with Banning, but the most extensive and entertaining treatment is given by Kevin Starr in *Inventing the Dream: California Through the Progressive Era* (1985).

JAMES ROSS MOORE

BARNES, Binnie (25 Mar. 1903–27 July 1998), film star, was born Gertrude Maud Barnes in North London, England, the daughter of William Barnes, a police constable, and Rose Sarah Noyes Barnes. Educated locally, she worked as a milkmaid, an asylum nurse, a chorus girl, a dance hostess, and (as "Texas Binnie" Barnes) the cabaret partner of a Will Rogers-style American comic before making her West End debut (as "Billie" Barnes) singing a languid torch song in André Charlot's 1928 revue. In 1931, after costarring in *Little Tommy Tucker*, a musical comedy about radio, Barnes gained further recognition opposite John Mills in *Cavalcade*, Noël Coward's musical love letter to the first thirty years of the century.

There followed a series of short films in which Barnes scrapped verbally with the comic Stanley Lupino. These caught the attention of director Alexander Korda, who cast her opposite Charles Laughton as the monarch's saucy fifth wife, Catherine Howard, in *The Private Life of Henry VIII* (1933). Korda's film brought her to the attention of Carl Laemmle, Jr., Universal Pictures' executive producer, and after another West End musical Barnes came to Hollywood in 1934.

Although her first American assignment, *There's Always Tomorrow*, was a contemporary tale, Korda's films and the 1934 *Private Life of Don Juan* (Douglas Fairbanks's last full-length effort) had associated Barnes with historical drama. For the rest of the golden age of American movies, Barnes's roles usually contributed to Hollywood's efforts to portray the history of the world. In *Diamond Jim* (1935), she played the queen of the American Gay Nineties musical stage, Lillian Russell, with Edward Arnold in the title role. The following year, again opposite Arnold, she portrayed a predatory Russian countess in *Sutter's Gold*, a tale of mid-nineteenth-century California. Barnes retreated to the eighteenth century as the fair Alice Monro in a 1936 adaptation of James Fenimore Cooper's *The Last of the Mohicans*.

Shortly thereafter Barnes became an early member of the Screen Actors Guild. She later told an interviewer, "In the scene [from *The Last of the Mohicans*] where we are crossing the river, I had high rubber boots on and there were snakes in the water. I was frightened and I didn't have a stunt woman. That was before the Guild had a contract. We did most of it ourselves. Back then I worked all hours of the day and night. Actors today, gosh, they have a good life, just look at what SAG has accomplished for us" (quoted at http://www.sag.com/fundmembers.html).

The Guild was recognized by Hollywood studios in 1937, but contract players were still worked hard. In 1938 alone, Barnes—eventually credited with fifty American films—made seven, including a trip to the thirteenth century in *The Adventures of Marco Polo* and forward to the seventeenth as Milady De Winter in a strange version of Dumas's *The Three Musketeers*, which was centered on the anarchic Ritz Brothers. One of her most notable historical efforts was one of her last—*The Spanish Main* (1945)—as the swashbuckling female filibuster Anne Bonney, a rival to Francisca, the role of the film's costar, Maureen O'Hara. Barnes commented later, "I trained for several months with a sword master. I could have beaten Errol Flynn. It was one of my best received performances" (quoted in Bergan).

Aside from strong historical women, Barnes frequently played the leading lady's witty but unprincipled rival. Thus in *Small Town Girl* (1936) she was a society woman luring the leading man, played by Robert Taylor, down the garden path; in *Three Smart Girls* (1937), an all-purpose gold digger; and in *Wife, Husband and Friend* (1939), the obvious role. The cool, blonde Barnes displayed unflagging glamour, recalling in 1990, "We were in the business of selling glamour. We went to parties in gowns the studios gave us. Look at TV series and films today which masquerade as glamour, and see how much they have fallen into tawdriness and cheapness" (quoted in Bergan).

In 1940, the year of a brief reprise of her past in British musical theater in André Charlot's *British War*

Relief Revue, Barnes, known as a "tart-tongued man's woman," married Mike Frankovich, a fledgling writer of screenplays whom she had met while playing poker "with the boys" at Clark Gable's house. She converted from Judaism to Catholicism. They had three children and remained married until Frankovich's death in 1992. During World War II Barnes's screen roles gradually altered; in 1943 she was reunited with Laughton in *The Man from Down Under*, playing what one writer called a "gorblimey Marjorie Main" character. She was briefly a regular panelist on a network radio show, "Leave It to the Girls," along with such stars as Constance Bennett and Lucille Ball, who reacted to a romantic topic suggested by a listener and then were countered by a guest male star putting forward the masculine argument.

Besides *The Spanish Main*, the last films in this part of Barnes's life were a "haunted house" comedy with Abbott and Costello called *The Time of Their Lives* (1946) and a tearjerker set in Britain, *If Winter Comes* (1947), with Walter Pidgeon, Angela Lansbury, and Deborah Kerr. Barnes left Hollywood when Frankovich became head of Columbia Pictures' international operations. They lived first in Italy and later in London, where Barnes appeared in *Shadow of the Eagle* (1950) and the Frankovich-produced *Decameron Nights* (1953), injecting into the latter, so wrote Ronald Bergan, "a modicum of sex." After appearing in *Malaga* (1954), she announced her retirement from the screen.

When Frankovich returned to Hollywood in 1963 as Columbia's executive producer, however, Barnes made a somewhat tongue-in-cheek comeback, playing a nun in both *The Trouble with Angels* (1966) and *Where Angels Go . . . Trouble Follows* (1968). Thereafter Barnes generally devoted herself to charitable work in Hollywood, though the film comedy *40 Carats* (1973) afforded her a brief dance with Gene Kelly. Barnes died in her Beverly Hills home.

• Among cinema reference works, *The American Film Institute Catalog of Feature Films: 1931–1940* (1993) and *The Complete Index to British Sound Film Since 1928* (1999) are authoritative. George MacDonald Fraser, *The Hollywood History of the World: From "One Million Years B.C." to "Apocalypse Now"* (1988), gives lively insight into Barnes's major roles. Obituaries of Binnie Barnes include Kathryn Shattuck's in the *New York Times*, 30 July 1998, and Ronald Bergan's in the (London) *Guardian*, 30 July 1998.

JAMES ROSS MOORE

BASQUIAT, Jean-Michel (22 Dec. 1960–12 Aug. 1988), painter, was born in Brooklyn, New York, the son of Gerard Basquiat, an accountant originally of Haiti, and Matilde Andradas Basquiat, of Puerto Rican descent. A precocious draftsman from childhood, Basquiat received little formal artistic training. The last school he attended was the experimental City-as-School program in Manhattan, where he befriended fellow artist Al Diaz.

Before quitting school altogether in 1978, Basquiat created SAMO (meaning "same old shit"), which was variously a pseudo-religion, a fictional logo, a nom de plume, and a persona. Basquiat and Diaz spray-painted original aphorisms with a copyright symbol next to the word SAMO on walls and in alleys in lower Manhattan. Their mock epigrams and mottoes included "SAMO as an end to mindwash religion, nowhere politics, and bogus philosophy," "SAMO saves idiots," and "plush safe he think, SAMO." Whereas other graffiti artists such as Fab 5 Freddy, Futura 2000, and Rammellzee painted multicolored and elaborately designed "tags" on subway cars and alleyways, Diaz and Basquiat focused on their concepts and text-based work rather than aesthetics. In the 11 December 1978 issue of the *Village Voice*, Basquiat and Diaz identified themselves as SAMO; soon thereafter, they parted ways.

Aside from his SAMO work, Basquiat drew and painted his own art on any available surface he could find, including refrigerator doors; he also made postcards and t-shirts, which he sold on the street. Using oil and acrylic paints, oil paint sticks, and collage materials, he blended roughly drawn visual elements and text. When asked about his subject matter, Basquiat responded that he painted "royalty, heroism, and the streets." Black male figures, skulls, crowns, and hobo symbols proliferated in his paintings. He sometimes included references to his personal heroes, such as musician Charlie Parker and boxer Joe Louis, as well as art-historical references such as Leonardo da Vinci's sketchbooks. Basquiat used words not as expanded captions but as crucial components in the composition and meaning of the work, sometimes repeating words or crossing them out, as in *Horn Players* (1983, Eli and Edythe L. Broad Collection, Los Angeles). In this painting, the artist painted Charlie Parker's name and the word "ornithology" (referring to the musician's nickname "the Bird") several times on the canvas, overlaid with more paint and next to his painted images of the musician. Basquiat once said, "I cross out words so that you will see them more; the fact that they are obscured makes you want to read them."

In 1980 Basquiat painted a large mural for his first group exhibition, the Times Square Show. Organized by Colab (Collaborative Projects Incorporated), the exhibition featured several artists early in their careers, including Jenny Holzer, Kenny Scharf, and Kiki Smith. The following year Basquiat took part in numerous exhibitions in New York, such as New York/New Wave at P.S. 1, along with artists Robert Mapplethorpe and Andy Warhol, and Beyond Words: Graffiti Based-Rooted-Inspired Works at the Mudd Club. The Galleria d'Arte Emilio Mazzoli in Modena, Italy, held Basquiat's first one-man exhibition in the spring of 1981.

In 1980 New York art dealer Annina Nosei began selling Basquiat's work and offered him her gallery basement to use as his studio. Despite this unusual arrangement (Nosei was criticized for having Basquiat "on exhibit"), she exposed Basquiat's art to several important collectors and gave him his first U.S. one-man exhibition in 1982. Although Basquiat changed dealers often in his short career, he maintained steady relationships with Los Angeles dealer Larry Gagosian and Bruno Bischofberger, who was based in Switzerland and was the artist's international representative.

Basquiat was the youngest artist in the prestigious Documenta 7 exhibition in Kassel, Germany (1982), and in the 1983 Biennial Exhibition at the Whitney Museum of American Art. The Museum of Modern Art included him in their International Survey of Recent Painting and Sculpture at MOMA (1983).

He continued to gain recognition when, in 1983, he became a close friend of Andy Warhol, who was also represented by Bischofberger. At the suggestion of the dealer, the two artists collaborated on several paintings in 1985. Warhol painted or silk-screened corporate logos such as those of GE and Arm & Hammer along with other images including Felix the Cat. Basquiat painted over and around Warhol's work with his repertoire of motifs and words. Their paintings, exhibited in New York at the Tony Shafrazi Gallery that same year, received mixed reviews. One *New York Times* critic wrote that Basquiat was an art world mascot and that Warhol used him to regain his own popularity. Warhol and Basquiat ended their friendship following the exhibition.

An article on Basquiat written by Cathleen McGuigan for the *New York Times Magazine* (10 Feb. 1985) exposed him to a popular audience but also posed questions about the consequences of an inflated art market for such a young career. Some critics claimed that Basquiat became more interested in making art that would satisfy his collectors than in creating innovative work. But many of his last works featured new developments, such as very dense accumulations of words and images, as in *Untitled (Stretch)* (1985, estate of the artist), or starkly powerful compositions, as exemplified by *Riding with Death* (1988, private collection), which shows a dark human skeleton riding a white skeleton of a horse.

Basquiat died of a drug overdose in New York at the age of twenty-seven. His death at such an early age commanded reflection in the art world, an environment where artistic ideals had been replaced by greed and the pursuit of fame due to a period of auspicious wealth and soaring art prices. Basquiat, who never hid his career aspirations, was hailed as the first African-American art star. Bearing the burden of this title, he was sometimes viewed as an exotic novelty or as a traitor to his race in the predominately white art world. But Basquiat refused to be labeled. He said, "I don't know if my being black has anything to do with my success. I don't think I should be compared to black artists but all artists."

Although not an organized movement, Basquiat and other painters grouped as "neo-expressionists"—including Julian Schnabel, Georg Baselitz, and Susan Rothenberg—returned a sense of bravura and improvisation to painting that harked back to the abstract expressionists. Influenced by pop art, Basquiat's wordplay and use of signs and symbols aligned him with other postmodern artists, particularly those like Robert Longo who combined specific and sometimes edited images inspired by the mass media to convey meaning. Basquiat also maintained a very personal vision in his work, painting his heroes (boxers and jazz musicians), his artistic influences (da Vinci and Warhol), and episodes from his own life (drug use and racism) in his idiosyncratic style. His poetic means of combining text with imagery and social issues with personal experiences resonates in the work of several contemporary artists such as Glen Ligon and Lorna Simpson.

• Phoebe Hoban's biography *Basquiat: A Quick Killing in Art* (1998) provides much information on the artist's personal life and his relationships with friends, lovers, dealers, and other artists. For critical essays and images of his work, see the catalog from the Whitney Museum of American Art's traveling retrospective *Jean-Michel Basquiat* (1992). Additional publications include *Basquiat* (1999), which offers previously published as well as new essays by Francesco Clemente, Keith Haring, and Bruno Bischofberger; the new catalogue raisonné *Jean-Michel Basquiat: Works on Paper* (1999); and *Jean-Michel Basquiat: Works on Paper* (1997), a catalogue from an exhibition at the Fondation Dina Vierny-Musée Maillol, Paris. Rene Ricard, "The Radiant Child," *Artforum*, Dec.1981, pp. 35–43, helped establish Basquiat's early fame in the art world. Obituaries are in the *New York Times*, 15 Aug. 1988, and *Art in America*, Oct. 1988. Posthumous evaluations of Basquiat's art and tragic death include Michael Wines, "Jean-Michel Basquiat: Hazards of Sudden Success and Fame," the *New York Times*, 27 Aug.1988; Greg Tate, "Nobody Loves a Genius Child," *Village Voice* (14 Nov. 1988): pp. 31–35; and Andrew Decker, "The Price of Fame," *Art News* (Jan. 1989): 96–101.

N. ELIZABETH SCHLATTER

BASS, Saul (8 May 1920–25 Apr. 1996), graphic designer, was born in New York City to Aaron Bass, a furrier, and Pauline Feldman Bass. He grew up in the Bronx and attended public schools, graduating from high school at the age of fifteen. From an early age, he was constantly drawing and sketching, and by his early teens he knew that he wanted to become what was then known as a commercial artist. After graduating from public high school in 1936 he received a scholarship to the Art Students League in New York City, where he studied until 1939. He had already launched his career as a freelance graphic designer after leaving high school, and he continued that career in New York until 1946. He also studied design at Brooklyn College during the academic year 1944–1945.

In 1946 Bass decided to move to the West Coast and settled in Los Angeles, where he established his own graphic design firm. He soon became prominent as a corporate designer, creating logos, trademarks, and other graphic images for a number of leading companies, including AT&T, Quaker Oats, Minolta, and the Bell Telephone Company. Bass also worked extensively for United Airlines, designing not only graphic images for the company but even taking a hand in the interior design of their planes. He played a similar multifunctional role for the Exxon Corporation, designing everything from logos to service stations.

Bass's work, though clever, projected simplicity and understatement and paired color with line to achieve its intended effect: striking memorability. Although his contributions to the design of the corporate landscape were considerable, he became best known for his work in the movies. He is credited with revolutionizing the presentation of film titles and opening credits—which traditionally had varied only in their typeface—by adding clever graphic elements, beginning with his dramatic designs for Otto Preminger's film *Carmen Jones* in 1954. Many memorable title sequences followed, including *The Man with the Golden Arm* (1955), which featured a moving cutout of a jagged arm, and *Anatomy of a Murder* (1959), whose credits were accompanied by silhouetted body segments. Bass went on to create the introductory frames for a number of successful movies, including *West Side Story* (1961), *A Walk on the Wild Side* (1962), *Around the World in 80 Days* (1956), *Spartacus* (1960), and Alfred Hitchcock's *Vertigo* (1958), *North by Northwest* (1959), and *Psycho* (1960). In some cases Bass designed scenes in the movies themselves, most notably in *Psycho*, for which he helped Hitchcock create the grisly shower stabbing.

Bass's professional helpmate and frequent partner was his second wife, Elaine Makatura, whom he married in 1961 and with whom he had two children; an earlier marriage, which also produced two children, ended in divorce. (His first wife's name is not known.) With his wife Elaine he made a series of short films on art and design; one of them, *Why Man Creates*, won an Academy Award for best documentary short subject in 1964.

By the late 1960s Bass, now among the nation's most celebrated designers, had withdrawn from film work to devote himself full time to his corporate clients. He returned to the movie industry in 1987 to design the credits for the film *Broadcast News*. In the years prior to his death Bass, together with his wife, created title sequences for several box-office hits, including *Goodfellas* (1990), *Cape Fear* (1991), and *The Age of Innocence* (1993), while continuing to work on corporate accounts.

Bass was often heralded as "the Picasso of commercial artists," and examples of his work were acquired for the permanent collections at the Museum of Modern Art in New York City and the Smithsonian Institution in Washington, D.C. A few months before his death, the School of Visual Arts in New York City honored him with a retrospective exhibition. Bass died in Los Angeles after a brief illness.

• Biographical information on Saul Bass is limited. See J. Stang, "Movie (Title) Mogul," *New York Times Magazine*, 1 Dec. 1957, pp. 86ff; *Who's Who in America*, 4th ed., 1992–1993; and his obituary in the *New York Times*, 25 Apr. 1996. For information on his work, see C. Sullivan, "The Work of Saul Bass," *American Artist*, Oct. 1954, pp. 28–31ff; "Definition for Creativity," *Design*, Mar. 1959, pp. 144–45ff;

"Saul Bass on Visual Excitement [interview]," *Popular Photography*, July 1964, pp. 108–9ff; and P. Haskin, "Saul, Can You Make Me a Title? [interview]," *Film Quarterly*, Fall 1996, pp. 10–17. For a posthumous appraisal of his contribution to film, see Martin Scorsese, "Saul Bass," *New York Times Magazine*, 29 Dec. 1996, pp. 44–45.

ANN T. KEENE

BATE, Walter Jackson (23 May 1918–26 July 1999), biographer and literary critic, was born in Mankato, Minnesota, the son of William G. Bate, a high school principal, and his wife, Isabel Melick Bate. The second of five children, he experienced two major crises while growing up in Mankato: at the age of four he was hit by a car and suffered permanent damage to his nervous system; and with the advent of the Great Depression seven years later his father's salary was cut in half, creating financial hardship for the family. To make matters worse, the elder Bate, a staunch Republican, was fired from his job altogether following the Democratic sweep in the elections of 1932. Despite the family's limited means, Walter's father urged his sons to get the best education possible, which to him meant attending an Ivy League college. Walter chose Harvard because of its proximity to Boston, where he could find work, and he enrolled there in the fall of 1935 with the intention of studying English literature.

To pay for his college education Bate worked thirty hours a week at dishwashing and other menial jobs. He walked regularly between his jobs and his rooming house in Boston and the Harvard campus, six miles away in Cambridge, to save the nickel subway fare. Despite this arduous schedule he emerged as a top scholar, focusing on English romanticism and becoming the prized student of such renowned Harvard academics as Douglas Bush, Robert Hillyer, and John Livingston Lowes. In particular, Bate was drawn to the poet John Keats, about whom he wrote his senior honors thesis. Bate's work received the Bowdoin Prize for the best undergraduate thesis, and he graduated summa cum laude in the spring of 1939; the thesis was published later that year by Harvard University Press as *Negative Capability: The Intuitive Approach in Keats*.

Although Bate felt like an outsider at the then-aristocratic Harvard—he was virtually penniless much of the time, ill fed and poorly clothed—his professors urged him to remain there for graduate work, and through the efforts of Douglas Bush he was given a small scholarship. It barely covered his tuition, however, and he had to continue struggling at various odd jobs to earn money for food, clothing, and personal expenses. Nevertheless, he managed to earn an M.A. within one academic year, receiving his degree in 1940 with a thesis on Jonathan Swift that earned him another Bowdoin Prize, this time for the best master's thesis. He continued in the graduate program for two more years, studying closely with Bush and Hillyer and writing his doctoral dissertation on the prosody of Keats. He received his Ph.D. in English literature

in 1942, and a chapter of his dissertation was awarded still another Bowdoin Prize. Upon graduation Bate was elected to the Harvard Society of Fellows, an honor that allowed him to do postgraduate research for five years at Harvard and gave him a small stipend in exchange for limited teaching duties.

Bate's appointment as a Harvard fellow gave him an opportunity to focus on what he enjoyed most: reading and writing about English literature, in particular that composed between 1660 and 1820—what he later termed "the extended eighteenth century." Bate believed this period, rather than the Renaissance, to be the true "Golden Age" of English literature, and he was especially attracted to the writings of authors who flourished after 1750, creating the early works of romanticism. He began his fellowship by revising his doctoral dissertation into a book, published in 1945 as *The Stylistic Development of Keats*, that offered a groundbreaking and painstaking analysis of the entire body of Keats's work. The book was well received by critics, including adherents of the so-called New Criticism that had emerged over the previous decade and would become the leading school of critical theory in the early postwar years. New Critics, reacting to what they considered the vagueness, subjectivity, and imprecision of traditional literary criticism, sought a more objective, even scientific, approach to the discipline, arguing that a critic should focus solely on the immediate text to interpret and evaluate a literary work and not be influenced by historical or biographical data.

But Bate did not find himself entirely in agreement with the tenets of the New Criticism, and an early important paper, "The Sympathetic Imagination in Eighteenth-Century English Criticism," also published in 1945, indicated the direction that his subsequent work would take. Eschewing both the strictly empirical and the exclusively subjective, Bate instead opted for a critical path that tempered empiricism with intuition and ultimately argued the importance of a historical approach to literary study—a method that would inform the entire body of his work over the next fifty years and establish him as both a major literary critic and an eminent literary biographer.

Another major work produced by Bate as a Harvard fellow was his third book, *From Classic to Romantic* (1946), a major history of criticism in the eighteenth and early nineteenth centuries that persuasively demonstrated the transition from neoclassicism to romanticism. Bate's extraordinary achievements were not lost on the Harvard faculty, some of whose most eminent members, including the philosopher Alfred North Whitehead, became personal friends and mentors, and from whom he absorbed the prevailing humanism that came to lie at the center of his life and career. At the conclusion of his fellowship in 1947, he was appointed an assistant professor at Harvard. Bate was to spend his entire career there, specializing in eighteenth-century English literature and the history of criticism. He was promoted to associate professor in 1949 and full professor in 1956; he was then appointed to two named chairs: Abbott Lawrence Lowell Professor in the humanities in 1962 and Kingsley Porter University Professor in 1977. He became an emeritus professor on his retirement in 1988.

One of Bate's major accomplishments as a Harvard professor was the successful championing of eighteenth-century English literature as a major body of work worthy of intense academic study; heretofore it had been virtually a poor stepchild of English departments throughout the country, seen only as a relatively unimportant transition between the Renaissance and Victorian eras. Another of Bate's accomplishments was the creation of a comprehensive course in literary criticism, dating from the writings of the ancient Greeks, which ultimately became a model for similar courses in other universities. As an outgrowth of that course he created an anthology, *Criticism: The Major Texts* (1952), representing the works of eighty critics, which soon became a major text in colleges and universities throughout the country. It was subsequently enlarged to include additional modern critics and has been reprinted many times. Bate's introductions to both the authors and the periods represented in the original edition were also collected and published in a separate volume, *Prefaces to Criticism* (1959), and therein offer a concise history of critical theory.

Although Bate had established himself by the mid-1950s as an authority on literary criticism, even greater recognition lay ahead for him as a literary biographer of both John Keats and Samuel Johnson, and his creation of a new kind of biography qualifies as his third major accomplishment. He came to the genre indirectly, however: like his first book on Keats, his initial study of Johnson—*The Achievement of Samuel Johnson* (1955)—was primarily an assessment of the man's work and thought, with an introductory chapter on Johnson's life, added almost as an afterthought, titled "The Life of Allegory" (the title comes from Keats, who wrote that the greatest writers, including Shakespeare, led "a life of allegory" and their "works are the comments on it"). The book was a critical success and its introductory biographical chapter, in which Bate considered Johnson's inner as well as his outer life, was singled out for particular praise as one of the best brief biographies ever written.

Writing the introductory chapter to his book on Samuel Johnson had convinced Bate that a literary biography treating both the life and the work of its subject was possible, and for his first attempt he turned again to John Keats. (Keats, having died at the age of twenty-five, perhaps seemed more manageable for such an initial effort than the septuagenarian Johnson.) Because of his academic duties, which now included chairmanship of the Harvard English department, it took Bate eight years to write the book. The resulting *John Keats*, more than 700 pages long, was published to critical acclaim in 1963. The first modern biography of the poet, it offered a seamless braid of Keats's life and work in a style echoing Bate's earlier study of Johnson. Bate showed particular skill at revealing how events in Keats's life were reflected stylistically in his poetry—an approach that was anathema to the New Critics but was nevertheless convincing. *John Keats* received several prestigious awards, most notably the 1964 Pulitzer Prize for biography—the first time the Pulitzer board had departed from its rule that the biography prize be given only to books with American subjects.

Bate next turned his attention to a much shorter study of another poet, Samuel Taylor Coleridge, written as part of a series of brief biographies of literary figures. The resulting *Coleridge*, published in 1968, also received critical praise and employed the same techniques that Bate had used to elucidate the life and works of Keats, though it did not attract the wide attention of the earlier biography. In his next book, *The Burden of the Past and the English Poet* (1970), which had developed from an essay and a subsequent lecture series at Harvard, Bate returned to the field of criticism, examining the role of historical precedent in eighteenth- and nineteenth-century British poetry. By this time Bate had already begun work on his second book about Johnson.

In undertaking a Johnson biography Bate faced a difficult challenge: he had to contend with the ghost of Boswell, Johnson's contemporaneous biographer who had been the revered authority for nearly two centuries, and he had to uncover the largely unknown story of the first half of Johnson's life. More than a decade of research and writing produced what many critics consider the most outstanding biography of the modern era and one of the best of all time. Bate's *Samuel Johnson* (1977) portrays the critic-dictionary maker-poet-conversationalist-moralist with both intellectual rigor and empathy, and—as he did in his biography of Keats—in an engaging style reminiscent of Johnson himself. *Samuel Johnson* won Bate a second Pulitzer Prize for biography in 1978, an exception to its award policy again having been made by the board; soon afterward the restriction was dropped altogether. *Samuel Johnson* also won a National Book Award and a National Book Critics Circle Award for its author, and it enjoyed a wide readership that extended well beyond academic circles.

Still another major accomplishment of Bate's career occurred in 1983 with the publication of a new and highly praised edition of Coleridge's *Biographia Literaria*, edited by Bate along with James Engell. During his years at Harvard, Bate also edited several other volumes, including the *Selected Works* of Edmund Burke (1960); Johnson's *The Idler and the Adventurer*, with John M. Bullitt and L. F. Powell (1963); and *Keats: A Collection of Critical Essays* (1964).

In addition to writing and research, Bate was one of Harvard's most popular professors. His courses "The Age of Johnson" and "The Function and Criticism of Literature" were always oversubscribed; his students praised him for his openness, availability, and kindly manner. In retrospect, Bate's affinity for Keats, the orphan who in Bate's words "pulled himself up by his own bootstraps," and Johnson, the hulking and ungainly poor boy who struggled against adversity enlightened and strengthened by high moral purpose, is not difficult to understand. It does not seem too far-fetched to suggest that Bate saw more than a little of himself in each man, and that Johnson, who survived to greatness in old age, was his lifelong hero.

Bate, who never married, had homes in both Cambridge, Massachusetts, and Amherst, New Hampshire. He died in a Boston hospital following a brief illness.

• For biographical information, see John Paul Russo, "Walter Jackson Bate," in *Dictionary of Literary Biography*, vol. 67: *Modern American Critics since 1955* (1988), and Robert G. Blake, "Walter Jackson Bate," *Dictionary of Literary Biography*, vol. 103: *American Literary Biographers, First Series* (1991). See also *Who's Who in America*, 53d ed. (1999). An obituary appears in the *New York Times*, 28 July 1999.

ANN T. KEENE

BATES, Ernest Sutherland (14 Oct. 1879–4 Dec. 1939), educator and author, was born in Gambier, Ohio, the son of Cyrus Stearns Bates, occupation unknown, and Laverna Sutherland Bates. After graduating from the University School of Cleveland, he entered the University of Michigan, where he received his B.A. and M.A. degrees in 1902 and 1903, respectively. He married Michigan alumna Florence Fisher on 6 August 1902 and a year later began his academic career as a lecturer in English at Oberlin College, remaining there until 1905. From 1907 to 1908 he was a tutor in English at Columbia University while completing his requirements for a Ph.D. His dissertation was later published as *A Study of Shelley's Drama "The Cenci"* (1908).

Bates's first full-time academic appointment was at the University of Arizona, where he became a professor of English in 1908. While in Arizona he occasionally spoke on behalf of the woman suffrage movement. In 1913, after the death of his first wife, he married Rosalind Boido, with whom he had one child, a son. He remained at Arizona until 1915, when he took a similar position at the University of Oregon. After his second marriage ended in divorce, Bates married Gladys Graham. He continued at Oregon until 1925, having switched in 1921 to the teaching of philosophy. After a controversy over the suppression of academic freedom erupted (the origins and particulars of which are now obscure), Bates left the relative security of academia and returned east.

With his academic career largely over—although he would later serve as a professor in the extension division of the University of Oregon in the years 1930, 1932, 1935, and 1936—Bates began the most productive period of his life. In January 1927 he became the first literary editor of the *Dictionary of American Biography*, which for many years served as the standard biographical reference work in American history. Bates contributed seventy-four articles to the project, concentrating his efforts on philosophic and literary figures of note. Long a casual critic of literature and widely admired for his wide-ranging grasp of social

topics, he began reviewing books for the New York Herald Tribune in 1929. In 1930 he joined the staff of the *Saturday Review of Literature* and from 1933 until 1936 served (along with V. F. Calverton) as associate editor of the *Modern Monthly*.

A quiet and unassuming man with a wide range of interests (he had considered the ministry before ultimately studying English and philosophy), Bates also produced a flurry of books in the latter part of his career. *The Friend of Jesus*, a biography of Judas Iscariot that was also published as *The Gospel According to Judas*, appeared in 1928 and was quickly followed by *The Land of Liberty* (1930), a study of the history of civil rights in America. He collaborated with J. V. Dittemore, a former "insider" at the Church of Christ, Scientist, to produce *Mary Baker Eddy: The Truth and the Tradition* (1932); this effort sought to apply the standards of modern scholarship to a balanced treatment of a controversial figure in American religious history. In the mid-1930s Bates focused on political history and produced *The Story of the Supreme Court* and *The Story of Congress*, both of which appeared in 1936; in that same year he collaborated with Oliver Carlson to produce *Hearst: Lord of San Simeon*, a biography that was critical of the newspaper magnate. The following year he published his final collaborative effort (this time with Alan Williams), *American Hurly-Burly*, a trenchant and witty review of political, social, and artistic events from the year 1936.

In the last years of his life, Bates's focus shifted yet again to religion. He served as editor for *The Four Gospels* (1932) and wrote *Biography of the Bible* (1937). His most influential work, *The Bible Designed to Be Read as Living Literature* (1936), became a best-seller. Seeking to make the King James version of the Bible more accessible to the average person, Bates eliminated much of the archaic language, updated both spelling and grammar, and eliminated most of the repetition and genealogies found within the original King James version. He also substituted the Revised Version of Proverbs, Job, Ecclesiastes, and the Song of Songs for their King James counterparts, and he made a point of presenting verse as verse, prose passages as prose, and letters as letters. Viewing the decline in Bible readership as both "deplorable" and "unnecessary," Bates noted in his introduction that "An edition for scholars is one thing; an edition for readers quite another. The latter should make use of the results of the former, but surely should not parade them" (p. xii). He had just finished writing another book when he was stricken with a fatal heart attack at his home, "Edgehill Inn," in the Spuyten Duyvil section of the Bronx; *American Faith* was published in 1940, the year following his death.

Although now almost forgotten, Ernest Sutherland Bates gained a niche in American cultural history because of his prodigious output. He was one of the last prominent examples of an academic who could address a wide range of topics—both in the classroom and in print—before the steadily increasing specialization of academia in the second half of the twentieth century made it nearly impossible to aspire to be a "renaissance man."

• The University of Arizona in Tucson holds a small collection of Bates's papers in its special collections department. Secondary information on Bates's life and career is scarce; the best sources are the entries about him in the 1940 edition of *Current Biography* and the Apr. 1940 edition of *Current History*. Obituaries appear in the *New York Times*, 5 Dec. 1939; the *New York Herald Tribune* 5, 6 Dec. 1939; the *Saturday Review of Literature*, 16 Dec. 1939; and *Time* and *Newsweek*, 18 Dec. 1939.

EDWARD L. LACH, JR.

BEIGHTLER, Robert S. (21 Mar. 1892–12 Feb. 1978), soldier, was born Robert Sprague Beightler in Marysville, Ohio, the son of William P. Beightler, a surveyor and executive with a cigar company, and Joana Sprague Beightler. He graduated from Marysville High School and attended Ohio State University for two years before leaving in 1911 to become an engineer for Union County, Ohio. In 1914 he married Anna Lawrence Porter; they would have two children and divorce in 1933.

While working as an engineer, Beightler also pursued a career as a National Guardsman. Impelled by patriotism and a passion for target shooting, he enlisted as a private in the 4th Infantry Regiment of the Ohio National Guard (ONG) in 1911. Three years later he was commissioned a second lieutenant. After the United States entered World War I in 1917, he went to France with his regiment (renumbered the 166th U.S. Infantry), serving first as a battalion adjutant and then, with the rank of captain, as regimental adjutant.

Between the world wars Beightler prospered in his civilian career. During the 1920s he worked for the Ohio Department of Highways, rising to the post of chief engineer in 1928. From 1930 to 1932 and from 1936 to 1939 he was a private contractor, earning a substantial income from road-building projects in Ohio and West Virginia. In January 1939 he was named director of the Ohio Department of Highways. At the time, the department was mired in charges of inefficiency and corruption, and during his twenty-month tenure he reformed many of its operating procedures and initiated a major program to upgrade the state's roads. Beightler married Claire Springer in 1939; they had no children.

Beightler's military career advanced in step with his civilian career. Commissioned a captain in the reorganized ONG in 1919, he was promoted to lieutenant colonel in 1924 and named G-2, or intelligence officer, of the ONG's 37th Division. Ambitious and committed to the mission of the Guard as the first-line reserve for the Regular Army, he worked hard to acquire military knowledge. In 1926 he completed the course for Reserve and Guard officers at the Command and General Staff School and in 1930 the G-2 course at the Army War College. From 1932 to 1936 Beightler served with the War Plans Division of the War Department General Staff, where he handled matters dealing with highways. Through these assignments he developed his military professionalism and gained experience in dealing with the highest levels of the army. He was promoted to colonel in 1939 when he was appointed chief of staff of the 37th Division; in 1940 he became a brigadier general after being named commander of the 74th Infantry Brigade. When the 37th Division was federalized in October 1940, Beightler was appointed commander with the rank of major general after the incumbent failed to pass his physical examination.

During the next sixteen months Beightler was under the close scrutiny of Regular Army officers while training the 37th Division at Camp Shelby, Mississippi. Regulars generally felt that in wartime Guard officers were poorly prepared for command above the battalion level, and in 1940–1942 many high-ranking Guardsmen were either retired or assigned to non-combat units because they did not measure up to the army's standards. Beightler was one of the few Guard generals to keep his command. Determined to demonstrate that Guardsmen could be as good at soldiering as regulars were, he put together an effective command team, established a command climate that emphasized rigorous training, discipline, and competence, and instilled a strong sense of unit cohesion.

Following the entry of the United States into World War II, Beightler's division was sent to Fiji in the South Pacific; he continued there with the division's training until the spring of 1943. In July and August 1943 he made a good showing against the Japanese in the costly operation to seize New Georgia in the central Solomon Islands. The next year he played a major role in stopping the Japanese offensive to eliminate the American bridgehead on Bougainville in the northern Solomons. Beightler hoped that his battlefield successes would lead to his being offered the command of a corps, but this was not to be; he would remain a division commander until the end of the war, a result, he felt, of the hostility regulars had for Guard generals.

On 9 January 1945 Beightler's 37th Division landed on Luzon in the Philippines, and during the next weeks he helped spearhead the American drive to Manila. Entering Manila on 4 February, the 37th Division bore the brunt of the fighting for the American Sixth Army in the ferocious month-long battle to liberate the city. Following the liberation of Manila, Beightler led his division in the seizure of Baguio in central Luzon and finished the war by driving the length of the Cagayan Valley in northern Luzon and eliminating Japanese resistance east of the Cordillera Mountains. After Japan surrendered in August 1945, he was appointed head of the Luzon Area Command, a temporary assignment that entailed taking the surrender of Japanese troops and processing American units returning to the United States.

In 1946 Beightler accepted a commission in the Regular Army in the expectation that it would lead to a high post in the postwar army and the rank of lieutenant general, which he thought his wartime service merited. His assignments were disappointing, however, perhaps because many regulars still saw him as a Guardsman. Beightler retired from the army in 1953 as a senior major general; from 1953 to 1955, as executive director of the Ohio Turnpike Commission, he oversaw the completion of the Ohio Turnpike.

Intelligent, confident, even-tempered, and a staunch advocate for the citizen-soldier, Beightler was an eminent Guardsman of the twentieth century and a successful combat leader. He overcame the obstacles that Guardsmen faced in the wartime army and molded his 37th Division into an effective fighting unit that never failed to carry out its mission. Beightler died in Columbus, Ohio.

• A small collection of Beightler's papers is in the Ohio Historical Society in Columbus. In *Minuteman: The Military Career of General Robert S. Beightler* (2000), John Kennedy Ohl examines Beightler's career within the context of Regular Army–National Guard tensions and his World War II accomplishments. Beightler's commitment to the National Guard is also examined in William M. Donnelly, "Keeping the Buckeye in the Buckeye Division: Major General Robert S. Beightler and the 37th Infantry Division, 1940–1945," *Ohio History* 106 (Winter-Spring 1997): 42–58. For additional discussions of Beightler's service during World War II, see Stanley A. Frankel, *The 37th Infantry Division in World War II* (1948); John Miller, Jr., *Cartwheel: The Reduction of Rabaul* (1959); and Robert Ross Smith, *Triumph in the Philippines* (1963). An obituary is in the *New York Times*, 13 Feb. 1978.

JOHN KENNEDY OHL

BELLAMY, Ralph (17 June 1904–29 Nov. 1991), actor, was born in Chicago, Illinois, the son of Rexford Bellamy, an advertising executive, and Lilla Louise Smith Bellamy. He later recalled that he developed a "colossal urge" to become an actor while attending New Trier High School in Winnetka, Illinois. The president of his school's dramatic club, he was expelled during his senior year for smoking a cigarette in the school theater. At the age of eighteen he began his acting career; one of his first professional acting jobs was playing two roles in Harold Bell Wright's *The Shepherd of the Hills*, which toured on the Chautauqua circuit during the summer of 1922. That year he married Alice Delbridge; they had no children and would divorce in 1931. His father, unhappy with Bellamy's decision to pursue acting, insisted that he take a job at his advertising firm; "but I was so careless that dad fired me," Bellamy told an interviewer (*Current Biography*, p. 29). In 1923 he was stage manager for a stock company in Madison, Wisconsin. He then joined the Beach and Jones Repetoire Company, a traveling group that performed plays in a tent. In 1924 he became the leading man with the Sherman Stock Company in Terre Haute, Indiana. Over the next five years he appeared in approximately 350 roles with stock companies throughout the Midwest and in New York State. An adept director and producer, he successfully operated his own troupe, the Ralph Bellamy Players, in Des Moines, Iowa, from 1926 to 1928.

In 1929 Bellamy moved to New York City, where he spent several frustrating months auditioning on Broadway. He later remembered that during this period he sometimes lived on a daily diet of a pound of peanuts and tap water. In October 1929 he made his Broadway debut in Marie Baumer's *Town Boy*, a play that closed after two performances. After touring with Helen Hayes in a production of George Abbott and Ann Preston Bridgers's *Coquette*, he won a starring role on Broadway as a strapping Texan in Lynn Riggs's comedy *Roadside* (1930). Although the play ran for only eleven performances, theater critics praised the "humorous sweep and gusto" of his portrayal, taking particular note of his "pipe-organ voice." These reviews drew the attention of talent scouts from Hollywood, which had recently introduced "talkies" and needed actors with distinctive speaking voices. Four studios approached Bellamy with contract offers; in late 1930 he signed with United Artists.

Bellamy later recalled that upon meeting Joseph Schenck, the head of United Artists, "I got the impression . . . that he felt he'd made a mistake" (Bellamy, p. 111). Bellamy never made a picture for the studio; rather, he was loaned out to Metro-Goldwyn-Mayer for his first film, *The Secret Six* (1931), in which he played a minor role as a gangster. In 1931 he married Catherine Willard, an actress; they had two children and would divorce in 1945. He was loaned out for two more films before his contract with United Artists expired in 1932, after which he signed a long-term contract with Columbia Pictures. His first role at Columbia was an important one, as a combative newspaper reporter in Frank Capra's drama *Forbidden* (1932), costarring Barbara Stanwyck. But for the next few years he appeared primarily in unexceptional action movies; for example, he played a deep-sea diver who fights a giant octopus in *Below the Sea* (1933) and a murderous flying-circus owner in *Flying Devils* (1933). In 1935 he was finally given an opportunity to display his versatility, turning in fine supporting performances as a boorish husband in King Vidor's *The Wedding Night* and as a kindly, handicapped millionaire in love with a manicurist (played by Carole Lombard) in Mitchell Leisen's comedy *Hands across the Table*.

In 1937 Bellamy hilariously portrayed a bashful, slow-witted Oklahoma oilman who courts a socialite (played by Irene Dunne), only to lose her to her suave ex-husband (played by Cary Grant), in Leo McCarey's screwball comedy *The Awful Truth*. He received an Academy Award nomination for his performance, but his success in the role caused him to be typecast. Over the next several years he played "the guy who doesn't get the girl" in a variety of films—the Fred Astaire–Ginger Rogers musical *Carefree* (1938), the suspense drama *Coast Guard* (1939), and the fast-paced comedy *His Girl Friday* (1940). Although he starred as the detective Ellery Queen in a series of "B" pictures during the early 1940s, he became frustrated with his repetitive assignments. His departure from Hollywood was precipitated by an incident in 1942, when he read a script that described a character as "a charming but naive fellow from the Southwest; a typical Ralph Bellamy part." "Then and there," he later remembered, "I decided to go to New York and try to find a play" (Bellamy, p. 140).

Bellamy found several challenging roles on Broadway during the 1940s, starring in three hit productions. In James Gow and Arnaud d'Usseau's *Tomorrow the World* (1943–1944) he portrayed a college professor who attempts to reform a member of the Hitler Youth whom he has brought to the United States from Germany. In 1944 he directed Claiborne Foster's melodrama *Pretty Little Parlor*, which ran for only eight performances. That year he guest-starred on twenty-seven major radio programs, including "The Philip Morris Show," "The Bing Crosby Show," and "Inner Sanctum," and made over a hundred personal appearances in an effort to sell wartime bonds. In 1945 he married Ethel Smith, a popular organist; they had no children and divorced a short time later. In 1945–1947 he played a presidential candidate in Howard Lindsay and Russel Crouse's political comedy *State of the Union*, a smash success that ran for 756 performances and won the Pulitzer Prize for drama. In 1949 he married Alice Murphy; they had no children. He did perhaps his finest stage work, as a police detective driven to savagery, in Sidney Kingsley's *Detective Story* (1949–1950). *New York Times* critic Brooks Atkinson wrote that his character was "magnificently played . . . with a kind of tired, lumbering, introspective passion." When *State of the Union* and *Detective Story* were made into successful films, Spencer Tracy and Kirk Douglas, respectively, were chosen for the roles that Bellamy had originated.

Bellamy starred from 1949 to 1952 on CBS in the live television series "Man against Crime," in a role very similar to the one he played in *Detective Story*. In 1952 he was elected president of the Actors' Equity Association and went on to serve four terms in that position. A vocal champion of actors' rights, he established the first actors' pension fund. In June 1953 he publicly decried the political blacklisting of the McCarthy era, and he led a commission that protected Actors' Equity members from unsubstantiated charges of Communist party membership (although actors who were proven to be communists were expelled from the union). In 1958–1959 he starred as a young Franklin Delano Roosevelt in Dore Schary's *Sunrise at Campobello*, a play that detailed the future president's struggle with polio. Theater critic Louis Kronenberger pointed out that "there was no trace of either virtuosity or tear-jerking vaudevillism" in the actor's "extraordinarily effective impersonation" of Roosevelt. Bellamy won an Antoinette Perry (Tony) Award and a New York Drama Critics award for the role; in 1960 he returned to Hollywood to star in a film version.

In the 1960s Bellamy starred in the television series "Frontier Justice"(1961), "The Eleventh Hour" (1963–1964), and "Harold Robbins's 'The Survi-

vors'" (1969–1970), which was a notorious flop. In 1968 he played a Satan-worshipping physician in Roman Polanski's film *Rosemary's Baby*. He appeared in twenty-one made-for-television movies during the 1970s and 1980s. In his last years he had small roles in the hit comedy films *Trading Places* (1983) and *Pretty Woman* (1990). He died in Los Angeles.

• Bellamy's *When the Smoke Hit the Fan: A Reminiscence of the Theater, Movies, and T.V.* (1979) contains a few autobiographical chapters, although the book is primarily concerned with relating show-business anecdotes. Useful overviews of the actor's life are in Robert Juran, *Old Familiar Faces: The Great Character Actors and Actresses of Hollywood's Golden Era* (1995), and *Current Biography* (1951). Doug McClelland, *Forties Film Talk: Oral Histories of Hollywood* (1992), includes a discussion by Bellamy of his role in *His Girl Friday*. An obituary is in the *New York Times*, 30 Nov. 1991.

THOMAS W. COLLINS, JR.

BENEDUM, Michael L. (16 July 1869–30 July 1959), oilman, was born Michael Late Benedum in West Virginia, the son of Emanuel Benedum, farmer and merchant, and Caroline Southworth Benedum. As a boy Michael worked on his father's farm and also at a general store his father owned in Bridgeport, West Virginia. He never had much formal schooling, but he did have access to many books at home, including the works of William Shakespeare and John Milton. Emanuel Benedum dreamed of one day sending his son to West Point.

Instead, Michael Benedum became an oilman as a young adult. In 1890 he met John Worthington, the general superintendent of the South Penn Oil Company, a subsidiary of Standard Oil of New Jersey, on a crowded train of the Baltimore & Ohio Railroad. Benedum had offered Worthington his seat in the passenger car, and before they had finished their ride together Benedum found himself hired as a land man. In 1896 he left his employment with South Penn and began to operate as an independent oil producer. In 1897 he had met Joseph Clifton Trees, soon to be his partner for fifty years until Trees's death in 1943. In 1900 the two men formed the Benedum-Trees Oil Company, the first of their many ventures in the oil business.

Benedum and Trees had their first big break in Illinois. They were invited to that state by J. J. Hoblitzell of Pittsburgh, Pennsylvania, who had opened the oil fields of Illinois, in Clark County, along the Wabash River, in 1904. Benedum and Trees were looking for a stake there by 1905. They found that the land of Clark County was already leased, so they ventured into Crawford County, contiguous on the south, and leased 50,000 acres, where they proceeded to drill the Robert Athey No. 1 well on the Athey farm in August 1905. This well came in as a gusher and thereby opened the first of the Crawford County fields, which were destined to be among the more prolific oil-producing areas in Illinois history.

By 1907, however, Benedum and Trees were ready to move on and sold all their Illinois holdings for between $7 million and $8 million, principally to Theodore N. Barnsdall of the Red Bank Oil Company and to the Ohio Oil Company. The two men then resumed their drilling operations, first in Oklahoma, then in Louisiana. In 1908 they opened the rich Caddo field in Louisiana's northwestern corner with the W. P. Stiles No. 1 well.

A year before the Stiles well came in, Benedum had changed his residence from West Virginia to Pittsburgh, Pennsylvania, the oil center of the United States in those days. He was accompanied there by his wife, Sarah Lantz Benedum, whom he had married on 17 May 1896 and with whom he had one child. In Pittsburgh Benedum built a fine home called "Greystone" in the fashionable East End.

A few years later Benedum and Trees made the first of their many oil discoveries abroad. In 1911, when Trees was in the seaport of Tampico, Mexico, he met on the street John Leonard, whom he had known in Pennsylvania. Leonard advised Benedum and Trees to prospect for oil along the Túxpam River, on the southern edge of the Golden Lane (a long stretch of land near the east coast of Mexico where prolific oil fields were found), which in fact they did. Benedum organized the Penn-Mex Fuel Company, and then Leonard negotiated a deal with the South Penn Oil Company in order to develop 25,000 leased acres of ranch land along the Túxpam. In about ten months the two companies—the South Penn having a 51 percent share in the venture—struck oil. It was the El Alamo No. 1 well, which gushed at the rate of 30,000 to 40,000 barrels per day. Shortly thereafter, El Alamo No. 2 came in producing 75,000 barrels per day.

Benedum and Trees, though, were soon to make even greater discoveries of oil in the jungles of Colombia. In 1916, on the urging of Leonard again, Benedum and Trees moved on to that country. Leonard, it should be added, while studying engineering in Paris, France, had previously met Roberto de Mares, a Colombian engineer, who had a large concession for oil in his homeland. Seepages there promised sizable petroleum reservoirs underground. Leonard had visited the de Mares concession, which certainly influenced Benedum and Trees to follow up on his lead. The two wildcatters went to work and formed the Tropical Oil Company, capitalized at $50 million. After striking oil, they sold their company in 1920 to the International Petroleum Company, owned by a subsidiary of the Standard Oil Company of New Jersey. Benedum and Trees came away from the transaction with 225,000 shares of International Petroleum Company common stock, valued at $33 million. The de Mares concession proved itself to be a superlative investment for all concerned because it delivered about 20 million barrels of oil annually for thirty years.

Back in the United States by the 1920s, Benedum and Trees sealed their fame and fortune. They opened the Big Lake oil field, the first in the Permian Basin of West Texas. To drill there the two men had organized the Plymouth Oil Company on 19 October 1923, which had acquired land leased by the Texon

Oil and Land Company in Reagan County. Undaunted by four dry holes, Benedum lent Plymouth Oil $800,000 to continue the drilling—a wise decision, as it turned out, for oil was finally struck at Big Lake on 24 June 1924. In 1962, three years after Benedum's death, Plymouth Oil, along with its subsidiary Big Lake Oil, sold out to the Marathon Oil Company (formerly the Ohio Oil Company).

An even greater discovery of oil followed that of Big Lake. On 28 October 1926 the Transcontinental Oil Company (owned by Benedum and Trees) and the Mid-Kansas Oil and Gas Company (a subsidiary of the Ohio Oil Company) jointly drilled the Ira G. Yates No. 1-A well in Pecos County, also in the Permian Basin, which hit oil at the rate of 450 barrels per day. That was nothing, however, compared with the Yates No. 30-A, completed 23 September 1929. Yielding initially 204,682 barrels per day, it became the second greatest oil well in history up to that time. (The greatest producer had been the Cerro Azul No. 4 in Mexico, a well owned by Edward L. Doheny that produced initially 260,858 barrels per day, after it blew in with a gusher 600 feet high on 10 February 1916.) By 1985 the Yates field had delivered a billion barrels of oil.

Benedum and Trees may be the greatest wildcatters who ever lived. Petroleum geologists generally believe that Benedum and Trees discovered more oil worldwide than any other oil operators in history; they found oil not only in several states in this country but also in Mexico, Colombia, Canada, Rumania (at the request of Queen Marie after World War One), Turkey, Peru, Brazil, and the Philippines.

Michael L. Benedum died peacefully at the age of ninety at his home, Greystone, in Pittsburgh.

To his credit, he never hoarded his earnings from oil. A philanthropist all his adult life as well as a devout Methodist, he gave away millions. For instance, on 27 December 1944, he and his wife established the Claude Worthington Benedum Foundation in memory of their only child, who had died of pneumonia on 18 October 1918 at an army hospital in Washington, D.C. When Benedum died, half of his estate of $100 million went to that foundation, which was created for religious, charitable, scientific, literary, and educational purposes, along with efforts to prevent cruelty to children and animals. Before her death on 11 August 1951, Benedum's wife had already contributed several million dollars to the foundation. It is worth adding that three-fourths of the income from this nonprofit foundation was earmarked for the benefit of Benedum's native state, West Virginia.

• Columbia University's Oral History Project possesses interviews with Michael L. Benedum, totaling some 60,000 words, covering much of his life. The standard biography is Sam T. Mallison, *The Great Wildcatter* (1953). For another good source of information, see "Benedum-Trees: I," *Fortune*, Dec. 1940, pp. 90–93, 118–22, 127–28, 130–32; and "Mike Benedum, Wildcatter: II," *Fortune*, Jan. 1941, pp. 72–76, 847–90. An obituary is in the *New York Times*, 31 July 1959.

KEITH L. MILLER

BERNARDIN, Joseph (2 Apr. 1928–14 Nov. 1996), Roman Catholic archbishop, was born Joseph Louis Bernardin in Columbia, South Carolina, the son of Joseph Bernardin, a stonecutter, and Maria Simion Bernardin, a seamstress. He attended both parochial and public schools in his hometown and, after graduating at sixteen, went on to the nearby University of South Carolina where he was a pre-med major. After working in a Catholic hospital, Bernardin decided to become a priest and transferred to St. Mary's College in Kentucky in time for the 1945–1946 academic year. He then transferred again, this time to St. Mary's Seminary in Baltimore, Maryland, where he earned a B.A. in philosophy in 1948. After receiving a master's degree in education from Catholic University in Washington, D.C., in 1952, he was ordained to the priesthood in the diocese of Charleston.

Bernardin spent the next fourteen years in that diocese, turning down opportunities for further study abroad in order to be near his ailing mother. He served the diocese as an assistant pastor (1952–1954), vice chancellor (1954–1956), chancellor (1956–1962), vicar general and diocesan consultor (1962–1964), and executive assistant to the bishop (1964–1966). He was consecrated as bishop and transferred to New Orleans in the latter year, where he served as auxiliary and assisted Archbishop Paul J. Hallinan in introducing many of the changes resulting from the Vatican II Council. In 1968 Bernardin went to Washington, D.C., and spent the next four years serving as general secretary of the National Conference of Catholic Bishops. Well regarded in Washington for his effectiveness in consensus-building, Bernardin put those skills to good use when he was appointed archbishop of Cincinnati in 1972.

During his ten-year-long administration in Ohio, Bernardin sought the views of both rank-and-file clergy and the laity when making decisions. Although the ultimate authority in all matters rested with him, he gained a reputation for fairness by allowing all sides in a dispute to vent their feelings. He solved one controversy over parochial school textbooks by delegating the responsibility for text selection to the individual parish, and went against traditional church positions by backing tax increases to support local financially strapped public schools. An indefatigable worker, he began his typical workday long before his staff arrived and usually stayed on the job until long after their departure; holidays often found him celebrating Mass among migrant workers or in prisons. In his efforts to remain in touch with the general population, Bernardin sold the archbishop's mansion, took up residence in a modest downtown apartment, and was often seen driving his own car. During the later years of his administration, he set up a $500,000 "emergency fund" in order to serve the indigent.

Bernardin gained additional duties in 1974, when he was elected president of the National Conference of Catholic Bishops; he was the first archbishop who was not a cardinal to be so honored. In that same year he also became a member of the International Synod of Bishops. Although not without his critics—some thought his ambition overweening—Bernardin remained especially popular among his fellow bishops and served as president of the NCCB until 1977. Usually identified with the left wing of the Catholic political spectrum—he had early issued a call against the Vietnam War and had a "basically positive" view of the Charismatic movement—Bernardin nonetheless stood firmly behind established church positions on issues such as abortion and the ordination of women.

In 1982 Bernardin was named by Pope John Paul II as the new archbishop of Chicago. The largest diocese in the United States at the time of his appointment, Chicago was also one of the most troubled; his predecessor, John Patrick Cardinal Cody, had antagonized both clergy and laity with his authoritarian style. More troubling still were allegations of financial impropriety within the archdiocese. Bernardin immediately took charge upon arrival and soon gained the trust of both clergy and laity alike. Shortly after the U.S. attorney in Chicago announced that the investigation into diocesan finances was being dropped in July 1982, Bernardin was elevated to the rank of cardinal. He again gained national notice in 1983, when he chaired a Catholic bishops' committee that produced "Challenge of Peace," a pastoral letter that unilaterally condemned the use of nuclear weapons. The letter, which earned Bernardin the Albert Einstein Peace Award for 1983, was widely discussed and read even in military circles.

A firm believer in applying a religious perspective to political and social issues of the day, Bernardin continually spoke out on topical issues. Again at odds with some of the more conservative elements in the Roman Catholic church, he assisted in drafting a 1987 statement urging toleration toward public school programs that promoted condom use in the prevention of AIDS. In light of the continuing problem of sexual abuse of minors by the clergy, he set up a committee charged with investigating allegations, punishing offenders, and providing support for victims. Largely staffed by laity, the program was considered a model to be emulated by other dioceses. Ironically, two years after the program was established in 1991, Bernardin himself was accused by a former seminarian, Steven Cook, who claimed that Bernardin had had a sexual relationship with him while he was archbishop of Cincinnati. Bernardin categorically denied the charges and claimed he had never even met Cook, whose memories of the incident supposedly resurfaced during hypnosis. The case was dismissed four months later, and Bernardin later met and effected an extraordinary reconciliation with his former accuser prior to Cook's death from AIDS in 1995.

Sadly, Bernardin soon faced yet another crisis: his own impending death from pancreatic cancer. During his very public last few months, Bernardin continued to work, creating the Catholic Common Ground Project, which sought to bring together Catholics of various ideological viewpoints, and ministered in particular to those facing imminent death, including hospital patients and a death row inmate. He also completed a book, *The Gift of Peace* (1997), and received the Presidential Medal of Freedom from President Bill Clinton. He died at his home in Chicago.

Joseph Cardinal Bernardin rose rapidly to the top of the Roman Catholic hierarchy, but he never really changed his primary ambition: to be an effective priest and a preacher of the Gospel. Although he led a life filled with accomplishments, he will be remembered for the manner in which he died as much as for the way in which he lived.

• Bernardin's papers are held at the Joseph Cardinal Bernardin Archdiocesan Archives in Chicago. He is the subject of John White and Eugene Kennedy, *This Man Bernardin* (1996). In addition to the book cited in the text, Bernardin authored a number of other works, including *Consistent Ethic of Life* (1988) and *A Blessing to Each Other: Cardinal Joseph Bernardin and Jewish-Catholic Dialogue* (1996). His career can also be traced through his column in Chicago's archdiocesan newspaper, the *New World*, and in a number of articles in *America*, most notably 8 June 1991, p. 613; 19 Mar. 1994, p. 3; and 11 Feb. 1995, p. 24. Obituaries are in most major papers, including the *New York Times*, the *Washington Post*, and the *Los Angeles Times*, 15 Nov. 1996.

EDWARD L. LACH, JR.

BETTMANN, Otto (15 Oct. 1903–1 May 1998), historian and photo archivist, was born in Leipzig, Germany, to Hans Bettmann, an orthopedic surgeon, and his wife, Charlotte Frank. The family was Jewish, and Otto grew up in a highly cultured environment, where he was especially drawn to his father's extensive collection of medical literature. As a child he enjoyed working in the darkroom of the elder Bettmann's clinic, where Hans Bettmann pioneered in the use of X-rays for diagnosis. Young Otto made copies of pictorial images he found in his father's books and collected from free publications offered by German medical firms, and in 1916, for his father's birthday, he presented a pictorial history of medicine that he had created from these images.

Otto Bettmann also had an early interest in music, particularly the works of Johann Sebastian Bach, which he pursued while attending the Oberreal Gymnasium in Leipzig. He went on to study at the Universities of Leipzig and Freiburg im Breisgau and in 1927 received a doctorate in history from Leipzig, with a dissertation on bookselling in the eighteenth century. After working briefly as an editor at the Carl Peters music publishing house in Leipzig, Bettmann returned to the university there to study library science and in 1932 received a diploma conferring upon him the status of "master librarian." For the next three years he worked at the Staatliche Kunstbibliothek, the state art library in Berlin. During this period, Bettmann refined his childhood interest in pictures as a tool for understanding the past. Inspired by an assignment from the library director to compile images from the collection relating to the history of books for a special exhibit, Bettmann went on to make his own collections of images in the three categories in which he was most interested: art, music, and medicine.

By 1935 Bettmann had accumulated an astounding 25,000 images, which he preserved on 35mm film. Forced from his job that year by the Nazis, he hastily packed his film into steamer trunks and fled Germany. He settled in New York City, hoping to establish an academic career, but he had little money and was forced to try earning a living in the midst of the Great Depression. Borrowing a friend's office, he unpacked his trunks and set up what became known as the Bettmann Archive, renting his pictures first to book publishers and eventually to other corporate clients, including newspapers and magazines as well as broadcasting companies and advertising agencies. Over the years Bettmann continued to increase his archive and to broaden its scope, acquiring new images from various sources, including private collections as well as newspapers and magazines that had gone out of business. He eventually amassed some five million images—paintings, drawings, cartoons, photographs, and other graphic material—representing virtually every imaginable field of human endeavor, reaching far back into history and continuing to the present day. Bettmann was especially known for acquiring the rights to some of the most famous photographs of the twentieth century, including celebrated shots of actress Marilyn Monroe and of British prime minister Winston Churchill. The Bettmann Archive became internationally known as one of the richest repositories of graphic images in the world, and it thrived at a time when public demand for visual information, fed by the popularity of picture magazines like *Life* and *Look*, grew almost insatiably. Bettmann's success also paralleled the growth and increasing prominence of advertising agencies, which were major users of his images.

While administering the archive, Bettmann also found time to write notable books that featured images from his collection. His first, *As We Were: Family Life in America, 1850–1900* (1946), written with Bellamy Partridge, was a pictorial history of U.S. life in the last half of the nineteenth century. Other Bettmann books included *A Pictorial History of American Sports* (1952), written with John Durant; *A Pictorial History of Medicine* (1956); and *A Pictorial History of Music*, written with Paul Lang (1960). *Our Literary Heritage* (1956), coauthored with literary historian Van Wyck Brooks, was a retelling in pictures of Brooks's five-volume work, *Makers and Finders: A History of the Writer in America, 1800–1915*. A selection of outstanding images from his collection was included in *The Bettmann Portable Archive* (1966).

All of Bettmann's books had more than respectable sales, but one in particular was a runaway bestseller: *The Good Old Days: They Were Terrible* (1974). Covering the period 1865 to 1914 in American life through pictures and text, the book demonstrated that the "good old days" were far from the Golden Age. Quite the contrary, according to Bettmann, who showed that this sentimentalized era was in fact char-

across the isthmus. It also provided for a resolution of the long-standing dispute over differential duties, the only issue that State Department communications—received after the treaty had been concluded—authorized Bidlack to act on. When he learned of Bidlack's actions, a surprised President Polk was at first inclined to view the treaty as an "entangling alliance," but he later threw his support behind the measure, which did not receive final ratification by Congress until 10 June 1848. Bidlack did not have long to bask in the congratulations of his government, as he died the following February in Bogotá, then the capital of New Granada and subsequently of Colombia.

Although memorialized by his fellow Americans in Bogotá with a statue, Bidlack's place in history has receded to that of a footnote. Nevertheless, his diplomatic initiative paved the way for the eventual construction of the Panama Canal, which was to revolutionize travel between the Atlantic and the Pacific.

• Bidlack's official correspondence is found among the State Department papers at the National Archives in Washington, D.C. His career receives attention in E. Taylor Parks, *Colombia and the United States, 1765–1934* (1935; repr. 1970); a sketch of his life in George B. Kulp, *Families of the Wyoming Valley*, vol. 3 (1890), pp. 1134–38, is still useful. See also Stephen J. Randall, *Colombia and the United States: Hegemony and Interdependence* (1992).

EDWARD L. LACH, JR.

BING, Rudolf (9 Jan. 1902–2 Sept. 1997), opera impresario, was born in Vienna, Austria, to Ernest Bing, an industrialist, and Stefanie Hoenigsvald Bing. Both parents encouraged their four children to share their interest in music, which included playing chamber music at home and regular attendance at the opera. Rudolf developed a particular love for both art and music and showed an inclination to pursue a musical career as a concert singer. After graduating from secondary school in Vienna, he studied voice with a private teacher, but his hopes of becoming a performer were dashed by the collapse of the Austrian economy following the country's defeat in World War I. He was forced to get a job quickly, and he found employment in a Vienna bookshop.

As it turned out, the bookshop also ran a concert booking agency, and Bing soon transferred to that branch of the business. His organizational skills and his musical knowledge quickly led to his appointment as head of the agency, and he established an opera division. Through his work there, he became well acquainted with artists of the Vienna State Opera, one of the best companies in the world. In 1927 Bing joined a leading theatrical agency in Berlin that placed singers in opera houses throughout Germany. A year later, he was appointed as an assistant to Carl Ebert, general manager of the Darmstadt State Theater, assuming duties that included casting and overall artistic supervision. In 1930, when Ebert was appointed head of the Charlottenberg Municipal Opera, near Berlin, Bing continued working as his assistant. A year earlier,

Bing had married a Russian-born dancer named Nina Schelemskaya, whose family had fled to Vienna following the Russian Revolution of 1917; the couple had no children.

In 1933, when Hitler came to power, Ebert and Bing left Germany and moved to England, where they joined the staff of the newly organized Glyndebourne Opera Company, an organization created to present summer performances of Mozart operas in Sussex. Under musical director and conductor Fritz Busch, Ebert became artistic and stage director, and his longtime assistant Bing was again hired to supervise casting. Under Bing's direction, outstanding opera singers from around the world were brought to Glyndebourne to inaugurate its opening season in 1934. The company enjoyed success, not only with audiences but through the sale of recordings of actual performances, and Bing was given much of the credit. In 1935 he was appointed general manager of Glyndebourne and served through the 1939 season. During their early years in England, both Bing and his wife became British citizens.

The outbreak of World War II at the end of the summer of 1939 brought a temporary halt to Glyndebourne's productions, and Bing found employment in a London department store, rising from a clerkship to an executive position. When Glyndebourne resumed in 1946, Bing was again at the helm as general manager. At this time he began to envision a British equivalent of Austria's Salzburg Festival that would include not only opera but also other forms of music as well as drama and ballet. Thanks to his efforts, and his persuasive gifts, the Edinburgh International Festival of Music and Drama opened in the summer of 1947. This event was a remarkable showcase of talent, including not only the Glyndebourne Opera but also the Vienna Philharmonic, directed by Bruno Walter; the Sadler's Wells Ballet; the Old Vic theater company; and such internationally known soloists as pianist Artur Schnabel, violinist Joseph Szigeti, cellist Pierre Fournier, and singers Lotte Lehmann and Kathleen Ferrier. The festival was an enormous success, and Bing continued as its artistic director for the next two summers while also serving as general manager of Glyndebourne.

Bing's accomplishments at both the Glyndebourne and Edinburgh Festival posts led to his appointment in May 1949 as general manager of the Metropolitan Opera in New York City, to succeed Edward Johnson at the end of the 1949–1950 season. At that time Bing was little known in the United States, and his appointment was something of a surprise, not only to veteran operagoers but to Bing himself. Soon, however, thanks to the media and their publicizing of Bing's impressive credentials, New Yorkers prepared to welcome Bing without reservation as an impresario with—to quote the *New York Herald Tribune*—both "taste and vision."

To prepare for his duties, which he was scheduled to assume on 1 June 1950, Bing arrived in New York in November 1949. He found the Metropolitan Opera in what he described later as "vast disarray" in virtually every area, from finances to stage management. In February 1950, after three months of study, he announced his plans for the next season, the first that he would oversee, with a fundamental change in policy: he reduced the number of operas being performed from two dozen or more to eighteen, and he extended the season by two weeks, from eighteen to twenty. He also declared that singers would have to reaudition each season and not simply be carried on the roster automatically from year to year. In addition, he broke the season in half for opera subscribers, offering them the option of two subscriptions instead of only one. Bing's strategy was intended to improve the quality of the opera company, allowing more time for rehearsals and guaranteeing that performances would not be hampered by inadequate casts, while at the same time encouraging more subscribers. At the time of his announcement, he was quoted as saying, "I will attempt to run this house, unmoved by promises or threats, on the principle of quality only."

Bing, who "ruled" as general manager for twenty-two years, is credited with vastly improving the structure of the Metropolitan Opera and restoring it to preeminence as one of the great opera companies in the world. He hired only the best singers and withstood frequent opposition to his choices. During his first season he brought to the Met the Norwegian soprano Kirsten Flagstad, one of the greatest Wagnerians of all time, in spite of her alleged Nazi sympathies, and in 1955, at the tail end of her career, he initiated the debut of Marian Anderson as the first black singer to appear on the Met stage. Eight years later he hired the young black soprano Leontyne Price, who enjoyed a long association with the company. Bing was also instrumental in hiring the temperamental soprano Maria Callas in 1956, but two years later, in the spring of 1958, he fired her for breaking the rules of her contract, an act that made headlines around the world and fueled Bing's growing reputation as something of an autocrat. (Contrary to the popular belief that he was never to let her perform at the Met again, he rehired her in 1965, to sing the title role in *Tosca*.) Although thwarted in his desire to hire a permanent full-time conductor at the Met—this did not come about until after his retirement—Bing was able to attract some of the world's greatest conductors to the orchestra pit, among them Karl Böhm, Herbert von Karajan, Erich Leinsdorf, Pierre Monteux, Sir Georg Solti, and Leonard Bernstein. In the fall of 1966 he helped the company settle into its spacious new home in Lincoln Center, and the following year he hired a friend, the renowned artist Marc Chagall, to design a new production of Mozart's *The Magic Flute*, one of his favorite operas. He also commissioned Chagall to paint the two massive murals illustrating scenes from the opera that now adorn the lobby of the opera house.

Like any artistic administrator, Bing was the target of criticism. He faced formidable obstacles in carrying out his job: not only resistance from temperamental performers but also the burden of escalating costs that could never tempt him to compromise on quality. During his tenure the Met barely survived two potentially disastrous labor strikes, in 1961 and 1969, and he was frequently taken to task for presenting "only the hits" of the operatic stage and not offering more modern works as well.

In 1971 Bing, who had remained a British subject, was knighted by Queen Elizabeth II. He retired from the Met a year later, in April 1972, at the age of seventy; the occasion was marked by a gala concert and a performance of Verdi's *Don Carlos*, the opera that had opened his first season at the Met. That same year he published a memoir, *5,000 Nights at the Opera*, and a year later a sequel, *A Knight at the Opera*. Bing was devastated by the death of his wife in 1983, and his mental health began to deteriorate. In 1987, against the wishes of friends, he married a young woman named Carroll Douglass, who had been married three times before to much older men and had a history of mental problems. The couple's travels in the United States and abroad and their often bizarre behavior made frequent headlines in supermarket tabloids. Finally, in 1989, Bing was diagnosed with Alzheimer's disease, and friends succeeded in having him admitted to the Hebrew Home for the Aged in Riverdale in the Bronx. They also succeeded in having his ill-advised marriage annulled, the judge concluding that Bing had "lacked the mental capacity" to enter into such a union. Bing lived at the home until a week before his death, when he was admitted to a nearby hospital for treatment of a respiratory ailment from which he did not recover.

• Biographical information on Rudolf Bing can be found in his two books of memoirs, *5,000 Nights at the Opera* and *A Knight at the Opera*. See also "Bing, Rudolf," in *Current Biography Yearbook* for 1950 and 1997. For a retrospective of his career, see James Oestreich, "For Rudolf Bing at 88, Operatic Drama Lingers," *New York Times*, 11 Mar. 1990. A lengthy obituary appears in the *New York Times*, 3 Sept. 1997; see also two corrections of that obituary in the *New York Times*, 11 Sept. and 19 Sept. 1997, p. A2.

ANN T. KEENE

BIRCH, John (28 May 1918–25 Aug. 1945), Baptist missionary and military officer, was born John Morrison Birch in Landaur, India, the son of George S. Birch and Ethel Ellis Birch. Both parents were Methodist missionaries under the auspices of the Presbyterian Church, U.S.A. George Birch was also an agricultural professor at Ewing Christian College, Allahabad, India, while Ethel Birch tutored English there and conducted women's Bible classes nearby. In 1920 the family returned to the United States. George Birch became a fruit farmer in Vineland, New Jersey, where John Birch first went to school. In 1930 the family, by then including seven children, moved to Rome, Georgia, where Birch attended high school. After graduating at the head of his class, he entered Mercer University; there, he deepened his religious convictions and evangelical passion and graduated magna cum laude in 1939. He completed a two-year

acterized by a high crime rate, economic catastrophe, and terrible living conditions. Despite its gloomy message, the public adored the book: it was reprinted ten times.

In 1981, well past normal retirement age, Bettmann finally relinquished control of his collection, selling it to the Kraus-Thomson Organization for an undisclosed price. Nine years later the Bettmann Archive, as it was still called, acquired an additional 11.5 million photographic images from the libraries of two news agencies, United Press International and Reuters. Another milestone in the history of the archive came in 1995, when Microsoft Corporation founder and chairman William H. Gates bought the entire archive, numbering more than 16 million items, through a subsidiary, the Corbis Corporation, intending it as the cornerstone of a projected library of digitized images for future sale over the Internet. The archive continued to provide images to its traditional clients, publishing and other media, under the name Corbis-Bettmann; rentals ranged from $75 to several thousand dollars or more.

After retiring from the archive in 1981, Bettmann moved to Boca Raton, Florida, and continued to write books. Among them was *The Delights of Reading* (1987), a collection of quotations and notations about books Bettmann had enjoyed during his life; proceeds from its sale were donated to the Library of Congress. *Bettmann, the Picture Man*, his autobiography, was published in 1992. Bettmann's last book was *Johann Sebastian Bach as His World Knew Him* (1995).

Bettmann became a naturalized American citizen in 1939, the year after he married Anne Clemens Gray, a Boston antiques dealer and interior decorator. The couple had three children before her death in 1987. Bettmann died eleven years later in Boca Raton after a brief illness.

• The best source of information on Otto Bettmann is his autobiography, *Bettmann, the Picture Man*. See also "Bettmann, Otto," in *Current Biography Yearbook* for 1961 and 1968, and in *Contemporary Authors*, vols. 17–20 (1976) and 167 (1999). For details of the purchase of the Bettmann Archive by William Gates, see Steve Lohr, "Huge Photo Archive Bought by the Chairman of Microsoft," *New York Times*, 11 Oct. 1995. An obituary appears in the *New York Times*, 4 May 1998.

ANN T. KEENE

BIDLACK, Benjamin Alden (8 Sept. 1804–6 Feb. 1849), lawyer, legislator, and diplomat, was born in Paris, Oneida County, New York, the son of Benjamin Bidlack, a pioneer farmer, and Lydia Alden Bidlack. After his family relocated to Wilkes-Barre, Pennsylvania, Bidlack completed his education at local public schools and the Wilkes-Barre Academy. Intent on a career in law, he studied law in the office of Garrick Mallery, a local attorney, and was appointed deputy attorney for Luzerne County shortly after gaining admittance to the state bar. After an early marriage to Fanny Stewart ended shortly after it began (for reasons that are not known), Bidlack married Margaret

Wallace on 8 September 1829. The couple had seven children.

In the early 1830s Bidlack moved to the Pocono region of Pennsylvania and entered the newspaper business, first as the publisher of the *Republican Farmer* in partnership with a Mr. Atherholt, and later—after selling the paper to Samuel P. Collins—establishing the *Northern Eagle*, which was the first newspaper published in Pike County, Pennsylvania. Bidlack then returned to Luzerne County and entered politics, serving as a Democrat in the state legislature in 1835–1836. In 1840 he was elected to the U.S. House of Representatives, where his most notable legislative achievement was the passage of a bill aiding Frances Slocum, who—after being abducted as a child by Native Americans in the Wyoming Valley of Pennsylvania—had become fully assimilated into the culture of the Miami tribe and in old age faced displacement and the loss of an annuity because of a new government treaty.

On losing his bid for reelection in 1844, Bidlack benefited from the influence of fellow Pennsylvanian James Buchanan—who had recently been named as the nation's new secretary of state—and was appointed by President James Polk in December 1845 as chargé d'affaires to New Granada, where he succeeded William M. Blackford. The country, located in Central America, had been formed from the dissolution of the United States of Colombia and was the current focus of American business interests, including an insurance claim involving the Insurance Company of the State of Pennsylvania. After settling in at his duty station—in the company of one son, having left his wife and the remainder of his family at home—Bidlack made rapid progress in the settling of American claims.

Although homesick and repeatedly denied requests to visit his family, Bidlack remained vigilant in his duties and soon became aware of the emerging issue of transoceanic transportation. Many nations and individuals had long sought a shortcut from the Atlantic to the Pacific Ocean that would enable ships to circumvent the long journey around South America, and attention increasingly came to be focused on the isthmus of Central America. Well aware of attempts on the part of both the British and the French governments to negotiate a right-of-way treaty (and equally aware of New Granadan concerns regarding sovereignty), Bidlack repeatedly requested instructions from the State Department regarding American plans in the area, only to experience frustration with both long communication delays and a government whose leadership was then currently absorbed with the Mexican-American War.

Convinced that delay only played into the hands of the British and the French, Bidlack initiated negotiations on his own and on 2 December 1846 concluded what later became known as the Mallarino-Bidlack Treaty. A general treaty that guaranteed neutrality in the area as well as the sovereignty of New Granada, the treaty also gave the United States a right-of-way

course at the Bible Baptist Seminary in Fort Worth, Texas, in one year and then left in July 1940 for China, sponsored by a World's Fundamentalist Baptist Missionary Fellowship.

Birch studied Chinese in Shanghai, quickly developed a moderate mastery of the language, and undertook missionary proselytizing in Hangchow. When Pearl Harbor was bombed and the United States and Japan went to war, in December 1941, Birch eluded a Japanese military detachment sent to arrest his group, fled 250 miles southwest to Shang-jao, Kiangsi Province, and continued to work, fearlessly, with diminishing numbers of free Chinese.

On 18 April 1942 Lieutenant Colonel James H. Doolittle led sixteen American B-25 bombers on a daring raid on Tokyo, Kobe, Yokohama, and other Japanese cities. By chance, Birch was at an inn near Shang-jao when a native of the area quietly spoke to him and led him to Doolittle and several other airmen, who had crash-landed or parachuted to safety and were being hidden by Chinese patriots in Chekiang Province. Birch led the survivors to safety. Having already applied to the American Military Mission in Chungking to be a chaplain, Birch was happy on 27 April to be ordered to that city. After an arduous trek, he arrived in June at Kuei-lin (Kweilin), Kwangsi Province, where he chanced to encounter Colonel (later Lieutenant General) Claire Lee Chennault, commander of the American Volunteer Group. He gave Birch, whom Doolittle had recommended to him, his first plane ride—to Chungking—and on 4 July commissioned him as a first lieutenant in his unit. Birch became Chennault's interpreter, intelligence officer, radio operator, and cartographer in Chungking and K'un-ming. In March 1943 Chennault's unit was renamed the 14th Air Force, and Birch worked as an air-ground liaison officer under Marshal Hsueh Yo, the Chinese War Area commandant. Birch saved many downed American airmen, trained Chinese soldiers as radio operators and cryptographers, transmitted valuable combat and political information to Chennault's headquarters, and learned to fly small planes.

The absence of detailed information about his activities made Birch a legend and, later, a convenient name on which to hang extremist views. Until mid-1944 Birch, promoted to captain, sent intelligence reports from Japanese-held spots north of the Yangtze River and organized supply drops to Chinese ground troops. On 17 July Chennault awarded him the Legion of Merit. By spring 1945 Birch was using two secret airfields he had planned and helped build for personnel-rescue and forward-supply missions. In May 1945 he was transferred to the Office of Strategic Services as an intelligence officer and continued his perilous work.

By the time Japan surrendered on 15 August 1945, the Soviet Union had tardily entered the war against Japan, and Communist Chinese forces were exerting political and military pressure in many parts of mainland China. Birch volunteered to lead a twelve-man

mission from an Anhwei Province airfield to a so-called "pocket of disturbance" in Tsingtao, on the Shantung Peninsula. On 25 August, after nine days of travel by air, horseback, boat, automobile, and railroad coach and handcar, they reached a point on the Lunghai railroad near Süshow. Birch encountered a squad of Communist guerrillas from the 8th Route Army engaged in sabotaging telephone wires. Surrounded, he was asked to turn over all or part of his equipment. When he refused, he and Lieutenant Tung, his Chinese aide, were escorted by two guerrillas to Huang-ko, a nearby village, to confer with the Communist officer in charge. The other members of Birch's unit were captured, disarmed, and, after hearing two shots, taken to pro-Communist Yenan—to be released two months later. Lieutenant Tung, shot in the leg and then bayoneted, was left for dead, but a friendly Chinese woman rescued him that night. Treated in Süshow and Chungking, Tung recovered but lost an eye and a leg. Birch, also shot in the leg, was repeatedly bayoneted and left to die; he was buried by friendly Chinese farmers. Nationalist forces, who soon received word of the incident, came and questioned the local people, and were shown Birch's temporary grave. They exhumed his body, identified its grievous wounds, and took it to Süshow. Delivered to American army personnel of the Air Ground Aid Service stationed there, it was wrapped in white silk, placed in a Chinese coffin, and reburied with full military honors in a mausoleum on a hillside overlooking the town.

The death of this American hero at the hands of Chinese Communists ten days after VJ-Day was hushed up, and to this day certain facts remain "classified." Even after a War Department internal memo dated 20 September 1945 said Birch was killed by Chinese Communists near Süshow on 25 August 1945, War Department officials told his parents he had been killed by a stray bullet, omitted mention of Communists, and said that addresses of his fellow American soldiers privy to details of his death had been lost or misplaced. Mao Zedong even averred that his forces had mistaken Birch and his party for Japanese in disguise. Robert H. W. Welch, Jr., a strident Christian anti-Communist, unearthed details about Birch, extolled him in a 1954 biography, and four years later founded the John Birch Society. It is through Welch's shadowy group that Birch's name entered the American political lexicon. No one can say whether he would have endorsed the John Birch Society's paranoid vision of Communist infiltration at the highest levels of American government. But he will retain a place in history because of the extremism promoted in his name.

• Robert H. W. Welch, Jr., *The Life of John Birch: In the Story of an American Boy, The Ordeal of His Age* (1954), is a laudatory biography. Birch's daring exploits in China are gratefully summarized in Claire Lee Chennault, *Way of a Fighter: The Memoirs of Claire Lee Chennault*, ed. Robert Hotz (1949), and in James H. Doolittle, with Carroll V. Glines, *I Could Never Be So Lucky Again* (1991). Measures of Birch's personal postwar anonymity, however, are his going unmentioned in both Jack Samson, *Chennault* (1987), and Lowell Thomas and Edward Jablonski, *Doolittle: A Biography* (1976). J. Allen Broyles, *The John Birch Society: Anatomy of a Protest* (1964), begins with a biographical sketch of Birch. See also James and Marti Hefley, *The Secret File on John Birch* (1995). Gerald Schomp, *Birchism Was My Business* (1970), is a tragicomic exposé of John Birch Society extremisms. The first notice of Birch's death appeared in a column by Constantine Brown in the *Washington Star*, 16 Nov. 1945.

ROBERT L. GALE

BIRD, Rose (2 Nov. 1936–4 Dec. 1999), chief justice of the California Supreme Court, was born in Tucson, Arizona, the daughter of Harry D. Bird, a salesman and chicken farmer, and Anne Bird, a factory worker. Her parents separated when she was five, and her mother moved Rose and her two older brothers to New York in 1950. Rose called her mother "my role model," an example of hard work, financial independence, and belief in education.

Bird attended Long Island University on full scholarship and graduated magna cum laude in 1958, intending to become a journalist. She worked as a secretary to save money before enrolling in 1959 at the University of California, Berkeley, to study political science. While serving as a state legislative intern under a Ford Foundation grant, she saw opportunities for making public policy in the legal profession and transferred to Boalt Hall School of Law. She received her J.D. with honors in 1965. During the next year she served as law clerk to the chief justice of the Nevada Supreme Court.

After passing the California bar exam in 1966, Bird applied for a job with the Sacramento county public defender to gain experience as a litigator but was rejected because she was a woman. The Santa Clara County public defender's office hired her as their first female lawyer. Between 1966 and 1974 she moved up to senior trial deputy and then to chief of its appellate division. From 1972 to 1974 she offered clinical training in criminal defense and a consumer protection course to Stanford law students.

Her involvement in the Democratic party had begun early in her life with neighborhood canvassing for Adlai Stevenson in 1952. In 1960 she volunteered for Dollars for Democrats. Bird, who had met Jerry Brown when they were students at Berkeley, worked on his campaigns (often as his chauffeur on the campaign trail) for school board in 1970, secretary of state in 1972, and governor in 1974. Upon his election as governor, Brown appointed Bird to his transition team and then to the Department of Agriculture and Services, making her the first woman in the California state cabinet. Her appointment caused disaffection among farm organizations, from whose leadership the agriculture secretary was usually chosen. She further alienated large-scale farmers by banning the short-handled hoe used by stoop labor and by shepherding through the legislature a bill protecting the secret ballot of field workers in union elections. Bird also

worked to strengthen the service sector of the department, which covered veterans' affairs, consumer protection, and industrial relations. She succeeded in placing "public" members on licensing boards against the wishes of professionals. She particularly encouraged the Occupational Safety and Health division to improve regulations of hazardous chemicals, an interest spurred by her mother's suffering from the environmental conditions in the plastics factory where she had worked.

When the chief justice position opened in 1977, Brown's nomination of Bird disappointed several judges who had hoped for the promotion. Female, lacking judicial experience, younger than her new colleagues, and with a reputation for extreme liberalism, she was an unconventional choice. Among opponents to her selection were the San Diego mayor (later governor of California) Pete Wilson, Bishop (later Cardinal) Roger Mahoney, and Los Angeles police chief Ed Davis. Supporters included the state bar association, the California Trial Lawyers Association, the California Women Lawyers Association, and former Chief Justice Phil Gibson. On the Commission on Judicial Qualifications with power to disapprove the nomination were senior Justice Mathew Tobriner, who favored her, senior appellate Justice Parker Wood, who did not, and Attorney General Evelle Younger, a Republican with aspirations for the governorship, who finally voted for her in the absence of disqualifying evidence.

At her swearing-in ceremony she described the state courts as "just another example of burgeoning bureaucracy, as places of cold rationality, inaccessible and unaffordable to the average citizen." Bird moved vigorously to promote judicial reforms. She alienated the director of the Administrative Office of the Courts, Ralph Kleps, who had served three chiefs and expected to guide the newcomer. He soon resigned, and she failed to win the loyalty of other Supreme Court staff. She introduced a civil-service-type procedure for selecting personnel of the Courts of Appeal, ending endemic nepotism. Her abrasiveness and imperiousness further alienated the court bureaucracy.

Bird appointed special commissions to study court congestion, pressed for the publicizing of court procedures, prohibited court employees from accepting gifts from lobbyists, and ended the practice of using central staff to draft tentative opinions for the justices. She pursued a plan to bring younger and nontraditional law workers into the system by choosing minorities and women for the Judicial Council (which she chaired), by assigning trial judges rather than appellate justices to temporary service on Supreme Court cases, and by bringing new trial judges to serve short-term needs of the Courts of Appeal. She favored televising some oral arguments but was outvoted by her colleagues. She discouraged publication of opinions without designated authors.

Bird was a moderate feminist who believed in equal opportunity and personally supported many professional women and organizations. She joined the new National Association of Women Judges, founded in Los Angeles in 1979, and gave many female judges temporary assignments to higher courts. When Joyce Kennard was chosen as the second woman on the California Supreme Court in 1988, she sent a note of congratulations and support. She noted in 1978 that a woman in public office lived under a microscope with no margin for error.

Bird managed to shield her private life from her public life. She gardened, baked, swam, saw movies, and read. Her simple lifestyle, with her small house and small car, reflected her personal philosophy. She was a populist who believed that government should serve and include ordinary people and that she should share their life style.

Bird's political ideology, however, made her an easy target for conservative groups. A movement to remove her from the court began with the November 1978 retention election, when voters had the opportunity to reject four justices. Three groups funded the advertising campaign against her: the "Law and Order Campaign Committee"; the "Vote No on Rose Bird Committee," serving agriculture interests; and the California Republican Central Committee. The anticrime committee charged her with extravagance, when actually she left her staff size unchanged, sold the court limousine, bought a used robe, and moved meetings of the Judicial Council from resorts to state buildings. She kept her office by only 52 percent, a record low for judicial retention. After 1978 the same conservative activists made five efforts to recall her but failed to gather enough signatures to reach the ballot.

Bird's notoriety rested on her consistent rejection of the death penalty when a substantial majority of the California public supported it. However, she also wrote opinions unpopular with conservatives in other significant cases: to protect tenants from eviction in retaliation for exercising their civil rights, to protect abortion funding for indigents, to prevent nightclubs from giving sex-based price reductions, to broaden the exclusionary rule for confessions and to narrow the test for double jeopardy, to give right to counsel to indigent defendants in paternity cases, to extend job protection to homosexuals, to require the highest standard of proof for the mentally disabled, and to protect a Democrat-drawn reapportionment of the state legislature. When the Court upheld the popular Proposition 13 limiting taxes for some home owners, she dissented alone on one issue, arguing for equal treatment for similar properties, and gained the enmity of antitax activist Howard Jarvis, who then raised money for a campaign to remove her from office.

Unlike other liberal judges, she warned that the court must not substitute its judgment for the legislature's. She opposed the creation of an intermediate level of scrutiny for equal protection claims, fearing that the test would invite judicial activism (*People v. Hawkins*, 22 Cal.3d 584, 608-9 [1978]).

Although voters reinstated the death penalty by ballot initiative in 1977, the year of Bird's appointment, there were no executions during her tenure. Bird voted to overturn every death sentence that came before the court, but she usually voted with the majority to uphold the guilty verdict. She voted to allow almost unlimited evidence in mitigation and to provide psychiatric and other experts and investigators for capital defendants. In one of her last death penalty cases, she argued that the state constitution required a comparative review of the proportionality of facts in death penalty cases (*People v. Allen*, 42 Cal.3d 1222 [1986]). In her dissents, she offered more radical arguments than her colleagues found palatable.

During her 1986 retention election, Republican officials, farm groups, and tax crusaders, calling themselves "Crime Victims for Court Reform" and "Californians to Defeat Rose Bird," spent $10 million to defeat Bird. In the last months of the campaign two pro-Bird groups organized, a coalition of women's associations and a citizens' committee to keep politics out of the courts. Trial lawyers and personal injury firms were her primary contributors. Her supporters raised less than $2 million, and, with one exception, Democratic candidates in the same election remained neutral.

Bird lost, receiving only 34 percent of the vote. Two other liberal justices, Cruz Reynoso (the first Latino justice) and Joseph Grodin, went down with her. Governor George Deukmejian, who was on the ballot for reelection, had campaigned vigorously for Bird's defeat; he won his reelection bid and gained three vacancies to fill on the court. The Brown period of populism was over. Deukmejian and future governors would take into account the attitude of nominees concerning the death penalty, and they changed the tenor of the court from liberal to conservative on crime, environment, and personal injury issues.

Bird faded from public attention and dropped her membership in the state bar. She performed briefly as a television commentator in 1988, taught courses at Golden Gate University School of Law in 1992–1993, and was a visiting law professor at the University of Sydney, Australia. Bird never married and shared her home and garden in Palo Alto, California, with her mother until her death in 1991. Out of public office she took pink-collar jobs and struggled with her health and finances. Bird had a mastectomy in 1976 and two more operations for cancer during her court tenure. She died in Palo Alto.

On the court Bird had continued her childhood pattern of hard work; she was always thoroughly prepared for oral arguments and court conferences. Her opponents faulted her choice of dispositions but could not fault the scholarship or reasoning of her opinions. Rose saw herself as part of the blue-collar class, like her parents, and in her judicial writings she acted as a spokesperson for the masses and the underdogs. This self-identification, along with her outspoken personality, did not fit the traditional image of a justice and alienated her peers. The California Supreme Court had flourished as a progressive institution in a liberal state after 1940, but by 1982 state politics and public opinion had turned conservative. To voters Rose was the symbol of liberal extremism. Her career was a classic tragedy; her fall from the chief justiceship was foreordained by the vigor, wealth, and persistence of her conservative opponents and by her own rigid integrity and blindness to court culture.

• A brief biography can be found in *The American Bench*, 3rd ed. (1985–1986), and a longer treatment is in Peggy Lamson, *In the Vanguard: Six American Women in Public Life* (1979). The *Los Angeles Daily Journal* provided regular profiles of her (see, for example, 2 Jan. 1984). The story of the Commission on Judicial Performance investigation is in Betty Medsger, *Framed: The New Right Attack on Chief Justice Rose Bird and the Courts* (1983). An early report is "Justice Rose Bird—Not One of the 'Good Old Boys'," *Los Angeles Times*, 6 Aug. 1978; see also the five-year report, "Rose Bird—A Study in Contrasts," *Los Angeles Times*, 20 May 1982. Summaries of her service are in "Bird Praised for Adminstration," *Los Angeles Times*, 20 Apr. 1986; and "Lone Justice," *Los Angeles Times Magazine*, 5 Oct. 1986, pp. 13–17, 42–43. Two political scientists, John H. Culver and John T. Wold, analyzed her role in state politics in "Rose Bird and the Politics of Judicial Accountability in California," *Judicature* 70 (Aug.–Sept. 1986): 81–89, and "The Defeat of the California Justices," *Judicature* 70 (Apr.–May 1987): 348–55. The 1986 retention campaign is covered by John A. Jenkins in "The Trouble with Rose Bird," *TWA Ambassador*, Nov. 1985, pp. 68–83. Bird offered her views to other jurists in "No Room for Error," *Judges' Journal* 19 (Spring 1980): 5 ff., and in "The Instant Society and the Rule of Law," *Catholic University Law Review* 31 (Winter 1982): 157–225. S. M. Wildman examined one of her administrative policies in "A Study of Justice Pro Tempore Assignments in the California Supreme Court," *University of San Francisco Law Review* 20 (Fall 1985): 1–11. For a critique of her death penalty opinions, see Stephen R. Barnett, "The Emerging Court," *California Law Review* 71 (July 1983): 1134–96. Obituaries are in the *Los Angeles Times*, the *New York Times*, and the *Washington Post*, all 6 Dec. 1999, and a report of her memorial service is in the *Los Angeles Times*, 18 Jan. 2000.

BEVERLY B. COOK

BLACKMUN, Harry A. (12 Nov. 1908–4 Mar. 1999), Supreme Court justice, was born Harry Andrew Blackmun in Nashville, Illinois, the son of Corwin Manning Blackmun and Theo Reuter Blackmun, whose family owned a flour mill in Nashville. Blackmun grew up in Minneapolis and St. Paul, Minnesota, where his father worked in a succession of enterprises, including wholesale and retail businesses, banking, and insurance. Blackmun was raised in a devoutly Methodist family with a strong work ethic. Although he was a serious, hardworking student, he had a healthy sense of humor and a well-rounded personality. He and Warren Burger, the future chief justice, first met in Sunday school at age four or five, attended the same elementary school, delivered newspapers and played tennis together, and remained close friends for life; when Burger married, Blackmun was his best man.

After high school, they took separate paths. Burger remained in Minnesota for college and law school, while Blackmun, with the help of a small scholarship award, attended Harvard, working as a janitor and tutor to supplement his income. An outstanding mathematics major, he graduated Phi Beta Kappa in 1929. Initially interested in becoming a physician, Blackmun ultimately decided to study law at Harvard, where his professors included Felix Frankfurter, one of America's preeminent jurists. After graduating from law school in 1932, Blackmun won admission to the Minnesota bar, then clerked for a year with Judge John B. Sanborn of the U.S. Court of Appeals for the Eighth Circuit, on which he would later serve before being elevated to the U.S. Supreme Court. In 1934, he joined a Minnesota law firm, eventually becoming a partner and specialist in tax law and estate planning. He was also a part-time instructor at the St. Paul College of Law (1935–1941) and the University of Minnesota Law School (1945–1947). In 1950 Blackmun, his wife (the former Dorothy E. Clark, whom he married in June 1941), and their three daughters moved to Rochester, where he was resident counsel at the Mayo Clinic until 1959.

A nominal Republican but never as active in politics as his friend Warren Burger, Blackmun was a supporter of Democrat Hubert H. Humphrey in his successful 1945 and 1948 campaigns for mayor of Minneapolis and a seat in the U.S. Senate. Although Humphrey endorsed the future justice when a vacancy arose on the Eighth Circuit appeals court in 1959, President Dwight D. Eisenhower probably relied more on the opinion of Warren Burger, whom he had earlier named to head the Justice Department's civil division and then to a seat on the District of Columbia Court of Appeals. Blackmun's Eighth Circuit record was moderately liberal on racial civil rights issues, relatively conservative in most other civil liberties fields, and markedly progovernment in cases involving the claims of criminal suspects and defendants.

In 1969 President Richard Nixon chose Burger to replace Earl Warren as chief justice of the Supreme Court. In 1970 the president had the opportunity to fill the vacancy left by Justice Abe Fortas, who had resigned under fire the previous year. After the Senate refused to confirm two nominees, Clement Haynsworth and G. Harrold Carswell, the president, at Chief Justice Burger's suggestion, had turned to "Old No. 3," as Blackmun thereafter regularly referred to himself. The Senate Judiciary Committee approved the nomination 17–0, and the full Senate concurred without a negative vote. Blackmun took his seat on 9 June 1970, over a year after Fortas's resignation.

Given their close friendship and Burger's apparent role in Blackmun's appointment, Court watchers quickly dubbed the pair the "Minnesota Twins," with Burger considered the dominant figure in their relationship. For a time, the label appeared apt. During Blackmun's first term, the two voted alike, and generally on the conservative side, in 95.8 percent of nonunanimous cases, including all but one criminal procedure ruling. In his first opinion, Blackmun rejected a search-and-seizure challenge to unannounced welfare home visits. He also joined Burger in dissent in the Pentagon Papers case (1971), supporting the Nixon administration's efforts to prevent the further publication of the Vietnam War–related documents on national security grounds and dismissing the First Amendment as merely "one part" of the Constitution. Later, he spoke for the Court in rejecting a constitutional challenge to a filing fee for federal bankrupts, even as applied to indigents.

From the beginning, however, the justice was more sensitive to civil liberties claims than Burger and William H. Rehnquist, the Court's most conservative activist justice. In 1973 Blackmun embraced a broad abortion right in his opinions for the Court in *Roe v. Wade* and *Doe v. Bolton* (1973), ultimately declining the chief justice's preference for a narrow ruling with little value as precedent. Beginning with the 1975 term, the Burger-Blackmun agreement rate declined steadily. By the early 1980s, Blackmun was more likely to be aligned with Justices William Brennan and Thurgood Marshall, the Burger Court's most liberal justices, than with Burger and other conservatives. That pattern continued on the Rehnquist Court.

Theories abound about the changing direction of Blackmun's voting record. Some suggest that his commitment to *Roe*, one of the most hotly disputed decisions in the Court's history, may have prompted a growing sensitivity to civil liberties claims generally, and especially to those of the most vulnerable in society. Others cite his well-known irritation at the "Minnesota Twins" label and particularly the degrading assumption that "Hip Pocket Harry" was a virtually certain vote for whatever position the chief justice adopted. Still others have contended that the ultimate outlines of Blackmun's jurisprudence were foreshadowed by the moderate record he developed on the circuit court. In truth, of course, a variety of factors were probably at work. Throughout his career, moreover, Blackmun displayed considerable disdain for dogmatic, inflexible positions and, with notable exceptions, a soul-searching lack of certitude uncommon among jurists. That such a justice's voting patterns might change markedly over a lengthy tenure is hardly surprising, if complicated to explain.

During his nearly quarter-century tenure, Blackmun played a major role in a number of issue areas. As *Roe*'s author, he established the rigorous trimester framework for judicial review of abortion regulations. When the Rehnquist Court, in *Planned Parenthood v. Casey* (1992), reaffirmed the "essence" of *Roe* but forbade only "undue" burdens on a woman's abortion choice, he expressed relief that *Roe* had not been discarded entirely but also vigorously defended its trimester framework. Although generally opposed to expansions in equal protection doctrine, he also spoke for the Court in adding discrimination based on alienage, or lack of U.S. citizenship, to the list of constitutional suspects subject to strict judicial scrutiny and often disagreed with later majorities willing to uphold certain forms of discrimination against noncitizens. He furnished the fifth vote when the Court, for the first time since 1936, struck down in *National League of Cities v. Usery* (1976) a congressional exercise of the commerce power on the ground that it violated state authority and principles of federalism. But Blackmun found *Usery* troubling and in *Garcia v. San Antonio* (1985) recanted his earlier position, thus relegating state sovereignty challenges to Congress's regulatory powers once again largely to the political arena. Increasingly over the years, Blackmun favored national authority over state prerogative in other fields as well. He also became more sensitive to criminal justice claims. When a 5–4 majority struck down a death penalty statute in 1972, Blackmun dissented, emphasizing his personal distaste for capital punishment but viewing its use as largely a matter of legislative discretion rather than an appropriate subject for judicial review. Over time, however, he became increasingly skeptical of capital punishment. In his final term, he concluded that no death penalty scheme could be devised that would eliminate the arbitrariness inherent in its imposition.

When he retired in 1994, Blackmun, at eighty-five, was the third-oldest person ever to serve on the Court. For several years after his retirement, he remained reasonably active. In 1997 he even played a cameo role— as Justice Joseph Story—in the film *Amistad*. But in March 1999, following a fall at his suburban Virginia home and hip replacement surgery, Justice Blackmun died, leaving behind a record that demonstrated the enormous impact that issues and events can have on a judge's initial predilections.

• The Harry A. Blackmun Papers are being organized for addition to the manuscript collections at the Library of Congress. They include an oral history conducted by Harold H. Koh, a former clerk to the justice. The *Hastings Constitutional Law Quarterly* 26, no. 1 (Fall 1998) contains articles on several important aspects of Justice Blackmun's jurisprudence. An obituary is in the *New York Times*, 5 Mar. 1999.

TINSLEY E. YARBROUGH

BLACKSTONE, Harry, Jr. (30 June 1934–14 May 1997), magician, was born Harry Bouton Blackstone, Jr., in Three Rivers, Michigan, the son of Harry Blackstone, a noted magician, and Mildred Phinney Blackstone, who assisted her husband in his shows. The younger Blackstone allegedly made his stage debut as an infant, carried on by his mother when she was unable to find a babysitter. By the age of four he was appearing regularly onstage as his parents toured the country, and like the children of most magicians he learned his father's tricks. He enjoyed performing, and it seemed natural that he, too, would become a magician; but throughout his childhood his father made it clear that young Harry was to get a formal education and prepare himself for a "real" profession.

At the age of seventeen Harry entered Swarthmore College but left after two years, later claiming that he had been asked to take a leave of absence after disrupting a psychology class with a faked demonstration of ESP. After a two-year stint in the army—during which he entertained fellow soldiers with magic tricks—he resumed his education, earning an undergraduate degree at the University of Southern California in 1958 and an M.F.A. in theater two years later at the University of Texas. Initially he followed his father's advice, eschewing magic—and avoiding the inevitable comparisons with the senior Blackstone—and working instead in television and theatrical production. During the 1960s he helped produce the "Smothers Brothers Comedy Hour" for CBS-TV; he then managed three West Coast touring companies of the musical *Hair*.

But the lure of performing remained. Sometime during this period Harry Blackstone, Jr., put together a small magic show and arranged a few bookings on the West Coast and in Las Vegas. The shows were a hit, and Blackstone Jr. began devoting himself increasingly to magic following his father's death in 1965. By the early 1970s he had established himself as a full-time magician, performing in well-known nightclubs and on network television. Departing from the classical magician's wardrobe of his father—white tie and tails, dramatized by a head of flowing white hair—the dark-haired and goateed Blackstone Jr. appeared in a glittering tuxedo, with a black silk scarf draped loosely under his collar. But his acts were updated versions of his father's "old-fashioned magic," comprising classic illusions, tricks, and sleight-of-hand maneuvers. The illusions, featuring a person or a large animal—usually, in Blackstone's case, a disappearing elephant—were complemented by tricks using small animals or objects, including playing cards, and sleight-of-hand presentations that combined distraction with manual dexterity. In one famous Blackstone example of sleight-of-hand, the magician would remove personal items and clothing, even the dress shirt under a suit jacket, from an unwitting participant chosen from the audience, keeping up a steady, entertaining patter all the while. Like his father, Blackstone pulled rabbits from hats and doves from spectators' pockets, made handkerchiefs dance and light bulbs float, and through it all kept his audience amused and distracted with witty commentary. Like his father, too, he developed a reputation as an adroit comic.

By 1980 Blackstone's showmanship had made him a household word in popular entertainment. In the spring of that year he opened a show in New York at the Majestic Theater on Broadway billed as a magical extravaganza and featuring hundreds of animals of all sizes, including an elephant and a camel; his wife, whom he sawed in half nightly; and fifty-five other human performers who performed in a series of fast-paced acts. Critics and audiences alike loved it, likening the show to a vaudeville production. *Blackstone!* ran for five months, a record for a magic show on Broadway, and was taped for later presentation on PBS.

Over the following years Blackstone continued to perform to great acclaim. In addition to his stage and television appearances, he created illusions for music videos by such groups as Earth, Wind, and Fire; magical effects for Sea World in Florida and Ohio; and an exhibit on magic at the Smithsonian Institution in Washington, D.C. He also wrote or coauthored several books on magic, including *There's One Born Every Minute* (1976); *The Blackstone Book of Magic and Illusion* (1985), written with Charles and Regina Reynolds; and *200 Magic Tricks Anyone Can Do* (1995). In the course of his career Blackstone was given many honors, including the designation "Magician of the Year" twice from the Academy of Magical Arts and Sciences, in 1979 and 1985, and the Masters Fellowship, the academy's most prestigious award, in 1994.

Harry Blackstone, Jr., was married twice. He had four children with his first wife, but her name and the date of their marriage are not known; it is assumed that they were divorced. In 1974 he married Arla Gay Blevins, with whom he worked onstage; the couple had one daughter.

Diagnosed with pancreatic cancer in the spring of 1997, Blackstone died a few weeks later at a hospital in Loma Linda, California.

• For biographical information, see "Blackstone, Harry (Bouton), Jr.," in *Contemporary Authors*, vols. 114 (1985) and 158 (1998), and *Who Was Who in America*, vol. 12 (1998). See also Tom Buckley, "Blackstone Conjures Up His Own Past," *New York Times*, 13 June 1980. An obituary appears in the *New York Times*, 16 May 1997.

ANN T. KEENE

BLOCK, Adriaen (fl. 1610–1624), Dutch mariner, explorer, and trader, was most likely born in Holland, but nothing is now known of his place of birth, parents, early education, or marital status. It is thought that he studied law but soon felt eager to go to sea. His opportunity came after Henry Hudson's fourth and final voyage in search of the Northwest Passage.

During his third attempt, financed by the Dutch East India Company in 1609, Hudson had discovered the river now named for him and sailed up it as far as the location of present-day Albany. His last voyage, financed by English enterprisers, took place in 1610–1611 and ended in mutiny and Hudson's being put ashore—to disappear from the historical record. Dutch merchants, eager to rediscover the Hudson River (which they called Mauritius, in honor of Prince Maurice of Nassau) and to trade with the Indians along its shores, soon sent out three unsuccessful expeditions for that purpose. After a voyage to the West Indies (c. 1611–1613), a Dutch skipper named Hendrick Christiansen (or Christiaensen; also called Hendrick Christiansen van Cleef) ventured near what is now the New York harbor; his ship was too heavily laden to approach land safely, but he reported details of the region upon reaching Holland. Christiansen and Adriaen Block chartered a ship, voyaged to the island that came to be named Manhattan, and returned to Holland with two sons of Indian sachems whom they called Orson and

Valentine. (Some authorities say that Orson and Valentine went to Holland later and that, when they returned to America, Orson caused Christiansen's death, for which he was shot and killed.)

A group of Dutch merchants financed yet another trip in search of the Hudson River. Although the date is uncertain, it was probably in 1613 that Christiansen, in charge of a fleet of four vessels, set sail as captain of the *Fortuyn* (*Fortune*). Block accompanied him as skipper of the *Tijger* (*Tiger*). The two vessels belonged to three Amsterdam merchants, named Hans Hongers, Paulus Pelgrom, and Lambrecht van Tweenhuysen. The other captains in Christiansen's fleet were Thijs Volkertsen (Volckertsen) Mosse, of the *Nachtegael* (*Nightingale*), and Cornelis Jacobsz May, whose vessel was also named the *Fortuyn* (*Fortune*). Block and Christiansen sailed together around Cape Cod, located the Hudson River, and ventured up it to Castle Island, near modern Albany. While wintering there, Christiansen built Fort Nassau, a combination redoubt and warehouse now regarded as the earliest such Dutch structure in America. It was garrisoned by a Dutch detachment and remained serviceable until 1617, when it was abandoned because of injuries done to it by freshets. Meanwhile, a fire accidentally destroyed Block's *Tiger* in New York harbor off the Battery. During the winter of 1613–1614, and on into the spring, he and his men built the *Onrust* (*Restless*) as a replacement. A small yacht, she was forty-four-and-a-half feet long and eleven-and-a-half feet wide, weighed only sixteen tons, and is said to have been the first decked vessel built in the New York area. Camping in huts they built on lower Manhattan, Block and his men were kept alive by the generosity of local Indians.

In 1614 Block and Christiansen, leaving a clerk named Jacob Eelkens in charge at Fort Nassau, sailed back down to Manhattan, went up the dangerous East River, through Hell Gate (which Block called Hellegat, meaning "Hell Gut" or "Hell Strait," because of its turbulence), and into Long Island Sound. Block alone, in his light *Restless*, safely visited New Haven harbor, which he called Roodenberg, from the red color of the hills nearby; entered the mouth of the Housatonic River; went up the beautiful Connecticut River, which he called Versche rivier (Fresh River), to a point probably somewhere between present-day Hartford and Windsor; visited a Nawaa Indian village and then a Pequot Indian village to the east along the Thames River; and perhaps crossed Fisher's Sound south to Block Island, which he called Adrianbloxeyland. If so, it was Block who discovered Block Island and not Christiansen (or Giovanni da Verrazzano, even earlier), as is sometimes recorded. Block continued south to Montauk Point, then called Visscher's Hook, and through Narragansett Bay, which he called Baye van Nassouwen and in which was a tiny island he called Roode (thus the name of present-day Rhode Island). He saw Martha's Vineyard (Texel), Nantucket (Vlieland), and Salem (now Nahant) Bay (Pyebaye), which he regarded as the northeasternmost extent of legitimate Dutch territory.

Block expertly surveyed and mapped Fisher's Sound, the Mystic River, Little Narragansett Bay, the Pawcatuck River, Point Judith, and Narragansett Bay. He crossed Buzzard's Bay and met Christiansen near Cape Cod (which Block called Kaep Bevechier), gave Cornelis Hendricksen the command of his *Restless*, and returned aboard Christiansen's *Fortune* to Holland. He probably arrived in July, or a little later, in 1614.

During part of the time while Block, Christiansen, and their two fellow skippers were trading with the Indians, they were joined by Jan de Wit (or With), captain of *het Vosken* (the *Little Fox*). Earlier, de Wit had served in these waters under Pieter Frenssen, who, along with two crew members, was murdered by hostile Indians. Taking command of the *Little Fox*, de Wit traded with the Indians for beaver and other skins and brought the *Little Fox* home to commercial success.

In October 1614 the merchants backing the five ships persuaded a government assembly, before which Block also appeared, to award them a charter granting them exclusive rights to trade in what was for the first time called New Netherland. Located between the fortieth and the forty-fifth parallels, the region was precisely shown on what is now known as "The Figurative Map of 1614." Block supervised the preparation of this map, on which was lettered "Nieuw Nederland" for the first time in cartographical history. The enterprisers—twelve men in all, including Hongers, Pelgrom, and Tweenhuysen—banded together as the New Netherland Company and were granted a three-year monopoly; interlopers were subject to enormous fines; and new expeditions began in January 1615.

It is unlikely that Block ever revisited America. In 1615 he accepted the offer of Tweenhuysen, who had helped organize a group called the Northern Company, to take command of a fleet of whalers heading for Spitzbergen. It is recorded that Block was still involved in the whaling industry as late as 1624, after which his name disappears from the historical record.

• Herbert Ingram Priestley, *The Coming of the White Man, 1492–1848* (1929), though not mentioning Block, provides a historical framework for his accomplishments by discussing late-sixteenth- and early-seventeenth-century Dutch voyages to America and the Dutch colonizing and trade that followed. The most substantial coverage of Block is in John Romeyn Brodhead, *History of the State of New York: First Period, 1609–1664* (1853). Brief discussions of Block are in E. B. O'Callaghan, ed., *The Documentary History of the State of New-York*, vols. 3 and 4 (1850, 1851); O'Callaghan, ed., *Documents Relative to the Colonial History of the State of New York*, vols. 1 and 2 (1856–1858); and Charles Deane, "New England," pp. 295–384, in Justin Winsor, ed., *Narrative and Critical History of America*, vol. 3 (1884). In J. Franklin Jameson, ed., *Narratives of New Netherland, 1609–1664* (1909), pp. 36–60, are substantial parts of *New World, or Description of West-India* [i.e., America] (1625) by Johan de Laet, who probably used Block's journals (now not extant) and also those of his associates, Hendrick Christiansen and Cornelis

Jacobsz May; and also in Jameson, pp. 293–354, is all of Adriaen van der Donck et al., *The Representation of New Netherland*, in which Block is mentioned as a trader. Material pertaining to Block appears in Nellis M. Crouse, "The White Man's Discoveries and Explorations," pp. 133–76, and Adriaan J. Barnouw, "The Settlement of New Netherland," pp. 215–58, in *Wigwam and Bouwerie*, vol. 1 of *History of the State of New York*, ed. Alexander C. Flick, 10 vols. (1933). I. N. Phelps Stokes, *The Iconography of Manhattan Island*, 6 vols. (1915–1928), includes (in vol. 2) a plate reproducing Block's "Figurative Map" and praise for its accurate and pioneering details. Block's original map is in the Algemeen Rijksarchief (ARA) at The Hague.

ROBERT L. GALE

BLORE, Eric (23 Dec. 1886–1 Mar. 1959), actor, was born in London, England, one of two children of Henry Blore, a schoolmaster, and his wife Mary Newton Blore. Blore was educated at the Mills School in Finchley. After selling insurance a while, he went on the stage in 1908, and by 1913 he had made his London performing debut.

Blore was one of the seemingly inexhaustible troupe of supporting players who gave the American screen during its golden decades of the 1930s and '40s its distinctive sheen. But during his British career, Blore was renowned as much for his writing as his comic acting. He wrote absurdist sketches that were incorporated into the bills of leading variety theaters and slightly saucy lyrics for a number of songs incorporated into musical revues. During World War I while serving in a Welsh regiment, he wrote "The Disorderly Room," a sketch based on the titles of popular songs, which throughout the interwar years was a regular part of the variety and radio repertoire. In 1917 Blore married Violet Winter. She died, childless, in 1919 during an influenza epidemic.

Wavy-haired and athletically built, Blore used his experience in Concert Party, the variety troupes popular at British seaside cities, and revue to create character in quick, broad strokes. By 1923 he had also created a revue, played his earliest film roles, and collaborated with Philip Braham on "How D'You Do?" (a song that served for many years as the opening number for the revues of André Charlot). Blore made his New York acting debut in 1923 as Bertie Bird in *Little Miss Bluebeard*, a starring vehicle for Irene Bordoni. One of the enduring theatrical stereotypes is the sillyass Englishman, and Bird was the first in a line of British fops and decayed nobles that kept Blore busy in nonmusical vehicles throughout the decade and effectively canceled his writing career. In 1926, the year of *The Ghost Train*, he married American actress Clara Macklin; they had one child and remained married until Blore's death. In the same year he made his American film debut as Lord Digby in the first screen version of F. Scott Fitzgerald's *The Great Gatsby*.

It was a return visit to the musical stage in 1932 that turned Blore's career toward its lasting achievement. By now virtually bald and owl-like in appearance, he played an officious, apoplectic waiter in *The Gay Divorce*, a resounding hit starring Fred Astaire and Claire Luce and featuring Cole Porter's music. Blore's arching eyebrows, oddly mincing yet rude obsequiousness and a general ability to draw attention to himself brought a contract from RKO–Radio Pictures and lasting fame in what became a virtual Fred Astaire–Ginger Rogers repertory company.

Blore's first supporting role with Astaire and Rogers came in *Flying Down to Rio* (1933) as Butterbass, a waiter suffering and seething under the command of the prissy hotel manager Franklin Pangborn. There followed *The Gay Divorcée* (1934), a partial reprise of his stage role in *The Gay Divorce* and his lone opportunity to dance on screen. Eleven films later, the role that catapulted Blore into fame came in *Top Hat* (1935).

Hollywood films of the Great Depression often seemed fascinated with the way the well-off lived, and men who could play valets were much in demand. Among the "Hollywood Raj" (as the constantly enlarging British colony came to be known) the tall, rather lugubrious Arthur Treacher had already established his credentials as an ideal Jeeves. Blore took a different line and created an incomparably eccentric comic character. He later wrote that his inspiration was a "batman" (orderly) who during his wartime service taught him "the whole art. . . . He had a way of putting out my studs that made them look worth at least 2 guineas." In *Top Hat*, equipped with a stylish script by Dwight Taylor (who had been responsible for *The Gay Divorce*), Blore played Bates, the disapproving manservant to bumbling, philandering Edward Everett Horton. Blore was regal ("WE are Bates, Sir," the film's catchphrase, caused the unsettled Horton to mumble about "all these plural personalities"). As Bates, Blore was also impish and coy; but his physical presence conveyed a menace that was not purely comic.

Blore made two more films with Astaire and Rogers: *Swing Time* (1936), as Mr. Gordon, the fussy manager of the studio where Rogers teaches dancing, who is ready to fire Rogers until he is almost literally blown away by the number ("Pick Yourself Up") danced by Fred and Ginger; and *Shall We Dance* (1937), as Cecil Flintridge, the floor manager in a hotel where the stars' on again–off again marital farce is played out. Although his characterization was broader than in *Top Hat*, Blore teamed with Horton in a classic sequence in which the principals engage in a furious shushing match with members of an irritated audience; it is worthy of Stan Laurel and Oliver Hardy's geometrically expanding tit-for-tat sequences.

Well before he had completed his work in the Astaire-Rogers films, Blore was making as much as $3,500 weekly. He eventually appeared in more than eighty films, never billed higher than third. He never improved upon Bates, most often playing a variation of him, memorably and at length as Diggs in the Warner Bros. semi-screwball comedy *It's Love I'm After* (1937), where he spat at a teenaged snoop: "If I were not a gentleman's gentleman, I could be such a cad's cad."

Blore showed up in such unlikely places as the Alps (*Swiss Miss*, 1938, with Laurel and Hardy) and vaguely tropical climes (*The Island of Lost Men*, 1939, and *South of Suez*, 1940), where, playing against stereotype, he made an oddly convincing down-at-the-heels expatriate grifter. He played the valet in more than one series of B pictures but often seemed out of place in melodrama; Blore was always most at home, most effective, in stylish, light-hearted films with music.

Having settled in Hollywood (he made one more British screen appearance as a thief in the 1939 mystery *A Gentleman's Gentleman*) and into his lucrative typecastings, Blore is said to have employed in everyday life excessively British turns of phrase, to have become "more English than the English." There were brief returns to the musical stage: in the Hollywood run of *André Charlot's British War Relief Revue* in 1940 and the nostalgic Broadway restaging of the *Ziegfeld Follies* in 1944. The demand for valets and butlers in films declined after World War II and with it Blore's vogue. In 1949, however, he proved an ideal choice for the voice of the manic, obsessed Toad in the animated Disney version of *The Wind in the Willows*. A year after his final film role in 1955, a stroke ended Blore's career; he died of a heart attack at the Motion Picture Country Home Hospital in suburban Los Angeles.

• The manuscripts of Blore's theatrical writing are on file in the Lord Chamberlain's Collection at the British Library, London; reviews and articles dealing with his British stage career are in the Theatre Museum, London. An invaluable source on the Astaire-Rogers films is Arlene Croce, *The Fred Astaire and Ginger Rogers Book* (1972). The details on many of Blore's films are in the *American Film Institute Catalogues 1921–1930* and *1931–1940*. The collection of the British Film Institute, London, is helpful. Something of Blore's life in Hollywood is gleaned from Sheridan Morley, *Tales from the Hollywood Raj* (1983) and papers held by the family of André Charlot in California. Blore's catchphrase from *Top Hat* is misquoted ("We are Jones, sir") in *Halliwell's Film Companion* (all editions). An obituary is in the *New York Times*, 3 Mar. 1959.

JAMES ROSS MOORE

BOMBECK, Erma (21 Feb. 1927–22 Apr. 1996), humorist and television personality, was born Erma Fiste in Dayton, Ohio, the only child of Cassius Fiste, a municipal laborer, and Erma Haines Fiste. Her father died when she was nine and her mother then went to work for General Motors in Dayton. Later her mother was remarried, to Tom Harris, who also worked at GM. Erma began her journalism career while attending Patterson Vocational High School, where she wrote a humor column for the school newspaper and worked part time in a secretarial position at the *Dayton Journal-Herald*. Following graduation in 1944 Erma worked full time at the *Journal-Herald* as a copy girl. After a year she entered the University of Dayton, where she majored in English and worked a variety of jobs, including writing for the student newspaper and magazine.

Upon receiving her B.A. in 1949, Erma Fiste went back to work for the *Dayton Journal-Herald*, this time as a reporter. At first relegated to obituaries and radio listings, she later wrote feature articles for the women's page as well as her own housekeeping column. In August of that year she married William Lawrence Bombeck, a former sportswriter for the paper; the couple would have three children.

With the arrival of their first child in 1953, Erma Bombeck quit work and became a full-time mother. After a decade at home with her children, she persuaded a nearby weekly newspaper, the *Kettering-Oakwood Times*, to allow her to write a humor column for $3 a week. Drawing on her experiences as a housewife, she soon attracted the attention of her former employer (the *Journal-Herald*), which hired her to produce two columns per week in 1965. Within a matter of weeks her column "At Wit's End" was syndicated by Newsday Specials. Featuring both self-deprecating humor and exaggeration, Bombeck stayed true to her core audience—stay-at-home wives and mothers who could identify with her.

Bombeck's first book, *At Wit's End*, appeared in 1967. By the late 1960s her column appeared in over two hundred newspapers, having moved first to Publishers-Hall Syndicate and then to the Field Newspaper Syndicate. Despite being in demand on the national lecture circuit, she put her family first, joking that she could not be away on a promotional tour for "more than two days because that's all the underwear we have" (*Current Biography Yearbook*, 1979). She began writing a humor column for *Good Housekeeping* in 1969, which along with articles in publications such as *Family Circle*, *McCall's*, *Reader's Digest*, and *Redbook* placed her attitudes, views on life, child-raising techniques, and household routines squarely within the American mainstream.

Her second book, *Just Wait till You Have Children of Your Own!* (1971), was produced in collaboration with cartoonist Bil Keane. In a chapter titled "Hide and Don't Seek Mother," Bombeck remarked on the teenage years and the need for separation at this age:

> The first time I realized my children were ashamed of me was at a PTA Open House. One of the teachers asked my son, "Is your mother here?" Instinctively, he jammed me into the locker, threw his body in front of it and said, "No, she couldn't come this evening. She's playing pillow bingo at the church." I was indignant. "Why did you say that? Have I ever laughed with cottage cheese in my mouth? Have I ever done my Gale Storm impersonations in front of anyone but family?" . . . He didn't answer. He just smiled and pretended he was giving me directions to the gym. (p.114)

Bombeck's third book, *I Lost Everything in the Post-Natal Depression*, appeared in 1973. While her previous books had sold well, her fourth offering, *The Grass*

Is Always Greener over the Septic Tank (1976), remained on the bestseller list for over a year and sold over half a million copies in hardback. In November of that year she began appearing twice weekly (as she would until 1986) on ABC-TV's "Good Morning America."

In the spring of 1978 her book *If Life is a Bowl of Cherries, What Am I Doing in the Pits?* was published, again to positive reviews. After a television adaptation of *The Grass Is Always Greener over the Septic Tank*, starring Carol Burnett as the "cinematic persona of Erma Bombeck" in the fall of 1978, Bombeck remained a successful author. By now syndicated in over 800 newspapers worldwide, her book production continued unabated, including *Motherhood, The Second Oldest Profession* (1983), *I Want to Grow Hair, I Want to Grow Up, I Want to Go to Boise: Children Surviving Cancer* (1989; with proceeds going to cancer societies worldwide), *All I Know about Animal Behavior I Learned in Loehmann's Dressing Room* (1995), and *Forever, Erma: Best-Loved Writing from America's Favorite Humorist* (1996).

During her most productive years, she worked from her home-office in Phoenix, Arizona, where she and her family had moved in 1971; her husband worked as a high school principal there. Bombeck received three honorary doctorates, and in 1978 she was appointed to the President's National Advisory Committee for Women.

Bombeck underwent a double mastectomy in 1992. After having suffered most of her life from polycystic kidney disease, she was placed on a waiting list for a kidney transplant soon after the surgery. She died in San Francisco, California, following complications from the transplant.

With uncommon wit, Erma Bombeck brought fresh insight into the tribulations of middle-class American family life. At a time when the traditional roles of women were being challenged by the rise of feminism, she celebrated motherhood and being a wife. Ironically, her very success as a syndicated columnist and author of bestselling books proved that a highly talented woman need not be bound by purely domestic concerns. But by not impugning domesticity Bombeck gave comic voice to the views of millions of Americans for whom the values of home and family were not in question.

• No collection of Bombeck's papers has been located. The best secondary source of information on her life and career is Susan Edwards, *Erma Bombeck: A Life in Humor* (1997). Also useful are feature articles in *Newsday*, 5 June 1969; *Life*, 1 Oct. 1971; *Christian Science Monitor*, 8 Aug.1973; and *People*, 21 Feb.1994. Obituaries appeared in the *New York Times* and *Variety*, both on 23 April 1996.

BARBARA BENNETT PETERSON

BONO, Sonny (16 Feb. 1935–5 Jan. 1998), entertainer, songwriter, and politician, was born Salvatore Phillip Bono in Detroit, Michigan, the son of Santo Bono, a truck driver, and Jean Bono (maiden name unknown), a beautician. Reared in a working-class environment, Bono was an average student and enjoyed playing the class clown. When he was seven the family moved to Los Angeles, California, where he finished his education. Bono married Donna Rankin in 1954, two years after his graduation from Inglewood High School. They had one daughter.

In 1956, eager for a career in the music business, Bono took a delivery job with the L.A. Meat Company, working the route that served Sunset Boulevard. At that time the business establishments on Sunset Boulevard included many independent record labels. Soon he was hired as a songwriter and A&R (artist and repertoire) man by Art Rube's Specialty Records, where he met Sam Cooke and Little Richard, two of the most popular rhythm-and-blues singers of the day. He left Specialty in 1961 and began assisting the influential record producer Phil Spector, for whom he worked as a publicist and wrote songs, including "Needles and Pins," which in 1964 became a hit record for the Searchers.

In the early 1960s Bono met a beautiful sixteen-year-old runaway, Cherilyn Sarkasian LaPier, who called herself Cher. They soon began living together (his first marriage having recently ended in divorce) and formed a musical partnership, capitalizing on Cher's powerful singing voice and Sonny's songwriting and production skills. Billed as Caesar and Cleo, they recorded "Baby Don't Go," "The Letter," and "Love Is Strange," without much success.

Bono finally achieved fame in 1965, when the couple, now performing as Sonny and Cher, released "I Got You Babe," which he wrote. Selling more than 3 million copies, it climbed to number one on the charts and became their signature song. "I Got You Babe" was followed by another hit, "The Beat Goes On" (1967). Building on the celebrity they enjoyed as a duo act, Bono wrote songs for Cher to record on her own, including "You Better Sit Down, Kids" (1967), which dealt with divorce, and "Bang, Bang (My Baby Shot Me Down)" (1966). By the late 1960s the public's tastes in music were changing, as psychedelic acid rock became more popular, and the antidrug, pseudo-hippie Sonny and Cher saw their success fade. Financial difficulties, in part caused by the failure of the Bono-produced film *Chastity* (1969), forced the pair to perform at nightclubs and in Las Vegas. They succeeded, though, in creating a comedy-musical act that made them the "Burns and Allen for the 1970s in which the husband was the brunt of the jokes" (*Newsweek*, 19 Jan. 1998). They married in 1969, after the birth of their daughter, Chastity, their only child.

In 1971 the couple introduced their Las Vegas show to Hollywood, starring in the weekly television variety show "The Sonny and Cher Comedy Hour," which blended slapstick comedy with musical performances. Each week Bono played the fool, as Cher's acerbic wit always got the best of him. The couple, dressed in quintessential 1970s fashion, with Cher in colorful, sequined Bob Mackie gowns and Sonny in bell-bottoms and paisley shirts, ended the show with a performance of "I Got You Babe," usually with Chastity in her parents' arms. But Sonny and Cher's on-screen harmony hid the dissolution of their real-life relationship. Both began having affairs, and their marriage was over by 1974, the same year their show left the airwaves; their divorce was finalized in July 1975.

After a brief solo attempt at television success and numerous guest appearances on such weekly series as "The Love Boat" and "Fantasy Island," Bono opened the first of several Italian restaurants in southern California. In the 1980s he had small roles in the films *Airplane II: The Sequel* and *Hairspray*. Following a brief third marriage, to Susie Coelho, he wed Mary Whitaker, whom he had met when she visited one of his restaurants after her college graduation, in 1986. They had two children together.

Bono's candidacy for mayor of Palm Springs was inspired by city zoning rules that frustrated his desire to hang a sign above his local restaurant. Although he had never voted in his life, he won election in 1988, serving a four-year term. As mayor he instituted an international film festival and supported antidrug efforts. In 1992 he lost the Republican primary in a run for the U.S. Senate. He blamed his defeat in part on his "Sonny Bonehead" image that lingered from his 1970s television series.

In 1994, overcoming the stigma of his celebrity, Bono was elected as a Republican to the U.S. House of Representatives, serving the Forty-fourth Congressional District in southern California. He took his place among the first Republican majority the House had seen in forty years. His election was a surprise—both to the media and to Bono. He told the Washington Press Club Foundation in 1995, "The last thing in the world I thought I would be is a U.S. Congressman, given all the bobcat vests and Eskimo boots I used to wear," referring to his fashion choices of the mid-1960s (*New York Times*, 7 Jan. 1998).

Bono supported both House Speaker Newt Gingrich and the Contract with America, as the Republican party agenda was called, finishing second only to the Speaker in fundraising. His conservative views on homosexual marriage strained his relationship with his daughter Chastity, who had become a prominent lesbian activist. But he managed to make friends across the aisle, charming opponents with his easygoing personality, frankness, and self-deprecating humor. Appointed to the House Judiciary Committee, he relished his "citizen-lawmaker" status in a House dominated by lawyers. Also a member of the National Security Committee, he was reelected in 1996.

Bono was killed in a skiing accident while on vacation with his family at the Heavenly Ski Resort in South Lake Tahoe, California. Both politicians and celebrities attended his funeral in Palm Springs, which generated bizarre newspaper photographs, such as the one of former president Gerald Ford consoling pop singer Tony Orlando. Among those delivering eulogies were California governor Pete Wilson, Newt Gingrich, and Cher, who told the 1,200 mourners that Bono "had the confidence to be the butt of the joke because he created the joke." In April 1998, four months after his death, Mary Bono won a special election to succeed her husband in the House.

Bono, who "made a career . . . of confounding people's expectations" (*Rolling Stone*, 19 Feb. 1998), was the quintessential American optimist, able to find success as a songwriter, music publicist, singer, television personality, restaurateur, small-town mayor, and Washington politician. Although—or maybe because—few took him seriously, he was a shrewd and savvy businessman. His nasal singing voice was little more than mediocre, yet he had the talent to produce a highly commercial form of popular music with overtones of contemporary youth culture and a sanitized aura of rock and roll. As a duo, Sonny and Cher could reach millions of working- and middle-class Americans for whom the likes of Jimi Hendrix, the Jefferson Airplane, and even the Beatles were anathema. A pop icon of the "Silent Majority" during the Vietnam Era and its aftermath, Sonny Bono lived a version of the American dream having wide appeal, which the final chapter of his life—as a conservative but genial member of Congress—seemed to validate.

• Sonny Bono's autobiography is *And the Beat Goes On* (1991). The *New York Times*, 31 May 1992, contains an article that discusses Bono's fight for political respect. The 1 Mar. 1995 edition of that newspaper features an interview with Congressman Bono; on 7 Apr. 1995 the *Times* published excerpts from some of his more humorous speeches. Obituaries are in the *New York Times*, 7 Jan. 1998; *Billboard*, 17 Jan. 1998; and *Time, Rolling Stone,* and *People*, 19 Feb. 1998. Accounts of the memorial service are in the *New York Times*, 10 Jan. 1998, and *Newsweek*, 19 Jan. 1998. "In His Absence," an article in the 26 Jan. 1998 issue of *People*, discusses the relationship of Cher and Mary Bono. The *New York Times*, 9 Apr. 1998, tells of Mary Bono's successful bid for her husband's seat in Congress.

STACEY HAMILTON

BONWIT, Paul J. (29 Sept. 1862–11 Dec. 1939), retail merchant, was born Paul Joseph (or Josef) Bonwit near Hanover, Germany, the son of Bernard Bonwit. His father's occupation and mother's name are unknown. He attended the local Gymnasium before moving to Paris at age sixteen, where he found work with a local export house as a clerk while continuing his academic studies at night. In 1883 Bonwit came to the United States. After a brief stay in New York City, he moved to Lincoln, Nebraska, where he worked in a department store. By now determined to enter the retail business world, he returned to New York and became affiliated with Rothschild & Company. Bonwit eventually became a partner in the firm, which was renamed Bonwit, Rothschild & Company. He married Sarah Woolf in 1893. The couple had two sons.

Eager to establish his own retail operation, Bonwit opened a store at Sixth Avenue and Eighteenth Street in 1895. Two years later he entered a partnership with Edmund D. Teller, and the two men relocated their establishment (now known as Bonwit Teller) to Sixth Avenue and Twenty-third Street. The partners incorporated their firm in 1907 as Bonwit Teller & Company and in 1911 relocated yet again, this time to the corner of Fifth Avenue and Thirty-eighth Street. They announced that this new location would provide consumers with "an uncommon display of wearing apparel from foreign and domestic sources . . . which will appeal to those who desire the unusual and exclusive at moderate prices." The firm continued to specialize in high-end women's apparel at a time when many of its competitors were diversifying their product lines, and Bonwit Teller became noted within the trade for the quality of its merchandise as well as the above-average salaries paid to both buyers and executives.

In 1930, sensing that the retail trade in New York City was moving uptown, Bonwit chose a new address farther up Fifth Avenue—the former Stewart & Company building at Fifty-sixth Street. Although the building had been remodeled as recently as 1929—with a "daringly modern" interior that consisted of separate, highly individualistic salons—Bonwit felt that the layout detracted from his merchandise, and he contracted with Ely Jacques Kahn for a complete overhaul. As the economic depression affecting the nation grew, such expenses did not add luster to the firm's bottom line. In 1931 the company attracted the attention of noted financier Floyd Odlum, who had shrewdly cashed in his stock holdings just prior to the stock market crash of 1929 and was creating a career for himself out of acquiring and turning around otherwise solid firms that were in financial distress. Bonwit agreed to let Odlum's wife Hortense serve as a consultant to the company in 1932, and two years later—dogged by poor health and saddened by the death of his wife—he sold the firm to Odlum's Atlas Corporation. Odlum promptly named his wife as the new president (she became in the process the first woman to hold such a position in New York), with Bonwit's son Walter staying on as vice president and general manager.

During his business career, Bonwit sat on the boards of both Harriman National Bank and A. Sulka & Company, while he also maintained an interest in philanthropies and the arts. He died in Manhattan after a brief illness. The firm bearing his name enjoyed something of a revival under the direction of the Odlums. Sold to the Hoving Corporation in 1946, the store underwent several changes of ownership, beginning with Genesco in 1956, then Allied Stores Corporation in 1979, and finally the Hooker Corporation in 1987. In May 1990 the developer Donald Trump demolished the Fifth Avenue store in order to make room for the Trump Tower, and the firm of Bonwit Teller no longer was in business.

In the history of retail trade, the name Bonwit Teller has remained synonymous with high quality in women's apparel, and through that association Paul Bonwit secured his niche in the annals of New York business.

• No collection of Bonwit's papers has been located, and secondary information on his life and career is scarce. Hortense M. Odlum's *A Woman's Place: The Autobiography* (1939) paints a grim picture of conditions at Bonwit Teller at the time of the Atlas Corporation takeover, while Robert Hendrickson's *The Grand Emporiums: The Illustrated History of America's Great Department Stores* (1979) gives a brief overview of the company's history. An obituary is in the *New York Times*, 11 Dec. 1939.

EDWARD L. LACH, JR.

BOWERS, Fredson (25 Apr. 1905–11 Apr. 1991), literary scholar, editor, and educator, was born Fredson Thayer Bowers in New Haven, Connecticut, the only child of Fredson Eugene Bowers, an executive of an automotive-parts manufacturing company, and Hattie May Quigley Bowers. He was educated at New Haven General High School (1917–1921), Brown University (Phi Beta Kappa, 1924; Ph.B., 1925), and Harvard (Ph.D., 1934), and during the next four years he taught as instructor in English at Harvard (1934–1936) and Princeton (1936–1938). During these years his marriage (1924–1936) to Hyacinth Adeline Sutphen, of a socially prominent New York family, produced four children but ended in divorce; it was also in his Harvard period that his interest in dogs was at its height, for he was then active as a breeder and judge of Irish wolfhounds, writing columns for the *American Kennel Gazette* and publishing as his first book *The Dog Owner's Handbook* (1936).

Nearly all of Bowers's professional life was spent in Charlottesville, Virginia, where he moved in 1938. His early years in Charlottesville were interrupted by World War II service (1942–1945) as Commander (USNR) in Naval Communications, Washington, D.C. In 1942 he married the novelist and short-story writer Nancy Hale (whose ancestors were Nathan Hale and Edward Everett Hale), and the happiness of their lives together lasted until her death forty-six years later. Bowers, celebrated for his teaching as well as his scholarship, quickly rose through the academic ranks at the University of Virginia (to associate professor in 1946, professor in 1948, Alumni Professor in 1957, and Linden Kent Memorial Professor in 1968); and in eight years of administrative service (department chair, 1961–1968; dean of the faculty, 1968–1969) his energy and devotion helped build Virginia into a major research institution. He also taught at the University of Chicago for sixteen summers (1949–1964). Among the honors he garnered were fellowships (such as Fulbright, 1952–1953, and Guggenheim, 1958–1959, 1970), honorary degrees (Clark, Brown, 1970; Chicago, 1973), and awards (notably the Gold Medal of the London Bibliographical Society, 1969, and election to the American Academy of Arts and Sciences, 1972). He retired in 1975 and died in Charlottesville sixteen years later.

At the time of Bowers's death, he had been the leading figure in the fields of bibliographical scholarship and textual criticism for three decades, succeeding to that title upon W. W. Greg's death in 1959. The idea that the texts of verbal works are affected by their passage through the printing process and that printed books hold physical clues to their own production history (clues that are therefore relevant to studying the intellectual content of the works transmitted by those books) had increasingly been recognized from the mid-nineteenth century onward; but no one before Bowers had been so aggressive in promoting the field nor so prolific in producing scholarly editions and fundamental theoretical statements. Over a career of some fifty-five years, he published about three million words of scholarly writing and over sixty edited volumes of the works of Christopher Marlowe, Thomas Dekker, Shakespeare, Beaumont and Fletcher, John Dryden, Fielding, Nathaniel Hawthorne, Walt Whitman, Stephen Crane, William James, and Vladimir Nabokov. His often insistent and uncompromising tone, contrasting with the courtliness of his demeanor, aroused controversy; but he did not seek argument for its own sake and was fair-minded and principled in his criticisms of others' efforts. The influence he exerted came not only from the solidity of his contribution to scholarship but also from the visibility he gave to his field.

His position of dominance was established in his forties by three publications. In 1948 he brought out the first volume of an annual, *Studies in Bibliography*, which rapidly became a prestigious organ for new approaches to bibliographical and textual scholarship; he continued as its editor until his death, and through it he profoundly affected the development of the discipline. The next year he published *Principles of Bibliographical Description*, which from that moment forward was regarded as a classic; it set out to codify and refine the methods for describing books as physical objects, and it remains the primary guide to its subject. And in 1953 the first volume of his edition of Thomas Dekker appeared, exemplifying a new editorial approach that, in the ensuing decades, influenced editors of all postmedieval literature. Following these early triumphs, he was asked to deliver the three major series of bibliographical lectures—the Rosenbach at the University of Pennsylvania in 1954, the Sandars at Cambridge in 1958, and the Lyell at Oxford in 1959—resulting in three major books, *On Editing Shakespeare and the Elizabethan Dramatists* (1955), *Textual and Literary Criticism* (1959), and *Bibliography and Textual Criticism* (1964). These books are eloquent statements of what he called "the bibliographical way," which recognized the vital role that artifactual evidence plays in establishing accurate texts. Although in the 1960s, 1970s, and 1980s he concentrated on producing editions rather than on writing books, he continued to publish essays, many of great significance, and gathered a substantial selection of them in 1975 as *Essays in Bibliography, Text, and Editing*.

Although Bowers's scholarly reputation will rest on his bibliographical studies and editions, his voluminous body of work includes literary history and criticism as well, from *Elizabethan Revenge Tragedy, 1587–*

1642 (1940), derived from his dissertation, to *Hamlet as Minister and Scourge* (1989), a collection of essays on Shakespeare and Milton. With the same discipline that underlay his scholarly and administrative productivity, he allocated time to many other enthusiasms: besides dogs, they included stamp collecting, music (he reviewed some 5,000 records in 1,162 columns for the *Richmond Times-Dispatch*, 1939–1966), sports cars, fox hunting, the stock market, and good food and wine (evident in the Bowerses' life at "Woodburn," their Charlottesville house with unobstructed views of the Blue Ridge Mountains, and at their summer place "Howlets," the Cape Ann stone cottage that had been Lilian Westcott Hale's studio). The intensity that Bowers brought to all his activities, professional and avocational alike, resulted in a lasting legacy: he not only came to personify bibliographical and textual scholarship in his own time, but his rigorous and powerful demonstration of the importance of physical evidence in books will continue to influence all who are concerned with the recovery of literature from the past.

• The principal collection of Bowers's papers is in the University of Virginia Library. The basic published source for details about his life is G. Thomas Tanselle, *The Life and Work of Fredson Bowers* (1993), which was published both in volume 46 of *Studies in Bibliography* and as a separate volume; it is accompanied, in both places, by a complete list of Bowers's writings compiled by Martin Battestin. Further information appears in David L. Vander Meulen, *The Bibliographical Society of the University of Virginia: The First Fifty Years* (1998). See also the substantial collections of tributes in *Papers of the Bibliographical Society of America* 79 (1985): 173–226; *Bibliographical Society of Australia and New Zealand Bulletin* 15 (1991): 45–102; *Dictionary of Literary Biography Yearbook: 1991*, ed. James W. Hipp (1992), pp. 224–53; and *Text* 8 (1995): 25–100; as well as George Walton Williams's article (with illustrations) in *American Book-Collectors and Bibliographers. First Series*, ed. Joseph Rosenblum (1994), pp. 13–21. A selection of photographs (including a reproduction of the 1946 oil portrait of Bowers by his mother-in-law, Lilian Westcott Hale) appear in *A Keepsake to Honor Fredson Bowers* (1974). Bowers's eldest son, Fredson T. Bowers, Jr., prepared a reminiscence for private circulation in 1993.

G. THOMAS TANSELLE

BOWLES, Paul (30 Dec. 1910–18 Nov. 1999), composer, fiction writer, and translator, was born Paul Frederick Bowles in Jamaica, New York, the son of Claude Dietz Bowles, a dentist from Elmira, and Rena Winnewisser Bowles, a native of Bellows Falls, Vermont. An only child, Bowles hated his father, a martinet who brooked no interference by his wife when it came to child-rearing. Bowles was three when he taught himself to read. A year later he was writing animal stories, recording personal impressions in a series of leather-bound notebooks, and drawing pictures of houses, streets, and imaginary railroad lines. Commanded to play for an hour daily within a fenced back yard with a view only of buildings and sky, Bowles never saw another child until he was five.

His formal education commenced at the Model School in Jamaica, where he was tested by the principal and placed in second grade shortly before reaching the age of seven. Taunted as a sissy until he beat up the neighborhood bully, Bowles was subtly rebellious. At school he refused to participate in any group activity and sometimes turned in class assignments with each word written backward. He was eight when his father brought home a phonograph and introduced him to classical music. "My mother found a teacher in the neighborhood from whom I took weekly lessons in piano technique, theory, solfeggio, and ear training. At this point I preferred jazz and the music of Paul Whiteman. I was nine when I composed what I thought was an opera, which I played on a zither and recited to anyone who would listen" (Bowles to Virginia Spencer Carr, Tangier, 11 Sept. 1996).

Bowles graduated from Jamaica High School, where he was president of the Poetry Society and editor of *The Oracle*, the school's literary magazine, in which he published over thirty poems and his first short story. Two of his poems, "Spire Song" and "Entity," written when he was sixteen, were accepted by an avant-garde journal, *transition*, published in Paris. Impatient to experience Paris firsthand, Bowles aborted his studies at the University of Virginia during his first semester and secretly fled to Paris, where he lived for four months. After a second partial semester at the University of Virginia in 1931, Bowles returned to Paris, where he was joined by Aaron Copland, who had agreed to work with him informally. By then Gertrude Stein had befriended Bowles, but told him that he was "no poet" and suggested that his creative impulses would be better served if he stuck to composing music.

In August 1931, upon Stein's advice, Bowles and Copland traveled together to Tangier, Morocco, where they rented a house on the side of a mountain with a stunning view of the Mediterranean. Bowles loved his new environment, but Copland found that he could not compose there, largely owing to the primitive conditions and a wretched piano, and was impatient to return to Berlin, where they had formerly worked together. After a week in Fez with Bowles, Copland left, and they did not see each other again until mid-December, in London, where Bowles's newly composed Sonata for Oboe and Clarinet was premiered in a concert of American music organized by Copland (reviewed by Henry Boys in *Modern Music* [Jan./Feb. 1932]: 92–93). Bowles composed a second sonata (Sonata no. 1 for Flute and Piano) in 1932 in Grenoble, France, upon his return from North Africa. A concert of his music in New York in 1936 prompted Copland to write that he much preferred "an amateur like Bowles" to a "well-trained conservatory product."

"Aaron described me as 'militantly non-professional.' . . . I thought I could do what I wanted to do without any rigorous training. Short, simple pieces were the most satisfying, perhaps because I didn't know how to appreciate long, complex ones" (Bowles to Virginia Spencer Carr, Atlanta, Georgia, 10 May 1994). Composer Phillip Ramey, a friend of both Bowles and Copland, declared: "Considering the determined way in which Paul resisted instruction, choosing instead to rely on his instincts, one finds it rather amazing that he achieved what he did as a composer. His music is fresh, spontaneous sounding, and delightful" (quoted in Schwarz, 1995). Another friend of Bowles, composer Ned Rorem, described Bowles's music as "nostalgic and witty, evoking the times and places of its conception—Paris, New York and Morocco during the twenties, thirties and forties—through languorous triple meters, hot jazz and Arabic sonorities. The intent of his music is to please." Bowles himself contended that "if there is no communication there is no music. Knowing that the 'average' listener has not had a musical education, [a composer] must have the courtesy to address his listener in terms which will not alienate him."

In February 1938, Bowles married Jane Auer, a writer best known for her novel *Two Serious Ladies* (1943), her play *In the Summer House* (1953), and a handful of short stories. Jane Bowles died in 1973 after a long illness. They had no children.

Living in the United States during much of the 1930s and 1940s, Bowles wrote music for several plays produced by the Federal Theatre and for more than a dozen films. He also wrote the theater scores for thirty-three Broadway plays, including William Saroyan's *My Heart's in the Highlands*; Lillian Hellman's *Watch on the Rhine*; Shakespeare's *Twelfth Night* and *The Tempest*; and Tennessee Williams's *The Glass Menagerie, Summer and Smoke, Sweet Bird of Youth*, and *The Milk Train Doesn't Stop Here Anymore*. Other compositions by Bowles include music for his wife's *In the Summer House* and for a number of plays produced by the American School of Tangier, including *Oedipus the King, The Bacchae, Caligula*, and *Hippolytus*.

With his wife's encouragement, Bowles began his first novel in Tangier in 1947, published as *The Sheltering Sky* (1949). A collection of seventeen short stories, *The Delicate Prey and Other Stories*, was published in 1950. Three novels followed: *Let It Come Down* (1952), *The Spider's House* (1955), and *Up Above the World* (1960); and a novella, *Too Far from Home* (1991). His publications also include four books of poetry, most notably *Thicket of Spring* (1972) and *Next to Nothing* (1981); an autobiography, *Without Stopping* (1972); *In Touch, The Letters of Paul Bowles* (ed. Jeffrey Miller, 1994); over two dozen translations of books by several Moroccan writers and storytellers and by the Guatemalan writer Rodrigo Rey Rosa; and many vocal compositions and other music, including several operas and ballets.

Bowles made his home in Tangier from 1947 until his death. A letter from Bowles to Charles Henri Ford in 1947 seemed as applicable in 1999 as when he wrote it: "Certainly I never meant to stay in Tangier again, but for no reason at all I have remained on and on, perhaps because one can get everything one wants here and the life is cheap as dirt, and travel is so damned difficult . . . and mainly the great fact that I haven't the energy to pack up and go anywhere else" (cited in Caponi, p. 220).

At Bowles's request, after his death his body was returned to the United States; his ashes were interred in Lakemont Cemetery, Lakemont, New York, which overlooks Seneca Lake and the community of Glenora, where Bowles spent most of his summer holidays as a youth. "Here [in Glenora] I was free to wander the woods and shore and could go alone to fetch the mail in a rowboat, all a source of supreme pleasure" (Bowles to Virginia Spencer Carr, Tangier, 28 Dec. 1998).

• A major collection of Bowles's papers is at the Harry Ransom Humanities Research Center of the University of Texas at Austin, and another, more recent, at the University of Delaware Library, Newark, Delaware. Much of the Delaware collection was acquired from Bowles himself a few months before he died. Valuable published interviews with Bowles include K. Robert Schwarz, "A Composer Long Ago, an American Far Away," *New York Times*, 17 Sept. 1995; Mel Gussow, "Music, His Music, Lures Bowles Back," *New York Times*, 19 Sept. 1995; and Phillip Ramey, "'You Didn't Even Want to Meet Prokofiev?,'" in Claudia Swan, ed., *Paul Bowles Music* (1995). See also Gena Dagel Caponi, *Paul Bowles: Romantic Savage* (1994). An obituary is in the *New York Times*, 19 Nov. 1999.

VIRGINIA SPENCER CARR

BOYD, John R. (23 Jan. 1927–9 Mar. 1997), air force officer, was born John Richard Boyd in Erie, Pennsylvania, the son of Hubert Boyd, a paper mill official, and Elsie Mae Beyer. When Boyd was three, his father died and his mother became a telephone-advertising salesperson. At Strong Vincent High School in Erie, Boyd was an honor student and a member of the swimming team. He received his diploma in absentia in 1945 because he was serving in the U.S. Army Air Forces. During his tour of duty in Japan (1945–1946), Boyd criticized the bivouacking of enlisted men in freezing tents and giving them cold K rations while officers enjoyed warm quarters and hot food. When Boyd and others dismantled and burned a wooden hangar for warmth, he was threatened with court-martial; but he ultimately helped to implement reform measures. His stubborn maverick personality was forming.

In 1947 Boyd was admitted to the University of Iowa on an athletic scholarship, joined the Air Force Reserve Officers Training Corps, received a B.A. in economics, and was commissioned a second lieutenant (1951). The year he graduated, he married Mary Ethelyn Bruce, with whom he would have five children. Trained at Columbus Air Force Base in Mississippi, and Nellis Air Force Base in Nevada, Boyd flew F-86 Sabrejets in twenty-nine combat missions (1953) from Suwon Air Base in Korea, where he was flight commander and assistant operations officer. He was successful fighting Chinese-flown MIG-15s over the Yalu River.

Boyd served as a tactical fighter instructor at Nellis Air Force base from 1954 to 1960, flying two to three sorties daily. Known as "40-second Boyd," he bet $40 that he could let a rival pilot fly on his tail and within forty seconds have him in his own gun sights. He never lost. His strategy was to get inside his adversary's "time-cycle loop." In his words, "quicker [maneuvering] is better than faster [aircraft speed]." His *Aerial Attack Study* (1960), published when he was a captain, analyzes all known dogfight strategies and his new ones. He taught his students to begin a second maneuver while the enemy was reacting to the first.

In 1960 the air force sent Boyd to the Georgia Institute of Technology, where he earned a B.S. in industrial engineering in 1963. Specializing in thermodynamics, he formulated theories that revolutionized American fighter aircraft designs. He studied combinations of potential energy (ability to change altitude), kinetic energy (airspeed), and turn rate (direction, radius) of every type of U.S. fighter plane, and compared each with other aircraft, whether American, Soviet, or those of other nations. He called his theory "energy maneuverability"; other specialists called it "maneuver warfare." His theory applies today in weapons design, battlefield tactics, and even business competition by foreign rivals. At Eglin Air Force Base, Florida (1963–1966), Boyd theorized that slow, heavy American F-86s dominated MIG-15s because of the F-86's superior roll rate and visibility from the cockpit. He developed his famous "OODA Loop"—meaning the sequencing of Observation, Orientation, Decision, and Action in each fast-cycle aerial combat encounter. A pilot will kill if he can OODA—see, conclude, climb, veer, and shoot faster than his enemy.

In 1966 Boyd, then a major, worked in the Pentagon at air force headquarters as research and development director. He continued to be frenetically active, abrasive, and addicted to blowing smoke at adversarial theoreticians, mainly aeronautical engineers opposing his energy-maneuverability notions. He and several fellow mavericks, soon dubbed the "Lightweight Fighter Mafia," wrote new computer programs, secretly proving that the F-4 Phantom jet was worse even than the obsolete MIG-17, and developed new Phantom tactics; in 1968 they also redesigned the FX, called the F-15, by changing its swing wing to a fixed wing and reducing its weight from 60,000 pounds to a nimble 40,000 (though wanting it even lighter). In 1969 Colonel Boyd was appointed Systems Command deputy chief of staff at Andrews Air Force Base in Maryland, where he co-designed YF-16 and YF-17 prototypes. After serving briefly as a combat support-group commander at the Royal Thai Air Force Base in Thailand, he returned to the Pentagon to supervise development plans (1973).

Boyd went nose-to-nose with entrenched bureaucrats who mistakenly felt that newer, more expensive weaponry was automatically better. Highly intelligent as well as brash, Boyd read widely—in anthropology, biology, business, economics, genetics, information theory, mathematics, physics, political science, psychology, and even Eastern philosophy. He developed a lecture on total battle, expanded from four to thirteen hours, called "A Discourse on Winning and Losing," and delivered it more than a thousand times to army and marine personnel, who dared not walk out, suggest cuts, or even yawn.

Economy-minded in his personal life, Boyd lived with his family in a basement apartment in Alexandria, Virginia, thus earning the nickname "Ghetto Colonel." When he retired from active duty (1975), he lived with his wife on his military pension, continued to read extensively, and never thought of taking high-paying jobs with defense contractors. Becoming a consultant in the Program Analysis Directorate, Office of the Secretary of Defense, he offered to work full time without a salary—but accepted one day's pay for every two weeks of work in order to have a Pentagon payroll pass to enter the building. He and his friends inveighed against $400 hammers, $600 toilet seats, and huge cost overruns in weapons procurement. He also finished "Destruction and Creation" (1973–1976), a twelve-page document in which he presented proof that analysis versus synthesis alternately creates-destroys-creates our images of reality. This idea underpinned his work on competition and conflict.

Until Boyd was advanced in age, he continued advising trusted cohorts and thus inspiring criticism of and improvements in U.S. defense systems. His influence has been incalculable. The Army's 1976 *Field Manual, 100-5, Operations*, based on the ineffective Vietnam-era firepower-attrition philosophy, was rewritten (1982, 1986) to incorporate Boyd's maneuver theory, which is also largely the basis of the U.S. Marine Corps's first *Fleet Marine Force Manual* (1989). The theory, put simply, is to shoot and engage in deception, creating maneuver opportunities, panicking adversaries, and capturing them from the rear. It paid off memorably during the Persian Gulf War (1991); but when it was incompletely followed, most of Iraq's Republican Guard escaped and thus helped Saddam Hussein retain power.

Boyd regularly advised his closest colleagues not "to be [an establishment success] but to do [something important]." He died of cancer at West Palm Beach, Florida, and is buried at the Arlington National Cemetery. Boyd Hall at the U.S. Air Force Weapons School at Nellis was dedicated 17 September 1999, thus beginning tangible official recognition to the brilliance of this cross-grained military wizard, the most revealing of whose several nicknames was "Genghis John."

• Boyd's service records are in the Military Personnel Records, National Personnel Records Center, St. Louis, Mo. His extensive personal papers and library are in the Marine Corps University Archives, Quantico, Va. James G. Burton, *The Pentagon Wars: Reformers Challenge the Old Guard* (1993), and James P. Stevenson, *The Pentagon Paradox: The Development of the F-15 Hornet* (1993), are technical, Stevenson highly so; both discuss Boyd's accomplishments, ex-

tol him as an uncontrollable genius, and analyze the insufficient application of his maneuver theory during the Gulf War. Burton calls Boyd an "intuitive, creative genius" and lists his library of 317 books and articles. Stevenson, who stresses Boyd's contributions to the lightweight fighter program, reports that several Vietnam War fighter pilots said Boyd's missile-evasion briefings saved their lives. Joseph J. Romm, "The Wisdom of Sun Tzu," *Forbes*, 9 Dec. 1991, pp. 154–62 *passim*, suggests that Japanese industrialists have flanked American competitors by innovative and flexible manufacturing techniques paralleling elements in Boyd's maneuver theory. *It Doesn't Take a Hero: General H. Norman Schwarzkopf, the Autobiography*, written with Peter Petre (1992), does not (but doubtless should) mention Boyd and the importance of his combat theories to the outcome of the Gulf War. Obituaries are in *Air Power History*, Summer 1997; the *New Statesman*, 4 Apr. 1997; and the *New York Times*, 13 Mar. 1997.

ROBERT L. GALE

BRADDOCK, Jim (7 June 1906–29 Nov. 1974), world heavyweight boxing champion, was born James Walter Braddock in the Hell's Kitchen neighborhood on the West Side of Manhattan, New York City, the sixth child of Joseph Braddock, an English-born furniture mover, and Elizabeth O'Toole Braddock. Soon after his birth, the family moved to Guttenberg (later North Bergen), New Jersey, where he attended St. Joseph Parochial School. His schooling ended at age thirteen after he knocked out another boy in a fight. He worked as a telegraph messenger, errand boy, printer's devil, and teamster and began his amateur boxing career at age seventeen, turning professional at age twenty, in 1926. He was managed throughout his boxing career by Joe Gould, who renamed him "James J. Braddock," after former heavyweight champions James J. Corbett and James J. Jeffries. (Gould's actual name was Joe Biegel.)

Fighting as a light-heavyweight, Braddock enjoyed immediate success as a professional boxer, winning fourteen fights in 1926, either by knockout or decision, with two draws. In 1927 he had seventeen bouts, winning all but two, and by midyear was fighting ten-rounders. In 1928 he became the leading contender for the light-heavyweight championship by scoring victories over two other contenders: by decision over former welterweight champion Pete Latzo and by a sensational two-round knockout over Tuffy Griffiths in Madison Square Garden.

In 1929, continuing to fight main events in Madison Square Garden, Braddock lost a decision to Leo Lomski but then knocked out former light-heavyweight champion Jimmy Slattery. This earned him a title fight with light-heavyweight champion Tommy Loughran on 18 July at Yankee Stadium. The clever Loughran decisively outboxed Braddock, winning nearly every one of the fifteen rounds.

With this loss Braddock's luck turned for the worse. He had invested his ring earnings in stocks and a taxicab company in North Bergen. In the stock market crash of November 1929 his stock investments were wiped out overnight and his taxicab company eventually failed. He continued his ring career but seemed to have lost confidence in his fighting ability after the Loughran defeat. His difficult financial situation prevented him from training properly, and he was often forced to fight heavier opponents and to take fights as a substitute, when suffering from ring-related injuries. He won only ten of thirty-three fights from the Loughran defeat to the end of 1933 and consequently his ring earnings declined greatly. But, having married Mae Fox in 1929, he had a wife and three children to support. On 25 September 1933 his career reached its lowest point when he suffered a broken hand while fighting Abe Feldman, causing the fight to be declared "no contest," with forfeiture of his purse. Unable to fight until the hand healed, he was forced to work on the docks as a stevedore and to go on welfare to support his family.

On 14 June 1934 Braddock, on short notice, fought John "Corn" Griffin in a preliminary bout to the Primo Carnera–Max Baer heavyweight title fight in the Long Island City Bowl. Griffin had put together an impressive record while boxing in the southern states and was to be built into a heavyweight contender, with Braddock to be his first victim before a big city crowd and sportswriters. Although Braddock was knocked down in the second round, he arose and floored his opponent four times before stopping him in the third. In his next two fights, for which he was well trained, he defeated John Henry Lewis, who had defeated him earlier, and badly trounced heavyweight contender Art Lasky. Weighing 190 pounds by now, the six foot three Braddock was then matched in a title fight with heavyweight champion Max Baer.

Braddock was given little chance to defeat Baer, and—on 13 June 1935 in Long Island City—he entered the ring a 10–1 underdog. Baer reportedly underestimated Braddock and did not train rigorously. Braddock carried the fight to Baer and outboxed his slugging opponent to win clearly, thereby becoming heavyweight champion. It was the greatest upset in the history of the heavyweight title. Although the fight itself was not especially exciting, the sportswriters and public were intrigued by Braddock's comeback from ring oblivion. Damon Runyon dubbed him "the Cinderella Man."

Throughout most of his ring career Braddock was a counterpuncher whose upright style and cleverness caused him to be compared to James J. Corbett, a "pretty picture to watch in action," to quote writer Francis Albertanti. He was a precise, hard hitter but tended to lack spontaneity in the ring, thereby failing to take advantage of his opponents' weaknesses. Beginning with the Griffin fight he became more aggressive in style yet still did not have the "killer instinct."

Now holder of the heavyweight championship, Braddock was content to make money from his sudden fame by personal appearances and testimonials. In the meantime Joe Louis, a sensational black contender, had appeared, and the two met for the heavyweight title in Chicago on 22 June 1937. The odds were 11–5 against Braddock, but he knocked Louis down in the first round and fought him on even terms until the fourth round. Combining to turn the fight against him, however, were his two years of ring inactivity and Louis's youth and terrific punching ability. Though having fought courageously, Braddock was put down for the full count in the eighth round, and so lost the title. Braddock received $320,000 for the Louis fight, by far his largest purse. He fought once more, outpointing British heavyweight contender Tommy Farr in 1938, and then retired.

A proud man, Braddock fully repaid the state of New Jersey for the welfare he had received and opened a restaurant, which was not a success. He had otherwise invested his earnings wisely, however, and continued to live comfortably.

During World War II, he enlisted in the army, rising to the rank of captain and serving in the Pacific theater. Quiet and unassuming, he performed many acts of charity without calling attention to himself. Braddock died in his sleep at his home in North Bergen.

• Braddock's record as a professional boxer is in the *1986–87 Ring Record Book and Boxing Encyclopedia*, ed. Herbert G. Goldman. There are two biographies: James L. Harte, *The Amazing Story of James J. Braddock* (1938), and Ludwig Shabazian, *Relief to Royalty* (1936). Useful articles in *The Ring* magazine are Francis Albertanti, "Braddock's Mother behind His Startling Rise," Feb. 1929, pp. 22–23, and Michael Silver, "Braddock: the Cinderella Man Whose Clock Never Struck 12," Nov. 1983, pp. 80–86. An obituary by Joe Nichols appears in the *New York Times*, 30 Nov. 1974.

LUCKETT V. DAVIS

BRADY, Diamond Jim (12 Aug. 1856–13 Apr. 1917), businessman and cultural icon, was born James Buchanan Brady in New York City, the son of Daniel Brady, a saloonkeeper, and his wife, whose name is not recorded. After attending local schools until the age of eleven, he left home and became a bellboy at the nearby St. James Hotel. While working there he befriended John M. Toucey, an official with the New York Central Railroad, who offered Brady (by then fifteen) a job in the firm's baggage department. After a few months of moving baggage by day and studying bookkeeping, at Paine's Business College, by night, he became a ticket agent at the Central's Spuyten Duyvil station in the Bronx. In 1874 Brady became a clerk in the home office, and in 1877 he was promoted to the position of Toucey's chief clerk. It was here that Brady began to display his love of fine clothing and nightlife, personal indulgences that would characterize his later lifestyle.

Brady lost his job—under circumstances that remain a mystery—after his older brother (whom he had helped to gain a position with the Central) unfairly blamed him for an office mishap. He quickly rebounded and took a sales job with the railroad supply firm of Manning, Maxwell, and Moore. Although unattractive in appearance and unschooled in both speech and manners, Brady was not only smart and ambitious but also possessed the ability to make people like him. He proved to be a capable salesman of the firm's handsaws, and was soon able to acquire his first diamond. A popular craze at the time, men wore diamonds to signify their social standing, and Brady, who was eager to make his mark in the world, soon became an expert on the subject and was given the nickname by which he is known to this day. With the nation's railroad lines booming as the country entered the 1880s, Brady began to sell the firm's entire product line and reaped enormous commissions. This income, combined with his expense account, was spent on the types of lavish dining and entertainment that Brady would enjoy for the rest of his life.

In 1888 Brady joined forces with Sampson Fox, an Englishman who had struggled to promote his idea of an all-steel undercarriage for railroad cars. While it was popular overseas, American railroad men had been openly skeptical of the design, feeling that it would not be adaptable to the American rail system. Brady shrewdly arranged for a demonstration of the design, and, with the skeptics now quieted, orders flew into the firm of the Fox Solid Pressed Steel Company. Brady, who also continued to work for Manning, Maxwell, and Moore, soon was wealthy beyond his dreams. Now able to indulge his love for theater, fine clothing, and fine dining to an unlimited extent, Brady became one of the best-known figures in New York. Throughout the "Gay Nineties" and the first decade of the new century, he was constantly a subject of press coverage as he attended opening nights at the theater decked out in impeccably tailored suits lavishly decorated with diamond displays; his parties became the stuff of legend, as did his gastronomic exploits, which often featured Brady enjoying numerous helpings of each item of a fourteen-course dinner. Although intimate with many leading figures of the day—including New York City police commissioner Theodore Roosevelt, who utilized Brady's influence in keeping boxer John L. Sullivan from drinking too much and getting into fistfights—Brady was never really accepted by polite New York society.

Despite his outsider status in the milieu of New York's "old money," Brady continued to live life on his own terms. Thanks to his near-legendary generosity with both the great and the common folk alike, he was perhaps the most widely known and recognized figure in New York society. Although he never married, he did establish a long-term relationship with Edna McCauley, which ended when she ran off with his best friend. More stable was his ongoing platonic relationship with actress Lillian Russell, who was his constant companion for years and the beneficiary of perhaps his most notorious gift, a gold-plated bicycle that featured a gem-studded frame and mother-of-pearl handlebars.

With the advent of all-steel railroad cars, Brady's second employer eventually merged with a competitor to form the Pressed Steel Car Company in January 1899. While Brady held no office in the firm—preferring the role of salesman—his abundant income continued. In the spring of 1901 he acquired a farm in South Branch, New Jersey (in addition to his lavishly furnished dwelling on Eighty-sixth Street in Manhattan), where he also entertained guests and where in his later years he dabbled in thoroughbred horses.

Never fully satisfied with working for Pressed Steel, Brady formed with engineer John M. Hansen the Standard Steel Car Company in the spring of 1902. Brady served as the firm's vice president in charge of sales, and, based on the industry-wide reputation of the two men, the firm was an immediate success.

As the years went by, Brady's body began to break down from decades of overindulgence. Overweight and suffering from high blood pressure as well as coronary disease, he had as his most serious problem a prostatic obstruction. He entered Johns Hopkins Hospital in Baltimore in 1912 and underwent an experimental operation for gallstones conducted by medical pioneer Hugh H. Young. Treated like a celebrity during his stay (and subject to a fluoroscopic examination that revealed a stomach six times the average size), Brady was so impressed by his treatment that he offered over $200,000 to Hopkins, which resulted in the establishment of the James Buchanan Brady Urological Institute.

Brady died in Atlantic City, New Jersey, after fighting a long battle with diabetes. Under the terms of his will, much of his estate went to charity, and the balance was split between Johns Hopkins Hospital and New York Hospital, which used the funds to establish a urological facility of its own. Diamond Jim Brady is remembered as an example of the wild excesses of his age. Although much of the wealth that he earned was dissipated in various forms of entertainment, his philanthropic generosity to medical research also remains a part of his legacy.

• Material relating to Brady's interactions with Johns Hopkins can be found within the Hugh H. Young Papers at the Alan M. Chesney Archives, Johns Hopkins School of Medicine, Baltimore, Md. For biographical information, see Parker Morell, *Diamond Jim: The Life and Times of James Buchanan Brady* (1934; repr., 1970), and John Burke, *Duet in Diamonds: The Flamboyant Saga of Lillian Russell and Diamond Jim Brady in America's Gilded Age* (1972). An obituary is in the *New York Times*, 14 April 1917.

EDWARD L. LACH, JR.

BRATTAIN, Walter H. (10 Feb. 1902–13 Oct. 1987), physicist, was born Walter Houser Brattain in Amoy, China, the eldest of five children of Ross R. Brattain, a teacher in a private school for Chinese boys, and Ottilie Houser Brattain. Early in Brattain's childhood the Brattain family returned from China and settled in Tonasket, Washington, a small town where the senior Brattain had grown up. On his return to the United States Ross Brattain switched from teaching to homesteading, cattle ranching, and flour milling. After completing his secondary education in the schools in Tonasket, Walter enrolled at Whitman College in Walla Walla, Washington, where he majored in mathematics and physics and received a B.S.

degree in 1924. He then entered the University of Oregon and in 1926 was awarded a master's degree in physics. In 1929 he transferred to the University of Minnesota, receiving a Ph.D. in physics. While studying for his Ph.D. Brattain worked at the National Bureau of Standards in Washington, D.C.; there, with Vincent E. Heaton, he designed a temperature-controlled oscillator and also worked on improving accuracy in measurements of time and vibratory frequency. Although Brattain enjoyed outdoor life and ranching, he attributed his becoming a physicist to his hatred of farming. He once stated, "following the horse and a harrow in the dust is what made a physicist of me."

In 1929 Brattain joined the Bell Telephone Laboratories in Murray Hill, New Jersey. At Bell he initially studied the influence of adsorbed films on electron emission from hot surfaces, electron collision in hot mercury, magnetometers, infrared phenomena, and frequency standards. When Dr. William Shockley joined the research staff of Bell Labs in 1936, Brattain had been working there seven years and had experience with investigation of semiconductors. The only amplifying device available in the 1930s was the three-electrode (triode) vacuum tube, invented in 1907 by Lee de Forest, which was based on an earlier discovery by Thomas A. Edison. Shockley was interested in finding a less bulky, sturdier, and cheaper substitute for the three-element vacuum tube. Research on a replacement for the vacuum tube triode had been discouraged until the development of radar demonstrated that vacuum tubes were unable to satisfactorily handle the extremely high frequency signals necessary for radar.

Shockley began his search for a vacuum tube replacement with a study of the properties of semiconductors, substances that have a conductivity between that of good conductors and insulators and are sensitive to the presence of small amounts of impurities. The crystal radio was the basis for beginning these studies because it consisted of a simple electrical circuit in which radio wave signals picked up by the antenna were rectified (transformed from alternating current to direct current) by a piece of galena (semiconductor) attached to a curl of wire (cat's whisker). To improve the crystal radio, Shockley began a search for a semiconductor that would amplify as well as rectify. As part of this investigation Brattain studied the electrical conductivity and rectification of semiconductors. In this work Brattain devoted most of his interest to a study of copper-oxide varistors, but he also studied the properties of silicon and germanium. In 1942 this work was interrupted when Shockley and Brattain were assigned to the division of war research at Columbia University to work on a vital World War II project: the magnetic detection of submarines.

Shockley and Brattain returned to Bell Labs in 1945 and Dr. John Bardeen joined their group. Upon resuming the experiments interrupted in 1942 Shockley concluded that the moving electrons within a semiconductor could be influenced by an electrical field imposed from outside. Shockley's idea was the genesis of the "transistor." The first attempts to put this idea to the test failed. To explain this problem Bardeen suggested that a layer of electrons trapped at the surface of the semiconductor prevented the applied electron field from entering the body. This possibility was investigated by studying the effects of light, heat, liquids, and metallic films on the surface of semiconductors. After gaining a better understanding of the surface behavior of semiconductors, Brattain and Bardeen built a device comprising two closely placed gold film contacts on one face of a germanium crystal containing a small amount of impurities and a third terminal on the opposite face of the crystal. A positive bias was placed between one gold contact (emitter) and the third terminal on the base, and a negative bias was placed between the base and the other gold contact (collector). Currents (signals) applied to the emitter flowed to the collector and amplified (increased) the current in the base collector circuit. This device provided the first observation of the transistor effect, and it represented the birth of the transistor that was announced in the summer of 1948. Although it amplified the signal as predicted, its mechanism of operation was unanticipated. The invention of the transistor is credited to Bardeen and Brattain. Shockley, who advanced the theory that led to the discovery, was the transistor's father.

To explain the unexpected mechanism of transistor operation these investigators studied how atoms are held together in crystals by electrons that are loosely bound to their nuclei. When these bonds are completely "filled" or "satisfied," a perfect crystal exists. The electrons in such crystals do not easily flow, because they are difficult to detach; therefore, such crystals are insulators. Introduction of foreign atoms into the crystal that do not fit into the crystal structure results in a surplus of electrons. These can produce a current or leave "holes" that move in the opposite direction, acting like positively charged electrons. "Holes" are spaces left by moving electrons and appear to move backward as the electrons move forward to fill the previously emptied spaces. These studies explained transistor action, showing that it involved a complex interplay of the type and concentration of impurities in semiconductors, the local contact between dissimilar materials, and the movement of electrons and holes. Brattain's contribution was to study the properties and behavior of the semiconductors used to construct the transistor, and to build the first experimental units.

The original transistor reported by Bardeen and Brattain was called a point contact transistor. This device was advanced by J. N. Shine's "photo" transistor in 1950, Shockley's "junction" transistor in 1951, and R. L. Wallace's "triode" transistor in 1952. In 1952 the transistor was perfected for commercial use. Its first application was in a "card translator" that was employed for routing long distance telephone calls. The transistor rapidly replaced the vacuum tube in all applications requiring amplification, rectification, and switching. It has not only replaced the vacuum tube in radios, television sets, hearing aids, and the like, but it has made possible modern computers, sophisticated medical equipment, rapid, reliable communication networks, and many industrial control devices.

On 1 November 1956 Shockley, Bardeen, and Brattain were awarded the Nobel Prize in physics for their "investigations on semiconductors and the discovery of the transistor effect." Other awards received by Brattain include the Stuart Ballantine Medal of the Franklin Institute (1952), the John Scott Award of the City of Philadelphia (1955), and the University of Oregon Distinguished Alumni Award (1976).

On 5 July 1935 Brattain married Keren Gilmore, a physical chemist, who also had a Ph.D. degree; they would have one child, William Gilmore Brattain. Keren Brattain died in April 1957, and a year after her death Brattain married Emma Jane Kirsch Miller. He retired in 1967 and joined the faculty of Whitman College, where he taught physics and worked on the surface properties of living cells. Brattain was known for his brusque, outspoken manner. He enjoyed golf, fishing, and reading. He died in Seattle and is buried in Pomroy, Washington.

• Three short biographies of Walter Brattain are in *Nobel Prize Winners*, ed. Tyler Wassen (1987); *Current Biography* (1957); and *National Cyclopedia of American Biography*, suppl. 1 (1960). Information about surface properties of semiconductors is given in Brattain's Nobel lecture "Surface Properties of Semiconductors," *Science* 126 (1956): 151–53. General information about the development of the transistor is in John Bardeen's Nobel lecture "Research Leading to Point-Contact Transistor" and in "To a Solid State," *Science* 84 (Nov. 1984): 105–12. An obituary is in the *New York Times*, 14 Oct. 1987.

DAVID Y. COOPER

BRENNAN, William J., Jr. (25 Apr. 1906–24 July 1997), Supreme Court justice, was born William Joseph Brennan, Jr., in Newark, New Jersey, the son of William Joseph Brennan, a politician, and Bridget Agnes McDermott Brennan. He grew up in Newark, one of eight children of Irish immigrants. His father shoveled coal in a brewery, gained prominence through union organizing, and became an immensely popular elected city official in charge of the Newark police and fire departments. Brennan attended Barringer High School in Newark and then the Wharton School of Finance at the University of Pennsylvania. Shortly before graduating with honors in economics in 1928, Brennan secretly married Marjorie Leonard (with whom he would have three children).

Brennan attended Harvard Law School where he was taught by Felix Frankfurter. After graduating in 1931, he returned to Newark to join the law firm of Pitney, Hardin and Skinner. He developed an expertise in labor law to serve the firm's corporate clients, his credibility enhanced as the son of a former union official; in 1938 he became a partner. He joined the Army in 1942 and served in administrative roles until 1945, specializing in military manpower problems

and earning the rank of colonel. In 1945 he returned to the law firm, which soon became known as Pitney, Hardin, Skinner and Brennan.

Brennan became involved in court reform efforts led by Arthur Vanderbilt, and in 1949 the two men accepted judicial appointments—Vanderbilt as chief justice of the New Jersey Supreme Court and Brennan as a trial judge on the state superior court. Brennan was a Democrat, but he was appointed by Republican governor Alfred E. Driscoll, the first of three judicial appointments for Brennan by Republican leaders. In little more than a year, Brennan was elevated to the appellate division of superior court, and in 1952 Governor Driscoll nominated him to the New Jersey Supreme Court. He developed a strong relationship with the senior Vanderbilt and became his close ally in efforts to clear up backlogs and delays in the New Jersey courts. Although the New Jersey Supreme Court had little occasion to deal with civil liberties issues or federal constitutional questions, Brennan wrote a handful of dissenting opinions previewing his belief that law and courts were essential to the furtherance of individual dignity.

When Justice Sherman Minton decided to retire from the U.S. Supreme Court in September 1956, a confluence of factors led President Dwight D. Eisenhower, a Republican, to select Brennan to fill the vacancy. Eisenhower and his staff were focused on the 1956 presidential campaign against Senator Adlai Stevenson of Illinois. They wanted a Catholic and Democratic Supreme Court nominee to appeal to Independent and Democratic voters in the northeast; they also wanted a product of the state courts to placate criticism from angry state chief justices that the federal system was encroaching on the states. Brennan fit the requirements and was known to Attorney General Herbert Brownell because of his participation a few months earlier in a Justice Department conference on court congestion and delays. Brennan took his seat on 16 October 1956 as a recess appointment because Congress had adjourned. He was not confirmed by the Senate until 19 March 1957, at which time Senator Joseph McCarthy of Wisconsin was the only audible "nay" in a Senate voice vote.

Brennan quickly displayed the talents that would become the hallmarks of his 34-year tenure on the U.S. Supreme Court. His expansive reading of the Constitution found new rights and broadened existing ones. He also showed a remarkable ability to function in a collegial institution, drafting opinions with compromises that could command the support of diverse Supreme Court majorities.

He wrote a number of important decisions pushing the boundaries of freedom of speech under the First Amendment. In *New York Times v. Sullivan* (1964), Brennan provided greater protection for criticism of public officials by making it more difficult for officials (and later for any public figures) to sue for libel. In a dissenting opinion in *Paris Adult Theatre I v. Slaton* (1973), he described how vague speech restrictions could silence free expression. In *Texas v. Johnson*

(1989) he wrote that burning the American flag as a protest was a form of protected speech. In these and other cases, he urged the Court and the people not to fear objectionable speech but to receive it as evidence of the strength of the exchange of ideas in a free society.

Brennan also helped to shape the contours of the Fourteenth Amendment guarantee of "equal protection of the laws." He wrote several major school desegregation decisions that were central to the Court's effort to enforce the mandate of *Brown v. Board of Education* (1954). He authored a number of decisions upholding the use of race and gender in national and local affirmative action plans, and his decisions continued to be debated even after he left the bench. His decision in *Baker v. Carr* (1962) opened up state legislatures to reapportionment challenges. He prevailed in *Eisenstadt v. Baird* (1972) in ruling that unmarried women were entitled to the same access to contraceptives as a matter of privacy that married couples enjoyed. He also led the Court in *Craig v. Boren* (1976) in deciding that discrimination based on gender in state and federal laws and policies required substantial justification to survive Fourteenth Amendment scrutiny.

Throughout his tenure he argued in speeches and later in opinions that the Constitution and the laws must be understood in ways that advanced human dignity for all. This emerged as a major theme for Brennan, one that tied together many aspects of his judicial career. His fight to make the provisions of the Bill of Rights apply to the states through the Fourteenth Amendment was one example of this commitment. He also wrote decisions that made it easier for individuals to sue for damages for misconduct of local governments and of federal officials. And he dissented in every death penalty case from 1976 until his retirement, arguing that it was "cruel and unusual punishment" for the government to execute people.

His life on the Supreme Court passed through different phases. During the tenure of Chief Justice Earl Warren, Brennan's influence was great because he developed a close bond of trust with Warren. He wrote or worked on many of the most important civil rights and liberties decisions of the period, and he had Warren's ear whenever he needed it. But with the retirement of Warren in 1969 and his replacement with Chief Justice Warren E. Burger, the dynamic changed, and Brennan found himself more often in dissent and having to work even harder to forge majorities. Soon after Burger joined the Court, Brennan's wife began a 13-year struggle with cancer; this battle made the gregarious and charming Brennan reclusive, devoted to caring for his wife and less willing to appear in public off the bench. His wife died in 1982, and the next year he married Mary Fowler, who had been his secretary for 26 years. The second marriage brought a new vigor to Brennan; he gave dozens of speeches in the mid-1980s, traveled the country and the world, and basked in the admiration of law schools and judges' groups.

In the Burger Court and after 1986, when William H. Rehnquist became Chief Justice, Brennan's expansive approach to the Bill of Rights and the Fourteenth Amendment became targets for young conservative lawyers and judges appointed by President Ronald Reagan. Brennan became a leading defender of the view that the Constitution was a broad, imprecise document that was intended to be adapted to the needs of each generation. His critics, while recognizing his success in his approach, argued with growing vociferousness that he was undermining the true meaning of the Constitution as defined by its words and by the intent of the Founding Fathers.

With this debate in full swing, Brennan vowed often that he would never retire from the Court, but after his doctor told him he had suffered a minor stroke, he retired on 20 July 1990. For a few years he taught and lectured, but his health deteriorated after he broke his hip in 1996, and he died the following year in Arlington, Virginia. His legacy to the Supreme Court was his views on individual rights and human dignity, issues that have played a pivotal role in shaping the Court's agenda.

• The William J. Brennan, Jr., papers are collected in the Manuscript Division of the Library of Congress. A biography is Kim Isaac Eisler, *A Justice for All, William J. Brennan, Jr., and the Decisions that Transformed America* (1993). A collection of essay tributes is E. Joshua Rosenkranz and Bernard Schwartz, eds., *Reason and Passion, Justice Brennan's Enduring Influence* (1997). Obituaries are in the *New York Times* and the *Washington Post*, both 25 July 1997.

STEPHEN J. WERMIEL

BRISTOL, Sherlock (5 June 1815–26 Sept. 1906), Congregationalist clergyman and frontier preacher, was born in Cheshire, Connecticut, the son of Gideon Bristol, the fourth generation of his family on the same Connecticut farm, and Julia Parker Bristol. His education began at a local school, and his religious education in a Sunday school class taught by a young lawyer who greatly influenced him. At age fifteen Bristol experienced an evangelical conversion and decided to pursue a career in the ministry. Needing a preparatory education, he attended an Episcopal academy in Cheshire and also learned Latin and Greek from Joseph Whiting, pastor of Cheshire's Congregational church, before entering, in 1833, Phillips Academy in Andover, Massachusetts, from which he was expelled in 1835 for his militantly abolitionist views. A benefactor enabled him to attend Oberlin College, where he came under the influence of Charles G. Finney and Asa Mahan, and from which he graduated in 1839. After one year of theological education at Yale Divinity School, he returned to Oberlin to finish at its theological school, graduating in 1842. That same year he married Emily Ingraham; after her death, he married Amelia Locke in 1865. He had six sons and three daughters.

During his last seminary year he preached at the Congregational church in Franklin, Ohio, where he remained as pastor until 1843, when Finney and Mahan persuaded him to become a fund-raiser for Oberlin College, a position he held for three years. Raising funds in New York City, he made the acquaintance of Arthur and Lewis Tappan, benefactors of evangelical and reform causes, and of Henry C. Bowen, publisher of the *Independent*. In 1846 he accepted a call as pastor to the Trinitarian Congregational Church of Fitchburg, Massachusetts, an antislavery congregation formed by seceders from other churches. There he stayed until probably late in 1847, when he was called to the Sullivan Street Church in New York City. During his year-long tenure at Sullivan Street, he was a delegate to the convention that formed the Free-Soil party in Buffalo, New York, in August 1848. From 16 October 1848 to 24 October 1849 Bristol was pastor of the Free Church in Andover, Massachusetts; while there, he addressed an antislavery convention in Boston.

Complaining of insomnia and nervousness, Bristol was advised by his physicians that he needed a more physically active life. So he left his family in Massachusetts after ending his Andover pastorate and joined the gold rush to California. He sailed from New York to Panama, crossed the isthmus on foot, and stayed two months on the other side awaiting passage to San Francisco. When his ship was delayed, remaining at anchor on the coast near San Simeon, he and some others disembarked and went overland to the mining camps, arriving there in early June 1850. He mined gold at several camps near Marysville and then moved near Downieville, where he and a partner operated a ranch and a store. He preached frequently in the mining camps. By late autumn 1851 he was in San Francisco, where he stayed briefly, and then returned to New York. After staying only a few weeks in Massachusetts with his family, he set off for the west again, so that he could invest his California gains in a homestead and preach on the frontier. He settled in Dartford, Wisconsin, where he was joined by his family, but he refused a proffered appointment by the American Home Missionary Society because it would have disallowed his working a farm at the same time, an occupation he felt necessary for his health. He served the congregational churches of Dartford, Green Lake, and Metomen concurrently from 1852 to 1858 and also led revivals in nearby towns, preaching in Methodist and Baptist churches as well as Congregational ones. In 1859 he received a call to the Congregational church in Elmwood, Illinois, where he remained until he returned to Dartford in 1861, suffering once again from nervousness. To improve his health he set out for the Oregon Territory in March 1862, joining a large wagon train of which he was elected captain, with the responsibility of scouting ahead to find suitable camps. His wagon train was several times under Indian attack, and Bristol led defensive sorties into the bush. Staying in Idaho, he mined gold near Idaho City and farmed in the Boise Valley. In December 1863 he traveled by boat down the Columbia River to Portland, Oregon, and returned to New York once more by way of San Francisco and Panama. In April 1864 he was back in Dartford, resuming his pastorate there for about a year until receiving a call from the Congregational churches in Brandon and Springvale (Ladoga), Wisconsin, where he stayed until late 1867.

When Bristol's nervousness resumed, he moved to California with his family. Locating in Ventura County, he bought a homestead, farmed, and for twelve years preached throughout the Santa Clara Valley. In these California years he turned to writing, publishing in 1887 an autobiography, *The Pioneer Preacher: Incidents of Interest, and Experiences in the Author's Life* (reprinted with an additional chapter in 1898), and a theological treatise with the title *Paracletos, or The Baptism of the Holy Ghost* in 1892. Fleming H. Revell, a major publisher of evangelical literature, published both books. Copies of *The Pioneer Preacher* were distributed to missionaries by the American Home Missionary Society, the American Board of Commissioners for Foreign Missions, and the American Missionary Association and placed on ships by the Seamen's Friend Society. Bristol also wrote articles for *The Pacific*, a Congregationalist publication. He died at Montalvo, California.

Bristol was a characteristic figure of nineteenth-century American evangelicalism and a promoter of many of its causes, with an ability to cross denominational boundaries to work with other evangelicals. He regarded a strict keeping of Sunday as the Sabbath as central to true piety; when he was captain of a wagon train headed for Oregon, he broke the group's Sabbath rest only once, to avoid an Indian attack. He committed himself to the cause of temperance while still a youth and early became an advocate of immediate abolition of slavery.

Bristol especially represented the evangelical Congregationalism of New England as it was shaped by the practices and beliefs of Charles G. Finney and Oberlin College. He took the preaching of revival as his prime task, adopting Finney's direct and argumentative style as he pressed the case for conversion. A published sermon of 1903, *The Sin of Not Doing*, argued, as Finney had, that since one has the ability to believe, one has the duty to be converted; refusal of conversion dishonors God. *Human Sinfulness*, published in the year of his death, emphasized each person's responsibility for his own moral record. Bristol enthusiastically adopted the Oberlin Perfectionism of Finney and Mahan while an undergraduate, arguing for it even against the theologian Nathaniel William Taylor during the year he was a theological student in New Haven. According to this Perfectionism, it is possible for believers to be freed of willful sin. His one theological book, *Paracletos*, asserted and defended this Perfectionism; it also expressed a postmillennial optimism that Christian perfection, empowered by the Holy Spirit, would lead to "Pentecostal revival" and the millennium, a time when the earth would become "a vestibule of heaven" (pp. 13, 36–37). A tract of 1903, *An Address to the Congregational Brotherhood*, attacked Congregationalist seminaries and associations for permitting "infidel" theology and biblical scholarship, as Bristol aligned himself with nascent fundamentalism's rejection of liberal theological trends.

Bristol's *Pioneer Preacher* is partly spiritual autobiography and an account of his reform and revival experiences, but it is also an account of exciting adventures. Bristol presented himself as a skilled woodsman, crack shot, and mighty hunter, chasing down alligators, pumas, and feral boars in Panama and California. He boasted of triumphs over local toughs as a boy in Connecticut, over an anti-abolitionist Irish mob in Massachusetts, over threatening bullies as a backwoods preacher in Ohio, over the Tammany Hall enforcer Isaiah Rynders in New York City, and over ruffians and robbers in the mining camps of California. On the way to Oregon and in Idaho he fought Indians. In short, Bristol was a rough-and-tumble freelance frontier preacher, whose ties with the ecclesiastical establishment were loose and whose restlessness led to a career of many brief pastorates interrupted by bouts of nervousness, which he relieved by physical labor and long trips westward.

• Dewey D. Wallace, Jr.'s 1989 edition of Bristol's autobiography, *The Pioneer Preacher*, the chief source for his life, is annotated and has an introduction that examines Bristol both as preacher and adventurer. *Services at the Dedication of the Free Christian Church, Andover, Massachusetts, September 19, 1908* helps sort out the chronology of his life. An obituary appears in *The Congregational Year-Book, 1907* (1907).

DEWEY D. WALLACE, JR.

BRODSKY, Joseph (24 May 1940–28 Jan. 1996), poet, was born Iosif Alexandrovich Brodsky in Leningrad (now St. Petersburg), Russia, the son of Alexander I. Brodsky, a commercial photographer, and Maria M. Volpert Brodsky, both of whom were secular Jews. As an adult he anglicized his first given name. Maria Brodsky worked as a language teacher and translator and provided most of the family's income. Although he grew up in a nonreligious household, young Brodsky was acutely conscious of being Jewish because of prevailing anti-Semitism, a factor he later blamed for his father's abrupt dismissal from the navy and his subsequent lack of success, and which made the son feel like an outsider from an early age.

Bored in school and conscious of his teachers' contempt, Brodsky left at fifteen to take a series of more than a dozen menial jobs, including work as a milling machine operator, a furnace stoker, and a corpse dissector in a morgue. At night he turned to literature for consolation, learning Polish to read the works of Czeslaw Milosz and English for the poetry of John Donne, and his language skills eventually earned him sporadic work as a translator. In his teens he also began to write poetry and became part of a fringe group of young artists and writers in Leningrad who published some of his verse in their journal. With other youthful poets he joined in the common practice of reciting his verse

on street corners, and his work eventually became widely known to the Russian literati, including the poet Anna Akhmatova, who praised him and whom Brodsky later cited as a major influence on his own poetry.

Brodsky's early verse lamented the drab materialism of Soviet Russia and posed the possibility of transcendence through a joyful apprehension of nature. While Akhmatova and other like-minded liberals commented favorably on his poems, more conservative writers felt threatened by Brodsky's growing popularity. Although his poetry was not, strictly speaking, political, his detractors alleged that it contained subversive themes, and in November 1963 he was openly attacked in the Leningrad newspaper as a "social parasite" who corrupted the young. The newspaper continued its attacks on Brodsky in the following weeks, doubtless encouraged by the government; during this time he was seized on several occasions and held briefly in a mental institution. Finally, the campaign of harassment culminated in a series of hearings in February and March 1964. Brodsky was formally charged with being a social parasite who failed to work consistently at an occupation appropriate to his background and training, the court declaring that he was not sufficiently educated to claim the status of a poet. Defiant throughout the proceedings, he was convicted of "not fulfilling the duties of a Soviet citizen" and sentenced to five years at hard labor.

Brodsky was sent north to a bleak state farm near Arkhangelsk, where he chopped wood, crushed rocks, hauled manure, and secretly read a copy of Louis Untermeyer's *New Modern American and British Poetry* (1950), which he had managed to bring with him to the farm. On the outside, protests against his sentence were being voiced by many leading Russian writers, and a transcript of the Leningrad hearings smuggled out of the country and translated into English had made his plight known in the West. The court's ludicrous questioning that challenged his qualifications to write poetry made the Soviet Union look ridiculous, and this was no doubt a major factor in the government's decision to release him after eighteen months of confinement.

Upon his return to Leningrad, Brodsky was allowed for a time to pursue, without government intervention, his activities as a poet and translator, and his poems began to be published in book form in Western countries—in the original Russian in the United States (1965, 1970) and in translation in Germany and France (both 1966). The first English translation of Brodsky, *"Elegy to John Donne" and Other Poems*, whose title reflected one of his earliest—and what would become one of his best-known—works, appeared in England in 1967. But harassment, now intensely anti-Semitic in nature, soon resumed—irrationally, since Brodsky did not identify himself as a Jew and wrote poetry reflecting in some instances a Christian sensibility.

During this period Brodsky was invited to attend several international poetry gatherings in Western

Europe, but the government prevented him from going. Then suddenly, in late 1971, he received several "invitations" from the government to immigrate to Israel. When he had not responded by the following May, he was ordered by the government to leave the Soviet Union. In short order his poems were confiscated, a visa was issued, and he was put on a plane for Vienna. Knowing that the American poet W. H. Auden had a summer home in Austria, Brodsky sought him out upon arrival. Auden put him in touch with other prominent Western writers and arranged for him to travel to England. Further efforts on Brodsky's behalf by Auden and other Western writers led to an invitation from the University of Michigan for Brodsky to become poet-in-residence there, and he entered the United States in 1972. He lived and taught in Ann Arbor for the next eight years but made frequent visits to other parts of the Western world, exploring New York City, Cape Cod, Mexico, London, Venice, and Florence. In the spring of 1980 he moved to Manhattan and first settled in Greenwich Village; he later moved to an apartment in Brooklyn Heights, where he made his home for the remainder of his life.

Beginning in 1970 and continuing intermittently over the next two decades, volumes of Brodsky's poetry were issued in their original Russian in limited editions by several small U.S. publishing houses. His popularity in this country grew following the publication in 1973 of the first collection of his verse to appear in English translation in the United States: *Selected Poems*, published by Harper & Row. The book's introduction, written by Auden, praised Brodsky as "a traditionalist" who pursued the dual themes of "lyric poets of all ages"—nature and the human condition. *Selected Poems* attracted wide attention, though critical responses varied: some were full of praise while others hesitated to voice unreserved approval; perhaps suspicious of the often tight rhyming schemes, they cautioned that Brodsky's apparent gifts might in fact be attributed to the translators.

During the 1970s, while teaching and traveling, Brodsky continued to write poetry, much of it reflecting the places he was visiting and focusing on what would become his signature themes: exile, wandering, and loss. Translated into English by well-known American writers, including the poets Richard Wilbur and Anthony Hecht, his poems were published frequently in such magazines as the *New York Review of Books* and the *New Yorker*. He also published verse in leading foreign periodicals, and anthologies of his work began appearing in translation in many other nations, East and West; by the end of the decade he had garnered a worldwide following. He had also become a U.S. citizen, insisting, however, that he remained a Russian in spirit and hoped—as it turned out, in vain—to return to his country one day. From his expulsion in 1972 until his death, he denied that he was an exile, preferring instead to refer to himself as "living abroad." But the persistent themes of his poems belied his claim.

When Brodsky moved to New York City in 1980, he accepted adjunct teaching appointments at both Columbia and New York universities. That same year saw the publication of *A Part of Speech*, the second collection of his verse to appear in English translation in the United States. Most of the poems had been published previously in American magazines, and many were rooted in perceptions formed during Brodsky's American travels; among the best known is his "Lullaby of Cape Cod," which praises the supremacy and endurance of the poet's voice over chaos and death. Like *Selected Poems*, the new volume was greeted with both praise and reservation, the latter again reflecting concern that the translations had enhanced the quality of the Russian originals. For many critics, however, including such prominent Western experts in Russian literature as Clarence Brown, Brodsky had emerged as the leading Russian poet of his time. One confirmation of his stature was his receipt in 1981 of a "genius grant" from the MacArthur Foundation, which provided him with a substantial stipend for five years.

Undoubtedly reflecting a growing confidence in his own fluency in English—and perhaps in part hoping to silence the voices of those who doubted his work's authenticity—Brodsky began providing his own translations into English in the early 1980s, adhering to the traditional rhymes and meters that were evident in his previously translated poetry. During this period, as he continued to publish verse in American and foreign periodicals, he also wrote a series of essays, part memoir and part reflection on his craft, that were published in 1986 as *Less Than One*, which won a National Book Critics Circle Award. Brodsky's meteoric rise to eminence received ultimate confirmation a year later, when he was awarded the 1987 Nobel Prize in Literature. When a third major collection of his verse in English, *To Urania: Selected Poems*, was published in 1988—with translations by Brodsky himself—critical praise was well-nigh universal. Three years later he received major recognition from his adopted country with his appointment to a one-year term as U.S. poet laureate.

In the remaining years of his life, Brodsky continued to contribute poetry to leading periodicals, but he published only one book-length work: *Watermark* (1992), an extended essay on Venice, which he had often visited and which remained one of his favorite cities. He also taught for brief periods at other American colleges and universities and beginning in 1990 served as the Andrew Mellon Professor of Poetry at Mount Holyoke College in Massachusetts. A chainsmoker, he suffered from heart trouble for many years, and open-heart surgery in 1979 and two subsequent coronary bypass operations did not appear to remedy his condition. He died suddenly of a heart attack at his Brooklyn apartment while preparing to return to Mount Holyoke for the spring term. At the time of his death, a new collection of his essays, *On Grief and Reason* (1995), had just been published. At his request, he was buried in Venice.

Several volumes of Brodsky's work have appeared posthumously, beginning with *So Forth: Poems* in 1996. This was followed by *Discovery* (1999), a children's picture book illustrated by Vladimir Radunsky, and a major anthology, *Collected Poems in English, 1972–1999* (2000). Brodsky was also the author of several plays, including *Mramor* (1984), *Marbles* (1988), and *Democracy* (1993). Brodsky was married to a woman named Maria (maiden name unknown) and had a daughter; he was also the father of a son born in the Soviet Union.

• For biographical information on Joseph Brodsky, see James Atlas, "A Poetic Triumph," *New York Times Magazine,* 20 Dec. 1980, pp. 32ff. See also "Brodsky, Joseph," in *Who Was Who in America,* vol. 11 (1996); *Current Biography Yearbook 1982* and *1996; Contemporary Authors,* vols. 41–44, First Revision (1979), pp. 95–96; *Contemporary Authors, New Revision Series,* vol. 37 (1992), pp. 51–55; and *Contemporary Authors,* vol. 151 (1996), p. 72. In addition, see the 1979 *Paris Review* interview with Brodsky by Sven Birkerts, reprinted in *Writers at Work,* Eighth Series (1988), pp. 373–412. See also Solomon Volkov, *Conversations with Joseph Brodsky: A Poet's Journey through the Twentieth Century,* translated by Marian Schwartz (1998). For critical assessments of Brodsky's work, see Valentina Polukhina, *Joseph Brodsky: A Poet for Our Time* (1989), and Lev Loseff et al., eds., *Joseph Brodsky: The Art of a Poem* (1999). An obituary is in the *New York Times,* 29 Jan. 1996.

ANN T. KEENE

BRONCK, Jonas (1600–1643), colonist, was born in Komstad, Småland, Sweden, the son of Jonas Bronck, a farmer. His mother's name is not recorded, and little is known of his early life. What is known is that he learned to read—most likely under the instruction of a local clergyman—and was influenced to forsake his homeland for the sea at a relatively early age, possibly by either the outbreak of the War of Kalmar between Sweden and Denmark in 1611 or the outbreak of local civil unrest due to excessive taxation of cattle herds in 1622.

While it is unclear where Bronck moved immediately after leaving Sweden—some sources place him in Denmark—he apparently finally settled in Amsterdam. After learning the sea trade, most likely self-taught, he eventually became a captain and amassed considerable wealth. On 6 July 1638 he married Teuntie Jeuriaens in Amsterdam; it is unclear whether the couple had any children.

Shortly after his marriage, Bronck made the decision to immigrate to the New World. His exact reasons for doing so are unknown; possible attractions may have included the potentially lucrative fur trade or the prospect of ample land with which to return to his farming roots. In the spring of 1639, Bronck and several other men chartered the ship *De Brant Van Troyen* (the Fire of Troy) and made arrangements to have their families, provisions, and livestock transported to New Netherland. In order to expand his land claim against the Dutch West India Company, Bronck hired three Germans, Carsten Pieter, Jacob Gever, and Jo-

chem Kaller, as indentured servants and also hired a servant girl, Clara Matthjis, for the benefit of his spouse.

On arriving in New Amsterdam in the early summer of 1639, Bronck faced an immediate crisis when he learned that his wife's servant girl was secretly engaged to be married, a direct violation of her terms of employment. After negotiating a settlement with her fiancé, Bronck set about the task of establishing himself. He arranged to settle in the southwest corner of what would become the borough bearing his name. His exact reasons for choosing the location—which comprised some 500 acres of wooded wilderness in a section later known as Morrisania—are unknown, as settlements in New Netherland had previously concentrated in New Amsterdam proper (now the lower tip of Manhattan Island) and Fort Orange, farther up the Hudson (or North) River at the site of present-day Albany, New York.

In addition to Bronck, his wife and their indentured servants, the new settlement included Pieter Andriessen and Laurens Duyts, two men whose board had been paid by Bronck, and two brothers, Cornelis and Jan Stille, with whom Bronck had struck a business deal. In exchange for land, a dwelling, and some livestock, the brothers were to share their produce with Bronck for the next six years, after which the land would revert to their name while Bronck reclaimed his original livestock and half of its progeny.

Bronck's house, called "Emmaus," was one of the finer examples of early colonial architecture in New Amsterdam; it featured exterior walls made of fieldstone and a tile roof (the material for which most likely came from the Netherlands). His home also contained possibly the finest library in the colony, numbering among its holdings manuscripts and published books written in Danish, Latin, and Dutch that covered subjects as varied as theology, navigation, and history. Well furnished, as befitted a man of his wealth, Bronck's home was the site of an important series of negotiations between Dutch officials and representatives of the Weckquasgeek tribe of Native Americans in 1642 that resulted in a temporary cessation of the hostilities that periodically sprang up between the local Native Americans and the Dutch. Ironically, it is unlikely that Bronck attended the negotiations, as he never ranked high in the counsels of local government.

The exact date of Bronck's death is not known; the cause is also unknown, but he must have died somewhere in New Netherland. Although there was a series of Native American uprisings around the time of his death, it is unlikely that he was killed in combat, as his farmstead remained unscathed. Following his death, his servants scattered and his widow married Arent van Curler, the business agent of the patroonship of Rensselaerswyck. (van Curler's wife appears in historical records as Anthonia Slachboom, but she is thought to have been the same person as Teuntie Jeuriaens.) After moving up the Hudson River with her new husband, Bronck's widow allowed her deceased husband's homestead to remain vacant for a number of years. It then disappeared from history.

Although unsuccessful in his attempt to found a permanent settlement in New Amsterdam, and largely forgotten today, Jonas Bronck will be remembered for the corrupted form of his name—Bronx—which belatedly, in 1898, became the name of the only portion of New York City that is located on the mainland.

• Although no collection of Bronck's papers is known to have survived, material relating to his life and activities can be found among the holdings of the Gemeentie Archief in Amsterdam, the Netherlands. The best secondary source of information on his life and career is Lloyd Ultan, *The Bronx in the Frontier Era: From the Beginning to 1696* (1993). He also receives mention in Edwin G. Burrows and Mike Wallace, *Gotham: A History of New York City to 1898* (1999). Older references such as J. H. Innes, *New Amsterdam and Its People: Studies, Social and Topographical, of the Town under Dutch and Early English Rule* (1902), remain useful as well.

EDWARD L. LACH, JR.

BROWN, Charles Oliver (22 July 1848–13 Mar. 1941), Congregationalist minister and popular lecturer, was born on a farm near Battle Creek, Michigan, to Oliver Brown, a blacksmith, and Celia Burrall Brown, a schoolteacher whose family had recently moved to Michigan from Connecticut. Soon after his birth, the family moved to Kalamazoo, Michigan, and then to Utah, Ohio, later incorporated into Toledo, where Oliver Brown operated a canal barge. The elder Brown was a devout Congregationalist and a supporter of temperance and abolition; his house at Utah was a station on the underground railway. Young Charles's schooling in Toledo was interrupted in 1861 when as an officer's valet he accompanied his father, who had volunteered and received a commission in the Third Ohio Cavalry to fight in the Civil War. Charles was at Shiloh the day after the battle and later was slightly injured in a skirmish with Confederate bushwhackers. In August 1862 he returned home and in the autumn of that year, with his mother and brother, moved to Oberlin, Ohio, to be educated at the college founded by Congregationalists. At Oberlin he first met the evangelist Charles G. Finney (with whom he claimed to have later spent many hours), who urged conversion upon him. In early 1864 Brown rejoined the Third Ohio Cavalry as a bugler and was in several skirmishes around Atlanta and in the assault on Selma, Alabama.

The war over, Brown studied in the preparatory department of Oberlin College during 1866–1867 but then moved to Olivet College in Michigan, where he received a B.A. in 1875 and an M.A. in 1876. (In 1888 he was awarded an honorary D.D. by Lenox College, a Presbyterian institution in Hopkinton, Iowa.) At Olivet he taught penmanship and bookkeeping and in his last year was an instructor in Greek. In 1866 he married Mary N. Wheat, whose family had moved to Oberlin to operate a boarding house for students. They had four sons but the marriage ended in divorce in about 1900; soon thereafter he married Mary Jane Jeremy (née Mallory).

At Olivet College Brown decided to enter the ministry; his first pulpit was at the Congregational church in Pittsville, Michigan. In 1876 he received a call to the First Congregational Church of Rochester, Michigan, where the membership almost doubled in his first year. In January 1880 Brown accepted a call from the Congregational church of Galesburg, Michigan, but a year later he left it for the more prominent First Congregational Church of Kalamazoo, which he left at the end of 1885 because of ill health. In January 1886 he began work as pastor of the First Congregational Church of Dubuque, Iowa, and in 1891 he moved to the First Congregational Church of Tacoma, Washington, where he also became a popular public lecturer. Brown's family background and his connections with Finney, Oberlin, and Olivet made him a proponent of revivalism and reform. His congregations at Rochester and Kalamazoo experienced revivals. In a sermon preached at Rochester on "The Problem of Satanic Influence Considered," Brown asserted, as Finney had, that human beings had the moral obligation and the power of choice to be converted and grow in holiness. At Kalamazoo he participated in a revival led by Dwight Moody's associate D. W. Whittle and later at Tacoma and San Francisco in revivals led by B. Fay Mills. Like Finney a postmillennialist who believed the second coming of Christ would follow the millennium, he rejected the premillennial return of Christ because he thought it discouraged revivals and reform. While at Kalamazoo he tried his hand at Christian apologetics through a series of Sunday evening talks published by Fleming H. Revell, Moody's brother-in-law, as *Short Talks to Young Christians on the Evidences* (1885), arguing that Christianity had improved the world's morals.

In 1886, the year of the Haymarket Riot, Brown published his best-known book: *Talks on the Labor Troubles*, based on lectures given at Dubuque, deals with problems of labor and capital. In these lectures Brown declared that although labor unrest was a danger to the Republic, supposedly inexorable economic laws should not prevent a search for economic justice and that America was a land of opportunity in which conditions for workers would be improved. He blamed much poverty on the use of alcohol. Years later, in 1895, when George D. Herron, Congregational minister and socialist, spoke in San Francisco, Brown denounced him for rejecting private property, stirring up class warfare, and promoting anarchy; a whole issue of *The Kingdom* (7 June 1895), a publication of Herron and his supporters, was devoted to refuting Brown's charges. While at Dubuque Brown also entered other controversies: a tract of 1888 (*Brown vs. Ingersoll: Did the Great Infidel Petition for Repeal of the Laws against Obscenity?*) attacked the noted skeptic Robert G. Ingersoll for undermining the American family, and in 1890 he defended the public schools against Roman Catholic criticisms in *The Public Schools and Their Foes*.

In late summer 1892 Brown moved to one of the largest Protestant congregations on the Pacific coast, the First Congregational Church of San Francisco, where he spoke out on racial issues. Having traveled in the South in 1886, he complained of the mistreatment of the freed blacks. The African-American activist Ida B. Wells referred to Brown as her strongest ally in an 1895 effort to get the clergy of San Francisco to condemn lynching. He remained in San Francisco until driven from his pastorate by a scandal involving charges of adultery and blackmail that appeared in the San Francisco newspapers in December 1895. His blackmailer was acquitted in a civil trial, and Brown was suspended from the ministry for unministerial conduct in April 1896 after an ecclesiastical trial by the Bay Conference of the Congregational Churches. In late 1896 he moved to Chicago, where he briefly served the Green Street Congregational Church before returning to San Francisco with a dramatic confession that he hoped would lead to reinstatement there. His effort failed and thereafter Brown lived in the Chicago area, mostly in Oak Park. He continued as a public lecturer, often at Chautauquas, speaking on such subjects as the Pilgrims, George Washington, Oliver Cromwell, and the Alaskan wonderlands (to which he had traveled while at Tacoma). He died in Chicago, notable by then as one of the last surviving Civil War veterans in the area.

Brown took pride in his denominational and national lineages. While pastor at Rochester, Kalamazoo, and Dubuque, he presided over semicentennial celebrations of these congregations' heritage, which, with its New England Pilgrim roots, democratic polity, and progressive outlook, he thought characteristic of what was best about America. Brown believed that northern victory in the Civil War achieved justice as well as unity and that great national progress was at hand—rum and Romanism he thought would go the way of rebellion. Later he considered the Spanish-American War a righteous cause and in a Chicago speech of 1915 favored military preparedness, citing the Civil War as an example of the good that can come from war. He remembered his participation in the Civil War fondly (perhaps because of his youth at the time), writing an account of his war adventures for his family in 1878, and in 1880 and 1885 he revisited battlefields where he had fought, publishing a narrative of these trips in 1886 as *Battlefields Revisited*. He was active in the affairs of the Grand Army of the Republic, which he served as a National Patriotic Instructor, often lectured on his war experiences, and gave speeches at the dedication of Civil War battlefield monuments. As late as 1931 he addressed the Chicago Sunday Evening Club on the subject of Abraham Lincoln. Thus veterans' activities and patriotic oratory helped fill his Chicago years.

Whether as preacher or lecturer, Brown was an impressive orator who loved the platform and expressed himself with flowery eloquence. In the Midwest and San Francisco, he was an articulate if restless spokesman for Protestant values, developing his own blend of Congregationalist pride, evangelical piety, Christian nationalism, moderately progressive reform, and millennial optimism. Representing the persistence of the legacy of Finney, he was largely untouched by the newer currents of theological liberalism and militant fundamentalism that were beginning to unsettle the Protestant consensus. In personality, Brown was restless and impetuous, and the scandal that drove him from the ministry tarnished his reputation and brought to an end his prominence and influence in Congregationalism and American Protestantism.

• Letters and manuscripts of Brown formerly belonging to his second wife are in the possession of the author of this *ANB* entry, including a "Brief Sketch of My Life" (1935) and an untitled memoir of his early life and Civil War adventures written in 1878. Information has also been gained from local church records. In addition to his writings listed above, he wrote or edited *Life and Character of Mrs. C. C. Wheat, of Oberlin, Ohio* (n.d.) and *Semi-Centennial Celebration of the First Congregational Church of Dubuque, Iowa, May 12th and 13th, 1889* (n.d.). See also *Professor George D. Herron: The Man and His Work on the Pacific Coast* (n.d.) and Alfreda M. Duster, ed., *Crusader for Justice: The Autobiography of Ida B. Wells* (1970). Dewey D. Wallace, Jr., "Charles Oliver Brown at Dubuque: A Study in the Ideals of Midwestern Congregationalists in the Late Nineteenth Century," *Church History* 53, no.1 (Mar. 1984): 46–60, discusses the high point of his ministry. See also *A History of the First Congregational Church United Church of Christ, Rochester, Michigan in the One Hundred Fiftieth Anniversary Year, 1827–1977* (n.d.). References to his role in the social gospel appear in James Dombrowski, *The Early Days of Christian Socialism in America* (1936); Henry F. May, *Protestant Churches and Industrial America* (1949); and C. Howard Hopkins, *The Rise of the Social Gospel in American Protestantism, 1865–1915* (1940). Brief obituaries are in the *Chicago Daily News*, 14 Mar. 1941, and the *Chicago Tribune*, 15 Mar. 1941.

DEWEY D. WALLACE, JR.

BROWN, Margaret Tobin (18 July 1867–26 Oct. 1932), social rights activist, philanthropist, actress, and *Titanic* survivor, popularly known as Molly Brown, was born Margaret Tobin in Hannibal, Missouri, the daughter of Irish immigrants. The real life of Margaret Tobin Brown has little to do with the myth of Molly Brown, a story created in the 1930s and 1940s that culminated in the 1960 Broadway hit *The Unsinkable Molly Brown*, starring Tammy Grimes, and Hollywood's 1964 Metro-Goldwyn-Mayer movie of the same name starring Debbie Reynolds. Margaret Tobin Brown was never called "Molly"; the name was invented by Hollywood.

Brown's parents had both been widowed; her father, John Tobin, worked in the Hannibal Gas Works and had a daughter named Catherine Bridget; her mother, Johanna Collins, had a daughter named Mary Ann. As a couple, they had four more children: Daniel (1863), Margaret, William (1869), and Helen (1871). Margaret Tobin attended the grammar school run by her aunt Mary O'Leary and as a teenager worked at Garth's Tobacco Factory. In 1883 Brown's stepsister

Mary Ann married a blacksmith and left Hannibal for the booming city of Leadville, Colorado. Daniel Tobin followed, and in 1886 Margaret joined them. She shared a cabin with her brother, who worked in a silver mine, and obtained a job in the carpets and draperies department of Daniels, Fisher, & Smith, a local mercantile store. In the spring of 1886 she attended a Catholic church picnic and met James Joseph "J. J." Brown, also the son of Irish immigrants and thirteen years her senior. She had hoped to marry well enough to help provide for her large family, but J. J., like her brother Daniel, worked in the mines. She wrote: "I thought about how I wanted comfort for my father and how I determined to stay single until a man presented himself who could give to the tired old man the things I longed for him. . . . I struggled hard with myself in those days. . . . Finally I decided that I'd be better off with a poor man whom I loved than with a wealthy one whose money had attracted me" (quoted in Iversen, p. 90).

Margaret Tobin and James Joseph Brown were married on 1 September 1886 and moved to a cabin in Stumpftown, a small, primarily Irish community close to the mines. Brown began to study with a tutor, helped establish soup kitchens for miners' families, and became interested in the formation of the National Woman's Party. The Browns had two children of their own and also raised the three daughters of Daniel Tobin, whose wife died in a mining camp.

J. J. Brown became superintendent of all the Ibex mining properties and was considered "a top flight mining man in Leadville when [Leadville] had the best mining men in the whole country" (quoted in Iversen, p. 99). In 1893, with the repeal of the Sherman Silver Purchase Act, J. J. Brown and his associates determined to make the Little Jonny Mine produce gold rather than silver but were prevented from reaching the gold at the bottom of the mine by slippery dolomite sand. J. J. Brown's practical solution was to use bales of hay supported by wooden timbers and baling wire to bolster the shaft. By October 1893, the Little Jonny was shipping 135 tons of ore per day. J. J. Brown was awarded 12,500 shares of stock and a seat on the board, and in 1894 the Browns moved to 1340 Pennsylvania Avenue in a fashionable neighborhood of Denver a few blocks from the state capitol.

The Browns were welcomed into exclusive Denver society by former governor James Benton Grant and his high-society wife, Mary Matteson Grant. They soon became an integral part of Denver society, although Margaret Brown's forthright opinions on the labor movement, feminism, and human rights issues sometimes created controversy. She became a founding member of the Denver Woman's Club, part of a national network of women's clubs dedicated to improving physical, intellectual, and moral conditions for women. The club established traveling libraries, art exhibits, community gardens, food banks, and public health clinics, and in 1898 Brown was elected chair of the art and literature committee. By 1905 more than 4,655 traveling libraries had been estab-

lished in 45 states. Also in 1898 Brown became a member of the Denver Women's Press Club and throughout her lifetime published numerous travel and literary articles.

Brown chaired a number of Catholic charities and raised funds to erect the Cathedral of Immaculate Conception and St. Joseph's Hospital in Denver. During this time she met Judge Ben Lindsey, the "kids' judge," and worked with him to assist destitute children through the Juvenile Aid Society and establish the first juvenile court in the country. In 1901 Brown became one of the first women to attend college at the Carnegie Institute in New York. Working with Alva Vanderbilt Belmont and the Political Equality League, she made several popular but ultimately unsuccessful bids for Congress and the Senate between 1909 and 1914. On 24 July 1914 Brown and Belmont organized an international women's rights conference in Newport, Rhode Island, which was attended by human rights activists from around the world. Following the 1914 Ludlow Massacre outside Trinidad, Colorado, Brown became a prominent advocate for labor. On 15 July 1927 she led a group of delegates from the National Woman's Party to appeal to President Calvin Coolidge for passage of the Equal Rights Amendment.

In 1912 Brown and her daughter Helen were traveling with the John Jacob Astor party in Cairo, Egypt. Upon receiving news that her grandson was gravely ill, Brown booked the next ship to America, the ill-fated *Titanic*. Few people knew she was on board. After the *Titanic* struck an iceberg, Brown helped load people into lifeboats and was forced to board lifeboat no. 6. She and the other women in the lifeboat banded together to keep rowing, despite problems presented by an emotionally overwrought man, Robert Hichens, who had been at the *Titanic*'s helm when the collision occurred. On the rescue ship *Carpathia*, Margaret not only used her fluency in several languages (French, German, and Russian) to comfort survivors but also organized and served as chair of the Survivors Committee, raising almost $10,000 before the *Carpathia* reached New York. On 29 May 1912 she presented a silver loving cup to Captain Arthur Henry Rostron of the *Carpathia* and a medal to each crewmember. In later years she helped erect a *Titanic* memorial in Washington, D.C.; commemorated the memory of *Titanic* victims in various ways; and continued to serve on the Survivors Committee. She was dismayed that, as a woman, she was not allowed to testify at the *Titanic* hearings. In response she wrote her own version of the event, which was published in newspapers in Denver, Newport, and Paris.

Although Margaret and J. J. Brown legally separated in 1909, they remained relatively close and never divorced. Following her husband's death in 1922, Brown was involved in a three-year court battle with her children over the estate despite the fact that most of the Brown fortune had been dissipated. By 1925 the family had reconciled. Fascinated by the work of Sarah Bernhardt, Brown traveled to France to study in the Bernhardt tradition, which emphasized conveying the psychological complexity of characters in drama, and she performed on stage in Paris and New York, often accompanied by her niece Helen Tobin.

In May 1929 Brown was awarded the Palm of the Académie Française for her dramatic interpretations of the work of Sarah Bernhardt. In April 1932 she was named to the French Legion of Honor in recognition of "overall good citizenship," which included her efforts on the *Titanic* and the *Carpathia*; her work with Judge Ben Lindsey on the Juvenile Court of Denver; her extensive volunteer efforts in France during World War I; and her work with the Alliance Française. She was recommended for the honor by Captain Arthur Henry Rostron of the *Carpathia* and the Maison Blerancourt, a museum near Paris that commemorates the volunteer efforts of American women during World War I.

Brown began to suffer from intense headaches and died suddenly at age sixty-five at the Barbizon Hotel in New York, where she had been working with young actresses. An autopsy revealed a brain tumor. Just before her death, she remarked to a reporter, "Money can't make man or woman . . . It isn't who you are, nor what you have, but what you are that counts." Brown is buried in New York with her husband.

The myth of "Molly" Brown began shortly before her death and grew to enormous proportions. In December 1930 *Fortune* magazine claimed that Brown was "as legendary as Paul Bunyan but as real as Pikes Peak." A year after her death, Gene Fowler, a flamboyant reporter for the *Denver Post*, published a fictional account of "the Unsinkable Mrs. Brown," a chapter in his novel *Timber Line* (1933). This account was republished, to much excited reaction, in *Reader's Digest*, and Fowler eventually sold the rights to this story to Metro-Goldwyn-Mayer. Caroline Bancroft, a Denver writer, perpetuated the myth in her popular 1956 tourist booklet, "The Unsinkable Mrs. Brown," still in print today. Bancroft believed that Margaret Tobin Brown's success was fabricated by the press and that Brown had purchased her French Legion of Honor medal in a pawn shop. In the 1940s a radio broadcast featuring Helen Hayes as "The Unsinkable Mrs. Brown" hit the airways. The story was further elaborated upon in the 1960 Broadway musical *The Unsinkable Molly Brown* starring Tammy Grimes, based on the book by Richard Morris with music and lyrics by Meredith Willson. The show was a smash hit on Broadway and resulted in the 1964 movie *The Unsinkable Molly Brown* starring Debbie Reynolds and Harve Presnell and directed by Charles Walters. James Cameron's 1997 film *Titanic* is a slightly more realistic portrait of Margaret Tobin Brown (played by Kathy Bates), although it perpetuates many of the myths, including the name Molly Brown, and presents an inaccurate account of the lifeboat scene. For many years, Margaret Tobin Brown's son, Lawrence, and her daughter, Helen, attempted to counteract the myth of Molly Brown but were unsuccessful.

• The chief source of biographical information is Kristen Iversen, *Molly Brown: Unraveling the Myth* (1999). Obituaries appear in the *New York Times*, the *International Herald Tribune*, published in Paris, the *Denver Post*, and the *Rocky Mountain News*, all in October 1932.

KRISTEN IVERSEN

BROWN, Ron (1 Aug. 1941–3 Apr. 1996), secretary of commerce and Democratic party leader, was born Ronald Harmon Brown in Washington, D.C., the son of William Brown, who worked for the New Deal–era Federal Housing and Home Finance Agency, and Gloria Elexine Brown. In 1947 the family moved to Harlem in New York City, where William Brown had been hired as the manager of the famed Hotel Theresa, the lodging of choice for celebrated black musicians, civic leaders, athletes, and writers. Ron spent much of his youth there, soaking up the rich cultural life of the hotel and meeting many of its famous residents. On graduating in 1958 from Rhodes, a private preparatory school in Manhattan, he entered Middlebury College in Vermont, becoming one of only three black students in the school and the first black to be initiated into his fraternity.

A fair student, Brown was popular and made friends easily. He received his degree in political science in 1962, the same year he married Alma Arrington. They had two children. In 1963 Brown began a tour of duty in the U.S. Army, serving in Germany and Korea. Although he contemplated a career in the military, he left the service with the rank of captain in January 1967 and accepted a position in New York with the National Urban League, a service agency that helped black people with housing, education, jobs, and job-related training. While attending St. John's University Law School in the evenings, Brown took on more responsibility at the Urban League and eventually became youth program administration specialist in 1970, when he also received his law degree from St. John's.

In 1971 Brown passed the New York State Bar exam and, at age thirty, was named general counsel for the Urban League. Two years later he moved his family to Washington, D.C., where he was appointed director of the Washington bureau, reporting to executive director Vernon Jordan. As head of the Washington office of the Urban League, Brown often was called to testify on Capitol Hill on issues related to African Americans, earning a reputation as a dynamic speaker and building relationships that served him well in his later endeavors. Despite his passion for civil rights, Brown was nonconfrontational, preferring to work within the system instead of against it.

In late 1979 Brown, eager to become involved in politics, left the Urban League to help manage Senator Edward Kennedy's unsuccessful campaign for the Democratic nomination for president. The following year Kennedy appointed Brown chief counsel to the Senate Judiciary Committee, of which the Massachusetts senator was chair. In April 1981, after the Republicans swept the Senate and White House,

Brown became deputy chairman to the Democratic National Committee (DNC), a position he held until 1985.

Also in 1981 Brown joined the powerful Washington lobbying and law firm Patton, Boggs and Blow, lured not only by a six-figure income but also by the prospect of becoming its first black partner. The pragmatic and affable Brown was a successful lobbyist. His client list included Japanese electronics firms; the telecommunications company MCI; the city of Denver, Colorado; and, perhaps most controversially, the Haitian government, then headed by the dictator Jean-Claude "Baby Doc" Duvalier. Brown's lucrative involvement with Haiti, during which he helped Duvalier's brother-in-law with a drug trafficking charge, ended when human rights abuses led to the dictator's exile in 1986. Brown retired from active practice with the firm in 1988 but remained an inactive partner until January 1993.

In 1988 Brown again entered national politics when he became convention manager for Jesse Jackson's bid to win the Democratic nomination for president. Although the campaign failed, Brown was successful in forcing the Democratic National Convention to accept elements of Jackson's strong civil rights platform. Buoyed by his success at the 1988 convention, Brown ran for the chair of the DNC in 1989. Overcoming conservative, southern, and Jewish opponents within the party who believed he was too closely allied with the liberal Jackson, Brown, in February 1989, became the first black to head a national political party. That April some black groups called the new chairman "Ron Beige" for supporting Richard Daley, Jr., for mayor of Chicago over a black opponent endorsed by Jackson. In his first real challenge as DNC chair, Brown calmed fears from within Democratic circles that he would steer the party even farther to the left.

Brown immediately began planning for the 1992 election, convinced that the Democrats could win the presidency for the first time in sixteen years. He recruited volunteers and staff from minority groups in large numbers and invigorated fund-raising efforts within the party. Under Brown's leadership the national party began making good on its promise to support local and state candidates; from 1989 to 1992 Democrats won all seven special congressional elections that were held. But his choice of New York City as the site of the 1992 convention was controversial because the selection coincided with the city's awarding a $210 million waste treatment contract to a company that Brown served as board member and in which he held stock.

In 1992, when Democrat Bill Clinton was elected president, much of the credit for his victory was given to Ron Brown. He had hoped to be rewarded by being named secretary of state, but instead Clinton offered him the top post in the commerce department, the fifth-smallest cabinet agency. Though some criticized Clinton's selection, in the belief that the president's image as a "Washington outsider" would be damaged by the appointment of a Washington power lawyer to his cabinet, Brown was easily confirmed, senators having remembered the contributions made to both Democratic and Republican campaigns by Brown's law firm. Brown revived and reinvented the agency and his position, becoming a "kind of commercial secretary of state" (*Newsweek*, 15 Apr. 1996). Tirelessly promoting American exports, Brown helped to secure agreements worth nearly $80 billion for U.S. businesses abroad, including a $1.4 billion contract for Raytheon to build a high-tech satellite system for the Brazilian rainforest and a $6 billion aircraft deal for Boeing in Saudi Arabia. U. S. exports increased 26 percent over his three-year term.

Despite the administration's praise of Brown's work as commerce secretary, scandal continually dogged him. In 1993 reports surfaced that he had promised to help lift the trade ban with Vietnam in exchange for a $700,000 bribe. Brown denied the charges, and later the Justice Department cleared him of wrongdoing. In May 1995 Attorney General Janet Reno appointed independent counsel Daniel S. Pearson to investigate charges that Brown had submitted "incomplete, inaccurate and misleading financial disclosure statements" and that he had accepted illegal payments from a former business partner. Also under investigation at the time of his death were charges that an Oklahoma company had paid his son Michael $160,000 in exchange for "influence with the Department of Commerce." Many believed that had Brown lived he would have been removed from office or perhaps even indicted.

In early April 1996, just as the independent counsel's investigation was getting under way, Brown and thirty-four others, including twelve executives from large U.S. corporations, were killed when the military plane used to transport them crashed in a storm in Dubrovnik, Croatia. The purpose of the trip, one of nearly twenty trade missions initiated by Brown during his tenure as secretary, was to promote American business investment in the former Yugoslavia, thereby rebuilding the war-torn area in the process. After a U.S. Air Force investigation, three military officers were relieved of command for allowing the plane to land with the knowledge that the airstrip had not been approved for bad weather landings.

Just days after the accident, controversy began to surround the circumstances of the commerce secretary's death. Air Force forensic examiner Lieutenant Colonel Steven Cogswell, who claimed to have viewed photographs and X rays of Brown's body, reported seeing a bullet-sized hole in Brown's skull. Although U.S. government officials assert that the wound was the result of blunt force trauma sustained during the crash, conspiracy theorists believe that Brown, whose body was not autopsied, was murdered because his indictment by Independent Counsel Pearson was imminent and administration officials feared he would implicate the president. Attorney General Reno declined to investigate, but rumors continued to circulate, spread by an unlikely alliance of black groups—including the National Association for the Advancement of

Colored People—and right-wing, anti-Clinton organizations.

Ron Brown may have been the most important commerce secretary in history but perhaps also the most controversial. In 1992 the Washington-based Center for Public Integrity said that no party chairman had "raised more questions about potential conflicts of interest than Ron Brown" (*Economist*, 19 Dec. 1992). Charges of conflict of interest soon carried over into his term in Clinton's cabinet. Although his roots were in civil rights advocacy, he also was shaped by his years as a lobbyist, during which he honed skills in risk-taking, scheming, and deal making, attributes that contributed to his success as commerce secretary. A remarkable conciliator and negotiator, Brown was respected by the white and the black establishments and was able to move with ease among both. In his eulogy, President Clinton said that Brown had "lived a truly American life."

• Tracey Brown wrote a memoir of her father, *The Life and Times of Ron Brown* (1998). Steven A. Holmes, *Ron Brown: An Uncommon Life* (2000), is a full-length biography. Articles criticizing Brown's DNC chairmanship include Edward T. Pound and Gary Cohen, "Living Well Is the Best Revenge," *U.S. News and World Report*, 7 June 1993, and Michael Kinsley, "Mr. Fix-It," *New Republic*, 22 Apr. 1991. A long interview with Brown before the 1992 election is in *Black Enterprise*, Mar. 1992. The *New York Times*, 7 Jan. 1993, details the Senate hearing for his appointment as commerce secretary. *Newsweek*, 11 Oct. 1993, contains an article about the Vietnam "sell-out," and an article in that same publication, 25 Oct. 1993, recaps his career. "The Commerce Secretary as Machine Pol: Sleazy Genius" is a long article in the *New Republic*, 15 May 1995. Obituaries and articles on his fatal plane crash appeared in most newspapers and magazines of the day. See especially the *New York Times*, 4 Apr. 1996; *Time*, *People*, and *Newsweek*, all 15 Apr. 1996; *Jet*, 22 Apr. 1996; *Business America*, Apr. 1996; and *Ebony*, June 1996. The *New York Times*, 14 Mar. 1998, discusses indictments that resulted from the grand jury investigation into Brown's finances.

STACEY HAMILTON

BROWNELL, Herbert, Jr. (20 Feb. 1904–1 May 1996), U.S. attorney general, was born in Peru, Nebraska, the son of Herbert Brownell, Sr., a college professor, and May A. Miller Brownell. As a child Brownell became interested in politics and excelled at debating and journalism while attending local public schools. Following graduation, he entered the University of Nebraska, where he edited the student newspaper and made Phi Beta Kappa. Although he taught journalism during his senior year at nearby Doane College, an offer of financial assistance from Yale Law School swayed him toward a legal career, and he traveled east after receiving his A.B. in 1924. While at Yale Brownell edited the *Yale Law Journal* and graduated cum laude in 1927.

Attracted by the professional opportunities in New York, Brownell began clerking at the firm of Root, Clark, Buckner and Ballentine in 1927. Admitted to the bar in the following year, he moved to the firm of Lord, Day and Lord in 1929 and became a partner in the firm in 1932. Disgusted by the dominance of local politics by the Democratic party machine, Tammany Hall, and by Republican acquiescence to its corrupt practices, Brownell joined a Young Republicans group and ran for the state assembly from Greenwich Village in 1931. Although he lost that election, he formed a lasting relationship with his campaign manager, Thomas E. Dewey. After successfully running again for the same office in 1932, Brownell served five terms in the New York State Assembly. While in the assembly Brownell championed legislation that established minimum-wage guidelines, reorganized New York City government, and liberalized New York's tough alimony laws. Brownell married Doris A. McCarter on 16 June 1934; the couple had four children.

After declining reelection, Brownell returned to his law firm (with which he would remain associated to the end of his career) and served as the general counsel for the American Hotel Association. Content to work behind the scenes, he managed Dewey's unsuccessful 1938 bid for the governorship, and in the following year became general counsel for the New York World's Fair. Successful in this post (his office lost only one case out of nearly a thousand lawsuits filed against the fair), Brownell soon achieved some notable triumphs in his political activities as well, directing a Republican win in the 1941 race for Manhattan borough president, Dewey's 1942 run for governor, and a 1942 Republican win in the New York lieutenant governor's race. Having proved his organizational mettle in dispensing patronage after Dewey's victory, Brownell managed Dewey's 1944 bid for the presidency. Appointed chairman of the Republican National Committee by Dewey during the course of the campaign, Brownell served in the post for two years, during which time he reorganized the national party and sought closer ties with precinct-level party organizations. Once again, and with the prospect of a victorious outcome, Brownell managed Dewey's presidential campaign in 1948, only to experience the disappointment of Dewey's loss to Harry Truman.

Following the 1948 debacle, Brownell returned to his law practice. When Dewey and his supporters pinned their hopes for 1952 on a candidacy by General Dwight D. Eisenhower, Brownell worked tirelessly behind the scenes at the Republican National Convention. After a series of stunning parliamentary maneuvers, Brownell secured the nomination for Eisenhower over Senator Robert Taft of Ohio; following Eisenhower's victory in November, he soon became one of the president-elect's closest advisers. After accompanying Eisenhower on a postelection trip to Korea, Brownell was named attorney general and assumed the post in January 1953.

As attorney general, Brownell generated controversy when he resurrected the case of Harry Dexter White, a Truman administration official accused of spying for the Soviet Union. After a series of heated charges and countercharges between Brownell and former president Truman, the matter quietly faded away. A hard-line anti-Communist, Brownell protested a stay of execution granted by the Supreme Court to Julius Rosenberg and Ethel Rosenberg, helping to expedite their deaths by electrocution. Pledging to "utterly destroy all" American Communist party activities, Brownell sought a variety of legislation from Congress, including increased penalties for seditious conspiracy and an amendment to the perjury law making the willful giving of contradictory testimony under oath a crime.

While being conservative on such issues as Communism and antitrust prosecution (a 1956 Justice Department decision allowed American Telephone & Telegraph (AT&T) to keep its Western Electric subsidiary), Brownell was consistently to the left of the Eisenhower administration on the issue of civil rights. He filed an amicus curiae brief in December 1953 that upheld the Supreme Court's authority to declare school segregation unconstitutional, and Brownell's recommendation helped to make Earl Warren the new chief justice of the Court. Brownell also played a key role in the creation and passage of the Civil Rights Bill of 1957, which, though approved by Congress in a watered-down version, did create a Civil Rights Commission and a civil rights division within the Justice Department. It was at Brownell's insistence that Eisenhower reluctantly ordered army troops into Little Rock, Arkansas, in the fall of 1957 to protect African American students attempting to integrate a local high school in the face of open defiance on the part of Governor Orval Faubus. Perhaps most importantly, Brownell prodded Eisenhower to appoint a score of federal judges throughout the South who were sensitive to the issue of civil rights; these judges carried out and in some cases even expanded on the impact of the Supreme Court's landmark decision in *Brown v. Board of Education*.

Brownell resigned as attorney general in October 1957. Although his counsel had been highly valued by Eisenhower, the president did not attempt to prevent his departure; many in the Republican party feared that his proactive stance on civil rights had become a political liability for the administration. In 1963 Brownell served as president of the Association of the Bar of New York City, and he was later an adviser to New York Mayor John Lindsay. At President Richard Nixon's request, Brownell served as a special envoy to Mexico from 1972 to 1974 on the issue of salinity of the Colorado River, and from 1975 to 1977 he chaired the National Study Commission on Records and Documents of Federal Officials. Brownell's wife, Doris, died in 1979; his second marriage—in 1987 to Marion R. Taylor—resulted in divorce. Brownell died at his home in Manhattan.

Although occasionally controversial, Brownell worked best behind the scenes. His role in aggressively seeking to have the Rosenbergs executed will continue to be debated, but he has not always been adequately recognized for his efforts to involve the Eisenhower administration in the cause of civil rights.

• Brownell's papers are held at the Dwight D. Eisenhower Presidential Library in Abilene, Kans. He was the coauthor (with C. W. Merritt) of *Manual of Laws Affecting Hotels and Restaurants in New York State* (1947). His autobiography (with John P. Burke) are *Advising Ike: The Memoirs of Attorney General Herbert Brownell* (1993). Secondary sources on his life and career include John Weir Anderson, *Eisenhower, Brownell and the Congress: The Tangled Origins of the Civil Rights Bill of 1956–57* (1964), and Stephen E. Ambrose, *Eisenhower: The President* (1984). An obituary appears in the *New York Times*, 2 May 1996.

EDWARD L. LACH, JR.

BUNDY, McGeorge (30 Mar. 1919–16 Sept. 1996), presidential foreign affairs adviser and philanthropist, was born in Boston, Massachusetts, the son of Harvey Hollister Bundy, a highly successful lawyer who served as a special assistant to Secretary of War Henry Stimson during World War II, and Katherine Putnam Bundy, who was related to several of Boston's most socially prominent families. He grew up in a noisy, high-spirited household where he and his siblings were encouraged to join their elders in debate about history and politics around the dinner table. (His older brother, William Bundy, would later become a high-ranking State Department official during the administrations of John F. Kennedy and Lyndon Johnson, serving these presidents at the same time that McGeorge did.) He attended Groton, an elite preparatory school in Massachusetts, where his classmates marveled at his intelligence and his sometimes brazen self-assurance. He became something of a school legend after one incident: when called upon to present a written assignment on the Duke of Marlborough, he stood up and read what sounded like an excellent composition, prompting a hail of giggles from his classmates; his perplexed instructor later found out that he had delivered the entire essay off the cuff, "reading" from a blank sheet of paper.

Following his graduation from Groton in 1936, Bundy entered Yale University, where he became the first student in the school's history to receive three perfect scores on his entrance exam. Although he majored in mathematics, his true interest was politics. A liberal New England Republican, he was actively involved in the Yale Political Union. As a columnist for the school's daily newspaper, he cultivated an image as an iconoclast, calling for the abolition of the Yale football program and mocking the ritualism and elitism of the school's secret societies; this did not prevent him, however, from joining Skull and Bones, Yale's most elite secret society, in 1939. During his senior year, he had an essay published in a collection entitled *Zero Hour: A Summons to Be Free* (1940), which included writings by poet Stephen Vincent Benét and journalist William L. White; Bundy's essay argued persuasively against American isolationism. Of another Bundy essay, entitled "Is Lenin a Marxist?," his professor, historian David Owen, remarked that he doubted "there were two men on the Yale faculty who could have written it" (Halberstam, p. 53). In June

1940 Bundy graduated first in his class and Phi Beta Kappa.

In 1941 Bundy received a rare honor when he became a junior fellow at Harvard University. This special nondegree graduate program permitted him to research whatever he wanted, with no exams or assigned papers, freeing him from the grind of typical graduate course work. That fall he ran unsuccessfully for the Boston city council. Initially rejected by his draft board during World War II because of his weak vision, Bundy memorized the eye chart and succeeded in joining the army in 1942, specializing in signal intelligence. He later became an assistant to a family friend, Rear Admiral Alan G. Kirk. Discharged as a captain in 1946, Bundy returned to Boston and became a research assistant for former secretary of war Henry Stimson, collaborating on his memoir, *On Active Service in Peace and War* (1948). He also ghostwrote for Stimson an important article for *Harper's* magazine that explained the decision-making process that led the United States to drop the atomic bomb on Japan ("The Decision to Use the Atomic Bomb," Feb. 1947). Published at a time when influential intellectuals were questioning the morality of the bombing, the article contended that using the bomb had been unavoidable, "our least abhorrent choice," the only alternative to an invasion of the Japanese home islands that might have cost a million American lives. Although revisionist historians have insisted that Japan was on the verge of surrendering and that the United States acted prematurely, Bundy's biographer, Kai Bird, points out that Bundy's essay "would stand for at least two decades as the definitive explanation of the decision to use the atomic bomb" (pp. 92–93).

During the late 1940s Bundy was aided by the patronage and friendship of several powerful establishment figures: Stimson, U.S. Supreme Court justice Felix Frankfurter, Judge Learned Hand, columnist Walter Lippmann, and poet and librarian of Congress Archibald MacLeish. In 1948 Bundy moved to Washington, D.C., where he served as a consultant for the Economic Cooperation Administration, which administered the Marshall Plan. That year he also worked for Republican presidential candidate Thomas Dewey's campaign, writing speeches on foreign policy.

Although Bundy had never taken an undergraduate or graduate government class, in 1949 he was appointed a lecturer in the government department at Harvard. The following year he married Mary Lothrop, who worked as an administrator at Radcliffe College; they had four children. In 1951 he published in the *Atlantic* magazine a scathing review of William F. Buckley's conservative manifesto *God and Man at Yale*. He also defended Secretary of State Dean Acheson, then under constant attack by Senator Joseph McCarthy, in *The Pattern of Responsibility* (1952), a collection of Acheson's speeches annotated and edited by Bundy. In these and other writings, he identified himself with what the historian Arthur Schlesinger, Jr., called "the vital center." Bundy supported a classi-

cally liberal government that was pragmatic rather than ideological; he believed that "the battle between right and left, on ideological terms, has become a battle in the clouds revolving around theoretical issues between socialism and capitalism which have little or nothing to do with the practical problem of effective economic organization in a free society" (quoted in Bird, pp. 102–3). Like many in the World War II generation, he supported a vigorous, interventionist U.S. foreign policy. Mindful of the threat of nuclear annihilation, however, he insisted that the Cold War should not be waged recklessly. He agreed with Acheson's "containment" approach toward the Soviet Union, which he summarized with these tenets: "Resist Communism, and build 'situations of strength'; work for an eventual settlement without war, accepting the fact that the course ahead is long, hard, and dangerous; stick to our ideals" (quoted in Bird, p. 112).

In 1953, at the age of thirty-four, Bundy was appointed dean of the faculty of arts and sciences at Harvard. In this capacity he oversaw a staff of more than 1,000 employees and the education of approximately 5,500 undergraduate and 1,800 graduate students. As an administrator, he was regarded by his colleagues as brash, arrogant, and highly effective. He was eager to dispel the school's image as a haven for blue bloods; as one professor noted, "Mac may have been a Yankee swell, but he went out of his way to surround himself with other kinds of people" (quoted in Bird, p. 133). During his administration, students began to be accepted based on merit rather than on family background: the percentage of applicants accepted dropped from 63 percent in 1952 to 30 percent in 1960, and more of these students were from public schools across the country, fewer of them "legacies" from New England preparatory schools. Bundy frequently clashed with the school's bureaucracy about faculty appointments. Over the objection of department committees, he brought intellectuals to the school who lacked traditional academic qualifications, including sociologist David Riesman, psychologist Erik Erikson, and playwright Lillian Hellman. These appointments reflected his philosophy that there "was no appeal beyond the test of excellence" (quoted in Bird, p. 136). Although Bundy was popular at Harvard, his few detractors pointed out that his approach to education encouraged an environment in which those who were flashily brilliant and competitive succeeded while others fared poorly. "I remember arguing with Mac about that all the time," Michael Maccoby, one of his assistants, later recalled. "I told him, 'The only thing you say about somebody is that they're bright or that they're not bright. It's like that's your only category.' His response was, 'Well, you're bright enough, what are you complaining about?'" (quoted in Bird, p. 144).

In December 1960 Bundy was appointed special assistant for national security affairs by newly elected president John F. Kennedy. Very quickly he became one of the most influential members of the administration. Observers noted that his "ability to move things" perfectly complemented the president's intensity, impatience, and pragmatism. Like the president, Bundy disdained lugubrious position papers filled with bureaucratic language, favoring brief memos in which he deftly summarized complex arguments. As journalist David Halberstam suggested, "To be a good memo writer in government was a very real form of power. Suddenly everyone would be working off Bundy's memos, and thus his memos guided the action, guided what the president would see" (p. 62). In keeping with Kennedy's wishes, Bundy modeled his national security staff after an academic faculty, putting together an informal, nonhierarchical group in which ideas could be discussed freely. The staff was intellectually diverse, including Walt Rostow, an eccentric advocate of guerrilla warfare, and Marcus Raskin, a 26-year-old pacifist. The idea was to expose the president to a wide variety of viewpoints on every issue. Bundy excelled at his own role as "traffic cop," making sure that the president heard good ideas and keeping his options open as much as possible. Bundy's staff became the dominant foreign policy group in the White House, usurping much of the influence traditionally wielded by the State Department, which was headed by the relatively unaggressive Dean Rusk. "Damn it, Bundy and I get more done in one day in the White House than they do in six months at the State Department," Kennedy reportedly told his wife (quoted in Bird, p. 189).

Historians have generally given mixed reviews to Kennedy's pragmatic approach to foreign policy, which tended to emphasize immediate action over long-term considerations. Although the president and his advisers were disgusted by Cold War jingoism and wished to reduce tensions with the Soviet Union, they also believed that they must stand firm against communism, in part because it was politically expedient to do so. In 1961 Bundy urged Kennedy to send limited combat troops to Vietnam, arguing that troop commitments had "become a sort of touchstone of our will" (quoted in Bird, p. 222). The president, dubious about American involvement in Southeast Asia but unwilling to abandon the region, chose to send military advisers instead.

In 1962, during the Cuban Missile Crisis, Bundy played devil's advocate, arguing for a surgical airstrike against Soviet missile silos even when many of Kennedy's other advisers supported a somewhat less confrontational naval blockade. When the crisis was resolved by reaching a compromise with the Soviets— in exchange for the removal of the missiles in Cuba, the United States agreed to withdraw NATO missiles from Turkey—Bundy and the few others in the administration privy to this information kept it secret. He later came to see this as a serious mistake: "Our colleagues, our countrymen, our successors, and our allies" were taught that "nothing responsive had been offered" and that only "unwavering firmness" could face down the Soviets, which only reinforced support

for a hard-line Cold War policy (quoted in Bird, p. 241).

Bundy also came to regret his enthusiasm for covert operations, by which the administration sought to achieve its objectives without taking responsibility. He urged the president to undertake the disastrous Bay of Pigs invasion of Cuba; authorized "Operation Mongoose," a sustained and unsuccessful Central Intelligence Agency (CIA) effort to oust Cuban leader Fidel Castro's regime after the invasion failed; and approved coup attempts against Dominican Republic dictator Rafael Trujillo and South Vietnamese president Ngo Dinh Diem, both of which ended in assassinations. Bundy later admitted that many covert operations were ill advised and uncontrollable, employing methods that were unauthorized and, at times, morally questionable.

Following Kennedy's assassination in 1963, his principal foreign affairs advisers—Bundy, Rusk, and Secretary of Defense Robert McNamara—agreed to stay at their jobs under the new administration of President Lyndon Johnson. Johnson's White House was a very different place from Kennedy's. An insecure man, especially regarding foreign policy matters, Johnson insisted on consensus and did not appreciate the give-and-take of ideas. Johnson's personality and his desire for consensus had repercussions for Bundy's performance as national security adviser; whereas he constantly confronted Kennedy with a diversity of foreign policy options, he rarely attempted to do so with Johnson. Some historians have castigated Bundy for this failure, particularly with regard to the president's conduct of the Vietnam War. Bundy's own view on Vietnam was subtle and complex, but generally hawkish. He did not agree with Johnson's and Rusk's adherence to the domino theory and other Cold War platitudes: "I always lose my temper," he later said, "at the notion that a series of complex political organisms can be understood by comparing them to an inanimate set of black tiles" (quoted in Bird, p. 17). But he did believe that the president needed to make a stand in Vietnam to maintain America's international credibility; he also feared political repercussions at home if Johnson gave up. In early 1965 he wrote of the administration's policy of sustained bombing in North Vietnam: "It may fail, and we cannot estimate the odds of success with any accuracy—they may be somewhere between 25 and 75 percent. What we can say is that even if it fails, the policy will be worth it. At the minimum it will dampen down the charge that we did not do all that we could have done, and this charge will be important in many countries, including our own" (quoted in Bird, p. 308). Critics have pointed to what they see as the flaw in Bundy's logic: if the administration merely intended to demonstrate its commitment to what seemed likely to be a lost cause, was this really worth American and Vietnamese lives?

Throughout 1964 and early 1965 Bundy advocated deepening the American commitment in Vietnam, including the use of air power and the introduction of limited ground troops; he believed that these "stiffeners" would give the South Vietnamese government an opportunity to stabilize the country. But when the situation continued to worsen and McNamara began advocating the introduction of 200,000 ground troops, Bundy registered his dissent. "This is a slippery slope toward total U.S. responsibility and corresponding fecklessness on the Vietnamese side," he argued. If the war was going so poorly, "do we want to invest 200 thousand men to cover an eventual retreat? Can we not do that just as well where we are?" (quoted in Bird, p. 331). Around this time, his relationship with Johnson deteriorated. Bundy was particularly disturbed by the president's refusal to seek congressional approval for widening the war and his failure to publicly explain the administration's rationale. In June, Johnson became furious with his adviser when Bundy engaged, without authorization, in a televised debate about Vietnam. Bundy later recalled, "He didn't want me to do it, and he knew that I knew he didn't want me to do it—and I did it anyway" (quoted in Bird, p. 322). During deliberations that summer, he felt that he was "holding onto the president's coattails," but he came around to supporting McNamara's plan for escalation. That fall he announced his intention to resign, although he continued to fundamentally support Johnson and the war effort, both publicly and privately.

While serving in the Kennedy administration, Bundy had ambitions to become secretary of state; by the time he left the White House in February 1966, his critics on the New Left were calling him a war criminal, and even his close friends felt that he had no future in government because of his association with Vietnam. That year he became president of the Ford Foundation, one of the largest private charitable trusts in the nation, with $3.7 billion in assets. The foundation had typically funded mainstream institutions such as hospitals and symphony orchestras, but Bundy radically remade its agenda, telling an interviewer, "I don't mind being a lightning rod for anger. Anyone serving that purpose is useful and important" (quoted in Bird, p. 377). His particular interest was combating racism, and the foundation funded dozens of civil rights organizations—from integrationist groups such as the National Association for the Advancement of Colored People (NAACP) to the Congress of Racial Equality (CORE), which was then moving toward a black-power philosophy. He provided money for community-development organizations in urban slums, such as the Bedford-Stuyvesant Development and Services Corporation in New York City. He also funded experimental community-control school boards in African-American neighborhoods.

Under Bundy's leadership, the Ford Foundation poured money into numerous public-interest law groups, including the Mexican-American Legal Defense and Educational Fund and the Women's Law Fund, organizations that sought to initiate legal actions on behalf of citizens who were typically poor and powerless. He funded environmental groups such as the Sierra Club and gave money for a lawsuit against the Environmental Protection Agency for failing to enforce antismog regulations. In 1967 he helped goad Congress into passing the Public Broadcasting Act; over the next several years the Ford Foundation gave hundreds of millions of dollars to the newly created Public Broadcasting System (PBS). His liberal crusading came with a cost: conservative congressmen passed legislation requiring all foundations to pay a tax on their investment income, and several Ford Foundation officials were placed on President Richard Nixon's "enemies list." Nevertheless, *Fortune* magazine wrote that Bundy had "led the way in making the private foundation a significant third force in American life—a powerful engine for social change independent of the dominant power centers of business and government" (quoted in Bird, p. 386).

In 1979 Bundy resigned from the Ford Foundation and joined the faculty of the history department at New York University; twenty-four professors protested his appointment because of his role in the Vietnam War. In 1982, along with former government officials George Kennan, McNamara, and Gerard Smith, he cowrote an influential essay in *Foreign Affairs*, arguing against America's long-standing policy of "first use" of nuclear weapons to stop a Soviet invasion of Europe ("Nuclear Weapons and the Atlantic Alliance," Spring 1982). During the 1980s he was a leading arms-control advocate and frequently criticized stepped-up defense spending by the administration of President Ronald Reagan. In 1988 he published *Danger and Survival: Choices about the Bomb in the First Fifty Years*. Critically acclaimed, the book analyzed the role of nuclear weapons in world politics. During these years Bundy rarely discussed Vietnam; he once admitted to an antagonist that he had made mistakes, then added snappishly, "But I'm not going to waste the rest of my life feeling guilty about it" (quoted in Bird, p. 401). In his final years, however, he worked on a memoir about his experiences during the war, which he never finished. He died in Boston.

Obituaries and editorials published upon Bundy's death suggested his mixed, controversial legacy. Arthur Schlesinger, Jr., writing in *George* magazine, praised him for "transcend[ing] the politics and complaisancies of his class" (p. 104). The *Washington Post* offered a defense of the Johnson administration's rationale for becoming involved in Vietnam: "The American role in the Vietnam War, for all its stumbles, was no accident. It arose from the deepest sources— the deepest and most legitimate sources—of the American desire to affirm freedom in the world" (18 Sept. 1996). *Time* magazine, taking a much more critical stance, said that Bundy personified "the hubris of an intellectual elite that marched America with a cool and confident brilliance into the quagmire of Vietnam" (30 Sept. 1996). Despite his distinguished career as a foreign-policy intellectual, educator, and philanthropist, he is best remembered as one of the chief architects of America's miserable failure in the Vietnam War.

• The best source of information on Bundy's life is Kai Bird's excellent dual biography, *The Color of Truth: McGeorge Bundy and William Bundy, Brothers in Arms* (1998). For Bundy's role in the Kennedy administration, see Lawrence Freedman, *Kennedy's Wars: Berlin, Cuba, Laos, and Vietnam* (2000). David Halberstam, *The Best and the Brightest* (1972), is a fine, impassioned history of the Vietnam War era. Like many writers, Halberstam is sharply critical of Bundy's role in the escalation of the war. For a particularly damning historical analysis of the Johnson administration, see Fredrik Logevall, *Choosing War: The Lost Chance for Peace and the Escalation of War in Vietnam* (1999). For sympathetic assessments of Bundy, see Arthur Schlesinger, Jr., "A Man Called Mac," *George*, Dec. 1996, and James Thomson, "A Memory of McGeorge Bundy," in the *New York Times*, 22 Sept. 1996. An obituary is in the *New York Times*, 17 Sept. 1996.

THOMAS W. COLLINS, JR.

BUNDY, William (24 Sept. 1917–6 Oct. 2000), presidential foreign affairs adviser, was born William Putnam Bundy in Washington, D.C., the son of Harvey Hollister Bundy, a highly successful attorney who served as special assistant to Secretary of War Henry Stimson during World War II, and Katherine Putnam Bundy, who was related to several of Boston's most socially prominent families. He grew up in Boston in a talkative, high-spirited household where the children joined in arguments about history and politics around the dinner table. Both he and his younger brother, McGeorge, were precocious, self-confident, and highly competitive. (McGeorge Bundy became national security adviser for John F. Kennedy and Lyndon Johnson, serving these presidents at the same time that William did.) William attended Groton, an elite prep school in Massachusetts. His passions as a student were history and current events; he graduated first in his class in 1935. He then attended Yale University, where he won the Snow scholarship (given by the faculty to a senior who combines "intellectual achievement, character, and personality") and the de Forest Prize for public speaking. He served as president of the Yale Political Union and was admitted into Skull and Bones, an elite social club that included many members who went on to successful careers in government and business. He received a B.A. degree in history from Yale in 1939. He then did graduate work in American history at Harvard University, earning an M.A. in 1940.

Bundy began studying for a law degree at Harvard in 1940, but after completing a year in school he decided to enlist in the U.S. Army Signal Intelligence Corps. He trained in cryptology and graduated from officer candidate school in 1942 as a first lieutenant. In early 1943 he married Mary Acheson, the daughter of Dean Acheson, who served as secretary of state under Harry S. Truman; Bundy and his wife had three children. They lived for a time in Washington, D.C., where he worked as a cryptologist. He later described his first significant assignment: "A hostile nation—which I should not name—was using a cipher based on pages from a book which the FBI knew had been checked out of the Library of Congress. My job was to use the same book, interpret the key and break this particular code. I and a very able colleague were successful" (quoted in Bird, p, 74). Afterward he was assigned to a top-secret code-breaking operation at Bletchley Park in England, where he was the commanding officer for a small group of American cryptologists. His daily assignment was to break the cipher used by the Luftwaffe, Germany's air force; his men typically learned the code each morning by breakfast time, and they deciphered tens of thousands of intercepted messages, which were forwarded to Allied commanders in the field. In recognition of his work, he was awarded the Legion of Merit and was made a member of the Order of the British Empire. He was discharged from the service in September 1945 with the rank of major.

Bundy returned to Harvard, where he earned his law degree in 1947. He practiced law for approximately three years with the influential Washington firm of Covington and Burling, but the work was boring to him. In 1951 he joined the Central Intelligence Agency, where he quickly advanced to become chief of the estimates staff at the Office of National Estimates. His analysts were responsible for providing intelligence reports on political, military, and economic trends in global hot spots; typical questions that they addressed included what might happen in the Soviet Union after Joseph Stalin's death and whether the French could hold Vietnam against the Communist insurgency being conducted by the Viet Minh. In 1952 Bundy was made principal assistant to Robert Amory, the CIA's deputy director of intelligence. The following year his career was almost derailed by Joseph McCarthy, who had decided to investigate "security risks" in the CIA: McCarthy had learned that Bundy contributed $400 in 1949 to help defend alleged Communist spy Alger Hiss. McCarthy's investigator, Roy Cohn, badgered the CIA with phone calls, insisting that Bundy had "contributed heavily" to the Hiss defense fund and was therefore unreliable. Bundy, for his part, pointed to his friendship with Alger's brother, Donald Hiss, who had been his supervisor at Covington and Burling; he admitted that he felt that Alger Hiss deserved a first-rate attorney. CIA director Allen Dulles, realizing that the Bundy case might become the first shot fired in a McCarthyite assault on his fort, pressured Republican Senate leaders and Vice President Richard Nixon to protect Bundy. They gave assurances that Congress would never authorize a full-scale investigation of the CIA. Nevertheless, Bundy was forced to testify before a loyalty board in February 1954; the board found no evidence of treason but recommended that he should be fired because his character rendered him "unsuitable" for intelligence work. Dulles chose to refer this decision to an internal CIA panel that dealt with "suitability" issues; it exonerated Bundy. "I did not thank

[Dulles] at the time," he later remembered, "but made my gratitude and respect amply clear over the years" (quoted in Bird, p. 170).

Bundy continued to work at the CIA until 1960. That year he was given a leave of absence to work as staff director for President Dwight Eisenhower's Commission on National Goals. The commission, which was composed of educators, corporate executives, and labor officials, published a report, *Goals for Americans* (1960), that called for increased funding for education and the arts, a full recognition of the rights of minorities and women, and dramatic steps to alleviate inner-city poverty. Bundy's biographer, Kai Bird, has called this report "a planning document . . . for what would become Lyndon Johnson's Great Society" (p. 182). In 1961 Bundy was appointed by President John F. Kennedy to serve as deputy to Paul Nitze, the assistant secretary of defense for international security affairs. In 1962 Bundy was responsible for providing military aid to northern India, where some disputed borderlands had been invaded by Chinese Communists. In November 1963 he replaced Nitze when Nitze became secretary of the navy. In early 1964 Bundy was appointed by President Lyndon Johnson to be assistant secretary of state for Far Eastern affairs. In this capacity he served as a crucial "pivot" in the State Department, providing the secretary and undersecretary with information he had received from lower-level experts, who "had 90 percent of their contact with him" (Halberstam, p. 379). Most significantly, he became one of the principal architects of U.S. policy regarding Vietnam.

Bundy's attitude toward U.S. involvement in Vietnam was complex and often wavering. He was one of the first hawks in the Kennedy administration, drafting a report in 1961 that urged the president to commit as many as 200,000 U.S. ground troops to prevent the fall of South Vietnam to Communism. His beliefs changed somewhat in September 1963, when he joined Secretary of Defense Robert McNamara and General Maxwell Taylor on a trip to Saigon. He later wrote that he left the country "with a lasting skepticism of the ability of any man, however honest, to interpret accurately what was going on. It was just too diffuse, and too much that was critical took place below the surface." He was convinced, however, that the unpopular regime of Ngo Dinh Diem, the South Vietnamese president who was backed by the U.S., "stood only a small chance of holding South Vietnam together" (quoted in Bird, p. 257). In the spring of 1964 he helped to draft what became known as the Tonkin Gulf resolution, which gave the president authority to undertake military activities without a congressional declaration of war. In policy debates later that year, he showed himself to be an ally of Undersecretary of State George Ball, the most dovish of President Johnson's advisers. Bundy flatly rejected Secretary of State Dean Rusk's assertion that if South Vietnam fell, more strategically important countries such as Thailand and India would be the next to go; to Bundy, the "falling domino" theory was overly simplistic. He also strongly disagreed with Johnson's decision to convene the "Wise Men"—a group of hardened Cold Warriors from previous administrations—for advice on Vietnam. "The men who met with the President . . . were bound to give him and his advisers every benefit of acceptance [of a war policy]," he wrote. "It was a poor way to proceed" (quoted in Bird, p. 338). Bundy in October 1964 wrote a memorandum proposing a policy that he described with a baseball adage, "Swing wildly at the first one, then bunt." He suggested that the U.S. strike hard by bombing numerous North Vietnamese targets, mining their ports, and establishing a naval quarantine; these steps would create pressure to reconvene the Geneva Conference, at which the U.S. should settle for a neutralist, coalition government, even with the knowledge that South Vietnam would probably soon turn Communist. The bombing campaign would harm Hanoi and give America a way out with honor, proving that it was "tough" on Communism, but no larger commitment would be necessary. Bundy's memorandum was circulated among Rusk, McNamara, and McGeorge Bundy, who all rejected it; a few weeks later he again approached Rusk and McNamara, suggesting that the United States simply negotiate a withdrawal, but was told "it won't wash" (quoted in Bird, p. 294).

A cautious man, Bundy quickly backpedaled from his dovish positions. In June 1965 Ball suggested that they coauthor a paper recommending American withdrawal, but Bundy refused. One state department official, Thomas L. Hughes, cited this as a crucial moment in the Johnson administration, claiming that if Bundy had thrown his support behind Ball, they might have swayed the other advisers. The documentary evidence suggests, however, that Johnson, Rusk, McNamara, and McGeorge Bundy had already made up their minds to expand American involvement and try to "waffle through" to victory. When Johnson announced in July 1965 that he was sending 100,000 troops to Vietnam, Bundy felt that it was his duty to support the president's decision. He spent much of 1966 working to strengthen the political stability of the regime of Nguyen Cao Ky (one of Diem's successors), although privately he regarded it as "absolutely the bottom of the barrel" (quoted in Bird, p. 349). Publicly he was quite optimistic about the war effort, and in the State Department many of his colleagues regarded him as a hawk. He was especially contemptuous of Johnson administration officials who broke ranks to criticize the war; when a former official wrote an antiwar essay in the *Atlantic* in 1968, Bundy dismissed it as "the voice of an inherently small man" (quoted in Bird, p. 374). In spite of his apparent confidence, though, his co-workers knew that he was under enormous pressure. Thomas L. Hughes commented: "Rusk just sat there listening and nodding his head like he was above it all. But Bill was the action officer on Vietnam; he had to deal with it every day. He could have done what McNamara did—he could have been for the war by day and against it at night.

But Bill Bundy wasn't like that. He was consistent" (quoted in Bird, p. 350).

Bundy left the government in early 1969, when Richard Nixon assumed the presidency. He then moved to Cambridge, Massachusetts, where he accepted a senior fellowship from MIT to write a history of the decision-making process that had led to the war. Experiencing a great deal of anguish and self-doubt as he attempted to write the book, he never finished it. In 1970 and 1971 his home was routinely picketed by antiwar demonstrators. In June 1971 a homemade bomb exploded at his office at MIT, planted there by a women's faction of the radical group the Weathermen; no one was injured, but the bomb caused $35,000 in damage. In 1972 he was attacked by the journalist David Halberstam in *The Best and the Brightest*, a bestselling examination of Kennedy's and Johnson's advisers that largely defined Bundy's public image. Halberstam characterized him as a "classic mandarin, abusive and rough on those who worked for him, obsequious to those above him"; he was criticized for failing to pass on the pessimistic war reports of lower-level State Department experts to his superiors (Halberstam, p. 396). This was an accurate portrayal of his job performance after 1965, when he permitted little debate among his subordinates about administration policy.

In 1972 Bundy was appointed editor of *Foreign Affairs*, a journal published by the Council of Foreign Relations. He surprised many of his critics when he frequently published their denunciations of the war. He continued at the journal until 1984, when he became a part-time faculty member at Princeton University. In 1989 he wrote about Vietnam: "I was never able to convince myself that there was a cost-free alternative course . . . or that any of the different strategies since proposed, especially those involving stronger military action, would have made sense. In a nutshell, my present feeling is that it was a tragedy waiting to happen, but one made much worse by countless errors along the way, in many of which I had a part" (quoted in the *New York Times*, 7 Oct. 2000). In his later years he researched and wrote a history of Nixon's foreign policy, *A Tangled Web: The Making of Foreign Policy in the Nixon Presidency*, which was published to critical acclaim in 1998. The book argues that Nixon and his national security adviser, Henry Kissinger, tended to act without consulting others and often used smokescreens to veil their true policy intentions, thus contributing to the general mood of frustration and anger that helped bring about Nixon's fall. Bundy died in Princeton, New Jersey.

• The best source of information on Bundy's life is Kai Bird's excellent dual biography, *The Color of Truth: McGeorge Bundy and William Bundy, Brothers in Arms* (1998). David Kaiser, *American Tragedy: Kennedy, Johnson, and the Origins of the Vietnam War* (2000), offers a careful scholarly appraisal of the early war years. The book presents a particularly valuable account of the disagreements about Vietnam within the Johnson administration in 1964 and early 1965; Kaiser fully documents Bundy's tentative alliance with George Ball during these years. Robert Dallek, *Flawed Giant: Lyndon Johnson and His Times, 1961–1973* (1998), describes Bundy's work for Johnson. David Halberstam, *The Best and the Brightest* (1972), is a fine, impassioned journalistic history of the Vietnam War era. For a thoughtful review of Bundy's history of Nixon's foreign policy, see Tony Judt, *New York Review of Books*, 13 Aug. 1998, pp. 54–58. An obituary is in the *New York Times*, 7 Oct. 2000.

THOMAS W. COLLINS, JR.

BURNS, George (20 Jan. 1896–9 Mar. 1996), comedian, was born Nathan Birnbaum in New York City, the son of Louis Philip Birnbaum, a kosher butcher and part-time cantor, and Dora Bluth. One of twelve children, Burns spent his childhood living in poverty in the tenements of Manhattan's Lower East Side. Indifferent to his parents' Orthodox Judaism, Burns adopted show business as his religion at age five when he got his first taste of applause by dancing to the music of an organ grinder. A natural entertainer, Burns had little interest in the rigors of education and quit school permanently after he failed the fifth grade. Even though he enjoyed enormous wealth and celebrity in later years, for the rest of his life Burns would never master basic reading skills.

Because his father died when Burns was only seven or eight, the street-smart child survived by working odd jobs in Lower Manhattan, including his first "booking" as part of a harmony act, the Peewee Quartet, which won a five-dollar group prize at a neighborhood theatre. Flush with success, the ambitious young entertainer resolved to learn everything he could about singing and dancing and set out to enter show business full time. Needing a stage name, he changed Birnbaum to Burns and borrowed George from his brother Izadore, who called himself George because he hated his own given name. Burns later said, "If George was good enough for Izzy, it was good enough for me."

The decade between 1910 and 1920 was difficult for Burns. When he wrote about his early years more than half a century later, Burns was good at "telling it cute," but in reality he lived hand to mouth and often went hungry. He later wrote, "I was in show business but I wasn't working. I had makeup, I had music, I had pictures but I had no job." In his darkest days between bookings, Burns resorted to making "soup" from ketchup and hot water.

In his teenage years, Burns became something of a ladies' man and often dressed like a dandy in plaid suits, with stickpins and spats. During this period, along with his friend Julius "Groucho" Marx, he acquired the habit of smoking his trademark cigar. By age eighteen, more through brains and determination than talent, Burns had succeeded in becoming a second-rate song-and-dance man in vaudeville, scrambling for bookings along with hundreds of other small-time acts. He would work anywhere (he defined a theater as "anything with a toilet"); he would work with anybody (he was half a tango team called "Pedro Lopez and Conchita"); and he even would work with animals: he did an act as "Maurice Valenti and His Wonder Dog" and another with a trained seal as "Flipper and Friend," giving himself second billing. Ironically, during these experimental years, it never occurred to Burns to work as a comedian. Furthermore, despite all his swagger, energy, and inventiveness, at age twenty-five Burns usually occupied the lowest spot on the theater's bill and he was still living at home. What was worse, despite his unrequited love for show business and his unfailing optimism and common sense, at this point in his career Burns did not seem to know what his act really was.

Burns's first break came when he and Hannah Siegel, his partner in a snappy dance routine, were offered a 26-week tour around the vaudeville circuit. However, they could accept the work only if they were married, since Siegel's parents were devout Jews. Although Burns was not in love, he agreed to the union, which he later called "a marriage of theatrical convenience." The couple were divorced at the end of the tour. Burns's next partner, Billy Lorraine, formed with him an all-purpose act that was mediocre at best. It lasted until the winter of 1923 when Burns met a young woman who would change his show business career—and his life—forever. She was Gracie Allen, a naive Irish Catholic actress from California who was also struggling to catch on in the theatre.

Burns was attracted to Allen for several reasons: she was pretty; she was always his best audience; she did not crave the limelight; and, because they had both failed at singing and dancing, she agreed to their becoming a comedy team even though Burns stipulated that she would do only the straight lines. From the beginning it was clear to Burns that Allen's straight lines, delivered in her sincere, high-pitched voice, were getting laughs while his own punch lines were falling flat. Moreover, there was something special about his new partner. Burns put it best in *Gracie: A Love Story* (1988): "Some kind of magical transformation had taken place. [The audience] loved her, I could feel it. It was the most amazing thing, and it happened just like that."

Burns quickly switched roles with Gracie, who now would deliver the jokes (which he wrote). From then on, Burns and Allen were a smash hit. George was not funny but the act was, and that was the only thing that mattered. Significantly, within weeks of beginning a lasting relationship with Gracie Allen, Burns met the other person with whom he would form a lifelong relationship: Jack Benny, a rising young comedian who immediately became Burns's best friend and confidant.

The Burns and Allen act first received serious notice in 1925, when it was booked for ten weeks on the Keith-Orpheum theater circuit, which stretched along the East Coast. With the success of their act, Burns and Allen grew closer personally. They were married in 1926 and adopted two children. By 1928, they were playing the best theaters in New York, including the famed Palace, and won the esteem accorded other Broadway stars like Benny, Fred Allen, Frank Fay,

Eddie Cantor, Fred Astaire and Adele Astaire, and the Marx Brothers. Burns and Allen toured European theaters in 1930 and made their radio debut on the newly established British Broadcasting Corporation.

Burns and Allen were among the first vaudevillians to capitalize on radio's booming popularity and soon became national stars. For the next twenty-six years, "The Burns and Allen Show" was an American entertainment staple, first on radio and then for eight years as a top-rated television situation comedy. To take advantage of multiple offers from Hollywood, the Burns family moved in 1936 to Los Angeles, where Burns became part of the establishment. He joined the exclusive Hillcrest Country Club and took a seat at the Round Table where the celebrity membership met for lunch. The regulars included Benny, Groucho Marx and Harpo Marx, Al Jolson, George Jessel, Edward G. Robinson, Eddie Cantor, Milton Berle, and the Ritz Brothers. When he was not out of town, Burns would lunch, joke and play bridge at the Round Table almost every day for the next sixty years.

Thanks to his good business sense, by 1951 Burns was a millionaire many times over. He and Benny also took on a series of mistresses. When Gracie Allen found out about these infidelities, Burns appeased her with an expensive mink coat. In later years the forgiving Mrs. Burns mused, "I wish George would find another girlfriend. I could use a silver fox jacket." In the mid-1950s, Allen's health began to fail. After she suffered a major heart attack in 1958, "The Burns and Allen Show" had to be canceled. At first Burns tried to work solo and then with several younger female partners, but without Gracie Allen he was again a failure. When she died in 1964, Burns was devastated. He regularly visited her crypt and carried on long conversations with her spirit. As many of Burns's old friends began dying off, he grew more depressed and believed his career was over.

Burns was slowed by heart bypass surgery in 1974, the same year that Jack Benny became gravely ill. Benny, who had won a major part in the movie adaptation of Neil Simon's *The Sunshine Boys*, recommended Burns for the role and in so doing resurrected his friend's languishing career. Burns broke down at Benny's funeral, but he realized that his friend had bequeathed him the one thing Burns had always sought: the opportunity to become a hit solo act. Burns won an Oscar as best supporting actor for *The Sunshine Boys* in 1975; at age eighty he was a bona fide movie star. He landed major roles in another half dozen popular light comedies including *Going in Style* (1978), the story of three geriatric bank robbers, and *Oh, God!* (1977) and its two sequels, *Oh, God! Book Two* (1989) and *Oh, God! You Devil* (1990), in which he portrayed the deity as a wisecracking little old man.

An elderly person becoming a star was an unprecedented phenomenon, and Burns's manager, Irving Fein, exploited it fully. "George Burns Celebrates Eighty Years in Show Business" (1993) culminated a series of television specials for CBS. A favorite guest on many late-night talk shows, Burns regularly sold out the biggest clubs in Las Vegas, Lake Tahoe, and Atlantic City. He disarmed his audiences by dryly telling old age jokes, such as "Nice to be here? At my age it's nice to be anywhere"; "I get a standing ovation just for standing"; and "I would go out with women my age, but there are no women my age." In fact, Burns had a number of relationships with younger women. The most serious were with Catherine Carr, a wealthy divorcée forty-five years younger than Burns, and Melissa Miller, a nineteen-year-old singer/actress fifty-two years his junior. Burns exploited his age to the fullest when, at age eighty-seven, his book titled *How to Live to Be 100—or More* (1983) was published and he announced that he wanted to celebrate his one-hundredth birthday by playing the Palladium in London.

Burns kept busy in other ways: recording in 1988 a hit album (with the title song of his movie *18 Again*); garnering a Grammy in 1990 for his "spoken word recording" of *Gracie: A Love Story*; and producing seven more bestselling books, including *Wisdom of the 90s* (1991) and *100 Years, 100 Stories* (1996). Although some of these books purport to be semi-autobiographical, Burns always goes for laughs, often at the expense of the facts. Late in life he quietly became a generous philanthropist, giving millions of dollars to the Actors Home and Cedars-Sinai Hospital in Los Angeles and to Ben Gurion University in Israel.

After his injury in a bathroom accident in his ninety-ninth year, Burns had to cancel his date at the Palladium. When journalists inevitably asked questions about his mortality, Burns would answer: "I'm not interested in dying—it's been done" or "I can't die. I'm booked." And he still was—at Caesar's Palace in Las Vegas. With his usual good timing, Burns did live to be 100 and died peacefully in Los Angeles just a month after his centennial birthday. He had made the most of his years, having given wit and charm to the condition of old age as few had done before.

• Burns's first book, *I Love Her, That's Why* (1955), is mainly about Gracie Allen and attests to her greater fame. *The Third Time Around* (1980) is perhaps Burns's best book and the most autobiographically accurate. Many of his ten books are available on audiotape, read by Burns himself. In 1989 he made a 45-minute videotape titled *The Wit and Wisdom of George Burns*. Together, Burns and Allen made more than two dozen Hollywood films. The best of an undistinguished group are *International House* (1932) and *The Big Broadcast* series of 1932, 1936, and 1937. The most complete biography is Martin Gottfried, *George Burns and the Hundred Year Dash*, published in 1996, the year Burns died. Melissa Miller wrote a book-length memoir, *Close but No Cigar: 30 Wonderful Years with George Burns* (1998). See also Cheryl Blythe, *Say Good Night, Gracie!: The Story of Burns and Allen* (1986). Even after his death Burns's show business career continued. In 1997 Scott Lane produced a computer-generated feature film, *Everything George*, starring a virtual George Burns interacting with live actors. Obituaries are in the *New York Times* and the *Los Angeles Times*, both 10 Mar. 1996, and in *Variety*, 18–24 Mar. 1996.

BRUCE L. JANOFF

BURROUGHS, William S. (5 Feb. 1914–2 Aug. 1997), author, was born William Seward Burroughs II near Forest Park in St. Louis, Missouri, the son of Mortimer Burroughs, an MIT graduate who ran a glass business, and Laura Lee Burroughs, a preacher's daughter and debutante intrigued by spiritualism. His later life would contrast sharply with his origins in what the Progressive-era theorist Thorstein Veblen called the "leisure class." A brother of Burroughs's mother, Ivy Ledbetter Lee, was a pioneer of public relations and advised John D. Rockefeller, Jr.; Burroughs's paternal grandfather, William Seward Burroughs, was an inventor who developed a practical adding machine.

At age four, Burroughs later claimed, he was sexually molested by a male friend of a beloved nanny. The incident purportedly left him with a long-repressed psychological injury. Shy and awkward, he read horror fiction and tales about cowboys and gangsters. At age eight he began writing his own stories, such as "The Autobiography of a Wolf." He was enthralled by a criminal's autobiography, which "sounded good to me compared with the dullness of a Midwest suburb where all contact with life was shut out" (quoted in Grauerholz and Silverburg, p. xxi). Young Burroughs "would break into houses and walk around without taking anything . . . Sometimes I would drive around in the country with a .22 rifle, shooting chickens" (quoted in Grauerholz and Silverberg, p. xxi). Afflicted with sinus troubles, he was sent at age fifteen to the dry atmosphere of New Mexico, where he entered a boy's academy, Los Alamos Ranch School. There he became a skilled marksman and knife thrower, developed a homosexual attachment to another boy, and experimented with drugs by swallowing a near-fatal dose of "knockout drops" (chloral hydrate).

In 1932 Burroughs entered Harvard. There he kept a loaded gun and a ferret in his room and was "just a completely beat down person with no idea of who he was or what he was" (quoted in Miles, p. 30). But he loved to read—especially Shakespeare, Coleridge, and Thomas De Quincy—and graduated with a bachelor's degree in American literature in 1936. He then traveled to Europe and entered the University of Vienna medical school, but left after one semester. In Dubrovnik, Yugoslavia, he became acquainted with gay intellectuals; a woman in their circle, Ilse Klapper, a German Jew hoping to escape the Nazis, persuaded him to marry her in 1937 so she could enter the United States. They separated after she moved to America and divorced after the war.

In Chicago in 1939 he attended lectures by Alfred Korzybski (1879–1950) on his iconoclastic linguistic doctrine of "general semantics." Also in the late 1930s Burroughs attended graduate school, studying psychology and anthropology at Columbia University and anthropology at Harvard. At Harvard he befriended Kells Elvins, a dark-humored man who helped inspire Burroughs's own bleak wit. Together they wrote a satirical article, "Twilight's Last Gleamings," which introduced the most famous recurring character in Burroughs's writings, "Dr. Benway," a darkly comic symbol of science gone berserk. While attending Columbia, Burroughs developed a crush on another man, who did not fully reciprocate the passion. Heartbroken, Burroughs deliberately used shears to cut off the end of his left little finger. He was committed to a psychiatric clinic, then sent home to his parents. After the United States entered the war in late 1941, Burroughs was drafted into the infantry; he managed to get out early, thanks to his mother's influential connections. In Chicago he worked as a door-to-door insect exterminator, saw a psychiatrist, and plotted (but did not undertake) robberies. In 1943 he followed two St. Louis friends, Lucien Carr and David Kammerer, to New York. At Kammerer's apartment Burroughs met the budding poet Allen Ginsberg. Carr introduced Burroughs to future novelist Jack Kerouac. Ginsberg, Kerouac, and Burroughs—later the three central figures of the 1950s "Beat Generation," which would defy orthodoxies in postwar American life and culture—became close friends who loved talking about literature. Being older and more erudite, Burroughs assigned Ginsberg and Kerouac "reading lists" that included Arthur Rimbaud, Oswald Spengler, and Jonathan Swift.

In August 1944, Carr knifed Kammerer to death, ostensibly to repel unwanted sexual advances. Although Burroughs and Kerouac were arrested for failing to report the killing, they were let off (Carr spent two years in prison); no publisher would take the mystery story that they based on the killing. Through Kerouac and Ginsberg, Burroughs met Joan Vollmer, a divorced single mother and journalism student at Columbia. Despite his homosexuality, Burroughs established a sexual relationship with Vollmer; by 1945 they shared an apartment with her young daughter, Julie. The couple, who eventually had a common-law marriage but were never formally married, heavily used the drug Benzedrine.

Burroughs also fenced stolen drugs, robbed drunks, and became addicted to heroin. He received a suspended sentence for obtaining narcotics with a faked doctor's prescription. With Joan and Julie, Burroughs then moved to New Waverly, Texas, where he grew marijuana in hopes of selling it; there, he and Vollmer had a son, William Seward "Billy" Burroughs, Jr. (III), born in 1947. After further run-ins with the law, Burroughs moved his family in September 1949 to Mexico City, where he entered Mexico City College, worked on a prospective novel, and had homosexual encounters. At a party in September 1951, while drunkenly trying to shoot a water glass off the top of Joan's head, he shot and killed her.

"I am forced to the appalling conclusion that I would never have become a writer but for Joan's death," Burroughs later wrote. "[T]he death of Joan brought me in contact with the invader, the Ugly Spirit, and maneuvered me into a lifelong struggle, in which I have had no choice except to write my way out" (quoted in Miles, p. 53). With the help of a nephew of A. A. Wyn at Ace Paperbacks, Burroughs

managed to sell the firm his first book, *Junkie* (later reproduced as *Junky*). It was double-bound with the memoirs of a narcotics detective and published under the pseudonym William Lee. *Junkie/Junky* offered a coldly clinical yet grimly witty view of an addict's life, neither apologizing for it nor whitewashing its ghastliness: "You become a narcotics addict because you do not have strong motivations in any other direction. Junk wins by default" (quoted in Grauerholz and Silverberg, p. 49).

After various travels—including a trip to South America, where he sought a powerful hallucinogen called *yage*—Burroughs settled in Tangier, Morocco, a haven for drug users and homosexuals (later the inspiration for his fictional dystopia, "Interzone"). Another resident was writer Paul Bowles, who later recalled Burroughs as a man who "lay in bed all day, shot heroin, and practiced sharpshooting with a pistol against the wall of his room" (Miles, p. 78). Burroughs subsequently said in *Naked Lunch*, "I had not taken a bath in a year nor changed my clothes or removed them except to stick a needle every hour in the fibrous grey wooden flesh of terminal addiction . . . I did absolutely nothing. I could look at the end of my shoe for eight hours." Eventually, he went to London to undergo Dr. John Yerbury Dent's "apomorphine cure" for addiction and then returned to Tangier where he wrote energetically. In 1958 he moved to Paris, staying at what was later called the "Beat Hotel." While in Paris Burroughs met the artist Brion Gysin, who would become a devoted friend and have a major creative influence on him.

Burroughs's career-making book was *The Naked Lunch* (1959, later republished without the definite article), which depicted the urban jungle of drug addicts "shivering in the junk-sick morning" (Skerl and Lydenberg, p. 137). It also satirized Americans' conformism, homophobia, Cold War anxieties, and the psychiatric establishment, symbolized by the sinister Dr. Benway. Many readers, baffled by the book's unorthodox structure and disjointed narrative style, were repelled by its grotesqueries, which included cannibalism and hangings with erotic overtones. Initially, *Naked Lunch* had trouble with American censors, and the U.S. Post Office refused to distribute magazines publishing extracts from the book. In a number of court cases, including one before the Massachusetts Supreme Court in 1966, it was deemed not obscene and thereby gained free distribution.

Reviewers quarreled over *Naked Lunch*. In a review in the *Times Literary Supplement* titled "UGH . . . ," John Willett said reading *Naked Lunch* is "not unlike wading through the drains of a big city . . . [It features] unspeakable homosexual fantasies . . . If the publishers had deliberately set out to discredit the cause of literary freedom and innovation they could hardly have done it more effectively" (Skerl and Lydenberg, p. 44). Dame Edith Sitwell compared reading such a book to having one's nose nailed to a lavatory. But Burroughs won praise from other writers, such as Norman Mailer, who called Burroughs the "only living American novelist who may conceivably be possessed by genius" (Miles, p. 17). The poet John Ciardi described Burroughs as "a writer of great power and artistic integrity engaged in a profoundly meaningful search for true values" (Skerl and Lydenberg, p. 22). To Marshall McLuhan, the assaults of Burroughs's critics were "a little like trying to criticize the sartorial and verbal manifestations of a man who is knocking on the door to explain that flames are leaping from the roof of our home" (Skerl and Lydenberg, p. 73). *Newsweek* called *Naked Lunch* "a masterpiece, but a totally insane and anarchic one" (Miles, p. 106).

In the early 1960s Burroughs's output included *The Soft Machine* (1961), *The Ticket That Exploded* (1962), and *Nova Express* (1964). These exploited "cut-ups," a technique that Burroughs learned from Gysin. After texts are literally cut up, unrelated lines are joined, resulting in hybrid passages that Burroughs sometimes found poetic: for example, "Raw peeled winds of hate and mischance blew the shot" (quoted in George-Warren, p. 214). Samuel Beckett reportedly dismissed cut-ups as "plumbing . . . not writing!" (Bockris, p. 214). But to Burroughs, it was a form true to the experience of life: "Every time you look out the window, or answer the phone, your consciousness is being cut by random factors. Walk down the street—bam, bam, bam" (quoted in George-Warren, p. 211).

Burroughs's reputation among the youthful avant-garde broadened after the Beatles included his face on the crowded cover of their record album, *Sgt. Pepper's Lonely Hearts Club Band*. Amid the student revolts of the 1960s, he depicted the young as the ideal agents of rebellion in his novel *The Wild Boys* (1971), which featured homosexual youth gangs in a futuristic, post-apocalyptic world. To the critic Alfred Kazin, Burroughs's work in general was solipsistic: "a world forever being reshuffled in the mind, a world that belongs to oneself like the contents of a dream" (Murphy, p. 142). Timothy Murphy, however, perceived a politically radical fantasy in *The Wild Boys*. One character says: "We intend to destroy all dogmatic verbal systems. The family unit and its cancerous expansion into tribes, countries, nations we will eradicate at its vegetable roots. We don't want to hear any more family talk, mother talk, father talk, cop talk, priest talk, country talk or party talk" (quoted in Murphy, p. 33).

After living rather reclusively in London for much of the period 1962–1974, Burroughs returned to the United States, taught at the City College of New York, and gave public readings. Contradicting his reputation as a drug fiend, he came across in public as a reserved, well-dressed man with a stone face and a dry, nasal voice. Admirers introduced him to such celebrities as Andy Warhol, Christopher Isherwood, and Tennessee Williams and to rock music stars including David Bowie, Kurt Cobain, and Deborah Harry; many of their conversations were tape-recorded and subsequently edited by Victor Bockris in *With William Burroughs: Report from the Bunker* (1996). Burroughs

had small roles in several films, including *Drugstore Cowboy* (1989) and *My Own Private Idaho* (1991). Despite his professed disdain for women, he befriended female writers, including Susan Sontag, and performed on stage with performance artist Laurie Anderson. In 1981, on the television show "Saturday Night Live," Lauren Hutton introduced Burroughs as the greatest living American writer. That same year he published the novel *Cities of the Red Night*, an apocalyptic blend of science fiction, detective fiction, boys' adventure tales, and other genres. A gun enthusiast, Burroughs earned substantial money by selling abstract paintings created by shooting cans of paint placed beside plywood panels. His successes were darkened, though, by his continued woes, including a recurrence of his heroin addiction. Doctors placed him on a methadone maintenance program. His grown-up son Billy, Jr., after a promising start as a writer, struggled with drug and alcohol abuse and died in 1981 at age thirty-four. Burroughs's worldview remained as bleak as his mask-like face: "There are no friends . . . There are allies. There are accomplices" (quoted in Miles, p. 138).

In 1983 Burroughs moved to Lawrence, Kansas, partly because land was cheap there and he could own a home; by settling in a small university town, he thought he could also get away from the big-city temptation of returning to drug abuse. In Lawrence, Burroughs wrote his last major books, among them *The Place of Dead Roads* (1983) and *The Western Lands* (1987). Thanks to Ginsberg's campaigning, he was elected to the American Academy of Arts and Letters. The French minister of culture designated him as a Commandeur de l'Ordre des Arts et des Lettres. In 1992 director David Cronenberg made a movie version of *Naked Lunch*, which was considered by some critics to be viscerally shocking. A deeply private man at heart, Burroughs kept numerous cats in his simple Kansas home, supported a foundation to protect lemurs, and took solitary boat trips on a lake. As he aged, he reflected on his tortured life: "People think of me as being cold—some woman wrote that I could not admit any feeling at all. My God. I am so emotional that sometimes I can't stand the intensity . . . I'm very subject to violent fits of weeping, for very good reasons" (quoted in Bockris, p. 248). He died in Lawrence.

Burroughs was a key figure in the Beat Generation, which laid the groundwork for much cultural dissidence in the United States during the second half of the twentieth century. According to Nicholas Zurbrugg, he was the "professional wicked uncle of postmodernism" (Skerl and Lydenberg, p. 177). In Burroughs's works, Cary Nelson said, "scatology becomes eschatology" (Skerl and Lydenberg, p. 127). Burroughs showed how to blend genres once scorned as trashy—science fiction, Wild West stories, boys' adventure tales, detective fiction, and pornography—to express avant-garde visions and radical worldviews. He urged his readers to question orthodox Zeitgeists that limit human freedom: "Storm The Reality Studio. And retake the universe" (quoted in Skerl and Lydenberg, p. 106).

• Burroughs's papers are divided among a host of repositories, including Butler Library, Columbia University; the International Center of Art and Communications, Vaduz, Switzerland; the George Arents Research Library, Syracuse University; and the Humanities Research Center, University of Texas, Austin. Burroughs often rewrote parts of his books for later editions; for example, *The Soft Machine* appears in three significantly different versions. He recorded his dreams and published them in *My Education: A Book of Dreams* (1995). Other works by him include *Exterminator* (with Brion Gysin, 1960), *The Yage Letters* (with Allen Ginsberg, 1963), *The Last Words of Dutch Schultz* (1970), *Exterminator!* (1973), *The Adding Machine* (1985), and *Queer* (1985). Major biographical accounts include Barry Miles, *William Burroughs, El Hombre Invisible: A Portrait* (1993) and Ted Morgan, *Literary Outlaw: The Life and Times of William S. Burroughs* (1988). Also see James Grauerholz's essays on different periods of Burroughs's life in *Word Virus—The William S. Burroughs Reader*, ed. Grauerholz and Ira Silverberg, with an insightful introduction by Ann Douglas (1998). Burroughs never wrote a formal autobiography, but a short memoir, "The Name is Burroughs," appears in his book *The Adding Machine*. Also see Burroughs's review of his life's work, "My Purpose Is to Write for the Space Age," *New York Times Book Review*, 19 Feb. 1984. John Tytell, *Naked Angels: Kerouac, Ginsberg, Burroughs* (1976), is a classic study of the Beats. Other assessments include Eric Mottram, *William Burroughs: The Algebra of Need* (1971); Robin Lydenberg, *Word Cultures: Radical Theory and Practice in William S. Burroughs' Fiction* (1987*); William S. Burroughs at the Front: Critical Reception, 1959–1989*, ed. Jennie Skerl and Robin Lydenberg (1991); and Timothy S. Murphy, *Wising Up the Marks: The Amodern William Burroughs* (1997). For Alfred Kazin's acute critique, see "He's Just Wild about Writing," *New York Times Book Review*, 12 Dec. 1971, p. 4. An obituary appeared in the *New York Times*, 3 Aug. 1997.

KEAY DAVIDSON

BURROWS, Abe (18 Dec. 1910–17 May 1985), author, comedian, and theatrical director, was born Abraham Solman Borowitz in New York City, the eldest of three children of Louis Borowitz, a businessman, and his wife Julia Saltzberg Borowitz. Burrows's high school education was spread among New York's boroughs. While working as a runner on Wall Street, Burrows attended City College of New York, New York University's school of finance, and the Pace Institute of Accounting.

In the early 1930s the Borowitz family changed its name to Burrows. Abe Burrows worked for several years at a Wall Street brokerage firm, from which he was fired in 1934. In 1936 he married Ruth Levinson; they were to have two children and divorce in 1948. In 1937 Burrows briefly entered the woven label business but was soon writing and performing comedy sketches in the Catskills. In 1939 he began writing for radio. In 1941, during the first of many assignments in California, Burrows helped create the program "Duffy's Tavern," remaining as its chief writer for five years.

"Duffy's Tavern," one of the most popular programs of its era, opened with the ringing of a telephone, which was answered by its star, Ed Gardner: "Duffy's Tavern, where the elite meet to eat, Archie the manager speaking, Duffy ain't here." Burrows made of Gardner a master of malapropism in the manner of a Damon Runyon character. After spending much of World War II in Hollywood, Burrows saw "Duffy's Tavern" become a musical film in 1945. Briefly listed by Paramount Pictures as a writer and producer, he collaborated with a friend, the songwriter Frank Loesser, on the film's theme, "Leave Us Face It," in which people "bandaged" others' names about and married in a French "chapeau" where an eternal love was "reincarcerated."

Between 1946 and 1950 Burrows wrote for several network radio shows, and in 1947–1948 hosted the "Abe Burrows Show," on which, as the "bald-headed baritone from Brooklyn," he performed monologues, played the piano, and sang his own satirical songs, including "The Girl with the Three Blue Eyes," a take on recently fashionable folk songs. After a tour in night clubs, in 1949 Burrows began a lengthy part-time career as television panelist, at first on "This is Show Business," which ran until 1956; in 1951 came "The Name's the Same," which ran till 1955. Burrows was thus simultaneously a "showbiz" insider and a satirist of the genre. In 1950 he married Carin Smith Kinzel; they remained married until Burrows's death.

His television popularity coincided with Broadway success in 1950. Theatrical producers Cy Feuer and Ernest Martin had been struggling to turn Runyon's fables of Broadway into a romantic musical with a score by Loesser. But after turning down the efforts of eleven librettists, they decided the material was better suited to comedy and hired Loesser's friend Burrows to write a fresh version. The show's director, veteran humorist and play "doctor" George S. Kaufman (one of Burrows's television co-panelists) tutored Burrows. The result was *Guys and Dolls*, an innovative blend of lyrical romance and genial cynicism often regarded as the best American musical of the second half of the twentieth century. Burrows began his directorial career with the revue *Two on the Aisle* (1951) and in 1952 coauthored and directed the gently Celtic musical *Three Wishes for Jamie*.

Burrows was summoned before the House Committee on Un-American Activities in open session beginning 12 November 1952, focusing upon "left-wing" meetings in wartime Hollywood. Via committee transcripts, these hearings found dramatic form in Eric Bentley's 1974 play *Are You Now or Have You Ever Been*. Burrows emerged as naive, unintentionally comic, essentially self-serving: the hearing's transcripts show that he admitted to "Communist" sympathies but said he had never "gone all the way"; he admitted that Communist party members, who had "poor senses of humor," regarded him as a Communist, although "in my heart" he never believed himself to be one; finally, he apologized to the committee for being "overvague." The theatrical portrayal of Burrows caused one reviewer to comment, ". . . the man's complex and often hilarious rationalizations are genuinely human if desperate contortions."

In 1953, after researching in Parisian archives, Burrows wrote the book for *Can-Can*, with music and lyrics by Cole Porter. Burrows directed the show as well as its 1981 Broadway revival. There followed another collaboration with Porter, *Silk Stockings* (1955), based on the 1939 Billy Wilder film *Ninotchka*. Burrows took over the libretto from Kaufman and his wife and soon was as renowned a play "doctor" as Kaufman. Burrows's libretti were generally followed for the screenplays of *Silk Stockings* (1957) and *Can-Can* (1960). In 1955 *The Abe Burrows Song Book*, a collection of satires and parodies, was published. He collaborated on the screenplay for *The Solid Gold Cadillac* (1956), based on Kaufman's original Broadway show.

Back on Broadway, Burrows directed the musicals *Say, Darling* (1958) and *First Impressions* (1959), the latter adapted from Jane Austen. His second collaboration with Loesser, *How To Succeed in Business without Really Trying* (1961), became the fourth musical to win the Pulitzer Prize for drama. It also won the Antoinette Perry (Tony) award for best musical and the New York Drama Critics award for best play. This time Burrows worked from an unproduced play by Jack Weinstock and Willie Gilbert, which had been sent to Feuer and Martin. As director, Burrows had the egotistical hero sing his song of praise ("I Believe in You") while looking at himself in the men's room mirror. The musical theater historian Gerald Bordman called Burrows and Loesser the true heirs to a tradition of satirical musicals that had begun with Kaufman, Morrie Ryskind, and George Gershwin and Ira Gershwin. The 1967 film version of *How to Succeed . . .* was extremely faithful to Burrows's book.

He also directed for the stage his adaptation of Budd Schulberg's novel *What Makes Sammy Run?* (1964) as a musical, which had moderate success, and the long-running comedy adaptation from the French, *Forty Carats* (1968).

Burrows made a brief (1965–1966) return to television as author of "O. K. Crackerby," a comedy-drama series for Burl Ives. The 1976 Martin Ritt film *The Front*, dealing in part with a nightclub comedian newly successful in television but willing to cooperate with witch-hunting congressmen, is sometimes compared with Burrows's experiences. In his 1979 autobiography, *Honest, Abe: Is There Really No Business Like Show Business?* Burrows made no mention of his appearance before the House Committee on Un-American Activities. He died in Manhattan of pneumonia. In 1991 the Abe Burrows Theater was established at the Tisch School of the Arts, part of New York University, through a gift from his son, James Burrows.

• The Billy Rose Collection at the New York Public Library, Lincoln Center, contains useful information. Aside from Burrows's own works, insight is gained from Eric Bentley, ed., *Thirty Years of Treason: Excerpts from Hearings before the House Committee on Un-American Activities, 1938–1968* (1971). Burrows's radio career is glimpsed in Frank Buxton and Bill Owen, *The Big Broadcast, 1920–1950* (1972), while his television years are chronicled in Tim Brooks and Earle Marsh, *The Complete Directory to Prime Time Network TV Shows* (1979). Among Stanley Green's useful books, see *Broadway Musicals Show by Show* (1985). Sylvie Drake's review of *Are You Now or Have You Ever Been* is in the *Los Angeles Times*, 1 Apr. 1975. The obituary by Robert D. McFadden in the *New York Times*, 19 May 1985, is a helpful source.

JAMES ROSS MOORE

C

CAEN, Herb (3 Apr. 1916–1 Feb. 1997), journalist, was born Herbert Eugene Caen in Sacramento, California, one of two children of Lucien Caen, a pool hall operator, and Augusta Gross Caen. He was educated in Sacramento schools and attended Sacramento Junior College (1934). Caen began writing sports for the Sacramento *Union,* where "Herbert" was jettisoned as not befitting a sportswriter.

In 1936, when Caen began to write about radio for Paul Smith's *San Francisco Chronicle,* that city was entering its most buoyant era—the Golden Gate and San Francisco–Oakland Bay bridges were being completed, and planning for the Golden Gate International Exposition (1939 San Francisco World's Fair) was under way—and the budding journalist found his home, claiming to have been at least conceived in San Francisco (during the 1915 Panama Pacific International Exposition). He got his own column in 1938 and embraced the city with gusto, helping to change its reputation from one rising from the ashes (after the great fire early in the century) to "the city that knows how." Patterning his journalistic style on Walter Winchell's (coining "Caenfidences" and "Herbasides"), Caen, "a brash kid with a Cadillac and a showgirl on each arm and more guts than a Butchertown slaughterhouse," waded in. His intimate, punchy delineation of San Francisco's foibles eventually won a special Pulitzer Prize (1996). In 1941 Caen married Beatrice Matthews, a showgirl. When they divorced, childless, in 1948, Matthews joked that the co-respondent was San Francisco.

During World War II Caen was assigned to communications in the U.S. Army Air Force and rose to the rank of captain. The dispatches emerging from his first visit to Paris on V-E Day in 1945 (he received the Médaille de la Libération de France, 1949) suggested a natural-born travel writer. On his return to civilian life, he rejected offers for a syndicated gossip column and turned his ability to evoke the spirit of place full upon San Francisco. Soon Caen's columns metamorphosed into books, and *Baghdad-by-the-Bay* (1949) established his national reputation and won an American Book Award. Caen marveled at San Francisco's innovative eccentrics (cafés called Joe's, New Joe's, Original Joe's, Original New Joe's), worshiping a city simultaneously cosmopolitan and parochial; he occasionally brought its proclivity for self-delusion up short: "San Francisco isn't what it used to be; yeah, but it never was."

In 1950, feeling himself underpaid, the high-living Caen left the *Chronicle* for its arch rival, the Hearst-run *San Francisco Examiner,* whose editorial policy sat uneasily alongside his New Deal politics. The *Chronicle*'s circulation dipped by 15 percent after his departure and gained 33,000 when he returned in 1958. Caen married Sally Gilbert in 1952; childless, they divorced in 1959.

By the time a 1957 *Time* profile called him "the Caliph of Baghdad," Caen had already perfected the "three-dot" method of writing a column. The print equivalent of Winchell's chattering telegraph key on the radio, the dots indicated the end of one burst of gossip, lyricism, or wisecracking and the nervous, urban transition to another. Caen confessed that his idea of a perfect column would be twenty-four short news items, all of them "scoops" that beat the city desk by at least a week. The friend of authors William Saroyan and Barnaby Conrad, bandleaders Benny Goodman and Artie Shaw, union leader Harry Bridges, physicist J. Robert Oppenheimer, crooner Frank Sinatra, and tycoon Louis Lurie, he introduced his readers to many regular informants, a little like Damon Runyon's cast of characters but a touch more real, less sentimental. A hotel doorman said that being mentioned in Caen's column meant "your name was good for a month." In 1963 Caen married Maria Theresa Shaw; they had a son and were divorced in 1974.

Although in his vision of San Francisco everyone was dressed to the nines and addicted to vitamin V (vodka, always Stolichnaya, with a twist), symphony, ballet, opera, baseball, and football, Caen proved to be both well placed and tolerant when the midcentury's scruffy youth rebellions arose in San Francisco. He coined "beatnik" to describe the 1950s phase that was focused on Lawrence Ferlinghetti's City Lights Bookstore and in the later 1960s shared anti-Vietnam war sympathies with the hippies of the Haight-Ashbury district. In the soul-searching aftermath of the assassinations of mayor George Moscone and supervisor Harvey Milk, Caen was credited with "civic psychotherapy."

In the art and craft of creating and embodying the image of a city, Caen paralleled his major journalistic contemporaries—Chicago's Mike Royko, New York's Jimmy Breslin, and his Los Angeles friend Jack Smith. In later years he ventured farther afield on special assignments to England, Egypt, and China and returned to what he perceived as a "yuppiefied" San Francisco vastly changed from the two-fisted bastion of privilege and unionism of prewar years. He criticized Mayor Dianne Feinstein in the 1980s for "Manhattanizing" the downtown area (and obscuring views of "golden hills") In 1992 he wrote, "It's always the end of an era. What they don't say is that it's the beginning of another. . . . What goes around comes around, then it goes away like the September fog that disappears with the blast of the noon siren and the evening cannon going off in the Presidio."

In 1986 Caen became the regular companion of Ann Moller, an investment consultant, who had two children from a previous marriage. Caen and Moller were married in 1996. In 1994 he was credited with helping to settle a Newspaper Guild strike at both local newspapers, convincing columnists that they should not resume their work until the lesser-paid employees could return. Caen received the Lifetime Achievement Award from the National Society of Newspaper Columnists and an award for distinguished achievement in journalism from the University of Southern California.

In 1996, Caen was awarded a special Pulitzer Prize for "extraordinary and continuing contribution as a voice and conscience of his city." Thanks to the San Francisco Board of Supervisors, a 3.2-mile waterfront promenade along the Embarcadero was renamed Herb Caen Way. Shortly thereafter Caen publicly acknowledged having lung cancer, and two months later 75,000 people celebrated Herb Caen Day. Caen died in San Francisco on a Saturday afternoon, missing the deadline for the obituary on file in the *Chronicle*, thereby granting the Sunday *Examiner* his last "scoop."

• Caen's writings are on file in the Bancroft Library at the University of California, Berkeley. In addition to *Baghdad-by-the-Bay*, he wrote the following books: *The San Francisco Book* (1948), *Baghdad, 1951* (1950), *Don't Call It Frisco* (1953), *Guide to San Francisco* (1957), *Herb Caen's New Guide to San Francisco and the Bay Area* (1958), *Only in San Francisco* (1960), *San Francisco, City of Golden Hills* (with Dong Kingman, 1968), *The Cable Car and the Dragon* (1972), *One Man's San Francisco* (1976), *The Best of Herb Caen 1960–75* (1991), *Herb Caen's San Francisco 1976–1991* (1992), and *The World of Herb Caen, San Francisco 1938–1997* (1997). There are various Herb Caen Web sites. Among many obituaries the fullest is by Larry Hatfield and Lance Williams (with Seth Rosenfeld) in the *San Francisco Examiner*, 2 Feb. 1997. A perceptive British obituary is by Christopher Reed in the *Guardian*, 5 Feb. 1997.

JAMES ROSS MOORE

CAESAR, Irving (4 July 1895–17 Dec. 1996), songwriter, was born Isidore Caesar in New York City's Henry Street settlement, the son of Morris Caesar, the owner of a secondhand bookstore, and Sophia Selinger Caesar. He attended the Chappaqua Mountain Institute, graduated from New York City's Townsend Harris Hall High School in 1914, and was briefly enrolled at the City College of New York before going to Detroit in 1915 to work for the Ford Motor Company as a mechanic. Caesar also served as secretary to Henry Ford's Peace Ship, the inventor's doomed attempt to end World War I. He was still working for Ford when his songs began to find acceptance on Broadway, beginning with the 1918 edition of Raymond Hitchcock's *Hitchy-Koo!*

Caesar, who claimed to have written his first poem at age five, eventually was credited with the lyrics of more than 1,000 songs, including several of the twentieth century's most popular. He came to embody the values of Tin Pan Alley, the area around New York's Twenty-eighth Street where popular music publishing was centered till midcentury. An advocate of simplicity, he frequently remarked, "Sometimes I write lousy, but I always write fast."

Although he never committed himself to a composing partner, the stocky, cigar-chomping Caesar soon achieved his career-confirming success with George Gershwin and Vincent Youmans. Gershwin was a demonstration pianist for the music publisher Remick's when he met the equally aspiring Caesar. Their "There's More to the Kiss Than the XXX," from *Good Morning, Judge!* (1919), has remained a peripheral part of the Gershwin repertoire. Caesar frequently retold the origin of "Swanee" (1919), the song that made both famous. He claimed to have convinced Gershwin in Dinty Moore's downtown restaurant that they should emulate "Hindustan," a current one-step. Next came a bus trip to the Gershwin home on Riverside Drive, "by which time the lyrics had been worked out. It took another fifteen minutes at the piano, while Gershwin's father noisily played cards in the next room."

The forceful "Swanee" achieved perfection in an idiosyncratic genre: the faux-bucolic southern song—always written by northern urbanites and performed by "show business legends" like Al Jolson and Judy Garland. (Caesar further enhanced the genre in 1936 with "Is It True What They Say about Dixie," with music composed by Gerald Marks.) "Swanee" received an immense production in Ned Wayburn's *Demi-Tasse Revue* and was soon adopted by Jolson, who made it a great hit. Caesar left the Ford Motor Company and in 1920 joined the fledgling American Society of Composers, Authors and Publishers (ASCAP), which he subsequently served for forty years as a director. While occasionally working with Gershwin ("Nashville Nightingale" was a modest hit in *Nifties of 1923*), Caesar continued to collaborate with others, eventually contributing lyrics or libretti to forty-four Broadway shows.

Caesar's collaboration with Youmans closely mirrored his experience with Gershwin. When they met in 1920, Youmans had recently given up song-plugging for Remick's and was trying to sell his compositions elsewhere. Caesar's lyrics pleased Youmans and in 1921 one was heard in the latter's *Two Little Girls in Blue*. It was early 1924, with Youmans and Otto Harbach's *No, No, Nanette* struggling to survive on the road, that at Harbach's request Caesar was asked to help enliven the show; thus began a successful Youmans-Caesar collaboration. Late one evening, so goes the never-challenged tale, the pair was working on songs for the show at Caesar's New York apartment. Caesar had fallen asleep, and Youmans woke him to listen to a new melodic line. Caesar found the new melody "monotonous" but in a few minutes fitted a "dummy" lyric to serve until they could work further on it the next day. They then left the apartment to attend a party at Gertrude Lawrence's, where, to much acclaim, they introduced their newly created song, calling it "Tea for Two." Caesar's boy-girl love lyric, in which few words contained as much as two syllables, perfectly enhanced Youmans's lilting line. Youmans suggested a title for another song: "I Want to Be Happy," and Caesar wrote the lyric. Both songs were added to *No, No, Nanette*. During its London run, the Prince of Wales insisted that both songs be repeated any time he saw the show. By its 1925 New York opening, the show was on track to becoming the most popular musical comedy of its era.

Nothing that Caesar wrote thereafter gained as much renown, although "Sometimes I'm Happy" (a new lyric to an old number by Youmans in *A Night Out*, 1925) has remained a standard. For Jolson he adapted the lyrics and libretto for the German original of *The Wonder Bar* (1931). Among other Americanizations were an adaptation of "Just a Gigolo," by the Austrian Lionello Casucci (1930), and the score of the German *White Horse Inn* (1936). Caesar also lyricized what he called pianist Oscar Levant's only hit song, "Lady, Play Your Mandolin" (1930), and shared credit for "Crazy Rhythm" in the Joseph Meyer–Roger Wolfe Kahn show *Here's Howe* (1928).

With the introduction of all-singing, all-dancing film musicals in 1928, Caesar, like most songwriters of his era, became a transcontinental peripatetic. In 1934, working with Ray Henderson and Jack Yellen, he produced two songs for Alice Faye in *George White's Scandals*. In 1935, with Henderson and Ted Koehler, Caesar created another song that became notoriously popular: "Animal Crackers in My Soup" for the film *Curly Top*. The song followed its tiny star, Shirley Temple, ever after. Later, in 1944 Caesar would help to create another signature: collaborating with the anarchic comic Jimmy Durante, he turned a catch line into the nonsensical "Umbriago." The song made its debut in the film *Music for Millions* and stayed with Durante for the rest of his life.

Beginning in 1938, Caesar regularly wrote words and music for what can only be called "public service" songs. In that year his volume of children's songs, *Songs of Safety*, included "Let the Ball Roll" and "Ice Skating Is Nice Skating." In that intensely patriotic time, he set the Pledge of Allegiance to music. For the federal government he created "Your US Mail Goes Through" and the symphonic "Pilgrim Suite" (both 1940). However, during the politically charged 1950s the government rejected his "Songs of Friendship"— including "Thomas Jefferski" and "Election Day." They were finally published by the Anti-Defamation League of B'nai B'rith.

Caesar was an early president of the Song Writers Protective Association (1936–1942). But, after the disastrous *My Dear Public* (1943), for which he wrote book, words, and music and served as producer (and was heard to complain about the reviews, "But why are they blaming *me*?"), he gradually assumed the role of elder statesman. He notably appeared on the first transmission of New York television station WOR-TV on 5 October 1949 and subsequently on American and British radio, retelling the insider's version of his era's history.

Caesar continued to visit his Manhattan office every day into his nineties, and late in life he married Christina A. Ballesteros. Caesar died in New York.

• Helpful information on Caesar can be found in David Ewen, *American Songwriters* (1987), and Warren Craig, *Sweet and Lowdown* (1978). Caesar's film songs are well covered in Clive Hirschhorn, *The Hollywood Musical* (1981). The Caesar-Youmans collaboration is detailed in Gerald Bordman, *Days to Be Happy, Years to Be Sad: The Life and Music of Vincent Youmans* (1982). The anecdote about Caesar's reaction to the slamming of *My Dear Public* appears in Bernard Delfont (with Barry Turner), *East End, West End: An Autobiography* (1990) Richard Severo's obituary of Caesar is in the *New York Times*, 18 Dec. 1996. An appreciation by Christopher Hawtree appears in the (London) *Guardian*, 19 Dec. 1996.

JAMES ROSS MOORE

CALDERONE, Mary S. (1 July 1904–24 Oct. 1998), physician and educator, was born Mary Steichen in New York City to Edward Steichen, a photographer, and Clara Smith Steichen. While Mary and her younger sister were growing up, living in both New York and France, their father emerged as one of the most acclaimed photographers in the world, and Mary Steichen later said that her father's ability to portray "human life and the human condition" made a deep impression on her at an early age. Her parents separated when she was ten, and Mary went to live with her father; she remained alienated from her mother for many decades, not restoring their relationship until Mary herself was in her sixties.

Mary Steichen was educated in private schools and at Vassar College, from which she graduated in 1925 with a degree in chemistry and several years of experience in amateur theatricals. With an aptitude for both science and dramatics, she decided to choose the latter as a career and spent several years studying with prominent actors at the American Laboratory Theater in New York City. However, by the late 1920s she had begun to realize that she would never be a first-rate actress, and she withdrew from the profession with a sense of failure. Compounding her unhappiness, she had married a fellow actor, L. Lon Martin, in 1926, and the marriage was not satisfying. The couple had two daughters, one of whom died of pneumonia, before divorcing in 1933.

During this troubling period, Mary Steichen searched for direction, reading widely, undergoing psychoanalysis, and taking a series of aptitude tests in an effort to discover what she should do with her life. She concluded that because of her skills in science she could probably become a first-rate doctor, and at the age of thirty she entered medical school at the University of Rochester. Five years later, in 1939, she received her degree. After interning at Bellevue Hospital in New York City for a year, she attended the Columbia University School of Public Health on a fellowship from the city's public health department and received the master of public health degree in 1942. A year earlier she had married

Dr. Frank Calderone, a public health physician under whom she worked while attending Columbia.

Mary S. Calderone, as she was now known, continued to work in the field of public health after receiving her M.P.H. degree. For more than a decade she served as a physician in schools in the suburbs of New York City, and her experiences led to a deepening interest in the medical aspects of human sexuality, particularly in contraception and the prevention of sexually transmitted diseases. In 1953 she became medical director of the Planned Parenthood Federation of America, headquartered in New York, which had been founded by Margaret Sanger earlier in the century to make birth control information available to the public. During Calderone's eleven years in the post she became an outspoken advocate of birth control, through lectures, media essays, and literature that was widely distributed by the organization. At the beginning of her tenure, the subject of birth control was still regarded as "indelicate" and rarely mentioned in public: contraceptive techniques were limited ("the pill" was not made available to the public until 1960) and most abortions were illegal. In many areas of the nation, physicians refused altogether to even discuss birth control—known euphemistically as "family planning"—with their patients, and sexually transmitted diseases were viewed with such shame that many people went untreated rather than acknowledge their condition.

One of Calderone's major accomplishments at Planned Parenthood was her success in persuading the American Medical Association to formally adopt a policy in 1964 that directed physicians to give birth control information to their patients as a matter of course. By this time Calderone had become aware, through thousands of letters she received at Planned Parenthood, that millions of Americans were woefully ignorant about all areas of sexuality, not just birth control. In 1961 she had participated in a wide-ranging conference on the family, sponsored by the National Council of Churches, and she and several other participants had subsequently formed a committee to look at existing studies on human sexuality. This group was the nucleus of the Sex (later Sexuality) Information and Education Council of the United States, Inc. (SIECUS), which Calderone and her colleagues founded in May 1964. Calderone resigned from Planned Parenthood to become the executive director of SIECUS (pronounced *SEE*-kuss), which had as its broadly defined goal "to define man's sexuality as a health entity."

Under Calderone, SIECUS undertook a massive education campaign throughout the nation, distributing information on all aspects of sexuality. Crusading for openness and frank talk about sexuality and its consequences, Mary Calderone became a revolutionary in the field of sex education. She traveled throughout the country, lecturing to audiences of all ages, her platform skills aided by her earlier dramatic training. Her major focus was the establishment of sex education programs in the nation's schools, and to this end

SIECUS created the publication *Guidelines for Sexuality Education: Kindergarten Through Twelfth Grade*; updated periodically, the guide is still in use.

In the early days of her tenure as the director of SIECUS, Calderone encountered opposition from all but the most liberal elements of the population, for at that time many people believed that sex was not an appropriate subject for discussion in the classroom. She remained undaunted, however, and by the time she stepped down as executive director in 1979, on her seventy-fifth birthday, some form of sex education had become the norm in most of the nation's schools.

From 1979 until 1982 Calderone served as president of SIECUS. After retiring, she became an adjunct professor for several years at New York University, teaching in its program on human sexuality. In addition to her writings for SIECUS and her many contributions to professional journals, she was the co-author of two bestselling popular books, *The Family Book About Sexuality* (1981, with Eric Johnson) and *Talking with Your Child About Sex* (1982, with James W. Ramey). She also edited several books on abortion and family planning.

Mary Calderone had two more daughters with her second husband, from whom she separated in 1979; he died eight years later. She retired from public life at the age of eighty, though she continued to contribute letters and op-ed pieces to newspapers from time to time on such issues as abortion rights, of which she was a strong proponent. That advocacy attracted wide attention and put her briefly at the center of controversy again when she published in the 16 September 1989 issue of the *New York Times* an op-ed piece called "Fetuses' Right Not to Be Born"; there she argued that terribly damaged fetuses had the God-given right to be aborted rather than suffer endless misery after birth.

Mary Calderone was a Democrat in politics and a lifelong Quaker. During the last years of her life she suffered from Alzheimer's disease and was confined to a nursing home in Kennett Square, Pennsylvania, where she died.

• For biographical information on Mary S. Calderone, see "Calderone, Mary S.," in *Current Biography Yearbook*, 1967 and 1998, as well as a profile in the *Washington Post Sunday Magazine*, 18 June 1967, pp. 14ff. Assessments of Calderone's accomplishments are in L. Gross, "Sex Education Comes of Age," *Look*, 8 Mar. 1966, pp. 20–23, and M. Vespa, "America's Biggest Problem?," *People*, 21 Jan. 1980, pp. 76–80ff. An obituary appears in the *New York Times*, 25 Oct. 1998; see also a correction to this obituary in the *New York Times*, 10 Nov. 1998, p. A2.

ANN T. KEENE

CALLAHAN, Harry (22 Oct. 1912–15 Mar. 1999), photographer, was born Harry Morey Callahan in Detroit, the son of Harry Arthur Callahan, a farmer turned factory worker, and Hazel Mills Callahan. Between 1934 and 1936 he studied engineering at Michigan State University. In 1936 he married

Eleanor Knapp and began working as a clerk for Chrysler Motor Parts Corporation.

An avid hobbyist in photography, Callahan credited a 1942 workshop by Ansel Adams with freeing him up for photography's possibilities. With his sharp 8'' × 10'' images of nature scenes, Adams proposed a new approach that emphasized the formal elements of black-and-white photography. Adams also showed Callahan that anything could be the subject of a photograph, from a blade of grass to traffic lights.

During the early to mid-1940s Callahan established major themes in his oeuvre: his wife, city streets, pedestrians, nature scenes, and building facades. His early 1940s series of light reflections on water and high-contrast images of weeds in the snow demonstrate his talent for exploiting formal elements such as tone, line, and texture through banal subject matter. A retrospective of painter Stuart Davis, which Callahan saw in New York in 1945, inspired the photographer to begin his series of torn sign photographs.

In the 1940s Callahan also began experimenting with photographic techniques such as extended exposure, multiple exposure in the camera, color photography, and various lens and camera formats. Like Adams, he shot photographs in sequences, such as his *Highland Park, Michigan* (1941–1942) series of people climbing an exterior staircase. He moved his camera during extended exposures to explore the effects of motion and light on film, as seen in his color images of neon lights, such as *Detroit* (ca. 1943).

In 1946 Callahan was invited to teach at the Institute of Design in Chicago, founded by Bauhaus artist László Moholy-Nagy and now part of the Illinois Institute of Technology. Callahan's style merged perfectly with the Institute's modern machine aesthetics and democratization of the arts. "We felt you should stop interfering with the machine and use it for what it can do best, and that was beautiful tone and beautiful texture," he said. Callahan, who had no formal training in photography, had his students explore different techniques such as shutter speeds, X rays, and photomontage. He also stressed that expressive subject matter should come from the photographer's life and environment and that a photographer should see photographically. He became head of the photography department in 1949.

Callahan had his first solo exhibition in 1947 at the 750 Studio in Chicago. His subsequent inclusion in exhibitions was greatly aided by the support of photographer Edward Steichen, director of the Museum of Modern Art's photography department. Steichen met Callahan in 1948 and included him in several MOMA exhibitions such as *In and Out of Focus* (1948), *The Family of Man* (1955), *Photographs by Harry Callahan and Robert Frank* (1962), a solo exhibition that traveled from 1968 to 1970, and a retrospective in 1976.

Building on the themes of everyday life and his surroundings, Callahan made several important series of works in the late 1940s and 1950s, including his photographs of pedestrians on Chicago's State Street and a large number of portraits of his wife, some of which included his daughter, Barbara, who was born in 1950. These images of Eleanor, naked, clothed, close up, or far away, became both a vehicle for Callahan's technical experimentation and an important record of his life and his devotion to his family. Around the same time he made two short 16mm movies about movement titled "Motions" and "People Walking on State Street."

Callahan also photographed during his many travels, which began with an extended stay in Europe in 1957, funded by a Graham Foundation Award for Advanced Studies in Fine Arts. Later trips resulted in images from Ireland, Spain, Asia, the Middle East, Latin and South America, and various regions of the United States. He remarked once that he valued his trips more for their impact on his perspective than the actual prints he produced, which often showed a continuum of his favorite subjects: streets, buildings, and anonymous pedestrians.

In 1961 the Rhode Island School of Design invited Callahan to establish a new photography department, which quickly gained a national reputation for its quality and emphasis on teaching in its graduate level. Aaron Siskind, who taught with Callahan at the Illinois Institute of Technology, joined him at RISD in 1971 and helped influence a generation of photography teachers who established photography departments in schools across the country.

In 1977, the year he retired from teaching, Callahan started working almost exclusively in color. Callahan credited everything from magazines to billboards to color television for his devotion to color, despite his having thousands of still undeveloped black-and-white images. Not only did color provide him with a new formal challenge, but the medium had recently gained critical acceptance while also becoming much easier and cheaper to use. Photographs of houses in Providence, Ireland, and Morocco from the 1970s and 1980s display his talent in depicting saturated planes of color.

In 1978 Callahan was the first photographer to ever represent the United States at the prestigious Venice Biennale. The American Academy of Arts and Sciences in Boston elected him a fellow in 1979, and RISD gave him an honorary doctorate of fine arts that same year. Solo exhibitions of his work were mounted at numerous museums, including the Center for Creative Photography (1979), the Art Institute of Chicago (1984), and the National Gallery of Art (1996). He died of cancer in Atlanta, having moved there in 1983.

Eschewing the popular but waning photographic styles of the 1940s—social realism and pictorialism—Callahan turned his attention to finding beauty and form in the seeming banalities of the everyday, the city, and his own family. His photographs, which ranged from near minimalist black-and-white studies to exuberantly cluttered, color, multiple exposures, displayed unrestrained experimentation in techniques and formalist analysis. One can see his legacy not only in his extensive body of images but also in the aesthetics and work ethic that he instilled in the many students who came under his influence during his lengthy teaching career.

• The Center for Creative Photography at the University of Arizona has the primary archive of Callahan's papers, color transparencies, and prints. The Archives of American Art in Washington, D.C., also has several papers and an interview with the photographer by Robert Brown from 1975. Publications of Callahan's work in volumes associated with exhibitions include Sherman Paul, *Harry Callahan* (1967); John Szarkowski, *Callahan* (1976); Sally Stein, *Harry Callahan: Photographs in Color/ The Years 1946–1978* (1980); Keith F. Davis, *Harry Callahan, Photographs: An Exhibition from the Hallmark Photographic Collection* (Hallmark Cards, 1981), which includes extended excerpts from an interview with Callahan; Anne Kennedy and Nicholas Callaway, eds., *Eleanor: Photographs by Harry Callahan* (1984); Keith F. Davis, *Harry Callahan, New Color: Photographs 1978–1987* (1988); and Sara Greenough, *Harry Callahan* (1996). Diane L. Johnson's interview with Callahan appears in *Callahan in New England* (1994), and Barbaralee Diamonstein's interview is in *Visions and Images: American Photographers on Photography* (1981); see also Melissa Shook, "Callahan," *Photograph* 1, no. 4 (July 1977): 1–4, 37, and Shook, *Picture Magazine*, no. 12 (1979): 6–10, 27–28. An analysis of Callahan's influence can be found in Andy Grundberg, "Photograph: Chicago, Moholy, and After," *Art in America*, Sept./ Oct. 1976, 34–35, 37–39. Louise E. Shaw et al., *Harry Callahan and His Students: A Study in Influence* (1983), includes work by several of Callahan's students. Informative obituaries are in the *New York Times*, 18 Mar. 1999, and *Art in America*, May 1999.

N. ELIZABETH SCHLATTER

CALVIN, Melvin (8 Apr. 1911–9 Jan. 1997), chemist, was born in St. Paul, Minnesota, the son of Elias Calvin and Rose Hervitz-Calvin. His father immigrated to New York from Kalvaria in Lithuania, and his mother came to the United States from the Georgian province of Russia. An excellent source of information about Calvin's early life is his autobiography, *Following the Trail of Light*, in which he states that "the name Calvin originated with the immigration authorities and was based on his [father's] birthplace in Europe." Calvin spent his early childhood in a middle-class neighborhood in St. Paul, where he played with his sister Sandra and cousins of his who had also emigrated from Lithuania. Calvin's father worked as a cigar maker in St. Paul and later as an auto mechanic in Detroit, when the family moved there at the time Calvin was entering high school. He attended City College of Detroit (later to become Wayne State University) and showed an early interest in chemistry. During the depression years Calvin's family could not afford having two children in college, which meant that his sister was unable to go.

Calvin received his undergraduate degree in 1931 from the Michigan College of Mining and Technology, where he was the first student to be awarded a B.S. in chemistry. Because the chemistry curriculum was in its infancy, Calvin was allowed to take various courses covering a broad range of topics in science,

which he came to feel contributed to his multidisciplinary approach to science later in his life. For financial reasons Calvin took a year off, after two years in college, and worked as a quality control analyst in a brass factory in Detroit. In his fourth year he began applying to various graduate programs and decided to attend the University of Minnesota. There he studied with George C. Glocker and wrote his thesis on the electron affinity of halogens; he received his Ph.D. in 1935. During his two years of postdoctoral study with Michael Polanyi at the University of Manchester in England, Calvin began to focus on coordination catalysis. In 1937, at the invitation of the well-known chemist Gilbert Lewis, he accepted a position as instructor of chemistry at the University of California at Berkeley. Ten years later, he was promoted to full professor. In 1942 Calvin married Genevieve Jemtegaard, the daughter of Norwegian immigrant parents. They were to have two daughters, Elin and Karole, and a son, Noel.

Calvin wrote *The Color of Organic Substances* in 1939 and *The Theory of Organic Chemistry* in 1940, both key texts. Calvin's interest in organic chemistry led him to join in 1946 the Bio Organic Chemistry Group at Berkeley's Ernest O. Lawrence Radiation Laboratory. Calvin had been introduced to Ernest Lawrence by Gilbert. His group assumed the title Laboratory of Chemical Biodynamics in 1960, when Calvin became the group's director. There is a long-standing legend at Berkeley that at the end of World War II Lawrence told Calvin that "now is the time to do something useful with radioactive carbon." Calvin dutifully followed this direction. Radioactive carbon in the form of carbon-14 became readily available in 1945. Calvin and his group began to develop methods of applying radioactive carbon to the study of photosynthesis, and he coauthored several books on the subject, among them *Isotopic Carbon* (1949), *The Path of Carbon in Photosynthesis* (1957), and *The Photosynthesis of Carbon Compounds* (1962).

Photosynthesis is the process by which plant organisms use energy generated by light from the sun to synthesize carbohydrates from carbon dioxide and water. Calvin used radioactive carbon-14 as a "tracer" to elucidate all of the pathways that carbon passes through in plant organisms from its absorption as carbon dioxide to its conversion to various sugars and other organic compounds during photosynthesis. Calvin and his group showed that sunlight acted via its absorption by the plant pigment chlorophyll and not, as was previously thought, by its interaction with carbon dioxide. Calvin's use of carbon-14 to decipher photosynthesis was the first instance in which radioactive isotopes were used to study biological pathways. The combined pathways identified by Calvin and his team came to be known as the Calvin Cycle, and in 1961 he was awarded the Nobel Prize in chemistry for this work.

Calvin was one of the first truly multidisciplinary scientists, and he populated his lab with people from various scientific backgrounds, including chemistry, physics, and biology. He was said to have preached the "laboratory without walls" philosophy and strongly encouraged cooperation among members of his group who were from different scientific backgrounds. When the old wooden Radiation Research Laboratory was torn down in 1959, Calvin played a central role in the design of a new structure. Completed in 1963, it was a round building with an open interior and radial lab benches, which he felt would promote interaction among the scientists working there. When Calvin retired from active research in 1980, the building was renamed for him.

Calvin's interdisciplinary approach to science was critical to his understanding of the "path of light" in plants, a problem that could be solved only by the cooperation of people from different disciplines. He spent his later years seeking a catalytic process for the photochemical production of oxygen from water and devising a way to use the plant pigment chlorophyll to convert solar energy to power. Throughout the remainder of his career he used the principles he learned from his study of photosynthesis to investigate new renewable resources of energy. He fostered many other research interests, including the biology of chemical carcinogens, the chemical evolution of life, and the possibility of life on other planets, and in each of these areas of investigation he made significant contributions. In the 1970s he was involved in NASA's lunar sample analysis program, which analyzed samples of dust and rock from the moon for various elements and molecules as well as for signs of life. His research group also conducted experiments in which organic molecules were exposed to simulated ancient atmospheric conditions that were thought to be present on earth at the time life evolved. He searched for clues to the evolution of life by studying organic substances found in ancient rocks and wrote a book on the subject, *Chemical Evolution*, published in 1969.

The author of seven books and five hundred technical publications, Calvin also held scores of patents. He consulted with many companies in industry and in 1964 he became a member of the Board of Directors of the Dow Chemical Company. He served on several scientific boards for the U.S. Government, including the President's Science Advisory Committee for Presidents Kennedy and Johnson. Calvin was the chairman of the Committee on Science and Public Policy of the National Academy of Sciences (1972-1975). In 1962–1976 he was chairman of the U.S. Editorial Board for the Joint U.S.-U.S.S.R. publication in planetary and space sciences facilitated by NASA and was the recipient of honorary medals too numerous to list.

Calvin had retired from being an active professor at Berkeley in 1980 but continued his scientific research until the time of his death. In 1987 his wife died of cancer. They had been together for forty-five years, and in that time her influence on his philosophical views of science was evident. When Calvin attended scientific meetings and gave lectures, she often accompanied him. Genevieve Calvin is listed as Mel-vin Calvin's coauthor on several scientific publications. A frequent participant in scientific discussions at international meetings, she was interested in promoting the use of plants as alternatives for fossil fuels. Calvin's health began to fail in the early 1990s; he died at Alta Bates Hospital in Berkeley at the age of eighty-five.

• The Melvin Calvin Papers are held in the Bancroft Library at the University of California at Berkeley. The best source of biographical information is his excellent full-length autobiography, *Following the Trail of Light: A Scientific Odyssey* (1992). Another source of biographical information is the entry on him in the *Current Biography* yearbook for 1962, which mainly concerns his early career. See also George B. Kauffman and Isaac Mayo, "Multidisciplinary Scientist--Melvin Calvin: His Life and Work," *Journal of Chemical Education* 73 (1996): 412. The *New York Times* obituary, 10 January 1997, contains a few incorrect dates.

RICHARD D. CALDWELL

CANTWELL, Mary (10 May 1930–1 Feb. 2000), writer, was born Mary Lee Cantwell in Providence, Rhode Island, the daughter of Leo Cantwell, a man of Scottish descent who worked as a production manager in a rubber plant, and Mary Lonergan Cantwell, a former teacher and the descendant of nineteenth-century Irish immigrants. As described in her nostalgic memoir *American Girl*, her upbringing in the town of Bristol, Rhode Island, was comfortable, though not without its stresses and strains. Bristol was a Protestant enclave whose founders had been seventeenth-century Puritans. The Lonergans and Cantwells were relative newcomers, and Roman Catholic to boot, which gave them the status of outsiders. Though they had roots in the town through friendships and participation in Bristol's rituals and festivities, family ties— she grew up in a household that included grandparents and a maternal aunt—rather than geographical identity were what seemed to hold them together and give them a sense of belonging.

Mary Cantwell was made aware of this difference at an early age, which she later characterized as being "a brown-eyed girl in the land of the blue-eyed." But religious and ethnic differences were not the only factors of separation: the fact that the Cantwells and Lonergans were middle-class, like their Protestant neighbors, and not blue-collar, like their local coreligionists, the recent immigrants who worked in Bristol's factories, made their place in the scheme of things even more problematic in young Mary's view. Sent, at her mother's instigation, to a private "Yankee" school for first grade, she flourished, only to be removed and enrolled in public school the following year because of her father's insistence on a "democratic" education. The experience seems to have been wrenching: she was harassed, bullied, and even beaten by classmates apparently because she was refined and well dressed, did her schoolwork, and enjoyed reading. But after several years she was able to find like-minded friends as well as sympathetic teachers who recognized her skill as a writer and encouraged her growth. Oddly enough, her trial by fire in the public schools did not diminish her love for her father, who remained her lifelong hero. Even more remarkable, her status as an outsider did not diminish her love for the Bristol of her early years, which, when she reached adulthood, came to stand in her memory and imagination for a vanished Golden Age of American life.

Cantwell loved books from an early age, and after finishing high school she entered Connecticut College in the fall of 1949, where she majored in English. Although she always wanted to be a writer, she believed that this was a field that didn't welcome women, so she settled on a career in magazine journalism. Following graduation in 1953 she moved to New York City, settling in Greenwich Village, and became a copywriter at *Mademoiselle*. Later that same year, on 19 December 1953, she married Robert Lescher, a literary agent; the couple subsequently had two daughters. Cantwell remained at *Mademoiselle* for much of the next three decades, editing features and ultimately serving as managing editor. During the late 1950s she worked for a time as a copywriter at *Vogue*.

Cantwell first came to wide public attention in 1980, when she was asked to be one of a series of guest contributors to "Hers," a weekly column for and by women in the *New York Times*. Writing about ordinary concerns and happenings, like the death of a cat or attending her daughter's high school graduation with her now-ex-husband, she struck a responsive chord in her readers, perhaps because she did not offer shrill rhetoric and the voice of certainty. Rather than proclaiming, as did some other women journalists of the period, that she had all the answers—or hinting that she knew them but refused to share—her observations expressed an appealing doubt and hesitation, a muddling through combined with a final uncertainty about the larger issues that all readers could identify with, including the poignant dilemmas faced by working mothers. Part of her skill lay in the personal tone that she projected, as though she were speaking to an individual and not addressing a collective audience: the reader felt that Cantwell was writing to *her* and to her alone. Readers felt comfortable with Cantwell and believed they would welcome her as a friend with whom they could talk over their concerns and troubles.

Cantwell's success as a columnist led to her appointment later the same year as a member of the editorial board of the *Times*. In both signed and unsigned editorials she addressed issues that especially concerned women, including contraception and abortion. Though she was liberal, her views seemed more commonsensical than political—as, for example, when she pointed out in a 1982 editorial that a government proposal to deny contraceptives to teenagers unless their parents gave permission would simply increase teenage pregnancies. Calling the proposed legislation "the squeal rule," she coined a term that was picked up by other commentators.

By the time of Cantwell's retirement from the *Times* in 1996, she had become widely known for two volumes of memoirs: *American Girl*, published in 1992

and covering her childhood, and *Manhattan, When I Was Young* (1995), an account of her early years in the city during the 1950s. In her second volume, Cantwell nostalgically portrayed a Manhattan as remote from the present as the Bristol she had described in *American Girl*, evoking a young woman's delight at discovering the glamour and sophistication of the big city for the first time. A third volume of memoirs, *Speaking with Strangers*, was published in 1998. Somewhat darker in tone—and reflecting the melancholy wisdom of old age—it covers a period during the 1970s when she was traveling extensively abroad for *Mademoiselle* while negotiating a painful divorce from her husband. Accounts of her travels are interspersed with recollections of a four-year affair with a famous writer whom she identifies only as "the balding man." At the time of publication Cantwell was reluctant to disclose his name, but later, after his death, she revealed to friends that—as many had guessed—the man was the poet and novelist James Dickey. All three volumes of Cantwell's memoirs received generous praise from critics and were widely read.

Throughout most of her years in New York, Cantwell remained a resident of Greenwich Village. She died of cancer at a Manhattan hospital.

• For biographical information, see the three volumes of memoirs discussed above. See also Wendy Smith, "Mary Cantwell: Tales of the City," an interview in *Publishers Weekly*, 6 Apr. 1998, pp. 53–54, and "Cantwell, Mary," in *Contemporary Authors*, vol. 140 (1993), p. 69. James Barron of the *New York Times* also provided information for this article. An obituary appears in the *New York Times*, 2 Feb. 2000.

ANN T. KEENE

CARAY, Harry (14 Mar. 1914?–18 Feb. 1998), baseball broadcaster, was born Harry Christopher Carabina in St. Louis, Missouri, the son of Christopher Carabina and Daisy Argint. Although most sources claim 1 March, in either 1919 or 1920, as his birthdate, Caray's birth certificate, examined by the *St. Louis Post-Dispatch*, gives a different date and a much earlier year of birth. Caray, whose Italian father abandoned the family early, lived with his French-Romanian mother and stepfather until her death before Harry was ten years old. He was then sent to live with his aunt.

Caray described his childhood growing up in a poor St. Louis neighborhood as "not particularly happy," and he turned to baseball for escape, making the trip to Sportsman's Park to see the Cardinals whenever he could. At Webster Groves High School he played baseball and basketball and was even offered a scholarship to play baseball at the University of Alabama, which he was forced to turn down because he could not afford the travel and living expenses. Kept out of World War II because of poor eyesight, Caray needed a job. Complaining that the Cardinals' broadcasts were as "dull and boring as the morning crop reports," in 1943 he lobbied for the job of calling the games for KMOX in St. Louis. He received an audition, but the station owner decided that he was too inexperienced for the large station and helped him get a broadcasting job at WCLC in Joliet, Illinois.

After a short period as an announcer with WKZO in Kalamazoo, Michigan, Caray (he had shortened his surname by this time) returned to St. Louis, where he briefly hosted a talk radio program. In 1945 he was hired by WIL-AM in St. Louis as an announcer for the Cardinals, and on 17 April he called his first game, a contest with the Cubs at Wrigley Field. Caray spent twenty-five years as the voice of the Cardinals and became popular throughout the Midwest, thanks in part to the 50,000-watt signal broadcast by KMOX, to which Caray had moved when Anheuser-Busch bought the team. In 1954 he was teamed with Jack Buck, who also became a renowned figure in Cardinals broadcasting.

In 1968 Caray broke several bones when a car hit him on a St. Louis street. The following year the Cardinals stunned Caray and his fans by firing the veteran broadcaster; rumors circulated of a romance between Caray and the wife of an Anheuser-Busch executive. At first annoyed by the gossip, he later felt flattered that people believed that a fifty-year-old man with huge, black, Coke bottle-thick glasses was being pursued by young women, asking "would you have gone around denying rumors like that?" Club officials, who called his dismissal a "marketing decision," telephoned him in a saloon to let him know he was being replaced. In his autobiography Caray, a lifelong heavy drinker, admitted that "it was probably appropriate, but I couldn't appreciate the irony at the time."

Caray accepted a job broadcasting for the Oakland Athletics, but he stayed only a year. In 1971 he moved to Chicago, where he spent the rest of his career. He called games for the American League Chicago White Sox for eleven volatile years and in 1982 angered Sox fans (some of whom subsequently became Cubs fans) by moving cross-town to become the lead announcer for the National League Cubs. It was with the Cubs that he enjoyed his greatest popularity, since their games were broadcast on Chicago "superstation" WGN-TV, which was carried over cable to homes throughout the nation.

Beloved by the fans in Chicago and around the country, Caray was not afraid to criticize players, fellow broadcasters, or team owners for their foibles and shortcomings but was quick to praise a good catch or a clutch base hit. In a ritual begun with the White Sox, during the seventh inning "stretch" of every home game he would bellow out his off-key rendition of "Take Me Out to the Ballgame," a tradition the Cubs continued after his death by inviting local and national celebrities to sing in tribute to Caray. Although the Cubs realized little success during the years he broadcast their games (the club's winning percentage topped .500 in only four of his sixteen seasons at Wrigley), Caray continued to entertain the intensely loyal Chicago fans with his animated announcing

style, becoming known for his trademark phrases "Holy Cow!" and "it might be . . . it could be . . . it is!" and for his habit of spelling players' names backward.

Nicknamed the "mayor of Rush Street" (for the city's nightlife district), Caray spent many nights in bars or restaurants, drinking and talking with friends and fans. In the late 1980s Caray became a spokesperson for Budweiser, which mounted a huge advertising campaign that featured the septuagenarian broadcaster in billboard ads and television commercials. He often held court at Harry Caray's, his restaurant in downtown Chicago, where the bar was appropriately sixty feet six inches long, the distance from the pitcher's mound to home plate.

As Caray aged, his skills as an announcer diminished, and he began to confuse players' names and call plays incorrectly, prompting the NBC television show "Saturday Night Live" to satirize his slurred speech and bungled play calling. His critics called on him to retire, but he refused. He suffered a stroke in 1987, missing the first game of his career. While out six weeks recuperating, celebrities, from Bill Murray to George Will, filled in, and his return in May 1987 was celebrated with a call from President Ronald Reagan. Two years later, on 23 July 1989, Caray won the Ford C. Frick Award and was inducted into the broadcasters' wing of baseball's Hall of Fame. In the mid-1990s, after fainting in the brutal Miami heat during a match-up against the Florida Marlins, he stopped calling away games.

On Valentine's Day 1998, while dining with his third wife, Dolores "Dutchie" Goldmann (whom he had married in 1975), at a Rancho Mirage, California, restaurant, Caray collapsed; he died in Rancho Mirage four days later. He was married three times and had five children. His son Skip Caray became the lead radio and television announcer for the Atlanta Braves, and his grandson Chip Caray followed in his grandfather's footsteps, becoming an announcer for the Cubs.

Arguably the most colorful character in broadcasting, Caray was one of the first announcers to become a star in his own right. Popular in St. Louis and an icon to Chicagoans, he was devoted to the fans, calling the games through a fan's eyes and sometimes even broadcasting Cubs games from the bleachers. He once said that if "a fan had a chance to get behind a mike like I do, he would sound like I do" (*St. Louis Post-Dispatch*, 19 Feb. 1998). Baseball fans continued to love Caray because he brought out the pure fun in baseball and prompted older listeners to remember a more innocent time, when the sport wasn't dominated by marketing gimmicks, oversized contracts, and bad player behavior. After Caray's death Cardinals Hall of Fame outfielder Stan Musial called the broadcaster "baseball's greatest salesman."

• Harry Caray's autobiography, written with Bob Verdi, is *Holy Cow!* (1989). Chicago Cubs announcer Steve Stone's book of reminiscences of Caray is *Where's Harry? Steve Stone Remembers His Years with Harry Caray*, written with Barry

Rozner (1999). See also Rich Wolfe and George Castle, *I Remember Harry Caray* (1998), which compiles reminiscences of Caray from broadcasters, baseball players, and family members. Excerpts from Caray's autobiography were published by the *St. Louis Post-Dispatch*, 22 Feb. 1998. Obituaries are in the *Chicago Tribune, New York Times*, and *St. Louis Post-Dispatch*, 19 February 1998, and *Sport*, May 1998.

STACEY HAMILTON

CARMICHAEL, Stokely (29 June 1941–15 Nov. 1998), civil rights leader, was born in Port-of-Spain, Trinidad, British West Indies, the son of Adolphus Carmichael, a carpenter, and Mabel (also listed as May) Charles Carmichael, a steamship line stewardess and domestic worker. When he was two, his parents immigrated to the United States with two of their daughters. He was raised by two aunts and a grandmother and attended British schools in Trinidad, where he was exposed to a colonial view of race that he was later to recall with anger. He followed his parents to Harlem at the age of eleven and the next year moved with them to a relatively prosperous neighborhood in the Bronx, where he became the only African-American member of the Morris Park Dukes, a neighborhood gang. But although he participated in the street life of the gang, he had more serious interests. "They were reading funnies," he recalled in an interview in 1967, "while I was trying to dig Darwin and Marx" (quoted in Parks, p. 80). A good student, he was accepted in the prestigious Bronx High School of Science. When he graduated in 1960 he was offered scholarships to several white universities, but a growing awareness of racial injustice led him to enroll in predominantly black Howard University in Washington,.D.C. Impressed by the television coverage of the protesters at segregated lunch counters in the South, he had already begun to picket in New York City with members of the Congress of Racial Equality (CORE) before he entered college in the fall of 1960.

Carmichael became an activist while still in his first year at Howard, where he majored in philosophy. He answered an ad in the newsletter of the Student Nonviolent Coordinating Committee (SNCC), a student desegregation and civil rights group, and joined the first of the interracial bus trips known as Freedom Rides organized in 1961 by CORE to challenge segregated public transportation in the South. He was arrested for the first time when the bus reached Mississippi. He was jailed frequently in subsequent Freedom Rides, once serving a 49-day term in Mississippi's Parchman Penitentiary.

After graduating in 1964, Carmichael joined SNCC full time and began organizing middle-class volunteers of both races to travel into the South to teach rural blacks and help them register to vote. From his headquarters in Lowndes County, Mississippi, he was credited with increasing the number of black voters of that county from 70 to 2,600. Lacking the support of either the Republican or the Democratic Party, he created the all-black Lowndes County

Freedom Organization, which took as its logo a fierce black panther. Growing impatient with the willingness of black leaders to compromise, he led his organization to shift its goal from integration to black liberation. In May 1966 he was named chairman of SNCC.

In June of that year, after James Meredith's "March Against Fear" from Memphis to Jackson had been stopped when Meredith was shot, Carmichael was among those who continued the march. On his first day, he announced his militant stand: "The Negro is going to take what he deserves from the white man" (quoted in Sitkoff, p. 213). Carmichael was arrested for trespass when they set up camp in Greenwood, Mississippi, and after posting bond on 16 June he rejoined the protesters and made the speech that established him as one of the nation's most articulate spokesmen for black militancy. Employing working-class Harlem speech (he was equally fluent in formal academic English), he shouted from the back of a truck, "This is the 27th time I've been arrested, and I ain't going to jail no more. The only way we gonna stop them white men from whuppin' us is to take over. We been saying freedom for six years and we ain't got nothing. What we gonna start sayin' now is Black Power!" (quoted in Oates, p. 400). The crowd took up the refrain, chanting the slogan over and over.

The term "Black Power" was not new with Carmichael—Richard Wright had used it in reference to the anticolonialist movement in Africa, and Adam Clayton Powell, Jr., had used it in Harlem—but it created a sensation that day in Mississippi, and Carmichael instructed his staff that it was to be SNCC's war cry for the rest of the march. The national press reported it widely as a threat of race war and an expression of separatism and "reverse racism"; Roy Wilkins, leader of the NAACP, condemned it as divisive; and Martin Luther King, Jr., pleaded with Carmichael to abandon the slogan. But although King persuaded SNCC to drop the use of "Black Power" for the remainder of the march, the phrase swept the country. Carmichael always denied that the call for black power was a call to arms. "The goal of black self-determination and black self-identity—Black Power—is full participation in the decision-making processes affecting the lives of black people and the recognition of the virtues in themselves as black people," he wrote in his 1967 book, written with Charles V. Hamilton, *Black Power: The Politics of Liberation* (p. 47).

In August 1967, Carmichael left SNCC and accepted the post of prime minister of a black militant group formed by Huey P. Newton and Bobby Seale in 1966, the Black Panther Party, which took its name from the symbol Carmichael had used in Mississippi. As its spokesman he called for the Southern Christian Leadership Conference (SCLC), the NAACP, and the Nation of Islam to work together for black equality. That year he traveled to Hanoi to address the North Vietnamese National Assembly and assure them of the solidarity of American blacks with the Vietnamese against American imperialism. In 1968 he married the famous South African singer Miriam Makeba; the couple had one child.

Carmichael remained with the Black Panthers for little more than a year, resigning because of the organization's refusal to disavow the participation of white radicals, and in 1969 left America for Africa, where he made his home in Conakry, capital of the People's Revolutionary Republic of Guinea. By then completely devoted to the cause of socialist world revolution emanating from a unified Africa, he became affiliated with the All-African People's Revolutionary Party, a Marxist political party founded by Kwame Nkrumah, the exiled leader of Ghana then living in Guinea as a guest of its president Sekou Touré. Carmichael changed his name, in honor of his two heroes, to Kwame Ture, and toured U.S. colleges for several weeks each year speaking on behalf of the party and its mission of unifying the nations of Africa. Divorced in 1978, he married Guinean physician Marlyatou Barry; the couple had one son. His second marriage also ended in divorce.

During the 1980s Carmichael's message of Pan-Africanism inspired little interest in the United States, and the attendance at his public appearances fell off. As Washington Post reporter Paula Span noted shortly before his death, "Back in the United States, there were those who felt Ture had marginalized himself, left the battlefield. His influence waned with his diminished visibility, and with the cultural and political changes in the country he'd left behind." He also came under criticism for anti-Semitism because of his persistent attacks on Zionism. A collection of fourteen of his speeches and essays published in 1971, *Stokely Speaks: Black Power Back to Pan-Africanism*, included such inflammatory assertions as "The only good Zionist is a dead Zionist," and was attacked in the press. The bulletin of the Anti-Defamation League of B'nai B'rith criticized his campus addresses, calling him "a disturbing, polarizing figure" who caused hostility between blacks and Jews.

In 1986, two years after the death of his patron Sekou Touré, Carmichael was arrested by the new military government on charges of subversive activity, but he was released three days later. Despite the continued fragmentation of Africa and the diminished influence of Marxism, he never lost his faith in the ultimate victory of the socialist revolution and the fall of American capitalism. To the last he always answered his telephone "Ready for the revolution," a greeting he had used since the 1960s. In 1996 he was diagnosed with prostate cancer, with which he believed he had been deliberately infected by the FBI. Despite radiation treatment in Cuba and at New York's Columbia-Presbyterian Medical Center during his last year, he died of that disease in Conakry.

Stokely Carmichael left a mixed legacy. His provocative rhetoric was widely opposed by black leadership: Martin Luther King, Jr., decried his famous slogan as "an unfortunate choice of words," and Roy Wilkins condemned his militant position as "the raging of race against race." But Carmichael's childhood friend Darcus Howe wrote of him in a column in *New Statesman*, "He will be remembered by many as the figure who brought hundreds of thousands of us out of ignorance and illiteracy into the light of morning."

• Balanced but generally sympathetic accounts of Carmichael's participation in the civil rights movement are in Lester A. Sobel, ed., *Civil Rights, 1960–66* (1967); Martin Luther King, Jr., *Where Do We Go from Here: Chaos or Community?* (1967); Harvard Sitkoff, *The Struggle for Black Equality, 1954–1980* (1981); Stephen B. Oates, *Let the Trumpet Sound: The Life of Martin Luther King, Jr.* (1982); Taylor Branch, *Parting the Water: America in the King Years 1954–1963* (1988); Gordon Parks, *Voices in the Mirror: An Autobiography* (1990); William L. Van Deburg, *Modern Black Nationalism: From Marcus Garvey to Louis Farrakhan* (1997); and Darcus Howe, "In Memory of Stokely, My Friend, Who Said, Get Guns," *New Statesman*, 27 Nov. 1998. Perceptive profiles of Carmichael during his most active years are "Inside Story of 'Black Power' and Stokely Carmichael," *U.S. News & World Report*, 15 Aug. 1966, p. 12, and Gordon Parks, "Whip of Black Power," *Life*, 19 May 1967, pp. 76–82. An interesting and sympathetic overview of his life and ideas is Paula Span, "The Undying Revolutionary," *Washington Post*, 8 Apr. 1998. An obituary is in the *New York Times*, 16 Nov. 1998.

DENNIS WEPMAN

CARTER, Betty (16 May 1929–26 Sept. 1998), jazz vocalist, was born Lillie Mae Jones in Flint, Michigan, the daughter of James Jones, a factory worker who also led a Baptist church choir, and Bertha Cox Jones. Carter grew up in Detroit, where she attended North Western High School. She later studied piano at the Detroit Conservatory, and it is rumored that she falsified her age to be admitted. In 1946 she began singing at local clubs and sitting in on sessions with Dizzy Gillespie's big band and Charlie Parker's quintet.

Carter, considered a bit of an eccentric, was much ahead of her time with her unique style of vocals. Unlike the comparatively smooth sounds of her predecessors Sarah Vaughan and Ella Fitzgerald, Carter's husky voice was then unusual; it was often described as having a saxophonelike quality. While touring with Lionel Hampton (1948–1951), Carter took the stage name "Lorraine Carter," but her flavorful improvisations and distinguishing scatting style inspired Hampton to give her the nickname "Betty BeBop." She eventually dropped "Lorraine" and adopted "Betty." The years with Hampton were difficult for the young singer. On several occasions, he fired her. Each time, Hampton's wife, Gladys, simply rehired Carter, insisting that she acquire some solid experience before going out on her own.

Carter also faced many obstacles working with various managers and recording companies. Never willing to conform to or imitate popular styles, she was labeled as troublesome and for many years went virtually unrecognized. After leaving Lionel Hampton's band in the early 1950s, she recorded the vocals on King Pleasure's *Red Top* in 1952. In 1955 she recorded *Meet Betty Carter and Ray Bryant*. In 1958 she worked with Miles Davis. In 1965 Carter married James

Redding; they had two sons and would eventually divorce. During this period, she toured and recorded with Ray Charles (*Ray Charles and Betty Carter*, 1961). Two of their most memorable duets—"Baby It's Cold Outside" and "Georgia on my Mind"—made Ray Charles a household name. Carter remained on the tour circuit, performing in Japan (1963), London (1964), and France (1968).

In 1969 Carter founded her own record label, Bet-Car Productions, and started hiring and mentoring aspiring jazz musicians. Her unselfish nurturing of young musical talent earned her the title "Godmother of Jazz." Her talented protégés included pianists John Hicks, Marc Cary, Mulgrew Miller, Benny Green, Stephen Scott, and Cyrus Chestnut; drummers Clarence Penn, Lewis Nash, and Jack DeJohnette; and bassists Buster Williams, Dave Holland, Chris Thomas, Michael Bowie, and Curtis Lundy. Her 1975 appearance in Howard Moore's musical *Don't Call Me Man*, as well as performances in 1977 and 1978 at the Newport Jazz Festival, gave rise to several club engagements through the mid-1980s. Audiences again were becoming enthusiastic over Carter's style. Her classic 1979 recording *The Audience with Betty Carter* eventually received a Grammy nomination. But it was her 1987 release *Look What I Got!* that earned her a 1988 Grammy Award and finally provided overdue recognition for her work in jazz. *Look What I Got!* became the first independently produced jazz album to achieve this honor. Over a career of almost fifty years, she recorded thirty albums.

In 1997 Carter received the National Medal of Arts Award from President Bill Clinton. She remained as fierce a supporter of music education as she was a critic of the commercial jazz market. Accusing producers of the inability to see beyond the available quick cash, Carter deplored the shift from original, intellectual jazz to an emphasis on producing hit records. She consistently pressured recording companies to create a larger budget for jazz and commit more marketing dollars to the production of upcoming artists instead of reissuing jazz classics from the 1930s and 1940s. She continuously reminded her students that "the Lord didn't stop giving out talent with Duke Ellington" (quoted in Marc Fisher, "Betty Carter, the Jazz Bringer," *Washington Post*, 28 Sept. 1998). Consistent with this philosophy was her creation in 1993 of Jazz Ahead (later adopted by the Kennedy Center), a music program that accepted twenty young students annually to develop their talent. Each year the program ended with a weekend of inspiring performances by the youthful musicians. She died in her Brooklyn home.

Betty Carter's vehement independence alienated some, but her originality advanced an innovative jazz, and her demand for excellence inspired a new generation of artists. While other jazz musicians enjoyed celebrity, she employed daring technique to transform her individuality into a distinctive sound.

• General information on Betty Carter is in Ian Carr, Digby Fairweather, and Brian Priestley, *Jazz, the Rough Guide: The Essential Companion to Artists and Albums*, 2d ed. (2000), and Leonard Feather and Ira Gitler, *The Biographical Encyclopedia of Jazz* (1999). Interviews and articles on Carter provide a more vivid and interesting depiction of the artist's life, such as Sonja Williams, "This Week's Profile: Betty Carter," National Public Radio (1999); Bob Blumenthal, "Personal Profiles: Betty Carter," *Boston Globe*, 2 Oct. 1998; Howard Reich, "Her Own Woman: Betty Carter," *Chicago Tribune*, 1 Oct. 1998; William Bauer, "Who Will Feed the Fire?," *Down Beat*, Dec. 1998; and Lawrence B. Johnson, "Jazz: Carter Does What She Can for Budding Jazz Musicians," *Detroit News*, 30 Oct. 1997. An obituary is in the *Washington Post*, 27 Sept. 1998.

NOLEN HARRIS

CARTER, Boake (28 Sept. 1898–16 Nov. 1944), broadcast journalist, was born Harold Thomas Henry Carter in Baku, then part of Russia (now the capital of Azerbaijan), the son of Thomas Carter, an oilman and British consul in that city, and Edith Harwood-Yarred Carter. He was educated at boarding schools in England and then spent a brief interval at Cambridge University, where he wrote for a student newspaper. Carter was impatient to enter the oil business with his father, and while making preparations to do so he worked as a stringer for the *London Daily Mail*. By this time England and most of Europe were fighting World War I, and Carter temporarily abandoned his ambition and joined the Royal Air Force, serving in the coast patrol.

By the time the war ended in 1918, the elder Carter had lost his stake in the oil business, and his son decided to try his luck in North American oil fields. For several years he traveled in Mexico and Central America, supporting himself as a freelance reporter for U.S. newspapers while searching unsuccessfully for an entrée into the oil business, and eventually moved north to the United States. After traveling around for a time he settled in Philadelphia, to which his parents had recently immigrated, and was soon hired to work on the city desk of the *Philadelphia Daily News*. In 1924 he married Beatrice Richter, assistant society editor of the *Philadelphia Bulletin*, and the couple moved to a farmhouse outside the city. They eventually had two children.

So far Carter's career in journalism had been confined to print, and it was not overwhelmingly successful. Carter found his real niche, in broadcast journalism, quite by accident, when WCAU, the CBS radio station in Philadelphia, sent out an urgent call for someone to broadcast a rugby match. Carter was their man, and his stint proved so successful that he was asked soon afterward to create a simulated broadcast of the Oxford-Cambridge rowing races: Carter read a "play-by-play" script while recorded sounds of British crowds were played in the background. This, too, was a hit, and Carter's career in radio broadcasting was born. At the suggestion of a radio official, who thought that "Harold Carter" did not sound interesting enough, he changed his first name to Boake, a family name on his mother's side.

At first Carter's radio appearances were limited because of his rather peculiar British accent, heavily colored by his years in Central America; some of his superiors felt that he was difficult to understand. Carter remedied the situation by reshaping his voice so that it conformed more closely to American speech but retained a distinctively British intonation. While continuing work for the *Daily News*, part of the Hearst newspaper chain, he became a news commentator for WCAU, writing his own scripts and delivering them in a dramatic tone. His local popularity got him a job as a commentator called "the Globe Trotter" in Hearst-sponsored newsreels, and soon his voice was known in movie theaters all over the country.

Carter made his nationwide broadcasting debut at the time of the Lindbergh baby kidnapping in March 1932, when he was hired by the national CBS network to report on the case from a mobile unit sponsored by WCAU. This opportunity, like so many others in Carter's life, came by chance: The president of WCAU was the brother-in-law of William S. Paley, the head of CBS in New York, and he persuaded a reluctant Paley to give the local journalist a chance. Carter proved that they had chosen the right man by scooping the competitors: leaving other journalists to report from the scene of the crime in Hopewell, New Jersey, where police restricted reporting, Carter established his headquarters at a hotel in Trenton, a dozen miles away, and was able to broadcast information freely, unhampered by the concerns of public officials. Often the information was incorrect, but that did not matter to his listeners, who were stirred by his dramatic delivery and made to feel that they, too, were getting an inside look at the sensational case, as one often baseless "clue" after another emerged. His up-to-the-minute coverage ended only with the discovery of the infant's body in May.

Covering the first months of the Lindbergh case made Carter a national media star, and he was hired by the Philco Corporation to do news commentary over the CBS network. This sudden rise in popularity encouraged him to become increasingly opinionated and sensationalistic in his presentations, and to his large following he also added detractors. Among them was the governor of New Jersey, who sued him for libel after Carter claimed that the governor was obstructing justice in the Lindbergh investigation. When Carter issued a statement denying that he had malicious intent, the case was dropped.

This episode did not cause Carter to become more restrained in his commentary. In fact, he soon became known for his crusades over the airwaves, finding possible dereliction of duty on the part of public officials whenever any disaster occurred. He became a regular syndicated columnist for the *Philadelphia Public Ledger*, commenting on the same issues that he discussed in his broadcasts. He also began writing books on public affairs, simplifying major issues of the day for a mass audience. They included *Black Shirt, Black Skin* (1935), about the war waged by Italy in Ethiopia; *Johnny Q. Public Speaks!* (1936), which attacked President Franklin D. Roosevelt's New Deal; *I Talk as I Like* (1937), *This Is Life* (1937), and *Made in U.S.A.* (1938), rehashes of some of his most popular radio topics, including crime and the glories of free enterprise; and *Why Meddle in the Orient?* (1938), which advocated an isolationist policy for the U.S. in the wake of Japanese aggression.

In June 1938 Carter was hired by the General Foods Corporation as a newscaster and advertiser of their cereals. On these broadcasts his criticism of the New Deal escalated, and he began attacking members of the administration and military officials at a time when support for the government was at an all-time high. Many of his remarks also suggested that he was a supporter of totalitarianism, and he made the additional mistake of attacking labor unions, perhaps not realizing that many in his audience were either members themselves or married to unionists. His listenership began to decline, and in December General Foods did not renew his contract. His response was to write another book, *Why Meddle in Europe?*, which urged the same isolationist stance he had advocated in his earlier book on Asia.

Carter returned to broadcasting in the fall of 1939, but by this time his popularity had fallen considerably. Ideally suited for a radio version of the Hearst style of yellow journalism, Carter had a know-it-all personality that ultimately began to grate on many of his listeners; provocative commentary that had been a welcome diversion from the despair of the Great Depression now began to seem inappropriate as the world moved perilously close to another war, which finally erupted. His broadcasts continued, however, this time on the Mutual network, as did his syndicated column, and he still maintained a following, albeit much reduced. The public that only a few years earlier couldn't get enough of Carter had turned its attention elsewhere.

In 1941 Carter divorced his first wife and moved to Los Angeles. The following year he announced unexpectedly that he had embraced an eccentric version of Judaism known as the "Biblical Hebrew" movement, advocated by a group called the Society of the Bible in the Hands of Its Creator founded by David Horowitz. "Obedience to the laws established by Moses," Carter now declared, was the answer to winning the war. Despite his earlier alleged sympathies for totalitarianism, he had apparently now concluded that Hitler, whom he described as "Satan," had to be defeated. In the summer of 1944 Carter married Paula Nicoll; several months later he died suddenly in Hollywood, apparently of a cerebral hemorrhage. By this time the man who had twice been voted "the most popular news commentator in the U.S."—and had in fact helped to invent the role of the radio commentator in American broadcasting—had become something of a has-been, and his death attracted only minor attention from the media. The publication *Current Biography*, which had featured him in a lengthy entry only two years earlier, did not even note his death until 1947.

• Biographical information on Boake Carter can be found in a number of popular publications that appeared during his heyday in the 1930s. The most reliable source is a profile by noted journalist A. J. Liebling in *Scribner's Magazine*, Aug. 1938, pp. 7–11ff. See also "Carter, Boake" entries in *Dictionary of American Biography*, suppl. 3 (1973), and in *Current Biography Yearbook*, 1942 and 1947. For an assessment of Carter's radio career, see Erik Barnouw, *A History of Broadcasting in the United States*, vol. II (1968). An obituary appears in the *New York Times*, 17 Nov. 1944.

ANN T. KEENE

CARTIER, Pierre (1878–27 Oct. 1964), jeweler, was born Pierre-Camille Cartier in France, the son of Louis-François-Alfred Cartier, also a jeweler; his mother's name is unknown. Pierre Cartier's grandfather Louis-François Cartier (1819–1904) founded Cartier, the renowned jewelry company, in Paris in 1847. Early on, Pierre Cartier and his brothers Louis-Joseph and Jacques-Théodule worked in the family business. Cartier's original clientele included French royalty as well as a burgeoning upper middle class, soon complemented by international customers traveling through the country. Aristocrats from all over Europe and Russia as well as wealthy Americans such as J. P. Morgan bought and commissioned work from the firm.

The coronation in England of Edward VII in 1902 brought so many commissions to Cartier that Pierre, along with Gaston Worth of the French fashion house called the House of Worth, established a branch in London that same year. Worth and Cartier often worked together to the advantage of their prosperous client base, as their stores were located near each other in Paris. They often displayed each other's wares in their windows, and occasionally their designers worked together to incorporate jewelry in clothing designs. By 1906 Pierre's brother Jacques took over the London branch.

Still looking to expand their business, Pierre Cartier traveled to Russia in 1904–1905. The Paris and London shops served several Russian aristocrats such as Grand Duke Alexis, Grand Duchess Vladimir, and Empress Marie Feodorovna. Cartier set up a temporary branch in St. Petersburg in 1908 and became a major rival of Fabergé before closing in 1914 at the outbreak of war. The connections that the firm forged during its time in Russia proved beneficial during the following years as many royal refugees sold their jewels to Cartier for resale, often to American consumers.

As a result of the increasing number of American clients, Pierre Cartier opened a New York branch in 1909 in a building at 712 Fifth Avenue. He offered jewelry with aristocratic pedigree, often reset to suit the latest fashions. In 1917 the company moved to banker Morton Plant's mansion at 653 Fifth Avenue. Cartier traded a double-strand pearl necklace, carved by Mrs. Plant and then valued at $1,000,000, for the building, which was designed by architect Welles Bosworth. The new store featured several showrooms including the Pearl room, the Silver room, the Wedge-wood room with its objects d'art, and the Blue room where they presented the most impressive and expensive jewels. Pierre Cartier married an American, Elma Rumsey, in 1909; they had one daughter.

Originally, all of the jewelry and related products were made in France and sent to the American branch. By the 1920s, however, the New York store established American Art Works, a workshop of up to seventy jewelers and goldsmiths, most from France. In 1941 the workshop closed and Cartier contracted out their work with the American firm of Wors & Pujol.

During the time Pierre Cartier presided at the New York store, he witnessed changes in jewelry fashions, while his company also helped start new trends. Cartier began the twentieth century selling stomachers, dog-collar necklaces, and epaulettes—items well out of style by the 1920s. The company excelled at modern and Art Deco designs in jewelry, clocks, and watches. A Cartier salesman once credited Pierre Cartier for inventing the idea of the clip brooch in the 1930s. Inspired by a clothespin, Cartier adapted the spring mechanism to brooches and ear clips. The opening of international markets affected Cartier's style: the firm began to create new jewelry inspired by designs from India, Japan, China, Russia, and Egypt. Cartier's refined taste extended to its publicity efforts. Advertisements were run in high-end magazines, and product placements were worked into fashion spreads for *Vogue* and *Harpers Bazaar*. But one of the most successful selling techniques was the loaning of jewelry to actresses and socialites, who wore the pieces to important events and often became too attached to the jewelry to return it.

Cartier's American elite clientele included the Vanderbilts, the Rockefellers, the Astors, Barbara Hutton, and Marjorie Merriweather Post. Pierre Cartier offered his customers the glamour and allure of unusual and historical pieces such as the marriage crown of the Romanov family and the silver service Napoleon ordered on his return from Elba. Perhaps the most famous of Pierre Cartier's transactions was the sale of the Hope Diamond to Evalyn Walsh McLean, who, wealthy in her own right, had married an heir to the company that published the *Washington Post*. In 1908 McLean bought from Cartier the Star of the East, a diamond of more than 90 carats, for $120,000. Two years later, Pierre Cartier and McLean were both in Paris, and he showed her the Hope Diamond, a blue diamond of just over forty-five carats. Pierre Cartier's sales pitch included a rich history of the stone passing through several generations of French royalty and carrying with it a legendary curse. Cartier and McLean returned to the United States without a sale; but soon thereafter he loaned the stone to McLean, and she became smitten. She bought the gem for $180,000. Cartier had the diamond set so it could be worn as a brooch or a pendant, and it became McLean's signature piece of jewelry. The diamond is now in the collection of the Smithsonian Institution's National Museum of Natural History.

In addition to his work for the company, Pierre Cartier served on the boards of Alliance Française in New York and the French Chamber of Commerce in the United States. In 1945, following the death of his two brothers, he moved to Paris to become president of Cartier International. He retired to Geneva, Switzerland, in 1947. Other members of the Cartier family ran the company until the branches were sold to different syndicates in the 1960s and 1970s.

Pierre Cartier helped turn his family's company into a truly international firm, small enough to maintain personal service yet large enough to accommodate the changing clientele's needs over the course of the twentieth century. In addition to forging ties with England and Russia, his greatest contribution to the company was opening and running the New York branch during times of unprecedented wealth in America. Although the fashions changed, Cartier strove to be a constant arbiter of taste while selling some of the most outstanding gems in the world.

• Hans Nadelhoffer, *Cartier: Jewelers Extraordinary* (1984), provides the most extensive information on the history of the firm as well as on Cartier's designs. Judy Rudoe, *Cartier: 1900–1939* (1997), was published in conjunction with an exhibition organized by the British Museum and the Metropolitan Museum of Art. Additional sources include Franco Cologni and Ettore Mocchetti, *Made by Cartier: 150 Years of Tradition and Innovation* (1993), Gilberte Gautier, *Cartier, the Legend* (1983), and Philippe Tretiack, *Cartier* (1997). *Biography of an Idea: Memoirs of Public Relations Counsel Edward L. Bernays* (1965) contains a chapter on Pierre Cartier and Bernays's work for him during the 1920s. For information on the Hope Diamond, see Evalyn Walsh McLean, *Father Struck It Rich* (1936), and the documentary on the diamond for the "Treasures of the World" series shown on PBS, produced by Stoner Productions (1999). Informative obituaries are in the *Washington Post* and the *New York Times*, both 29 Oct. 1964.

N. ELIZABETH SCHLATTER

CASTANEDA, Carlos (15 Dec. 1925?–27 Apr. 1998), anthropologist and writer, was born, according to his own report, on 25 December 1931 in São Paulo, Brazil, the son of a professor of literature; according to U.S. immigration records, he was born Carlos Cesar Aranha Castaneda on 15 December 1925 in Cajamarca, Peru, the son of C. N. Castaneda, a goldsmith and jewelry store owner, and Susana Aranha Castaneda. (Carlos Castaneda identified this couple as his adoptive parents rather than birth parents.) He claimed to have attended a boarding school in Buenos Aires, Argentina, studied sculpture in Milan, Italy, and served in the U.S. Army in Spain during World War II, but neither Italian school records nor American military records confirm his account. In fact, it appears he attended high school in Cajamarca and in 1948 moved with his family to Lima. There he attended the National College of Our Lady of Guadalupe and the National Fine Arts School of Peru, where he studied painting and sculpture. The immigration records indicate that he married in 1951 in Peru (although his wife's name is not known) and that the couple had one child.

Castaneda's version and the official records come together in 1951, when he immigrated to the United States. In 1956 he entered Los Angeles City College, where he majored in psychology and studied journalism and creative writing. That same year he married Margaret Runyon; they had no children, although Castaneda put his name as father on the birth certificate of a boy born to his wife. Castaneda was divorced in 1973 and, according to one account, married Florinda Donner in 1993. There were no children from the latter marriage.

In 1959 Castaneda entered the University of California at Los Angeles, where he studied anthropology. Funded in part by the anthropology department, he traveled to the Mexico-Arizona border the next year to study the medicinal use of plants by the local Indians. As he subsequently reported, while waiting in a bus station in Arizona he met Juan Matus, an elderly Yaqui Indian shaman who agreed to instruct him in the principles and methods of Yaqui sorcery and introduce him to an alternative perception of reality. His four-year apprenticeship included contact with other native holy men and the use of several local psychotropic plants, including peyote and hallucinogenic mushrooms. Castaneda prepared a report on his experience that was accepted as his master's thesis by UCLA in 1964. The following year, he withdrew from Don Juan's exacting tutelage. His account was published by the University of California Press in 1968 as *The Teachings of Don Juan: A Yaqui Way of Knowledge*. The next year it was reissued in a psychedelic dust jacket by a trade press and became an immediate bestseller. A blend of anthropology, allegory, and fantasy, it struck the exact note for the period with its validation of drugs as a ritual element of an ancient and spiritual culture; the counterculture of the period embraced it wholeheartedly. The book's critical reception, however, was mixed: Theodore Roszak, in the *Nation*, called it "a uniquely important contribution to our burgeoning psychedelic literature" (p. 184), but Dudley Young in the *New York Times* described it as "unsatisfying because it falls uneasily between ethnography, spiritual autobiography, and travel literature" (p. 30).

Castaneda renewed his contact with Don Juan in 1968 and published his further conversations with the sorcerer as *A Separate Reality* in 1971. Like its predecessor, it related many weird experiences and delved deeper into the hidden powers that a Yaqui "man of knowledge" could invoke. His third book, *Journey to Ixtlan: The Lessons of Don Juan*, served as his doctoral dissertation in 1970 and, when it was published in 1972, made him a millionaire. A steady stream of reports detailing his further progress on the road to illumination flowed from his pen until his last year. His eleven books sold over eight million copies in seventeen languages during his lifetime; they enticed many to follow his path into the Sonora Desert in search of enlightenment. In 1993 Castaneda emerged from a lifelong reclusiveness to promote a system of body exercises he trademarked "Tensegrity" (a term borrowed from architecture incorporating tension and integrity), which he claimed would bring an increased level of awareness and which he marketed profitably at seminars and workshops. He died at his home in Los Angeles.

One of the godfathers of the New Age movement, Castaneda was a controversial figure from the beginning of his career, described by some as more "shaman" than shaman but by Joseph Chilton Pearce, in 1971, as "the principal psychological, spiritual, and literary genius of recent generations" and by his teacher Don Juan as "the most important paradigm since Jesus" (quoted in Noel, pp. 13–14). His books were generally received with respect, but critical doubt of their authenticity grew with each succeeding publication. Castaneda never permitted his field notes to be examined; there were many internal contradictions in his books and no evidence that the worldview he presented was rooted in Yaqui culture; and investigation failed to locate his Indian mentor. Castaneda always insisted that his reports were meticulously recorded from his experience, but his work came increasingly to be regarded as fiction. His fall from grace in the academic world, however, did nothing to reduce the ardor of his followers or the commercial success of his books. As one admirer noted in 1973, it didn't matter if Don Juan was real or not. "Either Carlos is telling the documentary truth about himself and Don Juan, in which case he is a great anthropologist. Or else it is an imaginative truth, and he is a great novelist. Heads or tails, Carlos wins" (quoted in *Time*, p. 37).

• An irreverent account of Castaneda's personal life is in a memoir by his former wife Margaret Runyon Castaneda, *A Magical Journey with Carlos Castaneda* (1996), which Castaneda tried unsuccessfully to suppress. For critical studies of his books, see Dudley Young, *New York Times Book Review*, 29 Sept. 1968, p. 30; Edward H. Spicer, "Early Praise from an Authority on Yaqui Culture," *American Anthropologist* (Apr. 1969): 320ff.; William and Claudia Madsen, *Natural History* (June 1971): 74ff.; and Paul Riesman, "A Comprehensive Anthropological Assessment," *New York Times Book Review*, 22 Oct. 1972, p. 7. For extremely negative evaluations of Castaneda's books, see Richard De Mille, *Castaneda's Journey: The Power and the Allegory* (1976), and *The Don Juan Papers: Further Castaneda Controversies* (1990). A chapter is devoted to Castaneda's work as a hoax in Kathryn Ann Lindskoog, *Fakes, Frauds and Other Malarkey* (1993). For a critical examination of Castaneda's academic career, see Jay Courtney Fikes, *Carlos Castaneda, Academic Opportunism and the Psychedelic Sixties* (1993). A balanced anthology of critical reactions to Castaneda's work is Daniel C. Noel, *Seeing Castaneda: Reactions to the "Don Juan" Writings of Carlos Castaneda* (1976).

An informative profile of Castaneda is "Don Juan and the Sorcerer's Apprentice," *Time*, 5 Mar. 1973, pp. 36–45. Illuminating interviews are Sam Keen, "Sorcerer's Apprentice," *Psychology Today* (Dec. 1972): 90–102, and "Don Juan's Power Trip," *Psychology Today* (Dec. 1977): 40–126. An obituary is in the *New York Times*, 20 June 1998.

DENNIS WEPMAN

CASTELLI, Leo (4 Sept. 1907–21 Aug. 1999), art dealer, was born Leo Krauss in Trieste, then a part of the Austro-Hungarian Empire, the son of Ernest Krauss, a Hungarian-born banker, and Bianca Castelli Krauss. Following World War I and the annexation of Trieste by Italy, the Krausses changed their last name to Bianca's family name, Castelli. After receiving a law degree at the University of Milan in 1924, Leo Castelli worked at an insurance company in his hometown. In 1932 he transferred to Bucharest, Romania, where he met and wed Ileana Schapira, daughter of a wealthy industrialist. The offer of a banking job in the mid-1930s took Castelli and his wife to Paris, where they met architect and decorator René Drouin.

The Castellis formed a partnership with Drouin to start their first art gallery, which was located on the Place Vendôme. Their inaugural exhibition opened in the spring of 1939 and featured furniture by Drouin and artwork by surrealists Meret Oppenheim, Leonor Fini, and Eugène Berman. With the outbreak of World War II, the gallery closed, and the Castellis immigrated with their young daughter Nina to New York in 1941.

From 1943 to 1946 Leo Castelli served in the U.S. Army in different cities in Europe including Bucharest. While in Paris he reunited with Drouin who was selling art by Wassily Kandinsky, Jean Dubuffet, and Piet Mondrian. When Castelli finished his military service and returned to New York, he acted as an American representative for Drouin. Castelli and his wife began to immerse themselves in the New York art world, getting to know particular artists, mainly abstract expressionists, and even hosting Willem de Kooning and Elaine de Kooning at their East Hampton house for two summers. In 1949 he quit working with Drouin and began selling art independently as well as with the New York dealer Sidney Janis.

Castelli opened his own gallery in his and Ileana's apartment at 4 East Seventy-seventh Street in 1957. Their debut exhibition featured work by European and American artists, including Dubuffet, Alberto Giacometti, Mondrian, Jackson Pollock, David Smith, and Willem de Kooning. Refusing to pry artists away from other dealers and convinced that abstract expressionism had run its course, Castelli sought out emerging artists, such as Robert Rauschenberg, whose work he had seen at a 1954 show at Egan Gallery, and Jasper Johns, who was included in a Jewish Museum exhibition in spring 1957.

Although pop art, a representational style based on popular culture, had been gaining momentum prior to Castelli's involvement, the dealer's commitment to the artists of this movement and their work ultimately offered them a firm presence in New York, across the country, and overseas. He gave Johns his first one-man exhibition in January 1958. That same month, *ARTnews* magazine ran a photo of Johns's painting *Target with Four Faces* on its cover and included a short article on the artist and a review of the exhibition. Alfred Barr, director of the Museum of Modern

Art, bought four works for his institution and the rest of the show all but sold out. Rauschenberg's first exhibition at the gallery (in March 1958) did not sell as well but nonetheless included several of the artist's landmark works such as *Odalisk* and *Bed* (which Castelli bought for himself and donated to the Museum of Modern Art in 1988). By the mid-1960s Castelli represented the titans of American pop art: Johns (who remained with Castelli until the dealer's death), Rauschenberg, Roy Lichtenstein, James Rosenquist, and Andy Warhol.

Castelli also became an advocate for minimalist artists such as Frank Stella, Donald Judd, Dan Flavin, and Robert Morris and the conceptualists Bruce Nauman and Joseph Kosuth. Representing this diverse group of artists entailed at first several financial challenges; Castelli helped pay for the production of their pieces and for their installations in his gallery, and he offered most of his artists a monthly stipend regardless of sales. Collectors and museums took a number of years before beginning to acquire minimalist and conceptualist art, developments that along with pop art contributed significantly, in Castelli's view, to the erosion of abstract expressionism's hegemony.

Thanks to his ties to Europe, Castelli successfully promoted American artists to museums, galleries, and collectors overseas. An aid to his crusade was Ileana, who divorced him in 1960, married family friend Michael Sonnabend, and opened a gallery in Paris that represented a few of Castelli's artists. With his tireless campaigning, Castelli also helped Rauschenberg become the first American to win the International Grand Prize for Painting at the Venice Biennale in 1964. Over the years Castelli cooperated with several dealers in Rome, London, and Düsseldorf, thereby establishing an appreciation and market for his artists on an unprecedented level.

Castelli is also credited for decentralizing the New York art world for American collectors by forming alliances with other galleries and dealers throughout the country, including the Ace Gallery in Los Angeles, John Berggruen in San Francisco, Ronald Greenberg in St. Louis, and Janie C. Lee in Houston. Although he took a cut in his commission, by sharing his inventory and stable of artists with these other dealers Castelli greatly increased his collector base and ultimately profited tremendously. His artists were also exposed to a wider public.

At the same time, Castelli was expanding his New York presence. Castelli Graphics, which sold prints and photographs, opened in 1969 and was run by his second wife, Antoinette "Toiny" Fraissex du Bost. (They married in the 1960s and had one son; she died in 1987). In 1971 Castelli was one of the first dealers to move to SoHo, the burgeoning art scene in Manhattan at that time.

By the 1980s Castelli's reign was eclipsed by other younger dealers capitalizing on the art boom and even by Ileana, who was attracting major new talents to the New York gallery that she opened in 1971. During the 1990s his gallery remained something of a powerhouse based on his reputation, yet he had lost almost all of his original artists except for Jasper Johns and Roy Lichtenstein. He received several awards during his lifetime for his contributions to the world of art, including the French Legion of Honor in 1987 and the Centennial Medal of Honor from the National Arts Club in 1998. Castelli died at the age of ninety-one; he was survived by his third wife, Barbara Bertozzi, an art historian whom he had married in 1995.

Most of the artists Castelli represented had already exhibited before joining his gallery. But Castelli's specialty was in presciently recognizing emerging talents and offering several of them their first one-man exhibitions as well as worldwide exposure. He once told a *New York Times* reporter, "Anyone can discover an artist, but to make him what he is, give him importance, that's really discovery." With his monthly stipends and his connections to other dealers, collectors, museum directors, and art critics, he provided immense support to dozens of artists who shaped the course of American art history after abstract expressionism had peaked in its success. Although he did not open his own gallery until the age of forty-nine, he worked tirelessly until his death. When asked once if he would ever slow down, he responded, "What would I do? As it is I'm bored on Mondays when I can't come into the gallery."

• The Archives of American Art, Smithsonian Institution, conducted two oral history interviews with Castelli between 1969 and 1973, and 1997; transcripts are available. The AAA has microfilmed copies of the galleries' records from 1958 to 1968. Interviews with Castelli are also included in *Leo Castelli: A Tribute Exhibition* (Butler Institute of American Art, 1987), *Castelli and His Artists: Twenty-Five Years* (Aspen Center for the Arts, 1982), *Inside the Art World: Conversations with Barbaralee Diamonstein* (1994), and Barbaralee Diamonstein's earlier book of interviews, *Inside New York's Art World* (1979). Also see *The Art Dealers: The Powers behind the Scene Tell How the Art World Really Works* by Laura de Coppet and Alan Jones (1984).

For an in-depth biographical essay on Castelli, see Calvin Tomkins, "Good Eye and a Good Ear," *New Yorker*, 26 May 1980, pp. 44–72, reprinted in Tomkins's *Post- to Neo-: The Art World of the 1980s* (1988). Castelli wrote essays introducing several of his own catalogs as well as for Gianfranco Gorgoni, *Beyond the Canvas: Artists of the Seventies and Eighties* (1985). For information on Castelli's discovery of and relationship with Jasper Johns, see Susan Brundage, ed., *Jasper Johns: Thirty-Five Years* (Leo Castelli Gallery, 1993); *Jasper Johns: Drawings and Prints from the Collection of Leo Castelli* (Butler Institute of American Art, 1989); and an interview with Jasper Johns, after Castelli's death, in *Vogue*, Nov. 1999, pp. 304–6. *Leo Castelli y Sus Artistas* (Centro Cultural, Arte, 1987) includes a list of all of Castelli's exhibitions from 1957 through 1986. For information on Castelli's own art collection, see *A View from the Sixties: Selections from the Leo Castelli Collection and the Michael and Ileana Sonnabend Collection* (Guild Hall Museum, 1991) and *Coleccion Leo Castelli* (Fundación Juan March, 1989). *Leo Castelli: XXXth Anniversary* (1988) is a video of an interview conducted in his gallery. Informative obituaries are in the

New York Times, 23 Aug. 1999, and *Art in America*, Nov. 1999.

N. ELIZABETH SCHLATTER

CHAMBERLAIN, Wilt (21 Aug. 1936–12 Oct. 1999), basketball player, was born Wilton Norman Chamberlain in Philadelphia, Pennsylvania, the son of William Chamberlain, a welder and handyman, and Olivia Ruth Chamberlain, a domestic maid and cook. Although his father was only five feet eight inches and his mother five feet nine inches, by age ten Chamberlain was already six feet tall, and he stood six feet three when he graduated from elementary school. His astonishing growth continued through adolescence and he reached a full seven feet by his eighteenth birthday. In addition to his extraordinary height, Chamberlain was a natural athlete with fierce competitive instincts. He was a fast runner and was selected to participate in the 1946 Penn Relays when he was just ten years old. His youthful ambition was to be an Olympian. In high school he was undefeated in the shot put; he ran the hundred-yard dash in 9.3 seconds; and he recorded a vertical leap of fifty inches. Later in life Chamberlain boasted that he was perfect for the decathlon and could have been known officially as the world's greatest athlete.

Chamberlain's attraction to basketball, however, drew him away from track and field. His native Philadelphia had a rich basketball tradition, producing star players like Tom Gola, Paul Arizin, and Guy Rodgers, whom the young Chamberlain admired. Furthermore, racial barriers were being broken in college and professional sports in the late 1940s just as Chamberlain was maturing. His favorite basketball court was at the rough-and-tumble Haddington Recreation Center in West Philadelphia. The Haddington competition was a boon to Chamberlain, who quickly realized the value of massive size and athletic skills. He rapidly developed an ego as large as his body and delighted in the adoring neighborhood crowds that turned out to see him play.

Chamberlain matriculated in 1951 to Philadelphia's Overbrook High School, where he became a basketball phenomenon in his first year. He was considered so dominating that an opposing coach ordered his tallest player to impersonate Chamberlain in practices by standing on a table in front of the basket while the whole team swarmed around him, waving their arms as a five-on-one defensive tactic. It did not work: Chamberlain seemed to be able to score at will and had record games of 74 and 90 points. Overbrook won so many games by 50 or 60 points that Chamberlain was often taken out by halftime, yet he averaged 37.3 points per game with a three-year total of 2,252, breaking Gola's state scoring record; his teams won 58 of 61 games during his high school seasons. While most sportswriters began to refer to him by his obvious nickname, "Wilt the Stilt," Chamberlain preferred "the Big Dipper" because he had to "dip" under doorways—and could slam-dunk basketballs through hoops.

As Chamberlain's reputation grew, both college and professional coaches took note of his prodigious but still raw physical skills. To polish those skills, a National Basketball Association (NBA) publicist arranged for Chamberlain to spend his summers working as a part-time bellhop and basketball player at Kutsher's Country Club in the Catskill Mountains for $13 per week. During those summers, Chamberlain held his own against many of the best college and professional stars in the country, including Neil Johnston, who had led the NBA in scoring for three years running. He also met Eddie Gottlieb, owner of the NBA's Philadelphia Warriors, and Arnold "Red" Auerbach, coach of the Boston Celtics. Because the NBA had a territorial rule that granted its teams rights to graduating collegians in their geographical areas, Auerbach tried to talk Chamberlain into attending a Boston-area school. The politically astute Gottlieb, however, managed to amend the rule to permit teams to use their first-round picks to draft high school graduates in their areas. Accordingly, the Warriors secured rights to Chamberlain as a professional while he was still a schoolboy.

During his senior year at Overbrook, Chamberlain began attracting national attention: *Sports Illustrated, Time, Newsweek,* and *Look* and *Life* magazines all ran feature stories on the eighteen-year-old's phenomenal athletic prowess, and every major college in the country tried to recruit him. He wanted to get away from home but ruled out western schools because he believed they did not play topflight basketball and southern schools because many were still segregated. He finally chose the University of Kansas because of its strong basketball tradition and its coach, Forrest "Phog" Allen, who had been tutored by the sport's inventor, Dr. James Naismith.

Even against the best college competition, Chamberlain dominated utterly, in his first year leading his freshman team to an exhibition win over the Kansas varsity and in his first varsity game in 1957 drawing 17,000 fans and breaking school records for points and rebounds. Kansas won its first twelve games before losing to Iowa State, which used extreme stall tactics. When Kansas lost again five games later and finished the season at 21–2, Chamberlain's myth of invincibility was shaken. In the NCAA tournament that determined the national champion, Chamberlain led his team to the title game against undefeated North Carolina. In a fabled triple-overtime contest, North Carolina outlasted Kansas 54–53. Although Chamberlain scored a game-high 23 points and was named the tournament's most valuable player, he was devastated by the loss and considered it the beginning of his unfair reputation as a "loser."

Chamberlain had never been happy with his choice of Kansas and only reluctantly returned to college for his junior year. His grades were poor; his close relationship with Phog Allen was broken when the coach was forced into mandatory retirement; and he was frustrated by many rules changes that the NCAA instituted to neutralize his natural superiority. The most important of these was the prohibition of offensive goal-tending, which prevented Chamberlain from guiding teammates' shots into the basket. He also felt the sting of segregation in the rural Midwest and was troubled by a scandal that broke over irregularities in his recruitment.

Many colleges had offered Chamberlain money, cars, phoney jobs, and other perquisites in 1955. Kansas was no exception. A lucrative slush fund was created for him by rich supporters; he was seen driving a Cadillac around campus, prompting Leonard Lewin of the *New York Daily Mirror* to cynically note, "I feel sorry for The Stilt when he enters the NBA four years from now. He'll have to take a cut in salary." Although no legal action was ever taken, later Chamberlain did admit that he received at least $20,000 in under-the-table payments during his college years.

After the 1957–1958 season, which ended with Kansas having an 18–5 record and missing an NCAA berth, Chamberlain announced that he would forgo his senior year and turn professional. Because he was not eligible for the NBA until his college class graduated, Chamberlain played with the Harlem Globetrotters for one year; he then signed with Gottlieb's Warriors in 1959. At this highest level of competition, Chamberlain still dominated. At seven feet one inch and a massive 250 pounds, he won the NBA scoring title and made history as the first player to win rookie of the year, all-star game most valuable player, and league most valuable player honors in the same season. His most spectacular individual statistics came in his third year when he totaled 4,029 points, *averaging* 50.4 points per game. On 2 March 1962 he scored an astounding 100 points in one game against the New York Knickerbockers, establishing a record that stands among the most remarkable in the history of professional sports. In 1962 Gottlieb sold the Warriors franchise to a group in San Francisco, where Chamberlain won two more scoring titles but no championships. In mid-1965 he was traded to a new Philadelphia franchise, the 76ers, and intensified his rivalry with Auerbach's Boston Celtics and their star center, Bill Russell. The Celtics had already won nine NBA titles in ten years. In the 1966 Eastern Division finals, Chamberlain outplayed Russell but suffered his fourth playoff defeat to Russell's Celtics in six years.

In 1967 Chamberlain was the centerpiece of the strongest team he had ever played for. Coached by the clever Alex Hannum, with forwards Luke Jackson and Chet Walker, guards Hal Greer and Wally Jones, and key sixth man Billy Cunningham, the 76ers won 45 of their first 49 games en route to a 68–13 record, the best in league history up to that time. Chamberlain dedicated himself to team play, recording more assists, rebounds, and blocked shots but averaging only 24 points. This time his team easily won the divisional finals, beating the Celtics and their player-coach, Russell, four games to one. Chamberlain finally won his world championship when the 76ers defeated the

Warriors in six games, inspiring many experts to anoint this 1967–1968 team as the NBA's finest ever.

As his celebrity grew, Chamberlain considered a variety of opportunities outside basketball. In 1960 he had thought seriously about entering the Olympics in the decathlon and high jump. He turned down offers from professional football, baseball, soccer, and wrestling, but he was intrigued at the prospect of boxing world heavyweight champion Muhammad Ali. Amid swirls of publicity, Chamberlain signed lucrative contracts in 1968 and 1971 to fight Ali in the Houston Astrodome, but both bouts fell through. He attracted more publicity when he opened high-profile restaurants, bought racehorses, Great Danes, and polo ponies, sponsored race cars, dated glamorous women, and campaigned for presidential candidate Richard Nixon. In 1968, at the height of his fame, he was traded to the Los Angeles Lakers and moved to Hollywood. In Los Angeles, Chamberlain built a luxurious million-dollar home with outsized dimensions to fit his outsized body and appetites. His neighbors were movie stars and film industry moguls. He titled his first autobiography *Wilt: Just Like Any Other 7-Foot Black Millionaire Who Lives Next Door* (1973). He starred in Clio-winning television commercials, acted in several movies, including *Conan the Destroyer*, and formed a lasting relationship with Jack Kent Cooke, the multimillionaire businessman and owner of the Lakers.

When Chamberlain joined the Lakers, the team already had two other superstars, Elgin Baylor and Jerry West, but had never won an NBA championship. Critics argued that this new team would never win because the stars were too individualistic and would need three basketballs. Cooke predicted that they would never lose with three all-time greats on the same team. For the first three years of Chamberlain's tenure, the Lakers did lose: in the 1969 NBA finals against Russell's aging Celtics in seven grueling games; in the 1970 finals to the New York Knicks in another dramatic seven-game series; and in the 1971 Western Division finals to the Milwaukee Bucks and their young seven-foot center, Kareem Abdul Jabbar. That year marked the ninth time one of Chamberlain's NBA teams had lost a playoff series to the eventual champion, and he was hurt by increasing criticism that he was the most infamous "loser" in sports.

Elgin Baylor had been the undisputed captain of the Lakers until Chamberlain arrived, and the two stars clashed from the beginning. In 1972 Baylor retired, and Cooke hired his third coach in four years, disciplinarian Bill Sharman. Supporting Chamberlain and West were the brilliant cast of Gail Goodrich, Pat Riley, Happy Hairston, Keith Erickson, and Jim McMillian. The Lakers suddenly became unbeatable. From 5 November 1971 to 7 January 1972 they won 33 straight games, one of the most remarkable sustained efforts in professional basketball, and ended the season with 69 victories and an .841 winning percentage. In the playoffs, Chamberlain dominated Jabbar as the Lakers defeated Milwaukee in six games. Despite a broken hand, Chamberlain led the Lakers to an easy five-game victory over the Knicks in the finals. Chamberlain had his second world championship, was named series MVP, became a hero in Los Angeles, and temporarily silenced his critics. After an injury-plagued 1973 season, he retired as the leading scorer and rebounder in NBA history. His fourteen-year regular season totals were 1,045 games, 31,419 points, 23,924 rebounds, and 4,643 assists. His playoff totals were 160 games, 3,607 points, 3,913 rebounds, and 673 assists.

Chamberlain's basketball peers continued to regard him so highly that into the mid-1980s NBA owners tried to lure him out of retirement, but he never played again. In 1973–1974 he spent a year coaching the San Diego Conquistadors of the American Basketball Association, played professional volleyball, and even produced a movie, *Go For It* (1976). He made major headlines one final time in 1991 when he published his second autobiography, *A View from Above*. He had never married, but among his many candid declarations the most controversial was his claim that he had had sexual encounters with twenty thousand women. "Yes, that's correct," he boasted (p. 251), "*twenty thousand different ladies. At my age, that equals out to having sex with 1.2 women a day, every day since I was fifteen years old. . . . I give these numbers here not to impress. I give them because it's like when I played basketball—many of my numbers were so unbelievably high that most people dismissed them as fables or found them impossible to relate to.*"

Chamberlain's entire career seemed unbelievable. He was literally a larger-than-life figure. His impact changed the rules of professional basketball: the NBA was forced to widen the lane and outlaw dunking from the free-throw line, and like the NCAA they banned offensive goal-tending. Because he was a poor free-throw shooter, defenses deliberately fouled him brutally, yet in his 100-point game he made 28 of 32. When he was criticized for shooting too much in 1968, he led the league in assists. His defensive strength and stamina were legendary: he was an awesome shot-blocker yet never fouled out of a game, and he led the league in minutes played eight times. Basketball annals are heavy with his additional achievements: Associated Press all-America twice; NBA all-star 13 times; League MVP four times; scoring champion seven straight times; rebounding champion 11 times; most rebounds in one game, 55; 50 or more points in one game, 118 times; elected to the NBA Hall of Fame in his first year of eligibility.

Beyond all the numbers that arguably make Chamberlain the most dominant player in basketball history, his legacy is bittersweet. His overpowering size, strength, and fearsome play often led the public to view him as a villain and take pleasure in watching him fail, inspiring his most famous quote, "Nobody roots for Goliath." When he was particularly irritated by the casual observer's obvious question, "How's the weather up there?" he would sometimes spit and answer, "It's raining up here" (*View*, p. 23). In his epic battles with the smaller but defensively superior Russell, he lost six of eight playoff finals and was continually branded a loser. In fairness, Russell's Celtic teams were almost always more talented than Chamberlain's, but, in the 142 games they played head to head, Chamberlain averaged 29 points and 28.7 rebounds to Russell's 24 and 14.5. Moreover, three of the six losses were in seventh games by one or two points, and in the 1969 finals coach Bill van Breda Kolff would not allow the injured Chamberlain to reenter the seventh game, which the Lakers lost 108–106. In his long NBA career Chamberlain was, indeed, a winner—of more than 700 regular season games and two world championships. When asked whether Chamberlain was the greatest basketball player ever, Hall-of-Famer Oscar Robertson replied simply, "The books don't lie." The irony of Chamberlain's life was that he was an outgoing, joyful man of intelligence and painful candor who never shrank from the limelight but was too often blinded by its glare. Dave Anderson of the *New York Times* spoke for many when he remembered Chamberlain as "a gentle, good-natured Goliath." At the time of his death in Los Angeles, Chamberlain still held more than eighty high school, college, and professional basketball records.

• Chamberlain's last book, *Who's Running the Asylum? Inside the Insane World of Sports Today* (1997), is a frank behind-the-scenes look at the business and politics of sports. Ron Frankl, *Wilt Chamberlain* (1995), and Bill Libby, *Goliath: The Wilt Chamberlain Story* (1977), cover his entire playing career; for an account of his early years on the court, see George Sullivan, *Wilt Chamberlain* (1960). Chamberlain is featured prominently in Eric Nadel, *The Night Wilt Scored 100* (1990); Merv Harris, *The Lonely Heroes: Professional Basketball's Great Centers* (1975); Nelson George, *Elevating the Game: Black Men and Basketball* (1992); Terry Pluto, *Tall Tales: The Glory Years of the NBA, in the Words of the Men Who Played, Coached, and Built Pro Basketball* (1992; repr., 2000); Miles Shapiro, *Bill Russell* (1991); and Alex Sachare, ed., *The Official NBA Basketball Encyclopedia* (1994). Obituaries are in the *New York Times* and the *Los Angeles Times*, both 13 Oct. 1999.

BRUCE L. JANOFF

CHANCELLOR, John (14 July 1927–12 July 1996), television reporter, anchorman, commentator, and documentarian, was born John William Chancellor and raised in Chicago, Illinois, the only child of E. M. J. Chancellor and Mary Barrett Chancellor, hoteliers. Despite comfortable middle-class circumstances and a pronounced appetite for learning, he had little patience with formal education, preferring to adventure into such blue-collar jobs as carpenter's assistant and Mississippi riverboat deckhand while still a teenager.

Chancellor served in the U.S. Army from 1945 to 1947. Upon his discharge, he married Constance Herbert. (The couple had a daughter, Mary, and were divorced in 1956.) Also in 1947, Chancellor registered at the University of Illinois, but dropped out in less than a year when he found work at the *Chicago Sun-Times*. Discovering his life's vocation in journalism, he quickly moved through the ranks as a proofreader, and became well known as a reporter and feature writer.

In 1952, when Chancellor was forced to leave the *Sun-Times* because of a restructuring shake-up, he was hired by WNBQ (later redesignated WMAQ), the Chicago television station owned by the National Broadcasting Company, which was building a local news division. He was excited by the possibilities of this new form of news reporting, especially its potential for speed and intimacy, and during his first year at WNBQ he received a commendation from Sigma Delta Chi, the national journalism fraternity, for his live, on-the-scene coverage of a street gun battle leading to the capture of a murderer by the police.

NBC News executives in New York took note of the young reporter and promoted him to national assignments in the mid-1950s. Over the next three decades he would work in virtually every aspect of NBC's worldwide operations and eventually become the network's chief public figure. He first achieved widespread viewer recognition with his coverage of the major Civil Rights movement stories that were blanketing the media. These included the 1957 integration of Central High School in Little Rock, Arkansas, where he was threatened with violence by segregationists for his hard-hitting on-the-scene reports. He was also exposed to personal danger as a war correspondent, reporting from the bloody battlefields of the Algerian and Lebanese civil wars of the 1950s. (In 1958 he married Barbara Upshaw, with whom he was to have two children, Laura and Barnaby.)

Chancellor quickly became a familiar figure in such spotlight assignments as coverage of the national political conventions. In a famous incident at the Republican National Convention in 1964, supporters of Senator Barry Goldwater, who perceived a liberal bias in Chancellor, had him forcibly removed from the convention building on the pretext that he had illegally positioned himself on the floor in violation of the fire code. As he was led away not too gently by armed officers, he signed off to his audience by saying poker-faced, "This is John Chancellor, somewhere in custody." His wry, cool-headed attitude and tone gained him favor among viewers.

Over the course of his career, he was taken out of the field several times by network executives who hoped to exploit his down-to-earth, no-nonsense image at the cost of his actual contributions as a journalist. In 1961 he was brought back to New York from European assignments to be made host of NBC's live morning program, "The Today Show." Dating back to its debut a decade earlier, "Today" had been a slapdash mixture of entertainment and news. Although the show had always featured hard-news segments, it had been something of a comedy-variety program, with a chimpanzee named J. Fred Muggs among its regulars. Television, however, was establishing itself as the nation's primary source of daily information, and network officials wanted to overhaul the format and give "Today" a clear identity as a news program.

Chancellor, with his professorial eyeglasses, studious expression, and low-key delivery, proved to have just the right screen image. Moreover, he took administrative charge of the program, thoroughly molding it to his personal standards. Even though network management would have liked him to stay on as "Today" host, he yearned to get back out in the field—and his success made him powerful enough to have his way.

John Chancellor's ability to bring public respect to broadcast news was called on again, this time by the U.S. government. President Lyndon B. Johnson came to admire Chancellor during the time the reporter served as NBC's chief White House correspondent. In 1965 Johnson offered him the directorship of the Voice of America, the overseas radio service of the U.S. Information Agency. The Voice of America had functioned largely as a Cold War propaganda instrument since the end of World War II, and Chancellor was charged with the job of turning it into a trustworthy news source for its listeners around the world. Taking a drastic pay cut for his trouble, he once again accomplished a difficult makeover of a news operation in a relatively short time. In addition to bringing a measure of objectivity to Voice of America news coverage, Chancellor won new listeners by expanding its cultural services, adding popular American entertainers to the program schedule. Never completely comfortable as a journalist in a government job, he resigned only when, as he told the *New York Times*, he was personally satisfied that tax dollars were now supporting "honest journalism" at the Voice of America.

When he returned to NBC in 1967, Chancellor extended his activities beyond reporting into documentary filmmaking for the network. Two of his most acclaimed hour-long programs concerned the Middle East: "Israel: Victory or Else" and "Rabin and Sadat: War or Peace?" In the latter, he pulled off a journalistic coup by interviewing both the Israeli prime minister and the Egyptian president on camera together. It is also worth noting that during his forty years on television Chancellor conducted one-on-one televised interviews with every sitting U.S. president from Dwight Eisenhower to Bill Clinton.

But Chancellor is remembered most widely for his years as the anchorman of "The NBC Nightly News." Since the mid-1950s, NBC News had built its national identity around the popular anchor team of Chet Huntley and David Brinkley. Huntley, however, was forced to retire for health reasons in 1970. The network experimented with several new replacement teams, but all the while it continued to lose ratings points to its archrival, "The CBS Evening News," whose anchor, Walter Cronkite, was building a legendary reputation as "the most trusted man in America."

As in the past, NBC turned to Chancellor and offered him the anchor chair. He accepted the job despite reservations and became the national face of the entire NBC News operation for the next dozen years, starting in 1970. In contemporary terms, he provided the network with the "brand" image it needed to compete with CBS. While Cronkite usually led in the ratings, Chancellor was rarely more than a fraction of a point behind. In the years before mass cable-television diffusion, this translated into an enormous audience, far greater than what a "first place" finish would garner in the cable era. Moreover, a significant number of viewers and critics preferred the forthright earnestness of Chancellor's screen persona to the sometimes avuncular Cronkite.

Though predictably restless in the anchor chair, Chancellor served his long-time employer and his millions of viewers dutifully until 1982, when he happily yielded the mantle to Tom Brokaw. For more than a decade, he continued to appear regularly on the "Nightly News," offering analytic and editorial news commentary until he retired from NBC in 1993.

In the years that followed, he remained professionally active. In 1994, he narrated all nine hours of "Baseball," a Public Broadcasting System miniseries on the history of the sport produced by Ken Burns. He collaborated with Walter Mears on *The New News Business* (1995), an updating and reconsideration of their 1983 book *The News Business*.

John Chancellor died of stomach cancer at his home in Princeton, New Jersey, just before his sixty-ninth birthday.

• Obituaries appeared in the *Washington Post*, the *New York Times*, and the *Los Angeles Times*, all on 13 July 1996, in *USA Today*, 15 July 1996, and in many international dailies, such as the *Guardian* of London on 15 July 1996.

DAVID MARC

CHEATHAM, Doc (13 June 1905–2 June 1997), jazz musician, was born Aldophus Cheatham in Nashville, Tennessee, the son of Marshall Ney Cheatham, a barber, and Alice Anthony. The elder Cheatham was descended from Choctaw and Cherokee Indians who had settled in Cheatham County, Tennessee.

Cheatham began playing music with a youth band, the BFRS Band (Bright Future Stars) at Philips Chapel in Nashville. Self-taught, he played several instruments, beginning on drums before playing the cornet and later the soprano saxophone. He appears to have acquired the nickname "Doc" from performing at the local Meharry Medical College, where his mother worked as a lab assistant.

By the early 1920s, Cheatham was playing tenor saxophone in Nashville's Bijou Theater, a TOBA (Theater Owners Booking Association) outlet and the local venue for many of the classic blues singers of the time, including Bessie Smith, Ethel Waters, Clara Smith, and Ida Cox. During a school vacation in 1924, he made his first trip out of Nashville to Atlantic City, New Jersey, and played a C melody saxophone with Charlie Johnson's Orchestra at the Paradise Club. A later road excursion in 1925 with a small group landed Cheatham in Chicago, where the show disbanded and Cheatham was left to scramble for employment. It was in Chicago that he first became aware of New Orleans musicians and came under the influence of cornetists Freddie Keppard, Joe Oliver, and Louis Armstrong; it was a discovery that would cause him to concentrate on the cornet to the exclusion of all other instruments.

But Cheatham soon learned that his opportunities for employment in Chicago were limited; the city's entertainment during the 1920s was dominated by New Orleans–born musicians. This prompted another move to Philadelphia in 1927 and then in 1928 to New York City, where he played briefly with Chick Webb's orchestra before accepting an offer from Sam Wooding, with whom he undertook his first tour of Europe (1929-1931). The Wooding tour established Cheatham as a "lead" trumpeter, a label that would identify and in some ways categorize him for the next thirty-five years. Lead trumpeters were the ex officio leaders of the band, but they often sacrificed greater recognition for anonymity since the star jazz soloists, the improvisers, usually claimed the public's attention.

Beginning in the 1930s Cheatham gradually solidified his reputation as a lead trumpet player with a number of big bands including McKinney's Cotton Pickers, led by Don Redman and later Benny Carter, as well as the orchestra of Cab Calloway (with whom he spent eight years, 1931-1939). By the late 1930s, however, the traveling, long nights, and an inadequate diet were beginning to take their toll on Cheatham's health. He was suffering from nervous exhaustion, and a routine physical examination toward the end of his stay with Calloway convinced him to take a hiatus from playing music. He returned to Nashville and began a convalescence that lasted for eight months. Even though he was still not fully recovered, he made his way back to New York and eventually accepted work with Teddy Wilson's band, although not in the lead trumpet position.

The public's diminishing interest in big bands and Cheatham's continuing problems with his own health led to another break from performing during World War II. Between 1944 and 1946, he took a job in a U.S. post office on Long Island handling G.I. wartime correspondence in lieu of active military service. While at the post office he played no music, but after leaving he gradually worked his way back playing with the Eddie Heywood Sextet, a small combo that included Mary Lou Williams, Vic Dickenson, John Simmons, Lem Davis, and Billie Holiday on vocals.

It was during this period that Cheatham began to devote more of his time to teaching. By chance, one of his students, a Cuban trumpeter and bandleader, Marcellino Guerra, invited him to join his small Latin band. Latin music presented a new challenge for Cheatham and would occupy much of his time for the next twenty years as he performed intermittently with orchestras led by Damaso Perez Prado, Machito, Ricardo Rey, and Bobbie Cruz. He also began a new chapter in his personal life. When touring Uruguay with Perez Prado in 1951, Cheatham met a young South American woman named Amanda (maiden name unknown), whom he married the following year on a return trip to Chile. Despite the great difference in their ages, the couple produced two children and remained married until the trumpeter's death. Cheatham's two earlier marriages, the first while he was still with Marion Hardy's group in Chicago in the late 1920s and the second to a Cotton Club chorine, were unsuccessful and childless. The names of his first two wives are unknown.

The 1950s were years of stylistic diversity when Cheatham performed with groups led by Wilbur de Paris, Sammy Price, and Herbie Mann. In 1952 he began a long and productive association with George Wein, who at the time was operating jazz clubs in Boston. But the most rewarding chapter in Cheatham's long career began in the early 1960s when the trumpeter continued a gradual transition from lead trumpeter and ensemble player to featured soloist, vocalist, and, eventually, leader. In 1966, at age sixty, he accepted an offer from Benny Goodman and remained with the clarinetist into 1967. Goodman was suffering with back problems during this time, so the group did little touring and Cheatham played only with the sextet, not with Goodman's big band.

The peripatetic Cheatham now seemed to be in demand everywhere he performed and was especially revered during his frequent European tours of the 1970s and 1980s. As he became more confident in his gentle, melodic style of improvising, he gradually added distinctive vocal interpretations that provided some much needed rest from his trumpet playing. Now firmly established as a leader, he assumed the role of elder statesman of jazz and drew younger musicians and older admirers around him. His seventeen years at Sweet Basil's in New York (1980–1997) must be seen as one of the most enduring tenures of any jazz musician. By the early 1990s Cheatham had renewed his interest in New Orleans music, a direction he first explored in the 1920s, and had formed a creative alliance with the young New Orleans trumpet star Nicholas Payton. The two had met by accident while performing with different bands on a cruise ship and developed an immediate rapport. Their celebrated 1997 recording, *Doc Cheatham & Nicholas Payton*, recorded two weeks before Cheatham's death, remains one of the most curious bigenerational collaborations in recent jazz history.

The story of Doc Cheatham parallels in many ways the diversity of jazz itself during its first century. His seventy-year-long career spans virtually every major development in the music, and his own development was a steady progression toward greater recognition as a jazz artist. During the last two decades of his life, in particular, he emerged as one of the most sought-after trumpeters and jazz personalities. As a slow starter and a truly humble individual (he waited until he was in his sixties before claiming to be a jazz musician), Cheatham was fortunate to have lived long enough to see his work recognized. The Cheatham/

Payton appearances toward the end of his life introduced him to new and younger audiences, and he was clearly at a peak in his career when he died suddenly one night after completing a performance with Payton at Blues Alley in Washington, D.C.

• The most complete account of Doc Cheatham's life and career can be found in his autobiography, *I Guess I'll Get the Papers and Go Home* (1995), edited by Alyn Shipton. This volume also contains an extensive discography of Cheatham's recordings (1926–1994) prepared by Howard Rye. In two articles for the *New Yorker*, "Jazz: A Burning Desire" (5 Feb. 1979, pp. 118–120) and "Profiles: Light Everywhere" (25 Jan. 1982, pp. 42–44, 47, 51–52), music critic Whitney Balliett surveys the trumpeter's life, both personal and musical, through the 1970s. Dan Morgenstern summarizes Cheatham's career and provides information on the Cheatham/Payton collaboration in the liner notes to *Doc Cheatham & Nicholas Payton* (Verve 314537 062-2). Other assessments of Cheatham's contributions appear in Phil Schaap, "A Walking History of Jazz," *Down Beat* 62 (June 1995): 26–29, and Chip Deffaa, "Doc Cheatham," *Coda Magazine*, Oct./Nov. 1990, pp. 31–33. Cheatham and other trumpeters—Roy Eldridge, Rex Stewart, Joe Newman, and Red Allen—can be seen in a classic CBS television broadcast, "The Sound of Jazz" (1957), which also features Billie Holiday performing her classic "Fine and Mellow." His obituary appears in the *New York Times*, 3 June 1997.

CHARLES BLANCQ

CLARK, Georgia Neese (27 Jan. 1900–26 Oct. 1995), U.S. treasurer, was born Georgia Neese in Richland, Kansas, the daughter of Albert Neese, a farmer and businessman, and Ellen O'Sullivan Neese. Her father, a self-made man, had prospered in the years before her birth and become the town's leading citizen, owning much of its property as well as the bank and general store. Although a Presbyterian, Georgia Neese briefly attended a small Catholic college in nearby Topeka after graduating from high school in 1917, then transferred to Washburn University in that city. She majored in economics at Washburn and was also active on campus, serving as president of several student organizations, including the drama club. Determined to become an actress, she moved to New York City following graduation in 1921 and enrolled at Sargent's Dramatic School.

After two years of study at Sargent's, Georgia Neese embarked on a ten-year career as an actress, performing throughout the United States with major traveling stock companies and appearing onstage with some of the leading actresses of the early twentieth century, including May Robson and Pauline Frederick. She acquired a manager named George M. Clark, who became her first husband in 1929. Although the marriage ended in divorce in the mid-1940s, she continued to be known as Georgia Neese Clark throughout her professional life. She married Andrew J. Gray, a journalist and press agent, in 1953. She had no children from either marriage.

Georgia Neese Clark's stage career ended abruptly in 1930 when she felt obligated to return home to Richland and care for her ailing father. She became his caretaker for seven years, and by the time of his death in 1937 few opportunities remained for her to resume her work in the theater: the new movie industry had supplanted traveling stock companies as the nation's primary source of popular entertainment. By this time, however, Clark had already begun new careers in both politics and banking. The Neeses were longtime members of the Democratic party—the perennial underdog in Kansas, an overwhelmingly Republican state—and Clark had become active in party affairs soon after moving back to Richland in 1930. By the time of the 1932 national elections she had risen to a seat on the junior national committee of the Democratic party. She was an active campaigner for Franklin Delano Roosevelt, and his election as U.S. president that fall—despite losing the Kansas vote—confirmed her commitment to the party. In 1936 she was named to the Democratic National Committee and retained that post until 1964. In that capacity she appeared often as a public speaker on behalf of Democratic candidates at all levels and was friendly with other prominent Democrats of the mid-twentieth century, in particular Eleanor Roosevelt, who was not only first lady but a powerful political figure in her own right.

Clark began her official banking career in 1935 as the assistant cashier at the Richland State Bank, founded by her father and an uncle. Three years later, following her father's death, she became president of the bank, one of only a handful of privately owned banks in Kansas. She also took over the management of the town's general store, another family property, as well as other family property and businesses, including a grain elevator. By the late 1940s, her business success, combined with her continuing prominence in Democratic politics, had made her a likely candidate for an appointed position in the national government, at a time when more women were emerging as leaders in both major political parties.

Clark was a close friend and protégée of India Edwards, another prominent Democratic politician. In her role as head of the women's division of the Democratic National Committee, Edwards had been instrumental in garnering the women's vote for President Harry Truman during his difficult but ultimately successful reelection campaign in 1948. Edwards was now urging Truman to appoint, as an expression of gratitude, more women to executive positions in the national government. When U.S. Treasurer William A. Julian died suddenly in the spring of 1949, banker Clark—who had campaigned for Truman and also been a strong financial supporter of his campaign—was proposed by Edwards as a likely successor. Truman obliged, and on 4 June 1949 the White House announced Clark's nomination. She was confirmed unanimously by the Senate five days later and sworn in on 21 June.

As the twenty-ninth U.S. treasurer, the first woman to hold that post, Clark became the nation's banker, overseeing the receipt and disbursement of, and accounting for, all public funds, issuing U.S. coins and currency, and directing a staff that then numbered 1,600. Although the treasurer's role was largely out of the public eye—the U.S. secretary of the treasury, who held a cabinet-level post, had more authority and prominence—Clark's name became known to millions through her signature on all U.S. currency issued during her term in office. She remained without controversy at her post until 20 January 1953, when Truman was succeeded by a Republican president, Dwight D. Eisenhower. As her successor, Eisenhower appointed another woman, Ivy Baker Priest, a Republican political leader from Utah.

After leaving the treasurer's post, Clark returned to Kansas to resume control of the various Neese family enterprises and continued in that role for several decades. She remained active in national Democratic politics until her resignation from the Democratic National Committee in 1964, the same year that she moved the family-owned bank from Richland to Topeka, renaming it the Capital City State Bank. In retirement she enjoyed reading and playing golf with her husband, who died in 1994. Clark spent her final years in a Topeka retirement community, where she died.

• For biographical information, see entries for "Clark, Georgia Neese," in *Current Biography Yearbook* for 1949 and 1996. See also G. F. McQuatters, "The Lady with Our Money," *Independent Woman*, Nov. 1949, pp. 322–24, and "People of the Week," *U.S. News and World Report*, 1 July 1949, pp. 44–45. An obituary appears in the *New York Times*, 28 Oct. 1995.

ANN T. KEENE

CLEAVER, Eldridge (31 Aug. 1935–1 May 1998), social activist and writer, was born Leroy Eldridge Cleaver in Wabbaseka, Arkansas, the son of Leroy Cleaver, a waiter and nightclub piano player, and Thelma Hattie Robinson Cleaver, an elementary school teacher. When Cleaver was ten the family moved to Phoenix, Arizona; three years later, they moved again, this time to Los Angeles, California. Soon after, his parents separated. At this time, Cleaver became involved in criminal activities. In 1949 he was arrested for stealing a bicycle and was sent to reform school. In 1952 he was arrested for selling marijuana and was sent back to reform school. In 1954, a few days after his release, Cleaver was again arrested for marijuana possession and was sent to Soledad State Prison for a term of two and a half years.

While in Soledad, Cleaver earned his high school diploma and studied the works of Karl Marx, Thomas Paine, Voltaire, and W. E. B. Du Bois. During this time he also became increasingly angry at the oppression of black people. According to Cleaver, upon his release in 1957, he began raping women as "an insurrectionary act. It delighted me that I was defying and trampling upon the white man's law, upon his system of values, and that I was defiling his women" (Cleaver, *Soul on Ice*, p. 14). He was soon arrested and convicted of assault with intent to murder. In March 1958 Cleaver was sent to San Quentin State Prison. There he began to write as a cathartic, self-redemptive process. "For the first time in my life, [I] admitted that I was wrong, that I had gone astray—astray not so much from the white man's law as from being human, civilized—for I could not approve the act of rape. . . . My pride as a man dissolved and my whole fragile moral structure seemed to collapse, completely shattered. That is why I started to write. To save myself" (Cleaver, *Soul on Ice*, p. 15).

At San Quentin, Cleaver became a Muslim. After a prison guard shot and killed Booker T. X, Cleaver's cellmate and the minister of Muslims of San Quentin, Elijah Muhammad's West Coast representative, Minister John Shabazz, selected Cleaver as leader of the San Quentin Mosque. In that capacity, Cleaver proselytized new converts and lobbied politicians and the United Nations to grant religious freedom to Muslim convicts. Prison officials considered Cleaver to be an agitator, which in 1963 led to his transfer to Folsom State Prison. Following the assassination of Malcolm X in 1965, Cleaver denounced Elijah Muhammad, which caused his excommunication. Cleaver soon renounced the Muslim faith, but swore that when he was released from prison he would put Malcolm X's vision for the Organization of Afro-American Unity into practice.

In 1965 Cleaver was moved to Soledad State Prison. While there, he wrote to Beverly Axelrod, a white civil rights lawyer in San Francisco, seeking her help in his bid for parole. The two eventually became lovers. Impressed by his talent and intelligence, Axelrod smuggled his writings out of Soledad and took them to Edward M. Keating, editor of *Ramparts*. Some of Cleaver's prison writings were published by *Ramparts* and were lauded by such luminaries as Norman Mailer, Maxwell Geismar, and Paul Jacobs. The assistance of Axelrod, and Cleaver's reputation as a published writer, led to his release from prison in December 1966. He was immediately hired as a staff writer for *Ramparts*. In 1967, a selection of his prison writings was published as *Soul on Ice*, which instantly became a national bestseller.

Once out of prison, Cleaver founded the Black House, a cultural center in San Francisco, with poet Marvin Jackmon, playwright Ed Bullins, and singer Willie Dale. Located in a Victorian house on Pine Street in the Fillmore District, the Black House featured black cultural figures such as playwright LeRoi Jones (later known as Amiri Baraka). At a meeting of the Bay Area Grassroots Organizations Planning Committee in early February 1967, Cleaver encountered Black Panther leaders Huey Newton, Bobby Seale, Bobby Hutton, and Sherwin Forte. In the wake of urban riots, the newly formed Black Panthers had pioneered a strategy of monitoring the police while carrying law books and loaded guns as a means of mobilizing low-income blacks against police brutality.

When Betty Shabazz, the widow of Malcolm X, came to town for his memorial, the Black Panthers provided security. Outside the *Ramparts* office following Shabazz's interview by Cleaver, a confrontation with the police ensued. Using a combination of legal knowledge, bravado, loaded shotguns, and an acute assessment of the situation, Newton forced the police to back down. In that instant, Cleaver saw Newton and the Black Panthers as the embodiment of Malcolm X's Organization of Afro-American Unity. Cleaver wrote: "Huey P. Newton is the ideological descendant, heir and successor of Malcolm X. Malcolm prophesied the coming of the gun to the black liberation struggle. Huey P. Newton picked up the gun and pulled the trigger" (*Post-Prison Writings and Speeches*, p. 38).

Immediately after the confrontation at the Ramparts offices, Cleaver joined the Black Panther Party. One of his first endeavors was to launch the *Black Panther* newspaper, first published in April 1967 to address the murder of Denzil Dowell, a black man, by police in Richmond, California. The second issue of the newspaper announced Cleaver's position as the Minister of Information. In May 1967, he was arrested along with other Black Panthers at an armed protest at the California State capitol against the proposed Mulford Act, which would make it illegal for the Panthers to bear loaded arms. Because he was on parole, Cleaver could have been sent back to prison without a trial, but when his supporters demonstrated that he was there in the capacity of a reporter for *Ramparts*, charges against him were dropped.

Cleaver proved to be a wildly charismatic leader. He edited the party's newspaper, gave classes on political education to fellow Panthers, and was a flamboyant speaker who fascinated audiences and the press. In October 1967 Huey Newton was arrested after a confrontation with Oakland police that resulted in the death of one officer. Cleaver played a leadership role in the Free Huey movement that made Newton and the Panthers internationally famous. The Black Panther Party attracted thousands of full-time members and opened chapters in forty states. Cleaver was instrumental in the formation of alliances between the Black Panther Party and radical whites. It distinguished itself from many black nationalist organizations by working closely with many other groups, including Students for a Democratic Society, the United Farmworkers of America, and the anti-Vietnam War movement, toward a shared vision of the liberation of all peoples. In 1968 Cleaver ran for president on the Peace and Freedom party ticket.

In December 1967 Cleaver married Kathleen Neal, whom he had met at the office of the Student Nonviolent Coordinating Committee (SNCC) in Nashville, Tennessee. After the wedding, she moved to San Francisco and joined the Black Panther Party.

As the Black Panther Party became the leading black political organization in the late 1960s, FBI Director J. Edgar Hoover labeled the Black Panther Party the "greatest internal threat to national security." From 1967 to 1971 more than three-fourths of all FBI counterintelligence actions against black organizations targeted the Panthers. A number of violent confrontations between police and the Black Panther Party ensued.. On 6 April 1968, two days after

Martin Luther King, Jr., was assassinated, Cleaver was involved in a shoot-out with the Oakland police. When seventeen-year-old Panther Bobby Hutton attempted to surrender, the police shot and killed the teenager. Cleaver stripped and surrendered to the police stark naked, an antic which may have saved his life. He was arrested, charged with attempted murder, and his parole was revoked. He was sent to Vacaville State Prison, but two months later was released when a judge ruled that his parole had been improperly revoked. In September of that year, the University of California at Berkeley offered a series of lectures by Cleaver. Governor Ronald Reagan ordered the Board of Regents to overturn the university's decision. Students responded by protesting and sitting in at the university administration building. Reagan's attempts to silence Cleaver only emboldened him. At several speaking engagements, including one to nuns at the College of the Pacific, Cleaver led the audience in chanting "Fuck Reagan!" In an address delivered at Stanford University in October, Cleaver challenged Reagan, whom he often referred to as Mickey Mouse, to a duel. "I challenge him to a duel to the death or until he says Uncle Eldridge. And I give him his choice of weapons. He can use a gun, a knife, a baseball bat or a marshmallow. And I'll beat him to death with a marshmallow" (*Post-Prison Writings and Speeches*, p. 133).

Cleaver's vocal and well-publicized condemnations of Reagan led to the second revocation of his parole, and he was once again ordered back to prison. On 24 November, three days before he was scheduled to turn himself in, he fled to Cuba with the help of members of the San Francisco Mime Troupe and Ralph Smith, a Los Angeles Panther who resembled Cleaver. In August of the following year, he and his wife were reunited in Algeria, where they were granted asylum. A few months later, their son Maceo was born. In Algeria, Cleaver established the International Section of the Black Panther Party, identifying the black community in the United States as part of an international decolonization struggle, the "colony within the mother country." From their embassy in Algiers, the International Panthers participated in the Pan African Cultural Festival and communicated with revolutionary governments and groups around the world. In October of 1970 they traveled extensively in North Korea, North Vietnam, and Peking (Beijing), China; they were received by high-level notables such as Chou En Lai, the premier of China, and Kim Il Sung, the premier of North Korea. The North Vietnamese government sent letters home to the families of prisoners of war (POWs) through Cleaver; they offered to trade the U.S. POWs for the release of Huey Newton and Bobby Seale from prison. During this trip, Cleaver's daughter was born.

Meanwhile, the FBI's counterintelligence efforts were taking effect. A U.S. congressional investigation revealed that the Chicago police, in cooperation with FBI infiltrator William O'Neal, assassinated Chicago Panther leader Fred Hampton while he slept in his bed. In another incident, two members of the United Slaves organization, on FBI payroll, were convicted of murdering Panther leaders Alprentice Carter and John Huggins in Los Angeles. With more than twenty-five Panthers killed, Huey Newton and the national leadership in Oakland, California, took the position that armed confrontation was not sustainable. After Newton's release from prison in 1970, the party increasingly emphasized community programs such as the Free Breakfast for Children Program and a campaign to test for sickle cell anemia. But the seeds of schism were cultivated by the FBI, which, forging inflammatory correspondence and utilizing well-placed agents provocateurs, played upon ideological and personal differences within the party. From his exile in Algeria, Cleaver sided with the New York chapter of the party in criticizing Newton's consolidation of power and de-escalation of armed conflict with the State. During a San Francisco television show in February 1971, which provided a telephone hookup with Cleaver, Newton expelled Cleaver and the entire International Section of the Black Panther Party. Cleaver responded by claiming that he was the legitimate leader of the party, and expelling Newton and Chief of Staff David Hilliard the following month. While Black Panther Party activities continued until 1980, its chapters remained divided.

In 1972 the Cleavers relocated to Paris, where they lived underground for several months until high French officials, including future president Giscard d'Estaing, arranged for them to remain there legally. Cleaver became a born-again Christian after having a vision in which all of his Communist heroes disappeared and the image of Jesus Christ appeared. His religious awakening motivated him to return to the United States, which he did in November 1975 after charges from the April 1968 shoot-out were reduced from attempted murder to assault. Back in the United States, he met Reverend Billy Graham and founded the Cleaver Crusade for Christ in 1979. In 1980 he formed his own religion, Christlam, a combination of Christianity and Islam, which included an auxiliary called Guardians of the Sperm. During this time he pursued a variety of business interests, most notably the creation of men's pants that featured a codpiece-like feature called the "Cleaver sleeve" that emphasized rather than concealed the male genitalia.

Cleaver's religious transformation was accompanied by a political about-face. He became a Republican and endorsed Reagan's bid to be reelected president in 1984. In 1986, he ran unsuccessfully for the U.S. Senate as a Republican on a platform that denounced affirmative action and recommended a peacetime draft. During the late 1980s, Cleaver began using drugs. He and his wife divorced in 1987. That same year he was arrested for possession of crack cocaine, the first of many such arrests. In 1994, police found him wandering the streets of Berkeley with a rock of crack in his pocket and a severe head wound inflicted by a fellow addict. With the help of his family, Cleaver eventually got off drugs and reimmersed himself in evangelical Christianity. At the time of his death in Pomona, California, he was working as a diversity consultant at the University of La Verne.

Cleaver will be remembered primarily as a leader of the Black Panther Party, the most powerful black political organization of the late 1960s and early 1970s in the United States. Always at the center of controversy, with his flamboyant brilliance Cleaver mobilized residents of the ghetto underclass to participate in an international struggle for liberation. In the end, having lost the war, Cleaver surprised everyone when he joined the victors and earned amnesty as a fundamentalist Republican.

• While no biography of Cleaver exists, he was extremely candid in writing about his own life. *Soul on Ice* (1968) is his best-known work; it highlights the formation of his political thought. *Post-Prison Writings and Speeches* (1969) explores his early involvement with the Black Panther Party. *Soul on Fire* (1978) discusses his childhood, exile in France, and religious conversion. For others' perspectives on Cleaver, see David Hilliard and Lewis Cole, *This Side of Glory: The Autobiography of David Hilliard and the Story of the Black Panther Party* (1993). Essays in Charles E. Jones, ed., *The Black Panther Party (Reconsidered)* (1998), give the best comprehensive discussion of the Black Panther Party to date. An obituary is in the *New York Times*, 2 May 1998.

Lauren Araiza
Joshua Bloom

COLBERT, Claudette (13 Sept. 1905?–30 July 1996), actress, was born Lily Claudette Chauchoin in Paris, France, the daughter of Georges Chauchoin, a banker, and Jeanne Loew Chauchoin. Some sources indicate that she was born in 1903. When her father's business failed around 1910, her family immigrated to the United States, settling in New York City. Her father died soon afterward, and her strong-willed grandmother became the head of the family. Colbert later recalled that her grandmother greatly influenced her own worldview: "My grandmother had taught me to avoid inferiority complexes, to go out and get what I wanted, to believe I could be and do anything I wanted. I think I was a very healthy-minded, positivist [young woman], and I can thank her for that" (quoted in Quirk, p. 7). She attended Washington Irving High School, studying design in preparation for a career in the fashion industry. She also dabbled in acting, and in 1918 she appeared in a Greenwich Village theater in *The Widow's Veil*, a play written by one of her teachers. Following her graduation, she attended the Art Students League and worked in several dress shops, supplementing her income by giving French lessons. In 1923 she met the playwright Anne Morrison at a party; Morrison, taken with her poise and good looks, cast her in a three-line role in her play *The Wild Westcotts*. Colbert (who adopted her stage name for her Broadway debut) found herself acting with established stars Cornelia Otis Skinner and Elliott Nugent; although the play flopped, she was exhila-

rated by the experience and decided that she wanted to make her career in the theater.

For the next few years she appeared in small roles in several forgettable plays, such as *We've Got to Have Money* (1923) and *The Cat Came Back* (1924). "In the very beginning, they wanted to give me French roles," she told an interviewer. "You know, cute little maids with dark bangs and an accent. That's why I used to say my name Col-ber*t* just as it is spelled instead of Col-baire. I did not want to be typed as 'that French girl'" (quoted in Quirk, p. 7). In 1925 she won good reviews in the farce *A Kiss in a Taxi*, which ran for over 100 performances. Her breakthrough role came in 1927 in *The Barker*, costarring with Walter Huston and Norman Foster as a carnival snake charmer. *New York Times* critic Brooks Atkinson suggested that her "superior" performance effectively conveyed "the earnestness under the tawdry exterior of a midway slut."

Colbert's success in *The Barker* drew the interest of First National Studios, which cast her in the silent film *For the Love of Mike* (1927), directed by Frank Capra. The director later called the cheaply made picture the worst of his career; Colbert, who hated the broad pantomiming required by the silents, which deprived her of the use of her throaty, charming voice, determined never to make another film. *The Barker* ran on Broadway for 172 performances through 1927 and was taken to London in 1928. That year she married her costar Norman Foster; they had no children and would divorce in 1934. In 1929 she returned to Broadway in a dramatic role in *Dynamo*, a lesser play by Eugene O'Neill, and in *See Naples and Die*, a failed romantic comedy by Elmer Rice.

Colbert was lured back to films by the advent of sound and a generous contract offer from Paramount's New York City–based Astoria Studios, which promoted her as one of the main stars on their lot. She starred in six pictures for Astoria between 1929 and 1931, often playing blandly virtuous heroines. Because the studio used inferior sound equipment, her pictures were poorly received by critics and the public and did little to build her screen career. In 1932 Paramount shut down its East Coast facilities and moved her to Hollywood, where she was reduced to playing supporting roles. In 1933 she was "discovered" by Cecil B. De Mille and cast as "the wickedest woman in the world," Nero's wife, Poppaea, in the epic *The Sign of the Cross*. One notorious scene featured her taking a bath in asses' milk while her cats lapped and mewed by the side of the pool; the hit film's publicity proclaimed her as Hollywood's newest sex goddess. But her stock at the studio dropped when she starred over the next two years in several box-office disappointments, including De Mille's disastrously bad deserted-island adventure *Four Frightened People* (1934).

In 1934 Colbert was lent to the poverty-row studio Columbia Pictures to star in *It Happened One Night*. The film's genesis was unpromising: Colbert and director Frank Capra had "ended up hating each other" while making the failed *For the Love of Mike* (McBride,

p. 304); six other actresses, including Myrna Loy and Carole Lombard, had turned down her part; and co-star Clark Gable was forced to do the project by MGM, which had loaned him to Columbia as punishment for demanding a salary increase. The film's simple story concerns a spoiled heiress (played by Colbert) who runs away from her millionaire father; while on a bus, she meets an unemployed reporter (played by Gable) with whom, after many traveling mishaps, she falls in love. Although the picture received tepid reviews and closed quickly in major cities, it was embraced in small towns and rural areas and through word of mouth became a national phenomenon. Audiences delighted at the costars' playful sexiness: in one famous scene, Gable unsuccessfully tries to hitch a ride with his thumb before grudgingly giving way to Colbert, who shows a bit of her leg and brings a passing automobile screeching to a halt. Critics today applaud the film's deft mixture of comedy and social commentary, with its charming hero and heroine on the road in a nation suffering through the calamity of dislocation and uprootedness brought on by the Depression. Grossing over $6 million, *It Happened One Night* swept the major Academy Awards—an unprecedented feat—including a best actress award for Colbert. A landmark picture, it cemented her stardom and established her gifts as a comic actress.

Over the next several years Colbert demonstrated her considerable versatility. She played a working mother in the melodrama *Imitation of Life* (1934), gave a campy performance as the title character in De Mille's *Cleopatra* (1934), and portrayed a dedicated psychiatrist in *Private Worlds* (1935), for which she received an Academy Award nomination as best actress. She also gave effective performances in historical dramas such as *Maid of Salem* (1937) and *Drums along the Mohawk* (1939). But her best work came in romantic comedies: Ernst Lubitsch's *Bluebeard's Eighth Wife* (1938), Mitchell Leisen's hilarious *Midnight* (1939), Woody Van Dyke's *It's a Wonderful World* (1939), and Preston Sturges's anarchic *The Palm Beach Story* (1942). In a genre dominated by zany screwball heroines, Colbert was unique: she played chic modern women who were keenly intelligent and self-assured. As the film critic Jeanine Basinger has pointed out, the opening scene from *Midnight* exemplifies the typical Colbert character: she arrives at a Paris train station in miserable weather, fast asleep and penniless. She has lost all of her money gambling in Monte Carlo; all she has is her gorgeous evening gown. She wakes up, wryly comments, "So this, as they say, is Paris, huh?," covers her head with a newspaper, and darts off into the rain to seek her fortune—the master of her situation.

Although Colbert was at the height of her stardom during the late 1930s, she made few good pictures thereafter. Film historians have speculated that her choice of roles was limited because she failed to establish a working liaison with a top-flight director—similar to Marlene Dietrich's relationship with Josef von Sternberg, or John Wayne's with John Ford. Although she was respected by her colleagues, she had a reputation for being "incredibly professional but not at all pliable" (quoted in Everson, p. 24); always diligent that she look her best on the screen, her contracts stipulated that she would not work after five p.m., when she became tired, and she generally refused to have the right side of her face photographed (she believed that her nose looked crooked from that angle). Her reputation for inflexibility probably impeded her film career in the 1940s, when she appeared primarily in mediocre comedies, including several with Fred MacMurray. Her most important film during the decade was *Since You Went Away* (1944), a typically glossy David O. Selznick production about the American home front during World War II; she was nominated for an Academy Award for her portrayal of a mother. But she also withdrew from two fine films that might have bolstered her career: *State of the Union* (1947), after a disagreement with director Frank Capra, and *All About Eve* (1950), after she injured herself shortly before the production began.

After making a handful of weak pictures in the early 1950s, Colbert turned her attention to television and the stage. She made guest appearances on several television programs and starred in a special production of Noël Coward's *Blithe Spirit* on CBS. In 1956 she returned to Broadway, replacing Margaret Sullavan in *Janus*. In 1958 she costarred with Charles Boyer in the hit play *The Marriage Go-Round*, which ran for 450 performances. During the late 1950s she hosted a television documentary program, "Women," which dealt with topical problems affecting American women. In 1961 she made an unfortunate final film, *Parrish*, a soap-operatic drama intended to build the career of Troy Donahue. In 1963 she announced her retirement from films and her intention to continue on stage. She divided her free time between her homes in Barbados and Manhattan, with her husband, Joel Pressman, a surgeon whom she had married in 1935; they had no children and remained married until his death in 1968. She continued to appear occasionally on Broadway until she was in her late seventies. Newspaper critics who commented on her performances invariably mentioned that she looked much younger than her years; after a lifetime of taking exquisitely good care of herself, she remained svelte and energetic. In 1987 she made a well-received television movie, *The Two Mrs. Grenvilles*. She died in Barbados.

• The only biography of Colbert is Lawrence J. Quirk's mediocre *Claudette Colbert: An Illustrated Biography* (1985). William K. Everson, *Claudette Colbert* (1976), is a fine critical analysis of her screen career. See also Stephen Harvey, "Claudette Colbert," in *Film Comment*, Mar./Apr. 1984, pp. 59–61. For Colbert's contributions to romantic comedy, see James Harvey's indispensable *Romantic Comedy in Hollywood from Lubitsch to Sturges* (1987). Also valuable is Elizabeth Kendall, *The Runaway Bride: Hollywood Romantic Comedy of the 1930s* (1990). For Colbert's rocky relationship with Frank Capra, see Joseph McBride, *Frank Capra: The Catastrophe of Success* (1992). For her much more cordial relationship with Mitchell Leisen, see David Chierichetti, *Hollywood Director: The Career of Mitchell Leisen* (1973). For her work with Preston Sturges on *The Palm Beach Story*, see Diane Jacobs, *Christmas in July: The Life and Art of Preston Sturges* (1992). An obituary is in the *New York Times*, 31 July 1996.

THOMAS W. COLLINS, JR.

COLBY, William E. (4 Jan. 1920–28 Apr. 1996), intelligence officer, was born in St. Paul, Minnesota, the son of Elbridge Colby, an army officer and educator, and Margaret Mary Egan Colby, an ardent Catholic who guided her son in the path of that religion. William Colby was also influenced by his father's liberal views and by the family's peripatetic movements to locations as diverse as China and Vermont, where he studied at Burlington High School. He attended Princeton University, where he felt himself to be an outsider, educated as he had been at public schools and presenting, at five feet, eight inches, topped by eyeglasses, the appearance of a young man unlikely to win acceptance through athletic prowess. He graduated with an A.B. in 1940.

In 1941 Colby joined the U.S. Army and in 1943 the Office of Strategic Services (OSS). The OSS trained him for special missions, and he served behind enemy lines in France and Norway. In an effort to prevent German troops from being redeployed through Norway to be used against advancing Allied forces in Germany, he led the raid to destroy the Tangen railroad bridge—a daring and spectacular success, though the bridge was soon rebuilt.

In 1945 Colby married Barbara Heinzen; they had four children. He obtained a law degree from Columbia University in 1947, the same year that Congress approved the formation of the Central Intelligence Agency (CIA). After working for a short time in a law firm, Colby in 1949 joined the new agency. He served in Stockholm (1951–1953) and then in Rome (1953–1958), where he helped to arrange the secret subsidization of political parties to prevent communist electoral victories. Most of the recipients were centrist or slightly left of center, a political alignment that proved effective in combating communism but that gave Colby the reputation of having endorsed the "opening to the Left."

Colby was CIA station chief in Saigon from 1959 to 1962 and headed the agency's Far East division from 1962 to 1967. Then from 1968 to 1971 he directed the Phoenix program in South Vietnam, which sought to identify and eliminate communist activists (the Viet Cong) at the village level. Colby felt that the program was superior to the use of military force, which he believed was too blunt an instrument and alienated the Vietnamese. Nevertheless, estimates of the number killed under Phoenix range as high as 60,000 people. (Colby put the number at 20,587.) Phoenix has also been defended on relativist grounds—the Viet Cong assassinated nearly 40,000 of their enemies in the period from 1957 to 1972. But none of these arguments could prevent the program from becoming a focal point of the antiwar movement. Although Colby maintained that the deaths

characteristically arose in combat and not as a result of cold-blooded murder, critics of Phoenix labeled it an assassination program and a crime against humanity.

After Phoenix, Colby rose within the CIA's Washington bureaucracy, and on 4 September 1973 President Richard Nixon appointed him director of the agency. During his tenure the press and Congress turned on the CIA, accusing it of crimes and misdemeanors ranging from assassination plots to espionage against Americans at home. When in 1975 both houses of Congress set up inquiries into the activities of the intelligence community, Colby offered significant if limited cooperation. For example, he handed over to the Senate committee chaired by Idaho Democrat Frank Church details of the CIA's recent operations against the left-leaning government in Chile. The agency's attempts to sabotage the Chilean economy had contributed to the downfall of South America's oldest democracy and to the installation of a vicious dictatorship. Colby's candor on such matters shocked colleagues in the CIA, some of whom never forgave him for opening up the activities of what was, after all, a secret agency. His only daughter, Catherine, had died after a painful illness in April 1973, and colleagues speculated that the tragedy unlocked what some regarded as Colby's already overdeveloped Christian conscience. Though he strenuously denied that his daughter had opposed Phoenix, perhaps Colby did want to atone for his part in the program. It is also clear that he disapproved of certain of the CIA's activities that he called "deplorable" and "wrong" and wanted them stopped. In any case, he realized that a display of flexibility in his dealings with Congress would increase the agency's chances of survival.

With CIA morale at a low ebb, Colby's enemies began to line up. On the Left, a coalition of muckraking journalists, Vietnam War critics, and ambitious legislators refused to give him credit for attempting to open up the agency. On the Right, conservatives such as Barry Goldwater disliked Colby's liberalism and concessions to the Church committee. Colby had become politically vulnerable, and on 30 January 1976 President Gerald Ford replaced him with George H. W. Bush. Colby had introduced some significant reforms, such as the prohibition of assassination as an instrument of national policy and the practice of informing select members of Congress about the CIA's activities, but his intelligence career was over.

Colby's life continued to be eventful. In 1978 he published his memoir, *Honorable Men*, in which he defended himself against the Left over Phoenix and against the Right over his decision to clear the air while director of the CIA. In 1982, following the enactment of stringent secrecy legislation in the administration of President Ronald Reagan, the U.S. government began proceedings against Colby for making unauthorized disclosures, in the French-language edition of his memoir, about American efforts to retrieve secret codes from a sunken Soviet submarine. His agreement to pay a $10,000 fine in an out-of-court settlement barely covered the cracks between Colby and his enemies on the Right.

In 1984 Colby divorced his first wife and married a former diplomat, Sally Shelton. He had resumed legal practice and lectured widely, taking up a new cause—the campaign for a freeze on nuclear arms. On a spring day in 1996, Colby went down to the waterfront near his weekend home in Rock Point, Maryland, and launched his canoe into a stiff breeze. Until his body was found several days later with no evident signs of foul play, the press had one more chance to speculate about the fate of a man whose manner of death seemed to conjure up the enigma of his life.

• The William E. Colby Papers are located in the Seeley G. Mudd Library, Princeton University; some of Colby's Vietnam papers are in the Vietnam Collection at Texas Tech University. Colby's autobiography, *Honorable Men: My Life in the CIA* (1978), was written in association with Peter Forbath. Colby's *Lost Victory* (1989; with James McCargar) further addresses his activities in Vietnam. Hal Ford of the CIA's history staff has written a monograph on Colby's tenure as director, but it has not yet been declassified. Context on key episodes in his life is in Douglas Valentine, *The Phoenix Program* (1990), and Loch K. Johnson, *A Season of Inquiry: Congress and Intelligence*, 2d ed. (1988). Obituaries are in the *New York Times*, the *Washington Post*, and the *Los Angeles Times*, 7 May 1996.

RHODRI JEFFREYS-JONES

COLEMAN, James S. (12 May 1926–25 Mar. 1995), sociologist and educator, was born James Samuel Coleman in Bedford, Indiana, the son of James Fox Coleman, a factory foreman, and Maurine Lappin Coleman. He spent his early childhood in Bedford, then moved to Louisville, Kentucky, with his family and attended Manual High School, where he was a member of the football and track teams. After graduating in 1944 he enrolled briefly at a small, nonaccredited college in rural Virginia but left to enlist in the U.S. Navy that same year and served in the Atlantic during the remaining months of World War II. Discharged in 1946, he enrolled at Indiana University, then transferred to Purdue University, earning a B.S. in chemical engineering in 1949.

After graduating from college, Coleman worked for two years as a chemist at the Eastman Kodak Company in Rochester, New York. During this time, when the Cold War had emerged as a national issue, prompting widespread public discussion and debate over the nature of democracy, Coleman's interest in social issues grew, and he decided that he wanted to change careers. In 1951 he enrolled at Columbia University to pursue graduate work in sociology. During his time at Columbia, he spent two years as a research associate with the Bureau of Applied Social Research (1953–1955) and contributed a chapter to *Mathematical Thinking in the Social Sciences* (1954), a book edited by Paul F. Lazarsfeld, one of the first scholars to apply statistics to sociological studies. Coleman was awarded a Ph.D. in sociology in 1955, and his doc-

toral dissertation became the basis of his first book, *Union Democracy: The Internal Politics of the International Typographical Union* (1956), which he wrote with two other sociologists, Seymour M. Lipset and Martin A. Trow.

Following Columbia, Coleman spent a year as a fellow of the Center for Advanced Study in the Behavioral Sciences at Palo Alto, California. In the fall of 1956 he joined the faculty of the University of Chicago as an assistant professor of sociology; during his three years there he wrote and published his second book, *Community Conflict* (1957). He also began work, in collaboration with two other sociologists, Kurt Jonassohn and John W. C. Johnstone, on a study of Illinois high schools that was commissioned by the U.S. Office of Education. Begun in 1957, the same year that Coleman joined the faculty of Johns Hopkins University as an associate professor of social relations, the study—which involved extensive on-site interviews with students, teachers, administrators, and parents and examined all aspects of school life, including the role of teenagers in the larger community—was published four years later as a government monograph titled *Social Climates in High Schools* (1961). A book based on the study was also published in 1961: *The Adolescent Society: The Social Life of the Teenager and Its Impact on Education*. A second book growing out of the study, *Adolescents and the Schools*, was published in 1965. By this time Coleman was a full professor at Johns Hopkins, having been promoted in 1959.

The research that Coleman and his colleagues had begun in the late 1950s showed that American teenagers overall valued social and athletic success more than academic achievement—a startling and disheartening conclusion at a time when the United States was challenging the Soviet Union's demonstrated superiority in space exploration. In his books Coleman suggested several changes that might promote classroom success, among them school competitions in academic subjects, the abandonment of coeducation in favor of single-sex schools, and improved teacher training. Coleman's work received generally favorable reviews, though it seems to have had little impact beyond provoking further debate on the nature and purpose of public education.

But Coleman himself was now recognized in the public eye as a leading authority on U.S. schools, and as such he was a likely choice to head a special study on race and public education mandated by the 1964 Civil Rights Act. Appointed by the U.S. Commissioner of Education, Coleman and his co-chairman, Ernest Q. Campbell of Vanderbilt University, began work in the fall of 1965. With Coleman designated as the chief designer and overseer, the study focused on the education offered to blacks, Native Americans, Mexican Americans, Puerto Ricans, Asians, and poor whites. It sampled 600,000 pupils in grades one through twelve, 60,000 teachers, and hundreds of administrators in some 4,000 schools throughout the United States. Pupils were given achievement tests that evaluated cultural skills then deemed necessary for social and economic success. The results of the $1.5 million study were published in the fall of 1966 as a 737-page report titled *Equality of Educational Opportunity*, which quickly became known as the "Coleman Report."

The findings of the study were disturbing. Racial segregation was seen to be still widespread in American schools, more than a decade after it had been banned by the U.S. Supreme Court, and pupils at predominantly nonwhite schools had, as expected, had lower achievement rates than those in predominantly white schools. But inferior material resources and larger classes were not the factors principally to blame for the low achievement levels. What seemed more likely to be at fault were the deprived social and educational backgrounds of most of the teachers in nonwhite institutions, as well as the deprived home environments of the pupils themselves. Among the startling findings in the study was the fact that nonwhite pupils in segregated schools fell further behind their white counterparts with each grade level attained. Furthermore, black children were found to have a dropout rate almost twice that of whites, and less than 5 percent of U.S. college students were black. The Coleman Report also found that in schools that were predominantly white and middle-class, nonwhite students from lower economic levels did somewhat better in the classroom without hurting the achievements of the white majority. The overall conclusion of the Coleman Report was implicit in its findings: spending more money on facilities would not improve performance at so-called ghetto schools, but integration—into schools where both teachers and pupils were middle-class—might.

Although there were some negative reactions to the report—some critics challenged the accuracy of Coleman's sampling techniques, others argued that in measuring achievement he placed too much stress on verbal ability, and some black leaders accused Coleman of being racist—it was largely accepted as groundwork for public policy on both sides of the political fence. Commissioned and accepted by the administration of Democratic president Lyndon B. Johnson, it later became the cornerstone of Republican president Richard M. Nixon's proposals for educational reform. Efforts to achieve integration were made a top priority, and several billion dollars were allocated for that purpose during the Nixon administration. Chief among the tools used for integration was busing—moving both white and nonwhite students from their neighborhood schools to achieve racial parity. Busing proved to be controversial and unpopular, however, and it often had the effect of forcing nonminority children out of the public schools altogether and, especially in the South, into newly founded all-white private academies—a phenomenon known as "white flight." After more than a decade of court efforts to enforce it, the policy was gradually phased out in most communities.

Although Coleman himself had been in favor of busing as a tool to achieve school integration, he was forced to acknowledge its failure in a second study, published in 1975, two years after his return to the University of Chicago as University Professor of Sociology. His abandonment of busing made Coleman the subject of virulent attacks from liberals, who accused him of abandoning the cause of integration. He was publicly censured by many of his colleagues, including leaders of the American Sociological Association, who tried unsuccessfully to have him expelled from the organization. (Sixteen years later, in 1991, Coleman was elected president of the ASA.) But Coleman continued, undaunted, to study the plight of minority students and offer proposals to improve their education. In another controversial study, published in 1981, he concluded that such students did better at Catholic and private schools, largely because of superior discipline.

Coleman wrote more than thirty books and published numerous articles in the course of his long career. He also created an educational corporation that developed and marketed "mental games" aimed at improving the abilities of disadvantaged students. At the time of his death, he was engaged in a long-term study titled "The High School and Beyond," which examined the lives and careers of 75,000 people who had been high school juniors and seniors in 1980. In addition to his strong interest in education, Coleman also specialized in the study of communities, the subject of his book *Foundations of Social Theory* (1990). He considered this analysis of the formation and behavior of communities of all sorts—ranging from towns to trade unions—to be his best book.

Coleman was married twice. His first wife, whom he married in 1949, was Lucille Richey; the couple had three sons before divorcing in 1973. That same year he married Zdzislawa Walaszek, with whom he had another son. Coleman died of prostate cancer at a Chicago hospital.

• For biographical information, see "Coleman, James S(amuel)," in *Current Biography Yearbook 1970* and an obituary from the *New York Times*, Mar. 1995, in *Current Biography 1995*. See also *Contemporary Authors*, vols. 13–16 (1975), pp. 171–72, and "Coleman, James Samuel," in *Who Was Who in America*, vol. 11 (1996). For an assessment of the Coleman Report, see Christopher Jencks, "A Reappraisal of the Most Controversial Education Document of Our Time," *New York Times Magazine*, 10 Aug. 1969, pp. 12ff; see also the follow-up discussions of this article, including reader responses, in the issues of 14 Sept. 1969, pp. 74ff., and 12 Oct. 1969, pp. 12ff. In addition, see H. M. Levin, "The Coleman Report," *Saturday Review*, 20 Jan. 1968, pp. 57ff. An obituary appears in the *New York Times*, 28 Mar. 1995; see also a correction of this obituary in the *Times*, 8 Apr. 1995.

ANN T. KEENE

COMEY, Dennis J. (26 May 1896–14 Oct. 1987), Roman Catholic clergyman and labor arbitrator, was born Dennis Joseph Comey in Philadelphia, Pennsylvania, the son of Dennis Joseph Comey, an iron worker at the Baldwin Locomotive Works, and Catherine Veronica Reagan Comey; the parents had been farmers who emigrated from Timoleague, County Cork, Ireland. The oldest of thirteen children, he excelled in studies and athletics at St. Joseph's College Preparatory School in Philadelphia. On 30 July 1914 he entered the Society of Jesus at St. Andrew-on-Hudson, Poughkeepsie, New York, and continued his classical studies. He earned his A.B. (1920), M.A. (1921), and Ph.D. (1929) in philosophy from Woodstock College, Maryland; he first taught Latin at Boston College High School (1921–1922) and then Latin, Greek, Spanish, and rhetoric at Georgetown University, Washington, D.C. (1922–1925). He pursued theological studies at Woodstock College, where he was ordained a Roman Catholic priest on 20 June 1928. A year's concentration on ascetical theology at St. Beuno's College, Wales, preceded his solemn profession of his Jesuit vows in Rome, Italy, on 15 August 1931. In 1931 the Gregorian University in Rome named him a doctor of theology and in 1932 *magister aggregatus*. From 1932 to 1937 he was professor of theology at Woodstock College and from 1937 to 1943 president of St. Peter's College in Jersey City, New Jersey.

Comey returned to Philadelphia to join the faculty of St. Joseph's College, where in 1935 Richard M. McKeon, S.J., had founded the first labor school in a Jesuit institution of higher learning. Comey implemented an academically demanding three-year curriculum exemplifying the Jesuit pedagogy of rational eloquence intended to equip union members for public speaking, informed discussion, and contract negotiations. Based on principles outlined in Pope Leo XIII's encyclical about improving working conditions throughout the world (*Rerum novarum*, 1891) and Pope Pius XI's call for reconstruction of the social order (*Quadragesimo anno*, 1931), the school stressed the rights of workers to organize, to receive just wages, and to negotiate regarding their working conditions. The new curriculum offered an alternative to Communism ("Workers of the world unite!") and laissez-faire capitalism. Comey believed that principled teaching should be "ruggedly practical" and that one-sided education is not true education. In 1943, insisting that the hyphen is the most important part of "labor-management relations" (Comey, *Waterfront Peacemaker*, p. 2), Comey named his program the Institute of Industrial Relations. His goal was to "replace emotion with reason, anger with decorum, self-seeking with ethics." Free night classes taught by volunteers from labor and management enrolled over 6,000 students. Edward F. Toohey, president of the Philadelphia Council of the AFL-CIO, said that hundreds of union officers and management executives "learned their lessons in labor-management cooperation through the Comey Institute and in his classes on ethics and moral law" (*Philadelphia Inquirer*, 15 Oct. 1987). Longshoremen's work stoppages sometimes added up to more than a third of the year. The cost was heavy for workers, man-

agement, and Philadelphia. In 1951 the Philadelphia Marine Trade Association (PMTA) agreed with the International Longshoremen's Association (ILA) that binding arbitration should replace labor-management confrontation. Comey was named "permanent arbitrator" with the right to inspect the docks at will. Philadelphia ceased to have the wildcat strikes that plagued other ports. Labor experts from Ireland, Denmark, Germany, Egypt, Japan, as well as from the United States and Canada came to study Comey's institute.

Margaret Bourke-White's photograph of Comey involved in dockside arbitration, which appeared in *Life* magazine, was captioned: "Both workers and shippers have such confidence in Father Comey, that by mutual agreement they have made him arbiter of the waterfront with unrestricted power to adjust all disputes" ("The Jesuits in America," *Life*, 11 Oct. 1954). The dispute she witnessed concerned a contractual agreement for extra pay in "unusually distressing circumstances." Comey went down into the holds to examine the damp, stained sacks of sugar and decided against the union. The workers were unhappy, but they knew that he had awarded them time-and-a-half pay even when no one had complained about filthy holds. The union soon asked Comey to supervise its elections. In 1958, convinced that the principles and procedures were now in place for labor and management to settle their own disputes, he resigned as permanent arbitrator but continued to mediate, arbitrate, and supervise elections. In 1976 he asked his associate William A. Dawson, S.J., to design an undergraduate major in industrial relations at St. Joseph's University—a program Comey directed until his retirement in 1981.

Comey served on many boards. In 1953 President Dwight D. Eisenhower named him to the Taft-Hartley Board when the longshoremen's work stoppages threatened to shut down East Coast shipping. In 1963 Governor William W. Scranton appointed him to the advisory board in the Pennsylvania Department of Labor and Industry. In 1964 James H. J. Tate, the mayor of Philadelphia and an alumnus of Comey's institute (1945–1946), named him to the Mayor's Commission of Transit Labor Relations and the City Board of Labor Standards.

His publications included a weekly column on social justice for the *Catholic Standard and Times* (1953–1962); "May Doctors Strike?" *Medical Science*, Feb. 1968, pp. 49–53; monographs such as *The Lonely Supervisor* (1979), *The Function of a Shop Steward* (1979), and *The Business Manager* (1980); and a personal narrative, *Waterfront Peacemaker* (1983). He was often honored for his contributions to improve industrial relations: from the 1955 Page One Award of the Newspaper Guild of Greater Philadelphia to a bronze bust presented to St. Joseph's University in 1992 by the United Food and Commercial Workers (UFCW).

Alfred Corry, executive secretary and later president of the PMTA, summed up Comey's achievement: "The PMTA and ILA are jointly proud to have established a unique and distinctive contribution to peace. We stand alone. There is no record that any other port dared to match the Philadelphia experience" (Foreword, *Waterfront Peacemaker*, p. x). Trusted by both sides as an impartial referee and an "unrelenting advocate of the law and order written into a labor agreement," Comey was the linchpin. As Pennsylvania governor Robert P. Casey said, "The inspiration and encouragement of Comey's legacy was to follow the principles of fairness, decency and justice" ("Address," 9 Dec. 1992).

Asked when he became interested in labor-management relations, Comey quipped, "From the beginning of my life. My father was labor and my mother was management." He maintained that honest collective bargaining, with both sides aware of the legal premises and economic pitfalls, was the most important principle in American industry.

• A fire in 1966 destroyed most of the Institute of Industrial Relations' records. Comey's surviving papers are preserved in the St. Joseph's University archives, and relevant material is in the Urban Archives of Temple University, Philadelphia, Pa. Comey's columns on labor relations for the Philadelphia *Catholic Standard and Times* (1953–1962) also appeared in the *Star-Herald* of Camden, N.J., and the *Monitor* of Trenton, N.J. For the best study of Comey's years as permanent arbitrator, see Patrick Connelly, "The Philadelphia Experiment: Dennis J. Comey and the Origins of Job-Site Arbitration in the Port of Philadelphia, 1951–1959" (M.A. thesis, Villanova Univ., 1999). See also Anon., "They Put No Limits on Philadelphia's Dock Priest," *Business Week*, 6 June 1953, pp. 158–61; John McCarthy, "Father Comey: Labor Umpire," *Readers Digest*, Aug. 1954, pp. 32–37; Irwin Ross, "All Quiet on the Philadelphia Waterfront," *Readers Digest*, Sept. 1955, pp. 107–10; John LaFarge, S.J., and Margaret Bourke-White, *A Report on the American Jesuits* (1956); Hans Knight, "St. Joseph's Father Comey," *Sunday Bulletin Magazine*, 7 Apr. 1963, pp. 4–5; Adrian Lee, "'Waterfront Priest' Had Humble Origins," *Catholic Standard and Times*, 13 Jan. 1983, p. 19; and Maureen H. O'Connell, "Jesuit Tradition: Philadelphia's Waterfront Priest," *Saint Joseph's University Magazine*, Fall 2000, pp. 16–17. An obituary is in the *Philadelphia Inquirer*, 15 Oct. 1987.

FRANCIS F. BURCH

COMMAGER, Henry Steele (25 Oct. 1902–2 Mar. 1998), historian, educator and editor, was born in Pittsburgh, Pennsylvania, the son of James Williams Commager and Anna Elizabeth Dan Commager. Orphaned as a child, Commager was raised by his maternal grandfather, of Danish origin, in Toledo, Ohio, and Chicago, Illinois. After graduating from high school in Chicago, he attended the University of Chicago. He received a Ph.B. in 1923, an M.A. in 1924, and in 1928 a Ph.D. in history, his dissertation, unpublished, being "[Johann Friedrich von] Struensee and the Reform Movement in Denmark." Later Commager studied at the University of Copenhagen, Cambridge University, and Oxford University. He taught American history at New York University, as instructor (1926–1929), assistant professor (1929–1930), associate professor (1930–1931), and professor (1931–1938). He then established long careers as professor at Columbia University (1939–1956) and Amherst College (1956–1972). Between 1941 and

1975 Commager, who enjoyed traveling and associating with American and foreign students, was guest professor at twenty or more universities in the United States and in Chile, Denmark, England, France, Germany, Israel, Italy, Japan, Mexico, and Trinidad. During World War II, he served in the War Department's Office of War Information (England, 1943; France and Belgium, 1945). In 1928 Commager married Evan Carroll, with whom he had three children; she died in 1968. Eleven years later, Commager married Mary E. Powlesland.

A man of great energy and self-assurance, extraordinary memory, and single-minded professional dedication, Commager interpreted the U.S. Constitution, American history, and American studies to and with responsive students for sixty-five years. He published, edited, wrote, coauthored, contributed to, or editorially supervised more than a hundred books. He wrote for popular and scholarly periodicals. His bibliography includes original interpretations of American democracy, biographies of American leaders, editions of source material, and textbooks for university and college students and juvenile readers as well. His unwavering ambition was to help scholars and ordinary readers to understand and learn from America's past, and hence to appreciate their heritage, in order to more knowledgeably advance the cause of freedom and democracy. Commager's style is down-to-earth, straightforward, unaffected, and persuasive.

It is difficult to choose among Commager's publications to demonstrate his main concerns and versatility. The following are representative: *The Growth of the American Republic* (1930), *Documents of American History* (1934), *Theodore Parker* (1936), *The American Mind: An Interpretation of American Thought and Character since the 1880's* (1950), *The Search for a Usable Past, and Other Essays in Historiography* (1967), *Jefferson, Nationalism, and the Enlightenment* (1975), and *The Empire of Reason: How Europe Imagined and America Realized the Enlightenment* (1977).

The Growth of the American Republic, written with Samuel Eliot Morison, was initially an expansion of Morison's *The Oxford History of the United States, 1783–1917* (1927). In plain style, this collaboration describes the formation of the national government, Western expansion and settlement, political activities, America's evolutionary foreign policy, the Old South, the Civil War and Reconstruction, and the emergence of the United States as a world power. Often revised (since 1969 partly by William Leuchtenburg), the work is enhanced by excellent maps, tables, and bibliographies.

Documents of American History originally contained almost five hundred documents illustrating the course of American history from the age of discovery, with introductory notes and a bibliography. Each document sheds light on its own era or later epochs, or both. Periodically updated to delete less vital items and make room for numerous additions, it is often referred to by grateful researchers as "Commager's Documents." He compiled a similar but more specialized documentary anthology titled *The Blue and the Gray: The Story of the Civil War as Told by Participants* (2 vols., 1950).

Commager's biography of Theodore Parker was at once recognized as a provocative, nonjudgmental account of the elusive antebellum preacher, reformer, and abolitionist, as he saw himself and as his contemporaries saw him. Parker emerges as tough-minded and brave in taking religion down from the pulpit and espousing his brand of practical idealism at ground level. Some reviewers faulted Commager for stressing Parker's energy more than its successful use, but the fact-crammed work deserved being reissued in 1960 with a new introduction.

The American Mind is Commager's most personally revealing book. He wished he could call it "Prolegomenon to an Interpretation of Some Aspects of American Thought and Character from the 1880's to the 1940's." To Commager, American thinkers, while hoping for the triumph of democracy, were caught between contrary impulses: admiring the heroes of, and feeling victimized by, social and economic Darwinism but also seeking through amelioristic governmental action to control ruthless robber barons and thus to improve the lives of ordinary people. Commager eruditely finds evidence in a range of American thought, from written words through religious to architectural achievements. Americans he especially admires are as diverse as Henry Adams, Oliver Wendell Holmes, William James, V. L. Parrington, Franklin D. Roosevelt, Louis Sullivan, Frederick Jackson Turner, Thorstein Veblen, Lester Ward, Woodrow Wilson, and Frank Lloyd Wright. Although praised as a synthesis of history and philosophy, *The American Mind* has been criticized for hedging conclusions and lacking originality. All the same, its sure and certain sweep is awesome.

A series of volumes published fairly late in Commager's career demonstrate his abiding interest in eighteenth-century European and American thought: two collections of essays, *The Search for a Usable Past* (1967) and *Jefferson, Nationalism, and the Enlightenment* (1975), both of which mainly collect previous essays, and *The Empire of Reason* (1977). Cheerfully eclectic, he suggests that New World leaders, notably Ben Franklin, Tom Paine, John Adams, and Thomas Jefferson, did not simply echo the Enlightenment theories of Old World thinkers but instead realized and fulfilled them in the Declaration of Independence, the Constitution, and other key documents and acts. While some reviewers lamented certain omissions, others applauded Commager's vigorous prose and detailed documentation. Toward the end of the twentieth century, revisionist historians have complained that Commager's Jeffersonian view of America ignores the significance of religion in the lives of the downtrodden, is inattentive to Native and African Americans, and remains overly optimistic and pragmatic. Such critics, however, ignore Commager's contention that 1890 was a watershed for Americans, after which, though resourceful in meeting horrific twentieth-century crises, they have declined creatively and morally.

Exigencies of space prevent more than passing mention of Commager's publications concerning the American Revolution; his 1947 anthology of descriptions of America by foreign observers over the centuries (*America in Perspective: The United States through Foreign Eyes*); his 1951 biography of Robert E. Lee for young readers; his criticism of tyrannical majorities and undemocratic Supreme Court decisions alike; his preferences for diplomacy over reliance on the atomic bomb; his faith in the United Nations; and his fear of Russia. Effective to the last, Commager, when ninety-one and nearly blind, published a book-length interpretation of *Democracy in America*, Alexis de Tocqueville's 1840 classic analysis of the country's ethos. Commager's professional friendships included the following coauthors (in addition to Morison): Eugene Campbell Barker, Brand Blanchard, Geoffrey Brunn, Elmo Giordanetti, Robert Ward McEwen, Richard Brandon Morris, and Allan Nevins. All have joined in regarding him as both fiercely dedicated and inspiringly amiable. Commager died in Amherst, Massachusetts.

• Commager's papers, including proof of a voluminous correspondence, are widely scattered. Considerable material is at Columbia University, Harvard University, the University of Illinois, Iowa State University, the Library of Congress, the State Historical Society of Wisconsin, and Yale University. John A. Garraty, *Interpreting American History: Conversations with Historians* (1970), includes his engaging exchange with Commager. In their preface to *Freedom and Reform: Essays in Honor of Henry Steele Commager* (1967), Harold M. Hyman and Leonard W. Levy, eds., describe their mentor as an "implacable rationalist" of "awesome" ability as teacher-lecturer and scholar-writer; an accompanying bibliography of Commager's publications lists 373 items through 1966. Commager's obituary, with an illustration, is in the *New York Times*, 3 Mar. 1998.

ROBERT L. GALE

CONDON, Richard (18 Mar. 1915–9 Apr. 1996), writer, was born Richard Thomas Condon in the borough of Manhattan, New York City, the son of Richard Aloysius Condon, a lawyer and aide to New York governor Alfred E. Smith, and Martha Pickering Condon, a secretary in her husband's firm. Richard was reared in Washington Heights, an upper-middle-class area of New York City. Overcoming a speech impediment and a poor academic history, he graduated in 1934 from De Witt Clinton High School, where he excelled as a swimmer.

After graduation, Condon began working in a hotel as an elevator operator, the first in a series of low-paying jobs. The publication of his first article in *Esquire* helped to secure him a position as a copywriter at an advertising firm. During this time Condon's "Mid-Summer Skiing in Chile" appeared in *Town and Country*; the article was favorably received even though its author had never visited South America. In 1938 he wed former model Evelyn Rose Hunt. Their marriage, which produced two daughters, lasted until Condon's death.

Soon after his marriage Condon was hired as publicity director at Walt Disney Productions, where he was responsible for promoting such Disney hits as *Fantasia* (1940) and *Dumbo* (1941). Gaining a reputation as an effective publicist, Condon over the next twenty years would work for several large Hollywood studios, including Twentieth Century-Fox, United Artists, and Paramount. In the early 1950s, with José Ferrer, he produced for the stage, among other plays, Donald Bevan and Edmund Trzcinski's *Stalag 17* and Ben Hecht and Charles MacArthur's *Twentieth Century*, both of which had successful runs on Broadway; *Men of Distinction*, written by Condon, failed, closing after four shows.

Leaving a position at United Artists, Condon in 1958 published his first novel, *The Oldest Confession*, his years in the movie business having instilled in him "an unconscious grounding in storytelling." The book, whose plot revolves around art thievery, was both critically and commercially successful and led to a 1962 movie adaptation, *The Happy Thieves*, which foundered at the box office.

While *The Oldest Confession* brought him critical acclaim and hefty royalties, Condon's next novel, *The Manchurian Candidate*, was deemed "a triumph of satire and knowledge" and established his reputation as a "master of conspiracy theories." Published in 1959, the darkly humorous, cynical cold war thriller tells the story of Raymond Shaw, a former prisoner of the Korean war who is brainwashed and becomes an assassin for the Communists. The subplot of the novel concerns Shaw's stepfather, a McCarthy-like politician whom Shaw ultimately murders. The film version of the novel, directed by John Frankenheimer and starring Frank Sinatra, was released in 1962 but was removed from circulation by Sinatra soon after President John F. Kennedy was assassinated. The film was rereleased in the 1980s and has since achieved "cult classic" status.

Flush with his success from *The Manchurian Candidate*, Condon left the United States, living in Mexico City, Paris, and Switzerland throughout the 1960s. During this time he produced a string of mainly forgettable novels, with the exception of the favorably reviewed *An Infinity of Mirrors* (1964), a tale of a Nazi-era marriage between a German soldier and a Jewish woman. In 1971 Condon and his family relocated to Ireland, where he wrote *Winter Kills*, considered by many to be his best book since *The Manchurian Candidate*. The subject matter of *Winter Kills*—presidential murder and a Central Intelligence Agency cover-up—was controversial; despite critical praise and box-office success, its film adaptation (1979) vanished after only three weeks, likely a victim of its eery resemblance to the Kennedy assassination. Condon wrote steadily while in Ireland, publishing, among other works, *And Then We Moved to Rossenarra; or, The Art of Emigrating* (1973), one of only two nonfiction books written by Condon (the other was *The*

Mexican Stove [1972], cowritten with his daughter); *Money Is Love* (1975); and *Death of a Politician* (1978).

Condon's return to the United States in 1980 revived his career. He settled in Dallas, near his daughter's family, and began work on *Prizzi's Honor* (1982), the first of four novels about a mob family. *Prizzi's Family* (1986), *Prizzi's Glory* (1988), and *Prizzi's Money* (1994) followed, all attracting favorable reviews and selling briskly. A 1985 movie adaptation of *Prizzi's Honor* by the legendary film director John Huston received several Academy Award nominations. The Prizzi saga has been compared to Mario Puzo's *The Godfather*, with Condon interjecting a satirical sense of humor that Puzo sometimes lacked.

Condon continued writing until his death, producing in his last years *Emperor of America* (1990), which, according to reviewer Herbert Mitgang, "combine[d] the styles of *The Manchurian Candidate* and *Prizzi's Honor*" in a satire of the U.S. presidency (*New York Times*, 14 Feb. 1990), and *The Final Addiction* (1991), an imaginative "Reagan-Bush-Quayle-era thriller." Condon died in Dallas.

The theme that runs through most of Condon's twenty-six novels is abuse of power. According to the author, he set out to show people "how deeply their politicians are wronging them." The power that Condon railed against took many forms: communism in *The Manchurian Candidate*, the CIA in *Winter Kills*, and the Catholic Church in his 1983 novel *A Trembling upon Rome*. He seemed to genuinely believe that the conspiracies he wrote about in his books were real; he blamed Senator Edward Kennedy for the disappearance of the *Winter Kills* film. But his inclination toward paranoia made for entertaining, if sometimes uncomfortable, reading. Fellow author Donald E. Westlake, in his review of Condon's *The Venerable Bead* (1992), wrote that Condon "reflect[s] the real world through a slightly distorting mirror in which our near future grins back at us, without comfort" (*New York Times*, 13 Dec. 1992).

• There is no biography of Richard Condon. A lengthy article on the author, written by William Cobb late in Condon's life, is "The Don of Dallas," *Texas Monthly* 22, no. 8 (Aug. 1994). Condon's obituary is in the *New York Times*, 10 Apr. 1996.

STACEY HAMILTON

CONN, Billy (8 Oct. 1917–29 May 1993), world light-heavyweight boxing champion, was born William David Conn in East Liberty, Pennsylvania, a suburb of Pittsburgh. He was the oldest son of William Robert Conn, a steamfitter, and Irish-born Margaret McFarland Conn. Billy attended Sacred Heart Parochial School but his education ended with the fifth grade. He took up boxing after his father asked a friend, former boxer Johnny Ray, to teach his son how to defend himself. Ray soon found the boy to be an apt pupil and became his manager. Billy Conn had his first professional fight in 1934 at age sixteen, never having boxed as an amateur.

For the first year and a half of his career Conn did not distinguish himself, winning only eleven fights out of nineteen. Many of his bouts were held in small towns and cities in eastern Pennsylvania and West Virginia. Although six feet tall, he lacked muscular development and fought as a lightweight and welterweight. He grew into a middleweight in 1936 and won all of his eighteen fights that year, including a victory over local rival Fritzie Zivic, a future welterweight champion.

In 1937 Conn won six of eight fights, including victories over Babe Risko, Vince Dundee, Teddy Yarosz, and Young Corbett III, all of whom had been world champions. In 1938 he won six of seven fights, ending the year with a decisive victory over a middleweight title claimant, Solly Krieger, to whom he had lost in 1937.

In 1939 Conn, whose fights had heretofore been mostly in the Pittsburgh area, began to fight regularly in New York City. Twice he decisively beat Fred Apostoli, another claimant to the world middleweight title. Now a light-heavyweight, he again defeated Krieger and then fought Melio Bettina for the light-heavyweight championship of the world. Bettina's unusual left-handed style troubled Conn at first, but the Pittsburgher gained control by the seventh round and overwhelmed his opponent thereafter. Conn ended the year by again successfully defending his title, winning decisively over rugged Gus Lesnevich.

Conn was an exceptionally clever boxer, a quick thinker who often taunted his opponents in the ring. Ted Carroll, who saw him fight many times, described Conn thus:

> He mastered the knack of arm blocking to a degree that left his features completely unmarked . . . His left hook while not numbing was like a whiplash . . . Few light heavies took a punch as well . . . He did not rely on leg speed to the extent (of some brilliant boxers), but when he made a move it meant something and the moves were quick. He was as game as they come and had the competitive spirit to get up steam as a tough bout progressed and outfinish the other fellow with a burst of action. There have been few better "stretch performers."

In 1940 Conn established himself as a heavyweight challenger. He again defended his title successfully against Lesnevich and then beat four heavyweight contenders, including, by a knockout, Bob Pastor, who had fought Joe Louis for the heavyweight title.

The Pastor victory set the stage for Conn's most famous fight, in which he challenged Joe Louis for the heavyweight title at the Polo Grounds in New York City on 18 June 1941. Boxing brilliantly, Conn built a good lead on points, and Louis seemed on the verge of being knocked out in round twelve. Throwing aside caution and clever boxing tactics, Conn unwisely waded into close reach of his much heavier and harder-hitting opponent in round thirteen, going for a knockout. Louis soon hurt him severely with a short right hand and followed with a relentless barrage that sent Conn down for the count with just two seconds remaining in the round, thus ending a great fight and narrowly averting a tremendous upset.

In 1942, after easily outpointing middleweight champion Tony Zale, Conn was matched again with Louis. The fight was scheduled for June but had to be canceled when Conn sustained an injury. He had married Mary Louise Smith a few days after his fight with Louis, much to the displeasure of her father, "Greenfield" Jimmy Smith, a former major league baseball player. At the christening of their first child Jimmy Smith struck Conn, and the boxer retaliated with a blow to the jaw of his father-in-law, which resulted in his breaking a bone in his hand.

The second Louis-Conn fight was rescheduled for 12 October in Yankee Stadium. By that time both Louis and Conn had been inducted into the army, and the cooperation of the War Department was needed for the fight to be held. It was originally intended that all the profits of the fight would go to the Army Relief Fund, but promoter Mike Jacobs and Louis's manager, John Roxborough, altered the arrangements so that some of the money would be diverted to themselves to pay off debts of the fighters. Also it was arranged for "additional expenses" to be paid out of the profits, which caused Secretary of War Henry Stimson to cancel the fight and order the boxers back to their units.

For years, during World War II, the second Louis-Conn fight was anticipated with great interest. It was Louis's first title defense after the war and occurred on 19 June 1946. The fight drew a gate of nearly $2 million. As it unfolded, it was seen that the years in service had robbed Conn of his reflexes; Louis, although slowed, had boxed many exhibitions during the war years and seemed to have retained considerably more of his abilities. It was an extremely disappointing battle, with little action and no effective hitting by the challenger, and ended with Conn taking the full count in round eight.

Conn never again entered the ring with serious intentions. He had received $700,000 for his second fight with Louis, and this purse together with his earlier earnings allowed him to retire from the ring in good financial shape. He invested his savings intelligently in oil, a used car business, and other enterprises, and supported his wife and three sons comfortably. Despite his considerable wealth, he continued to live in the same house he purchased soon after his marriage. An inaugural inductee into the International Boxing Hall of Fame in 1990, he was to die of pneumonia in a Veterans Hospital in Pittsburgh.

• Conn's record as a boxer is given in Herbert G. Goldman, ed., *The Ring 1986–87 Record Book and Boxing Encyclopedia*. A short biography is available in *Current Biography: Who's News and Why 1941*, ed. Maxine Bloch, pp. 165–67. Several useful articles on Conn have appeared in *The Ring* magazine including Ted Carroll, "Billy Conn: The Collar Ad Hero,"

Aug. 1961, pp. 22–23, 45; Sam Andre, "Billy Conn: Boy Millionaire," Mar. 1963, pp. 16–19; and Joseph C. Tintle, "50 Years After Louis-Conn I: Remembering the Greatest Upset That Almost Was," Aug. 1991, pp. 43–45, 75. Also in *The Ring*, the column "Nat Fleischer Says," Dec. 1942, pp. 8–9, gives details of the cancelation of the second attempt to hold a Louis-Conn rematch. An obituary appears in the *New York Times*, 30 May 1993.

LUCKETT V. DAVIS

CONRAD, Pete (2 June 1930–8 July 1999), astronaut, was born Charles Peter Conrad in Philadelphia, Pennsylvania, the son of Charles Conrad, an investment broker, and Frances V. Sargent Conrad. He was called "Pete" from an early age because his mother liked the name. He was educated at the Haverford School in Haverford, Pennsylvania, and received his high school diploma from the Darrow School, New Lebanon, New York, in 1948. Like his father, who had served as a balloonist in World War I, Conrad was intrigued by flying. As a child, he built model airplanes. As a teenager, he hung around local garages and airfields, neglecting his schoolwork. He worked part time sweeping up in a machine shop to finance flying lessons and flew solo when he was sixteen. Encouraged by his father, he entered Princeton University in 1948 and earned a bachelor of science degree in aeronautical engineering in 1953.

Also in 1953 Conrad married Jane DuBose of Uvalde, Texas, whom he had met at Princeton. They had four sons, one of whom, Christopher, died of bone cancer at the age of 30. Conrad's first marriage ended in divorce in 1990; he then married Nancy Crane of Huntington Beach, California.

Conrad entered the U.S. Navy following his graduation from Princeton and became a naval aviator. In less than a year he went to the navy's test pilot school at Patuxent River, Maryland, and on completing that course of instruction in 1954 he was assigned as a project test pilot to the armaments test division. Although he applied, he was not chosen to be in the first group of American astronauts, the Mercury Seven, formed in 1958–1959. He always believed that he failed because he was too flippant when meeting psychologists who were screening the candidates. He relished telling the story of being asked to describe what he saw when shown a blank white card; his reply being that it was "upside down." In September 1962, however, he was accepted into the second class of NASA astronauts, who were assigned to Project Gemini. At the time, he was a safety officer with Fighter Squadron 96 at what was then Miramar Naval Air Station in San Diego, California.

Conrad flew his first space mission aboard Gemini V. Launched on 21 August 1965, he and command pilot L. Gordon Cooper flew 120 revolutions and covered a total distance of 3,312,993 statute miles. Terminated on 29 August 1965, the mission earned Conrad and Cooper space endurance records and enabled the United States to supplant the Soviet Union as leader in total flight hours in space. On 18 September 1966 Conrad flew as command pilot for the Gemini XI mission. In less than one orbit he was able to rendezvous with a previously launched Agena upper stage and practiced rendezvous and docking techniques that were necessary prerequisite steps in reaching the Moon during Project Apollo. He and his close friend Richard F. Gordon, Jr., piloted Gemini XI during extravehicular activity, set a new space altitude record, and completed the first fully automatic controlled reentry.

In November 1969 Conrad served as spacecraft commander for Apollo 12, the second lunar landing mission. Again, Richard Gordon was command module pilot, while Alan L. Bean served as lunar module pilot and accompanied Conrad to the Moon's surface. Although Apollo 12 was enormously important in the larger context of the lunar landing program, it has not received the attention it deserves. In July 1969 Apollo 11 had satisfied John F. Kennedy's mandate that the United States be the first to put a human on the Moon. Now the goal was to examine the lunar environment scientifically. Seemingly marked for disaster at the outset—it was struck twice by lightning on the launch pad—the crew of Apollo 12 put in a textbook mission, demonstrating that they could land precisely where they wanted to on the lunar surface. Having guided *Intrepid*, their lunar module, to the Ocean of Storms, Conrad and Bean spent more than seven hours traversing the moonscape. They collected rocks and set up an Apollo Lunar Surface Experiment Package to measure the Moon's seismicity, solar wind flux, and magnetic field. They also brought back for analysis pieces of the Surveyor 3 that remained from its landing there more than two years earlier. Meanwhile Gordon, in the loneliest job in the space program, was aboard the *Yankee Clipper* taking multispectral photographs of the lunar surface. The results were so stunning that the crew stayed in lunar orbit an extra day to take photographs. The data from these scientific activities continue to be analyzed, thus contributing to an emerging understanding of the workings of the universe.

Pete Conrad flew his fourth and final space mission in 1973 as a member of the inaugural crew of Skylab, the orbital workshop that would pave the way for a permanent human presence in space. The 100-ton spacecraft was launched, unmanned, into orbit on 14 May 1973, the last time the giant Saturn V launch vehicle would be used. Vibrations during liftoff almost immediately caused technical problems. Sixty-three seconds after launch, the meteoroid shield—designed also to shade Skylab's workshop from the Sun's rays—ripped off, taking with it one of the two solar panels; another piece wrapped around the other panel to keep it from properly deploying. In spite of this setback, the space station achieved a near-circular orbit at the desired altitude of 270 miles. NASA's mission control personnel maneuvered Skylab so that its Apollo Telescope Mount (ATM) solar panels faced the Sun to provide as much electricity as possible, but in the absence of the meteoroid shield this positioning caused workshop temperatures to rise to 126 degrees Fahrenheit.

While NASA technicians worked on a solution to Skylab's problem, Skylab 2, the first mission with astronauts, was postponed. Finally on 25 May 1973 astronauts Conrad, Paul J. Weitz, and Joseph P. Kerwin lifted off from the Kennedy Space Center in an Apollo capsule atop a Saturn IB to rendezvous with the orbital workshop. After substantial repairs requiring extravehicular activity (EVA), the workshop was habitable by 4 June. On orbit Conrad and the other two crew members conducted solar astronomy and Earth resources experiments, medical studies, and five student experiments, making three EVAs totaling six hours and twenty minutes. The first group of astronauts returned to Earth on 22 June 1973.

On 1 February 1974 Conrad retired from the U.S. Navy, from which he had been assigned to NASA. During a twenty-year navy and NASA career he had logged more than 6,500 hours flying time, with more than 5,000 hours in high-performance jet aircraft. He had logged forty-nine days, three hours, and thirty-seven minutes in space, a record at the time. He had not only walked on the Moon but had also set what was then a space endurance record of 672 hours and forty-nine minutes on Skylab.

Conrad accepted a position as vice president, operations, and chief operating officer of American Television and Communications Corporation (ATC) in Denver, Colorado. In March 1976 he joined the McDonnell Douglas Corporation in St. Louis, Missouri, as a vice president of international commercial sales; in 1978 he was promoted to vice president and then senior vice president of marketing for the Douglas Aircraft Company. He then became staff vice president and worked on the Delta Clipper launcher project.

In addition to flying his own private plane, Conrad piloted jets owned by his new employers, ATC and McDonnell Douglas. He also remained active in space-related affairs and auto and motorcycle racing, always expressing a love for "fast bikes, fast cars, and anything that moves." As a spokesperson for space exploration, he often testified on Capitol Hill in favor of opening the space frontier to average Americans and lobbying for space tourism and easier access to Earth orbit. In 1995 Conrad founded the Universal Space Lines and several sister companies with the goal of commercializing space. He intended to go back to space as an entrepreneur, to create inexpensive satellite and rocket launching methods. His fondest wish, he told many people, was to circumvent the governmental spaceflight bureaucracies to return to the Moon.

Conrad was a rare individual who combined a strong sense of duty and camaraderie with a mischievous sense of humor that became legendary at NASA. Small and wiry, he stood a mere five feet six and one half inches and weighed only 135 pounds at the time of his graduation from Princeton. His receding hairline, which later left him virtually bald, and the gap between his two front teeth suggested a comical figure, but he soon proved himself equal to anyone flying spacecraft for NASA in the 1960s. His first words as he stepped onto the Moon captured both the tenor of his humor and his excitement at flying in space. "Whoopee!" he shouted, "That may have been a small one for Neil, but that's a long one for me." Perhaps it was not exactly as memorable as Neil Armstrong's famous phrase—". . . one small step for [a] man, one giant leap for mankind"—but it expressed better than just about anything the sheer joy and excitement of exploring a foreign world.

While on a trip to Monterey, California, with his wife and friends, on 8 July 1999 Conrad was critically injured in an accident aboard his 1996 Harley Davidson. Near Ojai, California, the motorcycle left the road on a curve and crashed into a drainage culvert, ejecting the rider onto the pavement. Although his condition did not appear serious at first, Conrad later died of internal injuries at a hospital near his home in Huntington Beach, California.

At the time of Conrad's death, President Bill Clinton remarked that the third person to walk on the Moon had been "a man of unusual warmth and spirit . . . Conrad's excitement at being involved in the Apollo effort was both irrepressible and contagious." The president added, "Taking his work, but not himself, seriously was Pete's informal motto. Well-known for his boundless energy and love of adventure, Conrad was a natural leader who laid the groundwork for many aspects of NASA's human spaceflight efforts through his work on the Gemini, Apollo, and Skylab programs."

• Sizable biographical files on Conrad are in the NASA Historical Reference Collection, NASA Headquarters, Washington, D.C., and at the National Air and Space Museum, Smithsonian Institution, Washington, D.C. Conrad's education has been profiled in Scott White, "Pete Conrad at Princeton," *Princeton Alumni Weekly*, 2 Dec. 1969, pp. 8–9. Excellent biographical accounts of Conrad at NASA can be found in Courtney G. Brooks, James M. Grimwood, and Loyd S. Swenson, Jr., *Chariots for Apollo: A History of Manned Lunar Spacecraft*, NASA Special Publication-4205 (1979); Roger E. Bilstein, *Stages to Saturn: A Technological History of the Apollo/Saturn Launch Vehicles*, NASA SP-4206 (1980); Andrew Chaikin, *A Man on the Moon: The Voyages of the Apollo Astronauts* (1994); James M. Grimwood and Barton C. Hacker, with Peter J. Vorzimmer, *Project Gemini Technology and Operations: A Chronology*, NASA SP-4002, (1969); Barton C. Hacker and James M. Grimwood, *On the Shoulders of Titans: A History of Project Gemini*, NASA SP-4203 (1977); and W. David Compton and Charles D. Benson, *Living and Working in Space: A History of Skylab*, NASA SP-4208 (1983). For the history of Project Apollo, see especially Walter A. McDougall, *The Heavens and the Earth: A Political History of the Space Age* (1985), and Charles A. Murray and Catherine Bly Cox, *Apollo: The Race to the Moon* (1989). Obituaries are in the *New York Times*, the *Los Angeles Times*, *Aviation Week & Space Technology*, *Space News*, and the *Washington Post*, all 10 July 1999.

ROGER D. LAUNIUS

CORNELL, Joseph (24 Dec. 1903–29 Dec. 1972), artist and designer, was born Joseph I. Cornell, Jr., in

South Nyack, New York, the son of Joseph I. Cornell, a traveling salesman of woolen goods, and Helen Ten Broeck Storms Cornell. Although Joseph Jr. was the sixth male in his father's family to bear the name, he was never told what his middle initial stood for, and he dropped both the I. and the Jr. as an adult. Joseph Sr. had come from a family of modest means; his wife's family, whose ancestors included Dutch families of colonial New York and New Jersey, was wealthy and socially prominent. Joseph Sr.'s income, combined with his wife's modest inheritance, allowed them to establish a comfortable upper-middle-class household for their family, which also included three younger children. High culture was not emphasized, however; instead of visiting museums and attending the opera and symphony, the Cornells often took their children to New York City, just across the river from their home, to attend vaudeville shows, amusement parks, and penny arcades.

The death of Joseph Sr. in April 1917 put an end to the family's domestic comforts, although money was provided by his employers to send Joseph Jr. to boarding school that fall at Phillips Academy in Andover, Massachusetts. There he played soccer and behaved, as some of his classmates later described him, like a typically extroverted and vigorous schoolboy. He showed no interest in art, nor was any instruction in the subject offered to him. While he was at Andover, his mother, finding herself in severely straitened financial circumstances, moved the family to the first of a series of rented houses in Queens, New York. Upon graduation in 1921, there being no money for college, Joseph Cornell took a job as a salesman with a Boston-based textile firm, the William Whitman Company, becoming their representative in New York City. He worked there for ten years, making the rounds, as his father had done, of menswear manufacturers in lower Manhattan. On his lunch hours he enjoyed browsing in secondhand bookshops, antique stores, and small galleries. He began reading widely, drawn especially to the works of the German writers Goethe and Heine and to the French poet and novelist Gérard de Nerval, and he developed a strong interest in art, in particular Surrealism and other new movements of the early twentieth century. During this time he converted to Christian Science, following recovery from an illness in 1925. In 1927 he settled with his mother and an invalid brother who suffered from cerebral palsy in a modest frame house she had bought on Utopia Parkway in Flushing, Queens, and lived there for the rest of his life.

The Great Depression forced Cornell's layoff from his job in 1931, and a chance encounter in November of that year launched him on a new career. Passing the newly opened Julien Levy Gallery, he was intrigued by a window display featuring Surrealist art. Cornell had already become interested in the collages of Max Ernst, a founder of Surrealism who had also been influenced by Nerval, and he had begun making similar works on his own. He took them to Levy, who exhibited them as part of a show on Surrealism in

January 1932. Not long afterward, as Cornell later recounted, he passed an antique shop with miscellaneous objects, including a collection of rare compasses, displayed randomly in the window, and a few blocks later saw another shop, this one selling empty boxes in all shapes and sizes. An idea for a new art form was born: the creation of a new type of shadow box by assembling seemingly random objects—pictures, small figures and objects, bits of text, fabrics—behind a glass-fronted frame. By November 1932 he had his first one-man show at Levy's, which included small circular and rectangular boxes he had bought and within which he had placed various objects he had collected. The show ran concurrently with an exhibit of Picasso engravings and attracted modest critical attention.

Cornell's life and work now appeared to settle into a happy congruence, his art reflecting what might be termed a chance-by-design philosophy that seemed to inspire and guide his daily life. He continued to create his assemblages over the next few years, using found boxes and small objects from a collection of thousands of items, including postcards, newspaper clippings, and photographs, that he was amassing. During this time he studied woodworking with a neighbor in order to create his own boxes, which he began using almost exclusively after 1936. In addition to his artwork, he was employed from 1934 to 1940 as a textile designer by one of his mother's friends, Ethel Traphagen, at the Traphagen Commercial Textile Studio in New York City. In the mid-1930s Cornell also began experimenting with film. His first feature, a Surrealistic version of a forgettable 1931 movie called *East Borneo*, was called *Rose Hobart*, after the star of the original film; his was a shorter, reedited version in which frames were shown out of sequence to transform the original narrative into a jarring series of visual images. It was completed at the end of 1936 and shown to the public for the first time at Levy's in 1939.

The first of Cornell's entirely handmade box assemblages, *Untitled (Soap Bubble Set)*, dates from 1936; it is one of his best-known creations and is typical of Cornell's mature work. The assemblage brings together what appear to be, at first glance, dissimilar objects with no connection among them: cylindrical weights, an egg in a wine glass, an ancient lunar map, a clay pipe, and a plaster cast of a child's head, displayed in separate compartments within a box measuring approximately 14 inches wide by 15.5 inches high by 5.5 inches deep. The unity of the piece, hinted at in the title, is provided by the inherent meaning of each of the objects and the visual association that each of them has with the others: the child's head, rounded like the other objects, is an obvious reference to childhood; the pipe implies blowing soap bubbles, a childhood pastime; the roundness of soap bubbles suggests the moon, which in turn directs attention to the cosmos; the egg symbolizes life; the cylindrical weights at the top of the box, representing eternity, appear to press down on the objects below.

Cornell began receiving wider public attention in 1936, when *Untitled (Soap Bubble Set)* was shown at the Museum of Modern Art in New York City as part of an exhibition titled *Fantastic Art, Dada, Surrealism.* Cornell himself, though obviously inspired by the Surrealists, did not consider himself one of their number and took pains to point out that he did not share the group's interests in eroticism and the unconscious. Nor did Cornell call himself an artist, preferring instead the designation "designer"—the occupation, he often pointed out, that he listed on his voter registration card. Despite his lack of professional training, he in fact did work for many years as a designer, turning to magazine illustration and design for such publications as *Vogue* and *House and Garden* to support himself and his mother and brother after his job ended at Traphagen in 1940. During the 1940s he also devoted time to writing, contributing articles on the arts to small periodicals.

But Cornell's primary interest remained the creation of his boxes, which were selling well enough by the late 1950s—at prices ranging from $5,000 to $15,000 apiece—to enable him to give up outside design work. Many of the boxes were continuations of and variations on a single theme, such as the *Soap Bubble Set* series and another called *Pharmacy,* which featured arrangements of old drug bottles refilled with different small objects. Another well-known Cornell creation is the *Medici Slot Machine* series, whose boxes feature a young Renaissance prince or princess. Ballerinas and birds were also favorite subjects for his constructions, which were often "busy" and colorful. One notable exception was a series of austere wooden boxes he created in the late 1940s and early 1950s, inspired by the modern Dutch painter Piet Mondrian; they were covered with a lath of simple wooden strips and painted white.

Cornell's boxes could be both serious and playful, by turns melancholy and whimsical, projecting a dreamlike fantasy; but they never failed to be interesting. This was true as well of Cornell's filmmaking, which had dwindled during the 1940s and resumed in the following decade; rather than using found film he now directed cameramen to shoot abstract footage that he in turn assembled and edited into several art shorts. Also in the 1950s he returned to the creation of collages, which, like his boxes, featured assemblages of random objects and were included in shows of his work at the Museum of Modern Art and other museums and galleries.

Active in New York art circles during the 1930s and 1940s, Cornell appeared to withdraw from the world by the early 1950s. Although he took great pains to deny to the occasional visitor that he was a recluse, he now rarely left his home in Flushing, which had become a vast storehouse for a random collection of odds and ends, ranging from kitsch animal figurines to Old Master engravings, and from all of which he appeared to derive pleasure. By the 1960s his output had decreased considerably, owing to declining health, and his works during his last years were mainly collages. The deaths of his mother and his brother at the end of the decade plunged him into a deep grief

from which he never fully recovered, although he continued to encourage the exhibition and sale of his work. Throughout his life he maintained a special love and affinity for children, and in 1972, at the opening of one of his last exhibits in New York, those under age fourteen were honored as special guests. Cornell died later that year after suffering a heart attack at his home. He had never married, though not apparently from want of trying: he had a series of unrequited romances, their failure perhaps a result of the strong attachment that existed between Cornell and his mother throughout her lifetime.

Cornell's intriguing boxes earned him a place in American art that can only be called unique. Despite his attempts to separate himself from Surrealism, he was the leading American exponent of that movement. While his collages and film work have been surpassed by other disciples, most of the box assemblages produced by hundreds of his imitators pale by comparison with his. He modestly refused to call himself an artist, yet that designation has rightfully appropriated *him.*

• For biographical information, see Deborah Solomon, *Utopia Parkway: The Life and Work of Joseph Cornell* (1997); see also Dore Ashton, *A Joseph Cornell Album* (1974), which includes reminiscences of those who knew Cornell, as well as excerpts from some of his favorite writings, ranging from the sermons of John Donne to the essays of the physicist Max Planck. In addition, see "Cornell, Joseph," in *Who Was Who in America,* vol. 5 (1973). For critical analyses of Cornell's work, see Diane Waldman, *Joseph Cornell* (1977); Lindsay Blair, *Joseph Cornell's Vision of Spiritual Order* (1993); and Jodi Hauptman, *Joseph Cornell: Stargazing in the Cinema* (1999); see also Kynaston McShine, ed., *Joseph Cornell* (1980), an illustrated catalogue of a Cornell exhibition at the Museum of Modern Art in New York City that includes essays on his work. Charles Simic, *Dime-Store Alchemy: The Art of Joseph Cornell* (1992), is a small book composed of vignettes and brief poetic critiques that seems to capture by its style of presentation the spirit of Cornell's art. An obituary appears in the *New York Times,* 31 Dec. 1972.

ANN T. KEENE

CORRIGAN, Douglas "Wrong Way" (22 Jan. 1907–9 Dec. 1995), aviator, was born Clyde Corrigan in Galveston, Texas, to Clyde Sinclair Corrigan, a civil engineer, and Evelyn Groce Nelson Corrigan, a former schoolteacher. When he was two years old, the family moved to Aransas Pass, Texas, where the elder Corrigan worked on the construction of a railroad causeway. Four years later, in 1913, the family, which now included a younger brother and sister, moved again, this time to San Antonio. There Clyde Corrigan, Sr., opened a bakery and soda fountain across the street from the Alamo. After several years the business foundered, and in 1916 Corrigan abandoned his family to pursue a career as an inventor. Evelyn Corrigan opened a rooming house to support her children; her eldest son, whom she had renamed Douglas after securing a divorce from her husband, supplemented the family income by delivering newspapers.

In 1919 the family moved to Los Angeles, where Evelyn Corrigan opened another rooming house and Douglas attended school as well as working part time in a cannery. In his early teens, he and his brother lived with his father in New York City for a year while his mother recuperated from surgery. He attended high school in Los Angeles while working full time, first at a bottling works, and then at a bank. When his mother died in 1922, he left school, took over the care of his brother, and found a higher-paying job with a housing contractor. During the next three years he helped build houses in the new suburbs springing up around Los Angeles while taking correspondence courses in architecture.

Corrigan's life changed dramatically in the summer of 1925 when he drove past a new airfield one evening on his way home from work and stopped to take a look around. There were only a few small planes there, flying on a limited schedule between Los Angeles and San Diego, as well as a two-seater biplane, a Curtiss JN4D, or "Jenny," that was used to take people up for a brief "spin." Aviation was still in its infancy, and flying for most people was a novelty. Corrigan was fascinated, and though flying was expensive, he was determined to take a ride. The following weekend he went to the field, paid $2.50 for a brief swing over Los Angeles—and was hooked.

Over the next year and a half, Corrigan returned to the airfield each weekend for a fifteen-minute flying lesson, all he could afford. He was now determined to become an airplane pilot, and to get more time in the air he joined a local squadron of the National Guard, which owned several types of small planes. In early February 1927, shortly after his twentieth birthday, Corrigan left his construction job and moved to San Diego to join the San Diego Airline Company, flying occasional short hops in southern California but working primarily as a mechanic at the local aircraft factory. Not long after his arrival, another young pilot named Charles Lindbergh showed up at the airfield, looking for a ship he could fly from New York to Paris. A special plane was designed for him, and Corrigan was one of several young men who worked on the construction of what became known as the *Spirit of St. Louis.*

Lindbergh's celebrated transatlantic flight in May 1927 inspired many young men, and some young women as well, to be pioneers in aviation, but none more than Douglas Corrigan, who later wrote in his autobiography that he considered Lindbergh the greatest man who ever lived ("even greater than Lincoln"). Corrigan's evident skill as a mechanic, however, made him even more valuable to his employers, and for several years his flying time was limited to weekends. During the week he built and serviced planes for the newly established San Diego Air Service and its affiliate, the Airtech Flying School, though occasionally he was allowed to fly during lunch hours. By the fall of 1929 he had reached his first goal: earning a transport pilot's license.

During the next nine years Corrigan worked as a pilot, mechanic, flight instructor, and airport manager at airfields in southern California and, for a time, in New York, alternately flying wealthy private passengers and entertaining Americans pinched by the Great Depression with stunt flights—"barnstorming"—in small towns along both coasts. In the early 1930s he also worked for several aircraft companies in California, including Northrop and Douglas. Corrigan's earnings during this period enabled him to buy a series of small used planes that he hoped would enable him to achieve what had become his new life's goal: making a solo nonstop long-distance flight, preferably across the Atlantic, that would capture the headlines and make him as renowned as his hero Lindbergh.

Corrigan began making flights of long duration in August 1936, when he attempted a nonstop flight from San Diego to New York, by way of St. Louis, piloting a made-over OX5 Curtiss Robin that he had bought secondhand for $325. Though engine trouble forced him to make several stops en route, he was determined to fly nonstop coast to coast in preparation for a transatlantic flight. He came close to achieving that goal two months later, in October 1936, flying nonstop from Floyd Bennett Field in New York to San Antonio, Texas, a distance of 1,900 miles, in nineteen hours. Corrigan returned to San Diego, where he worked as a flight instructor while overhauling the Robin and installing additional gas tanks to extend her time in the air. In 1937 he made two flights to the East Coast, neither of them nonstop, expressly to seek permission from several New York airfields to fly to the British Isles. He was turned down, however, because neither he nor his plane was licensed for ocean flight.

In fact, Corrigan's plane was not even licensed to make transcontinental flights, and on his bicoastal hops he was forced to use out-of-the-way airfields so that his illegal takeoffs and landings would not attract attention. And after the disappearance of aviator Amelia Earhart over the South Pacific that summer, the government suspended the issuance of licenses for ocean flying. Broke and frustrated but still hopeful, Corrigan returned to work at Northrop in California in the late fall of 1937 and during the following winter and spring prepared his Robin for another try at a long-distance flight.

That opportunity finally came on 8 July 1938 when Corrigan, who had managed to acquire a so-called experimental (temporary) license for a nonstop cross-country flight, took off from an airfield in Long Beach, California, telling the airport manager that he was taking a "test hop" to El Paso, Texas. In fact, Corrigan had every intention of flying nonstop to New York, which is where he arrived, less than twenty-seven hours later, at sundown on 9 July after a nonstop journey of 2,700 miles.

By the summer of 1938 other pilots had already equaled Corrigan's feat, though none had done so in a plane as marginal as his Robin. But the fact that he was not the first to succeed, and the additional fact that the newspapers were filled with accounts of Howard Hughes's impending round-the-world flight, explained why Corrigan's arrival at Roosevelt Field on Long Island attracted relatively little attention. For that matter, even transatlantic solo flights now seemed almost old hat: at least half a dozen had been made since Lindbergh's. Despite his disappointment, the stubborn Corrigan resolved to keep on going, and after a few days' rest in New York he dutifully applied for permission to make a transatlantic flight. Again he was turned down.

Early on the morning of 17 July 1938 Douglas Corrigan took off in the Robin from Floyd Bennett Field after filing a flight plan indicating that he was returning to California. Observers on the ground were therefore surprised to see him heading not west but east—out across the Atlantic. Twenty-eight hours and thirteen minutes later, Corrigan landed the Robin at Baldonnel Airport in Dublin, Ireland. After introducing himself to airport authorities, he reportedly said, "Just got in from New York. Where am I? I intended to fly to California."

Whether or not Douglas Corrigan knew he was flying to Ireland has long been debated. Corrigan himself stoutly maintained that California was indeed his destination and that he had somehow misread his instruments. Aviation authorities did not agree: his pilot's license was instantly suspended and his plane was impounded. But he had achieved the renown he had dreamed of: instantly dubbed "Wrong Way Corrigan" by the press and by radio commentators, he and his escapade were front-page and broadcast news for days, and he became an instant American folk hero. On his return to New York on 4 August—via the ocean liner *Manhattan*, accompanied by his crated Robin—he was feted with a ticker tape parade along Broadway that drew an estimated million onlookers and was said to have been even greater than Lindbergh's in 1927.

Corrigan's instant fame led to a nationwide tour in the weeks following his return, as well as book and movie contracts. His autobiography, *That's My Story*, ostensibly written alone, was published before the end of the year, and he played himself in the film version of his life that soon followed, called *The Flying Irishman*. Though the book and the movie and Corrigan himself were ultimately forgotten amid the growing crisis in Europe, his famous epithet permanently entered the national lexicon: henceforth any wrongheaded maneuver was likely to be described as a "Wrong Way Corrigan."

The remainder of Corrigan's life was ordinary, and he failed to reach the stature of his hero Lindbergh, although from time to time brief newspaper features would appear on the anniversary of his famous flight. His license had been reinstated after his return to the United States from Ireland, and he went back to work in the growing aviation industry in California, serving as a test pilot during World War II. After the war he operated an air freight service and later bought an orange grove that he was eventually forced to sell. Corrigan was married to a woman named Elizabeth (full name unknown) and had three sons; his wife died in 1966. He continued to fly until the early 1970s, when he became a recluse after the death of one of his sons in a plane crash. He emerged from seclusion in 1988, the fiftieth anniversary of his errant flight, to appear with his famous Robin at a local airshow, and that summer he also visited Ireland. He died at a hospital in Orange, California.

• Biographical information on Douglas Corrigan can be found in *That's My Story*. See also accounts of Corrigan's flight and its aftermath in the *New York Times*, beginning 19 July 1938 and continuing for several weeks thereafter. An obituary appears in the *New York Times*, 14 Dec. 1995.

ANN T. KEENE

COWELL, Henry (11 Mar. 1897–10 Dec. 1965), composer, pianist, writer, and educator, was born Henry Dixon Cowell in Menlo Park, California, the son of Harry Cowell and Clarissa Dixon Cowell. Both parents were aspiring poets and writers; Harry, an Irish immigrant, worked as a linotypist. At the age of five Cowell began studying violin and showed signs of talent, but the lessons seemed to affect his health adversely and were discontinued. His parents divorced in 1903. Between 1907 and 1910 he and his mother lived in New York, penniless while she tried to earn a living by her writing, and stayed with relatives in Iowa and Kansas. In 1910 they returned to Menlo Park, where Cowell took jobs such as herding cows to support himself and his mother. Around this time Cowell came to the attention of the psychologist Lewis M. Terman, who wrote him up in a study of gifted children. Cowell also received encouragement from Samuel Seward, the literary scholar, and Ellen Veblen, wife of the economist Thorstein Veblen.

By 1912 Cowell had saved enough to buy a piano. He studied with local teachers and began to compose piano pieces characterized by the use of tone clusters, which he defined as "chords built from major and minor seconds," often played with the fist, flat hand, or forearm. Such chords were not completely new, but Cowell discovered them independently and integrated them into his work to such a degree that Béla Bartók later requested Cowell's permission before using the device. Many of Cowell's early works depict scenes from Irish mythology, reflecting an interest kindled in Cowell by his friendship with the poet John Varian.

Cowell made his debut as a composer-performer in March 1914 under the auspices of the San Francisco Musical Society. That year, too, he began studying composition with the pioneering musicologist and theorist Charles Seeger. With Seeger's encouragement, Cowell wrote in 1917–1918 a manuscript he would publish in 1930 as *New Musical Resources*, sketching a conceptual basis for unconventional approaches to counterpoint and rhythm as well as harmony, and inviting fellow composers to join him in exploring them. Cowell later introduced to Seeger the woman the latter would marry, Ruth Crawford (Ruth Crawford-Seeger).

Cowell served in the army in 1918–1919, mostly as a band musician. In the 1920s he performed extensively, making yearly concert-lecture tours of the States and several European tours. He also continued to explore new techniques, writing pieces in which the performer reaches inside the piano to strike, brush, or pluck the strings in various ways. In addition, Cowell began to exercise professional leadership among the "ultra-modern" wing of American composers. In 1925 he founded the New Music Society of California to promote performances of works by composers such as Dane Rudhyar, Edgard Varèse, Carl Ruggles, Arnold Schoenberg, and Leo Ornstein. In 1927 Cowell joined with Varèse to found the Pan American Association of Composers, which became identified with the view that American composers should create their own modernist musical culture independent of developments in Europe. Also that year he expanded the New Music Society's activities to include publication of *New Music*, subtitled *A Quarterly of Modern Compositions*. Charles Ives, whom Cowell met in 1927, became a close friend and the quarterly's principal sponsor. *New Music* helped to disseminate the work of experimentally minded composers for thirty-one years.

In 1929 Cowell joined the faculty of the New School for Social Research in New York City. In 1931 he went to Berlin to study comparative musicology with Erich von Hornbostel. From that time on, his composing increasingly reflected the influence of exotic music cultures, and he became a prominent educator in the largely neglected field of world music. Lou Harrison attended Cowell's course "Music of the Peoples of the World" in 1935 when Cowell gave it in San Francisco; he later studied composition with Cowell and became a friend and disciple. Another student of Cowell's who became an influential composer was John Cage.

Cowell's personal life suddenly became public in 1936 when he was arrested for engaging in "oral copulation," prohibited in California since 1921. His accuser was a seventeen-year-old boy, apparently his partner in the act. Cowell pleaded not guilty, on the grounds that he had not initiated the encounter, but later changed his plea to guilty. In the context of a nationwide crusade against lifestyles seen as deviant, he received a sentence of one to fifteen years in San Quentin. For the first thirteen months, he labored in a jute mill and was hard put to keep up his writing and composing in a cell without a desk or table. He was then transferred to the prison's education department and given the opportunity to work with the prison band and organize courses in musicianship.

In 1940 Cowell was paroled with the sponsorship of his friend and fellow composer Percy Grainger, who hired him as a secretary and research assistant. Cowell's civil rights were restored in 1941; the government engaged him to run a score-exchange program between the United States and South American countries, and he resumed teaching at the New School and elsewhere. Also in 1941 Cowell married Sidney

Robertson, an ethnomusicologist and a longtime friend to whom Cowell had grown closer during his incarceration. A side effect of the marriage was that Charles Ives renewed contact with Cowell, which he had broken off since Cowell's arrest; this had been painful for Cowell, who wrote, "I regard Ives the same as a father." In 1942 Cowell requested and received a full pardon from California governor Culbert Olson.

Cowell pursued a distinguished career as composer, writer, and teacher for the remainder of his life. In 1955 he and Sidney Cowell published the first comprehensive study of Ives's life and works; in 1956–1957 they toured the world, studying the music of various cultures. Cowell died in Shady, New York. He had composed something like 700 works, including symphonic, chamber, and vocal music as well as music for piano. Besides his output as a composer, he is remembered for the spirit of adventure and creative energy he exemplified.

• An extensive archive of Cowell's papers is held at the Music Division of the New York Public Library. *Henry Cowell: Piano Music* (Smithsonian Folkways 40801) is a recording of Cowell playing and discussing twenty of his works. Rita H. Mead, *Henry Cowell's New Music, 1925–1936: The Society, the Music Editions, and the Recordings* (1981), is a valuable resource. Michael Hicks, "The Imprisonment of Henry Cowell," *Journal of the American Musicological Society* 44 (Spring 1991), corrects errors found in earlier accounts. Bruce Saylor, "Henry Cowell," in *The New Grove Dictionary of Music and Musicians* (1980), offers a helpful overview. Carol Oja devotes a chapter to Cowell in *Making Music Modern: New York in the 1920s* (2000). Nicolas Slonimsky's autobiography *Perfect Pitch* (1988) records his friendship and professional alliance with Cowell. An obituary is in the *New York Times*, 11 Dec. 1965.

JONATHAN WIENER

COYNE, Joseph (27 Mar. 1867–12 Feb. 1941), actor, was born in New York City; his parents' names and occupations do not appear in readily available sources of information. By age sixteen he was performing as a singer and dancer at Niblo's Gardens. Before making his Broadway acting debut in 1895, he had been half of a vaudeville song-and-dance team (Evans and Coyne) and a member of the Rose Lyall Dramatic (repertory) Company. The first dozen years of Coyne's career on the legitimate stage were spent in a variety of roles in dramatic and musical entertainments. Following his dramatic debut in *The District Attorney* (1895), he worked into a starring role in *A Stranger in New York* (1897) and showed skill as a parodist in *Star and Garter* (1900). In 1901 Coyne made his first London appearance for American producer Charles Frohman, supporting Frohman's star Edna May as the foppish Bernie Tappertit in *The Girl from Up There*.

Returning to the United States after a successful run in the British musical comedy *The Toreador* (1902), Coyne found himself cast as a "traditional British nincompoop" in the musical *In Newport* (1904). Such impersonations of Englishmen were suddenly all that Coyne was offered. This was true for straight plays, such as *Abigail* (1905), and musicals, *The Rollicking Girl* (1905), for example. In 1906, by then almost forty and thoroughly grounded in his craft, Coyne returned to London to see if he could do better. His next appearance—in London in *Nelly Nell* (1907), Edna May's farewell production—was inconclusive. Even after producer George Edwardes had hired him to play the central role of Prince Danilo in the first English version of *The Merry Widow* (1907), it was not long before the constitutionally insecure Coyne was telling other cast members he would soon be returning to New York.

The "problem" was composer Franz Lehár's beautiful music: although Coyne's presence, particularly when dancing, was graceful, his voice was simply not beautiful. Finally, at one rehearsal, with Lehár present, Coyne decided to recite instead of sing the words to a song. The effect was stunning; Edwardes barred Lehár from future rehearsals and told Coyne to recite all his songs. When Lehár finally did overhear what was going on, Edwardes squelched his rage, saying, according to Alan Hyman: "That man will put a fortune in your pocket even if he does not sing your beautiful music." When *The Merry Widow* opened, the audience must have been surprised to see Coyne, an ordinary-looking man with an odd-shaped face and a beautiful smile, instead of the tall, handsome prince many had imagined. Then he "sang" about going to Maxim's, and the audience was won. Coyne may not have been the first performer to find this alternative, but his example established an approach to musical comedy lyrics that echoed through the century. (Lehár subsequently insisted that all Danilos should recite his songs.) Later in the show, Coyne and the "widow," Lily Elsie, danced the Merry Widow Waltz, dreamily and in the Viennese style, moving backward; during the first chorus Coyne held Elsie around the waist, during the second around the neck. When the dance ended, the audience made them do it again and again. Coyne parodied this legendary dance in a late 1907 edition of the satirical *Follies*, dancing the number with a rope slung around the neck of his dancing partner. He made a brief return to Broadway in 1908 with Alexandra Carlisle in a British comedy, *The Mollusc*, playing an Englishman invigorated by a long stay in the United States. He was not well received by the critics and returned to London and *The Merry Widow*.

From 1907 through the mid-1920s, the history of London's most popular musical comedies is generally a chronology of Coyne musicals. Now that he was established in England, he was allowed to portray an American, which he did with considerable impact. In *The Dollar Princess* (1909), opposite Elsie once more, he played an eccentric but loveable American oil baron. In *The Quaker Girl* (1910), one of the best-loved "Gaiety" (theater) musical comedies, his role was a young American naval attaché to the Paris embassy ("a bad, bad boy like me") who falls in love with "the Quaker girl" ("a good, good girl like you"). Coyne's "The Dancing Lesson," with costar Gertie

Millar, revived memories of *The Merry Widow* and retains much of its charm on a gramophone recording. In the role, Coyne was called by W. Macqueen-Pope "the beau ideal of young American manhood."

In succession Coyne, often as an American, starred in *The Dancing Mistress* (1912), *The Girl from Utah* (opposite Ina Claire, 1913), the Irving Berlin shows *Watch Your Step* (1914) and *Follow the Crowd* (1916), *The Bing Girls Are There* (1917), *Arlette* (1917), and Louis Hirsch's aviation lark, *Going Up!* (1919). In all of these Coyne danced and "sang" about dancing. Interspersed were leading roles in several nonmusical comedies. By the time he costarred with the young Gertrude Lawrence in a musical adaptation of the French *Dede* (1922) he had become an old reliable friend to the theatergoing audience. Offstage, Coyne, who never married, gradually acquired the reputation of a miserly eccentric, living in the cheapest room high atop one of London's finest hotels, washing his own underwear and dining out on teas and ice cream.

While starring in Rudolf Friml and Otto Harbach's *Katinka* in 1923, Coyne developed a serious ear infection that required an operation. A long recuperation delayed his return, but in 1926 he played the philandering Billy Smith in a memorable London version of the Vincent Youmans–Irving Caesar musical *No, No, Nanette!* (1925) in advance of its New York opening. Aside from the show's dancing songs, Coyne sang with London's new star Binnie Hale the classic "I Want to Be Happy." After *Queen High* (1926), Coyne's energy and popularity began to wane. His last London appearance was as Ezra Hunniwell in the comedy *Apron Strings* (1931). Coyne suffered major losses in the Wall Street crash. His health gradually worsened and he entered a nursing home in 1939, dying there of pneumonia two years later.

A true transatlantic figure, Joseph Coyne was a major player in the early-twentieth-century British musical theater. Of greater importance was the option he created—of necessity, but no matter—for future performers: reciting or only "semisinging" the words of a song. In the right dramatic situation, in the hands of real actors, it has enriched musical theater.

• Details of Coyne's London performances are in the archives of the Theatre Museum, Covent Garden, London. Coyne is glimpsed in two of W. Macqueen-Pope's reminiscences on theater: *Nights of Gladness* (1956) and *Ghosts and Greasepaint: A Story of the Days that Were* (1951). Alan Hyman, *The Gaiety Years* (1975), gives a good account of *The Merry Widow*. Gerald Bordman, *American Theatre: a Chronicle of Comedy and Drama 1869–1914* (1994), covers Coyne's nonmusical American career, while Bordman, *American Musical Theatre: A Chronicle*, 2d ed. (1992), deals with the musicals. Obituaries appear in the (London) *Times* and the *New York Times*, both 21 Feb.1941.

JAMES ROSS MOORE

CRATER, Joseph Force (5 Jan. 1889–1930?), jurist, was one of four children born in Easton, Pennsylvania, to Frank E. Crater, orchard owner and the operator of a produce market, and his wife (whose name cannot be ascertained). The family was comfortable financially, but Joseph learned the value of hard work from an early age by working long hours for his father. He also loved music, and encouraged by his mother he became a skillful pianist. After attending local public schools, he enrolled at Lafayette College, also in Easton, graduating with honors in 1911. He went on to law school at Columbia University and received his degree in 1916.

In 1912, while attending law school, Crater had met a young woman several years older who at that time was separated from her husband and had resumed using her maiden name, Stella Wheeler. Over the next five years Crater and Wheeler were inseparable; Crater helped her obtain a divorce, and they finally married in the spring of 1917. At that time Crater had been working as a low-paid law clerk in New York City since graduating from law school. To earn extra money, he began teaching legal classes at Fordham and New York Universities and at City College of New York. After several years of long hours and an income that he felt was too low, Crater announced to his wife that he was going into politics in order to "get ahead." At that time "going into politics" in any meaningful way in New York City meant joining the Democratic party, a powerhouse in Manhattan since the establishment of its headquarters, Tammany Hall, in the nineteenth century. Crater duly joined a local Democratic club, and his gregarious personality soon put him in good stead with party leaders. His efforts quickly paid off: in 1920 he received his first political appointment, as secretary to New York State Supreme Court justice Robert F. Wagner, Sr.

The fortunes of the Craters noticeably improved. Soon they were socializing with Tammany's top echelon, including future mayor Jimmy Walker and future governor and presidential candidate Al Smith. Although they continued to live in their same small apartment on Manhattan's Upper West Side, they became regulars at the city's top theatres, night clubs, and musical events. Crater remained with Wagner through his successful 1926 campaign for the U.S. Senate and left his service only after the new senator went to Washington, D.C., in 1927. Crater then set up his own law practice, which was so successful that by October of that year he was able to buy an elegant cooperative apartment on lower Fifth Avenue and fill it with expensive furnishings, including a baby grand piano. He also hired a maid, a cook, and a chauffeur, and the couple began to entertain lavishly. When his wife, according to her later account, asked how they could afford such a lifestyle, he assured her that his practice was thriving. When the Wall Street financial collapse occurred in October 1929, wiping out many of their friends and associates, Crater was apparently unaffected and explained to his wife that prudent money management had kept him from suffering major losses.

In April 1930, in an announcement that surprised many, Governor Franklin D. Roosevelt appointed Joseph Crater to the New York State Supreme Court to fill the unexpired term of a justice who had resigned. Crater was to serve until the fall, when an appointment for a full fourteen-year term would be made, and Crater told his wife that he had been assured by Roosevelt that he would be nominated. According to the governor, so he claimed, even bigger things were in store: he was likely one day to be appointed to the U.S. Supreme Court.

As Crater assumed his new duties on the bench, however, potential trouble for Tammany Hall was brewing. The New York state legislature began an official inquiry into alleged corruption by Democratic party officials in the city, which had been under the firm control of Tammany for many years. A retired state supreme court justice, Samuel Seabury (1873–1958), was appointed chief counsel to the investigating committee. Among various allegations that the committee was charged with tracking down were rumors of large-scale bribery, the selling of high-placed municipal jobs, and improper property transactions that allowed politically connected owners to make large profits at taxpayers' expense. Crater had reason to be concerned about the Seabury Investigation, as it came to be called, for in early 1929 he had been appointed receiver of a foreclosed hotel on the Lower East Side. This required him to handle the sale of the property and manage all moneys received as a consequence. In late June, under his administration, the hotel had been sold to the American Mortgage Loan Company for $75,000; six weeks later, in early August, the company sold it to the city, which wanted it condemned for a street-widening project, for $2.85 million dollars.

As Seabury began looking into the Liberty Hotel sale and other suspicious financial dealings by the city in the spring of 1930, Crater maintained his composure, telling his wife and friends that he himself had done nothing illegal in that transaction or in any other facet of either his public or private life. In fact, Seabury was never able to prove any wrongdoing in the Liberty affair, and his committee report, which resulted in the ultimate ouster of Mayor Jimmy Walker, the removal of several magistrates, and prison terms for a number of policemen, did not implicate Joseph Crater in any wrongdoing.

By that time, however, Judge Crater was nowhere to be found. He had vanished suddenly on the evening of 6 August 1930, after dining with friends and then climbing into a taxi near Times Square. Curiously, his disappearance was not announced until early September, the delay caused in part by his wife's failure to report him missing for several weeks. She had been spending the summer at their vacation cottage in Maine while her husband remained at work in the city, and she later claimed that while she expected him to come up for her birthday on 9 August, she was not completely surprised when he did not appear, assuming that "politics" had detained him. Only on 29 August, after receiving a call from one of her husband's judicial colleagues inquiring as to his whereabouts, did she return to the city. She later claimed that she then called his political associates at Tammany, and it was they who apparently alerted the police several days later. Senator Wagner, traveling in Europe, was also notified, and he returned immediately. On 4 September 1930, newspaper headlines told all of New York City that Judge Crater had vanished, and in the next few weeks the puzzling case made the news throughout the nation.

For the first few months following Crater's disappearance, many people around the country reported "sightings"; all proved false. Numerous rumors circulated about him. While some people believed that he had fled the country, as other Tammany appointees were doing, to avoid prosecution, others thought that he had been "bumped off," either because he himself had been involved in wrongdoing or because he knew too much about those who had—and in either case might be forced to tell what he knew to the Seabury committee. His involvement with the Liberty Hotel was the subject of many newspaper articles; so was his past legal representation of notorious gangsters. Though his wife vehemently denied it, he was also rumored to have been seen in the frequent company of showgirls with underworld associations. Stella Crater herself was believed by many to know more about the case than she had revealed to the police.

First months, then years went by, but there were no solid clues to explain Crater's disappearance, even though the New York City police department had offered a then substantial award of $5,000 for information. The case remained an evergreen media favorite, the most famous missing-persons case in the nation's history, and each year when 6 August rolled around, newspapers would run the story yet again. Somewhat oddly, the judge himself, rather than engendering sympathy, became the butt of jokes. A new expression, "to pull a Crater," entered the national lexicon, reflecting what became one prevailing view: that he had simply "taken a powder" and walked away from a troubling situation. Others assumed he had been the deserving victim of a gangland killing—one of so many occurring during Prohibition that it hardly merited special concern.

Interest in the Crater case declined considerably over the years as the chances of his still being alive seemed increasingly remote, given the year of his birth. A brief flurry of renewed interest occurred in 1961, following the publication of Stella Crater's memoir, *The Empty Robe*, but no new information was forthcoming. In 1985 the New York City police department declared the case officially closed.

• Biographical information on Judge Crater abounded in the press in the weeks following the announcement of his disappearance. The most reliable accounts are in the *New York Times*, beginning on 4 Sept. 1930, and continuing almost daily for several months. See also "Missing a Year; Search Still Going On," *New York Times*, 6 Aug. 1931, a summary of the status of the case on the first anniversary of Crater's disappearance. A readily accessible source of information is Stella Crater's memoir, *The Empty Robe*, though it is not, understandably, objective. For a summation of the case fifty years later, see R. Garrett, "Good Night, Judge Crater, Wherever You Are," *New York*, 11 Aug. 1980, pp. 11–12. See also James Barron, "60 Years Ago Tonight, Judge Crater Stepped into a Taxi," *New York Times*, 6 Aug. 1990.

ANN T. KEENE

CRAWFORD, George Gordon (24 Aug. 1869–20 Mar. 1936), a leading New South industrialist and designer of one of the nation's largest welfare capitalism programs, was born in Madison, Georgia, to George Gilmore Crawford, a physician, and Margarette Reed Howard Crawford of Savannah, Georgia. After Crawford's mother died giving birth to a daughter in 1874, he and his sister spent much of their childhood with relatives on their grandfather's 5,000-acre plantation south of Atlanta. A member of the first graduating class of the Georgia Institute of Technology in 1890, Crawford earned a degree in mechanical engineering, which he augmented with two years of study in technical chemistry at the Karl-Eberhard University in Tübingen, Germany. In addition to the knowledge gained in the chemistry laboratory, he had an awareness of efficiency as a factor in industrial development when he returned to the United States in 1892.

After a short period of employment as a draftsman at Sloss-Sheffield Iron and Steel Company in Birmingham, Alabama, Crawford became a chemist at the Edgar Thomson works of the Carnegie Steel Company near Pittsburgh, Pennsylvania. Having gained experience in several departments, he was assistant superintendent of the blast furnaces at Edgar Thomson when he left Carnegie Steel in 1897 to become superintendent of blast furnaces and steel works at the National Tube Company at McKeesport, Pennsylvania. Two years later Carnegie Steel brought him back to Edgar Thomson as the superintendent of what was then the largest blast furnace plant in the world.

In 1901 Carnegie Steel became the core of the newly organized United States Steel Corporation (USSC), and Crawford was made manager of the National Department of the National Tube Company, a complex organization of blast furnaces, steel works, and various mills at several different locations. In the short span of nine years in the industry, the young southerner had advanced to a position of responsibility for one of the three largest plants of USSC and began service on a variety of important committees of the giant corporation. Though tempted by several offers from other steel companies, he remained with U.S. Steel. During his time in Pennsylvania, Crawford met and married Mary Childs; they had one daughter, Maury. After Mary's death from tuberculosis, Crawford arranged for his daughter to live on the Georgia cotton plantation of his sister, who had children near her age.

Crawford's career took an unexpected turn during the panic of 1907 when U.S. Steel rescued a New York brokerage firm by purchasing the majority stock of the Tennessee Coal, Iron and Railroad Company

(TCI). Based in Birmingham, Alabama, the south's largest iron and steel company was thought by some industry experts to be an up-and-coming competitor to the Pittsburgh-based steel industry. Founded in 1871, the city of Birmingham boasted the presence of all the basic materials for the making of iron and steel within an eight-mile radius, but lack of capital and the high phosphorous content of the local ore stymied the potential of the region's industry. Eager for U.S. Steel capital, New South boosters hailed the purchase as a giant step forward for southern industry. In later years, however, southern critics spoke of the handicaps of a "colonial economy" controlled by outside interests, and in 1911 the federal government brought an unsuccessful suit against USSC for violation of the Sherman Antitrust Act based in part on charges of monopoly because of the TCI purchase.

At the insistence of U.S. Steel corporate executives, Crawford reluctantly returned to the south in 1907 as president of the new USSC subsidiary. Ironically, in light of his initial hesitation, he remained at the helm of TCI until 1930 and became known as one of the leading New South statesmen of the region. At TCI Crawford faced two major challenges: technical problems associated with the low-grade ore and the problem of obtaining a steady, efficient labor supply. Crawford's technical background and wide-ranging experience served him well in addressing the technological problems, although his task was compounded by the scope of TCI's endeavors. It was the only corporation subsidiary that included not only the production of steel and steel products but also the mining and transportation of coal and ore. As important as his steelmaking expertise, however, was Crawford's dogged determination to gain the necessary appropriations from USSC. Crawford not only met with U.S. Steel executives at corporate headquarters in New York but also encouraged company officials to visit Birmingham. With local businessmen, Crawford helped finance the building of an opulent hotel, The Tutwiler, where the USSC executives could stay during such trips. Crawford's second wife, Margaret Richardson (a New Orleans belle and former Mardi Gras queen whom he married in 1911) proved to be a valuable asset in entertaining the northern capitalists on their southern visits. Crawford's second child, Margaret Gordon, was born in 1913.

During Crawford's long tenure at TCI, extensive remodeling, expansion, and innovations marked each year. New coal mines were opened; additional open-hearth furnaces were added at existing plants; production began of by-products such as slag and phosphate fertilizer; a by-product coke plant was installed; and an industrial water supply was created with the construction of Bayview Lake. In 1917 the World War I demand for steel allowed Crawford to win approval of an $11 million appropriation for the building of a new group of mills known as Fairfield Steel Company.

Although TCI was involved in several labor strikes during Crawford's presidency, he did succeed in re-ducing labor turnover and molding a healthier work force anchored by family men rather than drifting laborers. Crawford's approach to the labor problem had to evolve within the framework of the policies of U.S. Steel. Under the leadership of Judge Elbert Gary, the steel corporation was experimenting with "welfare capitalism," defined by Gary as including fair wages, good working conditions, pensions, and school and recreation facilities but decried by organized labor as paternalistic and anti-union. Gary claimed that the system was not motivated by hostility to unions—although the last vestiges of unionism in U.S. Steel plants were eliminated in 1909—but by a mature social conscience within the industry.

Despite the opposition of many of his operating managers, Crawford utilized welfare capitalism more extensively than any other subsidiary president, creating one of the most complex and extensive systems in the nation. His programs included a rapid cleanup of environmental conditions in company towns, the remodeling of existing villages, and the building of new towns that included school buildings, playgrounds, community houses, bathhouses, and churches. In the segregated South, separate facilities were provided for black and white workers within the villages. Crawford hired an experienced social worker, Winifred Collins, who had worked in a Chicago settlement house, to head a large department of social science. Her cadre of employees developed a wide range of activities for the families of the workers, including domestic science classes, women's clubs, village bands, sports teams, and libraries. Through arrangements with local authorities, TCI funded and ran a school system of eight white and fourteen black schools from 1914 to 1933, providing equal facilities and equipment for both races. The TCI schools earned praise from several sources, including the U.S. Bureau of Education.

Crawford hired Dr. Lloyd Noland, an industrial physician with experience in the Panama Canal Zone, to create and operate a department of health that dealt with the eradication of malaria, typhoid, smallpox, and hookworm, and offered family health care as well as tending to work-related accidents. In addition to village dispensaries, Noland eventually built a large, well-equipped company hospital. The welfare and health programs contributed to a reduction of the annual worker turnover from 400 percent annually to 5.1 percent in 1930. The average work attendance was doubled, and the standard of living for TCI employees was higher than for other workers of the area.

In 1930 Crawford unexpectedly resigned to accept the presidency of Jones and Laughlin Steel Corporation of Pittsburgh, which had offered him a contract that he felt would make his family financially secure. Instead of directing an anticipated expansion program, however, Crawford spent five stressful years helping the company survive the Great Depression. His wife and second daughter continued to spend most of their time in Birmingham. Broken in health, Crawford resigned in 1935 at the age of sixty-five and returned to Birmingham where he died the following year.

Despite his corporate loyalty, Crawford was an astute analyst of the problems and potential of the South and worked to eliminate discriminatory freight-rate and product pricing systems, such as Pittsburgh Plus and the Birmingham Differential, which gave an advantage to northern steel mills even in selling to markets closer to Birmingham than Pittsburgh. His interest in bettering the economic development of the region led him to promote diversified agriculture, improvement of the state docks at Mobile, development of the state's river system, and creation of a state industrial development board. Trained as an engineer, he brought valuable technical skills to his career in the iron and steel industry, which particularly benefited struggling southern industry, but the unique problems associated with the southern work force and U.S. Steel's labor policy thrust him to the forefront of the early-twentieth-century experiment with welfare capitalism. Although criticized by organized labor, the programs measurably improved the quality of life for workers and their families in the years before the New Deal enabled unionization. Crawford's active and avid work to promote regional economic development beyond iron and steel made him one of the more realistic New South spokesmen.

• A collection of Crawford's personal papers, newspaper clippings, and scrapbooks is located in the Special Collections at Davis Library, Samford University, Birmingham, Ala. Company records of the Tennessee Coal, Iron and Railroad Company are not generally available to researchers but were used by Marlene Hunt Rikard in "An Experiment in Welfare Capitalism: The Health Care Services of the Tennessee Coal, Iron and Railroad Company" (Ph.D. diss., Univ. of Alabama, 1983). For an overview of Crawford's activities at TCI, see Rikard, "George Gordon Crawford: Man of the New South," *Alabama Review* 31 (July 1978): 163–81. More detail on his personal life and on the technological developments at TCI can be found in the M.A. thesis of the same title and by the same author (Samford University, 1971). Contemporary books and articles that include descriptions of Crawford's social work programs include Edwin Mims, *The Advancing South: Stories of Progress and Reaction* (1926; repr. 1969); Rose Feld, "Way Down in Alabama," *Success* 8 (Jan. 1924); and Hastings H. Hart, *Social Problems of Alabama* (1918). For a discussion of the TCI educational system, see Horace Mann Bond, *The Education of the Negro in the American Social Order* (1966) and U.S. Bureau of Education, *An Educational Study of Alabama* (1919). Crawford and TCI are included in several articles in the 6 Jan. 1912 issue of *Survey*, which focused on the conditions of labor in the Birmingham industrial district. Dr. Lloyd Noland contributed numerous articles to medical journals describing facets of the TCI health program, including "The Organization and Operation of an Industrial Health Department: A Description of the Work of the Department of Health of the Tennessee Coal, Iron and Railroad Co.," *Transactions of the Southern Surgical Association* 38 (1926): 275–84. Though sponsored by the Birmingham Chamber of Commerce, Ethel Armes's *The Story of Coal and Iron in Alabama* (1910; repr. 1973), is valuable for its contemporary interviews of southern industrialists, including

Crawford. An obituary appears in the Birmingham *Age-Herald*, 21 Mar. 1936.

MARLENE HUNT RIKARD

CRAWFORD, Isabel (26 May 1865–18 Nov. 1961), Baptist missionary, was born Isabel Alice Hartley Crawford in Cheltenham, Ontario, Canada, the fifth and youngest child of John Crawford, a Baptist minister and educator born in Northern Ireland, and Sarah Louise Hackett Crawford, originally from London.

Following his graduation and ordination from Edinburgh University and Stepney College, John Crawford felt called upon to work among the poor of London, preaching from a wagon chapel. In 1858 he moved his family to Canada and, as pastor of the Baptist church in Cheltenham and later as lecturer in biblical studies and church history at the Canadian Literary Institute at Woodstock, gained recognition for his advocacy of theological education. In 1880 Crawford founded Prairie College in Rapid City, Manitoba, for the purpose of training men for a frontier ministry. After the failure of this ambitious undertaking, Crawford served as pastor of Baptist churches in St. Thomas, North Dakota, and Wingham, Ontario. He died in Toronto in 1892.

Because her family moved so frequently, Isabel's formal schooling was sporadic. She attended Woodstock Central School and the Canadian Literary Institute, and she taught Sunday school in Rapid City. Her parents, however, were more important in the education of their daughter than the schools were. Her mother instructed Isabel in music, painting, writing verse and prose, and reading and interpreting the works of Shakespeare. Isabel served as her father's factotum in North Dakota, studying theology, church history, and church management under his direction.

Canada's western frontier with its frequent storms, prairie fires, and other natural disasters toughened Isabel Crawford. In Rapid City she developed a passion for hard work, often overextending herself. At the age of seventeen she fell victim to tuberculosis, leaving her almost totally deaf for the rest of her life. While convalescing Crawford decided on a career as a missionary. In North Dakota she taught painting to the neighborhood girls, earning the tuition to take the two-year program of study at the Women's Baptist Missionary Training School in Chicago. In 1891 she left Toronto for Chicago.

Crawford did not find her formal studies demanding, since she had learned church history and theology from her father. She managed to follow classroom exercises with a crude hearing device and by reading lips. What she learned by visiting the slums of Chicago was challenging and disturbing. Every Thursday the young trainees went out in pairs, bringing food, clothing, and the message of Christianity to the slum dwellers. Everywhere she came in contact with prostitutes, alcoholics, roughnecks, abandoned waifs, and starving people. On the Canadian frontier she had known poverty but not hopelessness. Her efforts to reach out to Chicago's slum dwellers frustrated her, and she was quick to blame capitalists and church groups for allowing such deplorable slum conditions to exist.

Crawford graduated from the Women's Baptist Missionary Training School in June 1893 and waited for the Women's American Baptist Home Mission Society to assign her to a mission field, preferably in China, India, or Africa. At the time of her graduation Chief Lone Wolf of the Kiowa Indians in the Oklahoma Territory issued an urgent appeal to the Baptists, indicating a strong interest in learning more about the Christian faith. Believing that Christianity might represent his people's last hope for salvation, he was prepared to welcome a missionary to his camp at Elk Creek. The Reverend George W. Hicks, who was part Cherokee, was ordered to go to Lone Wolf's camp at Elk Creek along with Isabel Crawford and Hattie Everts, another recent graduate of the Missionary Training School. Hicks, who knew Kiowa culture and language, soon made it clear that he could not immediately take up residence at Elk Creek because of family obligations. The Indians at Elk Creek were disappointed since neither Crawford nor Everts knew the customs of the people. They were provided with an interpreter named Paul, an Indian from the more populated Kiowa camp at Saddle Mountain, forty miles away. The inhabitants of Elk Creek looked upon the missionaries with suspicion.

Famine took hold of the reservation in the winter of 1894. On 30 March 1894 Crawford wrote in her journal: "Old journal, I am hungry and would eat you if you were beef." Supplies began arriving regularly by April. The Indians, Crawford wrote, "know more about starvation than any other people on the earth I believe and after this winter I have a sympathy for them that will always be ripe for action." Everts soon left the camp to continue her education. But Crawford, gregarious and energetic, remained, and the Kiowa Indians had already accepted her as one of their own.

When Hicks assumed his duties at Elk Creek, Crawford began her first lecture tour, soon establishing a national reputation among Baptists as an advocate of Christian justice for Native Americans. Wherever she went she said that only Jesus could save and uplift the Indians—but were they and the whites ready to accept this point of view? The Kiowa Indians at Elk Creek converted to Christianity. Following her whirlwind lecture tour, Crawford became a U.S. citizen. She was invited by the Kiowa Indians at Saddle Mountain, part of the Wichita Mountain range, to preach among them. Under her ministry conversions were made, and a congregation of one hundred members established the Saddle Mountain Baptist Church, which opened on Easter Sunday 1903. The Kiowa Indians became missionaries themselves, establishing the Sunlight Mission for the Hopi Indians of Arizona. Eventually, Lucius Aitsan, a Kiowa Indian and close friend of Crawford, became an ordained minister and pastor of the Saddle Mountain Baptist Church. Years later Crawford expressed satisfaction that many children and grandchildren of the original Kiowa Baptists had completed their college education.

A controversy swirling over Crawford's acquiescence and participation in celebrating the Lord's Supper without the officiating presence of an ordained minister forced her to leave her post at Saddle Mountain. From 1908 to 1913 Crawford traveled throughout the United States, lecturing to thousands of Baptists. A rousing speaker dressed in Indian costume, she brought the concerns of Native Americans to the attention of white audiences. After each talk she presented the Twenty-third Psalm in Indian sign language. In her later years Crawford worked among the Indians of western New York. She charged the New York Baptist churches and Albany with "criminal neglect" in dealing with the inhabitants of the Tonawanda, Tuscarora, Cattaraugus, and Allegheny reservations. She led a successful effort to prevent white Baptists and Presbyterians from making the Baptist church on the Allegheny reservation a Presbyterian church and changing the Presbyterian church on the Tuscarora reservation to a Baptist church solely for administrative purposes and without the consent of the Indians. She lectured frequently throughout the Northeast on behalf of justice for the Indians of New York.

A serious leg injury forced Crawford into retirement beginning in 1930. She spent the last years of her life in Orlando, Florida, and later with her two nieces in Grimsby, Ontario. In keeping with her wishes she was buried in the cemetery at Saddle Mountain. Her unwavering efforts to extend social justice to the Indians place her among the leading advocates of the American Social Gospel movement of the late nineteenth and early twentieth centuries. A lifetime of close relationships with Native Americans gave Crawford a Christian cultural perspective perhaps unique in modern American church history.

• The Isabel Crawford Papers are in the collection of the American Baptist Historical Society in Rochester, N.Y. See her delightful autobiography, *Joyful Journey, Highlights on the Highway* (1951). Also see Salvatore Mondello's three articles in the journal *Foundations*: "Isabel Crawford: The Making of a Missionary," 21 (Oct.–Dec. 1978): 322–39; "Isabel Crawford and the Kiowa Indians," 22 (Jan.–Mar. 1979): 28–42; and "Isabel Crawford, Champion of the American Indians," 22 (Apr.–June 1979): 99–115.

SALVATORE MONDELLO

CRAY, Seymour (28 Sept. 1925–5 Oct. 1996), electrical and computer engineer, was born in Chippewa Falls, Wisconsin, the son of Seymour Cray, a civil engineer, and Lillian Cray. Influenced by his father, Cray became interested in technology at an early age, building a variety of electronic gadgets before he reached his teens. In high school he won the school's science prize for his work in chemistry. Immediately after graduation in 1943, Cray joined the army and went to Europe and the Philippines to operate radio communications equipment during World War II. A year after his discharge he returned to Chippewa Falls and in 1947 he married Verene Vole; they would have three children.

The couple soon enrolled at the University of Wisconsin, but after a year transferred to the University of Minnesota. In 1951 Cray received a B.S. degree in electrical engineering and a master's in applied mathematics. He immediately began work at Engineering Research Associates (ERA), an electrical design and pioneering digital computer firm in St. Paul that had produced the Atlas, and a commercial version of this computer, the ERA 1101 (also known as the UNIVAC 1101). Cray developed a sophisticated control system to analyze and sequence programming instructions for this machine's successor, the ERA 1103 (UNIVAC 1103). He rapidly progressed from senior engineer to supervisor engineer at Remington Rand, an office machine firm that acquired ERA in 1952.

In 1955 Remington Rand merged with Sperry Corporation and Cray led the St. Paul division of Sperry-Rand's design team for a U.S. Navy computer project. Sperry-Rand, however, often failed to come through with sufficient funds for computer development projects, frustrating many top engineers, including ERA founder William Norris. In 1957, the company's bureaucracy and inadequate resources for computer development led Norris to resign. Frank Mullaney and several other engineers joined him in forming the Control Data Corporation (CDC) in Minneapolis. After completing some critical navy contract work, Cray followed several months later and became the firm's director of engineering and top computer designer. He immediately began work on a solid-state computer, the CDC 1604.

Cray's engineering colleagues were amazed by his mastery of nearly every aspect of the 1604's design and development, from the processors and power systems to the circuits and coding. He was indefatigable, frequently joining his wife and children for dinner and then returning to CDC to work until the early morning. When the 1604 hit the market in 1960 it was the fastest computer in the world with a clock speed of five microseconds. This established the 1604 as the computer of choice for many advanced scientific applications and gave CDC a market niche in an industry that was otherwise dominated by IBM.

The success of the 1604 allowed Cray to gain approval for a far more ambitious computer, the CDC 6600. To give him quiet and freedom, CDC President William Norris allowed him to start a new facility eighty miles away in Chippewa Falls and move the 6600 project there. The 6600, completed in 1963, was faster than its predecessor by a factor of fifty. Within a year more than a hundred 6600s were sold at roughly $8 million apiece. The supercomputer was born and CDC had established itself as the clear leader in this field. From the CDC 1604 through the CDC 6600 and his many other supercomputers, Cray was able to design machines of unprecedented speed through his innovative choice of smaller, more reliable materials, his great skill at building logic circuits for optimal efficiency, and his development of sophisticated cooling systems.

Cray completed the evolutionary 7600 before beginning design work on another revolutionary computer, the CDC 8600. The 8600, designed for unparalleled speed through incorporation of multiple processors, was the most ambitious computer development project to date. The machine, however, had a number of technical problems that, despite years of intense work by Cray, remained unsolved. CDC, involved in an expensive antitrust lawsuit against IBM, was forced to cut expenses. In 1972 Cray, frustrated with corporate power struggles, funding problems, and his failure to get the 8600 running, resigned to form his own company, Cray Research, taking a half dozen CDC engineers with him.

Cray Research set up shop in a small Chippewa Falls laboratory and Cray began work on the Cray-1, which was less ambitious than the 8600 but would be the fastest computer in the world. A critical factor facilitating the machine's speed was the use of integrated circuits instead of transistors. In 1976, prior to the computer's completion, Cray Research made an initial public stock offering, raising more than $10 million. Cray's goal of selling two machines a year easily was surpassed as government agencies competed to get Cray computers for defense, meteorological, and other scientific and engineering applications.

In 1975 Cray divorced his first wife. Five years later he was remarried, to Geri M. Harrand, and in this marriage he began to spend more time on recreation.

In 1981 Cray resigned as chair of the company and began to work as a contractor, which allowed him to follow his design interests unhindered and to have a more flexible schedule. As development of the Cray-2 bogged down, Steve Chen, a brilliant parallel-processing specialist who had joined Cray Research in 1979, developed a highly successful Cray computer, the X-MP. Others worked on completion of the Cray-2 in the mid-1980s as Cray switched to design work on the Cray-3, a computer that was also fraught with delay and difficulties. In 1987 the firm suffered a major blow when Steve Chen left to start his own company, Supercomputer Systems, Inc., taking more than 40 Cray engineers with him. To rejuvenate the CRAY-3 project, Cray incorporated a new firm, Cray Computer, in Colorado Springs, Colorado. Delays resulted in the company's losing some key contracts, however, and other projects lagged; Cray Computer declared bankruptcy in 1995. The following year Cray died near Colorado Springs from complications following an automobile accident.

Cray's creativity, tenacity, and overall capabilities led him to the forefront of supercomputer design, a field he then dominated for more than a decade and a half. His disinterest in commercial issues and disdain for the demands of corporate culture clearly were overshadowed by his intense focus on engineering and his great success in pushing the boundary for designing and building computers of unprecedented speed.

• Several corporate manuscript collections contain primary source material on Cray's work with ERA, Remington Rand, Sperry-Rand, and CDC. These include the Sperry-Rand collection at the Hagley Museum and Library, Wilmington, Del., and the Control Data Corporation Collection housed at the Charles Babbage Institute, University of Minnesota, Minneapolis, Minn. The Cray Museum in Chippewa Falls provides information on some aspects of Cray's work, especially projects at Cray Research and Cray Computer. The most important secondary source is Charles J. Murray, *The Supermen: The Story of Seymour Cray and the Technical Wizards behind the Supercomputer* (1997), a well-documented and balanced account of Cray's life and his achievements and their context. Works about Cray's colleagues also offer important perspectives, such as James C. Worthy, *William C. Norris: Portraits of a Maverick* (1987). Useful biographical sketches include James E. Tomayko, "Seymour Cray," Anthony Ralston, et al., *Encyclopedia of Computer Science*, 4th ed. (2000), pp. 466–67.

JEFFREY R. YOST

CROCKETT, James Underwood (9 Oct. 1915–11 July 1979), gardener and writer, was born in Haverhill, Massachusetts, the son of Earle Royce Crockett and Inez Underwood Crockett. After attending area public schools, he studied horticulture briefly at the University of Massachusetts. By 1935 he had moved to Long Island, New York, where he became an employee of Oak Park Nurseries, in East Patchogue. Four years later he moved again, this time to Texas, and became the superintendent of the Japanese Nursery Company in Houston. During his two years in Texas he studied horticulture part time at the state Agricultural and Mechanical College, now known as Texas A&M University.

During World War II, from 1941 to 1945, Crockett served in the U.S. Navy, rising to the rank of lieutenant. In 1943, on leave, he married Margaret Williams; the couple subsequently had four children. After the war ended, he moved back to Massachusetts and in 1946 opened a small business, Crockett's Flower Shop, in Lexington. A year later he began publishing *Flowery Talks*, a newsletter that included helpful hints for florists. Crockett sold the shop in 1948 but continued to publish the successful newsletter until his death more than thirty years later. During that time he made several lengthy trips to Europe, Latin America, the Caribbean, Hawaii, and Canada to search for botanical specimens.

Crockett's first book, *Window Sill Gardening*, was, as its title suggested, a how-to book for gardeners with modest abilities who wanted to grow plants in the windows of their homes. Published by Doubleday in 1958, it was a success and led to a more ambitious volume—for more ambitious gardeners—three years later: *Greenhouse Gardening as a Hobby* (1961), again published by Doubleday. Its further success led the Brooklyn Botanic Garden to hire him as the editor of a book on greenhouse gardening for their prestigious and widely praised how-to series; the result was *Greenhouse Handbook for the Amateur*, published in 1963.

This was followed by another book for Doubleday, *Foliage Plants for Indoor Gardening* (1967).

Working from his suburban home in Concord, outside Boston, Crockett was hired in the late 1960s to write and edit the *Time-Life Encyclopedia of Gardening*, a series of fifteen volumes issued at regular intervals during the following decade. Volume 1, *Annuals* (1971), was succeeded by books about roses, landscape gardening, lawns and ground covers, flowering house plants, bulbs, evergreens, perennials, flowering shrubs, trees, foliage house plants, vegetables and fruits, herbs, and wildflower gardening. *Greenhouse Gardening*, the fifteenth volume, was published in 1977, the same year that yet another Crockett book, *Crockett's Victory Garden*, was issued by Little, Brown. The latter was a companion volume to a weekly show by the same name that Crockett had begun hosting two years earlier on public television, through the local PBS station, WGBH in Boston.

The television program "Crockett's Victory Garden," which offered gardening tips to novices and professionals alike, was an immediate success, in large part because of the easy, reassuring manner of its host. Dressed in a denim work shirt and khaki pants, the bespectacled, graying Crockett beamed out upon his audience like a cherished uncle or trusted family doctor. Anyone, Crockett told his viewers, could grow anything, provided that care and patience were shown—and they believed him. The program proved such a hit locally that it was soon being broadcast throughout the country, reaching at least four million viewers each week, and the publication of a companion volume to the show was a testament to its popularity. The book became a bestseller, and Crockett arguably became the best-known gardener in America.

The show's title—and the name of the book—were derived from a common practice during World War II among city and rural dwellers alike: tending so-called "victory gardens" that were planted with fruits and vegetables to supplement the restricted diets caused by wartime food shortages. *Crockett's Victory Garden*—the book and the show—cashed in on the rebirth of interest in gardening that had occurred in the 1970s, in the wake of the back-to-the-land movement inspired by hippies and environmentalists, beginning in the late 1960s. Crockett's show—and two subsequent bestselling companion volumes, *Crockett's Tool Shed* (1979) and *Crockett's Flower Garden* (1981)—came to embrace both edible and ornamental plants.

Unfortunately, Crockett did not live to finish writing *Flower Garden*. He died while on vacation in Jamaica, not long after being diagnosed with cancer, and the book was completed by Marjorie Waters. The television series was abruptly canceled, although it was subsequently made available in reruns to PBS member stations.

In addition to his television appearances and book authorship, Crockett was also a syndicated columnist for United Press International during the 1970s. As a resident of Concord he was active in community affairs, including the local Congregational church. He was a member of, and active in, numerous professional organizations as well, including the Massachusetts Horticultural Society and the Garden Writers of America.

• Biographical information on Crockett is limited. See "Crockett, James Underwood," in *Contemporary Authors*, vols. 33–36, First Revision (1978), p. 217; *Contemporary Authors*, vols. 89–92 (1980), p. 115; and *Contemporary Authors: New Revision Series*, vol. 13 (1984), pp. 132–33. An obituary appears in the *New York Times*, 14 July 1979.

ANN T. KEENE

CUNLIFFE, Marcus (5 July 1922–2 Sept. 1990), historian, was born Marcus Falkner Cunliffe in Rochdale, Lancashire, England. His father, Keith Harold Cunliffe, was born and bred in Lancashire; his mother, Kathleen Eleanor Falkner Cunliffe, was an Anglo-Scot. Cunliffe attended the Royal Grammar School at Newcastle-upon-Tyne, where he was first introduced to American literary culture. He entered Oriel College in 1940, was commissioned lieutenant in 1942 in the British Army, earned his B.A. in 1944, and then served as an intelligence officer in the 4th Royal Tank Regiment—seeing action in France, Holland, and Germany in 1944 and 1945. After Germany's surrender, Cunliffe worked briefly with a military history team under Field Marshal Montgomery. Returning to Oxford early in 1946, he obtained an M.A. in 1946 and a B.Litt. a year later. His interest in the United States was furthered when he had fellowships at Yale University (1947–1949), the University of Chicago (1954), and Stanford University (1957–1958). Cunliffe taught courses in American studies, history, and institutions at the University of Manchester (1949–1964) and at the University of Sussex (1965–1980). In 1949 Cunliffe married Mitzi Solomon, a sculptor and designer; they had three children and were divorced in 1971.

Early in the 1950s, Cunliffe began to publish prolifically. Two of his first three books were on military subjects. *The Royal Irish Fusiliers, 1793–1950)* (1952) and *History of the Royal Warwickshire Regiment, 1919–1955* (1956) are both highly regarded by military historians for their attention to detail and for their graphic passages. Between these two books came Cunliffe's most famous and enduring work, *The Literature of the United States* (1954). In it, he conservatively theorizes that American literature is best when it blends autobiographical, biographical, and sociocultural data into realistic, aesthetically pleasing observations. Especially fine are his treatments of Herman Melville, Walt Whitman, and later expatriates. Cunliffe revised and enlarged this classic, the last time for a fourth edition (1986). It has been translated into Chinese, French, German, Italian, Japanese, and Portuguese.

Cunliffe combined lecturing, teaching, and writing, mostly in England, until 1980. During these years, he published *The Nation Takes Shape, 1789–1837*

(1960), *Soldiers and Civilians: The Martial Spirit in America, 1775–1865* (1968; rev. ed. 1974), *The Age of Expansion, 1848–1917* (1974), and *Chattel Slavery and Wage Slavery: The Anglo-American Context, 1830–1860* (1979), among less significant books. *The Nation Takes Shape* is a historical study of men and events that created changing patterns for America's early growth in western settlement, industry, and politics. Cunliffe suggests that America survived various tensions—city/countryside, nation/region, conservatism/experimentalism—by evolving into contentiousness rather than homogeneity. *Soldiers and Civilians* traces the origins and development of the American military tradition and comments interestingly on the American military ethos vis-à-vis the antimilitarist, the amateur, and the professional, which Cunliffe labels, respectively, Quaker, rifleman, and cavalier. Cunliffe daringly sees First Bull Run, the early Civil War engagement, as symbolizing America's simultaneous like and dislike of both professional and amateurish military units—with both groups split into the apathetic and the enthusiastic. This complex work has been praised for its sophisticated approach to military history, showing as it does the interdependence of soldiers, politicians, and civilians. *The Age of Expansion* portrays technological advances, demographic changes, and nationalism as fueling American dynamism, but the author also sees irony in the reversal of American social dynamism resulting from the contrary dynamism of European military institutions. In *Chattel Slavery and Wage Slavery*, Cunliffe shows how the concept of wage slavery in Europe influenced the theories of human slavery in the United States and, further, how U.S.-British relations were consequently strained. This study was faulted by some early reviewers for ignoring pro-British abolitionists in the northeastern United States.

By this time, Cunliffe was thoroughly fascinated by George Washington and the myths and truths surrounding him. In *George Washington: Man and Monument* (1958; rev. ed. 1982), Cunliffe presents his hero as "a true American" who at the same time pleased his Congress by acting like a European-style field marshal; he concludes that "[t]he man *is* the monument; the monument *is* the man." This book was only the first of several treatments of Washington by Cunliffe, who gradually expanded his study of the first president to include the ever-evolving office of the presidency itself.

In 1971 Cunliffe married Leslie Hume, a journalist; they were divorced in 1980. Also in 1980, Cunliffe moved permanently to the United States, where he became University Professor at George Washington University, in Washington, D.C. He held this position, though in poor health, until his death. In the light of his professional interests, his permanent change of residence was not surprising; moreover, by this time he had been a popular visiting professor at seven or more American universities, beginning in 1958, and had enjoyed a fellowship at the Woodrow Wilson International Center in Washington (1977–1978).

Exigencies of space prevent more than a brief indication of the scope of Cunliffe's editorial work and article writing. In *Pastmasters: Some Essays on American Historians* (1949; repr. 1979), he collected biocritical essays on thirteen prominent specialists. His edition of *The London Times History of Our Times* (1971) assembles critical essays, first, on aspects of world history since 1945 and, second, on separate worldwide geographical units. Cunliffe edited reprints of works by Jonathan Swift (1960), Rudyard Kipling (n.d.), St. Jean de Crèvecoeur (1978), and Mark Twain (1982). He published at least forty articles in books largely by others and upward of a hundred articles and reviews. Of special delight is his "European Images of America," in *Paths of American Thought*, edited by Arthur M. Schlesinger, Jr., and Morton White (1963). In it Cunliffe brings his Anglo-American approach to bear on a consideration of imaginary and real visions of America, the noble and ignoble savage, and liberty and libertinism. His love of the United States is evidenced by his asking in regard to Benjamin Franklin, George Washington, and Abraham Lincoln, "What European nation even in a history ten times as extensive as that of the young United States could claim a trio which held any comparable significance for mankind?"

Everything Cunliffe wrote or edited bears the stamp of professional skill, care, and readability. His point of view is not unique, but it is engagingly rare. His conservatism is manifest. His approach is historical and biographical, not often startlingly revisionist, but uniformly indifferent to modern and postmodern anticolonial, quasi-Marxist, and deconstructionist interpretations. He was a friendly, well-trained, ex-military European who viewed and defined American life, history, and letters as largely growing out of but distinct from pervasive and often restraining Old World influences. As an "outsider," he was never a victim of American ethnocentricity. And though an "insider" within a coterie of specialists studying American culture, he was fortunate in having an unusually broad intercultural base. He saw America, to quote him, as "a nation which has held in suspension all the extreme possibilities—hopes and fears alike—for the future of mankind under democracy, and which continues to enact them for itself and for much of Europe and the rest of the world . . ."

In the last several years of his life, Cunliffe suffered from the debilitating effects of leukemia. The disease slowed his professional activities only to a degree but ultimately was the cause of his death, which occurred in Washington, D.C.

• Marcus Cunliffe's papers are deposited in the Gelman Library at George Washington University. His "Backward Glances," *Journal of American Studies* 14 (Apr. 1980): 83–102, is a lively intellectual autobiography telling of his being challenged by American culture, especially its literature and history, not only to analyze it but also to defend it against several anti-American British critics. Cunliffe, *In Search of America: Transatlantic Essays, 1951–1990*, ed. Robert H. Walker (1991), is a posthumous republication of twenty-one of his best and most representative essays. *American Studies: Essays in Honour of Marcus Cunliffe*, ed. Brian Holden Reid and John White (1991), is a festschrift containing sixteen essays by British scholars, most of whom knew Cunliffe personally and all of whom knew and valued his writings. Both *In Search of America* and *American Studies* include extensive bibliographies of Cunliffe's books and pamphlets, books he edited or coedited, articles in books, and articles and review articles, and many reviews. An obituary is in the *New York Times*, 5 Sept. 1990.

ROBERT L. GALE

CURTI, Merle (15 Sept. 1897–9 Mar. 1996), historian, was born Merle Eugene Curti in Papillion, Nebraska, near Omaha, to John Eugene Curti and Alice Hunt Curti. His father was of Swiss origins while his mother's roots lay in New England. After high school in Omaha, Curti attended Harvard College, graduating summa cum laude in 1920. Entering Harvard's graduate history program, he studied with Frederick Jackson Turner, Charles Homer Haskins (whose course in medieval intellectual history influenced him), and the literary scholar Bliss Perry. His first publication, a 1922 essay stressing the value of literature as a source for historians, anticipated his future career. He received his Ph.D. in 1927; his dissertation on the antebellum American peace movement, written under Arthur Schlesinger, Sr., and published in 1929 as *The American Peace Crusade, 1815–1860*, reflected his own post–World War I disillusionment and antimilitarism. After a year at Beloit College (1921–1922) and study at the Sorbonne (1924–1925), Curti taught at Smith College (1925–1937), Teachers College of Columbia University (1937–1942), and the University of Wisconsin–Madison (1942–1968), where in 1947 he was named Frederick Jackson Turner Professor of History.

Curti's best-known work, *The Growth of American Thought* (1943), received the Pulitzer Prize in history. A magisterial survey of thinkers and writers from the Colonial era through the 1930s, it helped define the new field of American intellectual history. *The Making of an American Community* (1959), a collaborative social profile of Trempealeau County, Wisconsin, using then-innovative techniques of quantification and analysis of census reports, tax lists, local records, and other demographic data, played a comparable role in launching the so-called new social history.

Curti's scholarly output encompassed some twenty books and edited works and more than fifty articles exploring many facets of American history from the peace movement and philanthropy to dime novels and world's fairs. With Vernon L. Carstensen he wrote a centennial history of the University of Wisconsin (2 vols., 1949). With the literary scholars Willard Thorp and Carlos Baker, he edited *American Issues* (1941), a documentary collection of historical and literary documents. His popular high school textbook, *Rise of the American Nation* (1950), went through many editions.

Curti played a key role in reorienting the study and teaching of American history in the mid-twentieth century. In the early 1940s he chaired a committee of the Social Science Research Council whose 1946 report, *Theory and Practice in Historical Study*, urged increased attention to methodology and theory. As a member and then chair of the program committee of the American Historical Association (AHA) in 1939–1940, he pushed for more sessions on theory, social-science methodology, and neglected topics ranging from women's history to folklore and photography, thereby anticipating the transformation of the profession in the 1960s and beyond. He was president of the Mississippi Valley Historical Association (MVHA), the forerunner of the Organization of American Historians, in 1951–1952 and of the AHA in 1953–1954; he also helped found the American Studies Association in 1951.

Kindly and soft-spoken in personal encounters and invariably measured in his public pronouncements, Curti, in the tradition of John Dewey, whom he deeply admired, was nevertheless a politically engaged intellectual fully involved with the public issues of his day. The depression-ridden 1930s called forth his most radical work. *The Social Ideas of American Educators* (1935; rev. ed., 1968), argued that the U.S. educational system had often served the interests of the capitalist class. In *Peace or War: The American Struggle, 1636–1936* (1936; repr. 1972), he criticized pacifists who ignored imperialism, social injustice, and class exploitation, and who "coming from the middle classes, have naturally accepted the existing economic order and have not seen the threats to peace inherent in it" (quoted in Wittner, "Merle Curti and the Development of Peace History," p. 76).

Although a backer of America's role in World War II, he warmly supported students who were conscientious objectors. Dismayed by the early Cold War anticommunist hysteria fomented by Wisconsin senator Joseph R. McCarthy, Curti supported a "Joe Must Go" recall petition campaign. An early recruit to the civil rights struggle, he helped spearhead a successful 1944 campaign against racial discrimination at the University of Wisconsin Faculty Club and in 1952 persuaded a bitterly divided MVHA executive board to shift the association's convention to Chicago from segregated New Orleans. He also helped end the anti-Semitic policies of the exclusive Madison Club, to which he belonged. As Kathryn Preyer has written: "Curti was not a scholar isolated in his study but a committed citizen who took an active role in the great issues of his time. . . . [He drew] no line between the active and contemplative life."

Though not a spellbinding lecturer, Curti was revered as a teacher, particularly of graduate students, to whom he gave himself unstintingly, directing eighty-six doctoral dissertations. Many former students became lifelong friends with whom he carried on a voluminous correspondence. "No teacher," his Wisconsin colleague E. David Cronon recalled, "could more deftly ask just the right question in such a way as to open a new vista before a discouraged or unimaginative student while at the same time leading

him to believe that he was somehow instructing and enlightening the master." He held visiting appointments at the University of Tokyo (1959–1960), the University of Melbourne (1964), and other institutions, and received numerous honorary degrees.

Curti in 1925 married Margaret Wooster (Margaret Wooster Curti), an experimental psychologist and noted scholar in her own right, whose influence he generously acknowledged. She assisted with the statistical aspects of *The Making of an American Community*, and Curti's final book, *Human Nature in American Historical Thought* (1980) began as a collaboration with her. A pacifist and socialist, she also encouraged his engagement in public issues. They had two daughters, Nancy Alice Holub, who died in 1994, and Martha (Mother Felicitas Curti, O.S.B.). Widowed in 1961, Curti married Frances Bennett Becker in 1968. She died in 1978.

Curti died in Madison, Wisconsin, where he had remained active in the intellectual life of the community after his retirement. His professional contributions are recognized by the Organization of American Historians' annual Curti Prize for the best book in American intellectual or social history. The University of Wisconsin–Madison history department sponsors an annual series of Curti Lectures, maintains an endowed Merle Curti professorship, and awards Curti fellowships to advanced graduate students to design and teach their own courses.

• The Merle Curti Papers at the State Historical Society of Wisconsin in Madison offer a rich trove of letters and other materials. See especially Curti to Michael Kammen, 20 June 1993, a long autobiographical letter. E. David Cronon, "Merle Curti: An Appraisal and Bibliography of His Writings," *Wisconsin Magazine of History* 54 (Winter 1970–1971): 119–35, includes a full bibliography of Curti's publications to 1970. Robert A. Skotheim, *American Intellectual Histories and Historians* (1966), discusses Curti's central role in that field. Biographical summaries and appreciations include Paul Boyer, "Merle Curti, 1897–1996," *Organization of American Historians Newsletter* 24, no. 2 (May 1996): 1, 14; Kathryn Preyer, "Merle Eugene Curti," *Proceedings of the American Antiquarian Society* 106, part 1 (1996), 26–31; John Pettegrew, "A Tribute: Merle Curti, Pragmatist Historian," *Intellectual History Newsletter* 18 (1996): 70–75; G. D. Lillibridge, "So Long Maestro: A Portrait of Merle Curti," *American Scholar* 66, no. 2 (Spring 1997): 263–70; and Lawrence S. Wittner, "Merle Curti and the Development of Peace History," *Peace and Change* 23, no. 1 (January 1998): 74–82. An obituary is in the *New York Times*, 17 Mar. 1996.

PAUL BOYER

CURTIS, Carl T. (15 Mar. 1905–24 Jan. 2000), educator, lawyer, and politician, was born Carl Thomas Curtis near Minden, Kearney County, Nebraska, the youngest of the eight children of Frank Oscar Curtis, a farmer and courthouse caretaker, and Alberta Mae Smith Curtis. His grandfather had changed the family name from Swanson to Curtis upon immigration to the United States from Sweden in the 1860s. After graduating from Minden High School in 1923, Carl

Curtis taught for a year in Danbury, Nebraska, then enrolled for a year at Nebraska Wesleyan. From 1925 to 1930 he taught at a Kearney County school and the Minden Elementary School, where he also served as principal. Meanwhile, he attended summer sessions at Nebraska Wesleyan in 1927 and the University of Nebraska in 1928 and studied at a local law office part time. Admitted to the Nebraska bar in 1930, he maintained a private practice at Minden until 1939. He married a local teacher, Lois Wylie Atwater, in 1931; the couple adopted two children. After his first wife's death in 1970, he married Mildred Genier Baker two years later.

Curtis was elected Kearney County attorney in 1930 as a member of the Democratic party but was defeated for reelection in 1934. Finding his party loyalty questioned and becoming disenchanted with Franklin D. Roosevelt's New Deal as the national debt continued to grow, he became a Republican. In 1938 he was elected to the U.S. House of Representatives from the Fourth District in Nebraska and served eight consecutive terms. In 1954 he was elected as U.S. Senator from Nebraska and served four consecutive terms. By 1979 Curtis was one of just over twenty senators or representatives to have served on Capitol Hill for forty years or more.

From the beginning of his career in Congress Curtis advocated neutrality for the United States and opposed what he considered interventionist policies of the Roosevelt administration, but following the Japanese attack on Pearl Harbor in 1941 he voted for the declaration of war. He also endeavored to restrain the growth of the American welfare state or to modify its consequences, for he believed that it created a special class of people dependent on government and that its economic demands resulted in overwhelming taxation, inflation of the currency, and depletion of capital goods by which the economy had been sustained. He also tried to end deficit financing and the increase of the national debt. In 1951 he introduced a resolution to amend the Constitution to require a balanced budget, but by 1978 his renewed proposal in the Senate included a provision that in time of war or a national emergency the requirement might be set aside for one year at a time.

Curtis's right-to-work proposal in 1942, aimed at amending the 1935 National Labor Relations Act, pointed the way for passage of the Taft-Hartley Act in 1947, which provided for restraining unfair labor union practices and for government intervention in an immense strike or lockout injurious to the public interest. Ten years later, as a member of the Senate Select Committee, chaired by John McClellan, he participated with John F. Kennedy, Barry Goldwater, and others in the investigation of labor union abuses. Thanks to the McClellan committee disclosures, over 100 individuals were indicted and convicted, including union leaders Dave Beck and Jimmy Hoffa. And several of Curtis's recommendations, including the outlawing of secondary boycotts, were enacted in the Landrum-Griffith Act in 1959; the legislation gave more union control to rank-and-file members, protected their dues and pension funds, required officials to be bonded, required accounting and reports, guaranteed periodic elections, and ended arbitrary control by top union officials. Later Curtis was a leader in the successful efforts in 1965 and 1966 to prevent repeal of Section 14(b) of the Taft-Hartley Act, which outlawed application of agreements requiring membership in a labor organization as a condition of employment in any state or territory in which such a requirement is prohibited by state or territorial law. And in the 1970s he introduced legislation giving employees the right to vote in a secret ballot so that they might decide for themselves any representation by a union or acceptance of a wage offer or a labor-dispute settlement.

Curtis's strong interests in agriculture and the conservation of natural resources increased after a 1935 flood on the Republican River in southern Nebraska claimed over one hundred lives. Thus he introduced in 1943 a flood control resolution for the Missouri River Basin with the help of Lewis Pick of the Corps of Engineers in Omaha and the involvement of W. Glenn Sloan of the Bureau of Reclamation. The result was the Flood Control Act of 1944, also known as the Pick-Sloan Plan. As one of the major writers, Curtis made certain the legislation provided that the power revenues from the large dams could be used to help finance irrigation development. After the Flood Control Act went into effect, more than 160 projects were completed or authorized in the Missouri River Basin, covering almost one-sixth of the area of the United States, and the vast development of flood control and irrigation, with recreation sites included, provided national benefits not only for agriculture but for commerce and industry as well. Curtis was also a coauthor of the Watershed Protection and Flood Prevention Act of 1954, which authorized the Department of Agriculture in association with the Soil Conservation Districts to build projects too large for an individual farmer or soil conservation district to handle alone. The program was initiated by sixty-two pilot projects for the entire nation.

As a consistent advocate of equity and fiscal reform in the social security system, Curtis believed Congress ought to achieve a just balance between those who pay and those who receive. In 1947 he proposed to amend the Old Age and Survivors Insurance Act of 1935 to extend coverage to self-employed persons, domestic workers, and employees of local and state government, including teachers. Many of his ideas were incorporated in the 1950 Social Security Act. During Dwight D. Eisenhower's administration, he was chairman of a subcommittee that recommended greater coverage, a pay-as-you-go provision, increased monthly benefits, and maintenance of an existing trust fund for reserve purposes. Much of the Curtis Plan was included in the 1954 and 1956 amendments to the Social Security Act, with the result that the program covered some 90 percent of the work force by the 1960s.

In 1962 Curtis proposed a supplement to the existing social security program that enabled workers and unemployed spouses not covered by an employer-sponsored pension or other qualified retirement plan to establish individual, tax-sheltered savings accounts that allowed them to deduct the annual amount deposited from their gross incomes for the year. Income tax was deferred on the deposit and the account's earnings until withdrawal. Although his name was not attached, Curtis's proposal—known as the Individual Retirement Account—became law in 1974.

Curtis supported a variety of farm legislation bills, including those relating to rural electrification and industrial uses of farm surpluses, such as the manufacture of motor fuel from corn. He also supported appropriation bills to implement educational programs enacted by the federal government, although he favored local control of the public schools. He supported virtually all legislation benefiting veterans enacted since 1945, the year of the original G.I. Bill of Rights Act, and all civil rights legislation, from a law against segregation in the armed services in 1949 to the Voting Rights Act of 1965. But he opposed the blanket coverage of Medicare legislation in 1965 because he believed persons who had sufficient income ought to pay for their own medical expenses.

In partisan politics, Curtis served as floor manager of Barry Goldwater's campaign for the presidential nomination at the 1964 Republican National Convention. Despite criticism by his colleagues and others during Richard Nixon's Watergate scandal of 1974, Curtis defended Nixon because he believed it was essential to protect the power of the executive office.

Diminutive, serious, dedicated, and not a seeker of publicity, Curtis nevertheless received recognition from a wide variety of sources: he was awarded honorary doctor of laws degrees from Nebraska Wesleyan in 1958 and Creighton University in 1971. He was also given a medal by the mayor of Athens, Greece, in 1974 and the Master Key to the Panama Canal in 1976. In Kearney County, Nebraska, U.S. Highway 6/34 was designated Carl T. Curtis Drive in 1998.

After Curtis retired from the Senate in 1979, he was associated with a Washington, D.C., law firm until 1983, when he returned to Nebraska to write his autobiography in Lincoln. He died in Lincoln and was buried in his hometown, Minden.

Curtis's significant accomplishments include his initiation of the Flood Control Act of 1944 because it was the first comprehensive plan that involved both the Corps of Engineers and the Bureau of Reclamation and became the basis for future protective measures in flood plains around the country. His effort to reform social security and expand coverage has benefited nearly everyone over the age of sixty-five, and his successfully proposed Individual Retirement Account set a precedent for subsequent retirement and health-care planning and legislation. His dedication to placing the federal government on a pay-as-you-go budget was partially rewarded in 1997, when an agreement calling for a balanced budget by fiscal year 2002 was signed.

• The Carl T. Curtis Collection, housed at the Nebraska State Historical Society in Lincoln, spans the years 1918 to 1994. It comprises more than 160 cartons of correspondence, speeches, legislative files, scrapbooks, and photographs. His autobiography, written with Regis Courtemanche, is *Forty Years Against the Tide: Congress and the Welfare State* (1986). Reviews of his accomplishments are in *Current Biography* (1954); George Douth, *Leaders in Profile: The United States Senate* (1975); and Eleanora W. Schoenebaum, ed., *Profiles of an Era: The Nixon/Ford Years* (1979). Short biographical articles appeared in the *Omaha World Herald Magazine*, 12 Dec. 1954, 11 Dec. 1960, 29 Dec. 1963, 30 Oct. 1977, and 30 Dec. 1984. See also the *Sunday (Omaha) World Herald*, 23 Oct. 1994. Obituaries are in the *New York Times*, the *Lincoln Journal Star*, and the *Omaha World Herald*, 26 Jan. 2000.

E. A. KRAL

D

DANIEL, Jack (5 Sept. 1850?–10 Oct. 1911), distiller, was born Jasper Newton Daniel in Lynchburg, Tennessee, the son of Calaway Daniel. His mother's name and the exact date of his birth are unknown, a fire in the Lynchburg courthouse having destroyed his birth records. He grew up as one of thirteen children in the small town of Lynchburg, the county seat of Moore County, about seventy miles southeast of Nashville. At the age of seven, "Jack," who had been raised by a family friend, was sent to work on a farm owned by Dan Call, a Lutheran minister who owned a whiskey still.

In 1863 Call, who wanted to devote himself full time to the ministry, sold his still to Jack Daniel, then barely a teenager. Through Call he learned the "Lincoln County process" of making whiskey, which includes straining ("mellowing") it through hard maple charcoal. The technique, which adds depth and smoothness to the whiskey's flavor but also adds days to the distilling process, is still practiced today. In 1866 Daniel registered his distillery with the U.S. government, and it remains the oldest registered distillery in the United States. In 1904, at the St. Louis Exposition and World's Fair, Daniel's Old No. 7 Tennessee sipping whiskey received the gold medal, being judged the best of nearly twenty whiskeys from around the world.

Jack Daniel, a handsome man who stood only five feet two inches tall, never married or had children. A dapper dresser who had a reputation of being a ladies' man, he was rarely seen without his knee-length coat and wide-brimmed hat. In 1892 he formed the Original Silver Cornet Band, which played at saloon openings and political rallies.

One day in 1905 Daniel, arriving at work before his bookkeeper, tried to open his safe and realized that he had forgotten the combination. Angry, he kicked the safe, severely fracturing his toe. Never fully healed, the broken toe eventually led to a blood infection that killed him. He died and is buried in Lynchburg. At his gravesite are two white chairs, ostensibly for the ladies to sit by his grave and mourn his passing. On his death his nephew Lem Motlow assumed control of the distillery.

Jack Daniel's whiskey-making business, which began as a one-man operation in a town of about 350 people, is now a major marketing enterprise. For sale are cookbooks, glassware, and clothing with the Jack Daniel's brand. In addition, the collection of Jack Daniel's bottles and commemorative whiskey decanters is a very popular and lucrative business. Daniel's Tennessee Whiskey, probably the best-known distilled spirit in the world, is consumed in nearly 139 countries worldwide.

• Very little biographical information concerning Jack Daniel is available. The distillery in Lynchburg, Tenn., is open for tours of the founder's office, where the few details of Jack Daniel lore can be gleaned. Ben A. Green, *Jack Daniel's Legacy* (1967), is out of print and hard to find.

STACEY HAMILTON

DANILOVA, Alexandra (20 Nov. 1903–13 July 1997), dancer, was born Aleksandra Dionisievna Danilova in Peterhof, Russia, near St. Petersburg; her parents, Dionis Danilov and Clavdia Danilova, died when she was three. Because of her love of dancing she was placed by her wealthy foster parents at the age of eight in the Imperial Ballet School attached to the Maryinsky Theatre, in the same class as George Balanchine. Being small, she was often cast as a child in ballets and operas until her schooling was interrupted by the October 1917 revolution. In 1920 she graduated and entered the company of what had been renamed the State Academic Theater for Opera and Ballet, advancing rapidly to soloist status, while also working with some of the younger experimental choreographers, especially Feodor Lopukhov and Balanchine. Her most influential teachers were Elizaveta Gerdt in Russia and later Lubov Egorova in Paris and Nicolas Legat in London.

In June 1923 Danilova joined a small group organized by Balanchine to tour Germany; when ordered to return to the Soviet Union, the four dancers chose not to do so. They were soon engaged by Serge Diaghilev for his Ballets Russes, where Danilova assumed increasingly important parts, eventually creating roles in ballets by Léonide Massine (*Mercure* and *Le Pas d'Acier*) and by Balanchine, who had become the company's principal choreographer (*Le Bal*, *The Triumph of Neptune*, *The Gods Go a-Begging*, and taking over the role of Terpsichore in *Apollon Musagète*). By the time of Diaghilev's sudden death in 1929, she was one of the company's stars.

In 1931, without another engagement, she danced in the operetta *The Great Waltz* in London (repeating the role in New York in 1934), but she soon joined the Ballets Russes de Monte Carlo assembled by Colonel Wassily de Basil and René Blum, with Massine as chief choreographer. Her partnership with Massine in his *La Boutique Fantasque* (as Can-Can dancers) and *Le Beau Danube* (as a Flower girl and a Hussar) became legendary, but she was also acclaimed as Odette in Act II of *Swan Lake* and in the Fokine repertoire, especially in the title role in *The Firebird*, the Doll in *Petrouchka*, and in *Les Sylphides*.

The de Basil Ballets Russes toured widely, in 1933 having a great success in New York that led to annual extended American tours. In 1938 Danilova left de Basil to join the Ballet Russe de Monte Carlo formed by Massine and Sergei Denham, where her Glove Seller in Massine's *Gaîté Parisienne* (with Frederic Franklin as the Baron and Massine as the Peruvian) became especially famous. Other notable roles included an icy Myrtha in *Giselle* (she danced the title role, but it did not suit her temperamentally), the Sugar Plum Fairy in their abbreviated *Nutcracker*, the vivacious Swanilda in *Coppélia* (which she and Balanchine were to recreate in 1973 for the New York City Ballet), and in the *Raymonda* of Marius Petipa she restaged with Balanchine. When Balanchine worked with the company, she created the ballerina role in his witty *Danses Concertantes*, atypically, the eerie Sleepwalker (rather than the Coquette) in his *Night Shadow* (later renamed *La Sonnambula*), and the concluding ballet in the musical *Song of Norway*. Although she was always a glamorous figure and widely acclaimed as a great dancer, it was on the endless tours of the Ballet Russe in the 1940s, with Frederic Franklin as her regular partner, that she became a beloved figure for American audiences and an inspiration to countless young girls.

In 1949 Danilova returned to England (where she was greatly admired) as a guest with England's Sadler's Wells (now Royal) Ballet and the London Festival Ballet. In 1952 she left the Ballet Russe and danced with the small Slavenska-Franklin Ballet and then with her own little company, Great Moments of Ballet (1954–1956), retiring from ballet in 1957 but performing on Broadway in the musical *Oh Captain!* (1958) and gradually beginning to teach and to choreograph for the Metropolitan Opera (1959–1961). In 1963 Balanchine invited her to join the faculty of the School of American Ballet, where she taught advanced students until her retirement in 1989 and also staged ballets, especially works by Petipa and Michel Fokine, for the annual SAB workshop. She thus became a valued coach and role model for several generations of New York City Ballet dancers.

Danilova made two films, one with the Ballet Russes of Massine's *Capriccio Espagnol* (Jean Negulesco, 1941 as *Spanish Fiesta*) and *The Turning Point* (Herbert Ross, 1977), in which she played a ballerina-turned-teacher much like herself. In 1958 she received the Capezio Award, in 1984 the Dance Magazine Award, and in 1989 both a Kennedy Center Honor and New York City's Handel Medallion, while her autobiography, *Choura*, received the de la Torre Bueno Prize for the best dance book of 1986.

From 1927 to 1931 she and Balanchine lived together but never married. Her first husband was Giuseppe Massera, an Italian engineer who died in 1936, and in 1941 she married the Ballet Russe dancer Casimir Kokitch, obtaining an annulment eight years later. The great love of her life, however, was apparently a wealthy Spaniard whose family objected to his marrying a dancer. She was quoted as saying, "I sacrificed marriage, children and country to be a ballerina, and there was never any misunderstanding on

my part: I knew the price" (*New York Times*, 15 July 1997).

Although strong technically and acclaimed as Odette and in virtuoso pas de deux by Petipa, Danilova was essentially a *demi-caractère* dancer, shaping and coloring a step rather than emphasizing academic perfection, and with her vivacious personality more at home in *allegro* than in *adagio* movements (as distinct from her friend Alicia Markova, the most acclaimed Giselle of the time). The American critic Edwin Denby, who in 1938 had praised "a personal wit and distinction [that] makes her the equal of any great actress," added in 1945 that Danilova's "noble clarity of execution, her mastery over the many resources of dance rhythm, can make her formal steps and phrases seem poignantly unique and spontaneous, like a happy event in real life. . . . And in watching her, you feel, in the sustained flow of Danilova's rhythm, the alert vivacity of her personal dance imagination, the bite and grace of her feminine temperament, and a human sincerity that makes an artist both unpretentious and great" (*Dance Writings* [1986], pp. 52 and 320).

In his *New York Times* obituary, Jack Anderson, who called her extraordinarily versatile, noted that "She was known to her friends as Choura, and admired for her Champagne-like sparkle and a stage presence so intense that she could command attention even when she was not moving. With her heart-shaped face and dark brown hair, she was striking to behold. She was also celebrated for possessing what were considered the most beautiful—and photogenic—legs in ballet. Lincoln Kirstein, the New York City Ballet's director, once called them 'legs like luminous wax.'"

Danilova did much to create the image of ballet as a glamorous yet vital art for American audiences in the 1930s and 1940s. Then through her teaching she worked to pass on to younger dancers the traditions of the Russian school in which she had been trained, the Diaghilev ballet company in which she first achieved fame, and the Ballet Russe. In her dancing and in her always elegant person, she exemplified *the ballerina* to audiences and friends in the United States, Great Britain, and Japan—indeed, anywhere she danced or taught.

• Her charming autobiography, *Choura: The Memoirs of Alexandra Danilova* (1986), written with Holly Brubach, is the primary source of biographical information, along with A. E. Twysden, *Alexandra Danilova* (1947), an account of her life by a longtime admirer. Notable among her many interviews are "A Conversation with Alexandra Danilova," in *Ballet Review* 4, no. 4: 32–51, and no. 5: 50–60, and "Alexandra Danilova: St. Petersburg, Then and Now," *Ballet Review* 24, no. 1: 27–29. Reminiscences by friends and colleagues are in *Ballet Review* 26, no. 1: 37–56. The best accounts of the companies with which she danced are Serge Grigoriev, *The Diaghilev Ballet 1909–1929* (1953; reprint, n.d.); Richard Buckle, *Diaghilev* (1979); Kathrine Sorley Walker, *De Basil's Ballets Russes* (1983); and Jack Anderson, *The One and Only: The Ballet Russe de Monte Carlo* (1981). An account of Danilova at the School of American Ballet can be found in Jennifer Dunning, *But First a School: The First Fifty Years of the*

School of American Ballet (1985). Jack Anderson's obituary in the *New York Times* is dated 15 July 1997.

GEORGE DORRIS

DAVIDSON, William Lee (c. 1746–1 Feb. 1781), revolutionary war soldier, was born in Lancaster County, Pennsylvania, the son of George and Margret Davidson (maiden surname unknown), Scotch-Irish immigrants from Ulster, northern Ireland, who settled in 1748 near Davidson's Creek in Rowan County (now Iredell County), North Carolina. His father, a farmer and tavern keeper, died in 1760 and left him under the guardianship of John Brevard and Alexander Osborne. Davidson attended the Sugaw Creek Academy near Charlotte, where he may have been influenced by the Reverend Alexander Craighead, minister of the Sugaw Creek Presbyterian Church, who has sometimes been called the "Father of Independence" in the Carolina Piedmont. Beginning his career as a small farmer and slave owner in the neighborhood of Centre Presbyterian Church near the site of his father's home, Davidson in 1767 married Mary Brevard, daughter of his guardian and sister of Dr. Ephraim Brevard, reputed author of the legendary Mecklenburg Declaration of 20 May 1775. Four sons and three daughters were born of this marriage.

"Devoted to the profession of arms," as his friend Henry "Light Horse Harry" Lee wrote many years later, Davidson served as a lieutenant in the Rowan County militia regiment that went in 1767 with Governor William Tryon into Cherokee country to settle a boundary dispute. His qualities of leadership and dependability had been recognized when he became a constable in Rowan County and a militia captain in 1772. With the development of colonial resistance to the British government and the collapse of Royal authority, Davidson was named in 1774 to the Rowan Committee of Safety. As the owner of town lots in Charlotte, Davidson was also associated with the meetings of the Mecklenburg Committee of Safety that adopted the Mecklenburg Resolves of 30 May 1775, which declared null and void the commissions that had been granted by King George III. In December of 1775 he served as adjutant to Colonel Griffith Rutherford of the Rowan militia regiment in the campaign against Loyalists in upper South Carolina.

Commissioned a major in the Fourth North Carolina Regiment of the Continental army in 1776, Davidson participated in the defense of Wilmington, North Carolina, and Charleston, South Carolina, against the invasion attempts by British forces under Sir Henry Clinton. In 1777 Davidson's regiment joined George Washington's army in New Jersey. Owing to his gallant conduct at the battle of Germantown, Davidson was promoted to the rank of lieutenant colonel in the Fifth North Carolina Regiment and endured the harsh winter of 1777–1778 with his Continentals at Valley Forge. There he became a friend of Henry Lee and Daniel Morgan, with whom he would later serve in the Carolina Piedmont. He was transferred to the Third North Carolina Regiment in 1778 after returning from recruiting duties in North Carolina. In 1779 the North Carolina regiments were ordered southward to aid in the defense of Charleston against another British attack. While he was on furlough at his home in Rowan County, the British so completely invested Charleston that Davidson was unable to rejoin his regiment, which surrendered in May 1780 with General Benjamin Lincoln's army.

After losing his regiment, Colonel Davidson then joined the militia forces of the Salisbury District as second in command to Brigadier General Griffith Rutherford. In July, while engaged in suppressing a band of Loyalists emboldened by British successes in the South, he was severely wounded in an encounter with them at Colson's Mill. During Davidson's convalescence, General Rutherford was captured in August 1780 when the American army under General Horatio Gates was defeated at Camden, South Carolina. Davidson then succeeded Rutherford as brigadier general commanding the Salisbury Militia District. During the next several months, his militiamen and other partisan bands continually harassed the Loyalists and the British troops advancing on Charlotte. Although Davidson's forces were unable to prevent Lord Cornwallis's occupation of Charlotte in September, the British found themselves isolated in what Cornwallis reputedly called "the hornet's nest" where his forces were constantly exposed to sniper attacks by Davidson's men, who disrupted his lines of supply and communication.

The partisan leaders in western North Carolina urged General Gates to name General Davidson commander of the forces being assembled to fight Major Patrick Ferguson's British legion, which was advancing into their region. Gates, however, decided that Davidson could not be spared from his duties around Charlotte. On the defeat of Ferguson at King's Mountain on 7 October 1780, Cornwallis withdrew from Charlotte and returned to South Carolina, while Davidson continued his harassment of the departing British. When General Nathanael Greene, the successor to Gates, arrived at Charlotte in December, he depended heavily on Davidson to recruit and rally the militia in the effort to delay Cornwallis's return to North Carolina. In January 1781, when Cornwallis returned in the region west of the Catawba River, Greene ordered Davidson to guard the river fords and delay the enemy's crossing. At Cowan's Ford early on the morning of 1 February 1781, as he rode forward to rally his men against the British troops who had reached the eastern bank of the Catawba, General Davidson was killed by the shot of a Tory guide. When his body was found late that evening, it was buried by torchlight in the graveyard of the nearby Hopewell Presbyterian Church. Although Davidson's militiamen had been unable to prevent the British from crossing the Catawba, they did slow Cornwallis's advance until Greene was able to make a stand at Guilford Court House on 15 March.

Davidson's greatest contribution as one of North Carolina's most outstanding partisan leaders was the recruiting, assembling, and rallying of the militia in the western region. In recognition of his distinguished service, the Confederation Congress recommended the erection of a monument to his memory for "fighting gallantly in the defence of liberty and independence." "Light Horse Harry" Lee, who knew him well and admired him greatly, attributed Davidson's success to his "popular manners and pleasing address" as well as to his being "active and indefatigable" and "devoted to the profession of arms and the great cause for which he fought." Although Davidson never commanded troops in a decisive action or had the opportunity to demonstrate his grasp of strategy, he was a dependable and zealous subordinate who, according to Lee, was in the "habit of executing his orders with the greatest precision" (Henry Lee, *Memoirs of the War in the Southern Department of the United States* [1869 edition], p. 586).

General Davidson was commemorated by the naming of Davidson County in Tennessee and Davidson County in North Carolina in his honor. Davidson College in North Carolina was also named in his honor by action of the Concord Presbytery in 1835 as "a tribute to that distinguished and excellent man General Davidson, who in the ardor of patriotism, fearlessly contending for the liberty of his country, fell universally lamented in the battle of Cowan's Ford (Minutes of Concord Presbytery, 26 Aug. 1835).

• General Davidson left no papers, but the Chalmers Gaston Davidson Collection in the Davidson College Library contains copies of numerous contemporary documents and letters as well as scattered writings pertaining to the general's career. Chalmers Gaston Davidson, *Piedmont Partisan: The Life and Times of Brigadier-General William Lee Davidson* (1951), the only full-length biography and an authoritative treatment, is based on extensive research in numerous archives. Henry Lee, *Memoirs of the War in the Southern Department of the United States* (1812), gives one of the earliest and most reliable evaluations of General Davidson's career and contribution.

MALCOLM LESTER

DE CAMP, L. Sprague (27 Nov. 1907–6 Nov. 2000), writer, was born Lyon Sprague de Camp in New York City to Lyon de Camp, a businessman, and Beatrice Sprague de Camp. He was the middle child of three, in a family that had been in the United States since 1664. The de Camps' marriage ultimately failed, though not before they instilled in their children a love of traveling: while young, de Camp saw much of the United States, Europe, and Japan, and he traveled extensively throughout his life; his 1996 autobiography is as much a recounting of his travels as it is of his accomplishments. In 1922 he became one of the 1,500 original subjects in Lewis Terman's intelligence tests measuring lifelong accomplishments of youthful high achievers, and in 1929 he was the driver in a car crash that claimed the life of his older brother, Crawford, a memory that haunted him for life. In 1930 he

received a B.S. in aeronautical engineering from the California Institute of Technology; in 1933, he earned an M.S. in engineering from Stevens Institute of Technology in Hoboken, New Jersey. In 1931 he married a woman identified as Viola, whose full name he never divulged; they divorced in early 1933. His second marriage, to Catherine Crook on 12 August 1939, lasted until her death more than sixty years later.

From 1933 to 1936 de Camp worked as an instructor at the Inventors Foundation in New York, after which he was principal of the School of Inventing and Patenting in Scranton, Pennsylvania. His first book was *Inventions and Their Management* (1937), a textbook coauthored with Alf K. Berle. From 1942 to 1945 he served as a lieutenant commander in the U.S. Naval Reserve at the Philadelphia Naval Yard, working as an engineer with fellow writers Robert A. Heinlein and Isaac Asimov; he wrote radio scripts for "The Voice of America" from 1948 to 1956.

Genus Homo, de Camp's first work of science fiction, was co-written with P. Schuyler Miller during 1936–1938 and ultimately appeared in *Super Science Stories* (Mar. 1941). "The Isolinguals," his first non-collaborative science fiction story, appeared in *Astounding Science Fiction* magazine (Sept. 1937); he became a freelance writer following publication of "Language for Time Travelers" (*Astounding*, July 1938), occasionally publishing work under the pseudonyms Lyman R. Lyon and J. Wellington Wells. Notable early books—all first published in John W. Campbell's magazine *Unknown/Unknown Worlds*—include: *Divide and Rule* (1948), whose titular story features feudal humans ruled by kangaroo-like aliens; *Lest Darkness Fall* (1941), a classic alternative history involving a contemporary man transferred to Rome shortly after it had fallen to the Goths; *The Wheels of If* (1948), many of whose stories have been anthologized; *Solomon's Stone* (1957), about a dream world in which magic functions; and *The Undesired Princess* (1951), which involves a world governed by strict Aristotelian logic. In collaboration with Fletcher Pratt (1897–1956), de Camp co-wrote *The Incomplete Enchanter* (1941), *The Castle of Iron* (1950), and *Wall of Serpents* (1960), humorous fantasies featuring the hapless Harold Shea, who is transported to and must learn to function in various fictional worlds. Starting in 1950 de Camp co-wrote with Pratt the "Gavagan's Bar" series, fantastic stories told in the titular bar. Late in his career, de Camp returned to the Harold Shea series with *Sir Harold and the Gnome King* (1991) and concluded it with *The Enchanter Reborn* (1992) and *The Exotic Enchanter* (1995).

In 1949 de Camp began his Viagens Interplanetarias series. In it, Brazil is Earth's dominant power, and adventures occur on worlds named for Hindu and Egyptian gods (Vishnu, Ganesha, and Krishna; Osiris, Isis, and Thoth) during the span from the late twenty-first to the late twenty-second centuries. Although many of his stories were obviously inspired by the works of Edgar Rice Burroughs, de Camp used the adventure story framework to explore political, social, and economic relations. Notable stories from this series include *Rogue Queen* (1951); *The Search for Zei* (1962); *The Hand of Zei* (1963); *Cosmic Manhunt* (1954; preferred version as *The Queen of Zamba*, 1977); *The Tower of Zanid* (1958); and *The Prisoner of Zhamanak* (1982). Late in life, with the assistance of his wife, de Camp wrote *The Bones of Zora* (1983), *The Stones of Nomuru* (1988); *The Swords of Zinjaban* (1991); and *The Venom Trees of Sunga* (1992).

In 1950 de Camp discovered the heroic fantasies of Robert E. Howard (1906–1936) and was instrumental in rewriting many of Howard's unpublished manuscripts, the first such posthumous collaboration being *Tales of Conan* (1955). Starting in the 1960s de Camp edited or coedited a number of fantasy anthologies, including *Swords and Sorcery* (1963); *The Spell of Seven* (1965); *The Fantastic Swordsmen* (1967); *Warlocks and Warriors* (1970); and *3000 Years of Fantasy and Science Fiction* (1972). He also became a partner in Conan Enterprises, a company formed to exploit Howard's writings. In 1973 their publisher went bankrupt, and the ensuing lawsuits were not settled for three and a half years, though the de Camps ultimately recovered their expenses.

The first of de Camp's five historical novels was *An Elephant for Aristotle* (1958), which recounts the results of Alexander the Great's command to deliver a war-elephant from India to Greece. It was followed by *The Bronze God of Rhodes* (1960), set in Greece shortly before Demetrios Poliorketes's siege, and by *The Dragon of the Ishtar Gate* (1961), set during the reign of King Xerxes (486–465 B.C.) and involving a quest for a dragon. De Camp's historical novels were critically well received but were not sufficiently profitable for him to continue writing them; the same was true of his poetry, three volumes of which were published.

De Camp remained a lifelong rationalist and was in 1976 one of the founding fellows of the Committee for the Scientific Investigation of Claims of the Paranormal (CSICOP), quipping at the establishing conference that "many people have developed minds that are not only open, but gaping." *Lost Continents: The Atlantis Theme in History, Science and Literature* (1954) remains valuable, as do such books as *Lands Beyond* (1952), a collection of essays about myths and legends. *Spirits, Stars, and Spells: The Profits and Perils of Magic* (1966), co-authored with Catherine de Camp, examines the histories and practices of occultism and magic in Western culture, and *The Ragged Edge of Science* (1980) and *The Fringe of the Unknown* (1983) describe fringe and occult groups and their beliefs. *Great Cities of the Ancient World* (1972) is a serious study of thirteen "queen cities," including Thebes, Jerusalem, Nineveh, Tyre, Babylon, Memphis, and Athens; and *The Ancient Engineers* (1963), one of de Camp's finest works, describes the ways in which premodern cultures erected large structures. Another of his notable nonfiction books is the *Science Fiction Handbook: The Writing of Imaginative Fiction*

(1953; rev. ed., 1975), one of the first analyses of science fiction as a professional market.

De Camp's first book-length work of literary criticism was *The Conan Reader* (1968), a study of the works of Robert E. Howard. It was followed by *Literary Swordsmen and Sorcerors: The Makers of Heroic Fantasy* (1976), a collection of essays, and such edited volumes as *The Conan Swordbook* (1969) and *The Conan Grimoire* (1972). In addition, de Camp wrote *Lovecraft: A Biography* (1975), the first significant biography of H. P. Lovecraft (1890–1937), and with the assistance of his wife and Jane Whittington Griffin he co-wrote *Dark Valley Destiny* (1983), the first significant study of Robert E. Howard. These last two books have been criticized for lacking sympathy toward their subjects, but they remain valuable.

In 1953 de Camp shared an International Fantasy Award for the nonfiction *Lands Beyond*, co-written with Willy Ley. He won the Gandalf Grand Master of Fantasy Award in 1976, the Science Fiction Writers of America Grand Master Award in 1979, a World Fantasy Life Achievement Award in 1984, and in 1996 a Sidewise Special Achievement Award. His 1996 autobiography *Time and Chance* won the 1997 Hugo Award for Best Nonfiction Work, and in 1998 he was awarded the Pilgrim Award by the Science Fiction Research Association in recognition of his scholarship. Until his last years, when he retired to Plano, Texas, he was a visible presence at science fiction conventions: tall, courtly, articulate, genial, always willing to sign autographs and to discuss subjects as varied as the possible nature of Greek fire, the feasibility of interstellar travel, and the construction methods used for the pyramids of Egypt. He remained an active correspondent until his last year.

Catherine Crook de Camp died on 9 April 2000, and L. Sprague de Camp suffered a stroke and died on 6 November 2000, shortly before his ninety-third birthday, on the date that would have been his late wife's birthday. He was survived by his brother Lyman Lyon de Camp; two sons, Lyman Sprague and Gerard Beekman de Camp; and numerous grandchildren and great grandchildren.

Although he took the business of writing very seriously, de Camp repeatedly denied that his fantastic fiction possessed any social significance, and much of his output was intended primarily to entertain, an attitude that was not lost on his contemporaries. Brian Aldiss remarked that "his books give the impression of being thrown off for fun while he equips himself for a second expedition to the delta of the Orinoco or wherever." Nevertheless, even de Camp's least works are notable for their reasonable tone, intelligence, wit, and refusal to condescend, and his best works have become acknowledged classics.

• The Harry Ransom Center at the University of Texas at Austin holds virtually all of de Camp's papers, though a number of manuscripts are also held by Boston University. The most comprehensive autobiographical statement by de Camp is *Time and Chance* (1996). De Camp is mentioned in most histories of American science fiction and fantasy, but significant criticism does not exist. He is profiled by Lin Carter in "Introduction: Neomythology" in de Camp's *Literary Swordsmen and Sorcerors: The Makers of Heroic Fantasy* (1976); by Malcolm J. Edward and John Clute in "L. Sprague de Camp," in *The Encyclopedia of Science Fiction*, ed. Clute and Peter Nicholls (1993); by Clute in "L. Sprague de Camp," in *The Encyclopedia of Fantasy*, ed. Clute and John Grant (1997); by Don D'Ammassa in "L. Sprague de Camp," in *St. James Guide to Science Fiction Writers*, 4th ed., ed. Jay P. Pederson (1996); by Damon Knight in *In Search of Wonder*, 2d ed. (1967); by Sam Moskowitz in *Seekers of Tomorrow: Masters of Modern Science Fiction* (1966); by Brian Stableford in "L. Sprague de Camp," in *St. James Guide to Fantasy Writers* (1996); and in "L. Sprague de Camp," in *Science Fiction Writers: Critical Studies of the Major Authors from the Early Nineteenth Century to the Present Day*, 2d ed., ed. Richard Bleiler (1998). The most comprehensive bibliography to date is Charlotte Laughlin and Daniel J. H. Levack, *De Camp: An L. Sprague de Camp Bibliography* (1983). Obituaries and appreciations of de Camp appear in *Locus* for Dec. 2000, on his family's website (www.lspraguedecamp. com), and in the *New York Times*, 11 Nov. 2000.

RICHARD BLEILER

DE KOONING, Willem (24 Apr. 1904–19 Mar. 1997), artist, was born in Rotterdam, the Netherlands, the son of Leendert de Kooning, a beverage distributer, and Cornelia Nobel de Kooning, a café proprietor. After his parents divorced in 1907, Willem lived first with his father and then with his older sister and his mother, after she contested the custody arrangements. Willem left grammar school in 1916 and apprenticed with the commercial art and decorating firm of Jan and Jaap Gidding. He also enrolled in evening classes at the Rotterdam Academy of Fine Arts and Techniques, which he attended until 1924. In 1920 he left Gidding to work with Bernard Romein, the art director of a large Rotterdam department store. He traveled to Brussels and Antwerp in 1924, supporting himself through commercial art jobs.

De Kooning immigrated to the United States illegally as a stowaway aboard the Argentina-bound SS *Shelley* in 1926. He landed in Newport News, Virginia, on 15 August. He then traveled to New Jersey, where he found lodging at the Dutch Seaman's Home and work as a house painter in Hoboken. The following year, he moved to a studio on West Forty-fourth Street in Manhattan; there he worked as a commercial artist, house painter, and carpenter, and painted in his spare time.

Visiting Manhattan galleries and artists' studios in the late 1920s and 1930s, de Kooning met modernist artists such as, in 1929, John Graham and Stuart Davis and, in 1930, David Smith and Arshile Gorky. He spent the summer of 1928 at the artists' colony in Woodstock, New York. In 1934 he joined the Artist's Union. In 1935 de Kooning worked for the mural division of the WPA Federal Art Project on several assignments including the Williamsburg Federal Housing Project in Brooklyn, New York. A year later, a small study for the Williamsburg mural (not completed) was included in his first group exhibition, *New Horizons in American Art*, at the Museum of Modern Art in Manhattan. In 1936 he left the Federal Art Project because he was not a U.S. citizen. Despite financial woes, he shifted priorities and decided to paint full time, supporting himself through commissions and art tutoring (Gaugh, p. 123). De Kooning's works of the late 1930s and early 1940s show his interest in two key subjects: on the one hand, a haunting series of seated and standing male figures and, on the other, interiors and still lifes demonstrating his experimentation with abstraction. He spent long periods of time on single works, often leaving paintings unfinished for years.

At the end of 1936 de Kooning moved from 143 West Twenty-first Street to 156 West Twenty-second Street. That year, he met neighbors Edwin Orr Denby, a poet, and Rudolph Burckhardt, a painter-photographer. Through Denby, de Kooning was commissioned to design costumes for Nini Theilade's ballet *Les Nuages*, with music by Claude Debussy, performed by the Ballets Russes de Monte Carlo at the Metropolitan Opera House on 9 April 1940. De Kooning received several other commissions: in 1937 he designed a ninety-foot section of the three-part mural *Medicine* for the 1939 World's Fair Hall of Pharmacy, and around 1940 he created a four-part mural called *Legend and Fact* for the library of the SS *President Jackson* of American President Lines, commissioned by the U.S. Maritime Commission (Zilczer, p. 190).

De Kooning met Elaine Fried (Elaine de Kooning) around 1938. She took private art lessons from him for a year, eventually sharing his studio on West Twenty-second Street. They married on 9 December 1943. Although in 1944 they moved to 63 Carmine Street, de Kooning maintained a separate studio on Fourth Avenue between Tenth and Eleventh Streets. De Kooning's circle of art world acquaintances was widening. He became friendly with Jackson Pollock after they both were included in the 1942 exhibition *American and French Paintings* at the McMillen Gallery in New York City. A year later, he met Franz Kline at Conrad Marca-Relli's studio.

In 1943 Helena Rubinstein purchased *Elegy* (c. 1939; private collection, New York), which, like his other postwar images, is boldly painted by comparison with his earlier work. Despite the acquisition of *Elegy*, de Kooning remained in financial straits and continued to support himself through commissions rather than sales. In January 1944 the Container Corporation of America commissioned *The Netherlands*, an abstracted cityscape picturing traditional street and waterway traffic in a small town in Holland, for a "United Nations" advertising series in support of Allied war efforts (Zilczer, p. 190). With Milton Resnick, he designed in 1946 a backdrop for Maria Marchowsky's *Labyrinth*, a dance performed at New York Times Hall on 5 April.

Between 1946 and 1949 de Kooning created a series of black and white paintings, a technique used by other abstract expressionists such as Kline, Robert Motherwell, and Pollock. These works suggest X rays as thin white forms emerge through saturated black. De Kooning varied his surface textures by mixing materials like pumice with ordinary commercial enamel (Gaugh, p. 27). The black and white works dominated de Kooning's first one-person exhibition, held in April 1948 at the Charles Egan Gallery in New York City.

Nineteen forty-eight continued to be an important year in de Kooning's career. He was included in the *Annual Exhibition of Contemporary American Painting* at the Whitney Museum of American Art in Manhattan (again in 1949, 1950, 1963, 1967, and 1972; and the Whitney Biennials in 1981 and 1987). That year he also met the critic Thomas Hess, a champion of the New York School, an *ARTnews* associate editor, and an early supporter of de Kooning's work. (Hess was to write the first major monograph on the artist in 1959 and organize a major exhibition of his work at the Museum of Modern Art in 1968.) In the spring of 1948 he went for the first time to East Hampton, Long Island—an important gathering place for critics and artists of the New York School—where he visited with Kline, Egan, Pollock, and Lee Krasner. He would spend summers there between 1951 and 1953 at the art dealer Leo Castelli's house. During the summer of 1948 de Kooning taught at Black Mountain College near Asheville, North Carolina, under the direction of Josef Albers and with fellow faculty members in other arts, including the composer John Cage, the visionary structural designer Buckminster Fuller, and the dancer Merce Cunningham. In October the Museum of Modern Art acquired *Painting* (1948; Museum of Modern Art, New York); one of de Kooning's most abstract works at that point in his career, the image combines calligraphic black lines with patches of pink, orange, and turquoise on a white background.

By 1949 de Kooning's black and white works had shifted from primarily black to mostly white. These new canvases led to two of his most important works: a black and white abstraction titled *Attic* (1949; Metropolitan Museum of Art, New York) and *Excavation* (1950; Art Institute of Chicago), an abstraction in color. At roughly 80 x 101 inches, *Excavation* is one of de Kooning's largest and most successful works. In 1950 it was exhibited at the Twenty-fifth Venice Biennale, de Kooning's first group exhibition abroad, and in 1951 it received the Logan Medal and Purchase Prize in the *Sixtieth Annual American Exhibition* of the Art Institute of Chicago. At midcentury he was internationally recognized as a leading artist in the United States, exhibiting again at the Venice Biennale in 1954 and 1956, the São Paulo Bienal in 1951 and 1953, and the *Documenta* exhibition in Kassel, West Germany, in 1959, 1964, and 1977.

De Kooning worked with Albers again in the fall of 1950 as a visiting artist-critic at Yale University's School of Fine Arts in New Haven. De Kooning produced several essays on art during this period. In 1950, for example, Motherwell delivered de Kooning's text "The Renaissance and Order" at Studio 35 in New York (published in *trans/formation*, 1951).

His response to the Museum of Modern Art's invitation to comment on "What Abstract Art Means to Me" was read at the museum's 5 February 1951 symposium on abstraction (published in *MoMA Bulletin*, Spring 1951).

In June 1950 de Kooning started painting *Woman I* (1950–1952; Museum of Modern Art, New York). He reworked this canvas for approximately eighteen months. Having turned to the theme of women as early as 1938 and again in 1947, he continued with this particular series of paintings and drawings of women into 1953. The new images, many of which were exhibited at the Sidney Janis Gallery in March of that year, stirred controversy (see Cateforis, "de Kooning's 'Women'"). The bold, agitated figures in these canvases contradicted postwar commercial images of the American woman, raising questions about de Kooning's perceptions of women in general. Moreover, artists and critics who believed abstract expressionists should adopt complete abstraction saw his concentration on the figure as a betrayal of their goals. (In 1974 the Australian National Gallery in Canberra was to purchase *Woman V* [1952–1953] for $850,000, at the time a record sum paid for a work by a living American artist.)

During the late 1950s and early 1960s de Kooning's paintings such as *Gotham News* (1955; Albright-Knox Gallery, Buffalo, N.Y.) and *Easter Monday* (1956; Metropolitan Museum of Art, New York) took an increasingly abstract and frenetic turn. His "art had become a near-volcano of raucous, nervous and uncontainable energy" (Kimmelman, *New York Times*, 20 Mar. 1997). It also was a period of upheaval for the artist. The birth of his daughter Johanna Lisabeth to the artist Joan Ward in 1956 sealed his existing separation from his wife. (They reconciled around 1978.) In 1958 de Kooning rented a large loft at 831 Broadway in Manhattan and sublet Conrad Marca-Relli's house in Springs, East Hampton. That year he traveled to Venice, visited David Smith at Bolton Landing, New York, and saw Josef Albers in New Haven. He spent the winter of 1959–1960 in Rome working in the artist Afro's studio on the via Margutta.

On 13 March 1962 de Kooning became a U.S. citizen. In June 1963 he moved permanently from the loft on Broadway to Springs, East Hampton, where two years earlier he had purchased a small house from his brother-in-law Peter Fried. In 1964–1965 he built a new studio close to the house; there, he created more images of women including a group of large paintings on laminated doors and a series of small oil drawings. In 1964 he received the Guggenheim International Award and the Presidential Medal of Freedom. His first American retrospective opened at the Smith College Museum of Art in Northampton, Massachusetts, in April 1965. In 1968 he had his first solo exhibition in Europe at M. Knoedler et Cie, Paris; he then returned to Holland for the first time since 1926 for the opening at the Stedelijk Museum in Amsterdam of a touring retrospective of his work organized by the Museum of Modern Art.

De Kooning worked with sculpture for the first time in 1969, modeling and casting small-scale works at Herzl Emmanuel's foundry in Rome. Guided by the British sculptor Henry Moore, de Kooning experimented with large-scale pieces in a variety of materials the following year in New York. In 1972 his sculpture was exhibited for the first time at the Baltimore Museum of Art and then at the Sidney Janis Gallery; the latter exhibition was part of the settlement from a 1965 lawsuit that de Kooning had brought against Janis for breach of contract. In addition to painting and sculpture, de Kooning had tried his hand at printmaking. His first solo exhibition of lithographs was held at M. Knoedler et Cie in 1971. He had created his first print in 1957, an etching published in 1960 by the Morris Gallery, New York, to accompany a poem by the art critic Harold Rosenberg. His first lithographs were created in 1960 at the University of California, Berkeley.

In the mid-1970s de Kooning resumed painting and created a series of large abstractions that reflect the landscape of East Hampton. In 1975 he received the Gold Medal for Painting from the American Academy of Arts and Letters in New York, to which he was elected in December 1978. On his seventy-fifth birthday in 1979, the Dutch government named him an Officer of the Order of Orange in Nassau. Later that year, he was awarded the Andrew W. Mellon Prize for work in his solo exhibition at the Carnegie International in Pittsburgh.

De Kooning continued to make new paintings into his eighties. These late images combine soft yet deliberate lines and shapes with clear, white backgrounds. Their structure varies significantly from his earlier, more loosely painted images. Questions surrounding the authenticity of these late works, executed as the artist experienced symptoms from Alzheimer's disease, were largely dispelled by the 1995 touring exhibition *Willem de Kooning, the Late Paintings, the 1980s* (see Kimmelman, *New York Times*, 20 Mar. 1997). Other important late exhibitions of his work included touring retrospectives organized in 1984 (New York, Berlin, and Paris) and 1994 (Washington, D.C., New York, and London).

In 1989 de Kooning's painting *Interchange* (1955; private collection) brought $20.7 million at auction, a record high at the time for a work of art by a living artist (Zilczer, p. 196). He died at his home in East Hampton at age ninety-two. In May 1999 the journal *ARTnews* named de Kooning one of the twenty-five most influential artists of the twentieth century.

• Statements by the artist are reprinted in *The Collected Writings of Willem de Kooning*, ed. George Scrivani (1988). For chronology, see Judith Zilczer, *Willem de Kooning from the Hirshhorn Museum Collection* (1993). For general biography and interpretation, see Thomas B. Hess, *Willem de Kooning* (1959); Hess, *Willem de Kooning* (1968); Harold Rosenberg, *de Kooning* (1974); Harry F. Gaugh, *Willem de Kooning* (1983); Zilczer (1993); Marla Prather, *Willem de Kooning: Paintings* (1994); and Sally Yard, *Willem de Kooning* (1997). For special topics, see B. Berkson and R. Downes, eds., "Willem de Kooning, on his Eighty-fifth Birthday," *Art Journal*, Fall 1989 (special issue); Diane Waldman, *Willem de Kooning in East Hampton* (1978); David Christos Cateforis, "Willem de Kooning's 'Women' of the 1950s: A Critical History of their Reception and Interpretation" (Ph.D. diss., Stanford Univ. 1991); and F. Lanier Graham, *The Prints of Willem de Kooning: Catalogue Raisonné, 1957–71* (1991). The *New York Times* of 20 Mar. 1997 has a two-page obituary by Michael Kimmelman, "Willem de Kooning Dies at 92; Reshaped U.S. Art."

TRACY SCHPERO FITZPATRICK

DELANY, Annie Elizabeth "Bessie" (3 Sept. 1891–25 Sept. 1995), and **Sarah Louise "Sadie" Delany** (19 Sept. 1889–25 Jan. 1999), were born in Raleigh, North Carolina, the daughters of Henry Beard Delany, an educator and Episcopal bishop, and Nanny James Logan Delany. Bessie was to become a dentist, and Sadie a schoolteacher; late in life, they gained fame for their published reminiscences. Descended from a mix of black, American Indian, and white lineages, the sisters grew up in a family of ten children in Raleigh on the campus of St. Augustine's, the African-American school where their father, a former slave, served as priest and vice principal. The sisters graduated from St. Augustine's (Sadie in 1910 and Bessie in 1911) at a time when few Americans, black or white, were educated beyond grammar school. "We had everything you could want except money," recalled Bessie. "We had a good home, wonderful parents, plenty of love, faith in the Lord, educational opportunies—oh, we had a privileged childhood for colored children of the time" (*Smithsonian*, Oct. 1993, p. 150).

After completing their studies at St. Augustine's, both Sadie and Bessie went on to teaching jobs in North Carolina. Their father had strongly urged his daughters to teach, since he was unable to finance further education at a four-year college. He also advised them to make their own way, warning them against accepting scholarships that would obligate them to benefactors. Bessie took a job in the mill town of Boardman, while Sadie became the domestic science supervisor for all of the black schools in Wake County. Although she received no extra salary, Sadie also assumed the duties of supervisor of black schools in the county. Both sisters were shocked by the conditions their students lived in. Bessie later said in the sisters' joint memoir, *Having Our Say*, that she found the families in Boardman "poor and ignorant" (p. 89). Sadie remarked that her students' families in Wake County were "in bad shape" and that they "needed help with the basics" and "didn't know how to cook, clean, eat properly, or anything" (p. 81). She therefore concentrated her efforts on teaching sanitation, hygiene, and food preparation. She also convinced many of her charges to continue their education.

In 1916 Sadie moved to Harlem in New York City and enrolled at Pratt Institute, then a two-year college. After graduating in 1918 she enrolled at Columbia University, where she earned a B.S. in 1920. She returned to North Carolina briefly with the intention of helping her people but, discouraged by the pervasive Jim Crow system, soon returned to Harlem. She encountered racism in New York but concluded that the North "was an improvement over the South" (p. 107). She began teaching in an elementary school in Harlem in 1920, and for several years she also ran a candy business. In 1925 she received her master's degree in education from Columbia. Beginning in 1930, she taught at Theodore Roosevelt High School, a white school in the Bronx. Having skipped the interview because she feared her color would cost her the job, Sadie stunned school officials on the first day of school; but as she later observed, "Once I was in, they couldn't figure out how to get rid of me" (p. 120). With her appointment, Sadie became the first African American in New York City to teach domestic science at the high school level.

In 1918, after teaching for a short time in Brunswick, Georgia, and taking science courses at Shaw University in Raleigh, Bessie joined her sister in New York, where she enrolled the following year in the dentistry program at Columbia University. She completed her D.D.S. in 1923 and became only the second black female dentist licensed in the state of New York, with a practice in Harlem. She was well known there as "Dr. Bessie" and her office was a meeting place for black leaders, including James Weldon Johnson and E. Franklin Frazier. During the depression of the 1930s she found herself twice evicted from her office, but she persisted in her work.

During their childhood the Delany sisters had encountered the segregation and the discrimination of the Jim Crow South and the threat of violence that underlay the system. Bessie remembered the first time she ran into Jim Crow when, as a child in the mid-1890s, she found she could no longer go to the park that she had previously played in, and she also recalled experimenting with drinking the water from a "whites only" fountain and discerning no difference in its taste. Yet, like her sister, she found that in the North, too, restrictions and dangers hemmed her in. Bessie's closest brush with the Ku Klux Klan came not in the South, however, but on Long Island.

Neither Bessie nor Sadie ever married. Nanny Delany had urged her daughters to decide whether they were going to marry and raise families or have careers. As Bessie said years later, it never occurred to anyone that a woman could have both a family and a profession, and the sisters decided on careers. Bessie and Sadie lived together for nearly eight decades in New York City and then in nearby Mount Vernon, and they were surrounded by family members. All but one of their siblings settled in Harlem, and after their father's death in 1928 their mother lived with them. The sisters were devoted to their mother, and it was largely to please her that after World War II they left Harlem and moved to a cottage in the north Bronx. In 1950 Bessie gave up her dental practice to care for their mother full time. After their mother's death in 1956, the sisters moved to Mount Vernon, where they purchased a house in an all-white neighborhood. Sadie retired in 1960. Both sisters died at their home in Mount Vernon.

Sadie was amiable by nature, having broken the color barrier in the New York City public schools through craft instead of confrontation. By contrast, Bessie was feisty and contentious, accustomed to speaking her mind. "We loved our country," she observed, "even though it didn't love us back" (p. 60). Asked her impression of the Statue of Liberty when she first entered New York harbor, she replied that it was important as a symbol to white immigrants but meant nothing to her. Regarding her experience at Columbia University, she noted: "I suppose I should be grateful to Columbia, that at that time they let in colored people. Well, I'm not. They let me in but they beat me down for being there! I don't know how I got through that place, except when I was young nothing could hold me back" (p. 115).

The Delany sisters might have escaped notice by the wider world had they not in 1993 coauthored a bestselling memoir with the assistance of Amy Hill Hearth. *Having Our Say: The Delany Sisters' First 100 Years* had its origins in an essay that Hearth had written for the *New York Times* on the occasion of Bessie's one-hundredth birthday. So enthusiastic were readers' responses to the article that Hearth continued her interviews and produced the book. Published when Bessie was 102 and Sadie was 104, *Having Our Say* offered a perceptive, witty review of the sisters' lives through the previous century. As Hearth observed in her introduction to the book, it was meant less as a study of black history or of women's history than of American history, but the sisters' age, race, and gender combined to provide a tart perspective on the past. These two black women spoke of their strong family, the racism and sexism that could have thwarted them, and their triumphs. They spoke of their experiences as teachers in the segregated South, their participation in the mass migration of African Americans from the South to the urban North, and—although more briefly—their recollections of the Harlem Renaissance in the 1920s and the Great Depression of the 1930s. *Having Our Say* remained on the *New York Times* bestseller list—first in hardback and then as a paperback—for seventy-seven weeks and was adapted for a Broadway play in 1995 and a television movie in 1999.

• The Delany family papers are at St. Augustine's College, Raleigh, N.C. By the time Bessie Delany died, *Having Our Say* had sold nearly a million copies in hardback or paper and had been translated into four foreign languages. Reviewers were generally enthusiastic about the book, but an unsigned commentary in the *Women's Review of Books* 11 (Jan. 1994): 9–10, questioned the role of Amy Hill Hearth as a white woman selectively pulling together the recollections of two elderly black women. Hearth wrote a summary of *Having Our Say* for *Smithsonian* 24 (Oct. 1993): 144–64. The Broadway production of *Having Our Say* was reviewed by Vincent Canby in the *New York Times*, 7 Apr. 1995. A follow-up book, *The Delany Sisters' Book of Everyday Wisdom*, was published in 1994. *On My Own at 107: Reflections on*

Life without Bessie (1997) was written by Sadie with Amy Hill Hearth after Bessie's death. Obituaries of Bessie are in the *New York Times* and the *Washington Post*, both 26 Sept. 1995, and of Sadie in the *New York Times*, 26 Jan. 1999.

RICHARD HARMOND
PETER WALLENSTEIN

DEL REGATO, Juan A. (1 Mar. 1909–12 June 1999), oncologist, was born Juan Angel del Regato in Camagüey, Cuba, the son of Juan del Regato, an electrical engineer, and Damiana Manzano del Regato. After attending both public and private schools in his native city as well as in Nuevitas and Santa Clara, Cuba, and Mérida, Mexico, he entered the University of Havana in 1926 as a premedical student. In Havana del Regato supported himself by working as an extern, a medical photographer, and later as an X-ray technician, and when the university was forced to close in 1930 because of political unrest, he continued his education at the University of Paris with the financial support of the Cuban League of Cancer.

Del Regato's years in Paris were both busy and fulfilling. In addition to his work at the University—where he focused on oncology—he also studied at the Radium Institute, where he was influenced by Antoine Lacassagne, Claudius Regaud, and, particularly, Henri Coutard. After interning at the institute in 1934–1935, he spent the following year as a research fellow at the Curie Foundation and also assisted Coutard in a series of lectures given in the Soviet Union. He returned to the Radium Institute as Coutard's assistant in 1937, the same year in which he graduated from the University with a doctor of medicine degree and a diploma of radiophysiology and radiotherapy. His thesis, concerning radiotherapy for inoperable maxillary sinus cancer, represented the first report on nonsurgical treatment of the disease, and del Regato also contributed to medical technology with his development of the Regato Localizer, a lighting device designed to facilitate X-ray directional guidance during radiation therapy. Although unpatented by del Regato—who actually donated the rights to his device to several radiotherapy machine manufacturers—the device was later adopted for use in both cobalt 60 radiotherapy machines and linear accelerators.

In 1938 del Regato came to the United States and served as Coutard's assistant at the Chicago Tumor Institute before relocating later in the year to Washington, D.C., where he worked with Edwin A. Merritt at the Warwick Cancer Clinic and developed a set of specula and adapters that enabled the development of a highly effective X-ray treatment of uterine cancer. (On 1 May 1939 he married Inez Gertrude Johnson; the couple eventually had three children.) In 1941— the year in which he became a naturalized citizen— del Regato moved to the National Cancer Institute at the U.S. Marine Hospital in Baltimore, Maryland, where he served for two years as a research fellow and radiotherapist. In 1943 he relocated yet again, this time to Columbia, Missouri, where he served as chief radiotherapist at the Ellis Fischel Cancer Hospital. In

January 1949 he became the first medical director of the newly established Penrose Cancer Hospital in Colorado Springs, Colorado. Established by philanthropist Julie V. L. Penrose in conjunction with the Sisters of Charity as a memorial to her husband, Spencer Penrose, the institution soon became a world-class facility under del Regato's leadership. In 1949 he established an annual seminar that featured fifteen cancer case studies under discussion by a panel of experts with the additional input of previously-submitted diagnostic opinions by a worldwide network of experts. In 1950 he began one of the first training programs for radiotherapists in the United States. During the first twenty years of its existence, Penrose produced twice as many radiotherapists as any other institution, and the program was soon emulated throughout the United States.

It was in the treatment of prostate cancer, however, that del Regato made his greatest impact. At the time he began working in the area in 1958, 95 percent of the diagnosed cases were inoperable, and radiation was considered an ineffective form of treatment. By careful observation, del Regato noticed that this type of cancer was not resistant to radiation treatment; rather, being slow-growing by nature, it was merely slow to respond to treatment. By 1966, the Committee for Radiation Therapy Studies had approved a protocol for treatment using del Regato's methods, and in the following year the National Cancer Institute sponsored an extensive study at forty-two medical institutions. All in all, over 300 cases received treatment, and, with results verified over a period of years, del Regato was able to present his findings at the International Congress of Urology in July 1973.

Having served as professor of clinical radiology at the University of Colorado Medical School since 1950, del Regato took a similar position at the University of South Florida in Tampa, where he remained until his retirement in 1983. The author of numerous professional articles, he also authored *Cancer: Diagnosis, Treatment, and Prognosis* (1947, with Lauren V. Ackerman), which went into several editions and became a standard text in the field (later titled *Ackerman and del Regato's Cancer: Diagnosis, Treatment, and Prognosis*). A member and a correspondent of numerous professional associations, he was a founder and later president (1974–1975) of what is now the American Society for Therapeutic Radiologists and Oncologists, and also served as president of the Inter-American College of Radiology (1967–1971), the American Radium Society (1968–1969), and the International Club of Radiotherapists (1963–1965). Del Regato was the recipient of a host of awards for his work, including the Gold Medal of the American College of Radiology (1968), the Janeway Gold Medal from the American Radium Society (1973), and the Bruninghaus Prize from the French Academy of Medicine in 1979. During his long career del Regato also served as a consultant for a variety of institutions, including the Veterans Administration, the Vincent T. Lombardi Cancer Research Center at Georgetown

University, and Denver's Milheim Foundation. After spending his final years in a Tampa retirement home, he died in Traverse City, Michigan, while visiting one of his daughters.

In a lifetime devoted to fighting cancer, Juan del Regato made or contributed to significant advances in diagnosis, treatment, and technical equipment. His leadership at Penrose Cancer Hospital resulted in perhaps his most valuable legacy: the many radiotherapists for whom his program at Penrose provided the template for training others.

• Del Regato's papers are held at the American College of Radiology Archives in Reston, Virginia. In addition to the text previously cited, he was the author of *Radiological Physicists* (1985) and *Radiological Oncologists: The Unfolding of a Medical Specialty* (1993); he also contributed six articles to the original print edition of the *American National Biography*. An obituary appears in the *New York Times* on 22 June 1999.
EDWARD L. LACH, JR.

DE MENIL, Dominique. *See* Menil, Dominique de.

DENVER, John (31 Dec. 1943–12 Oct. 1997), singer, songwriter, and environmental activist, was born Henry John Deutschendorf, Jr., in Roswell, New Mexico, the son of Henry John "Dutch" Deutschendorf, an air force pilot, and Erma Swope Deutschendorf. Dutch Deutschendorf's military career forced the family to move often, and John grew up a shy, self-conscious loner with few friends. He began taking guitar lessons when he was eleven, and in high school he used his natural talent for playing and singing to gain popularity. From 1961 to 1964 he studied architecture at Texas Tech University, but he quit school in his junior year and moved to Los Angeles, where he hoped to devote himself full time to a music career. Taking the name "John Denver," he began playing at small folk clubs in the area with some success. He became a member of the "Backporch Majority," which played on the back porch of Ledbetter's, a club owned by Randy Sparks of the New Christy Minstrels, a popular folk group. But folk music was in transition at this time, as electric guitars and drums were more often being used, much to the dismay of traditionalists.

In 1965 Denver joined the folk group the Mitchell Trio, replacing Chad Mitchell, who had left for a career on Broadway. The Mitchell Trio's liberal leanings led them to perform antiwar songs and political satires, and it was during this time that Denver's political and social views were solidified. While with the Mitchell Trio, Denver composed a song he called "Oh, Babe, I Hate to Go," which later became immensely popular as recorded by the folk group Peter, Paul, and Mary as "Leaving on a Jet Plane." In 1967 Denver married Ann "Annie" Martell, and the following year the Mitchell Trio disbanded.

Denver finally secured a record deal in 1969, when RCA Records signed him to a two-year contract. His first album, *Rhymes and Reasons* (1969), included his version of "Leaving on a Jet Plane." In 1971 "Take Me Home, Country Roads," written with Bill and Taffy Danoff, became his first gold single. At about this time he hired a new personal manager, film producer Jerry Weintraub, who helped create the "image" of John Denver, the "granny glasses, the long hair, the slightly Western twang, the slightly self-deprecating sense of humor" (*Take Me Home*, p. 99). Weintraub began to promote his young star aggressively, and Denver made the rounds of the talk shows and variety specials on television, including appearances with celebrities as diverse as Frank Sinatra and Jim Henson's Muppets. In 1977 he starred with George Burns in the hit movie *Oh, God!*, playing a goofy supermarket manager visited by God (Burns). Though Denver was often overshadowed by Burns's hilariously deadpan style, the young singer was favorably reviewed for his comic portrayal of an average man plunged into extraordinary circumstances.

Denver recorded twenty-five albums for RCA over the next fifteen years and released a series of top-ten singles, including "Rocky Mountain High" (from the album by the same title, 1972), "Annie's Song" (written for his wife; from *Back Home Again*, 1974), and "Thank God I'm a Country Boy (from *An Evening with John Denver*, 1975). *John Denver's Greatest Hits*, which at his death had sold more than 10 million copies, and *John Denver's Greatest Hits, Volume Two* were released in 1973 and 1977, respectively.

Considered primarily a pop or folk artist, Denver also appealed to country music fans. Some performers, however, did not accept him as an authentic country singer/songwriter. When singer Charlie Rich opened the envelope revealing Denver as the 1975 Entertainer of the Year at the Country Music Association awards ceremony, he immediately set fire to the paper on which Denver's name was written, disclosing his disgust with the pop singer on national television. (Fortunately, Denver was in Australia at the time.) Despite this embarrassing incident, Denver continued to sell records. He had fourteen gold and eight platinum releases and won an Emmy Award for his 1976 television special "Rocky Mountain Christmas." In 1975 he started his own record label, Windstar. At his death he was the second bestselling artist in RCA Records history, finishing behind Elvis Presley.

Although Denver's music found popular appeal, critics scorned it as saccharine. He was denounced for his "decent mediocrity" and as a "quintessentially safe pop icon for the post-Vietnam, back-to-nature '70s" (*Rolling Stone*, 27 Nov. 1997). After the release of "Annie's Song," a critic for the *New York Times* wrote that Denver "settles for a corny sentimentality that just doesn't register on any deep level" (25 Aug. 1975). But his fans loved him for the very qualities others hated. His music evoked simplicity, a desire to escape to nature, to live where there were no wars, pollution, or cynicism.

In the early 1980s, as his star in music began to fall because of shifting tastes, Denver concentrated more on the social activism he had pursued in the previous decade. In 1976 he had formed an environmental research organization, the Windstar Foundation, whose causes included wildlife preservation. A founder of the World Hunger Project, he was appointed by President Jimmy Carter to the Commission on World and Domestic Hunger in 1977. He remained popular internationally, especially in Asia, making history in 1994 by becoming the first American singer to tour China and Vietnam. In the mid-1980s he performed in the Soviet Union and even recorded a song with Russian singer Alexandra Gradsky, "Let Us Begin (What Are We Making Weapons For?)." And he turned down an offer to ride on the Russian space shuttle

As the popularity of his music decreased, his personal life also began to deteriorate. His marriage to Annie had ended in a painful divorce in 1982 (they had adopted two children together) as a result of his infidelity. His 1988 union with his second wife, Cassandra Delaney, with whom he had one child, ended similarly in 1993. On the night of the final hearing of his divorce from Cassandra, Denver was arrested for drunken driving. An arrest for the same offense followed one year later.

Denver had begun to put his life back together when he was killed as the two-seat, homemade airplane he was piloting crashed off the coast of California, near Monterey Bay. Because of his drunken driving arrests, rumors immediately began to circulate that he was intoxicated at the time of the accident or that he had committed suicide. An investigation revealed, however, that Denver was sober and that the plane simply ran out of gas.

Denver will be remembered as representative of a particular strain in American popular culture of the 1970s, when his success as a performer was at its peak. Despite much cynicism about his "feel-good" music, his wholesome image appealed to a diverse audience, which included many older people who were charmed by his light lyricism and his smooth tenor voice. But perhaps his greatest talent lay in songwriting. For Denver, the creative impulse sprang from a desire "to take the personal experience or observation that inspired [the song] and express it in as universal a way as possible."

• John Denver's autobiography, *Take Me Home*, written with Arthur Tobier (1994), provides inclusive information on his early years, until about the time of his divorce from his first wife. The rest of the book seems self-absorbed and accusatory, written as it was during what he called his time of the "dark night of the soul." *Billboard*, 2 Apr. 1994, has an article about his upcoming performance in Vietnam. A long article about his life and death is in *People*, 27 Oct. 1997; a follow-up story on his memorial service is in the same publication, 3 Nov. 1997. Lengthy obituaries appear in the *New York Times*, 14 Oct. 1997; *Entertainment Weekly*, 24 Oct. 1997; *Billboard*, 25 Oct. 1997; and *Rolling Stone*, 27 Nov. 1997.

STACEY HAMILTON

DESMOND, Paul (25 Nov. 1924–30 May 1977), jazz saxophonist, was born Paul Emil Breitenfeld in San Francisco, California, the son of Emil Breitenfeld and Shirley King Breitenfeld. His father played organ for silent films and vaudeville acts at the Golden Gate Theater in San Francisco and wrote arrangements for local bands. (Later, as a teenager, Paul would select the surname Desmond from the San Francisco telephone book for use as a professional name.) The product of a troubled marriage, at the age of five Paul was sent to live with relatives in New Rochelle, New York, where he had his first six years of schooling, including a hands-on musical education with rudimentary instruments.

By 1936 family conditions in San Francisco enabled him to return. When he entered Polytechnic High School there he took music lessons, first violin and later clarinet, under the auspices of the school, played in the Polytechnic band, and served as editor of the school's newspaper. By age fifteen the thought had crossed his mind that he could actually make a living as a musician. This potential for gainful employment probably influenced his decision later, around the age of nineteen, to forsake the clarinet, replacing it with the alto saxophone. The saxophone was just then coming into its own as a solo jazz instrument, with artists such as Johnny Hodges, Ben Webster, Lester Young, Coleman Hawkins, and Charlie Parker establishing formidable benchmarks of virtuosity.

In 1943 Desmond was inducted into the army and stationed for three years with the 253rd Army Ground Forces band at the Presidio in San Francisco. He first met pianist-composer Dave Brubeck that year through a mutual friend and fellow musician, Dave van Kreidt. Brubeck and Desmond felt an immediate musical affinity that unfolded in a productive way as they worked together in an octet formed by Brubeck with Bay Area musicians in the mid-1940s.

That creative symbiosis continued in a trio led for a short time by Desmond himself, with Brubeck on piano and Norman Bates on drums. But it really grew and developed an impressive solidity when they first played together regularly, at a small club in Palo Alto, The Bandbox. By this time Desmond was studying to be a writer (but taking music courses as well) at San Francisco State College, while Brubeck was studying composition with Darius Milhaud at Mills College. After a brief hiatus, when Desmond left for an abortive sideman fling in New York City (with the bands of Jack Fina and Alvino Rey), the Dave Brubeck Quartet was formed in 1951. During its sixteen years of life it became one of the most successful jazz groups in the world, owing as much to Desmond's incomparable artistry as to Brubeck's considerable playing and writing talents.

Some critics thought the work with the quartet had a confining effect on Desmond. Others thought the quartet and Brubeck's individual genius—as well as the incomparable musical support of drummer Joe Morello (from 1956) and bassist Eugene Wright (from 1958)—gave him a context in which his talents could flourish uniquely. Whichever argument one accepts, both Desmond and the quartet became house-hold names in music by the end of the mid-twentieth century. Perennial jazz poll winners, the two main so-loists became one of the most popular and critically acclaimed duos in jazz history. Even they referred to their relationship as "a limited partnership."

Every critic who describes Desmond's playing speaks of his lyricism, his superior knack for building melodic bits into extended gestures of structural so-lidity. With trumpeter Harry "Sweets" Edison and guitarist Charlie Christian, he was unsurpassed in his talent for creating linked linear mosaics from the raw material of American popular song. But he enjoyed another special mark of excellence: the tone he got from a saxophone can be best compared to that of the most accomplished soloists within the classical rep-ertoire. Each separate tone begins as if there were no attack, as if its beginning were a seamless whole with its middle and end, a solid stream of sound that is both pure and precisely pitched. (However, some listeners, including jazz musicians such as Miles Davis, consid-ered Desmond's sound inappropriate for jazz.)

Desmond's recorded output is impressive because of the absence of such improvisatory clichés as the extended flood of notes—the "sheets of sound" that often infected post-bebop saxophone solos. Although he very early developed the alto's extra-high register, at no time did he stoop to the wailing screeches too readily invoked by lesser talents in fabricating emo-tions beyond the purely musical. His style was built on an enormous reservoir of technical knowledge. His "call and response," or canonic, exchanges in the heat of improvisation, with pianist Brubeck and later with Jim Hall and Gerry Mulligan, his self-answered fugal play in different registers with his own lines, and his sneaked-in quotations from other works all indicate an extraordinary musical mind. Desmond was adept even as a composer; his "Take Five," issued on the famous album *Time Out* (1959), was the quartet's greatest hit.

Desmond's playing arose naturally from an ele-gantly distinctive personality. His writing major in col-lege was only an early outcropping of a lifelong de-votion to the literature of high culture. He even aspired to writing a novel, but the product never made it past spasmodic manuscript stages. After his depar-ture from the Brubeck quartet he seemed on the verge of developing a career as a humorist; a symptomatic piece appeared in *Punch* (10 Jan. 1973). But his criti-cal acumen proved to be too strong for his creative motivation.

Blessed with a wry and sensitive wit, Desmond was admired by friends for his lively and recondite con-versation that brimmed over with allusions to and quotations from film and literary masterworks. But he was no intellectual stuffed shirt. After jobbing with him intermittently and then living with him in the quartet setting for sixteen years, Brubeck still re-garded him as a charming man. His insight, his artic-ulateness, and his hip perspective are encapsulated in his self-described musical aspiration: "I want to sound like a dry martini." Typically well-dressed on stage, he was described in his *Village Voice* obituary by Nat Hentoff as seemingly in a kind of reverie amid all the action, "an amiable solitary at the revival meeting." He was a tall, thin man in horn-rimmed glasses. His stage image, leaning into the crook of Brubeck's piano with legs crossed and arms folded over an idle horn, became coded among intimates as "the Stork."

Desmond's attraction to and for women was leg-endary, but he married only once, and then but briefly, to a woman whose first name was Duain. Left heartbroken by the failure of that relationship, he re-mained a free-wheeling bachelor for the rest of his life. During later years, his heavy drinking and a daily three packs of cigarettes began to eat away at his vi-tality. In the end, it was lung cancer that claimed his life.

After the Brubeck Quartet disbanded in 1967, Des-mond did not find a steady home for his playing. But there was no shortage of opportunities to perform and record with some of his favorite colleagues, Canadian guitarist Jim Hall and saxophonist-composer Gerry Mulligan above all others. He played festivals, toured Europe, Australia, and Japan, worked such prime jazz spots as the Half Note in Manhattan, and for a while played Toronto's Bourbon Street with his own quar-tet. On occasion he returned, at Brubeck's special call, to make tours and play isolated concerts with the quartet. His last public concert, with the help of blood transfusions to support his ebbing body, was with the quartet at Lincoln Center in 1976. In February 1977 he cut his final recording, *You Can't Go Home Again*, with Chet Baker. He died at his home in New York City in late May.

• Paul Desmond, "How Many of You Are There in the Quartet?" (*Punch*, 10 Jan. 1973), recounts an episode from his life with the Brubeck quartet. Coverage of his career is found in Dave Bittan, "Dave Brubeck-Philadelphia Sym-phony Orchestra," *Down Beat*, January 14, 1965; Nat Hen-toff, "The Solitary Floating Jazzman," *Village Voice*, August 22, 1977; Marian McPartland, "Perils of Paul: A Portrait of Desperate Desmond," *Down Beat* 27, no. 19 (1960): 15 (also in her book, *All in Good Time* [1987]); Arnold Jay Smith, "A Quarter of a Century Young: The Dave Brubeck Quartet," *Down Beat* 43 (25 Mar. 1976): 18–20, 45–46; L. Tompkins, "Giant Jazzman, Gentle Wit: Paul Desmond," *Crescendo International* (*CI*) xii/12 (1974) and xiii/1 (1974); and Whitney Balliett, "An Insouciant Sound," in *American Musicians II* (1996). Additional information appears in Joe Goldberg, *Jazz Masters of the Fifties* (1965), and Martin Wil-liams, *Jazz Masters in Transition, 1957–69* (1970). An infor-mative and engaging "76th Birthday Tribute to Paul Des-mond," featuring live and recorded comments by Dave Brubeck, Gene Lees, Jim Hall, John Snyder, Eugene Wright, Doug Ramsey, Nancy Wilson, and even a jovial 1954 ex-change between Charlie Parker and Desmond, was broad-cast over National Public Radio (*Jazz Profiles*), November 2000. An obituary is in the *New York Times*, 1 June 1977.
WILLIAM THOMSON

DICK, Gladys (18 Dec. 1881–21 Aug. 1963), medi-cal researcher and physician, was born Gladys Rowena Henry in Pawnee City, Nebraska, the daughter of William Chester Henry, a house and grain dealer, and Azelia Henrietta Edson Henry. Her family relocated to Lincoln, Nebraska, following her birth, where she attended local public schools before entering the University of Nebraska. After earning her B.S. in 1900, she had hoped to attend medical school, but faced her mother's stern opposition to the idea, which few women at that time pursued. She spent the next two years teaching high school biology in nearby Kearney, Nebraska, and took additional graduate course work at her alma mater. After finally gaining parental approval, she left Nebraska and journeyed east to the Johns Hopkins University School of Medicine.

Although Hopkins admitted women to its medical school—a novelty at the time—it provided no residential facilities. Henry solved this problem by purchasing a dwelling with the assistance of her fellow female students. After graduating in 1907, she remained in Baltimore for a year as an intern before venturing overseas for a year of postgraduate training in Berlin. It was during these years that Henry first became involved in higher-level medical research, studying subjects as diverse as blood chemistry and cardiac surgery with several leading members of the American medical establishment, including W. G. MacCallum, Harvey Cushing, and Milton Winternitz.

Henry relocated to Chicago in 1911 and worked with H. Gideon Wells on kidney pathochemistry at the University of Chicago. A working partnership in the field of scarlet fever etiology with George Frederick Dick brought additional benefits; the two married on 28 January 1914 and settled in Evanston, Illinois, after a lengthy honeymoon. Once settled, Gladys Dick practiced medicine and worked as a pathologist at Evanston Hospital. In the latter part of 1914 she joined her spouse at the John R. McCormick Memorial Institute for Infectious Diseases. During World War I she served as a bacteriologist with the U.S. Public Health Service and filled in for her spouse as a staff member at St. Luke's Hospital (now Rush-Presbyterian–St. Luke's Medical Center) in Chicago.

Dick remained at the McCormick Institute, which had been founded as a memorial to the son of Harold F. and Edith Rockefeller McCormick in 1902, until her retirement in 1953. (During this time she also became head pathologist at St. Joseph's Hospital in Chicago.) Working as a team, Dick and her husband made their greatest achievements in the identification, prevention, and treatment of scarlet fever, a disease that at the time was little understood and endemic to both Europe and North America. One problem faced by researchers everywhere was the fact that animals could not contract the disease and hence were useless for research purposes. Faced with the need for human subjects, the Dicks used hundreds of war veterans as test subjects, paying them a thousand dollars apiece. With the support of medical staff director Dr. Ludvig Hektoen, they identified the causative agent as a hemolytic streptococcus in 1921 and in October 1923 successfully produced the disease in volunteers who had been injected with an active scarlet fever culture. Shortly thereafter, the Dicks managed to identify and isolate the toxin (produced by scarlet fever bacteria) responsible for generating the characteristic red rash so long associated with the disease. They developed a skin test, later known as the Dick Test, which was soon used worldwide as an indicator of individual susceptibility to the disease. This breakthrough later led to the development of both immunization procedures and antitoxin production methods.

Although their success in scarlet fever research led to widespread publicity for the Dicks, troubles loomed. The couple was nominated for the Nobel Prize for medicine in 1925, but no prize was awarded that year. Even more troubling was the controversy that erupted over the originality of their research, especially after the team secured patents in 1924 and 1926 covering the production of toxin and antitoxin. In the highly competitive world of medical research, several other individuals—most notably A. Raymond Dochez, a former medical school classmate of Gladys Dick—had been conducting research along similar lines, and the Dicks' pursuit of patent protection smacked of commercialism to many, including the medical press and even the League of Nations health organization. The Dicks countered these charges by stating that their interests were more proprietary than monetary, with the quality of serum preparation being of paramount concern. Efforts to assert authority over the production process even led to a lengthy but ultimately successful lawsuit against Lederle Laboratories (*Dick et al. v. Lederle Antitoxin Laboratories*, 1930). Compounding the Dicks' difficulties were the growing financial problems of the McCormick Institute itself, which was ultimately renamed for Dr. Hektoen and taken over by Cook County General Hospital in 1943.

Despite their difficulties, the Dicks did receive recognition for their work, including the Mickle Prize of the University of Toronto (1926), the Cameron Prize of the University of Edinburgh (1933), and several honorary degrees.

Long interested in child welfare, Gladys Dick became involved in 1928 in the Cradle Society of Evanston, Illinois, and with her husband adopted a son and a daughter late in life. The Dicks retired to Palo Alto, California, in 1953, after which the formerly energetic Gladys suffered declining health. She died in Menlo Park, California.

Gladys Dick entered the medical profession at a time when few women even considered pursuing the profession and persevered in establishing a long and successful career. In association with her husband, she conducted research of a pioneering nature and of lasting consequence.

• Gladys Dick and her husband were the co-authors of *Scarlet Fever* (1938). Articles by Dr. Dick on her work appeared in the *Journal of the American Medical Association* 81 (1923): 1166–67; 82 (1924): 265–66, 301–2, 544–45, 1246–47; 84 (1925): 802–3; 115 (1940): 2155–56. Secondary sources on her life and work are scarce; the best are uncredited articles in *Science News-Letter*, 22 Oct. 1927, and the *Nebraska Alumnus*, June 1937, p. 27; June 1940, p. 6; and Dec. 1940, p. 19. Obituaries are in the *Chicago Tribune*, 23 Aug. 1963, and the *Journal of the American Medical Association*, 28 Dec. 1963.

EDWARD L. LACH, JR.

DICKERSON, Nancy (27 Jan. 1927–18 Oct. 1997), television news correspondent and producer, was born Nancy Conners Hanschman in Wauwatosa, Wisconsin, the daughter of Frederick R. Hanschman and Florence Conners Hanschman. Reared in the suburbs west of Milwaukee, she enrolled after high school graduation in Clarke College, an all-women's Catholic school in Dubuque, Iowa. After two years Hanschman transferred to the University of Wisconsin, where she pursued a liberal arts degree, studying English and foreign languages. She graduated in 1948.

After earning her bachelor's degree, Hanschman taught school in Milwaukee for two years but soon moved to New York City and then to Washington, D.C., in search of a more engaging career. In 1951 she accepted a position as a registrar at Georgetown University and began doing research for the U.S. Senate Foreign Relations Committee, which sparked her interest in politics, current events, and journalism. Though possessing no training in news reporting, Hanschman was hired as a producer for the CBS News radio program "The Leading Question." Despite her inexperience, she was successful in her new position, and she was named associate producer of CBS's long-running news interview program "Face the Nation," which premiered in late 1954. She was later promoted to producer for CBS News and Special Events.

CBS was impressed with Hanschman's 1959 feature on the Women's Army Corps in Europe, which was broadcast on "The World Tonight" radio program, and in 1960 she was named the network's first female correspondent. Thus began her long, successful association with television broadcast journalism. During the first months in her new position, she covered the presidential campaigns of both Democratic senator Hubert Humphrey and then Lyndon B. Johnson, becoming the first woman television correspondent on the floor of a national party convention. In late 1960 CBS rewarded her with her own radio program, "One Woman's Washington," which featured stories thought to be of interest to American women. In 1962 she married real estate investor C. Wyatt Dickerson; they had five children.

Nancy Dickerson remained with CBS until 1963, when she moved to the Washington Bureau of NBC News. During the 1960s she covered presidential inaugurations, political conventions, world affairs, and Martin Luther King, Jr.'s March on Washington. She left NBC in 1970 to become an independent news broadcaster and from 1971 to 1974 hosted "Inside Washington," a daily news program. Traveling exten-

sively, she collected friendships like autographs, using those connections to her professional advantage. During her long career, she interviewed, among others, Speaker of the House Sam Rayburn, President Richard Nixon, presidential candidate Barry Goldwater, Egyptian president Anwar Sadat, Israeli prime minister Menachem Begin, and Saudi Arabian foreign minister Prince Saud al-Faisal (the last three interviews appeared in the 1980 Public Broadcasting System special "Nancy Dickerson, Special Assignment: Middle East").

In 1980 Dickerson formed the Television Corporation of American, for which she produced documentaries and specials to sell to cable networks and for syndication. One of her best-known works is her 1982 documentary "784 Days That Changed America—From Watergate to Resignation," which took an in-depth look at the scandal that forced President Richard Nixon to resign his post. For this production she was awarded the University of Georgia's George Foster Peabody Award and the American Bar Association's Silver Gavel Award. Other documentaries produced by Dickerson include "Islam: The Veil and the Future," about women in the Middle East; "Being with John F. Kennedy" (in her memoirs Dickerson claims to have had an affair with Kennedy in the 1950s); and "Nancy Dickerson and the New Woman," a television special about the woman's movement. In 1983 she and her husband divorced. Six years later she married John C. Whitehead, an investor and former deputy secretary of state during the Ronald Reagan administration.

During the last decade of her life Dickerson served as an analyst for Fox News (1986–1991) and remained active until felled by a stroke in January 1996. She died in New York City and is buried in Arlington National Cemetery, her second husband having served in the military in World War II. In the year following her death Clarke College established the Nancy Dickerson Whitehead Medallion for Excellence in the Field of Mass Communication; recipients include "60 Minutes" reporter and former CBS News White House correspondent Leslie Stahl.

At the beginning of her career as a newswoman, Dickerson was asked by a major Washington newspaper to become the women's editor. She refused the offer, sensing (chances are, correctly) that she would spend her life writing "shopping and food columns." Instead, she spent her career covering most of the major stories of the 1960s and 1970s, using her social ties to gain access to newsmakers and collect story leads, perfecting the methods that male reporters had used for decades. Dickerson opened the way for women in television journalism and held her ground in a field that well after 1960 continued to be dominated by men. At the time of her death, however, women reporters had—to a large extent—attained parity with their male counterparts.

• Dickerson's memoir, *Among Those Present: A Reporter's View of Twenty-Five Years in Washington*, was published in

1976. She was at work on a follow-up to this autobiography when she died. A biographical entry on Dickerson, written by Christine L. Ogan, can be found in *Women in Communication: A Biographical Sourcebook*, ed. Nancy Signorielli (1996). An obituary is in the *New York Times*, 19 Oct. 1997.

STACEY HAMILTON

DICKSON, Dorothy (25 July 1893–25 Sept. 1995), dancer and musical actress, was born in Kansas City, Missouri, to William Dickson, a journalist, and his wife Clara Barrett Dickson. She was educated in Chicago schools. Her career as a ballroom dancer effectively began there when she partnered Carl Constantine Helson in a charity dance after Helson's father's business speculations went awry.

Dickson and Helson, whose professional name was Carl Hyson, were married in 1914. They had one child, were separated in 1923, and divorced in 1936. Contemporaries of Vernon and Irene Castle, Dickson and Hyson were quickly recognized in their own right. Booked at the fashionable Chicago nightclub Rector's, they were signed for a specialty number, dancing over a stage full of furniture to "Till the Clouds Roll By" from the Jerome Kern–P. G. Wodehouse–Guy Bolton Broadway musical comedy *Oh, Boy!* (1917). Soon they were also dancing in the *Ziegfeld Follies* as well as at the Coconut Grove nightclub.

In 1918 Dickson acted in *Girl O' Mine*, a frothy musical by Frank Tours and Philip Bartholomae, as well as Kern's *Rock a Bye Baby*, in which her original dance cameo was gradually built into a full speaking role. She danced in George M. Cohan's *The Royal Vagabond* (1919) and in 1920 teamed with Hyson in *Lassie*, to music by Hugo Felix. By then Hyson and Dickson had their own nightclub, the Palais Royal.

The 1920s and 1930s were a golden age for American musical theater, and it was Dickson who personified it to the British public. After the English impresario Charles B. Cochran imported Dickson and Hyson for his revue *London, Paris and New York* (1921), the feathery-dancing, fragile-voiced Dickson played the Cinderella heroine of Kern, Wodehouse, and Bolton's *Sally*. That was followed by two Kern-Wodehouse originals with virtually the same casts. In *The Cabaret Girl* (1922) Dickson portrayed a star of London's newest entertainment craze, while in *The Beauty Prize* (1923) she won a husband in a beauty contest.

Hair bobbed, wearing golden pumps, and sipping champagne, Dickson was *Patricia* (1924) in a British musical imitative of its American predecessors. *Patricia* and Dickson made radio history when one act was broadcast over the fledgling British Broadcasting Company. Of Dickson, London's *Tatler* said, "Whenever she is onstage the whole entertainment becomes 'alive.'" When the hottest show in town, *Charlot's Revue*, embarked on its monthly editions in 1925, Dickson introduced Harry Warren's "A Cup of Coffee, a Sandwich and You" a year before the show came to New York.

Perhaps the prototype of Jazz Age musicals, George Gershwin and Ira Gershwin's jazzy *Tip-Toes* opened in London in 1926 with Dickson in the title role as a dancing vaudevillian. Since the show had not been recorded during its New York debut, it fell to Dickson to first record the Gershwins' "Looking for a Boy" and "That Certain Feeling." Also in 1926 she made her first appearance in the form of a pantomime as Peter Pan and her first nonmusical role in Edgar Wallace's suspenseful *The Ringer*.

By this time, Dickson, with pale blonde hair, immaculate dress sense, and a dancer's physique, had outgrown flapperdom and was generally regarded as the most glamorous woman on the British stage, possessing, as described by an unidentified obituarist in the *Times* (London), 27 September 1995, "supremely photogenic beauty." In 1927 she took the title role in the British version of Richard Rodgers and Lorenz Hart's *Peggy-Ann*, a Cinderella story largely told in the lovelorn dreams of the heroine ("Where's That Rainbow?"). After another dramatic role, there followed *Hold Everything!* (1929), with the songs of B. G. DeSylva, Ray Henderson, and Lew Brown, including "You're the Cream in My Coffee." The André Charlot production of the dark musical *Wonder Bar* (1930) took the risk of keeping Dickson offstage for its first fifty minutes and its producer subsequently went bankrupt.

In 1930 Dickson resumed a cinematic career that had begun with four American films between 1919 and 1921. In a way, these motion pictures filmed in England returned her to her theatrical beginnings, for in the film *La Route est Belle* she played a dancer guest. Subsequent films included *Channel Crossing* (1932), *Danny Boy* (1934), *Sword of Honor* (1938), and *Paying the Piper* (1949). Although her still photographs were worthy of a model, her films were unmemorable.

Next came the long-running operetta *Casanova* (1932) and the Ivor Novello drama *Flies in the Sun* (1933). A photograph taken during its run showed Dickson and her daughter Dorothy Hyson, later herself a star, looking like twins. In 1935 Dickson took the lead in *Stop Press*, the English version of Irving Berlin's revue *As Thousands Cheer*, introducing to London "Easter Parade" in a sepia setting that evoked rotogravure. Her public influence was shown when she successfully persuaded the nation's censor to withdraw his objection to one of the show's sketches, which he claimed had been "sanitized" at a preview to ensure his approval.

In April 1936 Dickson teamed with the lithe, sardonic expatriate Walter Crisham in the revue *Spread It Abroad*, introducing by word and dance Eric Maschwitz's classic "These Foolish Things." The Crisham-Dickson partnership continued later in the year with *Careless Rapture*, a Novello extravaganza. A characteristic of any Novello musical was a show within a show: in this case a turn-of-the-century musical comedy called "The Rose Girl," with Dickson, its star, marrying into the aristocracy. Novello, Dickson, and

Crisham combined once more in 1937 for *The Crest of the Wave*.

Dickson sometimes complained, "My dancing has . . . so often kept me from getting the parts I wanted," but with the passage of time she turned away from the musical stage. At the outbreak of World War II, however, she teamed with Crisham in *Diversion*, an eclectic all-star revue. The comedienne Joyce Grenfell wrote that during that show the Shakespearean actress Edith Evans shared a dressing room with Dickson: "Dorothy advised Edith about makeup and clothes. Edith talked to Dorothy about books and poetry. . . . One day I . . . found them deep in a discussion about the story of Elisha and the Shunamite woman." Dickson then went on a number of tours to entertain troops around the Mediterranean basin, and at the age of fifty-one she played Helen of Troy on stage. In 1944 she was instrumental in creating the London version of the Stage Door Canteen, a type of food and entertainment venue established in America two years earlier, which allowed ordinary servicemen to mingle—even dance—with famous entertainers. At its opening, Fred Astaire and Jack Buchanan danced on the same bill.

Dickson went back to the United States in 1946, for several months writing a theater column for *Show Business*. After her return to London, her onstage appearances gradually decreased. In 1953 Dickson costarred in the domestic comedy *As Long as They're Happy*, Buchanan's last stage appearance. Dickson had become an international socialite, traveling in the set of Buchanan, Noël Coward, Beatrice Lillie, and Gertrude Lawrence, as well as joining the circle of Queen Elizabeth (the wife of George VI, later Queen Mother to Elizabeth II).

At a 1980 gala celebrating the seventy-fifth anniversary of *Peter Pan*, the 86-year-old Dickson was described as "shimmering in gold lamé and stiletto heels, the personification of timeless glamour." By 1986 she was said to have reached World War II in her autobiography, "Silver Linings," which was never published. A devout Christian Scientist, she refused to acknowledge her 100th birthday. Dickson died in London.

During the years between World Wars I and II, Dickson and other expatriates to Great Britain, including Edith Day, Mary Ellis, Bebe Daniels, and Ben Lyon, served as cultural ambassadors, showing that the products of the American musical theater were truly international. While Day and Ellis stood for American operetta and Daniels and Lyon for American film and vaudeville, Dickson was the personification of light-hearted, optimistic American musical comedy.

• Dickson's papers are held by family members and by Eric Braun, the collaborator on her unfinished autobiography, although the collections of the Theatre Museum, London, shed much light on her public image and career. Her American theatrical career is detailed in Gerald Bordman, *American Musical Theatre: A Chronicle* (2d ed., 1972). *The Noël Coward Diaries*, ed. Sheridan Morley and Graham Payn (1982), document some of her social life. Dickson emerges in biographies and studies of most of the composers of America's golden age of stage musicals and popular song: Gershwin, Kern, Berlin, Rodgers. The BBC archives hold several radio documentaries dealing with Dickson's career. Dickson's British films are catalogued at the British Film Institute, London. Obituaries appear in the *Times* (London) and the *Guardian* (London), the latter by Patrick O'Connor, both 27 Sept. 1995.

JAMES ROSS MOORE

DIMAGGIO, Joe (25 Nov. 1914–9 Mar. 1999), baseball player, was born Joseph Paul DiMaggio in Martinez, California, the son of Giuseppe Paulo DiMaggio, a fisherman, and Rosalie DiMaggio (maiden name unknown). He was the fourth of five sons and the eighth of nine children of immigrants who came from Sicily in 1898 and shortly after his birth settled in San Francisco's predominantly Italian North Beach area. Two brothers fished with their father, while Vince, Joe, and Dominic DiMaggio all became major league center fielders. After Joe dropped out of high school, having attended for one year, his brother Vince got him a tryout, and he signed to play baseball with the San Francisco Seals in the Pacific Coast League.

Three games as a shortstop at the end of 1932 were followed by the launching of DiMaggio's career in 1933 with a season that made him the most talked-about minor leaguer in the country. He batted .340, hit 28 home runs, and drove in 169 runs as an 18-year old "phenom," while also maintaining a 61-game hitting streak. The next two seasons he batted .341 and .398; complementing his 1935 average were 48 doubles, 18 triples, 34 homers, 154 runs driven in, and brilliant play in center field. Although some teams were scared away by his having suffered a knee injury, the New York Yankees sent the Seals five players and $25,000 for DiMaggio. The young center fielder was an instant sensation with the Yankees. Babe Ruth had been released after the 1934 season; the Yankees had lost three straight pennants; and even with Lou Gehrig, the game's best first baseman, the team needed the spark of inspiration the newcomer provided. Despite missing the first few weeks with a foot injury, DiMaggio took the American League by storm, batting .323 with 29 homers and 125 RBI and becoming the first rookie to start in an all-star game.

The next year DiMaggio was even better, leading the league with a personal high of 46 home runs while batting .346, scoring a league-best 151 runs and driving in 167. When he held out for a $40,000 salary the next spring, he began a yearly ritual, with the Yankees general manager Ed Barrow consistently underpaying him. Before free agency, players had little leverage, and DiMaggio finally signed for $25,000. In his first five seasons, he missed four openers because of injuries or holdouts.

DiMaggio's struggles for more money did not seem to limit his on-field performance. In 1938 he hit .324 with 32 home runs and 140 RBI, and in 1939 he won the first of his three most valuable player awards when he led the league at .381, with 30 homers and 126 RBI in only 120 games. He repeated as batting champion in 1940 with a .352 average, walloped another 31 homers, and drove in 133 runs. Yet that season was an oddity: the only one in the seven leading up to DiMaggio's military service in which the Yankees failed to win the pennant. He was, quite simply, a winner, and four straight pennants and World Series victories in his first four years set a record, which later was surpassed by the Yankees of 1949–1953.

The year 1941 helped make Joe DiMaggio a legend. That season he won his second MVP award, batting .357 with 30 home runs and a league-leading 125 RBI. More historic, he demolished Wee Willie Keeler's 1897 record of hitting safely in 44 consecutive games when he reeled off a streak of 56 straight, capturing the imagination of the nation with his daily pursuit. The record stopped on a dramatic note: Cleveland third baseman Ken Keltner made two brilliant backhand stabs to throw DiMaggio out; he was walked intentionally once; and shortstop Lou Boudreau survived a tricky hop to get DiMaggio in his final time at bat. Incredibly, he launched a new 16-game streak the next day. He came that close to a 73-game string. That was the year Ted Williams hit .406, the last .400 season of the twentieth century, but the Yanks won the pennant again and DiMaggio had his MVP award. He tailed off a bit in 1942, batting a modest .305 with 21 homers and 114 runs driven home. On 3 December 1942, he joined the Army Air Forces and spent the next three seasons playing baseball in the service. Tellingly, the Yankees lost two of the three pennants in his years away.

DiMaggio's favorite haunt in New York was Toots Shor's restaurant, where he sat at a back table and spent a good deal of time socializing with reporters, who—in an era of less intrusive journalism—did not write about his private life. DiMaggio early on developed a penchant for blond showgirls, and on 19 November 1939 he married Dorothy Arnold, a blond Universal actress he had met while she was making a movie in 1937. They had a son, Joe, Jr., in October 1941, but the marriage crumbled and ended in divorce in 1944. DiMaggio was later estranged from his son as well.

His brothers, meanwhile, were compiling impressive records in their own careers. Vince, two years older, played from 1937 to 1946 on five National League teams, batting .249 with 125 homers, two all-star game appearances, and six years as league leader in strikeouts. Dominic, two years younger, played from 1940 through 1953 with the Boston Red Sox, with three years off in the navy during the war. The "little professor," nicknamed for his glasses, was, according to a song popular in Boston, "better than his brother Joe, Dominic DiMaggio." He batted .298 for his career, though at 5 feet 9 inches and 168 pounds he was far smaller than Joe's 6 feet 2 inches and 193 pounds and lacked his more famous sibling's power.

When he returned from the service, DiMaggio's skills had declined a bit from his first seven seasons. He played another six years and led the Yankees to four pennants during that stretch. In 1946 he hit .290 with 25 homers and 95 RBI, his poorest season to that point, and the Yanks finished third. Then in 1947 he won his third MVP award with another subpar but pennant-winning year—a .315 average, 20 home runs, 97 RBI. His only postwar season on a level with his earlier glory came in 1948, when he hit .320 and led the league in homers with 39 and runs batted in with 155. The following year he missed the first half of the season with painful bone spurs in his right heel, returning for a crucial three-game series with Boston at Fenway Park. He led a Yankee sweep with four home runs in the three games and later helped his team capture the pennant by beating Boston in two must-win games to conclude the season. He averaged .346 with 14 homers and 57 RBI for the half season. In 1950 he hit .300 for the last time, but his .301 average included an impressive 32 homers and 122 RBI as he led the Yankees to another flag. He was clearly slowing down in 1951—his average dipped to .263 with 12 homers and 71 RBI as the Yankees won their third straight pennant. DiMaggio's successor as the team's center field super hero, Mickey Mantle, flanked him in right field as a rookie. On the eve of the World Series against the Giants, the Dodger scouting report on DiMaggio was leaked to *Life* magazine; its unflattering portrait of a player on the downward slope of his career helped move DiMaggio to decline a $100,000 contract for 1952 and retire before he embarrassed himself, a move consistent with the class for which he was famous. In his thirteen seasons, he compiled a .325 batting average, played in eleven all-star games, and led the Yankees to nine wins in ten World Series.

DiMaggio on the field was the picture of grace, both as a fielder and as a batter. In his distinctive batting stance, his legs were spread so wide that the right-handed hitter took only a short step with his left foot before swinging; an approach that allowed him to wait longer than most batters to commit himself to swinging at a pitch. As a result, he rarely struck out—his career marks of 361 home runs and 369 strikeouts are astoundingly close compared to the figures for any other slugger. In the field, he combined good positioning with quick reflexes and deceptive speed. He never seemed to crash into a fence or dive for a ball—he just glided and was there when it came down. DiMaggio was an ideally versatile player: he could hit, hit with power, field, throw, and run. Although he did not steal many bases, reflecting the style of the game at that time, he was as good as anyone at going from first to third or second to home on a hit and reputedly was never thrown out trying to take an extra base. He wasn't the best ever at any one thing, but he transcended statistics. The *New York Times* eloquently summed up his special quality in an editorial when he retired: "The combination of proficiency and exquisite grace which Joe DiMaggio brought to the art of playing center field was something no baseball averages can measure and that must be seen to be believed and appreciated" (quoted in the *Times* obituary).

On and off the field, he cultivated an image of consistent professionalism, pride, and courtliness that captivated the nation. He was sure of himself, cool, and seemingly emotionless—his stoicism just added to his mystique. When Al Gionfriddo robbed him of a hit in the 1947 World Series, the disgusted DiMaggio kicked at the dirt between first and second base, an action so rare that it became a major news story. He struggled to protect his privacy and maintain his reserve, yet he quietly reveled in being the center of attention. When he attended Old Timers games after his retirement, he insisted on being the last player introduced, assuring himself the biggest ovation. During his playing days, the custom-tailored star was, in the words of sportswriter Roy Blount, "the class of the Yankees in times when the Yankees outclassed everybody else" (quoted in the *Times* obituary).

In retirement, he pursued his second career: Joe DiMaggio, legend. He had some cameo roles to play in baseball, such as occasional appearances at Yankee Stadium, the Hall of Fame, and all-star games; he earned a lot of money making appearances, signing autographs, and later being a television pitch man for a bank and the Mr. Coffee brand of coffeemaker. He also served on the board of directors of the Baltimore Orioles. He was to leave at his death an estate estimated at $40 million. But the DiMaggio legend was most burnished by his marrying Marilyn Monroe, the Hollywood sex goddess, on 14 January 1954. While DiMaggio was a buttoned-down type who made a devoted practice of being a gentleman and hardly ever showed emotion in public, Monroe remained the extravagant exhibitionist wholly at odds with quiet domesticity. The stormy marriage lasted just nine months. They divorced amicably and remained close friends. After Monroe's death in 1962 from a drug overdose, a grief-stricken DiMaggio arranged for her funeral, and he nursed the feeling that had she lived she would have taken him back. He had roses delivered to her grave weekly for over twenty years. The legendary status that continued to cling to DiMaggio reflected his having become, in 1949, the first ballplayer to command an annual salary of $100,000. His competition with Ted Williams of the Red Sox, both in batting and in earnings, enhanced both their reputations. In later years Williams said he believed he was a better hitter than DiMaggio, but he acknowledged the "Yankee Clipper" as the greatest player of his time—he could do it all. Baseball observers noted the irony of where they each played: DiMaggio in Yankee Stadium, a park built for Babe Ruth and greatly favoring left-handed hitters, and Williams at Fenway Park, where right-handers had the advantage. Perhaps their rivalry would have reached an even higher plane had they been traded for each other.

The larger-than-life DiMaggio image was reflected in Les Brown's 1941 hit song "Joltin' Joe DiMaggio," Ernest Hemingway's Cuban fisherman ruminating on "the great DiMaggio" in *The Old Man and the Sea*, and Paul Simon's haunting lyrics in his song "Mrs. Robinson" from the movie *The Graduate* (1967): "Where have you gone, Joe DiMaggio? / A nation turns its lonely eyes to you . . ." In fact, the lonely legend lived for years in San Francisco with his widowed sister Marie, but his arthritis needed a warmer climate, so he made a new home in Hollywood, Florida. For many years a chain smoker of the Camels he endorsed, he finally kicked the habit, but surgery for lung cancer in 1998 led to lung infections and pneumonia. He died of those complications at his home in Hollywood.

• Noteworthy among biographical treatments are Glenn Stout, *DiMaggio: An Illustrated Life* (1995); *Joe DiMaggio: An American Icon* (1999), a *New York Daily News* compilation (1999); and Richard Ben Cramer, *Joe DiMaggio: A Hero's Life* (forthcoming). Obituaries on 9 Mar. 1999 include Joseph Durso's in the *New York Times* and Roger Kahn's in the *Los Angeles Times*, and Cramer's lengthy article in *Newsweek* of 22 Mar. 1999 is especially good.

JOHN R. M. WILSON

DIXON, Jeane (3? Jan. 1918–25 Jan. 1997), psychic and astrologer, was born either 3 or 5 January in Medford, Wisconsin, the daughter of German immigrants Frank Pinckert and Emma Von Graffee Pinckert (Dixon's *Washington Post* obituary lists her father's given name as Gerhart). Having become rich in the lumber industry, Frank Pinckert moved the family, which eventually included seven children, to Santa Rosa, California, when Jeane was a young girl. She received her early education from a governess at home and showed psychic talent early. According to *A Gift of Prophecy* (1965), the bestselling book by journalist Ruth Montgomery, as a child Jeane predicted that her brother Erny would become a great athlete (he later became an all-American football player) and foresaw the arrival of a mysterious black-edged letter; a few days later a letter was delivered that informed the family of the death of her maternal grandfather.

Recognizing the girl's abilities, Emma Pinckert took her eight-year-old daughter to see a gypsy who was encamped on horticulturist Luther Burbank's farm. According to Jeane, the gypsy examined her hands and immediately recognized rare palm markings (including a Star of David and a half-moon), which convinced her that the girl was "blessed with the gift for prophecy" (*A Gift of Prophecy*, p. 15). The gypsy gave her a crystal ball, which she used for many years as an instrument of meditation. Soon afterward the family moved to Los Angeles, where Jeane amazed her parents' friends with her "readings," entertainments that were encouraged by her deeply religious mother, who believed that God-given talents should be allowed to flourish.

After graduating from high school, Jeane pursued a short-lived career in the theater but in 1939 married family friend James Lamb "Jimmy" Dixon, a Los Angeles auto dealer whose business partner was "Our

Gang" producer Hal Roach. They had no children. After the United States entered World War II, the couple moved to Washington, D.C., where Jimmy Dixon, a divorcé twenty years Jeane's senior, handled real estate deals for the War Department while Jeane did volunteer work with the Home Hospitality Committee, giving psychic readings for U.S. servicemen. It was during this time that Jeane Dixon became well known in the Washington area for her extrasensory abilities. According to Dixon, she met with Franklin Roosevelt twice in 1944–1945, supposedly warning him of his impending death and advising him on U.S. relations with the Soviet Union and on the "race problem"; in the latter case she counseled that the United States "must not pamper the colored people."

As Dixon's local celebrity grew, she was inundated with requests from people seeking knowledge of their future or where their hidden talents lay. Finally, in the late 1940s, in the hope of giving her psychic abilities a much-needed rest, she joined her husband's Washington real estate firm, the James L. Dixon Agency, which he had started after the end of the war. She worked for many years at her husband's firm, eventually serving as secretary-treasurer. Although she assumed new responsibilities with the company, Dixon did not completely abandon her psychic work. During the 1940s and 1950s she prophesied that China would become a communist country, India would be partitioned, Mahatma Gandhi would be assassinated, and Harry S. Truman would defeat Thomas Dewey in the 1948 presidential election. Because many of these predictions were revealed after the fact in books and articles by either Dixon herself or through her friends and associates, there is little proof that she actually foretold these events.

In 1956, however, Dixon told *Parade* magazine that she had had a vision in 1952 that the Democratic president elected in 1960 would be tall, have dark hair and blue eyes, and die in office. (Dixon claims she told the reporter that the president would be assassinated but *Parade* refused to print such a shocking prognostication.) When John F. Kennedy was murdered in Dallas in November 1963, Dixon gained national recognition. But the media ignored her prediction, revealed in the months preceding the election, that Kennedy would lose the presidency to Republican Richard M. Nixon. She defended her incorrect forecast, claiming that she had had a vision several days before the election that she interpreted as a warning of ballot-box fraud: "unless the Republicans police every poll the victory will be stolen from them" (*A Gift of Prophecy*, p. 103).

It was Dixon's supposed foretelling of the Kennedy assassination that led journalist Ruth Montgomery to write *A Gift of Prophecy*, a litany of the Washington seeress's correct divinations. For nearly a decade Montgomery had been writing a New Year's Day column on Dixon's predictions for the coming year. The book, which became a bestseller, was followed that same year by the appearance in newspapers nationwide of a daily syndicated horoscope feature, "Jeane

Dixon's Horoscope Column," which Dixon began ostensibly because she could not respond to all of the personal requests for guidance. Dixon reported that by 1969 she was receiving approximately 3,000 letters a week seeking psychic advice. Beginning in the late 1970s, Rupert Murdoch's tabloid *Star* began publishing her predictions for the new year. Read by millions worldwide, the feature continued until her death.

A devout Roman Catholic, Dixon believed that she was an "instrument of God" and that most of her visions of the future came from a higher power. In her autobiography, *My Life and Prophecies* (written with Rene Noorbergen, 1969), in an author's note she compared herself to biblical prophets and claimed that the "purpose of this book is to show that as God spoke through the prophets so does He convey a message through each one of us." She blamed her incorrect predictions not on the signs God revealed to her but on her inability to interpret them accurately.

The Dixons became wealthy. They lived in a large townhouse in northwest Washington, and with wealth came friendships with celebrities and politicians. She was especially connected to the Republican party, serving as godmother to Senator Strom Thurmond's son and contributing at least $30,000 to the party in the last ten years of her life. But Dixon claimed that every dollar she earned with her psychic work went to charities, including the Damon Runyon Cancer Fund and, later, Children-to-Children, Inc., which she founded in 1964 to help children spiritually and physically. Her critics were uncomfortable with her far-Right views, which she disseminated through her books and columns. Several chapters in her autobiography are devoted to her belief that communist conspiracies were behind the civil rights movement, the anti–Vietnam War demonstrations, and the assassination of Martin Luther King, Jr. According to the news website apbnews.com, Dixon was an "FBI stooge," a "mouthpiece" who, through her speeches and columns, assisted the bureau in its efforts to discredit leftist protesters during the turbulent 1960s and 1970s.

In her later years, Dixon remained physically healthy, but a few longtime supporters believed her psychic powers had diminished. Having told Ronald Reagan in 1962 that he would be president someday, Dixon served as Nancy Reagan's astrologer during her husband's presidency until the first lady, believing that Dixon had lost her gift, turned to astrologer Joan Quigley for advice. When Dixon died in Washington, skeptics wondered why she had not included a hint of her imminent expiration in her 1997 *Star* magazine predictions.

Although some of Dixon's predictions came true, such as her uncanny ability to foretell winners in U.S. presidential elections (save Kennedy in 1960 and Bill Clinton in 1992), many more did not: World War III did not begin in 1958, the "end of an president Fidel Castro" was not in sight in 1969, at the turn of the century the United States still had not elected a woman president, and the comet that was to hit Earth in the mid-1980s, becoming "one of the worst disasters of the twentieth century" (*My Life and Prophecies*, p. 151), must have missed. Most of Dixon's prophecies were vague and imprecise enough so that they did come true somehow, somewhere—such as when she predicted that "great changes in medicine and welfare will facilitate our health, economy, and way of life"—and when they *were* more specific they were often utterly wrong or intended to advance a political agenda. For centuries, societies have craved information about the future, and soothsayers, oracles, prophets, or tabloid psychics have provided it to them. Although Dixon's psychic abilities are questioned, she fostered a successful career as a twentieth-century Nostradamus.

• In addition to *My Life and Prophecies*, Jeane Dixon's books include *The Call to Glory: Jeane Dixon Speaks of Jesus* (1972); *Yesterday, Today and Forever* (1975); *Jeane Dixon's Astrological Cookbook* (1976); *Horoscopes for Dogs* (1979); *A Gift of Prayer: Words of Comfort and Inspiration from America's Most Beloved Prophet* (1995); and the posthumous *Do Cats Have ESP?* (1998). The *Washington Post*, 25 July 1996, includes an article detailing her connections to the Republican Party. Obituaries are in the *New York Times* and the *Washington Post*, both 27 Jan. 1997.

STACEY HAMILTON

DONNER PARTY, a group of pioneers, earned its legendary name as the result of a notorious trek to California in 1846–1847. The party, which initially numbered thirty-two men, women, and children, assembled in Springfield, Illinois, in early April 1846 to begin the 2,500-mile journey westward. It comprised the families and servants of James Frazier Reed, the initial organizer of the group, and George and Jacob Donner; both the Donner men and Reed had settled in Illinois some years earlier and had made their fortunes, the Donners as farmers and Reed as a businessman. But the prevalence of sickness, including tuberculosis, cholera, and malaria, coupled with financial panic in the East in the early 1840s had fueled the desire of many, including the Donners and the Reeds, to move farther west, joining an exodus across the Mississippi River that would amount to more than half a million by the end of the decade.

The Donners and the Reeds left Springfield on 16 April 1846 in nine covered wagons. The first leg of their journey was the well-traveled route to Independence, Missouri, which they reached the second week in May. Beyond Independence lay what were only rarely used trails, for the great migration westward was still in its infancy. By 12 May, days after their arrival, they had secured enough provisions to begin the next leg of the journey, joined by other wagons; their next destination was Fort Laramie, a trading post in the foothills of the Rocky Mountains and the site of present-day Laramie, Wyoming. This part of the journey proved only a bit more difficult than the first, although drenching rains delayed their anticipated arrival date by one week, to 27 June. At Fort Laramie the party first learned of an event that later would have dire repercussions for their emigration: the United States had declared war on Mexico on 11 May.

The party slowly made its way over the Rocky Mountains toward the Little Sandy River, the next milestone on their journey. Here they would have to make a fateful decision: whether to head north to Fort Hall, following the known trail, or instead to turn south and travel a new route that passed through Fort Bridger. This new route, known as Hastings' Cutoff, was the brainchild of one Lansford Hastings, a young Ohio lawyer and entrepreneur who had traveled to California a few years earlier, been amazed by its possibilities for settlement, and published a bestseller called *The Emigrants' Guide to Oregon and California*. Hastings had recently proposed a new route to the West that took emigrants south around the Great Salt Lake and through the Great Salt Desert, claiming it was as much as four hundred miles shorter than the conventional northern trail. Indeed, Hastings himself promised to meet the Donner and Reed group when they reached Fort Bridger and to lead them the rest of the way to California.

Reed had intended from the outset to follow Hastings' Cutoff; even though he had been warned at Fort Laramie by experienced mountain men not to take it, he was determined to save time. Time, in fact, was of the essence because the party had to make its way across another rugged mountain range, the Sierra Nevada, before snows began in late fall. Otherwise, they risked being trapped there over the winter. On 20 July the long wagon train reached the Little Sandy River, and the next day most of the wagons headed north, opting for the conventional route; twenty, including the nine belonging to the Donners and the Reeds, headed south toward Fort Bridger and Hastings' Cutoff, persuaded by Reed to follow the new route. Their number, which would grow, with the addition of more hired men, to eighty-seven, elected George Donner as the head of the party, passing over James Reed, who had already begun to irritate some in the group with what some felt was too haughty a manner.

When what was now known as the Donner Party arrived at Fort Bridger a week later, Lansford Hastings was not there to meet them as promised. He had gone on ahead with another party, leaving instructions for those who chose to follow his path. After four days spent resting their oxen, making repairs to the wagons, and stocking up on provisions, the Donner Party began the next leg of their journey, through Hastings' Cutoff, on 31 July. They discovered, to their dismay, that the route passed through a tangled warren of canyons and brush, proving nearly impossible to follow. The wagons, which had to be double-teamed with oxen to get them across the unwelcoming terrain, were able to move at best only two miles a day, and the journey to the shores of the Great Salt Lake, their next outpost and a destination that should have taken only a week to reach, took more than three.

When they finally arrived at the lake on 22 August, the emigrants were exhausted and embittered, but they kept forging ahead toward the Great Salt Desert, which they reached on 30 August. They had expected the eighty-mile desert crossing to be simple by comparison, but it proved an even greater nightmare: an oven by day, a sticky mass by night, the desert took nearly a week to get over. The wagons got stuck up to their hubs in the gooey sand, oxen died or fled, and the water supply ran out before they had made it to the other side. Initial good humor had now given way to grumbling, for many of the exhausted emigrants had been forced to abandon their wagons and many of their possessions along the way. Worst of all, snow had now appeared in the foothills ahead, and the emigrants realized that they did not have enough provisions to get all the way to California, a distance of six hundred miles.

Two men in the party were sent ahead on horseback to find relief at Sutter's Fort, their ultimate destination in California, while the rest struggled on. The Donner Party finally reached the Humboldt River, where Hastings' Cutoff rejoined the older route, on 26 September. The so-called shortcut had in fact proved to be 125 miles longer than the other trail. Still they continued, trying to get as far as possible before the snows began in earnest, and hoping to encounter a relief party along the way. Tempers grew even more frayed, and on 5 October violence finally erupted: when James Reed tried to stop an enraged teamster from beating his oxen, the teamster turned on Reed with his whip, and Reed stabbed him in self-defense. The wounds were fatal, and the party demanded retribution. They settled on banishment for Reed, and he was forced to leave his family behind. He chose to ride on ahead, with the intention of getting help.

The party stumbled on, most of them now walking to spare the remaining oxen. By the time they reached the Truckee River, the gateway to the Sierra Nevada mountains, on 16 October, they had been menaced by Indians and lost several of their number to cold, sickness, and exposure. They camped there for several days, unsure of how to proceed, until 19 October, when Charles Stanton, one of the men who had gone to Sutter's Fort for help six weeks earlier, arrived with two Indian guides and mules loaded with fresh provisions. He also brought encouraging news: that the mountain pass would be clear of snow for another month.

After several more days of rest, the Donner Party resumed their journey, reaching Truckee Lake in eastern California by the end of October. But when they attempted to make a last effort to push over the mountain, they found the pass completely blocked by snow. Discouraged, angry, and frustrated—they were now only 150 miles from Sutter's Fort—they realized that they would be unable to continue until spring. They returned to Truckee Lake, built a winter camp, and settled in for what would become a nightmare of starvation and horror.

The events that transpired at the Truckee Lake camp over the next few months were recorded by some of the emigrants, including Patrick Breen, in their diaries. Other details came from survivors of the long ordeal and from their rescuers. After creating crude shelters and building fires to keep warm, obtaining food became the primary concern. Supplies gave out quickly, and the emigrants foraged for anything edible, including twigs and bark. One by one all the animals were killed off, including pet dogs, for meat, and when people began dying of starvation their corpses became a source of food as well. The first recorded instances of cannibalism appear to have occurred in late December, among a group of fifteen emigrants known as "the Forlorn Hope" who had left Truckee Lake a few weeks earlier to make another attempt to cross the mountains. They were soon snowed in and forced to make camp. After a week or more without food, members of the group began to die, five in all. With some reluctance, the survivors butchered their friends, roasted and ate some of the flesh, carefully wrapped the rest for future use—identifying it so that no one would have to eat a relative—and continued onward. Seven of the Forlorn Hope survived, making it as far as a cabin in the foothills on the other side of the Sierra Nevada by 17 January. Hearing the survivors' stories of not only their own plight but also of those back at Truckee Lake, the cabin dwellers sent out an alarm for help. By early February a relief party was heading from Sutter's Fort toward the mountains. Behind them came a second relief party, headed by James Reed, who had made it to the fort in late October and spent nearly three months trying to amass enough able-bodied men to help him; most had gone south to fight in the Mexican War, which had finally ended in January 1847.

At the Truckee encampment, conditions had gone from bad to worse as more emigrants had slowly starved to death. The first relief party, which arrived at Truckee on 19 February, was shocked to find blanket-covered corpses strewn about the snow and crazed survivors who were barely alive. Three days later, the relief party managed to take out twenty-four of the living, leaving the remaining thirty-one behind with scanty rations and the promise that the second relief party would arrive shortly. When Reed's rescue group arrived some days later, ten more emigrants had died, and many—but not all—of the survivors had now resorted to eating the flesh of the deceased. A notable exception was the Reed family, whose titular head in her husband's absence, Margaret Reed, had managed to keep herself and her four children alive by carefully rationing their provisions; several other women had managed to do the same for their own families.

It took two more rescue parties to bring out the remaining survivors. The third rescued Reed's party, which had been stranded in the mountains by a heavy snowstorm on the return journey; the fourth came to take out any remaining survivors and looked in vain for large sums of cash reportedly left there by the Donners. By the last week in April, more than a year after the Donners and the Reeds left Springfield, all of the forty-six surviving emigrants were safely in

California and eager to get on with their lives. But the story of the Donner tragedy—which had claimed both Jacob and George Donner, their wives, and four of their children but spared the Reeds—quickly spread back East as newspapers published sensational and lurid accounts, mostly derived from rescuers, of hardship, savagery, and cannibalism. Emigration to California fell off sharply as a consequence, and it did not resume full throttle until 1849, prompted by news of the discovery of gold near Sutter's Fort a year earlier. The Gold Rush was now on, and the Donner emigrants passed into history; the trail they forged through the Sierra Nevada was subsequently named Donner Pass to commemorate their journey, and the name "Donner" was given to several other local landmarks. Most of the survivors prospered, and some of them, years afterward when notoriety had faded, wrote their memoirs with varying degrees of accuracy. The last survivor of the Donner Party, an infant at the time of emigration, died in 1935.

• Many accounts have been written of the Donner Party, and new ones, often with dubious claims to accuracy, continue to appear. The most accurate and compelling source remains George R. Stewart's *Ordeal by Hunger*, first published in 1936, revised in 1960, and still in print. Stewart, a longtime professor of history at the University of California, Berkeley, wrote an account of the tragedy that is both highly readable and meticulously documented; the book includes maps, illustrations, and an appendix with excerpts from some of the more credible memoirs of survivors. The only recent book to offer new information is Donald L. Hardesty's *The Archaeology of the Donner Party* (1997), an account of studies made by archaeologists and anthropologists at the sites of the emigrants' cabins at Truckee Lake. For an account of the Donner Party in the context of nineteenth-century westward migration, the standard remains Bernard DeVoto's *The Year of Decision: 1846*, first published in 1942; for a briefer history, see Timothy Foote, "1846: The Way We Were—and the Way We Went," *Smithsonian*, April 1996, pp. 38ff.

ANN T. KEENE

DOUGLAS, Marjory Stoneman (7 Apr. 1890–14 May 1998), author and environmentalist, was born in Minneapolis, Minnesota, the daughter of Florence Lillian Trefethen Stoneman, who went by the name of Lillian, and Frank Bryant Stoneman, a businessman and newspaper editor. When Marjory was three her father's business failed, and the family moved to Providence, Rhode Island. Further business reverses took a toll on Lillian Stoneman's mental health and resulted in a nervous breakdown. Not long thereafter, Lillian separated from her husband and, with her six-year-old daughter, traveled to Taunton, Massachusetts, to live with her parents and unmarried sister.

Marjory was educated in the Taunton schools and graduated from high school in 1908. With funds scraped together by her aunt and grandmother, she was able to attend Wellesley College, where she majored in English. She enjoyed her college experience and formed lasting female friendships. She also showed an interest in women's rights; in her junior year, with some of her classmates, she joined a club to support a woman's right to vote.

Marjory Stoneman graduated in June 1912. The happy occasion turned grim, however, when she learned after graduation ceremonies that her mother was dying of cancer. She returned home to be with her mother, who died a few weeks later. Lonely and unsure of herself, she took a job in a department store in St. Louis to be near her closest friend, and after a year she moved to Newark, New Jersey. There she met Kenneth Douglas, an editor on the *Newark Evening News*, and their three-month courtship led to marriage. But the union proved to be an unhappy one. At the outset, Marjory knew little about Douglas, who was some thirty years her senior. After learning that he was forging bank drafts in her name and drinking heavily, she followed the advice of her uncle and left her husband. (Although she later divorced Douglas, she retained his surname.) In September 1915 she departed for Miami, Florida, to be reunited with her father, whom she had not seen since she was six years old.

Frank Stoneman had move to Florida in 1896 and in 1908 founded the *Miami News Record*, named the *Herald* in 1910. Marjory Douglas began working for her father's paper as the society editor and occasionally took assignments as a reporter. After the United States entered World War I, she joined the naval reserve, becoming the first woman from Florida to do so. She resigned in 1918 to volunteer for the American Red Cross, serving in France, Italy, and the Balkans. On her return to the *Herald* after the war, Douglas edited a literary column and wrote editorials. One project she supported in print was the proposal of Edward F. Coe, a landscape architect and Miami resident, to create an Everglades National Park. For several years she also served on a committee formed to advance the park proposal.

Having grown tired of the grind and mental strain of newspaper work, Douglas left the *Herald* in 1924 to become a freelance writer. With the income from her short stories, which appeared in popular publications like the *Saturday Evening Post*, she was able to support herself, and in 1926 she moved into a small house she had built for herself in Coconut Grove.

In 1942 Hervey Allen, an old friend and author of the bestselling *Anthony Adverse*, asked Douglas if she wanted to contribute to a series of books he was editing on the rivers of America. When she asked if she could write about the Everglades, Allen assented. Despite her familiarity with the area, she knew little about its history or dynamics. After roughly three years of research, she published in 1947 *The Everglades: River of Grass*, which was soon recognized as a classic and altered the public perception of wetlands as useless swamps.

The Everglades was first of all a natural history of the unique southern Florida saw grass wetlands, home to ibises, spoonbills, manatees, saltwater crocodiles, freshwater alligators, and numerous other species. But the book also told the shocking story of the waste of the area's natural resources—from the slaughter of its wildlife to the building of dams and canals to drain the wetlands for flood control, ranching, and farming. Douglas emphasized that denying water to the Everglades would destroy it. But despite the evidence of greed and irresponsibility forcefully presented in what one reviewer called a "beautiful, and bitter, sweet and savage book" (*New York Herald-Tribune Weekly*, 30 Nov. 1947), *The Everglades* closes with the hope that the public would at last act to salvage this "vast, magnificent, subtle and unique region."

The year *The Everglades* was published, President Harry S. Truman formally opened Everglades National Park. The new park, which Edward Coe had proposed more than twenty years earlier, embraced only 10 to 15 percent of the original Everglades. Nonetheless, Douglas was pleased, calling it a "great accomplishment." The U.S. Army Corps of Engineers, however, subsequently built levees for flood control, causing the water level in the park to shrink. And, in the late 1960s, plans to build a jetport near the park's northern edge further threatened the ecological health of the park.

The projected jetport elicited strong opposition from environmentalists and galvanized Douglas to act in 1969. At the urging of Joseph Browder of the National Audubon Society, Douglas, then seventy-nine years of age and with falling eyesight, helped found Friends of the Everglades. As the group's first president, she traveled throughout central and southern Florida to deliver speeches against the jetport. Responding to pressure from environmental groups, including Friends of the Everglades, the state decided in 1970 to situate the jetport elsewhere.

In the 1980s efforts were made by the state government to restore the water flow to the Everglades, and the U.S. Congress authorized the acquisition of over 100,000 acres to expand the park. But another serious threat to the park's ecosystem emerged: the quality of the water redirected to the Everglades was being compromised by pesticides and other agricultural pollutants. To address this issue, the state passed in 1991 the Marjory Stoneman Douglas Everglades Protection Act, which financed the construction of facilities to treat the wastewater from farms. The official signing ceremony was held in Douglas's front yard. (She subsequently expressed displeasure with the law's ineffectiveness.)

Douglas received many other honors. In 1975 she was named Conservationist of the Year by the Florida Audubon Society; a year later she received the same honor from the Florida Wildlife Federation. In 1989 she was named honorary vice president of the Sierra Club, and in 1993 President Bill Clinton presented Douglas with the Presidential Medal of Freedom for her work in preserving the Everglades. "Long before there was an Earth Day," said the president, "Mrs. Douglas was a passionate steward of our nation's natural resources and particularly her Florida Everglades" (*New York Times*, 15 May 1998).

Douglas continued to pursue her writing career along with her environmental activities. Among her later books are *The Joys of Bird Watching in Florida* (1969) and *Adventures in a Green World* (1973), an account of the work of David Fairchild and Barbour Lathrop. At the time of her death she was working on a biography of W. H. Hudson, the British naturalist and author. Douglas, the "Guardian of the Glades," died at her home in Coconut Grove.

• The Marjory Stoneman Douglas Papers are located in the Archives and Special Collections Department, Otto G. Richter Library, University of Miami, Miami, Fla. The basic source on Douglas's life is her autobiography, written with John Rothchild, *Voice of the River* (1987). Jennifer Bryant, *Marjory Stoneman Douglas: Voice of the Everglades* (1992), is a brief biography. Ann Vileisis, *Discovering the Unknown Landscape: A History of America's Wetlands* (1997), provides valuable background on the problems that beleaguer wetlands, including the Everglades. An obituary is in the *Miami Herald*, 15 May 1998.

RICHARD HARMOND

DRAPER, Paul (25 Oct. 1909–20 Sept. 1996), dancer, was born in Florence, Italy, to Paul Draper, a lieder singer, and Muriel Sanders Draper, author and lecturer. His aunt was the monologist Ruth Draper. In 1911 the Drapers moved to London and in 1915 to the United States. After his parents' divorce, Draper attended schools and colleges in Massachusetts, New York, New Jersey, Virginia, and Connecticut without obtaining a degree.

Eventually Draper dug ditches and served as assistant music critic for the *New York World-Telegram*. In 1930, while working as an instructor for the Arthur Murray Dance Studios, Draper learned the "time step" from the tap dancer Tommy Nip. A mostly self-taught tap dancer, Draper began to study ballet in 1931. He was accepted in 1933 by George Balanchine's new School of American Ballet, where, alongside nine- and ten-year-olds, he studied with Anatole Oboukhoff.

Draper's uniqueness was his combination of tap and ballet, which soon earned him titles such as "the aristocrat of tap" and "the dancing Hamlet." At Radio City Music Hall, his specialty was a "One Man Flash Act" performed on a marble pedestal. He quickly moved to more appropriate venues in Manhattan such as Cobina Wright's supper club, the Persian Room of the Plaza Hotel, and the Rainbow Room atop Rockefeller Center. In 1934 he made his Broadway debut in the revue *Thumbs Up*.

A performer of considerable intellectualism, Draper, often dressed in a fashionably short dinner jacket, performed what might be called "dance monologues" to classical music that was not usually considered suitable for tapping. The French critic Jacques Porel remarked, "[He] has succeeded in combining Russian choreography with the purely American form. From floor to waist he is American, but the upper part of his body has gone abroad." Draper later explained that while tappers strove to "lay down time," making heavy sounds, he wanted to make a lighter impression; so he rethought the shoe, using a very thin, small tap on the toe and a half-moon on the heel, filing the toe-tap to be paper thin. Sometimes coached by the jazz choreographer Buddy Bradley, he began to influence jazz (and eventually theatrical) dancers with his innovative steps.

In 1939 Draper was performing at the Cocoanut Grove in the Ambassador Hotel in Los Angeles when he encountered an old friend, the harmonica virtuoso Larry Adler, another artist with an eclectic repertory. Adler and Draper formed a double act and for the next decade regularly earned $100,000 per year performing in large theaters and night clubs. In a typical performance, Draper would dance to the music of Johannes Brahms, George Frideric Handel, and Domenico Paradies and Adler would play J. S. Bach, Isaac Albéniz, Claude Debussy, and George Gershwin. At the end of each half of the performance, they would join forces and ask audiences to suggest song titles they could play and dance to. By this time Draper had also developed his "Sonata for Tap-Dancer," in which the musical sounds came from his tapping feet.

In 1941 Draper married Heidi Vossler, a ballerina in George Balanchine's American Ballet. They had three children and remained married until Vossler's death in 1992. Draper's most significant film appearance came in 1948, when he played the role of Joe, a dancer longing to become a comedian, in William Saroyan's eccentric play *The Time of Your Life*. That year, *New York Times* dance critic John Martin likened Draper's feet to fingers on a keyboard: "His touch is sensitive . . . his phrasing beautifully free and rhythmic . . . with the most delicate and rapturous counter phrases."

Draper's and Adler's lives were soon dominated by the era's political climate. In 1948 one of Draper's original works, "Political Speech," in which he kissed imaginary babies and walked a tightrope, was booed by an audience. A woman in Greenwich, Connecticut, claimed that Draper and Adler were "pro-Communist" and should not be allowed to perform in the town. Columnists Igor Cassini and Walter Winchell took up the cause of denouncing the pair. With their bookings suddenly falling away, Adler and Draper sued for libel. Much of the trial dealt with the left-leaning sympathies of Draper's mother. Although Draper and Adler were never called before any investigative committee and both swore oaths that they were not—nor had ever been—Communists, the jury could not reach a verdict. In January 1950 Draper danced "Yankee Doodle Dandy" on the "Toast of the Town" television show, but complaints caused its host, Ed Sullivan, to apologize to sponsors. Draper's number was erased from the kinescope record.

Draper was blacklisted, and in 1951, after a tour of Israel with Adler, he moved to Switzerland. He returned to the United States in 1954, performing a solo concert at the 92nd Street Y and joining his aunt for a stage performance. Settling in Pittsburgh, where be-

tween 1967 and 1978 he taught theater at Carnegie-Mellon Institute, he began to write a regular column for *The Dancer*. In 1955 he choreographed Igor Stravinsky's *Histoire du Soldat* for a performance at the Phoenix Theatre. Among his 1960s appearances were *Gentlemen, Be Seated!* for the New York City Opera, choreographing *Archy and Mehitabel* for the Goodspeed Opera House in Connecticut, and a rare Broadway outing in *Come Summer*. He continued to develop satirical sketches such as "A Sharp Character" and "Dance Hall." Episode twenty-seven of Pete Seeger's television series *The Rainbow Quest* was devoted to his work.

In 1979 Lee Theodore, director of the American Dance Machine, invited Draper to New York, where he revived some of his vintage routines for the ADM's project to preserve great American dance on videotape. For two months a documentary team followed Draper's teaching, during which time he created a ballet tap barre adapted to accommodate the footwork and rhythmic application of tap, which subsequently influenced teachers who trained Broadway dancers. Bob Boross, a dance writer who attended the workshop, recalled "a constant stream of sound that never failed to make tap dancers as well as non-tap dancers sit forward to see where all of those sounds came from" (*The Dancer*, Dec. 1996). The documentary was broadcast on the Public Broadcasting System (PBS) in 1980.

Draper's later years were spent in Woodstock, New York, where he was involved in a serious automobile accident in 1995. The following year, Draper died of emphysema. The theatrical choreographer Bob Fosse, himself a prime blender of jazz and classicism, said simply that Draper "had many imitators—but none who could equal his artistry" (quoted from *The American Dance Machine*, PBS, 1980).

• The whereabouts of any Draper papers is unknown. Adler writes extensively of Draper in his autobiography *It Ain't Necessarily So* (1984). Bob Boross's critical memoir is in *The Dancer*, Dec. 1996. Jane Goldberg's "Conversations with Paul Draper" is in *Ballet Review* 5, no. 1 (1975–1976). A chapter on Draper is found in Rusty Frank, *Tap!* (1994). Draper's American Dance Machine work is in the Dance Collection of the New York Public Library, Lincoln Center; Roger Englander's film "Paul Draper on Tap" focuses on the same workshop. Muriel Draper, *Music at Midnight* (1929), is written from a mother's standpoint. An obituary by Jennifer Dunning appears in the *New York Times*, 21 September 1996; another by Larry Adler is in the (London) *Guardian* of the following day.

JAMES ROSS MOORE

DRYSDALE, Don (23 July 1936–3 July 1993), baseball player, was born Donald Scott Drysdale in Van Nuys, California, the son of Scott Drysdale, a repair supervisor with a telephone company, and Verna Ley Drysdale. His father, who had briefly pitched in the minor leagues in the early 1930s, taught him to catch and throw when he was five years old. He later recalled that both his parents spent hours tutoring him on how to play baseball and that his grandmother sometimes took over his paper route so that he would not miss neighborhood games. He began playing in organized leagues in 1945. His father, aware that adolescent pitchers often develop "Little League elbow," refused to allow him to pitch until he was sixteen. During his senior year at Van Nuys High School, he won ten of eleven pitching decisions and was named to the Los Angeles All-City team. Stanford University and the University of Southern California offered him baseball scholarships, and every major league team bid for his services. The Brooklyn Dodgers, who hired his father to work as a part-time scout, signed him to a contract in June 1954.

Drysdale progressed quickly through the Dodgers' minor league organization, spending 1954 with Bakersfield in the Class C California League and 1955 with Montreal in the Triple A International League. He made the Brooklyn Dodgers' opening day roster in 1956—at the age of nineteen, the second youngest player in the major leagues. In his first start, he struck out nine batters and pitched a complete game victory against the Philadelphia Phillies. He was used as a spot starter throughout the season, finishing with a 5–5 won-lost record and an earned-run average of 2.65. He also appeared as a relief pitcher in the World Series against the New York Yankees, which the Dodgers lost. At season's end, Brooklyn sportswriters named him Dodger Rookie of the Year.

In 1957 Drysdale established himself as the team's best starter, compiling a 17–9 record and a 2.69 earned-run average. The following year he married Ginger Dubberly, a professional model; they had one child and divorced in 1983. The Dodgers moved to Los Angeles in 1958, and for the next few seasons he turned in relatively disappointing performances. Although he led the league in strikeouts twice, between 1958 and 1961 he won only a few more games than he lost. One of his problems was the dimensions of Los Angeles Coliseum, a converted football stadium with a left-field fence that was only 251 feet from home plate. As he told a reporter, "A man could hit a ball with his knuckles, and ping! Over the fence she went" (quoted in Horn, p. 26). He also gained a reputation for having a temper that sometimes got the best of him. He quarreled with umpires, got into shouting matches with opposing players, and denounced the stadium to newspaper reporters. Chuck Dressen, a Dodgers coach, commented: "Some pitchers think too much. They should just throw. Drysdale worries about the size of the ballpark, the umpires. . . . A fellow like Warren Spahn never worries about anything except the man at the plate. With his natural ability, Drysdale could be a thirty-game winner" (quoted in Durslag, p. 56).

A right-hander who stood at six feet six inches, Drysdale featured a fastball that was regularly clocked at ninety-five miles per hour. His sweeping sidearm motion caused his pitches to run in perilously close to right-handed batters at the plate; as Willie Mays observed of him, "Until you get used to looking at this guy, you'll swear that every pitch is going to crack you on the head" (quoted in Durslag, p. 55). Although he always denied that he deliberately threw at hitters, he also adhered to a no-holds-barred pitching philosophy: "You do everything possible to get the win, everything possible to get that edge. . . . Take no prisoners, and if you were going to lose, take down the son-of-a-bitch who beat you, too. Make him feel the cost of victory" (Drysdale, p. 180). In 1957 he touched off a famous bench-clearing brawl when he hit Johnny Logan, the shortstop for the Milwaukee Braves, twice in the same inning—first with a fastball and then with a pick-off throw when Logan took his lead off first base. In 1959 he publicly threatened to sue the National League for "character assassination" when an umpire warned him about throwing beanballs. Two years later, he hit twenty opposing batsmen, the most by any National League pitcher since 1909.

In 1962 the team moved to the newly built Dodger Stadium and Drysdale enjoyed his best season. He led the major leagues with 25 wins, 314 innings pitched, and 232 strikeouts; for his performance, he was honored with the Cy Young Award and named the *Sporting News* Major League Pitcher of the Year. The same season, Sandy Koufax emerged as a dominant left-hander. Drysdale was often overshadowed by his teammate: for instance, in 1965, when he posted a 23–12 record with 210 strikeouts, Koufax went 26–8 and struck out a major-league record 382 batters. Nevertheless, the two pitchers formed one of the most potent tandems in baseball history, and the Dodgers won three pennants and two World Series between 1963 and 1966. During spring training in 1966, Drysdale and Koufax engaged in a highly publicized joint holdout, demanding three-year contracts and $1.05 million to be split between them. Their holdout—a pioneering effort at collective bargaining in major league baseball—ended unsuccessfully and only netted Drysdale a $25,000 raise.

In 1968 Drysdale had his most memorable season when he set a major-league record by pitching 58.2 consecutive scoreless innings. During his streak, he threw six straight shutouts and twice outdueled future Hall of Famer Bob Gibson. In 1969 he was abruptly forced to retire when he tore a rotator cuff in his right shoulder. His lifetime record for fourteen seasons included 209 wins, 166 losses, 2,486 strikeouts, 49 shutouts, and a 2.95 earned-run average. He made nine All-Star teams and appeared in five World Series. A good hitter, he led National League pitchers in home runs four times, twice tying the league record by hitting seven home runs in a season. He was remarkably durable, never missing his turn in the rotation during his entire career. He also set a National League record by hitting 154 batters. In 1984 he was elected to the National Baseball Hall of Fame.

Although he was the one of the game's most feared pitchers, Drysdale was well liked off the baseball diamond, becoming especially close friends with the Dodgers' amiable first baseman, Gil Hodges. During his playing career, he frequently appeared in television commercials; he also guest-starred on television programs such as "You Bet Your Life," "The Donna Reed Show," and "The Brady Bunch." After he retired, he began a second career as a sports broadcaster, announcing games for the Montreal Expos, Texas Rangers, California Angels, and Chicago White Sox. He later remarked that his only difficulty in making the transition from playing to broadcasting baseball games was learning to conduct interviews: "I felt so damn funny asking players questions when I already knew the answers." From 1978 to 1986 he worked as a commentator for ABC Sports. In 1986 he married Ann Meyers, a professional basketball player; they had two children. In 1988 he fulfilled a long-time ambition when he became an announcer for the Dodgers, teaming with Vin Scully. He died of a heart attack in Montreal, shortly before he was supposed to broadcast a Dodgers game.

• A clipping file on Drysdale is at the National Baseball Library, Cooperstown, N.Y. The most valuable source for information on his life is his autobiography, *Once a Bum, Always a Dodger* (1990). Colorful profiles are Melvin Durslag, "L.A.'s Fiery Strike-Out Artist," *Saturday Evening Post*, 1 July 1961, pp. 25, 55–56; Huston Horn, "Ex-Bad Boy's Big Year," *Sports Illustrated*, 20 Aug. 1962, pp. 24–29; and "Departure of Big D," *Time*, 2 Aug. 1969, pp. 59–60. For Drysdale's career within the context of the Dodgers' history, see Donald Honig, *The Los Angeles Dodgers: The First Quarter Century* (1983), and Neil J. Sullivan, *The Dodgers Move West* (1987). An obituary is in the *New York Times*, 5 July 1993.

THOMAS W. COLLINS, JR.

DUNCAN, Todd (12 Feb. 1903–27 Feb. 1998), singer and teacher, was born Robert Todd Duncan in Danville, Kentucky, the son of John Duncan, a garage owner, and Lettie Cooper Duncan, a music teacher. Duncan's B.A. (1925) came from Butler University; his M.A. (1930) from Columbia University's Teachers College.

Duncan taught music at the University of Louisville's Municipal College for Negroes from 1926 to 1929. While working on his master's degree, he studied voice with Sara Lee, Edward Lippo, and Sidney Dietch. In 1931 Duncan took a position at Howard University in Washington, D.C., where before retiring in 1945 he became head of the public school music and professional voice departments.

Duncan's singing career blossomed after a one-night, all–African-American production of *Cavalleria Rusticana* at New York's Mecca Temple in 1934, the year he married Gladys Jackson. (They had one child and remained married until Duncan's death.) More than one person claimed credit for spotting the tall, commanding baritone and recommending him to George Gershwin, then casting his opera *Porgy and Bess*.

The story of Duncan's audition for Gershwin is legendary. The classically trained Duncan was less than flattered by being courted by a "Tin Pan Alley" composer. Miffed at having to spend money on traveling from Washington to New York (the producers of *Cavalleria* had left town without paying his fee), Duncan did not bring an accompanist and asked Gershwin if he was able to play. Gershwin obliged at the piano as Duncan performed his choice, "Lungi dal Caro Bene," a nineteenth-century Italian art song. Gershwin requested that Duncan sing without the sheet music so he could watch his face and after a few bars asked, "Will you be my Porgy?" With money from Gershwin, Duncan and his wife returned the next week, running the gauntlet of the Theatre Guild, which was committed to producing Gershwin's opera but favored Paul Robeson.

Duncan recalled, "I was supposed to sing three or four songs . . . I sang opera, I sang Negro spirituals, I sang German lieder, French chansons. . . . I sang an hour, an hour and a half"—no show tunes, because, he said, he didn't know any. Then George and his brother Ira Gershwin performed the score. Duncan recalled, "When he started the opening music, I said to myself: 'All this chopsticks—it sounds awful.' I looked at my wife and said quietly, 'This stinks.' . . . By the time twenty minutes or a half hour had passed I just thought I was in heaven. These beautiful melodies in this new idiom—it was something I had never heard. I just couldn't get enough of it."

Before "I Got Plenty o' Nuthin'," the composer turned to Duncan and remarked, "This is your great aria. This is going to make you famous." Duncan recalled, "I said 'Yes?' He said 'Listen hard.' He started off—ump-pah ump-pah. And I just thought 'Aria?'" Duncan would sing "I Got Plenty o' Nuthin'" and the other songs from *Porgy and Bess* around the world for the next forty years.

After some visits to South Carolina so that the cultivated Duncan could learn how the inhabitants of "Catfish Row" really sounded, the opera opened in New York on 10 October 1935 with Anne Brown as Bess. Although criticism was at first divided, *Porgy and Bess* eventually took its place as the premier American operatic work with the crippled Porgy's persona created by Duncan: dignified and openhearted.

The short post-Broadway tour of *Porgy and Bess* was to conclude at Washington's National Theater in March 1936. But the theater's policy banned African Americans from attending alongside whites, and Duncan refused to perform where such a policy existed. In the face of the Musicians' Union threat of a $10,000 fine and a year's suspension, Duncan held firm and the theater's manager, S. E. Cochran, gave in. It was the first desegregated audience in the National Theater's history. The first songs recorded from *Porgy and Bess* were sung, however, by white singers, Lawrence Tibbett and Helen Jepson. (Duncan and Brown sang the 1940 Decca version, and other recordings by them were later located, including a 1935 rehearsal of *Porgy*.)

Duncan re-created Porgy in a California revival of the opera in 1938. Though racially stereotyped, he came to be in demand in musical theater. In 1938

Duncan played an African chief in a London production of *The Sun Never Sets*, a reworking of Edgar Wallace's story "Sanders of the River." That same year he received an honorary doctorate from Howard University. Duncan returned to Broadway in 1940 in the all–African-American production of the Vernon Duke–John LaTouche musical *Cabin in the Sky* as De Lawd's General, a dignified symbol of good fighting evil for the soul of a charming rascal. Duncan was miscast as a drummer in the 1942 film *Syncopation*, an attempt at jazz history.

The 1942 New York revival of *Porgy and Bess*, produced by Cheryl Crawford, with much of the original recitative trimmed, ran more than two years in New York and on tour. It is generally credited with cementing the opera's reputation as well as confirming Duncan's place in musical history. One critic praised his "sunnily haphazard disposition that warms the stage and radiates through the reaches of the house."

In 1944 Duncan made his concert debut in New York. He confessed to the "thrill of holding an audience even on your faintest note . . . [as] a violinist keeps his listeners silent even on the thin last stroke . . . they can hardly hear." In 1945 the New York City Opera signed Duncan to a contract, making him the first African American to be engaged by an American opera company. In his first year he sang Tonio in *I Pagliacci* and Escamillo in *Carmen*. In the same year Duncan received the president of Haiti's Medal of Honor and Merit. Also in the 1940s Duncan and Brown began to tour Europe with productions of *Porgy and Bess*. Duncan ultimately claimed to have performed more than 2,000 times in fifty-six countries.

While on a concert tour in Australia and New Zealand in 1949, Duncan was offered the role of Stephen Kumalo, a principled black minister whose son accidentally kills a white in Johannesburg, in the musical version of Alan Paton's tale of South African apartheid, *Lost in the Stars*. His moving interpretation of the role—from the skepticism expressed in the lyrics of "Lost in the Stars" to ultimate reconciliation in the tragic denouement—won Duncan in 1950 Antoinette Perry (Tony) and New York Drama Critics awards. He retired from show business the following year.

Duncan in later years taught voice in Washington and at the Curtis Institute of Music in Philadelphia. He was cited by the National Association for the Advancement of Colored People for his contributions to theater. The George Peabody Medal came his way in 1984. In 1985, fifty years after the premiere of *Porgy and Bess*, Duncan and Brown were guests at the first Metropolitan Opera production. Duncan died in Washington.

• Todd Duncan's "recollections" are included in Robert Kimball and Alfred Simon, *The Gershwins* (1973), pp. 179ff. Duncan's antisegregation stand is covered in Hollis Alpert, *The Life and Times of Porgy and Bess: The Story of an American Classic* (1990). Also useful is Allen Woll, *Black Musical Theatre: From "Coontown" to "Dreamgirls"* (1989). Informative newspaper articles are found in the *New York Herald Tribune*, 8 Dec. 1935, and the *New York Times*, 26 Apr. 1942. Duncan appeared in the 1998 PBS television documentary *Porgy and Bess: An American Voice*. Patrick O'Connor's obituary of Todd Duncan is in the (London) *Guardian*, 28 Feb. 1998, and a substantial obituary appears in the *New York Times*, 2 Mar. 1998.

JAMES ROSS MOORE

DURR, Virginia Foster (6 Aug. 1903–24 Feb. 1999), civil rights activist, was born in Birmingham, Alabama, the daughter of Stirling Johnson Foster, Presbyterian minister, and Anne Patterson Foster. She grew up in a traditional middle-class southern household that experienced a decline in its financial fortunes following her father's removal from his pulpit. While he drifted through a series of largely unsuccessful efforts in the business world, Virginia Foster attended local public schools and finishing schools in Washington, D.C., and New York. Concerned that his bookish younger daughter might not "marry well," her father sent her to Wellesley College in 1921. Although forced to drop out after her sophomore year for financial reasons, Wellesley proved to be a lasting influence on Foster. There she learned firsthand that women could make a difference in the outside world and how economic difficulties challenged the less fortunate in society. Perhaps of more importance, however, was the college's insistence that she dine with a young African American student at a time when such social contacts violated traditional southern mores. This and other similar social situations forced Foster to question many of the assumptions about society and life that she had accepted in her youth.

On returning to Birmingham, Foster made her "debut," served as maid of honor in her older sister Josephine's wedding to future Supreme Court justice Hugo Black, and began working at a law library. She married Clifford Durr, an attorney, in April 1926 and was to have five children with him. Following the onset of the Great Depression, local economic conditions deteriorated, especially among Birmingham's poor, and Durr became active in relief work. She organized a drive to provide free milk to poor children through the Junior League and later helped organize free concerts for local residents. Family efforts on behalf of Franklin Roosevelt's 1932 presidential campaign helped her husband gain a position in Washington with the Reconstruction Finance Corporation, and the couple relocated in 1933, settling in Seminary Hill, Virginia.

While her husband struggled with insolvent banks, Durr began serving as a volunteer with the Women's Division of the Democratic National Committee. She became particularly interested in abolishing the poll tax, which was used to keep poor whites and African Americans from voting in the South. She was a delegate at the November 1938 founding meeting of the Southern Conference for Human Welfare in Birmingham, which brought together a wide coalition of New Dealers, African Americans, and other political activists. Durr lobbied tirelessly on behalf of the conference's Civil Rights Committee (which became the National Committee to Abolish the Poll Tax in August 1941) despite years of legislative frustration at the hands of reactionary politicians in Congress. In 1948 both the Southern Conference and the NCAPT shut down, largely as a result of internal divisions caused by the increasingly pernicious red-baiting of the post–World War II era. Her husband, who had moved to the Federal Communications Commission in 1941, declined renomination to his position in 1948 in protest over the loyalty oath that Harry S. Truman's administration imposed on executive branch appointees. After he opened his own law practice, the couple struggled to survive. Clifford Durr defended individuals accused of Communist sympathies for modest fees; Virginia taught English to foreign diplomats. Disillusioned with Truman administration policies, Virginia became briefly interested in Henry Wallace's Progressive party and even stood for election to the U.S. Senate in 1948 as that party's candidate.

Eager to leave Washington, the couple relocated to Denver in the summer of 1950. Clifford became the general counsel of the Farmers' Union Insurance Corporation, but political trouble soon followed. After Virginia signed a statement opposing United States military action above the Yalu River during the Korean War, the story appeared in the *Denver Post*. When Virginia refused to sign a humiliatingly worded retraction, her husband lost his job. In addition to the political disappointments and setbacks the couple had experienced, Clifford Durr was suffering from a chronic back problem. Under these difficult circumstances, in 1951 they decided to move in with Clifford's family in Montgomery, Alabama. Clifford Durr slowly recovered and in 1952 reopened his law practice. Virginia served as his secretary, and the two represented mostly poor clients in loan-sharking and police brutality cases. Many of their clients were African Americans, some of whom had been referred to the couple by Ed Nixon, the local head of the NAACP.

After several years marked by financial struggles but little controversy, the Durrs again encountered trouble in March 1954 when Virginia and an associate, Aubrey Williams, were summoned to New Orleans to testify before Mississippi Senator James Eastland's Internal Security Subcommittee. At the hearing, held during the height of the McCarthy-era hysteria, the Durrs were questioned about their activities with the Southern Conference. Virginia simply refused to testify, contending that the committee and its activities were a charade. The experience galvanized the couple, who again became active in the civil rights movement despite suffering the opprobrium of their neighbors. They became friends with Martin Luther King, Jr., and his wife as well as with a local seamstress named Rosa Parks. When Parks was arrested in December 1955 for failing to comply with local bus-line segregation laws, the Durrs helped bail her out of jail and conferred with her before the decision was made to turn the incident into a legal test case. The ensuing boycott of the bus line lasted a year and eventually resulted in the desegregation of the city's buses; the event is considered the beginning of the modern-day civil rights movement.

During the 1960s the Durrs continued to support the civil rights movement. They often hosted Freedom Riders and members of the Student Nonviolent Coordinating Committee as well as visiting journalists and northern academics. Although the couple was disheartened by the shift toward militancy in the movement as the 1960s closed, they cherished the achievements they had helped bring about, such as the end of the poll tax and the passage of the Voting Rights Act of 1965. Clifford Durr died in 1975, and Virginia Durr died twenty-four years later in a nursing home in Carlisle, Pennsylvania.

Although not as well known as some leaders of the civil rights movement, Virginia Durr was at the forefront of the struggle from its very beginnings, and her courage and determination in the face of social ostracism stands in stark counterpoint to the stereotypical white reaction to the changes taking place in those years.

• *Outside the Magic Circle: The Autobiography of Virginia Foster Durr*, ed. Hollinger F. Barnard (1985), is the best source of information on her life and career. The most comprehensive study of the Montgomery bus boycott is J. Mills Thorton, III, "Challenge and Response in the Montgomery Bus Boycott of 1955–1956," *Alabama Review* 33 (July 1980): 163–235. Durr was also profiled in "Old Terrorist," *New Yorker*, 6 Sept. 1993, pp. 3132. The *New York Times* of 26 Feb. 1999 has an obituary.

EDWARD L. LACH, JR.

DUVALL, Gabriel (6 Dec. 1752–6 Mar. 1844), U.S. Supreme Court justice and congressman, was born at "Marietta," his family's plantation in Prince Georges County, Maryland, the son of Benjamin Duvall and Susanna Tyler Duvall. The descendent of an old, affluent Maryland family, Duvall (whose surname in some sources is spelled "Duval") was well educated in both the classics and the law and was admitted to the bar in 1778. A fervent believer in colonial independence, he served in the revolutionary war, enlisting as a muster-master in Maryland and later seeing action as a private in the militia at Morristown and Brandywine. In 1787 he married Mary Bryce, with whom he had his only child, a son. She died in 1790, and five years later he married Jane Gibbon; she also predeceased him.

Duvall began his career of public service in the early 1770s, when he served as a clerk to the General Court in Annapolis. Thereafter he secured positions of increasing responsibility and importance: clerk to Maryland State Convention (1775–1777); clerk to the Maryland House of Delegates (1777); election to the Maryland State Council (1782); and election to the Maryland House of Delegates (1787). Chosen a delegate to the Constitutional Convention in 1787, he refused the appointment for unknown reasons. Duvall served in the House of Delegates for eight years, until 1794, when he was appointed as a Democratic-Republican to a recently vacated seat in the Third U.S. Congress.

Reelected to a second term in Congress in 1796, Duvall soon left to become chief justice of the General Court of Maryland, holding this position until 1802. Throughout the 1790s he helped the Democratic-Republicans organize in his home state and supported Thomas Jefferson's bids for the presidency in 1796 and 1800, serving as a presidential elector in both elections. When Jefferson assumed the office in 1801, he rewarded Duvall by appointing him the first comptroller of the U.S. Treasury, a position he held from 1802 to 1811.

In 1811 President James Madison nominated Duvall for the U.S. Supreme Court to replace the retiring Samuel Chase, a fellow jurist from Maryland with the unfortunate distinction of being the only justice ever to have been impeached (although he was not removed). Duvall's nearly twenty-four years on the bench are unremarkable, as he sided in most decisions with John Marshall, who served as chief justice throughout Duvall's term. *Dartmouth College v. Woodward* (1819) is a notable exception; Duvall was the lone dissenter in this case, which defined the notion that a charter of a private corporation was a contract and, in effect, expanded the Constitution's Contract Clause to cover private, corporate charters. Duvall, however, wrote no opinion that supported his dissent.

Although Duvall wrote few opinions of his own, he did support Marshall and fellow justice Joseph Story in some of the most celebrated cases of the early nineteenth century, including *McCulloch v. Maryland* (1819), *Brown v. Maryland* (1827), and *Martin v. Hunter's Lessee* (1816), in which Story wrote an argument that has been called a "landmark in the history of federal judicial supremacy." Duvall did distinguish himself with his opinions against slavery, however. In *Mima Queen and Child v. Hepburn* (1813), Duvall alone dissented against a Court ruling that disallowed hearsay evidence in a case involving two enslaved African Americans who claimed that their ancestors

were free. Duvall, in his opinion, wrote, "It will be universally admitted that the right to freedom is more important than the right to property." He also wrote the opinion of the Court in *Le Grand v. Darnall* (1829) that if a slaveowner bequeathed property to his slave, then the slave was therefore free.

By most accounts, Duvall was ineffective during his last ten years on the bench. Afflicted by old age and illness and virtually deaf, the justice was often absent and was unable to hear arguments before the Court. Despite the pleas of his fellow justices, who asked him to step down, he refused to resign until he was sure that an acceptable replacement would be named. Duvall finally retired in early 1835, after learning that President Andrew Jackson would appoint Duvall's friend Roger B. Taney, a fellow Marylander, as Marshall's successor (Marshall resigned as chief justice in July of that year). Philip P. Barbour was selected to fill Duvall's seat. Duvall lived for nearly ten years after his retirement, dying at "Marietta" at the age of ninety-two.

Despite his longevity on the Court, Duvall wrote few important opinions and is now remembered more for being stubborn and deaf than for shaping the future of the young Supreme Court. Duvall, one of three "silent justices" of the Marshall Court (along with Thomas Todd and Brockholst Livingston), "steadfastly support[ed] . . . the constitutional doctrines which Mr. Chief Justice Marshall promulgated, in the name of the court" (Joseph Story, quoted in Bernard Schwartz, *A History of the Supreme Court* [1993]). His importance lies in his acquiescence to the views of Marshall, in helping give the "Great Chief Justice" the scope to define the Court as the powerful institution it is today.

• Duvall's papers are in the Library of Congress. Brief mentions of his work on the Court can be found in studies of Marshall and the Marshall Court. See also Dillard Irving, "Gabriel Duvall," *The Justices of the United States Supreme Court (1780–1969),* ed. Leon Friedman and Fred L. Israel, vol. 1 (1969).

STACEY HAMILTON

E

EBERHART, Mignon G. (6 July 1899–8 Oct. 1996), novelist, was born Mignon Good in Lincoln, Nebraska, the daughter of William T. Good and Margaret Hill Bruffey Good. She was educated in local schools and attended Nebraska Wesleyan University from 1917 until 1920. Three years later she married Alanson C. Eberhart, a civil engineer; she divorced him in 1946 to marry John P. Hazen Perry (occupation unknown) but divorced Perry in turn two years later and remarried Alanson Eberhart. There were no known children from either marriage.

As a young, well-to-do matron, Mignon Eberhart had little to occupy her time and turned to writing, she said, to amuse herself. Although she hardly needed the money, she decided to write detective stories after reading in a textbook that the mystery genre was the most lucrative. As a model, she chose popular mystery novelist Mary Roberts Rinehart, whose work she had come to admire. Alanson Eberhart's job called for frequent travel at home and abroad in the early years of their marriage, and his wife usually accompanied him, writing on boats and trains and in hotel rooms. In the early 1930s the couple settled in Chicago and remained there for a decade before moving to New Canaan, Connecticut. They returned to Chicago after World War II.

Mignon Eberhart's first published work, a novella called *The Dark Corridor*, appeared in the detective magazine *Flynn's* in 1925. Four years later Eberhart's first full-length mystery novel, *The Patient in Room 18*, was published by Doubleday. The book embodied what would become standard ingredients of the classic Eberhart mystery: murder and romance in a contemporary, often glamorous setting, with an attractive and determined female sleuth as its heroine. Eberhart's first novel introduced that sleuth as nurse and amateur detective Sarah Keate—one of the first female crime solvers in mystery fiction.

The Patient in Room 18 was an instant success, attracting a wide readership and earning critical praise from reviewers at major publications, including the *Saturday Review of Literature* and even England's prestigious *Times Literary Supplement*. What critics found especially noteworthy in her first as well as subsequent novels was Eberhart's attention to the emotional underpinnings of her characters and her exploration of their inner motivation. At a time when many popular detective stories were two-dimensional constructions of clues and stereotypical characters fitted together like a jigsaw puzzle, Eberhart's psychological penetration was received as a welcome innovation in the genre, and over the years she attracted legions of fans, including such disparate admirers as Gertrude Stein and President Harry S. Truman.

Over a career that spanned nearly six decades, the prolific Eberhart produced fifty-eight more novels, an average of one a year and nearly all of them bestsellers. Early on, she also wrote a collection of short stories featuring another female sleuth, a mystery writer named Susan Dare; these were published as *The Cases of Susan Dare* (1934). Nurse Sarah Keate, along with her friend, detective Lance O'Leary, reappeared as the protagonist in many of Eberhart's earliest novels, beginning with *While the Patient Slept* (1930), which was made into a successful movie in 1935. This was the first of half a dozen film adaptations of Eberhart's works during the 1930s and 1940s; other Eberhart novels that were filmed during this period included *The Patient in Room 18* as well as *Murder by an Aristocrat* (1932) and *The White Cockatoo* (1933). *The Mystery of Hunting's End* (1930) was turned into the movie *Mystery House* (1938), *From This Dark Stairway* (1931) was adapted for the screen as *The Dark Stairway* (1938), and *Hasty Wedding* (1938) was made into the movie *Three's a Crowd* (1945). An untitled Eberhart short story became the basis for still another movie, *The Great Hospital Mystery* (1937). Eberhart also wrote an original screenplay for the 1939 film *The Murder of Dr. Harrigan*.

Although Eberhart was reticent about discussing her private life, her continuing penchant for travel was well known. Beginning in the 1940s, her novels were often set in some of her most frequent (and then-exotic) destinations, including the Far East, the Caribbean, and some of the then lesser-known European capitals, such as Lisbon, as well as more conventional locales in America and England. Peopling these atmospheric settings were a mix of wealthy and often aristocratic characters, but her sleuths were usually from rather ordinary backgrounds and almost always women, in the mold of her first detective heroine, Sarah Keate.

Eberhart maintained her preeminence as the queen of American mystery throughout three postwar decades and well into a fourth, offering a new book to millions of devoted fans on a nearly annual basis with such suggestive titles as *Postmark Murder* (1956), *Message from Hong Kong* (1969), *The Bayou Road* (1979), and *The Patient in Cabin C* (1984). Critics remained favorable to Eberhart's work over the decades, citing her ability to tell an entertaining story in compact prose with psychologically believable characters. Eberhart was often hailed as an American Agatha Christie, the hugely popular British detective story writer and her contemporary, whom Eberhart herself greatly admired. She was also credited with inspiring a new generation of female mystery writers in the second half of the twentieth century, most significantly the bestselling popular novelist Mary Higgins Clark. Eberhart maintained her prolific output until her eighty-ninth year, publishing her last mystery, *Three Days for Emeralds,* in 1988.

During her long career Eberhart also published several collections of short novels that she termed "novelettes," including *Mignon Eberhart's Mystery Book* (1945) and *Five of My Best: Deadly Is the Diamond, Bermuda Grapevine, Murder Goes to Market, Strangers in Flight, Express to Danger* (1949). The collections *Deadly Is the Diamond* (1958) and *The Crimson Paw* (1959) include novelettes from *Five of My Best* as well as previously unpublished work. Some of Eberhart's novelettes were also included in several bestselling crime anthologies along with works by other prominent mystery writers, including Erle Stanley Gardner and Georges Simenon. In addition, Eberhart coauthored and published two plays, both of which were adaptations of early novels and had brief runs in New York: *320 College Avenue* (1938, with Fred Ballard) and *Eight O'Clock Tuesday* (1941, with Robert Wallsten).

Eberhart, who had resettled on the East Coast sometime during the final decades of her life, died at a nursing home in Greenwich, Connecticut.

• For biographical information, see the entries for "Eberhart, Mignon G(ood)," in *Contemporary Authors,* vols. 73–76 (1978), p. 180; *Contemporary Authors,* vol. 154, p. 123 (1997); and *Contemporary Authors New Revision Series,* vol. 60, pp. 134–38. See also the entries for "Eberhart, Mrs. Mignon (Good)," in *20th Century Authors* (1942) and *20th Century Authors: First Supplement* (1955), both edited by Stanley Kunitz. Eberhart's papers are at the Mugar Memorial Library, Boston University. An obituary appears in the *New York Times,* 9 Oct. 1996.

ANN T. KEENE

ECKMAN, Frederick (27 Oct. 1924–28 Oct. 1996), poet, editor, scholar, and teacher, was born Frederick Willis Eckman in Continental, Ohio, the son of Hector B. Eckman, a mechanic, and Helen E. Osborn Eckman. Fred Eckman grew up in the environs of small-town, rural Ohio and attended public schools. His affinity for language and the dramatic emerged early. He read voraciously, and schoolmates recall impromptu dramatic productions in barns and garages. During World War II, he served as a surgical technician in the U.S. Army and enrolled in premedical courses at the University of Florida. Following his discharge in 1946, Eckman enrolled at Ohio State University, majoring in English. He married Mary Louise Drummer Campbell in March of 1947; a son, Thomas Frederick Eckman, was born the following October.

At Ohio State, Fred joined the editorial staff of *Cronos,* which published an early version of his *XXV Poems.* In 1947 *Cronos* was renamed *Golden Goose,* with Richard Wirz Emerson and Eckman as chief editors. *Golden Goose* and Golden Goose Press were vital and influential small-press endeavors during the postwar era, publishing established writers such as Ezra Pound, William Carlos Williams, and Kenneth Rexroth, as well as newer poets such as Robert Creeley and Denise Levertov. Golden Goose Press also issued a revised edition of *XXV Poems* in 1949. Significantly, Eckman retained none of the work from *XXV Poems* in later collections, many of which seem forced, highly rhetorical imitations of other poets. Yet, as early as in "Song" (1948), Eckman had begun to write the kind of elegant, precise, and evocative poem that would characterize his later work. *Golden Goose* ceased publication in 1954.

Eckman received his B.A., cum laude, from Ohio State in 1948 and his M.A. in 1949. Also in 1949, he began his teaching career at Glenville State College in West Virginia. In 1952 Eckman returned to Ohio State to teach and pursue his Ph.D., which he received in 1954. His dissertation was titled "The Language of American Poetry: 1900–1910."

In 1954 Eckman was named an assistant professor at the University of Texas at Austin. There he continued editorial work with *University of Texas Studies in English* and *Texas Quarterly.* His second book of poetry, *The Exile* (1956), contained such notable poems as "The Starlings," "Child's Drawing," and "The Dream." Meanwhile, Eckman championed the writers and modes of expression in modernist poetry, at that time still poorly received within academe. Major critical essays from this period include "Moody's Ode: The Collapse of the Heroic" and "Karl Shapiro's *Adam and Eve.*" Eckman's poems and reviews began to appear regularly in *Poetry* magazine, including the first treatment of Allen Ginsberg's *Howl* in a major publication. In 1958 Eckman published *Cobras and Cockleshells: Modes in Recent Poetry,* a critical booklet that Hazard Adams has called "the most helpful orientation to the poetry of Fred's generation that there is." Eckman had no rigid critical orientation; such approaches were antithetical to his character and his writing. Rather, he classified poems into three stylistic modes: decorative, substantive, and kinetic. These modes correspond to the emphasis on modifiers, nouns, and verbs, respectively.

And yet 1958 also brought increasing disaffection in his marriage (he would be divorced in 1960) and his estrangement from what he considered a narrow, high-cult view of literature at the university. A new volume of his poetry, *Hot & Cold: Running* (1960), which included "Old Man, Phantom Dog," "La Solita," and "Love Lies A Bleeding," displayed the tight lines and jazz-based rhythms used by many poets of his generation. During this time, he met and fell in love with Martha Frances Campbell, whom he would marry in 1961. Despite promotion to associate professor in 1959, Eckman resigned from the University of Texas in 1960 and returned to Ohio in 1961 to teach at Bowling Green State University, where he remained until his retirement in 1980. His return to Ohio paralleled the refinement of a style begun in the signature poem "To Sherwood Anderson in Heaven" (1960) as he sought to employ in his poetry the rhythms and content of mid-American speech, particularly the everyday concerns and dreams of the farmers and residents of small towns in the Midwest, as evidenced in *The Epistemology of Loss* (1963).

On 1 August 1966 Eckman's son, Tom, was among those killed by a sniper at the University of Texas. His struggle with the grief of this loss would haunt the rest of his life. Still, he continued to write, as always, in creative bursts, publishing *The Noon-Day Devil* (1967) and *Sandusky & Back* (1970). *Nightmare Township* (1977), perhaps his most singular and characteristic work, contained a series of poems about railroads and rural Ohio, as well as several prose poems that combined his lyric and narrative talents.

In the summer of 1978, Eckman stopped writing poetry altogether, telling friends that he had said all he had to say as a poet. Yet he continued to produce critical writing that reflected his eclectic taste, including notable essays on Lorene Niedecker (1975) and Edna St. Vincent Millay (1976). In 1980 Fred and Martha Eckman retired and moved to El Paso, Texas, where he lived until his death. For nearly fifteen years after that move, he wrote regular poetry reviews for the *Minneapolis Star-Tribune*. He also published, in the *Continental News-Review* (the newspaper of his birthplace), a long essay on the role of the small town in American literature. Frederick Eckman died of cancer at age seventy-two, one day after his birthday.

Working across nearly half a century, Eckman was, in the words of Burton Hatlen, director of the National Poetry Foundation, "... a superlative poet ... and an indefatigable servant of poetry." His virtues as a poet include an unfailing ear for the music in a line and an ability to overlay that music with the drama and rhythms of American speech, striking imagery, and an earthy and mordant wit. At their best, his poems combine technical skill with a deep appreciation of the paradoxes and complexities of living—whether observing migrant-worker children in an ice cream store, wrestling with Jacob's Angel, retelling the nightmares of a lonely farmwife, or parsing the austere phrases of a favorite cousin's letter into a moving poem. His work serves as a reminder that important poetry often thrives at the margins of the literary landscape.

• Frederick Eckman's papers, literary correspondence, and the bulk of his personal library are housed in the Thomas and Frederick Eckman Collection at the Jerome Library at Bowling Green State University. There is no biography. A partial bibliography appears in Eckman's *The Continental Connection: Selected Writings 1947–1980* (1980). Prior to 1999, other than book reviews, commentary on Eckman's poetry was limited to a brief mention in Lucien Stryk's introduction to *Heartland: Poets of the Midwest* (1967) and in Carol Pierman's introduction to *The Continental Connection*. An extensive selection of Eckman's poetry and prose appears in *Over West: Selected Writings of Frederick Eckman with Commentaries and Appreciations* (1999); in addition to introductions by Linda Wagner-Martin and David Adams, this volume includes evaluations of Eckman's literary legacy by Hazard Adams, Maxine Cassin, Robert Creeley, Theodore Enslin, David Oliphant, Carol Pierman, and others.

DAVID J. ADAMS

EDEL, Leon (9 Sept. 1907–5 Sept. 1997), biographer, theorist of biographical literature, and literary historian, was born in Pittsburgh, Pennsylvania, to Simon Edel and Fannie Malamud Edel. His family moved to Saskatchewan, Canada when he was about two years old and he remained in Canada for his college education, receiving his B.A. in 1927 from McGill University in Montreal, and continued there for the start of his graduate studies, obtaining an M.A. in 1928 with honors, having written a thesis on the writer Henry James, the first step in his becoming the preeminent authority in the world on James's life and work. Along with friends in the arts community of Montreal, Edel helped to found the *McGill Fortnightly Review*, a literary publication. As a reward for the excellence of his thesis on James, he received a Province of Quebec scholarship to study abroad. Electing to attend the University of Paris, he was awarded his Ph.D. (*docteur ès lettres*) in 1931. Originally written in French, his dissertation on Henry James was "Les Années Dramatiques" and it was translated into English. In 1932 Edel took a post at Sir George Williams University in Montreal, where he was an assistant professor of English until 1934. He held a Guggenheim fellowship from 1936 to 1938. During the Great Depression and World War II, he also worked in broadcasting and journalism in Canada because at the time positions at American universities were difficult to obtain, especially with a foreign degree. He then served in the U.S. Army, rising from sergeant to first lieutenant, and was awarded the Bronze Star, having been a specialist in psychological warfare following D-Day. After the war, he worked as a journalist, first in Canada and then in New York. In 1950 he married Roberta Roberts, from whom he was to be divorced in 1979; the marriage was childless.

In 1953 Edel was named an associate professor of English at New York University and became a full professor in 1955. During his tenure at NYU, where he remained until 1966, he was honored with the title Henry James Professor of English and American Letters. Edel retired to Hawaii and taught at the University of Hawaii, where he was named the first Citizen's Professor of English in 1974. He married Marjorie Putnam Sinclair in 1980. He died in Honolulu at age eighty-nine.

Edel's enduring fascination with the life and work of Henry James took its most notable form in the magisterial five-volume biography that he began after World War II. *Henry James: The Untried Years, 1843–1870*, appeared in 1953. The subsequent volumes, all published by Lippincott, were subtitled *The Conquest of London, 1870–1883* (1962), *The Middle Years, 1882–1895* (1962), *The Treacherous Years, 1895–1901* (1969), and *The Master, 1901–1916* (1972). He was at work on the second and third volumes in 1959–1960 while a visiting professor at Harvard University, where he had the opportunity to examine James's private papers, given to Harvard Library upon the writer's death in 1916. Those two volumes were awarded the Pulitzer Prize for biography in 1963; that same year, Edel was also the recipient of a National Book Award. In an assessment of the full five-volume work, James Atlas wrote in the *New York Times Book Review* (6 Feb. 1972): "Edel manages to sustain interest in a figure who was sedentary, verbose, self-concealing; he maintains a swift narrative pace through ingenious organization of his material . . . and . . . gives us a rich tapestry of James's life and times that reads like a novel." The vastness of this landmark in literary biography reflected Edel's conviction that James was the "largest" literary figure to emerge from the United States during the latter half of the nineteenth century. The biographer saw in his subject the first great psychological realist in the history of the novel, a bridge between Romanticism and modernism, who surpassed in his range and fineness of insight the European writers of stature whom he admired and befriended, including Gustave Flaubert, Émile Zola, George Eliot, and Ivan Turgenev. As an American who spent most of his adult years in England and Europe, he developed in his numerous novels and stories "international" themes concerning the encounters of European and American characters and the conflicts between Old World and New World sensibilities and attitudes. Edel saw in the sweep of James's oeuvre as a whole—from such early masterpieces as *Daisy Miller* and *The Portrait of a Lady* and his subsequent novels on social themes, particularly *The Bostonians* and *The Princess Casamassima*, to the major achievements of his later years, including *The Wings of the Dove* and *The Golden Bowl*—a capacious imagination akin to Shakespeare's.

The matching of biographer and subject seems especially apt in Edel's case because he pioneered the psychological approach to the reconstruction of a writer's life in the course of studying in minute detail how Henry James developed into a master of psychological nuance in fiction. As early as his doctoral studies in Paris, Edel had pursued an interest in psychology and psychoanalysis by visiting in Vienna the psychiatrist Alfred Adler, a former associate of Sigmund Freud. Edel himself underwent psycholoanalysis following World War II and believed that the experience had heightened his intellectual skills. As summarized by Arnold M. Ludwig, the Edelian approach emphasizes the kind of piecing together of disparate details that a psychoanalyst would bring to formulating the personality profile of an analysand: "The task of the biographer is to detect the patterns and modes of a person's works and productions, or, to use Edel's own analogy, *the figure on the underside of the carpet*. Only by grasping the private mythology hidden behind the person's public mask can you depict the real person" (Ludwig, *How Do We Know Who We Are?* [1997], p. 57). In *Writing Lives: Principia Biographica* (1984), Edel proposed a set of premises that should be operative for the "new biography," including the need for biographers to "be familiar with the basics of psychoanalytical psychology" and to "be imaginative in dealing with the form and structure of their works as novelists are, feeling free to use the same techniques that give narrative to fiction—flashbacks, retrospective chapters, summary chapters . . . [and] glimpses into the future."

Edel was to condense his massive original study of James into, first, a two-volume biography, *The Life of Henry James* (1977), and, then, an even more accessible single volume, *Henry James, A Life* (1985). The latter was translated into several languages and won for the author international recognition. He was no less tireless as a compiler of James's work, bringing out editions of the author's neglected plays, his stories, portions of his correspondence, and his significant critical writings, including the prefaces to the novels. Edel's *A Bibliography of Henry James*, prepared in association with Dan H. Laurence, appeared in 1957.

But Edel by no means limited himself to Henry James. He also published studies of James Joyce (1947) and Willa Cather (1953; largely written by E. K. Brown and completed by Edel) and edited the diary of Alice James (1964) and the notebooks and journals of Edmund Wilson, which appeared under the titles *The Thirties* (1980), *The Forties* (1983), and *The Fifties* (1986). (Lewis M. Dabney completed the Wilson project by publishing *The Sixties* in 1993.) As a leader of the psychological approach to literary and biographical analysis, he advanced his ideas in *Literary Biography* (1959), *The Psychological Novel, 1900–1950* (1955), *Stuff of Sleep and Dreams* (1982), and contributed important articles to *Biography as an Art* and *Varieties of Literary Experience* (both 1965).

Numerous honors were bestowed on Edel. From 1957 to 1959 he was national president of the American chapter of P.E.N. and in 1972 was elected to the American Academy of Arts and Letters, which awarded him its Gold Medal for biography in 1976. The following year, he was selected to be the Vernon Visiting Professor of Biography at Dartmouth College, which served to acknowledge the influence Edel had come to exert on the genre of literary biography both in the United States and abroad. In 1977 he was also given the Hawaiian Writers' Award, and in 1981 he was designated a "Living Treasure" by the Honpa Hongwanji Temple.

Along with Richard Ellmann's *James Joyce* (1959; rev. 1982), Leon Edel's *Henry James* will endure as one of the seminal literary biographies written in the English-speaking world during the twentieth century. Like Ellmann, he vivified his subject and made of him a central canonical figure in the evolution of modernism in Western literature. His exhaustive research on James will remain a monument unlikely to be superseded.

• Edel, *Writing Lives: Principia Biographica* (1984) offers an excellent description of his writing methods and philosophy. There is an excellent review of Edel's editing and comments on the Wilson journals in the *New York Times Book Review*, 31 Aug.1986, by Joseph Epstein, the editor of the *American Scholar. Contemporary Authors*, New Revision Series, 22, pp. 110–17 has an excellent updated biographical sketch of Edel and integrates literary analysis with his life story. Lyall H. Powers, *Leon Edel and Literary Art* (1988), describes the techniques and literary conventions that Edel used in researching and writing biographies. Gloria G. Fromm, *Essaying Biography: A Celebration for Leon Edel* (1986), is a laudatory collection illuminating his works and contributions to the field of biography. John Batchelor, ed., *The Art of Literary Biography* (1995), includes critiques of Edel's methodology, reflecting the increasing skepticism among some scholars about the efficacy of psychoanalysis in understanding personality and the processes by which an author creates fiction. See also *Book World*, 6 Feb. 1972; *Globe and Mail* (Toronto), 3 May 1986; *New York Times Book Review*,19 June 1955, 4 Nov.1962, 6 Feb. 1972, 13 May 1979, 1 July 1979, 31 Aug. 1980, 14 Dec. 1980, 25 July 1982, 19 May 1982, 15 Apr. 1984, 28 Oct. 1984, 26 Jan. 1985, and 24 Nov. 1985.

BARBARA BENNETT PETERSON

EDMONDS, Walter D. (15 July 1903–24 Jan. 1998), author, was born Walter Dumaux Edmonds near Boonville, New York, at "Northlands," the family's farmhouse and summer retreat near the Black River. His father, Walter D. Edmonds, Sr., was a patent lawyer with an office in New York City, where the family regularly wintered. His mother, Sarah May Edmonds, was a descendant of seventeenth-century New England Mays. Edmonds attended the Cutler Day School in New York City (1914–1916); St. Paul's Academy in Concord, New Hampshire (1916–1919), which he disliked; and Choate School in Wallingford, Connecticut (1919–1921), which he delighted in. Proofs of his early interest in writing are, first, his tackling a short story when he was twelve and, second, his election to membership on the board of the *Choate Literary Magazine*. He happily spent boyhood summers on the family farm. He entered Harvard in 1921. While there, he was associated with the *Harvard Advocate*, as an editor, a secretary, and finally president. He also contributed twenty-one short stories, in addition to several poems, articles, and reviews, to the *Advocate*. Some of his early fiction is set in upstate New York, including the canal region. In his junior year, Edmonds attended an advanced composition course taught by Professor Charles Townsend Copeland, the legendary teacher of many future writers, and received encouragement from him. For Copeland, Edmonds wrote "The End of the Tow-Path," which concerns the Erie Canal and which was published, two years after he wrote it, in *Scribner's* magazine (July 1926). Edmonds graduated from Harvard in 1926 with a B.A. in English.

During the winter of 1926–1927, Edmonds engaged the well-connected Paul R. Reynolds as his literary agent. His writing in 1927 netted only $800. He had to earn better pay, even though after "The End of the Tow-Path" he sold eight stories, published in the *Atlantic Monthly*, the *Dial*, *McCall's*, and *Scribner's* (1927–1928). So he asked Ellery Sedgwick, editor of the *Atlantic Monthly*, for a position in his office. Instead, Sedgwick persuaded him to get a room in Cambridge and write a novel about the Erie Canal, for which he guaranteed publication by Little, Brown. The result, *Rome Haul* (1929), composed in four months and dedicated to Copeland, is a regional chronicle of the halcyon pre-railroad 1850s of the canal, based on newspaper files, oral traditions, and Edmonds's personal observations; it features a hero who rises from farm lad to towpath driver boy to boat owner, and—not least—winner of the heroine. *Rome Haul* was dramatized by Frank B. Elser (1932); retitled *The Farmer Takes a Wife*, it became a play by Elser and Marc Connelly (1934), then a movie starring Henry Fonda in his screen debut (1935), and finally a musical comedy starring Betty Grable (1953).

The Big Barn (1930), Edmonds's second novel, was less successful. It concerns the determination of a cruelly stubborn patriarch, aptly named Wilder, to build a domineering structure on his upstate New York family farm shortly before the Civil War. In 1930 Edmonds married Eleanor Livingston Stetson; they had three children. He complained to Harold Ober, his devoted agent from 1929 until Ober's death three decades later, that he needed a steady income while he crafted his next novel. Ober introduced him to George Horace Lorimer, editor of the *Saturday Evening Post*. Lorimer so admired Edmonds's fiction that he let him write unformulaic short stories—a rarity in slick magazines—for *Post* publication at good pay. Meanwhile, Edmonds was pinning his hopes on another, bigger novel about the Erie Canal. The result was *Erie Water* (1933), a love story underpinned by the history of the building of the canal from Rome, New York, in 1817 to Lockport in 1825, with a colorful portrayal of pungent regional folkways.

Edmonds's prolific career was under way. In all, he wrote some thirty-four books. Many are historical novels. About half are for children. A few are plain histories. And some are collections of short stories, of which he wrote more than seventy.

In an autobiographical essay, Edmonds called the years from 1933 to 1943 his most prolific. In addition to *Erie Water*, he wrote *Drums along the Mohawk* (1936), *Chad Hanna* (1940), *The Matchlock Gun* (1941), and many short stories collected in book form later. *Drums along the Mohawk*, clearly his finest work, was a bestseller second only to Margaret Mitchell's *Gone with the Wind* in 1936 and in 1937. It deals with the difficulties that settlers in the disputed Mohawk Valley experienced in their encounters with Indians, Tories, British troops, and colonial politicians and soldiers from 1776 to 1784. While being episodic and panoramic, the novel often centers on Gilbert "Gil" Martin and his wife Magdelana "Lana" Borst Martin—tough farmers on the disputed frontier. Edmonds is at his best when depicting his beloved valley and its sturdy people—their land, weather, food, crops, game, tools, speech patterns, and customs, and their acts of violence, love, suffering, failure, faith, endurance, and triumph. Fictive characters, though well limned, are sometimes overshadowed by historical personages such as General Nicholas Herkimer (and Petry, his doctor), Colonel Peter Gansevoort, and Lieutenant Colonel Marinus Willett. In a modest "Author's Note," Edmonds names some of his historical sources. *Drums along the Mohawk* was made into a movie in 1939 and starred Henry Fonda and Claudette Colbert. *Chad Hanna* is a rollicking novel about a traveling circus plying its trade in central New York. Emerging from *Post* pieces, like many other books by Edmonds, it is valuable not for its triangular love plot—hero, heroine, and female bareback rider—but, once again, as regional realism. The 1940 movie version starred Fonda, Linda Darnell, and Dorothy Lamour.

During these years, some of Edmonds's stories having juvenile themes did not appeal to Little, Brown, his only publisher through 1940. So Ober sent Edmonds's short story titled "The Spanish Gun," which first appeared in the *Saturday Evening Post* (17 July 1937), to the editor of the juvenile department at Dodd, Mead. Expanded as *The Matchlock Gun* (1941), this story about a ten-year-old boy who defends his home against Indians in colonial New York won the 1942 Newbury Medal for Children's Literature and, soon deemed a classic, remained in print for the next half century.

Although Edmonds said that the years from 1941 to 1956 were dry for him and that he suffered from writer's block, he did continue to produce. He mainly wrote fiction for younger readers and published collections of short stories that earlier appeared in magazines. He also wrote two full-length histories. To commemorate the utopian community in upstate New York that became the center of a silverware-manufacturing company with commendable labor relations, he wrote *The First Hundred Years, 1848–1948: 1848, Oneida Community; 1880, Oneida Community, Limited; 1935, Oneida Ltd.* (1948). For *They Fought with What They Had: The Story of the Army Air Forces in the Southwest Pacific, 1941–1942* (1951), Edmonds interviewed American soldiers who survived, though overmatched, battles against the Japanese early in World War II. Also dating from this period of Edmonds's career is his novel *The Boyds of Black River* (1953), a beautifully presented tangle of yarns concerning a patriarch and a talkative old friend, servants and workers, young lovers, a naughty flirt, an elopement, horses, an automobile, a dog, a pregnant pig—all strung along the unforgotten river of Edmonds's youth.

Eleanor Edmonds died in 1956. Later that year, Edmonds married Katharine May Howe Baker-Carr, whom he praised as a source of spiritual and creative inspiration. The popularity of *Three Stalwarts*, a 1962 one-volume reprint of *Drums along the Mohawk, Rome Haul*, and *Erie Water*, attests to Edmonds's continuing appeal during his lifetime. His final history book, *The Musket and the Cross: The Struggle of France and England for North America* (1968), narrates events from 1609 to 1689, with emphasis on fur-trade competition, French hunters, priests, and politicians, New England Indian wars, and military actions climaxing at Quebec. Readable though this busy book is, it does not add substantially to the more thoroughly researched historical classics by historian Francis Parkman. Then followed Edmonds's *Time to Go House*

(1969), which he claimed was the first book he ever designed from the outset for children. Its story, a pure delight, tells about a field mouse taking up residence in the author's home and falling in love with a house mouse there. *Bert Breen's Barn* (1975), which won a National Book Award, is a better novel on the subject than *The Big Barn*; its tough hero buys, takes apart, transports, and reassembles a barn.

In 1976 Edmonds sold Northlands, the old family place, and began to live year round in Concord, Massachusetts, where he and his wife had already settled on a part-time basis. Katharine Edmonds died in 1989. Edmonds's last book was *Tales My Father Never Told* (1995). It is a bittersweet memoir, warmed by generous humor, about a narcissistic father, distant but loving. He wanted his son to be an engineer and succeed in life, and he warned him that trying to be a writer might lead him to alcoholism and suicide. Edmonds, who did not succumb in the manner prophesied, died in Utica, New York.

Inviting comparisons with the humor of Mark Twain's works dealing with the Mississippi River and with the Yoknapatawpha family sagas of William Faulkner—but without their dark depravities—the best works of Edmonds will long endure. For seven full decades he entertained and instructed millions of readers. At their best, his books carefully depict upstate New York, the region of his birth and the place he especially loved.

• An autobiographical essay is "Walter D. Edmonds," *Something about the Author: Autobiography Series*, ed. Adele Sarkissian, vol. 4 (1987), pp. 167–80. Lionel D. Wyld, *Walter D. Edmonds, Storyteller* (1982), is a critical biography and includes a bibliography of Edmonds's books, stories, and miscellaneous pieces. J. Donald Adams, *Copey of Harvard: A Biography of Charles Townsend Copeland* (1960), quotes Edmonds's high praise of Copeland. Dayton Kohler, "Walter D. Edmonds: Regional Historian," *English Journal* 27 (Jan. 1938): 1–11, analyzes Edmonds's accurate use of historical detail. Alice Payne Hackett, *60 Years of Best Sellers: 1895–1955* (1956), reports that Edmonds's *Drums along the Mohawk*, on the bestseller lists in 1936 and 1937, added to the growing trend of big historical novels started by Hervey Allen's *Anthony Adverse* (1933) and continued by Margaret Mitchell's *Gone with the Wind* (1936). Obituaries are in the *Los Angeles Times*, the *New York Times*, and the *Washington Post*, all 28 Jan. 1998.

ROBERT L. GALE

EHRLICHMAN, John D. (20 Mar. 1925–14 Feb. 1999), a prominent figure in the Watergate scandals and assistant to President Richard Nixon, was born in Tacoma, Washington, to Rudolph I. Ehrlichman, a pilot, and Lillian C. Danielson Ehrlichman. His parents had emigrated from Austria to America; originally Orthodox Jews, they became adherents of Christian Science. In 1941 John's father died while flying for the Royal Canadian Air Force. Two years later Ehrlichman enlisted in the United States Army Air Corps, flew twenty-six bombing missions over Germany, and won the Distinguished Flying Cross and the Air Medal with clusters.

Ehrlichman attended the University of California at Los Angeles, where he met two fellow students who played major roles in his life, Harry Robbins "Bob" Haldeman, a fellow Christian Scientist, and Jeanne Fisher. Ehrlichman and Fisher married in 1949; they would have three children. After receiving his B.A. in 1948, Ehrlichman studied law at Stanford from 1948 until 1951. He then entered into a partnership in a Seattle firm specializing in property law, Hullin, Ehrlichman, Roberts, & Hodge, a relationship that lasted from 1952 until 1968. Through Haldeman, he became an activist in Republican presidential campaigns starting in 1956, and he worked as an organizer in Nixon's successful run for the presidency in 1968.

Nixon was impressed by Ehrlichman, a staunch loyalist, and named him as a special assistant. He and Haldeman (who served as chief of staff) appeared to some as Nixon's "Berlin Wall." Nixon admired Ehrlichman for being "tough as nails." White House counsel Leonard Garment considered Ehrlichman "more substantive" than Haldeman and less of an "instrument" of the president's desires, one who expedited a wide variety of domestic matters (interview with Leonard Garment, 27 Feb. 1985).

Ehrlichman preferred to think of himself as a moderate who was "all across the spectrum" politically. For the right, he was too liberal, for the left, too conservative. Liberals on the White House staff generally tended to be passive, Ehrlichman explained in his 1982 account *Witness to Power* (p. 212).

Ehrlichman's work as assistant to the president, and Nixon's desire to streamline his own policy-making machinery and strengthen his hand on the executive branch, led to Ehrlichman's appointment as Assistant to the President for Domestic Affairs, a newly created position and title. While serving in this capacity, he became director of the recently established Domestic Policy Council.

Clean air, clean water, pension reform, urban parks, land-use initiatives, and increased support for the arts and humanities were Ehrlichman's legislative responsibilities. The administration sought to reform welfare with its Family Assistance Plan, a minimum-income scheme intended to replace the New Deal–era Aid to Families with Dependent Children program, but this attempt was ultimately abandoned. Always a true Nixonian in his sensitivity to the political ramifications of domestic policies, Ehrlichman once explained White House initiatives on such matters as welfare reform and preferential job treatment in a memorandum that stated, "Some non-conservative initiatives [have been] deliberately designed to furnish some zigs to go with our conservative zags in the same way we have included [Daniel Patrick] Moynihans with our [Harry] Dents rather than trying to recruit only those non-existent middle-of-the roaders." He added that the welfare "reform effort has been a good zig, without damage to the Social issue, with promise of strong

blue-collar appeal." Labor both understood and hated the Philadelphia Plan (a program for minority employment in construction that included a system of affirmative action), he also wrote, because it was both "anti-labor and pro-black" and succeeded in driving "a wedge between the Democrats and labor," an administration goal. "In due time," Ehrlichman added, "if we administer it without undue zeal it can become a 'slow and reasonable' approach to civil rights" (John Ehrlichman to Nixon, 21 Oct. 1970, Ehrlichman Papers, Library of Congress). Ehrlichman's more lasting mark lay in designing legislation that led to the creation of the Environmental Protection Agency. One scholar later called him "the most effective environmentalist since Gifford Pinchot" (Hoff, *Nixon*, p. 21).

Ehrlichman's need to satisfy Nixon's demand to guard against leaks led him to create a White House intelligence unit. Funded by support from the Committee to Re-Elect the President, such specialists (later dubbed the "plumbers") were hired to provide "investigative support" for the White House. Ehrlichman was also tied to an "enemies list" designed to target administration opponents. A key covert operation of the plumbers, traceable directly to Ehrlichman, was the break-in at the offices of Dr. Lewis Fielding, Daniel Ellsberg's psychiatrist. Ehrlichman later contended that advance knowledge of the Fielding affair "encouraged" the White House–supported operatives to believe they had a "license" from Nixon, largely, he insisted, because the president was aware of the first intrusion (interview with John Ehrlichman, 17 June 1985). The scandal that became known as Watergate began when five members of the plumbers unit were apprehended breaking into the offices of the Democratic National Committee on the night of June 16–17, 1972.

Investigations by *Washington Post* reporters and Senate committees made John Ehrlichman a major defendant. He became known as the man who had suggested that L. Patrick Gray III, then acting director of the FBI, should become the fall guy for Watergate and should be left "twisting slowly, slowly in the wind." Under intense questioning, Ehrlichman justified White House intelligence operations even though they ignored the FBI and constitutional guarantees of privacy. "Because of the emphasis I put on the crucial importance of protecting the national security I can understand how highly motivated individuals could have felt justified in engaging in specific activities that I would have disapproved had they been brought to my attention," he told Senator Herman Talmadge of Georgia (Gold, *Watergate Hearings*, p. 522). It was, moreover, Nixon, not he, he argued, who had known about the break-in, so he had never given his advance approval. Later, he acknowledged that his testimony was a public relations disaster. On 30 April 1973, after Nixon had decided to force his two key aides out in an effort to save the presidency, Ehrlichman and Haldeman resigned. Shortly afterward, presidential counsel John Dean gave the committee his own explicit and damaging account.

At his own trial, which began on 14 October 1974, Ehrlichman broke with Nixon when his lawyer said that "Richard Nixon deceived, misled, lied to and used John Ehrlichman to cover up his own knowledge and his own activities. . . . In simple terms John Ehrlichman has been had by his boss, who was President of the United States." He had been deceived by the president, he added on 10 December (Schoenebaum, *Profiles of An Era*, p. 188).

The jury rejected Ehrlichman's denials of complicity in the Fielding break-in, holding that he was responsible for "a willful, arrogant act of men who took the law into their own hands and felt above the law." Found guilty on three counts of perjury as well as conspiracy and obstruction of justice, he was sentenced to serve from two and one-half to eight years in prison. He actually served eighteen months in the minimum security facility of the Federal Prison Camp at Safford, Arizona. "That man enjoyed life in San Clemente while I sat in jail for something he had done," Ehrlichman said bitterly about Nixon while regretting the abdication of his own judgment (author's interview, 17 June 1985). He also explained that, when confronting the Senate committee, he "saw these folks as adversaries, partisan adversaries, and so I didn't give them much quarter" (Ehrlichman interview, George Washington University National Security Archives). Before and after his jail term, Ehrlichman seemed to assume a more thoughtful and introspective demeanor. Old White House acquaintances, mainly Nixon loyalists, thought he underwent a "personality change" and became embittered, distorted and tragic. Diagnosed with late-onset diabetes while still in prison, he had to monitor the condition for the rest of his life. After his release, disbarred and unable to practice law, he left his wife Jeanne and children to find a new life in Santa Fe, New Mexico. Finally, after an extended separation, their marriage "was allowed simply to die, like a garden when people neglect it," as he put it (Ehrlichman, *Witness*, p. 416).

The former half of the "Berlin Wall" grew a beard, worked hard at softening his earlier image, plunged into environmental issues, became a consultant with local Native Americans, did some radio and television commentary, and devoted himself to a new career as a writer, which he enjoyed. He remarried in 1978, this time to Christy McLaurin, and they had a son. His faith in Christian Science lapsed. Two best-selling novels, *The Company* and *The China Card*, published in 1976 and 1986, respectively, drew from his White House experience. Additional accounts, *The Whole Truth* (1979) and *Witness to Power: The Nixon Years* (1982), contained his renditions of Watergate. He also co-authored *The Rigby File* in 1989.

After divorcing his second wife in 1990, he moved to Atlanta, where he became a senior vice-president of a company called Law Environment. In 1995 he married Karen Hilliard, a restaurateur; they had no children. After coping with complications from diabetes, he died at the Grace Community Assisted Living Center in Atlanta while working on a documentary video of Watergate called "The Eye of the Storm."

• Accounts of John D. Ehrlichman, and especially of Watergate, are rich and abundant. Jonathan Schell's early work *The Time of Illusion* (1975) remains most readable and useful, as is *The Watergate Hearings: Break-In and Cover-Up; Proceedings as Edited by the Staff of the New York Times*, edited by Gerald Gold (1973). The best source for Ehrlichman is his own book, *Witness to Power: The Nixon Years* (1982). The Watergate incident is analyzed most accurately and effectively by Stanley Kutler in *The Wars of Watergate: The Last Crisis of Richard Nixon* (1990) and in his *Abuse of Power: The New Nixon Tapes* (1997), which contains transcribed excerpts from Nixon White House tapes. J. Anthony Lukas, *Nightmare: The Underside of the Nixon Years* (1976), should not be overlooked as the first penetrating look into Nixon and Watergate, along with the two journalistic reports by Bob Woodward and Carl Bernstein, *All the President's Men* (1976) and *The Final Days* (1976). Ehrlichman's administration role is also described in *The Haldeman Diaries: Inside the Nixon White House* by H. R. Haldeman (1994). See also Joan Hoff's detailed attention to the administration's legislative history in *Nixon Reconsidered* (1994) and Herbert S. Parmet's *Richard Nixon and His America* (1990). Obituaries are in the *New York Times* and the *Washington Post*, both 16 Feb. 1999.

HERBERT S. PARMET

EISSLER, K. R. (2 July 1908–17 Feb. 1999), psychoanalyst, was born Kurt Robert Eissler in Vienna, Austria, the son of Robert Joseph Eissler and Alice Wurmfeld Eissler. (It is not known what his parents did for a living.) He earned a Ph.D. in psychology from the University of Vienna in 1934, with a thesis on the constancy of visual configurations in the variations of objects and their representation. Eissler continued his academic studies—in medicine—at the university, and was awarded a medical degree in 1937. He married Ruth Selke in 1936; the couple had no children.

Upon finishing medical school, Eissler undertook training at the renowned Vienna Psychoanalytic Institute, coming into contact with prominent practitioners such as Paul Federn, Richard Sterba, and August Aichorn. He became a member of the Vienna Psychoanalytic Society in 1938, only to see a promising career interrupted by the Nazi takeover of Austria, which engendered a murderous hostility toward both Jews and psychoanalysis, as illustrated by the misfortunes of another student at the institute, Bruno Bettelheim. After immigrating to the United States, Eissler settled in Chicago and became qualified for practice by the American Board of Psychiatry. He caused a sensation by challenging the dominance of Franz Alexander within the psychoanalytic community. In 1943 Eissler volunteered his services to the U.S. Army and entered the medical corps, in which he served until the end of the war with the rank of captain.

Following his discharge from the army, Eissler relocated to New York City, where he quickly developed a reputation for soundness in his clinical practice as well as for solid scholarship. Having served as August

Aichorn's assistant during his Vienna days, Eissler edited *Searchlights on Delinquency* (1949), a collection of articles that was dedicated to Aichorn in recognition of his pioneering work in the area of juvenile delinquency. He also continued to be critical of many members of his profession, indicting, for example, the German psychiatric community for its reluctance to recognize the validity of claims of psychological damage among Nazi concentration camp victims. Eissler himself lost a sibling in one of the camps.

Eissler's professional criticism had definite limits, however. Although he had never worked with or even met Sigmund Freud, he became known within his profession as the most ardent of Freudian admirers and defenders. Spurred by his inability to locate a minor document of Freud's and concerned about the loss of irreplaceable material in the aftermath of the war, Eissler took a leading role in setting up the Sigmund Freud Archives in 1952. He obtained an agreement with the Library of Congress to house the accumulated material and set about collecting correspondence, photographs, and taped interviews with former patients and associates of Freud.

Assisted in his task by Freud's daughter Anna (with whom he enjoyed a pleasant if not particularly warm relationship), Eissler amassed an impressive collection. Although some scholars complained about what they viewed as excessive restrictions on the collection, parts of it sealed for over 100 years, Eissler defended his policy as necessary to protect donor confidentiality. In 1952 Eissler also set up the Anna Freud Foundation, which facilitated the transfer of tax-free American contributions to the recently founded child therapy clinic that Anna had set up in Hampstead, England.

While the Freud Archives consumed much of his time—Eissler served as its secretary and sole employee for many years—his own scholarship continued to flourish. The author of numerous papers on subjects as diverse as juvenile delinquency, schizophrenia, and the vaginal orgasm, he also wrote several books, including *The Psychiatrist and the Dying Patient* (1955), *Leonardo da Vinci: Psychoanalytic Notes on the Enigma* (1961), *Goethe: A Psychoanalytic Study, 1775–1786* (2 vols., 1963), and *Medical Orthodoxy and the Future of Psychoanalysis* (1965), which deplored the trend toward medicalization within the profession.

Eissler continued in his role as unofficial Freudian defender to the end of his career. He spent a tremendous amount of time and energy in the early 1970s, for example, attempting to discredit a book, *Brother Animal: The Story of Freud and Tausk* (1969) by Paul Roazen, which dealt with Freud's alleged culpability in the suicide of Victor Tausk, an early disciple. Eissler's response, *Talent and Genius: The Fictitious Case of Tausk contra Freud* (1971), was as systematic a rebuttal of a claim against Freud as the psychoanalytic profession has ever seen.

At a spring 1974 meeting of the American Psychoanalytic Society in Denver, Eissler had a fateful encounter with Dr. Jeffrey Moussaieff Masson, a charismatic and charming Harvard-educated Sanskritist who was on the faculty of the University of Toronto and had become interested in psychoanalysis. (Contrary to most accounts, Masson says in his book *Final Analysis* that he first met Eissler in 1973.) Determined to enter the field, Masson pursued training in psychoanalysis and later attempted to set up his own clinical practice while a visiting Sanskritist at the University of California at Berkeley. The two men immediately became friends based on their mutually intense interest in Freud. Eissler lent Masson a considerable body of tapes and manuscript material on Freud, and in the fall of 1980 he named Masson as his successor at the Freud Archives, despite numerous warnings from colleagues that Masson was too brash and immature.

As projects director at the archives, Masson soon gained access from Anna Freud to a collection of previously unpublished letters between her father and Wilhelm Fliess, a Viennese physician to whom Sigmund Freud often referred patients, and it was assumed that Masson would publish a collection of correspondence that would add to Freud's luster. Masson, however, shocked the psychoanalytic community in the spring of 1981 when he delivered a paper before the Western New England Psychoanalytic Society in New Haven, Connecticut, that not only lamented the "present-day sterility" of the profession but also attempted to discredit Freud. The central point was Masson's allegation that Freud had abandoned his "seduction theory"—which held that all adult neuroses are based in sexual abuse during childhood—for nonscientific reasons related to Freud's personal anxieties. The controversy exploded when two articles that outlined Masson's views appeared in the *New York Times* in the summer of 1981, bringing Masson's charges—which he viewed as threatening the very foundation of psychoanalysis—to a much wider audience.

Following the appearance of the articles, Eissler felt personally and professionally betrayed. Angered and saddened by what he viewed as ingratitude toward himself and apostasy from the Freudian gospel, he fired Masson, commenting at the time, "Would you make director of the archives someone who writes plain nonsense?" (*New York Times*, 20 Feb. 1999) After charges and countercharges flew between the two men, Masson filed in April 1982 a $13 million lawsuit against Eissler and the Freud Archives, which was eventually settled out of court, with Masson receiving two lump-sum payments totaling $150,000. Though he suffered from distress and discouragement, Eissler continued to write and practice until shortly before his death in New York City.

Eissler's clash with Masson unfortunately overshadowed in the public eye the high regard that Eissler retained in the psychoanalytic community, both as a practitioner and as a scholar. Despite the decline in interest in classical Freudian analysis, Eissler's efforts to establish and maintain the Freud archives will be an enduring legacy, especially of benefit to historians seeking to trace the evolution of what was once the chief analytic tradition.

• There is a small collection of Eissler's papers at the Library of Congress in Washington, D.C. The two *New York Times* articles that precipitated Masson's firing are by Ralph Blumenthal: "Scholars Seek the Hidden Freud in Newly Emerging Letters," 18 Aug. 1981, and "Did Freud's Isolation Lead Him to Reverse Theory on Neurosis?" 25 Aug. 1981. The controversy received full coverage in Janet Malcolm's two-part article, "Annals of Scholarship: Trouble in the Archives," *New Yorker*, 5 Dec. 1983, pp. 59–152, and 12 Dec. 1983, pp. 60–119, which Malcolm later turned into a book, *In the Freud Archives* (1984). Masson published *The Complete Letters of Sigmund Freud to Wilhelm Fliess, 1887–1904* (1985), and addressed his side of the controversy in *The Assault on Truth: Freud's Suppression of the Seduction Theory* (1984) and *Final Analysis: The Making and Unmaking of a Psychoanalyst* (1990). An obituary for Eissler is in the *New York Times*, 20 Feb. 1999.

EDWARD L. LACH, JR.

ELDRIDGE, Roy (30 Jan. 1911–26 Feb. 1989), musician, was born David Roy Eldridge in Pittsburgh, Pennsylvania, the younger son of Alexander Eldridge, a contractor, and Blanche Oakes Eldridge, who ran a local restaurant. Eldridge was playing drums at the age of six and, finding that he could play anything he could hear, subsequently taught himself trumpet, flugelhorn, and piano. He dropped out of David B. Oliver High School at age fifteen and joined his saxophone-playing brother Joe's band as drummer.

After briefly fronting his own local band in 1927, Eldridge played trumpet in carnival and theater circuit bands before moving to the Chocolate Dandies, Hot Chocolates, the Dixie Stompers, the Night Hawk Syncopaters, the Midnite Ramblers, and the variously-named bands led by Don Redman. By the time he arrived in New York in 1930, first with Cecil Scott and then Elmer Snowden's band, he had developed a remarkable trumpet style that imperfectly fused two elements.

Perhaps the most competitive of jazzmen, addicted to after-hours "cutting" contests with every famous trumpeter he met, Eldridge could play higher and more "on the rim of chaos" than anyone else of his generation. Whitney Balliett wrote that his fingers released notes "the way a dog shakes off water." Contrarily, Eldridge, who idolized saxophone players Coleman Hawkins, Benny Carter, and Lester Young, could remove the hard edges, saying he liked to "play nice saxophone on the trumpet."

Later called by Dizzy Gillespie "the Messiah of our generation" and by jazz critics the link between Louis Armstrong's hot jazz and Gillespie's nervous bebop, Eldridge confessed to being influenced by Armstrong in 1932: "He taught me how to tell a story." Eldridge was with the Teddy Hill orchestra in 1935; the next year he joined Fletcher Henderson's orchestra as lead trumpeter and occasional singer, then formed an eight-piece band with his brother as saxophonist-arranger and began a lengthy recording career. He mar-

ried in 1937 Viola Lee Fong, a hostess at the Savoy Ballroom; they would have one child and remain married for the rest of their lives, Eldridge dying three weeks after his wife. In 1939 Eldridge, who had quit music for a year because of its emotional demands and according to some accounts because of racism and low pay, was playing "mild dance music" at the Arcadia Ballroom on New York's Broadway. By 1940 he was at Minton's in Harlem, where he encouraged the young drummer Kenny "Klook" Clarke to play the top cymbal, "superimposing rhythms with his left hand" (Shapiro and Hentoff, *Hear Me Talkin' to Ya*). Clarke, in time the preeminent drummer of the bebop era, said that "with Roy I got everything I'd been trying to do together." Gillespie, arguably the founder of bop, was there too, listening, soaking up everything Eldridge did.

All the bands mentioned above were entirely African American. But in the later 1930s the strict color line in popular music was sometimes breached—Billie Holiday singing with the Artie Shaw band, Henderson writing arrangements for Benny Goodman's orchestra, for which vibraphonist Lionel Hampton was a "special attraction." In April 1941 Eldridge joined Gene Krupa's orchestra as a "featured soloist." After trumpeter Shorty Sherock left, Eldridge became one of the first African Americans to play regularly with a "white" band.

During Eldridge's two years with the Krupa band, he proved to be a brilliant soloist and an engaging singer, combining with the young Anita O'Day on several of the swing era's most memorable duets. He later said, "I would sit in my dressing room and run over in my mind what I was going to do. But when I got out there I didn't try and make the B-flat or whatever I was thinking of, because I'd go right into a void where there was no memory—nothing but me—riding up on that stage at the Paramount Theatre with the Krupa band scared me to death. I'd shake like a leaf, and you could hear it. Then this light would surround me."

It was especially on the Pacific Coast that Eldridge encountered a racism he could not handle. When the Krupa band played the Hollywood Palladium, Eldridge was not permitted to stay with the others and had to find lodgings in the "colored" section beyond downtown Los Angeles. Under such pressure, in the midst of one of his most famous solos, "Rocking Chair," Eldridge ran offstage and vomited. He took to carrying a gun. When Krupa was jailed for a drug offense, Eldridge led the band until it broke up.

Although Krupa was supportive and Shaw, Eldridge's next white leader (Oct. 1944–Sept. 1945), even more so, racism continued to oppress Eldridge. Yet his reputation skyrocketed. His signature tune "Little Jazz" (a nickname laid on the barely five-foot-tall Eldridge by Duke Ellington's reed player Toby Hardwick) was recorded with Shaw. He won the *Metronome* magazine poll as top trumpeter in 1944 and 1946, was *Esquire* magazine's top trumpeter in 1945, and was named America's top trumpeter in the 1946

Down Beat magazine poll. (Eldridge was later named to the *Down Beat* Hall of Fame.)

After leaving Shaw, Eldridge had his own band again (1946–1948). Ensconced at New York's Three Deuces while Gillespie was at the Onyx, he engaged Gillespie in after-hours contests that became legendary. When the Krupa band re-formed in 1949, he joined it for several months, leaving to join the first of Norman Granz's yearly Jazz at the Philharmonic tours.

Eldridge's last stint with a white band came in 1950, when he joined the Goodman band for a European tour. When the band hit Paris, he was particularly acclaimed; he later said he had felt no racial prejudice there or anywhere else on the continent. He made a number of recordings, singing in English and French. (When the recordings were rereleased thirty years later, they caused a revival of interest in Eldridge.)

Back in the United States at Birdland in New York (1951), Eldridge told jazz writer Leonard Feather he would never join a white band again: "Man, when you're on the stage, you're great, but as soon as you come off, you're nothing. It's not worth the glory, not worth the money, not worth anything. Never again!"

Subsequently Eldridge led the group that accompanied Ella Fitzgerald's international concert appearances from 1963 to 1965 and in 1966 spent a year with Count Basie's orchestra, which was still playing swinging jazz. He frequently returned to Europe and appeared at various jazz festivals in the United States, including a miniature festival for President Jimmy Carter on the White House south lawn. From 1969 to 1979, when he gave up playing in public, he led a small swing band at Jimmy Ryan's on West Fifty-fourth Street in New York. In 1980 he suffered the first of several strokes. There followed many concerts honoring him. Suffering from emphysema, Eldridge, a giant of jazz blessed and tortured by extreme sensitivity, died in Valley Stream, New York.

• Leonard Feather's article detailing Eldridge's quitting of white bands is in *Down Beat*, 18 May 1951. A wide-ranging essay is Whitney Balliett's "Little Jazz" in *American Musicians: Fifty-six Portraits in Jazz* (1986). Various personal perspectives on Eldridge are found in Nat Shapiro and Nat Hentoff, *Hear Me Talkin' to Ya: The Story of Jazz as Told by the Men Who Made It* (1955). Also useful are James Lincoln Collier, *The Making of Jazz* (1978), and Dizzy Gillespie, *To Be or Not . . . to Bop* (1979). Eldridge's trumpet pyrotechnics are showcased in Jean Bach's 1994 film documentary *A Great Day in Harlem*, dealing with the famous 1958 photo shoot that united fifty-nine of America's greatest jazzmen. An obituary is in the *New York Times*, 28 Feb. 1989.

JAMES ROSS MOORE

ELION, Gertrude (23 Jan. 1918–21 Feb. 1999), biochemist, was born Gertrude Belle Elion in New York City, the daughter of Robert Elion, a dentist, and Bertha Cohen Elion. Both of her parents were immigrants: her father had emigrated to the United States from Lithuania at the age of twelve and her mother from Poland at the age of fourteen. Until the time she

was seven years old, the Elion family lived in a large apartment adjoining her father's dental office in Manhattan.

Her family then settled in the Bronx, where, Elion said, "[M]y brother and I had a happy childhood. We went to a public school within walking distance of our house" (quoted in *Les Prix Nobel 1988*). As a child, she demonstrated a keen intelligence and excelled in school. As she noted, "I was a child with an insatiable thirst for knowledge and remember enjoying all of my courses almost equally." She skipped several grades in school and, as a result, graduated from high school at the age of twelve.

When she was only fifteen, she decided it was time to attend college, despite the financial setback suffered by her father during the stock market crash of 1929. Finances, however, were not the only problem she encountered. She was also undecided on which career she ought to pursue. As she later recalled, when she finally did determine what she wanted to do, "one of the deciding factors may have been that my grandfather, whom I loved dearly, died of cancer when I was 15. I was highly motivated to do something that might eventually lead to a cure for this terrible disease" (*Les Prix Nobel 1988*).

In 1933 she entered Hunter College, choosing to major in science and eventually narrowing her choice to chemistry. She always believed that if it had not been the case that Hunter was a free college and that "my grades were good enough for me to enter it, I suspect I might never have received a higher education" (*Les Prix Nobel 1988*). Elion fit in nicely at Hunter College, where she made many friends and felt challenged academically. As she later explained, she was influenced by the fact that it was an all-women's school and her feeling that the teachers did not expect most of the students to seriously pursue a career. She set out to prove them wrong, and she did so by graduating Phi Beta Kappa with an A.B. degree summa cum laude in 1937.

She then began a lengthy and frustrating search for work. The Great Depression made it impossible for her to immediately go on to graduate school because "jobs were scarce and the few positions that existed in laboratories were not available to women," she later recalled. Her luck changed when she met a chemist who was in need of a laboratory assistant. Unfortunately, he was unable to pay her. Feeling that the experience would be worth it, she took the position, remaining there for a year and a half and finally earning $20 a week by the time she left.

During this time, Elion saved up her money and received help from her parents so that she could enter graduate school at New York University in the fall of 1939. As she recalled, "I was the only female in my graduate chemistry class but no one seemed to mind, and I did not consider it at all strange." Elion completed her required courses after only one year of graduate studies. She then began working on her research requirements at night and on weekends, so that she could take a position as a teacher-in-training and as a substitute teacher in New York City secondary schools. There, she taught chemistry, physics, and general science for two years.

She obtained her master of science degree in chemistry in 1941. Because of the outbreak of World War II, there was a shortage of chemists in the industrial sector, which meant that Elion was finally able to find work in a laboratory, although not in research. Her first position involved analytical quality control work for a major food company. She stayed there for a year and a half, but, as she later commented, "I became restless because the work was so repetitive and I was no longer learning anything" (*Les Prix Nobel 1988*).

In 1944 she found her true calling when she was hired by the pharmaceutical firm Burroughs Wellcome (later Glaxo Wellcome) to work as an assistant to Dr. George Herbert Hitchings, a medical researcher who was studying the structure of DNA with the hope of developing new drugs that could control the division of cancerous cells. She and Hitchings made a good team, and Elion was happy because of the opportunities she thereby gained: "Dr. Hitchings permitted me to learn as rapidly as I could and to take on more and more responsibility when I was ready for it . . . I never felt constrained to remain strictly in chemistry, but was able to broaden my horizons into biochemistry, pharmacology, immunology, and eventually virology" (*Les Prix Nobel 1988*). Her talent and persistence in following tedious procedures paid off, as she quickly improved synthesizing methods and created new compounds.

Eventually equals, Elion and Hitchings maintained a 44-year scientific partnership researching cures for several deadly diseases, including leukemia and cancer. Their methods were unique because they were the first to create new medicines by studying the chemical composition of diseased cells. In 1953 Elion and Hitchings developed the first two successful drugs for the treatment of acute leukemia. By interfering with the reproductive process of cancer cells, these drugs caused remissions in childhood leukemia. In 1957 Hitchings and Elion created the first immunosuppressive agent, which stopped the immune system from rejecting foreign tissue and which led to successful organ transplants. As a result, kidney transplants between unrelated donors became possible for the first time in history.

The two researchers continued their joint pioneering work throughout the 1960s. In 1963 Elion became director of the chemotherapy division at Burroughs Wellcome and in 1967 was named head of the department of experimental therapy. She received the Garvan Medal from the American Chemical Society in 1968.

During the 1970s Elion and her team began to work toward the goal of creating a compound that would successfully block viral infections. In 1977 they succeeded by creating the world's first antiviral medication, a drug used to combat viral herpes.

In the 1980s Elion oversaw the development of the AIDS drug AZT, and her design led to its creation in 1983. During that same year, she officially retired and was named emeritus scientist. In her later years, she continued her work toward the advancement of science through the World Health Organization and by assisting students in medical research. As she put it, "my career appears to have come full circle from my early days of being a teacher to now sharing my experience in research with the new generations of scientists" (*Les Prix Nobel 1988*). In 1984 she was appointed to the National Cancer board and in 1988 Elion shared the Nobel Prize in Medicine or Physiology with George Hitchings and researcher Sir James Black for codiscovering many important principles of drug treatment.

Elion was elected to the National Academy of Sciences in 1990, and although she never completed her doctoral degree, she received twenty-five honorary doctorates; her name appears on forty-five patents. In 1991 she was chosen for the National Women's Hall of Fame, became the first woman inducted into the National Inventors Hall of Fame, and was awarded the National Medal of Science. She was honored with membership in the Women in Technology International (WITI) Hall of Fame in 1998.

Elion never married, preferring to devote herself almost solely to her work and related activities. She did find time for some hobbies, however: most notably, photography, music, and international travel. She died at the University of North Carolina Hospital in Chapel Hill at the age of 81.

In her research partnership with Hitchings, Elion fulfilled her dream of becoming a lifesaving scientist. She persevered through economic hard times and in the face of formidable barriers to the advancement of women in her chosen field. Working for a leading pharmaceutical firm allowed her to conduct lengthy, expensive research aimed at practical results. Linked to pioneering treatments of cancer, viral diseases, transplant rejection, and AIDS, Elion established herself as a world-class biochemist.

• Elion's autobiography, originally published in *Les Prix Nobel 1988*, is available at www.nobel.se/medicine/laureates/1988/. A brief interview appears in Marguerite Holloway, "The Satisfaction of Delayed Gratification," *Scientific American*, Oct. 1991, which highlights the work that led to her Nobel Prize. Stephanie St. Pierre, *Gertrude Elion: Master Chemist* (1993), is a fairly brief biography. Other profiles highlighting the awarding of the Nobel Prize to Elion and Hitchings include Ingrid Wickelgren, "Two Americans, Briton Share Medical Nobel," *Science News*, 22 Oct. 1988; Jean L. Marx, "The 1988 Nobel Prize For Physiology or Medicine," *Science*, 28 Oct. 1988; and Peter Gwynne, "Nobels in Science Recognize Research Done Decades Ago," *Research and Development*, Dec. 1988. Consult the *Wall Street Journal*, 27 Feb. 1991, and Edmund Andrews, "First Woman in Inventors Hall of Fame," *New York Times*, 2 Mar. 1991, for discussions about her being the first woman inducted into the Inventors Hall of Fame. The *New York Times* of 23 Feb. 1999 has an obituary; see also Renee Goucher, "In Memorium," *InfoWorld*, 3 May 1999.

JUDITH B. GERBER

ELLIOTT, Carl A. (20 Dec. 1913–9 Jan. 1999), U.S. congressman, was born Carl Atwood Elliott in Gober Ridge, Franklin County, Alabama, the son of G. W. "Will" Elliott, farmer, and Nora Massey Elliott. The oldest of nine children, he grew up on a hardscrabble tenant farm and became interested in politics at an early age. After attending local public schools, he entered the University of Alabama in Tuscaloosa on a shoestring budget in 1930. His first night on campus was spent sleeping under a truck; he then lived in an abandoned building during his first year and a half of college. Despite his lack of means, Elliott managed to support himself by working a variety of odd jobs. His success on campus was marked by his election as class president during his senior year. Upon graduating in 1933, he entered law school at Alabama and received his law degree in 1936.

Elliott entered the legal profession in Russellville, Alabama, at a time when many of his clients could pay him only in trade. Sensing greater opportunities elsewhere, he relocated to Jasper, Alabama, in December 1936 and built up his legal practice while making plans to enter the political arena. Although he lost his first race—for Walker County Court judge in 1940—Elliott remained active in politics. In June 1940 he married Jane Hamilton; the couple was to have four children.

During the 1940s Elliott served as judge of Recorders Court (1942 and 1946), became a member of the Alabama State Democratic Executive Committee (until 1950), and was city attorney for a number of local communities, including Carbon Hill, Parrish, and Cordova. With the advent of World War II he entered the U.S. Army as a private in 1942 and rose to the rank of first lieutenant before a training injury led to discharge in 1944. On returning to Jasper, he resumed the practice of law and became a city judge in 1945. In 1948 he challenged Carter Manasco, a four-term incumbent congressman, for a seat in the U.S. House of Representatives. Elliott's tireless campaigning and his opponent's overconfidence resulted in his victory in the Democratic primary (then tantamount to election), and he took his seat in January 1949.

During his first term in Congress, Elliott served on the Veterans Affairs Committee and supported moderately liberal legislation such as the 1949 National Housing Act and statehood for Alaska and Hawaii. Closest to his heart, however, was the cause of education. Mindful of the obstacles that he had faced in pursuing his own education, Elliott was determined to provide better opportunities for Americans of all economic and social backgrounds to obtain a higher education, and he labored for a federal educational aid bill from his first day in office. Named to the Committee on Education and Labor in October 1951, he faced a reactionary chairman, Graham A. Barden of North Carolina, and a long history of failed attempts to involve the federal government in the educational field. Despite the long-standing opposition of conservatives such as Barden, Elliott managed to secure funding for badly needed rural libraries through his sponsorship of the Library Services Act of 1956. Appointed to the chairmanship of a special subcommittee on education following the 1956 elections, Elliott at last had the legislative wherewithal to realize his dream of comprehensive federal aid to education. Aided in his fight by the public sense of unease ensuing from the Soviet Union's 1957 launch of Sputnik, Elliott and his allies carefully crafted the wording of the proposed bill, emphasizing the role of education in the area of national defense. After a protracted struggle to ease the bill past yet another fiercely conservative power in the House—Howard Smith of Virginia, head of the House Rules Committee—Elliott was able to see the National Defense Education Act of 1958 signed into law by President Dwight D. Eisenhower.

Like many southern progressives of that era, Elliott had to tread carefully in dealing with the subject of race. He reluctantly signed the infamous "Southern Manifesto" of 1956, believing that failing to do so might deprive him of his seat and the chance to better the lot of all Americans, including African Americans, through education. Nevertheless, Elliott did speak out repeatedly against such hate groups as the John Birch Society and the Ku Klux Klan. He also campaigned for John F. Kennedy, a former fellow congressman, in Alabama during the 1960 presidential election in the face of considerable anti-Catholic sentiment. After Kennedy became president, House Speaker Sam Rayburn sought to facilitate Kennedy administration legislation by expanding the Rules Committee (and hence reducing Smith's influence) by three members. Elliott became one of the new members of the Rules Committee, much to the chagrin of many archconservatives in the South, who viewed any lessening of Smith's influence as an invitation to an avalanche of new civil rights legislation.

Elliott faced an unusual challenge to his bid for reelection in 1962. Following the 1960 Census, Alabama had lost a congressional seat, and the state legislature had failed to come up with a redistricting plan. Hence, all nine incumbent members of Congress had to run statewide at-large campaigns. Although Elliott survived this challenge, the same situation prevailed in 1964, by which time he had incurred the wrath of Governor George Wallace and his followers. A bitter campaign marked by "dirty tricks" led to Elliott's defeat.

Determined to vindicate himself, Elliott then ran for governor in 1966 against Lurleen Wallace, a stand-in for her husband, who was, constitutionally, barred from succeeding himself. Yet another nasty campaign, however, ended with Elliott's finishing third in the Democratic primary. He retired from public life heavily in debt, having cashed in his congressional pension in order to pay bills. Denied a teaching position at state colleges that feared the Wallaces' retribution, Elliott practiced law for several years until ill health forced him to stop working altogether. He remained broke and nearly forgotten until he won the first John F. Kennedy Profile in Courage Award in 1990. Elliott died in Jasper, Alabama.

Although he paid a high personal price for his principles, Elliott lived long enough to see many of his values honored. He took great (and justifiable) pride in his work on higher education, which enabled thousands of Americans to achieve an education that might otherwise have been out of their reach.

• Elliott's papers are held at the W. Stanley Hoole Special Collections Library, University of Alabama, Tuscaloosa. Elliott was the author of *Annals of Northwest Alabama*, 2 vols. (1958–1959). The best published source of information on his life and career is his autobiography, written with Michael D'Orso, *The Cost of Courage: The Journey of an American Congressman* (1992). His Profile in Courage Award received coverage in the 24 May 1990 edition of the *Tuscaloosa News*. An obituary appears in the *New York Times*, 12 Jan. 1999.

EDWARD L. LACH, JR.

ELLIS, Edward Robb (22 Feb. 1911–7 Sept. 1998), journalist, author, and diarist, was born in Kewanee, Illinois, the son of John Talcott Ellis, an improvident musician, and Lalla Robb Ellis. In 1912 his parents divorced. When he was a sophomore in the Kewanee High School, he and two friends held a contest to see who could keep a diary the longest. The two friends soon quit, but Ellis kept his, beginning on 27 December 1927, for the next sixty-eight years. He edited the high school newspaper and graduated in 1929.

Attracted by its journalism school, Ellis enrolled at the University of Missouri in 1929, worked at several jobs after the stock market crash caused family financial reverses, became a part-time reporter for the *Kewanee Daily Star-Courier* beginning in June 1933, and graduated from Missouri with a B.J. in 1934. Beginning a career as a reporter and feature writer, he worked for the New Orleans bureau of the Associated Press (1934), the *New Orleans Item* (1934–1936), and the *Oklahoma City Times* (1936–1938). In 1938 Ellis married Leatha Sparlin, a symphony orchestra violinist; the couple had one child. Ellis worked for the *Peoria Journal-Transcript* (1939–1942) and the Chicago bureau of the United Press (1942–1943). In his early years as an aggressive, observant journalist, he interviewed Huey Long, Thomas Mann, Sinclair Lewis, Eleanor Roosevelt, and many other celebrities. He also drew skillful caricatures of some of his subjects.

During World War II, Ellis served in the U.S. Navy (1943–1945), including duty on Okinawa (Aug.–Nov. 1945), where he helped publish a daily paper for naval personnel. On his return home, he was surprised by his wife's decision to divorce him (1945). Though melancholy, promiscuous, and sometimes thinking of suicide, he worked hard, again for the United Press bureau in Chicago (1946–1947), then moved to New York City and fell in love with Manhattan. He obtained employment with the *New York World-Telegram* (1947–1962), writing brilliant features on many events—not least, a prison execution—and prominent people, such as Senator Joe McCarthy, Grace Kelly, and Harry S. Truman. A 1950 assignment took him

briefly to Europe; his friend, Ruth Kraus, representing the *New York Herald-Tribune*, went there as well. The two, married in 1955, were wonderfully happy.

Ellis continued to cover many different beats, from political conferences to morgue scenes after fires and airplane crashes, and interview celebrities of all kinds, important people from different walks of life, including the conductor Arturo Toscanini, the actress Mae West, General Douglas MacArthur, the poet E. E. Cummings, the Reverend Adam Clayton Powell, and the popular singer Barbra Streisand. In 1961 Ellis and George N. Allen, a *New York Sun* reporter, published *Traitor Within: Our Suicide Problem*. Based on fifteen years of research and thousands of newspaper clippings, it is a survey of suicides in the United States compared with those in other countries. The authors see suicide as a worsening national mental-health problem and appeal for more research and prevention organizations. Certain parts smack of black humor—for example, anecdotes describing unsuccessful attempts at suicide.

In 1962 Ellis argued with his *World-Telegram* editor, told him off, and abruptly quit. While Ruth Ellis worked as a secretary to support him, then quit to help him, he laboriously researched, wrote, and partly dictated to his wife *The Epic of New York City* (1966; repr. 1989). Ruth had a fatal heart attack in 1965, shortly after the thousand-page manuscript was completed. Characteristically, after an episode of writer's block, Ellis recorded in a 5,000-word diary entry every agonizingly observed detail of his wife's suffering, hospitalization, and death. *The Epic of New York City*—a critical, but not financial, success—narrates the city's history from its discovery and first settlement to the present. Chapter by chapter, it focuses on single events of particular significance. Allan Nevins, the Pulitzer Prize–winning historian, called it "admirably planned and proportioned, . . . accurate and full, and . . . written in a vibrant, graphic style" (quoted in Ellis, *A Diary of the Century*, p. 378).

In 1967 Ellis moved permanently to a four-room apartment at 441 West 21st Street in lower Manhattan, where he had bookshelves built to accommodate his personal library ultimately numbering 12,000 volumes. He published *A Nation in Torment: The Great American Depression, 1929–1939* (1970; repr. 1995), an impressionistic, loose narrative of a terrible period in American history. The book was enthusiastically reviewed, received the 1970 Friends of American Writers Literary Award, and merited Ellis's being sent on publicity tours to promote sales.

After four years of research, Ellis published *Echoes of Distant Thunder: Life in the United States, 1914–1918* (1975; repr. 1996). It demonstrates the existence of what Ellis calls the "reign of terror" during Woodrow Wilson's presidency. Ellis discusses such controversial issues as military preparedness, neutrality, pacifism, propaganda, and the consequences of violent philosophical, ethical, and political disagreements, including labor-union struggles, racial animosities, and war-altered social behavior. He sets pro-war Senator Henry Cabot Lodge, ex-president Theodore Roosevelt, and their formidable cohorts against Senator Robert La Follette and others favoring neutrality. A major theme is Ellis's tracing of President Wilson's uncertainties until events propelled the nation into war. Although exciting and erudite, *Echoes of Distant Thunder* has been criticized for the author's learned but inharmonious digressions and his obvious reliance on secondary sources without footnotes. Undisguised are his biases against capitalism, the industrial-military complex, and Republican policies and in favor of peace, free speech, labor, and the rights of minorities. As he prepared to write this book, Ellis sought the advice of Roger Nash Baldwin, jailed World War I conscientious objector and later a co-founder of the American Civil Liberties Union.

Short of money by 1975, Ellis began to work part-time tape-recording his interviews of famous people for the Oral History Collection at Columbia University. He planned but never wrote other books. In 1985 he was invited to appear on television in Tokyo, with all his travel expenses paid, to discuss and show a sample of his diary, by then listed in the *Guinness Book of World Records* as the longest ever kept by an American, but he refused out of fear that something would be lost or an intimate passage exposed. In 1991 an interview of Ellis by a BBC reporter, mainly about his diary, was widely broadcast. In 1993 he formulated plans to donate his diary to New York University, to which, in 1995, two trucks hauled the sixty-six volumes.

A Diary of the Century: Tales from America's Greatest Diarist (1995), totaling 578 pages, contains generous excerpts, amounting to only about 1 percent of the original, which has been processed and is available for social historians to consult. They may also request copies of specific parts by fax. *A Diary of the Century* is a unique, fascinating volume, combining personal anecdotes, Ellis's analyses of his dreams, reports of both comic and tragic events, and descriptions of encounters with famous or notorious personalities. Ellis, alternately the bon vivant and the bookish hermit, emerges as self-centered and selfless, conceited and humble, joyful and depressed, opinionated and uncertain, acting as his own confessor and jury, and rubbing elbows with people from all strata of American society. Among the highlights of this astounding book are his interviews with Paul Robeson, Robert Moses, and Alger Hiss, his experimenting with marijuana, and his participation in Alcoholics Anonymous meetings, although those examples are too few to be indicative of the rich variety found in the pages of the published abridgment of Ellis's record of his insatiable curiosity. He planned to assemble his "advice" in a book to be called *Infinity and Three Doors Beyond* but managed only to pack his best maxims into four diary pages, dated 22 February 1978. If distilled, they would say that one lives best who seeks knowledge, transmutes it into wisdom, and practices kindness to everyone. Long suffering from emphysema, Ellis died in a hospital in his beloved Manhattan.

• The best available source of information on Ellis is *A Diary of the Century*, in which he interpolates innumerable explanatory notes here and there; some extensive, some short, they constitute an autobiography within diary selections. An entire issue of *Diarist's Journal*, July 1988, pp. 1–16, is devoted to Ellis's diary, which, totaling about 22 million words and filling 50 cartons, is deposited in the Fales Library of New York University. An obituary is in the *New York Times*, 9 Sept. 1998.

ROBERT L. GALE

ETTING, Solomon (28 July 1764–6 Aug. 1847), Jewish merchant and Baltimore civic leader, was born in York, Pennsylvania; he was the second oldest of the eight children of Elijah Etting, a Frankfurt merchant who came to York in 1758, and Shinah Solomon of Lancaster, Pennsylvania. As a boy, Solomon acquired business skills, working in the family store. After Elijah Etting, who was an Indian trader, died in July of 1778, Solomon did not go to Baltimore with his mother and his sisters. Along with his brother Reuben, he stayed in York, evidently to protect and preserve the family's business interests. Solomon in 1782 also became an authorized slaughterer of kosher meats (*shohet*). The next year he married Rachel Simon, the daughter of Joseph Simon, a prominent Indian trader and merchant from Lancaster.

Between 1784 and 1790 Etting lived in Lancaster and worked with his father-in-law in a partnership known as Simon and Etting. Located at East King Street and Center Square, this firm sold to Indians apparel, food, kettles, and guns and primarily purchased furs from them. Rachel Simon Etting, who had four children, died on 14 January 1790. After her passing, Etting in 1790 dissolved his partnership with Joseph Simon and went to Philadelphia. That year, he met Rachel Gratz, the daughter of eminent Philadelphia merchant Barnard Gratz; Etting married her on 26 October 1791, and they were to have eight children.

Etting moved his family to Baltimore in 1791 and actively participated in the city's business community until 1816. His first Baltimore business venture was a hardware store. This profitable firm, which operated between 1791 and 1806, was located on Calvert Street at Lovely Lane and offered a wide assortment of products: frying pans, pots, brooms, shovels, axes, hoes, hammers, nails, bolts, screws, locks, and hinges. In 1795 the ambitious Etting entered the merchant-shipping business and the next year was appointed a director of the Union Bank of Maryland, an institution dominated by Baltimore Jeffersonian Republican leaders. The firm of Rutter and Etting, which obtained credit and loans from the Union Bank, developed markets in many places between 1796 and 1807. Etting sent ships that contained hardware products, food, flour, tobacco, hides, and apparel to Caribbean and European ports, and he helped to organize the Baltimore East India Company in 1807. The year before, his prospering firm had moved to Market Street between Howard and Eutaw and continued to supply a variety of goods to domestic markets; food, cigars, brandy, apparel, and cotton textiles from India and China were sold to merchants in New York, Charleston, and Pittsburgh.

Etting during these years also was associated with significant political and military developments. In 1794 he was named a member of the standing committee of the Baltimore Republican Society, a Jeffersonian organization that attempted "to promote Republican principles and the rights of humanity." That same year, along with David Stodder, Alexander McKim, and four other prominent Baltimore Jeffersonian leaders, Etting was appointed to a committee to present to President George Washington resolutions expressing opposition to the provisions of the Jay Treaty. In his opinion, the treaty did not help American businessmen who traded with merchants in the West Indies. In 1797 Etting presented to the Maryland legislature a significant memorial stating that a Maryland law that required the taking of a Christian test oath to hold state offices and to practice law should be abolished; he also claimed that this Maryland law denied Jews their basic citizenship rights. The next year, when the repressive Alien and Sedition Acts of the Federalists were passed, the leadership of the Maryland Assembly refused to take action on Etting's memorial. Even during the presidency of the liberal spokesman Thomas Jefferson, however, the assembly in 1802 and in 1804 decisively voted to defeat Etting's petitions to terminate Jewish disabilities in Maryland.

Despite these setbacks, Etting continued to be a civic leader. He helped in 1804 to establish the Baltimore Water Company and was elected that year as one of its board members. Of more importance, he played an active role during the War of 1812 (which went on for two and a half years). When the British in 1814 attacked Baltimore, Etting, who had been elected as a member of the city's Committee of Vigilance and Safety, promptly acted to find hospital facilities for the wounded and sick. That same year, he headed a committee to consider ways of protecting Baltimore's harbor and corresponded with Robert Fulton about building a large paddle-wheel-driven warship. Etting, however, was unable to secure funding for the construction of Fulton's costly steam frigate. After the war, he actively served in 1816 on a committee that called for the allocation of monies for the building of many new streets in Baltimore.

Between 1816 and 1826 Etting focused his attention again on what was for him the salient issue of Jewish emancipation in Maryland. Despite his lobbying efforts and those of his friend Jacob I. Cohen, Jr., the Maryland Assembly, for various reasons, refused to grant political privileges and civic rights to Jews between 1816 and 1821. Stymied by the opposition of many Maryland Federalists to the passage of a so-called Jew Bill, the split between rural and urban Republicans over this proposed legislation, and the resentment of some Catholic and numerous Protestant groups to the bill, the supporters of Etting in the Maryland legislature met with failure during these five years. In 1822, with the sponsorship of the Hagerstown Jeffersonian Thomas Kennedy, who was an ardent advocate of religious and political liberties, a new bill, which called for the repeal of the Christian test oath, the acknowledgment of a belief in the afterlife, and the granting of Jewish political and citizenship rights, was introduced in the Maryland legislature in 1822 and was approved by seven votes. The proposed reforms, however, would effectuate a change in the Maryland constitution and thus required a majority vote during two consecutive sessions of the assembly. The state legislature defeated the bill in 1823 but passed it in 1824. After the first vote, Etting, in an 1824 memorial to the assembly, argued that Jews had served as patriots during the American Revolution and the War of 1812 and that the Federal Constitution had extended to them religious and political liberties; moreover, if the legislature were to approve the bill, Jews would especially contribute to the fostering of business, industry, and trade in Maryland. His memorial evidently was significant to the outcome of the second vote, for the Jew Bill was passed by the Maryland Assembly on 26 February 1825 and became law on 5 January 1826.

The enacting of this significant law appeared to produce, in numerous ways, a preponderant impact on Etting's later career. Between 1826 and 1830 he continued to provide Baltimore with leadership. Along with Cohen, Etting was elected in October 1826 as a member of the First Branch of the Baltimore City Council, and he later served as its president. Appointed a director of the Baltimore & Ohio Railroad in April 1827, Etting believed that this carrier was essential for the business and industrial expansion of the city. He also worked to improve Baltimore's medical institutions, serving in 1830 as chairman of the Baltimore Infirmary Committee. During the early 1830s Etting championed the cause of both African Americans and Jews. When he was elected a director of the Maryland State Colonization Society in 1831, he helped to fund a Maryland colony for freed slaves at Cape Palmas along the coast of Liberia. He then became involved with an issue concerning political anti-Semitism. After Senator Henry Clay in 1832 made a derogatory comment about a Jew during a speech concerning the tariff, Etting asked in a letter for an explanation from the senator. He received a letter of apology from Clay, who was a distant relative of the Lexingtonian lawyer and businessman Benjamin Gratz.

Throughout his adult years, Etting was associated with fraternal and religious organizations. In 1785 he became a charter member of Lancaster Masonic Lodge number 43 and later served as its treasurer and its master. Established in 1781 by Moses Michael Hays, the Philadelphia Masonic Lodge of Perfection extended membership to Etting in 1785. This Scottish Rite body was important to him because most of its members in the early 1780s were Jewish patriots during the American Revolution; through its rituals, this lodge emphasized republicanism, natural liberties, and civic equality. Etting, who never affiliated with a synagogue in Baltimore, held membership in Philadelphia's Mikveh Israel congregation. He died in Baltimore and was buried in that city next to his second wife, who had passed on sixteen years before him.

Although not a national figure, Etting contributed to the maturation of the early American republic. A civic booster and leader, he became an eminent Baltimore merchant-capitalist and was identified with the city's business aristocracy. He is best remembered for his lengthy yet successful struggle for Jewish citizenship rights in Maryland.

• The Maryland Historical Society, the Historical Society of Pennsylvania, the American Philosophical Society, and the Jewish Theological Seminary house primary sources concerning Etting's lengthy career. The best account of Etting's life can be found in Isaac M. Fein, *The Making of an American Jewish Community: The History of Baltimore Jewry from 1773 to 1920* (1971). Aaron Baroway, "Solomon Etting, 1764–1847," *Maryland Historical Magazine* 15 (1920): 1–20, presents a detailed profile but should be used with caution. Jacob R. Marcus, *United States Jewry, 1776–1985*, vol. 1 (1989), offers a fine account of Etting's business career. On Etting's life in Lancaster and his involvement in Freemasonry, consult Frederic S. Klein, *A History of the Jews in Lancaster* (1955). Edwin Wolf II and Maxwell Whiteman, *The History of the Jews of Philadelphia from Colonial Times to the Age of Jackson* (1956), mentions his brief stay in Philadelphia. Major reasons concerning Etting's involvement in Baltimore politics and business during the 1790s are suggested in Norman K. Risjord, *Jefferson's America: 1760–1815* (1991), and in Gary L. Browne, *Baltimore in the Nation, 1789–1861* (1980). Joseph L. Blau and Salo W. Baron, eds., *The Jews of the United States, 1790–1840: A Documentary History*, vol. 1 (1963), describes Etting's role as a municipal leader during the War of 1812. His importance to Jewish civic emancipation in Maryland is explained in Edward Eitches, "Maryland's 'Jew Bill,'" *American Jewish Historical Quarterly* 60 (1970–1971): 258–79; in Morton Borden, *Jews, Turks, and Infidels* (1984); in Naomi W. Cohen, *Jews in Christian America: The Pursuit of Religious Equality* (1992); and in Frederic C. Jaher, *A Scapegoat in the New Wilderness: The Origins and Rise of Anti-Semitism in America* (1994). J. Thomas Scharf, *History of Maryland from the Earliest Time to the Present Day*, vol. 3 (1879; repr., Tradition Press, Harboro, Pa., 1967), alludes to Etting's role on the Baltimore City Council. For his participation in the Maryland State Colonization Society, see Robert J. Brugger, *Maryland: A Middle Temperament, 1630–1980* (1988). An obituary is in the *Baltimore Sun*, 9 Aug. 1847.

WILLIAM WEISBERGER

EVERS, Johnny (21 July 1881–28 Mar. 1947), baseball player, was born John Joseph Evers in Troy, New York, the son of John Evers, a city government clerk, and Ellen Keating Evers. Details of his early life are unknown. He graduated from St. Joseph's Christian Brothers Teachers School in 1898 and thereafter worked in a collar factory. He began playing professional baseball in 1902 with a team in his hometown and joined the Chicago Cubs before the end of the season. Because he stood at five feet nine inches and weighed only 119 pounds, several of his teammates initially scoffed at his diminutive size and refused to take the field with him. According to Evers, "As I

climbed aboard the team bus [on his first day with the Cubs], 'Jack' Taylor, the pitcher, looked me over very carefully and cut me to the quick with, 'He'll leave in a box car tonight'" (quoted in Golenbock, p. 98). On 13 September 1902, the Chicago lineup featured for the first time second baseman Evers, shortstop Joe Tinker, and first baseman Frank Chance—a trio that would become one of baseball's most celebrated double-play combinations.

Evers established himself as a star in 1903, when he hit .293 and stole 25 bases. A quintessential dead-ball-era player, he excelled at defense, bunting, and base running. Nicknamed "the Crab" for his acerbic tongue and his penchant for fistfights, he also gained a reputation for being one of the quickest-thinking players in the game. He reportedly studied the baseball rule book and the *Sporting News* every night before he went to bed. He was considered a master at scrutinizing the body language and vocal inflections of players on opposing teams in order to learn their signals. Together with Tinker, he devised a number of trick defensive plays. He later described one of them:

> When a hit and run play is attempted and the batter hits a fly to the outfield, the base runner hearing the crack of the bat, must judge from actions of the fielders in front of him what has happened. When such a situation came up Tinker and [I] went through all the motions of trying to stop a grounder, or diving for a hit. The runner would fear being forced out at second and tear along under the impression the ball had gone through the infield. Sometimes he would be nearly to third base before the outfielder . . . would toss it to the first baseman and complete the double play. (Evers, p. 205)

Although Evers and Tinker played side by side for the Cubs for eleven seasons, they despised each other. Following an incident in 1905 when Evers stole a cab from Tinker outside an Indiana hotel, they refused to speak to each other off the field; their silence was finally broken thirty-three years later, when they met by chance at a World Series game and tearfully embraced.

Evers helped the Cubs dominate the National League between 1906 and 1910, a period during which they posted a .693 winning percentage in regular-season play and won four pennants (1906–1908, 1910) and two world championships (1907–1908). In 1908 he led the club with a .300 batting average. During the pennant race that season, he was a central participant in the famous "Merkle boner" play. In a crucial September game against the New York Giants, he alertly noticed when a Giants base runner, Fred Merkle, failed to advance all the way to second base on a game-winning hit by Al Bridwell. As New York fans swarmed onto the field to celebrate their apparent victory, he called for the ball and forced Merkle out. Because of the near-riot conditions that ensued at the stadium—Evers later recalled that Cubs manager Frank Chance left the field under a police escort and

$5,200 was stolen from the team's dressing room—the game could not be continued and was declared a tie. A few weeks later, the Cubs defeated the Giants 4–3 in a replay of the game to win the pennant.

Off the baseball diamond, Evers ran two successful shoe stores, one in Troy, New York, and the other in Chicago. In 1910, however, he went broke when his business partner gambled away $50,000 in profits and stock and creditors seized the stores. That year he was involved in an automobile accident that killed a close friend, and in September he broke his leg sliding into home plate during a game against Cincinnati. Afterward he suffered a nervous breakdown, and in 1911 he was able to play in only 46 games. The following year he rebounded with his best offensive season, finishing fourth among National League hitters with a .341 batting average. In 1913 he replaced the popular Chance as the Cubs' manager and led the team to a third-place finish and a respectable 88–65 record. However, he frequently clashed with team owner Charles Murphy and was fired during the off-season. In 1914 he was traded to the Boston Braves, where he was named team captain. That year the "Miracle Braves," buried in last place in mid-July, won the pennant by ten and a half games and defeated the Philadelphia Athletics in the World Series. When a Philadelphia player congratulated him, Evers reportedly spat at his feet. He batted .438 in the series and was named the National League's Most Valuable Player.

Evers retired in 1917 after eighteen major league seasons. During his career he compiled a .270 batting average, made 1,658 hits, scored 919 runs, and stole 324 bases. He stole home 21 times, to rank fourth in major league history. In twenty World Series games, he batted .316. In 1946 he and his teammates Tinker and Chance were elected to the National Baseball Hall of Fame.

Evers was married to Helen Fitzgibbons; they had two children. Following his retirement, he managed or coached with several teams, including the New York Giants (coach, 1920), the Cubs (manager, 1921), the Chicago White Sox (coach, 1922–1923; manager, 1924), and the Boston Braves (assistant manager, 1929–1932; scout, 1933–1934). During the late 1930s he served as vice-president and general manager of a minor league club in Albany, New York, where he later operated a sporting goods store and was superintendent of a municipal sports stadium. He died in Albany.

• A clipping file on Evers is at the National Baseball Library, Cooperstown, N.Y. Evers's memoir, *Touching Second* (1910), written with Hugh Fullerton, provides an invaluable colorful portrait of the early Chicago Cubs. He describes his participation in the "Merkle boner" play in John Carmichael, *My Greatest Day in Baseball* (1963). Peter Golenbock, *Wrigleyville* (1996), is an excellent history of the team. Warren Brown, *The Chicago Cubs* (1946), is useful but somewhat dated. For brief overviews of his career, see Donald Dewey and Nicholas Acocella, *The Biographical History of Baseball* (1995); and Lowell Reidenbaugh, *Cooperstown: Where Baseball's Legends Live Forever* (1983).

THOMAS W. COLLINS, JR.

F

FABER, John Eberhard (6 Dec. 1822–2 Mar. 1879), pencil manufacturer, was born in the town of Stein, Bavaria, near the city of Nuremberg, the son of Georg Leonhard Faber, a pencil manufacturer, and Albertina Frederika Kupfer Faber. The family pencil company, A. W. Faber, had been founded in Stein in 1761 by John Eberhard's great-grandfather Kaspar Faber and had become one of the most successful in Europe—so successful, in fact, that the very name "Faber" had come to be used as a generic term for pencil.

John Eberhard Faber grew up in a wealthy household, and as the youngest son he was encouraged by his father to pursue a career in law rather than going into the family business, whose ownership would pass to the eldest son following the father's death. After graduating from secondary school in Nuremberg, John Eberhard studied law at the universities of Heidelberg and Erlangen, but there he also pursued his deepening interest in classical literature and history, eventually becoming an expert in the field. Business attracted him even more than law or scholarship, however, and in 1849, in the wake of revolution and upheaval in western Europe, he immigrated to New York City and became an agent for his family's pencil company in Stein. He also began selling stationery and other business supplies imported from other companies in Germany and England.

As Faber's import business prospered, he turned his attention to providing wood for his own and other European pencil factories. He bought large tracts of cedar-forested land in Florida and initially harvested and shipped the logs abroad. After a few years he built a sawmill on one of the Cedar Keys, a group of small islands off the Gulf Coast of Florida, where he had the logs cut into segments suitable for pencil making before shipping them to Europe. Faber eventually decided that he could manufacture pencils more cheaply in the United States, rather than shipping the wood abroad. He would still have to import the leads, made of Bohemian clay and Austrian graphite, from the factory in Stein, but by assembling the finished product in New York he could avoid the high tariffs being imposed on his imported pencils.

In 1861 Faber opened a factory in New York City, soon after the Civil War began, and started manufacturing pencils under the name E. Faber. Initially he had difficulty in importing the necessary cedar wood because the South was now in Confederate hands. Through hard work, however, he slowly began producing his own pencils while continuing to import pencils from the family factory abroad, and after the Civil War ended in 1865 his pencil manufacturing business grew rapidly to become a leader in the field.

He suffered a brief setback in 1872, when his New York factory on the East River was destroyed by fire, but he built a larger factory in Brooklyn and continued to prosper. Part of his success was a consequence of his ingenuity: shortly after going into manufacturing in 1861 he perfected and patented an attached rubber eraser and also introduced and patented metal point protectors, using a nickel-plating process that he developed. He also expanded his business into other areas, establishing a factory in Newark, New Jersey, that manufactured rubber bands and separate erasers as well as penholders.

E. Faber had competitors from the outset and was not, as it claimed, "the oldest pencil factory in America"—several other companies, though much smaller in output, rightfully vied for that claim, including one started by Henry David Thoreau's father well before the Civil War. But it grew to become arguably the best-known pencil manufacturer in the United States, and its name became synonymous with quality. In 1904, to resolve a family dispute over use of the Faber name (two separate Faber companies, A. W. Faber and J. Faber, were now operating back in Stein and exporting their pencils to the United States), the American company E. Faber changed its named to the Eberhard Faber Pencil Company. Eberhard Faber pencils were manufactured in Brooklyn until 1956, when the factory there was closed and a new plant opened in Wilkes-Barre, Pennsylvania.

Faber married Jenny Haag of Munich during a trip home in 1854; the couple eventually had several children, including two sons who succeeded their father in running the pencil company. From the late 1860s onward Faber made his home on Staten Island, where he died.

• Biographical information on John Eberhard Faber, as well as a history of the company he started, can be found in *The Story of the Oldest Pencil Factory in America*, published by the Eberhard Faber Pencil Company in 1924. The definitive work to date on pencils, which includes an account of early pencil manufacturing in America, is *The Pencil: A History of Design and Circumstance* (Knopf, 1990) by Henry Petroski, a professor of civil engineering at Duke University. An obituary for Eberhard Faber is in the *New York Times*, 4 Mar. 1879.

ANN T. KEENE

FACTOR, Max, Jr. (18 Aug. 1904–7 June 1996), cosmetics inventor and businessman, was born Frank (some sources say Francis) Factor in St. Louis to Max Factor, Sr. (originally Faktor) of Poland and Esther Rosa Factor from Russia. Frank Factor was born after the family immigrated to America and settled in St. Louis in 1904. He later changed his name to Max Factor, Jr., upon his father's death in 1938.

In 1908 the family moved to Los Angeles and soon after Max Factor, Sr., started Max Factor & Company to create and sell wigs and makeup. The company immediately began providing makeup and hair goods for actors and actresses in Hollywood (clients included Charlie Chaplin and Buster Keaton). Factor, Jr., and his siblings worked in the family business from an early age, helping with deliveries, assisting behind the counter at the company store, and sometimes appearing in movies (particularly westerns made between 1913 and 1916). For *The Squaw Man* (1914), Factor, Sr., rented hairpieces and wigs made of human hair (a first in the industry) to director Cecil B. De Mille. The Factor boys, who worked as extras, also were responsible for retrieving all of the hairpieces following the mob scenes.

As he became more involved in the company, Factor, Jr., developed new formulas and application processes with his father. For the 1929 movie *Noah's Ark*, the Factors were faced with applying body makeup to over 2,000 extras. They decided to add a liquid solvent to the formula that could be sprayed onto the actors' bodies and faces, making application faster and more efficient. Perhaps their most revolutionary invention, however, was Pan-Cake makeup. Instigated by the development of Technicolor film, Pan-Cake came in flattering tones that would be lighter than greasepaint but extremely durable under the intense studio lights. Pan-Cake, so called because of its pan-like container and cake-like form, was applied with a sponge and provided a matte but flexible surface. Invented in 1937, Pan-Cake was applied to the entire cast of the movie *Vogues of 1938* (1937), the first film for which Max Factor received a screen credit for makeup. Highly praised by actors and actresses, Pan-Cake makeup became the formula of choice on Technicolor productions. During World War II, even the U.S. Marines turned to Factor for help with cosmetics, asking him to invent camouflage makeup for troops in the South Pacific.

After his father's death, Factor, Jr., became president of the company in 1938 and remained active on the business side as well as in the laboratories. Following the success of his makeup inventions in Hollywood, the company began marketing their products to American consumers. Utilizing the company's movie connections, Max Factor recruited celebrities to endorse its latest products, such as Pan-Cake makeup, Tru-Color lipstick (1940), and the automatic, refillable Mascara Wand (1958). Advertisements featuring Veronica Lake, Lana Turner, and Elizabeth Taylor suggested that any woman could look like a star with the right cosmetics. A typical slogan read "For that heavenly look of star-like loveliness . . . the one and only Pan-Cake Make-Up." The company sold its cosmetics at drugstores, thereby implying the endorsement of the local pharmacist in addition to the latest celebrity.

Actresses (and actors) such as Judy Garland and Rosalind Russell often tested new products such as Pan-Stik, a kind of cream makeup used in the movie *That Forsyte Woman* (1949). Factor also created special-effects cosmetics that were used in movies like *Frankenstein* (1931) and *Cyrano de Bergerac* (1950). In 1946 the company produced a special formula for black-and-white television, which at the time transmitted images in negative. After the arrival of color television in the mid-1950s, Factor invented a new line of makeup that flattered skin tones under the intense lights and sensitive cameras of this new medium. The company continued to provide high-quality hair goods and products to Hollywood until 1973, by which time synthetic materials had become cheaper to use than real human hair.

Prior to the 1940s the company conducted some business overseas, but following the war it began a worldwide expansion and by 1950 distributed products in over 100 countries on six continents. In 1961 the company acquired Parfumeri Internationale Corday. Nicknamed "the nose" for his acute sense of smell, Factor again sought celebrity spokespersons for his products, such as the actress and singer Joey Heatherton for Jet Perfume. Also in 1961 Max Factor was listed on the New York Stock Exchange. The company continued inventing new products throughout the 1960s and 1970s, including Sheer Genius liquid makeup (1960), Nail Satin nail polish (1961), and Ultra Lucent Waterproof makeup (1971). In the late 1960s, the third generation of Factors gained several top management positions in the company, and in 1973 they merged the firm with Norton Simon, Inc. Ron Perelman/Revlon acquired the merged company in 1986, and it was bought by Proctor & Gamble in 1991.

For his continuous contribution to the entertainment industry, Factor received the Distinguished Services Medallion from the Academy of Television Arts and Sciences in the mid-1950s. A star on Hollywood's "Walk of Fame" was dedicated to him and his father in 1969. The Max Factor Beauty Museum opened in 1984 in the old company headquarters on Hollywood Boulevard, featuring wigs, makeup, advertisements, photographs, and unusual inventions, such as the Beauty Calibrator (1932), which measured a person's facial features, and the Kissing Machine (1939), which tested lipstick durability with two sets of pressurized rubber lips. The museum closed in 1996, the same year that Factor died in West Los Angeles of heart failure.

Having retired from the company in 1973, Factor filled his last two decades with continued experimentation in the laboratories; he also became a racehorse owner and a philanthropist. Along with his family and company, Factor gave money to several causes, including Cedars-Sinai Hospital, the Devereaux Foundation of Santa Barbara, and UCLA. Factor had survived his wife Milly (maiden name unknown), whom he had married in the early 1930s and with whom he had two sons.

Although much of the family worked for the company, Factor and his father are in particular often credited with literally changing the female "face of America," and of the world, in the twentieth century. Continuously improving his company's products by adapting to new film and television technologies and responding to the beauty needs of the typical American woman, Factor, Jr. was instrumental in extending the world of cosmetics from Hollywood to the home, combining the glamour of the screen with practicality and affordability. Regarding his impact on the role of cosmetics in society, Factor once said, "It gives me a fine feeling to see all the beautiful women in the streets and to know that I had a part in making them beautiful" (*Time*, 23 Aug. 1954).

• Fred E. Basten with Robert Salvatore and Paul A. Kaufman, *Max Factor's Hollywood: Glamour, Movies, Makeup* (1995), provides a general overview of Factor, Sr., and Factor, Jr., as well as the development of the company. Jack Stuart Knapp, *The Technique of Stage Make-up* (1942), includes a short foreword written by Factor, Jr. Articles on the Factors and the company include "Make-Up Man," *Time*, 9 Dec. 1935; "Glamour for Sale," *Time*, 23 Aug. 1954; "Playing It Cozy," *Forbes*, 1 June 1968; "Women Are the Same the World Over," *Nation's Business*, Feb. 1972; and "The Max Factor in Mahoney's Life," *Business Week*, 18 Nov. 1972. Informative obituaries are in the *New York Times*, 14 July 1996; *The Economist*, 15 June 1996; and the *Los Angeles Times*, 9 June 1996.

N. ELIZABETH SCHLATTER

FADIMAN, Clifton (15 May 1904–20 June 1999), literary critic, anthologist, and radio personality, was born Clifton Paul Fadiman in Brooklyn, New York, the son of Russian-Jewish immigrants Isidore Michael Fadiman, a pharmacist, and Grace Elizabeth Fadiman (maiden name unknown), a nurse. Fadiman, who was known to friends and family as "Kip," began his lifelong passion for reading at age four, when he reportedly read his first book. By the time he was a teenager, he had read most or all of Sophocles, Dante, and Milton, among others. Fadiman later remembered that "by the end of high school I was not of course an educated man, but I knew how to try to become one" (quoted in Cross).

Fadiman was too young to enter college after graduation from Brooklyn Boys High School, so he worked for two years as a clerk before entering Columbia University. At Columbia his instructors included Mark Van Doren, and he numbered among his classmates Jacques Barzun, Mortimer Adler, and Whittaker Chambers, whom he advised to read *The Communist Manifesto*. Fadiman worked his way through school by writing book reviews for the *Nation*; lecturing, beginning in 1923, at the People's Institute; and, as he later told his daughter, by breaking in smoking pipes for the more prosperous students. Becoming something of a legend in Columbia's English department, he was hired by the Modern Library to translate Friedrich Nietzsche's *Ecce Homo* and *The Birth of*

Tragedy (*Die Geburt der Tragödie*) while still an undergraduate.

After graduating Phi Beta Kappa in 1925, Fadiman began teaching at the Ethical Culture High School (now known as Fieldston) in the Bronx. Two years later, after working with William Drake on an English translation of Franz Werfel's *The Man Who Conquered Death* (*Der Tod des Kleinbürgers*; 1927), he joined Simon and Schuster as manuscript reader and assistant editor. Promoted to general editor in 1929, he is said to have interviewed more than 2,000 authors and reviewed more than 25,000 book manuscripts while with the publisher. Having for years written book reviews for the *Nation*, *Stage*, and *Harper's Bazaar*, Fadiman became well known in literary circles for his refined, erudite opinions and in 1933 became book reviewer for the weekly *New Yorker*, where he remained for ten years. In 1927 he married Pauline Elizabeth Rush; they had one son together.

In 1935 Fadiman resigned his position at Simon and Schuster, and three years later he became moderator for NBC radio's quiz show program "Information, Please!" which featured questions submitted by listeners in an attempt to outwit a panel of experts. The winners fittingly were awarded sets of the *Encyclopaedia Britannica*. The show was enormously successful, reaching more than nine million listeners by 1942. Although taken off the airwaves in 1948, "Information, Please!" was briefly resurrected for television in the 1950s, with Fadiman as host. Throughout the 1940s and 1950s he was a familiar figure on television and radio, serving as host of a variety of programs, including "Keep 'Em Rolling," "This Is Show Business," "What's in a Word?" and "Conversation."

In 1944, the year after he left the *New Yorker*, Fadiman joined the board of judges for the Book-of-the-Month Club (BOMC), a position he held for the remainder of his life and which arguably brought him the greatest recognition. Through the club, he was able to influence the reading habits of millions of Americans. BOMC, which continues to reach a wide audience with its direct mail campaigns, brought literature and popular fiction to members' homes. But not everyone extolled its benefits. Believing that BOMC contributed to the dumbing down of American readers, Dwight Macdonald accused it of "supplying its readers with reading matter of which the best that can be said is that it could be worse" (quoted in the *Wall Street Journal*, 2 July 1999).

A master anthologist, Fadiman published more than twenty essay and story collections, on subjects ranging from anecdotes to mathematics to children's literature, an early example being *I Believe: The Personal Philosophies of Certain Eminent Men and Women of Our Time* (1939). *I Believe* was followed two years later by *Reading I've Liked: A Personal Selection Drawn from Two Decades of Reading and Reviewing*, a precursor to his *Lifetime Reading Plan*, first published in 1960 and updated in 1978, 1988, and 1997. Fadiman described *The Lifetime Reading Plan* as "not for the highly educated or even (not always the same thing)

---

the very well read" (3d ed., p. 2); it presents tips for reading the works Fadiman judged essential to understanding Western civilization. Immensely popular, the work has remained in print for more than forty years.

Many readers became acquainted with Fadiman through the introductions he wrote to classic works for the Modern Library and for other publishers, including the 1942 edition of Tolstoy's *War and Peace*. A member of the board of the *Encyclopeadia Britannica*, he claimed to have read or skimmed every edition of the encyclopedia's 200-year history, which resulted in the 700-page *Treasury of the "Encyclopaedia Britannica"* in 1992.

Fadiman and Pauline Rush divorced in 1949, and the following year he married writer Annalee Whitmore Jacoby. They had two children, both of whom became avid readers. His daughter, Anne Fadiman, became editor of the Phi Beta Kappa quarterly *American Scholar* and published a collection of essays concerning her bibliophilism as *Ex Libris* (1998). In the book she remembers as a toddler building castles from her father's 22-volume pocket edition of Trollope and participatory family viewing of the television quiz show "G.E. College Bowl" (a kind of "Information, Please!" for college students), noting that "Fadiman U." over the years "lost only to Brandeis and Colorado College" (*Ex Libris*, p. 15).

At the age of eighty-eight Fadiman lost his eyesight, the result of acute retinal necrosis. Although at first he believed he was "finished" (*Ex Libris*, p. 34), he learned to improvise. With the help of his son, who recorded books on tape for him, and his secretary, who transcribed his thoughts, he was able to continue evaluating books for the BOMC until the last year of his life. Fadiman died on Sanibel Island, Florida.

In his 1960 essay "Masscult & Midcult," Dwight Macdonald denounced Fadiman for his role as purveyor of all things intellectual, charging him with promoting "midcult," which the critic said "pretends to respect the standards of High Culture but waters them down and vulgarizes them" (quoted in the *Wall Street Journal*, 2 July 1999). The time during which Fadiman thrived has passed, however, and Eric Gibson, writing in the *Wall Street Journal*, is probably right when he says that Fadiman "would today be labeled an elitist" (2 July 1999). Fadiman, who confessed that he was "not a profound thinker" (*New York Times*, 21 June 1999), believed himself instead to be "a guide to the wisdom of others" (quoted in Cross). After Fadiman's death National Public Radio's "All Things Considered" program praised him as someone who "took joy in bringing ideas to a broad audience" (quoted in Cross).

• The Library of Congress lists sixty-nine books that Fadiman wrote, edited, or contributed to. For the history and influence of BOMC, see Janice A. Radway, *A Feeling for Books: The Book-of-the-Month Club, Literary Taste, and Middle-Class Desire* (1997). Eric Gibson's *Wall Street Journal* article is in the 2 July 1999 edition. An article on Fadiman is in the *New York Times Magazine*, 2 Jan. 2000. An obituary is in the *New York Times*, 21 June 1999.

STACEY HAMILTON

FAIRBANKS, Douglas, Jr. (9 Dec. 1909–7 May 2000), actor, was born Douglas Elton Fairbanks, Jr., in New York, the only child of Douglas Fairbanks, an actor, and Anna Beth Sully Fairbanks. At first because of the demands of his father's career and after his parents' 1918 divorce because of his mother's international lifestyle, Fairbanks never stayed in one school longer than two years, his time largely divided between New York and Hollywood (he completed eighth grade at Pasadena Polytechnic); later he was privately tutored in Paris.

It took Fairbanks decades to escape his father's shadow, and his "decision" to enter motion-picture acting was clearly an attempt, engineered by his financially strapped mother, to cash in on the elder Fairbanks's unsurpassed popularity. (Fairbanks Sr., emotionally remote, strongly opposed the decision and cut off financial support.) Although *Stephen StepsOut* (1923), a boy's adventures in the Orient, was not a success, young Fairbanks stayed on in Hollywood, writing titles, learning to run a camera and occasionally appearing on stage. Between 1925 and 1928, already tall and pencil-mustached, Fairbanks appeared in fifteen films, notably as the young society heir in *Stella Dallas* (1925) and, fourth-billed, as Greta Garbo's younger brother in *A Woman of Affairs* (1928).

In 1929 Fairbanks married actress Joan Crawford, a 1927 co-player in *Women Love Diamonds*. They had no children and were divorced in 1934. Fairbanks gained critical stature as a World War I pilot in *The Dawn Patrol* (1930) and as a hit man in *Little Caesar* (1931). He was the love interest of Katharine Hepburn's character in *Morning Glory*, the actress's 1933 film debut and the source of her first Academy Award.

Fairbanks's internationalist future became clearer after a brief return to Europe in the early 1930s, when he was swept up by friends of his father such as Noël Coward. In 1934 he appeared opposite Elisabeth Bergener as the future Czar Peter III in Alexander Korda's British film *Catherine the Great*. Staying on in London, he appeared on stage opposite his amour, Gertrude Lawrence, in two plays and, in 1936, an unsuccessful, nonmusical film adaptation of *La Bohème* called *Mimi*. An affair with Marlene Dietrich followed. An early attempt at his own production company, Criterion Films Ltd. was abandoned after three films, one of which, *The Amateur Gentleman*, was called the most opulent of its era.

Summoned to Hollywood in 1937 by producer David O. Selznick, Fairbanks embarked on the most successful years of his film career. Playing a villainous, dueling opponent of Ronald Colman's character in *The Prisoner of Zenda* (1937) and a rollicking soldier on India's Northwest Frontier in *Gunga Din* (1939) rescued Fairbanks from drawing-room roles. The elder Fairbanks died in 1939, the year of young Doug's marriage to Mary Lee Hartford. They had three children and remained married until her death in 1988. In *The Corsican Brothers* (1941) Fairbanks gave his most swashbuckling performance, as well as participating in one of the screen's longest duels—more than three minutes in a single take. By the time that film was released, Fairbanks, active between 1939 and 1941 in organizations supporting the Allies, had been commissioned a lieutenant junior grade in the U.S. Navy Reserve. Following a fact-finding "mission" to South America personally authorized by President Franklin Roosevelt, Fairbanks went on active duty (a biographer later suggested that Fairbanks, whose personal contacts seemed endless, could have been a diplomat).

Fairbanks's World War II exploits, often as part of international task forces, ranged from the mundane to the tragicomic to the heroic—from commanding a minesweeper off Staten Island to taking part in the war's worst convoy disaster (in which two-thirds of the merchant ships bound for Murmansk were lost in the North Sea) to landing troops on the coasts of Sicily and Italy, commanding armed reconnaissances near Capri, and, as part of Operation Anvil, landing the first invading French troops to return to France. Amid all of this, he was never long out of touch with his friends on both sides of the Atlantic. He even submitted a plan for ending the Japanese war based on exercising diplomatic efforts among his personal contacts. Among his awards were the American Silver Star, the French Chevalier Légion d'Honneur and the Distinguished Service Cross from the Royal Navy. At the end of the war he was a commander and retired as a captain.

From 1946 onward Fairbanks was involved in a number of organizations supporting the United Nations and facilitating war relief in countries including China and Korea, where, of course, he had personal contacts. He undertook several missions in connection with the Marshall Plan. His years with the Co-Operative for American Remittances to Europe (CARE) helped get $150 million in food packages abroad. For "furthering Anglo-American amity" Fairbanks received an honorary knighthood of the British Empire in 1949. His semidiplomatic years apparently ended with the Truman administration.

Fairbanks resumed his Hollywood film career with *Sinbad the Sailor*, a 1947 film highly evocative of his father's *The Black Pirate*; the droll comedy *That Lady in Ermine* (1948); and, as an Irish musketeer, *The Fighting O'Flynn* (1949). Back in England in 1949, he appeared once more for Korda in *State Secret* (U.K., 1950). In 1952 Fairbanks declared his retirement from motion picture acting and moved his family to London, where, though denying that he was a socialite, he was quickly accepted into the highest levels of society, including royalty. He formed another production company, creating television films largely aimed at the United States, and often appearing as the host of televised anthologies. One of these, the "Rheingold

Theatre," won a *Billboard* magazine award in 1954, while a 1960s series, "Douglas Fairbanks Presents," ran for many years. His part in a 1963 aristocratic divorce scandal was alleged in 1992, though he denied it for the rest of his life.

The Fairbanks family moved to Palm Beach, Florida, in 1973. In 1975 he edited (with Richard Schickel) *The Fairbanks Album*, a sourcebook on the life of his father, the rights to whose films he now possessed. He went on to write occasional poetry and volumes of autobiography, notably *Salad Days* (1988) and *A Hell of a War* (1995). In his later years, Fairbanks manufactured popcorn and ballpoint pens, developed land and returned regularly to the stage, notably as the urbane Professor Henry Higgins in touring productions of *My Fair Lady* well into the 1980s. In 1976 he returned to London as a witty globetrotter in *The Pleasure of His Company*. By now one of the screen's most recognizable faces, the benign image of comic aristocracy, he played frequent small roles in American television series. His last film was the made-for-television *Ghost Story* (1981). Fairbanks married Vera Shelton in 1990; they remained married until his death.

Although he lived sixty years beyond his father's death and his father's identity faded from general memory, Douglas Fairbanks, Jr., was never known simply as Douglas Fairbanks. This did not finally seem to trouble him, nor did the fact that during the last half of his life most Americans believed he was a British gentleman. It would be unsurprising if documents someday revealed further amateur diplomatism. Or maybe not.

• Fairbanks's own autobiographical works are readable and detailed. He is glimpsed in various memoirs and histories, including Sheridan Morley, *Tales from the Hollywood Raj* (1983). Brian Connell's *Knight Errant* is a sympathetic biography. Excellent obituaries include those by Ronald Bergan in the *Guardian* (U.K.) and Myrna Oliver in the *Los Angeles Times*, both 8 May 2000.

JAMES ROSS MOORE

FARMER, James (12 Jan. 1920–9 July 1999), founder and national director of the Congress of Racial Equality (CORE), civil rights activist, and educator, was born James Leonard Farmer, Jr., in Marshall, Texas, the son of James Leonard Farmer (known as "J. Leonard"), a Methodist minister and the son of ex-slaves, and Pearl Houston Farmer, who had been a teacher. Farmer's father, who earned a doctorate of religion from Boston University, was one of the first blacks in Texas to hold a Ph.D. When Farmer was six months old the family, which included an older sister, moved to Holly Springs, Mississippi, where his father had accepted teaching and administrative posts at Rust College. Able to read, write, and count by the age of four and a half, Farmer was accepted into the first grade. The family soon moved again, as Professor Farmer joined the department of religion and philosophy at Samuel Houston College in Austin, Texas.

Farmer's outstanding academic and oratorical skills won him a four-year scholarship, and at the age of fourteen he entered Wiley College in Marshall. He was fortunate in his mentor, the poet Melvin B. Tolson. Farmer was captain of the debating team and president of his fraternity. After his graduation in 1938, he enrolled at Howard University in Washington, D.C., to study for the ministry. Among others, the staff at Howard included Sterling Brown, Ralph Bunche, Carter G. Woodson, Benjamin Mays, and, most notably, Howard Thurman. Poet, philosopher, and preacher, Thurman introduced Farmer to Mohandas K. Gandhi's philosophy on the use of nonviolence to effect social change. At this time Farmer became the part-time student secretary for the Fellowship of Reconciliation (FOR), a Quaker pacifist organization.

During his years at Howard's School of Religion, Farmer focused on the interrelatedness of religion, economics, and race, and he wrote his master's thesis on this theme. As a result of his studies, Farmer decided not to be ordained, as the racial segregation in all denominations was repugnant to him. Close to graduation in 1941 when his father asked him what he then planned to do, he replied, "Destroy segregation." Asked how, Farmer told him it would involve mass mobilization and the use of Gandhi's principles.

Farmer began the grand mission of his life by continuing to work at FOR, first in Chicago, giving antiwar speeches there and in other midwestern cities. In Chicago he used Gandhi's technique for the first time to integrate a coffee shop where Farmer and a friend had been refused service. With added insult, they had been asked to pay $1 for a nickel doughnut and had had their money thrown to the floor. In May 1942 they returned with a group of twenty-eight others and staged a sit-in that succeeded.

At this time, under the auspices of FOR, Farmer cofounded CORE (Committee of Racial Equality). The acronym came before the name, to indicate its purpose: that racial equality is the core of a just society. In little over a year CORE had chapters in New York, Philadelphia, Detroit, Seattle, and Los Angeles. Its appeal was broad because CORE had always stressed its interracial aspect, mirroring the belief that the "race problem" concerned all Americans, black and white. At its second annual convention in 1944, "Committee" became "Congress," reflecting its rapid growth. Peak membership came in the 1960s when CORE had 82,000 members in 114 chapters. But Farmer described their efforts during the 1940s at integrating housing, banks, amusement parks, and barber shops as "a flea gnawing on the ear of an elephant" (*Lay Bare the Heart*, p. 153), for the lack of publicity CORE received.

In 1945 Farmer worked as a union organizer for furniture workers in the South. He also recruited college students for the League for Industrial Democracy, a socialist organization; organized and led strikes

for the New York arm of AFSCME (American Federation of State, County, and Municipal Employees); continued to participate in CORE's activities; and became program director for the National Association for the Advancement of Colored People (NAACP), under the leadership of Roy Wilkins. In 1945 Farmer married Winnie Christie; they had no children and divorced the following year. In 1949 he married Lula Peterson; they had two daughters.

In February 1961 Farmer took the helm of CORE, the organization he had founded, as its first national director. "The dream that made our hearts beat since 1942 was in 1960 a reality," Farmer recalled in his autobiography. The Montgomery Bus Boycott of 1956 had been successful, and a lunch counter sit-in, which four students in Greensboro, North Carolina, staged on 1 February 1960, soon became the catalyst for the formation of the national Student Non-Violent Coordinating Committee (SNCC).

In May 1961 Farmer launched the Freedom Rides to the South to end desegregation in interstate transportation and in station waiting rooms. A participant as well as CORE's director, Farmer faced terrifying episodes, and he was in a Louisiana jail on the day of the March on Washington in 1963. The demands for civil rights were answered with bus and church burnings and beatings by mobs and police. The violence escalated into the murders of CORE members James Chaney, Andrew Goodman, and Michael Schwerner in Mississippi in 1964. Such violence, coming a year after the Birmingham church bombing, in which four young girls died, and the murder of Medgar Evers, motivated civil rights workers to challenge the idea of nonviolence, as well as the large role played by whites within CORE. The preference for more confrontational action undermined Farmer's tenure, and he resigned in 1966.

Farmer then taught at Lincoln University in Pennsylvania and at New York University. In 1968 he ran for a Brooklyn congressional seat but lost to Shirley Chisholm. President Richard Nixon appointed Farmer assistant secretary in the Department of Health, Education, and Welfare in April 1969. "Chaf[ing] in the ponderous bureaucracy and long[ing] for my old role as advocate, critic, activist," Farmer resigned in December 1970. During the 1970s he worked with the Council on Minority Planning and Strategy, a think tank, and with organizations of public employees that made mortgage loans for integrated housing.

In 1985, despite failing eyesight, Farmer completed and published his autobiography, *Lay Bare the Heart*. He then taught history at Mary Washington College in Fredericksburg, Virginia, where he died.

To an enormous degree, James Farmer accomplished the goal he set for himself at the age of twenty-one, to "destroy segregation." His vision and energy challenged the social status quo and eliminated many injustices in American life. As Farmer summed up, "In movement days . . . the grasping at liberty . . . ennobled life for this nation" (*Lay Bare the Heart*, p. 351).

• The James Farmer Papers are at the Center for American History at the University of Texas at Austin, comprising forty-three feet. Tapes relating to his run for Congress in 1968 are held at the Schomburg Center for Research in Black Culture, New York Public Library. Farmer's *Lay Bare the Heart* (1985) is an exceptionally gripping and frank autobiography. Jeff Sklansky, *James Farmer: Civil Rights Leader* (1992), provides a skillfully condensed biography. For a description of Farmer's teaching life, see Michelle NK Collison, "One of the 'Big Four,' a Civil Rights Leader Keeps History Alive," *Chronicle of Higher Education*, 22 Feb. 1989, p. A3. Obituaries are in the *New York Times*, 10 July 1999, and *Jet*, 26 July 1999.

BETTY KAPLAN GUBERT

FAYE, Alice (5 May 1915–9 May 1998), singing actress, was born Alice Jeanne Leppert in New York to Charley Leppert, a policeman, and his wife Alice Moffat Leppert. Educated in New York schools and lying about her age, she began her professional career in 1928 as a dancer for the Chester Hale Troupe and the night-club entrepreneur Nils Thor Granlund. Faye (who legally changed her name in 1935) was a chorine in the eleventh *George White Scandals* (1931), when one of its stars, the singing bandleader Rudy Vallee, signed her to tour with his band, introducing her to radio in late 1932 on his "Fleischmann Hour," at the time America's most popular variety program.

Her connection with Vallee continued for several years, including in her 1934 film debut in the Fox Studios' *George White's Scandals*, in which she emerged as a sultry, deep-voiced blonde singer with an arrestingly straightforward face characterized by glistening eyelids and a snub nose. The songs she introduced became permanently identified with her. These included Ted Koehler and Jimmy McHugh's "I'm Shooting High" in *King of Burlesque* (1935) and, after the merger of Fox with Darryl Zanuck's Twentieth Century, "Goodnight, My Love" (by the studio's staff writers, Mack Gordon and Harry Revel) in *Stowaway* (1936), nominally a showcase for Fox's major star, Shirley Temple.

Faye eventually occupied a unique niche in American show business, a quality recognized in the title of a television documentary late in her life: "The Star Next Door." One of the best-loved stars of a golden age in American musical film, she also helped define a genre of radio situation comedy and embodied a particular brand of independence.

As a contract player during an era of unfettered studio power, Faye averaged five films per year. In 1936, the year she made *Sing, Baby, Sing*, a tale of radio, and *Poor Little Rich Girl*, again with Shirley Temple, Faye married singer Tony Martin, a frequent costar; their childless marriage ended in 1940.

Several 1937 films established Faye as Fox's top musical star, including *Wake Up and Live* and *You Can't Have Everything* (both with songs by Gordon and Revel) and *On The Avenue*, another contempo-

rary show-business story with an original score by Irving Berlin, who called her the best female singer in Hollywood. That same year Zanuck gave her the lead in *In Old Chicago*, a show-business story wrapped around the 1871 Chicago fire; nominated for a Best Picture Academy Award, it marked a divide in Faye's career. *Alexander's Ragtime Band* (1938), based on Berlin's life, also won a Best Picture nomination. In these films, lavishly dressed by such glamour-conscious designers as Travis Banton, Faye had become the usually good-hearted (but not always rewarded) and undeniably classy heroine of films recalling those "good old days." One critic called her a "luscious marshmallow sundae of a girl."

The string included *Sally, Irene and Mary* (1938), the film version of a 1923 Cinderella musical comedy, and *Rose of Washington Square* (1939), largely based on the 1910–1925 phase of Fanny Brice's stage career. In 1939 Faye was named the leading female box office star of the year by the Association of Motion Picture Distributors. At that time, the same association voiced its alarmed disapproval of the rising popularity of "radio theater" versions of musical films emanating from Hollywood--where most stars now lived. Metro-Goldwyn-Mayer canceled its radio show, and Zanuck quickly bought up the radio contracts of Faye, Tyrone Power, and other Fox stars.

Faye's "good old days" continued with *Lillian Russell* (1940), which fictionalized the career of the tempestuous 1880s vaudeville star Lillian Russell, and *Tin Pan Alley* (1940), with an Academy Award-winning score by Alfred Newman, which evoked the 1915–1935 era of popular song. The latter film also marked the Twentieth Century–Fox debut of the sassy Betty Grable, destined for fame as a World War II "pin-up girl." Faye was gradually shifted to "modern" escapist musicals. In two 1941 films, *That Night in Rio* and *Weekend in Havana*, Faye competed with the clamorous "Brazilian Bombshell," Carmen Miranda, but once more in a movie evoking the past, *Hello, Frisco, Hello* (1943), she sang Mack Gordon and Harry Warren's Academy Award-winning song, "You'll Never Know."

In 1941 Faye married Phil Harris, a bandleader and growling singer of novelty songs. (They had two daughters, and their marriage lasted until Harris's death in 1995.) *The Gang's All Here* (1943), with songs by Warren and Leo Robin, produced two major recorded hits sung by Faye: "A Journey to a Star" and "No Love, No Nothing." Following the birth of her first child, Faye had a cameo appearance in *Four Jills in a Jeep* (1944), about entertaining troops overseas, and she made a number of broadcasts for the Armed Forces Radio Service. Faye was cast in a highly dramatic role in *Fallen Angel* (1945), but it was edited harshly in order to highlight the film's leading lady, Linda Darnell. Faye quit, later writing, "I didn't even go to my dressing room to collect my personal belongings. I couldn't see anything coming for me but the same old dumb things."

On radio, Phil Harris had developed a popular character as the wise-cracking bandleader on "The Jack Benny Show." In 1946 Harris and Faye became the stars of "The Fitch Bandwagon," a long-running variety show adjacent to Jack Benny's Sunday night slot. The new comic format, based on their everyday lives and mainly written by Ward Byron, cast Harris as a bandleader and Faye as his (nonsinging) wife. In 1948 it was renamed "The Alice Faye and Phil Harris Show," continuing for nearly 300 broadcasts, and ending in 1954.

As a radio character, Faye, her fluty voice ideally complementing Harris's rasp, was the no-nonsense, tolerant but sharply humorous anchor of a company of "characters," including a drunken guitarist played by Elliott Lewis and one of Arthur Q. Bryan's lisping zanies. Although not the first of its genre—"The Adventures of Ozzie and Harriet" began in 1944—the show rarely stooped to the level of "dumb dad, long-suffering mom."

The situation on the radio show was very close to the real life Faye had made for herself with Harris. She wrote of her postmovie days, "I equated independence with seeing daylight during the week and learning how to drive a car." Later, Aljean Harmetz wrote of her "attitude of taking life as it came." Faye made few professional appearances after the end of the series until 1962, when she played Pat Boone's mother—singing one song—in the remake of the film *State Fair*. In 1973 she made a national tour in a stage revival of *Good News* (music and lyrics by B. G. DeSylva, Lew Brown, and Ray Henderson) alongside John Payne, a frequent costar in the Fox days.

Faye and Harris were honored with stars in the Walk of Fame of their hometown, Palm Springs, California. In 1984 Faye became a spokesperson for the Pfizer pharmaceutical company, urging "young elders" to live a healthy lifestyle. Along these lines, in 1990 she published (with Dick Kleiner) *Growing Older, Staying Young*. Faye died in Rancho Mirage, California.

• For details of Faye's life and work, see Barry Rivadue, *Alice Faye: A Bio-bibliography* (1990). Her films are well described in Clive Hirschhorn, *The Hollywood Musical* (1981). Valuable LP liner notes by Miles Kreuger are on Cameo CBS 32316, *Alice Faye in Hollywood: 1934–1937*. The Faye-Harris radio show is noted in Frank Buxton and Bill Owen, *The Big Broadcast, 1920–1950* (1972). Useful information is found in Michael Pitts and James Robert Parish, *Hollywood Songsters* (1991). Harmetz's obituary of Faye is in the *New York Times*, 10 May 1998; Ronald Bergan's is in the (London) *Guardian*, the same date.

JAMES ROSS MOORE

FEININGER, Andreas (27 Dec. 1906–18 Feb. 1999), photographer, was born Andreas Bernhard Lyonel Feininger in Paris, France, the son of American painter Lyonel Feininger and Julie Lilienfeld Berg. In 1925 Feininger received a diploma in cabinetmaking from the Bauhaus in Weimar, Germany, where his father taught. He graduated with a degree in architec-ture in 1928 from the Bauschule in Zerbst, Germany, and subsequently held several architectural positions throughout Europe, including one in Paris assisting Le Corbusier between 1932 and 1933. In 1933 Feininger and his future wife, Gertrud Wysse Hägg, moved to Stockholm, Sweden, where he worked as an architectural photographer. They married later that year and had one son, named Tomas, who was born in 1935.

In the mid-1920s Feininger taught himself the basic techniques of photography. His subjects included his car, the female form, and objects from nature, such as dandelion seeds and feathers. He explored solarization, reticulation, and bas-relief printing methods. In Stockholm, Feininger built a telephoto camera and photographed the city, particularly scenes of boats entering or docked in the harbors. His images from this period show the hallmarks of his style: emphasis on pattern and line, compressed space, powerful compositions, and monumentalized subject matter. In his close-ups of ears of corn and of leaves, he studied the geometric patterns of natural forms. During the 1930s Feininger wrote about his techniques for the magazine *Foto-Beobachter*. He also published his first book, *Menschen vor der Kamera* (1934), on how to photograph people, and the picture book *Stockholm* (1936).

In 1939 Feininger moved to New York City and quickly acquired work with the Black Star Agency. He photographed a variety of subjects for the agency, from the unemployed to automobiles to artists. He wrote of his Black Star experience, "It was the hardest possible school for any young photographer—a sink or swim proposition—but I learned fast and by the end of that year, there was nothing I couldn't photograph and photograph well." In 1942 he completed for the U.S. Office of War Information a series on the production efforts on the home front, particularly in factories, oil fields, and mines.

Life magazine hired Feininger as a staff photographer in 1943. During his twenty years at *Life*, he completed 346 assignments, the majority in black-and-white. For one of his favorite subjects, New York City, Feininger used a super-telephoto camera that he built himself to capture the city's density and dynamism in images such as the pedestrian- and car-clogged photograph "Traffic on Fifth Avenue" (1950). His image of Coney Island on Independence Day (1949) similarly flattens out the long expanse of shoreline packed with men, women, and children, who visually merge into one giant human mass.

Feininger originated many of his *Life* essay topics, including the series "Man-made Landscape" (5 June 1948), which showed major constructions that altered the countryside, such as highways, oil fields, and dams. For "Occupational Faces—Speaking of Pictures" (27 June 1955), Feininger included a striking 1951 photograph of photojournalist Dennis Stock holding his camera on its side in front of his face, so that the camera's viewfinder, which is round and relatively large, and the lens become in effect his eyes.

Feininger continued his unique nature studies in "Insect Engineers" (29 Aug. 1949), "Pest Portraits" (20 Mar. 1950), and "Bones" (6 Oct. 1952). In regard to his natural subject matter, he said, "I am awed by the degree of perfection of their structural elements relative to their functions, and moved by the exquisite beauty of many of their forms." He usually photographed his subjects in extreme close-ups viewed from below against monotone backgrounds, sometimes rendering the subject unrecognizable in favor of a compelling composition.

While at *Life* and after he left the magazine in 1962, Feininger published more than thirty books. Many of his picture books expanded on themes he explored at *Life*, including *New York* (1945), *Changing America: The Land As It Was and How Man Has Changed It* (1955), and *Feininger's Chicago, 1941* (1980). Additional picture books include *Maids, Madonnas, and Witches* (1961), with text by Henry Miller; *Trees* (1968); and *Shells* (1972). In his technical books, such as *Feininger on Photography* (1949), *Photographic Seeing* (1973), and *Andreas Feininger: Experimental Work* (1978), he stresses how the eye and the camera "see" differently; realizing these differences would help the photographer create a unique image rather than just a technically sufficient one. Feininger was a columnist for *Modern Photography* magazine from 1957 to 1972, and in 1972 he taught a course on photocommunication at New York University.

Throughout his career Feininger participated in several exhibitions, including the Museum of Modern Art's "In and Out of Focus" (1948) and "The Family of Man" (1955). His solo shows include a traveling exhibition, "The Anatomy of Nature," organized by the American Museum of Natural History (1957), "The World through My Eyes" at the Smithsonian Institution (1963), and a traveling retrospective organized by the International Center for Photography (1976). In 1965 he won a Gold Medal Award from the Art Directors Club of Metropolitan Washington, and in 1966 he received a Robert Leavitt Award from the American Society of Magazine Photographers. He died at age ninety-two in New York.

Feininger's oeuvre captured the specifics of his era—the photos of Manhattan in the 1940s and 1950s, for example—and reflected timeless form in studies such as his series on bones and shells. Inherent to his images is an appreciation for good design, both natural and man-made, which reveals his Bauhaus and architectural training. In his *Nature in Miniature* (1989), he wrote, "Photography allows me to communicate with anyone regardless of differences of alphabets, letters, or speech." With his camera as his "tool," Feininger explored photography as a "universal language" of the twentieth century.

• The Center for Creative Photography at the University of Arizona has the primary archive of Feininger's papers, prints, and negatives. The George Eastman House in Rochester, New York, has an extensive collection of Feininger's prints from 1928 to 1977. His autobiography, *Andreas Feininger: Photographer* (1986), provides biographical and stylistic information in addition to large reproductions of his work and a list of his favorite *Life* essays. In addition to the publications mentioned above, some of his notable books include *The Face of New York* (1954), *The Anatomy of Nature* (1956), *Successful Color Photography* (1954), *The World through My Eyes: 30 Years of Photography* (1963), *The Complete Photographer* (1965), *Forms of Nature and Life* (1966), and *Nature in Miniature* (1989). Feininger and his brother T. Lux Feininger collaborated on *Lyonel Feininger: City at the Edge of the World* (1965), a book about toys made by their father. Interviews of Feininger appear in Miriam Berkley, "The Quiet Man," *American Photographer*, Mar. 1987, pp. 50–58, Franklin Cameron, "Meet the Masters," *Petersen's Photographic*, Mar. 1987, pp. 38–40, and "Relativity," *Petersen's Photographic*, Oct. 1988, pp. 26–30. An obituary is in the *New York Times*, 20 Feb. 1999.

N. ELIZABETH SCHLATTER

FELDMAN, Morton (12 Jan. 1926–3 Sept. 1987), composer, was born in Brooklyn, New York. (His parents' names are not known; nor is there readily available information about how they made a living.) As a small child, Feldman was introduced to music by his mother, who helped him pick out traditional Jewish songs on the piano, and he was soon taking piano lessons; he wrote his first compositions at the age of eight. After attending public primary and secondary schools, he studied composition privately in New York with composers Wallingford Riegger and Stefan Wolpe. During his early years, Feldman had been especially drawn to the music of Edgard Varèse and Anton Webern, but the composer who was to have the greatest influence on him was John Cage, whom he met at a Carnegie Hall concert in 1949. Through Cage he became part of the social and intellectual circle of the so-called New York school of abstract expressionist painters then flourishing in Manhattan.

In an interview published in the *New York Times* several years before his death, Feldman clarified his artistic relationship to Cage as well as to abstract expressionism. Cage, the quintessentially "cool" composer whose scores seemed to reflect the dispassionate personality of Cage himself, had not provided him with a compositional template, Feldman said. He had done something better, in Feldman's view: he had given Feldman "a green light," conferring upon him permission to follow whatever creative urge possessed him. Although Feldman's music was as spare as that of Cage, and the two men, like Cage associates Earle Brown, Christian Wolff, and David Tudor, wrote music that is often lumped together as "minimalist," Feldman himself rejected that term. Indeed, Feldman's was a unique compositional voice in American music, and though he refused to define himself as part of any school or movement, he did not seem to object to music critic John Rockwell's characterization of him as "an old-fashioned post-Cageian avant-gardist." In contrast to the spareness of his music, his personal life expressed an exuberance for life and its pleasures. Often described as "Rabelaisian," Feldman seemed the antithesis of Cage, but the men remained friends and part of the same artistic circle for many years.

As for the influence of abstract expressionism on Feldman's work, it came, like Cage's, in the form of a "permission" to do things differently. In particular, it was painter Philip Guston, Feldman said, who showed him that he did not have to obey any established style or "historical vested interest." He could shape sound in as many ways as a painter was free to shape paint, and "plasticity" and "clarity" became his musical goals. In his studio in lower Manhattan, Feldman turned out his earliest works surrounded by Guston's paintings, as well as canvases by other abstract expressionists, including Franz Kline, Robert Rauschenberg, and Jackson Pollock.

Feldman's attempt to compose abstract musical paintings led him to devise several new forms of notation. The earliest was so-called graph notation, which he used in his first major work, *Projections* (1950–1951). Feldman's score for this series of integrated compositions for mixed ensemble did not specify pitches and rhythms; instead he identified a broad range for each instrument—upper, middle, or lower—and used different-sized rectangles and numerals to indicate the duration and number of notes to be played, almost always ranging from *piano* to *pianissimo*. He used graphic notation in other early works, including *Extensions III*, in 1952, but then abandoned it briefly to return for several years to conventional notation.

Soon dissatisfied because such notation restricted him, Feldman began creating other notational forms. His so-called free-rhythm notation was used in several compositions, including *Piano (Three Hands)*, written in 1957, in which chords are struck in succession to a slow tempo and are allowed to recede of their own accord. Another form of notation devised by Feldman and used in his composition *Piece for Four Pianos* (1957) gave players identical parts and requested only that they create "a series of reverberations." Feldman also began combining different forms of notation in a single work. By the early 1960s, in such compositions as *Durations* (1960–1961), he was using "race-course" notation, in which he notated each instrument's individual part conventionally but did not specify duration and coordination of parts. After nearly two decades of experimenting, however, Feldman had gradually returned to conventional notation by the late 1960s. Yet throughout his adult composing career, he created works with a hushed, quiet sound that became his trademark.

The titles of Feldman's compositions were often dedications to his friends, such as the ensemble pieces *De Kooning* (1963), which paid tribute to painter Willem de Kooning, and *For John Cage* (1982). Sometimes his titles are comments on personal experience, like *The Viola in My Life* (1970–1971). In addition to ensemble works, he wrote pieces for voice and chorus, usually using texts by writers that he knew, among them the poet Frank O'Hara. His friendship with the playwright Samuel Beckett resulted in a seventy-minute opera called *Neither* (1977), based on a brief text by Beckett and commissioned by the Rome Opera.

For many years he wrote relatively short compositions, most of them ranging from ten to twenty-five minutes in duration. But by 1979 he had begun to write longer instrumental works, beginning that year with the hour-long First String Quartet. His very lengthy Second String Quartet, written in 1983, can last as long as six hours in uninterrupted performance; at its premiere in Toronto in 1984 by the Kronos Quartet, it took nearly five. A notable long vocal work by Feldman is the ninety-minute *Three Voices* (1982), written for soprano soloist, accompanied by two tapes of her voice and using as a text several brief lines from a Frank O'Hara poem.

In 1972 Feldman had joined the faculty of the State University of New York at Buffalo and held the Edgard Varèse Chair, named in honor of a composer whose music had inspired him as a young man; he taught there until his death. Feldman's works did not appeal to a wide public, though for years this did not bother him; he claimed he was happy to be writing for what he perceived as a small but eagerly receptive and "discriminating" audience in both the United States and Europe. But this audience in America, he believed, had declined by the mid-1980s, and he lamented this to more than one interviewer. Critics, on the other hand, were another story. He was almost universally praised for his distinctive musical voice, and he is recognized as a major, if singular, figure in twentieth-century American music. Since his death, both recordings and concert performances of his music have steadily increased.

Feldman was married (to a woman named Barbara, maiden name unknown), but he had no children. He died in a Buffalo hospital while being treated for pancreatic cancer.

• Biographical information on Morton Feldman is limited. Although his life was the subject of speculation and gossip, he volunteered no personal information to interviewers, and his brief entry in several editions of *Who's Who in America* offers little beyond his date of birth and his major works. For discussions of his music that also include a few details of his early life, see the entry "Feldman, Morton" in *The New Grove Dictionary of American Music* (1986); see also the chapter about Feldman in David Ewen, *Composers since 1900: First Supplement* (1981). More on Feldman's music can be found in several interviews that he gave to critics over the years, especially P. Dickinson, "Feldman Explains Himself," *Music and Musicians*, Nov. 1966, pp. 22ff; C. Gagne and T. Caras, "Morton Feldman," in *Soundpieces: Interviews with American Composers* (1982); and John Rockwell, "A Minimalist Expands His Scale," *New York Times*, 7 Apr. 1985. For an assessment of Feldman's place in modern music, see Michael Nyman, *Experimental Music* (1974), and Michael Kimmelman, "The Abstract Expressionist of Music," *New York Times*, 28 July 1996. An obituary appears in the *New York Times*, 4 Sept. 1987.

ANN T. KEENE

FEREBEE, Thomas (9 Nov. 1918–16 Mar. 2000), U.S. Army Air Forces bombardier who released the first atomic bomb used in warfare, was born Thomas Wilson Ferebee just outside Mocksville, North Carolina, the son of William Flavious Ferebee, a farmer, and Zella Ward Ferebee. Their third child, he was born just two days before Germany signed the armistice effectively ending World War I. The parents raised tobacco, cotton, and corn with the help of the eleven children they would eventually have on their 150 acres near Winston-Salem. The Ferebees and their neighbors were skilled hunters and students of the natural wonders of Davie County, but in spite of the pride and joy that Ferebee derived from these activities, he was determined to escape from farming. Sports were an important diversion for him early on and formed the essence of his exit strategy. During the summers of his high school days Ferebee pitched or played outfield for mill teams, and during the school year he played baseball, football and basketball, and ran track. He essentially maintained this pattern at Lees-McRae College in Banner Elk, North Carolina, but lamented that the price he paid for unending athletic activities was a very poor education. In 1939, one year before he graduated, he tried out for the St. Louis Cardinals in Albany, Georgia. Told that he needed more experience, he returned to school to take his degree. He journeyed to Charlotte to join the U.S. Army Air Corps (later, the U.S. Army Air Forces) in 1940.

Hard work and athletics had rendered Ferebee a strong, handsome, and vibrant young adult. With his sights set on becoming a pilot, he was sent to Texas to enroll in aviation cadet school. The experience proved an unhappy one for Ferebee, and much of his frustration was bred by circumstances that he simply could not control. In high school, he had torn his left knee ligaments while playing football. He now discovered that high altitudes reawakened this old injury, making it very difficult for him to negotiate the plane's rudder pedals, an essential skill he needed in order to fulfill his ambition. His instructor, furthermore, was convinced that he was bent on forcing his plane through maneuvers that exceeded its design capability. This inauspicious beginning to Ferebee's military career paved the way to his place in history. With his aspirations apparently thwarted, he was at a precarious turning-point in his young life and could have succumbed to the pressures of being trained as a bombardier. Yet, while he was just beginning to build his formidable reputation as a poker player, he quickly demonstrated an ability to manifest a calmness at 12,000 feet in the air that allowed him to come within 500 lateral feet of a target.

Ferebee's talent was such that he was made an instructor. After his training at Maxwell Field in Montgomery, Alabama, and later at Albuquerque, New Mexico, was completed, Ferebee was assigned to the 97th Heavy Bombardment Group, 340th Squadron. His squadron leader was a young captain named Paul W. Tibbets, Jr., who impressed Ferebee as decisive—but with a thoughtful leadership style that suggested a fraternal concern for his men. Ferebee's understated professionalism, plus his knowledge of ballistics and the effect of wind on bombing, would

impress his captain, but another factor was at work. During his career, a characteristic of his would be spoken of almost in the form of a mantra, except that the words would vary slightly from different voices: action initiated a serenity that focused Ferebee's concentration.

In June 1942 his squadron shipped out to England, and for thirty missions over Europe and North Africa the bond between Tibbets and Ferebee and navigator Theodore "Dutch" Van Kirk would grow. Fellow poker enthusiast Van Kirk would also serve on the *Enola Gay* over Hiroshima under Tibbets. Before their commander would come to judge them as problem-free professionals, they had to prove themselves in the skies over a continental Europe all but strangled by the Axis and a North Africa that tottered precipitously close to the same state of affairs. With Tibbets at the controls and Ferebee stationed at their B-17's Norden bombsight, they hit targets from German war factories in occupied France to the Tunisian seaport of Bizerte. Along the way they dodged Messerschmitt fighters, participated in the first daylight raid on France, watched crew members such as Gene Lockhart suffer terrible mutilation from penetrating German shells, and ferried such eminences as Generals Mark Clark and Dwight Eisenhower to critical North African missions.

At the end of 1942, Tibbets and Van Kirk took on new assignments in Algeria and stateside. Ferebee continued making bombing runs. After sixty-four missions, the newly promoted major was sent home with a recommendation that he be given a vacation and another shot at becoming a pilot. General Hoyt Vandenberg told Ferebee, however, that another task might take precedence. After a tour of duty in Texas and Oklahoma, he was summoned to Wendover Air Base in the isolated Utah desert, where an already stringent security was tightening even more. Here, the 509th Composite Group—fifteen B-29 crews under the command of Paul Tibbets—was activated on 17 December 1944.

At Wendover, the bombing training was conducted at an unusually elevated 32,000 feet or nearly six miles—the altitude at which the drop over Hiroshima would be made. Ferebee's work was predominately supervisory but also entailed close collaboration on ballistic and ordnance matters with others attached to the Manhattan Project. The painstaking process included drops with units containing proximity-fuse firing mechanisms and resulted in models that would eventually look and aerodynamically behave like the atomic bomb. In June 1945, with Germany defeated and Harry S. Truman in the White House, Ferebee flew to Tinian in the Mariana Islands to join his unit. On 16 July a test firing of an atomic bomb in New Mexico was successful, and the USS *Indianapolis* left San Francisco for Tinian with a U-235 gun assembly for another bomb. Ten days later, the carefully worded Potsdam Declaration presented Japan a choice between unconditional surrender and utter destruction, without reference to atomic bombs. On 31 July Truman gave the final go-ahead to proceed with a mission meant to force the enemy to begin to capitulate. Meanwhile, the *Indianapolis* was torpedoed as it returned from Tinian to Guam; only 316 of its 1,199 crew survived the attack and ensuing 84-hour struggle against sharks and exposure.

The morning after they had christened their specially modified B-29 the *Enola Gay*, named for Tibbets's mother, Ferebee joined the crew for the 2:45 a.m. takeoff, surprised at the floodlights, movie cameras, and photographers that posterity-minded Manhattan Director Leslie Groves had arranged. After takeoff Tibbets, who carried a cyanide capsule for each of them in a box in his knee pocket, announced to the rest of the crew while Ferebee was napping that they had on board an atomic bomb. Two other B-29s assigned to record the event and take measurements joined them over Iwo Jima, while three weather planes ahead scouted the targets. The *Enola Gay*'s crew was augmented by Captain W. B. Parsons and his assistant who armed the 9,000-pound uranium bomb during the otherwise uneventful flight.

Ferebee had selected the aiming point at the city's center where the Aioi Bridge crossed a smaller bridge to the south and formed a perfect T. Until then largely unscathed, Hiroshima housed some 43,000 soldiers and did not have a P.O.W. camp; it was the main port for the shipment of men and supplies between the island of Honshu and Kyushu to the south, where an American invasion was expected to start. Hiroshima came into Ferebee's viewfinder, unencumbered by the protective Polaroid goggles that shielded the eyesight of all save himself, Tibbets, and Lieutenant Jacob Beser, who could not have done their work otherwise. At 8:15 a.m. the bomb was dropped, and it detonated less than a minute later at 1,900 feet over the courtyard of the Shima Hospital, an insignificant distance southeast of the aiming point.

Ferebee did not know for some time that out of a city of 343,000, some 60,000 to 80,000 had perished instantly, nor did he immediately realize that 60 percent of its area had been wiped out. A stunning 50,000 to 70,000 more of its inhabitants, suddenly without some 80 percent of its doctors and nurses, died in the coming months in that apocalyptic wasteland.

Twelve and a half hours after takeoff, the *Enola Gay* touched down in Tinian. Only then was Ferebee informed that the bomb had been an atomic weapon. Although Tibbets had been allowed to tell him that they were dealing with weapons of highly unusual destructive power, and Ferebee had slowly grasped that reality and its potential for ending the war, the true magnitude of their endeavor was just starting to sink in. After he, Tibbets, and Van Kirk flew over Hiroshima on their way to Nagasaki in early September, Ferebee was left to contemplate the horrible reality of the destruction that had been wrought.

Ferebee married Ann Elizabeth Gwin in 1945; they would have four sons. He became deputy wing commander for maintenance with several B-47 Stratojet bomber groups, was the U.S. NATO representative in France, and thereafter assumed command of an armament electronics unit. In 1966 he began observing American bombing in Vietnam; later he was stationed in Orlando, Florida, where in 1979 he retired with the rank of colonel. He sold real estate and grew roses; was married for a second time, to Mary Ann Conrad, in 1981; and in 1989 mourned the death of Kermit Beahan, who served as bombardier on the Nagasaki mission. He had convinced Tibbets to bring Beahan into the 509th. For the next eleven years, until his death at eighty-one, Ferebee would be the world's sole surviving atomic bombardier.

Largely because of his unshakeable coolness, Ferebee was selected to play a key role in the most secret project of the war. It would be the defining event of his life. Although he never wavered in his conviction that the two bombs had saved lives on both sides, he felt equally strongly that nuclear weapons should never be used again.

• The best overview of Ferebee's life is in an article by David Perlmutt, "This Can't Happen Again," *Charlotte Observer*, 6 Aug. 1995. David M. Kennedy's *Freedom from Fear* (1999) contains good descriptions of some of the harrowing missions Ferebee participated in, including the 1943 raid on the Rumanian oil refinery complex at Ploesti. An interesting overview of his relationship with Paul Tibbets, as well as the rest of the *Enola Gay*'s crew, is provided in Gordon Thomas and Max Morgan Witts, *Enola Gay* (1977). An excellent description of both Japan's position at the end of the war and the mission over Hiroshima is contained in Richard B. Frank, *Downfall: The End of the Imperial Japanese Empire* (1999). Ferebee's death occasioned a number of obituaries, including one in the *New York Times*, 18 Mar. 2000; among the most thoughtful was Nigel Fountain's in the *Guardian* (U.K.), 20 Mar. 2000.

PAUL T. SAYERS

FEYERABEND, Paul K. (13 Jan. 1924–11 Feb. 1994), philosopher, was born Paul Karl Feyerabend in Vienna, Austria, the son of a civil servant and a seamstress. "In the late twenties the streets and backyards of Vienna looked like amusement parks with organ grinders, animal acts, magicians, dancers, singers—entire bands," he later wrote (*Killing Time*, p. 7). As a child he regarded the world as a mysterious, unexplainable place. He suffered from "a nervous affliction, similar to epileptic fits" (*Killing Time*, p. 16). The father encouraged his son's personal flamboyance by taking him into restaurants where the child would stand on a table and sing: "And for that, Papa would get a beer!" In school he excelled at physics and mathematics and enjoyed astronomy, building a telescope "from a bicycle and an old clothing stand" (*Killing Time*, p. 29). He discovered philosophy "by sheer accident": when he bought bundles of cheap books, he occasionally found in them, and read, philosophical works such as René Descartes's *Meditations*.

Hitler marched into Austria in 1938. In 1942, as World War II raged, Paul was drafted into a Nazi-run work service. He later fought on the Russian front and won an Iron Cross for bravery. In January 1945, on the brink of adulthood, he was shot in the spine, leaving him permanently disabled. Thereafter he would rely on crutches and painkilling drugs.

After the war he attended the University of Vienna. His academic studies ranged from singing and theater to history, physics, and astronomy. He had a small part in a German feature film directed by G. W. Pabst and later lamented that "one of the biggest mistakes of my life" was rejecting an opportunity to become a production assistant for Bertolt Brecht. In 1948 he married the first of his four wives, a woman named Edeltrud (maiden name unknown), who preferred to be called Jacqueline. That same year he attended a summer seminar in Alpbach, Austria, where he met the philosopher Karl Popper. Popper's feisty, unpretentious manner impressed Feyerabend and perhaps encouraged him subsequently to affect a combative style of his own. At the university, Feyerabend was particularly intrigued by a controversial physicist and friend of Albert Einstein, Felix Ehrenhaft, whose iconoclastic views appear to have influenced the young philosopher's conviction that science did not advance in the inhumanly smooth, logical manner depicted in textbooks. Frustrated by his own physics research, Feyerabend switched his career plans to philosophy and obtained a doctorate in that subject in 1951.

The next year he traveled to England, intending to study with Ludwig Wittgenstein. By the time he arrived in the country, however, the great philosopher had died, and Feyerabend instead fell under the sway of Popper at the London School of Economics. Popper would soon become one of the best-known philosophers of the Cold War era; his antitotalitarian body of thought grew at least partly out of his iconoclastic philosophy of science. That body of thought did not keep him from being domineering to the point of eventually driving away some devotees, including Feyerabend. The younger man's later philosophy would nevertheless be clearly marked by Popper's advocacy of the virtue of repeatedly trying to disprove ("falsify") hypotheses by generating alternate hypotheses—the more outrageous, the better.

While in England Feyerabend taught at the University of Bristol from 1955 to 1958; by then he had won a reputation as a forceful philosophical commentator on quantum mechanics. At Bristol his concern about what he viewed as the dogmatic tendencies of science was influenced by another iconoclastic thinker, the physicist David Bohm, who had upset orthodoxy by arguing against the standard "Copenhagen" interpretation of quantum mechanics championed by physicist Niels Bohr. Feyerabend's discussions with the philosopher Philipp Frank and the physicist C. F. von Weizsäcker also helped persuade him that in the traditional philosophy of science, and even in Popper's comparatively radical thesis, the role of logic and reason in guiding scientists' thinking was overstated. While at Bristol Feyerabend married Mary O'Neill, his second wife; the relationship lasted only a year or two.

In the 1950s and early 1960s, Feyerabend was one of a number of scholars—among them Thomas S. Kuhn, N. R. Hanson, and Stephen Toulmin—who claimed that standard philosophical conceptions of how science worked contradicted actual historical examples of scientific discovery. Feyerabend was appointed to a post at the University of California at Berkeley in the late 1950s, where Kuhn was also teaching, and they would debate vigorously in a Berkeley coffeehouse. Feyerabend and Kuhn independently hit on the concept of "incommensurability." Positivist philosophers had long hoped to develop a neutral "observation language" that could be used to describe the contents of even significantly different theories. But Kuhn, Feyerabend, and other scholars emphasized that scientific observations are "theory-laden"—that even seemingly straightforward observations of nature can have ambiguous interpretations, which can vary according to the underlying theory used to interpret the observations. One extreme interpretation of this view is that the same terms (say, "mass") may have such different meanings in different theories (for example, in Newtonian and Einsteinian physics) that the theories cannot be meaningfully compared: they are incommensurable. Feyerabend read and critiqued Kuhn's manuscript for his soon-to-be-published *The Structure of Scientific Revolutions* (1962), the best known of the books from that decade and the next that questioned traditional conceptions of the evolution of scientific ideas. Although scholars would in time pair Kuhn and Feyerabend as challengers to orthodox notions of science who shared similar views, it is important to note that the two men had major disagreements on certain topics. Feyerabend in fact would come to be seen as by far the more radical philosopher of the two. To begin with, he was uncomfortable with Kuhn's notion of "normal science," according to which scientists tend to operate within the rules and concepts of a "paradigm" (a governing body of ideas and methods); they abandon it, Kuhn thought, only when the foundational principles of a science have accumulated an unbearable number of "anomalies" (contradictions between the paradigm and scientific observations), leading to a worldview-shattering scientific "revolution." By contrast, Feyerabend maintained that some important advances in the history of science came about precisely because iconoclastic scientists *refused* to abide by paradigmatic rules. For example, Galileo Galilei's argument for Copernican astronomy in the seventeenth century sometimes involved logical leaps that could not be justified by empirical data then available.

Amid the "countercultural" ferment of the 1960s and 1970s, Feyerabend's classes at Berkeley attracted huge student audiences. He limped on his crutches into the classroom, where he implored the young to question orthodoxy, even its most cherished shibboleths such as "knowledge." In his celebrated book *Against Method* (1975, eventually translated into more than a dozen languages), he presented highly readable yet exquisitely detailed analyses of episodes in the history of science—especially Galileo's research—that upheld his idea that there is no consistent scientific "method" or logical procedure such as that envisioned by the early logical positivists or their most voluble critic, Popper. Feyerabend half-jokingly said that when it came to picking a scientific methodology, a scientist might as well assume there is no such thing and should adopt the slogan "Anything goes." Although not a political anarchist, Feyerabend called himself an "epistemological anarchist." In the culturally heated atmosphere of the 1960s and 1970s, orthodox philosophers of science charged that Feyerabend was defending "irrationalism." He enjoyed such intellectual combat, though, and engaged in a particularly fertile exchange with his close friend, the philosopher Imre Lakatos, who tried to merge the best of Kuhn's and Popper's ideas. The correspondence between Feyerabend and Lakatos apparently inspired much of *Against Method*.

Feyerabend also upset the orthodox by defending the right of ordinary citizens to decide how science should be presented in schools, such as opting for the teaching of creationism (anti-evolutionism). If that was what citizens wanted, he maintained, then they were entitled to it. He drew support for this thesis from the nineteenth-century philosopher John Stuart Mill's *On Liberty*, a classic defense of free speech and the proliferation of viewpoints. In a similar vein, Feyerabend argued that modern medicine could benefit from exploring alternative medical procedures of other cultures, such as acupuncture. He maintained that he had personally benefited from medical treatments deemed unorthodox by Western standards. He appears to have viewed all belief systems, including rationalism and science, as destined to rigidify and lose the vigor and value they originally had as dissenting ideologies; hence they must never enjoy complete dominance and must always be forced to defend themselves against a "proliferation" of competing views. Scientists, Feyerabend said, have "more money, more authority, more sex appeal than they deserve, and the most stupid procedures and the most laughable results in their domain are surrounded with an aura of excellence. It is time to cut them down in size" (Broad, p. 534).

Feyerabend was an academic itinerant; he taught at numerous campuses around the world, sometimes holding simultaneous appointments, and restlessly changed jobs. In addition to his posts at Bristol and Berkeley, he had teaching positions at the University of Berlin, University College London, Yale University, the University of Sussex at Brighton, the University of Kassel (Germany), the University of Auckland (New Zealand), and the Federal Institute of Technology (now Zurich Polytechnic).

An article in the science journal *Nature* in 1987 labeled him—along with Kuhn, Popper, and Lakatos—a "betrayer of the truth." The same article identified Feyerabend as, "currently, the worst enemy of science." But Feyerabend eloquently denied the charge that he was "anti-science" (the label that would later

appear atop his obituary in the *New York Times*). On the contrary, he was trying to make science better by making it more humble, more aware of its limitations, and thereby open to a more imaginative multitude of possibilities and methodologies. Admirers depicted him as carrying on the noble tradition of philosophical Scepticism identified with Sextus Empericus and Michel de Montaigne. Even the journal *Science* acknowledged: "Compared with the stiff and sober work that is often done in the philosophy of science, his views are a breath of fresh air" (Broad, 1979).

In 1990, frightened by a major earthquake in the San Francisco Bay Area, Feyerabend fled Berkeley for his native Austria. He married the physicist Grazia Borrini, his fourth and last wife. Despite the physical pain from his wartime injuries, he continued to write numerous articles and books, including new, substantially revamped editions of *Against Method*. In 1994 he died in Geneva, Switzerland from a brain tumor.

Paul Feyerabend was one of the most controversial philosophers of science of the twentieth century, second perhaps only to Kuhn. With wit and zeal, Feyerabend raised fundamental questions about the reliability and limits of science and its most enthusiastic champions' depiction of it as the royal road to truth. Humanity, Feyerabend countered, was a "one-day fly," a "little bit of nothing" that foolishly thought it could answer ultimate questions of reality, while "the reality that is behind this is laughing, 'Ha ha! They think they have found me out!'" (Horgan, p. 37).

• Feyerabend's memoir, *Killing Time* (published posthumously in 1995), is an amiable, impressionistic and sometimes sharply self-critical autobiography finished on his deathbed. Besides *Against Method*, Feyerabend's other major books are *Science in a Free Society* (1978), *Farewell to Reason* (1987), and *Conquest of Abundance* (1999), as well as three volumes of his philosophical papers published by Cambridge University Press between 1981 and 1999. Feyerabend and Lakatos's correspondence is in *For and Against Method* (1999), edited by Matteo Motterlini. For a detailed critique of Feyerabend's ideas, with limited biographical information, see John Preston, *Feyerabend: Philosophy, Science and Society* (1997). Preston, along with Gonzalo Munévar and David Lamb, edited a valuable festschrift, *The Worst Enemy of Science? Essays in Memory of Paul Feyerabend* (2000), which includes personal reminiscences of the philosopher. Articles profiling Feyerabend include William J. Broad, "Paul Feyerabend: Science and the Anarchist," *Science* 206 (1979): 534–37; John Horgan, "The Worst Enemy of Science," *Scientific American* 268, no. 5 (1993): 36–37; Ian Hacking, "Paul Feyerabend, Humanist," *Common Knowledge* 3, no. 2 (1994): 23–28; and Roy Edgley, "Paul Feyerabend, 1924–1994: A Personal Memoir," *Radical Philosophy* (Summer 1994): 1–2. The *New York Times* of 8 Mar. 1994 has an obituary.

KEAY DAVIDSON

FINLEY, Charles O. (22 Feb. 1918–19 Feb. 1996), baseball team owner, was born Charles Oscar Finley in Ensley, Alabama, the son of Oscar Finley, a steelworker, and Burmah Finley (maiden name unknown). A born salesman, he later recalled that as a child he devised a scheme by which he purchased discolored eggs for five cents a dozen and resold them for fifteen cents a dozen. One year he won a bicycle from a publishing company for selling 12,000 *Saturday Evening Post* subscriptions. In 1931 he served as a batboy for the Birmingham Barons, a minor league baseball team. In 1934 his family moved to Gary, Indiana, where his father worked for U.S. Steel. Following his graduation from Horace Mann High School in 1936, the younger Finley also worked for U.S. Steel, and he organized and played first base for the Gary Merchants, an industrial league baseball team. In 1941 he married Shirley McCartney; they had seven children and would divorce around 1974. Rejected for military service during World War II because of an ulcer, he was assigned to an ordnance plant in Kingsbury, Indiana, where he eventually became a division supervisor in charge of 5,000 workers.

Following the war, Finley became a salesman for the Travelers Insurance Company and in 1946 set a company sales record. He paid for his relentless work ethic, however, when he collapsed on the job in December; he was then admitted to a sanitarium in Crown Point, Indiana, suffering from pneumonic tuberculosis. He remained there, bedridden, until early 1949. With time on his hands, he contemplated the irony of his predicament: because he had failed to sell himself health insurance, his illness caused his financial ruin. "I figured it was a bad enough situation for the average guy," he later recalled, "but what a calamity it'd be for a fellow with a big income who suddenly found himself without money to meet his high standards of living. . . . I thought of doctors. You know, suppose a surgeon loses a finger or gets crippled?" (quoted in Clark, pp. 7–8). Seizing on this train of thought, he developed a plan to sell group disability insurance to doctors. Following his release from the sanitarium, he immediately set about selling his new program through the Continental Casualty Company. Over the next few years he sold the insurance to 92 percent of the doctors in the Chicago area. By 1951 he made his first million dollars, following a particularly lucrative sale to the American College of Surgeons. He subsequently founded his own business, Charles O. Finley & Company of Chicago. By 1961 his company had sold $40 million in premiums annually, and his clients included the Southern Medical Association and the American Medical Association.

Beginning in 1954 Finley pursued a long-held ambition to own a major league baseball franchise. He bid on several teams, including the Detroit Tigers and the Chicago White Sox, but was continually put off by baseball's clubby, "old money" owners, who tended to view him as a *nouveau riche* upstart. In late 1960 he was able to acquire a controlling interest in the Kansas City Athletics in the American League; the following year he bought out the team's minority shareholders. During his first season as owner, Finley fired the team's general manager, reasoning that he could handle the job just as well. He also established himself as the team's de facto manager, pestering the

official manager, Joe Gordon, with phone calls during ball games, suggesting pinch hitters and pitching changes in language that was "acerbic, tough, profane, direct, suspicious" (Twombley, p. 42). Gordon blanched at Finley's intrusiveness and was fired in June 1961; over the next six years the owner hired and fired six additional managers, and during this period the team averaged 96 losses per season, finishing dead last three times. In order to bolster the club's poor attendance, he instituted several promotional ideas that he thought would appeal to the rural population around Kansas City. For example, a flock of sheep was installed behind the right field fence, with a shepherd to tend them; a mechanical rabbit popped up behind home plate to hand balls to the umpire; and the team's mascot was a mule named Charlie O. In spite of these efforts, the club often drew fewer than 5,000 fans to games.

Disgruntled, Finley began in 1964 to publicly explore the possibility of moving the Athletics to a different city. He also diverted money away from his major league team, using it instead to develop an excellent scouting and farm system. Between 1964 and 1966 he signed several "bonus babies" who would become major league stars, including three future Hall of Famers: outfielder Reggie Jackson, relief pitcher Rollie Fingers, and starting pitcher Jim Hunter. (Hunter was given a fake childhood nickname, "Catfish," by the owner, who wanted to play up Hunter's "folksy" North Carolina background.) Following the 1967 season, Finley was granted permission by the American League to move his franchise to Oakland, California.

As Finley's young prospects reached the major leagues in the late 1960s, the team improved dramatically: in 1968 they posted their first winning record in sixteen seasons, and they finished in second place in the American League western division the following two years. Between 1971 and 1975 they established themselves as one of baseball's great dynasties, winning five consecutive division championships and three consecutive world championships (1972–1974), only the second team in baseball history (following the New York Yankees) to accomplish this feat. Yet they were as famous for their dysfunctionality as for their victories. Encouraged by Finley to grow long hair, exotic mustaches, and mutton-chop sideburns, the Athletics were portrayed by the media as brash iconoclasts in a tradition-minded sport; during the 1972 World Series against the clean-shaven Cincinnati Reds, one sportswriter described the match-up as "the Bikers against the Boy Scouts" (quoted in Markusen, p. 171). Although the players often argued and brawled with each other, observers pointed out that they seemed to find a "common bond in their collective hatred of [Finley]" (quoted in Clark, p. xi). Stars Reggie Jackson and Vida Blue engaged in bitter, protracted disputes with the owner when they sought salaries commensurate with their market value; baseball commissioner Bowie Kuhn was forced to intervene to end Blue's holdout in 1972. Jackson later suggested the reason for the owner's difficulties with his players: "I told Dave Duncan [an Oakland player] that Finley treated his black players like niggers. Dave told me not to worry or feel hurt. He said Charlie treats his white players like niggers too." During the 1972 World Series, after infielder Mike Andrews made two errors in a game, Finley forced him to fake an injury so the team could place him on the inactive list and use a different infielder. When the truth leaked out, manager Dick Williams quit the team in protest and Kuhn reprimanded and fined the owner. In 1974 Finley signed a contract with Jim Hunter that provided a $50,000 insurance annuity, then refused to pay the annuity when he found out that it was not tax-deductible. The Major League Baseball Players' Association filed a grievance on behalf of Hunter; in December 1974 a labor arbitrator ruled that Finley had breached the contract and that the pitcher could freely negotiate with other clubs. Thus, the owner unwittingly hastened baseball into the high-salaried free-agency era.

Unwilling to pay such salaries, Finley decided in 1976 to sell off or trade his best players and start from scratch, rebuilding through his farm system; however, a deal to send Fingers, Blue, and outfielder Joe Rudi to the Boston Red Sox for $3.5 million was vetoed by Kuhn. The commissioner later commented that he could not trust Finley's motives: rather than rebuild the team, the owner may have intended to hold a "fire sale" and then pocket the money. In return, Finley called Kuhn "the village idiot" and filed an unsuccessful $10 million lawsuit against him. In 1976 the Athletics lost many players via free agency, and in 1977 they finished in last place. In 1979 they posted a pitiful 54–108 record, often drawing fewer than 1,000 fans to games. In 1981 Finley sold the club to the Haas family, which owned Levi Strauss & Company. After attempting to buy the Chicago Cubs in the early 1980s, he ended his affiliation with baseball. In his later years he continued to operate his insurance firm and served as president of a Canadian company, Century Energy Corporation. He died in Chicago.

Finley was a catalyst for change in major league baseball, sometimes for the good but more often for the worse. A master salesman, he was remarkably far-sighted in some of his promotional strategies: for example, during the early 1960s he argued for night World Series games, a designated hitter to bat for the pitcher, and interleague play that focused on regional rivalries—all ideas that have since been implemented. But more significant was the precedent he set through his contentious, often crass behavior. At the end of the twentieth century, major league baseball—thanks to its labor wars, the obsession with salaries, and the petulance of ballplayers—bore a striking resemblance to Finley's Athletics.

• The best history of Finley's Athletics is Tom Clark, *Champagne and Baloney: The Rise and Fall of Finley's A's* (1976). Also useful is Bruce Markusen's carefully researched *Baseball's Last Dynasty: Charlie Finley's Oakland A's* (1998). John Helyar's history of the sport's labor relations, *Lords of the Realm: The Real History of Baseball* (1994), suggests Finley's enormous impact on the free-agency era. For Finley's acrimonious relationship with Kuhn, see Bowie Kuhn, *Hardball: The Education of a Baseball Commissioner* (1987). For journalistic appraisals of his personality, see Wells Twombley, the *New York Times Magazine*, 15 July 1973, pp. 12ff., and Ron Fimrite, "The Finley He Knew," *Sports Illustrated*, 4 Mar. 1996, p. 28. An obituary is in the *New York Times*, 23 Feb. 1996.

THOMAS W. COLLINS, JR.

FITZGERALD, Ella (25 Apr. 1917–15 June 1996), singer, was born Ella Jane Fitzgerald in Newport News, Virginia, the illegitimate daughter of William Fitzgerald and Temperance (Tempie) Williams. The common-law marriage ended soon after her birth, and when Fitzgerald was three she moved with her mother to the mill town of Yonkers, New York, where they settled in a neighborhood composed of European immigrants and African Americans. In 1923, her mother began living with Joseph Da Silva, a Portuguese immigrant, with whom she had another daughter, Frances Da Silva. Ella Fitzgerald remained close to her half-sister, her only sibling, all of her life—one of her few enduring intimate relationships. Although she never divulged the facts publicly, it is known that Fitzgerald suffered some form of abuse from Da Silva, her stepfather, during the years when the girls were growing up in Yonkers.

When Fitzgerald was fifteen, her mother died suddenly at the age of thirty-eight. Not long after, Fitzgerald moved with her half-sister to Harlem to live with her mother's sister Virginia, and Joseph Da Silva died not long after that. Life with her aunt was not much of an improvement on her upbringing with Da Silva: unsupervised and impoverished, Fitzgerald began to hang out on the streets, picking up change by performing as a tap dancer and taking numbers for the ubiquitous illegal lottery popular throughout African-American communities. One bright spot, however, was the close friendship she formed with her cousin Georgiana "Georgie" Henry, who would became her companion until Henry's death in the mid-1960s.

But her mother's death had set in motion an unhappy and turbulent period in Fitzgerald's life. Despite her teachers' descriptions of her as a "model student," Ella Fitzgerald was often truant, so much so that she was placed as a foster child by the city of New York into the Colored Orphan Asylum in Riverdale. The orphanage was overcrowded—it was the depths of the Great Depression—and Fitzgerald was sent upstate to the segregated New York State Training School for Girls in Hudson in 1934. She soon ran away, however, returning to the streets of Harlem.

Ever since she was a young child, despite deepset shyness, Fitzgerald had dreamed of a career in show business. Although she joined the glee club at her local elementary school, her ambition was to become a dancer. And, on 21 November 1934, on a dare from friends, she decided to take a step in that direction by competing in an amateur talent contest at Harlem's newly opened Apollo Theatre. Although she had intended to dance, she changed her mind when she saw that she would be following a dance number and decided to sing instead, choosing a song she had heard often on the radio recorded by her favorite vocal group, the rhythmically swinging Boswell Sisters. So it was that Ella Fitzgerald, an unprepossessing teenager dressed in hand-me-downs—the very antithesis of the sexy big band "canary"—wowed the audience and won first place. Her abundant musical gifts were there from the start: a beautiful, clear voice, both perfect and relative pitch (the latter allowing her to easily hear the relationship of one note to another, highly useful for an improvising musician), a built-in metronome, excellent diction, and, finally, infectious enthusiasm and warmth. In the words of her biographer Stuart Nicholson, she embodied "the hallmark of innocence, the fresh young girl poised just this side of her womanhood."

Although Fitzgerald's talent had impressed other musicians who were present—Benny Carter for one, who recommended her to bandleader Fletcher Henderson—nothing more came of her debut. Henderson saw no need for a gawky, unstylish female singer, and her second amateur contest the next month, at the nearby Lafayette Theatre, was, according to the singer, a fiasco when the pianist switched keys, leaving the singer literally flat. Years later she could joke about being booed off the stage, but her determination to keep performing prevailed, and she tried out a third time at the Harlem Opera House. This time, she not only took first prize but also won a week's singing engagement with Tiny Bradshaw's orchestra.

By March of 1935, drummer Chick Webb, who led an extremely popular band at the Savoy ballroom, was persuaded to give Fitzgerald a try. Webb too was reluctant at first, but he decided to buy her an evening gown and test her at a Yale prom, where she was a sensation. Now seventeen, Fitzgerald became a regular with Webb, singing novelty and "jive" numbers as well as the ballads she loved. And although she was not formally adopted by Webb and his wife, the band became her family. Her first recording, "Love and Kisses" and "I'll Chase the Blues Away," was made with the orchestra on 12 June 1935, and she was on her way to becoming the most popular female singer in America. There followed many hits, including in 1938 "A Tisket, A Tasket," a novelty arrangement Fitzgerald contributed to, and many others, notably "Mr. Paganini," in which she used Louis Armstrong-style scat singing (swinging wordless vocalese). Then in June 1939 Chick Webb, who was crippled by tuberculosis of the spine, died. Fitzgerald was then chosen to front the band, and although it disbanded in 1942 as the big band era waned, her popularity continued. In 1940 she was among the very first African-American women invited to join ASCAP, and she performed in the early forties with such vocal groups as the Three Keys and the Ink Spots before going out on her own.

Ella Fitzgerald's personal life was less successful. Insecure about her looks because of her weight, she craved romance and affection. In 1941, on the day after Christmas, she eloped with Benjamin Kornegay, described as a band hanger-on. Crushed at revelations of Korengay's unsavory past, Fitzgerald consented to have the marriage annulled a few months later.

But Fitzgerald's career continued to build. She began a long association with Decca Records' Milt Gabler in 1943, with whom she made a series of hits. In October 1945 there was "Flyin' Home," showcasing her ability as a scat singer. The next year she went on tour with Dizzy Gillespie's bop-oriented big band, developing as one of the most proficient singers in the new modern jazz idiom. Her bop versions of "Lady Be Good" and "How High the Moon" in 1947 caused a sensation. Fitzgerald never was able to get a radio show (or, later, a television show) of her own, but she did appear in a number of films, which was rare for black artists until the 1960s. As early as 1942, she had a cameo role as a maid in an Abbott and Costello comedy called *Ride 'Em Cowboy* and was to have parts subsequently in *Pete Kelly's Blues* (1955) and *Let No Man Write My Epitaph* (1960).

The year 1947 was significant for Fitzgerald personally. On 10 December she was married again, to bassist Ray Brown, and the couple adopted her half-sister Frances's son. The boy, whom they named Raymond Brown, Jr.—also called Ray—grew up to become a musician himself. In 1949 another extremely important relationship, which endured for the rest of her life, began: she joined producer Norman Granz's newly formed organization Jazz at the Philharmonic (JATP). By 1954, Granz had also become her personal manager. The wide exposure she gained from the large-scale JATP tours, Granz's strong stand against racial discrimination on behalf of musicians in his troupe, and his understanding of Fitzgerald's artistic worth ensured worldwide fame and prosperity for her. The Granz-Fitzgerald relationship was not always smooth sailing: their shouting matches were well known, but his careful management of her career paid off. Leaving Decca Records in 1956, she signed with Granz's new label, Verve, and the result was a series of stunning albums. Best known are the composer songbooks. Beginning with an album of Cole Porter material, Fitzgerald made memorable recordings by George Gershwin, Harold Arlen, Johnny Mercer, Jerome Kern, Cole Porter, Irving Berlin, and Duke Ellington.

Despite the fact that Fitzgerald was at the top of her game professionally and artistically, and making a lot of money, to many who knew her during these years the singer seemed lonely. Never an extrovert until she hit the stage, her social life was spare and her romances fizzled. After she was divorced from Ray Brown in 1953, Fitzgerald announced a third marriage in 1957, this time to Norwegian Thor Larsen. But like the Kornegay liaison, this "marriage" (never actually confirmed) ended abruptly with the groom's reputation under a cloud. Again, Fitzgerald poured her energies into her work, with fine results. From the late fifties onward she toured constantly and produced a stream of recordings. Many of her devotees think her best recordings fall mainly in the decade between 1956 and 1966, during which she made not only the composer songbooks but also the album *Porgy and Bess* with Louis Armstrong in 1957 and exceptional live albums such as *Ella Fitzgerald at the Opera House* in 1957 and *Ella in Rome* in 1958. In 1960 there was the live album *The Complete Ella in Berlin* and the studio production *Let No Man Write My Epitaph* (entitled *The Intimate Ella* on CD), and in 1963 a wonderful *Ella and Basie* disc. But the grand Verve Records years were followed by a low period from 1967 to 1973, during which her new contract with Capitol Records tended to feature mostly ephemeral pop music (though a high point was her appearance on Frank Sinatra's television special in 1967, *A Man and His Music + Ella + Jobim*). When Fitzgerald left Capitol to sign on with Pablo Records, Norman Granz's latest label, she went back to recording the standards and jazz material her aficionados had loved. Among the many fine albums she made on Pablo were recordings with guitarist Joe Pass and *Ella at Montreux* in 1975, with pianist Tommy Flanagan.

But the years of constant work were causing stress and strain. There was another failed love affair in the early 1960s, this time with a young Dane. Although she went so far as to buy herself a house or apartment in Copenhagen and set up housekeeping there, she moved back to California in 1963; the romance was over. And her constant touring put a strain on her professional relationships; many of the finest pianists then in the business, who continued to love Fitzgerald's music, quit working for her out of sheer exhaustion. And she herself was slowed down by health problems, particularly complications from diabetes. Hospitalized from time to time for exhaustion and suffering from deteriorating vision (she had eye surgery several times, beginning in 1971) and a voice that was noticeably beginning to fray, Fitzgerald still retained a furiously fast, ebullient scat singing ability on her increasingly rare appearances. Despite open heart surgery in 1986, and amputation of both legs below the knees in 1987 due to complications from diabetes, she continued to perform and to record, albeit at a much slower pace.

When at last the indefatigable performer retired completely in 1994, two years before her death, Fitzgerald had reached permanent legendary status and was widely regarded as the most admired jazz singer in America. Wealthy and showered with countless awards and honors, she received numerous honorary doctorates in music and humane letters. Yet Fitzgerald never lost the modesty and humility that belied her achievements, and she remained a generous contributor to charities, notably to the organization in Los Angeles named in her honor, the Ella Fitzgerald Child Care Center.

Considered the epitome of jazz singing by many, to others she remains the nonpareil of pop vocalists.

Subsuming text to music, she projected charm rather than passion, the sunny, pure, and innocent sound of the honey-toned, endlessly swinging singer.

• Stuart Nicholson, *Ella Fitzgerald: A Biography of the First Lady of Jazz* (1993; repr. 1995), is the most complete biography to date of the singer. Among other biographies of Fitzgerald are Jim Haskins, *Ella Fitzgerald: A Life through Music* (1991), and Geoffrey Mark Fidelman, *First Lady of Song: Ella Fitzgerald for the Record* (1994). A collection of the best writings about Fitzgerald is contained in Leslie Gourse, ed., *The Ella Fitzgerald Companion: Seven Decades of Commentary* (1998). For information on Fitzgerald the singer, see Will Friedwald, *Jazz Singing* (1990; repr. 1996). Two very good videos are available about the singer: *Forever Ella*, of the A&E biography series on television, is a straightforward account; more insightful is *Ella Fitzgerald: Something to Live For*, directed by Charlotte Zwerin and narrated by Tony Bennett. An obituary notice, "'Mama Jazz' Bows Out," is on the editorial page of the *New York Times*, 18 June 1996.

LINDA DAHL

FLEXNER, Anne Crawford (27 June 1874–11 Jan. 1955), playwright, was the daughter of Louis G. Crawford and Susan Farnum. Born in Georgetown, Kentucky, while her parents were visiting relatives, she was named Anne Laziere Crawford after her paternal grandmother, a woman of French descent who was noted for vivacity, charm, and intelligence—qualities that also characterized her namesake. Anne Crawford spent her earliest years on the family farm in northern Georgia, but the Crawfords later moved to Louisville, Kentucky, where John M. Atherton, a relative, was a prominent businessman and civic leader. When Atherton hired Abraham Flexner, a noted local educator, to tutor his favorite niece, she soon met the requirements for admission to Vassar, from which she was graduated in 1895. After returning to Kentucky, she became a tutor in Flexner's preparatory school; she also wrote stories for *Southern Magazine*, a Louisville publication.

In 1897, with $300 in savings, the ambitious Anne Crawford moved to New York City, where she took a course in short story writing; to earn money, she sent theater reviews to the *Louisville Courier-Journal*. Finally realizing that her talent was in creating dialogue, she studied playwriting and began her first play, *A Man's Woman*.

A year earlier, in 1896, Anne Crawford and Abraham Flexner had become engaged, but they postponed marriage because of his financial obligations. On 23 June 1898 the couple were married in Louisville at the home of the bride's parents, then left for their first of many trips abroad. That fall, Abraham was again running his highly successful school; Anne finished *A Man's Woman*, paid for its 1899 publication, and had a copy sent to actress Minnie Maddern Fiske. Although Mrs. Fiske did not accept the play, she encouraged the young playwright by asking her to write a drama based on *Miranda of the Balcony*, an

1899 novel by A. E. W. Mason. The adaptation was finished in less than a year.

On 24 September 1901 *Miranda of the Balcony* opened in New York City's newly renovated Manhattan Theatre. Despite five ornate stage sets, a talented cast of thirty-five, and Minnie Maddern Fiske's elegant gowns (one was of pearls and gold, weighing forty pounds), reviewers complained of too much talk and too little action. Noted critic William Winter dismissed *Miranda* as mere social comedy—"a mixture of millinery with fatuous prattle." Its replacement soon went into rehearsal.

In Louisville, one of Flexner's friends was Alice Hegan Rice, whose first novel, *Mrs. Wiggs of the Cabbage Patch* (1901), was a national bestseller; *Lovey Mary*, its 1903 sequel, also sold thousands of copies. When Flexner asked if she could create a play from the two short novels, Rice thought the idea absurd but gave reluctant permission, later admitting that the "independent and determined" Flexner deserved full credit for the play's eventual success.

On 5 October 1903 *Mrs. Wiggs of the Cabbage Patch* premiered at Macauley's Theater in Louisville. Local critics tried to be objective—one even pointed out the "plethoric confusion" of so much novelistic material—but they praised the comedy and its creator. Flexner, however, kept tinkering with the dialogue before the play opened in other major cities, including St. Louis and Chicago. Despite the shabby costumes and ramshackle stage setting, the play was an immediate hit. On 3 September 1904 it began a run of 150 performances in New York's Savoy Theater; Madge Carr Cook starred as the indomitable Mrs. Wiggs, whose homespun optimism couched in pithy sayings was already well known to a multitude of uncritical readers.

Flexner's 50 percent share in the play's profits meant that her husband could close his school in June 1905, spend a year at Harvard, and then in 1906 again move his family, this time to Europe where he studied at German universities. Flexner herself was now free to get *Mrs. Wiggs* ready for its London opening at Terry's Theatre on 27 April 1907. She was afraid a sophisticated English audience would heckle the players, and in fact critics were prepared for the worst; instead, Londoners considered the play an important revelation of American character. Although a duchess complained that the actors were "wretchedly gowned," audiences were genuinely amused by the comical plot and folksy humor. For Flexner, the success was encouraging, yet what followed were discouraging periods of lesser theatrical achievement.

The Flexners returned to America in 1908, making their home in a New York City apartment and living partly on play royalties. While her husband traveled throughout the United States and Canada for a Carnegie study on medical education, Flexner was busy raising their two young children and working on *A Lucky Star*, a farce in four acts—"a crisp little laughmaker," according to the *New York Times* of 19 January 1910, but "mostly froth and bubbles." Later in

1910 came the publication of her husband's famous report that exposed the inadequate training of American physicians; then the family again went overseas so he could study European medical education.

In a letter of 28 August 1913, Abraham Flexner assured his wife that however difficult it was for a married woman to manage both family and a career, she had not only succeeded in both roles but her career had immensely enriched their lives. This praise was prompted, perhaps, by her next play, *The Marriage Game*, which opened in New York on 29 October 1913. Others might consider the comedy a revelation of the female mind at work, but for its author, the play had a moral: when a woman marries, the game is not won; it has only begun. For some, the play was immoral: the heroine—a charming paramour—made her virtuous rivals appear to be the cause of their own marital problems, thereby exonerating their wayward husbands.

Apparently, *Wanted—An Alibi* never survived its Albany tryout in June 1917. The following year, *The Blue Pearl* opened in New York City at the Longacre on 8 August; lightly praised for its unusual solution, the mystery catered to a wartime public's need to escape reality. Next, on 12 May 1920, the four-act *All Souls' Eve* was staged at the Maxine Elliott Theatre. A *Times* reviewer found the play "interesting throughout," but thought it failed as "a serious inquiry into spiritualism . . . because Mrs. Flexner has somewhat muddied her theses."

During the twenties, the Flexners traveled extensively, visiting, among other places, Egypt and the Middle East. From 1930 to 1939 they lived in Princeton, New Jersey, where Abraham Flexner headed the Institute for Advanced Study. Despite more travel, summers at "Ingleside," the family's Canadian retreat, and increased social obligations, Flexner continued her playwriting. Finally, on 21 December 1936, *Aged 26* opened at New York's Lyceum Theater. Chronicling an important year in the life of poet John Keats, *Aged 26* was described in the *Theatre Arts Monthly* (Feb. 1937) as "a thing of beauty and, if not a joy forever, at least a pleasure most of the time." In the June 1937 issue, Flexner was praised for having written a play "both dignified and touching."

In addition to those already mentioned, three other plays have been attributed to Flexner: *Bravo! Maria* (1925); *Love among the Ruins* (1935), reportedly the property of Katharine Cornell but never performed; and *The Lawbreakers* (early 1940s), an adaptation of Ferdinand Bruckner's *Die Verbrecher*.

By 1947 Abraham Flexner was living alone. "Not suddenly, but gradually, bereavement came in the loss of my wife," he wrote in his 1960 autobiography. Anne Crawford Flexner, in slow but steady mental decline, spent her final years in seclusion, under medical care. Early in 1955, at eighty years of age, she died in a Providence, Rhode Island, hospital.

Historian Eleanor Flexner credited her mother's financial success for making her own career possible. Never a prominent name in American theatrical history, playwright Flexner helped organize fellow dramatists into a professional association; for many years she was an officer in the Dramatists Guild of the Authors League of America. Of her seven Broadway plays, only *Mrs. Wiggs of the Cabbage Patch* achieved worldwide fame; in addition to being performed numerous times in America, Great Britain, Australia, and Asia, the play was also made into at least four movies: the 1914, 1919, 1934, and 1942 versions, with Flexner given a credit line in each. (The 1934 talkie, starring Pauline Lord, W. C. Fields, and ZaSu Pitts, remains a cinematic classic.) For both stage and screen, Anne Crawford Flexner interpreted the American character with wit and understanding, thereby entertaining a large segment of the population in the United States and overseas.

• The details of Flexner's career must be traced through family letters now housed at the Library of Congress (Abraham Flexner Papers), the American Philosophical Society in Philadelphia (Simon Flexner Papers), and Radcliffe's Schlesinger Library (Eleanor Flexner Papers). The last of those collections also includes Anne Crawford Flexner's 1903 journal plus newspaper clippings and photographs. The Eskind Biomedical Library at the Vanderbilt University Medical Center in Nashville, Tennessee, has a Flexner Family Collection that includes correspondence, biographical material, photographs, manuscripts, reprints, and a copy of the privately printed *A Family Memoir, 1899–1989*, a book written by Anne and Abraham Flexner's daughter, Jean Atherton Flexner Lewinson. Other biographical information can be found in Abraham Flexner's *I Remember* (1940), which is replete with photographs; the revised 1960 edition, titled *Abraham Flexner: An Autobiography*, is useful for the years after 1940. See also chapter 44, titled "Abraham and Anne," in *An American Saga* (1984) by the Flexners' nephew, James Thomas Flexner. Alice Hegan Rice's autobiography, *The Inky Way* (1940), has a discussion of Anne Flexner's role in the stage production of *Mrs. Wiggs of the Cabbage Patch*. An obituary is in the *New York Times*, 12 Jan. 1955.

MARY BOEWE

FLOOD, Curt (18 Jan. 1938–20 Jan. 1997), baseball player, was born Curtis Charles Flood in Houston, Texas, the son of Herman and Laura Flood (maiden name unknown), both of whom worked as hospital menials. In 1940 his family moved to Oakland, California. He later recalled that his childhood was disadvantaged but stable: "That is, we ate at regular intervals, but not much. We were not ragged. Both parents lived at home. In the conventionally squalid West Oakland ghetto where I grew up, most other households seemed worse off" (Flood, p. 19). As a teenager, he played on American Legion teams coached by George Powles, who developed a number of outstanding athletes in the Oakland area. One team featured three future major league stars in the outfield—Flood, Frank Robinson, and Vada Pinson. Although at five feet nine inches and 140 pounds he lacked the build to be regarded as a top baseball prospect, Flood was nonetheless given a contract with the Cincinnati Reds following his graduation from Oakland Technical High School in 1956.

Flood spent two seasons playing minor league baseball in the Jim Crow South, an experience that profoundly disturbed him. He later recalled that, while traveling, he often had to relieve himself by the side of the road behind the team bus because he was not allowed to use public restrooms. When playing in Georgia, state law forbade him to dress in the same room as his white teammates. For the first few weeks of his career, he wept every night after games; he also determined, however, "to solve my problem by playing my guts out" (Flood, p. 39). In 1956, with High Point–Thomasville in the Class B Carolina League, he hit .340 and drove in 128 runs; the following season, with Savannah in the Class A South Atlantic League, he batted .299 and made the all-star team. In 1958 he was traded to the St. Louis Cardinals, where he made the major league roster and batted .261 during his rookie year. His next two seasons were disappointing, however, in part because he got along poorly with manager Solly Hemus; Flood believed that Hemus was prejudiced and therefore unwilling to give him adequate playing time. He also had a bad habit of swinging for the fences, but under the tutelage of teammate George Crowe he adjusted his batting stroke and became a versatile line-drive hitter.

When Hemus was fired at midseason in 1961, Flood was immediately inserted into the Cardinals' starting lineup; by the end of the year, he had amassed a .322 batting average. During the next decade, he hit above .300 five times. He led the National League with 211 hits in 1964, and in 1967 he finished fourth in the league with a .335 batting average. But his hitting achievements were often overshadowed by his elegant play in the outfield—baseball scholars debate whether he or Willie Mays was the finest defensive center fielder of their generation. Possessing exceptional speed and sure instincts, Flood won a Gold Glove award every year between 1963 and 1969. From 3 September 1965 to 4 June 1967 he fielded 568 consecutive chances without committing an error, establishing a major league record for outfielders. He was named to five all-star teams, and he appeared in three World Series with the Cardinals. Ironically, the defensive play for which he is best remembered occurred in the seventh game of the 1968 World Series against the Detroit Tigers, when he misjudged a long fly ball, enabling two runs to score and ultimately costing the Cardinals the series.

In the fall of 1969, after a mildly sub-par season in which he batted .285, Flood was traded to the Philadelphia Phillies. He was devastated by the trade: he had lived in St. Louis for twelve years, run a successful portrait and photography studio in the city, and had close friends, such as his long-time roommate Bob Gibson, on the Cardinals team. In December he wrote baseball commissioner Bowie Kuhn, "I do not feel I am a piece of property to be bought and sold irrespective of my wishes" (Flood, p. 194). With retired Supreme Court justice Arthur Goldberg as his attorney, he proceeded to sue Major League Baseball, challenging the "reserve clause" inserted in players' contracts that forbade them to negotiate their employment in an open market. He explained his reasoning: "A salesman reluctant to transfer from one office to another may choose to seek employment on the sales force with a different firm. . . . But the baseball monopoly offers no such option to the athlete. If he elects not to work for the corporation that 'owns' his services, baseball forbids him to ply his trade at all" (Flood, p. 15).

Although many sportswriters believed that his suit was a cynical negotiating ploy to win a higher salary, Flood proved his seriousness by turning down a $110,000 contract offer from the Phillies and sitting out the 1970 season. While his case wound slowly through the federal courts, he found himself at loose ends. He later acknowledged: "As much as anything, I'm a baseball person, and to take that away from me cold turkey like that was not easy for me" (quoted in Eisenbath, p. 181). He moved to Copenhagen, Denmark, drank heavily, and received hate mail from fans. With the assistance of journalist Richard Carter, he wrote his autobiography, *The Way It Is* (1970), in which he offered an eloquent, angry indictment of the racism that he encountered throughout his career. In 1971 financial difficulties brought on by the lawsuit led him to return to baseball with the Washington Senators; but his heart was no longer in the game, and he retired in April. During his career he compiled a .293 batting average with 1,861 hits and 851 runs scored.

In 1972 the U.S. Supreme Court ruled against the plaintiff in *Flood v. Kuhn* by a vote of 5–3. In his majority opinion, Justice Harry Blackmun waxed rhapsodic about the virtues of baseball, listing the names of eighty-eight old-time stars; many of the other justices reportedly found his opinion "an embarrassment" (Lowenfish/Lupien, p. 213). But the Court also avowed its "grave reservations" about baseball's exemption from the Sherman Antitrust Act and suggested that Congress or a federal labor arbitrator might overturn the reserve system. In December 1972 an arbitrator ruled that the reserve clause was illegal, and in 1975 baseball players were guaranteed their individual bargaining rights through free agency. As a result, players' salaries rose dramatically in the ensuing decades: in 1969 the average annual salary was $24,909, while in 1993 it was $1.1 million, considerably more money than Flood made in his entire career.

During his playing days, Flood led a troubled private life. His 1959 marriage to Beverly Collins, with whom he had four children, led to a divorce, a remarriage, and a second divorce in the late 1960s. One of his closest friends was murdered in Oakland in 1966, and his brother Carl was sentenced to prison for bank robbery. Following his retirement, he lived for several years in Barcelona, Spain, and on the island of Majorca, where he operated a bar. A talented artist, he received numerous commissions to paint portraits and still lifes; his portrait of Martin Luther King, Jr., hung for more than thirty years in the living room of King's widow, Coretta Scott King. In a 1978 *Esquire* magazine profile he expressed his bitterness at being remembered as "the little black son of a bitch who tried to destroy baseball, the American Pastime" (Reeves, p. 42). That year he worked as a television commentator for the Oakland Athletics. During the 1980s he ran a public relations firm in Los Angeles. In his last years he suffered from throat cancer. He died in Los Angeles.

• Flood's autobiography, *The Way It Is* (1970), with Richard Carter, is regarded as a classic of baseball literature. For his experiences with racism, see Jules Tygiel, *Baseball's Great Experiment: Jackie Robinson and His Legacy* (1983). For a profile of Flood at the height of his playing career, see William Leggett, "Not Just a Flood, but a Deluge," *Sports Illustrated*, 19 Aug. 1968, pp. 18–21. For his landmark lawsuit against Major League Baseball, see two excellent histories of the sport's labor relations: John Helyar, *Lords of the Realm: The Real Story of Baseball* (1994), and Lee Lowenfish and Tony Lupien, *The Imperfect Diamond* (1980). For his post-baseball activities, see Richard Reeves, "The Last Angry Man," *Esquire*, 1 Mar. 1978, pp. 41–48. George F. Will, *Bunts: Curt Flood, Camden Yards, Pete Rose and Other Reflections on Baseball* (1998), and Mike Eisenbath, *The St. Louis Cardinals Encyclopedia* (1999), offer useful overviews of his life. An obituary is in the *New York Times*, 21 Jan. 1997.

THOMAS W. COLLINS, JR.

FOLLETT, Wilson (21 Mar. 1887–7 Jan. 1963), author and editor, was born Roy Wilson Follett in North Attleboro, Massachusetts, the son of Charles William Follett, a worker in a jewelry-manufacturing shop, and Cordelia Adelaide White Follett, a former teacher. After attending public schools in North Attleboro, he was an exemplary student at Harvard College, earning his B.A. in 1909, with a major in English and valuable study under Charles Townsend Copeland, a legendary professor there. While still a student, Follett studied piano assiduously and upon graduation had to choose between academe and a career as a concert pianist. In 1909 he married Grace Parker, who died in 1911 while giving birth to their only child.

From 1909 until 1918 Follett taught English at Texas Agricultural & Mechanical College (1909–1912), Dartmouth College (1912–1914), and Brown University (1914–1918). While at Brown, he taught a writing course at Radcliffe College. In 1913 he married Helen Thomas, a writer (as Helen Thomas Follett); they had two children and were divorced, probably in 1931. When Follett quit teaching, it was to commence an illustrious career as an editor. He worked in that capacity for Yale University Press, beginning in 1918, and later for Alfred A. Knopf, until 1929. In the early 1930s Follett moved to Culver City, now part of Los Angeles, where he was a freelance for motion picture studios. In 1932 he married Margaret Whipple; they bought a farm in Bradford, Vermont, had three children, and separated in 1947 but were never estranged. Soon after World War II began, Follett returned to Knopf as an editor replacing younger men serving in the armed forces (1943–1946). His last editorial work was accomplished with the New York University Press (1953–1958) and finally with Hill & Wang (1958–1963), during which time he wrote *Modern American Usage: A Guide*, which was posthumously published in 1966. Follett died in New York City.

Although Follett is most famous for his magisterial *Modern American Usage*, it was simply the culmination of a versatile career as a man of letters. As a critic, he wrote several books. The title of his *Joseph Conrad: A Short Study of His Intellectual and Emotional Attitude toward His Work and of the Chief Characteristics of His Novels* (1915), a "privately printed" monograph distributed by Doubleday, Page & Company, sufficiently indicates its scope. *The Modern Novel: A Study of the Purpose and the Meaning of Fiction* (written jointly with his wife, Helen Thomas Follett, 1918) analyzes novelists from Daniel Defoe to Thomas Hardy for their originality, realism, degree of representation, and harmony, as four gauges of their creative power. *Some Modern Novelists: Appreciations and Estimates* (again with Helen Thomas Follett, 1918), cleverly pairs several contrasting novelists to elucidate the values of each. For example, Henry James is seen as cosmopolitan, while William Dean Howells is provincial; Joseph Conrad is realistic, Edith Wharton, ironic. *Zona Gale: An Artist in Fiction* (1923) and *Arnold Bennett* (with Helen Thomas Follett and others, 1924) are relatively minor efforts.

In 1933 Follett published a novel, *No More Sea*, that is set in part on the Maine coast, where he lived in 1929–1930. It follows five generations of a family of seafaring men. The embittered heroine, having lost both father and husband to the sea, tries unsuccessfully to have her son live inland, but she cannot prevent his answering the lure of the sea.

Follett, competent in French and German, among other languages, was also a skillful translator. He published *Seedtime* (1947), his translation of a German novel by Leo Katz, about a 1907 Romanian peasant revolt; *Plato and Dionysius: A Double Biography* (1947), from the German of Ludwig Marcuse; and *Molière: The Man Seen through the Plays* (1958, repr. 1980), from Ramón Fernández's 1929 classic biography, originally in French. For his translations of the books by Katz and Marcuse, Follett used Joel Ames as his pen name. He edited *The Work of Stephen Crane* (12 vols., 1925–1926) and *The Collected Poems of Stephen Crane* (1930). Of less importance were his editions of Thomas Beer's *Mrs. Egg and Other Americans: Collected Stories* (1947) and Sidney W. Dean's *Cooking American* (1957).

From 1916 until 1962 Follett contributed almost innumerable articles, stories, and poems, some signed, others not, to the following magazines and periodicals, among others: the *Atlantic Monthly*, *Bookman*, the *Dial*, *Harper's Magazine*, the *New York Times Book Review*, the *Saturday Review*, the *Virginia Quarterly*, and the *Yale Review*. His ranging mind impelled him to write on subjects as varied as Ambrose Bierce, James Branch Cabell, Joseph Conrad, education, grammar, history, Henry James, politics, tools, and war.

Follett's *Modern American Usage* is the work for which he will be remembered longest. Together with a handful of other such reference books, including Henry W. Fowler's *A Dictionary of Modern English Usage*, William Strunk, Jr., and E. B. White's *The Elements of Style*, and Edwin Newman's *Strictly Speaking*, Follett's bible for the would-be literate is indispensable. As he was beginning his *Modern American Usage*, he wrote, "It is time we had an American book of usage grounded in the philosophy that the best in language—which is often the simplest—is not too good to be aspired to." His twin purposes were these: to analyze structural errors and ambiguities and thereby encourage writers and speakers to avoid flouting accepted norms, and to discuss certain words and idioms and thus provide tactful distinctions and suggestions. When Follett died, he left a manuscript draft of his book more than two-thirds complete. Jacques Barzun, the distinguished Columbia University professor and accomplished writer, put it into publishable form with the assistance of six eminent collaborators. An introduction invites the reader uncertain about a particular word or phrase to look it up in its alphabetical place. Examples, among hundreds, would be "hopefully" and "in terms of." Grammatical questions are also answered—for example, those concerning antecedents, "fewer" and "less," "lay" and "lie," "that" and "which," danglers, and voice. Long entries, often wittily erudite and with apt examples, are devoted to more complicated topics—for instance, the metaphor, the sentence, and the foreword (introduction, preface, and the like). One indication, among many, of thoroughness is the 43-page appendix on punctuation, offering not only basic rules but also polite suggestions. Although some reviewers quibbled at Follett's alleged subjective quirkiness, most found the book both delightful and helpful. It has stood the test of time sufficiently well to have gone into a second edition (1998, ed. Erik Wensberg).

Follett was no mere bookworm and writing machine. He was a brilliant and sympathetic conversationalist and had many enduring friendships. He mastered a great range of practical skills, from snowshoeing and fence-building to growing vegetables and making bread. He relished the quiddity of ordinary things: knew the plant and animal life of New England, was a fierce poker player and casino player, and followed major league baseball intently. He reserved a special fondness for classical music.

• Since Follett habitually destroyed manuscripts, letters, and other papers of various sorts, almost none of his personal papers has survived. Minor correspondence from him, however, is in the Anne Goodwin Winslow papers at the Memphis State University Library. John Tebbell, *A History of Book Publishing in the United States*, vol. 4, *The Great Change, 1940–1980* (1981), details the lexicographers' dispute over G. & C. Merriam Co.'s publication in 1961 of its "Webster Third" dictionary and Follett's vitriolic denunciation of it in his "Sabotage in Springfield," *Atlantic Monthly*, Jan. 1962. An extensive bibliography of his works is in private family archives. An obituary is in the *Boston Globe*, 9 Jan. 1963.

ROBERT L. GALE

FRANKOVICH, Mike (29 Sept. 1908–1 Jan. 1992), film producer, was born Mitchell John Frankovich in Bisbee, Arizona, one of four children of Yova Frankovich and Melica Frankovich (maiden name unknown), immigrant Yugoslavians. When all the children were small, the Frankovich family left the copper-mining town of Bisbee en route to California but stopped in Tonopah, Nevada, for several years after the elder Frankovich won its casino in a card game. They moved on to Long Beach, California, where he owned a fishing fleet. After Yova Frankovich abandoned the family, his wife moved to Los Angeles, where Mike and a brother excelled in high school football, gaining scholarships to the University of California, Los Angeles, on the recommendation of comedian Joe E. Brown. Frankovich starred in baseball and football; his 93-yard touchdown run during the 1932 season set a UCLA record. He graduated in 1935 and was inducted into UCLA's Hall of Fame in 1986.

Blessed with a pleasingly edged voice, a stock of stories and information, and boundless enthusiasm, Frankovich was soon broadcasting local baseball and football games as well as producing radio programs. He served as technical adviser on several sporting films. He was writing film scripts on speculation when he met the British actress Binnie Barnes at a poker game at Clark Gable's house. Frankovich and Barnes married in 1940, had three children and remained married until Frankovich's death. In 1941 Frankovich acted in several films including Frank Capra's *Meet John Doe*, always essentially playing himself as a sports broadcaster.

A deal struck among Republic Pictures, Barnes, and Frankovich gave him his first chance at producing in exchange for Barnes's accepting roles opposite the rising star John Wayne in the films *In Old California* (1942) and *In Old Oklahoma* (1943). World War II intervened and Frankovich joined the U.S. Army Air Forces, rising to the rank of colonel. Frankovich received multiple decorations. Shot down over China, he walked out to freedom, losing 100 pounds en route. In Europe, he commanded a bomber squadron and dropped weapons to Yugoslav insurgents under Marshal Tito. Upon his return, he found himself assigned by Republic to producing serials—the (usually) thirteen-episode potboilers made for unruly Saturday matinee audiences. After "G-Men Never Forget," "The Black Widow," and two of a similar stripe in 1947-1948, Frankovich decided on a wild gamble that turned out to be a stroke of genius. Fluent in three dialects of Serbo-Croatian as well as Spanish and Russian, Frankovich left for Europe in 1948 in search of financing for independent production. He moved his family to Italy, where in 1949 *Fugitive Lady*, starring Barnes, became his first solo production. In 1950 he made a deal with British Lion Films for several films, one of which, *Decameron Nights* (1952), shot in Spain and England, drew the attention of Columbia Pictures. Frankovich had perfectly anticipated American films' era of runaway production, a result of rising domestic costs and falling income, the latter due to

the impact of television. The Frankovich family moved to London and several films later, in 1955, the year of his *Joe MacBeth*, a Shakespearean remake, Leo Jaffe, heir apparent to Columbia's boss Harry Cohn, signed Frankovich as head of Columbia (Great Britain) Productions.

Between 1955 and 1963 Frankovich, a deal-maker willing to take a chance, produced from his British base films that burnished Columbia's reputation. *The Bridge Over the River Kwai* (1957), with five Academy Awards and a nomination, led a string of essentially serious, immensely entertaining big-budget epics that became Frankovich's signature. In 1959, with Columbia (Britain) producing 80 percent of the studio's European releases, Frankovich took charge of all European production. In the same year he advised Marshal Tito to help create a Yugoslav film industry. *The Guns of Navarone*, an exhilarating World War II adventure made in 1961 and the recipient of three Academy Award nominations, and *Lawrence of Arabia*, a complex and visually ravishing biography made in 1962, winner of four Academy Awards, were both financed by Columbia only when Frankovich threatened to make them independently. They immediately preceded his recall in 1963 to Hollywood, where he became vice president in charge of Columbia's worldwide production.

Columbia's long-time home on Gower Street, then essentially a television studio, was a salable asset. But the persuasive Frankovich seems to have convinced film unions that altering some of their codes might help save the industry. Columbia's domestic production resumed and prospered. *Cat Ballou* (1965, one Academy Award) was an apparently serious western script when Frankovich passed it to the film's eventual director, Elliot Silverstein, urging him, "Read it as a comedy." On familiarly epic scale was the weighty (and British-based) biography of Sir Thomas More, *A Man for All Seasons* (1966, five Academy Awards, two nominations). Frankovich was instrumental in identifying Sidney Poitier's talent and promoting his career in *The Bedford Incident* (1965), *Guess Who's Coming to Dinner?* (1967, two Academy Awards and five nominations), and, set and filmed in Great Britain, *To Sir, With Love* (1967). Poitier later wrote of his role (not designed for an African-American) as a newspaperman in *The Bedford Incident*, "The reins of a major studio were seldom to be found in the hands of men with such a sense of fair play."

In 1967 Frankovich moved off the top, telling the *Los Angeles Times*, "I wanted to make only the kind of pictures I myself was interested in—as opposed to the 30 or 32 pictures a year I had supervised for the good of the company." Releasing through Columbia, the output of Frankovich Productions proved generally of lighter weight, though it included the ironic lifestyle comedy *Bob and Carol and Ted and Alice* (1969, four Academy nominations). There were many adaptations of stage comedies often with the kooky Goldie Hawn, including *Cactus Flower* (1969, one Academy nomination), *There's a Girl in My Soup* (1970) and

Butterflies are Free (1972, one Academy Award). *Marooned* (1969) was a tale of space heroism. In 1972 Columbia left Gower Street forever. *The Shootist* (1976) was a moving elegy for the western as genre and the last film of Wayne, its star. One of Frankovich's last productions was the television film *Ziegfeld: The Man and His Women* (1978).

A long-time supporter of the American Film Institute, Frankovich also served as president of Variety Children's Charity and on several hospital boards of trustees. As the president of the Los Angeles Coliseum Commission, he helped lure the Oakland Raiders football franchise to Los Angeles.and negotiated the use of the Coliseum for the 1984 Olympics. In 1984 he received the Academy of Motion Picture Arts and Sciences' Jean Hersholt Humanitarian Award for "varied and extensive record of humanitarian activities." Frankovich, a member of the UCLA Foundation's board, continued as an unofficial scout for UCLA athletics. After suffering from Alzheimer's disease, Frankovich died in Los Angeles of pneumonia.

During years when control of the American film industry generally passed from its pioneer-tyrants to financial institutions here and abroad, when authority leaked from studios to performers, it was persuasive, visionary, and sometimes ruthless deal-makers such as Mike Frankovich who coddled Hollywood film, kept it identifiable, and eventually saved it.

• Frankovich's papers are dispersed among libraries at Brigham Young University, Provo, Utah; the Academy of Motion Picture Arts and Sciences, Los Angeles; the American Film Institute, Los Angeles; and the University of California, Los Angeles. Frankovich's film producer sons Mike Jr. and Peter provided family background for this essay, as did his brother Lee Frankovich. A negative view of Frankovich as a ruthless manipulator is part of Frank Capra, *The Name above the Title* (1971). Obituaries include Myrna Oliver's in the *Los Angeles Times*, 3 Jan. 1992, and William Grimes's in the *New York Times*, 4 Jan. 1992.

JAMES ROSS MOORE

FRIENDLY, Fred W. (30 Oct. 1915–3 Mar. 1998), broadcast journalist and television producer, was born Ferdinand Friendly Wachenheimer in New York City, the son of Samuel Wachenheimer, a jewelry manufacturer, and Therese Friendly Wachenheimer. Around 1926 his family moved to Providence, Rhode Island. Although he was an undistinguished student, he was fervently interested in radio and history during his youth. After graduating from Hope Street High School, he attended Nichols Junior College in Dudley, Massachusetts, majoring in business administration. In 1937 he was hired as a radio announcer and newscaster at a station in Providence, where his employers insisted that he change his name to Fred Friendly. During his tenure at the station he wrote and narrated five-minute documentaries about men such as the inventors Thomas Edison and Guglielmo Marconi; these were broadcast in 1942 as an ongoing series, *Footprints in the Sands of Time.*

During World War II Friendly served in the China-Burma-India theater as a correspondent for *CBI Roundup*, an Army newspaper. Pursuing his assignments aggressively, he proved adept at "making generals do what he, rather than they, wanted" (Swados, p. 31). He was permitted to fly on night missions with the first P-61 Black Widow fighters, and he rode in the first convoy along the Stilwell Road, a rugged combat-support highway that connected northern India and Burma. While stationed in Bombay, India, he helped to rescue several survivors of a dock explosion. Following V-E Day, he was granted a three-month leave of absence to travel in Europe, where he experimented with audiotape techniques while making a documentary about G.I.s. By the time he was discharged, as a master sergeant, he had been awarded four battle stars, the Legion of Merit, and the Soldier's Medal.

Following the war, Friendly moved to New York City, where he had "a tiny bank account, big plans, and fresh ideas about the use of sound" (Sperber, p. 320). In 1947 he married Dorothy Greene, a researcher for *Life* magazine; they had three children and would later divorce.

Friendly was particularly interested in using sound to explore history; influenced by Frederick Lewis Allen's colorful social history of the 1920s, *Only Yesterday*, he wanted to develop an aural equivalent. With typical salesmanship and chutzpah, he convinced the acclaimed radio journalist Edward R. Murrow to narrate the project. The pair collaborated on *I Can Hear It Now* (1948), an innovative record album that provided an oral history of the years 1933 to 1945. Unlike previous sound documentaries, which had utilized recreations by actors, mood music, and sound effects, *I Can Hear It Now* relied only on indigenous sound. The album skillfully juxtaposed major speeches by world leaders with small, offhand vignettes, such as New York City mayor Fiorello La Guardia reading the comics over the radio during a newspaper strike. Friendly called the project a "labor of love" and worked on it for eighteen months; the record proved to be a surprise hit, eventually becoming a staple of the Columbia Records catalog. In 1949 and 1950 he created two successful radio series for NBC, *Who Said That?*, an erudite panel quiz program, and *The Quick and the Dead*, a four-part documentary about the development of the atomic bomb.

In 1950 Friendly joined Murrow at CBS, where they collaborated on *Hear It Now*, a radio series based on their record. Around this time Friendly became intrigued by the possibilities of television. Knowing nothing about film techniques, he spent several months studying newsreel documentaries at the Museum of Modern Art in New York City. Murrow was wary of the fledgling medium; although he believed that television might become a powerful means of communication, he also felt that it was too closely linked to the world of show business. Nevertheless, in the fall of 1951 they introduced a program on CBS, *See It Now*, that would become a landmark in broadcast journalism—"the prototype of the in-depth quality television documentary" (Bluem, pp. 99–100). Observers noted that the two men complemented each other well; Murrow possessed great journalistic integrity but was somewhat staid and aloof, while Friendly was more flamboyant and hustling, an expert at wielding Murrow's name to get things accomplished. *See It Now* proved to be innovative from its first episode, which relied on new microwave technology to show live shots of the Golden Gate Bridge in San Francisco and the Brooklyn Bridge in New York City simultaneously—"the first time in the history of man," Murrow informed his viewers, "we are able to look out at both the Atlantic and Pacific coasts . . . at the same time" (quoted in Rosteck, p. 20). During its first two seasons, the program took a news-magazine approach, dealing with several topics briefly in each half-hour; by 1953 the show settled on a more substantive format in which only one topic was examined. A typical telecast included both live interviews and filmed segments, which were shot on 35-millimeter film with fully synchronized sound, giving them the high quality of a motion picture. Similar in style to *I Can Hear It Now*, the television program made remarkable use of small, evocative details; for instance, for a Christmastime report on the Korean War in 1952—the first combat report via television—the opening simply showed a soldier digging a foxhole, focusing on his boots, his hands gripping the shovel, and the shovel scraping against the frozen ground. Friendly and his staff mastered the close-up for their interviews, seizing on television's unique ability to telescope personal characteristics. As one critic suggested, "Every facial movement or gesture is heightened in effect, and every accompanying vocal inflection is correspondingly stressed, with the result that the whole personality of the man is peculiarly concentrated and revealed" (Whiteside, p. 54).

During its early seasons, *See It Now* typically dealt with nonpolitical subject matter; as Friendly later admitted, "The missing ingredients were conviction, controversy, and a point of view" (*Due to Circumstances beyond Our Control . . .*, p. 3). In 1953 and 1954, however, *See It Now* became perhaps the most politicized program in television history when it aired a series of broadcasts dealing with the impact of Senator Joseph McCarthy and his investigation of alleged communists in the United States government. In "The Case of Milo Radulovich, A0589839," shown in October 1953, Murrow examined the plight of a lieutenant in the Air Force Reserve who had been discharged as a security risk because of hearsay evidence that his father and sister read pro-communist newspapers. "An Argument in Indianapolis," broadcast a month later, looked at an effort by the American Legion and the Minute Women to prevent the left-leaning American Civil Liberties Union from holding public meetings in the city. In both instances, Friendly later told an interviewer, the *See It Now* staff sought out "the right incident . . . [a] shorthand for a real situation which would illustrate a national issue"

(quoted in Rosteck, p. 56). In March 1954 the program aired a bold attack on McCarthy, "Report on Senator Joseph R. McCarthy"; distilled from more than fifteen thousand feet of film, the report provided a wide-ranging investigation of the senator's techniques, showing him, for example, browbeating Voice of America deputy Reed Harris and making a joke about "Alger . . . I mean Adlai Stevenson" (a reference to convicted communist spy Alger Hiss). Eschewing any pretense to impartiality, the program ended with Murrow's insistence that "this is no time for men who oppose Senator McCarthy's methods to keep silent" (quoted in Friendly, p. 41). During the following days CBS received more than 100,000 phone calls about the broadcast, almost all of which were favorable. A week after the McCarthy program, *See It Now* aired "Annie Lee Moss before the McCarthy Committee," which showed the proceedings against an apparently innocent woman who had been fired from her government job. Cumulatively, these broadcasts helped to galvanize the public against McCarthy and contributed to his downfall as a political force. Although several journalists had criticized the senator previously, Murrow and Friendly were the first to use the power of television to condemn McCarthyism.

The CBS management was embarrassed by the controversial nature of the *See It Now* broadcasts on McCarthy and forced Murrow and Friendly to pay for advertisements for two of the shows out of their own pockets. Friendly later recalled that the day after the McCarthy show, "when the newspapers were running banner headlines about it and the CBS switchboard and mail rooms were jammed," he had ridden up an elevator with an executive who pointedly ignored the subject—"just asked me how I'd been" (quoted in Whiteside, p. 83). In subsequent years the program continued to deal with inflammatory subject matter, including reports on the impact of the *Brown v. Board of Education* Supreme Court decision in the South and the link between tobacco use and lung cancer. A 1955 broadcast about a Texas land scandal caused the program's sponsor, Alcoa, to cancel its sponsorship; the company had been expanding its installations in Texas. Afterward, the show lost its weekly lineup slot and was aired only occasionally. In 1958 it was cancelled, despite having won thirty-five major broadcasting awards.

Following the demise of *See It Now*, Friendly and Murrow coproduced an unsuccessful public affairs program, *Small World*, which filmed people in different areas of the world while they carried on a four-way conversation over the telephone. During the late 1950s the television industry suffered through a number of scandals involving rigged game shows; seeking to regain credibility with viewers, CBS invited Friendly in 1960 to become the executive producer of a new documentary program, *CBSReports*. Although he initially assumed that the series would be a Murrow-Friendly production, he was told that this would create "problems." Instead, Murrow was allowed to narrate a few episodes, but he became increasingly peripheral at the network and resigned in 1961. With Murrow's blessing, however, Friendly took the job and quickly built *CBSReports* into one of the most respected news shows on television. Featuring a staff of ten full-time producers, each of whom was responsible for two shows per season, the show was able to carry on lengthy, painstaking investigations; for example, producer David Lowe lived with migrant farm workers for a full year while assembling footage for the celebrated documentary "Harvest of Shame." Other significant documentaries included "The Population Explosion," "Biography of a Bookie Joint," "Biography of a Missile," and "The Business of Health: Medicine, Money and Politics." Friendly's colleagues saw him as a strong-willed perfectionist whose full-blown enthusiasm for each of his projects could become exhausting. The poet Carl Sandburg said that he was a man who "always looks as though he had just dismounted from a foam-flecked horse" (quoted in Schoenbrun, p. 165). "He was the one guy who sensed when to do a show so that it was ready for a news break," producer Gene de Poris recalled. "And in order to do it, he pushed mercilessly. When he'd phone me at midnight, at 1 a.m., at 2 a.m., my wife would ask, 'What can there be left to say that you didn't get said in 12 hours at the office?'" (quoted in Swados, p. 102).

In 1964 Friendly was appointed president of CBS News, a promotion that he came to regret. One of his first tasks was to remove Walter Cronkite from the anchor chair for the network's coverage of the 1964 Democratic National Convention. The move was made at the insistence of CBS chairman William Paley, who was unhappy with Cronkite's poor ratings during the Republican National Convention earlier that year, but Friendly believed that he humiliated Cronkite and later called it "the worst thing I've ever done" (quoted in the *New York Times*, 5 March 1998). In 1966 he became embroiled in a bitter dispute with his superiors when he attempted to provide gavel-to-gavel coverage of Senator William Fulbright's public hearings on the Vietnam War. His decision to show the testimony of former government official George Kennan was overridden by a newly appointed CBS group vice-president, John A. Schneider, who told him that housewives weren't interested in Vietnam. While Kennan testified, the network showed its regular daytime schedule, including a rerun of *I Love Lucy*. In protest, Friendly offered to resign, although he apparently intended this as a symbolic, nonbinding gesture; he also submitted his letter of resignation to the *New York Times*. The network president, Frank Stanton, angry that Friendly had gone public with the conflict, insisted that his resignation be accepted. Friendly later wrote that the network's choice had been "between interrupting the morning run of the profit machine—whose only admitted function was to purvey six one-minute commercials every half-hour—or electing to make the audience privy to an event of overriding national importance taking place in a Senate hearing room at that very moment" (p. 213). He was appalled that CBS, which had long fought for access to congressional hearings, chose to renege when given the opportunity to cover a vital debate.

The day after his resignation, Friendly was invited to join the Ford Foundation as an adviser on communications. In 1966 he and foundation president McGeorge Bundy devised an ambitious plan for funding a public television network devoted to educational programming. The plan called for the creation of a nonprofit domestic satellite system; under this plan commercial television networks would be charged for transmission services and the proceeds would be used to fund public television. Although their proposal was successfully opposed by commercial interests, Congress was spurred to pass the Public Broadcasting Act in 1967, which led to the formation of the Public Broadcasting System (PBS). In 1967 Friendly published a fine memoir, *Due to Circumstances beyond Our Control . . .*, in which he denounced the "mercantile advertising system" that held much of television in thrall. In the book he wrote that "because television can make so much money doing its worst, it often cannot afford to do its best." In 1968 he married Ruth Mark, a former schoolteacher; they had no children. That year he was appointed to serve in two positions at Columbia University, as Edward R. Murrow Professor of Journalism and as the chairman of the broadcast program. In 1974 he initiated a series of conferences about ethical issues in journalism; these conferences evolved into "The Fred Friendly Seminars," which were broadcast on public television into the 1990s. In 1976 he published a book that dealt with the history of the Federal Communications Commission's fairness doctrine, *The Good Guys, the Bad Guys and the First Amendment: Free Speech vs. Fairness in Broadcasting*. In 1981 he published *Minnesota Rag: The Dramatic Story of the Landmark Supreme Court Case that Gave New Meaning to Freedom of the Press*. The book explored a 1931 decision involving a bigoted newspaper publisher in Minnesota whose publication had been shut down under a public nuisance act. During his later years he continued to be passionately interested in constitutional issues; as CBS reporter Andy Rooney noted, "on the slightest provocation, or none at all, he will whip out the Constitution and read it to anyone he happens to be talking to." He died in New York City.

• There is no biography on Friendly. The best source for information on his career is his memoir, *Due to Circumstances beyond Our Control . . .* (1967). Revealing magazine profiles are Thomas Whiteside's colorful "The One-Ton Pencil" in the *New Yorker* (17 Feb. 1962; pp. 41–88); and Harvey Swados's somewhat negative "Fred Friendly and Friendlyvision" in the *New York Times Magazine* (April 1967; pp. 13, 102–121). Also useful are A. M. Sperber, *Murrow: His Life and Times* (1986); and David Halberstam, *The Powers That Be* (1979). For scholarly appraisals of *See It Now*, see A. William Bluem, *Documentary in American Television* (1965); Thomas Rosteck, *"See It Now" Confronts McCarthyism: Television*

Documentary and the Politics of Representation (1994); and Michael D. Murray, *The Political Performers: CBS Broadcasts in the Public Interest* (1994). For views of Friendly by his peers, see David Schoenbrun, *On and Off the Air: An Informal History of CBS News* (1989); and Bill Leonard, *In the Storm of the Eye: A Lifetime at CBS* (1987). An obituary is in the *New York Times*, 5 March 1998.

THOMAS W. COLLINS, JR.

FROMKIN, Victoria A. (16 May 1923–19 Jan. 2000), linguist and university administrator, was born Victoria Alexandra Landish in Passaic, New Jersey, the daughter of Henry Landish, a set designer for the theater, and Rose Lillian Ravitz Landish. The family moved to Los Angeles where Fromkin graduated from Belmont High School. She continued her education at the University of California, Berkeley, receiving a bachelor of arts degree in economics in 1944. A self-described "professional radical revolutionary" (quoted in Cheng and Sybesma, p. 1), Fromkin worked without pay for liberal and radical causes before and after she married Jack Fromkin in 1948. They had one child.

In late 1961 Fromkin returned to school, enrolling at the University of California, Los Angeles. Here, at the height of the great surge in Chomskyan generative grammar, she began to study linguistics. Her first linguistics professor was Harry Hoijer, but she considered her earliest mentor in linguistics to be Paul Garvin, who was working on machine translation and who nominated her for a two-week NATO-sponsored institute on machine translation in Venice, Italy. Neither Hoijer nor Garvin worked in generative grammar, but in Venice Fromkin met Yehoshua Bar-Hillel, a philosopher and colleague of Noam Chomsky. From their discussions Fromkin's linguistic interests turned to the nature of linguistic theory and its close connection to questions of how human beings acquire and process language.

Fromkin received a master of arts degree from UCLA in 1963. Her doctoral dissertation, published as *Some Phonetic Specifications of Linguistic Units: An Electromyographic Investigation* (1965), was directed by the UCLA linguist and phonetician Peter Ladefoged. For several years Fromkin's research and publications drew largely on her work in phonetics. Her interest in the physical production of speech led Fromkin to research on speech errors such as slips of the tongue. She sought to determine the implications of such errors for a theory of the mental representation of language and a model of language production. Her first paper on the topic in the journal of the Linguistic Society of America was widely read. "The Non-Anomalous Nature of Anomalous Utterances" (*Language* 47 [1971]: 27–52) demonstrated that speech errors are not random. Rather, they involve discrete units of a language (such as sounds, syllables, words) and processes of substitution, omission, transposition, and addition, and they follow the same rules of a language as do other types of linguistic performance. An English speaker, for example, might say "plit spea soup" for "split pea soup." In this error, the consonant

clusters *pl* and *sp* are normal sequences in the language. No speaker of English, however, would produce a speech error such as "slpit pea soup" because the sound pattern of the English language never allows the consonant cluster *slp* at the beginning of a word. The mental representation of the language and the processes of language production permit only those errors that obey the rules of the language.

Fromkin's 1971 article was based on 600 errors that she had collected. She was soon able to provide 1,000 English speech errors as the appendix to her edited volume *Speech Errors as Linguistic Evidence* (1973). Her second edited volume on the topic was *Errors in Linguistic Performance: Slips of the Tongue, Ear, Pen, and Hand* (1980), a compilation drawn from an international symposium she had conducted in Vienna, Austria, in 1977. Throughout the rest of her life she carried with her a small notebook in which she continued to record the speech errors she heard. The collection eventually contained over 12,000 examples.

Fromkin's later work was focused almost entirely on issues of brain and language. She studied language use and loss in aphasia, dyslexia, and Parkinson's disease, and she was involved in promoting the investigation of language acquisition in children deprived of language input. In all of these studies, she found evidence for language universals, the linguistic capacity of the human brain, and the modularity of language (a language faculty in the mind that is distinct from other cognitive systems and abilities). Her support for the theory of a genetically determined language faculty placed her within the broad framework of Chomskyan generative linguistics. However, because so much of her work was on the bridge between linguistics and other fields (phonetics, psychology, neurobiology), she rarely became embroiled in the controversies that attended the debates in theoretical linguistics during the last decades of the twentieth century.

Bridge-building between linguistics and other disciplines was of special importance to Fromkin. She wanted linguists to contribute their understanding of language to other fields, and she sought in those fields evidence for the claims linguists made about how the brain must be organized for language. Neuroscientific research involving brain imaging shows, Fromkin said, "that there are actually separate brain mechanisms that provide additional neural support for claims that we [linguists] make about the organization and processing of the grammar," in this case the modularity of lexical categories, such as unique names, animal names, and tool names, each of which is stored in a different area of the brain (quoted in Cheng and Sybesma, p. 23).

Fromkin was active in professional organizations. She served as president of the Linguistic Society of America (1985), chair of the board of governors of the Academy of Aphasia (1991–1993), and secretary and then chair of Linguistics Section Z of the American Association for the Advancement of Science (1993–1996, 1997–1998). Her achievements were recognized by her election to the National Academy of Sciences.

Appointed to the UCLA faculty upon completion of her doctorate, Fromkin remained there throughout her career. She chaired the linguistics department in 1970–1971 and again from 1973 to 1977 and then served as dean of the graduate division (1979–1989) and vice chancellor of graduate programs (1980–1989), the first woman to hold the rank of vice chancellor in the entire University of California system. She also became the first woman president of the Association of Graduate Schools in the American Association of Universities (1988). A highly regarded teacher, she earned a UCLA Distinguished Teaching Award (1974) and taught at the Linguistic Institutes of the Linguistic Society of America in 1966, 1976, 1977, and 1983. She served as visiting fellow at Wolfson College, Oxford University (1983, 1987) and as a visiting professor at many institutions, including Cambridge University (1977) and the University of Stockholm (1977). Her textbook *An Introduction to Language*, coauthored with Robert Rodman, was read by millions of students over the course of six editions (1974, 1978, 1983, 1987, 1992, 1998). At the time of her death in Los Angeles, she had just completed editing another textbook, *Linguistics: An Introduction to Linguistic Theory* (2000).

• An important interview with Fromkin by Lisa Cheng and Rint Sybesma appeared in *Glot International* 2 (May 1996): 1, 22–24. Larry M. Hyman and Charles N. Li, eds., *Language, Speech and Mind: Studies in Honour of Victoria A. Fromkin* (1988), contains her curriculum vitae and publications list to 1988. Obituaries are in the *Los Angeles Times*, 24 Jan. 2000, and the *New York Times*, 30 Jan. 2000.

JULIA S. FALK

FUJIKAWA, Gyo (3 Nov. 1908–26 Nov. 1998), illustrator and graphic artist, was born in Berkeley, California, the daughter of Hikozo Fujikawa, an interpreter, and his wife, Yu Fujikawa (maiden name unknown), a journalist and poet. Her Japanese father gave her a male first name, after an ancient Chinese emperor whom he admired. Raised in a bicultural atmosphere—the Fujikawa household was traditionally Japanese, but young Gyo attended American schools—she displayed artistic talent at an early age and began winning prizes for her artwork as a teenager. In high school she decided that she wanted a career as an artist for children, and with encouragement from her teachers she won a scholarship to the Chouinard Art Institute in Los Angeles, where she enrolled following graduation in 1926.

Fujikawa studied full time at Chouinard for several years and then became a freelance illustrator, drawing children and child-appealing images for magazines and advertising agencies. In the early 1930s she traveled to Japan to learn more about Japanese culture, an experience that she later claimed was an important milestone in her life. In particular, she was drawn to the art of Hiroshige, Utamaro, Sesshu, and Korin, and

they were to have a pronounced influence on her own work. Beginning in 1933, Fujikawa taught art at Chouinard while pursuing her freelance career, and she remained on the staff for six years. In 1939 she was hired by the Walt Disney Studios in Anaheim, California, as an artist in the promotion department; among her projects was the design of promotional material for Disney's groundbreaking semi-animated film *Fantasia*.

Fujikawa was sent by Disney to New York City in 1941 to design promotions for various Disney materials, including several mass-market Golden Books, and worked out of an office at the Western Printing and Publishing Company. There she became closely acquainted for the first time with children's publishing, and this renewed her long-held dream of concentrating on art for children. When her assignment with Disney ended in the fall of 1941, she remained in New York, hoping to find a job in the then relatively new field of children's books, but when this did not materialize she joined the motion picture advertising staff of the Hal Horne Organization, providing illustrations for film ads and posters. In 1942 the company became part of the advertising department in the New York offices of Twentieth Century–Fox. Only months earlier, in December 1941, the Japanese had bombed Pearl Harbor, and the United States was now at war with Japan. Prejudice against Japanese Americans swelled, and Fujikawa realized that she was lucky to have a job as well as her personal freedom. Back home in California, her parents and brother, like other Japanese Americans there, were forced to relocate to an internment camp, where they lived throughout the war. Abandoning her plans to return to the West Coast, she settled permanently in New York.

In 1943 Fujikawa became art director at the William Douglas McAdams advertising agency, which specialized in medical and pharmaceutical accounts, and she remained there for eight years. Finally, in 1951, she was able to leave the agency to freelance once again, with the hope that she might eventually move into children's publishing. In addition to specializing in illustrations of children, Fujikawa had also developed an interest in and aptitude for illustrating the natural world—birds and other animals, trees, flowers—and she became a major contributor of artwork to such leading publications as *Reader's Digest*, *McCall's*, *Ladies' Home Journal*, and the *Saturday Evening Post*. She also continued her work in advertising, creating such graphics as the babies for Beech-Nut Baby Foods and the Eskimo child for Eskimo Pies, the ice cream novelty product. An opportunity to do work aimed at entertaining children came at last in 1955, when the children's editor at Grossett & Dunlap, the book publishing company, asked her to illustrate a new edition of the children's classic *A Child's Garden of Verses* by Robert Louis Stevenson. Published two years later, the book was an instant success and earned Fujikawa critical praise.

While continuing as a freelance illustrator, Fujikawa turned her attention to the creation of her first children's picturebook, *Babies*, which was published in 1963 by Grosset. Using minimal text and appealing watercolors of infants, the book introduced the very youngest children to babies and what they do each day. What was especially notable about *Babies* was its multi-ethnic cast: Fujikawa's infants were not only white but also of Asian and African descent. When the head of the sales department asked Fujikawa to remove the "black babies," claiming that the book would not sell in the South if they remained, Fujikawa adamantly refused. She was vindicated: *Babies* became a bestseller and was widely praised not only for its gentle story and illustrations but also because its multicultural approach became a milestone in children's publishing. A sequel by Fujikawa, called *Baby Animals*, was also published in 1963. It, too, was a bestseller and, along with *Babies*, is still in print. By the end of the twentieth century, some 1.3 million copies of both books had been sold.

Despite this success, during the next decade Fujikawa continued with other freelance work for magazines and ad agencies and also designed several U.S. postage stamps. She did find time, however, to illustrate several collections of fairy tales and Mother Goose rhymes for children. Only when she had reached what was then considered standard retirement age—sixty-five—did she finally turn her attention to writing and illustrating children's books full time. Beginning in 1974 with the publication of the *A to Z Picture Book*, Fujikawa created an astonishing forty-four original picturebooks for children over the next sixteen years and illustrated an additional four. In 1981 alone, sixteen works by Fujikawa were published. Several of her books became bestsellers, including the *A to Z Picture Book*, reissued in 1981 as *Gyo Fujikawa's A to Z Picture Book*, and *Oh, What a Busy Day!*, first published in 1976 and also reissued in 1981 as *Gyo Fujikawa's Oh, What a Busy Day!* Many of her books, like *Millie's Secret* (1978), told simple realistic stories about small children; others presented tales of fairies, elves, and other fantasy creatures, including the bestselling *Come Follow Me*, first published in 1979 and reissued ten years later as *Gyo Fujikawa's Come Follow Me*.

Fujikawa used both watercolors and black-and-white detailed drawings to illustrate her books, creating a style that often combined realism with whimsical fantasy. Babies and children were identifiably human but frequently verged on the "cute," with smiling, round faces and black dots for eyes. This tendency toward cuteness, reinforced by Fujikawa's relentless pastel cheerfulness, probably caused her work to be passed over for major children's book awards, most notably the Caldecott Medal. Yet her illustrations were emotionally appealing to the young and offered bedtime comfort not only to small children but also to the adults who read to them.

Fujikawa, who never married, stopped painting in 1990, at the age of eighty-two. She died in New York City a few weeks after her ninetieth birthday.

• Biographical information on Gyo Fujikawa can be found in *Contemporary Authors: New Revision Series*, vol. 46 (1995) and in *Something about the Author*, vol. 76 (1994). See also profiles of Fujikawa in *Publishers Weekly*, 4 Jan. 1971 and 4 Sept. 1982. For an assessment of Fujikawa's early work, see Selma G. Lanes, *Down the Rabbit Hole* (1971), a study of children's book illustrators. An obituary appears in the *New York Times*, 7 Dec. 1998.

ANN T. KEENE

FUNT, Allen (16 Sept. 1914–5 Sept. 1999), radio and television producer, was born in Brooklyn, New York, the son of Russian immigrants Isadore Funt, a diamond importer and dealer, and Paula Saferstein Funt. A serious student, he graduated from New Utrecht High School in Brooklyn at the age of fifteen, spent a year at the Pratt Art Institute in Brooklyn, and went on to receive a B.A. in fine arts at Cornell University in 1934. Hoping to become an artist, he spent another year at Pratt, and in 1935 he began his working career in the art department of an advertising agency in New York. There he served first as a copywriter but within a year moved to the agency's radio department. In 1940–1941 he wrote the continuity for Eleanor Roosevelt's Sweetheart Soap chat show, but as the medium explored new avenues of entertainment in the 1930s, he became the agency's "gimmick" man, thinking up new ideas and producing audience-participation shows. His most successful was *The Funny Money Man*, which paid him $1,200 a week. Based on the idea of a scavenger hunt, it paid listeners random sums of money for miscellaneous items they sent in to the show. Funt called it "the stupidest show on radio" and later described his audience-participation days as "a degrading, lackluster period" of his life (quoted in Flagler, p. 79).

Funt joined the army in 1943 and was assigned to the Army Signal Corps in Oklahoma, where he recorded soldiers' messages to their families back home. After reading the gripe column in the army newspaper *Yank*, he tried recording the men's comments for broadcast but found that they froze up before the microphone. It was then that he got the idea that was to make him famous. He secretly activated the microphone ten minutes before he let his subjects know so that they talked informally with him, and thus he received spontaneous, natural recordings.

In 1946 he married Evelyn Kessler; the couple had three children. They divorced in 1964 and a month later Funt remarried, to Marilyn Ina Laron; they had two children together.

When he was discharged in 1946, Funt approached the Mutual Broadcasting System to finance an experiment: he proposed to secretly record conversations with people in public places that would be used for broadcast. The network advanced him a small sum, and he used the money to hide bulky two-part wire recorders, weighing more than 100 pounds, in restaurants and professional offices. He recorded natural interaction in everyday situations, capturing spontaneous exchanges between typical customers and waiters or clerks. For six months he didn't produce anything very amusing. The turning point came when by chance Funt was in a dentist's office and a patient took him for the dentist. Seizing the opportunity, Funt turned on his microphone and played the part, contradicting the patient and telling her he could not find a wisdom tooth in her mouth, and he captured her angry response on wire. He wasn't able to sell the idea to Mutual, but in 1947 the American Broadcasting Company agreed to present his work. Launched on 28 June of that year, his weekly thirty-minute show was called *The Candid Microphone*.

The radio program ran on ABC until August 1948, when it became a television show, still called *The Candid Microphone*. In May 1949 it switched to the National Broadcasting Company, which renamed it *Candid Camera*. It lasted only four months with NBC and then ran for a year over the Columbia Broadcasting System, from September 1949 to September 1950. The show had a two-month run again with NBC in 1953, and then it languished until October 1960, when CBS decided to try it again. This time it was a hit; in the 1960–1961 season it was ranked the seventh most popular show on American television, and it continued to reach a wide audience in many countries until 1967. As his show progressed, it evolved from stunts like breaking an egg in a man's hat or coasting into a garage and asking a mechanic to check the oil of a car that had no motor, to a sometimes serious study of human behavior, such as the "observation" films in which he examined the different gaits of people walking up and down stairs or different ways in which people puff cigarettes or eat spaghetti. In a more serious vein, Funt sometimes undertook to expose the verbal trickery of used-car salesman or created what he called "mood spots," such as recordings of a father telling his son a bedtime story or of a child playing with a kitten.

From 1974 to 1978 Funt produced *The New Candid Camera*, a weekly syndicated series, and several specials for NBC and CBS, as well as adult versions of the show for cable television. Episodes from *Candid Camera* were assembled into two feature films: the sexually suggestive *What Do You Say to a Naked Lady?* (1970), which received an "X" rating and lost money, and *Money Talks* (1972), a pastiche of people's reactions to odd situations involving cash. In the latter he had one of his employees sit at a restaurant counter, calmly salt and pepper a plateful of dollar bills, and eat them. "The man next to him tried not to look," he recalled in 1987, "but he did, his face showing he thought the money-eater was completely mad" (quoted in Hale). Funt also produced over forty movie shorts for Columbia Pictures, seven record albums, and more than 100 sales training films for major corporations. He published three autobiographical books: *Eavesdropper at Large* (1952), *Candid Kids* (1964), and *Candidly, Allen Funt* (1994).

In 1978 Funt moved to California, where he bred cattle and horses on a 1,100-acre ranch, but he never gave up *Candid Camera*. In 1989–1990, he produced several specials co-hosted with his son Peter, and in 1991 he created a new version of the show with Dom DeLuise as host, which he supervised until he suffered a stroke in 1993. He died at his home in Pebble Beach, California, of complications following that stroke.

Funt donated his entire library of *Candid Camera* recordings and films to his alma mater Cornell, along with a research grant, and also established a fellowship at Syracuse University for black students of radio and television. A pioneer of reality-based TV, he always considered himself as much an educator and sociologist as an entertainer and felt that his techniques had multiple uses. "When people are smiling," he once observed, "they are most receptive to almost anything you want to teach them. I think that can be applied industrially, academically, technically, and almost every other way" (quoted in Buck). Also a firm believer in the medical value of laughter, he established the Laughter Therapy Foundation to make videocassettes of his shows available at no charge to seriously ill people.

• Besides Funt's three autobiographical books and the archive at Cornell University, good sources of information about his life and work are J. M. Flagler, "Student of the Spontaneous," *New Yorker* (10 Dec. 1960), pp. 59–92; and Pete Martin, "I Call on the Candid Camera Man," *Saturday Evening Post* (17 May 1961), pp. 27–94. The history of *Candid Microphone* is well covered in Thomas DeLong, *Radio Stars* (1996); and John Dunning, *On the Air: The Encyclopedia of Old-Time Radio* (1998). The history of *Candid Camera* is summarized in Tim Brooks and Earle Marsh, *The Complete Directory to Prime Time Network TV Shows* (1992). Useful newspaper articles on his career include Wanda Hale, "Allen Funt Looks Candidly at Money," New York *Daily News* (20 Aug. 1972), "Funt Psychology," *New York Times* (6 June 1982), and Jerry Buck, "Focusing on People for 40 Years," New York *Daily News* (17 February 1987). An obituary appears in the *New York Times*, 7 September 1999.

DENNIS WEPMAN

G

GADDIS, William (29 Dec. 1922–16 Dec. 1998), novelist, was born in New York City, the son of William Gaddis and Edith Charles Gaddis. Gaddis grew up in Massapequa, Long Island, and his early life was disrupted by his parents' divorce when he was three. His mother gained custody of Gaddis, an only child, and to support the family she began work as a secretary at the New York Steam Corporation. But she was unable to care for Gaddis, and he was sent to a Connecticut boarding school, where he stayed until he was thirteen.

In 1941 Gaddis entered Harvard University to study English literature. The next year, illness forced him to drop out of school temporarily and dashed his hopes of entering the service to participate in World War II. Returning to Harvard in 1943, he joined the *Harvard Lampoon* staff and later became its editor. There, he experimented with every kind of writing: playlets, essays, fiction, and verse parodies. In 1945, after he and a drinking companion got into trouble with the Cambridge police, he was asked to leave Harvard.

Gaddis moved to New York's Greenwich Village, where he joined the *New Yorker* as a fact checker, a job he described as excellent training for a writer. He met many of the Beat writers and poets, including Jack Kerouac, William Burroughs, Allen Ginsberg, and painter Sheri Martinelli. (Gaddis appears as the character Harold Sand in Kerouac's 1958 novel *The Subterraneans*.) In two years, he saved enough money so that, supplemented by a stipend from his mother, he could spend five years traveling and gathering material for a first novel.

In 1947 he traveled to Mexico and then to Panama City, where he worked as a machinist's assistant on the canal. The next year, he went on to Costa Rica, where, during a brief civil war, he helped build an airstrip used to deliver arms and supplies from Guatemala. After spending two years in Spain, studying art and Christian church history, subjects that would play a major role in his book, he returned to New York in 1951.

In 1955 Gaddis's first book, *The Recognitions*, was published. Running to 956 pages in its original edition, this complex, multilayered novel tells the story of Wyatt Gwyon and his quest to find an authentic art amid a society so full of counterfeits that "recognitions" of authenticity are nearly impossible. He expected the novel to become an instant success. "I thought," he said, "with the naive kind of confidence that youth has, that the world is made up of falsehood and fraud, and I'm going to expose it. And everyone will be amazed" (*Publishers Weekly*, 12 July 1985 interview with Miriam Berkley). But the book was long and its prose style—which mixed realistically rendered dialogue and narrative without the use of quotation marks—proved too challenging for the critics. *The Recognitions* ran into a firestorm of negative reviews.

Gaddis married Pat Black shortly after publication of *The Recognitions*, and over the next three years the couple would have two children. (They were divorced in 1967; Gaddis's later marriage to Judith Thompson also ended in divorce in 1977.) The family suffered severe financial problems, and he began a series of public relations jobs for Pfizer International, the U.S. Army, and Eastman Kodak. At one point, he ghostwrote professional articles for a dentist in return for root-canal work.

In the meantime, the reputation of *The Recognitions* as an important novel grew. To some, it was the most important American novel of the post–World War II era. The literary scholar George Stade wrote that "contemporary fiction makes no real sense without the presence of this strange, perverse, confusing and ultimately sane book."

Gaddis's second novel, *J R*, was published in 1975. The hefty novel (725 pages in its original edition), based on Gaddis's extensive research on capitalism in the United States, is centered on eleven-year-old J. R. Vansant, from his hustling activities as a schoolboy to his rise and fall at the helm of a business empire built on paper. Louis Auchincloss, a writer familiar with wealth and its discontents, captured accurately the feel of the book, writing that, "reading *J R*, I feel at times as if I were lying alone on a desolate plain under a dark cloudy sky from which come the mumbles and throbs of human speech in every sort of dialect and slang, replete with self-pity, smugness, officiousness, swagger—in short, every banality the brain of man can devise to evade thought." *J R* won Gaddis his first National Book Award for fiction.

Although he gained respect as a novelist, Gaddis's readership and sales still were small, partly because of the demands his prose put on the reader but also because of his abhorrence of publicity. He felt that the work is more important than its author, or, as Gaddis would quote from *The Recognitions*, "What is any artist but the dregs of his work?" It was not until he received a MacArthur Foundation "genius award" in 1982 that he achieved a degree of financial security.

In 1985 *Carpenter's Gothic* was published. Named for the architectural style of the home the characters inhabit, "gothic" could also describe the genre Gaddis recasts in a new, metafictional form, as the novel describes a woman's disintegration at the hands of her husband. At 262 pages when first published, *Carpenter's Gothic* is considerably shorter than Gaddis's previous two novels, but it is no less complicated, with themes of Christian fundamentalism, imperialism in Africa, and nuclear Armageddon feeding the story's menacing atmosphere.

Gaddis's last novel to be published in his lifetime, *A Frolic of His Own* (1994), takes on the U.S. legal system, as its memorable first sentence makes clear: "Justice?—You get justice in the next world, in this world you have the law." The frolic refers to a lawsuit over a charge of plagiarism involving an unpublished Civil War play and a feature film that spirals into multiple lawsuits. The story is told with accurate legal terminology and a logic that veers into farce. The book won Gaddis his second National Book Award. A novella, "Agapé Agape: A Secret History of the Player Piano," was completed but not published when Gaddis died in East Hampton, New York.

Gaddis is the great unread novelist of the postwar era. His works trace the attempts of individuals to hold their lives together in the face of a steadily decaying and chaotic world. While he has been placed with such modernists as James Joyce and Thomas Mann and postmodernists like Thomas Pynchon and John Barth, he saw himself as kin to the Russian novelists of the nineteenth century, who attempted to preserve a vision of what their country could become rather than of what it had become.

• Gaddis's papers are not available at this time, and no biography exists. Gaddis gave two lengthy interviews about his art in the *Review of Contemporary Fiction*, Summer 1982, and the *Paris Review*, no. 105, Winter 1987. His study of failure in American life, "The Rush for Second Place" (*Harper's*, Apr. 1981), reiterates many of his themes. He was profiled in *Contemporary Authors*, new rev. ser., vol. 21 (1987), and *Current Biography 1987*. *In Recognition of William Gaddis*, ed. John Kuehl and Steven Moore (1984), is an overview of the man and his work. See also two books by Moore: *William Gaddis* (Twayne's United States Authors Series, no. 546, 1989) and *A Reader's Guide to William Gaddis's* The Recognitions (1982). A description of the hostile reviews of *The Recognitions* and a defense of the book can be found in Jack Green (pseudonym), *Fire the Bastards!* (1992). An obituary appears in the *New York Times*, 17 Dec. 1998.

BILL PESCHEL

GANSEVOORT, Peter (1749–2 July 1812), revolutionary war officer and merchant, was born in Albany, New York, the son of Harmen Gansevoort, a brewer, merchant, and member of the Albany Common Council, and Magdalena Douw Gansevoort, a member of an Albany Dutch patrician family. Gansevoort attended schools in New Jersey. In 1773 he and his father were charged with visiting a tavern in Albany in an effort to influence voters in an election, but the complaint was dropped when it could not be proved that they had given over any money.

On 19 July 1775, soon after the American Revolution began, Gansevoort was commissioned a major in the Second New York Regiment of the Continental army, which in August marched to Fort Ticonderoga and went on from there to the northern end of Lake Champlain. Though briefly ill because of unsanitary camp conditions, he helped in November to capture St. Johns, southeast of Montreal, and to attack Quebec successfully, while serving under Brigadier General Richard Montgomery, who was killed there. Ill again, Gansevoort joined American forces in retreat early in 1776. Promoted to lieutenant colonel on 19 March, he was placed in command at Fort George in June. By giving troops generous furloughs and holding military ceremonies, he pleased his demoralized men. On 21 November he was appointed colonel of the Third Regiment of the Continental army.

In the winter of 1776–1777, he returned to Albany to seek recruits for his depleted regiment, which by March was reconstituted as the Third New York Continentals. He was then appointed commander of Fort Stanwix (earlier and again later called Fort Schuyler). At the site of present-day Rome, New York, this fort was strategically located in the western part of the Mohawk Valley. Commanding some 500 Continental soldiers, aided briefly by 200 militiamen and reinforced by 250 soldiers from Massachusetts, Gansevoort repaired the fort and prepared to defend it. When the British attack under Colonel Barry St. Leger began on 3 August 1777, with a force of 1,700 regulars, Tories, and pro-British Indians, Gansevoort had 750 men, a six-week supply of food, and little ammunition. On 6 August Gansevoort declined St. Leger's invitation to surrender. On 11 August the British diverted the creek supplying water to the fort. Gansevoort countered by reopening old fort wells and ordering extraordinary sanitation measures. The British shelled the fort at a range as close as 150 yards, in an effort to breach its timber and turf walls. When St. Leger learned that General Benedict Arnold, then still loyal to the American cause, was heading up the valley with more than a thousand Continentals, he began to retreat on 22 August back to Canada. Gansevoort wisely decided not to pursue him, for fear of possible ambush. Gansevoort's brave steadfastness prevented the British from reinforcing General John Burgoyne before he attacked colonial forces at Saratoga and probably also saved Albany from being captured. In a letter to his wife Abigail Adams dated 2 September 1777, John Adams praised Gansevoort. On 4 October 1777 he was named colonel commandant of Fort Stanwix with a vote of thanks from Congress.

Gansevoort was assigned a command in Albany but returned as colonel commandant of Fort Schuyler from May to the fall of 1778. During this time he recaptured more than two dozen deserters and had five of them executed. General George Washington ordered Gansevoort to Schenectady in the fall of 1778. After wintering there and at Saratoga with his regiment, he and his men punished the pro-British Iroquois in the spring and summer of 1779 as far east as the Finger Lakes. He was ordered back to Albany that fall and soon fell ill again. By the spring of 1780 he was with Washington's army and served with his own regiment at West Point; from the fall until January 1781 he commanded at Fort Saratoga. He returned to Albany, was named brigadier general of the militia, and went into temporary retirement owing to a reduction in the army. As a civilian, he began to do his part to rebuild the Gansevoort family's war-depleted fortune.

On 12 January 1778 Gansevoort had married Catherine Van Schaick and was with her in Albany between his assignments at Fort Stanwix. They were together again at West Point. The first two of their five children surviving infancy were born during the war. (Maria Gansevoort, their last child, and only daughter, married Allan Melvill in 1814. The Melvills' first two children were Gansevoort Melville and Herman Melville, the illustrious author, who was named after Peter Gansevoort's first son, Herman. The *e* was added to the surname after Allan Melvill's death.)

When peace was declared in 1783, Gansevoort bought property in Saratoga County, New York. He had scouted there while on duty at Fort Saratoga. His holdings included a dilapidated sawmill built at Snock Kill Falls about 1770 by Hugh Munro, a Tory who fled to Canada during the Revolution. The Commissioners of Forfeitures confiscated Munro's property and released it to Gansevoort as a reward for his military services. He moved to Snock Kill in the spring to 1784, hired some men, built a mill and also a hut to live in with them, and began selling boards and planks. In 1787 he built a two-story house, hired some New Jersey millwrights, and contracted to market his lumber in Albany. In 1788 he was a member of the Albany Federal Committee voting to support ratification of the Federal Constitution and was also made an Indian commissioner by the Confederation Congress. By 1790 his lumber business, together with an adjacent farm, was such a going concern that Gansevoort often left it to his associates to manage. At this time he and his wife owned several black slaves. In 1790 Gansevoort was appointed sheriff of Albany. Gilbert Stuart, about 1794, painted Gansevoort's portrait. In 1802, by then an active state militia general, Gansevoort was appointed by President Thomas Jefferson military agent for the northern department of the United States, mainly to supervise the transportation of clothes, hospital supplies, and Indian subsidies to Fort Niagara and beyond. In 1809 he achieved his final military ambition when President James Madison appointed him a brigadier general in the U.S. Army. His main duties were to review courts-martial sentences occasioned by justifiable dereliction of duty among soldiers neglected during Jefferson's administration and later. Late in 1811 Gansevoort presided over the court-martial in Frederick, Maryland, of General James Wilkinson, who was acquitted on charges of nearly treasonous machinations in Louisiana. Returning home, Gansevoort caught a cold from the lingering effects of which he never recovered. At the time of his death, he was a director of the Albany Insurance Company and the New York State Bank.

Herman Melville and his wife named their second son Stanwix, in honor of the boy's great-grandfather, defender of Fort Stanwix. When Melville composed *Pierre; or, The Ambiguities* (1852), he used General Peter Gansevoort, his grandfather, as the model for General Pierre Glendinning, the deceased grandfather of young Pierre Glendinning, the hero of the novel.

• The bulk of the Gansevoort family papers is in the Gansevoort-Lansing Collection, New York Public Library, New York City; they were donated by Catherine Gansevoort Lansing, one of Peter Gansevoort's granddaughters. A brief, laudatory biography of Gansevoort is in Thomas J. Rogers, *A New American Biographical Dictionary; or, Remembrancer of the Departed Heroes, Sages, and Statesmen, of America*, 3d ed. (1824). An early account of Gansevoort's defense of Fort Stanwix, available to his descendants, is in William L. Stone, *Life of Joseph Brant—Thayendanegea: Including the Border Wars of the American Revolution, and Sketches of the Indian Campaigns of Generals Harmar, St. Clair, and Wayne* (2 vols., 1838). Amasa J. Parker, *Landmarks of Albany County, New York* (1897), and Alice P. Kenney, *The Gansevoorts of Albany: Dutch Patricians in the Upper Hudson Valley* (1969), detail the history of the Gansevoort family. Jay Leyda, *The Melville Log; A Documentary Life of Herman Melville, 1819–1891* (2 vols., 1951), contains primary materials relating novelist to grandfather. Herman Melville, *Pierre; or, The Ambiguities*, ed. Harrison Hayford et al., vol. 7 (1971), and Herman Melville, *Correspondence*, ed. Lynn Horth, vol. 14 (1993) of *The Writings of Herman Melville* (1968–), annotate, respectively, Melville's use of Gansevoort for fictive purposes in *Pierre* and Melville's several tangential comments on Gansevoort; Horth also includes a Gansevoort family tree, containing twenty-six names and sets of dates.

ROBERT L. GALE

GARSON, Greer (29 Sept. 1904–6 Apr. 1996), actress, was born Eileen Evelyn Greer Garson in London, England, the daughter of George Garson, a clerk for an importing firm, and Nancy Greer Garson. After Garson's father died in 1906, her mother managed a row of townhouses that she inherited from her husband. An extremely sickly child, Garson suffered from a heart malady and frequent fainting spells, and her doctors doubted that she would survive to maturity. She later recalled that she was "ill regularly, six weeks every autumn, six weeks every spring, ill enough to be put to bed for those intervals. . . . Every winter was a nightmare of long woolen underwear and colds, bronchitis, and cod-liver oil." Not healthy enough to play with other children, she became an avid reader and an excellent student. In 1921 she won a scholarship to the University of London. While at the university, she spent much of her free time attending plays in the city's West End. As she later explained, an acting career held a powerful appeal for her: "I was an introvert because of my shut-in life, and I longed to break out of it" (quoted in Troyan, p. 18). She received a bachelor of arts degree with honors in English in 1926 and then spent a year in France studying ecclesiastical architecture at the University of Grenoble.

In 1927 Garson returned to London, where she began a promising career as the manager of the research department for an advertising firm. She quit her job, however, in 1932 after successfully auditioning with the Birmingham Repertory Theatre. She spent eight months performing in a variety of plays, but was forced to quit the company when she became ill with pneumonia. In September 1933 she married Alec Snelson, a childhood sweetheart who had become an attaché with the British government in India. During their honeymoon, he insisted that she join him at his post, suggesting that she could act in the amateur theatricals put on by the wives of British officers. She refused and left him at the end of their honeymoon; they officially divorced in 1941. In 1935 she was cast in her first significant leading role in Sylvia Thompson and Victor Cunard's *Golden Arrow*, a play directed by and costarring Laurence Olivier. For the next three years, she starred in a number of plays in London, specializing in sophisticated comedies such as an adaptation of Alexander Engel's *Vintage Wine* (1935), with Sir Seymour Hicks, and an adaptation of Jacques Deval's *Mademoiselle* (1936), produced by Noël Coward. In late 1937 Metro-Goldwyn-Mayer vice president Louis B. Mayer, on a whirlwind tour of Europe to scout talent, signed her to a one-year film contract.

Garson called her first twelve months in Hollywood the most unhappy year in her life. She wanted to play the same kind of witty, vivacious roles that she had played in London, but no such work was forthcoming. MGM executives wanted to cast her in the Marx Brothers' comedy *A Day at the Races*, where her major scene would call for her to be wallpapered to the wall. She declined the role, feeling that it was beneath her, and for several months she received no assignments. "The trouble . . . was that I didn't fit into any established category," she later said. "No glamour girl, no cheesecake, the oddly-boned face and the tallness. It didn't charm people. It worried them" (quoted in Troyan, p. 80). In October 1938, with her contract about to expire, she was given a small but pivotal supporting role as a schoolmaster's wife in *Goodbye, Mr. Chips*. The film concerns a strict disciplinarian (played by Robert Donat) at an English boys' school who weds a graceful, gently humorous woman; he mellows under her influence and, after her death in childbirth, goes on to become a much-beloved headmaster. An excellent sentimental film, *Goodbye, Mr. Chips* earned seven Academy Award nominations in 1939, including one for Garson's first screen portrayal.

Following the success of *Mr. Chips*, MGM rewarded Garson with a long-term contract and began to assign her to several of their most prestigious productions. In 1940 she played Elizabeth Bennet, with Laurence Olivier as Mr. Darcy, in a fine adaptation of Jane Austen's *Pride and Prejudice*. In *Blossoms in the Dust* (1941), the studio's first Technicolor drama, she appeared in a biographical role as Edna Gladney, a woman who had worked tirelessly for the welfare of orphan children in Texas. The film costarred Walter Pidgeon as Gladney's husband; he would be reteamed with Garson in seven additional pictures. In 1942 she played the title role in *Mrs. Miniver*, a film that depicted the courage of an ordinary, if idealized, middle-class family during the Battle of Britain. Garson had been reluctant to accept the part, worried that Mrs. Miniver was too much like Mrs. Chips. When critics praised her characterization of a woman who was "brave, wifely, maternal, and a pillar of civilian morale," they merely reemphasized her concern. Nevertheless, *Mrs. Miniver* was a cultural phenomenon, becoming the second-highest grossing Hollywood movie to that date, behind only *Gone with the Wind*. Winston Churchill called the film "propaganda worth a hundred battleships." Franklin D. Roosevelt ordered a speech from the film to be printed in leaflets and dropped over German-occupied territory. Garson was vaulted to superstardom: she won the Academy Award for best actress, received over a thousand fan letters a day, and served as the inspiration for a popular line of Greer Garson paper dolls and coloring books.

During the filming of *Mrs. Miniver*, Garson began a courtship with the actor Richard Ney, who played her college-age son. Their behavior panicked Louis B. Mayer, who forbade the couple to date publicly until after the film had premiered. Garson married Ney in 1943; they divorced in 1947 and had no children. Always concerned about being typecast, she found herself assigned to a string of parts in the Mrs. Chips/ Mrs. Miniver mode. In *Random Harvest* (1942), she gave perhaps her best performance opposite Ronald Colman as a woman who falls in love with a war-shattered amnesiac. She was nominated regularly for best actress Academy Awards—for her roles in *Madame Curie* (1943), *Mrs. Parkington* (1944), and *The Valley of Decision* (1945). During this period, she complained to an interviewer: "Here I am, possibly the only natural redhead in Hollywood, mildewing away the years in shawls, shrouds, and chignons in unrelieved black and white" (quoted in Troyan, p. 157). Critics tended to agree with her: in the *New York Times*, Bosley Crowther noted of *Valley of Decision* that "the constant reiteration of the same righteous character not only makes movies tend to monotony but wastes the talents of a capable star." In 1946 MGM finally decided to retool her screen image by casting her as a sailor's pick-up in *Adventure*, costarring Clark Gable. The expensive film was a critical and commercial flop. During the late 1940s, the studio experienced serious financial difficulties and struggled to find her suitable roles. In 1949 she married E. E. "Buddy" Fogelson, a millionaire Texas oilman; they had no children. In 1950 she appeared in *The Miniver Story*, a wan sequel to her greatest success.

As her career in Hollywood declined, Garson focused her energies on her home life in Dallas, Texas, and on her husband's sprawling ranch outside Santa Fe, New Mexico. Highly visible members of the Dallas social elite, she and her husband were active philanthropists, making large donations to St. Michael's College in Santa Fe and establishing a permanent endowment for the Dallas Theater Center. In 1957 she declined an invitation from Texas Republicans to run for state congress. That year, she replaced Rosalind

Russell in *Auntie Mame* on Broadway. During the later 1950s, she starred in several television movies. In 1960 she received a final Academy Award nomination for her role as Eleanor Roosevelt in *Sunrise at Campobello*. During her later years, she became active in the breeding and training of racehorses. In 1992 the Greer Garson Theater, to which she donated $10 million, opened at Southern Methodist University in Dallas. She died in Dallas.

• A valuable interview with Garson is Gladys Hall, *Silver Screen*, 20 July 1942. Michael Troyan, *A Rose for Mrs. Miniver: The Life of Greer Garson* (1999), is a lengthy, occasionally insightful biography. Profiles of Garson published during her screen career include Mona Gardner, "The Glorified Mrs.," *Ladies Home Journal*, Sept. 1944, and Pete Martin, "Hollywood's Fabulous Female," *Saturday Evening Post*, 26 Dec. 1946. For information on Garson at MGM, see Gary Carey, *All the Stars in Heaven: Louis B. Mayer's MGM* (1981), and Charles Higham, *Merchant of Dreams: Louis B. Mayer, M.G.M., and the Secret Hollywood* (1993). Roy Hoopes, *When the Stars Went to War: Hollywood and World War II* (1994), and Thomas Doherty, *Projections of War: Hollywood, American Culture, and World War II* (1993), both discuss *Mrs. Miniver*. For an excellent scholarly discussion of the Hollywood "woman's picture," see Jeanine Basinger, *A Woman's View: How Hollywood Spoke to Women, 1930–1960* (1993). An obituary is in the *New York Times*, 7 Apr. 1996.

THOMAS W. COLLINS, JR.

GASTON, A. G. (4 July 1892–19 Jan. 1996), entrepreneur, was born Arthur George Gaston in Demopolis, Alabama, the son of Tom Gaston, a railroad worker, and Rosa Gaston (maiden name unknown), a cook. He grew up in poverty in rural Alabama before he and his mother moved to Birmingham, Alabama, after his father's death. He attended, and for a time resided at, Tuggle Institute, where he received a moral and industrial education. In 1910 he graduated from the school with a tenth grade certificate. Before and after graduation, he worked at a variety of part-time jobs, including selling subscriptions for the *Birmingham Reporter*.

Gaston served in World War I in France as a sergeant in the 317th Ammunition Train of the all-black Ninety-second Division of the U.S. Army. On returning to the United States, he briefly worked at a drycleaning factory for five dollars a day before landing a job at the Tennessee Coal and Iron (TCI) plant in Westfield, Alabama, constructing railroad cars. Always searching for a means of making more money, he supplemented his daily wage of $3.10 by selling his mother's homemade sandwiches and loaning money to colleagues who did not share his obsession for saving money.

Gaston early on exhibited signs of ambition and enterprise. As a young man he joined several fraternal organizations, where he gained visibility among members of the black community and nurtured relationships that helped him to develop a large client base when he started his own businesses. Birmingham's budding and segregated economy provided the opportunity for several black entrepreneurs looking for an opening to establish a business. Early in the twentieth century, Thomas W. Walker, William R. Pettiford, Oscar Adams, and Thomas C. Windham were all enterprising men who parlayed their energies into successful businesses that catered almost exclusively to Birmingham's black residents. They served as role models for Gaston who combined their business strategies with Booker T. Washington's self-help philosophy to engineer a modest business empire.

Gaston followed in the footsteps of his predecessor and competitor, Charles M. Harris, who founded the venerable Davenport and Harris Funeral Home in 1899 and then the Protective Burial Association in the 1920s. During the 1920s and 1930s numerous black entrepreneurs established burial and insurance companies to ensure members of their own race a respectable funeral. In the early 1920s Gaston married Creola Smith, who died during their first years of marriage. In 1923 he resigned his position at TCI and founded, with his father-in-law, Abraham Lincoln "Dad" Smith, the Booker T. Washington Burial Society and later the Smith and Gaston Funeral Home. In 1932 they incorporated the Booker T. Washington Burial Insurance Company in Fairfield, Alabama, when legal complications forced him to abandon the burial society. Gaston financed all his subsequent business ventures through this corporation. The company not only weathered the Great Depression; it also enjoyed a longevity that many of its competitors did not.

Gaston's carefully designed business tactics enabled his companies to survive the ravages of the depression that felled thousands of businesses throughout the nation. In Birmingham alone, all the black-run newspapers failed, and of the 200 black-owned retail stores in 1929, only 132 remained in 1935. Gaston accurately read the market and created businesses that served the black community's needs. He established diverse businesses that both trained blacks for future employment and provided them with essential services. In 1939 he and his second wife Minnie Lee Gardner (with whom he had one son) established the Booker T. Washington Business College to teach black students clerical skills. Gaston hired graduates of the college to fill the vacancies in his own companies, positions that were previously held by out-of-state blacks. He filled another void in 1954 when he constructed the Gaston Motel, which served blacks who otherwise were denied access to public accommodations in Alabama. Hailed as "one of the finest in the Southeast" by white hotel owners and praised as a wonderful symbol by blacks, the motel earned for Gaston the respect of representatives from both races. This facility later served as a meeting place during the civil rights movement.

While Gaston was creating his business empire, he chose a route that would benefit not only him but other members of the black community as well. Wanting to enable black homeownership, he founded the Citizens Federal Savings and Loan Association in

1957, later Citizens Federal Savings Bank. By and large, Birmingham's white-owned banks had discriminatory lending practices that successfully kept blacks out of the housing market. Members of the black community rallied behind Gaston's newest venture and helped the bank realize a steady growth in profits. By 1961 it ranked eleventh among all black-managed savings and loans, with assets totaling $5,120,633.85. By 1968 more than $6 million had been invested in home and church mortgages owned by blacks. In 1989 it was rated the safest savings and loan in Birmingham. Despite the savings and loan controversy that damaged the industry in the 1980s, and the loss of twenty-six of the forty-three black-owned thrifts, Gaston's company weathered the industry's dismantling and experienced growth. In 1991 it declared assets of $72,084,000 and deposits amounting to $65,563,000. Despite a decline in assets by 1995 to $58 million, it remained the largest black-owned bank in Alabama and the eighth largest in the country. Gaston remained chairman of the bank until his death.

In 1987 Gaston unexpectedly sold his insurance company and almost all of his other investments to his 400 employees for $3.5 million—a nominal sum, given the company's $34 million in assets and $726 million worth of insurance in force. He owned 97 percent controlling interest in Booker T. Washington Insurance (the remaining 3 percent was held by his wife, Minnie Gaston, and his employees). Gaston was determined to give something back to the community that had given him so much. Included in the transaction were his Booker T. Washington Broadcasting, which owned Birmingham-based radio stations WENN and WAGG; the A. G. Gaston Construction Company; Zion Memorial Gardens and New Grace Hill cemeteries; A. G. Gaston Senior Citizens Home; and Vulcan Realty and Investment Corporation. He only retained ownership of Citizens Federal Savings Bank and the Smith and Gaston Funeral Homes.

Gaston also played an important role in the civil rights campaign that rocked Birmingham in 1963, when protests against racial discrimination, led by Martin Luther King, Jr., met with violence from Birmingham's white residents and police. Gaston adopted a low profile during the demonstrations, although he openly criticized how the movement used children to draw greater sympathy for its cause. But his apparent fence-sitting belied what he was doing behind the scenes. He opened his motel for King and other Southern Christian Leadership Conference officials to plot their strategies, supplied them with the necessary office materials, put up bail, and secretly met with the city's white power structure to "broker for every citizen's basic rights" (*Birmingham News*, 20 Jan. 1996). His motel and home were bombed; yet he continued his effort to make peace with Birmingham's white community and opposed a plan to dispatch troops to the city, believing that local residents could come to terms without federal interference.

Gaston's negotiating with the white power structure and his criticism of King's use of small children in the demonstrations did not win him favor among many blacks. Yet, as Joseph Lowery, a longtime civil rights activist, declared, "Without A. G. Gaston, we would have been up the creek without a boat or a fishing pole. The motel, and his money for bond, were effective tools in the struggle against segregation in Birmingham" (*Birmingham News*, 20 Jan. 1996). Gaston defended his actions: "I was convinced it was now time to use the conference table instead of the streets to try to settle differences. If wanting to spare children, save lives, bring peace is Uncle Tomism, then I wanted to be a Super Uncle Tom" (*Green Power*, p. 125). Following the demonstrations, Gaston continued to engage in meetings with influential whites to effect change. He was a moving force behind the creation of Operation New Birmingham's Community Affairs Committee, which was credited with promoting cooperation and reconciliation between the races. Although his involvement in these types of organizations drew criticisms from many members of the black community, he moved ahead.

Gaston recognized that he had achieved something that others could not and was willing to share his expertise, time, and philosophy with those less fortunate. In 1966 he founded the A. G. Gaston Boys' Club of America, donating $50,000 as well as the proceeds from the sale of his autobiography, *Green Power*. He declared the Boys' Club "one of the greatest things I've done" (*Birmingham News*, 20 Dec. 1987).

Gaston created a business empire in spite of the prevailing race prejudice, relying on "green power" (the power of money) to seize the opportunities available to him. Inspired by Booker T. Washington, he became a role model for others. In 1992 *Black Enterprise* named him "Entrepreneur of the Century." He died in Birmingham.

• Gaston's personal papers are not available. However, there are abundant newspaper and magazine articles that chronicle his career. These are in the office of the Booker T. Washington Insurance Company and in the clipping file of the Birmingham Public Library. Gaston's autobiography *Green Power: The Successful Way of A. G. Gaston* (1968) is useful, as is an account he wrote entitled "Investment in Life" in *Many Shades of Black*, ed. Stanton L. Wormley and Lewis H. Fenderson (1969). The University of Alabama at Birmingham holds an oral history of Gaston conducted in 1976 and 1977. By far the most comprehensive and objective account of Gaston's life and career is found in John N. Ingham and Lynne B. Feldman, *African-American Business Leaders: A Biographical Dictionary* (1994), which also has a detailed bibliographical essay. Several *Black Enterprise* articles focus on Gaston's business career, especially in the June 1984 issue. For his role in the civil rights movement, see Howell Raines, *My Soul Is Rested: The Story of the Civil Rights Movement in the Deep South* (1977); Taylor Branch, *Parting the Water: America in the King Years, 1954–1963* (1988); and David J. Garrow, *Bearing the Cross: Martin Luther King, Jr., and the Southern Christian Leadership Conference* (1986). Obituaries are in the *Birmingham News*, 19 and 20 Jan. 1996.

LYNNE B. FELDMAN

GILPATRIC, Roswell L. (4 Nov. 1906–15 Mar. 1996), lawyer and presidential aide, was born Roswell

Leavitt Gilpatric in Brooklyn, New York, the son of Walter Hodges Gilpatric, a lawyer, and Charlotte Elizabeth Leavitt Gilpatric. He entered Yale University in 1924, was elected to Phi Beta Kappa, and received his B.A. with honors in 1928. He then entered Yale Law School, was an editor of the *Yale Law Journal,* and graduated in 1931.

On graduating from law school, Gilpatric joined Cravath, Swaine & Moore (which at that time was called Cravath, De Gersdorff, Swaine & Wood), where—with the exception of his service in the Truman and Kennedy administrations—he spent his entire professional life. Gilpatric came to this leading New York firm with letters of recommendation from, among others, William O. Douglas, later a prominent U.S. Supreme Court justice, who had worked as a Cravath associate (interview, 20 Nov. 1995, p. 22). Gilpatric was put to work on bankruptcies, such as that of the United Cigar Company. Early in his professional career, he began to make his mark in corporate and financial law, an area of growing importance since the late nineteenth century. He preferred not to engage in adversarial battles in court: "Once I'd been [at Cravath] a while, I made up my own mind that I'd be better off as a corporate lawyer, negotiator, etc. than I would as a courtroom litigator." As he developed skill in "the building up of small companies," he "gradually became . . . a corporate specialist" (interview, 20 Nov. 1995, p. 23). In 1932 he married Margaret Fulton Kurtz; they had three children.

In 1940 Gilpatric became a Cravath partner, and during this period he was a Visiting Sterling Lecturer at Yale Law School (1939–1942; 1946–1948). Like partners of other leading New York firms of his generation, Gilpatric was active in public service and performed pro bono work on behalf of cultural institutions, carrying on a practice with roots in the nineteenth century. During the World War II period, he was involved in advising corporations on legal matters relating to financing facilities for war production efforts. His work brought him to the attention of the Washington establishment (noted in *Current Biography 1964*). In 1945 he was divorced, and in 1946 he married Harriet Heywood.

Gilpatric served as a consultant to the Pentagon, was an active Democrat, and, through the recommendation of Robert Lovett and Thomas Finletter (interview, 30 Nov. 1995, p. 42), joined the Truman administration as assistant secretary of the air force and then as undersecretary (1951–1953). Regarding his acceptance of the assignment, Gilpatric noted that "the firm had a record, going back through World War I, of partners leaving the firm temporarily to take government positions" and "it was felt that the government experience would be helpful." He "thought it was a very profound experience, not only doing something worthwhile for my country, but I was learning a lot. . . . It broadened my whole horizon in the business community" (interviews, 1995: 30 Nov., p. 43; 20 Nov., p. 24; 30 Nov., p. 43).

Gilpatric oversaw procurement and production and material requirements for the air force. He became a critic of defense practices, especially during the Eisenhower administration, and gave speeches and wrote articles relating to duplication and the need for better research and development in regard to weapons and aircraft (*Current Biography 1964*, p. 150). Gilpatric returned to Cravath in 1953. He served as a member of the Rockefeller Brothers Special Studies Program (1956–1957), which issued a report critical of defense capability, and as a member of the Yale Council (1957–1964). In 1958 he and Harriet Heywood were divorced, and he married Madelin Thayer Kudner.

In 1961 Gilpatric joined the Kennedy administration as deputy secretary of defense. Well respected and personally known to John F. Kennedy, whom he had met while serving as undersecretary of the air force (interview, 20 Nov. 1995, p. 24), Gilpatric was invited to join a group of advisers that became known as the Executive Committee of the National Security Council (later called ExComm), which played a pivotal role in the Cuban Missile Crisis of 1962. Recognizing that the president wanted a forceful response to Soviet leader Nikita S. Khrushchev's installation of offensive nuclear weapons in Cuba, but opposing a secret air strike, Secretary of Defense Robert S. McNamara and Gilpatric argued for a naval blockade (Allison, p. 202). At an important point in the discussions, there was silence as President Kennedy reflected upon all the presentations. Gilpatric broke the silence and homed in on a key point: "Essentially, Mr. President," he said, "this is a choice between limited action and unlimited action; and most of us think that it's better to start with limited action" (quoted in Sorensen, p. 694). President Kennedy decided in favor of a naval quarantine; the Soviets agreed to remove the missiles; and the crisis was ultimately averted. Gilpatric was also involved in efforts in the administration to reorganize the defense establishment, national security, and defense policy. In 1962 Gilpatric, a Hotchkiss graduate, was named Hotchkiss Man of the Year; he received a Citation of Merit from Yale Law School the same year and in 1962 and 1963, respectively, he received honorary L.L.D. degrees from Franklin and Marshall College and Bowdoin College.

After returning to the Cravath firm in 1964, Gilpatric served as presiding partner from 1967 to 1977, when he officially retired but stayed on as counsel for three more years. In his later years, he continued to go to the office to provide advice and counsel. Highlighting his reputation "as a rainmaker whose extensive business contacts brought business to the firm," Gilpatric, by his own account, "did major work for eighteen companies . . . Of that eighteen, fourteen were a response to my own efforts" (interviews, 1995: 20 Nov., p. 9; 30 Nov., pp. 43–44). His clients included General Dynamics, CBS, Olin, and Fairchild Camera. Gilpatric served on the boards of several major corporations, including Eastern Airlines (1964–1985), Corning Glass (1965–1977), Fairchild Camera and Instrument Corp. (1965–1979; chairman 1975–1977), the Washington Post Company (1968–1970), and CBS (1970–1990). From 1972 to 1975, he was chairman of the Federal Reserve Bank of New York. While Cravath's litigation department grew during his tenure as presiding partner and the firm's corporate practice became more transactional, Gilpatric attempted to moderate Cravath's growth because he wanted "to keep the collegial character of the firm" (interview, 30 Nov. 1995, p. 61). In 1970 he and his third wife divorced, and he married Paula Melhado Washburn.

Gilpatric continued his work in cultural institutions and his interest in reorganizing and reforming the defense establishment. He was a trustee of New York University's Institute of Fine Arts (1965–1975), the New York Public Library (1972–1975), and the Metropolitan Museum of Art (1970–1984, where he was vice chair of the board). Regarding this involvement, he noted, "My work at the Metropolitan Museum was one of the most interesting phases of my whole career" (interview, 30 Nov. 1995, p. 81). Divorced again in 1985, Gilpatric was to marry Miriam R. Thorne in 1991. He served as chairman of the Commission on Fundamental Defense Management Reform and in 1993 received the Eisenhower Award from Business Executives for National Security. To eliminate wasteful spending and to enable the country to meet security challenges in the future, he advocated trimming the defense budget, reorganizing the Defense Department, and cutting the bureaucracy. He died at his home in Manhattan.

Gilpatric may be best known for his role in the Cuban Missile Crisis, but his legal career is also significant. He exemplified a type of New York attorney of his era: while embracing the modern conception of corporate counsel and its attendant power and privileges, he viewed public service and involvement in cultural institutions as integral to the responsibilities and performance of his legal practice.

• Transcripts of Roswell L. Gilpatric interviews by Laura Strauss, 20 and 30 Nov. 1995, for the Cravath, Swaine & Moore Oral History Project, contain information regarding his legal career not available in other sources (courtesy of Cravath, Swaine & Moore). For Gilpatric's continuing interest in reform of the defense establishment in his later years, see, for example, Roswell L. Gilpatric, "Revamp Defense Thinking," *New York Times*, 10 Apr. 1992. For biographical information regarding his family background and early career at the Cravath firm, see Robert T. Swaine, *The Cravath Firm and Its Predecessors, 1819–1948* (1946–1948). His professional life is noted in *Current Biography 1964*, and reflections on his family life and his professional and public careers are contained in "In Thanksgiving for the Life of Roswell Leavitt Gilpatric, November 4, 1906–March 15, 1996" (Memorials, St. James Church, New York). Gilpatric's role in the Cuban Missile Crisis and the Kennedy administration are discussed in Theodore C. Sorensen, *Kennedy* (1965); Robert F. Kennedy, *Thirteen Days: A Memoir of the Cuban Missile Crisis* (1969); Graham T. Allison, *Essence of Decision: Explaining the Cuban Missile Crisis* (1971); Arthur M. Schlesinger, Jr., *A Thousand Days: John F. Ken-*

nedy in the White House (1965); and David Detzer, *The Brink: Cuban Missile Crisis, 1962* (1979). An obituary appears in the *New York Times*, 17 Mar. 1996.

MARILYN TOBIAS

GINSBERG, Allen (3 June 1926–6 Apr. 1997), poet, was born in Newark, New Jersey, the younger son of Louis Ginsberg, a high school English teacher and poet, and Naomi Levy Ginsberg. Ginsberg grew up with his older brother Eugene in a household shadowed by his mother's mental illness; she suffered from recurrent epileptic seizures and paranoia. An active member of the Communist Party–USA, Naomi Ginsberg took her sons to meetings of the radical left dedicated to the cause of international Communism during the Great Depression of the 1930s.

In the winter of 1941, when Allen was a junior in high school, his mother insisted that he take her to a therapist at a Lakewood, New Jersey, rest home, a disruptive bus journey he described in his long autobiographical poem "Kaddish." Naomi Ginsberg spent most of the next fifteen years in mental hospitals, enduring the effects of electroshock treatments and a lobotomy before her death at Pilgrim State Hospital in 1956. Witnessing his mother's mental illness had a traumatic effect on Ginsberg, who wrote poetry about her unstable condition for the rest of his life.

Graduating from Newark's East Side High School in 1943, Ginsberg later recalled that his most memorable school day was the afternoon his English teacher Frances Durbin read aloud from Walt Whitman's "Song of Myself" in a voice "so enthusiastic and joyous . . . so confident and lifted with laughter" that he never forgot the image of "her black-dressed bulk seated squat behind an English class desk, her embroidered collar, her voice powerful and high" (quoted in Schumacher, p. 17). Despite his passionate response to Whitman's poetry, Ginsberg listed government or legal work as his choice of future occupation in the high school yearbook.

Attending the college of Columbia University on a scholarship, Ginsberg considered his favorite course the required freshman great books seminar taught by Lionel Trilling. Later Ginsberg also cited the renowned literary critics and biographers Mark Van Doren and Raymond Weaver as influential professors at Columbia. But Ginsberg's friends at Columbia were an even greater influence than his professors on his decision to become a poet. As a freshman he met undergraduate Lucien Carr, who introduced him to William S. Burroughs and Jack Kerouac, part of a diverse (and now legendary) circle of friends that grew to include the Times Square heroin addict Herbert Huncke, the young novelist John Clellon Holmes, and a handsome young drifter and car thief from Denver named Neal Cassady, with whom Ginsberg fell in love. Kerouac described the intense encounter between Ginsberg and Cassady in the opening chapter of his novel *On the Road* (1957).

These friends became the nucleus of a group that named themselves the "Beat Generation" writers.

The term was coined by Kerouac in the fall of 1948 during a conversation with Holmes in New York City. The word "beat" referred loosely to their shared sense of spiritual exhaustion and diffuse feelings of rebellion against what they experienced as the general conformity, hypocrisy, and materialism of the larger society around them caught up in the unprecedented prosperity of postwar America.

In the summer of 1948, in his senior year at Columbia, Ginsberg had dedicated himself to becoming a poet after hearing in a vision the voice of William Blake reciting the poem "Ah Sunflower." Experimenting with drugs like marijuana and nitrous oxide to induce further visions, or what Ginsberg later described as "an exalted state of mind," he felt that the poet's duty was to bring a visionary consciousness of reality to his readers. He was dissatisfied with the poetry he was writing at this time, traditional work modeled on English poets like Sir Thomas Wyatt or Andrew Marvell whom he had studied at Columbia.

In June 1949 Ginsberg was arrested as an accessory to crimes carried out by Huncke and his friends, who had stored stolen goods in Ginsberg's apartment. As an alternative to a jail sentence, Ginsberg's professors Van Doren and Trilling arranged with the Columbia dean for a plea of psychological disability, on condition that Ginsberg was admitted to the Columbia Presbyterian Psychiatric Institute. Spending eight months in the mental institution, Ginsberg became close friends with the young writer Carl Solomon, who was treated there for depression with insulin shock.

In December 1953 Ginsberg left New York City on a trip to Mexico to explore Indian ruins in Yucatan and experiment with various drugs. He settled in San Francisco, where he fell in love with a young artist's model, Peter Orlovsky; he took a job in market research, thinking that he might enroll in the graduate English program at the University of California in Berkeley. In August 1955, inspired by the manuscript of a long jazz poem titled "Mexico City Blues" that Kerouac had recently written in Mexico City, Ginsberg found the courage to begin to type what he called his most personal "imaginative sympathies" in the long poem "Howl for Carl Solomon"(*Original Draft Facsimile* Howl, p. xii). As his biographer Bill Morgan stated, in the poem "Allen finally accepted his homosexuality and stopped trying to become 'straight'" (*Allen Ginsberg and Friends*, p. 31).

In October 1955 Ginsberg read the first part of his new poem in public for the first time to tumultuous applause at the Six Gallery reading in San Francisco with the local poets Kenneth Rexroth, Gary Snyder, Michael McClure, Philip Whalen, and Philip LaMantia. Journalists were quick to herald the reading as a landmark event in American poetry, the birth of what they labeled the San Francisco Poetry Renaissance. Lawrence Ferlinghetti, who ran the City Lights Book Store and the City Lights publishing house in North Beach, sent Ginsberg a telegram echoing Ralph Waldo Emerson's response to Walt Whitman's *Leaves of Grass:* "I greet you at the beginning of a great career. When do I get the manuscript?" Later Ginsberg wrote that "in publishing 'Howl,' I was curious to leave behind after my generation an emotional time bomb that would continue exploding in U.S. consciousness in case our military-industrial-nationalist complex solidified into a repressive police bureaucracy" (*Original Draft Facsimile* Howl, p. xii).

Early in the following year *Howl and Other Poems* was published with an introduction by William Carlos Williams as number four in the City Lights Pocket Poets Series. In May 1956 copies of the small black-and-white stapled paperback were seized by the San Francisco police, who arrested Ferlinghetti and Shigeyoshi Murao, his shop manager, and charged them with publishing and selling an obscene and indecent book. The American Civil Liberties Union took up the defense of Ginsberg's poem in a highly publicized obscenity trial in San Francisco, which concluded in October 1957 when Judge Clayton Horn ruled that *Howl* had redeeming social value.

During the furor of the trial, Ginsberg left California and settled in Paris with Orlovsky, who was to remain his companion for the next forty years. Living on Ginsberg's royalties from *Howl* and Orlovsky's disability checks as a Korean War veteran, they traveled to Tangier to stay with Burroughs and help him assemble the manuscript later published as his novel *Naked Lunch* (1959). In 1958 Ginsberg returned to New York City, still troubled by his mother's death in the mental hospital two years before, haunted by the thought that he had never properly said goodbye to her. Using various drugs to explore his painful memories of their life together and confront his complex feelings about his mother, Ginsberg wrote his greatest poem, "Kaddish for Naomi Ginsberg," modeling his elegy on the traditional Jewish memorial service for the dead.

Continuing to experiment with various psychedelic stimulants to create visionary poetry, Ginsberg traveled to South America, Europe, Morocco, and India with Orlovsky in 1962. It was the most important trip of his life. Staying in India for nearly two years, he met with holy men in an effort to find someone who could teach him a method of meditation that would help him deal with his egotism and serve as a vehicle for heightened spiritual awareness. On a train in Japan, Ginsberg recorded in his poem "The Change" his realization that meditation, not drugs, could assist his enlightenment. He returned to North America in the fall of 1963 to attend the Vancouver Poetry Conference with Charles Olson, Robert Duncan, Robert Creeley, Denise Levertov, and many other poets who felt that they formed a community of nonacademic experimental writers.

In 1968 Ginsberg received wide coverage on television during the Democratic National Convention when he and the members of the National Mobilization Committee who were against U.S. participation in the war in Vietnam confronted the police in Chicago's Grant Park. The poet stayed on an impromptu stage and chanted "Om" in an attempt to calm the crowds being brutally attacked by tear gas and billy clubs. Ginsberg's courage, his humanitarian political views and support of homosexuality, his engagement in Eastern meditation practices, and his charismatic personality made him one of the favorite spokesmen chosen by a younger generation of radicalized Americans known as "hippies" during the end of this turbulent decade.

In the early 1970s Ginsberg's serious, bearded image with black-rimmed glasses, a tweed jacket, and an "Uncle Sam" paper top hat became a ubiquitous poster protesting the Vietnam War. In 1971 Ginsberg met Chögyam Trungpa Rinpoche, who became his meditation teacher at the Naropa Institute, a Buddhist college in Boulder, Colorado. Three years later, Ginsberg, assisted by the young poet Anne Waldman, founded a creative writing program called the Jack Kerouac School of Disembodied Poetics at Naropa. Ginsberg taught summer poetry workshops there and lectured during the academic year at Brooklyn College as a tenured distinguished professor until the end of his life.

In his remaining years, publishing steadily and traveling tirelessly despite increasing health problems with diabetes and the aftereffects of a stroke, Ginsberg gave readings in Russia, China, Europe, and the South Pacific. In the bardic tradition of William Blake, who played a pump organ when he read his poetry, Ginsberg often accompanied himself on a portable harmonium bought in Benares for fifty dollars. He was the archetypal Beat Generation writer to countless poetry audiences and to the general public. Unlike Kerouac, who died in 1969, Ginsberg remained a radical poet, the embodiment of the ideals of personal freedom, nonconformity, and the search for enlightenment. As a member of the American Academy and Institute of Arts and Letters, he unabashedly used his prestige to champion the work of his friends. Two months short of his seventy-first birthday, he died of liver cancer at his home in the East Village, New York City.

• Along with Ginsberg's many awards and honors, his list of publications encompasses hundreds of items. Most notably, in addition to those mentioned above, they include the collections *Reality Sandwiches, 1953–1960* (1963); *Planet News, 1961–1967* (1968); *Indian Journals: March 1962–May 1963* (1970); *The Fall of America: Poems of These States, 1965–1971* (1972), which won the National Book Award; Gordon Ball, ed., *Allen Verbatim: Lectures on Poetry, Politics, Consciousness* (1974); *Mind Breaths: Poems, 1972–1977* (1978); *Plutonium Ode: Poems, 1977–1980* (1982); *Collected Poems: 1947–1980* (1985); Barry Miles, ed., *Howl: Original Draft Facsimile, Transcript & Variant Versions, Fully Annotated by Author, with Contemporaneous Correspondence, Account of First Public Reading, Legal Skirmishes, Precursor Texts & Bibliography* (1986); *White Shroud: Poems, 1980–85* (1986); *Cosmopolitan Greetings: Poems, 1986–1992* (1994); *Selected Poems, 1947–1995* (1996), and *Death and Fame: Last Poems, 1993–1997* (1999). The front dust wrapper of this last book is a color photograph of the poet standing in his apartment next to a portrait of Walt Whitman, both white-bearded. The list of the forty most important Ginsberg titles in his posthumously published *Death and Fame* was gathered by his editors Bob Rosenthal, Peter Hale, and Bill Morgan into the categories of Poetry, Prose, Photography, and Vocal Words and Music. Bill Morgan compiled the 456-page descriptive Ginsberg bibliography, *The Works of Allen Ginsberg, 1941–1994* (1995). J. W. Ehrlich edited *Howl of the Censor* (1961), an account of the 1957 San Francisco trial investigating obscenity in Ginsberg's poem. Jane Kramer, *Allen Ginsberg in America*, was an early biography, followed by two full-length biographies: Barry Miles, *Ginsberg* (1989), and Michael Schumacher, *Dharma Lion: A Critical Biography of Allen Ginsberg* (1992). Bill Morgan, archivist for the estate of Allen Ginsberg, prepared the biographical text in *Allen Ginsberg and Friends* (New York: Sotheby's Catalog for Sale 7351, Oct. 7, 1999). An obituary is in the *New York Times,* 7 Apr. 1997.

ANN CHARTERS

GOETZ, William (24 Mar. 1903–15 Aug. 1979), film producer, was born in New York City, the youngest of the eight children of Theodore Goetz, a ship's purser, and Fanny Goetz (maiden name unknown). After his mother's death in 1913 and his father's subsequent abandonment of the family, Goetz was raised by his elder brothers and educated locally.

All of Goetz's five brothers eventually found niches in film: two of them cofounded Republic Pictures, and in 1924 another brought him to Hollywood, where Goetz became a crew member for Corinne Griffith Productions. Known there as a fast talker with an earthy sense of humor, Goetz rose to the position of associate producer by 1927, when he moved in succession to Metro-Goldwyn-Mayer and Paramount. In March 1930, the year he became associate producer at Fox Films, the "young, dashing" Goetz married MGM boss Louis B. Mayer's daughter Edith in the film colony's wedding of the year. They had two daughters and remained married until Goetz's death. Two years later, Mayer and his partner Nicholas Schenck capitalized Twentieth Century Films as a partnership among Joseph Schenck (Nicholas's brother), Darryl Zanuck, and Goetz. The 1933 merger with Fox Films that created Twentieth Century–Fox placed Goetz as vice president, though Zanuck headed production.

When Zanuck entered military service during World War II, Goetz took his place and quickly turned out a number of prestigious films, including the musical *Hello, Frisco, Hello*, the starkly realistic *Guadalcanal Diary*, and the uplifting Academy Award–winning *The Song of Bernadette* (1942). In these films, his trademark of quality—never cutting corners—became obvious. Shortly thereafter Goetz reportedly turned down an offer from Zanuck to stay on and his father-in-law's offer to take MGM's creative development post (he was quoted as telling his wife he had turned it down because the first thing he would have done was fire Mayer). Having run a studio, Goetz simply could not backtrack. He joined with Leo Spitz to invent International Pictures in 1943. In 1945, the firm merged with the ailing Universal Pictures, and Goetz, called in the gossip columns "the most talked about young man in Hollywood," became production chief of Universal International.

Under Goetz, the new venture forged international alliances, linking up with Britain's J. Arthur Rank organization, for example. UI prospered with well-made, well-judged "family entertainment" including the series of B pictures about the adventures of hicks Ma and Pa Kettle and another series starring the talking mule Francis, as well as "biopics" such as *The Glenn Miller Story*. That film's star, James Stewart, joined with Goetz for *Bend of the River* (1952), a production that changed the way movies were financed.

Although he was a product of the studios, Goetz now took a step that would hasten the studio system's downfall. He asked Stewart to take a gamble by accepting a 50 percent stake in *Bend of the River*—and forgoing a fixed fee for his performance in the film. Stewart and UI each cleared more than $750,000, and their precedent soon shifted the industry's balance of power. Goetz said, "The Jimmy Stewart treatment was . . . an initial caraway seed I helped plant which blossomed into a financial pastry shop for actors." Politically a Democrat (one reason why the right-wing Mayer eventually disinherited his daughter), Goetz was instrumental in allowing creative personnel to share in the profits of their work.

After the Academy Award–winning *From Here to Eternity* (1953), Goetz left UI in 1954, forming William Goetz Productions. He claimed, "You can do a lot of things as an independent that can't be attempted by a studio." Although the studios' absolute power over personnel and distribution had been weakened, they retained the "hardware," and independents still turned to them for production facilities. The company, which released its films through Columbia Pictures, continued until 1961. In 1964 the restless Goetz became vice president for Seven Arts.

As someone who enforced a "no relatives" rule in his place of work, Goetz enjoyed an unusual reputation in Hollywood. Although part of the town's royal family, he drove his own car, helped employees with personal problems, and had his personal chef prepare studio fare. He displayed taste, erudition, and manners. The director Billy Wilder said he was "the very antithesis of being pompous. . . . He had a funny cynicism." Goetz didn't win all his gambles. He acquired some of Mayer's thoroughbreds and won the 1950 Santa Anita Derby with Your Host, but the horse later broke down and rather than keep him for stud purposes Goetz collected the insurance. Your Host subsequently sired Kelso, one of the all-time money winners.

Starting in 1946, Goetz and his wife became Hollywood's most successful art collectors, specializing in the impressionists and postimpressionists. Part of his Van Gogh collection was used in the 1956 film *Lust for Life*. During the film's production, Goetz countered skeptics who thought it would be too intellectual: "If everyone who owns a Van Gogh goes to see the picture, it should be very successful."

Goetz became a director of the City National Bank of Beverly Hills and trustee for Reed College in Portland, Oregon. His last film released through Paramount was *Assault on a Queen* (1966). After cancer treatment at the Mayo Clinic, Goetz died at home.

• Of particular value is Angela Fox Dunn, "Bill Goetz: The Greatest of Them All," *Los Angeles Times*, 20 Apr. 1980. Goetz is glimpsed in such works as Neal Gabler, *An Empire of Their Own: How the Jews Invented Hollywood* (1988), and John Robert Colobo, ed., *Wit and Wisdom of the Moviemakers* (1979). The disposition of the Goetzes' art collection is the subject of many 1988 newspaper articles following Edith Goetz's death. Some personal reminiscences of Joan Midwinter of Pacific Palisades, California, William Goetz's longtime private secretary, aided in the writing of this *American National Biography* entry. Obituaries are in the *New York Times* and the *Los Angeles Times*, both 16 Aug. 1969, and *Variety*, 20 Aug. 1969.

JAMES ROSS MOORE

GOIZUETA, Roberto (18 Nov. 1931–18 Oct. 1997), business executive, was born Roberto Crispulo Goizueta in Havana, Cuba, the son of Crispulo Goizueta, an architect who owned a construction and hardware business, and Aida Cantera Goizueta. His maternal grandfather, Marcelo Cantera, a Spanish aristocrat, had moved to Cuba soon after the turn of the century and owned a sugar refinery. The Goizuetas lived in his mansion, and the young grandson idolized his grandfather, often repeating his aphorisms in later life.

A slim, serious young man, Goizueta attended Belen, a private Catholic second school in Havana. In 1948 the eighteen-year-old, who knew only a smattering of English, spent his senior year at the prestigious Cheshire Academy in Connecticut. He learned the new language by going to the same movies over and over again, absorbing American values along with the lingo. His discipline, combined with a photographic memory, served him well. "My professor said that my sentence structure was textbook-perfect," Goizueta recalled. "It should have been; it came right out of the textbook! The only way I could accurately convey a thought was to memorize, word for word, entire passages" (quoted in Pendergrast, p. 329). He graduated as class valedictorian, going on to Yale University, where he studied chemical engineering.

The collegiate Goizueta was not terribly memorable. "When I first saw this intelligent, shy, well-mannered young man walking down the dormitory hall," recalled his Yale roommate, "I never thought he would become the CEO of the number one ranked company in America" (quoted in *Life and Legacy*, n.p.). Goizueta played squash and soccer and graduated tenth in his 1953 class.

Returning to Cuba, where he married Olga Casteleiro on 14 June 1953, Goizueta displayed his first independent streak, turning down his father's offer to join the family firm. "I wanted to see if I was more than my father's son," he recalled (quoted in *Life and*

Legacy, n.p.). Instead, he answered a blind newspaper advertisement for a bilingual chemist, which turned out to be a position with the Havana subsidiary of the Coca-Cola Company. He began work for $500 a month on 4 July 1954. Rising quickly to a management position as chief technical director for Coca-Cola's five Cuban bottling plants, Goizueta appeared set for a comfortable mid-level career when Fidel Castro's revolutionary forces took over in January 1959.

Over the next year, it became clear that Castro might nationalize Coca-Cola. In May 1960 the Goizuetas sent their three children to live with relatives in the United States. In August Roberto and Olguita, as he called his wife, went to Miami for a two-week vacation and never returned. Two months later Castro seized Coke's Cuban branch. When he defected, Goizueta had $40, 100 shares of Coca-Cola stock, and the promise of a job. For a few months, he and his family lived in a single motel room divided by a curtain.

Those living arrangements did not last long. In 1961 Coke moved Goizueta to Nassau as area chemist for the Caribbean. In 1963 he became staff assistant to the senior vice president for Latin America. The following year he was transferred to Atlanta headquarters and in 1966 was promoted to vice president in charge of technical research and development, making the 35-year-old the youngest executive to reach that level within the company.

Coca-Cola associates knew Goizueta as a dedicated, impeccably dressed executive who left a bare desk every night. An able administrator, he was a notorious perfectionist. "He knew where every grain of sand was in the office," a fellow worker recalled (quoted in Pendergrast, p. 329). Goizueta's courtly, affable manner and Latin good looks hid what some called ruthlessness, but he rewarded results and never assumed an absolute position, quoting one of his grandfather's proverbs: "The quality of one's compromises is much more important than the correctness of one's position" (quoted in Pendergrast, p. 329). Although Goizueta kept his emotions under a steely, logical control, the surface tranquillity was belied by his chain-smoking. Outside of work and family, he had few interests aside from swimming laps and reading voraciously. He rated his best characteristic as persistence, his greatest fault impatience.

In 1974 Goizueta was initiated as one of the two men in the company who knew the secret "7X" formula that flavored the soft drink. During the late 1970s Goizueta lunched frequently with Robert W. Woodruff, known as "The Boss," the legendary Coca-Cola manager who, even in his eighties and nineties, had to approve every major decision within the company. In Woodruff, Goizueta found another wise old man, like his grandfather.

By 1979 the Coca-Cola Company was stumbling, its stock worth less than at the beginning of the decade, with archrival Pepsi gaining in market share. Chief Executive Officer Paul Austin, who had undiagnosed Alzheimer's disease, appointed six vice chairmen, any of whom might assume control of the company when Austin stepped down. Although Goizueta was one of them, he seemed the least likely to succeed, since he had no operating or marketing experience. In the company's long history, no foreigner—indeed, only Georgians—had ever run the company.

Yet in May 1980 Goizueta, who spoke in a halting Cuban-Dixie accent, was appointed the president of the company, almost certainly through the influence of Woodruff. In March 1981 he assumed the chairmanship from Austin, making gregarious Don Keough his chief operating officer. Within a month he summoned the top fifty Coca-Cola managers from around the world to a five-day conference in Palm Springs at which he passed out his carefully crafted "Strategy for the 1980s." He told them flatly that "there are no sacred cows" and that he would consider "the reformulation of any or all of our products" to jump-start the moribund company (quoted in Pendergrast, p. 336). Goizueta was about to act on his oft-quoted Spanish proverb: "Just because a man is courteous, don't think he isn't brave" (quoted in Allen, p. 403).

Goizueta cleaned house, forcing out those who did not agree with his vision and installing his own executives. He replaced cane sugar in the Coke formula with less expensive high fructose corn syrup; approved a joint venture to turn around the ailing Philippines bottler; ended a human rights disaster in Guatemala by arranging the buyout of a right-wing bottler; oversaw an aggressive new ad campaign ("Coke Is It"); diversified by purchasing Columbia Pictures; jettisoned money-losing enterprises such as shrimp farming, wine production, and water desalinization; took on reasonable corporate debt for the first time; and spearheaded the introduction of Diet Coke—a heretical move since it was the first product to take the sacred Coca-Cola name, other than the flagship brand. Some analysts questioned the wisdom of this flurry of activity, but by the end of 1984 Goizueta appeared to have the golden touch. Coke stock had appreciated 95 percent, including dividends, since he took over. Still, Goizueta was uneasy. "There is a danger when a company is doing as well as we are. And that is, to think that we can do no wrong. I keep telling the organization: We can do wrong and we can do wrong big" (quoted in Pendergrast, p. 346).

As if to illustrate his point, Goizueta oversaw the introduction of what came to be called "New Coke" in April 1985. The boldest of moves, changing the sacred formula made sense in many ways. Blind taste tests showed that Pepsi beat the old Coke formula by a small margin, and Pepsi's market share had been gradually creeping up on Coke for twenty years. Goizueta's flavor gurus had developed a new formula that beat Pepsi in taste tests. But the company badly miscalculated when it took away the public's favorite drink. "Would it be right to rewrite the Constitution? The Bible?" wrote one typical consumer. "To me, changing the Coke formula is of such a serious nature" (quoted in Pendergrast, p. 356). The company received more than 40,000 such letters of protest, in addition to 8,000 daily phone calls. Finally, Goizueta capitulated in July and brought back the old formula as Coca-Cola Classic. Ironically, the old Coke then began to gain ground on Pepsi, and the marketing disaster turned into a coup, so that some people thought that Goizueta had planned the entire thing.

The final ten years of Goizueta's life and career were largely triumphant. In 1989, after a few box-office bombs, Coke sold Columbia Pictures to Sony for a substantial profit, and the company refocused solely on highly profitable soft drinks. Taking his cue from the success in the Philippines, Goizueta approved joint bottling ventures around the world, including the creation of Coca-Cola Enterprises in the United States, with Big Coke holding a 49 percent share. Previously, the company had simply provided the flavor concentrate, and independent bottlers sold the beverage. Goizueta's more proactive stance assured better management, he asserted, although critics complained that the company overcharged its captive bottlers while boosting its own bottom line.

With the fall of the Berlin Wall in 1989, and the general triumph of free trade, Goizueta oversaw a worldwide cola blitzkrieg, penetrating the former Soviet bloc and communist China while profiting in Latin America. He also expanded company offerings with drinks such as Fruitopia, the failed OK Soda, and PowerAde. Goizueta was only half joking when he said, "If you look in your kitchen sink, there's one spigot that has a C and another spigot that has an H. That spigot that has a C should be used for what God intended" (quoted in Pendergrast, p. 390). In 1996 Goizueta beamed as the "Coca-Cola Olympics" took place in hometown Atlanta, followed by a deal in Venezuela that gave Coca-Cola control in one of the few countries that had always belonged to Pepsi.

In 1997, for the second year running, *Fortune* magazine named Coca-Cola the most admired American company, but in August Goizueta was diagnosed with advanced lung cancer. He died in Atlanta, leaving an astonishing business record. The Coca-Cola Company's market value had soared under his leadership—from $4.3 billion to $145 billion at the time of his death. Worldwide, Coke's soft drink share had grown from 35 to 50 percent.

During Goizueta's reign, critics claimed that Coca-Cola was contributing to the homogenization of world culture with ubiquitous advertising that promoted a fizzy, illusory lifestyle in order to sell non-nutritional soft drinks. Although profits always came first with Goizueta, he argued that by boosting the share price, he had done more good than most charities, since so many foundations held Coke stock. Goizueta could be thin-skinned, firing off corrective letters to analysts, but he also stressed the need for multinationals to be good corporate citizens: "We cannot for the long term exist as a healthy company in a sick society" (Goizueta, "Real Essence," p. 199). Two years before his death, Goizueta addressed a group of immigrants who had just taken the oath of American citizenship, as he

had in 1969. "You must sense the opportunity in your nostrils with every breath," he told them, clearly thinking of his own experience, "and you must see it in your dreams when you are asleep" (quoted in Pendergrast, p. 423).

• A few months before he died, Roberto Goizueta gave a speech about his business philosophy, "The Real Essence of Business," *Vital Speeches*, 15 Jan. 1997. David Greising's *I'd Like the World to Buy a Coke: The Life and Leadership of Roberto Goizueta* (1998) is a useful biography. Two comprehensive histories of Coca-Cola also contain substantial information about Goizueta: Mark Pendergrast, *For God, Country and Coca-Cola: The Definitive History of the Great American Soft Drink and the Company That Makes It*, 2d ed. (2000), and Frederick Allen, *Secret Formula: How Brilliant Marketing and Relentless Salesmanship Made Coca-Cola the Best-Known Product in the World* (1994). *The Life and Legacy of Roberto C. Goizueta* (1998), published by the Coca-Cola Company, is a good biographical pamphlet. "Goizueta, Roberto C.," in the *Current Biography Yearbook 1996*, pp. 166–69, provides an excellent overview. Thomas Oliver, *The Real Coke, the Real Story* (1986), covers the New Coke fiasco. Good articles include "Coke's Man on the Spot," *Business Week*, 29 July 1985; Neil Shister, "The Man Who Changed Coke," *Atlanta*, June 1986; "Roberto's World," *Southpoint Magazine*, Oct. 1989; "He Put the Kick Back into Coke," *Fortune*, 26 Oct. 1987; John Huey, "The World's Best Brand," *Fortune*, 31 May 1993; J. P. Donlon, "The Eighty-Nine Billion Dollar Man," *Chief Executive*, July 1996; and Greg W. Prince, "Goizueta's Legacies," *Beverage World*, Dec. 1997. An obituary is in the *New York Times*, 19 Oct. 1997.

MARK PENDERGRAST

GOLDWATER, Barry (1 Jan. 1909–29 May 1998), U.S. senator and presidential candidate, was born Barry Morris Goldwater in Phoenix, Arizona, the son of Baron M. "Barry" Goldwater, a businessman and retailer, and Josephine Williams Goldwater. Although raised an Episcopalian, Goldwater was the grandson of a Jewish immigrant from Poland, Michel Goldwasser, who had prospered in the "dry goods" business. Goldwater's father, Baron, eventually settled in Phoenix, where he opened a successful women's clothing store. Young Barry's unimpressive school record led his father to enroll him, at age fifteen, at Staunton Military Academy in Virginia, where Goldwater graduated as top military cadet in 1928. After his father's death in 1929, Goldwater dropped out of the University of Arizona and joined the family department store business. In 1934 he married Margaret "Peggy" Johnson; the couple had two sons and two daughters.

By 1937 Goldwater had become president of Goldwater's Inc., but in addition to retailing he pursued a number of other interests—aviation, photography, and Arizona history and culture—that became lifetime passions. Although over thirty and hampered by poor vision, Goldwater was accepted for active duty in the U.S. Army Air Forces during World War II. By the end of the war he had risen to the rank of colonel and later became a brigadier general in the Air National Guard.

Back in Phoenix after the war, Goldwater embarked on a political career. In 1949 he was persuaded to run for the Phoenix city council as part of a successful reform slate of candidates. On the city council, Goldwater gained a lasting reputation for candor, integrity, and humor. He further enhanced his political visibility by managing the successful gubernatorial campaign of Republican Howard Pyle in 1950. Technology (particularly air-conditioning), economic development, and immigration were transforming Arizona into a Republican bastion, and Goldwater's political rise paralleled the transformation of the state from old western Democratic populism to Sunbelt Republican conservatism. In 1952 Pyle encouraged Goldwater to run for the U.S. Senate against incumbent Democrat (and Senate majority leader) Ernest McFarland. Although regarded as an underdog, Goldwater conducted a hard-hitting campaign against the unpopular administration of Harry Truman and rode Dwight Eisenhower's coattails to an upset victory.

Once in the Senate, Goldwater quickly revealed himself to be a hard-line anticommunist (he was one of twenty-two senators who voted against the Senate censure of Joseph McCarthy) and staunch advocate of free enterprise and states' rights. In 1958 he won a relatively easy reelection against McFarland in a miserable Republican year, and the rising conservative forces within the Republican party began to look toward the charismatic Arizonan as a potential presidential candidate. While declining nomination at the 1960 Republican convention, Goldwater delivered a ringing oration that served as a rallying call to Republican conservatives and an implicit critique of Vice President Richard Nixon's accommodations with moderate northeastern Republicans such as New York governor Nelson Rockefeller. The defeat of the Nixon-Lodge ticket in the fall opened the door for a serious conservative challenge for the nomination in 1964 by Goldwater, whose political credo, *The Conscience of a Conservative* (1960), had become a bestseller thanks largely to his following among grassroots conservatives.

The impetus for Goldwater's 1964 campaign came from a devoted group of conservative activists led by F. Clifton White, rather than the candidate himself. But concern that the nomination might go to Rockefeller by default prompted Goldwater to permit White and his allies to build a nationwide grassroots conservative network dedicated to his nomination. In fact, following the controversy over Rockefeller's recent divorce and remarriage, Goldwater was catapulted to front-runner status, and the Arizonan eagerly anticipated pitting his libertarian, conservative philosophy against the established New Deal liberalism of President John F. Kennedy. The Goldwater camp's calculations were upset by Kennedy's assassination and his being replaced as president and as the 1964 Democratic nominee by Texan Lyndon Baines Johnson, a fellow southwesterner with a more moderate political profile.

White's efforts paid off spectacularly, however, as the Arizonan built up a formidable lead in convention delegates. Goldwater had particular strength in the South, where serious state and local Republican parties were emerging for the first time since Reconstruction. By the time the moderate, northeastern Republican establishment that had dominated the party since 1940 realized that Goldwater was on the brink of winning the 1964 presidential nomination, it was too late to stop him. Rockefeller staked his hopes on the critical California primary in June, but, despite intense campaigning by the New York governor, Goldwater's forces eked out a narrow but decisive victory. The charges of "extremism" hurled against Goldwater by Rockefeller and other establishment Republicans further alienated conservatives and led to a bitter and divisive Republican convention in San Francisco in July 1964. True to his image as a man of uncompromising principle, Goldwater chose conservative New York congressman William E. Miller as his running-mate, and his rousing acceptance speech took on his moderate critics directly: "Extremism in the defense of liberty is no vice, and . . . moderation in the pursuit of justice is no virtue."

Goldwater's general election campaign was a disaster. Johnson successfully wrapped himself in the mantle of his martyred predecessor by maintaining a booming economy and securing passage of the 1964 Civil Rights Act. Goldwater's outspoken nature, uncompromising southwestern conservatism, and hardline anti-Soviet stance also made it easy for the incumbent's campaign to depict him as an intemperate ideologue who could not be trusted with the huge U.S. nuclear arsenal. On the domestic front Goldwater's votes against the 1964 Civil Rights Act (on grounds that it violated states' rights) and his public speculations about privatizing the Tennessee Valley Authority were used to corroborate the extremist image. This highly unfair but effective strategy stifled the Arizonan's hopes for a principled debate on the issues and led to a landslide defeat in the fall, with Goldwater winning only 38.5 percent of the popular vote and carrying only six states (Georgia, Alabama, Louisiana, Mississippi, South Carolina, and his home state of Arizona) with a combined total of fifty-two electoral votes to Johnson's 486.

Goldwater returned to the Senate in 1968 and reestablished himself as a leader of Republican conservatives in that body. In 1974 he played a decisive role in the Watergate drama when he informed President Nixon that he would likely be convicted in a Senate impeachment trial. Having lost Goldwater's support, Nixon realized that his position was hopeless and resigned the presidency. As chair of the Senate Select Intelligence Committee during the 1980s, Goldwater was frequently critical of the Ronald Reagan administration, but his positions became even more idiosyncratic after his final retirement from the Senate in 1986. The ex-senator publicly attacked the growing influence of the religious right over the Republican party and spoke out in defense of abortion rights, gay rights, and even President Bill Clinton and his wife Hillary, anathema to contemporary Republican conservatives. These remarks only added to his reputation for candor and integrity and brought him sympathy from a broader ideological audience. Goldwater's wife Peggy had died in 1985, and in 1992 he married Susan Schaffer Wechsler. Barry Goldwater died of natural causes at his home in Paradise Valley, Arizona, at age eighty-nine.

Despite the decisive repudiation of Goldwater in 1964, his campaign revealed the outlines of a future Republican conservative electoral majority anchored in the South and West. As the New Deal electoral coalition unraveled in the face of the Vietnam war, racial strife, and the emergence of the campus counterculture, conservatism consolidated its grip on the Republican party and found a more receptive audience in the wider public. The final triumph of this "new right" conservatism was confirmed by Ronald Reagan's sweeping presidential victories in the 1980s. The electoral, economic, and social base of the Republican party shifted decisively in 1964, and Barry Goldwater ultimately proved to be one of the most influential losing presidential nominees in U.S. history.

• Goldwater's papers are at the Arizona Historical Foundation, located on the campus of Arizona State University in Tempe, Ariz. The clearest statement of his political beliefs remains *The Conscience of a Conservative* (1960). Goldwater also published two volumes of autobiography, *With No Apologies: The Personal and Political Memoirs of United States Senator Barry M. Goldwater* (1979) and, with Jack Casserly, *Goldwater* (1988). The major biography is *Barry Goldwater* (1995) by Robert Alan Goldberg. Peter Iverson, *Barry Goldwater: Native Arizonan* (1997), views Goldwater in the context of Arizona history, society, and politics. On the 1964 election, the best account of the nominating campaign is Robert D. Novak, *The Agony of the G.O.P. 1964* (1965), and on the general election, Theodore H. White, *The Making of the President: 1964* (1965). Goldwater's long-term impact on the Republican party and American politics is discussed in Mary C. Brennan, *Turning Right in the Sixties: The Conservative Capture of the GOP* (1995), and Nicol C. Rae, *The Decline and Fall of the Liberal Republicans* (1989). An obituary is in the *New York Times*, 30 May 1998.

NICOL C. RAE

GOLDWATER, John L. (14 Feb. 1916–26 Feb. 1999), publisher and writer, was born John Leonard Goldwater in New York City, the son of Daniel Goldwater and Edna Bogart Goldwater, who died during childbirth; the father, reportedly overcome by grief, abandoned the child and died soon afterward. Growing up in a foster home, Goldwater attended the High School of Commerce where he developed secretarial skills and some facility as a writer. At seventeen, he hitchhiked across the country, stopping at Hiawatha, Kansas, where he took a reporting job on the local newspaper. He subsequently moved to Kansas City, Missouri, where he found a position as secretary to the administrator of Grand Canyon National Park, then to Arizona, and eventually on to San Francisco

and jobs with the Missouri-Pacific Railroad, and, in rather rapid succession, other employers. After a year or so, he returned to New York. In later years, recounting his youthful employment experiences, Goldwater usually explained that he moved often from job to job because his attentions to young women in each location resulted in his being fired. Back in New York, he worked for various publishers and then became an entrepreneur, buying unsold periodicals, mainly pulp magazines, from publisher Louis H. Silberkleit and exporting them for sale abroad. Observing the success of the Superman character in the infant comic book industry in 1939, he joined Silberkleit and Maurice Coyne in launching a comic book publishing firm with himself as editor (while continuing as president of Periodicals for Export, Inc.), Silberkleit as publisher, and Coyne as bookkeeper.

MLJ Comics (derived from the initials of the partners' given names) produced its first comic book, *Blue Ribbon Comics*, with a cover date of November 1939. *Top-Notch Comics* followed in December, then *Pep Comics* in January 1940 and *Zip Comics* in February. These titles featured a cast of heroic characters similar to those in other comic books of the period: The Shield (the first patriotic comic book superhero), The Black Hood, Steel Sterling, Mr. Justice, The Comet, The Rocket, Captain Valor, Kardak the Mystic Magician, Swift of the Secret Service, and so on. None of the MLJ costumed crime fighters achieved the success enjoyed by rival publishers with Superman, Batman, Captain Marvel, and Captain America. But in 1941 MLJ published the first story about the character who would make the company's fortune. Concocted at the instigation of Goldwater (according to Goldwater), Archie Andrews, an irrepressible freckle-faced, carrot-topped teenager, debuted in the back pages of *Pep Comics* in issue no. 22, and, almost simultaneously, in *Jackpot Comics*, no. 4, both dated December 1941.

Drawn by cartoonist Bob Montana, Archie quickly became the most popular character in the MLJ lineup and would eventually become the archetypal American teenager. Within a year, he was the eponymous star of his own comic book, and in 1943 the radio program "The Adventures of Archie Andrews" began on 31 May (to continue, on different networks, until September 1953). The syndicated newspaper comic strip version, produced independently by Montana, started on 4 February 1946 and ran through the rest of the century and into the next. In 1946, the comic book company officially became Archie Comics Publications. Archie subsequently appeared in a television animated cartoon series (1969–1977) and in two live-action television movies. For a brief time in the 1970s, the character lent his name to a chain of restaurants.

In the early 1950s, as the nation experienced an increase in juvenile crime, an assortment of critics—psychiatric, literary, and political—charged that comic book stories bred youthful miscreants. Alarmed as the critics appeared to enlist greater and greater public support (particularly in governmental bodies with the power to produce controlling legislation), comic book publishers formed in 1954 a voluntary association to cleanse their product of objectionable content. The Comics Magazine Association of America was incorporated in September 1954 with Goldwater as president. "I was its prime founder," Goldwater said. "Its purpose was to adopt a code of ethics to eliminate editorial and advertising material which was inimical to the best interests of the comic book industry as well as its readers. I . . . succeeded in cooperation with industry leaders to quell the uproar and eliminate legislation which it is said could have put the comics industry in dire straits if not out of business altogether" (Smith, p. 9). Goldwater was one of the principal authors of the Comics Code, which consisted of forty-one prohibitions concerning the portrayal of crime, violence, religion, sex, horror, nudity, and the like, in both editorial and advertising pages. ("No unique or unusual methods of concealing weapons shall be shown"; "Profanity, obscenity, smut, vulgarity, or words or symbols which have acquired undesirable meanings are forbidden.") The Comics Code soon drove out of the industry several comic book publishers whose product could not adhere to the code and still retain its essential appeal. The most celebrated of these was EC Comics, which had inaugurated an industrywide trend toward horror comic books. Goldwater served as CMAA president for twenty-five years until he relinquished the office, whereupon the board of directors created the position of chairman of the board, in which capacity Goldwater served for several years. Goldwater married twice, the second time to Gloria Freidrun, with whom he had two children. His son from his first marriage, Richard, became an executive at Archie Comics. In addition to his involvement in the comic book industry, Goldwater was national commissioner of the Anti-Defamation League of B'nai B'rith, president of the New York Society for the Deaf, and a past master of the Masonic fraternity. In 1971, Archie Comics went public, but Goldwater's son bought the company back in 1983 and installed his father as honorary chairman, a role he filled until he died of a heart attack at his home in Manhattan.

The issue of who created the Archie character is clouded by rival claims from Montana and Goldwater. In histories of Archie Comics, Goldwater is credited with inventing the characters and Montana with envisioning them, but Montana (according to his daughter quoting her mother) had been sketching ideas for a teenage comic strip for some years before he began freelancing with MLJ Comics in 1941. When Goldwater asked for ideas about a comic book character that was not a costumed superhero, Montana and another MLJ artist, Joe Edwards, produced the Archie menage—Archie and his pal Jughead (Forsythe P. Jones) and Betty Cooper, the romantic interest; they worked, presumably, with editor Harry Shorten. Their creation may have appealed to Goldwater because of the current popularity of teenagers Andy Hardy in movies and Henry Aldrich on radio. Vic Bloom wrote the first story, perhaps guided some-

what by the Popular Comics character Wally Williams, who had a sidekick named Jughead. The nuclear cast expanded in April 1942 to include Veronica Lodge, a dark-haired vamp who contrasted with Betty's blonde wholesomeness. Goldwater would later imply that it was his own youthful adventures out West with the opposite sex that inspired what became the feature's chief plot mechanism—the ongoing competition between the two girls for Archie's favors (a canny reversal of the traditional situation in which two men vie for one woman) and Archie's ambivalence about which of the girls he desired most.

By the mid-1950s most teenager characters in comics had faded away, leaving Archie as the embodiment of the nation's perennial adolescent, and his high school adventures, romantic frustrations, and high-spirited juvenile pranks as a stereotypical model of teenage life in popular culture for generations to come. While Montana, until his death in 1975, was solely responsible for the newspaper comic strip version of Archie, Goldwater continued to oversee the unfolding of Archie's fate in an ever-lengthening list of teenage comic book titles from Archie Comics. He is more likely to be remembered, however, for his role in the CMAA than for his participation in the life of Archie Andrews.

• Goldwater wrote a history of the CMAA, *Americana in Four Colors: A Decade of Self-Regulation by the Comics Magazine Industry* (1964), and collaborated on *The Best of Archie* (1980), chiefly a collection of reprinted comic book stories. The most complete biographical account was obtained by Mary Smith in interviews with Goldwater and is published in Smith's *The Best of Betty and Veronica Summer Fun* (1991), a publication of the *Archie Fan Magazine*. The creation of Archie is rehearsed in Charles Phillips, *Archie: His First 50 Years* (1991). The story of the founding of MLJ is given in Ron Goulart, *Over 50 Years of American Comic Books* (1991), and the birth of the Comics Magazine Association of America and the criticism of comic books that prompted its creation are discussed at length in Amy Kiste Nyberg, *Seal of Approval: The History of the Comics Code* (1998). An obituary appears in the *New York Times*, 2 Mar. 1999.

ROBERT C. HARVEY

GORE, Albert, Sr. (26 Dec. 1907–5 Dec. 1998), U.S. senator, was born near Granville, Tennessee, the son of Allen Gore, a farmer, and Margie Denny Gore. He attended local one-room country schools and graduated from high school in nearby Gordonsville, after which he taught high school in Smith and Overton counties. He graduated with a B.S. from Middle Tennessee State Teachers College (now Middle Tennessee State University) in 1932 and in that same year lost his first attempt at elective office (superintendent of schools for Smith county). When his opponent died after a year in office, Gore was named to the post and served until 1936. By this time smitten with politics, Gore furthered his education by attending night law school at the Nashville YMCA. After three years of long-distance commuting from Carthage, he received his LL.B. in 1936. Admitted to the bar that year, he began practicing law in Carthage with his future wife, Pauline La Fon, whom he had met in Nashville while she was waitressing her way through Vanderbilt University Law School. Married on 27 April 1937, the couple had two children.

Driven and ambitious, Gore entered statewide politics early. He provided yeoman assistance to Franklin Roosevelt's 1932 presidential campaign with his organizational efforts among the state's Young Democrats. An effective orator, he became chairman of the state Democratic party's speakers' bureau in 1934 and was rewarded for his efforts with an appointment as state commissioner of labor in 1936. After two years in office—during which he took the lead in setting up "a model unemployment-compensation plan"—he resigned in order to run for the U.S. Congress. Claiming inspiration from the example of fellow Carthagite Cordell Hull, Gore mortgaged his farm to finance his campaign and spoke tirelessly throughout the Fourth District, accompanied by a bluegrass band in which he often was the featured fiddle player. After besting five other candidates for the Democratic nomination, Gore gained election to the House in 1938.

Assigned to the Banking and Currency Committee on his arrival in Washington, Gore soon displayed the independent streak that would characterize his entire legislative career. An internationalist in outlook, he consistently supported the foreign policy initiatives of both the Roosevelt and Truman administrations, including the Lend-Lease Act of 1941, the 1946 loan to Great Britain, Greek-Turkish aid, and the Marshall Plan. Gore also favored liberal trade policies and provided unwavering support to the extension of the reciprocal trade agreements that had been set up by his mentor Hull. On domestic matters, however, Gore was far less reliable as a presidential ally. He fought (and lost) a battle against what he termed a "weak-kneed" price control bill in 1941, and in 1949 he led a successful revolt against Secretary of Agriculture Charles Brannan's experimental farm price support plan. Although he did support Harry S. Truman's public housing plan, he drew the president's ire with his support for the Taft-Hartley bill. Gore also supported initiatives that were important to his home state, including the Tennessee Valley Authority and the Atomic Energy Commission.

A consistent foe of Ed "Boss" Crump's Memphis-based political machine, Gore challenged and beat incumbent Democratic Senator Kenneth McKellar, a long-time Crump ally, in the 1952 primary. In his three terms in the Senate, Gore and fellow Tennessean Estes Kefauver became leading southern voices of moderation on the issue of civil rights. Although, as a member of the House, Gore had voted against the establishment of a Fair Employment Practices Commission, which was meant to give blacks an even chance in the labor market, he was a consistent foe of the poll tax. He also was one of only three southern senators (Kefauver and Lyndon Johnson were the others) who refused to sign the 1956 "Southern Manifesto," which advocated resistance to desegregation activity, and in the following year he voted for the Civil Rights Act of 1957.

As a senator, Gore continued to support public utilities in general and the TVA in particular. His was a leading voice of opposition when southern utility company presidents Edgar Dixon and Eugene Yates sought a government contract to supply western Tennessee with power in 1954. Charging that the entire contract amounted to a sweetheart deal, Gore generated so much negative publicity that President Dwight D. Eisenhower eventually ordered the Atomic Energy Commission to cancel the contract. He was less successful in numerous attempts at tax reform. Although he and Senator Paul Douglas of Illinois fought for years to close what they considered unfair loopholes that favored the wealthy and businesses, their proposals seldom were reported out of the conservative Senate Finance Committee.

Gore's greatest achievement in the Senate came in the area of highway construction. He was the leading force behind both the Federal Highway Aid Act of 1956 and the Highway Revenue Act of 1956; together, these bills provided for the construction of 42,500 miles of interstate highways. Generally supportive of President Johnson's Great Society programs, Gore produced the first Medicare bill to pass either house of Congress. Toward the end of his Senate tenure, Gore became more consistently liberal. He supported the Civil Rights Act of 1965, voted against the school prayer amendment of 1966, and voted in favor of the Civil Rights Act of 1968. Despite his proposal as a House member to use nuclear weapons during the Korean War in order to create a radioactive demilitarized zone, by 1963 Gore supported the test ban treaty and was an early, vocal opponent of the Vietnam War. His opposition to President Richard M. Nixon's Vietnam policies and his refusal to support either Clement Haynsworth or G. Harrold Carswell, two southern Supreme Court nominees, led the Republican president to make Gore his number one target for defeat in the 1970 elections. Both Nixon and Vice President Spiro Agnew campaigned in Tennessee on behalf of their hand-picked candidate, four-term Congressman William Brock III, and their efforts helped Brock to a narrow victory.

After leaving office, Gore taught law at Vanderbilt University, and in 1972 he became chairman of the Island Creek Coal Company. He died in Carthage, Tennessee.

Although his legislative career defied neat categorizations, Gore was a leading voice of southern progressive politics in his era. His bitter defeat in 1970 notwithstanding, he must have gained a sense of retribution when his son Albert, Jr., won election to the U.S. House and Senate before becoming vice president in 1992.

• Gore's papers are at the Albert Gore Research Center at Middle Tennessee State University, Murfreesboro, Tenn. He was the author of *Let the Glory Out: My South and Its Politics* (1972). His career can be traced through Neal R. Peirce,

The Border South States: People, Politics and Power in the Five Border South States (1975), and Joseph Bruce Gorman, Kefauver: A Political Biography (1971). Obituaries appear in the Los Angeles Times and the Washington Post, 6 Dec. 1998, and in the New York Times, 7 Dec. 1998.

EDWARD L. LACH, JR.

GOSDEN, Freeman (5 May 1899–10 Dec. 1982), producer, writer, and performer on radio, was born Freeman Fisher Gosden in Richmond Virginia, the son of Walter Gosden and Emma L. Smith Gosden. His father had been a Confederate army officer, and—in a familiar pattern of nineteenth-century southern life—the once-prominent family found itself in modest circumstances following the Civil War. One of five children, Freeman began appearing as a carnival performer at the age of ten. He worked in traveling shows around the South as a magician's assistant, a clog dancer, a ukulele player, and a singer. After only a minimum of formal schooling at a military academy in Atlanta, he dropped out to become a tobacco agent and then a used-car salesman. When the United States entered the First World War in 1917, he joined the navy and was trained as a radio operator.

Upon his discharge in 1919, he decided to resume his boyhood career as a performer and found work on the vaudeville circuit with a regional troupe of the Joe Bren Company. While appearing in Durham, North Carolina, he met Charles Correll, another Bren performer, who would become his lifelong friend and partner. Gosden and Correll both had more success as production managers than as performers, and by 1924 they were working in management for Bren, sharing an apartment in Chicago.

As executives, Gosden and Correll missed the satisfactions of the vaudeville stage, and so, almost as a hobby, they developed a musical comedy act, which they performed over radio station WEBH in return for dinners at the hotel that owned the station. The broadcast consisted mainly of musical pieces and storytelling, much of which concerned the South and contained "Negro dialect" humor. In 1925 WGN, the most powerful radio station in the city, offered them salaried staff positions. Here they created, wrote, and produced a daily comic serial, "Sam 'n' Henry," in which they starred as two teenage African-American boys.

"Sam 'n' Henry" did well, but following a disagreement with management Gosden and Correll left WGN. Since the station owned the copyright, they were forced to abandon their successful program concept as well. Moving over to Chicago station WMAQ in 1928, they created a similar show, "Amos 'n' Andy," which would make them national stars and dominate the rest of their careers.

"Amos 'n' Andy" is the story of two black men from Georgia who come to the North to seek their fortune. Settling in Harlem, they establish the Fresh-Air Taxicab Company, named for its only property, a broken-down roofless jalopy. The paper-thin plots of the Monday-through-Friday serial were built around the characters' lack of intelligence or even common sense. The jokes were mostly malapropisms and mispronunciations. "That's downright re-scusting!" was a recurring line. Gosden's Amos, a low-key trusting soul, provides contrast to Correll's Andy, a boisterous loudmouth. Gosden and Correll played all the other characters, male and female, as well. It is estimated that over the years they played more than 500 different roles in this updated audio version of a "blackface" minstrel sketch.

The series was an instant and long-term success. In a technical and marketing innovation, Gosden and Correll made wax recordings of these programs and sold them to more than forty radio stations around the country, making "Amos 'n' Andy" one of the first nationally syndicated series. The National Broadcasting Company took quick note of this, however, and in 1929 signed Gosden and Correll to a $100,000-per-year contract to air the show on one of its coast-to-coast radio networks. It remained on national radio for the next twenty years, changing to a weekly half-hour format in 1943. "Amos 'n' Andy" was consistently among the ten most popular shows on the air, according to the authoritative Hooper ratings.

Gosden and Correll were also innovators in cross-media product tie-ins. In the 1930s they produced and starred in three "Amos 'n' Andy" movies: Check and Double Check (1930), The Rasslin' Match (1934), and The Lion Tamer (1934). In the first of these, they played the roles in blackface. In the latter two, actors were used with the voices of Gosden and Correll dubbed in to accentuate the dialect jokes they had developed in radio. Over the years the radio show spawned an Amos 'n' Andy daily comic strip, a book of Amos 'n' Andy sketches titled Here They Are—Amos 'n' Andy, and a series of records produced by RCA Victor.

Some dissatisfaction had always been registered against "Amos 'n' Andy," primarily from black newspapers such as Amsterdam News and the Chicago Defender. The critics believed that the radio show and the atmosphere it created constituted the plainly racist denigration of African Americans. The protests seemed to have little effect, however, until the show was adapted for television by CBS in 1951, at a time when the civil rights movement was beginning to gather steam. Despite the fact that black performers now played the television characters, "Amos 'n' Andy" came to epitomize the race stereotypes that had dominated American popular culture for the past century.

The NAACP, whose ranks had been increased with a generation of upwardly mobile black war veterans and by growing white support for an end to Jim Crow laws, took the lead in the fight to get the new television show off the air. CBS headquarters in New York was picketed, and product boycotts were threatened against sponsors. Even with good ratings, "Amos 'n' Andy" was canceled in 1953 after only two seasons. Following the cancellation, reruns were aired until 1961, when the show was finally withdrawn from domestic syndication. (It was syndicated abroad until 1966.) There would not be another network television show starring an African American until "I Spy," with Bill Cosby, which premiered in 1965.

Gosden and Correll claimed a kind of bewildered innocence in the midst of all this, preferring to see their work as a folksy celebration of "Negro life" that was otherwise ignored by the mass media. After the cancellation of the show on television, they attempted to revive it on radio. Although revamped several times, the show never achieved national distribution, and the final "Amos 'n' Andy" radio broadcast was aired on 25 November 1960.

Gosden and Correll's final effort to revive their careers began in 1961, with the premiere of "Calvin and the Colonel," a half-hour animated sitcom, which they wrote and produced and in which they starred as the principal voices. It concerned two southerners—a fox and a bear—who move to a northern city. The show did poorly in prime time, and the following year ABC-TV gave it a slot in its Saturday morning children's programming. The change in scheduling was to no avail; the show was canceled in September 1962.

In 1927 Gosden had married Leta Marie Schreiber, with whom he had a son and a daughter; they divorced in 1943. The following year Gosden married Jane Stoneham, daughter of the owner of the New York Giants baseball team, Horace Stoneham; this second marriage produced a son and a daughter as well.

Gosden and Correll remained friends until the latter's death in 1972. Living out his retirement in Palm Springs, Gosden played golf regularly with former president Dwight D. Eisenhower, and he became an active fundraiser for the Eisenhower Medical Center. At age eighty-three, he died of heart failure at the UCLA Medical Center.

Freeman Gosden claimed throughout his career to be an innocent lover of the Old South, whose characters and stories reflected a past era of American life. While he entertained millions, however, he also helped perpetuate racial attitudes and stereotypes that were increasingly at issue in a society attempting to make up for its past injustices. His failure to recognize the effects of his work eventually became far more significant than his intentions. The success of "Amos 'n' Andy"—and its demise—remains for the "Age of Information" a cautionary tale about the power of mass communication to insult as well as to entertain.

• Although relatively little has been written about Freeman Gosden per se, much has been written about "Amos 'n' Andy," especially in the context of the racial uproar it caused. See, for example, Melvin Patrick Ely, *The Adventures of Amos 'n' Andy: A Social History of an American Phenomenon* (1991), and J. Fred MacDonald, *Blacks and White TV: Afro-Americans in Television since 1948* (1983). The 11 Dec. 1982 issue of the *New York Times* has an informative obituary.

DAVID MARC

GOULD, Milton S. (8 Oct. 1909–21 Mar. 1999), lawyer, was born in New York City, the son of David H. Gould and Ida Gould. (His full middle name—if indeed he had more than an initial—is unknown; also missing from publicly accessible records is mention of his father's occupation and his mother's maiden name.) As a child Gould loved reading classics in Latin and Greek; following graduation from George Washington High School in Manhattan, he entered Cornell University in Ithaca, New York, with the hope of becoming a college professor. He earned his bachelor's degree in 1930, but he decided to study law rather than pursue graduate work in the humanities. After graduating from Cornell's law school in 1933, Gould joined the New York City firm of White & Case. His joy at finding even an entry-level job in the depths of the Great Depression was short-lived, however, when he encountered the anti-Semitism that at the time was rampant among major New York law firms. Disgusted at being consigned to a back room in which he was charged with drafting memos and forbidden contact with potential clients, Gould soon quit and joined a newly formed firm, Kaufman, Weitzner & Celler.

Gould thrived in his new environs and spent the preponderance of his career (save for a few years during which he prosecuted immigration corruption cases) with the firm whose founders included Emanuel Celler (who served as a U.S. congressman from Brooklyn) and Samuel H. Kaufman (who later served as a federal judge). He married Eleanor Greenburg in 1937; the couple had three children.

At a time when the legal profession was becoming increasingly specialized, Gould developed a reputation as a masterful litigator who handled a wide variety of cases, including libel, white-collar crime, real estate, and admiralty matters. Wily, charming, and "deceptively low-key" (*New York Times*, 24 Mar. 1999), Gould was a master at cross-examination, able sometimes to win cases by lulling his opponents into complacency. His client list included major names of the corporate world: Columbia Pictures, Curtis Publishing, Texas Oil and Gas, and Twentieth Century–Fox. In 1962 Gould won millions for the stockholders of the former Fifth Avenue Coach Lines when, after a bitter labor struggle, the city of New York took over the privately owned company. He eventually became a partner within his firm and in 1964 led it (by then known as Gallop, Climenko & Gould) into a merger with Manning, Hollinger & Shea. The merger created the firm of Shea, Gallop, Climenko & Gould and reunited Gould with former high school classmate William Shea, a politically powerful lawyer who had been instrumental in returning National League baseball to New York City.

Originally consisting of twenty-two lawyers, the new firm, which later became known simply as Shea & Gould, was notable for its diversity. Immediately nicknamed "Blarney & Chutzpah," the two managing partners (both of whom had experienced religious bigotry earlier in their careers) made sure that theirs was a pluralistic organization. Gould and Shea also brought their individual strengths to the firm. While an office joke held that Shea did not even know where the courthouse was located and that he was (in Gould's words) "incapable of parsing a sentence" (*New York Times*, 4 Feb. 1994), his political connections were impeccable, and few could maneuver as ably amid the smoke-filled back rooms of New York City. Gould contributed his courtroom skills, and both men worked to develop a firm that was brash, scrappy, and defiant of the mores that had been established by traditional Wall Street law firms. Spending considerable time training new associates, Gould helped create an atmosphere that a former associate who joined the firm in the mid-1970s remembered as ". . . a lot of running up and down halls, screaming and yelling. The firm hired some people who were visibly crazy but were brilliant and hardworking—and got results. We were team players" (*New York Times*, 7 Feb. 1994).

Gould and Shea drove in to work together each day and ran the firm like a benevolent dictatorship. It continued to grow even as its two managing partners aged. In 1979 they set up a five-man executive committee and until 1984 retained veto power. In the latter year Gould, despite having undergone triple-bypass surgery, argued perhaps his most famous case when he won a verdict (but no damages) for former Israeli defense minister Ariel Sharon in his libel suit against *Time* magazine. The firm opened new offices in Los Angeles (1985) and Miami (1986), and by the end of the decade it employed nearly 350 lawyers and enjoyed gross revenues of $100 million.

Yet Shea and Gould's success proved evanescent. In 1989 Shea suffered a stroke, the Los Angeles office collapsed, and the Miami office was operating in the red. Nationwide recession, greed among the younger partners, and excessive overhead eventually led the firm to dissolve itself in 1994. Although disgusted and heartbroken by this turn of events, Gould placed the blame for the debacle on his own shoulders, noting that ". . . I can't escape responsibility for the fact that I gave them the power to do what has been done" (*New York Times*, 7 Feb. 1994). He continued his legal career as a member of the firm of LeBoeuf, Lamb, Green & MacRae until his death at his home in Manhattan.

Although not as well known as his more gregarious partner, Milton Gould played a key role in the creation of one of New York City's leading legal firms. Along with William Shea, he contributed to the erosion of religious and ethnic barriers within the realm of corporate law. But the overreaching that he and his partner succumbed to can serve as a cautionary tale about the unconstrained business boom of the 1980s.

• Information on Gould's life and career is scarce: aside from a brief mention in Jack Newfield and Paul Du Brul, *Permanent Government: Who Really Rules New York?* (1981), the best source of information is Jan Hoffman, "An End to a Law Firm That Defined a Type," *New York Times*, 4 Feb. 1994. An obituary is in the *New York Times*, 13 Mar. 1999.

EDWARD L. LACH, JR.

GOULD, Morton (10 Dec. 1913–21 Feb. 1996), composer and conductor, was born in Queens, New York, to James Gould, a real estate agent, and Frances Arkin Gould. His parents had immigrated to America as children, his father from Vienna, his mother from Russia. He grew up in Queens and remained a resident of that borough for the rest of his life, living as an adult in Great Neck, only a few miles from his childhood home.

In the Gould household a player piano in the parlor was a major attraction for young Morton, who closely watched the automatic movement of the keys. According to family legend he was able to reproduce complete songs on the piano by the age of five. He was soon taking formal piano lessons and at the age of six wrote his first composition, a waltz. Two years later he was admitted with a full scholarship to the Institute of Musical Art, now the Juilliard School, in Manhattan. In his early teens Gould went on to study at the New York University School of Music, completing the curriculum in only two years, at the age of fifteen. As a teenager, Gould became well known in New York as a gifted and entertaining recitalist, giving numerous concerts and often improvising on themes suggested by members of the audience. In his studies he became drawn to American music, especially jazz, and even his earliest compositions written during his school days reflect this influence. Two of his first mature works were published during his teenage years: his piano suite *Three Conservative Sketches* (1927) and the orchestral work *Chorale and Fugue for Jazz* (1930).

Gould came of age at the height of the Great Depression of the 1930s, and that undoubtedly influenced his decision to focus on the commercial side of music-making rather than to pursue a career as an academic composer of "serious" music that might not have wide appeal: above all he wanted to create and play music that people would listen to again and again. He also needed to earn a living: because of his parents' financial difficulties, he had been forced to drop out of public high school in order to concentrate on finding a steady demand for his music-making. After playing for a while in various bands and orchestras, he turned to radio, which was in its heyday in the early 1930s and provided a steady demand for live musicians. In 1935 he was hired by WOR-AM, the Mutual network station in New York City, as a conductor, composer, and arranger. That same year he first gained national recognition when his *Chorale and Fugue for Jazz* was played by the Philadelphia Orchestra, with Leopold Stokowski conducting. Combining composition with his radio work, Gould had a number of original works to his credit by the end of the 1930s, including three piano sonatas, a piano concerto, and a violin concerto, as well as an orchestral arrangement of Stephen Foster songs (*Foster Gallery*, 1938) that entered the American symphonic repertoire.

Gould remained at WOR for seven years, producing and hosting a weekly music program, "Music for Today." When his stint ended in 1942 he went on to perform the same functions at CBS in New York for the next three years, directing the weekly shows "Cresta Blanca Carnival" and the "Chrysler Hour." During his decade in radio, Gould wrote a number of orchestral pieces specifically for broadcasting, including *Second American Symphonette* (1938), *Latin-American Symphonette* (1941), and *American Concertette* (1943), which became popular works in the orchestral repertory. *American Concertette* was also turned into a popular ballet called *Interplay* by choreographer Jerome Robbins in 1945. Two other works written by Gould during this period that became concert favorites were the *Boogie Woogie Etude*, composed for pianist José Iturbi, and the symphonic work *American Salute* (both 1943). During World War II he also composed his first score for a Hollywood movie—*Delightfully Dangerous* (1945)—as well as music for several documentaries made by the U.S. Office of War Information.

By the end of the 1940s Gould had achieved recognition as a leading composer of American music based on American themes, both musical and historical. During the decade he had produced nearly two dozen major compositions. Among them were three symphonies—the second, *Symphony on Marching Tunes* (1944), had been commissioned by the YMCA to commemorate its centenary—and the *Concerto for Orchestra*, commissioned by Erich Leinsdorf and premiered by the Cleveland Orchestra in 1945. Other compositions of the period included three premiered in 1942: *Cowboy Rhapsody*, based on cowboy folk songs and written for band, and the orchestral pieces *Lincoln Legend* and *Spirituals for Orchestra*. In 1945 he collaborated with Betty Comden and Adolph Green to write the musical *Billion Dollar Baby*. The following year his choral work *Of Time and the River*, based on the novel by Thomas Wolfe, was first performed. In 1947 he provided music for the premiere of Agnes de Mille's ballet *Fall River Legend*; arranged two years later as an orchestral suite, it remains one of Gould's most often played works.

To provide the widest possible audience for his music, Gould had formed his own touring orchestra in the late 1940s. With, in addition, his own recording studio and music publishing firm, he was now a real presence on the American musical scene. More Gould compositions were created, performed, and published in the 1950s, including a fourth symphony (1952), *Concerto for Tap Dancer and Orchestra* (1952), and the *St. Lawrence Suite* (1958), commissioned to commemorate the opening of the St. Lawrence Seaway. He also wrote the score for another musical, Herbert and Dorothy Fields's *Arms and the Girl* (1950), and provided scores for two Hollywood movies, *Cinerama Holiday* (1955) and *Windjammer* (1958).

During the 1960s and 1970s Gould's output was less prolific, but he remained active, not only leading his own orchestra in concert hall and radio performances as well as recordings but also acting as guest conductor of several orchestras, including the Pittsburgh, Chicago, and National symphonies. Noteworthy pieces by Gould during this period included the orchestral works *American Ballads* and *Symphony of Spirituals* (both 1976), as well as the musical scores for a television series on World War I (1964–1965) and the made-for-television film *Holocaust* (1978). In the 1980s and early 1990s he continued to conduct and compose while being involved in music organizations. He served as president of the American Society of Composers, Authors and Publishers (ASCAP) from 1986 to 1994, and held various positions with the American Symphony Orchestra League and the National Endowment for the Arts. His later compositions included two orchestral pieces, *Classical Variations on Colonial Themes* (1986) and *Stringmusic* (1995); the latter, commissioned by the National Symphony in honor of its conductor, Mstislav Rostropovich, won the Pulitzer Prize in music.

During his long career Gould made more than one hundred recordings, some of which have been reissued on compact disc. His own works, including both original compositions and arrangements, number in the hundreds. They are all characterized by vigorous rhythms, by engaging themes that seem to bind together the performer and the listener, and by harmonies that are distinctly American. Gould is also remembered as a major contributor to innovative music literature for school bands, a role that he tirelessly sought out beginning in 1938, when his band composition *Jericho*, with its diverse harmonies and rhythms for different performers, was introduced; prior to that time, members of school bands usually played the same tune simultaneously on their instruments.

In the early 1950s, at the height of his career, Gould was considered one of the three most popular native American composers, after George Gershwin and Aaron Copland. The ascendancy of Leonard Bernstein later in that decade, especially following the overwhelming popularity of *West Side Story* (1957), probably moved Gould into fourth place in popularity among twentieth-century American composers, but it did not diminish his stature as a composer.

Gould married Shirley Bank in 1944; they had two daughters and two sons. He died suddenly in Orlando, Florida, where he had been attending a festival of his music sponsored by the Disney Institute.

• Biographical information on Morton Gould can be found in *Current Biography Yearbook 1945* and *Current Biography Yearbook 1968*. See also the entry "Gould, Morton," in the *New Grove Dictionary of American Music* (1986), and L. Evans, "Morton Gould: His Life and Music" (Ph.D. diss., Columbia University Teachers College, 1978). An obituary appears in the *New York Times*, 22 Feb. 1996.

ANN T. KEENE

GRAHAM, Bill (8 Jan. 1931–25 Oct. 1991), rock concert producer, was born Wolfgang Grajonca, sixth child and first son of Jacob and Frieda Grajonca, middle-class Russian Jews living in Berlin, Germany. Wolfgang was two days old when his engineer father died in a construction accident, and he grew up in an orphanage where the children had to give the Nazi salute. When the war began in 1939 his group, by chance, was at a French orphanage on exchange. Facing deportation to the labor camps, the sixty-four Jewish boys and one teacher started walking to Lisbon. After stops in Casablanca and Dakar, Wolfgang and ten other boys made it to New York in September 1941.

A Bronx family took Wolfgang in and renamed him Billy. Kids teased the boy by calling him a Nazi, so he taught himself English with no accent. Billy grew up an athlete and crapshooter who wore the green and yellow of the Pirates Social club; he would later decorate his Fillmore concert venues in green and yellow. At eighteen he became a U.S. citizen and changed his name to William Graham (a change he later regretted: "Bill Graham is a nothing name"). Graham fought in Korea, where he was court-martialed for insubordination but also won the Bronze Star. Discharged in 1953, he studied business administration at City College of New York while driving a cab to pay the rent. His first job, as paymaster for a railroad, took him to San Francisco and taught him that money was not enough: he wanted to act.

Graham enrolled in acting school and for a decade alternated between business and acting. During this time he married Bonnie Maclean, whom he had met when he hired her as a secretary. In 1964 Graham combined his passions for commerce and the arts by becoming manager of the San Francisco Mime Troupe. Graham's rough manner grated on the radical actors, but on the eve of quitting he staged a benefit for the Troupe on 6 November 1965 that became a night-long meeting of San Francisco's underground scenes. The Jefferson Airplane and the Fugs (in from New York) played rock music; Lawrence Ferlinghetti read poetry; and Allen Ginsberg chanted mantras with the crowd of 3,000 radicals, students, artists, old beatniks, and new hippies.

The benefit raised so much money that Graham staged a second, and for a hall he found the Fillmore Auditorium in the heart of San Francisco's black neighborhood. "At 9:30 there was a double line around the block outside," jazz critic Ralph Gleason wrote in his *San Francisco Chronicle* column. "Inside, a remarkable assemblage of humanity was . . . frigging, fragging, and frugging [to the Grateful Dead, the Great Society, and the Mystery Trend]." Sensing that this was the art-business enterprise he had been looking for, Graham took over the Fillmore's lease and began presenting dances every weekend. Wes Wilson printed his first swirling Fillmore poster in February 1966, and the San Francisco psychedelic ballroom scene boomed. In 1967 Graham began booking concerts at the larger Fillmore West on Market Street and at the cavernous Winterland auditorium. In March 1968, he opened his Fillmore East in New York's East Village. Successive waves of rock stars—Janis Joplin, Eric Clapton and Cream, Jim Morrison and the Doors, Jimi Hendrix, Creedence Clearwater Revival—first met their mass audience at the Fillmores.

On his way to the top, Graham battled with police and bureaucrats, using his knowledge of the "straight" world to defend his "hip" enterprise, and he battled with hippies who sneered that he turned groovy psychedelic dances into a commercial formula. "Bullshit!" Graham responded in a typical office-pacing soliloquy. "Who needs all that crap about vibes? Hippies have to learn that we live in a business world. You want to rebel, great, but rebel *for* something!"

Gaunt and tall, Graham swept through his ballrooms like the Phantom of the Opera, his bony head thrust out in a nonstop showdown with an invisible opponent, his five-o'clock shadow and black brows adding to his menacing aura, his thick-lipped mouth always talking. On his desk stood two wooden hands giving the world the finger—his trademark, said an employee. Graham worked twelve- and seventeen-hour days—"God blessed me with a big adrenalin supply"—and described his leadership style as a "dictatorship without time clocks or rules. You do your work, great; don't, get out!"

On 4 July 1971, after only five years, Graham closed the Fillmores, but by then he had graduated to producing concerts at Oakland's Paramount theater that launched Boz Scaggs and the Pointer Sisters, and to coordinating Rolling Stones, Rod Stewart, and Elton John tours that crisscrossed the country, playing rock arenas from New York's Madison Square Garden to the Inglewood Forum in Los Angeles—most notably Bob Dylan's historic return tour in 1974. As his arena business continued to expand in the 1980s, Graham kept in touch with his roots by opening the Old Waldorf in San Francisco, a jewel-box club for up-and-coming talent. In 1987 he presented Santana, James Taylor, and Bonnie Raitt in Moscow.

Years of success and industry respect mellowed Graham, said intimates, but his perfectionist edge never dulled. "Am I a good producer?" he shouted at one reporter. "Goddam right I'm good! We have the best shows, the best lights, the best posters. I want that Oscar every night." His greatest dream, one that never came true, was to produce the Beatles. "I wake up in the middle of the night," he said in one interview as phones rang off the hook around him. "I can see the show. Easy, cool, no pressure, a week on each coast, I'd supply everything, they could just play. I'd do it free, nothing for myself. I mean, I might have to tie it in with a TV show, maybe closed circuit to college campuses." Graham interrupted that interview to grab his phone and answer it: "Yeah? No. Don't worry about me, worry about yourself!" He slammed down the receiver with an expletive. "L.A. bastards think they're tough!"

Graham and Maclean divorced in 1971, after having one son, David. Graham had another son and a daughter with other women. He was still in his prime and happy with girlfriend Melissa Gold on October 25, 1991. That day, while flying through rough weather to his Marin County home from a Huey

Lewis and the News concert in Concord, California, his helicopter ran into power lines north of San Francisco Bay. Graham, Gold, and pilot Steve Kahn were killed instantly in a fireball explosion.

Graham's life tells a classic American success story. Backed only by indomitable will, Wolfgang Grajonca landed in America as a ten-year-old Jewish orphan and turned himself into Bill Graham, the top rock concert producer of the 1960s, 1970s, and 1980s. Graham made the fame and fortune of countless rock stars (and his own) through three decades of explosive growth in American popular music. He will be remembered for the exposure he gave to the superstars of psychedelic rock, and for presenting a spectrum of music that included jazz, blues, and other genres alongside rock. Count Basie, Buddy Rich, Roland Kirk, Cannonball Adderley, Sun Ra, Miles Davis, Buck Owens, Willie Bobo, John Lee Hooker, Johnny Cash, Big Black, the Staple Singers, Aretha Franklin, Ray Charles all appeared on Bill Graham's stages.

• *Bill Graham Presents: My Life Inside Rock and Out* (1992) is a vigorous autobiography; *Rage & Roll: Bill Graham and the Selling of Rock*, by John Glatt (1993), a concise biography. Articles on Graham and the Fillmore appeared regularly in *Rolling Stone* from its first issues. An extensive profile of Graham by the author of this piece appeared in the *New York Times Magazine*, 15 Dec. 1968. An obituary is in the New York Times, 27 Oct. 1991.

MICHAEL LYDON

GRAHAM, Shirley (11 Nov. 1896–27 Mar. 1977), musical composer and director, author, and political activist, also known as Shirley Graham Du Bois, was born Lola Bell Graham in Indianapolis, Indiana, the daughter of the Reverend David A. Graham, an African Methodist Episcopal minister, and Etta Bell. She accompanied them when her father held pastorates in New Orleans, Colorado Springs, and Spokane. He delighted her with stories about important blacks in American history. In his churches, she learned to play the piano and the pipe organ and to conduct choirs. In 1914 she graduated from high school in Spokane, took business school courses, and worked in government offices in Spokane and Seattle. After she married Shadrach T. McCanns in 1921, she gave private music lessons and played the organ in white movie theaters, hidden backstage. She had two sons, Robert and David, and was either widowed in 1924 or obtained a divorce in 1929. (In many respects, biographical data concerning Graham are in dispute.)

In 1926 her father became president of Monrovia College, Monrovia, Liberia, and Graham accompanied both parents as far as Paris, where she studied music, met West African students, and shared their love of African music. On her return to the United States, she studied music at Howard University and then taught at Morgan College (now Morgan State University) from 1929 to 1931. Entering Oberlin College as a sophomore, she earned her A.B. in music in 1934, her M.A. a year later. While there, she wrote

Tom-Tom, a one-act play, and converted it into a three-act opera titled *Tom-Tom: An Epic of Music and the Negro*, writing both the libretto and the music. It was produced in Cleveland (summer 1932), the first opera by a black about blacks. The opening act features African music and jungle life in 1619; the second, America during the slave trade; the third, life in Harlem.

Graham headed the fine arts department of the Tennessee Agricultural and Industrial State College, Nashville (1935–1936). In 1936 she was appointed director of the Chicago Negro Unit of the Federal Theatre Project, part of the Works Progress Administration. She directed some plays, converted others into musicals, and taught classes. Perceived as curt, uncooperative, and aggressive by members of the unit already there, she resigned in 1938 and entered the Yale School of Drama on a scholarship in creative writing. While there (1938–1940), she wrote four plays. One was a revision of her first full-length effort, *Coal Dust* (produced at Morgan, 1930), retitled *Dust to Earth* (produced at Yale, 1941), a drama about racism in a West Virginia mining community and with well-managed black dialect. Her one-act *It's Morning* (produced at Yale, 1940) features a slave woman who kills her daughter after the child has been sold.

Graham left Yale without completing her Ph.D. to direct YWCA theater work in Indianapolis (1940–1941). In 1941 she supervised a YWCA-USO theater group at Fort Huachuca, Arizona, where 30,000 black soldiers were stationed. Witnessing racial discrimination, she began to agitate for civil rights, which caused her to be discharged in 1942. Her son Robert's death in 1943 at an Indiana army recruiting station owing to negligent medical treatment increased her outspokenness. She appealed for employment leads to W. E. B. Du Bois, the distinguished African-American educator, author, and civil rights leader, whom she had met in her parents' home in Colorado (in 1918 or 1920) and with whom she had corresponded since 1936. She became an NAACP field secretary in New York City (1943–1944). While also contributing to liberal magazines, she began at this time to write biographies aimed primarily at teenage and young-adult readers, including ones on George Washington Carver (1944, with George Dewey Lipscomb), Paul Robeson (1946), Frederick Douglass (1947), Phillis Wheatley (1949), and Benjamin Banneker (1949). Each of these figures was a notable person of African-American extraction, who could serve as role models and as inspirations to the youth whom Graham was seeking to reach. Her Douglass and Banneker books won awards.

On 14 February 1951, at age eighty-three, W. E. B. Du Bois married Shirley Graham, his first wife, Nina, having died the year before. In his autobiography, published in 1968, Du Bois wrote of Nina's death and added the following: "To fill this great gap, and let my work go on, I married again near the end of my days. [Shirley Graham] was a woman 40 years my junior but her work and aim in life had been close to mine because her father had long believed in what I was trying to do. The faith of Shirley Graham in me was therefore inherited and received as a joy and not merely as a duty. She has made these days rich and rewarding." On 9 February 1951 Du Bois had been indicted under the 1938 Foreign Agents Registration Act as an unregistered agent of anti-American pacifist organizations. Hence his marriage to Graham was conducted in secret to ensure her visiting rights if he were jailed (which he was not). A formal public marriage was held 27 February. Graham's surviving son changed his name to David Du Bois.

Graham long remained in the shadow of her husband, who was controversial because of his left-wing positions, which she shared. She helped him devotedly, traveled widely with him, and in 1961 moved with him to Ghana, where they worked together on an *Encyclopedia Africana*. After he died there in 1963, she became a director of Ghana Television (1964–1966). She moved to Cairo in 1967. Long barred from the United States because of her communist sympathies, she was allowed to visit in 1971 and again in 1975.

During her marriage with Du Bois and following his death, Graham continued to write (under the name Shirley Graham Du Bois), publishing still more biographies of people whom she deemed exemplary: Jean Baptiste Point du Sable (whom she identified as Jean Baptiste Pointe de Sable; 1953), Pocahontas (1953), Booker T. Washington (1955), Gamal Abdel Nasser (1972), and Julius K. Nyerere (1975). She also published *His Day Is Marching On: A Memoir of W. E. B. Du Bois* in 1971 and *Du Bois: A Pictorial Biography* in 1978.

Although Graham's biographies are enthusiastic and laudatory, they are readable because of their skillful combination of salient facts and fictional dialogue. Her book on Carver covers his whole life, from harsh childhood to successful experiments, and includes recipes for dishes with peanuts. The Robeson biography has been criticized as shallow and lacking in analysis. Her books on Douglass and on Wheatley, perhaps her best, combine sympathy, objectivity, and an awareness of sociocultural issues. Graham rescued Banneker and du Sable from neglect. Banneker invented a clock, helped plan Washington, D.C., and bravely wrote Thomas Jefferson to remind him of African-American rights. Du Sable left Santo Domingo for America in 1764 and after many difficulties built a trading post at a locale that became the city of Chicago. Graham's well-researched works on Booker T. Washington and Nyerere retain value. Her story of Washington is warm, emotional, and dramatic, with vivid renderings of historical events. The Nyerere book narrates the life of the hard-working leader who helped liberate Tanganyika and Zanzibar and make them into Tanzania. She presents Nyerere's vision of society as an extended family combining tribal pride and African tradition. Graham's memoir of her years with Du Bois combines respect, affection, and autobiographical details; some readers find it too romantic,

even worshipful, for overemphasizing domestic details and minimizing political commentary.

Graham's only novel, *Zulu Heart* (1974), has a startling plot, worthy of Hollywood exploitation. A rich white South African physician is in the process of dying until he receives a transplant of the heart of a black Zulu chief's son. He begins to feel tom-tom rhythms in his blood and feet, dreams about black experiences, visits "his" native village, speaks Zulu, and becomes a freedom fighter.

In 1973 Graham sold Du Bois's papers to the University of Massachusetts for $150,000. Having visited China four times, she returned there in 1976 to be treated for breast cancer in Beijing, where she died at the age of eighty. Because she regularly said she was ten or eleven years younger than she was, several biographical accounts, including obituaries, are incorrect.

In the face of discrimination, both blatant and subtle, Shirley Graham built a writing career with uncompromising dignity. After breaking new ground in the theater, by opening up opera and drama to a bold African-American perspective, she introduced young people, through her biographies, to notable Americans who—at the time she was writing—were not necessarily among the canonical figures of the country's history. Although she was overshadowed in her later years by being the spouse of a towering intellectual, W. E. B. Du Bois, she retained her drive to be a productive author in her own right. Her publications are perhaps not enduring works of literature, but her life serves as a lasting example of how a woman of color stood on her own feet at a time when her gender and race were viewed as disadvantages.

• Graham's papers are deposited in collections at Fisk University, Howard University, George Mason University, and the University of Massachusetts. Kathy A. Perkins, "The Unknown Career of Shirley Graham," *Freedomways* 25 (1st quarter 1985): 6–17, is a succinct biography. Touching on Graham are passages in *The Autobiography of W. E. B. Du Bois: A Soliloquy on Viewing My Life from the Last Decades of Its First Century* (1968); *The Correspondence of W. E. B. Du Bois*, ed. Herbert Aptheker (3 vols., 1973–1978); Jack B. Moore, *W. E. B. Du Bois* (1981); and Manning Marable, *W. E. B. Du Bois: Black Radical Democrat* (1986). An obituary is in the *New York Times*, 5 Apr. 1977.

ROBERT L. GALE

GREENFIELD, Meg (17 Dec. 1930–13 May 1999), editorial columnist, was born Mary Ellen Greenfield in Seattle, Washington, the daughter of Lewis James Greenfield, an antiques dealer, and Lorraine Nathan Greenfield. She attended Smith College, where she majored in English, was elected to Phi Beta Kappa, and graduated summa cum laude in 1952. After spending a year overseas at Cambridge University (where on a Fulbright scholarship she studied the writings of William Blake), Greenfield apparently spent additional time touring the continent before returning to the United States. She settled in New York and became the director of research for the New York committee of Adlai Stevenson's 1956 presidential campaign.

Although Greenfield had once contemplated a career in academia, she found herself drawn to the field of journalism and went to work for *The Reporter*, a journal of political commentary, in 1957. Assigned to its Washington bureau in 1961 as a staff writer, she became its Washington editor in 1965 and remained in that position until the magazine folded in 1968. That year, Greenfield joined the *Washington Post* as an editorial writer. Promoted to deputy editor of the editorial page in 1969, she soon made a name for herself with the insight, wit, and humor that her columns typically displayed. In 1974 Greenfield also began writing a biweekly column for *Newsweek* magazine that largely focused on life within the confines of Washington, an arena that, she later wryly explained, "contrary to widespread belief does not exclude everything human."

Greenfield remained at the *Post* for the balance of her career. Although she loved parties, she was essentially a private person by nature and eschewed much of the Washington media scene. She rarely made public appearances, usually restricting herself to university settings, and, as one who detested talking about herself, avoided television and print media interviews. Content to let her writing speak for itself, Greenfield addressed a wide range of topics in her column but placed particular emphasis on civil rights, the arms race, and politics.

In 1978 Greenfield achieved the ultimate recognition for a journalist, winning the Pulitzer Prize for a series of *Post* editorials on the press, international affairs, and civil rights. In a column titled "The Ford Years," she wrote, "The President who will leave office this week brought precisely the needed temperament, character and virtues to the high offices he has temporarily held ... Decency, in this context, becomes as an attribute something roughly comparable to good posture or punctuality. How odd that so few of us have been willing to acknowledge that decency in the White House can be regarded as a luxury or a bonus or a fringe benefit only at our peril. It is central. And its absence was central to the sorrows this country endured in the years preceding Mr. Ford's presidency" (16 Jan. 1977). In another *Post* column, with the title "The Savagery Stakes," she noted: "That black Africans have been known to be vicious to each other on a grand scale is not open to dispute. What is open to dispute is whether their depredations have somehow been distinctive in the sorry march of history. We think they have not come anywhere near such distinction, and that that is the point to be kept in mind about the ineffable Idi Amin" (1 Mar. 1977).

Greenfield became editorial page editor of the *Post* in 1979, replacing Philip Geyelin, who had originally hired her. Although physically diminutive (she stood five feet one), Greenfield ran her department with a firm hand, noting with typical humor that there was a "little Mussolini in every editorial writer." A perfectionist and remarkably hard worker, Greenfield was

nonetheless realistic about the range of influence that her editorials held: "What we tend to notice here is the great number of wise suggestions we make that are rejected at the polls, and in the agencies, and in the U.S. Congress, and in the District school board, and if there's someplace else I've left out, remind me—so that we don't feel the Republic or the environs are in any terrific danger of being [controlled] by the Washington Post editorial page. Much as we try" (quoted in *Post* obituary, 14 May 1999). While her career unfolded during a time of unprecedented change in women's roles, she viewed her rise to the top of a male-dominated profession as a series of "accidents and non-decisions," explaining, "I was an English major who couldn't decide what to do ... I wasn't trying to strike a blow for sisterhood" (quoted in *Post* obituary, 14 May 1999). Politically liberal herself, Greenfield prided herself on maintaining a detached evenhandedness in both her writing and her work relations. She also boosted the careers of many aspiring journalists, among them Michael Kinsley, Roger W. Wilkins, Charles Krauthammer, and George Will.

Despite her private nature, Greenfield—who never married—enjoyed a wide range of acquaintances; she claimed responsibility for introducing the enormously successful investor Warren E. Buffett to Microsoft Corporation founder Bill Gates. She also enjoyed volunteering at a local hospital, gardening, and studying Latin. Personally and professionally close to *Post* publisher Katharine Graham, she would occasionally slip away with her from work to enjoy a movie. Greenfield served from 1986 until 1995 on the Pulitzer Prize board and was also a member of the American Society of Newspaper Editors. She died at her Washington home following a lengthy battle with cancer.

Lauded on the editorial page of her paper as "one of the most accomplished and influential journalists of her time" following her death, Meg Greenfield was, by most accounts, just that. She will be remembered for her incisive wit and precise prose, as well as for her stature as a role model for many up-and-coming journalists, both male and female.

• Although no organized collection of Greenfield papers is known to exist, her alma mater, Smith College in Northampton, Massachusetts, maintains an extensive biographical file on her. She is the subject (along with two other women journalists) of an unpublished master's thesis by Gioia E. Diliberto, "Profiles of Three Newswomen" (University of Maryland, College Park, 1975). She also receives mention in Katharine Graham's *Personal History* (1997). Written in the last years of Greenfield's life and published posthumously, *Washington* (2001) contains her observations and insight into life in Washington, D.C. Extensive obituaries appear in the *New York Times*, *Washington Post*, and *Baltimore Sun*, all 14 May 1999.

EDWARD L. LACH, JR.

GREENWOOD, Charlotte (25 June 1893?–18 Jan. 1978), star of stage and screen, was born Frances Charlotte Greenwood in Philadelphia, Pennsylvania, the daughter of Frank Greenwood, a barber, and Annabella Jacquet Higgins Greenwood. Not long after her birth (the exact year of which is disputed in some sources), her parents separated and she moved first to Boston, Massachusetts, and then to Norfolk, Virginia, where she attended school; but she left school in the seventh grade when she moved to New York City. By the age of eleven she reached her adult height of five feet ten inches. While still in her early teens, Greenwood got a job in the chorus of *The White Cat* at the New Amsterdam Theatre. After a few more minor roles in such plays as *The Rogers Brothers in Panama* (1907) and *Nearly a Hero* (1908), she became a vaudeville performer, first in an act with Eunice Burnham, then in a high-kicking duet with Sidney Grant.

Greenwood continued her stage appearances in such presentations as *The Passing Show of 1912* and the Franz Lehár musical *The Man with Three Wives* on Broadway. After touring in *The Tik-Tok Man of Oz*, she finally achieved prominence in 1914, when she was the tall, lanky Letitia Proudfoot in the musical comedy *Pretty Mrs. Smith*, in which her farcical dancing and her rendition of the song "Long, Lean, Lanky Letty" brought her critical attention. Her performance also encouraged producer Oliver Morosco to build a musical around her talents, called, after her previous success, *So Long, Letty*, the first in a series of "Letty" shows, which included *Linger Longer, Letty* (1919) and *Let 'er Go, Letty*. The last of these plays was renamed because Greenwood opted out of the production to star in *Letty Pepper* (1922), a musical adaptation of Charles Klein's *Maggie Pepper*.

During the run of *So Long, Letty*, Greenwood married the production's stage manager, Cyril Ring. They were divorced in 1922. In December 1924 she married songwriter Martin Broones. There were no children from either marriage.

After her various appearances as "Letty," Greenwood appeared in musical revues, including Irving Berlin's second *Music Box Revue* (1922), *Hassard Short's Ritz Revue* (1924), and *Rufus LeMaire's Affairs* (1927). She moved to London for new challenges while her second husband pursued a career as a composer of musical comedy songs. On the British stage she appeared in *Wild Violets* (1932) at the historic Drury Lane Theatre and filmed *Orders Is Orders* the following year in England before returning to San Francisco to appear in Sidney Howard's *The Late Christopher Bean* (1933). Returning to Drury Lane, Greenwood was Tiny Barbour in the Jerome Kern and Oscar Hammerstein II musical *Three Sisters* (1934) and Aunt Isabel in *Gay Deceivers* (1935). She then returned to the United States, touring in *Leaning on Letty* (1935), which was her final "Letty" stage show. Greenwood took *Leaning on Letty* to Australia and performed a backstage radio broadcast over station WIP from the Chestnut Street Opera House in Philadelphia. When she finally retired Letty, she signed a film contract with Twentieth Century–Fox, but she still appeared in two more stage presentations, a national tour as Mama in *I Remember Mama* (1947–

1949), for which she was given the San Francisco Drama Critics Award, and Cole Porter's *Out of This World* (1950), her last Broadway appearance.

Greenwood began her film career in the silent era when a stage play brought her to the old Morosco Theatre in Los Angeles. Her first film was *Jane* (1915), in which she played the title role and was supported by her leading man on stage, Sidney Grant. The comedy *Baby Mine* (1928) followed. Next, she reprised her famous character Letty in the film version of *So Long, Letty* (1930), whose story line differed from the successful stage production. Other Greenwood film efforts included such comedy shorts as *Love Your Neighbor* (1930) and *Girls Will Be Boys* (1931). Her talent for broad comedy surfaced in films such as *Parlor, Bedroom and Bath* (1931), in which she romped on furniture with Buster Keaton; *Palmy Days* (1931), with Eddie Cantor; and *Flying High* (1931), with Bert Lahr. Later film roles included *Star Dust* (1940), with Shirley Temple; *Down Argentine Way* (1940), with Carmen Miranda; *Tall, Dark and Handsome* (1941), with Milton Berle; *Moon over Miami* (1941), with Betty Grable; *Springtime in the Rockies* (1942); *The Gang's All Here* (1943); *Home in Indiana* (1944), which she repeated on Lux Radio Theatre; *Up in Mabel's Room* (1944); *Driftwood* (1947); *Young People* (1948); *Oh, You Beautiful Doll* (1949); *Peggy* (1950); and *Dangerous When Wet* (1953).

Greenwood's best-known film role is probably that of Aunt Eller in the Rodgers and Hammerstein milestone musical *Oklahoma!* (1955), which is frequently shown on television and is widely available on video. Oscar Hammerstein had offered her the role in the Broadway production when the musical was premiered in 1943, but she was unable to accept it because of other professional commitments. Her final films were *Glory* (1956); *The Opposite Sex* (1956); a musical version of Clare Boothe Luce's classic play *The Women*, in which she played Lucy; and *The Sound of Laughter* (1963).

In 1944 Greenwood started in radio when Pepsodent toothpaste signed her as Bob Hope's replacement for a new program called "Life with Charlotte," in which she starred in a variety show set against the background of a boarding house, with Arthur Q. Bryant, Shirley Mitchell, and Matty Malneck's orchestra. That same year she appeared in the comedy-drama "The Charlotte Greenwood Show," as a cub reporter on a small-town newspaper who was trying her best to get to Hollywood. The show ran briefly on ABC radio.

Tall and lanky, Greenwood was a physical comedienne who used her limber body to get laughs as she flailed her long arms and legs and walked about on all fours, her palms flat on the floor. In 1950 Greenwood explained to an interviewer how she overcame insecurity about her height: "I capitalized on the gawky movements of my long legs and made a success on the stage. That cured my sensitivity. I haven't been sensitive about my height in forty-five years." She often commented that she was "the only woman in the world who can kick a giraffe in the face."

Greenwood was a devout Christan Scientist who ministered her faith to celebrities such as Doris Day. A very private woman who made her home in Beverly Hills, she cherished several dogs as dear companions. Living in California, she was able to stay active, playing golf and tennis and swimming year-round. Although she died in Beverly Hills in January 1978, the news was not announced until several weeks later, probably because her aversion to being in the public eye kept news organizations from noticing her death right away.

In most of her earlier roles Greenwood portrayed a gawky woman in hot pursuit of a man; her schemes to find romance with a routine of high kicking and waving her arms windmill style delighted audiences. Elements of her physical comedy can be seen in women performers of later decades, including Carol Burnett, Gilda Radner, and Lily Tomlin. That Greenwood could find success in four genres, from vaudeville to stage, screen, and radio, marks her as unique among American entertainers.

• The Library for the Performing Arts at the New York Public Library, Lincoln Center, and the Motion Picture Academy of Arts and Sciences Library, Beverly Hills, Calif., have files on Greenwood's career. The Motion Picture and Recorded Sound Division, Library of Congress, Washington, D.C., has some of her early films. The Cinema-Television Library and Archives of Performing Arts, Edward L. Doheny Library, University of Southern California, has a personal collection of papers and pictures. Greenwood is credited in several biographical sources with an autobiography, *Just for Kicks* (also listed in some sources as *Never Too Tall* [1947]), but it is hard to verify a published copy of this book. It is most likely an unpublished memoir with only limited circulation. Most of Greenwood's films from the 1940s and 1950s are on videocassette, and in 1950 Sony Classical released the original cast recording of *Out of This World*. The most complete sketch of Greenwood's life is in James R. Parish and William T. Leonard, *The Funsters* (1979). Short biographical essays can be found in Kurt Gänzl, *Encyclopedia of the Musical Theatre* (1994), Alfred E. Twomey and Arthur F. McClure, *Versatiles: A Study of Supporting Character Actors and Actresses in the American Motion Picture, 1930–1955* (1969), and in Mary Unterbrink, *Funny Women: American Comediennes, 1860–1985* (1987). Pictures of Greenwood in some of her stage roles are in Daniel Blum, *Great Stars of the American Stage: A Pictorial Record* (1952). See also Thomas A. DeLong, *Radio Stars: An Illustrated Biographical Dictionary of 953 Performers, 1920 through 1960* (1996), and David Quinlan, *Illustrated Encyclopedia of Movie Character Actors* (1985). Obituaries are in the *New York Times*, 14 Feb. 1978, and *Variety*, 8 Feb. 1978.

MARTIN J. MANNING

GREY, Clifford (5 Jan. 1887–25 Sept. 1941), librettist, lyricist, and bobsledder, was born Percival Davis in Birmingham, England, the son of George Davis, a whip manufacturer, and Emma Lowe Davis. He was educated at the Camp Hill School for Boys, one of the schools of King Edward the Sixth in Birmingham,

winning Latin and English prizes and becoming interested in theatrics.

Percival Davis became a performer in the type of seaside variety troupe known as Concert Party, and by 1907 he went by the name of Clifford Grey. In 1912, when he began to contribute to British musical theater, he married Maud Mary Gould; they had two daughters (he adopted Gould's daughter as well) and remained married until Grey's death.

Ultimately credited with more than 3,000 lyrics, Grey first gained renown for his lyric to the American Nat Ayer's "If You Were the Only Girl in the World" (*The Bing Boys Are Here*, London, 1916). While particularly cherished by British soldiers on leave, the song gained an enduring popularity in America. Grey was shortly the librettist most in demand in London, and in 1920 he was invited to New York by composer Jerome Kern, an earlier London collaborator, to help out P. G. Wodehouse and Guy Bolton on the new musical comedy *Sally*. Grey later wrote with some exaggeration that this American assignment of supposedly several weeks lasted twenty years.

Along with Wodehouse, Bolton, and (among others) Fred Thompson, Grey was of the particular tribe that dominated the central tradition of transatlantic musical theater between the two world wars. Sometimes as sole or dual authors, sometimes as "doctors" to each other's (or someone else's) ailing librettos, these peripatetics interacted to such an extent that the published credit for their melodies, books, and lyrics often obscured a collaboration that was sometimes generous and sometimes contentious and unwilling. Wodehouse thought Grey got many of his credits by simply changing a word here and there; Grey claimed to have invented tunes that turned into various songs attributed to others, including "Look for the Silver Lining." Like the others, Grey was constantly on the go, at first between London and New York; when sound was added to motion pictures in the later 1920s, the entire group added Hollywood to their itineraries and were largely responsible for the words of that first generation of film musicals.

After the production of *Sally* in 1920, Grey did indeed stay on, establishing residence on Long Island, working with various composers throughout the 1920s on a number of musicals and the occasional straight dramatic adaptation as well. He made one of his occasional leaps back to Britain for *The Rainbow* (1923), a revue whose original score came from George Gershwin. Grey's subsequent Broadway shows and some of his musical collaborations included *The Hotel Mouse* (1922, Ivan Caryll), *Lady Butterfly* (1923, Werner Jenssen), *Marjorie* and *Annie Dear* (both 1924, Sigmund Romberg), *June Days* and *Mayflowers* (both 1925, J. Fred Coots), *A Night Out* (1925, Vincent Youmans), *Hit the Deck!* (1927, Youmans), *The Madcap* (1928, Maurice Rubens), *Sunny Days* (1928, Jean Schwartz), *The Three Musketeers* (1928, Rudolf Friml), and *Smiles* (1930, Youmans). The most fruitful of these collaborations was *Hit the Deck!* The score included Grey's lyric to "Hallelujah!"

a rousing contemporary spiritual that showed how deeply Grey had tapped into American culture.

In an era when American law made dual citizenship impossible, Grey found various ways of expressing his enthusiasms for the United States. Undoubtedly the most remarkable of these came in 1928 and 1932. Calling himself "Tippi" Gray and inventing an American collegiate background, this bespectacled and apparently sedentary forty-one-year-old joined Billy Fiske, Geoffrey Mason, and Nion Tucker on the four-man American bobsled team that won the gold medal at the 1928 Winter Olympics in St. Moritz. Although Norway scored the most points for a national team in this early Olympiad, it was noted that bobsled teams accounted for more than half the overall total, which took the United States into second place. Grey won another gold medal in the four-man bobsled event in the 1932 games at Lake Placid, New York, joining Fiske, Eddie Eagan, and Jay O'Brien. The full dimensions of Grey's secret life remain to be established.

Between 1929 and 1931 Grey still shuttled across the Atlantic to work on British musical comedies (his collaboration on *Mr. Cinders*, 1929, with Vivian Ellis, resulted in some of British musical theater's most loved songs), while he also wrote screenplays and/or lyrics for fourteen American films, adapting some of his own musicals to the screen and working on original scores with a number of composers, including Oscar Straus, Herbert Stothart, and Bruno Granichstaten. Perhaps his most noted set of lyrics was created for director Ernst Lubitsch's *The Love Parade* (1929). Writing for Maurice Chevalier to Victor Schertzinger's music, Grey created, in "Nobody's Using It Now," the first musical soliloquy in talking pictures; for several years the song was a popular number with dance bands. (He also wrote *The Smiling Lieutenant* for Chevalier in 1931.)

Although most of Grey's family chose to stay in the United States after 1932 and he himself maintained an American residence, Grey worked mainly in Great Britain. There he wrote a number of nonmusical screenplays, including the acclaimed thriller *Rome Express* (1932), while as a theatrical lyricist he continued to collaborate with American composers including Oscar Levant and Johnny Green. "Got a Date with an Angel," with Grey's lyric to Jack Waller's melody in a 1931 London musical comedy, was popular in the United States and became the theme song of an American dance band led by the breathy-singing Skinnay Ennis.

When World War II broke out, Grey joined the British ENSA (Entertainment National Service Administration) to entertain servicemen. One of his performances in Ipswich was immediately followed by a German bombing raid, and as a result Grey died of an asthmatic attack.

• Grey's papers, including a biographical fragment, are held by family members, mainly in the state of Washington. Scripts of Grey's British theatrical work are held in the Lord Chamberlain's Collection at the British Library, London. The Billy Rose Collection of the New York Public Library holds a file on Grey. Data on Grey's films are found in the *American Film Institute Catalogues* for 1921–1930 and 1931–1940 and at the British Film Institute, London. Mark Steyn, "He Spread a Little Happiness," BBC Radio 4, 23 July 1988, is a useful source. Aspects of Grey's life surface in various biographies by Gerald Bordman as well as in autobiographies by contemporaries, including Vivian Ellis, *I'm on a See-Saw* (1953). Grey's Olympic exploits are partly catalogued in Tim Clark, "When Winning a Gold Medal Was a Lark," *Yankee*, Feb. 1980, pp. 88–159, and Geoffrey T. Mason, "Going for Gold in 1928," *Bowdoin Alumnus*, Late Winter 1976, pp. 8–9, as well as in personal letters to the author. The U.S. Olympic Committee's records on Grey are inaccurate. Useful obituaries appear in *The Stage*, London, 2 Oct. 1941; the *New York Times*, 27 Sept. 1941; and the *Times* (London), 27 Sept. 1941.

JAMES ROSS MOORE

GRIFFITH, Calvin (1 Dec. 1911–20 Oct. 1999), baseball executive, was born Calvin Robertson in Montreal, Quebec, to Jimmy Robertson and Jane Robertson (maiden name unknown). He was the second of seven children and the oldest of five boys. When his father became ill in 1922, he and his sister Thelma moved to Washington, D.C., to live with their uncle, Clark Griffith. After their father's death the following year, Griffith adopted the two children. Clark Griffith, later elected to baseball's hall of fame, had been a major-league pitching star and a successful manager, and by 1920 he had gained controlling interest of the Washington Senators of the American League. In 1924, when baseball legend Walter Johnson pitched the Senators to their only World Series title, young Calvin was the team batboy.

Calvin went away to Staunton (Va.) Military Academy (1928–1932) and then to George Washington University for three years, where he was catcher on the baseball team. He soon dropped out, however, to learn the baseball business from the inside, working his way up through the Senators' minor league chain—running the Chattanooga team from 1935 to 1937 and then the Charlotte club from 1938 to 1941. He managed some, played a bit, and served as club president. In 1941 he joined the Senators to run the concessions operation and gradually moved up to the front office. When Clark Griffith died in 1955, he left to Calvin and Thelma each 26 percent of the club. At that point, Calvin Griffith became the president of the team, a position he held until 1984.

The Senators baseball team had not won a pennant since 1933 and perennially finished in the second division, earning them an enduring barb: "Washington—first in war, first in peace, and last in the American League." Griffith Stadium was too small; parking was inadequate; broadcast revenues were meager; and attendance matched the team's mediocrity. Though he had made public promises both to Washington fans and to Congress that he would not move the team out of the nation's capital, Griffith announced on 26 October 1960 that he was relocating the team to the Twin Cities (Minneapolis-St. Paul) in Minnesota, where it would be known as the Minnesota Twins. (The American League simultaneously granted Washington an expansion franchise, again to be named the Senators, but after the 1971 season that team also moved and became the Texas Rangers, leaving the capital without major league baseball.) Griffith had received an offer he could not refuse; the Twin Cities built Metropolitan Stadium in suburban Bloomington with a low rental rate, guaranteed him a million fans for the first three years, and granted him full concession rights. The Twins succeeded on the field their first decade in the upper Midwest, winning the pennant in 1965 and earning Griffith the major league executive of the year award. Behind stars like Harmon Killebrew, Tony Oliva, Bob Allison, Zoilo Versalles, Jim Kaat, and Mudcat Grant, the Twins captured the American League's West Division title in 1969 and 1970 before reverting to playing .500 ball during the seventies. The failure to be competitive in pennant races undercut yearly attendance, which only twice surpassed one million between 1971 and 1983.

Attendance was crucial to Griffith. He was a throwback to the days when owners made baseball their life and living. Griffith was famous for his penuriousness, throwing nickels around like manhole covers, according to one player. His father had taught him not to commit money he did not have, and with the advent of free agency in 1976 it became clear that the tightfisted Griffith was not going to be able to compete with the new breed of owners who had made their fortunes in other areas and could write off baseball losses. He packed the Twins front office with family members, denying charges of nepotism by saying that they were a baseball family. His money woes were aggravated in September 1978 when he told a Waseka, Minnesota, civic group that he had moved the team from Washington because there were only 15,000 blacks in the Twin Cities, that blacks did not attend baseball games, and that he liked the hard-working white people of the area. Civil rights groups and the press never let Griffith forget his insensitive remarks. Future Hall of Famer Rod Carew said he did not want to keep playing for Griffith's "plantation" and left for the California Angels as a free agent a year later. Nevertheless, in 1982 the Hubert Humphrey Metrodome was built with public funds in downtown Minneapolis to free the Twins from weather problems, and attendance began to rebound—as did the team's performance behind its new stars, Kent Hrbek and Kirby Puckett. In 1984, amid rumors that Griffith might sell the team to interests that would move it to another city, a business task force developed a marketing plan to win back the fans and asked him for $125,000 to implement it. Disdainful of marketing, the owner refused. The aging Griffith finally gave up trying to compete, and after the 1984 season, in a move symbolic of the evolution of management, he sold the team to billionaire (and baseball neophyte) Carl Pohlad, under whose ownership the Twins won world championships in 1987 and 1991, largely with players developed by Griffith. Family ownership was over, after seventy-five years.

Griffith had married Natalie Niven on 1 February 1940; they had three children: Clark, Corinne, and Clare. The couple separated in 1974. Following his sale of the team, Griffith married Belva Block, who survived him. His son Clark felt that Griffith should be remembered for two things: recognizing the Twin Cities' sports potential and assembling skilled teams, even if he could not keep them together in the era of free agency. Griffith maintained homes in Edina, Minnesota, and Melbourne, Florida, the former site of the Twins' minor league spring training camp, where he died of heart ailments and a kidney infection.

• Obituaries are in the 21 Oct. 1999 issues of the *Minneapolis Star Tribune*, the *Washington Post*, and the *New York Times*.
JOHN R. M. WILSON

GRIFFITH-JOYNER, Florence (21 Dec. 1959–21 Sept. 1998), track and field star, was born Delorez Florence Griffith in Los Angeles, California, the daughter of Robert Griffith, an electrician, and Florence Griffith (maiden name unknown), seamstress. When "Dee Dee" (as she was nicknamed) was four, her parents divorced and she moved with her mother and siblings to a housing project in the Watts section of Los Angeles. She began running while in elementary school at meets sponsored by the Sugar Ray Robinson Youth Foundation, and by the age of fifteen she had won two consecutive Jesse Owens National Youth Games. As a member of an impoverished but disciplined family, Griffith learned from her grandmother how to style hair and fingernails, and she continued to excel in track and field at David Starr Jordan High School, from which she graduated in 1978.

In 1979 Griffith enrolled at California State University, Northridge, where she hoped to major in business. After being forced to drop out of school following her freshman year, she took a job as a bank teller but was able to return to school when assistant track coach Bob Kersee helped her obtain financial aid. When Kersee accepted a similar position at UCLA, Griffith followed him there and soon found that her running benefited from competing against some of the best track and field athletes in the country. Having barely missed making the 1980 U. S. Summer Olympics team, she was named to the 1981 World Cup team and helped the 400-meter relay team set an American record of 42.82 seconds. The following year, she won the 200-meter event at the NCAA nationals, and at the 1983 NCAA nationals she led the field in a then-record-setting time of 50.96 seconds in the 400-meter event.

After withdrawing from UCLA (commonly reported accounts of her graduating in 1983 with a degree in psychology are incorrect), Griffith set her sights on the 1984 Olympic Games. Amid a heavy training schedule, she supported herself by working as a hairdresser while dabbling on the side in clothing design and the writing of children's books. She made the 1984 U.S. Olympic team and won a silver medal in the 200-meter event, finishing second (as she had before) to an old rival from her high school days, Valerie Briscoe-Hooks, who had edged her out in the 1980 Olympic trials. Disappointed by the results at Los Angeles, Griffith sank into depression and began to gain weight. She took a job as a customer service representative with Union Bank and ended her engagement to fellow Olympic team member Greg Foster.

By 1987 Griffith had decided to attempt another bid for the Olympics, and she asked Bob Kersee to help her return to top form. Under his tutelage Griffith trained rigorously and continued to work at a bank and as a hair- and nail-stylist. She also received support from a new boyfriend, Al Joyner, who became her husband in an October 1987 Las Vegas ceremony. Having long excelled in the shorter events, Griffith-Joyner, with Kersee's help, prepared for the 1988 Olympic trials with longer-distance events in mind as well.

As the 1988 Olympic trials opened in Indianapolis, Griffith-Joyner soon grabbed the spotlight with a series of athletic performances and fashion statements that were equally spectacular. During a span of forty-eight hours, she shattered the previous world record of 10.76 seconds in the 100-meter dash no fewer than four times, clocking in at 10.60, 10.49, 10.71 and 10.61 seconds, respectively. Although the first heat result was later invalidated because of a tailwind of 3.2 meters per second, Griffith-Joyner astonished the track world (and herself) with her time of 10.49 seconds in the second heat, which beat the previous world record by more than a quarter of a second. Later that same week, she set a new American record in the 200-meter trials with a time of 21.77. Although her coach attributed her results to hard work, Griffith-Joyner said that she had simply learned to relax while running; trying too hard was counterproductive. Long known for eye-catching apparel, she wore during the heats brightly colored leotards with one leg cut out paired with contrasting bikini bottoms. Griffith-Joyner claimed that she had designed the outfits with greater physical comfort in mind, but she left little doubt that she enjoyed the public reaction as well, claiming that "looking good is almost as important as running well . . . It's part of feeling good about myself."

Griffith-Joyner created a minor stir when she fired Kersee after the Olympic trials and replaced him with her husband, a veteran Olympic track star, as her coach; she explained that Kersee had spread himself too thin among too many different athletes. She shook off the controversy to provide a memorable performance at the 1988 Olympic Games in Seoul. She won the gold medal in the 100-meters with an Olympic record time of 10.54 seconds. She then broke the world record while winning another gold medal in the 200-meters with a time of 21.71 seconds and garnered a third gold medal as a member of the 400-meter relay team. As a last-minute addition to the 1600-meter relay team, she helped the United States finish second to the Soviet Union in the national team standings. Her overall performance in Seoul broke Wilma Rudolph's 1960 record of three gold medals, and Griffith-Joyner, now popularly known as "FloJo," became a full-fledged media sensation.

Faced with a deluge of commercial offers, Griffith-Joyner retired from track in 1989 and dedicated herself to numerous outside interests, including motivational speaking at firms such as IBM, commercial endorsements, and the founding of the Florence Griffith-Joyner Youth Foundation. She and her husband became the parents of a daughter in 1990, and she also co-chaired the President's Council on Physical Fitness. The world reacted with shock when she was discovered dead at her home in Mission Viejo, California. Although her death resulted from an epileptic seizure, it generated renewed allegations, always vigorously denied by Griffith-Joyner, of illegal steroid use on her part.

In a short lifetime, Florence Griffith-Joyner set new standards of excellence in the world of track and field. She reached a level of commercial success hitherto almost unknown among African-American women, and her flamboyant style and appeal demonstrated that female athletes could combine physical attractiveness with athletic excellence.

• Griffith-Joyner's life and career are the subject of Nathan Aaseng, *Florence Griffith-Joyner: Dazzling Olympian* (1989); April Koral, *Florence Griffith-Joyner: Track and Field Star* (1992); and Mark Stewart, *Florence Griffith-Joyner* (1996). Media coverage of her athletic feats was extensive, and she was the subject of articles in publications as diverse as *People* magazine, *Sports Illustrated*, the *Sporting News*, *Time*, *Newsweek*, and *Ebony*. Obituaries can be found in major newspapers, including the *New York Times*, *Washington Post*, *Chicago Tribune*, *Los Angeles Times*, and the *Times* of London, all 22 Sept. 1998.

EDWARD L. LACH, JR.

H

HAHN, E. Adelaide (1 Apr. 1893–8 July 1967), classicist, philologist, and linguist, was born in New York City, the daughter of Otto Hahn, occupation unknown, and Eleonore Funk Hahn, a teacher. Hahn never used her first name and left no written record of what the first initial stood for. She was home-schooled by her mother until she was thirteen years old, when she was sent to the elementary school run by Hunter College so that she could become accustomed to the ways of a classroom. This began her lifelong affiliation with Hunter, following in the footsteps of her mother, a Hunter graduate and editor of the college's *Alumnae News* for three decades, a post that Adelaide Hahn assumed upon her mother's death. Hahn graduated from Hunter College High School and then, in 1915, from Hunter College, with majors in Latin and Greek. She received her master of arts in the classics in 1917 from Columbia University and in 1929 completed the Ph.D., also at Columbia, with a philological dissertation on the Roman poet Vergil, published the following year with the title *Coordination of Non-Coordinate Elements in Vergil*.

Hahn began teaching French at Hunter College in 1917, but in 1921 she received a regular appointment in Latin and Greek. Here she remained until her mandated retirement at age seventy in 1963. The intellectual center of the classics program at the college, she chaired the program from 1936 until she retired. From the beginning, Hahn was an active promoter of the classics at a time when they were threatened by twentieth-century modernism and the increasing emphasis on the relevancy of academic disciplines. In the first decade of her career she published frequent notes in the *Classical Weekly*, many pointing to parallels between some line from a classical author and a phrase from a modern one. She delighted in demonstrating how knowledge of the classics could enrich appreciation of modern literature, film, and current events. Her letters to the editors of the major New York daily newspapers also developed this theme. In addition to regular courses, her teaching included the production of plays and skits, many of which she wrote herself. All of this was designed to enhance interest in the classics, and the program at Hunter for many years flourished under her leadership.

Most of Hahn's early scholarly studies on Greek and Latin literature, especially poetry, were presented as oral papers and then published in *TAPA* (*Transactions and Proceedings of the American Philological Association*). However, following the founding of the Linguistic Society of America (LSA) in 1924, she moved increasingly toward a more linguistic orientation in her work. Literary studies on Vergil's "habit of siding with the 'under-dog'" (a paper in 1925) or his contrast between Latin *pius* and *pietas* (the English notions of piety and righteousness) on the one hand and *violentia* (violence and violation) on the other (a 1931 paper) gradually gave way to studies of language, not only Greek and Latin but also Hittite. For a full decade between 1946 and 1956, at the height of her career, Hahn published no literary studies at all; her work was entirely linguistic.

The LSA held four summer Linguistic Institutes in the years 1928 through 1931. At the last of these, Hahn studied Hittite with Edgar Howard Sturtevant, and a year later she presented her first paper on Hittite at the annual meeting of the LSA in New Haven, Connecticut. The paper, on possible historical relationships between the indefinite in Hittite and Latin, was published in *TAPA* two years later, the first of Hahn's two dozen articles and books on Hittite and its historical linguistic relationship to Latin and Greek.

Hahn regularly attended meetings of the Classical Association of the Atlantic States, the American Oriental Society, and the American Philological Association. She was pleased to be among the first women members of the New York Oriental Club in 1940, the first year women were admitted; when elected vice president of the American Oriental Society in 1952, she noted for the record at Hunter College that she was "the first woman to hold any office in this body in the course of its 110 years of existence." But active as she was in the classical and philological societies, it was the Linguistic Society of America that became the mainstay of her professional life. She was a Founding (charter) Member, the first woman to serve on the LSA Executive Committee (1930, 1934), vice president for 1940, and the first woman president (1946). In 1951 she filled the prestigious Hermann and Klara H. Collitz Professorship at the LSA Linguistic Institute held at the University of California, Berkeley. The records show Hahn in attendance and presenting a paper at nearly every annual (winter) and summer LSA meeting for more than forty years, from 1924 until the winter before her death.

Hahn's linguistic scholarship was criticized by some younger colleagues as old-fashioned and uninformed by the principles of a modern science of linguistics. After a negative review of her 1953 book *Subjunctive and Optative: Their Origin as Futures* in the LSA journal *Language* (vol. 30, pp. 389–99), she returned to the literary studies of the classical authors that had occupied her earlier in her career. In part her problems with linguists came about because the rigid methodology approved by American structural linguists in the 1940s and 1950s had little room for the diachronic studies of meaning in which Hahn engaged. (Leading American structuralists of the time were largely focused on the creation of synchronic descriptions developed from distributional patterns, primarily of the sound systems of modern languages.)

In an address to the International Congress of Linguists in Oslo, Norway, in 1957, Hahn praised the "diversity in unity" of the discipline of linguistics, both within the United States and transatlantically. She maintained that "scholarship advances not by agreement but by disagreement. . . . We are *all* linguistic scientists together . . ." (*Proceedings of the Eighth International Congress of Linguists*, p. 857). With her insistence on the value of classical languages for modern linguistics, her humanistic concern for written texts, and her repeated argument that the usage of native writers of a language must be honored over and above the artificial rules of grammarians and the changes made by academic editors, Hahn was a model scholar in both philology and linguistics at a time when the two disciplines were undergoing a separation. Her impressive command of the details of Greek and Latin texts and scholarship, her erudite writing, and her articulate presence at academic meetings made her a woman to be reckoned with at a time when few women had risen to such prominence within the fields she worked in.

Following Hahn's death in New York, she was named "a glory of Hunter" (*Hunter Alumni News*, Oct. 1967). She had maintained a vital classics program in the face of modernist pressures, and beginning in 1953 she created a pioneering undergraduate specialization in linguistics, an interdepartmental major that she later characterized as "a pre-Linguistics major," designed to prepare students for graduate work in linguistics. With her retirement, both the linguistics major and the Hunter College classical language requirement disappeared from the curriculum. Hahn continued her scholarship; her final book, *Naming-Constructions in Some Indo-European Languages* (1969), was published posthumously by the American Philological Association.

• Hahn's papers have not survived, but there is extensive correspondence between her and the longtime editor of the LSA journal *Language* in the Bernard Bloch Papers, Manuscripts and Archives, Yale University Library. Some material on her life and role at Hunter College can be found in the Distinguished Alumni Series, Box 145, of the Alumni Association Collection in the Hunter College Archives. The Hunter College Archives also contain Hahn's personnel records and her annual reports on her professional activities and those of the Department of Classics. The most complete biography appears in Julia S. Falk, *Women, Language and Linguistics: Three American Stories from the First Half of the Twentieth Century* (1999), pp. 185–264. See also Julia S. Falk, "Portraits of Women Linguists: Louise Pound, Edith Claflin, Adelaide Hahn," in Kurt R. Jankowsky, ed., *History of Linguistics 1993* (1995), pp. 313–20. An obituary with a bibliography of Hahn's scholarly publications is in *Language* 43 (1967): 958–64.

JULIA S. FALK

HAINES, Jackson (c. 1840–1879), ice skater, was born in either the United States or Canada to Alexander Frazee Haines, a cabinetmaker, and Elizabeth Terhune Earl Haines. His exact date of birth is unknown, and his birthplace is still in dispute: among American cities, Chicago, New York, and Troy (New York) are often mentioned. Most sources agree, however, that he came from a prosperous family and was well educated. Young Haines left North America when he was ten years old, accompanied by a relative, and traveled to Europe to study dancing. There he not only mastered ballet but also became a skilled ice-skater. He returned to the United States a few years later because his father wished him to apprentice as a cabinetmaker, but Haines was irresistibly drawn to the stage and left home in his late teens to become a performer.

Haines toured the eastern United States and Canada with several troupes, giving dance and skating exhibitions as well as appearing in juggling acts and acting as a ballet master for touring dance companies. But skating emerged as his passion, and he practiced for hours at a time. When he decided that the ice skates of the day—straight runners strapped on to ordinary boots or shoes—needed improvement, he built a new kind of skate: blades gracefully upturned at the toe that were forged to toe and heel plates screwed on to a special skating boot. Haines's elegant skates eventually became the prototype for ice-skaters everywhere and were in use until well into the twentieth century.

Haines's skating ability earned him two American national championship titles in the early 1860s, but these accomplishments gained him little recognition at that time. For one thing, ice-skating had not yet become a widely popular and regulated sport in the United States. For another, Haines had developed a new style of skating based on graceful, dancelike movements, a kind of ballet on ice, rather than confining himself to a demonstration of routine figures. Though he excelled at the basic figures, an accomplishment that had won him his titles, he was frowned on in conservative American skating circles, where he was considered too theatrical.

Recognizing that his chances for advancement in the United States were limited, Haines hoped to find Continental audiences more receptive to his skating. In late 1864 he left for a tour of Europe, beginning with a series of exhibitions in England. There he met with a cool response from Victorian audiences who were shocked by what seemed to them extravagant and flamboyant poses and gestures. In Stockholm, however, he was warmly welcomed, and after performing there to great applause he went on to a triumphal tour of major cities throughout northern and central Europe. In Vienna, where dancing was a craze, he was especially welcomed, skating to waltzes as well as mazurkas, quadrilles, and marches. Henceforth, music played a major role in his performances.

For his skating exhibitions, Haines always wore exotic costumes, appearing as royalty, as figures from drama and fairy tales, and sometimes as a polar bear. He especially enjoyed disguising himself as a woman, and he often skated on stilts. By 1870 he had become an internationally known celebrity—the first ice skater to be so recognized—and enjoyed the friendship of many of the crowned heads of Europe, including Czar Alexander II of Russia. His popularity created a craze for ice skating on the Continent, and many rinks, often named after him, were built to accommodate the demand for skating facilities.

Haines's performing career ended abruptly in the mid-1870s, probably for physical reasons, and he spent the remainder of his life as a skating instructor, primarily in Scandinavia. According to some accounts, he contracted a fatal case of pneumonia while traveling by sled from St. Petersburg, Russia, to Stockholm. He died in the small town of Gamla-Karleby, Finland, and is buried there, under a tombstone with the inscription "The American Skating King."

Haines was married as a young man to Alma Bogart, the daughter of a New York judge, and had three children. His two sons drowned in the Hudson River while Haines was abroad, and his daughter died in her teens.

Today Jackson Haines is considered the founder of modern ice skating. Haines's ballet-based technique was first known as the Viennese school of skating and subsequently renamed the international style in the years following his death. It was studied in Europe in the late nineteenth century by an American skater named Irving Brokaw, who first introduced it to the United States in 1908 in a series of exhibitions on the East Coast. The international style became increasingly popular, supplanting the more rigid American style by the 1920s, and is still in use today. Many of Haines's original movements on ice still survive, most notably the sit spin, also known as the "Haines spin."

• The most reliable source of biographical information on Jackson Haines is the account of his life and career in chapter 9 of Nigel Brown, *Ice-Skating: A History of the Sport from the Earliest Times to the Present* (1959). See also chapter 3, "Jackson Haines," in Irving Brokaw, *The Art of Skating* (1926). In addition, both books provide an informative history of ice-skating. Information for this essay was also provided by the U.S. Figure Skating Association in Colorado Springs, Colo.

ANN T. KEENE

HALL, Gus (8 Oct. 1910–13 Oct. 2000), Communist leader, was born Arvo Kusta Halberg in Iron, Minnesota, a small town near Hibbing on the Mesabi Range, the fifth of ten children of Matt Halberg and Susannah Halberg. Both parents were Finnish immigrants and before World War I had been members of the Industrial Workers of the World. Hall's father was a blacklisted miner and, like thousands of his fellow Finns, a charter member of the American Communist party. Gus left school after eighth grade to work in a logging camp in northeastern Minnesota; two years later, in 1927, he joined the Young Communist League and within a year had become an organizer for the YCL in the Upper Midwest.

In 1931 he was selected by the Communist Party-USA (CPUSA) to attend the Lenin School in Moscow for training in revolutionary theory and tactics. Several thousand "Red Finns" from Canada and the United States emigrated in the same period to Soviet Karelia to help build a socialist society and were later caught up in Stalin's purges; Halberg, however, returned to the United States in 1933 and was assigned to Minneapolis, where he participated in a series of protests and spent six months in jail in 1934 for inciting a riot during a Teamsters strike.

Assigned to the Pennsylvania-Ohio area by the YCL in 1935, he adopted the more American-sounding name of Gus Hall and went to work at Youngstown Sheet and Tube where he served as a union organizer. That same year he married Elizabeth Turner, a fellow-member of the YCL from a Hungarian-American family, with whom he had two children. As part of an arrangement with the fledgling Congress of Industrial Organizations (CIO), the CPUSA turned over dozens of its best organizers to the Steel Workers Organizing Committee (SWOC) in 1936, and Hall became a field organizer for SWOC. During the 1937 Little Steel Strike, he led SWOC forces against Republic Steel in Warren, Ohio, and was charged with plotting to dynamite company property and bomb the homes of scabs. He pleaded guilty to reduced misdemeanor charges, was fined, and soon resigned his union position to lead the CPUSA in Youngstown; two years later he became head of the party in Cleveland.

During World War II Hall served in the U.S. Navy as a machinist's mate on Guam. He was elected to the party's National Committee in 1944 while still overseas. Two years later he was elevated to the National Executive Board, one of several young veterans being groomed for national leadership who were not affected by the rancor over the ousting of Earl Browder as party leader in 1945.

As the Cold War developed, the government began a series of legal attacks on the CPUSA. The opening salvo was the indictment of the national leadership in 1948, including party general secretary Eugene Dennis and Hall, for violating the Smith Act by conspiring to promote the violent overthrow of the U.S. government. After a contentious 10-month trial in New York, ten defendants were found guilty, and Hall was sentenced to five years in prison. While the case was on appeal, Hall was elected to the party's second-highest position, national secretary. After the Supreme Court upheld the convictions in *Dennis v. U.S.* (1951), Hall and three other defendants jumped bail. He fled to Mexico but was captured within a few months, returned to the United States, and sent to Leavenworth Penitentiary in Kansas to serve his original sentence plus three years for jumping bail.

Hall's release from prison in 1957 coincided with a major crisis within the CPUSA occasioned by Nikita Khrushchev's speech denouncing Stalin's crimes, revelations of Soviet anti-Semitism, and disillusionment caused by the Soviet suppression of the Hungarian revolution. He quickly challenged Eugene Dennis's leadership of the CPUSA, telling party members he met on a cross-country trip that Dennis had violated party discipline and exhibited cowardice by surrendering in 1951 rather than going underground. Terminally ill and wary of further weakening an already decimated organization, down to 3,000 members from its prewar high of close to 80,000, Dennis stepped aside and Hall was elected general secretary in 1959.

Hall was, however, never able to rebuild the Communist party. In 1962 he was arrested and indicted for failing to register the CPUSA with the Subversive Activities Control Board as required under the McCarran Act, but the charges were dropped after major portions of the act were ruled unconstitutional. But even the end of legal attacks on the party did not improve its fortunes. The New Left that emerged in the 1960s scorned the Soviet Union as a bureaucratic, conservative power and viewed the CPUSA as a stodgy relic of the past. Hall's fervent pro-Soviet orientation led him to remove California Communists Dorothy Healey and Al Richmond from their party offices for opposing the Soviet invasion of Czechoslovakia in 1968, and he engineered in 1973 the removal of the long-time editor of the Yiddish-language *Freiheit*, Paul Novick, for pro-Zionism. The party continually denounced both Euro-Communism and Maoism.

Hall ran for president of the United States four consecutive times, beginning in 1972. His best showing came in 1976 when he received 59,000 votes. While he garnered few plaudits in the United States, he received a variety of honors from Communist countries. He visited the Soviet Union frequently; in 1981 he addressed the twentieth Soviet Party Congress at the invitation of Leonid Brezhnev.

While Hall's pro-Soviet posture rested on an ideological foundation, it was buttressed by Soviet subsidies. In 1987 Hall wrote to the Soviet Politburo asking that the subsidy it annually provided to the CPUSA be increased from two to four million dollars a year, claiming that opportunities had never been brighter for a communist breakthrough in American life. Despite its tiny membership and minimal influence in American political and cultural life, Soviet money helped finance party institutions and salaries.

The 1980s were difficult years for Hall. One of his closest advisers, Morris Childs, turned out to be a long-time FBI informant. Even though Childs came under government protection, Hall refused to admit that he had been an informant and squelched an internal party investigation. After the death of the party's second-in-command, Henry Winston, in 1986, Hall resisted demands from African-American members that another black be appointed to the post and was subjected to charges of racism. As Communist regimes in Europe began to disintegrate in the last half of the decade, Hall insisted that nothing was wrong with Soviet-style communism and that it was still thriving. His growing attacks on Mikhail Gor-

bachev's policies of *glasnost* and *perestroika* led to the end of Soviet subsidies, forcing the party's daily newspaper to become a weekly.

Following the attempted coup d'état against Gorbachev in 1991, Hall initially hailed the plotters but quickly retreated after their defeat. Hundreds of CPUSA members launched an effort to depose Hall, objecting to his dogmatic views and the absence of internal party democracy. At the CPUSA's 1991 convention in Cleveland, his supporters controlled the credentials committee and refused to seat many dissident delegates. A number of prominent dissidents, including Angela Davis, were either expelled from the party or quit, with hundreds joining a rival radical organization, the Committees of Correspondence. For the rest of the decade Hall boasted that the CPUSA was the most rapidly growing political party in America, but most observers doubted that it had more than a thousand members, even fewer than when he had become party leader in 1959. In 2000, shortly before his death in New York City, Hall resigned as national chairman and was appointed senior chair.

• Accounts of Hall's political activities can be found in Dorothy Healey and Maurice Isserman, *Dorothy Healey Remembers a Life in the American Communist Party* (1990), and Peggy Dennis, *The Autobiography of an American Communist* (1977). For his receipt of Soviet money, see Harvey Klehr and John Haynes, "Moscow Gold, Confirmed at Last?" *Labor History*, vol. 33 (Spring 1992), pp. 279–293. For a summing-up of his career, see Klehr and Haynes, "Hanging Up on the Hammer and Sickle," *Heterodoxy*, vol. 8 (June–July 2000), p. 9. For the CPUSA's account of his life, see the *People's Weekly World*, 21 Oct. 2000. An obituary is in the *New York Times*, 17 Oct. 2000.

HARVEY KLEHR

HALL, James Norman. See Nordhoff, Charles Bernard, and James Norman Hall.

HALL, Wendall (23 Aug. 1896–2 Apr. 1969), singer, composer, music publisher, and advertising executive, was born Wendall Woods Hall in St. George, Kansas, the son of Rev. George Franklin Hall and Laura Woods Hall. (His mother's lineage can be traced back to *Mayflower* passenger William Brewster). After living in the South, where he learned dialects he would use later in his singing career, Hall moved with his family to Chicago where he began entertaining at local events and singing in church. In 1914 he became part of a singing quartet and also played several musical instruments, including clarinet, guitar, saxophone, trombone, and ukulele. By 1917 he was working in vaudeville as the "Singing Xylophonist" and during 1918-1919 he served as a bugler with the American Expeditionary Force (AEF) in Europe. He returned to vaudeville in 1919 where he played xylophone and was a slide-whistle soloist with several orchestras, including Isham Jones.

In 1923 Hall recorded his compositions "It Ain't Gonna Rain No Mo'" and "Red Headed Music

Maker" for Gennett Records and soon after for Victor Records. The latter song became a major hit, selling over one million copies in both recordings and sheet music. "It Ain't Gonna Rain No Mo'" was to be Hall's most successful song and the one that catapulted him to show business stardom. As a result of its popularity he became an exclusive Victor recording artist and a vaudeville headliner. It was in radio, however, that Hall achieved his greatest fame. He first broadcast over station WEAF in Chicago in 1922 and the next year switched to WGN, after which he began a tour of American radio stations. Early in 1924 he signed radio's first national advertising contract with Eveready batteries, and on 4 June 1924 he and Marion Merchant Martin were married in the first wedding ceremony carried on radio. After a radio tour of Canada, he joined Will Rogers as cohost of the first presidential election radio chain broadcast in November 1924. In 1925 Hall toured radio stations in England, Scotland, France, Canada, Cuba, and Hawaii, and that year he also signed with Brunswick Records.

Hall was not only a major figure in popularizing radio; he also helped to bring the ukulele to prominence and have it recognized as a musical instrument by the Musicians' Union. He compiled a half-dozen songbooks as well as a volume of verse, *Love Poems* (1945), and founded several music publishing companies, including Dellwoods Music House, Music Maker Productions, and Wendall Hall Music Publishers. Hall also composed over 700 published songs, including the successfully recorded "Underneath the Mellow Moon," "Land of My Sunset Dreams," "My Carolina Rose," "Swanee River Dreams," "Lonely Lane," "We're Gonna Have Weather (Whether or Not)," "Lonely Russian Rose," and "Whispering Trees, Memories and You." His 1937 composition "The Rhythm of State Street" was adopted by the Chicago State Street Council as its official song. Although he wrote most of his songs by himself, Hall also collaborated with a number of other composers, including Carson J. Robison, Harry Woods, Peter DeRose, Frank Condon, May Singhi Breen, Gayle Grubb, and Ray Hibbeler. In 1930 he published a radio magazine, *What's on the Air.*

Early in 1929 Hall became the producer, director, and master of ceremonies of the Columbia network's "Majestic Theatre of the Air," a one-hour radio series broadcast in both the United States and Canada. In 1930 he headlined "At the Sign of the Shell" on the NBC Red network and the next year he was "The Pineapple Picador" on NBC radio. Hall also starred on NBC's "The Fitch Bandwagon," which continued into 1936. He then hosted "Gillette's Community Sing" on the CBS network from 1936 to 1937. He also directed and promoted talent shows, and among his discoveries was Grandpa Jones. While not a country music singer, Hall was popular with genre fans and often appeared on the "National Barn Dance" radio show in the 1940s and 1950s, and later he was a member of the Country Music Association. In 1937 Hall

also appeared in two short movie musicals in Columbia Pictures' "Bouncing Ball Community Sing" series.

Throughout his career, Hall was headquartered in Chicago, where he starred in "Thoughts of Romance" on WGN radio in 1945 and started in the early 1940s an advertising agency, Adsongs, which developed transcribed commercials sung and played by Hall. In 1949 he became sales manager for J. C. Deagan, Inc., and that year he also hosted a television program on WBKB-TV. In 1951 he starred in the series "Wendall Hall Reflections" on WBBM-TV. During the 1950s and early 1960s he remained an active entertainer, but after his wife died in 1964 he moved to Alabama to be with his son Lowell and was semiretired. He died in Mobile, Alabama, and was survived by two sons, Wendall, Jr., and Lowell Hall.

Wendall Hall was a major figure in the entertainment industry in the 1920s and 1930s. He was a pioneer in radio and television and a master self-promoter, calling himself the "Red Headed Music Maker," the "Modern Minstrel," "Dean of American Music," and "Mighty Monarch of the Air." Hall's music was both comic and romantic, and he popularized songs in both areas. His enthusiastic style of singing and his use of the ukulele made him a symbol of the raccoon-coat-wearing songsters of the Jazz Age. His composition "It Ain't Gonna Rain No Mo'" was one of the most successful songs in the history of popular music. Many consider him an influential figure in country music. Hall's music was both comic and romantic, and he popularized songs in both areas. His enthusiastic style of singing and his use of the ukulele made him a symbol of the raccoon-coat-wearing songsters of the Jazz Age.

• Hall's sheet-music collection and some memorabilia are housed in the Anderson Public Library, Anderson, Ind. Short biographies of Hall appear in *The ASCAP Biographical Dictionary of Composers, Authors and Publishers* (1966); Roger D. Kinkle, *The Complete Encyclopedia of Popular Music and Jazz, 1900-1950* (1974); Brian Rust, *The Complete Entertainment Discography from 1897 to 1942*, 2d. ed. (1989); Peter Gammond, *The Oxford Companion to Popular Music* (1991); Barry McCloud, *Definitive Country: The Ultimate Encyclopedia of Country Music and Its Performers* (1995); Paul Kingsbury, *The Encyclopedia of Country Music* (1998); and Colin Larkin, *The Encyclopedia of Popular Music*, 3d ed. (1998). Among articles about Hall are "Wendall Hall Praises Stromberg-Carlson Console Set," *Talking Machine World*, 15 Feb. 1925; "Wendall Hall to Record for Brunswick," *Talking Machine World*, 15 Feb. 1926; "Hall after Newspaper Tieup," *Billboard*, 7 May 1927, p. 21; "Popular Favorite Heads Program," *Anderson (Ind.) Daily Bulletin*, 23 Feb. 1929, p. 5; "Hall Hailed as Artist Finder," *Springfield (Il.) Journal*, 6 July 1930; and George Blacker, "Disco-ing In," *Record Research*, Mar.-Apr. 1982, p. 2. A front-page obituary, "W. W. Hall, Song Writer, Dies at 72," appears in the *Mobile (Ala.) Register*, 3 Apr. 1969.

MICHAEL R. PITTS

HARRIMAN, Pamela (20 Mar. 1920–5 Feb. 1997), ambassador, socialite, and political fundraiser, was born Pamela Beryl Digby in Farnborough, England, the daughter of Edward Kenelm "Kenny" Digby, the eleventh Baron Digby and an officer in the Coldstream Guards, and Constance Pamela Alice "Pansy" Bruce Digby. A few months after Pamela was born she moved with her family to Australia, where Baron Digby had accepted a position as military secretary to the governor general. She spent the first three years of her life there, returning in 1923 to England, where the family settled into the quiet life of lesser British aristocracy at "Minterne Magna," a 1,500-acre estate in the English countryside. Educated primarily in the arts and foreign languages, Pamela lived a relatively isolated existence, riding and hunting on the Minterne grounds, until 1935, when she spent a year in boarding school at Hertfordshire. She then lived for several months with a family in Paris for her "finishing," which for the most part ended her formal education.

By 1939, when she married Randolph Churchill, the son of the renowned British politician Winston Churchill, Pamela Digby had developed the charm and social skills for which she would become well known. The younger Churchill, convinced that he would perish in the war and desiring an heir, proposed to Pamela their first evening together. Problems surfaced in the wartime union from the beginning, stemming from Churchill's drinking, carousing, gambling, and generally boorish behavior (Pamela later admitted that the marriage was essentially over in 1941), but she developed a strong bond with her father-in-law, seeking shelter from the worst days of the Battle of Britain in the wine cellar at 10 Downing Street, the prime minister's residence. In October 1940 Pamela gave birth to her only child, Winston Spencer Churchill.

Through her famous father-in-law Pamela Churchill met newspaper publisher Max Beaverbrook, who hired her as a reporter for his *Daily Express* and *London Standard*. When her husband was shipped to Egypt for military service, Pamela began seeing other men, most notably Averell Harriman, who was serving as U.S. envoy to England at the time. The diplomat provided her with an apartment in Grosvenor Square in London and a $25,000 annual allowance. In return she reportedly was able to pass U.S. intelligence information to her father-in-law, who was trying to convince the United States to enter the war. After Averell Harriman left England, Pamela began an affair with Edward R. Murrow, the CBS war correspondent, and also had a fling with his boss, CBS founder William Paley.

Pamela Churchill soon established a reputation as a femme fatale and gained several enemies, since most of her lovers, including Averell Harriman, were married. Rumors circulated that she was searching for a wealthy husband when she moved to Paris after her divorce from Churchill in 1945 and began affairs with Elie de Rothschild and the wealthy Italian businessman Gianni Agnelli, for whom she converted to Catholicism. It seems more likely that she was instead cultivating friendships that she could use to her benefit later. In the late 1950s she began an affair with

Broadway producer Leland Hayward, who also happened to be married. But, according to her obituary in *Newsweek*, she "readily detected the vulnerability" in Hayward's relationship with his wife, and the producer soon divorced and in May 1960 became Pamela's second husband. Through her new spouse, Pamela Hayward made connections in both Hollywood and New York. She also became a naturalized U.S. citizen.

In 1971, just months after Hayward's death, she married her former paramour Averell Harriman, then seventy-nine years old, who had served as governor of New York and had run as a Democratic presidential candidate. In the 1980s, after the landslide victory of Republican Ronald Reagan, Pamela and Averell Harriman helped to raise millions for the Democratic party, hosting "issue evenings" at their Georgetown home to which potential donors, union leaders, and politicians were invited. She and Averell even set up their own political action committee (affectionately known as PamPAC), on which a young Arkansas politician named Bill Clinton served. When the 94-year-old Averell Harriman died in 1986, he left his widow an estate worth more than $100 million, but at her death only a fraction of that amount was left. In 1994 Averell Harriman's heirs sued his widow for "squandering" his estate but settled out of court, forcing Pamela Harriman to sell several expensive pieces of artwork.

Although first favoring Jay Rockefeller and Mario Cuomo for the Democratic presidential nomination in 1992, Harriman soon threw her support behind front-runner Bill Clinton. After winning the election, Clinton rewarded Harriman, by now considered in Washington a "serious political operator," with the ambassadorship to France, which enabled her to cultivate friendships and relentlessly entertain thousands at the U.S. embassy. Fluent in French since her teenage years, Harriman earned respect and admiration by skillfully soothing tense relations between the United States and France over the war in Bosnia and promoting U.S. commercial interests. But perhaps her greatest strength as ambassador was her ready access to the president, who, recognizing her contribution to his election, rarely refused her phone calls.

In February 1997, a few months before her planned retirement, Harriman suffered a cerebral hemorrhage while swimming laps at the Ritz Hotel in Paris, dying in a nearby hospital shortly thereafter. Her memorial service at the National Cathedral in Washington, D.C., deemed by the *New York Times* (14 Feb. 1997) the "closest thing to a state funeral Washington has seen in years," was attended by more than 1,200, including President Clinton. Earlier that week French president Jacques Chirac memorialized her as a "peerless diplomat" in the ranks of Thomas Jefferson and Benjamin Franklin and honored her with the Grand Cross of the Legion of Honor.

By most accounts Harriman was not a great wit or an intellectual (she once described her influence in politics as that of a "backroom girl"), but she successfully used her cultivated charm, determination, and political savvy to her advantage, as well as to the benefit of the Democratic party. Russell Baker of the *New York Times* compared Pamela Harriman's life story to "one of those bad novels in which women with gumption to spare come from nowhere and make the world their private property." The fact that she was able to succeed in this manner was to him wonderful, however, "because the real world's deck is so heavily stacked against real women" (9 Feb. 1997). Today, the great strength of the "real woman" is generally not deemed to lie in the ability to seduce rich and powerful men to her advantage, but in the 1940s and 1950s the opportunities for ambitious women to succeed in public life were limited. Extraordinarily able to adapt herself to changing circumstances, Harriman was courtesan, adviser, wife, political fundraiser, and, finally, successful diplomat.

• Two biographies of Harriman are Sally Bedell Smith, *Reflected Glory: The Life of Pamela Churchill Harriman* (1996), and Christopher Ogden, *Life of the Party: The Biography of Pamela Digby Churchill Hayward Harriman* (1994), which was made into a television movie starring Ann-Margret for the Lifetime cable network (1998). Both books have extensive notes and bibliography, but Harriman authorized neither. Ogden's book was commissioned by Harriman, but she later withdrew her approval after she realized that her sexual exploits would be central to the story. A long interview with Harriman about U.S.-French relations, among other topics, appears in *Europe* 343 (Feb. 1995). See also "Pamela Takes on Paris," *Town & Country*, Feb. 1994. A *New York Times* article by Michael Gross, 16 Feb. 1997, includes excerpts from an interview with Harriman conducted in late 1992. Obituaries are in the *New York Times*, 6 Feb. 1997; the *Economist*, 8 Feb. 1997; and *Newsweek* and *Time*, both 17 Feb. 1997.

STACEY HAMILTON

HAVEMEYER, Henry Osborne (18 Oct. 1847–4 Dec. 1907), sugar merchant and investor, was born in New York City, the son of Frederick Christian Havemeyer, Jr., a sugar merchant, and Sarah Osborne Townsend Havemeyer. From childhood on he was known as Harry. By the time of his birth the extended Havemeyer family, whose antecedents, originally from Germany, had emigrated from England in the late eighteenth century, was one of New York's wealthiest and most prominent, making their fortune in sugar refining. A substantial part of that fortune had been made by Harry's father, in partnership with his cousin William Frederick Havemeyer, who later served as a reform mayor of New York City.

Harry's mother died in his fourth year, and he—as the youngest son of ten children—was largely brought up by his eldest sister, Mary. In 1858 Mary married Lawrence Elder, a member of another prominent New York family, and Harry spent considerable time in their home. When he was fifteen he came under the care of Lawrence Elder's brother George and his wife, Matilda. In the Elder households Harry became well acquainted with both of his future wives: Mary Louise

Elder, the younger sister of Lawrence and George Elder, and Louisine, George's daughter. Harry was privately tutored and ultimately sent to boarding school in Stamford, Connecticut, but instead of attending college he was brought into the sugar refining business as an apprentice at the Havemeyer refineries on the Brooklyn waterfront, joining an older brother, Theodore.

Harry Havemeyer's apprenticeship in the era immediately following the Civil War coincided with a surge of growth in the sugar business, and he learned quickly, mastering not only the commercial side but also the technology of production. He and his brother quickly rose to positions of authority, overseeing the expansion of the family-owned refineries. In 1887 they brokered a merger of fifteen major refineries in the New York area and formed the Sugar Refineries Company, with Harry as president. However, the new corporate entity soon became the target of an antitrust suit brought by the state of New York, and in 1890, after several years of litigation, the court of appeals ordered its dissolution.

In 1891 the Havemeyer firm was reorganized as the American Sugar Refining Company under a charter from New Jersey, with Harry Havemeyer as its president and chief financial officer. It emerged more vigorous than ever, and Havemeyer achieved recognition as a major power on Wall Street whose company regularly produced high dividends. As a leader in the sugar refining industry, he fought, often successfully, for lower tariffs on the importation of raw sugar; conversely, he also sought high tariffs on refined sugar imports, in order to protect domestic manufacturers like himself.

The Havemeyer company remained free of further antitrust suits, but in the late 1890s it was embroiled in a lengthy dispute with John Arbuckle, a Brooklyn-based merchant and shipping magnate who had patented a packaging process for ground coffee. Under an agreement between them, Arbuckle began packaging and selling Havemeyer sugar, but when he started to make what Harry Havemeyer considered too high a profit, Havemeyer retaliated by going into the coffee business. Arbuckle responded in turn by establishing his own sugar refinery in Brooklyn, selling his product at lower prices and thereby making serious inroads in Havemeyer's business. Something of a truce was finally reached in 1901, ending several years of haggling that had cost both men an estimated $25 million: Havemeyer left the coffee business to devote his full attention to sugar refining, while Arbuckle cut back on sugar production to concentrate on coffee. At his death, which occurred in New York City, Havemeyer owned more than two dozen sugar plants that were responsible for providing close to 50 percent of the sugar used in the nation.

In private life Havemeyer enjoyed a luxurious lifestyle, centered primarily at his estate in Great South Bay, Long Island, and also, during his second marriage, at elegant homes in New York City and Greenwich, Connecticut. His first marriage, to Mary Louise

Elder in March 1870, was childless, and it ended in divorce a decade later, in large part, it was rumored, because of his heavy drinking. On 22 August 1883 Havemeyer married his first wife's niece, Louisine Waldron Elder (Louisine Waldron Havemeyer), after she had extracted a promise from him never to drink again. According to all reports, he remained true to his vow for the rest of his life. The marriage was a happy one, producing not only three children but also one of the most important art collections in the country.

Havemeyer's interest in art had been spurred by his second wife, whose own interest had been kindled during an extended visit to Paris in the 1870s. There she had met American painter Mary Cassatt, who became a lifelong friend and introduced her to many of the leading artists of the day, including Edgar Degas and Claude Monet, several of whose works Louisine had purchased. In 1889, following the birth of their last child, the Havemeyers began developing their art collection, journeying first to Paris to enlist the aid of Mary Cassatt in making their purchases and eventually traveling to other parts of the world to acquire art objects. Harry Havemeyer became especially attracted to Japanese porcelain and Chinese textiles, as well as Old Master paintings; both he and his wife shared a taste for impressionist paintings as well. Louisine Havemeyer continued to add to their collection after her husband's death, and much of it was bequeathed to the Metropolitan Museum of Art in New York City after her own death in 1929. The Havemeyers' youngest child, Electra Havemeyer Webb (1888-1960), also became a well-known art collector and benefactor of the Metropolitan Museum and other institutions.

• For biographical information, see Robert N. Burnett, "Henry Osborne Havemeyer," *Cosmopolitan*, Apr. 1903, pp. 701–4. See also Frances Weitzenhoffer, *The Havemeyers: Impressionism Comes to America* (1986), and Alice Cooney Frelinghuysen et al., *Splendid Legacy: The Havemeyer Collection* (1993), both of which include biographical information about Harry Havemeyer as well as his wife Louisine. In addition, see Henry O. Havemeyer, *Biographical Record of the Havemeyer Family, 1600–1945* (1945). See also Louisine W. Havemeyer, *Sixteen to Sixty: Memoirs of a Collector* (1961; repr. 1993). A history of the Havemeyer sugar business can be found in Gustavus Myers, *History of the Great American Fortunes*, 3 vols. (1910; repr. 1936).

ANN T. KEENE

HAWKES, John (17 Aug. 1925–15 May 1998), fiction writer and dramatist, was born John Clendennin Burne Hawkes, Jr., in Stamford, Connecticut, the son of John Clendennin Burne Hawkes, a businessman and prospector, and Helen Ziefle Hawkes. From 1935 through 1940 the Hawkes family lived in Juneau, Alaska, where the father sought to recover business losses from the Great Depression in the prospecting industry. After graduating from high school in Pawling, New York (1943), Hawkes began college at Harvard University but left to serve as an ambulance driver for the American Field Service in Germany and Italy during 1944 and 1945 (an experience informing his first novel, *The Cannibal*, published in 1949).

After working at the Fort Peck Irrigation Dam in Montana following the war, in 1947 Hawkes married Sophie Goode Tazewell (with whom he would have four children) and resumed his work at Harvard, studying creative writing with Professor Albert Guerard. His graduation in 1949 coincided with the start of his career as a published writer, with the New Directions Publishing Corporation issuing his work for a quarter century before academic noteworthiness brought him a larger commercial readership. After working for Harvard University Press, Hawkes joined Harvard's English Department in 1955, where he taught until 1958, when he assumed a similar post at Brown University, of which he was a member of the faculty until his death.

John Hawkes's career was defined by the university, the level at which he taught for more than forty years and the audience for which his novels, stories, and plays were intended. Never a popular author, he courted the interest of the postwar intelligentsia open to philosophically challenging novels by writers who were sometimes philosophers themselves; it is the world of Jean-Paul Sartre's *Nausea* and Albert Camus's *The Stranger* that welcomed Hawkes's work, which in turn made existential pondering a fact of life for readers of serious fiction in America for half a century to come. *The Cannibal* occupies the blasted landscape of Europe at the end of World War II. In stark contrast to other serious writers emerging from the war, such as Norman Mailer and James Jones, Hawkes treated his subject with oblique indirection; because homosexuality was still somewhat of a taboo subject, he displaced it with considerations of something considered fully unspeakable, cannibalism, with both homosexuality and cannibalism serving as reflections of the war's dislocation of humanistic culture. In *The Beetle Leg* (1951) and *The Goose on the Grave* (1954) Hawkes uses the novella format to show how the setting, whether the American West or Italy, is less material to his purposes than the inner landscape of violence and sudden death.

For Hawkes, any terrain is hostile, given the dislocations that postmodernity have visited upon the world. Such tendencies are given their fullest expression in *The Lime Twig* (1961), the author's most famous work. This novel, set in the horse-racing world of a postwar England just emerging from economic and cultural austerity, features violence not as a demonstrated subject but as a stylistic insinuation, an undercurrent that haunts readers in a subliminal way. The lushly tropical *Second Skin* (1964) nearly won the National Book Award, second only to Saul Bellow's *Herzog*; as a pair, Bellow's and Hawkes's novels spoke for a commanding seriousness in American fiction that made it the equal of the most intellectually imposing world literature.

The writing of John Hawkes earned its first substantial recognition as part of the innovative fiction movement starting in the 1960s. Much like his friend John Barth, he had begun his career a decade before the exuberant disruptions of literary tradition that would bring fame to such novelists as Donald Barthelme, Richard Brautigan, Ishmael Reed, and Thomas Pynchon. Hawkes's canon was now reevaluated and seen to be not only philosophically significant but also stylistically and formalistically challenging. Fiction that had once seemed simply intellectual was now read as disruptive of convention, particularly the conventions that gave primacy to character and strongly thematic narrative action. *Second Skin* became one of the first classics in this movement, its multiplicity of sexual relations reflecting the fragmentations of its development, the whole of it underpinned by Hawkes's trademark subliminal violence.

In the 1970s Hawkes's fiction reembraced European settings and deeply philosophical concerns. Although this Europe was a prosperously rebuilt one, the author's clear intent remained that of shattering all illusions of order, be they emotional (*The Blood Oranges*, 1971), physically sexual (*Death, Sleep, and the Traveler*, 1975), familial (*Travesty*, 1976), or mental (*The Passion Artist*, 1979). Because of repeated violence toward women (sometimes in fact, more often in fantasy), these works drew complaints about possible misogyny, but with *Virginie: Her Two Lives* (1982) Hawkes allays such fears by enriching his narrator's voice with a wit, insight, and tenderness well beyond that of his more familiar male spokesmen. As a nine-year-old telling of her two parallel adventures (as a sexual novice in 1740 and as a Parisian brothel dweller in 1945), Virginie maintains a fresh innocence that speaks against any pornographic intent. Indeed, better so than any of his novels this work establishes how John Hawkes creates his own fictive world that eclipses material considerations, sexual or otherwise.

Adventures in the Alaskan Skin Trade (1985), *Whistlejacket* (1988), *Sweet William: A Memoir of Old Horse* (1993), *The Frog* (1996), and *An Irish Eye* (1997) confirm the appraisal of one of Hawkes's first critical advocates, Robert Scholes, who saw him as an essentially "fabulative" author—that is, as one for whom the manner of the telling is as important as the story's substance (if not more so). For Hawkes, the manner *is* the substance; although other novelists would be more overtly metafictive (in foregrounding the making of fiction as its own subject), his were the works that helped bring American fiction to the stage of world literature, a stage shared with such fellow fabulists as Italo Calvino, Peter Handke, and Gabriel García Márquez. A member of the American Academy of Arts and Letters and a winner of most of the national and international prizes for fiction writers, Hawkes was, at the time of his death (in Providence, Rhode Island, following heart bypass surgery) a major figure in American fiction's development into postmodern form.

• Hawkes's papers are in the Houghton Library, Harvard University. Carol A. Hryciw, *John Hawkes: A Research Guide* (1986), is the principal bibliographical study. Major critical studies include Robert Scholes, *The Fabulators* (1967) and *Fabulation and Metafiction* (1979); Donald J. Greiner, *Comic Terror: The Novels of John Hawkes* (1973) and *Understanding John Hawkes* (1985); Patrick O'Donnell, *John Hawkes* (1982); Rita Ferrari, *Innocence, Power, and the Novels of John Hawkes* (1996); and Lesley Marx, *Crystals Out of Chaos; John Hawkes and the Shapes of Apocalypse* (1997). An obituary by John Barth is in the *New York Times Book Review*, 21 June 1998.

JEROME KLINKOWITZ

HAYCOX, Ernest (1 Oct. 1899–13 Oct. 1950), author, was born Ernest James Haycox in Portland, Oregon, the son of William James Haycox, an itinerant farmer, woodsman, and steamboatman, and Bertha Burghardt Haycox. Haycox's parents divorced before he was eleven, and thereafter his attendance at various schools became irregular and was interrupted by his having to hold menial jobs. In 1915 he withdrew from high school in Portland to join the Oregon National Guard, and in 1916 he served in the infantry along the Mexican border; but he then reentered high school and graduated in 1917. After duty with the U.S. Army in France (1917–1919), he returned home, ambitious to become a writer. Haycox attended Reed College in Portland (1919–1920) and then transferred to the University of Oregon, where he graduated with a degree in journalism in 1923. He had already written for high school and college publications. At the university he was encouraged by W. F. G. Thacher, a creative-writing professor and lifelong friend, to emulate popular magazine fiction, including some in pulps where his stories had already appeared.

Haycox, employed as a reporter for the *Portland Oregonian*, went to New York City in unsuccessful efforts to sell his stories to eastern publishers but doggedly continued to turn out western fiction. In 1925 he married Jill Marie Chord, with whom he was to have two children. By 1931 Haycox had placed 102 stories in *Western Story, Detective Story*, and *Short Stories* and had published three novels. The early stories are weak because of tell-not-show plots and prim heroines. He hit his stride, however, with his first novel, *Free Grass* (1929), cast in Dakota Territory and contrasting the effete East and the vigorous West, partly through two women—one from the East, the other from the West. The hero expresses a classic Western code: "Play your own hand, ask no favors, ride straight, shoot fast, keep all obligations."

Once *Collier's* magazine accepted "Dolorosa, Here I Come" (1931), Haycox was on the road to national recognition. *Collier's*, known as a "slick" in the parlance of the day, published upward of fifty of his stories and serials in the next six years, including *Rough Air* (1934), *The Silver Desert* (1935), and *Trouble Shooter* (1937). *Rough Air* concerns aviation and Hollywood, while the film industry dominates *The Silver Desert*. *Trouble Shooter* features the dramatic 1868–1869 construction of the Union Pacific Railway; the book served as the basis of Cecil B. De Mille's movie

Union Pacific (1939). These novels, especially the well-researched *Trouble Shooter*, signal Haycox's determination to shift, partly at least, from formulaic westerns. "Stage to Lordsburg" (1937), Haycox's most famous short story, shows in startling clarity his ability to handle psychologically diverse characters. *Stagecoach*, the 1939 movie adaptation of the story, directed by John Ford and starring John Wayne, has become a classic.

Several of Haycox's novels feature what critics have called his Hamlet hero, who suffers from doubt and is often touched by a sense of fatalism. In *Saddle and Ride* (1940), for example, the hero, a widower during the past decade, vacillates not only in situations demanding quick action but also in wondering which of two women he should prefer. Even while continuing to produce ordinary westerns for ever-increasing pay, Haycox began to aim higher, succeeding best with *The Border Trumpet* (1939), *Alder Gulch* (1942), and *Bugles in the Afternoon* (1944). These novels are historically sound, combine fact and fiction smoothly, and have an ambitious panoramic sweep. *The Border Trumpet* dramatizes army life in Tucson and Apache territory in the 1870s. *Alder Gulch* concerns the clash of the real-life crooked lawman Henry Plummer, his henchmen, and bloodthirsty vigilantes in Montana's 1863–1864 gold fields. *Bugles in the Afternoon* is a superlative fictional re-creation of General George Armstrong Custer's famous last stand. *Alder Gulch*, serialized in *Collier's*, and *Bugles in the Afternoon*, in the *Saturday Evening Post*, together earned Haycox $50,000. A distinct falling off is apparent in his last serial novel, *Canyon Passage*, *Saturday Evening Post*, 1945. It concerns the discovery of gold in 1849 along Montana's Rogue River and the settlers' ensuing conflict with Rogue Indians, whose justifiable opposition Haycox presents inaccurately. Nevertheless, in 1946 it was made into a popular movie with the same title, which premiered in Portland, where Haycox was showered with honors.

Turning away from what he called his "sagebrush novels" to Oregon's pioneering past, Haycox wrote, among much else, three beautiful short stories dealing with a homesteading family in the 1840s: "Cry Deep, Cry Still" (*Collier's*, 20 Nov. 1948), "Call This Land Home" and "Violent Interlude" (*Saturday Evening Post*, 4 Dec. 1948; 17 May 1952). On a grander scale, however, he envisioned in 1949 what he hoped would crown his literary career: eight novels depicting Oregon life from 1840 to roughly 1900 with extensive historical and social details. The main result was *Earthbreakers*, which shows Haycox at his best. Published posthumously in 1952, it follows a band of pioneers going to Oregon in 1845, clearing and building, cooperating and clashing. The hero, ex-trapper Rice Burnett, builds a grist mill. A "squaw man" and an ex-mountain man complicate the process of settlement formation, while two contrasting women present Burnett with difficult choices; in the process Burnett becomes Haycox's most thoroughly rounded hero.

Haycox underwent surgery in 1950 for what proved to be incurable stomach cancer. He died at his home two months later. A loyal Oregonian, he was active in conservative movements, for which he was esteemed in Portland and also in Washington, D.C. His solid portrayals of westward pioneers, cowboys, ranchers, miners, lawmen, outlaws, and brave frontier women of various sorts endeared him to millions of readers. Scholars have regularly praised him for his ever-evolving attempts to raise western fiction above the formulaic pattern inherited from traditionists, such as Owen Wister, Zane Grey, and Max Brand. Haycox challenged critics to see that the best "westerns," assuredly including his own, deserve to be called not "horse operas" and "oaters" but mature, nuanced novels about the Old West. He was a pioneer in his field fully as much as were those sturdy men and women facing west in his writings.

• Most of Haycox's papers, as well as his personal library, are in the Haycox Room at the library of the University of Oregon, Eugene. Twenty-two collections of short stories by Haycox, who wrote 250 in all, have been published, beginning with *By Rope and Lead* (1951). Jill Haycox and John Chord provide a bibliography in "Ernest Haycox Fiction—a Checklist," *Call Number* 10 (fall 1963–spring 1964): 4–17. For critical studies, see Richard W. Etulain, "The Literary Career of a Western Writer: Ernest Haycox, 1899–1950" (Ph.D. diss., Univ. of Oregon, 1966), which Etulain compressed into his crisply informative *Ernest Haycox* (1988); and Stephen L. Tanner, *Ernest Haycox* (1966). Robert L. Gale, "Ernest Haycox," in *Fifty Western Writers: A Bio-Bibliographical Sourcebook*, ed. Fred Erisman and Etulain (1982), pp. 183–93, outlines Haycox's life, major themes in his work, and criticism of it. Brian Dippie, *Custer's Last Stand: The Anatomy of an American Myth* (1976; repr. 1994), places Haycox's *Bugles in the Afternoon* in context. Jim Hitt, *The American West from Fiction (1823–1876) into Film (1909–1986)* (1990), and Jon Tuska and Vicki Piekarski, eds., *Encyclopedia of Frontier and Western Fiction* (1983), discuss ten movies adapted from fiction by Haycox. Tuska and Piekarski also discuss adaptations of Haycox plots for television and radio plays. An obituary is in the *New York Times*, 14 Oct. 1950.

ROBERT L. GALE

HAYS, Moses Michael (9 Mar. 1739–9 May 1805), Jewish merchant and Masonic leader, was born in New York City, the oldest of the eight children of Judah Hays, a Dutch merchant who had come to that city in 1733, and Rebecca Michaels Hays, the daughter of New York merchant Moses Michaels. Judah Hays, who became a freeman in 1735 and was naturalized in 1740, took his son Moses Michael into his prospering export and import business during the late 1750s. The young Moses acquired business skills from his father, for Judah purchased and sold food supplies and guns to the British during the French and Indian War and accrued profits from transporting such goods on his ship, the *Duke of Cumberland*, during the war.

The year after the war ended, Judah Hays died, and for the next two years Moses continued to manage his father's firm. On 13 August 1766 he married Rachel Myers, the daughter of the prominent New York silversmith Myer Myers; the couple was to have five daughters and two sons. By 1766 Hays had started his own business and marketed several kinds of products, including watches that he made and sold in the New York vicinity; that year, he also sold flour and other food products to Barnard and Michael Gratz of Philadelphia. In 1767 he began to deal with Aaron Lopez of Newport; Hays sold to the Rhode Island merchant linens, woolen goods, and barrel staves and bought from him spermaceti oil for distribution in New York markets. In the year that the aggressive Hays was made a freeman, 1769, he made a lucrative return in the same markets by selling sugar from the West Indies.

Hays, who considered the business climate of Newport to be superior to that of New York, moved his family in 1769 to Rhode Island and remained based in Newport for about twelve years. In the year of his arrival there, he established a partnership with Myer Polock. Hays and Polock built ships that transported large cargoes of fish, meats, and other foods from the American colonies to ports in Europe and in the Caribbean. Because of the acute decline of the colonial economy, which resulted from the imposition of the British taxes associated with the Townshend Acts, the firm of Hays and Polock suffered severe setbacks and was constrained in 1771 to declare bankruptcy. The next year, Hays obtained credit and loans and started a new business. For approximately the next eight years, he successfully operated a general merchandising store, which sold to Newport customers stationery, candles, clothes, groceries, liquor, and hardware.

Hays became involved with matters relating to the American Revolution in several ways. Having previously signed a statement of loyalty to the united American colonies in their war against Great Britain, he at first refused to take an oath of allegiance to the revolutionary cause required by an act of the Rhode Island Assembly in June 1776. Hays sent to the assembly on 17 July a detailed letter explaining that he objected to the administering of the loyalty oath because, according to his argument, both the Second Continental Congress and colonial legislatures had failed to extend natural liberties and citizenship rights to Jews. He proposed that the Rhode Island Assembly should empower Jews with the right to vote and grant them privileges conferred on other free citizens before compelling them to take the oath. Hays ultimately yielded and not only took the loyalty oath but also became an ardent supporter of the revolutionary cause, unlike other Jewish merchants in Newport, such as Myer Polock and Isaac Hart, who held to their Tory sympathies. Between 1777 and 1779, Hays provided the Continental army with food supplies and with military clothing and equipment. In 1779 he left Newport, which was occupied by the British, and lived for about a year in South Kingston, Rhode Island. Hays at this time purchased shares in the *Iris*, an armed Massachusetts ship that carried goods to be used by soldiers in the revolutionary army. In 1780 he returned to Newport to reside.

Hays went to Boston in 1782 and spent the later years of his active career there, becoming a wealthy man through his various endeavors. During the early 1780s, he developed a lucrative import and export business. With his headquarters on Boston's Long Wharf, he imported sugar and molasses from the West Indies and profitably exported fish, whale oil, and lumber products to merchants in European ports. He even began in 1783 to trade with merchants in China. That same year, he became a broker, engaging in foreign currency trading, extending loans to exporters and importers and purchasing and selling discounted notes. As a result of his familiarity with financial matters, Hays in 1784 participated in the founding of the Bank of Massachusetts. During the early 1790s, the ambitious Hays turned to insurance and became a successful underwriter of fire and marine insurance; in 1798 he became one of the founders of the Massachusetts Fire Insurance Company.

Hays also helped to foster religious and fraternal institutions. In 1767–1768 he served as second *parnas*, or vice president, of New York's Shearith Israel Congregation. Later, he became an active member of Newport's Yeshuat Israel Congregation. Freemasonry was similarly of great importance to Hays. Involved in low-degree Masonry, which consisted of the order's first three degrees, he served in 1769 as the first master of King David's Lodge of New York and eleven years later reestablished the lodge in Newport. During his years in Rhode Island, he succeeded in recruiting to the ranks of Freemasonry Moses Seixas and other prominent Jews who backed the cause of the American Revolution. Thereafter, he was affiliated with the Grand Lodge of Massachusetts, serving between 1788 and 1792 as its grand master.

Hays likewise played an important role in high-degree Masonry, a movement with dramatic ceremonies that provided both Jewish and Christian Masons with new roles and titles. On 6 December 1768 he was named in Albany a deputy inspector general for North America and the West Indies and was authorized to name others to the same position. On 25 June 1781 he presided over an important session of the Philadelphia Lodge of Perfection, which then consisted primarily of Jewish members but would become during the 1780s religiously assimilated. Empowered to confer degrees four through fourteen, Hays appointed as deputy inspectors on this occasion Isaac DaCosta, Samuel Myers, and other prominent Jewish refugees who came to Philadelphia to escape British persecution during the War of Independence. The high degrees conferred by Hays accentuated salient events, themes, and legends from ancient Jewish history. Moreover, they provided meaningful and vivid explanations of Masonic doctrines concerning natural liberties, religious toleration, and civic equality.

Hays died in Boston. He was buried in the family plot in Newport's Jewish Cemetery five years before his wife was laid to rest there.

As an energetic and enterprising person engaged in trade, Hays developed ties with a network of merchants who fostered the exchange of goods both within the American colonies and overseas. Keen to sense opportunity following the American Revolution, he expanded his activities into finance and insurance. The candid, cordial Hays was, however, as notable for his convictions as he was for his business acumen. Although he tried in vain to persuade the Rhode Island legislature to extend the full complement of civil rights to Jews within the boundaries of the colony (and later the state), his allegiance to the revolutionary cause was unstinting. (Rhode Island did not grant complete emancipation to Jews until 1842.) But Hays is known above all for his role in the Freemasonry movement during revolutionary times and in the early years of the Republic. Even as he helped make Freemasonry an effective conduit for the assimilation of Jews, he saw it as a significant means of achieving Jewish civic emancipation, itself a revolutionary doctrine.

• The American Jewish Archives, the American Jewish Historical Society, and the American Philosophical Society house some of Hays's business letters. For adequate accounts of his life, see Jacob R. Marcus, *Early American Jewry: The Jews of New York, New England, and Canada, 1694–1794,* vol. 1 (1951), which effectively describes his business activities, and Harry Smith and J. Hugo Tatsch, *Moses Michael Hays: Merchant, Citizen, and Freemason, 1739–1805* (1937), which contains some information about his business activities. Some information about Hays's involvement with his father in New York business affairs appears in Harold Korn, "Receipt Book of Judah and Moses M. Hays, Commencing January 12, 1763, and Ending July 18, 1776," *Publications of the American Jewish Historical Society* 28 (1922): 223–29. Several fine works offer an assessment of Hays's business and political achievements during the American Revolution: Morris A. Gutstein, *The Story of the Jews of Newport: Two and a Half Centuries of Judaism, 1658–1908* (1936); Lee M. Friedman, *Jewish Pioneers and Patriots* (1942); Samuel Rezneck, *Unrecognized Patriots: The Jews in the American Revolution* (1975); and Naomi W. Cohen, *Jews in Christian America: The Pursuit of Religious Equality* (1992). Hays's later life in Boston is examined by Jacob R. Marcus, *United States Jewry, 1776–1985,* vol. 1 (1989). Several studies mention in passing the contributions of Hays to Freemasonry: Edwin Wolf II and Maxwell Whiteman, *The History of the Jews of Philadelphia from Colonial Times to the Age of Jackson* (1956); Laurens R. Schwartz, *Jews and the American Revolution: Haym Salomon and Others* (1987); and William L. Fox, *Lodge of the Double-Headed Eagle: Two Centuries of Scottish Rite Freemasonry in America's Southern Jurisdiction* (1997). An obituary appears in the *Boston Columbian Sentinel,* 11 May 1805.

WILLIAM WEISBERGER

HELLER, Joseph (1 May 1923–12 Dec. 1999), novelist, playwright, and memoirist, was born in New York City, the son of Isaac Heller, a delivery truck driver, and Lena Heller (maiden name unknown). His father died when Heller was five. Heller's childhood centered on the streets of Coney Island, where he became known for his acerbic one-liners and practical jokes. His reading choices were typical for his age—books such as *The Rover Boys* and *Tom Swift*—but it was an early encounter with Homer's *Iliad* that would play a role when he became a writer and particularly in the development of his most acclaimed novel.

After graduating from high school in 1941, Heller became a blacksmith's helper at the Norfolk Navy Yard in Virginia. When the United States entered World War II, he enlisted in the Army Air Forces and was sent to armorers school; but on hearing rumors that armorers were going to be trained as gunners in bombers, Heller decided to make a change. "A gunner's life was supposed to be worth no more than three days," he said, "so I went to cadet school." He spent two years learning to be a bombardier. Graduating in 1944, he was shipped to the island of Corsica, where he flew B-25 bombing missions over France and Italy.

Heller admitted later that he was naive about the reality of combat. "I was so brainwashed by Hollywood's image of heroism that I was disappointed when nobody shot back at us," he recalled. Then, on his thirty-seventh mission, his plane was hit by flak, wounding a gunner, and he saw planes flown by his friends destroyed. "People go to fight wars because they don't understand the seriousness of what they're doing. When I finally did, I wanted out." Heller would fly sixty missions before he was discharged in 1945, and his experiences in battle would supply the background for *Catch-22.*

Heller married Shirley Held in 1945, entered New York University under the G.I. Bill, and in 1948 graduated Phi Beta Kappa with a bachelor's degree in English. In 1949 he received a master's degree in English from Columbia University and spent a year at Oxford as a Fulbright scholar. After graduation, Heller moved from job to job: teaching English to university freshmen, writing advertising copy for *Time* magazine, and then becoming an advertising manager for *Time, Look,* and, in 1958, *McCall's* magazine.

During this period, Heller also wrote short stories that were published in *Esquire* and the *Atlantic Monthly,* but he was inclined to dismiss them as "imitations of the type of stories that were being written then." One short story about his wartime experiences showed promise, however, and he spent the next eight years expanding it into a novel. It was originally meant to be called "Catch-18," but Heller changed the number after Leon Uris published his novel *Mila 18.*

The World War II books published at that time ranged from the detailed "war is hell" realism of Norman Mailer, Gore Vidal, and James Jones, to the lighthearted, almost nostalgic, "war is a hell of a party" novels by Marion Hargrove and Thomas Heggen. *Catch-22* was different. Its antihero is bombardier Captain John Yossarian, who, realizing the madness of war, tries everything he can to escape. Yossarian attempts to get out of the Army Air Forces by claiming that he is crazy. But, under the rule called Catch-22, anyone who asks to stop flying combat missions because he fears getting killed is inherently not crazy and therefore cannot leave.

Catch-22 was more than an antiwar book. Couched in humor reminiscent of a vaudeville act, it satirized militarism, nationalism, patriotism, discipline, ambition, loyalty, money, big business, sex, religion, mankind, and God. It questioned the values deeply held by the post–World War II generation by stating that dying for your country was futile, that leaders are fools who cannot be trusted, and that capitalism made victims of us all. Heller's combination of black humor and absurdity is exemplified by Milo Minderbinder, a war-profiteer who engages in a highly convoluted scheme for making money on the sale and resale of eggs, then forms a private air force and bombs his own airfield under contract with the Germans.

Catch-22 was published in 1961 to mixed reviews. Although it was admired for its dark comedy and its realistic depiction of the chaos and terror experienced during bombing missions, some critics objected to the novel's substantial length, its episodic structure, and the scattershot satire directed at too many targets. But the prevailing opinion, which grew over time, was best expressed by John W. Aldridge, writing in the *New York Times* on the novel's twenty-fifth anniversary (26 Oct. 1986):

> Mr. Heller was saying something outrageous, unforgivably outrageous, not just about the idiocy of war but about our whole way of life and the system of false values on which it is based. The horror he exposed was not confined to the battlefield or the bombing mission but permeated the entire labyrinthine structure of establishment power. It found expression in the most completely inhumane exploitation of the individual for trivial, self-serving ends and the most extreme indifference to the official objectives that supposedly justified the use of power.

In retrospect, it seems as if Heller had been writing less about the still-idealized World War II era than about the divisive and cynicism-engendering Vietnam War years. During the late 1960s and early 1970s, when opposition to American involvement in Vietnam was growing, *Catch-22* exploded in popularity, eventually selling ten million copies. With such enormous success, however, came a curse. Heller wrote six more novels and three plays, each of which would be compared, often unfavorably, to *Catch-22*. Heller did not seem bothered by the comparison. When an interviewer told him he had never written anything as good as *Catch-22*, Heller shot back, "Who has?"

As a final measure of its penetration into American culture, the word "Catch-22" entered the 1993 edition of the *New Shorter Oxford English Dictionary*, defined as "a condition or consequence that precludes success, a dilemma where the victim cannot win." Financial success was slow in coming to Heller. During the 1960s he wrote scripts for television shows such as "McHale's Navy" (under the pseudonym Max Orange) and screenplays for *Casino Royale* (an unsuccessful James Bond pastiche) and *Dirty Dingus McGee* (a satirical western starring Frank Sinatra).

Heller's work after *Catch-22* exhibited the same combination of acerbic commentary on society with a stand-up comedian's one-liners. *Something Happened* (1974) examines a man's discovery that because "something happened" in his past he has become no more than a family man with little passion or love for life. *Good as Gold* (1979) follows Dr. Bruce Gold's rise in Washington power circles in his quest to become the first Jewish cabinet official. Heller's savage portrait of Henry Kissinger, castigated as a "non-Jewish Jew," and his use of Jewish stereotypes caused controversy among Jewish groups who accused him of anti-Semitism, despite his being Jewish himself. *God Knows* (1984) has been described as the story of King David told in the voice of Mel Brooks.

In 1986 Heller came down with Guillain-Barré syndrome, a neurological disorder that left him nearly paralyzed. He recovered with the help of his friend Speed Vogel, with whom he wrote *No Laughing Matter* (1986) about his illness. In 1987 he married Valerie Humphries, the nurse who cared for him. In *Picture This* (1989), Heller uses Rembrandt's painting "Aristotle Contemplating the Bust of Homer" as the framework for a collection of reflections on the futility of war, injustice, money, and government.

In 1994 Heller brought back Yossarian and other characters from *Catch-22* for *Closing Time*, set in New York City fifty years after the war. He also wrote three plays based on his military experiences: *We Bombed in New Haven* in 1969 and two one-act plays drawn from *Catch-22*. He also published in 1999 *Now and Then*, a memoir.

Heller died in East Hampton, New York.

Heller's final novel, *Portrait of an Artist, As an Old Man*, was published posthumously to mixed reviews in 2000. Heller may have meant this character study of a writer nearing the end of his life, who searches futilely for the inspiration that fueled his early success, to be a reflection of his own frustrations as a writer. It was an accurate assessment; the tributes that appeared after Heller's death considered *Catch-22* to be his only major achievement. It remains, however, a landmark in American satire.

• Heller's papers are available at the University of South Carolina's Thomas Cooper Library. See Robert Brustein's analysis of *Catch-22* in the *New Republic*, 13 Nov. 1961. A lengthy interview and a biography of Heller can be found in the 4 Mar. 1979 and 28 Aug. 1994 issues of the *New York Times*. An obituary appears in the *New York Times*, 13 Dec. 1999.

BILL PESCHEL

HELMS, Bobby (15 Aug. 1936–19 June 1997), singer and songwriter, was born Robert Lee Helms in Bloomington, Indiana, the son of Fred R. Helms and Hildreth "Helen" Adams Helms. At an early age he showed a talent for music, and by the mid-1940s he and his older brother Freddy were singing as a duo called the Smiling Boys on WTTS, a local radio station. Their father founded a weekend stage show,

"The Monroe County Jamboree," to showcase his sons, and in 1949 they were featured on "The Happy Valley Show" on WTTV, Channel 4, in Indianapolis. The next year they became regulars on that station's "Hayloft Frolics." When his brother left the act in 1953, "Bouncing" Bobby Helms, as he was known, went solo and joined the Bob Hardy Country Show. The show toured the tri-state area of Indiana, Kentucky, and Ohio, where Helms developed a big following. He married Esther Marie Hendrickson in 1953, and in 1955 he recorded four original songs for Speed Records.

Helms's climb to international stardom began in 1956 when Ernest Tubb invited him to appear on his "Midnight Jamboree" radio show in Nashville, Tennessee. Helms then signed with Decca Records. His first release for the company, recorded in 1956, was "Tennessee Rock 'n' Roll," which was a moderate success. His next release, however, was a huge hit: "Fraulein" was voted the top country song of 1957 by both *Billboard* and *Cashbox* magazines and remained on the country charts for fifty-two consecutive weeks, a feat no other song has ever accomplished. Helms toured with Ernest Tubb for a time, but after his record success he formed his own band, the Golden Hawks. In 1957 Helms also recorded "My Special Angel," which was a multimillion seller, and he closed out the year with "Jingle Bell Rock," one of the all-time top selling Christmas songs. He appeared in *Billboard*'s chart of the 100 top-selling records with "Jingle Bell Rock" every year from 1957 to 1962, excepting 1959. In 1957 Helms was named male vocalist of the year by *Cashbox* and most promising new vocalist by *Billboard*, which also gave him its Disc Jockey Award. The year 1958 had him recording "Just a Little Lonesome" (his fourth gold record), "Schoolboy Crush," and "I Guess I'll Have to Miss the Prom"; that year he also appeared in the Columbia film *The Case against Brooklyn*, singing "Jacqueline," which became his fifth million-selling single. During this time, Helms began to make guest appearances on television programs such as "The Ed Sullivan Show," "The Patti Page Show," "Ozark Jubilee," and "American Bandstand" and on radio shows like "Grand Ole Opry" and "Country Music Time." In addition to being a country music headliner, he toured with pop stars like Fats Domino and the Four Preps.

In the late 1950s and early 1960s, Helms continued to tour constantly, playing over 300 days each year from 1957 through 1961. The steady stream of his bestselling records for Decca included "New River Train," for which he received a sixth gold record; "My Lucky Day"; "Hurry Baby"; "The Fool and the Angel"; "Lonely River Rhine"; "Let Me Be the One"; "Someone Was Always There"; "I Guess We Thought the World Would End"; "My Greatest Weakness"; "Then Came You"; "Yesterday's Champagne"; and "One Deep Love." When he signed with Columbia Records in 1963, his recut of "Fraulein" returned the song to the record charts. The next year he and his wife, Esther, divorced, and he married

Doris Young Huggins, who sang professionally as Dorie Carroll. Continuing to tour in the United States and Europe, Helms joined Kapp Records in 1965 and had hits in 1966 with "I'm the Man," "Sorry My Name Isn't Fred" and "Where Does a Shadow Go?" After he signed with Little Darlin' Records in 1967, he remained prominent on the charts for the next two years with "He Thought He'd Die Laughing," "The Day You Stopped Loving Me," "I Feel You, I Love You," and "So Long." In 1970, having switched to the Certron label, he had another hit with "Mary Goes 'Round." For Certron he also recorded the album *Jingle Bell Rock*, which has been reissued annually on a number of different labels, including Mistletoe, Holiday, Pickwick, Audio Fidelity, Phoenix, Pliz, Unison, and Collectables.

During the 1970s Helms worked as a solo act and recorded for various labels, such as Capitol, Larrick, Gusto, Ashley, Million, American National, and Stardom. In 1979 he opened the Special Angel Club in Plainfield, Indiana, but the night club venture was not a success; nor were his investments in a nursing home and a recording company. He also performed on radio and television commercials and in 1980 did a 20-song record to be sold by direct television marketing, *My Special Album*, for the Blue Diamond label. By the mid-1980s he had lost the vision in his right eye because of a rare ailment that was aggravated by harsh stage lights, forcing him to wear an eye patch. Nevertheless, he continued to work 150 tour dates each year in the United States and abroad. In 1987 his Kapp recording of "Jingle Bell Rock" was used as the title music in the film *Lethal Weapon*, starring Mel Gibson and Danny Glover, and in 1988 he returned to the record charts with "Somebody Wrong Is Looking Right" on Playback Records. Although a motion picture about Helms's life was planned in 1989, for which he re-recorded several of his hits for Capitol Records, the feature was never made. In the late 1980s he made guest appearances on the television shows "Fandango," "New Country," and "You Can Be a Star" on the Nashville Network.

In 1990 Helms did a ten-song video, "Greatest Hits and More." The following year, he starred in the weekly series "Bobby Helms & Friends" on WHMB-TV in Indianapolis, Indiana; made a holiday video, "Jingle Bell Rock"; and recorded two songs he had written, "Soldier's Prayer" and "In the Middle of a Love Affair," for his own company, Special Angel Records. In 1993 he opened the Special Angel Theatre in Myrtle Beach, South Carolina, and appeared for several weeks in Branson, Missouri, the resort and entertainment area that seemed likely to rival Nashville in the early 1990s. In 1994, in addition to touring England, he took part in a number of oldies and pop stage shows. Although plagued by ill health, Helms continued to perform until just a few months before his death at his Martinsville, Indiana, home. He was survived by his third wife, Rita Long, whom he married in 1997, and eight children from his first two marriages: Bobby Lee, Randy, Robert Lee II, Debbie, Tyeanne, Angel, Sharon and Melinda.

Bobby Helms was one of the most popular singing stars of the late 1950s. His full voice and straightforward way of singing (sometimes compared to Webb Pierce's) enabled him to become one of the first performers to transcend music barriers, selling tremendous numbers of recordings in both the pop and country markets. With his lack of affectation, down-home style, and boyish appearance, Helms appealed to a wide-ranging audience at the start of the rock 'n' roll era. To teenagers he exemplified this new musical genre, while still retaining his appeal for country fans and adult popular music listeners. His huge fan following was not limited to the United States; he was also very popular in Europe, especially in West Germany. Owing to poor management and unsuccessful financial ventures, Helms's career dimmed considerably after the 1960s, but he continued to be a popular drawing card for the rest of his life. His greatest contributions to music are threefold: his record of "Fraulein" stayed on the record charts longer than any other song; "My Special Angel" became a perennial golden oldies favorite; and "Jingle Bell Rock" was second only to Bing Crosby's "White Christmas" as a holiday bestseller.

• Lisa E. Brown and David Ward Davis's *Jingle Bell Rock* (1998) is a full-length biography of Helms. Brief biographies appear in Barry McCloud, *Definitive Country: The Ultimate Encyclopedia of Country Music and its Performers* (1995); Paul Kingsbury, ed., *The Encyclopedia of Country Music* (1998); and Colin Larkin, ed., *The Encyclopedia of Popular Music* (1998). His early recording career is detailed in the booklet by Jimmy Guterman in the two-disc Bear Family Records album *Fraulein—The Classic Years* (1992). Articles about Helms following his death include "Famous Country Singer Dies at His Home Here," *Martinsville* (Ind.) *Daily Reporter*, 20 June 1997, and Jim Asher, "Bobby Helms' Extraordinary Career, Private Self Given Tribute at Funeral," *Martinsville* (Ind.) *Daily Reporter*, 24 June 1997.

MICHAEL R. PITTS

HENDERSON, Virginia (30 Nov. 1897–19 Mar. 1996), nurse, was born in Kansas City, Missouri, the daughter of Daniel Brosius Henderson and Lucy Minor Abbot Henderson. Named for her mother's home state, she returned there at age four and began her schooling at Bellevue, a boys' preparatory school owned by her grandfather William Richardson Abbot. Her father, a former teacher at Bellevue, was an attorney who represented American Indians in disputes with the U.S. government, winning a major case for the Klamath tribe in 1937. Though Henderson's schooling was thorough, it did not yield a diploma, delaying her entry into nursing school. Patriotism stimulated her decision to enlist in the Army School of Nursing at Walter Reed Army Medical Center in Washington, D.C., where the students were treated as if they were cadets in the U.S. Military Academy. In 1921 Henderson graduated and began working as a nurse at the Henry Street Settlement in New York

City. Later, she studied at Teachers College, Columbia University, under the direction of her mentor, Annie Goodrich.

Henderson began her career as a nurse educator in 1924 at the Norfolk Protestant Hospital in Virginia, where she became the first and only teacher in the school of nursing. Library resources were nonexistent and money so scarce that she stocked shelves with free government publications from Washington. Henderson used Bertha Harmer's *Principles and Practice of Nursing*, the first textbook to employ physiology as the basis for teaching nurses. After five years she returned to New York to study for a bachelor of science degree in nursing at Teachers College, but she interrupted her studies for a year when she practiced nursing at the outpatient clinic at Strong Memorial Hospital in Rochester, New York. She later returned to Teachers College to complete her B.S. in 1932 and her master's degree in 1934 with financial aid from a Rockefeller Scholarship for academic excellence.

For sixteen years Henderson taught nursing at Teachers College and practiced nursing at major New York hospitals. In 1939 Macmillan Publishing Company asked her to write the fourth edition of *Textbook of the Principles and Practice of Nursing*, already a standard nursing text. In 1948 Henderson left Teachers College after a dispute over the importance of research as the basis for clinical teaching in nurse education.

With royalties from the fourth edition to support her, Henderson took five years to completely revise *Textbook of the Principles and Practice of Nursing* for publication in 1955. With the advent of antibiotics, Florence Nightingale's nursing care concepts of cleanliness, nutrition, rest, and ventilation had diminished importance. Henderson's new edition was organized around a view of nursing in which "nurses assisted individuals, sick or well, in the performance of those activities contributing to health, its recovery (or to a peaceful death), that they would perform unaided if they had the requisite strength, will or knowledge." This description of nursing concluded with the objective for giving nursing care: to enable individuals to be freed from the need for help as rapidly as possible. While physicians also sought independence for their patients using medicine and surgery, Henderson believed that nurses uniquely used physical strength, encouragement, and education to achieve the same result. The textbook was used uniformly throughout North America and served to standardize nursing practice.

The International Council of Nurses (ICN) commissioned Henderson to write *Basic Principles of Nursing Care* (1960) for nurses who had neither access to technology nor the medical expertise required to diagnose disease. *Basic Principles of Nursing Care* has been translated into thirty languages and continues to be used throughout the world.

Henderson joined the Yale School of Nursing in 1953 as a research associate to work on a critical review of nursing research. Leo Simmons and she published *Nursing Research: Survey and Assessment* in 1964 and wrote that most nursing research focused on nurses, not nursing care. A series of editorials that she wrote for professional journals helped stimulate the reorientation of nursing research, which subsequently became more clinical. Nowhere did that change take place so quickly as at the Yale School of Nursing, where faculty and students soon engaged in clinical practice research.

Noting the absence of an organized literature on which to base clinical studies, Henderson embarked on a project to annotate nursing literature. In 1972 she completed the four-volume *Nursing Studies Index*, which was hailed as her most important contribution to nursing science.

At the age of seventy-six Henderson began the sixth edition of *Principles and Practice of Nursing* (the title was shortened for this new edition). Over the next five years she led Gladys Nite and seventeen contributors to synthesize the professional literature she had just indexed. With the wisdom gleaned from over fifty years in the nursing profession and the opportunity to review the writing of all of the principal authors who wrote in English, Henderson fashioned a work that criticized health care and offered new techniques that would help nurses correct the problems. The book addressed issues that concerned both the individual and the health care industry as a whole. She argued that health care could be reformed if nurses would encourage their patients to be educated and not to be passive participants in their treatment. She eliminated medical jargon from her text and wrote in a style understandable to the layperson. Henderson died in Branford, Connecticut and was buried in Bedford County, Virginia. She had never married.

Henderson, by all accounts warm and vivacious, traveled the world, speaking to societies, universities, and governments and promoting the scientific basis of the nursing profession. She spoke of the necessity of a universal, comprehensive health service for all Americans and of the absurdity of for-profit health care. Equally important, she urged patients to be proactive in their treatment and in possession of their medical records. A prolific writer and tireless researcher, Henderson changed the public's perception of nurses and helped the profession document the scientific basis for nursing practice.

• Many of Henderson's ideas are in the sixth edition of *Principles and Practice of Nursing*, written with Gladys Nite (1978), which was translated into French, Spanish, and Japanese and reprinted by the ICN in 1997. Using information from recorded interviews, James P. Smith wrote *Virginia Henderson: The First Ninety Years* (1989). Edward Halloran compiled selected periodical articles for *A Virginia Henderson Reader: Excellence in Nursing* (1995). An obituary is in the *New York Times*, 22 Mar. 1996.

EDWARD HALLORAN

HESS, Leon (14 Mar. 1914–7 May 1998), businessman and owner of a football team, was born in Asbury Park, New Jersey, the youngest of four chil-

dren of Mores Hess, a businessman (his mother's name is not known). Leon attended public schools in Asbury Park. His parents were Jewish immigrant Lithuanians. His father established a coal and fuel oil delivery business. In 1933, unable to afford college, Leon took over his father's fuel delivery business, which was failing. He found success by marketing a substance that other companies considered a waste product: the thick residual oil that remained after lighter products, such as gasoline and kerosene, were distilled. Residual oil quickly hardened in the bottoms of barrels, but it had certain industrial uses and could be burned in some boilers. When the residual oil hardened before he could pump it from his truck on one delivery, Hess used a blowtorch to heat the oil so that it flowed. In this experience Hess recognized a business opportunity. He could buy residual oil at prices cheaper than coal, which was then the dominant fuel, and deliver it to his industrial customers in heated tankers. His customers found residual oil economical because it left almost no ash to be hauled away, thus cutting their costs. As coal customers switched to Hess oil, his business grew. By 1938 the company had grown to twelve trucks and a storage facility.

During World War II Hess served in the U.S. Army (1942–1945) in a capacity that drew upon his expertise in the fuel oil business. Hess helped to coordinate the delivery of fuel to General George Patton's tank corps.

Following the war Hess returned to the family oil business and continued its expansion. In 1958 Hess Inc. opened a refinery in Woodbridge, New Jersey, that became the headquarters for the company's retail and marketing operations. In 1960 Hess opened its first gas station, with prices lower than those of his competitors. By January 1961 it had twenty-eight service stations, eighteen oil terminals, and seven oceangoing tankers, in addition to the refinery. Sales for 1960 were more than $249.5 million, returning a net income of just over $7 million.

During the 1960s Hess made several shrewd moves that vastly expanded his flourishing business. In 1961–1962 he engineered the takeover of a fading business, the Cletrac Corporation, a former farm equipment manufacturer. Cletrac was "virtually a corporate shell," reported the *New York Times*, but the publicly traded company had a net working capital of $33 million. Hess Inc. was merged into Cletrac, which changed its name to the Hess Oil and Chemical Company, of which Leon and Mores Hess owned 69 percent. The stock of the new company was traded on the New York Stock Exchange.

With the Democrats in control of the federal government in the 1960s, Hess, a lifelong Democrat, cultivated political ties that had business benefits. Critics argued that when Hess sought preferential treatment in building refineries on the Virgin Islands he was "treated well" by Secretary of the Interior Stewart Udall and President Lyndon Johnson (Engler, *Brotherhood of Oil*, p. 65). Hess also cultivated relations with Senator Henry Jackson, an influential voice on energy matters. Pointing to the power of campaign contributions to influence public policy, critics suggested that the $250,000 that Amerada Hess executives and corporate allies reportedly gave to President Richard Nixon's reelection campaign in 1972 influenced the administration's decision to increase the company's import allocations and to quash the Interior Department's efforts to revoke its special import license.

In 1969 Hess realized his dream of creating a fully integrated oil company when he pulled off an industrial coup by merging with Amerada Petroleum, a leader in oil exploration and production. Amerada's officials rejected a better offer from Philips Petroleum in order to merge with Hess, fearing that the much bigger Philips would swallow up Amerada, but by the fall of 1972 the former Amerada executives had been deposed and Leon Hess was in control of the new company, Amerada Hess. During the 1970s Hess was a partner in the Alaska pipeline construction and negotiated oil deals face-to-face with Arab leaders, such as Libyan leader Moammar Qaddafi.

Hess's personal ten-hour work days, his detailed knowledge of all facets of his business operations, his dedication to quality, and his expectations of his employees led some Hess workers to joke that the letters in the Hess name stood for the expectation that they would work Holidays, Evenings, Saturdays, and Sundays. One writer described his management style as that of a "paternalistic tyrant" (quoted in Rich Cimini, "The Last Tycoon," *New York Daily News*, 9 May 1999). But Leon Hess also had a sentimental and playful side. In 1964 Hess introduced the first of an annual series of toy replicas of Hess tanker trucks and other equipment. Released in time for the Christmas shopping season, the promotional toy replicas were quite popular and soon became collector's items.

In 1954 Hess established a foundation to manage his charitable giving. Incorporated in Delaware in 1954, the Hess Foundation, Inc., focused its giving in New Jersey, New York, and other areas where Hess had business interests, including the Virgin Islands. Hess's giving favored education, hospitals, medical research, religious welfare funds, and temple support. Between 1975 and 1992 its assets grew from $18.5 million to $99 million and its annual grant-making increased from more than $1.4 million to more than $5 million. While he made donations to large cultural projects such as the Lincoln Center and the New Jersey Performing Arts Center, he also gave to smaller local charities in towns where he got his start in business.

In addition to the oil business and charity, Hess was involved in the business of horse racing and professional football. He was a major stockholder and member of the board of the Monmouth Park Jockey Club, which owned the Monmouth Park race track until it was sold to the New Jersey Sports and Exposition Authority in 1986. But his major sports passion was the New York Jets.

In March 1963 Hess and four other men paid a total of $1 million to purchase the bankrupt New York franchise of the young American Football League (AFL), which had been formed in 1960 to challenge the established National Football League. Hess's stake in the franchise was $250,000. The new owners soon changed the team name from the Titans to the New York Jets and the colors from blue and gold to white and green. To coach the team they hired Weeb Ewbank and the following year selected quarterback Joe Namath in the college draft. The team gradually improved under the new leadership, recording its first winning season in 1967. In the 1968 season the Jets won their first AFL championship and became the first AFL team to win the Super Bowl, defeating the NFL's Baltimore Colts, 16–7.

For the next thirty years, Hess waited and hoped in vain for the opportunity to return to the Super Bowl. As his partners faded from the scene, Hess remained a member of a dwindling ownership group. In February 1984 Helen Dillon sold Hess her 25 percent interest in the team, and he became the sole owner of the New York Jets. The hardnosed, shrewd businessman took a hands-off approach to the football operations, although he liked to be kept informed about developments and plans. Unhappy with the cleanliness and physical condition of Shea Stadium and the Jets' lease agreement there, Hess moved the Jets' home games to Giants Stadium in the Meadowlands in New Jersey beginning with the 1984 season.

Hess approached his relationship with the players and coaches as a paternalistic gentleman. As emotionally involved in the game as any fan, he liked being around the players and coaches. In 1984 he began his annual tradition of visiting the team's practice on Thanksgiving Day and giving the players a pep talk. Tall and lean himself, he was dwarfed by the players. Hess valued loyalty in his business associates, his friends and family, and in his football team, and he stood by his people. When defensive end Dennis Byrd suffered a broken neck and partial paralysis during a game in November 1992, Hess visited him every night in the hospital and provided the necessary resources to facilitate Byrd's recovery, even honoring the last two years of his contract.

Circumstances forced Hess to take charge of Jets' personnel decisions on two occasions. After the Jets' general manager was diagnosed with cancer, Hess stepped in and replaced unsuccessful first-year coach Pete Carroll with Rich Kotite, a personal favorite. "I'm 80 years old," Hess explained at a rare news conference. "I want results now" (Eskenazi, *Gang Green*, p. 281). But the Jets fared worse under Kotite, winning only three of sixteen games in 1995 and only one in 1996, and Kotite resigned. Hess now tacked in a different direction: rather than looking for loyalty, he hired someone with a record of coaching success, Bill Parcells, who had taken teams to the Super Bowl on three occasions, winning twice. Because Parcells was under contract to the New England Patriots, NFL Commissioner Paul Tagliabue mediated an agreement between the two teams that allowed Parcells to coach the Jets.

Parcells transformed the poor team he inherited into a winner in 1997. The Jets' record of nine wins and seven losses was its first winning season in nine years. The next season was the Jets' most successful season since the Super Bowl victory in January 1969. The team finished first in their division with a record of twelve wins and four losses, then won an exciting playoff game to advance to the conference championship game.

As the 1998 football season ended, Hess's health deteriorated. Suffering from a blood disease, Hess did not travel to Denver to see the Jets play the Broncos in the AFC championship game, watching instead on television in his Park Avenue apartment as the team lost 23–10, and ended that season's quest for another Super Bowl appearance. Hess decided to greet the players and coaches upon their arrival back in New York. Many players and coaches were surprised to see the 84-year-old owner at the airport after midnight on a cold January night to shake their hands, but it was a typically supportive gesture by Hess. It was the last time that many in what he called "the Jets family" saw him. He died four months later in New York City.

In 1947 Hess had married Norma Wilentz, the daughter of David T. Wilentz, then New Jersey's attorney general and later a national Democratic party leader. Together they had a son, John, and two daughters, Marlene and Connie. John B. Hess succeeded his father as the head of Amerada Hess in 1995, while Connie built upon her father's interest in politics as a member of the Pennsylvania House of Representatives.

In October 1998 *Forbes* magazine estimated Leon Hess's net worth at $720 million. His business, one of the nation's largest independent oil companies, was valued at $6.5 billion at the time of his death; his football team at $500 million. He built profitable organizations in his own unique way. Shrewd and aggressive in business, Leon Hess indulged his interests in people through his philanthropy and his ownership of the Jets, where some observers thought that the importance he placed on loyalty thwarted the pursuit of excellence and success that he demonstrated in business.

• No collection of Leon Hess's papers is available. Hess avoided publicity as much as possible, and even his entries in *Who's Who in America* are sparse, lacking certain standard information, such as the names of his parents, wife, and children. The business press, especially *Business Week* and *Forbes,* and major newspapers are helpful in tracing Hess's career. See especially the *New York Times,* 11 Jan. 1962, p. 43; 18 April 1969, p. 62; and 7 Aug. 1972, p. 39; as well as other articles listed in the *New York Times Index.* On his ownership of the Jets, see Gerald Eskenazi, *Gang Green* (1998). Hess's business activities, especially their furtherance through his political contacts, are mentioned in Robert Engler, *The Brotherhood of Oil: Energy Policy and the Public Interest* (1977). On the Hess Foundation, see Harold M. Keele and Joseph C. Kiger, editors, *Foundations* (1984), pp. 178–79; and various editions of the *Foundation Directory.* Obituaries and appreciations appeared in a wide range of newspapers in the metropolitan New York City region on 8 May 1999, including the *New York Times, Newsday,* the *New York*

Daily News, and the *Asbury Park Press*; many of the same papers covered the funeral service in stories and columns on 11 May 1999. Even the the *Voice of St. Lucia* carried an appreciation of Hess by former Prime Minister Sir John Compton on 15 May 1999.

KENNETH W. ROSE

HIGMAN, Howard (25 Apr. 1915–2 Nov. 1995), educator, was born William Howard Hunter Higman in Boulder, Colorado, the son of Joseph Henry Higman, a building contractor, and Clara Jones Higman. After attending local public schools, he entered the University of Colorado and received his B.A. in art in 1937. Having become interested in sociology, he obtained his masters degree in that discipline from Colorado in 1942. The previous year (1941), he had married Marion Hackstaff; they were to have three daughters.

When the United States entered World War II, Higman interrupted his Ph.D. studies at Colorado and, after failing his army physical, went to work in Washington, D.C., at the War Production Board. After serving as an economist with the Wage Analysis unit of the Statistics Division (1942), as a compliance officer with the Labor Division (1943), and as deputy chairman of the Shipbuilding Stabilization Committee (1944–1945), Higman moved to the Department of Labor, where he served as deputy director of the Shipbuilding Division from 1945 to 1946. Although he held a permanent civil service position and had attractive offers from private industry, he took a chance on an academic career and in 1946 went back to the University of Colorado to be a modestly paid lecturer in sociology.

Higman's return to his hometown proved to be permanent. He spent the balance of his career teaching at his alma mater, where he became an associate professor in 1954 and held a full professorship from 1961 until his retirement in 1985. Despite not having completed his Ph.D., Higman also chaired the sociology department from 1970 until 1974. An immensely popular instructor among his students—*Esquire* magazine had listed him among the most popular college professors in the country during the 1950s—Higman published relatively little and never developed a "school" of thought. He might well have remained an obscure figure had a chance mishap in 1948 not created the opportunity for him to make his mark.

In 1948, in collaboration with Henry Ehrman, a faculty member from the political science department, Higman conceived of the idea for a "United Nations Conference" that would feature an out-of-town speaker, several local speakers, and a model "UN" made up of University of Colorado students. When the featured speaker canceled at the last minute, Higman was forced to scramble for a substitute. The replacement speaker—James Warburg, a polemical critic of American Cold War policy—gave a speech that electrified the campus, and, much to his surprise, Higman was informed the following year by university president Bob Sterns that the "United Nations Conference on World Affairs" would be an annual event.

The Conference on World Affairs, as it soon came to be known, took on a life of its own. Held annually in Boulder, it differed radically from any other academic meeting. Participants (who were often returnees from previous years or recruited by previous participants) traveled to the Boulder campus from around the world at their own expense for the weeklong meeting and were housed in private dwellings. The presentation of formal papers was forbidden, and there were no local speakers (on the theory that they already had access to the eyes and ears of Boulder citizens). The conference featured panel discussions that allowed a variety of experts from a wide range of fields to discuss topics wholly unrelated to their particular areas of expertise.

Although the early conferences generally emphasized such topics as international affairs and politics, as the years went by the subject matter expanded to include matters not necessarily related to government and policy, such as pop culture and the arts. Among the featured speakers were Ralph Nader, Ted Turner, Buckminster Fuller, Timothy Leary, Roger Ebert, Henry Kissinger, Eleanor Roosevelt, and Marshall McLuhan. Much of the appeal of the conference came from its free-for-all format, which provided the potential for military generals debating with street poets on the use of nuclear force, witches expressing their views on foreign policy to former CIA operatives, or rock stars discussing Middle Eastern politics. As Higman himself put it, "In other conferences, this kind of stuff goes on in the bar. . . . You read your paper, and if you have any excitement, it's in the hotel room, not on stage. We try to put the excitement on stage."

Although the conference generated a great deal of good publicity for the University of Colorado at minimal cost to the school, by the early 1990s many were questioning its continued usefulness. Some faculty members remained skeptical about its scholarly value, while others criticized the predominance of white male speakers at a time when the concept of "diversity" on campus was being increasingly advocated. Much antipathy was focused on Higman, who remained the driving force and organizer of the conference throughout his life. Possessed of considerable charm, he was nevertheless difficult to get along with, and his personality as well as his outspoken opinions generated enemies throughout his tenure at the head of the CWA. After a 1990 task force recommended changes in the conference, Higman pointed out that the conference had in fact become more open to women and minorities in recent years. The changes, however, were insufficient to quiet Higman's most severe critics, and in 1994 university chancellor Jim Corbridge cut the funding for the next year's event. While the conference remained in limbo, Higman, who had suffered from declining health, died in Boulder. With his death, much of the opprobrium attached to the conference dissipated, and, heeding strong demand for its revival, the university restored funding in time to provide for the 1996 edition under a new director.

Without either a Ph.D. or significant publications to his name, Higman succeeded to a highly unusual degree in the academic world. The Conference on World Affairs, which proved to be unique among events sponsored by American universities, was a sufficiently powerful idea to survive the death of its creator.

• No collection of Higman's papers is known to exist. The best source of information on his life and career is the semi-autobiographical *Higman: A Collection*, ed. Tom Adams and Betty Brandenburg (1998). A lengthy discussion of Higman and the Conference from the perspective of his later years appears in Alan Prendergast, "Howard's End," *Denver Westword*, 26 Jan.–1 Feb. 1994, pp. 16–26. The *Denver Post* of 24 Nov. 1995 and the *New York Times* of 1 Dec. 1995 have obituaries.

EDWARD L. LACH, JR.

HINDEMITH, Paul (16 Nov. 1895–28 Dec. 1963), composer, was born in Hanau, near Frankfurt, Germany, the son of Robert Hindemith, a house painter, and Marie Warnecke Hindemith. He began violin lessons in 1904 and was admitted to Frankfurt's Hoch Conservatory in 1909, where he studied violin and composition. In 1914 Robert Hindemith volunteered to serve in the army; he was killed fighting in France, and Paul took responsibility for supporting his mother, brother, and sister. He joined the orchestra of the Frankfurt Opera in 1915 and was soon made concertmaster; he also played viola in a quartet led by his violin teacher. From 1917 to 1919, he served in the army as well.

Hindemith was a prolific composer in many genres throughout his life. He first became known for his chamber music; during the 1920s he rose to prominence with modernistic operas and other works and was a key figure in establishing the Donaueschingen festival of contemporary music. In 1924 he married Gertrud Rottenberg; they remained together until his death but had no children.

In 1927 Hindemith joined the faculty of the Staatliche Hochschule für Musik in Berlin. He found teaching a rewarding experience and also became interested in musical education for the general public; for a time he maintained that the composer's primary responsibility was to create works that amateurs could perform, and he wrote many such compositions. Hindemith's teaching activity also prompted him to write an important theoretical work, *Unterweisung im Tonsatz* (2 vols., 1935, 1937; translated as *The Craft of Musical Composition*), and other textbooks.

Hindemith's reactions to the coming of the Nazi regime may seem inconsistent from a present-day perspective. He was married to the daughter of a Jew, chose Jewish musicians as partners in performance, and opposed anti-Semitic attitudes in his teaching. But when a Nazi organization attacked him in 1933 as a "cultural bolshevist," he responded by meeting with its officials to discuss collaborating on educational projects, first establishing that he "was neither a half nor any other fractional Jew." Friends of Hindemith's tried at length to win support for the composer among influential Nazis, including Hitler himself. Over time, however, the Nazi apparatus settled into a hostile attitude toward Hindemith and made it virtually impossible for his works to be performed in Germany.

During these years Hindemith composed the opera *Mathis der Maler* ("Mathis the Painter"), perhaps his finest work, to his own libretto about the painter Matthias Grünewald and the Peasants' Revolt in sixteenth-century Germany. *Mathis* has been understood as a condemnation of tyranny, especially the scene in which church authorities burn "dangerous" books, as the Nazis also did. However, Hindemith thought in 1934 that Hitler would approve the libretto if he could be induced to read it.

Hindemith gradually withdrew from his involvements in German musical life, resigning from the Hochschule in 1937. Among other engagements outside Germany, in 1937, 1938, and 1939 he toured the United States as a violist, and in 1938 he and his wife emigrated to Switzerland. Serge Koussevitzky, conductor of the Boston Symphony Orchestra, who had known Hindemith since 1928, engaged him to teach composition at the summer 1940 session of the Berkshire Music Festival (where Leonard Bernstein would be one of his students). Meanwhile, with the outbreak of war, Hindemith was technically liable to be forced back to Germany and drafted. Nicolas Nabokov of Wells College had become friends with Hindemith during his American tour of 1939. Concerned for his safety, Nabokov and Cameron Baird, an acquaintance from the Hochschule who headed the University of Buffalo music department, arranged academic appointments for spring 1940 at Buffalo, Wells, and Cornell for Hindemith, who accepted after some hesitation and sailed for New York in February 1940. His arduous schedule that semester intensified when Yale University engaged him for a series of master classes and lectures, in the course of which he agreed to join the Yale faculty for the coming year.

Hindemith taught at Yale through 1953, working with some 250 graduate students, of whom twelve received master's degrees in composition and thirty-five in theory. A dedicated teacher by all accounts, he also composed steadily and received many commissions. Works of his American period include the popular *Symphonic Metamorphosis of Themes by Carl Maria von Weber* (1944), which originated in sketches for a ballet project with Léonide Massine that did not come off. Shortly after receiving American citizenship, Hindemith began *When Lilacs Last in the Door-Yard Bloom'd* (1946), a setting of Walt Whitman's poem, subtitled *A Requiem for Those We Love* and dedicated to the memory of Franklin D. Roosevelt and Americans who died in World War II. It was first performed in New York by the Collegiate Chorale under the direction of Robert Shaw.

Hindemith's later years at Yale were interrupted by absences, as he pursued various interests. He took sabbatical leave in the fall of 1948 for a conducting tour of Europe, then was asked to spend 1949–1950 as Charles Eliot Norton Professor at Harvard. Increasingly interested in a conducting career, which he could pursue more easily in Europe, he then arranged to spend alternate years at Yale and the University of Zurich, where he taught in 1951–1952. In the end, he left Yale to teach full time at Zurich, then retired to Blonay, Switzerland. Though living in Switzerland, he kept up American connections and thus came to write *Pittsburgh Symphony* (1958), in honor of the city's bicentennial, and *The Long Christmas Dinner* (1960), a one-act opera with a libretto by Thornton Wilder based on his play. He continued composing and conducting until shortly before his death, of acute pancreatitis, in a Frankfurt hospital.

A significant figure in twentieth-century music, Hindemith was one of those composers who discovered new means of expression while holding fast to the basic structure of tonality; he often spoke out against the atonal and serialist strategies associated with Arnold Schoenberg. His feelings for his adopted homeland were characterized by gratitude and affection, tinged in the end with disappointment. "Nobody ever bothered to call me an American musician," he wrote in 1956, "I always remained for them a foreigner."

• Hindemith's manuscripts, correspondence, and other papers are in the archives of the Paul Hindemith Institute, Frankfurt. The Paul Hindemith Collection at Yale University holds documents relating to Hindemith's life and work in the United States. His published writings include *A Composer's World: Horizons and Limitations* (1952), based on his Norton lectures at Harvard. Valuable sources of information are Geoffrey Skelton, *Paul Hindemith* (1975); Luther Noss, *Paul Hindemith in the United States* (1989); Skelton, trans. and ed., *Selected Letters of Paul Hindemith* (1995); and Ian Kemp, "Paul Hindemith," in *The New Grove Dictionary of Music and Musicians*. Michael Kater's chapter on Hindemith in *Composers of the Nazi Era* (2000) is useful as a guide to recent literature. An obituary is in the *New York Times*, 30 Dec. 1963.

JONATHAN WIENER

HISS, Alger (11 Nov. 1904–15 Nov. 1996), government official convicted of giving false testimony about Soviet espionage, was born in Baltimore, Maryland. His father, Charles Alger Hiss, a dry-goods importer, killed himself when Alger was two. His mother, Mary Lavinia Hughes Hiss, raised Alger and four siblings with the support of her husband's family. Hiss attended Baltimore public schools and Powder Point Academy in Massachusetts. He graduated from Johns Hopkins University in 1926 with an exemplary record. Similar success at Harvard Law School led to his selection in 1929 as a law clerk for Supreme Court Justice Oliver Wendell Holmes. In the same year he married Priscilla Fansler Hobson. They had two children: stepson Timothy Hobson and son Anthony.

In 1930 Hiss joined the Boston law firm of Choate, Hall and Stewart but in 1932 moved to the New York firm of Cotton, Franklin, Wright & Gordon. In 1933 he became an attorney in Washington, D.C., for the Agricultural Adjustment Administration and later served with the U.S. Senate's Nye Committee (investigating munitions firms) and the Justice Department. He joined the State Department in 1936 as an aide to Assistant Secretary of State Francis Sayre, who dealt with international economics. Hiss moved to the Far Eastern Division in 1939 and in 1944 to the Office of Special Political Affairs, where he worked closely with Undersecretary of State Dean Acheson and Undersecretary of State Edward Stettinius, who became secretary of state in November 1944. Named director of the Office of Special Political Affairs in March 1945, Hiss also served as executive secretary of the 1944 Dumbarton Oaks Conference that planned the United Nations, accompanied Stettinius to the February 1945 Yalta Conference, and served as secretary-general of the U.N. organizing conference in April 1945. In 1946 security officials informed Secretary of State James Byrnes of evidence indicating Hiss's cooperation with Soviet intelligence. Quietly encouraged to leave government service, Hiss in early 1947 became president of the Carnegie Endowment for International Peace.

Suspicions of Hiss's loyalties became public in August 1948 when an editor of *Time* magazine, Whittaker Chambers, appeared before the House Committee on Un-American Activities to corroborate testimony by Elizabeth Bentley, a former Soviet spy. Chambers named Hiss as one of the government officials he had known in a Communist group in the 1930s. Hiss in separate testimony emphatically denied association with Communism or acquaintance with Chambers. Initial public reaction supported Hiss, and the committee intended to drop the matter. However, Representative Richard Nixon, a freshman Republican, successfully urged that the conflicting testimony be pursued.

After a face-to-face confrontation, Hiss stated that earlier he had not recognized Chambers from photographs but now recognized him as a journalist he had known casually under the name Crosley in 1934 and 1935. Under questioning he stated that he had subleased an apartment to Chambers, loaned him money, and driven him to New York, and that the Hiss family had shared an apartment with Chambers and his wife for a few days. Some sections of Hiss's story fell apart. Chambers testified that Hiss, after purchasing a new car, had given his old one to the Communist party in 1936. Hiss countered that he had given his extra car to Chambers as part of the apartment sublease in the summer of 1935. But auto transfer records showed that Hiss had not bought his new car until September 1935, two months after Chambers's sublease had ended in June, and that in July 1936, a year after the sublease, Hiss had personally signed ownership of the old car over to a dealer who on the same day signed ownership over to a Communist activist.

These incongruities damaged Hiss's credibility, but he continued to firmly deny association with Communism and to have the support of many respected Washington figures. When Chambers repeated his charges outside the immunity provided by congressional testimony, Hiss sued. On 17 November 1948 Chambers produced four pages in Hiss's handwriting and sixty-five typed pages, some with annotations in Hiss's handwriting, which summarized or copied confidential 1938 State Department cables. A few weeks later Chambers produced microfilm of 1938 State Department cables and memoranda with Hiss's office stamp and handwritten initials on the documents. Chambers explained that Hiss's suit had forced him to produce documents showing that he and Hiss had carried out espionage for the Soviet military intelligence agency.

A grand jury examined the documents and heard testimony from Chambers, Hiss, and others and indicted Hiss on two counts of perjury, one for denying he had given documents to Chambers and another for denying he had met with Chambers in 1938. In the trials, held in New York, technical experts testified that the handwritten documents were in Hiss's hand and that all but one of the typed documents had been typed on a typewriter owned by the Hisses in the 1930s and kept in their home. The defense's own experts confirmed those findings privately. Parts of Chambers's story were corroborated by Julian Wadleigh, another State Department official who had spied for the Soviets and furnished Chambers with material, and Hede Massing, who had also worked for Soviet intelligence and had been aware of Hiss's cooperation. Separate from the trials two other participants in Chambers's espionage apparatus also confessed. Hiss continued to state that his relationship with Chambers had been casual, brief, and benign and to deny contact after 1935 except for possible fleeting encounters in 1936. Many prestigious character witnesses testified for Hiss, including Supreme Court Justices Felix Frankfurter and Stanley Reed. Hiss's defense argued that Chambers, motivated by a homosexually based pathological hatred of Hiss developed in 1934–1935, had stolen the documents from Hiss's State Department office in 1938 and by unknown means had gotten access to the Hiss family typewriter to prepare the typed material.

The initial trial ended in a hung jury but with a majority for conviction. A unanimous jury in a second trial convicted Hiss on both counts on 21 January 1950. An appeals court affirmed conviction and the Supreme Court denied appeal in March 1951. A 1952 petition for retrial was similarly rejected by district, appellate, and supreme courts. Hiss's conviction gave substance to public fears that Soviet espionage was a serious problem, and Republicans pointed to the case as evidence that the Franklin Delano Roosevelt and Harry S. Truman administrations had been lax in regard to Communism and espionage. Richard Nixon's role in the case gave him standing to win a U.S. Senate seat in 1950 and to become vice president in 1953. Hiss's defenders depicted the conviction as a frame-up aimed at tainting the New Deal with treason and fanning anti-Communist hysteria.

After serving three years and eight months of his five-year sentence, Hiss was released in November 1954. He separated from his wife, Priscilla, in 1958; in 1985 after Priscilla's death he married Isabel Johnson. During the 1970s he lectured widely, maintaining his innocence and arguing that he had been the victim of a conspiracy. Support for Hiss's innocence, once limited to his associates and the radical left, became widespread in the 1970s and 1980s. Opposition to the unpopular Vietnam War shattered the Cold War political consensus and gave credibility to Hiss's argument that he had been the victim of anti-Communist hysteria. The Watergate scandal discredited Richard Nixon, one of Hiss's chief antagonists, and made plausible the idea that a government conspiracy had forged evidence and coerced false testimony against him. Hiss's conviction became to many a symbol of anti-Communist excess and government abuse of power.

In 1972 Hiss gained a federal pension when he successfully sued on the grounds that the law denying pensions to persons convicted of his crimes was unconstitutional. The Massachusetts Supreme Judicial Court in 1975 readmitted Hiss to the practice of law, citing his blameless life since prison but adding that "nothing we have said here should be construed as detracting one iota from the fact that . . . we consider him to be guilty as charged." In 1978 Hiss submitted a detailed writ asking that his conviction be overturned. A federal district court in 1982 ruled that "the jury verdict rendered in 1950 was amply supported by the evidence . . . and nothing presented in these papers . . . places that verdict under any cloud." An appeals court and the Supreme Court also rejected Hiss's writ. Hiss died in New York in 1996.

In 1992 a Russian historian, Dimitri Volkogonov, announced that a search of Russian archives showed that neither Hiss nor Chambers had ever spied for the USSR. The claim faded when Volkogonov explained he had been allowed only two days' access at the archives of one Soviet intelligence agency, the KGB, and had had no access to the archives of the Soviet military intelligence agency for which Chambers and Hiss had worked. Subsequently, documents corroborating Hiss's espionage have been found in the KGB's archives by American historian Allen Weinstein and his Russian associate, Alexander Vassiliev, and by a Hungarian historian, Maria Schmidt, in the archives of the Hungarian Communist security service.

• A large body of journalistic and polemical literature exists on the Hiss case. Hiss's *In the Court of Public Opinion* (1957) is a lawyerly brief for his innocence, while his autobiographical *Recollections of a Life* (1988) describes his life and reasserts his innocence but has few new details concerning the case. John Chabot Smith's *Alger Hiss: The True Story* (1977)

advances explanations built around various conspiracies to argue for Hiss's innocence. The most thorough scholarly study is Allen Weinstein, *Perjury: The Hiss-Chambers Case* (1978; rev. ed. with new material, 1997). Weinstein finds that on the essential points regarding espionage the evidence shows that Chambers told the truth and Hiss did not. A similar conclusion is in Sam Tanenhaus, *Whittaker Chambers: A Biography* (1997; rev. ed., 1998). An obituary is in the *New York Times*, 16 Nov. 1996.

JOHN EARL HAYNES

HOBBY, Oveta Culp (19 Jan. 1905–16 Aug. 1995), publisher and government official, was born Oveta Culp in Killeen, Texas, the daughter of Isaac William Culp, a lawyer, and Emma Hoover Culp. As a child, Oveta was close to her father and with his encouragement developed an early interest in law. She was educated in the local schools as well as tutored at home, and after graduation from high school she studied at Mary Hardin Baylor College in Belton, Texas, and at the University of Texas Law School in Austin. As a law student she became parliamentarian of the Texas House of Representatives, serving in that post from 1925 until 1931 and later from 1939 to 1941. In her early twenties she also served as a legal clerk in the Texas State Banking Department, and in that capacity she helped to codify Texas banking laws. In addition, in 1930 she served as an assistant to the Houston city attorney.

By this time Oveta Culp had become active in the Democratic party, both locally and at the national level, and was a delegate to the National Democratic Convention held in Houston in 1928. A year later she ran for a seat in the state legislature but was defeated. About this time she began working in the circulation department of the *Houston Post* newspaper, and in 1931 she married *Post* publisher William Pettus Hobby, a widower twenty-seven years her senior who had served as the governor of Texas from 1917 to 1921; the couple eventually had two children, a son and a daughter. Their son, William P. Hobby, Jr., later served as the lieutenant governor of Texas for eighteen years.

Following her marriage, Oveta Culp Hobby turned from law and politics to a full-time career in journalism, beginning as a research editor at the *Post*. Between 1933 and 1938 she was book editor and then assistant editor of the *Post*; in 1938 she was named vice president of the paper. During this period she was credited with making a number of positive changes at the *Post*, restructuring its format and departments and giving greater prominence to women's news. By the end of the decade, as her husband gave increasing attention to his other business interests, including banking and radio, Hobby had become the de facto head of the newspaper. She had also revamped her image, transforming herself from a somewhat dowdy small-town girl with a Texas drawl into a well-spoken, impeccably dressed sophisticate who mingled comfortably with Houston high society.

Combining a full-time career with a family seemed to pose little difficulty for Hobby, who was also active in many local and state civic groups. She served as president of the Texas League of Women Voters and as a regent of the Texas State Teachers College, also becoming executive director of a Houston radio station and a director of a local bank. She even found time to write a book on parliamentary law, *Mr. Chairman* (1937), which was used for many years as a textbook in Texas and Louisiana.

In the summer of 1941, as the United States prepared for its eventual entry into World War II, Hobby was named by President Franklin D. Roosevelt to a dollar-a-year post in the War Department's Bureau of Public Relations. She became the first head of its new women's division, and in that capacity she had the responsibility of keeping wives and mothers of servicemen informed about their loved ones in the military. Later that year she was asked by General George C. Marshall, then chief of staff, to explore setting up a women's auxiliary army. With her recommendations, the Women's Auxiliary Army Corps (WAAC), the first American women's army, was established in May 1942, five months after the United States entered the war, and Hobby became its first director. Initially, she was given the rank of major but was quickly promoted to colonel.

Hobby's first job as head of the newly formed WAAC was to recruit officer candidates for administrative work. When this task was completed by early fall, she then began looking for volunteer recruits, initially some 12,000 and ultimately more than nine times that number. As part of her preparation for her new role, she visited England in October 1942 with Eleanor Roosevelt, the first lady, to assess the war efforts and activities of British women, including the inspection of the Women's Royal Navy Service (WRENS) and the Auxiliary Territorial Service (ATS). Back in Washington she streamlined her organization's name, dropping the word "Auxiliary" in 1943 and giving the renamed WAC status equal to the all-male U.S. Army. By then, WACs, as WAC soldiers were known, were serving in noncombat posts throughout the United States and in the European and Pacific theaters, and by the time the war ended in 1945 there were 100,000 WACs on active duty.

Retiring from her position as head of the WACs in the summer of 1945, Hobby returned to Houston, where she resumed her duties at the *Post* and enlarged her involvement in civic activities, both local and national. In the late 1940s she served as a consultant to the Hoover Commission, headed by former President Herbert Hoover; the commission studied the obvious need for administrative changes in the Executive Branch of the national government, and Hobby helped draft the report that summarized the commission's findings. She was also active as a leader during the postwar period in several national newspaper organizations as well as the recently formed American Cancer Society. In 1952 she was named coeditor and publisher of the *Houston Post*.

Although Hobby had been a lifelong Democrat, she broke with the party in 1948 to support the unsuccessful Republican presidential candidate, Thomas E. Dewey. Early in 1952, before the Republican National Convention, she announced her support for one of the likely Republican presidential nominees, General Dwight D. Eisenhower, and used editorials in the *Post* as a means of gaining the support of the Texas delegation for his eventual nomination at the national convention that summer. In the election campaign that followed, she became active at the national level on behalf of Eisenhower, often working at Republican headquarters in New York City. Following his election in November, Hobby was named by Eisenhower to head the Federal Security Agency (FSA) in Washington, D.C., and assumed the post on 21 January 1953.

The FSA had been created in 1939, and by the time of Hobby's appointment it was the umbrella organization for all departments in the federal government that dealt with the health, education, and social and economic security of Americans. These included the Public Health Service, the Food and Drug Administration, the Office of Education, and the Bureau of Old Age and Survivors Insurance. When Eisenhower took office, however, plans already were under way—in large part as a consequence of the Hoover Commission Report—to reorganize the FSA into a new department with cabinet-level status. On 30 March 1953, barely two months after Hobby took office, the FSA was renamed the Department of Health, Education, and Welfare (HEW) by an act of Congress. Hobby, now a member of Eisenhower's cabinet, took a new oath of office as the first secretary of HEW on 11 April, becoming the second woman in U.S. history to hold a cabinet post (the first having been Frances Perkins).

Hobby served without controversy as head of HEW until July 1955, when she returned to Houston at the behest of her husband to become editor and publisher of the *Post* and to help run his other business interests. She became chairman of the board of the *Post* following his death in 1964, continuing in that capacity until she sold the newspaper in 1983. In the following decade she sold most of the family's other business interests, including television stations, but retained ownership of radio station KPRC-AM in Houston. She died at her home in Houston several months after suffering a stroke.

• For biographical information, see "Hobby, Oveta Culp," in *Current Biography Yearbook* for 1942, 1953, and 1995. See also *Who Was Who in America*, vol. 11 (1993–1996). In addition, see "Mrs. Oveta Culp Hobby: The First Secretary of the Department of Health, Education and Welfare," the cover story in the *Journal of the American Pharmaceutical Association*, Apr. 1953. An obituary appears in the *New York Times*, 17 Aug. 1995.

ANN T. KEENE

HOFFMAN, Al (25 Sept. 1902–21 July 1960), songwriter, was born Alexander Hoffman in Derevno, near

Minsk, Russia, one of two sons of L. (possibly Louis) Hoffman, a cantor, and his wife, whose name has not survived. In 1908 the family emigrated to Seattle, where Hoffman attended Franklin High School, graduating in 1921. In his school annual, Hoffman listed his future as popular song composer and his motto as "Music washes away from the soul the dust of every day life."

In 1928, after leading his own band in Seattle, Hoffman moved to New York, where he played drums while pursuing his Tin Pan Alley dream. He first published songs in 1929 and in 1931 had his first hit, "Heartaches," written in collaboration with John Klemmer. Recorded by Ted Weems's orchestra in a rapid-fire manner that emphasized its novelty qualities (one entire chorus was whistled by Elmo Tanner), the number was rediscovered in 1947 and became a major hit all over again. In 1930 Hoffman became a member of ASCAP. Although Hoffman can be seen as the prototypical Tin Pan Alley writer, always the collaborator, always seeking the contemporary angle that would make a tune or lyric salable (and often forgettable), the course of his career was anything but typical. Popular tunes such as "Auf Wiedersehn, My Dear" (1932), "I Saw Stars" (he said the idea for this one had come to him when a dentist struck a nerve) and "Little Man, You've Had a Busy Day" (both 1934) preceded Hoffman's summoning by the Gaumont British studio in 1934.

Spurred by the success of American musicals in Britain, Gaumont planned a series of big-budget films that could compete with Hollywood's on their own terms. Although the singing, acting, and dancing talent of these musicals was British, the songs were almost exclusively American. Between 1934 and 1937 Gaumont made two successful series, one starring Jessie Matthews, the other starring Jack Buchanan. The songs for all but one of these films (Mack Gordon and Harry Revel wrote that one) were co-written by Hoffman with three fellow Americans. Al Goodhart was Hoffman's main collaborator, sometimes joined by Maurice Sigler and sometimes by Sammy Lerner. What made the songs remarkable was how the writers tailored the songs not only to British sensibilities but also to the stars' personalities. "Everything's in Rhythm with My Heart," emphasizing Matthews's poignant brightness, was for the rest of her career a signature tune. "I'm in a Dancing Mood" perfectly suited Buchanan's diffident smoothness and likewise became identified with him. The comic "Everything Stops for Tea" was a wry glance at a British institution that only an American perspective could achieve. Unfortunately, the films and their music were so successfully British that they had no future in the U.S.

In 1935, while in Britain, Hoffman, who was a clear-voiced singer, recorded several songs—though none of his own—with the Lew Stone Orchestra, at the time probably Britain's outstanding dance band. In 1936 and 1937 Hoffman and his collaborators wrote the scores for three London theatrical musicals. The British composer Vivian Ellis, whose music was

featured in one of them, was not pleased by the Americans' habit of "selling" their songs at the piano.

Hoffman married Nancy Kronberg in 1936; they had no children and remained married until Hoffman's death. Back in the United States, Hoffman began to divide his time between Tin Pan Alley and Hollywood, where he wrote film songs for Donald O'Connor, Peggy Ryan, and, on one occasion, Judy Garland and Freddie Bartholomew. He collaborated frequently with Jerry Livingston, producing "The Story of a Starry Night" (1942, melody borrowed from Tchaikovsky), "Mairzy Doats" (1944), most of the score of Walt Disney's *Cinderella* (1950, including the Academy Award-nominated song "Bibbidi-Bobbidi-Boo"), and some of the songs from Disney's *Alice in Wonderland* (1950).

Both "Mairzy Doats" (i.e., "Mares eat oats") and "Bibbidi-Bobbidi-Boo" (possibly an expansion of a long-remembered Russian song for children) illustrate a particular strength of Hoffman's: the creation of fanciful, often meaningless phrases. According to his nephew Jeff Kane, Hoffman, having thought up a catchy title, liked to compose in pajamas and slippers, "pacing, chain-smoking, and reciting nonsense words and silly sounds, testing them for rhythm." Other notable Hoffman ventures into nonsense included "Gilly Gilly Ossenfeffer Katzenelenbogen by the Sea" and "Chi-Baba, Chi-Baba Chihuahua," both major hits during the 1950s.

"Chi-Baba" (inspired, Hoffman claimed, by a radio news report, featuring the lengthy name of an Asian river, half-heard while he was dozing) was one of many Hoffman songs popularized during the 1950s by the television personality Perry Como, who had earlier begun his own singing career with the Weems orchestra. Others included "Papa Loves Mambo," "Hot Diggity," "There's No Tomorrow" (borrowed from "O Sole Mio"), and "If I Knew You Were Comin' I'd've Baked a Cake" (presumably inspired by Hoffman's driving one day into wholesome Oxford, Ohio.) Other hit songs, characterized mainly by their variety and sheer good-natured catchiness, included "I'm Gonna Live till I Die," "I Apologize," "Allegheny Moon," "Takes Two to Tango," "Oh, Oh, I'm Falling in Love Again," and the "Hawaiian Wedding Song." During the final decade of his life, it was a rare month when a song by Al Hoffman was not on the Hit Parade.

Hoffman died of prostate cancer at home in New York. Perhaps the best creator of novelty songs produced in America and a model of unpretentious popular songwriting, he also contributed significantly to the British musical film. And he lived out his high school dreams.

• Al Hoffman's papers, including many unpublished songs, are held by family members. His nephew Jeff Kane, of Nevada City, California, helped with this sketch considerably. Hoffman is listed in such works as Mark White, *You Must Remember This: Popular Songwriters 1900–1980* (1983), and the *ASCAP Directory*. The published obituaries are, in general, not particularly informative.

JAMES ROSS MOORE

HOGAN, Ben (13 Aug. 1912–25 July 1997), professional golfer, was born William Ben Hogan in Stephenville, Texas, the son of Chester Hogan, a blacksmith, and Clara Williams Hogan, a seamstress. When Hogan was nine, his father shot himself, a trauma that may have contributed to his subsequent reputation as a loner. His mother moved the family to Fort Worth after his father's death, and he and his two siblings worked to help her make ends meet. At age twelve he began caddying and developing his skills as a golfer. Three times—in 1930, 1931, and 1934—he tried to make it as a professional golfer and failed. In 1935 he married Valerie Fox, though his mother did not attend the wedding and never got along with his wife. They had no children.

In 1937, just before he exhausted the family's savings in a fourth attempt at the pro tour, he won $285 in the Oakland Open in California, the turning point in his career. He immediately landed a job as a club professional outside New York City and in 1938 won his first tournament in Hershey, Pennsylvania. Much of his success derived from his intensive practice sessions—he is said to have "invented" practice for touring pros. That enabled him to overcome a serious hook and to develop a left-to-right fade that became, along with his unmatched precision shot making, the key to his mastery. He became known as "Hawk" for his intense concentration and expressionless stare while playing, a concentration aided, according to him, by smoking two packs of cigarettes a day all his life. His intensity was exemplified by a characteristic moment in the 1947 Master's. Hogan was paired with his good friend Claude Harmon, who aced the twelfth hole. Hogan sank a birdie putt of his own—and failed to even acknowledge his friend's hole-in-one. On the course, Hogan was easily recognizable because of his slight stature at five feet eight-and-a-half inches and 150 pounds, which was crowned with his trademark flat white linen cap, and the perfection of his swing, which drew more admirers than that of any other player.

He golfed well in 1940, 1941, and 1942, arguably winning his first major in the latter year when he captured the Hale America Open, sponsored by the U.S. Golf Association (USGA) in place of the U.S. Open, which was suspended during the war. Hogan earned a medal identical to his U.S. Open medals, so one could make a good case for this being in effect the 1942 Open. Although he spent three years in the Army Air Forces stationed in Texas, emerging as a captain, he managed to do a lot of golfing. After the war, at age thirty-three, he became the dominant golfer on the pro circuit, winning nine major titles over the next eight years, beginning with the Professional Golfers' Association (PGA) title in 1946. A second PGA title and his first official U.S. Open title followed

in 1948. On 2 February 1949 he was severely injured when a Greyhound bus passing in the fog hit his Cadillac head on; by throwing himself in front of his wife to protect her, he avoided being impaled by the steering column. After his recovery he was never able to walk without pain, and his left shoulder hurt continually. His comeback and triumph in the 1950 U.S. Open at Merion, Pennsylvania, was the most satisfying victory of his career. That triumph inspired Hollywood to make its first golf film, *Follow the Sun* (1951), a syrupy biographical portrait starring Glenn Ford, for which Hogan was a major adviser.

In 1951 he won his first Master's and his third U.S. Open, a legendary triumph at Oakland Hills in Michigan. That course had been made almost impossibly difficult for the tournament, and when Hogan shot a 67 on his final round, arguably the finest round of golf in history, he exulted that he had tamed "the Monster." Two years later his career reached its summit when he became the only golfer ever to win three of the current four "majors" in the same year—the U.S. Open, the Master's, and the British Open. (Bobby Jones had won the U.S. and British Opens and the U.S. and British Amateurs, then considered the four majors, in 1930.) Because of ongoing pain from his accident, he had reduced the number of his tourney appearances, but he won five of the six he entered in 1953. He impressed the Scots that year by winning the only British Open he ever entered; his exploits and his intensity won him the title "the Wee Icemon."

Later in 1953 he started a golf equipment company, and the Ben Hogan line of golf clubs sold well into the 1990s. Though he sold the company to AMF in 1960, he remained as president for many years. His highly regarded instructional book, *Five Lessons: The Modern Fundamentals of Golf* (1957), was a commercial and pedagogical success. After losing the 1955 U.S. Open in a playoff, he cut back his playing drastically, and, despite a last hurrah at the 1967 Master's when he shot a third-round 66, he faded from the scene, finally retiring officially in 1971. He played his last 18-hole round in 1980 and took his last golf swings toward the end of the decade.

Hogan achieved a remarkable record as a golfer. Five times in the 1940s he led the pro circuit in winnings; three times he won the Vardon Trophy for lowest average score; and he earned his first of four PGA Player of the Year awards. He was one of only four twentieth-century golfers, along with Jack Nicklaus, Gary Player, and Gene Sarazen, to win all four Grand Slam titles during their careers. In all, he won nine majors and a total of 63 tournaments, trailing only Sam Snead (81) and Jack Nicklaus (70) for most victories. In 1988 he was named runner-up to Nicklaus as golfer of the century. Hogan died in Fort Worth.

• There have been few significant treatments of Ben Hogan's life. A "coffee table" compilation by Jules Alexander of photographs and articles, *The Hogan Mystique*, appeared in the mid-1990s. Curt Sampson, *Hogan* (1996), is the best biographical source; it provides a detailed account of the golfer's life and corrects some misconceptions. An obituary is in the *New York Times*, 26 July 1997.

JOHN R. M. WILSON

HOLLAND, Josiah Gilbert (24 July 1819–12 Oct. 1881), editor and writer, was born in Belchertown, Massachusetts, the son of Harrison Holland, a hardworking but unsuccessful mechanic and inventor, and Anna Gilbert Holland. The father's jobs took the family to Heath, South Hadley, Granby, and Northampton, and elsewhere in central and western Massachusetts. During his early years, Holland worked in small factories and attended district schools irregularly and Northampton High School briefly, leaving because of illness. While a teenager, he taught school, taught penmanship, and made daguerreotypes. After studying the rudiments of medicine with two physicians in Northampton beginning in 1840, Holland attended the Berkshire Medical College in Pittsfield, graduated in 1844, but was unable in the following three years to develop a practice in Springfield. He married Elizabeth Luna Chapin in 1845; the couple had three children. He tried his hand sporadically at writing and founded a short-lived weekly magazine in 1847. He was a school superintendent briefly in Richmond, Virginia (1848), and then in Vicksburg, Mississippi (1848–1850).

Returning to Springfield in 1850, Holland began a long association with Samuel Bowles, the distinguished editor of the *Springfield Republican*. Holland had already published minor pieces in the *Knickerbocker Magazine* and the *American Whig Review*, but now his literary career began in earnest. While Bowles was business manager of the *Republican*, Holland was its editor and principal writer, and bought into a money-making partnership with Bowles in 1852. Holland wrote moralistic, human-interest essays as letters from "Max Mannering to his sister in the country," contrasting town and rural life. He wrote three huge items in serial form for the *Republican*, all republished as books: *History of Western Massachusetts* (2 vols., 1855); *The Bay-Path: A Tale of New England Colonial Life* (1857), a novel about theological intolerance in seventeenth-century Connecticut; and *Titcomb's Letters to Young People, Single and Married* (1858), which evolved from his Timothy Titcomb newspaper essays on social and domestic morality. In 1857 Holland gave up editing the *Republican*, profitably resold his interest in it to Bowles, but continued contributing items until 1866.

Titcomb's Letters, published by Charles Scribner's "book-house," was such a nationwide success that Holland was soon in demand as a lyceum speaker. Through Scribner, he issued *Bitter-Sweet: A Poem*, a long, popular narrative (1858; 30th ed., 1877); more books of fiction and advice; and a profitable biography of Abraham Lincoln (1866). Holland's most successful book was *Kathrina: Her Life and Mine, in a Poem* (1867). William Dean Howells reviewed it scathingly in the *Atlantic Monthly* (Dec. 1867). Already advo-

cating realism rather than didactic sentimentality in literature, Howells first summarized the plot of *Kathrina*—a lad is led by a beribboned lamb to the "heroine" and religious faith—and then pronounced the work "puerile in conception, destitute of due motive, and crude and inartistic in treatment." Nevertheless, Holland knew how to appeal to genteel readers of his time, and *Kathrina* (50th ed., 1877) outsold everything in its class except Henry Wadsworth Longfellow's *The Song of Hiawatha* (1855); by 1881, ninety-nine thousand copies of *Kathrina* were in print.

Holland went with his family to Europe for two years, beginning in 1868. In Geneva in 1869 he conferred with his friend Roswell Smith, a rich, retired western-land speculator. Scribner had asked Holland to edit his family magazine, *Hours at Home*; Holland declined and, instead, with Smith formulated plans for a new magazine to encourage American art and literature. When they returned home, the two, together with Scribner, founded *Scribner's Monthly*, with stock divided at 40 percent for Scribner, and 30 percent each for Holland and Smith. Holland would edit the magazine, with the assistance of Richard Watson Gilder, editor of *Hours at Home*, while Smith would be business manager and Scribner would provide imprint and title. *Hours at Home* terminated in November 1870, and *Scribner's* began at once. Holland helped with its fine design, readable format, attractive illustrations, and writings by well-known and highly paid authors. He arranged for the following, among others, to publish serial novels in the magazine: Frances Hodgson Burnett, George Washington Cable, Rebecca Harding Davis, Edward Everett Hale, Bret Harte, and Henry James. The best of Holland's short-story writers were Julian Hawthorne, Helen Hunt Jackson, Frank Richard Stockton, and Constance Fenimore Woolson. Holland also accepted works by good essayists, notably John Burroughs, John Muir, and Charles Dudley Warner, whereas the poetry he selected was often sentimental, didactic, and hence ephemeral.

Holland serialized three of his own novels in *Scribner's*, all reissued in book form. *Arthur Bonnicastle* (1873) is about a New England lad, partly based on Holland himself, who goes to Yale College and though tempted in New York City remains acceptably decent. *Sevenoaks: A Story of To-day* (1875), Holland's best work, features a gilded-age mill owner whose ruthless greed leads to total ruin. *Nicholas Minturn: A Study in a Story* (1877) is a realistic narrative of a wealthy young man who admirably attempts social and economic reforms. By 1878 Holland's health, never robust, had deteriorated. His poetry, now virtually forgotten, was assembled in book form in 1879. He died suddenly in New York City of heart disease.

Holland is a typical example of the self-made nineteenth-century man of letters. He knew what his reading public wanted, and he provided it in preachy prose and didactic verse. On occasion, aspects of his fiction rise almost to the level of that of Charles Dickens, whom he admired and emulated. As an editor, Holland sought out the best, and usually safest, authors. He lived an admirably moral life, of the sort he advised others, by word and example, to lead.

• Most of Holland's scattered papers are at Harvard University, the Library of Congress, Yale University, the University of Virginia, Columbia University, the Pierpont Morgan Library of New York City, the Henry E. Huntington Library, the American Antiquarian Society in Worcester, Massachusetts, and Cornell University. Holland's works are listed in Jacob Blanck, comp., *Bibliography of American Literature*, vol. 4 (1963), pp. 204–18. Biographical material concerning Holland is in "Josiah Gilbert Holland," *Century Magazine* 23 (Dec. 1881): 160–67; Robert Underwood Johnson, *Remembered Yesterdays* (1923); and H. M. Plunkett, *Josiah Gilbert Holland* (1894). Richard Hooker, *The Story of an Independent Newspaper* (1924), and Stephen G. Weisner, *Embattled Editor: The Life of Samuel Bowles* (1986), discuss Holland's admirable relationship with Bowles. Frank Luther Mott, *A History of American Magazines: 1865–1885* (1957), and Herbert F. Smith, *Richard Watson Gilder* (1970), evaluate Holland's work as an editor of *Scribner's Monthly*. Mott says Holland "should be named in any list of the half-dozen greatest American magazine editors"; Smith, however, praises Gilder at Holland's expense and calls Holland didactic and prudish. The most laudatory discussion, brief though it is, of Holland's novels is Arthur Hobson Quinn, *American Fiction: An Historical and Critical Survey* (1936). In his *Cavalcade of the American Novel* (1952), Edward Wagenknecht calls Holland's best novels "still extremely readable" and praises their Dickensian "humor, . . . methods of characterization, and . . . themes, and most of all . . . humanitarianism." Robert J. Scholnick, *Edmund Clarence Stedman* (1977), contrasts Stedman, a comparatively liberal critic and editor, and Holland, who was well known for branding such poets as Lord Byron, Edgar Allan Poe, Algernon Swinburne, and Walt Whitman as nasty. In "Our Garnered Names," *Scribner's Monthly*, (Oct. 1878): 895–96, Holland makes his likes and dislikes abundantly clear. Obituaries are in the *New York Tribune* and the *Springfield Republican*, both 13 Oct. 1881.

ROBERT L. GALE

HOLMES, William Henry (1 Dec. 1846–20 Apr. 1933), artist, scientist, and administrator, was born on a farm near Short Creek in southeastern Ohio, the youngest of three sons of Joseph Holmes and Mary Heberling Holmes. In 1856 Holmes's mother died and his grandparents, John and Mary Heberling, raised him in nearby Georgetown until 1860, when his father married Sarah I. Moore. At eighteen, Holmes entered McNeely Normal School to prepare for a teaching career. While excelling in drawing, geography, and natural history and immersing himself in the student life of McNeely, Holmes taught temporarily in the Harrison County schools. In 1870 he was asked to join the McNeely faculty to teach art and science. Art was Holmes's real passion, however; not teaching. Restless, he decided to go to the nation's capital between terms to study under Theodore Kaufmann. When not in the studio, Holmes was at the Smithsonian Institution drawing birds and, perhaps, also drawing attention to himself. He was discovered there by a Costa Rican ornithologist, José Zeledon, and hired on the spot as one of the Smithsonian's contract illustrators.

Holmes liked his new work but learned that there was a difference between art and illustration when Assistant Secretary Spencer F. Baird looked at one of Holmes's birds and then asked what species it was.

In 1872 Holmes's talent took him to the newly designated Yellowstone National Park as an artist and geologist participating in Ferdinand V. Hayden's famous survey of the western territories. At the Lower Falls of the Yellowstone, he compared the magnificent scene before him with his memory of Thomas Moran's great (and recently unveiled) oil painting *The Grand Cañon of the Yellowstone*. (Moran had been on Hayden's survey team the previous year.) Thereafter, Holmes strove to realize the ideal of being faithful to nature and true to art.

Beginning in 1873, Hayden's survey undertook the mapping of the Colorado Rockies. From mountain station to drafting table, Holmes was intimately involved in this project and deserves much of the credit for the aesthetic brilliance of the cartographic masterpiece that resulted, the *Geological and Geographical Atlas of Colorado* (1877). While in the Four Corners region, Holmes discovered a new mountain type, the laccolith (a bulge in the earth's surface produced by the intrusion of igneous matter) and applied the geological theory of uniformitarianism to archaeology, leading to the still accepted view that the cliff dwellings of Mesa Verde were built by ancestors of the contemporary Pueblo peoples. Holmes returned to Yellowstone in 1878 and found evidence there of past glaciation. Later that year, with John W. Powell and Clarence E. Dutton, Holmes was a founding member of the Cosmos Club of Washington; he served as its president in 1907.

In 1879 Congress replaced the great field survey teams that charted the West with two permanent agencies based in Washington, D.C., the U.S. Geological Survey (USGS) and the Bureau of American Ethnology (BAE). During this bureaucratic transformation, Holmes left for Europe to study museum organization and exhibition. He also resumed his formal art training in Munich under the American Frank Duveneck. In 1880 he went west again, this time with the new USGS. Through powerful line drawings for Dutton's *Tertiary History of the Grand Cañon District, with Atlas* (1882), Holmes portrayed the Grand Canyon of the Colorado as a complete geological and topographical ensemble. Now, feeling secure in his profession, Holmes married Kate Clifton Osgood, an artist, in 1883; they had two sons, Osgood and William.

Despite Holmes's own unrivaled success in synthesizing documentation and embellishment, in 1884, as head of the USGS's division of illustrations, he instituted a new set of principles for scientific illustration. From now on, government illustrators were to report—in visual form—scientific facts and concepts, not create artistic visions. Holmes found an outlet for his own purely artistic impulses in the local Washington art scene, where he distinguished himself as a watercolorist of genteel themes. With regard to public displays of scientific information, Holmes similarly stressed education over entertainment, whether for the Smithsonian's museums in Washington or its exhibits at numerous international fairs, including the famous World's Columbian Exposition in 1893. Still, Holmes's art was evident in his imaginative arrangements of life-size models of Native Americans in recreated culture areas, a display concept that proved very popular and influential.

As a curator for the Smithsonian's National Museum, Holmes became concerned, if not obsessed, about the growing traffic in fake or mistakenly identified artifacts, especially those represented as crude stone implements dating back to a supposed American Paleolithic age. In 1889 Holmes went to work full time at the BAE on the antiquity problem, or "antiquity phantom," as he once called it. With the government's resources fully at his disposal, he persuasively argued in numerous presentations and articles that what the untrained eye saw as finished Old-Stone-Age tools were, in fact, nothing more than the rejects of relatively recent Native American toolmakers. It was not until 1926—with Jesse D. Figgins's carefully documented discovery near Folsom, New Mexico, of fluted points tightly wedged between the ribs of an extinct bison—that such a claim finally met Holmes's exacting tests of verification, an event that revolutionized the study of pre-Columbian America.

Holmes's contributions to American archaeology did not end here. His reductionist idea that primitive art evolved by "imperceptible steps," beginning with instinct, served as the basis for his works that became classics in the literature: *Origin and Development of Form and Ornament in Ceramic Art* (1886); "Natural History of Flaked Stone Implements" (1894); *Archaeological Studies among the Ancient Cities of Mexico* (1895–1897), a study of aboriginal architecture with panoramic foldouts; *Stone Implements of the Potomac-Chesapeake Tidewater Province* (1897); and *Aboriginal Pottery of the Eastern United States* (1903).

After an unhappy tenure as a curator with the Field Columbian Museum and as a professor at the University of Chicago from 1893 to 1897, Holmes returned to the National Museum. In 1902 he reluctantly succeeded Powell as chief of the BAE, which he headed until 1909. He brought Powell's maverick agency back to the fold of the Smithsonian Institution, before gladly returning to the National Museum as head curator of anthropology. During the First World War, Holmes served on the National Research Council, and in the hyperpatriotic, divisive aftermath of the war he used his influence within the American Anthropological Association to censure Franz Boas for publicly criticizing President Woodrow Wilson. In 1920 he left anthropology to direct the Smithsonian Institution's National Gallery of Art (now the National Museum of American Art). Holmes believed that art had degenerated since the days of Frederick Church, Sanford Robinson Gifford, and Thomas Moran and looked forward to the passing of modernism. He retired in 1932 at eighty-six and died the next year in the comfort of the home of his son William, in Royal Oak, Michigan.

• Kevin J. Fernlund, *William Henry Holmes and the Rediscovery of the American West* (2000), is a full-length biography. Shorter biographical treatments are Clifford M. Nelson, "William H. Holmes: Beginning a Career in Art and Science," *Records of the Columbia Historical Society* 50 (1980): 252–78; the chapter on Holmes in Joan Mark, *Four Anthropologists: An American Science in Its Early Years* (1980); John R. Swanton, "Biographical Memoir of William Henry Holmes, 1846–1933," *National Academy of Sciences Biographical Memoirs* 17 (1937): 223–52; and a sketch (probably written by Holmes himself), "Brief Biography of William Henry Holmes: Artist, Geologist, Archaeologist and Art Gallery Director, 1846–19—," *Ohio Archaeological and Historical Society Publications* 36 (1927): 493–527. David J. Meltzer and Robert C. Dunnell, eds., *The Archaeology of William Henry Holmes* (1992), which contains four reprints of Holmes's archaeological classics, also provides a short biographical overview and analysis. Insightful profiles may be found in Stephen J. Pyne, *How the Canyon Became Grand: A Short History* (1998); William H. Goetzmann, *Exploration and Empire: The Explorer and the Scientist in the Winning of the American West* (1966); and Wallace Stegner, *Beyond the Hundredth Meridian: John Wesley Powell and the Second Opening of the West* (1954). Curtis M. Hinsley, Jr., *Savages and Scientists: The Smithsonian Institution and the Development of American Anthropology, 1846–1910* (1981) analyzes Holmes's administration of the Bureau of American Ethnology, and Mary C. Rabbitt, *Minerals, Lands, and Geology for the Common Defence and General Welfare*, vol. 1: *Before 1879* (1979) and vol. 2: *1879–1904* (1980), evaluates Holmes's work as an artist and geologist in the federal surveys.

KEVIN J. FERNLUND

HORST, Horst P. (14 Aug. 1906–18 Nov. 1999), photographer, was born Horst Paul Bohrmann in the eastern German town of Weissenfels-an-der-Saale, the son of Max Bohrmann and Klara Schonbrodt Bohrmann, owners of a hardware store. Horst rarely used his surname during the early part of his career and dropped it formally in 1943, after he became a United States citizen, in order to avoid questions of a possible relationship to Nazi official Martin Bormann. He had a strained relationship with his parents, who favored their older son, Heinz. His mother was perhaps mentally unbalanced; on one occasion she arrived at the dinner table carrying a revolver and announced to her family, "I am going to shoot you all." Her sons dived under the table, and she was disarmed by her husband without shots being fired. Following that incident she was committed to a sanitarium for a period of time. Horst himself, because of a mild case of tuberculosis, spent a year in a sanitarium in Switzerland in the early 1920s, which effectively ended his formal public school education.

Growing up under the strict discipline and watchful eyes of parents and maternal grandparents (whom Horst described as "God-fearing Protestants"), Horst enjoyed his visits during school vacations with an aunt on his father's side, Grete Bohrmann, who lived in the city of Weimar. At her house a variety of artists congregated, some of whom were connected to the Bauhaus, a school of modernist art and architecture founded in Weimar in 1918. It was at her house that Horst developed his lifelong interest in the arts and, especially, with people in the arts.

For a year after leaving the sanitarium, Horst worked in an import-export firm in Hamburg, filing correspondence, orders, and receipts. He then enrolled in the Hamburg Kunstgewerbeschule, or School of the Applied Arts, where he hoped to regain contact with Bauhaus artists. That connection began in earnest when the noted architect Charles Edouard Jeanneret, known as Le Corbusier, invited him to apprentice at his studio in Paris. Horst moved to Paris in 1930, supported by an allowance from his parents. At Le Corbusier's studio Horst met painter Amedee Ozenfant, and in a Parisian cafe he met George Hoyningen-Huene, a Russian émigré and photographer for Vogue magazine. Horst occasionally served as a model for Huene, and through Huene he met fashion photographer Cecil Beaton and Mehemed Agha, art director at *Vogue*. In 1931, Agha invited Horst to the *Vogue* studio in Paris to learn how to photograph fashion models. At long last, Horst found something he wanted to do, a means of meeting artists, and an introduction to high society.

After a brief period of freelancing, Horst was hired by *Vogue*, for whom he continued to work off and on for the next sixty years. At first, Horst's work echoed the cool classicism of Huene, with plain or geometric backgrounds, artificial lights that emphasized chiaroscuro, and an occasional reference to ancient Greek or Roman sculpture. Within a few years, however, Horst developed a more personal and decorative style, complete with fantasy elements and a variety of background fabrics with patterns of undulating lines. His most famous picture was of a model wearing an unraveling Mainbocher corset; seen from behind, the model's body angles this way and that, focusing the viewer's attention on her and the abstract form she presents, while her corset appears to be coming undone on its own. This photograph was his last before leaving Paris for the United States in the summer of 1939, and he later described the picture as summing up his feelings about the period between the two world wars: "We all felt that war was coming. Too much armaments, too much talk. And you knew that whatever happened, life would be completely different after. . . . This photograph is peculiar—for me, it is the essence of that moment" (quoted in Lawford, p. 185).

Over the years, Horst met and made portraits of a variety of writers, artists, performers, and members of the elegant society, including Coco Chanel, Jean Cocteau, Noël Coward, Salvador Dali, Bette Davis, Marlene Dietrich, Janet Flanner, Katharine Hepburn, Cole Porter, Andy Warhol, and the Duke and Duchess of Windsor (Wallis Warfield Simpson). In 1935, after the temperamental Huene departed in a huff at imagined slights, Horst became the leading photographer for Vogue. The 1930s comprised the high point in his career in photography. His photographs, rooted in surrealism, emphasized mystery and odd combinations of people and objects, but they also added allure and glamor to his subjects. In later years, magazine editors sought a less studied, more natural look, and Horst fell out of favor. Yet he continued to work for magazines and private clients, including clothing designers Bill Blass and Calvin Klein.

In 1938 Horst met Valentine Lawford, who became his longtime companion and biographer. Horst was also survived by an adopted son, Richard J. Horst, who acted as his manager and archivist. Horst's work has been exhibited at art galleries that feature photography, including Sonnabend Gallery in New York City and Galerie Contretype in Brussels, Belgium. In 1984, the New York-based International Center for Photography organized a retrospective of his work, which traveled to Montreal, London, Florence, and Venice. He died at his home in Palm Beach Gardens, Florida.

• Publications by and about Horst include Horst P. Horst and Barbara Plumb, *Horst: Interiors* (1993); a fifty-minute documentary from Checkerboard Films, *Portrait of an Artist: Horst P. Horst—60 Years and Still in Vogue* (1993); Valentine Lawford, *Horst: His Works and His World* (1984); and Richard J. Horst and Lothar Schirmer, eds., *Horst: Sixty Years of Photography* (1996). An obituary is in *Art in America*, Jan. 2000, p. 142.

DANIEL GRANT

HORTON, Edward Everett (18 Mar. 1886–29 Sept. 1970), actor, was born in Brooklyn, New York, the son of Edward Everett Horton, Sr., the foreman of the *New York Times* composing room, and Isabella Diack Horton. After graduating from Boys' High School in Brooklyn, he attended classes at the Polytechnic Institute of Brooklyn, at Oberlin College in Ohio, and at Columbia University in New York City, where he studied history and German. He did not receive a degree from any of these institutions. Although his family wanted him to become a teacher, he preferred the theater from his earliest years. He made his acting debut in a Columbia dramatic club as a corseted lady. He was featured in a Newport, Rhode Island, show, which he later said gained him nothing but several cuts from classes, resulting in his expulsion from college. He sang baritone roles in 1907 on Staten Island with the Dempsey Light Opera Company in *The Bohemian Girl* (Michael William Balfe's classic) and *The Mikado* by William Gilbert and Arthur Sullivan. In 1908 Horton garnered a walk-on part in the production of Jules Eckert Goodman's *The Man Who Stood Still* by the Louis Mann troupe, in which he subsequently acted for the next three years and for which he also served as stage manager.

Horton developed his acting skills in Philadelphia with the Chestnut Street Stock Company and Beulah Jay's Little Theater, with a stock company in Portland, Maine, and for six years with the Wilkes Stock Company in Los Angeles. He formed his own stock company there, managed the Majestic Theater with his brother, George Horton, and combined acting before live audiences and making silent movies. Earning as much as a thousand dollars a week, he played the lead in Booth Tarkington's *Clarence* (1923) and the lead in Benn Wolfe Levy's four-character farce, *Springtime for Henry* (1932), among other successes. Over the decades, he tirelessly played Henry Dewlap, Levy's philandering bachelor, at least 3,000 times across the United States and in Canada and Cuba. Its profits enabled him to purchase a summer home in the Adirondacks on Lake George, near Glens Falls, New York. He was also featured in the following silent movies, among others: *A Front Page Story* (1922), *Ruggles of Red Gap* (1923), *Beggar on Horseback* (1925), and *La Bohème* (1926). Although most were financial failures, Horton's value steadily rose; and when sound was introduced, his well-modulated voice proved to be immediately attractive. He played the leading role in *The Terror* (1928), billed as the first "titleless" all-talking film. His performance earned him a long-term Hollywood contract.

Horton was almost never a star; nor was he, however, ever out of work. Among the most memorable movies in which he appeared in the 1930s were *Trouble in Paradise* (1932), *Design for Living* (1933), *The Merry Widow* (1934, with Jeanette MacDonald and Maurice Chevalier), and *Bluebeard's Eighth Wife* (1938), four of the many fast-paced comedies directed by Ernst Lubitsch; *The Gay Divorcée* (1934), *Top Hat* (1935), and *Shall We Dance?* (1937), three of several Fred Astaire–Ginger Rogers musicals, with Horton as Astaire's bustling sidekick; *Alice in Wonderland* (1933), as the whimsical Mad Hatter; and *Lost Horizon* (1937), directed by Frank Capra, as a crooked, befuddled anthropologist providing comic relief. He was often typecast as a fidgety, jittery, fussy Nervous Nellie Milquetoast, high-strung, exasperated, with a clever grimace and a crowd-pleasing double-take. Acting the incompetent comic, he adopted "Oh, dear, oh dear" as a tag line, mild but uttered as though the sky were falling. Through the 1930s Horton earned as much as $80,000 to $100,000 annually. Never marrying, he bought property at Encino, California, christened it "Belleigh Acres," repeatedly expanded the home there for himself and his mother, built adjacent houses for his brother (his business manager) and his sister and their families, and added a community barn, a ten-room doghouse, and a swimming pool and lighted tennis court. He spent lavish sums on rare flowers, dogs, and especially antiques (his collection was ultimately valued at $500,000).

In a 1945 interview, Horton offered an explanation for his success: "I have my own little kingdom [in the movies]. I do the scavenger parts no one else wants, and I get well paid for it." His best parts in the 1940s were in *Ziegfeld Girl* (1941), as Florenz Ziegfeld's agent; *Here Comes Mr. Jordan* (1941), as Celestial Messenger 7013, who makes a mess trying to get souls to heaven; *I Married an Angel* (1942), starring Jeanette MacDonald and Nelson Eddy; *The Magnificent Dope* (1942), opposite Henry Fonda; *Arsenic and Old Lace* (1944, directed by Capra), opposite Cary Grant and

Raymond Massey; *Summer Storm* (1944), in which he upstages George Sanders and Linda Darnell as a dissolute Russian aristocrat; and *Down to Earth* (1947), a musical comedy, based on *Here Comes Mr. Jordan*.

As Horton aged, he continued to perform effectively. His final credits include *All My Sons* (1957), *The Story of Mankind* (1957), *Pocketful of Miracles* (1961), *It's a Mad, Mad, Mad, Mad World* (1963), *Sex and the Single Girl* (1964) as a girlie-magazine publisher, *The Perils of Pauline* (1967), and *2000 Years Later* (1969). Beginning in 1950, Horton branched into television work, appearing on at least fifty shows, with Steve Allen, Lucille Ball, Johnny Carson, Jack Paar, and Red Skelton, among others; acting in "Burke's Law," "The Cara Williams Show," "F Troop," and "Holiday Hotel"; and narrating "Fractured Fairy Tales" on the Bullwinkle cartoon show. He also returned to the straw-hat circuit with *Miss Pell Is Missing* (1963) and on New York City stages was featured in *A Funny Thing Happened on the Way to the Forum* (1962) and in a revival of *Carousel* (1965). Seemingly indefatigable, Horton provided the off-screen voice for television commercials and was once the master of ceremonies at a dog show of the Westminster Kennel Club in Madison Square Garden, New York City.

Two weeks after he died of cancer in Encino, his last television appearance, in "The Governor and J.J.," was broadcast. *Cold Turkey*, the final one of the more than 150 movies in which he appeared, was released in 1971. When a friend asked Horton, at a time when he was over eighty, the secret of his longevity, his amusingly indirect answer was this: "Right now I'm on my way to my mother's birthday party." She was his hostess until her death at age 101. In the 1960s, residents of the San Fernando Valley gratefully made him their honorary governor and named his street, on which he alone resided, Edward Everett Horton Lane.

• Ephraim Katz, *The Film Encyclopedia*, 3d ed. (1998), lists films in which Horton appears. David Inman, *The TV Encyclopedia* (1991), lists shows in which Horton was featured. Filmographies having minimal biographical information about Horton include Evelyn Mack Truitt, *Who Was Who on Screen*, 3d ed. (1983); David Quinlan, *The Illustrated Directory of Film Stars* (1981); David Ragan, *Who's Who in Hollywood: The Largest Cast of International Film Personalities Ever Assembled* (1992); Leonard Maltin, ed., *Leonard Maltin's Movie Encyclopedia* (1994); and Martin S. Quigley, *First Century of Film* (1995). Movie books having illustrations featuring Horton include Deems Taylor et al., *A Pictorial History of the Movies* (1943); Benjamin B. Hampton, *History of the American Film Industry from Its Beginnings to 1931* (1970); Tom Shales, *The American Film Heritage* (1972); and Charles Higham, *The Art of the American Film, 1900–1971* (1973). Kyle Crichton, "Comedy—Six Days a Week," *Collier's*, 18 July 1936, pp. 22, 30, discusses Horton's early life, quick success, and lavish home in Encino, California. "The Theatre: Tour," *Time*, 22 July 1940, pp. 62–63, concerns Horton's 1939–1940 revival of *Springtime for Henry*. Sara Hamilton, "Roundup of Characters," pp. 90–91, 290–95 passim, in Richard Griffith, ed., *The Talkies: Articles and Illustrations from Photoplay Magazine 1928–1940* (1971), contains an affectionate personality sketch of Horton. Kevin Brownlow, in *The Parade's Gone By* (1968), quotes comic-actor Reginald Denny's comment that Horton was "a great farceur." Obituaries are in the *New York Times*, 1 Oct. 1970, and *Variety Obituaries 1969–1974* (1988).

ROBERT L. GALE

HOWARD, Robert E. (22 Jan. 1906–11 June 1936), fiction writer, was born Robert Ervin Howard in Peaster, Texas, the only child of Isaac Mordecai Howard, a physician, and Hester Jane Ervin Howard. The first nine years of Howard's life were spent in numerous small Texas towns as his father sought to establish a practice. The Howards moved to Cross Plains, Texas, in 1915; apart from brief periods in San Antonio, Brownwood, and New Orleans, Howard spent virtually his entire life there. Unable to start formal schooling until he was eight, he was nevertheless addicted to reading and learning. Paralleling his love of learning was a love of the physical, and through intense exercise Howard developed himself until, at nearly six feet, he weighed 200 pounds and was an enthusiastic amateur boxer. He graduated from high school at age seventeen and took bookkeeping courses at nearby Howard Payne College in Brownwood; upon returning to Cross Plains, he lived with his parents and worked at a variety of menial jobs while writing. His first professional sale was "Spear and Fang" (*Weird Tales*, July 1925), a caveman adventure.

From the late 1920s until his death, Howard worked as a professional writer, drawing on dreams, his beliefs in reincarnation and racial memories, his knowledge of Irish history, his conviction of the superiority of the white race, and local culture (Texas, southern, and western) as the basis for his fiction. He counted among his favorite authors Sir Arthur Conan Doyle, Jack London, Mark Twain, Sax Rohmer, Jeffery Farnol, R. W. Chambers, H. Rider Haggard, Ambrose Bierce, Arthur Machen, Edgar Allan Poe, and H. P. Lovecraft. Traces and occasional imitations of all of these writers can be found in Howard's fiction, some of which is crude and unabashedly racist; most is also compulsively readable. In 1930 Howard began to correspond with Lovecraft and other contributors to the magazine *Weird Tales*, including the poet Clark Ashton Smith and the writers August Derleth and E. Hoffmann Price.

Howard's most durable literary creation is undoubtedly the "Conan the Barbarian" series, but his other writings are not without interest. Two of his finest stories are "The Valley of the Worm" (*Weird Tales*, Feb. 1934) and the posthumously published "Pigeons from Hell" (*Weird Tales*, May 1938). The former purports to be the story behind the legend of the dragon slayer; it is grim and powerful, mixing muscular exuberance and Lovecraftian horror to great effect. The latter, based on folktales Howard heard from his maternal grandmother, features zombies and a haunted house, and is remarkably atmospheric.

Several fictional series preceded "Conan," the earliest of which concern Solomon Kane, a sixteenth-century Puritan; unbeatable with a rapier, Kane goes on adventures from England across Europe to Africa, where he acquires the Staff of Solomon from the witch doctor N'Longa, battles vampires and gorillas, and explores strange and forgotten cities. The series began in 1928 and improved as Howard's writing skills developed: the last of the series, "Wings of the Night" (*Weird Tales*, July 1932), describes Kane's attempt at assisting a small African tribe held hostage by a frightful band of harpylike creatures. Kane fails to save his new friends, and his vengeance is ferocious; the story itself carries a frightening internal conviction.

Following Kane, Howard began a series featuring King Kull, a massive Atlantean who has usurped the throne of Valusia in about 100,000 B.C. Kull is introduced in "The Shadow Kingdom" (*Weird Tales*, Aug. 1929), a story describing his battle against the shape-shifting serpent men who wish to steal his identity and take his throne. Reality itself is questioned in "The Mirrors of Tuzun Thone" (*Weird Tales*, Sept. 1929), which is perhaps the best story to feature Kull.

Obsession with the Picts of Britain led Howard to write stories featuring Bran Mak Morn, a Pict living at the time of the Roman invasion of Britain. The finest Bran story is unquestionably "Worms of the Earth" (*Weird Tales*, Nov. 1932), which describes his vengeance on the governor of a Roman frontier post. Bran Mak Morn never achieved the popularity of Kane, Kull, or Conan, but he remains interesting, a man of honor and compassion forced to fight for his country.

Howard's liveliest work is a series of slapstick westerns narrated by Breckinridge Elkins, an enormous, indestructible, and none-too-intelligent mountain dweller. The narratives tend to follow a pattern in which Elkins, seeking to placate a family member and/or to obtain the favors of an attractive woman, leaves the safety of the mountains and becomes disastrously involved in "civilization," often in the form of the law or bandits. These stories were popular with Howard's contemporaries, and Howard's first book was *A Gent from Bear Creek* (1937), a collection of Elkins adventures rewritten as a novel.

In a 1935 letter to Clark Ashton Smith, Howard claimed that Conan—who starts as Conan the Barbarian and becomes Conan the Conqueror and finally Conan the King—effectively emerged as a complete creation and was "the most realistic character I ever evolved . . . a combination of a number of men I have known . . . [with] the dominant characteristics of various prizefighters, gunmen, bootleggers, oil field bullies, gamblers, and honest workmen I had come in contact with." Conan, who is literally born on a battlefield, grows to massive manhood in a preglacial Europe of about 10,000 B.C. He is variously a thief, a soldier, a bravo, and a pirate, before emerging as a military leader and strangling the king to become ruler, but his reign is uneasy, as foes and forces always seek his life and throne.

Conan's first appearance is in "The Phoenix on the Sword" (*Weird Tales*, Dec. 1932), a rewritten Kull story involving supernatural vengeance; the character appears in seventeen additional stories published during Howard's lifetime. Among the best are "Queen of the Black Coast" (*Weird Tales*, May 1934), the only Conan story based on something other than hatred, greed, or lust; "Shadows in Zamboula" (*Weird Tales*, Nov. 1935), which describes Conan's adventures in a proto–Middle Eastern town that is terrorized by black cannibalistic slaves and dominated by a lethal priest; and "A Witch Shall Be Born" (*Weird Tales*, Dec. 1934), in which a crucified Conan seizes the neck of an attacking vulture with his teeth and bites it to death. "The Hour of the Dragon" (*Weird Tales*, Dec. 1935– Apr. 1936; book title: *Conan the Conqueror*), Howard's only novel featuring Conan, has a mythic theme, the Return of the King. The last story to feature Conan, the posthumously published "Red Nails" (*Weird Tales*, July–Oct. 1936), describes the folly of living for hatred and vengeance.

E. Hoffmann Price recalled Howard as a highly intelligent and kindly yet mercurial individual who carried a gun, held grudges against possibly imagined slights, and feared retaliation from nonexistent enemies hiding in scrub-oak thickets. Price's recollections also reveal that Howard's father was a domineering personality and that Howard was close to his mother. As Howard's financial success grew, his home life deteriorated to the point where his overprotective and physically debilitated mother would refuse to tell him when women had called. Although he was earning a good living as a writer, could well afford his own dwelling, and had the potential of a romantic future with Novalyne Price Ellis, a schoolteacher, Howard refused to leave his parents' house and spoke of committing suicide when his mother died. Concerned friends quietly confiscated his firearms, but it made no difference. On 11 June 1936, when Howard learned that his hospitalized mother had entered a terminal coma, he shot himself to death in his car. His mother survived him by less than one day; their funeral services occurred simultaneously.

In the decades following Howard's death his published stories were exhumed from the pulps and reprinted by small specialty presses, in particular Arkham House and Gnome Press; the stories were reissued in various formats, including comic books, mass-market paperbacks, and big-budget motion pictures. A significant industry has grown from his writings, and the number of sequels, pastiches, and adaptations involving his characters and story lines is enormous. Cross Plains, Texas, turned the Howard family home into a museum. Directly or indirectly, Howard remains an influence on virtually all writers of heroic fantasy. His fictional creations, in particular the massive Conan the Barbarian, revitalized American fantasy and are directly responsible for the popular literary genre known variously as "sword and sorcery" and "heroic fantasy."

• Howard's surviving letters have been collected in *Selected Letters 1923–1930* and *Selected Letters 1931–1936*. The most comprehensive bibliography of Howard remains Glenn Lord's *The Last Celt: A Bio-Bibliography of Robert Ervin Howard* (1976). Published texts by Howard remain problematic. Paperback editions of his works, in particular those published by Centaur Press, have been heavily edited to remove potentially offensive language and attitudes, and subsequent publishers unwittingly have used these texts. Others have attempted to publish Howard's texts as he wrote them, with varying success; even the supposedly correct 1995 Baen Books edition of *Solomon Kane* is not without error. This problem is documented in Steve Trout, "The Expurgated Solomon Kane," in *James Van Hise Presents the Fantastic Worlds of Robert E. Howard*, ed. James Van Hise (1997). The most comprehensive biography of Howard is L. Sprague de Camp, Catherine Crook de Camp, and Jane Whittington Griffin, *Dark Valley Destiny: The Life of Robert E. Howard* (1983), an expansion of L. Sprague de Camp's *The Miscast Barbarian: A Biography of Robert E. Howard (1906–1936)* (1975), which was later reprinted in *Literary Swordsmen and Sorcerors: The Makers of Heroic Fantasy* (1976), by the same author. Although he provides an enormous amount of factual data, de Camp's conclusions are occasionally suspect. Howard's love interest, Novalyne Price Ellis, provides her account of Howard in *One Who Walked Alone* (1986). Serious criticism of Howard began with de Camp's *The Miscast Barbarian* and Robert Weinberg's *The Annotated Guide to Robert E. Howard's Sword and Sorcery* (1976) and continued with Darrell Schweitzer's *Conan's World and Robert E. Howard* (1978). Weinberg described the "Conan" series in *Survey of Modern Fantasy Literature*, ed. Frank N. Magill (1983); see also *Dark Barbarian: The Writings of Robert E. Howard, a Critical Anthology*, ed. Don Herron (1984), and the biocritical article by E. F. Bleiler in *Supernatural Fiction Writers: Fantasy and Horror*, ed. Bleiler (1985).

RICHARD BLEILER

HRUSKA, Roman (16 Aug. 1904–25 Apr. 1999), attorney, representative, and U.S. senator, was born Roman Lee Hruska in David City, Butler County, Nebraska, the son of Joseph C. Hruska, a schoolteacher, and Caroline L. Dvorak Hruska. He attended local public schools before entering the University of Omaha (now the University of Nebraska–Omaha) where he took a prelaw course. Hruska also studied at the University of Chicago before finally, in 1929, receiving his LL.B. from Creighton University School of Law and passing the state bar. On 24 September 1930 he married Victoria E. Kuncl of Omaha; the couple had three children.

Hruska established a private legal practice in Omaha and became active in local fraternal and civic activities. Politics proving to be an irresistible lure, he served as a delegate to a series of state Republican conventions (1942, 1944, and 1946). In 1944 Hruska gained an appointment to the Douglas County, Nebraska, board of county commissioners. After completing the term that had been vacated by an incumbent, he won reelection to the post in 1946 and again in 1950. Respected by his peers, he chaired the board from 1945 until 1952 and served as president of the Nebraska Association of County Officials (1950–

1951) as well as vice president of the National Association of County Officials (1951–1952). He was elected in 1952 to the U.S. House of Representatives, where he served on the Appropriations Committee for two terms.

In 1954 another vacancy in public office again opened the door for Hruska, this time in the U.S. Senate, when the powerful incumbent Hugh Butler's sudden death a few hours after the election filing deadline threw the state's politics into turmoil. Both major parties scrambled to field candidates; Hruska's selection by the Republicans was based at least partly on the ongoing tradition of choosing a resident of Omaha as one of Nebraska's senators. Easily elected in the fall, Hruska arrived in Washington just in time to vote with a minority of senators who opposed the resolution of censure of Senator Joseph R. McCarthy of Wisconsin for his conduct as a rabid anti-Commnist.

As he had done in the House, Hruska continued to be a loyal supporter of nearly all initiatives put forward by Dwight D. Eisenhower's administration. Reelected in 1958, he served on the District of Columbia, Public Works, Appropriations, and Judiciary committees and quickly gained a reputation as a solid conservative. Consistent with his earlier firm anti-Communism stance, he was a steadfast supporter of the country's Vietnam War effort as well as of Cold War programs such as Radio Free Europe. For many years the ranking Republican on the Judiciary Committee, he sought to keep big business unfettered and used his power to thwart initiatives such as a 1961 investigation into the possible regulation of prescription drug prices. Although he could be counted on to vote for federal farm programs (many of which were of direct benefit to his constituency), he opposed nearly all the new domestic social legislation that emerged during the administrations of John F. Kennedy and Lyndon B. Johnson including Medicare, federal housing programs, and urban aid; he did support, however, the Civil Rights Act of 1964. Disturbed by what he viewed as excessive violence and sexual content within the television and motion picture industries, he sponsored several measures aimed at containing the trend. A major opponent of gun control legislation, Hruska took a leading role in shaping the Omnibus Crime Control and Safe Streets Act of 1968 (effectively deleting a provision that would have prevented mail-order sales of rifles and shotguns) as well as the Omnibus Crime Control Act of 1970.

By the late 1960s Hruska was a leader among Senate conservatives, having earned a 100 percent rating from the conservative Americans for Constitutional Action group. He had also earned the appreciation of President Richard Nixon, who while campaigning for Hruska's reelection in 1970 referred to him as "Mr. Law Enforcement." Earlier that year, Hruska had gained national notoriety for his dogged support of Clement Haynsworth and G. Harrold Carswell, two conservative southern Supreme Court nominees who ran into stiff opposition during their Senate conformation hearings. Angered by the lack of liberal support for the two men after he had grudgingly supported liberal judicial nominees during the Johnson administration, he lashed out at Carswell's critics, stating that he found Carswell to be "well qualified and well-suited for the post" and "a man of integrity." Responding to charges that Carswell was a mediocre choice at best, Hruska complained (he later said "facetiously"), "Even if he were mediocre there are a lot of mediocre judges and people and lawyers, and they are entitled to a little representation, aren't they? . . . We can't have all Brandeises, Frankfurters, and Cardozos." Despite Hruska's efforts, the Carswell nomination went down to defeat; the more respected Harry Blackmun won the appointment instead.

Even with President Nixon's active backing, Hruska barely won reelection in 1970. During his last term he remained an enthusiastic supporter of defense measures, including the ABM weapons system, and in 1974 he led the fight to restore the death penalty for a variety of federal crimes. He decided against running for reelection in 1976 and spent his remaining years in Omaha, where he died.

Roman Hruska's career was a notable example of the conservative reaction to the political and social upheavals of the mid-twentieth century. Although he is remembered for his defense of a nominee thought to be unworthy by many to sit on the Supreme Court, his positions on such issues as gun control and media content continue to ring true with a sizable portion of the American public.

• Hruska's papers are held at the Nebraska State Historical Society in Lincoln, Nebraska. Secondary material on his life and career is scarce. The best sources are newspaper accounts; see, for example, articles in the *New York Times*, 4 Jan. 1955, and the *Omaha World Herald* Sunday magazine, 10 Mar. 1963. See also the entry on Hruska in *Current Biography*, 1956, and George Douth, *Leaders in Profile: The United States Senate* (1975). Obituaries appear in the *Omaha World Herald*, 26 Apr. 1999, and the *New York Times*, 27 Apr. 1999.

EDWARD L. LACH, JR.

HUDSON, J. L. (17 Oct. 1846–5 July 1912), merchant, was born Joseph Lowthian Hudson in Newcastle-on-Tyne, England, the son of Richard Hudson, a businessman, and Elizabeth Lowthian Hudson. In 1855 he immigrated with his family to Hamilton, Ontario, Canada, where his father—who had previously run a tea and coffee business—entered the employment of the Grand Trunk Railway Company of Canada as a telegrapher. The younger Hudson began his schooling in Hamilton and briefly continued his education when his family again relocated, this time to Grand Rapids, Michigan. At age thirteen he became a telegraph messenger for the Grand Trunk, and he later worked nearby as a grocery store clerk and an orchard laborer.

At fifteen Hudson moved to Pontiac, Michigan, where he took a job as a clerk in a clothing store operated by Christopher R. Mabley. Five years later, in 1866, Hudson's father joined Mabley in a partnership operating a retail clothing store in Ionia, Michigan, and later made his son store manager after buying out Mabley's interest in the operation. In the post–Civil War era the firm of R. Hudson & Son thrived, and the partners soon added a flour mill and timberlands to their holdings. In 1873 the younger Hudson suffered a devastating double blow: not only did his father die, but the financial panic of that year drove the firm (of which he had inherited his father's half share) into bankruptcy. By dint of hard work, he eventually managed to return the firm to prosperity, and in 1877 he turned over its management to his brothers William and James.

That same year (1877), Hudson made what proved to be a wise decision when he relocated to Detroit and entered into another retail operation with his former partner Mabley. By the following year he had been promoted to store manager and was a partner in the firm as well. Eager to strike out on his own, Hudson finally established his own outlet in 1881, when J. L. Hudson, clothier to men and boys, opened for business in the Detroit Opera House Building. As was the case with several of his progressive business contemporaries, Hudson made a practice of clearly marking his merchandise with one low, fixed price and offered a generous return policy. He also made it a practice to maintain adequate supplies (which cut down on the delays associated with back-ordering) and spent considerable time and effort on the recruitment and training of his sales staff. With his business volume on the rise, Hudson added a variety of different departments from time to time, the first of which handled both furniture and floor coverings.

Hudson incorporated his firm as the J. L. Hudson Company in 1891 and, against the advice of many of his contemporaries, moved his store to what was then an outlying area of Detroit. Continued growth in sales soon justified his decision, and the building eventually expanded to eight floors in size. Despite the generally poor business conditions that marked the 1890s, Hudson's firm continued to flourish, and by 1896 he also operated stores in Cleveland, St. Louis, Toledo, and Buffalo.

While heavily involved in his own establishment, of which he was president for the rest of his life, Hudson also served as vice president of the American Vapor Stove Company and the Dime Savings Bank, Detroit. Perhaps his greatest contribution to commercial posterity (besides his own firm) was his contribution of capital in 1909 that resulted in the formation of the Hudson Motor Company, with Hudson as chairman of the board. The company successfully produced automobiles for many years before merging with Nash-Kelvinator to create American Motors in 1954. In addition, Hudson served as a director for a number of businesses, including the American Exchange National Bank, the Detroit City Gas Company, and the Third National Bank of Detroit. When the Third National Bank closed as a result of the depression of

1893, Hudson felt personally responsible for the losses of many depositors (believing that they had placed their money in the bank as a result of his directorship) and repaid the lost funds out of his own pocket at a cost of $265,000.

Like many businessmen of his time, Hudson took a keen interest in civic affairs. He was a founder and director of the Detroit Municipal League (later the Citizens League), a nonpartisan organization dedicated to improving local government and the public interest. His leadership was notable in the acquisition of the State Fair Grounds and in the activities of the Michigan Anti-Saloon League, the Municipal Lighting Commission, the Detroit Playground Association, and the Michigan Fresh Air Society, to name but a few of his civic commitments. An Episcopalian who had never married, Hudson died in Worthing, England.

J. L. Hudson was one of a handful of retail pioneers, a group that included John Wanamaker and Marshall Field, who created a mainstay in nineteenth- and twentieth-century American life: the department store. His most lasting legacy is the retail establishment that continues to bear his name.

• No collection of Hudson's papers has been located, and secondary information on his life and career is scarce. The best source remains Tom Mahoney and Leonard Sloane, *The Great Merchants* (1955; rev. eds., 1966, 1974). An obituary is in the *New York Times*, 6 July 1912.

EDWARD L. LACH, JR.

HUNGERFORD, Bruce (24 Nov. 1922–26 Jan. 1977), concert pianist, was born in Korumburra, Victoria, Australia, the son of Frank Pomeroy Hungerford, secretary of the shire of Korumburra, and Anna Maria Sinclair. He was given the name Bruce as an infant, although he was later christened Leonard Hungerford. In 1958 he formally changed his name to Bruce for personal and professional reasons. Hungerford's mother, a gifted violinist, was his first music teacher, and Daisy Hardwick of Korumburra his first piano teacher.

Hungerford began his serious music study at the age of twelve in Melbourne, Australia, with Roy Shepherd, who had been a pupil of the noted French pianist Alfred Cortot. In 1939, at the age of seventeen, he won a full scholarship to the Melbourne University Conservatorium, where he also won the school's highest awards. After his graduation he made his first important public appearance playing the Liszt E-flat Concerto with the Melbourne Symphony Orchestra.

During the years in which Hungerford was developing musically, he was also absorbed in the study of archaeology, paleontology, photography, and the history of ancient Egypt. Hungerford's lifelong fascination with the pyramids and the Great Sphinx of Egypt began when he was a very young child reading Arthur Mee's *Children's Encyclopedia* (1910). Dr. Alvin Bartlett, the local school district's physician, taught him the rudiments of photography as a teenager and encouraged his enthusiasm for the art. Hungerford's later intense preoccupation with the metaphysical aspects of life, especially the ancient Egyptian doctrine of reincarnation, was also fostered by Bartlett, who became his lifelong friend and mentor.

By 1943 Hungerford had absorbed all that was musically and artistically available to him in his native Australia. After a brief period of study in Sydney with the noted Polish pianist Ignaz Friedman, conductor Eugene Ormandy helped him travel to New York in 1945 for graduate study at the Juilliard School of Music with Ernest Hutchinson, president of the school.

In 1948 Hungerford met and played for the celebrated English pianist Dame Myra Hess, who became an important artistic influence in his life until her death in 1965. She enthusiastically recommended him as a pupil to Carl Friedberg, who had studied with Clara Schumann. After hearing Hungerford play Schubert's *Wanderer* Fantasy at his first lesson, Friedberg said, "There is not the slightest doubt that you will be one of the great pianists." Under Friedberg's tutelage from 1948 to 1955, Hungerford became a master of the German classical piano literature, the music for which Hungerford said he had the strongest personal conviction and to which he wanted to dedicate himself as a musician.

During the 1950s Hungerford furthered his passion for Egypt by studying hieroglyphics with William C. Haynes, curator of Egyptian art at the Metropolitan Museum in New York. At this time he also studied vertebrate paleontology at the Museum of Natural History and dug for dinosaur tracks whenever he could organize an expedition to local shale beds, such as those found in the Connecticut River valley. His home soon became known as "Dinosaur Haven" to colleagues and friends. To these studies Hungerford brought the same prodigious concentration, energy, and intensity that he demonstrated in his study of music.

Hungerford's second Town Hall recital in New York in 1953 brought him acclaim, and his third recital there two years later, which he devoted to the works of Bach, Beethoven, and Brahms, prompted a *New York Herald Tribune* reviewer to write: "One wonders how many pianists of Hungerford's generation can compare with him in perceiving the substance of music like this, and in making it compelling and comprehensible to others. How many indeed in any generation?" Meanwhile, a private law enacted by Congress granted Hungerford permanent residence in the United States without passport, a privilege given in recognition of his cultural contributions to the nation.

In 1957 Hungerford toured his native Australia. In 1958 he embarked on his first European tour and was hailed as "an outstanding pianist of international rank" by the German press. Critics compared him favorably with two of the great German pianists of the first half of the twentieth century. Edwin Fischer and Artur Schnabel, as his approach to the German classical repertoire was one of impressive conviction.

In 1959 Friedelind Wagner, granddaughter of the composer Richard Wagner, invited him to teach a master class in piano and to become pianist-in-residence at the Bayreuth Festival, a position he held from 1959 to 1966. At the invitation of the Wagner family, he recorded in 1960 the complete piano works of Richard Wagner, many of which had never been published and were unknown to the public. During these years in Europe he became a resident of Ambach, Germany, on Lake Starnberg in Bavaria, where he taught a select number of students.

In the midst of his European tours and concerts, Hungerford was invited in 1961 to be the still photographer for the National Broadcasting Company's River Nile Expedition. The mission of the expedition was to photograph the great temples and statues at Abu Simbel and other sites along the Nile, which were about to be dismantled and moved to higher ground to prevent their being submerged by the waters of the new high dam at Aswan. As the riverboat proceeded down the Nile, Hungerford practiced on a silent keyboard, preparing for a performance of Beethoven's Fourth Piano Concerto in Wigmore Hall in London, which would take place only one week after his return from Egypt.

After a triumphant Carnegie Hall concert in New York in 1965, the Vanguard Recording Society invited him to record the thirty-two Beethoven sonatas as well as piano works of Schubert, Brahms and Chopin. To better pursue this project, he returned to the United States and settled in New Rochelle, New York. He ultimately recorded twenty-two of the Beethoven sonatas before his untimely death.

In 1966 and 1967 Hungerford went back to Egypt for further study as the guest of the American University in Cairo, and in the spring of 1967 he gave a series of concerts at the University. In 1968 he was made a fellow of the American Research Center in Egypt, receiving from the Center a grant enabling him to complete a comprehensive study and a dazzling photographic record of the monuments of the Pharaonic civilization. In 1971 he wrote and recorded a series of seventeen half-hour lectures illustrated by 1,100 of his slides, which traced Egyptian history from the earliest known appearance of written language in the Nile Valley around 3100 B.C. to the start of the great decline early in the eleventh century B.C. This audiovisual production, entitled *The Heritage of Ancient Egypt*, was subsequently incorporated into the educational programs of museums and universities throughout the United States.

The following year he accepted an invitation to join the faculty of the Mannes College of Music in New York. In 1974 he became a United States citizen, and for the next three years he led a demanding life concertizing, teaching, recording, and lecturing. On 26 January 1977, his life came to a tragic end when, on his way home to New Rochelle after giving a slide lecture on Egypt at Rockefeller University, he was instantly killed in a head-on automobile collision. Also killed were his mother, a niece of his, and her husband.

Hungerford was an acknowledged master of the piano music of the German classical period. Although he was never accorded celebrity status by the general public, his work has been highly acclaimed by critics, such as Richard Dyer of the *Boston Globe*, who wrote that Hungerford's Beethoven sonata set "might well have stood as the finest contemporary cycle" if completed. He was exceptional among musicians for the breadth and intensity of his extramusical interests. He was deeply spiritual by nature and had a lifelong interest in reincarnation as well as the theories of the American psychic Edgar Cayce. Henry Fischer, curator of Egyptology at the Metropolitan Museum, recalled that Hungerford's love of Egypt was a "longstanding, deep-rooted passion, a passion that makes the interest of many full-time Egyptologists seem pale by comparison. . . . [Hungerford] could impart a feeling of awe in the presence of the great Pharaonic monuments: his voice seemed to echo down the corridors of time with all the vibrant and controlled intensity with which he played a Beethoven sonata." "Hungerford was strongly convinced that music is, in essence, an expression of spirituality," recalled his close friend and former student Thomas Stanback III. "He once told me that he devoted several hours a day to meditation and prayer and that these provided the basis for his life and art."

• Hungerford's personal papers, correspondence, newspaper clippings, and audio tape recordings of recitals and of his lessons with Carl Friedberg are housed at the International Piano Archives at Maryland (IPAM), a facility of the University of Maryland at College Park. Much biographical information on Hungerford can be found in the album notes by Thomas Stanback III that accompany *Bruce Hungerford in Live Performances of Piano Works by Franz Schubert*, a compact disc issued by the International Piano Archives (IPAM 1203). The Association for the Hungerford Archives, Inc. (AHA), composed of former students of Hungerford's, seeks to advance and promote Hungerford's artistic and intellectual legacy through publications and collaborative efforts with other organizations. Hungerford's recordings are available on the Vanguard Classics label (Omega Record Group) and from the International Piano Archives. A copy of *The Heritage of Ancient Egypt* can be found in the Egyptian Department of the Metropolitan Museum in New York, which also holds Hungerford's collection of approximately 12,000 color and black-and-white slides covering the entire period of Pharaonic civilization. Information for this article has been supplied by Paulina Hungerford, Hungerford's sister, and Thomas Stanback III, executive director of the AHA. Obituaries appear in the *News Times* of Westchester County, N.Y., 26 Jan. 1977, and in the *New York Times*, 27 Jan. 1977. See also *Time*, 7 Feb. 1999.

MARGARET MORELAND STATHOS

HUNTER, Jim "Catfish" (8 Apr. 1946–9 Sept. 1999), baseball player, was born James Augustus Hunter on a farm near Hertford, North Carolina, one of eight children of Abbott Hunter, a tenant farmer, and Millie Hunter (maiden name unknown). His older brothers taught him to pitch with control as they threw a ball at a hole in the barn door—the last brother

to hit the hole had to do the chores. The family occasionally traveled to Baltimore to watch major league baseball games, and veteran pitcher Robin Roberts, who was still winning with control and guile, became a model for Hunter. A hunting accident during his senior year at Perquimans High School cost him the little toe of his right foot, but Clyde Kluttz signed him to a contract with the Kansas City Athletics for a $50,000 bonus.

After surgery and a year of recuperation, Hunter debuted in 1965 with the mediocre Athletics, never having pitched in the minor leagues, and compiled an 8–8 record. Meanwhile, the team's flamboyant owner Charles O. "Charlie" Finley had dubbed him "Catfish," creating a story about his boyhood to make him more marketable. Back home, folks called him Jimmy all his life. Though Hunter's record over the next four years never topped .500 (9–11, 13–17, 13–13, 12–15), he was twice named to the American League all-star team. In 1968 the A's moved to Oakland, and on 8 May of that year Hunter pitched the first perfect game in the American League since 1922; after Rich Reese fouled off five 3–2 pitches with two out in the ninth, the budding star struck him out in a dramatic finish.

In Oakland, the young A's rapidly became competitive. They were the best team of the early seventies, and Hunter's records of 18–14, 21–11, 21–7, 21–5, and 25–12 provided a dependable base for the team's exploits. With other stars like Joe Rudi, Reggie Jackson, Bert Campaneris, Sal Bando, Vida Blue, and Rollie Fingers, the colorful green-and-gold-clad "mustache gang" won three straight World Series from 1972 through 1974, a feat no team but the Yankees had ever managed. In seven Series games over those three years Hunter racked up a 4–0 mark. His exploits in 1974 won him the Cy Young Award as baseball's outstanding pitcher.

At that point he carved a special place for himself in baseball history. His 1974 contract with the A's included a provision that in addition to his being paid $50,000 in salary another $50,000 would be paid on a deferred annuity at a North Carolina bank. When Finley, an insurance man, belatedly figured out that he would not be able to deduct the annuity payments, he balked. As the season wound down, the Major League Players Association charged Finley with violating the contract and gave him ten days to make good its terms. When he did not reply, the MLPA proclaimed that Hunter was a free agent, able to sign with any team he wished; an arbitrator confirmed that judgment. For the first time, a major league star at the peak of his career found out what value free-market economics placed on his abilities. Twenty-three of the twenty-four teams bid on him. Finley later claimed Hunter would have rejoined the A's for $200,000, but George Steinbrenner of the Yankees won the prize with a package totaling $3.75 million over five years, with the multiyear contract a first. The new deal easily dwarfed Dick Allen's record $250,000 1974 salary with the White Sox. A year later Andy Messersmith and Dave McNally successfully challenged the reserve clause, and Hunter, an anomaly in 1974, became the precedent for an era of salary escalation that reached $15 million a year for one player, Kevin Brown, by the end of the century.

As a Yankee, Hunter led a new team out of mediocrity. New York had not won a pennant since 1964; with Hunter on the roster, they won in 1976, 1977, and 1978, and captured the World Series in the last two of those seasons, giving Hunter five championship rings in seven years. Hunter's record with the Yankees began with a 23–14 mark in 1975, then 17–15 in 1976, an injury-plagued 9–9 the following year, and a resurgent 12–6 in 1978 after a midseason treatment revived his sore arm. At the young age of thirty-three, he retired at the end of his five-year contract after his sore arm flared up and dropped him to a 2–9 season in 1979. His career totals featured a 224–166 won-lost record and a 3.26 earned run average. But he also gave up 374 home runs, an American League record, which paradoxically derived from his impeccable control. Like his idol Robin Roberts, he kept the ball around the plate, leading to a lot of home runs but also many more harmless flies to center field. His pitching style was characterized by his control (954 walks in 3,449 innings), a middling number of strikeouts (2,012), and a lot of innings pitched; he led the league with 30 complete games in 1975. The six-foot,

190-pound right-hander batted a respectable .226 for his career, including .350 in 1971, when he became the only American League pitcher ever to win 20 games and bat .300 in the same year.

Hunter was very popular with his teammates, who looked up to him as a leader even when he was in his mid-twenties. He had a lively sense of humor, enjoyed practical jokes, and contributed some back-country aphorisms to the game. After losing a game in the 1977 World Series, he noted that "The sun don't shine on the same dog all the time." He did not let his athletic and financial success go to his head, remaining a "regular guy" despite the temptations of fame and fortune. When he retired, he returned to his farm in North Carolina and lived out his days with his wife, the former Helen Overton, the high school sweetheart he married on 9 October 1966, and their three children. In September 1998 he was diagnosed with amyotrophic lateral sclerosis, commonly known as Lou Gehrig's disease. His health deteriorated rapidly after that, and he died of ALS in Hertford at age fifty-three.

• Hunter shared his own story in the folksy *Catfish: My Life in Baseball* (1988), written with Arman Keteyian. Bill James assesses his place in baseball's pantheon in *The Bill James Historical Baseball Abstract* (1985), and Marvin Miller provides insight into his free agency in *A Whole Different Ball Game: The Sport and Business of Baseball* (1991). The *New York Times* of 10 Sept. 1999 has an obituary.

JOHN R. M. WILSON

IWERKS, Ub (24 Mar. 1901–7 July 1971), animator, was born Ubbe Ert Iwwerks in Kansas City, Missouri, the son of Dutch immigrant Ert Ubbe Iwwerks, who worked primarily as a barber and briefly as a photographer, and Laura May Wagoner Iwerks; he shortened his name when he was in his twenties. Iwerks grew up in Kansas City, attending Ashland Grammar School, from which he graduated in 1914. He then attended Northeast High School and worked part time as an apprentice with the Union Bank Note Company. He left school in 1916, without graduating, to work for the company full time and two years later tried his hand at farming in Scotland, Arkansas.

In the fall of 1919, when Iwerks was eighteen years old, he got his start in commercial art with a job at the Pesmen-Rubin Commercial Art Studio in Kansas City doing lettering and airbrush work for fifteen dollars a week. A month later, the studio hired another letterer, a young man of the same age named Walt Disney. The two budding artists quickly became friends as they churned out advertisements for catalogs, department stores, and theaters. When both were laid off following the preholiday rush, they decided to go into business together, establishing Iwerks-Disney Commercial Artists in January 1920. Iwerks excelled in straight drawing and lettering and Disney at cartooning and sales, and their company netted $135 in its first month, more than they had been earning at Pesmen-Rubin.

A month later, Disney landed a lucrative full-time position as a cartoonist for the Kansas City Slide Company. Iwerks tried to keep their business going, but because he lacked his partner's sales ability, the business faltered, and by March Iwerks, too, was working as an artist at Kansas City Slide. The company subsequently moved to a new location, changed its name to the Kansas City Film Ad Company, and became more involved in filmmaking, using animation and live action as media. Both Iwerks and Disney became intrigued with cartoons that moved, and in 1922 Disney left the company in order to form an animation studio of his own and convinced Iwerks to join him. The new studio, called Laugh-o-Gram, produced a series of cartoons based on fairy tales and one experimental film, *Alice's Wonderland*, which featured a live-action girl (played by Virginia Davis) acting with animated animals; but the firm went bankrupt the following year.

Iwerks returned to his old job at the Kansas City Film Ad Company, now renamed United Film Ad Company, for a salary of $50 a week, and Disney left Kansas City to seek his fortune in Hollywood. By 1924 Walt Disney was back in business, setting up contracts to market a series of cartoons featuring his Alice character, and persuaded Iwerks to move west to join his new company, Disney Productions, as an artist-cartoonist. At Disney Productions, Iwerks began working on the Alice cartoons as well as a new character, Oswald the Lucky Rabbit, which Disney eventually lost when his New York distributor, Charles Mintz, appropriated the character and raided Disney's animation staff. Iwerks remained loyal to Disney, signing a new contract in March 1928 and at the same time gaining a 20 percent partnership in the company.

Needing a new character to replace Oswald, Disney began discussing ideas with his staff, leading to his and Iwerks's collaboration on what has become the best-known character in animation history: Mickey Mouse. Iwerks gave Mickey his visual form, Disney his personality. Working single-handedly and at breakneck speed, Iwerks animated the first Mickey Mouse short, *Plane Crazy* (1928), a parody of Charles Lindbergh's exploits, in only two weeks, completing as many as seven hundred drawings in one day. "I've always had a competitive nature," Iwerks observed. "I'd heard that Bill Nolan, who was doing *Krazy Kat*, had done five hundred or six hundred drawings a day, so I really extended myself." In addition to being a fast animator, Iwerks was also skillful. Animator Friz Freleng, who joined the Disney staff in 1927, recalled that at a time when just making a character move was an accomplishment, Iwerks "could move a house in perspective. I thought he was a genius when it came to the mechanics of animation."

Following *Plane Crazy*, Iwerks began work on a second Mickey Mouse short, *Gallopin' Gaucho* (1928), but before it was completed, he began a more important project, the first animated talkie, *Steamboat Willie* (1928), which showcased Cinephone, a sound synchronization process that Iwerks refined; the other Mickey Mouse films were also eventually released with sound. Iwerks continued work on the Mickey series films as well as on Disney's Silly Symphony series, most notably *The Skeleton Dance* (1929), celebrated for its smoothly synchronized movement, and proved himself so indispensable to the studio that his salary exceeded Disney's.

After spending six landmark years with Disney, Iwerks resigned and sold his partnership in the company for $2,920, accepting film distributor Pat Powers's offer to finance him in his own studio at a salary of $300 a week. In 1930 his studio released its first film, *Fiddlesticks*, featuring Flip the Frog, a character that became more anthropomorphized and appealing in later films but remained dependent on the visual gags of silent film at a time when audiences embraced verbal humor. Flip cartoons hit their peak of popularity in 1932; by the following year the series ended, and Iwerks unveiled his replacement character, Willie Whopper, a little boy who tells great lies. Iwerks's third series, ComiColor Cartoons, satirized traditional fairy tales and utilized a Cinecolor process. Iwerks also directed two Porky Pig cartoons for Warner Bros. and worked on the Color Rhapsody series for Columbia.

It became readily apparent, though, that Iwerks's greatest talent in animation was technical rather than narrative. In 1934 he developed a horizontal multiplane camera, which enabled various layers of images to be filmed simultaneously, creating greater visual depth and realism. In 1940 Iwerks returned to Walt Disney Productions as creative technical director for the studio's Production Control Department and, later, the Optical Printing Department, developing photographic effects for *The Reluctant Dragon* (1958) and creating a sophisticated multihead optical printer utilized for the scenes combining animation and live action in *The Three Caballeros* (1944) and, later, *Mary Poppins* (1964) and *Bedknobs and Broomsticks* (1971). His subsequent positions included development engineer, responsible for reducing animation costs; head of the Special Processes and Camera Department; and Studio Technical Research Director. In Iwerks's last position, which he held until his death in 1971, he helped to design animated attractions at Disneyland, including It's a Small World, Pirates of the Caribbean, the Hall of Presidents, and the Haunted Mansion, and was in charge of technical design for new attractions being planned for Walt Disney World.

In 1962 Iwerks produced special effects for Alfred Hitchcock's film *The Birds*, and in 1964 he invented a panoramic camera that produced a continuous image on a screen encircling the camera. He won two Academy Awards: in 1959 for his improved design of the optical printer and in 1964 for his innovations in color traveling matte composite cinematography. He also was awarded the Herbert T. Kalmus Gold Medal Award for technical contributions to filmmaking.

In 1926 Iwerks married Mildred Sarah Henderson; the couple had two sons, Donald and David, both of whom would work as technicians for Walt Disney Productions. Iwerks's hobbies included bowling and collecting mechanical devices, firearms, and classic cameras. He died in Burbank, California. Regarded as animation's forgotten man, Iwerks never attained the fame of his collaborator, Walt Disney, but, like Disney, he helped to establish and refine the fledgling medium of animation.

• The single best article on Iwerks is David R. Smith, "Ub Iwerks, 1901–1971: A Quiet Man Who Left a Deep Mark on Animation," *Funnyworld*, Spring 1972, pp. 33–37+. Other useful sources include Jeff Lenburg, *The Great Cartoon Directors* (1993); Leonard Maltin, *Of Mice and Magic: A History of American Animated Cartoons* (1980; rev. ed., 1987); Bob Thomas, *Walt Disney: An American Original* (1976); Stefan Kanfer, *Serious Business: The Art and Commerce of Animation in America from Betty Boop to Toy Story* (1997); and Jeff Rovin, *The Illustrated Encyclopedia of Cartoon Animals* (1991). A recent biography is Leslie Iwerks and John Kenworthy, *The Hand behind the Mouse* (2001). An obituary is in the *New York Times*, 10 July 1971.

KATHY MERLOCK JACKSON

J

JACOBS, Helen Hull (6 Aug. 1908–2 June 1997), tennis player and author, was born in Globe, Arizona, the daughter of Roland H. Jacobs, a businessman, and Eula Hull Jacobs. Her mother, a Missourian with roots in the South, was a direct descendant of Carter Braxton, a Virginia signer of the Declaration of Independence; her father had come to Globe from the East Coast as a major investor in Miami Copper, the parent company of a huge copper mine that had been discovered several years before Jacobs's birth. She lived in Globe until 1914, when the copper company failed and Roland Jacobs moved his family to San Francisco, where he found work as a newspaper advertising executive.

As a teenager Jacobs began playing tennis with her father; advised by his doctor to take up the game as a healthy pastime, Roland Jacobs had bought his daughter a racket as well. Soon she was beating him, and with his encouragement she began entering local tournaments and winning. In the spring of 1923 a match was arranged for her in nearby Berkeley with Helen Wills (later Helen Wills Moody), a tennis prodigy and former national junior champion who was three years her senior. The man who had set up the match was William Fuller, Wills's coach, and Jacobs did well enough in the encounter to persuade Fuller to take her on as a pupil. At first Jacobs was reluctant to pursue the sport this seriously: until this time, writing had been her major interest, inspired by stories of her paternal grandmother, a minor but successful English author. But when Helen Wills went on to win the U.S. Open at Forest Hills, Long Island, that summer, Helen Jacobs decided that she, too, would become a tennis star—in large part to escape from San Francisco, a city she disliked intensely.

The Jacobses were able to lease a house in Berkeley recently vacated by the Wills family, and their daughter enrolled at the Berkeley Tennis Club and at Berkeley High School. Practicing at the club every afternoon after school, Jacobs improved her game considerably, and she began entering major tournaments. Her rise was meteoric: following in Helen Wills's footsteps, Jacobs won the national junior championship in 1924 and again in 1925. Continuing to combine tennis with her studies, Jacobs entered the University of California at Berkeley in 1926. She joined the American Wightman Cup team a year later and remained with the team for twelve years.

Jacobs left the university in 1929 to concentrate more fully on tennis and three years later won the first of four consecutive U.S. singles champion titles. Teaming with Sarah Palfrey, Jacobs also won the doubles championship in 1932, 1934, and 1935 and with George Lott won the mixed doubles championship in 1934. Jacobs was a finalist at Wimbledon half a dozen times, winning the women's singles championship once, in 1936, and leaving her lasting imprint on the tournament by being the first woman to play there in shorts. Over the course of her tennis career, Jacobs won nine Grand Slam titles, as well as playing in and winning tournaments in Austria, Egypt, Greece, and Switzerland. From 1928 through 1939 she was ranked among the top ten players in the world, and she headed the list in 1936.

Throughout this time, Jacobs was inevitably compared to her fellow Californian Helen Wills. But she was always in her slightly older rival's shadow. Wills, later known as Helen Wills Moody following her marriage, was a far more skillful player, setting records that remained unchallenged for decades. In eleven matches with Jacobs, Wills won all but one—the well-publicized U.S. Open championship at Forest Hills in 1933, in which she defaulted to Jacobs, alleging a back injury. Wills was also celebrated as a more graceful player, and she intrigued spectators with her trademark calm and aloofness. But the more outgoing and gracious Jacobs commanded a large and loyal following as the frequent runner-up who always smiled when she lost and never betrayed a grudge.

During World War II Jacobs withdrew from tennis to serve as an intelligence officer with the U.S. Navy in Washington, D.C., preparing for her duties by attending classes at the College of William and Mary in Williamsburg, Virginia, in 1942 and becoming a member of the women's naval unit known as the WAVES. After the war ended, she became a member of the naval reserves, still playing tennis occasionally and also working as a sportswear designer in New York City, where she had settled. She returned to active duty with the navy in 1950, during the Korean War, serving once again in Washington. After that war ended three years later she rejoined the reserves, retiring from the navy in 1968 with the rank of commander. By this time Jacobs had become well established in the career she had chosen for herself as a young girl: writing.

Jacobs had begun publishing short stories with the McClure Syndicate in the late 1920s. Her first book, a nonfiction work called *Modern Tennis*, appeared in 1932. A manual, *Improve Your Tennis*, followed in 1936, the same year that she published her autobiography, *Beyond the Game*. This was followed by another nonfiction guidebook, *Tennis*, in 1941. Jacobs went on to write fifteen more books, nearly all of them for teenagers; on occasion she used the pseudonym H. Braxton Hull. Her works include the novels *Storm Against the Wind* (1944), *Laurel for Judy* (1945), and *The Tennis Machine* (1972), as well as a number of works of nonfiction, among them a memoir, *Proudly She Serves: The Realistic Story of a Tennis Champion Who Becomes a WAVE* (1953), as well as *The Young Sportsman's Guide to Tennis* (1961), *Famous American Women Athletes* (1964), and *Better Physical Fitness for Girls* (1964).

In addition to writing books, Jacobs contributed numerous articles to major magazines and newspapers in the United States and abroad. She also worked for many years as a senior editor at the Grolier Council for Education Research in New York City. In private life, Jacobs, who never married, was a lifelong Episcopalian and enjoyed running a small farm on Long Island. She died at her home in East Hampton, Long Island, of a heart attack.

• For biographical information, see Jacobs's autobiography, *Beyond the Game*. See also the entries for "Jacobs, Helen Hull," in *Contemporary Authors*, vols. 9–12 (1974) and vol. 159 (1998); in *Something About the Author*, vol. 12 (1977); and in *Who Was Who in America*, vol. 12 (1998). For a history of American women's tennis, see especially Parke Cummings, *American Tennis: A Story of a Game and Its People* (1957); see also Richard Schickel, *The World of Tennis* (1975). An obituary appears in the *New York Times*, 4 June 1997.

ANN T. KEENE

JARRICO, Paul (12 Jan. 1915–28 Oct. 1997), screenwriter, was born Israel Shapiro in Los Angeles, the younger of two children of Russian immigrants Aaron Shapiro, a socialist lawyer who specialized in defending trade unionists and immigrants threatened with deportation, and Jennie Bernstein Shapiro. Israel Shapiro attended branches of the University of California in Los Angeles and Berkeley and received his B.A. from the University of Southern California in 1936, the year of his marriage to Sylvia Gussin. (The couple had one son.)

On the advice of an agent who was trying to sell one of his stories and who suggested that the author's plainly Jewish name was a disadvantage, Israel Shapiro became "Paul Jarrico" in 1937. Jarrico later explained that the surname had the same vowels as Shapiro and sounded "memorable, distinctive." In 1937, as Jarrico, he got a job with Columbia Pictures, where his first B-movie script was "No Time to Marry." For the next three years, Jarrico worked at several studios, turning out stories and scripts for produced and unproduced films. In 1939 the young director Garson Kanin, who had met Jarrico while both were briefly at Goldwyn Studios, hired him to work at RKO Pictures on the story for *Tom, Dick, and Harry*. Jarrico, credited with both story and script, said, "Kanin kept me with him all through the shoot and even the editing—unprecedented. . . . [H]e really seemed to believe that the writer was to the director as the composer was to the conductor, or the architect to the builder."

By conventional Hollywood standards, *Tom, Dick and Harry* (1941) was the peak of Jarrico's career. His screenplay was nominated for an Academy Award but lost out to Herman Mankiewicz and Orson Welles for *Citizen Kane*. The film was a charming Cinderella tale of three suitors in pursuit of the same young woman, played by Ginger Rogers. But its young socialist author intended it partly as an attack on the American success myth. One of the "controversial" lines written by Jarrico, who was destined to become a hero of the motion picture blacklist era, was "I don't believe in every man for himself—I get lonesome." By 1943 Jarrico was at Metro-Goldwyn-Mayer, where he co-wrote (with Richard Collins) two highly uncharacteristic screenplays—the frothy patriotic musical *Thousands Cheer* and *Song of Russia*, in which happy collective farmers dance, sing, and rarely farm. The latter movie, probably made under government pressure to promote Allied unity in the difficult wartime years, became one of three pro-Soviet films targeted by the House Committee on Un-American Activities as examples of "communist infiltration of the motion picture industry." (The other two films were *Mission to Moscow* and *The North Star*.)

In late 1943 Jarrico volunteered for the merchant marine, serving in North Africa and Italy before shipping home. Shortly before the end of the war, he was drafted into the navy but saw little service before being discharged. Between 1945 and 1951 few of Jarrico's story ideas at RKO were approved and only four movies on which he worked reached the screen. Jarrico came to believe that these slights stemmed from his membership in the Communist Party USA. He had joined the Young Student League at UCLA in 1933 and the CPUSA in 1937. Throughout his life he remained true to his belief that the party had done good work in Hollywood, particularly during the later Depression and wartime, combating "white chauvinism" and sexism and driving the creation of the industry's three major trade unions and the Anti-Nazi League.

From 1945 on, Jarrico edited the *Hollywood Review*, an occasional journal examining political ideas in film. During the original investigation of the film industry by the House Committee on Un-American Activities (or House Un-American Activities Committee; hence, HUAC) in 1947, he produced a twenty-minute documentary film, "The Hollywood Ten," which generally had to be distributed by hand. Jarrico's turn before HUAC came during the second phase of its Hollywood investigations in 1951. Identified as a CPUSA member by Collins, among others, he stood with screenwriter Michael Wilson in defying the committee, refusing to answer questions under the Fifth Amendment. He was, however, allowed to make a statement before HUAC, criticizing it and its methods. Howard Hughes, then the RKO boss, immediately fired Jarrico and removed his credit from the just-released *The Las Vegas Story*. A suit brought against Hughes by the Writers Guild of America failed. The restoration of credits to blacklisted writers became one of the driving forces behind Jarrico's later career.

Bereft of his passport, as a result of a State Department ruling, and having become technically unemployable in Hollywood (though black-market work was soon available), Jarrico took his most audacious step, forming the Independent Productions Corporation. In cooperation with Herbert Biberman and Adrian Scott, he planned an agenda of socially conscious films. In the end, only one, *Salt of the Earth* (1953–1954), was made. Wilson wrote the script, Biberman directed, and Jarrico found himself in the unfamiliar post of producer.

Shot on location in New Mexico using members of the International Union of Mine, Mill, and Smelter Workers and their wives as cast members, *Salt of the Earth* concerns the true story of a strike by Chicano workers against an exploitative zinc corporation, wherein the decisive factor was the "manning" of picket lines by the workers' wives, who thus expressed a willingness to be jailed. The film was nearly harassed out of existence during shooting. Its Mexican leading lady was deported; many film laboratories refused to process the film (Jarrico regularly drove long distances with cans of film looking for outlets); armed vigilantes regularly disrupted the filming; and film industry publications frequently attacked it. It was finally shown in only thirteen theaters, and the company went bankrupt. In 1955 *Salt of the Earth* was awarded the Grand Prix International as best film exhibited in France and the Karlovy Vary award at the Czechoslovakian Film Festival. The film, the only independent production made by blacklisted artists in the United States, was a milestone in American filmmaking and a symbol of resistance to the blacklist. It has been committed to videotape and DVD and preserved by the Library of Congress.

In 1958 the State Department's passport ruling was overturned, and Jarrico, who had quit the Communist party in 1956, left for Europe, where he moved from country to country, often writing scripts under the name Peter Achilles. After his divorce from Sylvia Jarrico in 1966, he married Yvette Le Floch; they were childless when they divorced. On his return to the United States in 1977, he met Lia Benedetti, whom he married in 1992.

Jarrico's later career included film scripts and a good deal of writing for television—comedy in the case of "The Phil Silvers Show" and realistic, socially aware drama in the instance of "The Defenders." He wrote a play, *Leonardo*, and frequently lectured at the University of California, Santa Barbara. A meticulous record-keeper, he provided young scholars with material for their work on the blacklist. In the 1990s he led a drive by the Writers Guild to complete the restoration of credits that had been erased from films written by the blacklistees. Tracking down long-missing persons, the tenacious Jarrico became the group's unofficial historian. As of 2001 the WGA had restored credits on ninety-four films. Some of his own credits may have gone unrestored; he said, "There'll be plenty of time for me."

Jarrico was killed in an automobile accident near Ojai, California, returning from the apology made to those blacklisted by the Writers Guild, the Screen Ac-tors Guild, and the Directors Guild. Jarrico and Ring Lardner, Jr., accepted the apology on their behalf. During the celebration, the actor Kevin Spacey portrayed Jarrico in a reenactment of the HUAC hearings. In 1999 the Writers Guild posthumously awarded Jarrico its Lieutenant Robert Meltzer medal for "singular acts of courage in the defense of freedom of expression and the rights of writers."

• Jarrico's papers are held by his widow, Lia Benedetti Jarrico, who contributed greatly to this entry, and the University of California, Los Angeles. UCLA also holds Jarrico's oral biography, recorded by Larry Ceplair between 1988 and 1990. Ceplair and Englund, *The Inquisition in Hollywood* (1980; rev. ed., 1991), is the standard work on the HUAC investigations of the film industry. A lengthy interview by Patrick McGilligan focusing on Jarrico's blacklisting is part of a general study of blacklisted screenwriters, *Tender Comrades* (1997). Herbert Biberman, *The Salt of the Earth* (1965), details that film's trials and triumphs. The screenplay and a full history are in Michael Wilson and Deborah Silverton Rosenfelt, *Salt of the Earth* (1978). An obituary is in the *New York Times*, 30 Oct. 1997.

JAMES ROSS MOORE

JIMMY THE GREEK. *See* Snyder, Jimmy "The Greek."

JOHNSON, Frank, Jr. (30 Oct. 1918–23 July 1999), U.S. district and circuit judge, was born Frank Minis Johnson, Jr., in Delmar, Alabama, the son of Frank M. Johnson, a postmaster and local Republican official, and Alabama Sivilla Long Johnson, a teacher. Growing up in mountainous Winston County, an area of few slaveowners that became a Unionist stronghold during the Civil War, he decided to become a lawyer after watching trials at the county courthouse, where his father served as probate judge. After becoming what he would term "a little rancorous" at sixteen, he was enrolled at Gulf Coast Military Academy and then attended Birmingham Southern College for less than a semester on a football scholarship.

On 16 January 1938, at nineteen, he married eighteen-year-old Ruth Jenkins; the union lasted until his death. After working a year and a half for the Works Progress Administration (WPA), he enrolled at the University of Alabama in the fall of 1939, graduating from the law school in 1943 near the top of his class. While there, he typed copies of lecture notes for his classmate and friend George C. Wallace. After receiving the Purple Heart and Bronze Star as a World War II combat infantry lieutenant in Europe, Johnson returned to Alabama and practiced law in Jasper. When General Dwight D. Eisenhower ran for president in 1952, Johnson became statewide leader of Veterans for Eisenhower.

Attorney General Herbert Brownell appointed Johnson U.S. attorney for the northern district of Alabama, where he attracted attention in the Justice Department by prosecuting the first successful peonage case in Alabama. He got convictions against two brothers, white planters who had paid fines for blacks convicted of minor crimes and then forced them to work as farm laborers; one had died after being horse-whipped following an attempted escape.

In October 1955, just before his thirty-seventh birthday, Johnson moved to the state capital, Montgomery, as the youngest federal judge in the country after a vacancy occurred in Alabama's Middle District. Six weeks later, the refusal of Rosa Parks to surrender her seat on a city bus to a white patron ignited a social revolution, as Martin Luther King, Jr.—the twenty-six-year-old minister of the Dexter Avenue Baptist Church located a few blocks from Johnson's courtroom—emerged as leader of the group that organized a city bus boycott.

Historian C. Vann Woodward later wrote, "Something very much like a panic seized many parts of the South toward the beginning of 1956, a panic bred on insecurity and fear. Race relations deteriorated in many areas, and as both races recoiled, old lines of communication between them snapped or weakened. On the white side, resistance stiffened into bristling defiance."

Because the bus boycott case involved a constitutional challenge to state law, Johnson called for a three-judge district court. In May 1956 he cast a decisive vote in a 2–1 opinion that extended beyond the realm of education the principles of the U.S. Supreme Court's landmark school desegregation opinion (*Brown v. Board of Education*). That vote signaled the trail-blazing direction he would follow as a trial judge hearing some of the nation's most important and far-reaching civil rights cases. In the storm that followed, Johnson stoically endured social ostracism, death threats, cross burnings, and a bombing of his mother's home in the belief of the perpetrator that it was Johnson's home. For nearly fifteen years, U.S. marshals provided him with round-the-clock protection.

During twenty-four years as a trial judge on the district court, Johnson issued orders desegregating Alabama schools and a host of other facilities, striking down barriers to voting and serving on juries, breaking new ground in gender discrimination and First Amendment issues, and extending constitutional protection to abused prison inmates and state mental patients. King would call him "the man who gave true meaning to the word 'justice.'" After having been threatened with contempt by Johnson in a case involving voter registration records, George Wallace launched a vituperative attack on the judge in his successful 1962 campaign for governor. He continued the attacks for more than a decade, once saying that Johnson needed "a barbed-wire enema."

On 7 March 1965 a watershed event occurred: national television depicted the "bloody Sunday" confrontation in which Alabama state troopers and a sheriff's posse assaulted civil rights marchers after they crossed the Edmund Pettus Bridge in Selma. Johnson held four days of hearings on a request by Martin Luther King and his Southern Christian Leadership Conference to enjoin the state of Alabama from interfering with a further attempt to march from Selma to Montgomery. The aim of such a march was to petition Governor Wallace to ensure that blacks be given due protection in seeking to register to vote. In rejecting the governor's position on the issue and authorizing a march that would block part of a major highway, Johnson wrote that his order "reaches . . . the outer limits of what is constitutionally allowed."

Johnson set precedent by applying to constitutional injury the traditional legal principle of proportionality—a larger award for a more serious personal injury or a harsher penalty for a more serious crime. "It seems basic to our constitutional principles that the extent of the right to assemble, demonstrate and march peaceably along the highways and streets in an orderly manner should be commensurate with the enormity of the wrongs that are being protested and petitioned against. In this case, the wrongs are enormous."

The Selma case offered a prime example of how Johnson improvised new forms of judicial relief to deal with the complexity and unprecedented nature of the constitutional issues involved in civil rights cases. Although his orders helped transform the social order in the South, the judge never viewed matters before him as societal issues. To him they were always legal issues. Johnson once explained in an interview:

> When you have a voting rights case and you find that there's been a pattern and practice of discrimination against the blacks in registering to vote, you don't register the blacks to vote so that they can gain political power. You are faced with some legal issues, and if they are entitled to relief you give them relief and you order that they be registered. Now the effect of their registering and voting and electing a sheriff and other county officials is something the court's not concerned with, and has no interest in it. . . . The role federal judges have played in the South has been one of effecting resultantly a social change. And there's no doubt about it. But that wasn't the motive and it wasn't the purpose and it wasn't the intent.

The Republican "Southern strategy" kept Johnson off the U.S. Supreme Court. His friend, Warren Burger, the chief justice, called him in from a fishing trip in the Gulf of Mexico to tell him that President Richard Nixon was about to appoint him to succeed Justice Hugo Black. Years later, a contrite Alabama congressman named William Dickinson confessed to Johnson that he and the state's other two Republican representatives had learned about the possible appointment and complained to Attorney General John Mitchell that such an appointment would hurt them politically. The congressman told Johnson, "We made a mistake and I want to apologize."

President Jimmy Carter nominated Johnson to become director of the Federal Bureau of Investigation. After a slow recovery from surgery for an aortal aneurysm discovered during a routine preconfirmation physical, Johnson withdrew. Carter subsequently appointed him to the Fifth Circuit Court of Appeals, and Johnson ended his career on the new Eleventh Circuit of Alabama, Florida, and Georgia after Congress split the Fifth Circuit.

Under a glass paperweight on his desk, Johnson kept this quote from Abraham Lincoln that served as his lodestar: "I'll do the very best I know how—the very best I can; and I mean to keep doing so until the end. If the end brings me out all right, what is said against me won't amount to anything. If the end brings me out wrong, ten angels swearing I was right would make no difference."

In the end he received not only the nation's highest civilian award, the Presidential Medal of Freedom, and recognition by Congress in naming the federal courthouse in Montgomery after him; he also was rewarded with acceptance into the Alabama Hall of Fame and a resolution honoring him from the state legislature, which twenty-five years earlier had called for his impeachment. He died in Montgomery.

• Johnson's professional papers are housed at the National Archives; scrapbooks and other materials are held by the University of Alabama Law School Library. There are four biographies: Robert F. Kennedy, Jr., *Judge Frank M. Johnson, Jr.: A Biography* (1978); Tinsley E. Yarbrough, *Judge Frank Johnson and Human Rights in Alabama* (1981); Frank Sikora, *The Judge: The Life & Opinions of Alabama's Frank M. Johnson, Jr.* (1992); and Jack Bass, *Taming the Storm: The Life and Times of Judge Frank M. Johnson, Jr., and the South's Fight over Civil Rights* (1993). The 24 July 1999 issue of the *New York Times* has a full-page obituary.

JACK BASS

JOHNSON, J. J. (22 Jan. 1924–4 Feb. 2001), trombonist, composer, and arranger, was born James Louis Johnson in Indianapolis, Indiana, the son of James Horace Johnson and Nina Geiger Johnson. In their early years, the church was a dominant influence in the lives of Johnson and his two younger sisters. His mother and father, who worshiped at a Baptist and a Methodist church respectively on the same street, insisted on bringing up their children in the traditions of both. Johnson's mother hired the church organist to teach him the piano at the age of nine. Later at Crispus Attucks High School, the only African-American public high school in Indianapolis, Johnson became passionate about music. Initially he was forced to play the baritone saxophone, but by the time he was fourteen he was appearing in the high school band and the YMCA marching brass band as a trombonist.

In the spring of 1942, against his father's wishes, Johnson joined a local band, the Snookum Russell orchestra, of which the trumpeter Fats Navarro was also a member. The group disbanded shortly thereafter, but Johnson's apprenticeship as a professional musician took off when, in October 1942, the visiting Benny Carter asked him to stand in for his absent trombonist. Carter and Johnson's musical relationship would continue for another two and half years as the band traveled extensively throughout the country; Johnson's earliest recordings are with the Benny Carter orchestra, although he was featured only as a sideman. His first recorded solo appears on a performance with Benny Carter of Cole Porter's "Love for Sale." During this time, Johnson was also asked to play at the very first Jazz at the Philharmonic concert.

By the mid-1940s Johnson felt confined and underutilized in Carter's big band format. He left the band to participate in the bebop revolution that was taking place on New York's Fifty-second Street. Johnson, whose fluid style and rapid-fire technique caught the attention of Charlie Parker and Dizzy Gillespie, pioneered the playing of the trombone in a bebop arrangement. His recording debut was on 26 June 1946 as leader of a quintet called Jay Jay Johnson and his Beboppers, which included Bud Powell and Max Roach. Before moving ahead with his work in bebop, Johnson that same year made one last recording with Count Basie's orchestra, a group he had been playing with sporadically.

On 23 September 1947 Johnson married Vivian Elora Freeman, a high school sweetheart; they would have two sons. In December of that year he sat in on recording sessions with the Coleman Hawkins, Illinois Jacquet, and Charlie Parker groups, as well as with his own quintet. By the early 1950s studio work for Johnson became less frequent, so he joined an all-star sextet led by Oscar Pettiford on a USO tour through Korea, Japan, and the South Pacific. He left the tour early—probably because of a drug habit. Like many jazz musicians in New York at the time, Johnson had his bout with drug addiction, but by all accounts he never developed a heroin problem as serious or prolonged as Charlie Parker's, Miles Davis's, or Stan Getz's. Nevertheless, in August 1952 Johnson left the jazz scene in New York and took a job as a blueprint inspector for Sperry Gyroscope in Long Island. This "self-prescribed rehabilitation" lasted for two years, and Johnson was seldom seen performing. He did manage to sit in with Miles Davis's sextet in a 1953 Blue Note recording session that included the titles "Tempus Fugit," "Ray's Idea," "C.T.A.," and Johnson's own compositions "Kelo" and "Enigma." In 1954, after leaving his job at Sperry Gyroscope, Johnson began playing with fellow trombonist Kai Winding. The collaboration marked the beginning of the most commercially and critically successful phase of Johnson's career. The Jay & Kai group, as they became known, recorded several albums that featured a unique duetting of trombone instrumentation.

Partly due to the influence of conductor/composer Gunther Schuller, Johnson's career began to move in other directions. Commissioned by the New York Classical Jazz and Classical Music Society to compose a piece for solo brass instruments and brass ensemble, Johnson recorded *Poem for Brass* in October 1956. The result of Johnson's growing familiarity with Central European modern classical music, especially the work of Paul Hindemith, *Poem for Brass* combined jazz and classical idioms and became a significant example of what Schuller called "third-stream music."

In June 1957 Johnson embarked on his first European tour, with concerts in Sweden, France, Belgium, Germany, and Holland. Back in New York in 1959, he was called as a key witness in one of the early "Police Card Cases." Since Prohibition, musicians in New York had been required by law to obtain a cabaret license from the New York Police Department before performing. The enforcement of the law by the NYPD was a grossly unfair and capricious use of power. Because of a 1946 conviction involving possession of a hypodermic needle, Johnson's card was revoked, and he was forced to apply for renewal every few months. Although the case did not overturn the licensing policy, Johnson's powerful testimony helped him get his card back and struck a heavy blow against the legality of the policy.

Later that year Johnson added trumpeter Freddie Hubbard and bassist Arthur Harper to his sextet, which went on to record one of his finest albums, *J.J. Inc.* The album contained some of Johnson's best-known compositions: "Shutterbug," "Fatback," "Aquarius," "In Walked Horace," "Minor Mist," "Mohawk," and "Turnpike," which was not issued on the original vinyl album but was included in the 1998 CD rerelease. The following year Johnson disbanded the sextet to devote more time to composing. The fruit of this labor was the 35-minute *Perceptions.* Commissioned by Dizzy Gillespie, the six-part work was recorded on 22 May 1961 with a large orchestra under the direction of Gunther Schuller. Of *Perceptions,* which was to be Johnson's most ambitious and extended composition ever, Schuller said: "Beyond all externals of form and technique, this music combines an eloquent musical imagination with a strongly disciplined mind, producing an enjoyable music of depth, pulsating warmth and infectious spirit."

In early 1965 Johnson's career again took a turn when he received an offer to play on Quincy Jones's soundtrack to the Sidney Lumet film *The Pawnbroker.* Emboldened by this experience, he moved to Los Angeles in 1970 and worked on the music for several television shows, including "Mayberry R.F.D.," The Danny Thomas Show," "That Girl," "Mod Squad," "Starsky and Hutch," "The Six Million Dollar Man," and "Mike Hammer." His movie credits, either orchestrating or composing, include *Man and Boy, Top of the Heap, Across 110th Street, Cleopatra Jones,* and *Shaft.*

In the late 1980s Johnson and his wife returned to Indianapolis. There he received an honorary Doctor of Music degree from Indiana University and the Indiana Governor's Art Award in 1989. In 1991 his wife died of a stroke, and Johnson recorded a dedicatory album entitled *Vivian.* On 11 September 1992 he married Carolyn Reid. Carolyn would act as his business manager until his retirement in 1996. Up until then, Johnson continued to perform and record actively. He died in Indianapolis on 4 February 2001.

Arguably the greatest of all jazz trombonists, Johnson will always be remembered, first and foremost, as the man who modernized the instrument. Through his virtuosity and technical innovations, Johnson made it possible for the trombone to assume as important a position in bebop and other subsequent jazz movements as the saxophone and trumpet. Johnson is also duly esteemed for his prolific and diverse body of compositions; over a span of fifty years, he recorded everything from big-band to experimental post-bebop works, and from hit musical arrangements for blaxploitation films to third-stream music.

• Published as part of Rutgers University's Institute of Jazz Studies series, Joshua Berrett and Louis G. Bourgois, III, *The Musical World of J. J. Johnson* (1999) is an indispensable biography and critical study of Johnson's music. An obituary appears in the *Indianapolis Star,* 8 Feb. 2001.

STEFAN VRANKA

JOHNSON, John (c. 1823–1900), mountain man, whose surname was originally Johnston, was known for his gory exploits, principally among the Crow Indians, which earned him the nicknames "Liver-Eating Johnson," "Liver-Eater," and "Crow Killer." His story, which became part of western frontier legend in the oral tradition of both white pioneers and Native Americans, inspired several modern fictionalized retellings, including the novel *Mountain Man* (1965), by Vardis Fisher, and the movie *Jeremiah Johnson* (1972).

Nothing is known about Johnson's life before the fall of 1843, when he traveled west on the Missouri River from St. Louis on the steamer *Thames* and disembarked at St. Joseph. After acquiring supplies and a pony, he set out for the area in and around the Rocky Mountains, with the intention of becoming a fur trapper and trader. Along the way he became partners with an experienced mountain man known as Old John Hatcher, who reportedly taught him not only how to trap but also how to scalp Indians who interfered. Johnson's early distrust of Indians, which was shared by trappers and settlers alike, developed at first from hearing many stories of their massacres and then after personally witnessing the aftermath of an Indian slaughter along the Musselshell River, in what is now Montana. The victims were a Connecticut farmer named John Morgan and his three children, who, along with Mrs. Morgan, had been heading west to Oregon. Morgan had been tomahawked and scalped by Blackfoot Indians while tending his oxen, his two sons murdered, and his daughter raped before she, too, was killed. As the Indians came for Mrs. Morgan, she raised an axe and counterattacked, killing four and scaring off the rest, but they still managed to carry off her wounded husband, leaving his scalp behind.

Inadvertently coming upon the scene a few hours later, Johnson tried to console Mrs. Morgan, helping her to bury her three children and her husband's scalp in separate graves. When she refused to leave the site, he built her a log cabin and helped her to settle there with her few belongings. This done, the obviously unhinged Mrs. Morgan drove Johnson off her premises and remained there for many years as a recluse until her death. The site became known as "Crazy Woman's Cabin" and was even marked thus on local maps. Johnson and other trappers continued to look after her, leaving food and clothing at her door, but she refused all human contact. The legend of Crazy Woman Morgan passed into western lore. For Johnson, it was an incident he never forgot, and sadly it proved to be a precursor of his own tragedy.

A few years after the Morgan murders, Johnson acquired a new trapping partner, Del Gue, and it was Gue who preserved the stories of Johnson's subsequent exploits. Despite Johnson's aversion to Indians, in the summer of 1847 he took as his bride a Flathead Indian girl called The Swan and brought her back to his cabin on the Little Snake River, near the present Wyoming-Colorado border. After living with her for some weeks, he headed into the mountains for a lengthy hunting trip, promising to come back early the following spring. Upon his return months later, he discovered the bones of his wife scattered on the ground, along with the remains of an unborn child. Nothing was left in the cabin except an old kettle. All signs pointed to a massacre by Crow Indians. Gathering his wife's and child's remains, Johnson placed them in the kettle and hid them in a secret cairn a short distance from the cabin; he would return to the site often over the following decades. Late that day he again set forth into the wilderness, vowing vengeance for the rest of his life against the Crows.

By the end of 1848 stories had spread far and wide of John Johnson's personal war against the Crows. In what is now Montana, Wyoming, and Colorado, bodies of Crow warriors were turning up, mutilated in a unique fashion: not only were they scalped; they had been cut beneath their ribs and their livers removed. According to Del Gue and other mountain men, it was Johnson who was doing the killing—and eating the livers of those he had killed. No one dared, or was even inclined, to challenge the big mountain man with his bushy red beard and Indian scalps dangling from his belt, but people were wary when he came riding into far-flung western settlements to trade his skins and buy supplies, and frontier children of that period grew up hearing from their mothers the admonition that if they didn't behave, then Liver-Eating Johnson would be called in to take care of them with his knife.

According to Gue, Johnson killed some 300 Crows over several decades. He also did battle with other tribes, including the Blackfeet, who briefly held him captive; and he was rumored to have cannibalized many of his other Native American victims, eating their limbs, however, in the tradition of many mountain men when food was scarce, rather than their internal organs. During the Civil War he also fought with the Union Army in Missouri, received an honorable discharge in September 1865, and subsequently helped government troops fight the Sioux, as well as Cheyennes, Arapahos, and other tribes, in the ongoing wars between settlers and Native Americans. Following one battle, he reportedly sampled, in the company of Del Gue and several other mountain men, the liver of a Sioux he had killed, perhaps to reinforce his reputation for fearsomeness.

Finally, sometime during the summer of 1869, Johnson quietly made peace with the Crows, personally meeting with their chiefs Gray Bear and White Badger and exchanging gifts to secure their agreement. According to Gue, Johnson had come to be impressed by the Crows' bravery and even their sense of honor, especially after discovering earlier that year that they had solemnly buried Crazy Woman Morgan after her death.

But Johnson continued to fight other Indians as well as hunt and trap. In the 1870s he took another wife, a young Piegan woman named Waving Grass, though apparently he did not remain with her for long. In the 1880s Johnson and his partner Del Gue parted company for a time when Johnson settled in Coulson, Montana Territory, as deputy sheriff of Custer County. But after a year he was restless for the wilderness. He resigned, then headed north along the Milk River into Alberta, Canada, accompanied by several other mountain men, and remained there for a time, trapping and fighting Indians. He subsequently rejoined Gue south of the Canadian border, and the pair spent several years working along the Yellowstone and Musselshell rivers. In 1888 the aging Johnson settled in Bear Creek, a Montana Territory settlement, where he built a cabin and continued trapping and hunting. He was soon elected the first marshal of nearby Red Lodge, about the time that Montana achieved statehood in 1889.

Johnson's health began to decline in 1895, and from then on he was looked after by area settlers. In December 1899 friends persuaded him to enter the Old Soldiers' Home, a Los Angeles institution for army veterans that had also been the last residence of Old John Hatcher. Johnson died there a month later and was buried in a nearby cemetery.

• The only known factual source of biographical information on John Johnson is *Crow Killer: The Saga of Liver-Eating Johnson*, by Raymond W. Thorp and Robert Bunker, first published in 1958 and reissued in 1969 with an introduction by folklorist Richard Dorson. The book is based on written and oral material amassed by Thorp on Johnson in the 1930s and 1940s, including oral accounts transmitted by Del Gue as well as Thorp's extensive interviews with White-Eye Anderson, another mountain man who had trapped with Gue. For nineteenth-century accounts of mountain men, see George Frederick Ruxton, *Life in the Far West* (1849; repr. 1983), and the diaries of W. A. Ferris, first printed in 1940 as *Life in the Rocky Mountains*. See also Stanley Vestal, *Mountain Men* (1937); the editors of American Heritage, *Trappers and Mountain Men* (1961); and Robert M. Utley, *A Life Wild and Perilous: Mountain Men and the Paths to the Pacific* (1997). In addition, see chapter 2, "The Mountain Man," in Bernard De Voto, *The Year of Decision: 1846* (1942), which offers a brief history of the earliest mountain men, beginning in the 1820s.

ANN T. KEENE

JOHNSTON, Annie Fellows (15 May 1863–5 Oct. 1931), writer of juvenile fiction, was born in Evansville, Indiana, to Albion Fellows and Mary Erskine Fellows. Her father, a Methodist minister, died when she was two years old; her mother then took her three children to nearby McCutchanville, where they spent two years with Erskine relatives. After five more years in Evansville, the family returned to McCutchanville to live in a house built for them on family property.

At age seventeen, the petite, dark-haired Annie Fellows began teaching in the country school she had recently attended; next, she studied for a year at the State University of Iowa (now the University of Iowa), where her uncle was a professor. She returned to Evansville and taught in the city's public schools for three years, followed by another three years as a private secretary.

In the summer of 1888, after becoming engaged to her cousin William Johnston, a widower with three children, Annie and her younger sister Albion made a long-planned trip to Europe; on 11 October the two women were married in a double ceremony at Evansville's Trinity Church, their father's former pastorate. Annie's happy marriage was soon over, for William Johnston died in 1892. After his estate was settled, so little money was left that "it drove me to writing in real earnest," his widow explained years later; that writing would soon become the family's main support.

Johnston's poems and stories had previously appeared in the *Youth's Companion* and other minor publications. In 1894 she published her first book, *Big Brother*, followed in 1895 by *Joel: A Boy of Galilee*, its details authenticated by the rabbi with whom she studied Hebrew.

In the meantime, her stepchildren were living with relatives near Louisville, Kentucky, in Pewee Valley, a village noted for its antebellum charm. There, on a visit, Johnston met an old Confederate colonel and his temperamental granddaughter, Hattie Cochran; she became the model for the main character in *The Little Colonel*, published in 1895 and the first of a series of thirteen books, all of which had numerous editions and translations.

During the next two years, Johnston went to Chicago to make a firsthand report on the Deaconess movement, which engaged in church-sponsored social work in the city's slums. In 1897 she again went to Europe, this time as a chaperone for a wealthy young American woman. They returned to the United States in mid-1898; in the fall she published *The Gate of the Giant Scissors*, a story set in France. It was followed by *Two Little Knights of Kentucky* in 1899. (That same year, those two books plus *The Little Colonel* reappeared in one volume as *The Little Colonel Stories*.)

A volume of poetry by Annie and Albion, titled *Songs Ysame* (1897), also bore the imprint of Boston's L. C. Page Company, now the sole publisher of the books of Annie Fellows Johnston. Eventually she would regret this contractual relationship, for the firm paid little but demanded full control over her work.

In September 1899 Johnston's stepdaughter Rena died after an operation for appendicitis; when her stepson John was diagnosed with tuberculosis, Johnston spent several months with him in the Catskills before their return to Kentucky in 1900. The next year they moved to the Southwest, finally settling at Boerne, Texas, in a home called "Penacres." During this period (1900–1910), Johnston published twenty-five books: a dozen for the Little Colonel series; six slim volumes, mainly short stories, for Page's Cosy Corner series; seven other books, including *In the Desert of Waiting* (1905), an allegory inspired by Arizona's Camelback Mountain, and *The Rescue of the Princess Winsome* (1908), a play in verse, with music by Albion.

After John's death in 1910, Annie Fellows Johnston and her stepdaughter Mary, an artist who designed *The Little Colonel Doll Book* (1910), moved back to Kentucky, making "The Beeches" in Pewee Valley their final home. Johnston had been a founding member of the Authors Club of Louisville in 1898. Now, after her return to Kentucky, she rejoined this group of women writers who met weekly to criticize their manuscripts and share publication information.

In October 1912 *Mary Ware's Promised Land*, one of the Little Colonel books, was published. In it, Mary Ware (a disguised Annie Fellows) leaves Texas for Indiana, where she becomes the personal secretary of Mrs. Blythe, a passionate advocate of housing reform. Though fictionalized, in reality this is an account of the activities and achievements of sister Albion Fellows Bacon, an Evansville socialite; influenced by Jacob Riis, she was one of Indiana's most vigorous campaigners for legislation to correct tenement evils and rebuild the cities' blighted areas. (The book's graphic slum descriptions, however, may have come from Johnston's early Chicago experiences.) Another important character in the book, reporter Sandford Berry, is remarkably similar in manner and appearance to poet James Whitcomb Riley, a longtime friend.

In all, eleven of Johnston's books were published during the last two decades of her life, years spent in Pewee Valley, with summer trips to Cape Cod, the setting for *Georgina of the Rainbows* (1916) and *Georgina's Service Stars* (1918). In 1931, the year of her death, *The Little Colonel Stories, 2nd Series*, was issued; *For Pierre's Sake and Other Stories* was published posthumously in 1934.

Johnston received daily some twenty to thirty letters from avid young readers, and was "deeply touched by their confessions and confidences." (At their insistence, she extended the Little Colonel series by adding the three Mary Ware books.) For nine years, she worked intermittently on her autobiography, *The Land of the Little Colonel* (1929), written to "satisfy the curiosity of my correspondents more fully than letters can do." Much earlier, she had published *The Little Colonel's Hero* (1902) specifically to answer the many questions to which she could not personally reply.

In her autobiography, the author whose books had sold over a million copies admitted that "it was my ambition to write the 'great American novel' some day, but it seemed as if everything conspired to keep me writing nothing but children's stories." Finally she realized that her reward—being a positive influence on young readers—was worth more than any "grown-up novel." And yet, *Mary Ware's Promised Land* is that adult work: in it, a compassionate but naive young woman reaches selfless maturity while striving to combat squalor, corruption, and the public's lack of interest in the plight of the needy.

During the last years of her life, Johnston was ill, reportedly from sleeping sickness and then cancer, so she was unable to finish projects begun with enthusiasm; yet in her lifetime she completed an "insignificant pile" of more than forty books. When Annie Fellows Johnston died, aged sixty-eight, she was "beloved by two generations of readers" and her stories "took their Kentucky setting to the corners of the earth," according to the front-page obituary in the *Louisville Courier-Journal* (6 Oct. 1931). After World War II, however, her books were no longer popular with teenagers and she was soon being faulted for writing that was unrealistic, sentimental, and often condescending toward race and class. Despite these criticisms, Johnston's books were a positive influence on several generations of readers who profited from their emphasis on good manners and moral integrity. These books are also worthy of study because they carefully describe many aspects of American life—economic, social, educational—that now belong to the historical past.

• Johnston's letters and documents are scattered, with the most useful located as follows: Regional and Family History Center, Willard Library of Evansville, Indiana; Lilly Library, Indiana University, Bloomington; Manuscripts Department, Berea College, Berea, Kentucky; Manuscripts Department, Filson Club Historical Society, Louisville, Kentucky; and Special Collections Department, Alderman Library, University of Virginia, Charlottesville. Because *The Land of the Little Colonel* (1929) was written in answer to questions repeatedly asked by readers, it fails as autobiography, for there are too many factual omissions. A literary couple (Johnston's lifelong friends) have written perceptively about her: Cale Young Rice, "Annie Fellows Johnston," in *Library of Southern Literature*, suppl. 1 (1923): 325–28, and Alice Hegan Rice, "An Appreciation," a foreword to *The Land of the Little Colonel*. For a comparative study of *Mary Ware's Promised Land* and relevant Johnston-Bacon biographical details, see Mary Boewe, "Annie and Albion: Reformers of Riverville," *Traces* 7 (Winter 1995): 4–11. (*Traces* is a publication of the Indiana Historical Society.) See also Elizabeth Steele, "Mrs. Johnston's *Little Colonel*," in Ray B. Browne et al., eds., *Challenges in American Culture* (1970), pp. 217–23. In it, Steele discusses the Little Colonel books as Americana, popular art, and children's literature. The *New York Times* of 6 Oct. 1931 has a long obituary.

MARY BOEWE

JOHNSTON, Frances Benjamin (15 Jan. 1864–16 May 1952), photographer, was born in Grafton, West Virginia, the sole surviving child of Frances Antoinette Benjamin Johnston, a journalist, and Anderson Dolophon Johnston, a bookkeeper with the U.S. Treasury Department. The family lived briefly in Rochester, New York, and then settled in Washington, D.C., where Johnston was privately tutored before she attended the Notre Dame Academy, near Baltimore, Maryland. In 1884 she went to Paris for two years of art training at the Atelier Julien. On her return to Washington, she supported herself by drawing illustrations for articles in the popular press. Aware that photography would revolutionize magazine illustration, Johnston got herself a Kodak camera and trained under Thomas Smillie at the Smithsonian Institution. Her work with Smillie's government team documenting the Chicago Columbian Exposition in 1893 was the first of her many world's fair commissions.

Opening her own Washington studio in 1895, Johnston photographed the city's political and society leaders, prompting *Life* magazine (in 1949) to dub Johnston America's "court photographer." The belle of Washington's bohemian set, the "Push," Johnston had a free-thinking, self-assertive style—seen in her famous 1896 self-portrait, with her cigarette and beer stein and hiked-up skirt—which came to symbolize the "New Woman." Self-supporting, single, but with a host of intimates of both sexes, she was the ultimate late-nineteenth-century liberated woman.

In 1899 Johnston took on three major projects that were shown in Paris in 1900, two of which won medals at the Paris World Exposition. The first, an exhibition she curated of 142 works by twenty-eight American women photographers, did much to advance the status of women in professional photography. A second project, a 350-image photo-survey of "progressive education" in Washington, D.C., gave a frame-by-frame view of the new educational techniques. Its success led the Hampton Institute in Virginia, established to educate newly freed African Americans, to hire Johnston to document their work as well. Johnston took some 150 photographs of education at Hampton, supplemented by "before" shots of the life of rural "unimproved" Virginians. While Hampton was criticized by some contemporaries as being too assimilationist, Johnston's Hampton survey not only raised financial support for the institution but also preserved a record of its work for later generations to ponder. (New York's Museum of Modern Art published excerpts, as *The Hampton Album*, in 1966, stimulating further debates.) Important commissions from the Carlisle School in Pennsylvania in 1901 and the Tuskegee Institute in Alabama in 1902 and 1906 followed; at Tuskegee Johnston worked closely with Booker T. Washington and George Washington Carver.

Meanwhile, with the encouragement of press agent George Grantham Bain, Johnston boarded Admiral George Dewey's battleship before it returned to the States from Manila Bay in 1899 and sent back candid photos of life on board. After that publicity coup, she segued into celebrity portraiture, feeding the American public's hunger for photos of the famous. Susan B. Anthony, Theodore Roosevelt, Joel Chandler Harris, Natalie Barney, Phoebe Hearst, and Mark Twain were some of her more popular subjects. Her portrait of President William McKinley in 1901, made seconds before he was shot, was one of her first mail-order gold mines, only to be surpassed a few years later by a lucrative sideline selling portraits of the ethereal Alice Roosevelt Longworth.

Johnston made a brief alliance with Alfred Stieglitz's Photo-Secession movement in the early 1900s but ultimately found its aesthetics too limiting for a self-supporting commercial photographer. In the building boom of the early twentieth century, she was drawn to the growing field of architectural photography and earned lucrative contracts from New York's leading architects. She and her then-partner, Mattie Edwards Hewitt, documented many of New York's important buildings, from the New Theatre to the Cathedral of St. John the Divine. Johnston's love of gardening together with the growing patronage of well-heeled 1920s socialites drew her into travel photojournalism, researching and photographing important European and American homes and gardens. Armchair gardeners could join her in exploring the villas of Europe or California and their stylish greenery at her "lantern" (slide) shows or in the pages of their Sunday newspapers.

In 1927, in the midst of a commission to photograph "Chatham," a restored Virginia estate, Johnston discovered a more compelling focus for her camera. The countryside around Chatham was filled with fascinating—and crumbling—older structures. Some were lovingly handcrafted colonial churches, others simple outbuildings and worksheds. Most would never be restored or even repaired, just removed. With her camera, Johnston could perform a sort of historic preservation, documenting these buildings on film for future study. She found a sympathetic ear at the Carnegie Foundation, which (along with the American Council of Learned Societies and the Old Dominion Foundation) sponsored her work with a series of grants in the 1930s and 1940s to document the vernacular architecture of the southern states. With the help of staff at the Universities of Virginia and North Carolina, as well as various real estate agents, librarians, and scholars, Johnston found her way to many abandoned treasures. Of the estimated 7,500 photos she made at this time, some were reproduced in monographs on individual southern states; some appear in Gwaltney's *Carnegie Survey of the Architecture of the South, 1927–1943;* and most can be found in Library of Congress collections that Johnston helped organize.

In her last years, Johnston moved to New Orleans, buying a Bourbon Street house where she gardened and photographed and drank and reminisced with other eccentrics, such as her great friend, photographer Joseph "Pops" Whitesell. A self-proclaimed "octo-geranium," Frances Benjamin Johnston died as she lived, an utterly liberated bohemian.

Johnston's career in photography spanned many genres: journalism, portraiture, architecture, landscaping, horticulture, and, finally, historic preservation. Although she was successful in each, her most enduring accomplishments remain the Hampton project early in her career and the historic preservation project of her last years.

• The personal papers and photographs of Johnston can be found at the Library of Congress, in the Manuscript Division and the Prints and Photographs Division. On her earlier work, see Pete Daniel and Raymond Smock, *A Talent for Detail: The Photographs of Miss Frances Benjamin Johnston, 1889–1910* (1974). For her full career, see Bettina Berch, *The Woman Behind the Lens: The Life and Work of Frances Benjamin Johnston, 1864–1952* (2000). An obituary appears in the *Times Picayune New Orleans States,* 17 May 1952, corrected 18 May 1952.

BETTINA BERCH

JONES, Thomas Goode (26 Nov. 1844–28 Apr. 1914), lawyer, politician, and judge, was born in Macon, Georgia, the first son of Samuel Goode Jones, a railroad builder and promoter, and Martha Ward Goode Jones; his parents were cousins. At the age of five he was brought by his family to Montgomery, Alabama. Educated there by private tutors, he then attended preparatory schools in Virginia prior to enrolling in the fall of 1860 at the Virginia Military Institute.

When the Civil War began, Jones supported the Confederacy, drilling volunteers in Richmond and serving with General Stonewall Jackson before joining the 53rd Alabama, with which he saw fighting in Mississippi and Tennessee. In the spring of 1863 he was assigned to the Army of Northern Virginia as an aide to General John B. Gordon. Wounded several times, he rose to the rank of major and was chosen to carry a flag of truce through the lines at Appomattox. After the war Jones would be a prominent figure in the Alabama state militia, serving on several occasions as an effective troop commander in actions against lynch mobs.

Following the surrender, Jones returned home and in 1866 married Georgena Bird of Montgomery. Seeking to live in antebellum style, he tried both cotton farming, which within a few years landed him seriously in debt, and journalism, editing the short-lived *Daily Picayune.* In 1868 he was admitted to the bar, having read law under former Alabama chief justice Abram J. Walker. Two years later, Jones, a loyal Democrat, was hired by the then Republican-dominated Supreme Court as its official reporter, a post he would retain for ten years.

In the following decades, Jones's legal career was both successful and distinguished. By the 1880s he would be a trusted advocate of large interests, including the Louisville & Nashville Railroad (L&N). A leading member of the Alabama State Bar Association, he was chosen to write its code of ethics. Approved in 1887, this document reflects Jones's bias as a member of the corporate bar, but it also sets forth a lawyer's duty to protect the friendless and to expose corruption. It was characteristic of Jones that, although he was a zealous defender of opportunistic, even predatory, clients, he had a profound respect for due process and equal justice before the law. Jones easily managed a similar contradiction in his approach to questions of race. A white supremacist, he was a sincere paternalist, working for what he considered the best interests of black citizens.

As a politician, Jones did yeoman service as a Montgomery alderman from 1875 to 1884. In the latter year he was elected to the legislature, where he risked the wrath of white planters by working against a contract labor bill that in its original form would have sent defaulting sharecroppers to prison for debt. Jones was elected Speaker of the Alabama house in 1886. Thereafter his rise was rapid in an increasingly turbulent political world.

Certainly Jones was unprepared for the rise of the Farmer's Alliance and kindred organizations. These agrarians attracted the support of tens of thousands of small farmers in Alabama, white and black, who were victims of the era's persistent trends—falling prices and high interest rates. Alliancemen promoted cooperative enterprise and criticized the power of merchants, lawyers, bankers, and industrialists. Yet these were among the chief groups who backed the ruling factions of the state Democratic party. In 1890, when the Alliance rallied behind the gubernatorial candidacy of Agriculture Commissioner Reuben F. Kolb, Jones was the least experienced of four conservatives who ran against him. Yet at the state convention he received the nomination when anti-Kolb managers decided to pool their votes.

After an easy victory in the general election, Jones advanced several ideas designed to correct abuses of the legal system. Over the course of two terms (1890–1894) he would discover that legislators were more interested in political survival than in bills to make sheriffs more accountable for lynchings. Jones's most notable legislative victory was an 1893 act that would have ended Alabama's brutal and long-entrenched "convict lease" system. Labor unions, women's groups, and many Democrats, including Reuben F. Kolb, had called for this reform—and under Jones's leadership lawmakers approved the removal of convicts from private hands by 1 January 1895. Yet the plan was repealed at the behest of Jones's successor in the midst of fiscal troubles brought on by the panic of 1893.

As a party leader Jones had the task of keeping the agrarians at bay. In 1892 Kolb ran for governor as a "Jeffersonian Democrat" backed by a coalition of Populists and Republicans. Jones was reelected after a racially charged campaign, his narrow victory (126,959 to 115,524) based on suspect majorities in Black Belt counties. Jones reacted to accusations of fraud with anguish and denial; but the following year he signed the Sayre Act, which made voting more difficult for illiterates and concentrated power in the hands of (Democratic) election officials. In the summer of 1894, Jones sent troops to the Birmingham area to thwart striking miners and railroad men whose political sympathies were decidedly Jeffersonian.

By the late 1890s many state Democratic leaders had embraced disfranchisement as a nonfraudulent method of crushing opposition. Jones supported suffrage restrictions, but in the 1901 constitutional convention he criticized the "grandfather clause" as a device aimed solely at blacks. Booker T. Washington, an old friend, appreciated Jones's combination of paternalism and legalism and used his influence with President Theodore Roosevelt to secure Jones an appointment as judge of Alabama's Middle and Northern Districts.

For Jones, the federal bench would be no safe haven. Beginning in 1903, he presided over a series of peonage trials, by which the government sought to end corrupt (but common) arrangements among local officials and employers. Peonage outraged Jones, yet he meted out mild punishments, convinced that public exposure would suffice to discourage the evil. From 1908 to 1910 Jones functioned as an unofficial judicial watchdog, assisting Booker T. Washington and Alabama circuit judge William H. Thomas to prepare a successful appeal of a 1903 contract labor law that deprived defendants of the presumption of innocence.

Jones's last great public enterprise was his involvement as principal trial judge in the long (1907–1914) regulatory war between the state of Alabama, led by Governor Braxton Bragg Comer, and a group of railroads led by the L&N. Unwilling to admit that he might be prejudiced in favor of his former client, Jones withstood popular anger and ruled consistently according to probusiness principles of jurisprudence. He died in Montgomery in April 1914, a mere two months after the two sides had reached a compromise settlement. Thus ended a life as complex and nuanced as the New South order that Jones so faithfully served.

• The Alabama State Department of Archives and History in Montgomery holds an extensive collection of Jones's private papers, as well as his gubernatorial papers. Records of his tenure as district judge are stored at the repository of the National Archives and Records Administration, East Point, Ga. For surveys of his career, see Paul M. Pruitt, Jr., "Thomas Goode Jones," in *Alabama's Governors: A Political History of the State*, ed. Samuel Webb and Margaret Armbrester (2001); Brent Jude Aucoin, "Thomas Goode Jones, Redeemer and Reformer: The Racial Politics of a Conservative Democrat in Pursuit of a 'New' South, 1874–1914" (M.A. thesis, Miami Univ., 1993); and Malcolm Cook McMillan, "Thomas Goode Jones, 1844–1914: Warrior, Statesman, and Jurist," *Alabama Lawyer* 17 (Oct. 1956): 376–81. For views of Jones's careers in various contexts, see Carolyn Ruth Huggins, "Bourbonism and Radicalism in Alabama: The Gubernatorial Administration of Thomas Goode Jones, 1890–1894" (M.A. thesis, Auburn Univ., 1968); William Warren Rogers, *The One-Gallused Rebellion: Agrarianism in Alabama, 1865–1896* (1970); Alliston Marston, "Guiding the Profession: The 1887 Code of Ethics of the Alabama State Bar Association," *Alabama Law Review* 49 (Winter 1998): 471–507; and Pete Daniel, *The Shadow of Slavery: Peonage in the South, 1901–1969* (1972; repr., 1990).

PAUL M. PRUITT

JORDAN, Barbara (21 Feb. 1936–17 Jan. 1996), lawyer, politician, and university professor, was born Barbara Charline Jordan in Houston, Texas, the daughter of Benjamin M. Jordan and Arlyne Patten Jordan. Her father, a graduate of the Tuskegee Institute, was a warehouse employee until 1949 when he became a minister at Houston's Good Hope Missionary Baptist Church, in which his father's family had long been active. Arlyne Jordan also became a frequent speaker at the church. The Jordans were always poor, and for many years Barbara and her two older sisters shared a bed, but their lives improved somewhat after their father became a minister. Barbara attended local segregated public schools and received good grades with little effort. She gave scant thought to her future, beyond forming a vague desire to become a pharmacist, until her senior year at Phillis Wheatley High School, when a black female lawyer spoke at the school's career day assembly. Already a proficient orator who had won several competitions, she decided to put that skill to use as an attorney.

Restricted in her choice of colleges by her poverty as well as segregation, Jordan entered Texas Southern University, an all-black institution in Houston, on a small scholarship in the fall of 1952. Majoring in political science and history, she also became a champion debater, leading the college team to several championships. She graduated magna cum laude in 1956 and went on to Boston University Law School, where she managed to excel despite rampant gender discrimination. Upon graduation she took the Massachusetts bar exam, intending to practice law in Boston, but ultimately decided to return to her parents' home in Houston. She used the dining room as her office for several years before setting up a downtown office, and she also worked as an administrative assistant to a county judge until 1966.

Jordan's first wholesale encounter with politics came during the 1960 national election campaign, when she became a volunteer for Democratic presidential candidate John F. Kennedy and his running mate, Texas senator Lyndon B. Johnson. She began at the Houston party headquarters by performing menial jobs but soon emerged as the head of a voting drive covering Houston's predominantly black precincts. The Democratic victory that fall changed Jordan's life in several ways: not only did it persuade her to enter politics; it also overturned her long-held sense that segregation was a way of life that had to be endured, and it convinced her that the lives of black people might be improved by political action.

Jordan began her political career by running for a seat in the Texas House of Representatives in 1962 and again two years later. She lost both elections but received an impressive number of votes. In 1966, following a Supreme Court–mandated electoral redistricting to allow fair representation for blacks and other minorities, Jordan won election to the Texas Senate from the newly created Eleventh District in Houston, becoming the first black state senator in Texas since 1883. Concerned that she might be branded a rabble-rousing liberal agitator, she determined to establish herself as a legislator working seriously for social change. She began by being an advocate for the ultimately successful passage of a bill establishing the state's first Fair Employment Prac-

tices Commission, to fight discrimination in the workplace. She also fought for passage of the state's first minimum wage law, for raises in workmen's compensation payments, and for the creation of a department of community affairs to deal with the problems of the state's rapidly growing urban areas. In addition, she blocked proposed legislation that would have made voter registration more difficult.

Named outstanding freshman senator during her first year in office, Jordan went on to reelection for two more terms, serving a total of six years and bringing to passage half of the bills she introduced. In March 1972 she became the first black woman in American history to preside over a legislative body when she was elected president pro tem of the Texas legislature. By that time she had decided to try for a seat in the U.S. House of Representatives from the state's new Eighteenth District, which was 50 percent black and 15 percent Mexican American. After winning a hard-fought primary against a black male state legislator, she ran for election that fall as the Democratic candidate and easily defeated her Republican opponent. Upon taking the oath of office in January 1973, she and another new representative, Andrew Young of Georgia, became the first two African Americans in modern times to sit as elected members of the U.S. House. Thanks to the assistance of former president Lyndon Johnson, who had become a friend during Jordan's years in the Texas legislature, she was appointed to a coveted seat on the House Judiciary Committee.

Jordan served three terms in the Congress, easily winning reelection in 1974 and 1976. She was a forceful presence, voting consistently for such liberal measures as increased federal aid to public schools and an extension of the guaranteed student loan program, legal aid for the poor, an increase in the minimum wage, and the continuation of the school lunch program. During her first term she also voted for several bills designed to limit U.S. involvement in the Vietnam War, and she voted against the construction of the Alaska oil pipeline because of concerns for the environment. But she first achieved a national presence in July 1974 as a member of the House Judiciary Committee.

On the opening day of the televised hearings held by the committee to consider articles of impeachment against President Richard M. Nixon, Jordan delivered a preliminary statement that moved to their very bones almost all who heard it. Speaking slowly and deliberately in a powerful deep and solemn voice, Jordan declared that despite not having been considered among "We, the people" when the Constitution was adopted, "the process of amendment, interpretation, and court decisions" had now guaranteed her inclusion. "Today, I am an inquisitor," she continued. "I believe hyperbole would not be fictional and would not overstate the solemnness that I feel right now. My faith in the Constitution is whole, it is complete, it is total. I am not going to sit here and be an idle spectator to the diminution, the subversion, the destruction of the Constitution." Speaking with authority, Jordan then set forth her reasons for believing that Nixon should be impeached, concluding that if the committee did not vote to do so, then the Constitution was worthless and should be sent through a paper shredder. Although she projected great control, Jordan later revealed that she was shaking with nervousness throughout the proceedings, and after casting her vote she wept.

Following Nixon's resignation not long afterward, Jordan's opening remarks, as well as her penetrating questioning during the committee hearings, remained in the public mind, and she was talked about as a candidate for higher office. In 1976, she was called upon to be a keynote speaker at the Democratic National Convention, along with Senator John H. Glenn, Jr., of Ohio. Following Glenn's unremarkable address, she electrified the convention with a speech delivered in a style part-William Jennings Bryan and part-hellfire Baptist preacher. Appealing for national unity, she declared that its achievement and the full realization of America's destiny lay only through the Democratic party.

In the 1976 fall presidential campaign, Jordan traveled the country, making speeches in support of the Democratic candidate, Jimmy Carter. Upon his victory in November, Carter discussed appointing her to the cabinet, but she was only interested in becoming attorney general, a post Carter was not willing to offer her. A year later, in December 1977, she surprised supporters by announcing that she would not seek a fourth term in Congress the following year. Although she was rumored to have health problems, she denied this, saying only that she wanted to devote herself to other concerns back in Texas. After leaving the House in early 1979, she was appointed to the Lyndon B. Johnson Chair in National Policy at the Johnson School of Public Affairs, a part of the University of Texas in Austin. Teaching courses in policy development as well as political values and ethics, she became one of the university's most popular professors, and students had to participate in a lottery to gain admission to her classes.

Jordan returned to the national political stage in 1988, when she delivered a rousing speech at the Democratic National Convention seconding the nomination of Lloyd Bentsen as the vice-presidential candidate. By this time, however, her physical ailment could not be denied: she was now confined to a wheelchair, the consequence, she said, of a "neuromuscular disorder." Later that summer she made national headlines again when she was found floating unconscious in the swimming pool at her home; she had gone into cardiac arrest while doing therapeutic exercises. She recovered, however, and by that fall was well enough to campaign for the national Democratic presidential ticket, headed by Michael Dukakis.

Jordan returned to the Democratic National Convention in 1992 as one of its keynote speakers, and again she riveted the audience with her call for support of presidential candidate Bill Clinton and his mandate for change. Although her health grew worse, she continued to teach at the university. She also served as chair of the Commission on Immigration Reform and in that capacity testified before Congress in 1995 on behalf of citizenship rights for children born in the United States to illegal immigrants.

Jordan, who never married, fiercely guarded her private life. Known to enjoy singing and playing the guitar, she was also a fan of the Lady Longhorns, the University of Texas women's basketball team, whose games she frequently attended. Following her death from viral pneumonia, which occurred at her home in Austin, it was disclosed that she had suffered from both multiple sclerosis and leukemia.

• For biographical information, see Jordan's brief memoir, coauthored with Shelby Hearon, *Barbara Jordan: A Self-Portrait* (1978). See also Mary Beth Rogers, *Barbara Jordan: American Hero* (1998), and James Haskins, *Barbara Jordan* (1977). In addition, see entries for "Jordan, Barbara C.," in *Current Biography Yearbook* for 1974, 1993, and 1996, and in *Who Was Who in America*, vol. 21 (1993–1996). An obituary appears in the *New York Times*, 18 Jan. 1996.

ANN T. KEENE

JUDD, Donald (3 June 1928–12 Feb. 1994), artist and art critic, was born Donald Clarence Judd in Excelsior Springs, Missouri, the son of Roy Clarence Judd, an executive for Western Union, and Effie Cowsert Judd. In 1946, just following high school, Judd served in the U.S. Army's Corps of Engineers in Korea. Near the end of 1947 he left the army and lived in New York while he attended the Art Students League. He briefly studied at the College of William and Mary in Williamsburg, Virginia, in 1948–1949. He moved back to New York in 1949 and enrolled in both the Art Students League and in Columbia University, where he received a bachelor's degree in philosophy in 1953 and later studied for an M.A. in art history until 1962. In 1964 he married Julie Finch; they had two children and later divorced.

In 1959 Judd began writing art criticism, mainly for *Arts Magazine*, then edited by art critic Hilton Kramer. Judd's exhibition reviews, written in a halting and somewhat dogmatic style, became a public means of developing his theories about art. In his writings, he decried artists such as Helen Frankenthaler and Philip Guston, who he thought perpetuated Abstract Expressionism well beyond its inventive stage, and he praised those moving art in a new direction, such as Frank Stella, Yves Klein, and Lee Bontecou, who were focusing on the primacy of the art object.

The same issues he discussed in his writings troubled him in his own paintings, which he called "half-baked abstractions." Rejecting the realist style taught at the Art Students League (which he attended until 1953), he painted broad areas of color on lightly hued backgrounds that later developed into thin lines crossing the canvas over colored rounds. Influenced by Stella and Klein, Judd's always "untitled" paintings rejected symbolism and illusionism.

Impressed by the three-dimensional reliefs of Bontecou and the sculpture of John Chamberlain and Claes Oldenburg, Judd began creating three-dimensional work around 1962. He preferred not to call his new work "sculpture," as the term suggested a process that was either additive (like molding clay) or reductive (like carving marble). Judd's early floor pieces consisted of painted plywood geometric shapes, such as boxes and triangles. By 1964 he started contracting out the production of his designs in industrial materials such as steel, aluminum, iron, and Plexiglas, thereby eliminating the role of the artist's hand in art.

In the mid-1960s he focused on making work in simple forms that rendered visible all aspects of the piece, that is, all the planes and joints of the shape. His pieces tended to be hollow or had tinted Plexiglas and never had more than two colors or materials. He often kept the surface of his mediums unaltered, or he painted the surfaces cadmium red, a tone that he felt highlighted all the parts of the piece. A signature work from this period consisted of seven identical galvanized iron boxes cantilevered on a wall. Later variations on this piece featured tinted Plexiglas or lacquered iron and an increased number of evenly spaced boxes.

By the mid-1960s Judd, Dan Flavin, Carl Andre, and Sol LeWitt, although not a formally cohesive group, began exhibiting together in several exhibitions at the Green Gallery and later the Leo Castelli Gallery in New York, at the Jewish Museum of Art in 1966, and the Los Angeles County Museum of Art in 1967. Critics called their work "ABC art," "Reductionist Art" and "Anti-art," but a January 1965 *Arts Magazine* article by Richard Wollheim is credited for naming it "Minimal Art" for its very low "art-content."

In 1965, the same year he stopped writing for *Arts Magazine,* Judd wrote an article for *Arts Yearbook* called "Specific Objects," in which he outlined several important aspects of minimalism. "Specific objects" were neither sculptures nor paintings. These three-dimensional pieces eliminated "the problem of illusionism and of literal space, space in and around marks and colors—which is riddance of one of the salient and most objectionable relics of European art." He lauded the use of new materials because they were "specific," "aggressive," and not "obviously art," and because "[t]he form of a work and its materials are closely related." Rejecting the concept of composition led him to argue: "The thing as a whole, its quality as a whole, is what is interesting. . . . In the new work the shape, image, color, and surface are single and not partial and scattered. There aren't any neutral or moderate areas or parts, any connections or transitional areas."

During the late 1960s and early 1970s Judd created larger pieces that related to architecture and landscape, such as an outdoor circular ring made of concrete commissioned by architect Philip Johnson in 1971. Also in the early 1970s, Judd bought a group of buildings in Marfa, Texas, that he renovated into living quarters and permanent exhibition spaces for hundreds of his own pieces as well as some by Flavin, Chamberlain, and others. Opened in 1986 and completed posthumously in 2000, the expanded compound is run by the Chinati Foundation, an organization originally presided over by Judd.

In Marfa, Judd made his own tables, chairs, beds, and benches for his home and studio. Although not strictly based on his previous work, the furniture shared several minimalist traits, such as open rectangular forms and wood or industrial materials. By the mid-1980s Judd was designing furniture executed by a Swiss factory and for sale to the public.

The first one-man show of Judd's "specific objects" was held at the Green Gallery in New York in 1963. The Whitney Museum of American Art gave him a retrospective as early as 1968 and mounted another in 1988. The Saint Louis Art Museum exhibited his furniture in 1991. He showed regularly at Castelli's gallery in New York as well as in numerous European galleries. Many museums have collected his work, including the Museum of Modern Art, the Hirshhorn Museum and Sculpture Garden, and the Art Institute of Chicago.

Judd worked continuously in the same style until his death from lymphoma at age sixty-five. Minimalism's heyday ended in the 1970s when artists and critics deemed the work antiseptic, subject to extremely rigid theory, and prohibitively expensive. Judd, however, was criticized for contradicting his own theories by using visually lush materials in his work, thereby including the notion of "beauty" in pieces that were supposed to be aesthetically neutral.

Emerging at around the same time as pop art, minimalism provided another influential alternative to the hegemony of abstract expressionism in the New York art scene. Embracing the purity of Piet Mondrian and Kasimir Malevich and the "all-overness" of Jackson Pollock's drip paintings, Judd stripped away the barrier between fine art and the viewer by placing his work on the floor (sans pedestal), making all parts of the piece visible, eliminating spatial depth, and utilizing new materials. Along with other minimalists, Judd paved the way for conceptual and installation artists of the 1970s and 1980s, further freeing the definition of art from craftsmanship, specific mediums, and aesthetic distance.

• Judd's writings have been published in *Complete Writings, 1959–1975* (1975) and *Complete Writings, 1975–1986* (1987). A transcript of a 1964 radio interview with Judd and Frank Stella, along with additional source material, is included in *Minimal Art: A Critical Anthology,* ed. Gregory Battcock (1968). For bibliographical information as well as critical analysis of Judd's work, see the catalogs of three retrospectives, *Don Judd* (Whitney Museum of American Art, 1968) with an essay by William C. Agee; *Donald Judd: Catalogue Raisonné of Paintings, Objects, and Wood Blocks: 1960–1974* (National Gallery of Canada, 1975) with an essay by Roberta Smith; and *Donald Judd* (Whitney Museum of American Art, 1988) with an essay by Barbara Haskell. For his graphic work, see *Donald Judd: Prints and Works in Editions 1951–1994* (Edition Schellmann, 1996). Additional catalogs include *Donald Judd: Eight Works in Three Dimensions* (Knight Gallery/Spirit Square Arts Center in Charlotte, NC, 1983), with an essay by Brian Wallis, and *Donald Judd: New Sculpture* (Pace Gallery, 1991) with an essay by Yve-

Alain Bois. For information on his furniture, see the exhibition catalog *Donald Judd Furniture: Retrospective* (DAP, 1993). For a recent reexamination of Judd's theories see Philip Leider, "Perfect Unlikeness," *Artforum*, Feb. 2000, pp. 98–103. Kenneth Baker, *Minimalism: Art of Circumstance* (1988), provides a general overview of the style. Informative obituaries are in the *New York Times*, 13 Feb. 1994, and *Art in America*, Apr. 1994.

N. ELIZABETH SCHLATTER

K

KANIN, Garson (24 Nov. 1912–13 Mar. 1999), author and director, was born in Rochester, New York, one of two sons of David Kanin, a builder, and his wife Sadie Levine Kanin. When Kanin was twelve, the family moved to Brooklyn, where he attended James Madison High School, dropping out in 1929. Before enrolling in the American Academy of Dramatic Arts in New York, Kanin had his own jazz band (Garson Kay and His Red Peppers), toured as a vaudeville comedian, narrated radio programs, and appeared in summer theater. He graduated in 1933 and was soon receiving good notices for high-energy comedy roles on Broadway. His appearances in the madcap farces *Boy Meets Girl* and *Three Men on a Horse* (both 1935) led to an association with the shows' director, George Abbott. Kanin directed touring versions of Abbott's productions and, on Broadway, *Hitch Your Wagon* (1936), a fictionalized version of one of John Barrymore's affairs, and the lynch-mob tale *Too Many Heroes* (1937).

In 1937, Beatrice Kaufman, the wife of Abbott's chief rival, George S. Kaufman, recommended Kanin to the office of Samuel Goldwyn. Although Kanin left Goldwyn halfway through his year's contract, the experience transformed Kanin from stage-struck to screen-struck and provided the earliest material—he even set the record straight on the legendary producer's "Goldwynisms"—for one of the best books ever written about the film capital, Kanin's *Hollywood* (1974). After six months' "learning the business" with Goldwyn, Kanin got his first directorial assignment with R-K-O, *A Man to Remember*, a 1938 B-movie about a small-town doctor thought (wrongly) by the world to be a failure. The film received good notices, and—after a less successful second effort—Kanin directed Barrymore in the gently satiric *The Great Man Votes* (1939). In the film gerrymandering has caused a pivotal city ward to be reduced to one voter—Barrymore—whose decision will swing the election. Subsequent directorial assignments provided material for further affectionate portraits—Charles Laughton and Carole Lombard (*They Knew What They Wanted*, 1940) and Ginger Rogers (*Bachelor Mother*, 1939, and *Tom, Dick and Harry*, 1941). Before entering the U.S. Army, Kanin also directed the screwball comedy *My Favorite Wife* (1940), lauded for both its "clockwork timing" and its spontaneity. By then Kanin had also shown himself to be a director who revered writers.

During World War II Kanin served in the U.S. Army Signal Corps, the Army Air Forces, the Office of Strategic Services, and the Supreme Headquarters of the Allied Expeditionary Forces in London, where he assisted British director Carol Reed in compiling "The True Glory," a documentary that was named best film of 1945 by the National Board of Review. In 1942 Kanin married actress-playwright Ruth Gordon; they had no children and remained married until Gordon's death in 1985. While on assignment with the OSS in Washington, Kanin gathered material on wartime profiteering that became the basis for his first play, *Born Yesterday*, written in London for a friend of his, the actress Jean Arthur. But Arthur withdrew just before the Broadway opening night, and Billy Dawn, who became one of Broadway and Hollywood's most memorable comic characters, was played by Judy Holliday. Opening in February 1946, *Born Yesterday* ran for 1,642 performances and received the Donaldson award for Best New Play, while Kanin was named Best Director of the 1945–1946 season. Kanin and Arthur C. Laurents shared the Sidney Howard Memorial award for playwriting. *Born Yesterday* illustrated Kanin's particular strength—quick, gritty, pungent, sophisticated dialogue. Later in the year, Kanin directed Ruth Gordon's autobiographical *Years Ago*, in which Fredric March won an Antoinette Perry (Tony) award for best actor.

After Kanin directed two more Broadway plays, the Kanin-Gordon screenwriting partnership lifted off with *A Double Life* (1948). Ronald Colman won an Academy Award for his performance in this melodramatic study of an actor who confuses real life with playing Othello. *Adam's Rib* (1949) was the first in a classic series of give-and-take, male-female tussles starring Spencer Tracy and Katharine Hepburn; the screenplay was nominated for an Academy Award. The Kanins' friendship with Tracy and Hepburn provided much of the material for *Tracy and Hepburn* (1971), Kanin's first piece of classic Hollywood nonfiction. *Adam's Rib* also contained a part for Holliday, "built up" by Kanin and Gordon to prove to Columbia's boss Harry Cohn, who had bought the film rights to *Born Yesterday*, that she deserved the screen role. Cohn finally agreed, and Holliday won the Best Actress Academy Award for 1951. The stormy relationship between Cohn and Kanin also provided some of Hollywood's most interesting reading.

Kanin's solo screenplays included *It Should Happen to You* (for Holliday and Jack Lemmon, 1953), and those with Gordon included *The Marrying Kind* (for Holliday) and *Pat and Mike* (for Tracy and Hepburn, another Academy Award nomination), both in 1952. Kanin's playwriting career continued until 1962, but he never repeated the success of *Born Yesterday*. His venture into musical theater yielded in 1960, however, the book for *Do Re Mi*, to music by Jule Styne, as well as a good deal of material for his novel *Smash* (1980), the day-by-day tale of the chaotic creation of a Broadway musical. Kanin's Broadway directorial career revived, and in 1955, having traveled to Amsterdam to meet Otto Frank, Kanin directed the Pulitzer Prize-winning *The Diary of Anne Frank*. In 1964 he directed the musical *Funny Girl*, Barbra Streisand's star-making vehicle.

A restless, prolific author ("I become physically ill if I don't write for three days"), Kanin produced in 1966 the first of his dozen books, *Remembering Mr. Maugham*, a memoir of the prolific British author-playwright. There followed *Tracy and Hepburn* and *A Thousand Summers* (1973), the first of Kanin's novels. But his success as a Hollywood screenwriter generally tended to obscure most of his subsequent literary work, including the novels *Smash* and *A Hell of an Actor* (the latter being the first of his novels to mix, in the fashion of the times, real people with fictionalizations); the semi-philosophical *It Takes a Long Time to Become Young* (1978), and the novels *Moviola* (1979), whose 92-year-old studio chief was based on Goldwyn and its narrator on Kanin, and *Cordelia?* (1982), a psychological tale evoking Alfred Lunt, Lynn Fontanne, and King Lear. After Gordon's death in 1985, Kanin said, "I'm half dead. . . . [W]ith Ruth no longer here . . . I don't feel completely with it." In 1990 Kanin married Marian Seldes, an actress; they remained married until Kanin's death.

Kanin wrote of moviemaking with an insider's knowledge and an outsider's curiosity. The British biographer Michael Freedland called Kanin "an icon to generations, truly a screenwriter's screenwriter," saying that writers of his generation regularly talked hopefully of "doing a Kanin"—telling a story with a particular kind of enviable wit.

• Kanin's papers are in the library of the Academy of Motion Picture Arts and Sciences. His books are the best measure of his mind and heart. Obituaries include Michael Freedland's in the (London) *Guardian*, 15 Mar. 1999, and a substantial one by Marilyn Berger in the *New York Times*, also 15 Mar. 1999.

JAMES ROSS MOORE

KAZIN, Alfred (5 June 1915–5 June 1998), literary critic, was born in Brooklyn, New York, the son of Charles Kazin, a house painter, and Gita Fagelman Kazin, a dressmaker. Both parents were Yiddish-speaking immigrants from Czarist Russia; and from both he happily absorbed middle-class, immigrant, Jewish, socialist values. Kazin received a B.S.S. at City College of New York in 1935 and an M.A. from Columbia University in 1938. While still an undergraduate, Kazin—already a voracious reader—wrote book reviews for the *New York Times*, the *New York Herald Tribune*, and the *New Republic*. From the beginning, he commanded a graceful, powerful style as he related contemporary literature to history, to contemporary political and cultural developments, and—often—subjectively to himself.

In 1937 Kazin was encouraged at Columbia by Professor Carl Van Doren to analyze post-1890

American literature and write a book on it. The result, with the help of a Guggenheim fellowship in 1940 and other grants, was *On Native Grounds: An Interpretation of Modern Prose Literature* (1942). Considered a ground-breaking, innovative work when it first appeared, this big book now seems limited both for attacking the so-called New Critics' stress on explications of textual diction and structure and for not considering American poets and dramatists. It still offers, however, valuable, clear discussions of premodernist American prose writers, both major and minor. With it, Kazin leaped to the forefront of vigorous young critics and enjoyed a celebrity that he felt hurt him later, as he evolved well beyond its limitations.

In 1938 Kazin married Natasha Dohn, a childless marriage that was later annulled. He lived in Greenwich Village and worked in New York City during most of the World War II years. In 1942 he became literary editor of the *New Republic*; in 1943 he became a contributing editor of *Fortune*; during the summer of 1944 he studied the works of William Blake at the Huntington Library in San Marino, California; and in 1944–1945 he taught at Black Mountain College in North Carolina, while continuing to contribute material to the *New Republic*. Early in 1945, supported by Office of War Information and Rockefeller Foundation grants, he studied labor and education in England, went on to Paris, and returned to Brooklyn the same year. In 1947 he married Carol Bookman, a novelist, and went back to Europe, combining a second Guggenheim fellowship and an assignment to teach at the American seminars in Salzburg, Austria. In 1951 he published *A Walker in the City*, which is partly autobiographical and partly defensive of his early leftist idealism, which had been challenged by wartime and postwar realities. In prose consciously emulating the poetry of Walt Whitman and Hart Crane, it is easily one of his finest works.

Kazin began an unsettled vocational and personal existence, though never one of intellectual uncertainty. In 1950 he and his second wife had a son but were divorced. He married Ann Birstein, a novelist, in 1952 and lectured at Harvard that year and the next. In 1953 he and his wife had a daughter, and he lectured that year and the next at Smith College. He taught in the American Studies program at Amherst College (1955–1957), at New York University (1957–1958), and at the New School for Social Research (1958–1962). In 1961 he presented the Christian Gauss lectures at Princeton University and also joined the editorial board of *American Scholar*, the journal of the Phi Beta Kappa Society. In 1962 he collected seventy-two of his essays and reviews, mostly published in periodicals earlier, as *Contemporaries*, which serves as a critical survey of modern literature. The following year Kazin began an appointment as distinguished professor at the State University of New York at Stony Brook, remaining until 1973. During these years he also lectured at the University of California at Berkeley (1963) and the University of California at Los Angeles (1969) and was also active as a senior fellow at the Center for Advanced Study in the Behavioral Sciences at Stanford University (1977–1978). He also published *Starting Out in the Thirties* (1965), a slim combination, structured chronologically, of intellectual autobiography and literary criticism, and *Bright Book of Life: American Novelists and Storytellers from Hemingway to Mailer* (1973), a controversial evaluation—called "quirky" by some reviewers—with especially perceptive comments on Saul Bellow and Isaac Bashevis Singer.

Next, Kazin taught at Hunter College and in the graduate school of the City University of New York (1973–1985). Meanwhile he published *New York Jew* (1978), another autobiographical volume, again including critical insights, but occasionally bitter in the view of some readers. In 1983, divorced since 1978, Kazin married Judith Dunford, a writer. His *An American Procession* (1984) is a companion piece to *On Native Grounds*—this time a reassessment in historical-survey form of American authors, whom he now saw as more defensive than rebellious. Thereafter, he lectured widely at institutions of higher learning in New York City and also out of state.

During these years, Kazin published *The Inmost Leaf: A Selection of Essays* (1978), a collection of some minor fugitive pieces; *A Writer's America: Landscape in Literature* (1988); and *Writing Was Everything* (1995), lectures delivered at Harvard. His *A Lifetime Burning in Every Moment: From the Journals of Alfred Kazin* (1996) is a generous, rambling, unindexed selection from his voluminous journals, begun in 1938, continuing through 1995, and described by his wife Judith as a place where he elaborated thoughts, worked up ideas, whined, rejoiced, and attacked. Kazin's last book, *God & the American Writer* (1998), which expresses his post-religious, individualistic faith, appeared shortly before his death in his Manhattan home of prostate and bone cancer.

It is difficult to sum up Kazin's achievement. He felt that literature, particularly realistic fiction, was as important as life itself, indeed, made life more understandable, more challenging to the mind and emotions. Paying scant attention to critical trends, he analyzed style and structure less than he related writer's meanings to their times and ours. He paid the most attention to what writers taught him about himself, about New York, and about the enigma of being Jewish. His autobiographical books, and the autobiographical touches in his more objective books, are most likely to be permanently judged to be his most valuable legacy to future readers. Incalculable must be the influence he had on listeners to his lectures and his conversation (which Judith Dunford compared to the gush of a flamethrower) and on readers of his short introductions to several textbook reprints of popular authors. His touchstone writers, about all of whom he held strong positions, were Sholom Aleichem, Saul Bellow, William Blake, Hart Crane, Ralph Waldo Emerson, Emily Dickinson, Theodore Dreiser, William Faulkner, Robert Frost, Nathaniel Hawthorne, William Dean Howells, John Keats, Abraham Lincoln, Herman Melville, Frank Norris, Harriet Beecher Stowe, Mark Twain, Nathanael West, and Walt Whitman.

In everything Kazin wrote—and sometimes overwrote—he took his emotions, thoughts, testiness, egoism, ambitions, and memories into personal account, if only implicitly; and he had the spirit to make his doing so worth his readers' attention.

• Kazin's journals, which are the heart of his private and critical comments, are housed in the New York Public Library. Robert Alter, "The Education of Alfred Kazin," *Commentary* 65 (June 1978): 44–51, praises Kazin's *On Native Grounds* and *New York Jew* but at the expense of much of his later work, especially *Bright Book of Life*. Cleanth Brooks, "Mr. Kazin's America," *Sewanee Review* 51 (Winter 1943): 52–61, deplores Kazin's adverse linking of southern formalists and Marxist critics. Paul John Eakin, "Alfred Kazin's Bridge to America," *South Atlantic Quarterly* 77 (Winter 1978): 39–53, is a superb essay on Kazin's first autobiographical writings. The chapter on Kazin in Sherman Paul, *Repossessing and Renewing: Essays in the Green American Tradition* (1976), pp. 236–94, praises him for being in the "green," that is, the positive Emersonian tradition. Kermit Vanderbilt, *American Literature and the Academy: The Roots, Growth, and Maturity of a Profession* (1986), downgrades the early Kazin, especially in the light of mounting criticism of *On Native Grounds*. Edmund Wilson, *Letters on Literature and Politics, 1912–1972*, ed. Elena Wilson (1977), contains many letters from the premier American critic to Kazin, praising, commenting on, and often correcting aspects of several of his colleague's books and essays. "Remembering Alfred Kazin," *American Scholar* 68 (Winter 1999): 13–35, is a collection of compassionate tributes by six personal acquaintances: Morris Dickstein, Michael Kazin (his son), Jonathan Rosen, Sean Wilentz, Antonio Dajer, and Judith Dunford (his fourth wife). An obituary is in the *New York Times*, 6 June 1998.

ROBERT L. GALE

KELLY, Gene (23 Aug. 1912–2 Feb. 1996), dancer, actor, choreographer, and director, was born Eugene Curran Kelly in Pittsburgh, Pennsylvania, the son of James Patrick Joseph Kelly, a Canadian-born salesman, and Harriet Curran Kelly. Both James and Harriet came from large Irish-Catholic families, and Eugene, as he was called until he entered high school, was the third of five children. In the interests of providing all of the Kelly children with refined middle-class backgrounds, Harriet made sure they had music, dance, and art lessons in addition to their regular schooling. Although Gene and his brothers Jim and Fred endured considerable taunting from friends and classmates who sneered that dancing was "for girls," it was quickly apparent that Gene and Fred, at least, found dancing very easy to do and enjoyed the attention it brought them.

In fact, despite, or perhaps because of, being "a little short"—he would top out at five feet nine inches—Gene was always aggressive physically, excelling in gymnastics and other things athletic. Throughout the 1920s, all of "The Five Kellys" (as they were billed for amateur theatrical performances in Pittsburgh) led hectic lives divided among dancing, athletics, and academics. In high school, the personable Gene played football, baseball, and ice hockey, did gymnastics, edited the school newspaper, served as his class social chairman, and acted and danced in school plays and talent shows. He graduated from high school at age sixteen, prepared to go on to college and, eventually, law school.

Kelly entered Pennsylvania State College in 1929, planning to major in economics. By the end of his freshman year he had developed a reputation as the college's "number one entertainer," and his summer job was as counselor for a YMCA camp at Lake Erie, where he also taught and staged shows. As the Great Depression caught up with the Kelly family—James Kelly lost his job as a salesman and was unable to find another—Gene was forced to work part-time in order to remain in college and transferred to the University of Pittsburgh in 1931. In addition to serving as a gas-station attendant, rolling tires for the Firestone Company, and teaching a few classes at a dance studio where his mother did clerical work, Gene began to dance professionally in a dance and acrobatics act worked up with his brother Fred. When Harriet Kelly decided to open her own dance studio in Johnstown, Pennsylvania, in 1931, Gene became her primary instructor. Although teaching was initially a "temporary means to an end," namely law school, by the time Kelly graduated from the University of Pittsburgh with a bachelor's degree in economics in 1933, he was well embarked on a thriving career as a dancer and teacher. For the next several years he ran what was now called the Gene Kelly Studio of the Dance, with one branch in Pittsburgh and another in Johnstown. He also choreographed amateur and professional shows in and around Pennsylvania. In the end, Kelly's legal career would consist only of three months in law school at the University of Pittsburgh.

In the summer of 1938 Kelly decided that his dance studios were so well established that they could be run without his active participation, and he bought a one-way ticket to New York City to try his luck on the Broadway stage. He was twenty-six years old, but his first job was as a chorus boy supporting Mary Martin in her Broadway debut in the Cole Porter show *Leave It to Me*. Kelly left the show three months after it opened for a featured role in a musical revue called *One for the Money*. His big break, however, came in 1939, when he was offered the role of Harry the Hoofer, a down-and-out dancer, in William Saroyan's play *The Time of Your Life*. Although Kelly's performance "stopped the show" on opening night, and his reviews were good, *The Time of Your Life* also became the crucible for Kelly's own development of a new dance language: "I realized," he said, "that there was no character—whether a sailor or a truck driver or a gangster—that couldn't be interpreted through dancing, if one found the correct choreographic language."

Kelly continued to develop his ability to find the "correct choreographic language" with which to act a character through dance in his next Broadway role, that of Joey in the Richard Rodgers–Lorenz Hart musical *Pal Joey*, which opened on 24 December 1940. *Pal Joey* had, as the *New York Times* put it, an "odious story," but Kelly managed to make Joey into what the *Herald Tribune* called "at once a heel and a hero." Although *Pal Joey* did not have a long Broadway run, Kelly's bravura performance ran, as one observer put it, "like an electric charge through the fabric of the show" and brought him to the attention of Hollywood talent scouts. Kelly signed a film contract with producer David O. Selznick, but before leaving *Pal Joey* for Hollywood Kelly managed to fit in one more Broadway job, that of dance direction for a new musical called *Best Foot Forward*. He also got married, on 24 September 1941, to a young actress named Betsy Blair. Six weeks later, the Kellys arrived in Los Angeles.

Gene Kelly's Hollywood career began with an enforced period of idleness that he found extremely frustrating. He was drawing a salary, but Selznick had no parts ready for him to play. And although America had entered World War II, Kelly was not allowed to enlist in the armed services. It would be five months before Kelly appeared in a film, and then it was as a loan-out to Metro-Goldwyn-Mayer producer Arthur Freed, to star opposite Judy Garland in a musical called *For Me and My Gal* (1942). Kelly was very effective in a role that was reminiscent of *Pal Joey*; the film was such a success that Freed persuaded Louis B. Mayer, the head of MGM, to buy Kelly's contract from Selznick. Thus in 1942 things finally seemed to be taking off for Kelly. His first child, a daughter, Kerry, was also born that year.

In 1943, however, Kelly once again faced a frustrating period. After his spectacular debut, Kelly's next several films—*Pilot No. 5*, a straight drama; the musicals *DuBarry Was a Lady* and *Thousands Cheer*; and another straight film called *The Cross of Lorraine*—seemed lackluster and trite. (He was thirty years old and a father, and although MGM had no particular plans for him, the studio continued to push, against Kelly's wishes, for a deferment from active duty.) MGM even loaned Kelly to the "poverty-row" studio Columbia in 1943 to make a Technicolor musical with Rita Hayworth. Because of Hayworth, the film was expected to be a box office success, which it was. What was not expected was the extent to which *Cover Girl* developed Gene Kelly's reputation as a star, as a male dancer, and as an innovative "choreo-cinema-maker," as he would come to be called by the end of the forties.

In *Cover Girl* Kelly experimented with how to transfer dance to the screen, how best to fit "a three-dimensional art into a two-dimensional medium." The "alter ego" number, which he devised with the help of Stanley Donen, is a cinematic tour de force in which Kelly's character dances in violent conflict with his own shadow image, something that could never be done on the stage. Kelly also began to think about his own screen persona: "On the stage," Kelly told Hermine Rich Isaacs in 1946, "I can walk around in rhythm for a minute or two doing nothing but grin at the audience or wink at someone in the first row orchestra, and they love it. They eat it up. I know because I've done it. But on the screen that sort of thing leaves them cold. The personality is missing." To replace "the impact that sheer presence provides on the stage," Kelly learned that he would have to transmute his "natural" energy as a personality into the kinetic energy of dance movement, choreographic patterns, color, camera work, and editing. How best to accomplish such a transmutation became the driving force behind Kelly's work in films over the next ten years.

Returning to MGM a musical star in 1944, Kelly was nevertheless loaned out again, this time to Universal, for another nonmusical, a Deanna Durbin film called *Christmas Holiday*. Finally, however, he was cast in a big-budget MGM musical, *Anchors Aweigh*, which paired Kelly with Frank Sinatra for the first time. But it was the combination cartoon and live-action dance that Kelly created using Jerry the Mouse that was the most memorable moment in the film. *Anchors Aweigh* was one of Kelly's biggest box-office successes of the 1940s, and his performance, playing a sailor, also earned him his only best-actor Oscar nomination. Equally important to Kelly, at the end of 1944 he was allowed, at last, to join the U.S. Navy. After training, he was inducted as a lieutenant (junior grade) into the photographic division of the naval air force.

Kelly's first MGM film after being discharged from the navy in 1946 was a low-budget musical comedy, *Living in a Big Way*, that did little to advance his career. His next film role was as himself, opposite Fred Astaire, in one number in the lavish Technicolor musical *The Ziegfeld Follies of 1946*. It was the only time in their MGM years that Astaire and Kelly appeared together; Kelly later remarked that he was the "Marlon Brando of dancers, and [Astaire] the Cary Grant," and the comparison does much to account for the "ordinary Joe" image of Kelly and the ineffable sophistication associated with Astaire. Astaire and Kelly switched roles, however, when Kelly broke his ankle playing volleyball in 1947. Astaire, who had retired from the screen in 1946, replaced Kelly in the Irving Berlin musical *Easter Parade*, with Judy Garland. Astaire with Garland was then followed by Kelly with Garland when Kelly joined the cast of Vincente Minnelli's stylized fairy-tale musical, *The Pirate*, as the swaggering acrobat Serafin. Although *The Pirate* now has its devotees, in 1948 audiences seemed unprepared for its mixture of satire, romance, and visual excess, and the film lost money.

Kelly's next 1948 film, *The Three Musketeers*, was much more successful. It was not a musical, but Kelly's exuberant physicality suited the role of D'Artagnan, and he arranged and performed most of his own stunts. After choreographing and dancing, with Vera-Ellen, the specialty ballet "Slaughter on 10th Avenue" in the all-star Rodgers and Hart biopic *Words and Music* (1948), Kelly again teamed up with Frank Sinatra for a period musical that Kelly cowrote with Stanley Donen, *Take Me Out to the Ball Game* (1949). The Sinatra-Kelly partnership continued to appeal to the public and led to one of Kelly's most important contributions to American musical history, the screen adaptation of the Broadway musical *On the Town*.

The story of three sailors on leave, *On the Town* (1949) was codirected by Kelly and Stanley Donen. Its innovations included location shooting on the streets of New York, the use of jump cuts to compress time and space, and, most important, the employment of dance as the overriding stylistic and aesthetic motivation for the film's design. "I really believed [*On the Town*] would be a milestone," Kelly later said, "because I set out to try to make it so," and it always remained the film closest to his heart. Roles in a drama, *The Black Hand*, and in Judy Garland's last MGM musical *Summer Stock* followed in 1950. Kelly then set out to make another milestone, a film that would be shot on location in Paris, feature the music of George Gershwin, and climax in a twenty-minute original ballet.

An American in Paris (1951), directed by Vincente Minnelli, ended up being shot in Hollywood, but it brought more honor and profit to MGM and to Gene Kelly than any other of his films before or since. Perhaps the quintessential product of the renowned "Freed Unit" at MGM, *An American in Paris* represents the advantages of the Hollywood producer–directed "stock company," in which the "self-consciously innovative" labor of the best obtainable writers, directors, composers, lyricists, designers, performers, and technicians was under contract and on call in the service of art as well as of commerce. *An American in Paris* was the first musical since 1929 to win the Academy Award for best picture; it won seven other Oscars as well, and it brought Kelly a special Oscar for his "extreme versatility as an actor, singer, director, and dancer" and "specifically for his brilliant achievement in the art of choreography on film."

The final film in what some critics have called Kelly's "great trilogy" at MGM was *Singin' in the Rain* (1952), again codirected by Kelly with Stanley Donen. Written around several song standards of Arthur Freed and Nacio Herb Brown, *Singin' in the Rain* was an affectionate look backward to the development of the movie musical itself during Hollywood's transition to sound in the late 1920s. Although it did not make as much money as *An American in Paris*, critics have since come to recognize *Singin' in the Rain* as "a nearly perfect film," one that appears on several lists of the best movies of all time. In 1989, it was one of the first twenty-five films chosen by the Library of Congress to be placed in its National Film Registry.

The breakup of the studio system by the mid-1950s also signaled the decline of the expensive and labor-intensive Hollywood musical as a genre, and Kelly's 1953 films were a thriller made in Germany called *The Devil Makes Three* and a comic melodrama shot in England called *Crest of the Wave*. Kelly also directed and performed in a three-part all-dance "prestige" film for MGM, shot in France and England in 1954, called *Invitation to the Dance* (another sign of the musical's downturn was that MGM shelved the film, giving it only limited release in 1956). Upon returning to Hollywood, Kelly made two more musicals, neither of which was financially successful—*Brigadoon* (1954) and *It's Always Fair Weather* (1955), both with Cyd Charisse. *It's Always Fair Weather* was a sequel of sorts to *On the Town*, and its dark and pessimistic mood—no romantic duets, and dances that usually burst from drunkenness and despair rather than joyful high spirits and happiness—exemplified many of the shifts in attitude taking place in American culture during the Cold War years. (A bit cheerier was the period number, "I Love to Go Swimmin' with Wimmin," that Gene performed with his brother Fred in Stanley Donen's 1954 tribute to Sigmund Romberg, *Deep in My Heart*.)

Fast approaching middle age in an entertainment industry that increasingly courted the "youth audience," Kelly starred in one more musical for MGM, *Les Girls*, and directed and performed in a straight film made in France, *The Happy Road*, both in 1957. He then began to freelance, playing dramatic roles in films like *Marjorie Morningstar* (1958) and *Inherit the Wind* (1960) and guest-starring in the Marilyn Monroe film *Let's Make Love* (1960), *What a Way to Go!* (1964), *The Young Girls of Rochefort* (French, 1968), and *Forty Carats* (1973). He continued to hone his skills as a director and producer with *The Tunnel of Love* (1958), a Doris Day film, and *Gigot* (1962), with Jackie Gleason as a mute French peasant. Kelly's biggest box-office and critical success as a director was the comic film *A Guide for the Married Man* (1967); this led to Kelly's being chosen to direct the film version of *Hello Dolly!* (1969), with Barbra Streisand, and the comedy-western *The Cheyenne Social Club* (1970), which he also produced.

In the late 1950s Kelly began to work again on the stage. In 1958 he directed the musical *Flower Drum Song*, which was a commercial if not a critical success. The Ballet Company of the Paris Opera also commissioned Kelly to choreograph a full-length dance work; the music he chose to use was George Gershwin's *Concerto in F*. The ballet, with the punning title *Pas de Dieux*, opened in Paris on 6 July 1960, and received a fifteen-minute ovation and twenty-seven curtain calls. Kelly, who would continue a love affair with France through the end of his life, was subsequently made a *chevalier* of the French Legion of Honor.

And, like many other Hollywood stars of the studio era, Kelly became a familiar face on television variety shows and specials. One of his most influential and popular television efforts was "Dancing Is a Man's Game" (1958), part of the "Omnibus" series, in which he choreographed dance routines that were performed by athletes as well as dancers in order to counter the "dancing is for girls" myth that Kelly had been fighting since his Pittsburgh days. "Jack and the Beanstalk," a combination of animation and live action that Kelly directed in 1967, won an Emmy as the outstanding children's program of the season. Kelly also starred briefly as Father O'Malley in the short-lived television series "Going My Way" (1962).

The 1970s were marked by a nationwide nostalgia for the sort of innocence and good times that the classic Hollywood musical represented, and Kelly was one of the stars whose work was prominently featured in the 1974 MGM compilation film, *That's Entertainment!* In the summer of 1974 he starred in a period stage musical, *Take Me Along*, in Dallas and St. Louis. *That's Entertainment! Part II*, for which Kelly choreographed new bridging sections for himself and Fred Astaire, appeared in 1976. Kelly's last feature film role was in the "futuristic" 1980 musical *Xanadu*, with Olivia Newton-John; although Kelly came to call the film "a mistake," it has since become a cult classic. Kelly also narrated *That's Dancing!* in 1985 and reminisced about his days in Hollywood for *That's Entertainment! Part III* in 1994.

Kelly's marriage to Betsy Blair had ended in 1957, and in 1960 he married Jeanne Coyne, whom he had known since she was a student in his Pittsburgh studio. They had two children, Timothy and Bridget. Coyne died of leukemia in 1973. In 1990 Kelly married Patricia Ward. Ill health had begun to plague him, and in 1994 and 1995 he suffered a series of strokes from which he never fully recovered. He died in his sleep at home in Beverly Hills.

In addition to Oscars and Emmys, the multifaceted career of Gene Kelly brought him other tributes and awards. In 1962, for example, the Museum of Modern Art presented a Gene Kelly Dance Film Festival. In 1981 he was the subject of a two-week film festival in France. On 5 December 1982 he was given a Lifetime Achievement Award in the fifth annual Kennedy Center Honors. In 1994, in a ceremony at the White House, President Bill Clinton presented Kelly with the National Medal of Arts. But these and other awards served only to stamp an official seal of approval on a perfectionist choreo-cinema-maker—an athletic, charming, and well-loved song-and-dance man who, dressed often in a sweatshirt and white socks and rolled up sleeves and blue jeans, happened to have a "unique ability," as one reviewer put it in 1962, "to appear not at all unique."

• Book-length biographies of Kelly include Clive Hirschhorn, *Gene Kelly: A Biography* (1974; rev. ed., 1984), and Jeanine Basinger, *Gene Kelly* (1976); entries about Kelly can also be found in most encyclopedias of film and film actors. Reliable information about Kelly's films can be found in Tony Thomas, *The Films of Gene Kelly, Song and Dance Man* (1991). Obituaries are in the *New York Times*, 3 Feb. 1996, and *Variety*, 5–11 Feb. 1996.

ADRIENNE L. MCLEAN

KEMPTON, Murray (16 Dec. 1918–5 May 1997), journalist, was born in Baltimore, Maryland, to James Branson Kempton, a stockbroker, and his wife, Sally Ambler Kempton. The senior Kempton died when Murray was three, and he was raised in a shabby genteel household whose atmosphere was dominated by his mother's Virginia relatives. He later recalled that their notions of honor, courtesy, and gentlemanly behavior were derived from the code of the Old South, and though Kempton became a social and political maverick he never lost his esteem for their values.

Kempton was educated at local schools and at Johns Hopkins University, where he wrote for the student newspaper, flirted with Communism, and became a member of the Socialist party. After graduating in 1939 with a degree in history and government, he first became a social worker in Baltimore and then was hired as an organizer by the International Ladies Garment Workers Union in Peekskill, New York. He subsequently worked as publicity director of the American Labor party in New York. His career goal, however, was journalism, and in 1942 he was hired by the *New York Post* as a labor reporter. Not long afterward he was drafted by the army and served for the next three years in the Pacific.

After the war ended in 1945 Kempton worked for several years as a reporter for a North Carolina newspaper, the *Wilmington Star*, before returning to the *Post* in 1947. His well-crafted stories about union activities, including the possible link of union officials to organized crime, earned him a promotion to labor editor of the *Post* two years later. While he continued to write about union affairs he also began doing articles on other subjects, including domestic and foreign politics, and during the 1950s civil rights and civil liberties became the focus of his concern.

This was the so-called McCarthy era, when the search led by Senator Joseph McCarthy of Wisconsin for Communist influence in government had mushroomed into what many feared was a wholesale attack on American democracy. National hysteria, fed by the Cold War, drove alleged Communist sympathizers from their jobs and often from their communities, and loyalty oaths became a requirement for employment. As a columnist at the then-liberal *Post*, Kempton was free to warn against the dangers of McCarthyism, which he did with both wit and eloquence. But he also took Communists to task for what he saw as their naiveté, in particular their blindness to Communism's ultimate betrayal of personal liberty, and he went on to expand his thoughts in his first book, *Part of Our Time: Some Ruins and Monuments of the Thirties* (1955), in which he examined the heyday of the American Communist party in the 1930s. The book was dismissed by conservatives, who felt that Kempton, though disdaining Communism, was still too radical in sentiment. It was also rejected by many on the left, who thought that Kempton had refused to recognize an important role in the radical movement played by these early Communists. However, the book received generous praise from critics who were liberal but staunchly anti-Communist—a category that best described Kempton himself, both as a journalist and as a private individual.

The 1950s also saw the birth of the civil rights movement, and Kempton wrote a number of articles that sympathetically chronicled its early years. He covered the national political conventions of 1952 and 1956 and the subsequent campaigns, ultimately mourning the two-time loss of the Democratic presidential candidate, Adlai Stevenson, his only political hero: Kempton had long since forsworn his allegiance to the Socialist party and was now a Democrat. He spent much of 1958 in Italy on a Fulbright grant, teaching journalism at the University of Rome. The following year he traveled with Soviet premier Nikita Khrushchev on his American tour, and in 1960 he again covered the American presidential campaign. In the early 1960s he continued to write about the civil rights movement in the South, especially the work of Martin Luther King, Jr., and briefly participated in the Freedom Rides.

Kempton's second book, a collection of his columns titled *America Comes of Middle Age*, was published in 1963 and was reviewed favorably by the critics as a fair assessment of the United States at midcentury. In the spring of that year he moved to Washington, D.C., to become an editor and columnist at the *New Republic*, then a liberal weekly, but remained there for little more than a year. He returned to New York in the fall of 1964 to become a columnist for the *New York-World-Telegram and Sun*, and when it stopped publication in the spring of 1966 he returned to the *Post* and resumed writing his old column. Kempton, who had eschewed participation in national politics for more than a decade following the defeat of Adlai Stevenson in 1956, became an active supporter of Democratic presidential hopeful Eugene McCarthy in the spring of 1968, amid growing opposition to the Vietnam War, and served as a delegate from New York to the Democratic National Convention in Chicago that August. Following the nomination of Hubert Humphrey on 29 August, Kempton joined an antiwar demonstration along Chicago's Michigan Avenue and was arrested for disorderly conduct. Although he claimed that he was participating in "a peaceful revolt" against government wrongdoing, he was convicted the following spring and fined $250; an appeal of his conviction was denied in March 1972.

Beginning in the mid-1950s Kempton contributed articles to a number of national magazines, including *Harper's*, the *Atlantic Monthly*, *Esquire*, and others, and from 1969 on was a frequent reviewer and essayist for the *New York Review of Books*. In 1973 he published his third book, *The Briar Patch: The People of the State of New York vs. Lumumba Shakur, et al.*, an assessment of the Black Panthers. He continued at the *Post* until 1981, when it became a conservative paper, and moved on to *Newsday*, writing a column for that paper until his death; its appearance was sporadic in his final years. His subjects were major and minor events in public life, and his rhetorical stance was invariably on the side of decency, fairness, and support for the underdog. He even found himself coming to Richard Nixon's defense in 1984, when the disgraced ex-president was denied the right to buy a co-op on Manhattan's East Side.

Kempton won a number of professional awards, including a Pulitzer Prize in 1985 for commentary. His last book, a collection of columns, titled *Rebellions, Perversities, and Main Events*, was published in 1994. He died of pancreatic cancer at a nursing home in New York City.

Kempton was married twice. His first wife was Mina Blumenthal, whom he married in 1942; they had four children. They were later divorced and he subsequently married Beverly Gary, with whom he had one son. In his final years he was the companion of Barbara Epstein, coeditor of the *New York Review of Books*.

Kempton's writing style was variously described as pungent, truculent, acerbic, and witty—adjectives that could also be applied to the work of a fellow Baltimorean, journalist H. L. Mencken. But it could also be opaque: unlike the usually terse Mencken, Kempton could generate elaborately constructed thickets of prose whose ultimate meaning often eluded readers and perplexed even admiring critics. In one famous incident he was acquitted in a libel suit brought by writer Victor Navasky because the court did not understand the meaning of the allegedly offensive article. His syntax aside, Kempton was long considered the conscience of American journalism. Throughout his career he was an outspoken supporter of fairness and decency in public life; and though both his audience and his popularity declined in the last two decades of his life, he was remembered at his death as a tireless champion of the poor and the powerless.

• For biographical information, see "Kempton, Murray," in the 1973 and 1997 editions of *Current Biography Yearbook*; *Contemporary Authors*, vols. 97–100 (1981), and vol. 158 (1998); and *Contemporary Authors: New Revision Series*, vol. 51 (1996). An obituary appears in the *New York Times*, 6 May 1997.

ANN T. KEENE

KENNEDY, John F., Jr. (25 Nov. 1960–16 July 1999), American icon, publisher, and lawyer, was born John Fitzgerald Kennedy, Jr., in Washington, D.C., the son of President John F. Kennedy, a descendant of a politically and socially prominent Massachusetts family, and Jacqueline Bouvier Kennedy, also from a socially prominent family. Born just seventeen days after his father was elected president of the United States, John-John (as he was nicknamed) was immediately thrust into the public eye and remained under its glare throughout his life. His early childhood was clouded by President Kennedy's assassination on 22 November 1963, which was believed to be a part of the so-called Kennedy curse, a long series of tragedies that has plagued the family. The murder robbed the president's only son of any first-hand recollections of his father. As a result, he said that he recalled very little about him. After the assassination, he, his mother, and sister Caroline moved out of the White House and settled in a colonial home in Georgetown.

Despite the constant public spotlight and the burden of being part of "America's Royal Family," Jacqueline Kennedy was determined to give her children as normal an upbringing as possible. She protected their privacy as much as she could, relocating the family in 1964 to New York City, where they moved into a large Fifth Avenue apartment overlooking Central Park. She also raised her children to be modest, hardworking, and well mannered. For John, however, there were constant reminders that he was not like other children, such as the fact that two Secret Service agents always accompanied him until he reached the age of sixteen.

In 1965 Kennedy began elementary school at St. David's, a private Catholic school for boys. He transferred in 1968 to Manhattan's Collegiate School, another exclusive boy's school. The Kennedy family was again beset by tragedy on 5 June of that year, when John, Jr.'s uncle Robert F. Kennedy was also assassinated. Fearing for her children's safety, his mother remarked, "If they're killing Kennedys, then my children are targets." Four months after Bobby Kennedy's death, Jacqueline Kennedy married Greek shipping tycoon Aristotle Onassis, but the family continued to live in New York most of the year so that John and Caroline could continue attending their regular schools. Their summers and vacations, however, were spent in Greece. When her second husband died in 1975, Jacqueline Kennedy Onassis and the children permanently relocated to New York City.

In 1975 John Kennedy enrolled in prep school at Phillips Academy in Andover, Massachusetts. Like his father, he was an average student, and he had particular trouble with spelling. His lack of academic interest often caused him to miss class, and as a result he failed one of his finals and had to spend an extra year at Andover. During his summer breaks his mother would send him on adventure and public-service vacations, including work in an earthquake-ravaged Guatemalan village, an Outward Bound wilderness course in Maine, and a stint on a Wyoming cattle ranch. She also taught him the value of public service, which she considered a large part of the Kennedy legacy. As a result, during the school year, he volunteered in Andover's community service program teaching English to disadvantaged immigrant children.

After finishing at Andover in 1979, Kennedy opted to go to Brown University rather than to Harvard, as his father, uncles, and sister had done. He enrolled at Brown in the fall of 1979, majoring in American history. While in college, he contemplated a career on the stage, appearing in several on-campus productions, including *The Tempest* and J. M. Synge's *The Playboy of the Western World*. His mother did not want him to be an actor, however, and, as he often did, he deferred to her wishes.

Kennedy graduated from Brown with a degree in history in 1983, and he spent the next three years traveling and working for several nonprofit organizations. In 1984 he took a job as a management and planning assistant in New York City's Office of Business Development. He also continued to act periodically in community theater productions.

In the fall of 1986 Kennedy began studying law at New York University Law School. The following summer he worked as a law intern in Los Angeles. In 1987 he was a law clerk with the Justice Department, and from 1988 to 1989 Kennedy, with the financial support of the Joseph P. Kennedy, Jr., Foundation, helped to develop the Mental Retardation and Developmental Disabilities Studies Programs, which awarded fellowships to needy students.

After he received his law degree in 1989, Kennedy took the New York State bar exam but failed it. Despite this early but well-publicized failure, he immediately was hired as an assistant district attorney in the New York district attorney's office. There he was responsible for intake duty, which entailed interviewing criminal defendants and people seeking to file complaints. In February 1990 he took the bar exam a second time and failed it again. When he took it for a third time in July 1990, however, he passed. He continued to work in the district attorney's office until 1993, when he resigned. During his short tenure he won all six of his cases and was regarded as an adequate attorney.

Despite the constant barrage of photographers and journalists following him, Kennedy carefully guarded his privacy, much as his mother did. As a result, many of his charitable acts were not publicized, and he was often portrayed in the media as a carefree, irresponsible playboy. In 1988, for example, he was named "Sexiest Man of the Year" by *People* magazine.

Kennedy took his legacy and responsibilities quite seriously, however, devoting himself to several nonprofit organizations and often reciting his grandmother's favorite quote, "Of everyone to whom much has been given, much will be required." He founded the nonprofit group Reach Up, an organization that helped those who care for the mentally disabled. Fearing that it would take away from the organization's mission, he often left his name out of its news releases. In 1991 Kennedy joined the Robin Hood Foundation, a group that fights poverty through food and after-school programs.

A member of President Bill Clinton's Committee on Mental Retardation, Kennedy also sat on the boards of the Institute of Politics at the John F. Kennedy School of Government at Harvard and the JFK Library Foundation. In 1989 he and his sister created the Profile in Courage Award, given out annually at the JFK Presidential Library in Boston. After the death of their mother in 1994, he and Caroline continued her work for the JFK Library and other charitable activities.

After discovering the law was not for him, Kennedy embarked on an entrepreneurial adventure. In September 1995 he launched his own publication, *George*, a political and popular culture magazine with the slogan "Not just politics as usual." The magazine, whose early covers featured celebrities and politicians dressed as famous historical figures such as George

Washington and Benjamin Franklin, received mixed reactions and never could secure for itself a fixed identity and a large subscription base.

As one of the country's most eligible bachelors, Kennedy won more press for his alleged involvements with women than he did for his work and charitable activities; he was romantically linked to, among others, the singer Madonna and actresses Julia Roberts, Sarah Jessica Parker, and Darryl Hannah. Once he entered into a lasting relationship with Carolyn Bessette, a Calvin Klein public relations executive, the media refocused its attention. They were married on 21 September 1996 in a private ceremony on an island off the Georgia Coast, and they then settled in the fashionable TriBeCa neighborhood of New York City. Unlike Kennedy, his wife rarely spoke to the media, and he implored the photographers and reporters surrounding their home to leave his wife alone.

From an early age, the athletic Kennedy had an adventurous spirit and enjoyed the outdoors. As a child, he took tennis lessons, learned to ski, and often rode his bike through Central Park. As an adult he could often be seen skating and biking to work through the streets of New York City or running in Central Park. He would take white-water-rafting, hiking, and parasailing vacations and was known to his friends as the "Master of Disaster" because of his fearlessness. Kennedy also developed a love for flying and earned his pilot's license in 1998.

Just one year after earning his pilot's license, on 16 July 1999, Kennedy embarked on an early evening flight in his Piper Saratoga with his wife and her sister, Lauren Bessette, on board. En route from New Jersey, they were approaching the island of Martha's Vineyard at dusk when the plane disappeared. An intense search-and-rescue mission involving the U.S. Navy was launched, although it was soon realized that the plane had to have gone down at sea and that its famous passengers must have perished. The extraordinary round-the-clock media coverage lasted for days, and throngs maintained a vigil outside Kennedy's residence in lower Manhattan. Once the bodies were recovered, the probable cause of the crash was thought to have been Kennedy's inability to fly the plane in low visibility without training and the use of navigational aids. The nationwide outpouring of grief culminated in the funeral held in New York, which, though closed to the public, drew numerous political and civic leaders. On 22 July 1999 the victims' bodies were cremated and their ashes strewn in the Atlantic Ocean, in part to ensure that there would be no gravesite to attract hordes of curiosity-seekers.

Kennedy experienced both the burdens and the privileges of birth in a famous political family and lived his life under constant media scrutiny, from the ridicule of his failed attempts to pass the bar exam to the grisly details of his death appearing in the tabloid *National Enquirer*. But he managed to create a dignified life of his own out of the shadow of the revered memory of his father, establishing himself as an independent thinker and remaining relatively unscathed by the incredible attention paid to him. Because he died at the age of only thirty-eight, however, questions about his ultimate legacy remain. Would he have entered politics? Could he have followed in his father's footsteps? We will never know for, as his uncle Senator Edward Kennedy said in his eulogy, John Kennedy "had every gift but length of years."

• Biographies are in Wendy Leigh, *Prince Charming: The John F. Kennedy, Jr. Story* (1993; rev. ed. 1994), and Stephen Spignesi, *The J.F.K. Jr. Scrapbook* (1997). Profiles of Kennedy's life appeared in special commemorative issues of *Time,* 26 July 1999; *Newsweek,* 26 July 1999; *People,* 2 Aug. 1999; and *People,* 31 Dec. 1999. Extensive obituaries are in *Nation,* 9 Aug. 1999; *Newsweek,* 2 Aug. 1999; *Time,* 2 Aug. 1999; *U.S. News and World Report,* 2 Aug. 1999; *New Republic,* 9 Aug. 1999; and *George,* Oct. 1999. Obituaries are also in the *New York Times,* 19 and 22 July 1999.

JUDITH B. GERBER

KENNER, Duncan Farrar (11 Feb. 1813–3 July 1887), businessman and Confederate legislator and diplomat, was born in New Orleans, Louisiana, the youngest son of William Kenner and Mary Minor Kenner. He was educated by private tutors and in private schools in New Orleans, where his father was a prosperous merchant, planter, and public official. Duncan's mother died at age twenty-seven when he was twenty months old, and his father died when he was eleven. Raised by relatives, Duncan attended Miami University in Oxford, Ohio, where he completed his studies in 1831. From the spring of 1832 to the fall of 1834 he traveled and studied in Europe; letters of introduction and social contacts brought him twice to the Austrian court, including a private meeting with Prince Klemens von Metternich, and to a ball for European royalty given by Baron Rothschild.

On his return from Europe he studied law in the New Orleans firm of John Slidell, a friend of his father. Having inherited a sizable estate, Kenner turned his attention to the development of his large sugar plantation, "Ashland," in Ascension Parish, Louisiana. A talented businessman and planter, he was able to develop Ashland into one of the largest and most profitable plantations in the state. By the eve of the Civil War, he maintained a slave force of 473, making him Louisiana's eleventh-largest slaveholder.

Kenner's financial success as a sugar planter permitted him to enjoy a grand lifestyle. The manor house he and his wife built at their Ashland estate was among the finest in Louisiana. (He married Anne Guillelmine Nanine Bringier, a member of one of Louisiana's most prominent French families, on 1 June 1839. They had two daughters and two sons.) Training and breeding thoroughbred horses on a private track at Ashland, Kenner earned a national reputation as his horses won prizes at New Orleans, Saratoga, and other prominent tracks.

In 1836, at the age of twenty-three, Kenner was elected to the Louisiana House of Representatives; he served several terms in the house and the state senate. Respected by his colleagues for his judgment and his serious, businesslike manner, he was a leader of the state's Whig party. An advocate of constitutional reform in antebellum Louisiana, he served as an active member of the state's 1844 Constitutional Convention and as president of the 1852 Louisiana Constitutional Convention. During his prewar political career, Kenner focused more on state issues than national problems, but as Louisianians became engaged in the sectional debate of the 1850s he maintained a hard-line position in favor of states' rights and favored secession following Abraham Lincoln's election in 1860.

With his sugar-growing neighbors opposing secession, Kenner lost in his effort to win election to Louisiana's secession convention. However, once the state broke its ties with the Union, he was one of seven Louisiana delegates sent by the state in February 1861 to the Montgomery convention, where the Confederate States were formed. At the meeting he was a strong supporter of Jefferson Davis and took a nationalist approach, advocating a national government similar to that of the United States. While he urged protective tariffs and subsidies for internal improvements, he called on the new nation to develop a more diversified economy.

As chairman of the House Ways and Means Committee, Kenner focused on the Confederacy's financing. Having studied and traveled in the North, he understood the massive power of the South's adversary and advocated conscription and all-out military preparation. As New Orleans fell to Union forces in April 1862 and a large part of Louisiana came under Federal occupation, he argued for impressment of slaves into military service and opposed exemptions from military duty, particularly the detested Twenty Slave Law. Early in 1863 he notified President Davis and Secretary of State Judah P. Benjamin, a close friend (and fellow Louisianian) with whom he shared lodgings while living in Richmond, that he was going to propose in Congress that, as a wartime measure, slaves should be emancipated and drafted as a way of bolstering the South's military and diplomatic efforts. Not only would the move provide needed men for the military, it would go a long way—or so Kenner thought—in winning diplomatic recognition from England and France. (It was widely believed that the slavery issue was the main obstacle preventing those nations from recognizing the South's independence.) Such recognition by the European powers, it was hoped, would soon lead to military aid for the floundering Confederacy. Otherwise, Kenner argued, the South could not win the war or remain an independent nation. Although Benjamin agreed with the reasoning, he felt the time was not right, and he and Davis quickly vetoed the notion and urged Kenner to say no more about it.

By late 1864, following Lincoln's reelection and a series of crushing reverses on the battlefield, and with several southern newspapers urging that slavery be sacrificed, if necessary, for national independence, Benjamin urged Davis to send Kenner to Europe on a secret mission to negotiate for diplomatic recognition in exchange for the abolition of slavery. Kenner possessed the conviction to speak persuasively and had the political acumen to carry out such a mission; further, he already had longtime relationships with the Confederacy's European emissaries John Slidell and James M. Mason, in France and England, respectively. To win support, Davis discreetly arranged a meeting with several leading congressmen, who violently objected that emancipation would ruin them financially. Kenner insisted that the Confederacy was in peril and pointed out that, as one of the South's largest slave owners, he was not requesting any greater sacrifice than he was willing to make himself. It was decided that Kenner would have plenary power to negotiate with England and France for recognition in exchange for emancipation and the authority to sell all of the South's cotton to finance arms purchases.

Kenner's bold crossing of enemy lines (in disguise) and sailing from New York City on a German passenger liner was a truly daring adventure. Five weeks after leaving Richmond, Kenner reached Paris on 24 February 1865. Slidell and Mason strongly opposed the plan until they understood that Kenner had both the president's and the secretary of state's backing and authority, which superseded their power. Slidell's meeting with Napoleon III on 4 March and Mason's with British prime minister Palmerston on 13 March, however, were to no avail; France would not act first, and Britain refused to risk a war with the United States. The British concluded that even if they wanted to assist the South, the Confederacy's military options were exhausted and beyond resuscitation.

Kenner was still in Europe when Richmond was evacuated by the Confederate government; a week later, Robert E. Lee surrendered to Ulysses S. Grant. At the United States Legation in Paris on 20 June, Kenner took an oath of loyalty to the United States and applied for an executive pardon. Having obtained a pardon from President Andrew Johnson, Kenner returned to his economically devastated Ashland estate. Unlike many of his fellow planters, Kenner survived the war with some resources. When confiscated by Federal forces, his Ashland estate had been leased by the government to individuals friendly to Kenner. Hence, when he returned home his holdings, though much reduced from their prewar grandeur, were substantial enough to permit the talented planter to regain quickly much of his prewar wealth. Faced with the many challenges of the postwar economy in Louisiana, Kenner resorted to innovative ways to rebuild his financial assets. He was probably the first in Louisiana to use the portable railroad to transport sugar cane from the fields to the mill. He used the very latest machinery in sugar production, including Norbert Rillieux's double-effect pans and the hydraulic pressure regulator developed by John McDonald. Kenner helped organize and was the first president of the Louisiana Sugar Planters' Association in 1877 and the Sugar Experimental Station in 1885.

Prominent in Louisiana politics during Reconstruction, Kenner played an active role in the Democratic party's attempts to regain control from Republican domination. He served in the state senate from 1866 to 1867 and again in 1878. While in the postwar legislature, he took the lead in preparing legislation that became known as the Black Code. Designed to return the former slaves in Louisiana to a status historian Roger Shugg has described as being somewhere between peonage and serfdom, the code was considered by people in the North and the U.S. Congress as an outrageous attempt to circumvent the Thirteenth Amendment and contributed to the imposition of Radical Reconstruction in the South.

During Radical Reconstruction, Kenner maintained amicable relations with both sides of the controversy, including a friendship with the controversial and corrupt Republican governor Henry Clay Warmoth. Because of his conciliatory attitude, Kenner became an active player for the Democratic party during the disputed presidential election of 1876, pitting Rutherford B. Hayes against Samuel J. Tilden, and he was instrumental in the Democrats' successful effort to regain control of the state's political machinery. Kenner eventually abandoned his hard line against the former slaves and worked for some political accommodations to be extended to black Louisianians.

Kenner continued to contribute his services to public endeavors for the rest of his life. In 1882 President Chester A. Arthur appointed him to the United States Tariff Commission, and Kenner also served on the Louisiana Levee Board. In 1884–1885 he served as chairman of the building committee for the World's Industrial and Cotton Centennial Exposition held in New Orleans. Continuing his passion for thoroughbred training and racing, Kenner was one of the founders of the Louisiana Jockey Club and served as president until his death in New Orleans in 1887 at age 74.

Although Kenner's most memorable action was his attempt to get the Confederacy to exchange emancipation for European diplomatic recognition and assistance, throughout his life he played a pivotal role in the political, economic, and social development of his state and region. Even though he uncritically accepted the racial assumptions of the antebellum South, Kenner contributed much to the development of Louisiana and the region. The breadth of his contributions across such a diverse spectrum of activities as state and national politics, diplomacy, large-scale commercial agriculture, science, business, and sports places him among the leading social and political architects of the nineteenth-century South.

• Duncan Kenner's travel diaries of his Grand Tour are collected (with notes and an introduction by Garner Ranney) in *A Man of Pleasure, And a Man of Business: The European Travel Diaries of Duncan Farrar Kenner, 1833–1834* (1991). The most abundant single source of Kenner's private papers is the Louisiana State University Archives, Baton Rouge, which holds the Duncan Farrar Kenner Papers, Kenner Family Papers, William Kenner Papers, an Ashland Plantation Record Book, and a half dozen other collections of family papers. The Historic New Orleans Collection has the Duncan Farrar Kenner Papers and an Ashland Plantation Journal, 1858, while the Louisiana State Museum's Archives and Manuscript Collection, New Orleans, has Duncan Farrar Kenner Papers. Tulane University's Manuscript Department, Special Collections Division, has a Duncan Farrar Kenner file and Benjamin Farrar Papers. The Library of Congress's Manuscript Division holds a Duncan Farrar Kenner Collection and the James M. Mason Papers.

The only full-length biography of Duncan Kenner is Craig A. Bauer, *A Leader among Peers: The Life and Times of Duncan Farrar Kenner* (1993). Bauer recounts Kenner's daring mission in "The Last Effort: The Secret Mission of the Confederate Diplomat, Duncan F. Kenner," *Louisiana History* 22 (1981): 67–95. A master's thesis by Grady Daniel Price, "The Secret Mission of Duncan F. Kenner, Confederate Minister Plenipotentiary to Europe in 1865" (1929), is at Tulane University.

CRAIG A. BAUER
MARK LAFLAUR

KESSEN, William (18 Jan. 1925–13 Feb. 1999), psychologist, educator, and historian, was born in Key West, Florida, the only child of Maria Lord Kessen, a third generation Key Wester, and Herman Kessen of Georgia, a ship's engineer with the Peninsular and Occidental Steamship line. The family moved to Fort Lauderdale when Kessen was ten; he graduated from high school at the precocious age of sixteen. The first in his family to attend college, Kessen pursued a variety of interests at the University of Florida, including history, acting, and radio announcing, but his undergraduate studies were interrupted by the outbreak of World War II.

Kessen was drafted in 1943 when he turned eighteen but spent the war as a clerk typist stationed in Litchfield, England. Meeting a wide range of other intellectuals in Colonel Killian's 10th Replacement Depot relieved the tedium of the work but also whetted his appetite for further study. He returned to Florida to study psychology in 1946, with support from the G.I. Bill. Psychologist David Spelt, Kessen's adviser at the University of Florida, encouraged him to apply to graduate school, and in 1948 he enrolled in the graduate program in psychology at Brown University. Later, in an autobiographical composition, he would place the move north in the context of a journey begun at age ten: "a flight from the values that defined my people . . . I was a committed Roosevelt liberal, a doubter of the heart values of the White South, and an unbeliever."

Like his peers at Brown, Kessen was a "rat-runner," working on a dissertation on response strength and stimulus intensity. Unlike many of his peers, he evinced an interest in methodology, an interest that slowly blossomed into a parallel career in history over the next forty years. At Brown, he met his "best and truest friend," fellow researcher Marion Lord; they fell in love and married in 1950; the couple would have six children: three daughters and triplet sons. Kessen finished the master's portion of his graduate

studies at Brown, but when his adviser, Gregory Kimble, was hired by Yale in 1950, Kessen transferred to Yale and wrote his dissertation there. His new colleagues at Yale engaged many of Kessen's broader interests. He frequented the classes of philosopher Carl Gustav Hempel, and social psychologist Carl Hovland provided an early model of the Socratic teaching and dedicated mentorship that Kessen himself soon exemplified. He began work on his first philosophical book with fellow student George Mandler, who would remain a lifelong friend and collaborator.

Kessen received his Ph.D. from Yale in 1952 and for two years worked as a postdoctoral fellow at Yale with child psychoanalyst Kaethe Wolf. Wolf had studied with Charlotte Buehler and Jean Piaget before fleeing her native Austria in 1940. She brought a radically different research sensibility to a department oriented toward positive science and impressed Kessen as a thinker, a writer, and a teacher. Perhaps owing to her influence, he began his career as an assistant professor at Yale (1954) with the study of infancy.

In the fifties, many of Kessen's studies concerned newborn sucking and movement, a research program that occupied a middle ground between the behaviorist research of his graduate career and the Piagetian study of intelligence. In 1960, he organized a conference for the Society for Research in Child Development that reintroduced Piaget to American psychology; a report on this conference was published in 1962. In the mid-1960s, with the first stirrings of the cognitive revolution, his own research took a cognitive turn. With Marshall Haith and P. Salapatek, he devised ingenious ways of studying infants' reception of visual events. In retrospect, Kessen's first two decades can be seen to have made remarkable advances in analyzing the psychology of very young infants. Unable to use many of the methods devised to study learning in adults, he derived from the animal literature ways of communicating in the language infants knew best: sucking, gazing, eating, and moving. These years were full and productive in many ways for Kessen. His involvement in the life of the university grew: he became associate professor in 1960 and professor in 1965.

Kessen's career as a historian of psychology began with his second book, *The Child* (1965). A documentary history of childhood, this book juxtaposes the quite varied perspectives of child experts from colonial times on; thus, *The Child* is also the first published record of Kessen's critique of expert knowledge. A subsequent series of trips abroad provided him with a firsthand sense of cultural variations in the construction of childhood. In the late 1960s he was one of the first Western scholars to conduct research in communist Czechoslovakia. In 1970–1971 he worked at the Ospedale degli Innocenti in Florence on a Guggenheim fellowship; he returned to Florence for the 1976–1977 academic year. In 1973 the State Department asked Kessen to lead a delegation of U.S. scholars to China, the first visit after the renewal of diplomatic relations. He published his observations in *Childhood in China* (1975), which was translated into

Danish, Swedish, and German. Kessen became the Eugene Higgins Professor of Psychology in 1976, and professor of pediatrics in 1978. He served as acting secretary of the university in 1980 and acting master of Calhoun College in the spring of 1989.

Kessen's more historical turn coincided with his presidency of Division 7 of the American Psychological Association (Developmental Psychology) in 1979–1980; his address, "The American Child and Other Cultural Inventions," took the discipline by storm and led to a symposium, The Child and Other Cultural Inventions (1981). He introduced a generation of psychologists to the methods and questions of social history and published a number of articles on the early history of psychology and its philosophical premises. His 1990 book, *The Rise and Fall of Development*, collects many of his insights into the field's history and philosophy. At the time of his death in New Haven, he was completing a study called *The Baby Book: 75 Years of Infant Care.*

In a half-century of research, Kessen pushed the boundaries of psychology forward in several ways. Early in his career, he developed ways of interrogating the psychology of very young children. In mid-career, he helped introduce developmental psychology to the cognitive revolution. Toward the end of his career, his historical research challenged developmental psychologists to consider their subject matter—the child—as a cultural rather than a natural object, and thus to consider their own work as a social as well as scientific enterprise.

• Useful publications by and about Kessen include Kessen and C. Kuhlman, eds., "Thought in the Young Child: Report of a conference on intellective development, with particular attention to the work of Jean Piaget," *Monographs of the Society for Research in Child Development* 27, no. 83 (1962). Kessen's address to the American Psychological Association is reprinted in *American Psychologist* 34 (1979): 815-20. The conference proceedings are published as F. S. Kessel and A. W. Siegel, eds., *The Child and Other Cultural Inventions* (1983). Kessen's autobiographical paper, "Nearing the End: A Lifetime of Being 17," is given in a Festschrift in F. S. Kessel, M. H. Bornstein, and A. J. Sameroff, eds., *Contemporary Constructions of the Child: Essays in Honor of William Kessen* (1991). See also Kessen's manuscript, "The Baby Book: 75 Years of Infant Care" (1998). An obituary is in the *New York Times*, 18 Feb. 1999.

JOSEPHINE J. FUESER

KIENHOLZ, Edward (23 Oct. 1927–10 June 1994), artist, was born Edward Ralph Kienholz in Fairfield, Washington, the son of Lawrence U. C. Kienholz, a farmer, and Ella Louise Easton Kienholz. Following his graduation from high school in 1945, Kienholz attended various schools in his home state, including Eastern Washington College of Education, Whitworth College, and Eastern Washington State College. During the late 1940s and early 1950s, he traveled throughout the country and supported himself with numerous jobs, such as buying and selling used cars, working as an attendant in a mental hospital, and managing a dance band. By 1953 Kienholz had settled in Los Angeles, where he met artists and dealers and soon began organizing exhibitions of his and others' work.

Although he received little formal training, Kienholz focused his energies and money on making art. His early work resembled abstract expressionist paintings, but after moving to Los Angeles he began using the debris he found in alleys and streets in his art. He mounted these found objects onto plywood to create three-dimensional wall reliefs coated with paint and resin. Many of his early paintings were simply identified as *Untitled*, but as his pieces became more elaborate, so did his titles, as in *George Washington in Drag* (1957; private collection). This early work explored the artist's concept of the founding father as actually the perverse mother of the country, imbued with a hollow, cynical patriotism rather than with the noble sentiments typically associated with the first president.

In 1957 Kienholz and art historian Walter Hopps opened the Ferus Gallery, which soon became an important showcase for emerging California avant-garde artists, such as Billy Al Bengston, Jay DeFeo, and Richard Diebenkorn. Kienholz himself exhibited at the gallery and maintained his studio in the back room. With his own art career booming, Kienholz sold his share of the gallery to Hopps, whom the artist commemorated in his sculpture *Walter Hopps Hopps Hopps* (1959; Lannan Foundation, Los Angeles). This freestanding sculpture made mainly of a gas station advertisement shows a male figure opening his lapel to reveal miniature Willem de Kooning, Jackson Pollock, and Franz Kline canvases for sale. The reverse side is constructed with pieces of vertebrae, telephone dials, and candy.

During the late 1950s and early 1960s Kienholz used his freestanding, three-dimensional assemblages of found objects often coated in resin to increasingly criticize American history, society, and traditions. *John Doe* (1959; Menil Collection, Houston) and *Jane Doe* (1960; private collection) feature severed mannequin parts presented on a child's stroller or on a table top. John Doe's armless torso stops at the hips and seems to bleed from his heart where a wooden cross resides. Jane Doe's head is bowed and soiled, and hidden beneath her lace "dress" the viewer finds fur minks wrapped around three drawers that represent stages of a woman's life: virginity, maternity, and menopause.

Roxys (1961–1962; private collection) was Kienholz's first constructed tableau. Inspired by a brothel in Nevada, the artist created a domestic interior populated by horrific figures representing prostitutes with titles such as "Miss Cherry Delight" and "Cockeyed Jenny." "Five Dollar Billy" is an assemblage with a woman lying on her back on top of a sewing machine table; her body consists of a life-size torso with a squirrel emerging from her breast. Kienholz revisited the theme of society's treatment of women in his tableau *The Illegal Operation* (1962; private collection), comprising a shopping cart bearing a bag of concrete that oozes out into a soiled bedpan containing various rusted medical instruments.

Kienholz's work became larger and more ambitious and somewhat autobiographical, as seen in *The State Hospital* (1966; Moderna Museet, Stockholm), which was based on his recollections of working in a mental asylum. An enclosed room with a barred window and a single light bulb on the ceiling reveals a naked man on a metal cot. He is trapped literally in his surroundings and figuratively in his head: above him lies the manifestation of his dreams, an identical figure also strapped to the bed.

The Los Angeles County Museum held a retrospective of Kienholz's work in 1966, and in 1968 he participated in the *Documenta 4* exhibition in Kassel, Germany. In 1972 he met photographer Nancy Reddin, who became not only his fifth wife but also his collaborative partner. In 1981 Kienholz announced that all of his work made since 1972 and in the future should bear both his name and his wife's. The couple adopted Reddin's daughter and Kienholz's son and daughter (whose mother was Mary Lynch Kienholz) from their respective previous marriages. Kienholz and Reddin remained together, working side by side, until Kienholz's death from a heart attack in Hope, Idaho, at age sixty-five.

By the early 1970s the Kienholzes had left Los Angeles to spend half the year in Hope and half in Berlin, West Germany. Inspired by their European environment, the couple made a series of assemblages that included *Volksempfänger*, cheap radios used largely to receive propaganda from the Nazi regime during the 1930s and 1940s. Caged, hanging, or displayed on tables, the radios symbolized for the artists the culture of war and an insight into how the dictatorship consumed home life and the workplace.

One of their most ambitious tableaux, *The Art Show* (1963–1977; L. A. Louver Gallery, Venice, Calif.) consists of cast figures with air-conditioning vents (blowing hot air) for faces, who are attending an art gallery opening where paintings by the Kienholzes hang on the walls. The vapid comments of the "viewers" that emanate from tape recorders inside each figure are full of art history rhetoric, showing that the creators of the tableau could turn their critical eyes inward to the hypocrisy of the art world.

During the 1980s the Kienholzes continued making assemblages and installations, several of which dealt with the issue of loneliness and old age. *Sollie 17* (1979–1980; private collection) recreates a room in a cheap residential hotel, occupied by a man perhaps in his seventies who fills his days reading books, playing cards, and staring out the window. *The Pedicord Apts.* (1982–1983; Frederick R. Weisman Art Museum, Minneapolis) consists of a lobby and hallway from a rooming house. The visitor walks into the installation and can hear conversations of the anonymous "occupants" when leaning toward the closed doors.

Kienholz participated in numerous national and international exhibitions, including two Venice Biennales (1977 and 1990) and shows at the Royal Academy of Arts in London and the Hirshhorn Museum and Sculpture Garden in Washington, D.C. The Kienholzes also had several "one-man" exhibitions abroad—in Germany, Denmark, and France—and in the United States at the San Francisco Museum of Modern Art (1984) and the Walker Art Center in Minneapolis (1985). A posthumous traveling retrospective was organized by the Whitney Museum of American Art (1996).

Kienholz's activities in Los Angeles (organizing exhibitions as well as creating artwork) added to the then-burgeoning art scene in that city. Like other artists of the era, such as Lee Bontecou and Louise Nevelson, Kienholz explored possibilities of assemblage made from debris. His work is also akin to that of George Segal, who similarly combined life-cast figures with created environments, but Kienholz's work remained true to a much darker vision than Segal's—one of loneliness, human cruelty and abuse, and extreme dissatisfaction with American society. Kienholz truly expanded on the notion of a tableau, an environment that viewers can enter and experience and where in many cases they can act as voyeurs. One of the few artists during the 1960s and 1970s who addressed contemporary political and social issues, Kienholz may sometimes seem pedantic, but his work was a precursor of the politicized art made in the early 1990s by Barbara Kruger, Lorna Simpson, and the Guerilla Girls.

• *Kienholz: A Retrospective* (Whitney Museum of American Art, 1996) includes extensive information on Kienholz's work as well as essays by Walter Hopps and an extensive chronology written by Nancy Reddin Kienholz. Robert L. Pincus, *On a Scale That Competes with the World: The Art of Edward and Nancy Reddin Kienholz* (1990), provides an extensive critical analysis and interpretation of their work. The catalog *Edward and Nancy Reddin Kienholz: Human Scale* (San Francisco Museum of Modern Art, 1984) includes a short essay written by the artist regarding the creation of the two tableaux *The Pedicord Apts.* and *Jesus Corner*. For Kienholz's early art, see the catalogs *Edward Kienholz* (Los Angeles County Museum of Art, 1966), *Edward Kienholz, 1954–1962* (Menil Collection, 1995, with an essay by Walter Hopps), and *Edward Kienholz: Sculpture 1976–1979* (Henry Art Gallery, University of Washington, 1979). *Edward and Nancy Reddin Kienholz: The Hoerengracht* (Museum of Contemporary Art, San Diego, 1994) is a catalog for the installation of the same title that represented a brothel from Amsterdam. Informative obituaries are in the *New York Times*, 12 June 1994, and *Art in America*, Sept. 1994.

N. ELIZABETH SCHLATTER

KIRKLAND, Lane (12 Mar. 1922–14 Aug. 1999), labor union leader, was born Joseph Lane Kirkland in Camden, South Carolina, the son of Randolph Withers Kirkland, a cotton buyer, and Louise Richardson Kirkland. He grew up in nearby Newberry, where many of his public school classmates had to work long hours after school in substandard conditions; Kirkland would later credit this exposure as the source of his interest in improving the lives of working men and women. Following the outbreak of World War II, he twice unsuccessfully tried to enlist in the Canadian armed forces—prior to the entry of the United States into the war—before returning to South Carolina, where he enrolled at Newberry College. In 1940 Kirkland dropped out of school and spent a year as a deck cadet with the merchant marine before enrolling in the U.S. Merchant Marine Academy. After graduating from the newly opened facility in 1942, he spent the remainder of the war as a chief mate on various cargo ships. In due course he received his master's license and subsequently joined Local 688 of the International Organization of Masters, Mates, and Pilots; it was to be his only direct experience as a rank-and-file union member.

At the end of the war Kirkland settled in Washington, D.C., where he spent his days drafting nautical charts at the U.S. Navy's Hydrographic Office while working toward a B.S. degree from the School of Foreign Service at Georgetown University at night. Upon graduating in 1948, he forsook a possible career in diplomacy and joined the American Federation of Labor (AFL) as a staff researcher. During the next several years he undertook a variety of tasks, including the preparation of a pamphlet on pension bargaining for member unions of the AFL. He also served as a speechwriter, first for Democratic vice-presidential candidate Alben W. Barkley in 1948 and later for presidential standard-bearer Adlai Stevenson in 1952 and 1956. Following the merger of the AFL and the Congress of Industrial Organizations (CIO) in 1955, Kirkland served as assistant director of the organization's Social Security Department before being named director of research and education within the International Union of Operating Engineers.

In 1960 Kirkland returned to the AFL-CIO as executive assistant to president George Meany, and for the next nine years he took an active part in the formation of the federation's policy and day-to-day operations. Often called upon to mediate disputes between member unions, Kirkland played a key role in ending the 1966 New York City transit strike. As one of labor's leading lobbyists on Capitol Hill, he urged the inclusion of a fair employment provision in the 1964 Civil Rights Act. At the end of the 1960s he also served as president of the Institute of Collective Bargaining and Group Relations, an organization that brought labor, management, and government together in an effort to promote the benefits of collective bargaining.

In May 1969 Kirkland was named secretary-treasurer of the AFL-CIO, a post previously held by Meany and considered by many as a springboard to the presidency. While the previous incumbent, William F. Schnitzler, had never earned Meany's trust or respect, Kirkland had in fact been carrying out many of the duties of the office for years. In his new post, he battled with the Nixon administration over its economic policies, earning for himself a spot on Richard Nixon's infamous "enemies list." As Meany's health declined, Kirkland assumed more of his duties, and in November 1979, following Meany's retirement, he became president of the AFL-CIO by acclamation.

As president, Kirkland made the reaffiliation of former AFL-CIO member unions such as the United Auto Workers (UAW) and the International Brotherhood of Teamsters (IBT) a top priority, noting in his acceptance speech that "all sinners belong in church . . . and all true unions belong in the American Federation of Labor and the Congress of Industrial Organizations." A longtime advocate of civil rights, he made the full inclusion of African Americans and women within union ranks a top priority. Kirkland also continued the legacy of his mentor Meany with his strong interest in both domestic political issues and foreign affairs. Previously a vigorous supporter of the American military's role in the Vietnam war (having backed Meany's 1972 decision to withhold labor support for Democratic presidential nominee George McGovern because of his antiwar stance), Kirkland remained an ardent anti-Communist and directed considerable AFL-CIO support to Poland's Solidarity movement in the early 1980s.

Despite successes abroad with Solidarity and at home—marked by an increased presence of women and minorities on union councils and the reaffiliation of both the UAW and the IBT—Kirkland presided over a troubled movement. Domestic union membership continued to decline as the American economy shifted from traditional "smokestack" industries to service-oriented enterprises, and a hostile Ronald Reagan administration in Washington meant that labor spent much of the 1980s fighting to hold onto previous gains. By the early 1990s Kirkland—long considered aloof and arrogant by many—faced an open revolt within labor's ranks; many felt his emphasis on overseas matters hurt the labor movement in the United States. Under heavy pressure, Kirkland resigned in August 1995, and that October he witnessed the defeat of his hand-picked successor, Thomas R. Donahue, at the hands of John J. Sweeney, one of the opposition leaders. Although embittered by the circumstances of his departure, Kirkland took considerable pride in the Presidential Medal of Freedom that he had received in 1994. In retirement he wrote and also worked with labor activists at the George Meany Center for Labor Studies.

Kirkland married Edith Draper Hollyday on 10 June 1944. They had five children, all daughters, but the marriage ended in divorce in 1972. The following year he married Irena Neuman, who survived him following his death from lung cancer at his home in Washington, D.C.

Intelligent and well spoken and with a demeanor suggesting more a college professor than a stereotypical union boss, Lane Kirkland led labor through some of its toughest times. Despite achieving considerable success, he was unable to reverse many of the trends that worked against organized labor in the latter part of the twentieth century. To his credit, he ably promoted union-building overseas, particularly in helping Solidarity overcome the Communist regime in Poland.

• Kirkland's papers are held at the George Meany Memorial Archives in Silver Spring, Md. While Kirkland awaits a biographer, information on his life and career can be gleaned from Joseph C. Goulden's *Meany* (1972) as well as Archie Robinson's *George Meany and His Times* (1981). Obituaries can be found in all major newspapers including the *New York Times* and the *Washington Post*, both 15 Aug. 1999.

EDWARD L. LACH, JR.

KIRSTEIN, Lincoln (4 May 1907–5 Jan. 1996), ballet director, dance historian, and arts activist, was born Lincoln Edward Kirstein in Rochester, New York, the son of Louis E. Kirstein, a businessman, and Rose Stein Kirstein. In 1911 his family moved to Boston where his father became an executive of the upscale Filene's department stores. Kirstein grew up in a world of beautiful visual expression: finely crafted public sculpture, home furnishings, paintings, objets d'art, architecture, and clothing. He attended Boston public schools until the ninth grade, then studied briefly at Exeter, and finished high school at the Berkshire School for Boys. He studied drawing, piano, and dance. Although he never particularly excelled in academics, he demonstrated a deep desire to learn and absorb information.

Kirstein's experience with dance began at age nine in summer camp. There he met one of Isadora Duncan's "Isadorables," whose lessons piqued his interest in dance. At age twelve he watched, with growing fascination, five successive performances given by Anna Pavlova, the famous Russian ballet dancer. At age fifteen, he began his annual summer trips to Europe that introduced him to Russian and European ballet. He spent time with the Bloomsbury group and had the opportunity to view Serge Diaghilev's ballets. He met the economist John Maynard Keynes and his wife Lydia Lopokova, a ballerina in Diaghilev's Les Ballets Russes. Kirstein writes that Keynes taught him to understand aesthetics as distinct from values and how to read visual art through many elements (*Thirty Years*, p. 7). E. M. Forster, Lytton Strachey, and Virgil Thomson also left strong impressions on him during his travels. These experiences sowed the seeds of what became his passion for creating a homegrown American ballet.

On graduating from high school, Kirstein spent a year apprenticing in a stained glass factory before entering Harvard in 1926. At Harvard, he founded and edited *Hound & Horn*, a literary magazine, funded by his father, whose contributors included Ezra Pound, E. E. Cummings, Katherine Anne Porter, and T. S. Eliot. Along with John Walker and Edward Warburg, a family friend and a future funder of the early incarnations of an American ballet, Kirstein helped found the Harvard Society for Contemporary Art, a forerunner to Manhattan's Museum of Modern Art. At this time, Kirstein was immersing himself in the study of art and artists and continuing to paint regularly.

After graduating from Harvard in 1930, Kirstein moved to his "second university," New York City, where he met many influential people in the arts.

Though "incapable of lifting a leg" (*Thirty Years*, p. 4), he briefly studied ballet with choreographer Michel Fokine, momentarily toying with the idea of using him to establish an American ballet. Then he met Muriel Draper, the mother of tap dancer Paul Draper. Muriel Draper bluntly informed Kirstein that he would never be a dancer, painter, or writer and that he should consider organization and management. Although she was not wholly correct, he credited her with giving him focus, meaning, and future direction (*Thirty Years*, p. 12). In 1931, he met Romola Nijinsky, the wife of ballet dancer Vaslav Nijinsky. Kirstein ultimately helped her write Nijinsky's biography, essentially receiving no credit for his efforts; however, he was grateful to Romola Nijinsky for opening the doors to Russian ballet and imbuing him with the skills to negotiate aesthetics, morality, and life with determination and confidence (*Mosaic*, p. 223).

Kirstein continued to travel abroad; he delighted in viewing Diaghilev's ballet performances and was greatly impressed with Diaghilev's young choreographer, George Balanchine. His first meeting with the future ballet revolutionary came through his relationship with theatrical designer Pavel Tchelitchev. Although Tchelitchev believed that to create an American ballet was completely foolish, he suggested Balanchine as the only possible choreographer for such an endeavor. When Kirstein and Balanchine finally met, at a party in London, Kirstein excitedly proposed his entire American ballet plan in thirty minutes. Balanchine said that he would think it over, and he added, famously, "But first a school." Kirstein began to forge relationships with friends and funders who could make it happen.

Before actually establishing a school in New York City, Kirstein lured Balanchine to America with the promise of a season in Hartford, Connecticut, at the Wadsworth Atheneum. The experiment in Hartford, however, soon failed. In 1934 Kirstein and Balanchine established the School of American Ballet on Madison Avenue in New York. Kirstein served as president and was instrumental in implementing his plan to create a space, a company, and a program that would further the growth of this art form in America.

The American Ballet was the first of five companies Kirstein and Balanchine would form together. Just prior to its dissolution in 1937, they created Ballet Caravan (later the American Ballet Caravan) to produce works by young, promising choreographers. Lew Christensen's *Filling Station* and Eugene Loring's *Billy the Kid* were both produced by this short-lived company, which toured in 1941 and then dissolved. That same year, Kirstein married Fidelma Cadmus, sister of the figurative and satirical painter Paul Cadmus, best known for his controversial painting "The Fleet's In." There were no children from the marriage, which lasted until her death in 1991. He then went to Europe to serve in World War II, working at one point to help recover art stolen by the Nazis. He returned to form Ballet Society in 1946. This troupe, which presented new work alone and with other organizations, showed dance films and encouraged new choreographers and dancers. It earned considerable respect and became the permanent company at New York's City Center in 1948, changing its name to New York City Ballet. In 1964, NYCB moved to its permanent home at the New York State Theater in Lincoln Center.

Throughout the years after the school and ballet company were established, Kirstein gave his money, imagination, time, and immense energy to the cultivation of ballet in America. He provided George Balanchine with an environment in which he could flourish, often deferring to Balanchine's desires and needs. "I know what my position is—which is subordinate which is the way I choose to be . . . My pleasure has been to make it possible for him to do what he wants" (quoted by Kisselgoff in "City Ballet's 'Arrival' Delights Kirstein").

Though he is primarily known as the man who brought ballet to America, Kirstein was also influential in the artistic and cultural education of the nation. He tirelessly assisted the careers of several artists. In 1932 he curated an exhibition for the Museum of Modern Art, *Murals by American Painters and Photographers*, an early attempt to bestow respect upon numerous American artists. He was influential in creating a career for photographer Walker Evans. Kirstein brought renewed interest to the work of sculptor Elie Nadelman, writing several laudatory articles about Nadelman and erecting two of his giant marble structures in the foyer of the New York State Theater. He cofounded the journal *Films* in 1939, produced several plays and founded the American Shakespeare Festival Theatre Academy in Stratford, Connecticut, wrote as an art critic for *The New Republic*, and also created and edited (1942–1948) *Dance Index*, one of America's first scholarly dance magazines. In 1959 he arranged a never-seen-before American tour for Gagaku, a traditional Japanese dance troupe.

His many writings include *Dance* (1935); *Ballet Alphabet* (1939); with Muriel Stuart, *The Classic Ballet* (1952); *Movement and Metaphor: 4 Centuries of Ballet* (1970); and *Thirty Years: The New York City Ballet* (1978). Kirstein was a master at depicting ballet in words. "Its filigrain of discrete steps; its speed, suavity, and flagrant tenderness; its metrical syncopation and asymmetry make visual superdrama on the broadest spectrum," he wrote in "Classic Ballet: Aria of the Aerial" (NYCB program, 1976).

Kirstein's multiple honors include the U.S. Government's highest civilian award, the Medal of Freedom, and New York City's highest cultural award, the Handel Medallion. He also received the National Medal of Arts and (with Balanchine) the National Gold Medal of Merit Award of the National Society of Arts and Letters, among other distinctions.

On 1 November 1989 Lincoln Kirstein retired as president of the School of American Ballet and general director of the New York City Ballet, remaining president and general director emeritus, respectively, at both organizations. He died at his home in New York City.

• Many of Kirstein's numerous program notes, essays, musings, correspondence, etc., can be found in the Dance Collection of the New York City Public Library. See Kirstein's clipping files there for a voluminous selection of articles about him, his NYCB program notes, essays, and obituaries. Two insightful autobiographies are *Mosaic: Memoirs* (1994) and *Thirty Years: The New York City Ballet* (1978 edition). For a deeper look into the School of American Ballet, see Jennifer Dunning's biography *"But First a School": The First Fifty Years of the School of American Ballet* (1985). Illuminating biographical articles include Anna Kisselgoff, "City Ballet's 'Arrival' Delights Kirstein," *New York Times*, 17 June 1971; Kisselgoff, "Kirstein—The Man Who Brought Us Balanchine," *New York Times*, 8 May 1977; Hilton Kramer, "Lincoln Kirstein as Critic and Patron," *New York Times*, 7 Jan. 1979; John Russell, "Lincoln Kirstein: A Life in Art," *New York Times Magazine*, 20 June 1982; Clive Barnes, "Lincoln in His Own Center," *Dance Magazine*, Mar. 1996; Joan Acocella, "The Lives They Lived: Lincoln Kirstein; The Impresario of Taste," *New York Times*, 29 Dec. 1996. For a more personalized account of his life see Nicholas Jenkins, "The Great Impresario," *New Yorker*, 13 Apr. 1998. For an extensive listing of Kirstein's writings until 1977, see Harvey Simmonds, *Lincoln Kirstein, the Published Writings, 1922–1977: A First Bibliography* (1978). A thorough obituary, by Jack Anderson, is in the *New York Times*, 6 Jan. 1996. Other obituaries are in *Dance Magazine*, Mar. 1996 (by Doris Perlman), and *Dance International*, Winter 1995/96.

JADA SHAPIRO

KLEINDIENST, Richard G. (5 Aug. 1923–3 Feb. 2000), government official, was born Richard Gordon Kleindienst on a farm near Winslow, Arizona, the son of Alfred R. Kleindienst, a railroad brakeman and local postmaster, and Gladys Love Kleindienst. His mother died when he was still a young boy, and his father hired a Navajo woman to serve as housekeeper for the family. She taught him the Navajo language, in which he became exceptionally proficient. Kleindienst later said that the diversified racial composition of Winslow—more Indians, Mexicans, and Asians than whites—gave him important lessons in respect for the rights of all human beings.

Kleindienst worked hard at home and in school, and to earn extra money he held two paper routes by the age of ten. As a teenager he joined his brother to run a gas station full time. He still managed to do well academically and to be popular as well, earning election as president of his high school class. After graduation in 1941 he enrolled at the University of Arizona, where he became an honor student as well as an honor cadet in the ROTC. In 1943, as World War II raged, he was called to active duty in the army and served as a navigator with the U.S. Army Air Forces in Italy. After leaving the army in 1946 he continued his education at Harvard, graduating magna cum laude a year later and becoming a member of Phi Beta Kappa. He went on to Harvard Law School, supporting himself as a law clerk in a major Boston firm during his studies.

On graduating from law school in 1950, Kleindienst returned to Arizona and joined the Phoenix law firm Jennings, Strouss, Salmon & Trask, eventually becoming a partner. There he became a specialist in commercial law, representing companies involved in industrial disputes. In 1958 he became a senior partner in another Phoenix law firm, thenceforth known as Shimmel, Hill, Kleindienst & Bishop, and remained there until 1969.

Kleindienst had been active in politics in college as president of the Harvard Conservative League, and back in Arizona he became friendly with Barry Goldwater, then a prominent businessman and conservative Republican leader, who encouraged him to enter local politics. Kleindienst took his advice, though claiming not to be as conservative as Goldwater, and ultimately became a precinct committeeman and a delegate to the 1952 Republican National Convention. There he joined the liberal wing of the party to nominate General Dwight D. Eisenhower for president. That fall he ran for a seat in the Arizona House of Representatives while campaigning for Eisenhower as well as Goldwater, who was running for the U.S. Senate. All three men were victorious in their election bids.

Following his single term in the state house (1953–1954), where he was the youngest member of that body, Kleindienst returned to his law practice and to partisan politics, joining with Goldwater to help make Arizona a solidly Republican state. He served as head of the Arizona Young Republican League, and in 1956–1960 and again in 1961–1963 he was chairman of the Republican State Central Committee and served on the Republican National Committee. Beginning in 1963 he worked arduously for the nomination of Barry Goldwater as president in 1964 and went on to serve as national director of field operations of the Goldwater for President Committee. In that role, while trying to mobilize convention delegates for Goldwater, Kleindienst reportedly tried to keep southern segregationist supporters at bay and succeeded in ousting the controversial and ultraconservative John Birch Society from the Goldwater campaign. A few liberal commentators later charged that Kleindienst, in securing the nomination for Goldwater, had used unethical tactics to sully the reputation of Goldwater's chief rival, Governor Nelson Rockefeller, but their allegations were never proved.

After the convention Kleindienst returned to Arizona to conduct his own campaign for the governorship. As predicted by most polls, Goldwater was defeated by the incumbent president, Lyndon B. Johnson, that fall. Although Republicans won most of the state offices in Arizona, Kleindienst unexpectedly lost his race to the Democratic candidate. Following this defeat, politics took a back seat in his life for several years, but he returned to the fray in 1966 as the director of John Williams's successful campaign for the governor's office. Kleindienst's demonstrated skills in running political campaigns for other Republicans had become well known in the party, and in 1968, as Richard M. Nixon pursued his quest for that year's Republican presidential nomination, Kleindienst was appointed national director of field operations for the Nixon campaign. Kleindienst was given much of the credit for securing the nomination for Nixon at the national convention that August, after which he became Nixon's deputy campaign director, serving under John Mitchell.

Following his victory in November, Nixon appointed Mitchell as attorney general and Kleindienst as deputy attorney general. Kleindienst took office on 31 January 1969, assuming duties that included administrative supervision of the Justice Department and its numerous departments as well as acting as a liaison with Congress. Kleindienst quickly developed a reputation as competent and articulate but also as heavy-handed and abrasive, often to the point of rudeness. Along with Mitchell he established, under Nixon's direction, an overall policy at the Justice Department that emphasized law and order rather than the protection of individual rights, especially as protests escalated against the ongoing Vietnam War. During an antiwar demonstration in May 1971 in Washington, Kleindienst drew heavy criticism from civil libertarians when he ordered the breakup of an encampment of demonstrators and mass arrests for alleged acts of civil disobedience. He drew further criticism when he made public his support for wiretapping, although under limited circumstances, and when he proposed extended detention in special camps for violent political dissenters, a policy later denounced by the Nixon administration. Kleindienst was also criticized initially for what were seen as strong-arm efforts to stop drug trafficking along the United States–Mexico border; eventually a more cooperative venture between the two governments was implemented.

Kleindienst did earn praise from liberals for his emphatic advocacy on behalf of minority hiring, especially for his determined efforts to recruit black lawyers for the Justice Department and for his successful recommendations of many black judges to federal courts. He played a major role in advising Nixon on judicial appointments and was personally responsible for hiring Arizona friend and protégé William H. Rehnquist as a department lawyer in 1969. Three years later Rehnquist was named an associate justice of the U.S. Supreme Court.

In early 1972, when John Mitchell resigned as attorney general to become the director of Nixon's reelection campaign, Kleindienst was named his successor. In the wake of his confirmation by the Senate Judiciary Committee on 25 February after three days of hearings, liberal columnist Jack Anderson charged that in 1971 the Justice Department, at Kleindienst's behest, had dropped an antitrust lawsuit against the International Telephone and Telegraph Company (ITT) after the company agreed to make a substantial contribution to the Republican party in the form of accommodations at several ITT-owned hotels. Kleindienst responded by asking that the Senate hearings be reopened so that he could deny the charges of wrongdoing. After a new series of hearings that stretched from 5 March to 27 April 1972—the longest confirmation hearings in U.S. history—Kleindienst's nomination as attorney general was finally approved, and he was confirmed by the Senate in early June. In the committee report and in the ensuing Senate debate, however, mention was made of many contradictions in Kleindienst's testimony as well as his possible involvement in several other antitrust suits that were dropped after the indicted companies made substantial Republican campaign contributions. Thus a cloud hung over Kleindienst as he assumed his new position.

After taking office as attorney general on 12 June, Kleindienst announced that his plans for the new post included strong enforcement of civil rights and antitrust laws and fights against organized crime and drug trafficking; he also promised full government support for prison reform. Five days later, however, the fateful break-in at Democratic party headquarters at the Watergate complex in Washington took place, and for the next ten months Kleindienst's Justice Department found itself in the eye of the storm in the ensuing uproar and investigation of the Nixon administration's involvement, with little time to pursue those lofty goals. Finally, on 30 April 1973, the embattled Kleindienst resigned, saying that he could no longer stay on when so many of his political associates were implicated in the scandal or under investigation. Although Kleindienst himself was suspected of involvement by many at the time, several years later reliable sources cleared his name, revealing that after hearing of the break-in he had in fact ordered—to President Nixon's dismay—full cooperation by the Justice Department with any subsequent investigation of wrongdoing, no matter who was involved.

Watergate nevertheless turned out to be Kleindienst's undoing in another way: secret White House audiotapes uncovered during the probe disclosed an April 1971 conversation between Nixon and Kleindienst during which Nixon had ordered Kleindienst to drop the Justice Department antitrust suit against ITT. In early 1974 Kleindienst was duly charged with refusing to testify accurately before the Senate during his confirmation hearings two years earlier; pleading guilty to the misdemeanor, he was fined $100 and given a thirty-day suspended sentence.

After leaving Washington in the spring of 1973, Kleindienst returned to Arizona and the practice of law. After his conviction in 1974 he remained out of the limelight, except for a brief period in 1981 when he was charged with, but later acquitted of, perjury in a case involving an Arizona client convicted of insurance fraud.

Kleindienst was married in 1948 to Margaret Dunbar; the couple had four children, all of whom, at their father's insistence, attended public schools. In private life he was active in civic and charitable organizations, played golf and chess, enjoyed classical music, and was a lifelong member of the Episcopal Church. In retirement, he wrote his memoirs, which were published with little fanfare in 1985. After suffering from lung cancer for four years, he died at his home in Prescott, Arizona.

• For biographical information, see "Kleindienst, Richard G(ordon)," in *Current Biography Yearbook* 1972; "Kleindienst, Richard Gordon," in *Who's Who in America*, 54th ed. (2000); and Kleindienst's autobiography, *Justice: The Memoirs of Attorney General Richard Kleindienst* (1985). See also "New Attorney General: His Views on Key Issues," *U.S. News and World Report*, 19 June 1972, p. 72. For information on the role of the Justice Department in the Watergate break-in and its aftermath, see especially Carl Bernstein and Bob Woodward, *All the President's Men* (1974); John Dean III, *Blind Ambition* (1976); and *Watergate: Chronology of a Crisis* (1975), an exhaustive compendium prepared by the staff of Congressional Quarterly Publications. An obituary appears in the *New York Times*, 4 Feb. 2000.

ANN T. KEENE

KOOPMAN, Karl (1 Apr. 1920–22 Sept. 1997), zoologist, was born Karl Friedrich Koopman in Honolulu, Hawaii, the elder child of Karl H. Koopman, a librarian, and Martha Brown Koopman. His family moved to Los Angeles when he was two years old, and young Koopman, along with his younger sister, attended elementary school there. He later said that his lifelong scientific interest in animals was kindled by frequent trips to the Los Angeles County Museum of Natural History as a child. When the elder Koopman was hired by Bard College in the early 1930s, the family moved to New York City, where Karl attended high school for several years. He also attended high school in South Carolina while his father served as the librarian of The Citadel, a military college.

Koopman's love of natural science led him to declare a major in chemistry when he entered Columbia University after graduation from high school. Undergraduate courses in evolution and vertebrate paleontology convinced him, however, that his true calling was zoology, and he majored in that field instead, graduating in 1943. He went on to earn a master's degree two years later and a doctorate in 1950.

As a graduate student at Columbia, Koopman worked closely with Theodosius Dobzhansky, one of the first scientists to study the genetics of fruit flies, and his dissertation was based on a series of experiments documenting natural selection in two fruit-fly species. An abbreviated version of Koopman's dissertation was published in 1950 as an article in the journal *Evolution* and became his first published work; it is still cited today as a groundbreaking paper in evolutionary studies. But fruit flies, and invertebrates in general, did not hold his complete attention. While completing his doctoral work, Koopman had also welcomed the opportunity to study vertebrates, specifically the natural history of mammals, an interest he fostered by frequent visits to the American Museum of Natural History in New York City.

Koopman had become especially fascinated by bats as an undergraduate at Columbia, and as a doctoral student he formally began his study of those mammals by focusing on species found in North America and the Caribbean. In the summer of 1949 he and a fellow graduate student, Ernest Williams, traveled to the West Indies to do research on bat species there. This was the beginning of a ten-year study by Koopman, during which he became an authority on West Indian bats. His work resulted in the publication of two seminal papers, "Land Bridges and Ecology in Bat Distribution on Islands Off the Northern Coast of South America" (*Evolution*, 1958) and "The Zoogeographical Limits of the West Indies" (*Journal of Mammalogy*, 1959).

In the mid-twentieth century, when Koopman began his research on bats, little was known about them and few zoologists had any interest in learning more about them. Koopman's pioneering work inspired a new generation of scientists to take a closer look at this often feared and loathed mammal, and the sudden availability in the 1960s of money from the federal government for scientific study was also instrumental in encouraging bat studies, especially in the West Indies, at that time an underexplored area for zoologists.

Koopman's formal academic career began in the fall of 1949, when he began teaching at the Middletown Collegiate Center in New York. After a year there he became an instructor in biology at Queen's College, also in New York. In 1958 he moved to Philadelphia, where he served as assistant curator of mammals at the Academy of Natural Sciences. A year later he moved on to Chicago, where he held the same position at the Field Museum of Natural History. Koopman returned to New York City in 1961 to become assistant curator of mammals at the American Museum of Natural History and was promoted to associate curator in 1966. He became curator in 1978, and upon his retirement in 1985 he was named curator emeritus.

During his years as a museum curator, Koopman was an acknowledged expert on all mammals, but bats remained the focus of his attention. By 1960 he had expanded his area of investigation to South America and Africa, and he went on to study bats in Australia, Asia, and the Pacific islands. At the end of the decade he had become an internationally recognized bat expert, and by the time of his death he was acknowledged as the world's leading authority on bat distribution and bat taxonomy. Over the years Koopman wrote a number of significant papers, primarily on bat systematics—the study of how bat species evolved over time and their relationship to one another—and bat classification, as well as bat biogeography, the study of the distribution of bat species. Several of Koopman's papers on bats became chapters in such basic mammalogy textbooks as S. Anderson and J. K. Jones, Jr., eds., *Orders and Families of Recent Mammals of the World* (1984), and D. E. Wilson and I. M. Reeder, eds., *Mammal Species of the World* (1993). He also contributed a major series of articles to *Bat Research News* between 1982 and 1985, and was the author of an important monograph, *Chiroptera: Systematics* (1994).

Koopman presented his findings at scientific conferences throughout the world, including annual meetings

of the American Society of Mammalogists, on whose board of directors he also served. At the time of his death he was associate editor of the society's journal, *Mammalian Species*. He was also active in the North American Bat Research Society and a participant in the annual North American Symposium on Bat Research, and, as an ardent conservationist, he was a longtime member of the Linnean Society.

Koopman was famous for his formidable memory and for his command of obscure and arcane facts about bat species. During his extensive travels he collected many bat specimens for museums, many of which were preserved entirely in alcohol for later study rather than—as had been customary among museum collectors—saving only the skins and skulls. Among mammalian morphologists he is recognized for perfecting a technique for extracting the skull from an alcohol-preserved bat without damaging the rest of the specimen.

Koopman, who never married, died suddenly at his New York apartment.

• For biographical information, see "Karl F. Koopman: 1920–1997," *Journal of Mammalogy* 79, no. 3 (1998): pp. 1070–75; Merlin Tuttle, "In Tribute: Karl F. Koopman, 1920–1997," *Bats*, Winter 1997 [*sic*]; and Helen Hays, "Karl Koopman: 1920–1997," *Linnean News-Letter*, Oct. 1997, pp. 1–2. For a layman's appreciation of Koopman's work, see Diane Ackerman, "Batman," *New York Times Magazine*, 4 Jan. 1998, p. 44. An obituary appears in the *New York Times*, 30 Sept. 1997.

ANN T. KEENE

KRISTELLER, Paul Oskar (22 May 1905–7 June 1999), philosopher and architect of the field of Renaissance studies in the United States, was born in Berlin, Germany, on the same day his father, Paul Oskar Gräfenberg, died. His mother, Alice Magnus, severed relations with the paternal family, and Kristeller did not later acknowledge his biological father. Descended on both sides from wealthy and distinguished Jewish families, Magnus raised the child with parental support. In 1911 she married Heinrich Kristeller, who formally adopted the six-year-old Paul Oskar. In 1914 the young Kristeller entered the highly competitive Mommsen-Gymnasium, where he mastered Latin, Greek, French, and English, as well as other academic subjects, and was graduated in 1923.

Kristeller proceeded to the University of Heidelberg, where he studied with, among others, the noted philosophers Karl Jaspers and Edmund Husserl, receiving his doctorate in 1928. After three years in Berlin studying classical philology, in 1931 he undertook postgraduate university work in Freiburg and Heidelberg with Martin Heidegger, another of the century's leading philosophers, with the aim of completing his *Habilitationsschrift*, a postdoctoral dissertation qualifying him to teach in a German university. The Nazi ascension in 1933, however, forced Kristeller to abandon his German university career. Heidegger—a Nazi party member and later an official of the regime—

provided him with letters of recommendation to scholars abroad.

In 1934 Kristeller left Germany for Italy. There, under the protection of Italy's premier philosopher Giovanni Gentile, a fascist ideologue and adviser to dictator Benito Mussolini, he attained a university-level position at Pisa's prestigious Scuola Normale Superiore. Meanwhile, he pursued his own research, laying the foundations for the important contributions he would make to Renaissance studies after 1939, when, forced a second time to escape dangerous anti-Semitic repression, he fled Italy for the United States.

Upon his arrival, Kristeller was assisted by American scholars, including Yale University church historian Roland Bainton, who had been instrumental in arranging for his visa. He taught at Yale in the spring of 1939 and received for 1939–1940 an adjunct appointment at Columbia University. He remained at Columbia thereafter, becoming a tenured associate professor in 1948 and in 1968 the Frederick J. E. Woodbridge Professor of Philosophy, a title he continued to hold, emeritus, after his retirement in 1973. In 1940, he married Edith Lind Lewinnek (d. New York City, 1992), whom he had met in Freiburg in 1931, and with whom he was reunited after her own separate escape from Europe. For more than fifty years, while Edith pursued her career as a medical doctor, the couple hosted students and friends but remained childless. In 1945, Kristeller became a U.S. citizen.

Kristeller's first major works emerged from his studies at Heidelberg and Freiburg, which resulted in monographs respectively on the third-century Neoplatonic philosopher Plotinus (published in German in 1929) and the fifteenth-century Italian Platonist Marsilio Ficino (prepared in German in 1938 but not published until 1943 in English; a revised edition appeared in 1953 in Italian). His work on Ficino brought Kristeller to the Renaissance, while the research it had required in Italian manuscript sources was preliminary to Kristeller's later codification of the European manuscript tradition. Kristeller continued those investigations of Italian libraries during 1934–1938, laying the basis for a major project that reached completion only in 1997: the *Iter Italicum*, described below. From the 1940s through the 1970s, Kristeller published a series of collections of studies that are the main vehicles for his original and powerful conceptions of the Renaissance, Renaissance humanism, and Renaissance philosophy. Among his important arguments are these:

Humanism should be distinguished from philosophy, in that it derives from the classical and medieval rhetorical traditions as they crystallized in a unique Italian civic setting. As a rhetorical movement, humanism had no single ideology and could not be linked to any single set of ideas such as "individualism" or "political liberty." Humanism was characterized by the large participation of laypersons (such as secretaries, bureaucrats, and amateurs) in the creation and circulation of texts, but it was not an anti-Christian or secularist movement, and many clerics also participated in the humanist movement. Scholasticism, the characteristic form of medieval philosophy, was by no means dead during the Renaissance; it was a vital intellectual tradition that coexisted with humanism, often in rivalry with it. The ancient Greek tradition of Platonism was fully revived during the Renaissance, within a Christian context, greatly affecting the character of Renaissance thought and literary production. It did not prevail to the exclusion of Aristotelianism, however, and both philosophical traditions continued to interrelate fruitfully. There was no single or novel Renaissance "concept of man," but the nature of humankind was one of several themes that Renaissance authors, both humanists and philosophers, considered. Renaissance humanism crystallized in Italy in conjunction with intensified artistic and literary activity, which together made Italy the leader of European culture for at least three centuries.

While Kristeller was elaborating these views about Renaissance thought, he also began the major projects that were to give a new, firm basis for Renaissance studies in the United States. In the 1950s, he launched the multivolume project *Catalogus translationum et commentariorum: Medieval and Renaissance Latin Translations and Commentaries*, a catalogue of the translations and commentaries of classical authors, Christian and pagan, of which he edited the first volume in 1960 as well as, in the same year, the fundamental reference tool, the modestly described "list" of *Latin Manuscript Books before 1600*.

Another multivolumed project began in 1945, based on notes taken in Italy in the 1930s: the *Iter Italicum: A Finding List of Uncatalogued or Incompletely Catalogued Humanistic Manuscripts of the Renaissance in Italian and Other Libraries*. Although the aim of this extraordinary project, the most important single enterprise related to Renaissance studies of the twentieth century, was to supplement existing manuscript catalogues, in its comprehensiveness and precision it actually supersedes them in many regards, making the uncatalogued manuscripts of Europe, ironically, more accessible than those already catalogued. The first two volumes, reflecting Kristeller's visits to Italian libraries in the 1930s through the 1960s, were published in 1963 and 1967. Over the next thirty years, five more volumes followed, based on subsequent investigations. The later volumes include entries on libraries, arranged alphabetically, from Australia to Yugoslavia, as well as supplements for Italy, and a comprehensive index. With these extended research projects, Kristeller not only reasserted his principle that knowledge of the Renaissance must be rooted in texts, but he also effectively guided the development of the research agenda for Renaissance specialists for the next decades.

Kristeller was active in several learned societies and associations, including the Medieval Academy of America and the American Council of Learned Societies, and helped launch the *Journal of the History of Ideas*. He was one of the founders of the Renaissance

Society of America (1954), which still represents the most important institutional embodiment of Renaissance studies in the United States. In addition, he tirelessly assisted other scholars, responding personally to inquiries till the end of his life. His long career came to an end when he died in his sleep at his home in New York City on 7 June 1999.

Kristeller brought a philosopher's precision and a classical scholar's sensitivity to language to the study of the Renaissance. He was among the most important, and last to survive, of the émigré scholars who fled European fascism. He was the single most important American scholar of the Renaissance in the twentieth century, and perhaps the most important anywhere since Jakob Burckhardt, whose *Civilization of the Renaissance in Italy* (published in German in 1860) first crystallized the concept of the Renaissance as a distinctive historical era.

• Kristeller commented on his own career in "A Life of Learning," an address that he delivered as the 1990 Charles Homer Haskins Lecture of the American Council of Learned Societies. A memoir of his early years, the "Iter Kristellerianum: The European Journey (1905–1939)," written in collaboration with Margaret L. King, was published in *Renaissance Quarterly* 47, 4 (1994): 907–29. A 1,080-page typescript of his memoirs is on deposit in the Columbia University rare book room, with additional materials. Kristeller published more than 500 items over seven decades. Of these the most important are, in the order of their publication, *Studies in Renaissance Thought and Letters* (4 vols.; 1956, 1985); *Renaissance Thought: The Classic, Scholastic, and Humanist Strains* (1961); *Eight Philosophers of the Italian Renaissance* (1964); *Renaissance Thought II: Papers on Humanism and the Arts* (1965); *Renaissance Concepts of Man, and Other Essays* (1972); *Medieval Aspects of Renaissance Learning: Three Essays*, ed. and trans. Edward P. Mahoney (1974); *Renaissance Thought and Its Sources*, ed. Michael Mooney (1979). In addition, the collection of sources Kristeller selected and translated together with his colleagues Ernst Cassirer and John Herman Randall, Jr., has been a classroom staple since its first printing, in 1948: *The Renaissance Philosophy of Man.*

Several volumes of studies by friends, colleagues, and students were compiled in tribute to Kristeller, including the *Itinerarium Italicum: The Profile of the Italian Renaissance in the Mirror of its European Transformations, Dedicated to Paul Oskar Kristeller on the Occasion of his 70th Birthday*, ed. Thomas A. Brady, Jr., and Heiko A. Oberman (1975); *Cultural Aspects of the Italian Renaissance: Essays in Honour of Paul Oskar Kristeller*, ed. Cecil H. Clough (1976); *Philosophy and Humanism: Renaissance Essays in Honor of Paul Oskar Kristeller*, ed. Edward P. Mahoney (1976), with a "Bibliography of the Publications of Paul Oskar Kristeller for the Years 1929–1974"; *Florilegium Columbianum: Essays in Honor of Paul Oskar Kristeller*, ed. Karl-Ludwig Selig and Robert Somerville (1987); and *Supplementum Festivum: Studies in Honor of Paul Oskar Kristeller*, ed. James Hankins, John Monfasani, and Frederick Purnell, Jr. (1987). Obituaries include two by his former students, Edward P. Mahoney, in the *Journal of the History of Ideas* 60, 4 (1999): 758–60, and John Monfasani, in *Renaissance News & Notes*, 11, 2 (1999) (published online at www.r-s-a.org/rsa/pub/rnn/11-2/kristell.html), also republished elsewhere, and one by Eric Pace in the *New York Times*, 10 June 1999.

MARGARET L. KING

KROL, John (26 Oct. 1910–3 Mar. 1996), Roman Catholic archbishop, was born John Joseph Krol in Cleveland, Ohio, the son of John Krol, a machinist, and Anna Pietruszka Krol. He grew up in a large, working-class family and attended local parochial schools. After graduating from high school, he started working as a meat cutter in a local supermarket. Following a series of thought-provoking religious discussions with a co-worker that turned his thoughts toward the priesthood, Krol began preparing for his ultimate career at St. Mary's College in Orchard Park, Michigan. He completed his studies at St. Mary's Seminary in Cleveland and was ordained in the Archdiocese of Cleveland on 20 February 1937.

After spending a year as curate at nearby Immaculate Heart of Mary parish, Krol journeyed to Rome, where he studied canon law at the Gregorian University. He received his licentiate from that institution in 1940 and because of the onset of World War II decided to return to the United States to finish his studies. Krol took a doctorate in canon law from Catholic University in Washington, D.C., in 1942 and then returned to his hometown and St. Mary's Seminary, where he taught canon law for a year. Blessed with an aptitude for foreign languages and exceptionally well organized (a talent that served him well as he concurrently held the additional posts of chaplain at the Jennings Home for the Aged and Defender of the Bond in the diocesan matrimonial tribunal), he soon caught the attention of his superiors. He became vice chancellor of the Diocese of Cleveland in 1943 and earned the designation of monsignor in 1945. Krol's work on canon law received national recognition in 1948 when he was elected president of the Canon Law Society of America. He became chancellor of the diocese in 1951 and in July 1953 was consecrated as auxiliary bishop of Cleveland. As auxiliary, he put his language skills to good use during religious radio broadcasts to the communist countries of eastern Europe.

In 1961 Pope John XXIII surprised nearly everyone (including Krol) when he designated the auxiliary as the new archbishop of Philadelphia following the death of the incumbent, John Cardinal O'Hara—such appointments typically went to local auxiliaries or to established bishops in smaller dioceses. Nevertheless, Krol soon proved to be a sound choice for the job. During his twenty-seven-year tenure, he oversaw sweeping changes in the nation's fourth-largest diocese. In the face of shifting population demographics among his flock, Krol oversaw the establishment of thirty-six new parishes (all but five of which were suburban in location) and the closing or consolidation of sixteen parishes (all but two of which were in the inner city). Intensely interested in education, Krol oversaw the building of eight new parochial high schools and also ensured the future financial stability of the entire system. When project enrollment increases failed to materialize and rising costs further threatened the schools, Krol gradually converted the formerly tuition-free system into one in which both parishes and parents contributed to the costs of education. He also successfully lobbied the state legislature for financial assistance with nonsectarian textbooks and transportation costs. In the face of declining enrollments, he made his greatest mark, perhaps, with the formation of Business Leadership Organized for Catholic Schools (BLOCS), a nonsectarian fund-raising organization that was formed by local businessmen.

In addition to his obligations in Philadelphia, Krol held an equally important role in the worldwide ecumenical council that would later be known as Vatican II. Having been named to the Preparatory Commission of Bishops and Government of Diocese on the basis of his grasp of canon law even prior to his appointment as archbishop, Krol also provided yeoman service to the council as a member of the central coordinating committee, which was responsible for keeping the proceedings on schedule as well as coordinating the work of various council commissions, and as the council's only American undersecretary. Krol's travels to Rome also gave him the opportunity to become fast friends with the Methodist bishop Fred Pierce Corson of Philadelphia, who served as the official Protestant representative at the proceedings. Their collaboration led to the formation in 1964 of the Archbishop's Commission on Human Relations, which sought to advance both ecumenical understanding and racial harmony. Krol received the Human Relations Award of the National Conference of Christians and Jews in 1968 for his role in this work.

In an era when change never came fast enough for some and entirely too fast for others, Krol faced numerous challenges. The diocesan seminary of St. Charles Borromeo was the scene of a walkout by seminarians protesting general conditions in 1966; when the local press obtained a "white paper" outlining the seminarians' grievances (an overly rigid curriculum, lack of personal autonomy, unduly strict living conditions), Krol issued an ultimatum to the students that ultimately restored order. In response to the crisis, he also upgraded the curriculum and facilities at the seminary. As a leader of the National Conference of Catholic Bishops (vice president, 1966–1971, and president, 1971–1974) and as chairman of the National Catholic Office for Motion Pictures, Krol often found his views at odds with what he perceived as an increasingly permissive society. Although considered by some a reactionary (Philadelphia was the last major diocese in America to allow Saturday evening mass as a means of meeting Sunday obligations), Krol's conservative reputation actually gave him credibility when he spoke out on such controversial issues as the SALT II treaty.

Krol rose to the rank of cardinal in 1967 on the same day that Bishop Karol Wojtyla of Cracow, Poland, received his red hat. They were fast friends, and when Wojtyla became Pope John Paul II in October 1978, there was speculation about Krol's role in his election. What is known for certain is that Krol exercised considerable influence among the American delegation (the second largest in number at the conclave) and that there was a general readiness for change among the cardinals to elect a non-Italian to the papacy.

After retiring in 1988, Krol spent his remaining years as the leader of the Papal Foundation, a fundraising organization that sought to create an endowment for the benefit of the Holy See. He died at his residence in Philadelphia.

• The papers of John Cardinal Krol are held at the Philadelphia Archdiocesan Historical Research Center in Wynnewood, Pa. His life and work are discussed in E. Michael Jones, *John Cardinal Krol and the Cultural Revolution* (1995), and in James F. Connelly, ed., *The History of the Archdiocese of Philadelphia* (1976). His career can also be traced in the pages of the archdiocesan newspaper, *The Catholic Standard and Times*, especially in the issues of 3 Apr. 1986, 14 Mar. 1996, and 17 Mar. 1996. An obituary is in the *New York Times*, 4 Mar. 1996.

EDWARD L. LACH, JR.

KUBRICK, Stanley (26 July 1928–7 Mar. 1999), film director, was born in New York City, the son of Jacques "Jack" Kubrick, a physician, and Gertrude Perveler. Because Kubrick was seen as a bright but extremely erratic student in the public schools of the Bronx, his father hoped to motivate the underachieving boy by buying him an expensive Graflex, a camera of professional quality. The concerned father also introduced Kubrick to his extensive personal library and taught him to play chess. The plan worked: the restless thirteen-year-old showed an instant affinity for photography, literature, and chess, and his early mastery of all three would be key in the realization of his skills as a movie director.

Kubrick's obsessive, driven personality manifested itself from his earliest teenage years. Immersing himself in the study of both the creative and technical sides of still photography, he landed a full-time job as a photographer for *Look* magazine by age sixteen. He also read virtually every book in his father's library and tried to see every movie that was released in New York City. Looking back on those early years, Kubrick told Joseph Gelmis that "I used to want to see almost anything. In fact, the bad films were what really encouraged me to start out on my own. I'd keep seeing lousy films and saying to myself, 'I don't know anything about moviemaking but I *couldn't* do anything worse than this'" (*The Director as Superstar* [1970], p. 315).

Poor grades and excessive absenteeism kept Kubrick from being accepted at any first-rate New York college. He briefly enrolled in evening classes at the City College of New York, but his natural intellectual inclination was for self-education, which he pursued with a passion. During the four years that he worked on high-profile feature articles as a photojournalist for *Look*, Kubrick became a relentless autodidact in every aspect of the history, art, and craft of filmmaking and transformed himself from an obscure staff photographer into a budding film director.

In 1948 Kubrick married his high school sweetheart, Toba Metz, and the couple moved into a Greenwich Village apartment among a bohemian community of artists and writers. During this period Kubrick began playing chess for money, and his mania for chess developed the logical, decisive side of his personality, which tempered his unbridled creativity. Influenced by the popular "March of Time" documentary news film series, the precocious Kubrick wrote, produced, directed, photographed, edited, and distributed two documentary shorts, *Day of the Fight* and *Flying Padre*, in 1951 before he was twenty-three years old.

Now committed full time to filmmaking, Kubrick completed his first two features, *Fear and Desire* in 1953 and *Killer's Kiss* in 1955. Both were financed on shoestring budgets mainly with money borrowed from a rich uncle; both were influenced by the fluid directorial style of Max Ophuls; and both displayed the raw beginnings of Kubrick's bleakly existential worldview, which acknowledged man's fundamental capacity for evil that the forces of goodness can never quite overcome. During this period of incessant work, Kubrick's marriage deteriorated. He quietly divorced and in 1954 married ballet dancer Ruth Sobotka.

A move to Hollywood led to commercial success when Kubrick teamed with producer James B. Harris to make his first studio picture, *The Killing* (1956), based on Lionel White's novel about a daring racetrack robbery gone bad. Film historians have found the film noir influential because of its nonlinear structure and innovative use of flashbacks. Kubrick's first classic film, *Paths of Glory* (1957), stars Kirk Douglas as a World War I colonel torn between obedience to the cruel indifference of his superior officers and loyalty to his men. Many have considered it one of the finest antiwar films ever made. During the shooting of *Paths*, Kubrick's second marriage collapsed, and he began a romance with Christiane Harlan, who had a small part in the film. Kubrick married Harlan in 1958 and adopted her young daughter. The couple, who stayed together until Kubrick's death, raised two more children of their own.

For the next two years, Kubrick tried to adjust to the pressurized, highly political environment of the Hollywood studio system, which he hated because of its "destructive competitiveness." He spent six agonizing months collaborating with Marlon Brando in preproduction of *One-Eyed Jacks*, but Brando eventually directed the movie himself. When Kirk Douglas fired his original director on the big-budget Roman epic *Spartacus*, Kubrick agreed to direct for a flat fee. A major box office success in 1960, the film established Kubrick's reputation as a bankable director. Nevertheless, he disliked his position as a hired hand in the Los Angeles movie colony and never again took on a project that did not give him full control.

After *Spartacus*, Kubrick became increasingly disillusioned with what he called the "undercurrent of low-level malevolence" in Hollywood and was alarmed by the violence of life in his native New York. Thus in 1961 he moved his family to a rural estate near London and made England the base for all his subsequent films. The first of these was *Lolita* (1962), adapted from Vladimir Nabokov's famous novel and as controversial as the book because of its strong sexual theme. The battle for the seal of approval for *Lolita* was the first of many encounters Kubrick had with the Legion of Decency and the British Board of Censors. Although compromised artistically by the censors, it stands as a fine cinematic rendering of Nabokov's classic narrative.

Reaching the zenith of his powers as a filmmaker in the decade following the release of *Lolita*, Kubrick produced and directed three consecutive masterpieces. In 1964 with the help of black humorist Terry Southern, he made the nightmare comedy *Dr. Strangelove, or: How I Learned to Stop Worrying and Love the Bomb*. Conceived at the height of the Cold War, the film satirizes the insanity of the nuclear arms race. The brilliant cast features Sterling Hayden, George C. Scott, and Peter Sellers, who plays three different roles, including the deranged scientist Dr. Strangelove. Perhaps the most absurd moment in the film comes when, during a scuffle between American and Russian officials, a worried U.S. president (Sellers) exclaims, "Please, gentlemen, you can't fight here; this is the War Room!" At the film's famous climax, a jingoistic American pilot, played by Slim Pickens, jubilantly rides a nuclear bomb down to its Russian target and triggers an atomic Armageddon.

In 1968 Kubrick collaborated with science fiction writer Arthur C. Clarke to create his most enduring film, *2001: A Space Odyssey*, which appealed to a large international audience moved by its deep, open-ended religious themes. The movie begins with an eerie depiction of a family of apes at the dawn of civilization and ends with an abandoned American astronaut being reborn in another galaxy. According to Kubrick, "the God concept is at the heart of the film," embodied in part by a black monolithic slab that appears at both the start and the climax of the film. The central portion of the film concerns the struggle between the robotlike astronauts and a neurotic supercomputer, HAL 9000, which dominates the humans until it has a breakdown when it cannot cope with its own fallibility. Throughout the film, Kubrick carefully preserves the mystery of the deity by minimizing dialogue, maximizing special effects, and by mixing sublime music by Richard Strauss and Johann Strauss during the film's most lyrical moments. As John Baxter notes, "Music had always been in the forefront of Kubrick's mind as he conceived *2001*. He 'intended the film to be an intensely subjective experience . . . that reaches the viewer at an inner level of consciousness, just as the music does'" (*Kubrick* [1997], p. 225). Kubrick won his only Oscar for the special effects in *2001*, setting the standard for science fiction movies for years to come.

After the huge success of *2001*, Kubrick quickly began work on another futuristic drama with his graphic adaptation of Anthony Burgess's dystopian novel, *A*

Clockwork Orange, which plays heavily on the themes of sex and violence in the postmodern age. The film's central figure, a brutal hoodlum named Alex (Malcolm McDowell), joyfully indulges in mindless gangland warfare and wanton eroticism, including a vicious rape-murder choreographed to the tune of "Singin' in the Rain." Kubrick's cold, unsparing portrayal of Alex's depraved antisocial behavior ignited controversy when the film was released in 1972, but in time it gained the "cult" status of Kubrick's other major films.

After the futuristic *Clockwork Orange*, Kubrick decided to reconstruct, with enormous attention to detail, the eighteenth-century world of William Makepeace Thackeray's novel *Barry Lyndon*. Although his 1975 adaptation is visually beautiful and earned seven Oscar nominations (in one scene, the set is lit entirely by candlelight), it amounts to a costume drama about an adventurer amid a corrupt aristocracy. As such, it is probably the least successful effort of Kubrick's mature period.

Never one to repeat himself, Kubrick next resolved to make the world's most frightening horror film. His adaptation of Stephen King's novel *The Shining* stars Jack Nicholson as a failed writer who slowly descends into madness as caretaker of a remote resort hotel in Colorado's Rocky Mountains. Despite King's criticism of Kubrick's adaptation, which deemphasizes some supernatural elements of the book, *The Shining* was a success both critically and commercially.

After the release of *The Shining* in 1980, Kubrick grew increasingly reclusive and eccentric. Able to complete only two more films in the last nineteen years of his life, he lived in a walled mansion and virtually never left home except to make movies. When he did, he refused to fly. He was reluctant to drive and ordered that no car in which he was riding travel more than thirty-five miles per hour, and he sometimes wore a crash helmet. Working most of the night and sleeping during the day, Kubrick shot and edited his later films in total secrecy. Uncompromising in his quest for perfection, he regularly frustrated his actors by retaking a shot up to a hundred times. He even rented weapons carriers to protect and transport unfinished film across London.

Kubrick's penultimate film, *Full Metal Jacket* (1987), is another indictment of war and military conduct, this time set in Vietnam. Because of Kubrick's reluctance to travel, the entire movie was made in an English studio except for the grisly battle scenes that were staged in an abandoned gasworks forty miles from his home. *Full Metal Jacket* explores once again the duality of good and evil in human nature, as illustrated by a cynical U.S. Marine private (Mathew Modine), whose helmet bears the slogan "Born to Kill," while on his battle fatigues he wears a "peace" emblem. The film ends with the victorious American troops marching through a barren battlefield singing "M-I-C . . . K-E-Y . . . M-O-U-S-E." The critical response to *Full Metal Jacket* was mixed but by and large favorable.

Kubrick's final film, *Eyes Wide Shut* (1999), is a cautionary tale of jealousy and sexual obsession adapted from *Traumnovelle* (Dream Story) by Arthur Schnitzler, a Viennese playwright and friend of Sigmund Freud. The movie's release attracted worldwide attention not only because it features in sexually charged scenes Tom Cruise and Nicole Kidman, husband and wife at the time of the film's making, but also because Kubrick died suddenly just days after he had completed postproduction. As usual, Kubrick presents a hard, unromanticized view of his subject, the danger and suffering of a marriage burdened by desire, voyeurism, and decadent eroticism. Critical reaction was disappointing, and Kubrick received no posthumous Oscar nominations for the project.

Kubrick completed only thirteen feature films during his career, but his careful records show that he had at least three more major projects deep in the planning stages: *AI*, a science fiction film about artificial intelligence; *Aryan Papers*, the story of a young Jewish boy who wanders through Nazi-controlled Poland during the most terrible days of World War II; and his pet project, a grandiose study of the obsessive genius of Napoleon, whom he greatly admired. Kubrick's films manifest an unsentimental, clean-burning intelligence unwilling to compromise with Hollywood convention. His pictures received thirteen Academy Award nominations in all. Among his other major honors are the Director's Guild of America's D. W. Griffith Award for lifetime achievement; the Venice Film Festival's Palme d'Or for career achievement; the Writer's Guild of America Award; and best director honors from the British Academy of Film and Television Arts, the National Board of Review, and the New York Film Critics.

Although Kubrick drove his casts and crews mercilessly, almost everyone he worked with marveled at his meticulous attention to detail and artistically pure approach to filmmaking. Most also acknowledged his dark philosophical outlook. Malcolm McDowell, star of *A Clockwork Orange*, said that Kubrick "is a genius, but his humour's black as charcoal." Reacting to Kubrick's death in London, his longtime friend and fellow director Steven Spielberg called him "the grand master of filmmaking" and commented that he "gave us complete environmental experiences that got more, not less, intense the more you watched his pictures. He copied no one while all of us were scrambling to imitate him."

• There is an abundance of material on Kubrick's personal life and films. Two exhaustive biographies are Vincent LoBrutto, *Stanley Kubrick* (1997), and John Baxter, *Stanley Kubrick* (1997). Norman Kagan, *The Cinema of Stanley Kubrick* (1989), analyzes all of the films through *Full Metal Jacket* and includes some biographical material. Alexander Walker, *Stanley Kubrick, Director* (1999), a revised edition of *Stanley Kubrick Directs* (1971), includes a complete filmography and many black and white photographs of every feature film. Thomas Allen Nelson, *Kubrick: Inside a Film Artist's Maze* (1982), is a scholarly interpretation of all the films through *The Shining*. Mario Falsetto, ed., *Perspectives on*

Stanley Kubrick (1996), is an anthology of more than three dozen articles and essays on Kubrick's work through *Full Metal Jacket* and includes a note by Kubrick, plus four in-depth interviews dating from 1960 to 1987. Michel Ciment, *Kubrick* (1984), is one of the few books that Kubrick actively helped to prepare, allowing himself to be interviewed at length and choosing many of the book's numerous stills and production photos. Several books focus on Kubrick's skill in adapting literature to film: Greg Jenkins, *Stanley Kubrick and the Art of Adaptation* (1997), on *Lolita, The Shining* and *Full Metal Jacket*; Niel Sinyard, *Filming Literature* (1986), on *Barry Lyndon*; and Geoffrey Wagner, *The Novel and the Cinema* (1975), on *A Clockwork Orange*. Danny Peary includes *The Killing* and *2001* in his *Cult Movies* (1981) and *A Clockwork Orange* in *Cult Movies 2* (1983). See also Wallace Coyle, *Stanley Kubrick: A Guide to References and Resources* (1982). Michael Herr, Kubrick's close friend and collaborator on the screenplay of *Full Metal Jacket*, wrote a highly personalized homage for *Vanity Fair*, Aug. 1999, pp. 137-50. Another of Kubrick's friends, Frederic Raphael, the principal screenwriter for *Eyes Wide Shut*, wrote a book-length memoir of Kubrick, *Eyes Wide Open* (1999). Obituaries are in the *New York Times* and the *Los Angeles Times*, both 8 Mar. 1999.

BRUCE L. JANOFF

KUHN, Maggie (3 Aug. 1905–22 Apr. 1995), social activist, was born Margaret Eliza Kuhn in Buffalo, New York, the daughter of Samuel Frederick Kuhn, an assistant manager for the Bradstreet Company (the company that later established Dunn & Bradstreet), and Minnie Louise Kooman Kuhn. The Bradstreet Company frequently transferred her father, requiring the family to move often. Before she was born, her parents were living in Memphis, Tennessee, but her mother was so uncomfortable with the racial segregation and discrimination prevalent in the South that she returned home to Buffalo to give birth to Maggie.

When she was five, Kuhn's family moved from Memphis to Louisville, Kentucky, where she excelled as a student in elementary school, particularly in reading, and even skipped a grade. After five years in Louisville her father was asked to manage the Bradstreet office in Cleveland, Ohio. Kuhn continued to do well in school after the family moved to Cleveland, remaining at the top of her class, and in 1922, at the age of sixteen, she graduated from high school with honors. Because her father wanted her to stay in Cleveland, she decided to attend the Flora Stone Mather College for Women at Case Western Reserve University, where she majored in English literature with a minor in sociology and French and joined the Gamma Delta Tau sorority in her sophomore year.

Kuhn graduated from Case Western in 1926 with honors and began working as a volunteer at the Cleveland Young Women's Christian Association (YWCA) with her aunt. She then became the assistant business and professional secretary. During this time, she was also active in the local Young Socialists League, being drawn to the group because they were working toward reforms not only within the labor movement but also on behalf of women. In 1929 she was sent for training

to the YWCA headquarters in New York, where she took courses in social work and theology at Columbia University's Teachers College and the Union Theological Seminary.

In 1930, at the age of twenty-five, Kuhn accompanied her family when her father was transferred to Philadelphia. Taking a position there as head of the professional department of business girls at the YWCA of Germantown, she was put in charge of programs for Germantown's young working women. During this time, she began an active role as a community organizer, reaching out to young women, trying to recruit them to come to the Y and to become active in women's and larger societal issues. As Kuhn's activism grew, she soon began giving classes for young women on marriage and sexuality. She invited members of the YWCA's African-American branch to organized meetings and discussions; she started an amateur theater group of men and women called the Play Shop; and she invited men from the YMCA to many of the YWCA's activities.

In 1941 Kuhn took a job at the National Board of the YWCA in New York City working as a program coordinator and editor for the YWCA's United Services Organization (USO) division, a civilian agency assisting in the war effort. The group's primary mission was to boost civilian morale and provide a sense of normalcy during war. Kuhn traveled around the country coordinating USO programs. In 1948 the USO division was phased out and Kuhn took a job as a program coordinator for the General Alliance for Unitarian and Other Liberal Christian Women in Boston.

Worried about her parents' declining health, Kuhn left Boston after just two years and took a job as assistant secretary in the social education and action department of the national headquarters of the Presbyterian Church of the USA in Philadelphia. In this role, she was responsible for analyzing public issues and lobbying on the church's behalf. She held this position for the next twenty-five years, throughout the 1950s and 1960s, during which her duties expanded to include coordinating programming in the division of church and race and editing and writing for *Social Progress*, the church magazine. She also encouraged churchgoers to take progressive stands on social issues such as desegregation, urban housing, the Cold War, and nuclear arms. She wrote pamphlets for the church, such as one in 1954 titled "The Christian Woman and Her Household," in which she preached responsible consumerism, encouraging women to boycott anything ethically wrong such as products produced under unfair labor conditions.

As each year passed, Kuhn became increasingly a social activist and worked in the early 1960s in support of Medicare, general health care, and public housing issues. She then began being an advocate for causes such as civil rights, peace, women's rights, and the welfare of the elderly. In the 1960s she was actively involved in protests against the Vietnam War. In the late 1960s she also worked as a Presbyterian observer for the church at the United Nations. In 1965 she was transferred to the church's New York office, where she worked on a program called Renewal and Extension of the Ministries. In 1969 she began work as a program executive for the church's Council on Church and Race as well as becoming involved in a subcommittee on the problems of the elderly. She was elected to the board of four of the church's retirement homes.

Kuhn's activism for the aged really began, however, about seven months before her sixty-fifth birthday when she was asked if she planned to retire that summer. Kuhn did not want to retire but in 1970 was forced to adhere to the church's traditional retirement age of sixty-five. Rather than letting forced retirement make her feel defeated and useless, she began to organize, recruiting several of her friends who were facing the same situation. As Kuhn recalled in her autobiography, "They gave me a sewing machine, but I never opened it. I was too busy." This informal group grew and in 1971 held a meeting on "Older Persons and the Issues of the Seventies." The event drew nearly 100 people, who agreed to join together to form a new social action organization and unanimously agreed that the first issue they needed to address was the Vietnam War. The group became active, attending antiwar demonstrations and holding fundraisers and large meetings.

The new group then began to focus on other issues such as specific problems of the aged and to advocate on behalf of a national health plan, pension rights, and the elimination of age discrimination in the workplace. They initially called themselves the Consultation of Older Persons. At the suggestion of a New York television producer, however, the group changed their name to the Gray Panthers because, in the view of the producer, they were similar to the militant Black Panthers, a group very active at that time. The Gray Panthers' aim was to encourage older people to take control of their lives and to get involved in larger social issues. In May 1972 Kuhn and her Gray Panthers garnered their first national attention when she spoke at a press conference following the annual meeting of the Presbyterian Church of the USA. As she spoke about retirement, senior citizens, nursing homes, sex after the age of sixty-five, and older activists, reporters became fascinated. The next day the story appeared in all major newspapers and was carried by all of the major wire services. She was invited to appear on the "Johnny Carson Show," the "Today Show," and the "Mike Douglas Show."

In 1973 the Gray Panthers merged with Ralph Nader's Retired Professional Action Group and began a study of nursing homes that produced *Nursing Homes: A Citizens' Action Guide* (1977). Through the group's Media Watch, she challenged the negative portrayal of the elderly on television. Eventually, the Gray Panthers advocated legislation that made health care free and available to all people. Kuhn was the one who coined the term "ageism," by which she meant the cultural bias toward the young and the devaluing of

the elderly, believing it was as poisonous a force as racism or sexism.

The first general convention of the Gray Panthers was held in 1975 and was attended by delegates from over thirty states. By 1977 the convention attracted over 350 delegates representing nearly seventy Gray Panther groups. Kuhn and the Gray Panthers were directly responsible for significant national measures to aid older Americans, including nursing home reform, ending forced retirement regulations, and combating fraud against the elderly in health care.

In later years, Kuhn also wrote numerous articles and books, drawing on her own experience in the church ministry, such as *Get Out There and Do Something about Injustice* (1972), *Maggie Kuhn on Aging* (1977), and her autobiography. Fiercely independent, she never married but spoke vividly of many passionate love affairs. She preferred to focus solely on her work and travels. Until her death at the age of eighty-nine, she continued to play a pivotal role in the Gray Panthers. She had been suffering from arthritis and osteoporosis for years and died at her home in Philadelphia in her nurse's arms.

Largely through her charisma, candor, and expressive style, Kuhn gained for the Gray Panthers media attention and successfully launched a social movement whose time had come. She served as a potent symbol of the power, strength, and energy that the elderly can muster on their own behalf.

• Kuhn's autobiography, *No Stone Unturned: The Life and Times of Maggie Kuhn*, was published in 1991. A profile of Kuhn and the Gray Panthers can be found in *Ms.* magazine, Jul./Aug. 1994. Obituaries are in the *Los Angeles Times*, the *New York Times*, and the *Washington Post*, all on 23 Apr. 1995, and the *Wall Street Journal*, 24 Apr. 1995.

JUDITH B. GERBER

KUHN, Thomas S. (18 July 1922–17 June 1996), historian and philosopher of science, was born Thomas Samuel Kuhn in Cincinnati, Ohio, the son of Samuel Lewis Kuhn, an industrial engineer, and Minette Stroock Kuhn. He attended Harvard University, receiving his bachelor of science degree in physics in 1943. Following two years of civilian service for the Office of Scientific Research and Development, he returned to Harvard to complete an M.A. in 1946 and a Ph.D. in 1949, both in physics. While completing his Ph.D., he taught general education as a junior fellow of the Harvard Society of Fellows. Kuhn married Kathryn Louise Muhs in 1948; they had three children and divorced in 1978. He remarried in 1982, to Jehane Robin Burns. In 1958 Kuhn went to the University of California at Berkeley, where he stayed until 1964, when he left to teach at Princeton University. He ended his professional career at the Massachusetts Institute of Technology, where he taught from 1979 to 1992.

Although Kuhn's academic degrees and earliest publications were in physics, his preparation to teach general education courses led him to the study of the history and philosophy of science, the fields in which he gained renown. By the early 1950s he had stopped writing on physics and begun writing on Isaac Newton, Robert Boyle, and other figures in the history of science, culminating in his first book, *The Copernican Revolution* (1957). This firmly established his credentials as a historian of science, but the work that made him well known among academicians was *The Structure of Scientific Revolution* (1962; 2d ed., 1970). In it he overturned the prevailing philosophical views of the nature of science, especially scientific changes and progress, and did so in such a compelling manner that philosophers of science came to speak of pre-Kuhnian and post-Kuhnian views.

In *Structure*, Kuhn introduced the notion of scientific paradigms. At the time, the prevailing theories were that science could be clearly demarcated from other kinds of knowledge because science (at least, good science) proceeded from an unbiased observational foundation, followed precisely defined procedures (the scientific method), and, as a result, made cumulative progress in modeling an independent, objectively known world. Good science, it was said, was a value-free, inductively based, cumulatively progressing means of gaining knowledge. Kuhn, armed with his understanding of the history of science, challenged this picture.

Change and progress in science, Kuhn claimed, are not the result of a cumulative collection of facts resulting from value-free observations and from theories inductively inferred from those observations. Rather, change and progress in science are a matter of the replacement of paradigms. Paradigms are defined sociologically from the perspective of scientific communities. A scientific community, for Kuhn, is defined in terms of actual communication linkages, such as sharing professional organizations and journals, attending conferences, or citing specific published works. A scientific community shares a particular paradigm in the sense that members of the community point to the same, or similar, scientific exemplars (or achievements) and the same, or similar, disciplinary matrices (or values, or theories). Science can be demarcated from nonscience because science is guided by a predominant paradigm at any given time. A Newtonian paradigm, for example, rests on a commitment to absolute space and time, whereas an Einsteinian paradigm does not. While a scientific community operates within the confines of a paradigm that gives structure to that community's work, nonscience and infant sciences are not governed or guided by a paradigm; instead many schools coexist, arguing from the fundamentals up, with no accepted methodology. Kuhn called paradigm-governed science "normal science," in which the scientific community engages primarily in solving particular puzzles, such as gathering more detailed data, or increasing the precision of agreement between observation and theoretical predictions, or determining more accurately the values of certain constants (such as the speed of light). Within normal science, the underlying paradigm is assured,

not tested. Scientists, not having to argue continually for the fundamentals, can specialize and focus on specific problems and details and thus make progress.

Inevitably, unexpected phenomena (or anomalies) occur. Often these anomalies can be resolved within the paradigm; sometimes, however, they build in number or strike at the heart of the paradigm. If many or particularly significant anomalies arise and persist, this can produce a crisis for the paradigm. Especially important for Kuhn is the fact that these anomalies can arise for nonscientific (political, social, or philosophical) reasons. When a crisis produces "profound professional insecurity," and rival paradigms are seriously considered, the community has shifted from normal science to revolutionary science. An example of this is the shift from the Ptolemaic, geocentric view of the solar system to the Copernican, heliocentric view. Such scientific revolutions abandon one paradigm for another; this occurs when the new paradigm resolves the old paradigm's anomalies and appears to hold promise to solve even more puzzles. A new normal science then emerges within the new paradigm.

Kuhn's views were striking for a number of reasons. First, he emphasized the revolutionary or discontinuous aspect of science, not the "normal," cumulative aspect. Science changes and progresses, he claimed, not because it steadily accumulates and assimilates more and more information, but because it makes sudden leaps. Second, these revolutions can be seen to have structure and stages. Third, truly revolutionary scientific changes are to a large extent nonrational. The observations made within normal science, said Kuhn, are theory-laden: what is accepted as legitimate observation is influenced by background theories and assumptions. In addition, what is seen as legitimate and what as anomalous can be motivated and justified on nonscientific grounds. Finally, the abandonment of one paradigm for another is often analogous to a conversion experience—in which one holistic view of things is supplanted by another—with the consequence that different paradigms are "incommensurable," such that scientists operating within rival paradigms understand the world differently.

Kuhn's model of scientific change was a conceptual earthquake. While many academicians hailed his "sociological turn," others were quick to criticize his views for portraying science as irrational and ideological. Kuhn spent much of the next three decades responding to critics and clarifying his views, insisting that he was giving a historically based description of scientific practice, not a normative prescription. Moreover, he insisted that science is not irrational and ideological but instead proceeds on the basis of rigorous checks and balances. Good science and the evaluation of rival theories can be characterized around values such as accuracy, consistency, breadth, simplicity, and fecundity. Nevertheless, his legacy lies in challenging the standard view of science as a value-free, cumulative process. Kuhn died in Cambridge, Massachusetts.

• Kuhn published almost 100 books, articles, and reviews. Besides the works cited in the text, Kuhn wrote *The Essential Tension* (1977) and *Black Body Theory and Quantum Discontinuity, 1894–1912* (1978). Hundreds of articles and several books have been written about Kuhn; those of note include Gary Gutting, ed., *Paradigms and Revolutions* (1980); Barry Barnes, *T. S. Kuhn and Social Science* (1982); Paul Hoyningen-Huene, *Reconstructing Scientific Revolutions* (1993); and Paul Horwich, ed., *World Changes: Thomas Kuhn and the Nature of Science* (1994). Obituaries are in the *New York Times*, 19 June 1996; the *Washington Post*, 21 June 1996; *Physics World*, Aug. 1996, pp. 50–51; and the *History of Science Society Newsletter*, Oct. 1996, pp. 3–4.

DAVID B. BOERSEMA

KURALT, Charles (10 Sept. 1934–4 July 1997), radio and television journalist, was born Charles Bishop Kuralt in Wilmington, North Carolina, the son of Wallace Hamilton Kuralt, a social worker, and Ina Bishop Kuralt, a teacher. An employee of the state, Wallace Kuralt did his work by traveling around eastern North Carolina, and young Charles often accompanied him. As they drove from county to county, Kuralt remembered, his father "would tell me little bits of history" (*New York Times*, 5 July 1997) about the places they visited. After spending a good part of his younger years on his maternal grandparents' tobacco farm in Onslow County, Kuralt moved with his family to Charlotte, North Carolina, in the mid-1940s. In 1948, at age fourteen, Kuralt began his radio career, broadcasting games for a minor league baseball club. He would later host a local music program and win a national Voice of Democracy speechwriting contest.

After graduation from Central High School in Charlotte, Kuralt entered the University of North Carolina at Chapel Hill, where he edited the student newspaper. In 1955, after fulfilling all the requirements for a history degree except the swimming test (in the mid-1960s the university waived the requirement and awarded him his degree), he left Chapel Hill to become a reporter for the *Charlotte News*, for which he wrote a regular human-interest column that in 1956 won the Ernie Pyle Memorial Award. Kuralt moved to New York City the following year when he was offered the job of newswriter for CBS radio's "Douglas Edwards with the News" program, thus beginning a 37-year association with that network. He married Sory Guthery in the 1950s (sources differ as to the date of their marriage, giving it variously as 1952, 1954, and 1957); they had two children and were divorced after a five-year marriage.

In 1959, at age twenty-five, Kuralt became the youngest news correspondent in CBS history at that time, covering the 1960 presidential election and serving as the first host of the television news program "Eyewitness to History." Named news chief for Latin America in 1961, Kuralt moved to Rio de Janeiro, where he reported on events from that part of the world, including the aftermath of Fidel Castro's rise to power in Cuba. Back in the United States, he subsequently served as West Coast news chief (1962-1963) and special assignment correspondent for the New York bureau (1964-1967), for which he produced documentaries on diverse topics. "Christmas in Vietnam" (1965) was filmed during one of four trips to the area, and "The Plaisted Expedition" (1967) covered a trek to the North Pole by Ralph Plaisted and resulted in his first book, *To the Top of the World* (1968).

In 1962 Kuralt had married Suzanna "Petie" Folsom Baird; they had no children together and remained married until his death.

In the late 1960s, tired of covering the war in Vietnam and the protests over it and hoping to "escape hawks, doves, gurus, and acid rock," Kuralt, as he put it, "took to the road" (*New York Times*, 5 July 1997). With only one technician and one camera operator to assist him, he began traveling the country in a motor home, reporting human-interest stories involving ordinary people. His "On the Road" segments began airing regularly on Walter Cronkite's "CBS Evening News" in late 1967. They continued until 1980, when Kuralt became the anchor for CBS's morning news program, a job he held for two years.

Kuralt liked to brag that he covered stories in his "On the Road" segments that the smallest of small-town newspapers wouldn't write about. With a distinct poetic flair, he covered, for example, Vermont foliage: "It is a death that causes this blinding show of color, but it is a fierce and flaming death. To drive along a Vermont country road in this season is to be dazzled by the shower of lemon and scarlet and gold that washes across your windshield" (quoted in *Christian Science Monitor*, 7 July 1997). Of equally keen interest to him were a man who hand-carved merry-go-round horses; a butcher who could balance thirty eggs in one hand; and a sharecropper with nine children, all college graduates—of whom he said, "whenever I hear that the family is a dying institution, I'll think of them" (quoted in *New York Times*, 5 July 1997).

As the segments gained popularity, people would line the roads waiting for the "On the Road" motor home to drive past, asking for autographs and photos with the beloved Kuralt. He admitted that the attention he received at times was ridiculous. At one point a PBS crew was covering the fanfare surrounding the filming of an "On the Road" segment in Michigan. Then, the local television station found out that Kuralt was in the area. He said, "While we shot our story, the Traverse City [Mich.] newsman shot us shooting our story, and the PBS crew shot a story about him shooting us shooting our story. I felt I was a character in some sort of Kafka nightmare" (*Saturday Evening Post*, Mar. 1991).

In 1980 Kuralt became the host for the laid-back news magazine "CBS News Sunday Morning," to which he contributed many "On the Road"-like pieces. In 1992 he anchored "America Tonight," CBS's answer to ABC's perennially successful late-night news program "Nightline." "America Tonight" was not a success. Kuralt retired from CBS in 1994, but his restless spirit did not allow him to stop working and traveling. He spent an enviable year traveling across America, finding the ideal spot to visit each month, from New Orleans in January to North Carolina in May and, lastly, to New York City in December; his account of his travels was published as *Charles Kuralt's America* (1995).

Kuralt was honored throughout his lifetime for his journalism. He was the recipient of three Peabody broadcasting awards and at least ten Emmy Awards; in 1980 he was awarded the George Polk Memorial Award for television broadcasting.

In the last year of his life Kuralt was diagnosed with lupus. He died from heart failure in New York City and was buried in Chapel Hill. After his death Patricia Shannon successfully contested his will, claiming that, as his longtime companion, he had intended that ownership of his fishing cabin in Montana be passed to her after his death. According to newspaper accounts, for nearly thirty years Kuralt had lived a double life. He had refused to divorce his wife, but he vacationed, spent holidays, and by all accounts lived as a family with Shannon and her children, whom he even helped put through college. The resulting scandal, which all parties tried to keep from the press, was a troubling footnote to what most believed was a life without shadows.

Called the "laureate of the common man" (quoted in the *Greensboro News Record*, 7 July 1997), Kuralt in his "On the Road" segments featured ordinary Americans who had not yet had, nor were likely to experience if not for him, their fifteen minutes of fame. After a decade of covering war and conflict he was glad to find in his travels that "the country . . . does not bear much resemblance to the one we read about on the front pages of newspapers or hear about on the evening news." His reportage served as an antidote to the cynicism that was already on the rise in television news and now is so prevalent. Kuralt truly "sought out and celebrated the poetry of everyday life" ([Raleigh] *News and Observer*, 9 June 1998).

• The Charles Kuralt Collection, which includes audio- and videotapes, photos, and papers, is in the Southern Historical Collection at the University of North Carolina at Chapel Hill. The best record of Kuralt's life remains his autobiography, *A Life on the Road* (1990). Other books by Kuralt include *Dateline America*, with photos by Mark Chester (1979); with Irwin Glusker, *Southerners: Portrait of a People* (1986); *Growing Up in North Carolina* (1993); and, with Loonis McGlohon (the composer of the "On the Road" theme song), *North Carolina Is My Home*, edited by Patty Davis (1998). Ralph Grizzle and Edwin M. Yoder, *Remembering Charles Kuralt* (2001), commissioned by the University of North Carolina, is a biography of the journalist told through remembrances by Kuralt's friends and colleagues. In "The Rocky Road to Popularity," *Saturday Evening Post*, Mar. 1991, Kuralt writes about becoming a minor celebrity. Obituaries are in the *New York Times* and the (Raleigh) *News and Observer*, both 5 July 1997; *USA Today*, Greensboro (N.C.) *News Record*, and *Christian Science Monitor*, all 7 July 1997; *Newsweek*, 14 July 1997; *People*, 21 July 1997; and *Quill*, Oct. 1997. "Charles Kuralt's Secret Life," an article in the (Raleigh) *News and Observer*, 9 June 1998, provides information on his relationship with Patricia Shannon.

STACEY HAMILTON

L

LAMARR, Hedy (9 Nov. 1913–19 Jan. 2000), actress, was born Hedwig Eva Maria Kiesler in Vienna, Austria, the daughter of Emil Kiesler, a director of the Bank of Vienna, and Gertrude Kiesler (maiden name unknown), a concert pianist. She was of Jewish extraction on both sides of her family, which proved fateful for her life and her career. As a child, she took ballet and piano lessons and was educated by tutors as well as at private schools. In 1929 she studied design in a Viennese finishing school. At Max Reinhardt's drama school in Berlin, she received both instruction and encouragement, which led to several roles in stage productions. Reinhardt served as both her coach and her mentor; she said of him: "Reinhardt made me read, meet people, and attend plays" (Lamarr, *Ecstasy and Me*, p. 18).

In 1931 Hedy Kiesler, as she called herself, visited Sascha Film Studios where director Georg Jacoby cast her in a bit part in *Die Blumenfrau von Lindenau*, also known as *Sturm im Wasserglas* (*Storm in a Water Glass*). Soon thereafter, she took an ingénue role (as a banker's daughter, a role she knew well) in the film *Man Braucht Kein Geld* (1931, released in English as *His Majesty King Ballyhoo*), which garnered good reviews. The director Alexis Granowsky then secured for her a part in a light comedy, *Die Koffer des Herrn O. F.* (1931, *The Trunks of Mr. O. F.*).

Hedy Kiesler's breakthrough performance came in 1932, when she starred in a film originally titled *Symphonie der Liebe* but better known as *Extase* (*Ecstasy*), a Czech production directed by Gustav Machaty. The film featured nudity and "the first explicit sex scene in a commercially distributed film" (*Entertainment Weekly*, 4 Feb. 2000, p. 76). Considered extremely daring at the time, the film caused a sensation in Europe and was deemed "obscene" by the U.S. Treasury Department when it was imported to the United States. (The distributors appealed the American ban on showing the film, which was lifted by Judge Learned Hand.) Such a stir was created that Hedy Kiesler's husband, a wealthy Austrian arms dealer named Fritz Mandl whom she married in 1933, reportedly attempted to purchase all extant copies of *Extase* in order to keep it out of circulation.

Despite being privy to numerous dinnertime discussions with leading political figures of the day, Hedy Kiesler reportedly found her husband, who openly sympathized with the Nazi cause, to be "dull" and divorced him in 1937. When Germany annexed Austria in 1938, she feared persecution at the hands of the Nazis and escaped to Paris disguised as a maid. Within a short time, she decided to emigrate to the United States. The film industry executive Louis B. Mayer signed her to a seven-year contract with Metro-Goldwyn-Mayer and changed her last name to Lamarr, in honor of Barbara La Marr, a screen star from the 1920s.

On arriving in the United States, Lamarr deliberately played down her sexually charged image by wearing ankle-length dresses. Determined to be taken seriously as an actress, she won good reviews for her first American film, *Algiers* (1938), in which she co-starred with Charles Boyer. Blessed with raven hair, almond eyes, and alabaster skin, set off by lustrous lipstick, she found herself in demand and quickly appeared in a number of films, including *Lady of the Tropics* (1939, with Robert Taylor); *Comrade X* (1940, with Clark Gable); *H. M. Pulham, Esq.* (1941, with Robert Young); *Come Live with Me* (1941, with James Stewart); *Crossroads* (1942, with William Powell); *White Cargo* (1942, with Walter Pidgeon); *Tortilla Flat* (1942, with John Garfield); and *Heavenly Body* (1943, again with Powell). Although her physical beauty undeniably opened doors for her (and was the source of female emulation and male admiration), Lamarr struggled to overcome her *Ecstasy* legacy and usually found herself typecast as a femme fatale; her thespian skills typically received no more than lukewarm praise. She did not advance her career by passing up leading roles in *Casablanca* and *Gaslight*, for both of which Ingrid Bergman won renown.

After moving to Warner Bros., Lamarr starred in *The Conspirators* (1944, with Paul Henreid); *Her Highness and the Bellboy* (1945, with Robert Walker); and *Let's Live a Little* (1948, with Robert Cummings). She also produced two of her films, *The Strange Woman* (1946) and *Dishonored Lady* (1947). Her later roles included *Samson and Delilah* (1949, with Victor Mature); *A Lady Without Passport* (1950, with John Hodiak); *Copper Canyon* (1950, with Ray Milland); and *My Favorite Spy* (1951, with Bob Hope).

An enthusiastic supporter of her adopted country, Lamarr tirelessly sold war bonds during World War II and even offered a noteworthy addition to warfare technology. A chance conversation with friend and composer-pianist George Antheil in 1940 concerning the war's progress led the two to collaborate on a sophisticated plan for a remote-controlled radio system that would let signals be transmitted at sea without fear of deciphering, detection, or jamming. Lamarr and Antheil gave the War Department diagrams and a description of the proposed technology, which received U.S. patent no. 2,292,387 in 1942, but it went unused by the time the patent expired in 1959, the year that Antheil died. Although it would later prove important to digital communications, Lamarr never made a penny from the technology.

Lamarr's personal life also proved frustrating. Although she adopted a son when she married screenwriter Gene Markey in 1939, divorce followed in 1940. She married actor Sir John Loder in 1943 and had two children with him, but the couple divorced in 1947. Her subsequent failed marriages were to nightclub owner Ted Stauffer (1951–1952), oil baron W. Howard Lee (1953–1960), and lawyer Lewis J. Boies (1963–1965). With her film career essentially over by the early 1950s, she drifted into television work and then gradually out of show business. In 1966 she unsuccessfully sued the ghostwriter of her autobiography for alleged inaccuracies. In her later years, while subsisting largely on Social Security and a Screen Actors Guild pension, she became legally blind.

Lamarr did gain a measure of vindication, however. In 1997 she and Antheil were honored with a Pioneer Award from the Electronic Frontier Foundation for having envisioned spread-spectrum communications, which was crucial, in particular, to the development of the cell phone industry. And in 1998 Lamarr was the recipient of the Viktor Kaplan Medal of the Austrian Association of Patent Holders and Inventors, considered the highest honor that Austria can bestow on an inventor. She made the news again in 1998 by suing the Corel Corporation for using an image of her from her prime Hollywood days to market a computer-graphics program; the matter was settled out of court. At age eighty-six, Lamarr died at her home near Orlando, Florida.

Although not as successful as some other European émigrées in Hollywood, such as Marlene Dietrich and Greta Garbo, Hedy Lamarr nevertheless created a legacy for herself as a stunning beauty who played opposite several of the most romantic leading men of the time. It was unfortunate, though, that she could not capitalize on her intellectual gifts, especially with regard to the patented frequency-hopping system. One can only wonder what direction her life might have taken if she had won recognition for that technology decades before she did.

• Lamarr's autobiography, *Ecstasy and Me: My Life as a Woman* (1966), contains a great deal of interesting information but should be relied on with caution. Her role in developing the "frequency-hopping" technology is succinctly covered by Anne Macdonald in *Feminine Ingenuity: Women and Invention in America* (1992); see also James W. Michaels, "Hedy Lamarr, Inventor," *Forbes*, 14 May 1990, and Mark Boslet, "Cast against Type: An Actress's Role in Wireless History," *Wall Street Journal*, 21 Feb. 1997. Obituaries can be found in the *Washington Post* and *New York Times*, both 20 Jan. 2000; *Time*, 31 Jan. 2000; *Entertainment Weekly*, 4 Feb. 2000; and *People*, 7 Feb. 2000.

BARBARA BENNETT PETERSON

LAMOUR, Dorothy (10 Dec. 1914–22 Sept. 1996), actress, was born Mary Leta Dorothy Slaton in New Orleans, Louisiana, the daughter of John Slaton, a waiter, and Carmen LaPorte Slaton, a waitress. (Although various sources list her surname at birth as Kaumeyer, Lamour states in her autobiography that it was Slaton.) Her parents divorced when she was a young child. (Her mother was subsequently briefly married to a man named Clarence Lambour. Mary Slaton, who was always called Dorothy, took Lambour's last name; she dropped the *b* when she became a professional singer.) She grew up in poverty—she later recalled that her home had newspapers in the windows because her mother could not afford curtains—and quit high school when she was fifteen. Thereafter, she briefly attended a secretarial college.

In 1930 Lamour's close friend Dorothy Dell, who also later acted in Hollywood, won first place in the "Miss Universe" beauty contest. When Dell signed a contract to appear as an "American Beauty" in a Fanchon and Marco vaudeville revue, she insisted that Lamour be hired as well. The two young women toured with Fanchon and Marco for several months in 1930. Lamour also appeared as "Miss Way Back When," attired in an 1890s-era bathing suit, in Mangel's Beach and Style Show, another vaudeville revue. In 1931 Lamour was named "Miss New Orleans" in a beauty contest. That year she moved to Chicago, hoping to make a career as a singer.

After working as an elevator operator for the Marshall Field's department store, Lamour joined the Herbie Kay band as their female vocalist. During the early 1930s, she toured throughout the Midwest and was featured on Kay's nationally broadcast weekly radio program. Around 1934 she moved to New York City, where she headlined at the fashionable Stork Club, appearing with such prominent bandleaders as Rudy Vallee and Eddie Duchin. In 1934 she was signed by NBC to star on a radio program, "The Dreamer of Songs," which aired three nights a week. She married Kay in 1935; they had no children and divorced in 1939.

In 1936 Lamour's radio program was relocated to Hollywood, and soon thereafter she signed a contract with Paramount Pictures. She later recalled her excitement upon reporting to the studio and learning that her wardrobes would be designed by Edith Head, who had provided gorgeous gowns and hairdos for Hollywood's leading actresses. To her disappointment, however, Lamour found that she was being fitted only for a sarong and that her long straight hair ("the longest tresses in the film colony," according to studio publicity) was not to be done up—thus becoming one of her trademarks. In her debut picture, *The Jungle Princess* (1936), she played an innocent native girl who lives in a cave and has as her best friends a chimpanzee and a 500-pound Bengal tiger. Although budgeted as a "B" picture, *The Jungle Princess* appealed to audiences at preview screenings, and Paramount's publicity department built the film into a popular success and Lamour into a promising new star. In 1937 she appeared in a major hit, John Ford's *The Hurricane*, a special-effects extravaganza in which she played the daughter of a Samoan island chieftain. Her screen image as an exotic beauty established, she went on to appear in several films of a similar mold, including *Her Jungle Love* (1938), *Moon over Burma* (1939), and *Aloma of the South Seas* (1941). In many of her films, she sang one or two songs; "Moonlight and Shadows" from *The Jungle Princess* became a number-one hit. She eventually grew tired of her repetitive "sarong" roles and hoped to stretch herself as an actress. Many of her serious dramatic efforts, as in *Disputed Passage* (1939) and *Chad Hanna* (1940), were, however, critically derided.

In 1940 Lamour reached the height of her popularity when she costarred with Bob Hope and Bing Crosby in *Road to Singapore*. Wartime audiences loved the silly, tune-filled comedy, described by *Time* magazine as a "marvelously shoddy" assemblage of ad-libs and old vaudeville routines. Four successful sequels followed in the next seven years. Typically cast in the series as a sultry princess who is wooed by both Hope and Crosby, Lamour called herself "the happiest and highest-paid straight woman in the business." In 1943 she married William Howard, a career military officer from a prominent Maryland family; they had two children and remained married until his death in 1977. Throughout the American involvement in World War II, she was one of Hollywood's busiest patriots, participating in camp tours and USO shows. Her popularity was such that during a four-day bond drive in New England, she helped raise over thirty million dollars. During this period, she introduced several songs in her films that became standards, including Johnny Mercer's "I Remember You" (*The Fleet's In*, 1942) and James ("Jimmy") Van Heusen's "It Could Happen to You" (*And the Angels Sing*, 1944) and "Personality" (*Road to Utopia*, 1946).

Lamour's film career declined in the late 1940s when she took several hiatuses to devote herself to her family. In 1952 she appeared as the "Girl with the Iron Jaw" in Cecil B. De Mille's circus epic, *The Greatest Show on Earth*; the following year she made a sixth "Road" picture, *Road to Bali*, after which Paramount ended her contract, and she and her family moved to Baltimore. In 1961 she developed a popular nightclub act, touring throughout the United States. In 1962 she was disappointed when Hope and Crosby reteamed for *Road to Hong Kong* but gave the female lead to Joan Collins; Lamour made only a cameo appearance in the film. However, she remained on friendly terms with her "Road" costars, and plans were in the works for an eighth picture when Crosby died in 1977. In 1967 she toured in a stage production of *Hello Dolly*, and throughout the 1970s she maintained a busy acting schedule in regional theater. During her later years, she was a frequent guest on Hope's television specials. She died in North Hollywood, California.

Possessing glamorous good looks and limited acting skill, Lamour appeared in several of Hollywood's biggest box office hits during World War II. Although her "jungle princess" films and "Road" comedies may seem corny to viewers today, they provided escapist entertainment for a nation at war.

• The best source for information on Lamour's life is her autobiography, *My Side of the Road* (1980). Randall G. Mielke, *Road to Box Office* (1997), analyzes the appeal of the "Road" series and provides a detailed description of the production of each of the films. The book also provides an overview of Lamour's film career. For information about her at Paramount, see James Robert Parish, *The Paramount Pretties* (1972). For views of her by her peers, see Bing Crosby, *Call Me Lucky* (1953); Ray Milland, *Wide-Eyed in Babylon* (1974); and Bob Hope, *Have Tux, Will Travel* (1954) and *The Road to Hollywood* (1977). An obituary appears in the *New York Times*, 23 Sept. 1996.

THOMAS W. COLLINS, JR.

LANDRY, Tom (11 Sept. 1924–12 Feb. 2000), football coach, was born Thomas Wade Landry in Mission, Texas, the son of Ray Landry and Ruth Coffman Landry. The members of the family were fixtures in their small-town community. Ray Landry owned a local garage and also acted as both the chief of the volunteer fire department and as superintendent of the First Methodist Church Sunday school. Tom Landry excelled in both academics and sports at an early age, and in high school he was not only a straight-A student but also president of his class and an outstanding football fullback. Graduating in the spring of 1942, only months after America's entry into World War II, he enrolled that fall at the University of Texas and joined the college football team; at the end of the semester he left college to enlist in the U.S. Army Air Forces. After training as a pilot, he flew thirty combat missions in Europe over the next three years with the Eighth Air Force.

At war's end in 1945, Landry returned to the University of Texas to study business administration. He also rejoined the college football team, playing quarterback and fullback and becoming co-captain in the fall of 1948, his senior year. The following January he married a college classmate, Alicia Wiggs; the couple eventually had three children. Upon graduating with a B.S. degree in 1949, Landry joined an American Football Conference team called the New York Yankees as a halfback. After one season the Yankees merged with the New York Giants, part of the National Football League (NFL), and Landry became a cornerback for the team. Between 1949 and 1952 Landry also attended the University of Houston in the off-season, studying mechanical engineering and eventually earning a second bachelor's degree in that field. During his six years with the Giants, Landry earned a reputation as a self-disciplined, well-grounded player who used his brainpower to master the game—he later acknowledged that his training as an engineer reinforced his approach to football—and in 1954 his skills received national recognition when he was named to the All-Pro defensive team. By this time he was also assisting the Giants' coaches.

In 1956 Landry ended his playing career to become the full-time defensive coach of the Giants. Over the next four years he was a major factor in the team's impressive 33–14–1 record, in large part by devising and implementing a new defense strategy. He replaced the traditional umbrella defense, which deployed a six-man line plus a roving linebacker, with what became known as the 4-3 defense. The new strategy called for ends to turn into linebackers, and it was ultimately adopted as the standard defense by all professional football teams. During Landry's tenure coaching the Giants, the 4–3 defense helped the team win two division titles and a world championship, and he was hailed as the best defensive coach in the business.

In 1960 Landry was offered the head coaching job with the Giants, but instead he opted to return to Texas as head coach of the Dallas Cowboys, a newly formed NFL expansion team owned by a friend, Clint Murchison, Jr. The Cowboys proved to have, at least initially, a conspicuous lack of athletic talent and a seeming inability to grasp even the most rudimentary strategies, offensive as well as defensive. The team posted a devastating 0–11–1 record their first season, but instead of giving up Landry rose to the challenge. Realizing that his cherished 4–3 defense, now practiced by all the Cowboys' opponents, was making a shambles of his team, he devised a multiple offense to counter it, using double and triple wings; he also revised the 4–3 into a new defense effort, an updated version of the umbrella called the flex. Persistence and ingenuity paid off, as did the acquisition of better players: in the 1965 season the Cowboys broke even in wins and losses for the first time; and in 1966, and again in 1967, they won the NFL Eastern Division title. They were playoff contenders thenceforth, playing in the Super Bowl for the first time in January 1971 and barely losing that game—by a 16–13 score—to the Baltimore Colts.

The team that had once invited comparison with the Marx Brothers in *Horse Feathers* was now on its way, thanks to Landry, to an NFL-record-setting twenty consecutive winning seasons and to four more Super Bowl appearances. Under Landry they won the Super Bowl twice, in 1972 and again in 1978. Over the years Landry became a readily recognizable figure on the sidelines, standing tall and trim, arms folded, in a sports coat and slacks, always wearing a fedora, and expressing little emotion. Indeed, in a sport where coaches were often foul-mouthed bullies who drove their teams through insult and abuse, Landry was a rare specimen, commanding respect and results through a dignified process of teaching that harnessed intellect and patience and motivated players to do their best. His demeanor reflected an inner strength that he attributed to a deep religious faith, and that faith appeared to sustain him in the 1980s when other teams began edging out the Cowboys in performance. Finally, after three consecutive losing seasons and the sale of the team, Landry was dismissed as their coach in February 1989.

Voicing neither bitterness nor regret, Landry expressed gratitude for the career he had enjoyed and pride in his twenty-nine seasons with the Cowboys, who had amassed 270 victories—the third highest number in NFL history—under his tutelage. In retirement he turned his full-time attention to the Fellowship of Christian Athletes, an organization he had been active in for years, and he traveled nationally on their behalf, often piloting his own small plane. In 1990 Landry was inducted into the Pro Football Hall of Fame. Four years later, at the age of seventy, he made news again when he successfully landed his plane in a dirt field in Texas after experiencing engine failure. In the late 1990s Landry was diagnosed with an acute form of leukemia, and he died of that disease at the Baylor University Medical Center in Dallas.

• For biographical information, see "Landry, Tom," in *Current Biography Yearbook* for 1972 and 2000; and Bob St. John, *Landry: The Legend and the Legacy* (2000). For a posthumous appreciation of Landry and an assessment of his years in coaching, see Dave Anderson, "Landry Was in Control as Cowboys' Coach," *New York Times*, 13 Feb. 2000; see also Bill Pennington, "Remembering Landry, the Thinker and Motivator," *New York Times*, 14 Feb. 2000. In addition, see Jennifer Briggs Kaski, *The Book of Landry: Words of Wisdom from and Testimonials to Tom Landry* (2000). An obituary appears in the *New York Times*, 13 Feb. 2000.

ANN T. KEENE

LANE, Burton (2 Feb. 1912–5 Jan. 1997), composer of popular music, was born Burton Levy in New York City, one of two sons of Lazarus Levy, a real estate salesman, and Frances Fink Levy, an amateur pianist who died when Burton was two. He attended the New York High School of Commerce.

The last of a particularly lyrical strain of twentieth-century songwriters, the composer known as Burton Lane was inspired by George Gershwin, who had earlier taken inspiration from Jerome Kern. Already under the spell of Gershwin's music, Burton Levy began composing when he was eleven. During a family holiday in Atlantic City, he was playing the piano when he was overheard by Gershwin's mother, who was also vacationing there. She arranged a meeting between Gershwin and the young composer, and Levy became a part of the Gershwin circle of friends. Gershwin introduced him to the music scholar Walter Damrosch, who urged him in vain to study classical composition. Levy published his first song, "Broken Butterfly," at age fifteen and was hired at sixteen by the Shubert brothers, for whom he wrote twenty songs for the next edition of the *Greenwich Village Follies*, a show canceled when its star fell ill. Levy then became pianist and song plugger for the music publishing house Remick's. Heeding a radio program host's advice, he changed his name to Lane.

Ultimately credited with more than 550 compositions, Lane composed almost exclusively for stage and screen. His first Broadway songs were written for *Three's a Crowd* (1930), to lyrics by Howard Dietz. Forming a partnership with Harold Adamson, an aspiring lyricist and family friend, Lane placed songs in *The Third Little Show* and wrote most of the score for Earl Carroll's *Vanities* (both 1931). In 1933 Lane and Adamson signed with Irving Berlin's music publishing company, which sent them to Hollywood to write for movie musicals. Lane and Adamson's first major hit was the haunting "Everything I Have Is Yours" in Metro-Goldwyn-Mayer's *Dancing Lady* (1933). The partnership, which produced film songs for Jimmy Durante, Maurice Chevalier, Ethel Merman, and Eddie Cantor, lasted until 1935. That year, Lane saw the Gumm Sisters in a vaudeville show at a downtown Los Angeles movie house, an act that closed with a song by the youngest sister, Frances. Lane met the Gumm family backstage, recommended Frances to MGM the next day, and played piano accompaniment for her audition, which lasted from ten in the morning until five in the afternoon. The studio then signed Frances Gumm, thus launching the career of Judy Garland.

In 1935 Lane married Marion Seaman, with whom he had one child; after a separation, they were divorced in 1961, when Lane married Lynn Daroff Kaye, who had three children from a previous marriage. They remained married till Lane's death. After working with Ralph Freed and Ted Koehler, Lane began one of his most fruitful periods in 1938 with Frank Loesser, a fledgling lyricist whom Lane had recommended for a job at Paramount Studios. Lane played melodies repeatedly until Loesser remembered them well enough to fit the words. The first Lane-Loesser score, for *Spawn of the North* (1938), included the bathetic "I Like Hump-Backed Salmon" sung by John Barrymore.

The best Lane-Loesser love songs, which became dance-band favorites and ultimately part of the standard popular repertoire, were understated combinations of musical and lyrical surprise. They were embedded in otherwise undistinguished films—"Says My Heart" in *Cocoanut Grove* (1938), "The Lady's in Love with You" in *Some Like It Hot* (1939), "I Hear Music" and "Dancing on a Dime" in *Dancing on a Dime* (1940). Apparently the collaboration convinced Loesser he could write his own melodies. Having been introduced to the politically liberal lyricist E. Y. "Yip" Harburg by George and Ira Gershwin, Lane returned to Broadway, writing the score of *Hold Onto Your Hats* (1940). The score included "There's a Great Day Coming Mañana," sung by Al Jolson, with Lane's buoyant melody counterpointing an ironic Harburg lyric—a portent of the more adventuresome and complex songs the pair would create for *Finian's Rainbow* (1947).

Lane returned to MGM, where in 1942 he wrote with Ralph Freed the Academy Award–nominated "How About You?" (sung in *Babes on Broadway*). Musicologist Alec Wilder called it "a marvelous, healthy, rhythmic ballad, a model of popular song writing . . . in thirty-two measures, a perfectly fashioned melodic line." Of one of Lane's stylistic hallmarks, Wilder added, "These uses of repeated notes . . . have . . . a considered quality. One feels that only repeated notes are right at this point." In the same year, Lane's "Poor You" for Frank Sinatra in *Ship Ahoy* reunited him with Harburg, thereafter his favorite collaborator. Harburg urged humor into Lane's writing, and Lane claimed his melodies always sounded better with Harburg's lyrics.

In 1946 Harburg recruited Lane for the Broadway version of James Stephens's Irish fable *The Crock of Gold*; Lane demurred, claiming that the project needed a Gershwin. Harburg prevailed, however, and turned the crock of gold into Fort Knox and the theme into brotherhood's triumph over prejudice; the result was *Finian's Rainbow*, the most musically varied of Lane's scores. To suit the wildly fanciful book, Lane wrote fey songs, rousing songs, playful songs, and soaring songs.

In Hollywood once more, Lane collaborated with Alan Jay Lerner on the score of *Royal Wedding* (1951). Its 34-bar "Too Late Now" was Lane's second Academy Award nomination. Wilder lauded its inventive release: "Once you have heard it, you would have it no other way." In Michael Feinstein's 1990 interview with Lane, the composer said that writing for Fred Astaire in this film was a lifelong dream, "to try and give Astaire what I saw Astaire do best, and that was wonderful rhythm beats in the music."

During the 1950s Lane, committed to the welfare of songwriters, became the first president of the Songwriters' Protective Association (later the Songwriters Guild), which was instrumental in forcing publishers to reveal their accounts. Lobbying congressional committees, he was an early advocate of intellectual property rights. Lane was a member of the American Society of Composers, Artists and Publishers (ASCAP) for more than sixty years and was on its board for more than eight.

In 1953 Lane collaborated with Ira Gershwin on *Give a Girl a Break*, a frustrating film project the collaborators called "Give a Song a Break." In 1955 he was reunited with Adamson once more to do *Jupiter's Darling*, a film starring Esther Williams, but another project with Lerner, *Huckleberry Finn*, fell through. Lane's only venture into television was *Junior Miss* (1957) with lyrics by Dorothy Fields.

Thereafter Lane entered a fallow period, claiming he could not write unless he was enthusiastic about a project; and when he was, Harburg often was not. But in 1965 he again teamed with Lerner on Broadway after that capricious lyricist had caused Richard Rodgers to abandon a collaboration. Lane and Lerner's musical about extrasensory perception, *On a Clear Day You Can See Forever*, includes the transcendent title song (". . . the magic of great professional writing," according to Wilder) as well as "Come Back to Me," a surging melody that underlines the lyrics by seeming to escape the boundaries of space and time. In 1966 Lane received the Sigmund Romberg Award from the American Guild of Authors and Composers. An early inductee into the Songwriters Hall of Fame, Lane received its Johnny Mercer Award for distinguished writing.

There was one more failed Broadway show with Lerner, *Carmelina* (1979), and a film collaboration with Sammy Cahn, *Heidi's Song* (1982). In 1990–1991 Lane recorded two volumes of *The Burton Lane Song Book*, playing piano and doing occasional vocals with the musicologist-singer Michael Feinstein.

Lane played at the December 1996 centenary tribute to Ira Gershwin at Carnegie Hall. He died in New York after a stroke; two days later, on 7 January 1997, the lights of all Broadway theaters were dimmed in his honor.

• The Burton Lane archives are held by the Library of Congress. The best discussions of Lane's songs are Alec Wilder, *American Popular Song: The Great Innovators 1900–1950* (1972), pp. 331–43, and Michael Feinstein's interview with Burton Lane packaged with *The Burton Lane Songbook* (Warner Communications, 1990). The most extensive listing of Lane's film credits is found in Clive Hirschorn, *The Hollywood Musical* (1981). Interesting information appears in various biographies of George Gershwin, as well as in Alan Jay Lerner, *The Street Where I Live* (1978), and Benny Green, *Let's Face the Music: The Golden Age of Popular Song* (1989). For obituaries, see Richard Severo's in the *New York Times*, 7 Jan. 1997, and Patrick O'Connor's in the *Guardian*, 8 Jan. 1997.

JAMES ROSS MOORE

LANGSTROTH, Lorenzo Lorraine (25 Dec. 1810–6 Oct. 1895), minister and apiarist, was born in Philadelphia, Pennsylvania, the son of John George Langstroth, occupation unknown, and Rebekah Aurelia Dunn Langstroth. After graduating from Yale in 1831, he began training for a career in the ministry and also served as a tutor in math at his alma mater between 1834 and 1836. In May 1836 he took over the pulpit at the South Congregational Church in Andover, Massachusetts, and on 22 August of that year married Anne M. Tucker of New Haven, Connecticut, with whom he was to have three children.

Forced by poor health to resign his office in 1838, Langstroth became principal of the Abbot Academy in Andover and remained there until 1839, when he moved to Greenfield, Massachusetts, and became principal of the High School for Young Ladies. In 1844 Langstroth returned to the ministry and became pastor of the Second Congregational Church in Greenfield, where he stayed for four years before going back to Philadelphia to serve as the principal of another girls' school.

After arriving in Philadelphia, Langstroth continued to experiment with beekeeping, a hobby that had long fascinated him. Although honey production had been practiced for several thousand years, beekeepers had long been frustrated with the cumbersome production methods then in use. Typically, bees were kept in straw baskets—known as skeps—within which bees attached honeycombs to the sides and roof. Numerous drawbacks accompanied this method: not only was it difficult to feed the bees or examine them for evidence of disease, but it was impossible to control the production of queen cells and drones. Worst of all in the view of many beekeepers was that they had to drive off or kill the bees each fall in order to harvest the honey. Langstroth carefully studied all of the available literature on the subject (much of which had been written by fellow clergymen in the United States and Europe) and experimented with a variety

of frame designs that would provide access and allow the beekeeper to overcome these limitations. In the fall of 1851 he determined that a gap of five-sixteenths of an inch between frames—and between the frames and the outer walls of the hive—was sufficient to allow bees to move about within the hive and not compel them to fill the gap with comb. His discovery of this "bee space" led to his constructing in the fall of 1851 the first truly movable beehive frame.

In 1852 Langstroth moved to Oxford, Ohio, and on 5 October of that year was granted a patent for the Langstroth hive, which featured two compartments: a lower one, which held food and allowed for the propagation of the swarm, and an upper one, which contained the removable frames and allowed for the extraction of honey. In 1853 he published *Langstroth on the Hive and the Honey-Bee*, in which he outlined the technical advantages of his new hive and the management techniques that enabled the production of new queen bees. (Subsequent editions sometimes appeared under the title of *Practical Treatise on the Hive and Honey-Bee*.) Having benefited from available literature during his experiments, Langstroth also became a tireless contributor to general publications on beekeeping in an effort to spread the results of his findings. By the time of the Civil War, Langstroth's hive was in common usage in the United States; it was introduced in England in 1862.

Unfortunately, like many inventors of his time, Langstroth initially had to struggle to achieve recognition for his efforts. Infringements on his patent became common, and he received little compensation. Although the contention over his achievements embittered him, he continued to revise his book and produced several subsequent editions. He also helped introduce into the United States Italian queen bees—a development that stimulated interest in beekeeping—and for several years produced them commercially. Langstroth spent the last years of his life in Dayton, Ohio, where he had the assistance of Charles Dadant, a French émigré and fellow apiarist whose revision (prepared with his son, Camille Pierre Dadant) of Langstroth's classic appeared as *Langstroth on the Hive and Honey Bee* in 1889. Dadant also arranged to have the work published in several foreign languages. In addition to his work with bees, Langstroth occasionally taught and preached in the years prior to his death, which occurred in Dayton.

Despite suffering the fate of numerous other inventors—that of being unable to gain just financial compensation for their efforts—Lorenzo Langstroth lived long enough to see his work achieve near-universal acceptance. His publication remains a classic in beekeeping literature, and his invention, one of a string of nineteenth-century inventions that made modern commercial honey production possible, earned him the title "father of modern beekeeping."

• A collection of Langstroth's correspondence and many editions of his classic work are held at the Cornell University library in Ithaca, N.Y. A biography by Florence Naile, *The Life of Langstroth*, was published in 1942 and reissued in a revised edition as *America's Master of Bee Culture: The Life of L. L. Langstroth* (1976), with a new foreword by Roger A. Morse. His accomplishments have received attention in a number of works, including Roger A. Morse, *Bees and Beekeeping* (1975), and Eva Crane, *The Archaeology of Beekeeping* (1983).

EDWARD L. LACH, JR.

LARSON, Jonathan (4 Feb. 1960–25 Jan. 1996), composer-lyricist-librettist of *Rent*, a rock opera inspired by *La Bohème*, was born in Mt. Vernon, New York, and raised in suburban White Plains, the second child of Allan S. Larson, a direct-marketing executive, and Nanette Notarius Larson. Both parents loved music and theater; show tunes and folk music were always playing in their home. Both Larson and his sister took piano lessons during elementary school. The boy could play by ear, and his teacher encouraged him to experiment with rhythm, harmony, and setting words. By high school, he was called the "Piano Man" after the enormously popular song of that title by Billy Joel. He also played tuba in the marching band. Active in school and community theater, Larson had major roles in several musicals.

In 1978 Larson entered the acting conservatory at Adelphi University with a four-year full-tuition merit scholarship. He told an interviewer in 1993 that the program was "an undergrad version of the Yale Rep [the theater where students of the Yale School of Drama work alongside veteran professionals]. And I was serious enough about theater to know that this was what I wanted to do." He earned his Equity card doing summer stock and received a BFA with honors in 1982. His favorite part of the curriculum was the original political cabarets. With classmates, Larson wrote rock-flavored attacks on the New Christian Right, Reaganomics, and the mind-numbing effects of television. He also scored *El Libro de Buen Amor* (1979) and *The Steak Tartare Caper* (1981), musicals with lyrics and libretti by faculty members. He had a knack for pastiche and for complex ensemble numbers that used themes in counterpoint. At Adelphi he could see his work on stage immediately and benefit from actor and audience response.

In class, Larson studied the theater of Bertolt Brecht and Peter Brook. Among his musical influences were *Jesus Christ Superstar*, the Beatles, Prince, and the Police. The writer he admired most was Stephen Sondheim, to whom he wrote during his last year in college. The distinguished composer-lyricist became an adviser to the young songwriter. After graduation, Larson moved to Manhattan, went on acting auditions, performed in a nightclub trio, and composed songs for a musical version of Rudyard Kipling's *Jungle Books*. In 1982 Larson adapted George Orwell's *1984* for the musical stage. Deeply affected by the novel, and unflappably confident, he completed book, music, and lyrics, recorded a "demo," sent a script to director Harold Prince, and wrote to Orwell's estate. The theatrical rights were not available. "So all the work that I had done on that transmogrified into *Superbia*, which was my own dystopia."

In the earliest drafts of *Superbia*, a young man with a music box wants to wake up an emotionally numb futuristic society. In later drafts, the hero never gets a chance to make his point. This shift seems to echo Larson's own experience with mounting a new musical. During the *Superbia* years, 1985–1991, Larson was chosen for ASCAP and Dramatist Guild development workshops. He lived on the edge of poverty, preferring to work as a waiter rather than divide his concentration with jingle- or copywriting. Organized and disciplined, he revised draft after draft of *Superbia* and submitted material to scores of regional theaters. In 1988 he won a $14,766 Richard Rodgers Development Grant, which funded a staged reading at Playwrights Horizons. Larson's belief in his work was just as large as his talent. An intense, soulful man with a long thin body and wild curly hair, he could say with a straight face, "I am the future of the American Musical" (and often did). But Larson's talent, devotion, connections, and persistence could not bring about a full-scale production of the show.

Larson addressed this disappointment in *tick, tick . . . BOOM!* (1990), an autobiographical "rock monologue" influenced by the work of Eric Bogosian and Spalding Gray. In the course of twelve songs and twelve stories, he told half-funny, half-bitter tales of bad readings and waiting tables; worried about turning thirty, whether to give up writing musicals, and if his current girlfriend was "the one"; and learned that his best friend was HIV-positive. *Tick* was deliberately easy to stage—"No sets, no costumes, no cast. Just me, a piano, and a band"—but Larson's hopes for a larger production or a record deal went unfulfilled. He did occasional downtown performances through 1994.

In 1989 the playwright Billy Aronson had asked Larson to collaborate on an update of *La Bohème*: a show about would-be artists of the present day coping with poverty, disease, and heartache. Larson suggested the multilayered title *Rent*. They wrote three songs and amicably separated. In 1991 three more of Larson's friends were diagnosed HIV-positive, and he returned alone to the project, with Aronson's blessings. In contrast to most Broadway shows of the time, which valued spectacle over meaning and technology over personal interaction, Larson envisioned a great rock opera that would bring people together, address social issues, and make musical theatre relevant to his generation: "*Hair* for the '90s."

Larson began the arduous dual development process again. While he did extensive research and tried out new material in friends' living rooms, he also applied for grants and looked for producers. In 1992 he approached the New York Theatre Workshop, a downtown theater specializing in new and avant-garde work. They expressed great interest in *Rent* and gave Larson an artistic home and rigorous feedback as he worked out the plot. Some of his characters were gay, others straight, some white and others shades of brown. Most were long on style, short on cash, and battling AIDS, addiction, or loneliness. Larson's score used pop music styles from heavy metal to gospel. When Larson won a $45,000 Richard Rodgers grant in 1994, the New York Theatre Workshop mounted a "studio production"; but the show still needed focus. Fall 1995 was a time of intense work and of passionate arguments about the show's shape and production timeline. Finally, just before Christmas, the show was cast and rehearsals began. Twice during "tech week," Larson went to hospital emergency rooms with severe chest pains but was released. The only full dress rehearsal was held on 24 January 1996. Anthony Tommasini, a music critic for the *New York Times*, attended, planning to mention *Rent* in an article about the centenary of *La Bohème*. Impressed by the score, Tommasini interviewed Larson that night and told him that the work was something special. A few hours later, alone in his apartment, Larson died from an undiagnosed aortic aneurysm.

After two weeks of previews, *Rent* opened on 13 February 1996 to rave reviews, and the original downtown run quickly sold out. A flood of publicity fueled the transfer of the show to Broadway on 29 April 1996. The show was an explosion of energy—with all the performers wearing small headset microphones as in a rock concert. Teenagers camped on the sidewalk outside the Nederlander Theatre for precious $20 tickets and testified in Internet chat rooms about how the show had changed their lives. Characters who happened to be homosexuals, people of color, infected, or homeless became familiar to audiences in a way that statistics or strangers never could. The 1996 Democratic Convention included a performance of the *Rent* song "Seasons of Love." Among other awards, the show and its author won the 1996 Pulitzer Prize for Drama and four Tonys. By the year 2000, *Rent* had been performed on five continents, spreading its message of tolerance and hope.

Also of interest are works that Larson created with collaborators. *Blocks* (1993), with lyrics by Broadway veteran Hal Hackady, is a revue about teen issues, which was performed in some New York City high schools. With songwriter Bob Golden, Larson wrote script and songs, directed, and produced a thirty-minute video for children called *Away We Go* (1994). *J. P. Morgan Saves the Nation* (1995) was a sardonic history lesson about capitalism, which Larson set to Sousa-style marches, grunge rock, and everything in between. The playwright Jeffrey M. Jones wrote the book and lyrics specifically for outdoor performances in New York City's financial district.

• The Larson family has an archive of manuscripts, correspondence, and "demo" recordings. In the winter and spring of 1996, numerous articles about Jonathan Larson and *Rent* appeared in New York City dailies, the *Village Voice*, *Time*, *Newsweek*, *Variety*, and other publications. Of particular interest is the set of articles in the *New York Times*, 17 Mar. 1996. *Rent: Book, Music, and Lyrics by Jonathan Larson . . .* (1997) is a lavishly illustrated volume containing the complete libretto, along with text and interviews by Evelyn McDonnell with Katherine Silberger, including anecdotes about Larson, *Rent*'s development, and the original cast. *US Magazine* published a lengthy profile by David Lipsky, Nov. 1996. John Istel wrote a feature on the composer for the *Village Voice*, 4 July 1995. A transcript of Larson and Istel's 1995 conversation was published in *American Theatre*, July/Aug. 1996. Barry Singer wrote about Larson in *New York Magazine*, 21 June 1993. An obituary is in the *New York Times*, 26 Jan. 1996.

AMY ASCH

LAUGHLIN, James (30 Oct. 1914–12 Nov. 1997), publisher and poet, was born James Laughlin IV in Pittsburgh, Pennsylvania, to Henry Hughart Laughlin and Marjory Rea Laughlin. His father was the president of Jones and Laughlin, a major steel mill founded by his great-grandfather, an Irish immigrant and the first James Laughlin. Although young James was expected to enter the family business, he rebelled at an early age, turning to art and literature, subjects that he later recalled received short shrift in the family household but to which he was attracted at school. He was educated privately, first in Pittsburgh and then at boarding schools in Switzerland and Massachusetts before entering the Choate School in Wallingford, Connecticut, where one of his teachers and mentors was Dudley Fitts, a noted translator of Greek poetry and drama. At Choate Laughlin wrote poetry and short stories and edited the school literary magazine. Another important mentor who encouraged his literary inclinations was an aunt who lived in Norfolk, Connecticut, and whom he visited regularly. Laughlin's literary ambitions received public recognition in his senior year at Choate, when one of his stories was published in the May 1933 issue of *Atlantic Monthly*.

Entering Harvard that fall, Laughlin chose to major in Latin and Italian and also studied English and American literature. He soon became impatient with the conservative views of many of his teachers, who had no use for the modern writers who most interested Laughlin, especially the poets Ezra Pound and T. S. Eliot. In early 1935 he left Harvard in the middle of his sophomore year to live for a time in Paris, which had become the literary and art capital of the world in the early decades of the century. Now determined to become a poet, he visited with the influential expatriate American writer Gertrude Stein and her companion, Alice B. Toklas. With their encouragement he wrote to Ezra Pound, who was then living in Rapallo, Italy, asking if he could visit with the poet. Receiving a favorable response, Laughlin headed for Rapallo and stayed with Pound for six months, writing poetry under his tutelage. Despite Laughlin's efforts, however, his poetry failed to pass muster with Pound, who cannily suggested that the young scion with a family fortune at his disposal might choose a career as a publisher of avant-garde literature instead.

Laughlin returned to Harvard to resume his studies in the fall of 1935, and while attending classes he took Pound's advice and founded a publishing company called New Directions with money borrowed from his father. Running the company out of a cottage on the grounds of his aunt's home in Norfolk and using his college dorm room as a warehouse, Laughlin launched his company in 1936 with a paperback collection of experimental writing called *New Directions in Prose & Poetry*, the first of what became an annual anthology. It included works by Pound as well as other distinguished but nonmainstream American writers, including William Carlos Williams, Wallace Stevens, Gertrude Stein, Marianne Moore, and E. E. Cummings, and a promising young poet named Elizabeth Bishop. There was also a poetic contribution from one "Tasilo Ribischka," the pseudonym of Laughlin himself. Laughlin printed seven hundred copies and took to the road on weekends to sell them at two dollars apiece from the trunk of his Buick. Thus was born what would one day become one of the most influential companies in the history of American publishing.

Laughlin remained at Harvard for four years, preparing a new edition of *New Directions in Prose & Poetry* each year while serving on the editorial board of the student publication the *Advocate* and completing course work for his undergraduate degree, which he received in 1939. Now able to devote himself full time to the press, Laughlin acquired a small staff and, continuing to work out of his cottage in Norfolk, began adding publications to his list, adhering always to his commitment to publishing high-quality works that would have been disdained as unprofitable by most commercial publishers, either because of their content and modernist style or because their authors were no longer in public favor. He began with a series called "Poets of the Year," which he launched in 1941 and which featured works by such new writers as John Berryman, Richard Eberhart, and Delmore Schwartz. Soon afterward he launched another imprint called "New Classics," which reissued out-of-print books by such prominent authors as Henry James, Evelyn Waugh, and F. Scott Fitzgerald. Still another series, "Makers of Modern Literature," featured assessments of major modern works by prominent critics, including Lionel Trilling's evaluation of E. M. Forster.

Modern American avant-garde writers as well continued to find a willing publisher in Laughlin, who issued volumes by Nathanael West, Gary Snyder, Kenneth Patchen, James Purdy, Djuna Barnes, Kenneth Rexroth, Denise Levertov, and the Beat poets Lawrence Ferlinghetti and Gregory Corso, among others. As one of his most important achievements, he published major foreign authors in translation, introducing many of them to the American reading public; they included Jorge Luis Borges, Hermann Hesse, Eugenio Montale, Pablo Neruda, Boris Pasternak, Octavio Paz, and Yukio Mishima. Laughlin also published works by contemporary foreign authors writing in English, notably Dylan Thomas and Vladimir Nabokov. Although Laughlin was both editor and publisher of his company—the staff grew over the years but he remained in charge—he appears to have exercised a gentle hand in the editorial process,

encouraging rather than trying to second-guess and rewrite others' material.

Subsidized by family money—Laughlin often noted that his father always willingly gave him money for his venture—New Directions began to turn a profit only in the 1950s, after twenty-three years of operating in the red. Its growing success was attributable in large part to an increasing demand for New Directions titles on college campuses as more and more professors assigned them in their classes. Laughlin continued to live in Norfolk but moved his office to New York City in the late 1940s; after several relocations in the city the company became permanently headquartered in Greenwich Village.

In addition to his activities as a publisher—and undeterred by the judgment of Ezra Pound—Laughlin continued to write and publish his own poetry, now under his own name. In composing his verse, which he described as "simple" and "often sentimental" and which members of his circle praised for its clarity, he often experimented with different poetical forms, though he remained under the stylistic influence of Pound and Williams. His verse appeared not only in his annual anthology but was also published separately in more than a dozen other volumes, beginning with *The River* (1938). He completed a volume of new poems, *A Commonplace Book of Pentastichs*, shortly before his death; it appeared posthumously in 1998. A final collection, *Poems: New and Selected*, was also published in 1998.

Laughlin served as president of Intercultural Publications, a publishing subsidiary of the Ford Foundation, from 1952 to 1969, and was a member of the U.S. Commission for UNESCO in the early 1960s. A longtime friend of Thomas Merton, whose early poetry he had published, Laughlin became a co-trustee of the Thomas Merton Legacy Trust, established after Merton's death in 1968, and coedited a posthumous Merton work, *The Asian Journal of Thomas Merton* (1973). He also published a book about his relationship with Ezra Pound (*Pound as Wuz*, 1987). In addition to his writing and editing, Laughlin acted as a quiet benefactor of many New Directions authors, paying their rents and medical bills and giving them loans when they were hard up. In private life he especially enjoyed skiing. He published articles about the sport in several national magazines, coauthored (with Helene Fischer) the book *Skiing: East and West* (1947), and even founded a ski lift company—a venture more profitable than New Directions.

Laughlin was married twice. His marriage in 1942 to Margaret Keyser, with whom he had two children, ended in divorce a decade later. In 1956 he married Ann Clark Resor and with her had two more children. He died en route to a hospital in Sharon, Connecticut, from his home in Norfolk after suffering a stroke.

• Some of Laughlin's papers, including his correspondence with William Carlos Williams, are at the Houghton Library, Harvard University; other Laughlin papers, including his correspondence with Ezra Pound, are at Yale University's Beinecke Library. For biographical information, see entries for "Laughlin, James," in *Current Biography Yearbook* for 1982 and 1998; *Dictionary of Literary Biography*, vol. 48 (1986); *Contemporary Authors: New Revision Series*, vol. 47 (1995); and *Contemporary Authors*, vol. 162 (1998). See also Donald W. Faulkner, "James Laughlin—Poet and Publisher," *Connecticut Artists*, Spring-Summer 1980, pp. 6–15; Susan Howe, "New Directions: An Interview with James Laughlin," in Bill Henderson, ed., *The Art of Literary Publishing: Editors on Their Craft* (1980); and Robert Dana, "James Laughlin: An Interview," *American Poetry Review*, Nov.-Dec. 1981, pp. 19–32. See also Hayden Carruth, *Beside the Shadblow Tree: A Memoir of James Laughlin* (1999). In addition, see various published collections of Laughlin's correspondence with New Directions authors, including *William Carlos Williams and James Laughlin: Selected Letters* (1989) and similarly titled collections featuring Laughlin's correspondence with Kenneth Rexroth (1991) and Delmore Schwartz (1993), among others. For an assessment of Laughlin's poetry, see especially Denise Levertov, "About James Laughlin," *Conjunctions*, Winter 1981–1982, pp. 68–69. An obituary appears in the *New York Times*, 14 Nov. 1997.

ANN T. KEENE

LAVEAU, Marie (1794?–16 June 1881), voodoo queen, was born in New Orleans about 1794, the illegitimate daughter, part black, part Native American, part white, of Charles Laveau and Marguerite Carcantel Laveau. This Roman Catholic "free woman of color" developed into a statuesque beauty with fine facial features and curly black hair. In 1819 she married Jacques Paris, a free quadroon Catholic carpenter from Santo Domingo (now Haiti). They lived in New Orleans in a house given her by her father. Paris soon disappeared and was reported dead. Calling herself "Veuve [Widow] Paris," she became a hairdresser for white and Creole women in New Orleans.

During this period, she was already participating in voodoo activities, well established in New Orleans as early as 1782. She encouraged indiscreet revelations from unhappy women while she was their sympathetic beautician. Intimate bits of gossip about husbands' quadroon mistresses, family alcoholism, insane aunts, and the like proved useful to her. Nearby Bayou St. John and Lake Pontchartrain marshes were locales of wild voodoo ceremonies, and downtown Congo Square was the scene of Sunday afternoon voodoo dances. In 1824 or a little later Christophe Duminy de Glapion, another Santo Domingo quadroon, moved in with Marie, remaining until his death in 1855. They had fifteen children.

Once Marie began her relationship with Glapion, she turned to practicing voodooism full time, becoming a voodoo queen by 1830. Her colorful ceremonies capitalized on traditional African and Caribbean elements such as spiders, black cats, roosters, blood-drinking, "the great Zombi" (her snake), and climactic acts of "possession" (fornication); but she added certain Catholic features—incense, statues of saints, holy water, and Christian music and prayers. Marie was one of the first queens to make their profession pay. She scared off, beat up, or hired as assistants

other voodooiennes. She sold invitations to lakeside rituals, permitted well-to-do white men to enjoy clandestine orgies, and bribed and otherwise charmed the police into ignoring her innumerable felonies. She presided over Congo Square slave dances for white spectators. She hired informants and pressured black girls to gather incriminating gossip, so as to persuade clients that she was a mind reader and a prophetess. She gloried in rumors—that she fed babies to her snakes, could cause white wives to turn adulterous, could accommodate pregnant women by inducing miscarriages. On one occasion she used her magic powers and paraphernalia, including pulverized lizard eggs, donkey hair, feathers, aphrodisiacs, brick dust, yellow ochre, and cayenne pepper, along with her *gris-gris*, the traditional red bag of voodoo amulets, to persuade a judge to acquit a wealthy man's rapist son. The grateful father deeded Marie a cottage on St. Anne Street, which became her permanent headquarters. In another coup, she succeeded in putting the leading New Orleans attorney under her control in order to gain legal advice and useful secrets from him.

By the 1850s "Mamzelle Marie" was undisputed head queen, in shawl, colorful satins, bejeweled necklaces, and accompanied by castanets, drums, fiddles, and flutes. She presided over waterside orgies. She built "Maison Blanche," half of which was a high-class brothel, the other half, a voodoo-rites scene, complete with torches, crocodiles, animal slaughters, and conversations with Lucifer. Until 1871 she also provided spiritual comfort to condemned prisoners in the parish jail. She visited them in their cells, brought them food, including her potent gumbo, and knelt in prayer with them. She donated an altar to the prison chapel and decorated it in a conventional manner. Just before one double execution, she was the cause, in her friends' eyes at least, of a violent storm that some devotees compared to the weather at the time of Christ's crucifixion. However, although the first attempt at hanging the condemned pair failed, the second succeeded.

In 1869 Marie reigned over her final voodoo conclave, after which her associates voted her into retirement. In 1875 she entered her little cottage and, according to one story, never came out again. A new Marie Laveau took over. She was most likely one of Marie's daughters, born in 1827 and christened Marie Laveau Glapion. In adulthood she bore an uncanny resemblance to her beautiful mother. She either was appointed by her mother to replace her as head voodoo queen or gradually assumed the role on her own. Known as Marie II, she had long been busy helping run her mother's bordello.

The legend developed that Marie Laveau never died. It was said by the faithful that she turned into a crow, a dog, a snake, and even a preternaturally old woman on the street or holding a log floating in St. John's Bayou. Rumors connected her with Aaron Burr, the Marquis de Lafayette, Louis Philippe, and even Queen Victoria. It is true that she knew Lafcadio Hearn, who interviewed her, and George Washington

Cable, who was anathema to conservative white citizens of New Orleans because of his liberal, pro-black writings. In *A Critical Dialogue between Aboo and Caboo*, an 1880 pamphlet signed "E. Junius," Abbé Adrien Emmanuel Rouquette accused Cable of consorting with Marie. This poet-priest wrote that "Savan Missié Kabri / . . . Li té dansé Kongo / Avek Mari Lovo" (Wise Mr. Goat [the bearded Cable] . . . he danced the Congo with Marie Laveau).

To this day, the crypts in which Marie I and Marie II supposedly repose, in St. Louis Cemetery No. 1, attract both suppliants and scoffers. Petitioners leave flowers, food, and coins; ask for assistance in matters of love, commerce, or combat; scratch crosses with red bricks; and stand and turn around thrice. To her critics, Marie Laveau was the devil incarnate; to her worshippers, she was a dusky saint.

• Raymond J. Martinez, *Mysterious Marie Laveau, Voodoo Queen, and Folk Tales along the Mississippi* (1956), is a biography. Henry C. Castellanos, *New Orleans As It Was* (1895), and Joy J. Jackson, *New Orleans in the Gilded Age: Politics and Urban Progress, 1880–1896* (1969), touch on Marie Laveau and her activities. Castellanos refers to Marie as a woman without scruples; Jackson is more tolerant. Edward Larocque Tinker, *Creole City: Its Past and Its People* (1953), presents Adrien Rouquette's unfounded accusations against George Washington Cable. Arlin Turner, *George W. Cable* (1956), and Jonathan Cott, *Wandering Ghost: The Odyssey of Lafcadio Hearn* (1991), discuss their respective subjects and Marie Laveau. Lafcadio Hearn, "New Orleans Superstitions," *Harper's Weekly*, 25 Dec. 1886, p. 843, mentions Laveau. Novels based on Laveau are Tallant, *The Voodoo Queen: A Novel*, and Francine Prose, *Marie Laveau* (1977). An inaccurate obituary is in the New Orleans *Daily Picayune*, 17 June 1881.

ROBERT L. GALE

LAWRENCE, Gertrude (4 July 1898–6 Sept. 1952), actress, was born Gertrud Alice (or Alexandra) Dagmar Klasen in London, England, to singing actor Arthur Klasen and his wife Alice Louise Banks Klasen. Incompletely educated in London, Lawrence adopted the professional surname of her father, Alf Lawrence, when in her early teens she decided on a theatrical career.

Lawrence, her era's most magnetic female stage star, was rescued from the chorus of a provincial troupe in 1916 by the American song and dance team Lee White and Clay Smith, who recommended her to André Charlot, the producer of their current London revue. For the next nine years, Lawrence's career was generally guided by Charlot, who repeatedly fired ("She was just a crazy kid") and rehired her. For Charlot, Lawrence became a star of intimate revue and made her debut (1923) in musical comedy. In 1917 she married Francis Howley; they had a daughter, separated, and in 1927 were divorced.

In January 1924 *Charlot's London Revue* opened in New York, ultimately transforming American musical revue but immediately making international stars of Lawrence, Beatrice Lillie, and Jack Buchanan.

Throughout the revue's run, Lawrence and Lillie, living together round-the-clock, filled their apartment with the nobility of New York's theatrical and musical communities. One result was George Gershwin and Ira Gershwin's *Oh, Kay!* (1926), written for Lawrence, whose waiflike performance of "Someone to Watch over Me" became part of Broadway legend. Slender and blonde, alternately willowy and gawky, never able to carry a tune confidently, she acted her songs in unforgettable and unpredictable style. When a subsequent Charlot revue played Hollywood in 1926, Lawrence, glorying in the sunshine, went barelegged and found herself a fashion trendsetter.

For a time Lawrence's career alternated uncertainly between the United States and Great Britain. In 1928, on her days off from the London run of *Oh, Kay!* she made her debut in straight drama for Charlot in Owen Davis's dour Pulitzer Prize–winning play *Icebound*. Back in New York later in the year, she led the cast of the Gershwins' *Treasure Girl*, which may have failed because audiences could not see in her a gold digger. The following year the composer Johnny Green wrote an "act" for Lawrence to perform for the British Broadcasting Corporation; it included "Body and Soul," which became one of the century's most renowned songs. In 1929 Lawrence starred in her first American musical film, "The Battle of Paris," with a score by Cole Porter. In the *International Revue* (1930), a stage revue by Lew Leslie, Lawrence introduced Jimmy McHugh and Dorothy Fields's "Exactly Like You." Later in 1930 Lawrence was scheduled to return to Charlot for a new revue when her childhood friend and fellow Charlot graduate Noël Coward (who had wanted her for his 1929 operetta *Bitter Sweet* but felt her voice wouldn't do) presented her with a new script, *Private Lives*. Thus Lawrence emerged as a unique presence in light drama and an ideal, coolly fragile and caustic foil for Coward. *Private Lives*, a four-handed version of the marriage game, which included "Somewhere I'll Find You," was a hit in London in 1930 and in New York in 1931.

For the next several years Lawrence appeared mainly in British plays and films, although in 1934 she starred in Porter's London musical comedy *Nymph Errant*. The show's choreographer was Agnes de Mille, who wrote of Lawrence's unique gift: "Her flair for improvisation being phenomenal, each performance, each rehearsal became in the great tradition a direct, fresh experience between her and the audience." Lawrence's notorious carelessness with money is frequently cited as the spur to her friend Coward's writing *Tonight at 8:30* (1936 both in London and New York) for the pair to perform. *Tonight at 8:30*, a tour-de-force series of nine one-act plays, some with music, presented in combinations of three, included "Still Life," which in a slightly expanded version became the classic British film *Close Encounter*. By the close of the run, which had a $4.40 top price, much higher than any other nonmusical show, Coward and Lawrence were established at the top of their profession in the United States.

Thereafter Lawrence rarely appeared outside the United States. In 1937 she began a lengthy New York and national run in Rachel Crothers's comedy *Susan and God*, as a woman who believes that being open with God and everyone else will help solve her problems, one of which is getting rid of an alcoholic husband; but life teaches her a tolerance that saves her marriage. This was followed in 1939 by *Skylark*, a bittersweet play by Samson Raphaelson about marriage, children, and making do that had begun its life in the small Cape Playhouse in Massachusetts run by Richard Aldrich. Called "luminous" in the role, Lawrence once more toured the nation. She married Aldrich in 1940; they had no children and remained married until her death.

In 1941 Lawrence starred as magazine editor Liza Elliott in the Kurt Weill–Ira Gershwin–Moss Hart musical *Lady in the Dark*, a venture highly unconventional for its time in subject matter (psychoanalysis) and method (the only music was in dream sequences). The show's hit was Danny Kaye's "Tschaikowski," a rapid-fire reeling-off of fifty Russian composers' names, which Lawrence had to immediately follow with a number of her own; but her competitiveness made "The Saga of Jenny" a classic of genteel bumping and grinding. Lawrence also starred on American radio in the 1940s in shortened versions of contemporary popular films and plays. She made several wartime tours entertaining servicemen for the British ENSA (Entertainment National Services Administration) and the American USO (United Service Organization). In 1945 she played Eliza Dolittle in a successful New York production of George Bernard Shaw's *Pygmalion*. Shaw had earlier refused to give his permission for a musical version, which might have starred Lawrence.

After World War II and the publication of her autobiography, *A Star Danced* (1945), Lawrence seemed to be retired, except for occasional revivals of earlier work and her appearances at Aldrich's Cape Playhouse. But in 1950 she was cast in an unusual role—the faded Southern belle Amanda Wingfield in Irving Rapper's film version of Tennessee Williams's *The Glass Menagerie*. For once in her career underplaying a role, she showed herself as an authentic actress. In 1951 she was named the head of the Columbia University School of Dramatic Arts. Having seen in Margaret Landon's book *Anna and the King of Siam* a fine vehicle for a musical, she persuaded Richard Rodgers and Oscar Hammerstein II to take on the project. Lawrence returned to Broadway in *The King and I* as the English governess to the Siamese king. The show ran for 1,246 performances and Lawrence won a Tony (Antoinette Perry) award for being Mrs. Anna, but midway through the run she died of previously undetected cancer in New York. The lights of all theaters on Broadway and in London's West End were dimmed in her honor. In 1968 Julie Andrews played Lawrence in the American biographical film *Star!*

• Gertrude Lawrence's life and career are partly documented in the holdings of the Billy Rose Theater Collection at the New York Public Library and the Theatre Museum, London, as well as in various papers held by family members in England and the United States. The papers held by the family of André Charlot in California and London reveal further details. In addition to *A Star Danced*, see the memoir by Richard Aldrich, *Gertrude Lawrence as Mrs. A* (1954), and the biography by Sheridan Morley, *Gertrude Lawrence, A Biography* (1981). Lawrence is glimpsed in many memoirs, biographies, and autobiographies, particularly Agnes de Mille, *Dance to the Piper* (1952) and Noël Coward, *Present Indicative* (1937). Many obituaries exist, including one that appears in the *New York Times*, 7 Sept. 1952.

JAMES ROSS MOORE

LEARY, Timothy (22 Oct. 1920–31 May 1996), clinical psychologist and psychedelic drug guru, was born Timothy Francis Leary in Springfield, Massachusetts, the son of Captain Timothy "Tote" Leary, a U.S. Army dentist, and Abigail Ferris Leary, a schoolteacher. Leary was an extremely bright, inquisitive, and outgoing child who inherited his family's Celtic flair for revelry and literature and a healthy disrespect for authority. Leary writes in his autobiography, *Flashbacks* (1983), that when he was ten, his paternal grandfather, the richest Irish Catholic in western Massachusetts, advised his favorite grandson, "[N]ever do anything like anyone else, boy. . . . Be the only one of a kind" (p. 24).

Leary never forgot his grandfather's advice. He was expelled from high school for writing inflammatory newspaper editorials and dismissed from the College of the Holy Cross for rebelling against its monastic Jesuit regimen. He was court-martialed for drinking and other offenses and "silenced" at the U.S. Military Academy at West Point, where he spent less than a year. In 1941 Leary enrolled at the University of Alabama, where he encountered psychology, a discipline that became the central academic interest of his life. Although he loved the intellectual challenge of higher education, Leary was again expelled, this time for spending a night in the girl's dormitory. He lost his student deferment and was drafted into service in 1943, but took college courses at night and earned a B.S. from the University of Alabama that year. While working as a psychological consultant in an army medical corps hospital in Butler, Pennsylvania, he met Marianne Busch, an army audio technician. The couple was married in 1944 and had two children. After the war the family moved to the West Coast, where Leary continued his studies in psychology. He earned an M.S. from Washington State University in 1946 and a Ph.D. from the University of California, Berkeley, in 1950.

Leary thrived in the open intellectual environment of the university community, succeeding as an assistant professor of psychology at Berkeley from 1950 to 1955. During these years Leary and his wife joined a wild, flirtatious party circuit, and both badly abused alcohol (Leary's alcoholic father had abandoned the family when Leary was fourteen). Marianne Leary became increasingly depressed and committed suicide in 1955. That same year Leary became director of psychiatric research at the Kaiser Foundation in Oakland, California. In 1957 he published his first important book, *Interpersonal Diagnosis of Personality*, named the year's best book in psychology by *Annual Review of Psychology* for its new approaches to human behavioral changes. Two years later he landed a prestigious position on the faculty of Harvard University.

In the summer of 1960 Leary took a vacation that changed his life. Frank Barron, a friend from graduate school and a leading psychologist, told Leary about a special kind of mushroom that induced mind-expanding visions and enhanced creativity. Consequently, with his children, Barron, and another young Harvard professor, Richard Alpert, Leary rented a house in Cuernavaca, Mexico, where he had his first hallucinogenic experience. He ingested six "magic mushrooms," washing them down with a bottle of Carta Blanca beer. In *Flashbacks* Leary recounts the altered state that followed: "I gave way to delight, as mystics have for centuries when they peeked through the curtains and discovered that this world—so manifestly real—was actually a tiny stage set constructed by the mind. There was a sea of possibilities out there (in there?), other realities, an infinite array of programs for other futures. . . . In four hours by the swimming pool in Cuernavaca I learned more about the mind, the brain, and its structures than I did in the preceding fifteen years as a diligent psychologist" (pp. 32–33).

When Leary returned to Harvard that fall, he re-evaluated his mission as a scientist and vowed to devote his professional life to the study of the mental health benefits of consciousness-expanding drugs. With Barron, Alpert, and another well-known psychologist, Ralph Metzner, Leary founded the Harvard Psychedelic Research Project and began administering mescaline, psilocybin (the active ingredient in the mushrooms), and other psychoactive drugs to colleagues and graduate students in a series of controlled experiments. Leary soon expanded the project to include volunteers at a prison and made real progress in treating alcoholism, schizophrenia, and other psychological disorders. During this time the group theorized that there was a relationship between drug-induced and naturally occurring religious experience. Leary believed that, in the proper social setting, psychedelics could be used to produce mystical states of revelation. In the midst of America's sexual revolution, he also reported that these drugs could act as powerful aphrodisiacs. Both of these radical propositions infuriated conservative antidrug groups, which were growing in step with the increasing popularity of the counterculture movement at Harvard and across the country.

With Leary at the forefront, the controversial Harvard project was heavily publicized and added to the political polarization of the nation. Among Leary's earliest supporters were the writers, philosophers, and artists of the Beat Generation, most notably Allen Ginsberg, Peter Orlovsky, Jack Kerouac, Neal Cassady, William Burroughs, and jazz musicians Thelon-ious Monk and Maynard Ferguson, all of whom had been using drugs for years. Other enthusiastic supporters were internationally renowned writers Aldous Huxley, Arthur Koestler, and Alan Watts. Early in 1962 Leary discovered LSD (lysergic acid diethylamide), a synthetic hallucinogen one hundred times stronger than psilocybin. On a visit to Los Angeles, he "dropped acid" with Hollywood celebrities, including Cary Grant and Steve Allen. That fall Leary's Harvard group relocated to a six-bedroom house called the Newton Center that became a hotbed for drug use as the counterculture gained popularity throughout the country and news of "bad trips" generated widespread negative publicity. Under pressure to resign from Harvard, Leary renamed his project the International Foundation for Internal Freedom (IFIF). In spring 1963 both Leary and Alpert were dismissed from the Harvard faculty when Alpert allowed undergraduates to join in the increasingly notorious experimentation.

After efforts to transplant the IFIF to Mexico failed, Leary opened the Castalia Center, a 64-room mansion on a 4,000-acre estate in Millbrook, New York, near Poughkeepsie. The estate, owned by the wealthy Hitchcock family, who were enthusiastic supporters of the Castalia Center, soon became commonly known as "Millbrook." Almost immediately Millbrook became a magnet for an ever-changing cast of pilgrims that included mystics, shamans, truth-seeking students, hippies, the original doctor feel-good (Max Jacobson), and Ken Kesey and his Merry Pranksters, who later were celebrated in Tom Wolfe's *The Electric Kool-Aid Acid Test* (1968). With Alpert and Metzner, Leary published *The Psychedelic Experience: A Manual Based on the Tibetan Book of the Dead* (1964), and his popularity with American youth soared. He called Millbrook "an earthly paradise," married New York model Nanette von Schlebrugge in 1964, and honeymooned in Japan and India, where he sought out holy men and studied Eastern religions.

While Leary was traveling, Alpert was left in charge of Millbrook, which spiraled out of control. Soon after Leary's return, Alpert left the Castalia Center, changed his name to Baba Ram Dass, and became a Hindu swami. Leary's marriage broke up. By the end of 1965 he was forced to shut down Millbrook and had been arrested in Laredo, Texas, for possession of less than an ounce of marijuana. Sentenced to thirty years in prison, he appealed the conviction. The case soon became a cause célèbre, and a defense fund was set up. While the case was being appealed Leary was able to reopen Millbrook, which was promptly raided by the county sheriff's office, led by G. Gordon Liddy, who would later gain notoriety in the Watergate scandal.

Now seen as a national leader of anti-establishment politics, Leary in 1966 argued before a Senate committee for the legalization of LSD and founded the League for Spiritual Discovery, a religious entity that sought constitutional protection for the right to use LSD as a sacramental substance. With an increasingly high profile, Leary consulted his friend Marshall Mc-Luhan, a future-oriented media expert, who advised him to think of himself less as a philosopher-reformer and more as a promoter-advertiser for his message. In response, Leary coined his famous phrase, "Turn on, Tune in, Drop Out," and became a celebrity on the lecture circuit and in multimedia liturgical shows. In 1967 he and Ginsberg drew fifty thousand participants at a "Human Be-In" in San Francisco. That same year he married Rosemary Woodruff. In 1968 Leary sang "Give Peace a Chance" with John Lennon and published *The Politics of Ecstasy* and *High Priest*, books that became bibles for hippies who began wearing "Leary Is God" buttons. At the height of his popularity in 1969, Leary announced his candidacy for the governorship of California. At the same time President Richard Nixon began calling him "the most dangerous man in America."

All of Leary's political plans crashed in January 1970, when a jury convicted him on a 1968 arrest for possession of two marijuana cigarettes. He was immediately remanded to jail in southern California, where he began serving a 31-year sentence for multiple state and federal drug felonies. Soon after he was incarcerated, Leary and Woodruff began planning his escape. With the help of the radical Weather Underground, on 13 September 1970 the 49-year-old Leary escaped from the state prison at San Luis Obispo by pulling himself across a twenty-foot-high cable and climbing down a telephone pole to a getaway car. In a scenario that played out like a B movie, Leary was given a disguise and a new identity and was spirited off to Algeria, where he joined fellow political exiles Eldridge Cleaver and his Black Panthers; the Panthers, however, did not trust Leary and placed him under house arrest. He found asylum in Switzerland, where he wrote *Confessions of a Hope Fiend* (1973). He eventually surfaced in Afghanistan with his new companion, Joanna Harcourt-Smith. In December 1972 Leary was arrested in Kabul by U.S. narcotics agents and extradited to the United States. He wound up in California's maximum security Folsom Prison where, for a time, he occupied a cell next to mass murderer Charles Manson.

Leary served more than three years in some forty different jails and penitentiaries during his protracted battle with the U.S. criminal justice system before he was paroled by California governor Jerry Brown in April 1976. Leary again became a success on the college lecture circuit and continued to grow intellectually. He studied computers, space migration, and methods for increasing human intelligence and life spans and wrote books that reflected these interests, including *Neuropolitics* and *Exopsychology* (both 1977), *Intelligence Agents* and *The Game of Life* (both 1979), and *Chaos and Cyber Culture* (1994). In 1978 Leary married Barbara Chase. In the last two decades of his life Leary organized Starseed, a cooperative aimed at colonizing space, and founded Futique, a software company that produced multimedia educational products in what Leary called "Cyberia." He

also staged a series of entertaining debates with his former nemesis Liddy. When Leary was diagnosed with prostate cancer in 1995, he even orchestrated his own death by writing *Design for Dying* (1997); appearing in the documentary film *Timothy Leary's Dead* (Strand) and the video *Timothy Leary's Last Trip* (Windstar); signing up for cryonic preservation of his head, a decision he later revoked; opening a website to monitor his last extravagant days; and arranging for his ashes to be shot into orbit around the earth. During his last illness, Leary remarried Rosemary Woodruff, who was with him when he died in Beverly Hills, California.

A born iconoclast, Leary emerged from the turbulent 1960s as one of America's most controversial figures for his outspoken leadership of the psychedelic crusade, which posed a serious threat to the status quo. In *High Priest* he argued that "the cause of social conflict is neurological. The cure is biochemical." As the Vietnam War raged and America was being torn apart by civil strife, many embraced Leary as a true visionary who argued for a hallucinogenic utopia, but many more were skeptical and saw him as a charming charlatan, a carnival barker for the counterculture. Critics accused him of hyping LSD as an easy path to pop mysticism spiced with Eastern religion and sex appeal. Perhaps Leary's sternest critic was his friend William Burroughs, who had experimented with drugs for most of his life. Burroughs had eagerly agreed to participate in the Harvard project but was disillusioned by Leary's starstruck message of instant enlightenment and believed that Leary was a politically naïve intellectual who was destined to fail. Allen Ginsberg, however, made this assessment of his fellow philosopher in the introduction to Leary's *Jail Notes* (1970): "Dr. Leary is a hero of the American consciousness. . . . It took innocent courage to explore his own unconditioned consciousness, to take LSD and other chemicals often enough to balance praxis with explanation, and to attempt to wed the enormity of his experience to Reason" (p. 10). While critical assessments like these run the gamut in characterizing Leary, no one can deny his unflagging courage, imagination, humor, and persistence in delivering his message to America's counterculture during a time of revolutionary social change.

• During Leary's imprisonment, he entrusted his personal archives to Michael Horowitz who, with Karen Walls and Billy Smith, compiled *An Annotated Bibliography of Timothy Leary* (1988), an exhaustive review of Leary's books, monographs, articles, interviews, sound recordings, computer software, and appearances in films and on television through 1987. Horowitz eventually gave Leary's papers to the Fitz Hugh Ludlow Library in San Francisco, one of the world's finest collections of documents on psychoactive drugs; however, public access to its holdings became problematic when it was placed in storage during the 1980s and later offered for sale. Other notable books by Leary published after 1988 are *Psychedelic Prayers and Other Meditations* (1997) and his collected writings on sexuality, *The Delicious Grace of Moving One's Hand* (1998). An audio version of *Flashbacks* read by Leary was produced by Hawkeye. In *Creativity and Psycho-*

logical Health (1963), Frank Barron relates how he introduced Leary to the Mexican magic mushrooms. See also Paul Krassner, "Dr. Leary—Or How I Learned to Transcend Ego and Expand My Consciousness," *The Realist,* Jan. 1965; Charles Slack, *Timothy Leary, the Madness of the Sixties and Me* (1974); and Arthur Kleps, *Millbrook* (1975). An account of Leary's cheerful preparations for his death is "Dr. Tim's Last Trip," *Time,* 29 Apr. 1996. Leary's official website is www.leary.com. Obituaries are in the *New York Times* and the *Los Angeles Times,* both 1 June 1996.

BRUCE L. JANOFF

LEE, Mabel (18 Aug. 1886–3 Dec. 1985), physical education teacher, advocate, and author, was born in Clearfield, Iowa, to Jennie Aikman Lee and David Alexander Lee, who was in the lumber business at the time. Although small, underweight, and often ill as a child, Mabel enjoyed physical games and activities that she called "natural gymnastics." These were especially important to her because organized physical education was not then part of the school system. In 1893, when Mabel's father joined his two brothers in the coal business, the family moved to Centerville, Iowa, where Mabel was to graduate from high school in 1904. Attending Coe College in Cedar Rapids, Iowa, she majored in psychology and minored in biology.

At a time when most women married, Lee was single-minded about her career. In her opinion, this left no room for marriage. She wanted to teach physical education, so after graduation from Coe, she enrolled in the Boston Normal School of Gymnastics, later acquired by Wellesley College. Here she was introduced to several concepts that influenced her significantly, the fundamental one being the study of health and hygiene and their impact on physical fitness. At most schools, these were not part of secondary or undergraduate curricula. Following a required physical examination, Lee was informed she needed corrective exercises for spinal curvature and a slight difference in the length of her legs. Through this experience, correctives became a focus for her own teaching, especially in the areas of posture and special needs. As a result of studying dance with an instructor who required his students to choreograph and perform for his classes, Lee learned to appreciate dance as a physical education activity; this practice helped her appreciate its educational value and gave her the courage as a teacher to develop and present pageants.

Lee also developed definite ideas about the purpose of physical education, ones that put her at odds with the intense competitiveness now characteristic of American athletics. Adamantly opposed to intercollegiate competition and its emphasis on developing a few elite players, she felt strongly that sports were essential for improving individual physical fitness and should be engaged in by people of all abilities. In her opinion, intramural sports were fine as long as all students who desired could participate equally.

With a Wellesley diploma in hand, Lee accepted a teaching position at Coe College in 1910. Undaunted by the straitlaced views of the time concerning the physical exercise of the female body, she instituted health and hygiene courses as requirements for freshmen women, whom she insisted be classified for corrective work by having them take comprehensive physical examinations. At Coe she also started a tradition of pageants that incorporated dance in several forms—in spite of some public outcry that dance was immoral in any form.

In 1918, lured by a better salary, Lee accepted a position with the Oregon Agricultural College in Corvallis (now Oregon State University). During the flu epidemic of 1919, however, she became seriously ill, resigned, and moved to her parents' home in Iowa for a lengthy recovery. Ready to resume work in 1920, she spent four years as director of physical education for women at Beloit College in Beloit, Wisconsin, where she instituted new programs and reorganized the physical education department.

Then Lee received an offer from the University of Nebraska, and in 1924 Lincoln became her home. Again intent on reorganizing and innovating, Lee exhibited a work ethic and held to standards that became those of the department. Once again, controversy dogged her efforts. She turned the established three-day-a-week class schedule into a five- or six-day schedule, annoying some instructors who had liked their relatively work-free days. Professors and parents who expected special favors for certain students because of their athletic prowess or social standing were disappointed to find that Lee would have none of it. She expected students to earn their grades and fulfill work requirements.

Under her guidance, a program that had consisted mainly of gymnastics expanded to include a variety of activities including team and individual sports, corrective exercises, and a program for special needs. Eventually there were nine full-time instructors. Some of her critics considered Lee to be a hard taskmaster, but she always took a keen personal interest in her students, listening to, counseling, and guiding them in diverse areas that included health concerns, professional aspirations, and proper deportment for young ladies. She was an outspoken crusader against smoking, always arguing from a health standpoint, years before the general public was aware of its hazards.

During the 1920s, Lee's leadership and organizational skills were extended to include professional physical education affiliations. Serving at various times as president of local, regional, and national groups, she reached a pinnacle when, in 1931, she became the first woman president of the American Physical Education Association.

As her reputation grew, Lee was considered to be *the* authority to consult about organization and administration of physical education departments. This led to her first book, *The Conduct of Physical Education* (1937), which was adopted as a text in most colleges and universities. Her second book, *Fundamentals of Body Mechanics and Conditioning,* written with Miriam Wagner, was published in 1949.

Throughout her career, Lee's influence on regional and national physical education was underscored by her involvement as a committee member of numerous national government-sponsored physical fitness programs. From 1941 to 1943 she served as a regional director of physical fitness for a program established by President Franklin Roosevelt. In 1942 she was the first woman president of the American Academy of Physical Education.

Having retired from the University of Nebraska–Lincoln in the spring of 1952, Lee spent the summer as a visiting professor at the University of Southern California. Then, as a Fulbright-funded professor, she was physical education consultant for Iraq's Ministry of Education in Baghdad (1952–1953).

Throughout her life, Lee kept copious notes about her work and the historical aspects of the physical education movement in the United States. For years, she had been urging the American Alliance for Health, Physical Education and Recreation (AAHPER) to establish archives. Now the officers responded by offering her the position of volunteer archivist. She accepted with the stipulation that she be provided with expenses for necessary research and travel. Thus in July 1960 she became AAHPER's first archivist and remained in that position until December 1969.

Meanwhile, Lee maintained an active schedule of speaking and writing. An Amy Morris Homans Fellowship Award from Wellesley College resulted in two books written over a period of twenty years: *Memories of a Bloomer Girl, 1894–1924* (1977) and *Beyond Bloomers* (1978). Although autobiographical in nature, they are also histories of the physical education movement in the United States. Lee completed the third draft of another memoir, "From Bloomers to Bikinis," but it remains unpublished. During this time, Lee worked on several other books about physical education and, at age ninety-seven, published *A History of Physical Education and Sports in the U.S.A.* (1983).

It may appear that Lee devoted herself solely to her profession. This was only partly true. In her books, she states that she had no social life as a student, yet she describes friendships and extracurricular activities with both men and women. Lee remained close to her parents and three sisters, visiting them often and sometimes traveling with them. After her father died, her mother spent the rest of her life with Lee in Lincoln.

Because Lee steadfastly stood up for her beliefs, and those beliefs did not always fit the public norm, she was not always liked by her peers, but she was universally respected for her knowledge, tenacity, and ability. She received many honors including an LL.D. degree from Coe College (1939); the Gulick Award from AAHPER (1948); an honorary doctor of physical education degree from George Williams College, Chicago (1956); and an honorary doctor of humanities degree from Beloit College (1977). In 1975 the AAHPER established the Mabel Lee Award, to be given to women under age thirty-six who show un-

usual promise in the field of physical education. In May 1977 the University of Nebraska's Department of Physical Education's new building was named Mabel Lee Hall. In October 1997, twelve years after her death in Lincoln, she was inducted into the Coe College Sports Hall of Fame.

• Other writings by Lee include *A Brief History of Physical Education*, 4th ed. (with Emmett A. Rice and John L. Hutchinson, 1958); *The History of the Middle West Society of Physical Education, 1912–1960* (1963); *History of Central AHPER, 1933–1963* (1966); *75 Year History of the American Association for Health, Physical Education and Recreation* (with Bruce L. Bennett, 1960); *A Brief History of Physical Education*, 5th ed. (with Emmett A. Rice and John L. Hutchinson, 1969); *Seventy-five Years of Professional Preparation in Physical Education for Women at the University of Nebraska–Lincoln, 1898–1973: Parts I–II* (with Dudley Ashton and Madge Phillips, 1973). She was also a contributing editor to the *Journal of Health and Physical Education* and the *Research Quarterly* of the American Association for Health and Physical Education. A short essay about her can be found in Robert E. Knoll's *Prairie University* (1995). An obituary that provides insight into Lee's personality and background is in the *Journal of Physical Education, Recreation and Dance* 57 (Mar. 1986): 24–26.

JEAN SANDERS

LEIPER, Henry Smith (17 Sept. 1891–22 Jan. 1975), Protestant Christian and international churchman, was born in Belmar, New Jersey, the son of Joseph McCarrell Leiper and Fanny Heywood Smith Leiper. A descendent of Scottish Presbyterians, Joseph McCarrell Leiper worked for the Dodd, Mead publishing company prior to attending Union Theological Seminary in New York. Fanny Leiper was a music and art teacher and the daughter of a former managing editor of the *Chicago Tribune* who became a Massachusetts legislator. Henry Leiper's parents moved in 1889 to do mission work in Indian Territory (later part of Oklahoma), where Joseph Leiper was ordained as a minister. When Fanny Leiper died in 1895, Leiper and his two brothers were raised by several McCarrell aunts. Leiper moved frequently, and for several years lived with his maternal grandmother in Worcester, Massachusetts.

In 1905 Leiper attended the preparatory school at Maryville College in Knoxville, Tennessee, before spending three years at the Blair Hall academy in New Jersey. At Amherst College, where he earned a B.A. in 1913, he became involved in the Student Volunteer Movement (SVM), studied organ and piano, wrote for the student paper, and decided on a career as a missionary. His studies at Union Theological Seminary were interrupted by his work for the national SVM, but he returned to Union in 1914, served the Rutgers Presbyterian Church, and was ordained a Presbyterian minister in 1915, when he also married Eleanor Lansing Cory. Influenced by Harry Ward, Norman Thomas, and Harry Emerson Fosdick, Leiper earned an M.A. in philosophy and ethics from Columbia University in 1917.

While the world was still reeling from World War I and the Russian Revolution, Leiper began missionary work in North China in 1918. Accompanied by his wife and their two young children, he settled in Beijing and began the tasks of famine relief, refugee work, and community service. Leiper's work took him beyond China to other parts of Asia and the Russian Far East. Continuing his interest in the SVM, he frequently worked with Chinese students. During this time, he transferred from the Presbyterian Church to the more liberal Congregational. In 1921 Leiper was elected auditor by the North China Mission, chaired the Mission Property Committee, and served as a delegate to the Japan Mission annual meeting. In several trips to Japan he aroused suspicion by aligning himself with critics of Japanese imperialism in Asia. The Leipers returned to the United States in 1922 after Eleanor Leiper developed heart problems and a nervous condition.

Most of Leiper's professional career was spent working in international church organizations. An indefatigable worker, he served as a secretary (executive director) for dozens of organizations, including the Congregational Commission on Missions (1923–1930), the American Missionary Association (1924–1927), and the Federal Council of Churches (1930–1938). Based in Leonia, New Jersey, Leiper made frequent trips to Germany in the early 1930s and, as a result, became an outspoken critic of Nazism and an opponent of the America First movement. His speeches, written dispatches, and journal articles warned of rampant anti-Semitism and neo-pagan aggression against Christian churches and pastors. At home he joined with Rabbi Stephen S. Wise in rallying America against Hitler's atrocities. His vast network of contacts in the United States and abroad enabled him to pursue these aims with vigor—and sometimes at some risk. He was part of an unsuccessful effort to initiate a U.S. boycott of the 1936 Olympic games in Berlin. His books from the 1930s and 1940s advocate a strong worldwide Christianity as a bulwark against nationalism.

In 1935 Leiper suffered the loss of his wife, Eleanor, whose health had deteriorated over the years. That same year, however, he married a family friend, Elizabeth "Elsie" Glover Olyphant; there were no children from this second marriage, and she died in 1978.

Among Leiper's major accomplishments for Christian unity was his role in forming the World Council of Churches (WCC) at Utrecht in 1938 from its predecessor, the Federal Council of Churches. World War II interrupted the work of the WCC, but after the war ended Leiper again served the council as associate general secretary. When the Geneva-based WCC expanded its operations throughout the world after 1945, Leiper worked on refugee projects, distributed bibles, and remained outspokenly committed to a common humanity and Christian unity. He became an expert at fundraising and was largely responsible for funding and organizing the WCC Conference in Amsterdam in 1948. But long-standing tensions

within the WCC, partly involving its head, the Dutch churchman W. A. Visser't Hooft, led to Leiper's dismissal from Geneva and his return to the organization's New York office, where he remained until 1952.

Leiper went back to work for the Congregational Church for the next several years, serving his last stint as an executive secretary, this time of the Missions Council, a position he held until 1959. In retirement Leiper remained active. He took the post of director of religion programs at Chautauqua in southwestern New York (1959–1967) and then as adviser to the American Bible Society.

Leiper's family was small but tight-knit. His first wife, Eleanor, shared her husband's interest in missions (the couple met at an SVM summer Bible camp) and often worked on her own projects. They had two children, Juliet McCarell (known as Carell), born in 1916, and Henry Martyn (known as Hal), born in 1918. Hal died in tragic circumstances, a ferry boat accident, in 1960 while a missionary in Japan.

Besides his work, Leiper was a talented musician and was fascinated by mechanical objects, especially cars and ships. He played piano and organ for many years, occasionally professionally. He designed and oversaw construction of the family's coastal summer house at Beidaihe east of Beijing (later taken over by Mao Zedong as a retreat), and during several of his transoceanic crossings he inspected the engine rooms of the ships he was on. Leiper died in Hightown, New Jersey, at the age of eighty-three. Leiper's writings identified racism and nationalism as the major evils of the twentieth century, while his ecumenical work paved the way for subsequent interreligious cooperation in the fields of international relief and human rights.

• Primary source material is in the Henry Smith Leiper Collection in the Burke Library Archives at Union Theological Seminary. Notable among his published works are *Blind Spots: Experiments in the Self-cure of Race Prejudice* (1929; rev. ed., 1944); *The Ghost of Caesar Walks: The Conflict of Nationalism and World Christianity* (1935); *Christ's Way and the World's, in Church, State and Society* (1936); and, with H. G. G. Herklots, *Pilgrimage to Amsterdam* (1947). A biographical exploration is William J. Schmidt and Edward Ouellette, *What Kind of a Man? The Life of Henry Smith Leiper* (1986). An obituary is in the *New York Times*, 23 Jan. 1975.

RICHARD CROUTER

LEMON, Bob (22 Sept. 1920–11 Jan. 2000), major league pitcher and manager, was born Robert Granville Lemon in San Bernardino, California, the second of two children of Earl Lemon, a gasoline station owner and former minor league ballplayer, and Ruth West Lemon. He grew up in Long Beach and signed a contract with the Cleveland Indians at age seventeen. He began as a third baseman and also played at shortstop and outfield, batting a solid .312 at Oswego (N.Y.) in his 1938 debut season. Moving up to New Orleans in the tough Southern Association the next year, he hit .309. He spent 1940 and 1941 at Wilkes-

Barre (Pa.) in the Eastern League, struggling at .256 in 1940 but bouncing back to .301 the next season and getting a "cup of coffee" with Cleveland at the end of the season. In 1942 he played with Baltimore in the International League, and despite a modest .268 average he hit 21 homers and seemed ready for a full trial with the Indians. Wartime service in the navy intervened, however, and pushed his big chance back three seasons. Playing service ball in Hawaii proved to be the break that made his career. He volunteered to pitch when his team ran low on hurlers, and his pitching impressed big-league catchers Birdie Tebbetts and Bill Dickey. While in the navy, on 14 January 1944, he married Jane McGee, with whom he was to have three sons (Jeff, Jim, and Jerry); they remained married until his death.

In 1946 Lemon got his chance with Cleveland, but manager Lou Boudreau soon benched him, convinced that he was not a good enough hitter. Tebbetts, catching for Detroit, suggested to Boudreau that he try Lemon as a pitcher, and Dickey, back with the Yankees, reinforced the idea. With help from coach Bill McKechnie and veteran pitching ace Mel Harder, Lemon made a relatively smooth transition to the mound, though he resisted the idea, still convinced that he could hit. He turned in a 4–5 won-lost record and 2.49 earned run average in 1946 and, after starting slowly in 1947, hit his stride in July, winning four in a row and finishing 11–5.

The 1948 season saw the six-foot, 180-pound Lemon blossom. He led the American League in innings pitched, threw a no-hitter against the Tigers, won 20 games (with 14 losses), and helped lead Cleveland to its first pennant since 1920. He capped his first of seven straight all-star seasons by winning two games in the World Series defeat of the Boston Braves. Lemon had established himself as one of the premier right-handed pitchers in baseball. Over the next five years, he won 22, 23, 17, 22, and 21 games, finished the majority of games he started, and led the league three times in innings pitched and once in strikeouts. He was not primarily a strikeout pitcher, though; for his career, he averaged about four strikeouts and four walks per game, with a curveball and slider his most effective pitches. His game was well rounded, too. Once he started pitching, his hitting improved to the point that he often pinch-hit. A left-handed hitter, he compiled a .232 lifetime batting average, and his 37 career homers rank second only to Wes Ferrell among major league pitchers. Beyond that, he was arguably the best fielding pitcher of his era.

The Indians finally broke through a Yankee five-pennant streak in 1954 when they won 111 games, an American League record for a 154-game season. Lemon led what many consider the best five-man starting corps in history: his 23–7 was complemented by Early Wynn (23–11), Mike Garcia (19–8), Art Houtteman (15–7), and Bob Feller (13–3). The dream season crashed in the World Series, though, when the underdog New York Giants swept the In-

dians, beating Lemon twice. Two more solid seasons ensued (18–10, 20–14) before a leg injury slowed him. He retired in 1958, having spent his entire 15 years with Cleveland. His career marks, which won him election to the Baseball Hall of Fame in 1976, were a 207–128 won-lost record with a 3.23 ERA.

After his playing career Lemon coached, managed in the minors, and then managed three major league teams with some distinction. From 1970 to 1972 he led the expansion Kansas City Royals, winning 85 games in 1971. In 1977 he took over a Chicago White Sox team that had won only 64 games the year before and guided the "South Side Hitmen," a collection of characters, to 90 wins and a second-place finish with his low-key approach to managing. Nevertheless, owner Bill Veeck fired him the next June, which freed him to be hired by Cleveland native George Steinbrenner, an old fan, to take over the New York Yankees in July. He managed the Yanks to one of baseball's famous comebacks: they trailed the Boston Red Sox by ten games when he took over, wound up in a tie, and beat the Sox in a playoff for the American League pennant on Bucky Dent's celebrated home run. To top off the 1978 season, the Yankees beat the Los Angeles Dodgers, four games to two, in the World Series. Steinbrenner fired him midway in the 1979 season, then brought him back again, "from the bullpen," as Lemon put it, to manage the last month in 1981 and lead the Yankees back into the World Series, which they lost to the Dodgers by the same 4–2 margin. Promised a full season of his own in 1982, Lemon instead was dismissed after a 6–8 start. Steinbrenner gave him a lifetime contract as a scout and adviser, but Lemon's days in the spotlight were over. He had compiled a 430–403 record as a manager, a .516 percentage, and excelled in his first year managing a team in his refreshingly easygoing manner.

A fine raconteur, Lemon was one of the game's most likable players. He had a hard time remembering names, so he called everyone "Meat." He famously said at his Hall of Fame induction that he never took the game home with him—he always left it in a bar along the way. Much of Lemon's *joie de vivre* faded when his youngest son, age 26, was killed in an auto accident shortly after the 1978 World Series victory. Lemon died in Long Beach, where he had grown up, succumbing to a stroke after several years of failing health.

• Information on Bob Lemon can be found in *Baseball Stars of 1954*, compiled by Bruce Jacobs, and *The Bill James Guide to Baseball Managers* (1997). Obituaries appear in the *Washington Post*, *New York Daily News*, *Chicago Sun-Times*, and *Cleveland Plain Dealer*, all 13 Jan. 2000.

JOHN R. M. WILSON

LEONARD, Buck (8 Sept. 1907–27 Nov. 1997), baseball player, was born Walter Fenner Leonard in Rocky Mount, North Carolina, the son of John Leonard, a railroad fireman, and Emma Sesson Leonard. Although his parents called him "Buddy," his younger brother mispronounced the name as "Buck," and that became his lifelong nickname. As a young child he learned about baseball while watching white minor league games through the gaps in a stadium fence. When a black ballpark was built in Rocky Mount around 1915, he became the batboy for a semipro team. Following his father's death during the influenza epidemic in 1919, he quit school to help his family financially. As a teenager he shined shoes, and from 1923 to 1933 he worked for the Atlantic Coastline Railroad shop, installing brake cylinders on boxcars. While working full time for the railroad, he played semipro baseball in the evenings. He quickly established himself as a hometown star, and at the age of seventeen he was named team manager. He later recalled that he began playing first base in 1931: "One reason why I did that was . . . I would be close to the umpire for some arguing and I wouldn't have to come all the way in from center field. That's a heck of a reason, but that's how I got started playing first base" (Leonard, p. 13).

In 1933, with the onset of the Great Depression, Leonard was fired from his job at the railroad shop. There being no other employment available, he decided to go on the road playing semipro baseball. He spent three months with the Portsmouth Firefighters and then jumped to the Baltimore Stars, whose manager promised him a percentage of the gate receipts for every game. But the team experienced serious financial difficulties and the players often went without food; when the team's two automobiles were impounded and auctioned off in New York City for failure to pay a hotel bill, he and his teammates were left stranded and almost penniless, which led him to join the Brooklyn Royal Giants. While in New York, he frequented a Harlem bar where Smokey Joe Williams, a former star pitcher in the Negro leagues, worked as a bartender. Williams saw Leonard play and recommended him to the Homestead Grays in the Negro National League in 1934.

With the Grays, Leonard played a grueling schedule of around 210 games per season, taking the field against both amateur and Negro league teams. He later recalled a typical itinerary: "A lot of times we would play three games in one day, and each one in a different town. We would play a ten-o'clock game in the morning, a three-o'clock game, and a twilight game at six-thirty. . . . [After a game] we changed sweatshirts and got in the bus, and the business manager would have a sandwich for everybody. . . . Now, we didn't change clothes, we just changed sweatshirts. We'd keep the uniform on and go out there and start the [next] game. The crowd was already there waiting for us when we got there" (Leonard, pp. 127–28). He estimated that in 1941 the Grays logged between 30,000 and 40,000 miles of road travel. During the winter, he usually played an additional ninety games with barnstorming teams in Cuba or Venezuela. In spite of the wearying effects of a year-round baseball season, Leonard gained a reputation for being one of the hardest-playing and most consistent Negro leagu-ers. He was named the Grays' captain during his rookie season, a position that he retained until the team folded in 1950.

A muscular left-hander with an exceptionally quick bat, Leonard often hit third in the lineup, with the slugging catcher Josh Gibson hitting fourth; they were known, respectively, as "the black Lou Gehrig" and "the black Babe Ruth." "Sometimes people asked us what the difference was between them and us," he later recalled. "Well, the only thing that we said was, they were white and we were black. . . . They were white and could play in the major leagues, and we had to play black baseball. That was the only difference" (Leonard, p. 107). He and Gibson helped the Grays to become the most dominant club in the Negro National League, winning nine straight championships between 1937 and 1945. Although statistics for the Negro leagues are notoriously incomplete, newspaper reports suggest that Leonard hit .500 during the first half of the 1937 season and .489 for the first half of 1938. His full-season batting average in 1939 was .363, and in 1940 he hit .372. Between 1936 and 1943 he averaged 34 home runs per season. In 1948, when he was forty-one years old, he led the Negro leagues with a .395 batting average. During his career he was selected eleven times to play in the annual East-West All-Star game, a major cultural event for black Americans that often drew 50,000 fans; no other Negro leaguer was chosen as frequently.

Although reporters from the Communist Party–USA newspaper *The Daily Worker* urged Leonard to agitate for the integration of major league baseball, he steadfastly refused. He reasoned that if white owners and white players were forced to accept blacks prematurely, conditions for blacks in the majors would be intolerable. In the handful of exhibition games that he played against major league barnstorming teams, which were led by stars such as Dizzy Dean and Lefty Grove, he batted .382. In 1936 he played on an all-black team in the "Little World Series," a tournament that featured several white players with major league experience; after winning seven straight games and the championship, the Negro leaguers were barred from future tournament play, and they were never awarded the $5,092 first prize. Around 1938 he and Gibson were called into the office of Washington Senators owner Clark Griffith, who told them that he was flirting with the idea of signing them to play for his last-place team; although they expressed their interest in the plan, they never heard back from him. In 1952, five years after Jackie Robinson broke the color barrier, St. Louis Browns owner Bill Veeck offered Leonard a major league contract, but he turned it down. "I knew I was over the hill," he later recalled. "I didn't try to fool myself" (Leonard, p. 222). The following season, at the age of forty-six, he played a few games of integrated baseball in the Class B minor league Piedmont League and batted .333. Two years later he retired after slugging 13 home runs in 62 games in the Central Mexican League.

Leonard was married twice: to Sarah Wroten, a schoolteacher, from 1937 until her death in 1966, and to Eugenia (maiden name unknown) in 1986. He had no children. After retiring from baseball, he delivered cigars for a tobacco company in Rocky Mount and then worked for twelve years as a truant officer. In 1966 he was licensed to sell real estate, and in 1970 he opened the Buck Leonard Realty Agency. A devout Christian, he was a member of the St. James Baptist Church in Rocky Mount for approximately seventy years. In 1972 he and Josh Gibson were inducted into the National Baseball Hall of Fame; along with Satchel Paige, they were the first Negro league players so honored. He proudly called his induction the greatest moment in his life. During his later years, he was actively involved in organizing reunions of Negro league players; although he suffered a stroke in 1986, he continued to attend Hall of Fame ceremonies in Cooperstown in his wheelchair. He died in Rocky Mount.

• A clipping file on Leonard is at the National Baseball Library, Cooperstown, N.Y. His autobiography, *Buck Leonard: The Black Lou Gehrig* (1995), as told to James A. Riley, provides a colorful, fascinating account of his life in the Negro leagues. For discussions of his career within the context of Negro league history, see Robert Peterson, *Only the Ball Was White* (1970), and Donn Rogosin's excellent *Invisible Men: Life in Baseball's Negro Leagues* (1983). Jim Reisler, *Black Writers/ Black Baseball: An Anthology of Articles from Black Sportswriters Who Covered the Negro Leagues* (1994), includes a few articles that portray Leonard at the height of his career. Jules Tygiel, *Baseball's Great Experiment: Jackie Robinson and His Legacy* (1983; rev. ed., 1997), discusses black stars such as Leonard who were "left behind" when major league baseball integrated during the late 1940s. For brief, valuable overviews of his life, see James A. Riley, *The Biographical Encyclopedia of the Negro Baseball Leagues* (1994), and Lowell Reidenbaugh, *Cooperstown: Where Baseball's Legends Live Forever* (1983).

THOMAS W. COLLINS, JR.

LEVERTOV, Denise (24 Oct. 1923–20 Dec. 1997), poet, was born in Ilford, Essex, England, to Paul Levertoff and Beatrice Spooner-Jones Levertoff; as an adult she reverted to the traditional spelling of her surname. Her father was a Russian Jew who had converted to Christianity in the late nineteenth century, ultimately becoming an Anglican priest. He traced his ancestry back to the founder of a mystical Hasidic sect that had flourished in Russia in the eighteenth century. Denise Levertov's mother was descended from a well-known Welsh mystic named Angel Jones. Levertov grew up feeling what she later described as "a sense of wonder" at the marvel of creation from the teachings of both of her parents, and although she was not conventionally religious as an adult, her upbringing was undoubtedly the source of a mystical strain underlying much of her poetry.

Levertov, along with her older sister, Olga, was educated at home and never attended school. For "instruction" her mother read aloud to the family daily from works by Dickens, Tolstoy, Conrad, and other great writers. Denise and her sister were encouraged to read widely themselves in the large family library, which included not only classical standards and scholarly books on a number of subjects but also many volumes of poetry. Their father was also a biblical scholar who was fluent in a number of languages, translated several Hebrew classics into English, and wrote a life of St. Paul. As a child Denise studied painting and ballet, and she began to write poetry. At the age of twelve she sent some of her poems to T. S. Eliot, who responded with an encouraging letter of advice, and by her early teens she had decided to become a poet.

Following the outbreak of World War II in 1939, Levertov trained as a nurse at St. Luke's Hospital in London and remained there for the duration of the conflict. Her wartime experiences, including the eight months in 1940–1941 when the city was under continual aerial bombardment from the Nazis, undoubtedly contributed to the strong antiwar stance that she was to take two decades later. Throughout the war years she wrote verse, some of which was published in local journals, and her first book of poetry, *The Double Image*, appeared in 1946. After the war ended in 1945, Levertov worked in an antiques store and a bookstore, then went to Europe, supporting herself by working at a hospital in Paris and teaching English in the Netherlands and in Geneva, Switzerland. There she met a young American writer, Mitchell Goodman, and the two were married in December 1947. They lived in Paris and Florence for several months then moved to New York in 1948; their son was born the following year, and she was naturalized in 1955.

Levertov had continued to write poetry during the postwar years, and her career was given an unexpected boost after some of her earlier verses were read by the American poet Kenneth Rexroth. Although he felt that both their neoromantic sentiments and their carefully rhymed and formally metered structure were old-fashioned, he believed that Levertov was a promising new writer, and he included her work in his anthology *New British Poets* (1949). Even more significant was her introduction to the poet Robert Creeley, a friend of her husband's who went on to teach at the celebrated Black Mountain College, an experimental school in Asheville, North Carolina. Creeley, along with the so-called Black Mountain Poets—including Charles Olson, Robert Duncan, and Edward Dorn—with whom he became allied, called for a new "projective," open verse that would supplant traditional "closed" poetry. They believed that most poetry from the recent past was centered in the poet's ego and expressed personal sentiments in arbitrarily constructed lines of constricted language: in a word, it sounded "affected" to contemporary ears. Projective verse, on the other hand, focused on nature and voiced the normal rhythms of human speech and breath. Among modern poets, the projectivists most admired William Carlos Williams, in whose verse could be heard the voices of ordinary people.

Levertov was impressed by Creeley's notions of poetry, and the verse that she now wrote reflected his influence, as well as that of Williams and another American poet, Wallace Stevens. Earlier she had claimed to be most inspired by the work of Gerard Manley Hopkins, Rainier Maria Rilke, and H.D. (Hilda Doolittle); now Williams and Stevens, and their distinctly American idiom, joined her pantheon. When Creeley moved on to become a member of the faculty at Black Mountain, Levertov began contributing poems to his new journal, the *Black Mountain Review*. Her second collection of verse, *Here and Now* (1957), represented a major departure from the style of her first.

Although *Here and Now* was published by the Beat poet Lawrence Ferlinghetti as part of his Pocket Poets series, Levertov claimed then and afterward that while admiring some of the work of Allen Ginsberg, Gregory Corso, and several other Beats, she never considered herself one of their number. She strove, she said, for poems with an "inner harmony in utter contrast to the chaos in which [many of the works of the Beats] exist." Poetry, she later noted, had a social function only to the extent that it should "awaken sleepers" rather than giving them violent shocks. Among the many admirers of her second book was Kenneth Rexroth, who later noted how pleased he was to see her move away from the sentimental "lassitude" of her earlier work.

Levertov published several more volumes in succession during the 1950s: *Overland to the Islands* (1958); *Five Poems* (1958); and *With Eyes at the Back of Our Heads* (1959). In these, as well as in *Here and Now*, she employed free verse to write about ordinary events in life and nature and the pleasure taken in their observation, leaving behind her early mannered style and announcing the birth of her true voice as a poet. Her next volumes, *Jacob's Ladder* (1961) and *O Taste and See* (1964), continued in this vein, conveying a delight in natural images and revealing the mystical strain that would become evident in most of her subsequent verse.

Levertov wrote several essays about her mature art, among them "Statement on Poetics" (1959), in which she made the paradoxical observation that while content determined form, "content is discovered only *in* form." Poets were seers, she wrote, conscious of the layered meaning of that word, and a poet had a "responsibility to communicate what he sees" so that "they who cannot see *may* see." Her 1965 essay, "Some Notes on Organic Form," which first appeared in *Poetry* magazine and has been widely anthologized, hazarded an explanation of how a poem came to be written: the poet, she said, had to have an experience so intense that it had to be "brought to speech."

By the early 1960s other critics besides Rexroth were applauding Levertov's poetry, though there were some dissenters who felt that she was following too consciously in the vein of the Black Mountain poets and lacked originality. Her critical and popular audience became increasingly polarized by the end of the decade as Levertov became an outspoken opponent of the Vietnam War. First drawn into opposition when the war escalated in 1965, she led the formation that year of the "Writers' and Artists' Protest against the War in Vietnam." For nearly a decade, until the last American forces were withdrawn in 1973, she was a leader of the antiwar movement, giving speeches and writing articles, some of which were included in her essay collection *The Poet in the World* (1973). A volume of her poetry, *The Sorrow Dance* (1967), decried the conflict while also mourning the death of her sister. In addition she visited Hanoi with an American antiwar delegation in 1972, a year that also saw the breakup of her marriage.

Levertov's collection *The Freeing of the Dust* (1975) included not only antiwar poems but also confessional verse in which she wrote about her present life and loneliness and narrated a spiritual journey that reflected the strong influence of Jungian psychology on her thinking. Levertov expanded on this theme in poems that she wrote during the final two decades of her life, by which time she had secured her status as an important American poet of the twentieth century. She published nearly a dozen volumes of verse during this period, including *Candles in Babylon* (1982) and the critically acclaimed *Breathing the Water* (1987), as well as two collections of prose: *Light Up the Cave* (1981) and *New & Selected Essays* (1992). Levertov's last book of poetry was *Sands of the Well*, published in 1996. In the course of her long career she also published translations of Bengali, Bulgarian, and French prose and verse and served as poetry editor of two prominent leftist periodicals, the *Nation* (1961–1963) and *Mother Jones* (1975–1978).

Levertov died in Seattle, Washington, of complications from lymphoma.

• For biographical information, see Linda W. Wagner, *Denise Levertov* (1967); "Denise Levertov," in Jean Gould, *Modern American Women Poets* (1985); and Carolyn Matalene, "Denise Levertov," in *Dictionary of Literary Biography*, vol. 5: *American Poets since World War II* (1980). For critical analyses of her work, see especially William Slaughter, *The Imagination's Tongue: Denise Levertov's Poetics* (1981); Harry Marten, *Understanding Denise Levertov* (1988); Linda W. Wagner-Martin, ed., *Critical Essays on Denise Levertov* (1990); Audrey T. Rodgers, *Denise Levertov: The Poetry of Engagement* (1993); and Albert Gelpi, ed., *Denise Levertov: Selected Criticism* (1993). An obituary appears in the *New York Times*, 23 Dec. 1997.

ANN T. KEENE

LEWIS, Janet (17 Aug. 1899–1 Dec. 1998), poet and novelist, was born in Chicago, Illinois, the daughter of Edwin Herbert Lewis, a novelist, poet, and teacher, and Elizabeth Taylor Lewis, who also taught college-level English. Lewis credited her father with being the first to teach her the fundamentals of style in writing poetry. The family spent most summers on Neebish Island in northern Michigan, where Lewis learned the history and legends of the Indians of the area. Her interest in Native Americans and her friendship with Molly Johnston, whose grandmother Neengay was the daughter of an Ojibway chief, is reflected in Lewis's early poetry and in her first novel, *The Invasion: A Narrative of Events concerning the Johnston Family of St. Mary's* (1932).

Lewis completed an associate of arts degree at the Lewis Institute (Chicago) in 1918 and a bachelor's degree with a major in French at the University of Chicago in 1920. During these years she began publishing poetry; "The Freighters," for example, won her entrance into the Poetry Club at the University of Chicago in 1918. In 1922 she published her first book of poems, *The Indians in the Woods*. The title poem establishes the form and tone for the entire collection. The poem contains only thirty-nine words, divided into ten short lines and three stanzas, beginning, "Ah, the woods, the woods / Where small things / Are distinct and visible." Perception, especially of the small, distinct, and visible, is a key preoccupation in all of Lewis's works. Like other imagist poets of the era, Lewis strove to convey meaning through the striking visual image. As Suzanne J. Doyle suggests, the early Indian poems intend "to capture the isolated perception with such precision, clarity, and harmony that it would suggest a considerable depth of conceptual content" (*Southern Review*, p. 531). *Poems Old and New, 1918–1978*, published in 1981, shows that during her long writing career Lewis developed lengthier and more overtly conversational or philosophical poems. Yet she never abandoned the imagist technique, exercising a vivid perception of the concrete elements of the real world in order to create in a few words an "image" that resonates visually in the reader's imagination, a technique used to great effect in all her writing.

Lewis's work generally accords with the literary tenets of the Gyroscope group, writers and scholars associated with the University of Chicago who favored classicism over contemporary modernism and romanticism. Lewis's poetry is spare and lyrical, her fiction often austere, with tragic plot arising out of a character's sense of moral rectitude. The members of the Poetry Club and the Gyroscope group supported Lewis's writing style. Many of them became her lifelong friends and were well-known writers themselves, including her husband, Yvor Winters, a noted literary critic who emphasized the importance of morality in art.

Although they had corresponded through letters, Lewis did not actually meet Yvor Winters until she had traveled and worked in France for several months and taught briefly at the Lewis Institute. She then discovered she had tuberculosis, and in 1922 she went to the Sunmount Sanitorium in Santa Fe, New Mexico, where Winters had gone earlier and was still recovering. Lewis was confined to bed rest for two years, and it was five more years before she was cured. Although she and Winters married on 22 June 1926, she was too ill to accompany him on his first teaching assignment. By the next year she could join him in Palo Alto, California, where he began his doctoral studies at Stanford University. In 1934 they bought a small house in Los Altos, where they wrote and gardened and raised Airedale show dogs. Winters taught at Stanford until his death in 1968. The couple had two children, Joanna Winters Thompson and Daniel Winters.

Lewis, who gave readings, conducted workshops, and was occasionally a visiting lecturer in creative writing, always thought of herself as a poet. Her collections include *The Wheel in Midsummer* (1927), *The Earth-Bound* (1946), *The Ancient Ones* (1979), and *The Dear Past* (1994). But she is most famous for her fiction, especially the brilliant short novel *The Wife of Martin Guerre* (1941).

The plot is taken from an actual case in sixteenth-century France. Martin Guerre and Bertrande de Rols are married at age eleven. Some years later Martin leaves and is not heard of again for eight years, when he returns after his father's death. Bertrande welcomes him back. Their estate flourishes under Martin's leadership, and their young son is joined by a new baby. But Bertrande increasingly believes Martin to be an impostor, since her remembered husband was never so kind and decent. Although she knows it will ruin all their lives if she acts on her suspicions, she cannot bear to continue what she now considers an adulterous relationship. A trial follows, with surprise witnesses and a tragic conclusion. Lewis used the same source, *Famous Cases of Circumstantial Evidence with an Introduction of the Theory of Presumptive Proof by S. M. Phillips* (editor unknown) (1873), for two other novels, *The Trial of Sören Qvist* (1947) and *The Ghost of Monsieur Scarron* (1959). She added rich historical details but let the plots stand without authorial comment. All deal with circumstantial evidence and moral choices.

Lewis wrote the libretto for *The Wife of Martin Guerre: An Opera*, with music by William Bergsma, which was first performed at the Juilliard School of Music in 1956, published in 1958, and reprinted as *The Wife: A Libretto for an Opera in Three Acts* in 1988. The French film *Le Retour de Martin Guerre* (1982), and a later American adaptation, *Sommersby* (1993), set in the post–Civil War South, owe to Lewis at least credit for having popularized the Martin Guerre story in the twentieth century, as do musical versions of the legend staged in America and Britain in the 1990s. Lewis wrote five other librettos for opera, one of which was *The Legend: The Story of Neengay, an Ojibway War Chief's Daughter, and the Irishman John Johnston: An Opera Oratorio* (1987) with music by Bain Murray, which was based on her first novel, *The Invasion*.

Lewis published to critical acclaim in every decade of the twentieth century after the first. She died at age ninety-nine in the home in Los Altos where she had lived for sixty-four years.

• Lewis's papers are in the Yvor Winters/Janet Lewis Collection at the Stanford University Library in Palo Alto, Calif. *The Selected Poems of Janet Lewis*, ed. R. L. Barth (2000), is the most readily available edition of her important poetry. A valuable interview appears in Richard Stern, "Janet Lewis,"

Virginia Quarterly Review (Summer 1993): 532–43. Vol. 41 of *Contemporary Literary Criticism* (1987) contains excerpts from numerous articles and reviews of her work, including Suzanne J. Doyle, "Janet Lewis's *The Ancient Ones*" from the *Southern Review* 16 (Spring 1980): 531–47. See also Charles L. Crow, *Janet Lewis* (1980); Brigitte Hoy Carnochan, *Landscape, Memory, and the Poetry of Janet Lewis* (1995); and Marilyn Yalom, ed., *Women Writers of the West Coast: Speaking of Their Lives and Careers* (1983). An obituary is in the *New York Times*, 5 December 1998.

LOIS A. MARCHINO

LEWIS, Shari (17 Jan. 1934–2 Aug. 1998), entertainer, was born Shari Hurwitz in New York City, the daughter of Abraham Hurwitz, college professor, and Ann Ritz Hurwitz, a public school music supervisor. She grew up in a household that encouraged artistic expression; after beginning piano lessons at the age of two, she also studied singing, acting, and dancing. Her father was also a professional magician, and Hurwitz accompanied him on USO tours during World War II. While convalescing from an injury, she also learned ventriloquism, which would later serve her well. After graduating from New York's Music and Art High School in 1950, she is said to have briefly attended nearby Columbia University, where she studied drama, although this cannot be confirmed. Her professional "break" came in 1951, when she appeared on the "Arthur Godfrey's Talent Scouts" television program and won a prize for a puppetry act.

Hurwitz enjoyed early success doing ventriloquist and vocal mimicry work on commercials, and she was soon featured on such early television programs as "Tinker's Toy Show," "Wonderama," and "Look To Win." She earned a show of her own, called "Facts 'n' Fun," on New York's WRCA-TV (now WNBC-TV) in 1953. This show (as well as others that followed such as "Kartoon Club" and "Shari and Her Friends") gave Hurwitz the chance to compose her own music, lyrics, and dialogue. The shows were interactive: live audiences of children could participate as they were entertained by a group of puppets with names like Randy Rocket, Pip Squeak, and Taffy Tink.

By the late 1950s Hurwitz was the host of two morning television programs in New York: "Hi, Mom," which ran on weekdays, and "Shariland," which appeared on Saturday mornings. While "Hi, Mom" was an hour-long mixture of children's entertainment and mothering advice, "Shariland" was largely a puppet show and featured some of her most famous characters, including Charlie Horse (a horse) and Wing Ding (a bird). Perhaps her most famous character was Lamb Chop, who first appeared on an episode of "Captain Kangaroo." The on-air relationship between Lewis and Lamb Chop was marked by intelligence and dry humor, and usually featured Lewis responding to Lamb Chop's antics, questions and interruptions in a gentle yet firm manner that suggested the two were equals instead of puppet and puppet master. After an early childless marriage to Stan Lewis failed, Shari Lewis married Jeremy Tarcher, a television producer, in 1958. The couple had one daughter.

Although Lewis garnered praise for her early work, including two Emmys—out of the twelve that she would win in her lifetime—for "Hi, Mom" and "Shariland," her greatest impact came as the host of NBC's "The Shari Lewis Show." A smash in the ratings, the show ran from 1957 until 1963 and was so successful that it hastened the demise of another legendary children's program, "The Howdy Doody Show." It received critical acclaim as well, earning Lewis the Peabody Award and the Radio-Television Mirror Award (both in 1960) and the Monte Carlo International Television Award in 1961. Although the program featured the same intelligence, wit, and nimble drawing-in of children that had made her previous efforts so successful, Lewis eventually fell victim to the trend in the mid-1960s toward animation, and her show was replaced by "The Chipmunks." Undaunted, Lewis—who had a background in summer stock as well as Broadway—recreated herself and spent the middle portion of the 1960s in touring productions of musicals such as *Bye, Bye Birdie, Funny Girl,* and *Damn Yankees.* She also formed a partnership with singer Donald O'Conner in a popular Las Vegas nightclub act that featured a number of puppets, including Lamb Chop.

In 1968 Lewis returned to television in Great Britain, where her "Shari at Six" became a Sunday night staple on the BBC until 1976. She also performed in a number of television specials that appeared in Australia and Canada and made her debut as a symphonic conductor (complete with her companion puppets) with the Dallas Symphony Orchestra in 1977. Eventually, Lewis—along with her puppets—served as guest conductor of more than 100 orchestras in the United States, Canada, and Japan. After maintaining a television presence through guest appearances on various shows such as "Hollywood Squares," Lewis made a triumphant comeback in the 1990s with her own PBS series. Although some of her older fans had wondered how Lewis might fare in the high-tech video age, her "Lamb Chop's Play-Along" was a huge success and earned Lewis another five Emmys in addition to the New York International Film Festival's Gold Award.

Never content to rest on past accomplishments, Lewis also produced several notable specials for PBS, including "Lamb Chop's Special Hanukkah" in 1995. She mined still another creative outlet through her authorship of sixty children's books, including titles such as *One-Minute Favorite Fairy Tales* (1981), *One-Minute Birthday Stories* (1995), and *Things Kids Collect* (1981). Much as she had mastered the new medium of television early in her career, by the mid-1990s Lewis had even produced an award-winning CD-Rom, *Lamb Chop Loves Music,* as well as a highly regarded series of home videos. Long active in the Girl Scouts organization, Lewis also campaigned tirelessly for high standards in children's programming and even testified (along with Lamb Chop) before the U.S. House Telecommunications Subcommittee in 1993 on behalf of the Children's Television Act of 1993.

Lewis collaborated with her husband for her last project, "The Charlie Horse Music Pizza," which made its debut on PBS in January of 1998. She was diagnosed with uterine cancer in June of that year and was forced to suspend the first year's production of the show while she underwent chemotherapy. Although initially thought to be responding to treatments, she died in Los Angeles that August from complications that resulted in pneumonia.

Despite occasional setbacks, Shari Lewis created a stellar career in show business that spanned fifty years. Although as a puppeteer she was decidedly "low-tech," the values that she brought to her shows were timeless. That enabled her to make a series of transitions in the evolving medium of television from its earliest days to the increasingly sophisticated use of video in the 1990s.

• Secondary sources on Lewis's life and career are limited. For her early career, see the *New York Herald Tribune*, 21 Nov. 1954, and the *New York World-Telegram*, 3 Dec. 1955. Articles about her later career can be found in *Newsweek*, 25 Apr. 1983; *People*, 23 May 1983; the *Wall Street Journal*, 18 Dec. 1991; and *Entertainment Weekly*, 27 Mar. 1992. Obituaries appeared in most leading papers, including the *New York Times*, the *Washington Post*, and the *Los Angeles Times*, all on 4 Aug. 1998.

EDWARD L. LACH, JR.

LICHTENSTEIN, Roy (27 Oct. 1923–29 Sept. 1997), artist, was born on the Upper West Side of New York City to Milton Lichtenstein and Beatrice Werner Lichtenstein. His father was a successful realtor, and the family, which included a daughter, enjoyed a comfortable lifestyle. During his years in local schools young Roy was especially interested in science, an interest that persisted throughout his life, but he also showed a marked aptitude for drawing, and after completing his secondary education at the Franklin School in 1940 he enrolled at Ohio State University to study fine arts. In February 1943, during World War II, he was drafted by the U.S. Army and served in Europe for three years with the 69th Infantry Division. He then returned to Ohio State to complete his education, earning a B.F.A. in 1946 and an M.F.A. three years later, specializing in both painting and sculpture.

During his years of graduate study Lichtenstein had been an instructor in the fine arts department at Ohio State, and he stayed on for several years after receiving his M.F.A. Failing to receive a faculty promotion, he left the university in 1951, the same year that he had his first solo art show in New York, and moved to Cleveland, where he married Isabel Wilson, the co-director of an art gallery there. The couple had two sons. In Cleveland Lichtenstein supported his family by creating window displays for a local department store as well as sheet-metal designs for Republic Steel,

painting as well as sculpting on evenings and weekends. While living there he made frequent trips to New York City to stay in touch with the contemporary art scene, then dominated by the so-called New York School of abstract expressionist painters, including Willem de Kooning, Jackson Pollock, and Franz Kline. He visited art shows, museums, and galleries, and frequented the hangouts of prominent painters, though he later said that he felt too shy to introduce himself.

From the 1940s onward Lichtenstein had experimented with various art styles and movements of the twentieth century, painting subjects that ranged from medieval artifacts to anthropomorphized plants to themes from American history, and by the late 1950s he was loosely categorized as an abstract expressionist. Consistently present in all his work, however, was the expression of a sly humor, often verging on parody. A few years after moving east with his family in 1957, first to join the faculty of the State University of New York at Oswego and later to teach at Rutgers University in New Jersey, Lichtenstein's style took a major turn. Drawing upon a long-standing interest in comic-strip art, he began painting large canvases depicting characters in the style of comics, complete with dialogue. His earliest ventures in this medium were produced to amuse his two young sons, most memorably a humorous large canvas, painted in 1960–1961 and called *Look, Mickey*, which featured Disney-like representations of Mickey Mouse and Donald Duck. He went on to create other large canvases in this style, painting images in bold, flat colors, heavily outlined in black, and stippled to replicate the Ben Day dots produced by mechanical printing to create the illusion of newspaper cartoon blow-ups. Many of them featured men and women in serious, even dramatic situations and bore such titles as *Drowning Girl, Frightened Girl*, and *In the Car*.

Until now Lichtenstein's work had attracted only modest attention in the art world, but when he began exhibiting his comics canvases at a New York gallery in 1962, he became an overnight sensation and introduced another dimension to the new pop art movement. Pop art—purportedly "serious" works that depicted subjects from popular culture in a style borrowed from commercial illustration—had emerged as something of a tongue-in-cheek rebellion against the high seriousness of abstract expressionism. As Lichtenstein himself later noted in a famous *ARTnews* interview with G. R. Swenson in 1963, American art had reached the point where "everybody was hanging everything." It was almost acceptable to hang a dripping paint rag" and call it art. "The one thing everybody hated was commercial art," which embodied "the most brazen and threatening characteristics of our culture." Jasper Johns, with his painted American flags and Ballantine Ale can sculptures, had pioneered the movement in the 1950s; and by the early 1960s other artists had come aboard, among them Claes Oldenburg, Robert Indiana, Andy Warhol, and George Segal. By this time Lichtenstein had overcome his shyness and had gotten to know some of them; Oldenburg, in particular, became a close friend.

The art establishment had its reservations about the eye-popping work of these upstarts, which it considered an affront to standards and taste. But though Lichtenstein acknowledged the rebellious genesis of the new movement, famously declaring himself "anti-" everything that characterized traditional art, he never agreed with critics and observers who saw his own work as part of pop art's ironic commentary on American art and culture. He argued—disingenuously, or so it seemed at the time—that he was only trying to demonstrate how all art is essentially an arrangement of colors and shapes. But as Lichtenstein went on to create more comics-style art during the 1960s, it increasingly reflected the world around him, in particular the culture of violence that exploded in American society during that decade. One of his most famous works, *Blam* (1962), which appears to be a frame lifted from an adventure comic, shows an up-ended fighter plane caught in a midair fire attack, its pilot falling from the cockpit, the word *"BLAM"* painted broadly against the explosions of light. Another work in the same vein is *As I Opened Fire* (1963), a three-frame sequence that shows a fighter plane making a strike, the words *"BRAT!"* and *"BRATA-TATATA!"* painted prominently on the canvas as sound effects.

Some critics have suggested that the distress and violence in Lichtenstein's art during this period reflected a crisis in his personal life: the breakup of his first marriage. He was divorced in 1965 and moved to a warehouse studio on the Bowery in New York. Three years later he married Dorothy Herzka, an employee at a Manhattan gallery; the couple had no children. By the end of the decade he had abandoned comic books as his models, though he would forever be associated with the art he produced in that style. He remained fascinated, however, with the notion of art-as-reproduction for the remainder of his career and produced works that were witty imitations of Pablo Picasso, Paul Cézanne, Piet Mondrian, and especially Claude Monet, whom he imitated in a series depicting Rouen Cathedral. Again Lichtenstein demurred when he was accused of put-downs, insisting that in his own way he was paying tribute to what had become major artistic icons. He also turned out abstract paintings of nudes, landscapes, and interiors, as well as abstract sculptures, prints, drawings, and giant murals, working on several pieces at once in his final studio, a loft on East 29th Street in Manhattan where he had moved in 1984. One of the best-known works of art from his later period is *Mural with Blue Brushstroke*, a five-story-high creation with Cubist elements that he painted in the mid-1980s for the lobby wall of the Equitable Insurance Company building in New York City.

In 1993 the Guggenheim Museum in New York City staged a major retrospective exhibition of Lichtenstein's work. Critical commentary ranged from adulatory to dismissive, reflecting the controversy that continued to surround Lichtenstein's art. Indeed, many critics still view Lichtenstein as an enigma. He was undeniably an artist who emerged at the forefront of a movement that exercised a major force in American art, but among the establishment there remains a certain wariness, as if Lichtenstein, like the unclothed emperor in the fairy tale, had somehow put one over on a gullible public and on museum curators and collectors alike who paid not-so-small fortunes for his work and hung it on their walls.

Shy and reticent to the end, Lichtenstein just kept on painting and appeared not to be too concerned about divided perceptions of his art, even as enthusiasm for the pop movement faded. He died at a New York hospital after being hospitalized with pneumonia.

• Biographical information is available from several sources. See the entry on "Lichtenstein, Roy," in *Current Biography Yearbook 1969*. See also Diane Waldman, *Roy Lichtenstein* (1971) and *Roy Lichtenstein* (1993); the first Waldman book covers Lichtenstein's early life and career, while the second, a catalogue of the retrospective exhibition at the Guggenheim, includes an essay with commentary on his later life and work. For Lichtenstein's own perspective on his art, see especially the interview with G. R. Swenson, "What Is Pop Art?" *ARTnews*, Nov. 1963, pp. 24ff. See also Calvin Tomkins and Bob Adelman, *Roy Lichtenstein: Mural with Blue Brushstroke* (1988), which includes an appreciative essay by Tomkins and an interview and photos by Adelman. Other useful evaluations of Lichtenstein's work and its significance include Lawrence Alloway, "An Examination of Roy Lichtenstein's Development," *ArtForum*, Mar. 1972, pp. 53–59, and Robert Rosenblum, *Roy Lichtenstein: Past, Present and Future* (1993), an exhibition catalogue for a Lichtenstein show at the Tate Gallery in London that includes an essay by Rosenblum. For commentaries on Lichtenstein's drawings, prints, and sculpture, see Diane Waldman, *Roy Lichtenstein: Drawings and Prints* (1970); Mary Lee Corlett and Ruth E. Fine, *The Prints of Roy Lichtenstein: A Catalogue Raisonné, 1948–1993* (1994); and Constance W. Glenn, *Roy Lichtenstein: Ceramic Sculpture* (1977). Major works on the pop art movement include Lucy Lippard, *Pop Art* (1966); John Russell and Suzi Gablik, eds., *Pop Art Redefined* (1969), which includes Swenson's interview from *ARTnews*; and Marco Livingstone, *Pop Art: A Continuing History* (1990). An obituary appears in the *New York Times*, 30 Sept. 1997; see also a correction to the *Times* obituary, 1 Oct. 1997, p. 2.

ANN T. KEENE

LILLIE, Beatrice (29 May 1894–20 Jan. 1989), comic actress, was born Beatrice Gladys Lillie in Toronto, Canada, the younger of two daughters of John Lillie, a schoolmaster, and Lucy Ann Shaw Lillie. Educated in Toronto and at St. Agnes College in Belleville, Ontario, Canada, Lillie was sometimes known as Gladys Monteil when appearing with her mother and sister Muriel onstage in Canada.

She followed them to London in 1914, appearing briefly in variety, or vaudeville, before auditioning for the revue producer André Charlot. Charlot was amazed by her ability to sing a sentimental song in a clear, uninflected voice, simultaneously pointing up its absurdity. This gift, allied with "working" an audience while appearing to ignore it, would become central to Lillie's reputation in the middle third of the twentieth century as "the funniest woman on earth."

After her revue debut in *Not Likely* (1914), Lillie worked—at first in male evening attire—almost exclusively for Charlot until 1926, a notable exception being her musical comedy debut in the 1919 London version of the Jerome Kern–Guy Bolton–P. G. Wodehouse *Oh, Boy!* (British title: *Oh, Joy!*). In 1920 Lillie married the exuberant and profligate baronet Sir Robert Peel; they had one son. Peel died in 1934, and Lillie never remarried, though her later decades were spent with John Philip Huck.

When Lillie first appeared in New York (*Charlot's London Revue*, 1924), her international fame, like that of costars Gertrude Lawrence and Jack Buchanan, was assured. But at a pre-opening party, a barrage of anti-British speeches had turned the mood ugly until it was Lillie's turn to speak. Charlot wrote, "She rose, holding her glass of champagne, and uttered a single syllable: 'Oh.' That single syllable was uttered so effectively that it seemed to bring our host and his friends suddenly to their senses. . . . she accompanied it with a swift upward movement of her glass which flung the champagne well over her shoulder. Perhaps it was this as much as the speech which made all the difference."

This flair for the unexpectedly apropos served Lillie well throughout her career. Although she often returned to Great Britain (from 1925, when Sir Robert's father died, onward as Lady Peel), most of her post-1925 career was spent in the United States, where, she once pointed out, "They spread the jam thicker." That she was now a titled lady probably helped her comic persona, which subverted pomposity.

After a reprise of *Charlot's Revue* in 1926, she took the lead in two Broadway musicals: *Oh, Please!* (1926), in which she parodied contemporary performers and introduced Vincent Youmans's "I Know That You Know," and *She's My Baby* (1928), singing Richard Rodgers and Lorenz Hart's "A Baby's Best Friend Is Its Mother." But she was always her best, most inventive self when in revue, where she could escape the bounds of "character." Lillie's silent motion picture debut came in *Exit Smiling* (1926).

Beginning in 1928, when she costarred in New York with her friend and fellow Charlot alumnus Noël Coward in his London revue *This Year of Grace* (in one notable number, "World Weary," as a Dickensian clerk sitting on a stool, munching an apple), Lillie was the acknowledged comic queen of American satirical revue. By 1929 she was appearing regularly on such popular radio shows as Rudy Vallee's Fleischmann hour. In 1930 she acquired an apartment on East End Avenue in New York, where she took up residence.

The Third Little Show (1931) found her singing Coward's "Mad Dogs and Englishmen" (in pith helmet) and a pompously sentimental Victorian number that became a signature song, "There Are Fairies at the Bottom of Our Garden," as well as parodying the trendy monologist Ruth Draper on a stage decorated

only by draperies: "In this little sketch I want you to imagine far too much." In *Walk a Little Faster* (1932), playing a "chantoosy" in a sketch by S. J. Perelman, she finished her elegant stint by picking up her skirt and roller skating offstage. In the same year she played the nurse in a production of George Bernard Shaw's *Too True to Be Good.*

Perhaps the most renowned American revues of the 1930s were *At Home Abroad* (1935) and *The Show Is On* (1936), both directed by Vincente Minnelli, both featuring scores by Arthur Schwartz and Howard Dietz, benefiting from sketches by Dietz, Marc Connelly, and Moss Hart, and both starring Lillie. In one of the sketches in *At Home Abroad* (written by Dion Titheradge and made famous in Britain by Cicely Courtneidge, from whom Lillie purchased the piece), Lillie tried in vain and a crescendo of malapropisms to purchase a dozen double damask dinner napkins. She repeated the sketch in the 1938 Bing Crosby film *Doctor Rhythm.* In *The Show Is On*, Lillie disrupted "The Reading of the Play" as a late arriver to *Hamlet* (in a production supposedly led by John Gielgud), muttering, "It is about a man and a woman: too much plot!"

After another New York appearance with Coward in his *Set to Music* (1939) Lillie returned to England for most of World War II. She appeared in cabaret at London's Cafe de Paris. When her son Robert was killed on naval duty in 1942, she heard the news between acts of a revue for Charles Cochran. For her wartime performances in the Middle East for the British ENSA (Entertainment National Service Administration) Lillie was awarded the African Star, the George VI Medal, and a Free French Medal by General Charles deGaulle.

Lillie returned to Broadway for *The Seven Lively Arts* (1944), for which she won the *New York Times*'s Donaldson Award. She divided the immediate postwar years between London and New York and made many radio appearances with Bing Crosby. The best revue of her later years was *Inside USA* (1948); in a Moss Hart sketch she ruins her actress friend's first night via snide remarks and a crass use of the actress's hairbrush to clean her own shoes.

By October 1952, when *An Evening with Beatrice Lillie*, a compilation based on her wartime tours, opened in New York, Lillie had become a regular guest on American television. *An Evening With Beatrice Lillie* won an Antoinette Perry (Tony) Award. In the same year Lillie was declared the Greatest Comedienne of All Time by the American Federation of Women's Philanthropics and she won a special commendation from the National Council of Christians and Jews. *An Evening with Beatrice Lillie* opened to acclaim in London in 1953; there followed a recording of its main numbers.

Lillie enlivened an otherwise moribund 1957 revival of the *Ziegfeld Follies* and in 1958 played the title character of *Auntie Mame* in both New York and London. Its author, Patrick Dennis, revealed that he had always intended the role of the madcap elder for Lillie.

When Lillie appeared as Madame Arcati, the spiritualist, in *High Spirits*, the musical version of Noël Coward's *Blithe Spirit* (1964), its author revealed that he had written the original role with Lillie in mind. As Madame Arcati, Lillie arrived onstage by bicycle, dismounted, removed the clips that had been holding her skirt in place, and turned them into bracelets, daring the audience to laugh. In 1967 she made her last film appearance in *Thoroughly Modern Millie*.

After suffering strokes in 1974 and 1975, Lillie generally remained in her "retirement apartment" on Park Avenue. But as her mental capacity declined, she eventually returned to Peel Fold, the family estate at Henley-on-Thames, England, where she died. John Philip Huck died thirty-one hours later. Three months later a public health facility in Toronto one block from her birthplace was renamed the Beatrice Lillie Building.

• Lillie's papers are dispersed, though good collections exist at the Theatre Museum and the Mander and Mitchenson Collection, both in London, as well as the Billy Rose Collection of the New York Public Library. The André Charlot archives held by family members in California and England, and by the University of California at Los Angeles, contain many references to Lillie. Beatrice Lillie's autobiography (with James Brough and John Philip) is *Every Other Inch a Lady* (1972). A biography is Bruce Arthur Laffey, *Beatrice Lillie: The Funniest Woman on Earth* (1989). Lillie's American stage career is well covered in Stanley Green, *The Great Clowns of Broadway* (1984). Also see Kenneth Tynan's appreciation of Beatrice Lillie, an essay titled "Beatrice Lillie, 1956" in *Show People: Profiles in Entertainment* (1979). Transcripts of radio broadcasts are held by the British Broadcasting Corporation and the Sound Archives of the British Library, London. Among many obituaries is Adam Benedick's in the (London) *Independent*, 23 Jan. 1989.

JAMES ROSS MOORE

LILLY, Eli (8 July 1838–6 June 1898), pharmaceutical manufacturer, was born the eldest of eleven children on a family-owned plantation in Baltimore County, Maryland, to Gustavus Lilly, a carpenter and building contractor, and Esther Elizabeth Kirby Lilly. He was named after his paternal grandfather. His father's family was descended from Swedish immigrants named Lillja who had come to Maryland in the eighteenth century. When Eli Lilly was an infant, the family moved west to Lexington, Kentucky, and lived there for more than a decade. In the spring of 1852 they moved north to Greencastle, Indiana, establishing themselves quickly in their new community as prominent citizens and staunch Methodists. After being educated at local schools, young Eli began working as a printer's devil for a local newspaper.

According to family legend, Eli Lilly was inspired to enter the drug business during a visit to an aunt and uncle in Lafayette, Indiana, in the summer of 1854. Walking around the town square one day, he noticed a local pharmacy called the Good Samaritan Drug Store. Drawn to the store by its name and the opportunity for doing good that it suggested, and also attracted by the store's aromas, he decided on the spot to become an apothecary, as pharmacists were then called, and secured a five-year apprenticeship with the store's owner, Henry Lawrence. At that time there were only three schools of pharmacy in the United States, and most aspiring apothecaries learned their trade through apprenticeship rather than formal schooling.

Drugstores then as now offered a variety of other items besides medicines, and nearly every drugstore also had a soda fountain that served not only soft drinks but also various tonics, some with liquor. In addition, drugstores, also called pharmacies, sold over-the-counter proprietary and patent medicines, for the most part useless bromides that were manufactured and prepackaged elsewhere, usually from patented formulas, and could be bought without a doctor's prescription. But the apothecary's principal and usually laborious job was to compound therapeutic mixtures of various substances as directed, or prescribed, by a physician; large pharmaceutical companies established for that purpose did not then exist.

As an apprentice, young Lilly spent his first year with Lawrence as a general helper, by day observing the work of his master while cleaning the premises, ordering supplies, restocking shelves, washing equipment, and running errands. Evenings were reserved for the study of chemistry as well as books on pharmacy, including the *United States Pharmacopoeia*, issued annually from 1820 onward, and the *American Journal of Pharmacy*. In his second and subsequent years of apprenticeship, Lilly learned to prepare and mix drugs from raw materials, using a mortar and pestle, a press, a special mill, and other devices. This could be arduous work, requiring not only considerable physical labor but also the memorization of hundreds of different substances and their uses. During his apprenticeship Lilly was given room and board and a dollar or two each week.

At the end of his five-year apprenticeship Lilly received a certificate of proficiency from his employer. After working for a time for another druggist in Lafayette, he returned to Greencastle in 1860 to open a small drugstore and soon afterward married a local resident, Emily Lemon. In November 1861 their only child, Josiah Kirby Lilly, was born. By the time of his birth, however, his father was far from home: he had joined the Union Army to fight in the Civil War, which had begun in April of that year. Lilly served for a while in the infantry and was then transferred to the artillery. As captain of the Eighteenth Indiana Battery, he participated in several major campaigns, including the battle of Chickamauga in 1863, before returning to Indiana to help organize the Ninth Indiana Cavalry. During service with that unit in the South he rose to the rank of colonel.

Upon receiving an honorable discharge from the army at war's end in 1865, Lilly chose to remain in the South. Together with a business partner he bought a cotton plantation near Port Gibson, Mississippi, and sent for his wife and young son. Postwar Mississippi was in chaos, however, and Lilly had to defend his property against roving bands that pillaged the countryside. By 1866 a drought had ruined his cotton crop, his partner had absconded, and his wife and young son were desperately ill with malaria. His wife soon died, and a disheartened Lilly, now and henceforth called "the Colonel" by all who knew him, abandoned the plantation and returned to Indiana.

Temporarily settling his son with his parents in Greencastle, Lilly moved to Indianapolis and went to work at H. Dailey and Company, a wholesale drugstore. After three years he had saved enough money to go into business on his own, and in 1869, in partnership with J. W. Binford, he opened the Red-Front Drug Store in Paris, Illinois. That same year he married Maria Cynthia Sloane and brought his son to Paris to live with them. Two years later, in 1871, the couple had a daughter; she died in her early teens. The drugstore was modestly successful, but Lilly, not satisfied with being a small-town druggist and believing that there was a business opportunity in the manufacture of prescription drugs, sold the store in 1873 and returned with his family to Indianapolis. In partnership with a dentist named Dr. Johnston, who furnished the capital, he soon opened a small laboratory in the city called the Johnston and Lilly Company. To help him he brought an employee from the Paris store, John Hurty, and made him chief chemist; Hurty would later go on to national prominence as a public health expert and crusader.

By the spring of 1876 Lilly's partnership with Johnston had floundered, and early that year the business was dissolved. Left with only a few pieces of equipment, scant supplies, and limited cash, Lilly nevertheless opened a tiny pharmaceutical plant in Indianapolis under the name "Eli Lilly, Chemist." Although the Indiana capital had become a flourishing and prosperous city, this was not an especially auspicious time to begin a business: economic hard times were descending upon the nation and were soon compounded by railroad strikes and a rash of corporate bankruptcies. Furthermore, drug manufacturing was a relatively new enterprise, trying to establish itself in the face of a boom in cheap patent medicines.

Nevertheless, through hard work and perseverance, and assisted initially only by two employees and the part-time help of his son, Josiah, Lilly slowly prospered. After two years the company moved to larger quarters in Indianapolis and added more employees; three years later, in 1881, Lilly incorporated his firm as Eli Lilly and Company and became its first president. Further expansion followed, including the establishment of a branch manufacturing plant in Kansas City, Missouri. Josiah Lilly, who had meanwhile enrolled at the Philadelphia College of Pharmacy, joined the company full-time upon graduation in 1882; he served initially as superintendent of production and became a director in 1887.

In the company's early years Eli Lilly personally supervised every aspect of the business, even taking his turn on the road as a salesman while also devising new methods of production, including the introduction of a special process to coat pills with gelatin. From its founding until Lilly's death two decades later, the firm grew into a major supplier of prescription medicines that were sold to drugstores throughout the region. Although competitors soon arose, the high quality of Lilly's goods and his reputation for honesty and fair dealing established the company as preeminent in its field.

By the late 1880s, the Lilly company, under Eli Lilly's leadership, had established a scientific research division and was beginning to develop new drugs, beginning with a treatment for venereal disease. It had also pioneered the manufacture of empty gelatin capsules in standard sizes, enabling pharmacists to dispense exact amounts of their own amalgamations—often foul-tasting—in an easy-to-swallow form. Although the company's sales diminished in the wake of a national depression in 1893, Lilly was able to keep it afloat through prudent management. As president of the Commercial Club, an alliance of Indianapolis businessmen, he also organized aid for the poor and unemployed during this period, establishing a public works program with the city as well as a food market.

Lilly was ill with stomach cancer in the last year of his life, and during this time he gradually withdrew from active involvement in the company. He died at his home in Indianapolis. A month later he was succeeded as president by his son, Josiah K. Lilly, who led the company into prominence as one of the largest pharmaceutical manufacturers in the nation.

• Biographical information on Eli Lilly is limited to three sources. The most accurate appears to be an extensive obituary in the *Indianapolis News*, 7 June 1898. The obituary provides most of the information included on Lilly in a company-commissioned history of the firm by Roscoe Collins Clark, *Threescore Years and Ten: A Narrative of the First Seventy Years of Eli Lilly and Company, 1876–1946* (1946); note, however, that this volume includes an incorrect death date. James H. Madison's *Eli Lilly: A Life, 1885–1977* (1989), a biography of Lilly's grandson, includes additional biographical information on "the Colonel." Additional information was provided by the Eli Lilly Company Archives in Indianapolis.

ANN T. KEENE

LINCOLN, Evelyn (25 June 1904–11 May 1995), secretary and author, was born Evelyn Maurine Norton in Polk County, Nebraska, the daughter of John N. Norton, a farmer and congressman, and Selma Josephine Floodman Norton. She moved with her family to Washington, D.C., when her father was elected as a Democrat to the seventieth Congress in 1927. She graduated from the University of Nebraska with a Bachelor of Arts in 1926. She attended George Washington University from 1933 to 1940; she took law courses but left before she received a degree. While in college, she met Harold W. "Abe" Lincoln, a fellow student at the university, whom she married. There is disagreement among sources as to the year of their marriage, but it appears to have been 1930, based on references in her obituaries to her husband of sixty-four years; they had no children. After they married, the couple moved to Albuquerque, where Harold Lincoln taught at the University of New Mexico. They then went to New York City when he was offered a teaching position at New York University. When he accepted a staff position with one of the committees of the U.S. House of Representatives, they returned to Washington.

Evelyn Lincoln's first job in Washington was in the office of the majority clerk of the House of Representatives, Truman Ward. Her next secretarial job was with Congressman Elijah Forrester of Georgia, but she was constantly looking for the opportunity of gaining a position with a presidential contender. In 1952 she interviewed for a job with John F. Kennedy, who was then a Massachusetts congressman running for the U.S. Senate. Lincoln volunteered to work evenings on the Kennedy senatorial campaign because, in her words, "I thought he might be going someplace; because I liked his philosophy" (Bergquist, p. 44). When Kennedy took his seat in the Senate in 1953, Lincoln became his personal secretary. Although she had quickly positioned herself to be a crucial assistant, she admitted later that Kennedy did not think they understood each other in the beginning. Evidently, he wanted to fire her but felt unable to do so.

Kennedy was for Lincoln the exact kind of promising aspirant for the presidency she had in mind. Presidential assistant Ted Sorensen wrote that Lincoln's "unfailing devotion and good nature more than compensated for a sometimes overly possessive attitude" (*Kennedy*, 1965). Smart and discreet, she nevertheless had no influence with Kennedy concerning political issues or his relations with others.

During Kennedy's near-fatal illness and long recuperation in 1955, Lincoln had an ulcer operation followed by major surgery for a spinal tumor, which impaired her ability to speak and to walk. After a slow but full recovery, she returned to Kennedy's office to the typing pool. In time, she would regain her former position.

With Kennedy's election to the presidency, Lincoln once again became his personal secretary. Because her office was strategically located in full view of the president's, it became a focal point for White House visitors unable to get through the president's appointments secretary, Kenneth O'Donnell. When Kennedy was assassinated in Dallas on November 22, 1963, Lincoln was riding in a bus that was part of the president's motorcade.

After leaving the White House, Lincoln worked on the presidential papers for the Kennedy Library, traveled around the United States giving lectures, and committed herself to maintaining what she considered Kennedy's golden image. The Lincolns' disillusionment with Washington, D.C., in the immediate post-Kennedy years led them to move to Sierra Leone, where the Kennedy image was revered and the Lincolns were able to be VIPs. After a short residence there, they returned to the Washington area.

Evelyn Lincoln's memoirs, *My Twelve Years with John F. Kennedy*, published in 1965, contained heartwarming anecdotes but nothing revelatory; the book proved she was not in fact an intimate of the president. She defended him against charges of extramarital liaisons and of secretly taping conversations in the Oval Office; the latter she considered just a recording of events.

From 1967 until 1973 Lincoln resumed work on Capitol Hill as a secretary for Representative James Kee, a Democrat from West Virginia, once again pursuing the chance to serve as an aide to a potential presidential candidate. (She eventually found that opportunity in Senator Gary Hart of Colorado, for whom she would campaign in 1982.) Lincoln's animus toward Lyndon Johnson became evident in her second book, *Kennedy and Johnson* (1968). Her account offered nothing new on the relationship between the two men but gave, Lincoln claimed, an insider's view of several important moments as both men campaigned for the presidential election in 1960. Not well received on publication, the book instigated a minor political controversy with the claim that Kennedy told Lincoln shortly before his death of his plans to replace Johnson with North Carolina governor Terry Sanford as his running mate on the 1964 Democratic ticket. For this and other undocumented statements, Lincoln was sharply criticized, and Robert Kennedy, embarrassed by the charges, was forced to deny them. The Johnson White House went so far as to investigate her allegations.

The full extent of Lincoln's devotion to the assassinated president's memory became apparent when conflict developed over ownership rights to her collection of Kennedy's personal belongings, memorabilia, and papers—including doodlings and even scraps of paper scavenged from wastebaskets. Lincoln claimed she had kept these items with the approval of Jacqueline Kennedy and Robert F. Kennedy. She contributed his papers to the John Fitzgerald Kennedy Presidential Library and Museum in Boston, but the legal question was whether Lincoln was permitted to keep other memorabilia as a permanent owner or simply maintain them as a custodian. After their mother died in 1994, President Kennedy's children, John F. Kennedy, Jr., and Caroline Kennedy Schlossberg, took exception to Lincoln's handling of the items she had kept. From their point of view, she had betrayed both the public trust and that of the Kennedy family. The family also accused Lincoln of giving material, including diaries and Kennedy artifacts, to Baltimore collector Robert White, who befriended her in the last years of her life. After Lincoln's death, White's auctioning off hundreds of Kennedy mementos brought the feelings of betrayal into public view and were widely discussed in the media.

Lincoln died in Washington, D.C. She epitomized the devoted personal aide who lives vicariously through a powerful figure and makes him a fulfillment of her own dreams. More important members of the Kennedy administration were equally given, however, to revering the thirty-fifth president and seeking to bask in his presumed glory. Until her death, she was one of the staunchest defenders of Kennedy the man, always denying his failings and willing to share sentimental anecdotes. A curious bit of assassination trivia in the saga of Lincoln's association with Kennedy has been noted: Abraham Lincoln, elected in 1861, had a secretary named Kennedy, and John F. Kennedy, elected in 1961, had a secretary named Lincoln.

• Material on Lincoln is in the John F. Kennedy Library, Boston, Mass., including an oral history interview and several feet of records that she had maintained. The Washingtoniana Division of the District of Columbia's Martin Luther King Memorial Library has relevant clipping files. The Senate Historical Office has brief, scattered recollections of Lincoln in its oral history collection. Patrick Anderson, *The Presidents' Men* (1965), contains a revealing chapter on Lincoln. See also Laura Bergquist, "Another Lincoln in the White House," *Look*, 9 Oct. 1962, pp. 36–38, 40, 44. Obituaries appear in the *New York Times* and in the *Washington Post*, both 13 May 1995.

MARTIN J. MANNING

LORD, Albert Bates (15 Sept. 1912–29 July 1991), folklorist, Slavist, and comparatist, was born in Boston, Massachusetts, the son of Robert Whiting Lord, a manufacturer of candy, and Corinne Bates Lord. After his high school years at Boston Public Latin School, he entered Harvard University, earning an A.B. in classics (cum laude, 1934) and an M.A. (1936) and Ph.D. (1949) in comparative literature, with graduate specialties in medieval English, ancient Greek, and Serbo-Croatian. On 24 August 1950 he married Mary Louise Carlson, later the long-time chair of Classics at Connecticut College, with whom he had two children: Nathan Eliot Lord, a high school English teacher, and Mark Edwards Lord, a potter and woodworker.

In 1934 Lord joined Milman Parry, his teacher, on an epoch-making expedition to the former Yugoslavia. Their plan was to test Parry's hypothesis about the oral tradition he envisioned behind the texts of Homer's *Iliad* and *Odyssey* by conducting an experiment in the "living laboratory" of South Slavic oral epic tradition. Toward that goal they recorded on aluminum discs hundreds of performances by nonliterate epic singers, called *guslari*, from six different regions or centers: Novi Pazar, Bijelo Polje, Kolašin, Gacko, Stolac, and Bihać. After Parry's death in 1935, Lord returned to those sites in 1950–1952 and more briefly during the 1960s. The resulting "half-ton of epic," as Lord often referred to it, became the basis of the Milman Parry Collection of Oral Literature at Harvard University, of Lord's editions and translations of selected performances (*Serbocroatian Heroic Songs*, 1953–), and, most important, of the comparative and interdisciplinary approach to the study of oral traditions that, in evolving far beyond Parry's original conception, was most centrally Lord's own creation.

Lord's 1949 dissertation, published in 1960 as *The Singer of Tales*, provided the foundation for this approach, which came to be known as the Oral-Formulaic or Parry-Lord Theory and was eventually to affect the study of scores of separate traditions from all over the world and from the ancient era through the present day. In this seminal manifesto he established the nature and functional role of traditional patterning at three levels of structure: the "formula," or recurrent phrase; the "theme," or recurrent typical scene; and the "story-pattern," or tale-type. Directing attention away from fixed, canonical documents and toward a flexible, multiform grammar of performance, he showed how the South Slavic *guslari*—and by extension myriad other performers in other traditions—composed in performance, depending not on texts or memorization but rather on the generative resources of a highly specialized language. Such singers do not repeat themselves verbatim, he showed, but keep their tales alive over generations by a verbal strategy of variation within limits. By drawing fluently on the specialized language, epic poets can compose and transmit tales of enormous length and richness without recourse to writing or reading. The comparative implications of this demonstration have had a revolutionary effect well beyond ancient Greek and South Slavic, in areas as diverse as medieval European works (for example, *Beowulf*, *The Song of Roland*, and *The Poem of the Cid*), a host of African traditions, central Asian epics along the Silk Roads, Native American narratives from a wide variety of tribes, both classical and modern poetry in Arabic, the Old and New Testaments of the Judeo-Christian Bible, Indian monuments from the *Mahabharata* to the *Siri Epic*, and many contemporary African-American genres.

The Oral-Formulaic approach draws its explanatory power from the combination of fieldwork and theory at its genesis, which took a number of forms. Lord collaborated with the composer Béla Bartók to produce *Serbocroatian Folk Songs*, an edition and translation of lyric poetry collected during the field expeditions of the thirties, which was published in 1951, six years after Bartók's death. Then, in 1953–1954, Lord published the initial two volumes of *Serbocroatian Heroic Songs*, consisting of performances from the Novi Pazar region. Here he presented multiple versions of the same epic tale from the same and different singers, illustrating as directly as possible how oral tradition relies not on absolute fixity but on rule-governed flexibility in performance and transmission. Some twenty years later his translation of Avdo Medjedović's *The Wedding of Smailagić Meho* (with the original-language version edited by David E. Bynum) appeared as part of the same series from the Parry Collection. Medjedović's master-performance, a fully developed poem of 12,311 lines by a *guslar* who could neither read nor write, is at once the culmination of what the Oral-Formulaic Theory predicted and an estimable artistic achievement in its own right. Here was a performance—unquestionably from an oral traditional source—that compared in length and elaboration to Homer's *Iliad* and *Odyssey*.

Alongside an extraordinarily wide-ranging series of articles starting in 1936 and continuing through the early 1990s, Lord's two final books magisterially summarize his comparative method and blaze a path for specialists in many fields. The first, *Epic Singers and Oral Tradition* (1991), combines reprinted and unpublished writings on ancient and modern Greek, South Slavic, medieval English, central Asian, and Finnish poetry that stem from oral tradition, tackling topics as diverse as the vexed term "oral literature," the dictation of the Homeric poems, the master *guslar* Avdo Medjedović, the traditional origin of the Old English *Beowulf*, and the oral traditional structure of the *Kalevala* and the *Digenis Akritas*. No less challenging is *The Singer Resumes the Tale* (1995), edited by Mary Louise Lord, in which he engages many of the debates that arose over issues of composition, transmission, and reception in oral and oral-derived traditions. Here the scope widens to include Latvian *dainas* and Anglo-American folk balladry in addition to many other areas, and special attention is paid to the crucial question of the "transitional text," the hybrid written composition whose author nonetheless employs an oral traditional style.

Lord served at Harvard as a lecturer from 1950 to 1952, an associate professor from 1952 to 1958, and a professor from 1958 to 1991; he occupied the Arthur Kingsley Porter Professorship in Slavic and Comparative Literature. He died in Boston.

Albert Lord's legacy is rich and many-sided. Throughout the disciplines of literature, anthropology, and folklore, and elsewhere, our understanding of verbal art is categorically different because of his seminal contributions. His and Parry's Oral-Formulaic Theory—well established as much more than a theory by the time of Lord's death—originally took shape from a unique blend of philology and fieldwork, of textual analysis and on-site recording, and for this reason it commands a singular authority. Scholars sometimes remark that the juxtaposition of Homer's ancient poems and the *guslar*'s modern performances was fundamentally Parry's insight, and Lord, who always honored his teacher's ideas, believed that as well. But the equally creative and groundbreaking extension of that original comparison to more than 150 language areas—an extension that changed the way we read and hear the works of ancient, medieval, and modern cultures—was Lord's particular gift to twentieth-century research and scholarship.

• In addition to Lord's editions (*Serbo-Croatian Folk Songs*, 1951, with Béla Bartók; and *Serbocroatian Heroic Songs*, 1953–), his trilogy of comparative studies defines the trajectory of his career from the initial description of the analogy between Homer and the South Slavic *guslari* (*The Singer of Tales*, 1960) through a highly developed extension to numerous other traditions (*Epic Singers and Oral Tradition*, 1991; *The Singer Resumes the Tale*, 1995). A short biography and a digest of his publications to date are available in "Obituary: Albert Bates Lord (1912–1991)," *Journal of American Folklore*, 105 (1992): 57–65. For a sense of the range and depth of Lord's influence, see Foley, *Oral-Formulaic Theory and Research* (1985, with updates in the journal *Oral Tradition*; see below for electronic version). For a history of the Oral-Formulaic Theory, see Foley, *The Theory of Oral Composition* (1988); for further analyses and developments, see Foley, *Traditional Oral Epic* (1990); *Immanent Art* (1991), *The Singer of Tales in Performance* (1995), and *Homer's Traditional Art* (1999). A brief obituary appears in the *New York Times*, 4 Aug. 1991.

JOHN MILES FOLEY

LORTEL, Lucille (16 Jan. 1900–4 Apr. 1999), producer, theater patron, and actress, was born Lucille Wadler, in New York City, the daughter of Anna Wadler and Harry Wadler, a clothing manufacturer. Her childhood was spent comfortably. Her father traveled often to Europe to buy designs that he would copy, and for a while her family lived in the Mayflower Hotel. Under the tutelage of her outgoing mother, she was raised among a circle of people who cultivated the arts. The family was close friends with the Gershwins—Anna Wadler and Rose Gershwin were contemporaries—and George Gershwin and Ira Gershwin's younger sister, Frances, was a girlhood chum of Lortel's who remained a lifelong confidante. The Wadler children (Lortel was a stage name that Lucille took as a young adult) were gifted. Her brother, Mayo, was a child prodigy as a concert violinist; her sister, Ruth, became a painter and would later marry the brother of bandleader Xavier Cugat.

Pretty, genial, and sociable, Lortel began her fascination with theater as a child and aspired to be an actress. After being tutored at home and later attending public school and, for a brief time, Adelphi College, she enrolled in the American Academy of Dramatic Arts. She later studied for a short time in Berlin with Max Reinhardt. In 1925 she made her Broadway debut in the Theatre Guild production of George Bernard Shaw's *Caesar and Cleopatra*, starring Helen Hayes. She also appeared in David Belasco's *The Dove*, with Judith Anderson; as Poppy in the touring company of John Colton's *The Shanghai Gesture* with Florence Reed; and in *The Man Who Laughed Last*, opposite Sessue Hayakawa—which the pair recreated on film in one of the first talking pictures.

Lortel's acting career was squelched when she met Louis Schweitzer in 1930 and married him the following year. Schweitzer was a wealthy chemical engineer who had earned his fortune in cigarette papers. She preferred her career to the prospect of marriage, but he convinced her, sending her a ticket to join him in Paris, where they were to be married. But on her arrival, the couple learned that by French law the marriage could not take place until it had been posted for several weeks. They sailed back together on the *Leviathan*, where they were married by the ship's captain, though Lortel would maintain, "I wouldn't have anything to do with my husband until we came back to New York." (In fact, she did not before there was another ceremony at City Hall and a religious service in Manhattan performed by the Jewish chaplain at West Point.)

Though Lortel appeared the next year in *The Man Who Reclaimed His Head*, with Claude Rains and Jean Arthur, Schweitzer did not want his new wife to work, least of all as an actress—a profession his mother disapproved of. Reaching a compromise, she was able to work during the rest of the 1930s in movie shorts filmed in Brooklyn, which allowed her to be home in the evenings. In her domestic life, Lortel became an energetic hostess—a role to which she was extraordinarily suited. Her parties, both at their apartment in the Plaza Hotel and at their country place in Westport, Connecticut, boasted the interesting and famous from New York's theatrical, literary, music, art, and business worlds.

The Schweitzers had no children. Louis, a ham radio enthusiast, spent hours holed up in the radio shack he had built on the Westport property. He also owned the FM radio station WBAI and founded the Vera Institute of Justice, which provides bail money to poor court defendants. By the mid-1940s, Lortel, having retired some years earlier, was restless. She missed the New York theater, which now, after World War II, was stirring in ways that would transform it from a center for Depression-era naturalism to an experimental playground for American and European theater artists.

In July 1947 the actor Canada Lee and the playwright Philip Huston needed a place to try out a new play, *Painted Wagon*. Lortel came to the rescue by offering them the use of the barn on her Westport property. The tractor and Ping-Pong table were removed, and on the night of 27 July seven actors, scripts in hand, performed a minimally staged reading of the play on a small raised platform before an invited audience seated in an array of camp chairs. Afterward, the audience—a mix of theater professionals and discriminating New York friends—gathered with the artists over coffee and sandwiches and discussed the ins and outs of what they had just seen.

Thus the White Barn Theatre was born. Word spread fast throughout the industry, as writers, performers, and directors eager to try out their own new material clamored for a similar opportunity. The second reading, *No Casting Today*, a musical revue by Alex Kahn with music by William Provost, was at the request of the agent Audrey Wood (who represented Tennessee Williams, among others). Before the end of that first summer, Lortel had presented four more such readings, with casts that included young performers Eva Marie Saint, Jo Sullivan, and Bibi Osterwald. The second summer saw the American premieres of Sean O'Casey's *Red Roses for Me*, with Kim Hunter and future film director George Roy Hill; William Saroyan's *Jim Dandy*, with Canada Lee and Zero Mostel; and choreographer Jack Cole's musical revue *Alive and Kicking*. All three shows would go on to the New York stage.

What was remarkable about Lortel's enterprise was that Off-Broadway, with its informal, experimental atmosphere, did not yet exist; and the notion of staged readings as performance was decades away from being commonplace. Additionally, apart from commercial Broadway, summer theater largely meant star-driven exports of New York hits, plus some conventional new works hopefully headed toward Broadway.

Westport, an hour's train ride from New York and noted for its community of celebrated actors, artists, musicians, and writers, was the perfect setting for Lortel's new theater. It was also only a stone's throw from what had perhaps become the nation's premier "straw hat" summer theater, the Westport Country Playhouse, headed by Theatre Guild founder Lawrence Langner, who supported Lortel's enterprise from the outset.

As an elite audience continued to stream in—from Marilyn Monroe and Arthur Miller to Rod Serling and Gian Carlo Menotti—the barn was gradually converted into a proper theater, with a full stage and an auditorium seating 150. Lortel specialized in innovative European and American plays that did not stand a chance under the box office–worshipping pressures of the commercial theater.

Over the next fifty years of her lifetime, many productions that Lortel nurtured in her barn advanced to Broadway and Off-Broadway, garnering countless awards while they plumbed uncommercial areas such as politics, race, multiculturalism, and new twists on the classics. She presented the Dublin Players Company, the Oxford University Players, and Geoffrey Holder's Trinidad Dance Troupe, and plays by Samuel Beckett, Edward Albee, Eugène Ionesco, and Sean O'Casey. Seasoned legends such as Mildred Dunnock, Peggy Wood, and James Coco worked alongside greenhorns such as Vincent Gardenia, Peter Falk, Sada Thompson, George Peppard, and Sidney Lumet.

After traveling to England and observing the British "club theatre" system—where audiences had regular ticket subscriptions—she instituted a similar setup at the White Barn. With her board members—the stage designer Ralph Alswang and the actress Eva Le Gallienne—she established a White Barn apprentice school and ran seminars on Chekhov, Ibsen, and Shakespeare, where Le Gallienne held forth.

Yet while embracing her role as theatrical innovator, Lortel was still first the hostess, treating the entire enterprise as a large house party. Almost as much care went into feeding, housing, and mothering the artists and tending to the audience—whom Lortel personally arranged in a painstaking seating plan—as into presenting the work onstage. And through the decades, the weekend-only performances were always accompanied by those greenroom sandwich-and-coffee receptions where patrons and artists could mingle.

The White Barn was not the only present Schweitzer lavished on his wife. He was the first foreigner in more than 400 years allowed to buy a gondola in Venice and—breaking with the tradition of identifying gondolas only by number—was permitted to name it "Lucille." When Lortel complained that it was hard to find a taxi after the theater, his answer was a gray Mercedes-Benz; and to drive it for her he found a cab driver actually named Louis Schweitzer, who used the car as an ordinary taxi when she did not need him. For some years, he also arranged for the couple to spend a part of each winter on a houseboat—a two-story villa—anchored off Miami Beach.

In 1955 Lou Schweitzer gave his wife another present. This time it was the Theatre de Lys on Greenwich Village's Christopher Street. Lortel immediately offered her new theatre to a struggling production, Marc Blitzstein's adaptation of Kurt Weill and Bertolt Brecht's *The Threepenny Opera*, starring Lotte Lenya. The production created an instant sensation and ran seven years, establishing Off-Broadway in the process.

Shortly afterward, restless because as a hit *The Threepenny Opera* was monopolizing her theater, Lortel convinced the American National Theatre and Academy to sponsor a matinee series at the de Lys as a "laboratory for innovation." The ANTA Matinee Series became a legend, over the next twenty years offering experiments such as Helen Hayes in a Shakespeare anthology; Siobhan McKenna as Hamlet; Anna Sokolow's dance reflections on Kafka's "Metamorphosis"; Godfrey Cambridge in "Shakespeare in Harlem," based on Langston Hughes's poems; a reading by Dame Sybil Thorndike and Sir Lewis Casson; Richard Burton in "An Afternoon of Poetry"; obscure works by O'Casey, Ionesco, Tennessee Williams, Edward Albee, and William Inge; and the work of new writers such as Terrence McNally and Adrienne Kennedy. In 1960 Lortel began sponsoring similar productions and seminars at the Library of Congress.

Lortel would eventually earn the nickname "the Queen of Off-Broadway" (a label she enjoyed) for shaping an arena that within a few decades would completely usurp Broadway's place as the staging ground for new American plays and innovative work. Turning to outside producing partnerships, at Circle in the Square in 1960 she presented Jean Genêt to American audiences with *The Balcony*, and in 1964 she was producer/midwife to the South African playwright Athol Fugard's first American production, *Blood Knot*, starring James Earl Jones and J. D. Cannon. Among the plays she introduced by Beckett was *Rockabye*.

The Theatre de Lys (renamed the Lucille Lortel Theatre in 1980) was home to plays such as David Mamet's *A Life in the Theater*, Sam Shepard's *Buried Child*, Marsha Norman's *Getting Out*, Caryl Churchill's *Cloud Nine*, Wendy Wasserstein's *Isn't It Romantic?*, Larry Kramer's *The Destiny of Me*, and Win Wells's *Gertrude Stein and a Companion*, the televised version of which won her an Emmy Award. Five of the approximately 500 plays Lortel produced were nominated for Tony Awards (although she never won), having either been produced directly for Broadway or moved after Off-Broadway success: William M. Hoffman's *As Is*, Lanford Wilson's *Angels Fall*, Fugard's *Blood Knot*, the South African import *Serafina*,

and Lee Blessing's *A Walk in the Woods*. This last, about nuclear disarmament talks between representatives of the United States and the Soviet Union, appeared in 1988, at the height of the senate debates on the INF Treaty; it was given a command performance at the Library of Congress for an audience that included the American secretary of state George Shultz and the Soviet ambassador Yuri Dubynin before going on to the London and Moscow stage.

Throughout her life, Lortel never failed to pursue compelling subject matter, be it disarmament, AIDS, or apartheid, while her artistic and business shrewdness only developed further with time. What made her an endearing figure (apart from her public and private generosity, particularly after her husband's death in 1971) was a contradictory personality in which high-minded artistic choices resided with an ongoing preoccupation with pragmatic details like what kind of cake icing to serve at a major opening. She addressed everybody as "Darling," and perhaps the only thing she loved more than the theater was a hot dog. On summer days at the White Barn, she favored shorts and sandals, while around New York she always could be spotted in natty suits with a hat at a rakish angle. Until shortly before the end of her life, almost every evening would find her at an Off-Broadway or Broadway theater. She died on Easter Sunday at New York Presbyterian Hospital at age ninety-eight.

During her lifetime she received numerous honors. Among her legacies are the Lucille Lortel Awards, which she established in 1986 and which are given annually for Off-Broadway achievement. She is the subject of a permanent tribute on display at the New York Public Library at Lincoln Center, where she sponsored the Theatre on Film and Tape archive; she also established the Lucille Lortel Fund for New Drama at Yale University (August Wilson's *Fences* being the first project to receive support) and various fellowships. "Honey, I've got a one-track mind and it's theatre, theatre, theatre," she liked to say. "I have no time for anything else." At the time of her death, both the Lucille Lortel Theatre and the White Barn were thriving.

• Valuable sources on the contributions of Lucille Lortel are the publications issued by the White Barn Theatre in Westport, Connecticut: programs, anniversary books, etc. (particularly commemorating its fiftieth anniversary in 1997). An extensive chronicle is also to be found in Sam McCready, *Lucille Lortel: A Bio-Bibliography* (1993). An obituary is in the *New York Times*, 6 Apr. 1999.

DEBORAH GRACE WINER

LOUGHRAN, Tommy (29 Nov. 1902–7 July 1982), light-heavyweight boxing champion, was born Thomas Patrick Loughran in Philadelphia, Pennsylvania, the son of John Loughran, a motorman for the city of Philadelphia, and Anna Haley. His father was an immigrant. The boy graduated from St. Monica's Parochial School and then attended the Roman Catholic School at Broad and Vine Streets for one year. Afterward he held various jobs, particularly at the Atlantic Refining Company and in a blacksmith shop for eighteen months. He tried to enlist in the army before finishing parochial school but was sent home for being too young.

At age sixteen Loughran got the urge to become a boxer and, with difficulty, persuaded a neighbor and former fighter, Joe Smith, to train and manage him. His relationship with Smith endured throughout his long career in the ring and formed a striking contrast to the usual exploitative manager-boxer relationship. Loughran made his professional debut in December 1919 and engaged in thirty-five fights in 1920 and 1921, gradually working his way to main event status. At first he tended to favor right-handed punching, as most young boxers did, but Smith made him spar with his right arm tied to his body, forcing him to learn to use his left hand. The result was that Loughran came to be known for his brilliant use of the left jab. Loughran was always a clever boxer who punched sharply but not with devastating effect; he employed clever footwork and deft shot-blocking to outscore his opponents. After the first two years of his boxing career, he rarely won by knockout.

In 1922 Loughran achieved a high ranking for the first time, even though losing close fights to two future champions, heavyweight Gene Tunney and middleweight Harry Greb. He defeated two other future champions, light-heavyweight Mike McTigue and middleweight Bryan Downey. From 1923 to 1925 he continued to fight tough opponents, including five more bouts with Greb, two with McTigue, and two with future light-heavyweight champion Jack Delaney. He lost some close fights and had several draws, but he always improved and learned to fight the best successfully. Loughran was unbeaten in 1926, his most notable win being at the expense of the famous French boxer Georges Carpentier, who had fought Jack Dempsey for the heavyweight title. The most successful year of his career, in which he won all ten of his fights, was 1927. He outpointed Young Stribling, to whom he had lost twice previously and, on 7 October, won partial recognition as world light-heavyweight champion by defeating McTigue in New York's Madison Square Garden, taking nearly every round by a wide margin. Only two months later, Loughran fought the other claimant to the light-heavyweight championship, Jimmy Slattery, also in Madison Square Garden. After a close, clean, hard-fought battle, Loughran became the undisputed titleholder.

In January 1928, Loughran defended his title against Leo Lomski, a hard hitter who floored Tommy twice in the first round. Loughran used his superb boxing ability and ring generalship, however, to fight a successful uphill battle and clearly win the fight. Later in the year he made two more successful title defenses against former welterweight champion Pete Latzo. In 1929, he beat Mickey Walker and Jim Braddock in light-heavyweight championship fights and then decided to relinquish that title and fight as a heavyweight. His first heavyweight fight, 26 September 1929 in Yankee Stadium, was a disaster. Matched with future champion Jack Sharkey, he was knocked out in the third round by a terrific right to the head. But he persevered and, in the next two years, he won several notable victories over other heavyweights, the best of which was the one-sided boxing lesson he administered in Madison Square Garden to another future champion, Max Baer. For most of this period Loughran was a ranked contender for the heavyweight title.

In January 1932, at the hands of Steve Hamas, a former college football player, Loughran suffered the second and last knockout of his career. Four months later he lost again to Hamas on a close decision and then, in the next year, defeated him twice. On 27 September 1933 he fought a rematch with Sharkey in Philadelphia and clearly outpointed him in fifteen rounds. This set the stage for his heavyweight title fight with the reigning champion, Primo Carnera of Italy. Loughran and Carnera fought in Miami on 1 March 1934. Loughran, at 184 pounds, was 86 pounds lighter and 6 inches shorter than his giant opponent. He boxed cleverly but could not overcome the physical disadvantages. As the fight proceeded, he weakened and was often trapped in the corners, where, unable to avoid Carnera's punches, he lost on points. Although Loughran continued to box until 1937, and won most of his remaining fights, he was never again a highly ranked contender. He fought in South America, Europe, Canada, and the western United States in the declining years of his career. His final record included nearly 180 fights. He fought fifteen world title holders and claimants, most of them more than once.

Loughran served in the Marine Corps in World War II as a physical conditioner. Later he worked on Wall Street as a sugar trader. He also became a popular after-dinner speaker and a sports commentator. After retirement he lived in Holidaysburg, Pennsylvania. In his personal characteristics, Loughran was almost the reverse of the stereotypical professional boxer. Although not highly educated, he was intelligent, urbane, and friendly. Because he was a clever boxer and avoided unnecessary punishment in the ring, he retained his handsome appearance. At no time in his long career was he accused of dishonesty or of giving less than his best. He was religious and attentive to his family, although he disappointed his mother by becoming a boxer instead of a priest. He never married. He was named to the International Boxing Hall of Fame in 1991. He died at home in Holidaysburg, Pennsylvania.

• Loughran's record as a boxer is available in Herbert G. Goldman, ed., *The 1986–87 Ring Record Book and Boxing Encyclopedia*. Articles in *The Ring* magazine include T. Carroll, "Loughran Boxing Master of Yore," Oct. 1958, and reprinted as "Last Requiem for a Light Heavyweight: Tommy Loughran," Oct. 1982; F. Albertanti, "From Newsboy to Champion," Dec. 1927; and G. T. Pardy, "Tommy

Loughran, Master Scientist and Ring Gamester Who Feared No Odds," June 1935. Another article is Q. Reynolds, "Alger Boys," *Collier's,* 17 Feb. 1934. His obituary appears in the *New York Times,* 10 July 1982.

LUCKETT V. DAVIS

LOWDERMILK, Walter Clay (1 July 1888–6 May 1974), soil scientist, geologist, soil conservation leader, and author, was born Walter Clay Lowdermilk in Liberty, North Carolina, the son of Henry Clay Lowdermilk, a businessman, lumberman, and rancher, and Helen Vashti Lawrence Lowdermilk. The family moved westward to Missouri, to Oklahoma, and finally to Arizona. Walter Lowdermilk graduated from the Park College Academy in Parkville, Missouri, in 1906 and then attended Park College (1908–1910). In 1910 he enrolled at the University of Arizona; after two years there he won a Rhodes Scholarship to Oxford University, where he earned a B.S. degree in forestry (1914); a B.A. degree in geology (1915); and an M.A. degree, granted in absentia (1922). While at Oxford he had an opportunity to study forestry in Germany. He also served on Herbert Hoover's Commission for Relief in Belgium (1914–1915).

He returned to the United States in 1915 and joined the U.S. Forest Service as a forest ranger at the Tonto National Forest, Arizona; the next year he transferred to the Santa Fe National Forest in New Mexico. This Southwestern experience greatly influenced his career, because it was here that he became interested in the processes of erosion on livestock range. He enlisted in the 10th Engineers of the American Expeditionary Force and scaled—that is, estimated the quantity of—timber cut by the military for war uses in France (1917–1918) and was later commissioned as a timber acquisitions officer in France (1918–1919). In 1919 he was assigned to the American Peace Commission to assess timber damage. When he returned to the Forest Service in 1919, it was as the regional research officer in Montana.

In 1922 Lowdermilk married Inez Marks, whom he had met during his college years in Arizona. A devout Methodist, she had graduated from the University of Southern California and had been a Methodist missionary in China since 1916. She became reacquainted with Walter while on leave in the United States. They returned to China in September 1922, where Lowdermilk had been appointed research professor of forestry at the University of Nanking, with a charge to use his talents in the interest of famine prevention along the Yellow River. Levees along the river were being built higher and higher as the river silted; this unstable condition caused the levees to break periodically. The resulting floods took lives and destroyed crops, which led to famine. Lowdermilk traveled upriver to the deep loess areas in Shansi (Shanxi) province—and perhaps to Shensi (Shaanxi) as well—where the heavy load of silt originated. He and his Chinese associates measured runoff and erosion and compared the bared hillsides to the ancient, and pro-

tected, temple forests, thereby bringing some attention to the ongoing need to safeguard Chinese watersheds from erosion.

The Communist uprising of 24 March 1927 in Nanking ended the Lowdermilks' stay in China. Leaving behind all their possessions, the Lowdermilks escaped to the United States. Before the departure from China, Lowdermilk had decided to study the processes leading to human-induced erosion. At the University of California he completed the requirements for a Ph.D. in the School of Forestry (with minors in soil science and geology) and also conducted research at the U.S. Forest Service's California Forest Experiment Station. The dissertation he completed in 1929 explained one of the basic processes in run-off and soil erosion: the raindrop falling on bared soil causes fine soil particles to seal the surface, resulting in reduced percolation and increased run-off; a covering of forest litter protects the soil, increases percolation, and keeps the water clean.

The Forest Service selected Lowdermilk to establish a research station at San Dimas, California, and to devise its research plan for understanding the impact of watershed management on water yield in the southern California climate. Before completing that work, Lowdermilk was recruited to be the vice-director of a temporary New Deal agency in the Department of the Interior, the Soil Erosion Service, in October 1933. After a congressional act of 27 April 1935 created its successor, the Soil Conservation Service, in the U.S. Department of Agriculture, he served as its associate chief (Dec. 1935–Mar. 1937), chief of the research division (Mar. 1937–Nov. 1939), and then head soil conservationist until his retirement.

The new service undertook operations through a group of watershed-based demonstration projects where the service hoped to get a majority of farmers to use soil and water conservation measures. Later the service expanded operations nationwide by assigning trained conservationists to work with locally organized conservation districts. Lowdermilk contributed to organizing all facets of the new service, but he especially concentrated on the research program. Furthermore, the demonstration projects afforded an opportunity to observe the effects of farmland conservation practices on the entire watershed. Thus Lowdermilk was instrumental in the new agency's contributions to understanding small watershed hydrology.

Lowdermilk was also a publicist for soil conservation, emphasizing the lessons to be learned from the historical land-use experience. From August 1938 until November 1939, he traveled in Europe, the Mediterranean area, and the Middle East studying past land-use practices and their results. Indeed, he often said his profession was to read "the records which farmers, nations, and civilizations had written in the land" and then to apply that knowledge to use but also conserve the land, so that it might be productive indefinitely. Lowdermilk wrote extensively on this topic and his travels. Some of his studies appeared in abbreviated form in a USDA pamphlet, *Conquest of the Land through 7,000 Years* (1953). The Soil Conservation Service has distributed over one million copies of the pamphlet in its educational efforts.

He also wrote *Palestine, Land of Promise* (1944), wherein he proposed a Jordan Valley Authority to provide power, water supply, and irrigation water. The book argued, as did his popular pamphlet *Palestine Can Take Millions* (1944), that the land there could support a much larger population. The message contravened the British and American foreign policy of the early 1940s that discouraged Jewish emigration to Palestine. During 1942–1943 he worked at the behest of the Chinese government on furthering the adoption of simple conservation practices in the Yellow River basin. After Lowdermilk's retirement from the Soil Conservation Service on 30 June 1947, he stayed active by consulting in French North Africa (1948) and in the British colonies in Africa (1949–1950). Following work with the U.S. Water Resources Policy Commission (1950) and the Supreme Allied Command in Japan (1951), he worked in Israel under the auspices of the Food and Agriculture Organization of the United Nations to organize a Soil Conservation Service. The young Israeli soil conservationists found him an inspiring teacher. Next he developed a school of agricultural engineering at the Technion (Israel Institute of Technology) in Haifa to train soil conservationists. It was eventually named the Lowdermilk School of Agricultural Engineering in his honor. The Israelis greatly appreciated Lowdermilk's contributions and in 1976 dedicated a grove of trees in Galilee in his memory. He was a fellow and president of the American Geophysical Union (1941–1944) and a fellow of the Society of American Foresters and of the Soil Conservation Society of America.

The Lowdermilks had two children, William Francis and Winifred Esther. In retirement the Lowdermilks had a home in the Berkeley, California, hills. Walter Lowdermilk died in Palo Alto, California, having spent his last years at the Veterans Hospital there. He had begun his career researching the basic processes of erosion and runoff, especially as influenced by humans. A leader in organizing government conservation agencies in the United States and abroad, he put research findings into action. As an author he spoke for the conservation movement, and in his international work served as a humanitarian by furthering conservation and the proper use of land to make and keep it productive.

• Walter Lowdermilk's papers can be found at the Bancroft Library, University of California, Berkeley; Hoover Institution Archives, Stanford University, Palo Alto, Calif.; and among Record Group 114, Records of the Soil Conservation Service, National Archives, College Park, Md. Lowdermilk wrote extensively in scientific and professional journals and in government publications, but he is perhaps best known for published works examining the interaction of humans with the land, cited above. A thorough oral history of Lowdermilk's life is an interview conducted by Malca Chall, *Wal-*

ter Clay Lowdermilk, Soil, Forest, And Water Conservation and Reclamation in China, Israel, Africa, and the United States (2 vols., 1969). Also valuable for information on his career is his wife's autobiography, Inez Marks Lowdermilk, *All in a Lifetime: An Autobiography* (1985), privately published by the Lowdermilk Trust in Berkeley, Calif. His career as a land conservationist is reviewed in J. Douglas Helms, "Walter Lowdermilk's Journey: Forester to Land Conservationist," *Environmental Review* 8 (Summer 1984): 132–145. For a general study of American agriculturists in China, see Randall E. Stross, *The Stubborn Earth: American Agriculturalists on Chinese Soil, 1898–1937* (1986). An obituary is in the *New York Times*, 9 May 1974.

DOUGLAS HELMS

LUCAS, Nick (22 Aug. 1897–28 July 1982), singer-guitarist-composer, was born Dominic Antonio Nicholas Lucanese in Newark, New Jersey, the son, one of nine children, of Otto Maria Lucanese, a gardener, and Bella Ermiania Lucanese. When he was four years old he began playing stringed instruments, and by the age of eight he and his older brother Frank were supplementing the family income by performing their music at various social events. He became so accomplished as a guitarist that in 1912 he and Frank made test pressings for the Edison Company, thus beginning a recording career that continued into the early 1980s.

Soon after graduating from school (the eighth grade being the highest in his school district), Lucas began appearing with various bands in Newark cabarets. He was also an accomplished banjo player, and in 1917 he made records with Earl Fuller's Jazz Band. That same year he married Catherine Cifrodella (who died in 1971); they had a daughter, Emily, born in 1918. With Ted Fio Rito, Lucas formed a vaudeville act, the Kentucky Five, which toured the country in 1918, and for the next several years he worked with the Vincent Lopez and Vernon Country Club orchestras. In addition to recording with the Vernon group, he made records with the Don Parker Trio and with his brother Frank, as the Lucas Ukulele Trio and the Lucas Novelty Quartet.

In the fall of 1921 Lucas joined Sam Lanin's orchestra as a banjo player, recording on Gennett Records as Bailey's Lucky Seven. At this point he began replacing the banjo with the guitar on his recordings. His guitar solos "Pickin' the Guitar" and "Teasin' the Frets," recorded for Pathé Actuelle in 1922, strongly influenced succeeding generations of guitar players, including Gene Autry, Merle Travis, and Chet Atkins.

In 1924, when Lucas went to Chicago to join Ted Fio Rito and Danny Russo's Oriole Terrace Orchestra, he also played the guitar and sang over radio station WEBH. Because the nationwide response was so great, he was signed by Brunswick Records, and his first record for the company, "My Best Girl," was a big seller. Billed by Brunswick as "the Crooning Troubadour," he became in the next several years one of the country's biggest record sellers. His major hits were "Brown Eyes, Why Are You Blue?," "In a Little Spanish Town," "I'm Looking Over a Four-Leaf Clover," "Looking at the World through Rose-Colored Glasses," "Sing Me a Baby Song," "Moonbeam, Kiss Her for Me," "Coquette," "You're Driving Me Crazy," "Always," "Side by Side," "Bye, Bye, Blackbird," "Among My Souvenirs," and "Lady, Play Your Mandolin." His record sales eventually totaled over eighty million copies.

In his 1926 debut on Broadway in *Sweetheart Time,* Lucas introduced "Sleepy-Time Gal." Later that year he scored a major triumph in London, where he appeared at several theaters, in addition to giving private performances for the prince of Wales and the queen of Spain. After appearing briefly in 1929 in the Broadway musical *Show Girl,* in which he sang George Gershwin's "Liza," he was featured in the Warner Bros. movie *The Gold Diggers of Broadway,* an all-talking Technicolor musical in which he introduced "Tiptoe through the Tulips with Me" and "Painting the Clouds with Sunshine." The record of the two songs sold more than a million copies and was his biggest hit; the sheet music for the two also sold exceptionally well. In 1929 he appeared in another Warner Bros. musical, *The Show of Shows,* in which he and Myrna Loy starred in a song-and-dance number called "The Chinese Fantasy." During the 1920s he was also a vaudeville favorite in the United States, often working with two-year advance bookings and eventually making $3,000 per week.

In the 1930s Lucas continued in vaudeville, starred in radio series for NBC (1931–1932) and CBS (1934–1935), and led his own band, Nick Lucas and His Troubadours. He also made short films for Master Art Products, Universal, Vitaphone, and Columbia. He appeared on Al Pearce's radio program from 1936 to 1938, and in 1939 he performed, for six months, in Australia, where he recorded for Regal Zonophone and had a weekday radio show in Melbourne.

Lucas worked frequently in nightclubs and vaudeville during World War II and took part in USO tours. He made short films for the Soundies Corporation of America in 1944, and after the war toured the Hawaiian Islands. In 1947 he began a two-year run in "Ken Murray's Blackouts" in Hollywood and stayed with the show when it appeared on Broadway as the "Blackouts of 1949." He made his national television debut in 1950 on "The Ken Murray Show" and the next year starred on the ABC radio series "Saturday Night at the Shamrock," made short TV films for Snader Telescriptions, and appeared in the musical movie *Disk Jockey.* Until the mid-1960s he remained active in nightclubs and on television while recording for a number of labels, including Diamond, Capitol, Cavalier, Crown, Accent, and Decca.

In the late 1960s Tiny Tim revived Lucas's 1920s hit "Tiptoe through the Tulips"; in 1969 Lucas performed the song at Tim's wedding to Miss Vicki on NBC Television's "The Tonight Show," that program's highest rated episode. In the 1970s Lucas sang on the soundtracks of the films *The Great Gatsby* (1974), *The Day of the Locust* (1974), and *Hearts of the West* (1975); continuing to make appearances across the country, he was a frequent guest on the West Coast radio and television programs hosted by Sam Yorty and Wally George. In 1980 he sang "Tiptoe through the Tulips" aboard a float of the same name in the Pasadena Tournament of Roses Parade. Thereafter he made appearances until late in 1981, when his health began to fail. He died in Colorado Springs, Colorado, where he owned a ranch.

Not only was Nick Lucas one of the most popular singers of his time; he can also be credited with bringing the six-string guitar into vogue. The Gibson Guitar Company manufactured the Nick Lucas Special from his own specifications, and the guitar pick that he helped design—and which carried his name—remained a favorite for several decades. The first of the so-called "crooners," his "intimate" style of entertaining—the directness and simplicity of only the voice and the instrument—allowed him to establish a personal connection with his audiences. Although he was primarily a vocalist on records, his guitar playing, along with his custom-designed instrument, his instruction books, and song folios, which included many of his own compositions, greatly aided in making the guitar the most popular musical instrument of the latter half of the twentieth century.

• Chapters on Lucas appear in Anthony Slide, *The Vaudevillians: A Dictionary of Vaudeville Performers* (1981); James Robert Parish and Michael R. Pitts, *Hollywood Songsters* (1990); Anthony Slide, *The Encyclopedia of Vaudeville* (1994); and Will Hoover, *Picks!: The Colorful Saga of Vintage Celluloid Guitar Plectrums* (1995). Among articles about Lucas are Michael R. Pitts, "Nick Lucas: The Crooning Troubadour," *Focus on Film* 20 (Spring 1975): 56–57; Lynn Simross, "Tiptoeing through a Comeback," *Los Angeles Times,* 5 Aug. 1975; Michael R. Pitts, "An Interview with Nick Lucas," *Screen Thrills* 6 (1976): 49–50; Mark Humphrey, "Nick Lucas: The Artist behind the Name," *Frets,* Apr. 1980, pp. 21–22; James Obrecht, "Nick Lucas: The First Star of Recorded Guitar," *Guitar Player,* Dec. 1980, pp. 44–50; Mark Humphrey, "The New-Fangled Guitar Sound of 1922," *Los Angeles Reader,* 21 Aug. 1981, pp. 1, 4–8; and Michael R. Pitts, "Nick Lucas on Film, Stage, Radio and Records," *Classic Images* 103 (Jan. 1984). Obituaries are in the *Los Angeles Times,* 31 July 1982, and *Variety,* 4 Aug. 1982.

MICHAEL R. PITTS

LUCKMAN, Sid (12 Nov. 1916–5 July 1998), football player and businessman, was born Sidney Luckman in Brooklyn, New York. Little information about his upbringing is available in the public record. In his autobiography, he refers to his parents as "Dad Luckman" and "Mom Luckman"; his mother's given name was Ethel. His father, an immigrant of German-Jewish extraction, ran a trucking business and became an avid football fan. Although the family business had gone into decline, "Dad" Luckman bought his son, before he was eleven years old, an expensive professional-style football, and the parents quarreled about the risks of Sid's playing an especially rough-and-tumble sport.

At Erasmus Hall High School in Brooklyn between 1931 and 1935, Sid Luckman came into his own as a tailback in the then-prevalent single-wing formation and led his team to a New York City championship. His prowess attracted thirty to forty offers of athletic scholarships from colleges nationwide, and Luckman was all but set to attend the U.S. Naval Academy, at the time a major football power. In his senior year at Erasmus Hall, however, he went to Manhattan to watch the college team of Columbia University practice and was introduced to the Lions' coach, Lou Little, whom he immediately saw as a future mentor. Although Columbia College did not offer football scholarships, Luckman happily chose to go there and worked odd jobs to pay his room and board.

As the pivotal player for Columbia, Luckman was a passer, runner, and receiver and also kicked extra points, punted, and played defense, a not-unusual degree of versatility in the days of one-platoon football. Luckman, though, was genuinely exceptional, despite the inability of Little's well-coached teams to achieve winning seasons. Luckman began his senior season by leading Columbia to upsets over Yale and Army, prompting *Life* magazine to put him on the cover of its 24 October 1938 issue with the tagline "Best Passer." Columbia nevertheless ended the season with only one more win, and Luckman's chance of earning the Heisman Trophy as player of the year faltered.

When he graduated, Luckman was wary of the punishing nature of National Football League play. He planned to join his brother in the family's trucking business, instead, and married his sweetheart from Erasmus Hall, Estelle Morgolin (with whom he was to have three children). To his surprise, the coach of the professional Chicago Bears, George Halas, asked to have dinner at the Luckmans' cramped apartment and offered him a contract. As Luckman was to recall, "Halas told me, 'You and Jesus Christ are the only two I would ever pay $5,000.' That was pretty big money then, and so I went" (King, *Greatest Quarterbacks*, p. 81).

Halas believed that Luckman had the superior mental tenacity needed to implement a revolutionary change in professional football. With the assistance of the ex-University of Chicago coach Clark Shaughnessy, Halas trained Luckman in the complexities of the T-formation, in which the quarterback would take the snap directly behind the center and serve as the field general in command of play-making. (By contrast, in the traditional single-wing formation, a quarterback in the modern sense was not used, and the ball might go first to any one of the backs.) In his initial professional season, however, Luckman was more a halfback than a quarterback and had limited success with the new system of offensive play.

But during the 1940 NFL campaign the Chicago Bears became a power to be reckoned with under the leadership of their now-confident quarterback, who had mastered a playbook of 350 offensive patterns. In the championship game of the season, the Bears met the Washington Redskins, to whom they had lost ear-

lier in the season. The result was the greatest rout in an NFL final, with the Bears winning 73-0. So dominant were the Bears that Luckman stayed on the bench for the second half. The "Monsters of the Midway" had been born.

In the following two seasons, Luckman established himself as one of the two premier passers in the NFL, the other being Sammy Baugh of the Redskins. His finest season came in 1943, when he was named Most Valuable Player of the Year. In October 1943, on "Sid Luckman Day" at the Polo Grounds in Manhattan, he engineered a crushing victory over the New York Giants with more than 400 yards in passing, a record at the time, and seven touchdown passes, a record since equaled but not surpassed. In the championship game that year, again against Washington, the Bears won handily, thanks to Luckman's five touchdown passes. (The Bears had also won the championship in 1941.)

Until then exempted from military service in World War II as a married man with children, Luckman enlisted in the Merchant Marine as an ensign stationed at Sheepshead Bay, New York. To the annoyance of some, he was released from duty every Sunday during the football season so that he could play with the Bears. He did, however, go on seven overseas voyages.

During the remainder of his career, the Bears won another championship, in 1946, and placed second in the NFL from 1947 to 1950, the year he retired. In his prime, Luckman was six feet tall and weighed 190 pounds. He had a lifetime passing percentage of 51.8 with 904 completions covering 14,683 yards; he passed for 137 touchdowns and 131 interceptions. He punted 156 times, rushed 204 times, kicked one extra point, returned 11 punts and three kickoffs, and, as a defensive back, had 14 interceptions, one of which he returned for a touchdown. (At a time when faceguards were not yet part of the equipment, he broke his nose perhaps a dozen times, too.) Named all-NFL quarterback in five of his twelve seasons, he was inducted into the College Hall of Fame in 1960 and the Pro Football Hall of Fame in 1965. In 1994 Erasmus Hall named its football field for him, an honor he particularly cherished.

While he played for the Bears, Luckman coached at spring practice at Columbia, Notre Dame, Army, and elsewhere to help collegiate quarterbacks learn the T-formation. He also developed a business career at an auto dealership in Chicago. After retirement, he continued to serve the Bears as a part-time coach and gave of his time gratis to Columbia as a quarterback coach. He enjoyed financial success during the latter part of his life as an executive with Cellu-Craft Products, a Chicago-based food-packaging company. At the end of his life he resided in Aventura (North Miami Beach), Florida, where he died. Funeral services were held at a synagogue in Chicago, and he was buried in Skokie, Illinois.

Historians of football agree with George Halas's assessment of Luckman's impact on the game: "With

Sid, we created a new type of football player—the T quarterback. Newspapers switched their attention from the star runner to the quarterback. It marked a new era for the game. Colleges used Luckman as their model for molding quarterbacks. In Sid's 12 years with the Bears, football was completely revolutionized" (King, *Greatest Quarterbacks*, pp. 83–84). Those who knew him emphasize that he was not only remarkably bright but also uncommonly thoughtful. He never ceased to express gratitude to those who helped him, especially Lou Little and Halas. More than one sportswriter has been moved to write that Luckman led the NFL in "class."

• The Pro Football Hall of Fame in Canton, Ohio, has a useful file on Luckman, with a year-by-year breakdown of his statistics. His autobiography, *Luckman at Quarterback* (1949), conveys the sense that Luckman was a Jimmy Stewart character come to life: a self-described "Jewish boy out of Flatbush" who fulfilled the American dream of 1940s Hollywood. Informative articles about his career include Ira Berkow, "I Remember It All as If It Were Yesterday'" [on the occasion of the Erasmus Hall football field being named for Luckman], *New York Times*, 2 Dec. 1994; Dave Anderson, "Luckman's Legacy: Classiness," *New York Times*, 12 July 1998; Paul Zimmerman, "Revolutionaries," *Sports Illustrated*, 17 Aug. 1998, pp. 78ff.; Ray Robinson, "Football Pioneer," *Columbia College Today*, Fall 1998, pp. 20–23; and the chapter on Luckman in Peter King, *Greatest Quarterbacks* (1999). The 6 July 1998 issue of the *New York Times* has an obituary.

PAUL BETZ

LUENING, Otto (15 June 1900–2 Sept. 1996), musician, was born into the deeply rooted German-American community of Milwaukee, Wisconsin. Both of his parents, Emma Jacobs Luening and Eugene Luening, were musical. His father taught music at the University of Wisconsin and was director of the Milwaukee Musical Society, later the Milwaukee Symphony (1879–1904). In 1912 Eugene Luening moved the family to Munich, where Otto received his early training in flute, piano, and composition at the Royal Academy of Music and gave his first public performance (on flute) in 1916.

After the outbreak of World War I in 1917, Luening moved to Switzerland and transferred to the Zurich Conservatory. He studied with Philip Jarnach and Volkmar Andreae and played flute in both the Tonhalle Orchestra and the Municipal Opera Orchestra under such notable conductors as Arthur Nikisch and Richard Strauss. While in Zurich he performed with a theatrical company, the English Players, founded by James Joyce who was in Switzerland waiting out the war. But his most important and lasting musical experiences came from his private lessons with the composer/pianist Ferruccio Busoni. It was under Busoni's influence that the young Luening's music developed a contrapuntal and harmonic clarity that would resonate throughout his compositions for the rest of his life. Luening's *Sextet* (1918) and *First String Quartet* (1919-1920) are products of this period.

In 1920 Luening moved to Chicago, where he supported himself as a freelance musician in various theater, vaudeville, and movie house orchestras. On Busoni's recommendation, he studied composition with the organist and theorist Wilhelm Middelschulte. He gradually gained a foothold in the Chicago musical scene and in 1922 helped to found and conducted the American Grand Opera Company. The company's first production was the Chicago premiere of Charles Wakefield Cadman's opera *Shanewis*. In 1925 Luening was invited to join the faculty of the newly formed Eastman School of Music in Rochester, New York, led by Howard Hanson. That same year he married Ethel Cod, who had been a voice student at Eastman; they had no children and would divorce in 1959. At Eastman Luening was a vocal coach and opera conductor. He helped found the Rochester American Opera Company and collaborated on various productions with other Eastman faculty members, which included conductor Eugene Goossens, Martha Graham, and theatrical director Rouben Mamoulian. Luening was later made executive director of the opera department.

Luening took a year leave from Eastman in 1928. In 1930 he received two consecutive Guggenheim fellowships (1930–1932), which allowed him to write his first opera, *Evangeline*, based on Henry Wadsworth Longfellow's poem about the migration of the Acadians out of Nova Scotia to New Orleans. By 1932 the Luenings were living in New York City and feeling the effects of the Great Depression when he was offered an assistant professorship at the University of Arizona at Tucson. After teaching there for two years he was selected to head the music department at the newly opened Bennington College in Bennington, Vermont. Luening thrived on the innovative atmosphere at Bennington; his natural talents as an administrator and advocate for the arts, combined with his work as an active performer, composer, and conductor both in Vermont and New York City, brought him into a sphere of activity that would ultimately shape twentieth-century American music. A firm believer in the arts for all Americans, Luening was instrumental in evaluating the role of the arts and humanities in this country. During his tenure at Bennington he was the force behind many of the Vermont state programs established by the Works Progress Administration's federal music project. Many of these projects involved innovative grass roots programs in the areas of music, dance, and the visual arts. In 1937, he was sent on a barnstorming mission by the Association of American Colleges (with a grant from the Carnegie Foundation) to visit colleges and universities around the country "to stimulate interest in music and the arts as integral parts of higher education" (quoted from his autobiography, *The Odyssey of an American Composer*, 1980, p. 407).

During the 1930s American composers mounted a concerted effort to attain a national voice, international recognition, and greater financial stability. Always a staunch advocate for American composers,

Luening was at the forefront of this movement when in 1937 he helped to found the American Composers Alliance. ACA's mandate was to promote the rights of American composers: together with Broadcast Music Inc. (BMI), composers were guaranteed royalty and licensing rights resulting from the commercial performance and broadcasting of their works. Under Luening's presidency the ACA became a resource for composers and made their works available to those interested in using new concert music for performance or broadcast purposes. ACA was also responsible for liaison activities with recording companies to record the works of their composer members; in 1954 Luening helped to found Composers Recordings Inc. for this specific purpose. (CRI still records contemporary music.)

The American Music Center was incorporated in 1939 by Aaron Copland, Otto Luening, Marion Bauer, and others as a nonprofit educational institution to house published and unpublished scores of American composers, assist in the commissioning of new works, and act as a clearinghouse for composers, conductors, and performers seeking information on contemporary American music. The center also acted as a postwar cultural information agency for the State Department. After more than fifty years, the AMC is still a vital part of the American music scene.

In 1944 Luening became Chairman of the music department of Barnard College and was made music director of Columbia University's Brander Matthews Theatre. In that post he conducted the premieres of Gian Carlo Menotti's opera *The Medium* (in 1946) and Virgil Thomson's *The Mother of Us All* (in 1947) as well as Luening's own opera *Evangeline*. In 1949 he was appointed professor of Music at Columbia University, where he became an early pioneer in the field of electronic music. Under the auspices of BMI and the ACA, the first public concert of electronic music (created on reel-to-reel tape recorders) was produced on 28 October 1952 at the Metropolitan Museum of Art. The program included Luening's *Fantasy in Space* and *Low Speed* as well as Vladimir Ussachevsky's *Sonic Contours*. Both *Fantasy in Space* and *Low Speed* are constructed of multitracked flute sounds recorded on magnetic tape. All of the layers are wedded by a deliberate acoustical (often tonal) relationship. Careful manipulation of the sound sources, combined with electronic reverberation, resulted in a rich, impressionistic, yet haunting contrapuntal texture. By to-

day's standards, these compositions seem primitive, but in their historical context, they were groundbreaking.

In 1959 Luening cofounded, with Ussachevsky, Milton Babbitt, and Roger Sessions, the Columbia-Princeton Center for Electronic Music at Columbia University, thus helping to establish electronic music as a viable art form and an accepted component of the university music curriculum. This pioneering work planted the seed for further technological advancements in electro-acoustic, synthesized, and digitized sound sources and helped to bring these advancements and their resulting products into the mainstream. Also in 1959 he married Catherine Johnson Brunson; there were no children from this marriage.

In 1970 Luening was made professor emeritus from Columbia University. Through the remaining decades of his long life he was a vital and active presence on the new music scene, particularly in New York City, writing music, attending concerts, and meeting and offering encouragement to younger composers.

Many of Luening's compositions were inspired by the simplicity and directness of the American landscape, resulting in a musical style innately lyric and fresh while at the same time beautifully informed by the music of the past. Some of his later works were written specifically to evoke the sounds and history of his native Wisconsin—for example, his *Wisconsin Symphony* (1976) and his *Potawatomi Legends* for chamber orchestra (1980). Luening always demanded clarity in his music and sought the same in the music of others. His compositions were at times less visible than those of other composer colleagues, which Luening attributed to a lack of sufficient self-promotion, but he could count an impressive number of major commissions and performances: the Los Angeles Philharmonic, the New York Philharmonic, the Jose Limón-Doris Humphrey Dance Company, and others. The many honors and awards bestowed on him include the National Institute of Arts and Letters, two NEA grants, the American Composers Alliance Laurel Leaf Award, the Brandeis Creative Arts Award and several honorary degrees.

• The major document on Otto Luening's life is his own autobiography, *The Odyssey of an American Composer* (1980). Ralph Hartsock, *Otto Luening: A Bio-Bibliography* (1991), is a comprehensive resource for work lists, performances, and articles by and about Luening. An obituary is in the *New York Times*, 5 Sept. 1996.

GEORGE BOZIWICK

M

MACK, Nila (24 Oct. 1891–20 Jan. 1953), radio writer-producer, was born Nila Mac in Arkansas City, Kansas, the daughter of Don Carlos Mac, a railroad engineer credited with the "first run over the tracks to Guthrie in Indian Territory" in 1889, and Margaret Bowen Mac, a dancing teacher. Her father's family name had apparently been MacLoughlin in a dim Scottish past; Nila was to add the "k" to her name when she entered show business. She attended the local high school, played piano for her mother's dancing school as well as at the local open-air theater, and "won 208 cakes in local cake-walking contests." After her father died as a result of a train derailment in 1907, her mother took her to New York for Chautauqua classes and in 1908 enrolled her at Ferry Hall finishing school in Forest Park, Illinois.

In 1909, with additional lessons in Boston in dancing, voice, and French, Nila Mack took a job with a touring repertory company. Playing leads, she toured, accompanied by her mother, and soon fell in love with Roy Briant, the company's male lead. When the company collapsed in a small Illinois town, Mack, her mother, and Briant started a theater there. It did not succeed and Mack and Briant went on tour again. They were married in Idaho in 1913; although there were no children from the marriage, it lasted until Briant's death.

In 1914 Mack and Briant settled in Chicago, where Briant wrote scripts for Paramount Pictures. Mack signed on with the Alla Nazimova theatrical troupe, appearing with Nazimova in the 1916 film *War Brides* and touring the country, while Briant moved permanently to Hollywood, where he died in 1927. After several years in vaudeville, Mack appeared in 1927–1928 in a number of New York shows—as disparate as the revue *Fair and Warmer* and Ibsen's *A Doll's House*. In 1929 she made her radio debut on the Columbia Broadcasting System, acting in Radio Guild productions that soon were known as the Columbia Workshop.

Because her mother was ill, in late 1929 Mack took the job of program director of the Arkansas City radio station. In 1930 she returned to New York to direct the weekly CBS children's program "The Adventures of Helen and Mary," which then starred Gwen Davies (Estelle Levy) and Patricia Ryan. The cast gradually increased, and in 1934 Mack changed the title to "Let's Pretend." Nila Mack's "Let's Pretend" became the most honored children's program in the history of American radio, as well as the longest-running, ending only when Mack died in 1953. It remained in its thirty-minute Saturday morning slot through two decades, and Mack wrote virtually every script.

"Let's Pretend" never paid much attention to trends and theories in children's literature or to contemporary popular culture in general. During the rise of comic book superheroes and radio adventures featuring heroic cowboys and spacemen, its stories— "Snow White [at times called Snow Drop] and Rose Red," "Hop o' My Thumb," as well as the perennial Cinderella, Red Riding Hood, and so on—were almost exclusively drawn from the popular fairy tales of the Grimms, Hans Christian Andersen, and Andrew Lang. Beginning in 1933, the annual Christmas program, an original script by Mack called "House of the World," recounted Good Will's triumph over Intolerance, Greed, Selfishness, and Poverty. There were other seasonal regulars, including "The Little Lame Prince," presented yearly in support of the March of Dimes and featuring an actor playing America's most famous polio sufferer, Franklin D. Roosevelt.

In the world of "Let's Pretend" there were kings and queens, princes and princesses, witches (often played by Miriam Wolfe) and fairy godmothers (frequently played by Marilyn Erskine), evocative sound effects, and a small orchestra directed by Maurice Brown, magically talking animals, and unfailingly happy endings. Mack later claimed that her sort of tale was particularly well suited to the years of the Great Depression, when a sense of wonderment and sound moral teaching were "good for people." Mack's "Let's Pretend" method also included reliance upon child actors, rather than grownups playing as children. She reasoned that they had the element "needed to produce the effect of magic and unreality best. . . . the childlike wonder." "Let's Pretend" was its own radio workshop, often taking a beginner and turning him or her into a professional. Yet, considering the lengthy run and the vast number of live performances, remarkably few of Mack's child protégés went on to greater things, though the twins Bobby and Billy Mauch had a brief vogue in film, Billy Halop became a Dead End Kid, Walter Tetley grew into a radio teenager, and Sidney Lumet became a major film director.

In the early 1940s CBS allowed Cream of Wheat to sponsor "Let's Pretend." A generation of listeners subsequently had imprinted forever on their inner ears the Cream of Wheat jingle: "Cream of Wheat is so good to eat / And I have it every day / We sing this song, it will make us strong / and it makes us shout Hurray!" Among Mack's original scripts during this period was "Castles of Hatred," a plea against racial prejudice, which also showed that not all stepmothers were evil. The program began to accumulate awards, eventually more than forty. These regularly arose from polls of radio editors across the United States Perhaps most prestigious was the George Foster Peabody/City College of New York Award in 1943 for "the most effective commercial program developed by a national network." That year, "Let's Pretend" was also acclaimed "the national program contributing most to education and public interest" by the American Schools and Colleges Association.

During her years at CBS, Mack also developed "The American School of the Air," "The March of Games," "Children's Corner," "Tales from Far and Near," and "Sunday Morning at Aunt Susan's." During World War II she directed "Let Freedom Ring," a patriotic series for the Department of the Interior. She wrote a children's book called *Animal Allies* (1942), and a story book based upon "Let's Pretend" scripts was published in 1948.

During the early 1950s Mack transformed a number of "Let's Pretend" stories into musical fantasies, but the underlying message was the same. "Let's Pretend" was still going strong when Mack died of a heart attack in her New York apartment. During subsequent decades, various attempts at regular radio or television series based on fairy tales failed; the particular magic of "Let's Pretend" died with Mack.

• The most thorough treatment of Mack's life is Betty Sybrant, "CBS's Nila Mack," in *Little Balkans Review* 3, no. 3 (Spring 1983): 1–15. Frank Buxton and Bill Owen, *The Big Broadcast 1920–1950* (1972), gives valuable program details. Obituaries, including the one in the 21 Jan. 1953 issue of the *New York Times*, provide little information.

JAMES ROSS MOORE

MACKAY, John W. (28 Nov. 1831–20 July 1902), miner and businessman, was born John William Mackay in Dublin, Ireland, the son of parents whose names and occupations are unknown. In the face of poverty, his family immigrated to the United States when Mackay was nine. He briefly attended public school, but his formal education ended when his father died. Faced with supporting his family, Mackay became apprenticed to noted New York shipbuilder William H. Webb. He gained a practical knowledge of tools during his apprenticeship that soon proved invaluable. After learning of the discovery of gold in California, Mackay joined the hordes of men making their way west in the hope of striking it rich.

On arriving in San Francisco, Mackay immediately proceeded to the gold mining fields that followed the Yuba River near Downieville, and for the next several years he enjoyed modest success in placer mining—otherwise known as "panning for gold." By the late 1850s Mackay had joined another rush, this time to Nevada, where the prospect of silver was driving the development of the soon-to-be-famous Comstock Lode. Hardworking and studious, Mackay benefited from taking a more prudent attitude toward financial matters than many of his contemporaries were wont to do, and he often took payment for his services in mining stock. After starting out in Nevada as a pickman, he soon mastered the technically demanding operations that the Com-

stock's deep vein mining demanded and became noted for his ability to construct the timber supports that were so critical to the development of the mines. Popular with fellow miners, Mackay insisted on working side-by-side with his men under the often horrific conditions within the mines, which included intense heat, bad air, and a constant danger from both floods and cave-ins. After advancing to the position of contractor, Mackay struck out on his own, but he experienced a series of discouraging failures before enjoying his first success in partnership with J. M. Walker at Gold Hill, Nevada.

Ironically, Mackay's first success came at a time when the Comstock's continuing vitality was seriously in question. By 1864, declining yields of the more easily reached veins had caused a financial downturn in the area, and a group of California bankers, led by William C. Ralston, had established a near-stranglehold on local operations by acquiring mines and ore mills at distressed prices. In 1864 Mackay and Walker formed a partnership with two San Francisco saloon-keepers, James C. Flood and William S. O'Brien. Walker soon retired and sold his share of the operation to Mackay; while Flood remained in San Francisco and handled business arrangements, the other partners sought to establish themselves in the face of opposition from Ralston and his associates. In the latter part of 1868 they were joined by James G. Fair, who later became a U.S. senator. In 1869, after quietly acquiring undervalued stock shares, the partners were able to gain control of the Hale & Norcross mine. With Fair serving as superintendent, the operation soon became a success. The partners immediately used some of the profits to purchase their own milling facility, thus freeing themselves from dependence on the Union Milling and Mining Company, which ran operations in the area for the Bank of California. Their speculation in two other local mines made them no money, however. In 1867 Mackay had married Marie Louise Hungerford Bryant, an impoverished widow with a young daughter; he later had two sons with her.

In the early 1870s Mackay and his partners acquired the Virginia Consolidated mine and spent considerable time developing it. By 1873 their efforts paid off spectacularly, as the mine began to produce fabulous amounts of gold as well as silver. The partners also acquired the adjoining California mine, which in combination with the Consolidated Virginia produced what came to be known as the "Big Bonanza" and resulted in Mackay and his partners becoming overnight millionaires.

Although the Mackays relocated to San Francisco in 1874 and then to New York in 1876, they spent much of their time in Europe, acquiring magnificent homes in both London and Paris. While Mackay remained involved with the Comstock Lode until the end of his life (and a generous donor to the surrounding community, helping to support, among other causes, a local orphanage and the Roman Catholic church, of which he was a member), he diversified his holdings, which came to include extensive tracts of

California real estate and the Bank of Nevada, which he helped found in 1878. As production on the Comstock generally declined after 1880, Mackay turned his attention in business to other areas, most notably the telegraph industry. In 1883, with the support of James Gordon Bennett, Jr., he founded the Commercial Cable Company, which in the following year laid two underwater cables to Europe. His entry into the telegraph industry pitted Mackay against Jay Gould, whose Western Union then dominated the industry. After an often bitter price war that lasted eighteen months, Mackay emerged victorious, and in 1886 he attacked Gould's land-based monopoly with the creation of the Postal Telegraph Cable Company.

Despite his spectacular successes, Mackay's last years were anything but tranquil. His stepdaughter's 1885 marriage to Don Fernando di Colonna, prince of Galatro, quickly crumbled and ended in divorce. When his old partner Flood attempted to corner the world market in wheat, the debacle resulted in a loss of ten million dollars and a great deal of embarrassment to Mackay. In February 1893 Mackay was shot and seriously wounded in San Francisco by William C. Rippey, a disgruntled speculator who blamed Mackay for his troubles. Although Mackay recovered, he suffered the further indignity of being overbilled by his doctors, who later settled with him out of court when he sought legal redress. A longtime Republican, Mackay turned down opportunities to serve in the U.S. Senate. He was planning a transoceanic cable across the Pacific when he died in London.

Mackay's life story was a classic American rags-to-riches tale. With his partners, he amassed wealth of legendary magnitude and made the Comstock Lode an enduring legend. The state of Nevada in effect grew out of the Comstock's bounty, and the money that flowed from the Big Bonanza into San Francisco helped to make the city the chief financial center in the West.

• No collection of Mackay's papers has been located. His life and career are covered in Oscar Lewis, *Silver Kings: The Lives and Times of Mackay, Fair, Flood, and O'Brien, Lords of the Nevada Comstock Lode* (1947; repr. 1986); Rodman Wilson Paul, *Mining Frontiers of the Far West, 1848–1880* (1963); Grant H. Smith, *The History of the Comstock Lode, 1850–1920* (1943; repr. 1998, with new title, *The History of the Comstock Lode, 1850–1997*, and new material by Joseph V. Tingley); and the still useful *Comstock Mining and Miners* by Eliot Lord (1883; repr. 1959). Mackay's battles with Jay Gould are covered in Maury Klein, *The Life and Legend of Jay Gould* (1986). Obituaries appear in the *Times* of London, 21 July 1902, the *New York Times*, 21, 22 July 1902, and the (New York) *Sun*, 21–23 July 1902.

EDWARD L. LACH, JR.

MACNELLY, Jeff (17 Sept. 1947–8 June 2000), editorial cartoonist, was born Jeffrey Kenneth MacNelly in New York City, the son of Clarence Lamont MacNelly, magazine executive and, later, portrait painter, and Ruth Ellen Fox MacNelly. Young MacNelly grew up on Long Island, attended Phillips Academy in Andover, Massachusetts, and enrolled in the University of North Carolina at Chapel Hill. There, he submitted occasional cartoons to the campus paper and to a local twice-weekly newspaper, the *Chapel Hill Weekly*. He married Marguerite Dewey Daniels on 19 July 1969 and left college without graduating to take a full-time job with the *Weekly*, where his editor was Jim Shumaker, already a picturesque figure in North Carolina journalism circles. MacNelly so valued his apprenticeship under Shumaker that he would later name and pattern his comic strip's title character Shoe after the Chapel Hill curmudgeon. In December 1970 MacNelly joined the *Richmond News Leader*, and sixteen months later, at age twenty-four, he won the Pulitzer Prize for editorial cartooning, proving that neither youth nor affiliation with a relatively small newspaper was an obstacle to winning. At about this time, he shattered another shibboleth—that only editorial cartoonists based at big city papers could be syndicated—when his cartoon started being distributed nationally by the Chicago Tribune Syndicate.

When *Shoe* debuted on 12 September 1977, MacNelly again broke new ground, becoming the first editorial cartoonist to simultaneously produce a widely syndicated daily comic strip. The strip's cast consisted entirely of birds (beginning with the cigar-chewing title character), giving MacNelly the perspective of an outsider from whence he could ridicule aspects of the human condition that his editorial cartoons (with their emphasis on public policy) ignored. As the strip evolved, its focus shifted slightly away from the Shumaker character to other birds, also taken from the cartoonist's life—chiefly, the "Perfesser," a writer on Shoe's newspaper, and the Perfesser's nephew, Skylar. Both were MacNelly: the unathletic Skylar was MacNelly at the age of twelve, and the Perfesser, distinguished by his paper-littered desk, was the mature and equally disheveled MacNelly.

In the spring of 1978 MacNelly collected his second Pulitzer, and the National Cartoonists Society named him the "best editorial cartoonist of the year" for 1977. A year later, NCS awarded him its "Oscar," the Reuben, for cartoonist of the year. And in 1980 he picked up his second Reuben (for 1979), this time specifically for *Shoe*. Then in June 1981 MacNelly announced that he was retiring from editorial cartooning to concentrate on the comic strip. At the time, his marriage was falling apart (after two children, Jeffrey Kenneth and Frank Daniels), and he felt his editorial cartoons were not up to the standard he had set for himself. But by the following March he was back, doing editorial cartoons for the *Chicago Tribune* in addition to *Shoe*. MacNelly won his third Pulitzer in 1985, and on 13 July 1985 he married Martha Scott Perry, with whom he had one child, Matthew Perry; but the marriage did not last long.

In 1987 MacNelly moved from Chicago to Washington, D.C., to be closer, he explained, to his many gag writers who inhabit the nation's capital, and he began illustrating Dave Barry's weekly humor column for the *Miami Herald* (also syndicated for national distribution), quickly establishing himself as a humorous illustrator par excellence. On 22 July 1990 MacNelly married Susan Spekin, and the couple began wintering in Key West, Florida, where the cartoonist took up sculpting and painting whimsical subjects. They bought a farm in Rappahannock County in the Blue Ridge Mountains of Virginia, and MacNelly worked at home, transmitting his cartoons to his syndicate electronically. On 4 January 1993 he launched another syndicated newspaper feature, a single panel gag cartoon called *Pluggers* for which readers submitted ideas. His oldest son, "Jake," assisted on this feature, but when he died in a mountain climbing accident in 1996, MacNelly, disheartened, gave up the cartoon to Gary Brookins, editorial cartoonist at the *Richmond Times-Dispatch*. Four years later, MacNelly was diagnosed with lymphoma; he died five months later but worked on his editorial cartoons and *Shoe* until the end.

Like many cartoonists of his generation, MacNelly initially fell under the influence of Pat Oliphant, an Australian who arrived in the United States in 1965. But for at least the last two decades of his life, MacNelly's work was distinctively his own. He demonstrated complete mastery of cartooning in four separate genres—comic strips, gag cartoons, humorous illustration, and editorial cartooning. But it is for his virtuoso performance in the last one that he is most noted.

Assuming the traditional posture of the authentic journalist, MacNelly was a spectator, more bemused by the passing show than outraged. Politicians may be craven power brokers with self-interest as their chief motivation, but to MacNelly—judging from his cartoons—these political leaders are merely bigger buffoons than the rest of the citizenry and therefore a greater inspiration to laughter. "The basis of effective humor in a political cartoon is ridicule," MacNelly wrote in *The Gang of Eight* (1985). "And ridicule is one of the most powerful and effective nonviolent weapons we humans possess. By subjecting the self-righteous and the pompous to derisive ridicule, we bring them down to earth with the rest of us where we can examine them on our own terms. It's even more fun when these guys have no sense of humor about it all."

One of the most influential cartoonists in the last quarter of the twentieth century, MacNelly inspired a generation of acolytes, among them, Nick Anderson (*Louisville Courier-Journal*), who said: "Editorial cartooning requires artistic talent, analytical thinking, insight, opinion, wit and an ability to think unconventionally. Most cartoonists are strong in only a few areas. MacNelly had them all, in spades. He was a master. But his greatest strength was [in] his [visual] metaphors. As a cartoonist, I can attest that these are the most difficult to conceive. It's easier to fall back on word play or hackneyed images, but MacNelly's metaphors were novel and enlightening" (*A Quiet Genius*).

President Bill Clinton's impeachment was a particularly rich vein of material for MacNelly. One cartoon depicts the GOP elephant firing a cannon labeled "Impeachment." The cannon fires with a massive "Bam!" but the cannon ball discharged is pebble-sized, and it seems to merely dribble out of the cannon's muzzle and bounce (but only once). As a splendid embellishment on both the picture and the message, the elephant is peering into a spyglass, suggesting that he believes his cannon is going to fire its missile a long, long distance. But, of course, it doesn't. MacNelly's metaphors were often cunningly contrived with more than one working part. In a cartoon showing Big Tobacco as a cow with its head in a guillotine, Congress, seated at the cow's side, seems about to milk it but has a hand on a string that, if pulled, would release the guillotine blade and behead Big Tobacco. "I wish he'd make up his mind," says the cow to itself.

MacNelly was more humorist than crusader. Others may be outraged, deploying humor as a weapon, but they are never detached enough to see the purely comic in the shenanigans of their targets. However detached MacNelly may have been, he was never disinterested: his comedy always had a point with which he deflated pretension and revealed the nudity of the emperor. His reaction to the Microsoft break-up showed a hooded medieval executioner labeled the Feds, axe in one hand, the head of a beheaded "Micro-goose" in the other, addressing the head: "We want you to lay smaller eggs—and make 'em square, so they fit in the box." The box is an egg carton labeled "Anti-trust." Of course, the goose, beheaded, won't be laying any more golden eggs.

Although an admitted conservative, MacNelly was essentially just anti-establishment. "I like to think I can call them as I see them," he said. "I don't make a conscious effort to infuse my work with my particular philosophy" (*Chicago Tribune*, 9 June 2000). Perhaps the best capsule summing-up of his latter-day attitude can be found in *Shoe* for 3 January 1997, in which the Perfesser at his cluttered desk muses: "When I first started out in journalism, I was going to be a one-man truth squad. But as time went on, my hair turned gray—and so did the truth."

• Only two collections of MacNelly's editorial cartoons have been published: *MacNelly: The Pulitzer Prize Winning Cartoonist* (1972) and *Directions* (1984). He illustrated *A Political Bestiary: Viable Alternatives, Impressive Mandates, and Other Fables* by Eugene J. McCarthy and James J. Kilpatrick (1978) and a collection of humor columns, *Dave Barry Talks Back* (1991). Reprints of the comic strip *Shoe* have appeared in numerous compilations, beginning in 1978 with *The Very First Shoe*, succeeded by such titles as *The Other Shoe*, *The New Shoe*, *On with the Shoe*, *A Shoe for All Seasons*, *The Shoe Must Go On*, *New Shoes*, *Play Ball*, and *From Couch Potato to Mouse Potato*. MacNelly was pictured on the cover of *Newsweek* for a special report on editorial cartooning (13 Oct. 1980), and he offers opinions on his craft in *The Gang of Eight* (1985), a book surveying the work of several editorial cartoonists. *A Quiet Genius: Remembering Jeff MacNelly*, a booklet compiling numerous articles by his colleagues, was published for the annual convention of the Association of American Editorial Cartoonists in June 2000. The most biographical information in one place can be found in the obituary published in the *Chicago Tribune*, 9 June 2000, and in "The MacNelly Gallery," a special section of the *Chicago Tribune* published on 25 June 2000.

ROBERT C. HARVEY

MACY, R. H. (30 Aug. 1822–29 Mar. 1877), retail merchant, was born Rowland Hussey Macy on Nantucket Island, Massachusetts, the son of John Macy, a merchant ship captain and retail merchant, and Elisa Myrick Barnard Macy. The fourth of six children, he received a meager formal education in his hometown before shipping out on a whaling ship at age fifteen. After four years at sea, Macy went to Boston and tried his hand at a variety of occupations with little success. In August 1844 he married Louisa Houghton, with whom he had a son and a daughter.

During his years in Boston, Macy made two unsuccessful attempts at running a dry goods store. After employment in still another local dry goods operation (this one run by his brother-in-law George Houghton) also proved unsatisfactory, Macy traveled to the West with his brother George in March 1849 and attempted to find fortune in the gold fields of California. When an attempt to set up a retail establishment in Marysville likewise ended in failure, Macy returned to the East and sought yet again to establish himself in the dry goods business, this time in Haverhill, Massachusetts, in April 1851. Although the store went under because of a limited market that was saturated with competition, it was here that Macy first used some of the techniques that would later bring him success: selling for cash (and usually buying with cash), the use of one price that was both cheap and fixed, and the extensive use of creative advertising.

After closing his Haverhill store in mid-1855, Macy briefly attempted to become a "stock and exchange broker" in Boston before heading west once again, this time to Superior City, Wisconsin, where he set himself up as a money and real estate broker only to meet once more with failure, this time as a result of the panic of 1857. Although at the time his prospects could hardly have seemed less promising, Macy was about to realize his greatest success. He opened a small "fancy" dry goods store on the corner of Sixth Avenue and Fourteenth Street in New York City in October 1858. In doing so, Macy faced several handicaps. He was an outsider in the highly competitive Manhattan marketplace, his credit history was made suspect by virtue of his previous business failures, and his store was both modest in appearance (measuring a mere 20 feet by 60 feet) and situated well north of the city's established retail district.

Despite the odds, Macy both survived and thrived in this venture. Although his finances dictated that he occasionally accept merchandise from wholesalers on credit, he held fast to his previous policies of selling at one low fixed price to all customers for cash only.

As he had done in Haverhill, he made extensive use of creative advertising that stood out from the drab pro forma announcements that typified retail advertisements of the day. His advertisements also quoted prices (another departure from conventional business wisdom) and tended to be larger in size than those of his competitors.

Perseverance and careful management carried the store through the difficult years prior to the Civil War. When the wartime spending boom commenced, Macy benefited, as he also did from the continued growth of the city northward. By 1861 the store conducted a mail-order business, and two years later it initiated its first annual clearance sale. Good employees proved to be a boon as Macy slowly expanded his staff. He appointed Margaret Getchell, a distant relative from Nantucket, as store superintendent. As one of the first women to hold such a position of responsibility, she not only ran the store efficiently but also influenced the selection of merchandise, the scope of which continued to expand as the business prospered. Perhaps the most important arrangement concluded by Macy was his agreement with L. Straus & Sons in March 1874, which permitted that firm to sell china, glassware, and silver out of the store's basement. The new arrangement resulted in increased sales and gave Isidor Straus and Nathan Straus their entry into the company that they would later run.

While Macy was firmly in control of his business, his family life became troubling. His main concern centered on his son Rowland's fondness for alcohol. After his son was disciplined for misconduct while a member of the Union Army during the Civil War, Macy took note of an officer, Abiel T. La Forge, who had befriended Rowland, Jr., and invited him to join the firm. La Forge was initially reluctant to join Macy's, but he fell in love with Margaret Getchell and went to work at the store following their marriage in 1869. Convinced of his son's incompetence, Macy made La Forge a partner in 1872 and further enlarged the partnership by adding a nephew, Robert Macy Valentine, in January 1875.

By the mid-1870s Macy's was thriving. In the face of war and economic depression, it generated receipts in the thousands of dollars each day, employed at least 400 people, and had physically expanded several times. Macy himself, however, became increasingly irritable and was dogged by poor health. A long trip overseas failed to restore his vigor, and he died in Paris.

Macy was typical of many contemporary businessmen—having to endure numerous failed ventures, relocations, and protracted struggles to achieve success. With perseverance and shrewd management, however, he became a pioneer in selling at retail large varieties of goods to an urban clientele. Although late in the twentieth century Macy's suffered through nearly fatal financial stress, it remains the world's largest department store. Now at Thirty-fourth Street and Broadway in Midtown Manhattan (a location known as Herald Square), the store that bears R. H. Macy's name is an enduring testament of his vision.

• The best source of information on Macy's life and career is Ralph M. Hower, *History of Macy's of New York, 1858–1919: Chapters in the Evolution of the Department Store* (1943). For more recent scholarship that makes mention of Macy and his role in the history of retailing, see Jeffrey A. Trachtenberg, *The Rain on Macy's Parade: How Greed, Ambition, and Folly Ruined America's Greatest Store* (1996), and Isadore Barmash, *Macy's for Sale* (1989). Obituaries appear in the *New York Times*, 31 Mar. 1877, and the Nantucket *Inquirer and Mirror*, 7 Apr. 1877.

EDWARD L. LACH, JR.

MADDOX, Rose (15 Aug. 1925–15 Apr. 1998), country singer, was born Roselea Arbana Maddox in Boaz, Alabama, the daughter of Charles Maddox and Lula Smith Maddox, sharecroppers. With the onset of the Great Depression, her parents, encouraged by dime-novel descriptions of California, decided to move west. With five of their children—four boys and one girl, ages seven to seventeen—they hitchhiked and rode freight trains across the United States. On arriving in Oakland, California, in April 1933, they lived for several weeks in a large culvert pipe; thereafter, they moved north to Tuolumne, where they unsuccessfully panned for gold. Between 1934 and 1936 the entire family worked as fruit tramps in the San Joaquin Valley. "We weren't going to school at the time, just following the crops," Maddox later recalled. "We'd camp out in the fields, in migrant camps, with all the other people who were in the same situation as us" (quoted in Whiteside, p. 25). Around 1937 the family settled in Modesto. Although only one of the Maddox children knew how to play a musical instrument, eighteen-year-old Fred decided that they should form a band, and he tried to convince the owner of a local furniture store to sponsor them on a Modesto radio station, KTRB. Rose later recounted how she became the band's singer: Fred "had no musical experience at all, but he had a long line of bull. [The furniture-store owner] said, 'I'll sponsor you . . . if you get a girl singer.' Fred said, 'We've got a girl singer.' . . . Fred said to me he didn't know if I could sing or not, but he could hear me a mile away belting out them songs when I'd do the dishes" (quoted in Dawidoff, p. 224).

Initially billed as the Alabama Outlaws, the Maddoxes were an immediate sensation on KTRB, receiving over a thousand fan letters during their first week on the air. Their shows featured wild hollers and yodels, cornpone clowning, and Rose's loud, rowdy vocals—all of which compensated for their lack of musicianship. For the Okies and Arkies who worked in California's agricultural regions, the Maddoxes "offered the music of home for people who no longer had a home" (Whiteside, p. 37). Because of the band's success, Rose dropped out of school halfway through the eighth grade to sing full time. During 1938 and 1939, now billed as the Maddox Brothers and Rose,

the band typically played at least fifteen shows each week, on the radio and at saloons, barn dances, and rodeos. In 1939 they were named the best hillbilly group at the Sacramento State Fair. As a result, they were given a radio contract with the McClatchy Broadcast Network, enabling them to reach all of California, Washington, Oregon, and much of Utah and Arizona. By 1940 they had become more musically sophisticated: they featured a wide-ranging repertoire of songs that included contemporary country hits, call-and-response blues, gospel hymns, lewd novelty numbers, and Woody Guthrie folk songs, playing many of them with a frenetic eight-beats-to-a-bar rhythm. During an era when popular country music was dominated by Hollywood singing cowboys, the Maddox Brothers and Rose were unique—the first hillbilly boogie band. As their "girl singer," the focal point of all their shows, Rose was a pioneer: one of the first women in country music to take center stage.

During World War II three of the Maddox brothers were drafted into the U.S. armed services, and the group temporarily disbanded. In 1942, at her mother's insistence, sixteen-year-old Rose married E. B. Hale, a serviceman and diehard fan of the band. When she gave birth to a son in 1943, Hale denied that the child was his and walked out on the marriage; they divorced a few years later. Following the war, the Maddox Brothers and Rose toughened their musical approach, using amplifiers and hiring side musicians who specialized in rhythm and blues. They also began to wear stage costumes created by Hollywood designer Nathan Turk—gaudy silk suits embroidered with cactuses, wagon wheels, or grapevines, the most eye-catching outfits in country music. In 1946 they signed a recording contract with 4 Star Records, unaware that the label was notoriously unscrupulous. Under the terms of their deal, the band agreed to surrender all royalties, retail proceeds, and song-publishing rights; in return, they were given unlimited quantities of their records to sell at personal appearances. The band recorded over seventy sides for 4 Star between 1946 and 1951. In 1948 they enjoyed a nationwide jukebox hit, the gospel tune "Gathering Flowers for the Master's Bouquet." Among their regionally popular records were a manic version of Hank Williams's "Honky Tonkin'," complete with donkey imitations; the ribald "Sally Let Your Bangs Hang Down," cowritten by Rose; and the proto-feminist "I Wish I Was a Single Girl Again" and "(Pay Me) Alimony." Williams, who wrote the song "How Can You Refuse Him Now?" for Rose, described his admiration for her 4 Star recordings: "When she sings those sacred songs like 'Gathering Flowers,' she sounds just like an angel that's as pure as the drifted snow. Then she'll turn around and do that song of mine, 'Honky Tonkin',' and she'll sound like a gal that's straight out of a cat house" (quoted in Whiteside, p. 101).

Beginning in 1948, transcriptions of the Maddox Brothers and Rose were broadcast from XERB, a giant border radio station in Rosarita Beach, Mexico; as a result, their music was heard as far east as the Mississippi River and as far north as Canada. Their broadening popularity won them an invitation to appear on the Grand Ole Opry in February 1949, billed as "the Most Colorful Hillbilly Band in America." Over the next two years they toured extensively in Texas and Oklahoma, headlined in Las Vegas, and participated in television broadcasts from southern California. In 1952 the band signed a lucrative contract with Columbia Records and made frequent appearances on the national radio program "Louisiana Hayride." Although they made almost forty sides for Columbia between 1952 and 1958, none of their records was a hit. Beginning in 1953, the label encouraged Rose to pursue a solo recording career, suggesting that her brothers' tomfoolery detracted from her own performances. In 1955 her solo single "Tall Men," with guitar accompaniment by Merle Travis, was a jukebox success. Rose felt especially constricted in the family band because of the domineering influence of her mother, the band's manager, who monitored her phone conversations, read her mail, and shooed away all potential suitors. In 1956 the family, with hard feelings all around, agreed to break up the Maddox Brothers and Rose.

As a solo artist for Columbia, Rose attempted a smoother vocal style and released several pop ballads backed with orchestral accompaniment, all of which sold poorly. When Columbia dropped her in 1959, she immediately signed with Capitol Records, and her first single for the label, "Gambler's Love," peaked at number 22 on the *Billboard* national charts. In 1959 she married James Brogdon, a club owner; they had no children and divorced around 1963. For Capitol she recorded a fine gospel album, *The Glory Bound Train* (1960), and had two top-twenty singles, "Kissing My Pillow" and "I Want to Live Again" (both 1960). She was also paired with Buck Owens for several duets dealing with the subject of divorce; "Loose Talk" and "Mental Cruelty" reached the top ten in 1961. The following year she was approached to record a bluegrass album by Bill Monroe, a long-time admirer who felt that her pure, uninhibited voice was poorly suited for contrived pop records. Monroe, Don Reno, and Red Smiley played on *Rose Maddox Sings Bluegrass*, her finest solo work and a groundbreaking effort, one of the few traditional bluegrass albums by a mainstream country star. In 1962 her pop single "Sing a Little Song of Heartache" peaked at number 3, and the following year *Cashbox* magazine named her their Top Female Country Vocalist.

With the rise of Beatlemania in 1964, Capitol Records lost interest in its country artists, and Rose was abruptly dropped from the label. During the late 1960s she toured with Buck Owens and Merle Haggard; she recorded the album *Rosie!* for Starday Records in 1967. Having begun to suffer from serious health problems, she underwent surgery in 1969 to remove half of her stomach. During the 1970s she toured almost constantly and was especially popular on the folk-festival circuit. In 1981 she recorded a crit-

ically acclaimed album, *This Is Rose Maddox*, for Arhoolie Records. Over the next decade she suffered several heart attacks; in 1989 she spent three months in a coma. Released from the hospital in September 1989, she returned to the stage in January 1990. In 1994 she recorded a final album for Arhoolie, *$35 and a Dream*. She died in Ashland, Oregon.

• For the 4 Star recordings of the Maddox Brothers and Rose, the best source is Arhoolie Records' *The Maddox Brothers and Rose, America's Most Colorful Hillbilly Band*, vols. 1 and 2 (1994; 1995). Bear Family Records has reissued their entire Columbia output on *Rockin' Rollin' Maddox Bros. & Rose* and *Maddox Bros. & Rose, Family Folks*. Rose Maddox's solo recordings on Capitol are available on Bear Family's *The One Rose: The Capitol Years* (1993). The best source for information on her life is Jonny Whiteside's fine biography, *Ramblin' Rose: The Life and Career of Rose Maddox* (1997). Nicholas Dawidoff, *In the Country of Country: People and Places in American Music* (1997), devotes a vivid chapter to her career. For articles about Rose Maddox, see Whiteside, "Cowgirl in a Cadillac," *LA Weekly*, 27 Apr.–3 May 1990, and Whiteside, "The Manifest Destiny of the Maddox Brothers & Rose," *Journal of Country Music* 11, no. 2 (1986): 6–15. For her career within the context of country music history, see Bill C. Malone's definitive study, *Country Music USA* (1968).

THOMAS W. COLLINS, JR.

MAHLER, Gustav (7 July 1860–18 May 1911), composer and conductor, was born at Kalište, Bohemia, the son of Bernhard Mahler, a distiller, and Marie Hermann Mahler. Gustav was one of fourteen children, the oldest of the seven who survived past childhood. He could play tunes on an accordion by the time he was four, and began piano lessons at the age of six. He entered the Vienna Conservatory in 1875, concentrating first on piano performance and later on composition. Already familiar with the scores of Richard Wagner's operas, he now sought out a circle of fellow Wagnerians, including the older composer Anton Bruckner, whose work he would acknowledge as an influence.

Mahler graduated from the Conservatory in 1878 and worked first as a piano teacher, then increasingly as a conductor. From 1880 to 1897 he progressed through conducting positions of increasing responsibility in Kassel, Prague, Leipzig, Budapest, and Hamburg. During this time he built a reputation as a masterly interpreter of Mozart and Wagner in particular, and as a passionate, often overbearing taskmaster.

Starting about 1894, Mahler expressed interest in obtaining a post as conductor at the prestigious Vienna Court Opera. Mahler was a Jew, albeit a secular one who was fascinated by Christian ideals, folklore, and mysticism. As such, he could not work for the Austrian imperial court. In 1896 he formally applied for the Vienna conductor's position and simultaneously declared himself a Catholic; he was baptized in February 1897. Mahler was engaged as conductor in Vienna in 1897 and subsequently appointed artistic director. For the next ten years he labored to establish a new standard of excellence at the Vienna Opera. At the same time, his working style aroused antagonism, and he remained a target for the anti-Semitism that flourished in Viennese public life.

Mahler also composed all this time, allocating this activity to the summer months as the demands on his time during the concert season intensified. Besides songs, which he wrote throughout his career, he composed a cantata, *Das klagende Lied*, completed in 1880; he finished a symphony in 1888 and went on to produce seven more over the next sixteen years, developing a distinctive approach to the form. Mahler wrote long symphonies for large orchestras, sometimes adding singers and choruses. His works are crowded with ideas yet highly organized, and they evoke a range of moods from deep dejection to great exaltation, with many shades of agitation and tranquility.

In 1902 Mahler married Alma Schindler, a 22-year-old musician, the daughter and stepdaughter of well-known painters. The Mahlers had two daughters, born in 1902 and 1904.

The year 1907 was a difficult one for Mahler: he began to experience heart trouble, his elder daughter died of scarlet fever and diphtheria, and he yielded to the pressure of criticism by resigning from the Vienna Opera. In June he accepted an engagement with Heinrich Conried, director of New York's Metropolitan Opera, to conduct there starting in January 1908. Mahler's initial experiences in New York were positive; he had the world's best singers to work with, including Enrico Caruso and Geraldine Farrar, and his *Tristan* was well received. However, Conried resigned in February 1908, Mahler turned down the offer of his job, and Otto Kahn, principal patron of the Metropolitan, recruited Giulio Gatti-Casazza from La Scala as director, along with Arturo Toscanini as conductor. Friction ensued between Toscanini and Mahler, who was apparently released from his Met contract in spring 1909. Meanwhile, he conducted two concerts with the New York Philharmonic Orchestra that season and signed a three-year contract to be its leader.

Mahler found the Philharmonic's players "untalented and phlegmatic" and set out to improve their training, a process that did not go smoothly. He also failed to cultivate harmonious relations with the orchestra's managing committee. Here as in Vienna, his performances encountered some hostile criticism, notably from Henry Krehbiel of the *Tribune*; but he also received supportive notices from other reviewers, such as Henry Finck of the *Post*.

While working primarily in the United States, Mahler returned to Europe for extended periods and continued his routine of off-season composing. In 1908 he completed *Das Lied von der Erde*, a work combining characteristics of a symphony and a song cycle for tenor and contralto or baritone, often labeled his masterpiece; in 1909 he finished his Ninth (numbered) Symphony. Mahler began a Tenth Symphony but completed only one movement in fully orchestrated form.

In February 1911 Mahler became too ill to continue working. His New York doctors diagnosed bacterial endocarditis and advised him to seek the care of specialists in Paris. Mahler accordingly went to a French sanatorium, but he obtained no relief and eventually returned to Vienna to die.

As a conductor in New York, Mahler did what he could to exert an influence on American musical life, demanding excellence from performers and often challenging audiences by programming the new music of the day. However, his efforts were frustrated to some extent by the politics of the New York music scene and, of course, his fatal illness. His interest in the work of contemporary composers extended to Americans: he led the Philharmonic in works of Edward MacDowell and Charles Loeffler, and planned to conduct Charles Ives's Third Symphony in the 1911–1912 season.

As a composer, Mahler was an important transitional figure who pursued the Romantic idiom to the limits of its possibilities while increasingly adopting strategies that would characterize the music of the twentieth century. Among modernists, Arnold Schoenberg in particular revered Mahler, who in turn offered Schoenberg moral and material support. In a different sphere, Mahler's use of the orchestra would be a model for Hollywood film composers such as Erich Wolfgang Korngold and Max Steiner (Mahler's pupil). Conductors who championed Mahler's works in the concert hall included Bruno Walter (his longtime associate), Leopold Stokowski, Otto Klemperer, and Dimitri Mitropoulos. From the 1960s through the 1980s Mahler's music surged in popularity, owing largely to the activities of Leonard Bernstein, who recorded each of the symphonies twice and promoted their entry into the standard repertory.

• Many of Mahler's autograph musical manuscripts and letters are in the Pierpont Morgan Library, New York City. Others are in the Library of the Performing Arts, New York, and at Yale, Harvard, Stanford, the University of Western Ontario, and the Moldenhauer Archive in Spokane, Wash. Alma Mahler Werfel's *Gustav Mahler: Memories and Letters* (1946) should be used with caution. The most comprehensive biography is Henry-Louis de La Grange, *Gustav Mahler* (French ed., 3 vols., 1973–1984; English ed., 4 vols., 1973–). Michael Kennedy, *Mahler* (1990), is a useful introduction. Edward Reilly, "Mahler in America," in Donald Mitchell and Andrew Nicholson, eds., *The Mahler Companion* (1999), has valuable information on Mahler's New York years and the American reception of his works. A dismissive obituary by Henry Krehbiel is in the *New York Tribune*, 21 May 1911.

JONATHAN WIENER

MARTIN, Don (18 May 1931–6 Jan. 2000), cartoonist, was born Don Edward Martin in Passaic, New Jersey, the son of Wilbur Lawrence Martin, a school supply salesman, and Helen Henrietta Husselrath Martin. He grew up in the almost idyllic pastoral environs of Brookside near Morristown, and—under the influence of his older brother Ralph, who drew his own comic books—Don began very early to draw, copying characters he saw in animated cartoons. When he was twelve years old, he and a friend produced a newspaper by hand, in single copy, which Martin illustrated; he also maintained an illustrated diary. On graduating from high school in Morristown in 1948, he pursued his artistic bent by enrolling in the Newark School of Fine and Industrial Art; after three years, he transferred to the Philadelphia Academy of Fine Arts, where he studied for a year.

When Martin left the Philadelphia Academy in 1952, he was planning on a career as a fine artist and went to live with his parents, working at various jobs during the day and painting in his spare time. By 1955, however, he was freelancing humorous drawings and doing illustrations, including designs for record album covers. He moved to New York City that year and found a position with a commercial art studio on Canal and Lafayette streets, where he worked for the next year or so. Encouraged by his supervisor, he took his portfolio of comic drawings around the corner and three blocks up Lafayette Street to the offices of *Mad* magazine, where he met the editor, Al Feldstein. Feldstein gave him an assignment and, after a couple of attempts, Martin completed it to the editor's satisfaction.

Making its debut in *Mad* in late 1956, Martin's work was an immediate hit among the magazine's adolescent readership. Before long, the cartoonist was known as "*Mad's* maddest artist," a sobriquet he would proudly carry with him the rest of his life. In association with *Mad*, Martin and a friend, writer E. Solomon Rosenblum, produced in 1962 the first of more than a dozen books of his cartoons, *Don Martin Steps Out*. After the third of these volumes, Martin used as a basis for his books some of his cartoon ideas that *Mad* had rejected, as well as longer stories by writers with whom he collaborated. These pictorial narratives are typically presented one picture to a page, an unusual feature in the genre and one that provides ample display of Martin's artwork. Altogether, his books have sold well over seven million copies worldwide in a dozen languages.

On the cusp of becoming a regular contributor to *Mad*, Martin married Rosemary Troetschal on 14 December 1956; the couple moved to Miami, Florida, in 1957, where they had one son, Max, and divorced in January 1976. Martin married Norma Haimes, a librarian, writer, and sculptor on 23 August 1979, and she became his creative partner thereafter.

In 1982 Martin collaborated on the choreography and designed the sets for a comic ballet, *Heads Up*, for the New World Festival of the Arts in Miami. In 1981 and 1982 the National Cartoonists Society named him the cartoonist of the year in "special features." In 1987 he severed his thirty-year association with *Mad* in a dispute over creators' rights. William Gaines, publisher of *Mad*, had always retained reprint rights as well as ownership of the original art he purchased for the magazine; without an unencumbered right to his work, Martin was unable to enhance his modest income from *Mad* through reprint royalties in the manner he believed he was entitled to. He then went to work for *Cracked*, a *Mad* simulacrum, and shortly thereafter, he and his wife collaborated on a comic strip, *The Nutheads*. Focusing on a typical Martin cast of crazies, the strip began in 1990 and ran until about 1993 but never achieved wide distribution.

Afflicted with a degenerative eye condition, Martin had corneal transplants late in his life, after which he could see to draw only with the aid of a magnifying glass and an uncomfortable contact lens that covered the entire eye. He and his wife became vocal advocates of creators' rights, and he continued to draw. He remained at home for most of his terminal struggle with cancer but died at Baptist Hospital in Miami.

The graphic insanity for which Martin is celebrated is readily discernible in almost any sample of his work. Virtually all of his characters have the same angular anatomy: limbs bent at right angles, toes turning up, pinky fingers elevated. They are nearly all anvil-jawed, jug-eared, bug-eyed, knock-kneed, and hinge-footed, with bulbous noses flattened onto their faces. Martin's affection for Charlie Chaplin's splay-footed stance can be seen throughout his work, and the influence of big-foot magazine cartoonists John Gallagher and Tom Henderson (favorites of his) can also be seen in the loose-limbed and bottle-nosed renderings. He admired Virgil Partch for his zaniness and Al Hirschfeld for his graceful line. Martin's sense of humor was aggressively physical. Inspired by the Three Stooges and Laurel and Hardy, he subjected his characters to a gamut of abuse, to which, after their initial comedic reaction, they seemed wholly impervious. A man at a bus depot sees a door marked "the quick way out," pulls the doorknob, and—SPLOP!—the door flattens him. A man goes up to a "Change" machine, inserts a bill, and—SPLIF!—becomes a woman. Even in the absence of abuse, the comedy was physical, depending heavily on the visual character of the medium. A woman in a French bistro nibbles at a dainty repast of frog legs only to—PAF!—see them become the disembodied legs of a prince. A hotel guest comes to the front desk to complain about cockroaches in his room and discovers that the desk clerk is a giant cockroach with four arms and quivering antennae.

Quoted in *Contemporary Graphic Artists*, Martin denied any high-flown satirical purpose in his cartoons: "The purpose of my cartoons [is] to be comical, both visually and in content. . . . The sillier the better. The anatomical distortions are the way they are because they strike me as funny. . . . I love Laurel and Hardy's slapstick and nonsense. Doors slamming in people's faces are fun. Pies in the face are fun." The madcap names Martin gave some of his characters reflect the same purpose: Fester Bestertester, often accompanied by the pin-headed Karbunkle, and the colossally inept superhero Captain Klutz, and the zany psychiatrist Dr. Fruitcake B. Fonebone. In pursuit of the same manic muse, Martin carefully concocted onomatopoeic sound effects. "Shklip" is the sound of construction workers tossing wet concrete at each other;

"splop" is a surgeon dropping body parts into a doggie bag; "fagroon" is a collapsing skyscraper. In an interview in *Cartoonist PROfiles*, Martin revealed something of his creative process for sounds: "I just did [a drawing] of somebody falling, and he goes 'splabadap.' But in this particular picture it seemed like the sound was too long, so I made it 'spwap.' Actually, a body falling down from a height of a few stories would go 'splabadap' because it would bounce a little bit whereas 'spwap' is like getting slapped in the face with a fish."

Although his cartoons were loud and boisterous, Martin himself was soft-spoken and mild-mannered—"the living antithesis of what he drew," according to Nick Meglin, an editor at *Mad*. Among Martin's favorite recreations were canoeing into the Everglades and camping in the silent wilderness.

• Martin's books include *Mad's Maddest Artist Don Martin Steps Out* (1962), *Mad's Maddest Artist Don Martin Bounces Back* (1963), and *Don Martin Drops Thirteen Stories* (1965), all with E. Solomon Rosenblum; with Dick DeBartolo, Phil Hahn, and Jack Hanrahan, *The Mad Adventures of Captain Klutz* (1967); with DeBartolo, *Mad's Don Martin Cooks Up More Tales* (1969), *Mad's Don Martin Comes On Strong* (1971), and *Don Martin Steps Further Out* (1975); with DeBartolo, Don Edwing, Mark Jacobs, and John Gibbons: *Mad's Don Martin Digs Deeper* (1979); *Mad's Don Martin Carries On* (1973), *The Completely Mad Don Martin* (1974, reprints), *Don Martin Forges Ahead* (1977), *Don Martin Grinds Ahead* (1981), *Captain Klutz II* (1983), *Don Martin Sails Ahead* (1986), and *Don Martin's Droll Book* (1992). The best single source of biographical data is *Contemporary Graphic Artists*, vol. 2 (1987). Extensive interviews appear in *Cartoonist PROfiles*, Dec. 1981; Mar. 1982; and Dec. 1990. Obituaries can be found in the *Miami Herald* and the *New York Times*, both 8 Jan. 2000.

ROBERT C. HARVEY

MARTIN, George Madden (3 May 1866–30 Nov. 1946), novelist and social activist, was born in Louisville, Kentucky, to Frank Madden, a bookseller, and Anne Louise McKenzie Madden. It has been said that she was christened Georgia May but later changed her first name to "George" for literary reasons. She herself explained in the postscript of her 29 March 1917 letter to Henry Watterson, editor of the *Louisville Courier-Journal*: "I almost wrote it Georgia or Georgie since you so dislike the masculine assumption—but you see I was named a surname for a cousin, a Dr. George."

As a child, young George frequently missed school because of illness and was tutored at home, where she had the full use of her father's library. At age fifteen she left school and was sent to health resorts in the Deep South. From 1890 to 1892, after her return to Louisville, she was a teacher at the Wellesley School.

On 15 June 1892 George Madden married Attwood R. Martin, a Louisville resident of French descent; their marriage lasted until the death of the husband, fifty-two years later, in 1944. The Martins were a congenial couple: he was a banker and real estate agent, prominent in civic affairs, and also interested in literature; she combined literary and educational interests in her writing and was deeply concerned about the role of women and blacks in southern society. Although childless, Martin created lovable little girls—the endearing but fictional Emmy Lou and Abbie Ann and Letitia.

Martin's first book, *The Angel of the Tenement* (1897), is only 134 pages long. The sentimental tale of a toddler named Angel, it tells how she suddenly appears in a tenement, is eventually found by her distraught mother, and thereafter comes under the wing of her tenement caretaker, who happily becomes her nanny. Martin never disavowed this apprentice work, yet she seldom mentioned it later as among her publications.

During the summer of 1898, in Pewee Valley, a village east of Louisville, George Madden Martin, Evelyn Snead Barnett, and Annie Fellows Johnston organized the Authors Club, which met weekly to criticize works in progress and share information on publishing opportunities. For the next three decades, club members met in Louisville, with the majority becoming highly successful authors. Out of this association came Martin's masterpiece, *Emmy Lou, Her Book and Heart*, serialized in *McClure's Magazine* with book publication in the fall of 1902. Emmy Lou immediately became "the most charming child in Kentucky literature, a genuine creation," according to bibliophile John Wilson Townsend. And Emmy Lou's troubles at school prompted educators nationwide to change their teaching methods.

One of Martin's early problems was her name. To avoid gender confusion, particularly in magazine publications, she usually put Mrs. Attwood Martin (frequently misspelled "Atwood") in parentheses below her name. (Unlike George Eliot, she had no need to disguise her gender.) Her masculine name was a handicap for this very feminine woman, who was described by Evelyn Snead Barnett as "fair-skinned, blue-eyed, sunny-haired, tall but delicately built." Barnett goes on to say: "Perhaps the keynote of her character may be found in her ever-present desire to be surrounded by an atmosphere of happiness. From a desire to make her friends happy and have things 'go smoothly,' she is ready on the instant to sacrifice her own comfort and predilections" (p. 3413). Martin appears serene and poised in a photograph taken in 1905 at Mark Twain's seventieth birthday celebration at Delmonico's restaurant in New York City.

Martin's next books were also serialized: *The House of Fulfilment* (1904); *Letitia, Nursery Corps, U.S.A.* (1907); and *Abbie Ann* (1907). In 1914 *Selina* appeared, with the title character the forerunner of the southern New Woman. Selina, who refuses to consider marriage as social security, fights for her independence, declaring, "How I'll get the independence I'm sure I don't know now, but I will get it." Readers never learn if Selina gains that independence for, as usual, Martin ended her story without a hint of its denouement, thereby illustrating the fact that life's problems cannot be resolved easily or quickly.

Two years later, a grown-up Emmy Lou reappeared in *Emmy Lou's Road to Grace* (1916), but this book was never as successful as its predecessor. *A Warwickshire Lad*, Martin's story of Shakespeare's boyhood, also came out in 1916 and was a fitting contribution to the Shakespeare tercentenary.

The first phase of George Madden Martin's career was now over, with World War I bringing abrupt change to her marriage and home life; no longer would writing, gardening, civic and social obligations be her full-time occupations. Attwood, she wrote her friend Ida Tarbell, was eager to join the army. At age fifty-one, her husband was ineligible for active service, but his business experience fitted him for a captaincy in the Quartermaster Corps, on the recommendation of Tarbell and others. Martin, with Tarbell's backing, then joined the staff of the *Red Cross Magazine*. By 1918, her husband was on duty in Washington, D.C., and she was in New York City.

After the war, Martin's fiction became a vehicle for various causes: *Children in the Mist* (1920) was her attempt, in eight sketches, to reveal the plight of black people; despite the book's authoritative tone, black leaders felt Martin's experience was based largely on a knowledge of her servants. The reviewer for the *Nation* (4 Sept. 1920), however, wrote that "Mrs. Martin avoids both sentiment and indignation" and "lets the stern implications arise in their bare and tragic force." *March On* (1921) is still a compelling novel about the experiences of women whose husbands were determined to go into battle. Each of these women displays an equally determined will to carry on alone in the empty aftermath of death.

Martin published three thoughtful articles in the *Atlantic Monthly*: "American Women and Public Affairs" (Feb. 1924), "American Women and Paternalism" (June 1924), and "The American Woman and Representative Government" (Mar. 1925). The lengthy article on paternalism is the most biographically significant, for in it she describes scenes from her childhood. The one on public affairs discusses her experiences while crisscrossing the United States. Through interviews and general conversation, she learned that American women, despite their being given the right to vote in 1920, continued to be apathetic about public affairs—a conclusion difficult for such a champion of causes to understand. She herself was heavily involved in representative government from 1920 through 1934: as an officer of the Women's Division of the Democratic National Committee, of the Kentucky Repeal and Regulation League, and of the Women's Organization for National Prohibition Reform. In 1920 she began a fourteen-year term on the Board of the Commission on Interracial Cooperation; in the 1930s she was chairman of the Association of Southern Women for the Prevention of Lynching.

Martin's last book, *Made in America*, was published in 1935. Its plot, the story of an immigrant who rose from rags to riches, is reminiscent of the rise to power of S. S. McClure, her early publisher and patron. The

likeness ends when hero Sheridan McNeill makes his vast fortune by illicit means.

In 1937, when her husband was forced to retire because of ill health, Martin had little time for writing. However, she did complete "Jane Todd Crawford, An Epic Tale" for Kentucky's Jane Todd Crawford Day, 13 December 1942. (In 1809 Crawford, the patient of Dr. Ephraim McDowell, had survived the first successful surgery for the removal of an ovarian tumor.) After her husband's death, Martin returned to New York, but soon was advised by her physician to go back to Louisville and await her own demise, which came as the result of myocarditis, a heart condition.

In her last years Martin was known best for her role in civic, state, and national politics. She was labeled a southern writer in the obituaries, but her writing was becoming dated: "just as fine wines are dated, and mellowed picture-painting, and silver with the patina on it," according to a Louisville friend, who added, "She remained all her life very truly a lady of letters." Today, the writing of George Madden Martin still has distinction and charm, revealing a southern mind at work in a long-ago world of the South.

• The papers of George Madden Martin were burned when a fire destroyed her Anchorage, Kentucky, home before World War I. Papers later placed in a bank vault were destroyed during the Louisville flood of 1937. Scattered letters by Martin can be found in the Manuscript Department, Ekstrom Library, University of Louisville; Tarbell Collection, Pelletier Library, Allegheny College, Meadville, Penn.; Bancroft Library, the University of California, Berkeley; and Houghton Library, Harvard University. There are snapshots in the Annie Fellows Johnston Papers, Regional and Family History Center, Willard Library, Evansville, Ind. Martin discussed her first publishing experiences in Gelett Burgess, ed., *My Maiden Effort* (1921), pp. 166–71. See also "George Madden Martin," in John Wilson Townsend, ed., *Kentucky in American Letters, 1784–1912*, vol. 2 (1913), pp. 198–202, and Evelyn Snead Barnett, "George Madden Martin," in the *Library of Southern Literature*, vol. 8 (1907), pp. 3413–16. An obituary is in the *New York Times*, 2 Dec. 1946.

MARY BOEWE

MATHEWS, Eddie (13 Oct. 1931–18 Feb. 2001), major league baseball player and manager, was born Edwin Lee Mathews in Texarkana, Texas, the son of Ed Mathews, a Western Union operator, and Eloise Hess Mathews. The family moved to Santa Barbara, California, where Eddie attended public school. His father, a former semiprofessional ballplayer, groomed him for a big-league career, and Eddie starred in football and baseball at Santa Barbara High School.

At one minute past midnight on the night of his graduation in June 1949, Boston Brave scout Johnny Moore signed Mathews to a contract for $6000 and shipped him across the country to begin his professional baseball career at High Point-Thomasville in the North Carolina State League. He hit .363 with 17 homers and 56 RBI in just 63 games, earning a promotion to Atlanta in the Double A Southern Association for 1950. There he clubbed 32 home runs and drove in 106 runs. With the draft looming over him, he joined the navy as the Korean War threatened to sidetrack his new career. His father, however, contracted tuberculosis and as an only son Mathews was granted a dependency discharge. He managed to play only 49 games with Milwaukee (American Association) and Atlanta late in 1951, but the Braves had seen enough to call him up to the major league club at age twenty in 1952.

His 25 homers, including the first three-homer game ever by a rookie, offset a .242 batting average and showed his promise as a bona fide slugger. At that propitious time, the Braves, upstaged by the Red Sox in Boston, ended fifty years of major-league franchise stability and moved to Milwaukee for the 1953 season. The 6'1", 190-pound Mathews and the new community hit it off from the start. He blossomed with a league-leading 47 home runs, a .302 average, and 135 RBI and helped make Milwaukee a huge success as a new baseball town. Mathews married a Milwaukee woman, Virjean Lauby, with whom he had three children: Eddie, Jr., John, and Stephanie.

When the inaugural issue of *Sports Illustrated* appeared in August 1954, Eddie graced its cover. He worked hard to overcome his early reputation as a mediocre defensive third baseman and became quite proficient with the glove, eventually leading the league in fielding in 1963. He drew praise for his solid work ethic and his competitive drive, which translated into constant hustle and a readiness to fight when it seemed appropriate. When Hank Aaron joined the team as a rookie in 1954, the Braves had a one-two punch that went on to hit 863 homers, beating Babe Ruth and Lou Gehrig by four as the most prolific teammates ever. While Aaron famously wound up with an all-time record 755, Mathews tapered off after 1959 and wound up with 512. During their years together, Aaron barely led, 442-421, with Mathews hitting over thirty homers for nine straight seasons.

Mathews's career flourished, as he and Aaron teamed up with Joe Adcock, Johnny Logan, Warren Spahn, Lew Burdette, and others to challenge the Brooklyn Dodgers as the best team in the National League in the late fifties. In many ways, the 1957 season was the high point of his career. Milwaukee won its first pennant and faced the New York Yankees in the World Series. Although Mathews went hitless in the first three games, he won game four with a homer in the ninth, scored the only run of game five to win that one, and wrapped it all up with a diving stop off Moose Skowron in the last game, turning a likely three-run double into a force-out to end the series with a 5-0 victory. It was, he said, "the biggest thing that ever happened to me."

The following season the Braves repeated as National League champs, but this time they lost the series to the Yankees and never made it back during the rest of Mathews's stay with the club. He had his last monster season in 1959, leading the league with 46 homers and batting .306. His output fell to 39 four-baggers in 1960 and never again topped 32.

Even though Mathews—with a sweet left-handed swing acclaimed one of the smoothest ever by Ty Cobb—had seemed the more likely of the Braves duo to beat Babe Ruth's career home run record, Aaron proved to have more staying power. After 1961, Mathews never hit over .265, and he was clearly on a downward trajectory.

In 1966, the Braves moved once again, this time to Atlanta. Mathews had the distinction of being the only Brave to play in all three of the franchise locations—Boston, Milwaukee, and Atlanta. In addition, he had played for minor league teams in both Milwaukee and Atlanta before making the big leagues, so he brought major league ball to two of his three minor league stops. However, following a modest .250 season in 1966, the Braves traded Mathews to the Houston Astros, who moved him to the Detroit Tigers late in the 1967 season. There he finished out his career in 1968, making his third World Series appearance as a bit player in the championship Tiger season. He greatly regretted that he was unable to finish his career as a Brave—hitting his 500th homer in a Houston uniform did not bring him the satisfaction that it might have.

Mathews ended his career with very impressive statistics. He was only the seventh player to amass over 500 home runs, and he collected 2,315 hits, drove in 1,453 runs, scored 1,509 runs (batting ahead of Aaron helped), walked 1,444 times, and struck out 1,487. His lifetime batting average over 2,388 games was .271, and he was a ten-time all-star.

In the seventies, divorced from his first wife, Mathews married and divorced twice more before marrying the former Judy King in 1981 and spending the rest of his life with her in Del Mar, California.

From late in the 1972 season until midway through 1974, Mathews managed the Braves, compiling a 149-161 record overall. The highlight of his managerial tenure came in April 1974 when his longtime teammate, Hank Aaron, hit his 715th home run to break Babe Ruth's mark. Despite a 50-49 team record, Mathews was fired in mid-season, in part because of excessive drinking. He held various positions with the Braves, the Milwaukee Brewers, and the Oakland Athletics following his managing career.

At millennium's end, as baseball sages pondered the state of the game, Eddie Mathews scored again. He had been elected to baseball's Hall of Fame in 1978. In 1999 the Society for American Baseball Research voted him the 31st greatest major league player in history. He trailed only Mike Schmidt, Brooks Robinson, and George Brett among all the third basemen ever to play the game. By this time, however, his health was failing. An accident in 1996 had crushed his pelvis, and he was never the same after that. He fought various ailments but finally succumbed in San Diego to complications from pneumonia.

• Information on Eddie Mathews can be found in his autobiography, *Eddie Mathews and the National Pastime* (1994). Obituaries are in *Sports Illustrated* and in the *Atlanta Constitution* and the *San Diego Union-Tribune*, 19 Feb. 2001.

JOHN R. M. WILSON

MATURE, Victor (29 Jan. 1915?–4 Aug. 1999), stage and screen actor, was born in Louisville, Kentucky, the son of M. G. Mature, an Austrian immigrant scissors grinder who later became a business executive, and Clara Mature (maiden name unknown), who was of French-Swiss ancestry. Sources differ as to his year of birth. Victor was their only surviving child, his brother and sister having died young. Educated first in public schools and then in parochial institutions, Victor completed his studies at St. Joseph's Academy, the Kentucky Military Institute, and the Spenserian Business Institute. He put his business school training to good use as early as the age of fifteen, when he made money as a candy wholesaler and invested his profits to become a restaurant owner. In 1935 Mature sold his restaurant and moved to California, where he began studying acting at the Pasadena Community Playhouse. Late the following year, in November 1936, he received his first stage acting part, in the World War I drama *Paths of Glory*. Mature, who had come to the Los Angeles area with very little money, secured a fellowship with the Playhouse, which paid his tuition and allowed him to work with his mentor, Playhouse director Gilmor Brown.

While working at the Playhouse, Mature was discovered by producer Hal Roach, who gave him his first film role, in *The Housekeeper's Daughter* (1939), which starred Joan Bennett. Although the role was small, it generated 20,000 fan letters for the new star. His first starring role, as a caveman in *One Million B.C.* (1940), also produced and directed by Roach, gave him a chance to display his remarkably muscular physique. Soon, through the efforts of studio promoters and his own flair for publicity, he became Hollywood's first real "hunk," described as "square-jawed," "intense," and "Mr. Beautiful." Mature, who enjoyed being admired for his looks and physical attributes, wryly said: "I don't mind being called 'Glamour Boy,' as long as that check comes on Friday."

In 1940 RKO picked up half of Mature's contract from Roach, for $250 a week, and he worked for that studio for seven years, starring in such films as *No, No Nanette* (1940), *Song of the Islands* (1942), and *My Gal Sal* (1942). Eager to generate more publicity for himself while displaying his acting talent, Mature appeared on Broadway during this time, starring in Moss Hart's production of *Lady in the Dark* (1941), opposite Gertrude Lawrence. The play received good reviews, with *New York Morning Telegraph* critic George Freedley noting that Mature played his role as a movie idol "in manly fashion." During one scene in the play, before Mature's character enters the room, he is described as "a beautiful hunk of a man," and the classification stuck. Soon critics and fans were calling him the "greatest matinee idol since Rudolph Valentino" (*Current Biography Yearbook 1951*, p. 417). David Thomson wrote in *Film Comment* (Nov. 1999, p. 74) that Mature "had a rare, adroit innocence, more musk than muscle, an ease and liberty" with the roles that he played.

In 1941, while on loan from RKO, Mature worked with Twentieth Century–Fox for the first time, appearing with Betty Grable in the mystery *I Wake Up Screaming*. For United Artists he starred in *The Shanghai Gesture* (1941). During World War II he returned to RKO, appearing in the musical comedies *Footlight Serenade* (1942, with Betty Grable) and *Seven Days' Leave* (1942, with Lucille Ball). Also in 1942 Mature enlisted in the U.S. Coast Guard and saw military duty in the North Atlantic, eventually rising to the rank of chief boatswain's mate. While in the service, he participated in war-bond tours and took advantage of assignment to shore duty to perform in the Coast Guard musical production *Tars and Spars* (1944–1945), a recruitment vehicle.

After the war, Mature was rewarded with a series of contracts from Twentieth Century–Fox, which had purchased his services from RKO in 1941. His first role after military service, as the consumptive gambler Doc Holliday in the classic John Ford western *My Darling Clementine* (1946), was perhaps his greatest performance. Starring as doomed parolee Nick Bianco in the film noir *Kiss of Death* (1947), Mature again gained recognition for his acting talent, allowing movie audiences to see beyond his good looks and winning smile. These successes were followed by the musical comedies *Wabash Avenue* (1950) and *Million Dollar Mermaid* (1952); action adventure tales *Dangerous Mission* (1954) and *Betrayed* (1954); and the western *Chief Crazy Horse* (1955). In the late 1940s and early 1950s Mature starred or costarred in several of the "great sagas" of the period. He played the title character in Cecil B. De Mille's *Samson and Delilah* (1949), the "captain" in *Androcles and the Lion* (1952), Demetrius in *The Robe* (1953), Horemheb in *The Egyptian* (1954), and the title character in *Demetrius and the Gladiators* (1954). All of these appearances confirmed his star quality but capitalized on his "beefcake" appeal at the box office, prompting film reviewers to claim that Mature was hired more for his good looks than for his acting ability.

By the mid-1960s Mature's career as a leading man was over, but he still found work in Hollywood, mostly by lampooning his "glamour boy" image. He played a has-been movie actor in the forgettable Peter Sellers satire *Caccia alla Volpe* (*After the Fox*; 1966) and appeared in the spoof comedy *Won Ton Ton, the Dog Who Saved Hollywood* (1976). In his last film role he played Samson's father in a made-for-television remake of *Samson and Delilah* (1984). All told, Mature appeared in more than fifty films, an impressive body of work by any standard.

Mature was romantically linked with some of Hollywood's most attractive stars, including Rita Hayworth and Lana Turner. He was married five times, to Frances Evans (married 1938, divorced 1941); Martha Stephenson Kemp (married 1941, divorced 1943); Dorothy Stanford Berry (married 1948, divorced 1955); Joy Urwick (married 1959, divorced 1969); and Lorey Sabena, an opera singer whom he married in 1974. His final marriage produced a daughter, Victoria, who trained to follow in her mother's footsteps. Mature died in Rancho Sante Fe, California.

Never taking himself or his acting too seriously, Mature liked to tell interviewers that he was a better golfer than actor. Indeed, many criticized him as "wooden" on screen, with an ever-present grin. But, like many of the female stars of his era, his talent was overshadowed by his good looks. He brought to his roles a low-key and casual disinterestedness, attributes desperately needed in sagas like *Samson and Delilah*. According to critic David Thomson, Mature had the particular ability to allow the viewer to "glimpse the abiding nonsense of a movie, hiding within its ponderous self-importance" (*Film Comment*, Nov. 1999). Combining sex appeal, versatility, and an understated acting ability, he thrived as a leading man in Hollywood for more than twenty years.

• A good early survey of Mature's life and film career can be found in *Current Biography Yearbook 1951*, pp. 417–19. Early career summaries appear in the *International Motion Picture Almanac, 1950–1951*; and *Winchester's Screen Encyclopedia* (1948). An article with photographs appears in *Life* 10 (7 Apr. 1941): 65–66. See also the *New York Daily News*, 7 Mar. 1941; *New York Herald Tribune*, 2 and 23 Feb. 1941; *New York Post Magazine*, 15 Dec. 1945, p. 12, 18, Oct. 1947, p. 12, and 10 Apr. 1949; *Photoplay*, Apr. 1942, p. 52, and May 1942, p. 57; and the *Saturday Evening Post*, 18 July 1942, pp. 24–25. David Thomson, *Film Comment* 35, no. 6 (Nov. 1999): 74, offers a laudatory obituary, as do the editors of *People*, 23 Aug. 1999, p. 137. See also the obituary in *Maclean's*, 23 Aug. 1999, p. 9.

BARBARA BENNETT PETERSON

MAXWELL, William (1733–3 Nov. 1796), revolutionary war general, was born near Newtonstewart, County Tyrone, in northern Ireland, the son of John Maxwell and Ann Maxwell (maiden name unknown), farmers. William Maxwell most likely descended from those members of the Maxwell clan of southwestern Scotland who were in Ireland since the late seventeenth century. At age fourteen he accompanied his parents to America, where they settled on a small tract of land in northwestern New Jersey, along the Delaware River, just south of present-day Phillipsburg in Morris (soon to be Sussex and later Warren) County. Maxwell appears to have had an elementary school education, probably at one of the parish schools in Ireland. A British officer referred to Maxwell as a former schoolteacher, which, however, was unlikely. Maxwell and his parents were staunch Presbyterians throughout their lives.

The traditional claim that Maxwell served in the ill-fated expedition of General Edward Braddock in 1755 is incorrect; he may have delivered flour to one of the army's staging areas. During the mid-1750s Maxwell probably had duty as one of 250 militiamen who by rotation maintained a blockhouse in Sussex County for the purpose of guarding against marauding Delaware Indians.

In 1758 Maxwell signed on as an ensign in the New Jersey Regiment (the Jersey Blues) and served in the New York campaign during the French and Indian War. Although present at the attack on Fort Ticonderoga on 8 July 1758, he was assigned to the rear and did not participate in the unsuccessful bloody assaults against the fort. After the French withdrawal, Maxwell had fort-building duty along Lake Champlain. The regiment returned home in November, and Maxwell later reenlisted for the period of April to November 1760 as a lieutenant. He and his regiment joined General Jeffery Amherst's Canadian expedition, and he was probably with the regular-provincial force at the capture of Montreal. Maxwell did not reenlist in the reduced New Jersey Regiment of 1761. Instead he accepted a position as a post commissary (strictly civilian status) with the British army. After brief duty at Schenectady and other forward posts, probably including Montreal (where he owned two small houses), Maxwell embarked on a long stint as commissary to a detachment of the Royal American (60th) Regiment at Fort Michilimackinac, at the straits between lakes Huron and Michigan.

At Michilimackinac, Maxwell profited on his own account by trade in goods with ever-present Indian groups and fur traders. A lifelong bachelor, Maxwell had an ardent desire to marry, but Michilimackinac, of course, presented scant opportunity; his reputedly unbecoming and slovenly appearance and his frugal Scottish ways and speech did not offer much enticement. Rather remarkably, however, he did have for a while a mistress, Sally Aisne, a middle-aged Oneida woman who was a prominent Indian trader in her own right and later a large landowner along the Thames River. Maxwell acquired as slaves several "Negro wenches," whom he soon sold.

When the Royal American Regiment was reassigned to duty in the West Indies in late 1772, Maxwell returned to New Jersey and soon enmeshed himself in the revolutionary movement, becoming a member of the Sussex County Committee of Safety and a delegate to the first and second New Jersey Provincial Congresses. On 29 October 1775 the Provincial Congress named Maxwell colonel and commander of the "Western Battalion," which was incorporated into the Continental army on 7 November 1775, with Maxwell commissioned as colonel and commander of what was now the Second New Jersey Regiment.

In March 1776 Maxwell and his troops joined the American force that, having invaded Canada, was retreating from its repulse at Quebec. As the New Jersey Continentals covered the rear of the American army, Maxwell skillfully fended off the enemy and avoided capture. Under the overall command of General John Sullivan, Maxwell and his regiment fought in the ill-fated assault on the British post at Three Rivers on 8 June. In anticipation of a British attack on Fort Ticonderoga during the summer and early fall of 1776, Maxwell and his troops were stationed at Mount Independence, across from Ticonderoga. On 23 October 1776 Congress elected Maxwell brigadier general.

With the British deferring further invasion from Canada during the winter of 1776–1777, Maxwell and most of the New Jerseyans connected with George Washington's army just before crossing the Delaware into Pennsylvania on 7–8 December. Maxwell performed a special assignment to secure or destroy boats along a 75-mile stretch of the Delaware River; he then was ordered to take charge of troops coming into Morristown before Washington's arrival there. On 5 January 1777 Maxwell led a small force that attacked a British foraging detail at Spanktown and on the next day the rear guard of the British army as it embarked from Elizabethtown.

During the Morristown encampment of 1777, Maxwell had virtually an independent command for the central coastal sector of New Jersey. When he engaged small British units at various times, he showed a mastery of tactical improvisation. A British officer referred to Maxwell's troops as a "nest of American hornets."

Maxwell gained distinction during the actions preliminary to the battle of Brandywine on 11 September 1777. Washington appointed him as commander of a temporary elite corps of light infantry to probe and harass the British advance. At Cooch's Bridge and Iron Hill, on 3 September, Maxwell's light infantry fought heated engagements, avoided being surrounded, and then conducted a measured retreat back and across Brandywine Creek. At the battle of Brandywine itself, Maxwell's troops brought on the initial action, again making a safe retreat. Maxwell received praise from all quarters, although a Virginian serving in the light infantry, Lieutenant Colonel William Heth complained: "He is to be sure—a Damnd bitch of a General."

At the battle of Germantown on 4 October, Maxwell and his New Jerseyans were mainly involved, on Washington's orders, with the unenviable and ultimately unsuccessful task of dislodging a British regiment from the thick-walled Chew house, which proved to be a costly diversion; fifty-three of Maxwell's brigade lay dead on the lawn. From a complaint by Heth, Maxwell faced a court-martial for incompetence and being drunk on duty. Maxwell won unanimous acquittal, although the court acknowledged his propensity for strong drink.

During the Valley Forge encampment, Maxwell commanded a thousand-man force for securing the area between Valley Forge and the Delaware and Schuylkill rivers. As General Henry Clinton's army left Philadelphia and headed for the New Jersey shore to sail to New York City and environs, Maxwell's brigade had the responsibility of annoying and impeding the enemy's march. At the battle of Monmouth on 28 June 1778, the brigade was soon involved in the inexplicable general retreat. As a prosecution witness at the court-martial of General Charles Lee, Maxwell testified to the confusion of orders. For the remainder of 1778 and in early 1779, Maxwell and his brigade had duty in guarding northeastern New Jersey, fighting a few skirmishes against British raiding parties.

Maxwell's brigade formed part of General John Sullivan's expedition against the Iroquois Indians in the summer and fall of 1779. Other than forcing warriors to retreat in brief encounters at Chemung, New York, on 13 August and Newton, near Elmira, New York, on 29 August, the invading force accomplished only the destruction of villages and crops. On its return eastward, the New Jersey brigade was assigned field duty in eastern New Jersey. Maxwell and his troops participated in the battles of Connecticut Farms (now Union) and Springfield, New Jersey, on 7 and 23 June 1780, against a British incursionary force led by General Wilhelm Knyphausen.

Meanwhile, several of Maxwell's officers pressured him to resign on the threat of court-martial. The actual complaint was never made public but probably had substance, such as the discontent caused by his drinking. Maxwell agreed to leave the army. After sending in his resignation, he reversed himself and decided to fight the charges; unfortunately, Washington had forwarded the resignation to Congress, which accepted it. At the heart of the matter, though, was the fact that Maxwell's senior officers, most of whom were from Elizabethtown's social elite and were related through kinship or marriage, had long favored having Maxwell replaced by Colonel Elias Dayton.

Maxwell returned to his parents' farm, which became his by partial inheritance and the sale of his brothers' shares to him. He then sold the northern New Jersey farm that he had leased out. Although elected to the New Jersey legislature in 1783, he was defeated in each of the two following years. During his brief legislative tenure, he voted for resumption of sales of confiscated Tory estates, relief for insolvent debtors, and pensions for New Jersey army widows. Maxwell subsequently stayed clear of politics despite sympathizing with those who opposed the Federalist party. He served on the Sussex County Board of Freeholders briefly and as trustee of the Greenwich Presbyterian Church. Maxwell frequently visited Colonel Charles Stewart at his Union farm (in neighboring Hunterdon County), where he died suddenly on 3 November 1796.

William Maxwell was one of Washington's best generals. He would undoubtedly have been promoted to major general had not Congress allocated only one position at that rank to the New Jersey Continental Line, which was held by General Lord Stirling (William Alexander). In exercising command in the field, "Scotch Willie" Maxwell exhibited dependability, sound judgment, resourcefulness, an understanding of military tactics, and the willingness to take calculated risks.

• Although William Maxwell's personal papers have not survived (destroyed by a fire in his house), there is ample correspondence in the public record, especially in the Papers of George Washington at the Library of Congress and the Papers of the Continental Congress at the National Archives. Many letters are also scattered among the papers of various military and political figures; of particular value are the papers of Colonel Israel Shreve at Louisiana Tech University.

The William Edgar Papers at the New York Public Library contain many letters by Maxwell, giving an in-depth look at the Michilimackinac years and Maxwell's own private concerns; Edgar was Maxwell's trade agent in Montreal. Numerous journals and diaries by members of the New Jersey brigade are informative on Maxwell and his relations with his troops. For a full biography, see Harry M. Ward, *General William Maxwell and the New Jersey Continentals* (1997). Daniel Morison (Surgeon's Mate), *The Doctor's Secret Journal*, ed. George S. May (1960), is a very amusing account of army life involving Maxwell at Michilimackinac. For brief sketches of Maxwell, though with inaccuracies, see Henry D. Maxwell, *The Maxwell Family, Descendants of John and Ann Maxwell* (1895); J. H. Griffith, "William Maxwell of New Jersey: Brigadier General in the Revolution," *Proceedings of the New Jersey Historical Society*, 2d ser., 13 (1894–1895): 111–13; and *Portrait and Biographical Record of Hunterdon and Warren Counties, New Jersey* (1898), 522–27. An obituary is in the *State Gazette and New Jersey Advertiser*, 8 Nov. 1796.

HARRY M. WARD

MCCAREY, Leo (3 Oct. 1898–5 July 1969), film director, was born Thomas Leo McCarey in Los Angeles, California, the son of Thomas McCarey, a prominent West Coast boxing promoter, and Leona Mistrot McCarey. His father intended for him to become a lawyer; after the younger McCarey graduated from Los Angeles High School, his father paid his way through the University of Southern California Law School. McCarey, however, aspired to be a songwriter. A fine piano player, he wrote tunes throughout high school and law school and in 1918 sold a song, "When the Eagle Flaps His Wings and Calls on the Kaiser." He later remembered that while he was celebrating his sale in a bar, he heard people outside cheering for the just-declared Armistice, which rendered his song instantly passé. While attending law school, he seriously injured himself when he fell down an elevator shaft; although he received a sizable settlement, he invested it in a copper mine that soon thereafter failed. He worked for several months as a mucker in Montana mines and served briefly as an attorney for a mining company. Although he opened a law practice in Los Angeles around 1918, he tried only three cases, losing all of them.

Deciding that he wanted to try a career in the movies, McCarey in September 1918 was introduced to the director Tod Browning. Browning hired him as "script girl" for *The Virgin of Stamboul* (1920) and a few other productions. In 1920 McCarey married Stella Martin; they had one child. With his limited experience, he was chosen in 1921 by Universal Studios to direct his first film, *Society Secrets*. "Because of my legal education I had developed quite a vocabulary," he later recalled, "and the heads of the studios in those days didn't have the advantage of advanced education. And they thought I was brilliant because I used big words. So they made a director out of me" (quoted in Bogdanovich, pp. 385–86). When his film proved to be a failure, however, he was fired.

In 1923 and 1924 McCarey worked as a gagman for the *Our Gang* series at Hal Roach Studios. Between 1924 and 1926 he directed dozens of successful comedy shorts for Hal Roach starring Charley Chase, and in 1926 he was named vice president and supervisor of comedy productions at the studio. In this capacity he sought to "slow down" silent comedy, relying on meticulously built gags and subtle acting rather than hyperkinetic slapstick. He later described the sort of gag he favored: "There's a royal dinner. All the royalty are seated around the table and somebody lets out a fart. Now everybody exchanges a *glance*, that's all" (quoted in Bogdanovich, p. 392). He based much of his comic writing on what he called "the ineluctability of incidents": an individual commits a single foolish act, and in trying to free himself from this difficulty only succeeds in getting into deeper and deeper trouble. Putting his comic theories into practice, McCarey introduced in 1927 perhaps the most successful comedy team in screen history, the skinny man/fat man duo of Stan Laurel and Oliver Hardy. Between 1927 and 1929 he supervised and wrote almost all of Laurel and Hardy's shorts, and he directed four that are considered by critics to be among the team's best, including *We Faw Down* (1928) and *Liberty* (1929).

In 1929 McCarey left Roach and turned to feature-film directing. Over the next several years, working for Fox Studios and Paramount, he directed many of the leading comedians of the era: Eddie Cantor in *The Kid from Spain* (1932); George Burns, Gracie Allen, and W. C. Fields in *Six of a Kind* (1934); Mae West in *Belle of the Nineties* (1934); and Harold Lloyd in *The Milky Way* (1936). In 1933 he made *Duck Soup* with the Marx Brothers, which is widely regarded by critics to be the group's funniest, best-directed film. Although the brothers specifically requested that McCarey be assigned to the project, he was initially unenthusiastic because they were, in his opinion, "completely mad . . . and also I couldn't get them all together at the same time—one was always missing" (quoted in Bogdanovich, p. 405). Forced by Paramount to accept the job, he decided to eliminate many of the elements found in other Marx Brothers pictures, such as a romantic subplot involving Zeppo and a harp-playing interlude featuring Harpo; the result was their most streamlined comedy, an almost nonstop procession of anarchic gags.

McCarey eventually became frustrated working with established comedians such as the Marx Brothers, who had already honed their personas and routines through years on stage; instead, he wanted to "take straight actors and make them do funny things," largely through improvisation on the set (Bogdanovich, p. 405). In 1935 he directed Charles Laughton, then best known for his dramatic work in *The Private Life of Henry VIII* (1933), in *Ruggles of Red Gap*, a delightful film about an English manservant who is transplanted to the rugged American West. In 1937, working for Columbia Pictures, he directed Cary Grant and Irene Dunne in the brilliant screwball comedy *The Awful Truth.* The film, about a divorcing couple who gradually realize their love for each other, won him an Academy Award for best director. Through improvisation, he helped Grant to craft his "first real Cary Grant performance"; indeed, film historians have suggested that the actor's screen persona—dapper, witty, casually zany—was largely modeled on McCarey's own urbane, humorous manner (Bogdanovich, p. 379). In both *Ruggles* and *The Awful Truth,* McCarey displayed his penchant for relaxed digressions, creating pictures that are character-rather than plot-driven, taking the time to explore even minor characters and to present them as funny and three-dimensional. The French film director Jean Renoir, discussing McCarey's humanistic approach, remarked that he "understands people better than anyone in Hollywood" (quoted in Harvey, p. 249).

During the late 1930s McCarey demonstrated his versatility when he directed two highly regarded dramas. *Make Way for Tomorrow* (1937) was his most personal work, inspired by the life and recent death of his father. The picture, featuring poignant performances by Beulah Bondi and Victor Moore, concerns an aged couple who become a burden on their children and must be separated for financial reasons. The critic James Harvey has pointed out that the film never becomes mawkish but is rather "one of the most delicately and unremittingly painful narratives a major Hollywood studio ever made" (p. 250); upon its release, however, it was a box-office flop. *Love Affair* (1939), costarring Dunne and Charles Boyer, is a deeply romantic story about a couple who fall in love on a transatlantic ship crossing, only to have circumstances sunder their relationship once they arrive ashore.

In 1940 McCarey was involved in a serious car accident that almost killed him; as a result, he was unable to be involved in the production of his screenplay for *My Favorite Wife,* a comedy that again teamed Grant and Dunne. In 1942 he directed Grant and Ginger Rogers in *Once upon a Honeymoon,* which was set in war-torn Europe. The film, an ambitious attempt to explore serious political issues through the conventions of romantic comedy, is generally viewed as an interesting failure.

A devout Catholic, McCarey made two sentimental films dealing with Catholicism, *Going My Way* (1944) and its sequel, *The Bells of St. Mary's* (1945). Both films starred Bing Crosby as a genial, songwriting priest. The pictures were enormously popular: in 1944 McCarey was listed as the highest-paid man in America because of his profits from *Going My Way,* and *The Bells of St. Mary's* became the highest-grossing film in the history of RKO Studios. With *Going My Way* McCarey won Academy Awards for best director and best original story, but the film seems rather uninteresting and hackneyed today and is held in low regard by many film critics. Although he was at the peak of his Hollywood success in the mid-1940s, his career afterward went into a precipitous decline. He later suggested that he suffered from "Academy Award poisoning" during these years, because no projects "came up to my standards, my image," and he therefore did no work for extended periods of time (quoted in Bogdanovich, p. 426). In addition, he developed a serious drinking problem. Some critics have suggested that his later films are unsuccessful because they offer a darker, less generous vision of human behavior. *Good Sam* (1948), a mildly amusing comedy that starred Gary Cooper as a do-gooder exploited by his neighbors, was a notorious box-office flop. *My Son John* (1952) is a lurid political drama about a mother who learns that her son is a Communist. McCarey's only box-office success during the 1950s was *An Affair to Remember* (1957), a soap-operatic remake of *Love Affair* that starred Grant and Deborah Kerr. In 1962 he directed his final film, *Satan Never Sleeps,* another heavy-handed exposé of Communism. In his later years he suffered from emphysema. He died in Santa Monica, California.

• For an in-depth interview with McCarey, see Peter Bogdanovich, *Who the Devil Made It* (1997); this interview is also available in McCarey's oral history file at the American Film Institute Library, Los Angeles, Calif. Another valuable interview appears in *Cahiers du Cinéma,* no. 163 (1965), pp. 11–21. There are no biographies of McCarey; the best short overview of his career up to the release of *The Bells of St. Mary's* is in *Current Biography* (1946). For McCarey's teaming of Laurel and Hardy and his influence on their comic style, see Wes Gehring, "Leo McCarey: The Man behind Laurel & Hardy," *Films in Review* (1980), pp. 543–49. An excellent critical overview of his career, with thoughtful discussions of *The Awful Truth* and *Make Way for Tomorrow,* is in James Harvey, *Romantic Comedy in Hollywood from Lubitsch to Sturges* (1987). Also recommended are Charles Silver, "Leo McCarey: From Marx to McCarthy," *Film Comment* (Sept. 1973), pp. 8–11, and Elizabeth Kendall, *The Runaway Bride: Hollywood Romantic Comedy of the 1930s* (1990). Robin Wood, "Democracy and Shpontaneity [*sic*]: Leo McCarey and the Hollywood Tradition," *Film Comment* (Jan.–Feb. 1976), pp. 7–15, offers a scholarly reading of *Once upon a Honeymoon.* An obituary appears in the *New York Times,* 6 July 1969.

THOMAS W. COLLINS, JR.

MCCAWLEY, James D. (30 Mar. 1938–10 Apr. 1999), linguist and East Asian specialist, was born in Glasgow, Scotland, the son of James Q. McCawley, a journalist, and Monica Maud Bateman McCawley, a physician. His full name originally was James Latrobe Quillan McCawley (Benjamin Latrobe, the distinguished architect and engineer who immigrated to the United States, was related to the McCawleys.) He changed his name to James David McCawley at the age of twenty-one, when he adopted American citizenship. He did not, however, renounce his ties to family and friends in Scotland and visited them on occasion.

McCawley enrolled at the University of Chicago in 1954 at age sixteen, earning an M.S. in mathematics in 1958. He then spent a year in Münster, Germany (1959–1960), where he attended classes at the Westfälische Wilhelms-Universität. In 1961 he finished the school year at Chicago one course short of a B.S. in biology, and that summer he attended the Institute of the Linguistic Society of America at the University of Texas. The following autumn, he enrolled in linguistics at the Massachusetts Institute of Technology, where he studied with Noam Chomsky, Morris Halle, and Paul Postal. In 1965 he earned his Ph.D. after submitting his dissertation, "The Accentual System of Modern Standard Japanese" (published in 1968 under the title *The Phonological Component of a Grammar of Japanese*). He then set about training himself in syntax, semantics, and pragmatics. He married Noriko Akatsuka in 1971; they were divorced in 1978. Although protective of his personal privacy, McCawley participated fully in the life of his extended family in the Chicago area.

With George Lakoff and John Robert Ross, McCawley developed the Generative Semantics approach for syntax, which prevailed in the late 1960s and early 1970s. He contended that semantics plays a significant role in determining syntactic structures and that an adequate representation of meaning not only entails breaking down the structures into smaller semantic features but also involves specifying the scope of quantifiers and negators. He could thus both continue to derive passive sentences from the same deep structure as the corresponding active sentences and explain why sentences such as *The boys did not like all the girls* and *All the girls were not liked by the boys* are not necessarily synonymous. These two sentences do not have the same deep structure because the quantifier *all* in the phrase *all the girls* and the negator *not* in the phrases *did not like* and *were not liked by* do not have identical scopes in them. *Not* has scope over *all* in the first, whereas under one interpretation *all* has scope over *not* in the second sentence. Thus, pragmatic considerations set aside, sentences such as *Mary upset Peter* and *Peter was upset by Mary* are still derivable from the same deep structure, since they denote the same state of affairs, unlike the preceding pair of sentences.

Several of his papers in which he propounded his approach to syntactic analysis were republished in his collections *Grammar and Meaning* (1973), *Adverbs, Vowels, and Other Objects of Wonder* (1979), and *Thirty Million Theories of Grammar* (1982). To show how logic can be used to advantage in linguistics, he published *Everything That Linguists Have Always Wanted to Know about Logic but Were Ashamed to Ask* (1981; 2d ed., 1993). He developed a logic framework proving that traditional formal logic models are too limited to account for various important linguistic distinctions (for instance, differences among universal quantifiers such as *all* and *every*). However, he preserved some traditional useful distinctions having to do, for instance, with modality and possible worlds (such as in conditional clauses) because they shed light on how speakers interpret sentence-meaning.

Perhaps because the abstractness of Generative Semantics caused it to fall into disfavor, McCawley shifted to an analysis of syntax that depended less and less on abstract semantic structures, unless this was absolutely necessary, and focused on many syntactic phenomena that deserve serious attention, articulating clearly what current approaches to syntax could account for and what they left unexplained. *The Syntactic Phenomena of English* (1988; 2d ed., 1998) exhibits his flair for presenting data in an interesting way, his perceptiveness in dealing with problematic cases and thorny issues, and at the same time his modesty in recognizing the limits of his own understanding of the facts. The same intellectual curiosity is evidenced in his *Linguistic Flea Circus* (1991), which he updated periodically and shared with his colleagues and students. It demonstrated how observation as a data-collection technique could be taken to the ultimate level, almost regardless of the kind of interaction he was engaged in. His passion for providing details, accuracy, and comprehensiveness are well reflected in his publications.

At the time of his death McCawley was the Andrew MacLeish Distinguished Service Professor in the Departments of Linguistics and East Asian Languages and Civilizations at the University of Chicago. His career as a teacher was marked by a willingness to reach beyond his academic home. He was invited to teach repeatedly at the summer Linguistic Institute of the Linguistic Society of America at several institutions: the University of Illinois at Urbana-Champaign (1968; scheduled to return in 1999), the University of Hawaii (1977), the University of New Mexico (1980), Maryland (1982), Georgetown University (1985), and the University of Arizona (1989). He also taught as a visiting professor, typically during the summer months, at other institutions, including the University of Michigan (1970), the University of California at Santa Cruz (1971), Australian National University (1973), the University of Illinois at Chicago (1978), the University of Delhi (1985), and National Tsing Hua University (Taiwan, 1994).

Among the honors McCawley received in his academic life were membership in the American Academy of Arts and Sciences (elected 1983), an honorary doctorate from the University of Göteborg (1991), the presidency of the Linguistic Society of North America (1996), and two festschrifts celebrating his accomplishments: *Studies Out in Left Field: Defamatory Essays Presented to James D. McCawley on the Occasion of His 33rd or 34th Birthday*, edited by Arnold M. Zwicky et al. (1971; repr. 1992), and *The Joy of Grammar*, edited by Diane Brentari et al. (1992). The essays included in both collections come close to representing the breadth of his intellectual interests. The first volume, which is light-spirited, captures the ambience of the period when Generative Semanticists disputed established positions on syntax and semantics. That was also the time in his career when McCawley did not hesitate to contribute to *Playboy* magazine an equally formative essay on the semantics of verbs associated with lovemaking.

McCawley's wisdom was indeed very much in demand. A voracious reader, he found time to peruse current publications and works in progress and commented on many of them. He wrote insightful reviews, especially on the most central or influential books in the field, including a long review article, published in the *International Journal of American Linguistics* 40 (1974): 50–88, on Noam Chomsky and Morris Helle's *Sound Pattern of English* (1968). McCawley attended more professional meetings than most scholars and was capable of commenting accurately, months or years afterward, on the contents of the papers presented. His ability to recall people's names was extraordinary and extended to those who would consider themselves minor figures in the ever-growing crowd of scholars, not only in linguistics but also in other fields; he could also recall names of restaurants and streets all over the world. He had an impressive knowledge of the scholarly history of a number of issues and could cite obscure references in fields that had a bearing on the topics he chose to discuss. Rare were those occasions when a colleague was better informed on a current topic in a given field. He did not abandon his own analytical framework but constantly adjusted it to an inspiring eclecticism.

When McCawley died of a heart attack in Chicago, he was about to complete the manuscript for a book on the philosophy of science as it applies to the development of linguistics. He was also interested in the history of linguistics. The work of Otto Jespersen fascinated him: he published a few papers on Jespersen's approach to the study of language, and he wrote the introduction to the 1984 reprint of the linguist's *Analytic Syntax*. McCawley spoke knowledgeably about many other earlier linguists, and one can only wish that he had lived longer to write his own history of the development of linguistics, in comparison with similar issues in the evolution of other disciplines in which he was equally versed. His wide-ranging interests included music (on which Yoko Sugioka's 1999 obituary is informative) and cuisine. He published *The Eater's Guide to Chinese Characters* in 1984.

Until his death, McCawley distinguished himself as a leading authority in the research areas of phonology, syntax, semantics, and pragmatics and showed a command of research issues in the philosophy of language and the philosophy of science. One of the most eclectic and encyclopedic linguists of his time and undoubtedly of the twentieth century as a whole, he was highly regarded even among those who did not practice his brand of linguistics.

• For overviews of McCawley's career, see the memorial notices by John Goldsmith and Jerrold M. Saddock, *Historiographica Linguistica* 26 (1999): 257–61, and by Yoko Sugioka, *English Linguistics* 16 (1999): 563–67.

SALIKOKO MUFWENE

MCCOY, Kid (13 Oct. 1873–18 Apr. 1940), world middleweight boxing champion, was born Norman Selby in Moscow, Indiana, the son of Francis Marion Selby, a farmer, and Mary Campbell Selby. Norman Selby took the name Charles "Kid" McCoy when he began his career as a boxer, evidently because his parents disapproved of boxing, and used that name until the later years of his life. In newspapers and other publications he was referred to simply as "Kid McCoy."

McCoy quit school after the fourth grade and later left home at age sixteen or seventeen, going to Louisville, Kentucky. There he worked in a department store, lived at the YMCA, and learned to box. Afterward he roamed for a few years and had his first recorded fight with Pete Jenkins in St. Paul, Minnesota, on 2 June 1891. Not until 1893 did he seriously pursue his boxing career, engaging in a dozen fights and serving as sparring partner to two world champions, Bob Fitzsimmons and Tommy Ryan. He won most of his fights easily until he was knocked out in one round by Billy Steffers on 10 May 1894. Subsequently he beat Steffers in a return bout and first gained serious attention in 1895 by beating Billy Maber. He then won several more significant victories but lost to Ted White in London, England, in 1895.

Nearly six feet tall, pallid and thin, McCoy looked too weak to be successful in the ring. But he was a hard puncher and often knocked out his opponents with an early round onslaught. He was an extremely clever boxer and tactician. On more than one occasion he is said to have tricked his opponents into taking him too lightly by feigning illness when he entered the ring, coughing and slumping down wearily in his corner. Yet he won most of his fights easily and his handsome face was unmarked when his career in the ring ended.

In 1896, soon after returning from England, McCoy persuaded Ryan, the welterweight champion, to fight him in an overweight bout at Maspeth, Long Island. Ryan, who had never been beaten, also claimed the middleweight title. He did not take McCoy to be a serious opponent and failed to train properly. In a tremendous upset, McCoy handed Ryan a severe beating, knocked him out in the fifteenth round, and claimed the middleweight championship himself.

Despite his claim, McCoy was not yet accepted as middleweight champion. After defeating Ryan he won a long series of victories, beating former welterweight champion "Mysterious" Billy Smith and middleweight contenders Dick O'Brien and Dick Moore, and traveled to South Africa where he knocked out Australian Bill Doherty. Finally the matter of the championship title was settled when McCoy knocked out Dan Creedon of New Zealand in fifteen rounds at Long Island City, New York, on 17 December 1897.

Soon becoming too heavy to fight as a middleweight, in 1898 McCoy defeated two highly regarded heavyweights, Gus Ruhlin and Joe Goddard, and thereafter mainly fought heavier men. On 10 January 1899, he suffered a ten-round knockout loss to heavyweight Tom Sharkey in New York City but then defeated the famous Joe Choynski in San Francisco. This latter fight is famous because it has been said to be the origin of the popular expression "the real Mc-Coy," used in a headline of the *San Francisco Examiner* after the fight, "Now You've Seen the Real Mc-Coy." (The headline referred to the fact that there were other fighters of the period named McCoy, but none of them were nearly so expert as Kid McCoy.)

Although losing by a one-round knockout to heavyweight Steve McCormick, McCoy continued to fight successfully in 1899 and 1900, winning again from Ryan and knocking out Peter Maher, Creedon, and McCormick in a return fight. He again defeated Choynski, this time unfairly by striking him from behind after the bell rang to end the third round; the referee failed to call a foul and Choynski could not continue.

On 30 August 1900 in New York, McCoy lost by knockout to former heavyweight champion James J. Corbett in five rounds. This fight was considered to be a fake by the newspapers; McCoy had been in the habit of betting on his own fights, and it seemed likely that he made wagers through other parties and arranged the outcome to win his bets. Thereafter he fought infrequently although he did box Jack Root for the world light-heavyweight title in 1903 and lost by decision in ten rounds.

Outside the ring, McCoy lived a chaotic existence and his name was prominent in the gossip columns for many years. He married many times, three times to the same woman, Mrs. Julia Woodruff. His marriages to Mrs. Woodruff, Mrs. Estelle Ellis, and Mrs. Edna Valentine Hein were all to wealthy, previously married women who provided him the money to open businesses, bet, drink, travel, and live in the upper reaches of society. He had no children.

Perhaps as a result of his South Africa trip in 1896, McCoy became interested in diamonds and around the turn of the century owned jewelry stores in New York. He made thirty-three trips to Europe and was suspected of smuggling gems. In 1912 he was accused of stealing jewels from the princess of Thurn and Taxis in Ostend, Belgium, although he was later absolved. At various times he operated a health farm, a detective agency, and an automobile agency.

In 1896 McCoy opened a bar and restaurant in the Casino Theater in the theatrical district of New York. Later he operated a similar business, "McCoy's Rathskeller," in the basement of the Normandie Hotel. He knew many famous actors, actresses, and other theatrical people, including Lillian Russell, Mack Sennett, DeWolf Hopper, D. W. Griffith, and William S. Hart. He taught boxing to wealthy men, most notably the author Maurice Maeterlinck in France. He was lampooned in a Broadway play, *The Other Girl*, in which Lionel Barrymore mimicked his mannerisms and speech.

In 1917 McCoy began a short but successful movie career as a supporting actor when he portrayed a detective in Maurice Tourneur's *House of Glass*. He appeared as an overaged boxer in Griffith's *Broken Blossoms*. In Los Angeles in 1924 he became involved with Theresa Mors, who was unhappily married to jeweler Albert Mors. After witnessing an altercation between Mrs. Mors and her husband, McCoy went with Mrs. Mors to her apartment, where she was fatally shot. He then went to Albert Mors's jewelry store and attempted to lure Mors there, eventually shooting three more people but not fatally. He was sentenced to forty-eight years in San Quentin prison but served only eight, being released to his former boxing pupil Harry Bennett, who promised that McCoy would have employment at the Ford Motor Company; his last years were spent as a gardener for Ford in Detroit.

In 1937 McCoy was married for the tenth time, this time to Sue Cobb Crowley. He died from an overdose of sleeping pills. Although his record is marred by a few doubtful fights, McCoy is regarded as one of the best middleweights in boxing history, winning 90 of 107 fights, 64 by knockout. He was elected to the International Boxing Hall of Fame in 1991.

• McCoy's boxing record is given in Herbert G. Goldman, ed., *The Ring 1986–87 Record Book and Boxing Encyclopedia.* The best source of information on his life, although not without errors, is Robert Cantwell's *The Real McCoy: The Life and Times of Norman Selby* (1971). Numerous articles on McCoy have appeared in *The Ring* magazine, all of doubtful accuracy, but the best are Dean Jennings, "There Was Only One Real McCoy," July 1980, pp. 74–81, and Daniel M. Daniel, "McCoy's Knockout of Ryan Was a Stunner," Feb. 1947, pp. 13–15. An obituary is in the *New York Times*, 19 Apr. 1940.

LUCKETT V. DAVIS

MCDOWALL, Roddy (17 Sept. 1928–3 Oct. 1998), actor, was born Roderick Andrew McDowall in London, England, to Thomas McDowall, an officer in the merchant marine, and Winifred Corcoran McDowall. Sensing an innate gift for acting in her son, Mrs. McDowall, who loved movies and stage entertainment, launched his career as an actor at an early age by enrolling him in elocution classes when he was five. At the age of seven, with his mother's encouragement, he appeared in his first movie, a British mystery titled *Murder in the Family* (1936), and went on to act in more than a score of other films in England over the next five years. Under British law he was too young to be working at all, but he avoided detection by crouching on the floor of the car that brought him to the movie studio.

Young Roddy's appearances had not gone unnoticed in Hollywood, and Darryl F. Zanuck, the head producer at Twentieth Century–Fox studios, encouraged his mother to bring him to California, promising a long-term contract. Mrs. McDowall, who had lived in the United States as a child, needed no further encouragement. In September 1940, as England waged war against Germany, she crossed the Atlantic in a convoy ship out of Liverpool with her son and his older sister and traveled on to Los Angeles, where the family settled. Roddy's first Hollywood movie was a mystery, *Man Hunt*, released in 1941. Not long after his arrival, he was also screen-tested for a movie version of the novel *How Green Was My Valley*, a heart-tugging story about the travails of a coal-mining family in Wales. After viewing the test, the casting director advised the director assigned to the project, William Wyler, not to use young Roddy because he was not a "cute and adorable" extrovert, as movie children then, in the manner of Shirley Temple, were expected to be.

After seeing the test, Wyler overruled the casting director and hired Roddy for the role of Huw, the youngest child in the family, who bears the brunt of much of the tragedy that ensues with heartrending bravery and compassion. Roddy, he felt, was a natural for the part, in particular because he was familiar with Welsh accents, having been reared by a Welsh nanny back in England. The picture—which starred Maureen O'Hara, Walter Pidgeon, and Donald Crisp— was put on hold for several months and then brought back into production, this time with John Ford as director. On its release in 1941 it became a box office success, thanks in large part to the compelling performance of its youngest major performer, and went on to win five Academy Awards, including one for Best Picture.

His success as a child actor now assured, McDowall went on to appear in prominent roles in a series of successful Hollywood movies, including *My Friend Flicka* (1943) and its sequel, *Thunderhead: Son of Flicka* (1945), the continuing saga of a boy and his horse in Wyoming, and *The White Cliffs of Dover* (1944), which depicted the courage and stoicism of a British family in wartime. But he is best remembered for his leading role in *Lassie Come Home* (1943), as the appealing and devoted young Scottish boy in search of his lost collie. Although he was in his fifteenth year when the film was made, McDowall, who was small for his age, looked much younger, and he continued to play juvenile roles in Hollywood films until his early twenties. Eager to learn more about movie-making, he served as associate producer in some of the films he appeared in during the late 1940s. During this period he also made his stage debut in the summer of 1946 at the Westport (Conn.) Playhouse in a production of John Van Druten's *Young Woodley*, and went on to star as both a singer and an actor in a vaudeville revue that made a cross-country tour several years later. Tour stops included a stint at the Capitol Theatre in New York City.

During his years in Hollywood, McDowall received the equivalent of an elementary and high school education at a school for child actors run by Twentieth Century–Fox on the studio lot. In 1951, in his twenty-third year and realizing that his days as a child star were numbered, McDowall decided to try for a full-time stage career and moved to New York City to receive formal training. Eschewing an audition at the Actors Studio, then the preeminent training ground for theater aspirants—he later recalled that he felt too nervous and incompetent—he chose to study privately with Mira Rostova. He began appearing regularly onstage on the East Coast in the early 1950s, initially playing supporting roles in a repertoire that included old standbys like *Charley's Aunt, The Doctor's Dilemma, Julius Caesar*, and *The Tempest*, as well as several new plays, among them *No Time for Sergeants*, which opened on Broadway in the fall of 1955. Two years later he had a starring role in the stage adaptation of *Compulsion*, Meyer Levin's novel about the Loeb-Leopold murder case (see Nathan F. Leopold, Jr., and Richard A. Loeb), for which he received rave reviews. But this success was followed by several years of appearances in plays that were box office flops, and McDowall returned briefly to Hollywood to appear in several more films, including *The Subterraneans* and *Midnight Lace*, both of which were released in 1960.

In the fall of 1959 McDowall returned to the New York stage in Jean Anouilh's *The Fighting Cock*, and his performance earned him not only excellent reviews but also a Tony Award for best supporting actor of the 1959–1960 Broadway season. He went on to play Mordred in the Lerner and Loewe musical *Camelot*, which opened in New York in December 1960, and again received positive reviews. (See Alan Jay Lerner and Frederick Loewe.) A year later he left the cast to return to Hollywood, this time to appear in the film *Cleopatra* (released in 1963), starring Elizabeth Taylor. Taylor, who had also been a child star and with whom he had appeared in *Lassie Come Home*, was one of his oldest and closest friends, and their relationship endured until his death.

Beginning in the late 1950s McDowall also acted on television, appearing in special productions of *The Tempest* and *Billy Budd* and on several network drama series, including "Playhouse 90," "Matinee Theater," and "Twilight Zone." In 1961 he won an Emmy for his supporting role in an October 1960 telecast of the play *Not Without Honor*. After appearing in several more Hollywood films during the 1960s, including such box office successes as *The Longest Day* (1962) and *The Loved One* (1965), McDowall made a series of celebrated science fiction and horror movies, starting with *Planet of the Apes* (1968) and three of its sequels. By the 1970s he was devoting more and more time to photography, an avocation he had enjoyed for many years. An avid observer with his camera of the Hollywood scene, he published five well-received collections of his work, beginning with *Double Exposure* in 1966. He was also a noted collector of old movies and film memorabilia.

All told, McDowall acted in 130 films over the course of his long career and made dozens of stage and television appearances. He never expressed any regrets about his upbringing and early entrance into the work force. Indeed, he claimed that he had absorbed the moral lessons implicit in the movies he had made as a child and that these had shaped his character. His assertion was borne out by his reputation: he was known and respected throughout his adult life as a man of intense loyalty and trustworthiness. He was also a celebrated storyteller, entertaining friends with memories of his six-decade-long career and offering impersonations—always kind—

of his many acquaintances over the years in films and theater.

McDowall continued to appear in the movies and onstage until he was diagnosed with cancer in the mid-1990s. His last film was *The Grass Harp*, released in 1996. McDowall, who never married, died at his home in Los Angeles.

• For biographical information, see entries for "McDowall, Roddy," in *Current Biography Yearbook* for 1961 and 1999; *Contemporary Authors*, vol. 167 (1999); *Contemporary Theatre, Film, and Television*, vol. 8 (1990); and Coral Amende, *Legends in Their Own Time* (1994). See also M. Nichols, "Child Stars Who Came Back," *Coronet*, Mar. 1958, pp. 82–83. An obituary appears in the *New York Times*, 4 Oct. 1998.

ANN T. KEENE

MCKELVEY, Vincent E. (6 Apr. 1916–23 Jan. 1987), geologist and ninth director of the U.S. Geological Survey (USGS), was born Vincent Ellis McKelvey in Huntingdon, Huntingdon County, Pennsylvania, the youngest son among the seven children of Ellis Elmer McKelvey, a Methodist minister, and Eva Rupert Faus McKelvey, an artist. After a year at Williamsport's Dickinson Seminary (later Lycoming College), young McKelvey transferred to Syracuse University. In a private ceremony in 1935, and a public one later, he married Genevieve Patricia Bowman, an elementary school teacher; they had two children, but only their younger son survived infancy. Influenced by Louis W. Ploger at Syracuse, McKelvey chose geology and earned a B.A. (with honors) in 1937.

Continuing his geological training with William H. Twenhofel and other professors at the University of Wisconsin, McKelvey received financial support from a graduate assistantship and intermittent work for the U.S. Soil Conservation Service (SCS) and the Wisconsin Geological and Natural History Survey. Twenhofel directed McKelvey's investigations of culturally accelerated sedimentation in the Coon Creek basin, southeast of La Crosse (as part of one of eight SCS-USGS erosion-control projects), and of freshwater lakes and bogs elsewhere in the state. In 1939 McKelvey received his M.A. degree and passed the USGS employment examination. He declined the agency's offer of water resources work to begin doctoral studies at the University of Wisconsin, intending to investigate the weathering of granitic rocks. In January 1941, however, McKelvey joined the USGS Section of Metalliferous Deposits, led by Twenhofel's colleague D. Foster Hewett, for work in its revived strategic minerals program.

McKelvey spent most of the next two decades assessing geology and mineral deposits in the Western United States. He initially aided Charles B. Hunt in studying manganese-bearing sedimentary rocks in Nevada and Arizona. In 1942 and 1943 he investigated vanadiferous shales in the Phosphoria Formation of the Idaho-Wyoming thrust belt as a member of William W. Rubey's project. While detailed to the

USGS Military Geology Unit (1944–1945) led by Hunt, McKelvey spent several months in Manila analyzing coastal areas for invasion planners. The USGS's postwar searches for uranium in the American West, funded by the U.S. Atomic Energy Commission, revived the Phosphoria project. McKelvey led the project starting in 1947, the year Wisconsin awarded him a Ph.D. for his studies of the stratigraphy of the Phosphoria's phosphatic shales. By 1960 McKelvey, Richard P. Sheldon, and their colleagues had established a structural, stratigraphic, paleontologic, and depositional framework for the Phosphoria Formation and other Permian-age rocks in the West. McKelvey also documented Aleksandr V. Kazakov's ideas about the chemistry and genesis of phosphorites. McKelvey ascribed their origin and the deposition of petroleum source beds to the nutrients in upwelling ocean currents, which led to new discoveries worldwide.

In the 1950s and 1960s the USGS increased McKelvey's managerial responsibilities, but at intervals the agency returned him at his wish to field-based research. He served initially (1950–1953) as chief of the trace elements program. In 1960 he became an assistant chief geologist, leading interagency programs and special services work in military and foreign geology, underground nuclear tests, and radioactive-waste disposal, and then (1962–1965) the economic geology unit's studies of metals, fuels, and engineering and foreign geology. McKelvey revived a USGS program to provide the Interior Department with needed estimates of U.S. petroleum reserves. His investigations of phosphate deposits in Mexico, Europe, the Middle East, and North Africa generated an abiding interest in the relations between natural resources and civilization. The "McKelvey Box," his diagrammatic classification of mineral deposits, portrays the dynamics of reserves (identified and recoverable) and resources (identified but not economically recoverable, or undiscovered) and is still widely used. He advised federal managers within and outside the Interior Department on energy resources and leasing policies for them. McKelvey represented the United States and advised groups in other countries about their mineral and energy resources. He served on the economic and technical subcommittee of the United Nations Committee on Peaceful Uses of Seabed and Ocean Floor beyond the Limits of National Jurisdiction, and helped to draft the initial U.S. convention for the Law of the Sea treaty.

McKelvey returned to administration as USGS chief geologist in June 1971, less than one month after Director William T. Pecora became undersecretary of the interior. McKelvey, who reluctantly assumed the directorship in December 1971, felt that he lacked his predecessor's political skills. He used humor and persuasion in leading the USGS and making known to a wider and more generalized audience the important role of USGS scientists in society and the value of their work to the nation. He chose Sheldon as chief geologist and Joseph S. Cragwall, Jr., as chief hydrologist. Under McKelvey's direction the USGS succeeded in significantly expanding funding for programs related to earthquake-hazards reduction, assessments of mineral and energy resources (especially those offshore), studies of the potential impacts of resource development on the environment, and other applied and basic work in the agency. In 1975 he founded, at the secretary of the interior's request, a Resource Analysis and Land Information (RALI) program, led by assistant director James R. Balsley, Jr., to provide information in readily usable form for solving environmental problems connected to land use and engineering projects, especially those in urban settings. McKelvey ascribed RALI's demise (1980–1982) to a lack of public interest and concern but also to opposition by Sheldon and other scientists and managers within the agency.

McKelvey traveled often and widely to speak before professional and general audiences to promote the USGS's role as an impartial agency for research and fact-finding, but he was better as a writer than as a speaker. In highlighting the growing depletion of mineral and energy resources, he emphasized that new resources could be found by improving and extending exploration techniques, developing deposits previously considered noneconomic, and discovering substitutes. After the embargo by the Organization of Petroleum Exporting Countries in the winter of 1973–1974, McKelvey chaired "Project Independence" for the federal Blueprint Interagency Oil Task Force, and he increasingly involved the USGS in long-range geologic estimates of oil and natural gas resources based on volumetric-yield assessments. These optimistic predictions of high ultimate production opposed those made by M. King Hubbert, a Shell Oil Company retiree then serving (1968–1976) as a USGS research geophysicist. Hubbert flailed McKelvey, the USGS, the Federal Energy Administration (FEA), and the petroleum industry for failing to heed his statistical predictions since the late 1950s that the production of U.S. oil from conventional sources would peak by 1971 (it did) and then decline to low ultimate yield (it did not). In the summer of 1974, when Hubbert testified before a Senate committee, McKelvey participated in an international research conference that the Association of American Petroleum Geologists (AAPG) convened at Stanford University to evaluate methods of estimating undiscovered oil and gas resources, and the FEA asked the USGS to reappraise the nation's recoverable share of these resources. In 1975 the nine authors of USGS *Circular 725* halved the agency's earlier estimates of the ultimate production of oil and gas from both conventional and unconventional sources. The new numbers, with levels of their probability, were still above Hubbert's forecasts, but close to 1974–1975 estimates by Mobil Oil Corporation and the National Academy of Sciences (NAS). Hubbert praised the USGS's new figures (*Science* 189 [1975]: 200). McKelvey supported them, predicting that large potential sources of gas, especially in geopressured zones underlying the

Gulf Coast region, would be found and developed in the coming decades.

In 1975 McKelvey, in his dual role as USGS Ethics Counselor, faced another vexing issue. The Government Accounting Office had claimed that forty-nine of the 223 USGS employees and consultants then required by the agency to file disclosure statements held financial investments that appeared to be in conflict with their federal duties, principally those persons in the Conservation Division's work of managing the leasing, fees, and royalties involved in producing energy and mineral resources from the public domain. The USGS's establishing legislation prohibited "personal or private interests in the lands or mineral wealth of the region under survey" and "surveys or examinations for private parties or corporations" (*U.S. Statutes at Large* 20 [1879]: 394). Some of the allegedly improper investments had been made many years before, but they had not been questioned during previous directorates. Subsequent reviews by the Interior Department's solicitor required divestitures by thirty of these persons but demonstrated that the other cases did not represent conflicts of interest. To reinforce his total commitment to preventing further conflicts of interest, McKelvey established a permanent position of deputy ethics counselor, who would report directly to him and oversee an annual review of all financial holdings and outside work of designated employees throughout the agency.

Early in 1977 members of President Jimmy Carter's administration decided to replace McKelvey, claiming he was "a poor administrator" (*Washington Monthly* 10 [1978]: 60); he would not, they felt, advance their energy policy of mitigating future shortfalls that depended partly on limited ultimate production of domestic natural gas. The president's science adviser convinced the administration to ask the NAS for a list of successor candidates, a procedure followed since 1943. When the five persons on the list declined the post, the administration selected H. William Menard, who had helped to compile the names, and announced McKelvey's resignation on 6 September 1977. In resigning effective 15 January 1978, McKelvey became the first USGS director to be relieved of his duties by an incoming administration. He remained with the USGS as a senior research geologist until he retired in 1980.

In 1978 ambassador-at-large Elliot L. Richardson asked McKelvey to become the senior scientific adviser in the U.S. delegation to the U.N. Law of the Sea Conference, returning him to activities he had left in 1975. McKelvey concentrated on the geology of continental shelves, maritime boundaries, and ocean-floor mineral resources. He also served as the U.S. delegation's senior deputy until 1981. There, as at the USGS, McKelvey emphasized reliable and impartial science.

McKelvey's contributions to science and society garnered honors and requests for additional service. He received a Rockefeller Public Service Award (1973) and honorary D.Sc. degrees from Syracuse (1975) and the South Dakota School of Mines and

Technology (1976). A hydrous, rare-earth uranium-carbonate mineral, an ammonite fossil, a peak in Antarctica's Thiel Mountains, a USGS building in Menlo Park, California, and the USGS Annual Forum on Mineral and Energy Resources all bear his name. Between 1967 and 1976 he served on the management boards or councils of the American Geological Institute, the Cosmos Club, the Geological Society of America, Resources for the Future, and the Society of Economic Geologists. McKelvey also advised academic departments at Harvard, Stanford, Syracuse, and the University of Virginia. The AAPG gave McKelvey its Human Needs Award for 1977. In 1980 he joined the Department of State for two years as a part-time foreign affairs officer. Between 1981 and 1984 he also counseled the Asian Development Bank, the Gas Research Institute, the National Oceanic and Atmospheric Administration, and Saudi Arabia's minister of mineral resources, and he served as an adjunct professor of marine mineral resources at the Florida Institute of Technology.

After a gallant two-year struggle with amyotrophic lateral sclerosis (Lou Gehrig's disease), during which he continued to write and publish, McKelvey died in St. Cloud, Florida.

• McKelvey's public papers are in Record Group 57 at the National Archives, except for the twelve field notebooks and related materials from his work in the West (1941–1952) now in the USGS Field Records Library at Denver. McKelvey's personal papers form Collection No. 5058 in the American Heritage Center at the University of Wyoming. Most of McKelvey's publications are listed in USGS *Bulletin* 937 (1944): 606, 959; 1049 (1957): 401, 445, 591, 925; 1195 (1965): 265, 308, 1035–36, 1553–54, 1777; and the successor volumes of the *Bibliography and Index of Geology*, issued yearly since 1960. These citations also are available on CD-ROM as part of the American Geological Institute's "GeoRef" online bibliographical database. His "Freedom, Objectivity, and Credibility," USGS *Administrative Digest* 625 (1973), remains a model for employee conduct. Typescripts of eighty-one of the speeches McKelvey delivered as director, and the 76-page transcript of Harold L. Burstyn's interview of him (1982), are in the USGS Library, Reston, Va. Biographical articles about McKelvey include Bernardo F. Grossling, *Geophysics: The Leading Edge of Exploration* 7, no. 9 (1988): 18–22; Richard P. Sheldon, *AAPG Bulletin* 71 (1987): 902; and Sheldon, in W. Roger Miller, ed., "The Thrust Belt Revisited," *Wyoming Geological Association Field Conference Guidebook* 38 (1987): 7. Mary C. Rabbitt evaluated McKelvey's directorate in "The United States Geological Survey 1879–1989," USGS *Circular* 1050 (1989); a scanned version of that publication is included in Clifford M. Nelson, ed., "Records and History of the United States Geological Survey," USGS *Circular* 1179 (CD-ROM, 2000). Prepared for the Senate Committee on Interior and Insular Affairs of the 94th Congress, the assessment of USGS oil and gas estimates in 1974–1975 and of McKelvey's coeval actions to eliminate alleged financial conflicts of interest by some USGS employees and prevent their recurrence appears in Allen F. Agnew's *The U.S. Geological Survey* (1975), pp. 91–99. Lawrence J. Drew, an energy resources analyst who joined the USGS in 1972, after three years with Cities Service Oil Company, also appraised the estimates dispute and its results in *Oil and Gas Forecasting:*

Reflections of a Petroleum Geologist (1990), pp. 27–28, 86–88, and in *Undiscovered Petroleum and Mineral Resources: Assessment and Controversy* (1997), pp. 2–5). Reactions to McKelvey's dismissal appear in the *Wall Street Journal*, 16 Sept. 1977; *Science*, 23 Sept. and 7 Oct. 1977; *Washington Post*, 13 Nov. 1977; *New York Times*, 1 Jan. 1978; and *Washington Monthly*, Apr. 1978. An obituary is in the *Washington Post*, 25 Jan. 1987.

CLIFFORD M. NELSON

MCNEILL, Don (23 Dec. 1907–7 May 1996), radio broadcaster, was born Donald Thomas McNeill in Galena, Illinois, one of two children of Harry McNeill, the president of a chair manufacturing company, and his wife Luella Weinberger McNeill. Reared in Sheboygan, Wisconsin, McNeill, who had hoped to become an editorial cartoonist, received his bachelor's degree in philosophy from Marquette University in 1930, by which time he had been working for a Milwaukee radio station for three years.

McNeill moved to Louisville, Kentucky, first as a staff announcer and then, with singer Van Fleming, as half of "Don and Van, the Two Professors." The team moved to San Francisco, where their show was broadcast on the West Coast via the National Broadcasting Company. At the end of the show's run, McNeill returned to Milwaukee, where in 1931 he married Katherine Bennett, who had been a secretary at Marquette when McNeill was a student. They had three sons and remained married until Katherine McNeill's death in 1985.

After an unsuccessful job search in New York, McNeill took a position at WSN in Chicago as a "schedule announcer" and writer for a Saturday program. In 1933 he also became master of ceremonies of an ailing daily morning show called "The Pepper Pot." McNeill was given carte blanche to revamp and rename the program. On 12 June 1933 the first edition of "The Breakfast Club" went on the air; soon it was carried by NBC's Blue Network, later the American Broadcasting Company.

McNeill's "Breakfast Club" was eventually credited with "almost single-handedly" turning early morning network radio into a profitable medium. It ran for more than thirty-five years, celebrating its last performance on 27 December 1968. Usually unscripted and unrehearsed, "The Breakfast Club," spreading a distinctively midwestern flavor across the land, was an unashamedly "corny" variety program. Of this aspect, McNeill wrote, "Corn is sentiment, sincere and unashamed. . . . Corn is the familiar, the tried and true. Every normal person likes corn. Cynics and sophisticates think they hate corn . . . but the tombstone of many a sophisticate bears a corny epitaph."

The show's formula evolved gradually. To a large orchestra and vocalist left over from "The Pepper Pot," McNeill added "characters"—among others, neighbors Ott Ort and the Beefbowers (in some ways, McNeill's humor prefigured that of Garrison Keillor, also enchanted by beautifully ugly Midwestern names), a clown and chief heckler (Sam Cowling, who contributed "Fiction and Fact from Sam's Almanac"), and a gossipy, sharp-witted rural spinster (Aunt Fanny, played by Fran Allison). The vocalist was transmogrified into the Cruising Crooner (Jack Owens among the audience). There was a bemused announcer—usually Durward Kirby.

Heeding the time (and commercial) demands made on morning programs, McNeill divided "The Breakfast Club" into fifteen-minute segments—but in a fresh way. A trumpet call and drum roll would signal the "First [or second, etc.] Call to Breakfast," followed by a musical "march around the breakfast table," which, though wholly imaginary in the large auditoriums from which it was broadcast, was probably enacted in kitchens and breakfast rooms across the land. As it matured, "The Breakfast Club" became known as a proving ground for radio talent. Jim and Marian Jordan, whose show "Fibber McGee and Molly" won them fame, were "Breakfast Club" graduates, as was the character actor Bill Thompson (in such roles as "The Old Timer," "Wallace Wimple," et al.). In its later years "The Breakfast Club" featured major guest stars from entertainment and sport without shunting aside its regular cast, who remained startlingly loyal. Allison and Cowling, who had joined in 1937, stayed to the end, as did bandleader Eddie Ballantine, on the show since 1933, and producer Cliff Petersen, from 1936 onward.

On the air, McNeill was a benign presence, popping aphorisms such as "Courtship makes a man spoon, but marriage makes him fork over," which could have come from the pages of the decidedly middlebrow *Reader's Digest*. During the "Memory Time" segment he regularly read out poems and essays sent in by listeners. When World War II broke out, there was a regular prayer: "Each in his own words, each in his own way, for a world united in peace, bow your heads and let us pray." His regular sign-off was "Be good to yourself."

McNeill often said that the audience really "wrote" his program; it responded to his "Sunshine Shower"—writing to shut-ins at his behest—and to requests for gifts to the needy. At its peak, the program received more than 100,000 poems and essays annually. A 1962 article in *The Voice of St. Jude* magazine, noting 410 stations in the United States and Canada and eighty on the Armed Forces Network, proclaimed "The Breakfast Club" the most popular radio program of all time. In 1947 McNeill received an honorary doctor of letters degree from St. Bonaventure in New York. In 1948, the year of McNeill's tongue-in-cheek "McNeill at the Wheel" presidential campaign, more than 190,000 visitors came to Chicago to watch "The Breakfast Club." McNeill's 1948 earnings topped $180,000, a monumental figure for the time. In the late 1940s McNeill settled in Winnetka, Illinois, where he remained for the rest of his life.

With television just around the corner, the ratings battle for network morning radio grew fierce, with Tom Breneman in Hollywood and Arthur Godfrey in New York contesting McNeill's preeminence. When television arrived, Godfrey proved to be the most successful on screen, though ABC experimented with "The Don McNeill TV Club" in an evening slot during 1950–1951, and during the 1954 season there was a daytime television version of "The Breakfast Club." But television was not McNeill's medium, and "The Breakfast Club" stayed with what was tried and true for it, even though the world around it changed gradually. As the United States became steadily more motorized, morning radio became "drive time" radio, filled by news and traffic bulletins.

After "The Breakfast Club" ended, McNeill taught communications at Marquette (1969) and the University of Notre Dame (1971). He served on the boards of the Sears Foundation and the Alzheimer's Disease and Related Disorders Association. In 1993 he was named to the Radio Hall of Fame of the Museum of Broadcast Communications. McNeill died in Evanston, Illinois. An obituary in the *Chicago Tribune* called his voice "as familiar to America as birds chirping, toasters popping, eggs sizzling and coffee perking."

• The Reverend Don McNeill of the Center for Social Concerns, the University of Notre Dame, contributed to this article, as did John Doolittle of American University, whose book on "The Breakfast Club" is due for publication in 2001. Among useful articles is "Corn for Breakfast," *Wall Street Journal*, 6 Mar. 1967. McNeill's radio years are also detailed in Frank Buxton and Bill Owen, *The Big Broadcast, 1920–1950* (1972). Obituaries include Kenan Heise's in the *Chicago Tribune*, 8 May 1996, and Myrna Oliver's in the *Los Angeles Times*, 9 May 1996.

JAMES ROSS MOORE

MEADOWS, Audrey (8 Feb. 1926–3 Feb. 1996), television personality, actress, and singer, was born Audrey Cotter in Wuchang, China, the daughter of the Reverend Francis James Meadows Cotter, an Episcopal minister, and Ida Taylor Cotter. Her parents had gone to China as Christian missionaries, and until she was five she lived in Wuchang and spoke both Chinese and English. The family returned to the United States in 1931 and first resided in Providence, Rhode Island, where her father had accepted a pastorate at St. John's Protestant Episcopal Cathedral. Following successive pastoral moves to Sewickley, Pennsylvania, and Pittsfield, Massachusetts, the family settled in 1935 in Sharon, Connecticut, where Rev. Cotter was rector of Christ Church until the late 1950s.

Audrey Cotter attended Miss Hill's School in Great Barrington, Massachusetts, and during her adolescence was much influenced by her older sister, Jane, who yearned to become an actress. Trained as an opera singer, while also taking acting lessons, Audrey displayed a beautiful coloratura soprano voice and began her career in light opera companies. At sixteen she appeared at Carnegie Hall in New York as a concert performer, winning glowing reviews. Although she planned to go on to Smith College, she was encouraged by her sister to move to New York. Jayne (now with a *y* in her name) and Audrey set their sights on stage and screen opportunities, frequenting casting offices in their search for work. Because of her impressive vocal range, which enabled her to hit E above high C, Audrey received numerous offers to act and sing with light opera companies all over the East Coast and Midwest during the late 1930s and early 1940s. After the United States entered World War II, she sang for the troops on USO tours of the South Pacific, where she contracted malaria and experienced several brushes with death, including three plane crashes. She remained ill for two years following her wartime service. Once she had regained her strength and verve, she changed her surname to Meadows (one of her father's middle names), which her sister had also done. Audrey Meadows began her career anew with a touring company that performed the musical *High Button Shoes*.

By successfully auditioning for the female roles on a televised comedy program on NBC, "The Bob and Ray Show," Meadows acquired a national audience starting in November 1951. Although the stars of the show, Bob Elliott and Ray Goulding, reorganized and renamed it "Embassy Club" in mid-1952, Meadows remained part of the ensemble, playing several different roles, for which she often made costume changes while still on the set, out of view of the camera. When "The Bob and Ray Show" was revived under its original name, she continued to gain audience appeal and garner excellent reviews. Her success on television won her the concurrent role of leading lady in the Phil Silvers Broadway musical *Top Banana* in 1952. These performances led to the role of a lifetime: that of Alice Kramden in "The Honeymooners" sketches on "The Jackie Gleason Show."

Although Jackie Gleason at first rejected Meadows for the part, she persuaded him that despite her youth and attractiveness she could effectively play a harried housewife. To prove her point, she posed for photographs with her hair ruffled and without makeup. But she was staking a lot to play opposite Gleason. "In a risky business," she later recalled, "the risk became all mine. I had bailed out of a surefire, long-running Broadway show to join a one-person-missing comedy quartet which had not yet played to a network audience. If we faltered, CBS surely had ten movies in the can. And with no annual contract, I would be at liberty to read for the ingenue's fruitcake sister or do crowd noises on radio. This was not part of my master plan. So I vowed to play the socks off Alice Kramden and prayed that the show would be a blockbuster hit, because the alternative was most depressing" (*Love, Alice*, pp. 30–31). With the trust resulting from genuine friendship, Meadows could handle the temperamental Gleason. Named "TV's Most Promising Star of 1953" by Television Magazine's writers, she then won an Emmy in 1954 for her role as Alice.

A classic situation comedy, "The Honeymooners" skits feature a New York bus driver and his wife, who yearn to get ahead in the world, an aspiration that the husband, Ralph Kramden, usually tries to fulfill by means of some offbeat "get rich quick" scheme. Inevitably entangled in such schemes are their neighbors the Nortons (played by Art Carney and Joyce Randolph). The longevity of the show can be largely attributed to the chemistry between Meadows and Gleason and the craftsmanship they brought to their respective roles. Meadows later said in her memoir: "The life of 'The Honeymooners' cast was rarely marked by order and precision . . . [W]hen our Mr. Gleason would experience distress at scripting or stage direction or find displeasure in things unknown, he would trash a scene in mid-performance and whisper that from here on out we would do it Civil War style!" (*Love, Alice*, p. 12). Alice serves as a perfect foil for Ralph's bragging, exaggerations, and temper, countering his putdowns with zingers of her own—whether in the script or not. A natural comic with an excellent sense of timing, Meadows was a genius at ad-libbing, a trait she shared with Gleason. As he put it, "Her unfailing instinct for comedy makes her an invaluable asset to my show" (*Current Biography 1958*, p. 279).

After 1955, Gleason abandoned his live one-hour variety format and revamped the show as "Jackie Gleason in The Honeymooners." Although the thirty-nine half-hour episodes that appeared in the 1955–1956 season later became classics that were perennially rerun, some critics at the time wondered why Gleason chose to replace his successful live format with a taped program. He did so because of the pressures of his schedule, but he soon realized that his style of comedy demanded greater spontaneity. When he reverted to a live format for the 1956–1957 season, however, he practically abandoned "The Honeymooners" in the process, even though Meadows still appeared in comedy sketches on the show. The latest incarnation of "The Jackie Gleason Show" performed poorly in the ratings against "The Perry Como Show" and was canceled in the summer of 1957.

Meadows's other television work included guest appearances with major comics of the day, such as Jack Benny, Carol Burnett, Sid Caesar, George Gobel, and Red Skelton. In addition to performing in a number of ABC television specials, she was an occasional contestant on various game shows, including "I've Got a Secret" (which featured Jayne Meadows as a regular panel member), "Name's the Same," "I'll Buy That," "What's in a Word," and "Take a Guess." In 1955–1956 she and her sister made several recordings for the RCA Victor label with a repertoire of songs like "Hot Potato Mambo," "Japanese Rumba," "Dear Ralph," and "Dungaree Dan and Chino Sue." Although she tended to work on the East Coast, she also had parts in several Hollywood movies, perhaps the best known of which is *That Touch of Mink* (1962), starring Doris Day and Cary Grant.

Meadows married Randolph D. Rouse, a Washington, D.C., builder, on 26 May 1956, but within a few years divorced him. She then married Robert F. Six, the president of Continental Airlines, in August 1961. In her later years she appeared on the television sitcoms "Too Close for Comfort" and "Uncle Buck." Upon her retirement from acting, she served as the first female director of the First National Bank of Denver and held an honorary position as vice president of sales for Continental Airlines. Meadows died of lung cancer in Los Angeles.

Alice Kramden gained for Audrey Meadows a measure of immortality in American popular culture. While other successful shows of the 1950s now seem so dated that they can only be viewed as historical artifacts, "The Honeymooners" retains the power to entertain because of the inimitable skill and vitality of its stars. Audrey Meadows staked her career on being cast by Jackie Gleason in the role of Alice, and she made the most of the chance given her.

• Meadow's autobiography, *Love, Alice: My Life as a Honeymooner* (1994), is the best source of information on her life and career. Also useful is her entry in the 1958 edition of *Current Biography*. Anita Gates's "Baby, You're the Greatest" is a book review of *Love, Alice* that appeared in the *New York Times Book Review*, 9 Oct. 1994, p. 28, and is supportive of Jackie Gleason and their work together. A special profile appears in the *New York Post Magazine*, 10 Mar. 1957, p. 3; articles in the 29 Sept. 1951 and 28 June 1955 issues of the *New York World-Telegram* offer insights into her career and roles. An obituary is in the *New York Times*, 5 Feb. 1996.

EDWARD L. LACH, JR.
BARBARA BENNETT PETERSON

MELLON, Paul (11 June 1907–1 Feb. 1999), philanthropist, art collector, horse breeder, and conservationist, was born in Pittsburgh, Pennsylvania, the son of Andrew W. Mellon, a banker, secretary of the treasury (1921–1932), and ambassador to Britain (1932–1933), and Nora McMullen Mellon. His parents divorced when he was five and his sister Ailsa was eleven. Under the terms of the divorce settlement, the children were to spend eight months with their father and four months with their mother, who was living in England. (When they reached the age of fourteen, the children were to decide how long they wished to stay with either parent.) As a child, Paul was afraid of his father, whom he described in his autobiography, *Reflections in a Silver Spoon*, as "inclined to be dry, and censorious and negative." He remembered, too, that he passed his "happiest days" with the servants who treated him "seriously" and talked to him "as one human being to another." In England with his mother Paul began to develop a lifelong affinity for the countryside.

After attending local Pittsburgh schools and Choate Academy, Mellon continued his education at Yale, earning an A.B. degree in 1929. At Clare College, Cambridge University, England, he received a second A.B. degree in 1931 and an M.A. in 1938. In his first year at Cambridge, when he was already an accomplished rider, he discovered fox hunting.

Mellon returned to Pittsburgh in late 1931 and, giving in to his father's wishes, commenced an internship at the Mellon Bank to gain an overall understanding

of its operations. His father also arranged for him to be a director of several companies, including Gulf Oil Corporation and the Pittsburgh Coal Company. His experience soured him on a business career. Although apprehensive about being rebuffed, he approached his father in November 1936 to apprise him of his intense distaste for business and his desire to live in the country and indulge his passion for horses. To Mellon's surprise, the father acquiesced in his son's wishes. Thereafter, Mellon and his wife made their home at "Rockeby," a Virginia farm he acquired from his mother. (He had married Mary Brown in 1935, and they were to have two children.) Originally comprising four hundred acres, Rockeby, located in Upperville, eventually encompassed over four thousand acres.

After the death of his father in August 1937, Mellon and his wife left for Europe. They studied with Carl Jung in Zurich and then traveled. But with Europe engulfed in war, they returned to the United States in 1940.

In the summer of 1941 Mellon joined the army as a private. At his request, he was assigned to the horse cavalry and sent to Fort Riley, Kansas, as an instructor in horsemanship. He attended Officers Candidate School and in 1942 was commissioned a second lieutenant. Anxious to see action, he secured a transfer to the Office of Strategic Services in 1944. He served in England, Belgium, and France and in early 1945 was promoted to major.

Discharged in August 1945 Mellon returned to Rockeby and to his unabated passion for fox hunting and trail riding. He had owned racehorses before the war but now became more serious about the breeding and racing of horses. It was his intention to try to run the enterprise at a profit, and so he decided to raise horses for flat racing rather than the less lucrative steeplechase. Rockeby Farms did manage to breed a number of outstanding horses, such as Arts and Letters, horse of the year in 1969, and Mill Reef, the winner of several races and sire of a remarkable string of successful offspring, including three Kentucky Derby winners.

Mellon was as serious about paintings as he was about horse breeding. As an Anglophile, he was drawn to collecting British art, starting in 1936 with the purchase of a horse painting by George Stubbs, at the time a largely forgotten eighteenth-century artist. In the 1950s he began to assemble an impressive collection of British art of the seventeenth and eighteenth centuries. To house the paintings, he built and endowed the Yale Center for British Art, which opened in 1977. He donated other works of art, both British and American, to the Yale Art Gallery and the Virginia Museum of Fine Arts, where he also served as a trustee.

No artistic institution benefited more from Mellon's generosity, however, than the National Gallery of Art in Washington, D.C. Endowed by his father, it was dedicated in 1941. At the ceremony, Mellon presented to President Franklin D. Roosevelt his father's entire art collection, a stunning gift that was accepted by Roosevelt in the name of the American people. Over the years Mellon made further contributions, as did his sister Ailsa, herself a serious collector, and his second wife, Rachel "Bunny" Lloyd Mellon (whom he married in 1948, two years after the death of his first wife). These were for the most part French and American paintings. Mellon, who served as president (1938–1939, 1963–1979) and a trustee of the National Gallery, also funded the construction of the museum's East Building.

Mellon's cultural interests were not confined to paintings. In 1945 he founded the Bollingen Foundation to translate and publish foreign works in English, as well as books devoted to art, anthropology, philosophy, and other subjects. The foundation also created the nation's top poetry prize. In 1969 he established the Andrew W. Mellon Foundation, which makes grants to educational, cultural, and medical institutions and to other organizations and causes.

Liberal though he was in funding the arts, education, and cultural causes, Mellon admitted that his contributions to conservation provided the "most heartwarming satisfaction" (quoted in *Reflections in a Silver Spoon*, p. 375). Through two foundations, the Avalon, founded by Ailsa in 1940, and the Old Dominion, set up in 1941 by Paul, the Mellons shared the cost of acquiring about 28,600 acres for inclusion in the Cape Hatteras National Seashore, dedicated in 1958. The foundations also funded the publication of *Our Vanishing Shoreline* (1956), a survey of Atlantic and Gulf coast areas worthy of preservation. The Andrew W. Mellon Foundation paid for the purchase of some 8,500 acres of the Cumberland Island National Seashore, and Paul Mellon acquired 1,100 acres near his home that were on the verge of being developed and gave the land to Virginia for Sky Meadows State Park.

Mellon's legendary philanthropy is the major reason for his historical significance. His largess is perhaps best identified with the National Gallery of Art, of which he was considered the "guiding spirit" (*People's Weekly*, 29 Mar. 1999, p. 147). The sum total of Mellon's beneficence during his lifetime totaled in excess of $600 million. Moreover, in his will he donated over $450 million to the National Gallery of Art, Yale, Clare College, and other universities and institutions.

There is no explanation for his extraordinary generosity in *Reflections in a Silver Spoon*. It has been suggested that in his sessions with Mellon, Carl Jung may have fostered "a useful sense of guilt" (*The Economist*, 20 Feb. 1999, p. 82). But Mellon may just as likely have derived the philanthropic habit from his father, the founder of the National Gallery of Art. Whatever the explanation, Mellon's immensely liberal giving was infused with a spirit of self-effacement. To exploit his philanthropy for power or public preferment never appealed to him. Like his father, what did attract this cultured, modest, and fastidious man was privacy, which he called in his autobiography the "most valuable asset that money can buy."

Mellon hardly neglected the advantages available to someone of great wealth. He owned five houses, traveled widely, and lived life to the full. He believed it was advisable "not to take life too seriously, to temper future responsibility with pleasure, and to take time out to smell the flowers." Mellon died at his Upperville, Virginia, home.

• Essential for an understanding of Mellon is his autobiography, *Reflections in a Silver Spoon: A Memoir* (1992), written with John Baskett. Brief summaries of Mellon's background and generosity are found in *House Beautiful*, July 1997, pp. 38f; *Daily Telegraph* (London), 3 Feb. 1999; *Los Angeles Times*, 6 Feb. 1999; *The Economist*, 20 Feb. 1999, p. 82; and *People's Weekly*, 29 Mar. 1999, p. 147. An obituary is in the *New York Times*, 3 Feb. 1999.

RICHARD HARMOND

MENIL, Dominique de (23 Mar. 1908–31 Dec. 1997), art patron, was born Dominique Schlumberger in Paris, France, to Conrad Schlumberger, an oil technology pioneer, and Louise Delpech Schlumberger. Dominique studied for an advanced degree in physics and math at the Sorbonne in the late 1920s before marrying John (at that time, Jean) de Menil, a banker in 1931. (They were to have five children.) In 1936 John de Menil began working for Schlumberger, Ltd., and soon thereafter he moved to Houston, Texas, to run the company's American branch. Dominique joined her husband in Houston in 1941, and they subsequently went to Venezuela to expand their business in South America. A few years later they resettled in Houston and commissioned architect Philip Johnson to create their primary residence, which was decorated by fashion designer Charles James. Dominique became a U.S. citizen in the early 1960s.

Although later renowned for their collection of modern art, their first acquisition came with trepidation. While still in Paris, the couple commissioned a portrait of Dominique by the surrealist Max Ernst. Displeased with the work, however, they kept it wrapped in a cupboard. Their second major purchase was a watercolor by Paul Cézanne, bought by John on the advice of Father Marie-Alain Couturier, a French Dominican priest living in New York during World War II. Convinced that modern art could play an important role in Catholic religion, Couturier was involved with the creation of several churches in Europe that featured work by twentieth-century artists, including the Chapel of the Rosary in Vence, France, commissioned from Henri Matisse.

Following Couturier's example, the de Menils began collecting art that they felt had a spiritual quality, such as Byzantine icons and African tribal worship objects. Dominique once wrote, "Through art, God constantly clears a path to our hearts." Despite their initial reaction to the Ernst portrait (which became one of their favorites), the couple also started to acquire surrealist art, including an astounding number of works by René Magritte and Ernst. In addition, they were purchasing modern art associated with the latest movements of the time, such as abstract expressionism, pop art, and minimalism.

Their passion for art extended beyond their home. In the late 1950s the de Menils became involved with the Basilian-run University of St. Thomas, located just south of downtown Houston. They bought and donated land around the campus to the university and commissioned Philip Johnson to create a master plan for the university's expansion, including the erection of several buildings designed by the architect. They funded the development of the institution's art department, initially headed by curator Jermayne MacAgy and later by Dominique, until they moved the entire department to Rice University (also in Houston) in 1969 to form the Institute for the Arts and the Rice Media Center. They also were actively involved in the Contemporary Arts Association (now the Contemporary Arts Museum), organizing exhibitions, serving on the board, and funding their operations.

In 1964 the de Menils commissioned Johnson to design a chapel originally intended for the University of St. Thomas. Named the Rothko chapel, the octagonal building houses a series of fourteen paintings made specifically for the location by artist Mark Rothko, who also influenced the final design of the structure. Outside the building, the de Menils placed "Broken Obelisk," a steel sculpture by Barnett Newman. The building was dedicated in 1971 "to meditation and peace," and in 1973 (the year that John de Menil died) it became home to an independent organization for interfaith worship and human rights. The chapel became the center of Dominique de Menil's humanitarian activities, which included the Commitment to Truth and Freedom Awards established in 1981 and the Carter-Menil Human Rights Foundation formed with former president Jimmy Carter in 1986. Since its completion, the chapel has hosted religious services for dozens of world religions, colloquiums, and award ceremonies for international figures including the Dalai Lama, Nelson Mandela, and Jonas Salk.

The de Menils had planned to open a museum designed by Louis Kahn for their permanent collection as early as 1972, but following her husband's death and Kahn's a year later, in 1974, Dominique de Menil halted the project. In 1980 she met Italian architect Renzo Piano, who had been co-architect for the Pompidou Center in Paris. Together they envisioned a museum that would be "small on the outside but be as big as possible on the inside." The collection would constantly rotate between public and nonpublic areas and pieces would be spaced physically in such a way that, in de Menil's words, "The public would never know museum fatigue and would have the rare joy of sitting in front of a painting and contemplating it." Opened in 1987 and called the Menil Collection, the building has an exterior made of gray cypress and white steel to blend into the surrounding neighborhood of bungalows also owned by the Menil Foundation. Inside, visitors enter galleries off a main long hallway with dark wood flooring and lit with interior spotlights and sunlight filtered through an unusual skylight system invented for the building. The museum features selections from the de Menils' collection, particularly ancient art, Byzantine and medieval art, arts of tribal cultures, and twentieth-century painting and sculpture including a large rotating exhibition on surrealism. Ample storage and office space supplements the galleries, which have also presented special exhibitions of work by leading artists such as Rothko, Franz Kline, Joseph Cornell, and Robert Rauschenberg—all organized by the museum's staff.

In the 1990s de Menil funded several different buildings for her collection: a chapel designed by her son François de Menil to house thirteenth-century Byzantine frescoes on long-term loan from the government of Cyprus and the Church of Cyprus; a separate building across from the Menil Collection to display the paintings and sculpture of Cy Twombly; and Richmond Hall, which houses late work by the minimalist artist Dan Flavin (1933–1996).

With her husband, de Menil also sponsored scholarly publications, such as catalogue raisonnés for Magritte by David Sylvester and for Max Ernst by Werner Spies and the ongoing multivolume work *The Image of the Black in Western Art* that was started in 1960 (published in four volumes from 1976–1989). Honors bestowed on her include the Order of Arts and Letters from the French government in 1984 and the U.S. Medal of Arts in 1986. Dominique de Menil died in Houston at the age of eighty-nine.

In addition to amassing an astounding private collection of more than 15,000 paintings, drawings, prints, sculptures, photographs, and rare books, John and Dominique de Menil left a firm imprint on Houston through their involvement with two universities, the city's art institutions, and finally their own museum. Friends and fellow art patrons were surprised that such an international couple remained in Texas. In defending her dedication to the city, Dominique de Menil said, "I always felt a kind of energy in Houston. I always felt that what didn't exist [here] would happen within a couple of years."

• Calvin Tomkins wrote an extensive biographical article on Dominique de Menil for the *New Yorker*, 8 June 1998, pp. 52–67. Additional biographical pieces can be found in the *Houston Post Magazine*, 31 May 1987, pp. 6–11, and the *Dallas Morning News*, 6 Apr. 1997. De Menil collaborated with Pie Duployé on a selection of writings by Father Marie-Alain Couturier called *Sacred Art* (1989). For reviews of the Menil Collection, see John Russell, "At Last, a 'Museum without Walls' . . . ," *New York Times*, 14 June 1987, and Reyner Banham, "In the Neighborhood of Art," *Art in America*, June 1987, pp. 124–129. The museum's opening was marked by the publication of *The Menil Collection: A Selection from the Paleolithic to the Modern Era* (1987). Susan J. Barnes, *The Rothko Chapel: An Act of Faith* (1989), provides information on the de Menils, the chapel's many plans, Rothko's commissioned series of paintings, and the subsequent history of the chapel itself. For earlier catalogs of the de Menils' collection, see *Look Back: An Exhibition of Cubist Paintings and Sculptures from the Menil Family Collection*, published for a traveling exhibition organized by the University of St. Thomas (1968); *Selection from the Menil Collection* (Institute for the Arts, Rice University 1971); *Transfixed by Light: Photographs from the Menil Foundation Collection* (1980); and *Reading Prints: A Selection of 16th- to Early 19th-Century Prints from the Menil Collection* (1985); the three latter books include short forewords by Dominique de Menil. Informative obituaries appear in the *New York Times* and the *Houston Chronicle*, both 1 Jan. 1998; *Art in America*, Feb. 1998; and *ARTnews*, Mar. 1998.

N. ELIZABETH SCHLATTER

MEREDITH, Burgess (16 Nov. 1907–9 Sept. 1997), actor and director, was born Oliver Burgess Meredith in Cleveland, Ohio, the son of William George Meredith, a physician, and Ida Beth Burgess Meredith, a Methodist minister's daughter. He called his childhood "grim and incoherent" because his father was a quarrelsome alcoholic. Meredith was a boy soprano in the choir of New York City's Cathedral of St. John the Divine and a four-year scholarship student in its school. He played the lead in its production of J. M. Barrie's *Peter Pan*. He spent three years at the Hoosac Preparatory School, Hoosick Falls, New York. After entering Amherst College in 1926 on an insufficient scholarship, he soon quit and held odd jobs, but he re-enrolled in 1927. He worked for room and meals, played Sir Toby Belch in Shakespeare's *Twelfth Night* at nearby Smith College, and left Amherst because of poor grades in 1928. More odd jobs followed, notably as cadet seaman to Venezuela. In 1929 through a former teacher he met Eva Le Gallienne, a theater-group manager in New York's Greenwich Village, where he appeared, unpaid, on stage. After summer theater work, he made impressive appearances on Broadway in 1933, and in 1934 acted in the first of seven plays with Katharine Cornell. He also started what became distinguished radio work as actor and host, including a 1937 performance as Hamlet.

Astounding success came when Meredith starred as Mio in Maxwell Anderson's *Winterset* in 1935, reprised the role in the 1936 movie version, and in 1937 appeared in *High Tor* (winning a Drama Critics award), also by Anderson, who became his surrogate father until they had a falling-out. Meredith was a Federal Arts adviser (1937) and an Actors' Equity Association Officer (1938). A dozen movies followed, the best being *Of Mice and Men* (1938), based on his friend John Steinbeck's novel, and as war correspondent Ernie Pyle, another friend, in *The Story of G.I. Joe* (1945). He also appeared with Paulette Goddard and Fred Astaire in *Idiot's Delight* (1939) and *Second Chorus* (1941), with Ginger Rogers in *Tom, Dick and Harry* (1941), and with Ingrid Bergman and Elia Kazan in *Liliom* (1942). His early assembly of other friends, their varied personalities complementing his mercurial nature, also included Tallulah Bankhead, Henry Fonda, Lee Strasberg, and Kurt Weill. During his leave-punctuated stint in the U.S. Army Air Force (1942–1945, rising to the rank of captain), Meredith

served in London but returned early in 1944 to make *Salute to France*, an indoctrination movie.

Meredith's postwar career was varied and spectacular. He not only continued acting but also was a director, writer, and producer—and occasionally a political activist. Among his seventy-five movies, several merit special comment. He appeared in *Magnificent Doll* (1946, as James Madison opposite Ginger Rogers's Dolley Madison) and *On Our Merry Way* (1948, with his friend Jimmy Stewart). His career suffered a setback when his liberal political views enflamed Senator Joseph McCarthy, who blacklisted him along with other Hollywood personalities alleged to favor communism. Otto Preminger helped restore Meredith to favor by casting and directing him in *Advise and Consent* (1962) and *The Cardinal* (1963, with Meredith's friend John Huston). More successful film appearances followed, notably in *Batman* as the Penguin (1966), in *Day of the Locust* (1973, receiving an Oscar nomination for his supporting role), in *Rocky* as Sylvester Stallone's trainer Mickey (1976, nominated for another supporting-role Oscar) and several *Rocky* sequels, in *True Confessions* (1980, with Robert De Niro), and as Jack Lemmon's father in *Grumpy Old Men* (1993) and its sequel.

Earlier, Meredith obtained what he called "a splendid revenge . . . [on] the McCarthy Gang" with his Emmy-winning performance as army counsel Joseph Welch in *Tail Gunner Joe* (1977), a telefilm ridiculing McCarthy's behavior during the 1954 army-McCarthy hearings. Meredith was better known as the Penguin on television's *Batman* series (1966–1968). Other TV work included co-hosting *Those Amazing Animals* (1980–1981) and filming the documentary *Myths of Ancient Egypt* (1981). Meredith's directorial skills were evidenced early and late, notably in the movie *The Man on the Eiffel Tower* (1950, filmed in Paris and starring actor-friends Franchot Tone and Charles Laughton) and in stage productions of *Ulysses in Nighttown* (1958, with Zero Mostel as James Joyce's Leopold Bloom), *A [James] Thurber Carnival* (1960), and *The Yin and the Yang of Mr. Go* (1970, which he also wrote and filmed in Hong Kong). Meredith's distinctive voice was in demand not only for continuing radio work but also as the narrator of movies, for example, *Afterglow* (1986, on the life of Robert Frost), and of TV productions, notably *Puff the Magic Dragon* (1979, in which he also sang); his distinctive voice-over could be heard on numerous TV commercials.

Despite punishing demands on his virtuosic talents, Meredith had an extraordinary personal life. He was married four times. He and actress Helen Derby, a divorcée with a child, were married in 1932; he divorced her in 1935, and she later committed suicide. In 1936 he married Margaret Perry, another divorcée; they were divorced in 1938. His marriage to Paulette Goddard, Charles Chaplin's ex-wife, lasted from 1944 to 1948. Meredith starred with Goddard in *The Diary of a Chambermaid* (1946), which he coproduced and for which he wrote the screenplay based on

Octave Mirbeau's novel *Celestine's Diary*. Meredith said that their marriage had ended without acrimony and simply because their separate careers caused them to spend many months apart. In truth, however, he sued her in 1952 for $400,000 of communal property; she countersued, and an out-of-court settlement favored her. In 1950 Meredith married Kaja Sundsten, a twenty-year-old Swedith dancer; they had two children and, again according to Meredith, were very happy. He died in Malibu, California.

Meredith owned a series of homes, including one called "High Tor" in Rockland County, near New York City, and later an estate in Malibu, where he was an admired wine connoisseur, amateur chef, and nonpareil host. His work gained him friends, and his friends gained him work. He will always be regarded as a genius of stage and screen.

• A source of substantial information about Meredith is his candid, chaotic autobiography, *So Far, So Good: A Memoir* (1994). Julie Gilbert, *Opposite Attraction: The Lives of Erich Maria Remarque and Paulette Goddard* (1995), has revealing information about Meredith, partly based on interviews. Lee G. Miller, *The Story of Ernie Pyle* (1950); Willi Frischauer, *Beyond the Scenes of Otto Preminger: An Unauthorized Biography* (1974); and Ginger Rogers, *Ginger Rogers: My Story* (1991), touch on Meredith and their respective subjects. James Robert Parish and Vincent Terrace, *The Complete Actors' Television Credits, 1948–1988* (1989), lists 112 TV shows featuring Meredith; Terrace, *Fifty Years of Television: A Guide to Series and Pilots, 1937–1988* (1991), describes eight shows (1949–1986) featuring Meredith, notably *Gloria* and *Mr. Novak*; Ephraim Katz, *The Film Encyclopedia* (3d ed., 1998), lists Meredith's seventy-five movie appearances. An obituary, with four photographs, is in the *New York Times*, 11 Sept. 1997.

ROBERT L. GALE

MERRICK, David (27 Nov. 1911–25 Apr. 2000), theatrical producer, was born David Margulois in St. Louis, Missouri, the youngest of six children of Samuel Margulois, a merchant, and Celia Margulois (maiden name unknown). He was educated at St. Louis's Washington University (where he finished second in a playwriting contest in which Tennessee Williams went unplaced) and the St. Louis University Law School. While studying law he met Leonore Beck; they were married in 1939 and moved to New York, where he began to practice law. In 1940 Merrick made his first investment in a Broadway show, putting $5,000 into Herman Shumlin's production of *The Male Animal*, a comedy by James Thurber and Elliott Nugent. He pocketed a $20,000 return. Later he claimed that his life had truly begun in 1940. It was then that Margulois became Merrick, saying he would need a new name if he ever had to practice law in his hated hometown.

Merrick had already rejected his earlier life; being at home with his warring parents, he said, had been like living on the set of *Who's Afraid of Virginia Woolf?* He soon made clear that his private life was no one else's business and that his "real" life was what happened in the theater. With this single-mindedness he would become his era's most successful theatrical producer. Astute investments such as *The Male Animal*, however, did not immediately elevate Merrick to a place on Broadway. Although he continued to practice law until 1949, he also worked for Shumlin, becoming his general manager in 1946. He made his debut as a producer with an English comedy called *Clutterbuck* (1949). The play broke even in the year of *Death of a Salesman*'s premiere, largely because of Merrick's use of the "stunts" that would characterize his career—hiring bellhops to walk through hotel lobbies and bars, calling for "Mr. Clutterbuck."

Merrick's breakthrough came in 1954 with his first musical, *Fanny*, which demonstrated his remarkable ability to spot and transform a "property." He flew to Monte Carlo unannounced to talk Marcel Pagnol, author of the trilogy of plays featuring Fanny, into granting rights to adapt the plays for the musical stage. Then he gradually persuaded Joshua Logan to be the director, but he failed to interest Richard Rodgers and Oscar Hammerstein II in writing the score (Merrick insisted on taking equal billing with them; decades of coolness followed). He eventually commissioned Harold Rome to write the music and lyrics. Once the show was set to open, Merrick had a full-size nude statue of the show's belly dancer erected in Central Park and posted notices ("Have you seen *Fanny*?") in men's restrooms all over town; he took out Broadway's first full-page advertisements. Once *Fanny* had begun its run, he made sure excerpts were regularly featured on the Ed Sullivan television show. *Fanny* was the hit of the season and stayed on for 888 performances, showing the largest profit of any Broadway production up to that time. The career of the man who became known as the "abominable showman" was firmly on track.

Merrick was the most interventionist of producers—he might, during a play's run, steal parts of a musical score he did not like—and he regularly set his employees at odds with each other, claiming that such friction produced the best results. But he was also responsible for significant positive changes in the way plays came to the stage; in 1957, for instance, he forced the racial integration of the backstage staff of the musical *Jamaica*. In 1958, while one of his conventional dramatic hits, *The World of Suzie Wong*, moved through its run, he took the first step in a single-handed "British invasion of Broadway" by importing the entire cast of playwright John Osborne's *Look Back in Anger*. In so doing he fought and won a battle with Actors Equity, noting that as a lawyer he knew "more about your rules and contracts than you do." During the run of *Look Back in Anger*, Merrick hired a woman for $250 to rush onstage from the audience and slap the loutish antihero. Criticized for such a tawdry tactic, he retorted, "If people can sell junk to the public that way, why can't I sell them a good play that way?" Late in 1958 he persuaded Laurence Olivier to repeat his role in Osborne's *The Entertainer* in a limited engagement on Broadway by telling Olivier that a rival producer of Merrick's was going to cancel a planned project with the actor.

Reading one chapter of stripteaser Gypsy Rose Lee's memoirs was enough to convince Merrick to get the rights and turn it into a musical. The result was *Gypsy* (1959), with music by Jule Styne and lyrics by Stephen Sondheim, generally regarded as the last great show of the American musical theater's golden age. During the 1960–1961 season Merrick opened back-to-back hits from abroad, the Irish play *A Taste of Honey* and an adaptation of the French play *Becket*. As the season went on, Merrick had six Broadway shows running simultaneously and received the first of his eight Antoinette Perry awards ("in recognition of a fabulous production record over the past seven years"). But he was disappointed with the lagging advance sale of tickets for the musical *Subways Are for Sleeping*; to draw attention to it, he hired ordinary people who bore the same names as the major theatrical critics to write rave reviews. Although major newspapers quickly caught on to the ruse, word got around, and the show enjoyed a moderately successful run.

Merrick's characteristic blend of "ruthlessness and vitality" reached one of its peaks in 1964 with *Hello, Dolly!* the musical version of Thornton Wilder's *The Matchmaker*, which Merrick had also produced in 1955. The musical's 2,844 performances made it at the time the longest-running broadway show on record. It was one of twelve shows, eight of them new, opened by Merrick during the 1963–1964 season, including Lionel Bart's *Oliver!* (the longest-running show in Great Britain) and one genuine flop, a revival of Tennessee Williams's *The Milk Train Doesn't Stop Here Anymore*, which had only four performances. One of several explosive collaborations with director-choreographer Gower Champion, *Hello, Dolly!* broke new ground when midway in its run Merrick brought in an all-African-American cast. In 1965 Merrick imported to New York Peter Brook's Royal Shakespeare Company production of Peter Weiss's intensely challenging play *The Persecution and Assassination of Marat as Performed by the Inmates of the Asylum of Charenton under the Direction of the Marquis de Sade*, and he squeezed a profit out of only 145 performances. The next year Merrick secured the first rights outside Ireland to Brian Friel's *Philadelphia, Here I Come*. By 1966 it was estimated by *Time* magazine that 20 percent of Broadway workers were in his employ.

Later in 1966 Merrick, frequently criticized for not encouraging new playwrights, produced the first play by stand-up comic Woody Allen. *Don't Drink the Water* was the season's most popular comedy, surpassing 500 performances. In 1969 Allen returned with the equally popular *Play It Again, Sam*, another Merrick show, in which Allen made his acting debut. The 1970–1971 Broadway season included seven new Merrick productions, with a half-dozen more in various stages of development. Perhaps most outstanding was the Royal Shakespeare Company's circuslike version of *A Midsummer Night's Dream*. In 1972 he pro-

duced the moderately successful musical *Sugar*, based on the film *Some Like It Hot*. Thereafter Merrick surprisingly decamped to Hollywood. The experience of coproducing *The Great Gatsby* (1974) was frustrating to him, but the film's reputation did grow in subsequent years. Merrick, the genius of publicity, seems genuinely to have been unprepared for the relentless glare surrounding the star-studded and apparently star-crossed Hollywood production.

When Merrick returned to Broadway in 1977, he found that his long-time rival Harold Prince was doing fine as a producer and director. Worse than that, however, "the Shuberts" (Bernard Jacobs and Gerald Schoenfeld, respectively president and chairman of the Shubert organization) had usurped his place at the top, even going so far as to import British dramatic successes and backing the musical show destined to break all long-run records, *A Chorus Line* (1975). Merrick's response was a classic demonstration of chutzpah. Determined to turn the Warner Brothers musical films of 1933–1935 into a show, he rehired Champion, and a grueling process of shaping and reshaping began, climaxing in a disastrous tryout at the Kennedy Center in Washington, which ran an hour overtime. As rumors of disaster swept about him, Merrick bought out all his investors ("This is my poker game"), threw out all the costumes and sets, plus the book, and virtually started from scratch. After a chaotic run-up to the premiere of *42nd Street* on 25 August 1980, the combative Champion (Merrick called him "a Presbyterian Hitler") sickened, dying of cancer on opening night. Merrick kept the news from his cast—and from everyone else. As *42nd Street* opened with the sound of dozens of tap shoes beating on a percussive stage, the audience responded with almost primitive joy. At the evening's close, Merrick stepped forward and announced Champion's death, to further outbreaks of emotion. The evening passed into Broadway legend; it was the poker player's last big stakes.

Although *42nd Street* ran on into 1989, the news thereafter created by Merrick was largely confined to courts of law. A near-fatal stroke in 1983 forced a portion of his marital history into the public eye, but a great deal of it remains obscured by Merrick's legal maneuverings. After the conclusion of his marriage to Leonore Beck (in 1960 according to Barbara Lee Horn in *David Merrick*), Merrick married Jeanne Gilbert, with whom he had one daughter. This second marriage ended in 1966, according to Horn, and in 1969 he wed Etan Aronson, secretly divorcing her only weeks later, although they too had a daughter. The divorce from Aronson surfaced when he married Karen Prunczik, a dancing actress from *42nd Street*. She was his wife at the time of the stroke. During court proceedings about the management of Merrick's estate (largely a struggle between Aronson and Prunczik) and about his mental competence, the stricken producer, who was supposedly bedridden, wheeled himself out of his convalescent home in a pouring rain. Handicapped by the aphasia that stayed with him for the rest of his life, he wrote out instructions to startled passersby to take to his lawyers. He thereupon divorced Prunczik and remarried Aronson, whom he may have divorced again in 1999, after he apparently had married Natalie Lloyd, a lawyer's receptionist.

Though lacking the power of speech, Merrick continued to be a producer—a revival of the Gershwins' *Oh, Kay!* and a stage version of the film *State Fair* (1996), which brought from him a final burst of scorn. When the score for *State Fair* was declared ineligible for a Tony because it was not original enough, Merrick declared he would shortly set up his own theatrical awards. Though he did create the Merrick Arts Foundation, he did not make good on that threat. He spent much of his last half-decade in his apartments at the Savoy in London, where he died. The commotion over his estate may yet be rumbling on. Undoubtedly the last of the flamboyant theatrical producers—and certainly the most financially successful of all—David Merrick was from one aspect a darkly melodramatic individual—almost always dressed in black, with a flourishing black mustache, frowning out from under a black homburg, lacking only a black cape. He never exhibited much interest in the literary side of drama and seemed entirely devoted to pleasing the most audiences. In Merrick's world there was not enough success to go around: "It's not enough that I should succeed—others should fail." (*Los Angeles Times*, 27 Apr. 2000). Offstage an apparently shy and insecure man (and one who inspired great loyalties among the staff he so regularly abused), Merrick once likened that success to climbing Everest: "And guess what there is when you get up there? Snow and ice" (*New York Times*, 27 Apr. 2000).

• Merrick's papers are so far unavailable. Howard Kissel, *David Merrick: The Abominable Showman, the Unauthorized Biography* (1993), is a rare attempt to penetrate the secrecy Merrick wove about himself. Of bibliographical interest is Barbara Lee Horn, *David Merrick: A Bio-Bibliography* (1992). Useful obituaries include those by Frank Rich, *New York Times*, 27 Apr. 2000; Michael Phillips, *Los Angeles Times*, 27 Apr. 2000; and Kevin Gregory, the *Guardian* (U.K.), 28 Apr. 2000. A sketch by Rhonda Geronimo is found at the website goodbyemag.

JAMES ROSS MOORE

MERRILL, James (3 Mar. 1926–6 Feb. 1995), poet, was born in New York City to Charles Edward Merrill, a stockbroker, and Helen Ingram Merrill, who published a small newspaper. The elder Merrill, who had two children from a previous marriage, was a founder of and senior partner in the brokerage firm Merrill, Lynch & Company. Young James was raised in an atmosphere of wealth and privilege, which continued even after his parents' divorce when he was twelve. A governess awakened his early interest in languages, teaching him both French and German, and he began writing poetry as a child, encouraged by his parents. A passion from childhood onward was music,

especially opera, to which he was introduced at the age of eleven.

Merrill was sent to exclusive private schools in the city and then to preparatory school at Lawrenceville, in New Jersey, where he continued writing poetry as well as short stories. With the help of his father he privately published a small collection of verse. After graduating in 1943 he entered Amherst College but took a leave of absence the following year to serve in the U.S. Army until the end of World War II, in 1945. Despite this interruption, Merrill excelled in his studies, majoring in literature. Having written a thesis on Marcel Proust, who became a major inspiration for his work, he graduated *summa cum laude* with a Phi Beta Kappa key in 1947.

During Merrill's years at Amherst his future career as a poet seemed all but assured. By the time of his graduation his verse had already appeared in *Poetry* and the *Kenyon Review*, and he had published his first book of poems, *The Black Swan* (1946). After college he moved back to New York to write—the enormous Merrill family fortune allowed him to pursue his interests without having to earn a living—but after a while he found the atmosphere too intense and distracting for serious work. He traveled for several years in Europe and Asia, reflecting on his life and family and apparently coming to terms with his homosexuality. He eventually settled in the small coastal town of Stonington, Connecticut, with David Jackson, who would become his longtime companion. During the 1960s Merrill bought a house in Athens and subsequently another residence in Key West, Florida, and divided his time among the three homes.

Merrill's first mature collection of verse was published as *First Poems* in 1951 and received mixed reviews; while a few critics praised his elegance and sensibility, most found his poetry to be technically polished but ultimately dull, without the necessary element of delight. Merrill responded by concentrating next on prose, including two plays: *The Bait* (1953), about a brother-sister relationship, and *The Immortal Husband* (1955), a retelling of the Greek myth of Tithonus. Both were produced in New York and received mildly favorable reviews. In 1957 he again received mixed reviews for his first novel, *The Seraglio*, the story of an aging businessman and his predatory female admirers. His inability to find definitive success as either a playwright or a novelist led Merrill to turn back to poetry. In 1954 he had published a limited edition of his poems, *Short Stories*, which was largely ignored by the critics, but he attracted wide attention in 1959 with the publication by Knopf of *The Country of a Thousand Years of Peace*. This time critics were almost all commendatory, calling it an important collection by a poet who had at last found his true voice, though some dismissed it as the work of a dilettantish aesthete and his subject matter—gardens, statues, Greek gods, and the like—as superficial.

There were few reservations about Merrill's collection *Water Street* (1962), which was praised for the very things his 1959 book had, for some, lacked: "a deeper compassion, a kind of humility," according to X. J. Kennedy in the *New York Times Book Review*, as well as self-irony. Indeed, Merrill had moved, as he later acknowledged, from a belief in "art for art's sake" to "art for life's sake." In the early 1960s he returned briefly to prose, writing his second—and what would be his last—novel, *The (Diblos) Notebook* (1965), the story of a Greek American returning to his homeland. Reviews were generally good, but Merrill now felt ready to commit himself full time to poetry. In 1966 he published another collection of verse, *Nights and Days*, that earned uniformly critical praise and received the National Book Award for poetry in 1967. With the publication of *The Fire Screen* in 1969, Merrill's place as an important American poet was now assured, and he was compared favorably with both W. H. Auden and Wallace Stevens. Two years later, in recognition of his stature, he was elected to the National Institute of Arts and Letters. That stature was reconfirmed in 1972 with the publication of his collection *Braving the Elements*. Critics extolled his gifts as a lyric poet, in particular as one who wrote both wittily and movingly about love. Merrill's receipt of American poetry's highest honor, the Bollingen Prize, in 1973, was still another confirmation of his significance.

In the final two decades of his life, Merrill's reputation as a major poet grew even greater as he published new collections of verse. His *Divine Comedies* (1976), which won a Pulitzer Prize, included "The Book of Ephraim," a long poem allegedly relating the messages of spirits from the other world, including deceased family members; Merrill claimed that he and David Jackson had received these messages through the use of a Ouija board. The Ouija poems continued and were published in two subsequent volumes, *Mirabell: Books of Number* (1978) and *Scripts for the Pageant* (1980). All three collections were included in a revised version in *The Changing Light at Sandover*, published in 1982. Although some readers and critics alike expressed initial skepticism at Merrill's foray into the occult, there was ultimate agreement that he had written a great and moving series of poems narrating the story of an individual's passage through time. Some reviewers compared his imaginative vision to that of Yeats, Blake, Milton, and Dante.

After *Sandover*, Merrill published several more verse collections, including *Late Settings* (1985) and *The Inner Room* (1988), and a collection of short prose, *Recitative* (1986). He also wrote a memoir, *A Different Person* (1994), in which he wrote candidly of his upbringing, his unhappiness as a child, and his transcendence of that unhappiness through his poetry. He died suddenly in Tucson, Arizona, while on vacation. A final collection of his poems, *A Scattering of Salts*, was published posthumously in 1995.

• For biographical information see *Contemporary Authors, New Revision Series*, vol. 63 (1998), and Willard Spiegelman,

"James Merrill," in *Dictionary of Literary Biography*, vol. 5: *American Poets and Writers since World War II* (1980). For critical evaluations of Merrill's work, see especially Stephen Yenser, *The Consuming Myth: The Work of James Merrill* (1987); David Lehman and Charles Berger, eds., *James Merrill: Essays in Criticism* (1982); and Guy L. Rotella, ed., *Critical Essays on James Merrill* (1996). See also David Kalstone, *Five Temperaments: Elizabeth Bishop, Robert Lowell, James Merrill, Adrienne Rich, John Ashbery* (1977). An obituary appears in the *New York Times*, 7 Feb. 1995.

ANN T. KEENE

MICHENER, James (c. 3 Feb. 1907–16 Oct. 1997), popular novelist and author of nonfiction works, was born James Albert Michener in circumstances that remain unverified. Reports vary concerning his parents and birth. Michener routinely said that when he was two weeks old he was saved from an orphanage and raised by Mabel Haddock Michener, a widowed laundress and seamstress in Doylestown, Pennsylvania. She had a five-year-old son, named Robert. Another account was that Edwin Michener, Mabel's husband, was also James's father, which Michener believed until he was nineteen, when his uncle Louis Michener told him Edwin died in 1902, leaving only Mabel and Robert. Before his death, Robert swore Michener was born in 1907 in Mount Vernon, New York, the second son of the then-unwed Mabel. Mabel, a Quaker, raised both boys—as well as numerous abandoned waifs—with loving care, in enduring poverty and illness, and alienated from her parents, in-laws, and neighbors. In the summer of 1921, Michener began hitchhiking forays that within six years took him into forty-five states. In 1925 he graduated from high school in Doylestown, its star basketball player, and on a scholarship entered Swarthmore College, where he earned a B.A. in English and history, summa cum laude, in 1929.

Michener taught English at a prep school in Pottstown, Pennsylvania (1929–1931), then traveled and studied abroad on a two-year Swarthmore fellowship, going to Scotland, England, Italy, and Spain. Home again, he taught at a Quaker school in Doylestown (1933–1936), and, in 1936–1939, at the Colorado State College of Education (now the College of Northern Colorado), where he also earned a master's degree. A visiting professorship at Harvard completed his academic career (1939–1940), by which time he had published widely in the field of education. In 1940 Michener began a nine-year association, interrupted by World War II, with the Macmillan publishing firm as a social-science editor.

In October 1942 Michener enlisted in the U.S. Navy reserve, was commissioned the following February, served for a year at desk assignments in Washington, D.C., and Philadelphia, and in April 1944 was sent to the Pacific theater of operations. He was partly an aviator inspector but mostly a publications officer. His visits to some fifty islands inspired his *Tales of the South Pacific* (1947). Although it won a Pulitzer Prize for fiction, it remained little known until *South Pacific*, the 1949 musical by Richard Rodgers and Oscar Hammerstein II, made him famous and rich. Then he began to write full time.

Michener and Patti Koon, a minister's tomboyish daughter, were married in 1935. She joined the U.S. Women's Army Corps, served in Europe, and returned home but never lived with Michener again. In 1948, they obtained a divorce, and he married Vange A. Nord, an attractive but unsuccessful writer. They built a home in Pipersville, Bucks County, Pennsylvania. She traveled with Michener only part of the time, and tensions mounted, leading to a divorce in 1955. That same year Michener married Mari Yoriko Sabusawa, a well-educated, gracious Japanese American who had been sent with her family to detention camps when World War II began. In 1960 Michener campaigned vigorously for presidential candidate John F. Kennedy. In 1962 Michener ran, unsuccessfully, for Congress as a Democrat. Until her death in 1994, Mari Michener established marital tranquillity, enabling her prolific husband to work at his own steady pace.

Nine of Michener's novels reached the top spot on the *New York Times* bestseller lists: *Hawaii* (1959), *The Source* (1965), *Centennial* (1974), *Chesapeake* (1978), *The Covenant* (1980), *Space* (1982), *Poland* (1983), *Texas* (1985), and *Alaska* (1988). *Hawaii*, the first to employ Michener's formula of intertwined multicentury, multiracial, and multigenerational plot strands, concerns Polynesian settlers, good and evil missionaries, and Chinese and Japanese migrants; it also includes another element that was to become formulaic: vignettes about historical themes, such as diseases, commerce, and squabbles. Michener's characterizations may sometimes seem flat and his dialogue thin, but his armies of readers loved the pattern set by the panoramic narrative of *Hawaii*. Rather like a blend of fiction and textbook, *The Source* presents layers of ancient-to-modern Jewish history in the land that is now Israel. *Centennial* chronicles events in Colorado, beginning with animals before the Indians came, then white hunters, traders, gold-seekers, railroaders, ranchers, and finally families surviving the 1930s drought only to confront contemporary social and environmental problems. *Chesapeake*, a four-century epic, involves the lives of three families as they impinge on Indians, African Americans, and Irish immigrants along Maryland's Eastern Shore. Too much backgrounding and foregrounding may seem to leave the characters in between a little thin. *The Covenant*, a heavily researched, five-century panorama, presents an African family, an Afrikaner family, and an English family, and their descendants, in South Africa—working together, competing, and fighting. Michener lovingly depicts their land. Fact and fiction are again woven together in *Space*, which portrays politicians, engineers, and astronauts in the U.S. space program against a tangled sociopolitical backdrop fraught with antagonism toward science; according to most reviewers, Michener leaves the reader with the message that science is an easy target of demagoguery but is in fact

a noble endeavor. Reverting to the long historical perspective, *Poland* reveals, in brief episodes, the life of a fictional village on the Vistula River from the thirteenth century to the present, with three families—one wealthy, one aristocratic, and one agrarian—on which to pivot the narrative. Reviewers familiar with Polish history found fault with Michener's omissions at several points. *Texas* is cleverly cast as the work of a fictional task force ordered by the governor to assemble materials for teaching schoolchildren about events leading to the state's 1986 Sesquicentennial celebration. Following a prehistoric prologue, *Alaska* narrates events from the eighteenth century forward, from Russian domination and the American purchase of the territory to the discovery and exploitation of oil, with episodes about gold-seekers, the salmon industry, the Alcan highway, and World War II. These nine blockbuster novels average 848 pages each.

Many of Michener's other works indicate his uncanny range. He wrote a novel about interracial marriage, *Sayonara* (1954); four books on Japanese art (1956–1962); with A. Grove Day, a collective biography of ten criminals in the Pacific region, *Rascals in Paradise* (1957); a novel about the 1956 Hungarian revolution, *The Bridge at Andau* (1957); a travel book on Spain and Portugal, *Iberia* (1968); nonfictional and fictional critiques of late-1960s violence, *Kent State* and *The Drifters* (both 1971); an indictment of the commercializing of college and professional athletics, *Sports in America* (1976); novels and travelogues set in regions south of the United States, including *Caribbean* (1989), *Six Days in Havana* (with John Kings, 1989), *Mexico* (1992), and *My Lost Mexico* (1992); a book of criticism, *Literary Reflections: Michener on Michener, Hemingway, Capote, and Others* (1993); and many other books and scores of essays. Michener ended his writing career with *Recessional* (1994), a novel about a congeries of elderly people in a posh retirement home, and *This Noble Land: My Vision for America* (1996), an expression of his old-age worries and undying optimism.

Michener undoubtedly resembled a writing machine. Some of his work has been dismissed by the elite as rambling, sentimental, thin, melodramatic, and didactic, with complex events too casually treated. But he carefully researched, sometimes with adoring assistants, the backgrounds for his many subjects, and he conscientiously familiarized himself with the locales he chose to portray. Some critics have also felt that, once he hit on his format, he uncreatively repeated success after success for profit. It is true that his manual typewriter, on which he typed using two fingers, was a money tree. Film and television rights to some of his novels added millions of dollars to his enormous royalties. It should be emphasized, however, that Michener, who had no children, donated $100 million to charity, $37 million to the University of Texas, vast sums to other schools, and millions of dollars in art works to several institutions. Innumerable readers revered him for his big books, with their exciting plot strands, their veins of information, and their encouraging espousal of the old-fashioned American virtues of self-reliance, common sense, patriotism, frugality, and the work ethic. At the end of his life, Michener practiced what he had preached in part of *Recessional*. Knowing that his renal failure was irreversible, he asked to be removed from a dialysis machine and soon died. His death occurred in Austin, Texas.

• Michener's papers, manuscripts, and miscellaneous items are scattered among various libraries. Leading repositories are in the University of Northern Colorado, the University of Hawaii, Swarthmore College, the University of Texas, and the Library of Congress. He also endowed and helped fill what became the James A. Michener Art Museum in Doylestown. His autobiography, *The World Is My Home: A Memoir* (1992), stresses his travels and his writing. His semiautobiographical novel, *The Fires of Spring* (1949), sheds light on his early years. F. X. Roberts and C. D. Rhine, *James A. Michener: A Checklist of His Works, with a Selected, Annotated Bibliography* (1995), and David A. Groseclose, *James A. Michener: A Bibliography* (1996), provide extensive coverage of primary and secondary sources. John P. Hayes, *James A. Michener: A Biography* (1984) is thorough and accurate. Three critical studies are A. Grove Day, *James Michener*, 2d ed. (1977); George J. Becker, *James A. Michener* (1983); and Marilyn S. Severson, *James A. Michener: A Critical Companion* (1996). Alice Payne Hackett and James Henry Burke, *80 Years of Best Sellers, 1895–1975* (1977), provides sales figures—slightly in excess of 50,185,000—of seven of Michener's most popular books. John Bear, *The #1 New York Times Bestseller* (1992), calling Michener "the all-time king of #1 bestsellers," lists nine by Michener and includes brief descriptive remarks. Obituaries are in the *Chicago Tribune*, the *Los Angeles Times*, the *New York Times*, and the *Washington Post*, all 17 Oct. 1997.

ROBERT L. GALE

MILES, Josephine (11 June 1911–12 May 1985), poet and educator, was born in Chicago, the daughter of Reginald Odber Miles, an insurance businessman, and Josephine Lackner Miles. Her father's work occasionally took the family to southern California, where the dry air of the nearby desert alleviated her chronic arthritis. After graduating from high school in Los Angeles, where she studied Greek and Roman classics, Miles studied at the University of California, Los Angeles (B.A., 1932), and at the University of California at Berkeley, majoring in the philosophy of language (M.A., 1934; Ph.D., 1938). Her dissertation, "Wordsworth and the Vocabulary of Emotion," was published in 1942. Appointed to the Berkeley faculty in 1940, she rose from instructor (1940–1941) to assistant professor (1941–1947), associate professor (1947–1952), and university professor (1972–1978).

Miles's dissertation foreshadows the type of criticism she would pursue during the course of her career: she analyzes the frequency of Wordsworth's word usages, relates his diction to his era, and discusses that era's general notions of style and his own views on style. The dissertation was reissued in *The Vocabulary of Poetry: Three Studies* (1946), to which Miles added a study of changing object-emotion in-

terconnections in nineteenth-century poetry and of major adjectives in English poetry from Sir Thomas Wyatt to W. H. Auden. Continuing her tabulation approach, Miles concentrated on key '40s decades in *The Continuity of Poetic Language: Studies in English Poetry from the 1540's to the 1940's* (1951; with a new introduction, 1965). In *Eras & Modes in English Poetry* (1957; rev. and enl., 1964), perhaps the most significant example of her approach to poetry, she replaces chronological and historical divisions by demarcating "eras" via distinctly changing "modes"— i.e., diction, rhythm, syntax, and form. While adducing wide-ranging evidence, she emphasizes key figures from John Milton to William Butler Yeats. Most reviewers found *Eras & Modes* stimulating, but others were puzzled because it combined detailed generalizations in some places with undue brevity elsewhere. As Miles explained in 1965, her purpose in these studies—to which she added *Renaissance, Eighteenth-Century, and Modern Language in English Poetry: A Tabular View* (1960)—is "to explore more systematically the full variety of the temporal span of five centuries, and in the spatial extension to America, discovering the levels [i.e., continuity] between the extremes [i.e., poetic individualities]." In *Poetry and Change: Donne, Milton, Wordsworth, and the Equilibrium of the Present* (1974), she continues this analysis of poetic language. Her range of reading is astounding; her purpose, to show that repetitions, recurrences, and patterns of key words constitute a kind of history of abiding values. She finds her evidence in the proportions of verbs, nouns, and adjectives, and she categorizes sentences thus created as clausal (or predicative), phrasal (adjectival), and balanced (classical). She does not ignore variety; for example, major words in Geoffry Chaucer are "wine" and "young"; in Ben Jonson, "friend" and "grow"; in Alfred, Lord Tennyson, "dreary"; in Browning, "blood"; in Wallace Stevens and Edna St. Vincent Millay, "own"; and in E. E. Cummings, "mountain."

More generally useful, perhaps, are *Criticism: The Foundations of Modern Literary Judgment* (1948; rev. ed., 1958) and *The Poem: A Critical Anthology* (1959). The volume on literary judgment, which Miles coedited with Mark Schorer and Gordon McKenzie, is an anthology of essays from Plato to the twentieth century, presenting a variety of principles and of texts analyzed. *The Poem*, edited by Miles alone, organizes the works of a hundred poets to show structure, sound, and substance and to present first-person, second-person, and third-person poems and poems of statement; the volume concludes with poems by five of her favorites: Donne, Alexander Pope, Samuel Taylor Coleridge, Walt Whitman, and Yeats.

Miles never slighted her professional responsibilities, even though her first love was probably writing poetry. She combined teaching, publishing, editing, and creative writing in an exemplary manner. Some of her first mature poems appeared in *Trial Balances* (1935), a collection featuring several young poets, edited by Ann Winslow. *Lines at Intersection* (1939), her first book, asserts the significance of ordinary events in a fifty-poem cycle from dawn through the day to the next morning. *Poems on Several Occasions* (1941) cyclically celebrates birth, love, and death and dramatizes the meaningfulness of the seemingly trivial. In *Local Measures* (1946), she continues to find significance in small, everyday matters. Given her interest in analyzing poetry, Miles not surprisingly begins with *Local Measures* to write poetry about poetic technique. *Poems, 1930–1960* (1960) reprints earlier poems, including some from *Prefabrications* (1955), and also offers new ones that express doubt, disbelief, and surprise that old psychological safeguards are disappearing—although perhaps only temporarily. A cause of dismay, she revealed later, was her fear that McCarthyism was threatening intellectual freedom and creativity. *Kinds of Affection* (1962) and *Fields of Learning* (1968) demonstrate her theories concerning, respectively, metaphor (attempts by figurative expression to dissolve denotations that separate) and what T. S. Eliot called "tradition and the individual talent" (as poetry moves through generational stages, the individual poet chooses subjects and a style to reflect and teach his era).

An excellent introduction to Miles's creative work is *To All Appearances: Poems New and Selected* (1974). It contains a selection of 106 poems from eight of her books and thirty new ones, the best of which is "Views from Gettysburg." In it she conflates historical images with present-day observations, citing both students and authors who recognize these intersections, and implicitly invites readers to extend the historical continuum projected by the poem with images from their immediate experience. "Walk over the plain ground / to parley . . .," Miles tells us in a call for the continuing renewal of "civil life" inspired by a place, Gettysburg, once synonymous with civil strife.

In *Coming to Terms* (1979) Miles offers poems summarizing her career; she images her retirement as a post-voyage landing. Her final volume, *Collected Poems, 1930–83* (1983), also presents many new works, in which she asserts that her public and private lives constitute one life and advises good-natured readers likewise to have big political and cultural concerns influence their personal decisions and vice versa. As though to validate her advice, Miles participated in many local Berkeley poetry groups, delighting and inspiring scores of admirers. Miles died at her home in Berkeley.

• Most of Miles's papers are at the libraries of the State University of New York at Buffalo, the University of Michigan, Washington University in St. Louis, and Yale University. Critical essays on Miles are Robert Beloof, "Distances and Surfaces," *Prairie Schooner* 32 (Winter 1958–1959): 276–84; Denis Donaghue, "The Habits of the Poet," *Times Literary Supplement*, 25 Apr. 1975; and Lawrence R. Smith, "Josephine Miles: Metaphysician of the Irrational," *Pebble*, no. 18-19-20 (1979): 22–35. Louise Bogan republished her 1956 review of Miles's *Prefabrications* in *A Poet's Alphabet: Reflections on the Literary Art and Vocation* (1970). Brief essays on Miles's poetry are included in James Dickey, *Babel to By-*

zantium (1968), and Randall Jarrell, *Poetry and the Age* (1953, repr., 1972); they object, respectively, to her obsession with small subjects and to her dry, minimalist style. Miles's typical verse has regularly been compared to that of Marianne Moore and William Carlos Williams. Obituaries are in the *New York Times*, 17 May 1985, and the *Los Angeles Times*, 18 May 1985.

ROBERT L. GALE

MINNESOTA FATS (19 Jan. 1913–18 Jan. 1996), pool player and hustler, was born Rudolf Walter Wanderone in Washington Heights, New York City, the only son of Rosa Wanderone (maiden name unknown) and Rudolf Wanderone, Swiss immigrants who also were the parents of three girls, Rosie, Julie, and Jerry. Rudolf the elder, according to his son, traveled the world as a soldier of fortune or military mercenary before coming to America to work odd jobs in blacksmithing, heating, and plumbing.

The son, called Roodle, graduated from Public School 132 at age thirteen in 1926. From that point on he spent his life in the pool hall subculture as a minor hustler, road player, and gambler. His early nicknames included New York Fatty, Brooklyn Fats, Chicago Fats, and just plain Fats. He was seriously overweight even as a teenager, and as an adult his weight varied from about 250 to 300 pounds on a five-foot ten-inch frame. He preferred games that depended on clever maneuvers and defensive plays rather than shot-making ability, games like one-pocket and bank pool. Because he never played in tournaments or in refereed matches where his skill could be assessed, it is impossible to determine how good he was in his prime.

In 1941, Wanderone married Evaline Inez; she divorced him in 1985.

While Wanderone was never in the top rank as a pool player, he was an effective hustler, much better than the local amateurs he encountered in his travels, and good at "making a game," that is, getting a favorable handicap from players better than he was. He was a compulsive talker and a master at distracting and irritating his opponents with braggadocio, needling, and asides. He sometimes was able to coax inferior players into money games by offering tricky handicaps that were not as onerous as they seemed. He played for money only when the odds were strongly in his favor. There are several stories about a well-rested Wanderone challenging superior players who were exhausted from marathon gambling sessions.

"Roodle" Wanderone metamorphosed from an obscure pool hustler of uncertain ability into Minnesota Fats, the greatest player of all time, shortly after the movie *The Hustler* appeared in 1961. A one-pocket tournament held that year in the tiny town of Johnston City, Illinois, attracted Fats along with other denizens of the shadowy hustling underworld: Johnny Irish, Cornbread Red, Handsome Danny, The Knoxville Bear, Boston Shorty, and Tuscaloosa Squirrely. Fats was semiretired at the time and living in his wife's hometown, Dowell, Illinois. The movie featured Jackie Gleason in the supporting role of a money player named Minnesota Fats. Wanderone, always an opportunist, claimed that the movie was about him, and perhaps he believed it even though he resembled the Gleason character only superficially. The movie, in fact, revealed nothing about the life of Minnesota Fats; it was centered on a young hotshot called "Fast Eddie" Felson, played by Paul Newman. One veteran hustler, Hubert "Daddy Warbucks" Cokes, speaking of Wanderone, told reporters at the time, "Don't call him Minnesota Fats. He don't even know where Minnesota is."

When an article about the tournament by sports columnist Tom Fox, titled *Hustlers' Holiday in the Lion's Den,* appeared a few months later in *Sports Illustrated,* Wanderone's rise to fame began. Offers for talk show appearances and trick shot exhibitions poured in. Whether his tall tales about beating everybody on the planet "for the cash" were true or not didn't matter. "I outdrew the Pope in Rome," he said, "and that ain't even good pool country." Other quotable lines, delivered in a kind of W. C. Fields drawl, included "When I was eight years old, I was a grown man, playin' cards or shootin' pool or chasin' broads," "I've never lost and I've been hustlin' since I was two or three years old," "I been hustlin' pool since Moby Dick was a guppy," "I won the Man of the Year in Industry Award even though I ain't worked a day in my life," and "All my life I've done nothin'. Done it better than any man alive." Name a pool or billiard champion from any country or any era and ask Wanderone if he knew him and he was liable to reply, "Know him? I beat him out of every nickel he ever had."

Not everybody was amused. Willie Mosconi, many times World Champion in straight pool, was infuriated when Fats claimed he had beaten him. Mosconi offered to play Fats any game for any amount of money and even offered odds. Fats ducked the showdown for years, preferring to repeat his boasts and to play eight-ball on his own television show, "Celebrity Billiards—Minnesota Fats Hustles the Stars." They finally met on ABC's Wide World of Sports in 1978. With Howard Cosell moderating, Mosconi drubbed Wanderone unmercifully, a televised slaughter that was repeated several times in the following years.

Also infuriated by Wanderone was author Walter Tevis, who insisted until his death in 1991 that the Minnesota Fats character was entirely fictional. "I made up Minnesota Fats," he said, "just as Walt Disney made up Donald Duck." In a 1968 letter to Bill Burns, a writer who was researching his life, Tevis wrote that Minnesota Fats is "a character of which I am quite proud. I worked carefully on his make-up—his dignity, his silence, his charisma, his astonishing physical grace—and I am as proud of him as I am of any character I have invented." Tevis said he had never seen or heard of New York Fats. "I am especially dismayed that Mr. Wanderone should appear on the scene, with his self-serving and dishonest flummery, to represent that aspect of the game that I take to be its worst: the 'pool shark' aspect . . . and of course, dammit, I don't want my 'Minnesota Fats' stolen from me." In his novel *The Color of Money,* a sequel to *The Hustler* set twenty-five years later, Minnesota Fats dies early on. The Fats character doesn't appear at all in the movie made from the novel.

For keeping the game of pool before the public—though in a negative way—Wanderone received the Industry Service Award in 1970 from the Billiard and Bowling Institute. The Billiard Congress of America inducted him into its Hall of Fame in 1984, not in the Great Player category but rather for "meritorious service," calling him "pool's foremost sideshow."

Wanderone, perhaps the only man ever to build a career around impersonating a character in a novel, died in Nashville, Tennessee. A few years before his death, he married Theresa Bell, a woman fifty years his junior. He had no children.

• For Wanderone's quirky opinions on a variety of topics, see "The World According to His Heaviness," *Billiards Digest,* Nov. 1983. The only source of information about Wanderone's early life is his as-told-to autobiography, *The Bank Shot and Other Great Robberies* (1966), by Tom Fox. See also John Grissim, *Billiards* (1979); Willie Mosconi and Stanley Cohen, *Willie's Game* (1993); George Fels, *Legends of Billiards,* a collection of player profiles from *Billiards Digest* magazine (1993); Robert Byrne, *Byrne's Wonderful World of Pool and Billiards* (1996); and W. W. Woody, *Buddy Hall: Rags to Rifleman,* a biography of a professional pool player (1995). Also helpful are the interview with Walter Tevis in *Billiards Digest,* Feb. 1984, and an article by Mort Luby, "Remembering Fatty," *Billiards Digest,* Apr. 1996. An obituary is in the *New York Times,* 19 Jan. 1996.

ROBERT BYRNE

MITCHUM, Robert (6 Aug. 1917–1 July 1997), actor, was born Robert Charles Duran Mitchum in Bridgeport, Connecticut, the son of James Mitchum, a shipyard and railroad worker, and Ann Gunderson Mitchum. When Mitchum was eighteen months old, his father was crushed to death in a switching-yard accident. Subsequently, Mitchum's mother found work as a linotype operator at a newspaper. An insolent and mischievous child, Mitchum was frequently in trouble at school for his fistfights and pranks. His mother, unable to handle him, sent him to live for several months with his grandparents in Felton, Delaware, where he was expelled from the local middle school after scuffling with a principal. Around 1930 he went to live with his older sister, who had broken into show business as a dancer in New York City. When he was a freshman at Haaran High School, he was expelled for exploding a firecracker during band practice. Afterward he decided to become a hobo. He later relished telling interviewers about his adventures on the road. One story had him being arrested for vagrancy in Savannah, Georgia, and then serving on a chain gang, shackled to a six-foot-eight-inch Creole murderer, with whom he escaped after striking a guard in the head with a shovel. But his family confirmed that many of his stories were "largely imaginary" and that there was "a bit of the con in brother Bob" (quoted in Eells, p. 25).

Between 1932 and 1937 Mitchum crisscrossed the United States, riding freights and working at a variety of jobs: as a ditch-digger for the Civilian Conservation Corps, a coal miner in Pennsylvania, a bouncer at a bar, and a professional boxer. In spite of his rough-neck lifestyle during these years, his ambition was to become a writer. In 1937 he settled in Long Beach, California, where his family had moved. His older sister, who hoped to cultivate his artistic interests, encouraged him to try out with a local "little theater" group, the Players Guild of Long Beach; over the next two years he worked as a stagehand and appeared occasionally in plays, including a starring role as Duke Mantee in Robert Sherwood's *The Petrified Forest*. He wrote two children's plays that were produced by the guild, several raunchy comedy routines and songs that were performed by local burlesque actors, and the text for an oratorio that was performed in 1939 at the Hollywood Bowl at a benefit for European Jewish refugees. In 1939 he spent several months working as a pitchman for a traveling astrologer. In 1940 he married Dorothy Spence, his boyhood sweetheart from Delaware whom he had courted intermittently during his journeys; they had three children.

In order to support his new wife, Mitchum took a job as a machine operator with the Lockheed Aircraft Corporation. He hated the monotony of factory work, however, and in 1942 explored the possibility of working as an extra in Hollywood films. After meeting William Boyd, the star of the "Hopalong Cassidy" series of westerns, he was hired to play a villain in *Hoppy Serves a Writ* (1943). With his barrel chest, deep bass voice, and heavy-lidded eyes, Mitchum exuded a rough but sensual masculinity on the screen. As "Hopalong" actor George Givot remarked, "Even in small parts in cheapie productions, he had . . . that certain something that makes people look at you when you're doing nothing, watch you, remember you and wait for you to come back" (quoted in Eells, p. 54). Several Hollywood studios took notice of Mitchum in his film debut, and in 1943 he played minor parts in thirteen pictures for six studios, as well as appearing in seven additional Hopalong Cassidy films for United Artists. After receiving positive critical notices for his supporting work in *When Strangers Marry* and *Thirty Seconds over Tokyo* (both 1944), he signed a seven-year contract with RKO Radio Pictures.

In 1945 Mitchum, on loan to United Artists, had his first important screen role, as a war-weary but resolute infantry officer in William Wellman's *The Story of G.I. Joe*. Critics regard the picture, which provides a grunt's-eye view of World War II, to be one of the finest war films of the era; for his performance Mitchum received his only Academy Award nomination, as best supporting actor. Such was his popularity following *G.I. Joe* that studios rereleased several of his earlier pictures, in which he had been typically billed eighth or ninth, and publicized his "starring" roles. In 1947 he appeared in three noteworthy films at RKO: Edward Dmytryk's *Crossfire*, a hard-hitting examination of anti-Semitism; Raoul Walsh's *Pursued*, an "adult" western with Freudian overtones; and Jacques Tourneur's masterful film noir *Out of the Past*. Of the last film, *New York Times* critic Bosley Crowther wrote: "Robert Mitchum is magnificently cheeky and self-assured as the tangled private-eye, consuming an astronomical number of cigarettes in displaying his nonchalance." Yet in spite of his self-sufficiency and physical impressiveness on the screen, he also managed to project a curiously passive quality, a "nearly listless, burdened feeling of having been-there-done-that" (Gross, p. 6). Film historians suggest that Mitchum in *Out of the Past* became one of Hollywood's first existential antiheroes, stoical, cynical, and doomed.

Although Mitchum was by now a major Hollywood star, he tended to shrug off his fame, living in a modest home, wearing clothes that he had stolen from the RKO wardrobe, and choosing as his friends gaffers, soundmen, and bit players rather than other celebrities. With typical self-deprecation, he enjoyed telling a story about so infuriating Katharine Hepburn on the set of *Undercurrent* (1946) that she yelled at him, "You know you can't act, and if you hadn't been good looking you would never have gotten a picture. I'm tired of playing with people who have nothing to offer" (quoted in Eells, p. 77). In August 1948 he was arrested by Hollywood narcotics officers for possession of marijuana; he served a sixty-day sentence at a prison farm in Castaic, California, joking to interviewers that it was "just like Palm Springs without the riffraff." Although he initially assumed that his acting career would be ruined, two of his films released soon after his arrest, *Rachel and the Stranger* (1948) and *The Red Pony* (1949), were box-office hits. His quick rehabilitation in the public eye was aided in no small part by influential gossip reporter Hedda Hopper, an archconservative who nevertheless liked Mitchum personally and defended him in her column. Between 1949 and 1954 he starred in over a dozen films for RKO, many of them mediocre action pictures in which he played the same role of a cynical, laconic tough guy. Critics routinely lambasted these films and accused him of sleepwalking through his performances, an accusation that he did not deny. He complained to Hopper: "I wear the same suit, speak the same lines, throw the same punches. All they do is change the girl. . . . When I'm interested, I know my lines and everybody else's. When I'm not, I go on the set and announce, 'Tell me what to say.' No fret, no strain, no pain. If you want my interest, interest me. If you just want my presence, pay me" (quoted in Marill, pp. 31–32). His finest performance at RKO during these years was as a washed-up rodeo rider in Nicholas Ray's *The Lusty Men* (1952), in which the director encouraged him to improvise many of his lines.

In 1955, following the expiration of his RKO contract, Mitchum set up an independent film company, DRM Productions, and also began to work on a freelance basis. That year he gave the best performance of his career, as a psychopathic preacher in Charles Laughton's idiosyncratic southern Gothic masterpiece, *The Night of the Hunter* (1955). Film critic Carrie Rickey has commented: "Is there an image more terrifying than the sight of Robert Mitchum . . . soulfully singing 'Leaning on the Everlasting Arm' on horseback as he soullessly stalks two young children?" Mitchum's preacher is not only menacing but also seductively soft-eyed and entirely at ease with himself; "he projects the alarming possibility that evil has its authentic moments of satisfaction and even of genuine reward" (Gross, p. 7). Unfortunately, *The Night of the Hunter* was a box-office fiasco, and afterward the actor returned to more conventional roles, churning out a series of uninspired action pictures for his production company. In 1957 he recorded a calypso album for Capitol Records; for his film *Thunder Road* (1958), he wrote and recorded the title song, "The Ballad of Thunder Road," which reached number sixty-two on the Hot 100 Chart. In 1960 he gave two excellent performances, as a libidinous Texan in Vincente Minnelli's *Home from the Hill* and as a boisterous Australian sheep drover in Fred Zinnemann's *The Sundowners*. He won best-actor honors from the National Board of Review for the latter film.

In 1962 Mitchum again proved his skill at playing predatory characters, as a southern "cracker" rapist in *Cape Fear*. During the 1960s he continued to star regularly in pictures, mainly westerns, although most of them were mediocre. He also turned down lead roles in significant films such as *The Misfits* (1961), *Patton* (1970), and *Dirty Harry* (1971), claiming that they would require too much effort. In 1970, in a departure from his usual screen persona, he appeared as a mild-mannered Irish schoolmaster in David Lean's *Ryan's Daughter*, which was generally dismissed by critics as a bloated epic. During the 1970s he starred in a trio of interesting crime films: *The Friends of Eddie Coyle* (1973), in which he gave a fine performance as an aging hoodlum; *The Yakuza* (1975), which dealt with organized crime in Japan; and *Farewell, My Lovely* (1975), as Raymond Chandler's private detective, Philip Marlowe. In 1982 he starred as a retired basketball coach in *That Championship Season*, a much-hyped drama that proved to be a critical and commercial flop (even though the play from which it was adapted, written by Jason Miller, had been a success on Broadway). In 1983 Mitchum gave a rather flat performance as a navy captain in the big-budget television miniseries *The Winds of War*. During his later years, he continued to play small parts in films, including Martin Scorsese's 1991 remake of *Cape Fear*. One of his final performances—in a career that spanned six decades and approximately 130 movies—was in Jim Jarmusch's acclaimed cult western *Dead Man* (1995). He died in Santa Barbara, California.

Mitchum insisted that his goals as an actor were to "learn your lines and don't bump into the furniture or other actors" (quoted in Eells, p. 186). His colleagues, however, maintained that he was deeply pas-sionate about his craft and that his nonchalance was a defensive pose. In his interviews he seemed to relish presenting himself as a foul-mouthed, two-fisted cynic, but Charles Laughton described a much gentler man: "All this tough talk is a blind, you know. He's a literate, gracious, kind man, with wonderful manners, and he speaks beautifully—when he wants to. . . . You know, he's really terribly shy" (quoted in Callow, p. 232). Although he often appeared in unremarkable films—by his own estimation, he made one good picture for every four that were trash—he nevertheless made a lasting contribution to cinema through his performances in *Out of the Past* and *The Night of the Hunter*.

• A helpful biography on Mitchum is George Eells, *Robert Mitchum* (1984). For a fascinating, less than complimentary profile of the actor, see Barry Rehfeld, "Robert Mitchum Gives a Rare Interview," *Esquire*, Feb. 1983, pp. 50–56. Valuable critical overviews of his career are Harlan Kennedy, "Mitchum," *Film Comment*, July-Aug. 1992, pp. 30, 34–35; and Larry Gross, "Baby, I Don't Care," *Sight and Sound*, Sept. 1997, pp. 6–9. Alvin H. Marill, *Robert Mitchum on the Screen* (1978), provides information on each of his films through 1978. *Out of the Past* is often discussed in books dealing with film noir; two good scholarly studies are James Naremore, *More Than Night: Film Noir in Its Contexts* (1998), and Nicholas Christopher, *Somewhere in the Night: Film Noir and the American City* (1997). For an excellent discussion of *The Night of the Hunter*, see Simon Callow, *Charles Laughton: A Difficult Actor* (1987). An obituary appears in the *New York Times*, 2 July 1997.

THOMAS W. COLLINS, JR.

MITFORD, Jessica (11 Sept. 1917–23 July 1996), writer and social critic, was born at Batsford Park, Gloucestershire, England, the daughter of David Bertram Ogilvy Freeman Mitford (the second Lord Redesdale) and Sydney Bowles Mitford. Since her parents felt that girls did not need to go to school, they tutored their six daughters at home but dispatched their one son to Eton. While her pro-Nazi sister, Unity, decorated their sitting room with swastikas and fasces, Jessica Mitford retaliated by scratching hammers and sickles in the windows with a diamond ring. In 1937 she eloped with Esmond Romilly, her second cousin and a nephew of Winston Churchill. After the couple briefly supported the Loyalist guerrillas in Spain, they were married in Bayonne, France. Home again in England, they worked for an advertising agency in London until 1939 then traveled to the United States and held a variety of jobs. Jessica Mitford became a union organizer, tended bar in a Miami restaurant, and clerked in a dress shop in Washington, D.C.

When World War II began, Romilly joined the Canadian Air Force. He was killed in action in 1941, leaving his widow with their one child, a daughter. In 1941 Mitford became an investigator for the Office of Price Administration. In 1943 she married Robert E. Treuhaft, a labor and civil rights lawyer, with whom she would have a son. The couple moved to Oakland,

California, and in 1944 Mitford became an American citizen.

Mitford's literary career began late. She once said that when she was thirty-eight she had concluded that writing was the only occupation requiring neither education nor skills. Her *Lifeitselfmanship, or How to Become a Precisely-Because Man* (1956), a privately printed pamphlet, wittily criticizes the imprecision of Communist rhetoric. Next came *Daughters and Rebels* (1960), published in Great Britain as *Hon(orable)s and Rebels*, in which she describes her parents and her six siblings but mainly responds to two of her sister Nancy Mitford's many novels, *Highland Fling* (1931; rev. ed., 1951) and *Pursuit of Love* (1945). In both, Nancy presents wicked, semiveiled portraits of their parents. *Daughters and Rebels*, briefly on bestseller lists and favorably reviewed, offers Mitford's own profiles of various family members, especially three of her sisters: Nancy; Diana, who married Sir Oswald Mosley, a fascist; and Unity, who traveled to Germany and was for Hitler—as were their parents—before the war. *A Fine Old Conflict* (1977) is another autobiographical volume. In it Mitford concentrates with saucy frankness on her activities, including fundraising, as a member of the American Communist party in the 1940s and 1950s, her disillusionment in the 1960s, and also the renewal of her friendship with her sister Nancy. *Lifeitselfmanship* reappears in this volume as an appendix.

In her early writing Mitford found her distinctive métier: muckraking. Five superb examples of investigative journalism followed, beginning with *The American Way of Death* (1963; rev. ed. 1978). Then came *The Trial of Dr. Spock, William Sloane Coffin, Jr., Michael Ferber, Mitchell Goodman, and Marcus Raskin* (1969); *Kind and Usual Punishment: The Prison Business* (1973); *Poison Penmanship: The Gentle Art of Muckraking* (1979); and *The American Way of Birth* (1992). She also published widely in many periodicals, including *Esquire, Ladies' Home Journal, McCall's,* the *Nation,* and the *Saturday Evening Post.*

The American Way of Death, generally considered her best book, is a thoroughly researched exposé of the greedy commercialism of the American funeral business. Mitford quotes from the industry's own brochures and advertisements to ridicule their syrupy hypocrisy. The book, ineffectively counterattacked by spokesmen for morticians, became a bestseller, helped bring about legislative changes, and inspired a television documentary ("The Great American Funeral," CBS, 1963). *The American Way of Death Revisited* (posthumously published, 1998) updates certain facts and figures and includes new chapters on prepayment plans, multinational corporations, and the failure of the Federal Trade Commission to enforce laws that Mitford's book helped create.

In *The Trial of Dr. Spock,* Mitford, who regarded the Vietnam War with disgust, chronicles the 1968 trial and conviction of the so-called Boston Five for conspiring to aid and abet persons trying to violate the Selective Service Act. She attended the trial and interviewed the accused men, the defense and prosecuting attorneys, other officials, and later some jurors. Her aim was to show the hazards to liberty that individuals can encounter when confronting conspiracy laws. Many reviewers praised her stand, while some either regarded her as almost hagiographic in presenting the five accused men or reviled her contempt for the American legal system.

Kind and Usual Punishment is a hard-hitting exposé of the American prison system as inhumane, costly, and ineffective. As a partial solution, Mitford recommends shorter sentences, elimination of indeterminate sentences, and abolition of paroles. Her analyses and conclusions are based on interviews with legislators, lawyers, prison administrators, criminologists, and ex-convicts. Reviewers generally found her descriptions of more value than her tentatively suggested remedies.

When Mitford taught a Yale workshop on her journalistic techniques in 1976, she was inspired to collect seventeen of her juiciest satirical attacks, appearing in various periodicals from 1957 to 1979, on chicanery and institutionalized lunacy, and republish them as *Poison Penmanship.* Her targets include truth-bending headlines, the funeral industry, cross-country touring, civil-rights violations in the South in the early 1960s, Hollywood's film version of Evelyn Waugh's *The Loved One,* and banning public use of the word "syphilis." She also skewers the Elizabeth Arden health and beauty resort in Maine, and the Famous Writers School, headed by Bennett Cerf and Faith Baldwin, which was forced to file for bankruptcy two years after Mitford's original essay was run in the *Atlantic* (July 1970). Other objects of Mitford's venom include the treatment of an unusually intelligent prisoner, the author of *Soledad Brother: The Prison Letters of George Jackson* (1970), who was later killed in a San Quentin shoot-out, and the loyalty oath and fingerprinting that were required of her to become a distinguished sociology professor at San Jose State University in the fall of 1973. She fixes her gimlet eye on "frenemies" (acquaintances, not "actual friends or outright enemies"); a tourist-trap restaurant in New York called the Sign of the Dove; a sneakingly admired criminal who conned sophisticated lawyers; and archaeologists (requiring her "caper" to Egypt). *Poison Penmanship* is Mitford's most revealing book. In it she defines her format as "straightforward narrative of . . . events as they unfold . . ." In his afterword, Carl Bernstein calls the book "as good a primer on reporting as I've read."

In *The American Way of Birth,* Mitford examines instances of the medical mismanagement of childbirth. She discusses the handling of pregnant women on welfare, inadequate prenatal care generally, and the ineffectiveness of sophisticated birthing technology. She deplores the downgrading of midwifery. The book is replete with anecdotes, some humorous, others harrowing.

Mitford died of cancer in Oakland, California. Having come from a sophisticated British family, she exemplified an American type: the self-made person in a vocation of her choosing. Deserving of her sobriquet "Queen of the Muckrakers," she brought to her work as a highly successful writer wit and fun to go with a dogged pursuit and exposure of facts of all kinds.

• Jonathan Guinness and Catherine Guinness, *The House of Mitford* (1984), exhaustively discusses Jessica Mitford's eccentric parents and their seven children. A short autobiography by Mitford, in addition to the books mentioned above, appears in *Contemporary Authors Autobiography Series*, vol. 17, ed. Joyce Nakamura (1993), pp. 137–51. Obituaries are in the *Los Angeles Times* and the *New York Times*, both 24 July 1996.

ROBERT L. GALE

MONDRIAN, Piet (7 Mar. 1872–1 Feb. 1944), painter, was born Pieter Cornelis Mondriaan in Amersfoort, the Netherlands, to Pieter Cornelis Mondriaan, artist and teacher, and his wife, Johanna Christina Kok Mondriaan. The upper-class Mondriaan family was well established in both artistic and political circles, and the senior Mondriaan was a well-known painter of prominent figures in Dutch history. An uncle, Frits Mondriaan, was also a noted artist. During young Pieter's childhood the family moved to a home near Winterswijk, where he began studying drawing with his father and his uncle. After qualifying as an art teacher through both secondary school training and private instruction, he entered the Academy of Fine Arts in Amsterdam in 1892. There he came under the influence of the so-called Hague school, a group of Dutch artists who painted landscapes in the tradition of the Barbizon school. He spent five years at the academy, painting mostly rural landscapes.

Beginning in 1894, while continuing to paint landscapes and occasional portraits, Piet Mondrian—he had shortened his name when he left home—earned his own living, working successively for more than a decade as book illustrator, tile painter, ceiling decorator, copier of paintings at the Rijksmuseum, painter of pulpit panels, and drawing instructor. The style of his paintings during that period began to depart from the conventions he had observed at the academy as he came under the influence of impressionism and symbolism. Seeking to depict natural scenes as metaphors for the life cycle of growth and decay, he turned to bright, even garish, colors—orange and purple were particular early favorites—to produce not only oil paintings but also watercolors and pastels that were increasingly bold and abstract.

About 1906 Mondrian became deeply interested in theosophy, a philosophical movement that emphasized the mystical relationship between man and nature. From his reading and study he concluded that artistic creation was largely a product of intuition, and that painting should express both the outward reality of nature and an inner, spiritual meaning. His artistic development was further influenced by his annual summer visits, beginning in 1908 and continuing until 1916, to the Dutch artists' colony at Domburg, on the island of Walcheren, where he came under the influence of neo-impressionism. By 1909, with the presentation at the Stedelijk Museum in Amsterdam of his first major show, Mondrian was considered an important painter in the new Dutch avant-garde.

Popular as well as critical acceptance in the Netherlands of the paintings of Mondrian and other Dutch neo-impressionists was aided considerably by the creation at this time of a new wing of the Rijks museum, one of Europe's leading art museums; the new wing was devoted entirely to the work of then-modern painters, including van Gogh, Cézanne, and Vuillard. Avant-garde artists, encouraged by the public's receptivity to their ideas, and seeking to counter the influence of the conventional Hague school, created a new movement, which they named Nieuwe Beelding (new plastic image). They formed a group called the Moderne Kunstkring (modern art circle), which Mondrian joined. The group's first show, at the Stedelijk Museum in 1911, not only exhibited Dutch artwork but also introduced cubism to the Netherlands through paintings by Picasso and Braque. Critics were quick to notice cubist influences in the works by Mondrian exhibited at the show, notably his *Church at Zoutelande* (1910–1911), pointing out how his use of broad swathes of color emphasized their geometric composition.

Cubism had been born in Paris, the mecca of so many artists, and Mondrian was drawn to that city as well. In 1912 he moved to a friend's studio there and after a brief stay rented his own space in a studio complex shared by a number of artists, including the much younger Diego Rivera, who became a close friend. Drawn quickly into the Paris art scene, he became friendly with many important artists of the period, including Fernand Léger and Georges Braque. As he had with impressionism, symbolism, and neo-impressionism, Mondrian used the basic premises of cubism—abstraction and fragmentation—to inspire his own vision rather than copying the style of cubist painters. Beginning with his move to Paris in 1912, he began calling his paintings "compositions" and designating them by number rather than giving them titles, which he believed narrowed a viewer's understanding of his work. The emergence of his distinctive mature style began in 1914–1915 with the so-called Pier and Ocean Series, paintings that offered varying patterns of horizontal and vertical lines with limited use of color.

At the conclusion of his annual summer trip to Domburg in 1914, Mondrian was forced to remain in the Netherlands following the outbreak of World War I in August. During the war years he lived in Laren, a town near Amsterdam favored by intellectuals, and became friendly with several composers and writers as well as other artists, including Theo van Doesburg and Bart van der Leck. Both men were to have a profound influence on Mondrian's work. Van der Leck had begun to use only white and black, plus the three primary colors—red, blue, and yellow—in his geometrical paintings, a palette that Mondrian would soon adopt. In 1917 Van Doesburg, the founder of a contemporary Dutch abstract movement called de Stijl, began publishing a journal with that title, and over the next three years Mondrian contributed several autobiographical essays on his development as a painter. In his *De Stijl* essays he also expressed a belief that henceforth painting should no longer be representational but should instead attempt to embody the order of the cosmos. Moreover, he said, this order could be achieved on canvas only by the use of clearly demarcated horizontal and vertical lines, and by limiting the palette to white, black, and the three primary colors to express "universal light."

Although Mondrian's pronouncements in his *De Stijl* essays defined his own mature style, he did not follow them entirely for several years, preferring instead to experiment with various arrangements of grids and with colors that were often blended. But the goals embodied in both Nieuwe Beelding and de Stijl remained uppermost in his mind, and on his return to war-weary Paris in 1919 he began to work for their acceptance there, writing about them in avant-garde journals. Among the most important of his published works was *Le Néo-plasticisme* (1920), a monograph that distilled the essence of his *De Stijl* essays and also gave a name to his own style: neoplasticism.

From 1922 onward Mondrian painted only canvases with strong horizontal and vertical lines, using only white, black, red, blue, and yellow. Most of them were grids of heavy black lines, usually asymmetrical, on a brilliant white background, and with some of the grid-created rectangles painted in blue, yellow, and red of an equally strong intensity. When Van Doesburg decreed in 1925 that followers of de Stijl could also use diagonals, Mondrian resigned from the movement and continued to paint only canvases with straight lines.

Mondrian, who never married, remained in Paris until 1938. That year, with the threat of war looming in Europe, he moved to London. When the Germans began bombing the city in 1940, he fled to the United States and settled in New York, where he died four years later. In his last paintings he tried to suggest some of the liveliness he found in Manhattan—and in jazz, a long-time interest that he came to appreciate even more in later life—by using colored lines instead of black and by creating many smaller rectangles that he filled with color.

Mondrian is considered a major figure in modern art and a leading practitioner of what came to be known as nonobjective art; his works are owned by many of the world's leading museums. Among his best-known and most frequently reproduced paintings is *Broadway Boogie Woogie* (1942–1943), which is on permanent display at the Museum of Modern Art in New York City. Departing from his usual practice of not giving his paintings descriptive titles, Mondrian named it as a tribute to the city that became his final home. Although he was known to the American artistic community while he resided in this country, general recognition of his stature occurred only posthumously, as is indicated by the brevity of the notice of his death in the *New York Times*. He died in New York.

• For biographical information, see Michel Seuphor, *Piet Mondrian: Life and Work* (1956), which also includes illustrations of nearly every known Mondrian painting; L. J. F. Wijsenbeek, *Piet Mondrian* (1968); and Frank Elgar (tr. Thomas Walton), *Mondrian* (1968). Mondrian's essays on art are found in *The New Art—The New Life: The Collected Writings of Piet Mondrian*, ed. and trans. Harry Holtzman and Martin S. James. For critical evaluations of Mondrian's work, see Carel Blotkamp, *Mondrian: The Art of Destruction* (1995), and Serge Fauchereau, *Mondrian and the Neo-Plasticist Utopia* (1994); see also Meyer Schapiro, "Mondrian: Order and Randomness in Abstract Painting," in Schapiro, *Modern Art—19th and 20th Centuries: Selected Papers* (1979). A brief obituary appears in the *New York Times*, 2 Feb. 1944.

ANN T. KEENE

MONROE, Bill (13 Sept. 1911–9 Sept. 1996), musician, was born William Smith Monroe in Rosine, Kentucky, an area of rolling hills about fifty miles south of the Ohio River in the western part of the state. The son of James Buchanan "Buck" Monroe, a successful farmer who was also involved in coal mining and logging, and Malissa Vandiver Monroe, he was the youngest of eight children. He grew up with chronically poor eyesight and an attendant shyness. As a youth he worked for his father, loading cross ties and hauling them to the train station, and developed a strict work ethic and self-discipline that would become a hallmark of his later career. He enjoyed listening to his mother's old Irish ballads and fiddle tunes and was inconsolable when she died in 1921 from a painful spinal disease. Seven years later his father died.

During these formative years in Rosine, Monroe was exposed to musical influences that would become a part of his bluegrass music. Perhaps the most potent influence was his uncle Pendleton Vandiver, a locally well-known fiddler who took young Monroe with him into the backwoods on horseback to play for square dances. These experiences gave Monroe a lifelong love of fiddle music and provided the inspiration for one of his most famous songs, "Uncle Pen." A second influence was shape-note gospel music (music printed in an old Southern notation in which the pitch of the note was indicated by its shape rather than its position on the staff); all the Monroe boys attended shape-note singing schools that were held in the area by agents of gospel music publishers such as James D. Vaughan and Stamps-Baxter. Here they learned rudiments of harmony and timing. A third influence was a local African-American guitar player named Arnold Shultz, who played with Monroe at dances and exposed him to the blues and to sophisticated instrumental techniques such as "passing chords." Although Monroe became adept at playing the guitar, his main instrument soon became the mandolin, which up until then had been known in American music primarily as a polite parlor instrument.

In 1929 Monroe followed his brothers Birch and Charlie Monroe north to the Chicago area, where they worked for the Sinclair oil refinery and found part-time jobs as dancers for a touring company of the "National Barn Dance," a popular radio show over station WLS in Chicago. The three brothers also began to play music around the area, and when fiddler Birch decided there was no future in it, Bill and Charlie decided to seek a radio career as a singing duo. Working for a patent drug company called Texas Crystals, they were sent to stations in Nebraska and Iowa before moving to Charlotte, North Carolina, in 1935. During this time, one of the most popular subgenres of country music was the close-harmony duet singing of acts such as the Delmore Brothers and Karl and Harty. Utilizing the new sensitive microphones of radio, the style permitted softer, more subtle singing and often emphasized sentimental or gospel songs. The Monroe Brothers, as they called themselves, soon became one of the most popular acts of this type in the South. From 1936 to 1938 they recorded sixty songs on RCA Victor's Bluebird record label, including what would be their career song, "What Would You Give in Exchange for Your Soul?" (1936). The act's forte was to deliver old gospel songs and folk songs at blistering tempos that featured Bill's virtuoso mandolin playing and the duo's rapid-fire harmony singing.

At the height of their popularity, in 1938 the brothers split up and each formed his own band. After floundering for several months, Bill Monroe finally got the kind of band he wanted and in September 1939 successfully auditioned for "The Grand Ole Opry" over Nashville station WSM. In tribute to his home state, he called the band the Blue Grass Boys (written originally as two words). During World War II they became one of the most popular acts on the Opry, and they toured widely with their own tent show; a sidelight was staging baseball games between the band and local teams. While the music was distinctive, many historians do not see in it the characteristics that were later to define bluegrass music as a genre.

These characteristics emerged in 1945, when Monroe added to his band the singing and guitar work of Tennessee native Lester Flatt and the innovative three-finger banjo playing of North Carolinian Earl Scruggs. When this band journeyed to Chicago to make its first records for Columbia in 1946, the new bluegrass sound—breakneck tempos, a high-pitched tenor voice (Monroe's), and individual instrumental solos in the manner of jazz performances—was spread across the country. Across the South young banjo players were trying to learn how to emulate Scruggs's rippling cascades of notes and pulls.

By 1950 Flatt and Scruggs had formed their own band, and Monroe began what was to be his long association with Decca Records. During the next two decades, he also began to hire superb musicians and singers, including singer Jimmy Martin, banjoist Rudy Lyle, singer Carter Stanley, guitarist Ed Mayfield,

banjoist Bill Keith, and fiddler Kenny Baker. He also continued to write autobiographical (he called them "true") songs such as "My Little Georgia Rose," "I'm on My Way to the Old Home," and "The Little Girl and the Dreadful Snake." He also composed a number of fiddle tunes that quickly became standards, such as "Scotland," "Big Mon," and "Cheyenne." By the early 1950s dozens of bands were performing what was now being called "bluegrass" music.

In 1963 he began to work with folklorist-musician Ralph Rinzler, who helped him get bookings at folk festivals, college campuses, and urban clubs. By 1967 Monroe had started his own festival at Bean Blossom, Indiana, and was enjoying cultlike devotion from many of his young followers. Throughout all of his new popularity he continued to work from his base at Nashville's Grand Ole Opry; he was elected to the Country Music Hall of Fame in 1970. Monroe was married twice, first to Minnie Brown (from 1936 until their divorce in 1959) and then to Della Streeter (1985; divorced 1987). His children, both with Minnie Brown, were Malissa (b. 1936) and James (b. 1941), both of whom were also involved in music.

In the last two decades of his life, Monroe wore proudly his title "Father of Bluegrass Music," toured widely overseas, and continued to write and record his music. In 1988 his album "Southern Flavor" won the first Grammy given for the bluegrass category. In 1995 he was summoned to the White House to receive the National Medal of the Arts. The following year, in April, Monroe suffered a stroke that forced him to curtail his touring and performing. A final album, comprising new instrumental tunes, was never completed. He was buried near his family homeplace in Rosine.

Historians have commented that Monroe was the only American artist who single-handedly created a new genre of music. But he was far more than the leader of a musical movement. He was a vital link between older southern folk music and twentieth-century commercial country music, and the musical standards he set were widely embraced. He was admired and emulated by artists as diverse as Elvis Presley, Vince Gill, Marty Stuart, Ricky Skaggs, Ray Charles, and young country bands like BR549. A genuine American original, his recorded legacy forms an important keystone in twentieth-century American music.

• A useful biography is Richard D. Smith, *Can't You Hear Me Callin': The Life of Bill Monroe* (2000). See also Tom Ewing, *The Bill Monroe Reader* (2000). An obituary is in the *New York Times*, 10 Sept. 1996.

CHARLES K. WOLFE

MONTAGU, Ashley (28 June 1905–26 Nov. 1999), anthropologist, was born Israel Ehrenberg in the East End section of London, England, the son of working-class Jewish immigrants Charles Ehrenberg, a Polish-born tailor, and Mary Plotnick Ehrenberg, who was born in Russia. Bright and ambitious from an early age, the young Ehrenberg determined that in order to get ahead in the world he would have to assume the name and persona of an upper-class Englishman. Meanwhile, he read widely, haunting secondhand bookshops to seek out works by major authors, especially biologists and natural historians like Charles Darwin and Thomas Henry Huxley.

According to the biography Ehrenberg submitted to interviewers after he adopted the name Montagu, he followed the completion of his secondary education with studies in physical anthropology at University College, London, in the early 1920s. He then ostensibly worked for several years as a researcher at the British Museum of Natural History and briefly studied anthropology and ethnology at the University of Florence. He came to the United States in 1927 or 1928 to study at Columbia University under Franz Boas and other distinguished anthropologists, then returned to London in 1929 to work for a year as curator of physical anthropology at a medical museum in London. He returned to Columbia in 1930 to resume graduate studies, receiving his Ph.D. in anthropology in 1937 and obtaining permanent residency. He became a U.S. citizen in 1940.

Precisely when Ehrenberg became Montague Francis Ashley Montagu—Ashley Montagu for short—is unclear. His full adopted name, he acknowledged years later, was borrowed from several English writers, including Lady Mary Wortley Montagu, an eighteenth-century writer and feminist whom he admired. With the publication in 1937 of his first book, *Coming into Being among the Australian Aborigines*, a reworking of his doctoral dissertation, he became publicly known as Ashley Montagu. His Oxbridge diction, as well as claims to a stockbroker father named Charles Plot and to other well-born relatives, were in evidence by the time he began providing biographical information to reference publications and interviewers in the 1940s, and he continued to pass himself off publicly as an English gentleman. Only in a revised *Who's Who in America* entry, submitted late in life, did he revise his biography to list his parents' real names. In private, however, his true identity was known to family and friends long before that, according to his authorized biographer, Susan Sperling.

Ashley Montagu began his American academic career in 1931, serving as an assistant professor of anatomy at New York University. After seven years at NYU, during which he earned his doctorate but failed to achieve tenure, Montagu moved to Philadelphia to become an associate professor of anatomy at Hahnemann Medical College. Montagu left Hahnemann in 1949 to become professor of anthropology and chairman of the department at Rutgers University in New Jersey. Six years later, in 1955, he left Rutgers to devote himself full time to writing.

By this time Montagu had published ten more books on topics in anthropology, beginning with *Man's Most Dangerous Myth: The Fallacy of Race* in 1942. At a time when the Western democracies were fighting aggressors who championed racial superiority and employed genocide to advance their claim, Montagu's book, grounded in scientific data yet gracefully written in a style accessible to laymen, argued that perceived racial differences were manufactured by society and not borne out by biological studies. The book, which has gone through numerous editions and remains in print, struck a sympathetic chord with the public and gained him a wide following. *Statement on Race*, a 1949 United Nations declaration drafted by Montagu that espoused the same philosophy, was published in 1952 together with an extended discussion of the declaration. During the 1940s and early 1950s Montagu's other published works included a well-received textbook, *Introduction to Physical Anthropology* (1945), which was revised and reprinted several times over the following decades, and several bestselling books about the habits and quirks of "the human animal," among them *On Being Human* (1950) and *On Being Intelligent* (1951).

Montagu's reputation grew in tandem with an increasing public interest in the relatively new field of anthropology; this interest had been fueled by the breakup of colonial empires in the wake of World War II and the emergence of third-world nations. Once-remote areas, heretofore visited only by explorers and scholars, were becoming increasingly accessible to journalists through air travel, and their reports, delivered in print and on the radio as well as through the new medium of television, whetted the curiosity of an educated public already forced to confront the meaning and implications of racial differences. A skillful writer, Montagu emerged as one of the first experts in the field of anthropology to bridge the gap between academia and the public. He was especially adept at making complex ideas understandable to the layman while preserving the validity and dignity of his subject matter, and he came to enjoy a popularity rivaling that of fellow anthropologist and writer Margaret Mead. Professorial without being pompous, the authorial voice that Montagu projected was wise and humane. Those qualities, coupled with the persona of an English gentleman and the fact that Montagu was also articulate, charming, and well-tailored, made him a natural for television.

Indeed, Montagu became a frequent presence on television news and public affairs shows as well as radio programs following the 1953 publication of his book *The Natural Superiority of Women*, in which he claimed that women were complete and perfect, enjoying physical and psychological superiority over men, whom he deemed the inferior sex. The book became a runaway bestseller, made Montagu famous throughout the nation, and earned enough money to enable him to retire from Rutgers. He went on to write or co-author nearly four dozen additional books, among them popular works on a variety of topics in anthropology and human behavior. He also became a frequent contributor to popular periodicals, offering his reflections on issues of everyday concern, including child rearing and relations between the sexes. A staunch feminist, Montagu was in even greater demand as a television commentator when the feminist movement gained ascendancy in the 1970s. He appeared often on the "Tonight Show" and other network broadcasts, as a dignified but genial and witty guest espousing a philosophy of tolerance and inclusion that, while liberal, did not arouse partisan animosity because it seemed more commonsensical than political.

Among Montagu's most notable later titles are *Man: His First Million Years* (1957); *Life before Birth* (1964); *The Anatomy of Swearing* (1967); *Touching: The Human Significance of Skin* (1971); and *The Nature of Human Aggression* (1975), in which he argued that man's environment, and not his innate nature, causes him to behave aggressively. Montagu's unswerving belief in the power of the environment to shape individuals was in fact a hallmark of all his work. His book *The Elephant Man: A Study in Human Dignity* (1971) reintroduced to the public the story of John Merrick, a nineteenth-century Englishman suffering from a disfiguring disease whose humanity was restored by the care of a compassionate physician. The book inspired a play about Merrick and became the basis for the movie *The Elephant Man* (1980). Montagu was also the co-author of widely respected textbooks on genetics and biological anthropology. In addition to his own books, he compiled and edited sixteen essay collections and anthologies, including *Man and Aggression* (1968), *Race and IQ* (1975), and *Science and Creationism* (1984). Under the pseudonym Academicus Mentor, he also wrote *Up the Ivy* (1966), a humorous commentary on academic one-upmanship. Like his earliest works, many of Montagu's later books were revised and reissued, and many remain in print. A new edition of *The Natural Superiority of Women* appeared in 1999, not long before his death.

While adhering to a prolific writing schedule and making frequent television appearances, Montagu continued to lecture at various colleges and universities, including the New School for Social Research in New York City, where he remained a part-time faculty member from 1948 until 1959. He joined the faculty of Princeton University in 1978, serving as a lecturer until 1983 and as a university fellow until his death.

Montagu was active in many professional organizations and received numerous honors in the course of his career, including the Charles Darwin Lifetime Achievement Award from the American Association of Physical Anthropologists in 1994. In private life he was an avid gardener and especially liked to grow vegetables. Montagu married Helen Marjorie Peakes in 1931, after settling in the United States, and the couple had three children. Montagu died at a hospital near his home in Princeton, New Jersey. Although his lifelong emphasis on the preeminent role of the environment in shaping human nature continues to have its detractors, Montagu remains one of the leading anthropologists of the twentieth century.

• For biographical information, see especially "Montagu, Ashley," in *Who's Who in America*, 53d ed. (1999). See also "Montagu, Ashley," in *Contemporary Authors: New Revision Series*, vol. 78 (1999), pp. 355-62, which includes the text of a 1981 interview. In addition, see entries for Montagu in *Current Biography Yearbook* for 1967 and 2000. An obituary is in the *New York Times*, 29 Nov. 1999.

ANN T. KEENE

MONTGOMERY, Elizabeth (15 Apr. 1933–18 May 1995), actress, was born in Los Angeles, California, the daughter of Robert Montgomery, a handsome actor, and Elizabeth Allen Bryan Montgomery, a beautiful actress. Elizabeth Montgomery graduated from the Spence School for actors and actresses, in New York City, and then studied at the American Academy of Dramatic Arts, also in New York. Following three years of strenuous training, she made her debut in 1951 in "Top Secret," a segment of "Robert Montgomery Presents," her father's popular television show. By the 1950s, Robert Montgomery was widely known not only as a versatile actor, director, and producer but also as the first president of the Screen Actors Guild (1935–1939) and as a decorated naval combat veteran. He even helped direct Dwight D. Eisenhower during his campaign for the presidency and was the first actor to be invited to the White House to prep a president for on-camera appearances. Her father's influence was of assistance to Elizabeth Montgomery, who, however, quickly became a success in her own right.

The young actress made her stage debut in 1953 in *Late Love*, at the National Theatre in New York. She continued in her father's show as a summer repertory player that year (and also in 1954 and 1956), meanwhile appearing as well on television's "Armstrong Circle Theater" (1953, 1954), the "Kraft Television Theater" (1954, 1955), and "Studio One" (1955). By this time she had won the 1954 David Blum *Theatre World* award as the most promising theatrical newcomer. Hollywood soon recognized her talents, and she was cast as the leading lady opposite Gary Cooper in the film *The Court-Martial of Billy Mitchell* (Warner Bros., 1955).

Montgomery continued to be in great demand as an actress, occasionally in movies but more frequently on television shows. She once remarked, "I guess you could say I'm a TV baby." The story of her public life is her unblemished record of professional successes. Her next movies were *Johnny Cool* (United Artists, 1963), a crime drama in which she played opposite Henry Silva, and *Who's Been Sleeping in My Bed?* (Paramount, 1963), a bedroom farce opposite Dean Martin. A sample listing of television shows in which she appeared, usually in starring roles, includes memorably vivacious performances in "Warner Brothers Presents" (1956), the "DuPont Show of the Month" (1958), "Alfred Hitchcock Presents" (1958), the "Loretta Young Show" (1959), "Wagon Train" (1959), "National Velvet" (1960), two Alcoa Company shows (1960, 1962), "The Untouchables"

(1960, for which she received an Emmy nomination), "Twilight Zone" (1961), "Burke's Law" (1963, 1964), "Rawhide" (1963), "77 Sunset Strip" (1963), and "The Flintstones" (1965, voice only). Noted for her versatility, she invigorated all these appearances with her beauty, clean sexiness, intelligence, and grace. Eventually she was featured in more than 250 television shows.

Montgomery's most phenomenal television success was in "Bewitched," as Samantha Stephens, a witch in delectable human form. This 254-episode ABC situation comedy was a spectacular success from 1964 to 1972. During its first season, it was rated highest of all new series. For its first five seasons, it was always in Nielsen's list of "Top Ten" television shows. By 1968 reruns had earned ABC $9 million. As Samantha, Montgomery is the suburban housewife of Darrin Stephens, who is an advertising executive and ideologically a sexist. He tries to suppress the powers of his sensual blond witch-wife, who is capable of altering time, space, and human situations. But on occasion after occasion Darrin needs and has to be properly grateful for her supernatural assistance. She is able to call up her potency merely by wiggling her nose, which became known as "the witch twitch." Several episodes feature Samantha's mother, Endora (played by Montgomery's scene-stealing friend, Agnes Moorehead), her uncle Arthur (played by Paul Lynde, with deliberate homosexual vibrations, a daring television innovation in the 1960s), and her daughter, Tabitha (also possessed of witch power). The success of "Bewitched" inspired two spin-offs, NBC's durable but less popular "I Dream of Jeannie" (1965–1970) and ABC's "Tabitha" (1977). Given the appeal of Montgomery's Samantha to the then-emerging women's liberation movement, it was off-putting for Jeannie, though well acted by Barbara Eden, to call her man "Master." After all, Samantha's gauche Darrin is uproariously demeaned by his female superiors, not least when Endora memorably, if briefly, makes good her rhyming threat to her earthling son-in-law: ". . . I do not like the way you gloat / So I'm turning you into a billy goat." In 1966, 1967, 1968, and 1970 Montgomery was nominated for Emmy awards; but by 1972 the zany show had run its course.

Declining to accept another television series, Montgomery turned instead to starring in made-for-television movies. Her most powerful performances were in *A Case of Rape* (1974) and *The Legend of Lizzie Borden* (1975), for each of which she was nominated for an Emmy. At this time, she was said to be the first actress to receive $1 million for a single television movie. In addition, she narrated two liberal television movies: *Coverup: Behind the Iran-Contra Affair* (1988) and *The Panama Deception* (1992), the latter an Academy Award recipient for best documentary. Her final success was in the role of Edna Buchanan, the brave, prize-winning crime reporter in *Deadline for Murder* (1995).

Montgomery had a mercurial marital career. In 1954 she married Frederick Gallitin Gammann; they had no children and were divorced in 1955. In 1957 she married movie actor Gig Young; they had no children and were divorced in 1963. In 1963 she married William Asher, who had directed the motion picture *Johnny Cool* and a year later began to produce and direct "Bewitched"; they had three children and were divorced in 1974. In 1973 Robert Heath Foxworth became Montgomery's devoted companion. Foxworth, divorced in 1974, was a television actor-director and the father of Bo Foxworth, an actor. In 1978 Montgomery appeared in "The Awakening Land" and was honored with her final Emmy nomination, as the best actress in a television miniseries. She married Robert Foxworth in 1993, two years before her death of cancer in Los Angeles. Ever the histrionic personality, she persistently—and for a time successfully—purported to be five years younger than she was, dying, according to several unpublished reports, at the age of fifty-seven.

• John Walker, ed., *Halliwell's Film & Video Guide* (rev. and updated ed., 1998), identifies Montgomery's numerous appearances. Montgomery and "Bewitched" are discussed in detail in Marc David, *Comic Visions: Television Comedy and American Culture* (1989; 2d ed., 1997); Herbie J. Pilato, *The Bewitched Book: The Cosmic Companion to TV's Most Magical Supernatural Situation Comedy* (1992); and Barry Putterman, *On Television and Comedy: Essays on Style, Theme, Performer and Writer* (1995). Obituaries are in the *Boston Globe* and the *New York Times*, both 19 May 1995, and the British *Daily Telegraph*, 20 May 1995.

ROBERT L. GALE

MOODY, Helen Wills (6 Oct. 1905–1 Jan. 1998), tennis champion, was born Helen Newington Wills in Centerville, California, to Clarence Alfred Wills, a physician, and Catherine Anderson Wills. She grew up in nearby Berkeley and was educated in area private schools; she also attended a boarding school in Vermont. Wills began playing tennis as a child, instructed by her father, and quickly demonstrated an aptitude for the game. When she turned fourteen in 1919, she was given a membership by her parents in the Berkeley Tennis Club, and a coach there began setting up daily matches for her. Soon she came under the tutelage of tennis champion Hazel Wightman, who was later acknowledged to have had a major influence on her game.

In 1921, after a series of local victories, Helen Wills entered the U.S. junior championship competition at the age of fifteen and won the national girls' title; a year later she again won the title. Her meteoric rise continued: after a series of wins at regional meets, the seventeen-year-old won the annual U.S. Open competition in Forest Hills, New York, in the summer of 1923, defeating the women's champion, Molla Mallory, and thus becoming the second-youngest player ever to hold the national adult women's title. Soon afterward Wills was ranked as the number-one female player in the nation, a distinction she would hold for a decade, and from 1927 to 1934 she was also the top-rated female player in the world.

Beginning in 1923, Wills won seven U.S. championships, a record that has never been equaled. She also established the record for a streak of victorious singles matches, racking up 180 wins and no losses from 1927 to 1933. In addition, Wills won eight Wimbledon titles, more than any other player until Martina Navratilova won her ninth at Wimbledon in 1990. For many years Wills also held the record for the greatest number of Grand Slam singles titles—nineteen—and today ranks second in that distinction only to Margaret Court, who had twenty-four. Wills was a championship doubles and mixed doubles player as well, winning a dozen U.S., French, and Wimbledon titles over the years with such prominent partners as Don Budge.

Wills was not only athletically gifted; she also had strong intellectual and artistic talents. While establishing her pre-eminence in tennis, she matriculated at the University of California at Berkeley in the fall of 1923, majoring in fine arts, and graduated with honors and a Phi Beta Kappa key four years later. In college she excelled in painting and drawing, and they remained lifelong avocations. She publicly exhibited her skill in these areas by illustrating some of the articles she wrote about tennis for national magazines during her championship years and by showing and selling a number of her paintings.

The rise of Helen Wills to national prominence came in the era of the so-called Roaring Twenties, when newsreels were increasingly shown in theaters across the country and gave most Americans their first "live" glimpses of celebrities in politics and entertainment as well as sports. Beginning with her first U.S. championship match in 1923, the petite Wills—with her hair in braids—captured national attention. The source of her appeal, however, did not come from any efforts on her part to please the crowd. On the contrary, she was so concentrated on the court, so seemingly oblivious to those observing her, and so much in control of her feelings that she quickly earned the nickname "Little Miss Poker Face." The public was fascinated by her, and as she matured into a classic but always somewhat remote beauty their fascination only increased. Soon her natural reticence and her display of cool aloofness amidst noisy displays of public attention had earned her a new title, "the Garbo of tennis," bestowed on her by one of her losing opponents, Alice Marble.

This very aloofness appeared to make Wills even more intriguing; she remained firmly in the public eye for nearly two decades and was a sought-after figure. The subject of countless magazine articles, she appeared on the cover of *Time* magazine twice, in 1926 and again in 1929. Acclaimed for her good looks as well as her athletic prowess, she agreed to sit for several prominent artists, including Diego Rivera, who used her as the model for the female figure in his mural *The Riches of California* at the San Francisco Stock Exchange. Her opinions were sought by many, in-

cluding the popular philosopher Will Durant, who included a chapter by her in his bestselling collection *On the Meaning of Life* (1931), and she inspired verses by several poets, including the American Louis Untermeyer.

As a tennis player, Wills combined great strength and endurance with rare grace, and in her signature white visor and smart knee-length costumes, she was a riveting figure on the court. One of her many admirers, Charlie Chaplin, once claimed that Helen Wills playing tennis was the most beautiful thing he had ever seen. Yet Wills was no "ladylike" player. Indeed, her major contribution to the game was her insistence that it be played by women as a real sport, and not with dainty hesitation. Moreover, she believed that sexist social expectations about "appropriate" female behavior were not the only hindrance to the development of the women's game; the primary culprit was the restrictive clothing that women players had up to this time been forced to wear on the court—long cumbersome skirts and high-buttoned, long-sleeved blouses. Although Wills is credited with being an innovator by wearing shorter, more practical tennis costumes, it should be noted, however, that her revolution in court fashions came at a time when considerations of comfort and practicality were replacing decorum and concealment as the standard in women's clothing—and when women in both America and Europe were increasingly exhibiting political and social independence.

Indeed, though Wills inspired many young women to pursue athletic accomplishment, she herself had a role model in Suzanne Lenglen, the legendary French champion only six years her senior. Following Lenglen's lead, Wills used men as practice partners in order to strengthen her endurance, and her own choice of attire was undoubtedly influenced by Lenglen's fashion chic on the court. The two were often compared in the media and actually met each other on several occasions, but they played together only once—in a challenge match in Cannes, France, in 1926 that was one of the most celebrated athletic events of the decade. Wills ultimately lost to Lenglen (6–3, 8–6), but she gained valuable insight into how to improve her game by focusing more on technique and less on simply battering opponents into defeat.

According to Wills, another benefit of her match with Lenglen was her introduction in Cannes to an American financier named Frederick Moody. The two were married in 1929, and henceforth she was known professionally as Helen Wills Moody, even after their divorce in 1937. She subsequently married a film writer and polo player named Aidan Roark; that marriage also ended in divorce. She had no children from either marriage.

Helen Wills Moody played her last professional match in 1938, winning her record eighth singles title at Wimbledon against her longtime American rival Helen Jacobs. She then retired to live the life of a well-to-do upper-class matron, first in the San Francisco Bay area and later in Southern California, as a member of the Junior League and her local Episcopal church, and she continued to paint and draw. In private, she was apparently given to periods of self-described "melancholy," which she said could be relieved only by artistic expression. The author of two previous books—*Tennis* (1928), an introduction to the sport, and *Fifteen-Thirty: The Story of a Tennis Player* (1937), a memoir published a year before her retirement—she also wrote, with Robert Murphy, a tennis mystery novel, *Death Serves an Ace* (1939). She continued to play tennis for recreation until 1987, when she turned eighty-two.

Throughout her life, Helen Wills Moody maintained a keen interest in the game and never hesitated to offer public comments on major players. (Not surprisingly, she was a strong admirer of Chris Evert and Pete Sampras, and decried the behavior of Jimmy Connors; she seemed to be genuinely in awe of Martina Navratilova.) After several years of failing health, Helen Wills Moody died at a convalescent home in Carmel, California.

• There are two major sources of biographical information on Helen Wills Moody: her memoir *Fifteen-Thirty*, as well as *The Goddess and the American Girl: The Story of Suzanne Lenglen and Helen Wills* (1988), a dual biography by Larry Engelmann. Engelmann's bibliography lists a number of contemporary articles about her; see, for example, John B. Kennedy, "Little Miss Poker Face: An Interview with Helen Wills," *Collier's*, 18 Sept. 1926, pp. 10ff. For a history of American women's tennis, see especially Parke Cummings, *American Tennis: The Story of a Game and Its People* (1957), and Richard Schickel, *The World of Tennis* (1975). The best popular history of the 1920s and the celebrity culture that it spawned remains Frederick Lewis Allen's classic work *Only Yesterday* (1931); see also its sequel, *Since Yesterday* (1940). For an equally absorbing account of American popular culture of the 1920s and 1930s, see *The Aspirin Age* (1949), a collection of essays edited by Isabel Leighton. An obituary of Helen Wills Moody appears in the *New York Times*, 3 Jan. 1998.

ANN T. KEENE

MOORE, Archie (13 Dec. 1913?–9 Dec. 1998), boxer, was born Archibald Lee Wright, the son of Thomas Wright, a farm laborer and drifter, and Lorena Wright. He always insisted that he was born in 1916 in Collinsville, Illinois, but his mother told reporters that he was actually born in 1913 in Benoit, Mississippi. His father abandoned the family when Archie was an infant. Unable to provide for him and his older sister, his mother gave them into the care of an uncle and aunt, Cleveland and Willie Pearl Moore, who lived in St. Louis, Missouri. Archie later explained why he was given their surname: "It was less questions to be called Moore." He attended all-black schools in St. Louis, including Lincoln High School, although he never graduated. His uncle and aunt provided him with a stable upbringing, but after his uncle died in a freak accident around 1928, Moore began running with a street gang. One of his first thefts was a pair of oil lamps from his home, which he sold so that he would have money to buy boxing gloves. He

later recalled of his stealing: "It was inevitable that I would be caught. I think I knew this even before I started, but somehow the urge to have a few cents in my pocket made me overlook this eventuality" (Moore, p. 19). After he was arrested for attempting to steal change from a motorman's box on a streetcar, he was sentenced to a three-year term at a reform school in Booneville, Missouri. He was released early from the school for good behavior after serving twenty-two months.

Around 1933 Moore joined the Civilian Conservation Corps, working for the forestry division at a camp in Poplar Bluff, Missouri. Having determined to become a boxer, he decided to make his work at the camp a form of training. He later recalled that the other boys constantly kidded him about one daily exercise—standing upright in the bed of a truck as it drove along primitive forest roads, waiting until the last possible moment before ducking or weaving away from tree branches. The captain of the camp permitted him to organize a boxing team, which competed in Golden Gloves tournaments in southern Missouri and Illinois. Many of his fights occurred in a racially charged atmosphere; he later described one of them, against a white boxer named Bill Richardson in Poplar Bluff:

> I knocked him down with a volley of head punches about one minute into round one. His brother . . . was the referee. He was furious at me and told me to keep my punches up. Since I had been hitting Bill in the head I would have missed him altogether if I threw my punches any higher. But the referee said I had fouled him. . . . I got steamed at this and offered to fight [the referee], too. I resolved not to hit Bill any place but his head. . . . In the second round I dropped him with a left hook that spun his head like a top. . . . I heard a man at ringside say, "For two cents I'd shoot that nigger." (Moore, p. 33)

After the bout, the boxing team was followed back to camp by a line of cars loaded with angry "townies." They dispersed only when the camp captain threatened them with a submachine gun.

Moore first boxed professionally as a middleweight. Sources differ about the circumstances of his first professional fight, which occurred either in 1935 against "Piano Mover" Jones or in 1936 against "the Poco Kid," who was knocked out in the second round. In 1936 Moore appeared in twenty-two fights, winning all but four of them, sixteen by knockout. In 1937 and 1938 he averaged a bout a month, winning twenty by knockout and losing only once. During these years he moved his base of operations from St. Louis to San Diego. He first gained prominence in 1938 when he twice fought Johnny Romero, a top-ranked middleweight contender. Romero beat Moore in a ten-round decision in the first match, but in the rematch Moore knocked Romero out in the eighth round. In 1940 Moore boxed in Australia, winning seven consecutive bouts, including two against Ron Richards, who at the time held the Australian light-heavyweight and heavyweight crowns. That year Moore married Mattie Chapman; they became estranged when he toured Australia without her and divorced soon after he returned to the United States. He had three more failed marriages during the 1940s and early 1950s, about which little is known; he had two children from these marriages. He later explained to an interviewer about his difficulties with women: "You've got to marry [boxing]. And so I did. Boxing was my lover. It was my lady. . . . When you're married to a career, as I was, your wife must be cognizant of that" (quoted in Deford, p. 105).

When he returned from Australia, Moore was ranked fourth among the world's middleweights. His career almost ended in February 1941, however, when he spent five days in a coma after undergoing surgery for a perforated ulcer. During his recovery he suffered complications from peritonitis and pneumonia, and when he was released from the hospital his weight had dropped from 163 to 108 pounds. By January 1942 he had returned to the ring, winning five consecutive fights by knockout. That year he was ranked as the world's top middleweight contender. He won the California middleweight title in 1943 by defeating Jack Chase in a fifteen-round decision. In 1945 he moved from San Diego to Baltimore so he could fight on the East Coast. After knocking out Lloyd Marshall in a fight in June 1945, he became the top-ranked light-heavyweight contender. Over the next few years he lost three times to Ezzard Charles, a former heavyweight champion, but he defeated such well-regarded boxers as Harold Johnson and Jimmy Bivins. Although he continued to be highly ranked, for a number of reasons he was unable to get a shot at the title. Boxing historians have suggested that during these years there was an effort by promoters to "freeze out" black challengers from title bouts against white champions. In addition, the nation's boxing capital was New York City, and because of incompetent or crooked management, Moore was able to secure only two matches there between 1945 and 1953. Relegated to fighting in out-of-the-way places—such as Flint, Michigan; North Adams, Massachusetts; and Cordoba, Argentina—he was not considered a marketable boxer. In 1949 he attempted to end his relationship with one manager, Charley Johnston, but in retaliation Johnston influenced promoters to boycott Moore. He recalled bitterly that in 1950, when he was the top-ranked contender, "I fought only twice and made my living with my pool cue, hustling for small bets in neighborhood pool rooms in whatever town I was in" (Moore, p. 132).

Determined to gain a title bout against the light-heavyweight champion, Joey Maxim, Moore mounted a letter-writing campaign to New York City newspapers. He wrote as many as thirty letters a night, winning the support of influential sportswriters, such as Red Smith at the New York Herald Tribune. Through the pressure of Moore's publicity efforts, he finally gained a match with Maxim, but only after guaranteeing him a $100,000 cut of the purse. On 17 December 1952, at the age of thirty-nine, he defeated Maxim in a fifteen-round unanimous decision. After the purse was divided, Moore was paid $800. He successfully defended his title against Maxim in June 1953 and in January 1954. In August 1954 he knocked out Harold Johnson in the fourteenth round to again retain his title. In 1955 he knocked out Bobo Olson, the middleweight champion, in three rounds. Moore next sought to fight the heavyweight champion, Rocky Marciano. He spent $50,000 on letter writing and advertising to prod Marciano into a bout; in a typical bit of showmanship, he put up "wanted" posters that offered a reward for the "capture and delivery" of the heavyweight champ to "sheriff Archie Moore." On 21 September 1955 the 41-year-old Moore met the 32-year-old Marciano. In one of his greatest moments in the ring, he knocked Marciano down in the second round—only the second time in Marciano's career that he went down to the canvas. Marciano, however, came back to batter Moore for the next six rounds. At the end of the eighth round, the referee told Moore that he was stopping the fight, but Moore insisted that he would only go out on his back like a fallen champion. In the next round, Marciano knocked him out.

A right-hander at five feet eleven inches, Moore looked unimposing and somewhat flabby in the ring. New Yorker writer A. J. Liebling described his "commonplace body" and his "serene and scholarly aspect," comparing his features in repose to those of the actor Orson Welles (Liebling, p. 297). He was an analytical, careful counterfighter rather than an aggressive puncher, spending much of his time in a bout in what he called his "shell defense" to ward off blows, taking only one step for his opponent's every two, waiting for his opponent to leave himself exposed or to wear himself out. Possessing expert timing and reflexes, he reportedly could hit the light bag at a gymnasium eight hundred times in three minutes—an average of almost five times per second. He was nicknamed "the Mongoose" because of his ability to strike suddenly and then backpedal. Loquacious and funny, he was well liked by other boxers and sportswriters; Red Smith sometimes published entire letters from Moore in his column. As a champion he proved to be a good entertainer, dressing flamboyantly in a homburg and a midnight-blue tuxedo for one weigh-in and often wearing a yachting cap because "it lends the impression that you own a yacht." He also made much of his "secret" diet that he used to make weight for matches, which he claimed he had learned from watching the aborigines in Australia. "I never saw a fat aborigine," he noted (Moore, p. 87). At his training camps he ate behind a screen, hidden from the prying eyes of reporters. A few years before his retirement, he revealed that the diet included drinking a cup of sauerkraut juice in the morning and chewing meat for its juices only, then spitting out the fiber.

In 1955 Moore married Joan Hardy, a model; they had five children and remained married for the rest of his life. In November 1956 he fought Floyd Patterson for the heavyweight title following Marciano's retirement; Patterson knocked him out in the fifth round. In 1958 he defended his light-heavyweight title against Yvon Durelle, in what boxing historians consider to be one of the most exciting fights of the 1950s. Durelle knocked Moore down three times in the first round and once more in round five, but Moore persevered and went on to knock Durelle out in the eleventh round. As a result of this fight, Moore was named Fighter of the Year by the Boxing Writers Association; his knockout of Durelle was the 127th of his career, setting the record for most knockouts by one fighter. In a rematch with Durelle in 1959, Moore won by a knockout in three rounds. He failed to defend his title in 1960 and 1961, and as a result his crown was stripped away by boxing's sanctioning boards in February 1962. Altogether he was light-heavyweight champion for nine successive years, longer than any other boxer. In 1962 he fought Cassius Clay (who later changed his name to Muhammad Ali) and was knocked out in the fourth round; Moore thus became the only boxer to fight both Marciano and Ali. In his final professional fight, he knocked out Mike DiBiase in three rounds in March 1963, a few months before his fiftieth birthday. His career record for 231 professional bouts was 196 wins, 26 defeats, eight draws, and one identified as "no contest." He won 143 fights by knockout and was himself knocked out only 8 times. In 1966 he was elected to the Boxing Hall of Fame.

Moore appeared as the slave Jim in Metro-Goldwyn-Mayer's *The Adventures of Huckleberry Finn* (1960), a film that received mixed reviews. He hoped to pursue an acting career following his retirement from boxing, and in subsequent years he won small roles in a few films, including *The Carpetbaggers* (1964), *The Fortune Cookie* (1966), and *Breakheart Pass* (1976). During the 1960s he founded an organization called Any Boy Can, which taught boxing to underprivileged youth in the San Diego area. In 1974 he helped train heavyweight boxer George Foreman for his famous "Rumble in the Jungle" title bout in Zaire against Ali. In 1976 he served as an assistant coach for the Nigerian Olympic boxing team. Actively involved in efforts to teach children about the dangers of drug abuse, he worked during the 1980s as a youth boxing instructor for the federal Department of Housing and Urban Development, assigned largely to ghettos in San Diego and Los Angeles. "I try to pass on the arts I know: self-control, self-reliance, self-defense," he told a reporter. In the early 1990s he again worked as a trainer for George Foreman. He died in San Diego.

• Moore's career professional boxing record is in Herbert G. Goldman, ed., *The Ring Record Book and Boxing Encyclopedia* (1987). The best source of information on his life is his autobiography, *The Archie Moore Story* (1960). Unfortunately, Marilyn Green Douroux's *Archie Moore, the Ole Mongoose: The Authorized Biography of Archie Moore, Undefeated Light Heavyweight Champion of the World* (1991) is amateurishly written. For a colorful profile, see Frank Deford, "The Ageless Warrior (Archie Moore)," *Sports Illustrated*, 8 May 1989, pp. 102–14. A. J. Liebling wrote for the *New Yorker* about Moore's 1954 bout with Harold Johnson and his 1955 bout with Rocky Marciano; Liebling's vivid, entertaining reports are collected in his book *The Sweet Science* (1956). In 1959 the author George Plimpton fought a three-round exhibition match against Moore as one of his experiments in "participatory journalism"; the fight is amusingly described in Plimpton's *Shadow Box* (1977). Peter Heller, "*In This Corner . . . !" Forty World Champions Tell Their Stories* (1973), includes a lengthy interview with Moore. An obituary is in the *New York Times*, 10 Dec. 1998.

THOMAS W. COLLINS, JR.

MORGAN, Barbara (8 July 1900–17 Aug. 1992), artist and photographer, was born Barbara Brooks in Buffalo, Kansas, to a family descended from seventeenth-century New England colonists. (Specific information about her parents is not available.) She grew up in southern California and studied art at UCLA, where part of her training included sketching and painting live dancers, trying to isolate and capture individual movements—a skill that she would put to good use many years later. She graduated in 1923 and two years later married Willard D. Morgan, a photographer who encouraged her to explore that medium as an art form. She resisted, however, preferring to paint. Moving to New York with her husband, she spent her early married life caring for the household and the couple's two sons in suburban Westchester County while Willard Morgan established a career in the fledgling discipline of photojournalism and popularized the use of the Leica camera. In the late 1930s he became the first photo editor of the newly founded *Life* magazine and later served as the first director of the photography division at the Museum of Modern Art in New York City. The marriage ended with his death in 1967.

By the mid-1930s, a reluctant Barbara Morgan had finally given in to her husband's urging and begun taking photographs, choosing various subjects with no intent to perfect the form. The turning point in her life came in 1935, when she attended a performance of dancer Martha Graham's "Primitive Mysteries," which centered on Native American rituals in the Southwest. Graham had founded her own company several years earlier and was slowly beginning to make a name for herself as the preeminent exponent of modern dance in America. Morgan was captivated by Graham's performance and went to meet her backstage. The two women felt an instant bond, based in part on certain surface similarities—they were close in age (Graham was only four years older than Morgan); had both studied in Los Angeles; had both traveled extensively in the American Southwest and been drawn to its culture and people; and had Pilgrim ancestors. But they also shared a deeply felt intuition that drew each instinctively to myth and ritual as the basis for art.

The rest, as they say, is history: Morgan asked Graham if she could photograph her, Graham readily assented, and a collaboration that would play a major role in the popularization of modern dance—and the emergence of Martha Graham as its leading exponent—was born.

Barbara Morgan often said in later interviews that a pivotal moment in her life had come at the age of five, when her father explained, to her delight, that even stationary objects were in constant motion because "atoms danced inside everything." She had tried in her own art to express that motion; now, in photographing Graham, she would try to capture the grace and movement and energy of the dancer's performance in two-dimensional black and white. She prepared herself by having long discussions with Graham in which they shared their similar thoughts and beliefs. Both women saw their art as a tribute to native cultures and as an atonement for the "sins of the fathers"—the wresting of the American landscape from its original inhabitants centuries earlier. Morgan also began attending all of Graham's classes and rehearsals as well as performances. For the actual photographing of Graham, however, Morgan decided not to shoot her live onstage, which had been traditional, but instead to pose her in empty theaters and studios, with special lighting that Morgan herself designed. Following a shared belief in a principle of Japanese painting known as *esoragato*, in which the painter empathetically identifies himself with his subject before he begins to paint, the two women began each session by sitting on the floor about ten feet apart and silently "becoming" the subject of the dance itself. When they felt ready to begin, they would raise their hands to signal each other.

What began as a small-scale endeavor grew into a project that took more than five years to complete as Morgan systematically photographed more than a dozen dances that Graham had created for herself and her company. Morgan took hundreds of photographs and together the women selected those they agreed were the best. Morgan later said that both of them knew instinctively what to choose and what to reject. Those they chose were published in 1941 as *Martha Graham: Sixteen Dances in Photographs* by Morgan & Morgan, a company formed in Dobbs Ferry, New York, expressly for this purpose by Barbara and Willard Morgan. In an accompanying essay Morgan described in simple detail the equipment she had used to take the pictures—a 4 × 5 Speed Graphic camera and multiple flashlights, using a Kalart focal plane synchronizer—and the techniques she had used to capture Graham and her dancers. "Light is to the photographer what movement is to the dancer," she wrote. "The best pictures in this book are portraits of energy; energy of imagination, generating motor energy and transfixed by light energy."

Martha Graham: Sixteen Dances in Photographs became an instant classic and a collector's item, and many of the images were subsequently used to promote Graham's work as her career blossomed. Several of the images, capturing Graham in motion, her draped skirts of undulating fabric swirling about her, are among the most famous photographs of the twentieth century. A facsimile edition of the book was printed in 1980 with an updated choreographic record and new forewords by Morgan and Graham. Morgan acknowledged some years later that she never charged Graham for taking the photographs, which she felt were a way of sharing in the "sense of affirmation" that she believed Graham was giving to the nation and the world during the Great Depression. She did, however, retain the rights to their use. Graham never forgot the debt she owed to Morgan and often paid tribute to her.

Morgan went on to take photographs of other subjects, specializing in children, trees, and plants, and had several exhibitions of her works, which were published by Morgan & Morgan in book form over the years: *Summer's Children* (1951), a collection of photographs of American children at summer camps; *Barbara Morgan*; and *Barbara Morgan: Photomontage*. She also worked as a freelance book designer and photo editor for several publishers, including her own firm. In addition, Morgan was a friend and frequent correspondent of many noted Americans of the twentieth century, including poet William Carlos Williams, anthropologist Margaret Mead, folklorist Joseph Campbell, and fellow photographer Edward Weston, and many of their letters survive (although not in a public repository).

Morgan, who lived in Scarsdale, New York, for many years, died at a hospital in North Tarrytown, New York.

• Biographical information on Barbara Morgan is limited. See an interview by Andrea Lublinski, "Photographer Recalls Martha Graham Years," *New York Times*, 1 April 1984, sec. 22, p. 26. See also the entry on Morgan in *Who's Who in America*, 38th ed. (1974–1975). Brief biographical information is also included in *Martha Graham: Sixteen Dances in Photographs*. See also Martha Graham, *Blood Memory: An Autobiography* (1991), for recollections of their collaboration. For comments by Morgan on her work, see "Discussion with Barbara Morgan," (author unknown) *Arts in Society*, Summer 1976, pp. 272–75. For assessments of Morgan's work, see Leonard Baskin, "Dialogue with Photographs," *Massachusetts Review*, Spring 1983, pp. 74–80, and B. Confino, "Barbara Morgan: Photographing Energy and Motion," *Saturday Review of Literature*, 7 Oct. 1972, pp. 62–66. An obituary appears in the *New York Times*, 19 Aug. 1992.

ANN T. KEENE

MORGAN, Garrett A. (4 Mar. 1877–27 July 1963), African-American inventor, was born Garrett Augustus Morgan on a farm in Claysville, Kentucky, the former black section of Paris, Kentucky. He was the son of Sydney Morgan, a railroad worker, and Elizabeth Morgan (maiden name unknown), a preacher's daughter. Young Morgan had few educational opportunities and left home with only a sixth-grade education. He became a handyman in Cincinnati, Ohio, and moved in 1895 to Cleveland, where he made his home for the rest of his life. Soon after he became a janitor in a sewing machine factory, he began to repair and adjust sewing machines. He invented a belt fastener for sewing machines in 1901 and sold rights to it for $50. His hard work and acumen enabled him to advance in the next few years to success as an independent businessman and inventor.

In 1907 Morgan opened his own shop, in which he sold and repaired sewing machines. He bought a house and invited his mother to live with him. In 1908 he married Mary Anne Hassek, with whom he was to have three children. In 1909 Morgan established a tailor shop, eventually hiring thirty-two employees and supervising the manufacture of suits, dresses, and coats.

In 1912 Morgan invented a gas mask, which he called a breathing device. It was a helmet, or safety hood, which enabled a fireman to enter a burning, smoke-filled building, breathe freely for a short time, and effect rescues without lung damage to himself. The invention was fitted with a portable attachment that sent the fresher air from ground level or floor level up through a tube. Another tube in the helmet, separate and valved, vented exhaled breath. The invention proved to be so effective that laborers, engineers, and chemists soon began to use Morgan's helmets to protect themselves from dust or toxic fumes in their work environments. In 1912 Morgan established the National Safety Device Company to manufacture gas masks.

Morgan had long noticed that the rapid up-and-down movement of a sewing machine needle through wool generated enough heat to scorch and "fuzz" the material. Experimenting with various chemical solutions, he discovered a combination that not only smoothed fuzzed fabric but also straightened human hair, and in 1913 he founded the G. A. Morgan Hair Refining Cream Company to produce and sell his solution.

In 1914 Morgan wisely patented his gas mask. Meanwhile, his National Safety Device Company was being skillfully managed by several officers, all of whom except Morgan were white. He persuaded many of his black friends to buy stock in his flourishing company. Between 1914 and 1916, the value of a share of his company's stock rose from $10 to $250, largely owing to Morgan's gift for displaying and marketing his product. For example, in October 1914 he demonstrated his gas mask in New Orleans. To get around racial prejudice in the city, he took along a white friend named George Mason to pose as "Garrett A. Morgan," the inventor, while he posed as George Mason, the inventor's helper, already advertised as "Big Chief" Mason, a full-blooded Indian. Inside a canvas tent they built a fire of tar, sulphur, formaldehyde, and manure. After the thick, stinking smoke was trapped inside the tent, in walked the helmeted "Big Chief." After twenty dramatic minutes, he emerged unharmed, removed his protective gear, and presented himself. The "chief" was Morgan himself. In 1914 several New York firemen, equipped with

Morgan's masks, rescued victims from a subway fire. News coverage was extensive and orders soon came in from cities in Ohio, New York, and Pennsylvania for Morgan's lifesaving helmets.

In 1916 an explosion in the Cleveland water works trapped eleven laborers five miles from the shore of Lake Erie and two hundred feet below its surface. The first ten would-be rescuers to take the elevator down into the smoke-, dust-, and gas-filled shaft all died. Morgan and his brother, Frank Morgan, answered a frantic appeal, donned helmets, repeatedly descended, saved trapped victims, and retrieved the bodies of the others. Morgan was honored with gold prizes, diamond-studded medals, and honorary membership in grateful organizations, and more orders poured in. Nevertheless, owing to continued racial prejudice, Morgan, ever quietly prudent, continued to hire white men to demonstrate his gas mask in the Deep South. Even so, when his identity was revealed, orders dwindled.

In 1923 Morgan patented another invention that he had been working on for some time. It was the first automatic traffic light and was designed to control the stop-and-go movements of horse-drawn and motorized vehicles at the intersections of public streets. The absence of traffic-controlling devices was resulting in countless accidents as vehicular traffic in major cities increased in volume. Morgan's invention in its first form was a stand containing two semaphore signals, one painted "Go," the other "Stop." The signals would be operated manually by an ingenious system of cranks, shafts, racks, and gears. When one signal was activated, the other would drop to a vertical position and be shielded from view. The flow of traffic would be changed by rotating the entire stand, usually by 90 degrees but depending on the intersection layout. For safety, all traffic could be stopped by placing both signals in the vertical position. At night, the system would be lighted by two mounted electric lamps, powered either by a battery inside the stand or by leads from an overhead line. Morgan sold all rights to this invaluable invention, for the then-goodly sum of $40,000, to General Electric.

Remaining busy, Morgan not only invented a fastener for women's hats, a round belt fastener, and a friction drive clutch; he also founded the *Cleveland Call* in the 1920s. Renamed the *Call & Post* in 1932, it featured news items of special interest to black readers, and it was soon issued in Cincinnati and Columbus, as well as in Cleveland. Morgan was a charter member of the Cleveland Association of Colored Men, was treasurer of the association beginning in 1914, and remained a member when it was absorbed by the National Association for the Advancement of Colored People.

In 1943 Morgan began to suffer from glaucoma, which his annual stays at the Mayo Clinic could not ameliorate; eventually he lost 90 percent of his vision. In 1960, though legally blind, he devised an electric hair-curling comb and also a pellet that could be put into a cigarette to extinguish it should the smoker fall asleep.

An astute inventor, Morgan was also a pragmatic businessman, who dealt with racial prejudice by trying to work around it. At a later time, he probably would have gained greater renown. His life is a measure of how far an enterprising person could advance despite the color barrier, yet it also serves to illustrate how far American society would have to progress before race would be much less of a factor in the judgment of someone's worth.

• The Garrett A. Morgan Papers are at the Western Reserve Historical Society in Cleveland; included is a copy of Morgan's "Traffic Signal" patent (no. 1,475,024; 20 Nov. 1923). Brief coverage of Morgan's life and achievements is in Russell L. Adams, *Great Negroes, Past and Present* (3d ed., 1969); Richard L. Green, ed., *A Salute to Historic Black Scientists and Inventors* (1985); Louis Haber, *Black Pioneers of Science and Invention* (1991); Robert C. Hayden, *Eight Black American Inventors* (1972); and Portia P. James, *The Real McCoy: African American Invention and Innovation, 1619–1930* (1989). An illustrated obituary is in the Cleveland *Plain Dealer*, 31 July 1963.

ROBERT L. GALE

MORGAN, William Wilson (3 Jan. 1906–21 June 1994), astronomer, world expert on the classification of the spectra of stars, and director of Yerkes Observatory, was born in Bethesda, Tennessee, the son of William T. Morgan, a Southern Methodist home missionary (later a minister and still later an inspirational lecturer), and Mary Wilson Morgan, a home missionary. His family moved about the South frequently, and young William and his sister Mildred were taught at home until 1915; after that he attended small village schools. His first two years of high school were at a junior college in Missouri, and the last two at Central High School, Washington, D.C. In 1923 he entered Washington and Lee University in Lexington, Virginia, and studied there for three years.

Morgan's professor in physics and astronomy got him a job as an observing assistant at the Yerkes Observatory of the University of Chicago, located in Williams Bay, Wisconsin, where he was to spend the rest of his life. As an assistant he became a special undergraduate student at Yerkes Observatory, and he earned his bachelor's degree in June 1927 without ever having set foot on the campus in Chicago until the previous month. He remained a graduate student for four and a half years, one of them spent in Chicago taking graduate courses in celestial mechanics, physics, and astronomy; he received his Ph.D. in astronomy in December 1931 during the Great Depression. In 1928 Morgan married Helen M. Barrett, the daughter of a senior professor at Yerkes Observatory; they had two children. Helen Morgan died in 1963, and in 1966 he married Jean Doyle Eliot.

After earning his Ph.D., Morgan remained at Yerkes as an assistant at the same low salary he had been earning as a graduate student; there were very few job openings for astronomers in those grim depression

years. In the summer of 1932 he was promoted to instructor and in 1936 to assistant professor. His research, like his thesis, was on stellar spectroscopy, especially spectral classification of stars. It is an empirical fact, known from earlier work in Europe and America, that purely on the basis of the appearance of their spectra the great majority of stars can be fitted, to a first approximation, into a single sequence of types, ranging (then) from O5 to M5. It is roughly a temperature sequence, as was then being proved.

Morgan became an expert first on the spectra of A stars (in his thesis), then on the spectra of all stars. With his critical, inquiring mind, almost completely unfettered by the astrophysical theories then being applied (in many cases erroneously) to interpret the spectral sequence, he saw several ways in which the accepted system then in use could be greatly improved. It was based on the early Harvard system of classification, modified by later work at Mount Wilson Observatory. Morgan cut through the historical and somewhat contradictory methods of defining the system then in use and gradually developed his own system, in which each spectral type was defined entirely by a few "standard stars" of that type; for instance, Vega (α Lyrae) was a primary standard of A0 V, and the Sun of G2 V. He thus introduced directly into the classification scheme a "luminosity class" such as Ia for a supergiant, III for a giant, or V for a main-sequence star. Thus he had a two-dimensional spectral classification scheme, ideal for use in finding the distances of stars, based on calibration of the luminosities (or absolute magnitudes) of nearby stars.

Morgan ran into resistance from astronomers with vested interests in the older systems and from some theorists of those days, whose simplified hypotheses his classification methods proved wrong. Morgan used only the best data, his own spectral classifications, and high-precision photoelectric measurements of stars' magnitudes and colors, which were mostly from Joel Stebbins and his associates at the University of Wisconsin and later from Stebbins's former students.

This system, published in 1943 as *An Atlas of Stellar Spectra: With an Outline of Spectral Classification*, by Morgan, Philip C. Keenan, and Edith Kellman (usually referred to as the MKK system), swept the field. Morgan published later revisions with Keenan in 1951 (MK system) and 1973 (revised MK system). He always emphasized that spectral classification is a *process* of matching stellar spectra with those that define the system, not *measuring* intrinsic properties of stars.

Morgan especially concentrated on O- and B-type stars, the hottest, most luminous stars that therefore were most useful in measuring large distances. In 1951 he succeeded in measuring in this way the distances to a number of "O-associations" (containing hot stars and gaseous nebulae) in our Galaxy, exactly the objects that outline the spiral arms of galaxies like M 31. In this way Morgan proved the long-held conjecture that our Galaxy *is* a spiral and mapped, for the first time, the nearest parts of its spiral arms. He also played a key role in setting up, with Harold L. Johnson, a new photoelectric-photometry system (UBV) based on the properties of the spectra of stars he knew so well.

Morgan next applied his same spectral classification methods to the wider field of stellar populations: stars of different ages in different regions of our Galaxy, globular clusters, and other galaxies. Much of this research he did as a visitor to Lick and Mount Wilson and Palomar Observatories, some of it in collaboration with Nicholas U. Mayall and George H. Herbig. Morgan showed that globular clusters have a wide range of heavy-element abundances, including "normal" abundances in the clusters closest to the galactic nucleus, and that the stars in the nucleus of M 31 also have normal abundances. These paradigm-shattering results conflicted with the accepted theories of the 1950s and therefore helped to correct them with more realistic ideas on galaxy formation. Similarly, Morgan overturned some of Edwin Hubble's widely used classification of the forms of galaxies.

After the success of the MKK system, Morgan went up the academic ladder rapidly to full professor. He was director of Yerkes Observatory for three years in the 1960s and became a distinguished service professor in 1966. Morgan had been elected to the National Academy of Sciences and had won all the medals and honors an American astronomer could hope for. He was elected to several foreign academies of science. Morgan died at his home very near Yerkes Observatory, where he had spent his entire academic life.

Throughout his career, Morgan concentrated entirely on describing rigorously "the thing itself," from the spectrum of a star to the form of a galaxy, and in doing so he greatly widened our understanding of our part of the cosmos.

• Many letters to, from, and about Morgan are preserved in the Yerkes Observatory Archives, Williams Bay, Wisc. Donald E. Osterbrock, "William Wilson Morgan 1906–1994," *Biographical Memoirs of the National Academy of Sciences* 72 (1997): 1–30, contains a selected bibliography of Morgan's published scientific papers and also a few references to other writings by or about him. See also Donald E. Osterbrock, *Yerkes Observatory, 1892–1950: The Birth, Near Death, and Resurrection of a Scientific Research Institution* (1997). Informative obituaries are in the *Milwaukee Journal*, 23 June 1994, and the *New York Times*, 24 June 1994, and a science-oriented obituary is in *Physics Today* 50, no. 12 (Dec. 1994): 82–83.

DONALD E. OSTERBROCK

MORRIS, Alice Vanderbilt (7 Dec. 1874–15 Aug. 1950), founder, benefactor, and writer in the international auxiliary language movement, was born Alice Vanderbilt Shepard in New York City, the daughter of Elliott Fitch Shepard, a lawyer, banker, and newspaper publisher, and Margaret Louisa Vanderbilt Shepard, socialite daughter of William Henry Vanderbilt and granddaughter of "Commodore" Cornelius Vanderbilt. Privately educated in New York City, Alice Shepard injured her back in a childhood fall, thereafter using a brace and requiring regular rest. When in 1888 John Singer Sargent asked to paint a portrait of the beautiful girl, her mother denied permission for the formal sittings that would have been too physically difficult. Sargent completed instead an elegant, vigorous sketch, which he showed at the exhibition of the Society of American Artists in New York in 1890.

On 10 June 1895 Alice Shepard married Dave Hennen Morris, and the couple moved to Boston while he completed his studies at Harvard. Alice Morris registered for the first time in college as a special student at Radcliffe. Several years later she attended a women's law class at New York University, where her husband had received his law degree. These brief associations with the world of higher education were her only academic preparation for the later role she was to play as an intellectual leader in the international auxiliary language movement in the United States and Europe.

Supervising the upbringing of their six children took much of Morris's time in the first two decades of the twentieth century. An essentially private woman, she was not much a part of the social scene that attracted some of the other Vanderbilt women of her generation. As an avocation, she studied the constructed language Esperanto.

In 1921 Alice Morris was resting at a Pompton Lakes, New Jersey, sanitarium when she met Jesse Fulton Cottrell, wife of Frederick Gardner Cottrell, a member of the National Research Council (NRC) who was at the time vigorously advocating the notion of an international auxiliary language. Cottrell sought a language for mutual understanding, especially in his area of interest, the sciences. It was to be an auxiliary language, for special purposes, not a replacement for existing natural languages. He believed that a language constructed scientifically and systematically might prove easier to learn than natural languages. The Morrises and the Cottrells joined forces and in 1923 sponsored a series of informational and organizational meetings in New York City to promote an international auxiliary language, with several hundred social, business, and academic leaders in attendance. The meetings resulted in the founding of the International Auxiliary Language Association in the United States (known by the acronym IALA) in 1924. Dave Morris was its treasurer. Alice Morris was honorary secretary, and it soon became clear that she was to be the moving force behind the activities of the organization, as well as a major source of its funding.

IALA sponsored university research into the need for an international auxiliary language, supporting the preparation and publication of a book on language use at international conferences—Herbert N. Shenton's *Cosmopolitan Conversation* (1933)—and funding research on the relative ease of learnability of constructed languages and natural languages. The latter work was conducted by Helen Eaton, an IALA researcher who proposed, in her *General Language Course* (1934), the use of a constructed language as an introduction to both foreign language study and the study of English.

Alice Morris's main interest was in the linguistic research program of IALA, and she worked diligently to attract two of the leading linguists of the time to IALA's work: the American Edward Sapir and the world-renowned Danish linguist Otto Jespersen. At her request, Sapir prepared a "Memorandum on the Problem of an International Auxiliary Language" (*Romanic Review* 16 [1925]: 244–56) with the hope of obtaining the signatures of leaders of the Linguistic Society of America (LSA). Several did cosign the document, but others refused and the LSA never adopted a position in support of either IALA or the concept of an international auxiliary ˌage.

Morris had begun with an interest in Esperanto, but her work with Jespersen and Sapir soon convinced her to abandon advocacy of that particular language and to look instead at research to determine commonalities of vocabulary and grammar among the languages most widely spoken in the United States and Europe—English, German, and the Romance languages French, Italian, Portuguese, and Spanish. IALA's linguistic research resulted in a number of comparative studies, including two written by Sapir and edited by Morris, published as monographs of the Linguistic Society of America with full subventions from IALA: *Totality* (1930) and *The Expression of the Ending-Point Relation in English, French, and German*, coauthored by Sapir and his student Morris Swadesh (1932).

Morris invited Jespersen to lead IALA's European efforts. In order to introduce him to the American public as a supporter of the movement, she prepared the outline of an article on international auxiliary language and paid him an honorarium to write it. IALA then arranged for its publication (Jespersen, "Nature and Art in Language," *American Speech* 5 [1929]: 89–103). Next, Morris organized a meeting in Geneva, Switzerland, in spring 1930, convened by Jespersen. The eighteen participants, creators and advocates of auxiliary languages, discussed ways in which they might cooperate toward a common goal. Morris arranged and funded such meetings throughout the 1930s, but true collaboration was never achieved. In the end IALA went its own way and constructed yet another international auxiliary language, which it named Interlingua.

In 1945 Morris presented to IALA a report on the proposed language, with a core international lexicon extracted from the vocabularies of modern English, French, Italian, Spanish, and Portuguese. In 1951, a year after Morris's death at her summer home in Bar Harbor, Maine, funds left to IALA in her will made possible the publication of two resources for the language produced by the IALA staff: *Interlingua-English: A Dictionary of the International Language*, by Alexander Gode, and *Interlingua: A Grammar of the International Language*, by Alexander Gode and Hugh E. Blair. IALA ceased its activities and was formally dissolved a few years later. Then in 1970 Morris's daughter Alice Morris Sturges cofounded a new organization, the Interlingua Institute, which actively promoted the Interlingua language until it, too, was dissolved at the end of the twentieth century.

In 1931 Alice Vanderbilt Morris was awarded an honorary doctor of letters degree by Syracuse University in recognition of her work toward an international auxiliary language. In addition to editing the two Sapir monographs, she wrote several unpublished comparative studies, numerous IALA reports, and popular articles ("Why Should We Cut Out Our Tongues?" *The Forum* 77 [1927]: 712–16; "A Voice in the World," *Quest*, Feb. 1936, pp. 15, 30–32). Bringing together American and European leaders in the movement, Morris dedicated twenty-five years of her life to the search for a common constructed language. Interlingua is still promoted by small groups in Europe, although it has all but disappeared in the United States. Nevertheless, Morris's ideas about commonalities of meaning survive in the semantic studies of Sapir, and her effort to link the IALA project to the field of linguistics was an important deterrent to the increasing academic isolation of the field as it developed in America during the late 1920s and the 1930s.

• Morris's IALA correspondence, as well as copies of IALA reports and publications, are in the Archives of the Interlingua Institute at the New York Public Library. Frank Esterhill, *Interlingua Institute: A History* (2000), traces the history of IALA and its successor organization with some discussion of Alice Vanderbilt Morris's role in the founding and development of IALA. On the relationship of professional linguists to the international auxiliary language movement, see Julia S. Falk, "Words without Grammar: Linguists and the International Auxiliary Language Movement in the United States," *Language & Communication* 15 (1995): 241–59. A reproduction of the portrait by John Singer Sargent and an account of the circumstances of its creation are given by Elaine Kilmurray, "Alice Vanderbilt Shepard, 1888," in *John Singer Sargent: Complete Paintings*, ed. Kilmurray and Richard Ormond (1998), pp. 136–37. The most complete biography appears in Julia S. Falk, *Women, Language and Linguistics: Three American Stories from the First Half of the Twentieth Century* (1999), pp. 31–92. An obituary is in the *New York Times*, 16 Aug. 1950.

JULIA S. FALK

MORRIS, Willie (29 Nov. 1934–2 Aug. 1999), writer and editor, was born William Weaks Morris in Jackson, Mississippi, the son of Henry Rae Morris, a gas station owner, and Marion Weaks Morris, a part-time piano teacher from a long line of Deep South gentility. Morris counted among his ancestors governors, senators, and the founders of Harpers Ferry, Virginia (now W.Va.). Born into the "old, impoverished, whipped-down South" (*North toward Home*, p. 9), Morris grew up in the time of Jim Crow, when blacks lived a separate existence from whites and nearly every experience was infused with a consciousness of race. When Morris was still an infant, his family moved to nearby Yazoo City, a small town northwest of Jackson on the fringe of the Mississippi Delta, which he famously described in his autobiography *North toward Home*. A well-liked and intelligent student, he was voted most likely to succeed and graduated as valedictorian of his Yazoo City High School class in 1952.

Before his father advised him to "get the hell out of Mississippi," the teenage Morris entertained fantasies about owning a plantation, where he would "preside there on the banks of the Yazoo over boll weevils big enough to wear dog tags" (p. 140). But instead of pursuing a degree at the University of Mississippi, "as all my friends planned to do," he chose to attend the University of Texas at Austin, where he became editor of the *Daily Texan*, the university newspaper. He was later fired for printing accusations that the governor and legislature of Texas colluded with oil interests. After graduating Phi Beta Kappa in 1956, he studied history as a Rhodes Scholar in Oxford, England; in 1958, while still in England, he married his college sweetheart, Celia Ann Buchan, with whom he was to have a son. He returned to the United States in 1960 to edit the *Texas Observer*, a weekly political newspaper based in Austin. In 1962 he left the publication and moved to California, where he briefly attended graduate school at Stanford.

In 1963 Morris moved to New York (the "big cave," as he called it) and was hired at the revered *Harper's Magazine*, since 1850 the longest continuously published magazine in U.S. history. Three years after he joined the magazine, in 1966, the 32-year-old Morris succeeded John Fischer, thus becoming the youngest editor-in-chief of *Harper's* to date. The following year he published *North toward Home*, which describes his childhood in Yazoo City, his work as editor of the *Texas Observer*, and other aspects of his life until his arrival in New York, interweaving personal experiences with the larger events that were shaping the nation in the mid-twentieth century. The *Times* of London called the work "the finest evocation of an American boyhood since Mark Twain," and the book received the Houghton Mifflin Literary Fellowship Award for nonfiction.

Many believe that Morris's years at the helm of *Harper's* were among the best in the publication's long history. He assembled a team of talented contributing editors, including former *New York Times* writer David Halberstam, a war correspondent who wrote scathingly of the mismanagement of the Vietnam War; Texan Larry L. King, who later found financial and critical success with the musical *The Best Little Whorehouse in Texas*; and author Marshall Frady; among many others. By all accounts an "author's editor," Morris drew the best writers of the time to the magazine, including fellow southerner William Styron, who contributed a long excerpt of *The Confessions of Nat Turner*, and Norman Mailer. Morris boldly devoted the entire March 1968 issue to Mailer's "The Steps of the Pentagon," a 90,000-word excerpt from what became the critically acclaimed *Armies of the Night*, an account of the October 1967 march on Washington protesting the Vietnam War.

Although Morris had given *Harper's* new cachet and boosted circulation, the relatively liberal fees he paid to contributing writers and editors undercut the gains in revenue. A simmering clash with management boiled over when Morris decided to excerpt at length Norman Mailer's *The Prisoner of Sex* in the March 1971 issue. *Harper's* majority stockholder, John Cowles, Jr., made it plain that he felt Morris was putting literary values ahead of profits and asked him incredulously, "Who are you editing this magazine for, a bunch of hippies?" Morris quit, and most of the in-house editorial staff followed suit. He was not to return to magazine publishing.

Thereafter, Morris lived for years on Long Island, in Bridgehampton, New York, with his black Labrador, Pete, whose death in 1983 made the nightly news (Pete was buried in the city cemetery in Oxford, Mississippi, where a Faulkner family member read the eulogy). During this time Morris wrote *Yazoo: Integration in a Deep-Southern Town* (1971), about school integration; a children's book, *Good Old Boy: A Delta Boyhood* (1971); and a critically panned novel, *The Last of the Southern Girls* (1973). When James Jones, the author of *From Here to Eternity*, died in 1977, Morris finished the last few chapters of his good friend's novel *Whistle*; the following year he wrote *James Jones: A Friendship*. During this period he also got divorced.

In 1980 Morris returned to Mississippi to, as he put it, "live and die in Dixie." Settling in Oxford, he became writer-in-residence and teacher at Ole Miss. His return to the South seemed to spark his creativity, and he published the critically acclaimed *The Courting of Marcus Dupree* (1983), which detailed the manic pursuit by colleges of a black high school athlete and illuminated the racial politics of collegiate football in the South. Several more books followed: *Homecomings* (1989), an essay collection; *After All, It's Only a Game* (1992), a collection of short stories concerning sports; *New York Days* (1993), a sequel to *North toward Home*; and *My Dog Skip* (1995), a book about his childhood dog. *New York Days* details Morris's years in magazine publishing and records his marveling about how, upon his being named editor-in-chief of *Harper's*, he became, almost overnight, "one of them," a distinguished member of New York's literary community. But he also writes about America in the 1960s and the hopes and failures of his generation, calling the decade "a time of immense and pristine hope and idealism, the last the nation would have for many years." The book received mixed reviews, as many critics complained about the endless name-dropping and the author's lapses in memory.

In the early 1990s Morris married JoAnne Prichard, an editor at the University Press of Mississippi with whom he had worked on *Homecomings*. After his marriage he moved to Jackson, where he spent the rest of his life. The couple had no children together.

In the mid-1990s Morris was an unofficial adviser on the Rob Reiner film *Ghosts of Mississippi*, which tells the story of the attempt to bring the assassin of civil rights activist Medgar Evers to justice. Although the movie was not a critical or commercial success, it inspired Morris's *The Ghosts of Medgar Evers: A Tale of Race, Murder, Mississippi, and Hollywood* (1998), which is part autobiography and part criticism of Hollywood for the box office failure of the film. *My Dog Skip* was also made into a film, which Morris screened a few days before his death.

A lifelong heavy drinker, Morris died from heart failure in Jackson. He was the first writer accorded the honor of having his body lie in state in the rotunda of the Old Capitol building. He was buried in the Yazoo City cemetery, one of his favorite childhood haunts and "the coolest place in town" (*North toward Home*, p. 31). In 2000 the University Press of Mississippi published *My Mississippi*, a collection of reminiscences and photographs of the state, with text by Morris and photographs by his son, photojournalist David Rae Morris.

Morris wrote eloquently about the complex struggle that most southerners face: how to celebrate their heritage without forgetting the sins and horrors of the past. He spoke of a "certain burden of memory and a burden of history" that most "sensitive southerners" feel. Having spent much of his life trying to distance himself from the world of his southern upbringing, he found himself ultimately drawn back to the place. But, as his account of Marcus Dupree's high school football career illustrates, that world had changed more than Morris could have imagined in his youth. A master storyteller and essayist, he was able to thrive at the center of the literary scene in New York and then, with renewed perspective, successfully go back home.

• Morris's "Going Home with Mark Twain," about Twain's *Life on the Mississippi* and its influence on his life, is in *American Heritage* 47 (Oct. 1996). Morris's article-length account of the filming of *Ghosts of Mississippi* is "Back to Mississippi," *George*, Jan. 1997. A profile of Morris, "The Yarn Spinner from Yazoo," is in *U.S. News and World Report*, 13 Sept. 1993. An article by a former editor at *Harper's* is Midge Decter, "Southern Comforts," *Commentary* 106 (July 1998). Reviews of *New York Days* are in *Esquire*, Sept. 1993, and *Progressive*, Feb. 1994. An article on the collaborative book *My Mississippi* is in *New Orleans Magazine*, May 2000. The special 150th anniversary issue of *Harper's Magazine*, June 2000, relates the history of the magazine and Morris's contributions to it. Obituaries are in the *Mississippi Business Journal*, 16 Aug. 1999, *Texas Monthly* 27 (Sept. 1999), and the *New York Times*, 3 Aug. 1999.

STACEY HAMILTON

MORRIS, Wright (6 Jan. 1910–25 Apr. 1998), writer, was born Wright Marion Morris in Central City, Nebraska, to William Henry Morris, a railroad employee and failed chicken farmer, and his wife, Ethel Grace Osborn Morris. His mother died when Wright was only six days old, and his father, who was something of a ladies' man, had a series of girlfriends who were indifferent to his son. When Wright was eight, his father married a teenage dancer who soon abandoned the family. Father and son then moved around the state several times before settling in Omaha in 1919.

At the age of fourteen Wright Morris, who had become something of a loner, left home to live on his own, settling in Prohibition-era Chicago and attending high school there. He supported himself throughout high school and during his brief attendance at Crane College by working at various office jobs and as an attendant at a YMCA. During the 1920s he also made several trips by car to California with his father.

Morris discovered what would become his life's passion—literature—in 1930, when he enrolled at Pomona College in Claremont, California, with the financial help of a relative. Under the guidance of professor and critic Leon Howard, Morris began writing short pieces about his personal experiences, including observations of Chicago gangsters. In 1933 he took a year off from college to travel in Europe, and after spending some time in Paris he decided to become a professional writer. He returned to California and married Mary Ellen Finrock, who supported the couple by working as a teacher. Many years later Morris told the story of his fateful year abroad in *Solo: An American Dreamer in Europe, 1933–1934* (1983).

Morris's first published writings were short prose pieces included in the annual collection *New Directions in Prose and Poetry* in 1940 and 1941. During this time he also worked on his first novel, *My Uncle Dudley*, a fictionalized and often comical account of his early years traveling in the American West with his father. It was published in 1942, the same year he won his first Guggenheim Fellowship to complete his book *The Inhabitants* (1946), a collection, accompanied by his own text, of photographs he had taken of rural vistas and locales during a series of journeys he made throughout the United States in the late 1930s and early 1940s. He won two subsequent Guggenheim grants for similar projects (1946 and 1954). Morris's interest in photography persisted throughout his life and resulted in the publication of three additional volumes of photographs and accompanying text: *God's Country and My People* (1968), *Love Affair: A Venetian Journal* (1972), and *Photographs and Words* (1982). Catalogues of several exhibitions of his photographs were also published during his lifetime: *Wright Morris: Structures and Artifacts, Photographs 1933–1954* (Sheldon Memorial Art Gallery, University of Nebraska, 1975), and *Time Pieces: The Photographs and Words of Wright Morris* (Corcoran Gallery, Washington, D.C., 1983).

My Uncle Dudley encompassed themes that would recur in his subsequent fiction, in particular the "on the road" odyssey of a renegade protagonist in search of the American dream. Although the book attracted little critical or popular attention, Morris forged ahead with his fiction, writing and publishing three more novels over the next seven years: *The Man Who Was There* (1945); *The Home Place* (1948), in which he included his own photographs of rural Nebraska as illustrations; and *The World in the Attic* (1949). All three also focus on a theme hinted at in his first novel: their protagonists return, full of yearning and expectation, to the small towns or country places where they grew up, only to discover that their idealizations do not match the realities they encounter. This theme, simply stated as "You can't go home again," became the centerpiece of much of his subsequent fiction.

Morris, who had moved from California to Pennsylvania with his wife in 1944, switched from the Great Plains to suburban Philadelphia for the setting of his fifth novel, *Man and Boy* (1951), which focuses on the relationship between a cold mother and her war hero son and explores the emptiness of the American dream of success. This notion is also explored in his next novel, *The Works of Love* (1952), which follows the strivings and ultimate failure of a character much like Morris's father as he tries to escape from the bleak loneliness of the Nebraska plains. *The Deep Sleep*, published a year later, is another exploration of the American dream, again centering on characters living in an upper-class Philadelphia suburb. *The Deep Sleep* was the first of Morris's books to receive major critical attention, including a nomination for a National Book Award. His next book, *The Huge Season* (1954), the story of a college friendship that endures and ultimately ends in tragedy, was followed two years later by a novel that finally won Morris the NBA: *The Field of Vision* (1956), which focuses on a group of Americans attending a Mexican bullfight who gather to assess their common past. A year later came *Love among the Cannibals* (1957), a story of two songwriters who move from Hollywood to Acapulco to reevaluate their lives.

Although he remained unable to acquire a wide readership, Morris was encouraged by winning the National Book Award and by the growing reception of such eminent literary critics as Wayne Booth, who, while acknowledging an unevenness in his work, praised him for his willingness to engage serious issues at the heart of the American experience and for his unique ability to "render the mystical relation of time and the timeless." But by the end of the 1950s, the increasingly allusive style and complicated structure of Morris's books, coupled with the ultimately sobering conclusions to be drawn from them, seemed to virtually guarantee that he be denied popularity. Often compared to Sherwood Anderson for his bleak depiction of American life, Morris did not find favor with a nation eagerly awaiting the buoyant promise of a new decade, ushered in by the election of the youthful John F. Kennedy to the presidency in 1960. Simply put, given the national mood, readers did not want to be reminded of depressing realities that offered little hope of redemption and urged resignation and reconciliation over delusion.

Though interviews with Morris at the time made it clear that he recognized he was out of step with the general public, his creative pace began to slacken only slightly during the sixth decade of his life, and in his fiction he remained committed to his now well-established themes of loss and emptiness. He published five novels over the next ten years: *Ceremony in Lone Tree* (1960), *What a Way to Go* (1962), *Cause for Wonder* (1963), *One Day* (1965), and *In Orbit* (1969). Four more appeared during the 1970s: *Fire Sermon* (1971), *War Games* (1972), *A Life* (1973), and *The Fork River Space Project* (1977). His critical reputation as "a writer's writer" now secure, he garnered other acknowledgments of his achievement in the last decades of his life, including election to the National Institute of Arts and Letters in 1970, a fellowship from the National Endowment for the Humanities in 1976, and the receipt in 1985 of one of the first Whiting Writers Awards.

Beginning in the 1960s Morris also increased his output of short stories, which he had been publishing in literary journals for more than a decade. Five collections appeared prior to his death: *Green Grass, Blue Sky, White House* (1970); *Here Is Einbaum* (1973); *The Cat's Meow* (1975); *Real Losses, Imaginary Gains* (1976); and *Collected Stories 1948-1986* (1986). In the last years of his life he continued to publish short stories, including several in the *New Yorker*.

Morris's last novel, *Plains Song*, was published in 1980 and won the American Book Award the following year. Generally acknowledged as the best work of his career—one typical review, by Lynne Waldeland in *Critique*, praised it as "a great hymn to the pioneer spirit"—*Plains Song* recounts the parallel life stories of a Nebraska farm wife, Cora Atkins, and her cousin Sharon Rose with whom she was raised. Cora endures adversity as she lives out her life on the Plains, while Sharon Rose rejects her rural background for a career and an ultimately lonely existence in Chicago; she makes a kind of peace with both her pioneer roots and the limitations of her future when she returns to Nebraska years later, after Cora's death. Morris garnered additional critical praise for three volumes of autobiography published during the 1980s: *Will's Boy: A Memoir* (1981); the aforementioned *Solo: An American Dreamer in Europe* (1983); and *The Cloak of Light: Writing My Life* (1985).

In addition to being a full-time writer, Morris taught at San Francisco State University for eleven years, beginning in 1963. He also lectured on writing at Princeton, Sarah Lawrence, and Swarthmore.

Morris divorced his first wife in 1961 and later that same year married Josephine Kantor, an art dealer. He had no children from either marriage. He died in Mill Valley, California, where he had lived since the 1960s.

• Biographical information on Wright Morris can be found in his three volumes of autobiography. See also David Madden, *Wright Morris* (1964); Leon Howard, *Wright Morris* (1968); and Michael Adams, "Wright Morris," *Dictionary of Literary Biography*, vol. 2 (1978), all of which include critical appraisals of Morris's work. For other major critiques, see Wayne Booth, "The Two Worlds in the Fiction of Wright Morris," *Sewanee Review*, Summer 1957, pp. 375–99; Booth, "The Shaping of Prophecy: Craft and Idea in the Novels of Wright Morris," *American Scholar*, Autumn 1962, pp. 608–26; G. B. Crump, *The Novels of Wright Morris* (1978); Robert E. Knoll, ed., *Conversations with Wright Morris* (1977); and "Interview: Wright Morris," *Great Lakes Review*, Winter 1975, pp. 1–29. An obituary appears in the *New York Times*, 29 Apr. 1998.

Ann T. Keene

MUDD, Samuel Alexander (21 Dec. 1833–10 Jan. 1883), alleged conspirator in the assassination of President Abraham Lincoln, was born in Charles County, Maryland, the son of Henry Lowe Mudd and Sarah Ann Reeves, tobacco planters. The ancestral Mudds of Maryland were among the most prominent citizens in Charles County, which they had named and inhabited since the 1600s. Samuel grew up on the tobacco plantation of his father, "Oak Hill," and was tutored at home for most of his early life, attending school in nearby Bryantown only briefly.

Beginning in 1849, Samuel spent two years at Frederick College in Frederick, Maryland, before transferring in 1851 to Georgetown College in the District of Columbia, where, despite the rigorous academic schedule, he found time to indulge his interest in music. Mudd graduated in 1854, then entered the Baltimore School of Medicine. After receiving his diploma two years later, he returned to Charles County and began practicing medicine with an older cousin, George Mudd. On Thanksgiving Day 1857 Samuel married Sarah Frances Dyer (affectionately known as "Frank"), who came from a family as well established as his, and they soon moved into a home of their own, "Rock Hill Farm," built on land in Zachia Swamp given to them by Henry Lowe Mudd. They had eight children who survived infancy.

Samuel Mudd's medical practice did not grow as he had hoped, and he began to plant tobacco to augment his income. By the beginning of the Civil War most of his earnings came in fact from tobacco farming, for which he used slave labor. According to Mudd, the idea of abolition was "unpatriotic," and he viewed slave ownership as essential to maintaining his way of life. Despite Charles County's secessionist bias, Maryland voted to remain a part of the Union, disappointing Mudd and his fellow planters, for most of their business was transacted with the South. But Mudd continued practicing medicine and planting during the war years as best he could, losing his slaves in November 1864 when abolition was achieved in Maryland.

By early April 1865, when the Confederate general Robert E. Lee surrendered the Army of Northern Virginia to his Union counterpart, Ulysses S. Grant, the war was effectively over. A few days later, on Good Friday, 14 April 1865, actor and Confederate sympathizer John Wilkes Booth assassinated the president at Ford's Theater in Washington. After shooting Lincoln at close range, Booth jumped from the president's box to the stage, breaking his leg in the fall. He managed to escape and, with his cohort David Herold, began the ride south that would change forever the life of Samuel Mudd.

Mudd later professed not to have recognized either man when he invited the injured Booth and Herold into his farmhouse at four o'clock the following morning. But just six months earlier, Booth had stayed overnight at Mudd's house, visiting Rock Hill Farm ostensibly with an interest in purchasing land from the doctor. Also, while in Washington on Christmas Eve 1864, Mudd had again run into Booth, who invited him for drinks and conversation in his room. According to Mudd, on the dark morning of 15 April, Booth had disguised himself with a shawl and a fake beard and said almost nothing, thereby making identification difficult. The pair had made this several-mile detour to Mudd's house on their way to Virginia because Booth's broken leg was causing him severe pain and because Mudd was the only doctor in the area whom Booth knew.

Mudd set Booth's broken leg, provided him a razor with which to shave, and rode into nearby Bryantown with Herold to inquire about a carriage to transport Booth. The two visitors, whom both Mudd and his wife termed "suspicious," left Rock Hill Farm on Saturday afternoon. It was later that day that Mudd learned of the president's fate, and on the following Sunday Mudd related the story of his dubious guests to his cousin George, who promptly informed the authorities.

Washington was in a state of panic following the president's assassination, and Secretary of War Edwin Stanton began taking into custody anyone with connections to Booth, including John Ford, the owner of the theater where the murder occurred (he was later released). It was in this climate that Samuel Mudd was arrested and taken to the Old Capitol Prison in Washington on 24 April, charged with the same heinous crimes as Booth and the other six conspirators. After Booth's capture and death two days later, Mudd and the others were moved to the Arsenal Penitentiary, where they would spend the duration of their military trial, which was slated to begin on 9 May.

Although as a "gentleman" Mudd received slightly better treatment in custody than the others did, he was shackled with leg irons and forced to wear a heavy canvas hood that made sensory experience nearly impossible. Very little time was given for defense preparations, and Mudd secured as his attorney Thomas Ewing, a former brigadier general in the Union army. Ewing served Mudd well under circumstances that were heavily weighted against the conspirators; many felt the proceedings were mere formality, a "court of conviction." The case against Mudd seemed strong on the surface, but with time and perhaps before a jury of his peers many of the charges against him would have been proved at best circumstantial. Mudd's disastrous mistake was in initially telling the authorities that he had never met Booth, a story that was easily refuted.

On 29 June Mudd was spared the gallows by one vote of the nine-man military commission and sentenced to life at hard labor. Feeling betrayed, Mudd would later write that his "case was prejudiced and I was already condemned on the strength of wild rumor and misrepresentation" (quoted in *The Riddle of Dr. Mudd*, p. 214). On 17 July Mudd and the other three alleged conspirators who were spared were sent to what was known as "Devil's Island," Fort Jefferson on Garden Key in the Dry Tortugas, Florida, which housed Confederate prisoners during the Civil War.

For nearly four years Mudd languished in squalid conditions, although, as the fort's most celebrated resident, he must have fared better than his fellow prisoners, as he was allowed to work in the prison hospital. He failed in an escape attempt early in his captivity, but his reputation was redeemed when, in the fall of 1867, he was named post physician during a yellow fever epidemic that ravaged Fort Jefferson, saving the lives of many prisoners and soldiers. Pardoned by Lincoln's successor, Andrew Johnson, in 1869, Mudd returned to Charles County to a diminished farm and very little money, legal fees having drained his savings.

Mudd lived his last fourteen years in virtual anonymity, fathering five more children (one of whom died in infancy) and returning to the life of a tobacco planter. Never regaining his health completely after his release from prison, Mudd died in Charles County of pleurisy at age forty-nine.

Since Mudd's death, historians have argued over Mudd's innocence, and many of his descendants have tried to restore his reputation. In 1990 the doctor's grandson Richard Dyer Mudd requested that Mudd's case be reviewed by the Army Board of Correction of Military Records, which two years later recommended that the conviction be removed from army records because he was tried improperly, before a military commission instead of in civilian court. The recommendation was rebuffed by army administration, and in 1997 Richard Mudd brought the issue before the U.S. District Court in Washington, which again left the decision with the army. In March 2000 the army ruled that the military commission was justified in trying and convicting the alleged conspirator, citing *Ex Parte Quirin* (1942), which held that a "military trial was justified . . . [for] those accused of committing offenses against the law of war" (*Oxford Companion to the Supreme Court of the United States*, ed. Kermit L. Hall [1992], p. 697). Mudd's case fit this definition, they ruled, because the assassination of the president was essentially a military act and the city of Washington, D.C., was at the time under "threat of invasion." Unfortunately the army's ruling shed no new light on Mudd's guilt or innocence, and the movement by Richard Mudd to clear his grandfather's name continues: two newsletters devoted to the efforts to exonerate Mudd still regularly circulate. But, as the truth ostensibly remains unrevealed more than a century later, what role, if any, Mudd played in the assassination of the president who held the country together during its most difficult time will likely never be known for certain.

• A few letters written by Mudd in prison exist; otherwise no material written by him can be found. The federal authorities seized many of his papers, and early information about him was lost when Oak Hill burned in 1881. Samuel Carter III, *The Riddle of Dr. Mudd* (1974)—a comprehensive biography—is generally favorable to Mudd. Edward J. Steers, however, presents a convincing argument of his guilt in *His Name Is Still Mudd: The Case against Dr. Samuel Alexander Mudd* (1997). Nettie Mudd, *The Life of Dr. Samuel A. Mudd* (1906), is a biography by his daughter. Many articles have appeared about his grandson Richard Mudd's fight to clear the doctor's name. Most interesting are Alan Bassin, M.D., and J. Patrick O'Leary, M.D., ". . . And His Name Was Mudd," *American Surgeon* 63, no. 9 (Sept. 1997): 842–43; "Appeal Could Clean up Mudd's Reputation," *Navy Times*, 21 Dec. 1998; and an article in the *Philadelphia Inquirer*, 18 Dec. 1998. Most books about the assassination of Lincoln contain information on Mudd, as does Samuel B. Arnold's autobiographical *Defense and Prison Experiences of a Lincoln Conspirator* (1943).

STACEY HAMILTON

MULLIGAN, Gerry (6 Apr. 1927–20 Jan. 1996), baritone saxophonist, composer, and arranger, nicknamed Jeru, was born Gerald Joseph Mulligan in Queens, New York City, the son of George Mulligan, a management engineer, and Louise Shannon Mulligan. The father's occupation required that the family move frequently up and down the East Coast and throughout the Midwest. Mulligan later claimed that his jazz career was spawned when he was in the third or fourth grade in Marion, Ohio, and saw Red Nichols's tour bus parked in front of a hotel; the small Greyhound, he recounted, came to symbolize for him travel and adventure.

Mulligan studied piano as a youth, and he also learned to play clarinet, trumpet, flugelhorn, and the various saxes on his own. A precocious teenager, he wrote his first arrangements for the band at his high school in Michigan, but the director rejected them. The family settled in Philadelphia when he was seventeen, and there he studied clarinet and arranging with a big band musician; still in high school, he sold two arrangements to a local radio station and organized his own dance band. By now he was playing reed instruments professionally, and in 1944 he left high school for a brief road job as an arranger with Tommy Tuck's band; he soon returned to Philadelphia for a job as a staff arranger for radio station WCAU. He played in the station's studio orchestra (led by Elliot Lawrence) when it appeared at a concert featuring Charlie Parker and Dizzy Gillespie; a hesitant and admiring Mulligan played tenor for Parker, who offered him encouragement. Mulligan moved to New York City in 1946 and joined Gene Krupa's band as staff arranger, also playing occasional tenor; by now he was listening closely to the innovative arrangements of the bop-incubating Earl Hines and Billy Eckstine bands. Krupa recorded two of his arrangements, most notably "Disc Jockey Jump," one of the first dance-band compositions to incorporate bop harmonies. Mulligan also began to write for the Claude Thornhill orchestra, and it was Thornhill's chief arranger, Gil Evans, who encouraged him to move permanently to New York. There he began to hang out in Evans's basement apartment, along with Miles Davis, John Lewis, George Russell, and others; together, these musicians founded the Birth of the Cool band. The recordings this group made in 1949 and 1950 included three Mulligan compositions and two additional arrangements, stellar examples of a renewed emphasis on collective interplay among the musicians. At the same time, Mulligan was perfecting his skills on the baritone saxophone, playing for several small groups and arranging for others (including Lawrence, Thornhill, and briefly, Stan Kenton). In August he recorded a short-lived tentette for Prestige, modeled after the "Birth" nonet.

In 1952 Mulligan moved to Los Angeles and established the first of his famed pianoless quartets, with Chet Baker on trumpet, and bassist Bob Whitlock and drummer Chico Hamilton. Mulligan's drug arrest in the summer of 1953 and subsequent six-month incarceration broke up this group; when he returned, Baker had become a star and the two split over the money. Trumpeter Jon Eardly took Baker's place from 1954 to 1956, trombonist Bob Brookmeyer stepped in from 1956 to 1957, and trumpeter Art Farmer replaced Brookmeyer from 1958 to 1959. Mulligan occasionally expanded the group: in 1953 alto saxophonist Lee Konitz joined briefly, resulting in a quintet, while in 1955 and 1956 Zoot Sims joined Eardly and Brookmeyer to form a sextet. Mulligan also formed a tentette in 1953 as a rehearsal band. Sometime in the early 1950s he married Arlyne Brown; the couple had one child, a son, and divorced in 1959.

Mulligan traveled widely throughout the United States and Europe with these groups and recorded them extensively. The best-known sessions are those he recorded in 1952 and 1953 for Pacific Jazz and Capitol Records with the Baker quartet, sessions that established his essential style for the remainder of his career. He and Baker played unison lines, set off from each other by the starkly different sounds of their instruments and by Mulligan's own written counterpoint, often a "very lightly accented rhythmic orientation" (Piazza, p. 73). The sound may have been somewhat homogenous and emotionally subdued, but it was also seductive and sinuous. And, as noted in the *New Grove Dictionary of Jazz* (1994), the absence of the piano's chordal underpinnings allowed the horn players to improvise "in delicate two-part counterpoint" (p. 814).

Mulligan recorded with each of the subsequent quartets, and with the Konitz quintet, the sextet, and the tentette. While adhering to the same basic formula, each group also had its own identity—certainly Brookmeyer's trombone, for instance, had a gutsier sound than Baker's whispy trumpet. Mulligan's genius as an arranger is impressive throughout the recordings, consistently combining harmonic complexity and lyrical simplicity in extended ensemble passages. The members of Mulligan's groups always listened to each other and always drew an unusual density of texture from their instruments.

Mulligan also continued to develop and extend his unique style on the baritone sax. Essentially a swing player (much like Adrian Rollini, whom he admired greatly, rather than the bop player Serge Chaloff), and the greatest exponent of the instrument since Harry Carney, Mulligan played with equal facility at all tempos and in upper and lower registers alike. The most notable feature, however, was his extraordinary lyricism; he often played with a light, airy tone and improvised his melodies in linear fashion, reminiscent of Lester Young.

Mulligan began to branch out further in the late 1950s. His stature was recognized when he played in the sax section (with Coleman Hawkins, Young, and Ben Webster) on the legendary 1957 television broadcast "The Sound of Jazz." He made a series of recordings with jazz luminaries, the best being those with Paul Desmond, Thelonious Monk, and Stan Getz, all in 1957, Ben Webster in 1959, and Johnny Hodges in 1960. He devised his best arrangements in a studio session in 1957, most of which were not released until years later. He also appeared in several films, most notably *Jazz on a Summer's Day*, filmed at the 1958 Newport festival, and *The Subterraneans*, in which he played a "beat generation" preacher who wins over his congregation through jazz. He recorded the first of several soundtracks, for the Susan Hayward film *I Want to Live!* (1958).

In 1958 Mulligan signed a recording contract with Columbia Records that produced at least two masterpieces. *What Is There to Say?* (1959), a reunion of sorts with Farmer; and *Jeru*, a quartet album of ballads that many consider to be Mulligan's finest effort. His most influential experiment during these years was his Concert Jazz Band, a thirteen-piece group that toured widely in the United States and Europe. The group recorded two albums for Verve Records, and the second in particular, a live session from the Village Vanguard, documents Mulligan's original approach to large-group arranging. Featuring a variety of exceptional soloists, including Sims, Brookmeyer, and trumpeters Clark Terry and Thad Jones, Mulligan arranged the tunes in concerto grosso style, "in which a small group is framed by the larger orchestra, with the listener's attention being passed back and forth" (Klinkowitz, p. 126). Two pieces, "Come Rain or Come Shine" and George Russell's "All About Rosie," are particularly strong examples.

During the early 1960s Mulligan also recorded for Mercury, Limelight, and Philips, and in 1963 he again recorded with a sextet, featuring Farmer and Brookmeyer, guitarist Jim Hall, and his favored rhythm section at the time, Dave Bailey on drums and Bill Crow on bass. Then inexplicably, he spent the next five years playing formulaic pop arrangements, all but disappearing from the jazz scene. It was also a time of personal turmoil: he had recently ended a long-time relationship with actress Judy Holliday, who died soon thereafter from cancer, and initiated a new relationship with actress Sandy Dennis.

In 1968 Mulligan appeared with the pianist Dave Brubeck at a concert, replacing the recently departed Desmond; a one-time appearance turned into a four-year relationship that produced five albums. In 1971 he produced one of his most innovative albums, and one of the few to successfully mix swing and fusion musicians, *The Age of Steam*, recorded with a fourteen-piece band. Rhythm dominated—but did not obscure—melody, and the electric piano and guitar reflected strong rock influences. Two of the best tracks reveal Mulligan's undiminished ability to merge styles. "Over the Hill and Out of the Woods" has a powerful solo by trumpeter Harry "Sweets" Edison, a swing giant no one would connect with jazz fusion, while "Grand Tour" is one of the most beautiful pieces Mulligan ever wrote, with haunting solos by Mulligan and Bud Shank on alto. Throughout the album, Mulligan sails above the other instruments, sounding, as always, completely contemporary.

Mulligan appeared with Charles Mingus at an Avery Fisher Hall concert in New York in 1972, released the next year as *Charles Mingus and Friends in Concert*. In 1974 he collaborated with the great Argentine tango player Astor Piazzolla and that same year was artist-in-residence at the University of Miami. From 1974 to 1977 he led a sextet, and from 1978 to 1979 a fourteen-piece big band. He continued to record prolifically. In 1980 he released *Walk on Water* with a twenty-piece big band, one of his best large-group efforts; the album opened with the notable "Unfinished Woman," written in honor of Holliday. In 1983 another large-group effort that included several fusion players, *Little Big Horn*, followed. In both cases, he continued to play in the essentially lyrical, swing mode that characterized his entire career. This was true even on the strangest album he ever had a hand in, a 1984 session, titled *2:00 AM, Paradise Cafe*, featuring pop crooner Barry Manilow. In 1986 he recorded *Soft Lights and Sweet Music* for Concord Records, with the young swing tenor saxophonist Scott Hamilton. Three years later he released *Lonesome Boulevard*, an excellent quartet album, and in 1992 *Rebirth of the Cool*, an attempt, only partly successful, to recreate the experience of the original classic sessions. During this time Mulligan did not abandon his predilection for musical experimentation; in 1987 he recorded *Symphonic Dreams* with the Houston Symphony Orchestra, an album of slightly jazzed-up classical pieces. His final recordings were for Telarc: *Paraiso-Jazz Brazil* (1993), *Dream a Little Dream* (1994), and *Dragonfly* (1995). Mulligan died unexpectedly in Darien, Connecticut, from complications after undergoing surgery for a knee infection; he had also been suffering from liver cancer. He was survived by his son and by his second wife, Franca Rota, whom he had married in 1985.

Dave Brubeck once noted, "When you listen to Gerry, you feel as if you were listening to the past, present, and future of jazz, all in one tune, and yet it's done with such taste and respect that you're not ever aware of a change in idiom. Mulligan gets the old New Orleans two-beat going with a harmonic awareness of advanced jazz, and you feel not that tradition is being broken, but rather that it's being pushed forward" (quoted in Hentoff, p. 106). The most catholic of jazz musicians, Mulligan was a warm, witty person who infused all of his music with those same qualities, no matter the style or era. In his last decade he constantly pursued his lifelong love of jam sessions and was an irrepressible presence at dozens of concerts and festivals. His honors are legion. He won the *Down Beat* poll for baritone sax every year from 1953 until his death; he contributed dozens of classic compositions to the jazz repertoire, including "Bernie's Tune," "Nights at the Turntable," "Limelight," and "Walkin' Shoes"; and his arrangements of standards like "Come Rain or Come Shine" made them irrevocably and uniquely his own. Finally, his own skills on the baritone made tunes like "My Funny Valentine" completely his own. Above all, Gerry Mulligan brought a combination of intellectualism and simple beauty to his playing that is immediately recognizable, a sense of linear grace that, except perhaps for Lester Young, has no parallel in the history of jazz.

• Raymond Horricks, *Gerry Mulligan* (1986), provides a thorough and perceptive, if brief, introduction to his career and music. Jerome Klinkowitz, *Listen: Gerry Mulligan, an Aural Narrative in Jazz* (1991), is a unique and fascinating effort that provides an album-by-album discussion of Mulligan's recordings, accessible even to the nonmusician. Ted Gioia provides extensive and informative liner notes for the 1996 Blue Note reissue, *The Complete Pacific Jazz Recordings of the Gerry Mulligan Quartet, with Chet Baker*. Whitney Balliett and Nat Hentoff contribute their typically insightful, personal comments in Balliett, *New York Notes: A Journal of Jazz in the Seventies* (1977), and Hentoff, *Jazz Is* (1976). See also Tom Piazza, *The Guide to Classic Recorded Jazz* (1995). The deaths of too many jazz musicians pass little noticed; this was certainly not so with Mulligan. See, for instance, the lengthy obituary in the *New York Times*, 21 Jan. 1996, and the appreciations by Gary Giddins, "Gerry Mulligan, 1927–1996," *Village Voice*, 13 Feb. 1996, and John McDonough, "Goodbye, Jeru," *Down Beat*, Apr. 1996.
RONALD P. DUFOUR

MUSKIE, Edmund S. (28 Mar. 1914–26 Mar. 1996), governor, U. S. senator, and secretary of state, was born Edmund Sixtus Muskie in Rumford, Maine, the son of Stephen Muskie, a tailor, and Josephine Czarnecki Muskie. The spelling of his immigrant father's surname, Marciszewski, had been distorted by an official at Ellis Island, and the new version was eventually adopted by the family. Quiet and studious as a boy, Muskie grew up in relative poverty and often felt isolated as a member of one of the few immigrant families in the area. He attended local schools before entering Bates College in Lewiston, Maine, from which he graduated cum laude with a B.A. in 1936. Awarded a scholarship for law school, Muskie received his LL.B. from Cornell in 1939 and gained admittance to the bar in both Massachusetts (1939) and Maine (1940).

With the entry of the United States into World War II, Muskie left a modest legal practice behind in Waterville and joined the U.S. Naval Reserve in 1942. While serving on destroyer escorts in both the Atlantic and Pacific theaters of operation, he rose to the rank of lieutenant before gaining his discharge in late 1945. On returning home, Muskie resumed his legal work, became active in local Democratic party politics, and was elected to the Maine House of Representatives in 1946. Although he lost an attempt to defeat the incumbent mayor of Waterville in 1947, he was reelected to the legislature and became Democratic floor leader in 1948. That same year, he married Jane Francis Gray; they were to have five children.

Bored with the legislature and eager to supplement his modest legal earnings, Muskie resigned in 1951 and became the state director of the Office of Price Stabilization. Even though he brought several skills to the unpopular post (which attempted to rein in both management and labor in the fight against inflation), the frustrations of the post led him to resign in 1952. Having been elected to the Democratic National Committee, he attempted to revive his legal practice, but a year later, in 1953, he fell and suffered a broken back. Once he recovered, Muskie planned to run for Congress in 1954. No other Democrat, however, was willing to run against incumbent Republican governor Burton M. Cross, and the task fell to Muskie. Initially considered an underdog in the race, he made skillful use of the relatively new medium of television, which, combined with Republican overconfidence, led to an upset victory.

Following his inauguration, Muskie dealt carefully with the legislature, which was still overwhelmingly Republican in makeup. With his first priority the state's economic revitalization, he sought to create an industrial development agency that might generate badly needed jobs. State government reorganization and expanded support for public education were other priorities of his. Following his reelection in 1956, Muskie continued to push for industrial expansion and obtained a sales tax increase to fund several of his programs.

Although Muskie had also secured from the legislature a longer term for the governorship, four years rather than two, he had set his sights on the U.S. Senate. Once again an underdog despite his popularity as governor, Muskie nevertheless defeated incumbent Republican Frederick G. Payne in 1958, becoming Maine's first popularly elected Democratic senator in the process. The campaign was bitterly fought and marked by Muskie's public outbursts of anger in reaction to what he considered unfair attacks by the scandal-plagued Payne.

On arriving in Washington, Muskie almost immediately drew the wrath of Senate majority leader Lyndon Johnson for his failure to support a cloture motion. As a result, he lost several key committee assignments. Even so, Muskie soon earned the respect of his peers (including Johnson) for his low-key but effective manner. Particularly noted for his efforts in urban renewal and federal-state relations, he made his greatest contributions in the emerging area of environmental legislation. Under his leadership, the Clean Air Act of 1963 and the Water Quality Act of 1965 became law, and he also secured a $428.3 million antipollution appropriation in 1967. Muskie's voting record was solidly liberal, and he generally supported most initiatives put forward by Presidents John F. Kennedy and Lyndon Johnson. Within the Senate hierarchy, he passed up races for the position of majority whip in 1965 and 1969.

Some thought that Muskie's lack of forcefulness marked a lack of ambition, but he did accept an opportunity for even higher office. In 1968 Democratic presidential nominee Hubert H. Humphrey badly needed to heal the breach within his party between liberal supporters of Eugene McCarthy and conservatives who backed George Wallace. He also needed to appeal to ethnic voters, and Muskie as a vice-presidential candidate seemed to be a perfect fit. Although Muskie's demeanor and rhetoric were credited by many as a highlight of an otherwise dreary campaign, the twin burdens of civil unrest and the Vietnam War proved too great for the ticket to overcome, and the Democrats were narrowly defeated by Richard Nixon and Spiro Agnew.

Despite the loss, Muskie returned to the Senate in an almost upbeat mood and prepared for his own presidential run. Massachusetts senator Ted Kennedy's claim on the Democratic nomination was seriously weakened by the Chappaquiddick incident of 1969 (in which a young woman staffer of Kennedy's drowned in a car that he drove off a bridge), and Muskie himself was easily reelected in 1970. By 1972 he had dropped all pretensions of supporting the Vietnam War and seemed poised to claim the nomination. However, another public display of anger—this time in the snows of New Hampshire during the primary season—made him appear not in command of himself. The incident had been precipitated when a local right-wing newspaper, the *Manchester Union-Leader*, accused him of using ethnic slurs and made derogatory remarks about his wife. It was later revealed that the story had been planted in the paper by Nixon operatives.

After withdrawing from the presidential race, Muskie returned to the Senate and served until 1980 as chairman of the Budget Committee. He resigned in May of that year and briefly served as secretary of state under President Jimmy Carter. Following Carter's defeat, Muskie left public office and practiced law in Washington, D.C. He also served on the Tower Commission, which investigated the Iran-Contra affair during Ronald Reagan's presidency, and headed up a Democratic think tank, the Center for National Policy. Muskie died in Washington, D.C.

Denied the nation's highest office by a series of missteps, Muskie nevertheless enjoyed a career of public service marked by several solid achievements. His victories as governor and senator helped build up the Democratic party in Maine, and in Congress he sponsored landmark legislation concerning water and air pollution that brought new attention to the environment as a matter of public policy.

• The papers of Edmund Muskie are held at Bates College, Lewiston, Me. Biographical information can be found in Theodore Lippman, Jr., and Donald C. Hansen, *Muskie* (1971), and David Nevin, *Muskie of Maine* (1972). His political career was the subject of extensive media coverage, most notably Stewart Alsop, "Muskie: No Foundation All the Way Down the Line," *Newsweek*, 8 May 1972, p.118. Obituaries are in the *New York Times*, the *Chicago Tribune*, and the *Times* (London), all 27 Mar. 1996.

EDWARD L. LACH, JR.

N

NELSON, Battling (5 June 1882–7 Feb. 1954), lightweight boxer, was born Oscar Matthew Nielsen in Copenhagen, Denmark. He came with his parents, Niels and Mary Nielsen, to the United States in 1883. The family lived briefly in New York City, Oshkosh, Wisconsin, and Dalton, Illinois, before moving in 1885 to Hegewisch, a community on the southeast edge of Chicago, which was annexed into the city in 1889. The family name soon became anglicized into "Nelson," and the family worked as truck farmers and, in the winter, as ice-cutters. Young Nelson attended Henry Clay school until he was thirteen years old then went to work as a meat cutter for G. H. Hammond Company, a local meatpacking firm.

In 1896 Nelson had his first boxing experience in the tent of a traveling circus. In the next few years he wandered about the Upper Midwest, holding various jobs, fighting twice in Sioux Falls, North Dakota, in 1898, and four times in the Chicago area, but his boxing career did not begin in earnest until the summer of 1900. From then until February 1904, he fought frequently, met many good midwestern fighters of his weight, and won most of his bouts. Nelson's nickname, "Battling," seems to have come from these early days, although he claimed that it was a given name.

In May 1904, Nelson traveled with his manager, Teddy Murphy, to San Francisco, and suddenly progressed from obscurity into contention for the lightweight title. In quick succession, he defeated four outstanding lightweights: Martin Canole; Eddie Hanlon; Aurelio Herrera in Butte, Montana; and former lightweight champion Young Corbett. His ten-round knockout of Corbett earned him a fight with Jimmy Britt for the vacant world lightweight title. They met in San Francisco on 20 December 1904, and the heavily favored Britt won a stirring twenty-round battle on points, proving to be a better boxer and ring general than Nelson.

In 1905 Nelson again knocked out Young Corbett then met Britt in a return lightweight title fight in Colma, California, on 9 September 1905. Nelson, relatively uneducated and from the working class, and the better-educated, fancy-dressing Britt thoroughly disliked each other. Their ring styles were equally in contrast, Britt being a clever boxer who wanted to keep the fight at long range, whereas Nelson was an aggressive slugger who preferred infighting. Britt clearly was winning the fight until the nineteenth round, when Nelson suddenly knocked him out with two powerful punches to the jaw—a dramatic conclusion to a great fight.

Nelson defended his lightweight title against Joe Gans on 3 September 1906, in remote Goldfield, Nevada, in one of the most famous fights of the era. It was the first fight promoted by Tex Rickard, who went on to become one of the most famous sports figures of the time. Gans, who had relinquished the lightweight title after a successful defense against Britt in 1904 because of difficulty in making the lightweight limit of 133 pounds, was an African-American boxer of great ability, as indicated by his sobriquet, the "Old Master." To publicize the city of Goldfield, and its mining industry, Rickard inveigled Gans into meeting Nelson in a fight of unlimited duration. As expected, Gans proved to be the cleverer boxer and cleaner hitter, and he punished Nelson severely. Nelson demonstrated, however, why he was called the "Durable Dane" by easily surviving the punishment and continuing to press the fight. He resorted to foul tactics, often butting Gans in the face. The fight continued until the forty-second round when Nelson struck Gans a low blow that caused the "Old Master" to collapse in pain, whereupon the referee awarded Gans the fight on a foul.

Having lost the lightweight title, Nelson had only one fight in 1907, a twenty-round loss to Britt in which he was cleverly outboxed. He got an opportunity to win back the lightweight title from Gans at Colma on 4 July 1908. By this time Gans was suffering from tuberculosis but had the better of the first ten rounds before Nelson's forceful style began to overcome him. Nelson scored a knockout in the seventeenth round and won back the championship. The two men met for the third and last time just three months later, on 9 September, in another title fight in which Nelson was the favorite for the first time. Gans did his best but suffered a bad beating and was knocked out in the twenty-first round.

George Barton, a famous sportswriter and referee of those days, described Nelson as "a unique champion. He was a fighter of the rough-and-ready school. As for boxing, he knew little about the science of the sport. He was . . . always boring in toward his opponent, fighting frequently in toe-to-toe, head-to-head mixing." His busy style, coupled with his endurance, ruggedness, and boundless self-confidence, account for Nelson's success in the ring.

Nelson defended his lightweight title successfully twice in 1909, knocking out Dick Hyland in twenty-two rounds and Jack Clifford in five, and again in January 1910, stopping Eddie Lang in eight. Just when he seemed almost invincible, he lost the title to Ad Wolgast in Point Richmond, California, on 22 February 1910. Giving and receiving terrific punishment, Nelson tired after thirty rounds and Wolgast beat him unmercifully until the fight was stopped in the fortieth round. Returning to action later that year, Nelson was counted out for the only time in his career in a fight with Owen Moran. He continued to fight until 1917, without ever again being a contender for the lightweight title.

After retiring from the ring, Nelson toured with a circus. He attempted unsuccessfully to enlist in the army during World War I. He made a fortune from boxing but lost most of his money through unrepaid loans. Notoriously eccentric, he made the Jack Dempsey–Jess Willard heavyweight title fight in 1919 the occasion for his most famous escapade: on a very hot day he was discovered bathing in a tub of lemonade made up for sale to the spectators. He was indigent from 1918 to 1925, when his father died and left him $125,000, which actually came from money that Nelson had given him from his own ring earnings. Bad investments consumed this second fortune by 1935, and he then worked at various low-paying jobs, most notably in the Chicago post office during the 1940s, and lived in squalor. Nelson's battered face betrayed his long ring career, but his mind remained clear until 1951, when he was beaten severely on the street by hoodlums.

In 1913 Nelson married Fay King, who later became a well-known cartoonist, but they were divorced in 1916. He married again late in life, and his second wife, Edna, died in 1953, just a month before his own death from lung cancer. He was elected to the International Boxing Hall of Fame in 1992.

• Nelson's quaint autobiography, *Life, Battles and Career of Battling Nelson: Lightweight Champion of the World,* (1908), is a useful but not completely reliable source of information. Helpful articles in *The Ring* magazine include Nat Fleischer, "Battling Nelson, the Durable Dane," Feb. 1931; George Barton, "Durable Dane Greatest Marathon Fighter," Nov. 1953; Francis Donegal, "The Wake of Battling Nelson," May 1954; Steven R. Nicolaisen, "When Battling Nelson Finally Mastered Joe Gans," June 1984; and P. N. Ehrmann, "Battling Nelson and Ad Wolgast: A Feud till the Bitter End," Nov. 1990. His boxing record appears in Herbert G. Goldman, ed., *The 1986–87 Ring Record Book and Boxing Encyclopedia.* An obituary is in the *Chicago Tribune,* 8 Feb. 1954.

LUCKETT V. DAVIS

NESS, Eliot (19 Apr. 1903–16 May 1957), law enforcement agent, was born in Chicago, Illinois, the son of Norwegian immigrants Peter Ness, a baker, and Emma Ness (maiden name unknown). His hardworking parents having instilled in him a solid work ethic, Ness graduated from high school with excellent grades. After briefly working at an automobile plant and a real estate office, he enrolled in the University of Chicago, taking courses in business and political science. In 1925 he received his bachelor's degree in business administration.

After graduation Ness investigated insurance applicants for the Retail Credit Company. He was then hired by the Chicago office of the U.S. Treasury Department and soon thereafter transferred to the corruption-ridden Prohibition Bureau, where he undertook the work that made him famous: enforcing the Eighteenth Amendment to the U.S. Constitution under the provisions of the 1920 Volstead Act, which banned the production and consumption of alcoholic beverages. The unpopular law created new opportunities for crime organizations to make huge profits selling illegal liquor and liquor-making supplies and operating speakeasies, where people could imbibe with relative freedom. In order to operate these illegal enterprises, many bribes were offered and accepted by Prohibition agents, as well as local law enforcement. To add to the lawlessness, Chicago's "beer wars," in which rival gang factions vied for control of the city's lucrative illegal liquor business, left many dead. A key figure in the violence was the notorious gangster Al "Scarface" Capone, who had set up shop on Michigan Avenue.

Naive but confident that he would be the agent to bring down Capone, the 24-year-old Ness began his career with the Prohibition Bureau, staking out speakeasies and liquor stills in Chicago Heights, even though he evidently disagreed with and on many occasions violated the Volstead Act. The young agent and his partners had quickly gained a reputation for being tough on offenders and not afraid to use violence during arrests. In 1928, soon after Capone was named "Public Enemy Number One," Ness was transferred to the Justice Department, where he was named special agent, heading a squad of men devoted to bankrupting the businesses of Capone and other mobsters. During this time, Ness married Edna Staley; they had no children.

Ness and his team went to work with a vengeance, carrying out numerous raids on mob-owned or -controlled liquor stills and breweries, speakeasies, and warehouses. Despite some early missteps, Ness soon found the publicity he craved: the Chicago newspapers heralded the work of Ness and his "Untouchables" (meaning evidently that they could not be intimidated or bought by the mob). When the squad acquired for their raids a large truck, they could drive right into barricaded warehouses and distilleries. Threats were made against the lives of Ness and his team, and there is evidence that Capone hired someone to assassinate Ness. But, as with other events of his Chicago years, Ness exaggerated the threat to his life in the book *The Untouchables.*

The work of the Untouchables began to pay off in the early 1930s, as mobsters were forced to scale back and/or conceal their bootlegging activities. Along with a large raise, Ness received a promotion to assistant special agent in charge of the Midwest region, reporting to the U.S. attorney general. In the summer of 1931 Capone, who was beginning his descent into syphilis-induced insanity, was found guilty of income tax evasion and failure to file a tax return; he was sentenced to eleven years in prison. Two years later Congress repealed Prohibition. The Untouchables were soon disbanded, and in August 1934 Ness became an investigator with the Alcohol Tax Unit in Cleveland, Ohio.

Ness's political career in Cleveland began in 1935, when he was appointed director of public safety, his "outsider" status appealing to the city's reform-minded mayor. As director he made the police department his top priority, investigating and dismissing officers found guilty of corruption and setting up a highly respected police academy. He also devoted money and time to the youth of Cleveland, lobbying the city for more and better playgrounds, ball fields, and other recreational opportunities. Ness was criticized during his term for his handling of the "torso murders" that terrorized Cleveland in the late 1930s. At least twenty victims were slain by a serial killer, who was never caught. During his term Ness also gained a reputation as a "union buster," calling out the police and authorizing force to break labor walkouts. In 1938 Ness and Edna Staley divorced, and the following year he married Evaline McAndrews. They too had no children.

In March 1942 Ness, who in recent years had begun drinking heavily, crashed his car, allegedly while drunk. As a result he resigned his position as public safety director and moved with his wife to Washington, D.C., where he worked with the Federal Social Protection Program, educating soldiers about the dangers of venereal disease. In 1944 Ness returned to Cleveland to become chairman of the board of the Diebold Safe and Lock Company. The following year, he was divorced from Evaline, and in January 1946 Ness married Elisabeth Anderson Seaver, a sculptor; they adopted a son together.

The last years of Ness's life were marred by disappointments and futile attempts to regain the glory he had enjoyed in Chicago. He served as treasurer and vice president of the Middle East Company, an import/export business that served Asia and the Middle East, but the company was troubled from the beginning, plagued by governmental restrictions and a crowded market. In 1947 Ness was soundly defeated in a race for mayor of Cleveland. Soon he lost his position at Diebold, having been demoted because of company politics. After peddling personal alarms and clerking at a bookstore, he secured a salary of $150 per week as president of the North Ridge Industrial Corporation, which produced checks and pioneered the watermarking process. When the company's headquarters were moved to Coudersport, Pennsylvania, in 1956, the Nesses made the move as well. That same year, Eliot Ness's account of his years fighting crime in Chicago, co-written with sportswriter Oscar Fraley, was purchased for publication.

Less than a month after seeing the galley proofs of *The Untouchables*, Ness died of an apparent heart attack at his home in Coudersport. Chicago newspapers did not run obituaries of the former crime fighter, and his estate was valued at little more than $1,000 at his death. *The Untouchables*, published in November 1957, did not sell well, but in 1959 a television series of the same name began airing on ABC. The critically acclaimed show, starring Robert Stack as Eliot Ness, ran for four seasons. Though forced off the air by complaints of excessive violence, "The Untouchables," which certainly exaggerated and sensationalized the work of the Prohibition Bureau, promoted the enduring interest in Eliot Ness's legendary career as a relentless pursuer of the mob. The story was revived, with even more embellishment, in 1987 by director Brian de Palma in the hit film *The Untouchables*, starring Kevin Costner.

Ness's story is as sad as it is common. Bright and ambitious, he was—in his prime—one of the best-known law enforcement officials in the country, praised for his pragmatism, determination, and honesty. But once his nemesis was jailed and Prohibition was repealed, Ness found himself without a focus, and his celebrity waned. He spent the rest of his life trying unsuccessfully to recapture the renown that he enjoyed in his younger years, drinking heavily and drifting from job to job until his early death. Yet soon thereafter his name was turned into a household word, thanks in large part to Hollywood's mythmaking power. The sensational depictions of his years with the Prohibition Bureau have given Eliot Ness a permanent place in the lore of American crime-fighting.

• Ness's *The Untouchables*, written with Oscar Fraley, was published in 1957. Paul W. Heimel, *Eliot Ness: The Real Story* (1997), is a complete biography. Steven Nickel, *Torso: The Story of Eliot Ness and the Search for a Psychopathic Killer* (1989), focuses on Ness's years in Cleveland, including his unsuccessful pursuit of the notorious "Torso Murderer." See also Paul Robsky and Oscar Fraley, *The Last of the Untouchables* (1962); Steven Nickel, "The Real Eliot Ness," *American History Illustrated*, Oct. 1987; Fraley, "The Real Eliot Ness," *Coronet*, Jan. 1972; and Peter Jedick, "Eliot Ness," *Cleveland Magazine*, Apr. 1976.

STACEY HAMILTON

NEWCOMB, Josephine (31 Oct. 1816–7 Apr. 1901), philanthropist, was born Josephine Louise Le Monnier in Baltimore, Maryland, the daughter of Alexander Le Monnier, businessman, and Mary Sophia Waters Le Monnier. Her father, a French émigré, was devoted to his three children and was financially able to provide an above-average education for them. After supervising their initial academic training, he sent them to Europe, where they lived with relatives who further expanded their education with travel throughout Europe and Asia.

After she returned to the United States in her teens, however, Le Monnier's life took a dramatic turn for the worse. In addition to losing her mother in 1831, she saw her family's finances undergo a severe reversal, and she moved to New Orleans with her widowed father, where they resided with her older, married sister. There she met Warren Newcomb, a promising wholesale grocery merchant from Louisville, Kentucky; following a long courtship, the two were married on 15 December 1845.

In the early years of their marriage the Newcombs split their time between New Orleans, Louisville, and New York City, where their second child, Harriott Sophie, was born in 1855 (their first child, a son, had died in infancy). Committed to giving their daughter the same benefits that Josephine had enjoyed as a child, Warren Newcomb retired in 1863 and took his family on an extended tour of Europe. He found life as a member of the idle rich uncongenial, however, and the couple returned to New York City, where, with the aid of a nephew, he opened a branch office of H. D. Newcomb & Brothers.

In a move that would foreshadow later events, Warren Newcomb entered into the field of philanthropy when, in cooperation with Cyrus McCormick, he endowed a chair at Washington and Lee University in Lexington, Virginia. After her husband's death in 1866, Josephine Newcomb inherited an income of $10,000 per year and turned all her attentions to her daughter, for whom a $200,000 trust fund was established. Sadly, Harriott contracted diphtheria at their summer home in Niagara Falls, New York, in 1870, and died the following December. Long estranged from her husband's relatives (who saw her behavior as eccentric and had sought to contest his will), Newcomb seemed to those who know her well to be in danger of losing her mind. She slowly got over her misfortunes, however, and began to search for a suitable memorial for her daughter (whose trust fund now came under Newcomb's control). In 1882 she donated $20,000 to Washington and Lee University, which was used to construct a library commemorating General Robert E. Lee, and in the same year contributed a like sum to the Confederate Orphan Home in Charleston, South Carolina. Newcomb also made a donation permitting the establishment of a school for impoverished seamstresses in Charleston. Her adopted hometown of New York also benefited from her largess, as she donated $10,000 to a school for the deaf and also endowed a bed at the Eye, Ear, Nose, and Throat Hospital in her daughter's name.

Generous as these gifts were, Newcomb still remained unsatisfied. Correspondence from a friend in New Orleans, however, set the stage for her most lasting donation of all. In 1886, at the urging of Ida Ann Slocomb Richardson, Newcomb began considering the establishment of a women's college that would be attached to Tulane University. After meeting with Tulane president William Preston Johnston, she arranged for a donation of $100,000 to be used toward the creation of H. Sophie Newcomb Memorial College, commenting at the time that her endowment was "large enough in case of failure, and small enough to allow additions in case of success." Newcomb placed few restrictions on the use of her gift, asking only that her daughter's birth and death anniversaries be observed with an Episcopal memorial service and that daily nonsectarian chapel be conducted. The college commenced operations in October 1887, and Newcomb was eventually convinced that she had created the perfect memorial for her daughter. In her later years, though, she began spending her winters in New Orleans, where her close supervision of college operations was not always appreciated by the administration. Despite her occasional misgivings (she once

threatened to remove her entire gift), Newcomb contributed nearly $1,000,000 to the college during her lifetime.

Forced by illness to spend the winter of 1900 at the home of the Episcopal minister John Chamberlain in New York City, Newcomb never recovered and died there on Easter Sunday, 1901. Fearing attempts by relatives to overturn her will (dated 12 May 1898), she had arranged to have her estate immediately probated, which resulted in Newcomb College receiving an additional $2.6 million as a residual. The college, which continues to be a vital part of Tulane University, is an enduring memorial not only to H. Sophie Newcomb but also to her mother, one of a number of nineteenth-century philanthropists who advanced the cause of American higher education, especially for women.

• Newcomb's papers have not survived, and secondary literature on her life is scarce. The best source remains Brandt V. B. Dixon, *A Brief History of H. Sophie Newcomb Memorial College, 1887–1919* (1928); John P. Dyer, *Tulane: The Biography of a University* (1966) is also useful. Obituaries appear in the *New Orleans Times-Picayune*, 7–9 Apr. 1901, and the *New York Daily Tribune*, 9 April 1901.

EDWARD L. LACH, JR.

NEWHOUSER, Hal (20 May 1921–10 Nov. 1998), baseball player, was born Harold Newhouser in Detroit, Michigan, the son of Theodore Newhouser, a wood patternmaker for automobile manufacturers, and Emlie Macha Newhouser. He played football and ice hockey as a child, but he did not begin playing baseball until he was approximately 13 years old. He first pitched in 1936 for the Detroit Baseball Federation, a sandlot organization. He later recalled that, from his very first game on the mound, he felt certain he would one day become a professional ballplayer. In 1937 he enjoyed a sensational season for an American Legion team, winning 15 games, striking out 24 batters in one game, throwing two no-hitters, and winning the Most Valuable Player award in a state tournament. The following year he struck out 163 batters in his first 10 games; during tournament play he pitched 65 consecutive scoreless innings. Such was his reputation that, when an opposing shortstop got two hits off of him, a Cleveland Indian scout immediately signed the shortstop to a contract.

Newhouser later described the circumstances of his own signing in the fall of 1938. Detroit Tiger scout Wish Egan, who had actively pursued him, offered him a $400 signing bonus. "Well, $400 was $400, and they were smart. If it had been a check, it wouldn't have looked like anything, but being dollar bills, I had never seen anything like that. I didn't have any money. And a salary of $150 per month. That was the first job I ever had outside of selling newspapers and setting pins in a bowling alley" (quoted in Jordan, p. 16). The young pitcher gratefully signed. But a few minutes after Egan left the Newhouser home, a Cleveland Indian scout pulled up in a Lincoln Continental and offered a $15,000 signing bonus and the keys to the car. Although his parents felt hoodwinked by the Tigers and wanted to have the contract annulled, Newhouser, loyal to his hometown team, decided to turn the Indians down.

A six-foot two-inch left-hander, Newhouser started the 1939 season in the low minors, pitching for Alexandria, Louisiana, in the Evangeline League, where he won eight of his 12 starts; he was then promoted to Beaumont in the Texas League, where he lost 14 games in 19 decisions. In spite of his losing record, the Tigers regarded him as their best pitching prospect, and in September he was called up to the big league team. On 29 September 1939, at the age of 18 and not yet graduated from high school, he made his debut, pitching five innings in a loss against Cleveland. The following season, working as a spot starter and relief pitcher for the Tigers, he won nine games and lost nine games. Although the team made the World Series, he did not see any postseason action; he later recalled, however, the unique thrill of sitting in high school classrooms in the mornings and sitting on the bench in series games in the afternoons. He graduated from Wilbur Wright High School around 1941. That year he married Beryl Steele; they had two children. He also became a full-time starter, but over the next three seasons he failed to live up to his potential.

The general consensus was that Newhouser had great "stuff"—a 90-plus-mile-per-hour fastball and a biting curveball—but was probably too high-strung to be a successful major league pitcher. Boston Red Sox infielder Lamar "Skeeter" Newsome suggested that he possessed every pitching skill "except control of himself" (quoted in Jordan, p. 46). In many games he would pitch brilliantly for several innings, only to come unglued after making one or two small mistakes. In spite of his reputation as a strikeout pitcher, he often was unable to throw strikes; for example, in 1941 he struck out 106 batters while walking a whopping 137. Moreover, he alienated many of his teammates with his behavior on the field. The young pitcher frequently chided the Tigers' aging star, Charlie Gehringer, for poor defensive plays, and that, said teammate Billy Sullivan, "was like blaspheming God" (quoted in Jordan, p. 46). A hard loser, he ripped up his uniforms, broke soda-pop bottles in the clubhouse, screamed at opposing players, and became known around the league for his "rotten stare." In 1943 he pitched well enough to make the all-star team, but he finished the season in a miserable slump, losing twelve of his last thirteen decisions.

After the 1943 season, a discouraged Newhouser contemplated quitting the game and made plans to work as a draftsman for Chrysler. The Tigers decided to put him under the tutelage of veteran catcher Paul Richards, hoping that he might help the young pitcher to mature. Richards patiently worked with Newhouser to improve his disposition on the field; he also helped the pitcher to dramatically improve his change-up, teaching him to throw it with the exact same delivery that he used for his fastball, thus making it undetect-

able by hitters. With this pitch added to his arsenal, his improvement was staggering: in 1944 he posted a 29-9 won-lost record with a 2.22 earned-run average, led the league with 187 strikeouts, and threw 26 complete games with six shutouts. In 1945 he was even more dominant, winning 25 games against nine losses and leading the league in eight categories: winning percentage (.735), earned-run average (1.81), strikeouts (212), innings pitched (313), complete games (29), shutouts (8), fewest hits per nine innings, and most strikeouts per nine innings. That autumn the Tigers won the world championship against the Chicago Cubs, with Newhouser winning two of his three decisions. In both 1944 and 1945 he won the American League's Most Valuable Player Award, becoming the only pitcher in major league history to win the award two years in a row. Some baseball writers suggested that Newhouser's statistics were inflated during these years, because many of the game's best players were away serving in World War II; for example, the *New York Journal-American* called him a mouse who "looked so good when the cats were away." (Newhouser had been declared ineligible for service because of a heart condition.) But his effectiveness continued in the postwar years: between 1946 and 1950, he averaged 19 victories per season. In 1946 in the MVP voting he finished second to Ted Williams, putting together a 26–9 record, leading the league with a 1.94 earned-run average, notching 275 strikeouts, and holding opposing hitters to a league-low .201 batting average. During the late 1940s his matchups with Cleveland's star pitcher Bob Feller were eagerly anticipated, pitting the league's best left-hander against its best right-hander. In one of his greatest games, on the final day of the 1948 season, suffering from a sore arm and pitching on short rest, he beat Feller 7–1 before 74,000 fans at Cleveland's Municipal Stadium; the loss dropped the Indians into a tie with the Red Sox for first place.

Beginning in 1948, Newhouser suffered from shoulder problems that ultimately cut short his career. He described the nagging pain as "worse than a toothache"; although he saw at least twenty-six specialists over the next few years, "not one of them could give me the reason for the pain" (quoted in Jordan, p. 218). After averaging 283 innings pitched per season between 1944 and 1950, he threw only 96 innings in 1951. In 1953 he managed to appear in only seven games. Following that season, only 32 years old, he announced his retirement. But former Tiger great Hank Greenberg, who was now the general manager for Cleveland, lured him out of retirement to pitch for the Indians in 1954. He later recalled that he could no longer throw a curveball, his fastball was no longer fast, and, because he had no fastball, his change-up was ineffective. Nevertheless, through sheer wiliness, he played a crucial role as a relief pitcher on the pennant-winning team, turning in a 7–2 record and a fine 2.51 earned-run average. He appeared in two games in 1955 and then retired for good. During his career, he appeared in 488 games and pitched 2,992.2 innings, winning 207 games and losing 150 with a 3.05 earned-run average. Always fiercely determined on the mound, he completed 212 of his 374 starts; "you couldn't get the ball away from him—he hated to be pulled from a game," Tiger catcher Joe Ginsberg remembered. He was named to six American League All-Star teams.

After his retirement, Newhouser became a top scout for the Baltimore Orioles between 1956 and 1961, signing several prominent players, including pitchers Dean Chance and Milt Pappas. From 1961 to 1964 he worked as a scout for the Indians. In 1964 he became a banker for Community National Bank in Pontiac, Michigan; he worked there as a vice president in charge of business development for twenty years. Following his retirement from the bank, he returned to baseball as a scout for the Houston Astros. For many years his name was passed over by Baseball Hall of Fame voters, who seemed determined to punish him for having his two best seasons during World War II. Many of his contemporaries—including Hall of Famers Ted Williams, Bill Dickey, and George Kell—were vocal in their insistence that he should be inducted. In 1992 he was finally selected by the Hall of Fame veterans' committee. In 1997 he became the only pitcher to have his uniform number retired by the Detroit Tigers. The following year he died in Southfield, Michigan.

• A clipping file on Newhouser is at the Baseball Hall of Fame in Cooperstown, New York. At the height of his success he wrote a book that described his pitching philosophy: *Pitching to Win* (1948). He appears in several interview segments in the film *The Life and Times of Hank Greenberg* (2000). The best source for information on his life is David M. Jordan's biography, *A Tiger in His Time: Hal Newhouser and the Burden of Wartime Ball* (1990). For his career within the context of Tigers' history, see Richard Bak, *A Place for Summer: A Narrative History of Tiger Stadium* (1998). An obituary is in the *New York Times*, 11 Nov. 1998.

THOMAS W. COLLINS, JR.

NEWLEY, Anthony (24 Sept. 1931–14 Apr. 1999), singer and songwriter, was born in the East End of London, the son of Frances Grace Newley, a single mother. It has been reported that Newley's father was a local building contractor who made himself known late in Newley's life, but his name has not been recorded. Educated mainly locally, Newley, like many London children during World War II, was evacuated to the countryside. A sojourn with a music hall performer introduced him to theater, and at age fourteen, while working as a tea boy for an advertising agency, he entered London's Italia Conti stage school.

Newley made an acclaimed film debut as the Artful Dodger in director David Lean's 1948 version of Dickens's *Oliver Twist*. Over the next decade, he played small parts in more than twenty British films. In 1955 he costarred in the pantomimic, scenery-free revue *Cranks* ("A Tribute to the Modern Spirit"), which, according to one obituarist, "ideally suited [his] idiosyncratic acting, singing and dancing." New-

ley first came to America with *Cranks*, a 1956 failure on Broadway. That same year, he married Elizabeth Anne Lynne, a dancer; he subsequently married actress Joan Collins (two children) and Dareth Dunn (two children); all of his marriages ended in divorce.

Newley achieved British celebrity through his role as Jeep Jackson, a conscripted rock-and-roll singer patterned on Elvis Presley, in the satirical 1959 film *Idle on Parade*. Its title song, intended as a parody, was the first of three years of British "chart" hits for Newley the singer. His ironically flippant, music hall–influenced recordings of "Strawberry Fair" and "Pop Goes the Weasel" introduced him to an American audience. A surrealistic 1960 British television series, "The Strange World of Gurney Slade," caught the attention of critics and intellectuals, who saw him as a major new comic talent.

In 1961 Newley talked British producer Bernard Delfont into backing a show he was writing with Leslie Bricusse, a 1954 product of the Cambridge University Footlights revue. According to Delfont, the resulting stage musical, *Stop the World—I Want to Get Off!* "was a fantastical view of life, reduced to clownish simplicity but it exactly caught the mood of the times—cynicism founded on hope." As the show's white-faced clown protagonist, named Littlechap, Newley rises to fame and fortune in a wicked, manipulative world (an on-stage circus tent) without finding happiness. Alone at the final curtain, he sings the classic "What Kind of Fool Am I?" A major hit (recorded more than 100 times, winning both the 1962 British Ivor Novello and the American Grammy awards for best song), it could serve as a metaphor for Newley's life, and perhaps for his generation as well. After a 555-performance London run, it was transferred to Broadway in 1962. Coproduced by David Merrick, it ran for 500 performances, followed by a national tour that established Newley as an American star, an unclichéd talent with a boundless future.

In 1964 Bricusse and Newley wrote lyrics to the theme of the James Bond film *Goldfinger*. The rampant popularity of their often buoyant score from *The Roar of the Greasepaint—The Smell of the Crowd* made that allegorical show, set on a huge gaming board, a moderate Broadway success in 1965; the self-pitying "Who Can I Turn To?"—sung onstage to God—was recorded 200 times. Newley played the central role (Norman Wisdom had played it in its unsuccessful British run, but Merrick insisted on Newley as a condition of producing the show) and later remarked, "With the Americans, it worked." His (London) *Guardian* obituarist wrote, "His public bleeding heart was to the American taste."

Newley's British fame soon faded. His and Bricusse's sweepingly romantic songs were out of step with the new wave personified by the Beatles, and his style of singing, characterized by remarkably flattened vowel sounds, had already invited parody by the rising pop star David Bowie. Newley moved to Hollywood in 1967, supporting Rex Harrison in the musical film adaptation of Hugh Lofting's Doctor

Dolittle stories. *Guardian* reviewer Eddie Fiegel ("British Cool Started Here," 5 May 2000) later noted that Newley was by then welcomed "as one of the three great ambassadors of British cool, alongside Michael Caine [an actor] and Tommy Steele [a musical performer]."

Newley's subsequent American film career included romantic comedies such as *Sweet November* (1968, costarring with Sandy Dennis). With Bricusse he created the score for a fantasy that became a children's classic, *Willy Wonka and the Chocolate Factory* (1971), adapted from Roald Dahl's book. The film's major hit, "The Candy Man," is frequently credited to Newley alone.

By this time Newley was thoroughly established in the United States as a singer, particularly in the large showrooms of Las Vegas, where his blend of romanticism and chutzpah, as well as his highly stylized versions of classic American popular songs, never seemed out of date. For the next two decades he made occasional film appearances and occasionally collaborated with Bricusse, including the moderately successful music-hall pastiche, *The Good Old Bad Old Days* (London, 1972). In 1983 his musical play *Chaplin* was performed in Los Angeles, but did not open on Broadway.

In 1985 Newley was diagnosed with renal cell cancer, which went into remission. In 1989 he and Bricusse were named to the Songwriters Hall of Fame, and a London revival of *Stop The World—I Want to Get Off!* failed. After some television appearances, including one with his ex-wife Joan Collins in Noël Coward's *Tonight at 8:30*, Newley returned to the United States and his singing career. His cancer reemerged in 1998, and he died in Jensen Beach, Florida.

Even after major success, Newley apparently saw himself as a streetwise boy—in later life he told a California newspaper that he would never feel older than eighteen—an artful dodger of life, cheerfully thumbing his nose at the fuddy-duddies who held power. His personal life was regularly wrecked by the same self-centered brilliance that made him an international idol. But a year after his death, compilations of his recordings began to appear, and his essential nature (". . . a singularly funny, tender-hearted, romantic soul") began to surface, finally liberating Newley from the 1960s.

• The Theatre Museum of the Victoria and Albert Museum (London) has a Newley file. Good evaluations of Newley's singing career are by Nigel Fountain, in the (London) *Guardian*, 15 Apr. 1999, and by Eddie Fiegel, also in the *Guardian*, 5 May 2000. Newley's career in American musical film is detailed in Stanley Green, *Encyclopedia of the Musical Film* (1981). An unflattering portrait of Newley is included in Joan Collins, *Past Imperfect* (1978). Useful information comes from Bernard Delfont with Barry Turner, *East End, West End: An Autobiography* (1990). Obituaries are in the (London) *Guardian* (by Dennis Barker), the *New York Times*, and the *Los Angeles Times*, all on 15 Apr. 1999, and the (London) *Times*, 16 Apr. 1999.

JAMES ROSS MOORE

NITSCHKE, Ray (29 Dec. 1936–8 Mar. 1998), football player, was born Raymond Ernest Nitschke in Elmwood Park, a suburban area of Chicago, Illinois, the son of Robert Nitschke, who worked for a Chicago streetcar line, and Anna Petersen Nitschke. Nitschke's father died in an automobile accident when he was three years old, and his mother died suddenly of a blood clot when he was thirteen years old, according to his autobiography. After his mother's death, Nitschke and his brother, Richard, were adopted by their elder brother, Robert, who was just twenty-one at the time. Ray took the loss of his mother hard, and he felt fate had robbed him of a normal childhood. He frequently tussled with others, taking on many who were older and bigger. Nitschke was able to channel his emotions through sports at Proviso High School in Maywood, Illinois. He excelled in football, baseball, and basketball. In his senior year, he led the Pirates to the 1953 Suburban League Football Championship as a quarterback and defensive lineman.

Nitschke graduated from high school in 1954 and passed up a professional baseball contract from the St. Louis Browns in favor of a football scholarship at the University of Illinois. Nitschke was a fullback and defensive linebacker for the Illini. He led his team in scoring as a senior, averaging 6.5 yards on 79 carries. His prowess on defense drew the attention of pro scouts, and he was drafted in the third round by the Green Bay Packers in 1958.

Nitschke had the opportunity to start in eight games at middle linebacker in his rookie year because of an injury to the veteran starter, Tom Bettis. Nitschke, however, was benched when Bettis returned.

Vince Lombardi became the coach and general manager of the Packers in 1959, bringing strict discipline and a winning attitude to the team. Nitschke was frustrated with the new coach, however, because he continued to see little playing time. The situation was aggravated by Nitschke missing practice time because he was called up for Army Reserve duty during the 1959 and 1960 seasons. Off the field, Nitschke was still having some trouble with his temper, especially after imbibing alcohol.

In the ninth week of the 1960 season Nitschke was promoted to starting middle linebacker. At the end of the following season the Packers defeated the New York Giants in Green Bay to win the 1961 NFL Championship. Nitschke was emerging as a leader on the defense. Coach Lombardi told the press, "He has learned his keys" (quoted in Nitschke and Wells, p. 80). The linebacker's film study and hard work on the practice field had led to accurate reading of the opposition's intentions. Nitschke's reputation around the league as a tough but clean tackler was growing as well. Nitschke hit hard and sought to make opposing players shyer each time they approached him. He had good lateral speed and was constantly in motion. At 6'3" and 235 pounds, Nitschke was tall enough to defend the passing lanes and strong enough to mix it up in the trenches with heavier linemen. Nitschke was just as aggressive on the practice field, causing Packer guard Jerry Kramer to lament that Ray "just didn't know what it was like to 'brother-in-law,' to ease-up" (Kramer and Schaap, p. 150).

There were some changes off the field for Nitschke in 1961 as he married Jacqueline "Jackie" Forchette, a waitress. Having someone to share his life mellowed Nitschke. He gave up drinking and began to build a family life—something he never had as a child. The couple eventually adopted three children.

1962 was a banner year for the Packers and for Nitschke. The team went 13–1 in the regular season, as the defense held their opponents to an average of 234 yards and less than 11 points per game. A bitterly cold December wind swirled through the New York Polo Grounds stadium when the Packers played the New York Giants in the 1962 NFL Championship game. Both teams were aggressive on defense from the opening series; the Giants defense was led by Sam Huff, the Packers by Nitschke. It would be Nitschke's day in the end, as he recovered two fumbles and deflected a pass that was caught by teammate Dan Currie for an interception. Nitschke was named Most Valuable Player in the 16–7 Packer victory.

In 1964 Nitschke bounced back from an injury-marred 1963 season and was selected for the Pro Bowl. The Packers returned to championship form in 1965, winning the NFL Championship 23–12 against the Cleveland Browns. The Packers were the NFL champions again in 1966. Nitschke had five tackles in Super Bowl I, as the Packers defeated the Kansas City Chiefs 35–10 and shut out the Chiefs' offense in the second half. The Packers won their third straight NFL title in 1967. They then throttled the Oakland Raiders in Super Bowl II, winning 33–14 as Nitschke made nine tackles. Nitschke, considered the backbone of the dominant Packer defense, was named All-Pro in 1964, 1965, and 1966.

The departure of Lombardi as coach and some injuries to key offensive players hurt the Packers in 1968 and beyond, but Nitschke persevered. In Nitschke's final years, the Packers began building for the future, and Coach Dan Devine opted to give the bulk of the playing time to the young middle-linebacker, Jim Carter. Nitschke, who felt he was still in prime playing condition, was unhappy with the decision but contributed to the defense from the sidelines, communicating with coaches in the booth.

Nitschke retired after the 1972 season, having played 15 years as a pro in 190 games. He finished with 25 interceptions, 20 fumbles recovered, and two touchdowns scored. His dominance at middle-linebacker throughout the 1960s was recognized in the many awards he received. He was inducted in the Green Bay Packers Hall of Fame in 1975 and in the Pro Football Hall of Fame in 1978. He was named to the NFL 50th Anniversary Team in 1970 and to the NFL 75th Anniversary Team in 1995. In 1983 the Packers retired his jersey number 66, and they named one of their practice fields the Ray Nitschke Field in 1997.

After his retirement Nitschke remained in Green Bay, raising his family in his suburban Oneida home. He was one of the founders of *Ray Nitschke's Packer Report* in 1973 and wrote a column in the weekly newspaper until he died. He was always accessible to fans and wrote countless autographs. Nitschke's home number was listed in the local phone directory, and it was not unusual for Ray to meet admiring fans who called him to share a story or ask for an autograph.

Nitschke's celebrity brought offers for movie and television commercial appearances. Nitschke had a small role in The Monkees' 1968 satirical movie, *Head*. In 1974 he played a tough prison guard in the Burt Reynolds comedy *The Longest Yard*. Nitschke's most famous commercials were in the Miller Lite All-Star series. Nitschke's first appearance in the series was in 1975 with Ben Davidson and Rosie Grier, and he continued his participation in the ad series into the 1980s. He also did regional commercials for Oldsmobile.

Nitschke was an affable spokesman for several Wisconsin businesses, and he was a national account representative for Clairmont Trucking. He also rolled up his sleeves for several charities, including serving twenty-two years as the honorary chairman of the local Cerebral Palsy Telethon. The Nitschkes' support for recovering alcoholics was so strong that the former Green Bay Samaritan House drug and alcohol treatment center was renamed the Jackie Nitschke Center.

After Jackie died of cancer in 1996, Nitschke rededicated himself to his family and his Christian faith. He died suddenly of a heart attack in Venice, Florida, while vacationing with his daughter and granddaughter. His life was memorialized in a ceremony at Bayside Christian Fellowship in Green Bay. On 2 October 1998 Green Bay's newly rebuilt Main Street Bridge was dedicated as the Ray Nitschke Memorial Bridge.

Although his competitors and teammates will not forget "Number 66" for his ferocious intensity on the playing field, those who met Nitschke off the field remember his warmth and caring spirit. Nitschke was a man who overcame his troubled youth to become a hero and role model to many fans.

• Ray Nitschke wrote an autobiography with Robert Wells, *Mean on Sunday* (1973; paperback ed., 1998). Nitschke's story after football is included in a chapter of *Distant Replay* (1985) by Jerry Kramer and Dick Schaap, and is also included in a chapter of *Downfield!: Untold Stories of the Green Bay Packers* (1996) by Jerry Poling. Frank Deford's *Lite Reading* (1984) profiles the Miller Lite All-Star series of commercials, including Nitschke's.

KEITH BREWSTER

NOBLE, Ray (17 Dec. 1903–3 Apr. 1978), popular composer and bandleader, was born Raymond Stanley Noble in Brighton, England, to Frank Stanley Noble, a neurosurgeon, and Maude Edith Poole Noble. Educated at South London's Dulwich College, Noble was early lured from classical music by the flood of "hot" American recordings by bands such as McKinney's Cotton Pickers and the Original Memphis Five that began to arrive in Britain circa 1925. In 1926 Noble, at the time playing piano and leading a small band, twice won the *Melody Maker* magazine's contest for dance band arranging.

Noble then became staff arranger for the music publisher that owned *Melody Maker*, as well as pianist-arranger for Debroy Somers, who led a top London hotel band. In 1927 Noble married Gladys Violet Childers; the couple had no children and remained married until Noble's death. In 1928 he was chosen to arrange for the new dance orchestra of the British Broadcasting Company. Some of his lush arrangements required an enlargement of the orchestra. In 1929 Noble became music director for His Masters Voice (EMI) records. Shortly thereafter, he took over the company's New Mayfair Dance Orchestra. This was a recording ensemble, and Noble enhanced it by recruiting from the major hotel orchestras. The orchestra often accompanied film and stage stars such as Jack Buchanan.

All of Noble's fame before he went to the United States was derived from the New Mayfair, which by 1934 had been renamed Ray Noble and His Orchestra. The band, which rarely assembled in public, used progressively more American material. Its style was uncloyingly sweet, often refreshed by bursts of jazz. From 1931 its most popular recordings were Noble's own compositions, usually sung by Al Bowlly. These included "Goodnight, Sweetheart" (1931), "Love Is the Sweetest Thing" (1932), and "The Very Thought of You" (1934.) The recordings of Ray Noble and His Orchestra, released in the United States under the RCA Victor label, were quickly seized upon by college students in the Northeast, and, sight unseen, Noble's was soon America's most popular British band.

Noble's American career began in some confusion. Invited to play an engagement with his band at New York's Rainbow Room in 1934 as well as leading a network radio show, Noble ran into trouble with organized labor: he was not cleared by the American Federation of Musicians (AFM), who argued that a British band would steal work from Americans and open the gates for even more competition. While the argument continued, Noble headed to California, where for the moment motion picture labor wielded less power. He wrote ("Why Stars Come Out at Night"), arranged scores, and made his first film appearance as a bandleader alongside George Burns and Gracie Allen, Bing Crosby, Jack Oakie, and other "radio" stars in *The Big Broadcast of 1936* (1935).

When Noble was cleared by the AFM in 1935, it was with the understanding that he would lead an "American" band—a solution that paralleled the experience of some American bands in Britain. Aside from Noble, there were only two Britons, vocalist Bowlly and drummer-manager Bill Harty. In Noble's absence the rest of the sixteen-piece ensemble had been assembled by trombonist Glenn Miller, who left his job with the Dorsey Brothers Orchestra to work with Noble. Miller, then decidedly of the Dixieland

persuasion, assembled an all-star lineup, the "hottest" Noble group of all. It included trumpeter Charlie Spivak, pianist Claude Thornhill, reed players Bud Freeman and Johnny Mince, guitarist George Van Eps, and trombonists Miller and Will Bradley. Considering the warmth and strength of Noble's arrangements, the big-band historian George Simon wrote that everything pointed to this being "one of the great all round bands of all time."

The Rainbow Room run, with Noble leading from a white piano that toured the floor-side tables, was extremely successful. When Noble revisited England briefly in 1936, Miller fronted the band, notably (and, of necessity, when trumpeter Pee Wee Erwin left) inventing what became known as the (clarinet-led) "Glenn Miller sound." In the normal way of sidemen, there were other defections; when Bowlly returned to England permanently at the end of 1936, Noble broke up the band after a brief tour and returned to Hollywood. There he formed a recording orchestra, often accompanying Fred Astaire.

In his first film appearance and some of the recordings made with his New York band, Noble, slim, diffident, and pencil-mustached, the very image of a gentleman, had found an "acting" persona—the harmless "silly ass" Englishman. For the rest of his noncomposing life, Noble played this part perfectly in American films particularly as an aristocrat with surprising wit and flair in *A Damsel in Distress* (1937) and on the Burns and Allen radio show, beginning in 1937. (The idea of a comic bandleader had just been pioneered by Jack Benny, who hired the garrulous Phil Harris as leader and foil.) Between Burns and Allen and the Edgar Bergen–Charlie McCarthy show, Noble, who then took up American citizenship, led radio bands and played the cheerful English idiot into the early 1950s, creating memorable moments such as the confrontation with Fats Waller in which Noble, in an exaggerated British accent, greeted the great stride pianist, "Well, if it isn't Fats Waller—lay that mess on me, man!"

When he was not on air or in film, Noble led a hotel band in Los Angeles. In 1938 one of the compositions on Native American themes that had come to him on the cross-country tour, "Cherokee," was recorded by the Charlie Barnet orchestra, becoming one of the swing era's most characteristic numbers and seen by some critics as a precursor of the nervous "bebop" movement that began during the war years. In the later 1940s, Noble teamed with singer Buddy Clark on several recordings that helped make Clark a star.

When the Bergen-McCarthy radio program ended in 1955, Noble retired and in the early 1960s moved to Jersey, one of the English Channel islands. In 1971 the Nobles returned to the United States, settling in Santa Barbara, California, where they lived for the rest of Noble's life. He died in London, where he had gone for cancer treatment.

In 1996 Noble was inducted into the National Academy of Popular Music's Songwriters Hall of Fame. Musicologist Alec Wilder, a man who often chided Jerome Kern for seeming too "English" in his melodies, said of Noble's compositions, they "are so American in style and so loved by Americans that he is musically American by adoption . . . they scarcely seem like importations." He characterized "Love Is the Sweetest Thing" as "very pure, as opposed to sensuous . . . the work of a distinguished melodist . . . the song was written as much to be sung as played, indeed, more." He called "I Hadn't Anyone till You" (1936) "stylish throughout, verse and chorus . . . no attempts to be clever rhythmically . . . smooth, direct, . . . a song with both great sophistication and a flavor of the past."

• Brian Rust, *The Dance Bands* (1972), Tony Staveacre, *The Songwriters* (1980), and Chris Hayes, *The Leader of the Band* (1994) are British publications filling in important details. Alec Wilder, *American Popular Song: The Great Innovators, 1900–1950* (1972), is, as usual, helpful. Obituaries include one in the *Santa Barbara News-Press*, 3 Apr. 1978, and John Wilson's in the *New York Times*, 4 Apr. 1978. The former newspaper ran a feature on Noble by Mary Every on 13 Feb. 1973. Appreciations include Leonard Feather's and Howard Lucraft's in the *Los Angeles Times*, both 23 Apr. 1978.

JAMES ROSS MOORE

NOLAN, Thomas B. (21 May 1901–2 Aug. 1992), geologist and seventh director of the U.S. Geological Survey (USGS), was born Thomas Brennan Nolan in Greenfield, Franklin County, Massachusetts, the only child of Frank Wesley Nolan, a physician, and Anna Sarah Brennan Nolan, a schoolteacher. When the Nolans separated in 1902, two years after their marriage, Anna and Thomas returned to her parents' home in New Haven, Connecticut. There young Nolan worked after school and during five summers at the Winchester Repeating Arms Company, rising from office boy to manager of a division's sales staff.

Nolan entered Yale, his father's university, in 1918 on a scholarship to its Sheffield Scientific School. Although he earned a Ph.B. degree in metallurgy in 1921, he had already embraced geology after taking the required introductory course from Alan M. Bateman. Nolan's graduate scholarship supported advanced studies with Bateman, Adolph Knopf, and Chester R. Longwell. In 1922 Bateman helped Nolan get a summer job in Alaska. Nolan spent the next summer in southern Nevada with Longwell, who mapped quadrangles for the USGS. Longwell guided Nolan's Ph.D. study, completed in 1924, of the stratigraphy and structure of the northwest part of the thrust- and block-faulted Spring Mountains, west of Las Vegas, a range mapped by Longwell and Yale-trained D. Foster Hewett. In 1929 Nolan used his dissertation's results to refute Andrew C. Lawson's idea that overthrust faults could not produce substantial horizontal displacements.

Nolan joined the USGS Section of Metalliferous Deposits in 1924 and spent the next two decades assessing the geology and ores at locales in the western United States. After assisting Knopf's investigation of the Mother Lode gold district in California, and

studying Utah's potash brines in 1925, Nolan centered his studies on the geologically complex Great Basin. He evaluated the mining district at Gold Hill in Utah and then those at Tonopah and Eureka in Nevada, where the use of his maps and isometric block diagrams revitalized production. In the 1930s Nolan also began training younger geologists in geologic mapping, which he preferred to the economic studies of mining districts and dam sites that he also taught. In 1933 the sixteenth International Geological Congress, held in Washington, D.C., awarded him its Spendiarov Prize as the most promising young geologist of the host country.

Nolan's growing stature as a scientist brought requests for service outside the USGS and managerial assignments within the agency. Between 1934 and 1937 Nolan served continuously in the National Research Council's Division of Geography and Geology. He twice briefly led the USGS metals section in the absence of Gerald F. Loughlin, who became chief geologist in 1935, and Loughlin's successor Hewett. In 1938 Hewett made Nolan his untitled assistant in the USGS's revived strategic minerals program. While Hewett cooperated with the U.S. Bureau of Mines and advised the war agencies, Nolan supervised onsite the program's operations in the West. Hewett gave Nolan special responsibility for the steel- and lamp-important tungsten project, the prelicensing examinations of mines for the War Production Board (WPB), coordination with the British Geological Survey's minerals program, and service on the Society of Economic Geologists' council. Contacts with the WPB's Metals and Materials Branch, led by Bateman, introduced Nolan to William E. Wrather, an independent oil geologist then serving as Bateman's deputy. Wrather became the USGS's sixth director in 1943, the year Nolan published his geologic synthesis of the Basin and Range province.

Wrather increased Nolan's administrative responsibilities in the USGS and brought him to Washington, D.C., to serve as acting director for three months while Wrather accompanied the Technical Oil Mission to the Middle East for Secretary of the Interior Harold L. Ickes. Wrather and Nolan then chose Yale-trained Wilmot H. "Bill" Bradley, who led the USGS Military Geology Unit, to replace Loughlin as chief geologist. They asked Bradley to concentrate postwar geological activities in the prewar regional centers and rebalance research to meet the agency's long-term view that applying science to human needs required science to apply. In December 1944 Ickes appointed Nolan assistant director, a new position established to increase efficient administration. In the next dozen years Wrather and Nolan functioned well as a team. Wrather dealt with Congress and the USGS's other constituencies, while Nolan led the USGS executive committee, managed the agency's daily operations, and represented the director on federal and other committees. Nolan also served as acting director when Wrather traveled and during the illness that led to Wrather's total disability in 1955.

Nolan succeeded Wrather as director in 1956 and founded an advisory committee of outside experts. As director Nolan continued to expect the best from himself, and he would not settle for less from others. He led by example in encouraging basic research in the agency's geologic and water-resources programs. During summer months Nolan mapped in Nevada and directed the USGS from there. Luna B. Leopold, appointed chief hydraulic engineer in 1957, and Charles A. Anderson, who succeeded Bradley as chief geologist in 1959 when Bradley returned to original studies at his own request, led balanced programs and continued their own research. Anderson resumed full-time studies in 1964; Nolan and Leopold made the same decision in 1965. As a scientist at the highest grade in the federal government until mandatory retirement in 1971, and as a reemployed annuitant until 1986, Nolan continued to work at Eureka, Nevada, extending his mapping, improving his initial synthesis of the mining district issued in 1962, and arranging with his colleagues to complete the area's geologic maps. He remained an avid ornithologist and a skilled bridge player.

Nolan's sensitive but firm leadership reshaped the USGS for operations increasingly expanded in content, funding, and scope to meet growing national needs. Continued USGS searches for uranium ores accompanied new evaluations of underground nuclear tests, geologic conditions affecting the peaceful uses of atomic energy, and the disposal of radioactive waste. When Congress authorized USGS work outside the national domain, the agency renewed its cooperative activities with other nations and began official work in Antarctica. Photogeologic studies of the moon and field-training astronauts in geology helped prepare the way for lunar landings. The rock-magnetics project, begun to solve practical questions arising from airborne surveys, supplied a time-scale based on the isotopic dating of magnetic-field reversals as a key part of the plate-tectonics model. Work at a new national center for earthquake research and prediction paralleled increased studies of volcanic hazards. New techniques of geochemical exploration determined that the distribution of some chemical elements adversely affected public health. A new marine-studies program concentrated on sea-floor mineral resources and coastal processes. The USGS and the Bureau of Mines assessed the mineral potential of areas designated for protection under provisions of the Wilderness Act. The new Office of Water Data Coordination met federal-wide responsibilities in collection and storage assigned by the Bureau of the Budget, which also made the USGS accountable for programming and coordinating all federal topographic mapping activities and producing the cooperative *National Atlas of the United States of America* (1970), edited by Arch C. Gerlach. Using orthophotogrammetric methods enabled the USGS in 1964 to promise complete topographic coverage of the conterminous United States in the 7.5-minute (1:24,000-scale) map series by 1980 [completed in 1990].

Nolan's modest ways sometimes obscured his contributions as an adviser in government and to universities, where he promoted the value of basic research and the role of scientists in formulating national policy. He traveled widely and as a government official spoke often, more effectively than he wrote, to explain the USGS's work. He believed that human ingenuity would negate Malthusian predictions of shortfalls in nonrenewable resources. With some success Nolan served on the Federal Council for Science and Technology and chaired its standing committee, but he did not favor establishing a separate department for those activities (George B. Kistiakowsky, *A Scientist at the White House* [1976], p. 65). He also advised other federal boards and commissions, the Massachusetts Institute of Technology, Harvard and Stanford Universities, the American Geological Institute, and the International Union of Geological Sciences, which he served as vice president from 1964 to 1972.

Nolan's contributions to knowledge and society earned him significant recognition. His peers elected him to the Cosmos Club (1943), the American Academy of Arts and Sciences (1950), the National Academy of Sciences (1951), and the American Philosophical Society (1957). He also served as president of the Society of Economic Geologists (1949) and the Geological Society of America (1961). Columbia University awarded Nolan the Li Medal (1954) for advancing the science of tungsten, and he received the Tokyo Geographical Society's Silver Medal (1965) for his role in developing research projects in Japan. Nolanite, an iron-vanadium mineral from Saskatchewan, several species of Paleozoic invertebrates, and a pinnacle in Antarctica's Thiel Mountains also honor him. Princeton University gave Nolan a Rockefeller Public Service Award (1961), and the University of St. Andrews in Scotland granted him an LL.D. (1962). President Ronald Reagan signed a special letter of commendation in 1984 on the sixtieth anniversary of Nolan's federal employment; in responding, Nolan emphasized that USGS's distinction depended on its continued commitment to public service and increasing an understanding of the significance of its work.

In 1927 Nolan married Mabelle Blanche "Pete" Orleman, a parasitologist with the U.S. Public Health Service. The Nolans, who had one son, were known for their cordial hospitality. Nolan died of a pulmonary thromboembolism in Washington, D.C.

• Nolan's public papers are in Record Group 57 at the National Archives, except for the thirty-one field notebooks and related materials from his work in the West (1924–1986) now in the USGS Field Records Library at Denver, where they are supplemented by his visual records in the Photographic Library. His personal papers are currently held by the USGS in Reston, Virginia, but they are intended for deposit in the American Heritage Center at the University of Wyoming. *U.S. Geological Survey Bulletin* 823 (1931): 452–53; 937 (1944): 420, 478, 531, 690–91, and 819; 1049 (1957): 676; 1195 (1965): 1100, 1185–86; and the successor volumes of the *Bibliography and Index of Geology*, issued yearly since 1960, list most of Nolan's publications. These citations also are available on CD-ROM as part of the American Geological Institute's "GeoRef" online bibliographical database. Unpublished transcripts of oral-history interviews of Nolan in 1988 by Ernest L. Hendricks, who succeeded Leopold as USGS chief hydrologist, and in 1989 USGS geologist Thomas W. Stern are at, respectively, the USGS Library in Reston and the Cosmos Club, Washington, D.C. Biographical articles about Nolan include those by Gerge B. Stewart in Delia Kuhn and Ferdinand Kuhn, eds., *Adventures in Public Service: The Careers of Eight Honored Men in the United States Government* (1963), pp. 137–43; David B. Stewart, *American Mineralogist* 79 (1994): 575–76 (with selected publications); and Luna B. Leopold and Arthur A. Baker, *Geological Society of America Memorials* 27 (1996): 33–34. Mary C. Rabbitt evaluated Nolan's directorate in "The United States Geological Survey 1879–1989," *U.S. Geological Survey Circular* 1050 (1989); a scanned version of that publication is included in Clifford M. Nelson, ed., "Records and History of the United States Geological Survey," *U.S. Geological Survey Circular* 1179 (CD-ROM, 2000). Obituaries are in the *Washington Post,* 5 Aug. 1992, and the *New York Times,* 6 Aug. 1992.

CLIFFORD M. NELSON

NORDHOFF, Charles Bernard (1 Feb. 1887–11 Apr. 1947), and **James Norman Hall** (22 Apr. 1887–6 July 1951), fiction writers, became famous for the work they did in collaboration.

Nordhoff, the son of Walter Nordhoff, a *New York Herald* foreign correspondent, and Sarah Cope Whitall Nordhoff, who came from a Philadelphia Quaker background, was born in London, England. He moved with his parents in 1890 to a rugged family ranch in Baja California and in 1894 to Los Angeles. While a student at a private classical school in Pasadena, he spent his free time near the ranch, hunting, sailing, and fishing. After the San Francisco earthquake he transferred from Stanford University, where he had taken classes in 1905–1906, to Harvard College, graduating in 1909. He worked two years in the sugarcane business in Mexico and joined his father to manufacture china products near San Diego until 1916. During the last two years of World War I, Nordhoff drove a French ambulance in combat, was a pilot with the Lafayette Escadrille, was commissioned in the U.S. Army, and chafed at a staff job in Paris. He wrote letters to his mother describing his ambulance work and air combat. She sent them to Ellery Sedgwick, the *Atlantic Monthly* editor, who published parts of them beginning in January 1918; Nordhoff's war correspondence was assembled in *The Fledgling* (1919).

Hall was born in Colfax, Iowa, the son of Arthur Wright Hall, a storekeeper and owner of a mineral-water business, and Ellen Young Hall. After finishing high school, he entered Grinnell College in Iowa, from which he graduated with a Ph.B. in 1910. The next four years he spent as a caseworker in Boston for the Massachusetts Society for the Prevention of Cruelty to Children. Vacationing in England when World War I began, Hall joined Lord Kitchener's "First Hundred Thousand" and served in the British army as a machine gunner in France; having requested a leave in 1915 to visit his ailing father, he was granted a discharge instead. In 1916 Sedgwick published in the *Atlantic Monthly* some of Hall's war essays, which became the basis for his *Kitchener's Mob: The Adventures of an American in Kitchener's Army* (1916). Back in France to write about the Lafayette Escadrille, he flew with it instead. He then became a captain with the American aviation forces, crashed, was imprisoned by the Germans, and gained his release after the Armistice. He published *High Adventure: A Narrative of Air Fighting in France* (1918).

Having met in Paris in 1919, Nordhoff and Hall went to Martha's Vineyard, where they wrote and edited *The Lafayette Flying Corps* (2 vols., 1920). With a contract to write articles for *Harper's Magazine* about the South Seas, they soon moved to Tahiti. In 1920 Nordhoff married Vahime Tua Tearae Smidt, a Polynesian, with whom he was to have seven children. While Hall was visiting the Tuamotu Archipelago (1920–1921), Nordhoff explored the Cook islands. The two men settled back in Tahiti and collaborated on *Faery Lands of the South Seas* (1921), about their experiences in the region. Nordhoff's chapters concern native adventures and myths; Hall's concentrate on impressions of the Polynesians as people. After restlessly traveling to the Marquesas Islands, the United States, and Iceland (1922–1923), Hall returned to Tahiti and wrote somewhat indifferently. Meanwhile, Nordhoff produced two exciting novels for juvenile readers, *The Pearl Lagoon* (1924) and, its sequel, *The Derelict: Further Adventures of Charles Selden and His Native Friends in the South Seas* (1928), and several minor items. In 1925 Hall married the daughter of a Tahitian woman and an English sea captain, Sarah Winchester, who became a beneficent influence on him. They had two children.

In Tahiti, the two authors drew on personal experience to write *Falcons of France* (1929), a novel based on their combat flying: the hero trains the way Nordhoff did and is shot down and imprisoned as Hall was. Casting about for ideas to develop into more fiction, Hall found Sir John Barrow's *The Mutiny of the Bounty* (1831), which Hall had bought in Paris during the war. The two men used it as a basis for their novel *Mutiny on the Bounty* (1932). An enormous popular and critical success, it narrates the cruelty of Lieutenant William Bligh (1754–1817), captain of H.M.S. *Bounty,* during his arduous mission to fetch Pacific breadfruit seedlings to the West Indies in order to produce cheap food for slaves. Led by Fletcher Christian, the master's mate, mutineers in 1789 seize the *Bounty* and set Bligh and most of his few loyal followers adrift in the ship's launch. Christian leads the others to Tahiti, and with some of them, as well as several friendly Tahitians of both sexes, sails on in quest of a permanent island home in the South Seas. Meanwhile, Bligh survives to wreak havoc on everyone who can be found. In writing the novel, Nordhoff and Hall were helped by Sedgwick, their editor, who supplied them with many historical documents. Although, in general, Nordhoff handled plot problems while Hall presented factual details, the two shared and revised each other's drafts and thus were genuine collaborators. *Mutiny on the Bounty* is notable for skillful use of documents, vigorous dialogue, and vivid descriptions of ship life, weather at sea, and lush islands.

A pair of fine sequels complete the Bounty trilogy: *Men against the Sea* (1934), about tough Bligh's real-life survival, and *Pitcairn's Island*, about violence in Christian's island colony, much fictionalized in the absence of historical documentation. The award-winning movie adaptation of *Mutiny on the Bounty* was produced in 1935 and featured Charles Laughton in one of his most memorable performances as Captain Bligh. (The enduring popularity of the story is evident from the fact that two more Hollywood productions of *Mutiny on the Bounty* were made in 1962 and 1984, although neither achieved the success of the original film.)

In the eleven years following the completion of the Bounty trilogy, Nordhoff and Hall wrote six more books together, of which *The Hurricane* (1936), sea fiction at its best, is especially notable. The two authors, having gained a pittance for movie rights to the Bounty story, now could command the much higher sum of $60,000 for *The Hurricane*; lavishly produced, the film appeared in 1937. Another collaborative effort deserving of mention is *Botany Bay* (1941), albeit Nordhoff had more of a hand in it than Hall; it bitterly fictionalizes the colonizing of part of Australia by British convicts.

For years Nordhoff had been a philanderer, but he divorced his wife in 1936 when he caught her with their native chauffeur; after his marriage ended he had three children with a native mistress. In 1941 he married Laura Grainger Whiley in Santa Barbara, California. Aware of his diminished talent, burdened by failing health, and drinking heavily, he died of cardiac disease. Hall, in California for his daughter's wedding, attended the cold, prayerless funeral. He returned to Tahiti and continued to write: *A Word for His Sponsor: A Narrative Poem* (1949), inveighing against nuclear war; *The Far Lands* (1950), a novel cast in early Polynesia; and *My Island Home: An Autobiography*, posthumously published in 1952 though incomplete. In 1950, after a visit to his home state of Iowa, where he attended the fortieth anniversary of his Grinnell class, Hall returned to his beloved Tahiti, where he died the following year.

Nordhoff and Hall separately wrote works that often exhibited excellence but occasionally are less inspired. At their best while working together, these skillful, cooperative collaborators produced historical fiction that both enthralled the millions and delighted the critics. Their Bounty trilogy remains a model of meticulous research, realistic plotting and dialogue, and romantic painterly description.

• All but a few of Nordhoff's papers are in the Manuscript Division, Library of Congress, Washington, D.C. Most of Hall's papers are in the libraries of Grinnell College and the University of Iowa. In *My Island Home: An Autobiography* (1952), Hall mainly focuses on himself but sheds much light on Nordhoff as well. In "Fern Gravel: A Hoax and a Confession," *Atlantic Monthly*, Sept. 1946, pp. 112–14, Hall tells how he wrote *Oh, Millersville* (1940), a collection of pseudo-childish poems putatively by Fern Gravel. Paul L. Briand, Jr., *In Search of Paradise: The Nordhoff-Hall Story* (1966), narrates the lives, often intertwined, of both men and also contains thorough primary and secondary bibliographies. Robert Roulston, *James Norman Hall* (1978), emphasizes Hall but includes information on Nordhoff. Murray D. Welch, "James Norman Hall: Poet and Philosopher," *South Atlantic Quarterly* 39 (Apr. 1940): 130–40, emphasizes Hall's love of solitude, silence, idleness, and reverie, with quotations from his minor works. Alice Payne Hackett and James Henry Burke, *80 Years of Best Sellers, 1895–1975* (1977), reports that *Mutiny on the Bounty* sold 3,556,694 copies by 1975 and that *The Hurricane* made the 1936 bestseller list. Details concerning the movie *Mutiny on the Bounty* are in Bob Thomas, *Thalberg: Life and Legend* (1969), and Patricia King Hanson and Alan Gevinson, eds., *The American Film Institute Catalog of Motion Pictures Produced in the United States: Feature Films, 1931–1940* (1993). There are obituaries in the *New York Times* on Nordhoff, 12 Apr. 1947, and on Hall, 7 July 1951.

ROBERT L. GALE

NORVO, Red (31 Mar. 1908–6 Apr. 1999), musician, was born J. Kenneth Norville in Beardstown, Illinois, one of four children of Joseph Norville, a railroad dispatcher, and Estelle Smith Norville. Because a railroad family moved a lot, Norvo was educated at various places in Illinois. He apparently studied mining engineering in 1926-1927 at the University of Missouri and later claimed he had also "tried college twice" at the University of Illinois and the University of Detroit.

When Norvo was fourteen, while visiting his brother who was in college in Rolla, Missouri, he became fascinated by a marimba player. The next year, he bought a table model xylophone and taught himself to play it. At seventeen, having joined a group called the Collegians, he taught himself harmony and for the rest of the decade was in vaudeville, singing and dancing and playing piano or xylophone. One evening the master of ceremonies, Paul Ash, who typically mispronounced his name, called him "Norvo." Norvo later told jazz writer Whitney Balliett that the show business daily *Variety* picked up "Norvo" and so he kept it. Eventually Norvo led house bands in Milwaukee, Kansas City, Detroit, and Minneapolis.

In 1929 Norvo got a job in Chicago radio, where he worked with composer-conductor Victor Young and played tympani and xylophone with Paul Whiteman's orchestra. Playing the xylophone, he made his first recording, "Moon Country," with Whiteman. Whiteman's vocalist was Mildred Bailey. Norvo and Bailey married in 1933 and divorced, childless, in 1945.

The first group to bear Norvo's name was a quartet including clarinetist Benny Goodman. Among the quartet's 1933 recordings was the Bix Beiderbecke composition "In a Mist." Commenting on its "odd harmonies and notes and arrhythmic collective passages," Balliett called it a precursor of "free jazz" and probably the first inkling of Norvo's eventual status as a jazz visionary—and of a kinship with the innovative cornetist Beiderbecke, about whom Norvo later said, "He had all the harmonies to play bebop, but the style then was to play melodic."

Norvo's next group included clarinetist Artie Shaw and saxophone player Charlie Barnet. When Bailey joined them at the Blackhawk in Chicago in 1936, the Red Norvo and Mildred Bailey band was formed; for the first time, according to Balliett, "a jazz vocalist had a first-rate jazz band built around her." It was with the Norvo band that Bailey introduced her signature tune, Hoagy Carmichael's "Rockin' Chair."

Courtesy of music writer George Simon, Norvo and Bailey soon were known as "Mr. and Mrs. Swing." The band continued until 1942, though Bailey retired with diabetes in 1940. The twelve-piece Norvo-Bailey band was perhaps the quietest, most thoughtful of the swing era. Although few knew it at the time, Norvo had suffered hearing loss as a child, and this handicap may have contributed to both the quietness and his characteristic stance while playing—crouched over his instrument, with "outrigger elbows," listening intently, blending his improvisations with what was going on around him. Norvo later remarked, "You listen about 12 feet around you." (Norvo suffered additional hearing loss in 1961, but operations eventually ameliorated the condition.)

After the demise of his "big" band in 1942, Norvo became identified with small New York clubs where new directions in jazz were under way. He gradually abandoned the xylophone in favor of the vibraharp (he always preferred its brand name to the generic "vibraphone"), a 1927 invention of the Deagan company that used electronic pulsators to enhance a xylophone, producing round, bell-like tones and a rolling vibrato. Norvo—who didn't use the instrument's motors—invented special vibraharp mallets as early as 1928. He was eventually acknowledged as the man who made it a seriously regarded instrument.

Norvo's small groups, playing what came to be known as chamber jazz, often improvising their way into counterpoint, and usually eschewing drums and piano, created fusions between swing and the nervous new bebop. In such originals as "Blues à la Red" (1944), Norvo's characteristic mixture of odd figures and streamlined swing was particularly on display. Briefly replacing vibraphonist Lionel Hampton in Benny Goodman's sextet, Norvo appeared on Broadway with Goodman's group in the 1945 Billy Rose revue *The Seven Lively Arts*. In the same year Norvo joined the first Woody Herman Thundering Herd, in particular its remarkable small group, the Woodchoppers—alongside Herman, saxophone player Flip Phillips, trombonist Bill Harris, trumpeter Sonny Berman, and others.

While playing with the Herman band, Norvo had met Eve Rogers, sister of another of Herman's trumpeters, Shorty Rogers. In 1946 they married; they had two children and remained married until her death in 1992. In the middle and late 1940s, Norvo won

awards from *Metronome* and *Esquire* magazines. In 1947 he moved to California, where two years later he formed a trio unique in its era. At the Haig jazz club in Los Angeles, Norvo, guitarist Tal Farlow, and bassist Red Kelly created brilliantly complex, swinging music characterized by rapid tempo changes. In 1950 Charles Mingus replaced Kelly. A later version of the trio had Jimmy Raney on guitar and Red Mitchell on bass. Balliett described Norvo's impact: "He picks out the best notes, suspending them briefly before the listener like a jeweler holding good stones up to the light. . . . In a solo, everything doubles in intensity. . . . Norvo's flow of notes [as in the group's jazz classic "Move"] is startling. . . . [H]is rhythms shift constantly, and his choice of notes and harmonies is daring."

The Norvo trio's great years were the 1950s, though Norvo again worked with Goodman as well as making memorable records with saxophone player Ben Webster, pianist Jimmy Rowles, and trumpeter Harry "Sweets" Edison. In 1951 Norvo's trio appeared in the films *Disc Jockey* and *Texas Carnival*, and in 1956 Norvo opened his own club in Santa Monica. In 1958 Frank Sinatra, who had in 1939 turned down an offer to be the Norvo band's vocalist because he had just signed with Harry James, hired Norvo to accompany his appearances at the Sands Hotel in Las Vegas. The association, which included international tours with Sinatra, lasted nearly twenty years. In 1959–1960 Norvo was a regular on the television series "Johnny Staccato." Staccato, played by John Cassavetes, was a jazz pianist who doubled as a private detective, and the show's main locale was a Greenwich Village jazz club where Norvo, guitarist Barney Kessel, drummer Shelly Manne, bassist Mitchell, and trumpeter-leader Pete Candoli held forth.

After the operations that saved his hearing, Norvo withdrew from music for two years but returned to work in Las Vegas and was rarely idle thereafter until a stroke caused his retirement in 1986. He died at a convalescent home in Santa Monica.

Father of the vibraharp as a jazz instrument, bridge between different generations of music, Red Norvo once said, "The vibraharp is a peculiar instrument because it tends to take on the characteristics of the people who play it. Vibraharp players in general are gentle, quiet people." He added, "The main thing is that jazz should be fun. After all, the *music* is more important than any of us musicians."

• Nothing is better than Whitney Balliett's essay "The Music is More Important" in his *American Musicians: Fifty-six Portraits in Jazz* (1986). For a British angle, see Bruce Crowther and Mike Pinfold, *The Big Band Years* (1988). Also useful are Ira Gitler, *Swing to Bop: An Oral History of the Transition in Jazz in the 1940s* (1985); Leonard Feather, *The Book of Jazz* (1957); John Chilton, *Who's Who of Jazz! Storyville to Swing Street* (1972); and Nat Hentoff and Nat Shapiro, *Hear Me Talkin' to Ya: The Story of Jazz as Told by the Men Who Made It* (1955). Norvo's TV career is chronicled in Tim Brooks and Earle Marsh, *The Complete Directory to Prime*

Time Network TV Shows 1946–Present (1979). Of many obituaries, Peter Watrous's from the *New York Times*, which is also on http://elvispelvis.com/rednorvo.htm, is particularly good.

JAMES ROSS MOORE

NYRO, Laura (18 Oct. 1947–8 Apr. 1997), popular singer-songwriter from the late 1960s onward, was born Laura Nigro in the Bronx, New York, the daughter of Louis Nigro, a piano tuner and jazz trumpeter, and Gilda Mirsky Nigro, a bookkeeper. A largely self-taught pianist and an avid reader of poetry who grew up listening to Leontyne Price, Billie Holiday, Debussy, and Ravel with her mother, Laura began composing songs at age eight. She credited the Sunday school at the New York Society for Ethical Culture with providing the basis of her education; she also attended Manhattan's High School of Music and Art. Among Laura's favorite musicians were John Coltrane, Curtis Mayfield and the Impressions, and performers of the so-called girl group genre of early 1960s rock music, such as Martha and the Vandellas and the Shirelles. While in high school, Laura sang with a group of friends in New York City subway stations and on street corners. She and her family spent summers in the Catskill Mountains, where her father played the trumpet at resorts.

The record company executive Artie Mogull became Laura's first manager in 1966. Her father, who tuned Mogull's piano, had convinced him to give his daughter an audition. That year Laura sold her first song, "And When I Die," to Peter, Paul, and Mary for $5,000 and recorded her debut album, *More Than a New Discovery*, for Verve Folkways. As a teenager she had experimented with different names, and Nyro (pronounced "Nero") was the one she was using at this time. The following year she appeared at the Monterey Pop Festival.

Curiously, nearly all of the many written accounts of Nyro's Monterey appearance describe her performance as a fiasco that culminated in her being booed off the stage. However, this appears not to have been the case. In 1997, D. A. Pennebaker, maker of *Monterey Pop* (1969), the original, highly acclaimed documentary film of the festival, released *Monterey Pop: The Lost Performances*. In it, Lou Adler, one of the organizers of the Monterey Pop festival, says that he and Pennebaker called Nyro after viewing the original Monterey footage preparatory to making the later film and told her that "the only thing close to a boo that we can hear is somebody yelling 'Beautiful.'" They invited her to Pennebaker's New York studio to see the footage for herself, but she died soon after receiving the invitation. Even the *New York Times*, in Stephen Holden's 10 April 1997 obituary of Nyro, perpetuates the booed-off-the-stage myth, although it corrects the record in an article by Deborah Sontag published on 26 October 1997.

Soon after her appearance in 1967 at Monterey, David Geffen heard Nyro and approached Mogull, who had negotiated her recording contract with Verve

and owned her music publishing rights, about taking over as her agent. Nyro successfully sued to void her management contract with Mogull and her recording contract with Verve on the grounds that she had entered into them while a minor. Mogull, however, retained ownership rights to the songs she had written thus far. Geffen became Nyro's manager, and the two established a new music publishing company, Tuna Fish Music, under which the proceeds from her future compositions would be divided equally between them. Geffen also arranged a new recording contract for Nyro with Clive Davis at Columbia Records and purchased the publishing rights to Nyro's early compositions from Mogull for $470,000. The second contract he negotiated for Nyro with Columbia, in which they sold all her music publishing rights to the record company, made both Geffen and Nyro millionaires and marked an early milestone in his rise to the top of the popular music business.

In 1968 Columbia Records released Nyro's second album, *Eli and the Thirteenth Confession*, which is widely considered to be one of her best works. It was followed in 1969 by *New York Tendaberry*, another highly acclaimed work. Nyro invited jazz great Miles Davis to the studio while she was recording *New York Tendaberry* and asked him to contribute to an instrumental section, but once he heard what had already been recorded he is reported to have replied, "I can't play on this. You already did it."

After her 1970 album, *Christmas and the Beads of Sweat*, Nyro released *Gonna Take a Miracle*, her only album of all nonoriginal material, in 1971. Recorded with the group Labelle, *Gonna Take a Miracle* features Nyro's interpretations of classic rhythm-and-blues songs previously performed by groups like Martha and the Vandellas. In 1973 Columbia re-released her first album, *More Than a New Discovery*, as *The First Songs* (Verve had also re-released it, as *Laura Nyro*, in 1969). In October 1971, however, Nyro had married David Bianchini, a carpenter, and embarked on the first of the several sabbaticals from recording and touring that would punctuate her career. By the time she returned, with the release of *Smile*, in 1976, the marriage was over. The following year a live album, *Season of Lights*, appeared. After the 1978 album *Nested*—recorded when she was pregnant with her only child, a son named Gil Bianchini—she again took a break from recording, this time until 1984's *Mother's Spiritual*. (Although she gave her son the surname of her former husband, David Bianchini was not, in fact, Gil's biological father.) She began touring with a band in 1988, her first concert appearances in ten years. These led to her 1989 release, *Laura Live at the Bottom Line*, which included six new compositions. Her final album of predominantly original material was *Walk the Dog and Light the Light* (1993), the first and last tracks of which are covers of several rhythm-and-blues songs she loved greatly, Phil Spector and Hank Hunter's "Oh Yeah, Maybe Baby" and a medley consisting of Curtis Mayfield's "I'm So Proud" and Lowman Pauling and Ralph Bass's "Dedicated to the One I Love." The 1997 release *Stoned Soul Picnic: The Best of Laura Nyro* is a 34-song compilation spanning her entire career. The new material and additional covers she recorded in her last years have not been released.

Laura Nyro had one sibling, a younger brother, Jan Nigro, who played acoustic guitar on *Mother's Spiritual*. Maria Desiderio, a Brooklyn-born painter whom Nyro met in 1977, was her companion until Nyro's death on 8 April 1997 at their home in Danbury, Connecticut. Like her mother, Nyro died of ovarian cancer at age forty-nine.

Nyro's own renditions of her songs never attained hit status, but between 1968 and 1970 a number of other singers had achieved significant successes on the charts with her works: the Fifth Dimension with "Wedding Bell Blues," Blood, Sweat, and Tears with "And When I Die," Three Dog Night with "Eli's Coming," and Barbra Streisand with "Stoney End."

Nyro's evocative vocal style mixed jazz and rhythm-and-blues with street pop, gospel, and Broadway, and her three-octave range has led her voice to be characterized as both "a blues soprano" and "a rich, charcoal-smudged alto." Her lyrics range from the breezy "Blowin' Away" to the tragic "Poverty Train" and "Buy and Sell" and the confessional "Lonely Women"; a number of her songs address social issues, including the antiwar "Save the Country," the feminist "Women of the One World," and the environmentalist "Lite a Flame (The animal rights song)." One of her most important songs of social protest was "Broken Rainbow," the title song for a documentary about the relocation of the Navajo that won the Academy Award for best documentary in 1985.

It would be difficult to overstate the extent of Nyro's influence on popular musicians from the 1960s to the present day, including Rickie Lee Jones, Jane Siberry, Phoebe Snow, and Suzanne Vega. Even the legendary Joni Mitchell, who has repeatedly expressed her distaste for being "lumped in with the women" and generally disdains acknowledging influences, conceded Nyro's impact on her in an interview published in the December 1994 issue of the British magazine *Mojo*. A tribute album, *Time and Love: The Music of Laura Nyro*, on which Nyro's compositions are performed by fourteen women singers and groups, appeared after her death.

• A full-length biography of Laura Nyro, written by Michele Kort, is forthcoming from St. Martin's Press. Articles about her life and music include Maggie Paley, "The Funky Madonna of New York Soul," *Life*, 10 Jan. 1970; John Rockwell, "From City Girl to Natural Woman," *Rolling Stone*, 8 Apr. 1976; and Deborah Sontag, "An Enigma Wrapped in Songs," *New York Times*, 27 Oct. 1997. Fred Goodman, *The Mansion on the Hill* (1997), and Stephen Singular, *The Rise and Rise of David Geffen* (1997), contain brief discussions of her relationships with Mogull and Geffen.

DAWN LAWSON

NYSWANDER, Dorothy B. (29 Sept. 1894–18 Dec. 1998), public health official, was born Dorothy Bird in Reno, Nevada, the daughter of Albert Dixon Bird, a businessman who later became an accountant, and Margaret Cowan Millar Bird. She grew up in Topaz, California, and after attending a local elementary school returned to Reno and completed high school before entering the University of Nevada. A precocious student, Bird skipped a year of high school and received both her B.A. and M.A. in mathematics in 1915. Following graduation, she taught high school English and mathematics in Elko, Nevada, for a year before going back to the University of Nevada for additional graduate work. Bird married James Nyswander, a mathematician, in 1916; the couple had one daughter, Marie Nyswander, before divorcing in 1922. In 1919 she moved to the University of California at Berkeley and continued to teach on the side while pursuing her new academic interest in educational psychology. Upon receiving her Ph.D. in that subject in 1926, she became an assistant professor at the University of Utah and eventually rose to the rank of full professor.

Nyswander conducted her first formal academic study between 1932 and 1933, when she undertook a diagnostic survey of New York City schoolchildren under the auspices of the American Child Health Association. With the effects of the Great Depression becoming increasingly evident, in 1933 she returned to Utah and was appointed by the governor to the state board of welfare, where she helped design work programs for women. Her efforts caught the attention of national Works Progress Administration head Harry Hopkins, who brought her to the WPA office in San Francisco in 1934. In the following year, Nyswander became WPA regional supervisor in charge of eleven western states.

In 1936 Nyswander returned to New York City and spent four years conducting research into the health of schoolchildren in eight public schools in the Astoria section of Queens. Sponsored jointly by the New York City Board of Education and Board of Health, her results—published in 1942 as *Solving School Health Problems: The Astoria Demonstration Study*—went through three printings. As director of the study, she created a blueprint that, in her own words, ". . . helped school administrators plan their school medical programs." The work remains influential to this day.

Nyswander stayed in New York from 1940 through 1942 and ran the Kips Bay–Yorkville District Health Education Demonstration, the results of which provided fresh data on nutrition to both home economics teachers and social workers. In 1942 she went to work for the Federal Works Agency, where she spent two years setting up nursery schools in the northeastern United States for the benefit of female wartime factory workers. In 1943 she married George T. Palmer, a health administrator; there were no children from the union. Frustrated with interference from local school boards that resented her influence and power, Nyswander resigned in 1943 and went to work in Washington, D.C., for the Inter-American Education

Foundation, which sought to provide health and educational assistance to Latin American countries (and also discourage any South American assistance to Nazi Germany). Charged with offering U.S. aid in the areas of health and physical education as well as home economics to any South American national government that asked for the help, Nyswander was hampered by the lack of interest on the part of targeted nations as well as by American bureaucratic meddling.

Eager to return to the western United States, Nyswander jumped at the chance to join the faculty of the University of California at Berkeley in 1946 with the rank of full professor. Recruited by Dean Walter Brown, Nyswander transformed a moribund Department of Hygiene into an internationally recognized School of Public Health with a first-rate faculty that she brought in. In addition to teaching classes, she developed a curriculum that reflected the profound influence of the work of Kurt Lewin, a leading social psychologist, on her own professional thinking, thus pioneering the use of behavioral sciences within the public health profession. She resigned from the faculty in protest over the loyalty oath controversy in 1957, although she was later persuaded to return on a part-time basis.

Nyswander first worked overseas in early 1945, when she briefly taught school health in Ecuador. In the latter portion of her career, she often traveled abroad, working for the U.S. Public Health Service in Panama (1954) and in Brazil (1958). She also consulted on the prevention of malaria in Jamaica (1959) on behalf of the Malaria Institute and in Turkey (1960) for the World Health Organization. Her most extensive overseas work occurred between 1961 and 1965, when she assisted in family planning efforts in Calcutta, India, as a visiting professor of health education at the All India Institute of Hygiene and Public Health (1961) and in New Delhi, where her work received support from the Ford Foundation.

A member of both Phi Kappa Phi and Sigma Xi and of numerous professional organizations, she was honored by the creation of the Dorothy B. Nyswander Annual Lecture in Public Health Education, which was held at the University of California beginning in 1957. She published extensively in such professional journals as the *Journal of Public Health Nursing*, the *Journal of the American Dietetic Association*, and the *New York State Journal of Dentistry*. For many years following her retirement from UC-Berkeley, she stayed active as a teacher and consultant. She retained her good health until shortly before her death at her home in Berkeley at the age of 104.

A major contributor to the field of public health, Nyswander made her mark within the profession without the benefit of formal medical training. Remembered primarily for her work in establishing UC-Berkeley's School of Public Health and the Astoria study, she had an impact on many institutions and countries, which benefited from her formidable skills as a researcher and administrator.

• No collection of Nyswander's papers has survived, although the University of California, Berkeley, has a comprehensive file on her in its archives. Nyswander was the subject of an extensive oral history project by Harriet Nathan, published in 1994 as *Dorothy B. Nyswander: Professor and Activist for Public Health Education in the Americas and Asia*. An obituary is in the *New York Times*, 29 Dec. 1998.

EDWARD L. LACH, JR.

O

OGILVY, David (23 June 1911–21 July 1999), advertising executive, was born David Mackenzie Ogilvy in West Horsley, about 30 miles southwest of London, England, the son of Francis John Longley Ogilvy, a stockbroker, and Dorothy Fairfield Ogilvy. Brought up in a cultured family—his father was a Cambridge-educated classics scholar and a cousin was the writer Rebecca West—Ogilvy nevertheless spent an impoverished childhood because of the failure of his father's business. At the age of thirteen, however, he won a scholarship to Fettes, an elite public school in Edinburgh, and at seventeen he won another to Christ Church, Oxford, where he studied modern history. After two years there Ogilvy concluded that he was not cut out for the scholarly life. "Perhaps it was impatience with academe and the itch to start earning a living," he later wrote. "Perhaps I was intellectually out of my depth. Whatever the reason, I failed every examination" (*Blood, Brains & Beer*, pp. 40–41).

In 1931, with no particular direction in his life, Ogilvy made his way to Paris, where he became an apprentice chef at the Hotel Majestic. After a year of the job's "slave wages, fiendish pressure, and perpetual exhaustion," he took a job selling Aga kitchen stoves in England and Scotland. Employing his recently acquired culinary skills during demonstrations of the stoves, he was so successful that he was commissioned to write a sales manual (described by *Fortune* thirty years later, according to Ogilvy, as "probably the best sales manual of all time"). On the basis of this composition, he secured a job through his brother Francis with the London advertising agency Mather & Crowther in 1935. As a promising account executive, he persuaded his firm to send him to the United States for a year to study American techniques in 1938. At the end of that year, from a love of adventure, a desire for independence, and the belief that he could make more money in the United States, he decided to emigrate.

Ogilvy soon found a job as assistant director of the Audience Research Institute of Dr. George Gallup, the nation's leading pollster. There he learned about America and the tastes of its people. He conducted 439 surveys and became expert in methods of research that he later employed in his advertising agency. In 1939 he married Melinda Street of Virginia; they had one son. The marriage ended in divorce in 1955. Two years later Ogilvy married Anne Cabot of Boston; they later divorced, and Ogilvy married again, this time to Herta Lans of Germany in 1973. No children resulted from his second or third marriage.

During World War II, Ogilvy joined the British intelligence service in the United States, becoming an aide to the English spy William Stevenson in 1942 and serving in 1944 as second secretary at the British Embassy in Washington. Having grown to love the rural life of the Amish farmers he observed in Pennsylvania, he and his wife bought a farm there, in Lancaster County, and grew tobacco. However, he soon found himself unsuited to the strenuous life of the farm, and, after three unremunerative years, he abandoned rural life. He later recalled that he had "no credentials, no clients, and only $6,000 in the bank" (*Blood, Brains & Beer*, p. 125), yet he moved to New York and opened an advertising agency. With the financial help of his brother Francis and the London agency Mather & Crowther, he founded Hewitt, Ogilvy, Benson & Mather in 1948. In the next three decades, the firm (later renamed Ogilvy & Mather) became one of the largest in the world, with offices in twenty-nine countries and an annual gross of nearly $800 million internationally.

Ogilvy's success was phenomenal. He numbered among his best-known campaigns the Hathaway Shirt ads using a model with a black eye patch, a series for Schweppes beverages that featured board member "Commander" Whitehead calling his product "curiously refreshing," and the famous boast for Rolls-Royce that "at 60 miles an hour the loudest noise in the new Rolls-Royce comes from the electric clock." He also persuaded Eleanor Roosevelt to make a television commercial advertising margarine. His clients included Lever Brothers, IBM, Merrill Lynch, Morgan Guaranty, General Foods, American Express, Shell Oil, Mercedes-Benz, and the governments of the United States, France, and Great Britain. He created extensive series of ads for the Tourist Board of Puerto Rico and the British Travel Association, and Sears, Roebuck used his services for their first national advertising campaign. "I doubt whether any copywriter has ever had so many winners in such a short period of time," Ogilvy later gloated. "They made Ogilvy & Mather so hot that getting clients was like shooting fish in a barrel" (*Blood, Brains & Beer*, p. 127). He wrote *Confessions of an Advertising Man* (1963) to attract new clients, hoping to perhaps sell 4,000 copies. It did bring business, and it also became a best seller, with sales topping 600,000 in eleven languages. His two later books, *Blood, Brains & Beer* (1978, named for the three foods his grandfather had urged him to eat to make him clever and strong) and *Ogilvy on Advertising* (1983), were also commercial successes.

In 1965 Ogilvy & Mather merged with its London backers Mather & Crowther and went public. Ogilvy remained as chairman, but in 1975 stepped down and retired to France. He purchased the Château de Touf-fou in the Loire Valley, which had 37 bedrooms, 17 bathrooms, stables with stalls for 19 horses, and vineyards that produced 6,000 bottles of wine a year. He came out of retirement in the 1980s to become Ogilvy & Mather's chairman in India because of his love for that country, and he also served for a year in the firm's Frankfurt office. Ogilvy & Mather was bought in 1989 by WWP Group for $864 million, and Ogilvy was made the company's non-executive chairman, a position he held until 1992. Throughout his long working career he contributed his services to many causes and institutions, including the Lincoln Center in New York, the World Wildlife Fund, the New York Philharmonic, and the United Negro College Fund. He died at Touffou.

A lean, handsome figure, Ogilvy was known for his worldly, aristocratic manner and shrewd wit. His influence on American advertising was profound and far-reaching. Known as "the father of the soft sell," he emphasized scrupulous research, respect for both his clients and his audience, and good taste. In his memoir *Blood, Brains & Beer* he laid down several rules for a successful agency that were to become a canon for American advertisers. Among the most quoted are: "Unless your advertising contains a Big Idea, it will pass like a ship in the night"; "You cannot *bore* people into buying your product. . . . You cannot save souls in an empty church"; "The consumer is not a moron, she is your wife. Try not to insult her intelligence"; and "Advertising should be true, credible, and pleasant. People do not buy from bad-mannered liars" (p. 149). Of all his advertising campaigns, he was proudest of his work for the Tourist Board of Puerto Rico, for which the image he created of serenity and beauty did much to bring tourism and foreign investment to the island.

• Ogilvy's professional career is documented in the files of Ogilvy & Mather, a unit of WWP Group P.L.C., in New York City. The best available source of information about his life is his three anecdotal volumes of autobiography mentioned above. An obituary appears in the *New York Times,* 22 July 1999.

DENNIS WEPMAN

OKAKURA Kakuzo (23 Dec. 1862–2 Sept. 1913), art historian, connoisseur, and author of *The Book of Tea,* was born in Yokohama, Japan, the son of Okakura Kanemon, a silk merchant and former samurai, and his wife, Kono. His eclectic upbringing and gift for languages fitted "Tenshin" (or "heart of heaven," the honorific name by which Okakura is known to the Japanese) for the role of cultural ambassador to the West. Okakura and his younger brother Yoshisaburo (later a professor of English and for a time a translator for Lafcadio Hearn) learned English at the local Christian mission school of Dr. James Hepburn, the inventor of the system for Romanization of Japanese words that is still in use. Okakura also studied classical Chinese at a Buddhist temple. An arranged marriage

with Motoko Ooka took place in 1879; the couple would later have a son and a daughter.

Okakura graduated in 1880 from the Faculty of Letters at the newly founded Tokyo Imperial University, where he studied with Ernest Fenollosa, a leader in the effort to preserve traditional Japanese arts in the face of the Westernizing Meiji government. Inspired by Fenollosa, Okakura published in 1882 a defense of calligraphy as a fine art. Fenollosa and Okakura carried out an extensive government-sponsored survey of the art collections of Buddhist temples. In 1886 the two men were appointed to the Imperial Commission of Enquiry to study methods of art education in Europe and the United States with a view toward establishing a national art academy in Japan. In his own writings and speeches, Okakura marked out a middle path between unquestioning preservation of Japanese traditions and the wholesale adoption of "European" methods and ideas. "Conformity is the domicile of bad habits," he wrote. "Art is a product of past history combined with present conditions. It develops from this fusion of past and present."

During the summer of 1886, the historian Henry Adams and the painter John La Farge visited Japan. Their hosts were Fenollosa, Okakura, and Dr. William Sturgis Bigelow (a significant collector and benefactor of the Japan collection at the Museum of Fine Arts, Boston). That fall, Okakura and Fenollosa joined Adams and La Farge on their return journey, to begin their official tour of Western art institutions. Through his close personal friendship with La Farge, Okakura helped develop the fusion of Japanese and Western motifs that emerged in such impressive works as La Farge's Church of the Ascension mural in New York City (where the background is a Japanese mountain landscape) and the Adams Memorial in Washington by the sculptor Augustus Saint-Gaudens. The latter was designed for the grave of Henry Adams's wife, Clover, who had committed suicide just before the Japan journey, and draws on Japanese conceptions of Kannon, the Buddhist deity of mercy.

After his return to Japan, Okakura rose rapidly in the arts establishment. In 1890, at the age of twenty-seven, he became director of the new Tokyo Art School (now the Tokyo National University of Fine Arts and Music), which he led for eight years. He also served as curator of art at the Imperial Museum (now the Tokyo National Museum) and helped conceive the Japanese pavilion for the 1893 World's Columbian Exposition in Chicago. Political and personal troubles, including his affair with the wife of a prominent colleague in the Ministry of Education, led to Okakura's resignation from his official posts. Many of his teachers joined him in the founding of an alternative private art school, the Japan Art Institute. Several of Japan's leading modern painters, including Yokoyama Taikan and Hishida Shunso, emerged from this school.

Okakura traveled to India in 1901, where he lived with the family of the Bengali poet, Nobel-prize winner, and partisan Rabindranath Tagore. This was the beginning of a new phase in Okakura's career: twelve years of nomadic wandering as international celebrity and writer of books for the English-speaking public. In India, Okakura drafted his first book in English, *The Ideals of the East* (1903), which opens with the famous and often quoted line: "Asia is one." On 10 February 1904, the day that Japan entered a war with Russia, Okakura boarded a ship in Yokohama bound for the United States. Dr. Bigelow, aware of Okakura's difficulties in Japan, had arranged for him to work as an adviser on Chinese and Japanese art at the Museum of Fine Arts, Boston, the department that Fenollosa had established in 1890. In September 1904 Okakura lectured on Japanese art at the St. Louis World's Fair.

From 1904 until his death in 1913, Okakura worked at the Museum of Fine Arts, Boston, then and now the most comprehensive repository of Japanese art outside Japan. In collecting ancient ritual jade implements and Taoist sculptures and paintings, Okakura went far beyond his contemporaries' taste for export porcelain, and his policy of filling gaps in the collection remains in place today. During this period, Okakura emerged as the very embodiment of Japan in dress and deportment, in the Boston of his close friend and patron, Isabella Stewart Gardner, who had just opened her eclectic museum on the Fenway. Gardner told Mary Berenson that Okakura was "the first person . . . who showed her how hateful she was, and from him she learnt her first lesson of seeking to love instead of to be loved."

In November 1904 Okakura published his second book in English, *The Awakening of Japan*. Nationalistic in tone and argument, the book celebrates Japanese prowess in the arts and on the battlefield. These themes recur in *The Book of Tea* (1906), Okakura's most popular book in English. Okakura linked Western incomprehension of the tea ceremony to the recently completed Russo-Japanese War. "The average Westerner . . . will see in the tea ceremony but another instance of the thousand and one oddities which constitute the quaintness and childishness of the East to him. He was wont to regard Japan as barbarous while she indulged in the gentle arts of peace; he calls her civilized since she began to commit wholesale slaughter on Manchurian battlefields." Okakura's philosophy of the "imperfect" and his sustained attack on "uniformity of design" are aspects of the *wabi* aesthetic of rustic poverty. This *wabi* taste for thatched roofs and unfinished beams was congruent with the American Arts and Crafts aesthetic—what Thorstein Veblen called in *The Theory of the Leisure Class* "the exaltation of the defective." Frank Lloyd Wright specified that it was in *The Book of Tea* that he first came across the idea of interior space that inspired his own "architecture of within."

Okakura's final years were marked by ill health, though he continued to travel to Japan and China in search of objects for the Museum of Fine Arts. In 1911 he was awarded an honorary degree from Harvard. Okakura's final months were spent completing an opera libretto called "The White Fox," about a vixen who takes human form to impersonate the lost

love of her benefactor. Okakura died at age fifty of kidney failure in the mountain village of Akakura, northwest of Tokyo.

• The major source for Okakura's books, articles, and correspondence is *Okakura Kakuzo: Collected English Writings* (1984), published by Heibonsha in Japan. *The Book of Tea* is available in several different editions. Yasuko Horioka, *The Life of Kakuzo* (1963), is published by Hokuseido in Japan. The catalog for an exhibition entitled *Okakura Tenshin and the Museum of Fine Arts, Boston* (2000)—especially the article by Anne Nishimura Morse, "Promoting Authenticity: Okakura Kakuzo and the Japanese Collection of the Museum of Fine Arts, Boston"—includes important information on Okakura as collector and connoisseur. "Tea with Okakura," by Christopher Benfey, *New York Review of Books*, 25 May 2000, pp. 43–47, provides an overview of Okakura's career. Stephen N. Hay, *Asian Ideas of East and West: Tagore and His Critics in Japan, China, and India* (1970), explores the friendship between Okakura and Tagore. Kevin Nute, *Frank Lloyd Wright and Japan* (1993), details Okakura's influence on Wright. For Okakura's relationship with Isabella Gardner, see Douglass Shand-Tucci, *The Art of Scandal: The Life and Times of Isabella Stewart Gardner* (1997). An obituary by William Sturgis Bigelow and John Ellerton Lodge, "Okakura-Kakuzo 1862–1913," appeared in *Museum of Fine Arts [Boston] Bulletin* 11, no. 67 (Dec. 1913): 72–75.

CHRISTOPHER BENFEY

OLAND, Warner (3 Oct. 1880–6 Aug. 1938), movie actor, was born Jonah Werner Ölund in Umea, Vesterbötten, Sweden. His father, Jonas Ölund, was Swedish; his mother, Maria (maiden name unknown), Russian. When he was thirteen, his family immigrated to the United States and settled on a farm in Connecticut. After graduating from a Boston high school, Oland gave up hoping to become a judge and entered Curry's Dramatic School, where he took voice lessons. He and other Curry students went backstage during a performance of Hall Caine's *The Christian*. This led to Oland's being offered the leading role of Jesus. His success enabled him to accompany the troupe on the road—at $18 a week.

For some years Oland acted with stock companies, went on tour throughout the United States and appeared on Broadway. The actress Alla Nazimova saw him with a touring Shakespeare company and added him to her 1906 repertory of Henrik Ibsen plays. Money thus earned he put into his own successful 1908 production of Ibsen's *Peer Gynt*, using his translation, but lost money trying to produce another work. In 1908 Oland married Edith Gardner Shearn, an artist recently back from Paris. She learned Swedish, and between 1910 and 1913 she and Oland, an accomplished linguist, published their translations of ten plays by August Strindberg. They translated more in the early 1920s.

There is disagreement as to when Oland made his film debut. Some authorities say it was when he played opposite Theda Bara in *The Jewels of the Madonna* (1909); others, when he portrayed John Bunyan in both *The Life of John Bunyan* and *Pilgrim's Progress* (1912). In 1913 Oland was on tour as the foolish husband in Porter Emerson Browne's *A Fool There Was*. After he played a villain opposite Bara in the five-reel *Sin* (Fox, 1915), he appeared in at least forty more silents, including six in 1916 alone. In the fifteen-chapter serial *Patria* (1917), designed to increase American patriotism and featuring Rudolph Valentino, Oland had his first Oriental role. (He contended that the Mongol invasion of Scandinavia centuries before the birth of his parents was responsible for his Oriental features.) Soon thereafter, he was a vicious Chinese menacing Pearl White in *The Fatal Ring* (Pathé, 1917). Although he grew discontent being typecast as a hissing villain, this and later serials paid him $1,000 a week. Many other roles provided both variety and challenge. For example, he appeared with Tom Mix in *Riders of the Purple Sage* (Fox, 1925), with Lon Chaney in *Tell It to the Marines* (MGM, 1926), and John Barrymore in *Don Juan* (Warner Bros., 1926).

Oland had a bit part in the first talkie, *The Jazz Singer* (Warner Bros., 1927), as Al Jolsen's unhappy father, a cantor. Oland played the title roles in Paramount's *The Mysterious Dr. Fu Manchu* (1929), *The Return of Dr. Fu Manchu* (1930), and *Daughter of the Dragon* (1931). Oland's Fu Manchu led to the role that made him famous, Charlie Chan, which he inaugurated in the now-lost *Charlie Chan Carries On* (Fox, 1931). A Spanish version of this movie followed the English version, was shot the same day using the same sets, and therefore provides insights into the missing English version. It is said that the Cuban actor playing Chan patterned his soft-spoken style on Oland's.

There had been three earlier Fox Chan films (two lost), but Chan's roles in them were played by Oriental actors. *Charlie Chan Carries On* was the first of sixteen Chan movies made between 1931 and 1937 in which Oland starred. He needed little makeup aside from a small goatee to go with his own mustache and seemingly Mongolian eyes and eyebrows. *The Black Camel* (1931), adapted from the Earl Derr Biggers novel of the same name, is the earliest surviving Chan film that features Oland. In it, Bela Lugosi had a major part and Robert Young made his screen debut.

Oland's next three Chan movies (Fox, 1932, 1933, 1934) are lost. *Charlie Chan in London* (Fox, 1934), which followed, survives. The first Chan movie not based on a Biggers novel, it showcases Oland at his best, as he appears onscreen almost continuously; Ray Milland costars here in one of his first film roles. The popularity of Oland's Chan venturing abroad (from his home in Hawaii) inspired his next three films, *Charlie Chan in Paris*, *Charlie Chan in Egypt*, and *Charlie Chan in Shanghai* (Fox, all 1935). During these years, Oland appeared in several movies having nothing to do with Charlie Chan; for example, in *The Painted Veil* (MGM, 1934), with Greta Garbo, and in *The Werewolf of London* (Universal, 1935). In the former, Keye Luke made his feature film debut; in 1935 he came to be "Number One Son" of Oland's Chan in Fox's *Charlie Chan in Paris*, the first of eight such

pairings. Critics uniformly praise Luke and regard the father-son relationship on the screen as charming and warm.

In 1936 Oland played Chan in three of his last seven movies, all following Fox's merger with Darryl F. Zanuck's Twentieth Century Company; they are *Charlie Chan's Secret*, *Charlie Chan at the Circus*, and *Charlie Chan at the Race Track*. Critics regard Oland's performance in *Charlie Chan's Secret* as perhaps his finest, owing in part to Zanuck's assigning Gordon Wiles as director. In the *Circus* movie, Oland's Chan delivers many of his famous neo-Confucian aphorisms, such as "Mind like parachute, only function when open" (later adapted for a bumper sticker promoting tolerance); he also graciously befriends a pair of dancing midgets, played by George and Olive Brasno. Oland's four 1937 Chan movies are *Charlie Chan at the Opera*, *Charlie Chan at the Olympics*, *Charlie Chan on Broadway*, and *Charlie Chan at Monte Carlo*. In the *Opera* movie, Chan is suitably pitted against a Boris Karloff character. In the *Olympics* movie, which memorably documents the Berlin Olympics and foreshadows World War II, the detective is gripping when tugged between duty and his kidnapped son. The *Broadway* movie is enriched by Oland's fine portrayal of a wily investigator maintaining calm amid whirlwind action. He had only a minor role in the *Monte Carlo* movie, a last foray abroad, and thus ended his career somewhat disappointingly.

On occasion in the later movies, Oland's acting had alarmed his associates, since it was criticized for fuzziness, which stemmed from a chronic drinking problem that was aggravated by his wife's filing for divorce in 1937. Production started on *Charlie Chan at the Ringside* in January 1938, but Oland was forced to bow out and was soon hospitalized. (The script was revised as *Mr. Moto's Gamble*, with Peter Lorre replacing Chan as Japanese secret agent Kentaro Moto.) Although Oland went to Sweden in April to rest, he developed pneumonia. His wife had agreed to try for a reconciliation and joined him in Sweden, but he soon died in a Stockholm hospital. A versatile, intelligent actor, Oland will be remembered most for only one role. He was "the complete Chan," as his friend Keye Luke correctly defined him.

• George A. Katchmer, *Eighty Silent Film Stars: Biographies and Filmographies of the Obscure to the Well Known* (1991), contains a biography of Oland and a descriptive list of ninety of his films. Ken Hanke, *Charlie Chan at the Movies: History, Filmography, and Criticism* (1989), and Charles P. Mitchell, *A Guide to Charlie Chan Films* (1999), summarize Oland's life and discuss his Charlie Chan movies. Obituaries are in the *New York Times*, 7 Aug. 1938, and *Variety*, 10 Aug. 1938.

ROBERT L. GALE

OWENS, Elisabeth (15 May 1919–15 Nov. 1998), educator, was born Elisabeth Ann Owens in Oxford, Massachusetts, the daughter of parents whose names and occupations cannot be readily ascertained. After graduating from Girls Latin School in Boston, she entered Smith College on a full scholarship and graduated summa cum laude in 1940 with a degree in economics. Intent upon earning a Ph.D. in the subject, she entered graduate school at the University of Chicago, but she dropped out and moved to Washington, D.C., after the United States entered World War II. Owens spent two years (1941–1943) helping to organize the Office of Price Stabilization (precursor to the Office of Price Administration), where she worked with the Reciprocal Trade Agreements Program on topics such as automobile and shoe rationing. She then worked (successively) at the State Department, the United Nations Relief and Rehabilitation Agency, and, from 1943 to 1945, at the Fiscal Division of the Bureau of the Budget. Although initially "more irritated than impressed by the lawyers" (Swiger, p. 141), she realized the importance of legal credentials and decided to pursue the study of law. Attracted to Yale by its willingness to admit female students, she moved to New Haven in 1948 and graduated from law school in 1951.

After undergoing numerous "sham" job interviews—where the firm in question merely wanted to be able to say they had interviewed female applicants—Owens landed a job with the Boston firm of Hill, Barlow, Goodale & Adams. After four years in general practice at the firm, she learned of an opening at Harvard University Law School's International Program in Taxation (ITP) and began working as a research assistant under Professor Stanley Surrey, a tax reform expert and the director of the three-year-old program. Originally supported largely by Ford Foundation funds, the ITP later also received financial support from legal and accounting firms (as well as corporations) with an interest in international tax concerns. According to Owens, it was Surrey who stimulated her interest in the field: "I think, at one point, Professor Surrey asked me, 'What is a creditable tax?' My answer turned into three books."

An indefatigable worker, Owens advanced steadily if not spectacularly within the ITP. She was annually re-appointed to her position until 1961, when she became associate in law and editor of publications. From 1963 until 1965 she served as lecturer on law and research associate in law; on 15 November of the latter year she became lecturer of international tax law and research director. Her career and reputation were both aided immensely by the publication of her first book, *The Foreign Tax Credit*, in 1961. An instant classic in a field that was badly in need of codification at the time of its publication, her 600-page reference work was hailed as the most useful book of its type in the last thirty years, and was still being used as a standard reference in the field at the time of her death.

Owens took a leave of absence from Harvard in 1963–1964 in order to join Surrey in Washington, D.C., where she served as a consultant to the special assistant for international tax affairs. On returning to Harvard, she began teaching full time at the law school in addition to her duties at the ITP. Her course, "International Aspects of U.S. Income Taxation,"

was a success, and in 1967 Owens was promoted to lecturer in law and senior research associate, which finally placed her on the tenure track. In 1972, as the result of a decision that her colleague (and one-time supervisor) Milton Katz described as "a very good thing for the School and a delayed justice to Professor Owens," Elisabeth Owens was granted tenure at the Harvard Law School, becoming the first woman to be granted such status. Many (including Owens) thought that the passage of the Higher Education Amendment (to the 1964 Civil Rights Act) of 1972 had greatly aided her cause. Although she readily admitted having faced discrimination owing to her gender—commenting that the granting of tenure ". . . was a decision that I . . . felt was overdue"—Owens never viewed herself as a crusader for women's rights.

Despite having to teach a course called "Women and the Law"—which covered discrimination issues in employment and other areas—for a year, Owens remained focused on her primary interests. In 1975 and 1979 she produced (with coauthor Gerald Ball) *The Indirect Credit*, which expanded on a chapter in *The Foreign Tax Credit* dealing with credit for foreign taxes paid by foreign subsidiaries of American shareholders. She was named a Henry L. Shattuck Professor of Law in 1976, and between 1980 and 1982 she published a three-volume casebook, *International Aspects of U.S. Income Taxation*. She also developed in mid-career an interest in the environment and environmental law, which led to her teaching courses on water rights, starting in 1970, and natural resources law (oil and gas), beginning in 1971. Even though Harvard students regarded her course in international tax as the toughest course in the law school, Owens never really relished her role as a teacher, claiming that she felt inadequate as a speaker. Although personally warm and helpful to colleagues and students, Owens rarely socialized and joined few if any organizations, preferring the solitary role of researcher and scholar. She never married.

Following her retirement in 1981, Owens served an additional year at ITP before relocating to Falmouth, Massachusetts. She enjoyed reading and gardening in her last years and died in Falmouth after a long bout with Parkinson's disease.

Although she had never originally envisioned herself as either an attorney or a teacher, Elisabeth Owens achieved much in both fields. She overcame considerable obstacles in becoming the first female tenured professor at Harvard Law School, which undoubtedly was facilitated by her pioneering work in the field of foreign tax credits. Ironically, the law itself—specifically the 1972 extension of Title VII of the 1964 Civil Rights Act to university campuses—finally allowed her to obtain the professional standing that was her due as a result of her formidable legal scholarship.

• Owens is one of twelve prominent female attorneys profiled in Elinor Porter Swiger, *Women Lawyers At Work* (1978). She was also the subject of profiles in Emily Newburger, "Elisabeth Owens: Tax Innovator," *Harvard Law*

Bulletin 30, no. 4 (Summer 1998): 23, 29, and "Elisabeth A. Owens 1919–1998," *Harvard Law Bulletin* 50, no. 2 (Spring 1999): p. 57. Tributes appear in the *Harvard Law Review* 112, no. 7 (May 1999): 1403–19. An obituary appears in the *New York Times*, 20 Nov. 1998.

EDWARD L. LACH, JR.

P

PACKARD, David (7 Sept. 1912–26 Mar. 1996), industrialist and philanthropist, was born in Pueblo, Colorado, the son of Sperry S. Packard, a successful lawyer, and Ella Graber Packard, a high school teacher. He knew at the age of ten that he wanted to be an engineer, and he never wavered from that ambition, despite his father's wish that the boy would follow him into the legal profession. The Pueblo of his childhood was something of a rough-and-tumble mining and industrial town, where Packard developed interests in the outdoors and in tinkering with things, especially radios and electronics. In school he was good in math and science, had difficulty with Latin, and excelled in sports.

Having visited and been impressed with Stanford University on a trip to California with his family in 1929, he applied and was accepted there for the fall of 1930. As an undergraduate, he set records in freshman track and lettered in varsity track, football, and basketball. In summers he returned to Pueblo where he worked at various manual labor jobs (mining, construction, brickyard, ice hauling). At Stanford's amateur radio station, he first encountered Fred Terman, son of Lewis Terman, inventor of the Stanford Binet IQ Test. Fred Terman, a young professor of "radio engineering," was to become a major influence in Packard's life. He also met his future business partner and friend, William Hewlett, in their freshman year together. They shared an enthusiasm for electrical engineering and rugged outdoor activities. As a senior, Packard served meals in a sorority dining room, where he met Lucile Salter, a student from San Francisco. They married in 1938 and had four children. They remained together until her death in 1987.

Packard graduated Phi Beta Kappa in 1934 and was offered a job by General Electric in Schenectady, New York. In the depths of the Great Depression, Terman encouraged him to go east for the employment and the useful experience it would afford him. Beginning in February 1935 Packard worked at GE, where he learned important lessons about manufacturing processes. On the side he played for a local professional basketball team and enjoyed hunting, fishing, and skiing. Terman then arranged for a graduate fellowship for Packard back at Stanford, and on unpaid leave but with GE's blessing, in August 1938 Packard and his wife drove back to California carrying in the car a used drill press that would soon be Hewlett Packard's first piece of equipment. He formally resigned from GE a year later.

Packard worked on his electrical engineering degree at Stanford while doing research at Litton Engineering Laboratories in Redwood City. Bill Hewlett had meanwhile earned a master's degree at MIT and was

also lured back to Stanford by Terman. The two friends, reunited, set to work on a plan to create an electrical engineering business. The Packards rented an apartment on Addison Avenue in Palo Alto, and Hewlett, still a bachelor, lived in a small building in the back. The property also had a one-car garage that became Packard's and Hewlett's workshop. In 1989 on Hewlett Packard's 50th anniversary, the garage was designated a California Historical Landmark and "the birthplace of Silicon Valley."

The early days of the Hewlett Packard company are legendary. A coin toss determined the order of names in the title. With Terman's encouragement, they began, with an initial $538, a West Coast firm in an industry dominated by East Coast giants such as GE and Westinghouse. Their first creations were essentially "inventions to order"; their first viable product was an audio oscillator. Whimsically, they planned to market it for $54.40 (inspired by the 1844 political slogan "fifty-four forty or fight!") until it became clear that this would not cover the production costs. The instrument sold for $71.50, well below the price of their nearest competitor. The celebrated buyer of the first eight units was Walt Disney Studios, which used the instrument in the production of the movie *Fantasia*.

The oscillator produced high-quality audio frequencies used in communications, geophysics, medicine, and defense. Until the late 1960s when HP entered the consumer electronics field with a desk calculator, the company focused on, and made its reputation on, measurement and testing equipment. Wartime brought HP's first growth spurt, and the Korean War produced another burst. The company incorporated in 1947, went public in 1957, and was listed on the New York Stock Exchange in 1961. HP introduced the pocket calculator (the model 35) in 1972, making the slide rule obsolete, and the LaserJet printer in 1984, permitting high-quality printing with personal computers. HP sales doubled between then and 1990 and again by 1995, the year it launched its own first personal computer. Alongside this growth in their business, the partnership between Packard and Hewlett extended to joint ventures in ranching, real estate, and family vacations.

Temporarily resigning as chairman of HP, Packard served as Deputy Secretary of Defense under Melvin Laird during the first Richard Nixon administration (1969–1971). (Conflict of interest laws compelled him to put his HP stock into a charitable trust, which earned some $20 million in appreciation and interest while he served.) Laird credited to their administration reform of the procurement process, an end to the military draft, and the policy of "Vietnamization" (gradual withdrawal of U.S. personnel from southeast Asia). Packard left at the end of 1971, in exasperation because the Pentagon did not operate with even the most basic business principles and in concern over the effect his public political life was having on his family; he returned to the chairmanship of HP. From 1973 to 1981 he served on the Trilateral Commission, a group of influential private citizens in North America, Europe, and Japan founded by David Rockefeller to foster closer cooperation among the industrialized nations. He retired from active management of the company in 1978 and devoted himself to public and philanthropic services. He served in 1980 on the Committee on the Present Danger (to deter Soviet expansion), and in 1983 on the Advisory Group on United States–Japan Relations, established that year by President Ronald Reagan. In 1982–1986 he chaired the Panel (of the White House Science Council) on the Health of U.S. Colleges and Universities. In 1985–1986, on Laird's recommendation, Packard chaired Reagan's Blue Ribbon Commission on Defense Management (also known as the Packard Commission). In 1990 Packard returned to revitalize HP, which was struggling through a recession. His final retirement as chairman came in 1993.

Packard's business philosophy, to a degree codified in his 1995 autobiography *The HP Way: How Bill Hewlett and I Built Our Company*, emphasized respect, trust, and openness toward employees and customers. He believed in decentralization, sustainable growth, and generous support of research and development, funding expansion through profits rather than leveraging. Two principles credited to Packard are the notions of "management by objective" and "management by walking around" (the plant, preferably in shirtsleeves).

During his lifetime Packard's principal beneficiaries were Stanford, to which he and Hewlett donated more than $300 million; a fellowship program for young scientists and engineers; grants to black colleges; the Lucile Salter Packard Children's Hospital at Stanford; the Monterey Bay Aquarium, under the direction of his daughter Julie; and the San Jose Museum of Art. He left his estate to the David and Lucile Packard Foundation, an endowment valued at about $9 billion in 1998. In a wide-ranging interview with the *Christian Science Monitor* in November 1986, Packard discussed his concerns for the twenty-first century that generally form the objects of his philanthropic legacy: world population control, the degradation of the environment, world energy supplies, support of scientific education and research, and economic relations among nations. He died in Palo Alto.

• David Packard's papers were to be transferred to Stanford University in 2002. Apart from the stylistically wooden but engaging autobiography *The HP Way* (1995) mentioned above, there is an interesting "Biographical Memoir of David Packard" by Melvin Laird in *Proceedings of the American Philosophical Society* 142, no. 1 (1998): 145 ff. The interview by R. M. Kidder in the *Christian Science Monitor*, 21 Nov. 1986, reveals a mind broader than that of a mere political ideo-

logue. David Devoss's interview (*Los Angeles Times*, 22 Feb. 1987) is a lengthy exploration of Packard's views on defense spending and national security in the Soviet era. A more personal account, "The Apricot Farmer's New Hospital," by Sam Whiting, appears in the *San Francisco Chronicle*, 12 Apr. 1991. Substantial obituaries, each with something of a regional bias, appeared the day after his death in the *Los Angeles Times*, by J. Pitta; the *New York Times*, by L. M. Fisher; the *San Francisco Chronicle*, by C. Burress and M. Simon; and the *Washington Post*, by B. Barnes.

KATHRYN LORIMER KOKEN

PACKARD, Vance (22 May 1914–12 Dec. 1996), journalist and social critic, was born Vance Oakley Packard in Granville Summit, Pennsylvania, to Philip J. Packard and Mabel Case Packard. He grew up in State College, Pennsylvania, where his father managed a farm owned by Pennsylvania State University. After attending local public schools, young Packard entered Penn State in 1932, majoring in English and working on college publications. Upon graduation four years later, he worked briefly for the local newspaper, the *Center Daily Times*, and then moved to New York City to attend the Graduate School of Journalism at Columbia University. Packard earned his master's degree in 1937 and soon afterward joined the staff of the *Boston Daily Record* as a reporter. After several years there he became a reporter for the Associated Press.

In 1942 Packard moved from newspaper reporting to join the staff of *American Magazine*, first as a section editor and then as a staff writer. When the magazine ceased publication in July 1956, he became a writer for *Collier's* and remained there until that periodical's demise five months later. By this time Packard had already published two books that were modest financial successes: *How to Pick a Mate* (1946), a guidebook written with the head of the marriage counseling service at Penn State; and *Animal IQ* (1950), a popular paperback on animal intelligence. At the time his job ended at *Collier's* he had begun work on a more ambitious project, an indictment of the American advertising industry. Its publication in 1957 as *The Hidden Persuaders* gained Packard national attention and launched his new career as a social critic.

Packard had been interested in the phenomenon of advertising for many years, and his interest had peaked by the 1950s, paralleling the post–World War II growth of the ad industry as a major force in American business. Packard saw a sinister side to advertising's emerging preeminence in society, believing that it was inducing millions of citizens to buy products they did not necessarily need or even want. He decried the manipulation of human behavior through the efforts of psychologists involved in so-called motivational research, which, in an allusion to the dystopian novel *1984*, he likened to "the chilling world of George Orwell and his Big Brother." In particular, Packard accused advertisers of using "subliminal projection": flashing split-second messages like "Drink

Coke" or "Buy Buicks" on television and movie screens to promote these and other products.

The Hidden Persuaders struck a responsive cord in the public, at a time when the ad-fueled postwar consumer boom had become a major force in American life, and the book quickly sold thousands of copies. Not surprisingly, the advertising industry struck back, accusing Packard of maligning them unfairly—ads, they claimed, provided a necessary service to consumers—and denying categorically that subliminal projection was ever used. However, their protests had little effect on the book's popularity: it remained on the *New York Times* bestseller list for a year, and the term "hidden persuaders" entered the national vocabulary as a synonym for unethical advertisers.

Packard's next book was *The Status Seekers* (1959), an indictment of what he viewed as increasing social stratification in American life. Ironically, widespread prosperity had not led to greater equality, he argued; instead, it had launched Americans on a frantic search for other, noneconomic ways to proclaim social superiority and to differentiate "the elect from the non-elect," creating a status-driven society. *The Status Seekers* was also a bestseller and earned Packard favorable critical attention as well. It was followed a year later by still another bestseller, *The Waste Makers* (1960), which took direct aim at American business for implementing a policy of "planned obsolescence," encouraging consumers to discard still usable products in order to buy newer and more expensive goods.

Undaunted by accusations of muckraking from the business establishment, Packard went on to write seven more bestselling books of social criticism during the next three decades, although his tone softened somewhat over the years, becoming more hopeful and losing its earlier stridency. They included *The Pyramid Climbers* (1962), which took a jaundiced look at the rigidly structured lives of corporate executives and the conformity required for their advancement in the hierarchy, and *The Naked Society* (1964), which examined the threat to privacy posed by the new technologies. In *The Sexual Wilderness* (1968), Packard focused on the sexual revolution of the 1960s and the not entirely beneficial changes in male-female relationships. *A Nation of Strangers* (1972) described the loss of communal structure created by frequent transfers of corporate executives and their families. *The People Shapers* (1977) took a critical look at the increasing reliance on psychological and biological testing and experimentation to manipulate human behavior and personality. In *Our Endangered Children* (1983) Packard warned that American society, increasingly preoccupied with money, power, status, and sex, was ignoring the needs of future generations. *Ultra Rich: How Much Is Too Much?* (1989) offered a critical examination of the lives of thirty American multimillionaires and their extravagances.

Packard's success during his four-decade career as a writer of social criticism lay not only in his timely subject matter but perhaps even more in his clear and engaging style, which overcame the resistance of even the most reluctant reader. Equally comfortable in front of an audience and behind a typewriter, he was a popular lecturer, making frequent public appearances on behalf of his books. He not only enjoyed a wide following among ordinary Americans but is also credited with inspiring other prominent social critics of the 1960s, including Ralph Nader, Rachel Carson, and Betty Friedan, whose groundbreaking book *The Feminine Mystique* (1963) was inspired by hearing one of his lectures. He is also credited with influencing public policy in at least one instance: President John F. Kennedy reportedly established the Office of Consumer Affairs after reading both *The Hidden Persuaders* and *The Wastemakers*.

In 1938 Packard married Virginia Matthews, with whom he had two sons and a daughter; he lived in suburban Connecticut for most of his adult life. He died at his summer home on Martha's Vineyard in Massachusetts.

• For biographical information on Vance Packard, see *Contemporary Authors, New Revision Series*, vol. 7 (1982), which also includes an interview with Packard; *Contemporary Authors*, vol. 155 (1997); and "Packard, Vance (Oakley)," in *Current Biography Yearbook 1958*. For an assessment of Packard's role in American culture in the second half of the twentieth century, see David Horowitz, *Vance Packard and American Social Criticism* (1994). An obituary appears in the *New York Times*, 13 Dec. 1996.

ANN T. KEENE

PARISH, Mitchell (10 July 1900–31 Mar. 1993), lyricist, was born in Lithuania to Meyer Peresz—pronounced "Parish" and thus Anglicized—and Rose Rosenstock Peresz. The family arrived in Shreveport, Louisiana, before Parish was a year old and three years later moved to New York City, where the elder Parish became a washer of skyscraper windows. An exceptional student in New York City schools, Parish won a $5 weekly grant from the Henry Street Settlement. He was editing his high school's literary magazine when lyrics he contributed to a hospital show brought him to the attention of Irving Mills, who arranged for him to be hired as a staff writer by Jack Mills Music Publishers. In 1923 Parish married Mollie Lillienfeld; they would have two children.

Plugging songs and writing on assignment, Parish achieved few successes until 1928, when he set lyrics to a Cliff Burwell melody that became "Sweet Lorraine," subsequently a jazz standard. The song's appeal led to Parish's putting words to a slower version of Hoagy Carmichael's "Barnyard Shuffle," retitled "Star Dust" by one of Carmichael's friends. Parish's lyrics included a verse that could not be accommodated by the original melody, so Carmichael wrote an additional one. "Star Dust" (c. 1933) became the most recorded song of the twentieth century, though its main popularity did not begin until 1940.

In keeping with his early staff-writing experience, Parish generally worked with melodies that had already been completed. In 1931 his lyrics graced one of Carmichael's loveliest compositions, "One Morning in May." In 1933 he set words to Duke Ellington's instrumental "Sophisticated Lady," following it in 1934 with "Stars Fell on Alabama" to Frank Perkins's melody. "Hands Across the Table," from *Continental Varieties* (1934), was a rare theatrical song. Parish entered the Hit Parade rankings with "Organ Grinder's Swing" (1936), to a tune by Will Hudson. Between 1935 and 1945 Parish supplemented his songwriting income by working as a court clerk in Manhattan, and in 1946 he entered New York University to study English literature; he was elected to Phi Beta Kappa in his junior year, ranked first in his class, and graduated summa cum laude in 1950.

Parish's golden years began in 1938, when he put words to Edgar Sampson's swinging "Don't Be That Way," virtually Benny Goodman's signature as a bandleader. The composer and writer Alec Wilder admitted in 1972, "Most of those buying it won't be able to sing it, but the tune is in the piano part and at least they'll have the pleasure of playing it, while I go on stubbornly trying to sing it."

In the following year Parish's lyrics dominated American popular song, beginning with "Deep Purple," a lush Peter DeRose melody from 1934 that became bandleader Larry Clinton's theme. This was followed by "Stairway to the Stars" to Matty Malneck and Frank Signorelli's cascading tune—both reaching number one on the Hit Parade. "Lilacs in the Rain" (also with DeRose) and "The Lamp is Low" (Clinton's borrowing from Maurice Ravel) contributed to Parish's seven 1939 Hit Parade lyrics.

In 1940 one of bandleader Glenn Miller's compositions had recently evoked a particularly neurotic lyric from Eddie Heyman, so the bandleader turned to Parish for help. "Moonlight Serenade" gained immortality as Miller's incomparably danceable theme song. In the same year Parish added words to "semi-classical" composer Leroy Anderson's sinuous "Blue Tango," but the song did not become popular for another decade. All the lyrics subsequently fitted to Anderson's melodies came from Parish. Parish also provided the words to the tune that bandleader Russ Morgan had written for his theme, "Does Your Heart Beat for Me?"

Parish next wrote for such large traveling ice-skating shows as the Ice Capades. "Take Me in Your Arms," with Fritz Rotter and Fred Markush, followed in 1943. As American popular song began to change radically with the fading of the big band era, leaving swing and jazz behind, Parish's collaborations were altered significantly. He put words to the dashing Israeli melody "Tzena Tzena Tzena," a Hit Parade number one in 1950. "Blue Tango" reached number one in 1951. In 1952 Parish lyricized Heinz Roemheld's theme for the moody Western film "Ruby Gentry"; recorded by the Harry James Orchestra as "Ruby," it was a major hit. Among Parish's ex post facto collaborations with Italian songwriters was "Volare," to Domenico Modugno's hopping melody. As "Nel Blu Dipinto di Blu" it gained American recognition, but with Parish's English lyrics it took the 1958 Grammy award for best new song.

After their original publication in Walter Winchell's *New York Journal-American* column, thirty-five of Parish's sonnets were collected in *For Those in Love* (1965, New York), arranged in sections charting a romantic lover's moods throughout a sleepless night. One was adapted from the French symbolist Paul Verlaine and others alluded to poets of a romantic bent such as Hart Crane and Thomas Chatterton. In 1949 Parish had told the *New York Times*, "You don't write lyrics for Tin Pan Alley like T. S. Eliot." The couplets closing these sonnets evolved from "You smiled and pressed my hand, and stroked my head / But did not understand a word I said" through "Yet if it's true we're better off apart / Why does the scent of lilacs haunt my heart?" to "So hush, little heartache, don't you cry / You'll be a torch song by-and-by." Accepting himself as a songwriter-poet, he alluded to singers Tony Bennett, Jo Stafford, Dinah Shore, Patti Page, Frank Sinatra, and Bing Crosby.

Among many tributes to Parish's achievements, in 1950 he was honored for a lifetime's work by the Chicago television program "Tin Pan Alley." He subsequently was awarded an honorary D.Litt. by Tusculum College of the University of Charleston and was elected to the Songwriters Hall of Fame.

Parish's lyrics to "Star Dust" typified the lifelong poeticism of this scholarly romantic, who was eventually credited with as many as 1,000 songs for 100 composers. His lines were filled with twilight, garden walls, mist and rain, heavenly bodies, and lost or unrequited love. He later commented, "Writing song lyrics was my deliverance from deprivation. . . . I sometimes think that all the lyrics I wrote about the moon and stars expressed a longing for what I couldn't see back then." In 1985 an off-Broadway tribute to Parish's career, *Star Dust*, was unsuccessful. In 1993 Dale Harris wrote in the (London) *Guardian*, "While the show was closing up someone somewhere was no doubt singing the title song." Parish died in New York of complications following a stroke.

• This article was prepared with the assistance of Parish's son, Dr. Lawrence Parish, of Millbrook, New York, and his nephew, also Dr. Lawrence Parish, of Philadelphia, Pennsylvania. They corrected contradictions found in all other biographical publications.
Hoagy Carmichael, *The Stardust Road* (1946), is somewhat helpful. Useful analyses and listings are found in Alec Wilder, *American Popular Song: The Great Innovators, 1900–1950* (1972); David Ewen, *American Songwriters* (1987); and Warren Craig, *Sweet and Lowdown* (1978). An obituary of Mitchell Parish is in the *New York Times*, 2 Apr. 1993, and a perceptive appreciation by Dale Harris is in the (London) *Guardian*, 10 July 1993.

JAMES ROSS MOORE

PARKER, George S. (12 Dec. 1866–26 Sept. 1952), inventor and businessman, was born George Swinnerton Parker in Salem, Massachusetts, the son of George Augustus Parker, a master mariner, businessman, and auctioneer, and Sara Hegeman Parker. Educated locally, Parker had intended to become a journalist, but at age fifteen he invented a game he called Banking for an informal club of fellow game-playing enthusiasts. This game, in which players borrowed their stakes from the Bank, rewarded the best—and luckiest—speculator, since 160 cards determined their "luck," while bankruptcy lay in wait. At the suggestion of his older brother Charles, Parker spent $40 having 500 sets made, and by the end of 1883 he had cleared a profit of $140. The George S. Parker Company became Parker Brothers in 1882 when Charles joined. The eldest brother, Edward, joined in 1892 and, with George Parker as president, Parker Brothers purchased a Salem game-making enterprise and leased a factory. Parker Brothers, later America's premier games maker, was soon publishing twenty-nine games.

Parker himself was eventually credited with inventing more than 100 games. Many of his early board games were well-illustrated variations on the popular chutes (or snakes) and ladders format. Usually by the throw of dice, players advanced toward a goal, but their progress could be accelerated or retarded by "luck"—i.e., landing on a good or bad space. Parker's variations, usually topical, are virtual chronicles of American history: the Railroad Game, Innocence Abroad (a play on the title of Mark Twain's popular travel book), Klondike, and the Battle of Manila. Parker also created board variations of golf and baseball and showed an interest in morally "improving" topics such as Presidential Proverbs and the Story of the Bible.

Parker's games were published only after extensive play-testing with friends and employees. Because of their topicality and simplified rules of play (almost always written by George Parker), Parker Brothers helped change American game-playing from what Parker called the "tedious and traditional" to a family institution. A Parker philosophy of games developed: a game should take no more than forty-five minutes and should produce a clear winner. Eventually a list of common "errors" guided the company in accepting or rejecting new ideas sent its way. Parker also innovated in game-publishing by advertising heavily in newspapers and magazines.

In 1896 Parker married Grace Mann; they had three children and remained married until Parker's death. In the early 1900s Parker Brothers entered the most creative phase of its existence. Parker invented Pit—a raucous bidding game based on the workings of the Chicago Grain Exchange—as an alternative to Contract Bridge, which he deemed an insidious game that promoted gambling. Pit was followed by Flinch, a versatile card game that for a time outsold all other card games; Flinch was followed in 1906 by another card game, Rook, which sold more than 55 million copies throughout the century.

Though Parker eventually abandoned inventing games, he proved to be an adroit and occasionally sharp businessman. In 1887 he introduced a ball-and-paddle game called Indoor Tennis, but the game did not become popular until he purchased in 1901 the rights to the name Ping-Pong from its English inventor. As marketed by Parker Brothers, Ping-Pong became an international craze. (In 1921 Parker's monopoly was finally broken when international competitions decided to save on royalties by retitling their sport "Table Tennis.")

One of Parker's fifteen visits abroad resulted in the importation of laminated French wooden jigsaw puzzles, which he marketed as Pastime Puzzles. The modern jigsaw puzzle, cut in such interesting patterns as lobsters and stars, was Parker's innovation. Perhaps the peak of the company's success during Parker's presidency was its acquisition in 1924 of the rights to Mah Johngg. This relatively expensive Chinese game (good sets were crafted of real ivory and bamboo) was the craze of the Roaring Twenties. Unfortunately, the craze ended almost as rapidly as it had begun, and by 1929 Mah Johngg was a major loser.

In 1934, two years after his daughter married Robert Barton, a trademark lawyer, Parker stepped up to chairman of the board of Parker Brothers, turning the presidency over to Barton, although during World War II Parker again assumed the presidency. Parker Brothers remained in Salem, run by a Barton or a Parker, until almost the end of the twentieth century. Parker was named to the Toy Industry Hall of Fame in 1986.

The company's greatest fame was gained with Parker as chairman of the board. This began in 1934 with the introduction of Sorry!—a variation on Chutes and Ladders that allowed players to send each other backward. In 1935 came the introduction of Monopoly, which became the world's most famous board game. Monopoly came to Parker Brothers from a variety of overlapping sources—among them Parker's own ancient Banking. Other ancestors of Monopoly included Lizzie Magie's 1904 Landlord's Game (which advocated Henry George's single tax theory and included Go to Jail cards), Dan Layman's Finance, and Charles Todd's Monopoly, itself the model for Charles Darrow's new Monopoly, which was in 1934 a minor success at Wanamaker's in Philadelphia and F. A. O. Schwarz in New York. It was Darrow's game that named the various "properties" for streets in his native Atlantic City, New Jersey.

Although by February 1935 Monopoly sets were being produced at a rate of 20,000 per week, the fad seemed to have run its course by late 1936. Parker himself ordered the end of production in early December of that year. But some sets remained in the stores when a new rush developed—this time because children had taken over the game from their elders. Monopoly was eventually marketed in seventy-five countries.

In 1949 Parker Brothers purchased from the English game makers Waddington's the rights to the detective game Cluedo, renaming it Clue for the American market. In the same year, Risk: the Game of International Strategy was adapted from a French original, Miro. Eventually, Parker Brothers published 1,800 games.

Beyond his corporate responsibilities to the company he founded, Parker was a director of the Salem Savings Bank, the Essex Institute, the Naumkeag Trust Company, the Naumkeag Steam Cotton Company, and the Pequot Mills. (Naumkeag was the name originally given to the settlement that became the town of Salem.) He also belonged to clubs in Salem, Boston, and Washington, D.C. Parker died at Massachusetts General Hospital in Boston.

• Various Parker family papers are on file at the Phillips Library of the Peabody Essex Museum, Salem, Massachusetts. The Parker Brothers company archives are stored at Hasbro Games, Pawtucket, Rhode Island. A standard version of the history of Parker Brothers' most notable game is Maxine Brady, *The Monopoly Book: Strategy and Tactics of the World's Most Popular Game* (1974). An alternative view is Burton H. Wolfe, "The Monopolization of Monopoly: The $500 Buyout," *San Francisco Bay Guardian*, 23 Apr. 1976. The best obituary is in the *Salem Evening News*, 27 Sept. 1952.

JAMES ROSS MOORE

PARKER, Tom (26 June 1909–21 Jan. 1997), music promoter, best known as manager of Elvis Presley, was born Andreas "Dries" Cornelis van Kuijk in Breda, Holland, the son of a liveryman. His parents' names are unknown. Dries dropped out of school while still a young teenager to work with his father, who died in 1925. After his father's death he began working for the Holland-America shipping line and ended up in New Jersey for a brief time, living with a Dutch family there. He returned to Breda in 1927, working in the shipping business for two years until leaving Holland in 1929. That same year he enlisted in the U.S. Army under the name "Andre van Kuijk" and was stationed in Hawaii under Captain Thomas R. Parker, likely the source of his assumed name. His family, still in Holland, began receiving letters and cash from the United States, signed by a "Thomas Parker." This correspondence continued until 1932, when Parker received a medical discharge from the army after being transferred to Pensacola, Florida, and suffering a knee injury.

Moving to Tampa in 1932, Parker, who as a child was fascinated with the circus, joined the Johnny J. Jones Exposition, a carnival that spent its winters in the area. After moving to Royal American Shows a couple of years later, Parker met Marie Mott, whom he married in about 1935. Parker left the carnival after his marriage, taking a position with the local humane society.

While living in Tampa, Parker began a career as a promoter, representing, among others, country and western stars Roy Acuff and Ernest Tubb, pop singer Gene Austin, and cowboy actor Tom Mix. In 1946 Parker moved to Nashville, Tennessee, where he began managing the career of singer Eddy Arnold. There is no doubt that Parker helped to launch Arnold's career, landing him casino bookings in Las Vegas and film roles. But his devotion to his clients manifested itself in an oppressive managerial style that prevented performers like Arnold and Elvis Presley from contributing to the artistic direction of their careers. When Arnold advised Parker to take up a hobby, like golfing or boating, Parker replied, "You are my hobby" (quoted in Guralnick, *Last Train to Memphis*, p. 167). In 1948 the governor of Louisiana bestowed on Parker the honorific "Colonel," and Parker demanded to be addressed as such for the rest of his life.

In 1953 Arnold fired his promoter. Devastated, but characteristically eager to rebound, Parker created his own management company, Jamboree Attractions, and began promoting the RCA Caravan, a tour starring singer Hank Snow, whose career Parker began to manage with success. It was in 1955 that Parker first saw the young, raw Elvis Presley perform, having been steered to him by Oscar Davis, a showy promoter who at the time was working as Parker's "advance man." Parker immediately recognized the twenty-year-old's unique attraction and booked him to open for Snow on a Jamboree Attractions tour.

Parker pursued Presley enthusiastically. On 15 August 1955, enlisting the help of Snow, he persuaded the young singer and his parents to sign a contract that named Parker as Presley's "special adviser," which some allege put the singer in debt to him immediately. That same year, with Parker's guidance, Presley left the Sun label, on which he had exclusively recorded, and signed with RCA Records. From the beginning, according to Guralnick, "the Colonel had [for Presley] a vision of success on a national scale that was shared by virtually no one else" (quoted in *People*, 3 Feb. 1997).

Parker began promoting his client heavily, signing him to the now-famous television appearances on "The Ed Sullivan Show" and laying the groundwork for Elvis to become a Hollywood star. Over and over the Colonel seemed to make the most financially advantageous decisions about Presley's career, knowing just when to hold out or give in when dealing with record companies, movie producers, or fans. He often restricted Presley's exposure to his fans, allowing "his boy" to make frequent public appearances but tightly limiting his public performances. He made sure that Presley was seen with the right people at the right time, whether it was the queen of Thailand or Pat Boone. Perhaps one of the keys to Parker's success as a manager was his image of being an uneducated "rube," easily hoodwinked or manipulated. But this was an image he cultivated to his own benefit—it was just part of his act.

Both Parker and Presley made millions from the singer's stardom. The savvy manager who looked like a carnival barker, with his rotund physique and ever-present cigar, certainly took his fair share of Presley's earnings. Parker maintained that he kept only 25 percent of the singer's proceeds, but others believe that it was more on the order of 50 percent. Presley biographer Peter Guralnick asserts that in later years Parker and Presley were essentially business partners, splitting down the middle profits from the many merchandising contracts that Parker negotiated. He allowed the singer's likeness to appear on everything from charm bracelets to whiskey decanters. Presley once joked that Parker stayed awake at night "thinking up ways to promote me."

Months before the singer's death in August 1977, reports surfaced that Parker wanted to sell Presley's contract, ostensibly because of heavy gambling debts. Though Parker vehemently denied the story, published in the *Nashville Banner*, it was true that the Colonel had begun to believe that the drug-addicted Presley "was more trouble that he was worth" (Guralnick, *Careless Love*, p. 632). At the time of the singer's death, Parker was named executor of the estate, receiving 50 percent of all income from merchandising rights related to the Presley name and image. This arrangement continued for several years, until a Memphis probate court, at the request of Presley's family, eliminated his rights to the estate.

After Presley died, Parker frequented Elvis conventions, signing autographs and promoting his client, whose fame only increased after his untimely demise. In 1980 Parker's wife passed away, and he moved to Las Vegas, where he continued to work in the entertainment business, becoming an adviser to Hilton Hotels. He was married a second time, to a secretary for RCA Records named Loanne (maiden name unknown). He died in Las Vegas.

Guralnick writes that Parker "remained something of an enigma. . . . He kept nearly everyone, even his closest associates, at arm's length" (*Last Train*, p. 168). He fabricated stories of his early life, claiming at times to have been an orphan from West Virginia who had spent his youth in the circus. Many believe that Presley's meteoric rise was largely due to Parker's managerial savoir-faire. Yet there is a persistent feeling that Parker took Presley for millions and cheapened his career, exploiting every facet of the singer's life in the quest for money.

• Information on Parker before he acquired Presley as a client is scant. See Peter Guralnick's two-volume Presley biography, *Last Train to Memphis: The Rise of Elvis Presley* (1994) and *Careless Love: The Unmaking of Elvis Presley* (1999), for reliable accounts of Parker's relationship with the "King of Rock 'n' Roll." See also Dirk Vallenga, *Elvis and the Colonel* (1988); Sean O'Neal, *My Boy Elvis: The Colonel Tom Parker Story* (1998); and James Dickerson, *Secret Life of Colonel Tom Parker* (1998). Obituaries are in the *New York Times*, 22 Jan. 1997; *People*, 3 Feb. 1997; and *Rolling Stone*, 20 Mar. 1997.

STACEY HAMILTON

PARKS, Lillian Rogers (1 Feb. 1897–6 Nov. 1997), White House seamstress and author, was born Lillian Adele Rogers, the daughter of Emmett E. Rogers, Sr., a waiter, and Margaret "Maggie" Williams Rogers. Source information is sketchy regarding her early years, but her godchild, Peggy Holly, believes that Lillian Parks was born in the District of Columbia and as a child spent summers with relatives in Virginia.

Her father—by Parks's account an alcoholic unable to hold a job—left his family when she was a child; in 1909 her mother took a job at the White House at the beginning of William Howard Taft's presidency and often found it necessary to take her daughter along with her when she went to work. A victim of polio at the age of six, Parks used crutches for the rest of her life. She attended St. Ann's Catholic School and Stephens Elementary School in the District of Columbia. As she got older, she enjoyed listening to her mother's accounts of the day's events at the White House. After dropping out of Phelps Business School because of ill health, she began taking in sewing jobs and accompanied her mother to the White House on Sunday nights to turn down the bedcovers for the first family. She also worked as a cashier in a movie theater, as a doctor's receptionist, and as a seamstress in a dress shop. In 1935 Lillian Rogers married Carlton Parks; there were no children, and the couple quietly divorced in 1946.

In the fall of 1929, the current first lady, Lou Henry Hoover, a fastidious woman who took pride in her appearance and knew the value of good tailoring, brought Parks to the White House as a seamstress and maid. In 1948 Parks expected to be transferred to the U.S. Department of the Treasury when the White House was closed for structural restoration, but instead she went with the Trumans to Blair House, the temporary presidential residence, where she maintained a sewing room on the top floor. Parks returned to the White House in 1952 when the renovation was completed and remained there until her retirement in 1959.

After reading a book that Frances Spatz Leighton cowrote with a former chef in the Eisenhower White House, Parks realized that she had many memories of her White House years that would be interesting to others. In 1961, she published *My Thirty Years Backstairs at the White House*, written with Leighton, as a series of personal vignettes of first ladies and their families as seen from the servants' viewpoint, beginning with the Tafts in 1909. The book contained the notes and recollections of both Parks and her mother, Maggie Rogers, who rose to the position of top White House maid before retiring in 1939. The memoirs constituted an inside view of life in the White House over fifty years. Parks admitted that she left out much of what she might have reported because she did not want to embarrass the eight first families she and her mother had worked for. The book received much attention, remaining on the *New York Times* bestseller list for more than six months, creating a certain notoriety for its author and prompting first lady Jacqueline Bouvier Kennedy to request that all White House domestic employees pledge to refrain from writing about the private lives of their first families. Many years later, in 1979, Parks's book was the basis of a television miniseries.

In spite of the concerns voiced in some circles, the book's anecdotal "revelations" were positive and benign. In general, Parks was complimentary to all of the first families that she or her mother served, but Bess Truman—of whom she said, "Bess is best"—was clearly a favorite of hers. Parks always felt comfortable with Mrs. Truman because the first lady had no fancy airs and knew who she was at all times: a midwestern matron in a happy marriage who appreciated the staff for their worth as human beings and for the work they did for her family. She respected them as equals and saw to it that they were well treated, often sending the maids home early Sunday afternoons, assuring them, over their protests, that she was perfectly capable of turning down beds by herself. Parks and Bess Truman continued to correspond with Christmas and birthday cards long after both had left the White House.

More evidence of how well Parks was treated in the White House is an incident she related in her book: during World War II, when White House domestic staff members were not allowed to use the elevator (to leave it free for the disabled president, Franklin D. Roosevelt, in case of an emergency), the handicapped Parks, who was only four feet ten inches tall, was given an exemption and allowed to use the elevator. Parks's recollection of her treatment by Roosevelt indicates that the polio they both had suffered from created a special bond between them, since no one else in the White House knew what it was like to walk with crutches and endure the hardships of living with such a condition. Although she respected and admired Eleanor Roosevelt, Parks felt free to voice criticisms in her next book, *The Roosevelts: A Family in Turmoil* (1981). She may have tried to set the record straight about the Roosevelts' long stay at 1600 Pennsylvania Avenue, but few of her apparent revelations were really new because books by two of the Roosevelts' children and by close friends of the family had brought to light more telling and personal details. Reviews of the book reflected this, generally praising the intimate tone of it but criticizing the lack of a more insightful view that her position as a White House insider presumably afforded her. Her third publication, *It Was Fun Working in the White House* (1969), was a children's book that contained much material from *My Thirty Years Backstairs at the White House*.

After her retirement, Parks lived in Takoma Park, Maryland, just outside Washington, D.C., in a home decorated with presidential mementos. She appeared on several radio and television talk shows to reminisce about her White House years and was active in Neighbors Inc. (a community organization in the Washington ward where Parks had resided), the National Association of Negro Business and Professional Women's Clubs, and Don't Tear It Down (a preservation society in the District of Columbia). On her eighty-fifth birthday, the Washington City Council bestowed the honor of declaring it Lillian Rogers Parks Day.

In the summer of 1992 Parks was one of several former White House employees who appeared at the Smithsonian Institution's annual American Folklife Festival on the Washington Mall to discuss her experiences at the White House. In 1994 the Smithsonian's Center for Folklife Programs and Cultural Studies, in cooperation with the White House Historical Association and the National Archives, mounted the exhibit "Workers at the White House" at the Charles Sumner School Museum and Archives in Washington; reproductions of scrapbooks maintained by Parks were displayed there. She died of a heart attack in Washington at Sibley Memorial Hospital.

In her retirement, Parks never expressed bitterness about the clearly defined "upstairs-downstairs" atmosphere that existed in the White House during her years there. She considered it a remarkable stroke of good fortune to have worked at 1600 Pennsylvania Avenue at a time when minorities in Washington, D.C., had few opportunities to advance. Whatever their failings, her books provided the first behind-the-scenes accounts of the domestic life of presidential families from the Tafts to the Eisenhowers; as such, they remain valuable documents.

• Personal information on Lillian Rogers Parks is difficult to find, especially with regard to the exact location of her birthplace. Her books have large gaps related to her own life. The records of the White House Office (Record Group 130), which contain material on housekeeping activities with reference to Parks, are in the National Archives, College Park, Md. The Washingtonia Collection, Martin Luther King Public Library, Washington, D.C., has a clippings file on Parks. The Smithsonian Institution produced a video of the 1994 exhibit at the Sumner School, "Workers at the White House," which includes an interview with Parks. There is a transcript of an oral history in the Moorland-Spingarn Research Center, Howard University, Washington, D.C. Obituaries appear in the *New York Times* and the *Washington Post*, both 12 Nov. 1997.

MARTIN J. MANNING

PATKIN, Max (10 Jan. 1920–30 Oct. 1999), baseball clown, was born in West Philadelphia, Pennsylvania, the son of Samuel H. Patkin, a delicatessen operator and later a repairman, and Rebecca Patkin (maiden name unknown); both parents were Russian-Jewish immigrants. He graduated from West Philadelphia High School; two years at Brown Prep confirmed his lack of academic promise. Since seeing Jimmie Foxx at an Athletics game at age eight, however, he had been set on baseball for a career; as a youth he never took his cap off except to sleep, and then it went under his pillow along with his glove. In school he showed promise as a baseball pitcher, and he signed with the Chicago White Sox organization.

He pitched two years in the Wisconsin State League (class D), compiling a 10–8 record with the Wisconsin Rapids in 1941 while striking out 134 in 178 innings, but he injured his pitching arm in a collision at home plate. In 1942 he was released by the Wisconsin Rapids and signed by Green Bay, but his arm had deteriorated, his control had gotten worse, and that same year Green Bay released him with a 3–4 record. He then joined the navy and spent the next three years in the service—mostly, it appears, playing baseball. While he was still in the navy, playing service ball, his career as a comedian began. It happened in a game when Patkin was pitching and Joe DiMaggio hit a mammoth home run: Patkin followed the Yankee slugger around the bases, mimicking his distinctive step and bringing down the house.

After the war, Patkin signed with Wilkes-Barre (Pa.) and split two decisions in 1946 before being released for the third and final time in his brief pitching career. However, his comic antics earned him several minor league appearances and caught the attention of master promoter Bill Veeck, owner of the Cleveland Indians. Veeck, famous for his lack of sensitivity in the finer points of baseball decorum, signed Patkin to coach the Indians and to keep the fans entertained at the same time. For the rest of 1946 and part of 1947, he helped keep fans in the seats; however, when the Indians became more competitive and drew crowds based on the merits of their ball playing, the clown act became superfluous and Patkin was cut loose by Veeck.

Although Patkin still fancied himself a pitcher, Veeck's connections helped him begin a career as a minor league attraction that lasted nearly half a century. By his own estimate, he had 90 to 100 engagements a year, over 4,100 in all, and he never missed a game despite numerous injuries along the way—until a severe sprained ankle sidelined him in 1993. That year he gave his final performance, in Glens Falls, New York. He had almost always performed for packed houses in the majors, but on 20 July 1969 he entertained an audience of only four people during a game in Great Falls, Montana—on that day most of the country was home watching Neil Armstrong and Buzz Aldrin become the first men to walk on the moon.

Much of Patkin's appeal derived from his appearance. At a gangly six feet three inches, he had a large nose, double joints that gave him the appearance of being made of rubber, and a madcap manner that was funny before he even began his act. Veeck once said that Patkin looked like he was assembled by somebody who had trouble reading the instructions. At age seventy-three he could still stretch his legs spread-eagle style and then bend at the waist until his nose touched the ground, which he did to pretend to steal the catcher's signs. As part of his act, he dressed in a baggy uniform with a question mark on the back, wore his cap sideways, and flapped his arms and walked like a bird.

During his minor league engagements he would often coach for two or three innings. He would mimic the first baseman's warm-ups, pretend to steal signals from the catcher, and show the third-base coach how to give signals while dancing to a raucous recording of "Rock around the Clock." His signature gag was to take a big drink of soda or water and then spew it into the air (or onto ballplayers), sometimes sending up dozens of geysers from one huge gulp. To cap his routine, he would carry as many as twenty bats to the plate, discard all but one, and slither under the catcher to take his spot in the batter's box. The first pitch in this choreographed sequence was a brushback. Then,

after he took a strike, he would push the catcher over. Finally, he would hit an easy pitch for a ground ball and run to third base, where he would stop short of the bag, point up toward the sky, and when the third baseman looked up he would slide under him. The umpire always called him out, provoking a huge argument and then ejection, his ticket back to the clubhouse.

He dubbed himself the "Clown Prince of Baseball," usurping the title from Al Schacht, a former Washington Senators pitcher and coach who was winding up his career as Patkin began his. He was perhaps the last of his ilk: later baseball entertainers like the Chicken and the Phillie Phanatic were less related to the game itself and more of a sideshow, unlike Patkin, who was part of the action. He was immortalized in *Bull Durham*, the 1987 movie about minor league baseball in which Patkin played himself.

Patkin's personal life was less successful than his career. In the early 1960s he married Judy Oberndorf, a lovely woman seventeen years his junior, following a seven-year courtship. Their tempestuous ten-year marriage was characterized by her unfaithfulness, and in a messy divorce Judy got most of the goods and Patkin got custody of their adopted daughter, Joy. The death of his brother in 1994 led to his hospitalization for depression, and he died in Paoli, Pennsylvania, of an aortic aneurysm.

• The best source of information on Patkin is his autobiography, *The Clown Prince of Baseball*, written with Philadelphia sportswriter Stan Hochman in 1994. An obituary is in the *New York Times*, 1 Nov. 1999.

JOHN R. M. WILSON

PATTERSON, Ada (5 July 1867–26 June 1939), newswoman, was born in Mount Joy, Pennsylvania, the daughter of John M. Patterson and Elizabeth Ellen McDannel Patterson, farmers. In 1877 Patterson moved with her family to Franklin County, Nebraska. After graduating from Franklin Academy in 1885, she taught school for four years in Riverton, Nebraska, and for one or two years in Lincoln, the state capital. By the early 1890s she had moved to Utah, where she was hired as the society editor for the *Salt Lake City Herald*, which was overseen by a grandson of the famed Mormon leader Brigham Young. (Some newspaper accounts erroneously place her in Utah as early as 1881.)

Growing weary of "describing madame, the bishop's frock or the poppy lunches of the woman's literary club," Patterson soon moved to San Francisco, California, where she was hired as a reporter for the *San Francisco Call*. There she was able to delve into "serious" journalism, covering murder trials, fires, and city scandals. Patterson's work with the *Call*, in her words, "fairly launched" her career as a reporter, and she traveled east to Missouri, becoming a feature reporter for the *St. Louis Republic*.

In St. Louis Patterson established her reputation as the "Nellie Bly of the West," as readers compared her to the celebrated muckraking journalist and author. In those days, she later said, "I did anything I was asked to." For instance, she took a precarious walk on a plank at the top of the St. Louis City Hall to describe the view, and she once "drove" a locomotive through the night from St. Louis to Chicago. The latter adventure led to perhaps her greatest journalistic coup: she was the only reporter to secure an interview with Judge Isaac Charles Parker of Fort Smith, Arkansas, who at the time held the distinction of having sentenced more men to death than any other judge. Parker acquiesced to Patterson's request for an interview, despite having turned down many male journalists, because he had also driven a locomotive once and wanted to compare experiences.

In 1897 Patterson became the first woman journalist to cover an execution, when she stood on the gallows with Dr. Arthur Duestrow, who had shot and killed his wife, then "bashed in the brains" of his hysterical daughter, the only witness to the crime. The resulting story, which was widely praised for its well-balanced but passionate coverage, led to a job offer from *New York Evening World* editor Bradford Merrill. On arriving in New York, however, Patterson learned that Merrill was on holiday and apparently had told no one else at the *Evening World* about offering her the job. Fortunately, the young newswoman met a former acquaintance who advised her to "come over to our shop," the *New York American*, where she was hired as a feature reporter.

Patterson's first story for the *American* told the tale of her excursion "down in the caisson of the bridge . . . being built across the East River." Several other dangerous assignments followed, including rides in a submarine and with a race car driver. Her widely praised coverage of the 1904 murder trial of Nan Patterson, acquitted of murdering her lover, presaged her reporting, for Arthur Brisbane's *New York Evening Journal*, on the celebrated murder trial in 1907 of Harry K. Thaw. Tried for shooting to death in a fit of jealousy famed architect Stanford White at a premiere at Madison Square Garden, Thaw eventually was found not guilty and sentenced to a term in a mental institution. During the long case, which became a media spectacle, newsmen sitting opposite Patterson and fellow female reporters Dorothy Dix, Winifred Black, and Nixola Greeley-Smith christened them the "sob sisters" for their emphasis on the dramatic elements of the trial and sympathy and compassion for Thaw's wife, Evelyn Nesbit. Unfortunately, the name stuck, becoming synonymous with female reporters for decades to come.

Patterson retired in 1923 to write magazine articles for women's and theater magazines. She had always been interested in the dramatic arts, having contributed stories and conducted interviews for *Theatre Magazine* in the early 1900s and in 1902 published *By the Stage Door*, a collection of short stories. She never married. Patterson died in Sarasota, Florida.

Patterson was quoted as saying that only "one woman in fifty is physically strong enough to endure" the life of a news reporter, acknowledging that the work is "exhausting to brain and body." Even though this view today would be considered dated and perhaps even sexist, Patterson understood that women had to be strong, detached, and energetic to survive in the newspaper business. Perhaps she was most skilled at interviewing, combining sympathy and cynicism to produce well-balanced stories. Although women at the turn of the twenty-first century have a strong presence in newspaper journalism, male reporters still dominate "hard news" writing, which usually includes politics, crime, and foreign affairs. But the gains that women have made in the field would not have been possible without the contributions of women like Ada Patterson and her fellow "sob sisters."

• Patterson published two full-length works, *Maude Adams: A Biography* (1907) and, with Victor Bateman, *By the Stage Door* (1902). There is no biography of Ada Patterson. Patterson's magazine articles include "Her First Appearance," *Ladies Home Journal*, Feb. 1904, p. 10; "They Stood on the Bridge," *Woman's Home Companion*, May 1905, pp. 13, 35; "Giving Babies Away," *Cosmopolitan*, Aug. 1905, pp. 405–12; "As the Actors Spend Christmas," *Ladies Home Journal*, Dec. 1906, p. 21; "Mother and I," *Delineator*, Oct. 1913, p. 7; "Man Who at 28 Suddenly Had a Great Idea," *American Magazine*, Oct. 1917, pp. 52–53; "Are We Happy?" *Independent Weekly Review*, 3 July 1920, pp. 22–23; and "That's Friendship," *Theatre Magazine*, Apr. 1931, p. 45. Information on her and the other "sob sisters" can be found in Ishbel Ross, *Ladies of the Press* (1974), and Phyllis Leslie Abramson, *Sob Sister Journalism* (1990).

STACEY HAMILTON

PAYTON, Walter (25 July 1954–1 Nov. 1999), NFL Hall of Fame football player, was born Walter Jerry Payton in Columbia, Mississippi, the son of Peter Payton, a factory worker, and Alyne Payton. Walter, or "Spider Man" as he called himself as a boy, was active in Boy Scouts, the church choir, camping with friends, and playing drums in the band before he finally turned to football his junior year in high school at the all-black Jefferson High School. Already bigger and stronger than most of his teammates, Walter was an instant starter.

Halfway through his junior year at Jefferson, the all-white Columbia High School was ordered to integrate, and Payton and several of his teammates transferred there. They were upset, however, when a white coach, Tommy Davis, was hired for the Columbia job instead of their Jefferson coach, Charles Boston. Already socially conscious at the age of sixteen, Payton boycotted spring practice that year to express his dissatisfaction, but, recognizing that the decision would not change, he joined the team for the start of his senior season.

Payton led his Columbia team to an 8–2 record that year and was named All State. But with just one year at the school and two years of high school football, he was not heavily recruited. He attended nearby Jackson State University, where he joined a team that featured a number of other future NFL players and Pro Bowlers, including Jerome Barkham, Vernon Perry, Ricky Young, Robert Brazille, and fellow Hall of Famer Jackie Slater. At Jackson State Payton rushed for 3,563 yards, achieved a 6.1 average, and became the NCAA's all-time leading rusher with 65 touchdowns. He majored in communications and graduated in 1975.

In the spring of 1975, the Chicago Bears made Payton the fourth player chosen on the first round of the NFL college draft. While it may have seemed strange at the time for the young man from rural Mississippi to leave the small city of Columbia for the second largest city in the country, the shift proved ideal. Payton spent his entire thirteen-year professional football career in Chicago, becoming one of the greatest players in the history of the game. And he did it as arguably the toughest and hardest-working player the game had ever seen, giving meaning and hope to the citizens of the "City of Big Shoulders" who flocked to Bears games to watch Payton carry his mediocre team week after week.

Payton played all but one game his rookie year. Over the player's strenuous objections, Rookie coach Jack Pardee forced his prize pupil with a sprained ankle to sit out the fifth week of the season. This game, with the Pittsburgh Steelers, was the only game Payton missed in his thirteen-year career, a record that perhaps more than any of his others raised number 34 to legendary stature.

Walter Payton married Connie Norwood in 1976; they would have a son, Jarrett, and a daughter, Brittney.

Over the next twelve seasons Payton averaged 1,337 yards rushing per season. He went to his first Pro Bowl in 1976 and then eight more in '78, '79, '80, '81, '84, '85, '86 and '87. In 1977, playing with a bad case of flu, Payton set an NFL record rushing for 275 yards in a game against the Minnesota Vikings. On 7 October 1984, he rushed for 154 yards against the New Orleans Saints, shattering what was believed to be Jim Brown's unassailable record of 12,312 yards. Payton finished his career with 10 NFL records including 3,838 rushes, 16,726 yards, most 1,000-yard seasons (10), and most 100-yard rushing games (77). He also set 28 Chicago Bears records and was the team's backup punter and placekicker. He even played quarterback in a game in 1984. He was inducted into the Hall of Fame on 31 July 1993, the first player in the history of the Hall to be presented by his son. His wife and daughter were also in attendance.

Payton was, however, far more than just a great football player. Mike Ditka, Payton's coach for the last five years of his career and during his only championship season in 1985, said of Payton, "I mean no disrespect to any player, because there've been a lot of great ones. I'll just say I believe he was the best I ever saw and probably the greatest ever." To millions of fans in Chicago and around the world he was known affectionately as "Sweetness," the name he earned for the way he both played on the field and carried himself off it. Payton was successful in business as well as sports; he had interests in restaurants, real estate, banking, construction, and, particularly, auto racing. One of his great disappointments was failing to become an NFL owner because of a failed bid to gain an expansion team in St. Louis when the clubs were awarded to Jacksonville and Carolina and the Rams then moved to St. Louis.

Late in 1998 it became obvious that something was wrong with the always robust Payton when he began losing weight and the whites of his eyes began to yellow. In February 1999 he went public with the news that he had primary sclerosing cholangitis, a rare disease of the liver. Fans everywhere expected to hear that the unstoppable Payton would be receiving a liver transplant, but when a trip to the Mayo Clinic in May revealed a tumor in his liver, all hope was lost. His last months were spent as a crusader for organ donorship and transplants. He died at home in South Barrington, Illinois.

• Sources of information on Walter Payton include Mike Towle, *I Remember Walter Payton* (2000), and the *Chicago Bears Media Guide* (1975, 1984, and 2000 eds.), as well as entries in *Current Biography* (1985) and *Who Was Who in America*, vol. 13 (1998–2000). Obituaries are in the *Chicago Tribune* and the *New York Times*, both 2 Nov. 1999; see also the special section on Payton in the *Chicago Tribune*, 7 Nov. 1999, comprising articles by Don Pierson and other writers.

HUB ARKUSH

PEABODY, Endicott (30 May 1857–17 Nov. 1944), educator, was born in Salem, Massachusetts, the son of Samuel Endicott Peabody, merchant banker, and Marianne Cabot Lee Peabody, the daughter of John C. Lee, also of Salem, the founder of Lee, Higginson and Company, Boston's leading merchant bankers. At age thirteen, Endicott, or Cotty as he was known to his family and friends, accompanied his family to England where his father joined the London banking establishment of his distant cousin George Peabody of Baltimore. Among George Peabody's other partners was Junius S. Morgan of Hartford, and thus began a close connection between the two families that redounded greatly to young Endicott's benefit during his long career as founder and headmaster of Groton School from 1884 to 1940.

While in England, Peabody attended Cheltenham College, a recently established public school, before going on to Trinity College, Cambridge. At Cheltenham, Peabody acquired his lifelong love of athletics and his unshakable confidence in their role in the character formation of adolescent boys, the "muscular Christianity" perfectly depicted in Thomas Hughes's novel *Tom Brown's Schooldays* (1857). Otherwise, Peabody described his experience at Cheltenham as entirely "negative," prompting him to eliminate fagging (junior boys performing menial tasks for seniors) as part of the prefect system at Groton and to insist on Groton's small size as more conducive of an intimate, "family" atmosphere best suited for education.

While in Britain, this scion of patrician New England was deeply influenced by the Christian socialism of Charles Kingsley and F. D. Maurice (though it may be safely said that Peabody was always worried more about making capitalism more Christian than Christianity more socialist).

Returning to the United States at age twenty-one, Peabody spent an uneasy year as a banker on Boston's State Street before consulting Phillips Brooks, the rector of Trinity Church, on the advisability of entering the ministry. Despite the fact that Peabody's family was staunchly Unitarian, Peabody entered the Episcopal Theological School in Cambridge the following autumn. In 1882 he spent a year as a temporary minister in Tombstone, Arizona, where Wyatt Earp and his brothers numbered among his parishioners. On his return to Cambridge, he began courting his first cousin Fanny Peabody, whom he ultimately married in the summer of 1885. She was his lifelong helpmate and an integral partner in the school they created.

Peabody served for a year as temporary chaplain at St. Mark's School in Southborough, Massachusetts, and was regarded by some as a candidate to be the next headmaster there when a friend suggested to the twenty-seven-year-old that he consider founding his own school. The idea took more concrete form during a visit to his relations-by-marriage Mr. and Mrs. James Lawrence of Groton, Massachusetts, who offered to buy for his school a ninety-acre farm on a nearby site, later approved by Frederick Law Olmsted, overlooking Wachusett and Monadnock mountains. Thanks to family connections, Peabody raised $34,000 for his project in a matter of weeks. Groton's first board of trustees included Phillips Brooks as its chair and his father, Samuel Endicott Peabody, as treasurer. Other founding members of the board included the future Bishop William Lawrence, a legendary fundraiser in his own right, and J. Pierpont Morgan. The announcement of the trustees declared that their school would make every endeavor "to cultivate manly Christian character," preparing boys not only for college but also for "the active work of life."

Groton School opened on 15 October 1884 with twenty-four boys and three masters: Peabody, the Reverend Sherrard Billings (like Peabody, just twenty-seven years old), and the twenty-one-year-old William Amory Gardner (a prodigious student of the classics and the nephew of art patron Isabella Stewart Gardner.) There was a relaxed informality about the early years of the school that Groton later lost as it grew in size and reputation, but there always remained, in the words of Peabody's biographer, "an intimacy at the heart of things that was the peculiar genius of the place" (Ashburn, *Peabody*, p. 71). Peabody knew every boy, his family and relations, and their circumstances. Throughout his long career, Peabody and his wife shook hands with each of the students as they filed by to say good night.

It was Peabody's lifelong endeavor, together with his close friend, distant relative, and ally Theodore Roosevelt, to attract the sons of America's newly minted plutocracy into careers of public service. Although Groton never generated as many clergymen as Peabody would have liked, his tiny school with fewer than a thousand graduates in its first fifty years produced one president of the United States (Franklin D. Roosevelt), two secretaries of state, three senators, one congressman, nine ambassadors, two state governors, two assistant secretaries of the navy, one secretary each of the treasury and the army, two lieutenant governors, a police commissioner of New York City, and a governor of the Federal Reserve Bank. Peabody himself did not vote for Roosevelt in 1932, but he stood side by side with his former student at the school's fiftieth anniversary to face down the opposition of many graduates who regarded the president as a traitor to his class.

On his retirement at the age of eighty-three, Peabody was succeeded by the Reverend John Crocker, his former student and protégé. He died in Groton.

One searches Peabody's writings in vain for any clue to his remarkable influence; his published sermons are almost entirely devoid of interest. The secret to the riddle surely lay in his extraordinary physical presence and implacable rectitude. Tall, handsome, and large-boned, Peabody had the size and shape to command instant respect from small boys. Those summoned to his study for a personal conference counted themselves fortunate to be told of the death of a near relation rather than face the rector's wrath for some disciplinary infraction. One student neatly summed up Peabody's demeanor by saying to his father, "The Rector would be a great bully, if he wasn't such a terrible Christian."

Despite its small size, Peabody's school has had a disproportionate impact on both American history and the public imagination. As one historian of American education writes, "For those Americans who were even aware of the institution, he *was* the private preparatory school; perhaps more than any other man in the twentieth century he fixed in the American consciousness the public image of the private preparatory school and its headmaster: vigorous, moralistic, and Anglophile—but withal, curiously attractive" (McLachlan, p. 244).

• Peabody's voluminous correspondence, his sermons, and his notes for talks to the faculty are part of the Groton School Archives, Groton, Mass. Other relevant sources include Frank D. Ashburn, *A Portrait of Peabody of Groton* (1944; repr., 1967) and *Fifty Years On: A Short History of Groton School* (1934); William Amory Gardner, *Groton Myths and Memories* (Groton, 1928); James McLachlan, *American Boarding Schools: A Historical Study* (1970); and *Views from the Circle: Seventy-Five Years of Groton School* (Groton, 1960); and Louis Auchincloss, *The Different Grotons* (1960).
JOHN W. TYLER

PEARL, Minnie (25 Oct. 1912–4 Mar. 1996), entertainer, was born Sarah Ophelia Colley in Centerville, Tennessee, to Thomas K. Colley, a lumberman, and Fannie Tate House Colley, a pianist and prominent suffragist. The youngest of five daughters, she grew up in a prosperous household, and her flair for dramatics and music, evident at an early age, was encouraged by the family. She sang and gave dramatic readings in public during her childhood, and by her teens she had decided to become a stage actress. She planned to attend a women's college in the East and then go on to drama school, but during her senior year in high school the stock market crash of 1929 occurred and her father was unable to pay for such an expensive education. Instead, she enrolled in the fall of 1930 at Ward-Belmont College, an exclusive girls' finishing school in Nashville that had an outstanding drama department. Although she felt initially out of place among her far more elegant classmates, she perfected her acting skills there, entertaining at campus events and becoming one of the school's most popular students.

After graduating in 1932, Sarah Colley moved back home to live with her parents until she turned twenty-one and could freely pursue an acting career. To pass the time she set up a small studio and gave lessons in dramatics, piano, and dancing to local children. The Great Depression was now fully under way, however, and a lack of both nerve and resources forced Colley to postpone her leave-taking even as she became of adult age. Finally, in the spring of 1934, impatient to start her career, she applied to the Wayne B. Sewell Production Company, an Atlanta-based organization that put on theatrical events throughout the South, using company-trained employees to find and direct local talent. She was hired as a producer/director, and for the next six years she traveled throughout the South, staging musical comedies. The work itself was often tiresome and unrewarding, but the experience enabled her to grow into a confident young woman who now had the poise and self-assurance to make her way in the wider world of the theater.

Sarah Colley had long suspected that her true gifts lay in comedy rather than in serious dramatic acting, and as a child she had been enthralled by the funny stories told by her father, a noted raconteur. Although reluctant nevertheless to give up her long-held dream of being a dramatic actress, she became increasingly drawn to southern hillbilly humor as she traveled through the South for the Sewell Company, interacting with "the locals." Out of her imagination grew a comic character she called "Minnie Pearl" (using two names commonly given to young women in the rural South), who was kindhearted, good-humored, and could laugh at herself. For Minnie Pearl's "hometown" Colley chose "Grinder's Switch," the name of the railway freight station where her father loaded his lumber. Donning a frilly dress, old black flat-heeled shoes, and a flower-bedecked battered straw hat with a cheap price tag dangling from its brim, Colley assumed the role of Minnie Pearl to create advance publicity for the Sewell Company shows, creating short stand-up routines and telling jokes on herself that evoked comfortable, knowing laughter. Colley gave her first paid performance as Minnie Pearl in the spring of 1939, at the request of a women's club in

Aiken, South Carolina, where a Sewell troupe had recently played.

By 1940 the Sewell Company was in decline as radio and the movies supplanted live performances, and Colley resigned to return home to her mother, who had been widowed and left nearly destitute three years earlier. Colley found work at a government-sponsored children's recreation center in Centerville while continuing to perform her Minnie Pearl routines at local gatherings. A family friend persuaded the manager of WSM, a radio station in Nashville, to audition Colley as Minnie Pearl for the "Grand Ole Opry," a country music and humor show broadcast nationally over the NBC network by WSM from Nashville every Saturday evening. Colley was at first reluctant, since she was not a fan of country music and had not envisaged such a venue as her route to stardom, but the promise of entering real show business—and making more money—induced her to try out.

WSM executives were also reluctant, even after hearing her audition, because they feared that Colley, who was obviously educated and upper class, would be resented by the show's regular listeners and accused of making fun of country people. They therefore scheduled her for a single appearance, late on the show one Saturday evening in November 1940. Their concerns were ill-founded: Sarah Colley as Minnie Pearl was an instant success, judging by the avalanche of letters the station received, and she was quickly hired as a comedienne to become a regular performer on the show at ten dollars a week. A month later, "Opry" performer and national country music star Roy Acuff hired her to become part of his weekly road show, which performed one-night stands six days a week and returned to Nashville each Saturday evening for the "Opry." This arrangement did not last, however, because, as Colley herself later acknowledged, she was not yet able to "loosen up" and present a more developed character.

The need for more money to support herself and her mother led Colley to work on her alter ego in earnest, hiring a sister to help her write new material, adding dancing to her act, and generally learning to "let go" with a torrent of silly humor. In the summer of 1941 she joined the road show of country music star Pee Wee King and as part of that act toured with the "Camel Caravan," a group sponsored by the R. J. Reynolds Tobacco Company that entertained American servicemen. Her participation continued through the war years, alternating with appearances on the "Grand Ole Opry."

Although long reluctant to wed, she finally accepted the proposal of a former air force pilot named Henry Cannon who ran a charter airline service, and the couple were married in February 1947; they had no children. For a time Sarah Colley Cannon dropped out of touring, remaining in Nashville to be a housewife and limiting her performances to Saturday night stints on "Opry." She soon began to miss the stimulation of full-time show business, however, and by 1948 was on the road again, this time with her husband flying her to performances. Soon he had sold his business and become her manager while continuing to fly her around the country. The focus of her career, however, continued to be her weekly appearances on "Grand Ole Opry," and over the following decades she allowed Minnie Pearl to change with the times, evolving into an ever more free-spirited, even raucous character as she appeared with such legends as Elvis Presley and Hank Williams. She became a national sensation, making frequent guest appearances on other television variety shows and also recording a number of albums that featured her comedy routines and music; one of her songs, "The Answer to Giddyap Go," was a Top Ten country hit single in 1966. That same year she was honored as "Woman of the Year" by *Billboard* magazine. In 1970, writing as Minnie Pearl, she published a cookbook, *Minnie Pearl Cooks*.

During the 1970s Cannon cut back on touring in order to enjoy more time at home with her husband, but she remained a fixture on "Opry" and also appeared regularly on two other shows, "Hee Haw" and "Nashville Now." In 1975 she was inducted into the Country Music Hall of Fame in Nashville, an achievement she considered her greatest single honor. Cannon as Minnie Pearl published her second book, *Minnie Pearl: An Autobiography*, in 1980. In 1984, under her supervision, the Minnie Pearl Museum opened in Nashville, offering displays of Minnie Pearl's clothing and videotapes of her performances. In the 1980s she also wrote a column for the *Nashville Banner* newspaper called "Minnie's Memories," which included anecdotes about country life in days of yore.

In the fall of 1992 the Nashville Network paid tribute to Cannon as Minnie Pearl with a televised country music and comedy special, "Hats Off to Minnie: America Honors Minnie Pearl." That same year she was also honored by President George Bush with the National Medal of the Arts. By this time, however, Cannon was in failing health and unable to attend either event. Although she had successfully overcome breast cancer diagnosed in 1985, eventually undergoing a double mastectomy, and had gone on to become a prominent spokesperson for the American Cancer Society, she suffered a major stroke in 1991 and had to withdraw from all public appearances. Complications from another stroke led to her death in a Nashville hospital five years later.

• The primary source for biographical information on Sarah Colley Cannon is her autobiography, co-authored with Joan Dew and published under the name Minnie Pearl. See also "Pearl, Minnie," in *Current Biography Yearbook 1992*; *Contemporary Authors*, vol. 129 (1990); *Contemporary Authors*, vol. 151 (1996); the entry on Minnie Pearl in Melvin Shestack, *Country Music Encyclopedia* (1974); and the chapter on Cannon/Minnie Pearl in Alanna Nash, *Behind Closed Doors: Talking with the Legends of Country Music* (1988). An obituary appears in the *New York Times*, 5 Mar. 1996.

ANN T. KEENE

PEATTIE, Donald Culross (21 June 1898–16 Nov. 1964), naturalist and writer, was born in Chicago, Il-

linois, to Robert Burns Peattie, a journalist, and Elia Wilkinson Peattie, a writer and literary critic for the *Chicago Tribune*. From an early age Peattie suffered from various respiratory ailments and turned to books for consolation; his interest in nature was kindled by an extended visit during his childhood to the Great Smoky Mountains in North Carolina, where he was sent to improve his health. As a teenager he wrote poetry with the encouragement of his mother, a published novelist. He was educated at the University of Chicago's Laboratory School, and after completing secondary schooling there in 1916 he went on to study French at the university.

In 1918 Peattie moved with his parents to New York City. There he got a job as a reader for George H. Doran, a New York publisher, with the intention of pursuing a writing career. A visit to the Bronx Botanical Garden reawakened his interest in nature, however, and in 1918 he entered Harvard, majoring in the natural sciences. While in college he did fieldwork in botany in the South and Midwest and published several papers on his findings in scientific journals. He also continued to write poetry and received the university's Witter Bynner Poetry Prize in his senior year.

On graduating with honors from Harvard in 1922, Peattie went to work for the U.S. Department of Agriculture in Washington, D.C., and spent a year in Miami studying frost resistance in tropical plants. In 1923 he married Louise Redfield, a novelist and former high school classmate; the couple eventually had three sons, as well as a daughter who died in childhood. A year later he left government service to embark on a career as a freelance writer. With encouragement and assistance from his wife, he began his first book, *Cargoes and Harvests* (1926), a study of the economics of botany. In 1925 he began writing a nature column for the *Washington Star* newspaper, a position he held for a decade. In addition, he wrote a number of entries during this period for the *Dictionary of American Biography* and also published magazine articles on a variety of topics. Among the several botanical studies he published in this period were *Down Wind: Secrets of the Underwoods* (written with his wife, published in 1929) and a handbook, *Flora of the Indiana Dunes* (1930).

Peattie wanted to concentrate on writing fiction, however, as did his wife, and in 1928, with the help of a loan from his mother-in-law, he moved abroad with his wife and children. They eventually settled in the south of France, which had become a popular refuge for expatriate writers. After living in Vence and Nice, they moved to Menton, where both he and his wife wrote a series of novels. None of them attracted much critical attention or public favor, though his wife's books were somewhat more successful than his own. The most acclaimed work to come out of Peattie's sojourn in France was an illustrated history published abroad in 1930 as *Vence: The Story of a Provençal Town through Two Thousand Years*; it was revised and published in the United States in 1945 as *Immor-*

tal Village and reprinted eighteen years later under the title *Vence: Immortal Village*.

By 1933 the Peatties' money had run out, and they were forced to return to America. They settled on a square-mile plot of land in rural Illinois, where Peattie wrote his first bestseller, *An Almanac for Moderns* (1935), a collection of daily meditations on nature that attracted national attention and critical praise. That same year he also published *Singing in the Wilderness*, a somewhat sentimental account of John James Audubon and his wife that was nevertheless a success. A year later Peattie published what became one of his best-known books, *Green Laurels: The Lives and Achievements of the Great Naturalists*, a series of profiles of men who studied the natural history of the earth, beginning with Aristotle and concluding with Jean-Henri Fabre. This was followed by the essay collections *The Book of Hours* (1937), *A Prairie Grove* (1938), and *Flowering Earth* (1939).

In the late 1930s Peattie moved west with his family, to a house he had built in Santa Barbara, California, with proceeds from the sale of *An Almanac for Moderns*. Over the next two and a half decades he produced nearly two dozen books, all but one nonfiction. These included several works for children: six volumes on world history, published in 1937, and *The Rainbow Book of Nature* (1957), his last major work to appear. Many of Peattie's books for adults, like the popular *Journey into America* (1943), combined observations about nature with histories of the region he was describing and biographies of area residents, the little-known as well as the famous. He also wrote a series of successful nature guides, including *A Natural History of Trees of Eastern and Central North America* (1950) and *A Natural History of Western Trees* (1953). In addition to writing books, Peattie was a frequent contributor to national magazines, including the *Reader's Digest*; he served as its roving editor from 1943 until his death. His autobiography, *The Road of a Naturalist*, was published in 1941.

Peattie's work won him several honors, including election to the National Institute of Arts and Letters in 1941, that reflected his stature as both a serious writer and a popularizer of nature study. Critics were not always kind, however, sometimes taking him to task for a prose style that could verge on the florid as he strove to communicate his enthusiasm for the natural world. Today his work is largely forgotten, although several of his books, including *Flowering Earth* and his guides to trees, have been reissued. His status, however, as a major nature writer in the middle decades of the twentieth century remains unchallenged. He taught millions of Americans to derive pleasure and solace from the natural world around them, distracting them, however briefly, from economic depression and war.

In his final years Peattie suffered from a variety of illnesses, including diabetes. He died at his home in Santa Barbara and was buried at the local cemetery.

• For biographical information, see Peattie's autobiography, *The Road of a Naturalist* (1941); information about the family is also included in *Incurable Romantic* (also 1941), a memoir by his elder brother, Roderick Peattie, a distinguished geographer. In addition, see entries for "Peattie, Donald Culross," in *Current Biography Yearbook* for 1940 and 1965, and in *Contemporary Authors*, vol. 102 (1981). An obituary appears in the *New York Times*, 17 Nov. 1964.

ANN T. KEENE

PERKINS, Carl (9 Apr. 1932–19 Jan. 1998), songwriter and rockabilly pioneer, was born Carl Lee Perkins in Tiptonville, Lake County, Tennessee, the son of Buck Perkins, a sharecropper, and Mary Louise Brantley. The second of three sons born to the only white sharecropping family in Tiptonville, Carl began picking cotton at age six, once gathering more than 300 pounds of cotton in less than seven hours for "an RC [Cola] and a Moon Pie." He was influenced musically by both country and bluegrass played on Grand Ole Opry radio broadcasts and by blues and gospel songs sung by the sharecroppers with whom he worked. His father fashioned his first guitar from a broom handle and an empty cigar box; later, after obtaining a secondhand Gene Autry model, Carl would play with his friend and fellow sharecropper "Uncle John" Westbrook, who taught him that real music comes from the soul, not the guitar.

When Perkins was fourteen his family moved to nearby Jackson, Tennessee, where he would live until his death. After arriving in Jackson, he quit school to support his family, which had become even more impoverished after leaving the sharecropping fields of Tiptonville. Soon he began writing songs, and Perkins and his brother Jay made their first appearances as the Perkins Brothers, playing at beer joints in and around Jackson, including the Cotton Boll and the Sand Ditch. It was in these dives that Carl developed his craving for drink, an addiction with which he struggled until the late 1960s, when he ceremoniously hurled his last liquor bottle into the Pacific Ocean.

The Perkins Brothers enjoyed increasing success, as honky-tonk patrons favored their up-tempo country and western repertoire. Soon the third Perkins brother, Clayton, joined the group, which by now was eager to expand its distinctive style of music out of rural western Tennessee. In 1953 Carl Perkins married Valda Crider. Their marriage lasted nearly forty-five years, through both hard luck and celebrity; they had four children together.

In 1954 Perkins first heard the young Elvis Presley's version of Bill Monroe's "Blue Moon of Kentucky" on the radio, immediately recognizing his own style in the young singer's Monroe-inspired bluegrass sound. For the rest of his life Perkins would be compared with an early Elvis Presley and, had bad luck not intervened, might have enjoyed the same measure of financial success. Presley was recorded by Sun Records producer Sam Phillips, and later that year the Perkins Brothers Band drove the seventy or so miles to Memphis to request an audition. Aware of the originality of their lively country rhythm, Phillips recorded the band, and in 1955 Perkins first heard himself on the radio, singing "Turn Around." The single was widely played on area country stations, and Perkins felt that his time had come.

Soon Perkins developed a friendship with Presley, and Phillips introduced him to the country-and-western star Johnny Cash, who suggested that Perkins "write . . . a song about blue suede shoes." Some time later, while playing a show at a supper club, he heard a young man admonish his date not to "step on my suedes!" Later that evening, in the small apartment he shared with Valda in the Jackson housing project, Perkins scrawled on a potato sack the lyrics that would secure his place in rock-and-roll history. Released on 1 January 1956 with "Honey Don't" on side B, "Blue Suede Shoes" became Sun Records' first million-selling record, and performers as different as Lawrence Welk and Presley began to include the song in their shows and release their own recordings of it.

In March 1956, just as Perkins's celebrity seemed to be overtaking Presley's, Carl and his brothers were seriously injured in a car accident while driving to New York to perform on "The Perry Como Show," which would have been the band's first nationally televised appearance. Jay Perkins broke his neck in the crash and would die two years later of an illness related to that accident. Despite the release of other hit singles after Jay's injury, including "Everybody's Tryin' to Be My Baby," "Dixie Fried," and "Matchbox," and a 1956 appearance on the Grand Ole Opry, Perkins's career never recaptured its energy and momentum. By the fall of that year, when Perkins played the Como show, it was, in his words, "useless [because] Presley had done knocked the nation cross-eyed with all his TV appearances" (*Go, Cat, Go!* p. 215).

For the rest of his career Perkins survived, sometimes thrived, as a songwriter and solo musician, although he never enjoyed the success he found with "Blue Suede Shoes." But he influenced such rock-and-roll stars as Eric Clapton and the Beatles, who in the 1960s would cover "Everybody's Tryin' to Be My Baby," "Honey Don't," and "Matchbox." He sustained himself financially with appearances at honky-tonks and Las Vegas nightclubs and by playing guitar in his old friend Johnny Cash's band. In 1964 he severely injured his guitar-playing hand in a freak ceiling fan accident, and a little more than a year later he nearly lost his foot in a hunting accident. Taken advantage of by Phillips and Sun Records during the 1950s, Perkins later sued both and received a large settlement in 1978. His songwriting credits include "So Wrong," which Patsy Cline recorded; "Daddy Sang Bass," taken to number one on the country charts by Cash; "Champaign, Illinois," co-written with Bob Dylan; and "Silver and Gold," which Dolly Parton recorded.

In his later years Perkins began performing with two of his sons as the C.P. Express, just as he had sung with his two brothers decades before (Clayton Perkins committed suicide in 1973). A mentor to the Beatles,

Perkins appeared on Paul McCartney's 1981 album *Tug of War*. That same year, moved by a photo of an abused child, he helped found in Jackson the Exchange Club–Carl Perkins Center for the Prevention of Child Abuse, to which he devoted money and energy until his death.

In 1986 Perkins won a Grammy Award for his "spoken-word" contribution to *Class of '55: Memphis Rock & Roll Homecoming*, an album featuring, in addition to Perkins, former Sun Records artists Roy Orbison, Johnny Cash, and Jerry Lee Lewis. Also in 1986 Perkins appeared in a Cinemax television special, "A Rockabilly Session: Carl Perkins and Friends," which featured the rockabilly king performing with George Harrison, Ringo Starr, Eric Clapton, and others. Later that year he received the Career Achievement Award from the Academy of Country Music and was inducted into the Rock and Roll Hall of Fame, thus validating his status as a rock-and-roll legend. After recovering from throat cancer in the early 1990s, Perkins died of a stroke in Jackson.

Perkins's music was rockabilly at its best, combining the country twang of bluegrass with a rock-and-roll beat accented by the sounds of Delta blues. In his words, rockabilly is "country with a black man's rhythm," the "blues speeded up" (*Guitar Player*, Mar. 1997). Perkins could make his guitar, according to John Fogerty of Creedence Clearwater Revival fame, "do it all"; his style of playing is now considered to be the way rockabilly guitar should be played. But Perkins is best remembered for his contribution to early rock and roll through his Sun sessions and for "Blue Suede Shoes," an anthem of youth in the 1950s, one of the first songs to be a cross-over hit on the rock, rhythm and blues, and country charts.

• David McGee, *Go, Cat, Go! The Life and Times of Carl Perkins, the King of Rockabilly* (1996), is a good biography. Although the book is written in the third person, Perkins himself is given credit as coauthor because of his extensive contributions to its writing. A review of *Go, Cat, Go!* is in the *Memphis Business Journal*, 20 May 1996, pp. 25–26. For interviews, see "A Conversation with Carl Perkins, *Oxford American*, no. 16 (n.d.): 97–99; *New York Times*, 10 Nov. 1996; "Talking with Carl Perkins," *People*, 13 Jan. 1997; and "Carl Perkins and the Roots of Rockabilly," *Guitar Player* 31 (Mar. 1997): 46–54. Bear Family Records issued a five-CD collection of his recordings, *The Classic Carl Perkins* (1990). Obituaries are in the *New York Times*, 20 Jan. 1998; *Billboard*, 31 Jan. 1998; *Rolling Stone*, 5 Mar. 1998; and *Guitar Player*, May 1998.

STACEY HAMILTON

PERKINS, Dexter (20 June 1889–12 May 1984), historian and educator, was born in Boston, Massachusetts, the son of William Perkins, an importer, and Cora Farmer Perkins. Thought by his parents to be too young for college following graduation from the Boston Latin School in 1905, he entered the Sanford School in Redding, Connecticut, and graduated in 1906. An excellent scholar, Perkins majored in history at Harvard and was named to Phi Beta Kappa prior to receiving his A.B. degree in 1909. He continued his education overseas and earned a diploma from the École des Sciences Politiques (Paris) in 1913; in the following year he also received his doctorate from Harvard. His dissertation, "The Monroe Doctrine, 1823–1826," was his first written analysis of this landmark in American foreign policy, which would serve as the focus of his career.

Perkins entered the teaching profession as an instructor at the University of Cincinnati in 1914. In the following year he moved to the University of Rochester at the same rank. He married Wilma Lois Lord, one of his former students, on 2 May 1918; the couple eventually had two sons. Following the entry of the United States into World War I, Perkins joined the U.S. Army infantry as a private in June 1918. By the end of the war he had risen to the rank of captain and managed to merge his interest in history with his military duties, serving from October 1918 until February 1919 in the historical section of General Headquarters in Chaumont, France. Perkins later attended the Paris Peace Conference (where he was charged with reporting on the proceedings to the American Expeditionary Force commander, General John Pershing) and was discharged in June 1919.

At the conclusion of the war Perkins returned to the University of Rochester, where he was promoted to assistant professor. He became an associate professor in 1922, and in 1925 he took on the additional duties of departmental chairman. In 1927 his dissertation was published under its original title and soon brought Perkins recognition for his insights into both the Monroe Doctrine's authorship (shared equally between John Quincy Adams and James Monroe) and its effect (while initially valueless—the European powers had not been a legitimate intervention threat in 1823—it set the tone for later American diplomatic strategies). Peer recognition came in 1928, when Perkins became secretary of the American Historical Association, a position he held until 1932 (he also served as corresponding secretary until 1939).

Perkins continued to work on the doctrine and its impact, producing *The Monroe Doctrine, 1826–1867* (1933), *The Monroe Doctrine, 1867–1907* (1937), and *Hands Off: A History of the Monroe Doctrine* (1941), later revised as *A History of the Monroe Doctrine* (1955). In addition to his work on the doctrine, which Perkins described as "perhaps the most important single document in American diplomatic history," he also wrote *America and Two Wars* (1944), *The United States and the Caribbean* (1947), *The Evolution of American Foreign Policy* (1948), *Charles Evans Hughes and American Democratic Statesmanship* (1956), *The American Way* (1957), and *The New Age of Franklin Roosevelt* (1957).

Well respected outside of academia, Perkins was appointed the city historian of Rochester (1936–1948) and held a panel chairmanship on the National War Labor Board during World War II. Near the end of that conflict he served as official historian at the Overseas Branch of the Office of War Information at the United Nations Conference in San Francisco, where he observed the birth of the United Nations organization firsthand. He was elected moderator of the Unitarian Churches of the United States and Canada in 1952 and chaired the council of the Harvard Foundation for Advanced Study from 1951 to 1956.

On the basis of his scholarly reputation, Perkins was invited to give lectures both abroad and at home. He was a Commonwealth Fund Lecturer at University College of the University of London in 1937 and was named the first visiting Pitt Professor in American History and Institutions at Cambridge (1945–1946). In 1946 he began lecturing at the National War College in Arlington, Virginia, and continued to do so until 1954. He returned to England for a series of lectures at the Royal Institute of International Affairs in 1948 and 1952, and in the spring of 1949 he delivered the Gottesman lectures at the University of Uppsala in Sweden, which were later published as *The American Approach to Foreign Policy* (1951). His longest affiliation was with the annual Salzburg Seminar in American Studies in Austria; after teaching there during the summer of 1949, he returned as the seminar's president each year from 1950 until 1961.

After spending much of the early 1950s building up the Ph.D. program at Rochester, Perkins moved in 1954 to Cornell University, where he held a chair as the first John L. Senior Professor of American Civilization until 1959. The crowning achievement of his professional career came in 1956, when he was elected president of the American Historical Association. Long troubled by what he considered to be an overemphasis on publication at the expense of classroom instruction in academia, Perkins argued in his inaugural speech, "We Shall Gladly Teach," that the "greatest challenge confronting historians today is the challenge of the classroom." Late in his career, Perkins argued that American foreign policy had been unique in its generally open and moralistic approach in dealing with other nations. He also spent a considerable amount of time attacking members of the so-called "revisionist" school of history. Deploring what he called "history by hypothesis," Perkins became a de facto spokesman for the "consensus" school in arguing that the United States had entered both world wars of the twentieth century on the basis of the need to preserve national security. Following a long retirement, Perkins died in Rochester, New York.

Although Perkins's conclusions about American diplomatic history were attacked during his later years (particularly during the 1960s), the good reputation of his scholarship has remained intact. His advocacy of a balanced approach to academic work—combining excellence in teaching with substantive research—has continued to be an ideal, especially as universities have had to reassess the criteria for tenure.

• Perkins's papers are held at the University of Rochester, Rochester, N.Y. His autobiography, *Yield of the Years* (1969), is an excellent source of information on his life and career. Also useful are Peter Novick, *That Noble Dream: The "Objectivity Question" and the American Historical Profession*

(1988), and Arthur J. May, *A History of the University of Rochester, 1850–1962* (1977). An obituary is in the *New York Times*, 16 May 1984.

EDWARD L. LACH, JR.

PETERSON, Roger Tory (28 Aug. 1908–28 July 1996), ornithologist and artist, was born in Jamestown, New York, to Charles G. Peterson and Henrietta Bader Peterson. Both his parents had emigrated to America from Europe: his father had been born in Sweden, his mother in Germany to parents of Slavic descent. His father, an intensely practical man, worked for a company that made office furniture. Though he admired the artistic talent his son exhibited at an early age, he was also skeptical of Roger's dreamy absorption in nature and feared that the boy would not come to a good end. From earliest childhood Roger Tory Peterson enjoyed being alone in the woods and countryside, observing animals and especially birds. He began to sketch what he saw, and at the age of fourteen won a prize for a drawing of a butterfly. His active membership in a Junior Audubon Club from the age of eleven onward gave a focus to his life that the activities of other children his age did not, and in old age he remembered himself when young as a rebellious loner for whom nature provided salvation.

Increasingly obsessed by birds during his teen years, Peterson earned money as a newspaper delivery boy to buy a camera and began photographing different species. Overall an average student in high school, he excelled at mechanical drawing but did poorly in industrial arts, which puzzled his craftsman father. He also did not do especially well in biology and never formally studied birds. He worked briefly as an engineering draftsman after graduation, then got a job painting pictures and designs on furniture. A friend encouraged him to seek further training in art, and in 1927 Peterson moved to New York to attend the Art Students League. After two years there he enrolled at the National Academy of Design, remaining there until 1931 under the tutelage of several distinguished painters, including John Sloan. In New York he also came under the influence of Louis Agassiz Fuertes, a noted wildlife painter, and the ornithologist Ludlow Griscom.

After leaving the Academy, Peterson moved to Brookline, Massachusetts, to teach art at a boys' school there. The paintings he had done of birds while a student in Manhattan attracted the attention of an editor at *Audubon* magazine, who suggested that he publish them in book form, perhaps even as a guide for bird-watchers. Peterson liked the idea and approached a series of publishers. At least four turned him down before Houghton Mifflin agreed to publish such a book in 1934, calling it *A Field Guide to the Birds, Including All Species Found in Eastern North America.* However, they had little hope of its success and printed only two thousand copies. Much to their surprise, and Peterson's, the first printing sold out within two weeks, and additional copies were bought as quickly as they arrived in bookstores. Peterson's book was an enormous success and launched him on a celebrated career as the most famous ornithologist in the United States.

The appeal of Peterson's book for bird-watchers was not difficult to understand. At that time bird guides were textbooks written for professional ornithologists, not for amateur birders, and were filled with mind-boggling illustrations and confusing details. Peterson's guide offered beautiful but simple illustrations in color, grouping birds similar in appearance together rather than by species, and describing them in uncomplicated ways with pointers for easy identification. What was indeed surprising was the number of Americans who were interested enough in birds to invest in a guidebook, at a time when the Great Depression had drastically reduced disposable income. The book continued to sell over the years, providing Peterson with a steady income and enabling him to leave his teaching job and set up a studio in Old Lyme, Connecticut. Four editions of *A Field Guide to the Birds* were published during his lifetime, selling more than five million copies, and he was working on a fifth at the time of his death; by then he had earned the praise of conservationists and scientists throughout the nation for making bird-watching a national pastime.

Peterson wrote other books on birds as well, including specialized guides to birds in the western United States, the Southwest, Europe, and Mexico. He also wrote and illustrated *A Field Guide to Wildflowers* (1968) and edited other Houghton Mifflin guides that focused on mammals, butterflies, shells, rocks and minerals, and other categories of nature; the collection, ultimately numbering twenty-one volumes, became known as the Peterson Field Guide Series. All told, Peterson wrote or edited nearly fifty books about nature and contributed articles to *Audubon, National Geographic, Reader's Digest,* and *Life,* among other publications. In addition to creating educational materials for the National Audubon Society and the Boy Scouts, he produced and narrated a series of films on nature for the National Geographic Society. Peterson received numerous awards for his work, both in the United States and abroad, including the Presidential Medal of Freedom from President Jimmy Carter and the gold medal of the Swedish Academy of Sciences.

Although writing and illustrating books occupied much of his time, Peterson still enjoyed painting birds and other wildlife for pleasure, exhibiting his artwork at galleries and museums and selling many of his prints to private collectors over the years. He also liked to travel, an interest he was finally able to pursue seriously beginning in 1953, when he journeyed extensively throughout the United States with a noted British naturalist, James M. C. Fisher, visiting wildlife refuges and rural areas and taking many photographs. As an outgrowth of their trip, the two men wrote *Wild America,* published in 1955. Over the next two decades Peterson traveled to every continent in the world, always in search of nature, and by 1974 had become such a noted world traveler that the Explorers Club awarded him their highest honor, the Explorer's Medal.

Peterson had three marriages. His first, to Mildred Washington in 1936, ended in divorce. He then married Barbara Coulter in 1943; the couple had two children. After their divorce he married Virginia Westervelt in 1976. He died at his home in Old Lyme following a stroke.

• The primary source of biographical information on Peterson is the authorized biography by John C. Devlin and Grace Naismith, *The World of Roger Tory Peterson* (1977). See also "Peterson, Roger Tory," in *Current Biography Yearbook 1959*; *Contemporary Authors, New Revision Series*, vol. 1 (1981); *Contemporary Authors*, vol. 152 (1997); and *Who's Who in America*, 50th ed. (1996). In addition, see Lisa W. Foderaro, "Reluctant Earthling: In the Studio with Roger Tory Peterson," *New York Times*, 26 Aug. 1993. An obituary appears in the *New York Times*, 30 July 1996.

ANN T. KEENE

PHILLIPS, Jonas (1736–29 Jan. 1803), merchant and Jewish civil rights leader, was born Jonas Phaibush in Buseck, Germany, the son of Phila Stein Phaibush and Aaron Phaibush (other spellings of this name found in the biographical literature include Faibush and Feibush), a clothing merchant. There is little known about the early life of Jonas in Buseck, a Rhenish village then under the dominion of Prussia. In 1756 he traveled to England, where he assumed an English surname, Phillips, which he retained thereafter. In November of that year, he sailed on the ship *Charming Nancy* to America and went to Charleston, South Carolina. There Phillips served as an indentured servant of Moses Lindo, a Sephardic Jew who ran one of the largest indigo plantations in the colony of South Carolina. Having fulfilled his obligations to Lindo, Phillips left Charleston in 1758 and by sometime the next year he was in Albany, New York. He was recognized on 13 August 1759 as a freeman of Albany and that year started his own business, which was located near the city's fort. As the French and Indian War raged, Phillips, between 1759 and 1761, sold a variety of goods, including European clothes and textiles, wines, brandies, tea, milk, and biscuits.

In late August 1761 Phillips dissolved his firm in Albany and moved to New York City to enhance his business opportunities, opening a store that sold food and clothes. On 10 November 1762 in Philadelphia, Pennsylvania, he married Rebecca Machado, a Sephardic Jew whose father, the late David Mendes Machado, had served as *hazan* or leader of New York's Congregation Shearith Israel. The couple had twenty-one children, the most prominent being the New York actor Aaron J. Phillips and the Philadelphia criminal lawyer Zalegman Phillips. Affected by the difficult economic conditions that arose at the end of the French and Indian War, Phillips went bankrupt in 1765. Between April 1765 and March 1770 he served as a *shohet* or a meat slaughterer for Shearith Israel.

During the early 1770s Phillips once again engaged in business activities. In 1770, with financial support from his friend Isaac Moses, he started a food and clothing firm in New York, while also serving as an auctioneer. Along with other New York merchants, the outspoken Phillips signed the 1770 nonimportation resolutions, which were directed against British taxation policies. In an effort to improve his prospects in the colonial business world, in 1774 he had moved his family to Philadelphia, where he opened on Market Street, near the courthouse, a retail firm offering a vast assortment of merchandise. In 1775 and in early 1776 his store sold, among other things, coats, raccoon and beaver skins, linens, Carolina indigo, writing paper, nutmeg and pepper, and wines. By June 1776 Phillips was doing fairly well in this business and looking for ways to make it more lucrative.

With the outbreak of the American Revolution, Phillips became a patriot, believing that an independent America would improve his business fortunes and that its leaders would grant to Jews the civil liberties that were their due. He helped in several ways to further the cause of the patriots. During the revolutionary era, he acquired merchandise from and sold goods to Europeans who backed the American cause. On 28 July 1776 Phillips sent a cargo of goods, a Yiddish translation of the Declaration of Independence, and a lengthy letter to one of his relatives, the Amsterdam merchant Gumpel Samson. In this letter he predicted that America would become a republic like Holland and that the revolutionary war would make England bankrupt. Phillips also informed Samson that profits as high as 400 percent could be derived in America from the sale of military clothing, woolen blankets, guns, and food supplies. Although the British seized the shipment to Samson, Phillips faired well as a revolutionary merchant-shipper. Before the end of the American Revolution, he became the second wealthiest Jewish patriot in Philadelphia. He was not, however, only a bystander who made profits. On 31 October 1778 he was mustered in the Philadelphia Militia as a private and served in Captain John Linton's company of Colonel William Bradford's battalion.

At the end of the War of Independence, Phillips concentrated on matters concerning Jewish citizenship rights. As a leader of the Philadelphia Jewish community, when he presented to the Pennsylvania Council of Censors in 1783 a petition to terminate civic disabilities against Jews in that state, the council chose not to act. Seven years later, however, the Pennsylvania legislature approved a state constitution that abolished a Christian test oath and allowed Jews to hold public offices. Phillips also voiced his concerns about Jewish civil rights to the Federal Constitutional Convention, which was held in Philadelphia. On 7 September 1787 he sent to members of this convention a lengthy letter in which he maintained that many Jewish patriots "fought and bled for liberty" and that all individuals should be endowed with the right to be "free in the Exercise of Religious Worship." He also argued that "the sons of Abraham, Isaac, and Jacob" should be permitted to vote wherever they lived and to occupy political positions in the newly created federal republic. The letter may have contributed to the momentum to produce a federal constitution free of religious bias, thereby guaranteeing to Jews full citizenship.

Like other merchants of the time, Phillips was active in fraternal and religious institutions. In 1760 he was made a Mason in New York City's Trinity Lodge# 4. His involvement in Freemasonry evidently enabled him to assimilate, to develop business contacts, and to acquire an interest in the ideologies of the American Revolution. Besides being a member of New York's Shearith Israel synagogue, Phillips played a prominent role in Philadelphia's Mikveh Israel congregation. In March 1782 he made a large donation for the construction of a new synagogue for Mikveh Israel, and the following September, as the newly elected president of the congregation, he participated in the dedication of the completed building in Cherry Alley. After retiring from business in 1799, Phillips remained as contentious as ever; a quarrel that he had with leaders of Mikveh Israel in 1801 led to his resignation from the congregation the following year. He died in Philadelphia and was buried in New York in the cemetery of Congregation Shearith Israel.

Aggressive and obstinate, Phillips is an early example of the classic American story of the penniless immigrant who eventually becomes exceptionally wealthy. As a retailer and wholesaler, he also exemplified the nascent American spirit of commerce that was eager to be free of colonial fetters. And in his determined advocacy of full citizenship for Jews he gave expression to the fundamental right guaranteed in the First Amendment.

• There are some primary materials and secondary sources relating to the career of Phillips. Letters of his are housed in the Library of the American Jewish Historical Society in New York and in the collections of the American Jewish Archives in Cincinnati. Short biographical accounts of Phillips appear in Samuel Rezneck, *The Saga of an American Jewish Family since the Revolution: A History of the Family of Jonas Phillips* (1980), and in David De Sola Pool, *Portraits Etched in Stone: Early Jewish Settlers, 1682–1831* (1952). For his career as a businessman in Philadelphia, consult especially Jacob R. Marcus, *United States Jewry, 1776–1985*, vol. 1 (1989). His business achievements during the American Revolution are evaluated in Samuel Rezneck, *Unrecognized Patriots: The Jews in the American Revolution* (1975), and in Laurens R. Schwartz, *Jews and the American Revolution: Haym Salomon and Others* (1987). In their *History of the Jews of Philadelphia from Colonial Times to the Age of Jackson* (1956), Edwin Wolf II and Maxwell Whiteman, assess the Phillips's contributions to the eighteenth-century Jewish civil rights movement and to Philadelphia's Mikveh Israel congregation. For his involvement in Freemasonry and his leadership role in the Jewish emancipation movement during the American Revolution, see William Weisberger, "Freemasonry as a Source of Jewish Civic Rights in Late Eighteenth-Century Vienna: A Study in Atlantic History," *East European Quarterly* 34 (Winter 2000): 419–445.

WILLIAM WEISBERGER

PIERCE, Bessie Louise (20 Apr. 1888–3 Oct. 1974), historian and educator, was born in Cairo, Michigan, the daughter of Clifton Jonathan Pierce, a dry goods store clerk, and Maria Carmelia Pierson Pierce. As a young child, she relocated with her family to Waverly, Iowa, where her father enjoyed a successful partnership in his own dry goods operation. After serving as president of her high school class for four years, Pierce graduated in 1905 and entered the State University of Iowa (now the University of Iowa). Although few women at that time undertook higher education, Pierce's family was supportive (an aunt had previously completed medical school), and she graduated Phi Beta Kappa with a degree in education in 1910. She then taught high school in Mason City and Sanborn, Iowa, but became frustrated because of the unlikelihood of promotion and decided to enter graduate school.

Pierce began study at the University of Chicago, which welcomed women, as a summer student. By 1916 she had become principal of the State University of Iowa's high school in Iowa City and earned her master's degree in 1918. The arrival of Arthur Schlesinger, Sr., on the campus at Iowa City proved fortuitous for Pierce. Interested in social history as well as the role of women in history, Schlesinger asked Pierce to be his first graduate student. Pierce received her Ph.D. in 1923 and immediately joined the faculty at Iowa. Initially interested in the history of education, she wrote a dissertation on the subject, which was published as *Public Opinion and the Teaching of History in the United States* in 1926.

Promoted to associate professor in 1926, Pierce acquired an academic reputation that soon spread, and in 1929 she faced a difficult choice: either to remain at Iowa and enjoy a sure promotion to full professor or to join the University of Chicago faculty with a three-year contract as an associate professor. Given the opportunity to complete a full study of Chicago history, Pierce jumped at the chance and remained at Chicago for the rest of her career. Her History of Chicago project benefited from access to a vast amount of scholarly material that the university's social scientists had accumulated in creating a new academic field—urbanology.

Charged with studying political, economic, cultural, and social forces as they applied to a single urban setting, Pierce soon grasped the enormous scope of her task. After setting up university course work in city history, she set about researching and writing. Many complications arose, not the least of which were the general lack of indexes for local newspapers and the loss of raw research material as a result of the Great Fire of 1871. With no significant grant money available, funding was initially a problem, although the ready availability of unemployed Ph.D.'s (due to the Great Depression) helped. The first product of the project was a lively collection of reminiscences by foreigners, *As Others See Chicago*, which appeared in 1933.

Having decided on dividing her history into several volumes, Pierce assisted with the Illinois Writers Project (which documented the lives of the state's African Americans) as well as with the Foreign Language Press Survey (which translated newspaper accounts from area ethnic presses), in addition to pursuing her own work on the History of Chicago Project. The first volume, *A History of Chicago: The Beginning of a City* (1937), covered Chicago history from 1673 until 1848. The second volume, *A History of Chicago: From City to Town, 1848–1871* (1940), appeared just as World War II began to take center stage. With military service claiming many of her assistants and much of the financial assistance that had belatedly arrived from various private foundations, Pierce served as a War Bond warden and also doubled up on her teaching load in the absence of many of her male colleagues. In 1942 she also chaired a committee of the American Historical Association charged with interpreting American history for wartime propaganda purposes.

Promoted to full professor in 1943, Pierce gained national attention when a group of rival railroad executives asked her to debunk a claim by the Santa Fe and Burlington Railroad that their transcontinental service had been largely responsible for Chicago's rise to prominence. She testified before the Interstate Commerce Commission in December 1946 that economic dominance, rather than transportation, had been the determining factor in Chicago's position of power. The case provided a side benefit to Pierce, enabling her to gather economic data for the third volume of her history. Given additional time to write following her retirement from Chicago in 1953, Pierce produced the third volume, *A History of Chicago: The Rise of a Modern City, 1871–1893*, which appeared in 1957. The beneficiary of numerous awards in her later years (including Guggenheim fellowships in 1956 and 1957, the Lou Kent Fink award from the American Association for State and Local History in 1958, and the American Association of University Women fellowship in 1965–1966), Pierce nevertheless was frustrated in her later years. Slowed by age, she found working increasingly difficult, and it became obvious to her associates that she would never complete all five planned volumes. Never having married, Pierce retired to Iowa City, Iowa, where she died.

Although the individual volumes of Pierce's magnum opus were well received at the time of their publication, the work as a whole was later criticized for its overemphasis on economic issues and its general lack of interpretive analysis. Nevertheless, Pierce will be remembered as one of the "second generation" of women professional historians who made their mark by pursuing major, long-term research projects.

• Pierce's papers are held at the Department of Special Collections, University of Chicago. The best secondary sources on her life and career are Perry Duis, "Bessie Louise Pierce: Symbol and Scholar," *Chicago History: The Magazine of the Chicago Historical Society*, Fall 1976, pp. 130–40, and Joseph Haas, "Historian's Secret: Bessie Pierce Loves Chicago," *Chicago Daily News*, 25 Mar. 1967. An obituary is in the *New York Times*, 5 Oct. 1974.

EDWARD L. LACH, JR.

POLK, Sarah Childress (4 Sept. 1803–14 Aug. 1891), first lady, was born in Murfreesboro, Tennessee, the daughter of Joel Childress, a merchant, planter, and land speculator, and Elizabeth Whitsitt Childress. When it was rare for daughters to be well educated, Sarah was an exception: after attending common school, she was tutored at Bradley Academy for boys after hours and then went to Abercrombie's Boarding School in Nashville. At an uncle's home there, she met Andrew Jackson. When she was about fifteen, Sarah entered the Moravian Female Seminary in Salem, North Carolina, where she studied practical subjects and the polite arts, took piano lessons, and became an avid reader. Joining her mother and siblings when her father died in 1819, she was in comfortable circumstances, served by thirty-four slaves, in a fine home with a sizable library.

James Knox Polk, the future president, may have first met Sarah at the Bradley Academy. They were certainly guests at a reception honoring William Carroll, the governor of Tennessee, probably in 1921. Present also were Jackson and Felix Grundy, a Nashville lawyer and former Kentucky Supreme Court justice. Jackson encouraged Polk to marry Sarah, saying she would help him settle down and advance his political career. Polk had read law in Grundy's office and was chief clerk in the state legislature. While Polk courted her, Sarah allegedly said she would not marry him unless he ran for the legislature, which he did successfully in 1823. Polk, a Methodist, and Sarah were married the following New Year's Day in her Murfreesboro Presbyterian church.

Sarah seldom saw Polk while he served in the legislature, at that time in Columbia, Tennessee. Elected to the U.S. House of Representatives in 1825, he went to Washington, alone, but in the fall of 1826 she insisted on living in Washington too. Although some biographers say that Sarah had a miscarriage during Polk's second congressional term, in truth he was probably sterile following major bladder surgery in 1812. Childless, Sarah became surrogate mother to her husband's two youngest brothers, whose wildness often taxed her patience.

Sarah not only followed national matters of concern to Polk but also complemented his austere manner in society: an affable and intelligent conversationalist and gracious hostess, she attended House sessions when he spoke and was more a confidante than a homemaker. Reelected to Congress in 1827, Polk, with Sarah's assistance, helped advance Jackson's successful bid for the presidency. During Jackson's two terms as Democratic president (1829–1837), the Polks were among his dearest friends. Other allies of the Polks included Franklin Pierce, a future president, and Joseph Story, a Supreme Court justice. When in 1834 Polk planned to move some of his slaves to his newly purchased cotton plantation in Mississippi, Sarah aided by ordering supplies and keeping the transfer private until the last minute. Like many southern politicians of the time, the Polks regarded their slaves, whom they regularly called their "servants," as money-earning property.

When Polk was Speaker of the House (1835–1839), Sarah did all she could to protect his already precarious health. In 1839 she aided his campaign for governor of Tennessee by mailing pamphlets, supervising his schedule, and handling his voluminous correspondence. When he was governor (1840–1842), she proved to be a sparkling hostess in the official Nashville mansion, acted as his secretary, and worried, as he did, about their inadequate income. She seemed relieved that his two bids for reelection failed, because practicing law in Columbia proved less stressful for him. She felt, however, that fate itself caused expansionist Jackson to oppose Martin Van Buren in favor of Polk as presidential nominee at the Democratic convention of May 1844. Most experts were certain that the Whig candidate, Henry Clay, would defeat Polk, but Sarah threw herself into the campaign, mainly by sending journalists statements about Polk's positions on key issues. Evidently, she never doubted the outcome.

After Polk's inauguration (March 1845), Sarah treasured the Bible used in the ceremony. During his administration, she was his unpaid secretary and evolved into the most powerful first lady since Dolley Madison, whom she admired and entertained. Polk told Sarah that he planned to reduce the tariff, have an independent treasury, settle the Oregon question, and acquire California. In reply, she prophetically warned him that Texas was still problematic. Although in public statements Sarah typically presented herself as the president's mouthpiece—"Mr. Polk thinks . . ."—in private she summarized correspondence and publications for him, debated policies with him, critiqued his pronouncements and those of his cabinet members, and became his only confidante. She conferred with members of Congress each Saturday, hosted receptions twice weekly, and preferred the conversation of key men to the companionship of socially important women. She supervised refurbishing the White House, prohibited dancing, card-playing, and hard liquor there, trained the staff but reduced their number by bringing in some of her slaves, usually declined politicians' gifts, and purchased her own costly Parisian gowns.

When Texas was annexed in December 1845, Sarah happily saw Polk's popularity increase, and when the Mexican War began in May 1946, she viewed the war, as well as expansion into the Northwest, as foreordained. She soon arranged for a daguerreotype, the first taken in the Executive Mansion, of Polk and the war cabinet. Once the war was over in May 1848, Sarah, worried about Polk's overtaxed and waning strength, journeyed alone to Nashville to start renovating their retirement home. In March 1849 she was hostess at the final White House party

of Polk's administration, at which Zachary Taylor, president-elect and Whig, was the honored guest. She told Polk that the dinner was a delight, whereupon Polk, who regarded Taylor as honest and brave but politically ignorant, replied that he would like to leave at once for home.

Their four-week, circuitous trip to Nashville exhausted Polk dreadfully, and Sarah agonized over his health. Both had been exposed to cholera between New Orleans and Natchez, and in June it killed him. For the remainder of her long life Sarah memorialized her husband, by preserving his study in Polk Place intact, having him interred in a marble tomb on the front lawn, and proudly exhibiting his papers and other possessions. Friends tried to be of solace, but—though welcoming them hospitably—she did not return their visits. As a rule, she went out only to church. Nevertheless, she managed their Mississippi cotton plantation astutely—by correspondence. In his will, Polk esteemed her for her "prudence, care, and economy." She died at home in Nashville.

Sarah Polk represents a type of southern woman of the antebellum era whose force of character evidently drew its strength from devotion to a prominent husband. Possessed of a lively intellect and an ingratiating charm, she was one of the most admired first ladies of the nineteenth century. In her zeal to watch out for her husband's interests and well-being, she was exceptionally well matched with one of the hardest-working presidents the nation has had.

• Anson and Fanny Nelson, *Memorials of Sarah Childress Polk: Wife of the Eleventh President of the United States* (1892; reprint 1974), contains reminiscences by close friends. John Reed Bumgarner, *Sarah Childress Polk: A Biography of the Remarkable First Lady* (1997), presents Sarah Polk's personality and political positions and includes pertinent medical details. Among several similar books, Paul F. Boller, Jr., *Presidential Wives* (rev. ed., 1998), and Betty Boyd Caroli, *First Ladies* (expanded ed., 1995), sufficiently describe Sarah's activities as first lady. Herbert Weaver et al., eds., *Correspondence of James K. Polk* (1969–), includes letters to and from Sarah and references to her in other letters, as do the Polk Papers in the Library of Congress. Augustus C. Buell, in *History of Andrew Jackson: Pioneer, Patriot, Soldier, Politician, President* (2 vols., 1904), summarizes Sarah's comments to Buell in 1875 regarding Jackson's attitude toward her and depicts her in old age as sensitive and keenly intelligent. Paul H. Bergeron, *The Presidency of James K. Polk* (1987), Charles Grier Sellers, *James K. Polk: Jacksonian, 1795–1843* (1957), and *James K. Polk: Continentalist 1943–1946* (1966), include much information concerning Sarah. *Pen and Sword: The Life and Journals of Randal W. McGavock* (1959), edited by Hershel Gower and Jack Allen, contains entries showing the respect for Sarah displayed from 1848 to 1860 by McGavock, Felix Grundy's grandson, a young Nashville politician who, as a Confederate Army colonel, was killed in 1863.

ROBERT L. GALE

POTTER, Clare (1903–5 Jan. 1999), fashion designer, was born Clare Meyer in Jersey City, New Jersey; her parents' names and occupations do not appear in readily available sources of information. Potter's ambition from her early years was to be an artist. By the age of fifteen, she was attending classes at the Art Students' League in New York City. After completing high school Potter studied at Pratt Institute in Brooklyn, New York, with every intention of becoming a painter.

It was the gentle persuasion of Pratt's director that led Potter toward another career. Her observation of Potter's paintings and the clothes she made and wore convinced her that Potter's skills were better suited to fashion. Potter then decided to study costume design (she later acknowledged that her paintings really were not all that good). She switched to a design course, took classes at a draping school, and began learning her new field. Before she had finished her course work, Pratt Institute sent her to a job at Edward L. Mayer, Inc., a prominent New York City dress manufacturer. Potter's job (which she couldn't believe she was being paid for) was to do research in museum collections and use her findings to create embroidery patterns for the beaded and embroidered dresses popular during the 1920s. Eventually Potter began offering her own suggestions for the dresses. Her efforts were well received by Mayer; Potter found herself working as a fashion designer. After staying with the firm for three years, she spent six months in Mexico, worked in another wholesale house, and then in 1930 began to design clothes for Charles W. Nudelman, Inc., on Seventh Avenue. Her clothes were sold during the 1930s and 1940s under the label "clarepotter."

At the outset of her career nearly all fashionable women's clothes manufactured in America were based on Parisian styles. While the names of many French couturiers were known around the world, American designers still worked in anonymity. One woman, Dorothy Shaver, is credited with changing that state of inequity and bringing designers like Potter to the public's attention. In 1932, Shaver, a vice president of the Lord and Taylor department store in New York City, initiated the store's promotion of American fashions and the people responsible for them. In 1936, Potter's clothes, along with those of Vera Maxwell and Helen Cookman, were featured in the store's Fifth Avenue windows and in interior store displays that showed photographs of Potter alongside her creations. As a result, Potter became one of the earliest American fashion designers known to the public by name.

Potter's approach to fashion design was thoroughly American, relying on her knowledge of the way women lived their lives—particularly the "town and country set." While vacationing in Paris, she avoided seeing the offerings of the French fashion houses. Instead, along with other American designers of the period, Potter focused on sportswear—then a fledging genre of clothes that came to define American style. Her pants ensembles, blouses and skirts, beach clothes, at-home outfits, and dresses smartly satisfied American women's wardrobe needs. Potter is credited with making evening clothes casual and sports clothes refined.

During the 1930s, 1940s, and 1950s, it was also her sophisticated sense of color, taken from her training as a painter, that distinguished Potter's stylish sportswear. Her clothes were seen in *Vogue, Harper's Bazaar, Women's Wear Daily*, and *Town and Country*, photographed by such leading photographers as Horst P. Horst, Dahl-Wolfe, and Hoyningen-Huene, often with captions that read "Clare Potter, colorist." She preferred to combine two or three fabric colors in one outfit rather than add ornamentation, which she disliked. In a 1940 Harper's Bazaar photograph, a Clare Potter blouse and skirt outfit is described as ". . . white, coral, acid green, and blackberry; turquoise earrings; a violent pink rose," illustrating Potter's emphatic use of a rich palette. Potter found, and copied, colors from everyday objects around her. She cut out a blue mailing label from an envelope on her desk and had the color matched by a textile manufacturer; paints she bought while on vacation in Bermuda were translated into fabric colors; and the hue of one rose-colored cloth was derived from a memo pad. Inspiration also came from the farm in West Nyack, New York, where she lived with her husband, J. Sanford Potter, an architect (the date of their marriage is unknown). On the farm, Potter kept turkeys, raised Dalmatian dogs, and rode horses. She once made a successful printed fabric using the Dalmatians' spots as a motif.

As American fashion came into its own, Potter continued making the clothes she was known for—straightforward dresses, evening pajamas, tailored pants, and chic beach outfits. She later sold clothes through the Timbertop firm, which she established in West Nyack. In the late 1950s, she and her husband moved from their farm to a Japanese-style house in Fort Ann, New York. Potter's active life of gardening and riding horses continued until her death at her home in Fort Ann.

Potter's achievements were recognized early in her career. In 1937 she received the Lord & Taylor award for distinguished designing in the field of sports clothes for women; in 1939 the Neiman-Marcus award for distinguished service in the field of fashion; and in 1946 the Coty Fashion Critics' Award. Examples of Clare Potter's clothes can be found in museum collections such as the Costume Institute at the Metropolitan Museum of Art. In the 1940s Potter was included in two Costume Institute shows, "A Designers' Exhibition of Costumes and Millinery Derived from Museum Documents" (1940) and "American Fashions & Fabrics" (1945). More recently, Potter's clothes were shown in "All-American: A Sportswear Tradition" (1985) at the Fashion Institute of Technology; "American Ingenuity: Sportswear 1930s–1970s" (1998) at the Metropolitan Museum of Art; and "Designing Women: American Style 1940–1960" (1998) at the Wadsworth Atheneum in Hartford, Connecticut.

• A profile of Clare Potter at work is featured in Beryl Williams Epstein, *Fashion Is Our Business* (1945). Discussions of Potter's role in the history of American fashion can be found in Caroline Milbank, *New York Fashion: The Evolution of American Style* (1989), and in Richard Martin's exhibition catalogues *All-American: A Sportswear Tradition* (1985) and *American Ingenuity: Sportswear 1930s–1970s* (1998). Potter's obituary is in the *New York Times*, 11 Jan. 1999.

DONNA GHELERTER

POVICH, Shirley (15 July 1905–4 June 1998), sportswriter, was born in Bar Harbor, Maine, the son of Nathan Povich, a furniture store owner, and Rosa Orlovich Povich. As a youngster, he attended local schools and also caddied at the Kebo Valley Golf Club. Bar Harbor was a well-known resort for the rich and famous, and Povich had the good fortune to serve as the long-term caddie for Edward B. "Ned" Mc-Lean, the owner of the *Washington Post*. Povich so impressed McLean that the latter offered him both a job at the paper and an expenses-paid education at Georgetown University, McLean's alma mater. During the train trip to Washington in the fall of 1922, Povich (who had never been outside of Maine in his life) stopped in New York and witnessed his first major league baseball game, a World Series victory by the New York Giants over the New York Yankees.

Upon arriving in Washington, Povich spent his first day caddying for McLean and President Warren G. Harding. He enrolled in law classes at Georgetown and began working as a copyboy at the *Post* in 1923. After quickly moving up in the ranks (from copyboy to police reporter and rewrite man), Povich left school and jumped at the chance to transfer to the sports department in 1924. Thrilled at seeing his name under a byline, Povich's first article described the crowd's reaction on the return of the Washington Senators baseball team (then in the middle of a rare—for that team—pennant race). When his editor, Norman Baxter, became managing editor of the paper two years later, Povich took over as the sports editor; at twenty-one, he was the youngest man in the country to hold this position on a major newspaper. Unfortunately, Povich had to face budgetary problems as well as deadlines because the *Post*'s circulation at the time badly lagged behind that of its major rivals in Washington, the *Herald* and the *Star*.

That same year, 1926, Povich began writing a regular column, "This Morning," which he continued for the rest of his life. He also attempted to boost the *Post*'s circulation; when the rival *Star* boasted of the famous guest authors that it would pay to cover the 1927 World Series—"ghostwriting" being a common practice at the time—Povich planted an advertisement in the *Post* touting its coverage of the event with actual sportswriters and featuring the headline REACH FOR A POST INSTEAD OF A GHOST.

A religious man who postponed his first train ride and skipped a game of the 1955 World Series because both fell on Yom Kippur, Povich delayed his marriage to Ethyl Friedman for a year, until February 1932, because he was in mourning following his father's death. The couple had three children, one of whom,

Maury Povich, became a controversial television personality often seen as a scandal-monger.

Povich stepped down as sports editor in 1933. During the course of his long career, he reported on some of the most notable events in the history of sports, including the Jack Dempsey-Gene Tunney "long count" heavyweight championship fight in 1927, Babe Ruth's famous "called home run" in the 1932 World Series (according to Povich, the story was a myth), Lou Gehrig's retirement at Yankee Stadium (1939), and Don Larsen's perfect game in the 1956 World Series. All told, he attended sixty World Series and twenty Super Bowls. In addition to writing his column, he covered the Senators for many years. As a columnist, his opinions occasionally drew the ire of Senators' owner Clark Calvin Griffith and his son Clark, who later moved the Senators to Minnesota, and (still later) Bob Short, who owned the reincarnated, expansion Washington Senators before relocating the franchise to Texas.

Povich encountered even greater controversy in his relationship with Washington Redskins owner George Preston Marshall. In 1942 Povich accused Marshall of pocketing an inappropriate share of the gate receipts of a charity football game played for the benefit of World War II orphans and widows. Marshall sued for libel but lost to Povich and the *Post* in court. Sensitized to the race issue after following boxer Joe Louis's career, Povich also badgered Marshall regarding the Redskins' racial policies. When the Cleveland Browns were led by their African-American star, Jim Brown, to a victory over the Redskins, Povich wrote, "Jim Brown, born ineligible to play for the Washington Redskins, integrated their end zone three times yesterday." He also took baseball to task regarding its whites-only policy. After covering Negro league spring training in 1941, he noted that the big leagues were missing out on "a couple of million dollars worth of talent. . . . They happen to be colored. [T]hat's their crime in the eyes of the big-league club owners."

Having persistently nagged his editor for the opportunity, Povich was sent to the Pacific in 1945 as a war correspondent. There, he covered the U.S. Marines and returned to the United States near the conclusion of the baseball season. In the postwar era he received numerous awards and honors, including the National Headliners Award (1947), the presidency of the Baseball Writers Association of America (1956), the E. P. Duttin prize (1957), the Grantland Rice Award (1964), the J. G. Spink Award (1976), and the Red Smith Award (1983). Winning the Spink award also placed Povich in the Sportswriters Wing of the Baseball Hall of Fame.

Although he officially retired in 1974, Povich remained active. He continued to write his column, taught at American University, and served on the Veterans Committee of the Baseball Hall of Fame, which gave previously overlooked old-time ballplayers another shot at membership in Cooperstown. Beloved by his colleagues—Ben Bradlee, former executive editor of the *Post*, once stated that "he was the sports section. For a lot of years, he carried the paper, and that's no exaggeration"—he was also regularly read by individuals (such as Dwight Eisenhower and Richard Nixon) who otherwise found the *Post* politically unpalatable. He died in Washington, D.C.

Although always critical of his work, Shirley Povich left behind a solid legacy of memorable sportswriting. In addition, his talent attracted levels of readership that helped make the *Washington Post* the dominant paper in the nation's capital, while his forthright statements on race made a genuine difference in the struggle for civil rights in the world of sports.

• Povich was the author of *The Washington Senators* (1954). His autobiography, *All These Mornings*, was published in 1969. He was also the subject of interviews in Jerome Holtzman, *No Cheering in the Press Box* (1974; rev. ed., 1995), and Dave Kindred, "Yes, Virginia, Baseball Should Expand," *Sporting News*, 21 Nov. 1994. Obituaries are in the *Washington Post*, 5 June 1998, and the *New York Times*, 7 June 1998.
EDWARD L. LACH, JR.

POWELL, Dawn (28 Nov. 1896–15 Nov. 1965), writer, was born in Mount Gilead, Ohio, to Roy K. Powell and Hattie Sherman Powell. (Later in life Dawn Powell insisted that the year of her birth was 1897, and this is the date that appears in most reference works, but her official biographer, Tim Page, has confirmed that 1896 is correct.) Her father, charming but feckless, held a series of jobs in area mills before settling into the life of an itinerant salesman, peddling everything from cookies to coffins, after Dawn and her two sisters were born. Following the death of their mother in 1903, the children were cared for by various relatives in villages and farms in the region. When Roy Powell eventually remarried six years later, the children joined him at his new wife's farm near Cleveland. But the life they found there was no better: the second Mrs. Powell proved to be a stereotypically mean stepmother, punishing them severely and subjecting them to endless humiliation. She was especially scornful of Dawn's attempts to write poems and short stories, burning every piece of writing that the child produced.

After more than a year of enduring the situation, Dawn Powell ran away to an aunt's house in Shelby, Ohio, where she was able to attend high school. Her aunt, who worked as a buyer for a major department store in Cleveland and had sophisticated tastes, recognized that Dawn was a thoughtful, gifted child and encouraged her interest in books and writing. With the help of her aunt, Dawn Powell entered Lake Erie College upon graduation from high school in 1914. There she was active in dramatics, edited the college magazine, and earned a bachelor's degree in literature in 1918. She immediately joined the naval reserve as a yeomanette, but after only a few months of service she decided to move to New York City to pursue a writing career, again with the encouragement of her aunt.

In New York Powell found work as a publicist for several organizations, including the Inter-Church World Movement. There she met an advertising executive named Joseph R. Gousha, and the couple were married in 1920. They settled in Greenwich Village, where Dawn Powell would live for the rest of her life, and had one son, born in 1921. The son, who may have suffered brain damage at birth, was exhibiting severe emotional problems by the age of three. Powell and her husband cared for him themselves, educating him at home, until it became impossible for Powell to handle the situation; he was ultimately institutionalized as an adult.

Powell's marriage had enabled her to quit her job as a publicist and devote herself to her own writing, and despite the upheaval caused first by her son's condition and then by her husband's alcoholism, she began to produce fiction, using the Children's Reading Room of the New York Public Library on Fifth Avenue as the place to write. What became the classic elements of Dawn Powell's work were in evidence from the outset. Her first novel, *Whither*, published in 1925, has the characteristic satiric tone, mordant wit, and unforgiving eye for the foibles of middle-class Americans, whether they lived in the Middle West, the setting for her early work, or were newly arrived midwestern émigrés to the big city of New York desperately seeking sophistication.

Fifteen more novels followed over the next thirty-seven years; her last, published in 1962, was *The Golden Spur*. Considered literary rather than popular novels and published by well-established and eminently respectable houses—Farrar and Rinehart, Scribner's, Houghton Mifflin, Viking—many of them received respectful critical notices. Her last novel even earned a favorable review in the *New Yorker* by the eminent Edmund Wilson, who pronounced her on a par with the British writers Evelyn Waugh, Anthony Powell, and Muriel Spark. None of her books, however, were widely read, and by the time of her death all were out of print. Thus to call her a forgotten writer misses the point: during her lifetime she had never been widely recognized. Though Powell's tart gifts earned her praise from the New York literati, they could never command a readership among most of her contemporaries: she was simply not a writer with whom even the most sophisticated readers could feel entirely comfortable. Her comic but ultimately lethal acerbity was simply too off-putting in the early and middle decades of the twentieth century. As the century drew to a close, with irony the watchword of its final decade, it was perhaps not surprising that Dawn Powell began to be discovered and applauded on a larger stage.

Powell seemed to be unhindered by her failure and by her family difficulties. She saw herself as a latter-day Petronius, the scathingly witty Roman writer, and the body of her work as a modern equivalent of his *Satyricon*. Though she suffered through periods of suicidal despair, she possessed a seemingly heroic ability to enjoy life despite its vicissitudes. She had a wide circle of friends and admirers, as well as a long-time lover, and when none of them were around she found diverse interests to keep her occupied, including jazz and modern music, and retained an appealing ability to see the quirky humor in almost every human undertaking. She was also a fan of radio crime dramas. In addition to her novels, she wrote ten plays, only one of which was published, and as many as a hundred short stories, a small collection of which was published as *Sunday, Monday and Always* in 1952.

Powell's health had begun to fail by the late 1950s, and not long after her husband's death in 1962 she was diagnosed with cancer. She was in and out of hospitals in Manhattan before finally succumbing to the illness. Her body was willed to the Cornell Medical Center, but a series of mixups prevented its return to her family in Ohio for final burial. Five years after her death, she was finally interred—in the New York City Cemetery on Hart Island, the final resting place of the city's unwanted and unclaimed dead. It was an ironic end that Powell herself would undoubtedly have appreciated.

The slow "resurrection" of Dawn Powell began in the fall of 1987, with the publication of a long, appreciative essay by Gore Vidal in the *New York Review of Books* and the subsequent reprinting over the next few years of four of her major novels: *The Golden Spur*; *Angels on Toast*, originally published in 1940; *The Locusts Have No King*, which first appeared in 1948; and *The Wicked Pavilion*, first published in 1954. All are quintessential Powell, peopled with comic New Yorker wannabes looking for both a fast buck and social cachet and animated by ultimately heartbreaking delusions. During the 1990s nearly all of her novels came back into print in paperback form, and their widespread distribution, together with their inclusion on many college reading lists, and the publication of her diaries and letters and a major biography seemed to guarantee an enduring recognition and readership denied to Powell during her lifetime.

• The Dawn Powell Collection at the Columbia University Library is the repository of her papers. The most accurate source of biographical information on Powell is Tim Page's biography, *Dawn Powell*, published in 1998. Powell's largely autobiographical novel, *My Home Is Far Away*, first published in 1944 and reprinted in 1995, gives an even more focused insight into her early years. See also Tim Page, ed., *The Diaries of Dawn Powell, 1931–1965* (1995), and *Selected Letters of Dawn Powell, 1913–1965* (1999). For appreciations of her work, see especially Gore Vidal, "Dawn Powell: The American Writer," *New York Review of Books*, 5 Nov. 1987, and Edmund Wilson, "Dawn Powell: Greenwich Village in the Fifties," *New Yorker*, 17 Nov. 1962. An obituary appears in the *New York Times*, 16 Nov. 1965.

ANN T. KEENE

POWELL, Lewis F., Jr. (19 Nov. 1907–25 Aug. 1998), Supreme Court justice, was born Lewis Franklin Powell, Jr., the son of Lewis Franklin Powell and Mary Lewis Gwathmey Powell, in Suffolk, Virginia,

but spent most of his life in Richmond. The descendant of one of the original Jamestown settlers, Powell graduated from McGuire's University School in 1925, then attended the college of Washington and Lee University, where he was manager of the football team, managing editor of the student newspaper, and student body president, while also compiling an outstanding academic record. Following graduation and election to Phi Beta Kappa in 1929, he remained at Washington and Lee for law school, earning an LL.B. and admission to the Virginia bar in 1931. Delaying law practice for a year, Powell received a master of law degree at Harvard, where his professors included Felix Frankfurter and Roscoe Pound.

On returning to Virginia, Powell practiced law for two years in a Richmond firm, then began a long association with what is now Hunton and Williams, one of the city's most distinguished firms. Becoming a partner in 1938, he combined trial practice with representation of a variety of large commercial interests, serving as a director in eleven major corporations, including Philip Morris. He also became a pillar of Richmond's civic and social life. (In 1936 he married Josephine Pierce Rucker, with whom he was to have three daughters and a son.) During World War II, he served in the U.S. Army Air Forces, rising to the rank of full colonel and serving as a combat and intelligence officer in Europe and North Africa. After the war, he resumed his active law practice and took on a variety of public service commitments—for example, chairing the commission that drafted the charter for Richmond's conversion to the city manager form of government and becoming president of the local chamber of commerce.

Powell performed his most significant public service during that period, however, as chairman of the Richmond school board from 1952 to 1961. Refusing to embrace massive resistance to school desegregation, Powell pursued a moderate course, overseeing without incident the admission of black students to formerly all-white Richmond schools. As a director of Miller & Rhodes, Richmond's largest department store, he also played a role in its decision to integrate its dining room before it became a target of sit-in demonstrations. Powell was hardly a racial liberal; on one occasion, in fact, a federal appeals court concluded that some of the school board's decisions during his stewardship helped to perpetuate segregation. He was also a member of all-white private clubs; and, at the time of his Supreme Court appointment, his law firm had never hired a black attorney. Even so, he was far more progressive than many of his contemporaries. Powell also rose to national prominence in the activities of his profession, holding a variety of positions before being elected president of the American Bar Association (ABA) for the 1964–1965 term. He worked tirelessly, moreover, in behalf of government-financed legal services for the poor.

When Justice Hugo L. Black of Alabama retired and died in the fall of 1971, Powell's superb professional credentials and southern roots made him an excellent prospect for a U.S. Supreme Court appointment. President Richard Nixon was no doubt impressed, too, with the Virginia native's generally conservative position on wiretapping, his fear that civil rights and antiwar protests could degenerate into violence, and his concern that the Warren Court had placed an undue emphasis on the rights of criminal defendants—the very sorts of considerations that had prompted the president to replace Chief Justice Earl Warren with Warren Burger two years earlier.

Whatever Nixon's motivation, his nomination of Powell on 21 October 1971 to fill Justice Black's seat was warmly received. Under other circumstances, the ABA might have been concerned about the nominee's advanced age (sixty-four at the time of his nomination). But it could hardly oppose one of its former national presidents, and its judiciary committee termed Powell "the best person available." Following a cursory hearing, the Senate Judiciary Committee unanimously endorsed the nomination. On 6 December the full Senate concurred 89–1, making Powell the first justice from Virginia since Reconstruction. Justice Powell would serve on the high court through its 1986–1987 term. As a justice he generally assumed the same sort of cautious, moderate stance he had followed as chairman of the Richmond board of education—a position that, combined with his considerable leadership skills and powers of persuasion, made him the most influential justice of the Burger era.

Powell's moderate, pragmatic jurisprudence at times resulted in his becoming the classic pivotal vote on controversial issues facing the Court. In *Regents of the University of California v. Bakke* (1978), the Court's first ruling on a challenge to an affirmative action program, the justice provided the fifth vote for holding a challenged university racial admissions quota invalid, but he also joined four other justices in approving the use of race and other "non-merit" factors to secure a diverse student body. Earlier, when the Court confronted the jury unanimity issue in *Apodaca v. Oregon* (1972), Powell also cast the pivotal vote. Faithful to precedent, he agreed that federal juries must continue to issue unanimous verdicts. But he was unwilling to embrace the thesis that the Fourteenth Amendment's due process clause imposed the same procedural standards on states that the Court required of federal proceedings under the Bill of Rights. He thus concluded that nonunanimous state jury verdicts satisfied the Fourteenth Amendment's more flexible due process standard. While Powell joined the 5–4 majority opinion in *Branzburg v. Hayes* (1972), rejecting a First Amendment privilege exempting newspersons from grand jury testimony, he suggested in a separate opinion that judges should weigh competing press and prosecutorial interests to determine whether a media subpoena should prevail in a given case—a stance that led some to conclude the *Branzburg* vote was 4½–4½ rather than 5–4.

Powell developed a mixed record in other areas as well. A leader in the Burger Court campaign to curtail litigant access to the federal judiciary, he harshly criticized the Warren Court's decision in *Flast v. Cohen* (1968), which granted litigants the ability to challenge federal spending programs under certain circumstances merely on the basis of the injury they suffered as federal taxpayers. In *United States v. Richardson* (1974), the justice not only joined the Court in rejecting a taxpayer challenge to secret congressional funding of the CIA but also filed a concurrence urging the Court to limit *Flast* to its facts and warning of the dangers inherent in allowing litigants to air broad policy issues in the courts rather than in the legislative arena. Powell also joined the Court in limiting application of the Fourth Amendment exclusionary rule and the warnings that police are required to give suspects under *Miranda v. Arizona* (1966). In *Stone v. Powell* (1976), for example, the justice held for a majority that state defendants given a full and fair opportunity to raise illegal search and seizure issues in the state courts cannot raise such claims in a federal habeas corpus suit. The justice was also generally reluctant to expand the scope of unenumerated rights extending constitutional protection or to enlarge beyond race and related factors the "suspect" or "quasi-suspect" classifications subjected to strict judicial scrutiny under the equal protection guarantee.

At the same time, Powell joined *Roe v. Wade* (1973) and also spoke for the Court in *Moore v. East Cleveland* (1977), favoring familial rights over a local zoning regulation. Although late in his career he joined a 5–4 majority in *Bowers v. Hardwick* (1986) upholding state authority over homosexual sodomy, he found the case troubling, later telling a law school audience his *Bowers* vote was probably a "mistake." In certain other civil liberties fields, he also assumed a liberal stance. He defended, for example, the controversial construction of the religious establishment clause the Court adopted in *Lemon v. Kurtzman* (1971), under which laws affecting religion were declared unconstitutional unless they had a secular purpose, a primary effect that neither advanced nor harmed religion and did not create an excessive entanglement between church and state.

Justice Powell retired in 1987, at the end of Chief Justice Rehnquist's first term in the Court's center seat. For a number of years following his retirement, he remained quite active, sitting on various court of appeals panels, chairing a committee on the use of habeas corpus proceedings in death penalty cases, and lecturing. As his health gradually declined, his pace slowed. In 1996 his wife, Josephine, died. In 1998 he died at his home in Richmond.

• The Lewis F. Powell, Jr., papers are on file in the law school at Washington and Lee University. For an outstanding biography and analysis of the justice's involvement in important cases, see John C. Jeffries, Jr., *Justice Lewis F. Powell, Jr.* (1994); Jeffries clerked for Powell. An obituary is in the *New York Times*, 26 Aug. 1998.

TINSLEY E. YARBROUGH

PRATT, Wallace E. (15 Mar. 1885–25 Dec. 1981), petroleum geologist and conservationist, was born

Wallace Everette Pratt in Phillipsburg, Kansas, the son of William H. and Olive Bostetter Pratt. As a boy Wallace began to take an interest in geology with a particular fascination for granite. When he was ready for college, he chose the University of Kansas in Lawrence, where he enrolled in 1903. Soon after his arrival, Pratt obtained a job as a night clerk at the New Eldridge House, for which duties he received free room and board. In 1905, while still studying at the university, Pratt began working for the Kansas University Geological Survey, testing rock samples and analyzing cement materials.

Pratt acquired four degrees from the University of Kansas: a B.A. in geology (this degree required a grounding in the humanities) and a B.S. in science in 1908; an M.A. in geology in 1909; and an engineer of mines degree in 1914. As early as 1909, however, Pratt took a job in the Philippines, where he worked until 1915 as a geologist for that country's Bureau of Science.

Pratt then found employment in the U.S. oil business. In 1916 he began work as a geologist for the Texas Company (Texaco), and in 1918 he found a new job as chief geologist for the Humble Oil & Refining Company, of which he became a director in 1924 and a vice president in 1930. In 1937 Pratt resigned his positions with Humble Oil to become a vice president and executive committee member with the Standard Oil Company of New Jersey, headquartered in New York City. He retired from Standard Oil in 1945, at which time he and his second wife built a small house in McKittrick Canyon, just east of the Guadalupe Mountains in West Texas.

Pratt was married three times. With his first wife, Pearl M. Stuckey, whom he married on 30 December 1912, he had three children. After Pearl died, he married Iris Calderhead on 3 January 1941. When she died some twenty-four years later, after they had left McKittrick Canyon for Tucson, Arizona, Pratt married Suzanne d'Autremont on 4 November 1966.

During the time Pratt lived at McKittrick Canyon, he worked as a consulting geologist. To reach his consulting business at Carlsbad, New Mexico, sixty-five miles from McKittrick Canyon, he flew his own two-seater plane. Pratt, it should be added, loved flying this open cockpit plane, which he continued to do until the age of eighty.

Petroleum geology was coming of age by the time Pratt had reached his mid-twenties. In 1917, for instance, the Southwestern Association of Petroleum Geologists was formed and then became the American Association of Petroleum Geologists the next year. A founding member in 1917, Pratt was the organization's fourth president in 1920.

Early in his career Pratt demonstrated an uncanny ability to find oil, if not gas. In 1921 he convinced Humble Oil to invest $400,000 for prospecting near Mexia in East Texas. The company had leased land in the vicinity, and Pratt—unlike other geologists, who favored drilling on the eastern edge of this block of leases—predicted oil was to be found along the western edge. His geological acumen was borne out: of the 180 wells drilled there, 175 produced oil.

Just as remarkable were his predictions for the huge King Ranch, where practically no one, except Pratt, believed oil and gas to exist. He proceeded to lease the land on the ranch in a campaign lasting fifteen years. Drilling once again confirmed Pratt's faith in a prospect: there came a time when the King Ranch had more than 600 producing oil and gas wells, in addition to having the world's largest natural gas processing plant.

Pratt's geological acumen in prospecting for oil and gas, especially the former, stemmed from his sound training and experience. As a student at the University of Kansas he worked closely with Erasmus Haworth, at that time the head of both the Department of Geology and the Kansas University Geological Survey. Then, in 1916, while working for the Texas Company, Pratt was sent to Mexico by the company's chief geologist, Elmer Grant Woodruff. There, for a year, Pratt learned much from the mapping of structures and from studies of the surface geology.

Pratt put his knowledge and geological hunches to good use. He was one of the first petroleum geologists to recommend drilling along fault lines, like the one near Mexia, referred to above. No later than the early 1940s he also saw the need to search for oil and gas with less emphasis on structure, particularly anticlines. In 1942 Pratt summarized four principles for guidance in prospecting: search in the deep parts of depositional basins at a distance from any anticlines located along the margins; drill near subsurface strata composed of marine organic shales or limestones; search along unconformities (associated with ancient erosion surfaces between some rock beds); and drill in relatively undeformed strata in the central portions of huge depositional basins.

Early in his career Pratt also became an ardent conservationist. He advocated the wide spacing of wells to limit the loss of gas in the oil reservoir, gas being needed for the expelling of crude from beneath the surface. The flaring of gas from wells, which was common in his day, was to Pratt a deplorable practice. To protect the environment he sought controls on water pollution by tankers and refineries.

Pratt's greatest contribution to the cause of conservation, though, concerned McKittrick Canyon and its environs. Over a period of many years, beginning in 1921, he purchased 5,632 acres in the canyon; he then proposed to donate all of it to the National Park Service if the federal government would acquire much of the surrounding land for a national park. The government acted on his proposal, buying 72,000 acres in the nearby Guadalupe Mountains. True to his promise, Pratt then deeded McKittrick Canyon to the federal government in 1961, which, with the other acreage, became the new Guadalupe Mountain National Park. It opened to the public in 1972.

Pratt wrote more than 100 geological papers, but he reached a wider audience than fellow petroleum geologists usually managed to do. His *Oil in the Earth*

(1942; 2d ed., 1944), derived in large part from four lectures he delivered in March 1941 to geology students at the University of Kansas, made the fundamentals of petroleum geology and the accomplishments of American oil-finding readily understandable to nongeologists. Pratt again reached a wide readership among intelligent lay readers with "Oil Fields in the Arctic," published in the January 1944 issue of *Harper's Magazine*. In this article he foresaw the finding of oil along the northern shores of Siberia, Alaska, and Canada, and he pinpointed the vicinity of Cape Simpson on the Arctic coast of Alaska's North Slope as a promising place for oil to be found. That geological hunch proved correct with the discovery in 1968 of the prolific Prudhoe Bay field, located about 200 miles east of Cape Simpson.

Several of Pratt's honors bear mention. In 1945 the American Association of Petroleum Geologists made Pratt the first recipient of its highest honor, the Sidney Powers Memorial Medal for distinguished service. In 1948 the American Institute of Mining and Metallurgical Engineers awarded him the Anthony F. Lucas Gold Medal for the art of petroleum exploration. In 1950 Columbia University gave Pratt the James Furman Kemp Medal for distinguished service to mankind in the field of geology. And in 1969 he was elected to the Permian Basin Hall of Fame as one of only twelve pioneers in petroleum prospecting initially selected.

Pratt died in Tucson; he was survived by his third wife and the three children by his first marriage.

• The Kansas Collection of the Kenneth Spencer Research Library at the University of Kansas, along with the University Archives, has much material on Wallace E. Pratt. His papers there amount to approximately fifteen linear feet, including, among other things, correspondence, diaries, photographs, and records of professional associations. Secondary sources of value include the following: *University of Kansas Alumni Magazine* 58 (Nov. 1959): 8; Keith Elliott, "Petroleum Pioneer Pratt," *Graduate Magazine of the University of Kansas* 69 (May 1971): 20–21; and W. L. Copithorne, "The Worlds of Wallace Pratt," *The Lamp* (published by Standard Oil), Fall 1971, pp. 11–15. For a brief obituary, see the *Graduate Magazine of the University of Kansas* 80 (Feb. 1982): 17.

KEITH L. MILLER

PURCELL, Charles H. (27 Jan. 1883–7 Sept. 1951), civil engineer and highway executive, was born Charles Henry Purcell in North Bend, Nebraska, a son of John Purcell, a grain merchant, and Mary Gillis. Despite his father's untimely death, the family remained in North Bend, where Charles attended the public schools, and was among only four graduates in 1900. Indecision about his future after one year at the University of Nebraska led him to Chicago the following year, where he was employed by the Bemis Bag Company and later the Grain Pit. After studying structural engineering at Stanford University for one semester, he transferred to the University of Nebraska in February 1903 following his mother's death. He studied at the university's Industrial College under such distinguished professors as DeWitt B. Brace, Charles R. Richards, and Oscar Van Pelt. During weekends and vacations he was a draftsman for the Burlington Railroad.

After receiving his bachelor's degree in 1906, Purcell spent most of his early career in the Pacific Northwest. As resident engineer with the Union Pacific Railroad in Wyoming, he built his first bridge: a 200-foot-long steel girder, concrete foundation structure over Bitter Creek. He then was design engineer for Nevada Consolidation Copper Company, followed by two and a half years as principal assistant chief engineer at the Cerro de Pasco mines in Peru, South America. After brief stints in California and Washington, he moved in 1911 to Portland, Oregon, where he built concrete bridges for a Columbia River logging railroad despite opposition from the builders of iron bridges. Two years later, he became the first bridge engineer of the newly organized Oregon State Highway Department; after promotion to assistant state highway engineer, he designed and constructed in Jackson County the state's first paved highway. In 1915 he was dismissed for exposing excessive bridge costs, but promptly became bridge engineer for Multnomah County and its Columbia River Highway Project, where his 170-foot-long concrete arch bridge across Moffett Creek gained the attention of engineers nationwide. After becoming bridge engineer in 1918 for the U.S. Bureau of Public Roads, he was promoted two years later to district engineer, supervising the expenditure of federal funds for national forest, park highway, and bridge work in Oregon, Washington, Montana, northern Idaho, and Alaska.

In 1928 Purcell took the position of California State Highway Engineer and was responsible for the proposed San Francisco-Oakland Bay Bridge, the first ever to cross San Francisco Bay. As a member of the newly created Bay Bridge Commission, he prepared preliminary plans and a design, was appointed chief engineer, and, assisted by President Herbert Hoover and others, secured the $77 million necessary. After a construction period of three and a half years, the 8.25-mile-long double deck structure opened ahead of schedule in November 1936, six months before the Golden Gate Bridge opened in May 1937.

The western portion of the Bay Bridge—from San Francisco to Yerba Buena Island—consists of four towers and two main suspension spans joined end to end and connected with a massive central anchorage. It crosses Yerba Buena Island through a 540-foot-long bore tunnel, and the eastern span to Oakland consists of one 1400-foot-long cantilever span and a series of through and deck trusses. An unprecedented feature is the depth of the central anchorage, a 500-foot-tall structure, 220 feet of which lie below the surface of the water. It is the world's largest pier. Another is the huge caisson, codesigned by Purcell and Daniel E. Moran, which was floated into position and sunk in 100 feet of water, in spite of swift tidal currents, and then another 120 feet of silt to bedrock below the bay.

The 51 piers that form the underwater foundation of the entire bridge are another unique feature. In November 1955 the American Society of Civil Engineers (ASCE) selected the Bay Bridge as one of the seven modern civil engineering wonders of the United States, making it the first bridge in the nation to receive the ASCE designation. Because of earthquake damage in 1989, the eastern span was scheduled for replacement, but little more than seismic retrofitting was needed for the western span, the world's only twin suspension bridge.

As State Highway Engineer, and later Director of Public Works under Governor Earl Warren, he also transformed the California State Highway system from 4,800 miles of rural main roads in 1928 into 14,000 miles of vastly improved rural and urban highways by 1950, including 630 miles of metropolitan freeways and the world's first four-level interchange, opened in 1953 in Los Angeles. By making the state's first commitment to modern freeway construction, which resulted in 1940 in the completion of the Arroyo Seco Parkway (now Pasadena Freeway), called "the first freeway in the West," and by brokering a compromise among his various constituencies, Purcell established California as a pioneer in metropolitan freeway development that anticipated interstate highway design standards by at least a decade. And he championed A. D. Edmonston's plan for construction of the California Aqueduct to transport Feather River water to the southern area of the state, which the California legislature approved in 1951, and voters funded in 1959.

Elsewhere, Purcell was from 1928 to 1951 a member of the Executive Committee of the American Association of State Highway Officials (AASHO), which worked closely with the U.S. Bureau of Public Roads (now Federal Highway Administration), and in 1937 he was appointed by U.S. Secretary of Agriculture Henry A. Wallace to the twelve-person Committee on Planning and Design Policies, whose recommendations on maximum safety and highway utility became, in effect, the national design policy for the United States. He was also the U.S. representative on the Permanent International Commission of the Permanent International Association of Road Congresses. And in 1941 he was selected by President Franklin Delano Roosevelt to serve on a seven-man National Interregional Highway Committee, whose final report in 1944 influenced Congress that year to authorize the establishment of a national system of interstate highways. Called the Eisenhower Interstate System, now comprising more than 42,000 miles, it was included in the 1994 update of the ASCE's list of the seven modern civil engineering wonders of the United States.

Purcell's major recognition included honorary degrees of Doctor of Engineering in 1935 from the University of Nebraska, his alma mater, and Doctor of Laws in 1937 from the University of California at Berkeley. He received the George S. Bartlett Award in 1944 from AASHO and other highway organizations for his contribution to highway progress. And the

ASCE elected him an honorary member in 1945, its most distinctive individual recognition (between 1853 and 1998 only 494 of its more than 100,000 members were accorded this honor). He died in Sacramento only five weeks after retirement from a 45-year career as one of the nation's great bridge builders and highway authorities. Surviving was Minnie Pullen, whom he married in 1914. There were no children.

• Materials on Purcell are housed in the California Department of Public Works Division of Highways Collection at the California State Archives and in the California Department of Transportation Library at Sacramento. For reliable accounts of the Bay Bridge, see *Engineering News-Record*, 20 Oct. 1932, 19 Oct. 1933, 22 Mar., 5 Apr., and 23 Aug. 1934, and 26 Nov. 1936. Assessments of Purcell's accomplishments are in J. Kip Finch, "Seven Modern Wonders Named," *Civil Engineering* (Nov. 1955): 33–45; Henry Petroski, *Engineers of Dreams: Great Bridge Builders and the Spanning of America* (1995); and a video originally presented on the Arts and Entertainment History Channel, "The Great Bridge, Eight Miles of Steel: The San Francisco-Oakland Bay Bridge" (1998), VH 42219. For insights into Purcell's role in highway development, see his "Annual Convention Address," *American Highways* (Jan. 1939): 1–5; Federal Highway Administration, *America's Highways 1776–1976* (1977); Bruce Seely, *Building the American Highway System: Engineers as Policy Makers* (1987); and David W. Jones, Jr., *California's Freeway Era in Historical Perspective* (1989). A biography with national tributes upon Purcell's retirement is in *California Highways and Public Works* (July/Aug. 1951): 1–4. The most comprehensive biographical article is E. A. Kral, "Charles H. Purcell: A Civil Engineering Immortal," *Wilber* [Nebraska] *Republican*, 2 June 1999. An obituary is in the *San Francisco Chronicle*, 8 Sep. 1951.

E. A. KRAL

PUZO, Mario (15 Oct. 1920–2 July 1999), author, was born near 30th Street and 10th Avenue, in the Hell's Kitchen section of New York City, the son of Antonio Puzo and Maria Le Conti Puzo, immigrants from Naples. Employed by the New York Central Railroad, his father was a track laborer whose behavior became increasingly erratic. Eventually he was diagnosed as a schizophrenic and was institutionalized for the remainder of his life, leaving his wife to care for seven children.

Puzo, who grew up in a family that he described as the "poorest of the poor," was possessed by "every desire to go wrong." That he avoided gangs and delinquency can be attributed, in good measure, to the formidable Italian family structure. He never came home from school or play to an empty house, since his mother or sister was there to greet him—or to chastise or punish him if necessary (*Godfather Papers*, p. 17). As Puzo remarked once, "I was raised by my mother and sister" (*New York Times*, 8 May 1997).

It was assumed by his mother that her son would go to work for the railroad, as had his father and other family members. But Puzo had a very different ambition; he wanted to be a writer, a goal his mother, who was illiterate, never understood. Puzo "escaped" from his mother by joining the Hudson Guild Settlement House (located on West 27th Street). He spent some "of the most exciting days" of his life at the Hudson Guild, where he played basketball and baseball, became captain of the football team, and for five successive years was elected president of a sports club called the Star Club, an honor he especially prized. An avid reader, he also availed himself of the Settlement House library. Each summer, too, the Guild arranged for him, as a Fresh Air Fund child, to be sent to a farm in New Hampshire. (The Fresh Air Fund remains a charity in New York City aimed at giving poor children a summer respite from urban life.) Puzo was to recall that this experience made him "happier than I have been before or since" (*Godfather Papers*, pp. 19–20).

The happy days of summer ended abruptly when at age fifteen Puzo became too old to be a Fresh Air Fund youngster. He then got a job as a messenger in the railroad freight office to help support his family. And at eighteen, having graduated from Commerce High School, he went to work full time as a switchboard attendant for the railroad. He "hated his life" and felt trapped, as he wrote, by "the steady job, the nice girl who would eventually get knocked up, and then by marriage and fighting over counting pennies to make ends meet" (*The Godfather Papers*, p. 29). His plan of becoming a writer seemed, at this point, fanciful indeed. The entry of the United States into World War II, however, "delivered" him from his mother, family, and girlfriend. He made an "innocent getaway" by joining the army (*Godfather Papers*, pp. 25–26). Initially rated 4F because of poor eyesight, he was accepted into the service on 15 July 1942. With the Fourth Armored Division, he was assigned to the military government of captured French towns and finished military service on 7 December 1945 never having fired a shot.

After the war Puzo worked as a public relations officer with the U.S. Air Force, and in 1946 he married Erika Lina Broske. When he returned to the United States in the late 1940s he took a job in New York as a government clerk. In the evenings he attended writing classes at the New School for Social Research and Columbia University on the GI Bill. In 1955 he published his first novel, *The Dark Arena*, which dealt with a World War II veteran who returned to Germany to find his former mistress. In 1960 Puzo was hired by Bruce Jay Friedman as an assistant editor for a group of men's magazines. He also contributed action stories for the magazines.

In 1964 Puzo published *The Fortunate Pilgrim*, an autobiographical novel. The book recounted the story of a poor Italian immigrant family in the late 1920s and 1930s living on Manhattan's West Side. The central character is Lucia Santa, an angry, strong-willed matriarch, who guides her family through economic adversity, emotional tumult, madness, and death. The novel was praised in the *New York Times* as a "small classic, lifted into literature by its highly charged language, penetrating insights and the mixture of tenderness and rage" (*New York Times Book Review*, 31

January 1965). Despite outstanding reviews, *The Fortunate Pilgrim* earned Puzo only $3,000. With a family to support and deeply in debt to relatives, banks, and bookmakers, he decided to abandon "art" and write a "commercial" novel (*Godfather Papers*, p. 34). During the roughly three years he worked on the book, Puzo met expenses by writing adventure stories, a children's book (*The Runaway Summer of Davie Shaw*, published in 1966), and magazine articles. The resulting novel, *The Godfather* (1969), which has to do with the rise to power of Don Vito Corleone, a Mafia chieftain, and his family, found favor with most critics. *Newsweek* on 10 March 1969, for example, described Puzo as an "extremely talented story teller," who had written a "valid and fascinating portrait of America's most powerful and least understood subculture, the Mafia." The novel rapidly ascended the *New York Times* bestseller list and remained there for sixty-seven weeks.

The paperback book rights to the novel were sold for $410,000, of which Puzo received half. He sold the film rights for $85,000, and for another $100,000 he agreed to go to Hollywood to adapt the book to the screen. Francis Ford Coppola assisted in composing the screenplay and directed the movie, which was released in 1972. More popular than the book, the film grossed $60 million, at the time a huge sum. At the Academy Awards ceremony in 1973, *The Godfather* won three Oscars, including ones for best picture and screenplay.

Puzo, again joined by Coppola, wrote the screenplays for *The Godfather Part II* (1974), which won an Oscar for best picture, and for *The Godfather Part III*. His other credits as a screenwriter include *Earthquake* and *Superman* (1978). At the same time Puzo continued to practice his craft as a novelist, writing *Fools Die* (1978), *The Sicilian* (1984), *The Fourth K* (1990), and *The Last Don* (1996). *Omerta* was published posthumously in 2000. In 1977 he also wrote a nonfiction volume, *Inside Las Vegas*. Puzo died at his Bay Shore, Long Island, home.

From a critical perspective, Puzo's reputation rests solidly on *The Fortunate Pilgrim*. In "its legend, force, insight, language, authenticity, and persuasion," writes Rose Basile Green, *The Fortunate Pilgrim* "is good enough to be the classic Italian-American novel and an important milestone in the mainstream of American literature" (*The Italian-American Novel*, p. 351).

In the realm of popular culture, however, Puzo's name will always be linked with *The Godfather*, which outsold every other novel of the 1970s. And in 1998, when the American Film Institute announced the hundred best American movies of the previous century, *The Godfather* was third on the list and *The Godfather Part II* earned the thirty-fourth place. Puzo's famous Mafia family has engendered numerous imitators, including such films as *Our Family Honor* (1985), *Married to the Mob* (1988), *Cookie* (1989), and *The Freshman* (1990), as well as the highly acclaimed television series "The Sopranos."

• Puzo's papers remain in the possession of his family. Although far from a full-fledged autobiography, *The Godfather Papers and Other Confessions* (1972) does provide information unavailable from other sources on Puzo's early years and his Hollywood experience. Camille Paglia's interview with Puzo in the *New York Times* of 8 May 1997 is especially helpful in understanding his career. An earlier interview worth consulting is in *Publishers Weekly*, 12 July 1978. A small cottage industry of literary criticism has grown up around *The Godfather*. Among the best is Marianna De Mario Torguvnick, "*The Godfather* As the World's Most Typical Novel," *South Atlantic Quarterly* 87 (Spring 1988): 329–53. For more on *The Fortunate Pilgrim*, see Rose Basile Green, *The Italian-American Novel: A Document of the Interaction of Two Cultures* (1973). The fullest obituary is in the *New York Times*, 3 July 1999, but several other obituaries are also informative, including those in the *London Daily Telegraph*, 5 July 1999, and the *Los Angeles Times*, 3 July 1999.

RICHARD HARMOND

Q

QUINTERO, José (15 Oct. 1924–26 Feb. 1999), theatrical director and teacher, was born José Quintero Palmorala in Panama City, Panama, one of the four children of Carlos Rivera Quintero, a businessman and politician, and Consuelo Palmorala de Quintero. After local schooling, in 1943 Quintero entered Los Angeles City College, a two-year school noted for its theater program. Quintero drank in the plays that toured to Los Angeles and transferred to the University of Southern California as a theater major, graduating in 1948. In 1948 he attended the Goodman Theatre and Dramatic School in Chicago and in 1949 moved to New York.

In that year Quintero and Theodore Mann formed twelve young actors into a group called the Loft Players, and by the summer of 1950 they were performing in repertory theater at Woodstock, New York, where for a total of $500 they staged a series including J. M. Synge's modern Irish classic *Riders to the Sea* and Tennessee Williams's recent *The Glass Menagerie*. When the Greenwich Village Inn, a nightclub at 5 Sheridan Square in New York, went out of business later that year, the Loft Players moved in—and the theater known as Circle in the Square was born.

Quintero was eventually responsible for the revitalization of off-Broadway theater, the rebirth of arena staging, and the revival of interest in the work of Eugene O'Neill. He became a major interpreter of contemporary playwrights as dissimilar as the poetic Williams and the black-humorist Jules Feiffer. With its in-the-round, or arena, staging, Circle in the Square was "physically conceived and artistically committed to the art of acting, producing great work and plays that deserve re-examination" (Richard E. Kramer, *Cambridge Guide to World Theatre*, 1988). Its first production, a revival of Howard Richardson and William Berney's 1945 melodrama about witch-hunting, *Dark of the Moon*, directed by Quintero, won four off-Broadway awards. The next, a revival of Williams's three-year-old *Summer and Smoke*, introduced and starred Quintero's Goodman School classmate Geraldine Page. The *New York Times* subsequently remarked, "Quintero successfully ignited footlights all over the Village. American theater expanded some 40 blocks." Quintero remained mainly with Circle in the Square through 1964, directing most of its offerings.

Against the mood of his time, Quintero believed that O'Neill, who died in 1953, had single-handedly elevated American theater from frivolity to seriousness. (Quintero eventually directed nineteen O'Neill plays). By 1956, when Quintero sought to direct a revival of *The Iceman Cometh*, O'Neill's lengthy 1939 play about the "pipe dreams" of derelicts in Harry Hope's Saloon, the playwright's works had been little performed for ten years. Finding rights "unavailable," Quintero sought out O'Neill's widow, Carlotta Monterey. Quintero recalled that Monterey soon "began to talk about her husband's work almost as though he was present." In 1977 Quintero told *Time* magazine that he felt "possessed" by O'Neill's spirit; he also wrote that he half believed that "permission to do the play had come from the dead dramatist himself." For the rest of her life, Monterey called Quintero "Gene."

Affinity with O'Neill came naturally to Quintero; both preferred slow pacing and passionate disclosures onstage. Quintero also understood O'Neill's haunted relationship with his father, a successful yet ruined actor; Quintero believed his own childhood to have been blighted by his powerful father's disapproval. Working closely with his performers to discover meaning from the play's text, Quintero coaxed the poetry of inadequacy, pride, failure. In his 1974 autobiography, he wrote, "You're after that shy, inner thing hidden in the woods of your being . . . the treasure of your blind heart. . . . Success is a terrible thing . . . You're afraid they will find you out."

The 1956 production of *The Iceman Cometh*, which ran for 565 performances at Circle in the Square and was a winner in the Drama Desk's Vernon Rice Awards, reestablished O'Neill and established Quintero and Jason Robards (in the role of Hickey, the evangelistic hell-raiser who makes the derelicts face reality with horrifying results) as O'Neill's major contemporary interpreters. Quintero told the *Los Angeles Times*, "I felt that he [O'Neill] was writing about me . . . the kind of landscape which I understood. I mean . . . I was one of the bums . . . he described me so completely." Set in a saloon, the play was ideally suited to staging in an arena theater, and Quintero likened it to "a complex musical form, with themes repeating themselves with slight variation, as melodies do in a symphony. . . . O'Neill has often been criticized by those who do not see the strength and depth of meaning the repetitious achieves."

Later in 1956, Quintero moved to Broadway for a production of O'Neill's tragic *Long Day's Journey into Night*, starring Fredric March and Florence Eldridge as the doomed couple based on O'Neill's parents, with Jason Robards essentially playing the young O'Neill. The production won an Antoinette Perry (Tony) award. Of the play, the *Times*'s Brooks Atkinson wrote, "It restores the drama to literature and the theater to art."

In 1959 Quintero directed his first television productions and in 1960 *Cavalleria Rusticana* and *I Pagliacci* at the Metropolitan Opera; in 1961 he made a rare venture into film, directing Vivien Leigh in Williams's *The Roman Spring of Mrs. Stone*. Before leaving Circle in the Square, he introduced future stars George C. Scott and Colleen Dewhurst, teaming them in O'Neill's expressionistic *Desire under the Elms*. This 1962–1963 production, fully embracing O'Neill's Freudian symbolism and finding the poetry in what others saw as clichéd or pseudorural dialogue, achieved 380 performances, the longest run in the play's history, dating from its premiere in 1924.

Among other Quintero-O'Neill productions in New York were the lengthy one-act *Hughie*, with Robards again, in 1964; *More Stately Mansions*, staged for the first time in 1967; *A Touch of the Poet* (revived in 1977, after being first produced in 1958 by Harold Clurman); *A Moon for the Misbegotten*, in 1973, resulting in another Tony award; and *Anna Christie* (1977). Quintero reestablished O'Neill in Los Angeles with several productions, beginning with *More Stately Mansions*, which opened the new Ahmanson Theatre in 1967. In 1981 Quintero received the O'Neill Birthday Medal "for enhancing the understanding" of O'Neill's work. In 1985 he was reunited with Robards in a national tour of *The Iceman Cometh*.

Quintero's 1980 production of Williams's last play, *Clothes for a Summer Hotel*, closed after fourteen performances. He gradually abandoned directing; in 1961 he had begun teaching at Circle in the Square in a program that offered a degree from New York University. His tenure, beginning in 1983 as teacher and artistic director of the Springold Theater at Brandeis University, ended in 1987 when cancer forced the removal of his larynx. From 1989 onward, fitted with a voice-box, he was theater director and chair of the department of performing arts at the University of Houston; he eventually divided his teaching year between Houston and Florida State University.

Quintero's longtime companion was Nicholas Tsacrios, who was credited by the director with helping him to recover from alcoholism. In 1996 Quintero directed two O'Neill works from 1917, *The Long Voyage Home* and *Isle*, at the Provincetown Repertory Theatre. The 93-seat former Kaufman Theater in New York at 534 West Forty-second Street was established in 1999 as the José Quintero Theater. When Quintero died in Manhattan, Geraldine Page said, "What made José a great director was that he would do everything by suggestion. He would give you the means without telling you what to do." Colleen Dewhurst had once similarly remarked, "He understands the fragile ego of the actor. I'd trust him with my life."

• Quintero's papers, mainly covering 1960 through 1998, are held by the M. D. Anderson Library at the University of Houston. Quintero's autobiography is *If You Don't Dance, They Beat You* (1974). Quintero's "Postscript to a Journey" is in *Theatre Arts*, Apr. 1957, pp. 27–29. A critical interview by Randolph Goodman (Brooklyn College, City University of New York) is in Goodman's *From Script to Stage* (1971), pp. 446–48. Among many perceptive articles by Brooks Atkinson in the *New York Times*, see in particular one in the 9 May 1958 issue. An obituary by Mervyn Rothstein and Richard Severo is in the *New York Times*, 27 Feb. 1999; another is in the *Los Angeles Times* issue of the same date.

JAMES ROSS MOORE

R

RADNER, Gilda (28 June 1946–20 May 1989), comedian, was born in Detroit, Michigan, the daughter of Herman Radner, the wealthy owner of a real estate business and a brewery, and Henrietta Dworkin Radner. She later recalled that her father, an amateur tap dancer and magician who "couldn't carry a tray to the table without tripping to make us kids laugh and make my mother nervous," spurred her own interest in performing comedy (quoted in Saltman, p. 37). An obese child, she learned to poke fun at herself before others could make fun of her: "If you can decide to be funny, I decided it at the age of ten. When I was ten, I said to myself, 'You're not going to make it on looks . . .' I just knew if people said I was fat, I'd laugh and make jokes about it and that would be my world" (quoted in *Current Biography*, p. 327). From the age of ten, Radner attended the Liggett School for Girls, where she excelled and was a member of the dramatics board. Following her graduation in 1963, she attended the University of Michigan in Ann Arbor for six years, majoring in drama but never completing her degree. She appeared in university and local theater productions of classic comedies such as *Lysistrata* and *The Taming of the Shrew* and gained her first experience working in radio, as a comic "weather girl" at the campus station.

In 1969 Radner moved to Toronto, Canada. For the next two years she worked for an avant-garde theater, starring in children's play productions in which her specialty was performing pantomime. In 1972 she gained her first professional acting experience when she was chosen for a role in the religious rock-musical *Godspell*. The following year she joined the Toronto company of Second City, an improvisational comedy troupe that was based in Chicago. In 1973 and 1974 she became well known in Canada when she appeared in several television productions for children, and she had a one-line role as a chanting Greenwich Village Buddhist in *The Last Detail* (1973), starring Jack Nicholson.

In August 1974 Radner moved to New York City, where she joined the cast of "National Lampoon Radio Hour." The syndicated program was an offshoot of the topical-humor magazine *National Lampoon*. Her mentor was John Belushi, an alumnus of the Chicago Second City troupe who had invited her to be on the show. The following year she appeared with Belushi in *The National Lampoon Show*, an Off Broadway revue that also toured college campuses in Canada and New England. Costar Bill Murray described one of her most popular characters, Rhoda Tyler Moore, "a blind girl trying to make it in New York," in a parody of the television program "The Mary Tyler Moore Show":

She set up the character by skipping onto the stage, swinging her cane, and singing her upbeat theme song: "Who's always the last one in the room? / The one who poked her eyes out with a broom; / Who's the girl who likes everyone she meets / 'Specially if they help her cross the streets . . ." John Belushi played her boyfriend, and he'd change his voice and pretend to be these thugs hitting her. . . . Then he'd change back to the boyfriend's voice and pretend to be saving her from the thugs. . . . She'd run, with a cane, full speed into this wall. To get a laugh. She was covered with bruises. You had to admire her. (Quoted in Saltman, pp. 112–13)

In 1975 Radner became the first cast member to join "Saturday Night," later renamed "NBC's Saturday Night Live." The late-night television show recruited many of its performers and writers from the ranks of Second City and *National Lampoon* and tapped the same vein of humor—hip satire with an anything-goes, rock'n'roll sensibility. The ninety-minute program premiered in October 1975, broadcast live from New York's Rockefeller Center; although the show's Nielsen ratings were initially poor, it quickly became a phenomenon among young audiences and by 1979 attracted more than 25 million viewers weekly. As one of the Not Ready for Prime Time Players (which included Belushi, Murray, and Chevy Chase), Radner introduced several memorable characters: Emily Litella, a hard-of-hearing elderly woman who delivers impassioned editorials on such topics as "violins on television" and "making Puerto Rico a steak"; Rhonda Weiss, a stereotypical Jewish-American "princess"; Debbie Doody, the wife of Howdy Doody; and Baba Wawa, a lisping takeoff on television personality Barbara Walters. Perhaps her most popular (and most often recurring) character was Roseanne Roseannadanna, a tough-talking news commentator who gives long spiels on disgusting minutiae such as nose hair. Radner was often called on to play wide-eyed children, including a Brownie who gets eaten by a land shark and a little girl whose parents won't believe there is a monster in her closet. Radner was also adept at a gentle kind of humor not usually evident on the show. In one of her best sketches, she and Steve Martin played a woman and a man whose eyes briefly meet across a crowded disco and who then fantasize about performing a graceful Fred Astaire–Ginger Rogers dance. By 1977 she and her "Saturday Night" cohorts had become national celebrities; writers on the program agreed that Radner and Belushi were the most visible and essential cast members, the "meat and potatoes" of the show (Hill and Weingrad, p. 277). In 1978 she received an Emmy Award for "outstanding continuing performance by a supporting actress in music or variety."

By 1979 Radner's career had begun to wear on her emotionally and physically. A compulsive eater and dieter throughout her life, she became bulimic while on "Saturday Night," admitting ruefully to an interviewer that she had "thrown up in every toilet in Rockefeller Center" (Hill and Weingrad, p. 323). The show's chaotic backstage atmosphere, characterized by a grueling production schedule, vicious ego clashes, and cocaine abuse by many performers and writers, added to her sense that television had "sucked enough . . . blood" and that she needed a change (quoted in Saltman, p. 193). In 1979 NBC president Fred Silverman, who envisioned her as the next Lucille Ball, made serious efforts to build a prime-time variety series around her, but she rejected his plan. Instead, she and "Saturday Night" producer Lorne Michaels developed an ambitious multimedia project, *Gilda Radner, Live from New York,* as a platform from which to launch her post-television career. Radner's sketch-comedy stage show ran for only a month on Broadway in 1979; a comedy album based on the show was also released, to tepid sales. A film version, *Gilda Live* (1980), directed by Mike Nichols, received a similarly negative reception. Several critics pointed out that Radner offered nothing new as an actress in *Gilda Live* by simply rehashing "Saturday Night" characters that she had already played numerous times. In the spring of 1980, following a series of disputes between Silverman and Michaels, NBC announced plans to retool "Saturday Night" with a new producer and cast, and Radner's affiliation with the program ended.

During the 1980s Radner made only sporadic efforts to continue her acting career. In 1980 she appeared in the film *First Family,* a political satire costarring Bob Newhart and Madeline Kahn, which was one of the year's most notorious flops. That year she married G. E. Smith, a rock musician; they had no children and divorced a short time later. In 1984 she married the actor Gene Wilder; they starred together in three disappointing comedies, including *The Woman in Red* (1984). Many show business observers were puzzled by her inability to capitalize on her "Saturday Night" success, but she seemed content to maintain a low profile. In 1986 she was diagnosed with ovarian cancer. She courageously battled her disease, and her doctors gave her a good prognosis for recovery. In March 1988 she was the subject of an upbeat cover story in *Life* magazine; later that spring she made a comeback cameo on the television program "It's Garry Shandling's Show." The following spring she died in Los Angeles.

• Radner's autobiography, *It's Always Something* (1989), released shortly before her death, offers a frank, powerful retelling of her struggles with cancer; the book offers only a few chapters detailing her acting career. She also cowrote, with Alan Zweibel, a "Saturday Night" writer, *Roseanne Ro-* *seannadanna's "Hey, Get Back to Work!" Book* (1983). Valuable portraits of Radner are Zweibel, *Bunny Bunny: Gilda Radner, a Sort of Love Story* (1994), and David Saltman, *Gilda: An Intimate Portrait* (1992). *Current Biography*, Feb. 1980, offers a useful short overview of her life. Doug Hill and Jeff Weingrad, *Saturday Night: A Backstage History of Saturday Night Live* (1986), offers the best history of the show. Radner's comedic style can be seen in numerous videotapes of "Saturday Night," including the video *The Best of Gilda Radner* (1989). An obituary is in the *New York Times*, 21 May 1989.

THOMAS W. COLLINS, JR.

RAND, Paul (15 Aug. 1914–26 Nov. 1996), graphic designer, was born Peretz Rosenbaum in Brooklyn, New York, to Itzhak Yehuda Rosenbaum, a Polish immigrant, and Leah Rosenbaum (maiden name is unknown). The family, which also included his twin brother, Fishel, and an older sister, were strict Orthodox Jews who made their home in the Brownsville section of Brooklyn, where the elder Rosenbaums ran a grocery store. Peretz and his twin were inseparable as children, attending both public school and yeshiva, and manifested independence from an early age, often venturing outside the neighborhood to explore the secular world and attempting to bend and break the rules of Jewish tradition. Peretz showed an artistic aptitude from the time he was a toddler, drawing and sketching whenever he could find pencil and paper. Newspaper cartoon strips, especially "Krazy Kat," were an early influence, and much to his father's disapproval he became a devotee of comic books. As he grew older, he found himself confronting and rejecting the strictures of his religious tradition at every turn, beginning with his insistence on drawing human figures—a forbidden act in the eyes of Orthodox Jewry.

Peretz Rosenbaum's desire to leave behind the world of his family grew insistently. He felt compelled to become a painter, and he seized every opportunity to display his talent in public school, creating signs for plays and murals to decorate barren walls. His father reluctantly allowed him to study art at the Pratt Institute at night if he attended public high school by day, and by 1932 he had earned two high school diplomas. But despite his perseverance, he believed that he had learned virtually nothing at either institution, and he had already begun to have doubts about becoming a painter. Moreover, the Great Depression was now under way and poverty surrounded him: he therefore had to find a practical way to make a living.

Browsing in bookshops and among the art collections at the New York Public Library on Fifth Avenue, Rand had already discovered the exciting new world of graphic design and modern typography emerging in postwar Europe. Journals like the British *Commercial Art* and Germany's *Gebrauchsgrafik* introduced him to new movements in art that were influencing design—he later claimed that he never heard of Picasso or Modernism during his years at Pratt—and when he discovered the Bauhaus, the influential state-run arts and crafts school founded in Germany a decade earlier, he was captivated by its goal of bringing high-quality modern design to the masses. Unable to move to Europe, he enrolled at the Art Students League in Manhattan. There he came under the influence of one of the drawing teachers, the German Dadaist George Grosz, who had recently fled the Nazis and settled in New York. Though Grosz spoke little English, Peretz Rosenbaum instinctively understood what the man was trying to teach him, and he realized for the first time that drawing skills were essential to all forms of art. Another important influence during his student years was the work of Paul Klee, who strongly influenced the way in which he would combine line and color.

In 1934, while still attending classes at the League, Peretz Rosenbaum became a part-time illustrator at a company that created stock graphic images for newspaper and magazine ads. The images were ordinary, even trite, but this on-the-job training gave him greater familiarity with graphic design techniques and increased his self-confidence. He then found work with George Switzer, a prominent package and industrial designer, and soon he was designing graphic materials for such leading companies as Hormel (the meatpacking firm) and Squibb (pharmaceuticals manufacturer). About this time Peretz Rosenbaum discarded his birth name and became Paul Rand, convinced that ultimate success could be achieved only by leaving behind this last vestige of his immigrant forebears.

Rand went on to work for the media company Esquire-Coronet, designing pages for *Apparel Arts* magazine. Promoted to art director of the company in 1936, he assumed new duties that included fashion and gift layouts for the sophisticated men's magazine *Esquire*. In 1941, when Esquire-Coronet partner William Weintraub left to found his own eponymous advertising agency, Rand joined Weintraub's company as creative director. Over the next thirteen years Rand collaborated with other designers on ads for Dubonnet, Lee Hats, and the Auto Car Corporation.

In 1954 Rand left the Weintraub Advertising Agency to work as a freelance designer at the home studio he had established in Weston, Connecticut, two years earlier. Over the following years he amassed a client list of some of the nation's most prominent concerns, including IBM, Cummins Engine, Westinghouse, United Parcel Service (UPS), and the American Broadcasting Corporation (ABC). The designs and logos he created became world-famous, and many of them are still in use today. With Eliot Noyes, the product and building design consultant at IBM, Rand designed the familiar corporate logo: the initials "IBM" in block letters broken into horizontal lines. For UPS he created a logo featuring a package tied with string, while for Westinghouse he made the initial "W" a distinctive emblem. The ABC trademark, a trio of encircled lowercase letters, was yet another example of how Rand grounded his designs in simple but strong typography to create a visual impact, and this approach became a major characteristic of all his future work.

Rand became even more widely known for the distinctive book covers he created for major book publishers beginning in the mid-1950s, most of his assignments being important quality paperbacks of a diverse range, such as *The Anatomy of Revolution* by Crane Brinton; E. H. Gombrich's *Art and Illusion*, and *The American Essays of Henry James*. All his covers featured a bold use of color, paired with a single striking image and the strong, clean typography that had become his trademark. The Rand style, unique as a fingerprint, commanded instant recognition, whether in a magazine layout, on a letterhead, or wrapped around a book, and it changed the look of twentieth-century graphics. Other designers strove to emulate his work, and "the Rand look" itself became an American icon.

In addition to his studio work, Rand taught in New York at Cooper Union (1938–1942) and the Pratt Institute (1946) before joining the Yale University faculty as a professor of graphic design in 1956; he remained at Yale for thirteen years. He also illustrated several children's books—a medium in which he was not entirely comfortable. Of more importance, he wrote several books on graphics, including *Thoughts on Design* (1946) and three heavily illustrated collections of reflections on his career: *Paul Rand: A Designer's Art* (1985); *Design, Form, and Chaos* (1993); and *From Lascaux to Brooklyn* (1996). In addition, he was a major contributor to *Looking Closer: Critical Writings on Graphic Design* (1994).

Rand was married three times. No biographical information about his first wife is available, though it is assumed that the couple divorced. His second wife, Ann, was an architect, and the couple had Rand's only child, a daughter, before they divorced. Rand married his third wife, Marion Swannie, in 1975, after she retired as the manager of IBM's graphic design department. He died from cancer at a hospital in Norwalk, Connecticut.

• For biographical information, see Steven Heller, *Paul Rand* (1999), which includes several hundred illustrations of Rand's designs. See also Rand's own books, mentioned earlier, for discussions of his design philosophy. In addition, see Yusaku Kamekura, *Paul Rand: His Work from 1946 to 1958* (1959), and *A Paul Rand Miscellany* (1984). See also one of Rand's last public pronouncements, "Failure by Design," an op-ed piece in the *New York Times*, 2 May 1993, in which Rand voices his concern that corporate America is not paying enough attention to good design in the late twentieth century. An obituary appears in the *New York Times*, 28 Nov. 1996.

ANN T. KEENE

RANDOLPH, Jennings (8 Mar. 1902–8 May 1998), U.S. congressman and senator, was born in Salem, Harrison County, West Virginia, the son of Ernest Randolph, a petroleum producer, attorney, and cattle shipper, and Idell Bingman Randolph. After attending local public primary school, he entered Salem

Academy and on graduating in 1920 enrolled in nearby Salem College (now Salem-Teikyo University). Interested in journalism, he served as president of the West Virginia Inter-Collegiate Press Association during his senior year. Randolph graduated in 1924 with a B.A. and became a reporter on the Clarksburg (W.Va.) *Daily Telegram*. The following year he served as associate editor of the *West Virginia Review*, based in Charleston.

In 1926 Randolph joined the faculty of Davis and Elkins College in Elkins, West Virginia; he remained there until 1932, eventually becoming head of the department of public speaking and journalism. The political arena soon beckoned, however, and after his first attempt (1930) to unseat Republican congressman Frank L. Bowman proved unsuccessful, Randolph ran again in 1932. He benefited from the Roosevelt landslide and entered the U.S. House of Representatives as a Democrat. On 18 February 1933 he married Mary Katherine Babb of Keyser, West Virginia; they were to have two sons.

Reelected six times, Randolph proved to be a loyal supporter of most New Deal and Fair Deal measures. While in Congress, he served on the District of Columbia and Civil Service committees and also gained a name for himself as a tireless advocate for aviation. In addition to sponsoring the Civil Aeronautics Act of 1938, he won federal financial assistance for such programs as airmail pickup and pilot training. Randolph was also instrumental in establishing the National Air Museum.

Defeated in his bid for reelection in 1946 when the Republicans prevailed, Randolph remained in Washington to work as the assistant to the president of Capital Airways and as the company's director of public relations. Still interested in aviation policy planning, Randolph served from 1947 to 1949 as chairman of the Aviation Planning Commission in Washington and beginning in 1953 chaired a Department of Commerce panel that studied the role of federal funding in airport contruction. He also continued to be a faculty member of Southeastern University in Washington, where he had held the chair in public speaking since 1935; in 1952 he became the dean of the university's School of Business Administration. Nor had he severed ties with West Virginia politics: he was a delegate-at-large from the state to the Democratic National Conventions of 1948, 1952, and 1956.

In 1958 Randolph returned to public office when he was elected to fill out the balance of the late senator Matthew Neely's term. The winner of a full term in 1960, he would be reelected three more times, serving on a variety of committees (including Civil Service, Labor and Public Welfare, and Public Works) until 1984. Although he described himself as a "Jeffersonian Democrat" who was mainly interested in acting on his fellow West Virginians' concerns, many of the issues he pursued were national in scope. Besides retaining a focus on aviation, he tirelessly supported an active federal presence in many areas of American life, including interstate highway construction, aid to the handicapped, and funding for economically distressed areas. Generally liberal in his views, he voted for the 1964 Civil Rights Act as well as the 1965 Voting Rights Act and was a strong supporter of President Lyndon Johnson's Great Society proposals.

Randolph further belied his image as a parochial senator with his work in two key policy areas: energy consumption and voting rights. As early as 1943, while still a member of the House, he had urged the country to explore alternative sources of energy—not because of actual supply shortages but out of a concern for wartime disruptions. Two decades later, in June 1961, he led sixty-three of his fellow senators in offering a resolution that called for a special study of fuel supplies in order to prevent an "energy gap." A leader in the movement to lower the voting age to eighteen, Randolph made his first attempt to push for a constitutional amendment in 1942. He resubmitted the proposal ten more times, and in 1971 the Twenty-Sixth Amendment was ratified. Finally rewarded for his efforts, Randolph was quoted as saying, "I believe that our young people possess a great social conscience, are perplexed by the injustices which exist in the world, and are anxious to rectify these ills" (*New York Times* obit.).

As chairman of the Public Works Committee after 1966, Randolph skillfully steered a great deal of "pork barrel" legislation toward his home state. A longtime supporter of the coal industry—a major employer in West Virginia—he engaged for many years in a fine balancing act between the needs of industrial development, the environment, and workers' health. Initially cool to the idea of compensating victims of "black lung" disease (a major health hazard among coal miners) on the grounds that the program's cost might put many small mine operators out of business, he relented under pressure from workers and sponsored a 1972 measure that liberalized eligibility standards for afflicted miners.

Dogged by allegations that he had received illegal campaign funds from Phillips Petroleum Corporation in 1975, Randolph appeared to be in trouble as the 1978 election season began. He benefitted, however, from campaign appearances by President Jimmy Carter and was reelected by state voters. Randolph's wife died in the early 1980s, and in 1984 he decided not to seek reelection. His own health began to decline soon after leaving the Senate, and he spent the last decade of his life in a nursing home in St. Louis, Missouri, where he died.

While Jennings Randolph portrayed himself as an adherent of the adage "All politics are local," he made his mark in fact as a legislator having genuinely national concerns. Perhaps his longevity in Congress can be attributed to his having always remembered that a successful politician must not distance himself from his constituents at home.

• Randolph's papers are held at Salem-Teikyo University in Salem, W. Va. With J. A. Bell, he wrote *Speaking That Wins* (1939), which was reissued in 1951 as *Mr. Chairman, Ladies and Gentlemen: A Practical Guide to Successful Speaking*. Secondary information on his life and career is scarce, the best source being a 1962 entry in *Current Biography* that covers his life up until his early years in the Senate. An obituary is in the *New York Times*, 9 May 1998.

EDWARD L. LACH, JR.

RANKIN, J. Lee (8 July 1907–26 June 1996), attorney and solicitor general of the United States, was born James Lee Rankin in Hartington, Nebraska, the son of Herman P. Rankin, occupation unknown, and Lois Gable Rankin. He attended public schools in Lincoln, Nebraska, before entering the nearby University of Nebraska, where he received an A.B. in 1928 and an LL.B. in 1930. Admitted to the bar that same year, he began his legal career in the local firm of Beghtol, Foe and Rankin. On 4 September 1931 he married Gertrude Carpenter, with whom he was to have three children. Named a member of the firm by 1935, he also became active in local Republican party politics and served as Nebraska primary campaign manager during New York governor Thomas E. Dewey's unsuccessful 1940 bid for the presidency.

Rankin enjoyed better success in 1949, when he oversaw Dewey's 40,000-vote win in Nebraska, and in 1952, when he ran Dwight D. Eisenhower's statewide campaign. Following Eisenhower's victory, Rankin was appointed assistant attorney general in charge of the office of legal council at the Department of Justice, largely through the influence of an old friend, Herbert Brownell, who became Eisenhower's attorney general. In his new position Rankin was responsible for drafting legal opinions for a number of administration officials, including Secretary of State John Foster Dulles, as well as advising Brownell on the formation of legal policy. His most important case occurred in his first year in office, when he appeared before the Supreme Court in December 1953 and argued that school segregation on the basis of race was unconstitutional under the Fourteenth Amendment to the Constitution and that the Court had both the power and the obligation to declare segregation unconstitutional. The presentation by the Justice Department helped bring about the historic decision of *Brown v. Topeka Board of Education* (1954) and earned Rankin high praise from Brownell, who later stated that "His preparation and argument were first class" (*Advising Ike*, p. 194).

While not well known outside the Department of Justice, within the department Rankin quickly gained a reputation as a hard worker with the ability to comprehend the most intricate and complex legal problems. After completing a study of the potential for trading surplus agricultural commodities within Soviet bloc countries in 1955, he then undertook a study of the presidential succession issue at Eisenhower's behest in 1956. When Solicitor General Simon Sobeloff resigned his post in order to accept a judicial position on the U.S. Court of Appeals, Rankin was a logical choice to succeed him. Despite some concern that Rankin might encounter resistance during his Senate confirmation hearings due to his role in civil rights issues, he was confirmed on 28 May 1957.

As solicitor general, Rankin served as the Eisenhower administration's "point man" on a number of issues, including state ownership of continental shelf oil repositories, federal control over the natural gas used in interstate commerce, Communist party membership, and the passport rights of American citizens. He also took a leading role in addressing the variety of legal disputes that arose over legislative reapportionment throughout the United States, and he created the Justice Department's principle of "one man, one vote." Rankin reentered the civil rights fray in 1959, when he filed a brief before the Supreme Court relating to a district court order that had postponed school integration in Little Rock, Arkansas. During the debate Rankin urged that citizens not be taught that "the courts will bow" to violence, which he argued would "destroy the whole educational process then and there." Constitutional rights must be upheld, Rankin further argued, "not just the rights that I like and want for me, or that you like and want for you, but all of them for every man and woman" (*New York Times*, 29 Aug. 1958) Holding what he termed the "aristocrat of legal jobs," Rankin controlled the government briefs and arguments in all cases that went before the Supreme Court; he also answered only to the attorney general in deciding which of the cases the government had lost should be carried before either the courts of appeals or the Supreme Court.

After leaving office in 1961, Rankin moved to New York City and resumed his private legal practice. Among the clients that he represented were the American Civil Liberties Union, in whose behalf he argued the landmark 1962 case *Gideon v. Wainwright*, which established the right of an indigent person to free legal representation; the case was the subject of a prize-winning book by Anthony Lewis, *Gideon's Trumpet*, which was the basis of a 1980 film with the same title, starring Henry Fonda. Rankin also served as legal counsel on the Warren Commission, which was created by President Lyndon Johnson to investigate the assassination of President John F. Kennedy. After helping to redraft and reword the prose of the extensive report (26 volumes, 800 pages), Rankin remained convinced of the accuracy of its findings; although he rarely spoke of it in public afterward, close associates confirmed that he was pained by what he viewed as crackpot conspiracy theories surrounding a national tragedy.

Rankin remained in private practice until 1978 but interrupted that work for one last stint in public life, this time as corporation counsel under New York City mayor John V. Lindsay from 1966 until 1972. As the head of a staff of 378 attorneys, he helped defend the city in a wide range of litigation cases as well as providing legal opinions on matters as divergent as the legality of school decentralization and the legality of John Birch Society membership among the city's police force.

After retiring, Rankin moved successively to Weston, Connecticut (1978), Los Gatos, California (1995), and Santa Cruz, California (1996), where he died in a nursing home after a period of declining health.

• Rankin's papers are divided between the Lyndon Baines Johnson Presidential Library in Austin, Texas, and the National Archives in Washington, D.C. He receives high praise from his friend and superior Herbert Brownell in Brownell's *Advising Ike: The Memoirs of Attorney General Herbert Brownell* (1993). He was also the subject of an entry in *Current Biography* (1959). An obituary is in the *New York Times* on 30 June 1996.

EDWARD L. LACH, JR.

RAY, Aldo (25 Sept. 1926–27 Mar. 1991), actor, was born Aldo Da Re in Pen Argyl, Pennsylvania, the son of Silvio Da Re and Maria Da Re. At age two he moved with his family to Crockett, in northern California, where his father worked in a sugar refinery; he was the oldest of seven children. After graduating from high school in 1944, he became a navy frogman and was involved in the invasion of Okinawa. Mustered out of the service in 1946, he attended Vallejo Junior College and the University of California at Berkeley, where a knee injury curtailed his plans for a career in football. He turned to politics and in 1950 was elected constable of Crockett but resigned the job after scoring a success as a college football player in Columbia Pictures' *Saturday's Hero* (1951). The studio signed him to a contract and changed his named to Aldo Ray.

In 1952 Ray caused a sensation as Chet Keefer in *The Marrying Kind*, a soap opera-comedy about the disintegration of a marriage. With studio chief Harry Cohn as his mentor, the actor had good roles in a succession of box office successes, including *Pat and Mike* (1952), *Let's Do It Again* (1953), *Miss Sadie Thompson* (1953), *We're No Angels* (1955), and *Nightfall* (1956). His greatest fame came during this period when he portrayed the epitome of the noncommissioned officer in such war epics as *Battle Cry* (1955), *Three Stripes in the Sun* (1955), *Men in War* (1957), and *The Naked and the Dead* (1958). He was also impressive as the loutish factory worker who lusts after his sister-in-law in *God's Little Acre* (1958).

After ending his Columbia contract in 1958, he appeared opposite Lucille Ball in the "Desilu Playhouse" production of "Kitty" on CBS-TV that year and then went abroad for several lucrative film assignments: *The Siege of Pinchgut (Four Desperate Men)* (1959), filmed in Australia; the British production *The Day They Robbed the Bank of England* (1960); an Italian swashbuckler, *Musketeers of the Sea* (1960); and a mystery, *Johnny Nobody* (1961), which was made in Ireland. Back in Hollywood, Ray guest-starred on a number of television shows, including "Frontier Circus," "Naked City," "The Virginian," "Alcoa Premiere," "Ben Casey," "Kraft Suspense Theatre," "Burke's Law," "Bonanza," "Voyage to the Bottom of the Sea," and "Daniel Boone." In the mid-1960s Ray

returned to the screen, receiving critical acclaim for his finely etched performances in *What Did You Do in the War, Daddy?* (1966), *Dead Heat on a Merry-Go-Round* (1966), and *Welcome to Hard Times* (1967), a western in which he expertly portrayed a crazed killer without speaking one line of dialogue. He also resumed making military action features, first going to Italy to headline *Commando Suicida* (1968) and then appearing as a tough sergeant in John Wayne's controversial but highly successful pro-Vietnam War production, *The Green Berets* (1968).

The actor's association with B movies began in 1967 when he starred in *Riot on Sunset Strip*. For the remainder of his career he would appear in such fare, although he also would do an occasional big-budget production, such as director René Clement's *La Course du Lievre à Travers Les Champs* (1972), filmed in Canada and issued in the United States as *And Hope to Die*. In it he was impressive as a punchy ex-boxer who accidentally brings about the downfall of his gang. Still, most of his film work was in low-budget efforts: he played crooked or racist cops in actioners like *Angel Unchained* (1970), *Tom* (1973), and *The Dynamite Brothers* (1975); a brutal prison guard in *The Glove* (1978); a neo-Nazi in *The Lucifer Complex* (1978); monster fighters in *Bog* (1978) and *Nightstalker* (1979); and badmen in westerns like *Seven Alone* (1974), *Gone with the West* (1975), and *Sweet Savage* (1978). The latter was a triple X-rated production shot in Texas for which Ray won the Adult Film Association Award as best actor even though he did not participate in any of the feature's nudity or sex sequences. During the 1970s he guest-starred on such television shows as "The Outsider," "Movin' On," "Police Story," "S.W.A.T.," "Marcus Welby, M.D.," "The Quest," "Delvecchio," "Sweepstakes," and "CHiPS," and he also appeared in TV commercials. In 1972 he did the voice of Muscle Mutt in the animated adventure spoof series "The Houndcats."

The 1980s found Ray continuing to appear in mostly low-budget horror and science fiction features like *Straightjacket (Dark Sanity)* (1980), *Human Experiments* (1980), *Mongrel* (1982), *Biohazard* (1984), *Evils of the Night* (1985), *Frankenstein's Great Aunt Tilly* (1985) and *Star Slammer—The Escape* (1986), although he did have good roles in A films, such as his voice-over in the animated classic *The Secret of NIMH* (1982) and as the police inspector in *To Kill a Stranger* (1983). By now, however, Ray's career was hampered by three divorces, money woes, and alcoholism; his drinking caused him to lose some jobs, including a role in *Dune* (1984). He left Hollywood in 1983 and returned to the family home in Crockett.

In 1986 the actor was expelled from the Screen Actors Guild for allegedly making a non-union feature, although the film in question, *Lethal Injection* (1985), was never released. It was claimed that the action was the result of a grudge against Ray by someone in the Guild, and one of its factions, Actors Working for Actors, protested the expulsion. It was also claimed that the dismissal was politically motivated, since Ray was considering a return to politics at the time. While the action may have cost the actor a few jobs, he got his full pension and medical coverage and continued to be very active on screen. In the year of his expulsion, he starred in the slasher melodrama *Terror on Alcatraz* (1986) as real-life escapee Frank Morris, and he played a priest in *Blood Red* (1988). In 1987 he acted in director Michael Cimino's "biopic" of Salvatore Giuliano, *The Sicilian*, and took the role of a mobster in *Hollywood Cop*. He then went to South Africa to appear in the action feature *Swift Justice* (1989). Back in Hollywood, he co-starred in the war games comedy *The Shooters* (1990) and portayed a nasty pizza parlor owner in *Shock 'em Dead* (1990). His final feature, *Foreign Agent* (1991), was issued posthumously.

The actor was diagnosed with throat cancer in 1990 but continued to work in films before a combination of the disease and pneumonia killed him. Ray died at the Veterans Administation Hospital in Martinez, California. He was married three times: to Shirley Green, actress Jeff Donnell, and Johanna Bennett, and was survived by three children, Clair, Paul, and actor Eric DaRe.

Much has been made of Ray's so-called slide from A pictures to B movies, but in more than eighty feature films his performances never wavered. Unlike most of his contemporaries who enjoyed success in the 1950s, the gravel-voiced actor remained active as a globe-trotting perennial with a big fan following. Still, the critical and popular acclaim of his early years caused him to be typecast. He told an interviewer in 1990, "In some ways the tough soldier role locked me in. There were no sophisticated roles for me. I never seemed to get past master sergeant, although I always thought of myself as upper echelon."

• Brief profiles of Ray appear in Ian Cameron and Elisabeth Cameron, *The Heavies* (1969); Danny Peary, *Cult Movie Stars* (1991); David Ragan, *Who's Who in Hollywood* (1992); Ephraim Katz, *The Film Encyclopedia* (1994); Leonard Maltin, *Leonard Maltin's Movie Encyclopedia* (1994); and David Quinlan, *The Film Lovers' Companion* (1997). Articles on Ray include Grover Lewis, "The Battle Cry of Aldo Ray," *Movieline Magazine*, Jan. 1991, pp. 44-48, 74-79; and Herb Fagan, "Aldo Ray: The Long, Hard Fall of a Hollywood Hero," *Films of the Golden Age*, Summer 1998, pp. 74-84. Obituaries appear in the *Los Angeles Times*, 18 Mar. 1991, and *Variety*, 3 Apr. 1991.

MICHAEL R. PITTS

RAYE, Martha (27 Aug. 1916–19 Oct. 1994), actress and singer, was born Margaret Theresa Yvonne Reed, in Butte, Montana, where her parents, Pete Reed and Maybelle Hooper Reed, Irish immigrants who had formed a vaudeville double act, were stranded at the time. Raye joined the act at age three. She was educated in Montana and Chicago and at the Professional Children's School in New York City.

Having taken her stage name from a telephone book, Raye turned professional in 1933, singing and dancing with the Benny Davis and Ben Blue companies, as well as playing the Loews vaudeville circuit.

She appeared in the Broadway revues *Calling All Stars* (1934) and the *Earl Carroll Sketchbook* (1935) and headed west in 1935. The jazz pianist Mary Lou Williams later recalled that the nineteen-year-old stopped "in Kansas City on her way to California. . . . She stayed close on to two weeks, and was down at the clubs digging the music and singing like mad, night after night. Martha hated to leave and nearly missed doing her picture."

"Her picture" was *Rhythm on the Range* (1936), and Raye got the part after being seen by producer Norman Taurog one Sunday night at the Trocadero nightclub on Hollywood's Sunset Strip, clowning with comics Jimmy Durante and Joe E. Lewis. In the film, which starred Bing Crosby, Raye played a cowboy's sister and sang "You've Got to Swing It" ("Mr. Paganini"), establishing herself as a swing singer of the first rank and typecasting herself as a loud- (and large-) mouthed knockabout.

Raye never got the chance to sing with a big band in the swing era's golden years, though between 1937 and 1941 her films always included at least one showcase for her scat-singing and sometimes, as in *The Big Broadcast of 1938*, ballads, often alongside the "Arkansas Traveler" Bob Burns. Mostly she was asked to make faces and expend her apparently boundless energy (Dorothy Lamour later said that Raye could sing and dance at Hollywood nightclubs till 3:00 a.m. and still be bright early mornings on the set). In 1937 Raye married Hollywood makeup man Hamilton "Buddy" Westmore; the marriage, the first of seven for Raye, lasted approximately three months. In 1938 she married composer David Rose; they were divorced in 1941.

In 1940 Raye returned to Broadway with Al Jolson in *Hold on to Your Hats*, singing two comic songs. She played the dissatisfied spouse Luce in the 1940 film of Richard Rodgers and Lorenz Hart's *The Boys from Syracuse*, and in 1941 Raye was much at home in the film of Ole Olsen and Chic Johnson's manic *Hellzapoppin*. In the same year she married hotelman Neal Lang; they were divorced in 1944.

When the United States entered World War II, Raye's second career emerged. For the rest of her life, she was an indefatigable entertainer of American troops around the world. A retired sergeant-major of the Rangers wrote in 1991, "She stepped down off that stage, in 1943, I guess it was, and gave me a hug and a kiss. She stole my heart. I was floating on a cloud." *Four Jills in a Jeep* (1944) was the film version of one of Raye's real-life USO tours. Along with Kay Francis, Carole Landis, and Mitzi Mayfair, Raye started out in England. After a week in Africa, the others went back to the United States, but Raye stayed for three and a half months, until yellow fever sent her home. Complications from her illness stayed with her, curtailing her participation in entertaining the troops in the Korean War. In 1944 Raye had married dancer Nick Condos; they had one child and were divorced in 1953.

Perhaps Raye's most notable (and least typecast) film role came in *Monsieur Verdoux* (1947). Vivacious and physically tough, Raye played the one victim that director Charles Chaplin, as the attractive serial killer Verdoux, could not finish off. Her first appearance with Milton Berle, the era's television king, in 1948 made the louder-than-life Raye a star of network television. In 1951 she led four episodes of an "All-Star Revue" and between 1954 and 1956 alternated with Berle, Bob Hope, and Steve Allen as hosts of a comedy hour. The *New York Herald Tribune* called her the country's number one comedienne of the 1953–1954 season. In 1954 Raye married dancer Edward Begley; they were divorced in 1956. In the 1955–1956 season she led "The Martha Raye Show," a musical variety show telling a new story every week, with prize fighter Rocky Graziano as her somewhat punch-drunk boyfriend. Raye performed in New York, Las Vegas, Chicago, and Tahoe nightclubs and for a time owned her own, the Five O'Clock Club in Miami. In 1956 she married bodyguard Robert O'Shea; they were divorced in 1962.

Raye returned to the screen in 1962 with Durante and Doris Day as the singing circus comedienne Madame Lulu in an adaptation of the Rodgers-Hart musical *Jumbo*. That year, however, she admitted she was often lonely: "My career is my whole life." When the American involvement in the Vietnam war increased, Raye was on the road again. She spent as many as six unpaid months yearly for the duration, and once, at Soc Trang in 1967, she aided thirteen consecutive hours of surgery. Raye was made an honorary lieutenant colonel ("Colonel Maggie of the Boondocks") in Special Services. One veteran said of her trips to Vietnam, "She never ran out of energy and could not stand to see someone depressed."

In 1967 Raye replaced Ginger Rogers in a Broadway revival of *Hello, Dolly!* At the 1969 Academy Awards, she received the Jean Hersholt Humanitarian Award. In 1970 the puppeteers Sid and Marty Krofft cast her as the raucous voice of Boss Witch in the stage version of their children's television program "H. R. Pufnstuf," which was followed two years later by the Kroffts' television program "The Bugaloos," in which Raye played Benita Bizarre. In 1972 she took the lead in the Broadway production of *No, No, Nanette!* and subsequently toured in the 1920s musical comedy throughout the country in regional theaters. Between 1969 and 1974 she was regularly seen on episodes of the television comedy anthology "Love, American Style" and between 1976 and 1977 played a rambunctious housekeeper on the comedy-drama series "McMillan and Wife." She was quoted as believing she was no longer welcome in films because of her "right-wing views."

In declining health, Raye lost a leg to cancer. In 1989 a Medals for Maggie campaign was launched, seeking formal recognition of her military service. In 1991 she married her agent, Mark Blufeld Harris; they would remain married until Raye's death. In 1992 she requested burial at the military cemetery at Fort Bragg, North Carolina, and a special exception to policy was granted. In 1993 she was awarded the Presidential Medal of Freedom by President Clinton. Raye, her energy at last spent, died in Los Angeles of a stroke, aggravated by circulatory difficulties.

• Noonie Fortin, *Memories of Maggie: Martha Raye, a Legend Spanning Three Wars* (1995) is a biography by the chairman of the Medals for Maggie committee. Mary Lou Williams's anecdote comes from Nat Shapiro and Nat Hentoff, *Hear Me Talkin' To Ya, The Story of Jazz as Told by the Men Who Made It* (1955). A revealing interview is Sidney Skolsky's in the *New York Post*, 8 July 1962. Tim Brooks and Earle Marsh, *The Complete Directory to Prime Time Network TV Shows, 1946–Present* (1979), lists Raye's television credits. Stanley Green, *Encyclopaedia of the Musical Film* (1981), is similarly comprehensive. Obituaries include Lawrence Van Gelder's in the *International Herald Tribune*, 21 Oct. 1994, and Ronald Bergan's in the (London) *Guardian* on the same date.

JAMES ROSS MOORE

RAYMOND, Arthur E. (24 Mar. 1899–22 Mar. 1999), aircraft designer, was born Arthur Emmons Raymond in Boston, Massachusetts, the son of Walter Raymond and Hattie Lewis Raymond, prosperous owners of Pasadena's Raymond Hotel, a favorite winter stomping ground of wealthy easterners. Raymond grew up in a cottage on the hotel grounds. His interest in aviation was sparked by his flight over Los Angeles in a dirigible when he was fifteen. That experience led to his experimenting with aerial photography by mounting a camera on a tethered balloon and a twelve-foot kite. He graduated from Pasadena High School in 1917 and went east to study at Harvard University, where he earned a bachelor of science degree in 1920. He spent the next year at the Massachusetts Institute of Technology (MIT), completing a master of science degree in aeronautical engineering in 1921. Unable to find work in his chosen field, Raymond returned to California where he went into the hotel business with his father. While there he met and married, in 1921, Dorothy Lee of Pasadena, California; they had one son, Stanley Walter. Both preceded Raymond in death. In 1989, Raymond married Mimi Hunt, who died in 1993.

Through career setbacks and family responsibilities, Raymond's love of aviation never wavered. In 1925, after taking additional courses at the California Institute of Technology (Caltech), he went to work for the Douglas Aircraft Company as a metal worker on the shop floor at its plant in Santa Monica, California. Within weeks, the firm's owner, Donald Douglas, called Raymond's mentor at MIT, Edward P. Warner, asking him to recommend a good young engineer to oversee stress analysis for his aircraft designs. Warner wired back, "He is Arthur Raymond. He works in your shop." Before the end of the year, Raymond had been moved from the shop floor to the engineering department to undertake stress analyses of pontoon struts on a Douglas amphibian aircraft then under development.

In the Douglas engineering department Raymond worked with about a dozen engineers, including Donald Douglas himself, and quickly made a name as one of the best and most creative aeronautical engineers in a department known for its innovative nature. In 1927 Donald Douglas promoted him to assistant chief engineer, and he became chief engineer in 1936. Three years later, he became vice president in charge of engineering at Douglas, a position he held until his retirement.

While Donald Douglas had enjoyed great success as a builder of navy pursuit planes, in 1932 he wanted to branch out and build a transport aircraft that would provide fast, reliable long-distance travel across the United States. Raymond received the nod to oversee development of what eventually became the DC-3. Discussing it with numerous aviation pioneers, including Orville Wright and Charles Lindbergh, Raymond embarked on a plan to build a plane that could carry thirty passengers in relative comfort during a nonstop transatlantic flight. The DC-1 first flew in July 1933, ten months after Douglas signed a contract with TWA for the delivery of the plane. Although the DC-1 met TWA's specifications, Douglas Aircraft built only one prototype and moved on to the next generation. "It wasn't a perfect airplane by any means," Raymond commented. The production model was the DC-2, which provided an additional row of seats and used a higher-octane fuel.

Although the DC-2 had only limited commercial success, it did well in a London to Melbourne air race. Its successor, however, was financially viable—a speedy, hardy aircraft that greatly shortened the time between destinations in the United States. By the time the DC-3 was introduced in 1935, Raymond and his design team were able to round out the fuselage to provide seating for three passengers in each row. That made the DC-3 "probably the first of the so-called wide bodies," Raymond recalled. Most important, it was the first aircraft to accommodate enough passengers to be profitable without carrying mail under government contract.

The DC-3 was the country's first reliable passenger plane; it proved to be an enormous winner for Douglas Aircraft, and the company could hardly keep pace with the orders. By 1939 the DC-3 dominated commercial aviation and contributed to the later success of such major airlines as United, American, and TWA. The aircraft remained widely in service into the 1960s. Douglas produced 10,926 DC-3s between 1935 and 1945, and with over 500,000 rivets the aircraft could withstand virtually anything. This was especially important for the DC-3's military variant, the C-47, as it became the workhorse and the mainstay of the air transport mission during World War II. The DC-3 in so many ways represented the pinnacle of aeronautical design for piston engine transports, and Arthur Raymond justifiably celebrated its long-standing success. More than fifty years after the first DC-3s were built, as many as 2,000 of the original 11,000 planes were still in use around the world.

In addition to managing the production of the DC-3 and thereby helping to revolutionize air travel, Raymond guided the company's early developments of rocket and missile technology, including the Nike Ajax and Hercules anti-aircraft missiles deployed around Los Angeles and other major cities during the 1950s, as well as the Thor ballistic missile. His last major commercial aircraft design project moved Douglas planes from propeller to jet power in the DC-8. He also served on a variety of boards and panels throughout his career. He served as a member of the Department of Defense's Steering Group for the Technical Advisory Panel of Aeronautics; between 1946 and 1956 he served on the National Advisory Committee for Aeronautics; and he was a member of the U.S. Air Force's Space Systems Division Advisory Group.

Raymond spent thirty-five years at Douglas Aircraft, overseeing the development of the DC-1 through DC-8 series of transport aircraft. After his retirement from Douglas in 1960, he served as a special consultant to the NASA administrator, James E. Webb, on a variety of aerospace issues and played an important role as an adviser on efforts throughout the 1960s to develop a supersonic transport. He also became a consultant to the Rand Corporation and was a trustee of the Aerospace Corporation (from 1960 until 1971), a member of the National Academy of Sciences (1964), and a past president of the Institute of Aeronautical Sciences, which became the American Institute for Aeronautics and Astronautics, 1963. He would have turned 100 years old had he lived two days longer. He died at the St. John's Hospital in Santa Monica, near his home in Bel-Air, California.

• Sizable biographical files on Raymond are in the Douglas Aircraft Company corporate records located at the Boeing Company, Seattle, Wash., and the NASA Historical Reference Collection, NASA Headquarters, Washington, D.C. Raymond profiled his role in the development of transport aircraft in "The Well-Tempered Aircraft," *The 39th Wilbur Wright Memorial Lecture*, Anglo-American Conference, Brighton, England, 10 Sept. 1951; "The Bouncing Crystal Ball," presented at the Semi-Annual Banquet of Air Industries and Transport Association of Canada, Victoria, B.C., 24 Apr. 1952; and "Air Transport History and a Glimpse into the Future," *Astronautics and Aeronautics*, July 1968, pp. 58–69. His work at Douglas and the aircraft he built have been discussed in Frank Cunningham, *Sky Master: The Story of Donald Douglas* (1943); René J. Francillon, *McDonnell Douglas Aircraft since 1920* (2 vols., 1988–1990); Henry M. Holden, *The Douglas DC-3* (1991); Douglas J. Ingells, *The McDonnell Douglas Story* (1979); and Arthur Pearcy, *Sixty Glorious Years: A Tribute to the Douglas DC-3 Dakota* (1995). An obituary is in the *New York Times*, 27 Mar. 1999.

ROGER D. LAUNIUS

REEDY, George E. (5 Aug. 1917–21 Mar. 1999), author and presidential press secretary, was born in East Chicago, Indiana, the son of George Edward Reedy, a newspaperman, and Mary Mulvaney Reedy. Intellectually curious from an early age, he attended the University of Chicago, where he dabbled in socialism and—according to family lore—learned Greek in order to read Aristotle in the original and thereby "one-up" university president Robert Maynard Hutchins. After graduating with a degree in sociology in 1938, Reedy took a job with the Washington bureau of the United Press, where he covered both Congress and the executive branch. In 1942 he joined the U.S. Army Air Forces and served as a radar intelligence officer in the Pacific theater of operations; he achieved the rank of captain before leaving the military in 1946.

After the end of World War II Reedy returned to Washington and his former employer. While covering the House of Representatives, he met Lillian Greenwald, a reporter with the International News Service, whom he married in March 1948 (the couple had two sons). His coverage of the Senate led Reedy to take an interest in Texas senator Lyndon B. Johnson, and in 1951 he became a member of Johnson's staff. Although Johnson was a notoriously tough and demanding man to work for, he and Reedy formed an effective working relationship, which even extended to Reedy and his wife occasionally babysitting Johnson's daughters. Reedy later denied the oft-repeated story that he took the job because he knew that Johnson was "going to be the President of the United States some day" (*New York Times*, 22 Mar. 1999), but he was certainly impressed with Johnson's intelligence, political skill, and ambition. In 1952 Reedy became staff director of the Democratic Policy Committee, where he remained until 1960. Following Johnson's election to the vice presidency that year, Reedy served as his special assistant and coordinated both speechwriting and press relations for his office.

When Johnson assumed the presidency following the assassination of John F. Kennedy, Reedy remained in Washington and in March 1964 replaced Pierre Salinger as White House press secretary after Salinger resigned in order to run for a Senate seat from California. Reedy's unhappy tenure was marked by steadily declining relations between Johnson and the press corps. He later claimed that "of all the LBJ weaknesses, perhaps the most important was his inability to understand the press. He was totally baffled by journalists who practiced an art that he regarded as a mystery and he never fully comprehended why they failed to respond to the type of treatment he practiced so successfully on other politicians and on government officials" (*Lyndon B. Johnson*, p. 59). Although Johnson could be exceedingly generous to his staff—he once apologized to Reedy by giving him a Lincoln Continental—he also had a cruel and vindictive streak and did not spare Reedy from occasional humiliations such as public disparagements of Reedy's weight and personal appearance. Their relationship completely fell apart after Reedy offered private criticism of the conduct of the Vietnam War to Johnson, and in July 1965 he was replaced as press secretary by Bill Moyers.

Although Reedy remained available to the White House, serving as a special aide to Johnson in late 1965 and 1968 as well as having stints on the National Advisory Committee on Selective Service and the Na-

tional Advisory Committee on Marine Science and Engineering Resources, his later career focused on writing and scholarship. He was president and director of Struthers Scientific and International Corp., a research and development firm, between 1968 and 1972 and held a fellowship at the Woodrow Wilson International Center for Scholars. His first book, *Who Will Do Our Fighting for Us?* was published in 1969, followed by the well-received *Twilight of the Presidency* (1970), in which Reedy noted that the White House was "becoming more and more of a royal court . . . a place where a president is so insulated and isolated from the people that he doesn't really know what's in their hearts" (*Milwaukee Journal-Sentinel*, 22 Mar. 1999). In 1971 Reedy published *The Presidency in Flux* and became dean of the School of Journalism and Nieman Professor of Journalism at Marquette University in Milwaukee. Well liked and respected in his new profession, Reedy remained dean of the journalism school until 1977 and continued to teach full time until 1990, when he became professor emeritus. His later writings included *The United States Senate: Paralysis or a Search for Consensus?* (1986), a thoughtful review of that body's inner workings; *Lyndon B. Johnson: A Memoir* (1982), a critical but balanced reminiscence about a man with whom Reedy did not speak from 1970 until his death in 1973; and *From the Ward to the White House: The Irish in American Politics* (1991). In 1988, four years after the death of his first wife, he married Ruth Brial Wissman. The couple had no children and separated several years before Reedy's death in Milwaukee.

A thoughtful and intelligent man, Reedy took on the challenge of advising and speaking for a politician with a huge but fragile ego. When Reedy fell out of Johnson's favor, he could have been shattered by the experience. Instead, he grew in stature—as a keen observer of the national political scene and as an educator of journalists with exceptional experience to call upon.

• Reedy's papers are divided between the Lyndon B. Johnson Presidential Library in Austin, Tex., and the Marquette University archives in Milwaukee, Wisc. Although a full-length biography of Reedy remains to be written, information about his career can be gleaned from books concerning the Johnson presidency, including Robert Dallek, *Flawed Giant: Lyndon Johnson and His Times, 1961–1973* (1998), and Irwin Unger and Debi Unger, *LBJ: A Life* (1999). Obituaries are in the *Milwaukee Journal-Sentinel* and the *New York Times*, both 22 Mar. 1999.

EDWARD L. LACH, JR.

REESE, Pee Wee (23 July 1919–14 Aug. 1999), baseball player, was born Harold Henry Reese in Ekron, Kentucky, the son of Carl Reese, a railroad detective, and Emma Reese (maiden name unknown). A few years after his birth, the family moved to Louisville. Pee Wee earned his nickname there by winning a city peewee marbles championship, although it has often been supposed that it resulted from his diminutive size. He was so small that he was afraid to go out for the baseball team at DuPont Manual High School, but in his senior year he made the team and earned a letter. Following graduation he continued playing on a Presbyterian Church League team, which won the city amateur title, and attracted the attention of the local Triple A Louisville Colonels. He had two good seasons with a batting average in the .270s and spectacular fielding, forcing the Boston Red Sox, who controlled the franchise, to decide between Reese and manager-shortstop Joe Cronin. Cronin's reluctance to promote a rival led Boston to sell Reese to the Brooklyn Dodgers of the National League for $40,000.

The Dodgers also had a shortstop-manager, Leo Durocher, but he saw the potential in Reese and made him a project, even moving the rookie in with him. A broken foot and a beaning marred Reese's rookie season in 1940, but he won the regular job in 1941, despite a .228 batting average and league-leading 47 errors, and helped lead the Dodgers to their first pennant since 1920. During spring training the next year, he married Dorothy Walton, with whom he had a son and a daughter. Like most of his ball-playing contemporaries, Reese interrupted his career in 1943 to enter military service, spending three years in the U.S. Navy.

When Reese returned for the 1946 season, he became a key ingredient in the greatest string of seasons in Dodger history. From 1947 through 1956 the team won six pennants and finished second three times and third once. Reese, named team captain, led the team both on and off the field. That leadership made itself felt most dramatically by the way he smoothed the path for Jackie Robinson to be accepted as part of major league baseball. Branch Rickey had signed Robinson to play at Montreal in 1946 with the idea that the next step would be for Robinson to break the color barrier that kept talented African Americans from playing at the highest level of the game. When Robinson looked like a good bet to make the Dodger team in the spring of 1947, a group of southern players led by Dixie Walker circulated a petition demanding that Robinson not be allowed to play for Brooklyn. But when Reese, who was from segregationist Kentucky, refused to sign the petition, along with a few other veterans, the movement died. He did much to put the black pioneer at ease. When Robinson received a letter from a man who threatened to shoot him at an Atlanta exhibition, Reese, warming up next to Robinson, kidded, "Jack. Don't stand so close to me today. Move away, will ya? The guy might be a bad shot!" (Kahn, p. 325; *Sporting News*, 30 Aug. 1999). Probably the most famous Reese-Robinson story concerns a game in Cincinnati on 14 May 1947. The fans and the Reds bench were heckling Robinson unmercifully when Reese stopped play and went over to the first baseman and, as if discussing strategy, casually draped an arm over his shoulder. That simple gesture of common humanity from a southern white man hushed the verbal sniping. It also exemplified two of the major themes of Reese's life: civility and a great desire to win. Support for Robinson was not just principled; it was pragmatic: here was an outstanding ballplayer who would help the Dodgers win.

During those golden years with "the boys of summer," as Roger Kahn famously dubbed them, Reese led a sparkling collection of players, including Roy Campanella, Duke Snider, Gil Hodges, Billy Cox, Carl Furillo, Don Newcombe, Preacher Roe, and Junior Gilliam. They readily called him captain and still did long into his retirement. Reese's statistics, however, were fairly modest. He batted .269 for his career, placing him among the weaker-hitting Hall of Fame shortstops. He led the league only three times in any offensive category: 104 walks in 1947, 132 runs in 1949, and 30 steals in 1952. His fielding average of .962 was unremarkable by later standards (infield accuracy having been enhanced by artificial turf); but his range was outstanding, and he was the best of his era at going back on pop flies. The culmination of those years came in 1955 when, after World Series losses to the Yankees in 1941, 1947, 1949, 1952, and 1953, "next year" finally came for the Dodgers. In the 2–0 finale, Reese threw out the last Yankee to nail down the victory. Two seasons later, turning 39, Reese had slowed down, his average plummeting to .224. He played part-time for the Dodgers after they moved to Los Angeles in 1958, then retired. After one year as a coach, he left the field forever, foregoing coaching and managing opportunities in part because of the stomach ulcers he had developed.

Following his playing days, Reese worked with Dizzy Dean for six years on the CBS Game of the Week telecasts, then three more with Curt Gowdy on NBC. He also did some broadcast work with the Cincinnati Reds and Montreal Expos. In 1971 he joined the Hillerich and Bradsby Company, makers of Louisville Slugger bats; during this time he also operated a bowling alley and was part owner of a bank. He died of cancer in Louisville.

Reese's Hall of Fame plaque, unveiled in 1984 after his election by the Veterans Committee, reads: "Shortstop and captain of the great Dodger teams of the 1940s and '50s. Intangible qualities of subtle leadership on and off field, competitive fire and professional pride complemented dependable glove, reliable base running, and clutch hitting as significant factors in 7 Dodger pennants. Instrumental in easing acceptance of Jackie Robinson as baseball's first black performer." Although Reese's skills on the playing field contributed to the Dodgers' success in the 1940s and 1950s, perhaps more important to the team was his moral leadership during a time of transition and controversy in major league baseball. Long-time Dodger broadcaster Vin Scully described him as "a remarkable human being, I think, more than a player" (*Sporting News*, 23 Aug. 1999).

• Chapter-length treatments of Reese can be found in Roger Kahn, *The Boys of Summer* (1971); Bruce Jacobs, ed., *Baseball Stars of 1950* (1950); and Donald Honig, *The Greatest Shortstops of All Time* (1992). Obituaries are in the *Louisville Courier-Journal*, 15 Aug. 1999; the *New York Times*, 16 Aug.

1999; the *Los Angeles Times*, 19 Aug. 1999; and the *Sporting News*, 23 Aug. and 30 Aug. 1999.

JOHN R. M. WILSON

RESTON, James (3 Nov. 1909–6 Dec. 1995), journalist, was born James Barrett Reston in Clydebank, Scotland, to James Reston, a machinist, and Johanna Irving Reston. When he was an infant the family tried to immigrate to the United States, but his mother's illness forced their return to Scotland. For much of the next eleven years the family, which also included an older sister, lived in Alexandria, Dumbartonshire, where the children attended local schools. The Reston household was poor but disciplined, and strict Presbyterianism ruled. In 1920 the Restons successfully immigrated to the United States and settled in Dayton, Ohio, where the senior Reston took a job with Delco, a subsidiary of General Motors. To earn extra money young James, nicknamed "Scotty," worked as a caddy at a local golf club and soon became proficient at the game; in his teens he won the state high school golf championship and was also a two-time Ohio public links champion.

Upon graduating from high school in 1927, Reston considered a career as a professional golfer, having long since given up his mother's dream for him of becoming a preacher. But he also enjoyed writing, and his mother persuaded him to go to college. To help pay for it, he edited a company publication at Delco for a year, then enrolled as a journalism major at the University of Illinois. Reston did not excel in his studies, but he shone in golf as well as soccer, lettering in both sports, and was also president of his fraternity. After graduating in 1932, he went to work for a year as a sportswriter for the *Springfield* (Ohio) *Daily News*. The job had been secured for him by former Ohio governor James M. Cox, the 1920 Democratic presidential candidate and publisher who owned the paper and for whom Reston had caddied some years earlier.

In 1933 Reston joined the sports publicity department at Ohio State University in Columbus and then took a job in the press office of the Cincinnati Reds baseball team. During a trip to New York with the Reds in 1934, he quit to become a reporter for Associated Press, where he prepared sports features and wrote a column about the city. After three years he was promoted and sent to London to help cover overseas sporting events as well as the British Foreign Office.

At a time when England was moving toward war, Reston proved to be an insightful reporter in his coverage of government affairs. His articles attracted the attention of the *New York Times*, and in 1939 the newspaper hired him as a reporter for its London bureau. Reston stayed there until mid-1941, covering the Blitz and other major news developments as World War II got under way. He was then transferred to the *Times*'s Washington, D.C., bureau, where for a time he reported on the State Department. In 1942, in the

wake of the U.S. entry into the war, Reston published his first book, a call to arms titled *Prelude to Victory* that encouraged all-out participation in the war effort. The book brought him to the attention of government authorities, and he was recruited for service in the U.S. Office of War Information in London. A year later, at the request of the publisher, Arthur Hays Sulzberger, he left that post and came to the *Times* offices in New York City, where he was assigned the task of acquainting Sulzberger's son-in-law and presumptive heir, Orvil Dryfoos, with the newspaper business. At the end of 1943 he went back to Washington as a diplomatic correspondent for the *Times*.

In 1944 Reston scored a scoop for the *Times* in the course of covering the Dumbarton Oaks Conference, a meeting of world leaders to establish the future United Nations. He was able to secure secret papers—leaked to him by Chinese delegates—detailing the positions of the Allies, and he published a series about them in the *Times*. The incident created a furor, not only among government officials but also with many of his colleagues in the press corps, who called the publication of such secret and sensitive material unethical. But the *Times* supported Reston, standing behind his assertion that "the people's right to know" was a fundamental principle of democracy. The series earned him a Pulitzer Prize in 1945 for national reporting.

His place in the *Times*'s journalistic firmament now assured, Reston went on to become the most knowledgeable and influential newspaperman in Washington, owing in no small part to his canny skill in rooting out sources. He became known as the ultimate Washington insider among the capital press corps, and his writings, including his interviews over the years with most of the world's major leaders, were not only a must-read for the educated American public but also were scrutinized by official Washington. Awards as well as other job offers became routine for Reston, and in 1953, fearing that the *Washington Post* might lure him away, the *Times* made him head of its prestigious Washington bureau. Over the following years Reston made the bureau undeniably the best in the nation, hiring a number of young reporters who went on to become national names themselves. Among his protégés were Russell Baker, David Halberstam, Anthony Lewis, Neil Sheehan, Hedrick Smith, and Tom Wicker, and in these years he established a lifelong reputation for treating young colleagues with respect and fairness. Continuing to write for the paper himself, he hired fledgling journalists to help him prepare news stories, book reviews, and a weekly unsigned gossip column, along with thought-provoking pieces on a regular basis for the Sunday edition.

In 1957 Reston won a second Pulitzer Prize, for distinguished reporting the previous year on the executive branch of the government. Three years later he began contributing to the paper a column on national politics titled "Washington," which appeared three times a week. The column continued for nearly three decades; it became a mainstay of the *Times* and was praised for its erudition and wisdom. Its inherent and consistently strong defense of American ideals and the democratic promise established Reston as something of a national conscience.

Following new publisher Arthur Ochs Sulzberger's reorganization of the *Times* in 1964, Reston turned over the helm of the Washington bureau to Tom Wicker and became an associate editor. While continuing to write his column and contribute other stories to the *Times*, he also began a study of the relationship between newspapers and government officials, especially as it affected American foreign policy. On a number of occasions since his Dumbarton Oaks scoop in 1944, an older and wiser Reston had been persuaded to see the merits of reshaping or even delaying stories that might affect national security. In one significant instance, he went along with a decision by then-*Times* publisher Orvil Dryfoos to play down the paper's scoop on the impending CIA-sponsored Bay of Pigs invasion in Cuba in the spring of 1961. A year later, on learning that the Soviet Union had secretly placed nuclear missiles in Cuba, he and the *Times* acceded to a request by President John F. Kennedy that the news not be published until after Kennedy addressed the nation; this reticence may have helped the United States gain the upper hand in what became known as the Cuban missile crisis.

Reston's ongoing study resulted in a series of lectures delivered in 1966 before the Council on Foreign Relations in New York, in the course of which he argued that in some cases unlimited freedom of the press posed a risk to national security. However, he stoutly reaffirmed then, as he did throughout his career, that the people's right to know was paramount and that the press had a responsibility to inform the public of the underlying causes of events considered newsworthy rather than merely reporting the events themselves. The lectures appeared in book form in 1967 under the title *The Artillery of the Press: Its Influence on American Foreign Policy*. During the 1960s Reston, now a national figure, had also become a sought-after public speaker, and some of his speeches, as well as articles and columns, appeared in a second book he published in 1967, *Sketches in the Sand*.

In May 1968 Reston moved to New York to become executive editor of the *Times*, and despite a short tenure in that post he strengthened both news reporting and commentary; in one of his most significant changes, prominent figures outside the newspaper business contributed engaging articles on their specialties, which included such diverse topics as art, humor, the nuances of law, and economics in Europe. By early 1969 Reston was back, at his own request, in Washington, continuing to write columns while serving as a vice president, responsible for overseeing news coverage and presentation. In 1971, having concluded that national security would not thereby be compromised, he played a major role in the *Times* publication of the so-called Pentagon Papers, a collection of stolen secret documents that related, in often disturbing detail, the role of the Defense Depart-

ment in the Vietnam War. That same year Reston also made international news with a series of articles detailing a visit to the People's Republic of China, at a time when hardly any Westerners were allowed to enter the country. The articles, surprisingly complimentary to the country, were crowned by an in-depth interview with Premier Chou En-lai and may have helped pave the way for President Richard M. Nixon's historic visit to China the following year.

Reston reasserted his position as the nation's moral compass during the Watergate crisis that began in 1972, staunchly criticizing President Nixon's efforts to keep the press from uncovering the facts behind the break-in and its aftermath. The Watergate affair, which culminated with Nixon's resignation in August 1974, was the last major event that Reston actively covered. Now in his sixty-fifth year, he stepped down as vice president of the *Times* to become a consultant to and director of the company. Another volume of his speeches and columns, *Washington*, was published in 1986. Though Reston continued to write his column until 1987, his influence on public opinion appeared to decline. No longer welcomed as a moral crusader—perhaps because such a stance no longer seemed fashionable—he was now dismissed by a new generation as a Washington insider who had become too cozy with the establishment to remain a prominent force in American journalism.

Sensing that time and events had passed him by, and welcoming retirement after decades of hard work, Reston left the *Times* on his eightieth birthday, in 1989. Two years later he published his autobiography under the title *Deadline: A Memoir* (1991). In preparing the book he was assisted by his wife, the former Sara Jane Fulton, nicknamed Sally, whom he had married in 1935 and who served as his closest confidante; the couple had three sons. In retirement, Reston and his wife continued to live at their home in Washington, D.C. Over the years they also maintained vacation residences in rural Virginia and on Martha's Vineyard, where they owned and operated the island's local paper, the *Vineyard Gazette*, as a hobby. In his final years Reston suffered from cancer, and he died of the disease at his Washington residence. At his death, he was remembered fondly and eulogized by many of his near-contemporaries, including influential *Washington Post* publisher Katharine Graham, who declared that "he helped lead postwar America from isolationism to internationalism."

• For biographical information, see entries for "Reston, James," in *Current Biography Yearbook* for 1943, 1980, and 1996. See also Reston's memoir, *Deadline* (1991), as well as *Contemporary Authors: New Revision Series*, vol. 58 (1997). For accounts of Reston's varying roles at the *New York Times*, see Gay Talese, *The Kingdom and the Power* (1969); Harrison Salisbury, *Without Fear or Favor: An Uncompromising Look at the New York Times* (1980); and Susan E. Tifft and Alex S. Jones, *The Trust: The Private and Powerful Family behind the New York Times* (1999). An extended obituary appears in the *New York Times*, 8 Dec. 1995.

ANN T. KEENE

RIBICOFF, Abraham (9 Apr. 1910–22 Feb. 1998), lawyer, politician, and statesman, was born in New Britain, Connecticut, the son of Abraham A. Ribicoff, a factory worker, and Rose Sable Ribicoff. Although he grew up in relative poverty, Ribicoff's family valued education and insisted that all his earnings from part-time boyhood jobs go toward his future schooling. After graduating from local public schools, he worked for a year at a nearby factory of the G. E. Prentice Company in order to earn additional funds for college. He enrolled at New York University in 1928, then transferred to the University of Chicago after the Prentice Company made him their Chicago office manager. While in Chicago, Ribicoff juggled school and work schedules and was permitted to enter the university's law school before finishing his undergraduate degree. Still a student, he married Ruth Siegel on 28 June 1931; they were to have two children. Ribicoff served as editor of the *University of Chicago Law Review* in his third year and received the LL.B. degree cum laude in 1933.

Upon graduation, Ribicoff returned to Connecticut and was admitted to the state bar. After practicing law in the office of a Hartford lawyer, he set up his own practice, first in Kensington and later in Hartford. By now interested in politics, he was elected to the Connecticut General Assembly in 1938 as a Democrat. Reelected the following year, he was named "most able representative" in a poll of local political correspondents.

In 1941 Ribicoff left the general assembly and was appointed a judge in the Hartford Police Court. He chaired the Connecticut Assembly of Municipal Court Judges in 1941–1942 and in 1943 headed a special state committee charged with studying crime and alcoholism. Reappointed to the bench by the governor, Ribicoff also served from 1945 to 1947 on the Hartford Charter Revision Commission, a bipartisan group that was influential in establishing both city-council and city-manager forms of government in the state capital. In 1947 Ribicoff began a two-year stint as the hearing examiner for cases brought about by the Connecticut Fair Employment Practices Act.

Ribicoff returned to partisan politics in 1948, when he was elected to the U.S. House of Representatives from the state's First District. He served two terms in the House, during which time he served on the Foreign Affairs Committee (a position usually reserved for members with more seniority) and generally proved to be a loyal supporter of Truman administration foreign and domestic policies. Generally liberal in his outlook, he surprised many by opposing a $32 million appropriation for the construction of a dam in Enfield, Connecticut, arguing that the money was better spent on military needs and foreign policy initiatives such as the Marshall Plan.

On the death of the incumbent U.S. senator Brien McMahon in 1952, Ribicoff sought to fill out the remaining four years of his term but suffered a narrow loss to Republican Prescott S. Bush. After returning to his legal practice for two years, he ran for governor against incumbent Republican John Davis Lodge, winning the election by a little over three thousand votes. As governor, Ribicoff soon faced the challenge of rebuilding his state in the wake of devastating floods that occurred in the late summer and fall of 1955, and he was able to lead bipartisan efforts to aid damaged areas. Ribicoff then successfully argued for increased state spending on schools and welfare programs. He also supported an amendment to the state constitution that enabled local municipalities to have greater governing powers. Easily reelected in 1958, Ribicoff had by now become active on the national political scene. A longtime friend of Senator John F. Kennedy, Ribicoff had nominated his fellow New Englander for vice president at the 1956 Democratic Convention and was one of the first public officials to endorse Kennedy's presidential campaign.

When Kennedy became president, Ribicoff was offered his choice of cabinet posts in the new administration. He reportedly turned down the position of attorney general, fearing that as a Jew he might create needless controversy within the emerging civil rights movement, and instead chose to be secretary of health, education and welfare (HEW). Although he did manage to secure a revision of the 1935 Social Security Act that liberalized requirements for aid-to-dependent-children funds from Congress, Ribicoff was unable to gain approval for the administration's medicare and school aid bills. Eventually he tired of attempting to manage HEW, whose very size made it, in his opinion, unmanageable.

Ribicoff resigned from HEW in 1962 and returned to Connecticut, where he launched a successful campaign for a seat in the U.S. Senate. Reelected in 1968 and in 1974, he served on the Finance Committee and continued to lobby for welfare and health insurance reforms. Having successfully led a traffic safety campaign that netted thousands of suspended or revoked licenses for convicted drunk drivers while he was governor, he continued to press for transportation safety in the Senate and was instrumental in passing the National Traffic and Motor Vehicle Safety Act in 1966.

Initially a supporter of Lyndon B. Johnson's programs, Ribicoff eventually turned against the Vietnam War and the president's management of it, believing that it drained badly needed resources away from domestic programs. He championed the unsuccessful presidential bid of Senator George McGovern in 1968; at the Democratic National Convention, he gained national attention when he took to the podium to denounce the "Gestapo tactics" used against demonstrators by Chicago police. Ribicoff spent the remaining years of his Senate career fighting for such liberal issues as school integration, welfare and tax reform, and consumer protection. Following the death of his wife, he married Lois Mell Mathes in 1972.

After retiring in 1980, Ribicoff served as special counsel to the New York City law firm of Kaye, Scholer, Fierman, Hays & Handier. He divided his time between homes in Cornwall Bridge, Connecticut, and Manhattan. Having suffered in his later years from the effects of Alzheimer's disease, he died at the Hebrew Home for the Aged at Riverdale in the Bronx, New York. A pragmatic supporter of moderate to liberal causes, Ribicoff was one of the first Jewish politicians to make major contributions on the state and federal levels of partisan politics.

• The largest portion of Ribicoff's papers is at the Library of Congress; material relating to his years as Connecticut's governor can be found at the Connecticut State Archives in Hartford. He was the author of *America Can Make It!* (1972) and, with Jon O. Newman, *Politics: The American Way* (1973). Coverage of his career is in Albert E. Van Dusen, *Connecticut* (1961), and Herbert F. Janick, *A Diverse People: Connecticut, 1914 to the Present* (1975). Obituaries are in the 23 Feb. 1998 issues of major newspapers, including the *New York Times*, the *Los Angeles Times*, and the *Chicago Tribune*.

EDWARD L. LACH, JR.

RICHARDSON, Elliot (20 July 1920–30 Dec. 1999), attorney and public official, was born Elliot Lee Richardson in Boston, Massachusetts, the son of Edward P. Richardson, a physician, and Clara Shattuck Richardson. The scion of an old and locally distinguished family with a long history of achievement in both medicine and politics, Richardson graduated from Milton Academy and entered Harvard, where he majored in philosophy and drew cartoons for the Harvard *Lampoon*. After graduating cum laude in 1941, he entered Harvard Law School, only to have his education interrupted by World War II. Richardson served as a lieutenant in the U.S. Army and participated in the Normandy invasion; by war's end he had earned a Bronze Star and two Purple Hearts.

On returning to law school in 1945, Richardson served as editor and president of the *Harvard Law Review* and graduated cum laude in 1947. After successively clerking for Justices Learned Hand (1947–1948) and Felix Frankfurter (1948–1949), he joined the firm of Ropes, Gray, Best, Collidge and Rugg. On 2 August 1952 he married Anne Francis Hazard; the couple eventually had three children. Although he later claimed that private practice "didn't match the satisfaction of doing a good job for the public," Richardson remained with the firm until 1957, except for a brief stint in 1953–1954 as an aide to U.S. Senator Leverett Saltonstall. He was then appointed assistant secretary for legislation in the Department of Health, Education and Welfare (HEW) by President Dwight D. Eisenhower. While in Washington Richardson played a leading role in creating the National Defense Education Act of 1958 and also briefly served as acting department head. In 1959 he returned to Massachusetts when Eisenhower appointed him to be a U.S. attorney. Quickly gaining a reputation as a tough prosecutor, his most famous case involved the tax evasion conviction of Bernard Goldfine, a textile manufacturer who had been implicated in the Sherman Adams scandal.

Following the 1960 elections, Richardson briefly returned to private legal practice, but it was clear that his future lay in public service. After losing the 1962 Republican primary for state attorney general to future Senator Edward Brooke, he was elected lieutenant governor of Massachusetts in 1964. Not content with the typical ceremonial duties usually associated with the post, Richardson formed an active partnership with Governor John Volpe in formulating policies in areas such as mental health reform, welfare, and education. Elected state attorney general in 1966, Richardson pursued a generally liberal agenda that included toughening consumer protection laws and combating unfair trade practices.

In 1969, following the recommendation of Secretary of State William P. Rogers, President Richard Nixon appointed Richardson as undersecretary of state. Although inexperienced in foreign policy, Richardson immersed himself in the job and was soon capably representing the Nixon administration at international conferences on subjects as diverse as free trade and strategic arms limitation (SALT). He also proved a capable administrator and gained credibility with his subordinates when he attempted a number of administrative reforms, most notably in revitalizing the Foreign Service Board, of which he became the head in June 1969. Of perhaps greatest importance, Richardson also served as an intermediary in the ongoing conflicts between Secretary Rogers and Nixon's increasingly powerful national security adviser, Henry Kissinger.

In June 1970 Nixon tapped Richardson to be the head of HEW. On returning to HEW, Richardson found a badly demoralized and disorganized bureaucracy that had greatly expanded in size and scope since the Eisenhower administration. In line with the Nixon administration's proposed "New Federalism," Richardson attempted to consolidate programs, streamline grant processing, and decentralize authority and decision making. He also had to deal with the controversial issue of school desegregation and faced criticism from civil rights activists when he announced in August 1970 that federal funds would no longer be cut off from school districts that refused desegregation; in typical fashion, Richardson offered the alternative of Justice Department prosecution, claiming that it was a more effective means of achieving the same goal.

In the aftermath of his 1972 reelection, Nixon shook up his cabinet assignments and named Richardson to replace the retiring secretary of defense, Melvin Laird. Richardson had hardly settled into his new post, however, when the burgeoning Watergate scandal made him the perfect choice—given his squeaky-clean image—to replace Richard Kleindienst as attorney general in April 1973. After guaranteeing an independent investigation of the scandal during his confirmation hearings before the Senate Judiciary committee, Richardson selected Harvard law professor Archibald Cox as special prosecutor but soon found himself in the middle of an increasingly bitter power struggle between Cox and the White House. When Richardson resigned rather than accede to Nixon's demands that he fire Cox on 20 October 1973, the resulting "Saturday Night Massacre" created a firestorm of controversy for the administration and made Richardson a folk hero in the eyes of many.

After dividing the next year between academia, writing, and speaking engagements, Richardson returned to Washington in December 1974 as President Gerald Ford's ambassador to Great Britain. Unhappy in this position, he was named secretary of commerce in November 1975 and spent the remainder of the Ford administration in that post. After serving as ambassador at large to the international Law of the Sea conference under President Jimmy Carter (1977–1980), Richardson returned to private legal practice in the Washington office of the law firm of Milbank, Tweed, Hadley, and McCloy. He remained active in public life, however, making an unsuccessful attempt to become the Republican nominee for the U.S. Senate from Massachusetts in 1984, as well as serving as a monitor of UN-sponsored Namibian (1988) and Nicaraguan (1989) elections. Awarded the Presidential Medal of Freedom in 1998, Richardson died in Boston while visiting relatives.

The only person ever appointed to four cabinet-level posts, Richardson often joked that he had "never held a job for more than two years." Aptly nicknamed "the man for all positions," he had an unshakable integrity that was put to the test during one of the most traumatic periods in American political history. His commitment to public service made him an exemplary figure in an era of increasing cynicism, and his ability to work in different capacities revealed him to be an intelligent generalist in a culture favoring specialization.

• Richardson's papers are held at the Manuscript Division of the Library of Congress in Washington, D.C. His memoirs, *Reflections of a Radical Moderate* (1996), is less concerned about the details of his life and career than his views on a variety of public and social issues. He was also the author of *The Creative Balance: Government, Politics, and the Individual in America's Third Century* (1976). Obituaries appeared in many leading newspapers—including the *Boston Globe*, the *New York Times*, and the *Washington Post*—on 1 Jan. 2000.

EDWARD L. LACH, JR.

RIGNEY, Bill (29 Jan. 1918–20 Feb. 2001), major league baseball player and manager, was born William Joseph Rigney in Alameda, California, the son of George "Deke" Rigney, who was in the tile business in Oakland, and Eleanor Connors Rigney. Following his graduation from Oakland High School, Rigney was discovered on the local sand lots and signed by the Oakland Oaks of the Pacific Coast League in 1938. The Oaks sent him to Spokane, Vancouver-Bellingham, and Topeka in the lower minors before he stuck with the PCL team in 1941 and 1942, hitting .208 and then a much-improved .288. In the minors he was known as "Specs" because he was one of the few infielders in baseball to wear eyeglasses. Rigney then spent three years in the navy, where he met Paula Bruen; they were married on 18 January 1944. The couple would have three children and remain together

until her death in 1998. In 1946, with the war over, Rigney joined the New York Giants for spring training. The slender (six-foot-one, 165-pound) young Irish Catholic had never been to New York or even been in a big league ballpark before.

His playing career, all with the Giants, lasted eight seasons—four as a regular and four as a utility player. He was better suited to playing third base or shortstop because of his strong arm, but he played more at second base than at either of those positions. He managed a modest .236 rookie season with three homers in the leadoff spot but did not draw enough walks to be a legitimate leadoff hitter. He became a noted chatterer and bench jockey, earning his Giant nickname—"Cricket." In 1947 he changed his batting stance and began pulling the ball, knocking 17 homers into left-field stands and contributing to a new National League team record, since eclipsed, of 221 home runs. His roommate, Johnny Mize, hit 51, leading Rigney to lay claim to a major league record for roommates. From 1947 to 1949 he batted .267, .264, and .278, and he played in the 1948 all-star game. He was reduced to a utility role from 1950 through 1953, appearing in only 179 games over that span. He later recalled that his career highlight was being a part of the Giants' famous comeback to beat the Dodgers in the 1951 playoff series, and he went one for four as a pinch hitter in the Giants' World Series loss to the New York Yankees. Rigney nostalgically remembered the late forties and early fifties as the time when baseball was played the best and New York's Giants, Yankees, and Dodgers were the epicenter of that excellence. He compiled a modest .259 average over his eight seasons and finished with 41 home runs.

Following the 1953 season, Rig, as he came to be called, took on his first managerial assignment, guiding the Minneapolis Millers of the American Association as a player-manager and winning the Little World Series against the International League champs in 1955. He had been tabbed as a potential manager as early as 1951, and with two years of minor league seasoning he was hired by Horace Stoneham to replace Leo Durocher at the helm of the Giants. He piloted New York to two sixth-place finishes, then moved with the team across the continent to San Francisco. Newly energized in their new city, the Giants finished third two years running, letting the 1959 pennant slip away in the season's final week. Despite Rigney's expertise as a baseball man and his ability to work well with talented young players like Orlando Cepeda, Willie McCovey, and Jim Davenport, his big star, Willie Mays, felt unloved. In June 1960 Stoneham fired Rigney and replaced him with Tom Sheehan, under whom the Giants fell from second to fifth.

Rigney bounced back in 1961 as the first manager of the expansion Los Angeles Angels in the American League. He skippered the Angels for over eight years, racking up some impressive achievements. The team won 70 and lost 91 in 1961, a record for a first-year expansion team. The next year the Angels shocked baseball by actually leading the league as late as 12

September, then slipping to third place with an 86-76 record but garnering a manager-of the-year award for Rigney. The bubble burst in 1963 and the Angels plunged to ninth, following that with fifth-, seventh-, sixth-, fifth-, and eighth-place finishes in the ten-team league. Early in the 1969 season the Angels fired the man who had become the senior manager in the league.

In 1970 the Minnesota Twins hired Rigney to replace the popular Billy Martin, who had won the West in the newly divided American League in 1969. Rigney repeated with the Twins, going 98-64 for his best record ever, only to be swept by the Baltimore Orioles in the play-offs. In 1971 the team slipped to fifth, twelve games below .500, and even a 36-34 start the following season could not save Rigney his job. Once again he was fired. Four years later, he had one more shot when his friend Chub Feeney brought him back to the Giants for the 1976 season. A 74-88 record and fourth-place finish ended that comeback, which he admitted later had been a bad idea. He scouted for the Angels until 1982, when he became a special assistant to Oakland A's President Roy Eisenhardt, a position he retained until his death. He received a good deal of credit for rebuilding the A's into a pennant-winning team in 1989, a pennant that Rigney never won as a manager.

Rigney was the quintessential career baseball man, spending 60 years as player, manager, coach, scout, broadcaster, and executive. He was a noted storyteller and humorist who, despite being fired by several close friends, never lost his positive outlook or became cynical. As a manager he kept an even keel and got along well with every player, although he was closest to those he had worked with in the early "fun" years with the Angels, especially future managers Jim Fregosi and Bob Rodgers. He compiled a 1,239-1,321 lifetime mark as a manager and left behind a legion of admirers and friends. He died in Walnut Creek, California, of cardiopulmonary complications after a long illness.

• Information on Bill Rigney can be found in Danny Peary, ed., *We Played the Game* (1994); in *The Bill James Guide to Baseball Managers* (1997); and in obituaries of 21 Feb. 2001 in the *San Francisco Chronicle*, the *Los Angeles Times*, and the *New York Times*.

JOHN R. M. WILSON

RILLIEUX, Norbert (17 Mar. 1806–8 Oct. 1894), inventor, chemical engineer, and first cousin of the painter Edgar Degas's mother, was born in New Orleans, Louisiana, the son of Vincent Rillieux, Jr., an engineer, and Constance Vivant, who belonged to a wealthy free black family of landowners and landlords. Vincent Rillieux, Jr., a businessman and inventor of a steam-operated press for baling cotton, was white, but Norbert and his mother belonged to the mainly Francophone and Catholic ethnic group of "free people of color" (often referred to as "Black Creoles" after the Civil War). Little is known of Norbert Rillieux's childhood from the time of his baptism

in the St. Louis Cathedral of New Orleans to the time he and his brother Edmond were sent, like many other young free men of color, to France to be educated. By 1830 Norbert was an instructor in applied mechanics at the École Centrale in Paris and is reported to have published several papers on steam power.

The following year, in 1831, Norbert Rillieux made an extraordinary discovery that prompted his return to New Orleans and would eventually transform the sugar-refining process in Louisiana and throughout the world. The traditional manner of reducing sugarcane juice for sugar production, called the "Jamaica Train," required the tedious and backbreaking labor of numerous slaves who, armed with long ladles, skimmed the boiling sugar juice from one open kettle to the next. Rillieux developed an ingenious apparatus, employing condensing coils that used the vapor from one vacuum chamber to evaporate the juice from a second chamber. The new invention—safer, more efficient, and less expensive than the open-kettle system—has been described as having been as significant for the sugar industry as Eli Whitney's cotton gin was for the processing of cotton.

Rillieux failed to interest French planters in his invention, but in 1833 he was invited back to New Orleans by the planter and banker Edmund Forstall to be chief engineer of a new sugar refinery. The appointment did not materialize, but Rillieux continued to perfect his apparatus and also made a fortune in land speculation, which he lost in the nationwide financial collapse of 1837. Some elegant architectural drawings that he produced with his brother Edmond during this period survive in the Notarial Archives in New Orleans. In 1843 two prominent planters hired Rillieux to install evaporators, Theodore Packwood at his plantation later known as Myrtle Grove, and Judah P. Benjamin at his Bellechasse plantation. Within three years Packwood won first prize and Benjamin and Packwood second prize for best sugar, the awards mentioning use of Rillieux's patent sugar boiling apparatus. On 26 August 1843 Norbert Rillieux was awarded his first patent from the U.S. Patent Office for a double effect evaporator in vacuum, followed by a patent in 1846 for a triple effect evaporator with horizontal tubular heating surface. Approval for a later patent (1857) was at first denied on the erroneous assumption that Rillieux was a slave and therefore not a U.S. citizen. "Now, I was the applicant for the patent and not the slave. I am a Citizen of the United States and made oath of the fact in my affidavit," Rillieux wrote.

Judah Benjamin, the brilliant Jewish jurist who later served as Jefferson Davis's secretary of state for the Confederacy, became Rillieux's major supporter in Louisiana sugar circles. He publicized Rillieux's apparatus in a series of articles in J. D. B. De Bow's popular commercial magazine (which came to be known as *De Bow's Review*). In 1846 Benjamin described the sugar produced by Rillieux's method as the best in Louisiana, its "crystalline grain and snowy whiteness . . . equal to those of the best double-refined sugar of our northern refineries." For ten years at least, Rillieux was a conspicuous figure in New Orleans manufacturing. Benjamin's earliest biographer, Pierce Butler, reported that "frequently, for quite long visits, came the dried-up little chemist Rillieux, always the centre of an admiring and interested group of planters from the neighborhood as he explained this or that point in the chemistry of sugar or the working of his apparatus." Rillieux was described by one contemporary as "the most sought-after engineer in Louisiana," but he was still, by Louisiana law, a "person of color," suffering under increasing legal and social restrictions as North-South tensions escalated.

It is not known exactly when Rillieux returned to France. He had many reasons, including the new restrictions imposed in 1855 on free people of color in New Orleans. Apparently Rillieux returned to France just before or during the Civil War and remained there until his death. There is no evidence that he knew his most famous relative, the Impressionist painter Edgar Degas, another Parisian. Late in life Rillieux became interested in Egypt, and in 1880 he was found deciphering hieroglyphics in the Bibliothèque Nationale by the Louisiana planter Duncan Kenner. During his seventies he was still working on refinements to various devices for beet and cane sugar production. Norbert Rillieux was buried in Paris's Père Lachaise cemetery, survived by his wife, Emily Cuckow Rillieux, who lived in comfortable circumstances for another eighteen years.

• Aside from a letter of Rillieux's published in the correspondence section of *De Bow's Review* 8 (1848): 291–93, and his correspondence with the U.S. Patent Office, little of Rillieux's writing seems to have survived. The sugar expert George P. Meade's article "A Negro Scientist of Slavery Days," in *Scientific Monthly* 62 (1946): 317–26, was a pioneering effort to recognize Rillieux's importance. It was reprinted with notes by Sidney Kaplan (on both George Meade and Rillieux) in *Negro History Bulletin* 20, no. 7 (April 1957): 159–63. The family connection of Rillieux and Degas was first announced in Christopher Benfey, "Degas and the 'Black World': Art and Miscegenation in New Orleans," *New Republic*, 21 Oct. 1996, pp. 25–30. A fuller version appeared in Benfey, *Degas in New Orleans* (1997). See also John A. Heitmann, *The Modernization of the Louisiana Sugar Industry 1830–1910* (1987). An obituary by Rillieux's secretary, Horsin-Deon, was translated and published in the *Louisiana Planter and Sugar Manufacturer*, 24 Nov. 1894, p. 331.

CHRISTOPHER BENFEY

ROBBINS, Harold (21 May 1916–14 Oct. 1997), novelist, was born in New York City. Evidently abandoned, he never learned who his parents were, but the name Francis Kane was on his birth certificate. He was first placed in a Roman Catholic orphanage in New York City's Hell's Kitchen and then in a series of foster homes. In 1927 he was adopted by a Manhattan pharmacist named Rubin and was called Harold Rubin. Later, when he became an author, he legally changed his name to Harold Robbins.

He dropped out of high school at fifteen, rented a room in Harlem, and shoveled snow when winter came. He ran numbers for a syndicate and was soon clever enough to counsel the oddsmakers. Going straight, he was a cook, a grocery-store clerk, and a cashier. On his savings, he took flying lessons and bought an old airplane. With an $800 loan, he flew to Virginia and the Carolinas, bought entire fields of unharvested crops, and sold the produce to New York stores. By age twenty, he was worth $1.5 million. In 1939 he sought to profiteer on sugar, buying shiploads at $4.85 per hundred pounds, but he was wiped out when the Roosevelt administration froze the price of sugar at $4.65 per hundred.

Losing his rented Manhattan hotel penthouse, Robbins returned to Harlem and worked as a shipping clerk at the Universal Pictures warehouse in New York. His discovery of $30,000 in overcharges paid by Universal gained him a promotion. Although he became director of the budget and statistical department (nominally until 1957), he falsely boasted of being Universal's youngest vice president. When he ridiculed the novels Hollywood was buying for film fodder, a Universal vice president challenged him to write a better one. He quickly churned forth a 600-page manuscript, which the publishing house of Alfred A. Knopf brought out in 1948 as *Never Love a Stranger*. Its hero, autobiographically named Frank Kane, tells of his Catholic orphanage beginnings, his being befriended by Jewish relatives, and his young adulthood in the 1930s. Because of its lurid passages—as judged by the standards of the day—*Never Love a Stranger* was part of a case brought against book dealers for offering obscene novels for sale; the non-jury trial, held in 1948, ended in an acquittal. Most of Robbins's later novels contain similarly trashy passages—for example, *The Storyteller* (1985) and *The Piranhas* (1991). By then, however, obscenity laws were almost nonexistent. Robbins's writings constantly present the competition for power and control, whether in boardrooms, bedrooms, or spicier locales. This holds true for *The Predators*, posthumously issued in 1998 and reprising much from *Never Love a Stranger* and *A Stone for Danny Fisher*, with which Robbins began his scramble to riches.

Robbins wrote twenty-four novels, each of which sold over 600,000 copies and several of which were turned into money-making movies. Although his writings were often savagely reviewed, he was sometimes praised for gritty plots, credible characters, and nimble dialogue. Knopf published his first five novels; Robbins then turned to Simon & Schuster and its subsidiaries Pocket Books and Trident Press. Robbins's most ambitious effort in fiction is his 1,500-page Hollywood trilogy: *The Dream Merchants* (1949), *The Carpetbaggers* (1961), and *The Inheritors* (1969). *The Dream Merchants* traces the rise of a young man in the movie industry, characteristically mixing melodrama, sentimentality, and lurid sexual episodes. *The Carpetbaggers* narrates the efforts of Jonas Cord, a vicious man's son, to gain wealth and power in Hollywood, aviation, and high finance. It is loosely patterned on Howard Hughes's career (which Robbins denied); its heroine, Rina Marlowe, resembles Jean Harlow (which the author also denied). *The Inheritors* involves a television programmer's struggles with media moguls and jet-setters and describes his escapades with many mindless females. The film *Nevada Smith* (1966), a formulaic western, capitalized on the popularity of *The Carpetbaggers* by taking a character from it and tracing his earlier life as a cowboy. This character also reappears in *The Raiders* (1994), a tardy sequel to *The Carpetbaggers* that continues the saga of the Cord family and features Jimmy Hoffa, Meyer Lansky, and other unsavory types.

Robbins's best novel, according to most critics, is *A Stone for Danny Fisher* (1952). It dramatizes a sensitive Jewish lad's fight to survive as a New York hustler-boxer in the 1930s and 1940s, at the expense of traditional moral and cultural values. An early example of Robbins's addiction to sleaze is *79 Park Avenue* (1955). Narrating the climb and fall of a slum-born New York prostitute, it partly echoes the sensational 1954–1955 Minot Frazier Jelke–Patricia Ward trial in New York, which had to do with the question of whether Ward was forced into prostitution. Robbins's most intriguing novel is *Where Love Has Gone* (1962). It features a beautiful sculptress named Lora, who stabs her lover to death and blames her young daughter for the deed. This novel created a furor because it appeared only four years after actress Lana Turner's Beverly Hills lover, Johnny Stompanato, was fatally stabbed—allegedly by Turner's young daughter. *The Betsy* (1971) offers an unsavory plot twist concerning an automobile magnate, his vapid son, and Betsy, allegedly the old man's granddaughter but in reality his daughter by his daughter-in-law; the title refers to a "wonder car" meant to last a lifetime.

Of the nine movies made from Robbins's novels and original scripts, *A Stone for Danny Fisher*, retitled *King Creole* (1958), is memorable for starring Elvis Presley in his third movie. *Stiletto* (1969), dramatizing well-dressed Mafioso violence, was the first of several films Robbins coproduced. His foray into television was most sensational in connection with *The Survivors* (ABC, 1969–1970), an expensive flop, though with Lana Turner in the costly cast.

Robbins enjoyed a spectacular career and a lavish lifestyle, but he also developed a gargantuan conceit. In 1967 he was interviewed by reporter Thomas Thompson in his Carlton Hotel office in Cannes, France, downhill from his Riviera villa and with his yacht bumping in the harbor. He boasted as follows: *The Adventurers* (1966), partly based on South American revolutionary Porfirio Rubirosa, earned him $1.5 million, and the movie would gain him $1.3 million. For each of his three most recent novels Trident guaranteed him a $500,000 advance. He had four novels in his head awaiting dictation. If he wrote nothing more, he would glean $300,000 to $400,000 annually until 1981. By his lights, he had wisely demanded, and received, a $5.5 million advance for writing the

wretched *Survivors*. So he did not mind recently losing $156,000 at the Monte Carlo tables. When in need of new suits, he would fly to the Parisian couturier of the film star Sean Connery and Sammy Davis, Jr. He also wisely kept in touch with America after the war, whereas the more celebrated writers James Jones, Norman Mailer, and Irwin Shaw did not. In 1975 Robbins revealed to interviewer Leslie Hascom that he was the best novelist alive, that he admired James T. Farrell, John O'Hara, and John Steinbeck, but that Ernest Hemingway never managed the novel form.

In his second home, formerly Gloria Swanson's Beverly Hills mansion, Robbins suffered a stroke in 1982 and was confined to a wheelchair, but he continued to publish. Oddly, he talked much about himself but revealed little about his three wives (some sources say five). His first marriage, to Lillian Machnivitz, was "dissolved." With his second wife, Grace Palerno, he had two daughters. His last marriage was to Jann Stapp in 1992. Dying of pulmonary arrest in a hospital in Palm Springs, California, he was survived by Jann Robbins and his two daughters. His celebrity continued worldwide thereafter because his books had been translated into thirty-nine languages.

• Robbins boasted that he never rewrote and kept neither notes nor manuscripts. Scot Haller, "The World's Five Best-Selling Authors," *Saturday Review,* Mar. 1981, pp. 14–20, names Robbins first, with Barbara Cartland, Irving Wallace, Louis L'Amour, and Janet Dailey following in order. But the number of Robbins's books that were sold through 1980, said at the time to have been 200 million, has been disputed; see the *Washington Post,* 26 Oct. 1997, where the more modest figure of 45 million up to 1975 is given; the *New York Times* obituary offers a lifetime figure of 50 million. Thomas Thompson, "A Tour through the Harold Robbins Industry," *Life,* 8 Dec. 1967, details his early life, success, and pride. Leslie Hascom interviewed Robbins for the *Pittsburgh Press,* 16 Mar. 1975. James B. Lane, "Violence and Sex in the Post-War Popular Urban Novel: With a Consideration of Harold Robbins's *A Stone for Danny Fisher* and Hubert Selby, Jr.'s *Last Exit to Brooklyn,*" *Journal of Popular Culture* 8 (Fall 1974): 295–308, brilliantly analyzes ingredients in *A Stone* . . . that make it "the forerunner of a bright new genre of realistic urban novels." Jane Ellen Wayne, *Lana: The Life and Loves of Lana Turner* (1995), reports the supposed facts of Johnny Stompanato's death, which Robbins fashioned into *Where Love Has Gone.* Leslie Halliwell, *Halliwell's Who's Who in the Movies,* ed. John Walker, 13th ed. (1997), and Alex McNeil, *Total Television: The Comprehensive Guide to Programming from 1948 to the Present,* 4th ed. (1996), list, respectively, Robbins's big- and small-screen successes. An obituary is in the *New York Times,* 15 Oct. 1997.

ROBERT L. GALE

ROBBINS, Jerome (11 Oct. 1918–29 July 1998), choreographer, dancer, director, was born Jerome Wilson Rabinowitz, the son of Harry Rabinowitz and Lena Rips Rabinowitz, owners of a delicatessen in New York City. When Robbins was still a preschooler, the family moved to Weehawken, New Jersey. The parents opened a corset factory in Union City.

Like many Jewish immigrants of that period Robbins's parents were eager for their offspring to be exposed to the arts. Little did they realize that their son, although his talents were wide-ranging, would become passionate about dance. The father took an especially dim view of this choice. At first, Robbins's older sister Sonia gave him dance lessons at home. She then encouraged him to audition for her teacher, Senia Gluck-Sandor. With his wife, Felicia Sorel, Gluck-Sandor maintained a school in New York called The Dance Center. It was a stimulating place, and within a year the fifteen-year-old Robbins became a member of the school's workshop company. He later maintained that the strongest influences on his artistic development were Gluck-Sandor and George Balanchine.

In 1936 Gluck-Sandor encouraged him to change his name to Robbins. In 1944, both he and his parents did so legally.

Dancing in the chorus of *Great Lady* (1938) was Robbins's first Broadway experience. It also marked the first time he encountered Balanchine. (Although William Dollar was credited with the show's choreography, Balanchine assumed most of the responsibility.) During this period (1937–1941) Robbins spent his summers working at Camp Tamiment, an adult resort in the Poconos that required its entertainment staff to put on two full performances a week. These were produced by Max Liebman, who later directed the popular "Your Show of Shows" on television and who presented the best of the Tamiment-1938 output on Broadway. It was called *The Straw Hat Revue* (1939), and Robbins was in the chorus.

The following year, he again encountered Balanchine, who was the choreographer for another short-lived show called *Keep Off the Grass*. Despite this, it was a banner year. American Ballet Theatre (then called Ballet Theatre) was formed, and Robbins was accepted into the corps. It was quickly apparent that as a dancer (and later as a choreographer) he had an unusual flair for humor. It was never slapstick, never pratfall. Instead, it emanated deftly from characterization and from the flavor of the movement.

During Robbins's second year with the company, choreographer Agnes de Mille chose him to portray the mischievous youth in her *Three Virgins and a Devil* (1941). It was a brief role, but his jaunty behavior galvanized the ballet's action. The following season, as Hermes in David Lichine's *Helen of Troy*, he drew laughter by insouciantly munching on an apple outside of Helen's boudoir during her love scene. The lonely puppet in Michel Fokine's *Petrouchka* (1941 revision) was to reveal Robbins's emotional range, as did Balanchine's *Prodigal Son* (revival, 1950), which he performed with New York City Ballet.

Despite his occasional featured roles with Ballet Theatre, Robbins was still in the corps. But he received permission from the company's artistic director, Lucia Chase, to begin work on a small opus of his own. Perhaps it was inspired by Paul Cadmus's painting *The Fleet's In*. But the Cadmus scene was lewd,

whereas Robbins's ballet, called *Fancy Free* (1944) had a sweetness and an innocence that were consistent throughout. He cast himself as one of three sailors on shore leave. The other participants in the rollicking search for girls were John Kriza and Harold Lang. Muriel Bentley, Janet Reed, and Shirley Eckl were their quarry. Rex Cooper portrayed a bartender.

When it opened at the Metropolitan Opera House, *Fancy Free* met with tumultuous approval. In addition to its sharply drawn characters, it drew on a spirited jazz score by Leonard Bernstein and a witty yet understated decor by Oliver Smith. At the end of the twentieth century, the ballet was still being enthusiastically applauded. Later in 1944, Robbins and Bernstein joined forces with three experienced Broadway creators, director George Abbott and writers Betty Comden and Adolph Green. They expanded on the sailors-on-shore-leave theme for *On the Town*, starring Sono Osato.

Between 1945 and 1949, Robbins's Broadway career outweighed his ballet output. On Broadway he created the dances for *Billion Dollar Baby* (1945), *High Button Shoes* (1945), *Look, Ma, I'm Dancin'* (1948), and *Miss Liberty* (1949). Especially memorable were his "Charleston" in *Billion Dollar Baby* and his "Mack Sennett Ballet" in *High Button Shoes*. Here he created a hilarious chase that propelled the dancers in and out of a row of bathhouse doors in pursuit of a family of burglars. It was a miracle of ingenuity and comic timing. His ballet output during this period included the lighthearted *Interplay* (1945), with a score by Morton Gould, and *Facsimile* (1945), his first attempt at serious choreography. Its tense commentary on loneliness pitted the dramatic ballerina Nora Kaye against two indecisive lovers. At the ballet's climax she was required to scream, "Stop! Stop!" The effect was melodramatic rather than tragic.

Robbins began to feel that his ballet career was moving too slowly. He wrote to George Balanchine, whose New York City Ballet had been launched in 1948, and offered his services as a dancer, choreographer, or whatever Balanchine required. The master welcomed him and in 1949 gave him the title of associate director. He was encouraged to make as many ballets as he wished, and Balanchine gave him performing roles that were well suited to his talents. In addition to *The Prodigal Son*, Robbins shone in Balanchine's *Bourrée Fantasque* (1949) and *Tyl Ulenspiegel* (1951). His own career as a New York City Ballet choreographer was firmly launched with *The Guests* (1949), *Age of Anxiety* (1950), *The Cage* (1951), *Afternoon of a Faun* (1953), and *Fanfare* (1953).

In the early '50s Robbins stopped performing. At this point, he was deeply immersed in psychoanalysis, principally as a way of resolving his sexual ambivalence. He was contemplating marriage with Nora Kaye, and it was for her that he created *The Cage*, a darkly brilliant evocation of a community of female insects whose novice, danced by Kaye, learns, spider-like, how to destroy her suitors. Impelled by Igor Stravinsky's terse Concerto in D for String Orchestra, and shadowed by a web of rope designed by Jean Rosenthal, the predominantly female cast was the very embodiment of savagery. Robbins's marriage to Kaye never took place. In fact, he never married. *The Cage* endured, as did *Afternoon of a Faun*, a poetic pas de deux that commented delicately yet wisely on narcissism and its effect on two dancers about to fall in love. Another crucial event in Robbins's life took place that same year. He was summoned to testify before the House Un-American Activities Committee, and he incriminated eight people. This action was a source of regret for him during the rest of his life. It also turned a number of people fiercely against him.

In 1951 Robbins had created the sparkling yet touching "Small House of Uncle Thomas" ballet for the Broadway production of *The King and I*. In 1954 he turned to pure fun with *Peter Pan*. But a peak in his Broadway career was *West Side Story* (1957), a poignant depiction of gang life in New York. In this "Romeo and Juliet" offshoot he joined with a nucleus of distinguished creative artists: Leonard Bernstein, score; Oliver Smith, decor; Stephen Sondheim, lyrics; Arthur Laurents, book; and Irene Sharaff, costumes. It was, however, the dances that gave *West Side Story* its full dimension.

In later years, Robbins was to return several times to the music of Chopin. His first attempt, *The Concert (Or, the Perils of Everybody)* (1956), dealt with the outlandish fantasies of concertgoers. In 1958 he was invited to form an ensemble called Ballets: USA, which made its debut that summer at the Festival of Two Worlds in Spoleto, Italy. Although he particularly enjoyed working with the company and created new works, including *NY Export: Opus Jazz* (1958) and *Moves* (1959), the project was disbanded after only two years. It was briefly reassembled in 1962 to appear before the shah of Iran at the White House.

Although still associated with the New York City Ballet, Robbins returned to American Ballet Theatre to stage *Les Noces* (1965). Set to Stravinsky's powerful score, the ballet was equally potent in its depiction of a Russian peasant wedding. For some, it seemed a logical outgrowth of the wedding dances in *Fiddler on the Roof* (1964), Robbins's beautifully crafted evocation of his own family's Russian shtetl background. After *Fiddler*, he needed time to think. So he obtained a grant from the National Endowment for the Arts, assembled a group of dancers and other collaborators, and formed the American Theater Laboratory. They were committed to experimentation rather than finished productions.

Renewed and refreshed, Robbins returned to New York City Ballet and turned out four of his most distinguished ballets: *Dances at a Gathering* (1969), *In the Night* (1970), *The Goldberg Variations* (1971), and *Watermill* (1972). For *Dances at a Gathering* and *In the Night*, he also returned affectionately to Chopin. Lasting a full hour, *Dances at a Gathering* was performed to eight mazurkas, five waltzes, three etudes, one scherzo, and a nocturne. The ballet became so deeply identified with Robbins at his most sensitive

that it was used to conclude his memorial service. The original participants were Patricia McBride, Edward Villella, Violette Verdy, Allegra Kent, Sara Leland, Kay Mazzo, Anthony Blum, John Clifford, Robert Maiorano, and John Prinz. During the American Theater Lab interlude, Robbins and his dancers had studied Japanese Noh and Kabuki. Echoing their formality, he created *Watermill*. Villella was entrusted with the principal role, that of a man contemplating his life.

The New York City Ballet has presented several festivals devoted to individual composers. For the Stravinsky Festival (1972), Robbins contributed five works; for the Ravel Festival (1975), he again turned out five. He did not contribute to the American Music Festival (1988) because he was preparing *Jerome Robbins' Broadway* (1989), a retrospective of his musical theater choreography. Although his rehearsal time for the show was longer than for anything he had created, it was a box office disappointment; and his characteristically irate rehearsal behavior reached extremes. Part of this may have come from a decline in his health. Yet he continued to create works for the New York City Ballet that often displayed new levels of elegance and sophistication. For pure theatricality, there were *The Four Seasons* (1979), to ballet divertissements from Verdi operas, and *I'm Old-Fashioned* (1983), which combined Fred Astaire and Rita Hayworth on film with company dancers on stage. The introspective Robbins was again called forth in *Opus 19/The Dreamer* (1979), *In Memory of . . .* (1985), and *Ives Songs* (1988). Minimalist composers Philip Glass and Steve Reich were treated with high imagination in *Glass Pieces* (1983) and *Eight Lines* (1985).

George Balanchine died in 1983. The company's board of directors subsequently named Robbins co-ballet master in chief, along with Peter Martins. In 1990, after a two-week Jerome Robbins festival consisting of twenty-seven of his ballets, he relinquished the post but continued to set new ballets and rehearse his existing ones.

As America's most distinguished, native-born ballet choreographer, Jerome Robbins received forty-eight awards during his lifetime. These included the City of New York Citation (1959), City of Paris Award (1971), Handel Medallion (1978), Kennedy Center Honors (1981), and France's Commander of the Legion of Honor (1993). He died at his home in New York City.

• Christine Conrad's *Jerome Robbins: That Broadway Man, That Ballet Man* (2000) is essentially a picture book. Greg Lawrence, *Dance with Demons: The Life of Jerome Robbins* (2001) gives extensive coverage, particularly in the depiction of his Broadway career and in observations about his personal life. *Ballet Review* 16 (Summer 1988) contains a many-voiced tribute. Doris Hering's "Jerry's Legacy" in *Dance Magazine*, Apr. 1989, includes a detailed account of *Jerome Robbins' Broadway*. See also Hering's "Robbins, Jerome" in the *International Encyclopedia of Dance*, vol. 5 (1998). Obituaries appear in the *New York Times* and the *Washington Post*, 12 Oct. 1998.

DORIS HERING

ROBERTS, Peter (26 Aug. 1859–2 Dec. 1932), minister, sociologist, and educator, was born in Dowlais, South Wales, Great Britain, the son of John Roberts and Elizabeth Davis Roberts. Information about his early life is extremely limited. According to one source, Roberts worked as a coal miner and as a blacksmith's apprentice in his youth. He went to school at Glangadog, South Wales, and received his B.A. at Brecon Memorial College, Wales, in 1883. In the same year, Roberts immigrated to the United States, where he attended Yale University. Graduating with a bachelor of divinity degree in 1886, he delivered the commencement address.

Ordained at Plymouth Congregational Church in Scranton, Pennsylvania, on 1 November 1886, Roberts served as minister in Scranton (1886–1891), Olyphant (1891–1899), and Mahanoy City (1899–1907). All three Pennsylvania communities counted large numbers of Welsh immigrants such as himself among their populations. And like other communities in the Pennsylvania anthracite mining region, all three had Welsh Congregational churches, which may have made the particular area especially attractive to Roberts.

In 1899 Roberts took a leave from the ministry and returned to Yale for a Ph.D. in sociology. Roberts completed his graduate studies in 1901 with a dissertation on the economic development of the anthracite coal industry in 1901 under the direction of William Graham Sumner, one of America's foremost sociologists and social Darwinist intellectuals at the time.

In April 1901 Roberts married Rachel Evans in New York City. Before she died in 1925, they would have ten children, some named in ways as telling as Roberts's social thought: for example, William Sumner Roberts (after his dissertation adviser) and John Ruskin Roberts (after the nineteenth-century British intellectual).

Eventually the author of numerous books and articles on immigration and Americanization, Roberts, while not unsympathetic to immigrants and their predicaments, was at times rather critical of their potential impact on American society. In *The Anthracite Coal Industry: A Study of the Economic Conditions and Relations of the Cooperative Forces in the Development of the Anthracite Coal Industry of Pennsylvania* (1901) and *Anthracite Coal Communities: A Study of the Demography, the Social, Educational and Moral Life of the Anthracite Regions* (1904; reprint, 1970), Roberts admonished employers for not exercising enough care for their workers; but he mostly scolded immigrants for what he saw as an inclination toward immediate gratification, and he urged them to practice forbearance and civilized self-restraint instead. In subsequent years Roberts modified his point of view to some extent.

In 1909 Roberts contributed a brief essay on Pittsburgh workers to *The Pittsburgh Survey*, the multivolume study directed by Paul Underwood Kellogg and funded by the Russell Sage Foundation. Roberts's offering reflected the often contradictory cultural perceptions and biases of the survey's participants. Sympathetic toward the downtrodden, exploited workers, and appalled and disgusted with the social and economic repercussions of urban, industrial society, Roberts, like his fellow writers and researchers, placed his hopes in the ameliorative effects of American civilization on the immigrants. Despite the urban squalor, poor working conditions, and exploitative landlords and employers that burdened them, it was up to the immigrants to accept the outstretched hand of moral uplift. This, Roberts had come to believe, could be facilitated through teaching them English.

While serving as the special secretary for immigration with the Young Men's Christian Association's Industrial Department from 1907 to 1921, Roberts coordinated the YMCA's Americanization programs and wrote lesson plans for the teaching of literature, the English language, and civics. The English lessons, textbooks, and teaching materials, combining language acquisition with practical advice, were intended to reinforce punctuality and diligence at work and frugality and forbearance in workers' consumer habits. Such counsel certainly meshed well with interests of such companies as International Harvester, Ford, and General Electric, which sponsored YMCA-run English lessons taught with the Roberts method on company premises. His method had some influence beyond company-sponsored worker education programs; in 1908 he copyrighted his textbooks and sold them to public and private schools.

Contrary to nativist advocates of immigration restriction, Roberts actually favored immigration as a boon to the country's economic development. He blended his appreciation of immigrants' contributions with racial notions of their group-specific character and capacities. In 1912 he wrote that "industry had a place for the stolid, strong, submissive, patient Slav and Finn, it needed the mercurial Italian and Roumanian; there was much coarse, rough and heavy work to do [in] mining and construction camps; in tunnel and railroad building; around smelters and furnaces. . . . The new immigrant has supplied the need" (quoted in Jacobson, p. 71).

Roberts approached immigrants with more understanding and sympathy than most of his contemporaries, such as Lothrop Stoddard or Madison Grant. As Roberts put it, "shun the foreigner, leave him to himself, let him alone in dirt and disease and unseen by an appreciative eye . . . and he will simply drift. We would do the same" (quoted in Korman, p. 143). Roberts hoped to uplift immigrants and facilitate their integration into American life. He wrote, "I believe in the immigrant. . . . He has in him the making of an American, provided a sympathetic hand guides and smoothes the path which leads to assimilation. The hand of the native-born can best do this" (quoted in *New York Times*, 4 Dec. 1932). Although Roberts saw immigrants as a potential source for social and cultural upheaval, he also perceived in them a potential boon because the assimilation of immigrants would serve to affirm American values while at the same time it carried a promise of cultural renewal and economic expansion.

In addition to using his language and civics programs, the YMCA relied on Roberts's skills and abilities to coordinate several important operations. During World War I, Roberts coordinated the YMCA's efforts at government-run plants. Available published sources on his life and career give no indication of what he did in retirement.

Survived by his children, ten grandchildren, and a sister, Mrs. Philip H. Warren of Scranton, Roberts died at his home in Mount Vernon, New York.

• There are no available private papers of Peter Roberts. Archival materials pertaining to Roberts as the YMCA special secretary for immigration can be found in the YMCA Industrial Department Records, Kautz Family YMCA Archives, University Libraries, University of Minnesota, Twin Cities. In addition to the publications mentioned above, Roberts's writings include *The New Immigration: A Study of the Industrial and Social Life of Southeastern Europeans in America* (1912) and *The Problem of Americanization* (1920). He also published a little-known article on Slavic people, "The Slavs," in Alfred Rambaud et al., *The Case of Russia: A Composite View* (1905), pp. 293–337. Roberts's language manuals include *English for Coming Americans: First Reader* (1911), *English for Coming Americans: Teacher's Manual* (1912), and *Civics for Coming Americans* (1914). For his contribution to the Pittsburgh Survey, see "Immigrant-Wage Earners [*sic*]," in Paul Underwood Kellogg, ed., *The Pittsburgh Survey*, vol. 6: *Wage-Earning Pittsburgh* (1914), pp. 33–60.

An uncredited article in a YMCA periodical—"The Outreach to Industrial Men," *Association Men* 32 (July 1907): 428—mentions Roberts's early work experience. On his language and civics programs, see also Gerd Korman, *Industrialization, Immigrants, and Americanizers: The View from Milwaukee* (1967); Edward George Hartmann, *The Movement to Americanize the Immigrant* (1948); Matthew Frye Jacobson, *Barbarian Virtues: The United States Encounters Foreign Peoples at Home and Abroad, 1865–1917* (2000); Paul McBride, *Culture Clash: Immigrants and Reformers, 1880–1920* (1975); and McBride, "Peter Roberts and the YMCA Americanization Program, 1907–World War I," *Pennsylvania History* 44 (1977): 145–62. For a brief examination of Roberts's contribution to the Kellogg-directed survey, see Ewa Morawska, "The Immigrants Pictured and Unpictured in the Pittsburgh Survey," in Maurine Weiner Greenwald and Margo Anderson, eds., *Pittsburgh Surveyed: Social Science and Social Reform in the Early Twentieth Century* (1996), pp. 221–44.

An obituary appears in the *New York Times*, 4 Dec. 1932; see also the Yale Obituary Record, Yale University Archives, Yale University, New Haven, Connecticut.

THOMAS WINTER

RODDENBERRY, Gene (19 Aug. 1921–24 Oct. 1991), writer and television producer, was born Eugene Wesley Roddenberry in El Paso, Texas, the son of Eugene Edward Roddenberry, railroad worker, and Carolyn Glenn Coleman Roddenberry. Seeking greater opportunities, his father relocated the family to southern California shortly after Gene's birth and became a policeman in Los Angeles. A voracious reader, the younger Roddenberry became an avid fan of pulp fiction novels and movie serials such as "Buck Rogers" and "Flash Gordon." He attended local public schools before entering Los Angeles City College, where he studied police science. Roddenberry also took flight instruction under the auspices of U.S. Army general Henry "Hap" Arnold's Civilian Pilot Training program, and after graduating with an A.A. degree in 1941 he immediately enlisted in the U.S. Army Air Corps. While in training in Texas, he married Eileen Anita Rexroat on 20 June 1942; they were to have two daughters.

After leaving Texas, Roddenberry spent the first part of World War II piloting B-17 bombers on reconnaissance and bombing missions in the South Pacific. He spent the latter portion of the war stateside investigating airplane crashes. He rose to the rank of captain before resigning from the military in early 1945. Although he spent the next several years as a pilot for Pan American World Airways, Roddenberry harbored a continuing desire to become a writer. His first published work, a poem, appeared on the op-ed page of the *New York Times* in 1945, and he took extension writing courses at both Columbia University and the University of Miami in order to hone his craft. Fascinated by the new medium of television, Roddenberry resigned from Pan Am in May 1948 and moved with his family to southern California in the hope of becoming a television writer. On his arrival, Roddenberry discovered to his chagrin that most television production at that time took place in the New York area—from which he had just departed. With few immediate prospects and no credits to his name, he joined the Los Angeles Police Department in January 1949. Initially assigned to traffic control, he later transferred to Public Information, where he was charged with drafting literature and writing speeches for Chief William H. Parker. He continued to write in his spare time, and he benefited from the close relationship between the police department and Jack Webb's "Dragnet" television series. Although he submitted several story ideas to the show, success was slow in coming. His first break came in 1953, when he became the technical adviser for the show "Mr. District Attorney." He soon sold his first television script to the program, writing under the name Robert Wesley, and shortly thereafter sold his first science fiction script, "The Secret Weapon of 117," to the Chevron Hall of Stars syndicated program. With continued success (he also wrote for the programs "Highway Patrol" and "I Led Three Lives"), Roddenberry resigned from the police force in 1956 and began writing under his own name full time.

By the early 1960s Roddenberry was engaged in producing as well as writing, and the success of his show "The Lieutenant" led to greater opportunities. In 1964 he began pitching an idea for an outer space drama, set in the future, that featured a multi-ethnic crew. After the idea was rejected by MGM, it caught the interest of Oscar Katz, the head of programming at Desilu Productions. Although CBS turned them down, Roddenberry and Katz sold the idea to NBC as a sort of "wagon train to the stars." The program, "Star Trek," had to undergo a long gestation period, including not just one but two pilot episodes before it made its debut on 8 September 1966. Despite failing to ever make it into the top-twenty ratings, the show quickly developed a fanatical following; viewers related not only to the show's characters (strong Captain James T. Kirk, logical half-Vulcan Mr. Spock, and emotional Dr. McCoy) but also to the show's subtle message that humankind, flawed and self-destructive, might yet have a glorious future. Roddenberry wrote several episodes of the series himself and rewrote several more. In the face of widespread protests, some of which were orchestrated by Roddenberry behind the scenes, the show was canceled after seventy-nine episodes in 1969. That same year, Roddenberry, after divorcing his first wife, married actress Majel Barrett; they had one son.

Roddenberry continued to write and produce, both for feature films, such as *Pretty Maids All in a Row*, and television, including "The Questor Tapes." In the meantime, old episodes of "Star Trek"—now seen in syndication and in translation worldwide—were enjoying increased popularity. The show provided the basis for numerous fan clubs as well as heavily attended conventions featuring Star Trek merchandise, memorabilia, and panel discussions with cast members. The show returned to television as an animated Saturday morning cartoon in 1973–1974, and after negotiations bogged down during attempts to revive the television series with the original cast members, the decision was made to produce "Star Trek" feature films. Roddenberry co-wrote and produced *Star Trek: The Motion Picture* (1979), and its box office success quickly prompted the release of *Star Trek II: The Wrath of Khan* (1982), *Star Trek III: The Search for Spock* (1984), *Star Trek IV: The Voyage Home* (1986), *Star Trek V: The Final Frontier* (1989), and *Star Trek VI: The Undiscovered Country* (1991), all of which featured Roddenberry as executive consultant. By now fully convinced of the franchise's commercial viability, the Fox Network brought the show back to television with a new cast as "Star Trek: The Next Generation" in the fall of 1987, with Roddenberry again serving as executive consultant.

Roddenberry died in Santa Monica, California, after a brief period of declining health. Having been honored with a star on the Hollywood Boulevard Walk of Fame in 1985, he achieved a legendary status equal to that of the show he had created. One of the few television writers and producers to become a widely celebrated figure, he (along with Arthur C. Clarke and several others) paved the way for an increased acceptance of serious science fiction in both television and films.

• A collection of Roddenberry's papers relating to his work on "Star Trek" is held at the UCLA Arts Library Special Collections. The best secondary source of information on his life and career is David Alexander, *"Star Trek" Creator: The Authorized Biography of Gene Roddenberry* (1994). See, in addition, Joel Engel, *Gene Roddenberry: The Myth and the Man behind "Star Trek"* (1994); and Yvonne Fern, *Gene Roddenberry: The Last Conversation: A Dialogue with the Creator of "Star Trek"* (1994; rev. ed., 1996). Also useful are Betsy Caprio, *"Star Trek": Good News in Modern Images* (1978), and Karin Blair, *Meaning in "Star Trek"* (1977). Obituaries appear in all leading U.S. newspapers of the time, including the *New York Times*, 25 Oct. 1991.

EDWARD L. LACH, JR.

ROGERS, Roy (5 Nov. 1911–6 July 1998), country singer and actor, was born Leonard Frank Sly in Cincinnati, Ohio, the son of Andrew Sly, a shoe-factory worker, and Mattie Womack Sly, who had become disabled after being stricken by polio. (During the early 1930s he began to use the name Leonard Franklin Slye, although no documentation has been found showing a legal name change.) When Leonard was an infant, his father built a makeshift houseboat on which the family lived on the Ohio River for approximately eight years; they spent much of that time moored near Portsmouth, Ohio. In 1919 they settled on a small farm in Duck Run, Ohio. His father continued to work in Portsmouth and lived away from home for two weeks at a time, so eight-year-old Leonard became responsible for running the farm and hunting with a slingshot in order to feed his mother and three sisters. He later recalled that "for the Slye family, about the most fun we could have together was singing. My whole family was musical. Pop played mandolin and mother played guitar, and my sisters and I all joined in" (Rogers and Evans, p. 25). He and his mother were also accomplished yodelers, using yodels as a form of communication: for example, when his mother wanted to call him in from the fields for dinner, she would use one type of yodel, and if a storm was approaching he would use another yodel as a warning. He learned to play mandolin as a boy and became skilled at calling square dances. Although his ambition was to become a dentist, he was forced to drop out of high school after two years because of financial difficulties. His family then moved back to Cincinnati, where he took a factory job at the U.S. Shoe Company alongside his father.

In 1930 Slye persuaded his father to move with him temporarily to Lawndale, California, where one of his sisters had moved. They drove gravel trucks for four months before returning to Ohio. Leonard, however, lured by the California climate and the promise of a permanent job as a truck driver, joined his sister again in late 1930. The rest of his family followed soon thereafter, but a few weeks later, the truck company went bankrupt. Father and son became migrant workers, picking peaches for Del Monte and living in the same camps that author John Steinbeck researched for his novel *The Grapes of Wrath*.

In 1931 Leonard and his cousin Stanley, billing themselves as the Slye Brothers, performed frequently at square dances. In August of that year one of his sisters convinced him to appear on an amateur show, "The Midnight Frolic," on a small radio station in

Inglewood, California. Based on this performance, he was invited to join a local country music group, the Rocky Mountaineers, as their vocalist and rhythm guitarist. Over the next two years he appeared with three additional bands, Benny Nawahi's International Cowboys, the O-Bar-O Cowboys, and Jack and His Texas Outlaws, none of which experienced any real success. He later recalled a particularly disastrous barnstorming trip with the O-Bar-O Cowboys in 1933, when they drove in a "rotten old heap of a car," pawned his wristwatch to pay for sleeping quarters, subsisted on hawks and blackbirds that he shot, and once played to a completely empty venue (Rogers and Evans, p. 61). In 1933 he married Lucile Ascolese; they had no children and divorced in 1936. During 1933 he also met his second wife, Grace Arline Wilkins, in Roswell, New Mexico, when she brought him a lemon pie after he sang "The Swiss Yodel" at her request on a local radio station. They married in 1936 and had three children (one of them was adopted); she died in 1946 from an embolism after giving birth to their third child.

In late 1933 Slye contacted two former members of the Rocky Mountaineers, Bob Nolan and Tim Spencer, both of whom had quit the music business in frustration because of financial problems. He convinced them to give up their steady jobs to form a new group, the Pioneer Trio. They moved into a boarding house in Hollywood and spent several weeks rehearsing for ten hours a day, perfecting a smooth, meticulous "block" harmony singing style in which their three voices blended as one. They were soon hired for a regular spot on radio station KFWB in Los Angeles, where they received positive critical notices in local newspapers. In early 1934 a virtuoso fiddler, Hugh Farr, joined the band. In March the group's name was changed to the Sons of the Pioneers. During 1934 they recorded approximately 300 songs as transcriptions for the Standard Recording Company; these transcriptions were distributed to radio stations across the country, spurring the group's popularity. In 1935 Farr's brother Karl, a guitarist, was added to the band, completing its sound. The Sons of the Pioneers featured mellow, syncopated harmony singing, vigorous trio yodeling, and fine hot-jazz musicianship (the Farr brothers were particularly influenced by jazz guitarist Django Reinhardt). Nolan and Spencer were talented songwriters and arrangers, and several of their western-themed songs are now regarded as classics: "Way Out There" (1934), "Tumbling Tumbleweeds" (1934), "Cool Water" (written in 1934; recorded in 1941, after Slye left the group), and "Blue Prairie" (1936). In 1935 the Sons of the Pioneers became one of the first acts signed by the newly formed Decca Records. The following year they played at the Centennial Exposition in Dallas at the invitation of the governor of Texas. They were featured in several films in 1936, including the Bing Crosby musical *Rhythm of the Range* and "B" westerns starring Charles Starrett and Gene Autry. In one of his first prominent roles, in *The Old Corral*, Slye,

billed as Dick Weston, played a villain who is forced by Autry to yodel at gunpoint.

In 1937 Autry became involved in a contract dispute with Republic Pictures and threatened to not report for the filming of his western *Washington Cowboy*. As a contingency, Republic producer Sol Siegel decided to groom another actor to play Autry's singing-cowboy role; Slye was chosen out of a large group of actors and signed to a studio contract in October 1937. He quit the Sons of the Pioneers at the same time. When Autry refused to appear in *Washington Cowboy* in early 1938, Slye was given the new stage name Roy Rogers and immediately placed in the starring role. The film, renamed *Under Western Stars* and heavily promoted by the studio, proved to be a nationwide hit. After Autry settled his dispute with Republic, Rogers was relegated to starring roles in smaller-budget pictures, including several action-packed historical westerns: *Billy the Kid Returns* (1938), *Days of Jesse James* (1939), and *Frontier Pony Express* (1939). In 1940 he gave a creditable supporting performance in an "A" western, Raoul Walsh's *Dark Command*, costarring John Wayne and Claire Trevor. Although Rogers's westerns during this period were highly profitable, he did not become a major star until 1942, when Autry left the studio to join the U.S. Army Air Forces. Promoted as "King of the Cowboys," Rogers was the number one cowboy box-office draw in America from 1943 to 1955.

Rogers starred in 48 "B" westerns for Republic between 1943 and 1951. These films were highly formulaic and often featured the same principal cast: Rogers as the low-key, kind, dependable hero; Trigger, his horse, a remarkably well-trained golden palomino who could smile, blow kisses, dance jigs, and sign his name with a pencil; Dale Evans, who played Rogers's love interest (although they never kissed on-screen for fear of offending his primary audience—young boys); George "Gabby" Hayes, a crusty comic sidekick; the Sons of the Pioneers, who continued to sing with Rogers in musical interludes; and Bullet, "the wonder dog." Some of his westerns had almost no action content. Films such as *Idaho* (1943) and *The Cowboy and the Senorita* (1944) were deliberately patterned after the smash-hit Broadway musical *Oklahoma*, featuring elaborately staged fiesta and nightclub sequences and the star outfitted in gaudy rhinestone suits festooned with cactuses, horseshoes, or yellow roses, created by western-wear designer Nudie Cohn. During the late 1940s, as the interest in musical westerns declined, Rogers's films became much more serious-minded, tackling issues such as wildlife preservation and national preparedness, and featuring an unusual amount of brutality and bloodshed. Western film historians generally suggest that his movies that struck a balance between music and action were his best: *Heart of the Golden West* (1942), *Silver Spurs* (1943), and *The Man from Music Mountain* (1943).

Because Republic paid him an extremely low salary ($150 per week in 1940), Rogers toured extensively to supplement his income, appearing at sold-out rodeos throughout the United States and the British Isles. The dramatic climax of his rodeo performances involved an elaborate stunt with Trigger. First, the announcer would explain to the audience that in the Old West wandering cowboys were often shot by outlaws. In his memoir, Rogers recalled what would follow:

> A gunshot then rang out and I slumped over in the saddle. A second shot followed, and Trigger shook like he was hit. He began to limp worse and worse, like he was about to die. Growing weaker with each step, he gradually went down, falling to his side, motionless, with me laying there next to him, also dead. ... The lights dimmed; "Taps" played over the loudspeaker. Let me tell you, I could hear the sniffles of the little ones, and they'd cry, "Get up, Trigger! Please!" We'd lie there till the last note of "Taps," ... at which point [Trigger] leapt to his feet and shook himself back to life. I swung into the saddle and we loped around the arena, waving to everyone, and galloped out of there. (Rogers and Evans, p. 145)

Rogers took his responsibilities to his young fans extremely seriously, giving up cigarettes and beer so that he would project a clean image. He later said that Republic refused to provide him with a staff to respond to his fan mail, suggesting that he throw the letters away; instead, he and his wife Arline answered every letter themselves, paying the postage out of their own pockets. He also made hundreds of appearances at orphanages and children's hospitals, accompanied by Trigger. At the peak of his success in the mid-1940s he received nearly 75,000 fan letters in one month (Trigger received 2,000 letters per week), and a *Life* magazine poll of children named him as one of the three Americans they most wanted to emulate, alongside Abraham Lincoln and Franklin Delano Roosevelt.

In December 1947 Rogers married his frequent co-star Dale Evans; they had one biological child and adopted three children, including a Korean War orphan and a boy who had suffered brain damage as the result of physical abuse. By the early 1950s he began to phase out his film work to concentrate on other entertainment media. First broadcast in 1944, his radio series, "The Roy Rogers Show," was carried by more than 550 stations in 1950 and continued on the air until 1955. Even more successful was his television program, also called "The Roy Rogers Show," which ran from late 1951 until 1957. The show, aired on NBC on Sunday evenings, was required viewing for millions of children. During the decade he became one of the most heavily merchandised stars in entertainment history, lending his name and image to more than 450 products. He appeared in advertisements for Post Cereal, Nestlé Quik, Magic Chef stoves, Quaker Oats, Friskies dog food, and Kodak film. Parents bought their children Roy Rogers alarm clocks, bedsheets, cameras, footballs, and lunch boxes. The 1955 Sears, Roebuck mail-order catalogue featured more

than a dozen pages of Roy Rogers–related items. Roy Rogers comic books sold 1.3 million copies per issue, and separate Trigger and Dale Evans comic-book lines were also popular. To assure the quality of every product that bore his name, he insisted that they all be tested in his own home; he later ruefully noted that his children became so inundated with Roy Rogers merchandise that his oldest son had dreams about carrying a Hopalong Cassidy lunchbox. By the end of the century, many of these items became valuable collectibles that sold for hundreds or even thousands of dollars, indelibly linked in the minds of the Baby Boom generation to the innocence of their childhood.

Rogers's family was struck by tragedy several times in the 1950s and 1960s. His and Evans's biological child was born with Down's syndrome and died shortly before her second birthday, and two of their adopted children died in accidents. Deeply committed Christians, the couple toured frequently with Billy Graham's crusades and with Bill Bright, the founder of the Campus Crusade for Christ. Although Rogers never achieved major success as a solo recording artist, in part because he was most comfortable as a harmony singer, he did introduce a few noteworthy songs during his film and television career, including Cole Porter's "Don't Fence Me In" (from the film *Hollywood Canteen*, 1944) and the Evans-penned "Happy Trails," the theme song for his television program. He also enjoyed several country hits during the early 1970s: "Money Can't Buy Love" (1970), "Lovenworth" (1971), and the nostalgic "Hoppy, Gene and Me" (1974). During the late 1960s he joined in a partnership with the Marriott Corporation to develop a chain of fast-food restaurants under his name; the chain eventually included 800 restaurants and was sold in 1990 to Hardee's. In 1970 California Republicans urged him to run for Congress, but he refused, noting that he had "so many Republican and Democratic fans that I wouldn't want to lose any of them." In 1976 he opened the Roy Rogers–Dale Evans Museum in Victorville, California, which displayed mementos from throughout their lives. In 1980 the Sons of the Pioneers were inducted into the Country Music Hall of Fame, and in 1989 Rogers was inducted as an individual. In his old age he still attempted to make daily appearances at his museum to visit with his fans. He died at his ranch near Victorville.

• The best source for information on Rogers's life is his coautobiography with Dale Evans, *Happy Trails: Our Life Story* (1994). An excellent short overview of his career is given in Laurence Zwisohn's liner notes to Rhino Records's three-CD compilation *Happy Trails: The Roy Rogers Collection, 1937–1990* (1999), which includes dozens of performances from his radio program. Also useful is Robert W. Phillips, *Roy Rogers: A Biography, Radio History, Television Career Chronicle, Discography, Filmography, Comicography, Merchandising and Advertising History, Collectibles Description, Bibliography and Index* (1995). Unlike many other published sources, Phillips includes information about Rogers's first marriage to Lucile Ascolese. For information on the Sons of the Pioneers, see Zwisohn and also Ken Griffis, *Hear My Song: The Story of the Celebrated Sons of the Pioneers*

(1974). For Rogers's film career, see Richard Maurice Hurst, *Republic Studios: Between Poverty Row and the Majors* (1979). An obituary is in the *New York Times*, 7 July 1998.

THOMAS W. COLLINS, JR.

RONELL, Ann (25 Dec. 1905–25 Dec. 1993), composer and lyricist, was born Ann Rosenblatt in Omaha, Nebraska, the third of four children born to Morris Rosenblatt, a coal dealer, and Mollie Rosenblatt (maiden name unknown). The year of Ronell's birth has appeared variously as 1903, 1906, and 1908; she was also known as Anne and Anna. She was descended from recent immigrants, her father being a Russian émigré who arrived in this country from Czarist Russia in 1890 and settled in Omaha. After graduating from Omaha's Central High School in 1923, she enrolled first at Wheaton College in Norton, Massachusetts, and then transferred following her sophomore year to Radcliffe College, where she could receive more intensive musical training. Her teachers at Radcliffe included Edward Ballantine, Archibald Davison, Edward Burlingame Hill, and Walter Spalding, all notable teachers of composition.

At Radcliffe she wrote songs and background music for college plays, and for one of the school's music publications she wrote reviews and interviewed composers who were in Boston for performances of their works by the Boston Symphony Orchestra. An interview with George Gershwin led to a friendship with the older composer and a decision to make music her career. Gershwin helped her become rehearsal pianist for his show *Rosalie*; in addition to playing at rehearsals, she coached the show's star, Marilyn Miller. During her early years in New York, she continued to coach and also taught music. Given her diminutive size (five feet two-and-a-half inches and, throughout her adult life, about 100 pounds), she was able to take odd jobs modeling children's clothes to help make ends meet. Gershwin eventually encouraged her to change her surname from Rosenblatt to Ronell (this at a time when Jews in show business were often adopting non-Jewish-sounding names), and she subsequently dedicated one of her early songs, "Willow Weep for Me," to him (which was unusual for a popular song).

As early as 1929, Ronell had placed a song in a show, *Down by the River*, for Radio City Music Hall. Two years later she was one of many contributors to *Shoot the Works* with "Let's Go Out in the Open Air." In 1932 she produced the two songs that made her famous, "Rain on the Roof" and "Willow Weep for Me," the latter quickly becoming a favorite of jazz performers and recorded by such singers as Billie Holiday and Dinah Washington.

In 1933 Ronell moved to Hollywood. She worked first at Disney Studios, where with Frank E. Churchill she elaborated, with new lyrics and music, the fragmentary version of the song "Who's Afraid of the Big Bad Wolf?" that was used in Disney's "Three Little Pigs" animated "short." While working at Disney Studios she met Lester Cowan, a film producer, who

would become her husband on 6 November 1935 in a wedding at sea on the *Santa Elena*. Also in 1935 she composed her first concert work, *The Magic of Spring*, a ballet/operetta for which she wrote both the words and the music. She would later write a second ballet, *Ship South*. Other "serious" works that she wrote or adapted during her Hollywood years include a folk opera based on the life of Stephen Foster, *Oh! Susanna* (1947), translations of Mozart's *The Magic Flute* and Pergolesi's *La Serva Padrona*, and—for the Metropolitan Opera—a translation of Johann Strauss's *The Gypsy Baron* for the 1959–1960 season, followed by a revision of her 1938 translation of Friedrich Flotow's *Martha* in 1961.

After leaving Disney, Ronell regularly worked on films as a production assistant and then as music director for Paramount and United Artists. She wrote songs and background music and was the first woman to conduct a major film sound track, *Tomorrow the World* (United Artists, 1944). Her film credits include *Down to Their Last Yacht* (1935), *The Big Broadcast* (1936), *Champagne Waltz* (1937), *The River Is So Blue* (1938), *Blockade* (1938), *Algiers* (1938), *You Can't Beat an Honest Man* (1939), *Magic in Music* (1940), *The Story of G.I. Joe* (1945), *One Touch of Venus* (1948), *Love Happy* (1949), and *Main Street to Broadway* (1953). *The Story of G.I. Joe* led to Ronell's two Oscar nominations in 1945: for best score and for the song "Linda."

Ronell's last film, *Meeting at a Far Meridian* (1964), was a joint Soviet/United States production by Lester Cowan Productions and Mosfilm Studio. She served as conductor for the film score and both adapted the music and supplied an English translation for the song "Moscow Windows" by Tikhon Khrennikov, which became "Take Me, Take Me to the Moon." Ronell took credit for other film "firsts." She said, "To the best of my knowledge, *G.I. Joe* was the first film drama to use a theme song sung over the title credits. Though it was a radical departure to score the picture this way, my collaborator Louis Applebaum and I set in motion a fashion which is more prevalent than ever today" (U.S. Information Agency interview, 1965). A pioneer in film scoring, she also was involved, again in her own words, in ". . . making a record album from *Ladies in Retirement* as the first recording of a complete film score for the public by a Hollywood producer." In 1942 Ronell returned to Broadway with *Count Me In*, for which she wrote both lyrics and music, making her the first woman to do so for a Broadway show.

After her Hollywood years Ronell served on the boards of the National Academy of Popular Music, the American Guild of Authors and Composers, the Dramatists Guild, and the American Society of Composers, Authors and Publishers (ASCAP). She also initiated a recording project of the recollections of the great songwriters of her era. In 1991 she was elected to the Song Writers Hall of Fame by the Board of Directors of the National Academy of Popular Music, "to honor you and your song 'Willow Weep for Me.'"

Throughout her career, Ronell consistently wrote both the words and music of her songs and contributed lyrics to other composers' work, often in the form of translations or adaptations. While musically not as innovative as her mentor Gershwin, Ronell always exhibited superb craftsmanship, which was innate and then refined by her training. As a lyricist she shared the best traits of her finest contemporaries: economy of words and the ability to set a scene and tell a story in ordinary yet nonetheless poetic language. Her skill as both lyricist and composer allowed her to take ideas and extend them beyond the obvious limits, without losing the listener's attention.

Among Ronell's best or most memorable songs are "Baby's Birthday Party" (1930), "The Candy Parade" (1931), "Who's Afraid of the Big Bad Wolf?" (1933), "You've Got It All" (1943), "Someone in the Know" (1943), "On Leave for Love" (1943), "The Woman behind the Man behind the Gun" (1943), "The Lullaby" (1953), "(Don't Look Now, But) My Heart Is Showing)" (1948), "My Week" (1948), "Beach Boy" (1934), "Andy Panda" (1939), "On a Merry-Go-Round" (1936), "In a Silly Symphony" (1933), "C'est la Vie" (1938), "Mickey Mouse and Minnie's in Town," which Walt Disney Studios "accepted as the official Mickey Mouse birthday song" (1933), "Love Happy" (1950), "Beloved" (n.d.), "The River" (1951), "You're Lovely" (n.d.), and "Dark Moon" (n.d.).

By the time Ann Ronell died in New York in her late eighties, she had suffered the same fate as many of her contemporaries in the field of popular music: their style had become overshadowed by rock and roll. Nevertheless, she was a pioneer as a woman composer and lyricist, and two of her songs have a permanent place in American popular culture: "Who's Afraid of the Big Bad Wolf?" and "Willow Weep for Me."

• Ann Ronell has an entry by Virginia Gratton in *American Women Songwriters* (1993). Her early relationship with Gershwin is covered in Joan Peyser's biography of George Gershwin, *The Memory of All That* (1993). Alec Wilder critiques "Willow Weep for Me" in *American Popular Song* (1990). See also Edward Jablonski, "Ann Ronell—Omaha's Musical 'Trailblazer,'" *Nebraska Life Magazine* 1, no. 4 (Fall 1997): 16–19. Newspaper articles of interest, most of which are found in the Archives of Radcliffe College, include Jessie Ash Arndt, "Song Writer as Plucky as Three Little Pigs," *Christian Science Monitor*, 3 Jan. 1955; Jerene Clair Cline, "Ann Ronell's Song Writing Dynamo," Omaha *Sunday World-Herald Magazine*, 28 Nov. 1948; and Edith Oliver's *The Theater* column, *New Yorker*, 26 July 1988. United Artists issued a biographical sketch around 1950, and in 1965 the U.S. Information Agency interviewed Ronell in connection with the film *Meeting at a Far Meridian* ("Little Lady of Song: An Interview with Composer Ann Ronell"). Other information can be gleaned from the Metropolitan Opera Archives. Obituaries are in the *New York Times*, 29 Dec. 1993, and *Variety*, 5 Jan. 1994.

BENJAMIN SEARS

ROOSEVELT, Kermit (16 Feb. 1916–8 June 2000), intelligence operative, businessman, lobbyist,

and writer, was born in Buenos Aires, Argentina, the first child of Kermit Roosevelt, Sr., a businessman, soldier, and explorer, and Belle Wyatt Willard Roosevelt, a businesswoman and political activist who came from a socially prominent family. He was a grandson of President Theodore Roosevelt and a distant cousin of President Franklin D. Roosevelt on his father's side; his mother's father was the American ambassador to Spain at the time of his parents' wedding in Madrid in 1912. Shortly after Kim, as he was usually known to family and friends, was born the family moved to Madrid. During World War I, his father served with the British and American armies in Mesopotamia and France while the rest of the family lived in Spain. After the war, his father led his wife and now two young sons back to Long Island, New York, and by 1925 young Roosevelt had two brothers and a sister. He followed in his father's and grandfather's footsteps by enrolling at Groton, the prestigious preparatory school in Massachusetts. There he wrote earnest adolescent poetry, sharpened his tennis skills, and missed his cats terribly. Disciplined by a rigorous curriculum that included German and Latin, Roosevelt developed into a promising student. Nurtured by loving parents and growing up in an age when letter writing was an everyday form of communication, his early correspondence revealed a keen sense of humor, which he retained throughout his life, and a patrician lifestyle including such activities as duck hunting in the country.

Roosevelt's parents were socially well connected, frequently entertaining the likes of Will Rogers and his wife as houseguests and routinely lunching with such notables of the day as journalist Walter Lippmann and New Deal cabinet members and power brokers Harold Ickes and Frances Perkins. And they were not above using these connections to advance their eldest son's way in the world. Roosevelt was astute enough to parlay these connections into increasingly responsible positions in the execution of his country's foreign affairs, but by young adulthood he had already demonstrated other attributes equally important in his rise. His intelligence and capacity for hard work would augment his sense of adventure, which was stimulated in large part by his father's stories about his adventures on African safari and the exploration of the River of Doubt (renamed Rio Roosevelt) with his own father. In fact, this appetite for adventure became such a driving force that in 1969 Miles Copeland would write that it had formed Roosevelt's frankly expressed motivation in embarking on a career with the CIA.

On his return from a trip to the Soviet Union in 1934, Roosevelt again followed in the footsteps of family tradition by enrolling at Harvard University. He completed the four-year course in three years and graduated cum laude. On 28 June 1937 he married Mary Lowe Gaddis, who was from a socially prominent Milton, Massachusetts, family. Polly, as she was known, had just completed her sophomore year at

Radcliffe; their marriage was a happy one, and they would have four children together.

Roosevelt taught history at Harvard and the California Institute of Technology while doing postgraduate work at both institutions. It was during this period that he began his study of propaganda during the English Civil War and began to compare it to contemporary propaganda. He argued that, when seen in its proper perspective, propaganda did not have to be only a force for evil but could also be inspirational and the source of hope and courage. During 1941 he made public addresses to small groups on problems connected with national defense and the war.

Roosevelt became an assistant section chief in the Office of War Information (OWI) during 1942. From January to November 1943, he served as Dean Acheson's assistant when Acheson was assistant secretary of state for economic affairs. Later he joined the Office of Strategic Services (OSS) and served in the Middle East. He was involved in a serious jeep accident in Italy just as the war ended and was hospitalized for almost a year. He directed preparation of the wartime history of the OSS, lamenting "the most horrible officialese language" that the Defense Department insisted on using. After its creation, he joined the CIA and served as the chief of its Near East and Africa division.

In late 1951 Roosevelt's former superior Dean Acheson, Harry Truman's fourth secretary of state, borrowed Roosevelt from the CIA. He assigned him to head a committee composed of individuals from government, academia, and business to investigate, prioritize, and devise solutions to problems in the Arab world. The first major project that this committee devised dealt with Egypt, a country Roosevelt knew well. The American intelligence community had been busy for two years with their identification of revolutionary currents in that country, centered on Islamic forces in one direction and Communists in the other. The committee had concluded that the best way to neutralize those forces that appeared to be on the brink of violent confrontation was to institute a peaceful revolution. By March 1952, however, Roosevelt's efforts in Egypt toward this end had fallen frustratingly short. In May, he returned to Washington to advise Acheson that the Egyptian army was going to grasp the political initiative in that country and that it would be done on the Egyptians', not the Americans', terms. His accurate summation of this situation and other political realities in Egypt was confirmed when in July of 1952 the Egyptian army sprang a bloodless and successful coup. In the future he would again play a pivotal role in Egypt's relations with the West.

In the meantime, political developments in Iran would claim Roosevelt's attention and gain him his most lasting notoriety. Immediately after World War II ended, the Soviets had earned the much-deserved mistrust of the shah, the Majlis (the Iranian parliament, which did not become bicameral until 1949), and much of the rest of Iran by making a number of aggressive moves. Rather than honor his commitment

to withdraw his 31,000 troops from Iran, Stalin instead doubled their number, demanded oil concessions, and attempted to force the creation of a communist state of Azerbaijan in northern Iraq. That crisis had been defused largely through the tenacious diplomacy of then-Secretary of State James F. Byrnes, who supported Iran's case before the Security Council of the new United Nations.

It was the British, however, whose long presence had engendered the deepest political resentment in Iran. The Anglo-Iranian Oil Company, most of whose stock was owned by the British government, had been paying Iran far less than the British government taxed it. The Truman administration's warnings to London to address the problem fell on deaf ears. On 7 March 1951 Ali Razmara, Iran's pro-Western prime minister, was assassinated, and Iran moved to nationalize its oil industry. The British response was a show of force by the British navy, the freezing of Iranian assets, and a spiraling descent in relations between the two countries.

At the end of April 1951 Mohammed Mossadegh was elected prime minister, and on 1 May nationalization of Iran's oil industry became law. The British were expelled from the country. Nine months later Roosevelt was approached by the British Foreign Office about organizing the overthrow of Mossadegh. He advised them that the outgoing Truman administration was unlikely to approve such an operation but that the new Republican administration under Dwight Eisenhower would likely take a different view. On 25 June 1953 Roosevelt met in the office of Secretary of State John Foster Dulles with a group of powerful figures in the new administration. He portrayed the proposed coup as a cooperative venture between Iranian sovereign Mohammed Reza Shah Pahlavi, the Americans, and the British that would remove Mossadegh, check the growth of the Tudeh (Iranian Communist Party) and Soviet influence in Iran, and restore the shah's political strength. In promoting the plot to remove Mossadegh, Roosevelt had in his favor John Foster Dulles's negative opinion of the elderly Iranian leader. The eccentric, emotional Mossadegh was a thorough nationalist whose theme was Iran for the Iranians. He was no puppet for Soviet interests, but his neutralism in the cold war was alone enough to damn him in Dulles's eyes, in addition to his tolerance of domestic communism in the form of the Tudeh and his obvious disrespect for free enterprise. Roosevelt's scheme was approved by the group with little critical analysis, and Dulles took it to Eisenhower for his approval.

Roosevelt secretly entered Iran on 19 July 1953 and directed the operation with methodical coolness. His aim was to force the Iranian people and the armed forces to choose between the shah and Mossadegh, whom he portrayed as a revolutionary figure backed by the Soviet Union. Roosevelt used two Iranian brothers (the so-called Boscoe brothers) for key advice and important intelligence. Through them and two other Iranian operatives nicknamed "Laughing

Boy" and "The Mad Musician" he controlled the mass of anti-Mossadegh street demonstrators in Tehran. He met clandestinely with the shah to coordinate strategy and assure him that he acted with the full authority of Eisenhower and Churchill. It was arranged for the shah to dramatize his plight, in line with Islamic tradition, by fleeing the country at a pivotal moment.

Although Mossadegh was still able to galvanize support in the streets, the street demonstrations on 19 August 1953 organized by Roosevelt's team prevailed. Key commanders in the army rallied to the shah's defense and that same day, just three days after he had taken flight, the grateful shah returned to his capital in triumph. Mossadegh was arrested and sentenced to three years of imprisonment. Fazlollah Zahedi was appointed the new prime minister. His appointment gave the British much discomfort, as they had arrested him in 1941 and interned him in Palestine, but they went along with the choice because they had little in the way of options. One year after the coup, the Iranian government completed a contract with an international group of oil companies: 40 percent of the business went to American firms, 40 percent to British, and the remaining 20 percent to firms of other nationalities.

The rest of Roosevelt's tenure with the CIA occurred in a period of complex and important developments in the Middle East. In late 1956, the Anglo-French-Israeli military assault on Egypt, despite American and Soviet opposition, sharpened Cold War lines and increased Gamal Abdel Nasser's anti-Western orientation and influence in the Arab world. Almost immediately after it was thwarted, in November 1956, the British SIS undertook an operation to assassinate Nasser in Operation Unfasten. John Farmer was instructed by his government to brief Roosevelt, on a visit to London, on the plan. Roosevelt, like Farmer himself, reportedly had a very low opinion of it. The plan did not come to fruition, but four months after it was hatched Nasser himself exposed it to the world. These events combined to make Roosevelt's work even more ticklish than usual.

Roosevelt left the CIA in 1958 and thereafter worked as director of government affairs for Gulf Oil for six years. His subsequent activities as consultant, businessman, and lobbyist were highly lucrative and dealt with such clients as the Iranian and Saudi Arabian governments and subsidiaries of the Northrop Corporation. His career as a writer was highlighted by his 1979 account of the coup in Iran, *Countercoup: The Struggle for the Control of Iran*, which had to be recalled by the publisher for revision after the British Petroleum Company maintained that the book included libelous statements to the effect that its predecessor firm had helped organize the coup. He died in Cockeysville, Maryland, of complications from a stroke.

Roosevelt served his country ably at many junctures of his career in the Middle East. His was often a voice of moderation and restraint, his advice frequently insightful. He maintained that the main reason American intervention in Iran was successful was because the people and the army welcomed it. He warned against other ventures where this might not be the case, such as the Guatemalan coup of 1954, the command of which he claimed he turned down. He gave little thought, either in the Cold War environment of 1953 or later, to the possibility that Mossadegh was not a tool of the Soviet Union and was what he appeared to be: an ardent nationalist determined not to have his country controlled by outside forces. Though the shah would strictly align himself militarily with the West, the price that the Iranian people paid for his police state was steep. Furthermore, the precedent established by violating Iran's sovereignty was arguably damaging to the United States' record in foreign policy and helped set the stage for other actions that were not in keeping with the ideals that had motivated the country during World War II.

• The Papers of Kermit and Belle Roosevelt are housed in the Manuscript Division of the Library of Congress in Washington, D.C. They contain a wealth of correspondence to and from their son at various stages of his life, rough drafts and finished manuscripts of lectures and articles written by the younger Roosevelt, and other biographical information that paints a picture of the intelligence operative outside of officially drawn portraits. Roosevelt himself edited the two-volume *War Report of the O.S.S.* (1976). His other books include *Arabs, Oil, and History* (1949), *A Sentimental Safari* (1963), and the previously mentioned *Countercoup* (1979). There is much insightful and highly opinionated commentary on Roosevelt's activities and postwar American diplomacy in the Middle East in Miles Copeland, *The Game of Nations* (1969). William Blum, *Killing Hope* (1995), offers a highly critical summary of American activity toward Iran in the Mossadegh era. In 2000, the CIA's secret history of the 1953 Iranian coup was discovered. It differed from Roosevelt's account in several respects, perhaps most notably in its less-positive portrayal of the shah. Because Roosevelt's activities involved so many major actors on the international scene, he is discussed in numerous books and articles, but he has not been the subject of a full-length biography. Of the several lengthy obituaries, the most comprehensive and helpful in defining his place in history was written by Bart Barnes for the *Washington Post*, 10 June 2000.

PAUL T. SAYERS

ROSTEN, Leo (11 Apr. 1908–19 Feb. 1997), writer, was born in Lodz, Poland, to Samuel C. Rosten and Ida Freundlich Rosten. (His full name was Leo Calvin Rosten.) His parents emigrated three years after his birth and settled in Chicago, where he was educated in the city's public schools and grew up in a traditional Jewish household. After high school he attended the University of Chicago, graduating with a degree in philosophy in 1930. He then taught English in night school to newly arrived immigrants and began contributing both comic pieces and serious articles on political issues to major magazines as a means of paying for graduate studies in political science at the university. He also studied briefly at the London School of Economics before receiving a Ph.D. from the University of Chicago in 1937.

The year 1937 was significant for Rosten for another reason as well: while working briefly as a screenwriter in Hollywood, he published his first two books. One was *The Washington Correspondents*, a study of the Washington, D.C., press corps that garnered critical praise. But the other, appearing under the pseudonym Leonard Q. Ross, made him famous: *The Education of H*Y*M*A*N K*A*P*L*A*N*, a collection of hilarious stories, written originally for the *New Yorker*, about the struggles of a fictitious German-Jewish immigrant named Hyman Kaplan to learn English in night school. The title reproduced one of Mr. Kaplan's many idiosyncrasies: writing his name in capital letters and embellishing it with asterisks. The critics and the public warmly embraced Ross/Rosten's collection, making it a bestseller, and over the ensuing years the book became a classic. During the 1950s it was even assigned reading in many urban American high schools to help students better understand the swelling population of displaced persons newly arrived from Europe in the postwar years, for underneath the humor of Mr. Kaplan's mangled syntax, misplaced idioms, and maddeningly logical mistakes (he believed, for example, that the opposite of "inhale" was "dead") lay a moving story of yearning and triumph—the cornerstones of the American dream.

The overwhelming popularity of *Hyman Kaplan* did not induce Rosten to become solely a comic writer, however. Indeed, many of the books, articles, and screenplays he produced were on serious themes, yet his accessible, entertaining manner and his ear for language—along with his eye for the comic possibilities in any situation—were evident in nearly everything he wrote. What his early success in writing did was to divert him from the academic career he had prepared for and launch him instead as a full-time professional writer. Undoubtedly, the limited number of academic jobs available during the 1930s and his coincidental discovery of a means of making a good living also influenced his decision as the Great Depression gave way to World War II.

After *Hyman Kaplan*, Rosten wrote a series of fiction and nonfiction books, most published under his own name but others under the pseudonyms Leonard Q. Ross or (simply) Leonard Ross. Among the first were the novels *Dateline: Europe* (1939) and *Adventure in Washington* (1940), as well as several nonfiction works, including *The Strangest Places* (1939), sketches of people and places in New York and other American cities, and *Hollywood: The Movie Colony, the Movie Makers* (1941), a study of the American film capital.

During the war years, Rosten worked in Washington, D.C., as a writer for various government agencies, including the Office of War Information, and his political expertise led to his working briefly for the Rand Corporation as a writer and consultant in the late 1940s. In the 1940s and 1950s he continued writing screenplays, published several thrillers, and contributed articles on the American scene to various periodicals, including *Look* magazine, where he became an editorial adviser in 1950. He also edited *A Guide to the Religions of America*, published in 1955. His creation Mr. Kaplan reappeared in a series of new adventures under the title *The Return of H*Y*M*A*N K*A*P*L*A*N* (1959). During the 1960s, Rosten published several more books, including a collection of his short pieces called *The Many Worlds of L*E*O R*O*S*T*E*N* (1964).

But much of Rosten's energy during the decade was devoted to writing the book that would make him even more famous than his Mr. Kaplan had done: *The Joys of Yiddish*, first published in 1968. Part lexicon, part joke book, this extensive compendium of Jewish humor and Yiddish words and expressions was the first of its kind and attracted Jewish and non-Jewish readers alike, offering definitions of everything from *Adonai* to *Zohar* (with more familiar words like *chutzpah*, *nosh*, and *shlemiel* in between) and usually including at least one joke for each to give an example of their use. Over the years *The Joys of Yiddish* has sold millions of copies; and even though Rosten wrote it as a popular guide, it is now considered the standard reference work on the Yiddish language.

During the remaining years of his life Rosten published more than a dozen books, most of them on light themes. They included *People I Have Loved, Known, or Admired* (1970), another collection of Hyman Kaplan stories called *O K*A*P*L*A*N! MY K*A*P*L*A*N!* (1976), and *Silky: A Detective Story* (1980), as well as *Leo Rosten's Treasury of Jewish Quotations* (1972) and a slight sequel to his *Joys of Yiddish* called *The Joys of Yinglish* (1989).

In addition to his career as a writer, Rosten taught and lectured in the course of his lifetime at several institutions, including Yale and Columbia universities, the University of California at Berkeley, and the New School for Social Research.

Rosten was first married in 1935 to Priscilla Mead, with whom he had three children. After her death he married Gertrude Zimmerman in 1960. Rosten died at his home in New York City, where he had lived for many years.

• For biographical information on Leo Rosten, see "Rosten, Leo C(alvin)," in *Current Biography Yearbook 1942*, as well as in *Contemporary Authors*, new revision series, vol. 6 (1982), which also includes an interview with Rosten. In addition, see *Who's Who in America*, 38th ed. (1974–1975). An obituary appears in the *New York Times*, 20 Feb. 1997.

ANN T. KEENE

ROUSE, James (26 Apr. 1914–9 Apr. 1996), mortgage banker and real estate developer, was born in Easton, Maryland, to Willard G. Rouse and Lydia Robinson Rouse. His father was a successful canned-foods broker on the Eastern Shore of Maryland, where the Rouse family made their home; though they were prosperous, the elder Rouse saw to it that all his children learned the value of work. Young James tended the family garden and as a teenager worked in the local canneries as well as caddying and selling Fuller Brushes. Both socially popular and an excellent student, James Rouse was elected president of his class as well as the student council at Easton High School, edited a school newspaper, and was active on the basketball and track teams.

Rouse's promising future appeared to be compromised in his mid-teens, however, when his mother and father died within a few months of each other in the winter of 1930. The Great Depression had begun following the Wall Street crash the previous fall, and his father left numerous debts and a foreclosed mortgage on the family home. Rouse nevertheless graduated from high school in June 1930 and with the help of relatives attended a college preparatory school in Port Deposit, Maryland, for a year. In 1931 he moved to Hawaii to live with a married sister and enrolled at the University of Hawaii. Returning to the mainland the following year, he was able to attend the University of Virginia on a scholarship, but a lack of money forced him to leave in the spring of 1933 to find a job.

Rouse moved to Baltimore, where he worked for a while parking cars in an apartment house garage. In 1934 he enrolled in night law school at the University of Maryland, supporting himself as a legal clerk at the Baltimore office of the Federal Housing Administration (FHA). In 1936, while still attending law school, he approached the Title Guarantee and Trust Company of Baltimore and persuaded them to create a mortgage department and hire him to run it. He did so for three years, meanwhile earning a law degree in 1937. Two years later, with the help of a loan from friends and family members, he opened a mortgage banking business with a real estate appraiser named Hunter Moss. Specializing in obtaining FHA loans for single-family houses, the Moss-Rouse Company was soon handling mortgages worth $6 million, a sizable sum at that time. In 1941 Rouse married Elizabeth J. Winstead, with whom he would have three children before the couple divorced in 1972.

Taking a leave of absence from his company, Rouse joined the U.S. Naval Reserve early in 1942, weeks after the nation entered World War II. He served with the Commander Air Force Pacific Fleet, rising to the rank of lieutenant commander by the time he was discharged in 1945. On his return to Baltimore after the war, Rouse began expanding his company to finance apartment houses and shopping centers. In the early 1950s he bought out his partner and renamed the firm James W. Rouse and Company, Inc. By 1970 the company's loan portfolio totaled a staggering $885 million, and Rouse was enjoying multimillion-dollar annual revenues.

At the same time that Rouse was growing his business, he was also becoming increasingly committed to the improvement of urban environments through the building of affordable housing. He served as chairman of the Mayor's Advisory Committee on Housing in Baltimore for three years, beginning in 1949, thereby spearheading the nation's first effort to upgrade urban slums. A supporter of Dwight D. Eisenhower during the 1952 presidential campaign, Rouse was named chairman of Eisenhower's Advisory Committee on

Government Housing Policies and Programs after his election. The committee's recommendations became part of the 1954 Housing Act, which provided federal funds for slum clearance and rebuilding.

By now a nationally recognized authority on urban housing, Rouse coauthored a book with Nathaniel Keith titled *No Slums in Ten Years* (1955), which proposed a plan to redevelop Washington, D.C., with federal funds. The plan was not implemented. But as a founder and vice-chairman of the Greater Baltimore Committee over half a dozen years, beginning in the mid-1950s, Rouse was able to propose and help implement the city's Charles Center redevelopment project, a major urban renewal program. He also served as chairman in 1961 of a state government subcommittee that established a city planning agency in greater Baltimore. In 1958 Rouse had also founded a national anti-slum group, the American Council to Improve Our Neighborhoods, composed of businessmen and housing industry leaders and known by the acronym ACTION. He served two nonconsecutive terms as its president before it was merged in 1970 with the Urban Coalition, a similar group led by John Gardner.

Rouse had begun building his own shopping centers in 1955, when he constructed the Mondawmin Mall in Baltimore. He created his first so-called shopping mall—an enclosed shopping center—in 1958 in Harundale, outside Baltimore, making it the second such construction in the United States. The first—Southdale, in Minneapolis—had opened a few months earlier, but it was Rouse's mall that attracted greater national attention and became the prototype for similar structures throughout the nation. By the end of the 1960s Rouse had built seventeen malls and shopping centers, and five more were under way. To run these ventures apart from his mortgage business, he created a new company, Community Research and Development, Inc.

Rouse was obviously a gifted businessman, and he had become one of the nation's leading developers. He was not motivated by making money, however. He wanted to serve people by creating environments where human beings could live and work and even play to their fullest capacities. He continually studied people in public settings, watching them walk city streets, do their shopping, and socialize, and in his real estate projects he tried to accommodate and encourage social interaction. Soon he was dreaming of creating an entirely new city, and he started, in the early 1960s, by working on such a project in miniature: the construction of Cross Keys, a small residential, business, and shopping complex on the north side of Baltimore. He also began quietly buying 14,000 acres of land in rural Howard County, Maryland, lying between Baltimore and Washington, D.C. He then assembled a panel of academic experts on human behavior to serve as consultants to the engineers and architects of his proposed model city. As a guiding principle, he decreed that the community would be integrated, both racially and economically.

The result of this enormous undertaking was the city of Columbia, Maryland, whose construction was launched in the summer of 1966 and whose homes began selling a year later. By the 1980s Columbia, with a projected population of 110,000, had grown to 56,000 residents, 20 percent of whom were black. In the late 1990s Columbia's population has grown to near maximum capacity while sustaining a racially diverse population. Although some nay-saying critics took Rouse to task for erecting what they called unimaginative structures and creating a cookie-cutter suburban ambience, most observers and urban experts praised his efforts and lauded his accomplishment.

The creation of Columbia would remain Rouse's best-known endeavor, but he continued to distinguish himself in urban redevelopment as well. In the 1970s and 1980s he created major shopping centers in formerly run-down areas of Philadelphia (the Gallery at Market Street East), Boston (Faneuil Hall Marketplace), Baltimore (Harborplace), and New York City (South Street Seaport), as well as in St. Louis, San Francisco, and Milwaukee, in many instances restoring historic structures to their former glory and incorporating them into a larger complex. In 1982, with the profits from these and other ventures, Rouse established the Enterprise Foundation to encourage the building of urban housing for the poor. During his lifetime the foundation aided several hundred groups in cities throughout the United States, offering advice and money that led to the construction of nearly 50,000 low-cost housing units. Rouse's second wife, Patricia Traugott, whom he had married in 1974, eventually became an active partner in the Enterprise Foundation; they settled in a large house overlooking one of Columbia's two man-made lakes. An avid outdoorsman and nature enthusiast, he served on the board of the Urban Wildlife Research Center and enjoyed watching waterfowl through a telescope set up in his living room. Rouse died at his home of complications from Lou Gehrig's disease.

• For biographical information on Rouse, see *Current Biography Yearbook 1982* and *Who's Who in America*, 38th ed. (1974–1975). See also "The New Entrepreneur: Romantic Hero of American Business," *Saturday Review*, 22 July 1978, pp. 12ff. For information on Rouse's development of Columbia, see J. W. Anderson, "A Brand New City for Maryland," *Harper's*, Nov. 1964, pp. 100ff; see also Gurney Breckenfeld, *Columbia and the New Cities* (1971). An obituary appears in the *New York Times*, 10 Apr. 1996.

ANN T. KEENE

ROYKO, Mike (19 Sept. 1932–29 Apr. 1997), newspaper columnist, was born Michael Melvin Royko, Jr., in Chicago, Illinois, the son of Michael Royko, Sr., a tavernkeeper, and Helen Zak Royko. He grew up in the predominantly ethnic working-class neighborhood of Humboldt Park, initially living on the second floor over his father's tavern and then shuttling back and forth between parents following their divorce; after the divorce his mother opened her own

tavern. Royko attended local public schools before dropping out of high school at age sixteen. He began working nights at Marshall Field's department store and eventually obtained the equivalent of a high school diploma after completing a special program run by the Central YMCA. After attending nearby Wright Junior College in 1951–1952, he spent four years in the air force, splitting his time between Korea (where he worked as a radio operator) and O'Hare Field (today's O'Hare Airport but then an air base), where he took the only position that interested him, editorship of the base newspaper, the *O'Hare News*. In 1954 he married Carol Joyce Duckman, with whom he was to have two sons.

Still uncertain as to the course of his career after returning to civilian life, Royko decided to give his new-found interest in journalism a test run by becoming a reporter with a chain of small Chicago neighborhood weekly papers. Within a few months he was hired by the Chicago City News Bureau—a local news-gathering and reporting service that enjoyed financial support from the city's four daily newspapers—and in 1957 became an assistant editor at the agency. Two years later Royko joined the Chicago *Daily News*, initially as a night police reporter. In September 1963, after several years of covering local government and the Illinois state legislature and having begun to write a weekly column concerning county government, he parlayed an offer from a rival newspaper into a twice-weekly column in the *Daily News* that reflected his views on topics of his own choosing. His byline soon appeared five times a week, and within a few years Royko became a Chicago institution. Addressing topical issues ranging from school busing to corruption in local governments, his columns featured straightforward writing and a finely developed social conscience that often championed the "little man" in his fight against societal or institutional injustices.

Royko's first collection of columns, *Up Against It*, was published in 1967, and its success provided the impetus for *I May Be Wrong, but I Doubt It* in 1969. The uproar surrounding the Democratic Party's 1968 National Convention in Chicago provided Royko with additional ammunition against a longtime foe, Chicago mayor Richard J. Daley, who used heavy-handed police tactics to disperse and arrest both peaceful protesters against the Vietnam war and radical activists. After winning the 1969 Heywood Broun Award of the American Newspaper Guild for "sardonic, bold and courageous" writing about the turmoil during the convention and on other topics such as the assassination of Dr. Martin Luther King and police raids without warrants, he took further aim at the mayor in 1971 with the publication of his only book not drawn from his columns. Although *Boss: Richard J. Daley of Chicago* met with mixed reviews, Royko achieved the ultimate recognition within his profession in 1972 when he was awarded the Pulitzer Prize for commentary.

A third collection. *Slats Grobnik and Friends*, appeared in 1973—Slats being a fictitious friend of Royko's who often made an appearance in his columns. After the *Daily News* folded in 1978 Royko moved to the rival *Sun-Times*, where his influential writing affected criminal investigations; one column, for example, indirectly led to jail sentences for several gangsters, exposure of corruption among officeholders, and a judge's suicide. But he also had an impact on political contests: his writings were widely credited with influencing the outcome of the 1970 Illinois race for U.S. senator as well as the election of anti-Daley candidate Jane Byrne to the mayor's office. Occasionally, Royko's work affected ordinary people. When his fourth collection of columns, *Sez Who? Sez Me*, appeared in 1982, the publicity generated by one of the columns—concerning the plight of a badly wounded Vietnam veteran who had been treated dismissively by the Veterans Administration—resulted in a reversed decision by the agency.

After the *Sun-Times* was purchased from the Marshall Field Company (which had also owned the *Daily News*) by international media magnate Rupert Murdoch in 1984, Royko reacted with disgust and moved to the crosstown rival *Tribune*. Welcomed with open arms by his newest employer, Royko also released another collection of columns, *Like I Was Sayin'*, that same year. After his wife died in 1979, Royko married Judith Arndt in 1985, with whom he had a son and a daughter. He closed the decade by issuing in 1989 still another collection, *Dr. Kookie, You're Right!* Proving that he had lost none of his wit, the book included perspectives on the furor over the film *The Last Temptation of Christ*, trendy restaurants, the impact of drug testing on baseball's spring training, and an art assessment ("My only reaction to the *Mona Lisa* is the thought that if she went into a singles bar, she'd spend the entire evening buying her own drinks").

Among the many honors that Royko received were the *Washington Journalism Review*'s Best Columnist in America award, the Erne Pyle Award, and the H. L. Mencken Award. By the time he died in a Chicago hospital, Royko's column ran in syndication in at least 600 newspapers nationwide, and he enjoyed a reputation as one of the most widely read and influential columnists of his day. Largely self-taught as a journalist, he developed a loyal following on the basis of years of witty, often caustic commentary that resonated with the public and delineated universal themes within situations both profound and commonplace.

• Royko's widow collaborated with Studs Terkel and Lois Wille to produce *One More Time: The Best of Mike Royko* (1999). He is the subject of Doug Moe, *The World of Mike Royko* (1999). He was profiled by William Brashler in *Esquire*, 8 May 1979, pp. 44ff., and by Jerry Talmer in the *New York Post*, 16 Apr. 1971, p.16. The 30 Apr. 1997 issues of all major newspapers, including the *Chicago Tribune*, have an obituary.

EDWARD L. LACH, JR.

RÓZSA, Miklós (18 Apr. 1907–27 July 1995), composer, was born in Budapest, Hungary, the son of Gyula Rózsa and Regina Berkovits. His father was a wealthy landowner à la Tolstoy who ran for parliament as a socialist but was not elected. Rózsa's mother had studied the piano at the Budapest Academy with two former students of Franz Liszt. When Rózsa was five, his great-uncle brought him a scaled-down violin from Paris. He immediately began to learn the instrument; at age seven, he composed one of his first pieces, "Student March." Rózsa played and conducted before the public dressed as a miniature eighteenth-century adult, the standard costume of European prodigies. Later, he studied the viola and the piano.

Rózsa attended the Realgymnasium in Budapest. After graduating in 1925, he moved to the Conservatory of Leipzig, Germany, where he studied with Sigfrid Karg-Elert, Theodor Kroyer, and Hermann Grabner. Initially, Rózsa's father objected to his son's wish to become a composer. A letter from Grabner convinced the elder Rózsa that although composing music for a living was a fanciful ambition, it was all his son wished to do, and that the young man had a talent for it. In 1929 he received his diploma *cum laude* from the Conservatory of Leipzig. That same year, he published his Rhapsody for cello and orchestra and *Variations on a Hungarian Peasant Song*. "I longed for the crystal clarity of Hungarian folksong as a basis for my music," Rózsa recalled (Rózsa, p. 41).

Rózsa moved to Paris in 1931, where he endured his share of shabby digs and trips to the pawnbroker. At his Paris début in the spring of 1931, a concert of his chamber music, Richard Strauss was in the audience and led the enthusiastic applause "like a cheerleader," Rózsa remembered. While in Paris, he wrote the score of his only ballet, *Hungaria*, which would run for two years in London, as well as a Theme, Variations and Finale for orchestra (1933), his best-received piece to date. In Paris he also discovered a new way to earn money: writing music for films. Initially, Rózsa composed fanfares for the Pathé-Journal newsreels. After he waited a year and half to be paid by Pathé, however, he decided that French business methods did not suit him, and decided to try London.

In 1935 Rózsa arrived in England with £16 in his pocket and virtually no command of English. He was hired by Alexander Korda, the flamboyant producer at London Film Productions, who was also Hungarian. Rózsa composed the score for Korda's *Knight without Armour*, starring Marlene Dietrich and Robert Donat. Scoring dramatic films presented a technical challenge that Rózsa referred to as learning "how to write music with a stopwatch." Rather than regarding this as a limitation, he saw it as a chance to explore a different idiom musically. In 1937 Rózsa tackled his most prestigious film assignment to date, *The Four Feathers* (1939). Ironically, it was the Hungarian Korda brothers and Rózsa who were responsible for the box office success of this quintessentially British story about the pitfalls of imperialism and the true nature of courage. Meanwhile, he kept up his production of concert music, winning the Franz Joseph Prize, Hungary's highest music award, in 1937 and

1938. His *Three Hungarian Sketches* was published in 1938.

The next year, when war broke out between England and Germany, Korda and his production team, including Rózsa, relocated to Hollywood. There Rózsa would complete the score of *The Thief of Bagdad* (1940), which earned him his first Academy Award nomination. The soaring romanticism of his next score, for *Lady Hamilton* (American title: *That Hamilton Woman*), released in 1941, perfectly matched this largely fictional story of Lord Nelson and his Emma, as played by Laurence Olivier and Vivien Leigh. In the film, the threat posed by Hitler is implicitly compared with the Napoleonic threat of the early nineteenth century. *Lady Hamilton* was explicitly produced to buck up English morale and to tempt American Anglophiles out of their isolationist shell. The film was a big hit. Korda was knighted; Winston Churchill declared it his favorite film (Walker, p. 160); and it established Rózsa as a top film composer. That year also brought him two Academy Award nominations, for *Lydia*, starring Merle Oberon, and *Sundown*. Another nomination followed in 1942 for *Jungle Book*.

When the commercial possibilities of recording film scores, in whole or part, became obvious to the big record labels, Rózsa's scores and the suites he arranged from then were among the most in demand. His *Jungle Book Suite* for narrator and orchestra was the first American film score to be recorded.

He married Margaret Finlason, an actress, in August 1943; they were to have two children. Nineteen forty-three also saw the premiere at Carnegie Hall of the Theme, Variations and Finale in a revised version, conducted by Bruno Walter and, at one memorable performance, by the 25-year-old Leonard Bernstein.

In the 1940s, at the height of his career, Rózsa wrote three or four film scores a year while also producing concert works such as the Concerto for string orchestra (1943) and the Sonata for piano (1948). *Five Graves to Cairo*, released in 1943, brought together Rózsa and mercurial director Billy Wilder. The two teamed up again for the 1944 film noir *Double Indemnity*, in which Rózsa's music put a chilling framework around the film's depiction of sexual obsession and the rotten underside of middle-class southern California life. The musical director of the film, however, accused Rózsa of writing music more suited to Carnegie Hall than a movie theater. "In *Double Indemnity* I introduced certain asperities of rhythm and harmony which wouldn't have caused anyone familiar with the serious musical scene to bat an eyelid, but which did cause consternation in certain musical quarters in Hollywood," Rózsa recalled (quoted in Palmer, p. 5). Wilder intervened and Rózsa's score was used as written; it earned him another Academy Award nomination.

His next score, for Alfred Hitchcock's *Spellbound*, won him his first Academy Award, for Best Music of 1945. *Spellbound* also marked Rózsa's first use of the theremin, an electronic instrument he employed to conjure up the delusional and psychotic states portrayed in that film. *Spellbound* remains the most recorded of Rózsa's film scores. In *The Lost Weekend* (1945), he exploited the theremin's eerie tremolo to produce the aural surrealism that underlined a realistic depiction of alcoholism. Later in the 1940s he dug more deeply into film noir territory with scores for *The Strange Love of Martha Ivers* (1946), *The Killers* (1946), *Brute Force* (1947), and *The Naked City* (1948). In *The Killers* Rózsa introduced a distinctive, four-note dum-da-dum-dum motif that was later used (without permission) in the theme of the television series "Dragnet" and the film derived from it.

In 1948 he earned his second Academy Award for *A Double Life*, "my last patho-psychological [*sic*] picture," as he called it (Rózsa, p. 156). He also joined the music staff at Metro-Goldwyn-Mayer that year and remained until 1962. From 1945 to 1965 he also served on the faculty of the University of Southern California, where he taught a groundbreaking course on film composition.

He lightheartedly labeled the 1950s his "historico-Biblical period" (Rózsa, p. 163). They began with *Quo Vadis* (1951) and ended with *Ben-Hur*. The latter film brought Rózsa his third, and most cherished, Academy Award for Best Music in 1959. Rózsa also wrote the scores for *The Asphalt Jungle*, directed by John Huston and released in 1950, *Ivanhoe* (1952), and *Julius Caesar* (1953), the last starring Marlon Brando. Always a prolific composer, in the year 1953 alone he scored five major films and wrote the Concerto for violin and orchestra. Jascha Heifetz had commissioned the Concerto, which Rózsa completed in six weeks.

Rózsa slowed down only slightly in his later years. *El Cid* (1961) was his last large-scale Hollywood epic, although he wrote scores for another dozen films; works of the 1960s not written for Hollywood included the *Notturno ungherese* written in 1964 and the 1966 Sinfonia Concertante. He won the French academy award, the César, in 1977, for his music in Alain Resnais's *Providence*. In spite of a debilitating stroke in 1982, he continued to compose until subsequent strokes and loss of sight compelled him to stop. He died at the Hospital of the Good Samaritan in Los Angeles, after suffering a final stroke some weeks earlier.

Rózsa was the last of the great composers of Hollywood's Golden Age. He brought to his work a European sensibility and a musical standard that helped to fashion the music of this favorite medium of American popular culture in its Golden Age and beyond. In 1974 Dennis Mann-Riley aptly described his achievement: "Miklós Rózsa succeeds in not only exposing the visual impact and essence of film art but, also, in revealing films' intrinsic architecture and dynamic logic. His music possesses amazing buoyancy and glimmers with an exigent inner imagery that sweeps along all kinds of audiences' imaginations" (quoted in *Films in Review*, June–July 1974).

• Rózsa's papers, including unpublished manuscripts, letters, and photographs, are in a collection at the George Arents Research Library at Syracuse University. For a comprehensive look at Rózsa's non-film music, see Christopher Palmer, *Miklós Rózsa, A Sketch of his Life and Work* (1975). Rózsa's autobiography, *Double Life* (1982, repr. 1989), provides behind-the-scene Hollywood anecdotes and fairly comprehensive documentation of his professional life. For an excellent study of film music from the silent era to the present, see Roy M. Prendergast, *Film Music, A Neglected Art* (1992). Another excellent source for the history and place of film music is Christopher Palmer, *The Composer in Hollywood* (1990). Interesting articles about Rózsa include David Beams, "The Sound Track," *Films in Review*, June–July 1959, pp. 367–370; Ken Doeckel, "Miklós Rózsa," *Films in Review*, November 1965, pp. 536–548; and Page Cook, "The Sound Track," *Films in Review*, June–July 1974, pp. 362–366. An obituary is in the *New York Times*, 29 July 1995.

ANDREA WEEVER

RUBELL, Steve (2 Dec. 1943–26 July 1989), entrepreneur and discotheque owner, was born in Brooklyn, New York, the son of Philip Rubell, a postman who later became a tennis pro, and Ann Hirschbein Rubell, a schoolteacher. He received his early education in local public schools before entering Syracuse University, where he captained the tennis team and first displayed the entrepreneurial talent that would distinguish the rest of his life. It was at Syracuse that Rubell first met Ian Schrager, who had, ironically, grown up a few blocks from where Rubell lived; the two men became fast friends and, later, business partners.

After graduating with a B.A. in history in 1965, Rubell took additional course work at Syracuse for a few more years and also completed a stint in the National Guard. An unhappy year at a Wall Street firm was followed by brief unemployment, until Rubell borrowed $13,000 from his parents and opened restaurants in New Haven, Connecticut, and Bayside, Queens, New York. While knowing nothing of the technical aspects of running a restaurant, Rubell possessed a knack for determining what people wanted. He reconnected with Schrager, who was practicing real estate law, and put him on retainer. The two men enjoyed modest success with a chain of Steak Loft restaurants, but they soon had bigger enterprises in mind. Schrager had noted the newly emerging energy in post-Vietnam, post-Watergate New York nightlife, and he introduced Rubell (previously something of a homebody) to the scene. When Rubell threw a wildly successful party for Schrager's fiancée at one of his restaurants, the two men were determined to enter the nightclub business. Although the two were opposites in nearly every way—Schrager was tall, retiring, and straight, while Rubell was diminutive, ebullient, and gay—their partnership proved to be a powerful one.

After an initial partnership with two other experienced club owners collapsed, Rubell and Schrager opened their first nightspot, the Enchanted Garden, next to a golf course in Douglaston, Queens, New York. The discotheque's success led the partners to want more. They set their sights on Manhattan and

soon acquired the services of well-connected socialite Carmen D'Alessio, who served as their entree into the celebrity-laden world of Manhattan nightlife. A friend of D'Alessio's, German male fashion model Uva Harden, had run into financial difficulties in his attempt to turn a former television studio at 254 West 54th Street into a discotheque. The partners bought out Harden for a token sum and acquired additional financial backing from a new silent partner, Jack Dushey. After extensive and expensive renovations, Studio 54 opened to the public on 26 April 1977.

What followed immediately was a cultural phenomenon. Instantly, Studio 54 became *the* place to be for celebrities and ordinary people alike. Rubell was the most visible partner and essential for the nightclub's success. He ensured that the club's design would be memorable: for example, a large man-in-the-moon figure equipped with a mechanical cocaine spoon that was lowered from the ceiling nightly. But he also employed a notorious, seemingly arbitrary selection process for individuals seeking admission to the club— "tossing the salad," as he put it. He often stood outside the club and personally determined who would gain admittance and who would not, and legendary stories of people being denied admission to the club made the throngs of people who gathered outside each evening even more eager to gain admission. In turn, celebrities such as Andy Warhol, Halston, Liza Minnelli, and Brooke Shields enjoyed a symbiotic relationship with the club; their presence added to the glamour of the place, and that glamour added to their own fame. Adding to Studio 54's notoriety were excesses of all kinds, including drug use and promiscuous, open sexual activity.

Despite occasional difficulties, such as losing its liquor license for five months in 1977, the club prospered. Never discreet, Rubell bragged during an interview for *New York* magazine that "Profits are astronomical . . . only the Mafia does better." The article, combined with inside information from a disgruntled former employee, led to an Internal Revenue Service raid on the club in December 1978. Despite the efforts of their attorney, the infamous Roy Cohn, in November 1979 Rubell and Schrager pled guilty and in January 1980 were each sentenced to three and a half years in prison for personal and corporate income tax evasion. After spending seven months at the nearby Metropolitan Correctional Center, the two were transferred to Maxwell Air Force Base in Montgomery, Alabama. In exchange for a sentence reduction, Rubell and Schrager agreed to testify against other club owners who had employed (in Rubell's words) "cash-in, cash-out, and skim" accounting methods. The two were released in February 1981.

Following their release, Rubell and Schrager faced new obstacles. Besides being shunned by many former friends, they were unable to obtain credit or even open a checking account. Nevertheless, they pressed on. They acted as paid consultants for the new owner of Studio 54, Mark Fleischman, and then became interested in the hotel business. After checking out various properties, they found a backer and purchased the Executive Hotel on Madison Avenue and Thirty-eighth Street in July 1983. It reopened as Morgans that October and was soon a success. Other hotels followed: the Century Paramount in Times Square and, on the Upper East Side, the Royalton and the Barbizon. Rubell and Schrager even managed a successful return to the nightclub world with the May 1985 opening of the Palladium. By the late 1980s Rubell, who had emerged from prison almost penniless, had a net worth in excess of $50 million.

Rubell's health, however, began to deteriorate from the effects of years of heavy drug use and hard living. He died in New York City after a period of intense illness. He will continue to be identified with Studio 54, a club that came to epitomize an era. His life serves as a cautionary tale regarding quick and easy money and as a textbook case of entrepreneurial spirit overcoming all obstacles.

• No collection of Rubell's papers is known to exist. Although it must be used with caution, Anthony Haden-Guest's *The Last Party: Studio 54, Disco and the Culture of the Night* (1997) is the best available source of information on Rubell's life and career. Studio 54 and Rubell were the subject of extensive coverage by the media, both in New York and nationally. See Henry Post, "Sour Notes at the Hottest Disco," *Esquire*, 20 June 1978, pp. 79–86, and Dan Dorfman, "The Eccentric Whiz Behind Studio 54," *New York*, 7 Nov. 1977, pp.14–15. For his post-Studio comeback, see Alix M. Freedman, "White-Collar Chic: Studio 54 Partners Are Even More Successful as New York Hoteliers," *Wall Street Journal*, 19 Jan. 1989. His obituary appears in the *New York Times*, 27 July 1989; the 28 July 1989 and 25 July 1990 issues of the *Times* have follow-up articles.

EDWARD L. LACH, JR.

RUTGERS, Henry (7 Oct. 1745–17 Feb. 1830), soldier and philanthropist, was born in New York City to Hendrick Rutgers, a wealthy landowner, and Catharine de Peyster Rutgers. Although details of his early education are sketchy, he most likely prepared for college under the tutelage of a learned clergyman; in any event he completed his formal education in 1766 by graduating from King's College (now Columbia University). As a direct descendant of Rutger Jacobsen Van Schoenderwoert, an early immigrant to New Amsterdam, Rutgers benefited from his forefathers' business savvy. Early investments in breweries had reaped for the family enormous profits, which were subsequently reinvested in land speculation. As a result, the Rutgers family owned a considerable tract of land stretching from today's Chatham Square to the East River, and income from this property guaranteed Henry Rutgers a lifetime income.

Despite his family's wealth and prominence, Rutgers openly sympathized with the revolutionary movement that was rapidly gaining momentum. A supporter of the Sons of Liberty (who sometimes met at the Rutgers farm), he backed up his political activity with military service in the cause of American independence. Although the exact date of his enlistment

is not known, he had risen to the rank of captain in the New York militia by the time the battle of White Plains was fought. He remained a member of the militia after the war and resigned the command of the First New York regiment as a colonel in 1795.

With the end of hostilities and the withdrawal of the British from New York, Rutgers regained his home (which had been used as a hospital and a barracks during the occupation) and turned his attention to public affairs and politics. He gained election to the state legislature in 1784 and was reelected several times. Rutgers also took a leading role in the raising of $28,000 toward the construction in 1811 of the first Great Wigwam of Tammany Hall, the political and benevolent organization that later became synonymous with corruption in New York City. Avidly interested in education, Rutgers also donated the land for the city's second free school (established for impoverished residents) and often made up the difference in that institution's operating deficits out of his own funds. He served as a regent of the University of the State of New York from 1802 to 1826 and was a trustee of the College of New Jersey (now Princeton University) from 1804 to 1817.

A religious man, Rutgers provided yeoman service to his own church (Dutch Reformed) and donated generously to a number of other local denominations as well. The Market Street Dutch Reformed Church, of which he was an elder, and the Rutgers Street Presbyterian Church both benefited from his gifts of land. Rutgers also served as an elder at the First Presbyterian Church, and by 1825 he had become president of the Dutch Reformed church's Board of Corporation. It was this position that eventually led to his most notable role. During Rutgers's tenure as a trustee of Queen's College in New Brunswick, New Jersey, from 1816 to 1821, the struggling institution (which had been chartered in 1766 and originally opened in 1771) was closed for the second time in its brief existence. Although most institutions of higher learning at that time endured similar struggles for both students and funding, Queen's College was in a particularly precarious position. Its sponsor, the Dutch Reformed church, had a relatively small membership and was riven with internal dissension, putting the college's future in doubt. When Rutgers's pastor and friend Philip Milledoler was named president of the newly reopened college, Rutgers donated $5,000 to the institution as well as a bell, which was subsequently hung in the main building (Old Queen's) on campus. In honor of this gift (and possibly to encourage further gifts from Rutgers), an effort was made to change the name of the college. On 5 December 1825 the New Jersey state legislature changed the name of Queen's College to Rutgers College; although no further gifts were forthcoming from Rutgers himself, the donated funds were sufficient to save the college.

Rutgers continued his philanthropic endeavors until the end of his life, spending the years from 1828 until 1830 as president of the Free School Society.

Although he never married, he adopted a relative, William Bedlow Crosby, as his son. He died in New York City. Although little known today, Rutgers will be remembered for his relatively small gift that allowed a struggling school to survive and later evolve into today's Rutgers University.

• A small collection of Rutgers family papers is held at the Rutgers University Library in New Brunswick, New Jersey, and a sample of Rutgers's correspondence can also be found in the William Edgar papers at the New York Public Library. Secondary sources on Rutgers's life and career are scarce, but information can be found in George H. Holsten, Jr., *Bicentennial Year: The Story of a Rutgers Celebration* (1968); Richard P. McCormick, *Rutgers: A Bicentennial History* (1966); and George P. Schmidt, *Princeton and Rutgers: The Two Colonial Colleges of New Jersey* (1964). An obituary appears in the *New York Daily Advertiser*, 18 Feb. 1830.

EDWARD L. LACH, JR.

S

SAGAN, Carl (9 Nov. 1934–20 Dec. 1996), space scientist, author, science popularizer, TV personality, and antinuclear weapons activist, was born Carl Edward Sagan in Brooklyn, New York. He was the son of Rachel Molly Gruber Sagan and garment industry worker Samuel Sagan, an immigrant from the Ukraine. Carl Sagan's Jewish background encouraged him "to ask questions early," as he later observed (Davidson, p. 57); so did his mother's skeptical, sometimes acidic personality. At age five, he became interested in astronomy when he read in a library book that the stars are distant versions of our sun. His interest in science soared when his parents took him to the New York World's Fair of 1939–1940, which offered an optimistic and (as he later acknowledged) "extremely technocratic" view of the future (Davidson, p. 14).

Sagan developed a passionate interest in mythology, rocketry, and science fiction, especially Edgar Rice Burroughs's tales about life on Mars. His family moved to Rahway, New Jersey, in the late 1940s, where he attended Rahway High School, participated in many student clubs, acted in school plays, and covered sports for the student newspaper. He also appeared in student debates on radio and TV. In 1947 he discovered *Astounding Science Fiction* magazine, which introduced him to more mature scientific speculations than those in Burroughs's fables. That same year inaugurated the "flying saucer" craze; young Carl suspected the "discs" might be alien spaceships. He graduated in June 1951. The yearbook named him the male students' "Class Brain" and "Most Likely to Succeed."

That autumn Sagan entered the University of Chicago. Hoping to become an astronomer, he majored in physics and ran the "theoretical" section of the campus astronomy club. He also obtained an unusually rich education in other subjects, especially biology. He would later credit his intellectual diversity to the campus's then-extant "Hutchins program" (named for former chancellor Robert Maynard Hutchins) of historically based, multidisciplinary education.

A decisive impact on Sagan's career was an experiment on the origin of life, the results of which were published during his sophomore year. The experiment was performed by an acquaintance, Stanley Miller, a graduate student in chemistry. Working under Nobel Prize–winning chemist Professor Harold C. Urey, Miller exposed a mixture of methane, ammonia, and water to electrical discharges; the result: amino acids, which are building blocks of living organisms. Miller's experiment dramatized the possibility of explaining life and its origins in purely scientific terms

without resorting to supernaturalism or mysterious "vital forces." The experiment thrilled Sagan, partly because he was a religious skeptic and partly because it reinforced his belief in extraterrestrial life. Miller's experiment implied that organic molecules form readily wherever the chemical conductions—in particular, a hydrogen-rich atmosphere—were right. Because hydrogen pervades the cosmos, this implied that alien life is common. Humans might not be alone in the cosmos.

Inspired, Sagan wrote his first published scientific paper, "Radiation and the Origin of the Gene" (1957), while still an undergraduate. He completed it with guidance from his first important mentor, Nobel Prize–winning geneticist H. J. Muller of Indiana University, for whom Sagan worked one summer as a lab assistant. The paper was published in the journal *Evolution*, an auspicious venue for a 22-year-old researcher still a few years shy of his doctorate. In 1954 Sagan obtained his A.B. degree with general and special honors, followed by his S.B. in physics in 1955 and, in 1956, his master's degree in the same subject, all at the University of Chicago. Then he entered graduate school at one of the astronomy department's two observatories, Yerkes Observatory in Williams Bay, Wisconsin. He spent the summer of 1956, ostensibly observing Mars, at the other campus observatory, McDonald Observatory at Fort Davis, Texas. His supervisor for that summer was noted astronomer Gerard Peter Kuiper, who complained that Sagan preferred to talk about extraterrestrial life rather than look through the telescope. Still, Kuiper eventually agreed to supervise Sagan's doctoral dissertation.

In June 1957 Sagan married Lynn Alexander of Chicago, with whom he was to have two children, both sons. They settled in Madison, Wisconsin, where she entered graduate school in biology at the University of Wisconsin. Sagan commuted to Yerkes to work on his doctorate. He gave public lectures on astronomy at Yerkes, ran an acclaimed science lecture series starring distinguished scientists (such as Urey, Muller, Kuiper and George Gamow) on the Chicago campus, and wrote his first popular article, "Life on Other Planets," for the *University of Chicago Magazine*.

At Wisconsin, Sagan met another crucial mentor, future Nobel laureate Joshua Lederberg. They shared a mutual interest in the possibility of extraterrestrial life. The "space race" between the United States and the USSR began in October 1957, when the Russians successfully launched the first satellite, Sputnik. Sagan and Lederberg feared that the superpowers would contaminate the moon and planets with rocket debris that accidentally included microorganisms; the "bugs" might proliferate and destroy extraterrestrial ecosystems, if any existed. Lederberg arranged Sagan's appointment to a National Academy of Sciences advisory board on "exobiology," the fledgling science of extraterrestrial life.

Sagan completed his doctoral dissertation in astronomy and astrophysics in June 1960. It discussed three questions: Might Miller-Urey–type processes have generated complex organic molecules, which in turn might have evolved into microbes, on the moon? Might the "gas giant" planet Jupiter contain complex organic molecules that could be remotely detected with astronomical spectroscopes? And why does the planet Venus emit intense microwave radiation? Sagan's answer to the first two questions was yes. As for the third question, he argued (expanding on a 1940 proposal by Rupert Wildt) that Venus emits intense microwave radiation because the planet is extremely hot, due to an atmosphere rich in carbon dioxide and water vapor that traps infrared radiation via the "greenhouse effect."

During his postdoctoral fellowship (1960–1962) at the University of California at Berkeley, Sagan helped to develop an infrared radiometer that would fly to Venus aboard Mariner 2, the first successful interplanetary robotic probe. His powerful imagination discomfited some colleagues. For example, he proposed ways in which humans might launch spaceships to the stars and "terraform" Venus into a habitable world. He was one of a small band of pioneers who met at a Green Bank, West Virginia, radiotelescope site in late 1961 to discuss ways to use the giant "dishes" to detect possible radio signals from alien civilizations. Some scientists, notably Urey, regarded Sagan as a bright but verbose, reckless thinker.

Science reporters, however, were intrigued by his erudition, good looks, and charmingly eccentric style of speech. In the early 1960s *Newsweek* magazine called him "brilliant." By now a UFO skeptic, he testified as an expert witness in a court trial of a UFO hoaxer-embezzler. About the same time, his marriage ended in divorce. (Lynn Sagan, later Lynn Margulis, would in time become a famous microbiologist.)

In 1963 Sagan began a joint appointment as a lecturer and assistant professor of astronomy at Harvard and as an astrophysicist at the nearby Smithsonian Astrophysical Observatory. During his five years on campus, he wrote a number of prescient papers on Venus and Mars with his first graduate student, the brilliant space scientist James B. Pollack (1938–1994). Until then, many astronomers, including Kuiper, had attributed brightness variations on the surface of Mars to seasonal vegetation changes. Sagan and Pollack suggested an alternative explanation: windblown dust. Also at Harvard, Sagan joined the antiwar movement. He quit an air force advisory board on UFOs in protest of U.S. policies in Vietnam.

Sagan's first important work of science popularization was *Intelligent Life in the Universe* (1966), which he cowrote with the Soviet radioastronomer I. S. Shklovskii. Despite his accomplishments, he was denied tenure at Harvard, at least partly because Urey

sent a harsh anti-Sagan letter to the Harvard tenure committee. In 1968 he began teaching at Cornell University in Ithaca, New York, and married again. His new wife was Linda Salzman, an aspiring artist, with whom he had another child, also a son.

In coming years Sagan, chemist Bishun Khare, and others simulated the formation of organic molecules in the atmospheres of other planets such as Jupiter. Also, Sagan and physicist George Mullen proposed that the early earth was warm enough for life because primordial ammonia gas trapped solar infrared radiation. Likewise, Sagan suggested, Mars—now extremely cold, with low air pressure—had perhaps once been warm enough for life. Might any of its prehistoric inhabitants have survived to the present? Sagan thought so. He became a prominent figure in NASA's project to send life-detecting robots to Mars. In 1972 he and his second wife designed plaques containing "messages" to aliens (including an image of a naked man and woman) that were affixed to the Pioneer space probes. These robotic spaceships were launched toward the outer planets; they would eventually escape the solar system and enter galactic space.

Sagan was an eloquent writer. His bestselling 1973 book, *The Cosmic Connection*, a highly personal account of his fascination with space science, impressed many critics. His ability to explain difficult ideas in entertaining ways won him a semiregular spot on Johnny Carson's "Tonight Show" on the NBC-TV network. Sagan's fame grew even as space missions disproved some of his scientific ideas—in particular, his belief that organic molecules or life might be found on the moon and Mars. His explanation for the great heat of Venus, however, was largely vindicated, although its atmosphere had much less water vapor than he expected. Another triumph came when space probes took close-up photos of Mars and found its surface changes were, indeed, caused by windblown dust.

Sagan's book *The Dragons of Eden* (1977) was a crazy salad of speculations about the brain and the possible value of myths and dreams as clues to human evolution. Another bestseller, it won a Pulitzer Prize. Also in 1977 NASA launched to the outer solar system the Voyager space probes, which carried audio records designed by Sagan, his wife, science writer Timothy Ferris, Ferris's fiancée Ann Druyan, radio astronomer Frank Drake, and artist Jon Lomberg. The records contained samples of terrestrial music, earthly sounds and voices, and acoustically coded pictures. Sagan fell in love with Druyan. Soon he left his wife Linda for Druyan, then twenty-eight, a political radical and aspiring writer. Sagan and Druyan would develop an intense emotional and intellectual partnership.

In 1980 PBS-TV ran Sagan's thirteen-part science series, "Cosmos." The show reached a global audience of at least 400 million and won major TV awards, including Emmys and the Peabody. The program offended some religious traditionalists and intellectuals, who were dismayed by Sagan's religious skepticism and what they regarded as his "scientistic" conviction that science is the royal road to truth, superior to other modes of inquiry. After Sagan and Salzman finally divorced in 1981, he married Druyan; they had two children, a daughter and a son.

Under Druyan's tutelage, Sagan's political views shifted overtly to the left. In the 1980s he was the best-known proponent of the "nuclear winter" hypothesis, which challenged the superpowers' nuclear war-fighting policies. Sagan and four other scientists (Richard Turco, Brian Toon, Thomas Ackerman, and Pollack, collectively known as TTAPS, with the "S" standing for "Sagan") calculated that even a "small" exchange of nuclear warheads could trigger vast urban fires. That, in turn, would gush massive clouds of soot into the atmosphere, blocking sunlight and triggering a global cooling—perhaps even widespread freezes. Hence it might be impossible to "win" a nuclear war, as some nuclear strategists had hoped: victory might be short-lived because the "victor" would succumb to a devastating climate change. The only sure way to avoid nuclear winter, Sagan concluded, was to radically shrink the size of U.S. and Soviet nuclear arsenals. He defended this view in numerous speeches and TV appearances, in a face-to-face meeting with Pope John Paul II, and at an antinuclear protest near a weapons testing site in the Nevada desert (where he was arrested).

In response, H-bomb co-inventor Edward Teller attacked the TTAPS theory in *Nature*. The conservative publication *National Review* called the nuclear winter hypothesis a "fraud from the start," and ran a cover story ridiculing its prime exponent as "Flat-Earth Sagan." Scientists also debated the validity of the nuclear winter hypothesis. Whatever its merits, it supposedly influenced the Soviet leadership's decision (under reformist leader Mikhail Gorbachev) in the late 1980s to seek major reductions in nuclear armaments (Kokoshin, p. 136).

Druyan helped Sagan to write his only novel, *Contact* (1985), about the quest for alien radio signals. The couple also developed (with film producer Lynda Obst) a movie version of the book. The Sagans jointly wrote two books, including the superb *Shadows of Forgotten Ancestors* (1992), which scrutinized the evolutionary roots of human behavior, especially society's self-destructive tendencies.

Some scientists resented Sagan's literary and financial success, as well as his political activism, taste for scientific speculation, and sometimes abrasive personality. In 1992, after an emotional debate, members of the National Academy of Sciences refused to admit him to their ranks. Ironically, two years later the same organization gave him its Public Welfare Medal in recognition of his energetic popularization of science. "No one has ever succeeded in conveying the wonder, excitement and joy of science as widely as Carl Sagan and few as well," the citation stated (Davidson, p. 397). In Seattle, Washington, on 20 December 1996, he died from pneumonia as a complication of a blood disease, myelodysplasia.

Sagan was one of the twentieth century's most "visible scientists" (Goodell, 1977), that is, a scientist who popularizes his or her work and, hence, is an unofficial liaison between scientists and laypeople. His imagination, literary skill, and showmanship captivated millions of readers and TV viewers. In the realm of science itself, he made a number of important contributions, especially to the study of Venus and Mars. As a teacher at Harvard and Cornell, he helped educate and inspire a generation of space scientists (Broad, p. D-5). As a political activist, he championed improved U.S.-Soviet scientific relations and led the nuclear winter debate, one of the last scientific controversies of the Cold War. At a funeral service for Sagan, Vice President Albert Gore, Jr., spoke of his friend's luminous personality: "Those of us who were privileged to bask in that light, however briefly, will never, ever forget its brilliance" (Gore, 1996).

• As of mid-1999, Ann Druyan of Ithaca, N.Y., was in possession of Sagan's voluminous private papers, including his 265-page résumé, an exhaustive record of Sagan's publications, speeches, and awards and honors and of articles about him. Sagan's doctoral dissertation, "Physical Studies of Planets" (1960), is available from University Microfilms, Ann Arbor, Mich. A uniquely valuable record is historian Ronald E. Doel's long tape-recorded interview in 1991 with Sagan, archived at the Niels Bohr Library, American Center for Physics, College Park, Md.

Sagan's scientific papers include "Indigenous Organic Matter on the Moon" and "Biological Contamination of the Moon," *Proceedings of the National Academy of Sciences* 46 (1960): 393–96 and 396–402; "The Planet Venus," *Science* 133 (1961): 849–58, which cites the possibility of turning Venus into a habitable world; "Microenvironments for Life on Mars" (with Joshua Lederberg), *Proceedings of the National Academy of Sciences* 48 (1962): 1472–75; "Direct Contact among Galactic Civilizations by Relativistic Interstellar Spaceflight," *Planetary and Space Science* 11 (1963): 485–98, which proposes sending humans to other stars and suggests aliens might have visited the earth in the past; "Life in the Clouds of Venus?" (with Harold Morowitz), *Nature* 215 (1967): 1259–60; "The Prospects for Life on Mars: A Pre-Viking Assessment" (with Lederberg), *Icarus* 28 (1976): 291–300; and "Particles, Environments, and Hypothetical Ecologies in the Jovian Atmosphere" (with E. E. Salpeter), *Astrophysical Journal*, suppl. ser. 32 (1976): 737–55, which speculates about the possibility of balloonlike creatures floating in the atmosphere of Jupiter.

Among Sagan's books not cited in the text are *Cosmos* (1980); *Comet*, with Ann Druyan (1985); *A Path Where No Man Thought: Nuclear Winter and the End of the Arms Race*, with Richard Turco (1990); *Pale Blue Dot: A Vision of the Human Future in Space* (1994); and *A Demon-Haunted World: Science as a Candle in the Dark* (1996). His last book, published posthumously, was *Billions and Billions: Thoughts on Life and Death at the Brink of the Millennium*, with an epilogue by Druyan (1997). The film version of *Contact*, starring Jodie Foster and directed by Robert Zemeckis, was released by Warner Bros. in 1997, several months after Sagan's death.

For an early biographical portrait, see Shirley Thomas, "Carl Sagan," in *Men of Space*, vol. 6: *Profiles of Scientists Who Probe for Life in Space* (1963). Posthumous assessments include Keay Davidson, *Carl Sagan: A Life* (1999), a detailed portrait of his career and often troubled personal life, and

William Poundstone, *Carl Sagan: A Life in the Cosmos* (1999). An especially astute profile appears in Henry S. F. Cooper, Jr., "A Resonance with Something Alive," *New Yorker*, 21 and 28 June 1976. Rae Goodell, *The Visible Scientists* (1977), assesses Sagan as an example of a social type—the scientist who popularizes his or her work. The impact of the nuclear winter hypothesis on Soviet military policy is cited in Andrei A. Kokoshin, *Soviet Strategic Thought, 1917–91* (1998). The *New York Times* article on Sagan's training of numerous space scientists is William J. Broad, "Even in Death, Carl Sagan's Influence Is Still Cosmic," 1 Dec. 1998. The *New York Times* of 21 Dec. 1996 has a front-page obituary.

KEAY DAVIDSON

SAMTER, Max (3 Mar. 1908–9 Feb. 1999), immunologist, was born in Berlin, Germany, the son of Paul Samter, a physician, and Claire Rawicz Samter. After studying at the Universities of Freiburg (1926) and Innsbruck (1928) and completing an internship at the Medizinische Universitätsklinik der Charité in Berlin (1931–1933), he received his medical degree from the University of Berlin in 1933. Samter began practicing medicine in the Berlin-Karow area, typically visiting his patients on a BMW motorcycle. The early years of his medical career coincided with the rise to power of Adolf Hitler. Although Samter was initially "curious" as to how Hitler's regime would evolve, it was soon clear that life as a Jew under the new order would not be pleasant. By writing a series of short novels that satirized the Nazis, he drew the attention of authorities, but he survived because of his friendship with a group of German storm troopers who shared his love of motorcycling and who gave him advance warning of periodic raids by the Gestapo.

By 1937 Samter realized that he had no future in Germany and accepted an offer to join the staff of the Johns Hopkins Hospital in Baltimore, Maryland, where he worked in hematology under Maxwell M. Wintrobe. Although he could not speak a word of English on arriving in the United States, Samter quickly adapted to his new surroundings and after a year and a half at Hopkins moved to the University of Pennsylvania, where he worked in the departments of anatomy (studying lymphocytes) and pharmacology and supported himself by translating *Biological Abstracts*. After briefly operating his own clinical practice in New Jersey (in order to afford to bring his parents over from Germany), Samter enlisted in the U.S. Army, rising eventually to the rank of captain and serving in a field hospital while a participant in such operations as the D-Day invasion and the Battle of the Bulge.

On leaving military service in 1946, Samter found his professional opportunities limited, and he also had to deal with the progressive loss of his hearing as a result of exposure to combat explosions. He secured, however, a position as a research associate in the biochemistry department at the University of Illinois College of Medicine in Chicago; when his deafness did not advance as quickly as he had first feared, he managed to treat patients as well. He married Virginia Svarz Ackerman, a medical illustrator and divorced mother of two, on 17 October 1947; the couple were to have one daughter of their own.

At the Illinois College of Medicine Samter—who had long been interested in research on allergies and clinical immunology and had authored a paper on asthma while still an intern in Germany—settled into his life's work. He spent twenty-eight years at Illinois, eventually serving as the associate dean for clinical affairs (1974–1975) and then as the first chief of staff of the University of Illinois Hospital. In the area of clinical research, his most notable contribution was the discovery that patients who suffered from both nasal polyps and asthma were at great risk—even to the point of death—if they were treated with aspirin. This condition, now known as Samter's syndrome, is not always readily apparent—indeed, susceptibility may not become evident even after decades of treatment—but its identification represented an important advance in the field of internal medicine. As an educator, Samter made valuable contributions to the literature: he wrote approximately seventy-five articles and several books. His books included *American Lectures in Allergy* (1950, with Oren C. Durham), *Regional Allergy* (1954, with Harry L. Alexander), *Excerpts from Classics in Allergy* (1969), and *Hypersensitivity to Drugs* (1972). His most heralded effort was *Immunological Diseases* (1965), which quickly became the standard text in the field of immunology. When the fifth edition appeared in 1995, it bore the revised title *Samter's Immunological Diseases*.

As Samter noted in an interview in his later years, ". . . while I enjoyed my years in the laboratory, I remained quite certain that I had become a physician because I wanted to treat patients. In fact, when people asked me, 'What kind of immunologist are you?' I usually said, 'I am an immunologist in general practice'" (*Asthma and Allergy Proceedings*, p. 332). A warm and friendly man, Samter believed that treating patients who had allergies also meant working with their families, and he often hosted tea parties at his home for his younger patients and their parents in order to gain a better understanding of their environment.

As the study of allergies continued to evolve into the specialty of immunology, Samter was active in the professional societies concerned with the subject. He served as president of both the American Academy of Allergy (1958–1959) and the International Association of Allergology (which were later renamed the American Academy of Allergy, Asthma, and Immunology and the International Association of Allergology and Clinical Immunology, respectively). He received many awards, notably the Asthma and Allergy Foundation of America's Allergist of the Year award in 1982. After retiring from Illinois in 1975 Samter moved across town to Grant Hospital, where until 1983 he directed what was later renamed the Max Samter Institute of Allergy and Clinical Immunology.

Samter continued to see patients until 1992. He died at his home in Evanston, Illinois.

Memorialized by the syndrome that bears his name, Samter helped to create the modern field of immunology.

• Samter's papers have not been located. He was the subject of an insightful review in Sheldon G. Cohen, M.D., and Guy A. Sttipane, M.D., "Max Samter, 1908–1999," *Allergy and Asthma Proceedings* 20, no. 5 (Sept.–Oct. 1999): 329–35, and an obituary in the *Journal of the American Medical Association* (*JAMA*) 281, no. 23 (16 June 1999): 2255–56. An obituary also appears in the *New York Times*, 15 Feb. 1999.

EDWARD L. LACH, JR.

SANFORD, Terry (20 Aug. 1917–18 Apr. 1998), governor, college president, and U.S. senator, was born James Terry Sanford in Laurinburg, North Carolina, the son of Cecil LeRoy Sanford, hardware merchant, and Elizabeth Terry Martin, schoolteacher. After receiving his early education in local public schools, he attended Presbyterian Junior College and then the University of North Carolina at Chapel Hill, graduating with a B.A. in 1939. After serving as a special agent with the Federal Bureau of Investigation for two years (1941–1942), Sanford resigned and enlisted in the U.S. Army. He married Margaret Rose Knight in July 1942; the couple had two children. Sanford saw service as a paratrooper in several European campaigns (including the invasion of southern France and the Battle of the Bulge) and was decorated with both the Bronze Star and the Purple Heart. Discharged as a first lieutenant in December 1945, he returned to his alma mater and received an LL.B. in 1946. Admitted to the bar that same year, he remained in Chapel Hill and served as assistant director of the Institute of Government until 1948.

Sanford moved to Fayetteville in 1948 and formed a law partnership (Sanford, Philips, McCoy & Weaver). After organizing a local unit of the North Carolina National Guard, he served as its commanding officer and also became politically active. He served as president of the state's Young Democrats in 1949, and in the following year Governor W. Kerr Scott appointed him secretary-treasurer of the state ports authority. He served in the North Carolina State Senate in 1953–1954; during the latter year he successfully managed Scott's bid for the U.S. Senate.

By now solidly schooled in the techniques of political organization and closely identified with the Scott wing of the Democratic Party, Sanford returned to his law practice following the campaign and planned his own race for governor. In 1960 he won the Democratic primary but failed to gain a majority of the vote. Pitted against hard-core segregationist I. Beverly Lake in the runoff primary, Sanford continued to preach the progressive gospel of economic development and educational improvement and soft-pedaled the racial issue, declaring that what the state needed was "massive intelligence, not massive resistance" (that is, resistance to federally mandated de-

segregation). Shortly after winning the runoff, Sanford joined a handful of North Carolina delegates at the national convention in supporting John F. Kennedy's bid for the Democratic presidential nomination, thereby securing Kennedy's appreciation and an open ear in the White House after both men won their respective races in the fall general elections.

Inaugurated in January 1961, Sanford soon made good on his campaign promises. Although his Quality Education Program was not without controversy—it was financed by placing a sales tax on food—the measure had results: more teachers with higher salaries, expanded libraries, and revamped curriculums. In 1963 Sanford sponsored the Higher Education Act; far-reaching in its impact, it created a statewide system of community colleges and technical institutes, established four-year universities within the state's University of North Carolina system at Asheville, Charlotte, and Wilmington, and upgraded existing colleges (Woman's College and North Carolina State College) to university status (UNC-Greensboro and North Carolina State University, respectively). Other institutions established by Sanford included the Center for Mental Retardation, Operation Second Chance (for dropouts), and the North Carolina School of the Arts in Winston-Salem.

In an effort to combat poverty, Sanford established the North Carolina Fund in 1963. Largely underwritten by the Ford Foundation, the program sponsored an experimental antipoverty program that became a model for antipoverty legislation nationwide. Concerned by the state's relative underdevelopment in manufacturing, Sanford also committed $1.2 billion toward new manufacturing facilities, which resulted in the creation of more than 120,000 jobs.

With racial tensions a key factor in the American political life of the time, Sanford set an example on becoming governor by sending his two children to the only integrated elementary school in Raleigh. He sought to eliminate job discrimination against African Americans in 1963 with the formation of the Good Neighbor Council, a biracial panel charged with creating ways "to give all men and women their best chance in life."

Constitutionally prohibited from running for reelection, Sanford left office in 1965 and returned to the practice of law. A position as director of Duke University's Study of American States led to a book—*Storm over the States* (1967)—and in late 1969 to the presidency of the university. Popular among students (who nicknamed him "Uncle Terry"), Sanford oversaw the continued development of Duke University (particularly its medical school) into a leading national institution. He attempted to reenter political life in 1972, but his campaign for the presidency foundered after he suffered an embarrassing defeat in his home state's primary by Alabama governor George Wallace.

After a second attempt at the presidency likewise resulted in early failure in 1976, Sanford returned to Duke and served as its president until 1986, when he surprised many observers by winning a U.S. Senate seat that had been vacated by the suicide of Republican incumbent John East. A freshman senator at age sixty-nine, Sanford learned the ropes of the institution quickly but made a notable display of indecision in 1987 when he reversed his vote three times before ultimately joining other Democrats in overriding President Reagan's veto of a highway bill. He also raised the ire of North Carolina's more conservative voters with his opposition to the Persian Gulf War. Initially considered a good bet for reelection, he could not overcome concerns regarding his health, which emerged when he was hospitalized with a heart condition in the middle of the campaign. He lost by a narrow margin to Lauch Faircloth, a former friend and former Democrat.

His life in public office over, Sanford returned to his law practice and also taught public policy and government at Duke. He died at his home in Durham, North Carolina, after a battle with cancer. Although his policies often were not fully appreciated by his constituents, Sanford built a career of solid achievement. In the vanguard of southern progressives during the pivotal years of the civil rights movement, he provided leadership in the face of intense racial unrest and helped North Carolina avoid some of the trauma that neighboring states experienced. His most enduring legacy remains in education, which he made a central concern of state government.

• Sanford's papers are divided between the North Carolina state archives in Raleigh, the Duke University archives in Durham, and the Southern Historical Collection at the University of North Carolina in Chapel Hill. Sanford published several books, including *Needed: A Comprehensive Policy for Public Education* (1964), *But What About the People?* (1966), and *A Danger of Democracy: The Presidential Nominating Process* (1981). Other writings of his appear in Sam Ragan, ed., *The New Day* (1964), and *Messages, Addresses, and Public Papers of Terry Sanford* (1966), ed. Memory Mitchell. Secondary sources on his life and career include Jack Bass and Walter DeVries, *The Transformation of Southern Politics: Social Change and Political Consequence since 1945* (1976); Earl Black, *Southern Governors and Civil Rights: Racial Segregation as a Campaign Issue in the Second Reconstruction* (1976); Howard E. Covington, Jr., and Marion Ellis, *Terry Sanford: Politics, Progress, and Outrageous Ambitions* (1999); and Neal R. Peirce, *The Border South States: People, Politics, and Power in the Five Border South States* (1975). An obituary is in the *New York Times*, 20 April 1998.

EDWARD L. LACH, JR.

SAVIO, Mario (8 Dec. 1942–6 Nov. 1996), social activist, was born Mario Robert Savio in New York City, the son of Joseph Savio, a machinist. His mother's name is unrecorded. Although physically frail, Savio early on displayed an intellectual precocity that would mark his entire life. After finishing at the top of his class at Martin Van Buren High School, he entered Manhattan College on a scholarship, but finding it "too parochial" he transferred to Queens College, where he served as president of the Fraternity of Christian Doctrine. By now deeply interested in social action, he spent the summer of 1963 in the Taxco area

of Mexico, where he helped local residents construct a laundry in an effort to combat outbreaks of cholera. After his parents relocated to Los Angeles, Savio enrolled at the University of California at Berkeley, where he began to study philosophy.

At Berkeley Savio continued to explore the world of politics, and after a brief association with the Young People's Socialist League, he became active with the Student Nonviolent Coordinating Committee (SNCC) and spent the summer of 1964 in Mississippi, where he taught at a Freedom School and also registered African-American voters. Outraged at the injustices that he witnessed in Mississippi, Savio returned to the Berkeley campus in the fall of 1964 and became Chairman of the University Friends of SNCC.

Determined to raise money and recruit new members for his organization, Savio soon ran afoul of the campus administration, which in the post-McCarthy era was loath to tolerate even a hint of what it considered rabble-rousing. Previously allowed a small patch of land immediately off campus from which they could distribute literature, all campus organizations lost even that privilege on 14 September 1964, when the Berkeley administration, bowing to pressure from the nearby *Oakland Tribune* (which had been subjected to picketing due to its racial policies), banned even that limited activity. Savio led several other student organizations in forming an ad hoc organization called the United Front and set out to test the university's resolve. On 1 October 1964 Savio and seven other students were suspended for distributing political literature; when Jack Weinberg, a nonstudent member of the campus chapter of the Congress of Racial Equality (CORE), was arrested by local police on the same charge, campus passions exploded. A large group of students surrounded the squad car and prevented the police from removing Weinberg. By delivering a fiery speech to a large crowd from the top of the squad car, Savio gained instant credibility as the leader of an emerging movement.

Soon thereafter, university officials formed a committee to address student concerns, tensions temporarily eased, and Savio became the de facto head of what came to be known as the Free Speech Movement (FSM). The crisis reappeared, however, when the University Board of Regents met on 20 November 1964 and upheld the suspensions of Savio and another student as well as placing further restrictions on student activity. In retaliation, the FSM leaders called for a massive student strike, and on 2 December 1964 over 2,000 students occupied the university's administration building following a massive rally in which Savio declared that "there is a time when the operation of the machine becomes so odious, makes you so sick at heart, that you can't take part . . . you've got to put your bodies upon the wheels and upon the gears, upon the levers . . . and you've got to make it stop." Eight hundred students remained in the building, Sproul Hall, until they were removed by police, and for the next five days the campus was paralyzed by a student strike. When university president Clark Kerr attempted to outline proposed reforms at a large outdoor meeting in the campus's Greek amphitheater on 7 December, Savio tried to join him on stage only to be forced off by campus police. The police actions further inflamed the already volatile crowd, and Savio was later allowed to speak. The next day, the faculty senate passed resolutions urging the removal of restrictions on expression and the lifting of disciplinary actions against Savio and others. Later that month, the Board of Regents, while refusing to grant disciplinary authority to the faculty, did reaffirm the First Amendment rights of students and also appointed a new university chancellor, who further eased student restrictions.

Although ultimately successful, the Free Speech Movement leaders paid a price for their actions, with Savio serving a jail sentence of four months in 1965. When the FSM disbanded nearly as quickly as it had formed, Savio largely dropped out of politics. He spent the next several years working at a bookstore in Los Angeles and teaching at an alternative school. He finally returned to higher education in the early 1980s, when he earned an undergraduate degree in physics summa cum laude from San Francisco State University in 1984 and a master's degree from the same institution the following year. After teaching at San Francisco State and at Modesto Junior College for a number of years, in 1990 he began teaching mathematics and philosophy at Sonoma State University. In the mid-1990s Savio reemerged politically when he challenged Proposition 187 (1994, which sought to limit public benefits for illegal immigrants) as a "know-nothing fascist law." In 1995 his was a leading voice against Proposition 209, which sought to overturn affirmative action.

After an early marriage to Suzanne Goldberg that produced two sons had ended in divorce, Savio married Lynne Hollander, with whom he had one son. Savio died in Sebastopol, California, where he suffered a heart attack while moving furniture into his new home.

Labeled variously a troublemaker and a self-aggrandizer at the height of the FSM's activity, Mario Savio's rapid descent into obscurity after a brief period in the spotlight seemed to confirm the criticism of his harshest denigrators. Nevertheless, the movement he led had a profound impact on political developments in the 1960s. Locally, it became a lightning rod issue in the 1966 California governor's race, where it led to the election of Ronald Reagan and ultimately to the dismissal of Clark Kerr from his university post. Nationally it served as a harbinger of much of the unrest that developed on other college campuses in the latter part of the decade, and Savio's role within the movement will remain his greatest legacy.

• The papers of the Free Speech Movement are at the Bancroft Library at the University of California at Berkeley. Savio's role in the FSM has been studied extensively; see Hal Draper, *Berkeley: The New Student Revolt* (1965); Max Heirich, *The Beginning: Berkeley 1964* (1968); W. J. Rorabaugh, *Berkeley at War: The 1960s* (1989); and David Lance Goines, *The Free Speech Movement: Coming of Age in the 1960s* (1993). Obituaries are in the *New York Times* and the *San Francisco Examiner*, 7 Nov. 1996.

EDWARD L. LACH, JR.

SAYÃO, Bidú (11 May 1902?–12 Mar. 1999), opera singer, was born Balduina de Oliveira Sayão into an independently wealthy family in Rio de Janeiro, Brazil, the daughter of Pedro de Oliveira and Maria José Costa Sayão. Her birth year has always been in dispute and has variously been reported as 1902, 1905, and 1906, although the earliest date seems the most probable. She was brought up in a society that frowned on upper-class women aspiring to a career of any sort outside the home, but like other girls of her background she was privately tutored in a variety of subjects and trained to play the piano. From an early age, however, she developed a passion for the theater, dressing up to act out roles from stories read to her by her nanny. Her obvious skill caught the eye of an uncle who was also a theater devotee, and he began writing monologues for her to recite at private charity benefits. By the time she was a teenager she had developed a good soprano singing voice as well, and her uncle, unbeknownst to her parents, suggested that she might combine her theatrical and musical skills by becoming an opera singer. He found her a teacher, soprano Elena Teodorini, a European émigré considered one of the best vocal coaches in Rio at the time, and she began taking lessons secretly.

After four years of lessons Sayão was declared by her teacher to be ready for more advanced training abroad, and her parents had to be told at last of her intention to become a singer. Initially horrified, they were persuaded to acquiesce by Mme. Teodorini, who told them their daughter had a great talent worth encouraging. In 1924 Sayão was sent to France to study with the great tenor-turned-teacher Jean de Reszke. De Reszke stressed interpretation rather than focusing on the mechanics of voice training, and with the assistance of another celebrated singer, Lina Cavalieri, and the composer Reynaldo Hahn at the piano, he acted out entire operas with great flair. Sayão was an attentive pupil, and after a year of training she had learned a sizable repertoire of arias as well as concert songs. She returned to Rio in 1925 to make her stage debut as a concert singer at the Teatro Municipal— and with that debut she created a sensation.

After further study in Rio, Sayão made her operatic debut a year later at the Teatro Municipal as Rosina in Rossini's *The Barber of Seville*. According to legend, her parents, who still opposed an operatic career for their daughter, tried to keep her from performing, and only with the intervention of her teacher was a compromise reached: She could sing one performance, and if it was a success, then she could continue in opera. If she failed, she had to give up her desire to become an opera singer. Fortunately for Sayão and for millions of future opera fans, she again triumphed, winning not only rave reviews but invitations to sing at major opera houses in Europe. After making her European debut not long afterward at the Teatro Costanzi in Rome, again singing the role of Rosina, she was soon appearing in major lyric and coloratura roles at both the Paris Opéra and the Opéra-Comique, Milan's La Scala, and houses in Naples and Genoa, as well as the Teatro Colón in Buenos Aires and the Royal Opera House of Brazil.

Sayão made her first stage appearance in the United States in December 1935, in a recital at New York's Town Hall that drew warm notices. The following April she appeared as soloist in several performances of Debussy's *La Demoiselle élue* with the New York Philharmonic, under the baton of Arturo Toscanini, and again was given favorable attention by both audiences and critics. But perhaps the greatest ovation of her career to date came following her North American operatic debut, which occurred in February 1937 at the Metropolitan Opera House in New York City. Singing the title role in Puccini's *Manon* as a successor to the newly retired and much beloved Lucrezia Bori, and dressed in stunning gowns as well as dazzling jewels from her own priceless collection, she was greeted with thunderous applause as well as effusions of praise from New York's major music critics. They not only raved about the skill with which she sang the role but also gloried in her enchanting presence onstage, proclaiming the petite, blue-eyed, golden-haired Sayão charming and adorable. She followed her debut in quick succession with acclaimed appearances at the Met as Violetta in Verdi's *La Traviata* and Mimi in Puccini's *La Bohème*, roles for which she was also declared ideally suited. Now in her thirties, Sayão had at last found her operatic home, and she remained with the Metropolitan Opera for the rest of her career.

Indeed, Sayão never sang outside the Western Hemisphere again. She starred at the Met for more than a decade, appearing in more than two hundred performances. She sang there in twelve major operas, most frequently in the roles of Mimi in *La Bohème*, Susanna in Mozart's *The Marriage of Figaro*, the title heroine in *Manon*, and Zerlina in Mozart's *Don Giovanni*. She sang similar repertory at the San Francisco Opera as well and also appeared in operas and on the concert stage in her native Rio, Buenos Aires, and other South American cities. In addition, Sayão made many recordings of both songs and operas; during World War II she also entertained American soldiers at army camps and hospitals and was decorated by the U.S. government for her efforts. Retiring from the Met in 1951—she sensed, she said later, that she would shortly be eased out by the new manager, Rudolf Bing—she nevertheless continued to appear in concerts and recitals in North and South America. Sayão abruptly left the stage for good in 1958, following an appearance at New York's Carnegie Hall in *La Demoiselle élue*.

Early in her career Sayão was married to Walter Mocchi, the head of the Teatro Colón in Buenos Aires, but the marriage eventually ended in divorce. In 1947 she married an Italian baritone, Giuseppe Danise, who retired from the stage to manage his wife's career. There were no children from either marriage. Sayão and her second husband maintained residences in both New York City and Lincolnville, Maine, and after his death in 1963 she continued to be a frequent and beloved presence at recitals and concerts in New York, diminutive and chic in high heels and her trademark chignon. She died at a hospital in Rockport, Maine, not far from her home in Lincolnville.

• For biographical information, see entries for "Sayão, Bidú," in *Current Biography Yearbook* for 1942 and 1999. See also an interview with Sayão in Lanfranco Rasponi, *The Last Prima Donnas* (1982). In addition, see Will Crutchfield, "A Met Manon in 1937 Visits a New Met 'Manon' in 1987," *New York Times*, 1 Feb. 1987, sec. 2, pp. 27ff. An obituary appears in the *New York Times*, 13 Mar. 1999. (Note that it contains contradictory information regarding Sayão's age: The headline and a first-paragraph text reference claim she was ninety-four at the time of her death, yet later in the article her birth date is twice given as May 1902, which would have made her ninety-six.)

ANN T. KEENE

SCHAPIRO, Meyer (23 Sept. 1904–3 Mar. 1996), art historian, was born Meir Schapiro in Siauliai, Lithuania, to Nathan Menachem Schapiro and Fanny Adelman Schapiro. The father, who was descended from a long line of Talmudic scholars, had abandoned Orthodoxy as a teenager and embraced both the secular Jewish Socialist Bund and an eastern European movement called the Haskala, which looked to the Western secular tradition for enlightenment. In 1904, about the time of Meir's birth, his father immigrated to the United States, leaving his family behind, and began teaching Hebrew at a Yeshiva on the Lower East Side in New York City to earn money for their transatlantic passage. Three years later, Nathan Schapiro was able to send for his family; and when they arrived on Ellis Island, young Meir's name was changed to Meyer.

The Schapiros moved to Brooklyn, where Nathan Schapiro supported the family as a paper-and-twine jobber while continuing to pursue the study and teaching of Hebrew language and literature. Meyer and his two siblings grew up speaking Yiddish and, reflecting their father's intellectual interests, reading contemporary Jewish periodicals as well as scholarly works on biblical history and Darwinism. Meyer himself exhibited wider-ranging interests, including sports and drawing, and also enjoyed making electrical gadgets and developing photographs. His parents encouraged him in all these areas, even enrolling him as the only child in a night-school art class taught by painter John Sloan. To support his various interests he worked at various odd jobs during the summer, including stints as a Western Union delivery boy and a clerk at Macy's.

Art became a passion for Meyer Schapiro. Although he excelled in every school subject, receiving top grades at Boys High School in Brooklyn, he hoped to make a career in that field. But a first-rate education was deemed mandatory by his parents, and Schapiro realized that he did not have the ability to become a truly great painter. After graduating from high school at the age of fifteen, he attended Columbia University on two prestigious scholarships and followed a liberal arts curriculum that was strong in languages, mathematics, and philosophy. He also took classes in art history, but he was disappointed in their quality. After receiving his undergraduate degree with honors in 1924 he decided to pursue graduate studies in anthropology at Columbia under the direction of Franz Boas, who had become a mentor to him. Schapiro's love of art proved greater than his eagerness to study under the great Boas, however, and after seeking unsuccessfully to enroll in Princeton University's art history department he reluctantly continued his studies in art at Columbia.

Schapiro's enthusiasm grew when he became a student and protégé of the noted medieval art historian Ernest DeWald, who had come to Columbia from Princeton, and under DeWald's guidance he began a rigorous study of the works of leading German historians of medieval art, in particular Wilhelm Voge and Alois Riegl. Reading their works in German, which he taught himself, Schapiro was especially struck by the ways in which works of art reflected changes in human perception over the centuries. For his doctoral dissertation, Schapiro studied sculptures dating from the twelfth century at Moissac, a Romanesque abbey near Toulouse, France, traveling there in 1926 and 1927 on a fellowship from the Carnegie Corporation. While in France Schapiro also studied other examples of Romanesque sculpture and architecture, noting in particular how it evolved from flatness and uniformity to a style more complex, intricate, and naturalistic.

Before Schapiro's study of Moissac, art historians had dismissed most Romanesque work as crude historical documentation or mere artifacts rather than art. Schapiro's groundbreaking dissertation on Moissac emphatically and convincingly laid that assessment to rest; when parts of it were published in the *Art Bulletin* in 1931, his reputation as a brilliant new art historian was assured. By this time, Schapiro had become a member of the Columbia faculty: he had begun lecturing there in 1928, soon after returning from France, and had received his doctorate a year later. Schapiro was to spend his entire academic career at Columbia, advancing up the ladder to assistant professor in 1936, associate professor in 1946, and full professor in 1952. He was named university professor in 1965 and retired as university professor emeritus in 1973.

Although Schapiro had established his reputation as a historian of medieval art and continued his research in that field, he also became known as an authority on modern European painting, in particular the works of Paul Cézanne, whom he greatly admired. Unlike many scholars, Schapiro was a brilliant classroom lecturer, and students flocked to his courses.

Some of them were young artists who became well-known painters, among them Robert Motherwell. Many others were inspired by Schapiro to become art historians themselves; still others became curators at major institutions in the United States and abroad. What lay at the heart of Schapiro's effectiveness as a teacher was his obvious enthusiasm for all forms and periods of art, and his ability to communicate their interrelatedness as well as their wider cultural significance. Underpinning Schapiro's effectiveness was his vast erudition combined with exceptional competence as a public speaker.

Schapiro had less facility as a writer. Although his prose was clear and competent, it was not imbued with the magic of his lectures, which may be why he published relatively little, given his stature by the middle of the twentieth century as arguably the best-known art historian in America. In fact, Schapiro's first book—a monograph on Vincent van Gogh that served as an introduction to a folio of the artist's paintings—did not appear until 1950, nineteen years after his seminal article was published in the *Art Bulletin*. Another monograph, this time on Cézanne, appeared in a similar format three years later. Another twenty years passed before the publication of Schapiro's next book, *Words and Pictures* (1973), in which he offered a semiotic analysis of illuminated manuscripts. Beginning in the late 1970s, when the retired Schapiro himself was in his seventies, his essays were collected and published in four volumes over the next two decades, beginning with *Romanesque Art* (1977) and followed by *Modern Art: 19th and 20th Centuries* (1978), *Late Antique, Early Christian and Medieval Art* (1979), and *Theory and Philosophy of Art: Style, Artist and Society* (1994).

Schapiro was a public figure in New York and one of the city's preeminent resident intellectuals. He maintained close friendships with many contemporary painters and writers and welcomed them to his apartment in Greenwich Village. Gatherings at the Schapiro home were cohosted by his wife, pediatrician Lillian Milgram, whom he had married in 1928 and with whom he had two children. In his youth and throughout the 1930s Schapiro and his wife were committed to left-wing politics and were active in several political organizations. After the Stalinist purges, they became disenchanted with Communism, and in 1940 Schapiro was a major organizer of the Federation of Modern Painters and Sculptors, an organization founded to promote progressive art and to counter the Communist-dominated American Arts Congress. Despite this, Schapiro was able to avoid the acrimonious political quarrels of the period and maintain his friendships with Communists and non-Communists alike.

In addition to teaching at Columbia, Schapiro lectured at New York University (1932–1936) as well as the New School for Social Research (1936–1952), where his talks became a focal point for artists active in the postwar movement that became known as Abstract Expressionism. In 1966–1967 Schapiro delivered the annual Charles Eliot Norton Lectures at Harvard, and during the following year he served as the Slade Professor of Art at Oxford University. In 1974, a year after his retirement from Columbia, he lectured at the Collège de France in Paris. That same year, in honor of his seventieth birthday, a dozen prominent American artists, including Jasper Johns, Ellsworth Kelly, Roy Lichtenstein, Robert Motherwell, Robert Rauschenberg, and Andy Warhol, produced a collection of lithographs, etchings, and screen prints that were sold in a limited edition; the proceeds were given to Columbia University to endow a chair in Schapiro's name.

Although Schapiro downplayed his own artistic skills, he continued to paint for pleasure throughout his life. His subjects included different views of his summer home in rural Vermont, as well as landscapes, seascapes, and portraits. Schapiro died at his home in New York.

• For biographical information, see especially Helen Epstein's two-part profile, "Meyer Schapiro: 'A Singular Need to Know,'" in *ARTnews*, May 1983, pp. 60ff, and Summer 1983, pp. 84ff. See also "Schapiro, Meyer," in *Current Biography Yearbook 1984*, and "Schapiro, Meyer," in *Contemporary Authors*, vols. 97–100 (1981). In addition, see Deborah Solomon, "Meyer Schapiro: A Critic Turns 90," *New York Times Magazine*, 14 Aug. 1994, pp. 22–25. For an assessment of Schapiro's career and its significance, see Hilton Kramer, "Columbia Honors Schapiro as the Model Art Historian," *New York Times*, 7 May 1975. An obituary appears in the *New York Times*, 4 Mar. 1996.

ANN T. KEENE

SCHINE, G. David (11 Sept. 1927–19 June 1996), government official and businessman, was born Gerard David Schine in Gloversville, New York, the son of J. Myer Morris Schine, millionaire owner of radio stations, movie theaters, and hotels, and Hildegarde Feldman Schine. After graduating from Harvard in 1949, Schine was appointed by his father to be president of his own company, Schine Hotels Inc.

In 1952 he published an error-filled pamphlet, *Definition of Communism*, and had it placed in all of his company's hotel rooms. Despite its inaccuracies, the pamphlet caught the notice of anti-Communists. Late in 1952 Schine was introduced to U.S. Justice Department attorney Roy Cohn, chief counsel for Senator Joseph McCarthy's Senate Committee on Government Operations, which tenaciously pursued any sign of Communist infiltration in the foreign service and the military. The two became friends, and Cohn soon persuaded McCarthy to hire Schine in February 1953 as the committee's "chief consultant," an unpaid position McCarthy created "to please Cohn" (Reeves, *Life and Times of Joe McCarthy*).

Schine assisted Cohn in an investigation of the Voice of America (VOA) in February and March, planning strategy and subpoenaing VOA employees. Those hearings brought to light the presence of "numerous Communist and pro-Communist publications" in European State Department libraries. Mc-

Carthy quickly sent Cohn and Schine abroad to uncover inefficiency and "subversives" within the International Information Administration (IIA). After arriving in Paris on 4 April, they traveled to nine European cities in eighteen days. The trip made both men and the anti-Communist cause they served objects of ridicule (as "junketeering gumshoes") and of fear (they caused hundreds to lose their jobs and inspired "book-burnings"). Although they exaggerated what they achieved and used Draconian methods, there was evidence of actual mismanagement and misuse of funds in both the VOA and the IIA.

Soon after they returned from Europe, other issues emerged that proved far more important to the legacy of McCarthyism. In his 17 July 1953 syndicated column, Drew Pearson reported on unpatriotic draft avoidance among McCarthy's staff. He obtained Schine's draft records and uncovered "questionable deferments." With Pearson applying pressure, the California draft board reevaluated Schine's case and eventually drafted him. Schine arrived at Fort Dix, New Jersey, on 10 November 1953. After failing to get his friend an officer's commission, an enraged Cohn began alternately cajoling and harassing U.S. Army officials on Schine's behalf.

At the time, Senator McCarthy was involved in an investigation of the army, partially justified by legitimate instances of "lax security" and officers suspected of Communist sympathies. William Klingaman has suggested that during the first two months of McCarthy's fishing expedition the army cooperated with him. When the Senator pressed to see confidential files, however, and verbally attacked the commander of Fort Monmouth, General Ralph W. Zwicker, "the campaign . . . to obtain special considerations for Schine provided Army officials with a weapon" to fight back.

On 16 March 1954, the Senate Committee on Government Operations created a Permanent Subcommittee on Investigations under Senator Karl Mundt of South Dakota to review the charge that McCarthy was trying "to punish the U.S. Army for drafting his former aide." The televised hearings ran from 22 April to 17 June, with thirty-six days of testimony seen by millions. Though McCarthy himself seemed to be only minimally involved in obtaining special treatment for Schine (he told Secretary of the Army Robert Stevens there was "nothing indispensable about [Schine]"), he was held responsible for Cohn's rabid crusade. Witnesses testified that Schine had been "released from drills to accept phone calls and . . . received passes every weekend and holiday." Stevens testified that he did give Schine privileges because he believed Cohn was "threatening" him. McCarthy, with Cohn whispering in his ear, denied any undue pressure and relentlessly badgered witnesses, prompting Army lawyer Joseph N. Welch to famously criticize the senator: "Have you no sense of decency, sir, at long last?" Though the hearings came to no definite conclusion, there was enough evidence for the Senate to vote to censure McCarthy on 2 December 1954.

Examinations of Cohn and Schine's relationship have attempted to explain Cohn's obsessive behavior over Schine's army service by pointing to rumors of their homosexuality. Though gay, Cohn denied any sexual relations with Schine. It seems most likely that, if there was an erotic attraction, it was only on Cohn's side. Others found the relationship purely mercenary: "Schine paid Cohn's expenses" (Ewald, *Who Killed Joe McCarthy?*). Whatever the truth, the fact remains that Cohn had a strong enough attachment to Schine to risk the destruction of McCarthy's anti-Communist movement for him.

Schine remained in the army until his discharge in 1955. In 1957 he married Hillevi Rombin; they had six children. Schine became a successful businessman, serving in his father's empire as a hotel president. He was also involved in the entertainment industry, most notably as executive producer of the film *The French Connection* (1971), winner of the Academy Award for best picture. In 1977 Schine and Cohn sued Universal Studios and NBC for defamation in a television movie about McCarthy, *Tailgunner Joe*, but an appellate court ruled they had no case. Schine died on his way to inspect a theater for a stage production of *Dr. Jekyll and Mr. Hyde* when the single-engine plane piloted by his son Berndt crashed shortly after takeoff from Burbank, California. His wife and son were also killed.

An eager participant in McCarthy's anti-Communist witch hunt, Schine nevertheless found his niche in history by unwittingly helping to bring about its downfall.

• Helpful government records include *State Department Information Program—Information Centers* (1954); *Foreign Relations of the United States, 1952–1954*, vol. 1, part 2: General Economic and Political Matters; and *Communist Infiltration in the Army* (1954). See also books on McCarthy: Fred J. Cook, *The Nightmare Decade: The Life and Times of Senator Joe McCarthy* (1971); William B. Ewald, Jr., *Who Killed Joe McCarthy?* (1984); Arthur Herman, *Joseph McCarthy: Reexamining the Life and Legacy of America's Most Hated Senator* (2000); William K. Klingaman, *Encyclopedia of the McCarthy Era* (1996); David M. Oshinsky, *A Conspiracy So Immense: The World of Joe McCarthy* (1983); Thomas C. Reeves, *The Life and Times of Joe McCarthy* (1982); Richard H. Rovere, *Senator Joe McCarthy* (1959). For Cohn and Schine's relationship, see Nicholas von Hoffman, *Citizen Cohn* (1988), and Tony Kushner's play "G. David Schine in Hell" in *Death and Taxes: Hydriotaphia and Other Plays* (2000). The Cohn-Schine overseas trip and Army-McCarthy hearings were covered in most major newspapers. An obituary is in the *New York Times*, 21 June 1996.

KRISTEN WILLIAMS

SCHULTZ, Theodore W. (30 Apr. 1902–26 Feb. 1998), economist, was born Theodore William Schultz on a farm near Arlington, South Dakota, to Herry E. Schultz, a farmer, and Anna E. Weiss Schultz. The eldest of eight children who were all expected to work on the family farm, young Theodore had a sporadic early education and never attended high school. Over his parents' objections, he enrolled at South Dakota State College when he was in his early twenties and earned a bachelor's degree in agricultural economics in 1926. He went on to graduate study in the same field at the University of Wisconsin, where he received a master's degree two years later and a Ph.D. in 1930. Schultz later noted that he had been born when times were especially hard for farmers, and from an early age he wanted to find a way to improve the situation of his parents and their farm neighbors. Understanding economics, he came to believe, was the key to improving their circumstances.

In the fall of 1930 Schultz joined the faculty of what was then Iowa State College (now University) as an assistant professor of agricultural economics. He was promoted to associate professor a year later, to chairman of the joint department of economics and sociology in 1934, and to full professor in 1935. Here he began making major contributions to the field of agricultural economics, becoming a pioneer in the study of human capital and in particular ways to improve the position of low-income groups in agriculture, rather than pursuing the discipline's heretofore traditional focus on land and other physical capital. His expertise came not only from books but from firsthand observation, and it was not confined to American agriculture: In 1929, as a graduate student at Wisconsin, he had traveled to Central Europe and Russia to study peasant agriculture; and in 1936, while at Iowa State, he toured farms in Scandinavia and Scotland. In 1941 Schultz traveled to South America as chairman of a U.S. government–sponsored agricultural development mission. His first book, *Redirecting Farm Policy*, was published in 1943, when the United States was embroiled in World War II and farmers were being asked to produce as much as they could for the war effort. At Iowa State, Schultz also edited the *Journal of Farm Economics* from 1939 to 1942.

When Schultz left Iowa State in 1943 to become a professor of economics at the University of Chicago, it seemed an obvious career move, but Schultz's resignation was prompted by more than the offer of tenure at a major American university: he was protesting the violation of a colleague's academic freedom. A fellow professor on the Iowa State faculty had written an article in a college publication supporting oleomargarine as a wartime substitute for butter, which dairy farmers were vigorously opposing. When the college administration withdrew the article as unpolitic, Schultz spoke out against the action to no avail and promptly resigned in protest.

During his long career at the University of Chicago, Schultz became an acknowledged expert on low-income groups in agriculture and a major authority on the agricultural economies of underdeveloped countries. His areas of expertise were reflected in the titles of the nine books he wrote over more than three decades; many of them became standard texts: *Agriculture in an Unstable Economy* (1945), *Production and Welfare of Agriculture* (1949), *The Economic Organi-*

zation of Agriculture (1953), *The Economic Value of Education* (1963), *Transforming Traditional Agriculture* (1964), *Economic Crises in World Agriculture* (1965), *Economic Growth and Agriculture* (1968), *Investment in Human Capital: The Role of Education and of Research* (1971), and *Human Resources/Human Capital: Policy Issues and Research Opportunities* (1972). Schultz was also the principal author of a major study for the United Nations, *Measures for Economic Development of Underdeveloped Countries* (1951).

In addition to his books, Schultz wrote numerous articles for academic journals, and he also contributed essays to major books on economic issues, including *Poverty amid Affluence*, edited by Leo Fishman (1966). Schultz remained at the University of Chicago until his retirement as an emeritus professor in 1972, serving as chairman of the economics department from 1946 to 1961 and holding the Charles L. Hutchinson Distinguished Service chair from 1952 until 1972. As an emeritus professor he stayed active as a prominent scholar in his field and was a familiar presence at the university, walking daily across campus to his office no matter how severe the weather. He continued to publish in academic journals and contribute essays to several book-length collections, including *Human Migration*, edited by William H. McNeill and Ruth Adams (1978). He also edited several collections of essays, including *Economics of the Family: Marriage, Children, and Human Capital* (1974).

Beginning in the 1950s, Schultz was active as a consultant to a number of U.S. government agencies, including the Federal Reserve Board, the Agency for International Development, and four cabinet departments. In addition, he served as a consultant to several United Nations agencies, including the Food and Agriculture Organization and the International Bank for Reconstruction and Development, and was also a consultant to the Ford and Rockefeller foundations, the Carnegie and RAND corporations, and the Brookings Institution. Between 1949 and 1967 he held a series of administrative posts with the National Bureau of Economic Research. For many years he was a trustee of both the Population Council and the International Agricultural Development Service.

Schultz received a number of awards over the course of his long career, the most important being the Nobel Memorial Prize in economic science when he was seventy-seven years old. He shared the 1979 prize with Sir Arthur Lewis, a West Indian economist who, complementing the work of Schultz, had devoted most of his professional life to the economic betterment of poor countries. In its citation, the Nobel Committee applauded Schultz for arguing strongly against "policies in developing countries that emphasized industry at the expense of agriculture and urban consumers at the expense of farm people and expanded food production. The rapid adoption by low-income countries in the mid-1960s of the new high-yielding varieties of rice and wheat was fully consistent with his conclusions."

Schultz was married to Esther F. Werth; the couple had two daughters and a son. He died at a nursing home in Evanston, Illinois.

• The Theodore William Schultz Papers are at South Dakota State University, Brookings, S.Dak. For biographical information, see William Robbins, "Theodore William Schultz," *New York Times*, 17 Oct. 1979; and "Schultz, Theodore William," in *Contemporary Authors*, vols. 85–88 (1980). See also "Nobel Economics Prize Shared by Two Professors," *New York Times*, 17 Oct. 1979; and Leonard Silk, "Human Capital Is Nobel Focus," *New York Times*, 17 Oct. 1979. An obituary appears in the *New York Times*, 2 Mar. 1998.

ANN T. KEENE

SCHULZ, Charles M. (26 Nov. 1922–12 Feb. 2000), cartoonist, was born Charles Monroe Schulz in Minneapolis, Minnesota, to Carl Schulz, a barber, and Dena Halverson Schulz. Young Schulz became a devotee of comics and cartoons at an early age, and from childhood onward he was known as "Sparky," after a horse named Sparkplug featured in one of his favorite comics, *Barney Google*. By the time he was in the first grade he was drawing accurate copies of cartoon characters and had decided to become a cartoonist himself.

Initially the path proved rocky, however. Schulz was an indifferent student, failing eighth grade as well as a series of academic subjects in high school and having little success in sports and social life. Even more discouraging to him was the rejection of his cartooning efforts by the high school yearbook staff. After graduation in 1940, he spent the next few years taking drawing courses from an art correspondence school. Early in 1943, as World War II raged, he was drafted into the army and joined U.S. forces fighting in France and Germany, rising eventually to the rank of staff sergeant in the 20th Armored Division. His years in the army were apparently undistinguished, though they did give rise to an incident often cited thereafter as an index to his character: called upon to throw a grenade into an enemy emplacement, he refused to do so after seeing a small dog walk inside.

When the war ended in 1945, Schulz returned to Minneapolis and began looking for cartooning jobs. He worked for a time lettering comics pages for an area religious magazine, contributed cartoons to local newspapers and even sold a few to the *Saturday Evening Post*, and also taught at his old correspondence school, Art Instruction, Inc. There he met Joyce Halverson, the sister of another staff member (and apparently no relation to his mother's family), whom he married in 1949; the couple eventually had five children. By 1950 he had begun drawing a comic strip called *Li'l Folks* for the *St. Paul Pioneer Press*, and that year it was bought by United Feature Syndicate for national distribution. Because another syndicated strip had a similar name, UFS—over Schulz's strenuous objections—renamed his cartoon *Peanuts*.

Peanuts offered wry commentary on the human condition through the antics and declarations of simply drawn child characters who in fact talked and acted like adults. Although readers and critics alike surmised that Schulz got his ideas from observing his own children, his own childhood may have provided sufficient inspiration for a lifetime. Heading the cast of characters in *Peanuts* was the non-achieving Charlie Brown, ostensibly named after a school friend of Schulz's. Clueless Charlie, forever trying to succeed, was doomed to lamentable—and usually hilarious (as well as poignant)—failure. He was a washout at all sports and games (even kite-flying was a disaster); his loves were always unrequited; and he seemed unable to negotiate even the simplest tasks (he got rocks when he trick-or-treated at Halloween, and when he tried to buy a Christmas tree the best he could get was a spindly assemblage of dead branches). Charlie, of course, was Everyman—or more precisely Sisyphus—and the world proved forever impossible to conquer. Yet he kept on trying, and that fact lay at the heart of the cartoon's appeal.

Poor Charlie Brown's chief antagonist was Lucy, a bossy neighborhood girl who seemed to exist solely for the purpose of reminding Charlie of how ineffectual he really was. Also featured in this Everyperson cast were Lucy's thumb-sucking, blanket-hugging little brother, Linus; Schroeder, a musical prodigy who played Beethoven on a toy piano missing its black keys; and Snoopy, a lovable beagle with a rich fantasy life that included stints as a World War I flying ace. Other child characters in the strip—no adults ever appeared, though they made occasional background noises—included Sally, Charlie's romantic little sister, and Peppermint Patty, a blustering neighborhood toughie with a crush on the hapless Charlie. There was also a whimsical bird named Woodstock, whose body language compensated for his lack of speech.

Peanuts first appeared in October 1950 in eight daily newspapers. The feature was immediately popular and was soon picked up by hundreds of other newspapers throughout the country. By the end of the decade Schulz had become arguably the best-known cartoonist in the United States, and Charlie Brown et al. had become household names; the strip was even responsible, thanks to Linus, for adding the term "security blanket" to the national lexicon. Schulz's *Peanuts* attracted admirers from every walk of life, including academics who found deep meaning in the utterances of its characters and assumed their creator was in fact a closeted intellectual—a supposition that Schulz, perhaps disingenuously, always took pains to deny.

The popularity of the strip was so great that it spawned a host of licensed products, ranging from toys to clothing to greeting cards, as well as a series of award-winning animated television specials, beginning in 1965 with "A Charlie Brown Christmas." The strip was also the basis for a series of feature films, and it inspired several musical compositions, including the popular stage musical *You're a Good Man,*

Charlie Brown. From the 1950s onward Schulz assembled and published his cartoon strips in book form, beginning with *Peanuts* in 1952, and followed by *More Peanuts* (1954) and *Good Grief, More Peanuts!* (1956). Thereafter new *Peanuts* collections appeared at the rate of more than one a year for nearly four decades. In addition, *Peanuts* characters were featured in both print and television advertising, most notably for the Metropolitan Life Insurance Company. Snoopy himself was the official mascot of NASA, and the lunar excursion module on the Apollo 10 mission was named after him.

By the time of Schulz's death he had drawn a total of 18,250 *Peanuts* strips, and the cartoon was syndicated in 2,600 newspapers worldwide, appearing in twenty-one languages in seventy-five countries. He had also become the recipient of a number of honors, including an unprecedented two Reuben Awards (1955, 1964) from the National Cartoonists' Society; that organization also bestowed upon him a posthumous Lifetime Achievement Award in 2000. The popularity of *Peanuts* and its spin-offs made Schulz a very rich man: by 1990 he had become one of the ten wealthiest entertainers in the world, with an annual income of some $32 million, and at his death he was said to be earning in excess of a million dollars a week.

From the 1950s onward Schulz lived with his family in Santa Rosa, California. In private life, he was a fundamentalist Christian who eschewed alcohol, tobacco, and rough language. His only personal crisis as an adult seems to have occurred in the early 1970s, when he left his wife after concluding that she no longer cared for him. He divorced her in 1972 and a year later married a local woman, Jeannie Clyde; there were no children from this marriage.

A man of simple tastes, Schulz was especially fond of all dogs (not just beagles) and always owned at least one. For recreation, he enjoyed golf, tennis, and bridge, as well as skating and ice hockey, a passion he shared with Snoopy. His devotion to skating led him to open the *Peanuts*-themed Redwood Empire Ice Arena in his adopted hometown in 1968, and he skated there frequently with his family and friends in the following decades. His life was otherwise uneventful as he continued to turn out strips and books and authorize related products. He rarely left Santa Rosa, attributing a virtually lifelong dislike of travel to the sudden death of his mother on the day that he left for army boot camp in 1943.

In later years Schulz suffered from palsy and other ailments but continued to draw the strip despite increasing hand tremors. Although many cartoonists have allowed others to continue their work after their deaths, Schulz was opposed to this idea and made an agreement with the syndicate to terminate the strip when he could no longer produce it. When he finally ceased working in the fall of 2000, after being diagnosed with terminal colon cancer, he had prepared two months' worth of new strips. By coincidence, the last one appeared on the day after his death, which occurred at his home in Santa Rosa. A 22,000-square-foot Charles M. Schulz Museum celebrating the cartoonist's life and work is under construction adjacent to the Redwood Empire Ice Arena.

• For biographical information, see Rheta Grimsley Johnson, *Good Grief: The Story of Charles M. Schulz* (1989; repr. 1995); see also "Good Grief: Why Did We Love Charles Schulz and His Unforgettable Peanuts Gang?" *Entertainment Weekly*, 25 Feb. 2000. In addition, see entries for "Schulz, Charles M(onroe)," in *Current Biography Yearbook* for 1960 and 2000; in *Contemporary Authors: New Revision Series*, vol. 6 (1982), which includes an interview with Schulz; in *Contemporary Authors*, vol. 187 (2001); and in *Something about the Author*, vol. 118 (2001), which has a complete listing of Schulz's numerous books. See also a National Public Radio interview with Schulz included in Charles Siegel, ed., *The NPR Interviews* (1994). M. Thomas Inge, ed., *Charles M. Schulz: Conversations* (2000), has excerpts of interviews conducted with Schulz over four decades on a variety of topics. For an assessment of Schulz's impact on American popular culture, see Arthur Asa Berger, *The Comic-Stripped American: What Dick Tracy, Blondie, Daddy Warbucks, and Charlie Brown Tell Us about Ourselves* (1973). For a posthumous appreciation of Schulz, see George Saunders, "Strip Mind," *New York Times Magazine*, 7 Jan. 2001, pp. 52–53. An extended obituary appears in the *New York Times*, 14 Feb. 2000; see also a correction to this obituary in the issue for 15 Feb. 2000, p. 2.

ANN T. KEENE

SCOTT, George C. (18 Oct. 1927–23 Sept. 1999), actor, was born George Campbell Scott in the Appalachian coal mining town of Wise, Virginia, the son of George Scott, a mine surveyor, and Helena Scott (maiden surname unknown). During the Great Depression, the father moved the family to Detroit, where he found a job on the Buick assembly line; he later became a businessman. Scott's mother was a sickly woman who wrote poetry and gave recitations as an elocutionist. She died when Scott was eight, leaving him to be raised mainly by his elder sister, Helen. But his mother's interest in the arts and literature apparently had a lasting influence. At Redford High School in Detroit, Scott not only pursued athletics but also aspired to write fiction.

In 1945 Scott graduated and enlisted in the Marines, too late for combat duty in World War II. Part of his four-year military service was spent behind a desk in Washington; the rest, burying the dead at Arlington National Cemetery. He said later of those days that he was drunk most of the time. "You can't look at that many widows in veils and hear 'Taps' that many times without taking to drink." His fabled alcoholism, of which he made no secret, also contributed to his trademark craggy profile: his nose was broken five times when he was with the Marines, four of them in barroom brawls.

Once discharged from the military, he enrolled at the University of Missouri School of Journalism, intending to become a writer. There, he happened to audition for a student production of Terence Rattigan's play *The Winslow Boy* and got the part. From the moment he stood before an audience, he knew he had found his calling. He left the university without a degree in 1950 and began acting in stock companies, playing more than 125 roles before moving to Washington, D.C., where he earned food and rent money as a construction worker. In 1956 he moved to New York. There he spent his nights operating a check-sorting machine in a bank while during the day looking with increasing desperation for acting jobs that didn't seem to exist. When he was at his lowest point and considering giving up acting altogether after his seven-year struggle, he heard about an audition for Shakespeare's *Richard III*, for Joseph Papp's newly formed New York Shakespeare Festival. He auditioned and was called back for the next round, but, in his own opinion, he did poorly. After begging for another chance, he was allowed to audition again and got the part.

His New York debut as Richard III, outdoors in Central Park, was a stunning success, and is still considered the performance of Shakespeare in the park against which all others are measured. Instantly, the thirty-year-old actor's career took off. That same year he took the roles of Jaques, in *As You Like It*, and the poisoning Lord Wainwright, in a revival of Edwin Justus Mayer's *Children of Darkness* at Circle in the Square. For those performances, he received Obie, Theatre World, Clarence Derwent, and Vernon Rice awards; a year later he was appearing on Broadway opposite Judith Anderson in Speed Lamkin's *Comes a Day*. In his role as a psychopath (for which he was nominated for the first of his four Tony Award nominations) he decapitated a pet bird onstage nightly; legend has it that this exhibition won him his role as a prosecutor in Otto Preminger's *Anatomy of a Murder*.

On film, Scott played so many lawyers, for both the defense and the prosecution, that in his obituary in the *New York Times* critic Mel Gussow wrote, "He could have taken up law as an alternative profession." *Anatomy of a Murder* was Scott's second film (his first, *The Hanging Tree*, cast him as a villain stirring up a lynch mob against Gary Cooper), and it made him a star. For his performance, he received an Academy Award nomination, again the first of four.

With his chiseled face, raspy voice, and magnetic personality, Scott displayed an intensity that seemed always on the edge of violence. He created a formidable parade of bad guys and antiheroes—both dramatic and comic: a gambler in *The Hustler*, the bomb-loving General Buck Turgidson in Stanley Kubrick's *Dr. Strangelove*, and—the defining role of his career—George S. Patton in the Academy Award-winning *Patton*. His peers considered him a maverick, similar to Marlon Brando in his powerful natural talent and intuitive acting. Unlike Brando, though, Scott deplored method acting and the Actors Studio. His instructors, he said, were tough guys James Cagney and Humphrey Bogart, whose movies he used to haunt as a means of escape.

Ironically, Scott never cared for making movies, a job he considered tedious, although he appreciated financial freedom (and the fame) that allowed him to work in the theater—a pursuit he credited with keeping him sane. A complex and difficult man, prone to temper tantrums, physical fights, and drunkenness that marred both his professional life and his personal life, he had great respect for the quest for dramatic excellence—his own and that of his colleagues. His erratic temper and penchant for violence kept odd company with his professional prowess. While doing Neil Simon's comedy *Plaza Suite* on Broadway in 1968, his costar Maureen Stapleton reportedly told director Mike Nichols, "I'm so frightened of George, I don't know what to do." To which Nichols, legend has it, replied, "My dear, the whole world is frightened of George." Yet those who worked with him also expressed their admiration. Jack Lemmon, who starred with him in television remakes of *Twelve Angry Men* and *Inherit the Wind*, called him "one of the greatest and most generous actors I have ever known."

Scott, however, held little respect for the movie business itself, with its call for career-jockeying and politicking. He considered the Academy Awards ceremonies "a two-hour meat parade, a public display with contrived suspense for economic reasons." While he simply ignored his first Oscar nomination, he responded to his second, for *The Hustler* (1961), by wiring back, "No thanks." Again, in 1971 he showed his contempt by refusing the Academy of Motion Picture Arts and Sciences' Best Actor nomination for *Patton*; his action had no effect on the Academy, which awarded him the Oscar anyway. He said later that he had spent Oscar night watching hockey. Scott was the first ever to refuse the honor; Brando would follow his example two years later. In 1972 Scott also refused an Emmy Award for his performance in a television adaptation of Arthur Miller's *The Price*.

In a frenetic career that bounced between stage, film, and television, Scott's credits also include the films *They Might Be Giants* (as a delusional judge who thinks he's Sherlock Holmes); Paddy Chayefsky's black comedy *The Hospital*; Larry Gelbart's spoof *Movie Movie*; *The Formula* (appearing with Marlon Brando); and *Day of the Dolphin*, *The Hindenburg*, *Taps*, and *Malice*. Going behind the camera, he directed *Rage* and *The Savage Is Loose*, which both failed. Television work included two short-lived series: the critically acclaimed *East Side/West Side* in 1963–1964 and the 1987–1988 sitcom *Mr. President*. On television, he played Scrooge, Mussolini, the Beast in Hallmark Hall of Fame's *Beauty and the Beast*, and reprised his role as General Patton in *The Last Days of Patton* (1986), which he himself commissioned. He had a penchant for theatrical adaptations: *The Price* (1971) costarred his wife, Colleen Dewhurst; they also appeared together in an adaptation of Miller's *The Crucible*. Scott won the second of his three Emmys for directing a television adaptation of Broadway's Civil War drama *The Andersonville Trial*, which he had performed onstage in 1959. His work on Broadway included *Uncle Vanya* (1974); Willy Loman in *Death of a Salesman*, which he also directed (1975); *The Merchant of Venice*, for the New York Shakespeare Festival; Eugene O'Neill's *Desire Under the Elms*, at Circle in the Square; and Lillian Hellman's *The Little Foxes*, at Lincoln Center.

His personal life could only be described as tempestuous: well-publicized romances with Ava Gardner, among others, and five marriages with four divorces. From 1951 to 1955 he was married to Carolyn Hughes, with whom he had a daughter. Later in the 1950s he married and divorced Patricia Reed; they had two children. He twice married and divorced actress Colleen Dewhurst (1960–1965, 1967–1972), whom he met onstage in *Children of Darkness*. They had two sons, including the actor Campbell Scott. In 1972 he married actress Trish Van Devere. They lived in both Los Angeles and Greenwich, Connecticut, and remained together until his death..

To the end of his life, though compromised by ill health, Scott remained a battler. In 1996, he returned to Broadway in a revival of *Inherit the Wind*, as the lawyer based on Clarence Darrow. Though he received his fourth Tony nomination, illness forced him out of the production. Simultaneously, a 26-year-old actress who had been his personal assistant filed a $3 million lawsuit against him claiming sexual harassment. Scott recuperated, coming back to appear in 1997 in a new television adaptation of *Twelve Angry Men*, with Jack Lemmon and Hume Cronyn, for which he won another Emmy. He starred again with Lemmon on television soon afterward, in a new adaptation of *Inherit the Wind*; this time, rather than the Darrow character he played Darrow's nemesis, the bombastic, bible-thumping Matthew Harrison Brady, based on William Jennings Bryan. The program aired some four months after Scott died as the result of a ruptured aortic aneurysm. A forceful and magnetic actor to the end, the ailing actor's performance was referred to by the *New York Times* as "impassioned . . . as he assailed 'this crime against man and God.'"

• A valuable source on the life of George C. Scott is the clipping file held by the New York Public Library of the Performing Arts at Lincoln Center. There is an entry on Scott in *Current Biography* (Apr. 1971). Additionally, Scott is discussed at length in *Colleen Dewhurst: Her Autobiography* (1997). An obituary is in the *New York Times*, 24 Sept. 1999.

DEBORAH GRACE WINER

SEABORG, Glenn T. (19 Apr. 1912–25 Feb. 1999), scientist and Nobel laureate in chemistry, was born Glen Theodore Seaborg in Ishpeming, Michigan, the son of Herman Theodore Seaborg, an iron worker whose parents were Swedish immigrants, and Selma Olivia Erickson Seaborg, who came to Ishpeming from Sweden at the age of 19. Glen learned Swedish before he learned English, and although he was proficient in English by the time he started kindergarten, he was so shy that he was afraid to raise his hand to ask the teacher's permission to go to the bathroom. A tall boy, he was known by the nickname "Lanky."

When Glen was ten years old the family moved to Home Gardens, California, near Los Angeles because his mother wanted to expand the opportunities for her children beyond those available in the rather isolated community of Ishpeming. (About this time he changed the spelling of his name from "Glen" to "Glenn.") After the move, however, his father was never able to find permanent employment at his trade, and the family remained very poor throughout Glenn's childhood. He attended the Wilmington Avenue Grammar School in the Watts District of Los Angeles and entered David Starr Jordan High School in 1925. In his junior year he was required to take a laboratory course. Chemistry was offered that year and was taught by Dwight Logan Reid, an outstanding teacher whose enthusiasm sparked Glenn's decision to become a scientist. As a senior he took physics from the same teacher and was as fascinated by physics as by chemistry.

Seaborg graduated from high school in June 1929 and found summer employment as a laboratory assistant. His earnings and the fact that he could live at home and commute by car with a friend enabled him to enroll at the tuition-free University of California at Los Angeles (UCLA) in the fall of 1929. He decided to major in chemistry because he thought it would be easier for a chemist than a physicist to get a position in industry. Because of his excellence in the quantitative analysis class, he was offered a chance to serve as laboratory assistant and work in the stockroom for six hours a week at 50 cents an hour, which enabled him to stay in school; in May 1931 he was awarded a $150 scholarship for the following year. In his senior year he took a course in modern physics and learned about the exciting new discoveries in nuclear science. Although he received his A.B. in chemistry in 1934, he decided to stay on for a fifth year in order to take more courses in physics.

Seaborg hoped that graduate work in chemistry might be instituted at UCLA, and he even went so far as to travel to Berkeley to urge University of California president Robert G. Sproul to initiate such a program at UCLA. This behavior was characteristic of Seaborg: if he was convinced of something's importance, he would go right to the top to state the case, regardless of how brash this might appear. Sproul treated him politely but was not encouraging, and Seaborg decided to go to UC Berkeley. He was accepted for graduate study and was granted a teaching assistantship of $50 per month. He began there in August 1934. He found the atmosphere at Berkeley to be exhilarating and stimulating. The faculty included Gilbert N. Lewis, dean of the college of chemistry. Seaborg earned his Ph.D. in chemistry in the spring of 1937 with a thesis on neutron scattering. Lewis invited him to stay on as his personal research assistant. The cyclotron was invented by E. O. Lawrence at Berkeley in 1931, and improved versions made it possible for Seaborg and collaborators during 1936–1938 to produce and chemically identify many new radioisotopes, including iodine-131 and technetium-99m, which are still widely used in nuclear medicine and biological research today.

Seaborg became an instructor at UCB in 1939 and assistant professor in 1941. He is probably best known for his leadership role in the discovery of plutonium in February 1941. His associates were Arthur C. Wahl, his first graduate student, fellow instructor Joseph W. Kennedy, and professor E. M. McMillan. They produced and positively identified the new element plutonium by chemically separating the isotope plutonium-238 from the products of bombardments of uranium with deuterons from the Berkeley 60-inch cyclotron. Soon thereafter, Kennedy, Seaborg, Emilio Segrè, and Wahl produced the much longer-lived isotope plutonium-239 and found that it was even more fissionable with thermal neutrons than uranium-235.

These discoveries led the United States to undertake a program to produce plutonium for use in its atomic bomb project. In April 1942 Seaborg took a leave of absence from UCB to go to the University of Chicago's Metallurgical Laboratory to head the chemistry group charged with devising plant processes for chemical extraction and purification of plutonium produced at the Hanford reactor. He returned to Berkeley in June 1942 to take Helen Griggs (then Lawrence's secretary) back with him; they were married en route to Chicago. They had six children and remained together until Seaborg's death.

The plutonium process chemistry was worked out by 1944, and Seaborg and his colleagues at Chicago tried unsuccessfully to produce the next elements, 95 and 96. In 1945 Seaborg came up with his then revolutionary "actinide" hypothesis of heavy element electronic structure. He proposed that elements heavier than actinium belong as a transition series under the lanthanide transition series in the periodic table of elements. This idea enabled him and his co-workers to chemically separate and discover these elements, americium (95) and curium (96), on the basis of their chemical similarity to the lanthanide elements. Americium was produced in 1945 by irradiation of plutonium-239 with neutrons in a reactor; curium was produced in 1944 by cyclotron bombardments of plutonium-239 with helium ions. At the time, Seaborg's actinide concept was viewed as a "wild" hypothesis that would ruin his reputation, but later investigations have proven him correct, and the actinide concept is incorporated in the modern-day periodic table.

Seaborg joined the Metallurgical Laboratory's Franck Committee in recommending that the atomic bomb not be used in Japan. However, he said later that he was able to accept the decision of people who know more than he did to drop bombs on Hiroshima and Nagasaki on 6 and 9 August, 1945. He is quoted as saying, "It saved hundreds and thousands of Americans' lives and maybe a million of Japanese lives, because otherwise they would have had to go on for months and months storming the beaches and so forth. . . . I had cousins who thanked me every time they saw me for saving their lives" (Graff, 18 Mar. 1996).

Shortly after the end of World War II in August 1945, Glenn Seaborg accepted an offer to return to the University of California, Berkeley, to be full professor of chemistry and head of the nuclear chemistry division in the Berkeley Radiation Laboratory. However, he remained at the Metallurgical Laboratory in Chicago until May 1946 to finish his duties there and provide for an orderly transition to new management. Seaborg and his coworkers, including many graduate students and postdoctoral fellows, went on to discover seven more elements beyond plutonium: elements 97 through 102, and element 106. The first of these, berkelium (97) and californium (98), were produced at the Berkeley 60-inch cyclotron in 1949-1950. In 1951 Seaborg and McMillan were awarded the Nobel Prize in chemistry for their research on the transuranium elements. Seaborg, only 39 at the time, was the youngest winner of the prize in chemistry.

Seaborg served as chancellor at UC Berkeley from 1958 until 1961 when president-elect John F. Kennedy asked him to chair the U.S. Atomic Energy Commission. Seaborg led negotiations resulting in the limited nuclear test ban treaty prohibiting the testing of nuclear devices in the atmosphere or under the sea, which was approved by the U.S. Senate in 1963. He strongly supported the use of nuclear energy as a source of electricity and led delegations to some sixty-three countries, including the USSR, to promote the peaceful uses of atomic energy.

In 1971 he returned to Berkeley as professor of chemistry and continued his teaching duties until 1979. Element 106 was identified in 1974 by a Berkeley-Livermore team that included Seaborg and was led by longtime coworker and friend Albert Ghiorso. After the discovery was confirmed by another group in 1993, the discovery team met without Seaborg and agreed to propose the name "seaborgium." Although the name was initially rejected by the International Union of Pure and Applied Chemistry on the basis that Seaborg was still alive, it was finally approved in August, 1997. He regarded having an element named after him as an even greater honor than the Nobel Prize.

Seaborg supervised the Ph.D. research of more than sixty-five students. He was the first director of the Lawrence Hall of Science and served as associate director-at-large of the Lawrence Berkeley National Laboratory until his death. He authored more than 500 scientific articles and numerous books, including editing the journals that he faithfully kept throughout his career. These formed the basis for a number of books, including an autobiography published in 1998 titled "A Chemist in the White House: From the Manhattan Project to the End of the Cold War." He maintained his involvement in science and mathematics education at all levels and always had time to meet with students.

He was active in the American Chemical Society (ACS), serving as its president in 1976. One of his last accolades was being voted one of the "Top 75 Distinguished Contributors to the Chemical Enterprise" over the last seventy-five years by the readers of *Chemical & Engineering News*. He accepted the award at a huge ceremony and reception on 23 August during the 1998 ACS national meeting in Boston. The following morning he gave the introductory comments at a symposium on the chemistry of the Manhattan project. That evening at his hotel he suffered a stroke and a fall from which he never recovered. He died at his home in Lafayette, California.

• *The Transuranium People: The Inside Story* (2000) by Hoffman, Ghiorso, and Seaborg provides details of Seaborg's early life and describes his contributions to the discovery of the elements. A detailed memoir including selected original publications from 1938 to 1995 was published in the National Academy of Sciences *Biographical Memoirs*, vol. 78 (2000). *The Plutonium Story—The Journals of Professor Glenn T. Seaborg 1939–1946* (1994) gives a day-by-day account of the discovery of plutonium and the amazing research and development program that revealed its chemistry and provided plutonium for the U.S. atomic bomb project. An excellent interview is Amy Graff, "UC Chemist Seaborg Finds the Elements of Scientific Success," *Daily Californian*, 18 Mar. 1996. Obituaries are in the *New York Times*, 27 Feb. 1999; *Nature*, Mar. 1999; *Physics World*, Mar. 1999; *Physics Today*, *Chemistry and Engineering News*, and *Chemical Educator* (all 2 Apr. 1999); and many other scientific publications and newspapers.

DARLEANE CHRISTIAN HOFFMAN

SEPKOSKI, J. John, Jr. (26 July 1948–1 May 1999), paleontologist, was born Joseph John "Jack" Sepkoski, Jr., in Presque Isle, Maine, the son of Joseph John Sepkoski, Sr., a chemist, and Sally Feuchtwanger Sepkoski, a part-time librarian. Sepkoski's father was transferred several times while working for the Allied Chemical Corporation, and his childhood years were spent in New Jersey, Iowa, and Syracuse, New York, where he graduated from high school in 1966. As a teenager Sepkoski was a drummer in a rock-and-roll band, and he maintained an interest in cutting-edge, alternative rock music throughout the rest of his life; he also built furniture as a pastime.

From the age of ten, Sepkoski enjoyed collecting fossils. By the time he applied to college, he had his heart set on a career as a paleontologist. He chose the University of Notre Dame, where he enrolled in 1966, partly because he was assured by the chairman of the department, Raymond Gutschick, that he would have the opportunity to pursue his paleontological interests. Gutschick served as Sepkoski's research advisor for an undergraduate thesis on the paleoecology of an ancient Silurian reef complex preserved near the town of Monon, Indiana.

By happenstance during Sepkoski's sophomore year he attended a short course on the computer application of statistical techniques to geological data, which influenced his entire approach to his studies.

He wrote computer programs for statistical analyses of the data collected at Monon and thus began to develop the intellectual tools that would place him at the vanguard of a paleontological revolution just a few years later.

Exhausted from the grind of his academic work, however, Sepkoski left college after the first semester of his senior year and went to live with his sister, Carol, in Boston. Prior to his departure, he sent applications to various graduate programs and applied for a National Science Foundation Graduate fellowship. When he was notified that he was accepted to study at Harvard University on an NSF Fellowship, he returned to Notre Dame, completed his degree in the summer of 1970, and enrolled at Harvard the following fall.

In 1971, after his first year as a graduate student at Harvard, Sepkoski married Maureen Meter; they had one son.

For his doctoral dissertation, Sepkoski focused on the Paleozoic rocks of Montana and adjacent states. The study was supervised by Bernhard Kummel and Raymond Siever and was not completed until 1977, long after Sepkoski had left Harvard to take his first faculty appointment. His high-resolution, descriptive account of Upper Cambrian strata in a three-state region further broadened Sepkoski's knowledge but was wholly unrelated to the research that contributed to his later prominence.

Even after his admission to Harvard, Sepkoski, unsure about the direction of his career, considered moving to the University of California, Santa Cruz. At about that time, however, he began to be influenced by a new, more synthetic approach to paleontology championed by a cadre of young researchers that included Harvard paleontologist Stephen Jay Gould, whose direct intercession was instrumental in keeping Sepkoski at Harvard. Gould's scientific pursuits, coupled with those of biologist E. O. Wilson, strongly influenced Sepkoski to pursue a second research agenda at Harvard virtually in isolation from his dissertation and ultimately to focus on the geological history of global biodiversity.

In the early 1970s Gould, David Raup, Thomas Schopf, and Daniel Simberloff developed a quantitative model that simulated the process of biological diversification: they began to investigate the possibility that changes through geological time in the number of taxa (*biodiversity*) within major evolutionary groups were caused by randomly arrayed processes rather than singular, identifiable, mechanisms. Recognizing Sepkoski's promise as a quantitative paleontologist, Gould invited Sepkoski to join this research group and to compile data from the paleontological literature that could be used to determine the global diversity trajectories, through time, of various evolutionary groups. The project that motivated this work was completed in the middle 1970s, but Sepkoski continued to compile fossil databases that could be used to reconstruct the overall history of global diversity.

In 1974, well before he completed his dissertation, Sepkoski joined the faculty at the University of Rochester, where Raup was also in residence, and began to focus not only on the calibration of global diversity trends but also on their meaning. Armed with R. H. MacArthur and E. O. Wilson's famous model describing the colonization of newly emergent islands, Sepkoski scaled up the model to describe the diversification of life on earth at the global level, arguing that the history of global diversity has been influenced throughout its history by the existence of upper limits, so-called *equilibrium levels of diversity*. At the same time, Sepkoski's empirical calibrations, by themselves, captured the imagination of paleontologists and evolutionary biologists, who sought explanations for the patterns he documented. His graphical depiction of the global history of marine animal family diversity, first published in 1981, is among the most frequently reproduced figures in the history of geology.

When he arrived at Rochester, Sepkoski began to work with Raup in the emerging field of macroevolution, particularly on the series of sudden, catastrophic *mass extinctions*, as they are known, that have punctuated the history of life. This collaboration continued at the University of Chicago, where Sepkoski joined the faculty in 1978 and where Raup later moved in 1982 after a stint at the nearby Field Museum. In 1983 Raup and Sepkoski presented a statistical analysis indicating that mass extinctions after the Paleozoic Era recurred regularly with a periodicity of 26 million years, a finding that sent shockwaves through the scientific community at large. At about that time, researchers were just coming to grips with the possibility that the impact of a comet or asteroid had caused the mass extinction at the end of the Cretaceous Period that killed off the dinosaurs. The suggestion of periodicity caused many scientists to explore in earnest the possibility that *all* mass extinctions were caused by large-body impacts recurring periodically in association with a previously unknown, astronomical mechanism.

Despite the intellectual excitement and attention that it brought to him, periodicity was for Sepkoski a double-edged sword. Already sensitive to the inevitable criticisms from older, more conservative paleontologists that accompanied his development of global fossil databases, Sepkoski was confronted with a larger wave of controversy concerning the methodologies used to diagnose periodicity, and the question of periodicity remains unsettled even today. Beyond that, he was forced to deal with a steady stream of press interviews and requests to present talks and publish review papers devoted to periodicity and mass extinctions. He noted on several occasions that he found these to be intellectually stifling, and the result can be observed clearly in his research output: while none were as groundbreaking as several that he published before 1988, he continued to publish well-regarded research papers throughout the remainder of his life.

During his growing prominence in the 1980s and 1990s, Sepkoski received important awards and appointments, most notably the Paleontological Society's Charles Schuchert Award (1983), coeditorship of the journal *Paleobiology* (1983–1986), the presidency of the Paleontological Society (1995–1996), membership in the Polish Academy of Sciences (1997), and the Medal of the University of Helsinki (1997).

Sepkoski's first marriage ended in divorce in 1987. In 1992, he married Christine Janis, a (vertebrate) paleontologist at Brown University. Over the next several years, Sepkoski spent time in Chicago and Rhode Island, where he enjoyed his waterfront home in Warwick. He died in Chicago.

Jack Sepkoski was a central force in the transformation of paleontology into a modern science that uses fossils as data to address questions of global significance in ecology and evolution. His legacy is evidenced by the extent to which his research on patterns and processes in global biodiversity continues to be cited and debated by his colleagues around the world.

The major threads of Sepkoski's research career can be gleaned from several of his research papers published in the primary literature. His documentation of marine animal biodiversity throughout the history of life is provided in "A Factor Analytic Description of the Fossil Record," *Paleobiology* 7 (1981): 36–53. A paper published in the same year arguing that the global diversity trajectory through time is biologically meaningful and not a spurious reflection of variations through time in the extent of the fossil record is "Phanerozoic Marine Diversity and the Fossil Record" (with R. K. Bambach, D. M. Raup, and J. W. Valentine), *Nature* 293 (1981): 435–37. The culmination of his application of equilibrium models to the history of marine life is presented in "A Kinetic Model of Phanerozoic Taxonomic Diversity III. Post-Paleozoic Families and Mass Extinctions," *Paleobiology* 10 (1984): 246–67. The case for periodicity is summarized in "Periodic Extinctions in Families and Genera" (with D. M. Raup), *Science* 231 (1986): 833–36.

• An autobiographical account of Sepkoski's foray into the evaluation of global biodiversity and mass extinctions is in "What I Did with My Research Career," in *The Mass Extinction Debates: How Science Works in a Crisis* (1994), ed. William Glen. A discussion devoted to Sepkoski and his scientific approach is provided by Michael Ruse, *Mystery of Mysteries: Is Evolution a Social Construction?* (1999), ch. 11. An overview of Sepkoski's research career, including a full list of his publications, is in D. M. Raup, "In Appreciation: J. John Sepkoski (1948–1999)," *Paleobiology* (1999): 424–29. A more informal reminiscence of Sepkoski's influence is A. I. Miller, "J. John Sepkoski, Jr.: A Personal Reflection," *Journal of Paleontology* (1999): 741–43. An obituary is in the *New York Times*, 6 May 1999.

ARNOLD I. MILLER

SHAMBAUGH, George E., Jr. (29 June 1903–7 Feb. 1999), otolaryngologist, was born George Elmer Shambaugh, Jr., in Chicago, Illinois, the son of George Shambaugh, Sr., a pioneering otolaryngologist, and Edith Capps Shambaugh. After graduating from the University High School of the University of Chicago, he attended Amherst College, from which he graduated in 1924. Shambaugh then entered medical school at Harvard and received his medical degree in 1928. He spent his internship at Peter Bent Brigham Hospital in Boston (1928–1930) and had residencies at the Massachusetts Eye and Ear Infirmary (1930–1932) and at Presbyterian Hospital in Chicago (1932–1933). During his residencies, Shambaugh discovered more effective means of detecting otosclerosis, a condition resulting from an abnormal growth formation within the bone structure of the inner ear that was present at birth and that eventually caused deafness. The study of its treatment would prove to be the focal point of his professional career. In 1927 Shambaugh married Marietta "Mitzi" Susan Moss, with whom he had two children.

With his formal training completed, Shambaugh joined his father in clinical practice. (George Shambaugh, Sr., was a founding member of the American Board of Otolaryngology and had been the first to describe a portion of the inner ear as Shambaugh's gland). George, Jr., also studied allergies under the direction of French Hansel, beginning what would come to be a lifelong interest. After hearing Julius Lempert present the details of his one-stage fenestration operation at the 1938 meeting of the American Otological Society—and realizing its potential implications for the treatment of otosclerosis—Shambaugh became Lempert's leading student. That same year he journeyed to Stockholm, Sweden, and worked with Leonard Holmgren, the first surgeon to have successfully made a fenestration in the lateral semicircular canal, and also met Maurice Sourdille, who had exteriorized the fenestra in a three-stage operation.

On returning to Chicago, Shambaugh opened the first otological research laboratory in the United States at Northwestern University's Medical School. Using rhesus monkeys for his study subjects, Shambaugh attempted to replicate the operation that would be needed on human subjects in order to reopen the small "window" between the middle and inner ear. Feeling that the equipment on hand was inadequate for the job, he began utilizing a Zeiss operating microscope—later known as the otomicroscope—with great success. Shambaugh also began using a technique called continuous irrigation, which kept bone dust from accumulating around the operating area. After compiling the results of hundreds of operations in 1945, he published his findings in an article titled "Fenestration Operation for Otosclerosis" in *Acta Otolaryngologica* (1949). Unfortunately, the latter part of the 1940s proved troubling for Shambaugh when his relationship with his former mentor Lempert collapsed over his work with fenestration and his first marriage ended in divorce in 1945. Shambaugh was remarried—to Genevieve Krum in 1946—and with his second wife adopted a son.

Shambaugh entered into a collaborative effort in 1946 when he initiated the Otologic/Audiologic Diagnostic Clinic at Northwestern in cooperation with a leading audiologist, Raymond Carhart. The weekly interaction between graduate students in otology and audiology proved to be a fertile source of cross-disciplinary inspiration for scores of residents. A tireless publisher who authored over 400 articles in his career, Shambaugh also made a major contribution to otology literature with the 1959 publication of *Surgery of the Ear*. The text went into three additional editions (1967, 1980, and 1990) and quickly became the standard reference work in the field.

In addition to carrying a heavy patient load in his own clinical practice, Shambaugh served his profession in a variety of administrative posts. He chaired the department of otolaryngology at Northwestern University's School of Medicine between 1951 and 1964, and also held presidencies in a number of professional organizations, among them the American Otological Society, the Otosclerosis Study Group, and the American Society of Ophthalmologic and Otolaryngologic Allergy. Following in his father's footsteps, Shambaugh also served as the editor of the *Archives of Otolaryngology* from 1960 until 1970.

In an effort to spread the combined knowledge and experience of otologists worldwide, Shambaugh organized the first Shambaugh International Workshop on Otomicrosurgery in 1959. That first workshop, which featured presentations on subjects as diverse as tympanoplasty and stapes surgery, proved so popular that it became a quadrennial event, with subsequent meetings being held until 1992. After reaching the status of professor emeritus at Northwestern in 1972, Shambaugh maintained an active schedule and continued to perform operations until at least 1982. Although he focused much of his attention in his later years on research into hearing loss caused by both allergic and environmental factors, Shambaugh was engaged in clinical practice until two weeks before his death, which occurred at his home in Sandwich, Illinois.

As a researcher, teacher, administrator, and clinical practicioner, George Shambaugh, Jr., not only escaped his father's considerable shadow within the same profession but made a number of lasting contributions in his own right. The continued development of the subspecialty of otology within the field of otolaryngology owes much to his efforts.

• No collection of Shambaugh's papers has been located. The best secondary sources of information on his life and career are Eugene L. Derlacki, Howard P. House, and John L. Shea, Jr., "George E. Shambaugh, Jr., MD: A Pioneer of American Otomicrosurgery," *Archives of Otolaryngology—Head and Neck Surgery* 122, no. 6 (June 1996): 596–99, and Shea and Derlacki, "George E. Shambaugh, Jr., 1903–1999," *Annals of Otology, Rhinology, and Laryngology* 108, no. 10 (Oct. 1999): 1016–17. An obituary is in the *New York Times*, 17 Feb. 1999.

EDWARD L. LACH, JR.

SHANKER, Albert (14 Sept. 1928–22 Feb. 1997), teacher and union leader, was born in New York City, the son of Morris Shanker, a union newspaper deliveryman and a former rabbinical student from Poland, and Mamie Burko Shanker, a sewing-machine operator. The son of immigrants whose first language was Yiddish, Shanker grew up in a working-class neighborhood in Queens, where he learned the benefits of trade unionism from his parents and the effects of prejudice from neighbors of predominantly Irish and Italian extraction. He attended local public schools and entered the University of Illinois in Urbana after graduating from Manhattan's prestigious Stuyvesant High School. While attending Illinois, Shanker became politically active by joining the Young People's Socialist League and picketing segregated restaurants and movie theaters in the community.

After graduating with a B.A. in philosophy in 1949, Shanker returned to New York and studied mathematics and philosophy at Columbia University. He earned an M.A. and completed all the requisite course work for a Ph.D. but took a teaching job before completing his dissertation. His first assignment came in East Harlem, where as a substitute he taught mathematics and, to motivate his typically impoverished and disaffected students, used unorthodox examples, such as "If it takes four ounces of poison to kill a person, how many ounces would it take to kill your mother, your father, your sister and your brother?" (*Current Biography Yearbook 1969*, p. 393). After transferring to a junior high in Long Island City, he became interested in trade unionism as a possible solution to the endemic problems that teachers then often faced, including low pay, large workloads, and unsupportive administrators. He joined the New York Teachers Guild, a small union that was the local branch of the national American Federation of Teachers (AFT). Shanker resigned his teaching position in 1959 and began organizing activities on behalf of the guild, which was but one of a host of small competing unions that sought to represent the city's teachers.

Tireless work by Shanker—he visited more than 700 of the 850 schools in the system—brought about a merger with another union splinter group and resulted in the formation of the United Federation of Teachers (UFT) in 1960. As the secretary of the new union, which won a certification vote in 1961 and became the sole bargaining unit for New York City's teachers, Shanker began editing its house paper, the *United Teacher*, in 1962. On 18 March 1961 Shanker wed Edith Graber, a teacher; the couple had three children (Shanker also had another child from an earlier marriage). In 1964 Shanker replaced the union's president, who had resigned in order to run for the presidency of the AFT, and found himself the leader of the largest local union in the AFL-CIO.

Soon after taking his new position, Shanker displayed the keen negotiating skills that would characterize his career by obtaining a new two-year contract from the New York City Board of Education. After protracted negotiations, a strike was averted, and

Shanker presented his rank and file with a contract that provided for an average increase in wages and benefits of about $800 a year. Two years later, Shanker led a two-week job action by teachers that produced mixed results; while the teachers earned higher wages, the union was fined and Shanker received a fifteen-day jail sentence for violating the state's Taylor Law, which forbade strikes by public employees.

Still greater troubles, however, loomed. Frustrated by years of inaction on the issues of desegregation and local control, many minority residents of New York favored the decentralization of the citywide school system. When Mayor John Lindsay obtained $54 million in additional state aid for education (with the stipulation that the city set up a decentralization plan) in 1967, the school board fretted over losing control over its operations, while the UFT worried about the plan's effect on teachers' rights. Three local experimental districts were set up, one of which was in the Ocean Hill–Brownsville section of Brooklyn, which was largely African American in makeup. When the local administrator, Rhody McCoy, summarily dismissed several teachers on charges of sabotaging the experiment in May 1968, the UFT reacted with alarm. Several hundred area teachers walked out in protest; and after McCoy refused to take the teachers back despite their having been cleared of all charges, a bitter citywide strike erupted in the fall, lasting fifty-five days. Although the dismissed teachers won reinstatement and the decentralization plan was put in abeyance—to be implemented later with certain provisos regarding teachers' rights—the union paid a high price (and Shanker went to jail again). In the social upheaval of the times, much of the public viewed the mostly white (and Jewish) union's actions as an attack on minorities, an accusation that Shanker, a charter member of CORE and a veteran of numerous desegregation matches, found galling.

Shanker became president of the American Federation of Teachers in 1974 and served in that position until 1997, while retaining his presidency of the UFT until 1986. As a national spokesman for educational reform in his later years, Shanker promoted his views through a weekly newspaper column, "Where We Stand." Following an abortive strike in New York City in 1975, he began to advocate that labor and management be collaborators rather than adversaries, and in 1982 he supported experimental programs in places like Toledo, Ohio, that weakened the concept of teacher tenure. The following year he shocked many fellow union leaders by endorsing the Reagan Administration's National Commission on Excellence in Education's report on public schools, which put forth such traditionally nonunion ideas as merit pay, longer school days, and tightened graduation standards. Shanker died of cancer in New York City.

Raised in a pro-union household, Albert Shanker came out of the classroom and enjoyed great success in building the UFT into the largest local union in the country. Although his early efforts on behalf of membership brought credible results, his leadership in the 1968 strike remained controversial long afterward. Similarly, many of the initiatives that he promoted during his tenure as a national labor figure generated strongly conflicting reactions among teachers as well as other interest groups.

• Shanker's papers are held at the UFT Archives in New York City. The records of the AFT are held at the Archives of Labor and Urban Affairs, Walter P. Reuther Library, Wayne State University, Detroit, Mich. Secondary sources that cover Shanker's union activities include Stephen Cole, *The Unionization of Teachers: A Case Study of the UFT* (1969); Robert J. Braun, *Teachers and Power: The Story of the AFT* (1972); and Philip Taft, *United They Teach: The Story of the UFT* (1974). See also the entry on Shanker in *Current Biography Yearbook 1969*. An obituary is in the *New York Times*, 23 Feb. 1997.

EDWARD L. LACH, JR.

SHAPIRO, Karl (10 Nov. 1913–14 May 2000), poet, was born Carl Shapiro in Baltimore, Maryland, the younger son of Joseph Shapiro, a man of several occupations, and Sarah Omansky Shapiro. He attended the University of Virginia, Johns Hopkins University, and the Enoch Pratt Free Library School in Baltimore without receiving a degree. While at Pratt he was drafted into the U.S. Army in 1941. During the time he was alternately dabbling in formal education and working at odd-jobs, Shapiro also read and wrote poetry, imitating classic and modern poets. His first (self-published but not self-financed) volume of poems appeared in 1935.

By the time he entered the army, assigned to the medical corps, Shapiro's work had already appeared in the era's leading poetry journals. He had won two awards from *Poetry* magazine and was included in *Five Young American Poets* (1941). Changing his given name from Carl to Karl (which he thought more fitting for a poet), he wrote throughout his military training period ("In the army one could be a poet without anybody knowing about it") and aboard the Queen Mary, heading for assignment in the South Pacific. His work was regularly mailed back to the United States, where his friend Evelyn Katz served as his editor and agent.

Shapiro's first important collection, *Person, Place and Thing*, was published in the United States in 1942, the year his erotic *The Place of Love* was published in Australia. In 1944 Shapiro was awarded a special Guggenheim fellowship reserved for servicemen doing creative work; he also received a commendation from the American Academy of Arts and Sciences for his book *V-Letter and Other Poems*, which subsequently won the Pulitzer Prize for poetry. Although one of only a handful of Americans who wrote with understanding about wartime, Shapiro rebelled at being called a war poet. He had referred to himself as "A poet in the Battle Zone, which he had seen almost nothing of, who was serenely writing good poetry." Once on the scene, his observations were clear ("Elegy for a Dead Soldier" manages both a tribute and an ironic unsentimental catalogue of the soldier's shortcomings), and for a time his war poems could be found in every major anthology.

In the long run Shapiro's poetic reputation rests, however, mainly on sharp snapshots of his era's everyday life--word pictures both elegant and colloquial; many were written during the war, far from their actual locales. "Auto Wreck" begins with "Its quick soft bell beating, beating" as the red-lighted ambulance, like a heart beating away its lifeblood, speeds toward the site of the sudden, terrible collision. The poem is in many ways as concrete as those of one of Shapiro's idols, the imagist William Carlos Williams, but it also comments, posing the unanswerable question of cause and effect. "Drug Store" shows Shapiro on favored American ground: "It baffles the foreigner like an idiom," introduces a nearly photographic image of the fast-disappearing corner drug store. This scene, where young men leaf through their girly magazines, drinking sodas and talking big, is portrayed as a cruelly unsatisfactory substitute for life. "Hollywood" preserves in multiple images the ambience of the pre–World War II Lotus Land, seen ambivalently by Shapiro as "A Possibly Proud Florence." "The Progress of Faust," a tour de force of historical allusion, equates the development of an atomic bomb with the Faustian bargain.

In these poems Shapiro found a place where proper metrics and form could coexist with the conversational. "An Essay on Rime," which gave its name to a 1945 volume, took up arms against most of modern poetry. Confessing a love of both "decasyllables and the conversational," Shapiro bemoaned "Confusions"—in prosody, language, and belief—among his contemporaries, ever since "the imagists tore rising rhythm [the iambic beat] apart." Even past heroes such as the experimentalist E. E. Cummings were chided ("Let us look twice before we adulate the alphabet"). In issuing "Essay" Shapiro joined the cutthroat world of literary criticism; he called his own brand "mad-dog criticism." As the years passed, Shapiro's critical writings outstripped his poetry. A typically humorous and hubristic sally was "Trial of a Poet," a mock-tragic "play" that was published as a book in 1947. This dialogue among a doctor, a priest, a public officer, and a chorus about the proper fate of a poet (Ezra Pound, in fact then awaiting trial and sentencing for treason because of the pro-Fascist broadcasts he made from Italy during the war) is concluded when the poet himself, roused from his stupor, assumes the role of judge and proclaims, "Therefore, for the crime of acting upon the sense of poetry as upon the sense of prose, I condemn the prisoner to be known hereafter as a dull poet and the lapdog of his age."

On returning to the United States, Shapiro married Evelyn Katz and was assigned to the Office of Strategic Services; the couple would have two children and divorce in 1966. After his discharge from the army Shapiro edited a poetry anthology and in 1947 became a consultant to the Library of Congress. In 1948, the year he voted against Pound ("an anti-Semite"), who won the Bollingen Prize anyway, Shapiro was invited to teach at Johns Hopkins University. He accepted and remained in academia for the rest of his working years. For six years beginning in 1950 Shapiro edited *Poetry*, often concurrently with editing the *Newberry Library Journal*. He expressed pride in opening *Poetry* to more Catholic and Jewish writers. In 1954 he left Johns Hopkins, spending some time in the University of Iowa's writing program (thus joining the trend to "Creative Writing") and lecturing at the University of California campuses in Berkeley and Davis. Two years later he became a professor at the University of Nebraska., where he also edited the journal *Prairie Schooner*. In 1960 the essays he contributed to *In Defense of Ignorance* particularly praised the spontaneous and sexually liberated writers Walt Whitman and D. H. Lawrence. In 1962 he published *Prose Keys to Modern Poetry* and in 1964 *The Bourgeois Poet*, a poetic examination of the relationship between society and the individual. Shapiro came to call himself a bourgeois poet, although he wrote increasingly of previously taboo subjects such as masturbation. (Commenting on such presumed inconsistencies in his makeup, Shapiro said that the social revolutions of the 1960s had split him into "a patriot with a West Coast hedonism.") Shapiro left Nebraska in 1966, ostensibly because *Prairie Schooner* had not been allowed to publish a poem about homosexuality.

Shapiro married Teri Kovach, a novelist, in 1967. They remained married until her death in 1982. In 1971 his only novel, *Edsel*, an erotic exposé of life in the Midwest, was published but foundered when its publisher went bankrupt. In 1968 Shapiro joined the English faculty at the University of California, Davis, staying on until 1986. While at Davis he married Sophie Wilkins; they were together until his death. Shapiro referred to his status at both Nebraska and Davis as that of "a mad guest," and in fact he was often away on lecturing trips around the world.

The Younger Son, the first volume of a proposed autobiographical trilogy called *Poet*, was published in 1988. The second volume, *Reports of My Death* (1990), got its title from a widespread belief that Shapiro was in fact dead. For one thing, his work had gradually vanished from anthologies of contemporary poetry. And twenty-five years earlier an article in the *Journal of the American Medical Association*, apparently prompted by a former student's disgruntlement, had listed Shapiro among famous poets who had committed suicide. Not long thereafter a *New York Times* crossword puzzle listed "Shapiro" as the answer to the clue "dead poet." Shapiro never took effective action to change these perceptions.

He died in Davis. An original and for a time highly disciplined voice in American poetry who seemed always to be dragged in two directions simultaneously (though not always the same two), Shapiro awaits a further verdict on his later, freer work. Until then, he remains a fresh source for those wishing to understand something of American life and culture just before World War II.

• In addition to works mentioned above, Shapiro published these volumes of poetry: *Poems 1940–1953* (1953), *Poems of a Jew* (1958), *Selected Poems* (1968), and *Adult Bookstore* (1976). Other works of criticism were *Beyond Criticism* (1953), *To Abolish Children* (1968), and *The Poetry Wreck* (1975). His papers are at the University of Maryland Libraries. Sources of commentary on his poetry include Joseph Reino, *Karl Shapiro* (1981). An obituary is in the (London) *Guardian*, 18 May 2000.

JAMES ROSS MOORE

SHARKEY, Jack (26 Oct. 1902–17 Aug. 1994), world heavyweight boxing champion, was born Josef Paul Zukauskas (the name he gave when he entered the U.S. Navy) in Binghamton, New York. His name at birth has been the source of much confusion; it has been given incorrectly in boxing record books and elsewhere as John Zukauskay, John Coccoskey, and Joseph Paul Cukoschay. His parents were Lithuanian immigrants; his father was a mechanic by occupation. Sharkey attended school until the eighth grade, when a family financial crisis forced him to seek employment. He worked in a shoe factory and as a construction worker, a glassblower, and a railroad brakeman before joining the navy.

Sharkey's boxing career began when he was in the navy. He engaged in more than 25 service bouts and became heavyweight champion of the Atlantic Fleet. In 1924, just before his discharge from the navy, while stationed in the Boston area, he changed his name and turned professional under the management of Johnny Buckley, a former Boston-area fighter. Sharkey's progress was rapid but not without setbacks. He lost his fourth fight on a poor decision, but he quickly avenged that loss and then was unexpectedly knocked out by Quintin Romero-Rojas of Chile in his tenth fight. He lost decisions to Jim Maloney of Boston, who became his arch Boston-area rival, to veteran Charley Weinert twice, and to Bud Gorman. But he defeated Maloney twice in rematches and beat two highly rated opponents, Johnny Risko and Jack Renault.

In the fall of 1926 Sharkey became famous by defeating two formidable black heavyweight contenders. First he decisively outboxed George Godfrey, who outweighed him by more than thirty pounds. That victory earned him a bout in Brooklyn with Harry Wills, who had long been the foremost contender for the title but had been unable to get a match with champion Jack Dempsey. Sharkey won every round and might have scored a knockout had Wills not been disqualified in the thirteenth round.

After three more victories, two of them at the expense of former light-heavyweight champion Mike McTigue and Maloney, Sharkey was matched with Dempsey, who had lost the heavyweight title to Gene Tunney. They met on 21 July 1927 at Yankee Stadium in New York City. For six rounds Sharkey punished Dempsey and was winning decisively. In the seventh Dempsey landed three low blows, and after the last

one Sharkey turned to the referee to protest, leaving himself unprotected. Dempsey took immediate advantage of the opening and knocked out Sharkey with a left hook to the chin.

Sharkey stood six feet tall and weighed 190–200 pounds. Promotor Tex Rickard said, "I've seen them all, big and little. But Sharkey stands out . . . because he is the fastest heavyweight in the ring, with a left like a piston and a right straight and hard as a ramrod." Sharkey was known for his boastfulness and said of himself, "I am a blowhard. Part of my business is bluster—and so long as I'm in this business I'll have all the fixings." However, as exemplified by the Dempsey loss, he gained a reputation for being temperamental and performing erratically at critical moments.

In 1928 and 1929 Sharkey won several major victories, knocking out former light-heavyweight champions Jack Delaney and Tommy Loughran and outpointing heavyweight contender W. L. Stribling (Young Stribling). A knockout of British heavyweight champion Phil Scott in Miami, in which Sharkey himself was accused of hitting low, earned him a fight with Max Schmeling of Germany for the vacant heavyweight championship. They met on 26 September 1930 before 77,000 fans at Yankee Stadium. Sharkey almost knocked out Schmeling in the third round, but in the fourth he landed a low blow that floored his opponent and caused him to lose by disqualification.

Now the foremost contender for Schmeling's heavyweight title, Sharkey fought a disappointing 15-round draw with former middleweight champion Mickey Walker, a much smaller man. Just when it appeared that he was losing his top contending position, however, he redeemed himself by decisively beating the Italian Primo Carnera, who was sixty pounds heavier. This forced Schmeling into giving Sharkey another chance at the heavyweight title, and they met on 21 June 1932 at the Long Island City Bowl, New York City. It was a close, well-fought battle, with Schmeling the aggressor and Sharkey boxing on the retreat. Spectators were about evenly divided as to the winner, but Sharkey received the split decision and won the championship, prompting Schmeling's manager, Joe Jacobs, to shout his famous, often-copied complaint into the ring microphone, "We wuz robbed!"

It was expected that Schmeling would be given a chance to win back the heavyweight title from Sharkey, but bad relations between Jacobs and Jimmy Johnston, the predominant New York City promoter, prevented the match from being made. Instead, Sharkey defended his title against Carnera at the Long Island City Bowl on 29 June 1933. Sharkey won the first five rounds with clever boxing and seemed well on his way to victory, but he changed his tactics in the sixth round and launched a reckless attack that Carnera met with a series of uppercuts, the last one of which knocked out the champion. Sharkey had lost the heavyweight title slightly more than a year after winning it.

After losing decisions to King Levinsky and Tommy Loughran, Sharkey was inactive for the next two years then made a comeback late in 1935. This soon led to a match with Joe Louis on 18 August 1936 at Yankee Stadium. Sharkey fought well, but Louis knocked him out in the third round. This was Sharkey's last fight.

A devoted family man, Sharkey married Dorothy Pike in 1925; they raised three children. He managed his ring earnings skilfully and was financially secure when his career ended. While continuing to live in Boston, he operated a bar and refereed boxing and wrestling matches. In later life he moved with his wife to Epping, New Hampshire, and hunted, fished, and became an expert fly casting angler. He lived comfortably until the end or his life and died in Beverly, Massachusetts, of a respiratory ailment.

• Sharkey's ring record appears in Herbert G. Goldman, ed., *The 1986–87 Ring Record Book and Boxing Encyclopedia.* Accounts of his major fights may be found in *The Ring* magazine, the *New York Times,* and in Gilbert Odd, *Kings of the Ring: 100 Years of World Heavyweight Boxing.* Articles on Sharkey include John B. Kennedy, "Loudspeaker," *Collier's,* 1 March 1930, pp. 27–28, 30; Heinie Miller, "Famous Navy Fighters," *The Ring,* July 1958, pp. 20–21, 59; Ray Grody, "Ex-Heavy Champion Sharkey Fly Casting Star at 70," *The Ring,* Jan. 1973, pp. 12–13; and Lawrence McNamee, "Former Champ Jack Sharkey: An Exclusive Interview," *The Ring,* July 1979, pp. 22–25, 57. An obituary is in the *New York Times,* 19 Aug. 1994.

LUCKETT V. DAVIS

SHAW, Robert (30 Apr. 1916–25 Jan. 1999), conductor, was born Robert Lawson Shaw in Red Bluff, California, to Shirley Richard Shaw, a Protestant clergyman, and his wife, Nelle Mae Lawson Shaw. As an ordained minister of a denomination then known as the Christian Church, the elder Shaw rarely stayed in one place for long, moving his family from town to town in California as he heeded the call to serve yet another congregation. As a consequence, each of his five children was born in a different locale, and young Robert, like his sisters and brothers, attended a series of public schools throughout the state. Rather than causing resentment and animosity, however, the Shaw family's peripatetic existence seemed to draw them closer, and from childhood onward Robert, imbibing the evangelistic fervor of the household, determined that he, too, would become a minister.

Music, along with religion, was a family staple, thanks to Robert Shaw's mother, a church choir soprano who apparently had more talent than the term usually implies, and all the Shaws enjoyed singing at home as well as at services. After enrolling in 1934 at Pomona College (which his father had also attended) as a literature and philosophy major, Shaw joined the college glee club and became the director of a local church choir, one of several jobs he took to support himself. Though he had virtually no formal education in music, his singing talent, along with his infectious enthusiasm for vocal performance and his ability to work easily with a group, led to his appointment as

conductor of the glee club, at an annual salary of $500. A performance by the group on campus in 1937 attracted the attention of the orchestra leader and choral conductor Fred Waring, who had brought his ensembles to Pomona to make a movie for Warner Brothers. Waring offered Shaw, now a junior at the college, a job on the spot, but Shaw initially declined, citing not only his desire to finish his education at Pomona but also his long-held dream of entering the ministry. Waring persisted, however, and by the spring of 1938, with the country still in the midst of a major depression, Shaw was ready to reconsider. He left college before graduation, intending to return the following fall, and moved to New York City to organize and direct a new ensemble, the Fred Waring Glee Club.

Shaw and the glee club were a perfect match, and he soon decided to forgo the ministry in favor of a career as a choral conductor. He continued his association with Fred Waring for seven years, and during that period he also took on assignments outside the Waring organization, including stints as an announcer at musical extravaganzas organized by the promoter Billy Rose. One such event brought him back to California in early 1940, and while working there he managed to complete the remaining requirements for his undergraduate degree at Pomona before returning to New York that summer.

Shaw's interest in religion had not abated, and an opportunity to combine it with his musical vocation arose spontaneously in 1941, when fellow members of the congregation at the Marble Collegiate Church in New York encouraged him to organize an amateur chorus for recreational singing of great choral classics. Shaw obliged by running a classified ad for additional singers in the *New York Times.* Out of some 500 respondents, Shaw culled a chorus of 200 that became known as the Collegiate Chorale, with the ambitious goal of bringing choral music to a wide audience by not only performing themselves but also encouraging the formation of other choral groups. The chorale soon moved from the church basement to its own rented rehearsal space at New York's City Center and early in 1942 appeared for the first time in public, performing with the National Orchestral Association at Carnegie Hall.

Within several years of its founding, the Collegiate Chorale had emerged as a major music-making organization in New York City, attracting large audiences and favorable critical attention for its presentations of such choral standards as the Brahms *Requiem,* Bach's B-minor Mass, and Beethoven's Ninth Symphony, as well as newer compositions by twentieth-century composers, including Paul Hindemith and Lukas Foss. The chorale also began appearing with the likes of Arturo Toscanini and the NBC Symphony and Serge Koussevitzky and the Boston Symphony, and its radio appearances brought it national recognition. Shaw's own rising stature as a choral conductor was acknowledged early in his career—the National Association of American Composers and Conductors cited him in 1943 as the most important American-born conductor. That same year saw the inauguration of what became a standard ritual for Shaw: the establishment of so-called choral clinics. These intensive sessions, several weeks in length, offered refresher training to both professional and amateur choral musicians and were held variously on college campuses and at prominent cultural sites around the country. The clinics, which usually focused on the preparation of a single major work that was presented at the end of the session, continued to be led by Shaw for fifty-five years.

Shaw organized the Collegiate Chorale as a not-for-profit group and ran it democratically—all decisions, including choice of repertoire and venue, were made by a vote of its members. Initially he financed the group out of his own pocket, supplemented by a donation from Fred Waring, modest dues from members, and proceeds from ticket sales. By 1945 the concerts had become sufficiently profitable to pay Shaw a full-time salary, and he was able to resign that year from the Waring organization. In addition to devoting himself to the chorale and to his choral clinics, Shaw served for a time in the 1940s as choral director at both the Juilliard School of Music and at the Berkshire Music Festival, held each summer at Tanglewood in Massachusetts, and he also became the conductor of a chorale formed by the RCA Victor recording company. During the mid- and late 1940s, initially financed by a Guggenheim Fellowship awarded in 1944, Shaw devoted time to an intensive study of music theory, conducting, and performance under the tutelage of a Juilliard faculty member; he took private piano lessons as well and also studied briefly with the noted conductor George Szell.

In the late 1940s, after taking a leave of absence from the Collegiate Chorale, Shaw organized a professional choral group of forty voices known as the Robert Shaw Chorale; the group began appearing in concert and on NBC Radio in 1948 and soon surpassed the Collegiate Chorale in eminence. In early 1952 Shaw launched the five-month-long Choral Masterworks Series at Carnegie Hall, which featured the Robert Shaw Chorale performing music from the seventeenth to the twentieth century. These highly praised performances led to a series of recordings and, most importantly, to annual national tours by the chorale, which in the ensuing years brought choral music to tens of thousands of people in communities both large and small across the country. Often the tours were financed by Shaw himself, who had developed into a somewhat messianic spokesman for choral music and the good he believed that it engendered in audience and performer alike. In addition to singing standard choral works by Beethoven, Brahms, Bach, Haydn, Mozart, and Verdi, the Robert Shaw Chorale commissioned and performed works by leading contemporary composers, among them Samuel Barber, Benjamin Britten, and Aaron Copland; they also performed American folk songs, spirituals, and Christmas carols. In the 1960s the chorale began performing

goodwill concerts in countries around the world, including the Soviet Union, under the auspices of the U.S. State Department.

Meanwhile, Shaw had formally resigned from the Collegiate Chorale in 1954, a year after becoming conductor of the San Diego Symphony. In 1956 he left the San Diego post to become associate conductor of the Cleveland Orchestra, one of the most prestigious organizations of its kind in the world, under George Szell, with special responsibility for the orchestra's chorus. While continuing to work with his own Robert Shaw Chorale, he transformed the Cleveland Orchestra Chorus into a distinctive musical organization during an eleven-year tenure. The chorale was disbanded in 1967, the year that Shaw left the Cleveland Orchestra to become music director of the Atlanta Symphony. During his tenure in Atlanta, Shaw turned the city's heretofore part-time ensemble into a major institution that made commercially successful recordings of both orchestral and choral standards; the symphony also began making annual appearances at Carnegie Hall and toured to great acclaim both domestically and overseas. He also founded two affiliated choral groups, the Atlanta Symphony Chamber Chorus and the Atlanta Symphony Orchestra Chorus, and he continued his close association with both groups following his retirement as music director of the orchestra in 1988.

Shaw was married twice. His first wife was Maxine Farley, a department store executive whom he married in 1939 and with whom he had three children; she subsequently became the librarian of the Collegiate Chorale. They were divorced in 1970, and four years later he married Caroline Saulas, with whom he had a son; she died in 1995.

In the last decade of his life Shaw continued to give choral workshops, including the Robert Shaw Carnegie Hall Workshop, established in 1990; he led the last workshop in performance in January 1998. Shaw was in failing health during the final year of his life and died at a hospital in New Haven, Connecticut, after suffering a stroke while visiting his youngest child at Yale.

Although in the later years of his career Shaw preferred to characterize himself as a symphony orchestra conductor—his listed occupation in *Who Was Who in America*—he will be remembered primarily as a choral conductor. His legacy in that field is undeniable: his tireless championing of choral music helped foster the growth and popularity on the concert stage of a genre that had once been confined largely to the sanctuary. While critics debated, sometimes prissily, the nuances of his presentations, Shaw remained oblivious to their fussing, leading his choral battalions ever onward as he communicated a love for music that stirred audiences and performers alike. Millions of listeners bought his recordings, and he earned more than a dozen Grammys during his career. To his great pleasure, scores of amateur choral groups sprang up around the nation, inspired by the chorales he founded. With the down-home earnestness of a country preacher, Shaw was an eminent crusader for the power of music to enlighten and delight.

• For biographical information, see Joseph A. Mussulman, *Dear People . . . Robert Shaw* (1979), an authorized biography. See also the entries for "Shaw, Robert (Lawson)," in *Current Biography Yearbook* for 1949, 1966, and 1999. The lengthy entry for "Shaw, Robert Lawson," in *Who Was Who in America*, vol. 13 (2000), includes a detailed résumé of Shaw's major professional activities. For interesting profiles of Shaw and discussions of his methods as a choral conductor, see especially A. M. Lingg, "Sing with Me!" *Recreation*, 19 Mar. 1949, pp. 536–539; C. Bird, "He's Got Everybody Singing," *Saturday Evening Post*, 25 Dec. 1948, pp. 34ff.; and Donal Henahan, "By Gosh and By Golly, It's Shaw," *New York Times*, 19 Oct. 1969. An obituary appears in the *New York Times*, 26 Jan. 1999.

ANN T. KEENE

SHEA, William (21 June 1907–2 Oct. 1991), lawyer, was born William Alfred Shea in New York City, the son of Ashley P. Shea, estate agent, and Olive L. Martin. He attended public schools in Brooklyn and Queens before returning with his family to the Washington Heights section of Manhattan, where he served as president of the student council at George Washington High School and excelled at both academics and basketball. After graduating, he attended New York University for a year (and played lacrosse and freshman football) before transferring to Georgetown University. Attracted to Georgetown by the offer of a four-year scholarship that would cover law school as well as undergraduate study, Shea received his LL.B. in 1931 and shortly thereafter gained admittance to the bar in both the District of Columbia and New York.

On returning to New York, Shea joined Cullen & Dykman, a firm whose clients included the Brooklyn Trust Company—which served as ownership trustee for baseball's Brooklyn Dodgers. He made the acquaintance of George V. McLaughlin, a powerful figure in Brooklyn Democratic politics, and fellow attorney Walter O'Malley (who later became owner of the Dodgers), and he soon displayed the talent for backroom negotiations that served him well throughout his career. Shea entered state government as first counsel to the Liquidation Bureau of the New York State Banking Department in 1934 and remained there until 1936, when he became assistant general counsel to the state superintendent of insurance. In 1937 he married Mary Nora Shaw, with whom he was to have three children.

Sensing greater opportunities in the private sector, Shea left government service in 1941 and formed the law firm of Manning, Hollinger & Shea. He soon rose to the top of his profession not as a trial lawyer (a running joke in his office suggested that he was unaware of the location of the local courthouse) but as the consummate broker of backroom deals between politicians, union heads, and corporate leaders. Usually content to stay out of the limelight, Shea came into prominence in December 1957 when New York

City mayor Robert Wagner appointed him (along with Bernard Gimbel, Clint Blume, and Jim Farley) to a special committee charged with returning National League baseball to the city. Local baseball fans had been stunned earlier that year when New York Giants owner Horace Stoneham and Brooklyn Dodgers owner Walter O'Malley had announced plans to relocate both teams to the West Coast in time for the 1958 season. Although Shea's only previous experience in sports during his adult years had been as a fan and as the owner of a short-lived minor league football team, his negotiation skills and combination of charm and bluster made him the perfect choice for the position.

Realizing that the city needed a new stadium to replace the antiquated former homes of the Dodgers and Giants (Ebbets Field and the Polo Grounds, respectively), Shea soon persuaded the city to commit resources to the building of a new facility in Flushing Meadows, Queens. He then unsuccessfully tried to convince existing National League teams in Cincinnati, Pittsburgh, and Philadelphia to relocate; he was also rebuffed by the National League owners when he suggested that the league create a new New York franchise via expansion. In the wake of these frustrations, Shea's negotiating skills came to the forefront. He teamed up with venerable baseball executive Branch Rickey and put forth a proposal to create a new, third major league in November 1958. Dubbed the Continental League, the new organization benefited from the pent-up demand for major league baseball in cities not then in possession of teams. The league formally came into existence on 27 July 1959 with franchises awarded to Houston, Toronto, Denver, and Minneapolis–St. Paul in addition to New York. Three additional teams (Buffalo, Dallas–Ft. Worth, and Atlanta) were added in January 1960, and a schedule was announced for the 1961 season. Existing American and National League team owners viewed these developments with dismay; a competing league had the potential to steal their star players and drive up the salaries of those who chose to remain with their present teams. Even more alarming, however, was the threat that the league posed to baseball's long-cherished exemption from federal antitrust laws. Rather than face that possibility, an agreement was reached in the summer of 1960 that resulted in four expansion baseball franchises (New York and Houston in the National League and Los Angeles and Washington in the American League) in exchange for the dissolution of the proposed Continental League.

New York's new National League team, the Mets, made their debut in the 1962 season. After playing their first two seasons in the Polo Grounds, they moved to the Flushing Meadows facility, which had been named the William A. Shea Stadium by a grateful city, in time for the 1964 season. Although Shea once joked that the stadium would probably be renamed fifteen minutes after his death, he was justifiably proud of the honor.

In 1964 his law firm merged with Gallop, Climenko & Gould to form Shea, Gallop, Climenko & Gould. The merger reunited Shea with Milton Gould, a former high school classmate; several name changes later the firm became in 1979 Shea & Gould, in time one of the most powerful and influential in New York. After helping to negotiate New York state's purchase of the Long Island Rail Road from the Pennsylvania Railroad in 1965, Shea was appointed by Governor Nelson Rockefeller to the Metropolitan Commuter Transportation Authority, an agency charged with operating the LIRR as well as working out an agreement to run the New Haven Railroad's commuter service. Although Shea's firm came under increased scrutiny in his later years—the journalists Jack Newfield and Paul De Brul termed it "a factory of legal graft"—it grew to include almost 300 lawyers by 1990. Content to delegate responsibility for the day-to-day management of his firm in later years, Shea died in his Manhattan home following a period of declining health.

• Shea is the subject of Roy Terrell, "3rd League Cities Pin Hopes on This Man," *Sports Illustrated*, 20 July 1959, pp. 30–32, and Nicholas Pileggi, "No Matter Who Loses the Elections, Bill Shea Wins," *New York*, 11 Nov. 1974, pp. 45–53. For a less flattering view of his career, see Jack Newfield and Paul Du Brul, *Permanent Government: Who Really Rules New York?* (1981). An obituary is in the *New York Times*, 4 Oct. 1991.

EDWARD L. LACH, JR.

SHEEAN, Vincent (5 Dec. 1899–15 Mar. 1975), journalist and author, was born James Vincent Sheean in Pana, Illinois, the son of William Charles Sheean and Susan MacDermot; he was nicknamed Jimmy. After high school in Pana, he attended the University of Chicago from 1916 to 1920, taking courses in English literature, Romance languages, history, and philosophy, and worked on the school newspaper. When his mother died in 1921, he lacked funds to continue at the university and, without a degree, moved to Greenwich Village in New York, where he became a reporter for the *Daily News*. In 1922 he bummed around France and Italy, then became a political correspondent out of Paris and London for the *Chicago Tribune* (1922–1924). In *Personal History*, his 1935 bestselling autobiography, he says that although he began reporting coldly and impersonally in "the pesthouse of Europe," "[t]his professional indifference to the material of journalism did not endure"; "political interest deepened to political passion, and I came in time to 'take sides' and have opinions . . ." Favoring the socialist left, a weak Germany over a vengeful France, and Greece over Turkey, he was alarmed by Mussolini's fascism in Italy, Primo de Rivera's Falange movement in Spain, Japan's early "fatal touch of reality" concerning its military power, and the impotence of the League of Nations.

In 1925 Sheean went east twice from Tangier through Spanish-French lines, which were allied against anticolonial insurgencies in Morocco, to interview the courageous, doomed Riffian rebel Abd el Krim (Abd-al-Krim)—once for the *Tribune*, then for the North American Newspaper Alliance—and described his adventures in *An American among the Riffi* (1926; published in Great Britain as *Adventures among the Riffi*). In 1926 he visited Tehran for the coronation of Riza Shah Pahlavi and studied international diplomacy and much else in Persia. Traveling to Moscow, he sympathized with "the Bolshevik effort" but not "its methods or results," haunted Moscow's art museums, and quickly wrote *The New Persia* (1927). Temporary Kuomintang successes in 1927 induced the North American Newspaper Alliance to send Sheean to China, where he dispatched colorful cablegrams from Shanghai, Nanking, Hankow, Peking (Beijing), and elsewhere; he applauded pro-coolie, antiforeign, anticapitalistic, anti-imperialist events, met Chiang Kai-shek and Sun Yat-sen's brave widow, among other leaders, and admired the Russian Mikhail Borodin (a leader of the Chinese Communists) and his fiery American-born assistant, Rayna Prohme. Ahead of Communist defeats, Sheean escaped to Moscow, witnessed celebrations of the Russian Revolution's tenth anniversary, and was with Prohme when she died after being forced to flee China with Borodin.

A period of vacillating in Paris and London and lecturing in America on Morocco and China was followed in 1929 by a trip to Jerusalem to work for an American Zionist periodical *New Palestine*. When he observed conditions, however, he refused further pay, broke with the Zionists, and adopted a pro-Arab, anti-British stance. Having witnessed and heard about Arab mob action against Jews, who he felt were deliberately inviting bloodshed, he concluded: "The country was tiny and already inhabited: why couldn't the Zionists leave it alone?" Sheean grew ill, stopped his inflammatory cables, testified before a British commission of inquiry, and returned indirectly home.

Between 1927 and 1938 Sheean published five novels. The most interesting are *Gog and Magog* (1930), about an American's romance in Moscow with a pro-Communist American strongly resembling Prohme, and *Sanfelice* (1934), his longest and perhaps best novel, a tragic historical romance with such background figures as Lord Nelson and his paramour, Lady Hamilton. *A Day of Battle* (1938) details French-English combat on 11 May 1745 at Fontenoy, Flanders, and is, like much of his fiction, more successful in suggesting the politico-historical background than in foregrounding characters, dialogue, and action.

In 1939 Sheean published *Not Peace but a Sword*, a sequel to his somewhat better *On Personal History*, which vividly covers the Spanish Civil War and the Nazis in Czechoslovakia. During World War II, Sheean served in the U.S. Army Air Force (1942–1944) in North Africa, Italy, India, and China, rising from captain to lieutenant colonel. He covered the 1945 United Nations conference in San Francisco.

This House against This House (1946) combines his wartime experiences and a plea for peace.

In 1947 Sheean visited India, which he always found spiritually nourishing, interviewed Mahatma Gandhi, and was a horrified witness of the holy man's assassination. *Mahatma Gandhi: A Great Life in Brief* (1954) is Sheean's undogmatic, factual biography. His *Nehru: The Years of Power* (1960), also based partly on interviews, is similarly insightful and sympathetic. One of Sheean's best later books is *Dorothy and Red* (1963), a rollicking biography of the disastrous marriage of two of his closest friends, novelist Sinclair Lewis and journalist Dorothy Thompson.

Sheean wrote five more novels. *Bird of the Wilderness* (1941) is a psychologically autobiographical fictional account of a sensitive Illinois teenager's confusion at the advent of World War I. Sheean's last novel, *Beware of Caesar* (1965), tediously concerns Nero and his demand that Seneca commit suicide. Sheean's lifelong love of music found literary expression in enthusiastic biographies of Oscar Hammerstein (1956) and Giuseppe Verdi (1958) and also in *First and Last Love* (1956), Sheean's history as a listener to music together with sketches of musical personalities.

Sheean married Diana Forbes-Robertson, the British actor Sir Johnston Forbes-Robertson's daughter, in 1935. Divorced in 1946, they remarried in 1949; they had two children. Sheean was semiretired in Arolo, Italy, near the Swiss Alps, where he was working on what would have been a rich and colorful autobiography, when he died of lung cancer.

A liberal, daring risk taker, Sheean seemed to gravitate toward many of the world's political hot spots. At its best, his subjective journalism was of a high order, enhanced by personal thoughts and feelings—and interlaced with gossip, too. His example influenced a generation of similarly ambitious reporters, especially in the 1930s and 1940s, and he was a generous friend of countless writers. As the gimlet-eyed observer of many of the most influential political leaders of his momentous epoch, he made the world overseas vivid to American readers.

• Most of Sheean's papers are in collections at the American Academy of Arts and Letters in New York City, Columbia University, Harvard University, and the New York Public Library. His relatively minor works include *The Pieces of a Fan* (1937), fourteen competent but shallow short stories; *Between the Thunder and the Sun* (1943), egocentric reminiscences about pre–World War II Cannes and Salzburg, the early London blitz, and much else; *Lead, Kindly Light* (1949), about finding spiritual guidance in traditional Hinduism; *Indigo Bunting* (1951), a biography of his close friend Edna St. Vincent Millay; a biography of Thomas Jefferson for juvenile readers (1953); and *Faisal: The King and His Kingdom* (1975), which is about Saudi Arabia. The best source of information on Sheean's early career is his *On Personal History*, for which he wrote a new introduction in 1969 and which he planned to update. He is represented, with a biographical note, in *Reporting World War II: Part One, American Journalism 1938–1944* (1995). Carlos Baker, *Ernest Hemingway: A Life Story* (1969), and Mark Schorer, *Sinclair Lewis: An American Life* (1961), treat their respective subjects' friendships with Sheean. David S. Woolman, *Rebels in the Rif: Abd el Krim and the Rif Rebellion* (1968), cites Sheean's *An American among the Riffi*. In his *Think Back on Us . . . A Contemporary Chronicle of the 1930s* (1967), Malcolm Cowley praises Sheean's *Personal History* as the best of the many "farewells" to Paris, southern France, Spain, Moscow, and China by any foreign correspondent from America. Rarely discussed in accounts of American fiction, Sheean's novels are briefly treated in *American Novelists of Today* (1951; repr., 1976), by Harry R. Werfel, who defines their common theme as "man's emergence from bondage." Obituaries are in the *New York Times* and the *Washington Post*, both 17 Mar. 1975.

ROBERT L. GALE

SHEPARD, Alan (18 Nov. 1923–21 July 1998), astronaut, was born Alan Bartlett Shepard, Jr., in East Derry, New Hampshire, the son of Alan B. Shepard, a retired Army colonel and insurance broker, and Renza Emerson Shepard. As a boy, Shepard loved to tinker with car and boat motors and spent many happy childhood hours building model airplanes. In his 1962 essay, "The Urge to Pioneer," Shepard recalled, "I was raised, if not exactly in an atmosphere of aviation, at least in the midst of mechanical things" (*We Seven*, p. 65). In high school at Pinkerton Academy in Derry where he excelled in mathematics, the fledgling aviator took odd jobs at the local airport in exchange for airplane rides and became obsessed with flying.

Influenced by his father's military background, Shepard studied for one year at Admiral Farragut Academy in New Jersey and earned an appointment to the U.S. Naval Academy in Annapolis, Maryland. After graduating in the middle of his class in 1944, Shepard was commissioned as an ensign, and during the closing months of World War II he served on the destroyer *Cogswell* in the Pacific theater. In 1945 Shepard married Louise Brewer; the couple had two daughters and raised a niece as their third child. After the war, Shepard took flight training at navy schools in Texas and Florida. He received his wings in 1947 and was assigned to Fighter Squadron 42 out of Norfolk, Virginia. In 1948 and 1949 he served two tours of duty flying fighter jets aboard aircraft carriers in the Mediterranean.

The major break in Shepard's career came in 1950 when, still a lieutenant, junior grade, he was one of only three junior officers chosen to attend the navy test pilot school at Patuxent River, Maryland. After qualifying as a test pilot, Shepard helped perfect advanced navy aircraft, experimented with high altitude flying, worked on in-flight refueling systems, and conducted suitability trials with F2H3 Banshee jet landings on angled carrier decks. After tours on carriers in the Pacific from 1953 to 1956, Shepard returned to Patuxent as an instructor for the test pilot school and won a prized appointment to the Naval War College. Upon graduation in 1958, he was assigned to the staff of the commander-in-chief, Atlantic Fleet. At this point during his rapid rise through the naval ranks, Shepard had accumulated some 37,000 hours' flying time—1,800 in jet aircraft—and became a prime candidate for the manned space flight program being planned by the National Aeronautics and Space Administration (NASA).

From the 110 top military test pilots invited to volunteer for NASA's Project Mercury, Shepard was one of seven elite flyers chosen to train as America's first astronauts. In the spring of 1959, along with John Glenn, Virgil "Gus" Grissom, Donald "Deke" Slayton, Scott Carpenter, Gordon Cooper, and Walter Schirra, Shepard began an intense two-year physical, psychological and scientific regimen covering every conceivable aspect of space flight, from astronomy, astrophysics, and astronautics to meteorology and aviation biology. Furthermore, under rigorous simulated conditions, he experienced virtually all physical sensations that could be involved in actual space flight, including the effects of excessive G-forces and weightlessness.

Shepard reached the pinnacle of his career on 21 February 1961 when Robert Gilruth, the director of Project Mercury, informed Shepard that he had been chosen as the prime pilot for America's first mission into space. The launch was scheduled for 12 March but because a test flight with a chimpanzee had gone badly, it was decided that another unmanned test of the massive seven-story Redstone rocket was necessary. In the meantime, on April 12, Russian cosmonaut Yuri A. Gagarin became the first human to enter space when his *Vostok I* spacecraft completed one full orbit around the planet. Shepard was bitterly disappointed by the delay, and he was even more frustrated when his next scheduled launch was postponed for three days due to bad weather. Finally, at 9:34 A.M. on 5 May, 1961, twenty-three days after Gagarin's historic flight, Shepard blasted off from Cape Canaveral, Florida, in his *Freedom 7* Mercury capsule, reaching an altitude of 115 miles and a velocity of 5,180 miles per hour, which pulled a maximum G-force of eleven. Moreover, in contrast to the Soviet policy of secrecy, the dramatic launch of *Freedom 7* was broadcast live around the world.

When, at the most critical moment, a cool and collected Shepard radioed NASA's Mission Control that "Everything is A-O.K.!" democratic societies everywhere rejoiced over this major technological triumph, and the 37-year-old naval commander became an authentic American hero. His entire suborbital flight was nearly flawless. It had barely penetrated the borders of outer space and had lasted just fifteen minutes and twenty-two seconds, including a five-minute period of weightlessness, but its symbolic political importance was incalculable. Although Gagarin had been in space for a longer time and had traveled at a much higher velocity, his flight was fully automated and he had been, in a sense, merely a passenger. In contrast, Shepard took over manual control of his spaceship and expertly conducted a series of precise maneuvers. His splashdown and recovery, viewed by millions on live television, were perfect. After a whirlwind round of debriefings and medical examinations, he was in-

vited to the White House, awarded the NASA Distinguished Service Medal, and was honored by ticker-tape parades not seen since the days of Charles Lindbergh. Twenty days after the flight, in the boldest of mission statements, President John F. Kennedy announced to Congress and the world that America "should commit itself to achieving the goal, before the decade is out, of landing a man on the moon and returning him safely to earth."

As a central figure in Kennedy's grand plan, Shepard was next assigned to be Mission Control's capsule communicator for Grissom's suborbital flight (a rerun of Shepard's *Freedom 7* mission) and for Glenn's famous triple orbiting of the earth aboard *Friendship 7* in February 1962. In May 1963 Shepard was scheduled to pilot the final Mercury mission, but NASA cancelled the flight in order to develop the new Gemini program, which featured a two-man crew. Shepard had just begun training for the first manned Gemini flight in 1963 when he developed a serious inner-ear disorder diagnosed as labyrinthitis (Meuniere's syndrome), which grounded him for eight years.

Still fully committed to the advancement of America's space program, Shepard became Chief of NASA's Astronaut Office and ruled all aspects of astronaut training and flight scheduling with an iron hand. In his autobiography, *Leap of Faith* (2000), Gordon Cooper complains bitterly that Shepard played politics in selecting crews for Gemini and Apollo missions (pp. 176–82). Shepard did play hardball as an administrator and never wavered from his ambition to return to space. After a successful operation on his inner ear in 1969, he found a place for himself as commander of the nine-day flight of *Apollo 14* (31 Jan.–9 Feb. 1971), and on 5 February he became the fifth human being to walk on the moon. With co-pilot Edgar Mitchell, Shepard spent thirty-three hours conducting experiments on the lunar surface. Moreover, with his knack for self-promotion, he made his lunar exploration memorable by driving a two-wheeled vehicle dubbed "Shepard's Rickshaw" while gathering moonrocks, and by hitting two golf balls in the one-sixth gravity with a makeshift six-iron which he had rigged from his lunar module, *Antares*.

Soon after the *Apollo 14* mission, President Richard M. Nixon appointed Shepard as a delegate to the twenty-sixth United Nations General Assembly. In 1974, having been promoted to the rank of rear admiral, Shepard retired from the navy and at the same time from NASA. Already a millionaire from investments in real estate and banking, he became chairman of Marathon Construction in Houston and founded his own business, Seven Fourteen Enterprises. In 1984 Shepard and the other surviving Mercury astronauts established the Mercury Seven Foundation to raise money for scholarships for science and engineering students. Among his many national honors, Shepard was awarded the Navy Distinguished Flying Cross, the Smithsonian Institution's Langley Medal, two honorary doctorate degrees, and the Congressional Medal of Honor for Space. He died in Monterey, California.

Shepard's influence on the history of America's space program is profound. As the natural leader of the seven original astronauts, he earned a reputation as a tough behind-the-scenes mediator on behalf of manned spaceflight. He could be by turns ruthlessly competitive and a charming jokester. In the tense early days of the Mercury program, Shepard brought in comedian Bill Dana as the quixotic "Spanish Astronaut," José Jimenez, to relax his six high-strung colleagues. He was a brilliant engineer who tested radical designs for future spacecraft and helped plan long-range missions to the moon and beyond. He is properly lionized for his courage and patriotism in sitting atop experimental rockets filled with explosive fuel in order to further America's ideological interests in the Cold War against the Communist bloc. Prior to his thrilling fifteen-minute flight witnessed by an expectant nation in 1961, the United States had absorbed a crushing series of setbacks, including the Russian launch of *Sputnik*, the world's first manmade satellite, in 1957; fiery booster rocket explosions; Gagarin's epic flight; and the Bay of Pigs fiasco in Cuba just five days after *Vostok I*. The timing was perfect, then, for Shepard's exhilarating success aboard *Freedom 7*, which galvanized the scientific community, renewed America's national confidence and international prestige, and proved to be a major step in the American drive to land a man on the moon and win the Cold War.

Perhaps Shepard himself best summarized his character and philosophy in a 1998 interview when he mused, "Standing on the surface of the moon, looking up in the black sky, at a planet which is four times the size of the moon, as we see it, and thinking about the millions of people that are down there . . . desperately trying to get along. . . .What a shame it is that they can't be put on the moon and let them look back at the planet Earth for a while, so they could say, 'Hey, look, we've got to take care of this place.'" In his groundbreaking book, *The Right Stuff* (1979), Tom Wolfe was speaking about Shepard as much as anyone when he characterized a brash young pilot in the U.S. space program as a patriot who possessed an ineffable quality beyond bravery: he flew "in a hurtling piece of machinery and put his hide on the line and then had the moxie, the reflexes, the experience, the coolness, to pull back in the last yawning moment—and then go back up again the next day, and the next day, and every next day, even if the series should prove infinite—and ultimately, in its best expression, do so in a cause that means something to thousands, to a people, a nation, to humanity, to God" (p. 24).

• Less than one month after Shepard's flight aboard *Freedom 7* in 1961, Martin Caidin produced a book-length re-creation of the entire mission, *Man into Space*. That same year Caidin also published *The Astronauts: The Story of Project Mercury*, and Jewel and Charles Smaus wrote *America's First Spacemen*, both featuring Shepard. In *We Seven: By the Astronauts Themselves* (1962), Shepard contributed four essays, including "The First American," a minute-by-minute account of his suborbital flight. In 1994, with Deke Slayton as coauthor, Shepard published *Moon Shot: The Inside Story of America's Race to the Moon*, a thorough review of the U.S. space program from its beginnings through Slayton's flight in one of the last Apollo missions in 1975. Shepard disliked *The Right Stuff* because he believed Wolfe concentrated too much on the astronauts' personal lives, and he therefore was pleased to write the foreword to Joseph Atkinson and Jay Shafritz's *The Real Stuff: A History of NASA's Astronaut Recruitment Program* (1985). Shepard also wrote the foreword to Stanley Goldstein's scholarly *Reaching for the Stars* (1987) on the importance of early astronaut training. Among NASA's many publications featuring Shepard are *Astronaut Fact Book* (1992) and Loyd Swenson, James Grimwood, and Charles Alexander, *This New Ocean* (1998), concerning the part of the NASA history series devoted to Project Mercury. See also Joseph Bell, *Seven into Space* (1960); Michael Cassutt, *Who's Who in Space: The First 25 Years* (1987); and Robin Kerrod, *The Illustrated History of NASA* (1988). Video recordings featuring Shepard are *Racing for the Moon: America's Glory Days in Space* (1989), and *Apollo 14: Mission to Fra Mauro* (1995). An obituary is in the *New York Times*, 23 Aug. 1998.

BRUCE L. JANOFF

SHEPHERD, Jean (26 July 1921–16 Oct. 1999), humorist and multimedia performer, was born Jean Parker Shepherd in Chicago, the son of Jean P. Shepherd, a white-collar worker for Borden Dairies, and Anne Heinrichs Shepherd. A good deal of confusion surrounds the date of Shepherd's birth: it has been reported as 21 or 26 July and with various birth years ranging from 1921 to 1929. Possibly the outgrowth of vanity (after all, it may have been more hip during his New York heyday in the late 1950s through the middle 1960s for him to be "twenty- or thirty-something" rather than "forty-something"), the lack of consistency in his claimed birth year accurately represents his unwillingness to reveal details of his personal life, something that he always claimed had nothing to do with his work. This may seem a strange position for him to have taken, given the fact that generations of Americans believe they know a great deal of Shepherd's life from the stories he told on the radio, wrote for magazine and book publication, and presented on television and in film.

Shepherd, with his younger brother Randall, grew up in the Hessville section of Hammond, Indiana. The "inverted bowl of darkness," one of the antinostalgic names he gave the Midwest, is present in virtually all of his stories, and at the center is Hammond, which he described as "tough and mean" and Chicago's "broad rear end." A prototypical industrial town, the fictionalized "Hohman" came to represent *home* for Shepherd and his fans: "Ours was not a genteel neighborhood . . . [n]estled picturesquely between the looming steel mills and the verminously aromatic oil refineries . . ." The family lived in a middle-class house on Cleveland Street, and Shepherd attended Harding Elementary School and Hammond High School, graduating in 1939. Given the consistency of the narratives Shepherd presents, it is fair to let one speak for his childhood: "My old man, my mother, my kid brother and I slogged along in the great tradition. The old man had his high point every Wednesday at George's Bowling Alley, where he once rolled a historic game in which he got three consecutive strikes. My kid brother's nose ran steadily, winter and summer. My mother made red cabbage, peanut-butter-and-jelly sandwiches, meat loaf and Jell-O in an endless stream. And I studied the principal exports of Peru at the Warren G. Harding School." When he was sixteen, Shepherd had his first radio experience doing weekly sportscasts for a local station. He also was a ham radio operator and worked part time after school as a mail boy in a steel mill.

From 1944 to 1946, Shepherd served in a U.S. Army Signal Corps radar unit. This experience provided the material on "army life" that he would later recount during his radio broadcasts and in several published stories. Following the war, he lived in Chicago, where he studied acting at the Goodman Theatre School on the GI Bill. He also attended Indiana University, but he left without completing a degree. In 1948 he held three different announcing jobs on Cincinnati radio stations; a late-night slot on WSAI lasted until 1951, foretelling what was to become his prime time broadcasting venue. In 1950 he married Joan Warner, an English major graduate of the University of Cincinnati. The couple had two children: son Randall, born in 1951, and daughter Adrian, born in 1957, after Shepherd had left Warner. In later years Shepherd would not refer either to his children or to his first wife, and at the time of his death several obituaries erroneously reported that he had no survivors, even though Warner and his children were still living.

A job at KYW radio took Shepherd to Philadelphia in 1951, but by January 1953 he had returned to Cincinnati to work for WLW. A "loose-cannon style" television comedy show, *Rear Bumper*, appeared first on WLWT in Cincinnati, where it attracted the attention of Steve Allen, who had suggested Shepherd for host duties on NBC's *Tonight* show. Although the *Tonight* job never materialized, New York beckoned, and Shepherd began what was to be a 21-year career on WOR. By 1956, he settled again into a late-night time slot, 1:00–5:30 A.M., and cultivated a devoted group of fans. The college students, shift workers, and insomniacs, whom he affectionately dubbed "the night people," came to his rescue when the station actually pulled him off the air at 2:30 A.M. on 16 August 1956 because he had done a promotion for Sweetheart soap, urging his listeners to buy the product, even though the company had not purchased commercial time. A mass protest of fans—and the gratitude of newly signed sponsor Sweetheart—forced WOR to reinstate Shepherd, and he continued his overnight broadcasts until 1961 when his programs were shortened to 45-minute shows airing in various time slots prior to midnight. The abbreviated format lasted until his retirement from regular broadcasting duties in 1977.

From the late 1950s through the 1960s, Shepherd became a kind of cult figure in New York, and in as many as twenty-seven states where the 50,000-watt clear-channel broadcasts of WOR reached at night. Hip, irreverent, "beat" observations on the passing scene and the foibles of contemporary urbanites alternated with warm, humorous anecdotes from a pseudo-autobiographical midwestern boyhood as Shepherd created a talk-show format in which he did all of the talking. Featured in articles appearing in *Mad* magazine, *Time*, and *Newsweek*, Shepherd began a truly multimedia career: he recorded "The Clown," a jazz-poetry piece with Charles Mingus (1957), wrote a regular column for the *Village Voice* (1956–1957), edited and wrote the introduction to *The America of George Ade* (1960), appeared in theatrical productions (1961), and performed live shows at clubs such as the Limelight. One of his most infamous escapades resulted from his impatience with the influence that critics and other cultural arbiters had on public taste. Urging his listeners to visit their local bookstore and ask for a nonexistent book titled *I, Libertine* by Frederick Ewing and to discuss it knowingly among friends and strangers alike, Shepherd pulled off a literary hoax that became international news. The fictitious book rose on the bestseller list over a period of seven weeks during the summer of 1956, and "Ewing" was mentioned in newspaper columns, as Shepherd and his fans manipulated the "system" until he finally allowed the *Wall Street Journal* to reveal the truth. Shepherd subsequently published a paperback version of *I, Libertine* under the Ewing pseudonym and donated the proceeds to charity.

Shepherd married actress Lois Nettleton in 1961, and their marriage would last six years until their divorce. In *Understanding Media* (1964), Marshall McLuhan wrote: "Jean Shepherd of WOR in New York regards radio as a new medium for a new kind of novel that he writes nightly. The mike is his pen and paper. His audience and their knowledge of the daily events of the world provide his characters, his scenes, and moods." Because his narratives proved so popular, Shepherd began to publish short fiction in *Playboy* and won the magazine's satire award in 1966, 1967, and 1969. In 1966 he published *In God We Trust, All Others Pay Cash,* a "novel" that included several of his previously published stories, and the subsequent book tour confirmed that he had found a national audience. *Wanda Hickey's Night of Golden Memories and Other Disasters* followed in 1971, and the title story about the puberty rite of a junior prom, which had originally appeared in *Playboy* (1969), proved to be his most popular narrative. Shepherd published two other books containing stories and essays that had originally appeared in periodicals: *The Ferrari in the Bedroom* (1972) and *A Fistful of Fig Newtons* (1981).

Meanwhile, Shepherd resurrected his interest in television programming. A series of twenty five-minute commentaries, "Rear Bumpers," appeared on WGBH (Boston) in 1969, and in 1971 his thirteen-episode series "Jean Shepherd's America" ran on PBS stations nationwide. The series featured segments on such topics as steel mills, beer, and Maine; it proved popular with audiences and won favorable reviews from critics. New Jersey Public Television's "Shepherd's Pie" (1978) and "Jean Shepherd on Route One" (1983), and the nine-episode second series of "Jean Shepherd's America" (1985) for PBS followed. But it was Shepherd's interest in feature-length narratives that created his most enduring productions. In December 1976 "The Phantom of the Open Hearth," based on the Wanda Hickey story and two other tales from *In God We Trust*, aired on the PBS series *American Playhouse*; a published version of the screenplay followed in 1978. This production earned Shepherd a Critic's Circle Award nomination and focused his interest at the time on developing new projects for television. In April 1977 Shepherd ended his radio broadcasting career at WOR, believing that his creativity was better served by television and film. ABC contracted with Shepherd to develop a pilot and six scripts for a television series in 1978, and he moved to Hollywood to oversee the filming. But the project never fully materialized. Instead, a sequence of feature-length works based on his stories appeared on *American Playhouse* (PBS): "The Great American Fourth of July and Other Disasters" (1982), "The Star-Crossed Romance of Josephine Cosnowski" (1983), and "Ollie Hopnoodle's Haven of Bliss!" (1989).

In 1977 Shepherd married his agent-companion-amanuensis, Leigh Brown, and he would share his life and creative chores with her until her death in 1998. They would collaborate with director Bob Clark on *A Christmas Story* (1983), a theatrical release that would become an enduring holiday classic on television. In many respects, this film was the most effective and coherent of Shepherd's efforts to capture both the frustrations and the small victories and satisfaction to be found in the kind of midwestern working-class world he had been describing for more than two decades in his radio monologues and in his published fiction. A later effort by the same team, *It Runs in the Family* (1994), did not succeed as well and was put immediately into videotape release under the title *My Summer Story*.

In his later years, after serving as a commentator on NPR's "All Things Considered" between 1981 and 1984, Shepherd came to disparage his work on radio, much to the dismay of his longtime fans. While he could still be heard in commercial voice-overs or interview segments on television and radio, he faded from public view as his once popular concert appearances at college campuses and other venues became less frequent in the late 1980s and the 1990s. Whereas he had once maintained a summer home in Maine, a New York apartment, a New Jersey farm, and a Florida condo, using his private plane to commute from one location to another, he and his wife moved to a house in a quiet Sanibel, Florida, neighborhood. Shepherd became increasingly reclusive in his last years except for infrequent radio interviews, and died of natural causes in a Fort Myers hospital.

Jean Shepherd's significance is twofold. First, his contributions to the medium of radio broadcasting are considerable. At a time when radio was in a state of transition, Shepherd offered an alternative to the ubiquitous disc jockey and recorded music format, and it is possible to trace the lineage of later "talk radio," "shock jock," and raconteur programming (such as Garrison Keillor's Lake Wobegon tales) to what Shepherd was performing on WOR. Even more important is his stature as a humorist. Without condescension, but with the wit characteristic of Mark Twain, he created a vivid and amusing portrait of middle-class American culture that lives in our collective memory.

• Scholarly appraisals of Shepherd's work can be found in Joseph Trimmer, "Memoryscape: Jean Shepherd's Midwest," *Old Northwest* 2 (1976): 357–69; Peter Scholl, "Jean Shepherd: The Survivor of Hammond," *Great Lakes Review* 5 (1978): 7–18; and James Smith, "Humor, Cultural History, and Jean Shepherd," *Journal of Popular Culture* 16 (1982): 1–12. *Current Biography Yearbook* (1984) contains an account of Shepherd's life through the early 1980s. Useful profiles of Shepherd and his work in various media appear in Edward Grossman, "Jean Shepherd: Radio's Noble Savage," *Harper's Magazine*, Jan. 1966, pp. 88–89, and Maralyn Lois Polak, "What's Jean Shepherd Got Against Woody Allen?," *Philadelphia Inquirer Sunday Magazine*, 9 Jan. 1983. Informative tributes include Charles Strum, "Remembering Jean Shepherd: Kabuki Radio: 'Creeping Meatballism' and Other Peculiar Riffs on America," *New York Times*, 26 Mar. 2000. An obituary appears in the *New York Times*, 18 Oct. 1999.

JAMES F. SMITH, JR.

SHEPPARD, Sam (29 Dec. 1923–6 Apr. 1970), osteopath and murder suspect, was born Samuel Holmes Sheppard in Cleveland, Ohio, to Richard Allen Sheppard, an osteopath, and his wife, Ethel Niles Sheppard. Young Sam's father had founded a flourishing osteopathic clinic in Cleveland, and the family, which included two other sons, enjoyed a prosperous, upper-middle-class life. After graduating in 1942 from Cleveland Heights High School, where he was a popular athlete and a good student, Sam Sheppard enrolled at the Los Angeles College of Osteopathic Physicians and Surgeons to prepare for a career as an osteopath. In February 1945, while still a student there, he married Florence Marilyn Reese, known as Marilyn, a high school classmate and longtime girlfriend then in her senior year at Skidmore College. The couple lived in Los Angeles for several years while Sheppard completed his medical studies, and during that time their only child, Samuel Reese Sheppard, was born.

In 1951 the Sheppards and their son moved back to Cleveland, settling in a large house on the shores of Lake Erie in the upscale suburban community of Bay Village. Sam Sheppard joined his father in practice at the family-run Bay View Hospital, and Marilyn Sheppard busied herself with her home, family, and occasional outings with friends. By all accounts the

Sheppards enjoyed a typical 1950s suburban social life, highlighted by cookouts, church socials, boating and water-skiing on the lake, and neighborhood get-togethers. Their apparently happy life changed dramatically in the early morning hours of 4 July 1954, when Marilyn Sheppard, four months pregnant with the couple's second child, was bludgeoned to death in the bedroom of their home. At six A.M., some hours after the crime was committed, police arrived on the scene, launching an investigation into what became one of the most notorious murder cases of the twentieth century.

Sam Sheppard's account of the crime never varied. He claimed that he had been asleep on a daybed in the living room when the murder was committed, and that his wife's outcries had awakened him. When he went upstairs to investigate, he said, he was knocked unconscious in the bedroom doorway by a blow to the head from an unseen assailant. Regaining consciousness, he crept into the bedroom and discovered that his wife was dead. Hearing noises below, he went downstairs and encountered a man he henceforth described consistently as "a bushy-haired intruder" who emerged from the darkness and knocked him out. Sheppard told police he was unconscious for several hours and awoke about five-thirty a.m. to find himself lying on the family's private beach. He then made his way back to the house and telephoned the mayor, a personal friend, who arrived with his wife shortly afterward and called the police.

After being questioned briefly, Sheppard was taken to Bay View Hospital for treatment of neck injuries he said he had sustained in the attack, and his seven-year-old son, who had been asleep in the house, was placed in the custody of an uncle. The house itself was a shambles, with furniture overturned and drawers pulled out, their contents strewn all over the floor, and blood stains spattered everywhere. Under sedation at the hospital, and without his lawyer present, Sheppard was interrogated over a five-hour period later that day by a series of investigators, including the coroner, the police chief, and several police officers. Sheppard offered the theory that the murder had been committed in the course of a robbery gone awry, but his questioners regarded his story with increasing skepticism, and by the end of the day at least one officer had accused Sheppard point-blank of killing his wife.

Over the next few weeks, as Marilyn Sheppard was quietly buried and her husband recovered from his injuries, investigators continued to search the Sheppard home for clues. But they were not moving rapidly enough in the opinion of Cleveland's three daily newspapers, for which the Sheppard case had become front-page news. From the outset the *Press*, the *Plain Dealer*, and the *News* all pointed the finger of suspicion at Sam Sheppard, and the *Press*'s editor, Louis B. Seltzer, was especially relentless, demanding that "Dr. Sam," as he was now publicly called, be given the third degree by the police. On 22 July a three-day inquest opened into Marilyn Sheppard's death amid hoopla and frenzy. Convened in the local high school

gymnasium to accommodate large crowds of reporters, radio and television crews, and a curious public, it opened with a body search of Sheppard and the presentation of a formal statement given by him to the police twelve days earlier; his lawyer was not allowed to give evidence and was forcibly removed from the proceedings when he attempted to participate. Sheppard gave no oral testimony at the inquest, and this whipped the local papers into an even greater frenzy as they continued to hint at the doctor's guilt, buttressing their claims with allegations that the police had targeted him as their leading suspect.

On 23 July the Cleveland police department took formal charge of the Sheppard case from the Bay Village police, and seven days later Sam Sheppard was arrested on suspicion of murder. After being held for more than two weeks, he was released on bail on 16 August, but the next day he was indicted for murder by a grand jury and rearrested. Attempts by defense attorneys to have the case tried outside the Cleveland area because of possible bias owing to adverse publicity were dismissed by the court and sneered at by the local papers, which continued to make Sheppard front-page news. During a three-month trial that began in October, editorials repeatedly called for his conviction. Jurors were not sequestered and were often featured, along with their pictures and comments, in the media. When it was revealed that Sheppard had indeed been having an affair with a young laboratory technician at his hospital, a palpable motive for the crime seemed evident, and the prosecution called for a first-degree murder conviction, which meant death in the electric chair.

To no one's surprise, the jury found Sam Sheppard guilty, but it did not give the prosecution the verdict it wanted, convicting him instead of second-degree murder. On 21 December 1954, he was sentenced to life imprisonment. Two weeks later his mother committed suicide, and in late January his father died after suffering severe stomach hemorrhages; eight years later Marilyn Sheppard's father also committed suicide.

As Sam Sheppard began serving his life sentence in a state penitentiary near Columbus, defense attorneys filed an appeal that was turned down by the state court of appeals in July 1955. That denial was appealed all the way to the U.S. Supreme Court, where it was ultimately upheld. But Sheppard supporters were appalled by what they believed to be a miscarriage of justice, citing the way in which the trial was conducted and in particular the suppression of evidence by a noted criminologist that suggested the presence of a third person in the house on the night of the murder. They pressed for another appeal, and in 1962 the noted criminal defense attorney F. Lee Bailey was persuaded to become their lead attorney. Public interest in the case was renewed in the fall of 1963 when ABC Television began running a weekly drama series called *The Fugitive*, featuring a doctor wrongfully accused of his wife's murder and therefore continuously in flight from the police; most observers believed the show was based on the Sheppard case. Bailey's efforts eventually resulted in the overturning of Sheppard's conviction by a federal district court, which ruled that he had been denied a fair trial, and on 16 July 1964 he was released from prison.

In June 1966 the U.S. Supreme Court upheld the federal district court's decision, citing among other inequities the carnival-like atmosphere that prevailed during Sheppard's trial. Their pronouncement paved the way for a retrial, which began in late October 1966; three weeks later the jury found Sheppard not guilty of the murder of his wife. In the wake of his acquittal, reports continued to surface of possible suspects, but most of these were quickly dismissed as hoaxes, and Sheppard himself, perhaps understandably, now seemed uninterested in trying to solve his wife's murder. In the fall of 1967 he regained his license to practice osteopathic medicine, and with his second wife, Ariane Tebbenjohanns, a German national who had corresponded with him during his imprisonment, he settled in Youngstown, Ohio. He joined the staff of the Youngstown Osteopathic Hospital and worked there for a year, resigning in December 1968 after two civil wrongful death suits were brought against him and the hospital.

Sheppard then moved with his wife to Gahana, Ohio, near Columbus, and started a private medical practice. Hardly had he begun to fade from public attention when he emerged once again in the public eye, this time by giving public wrestling exhibitions with a newly acquired friend-turned-business-manager named George Strickland. Claiming that he was performing a public service by demonstrating a physical fitness routine for middle-aged men, he denied reports that he badly needed additional income and reportedly donated some of his earnings to the Sloan-Kettering Cancer Research Foundation. In October 1969, now living in Columbus, he divorced his second wife and married George Strickland's twenty-year-old daughter, Coleen.

Sheppard's unexpected death six months later—at his home in Columbus after complaining of nausea and apparently injuring himself in a fall—sparked a brief flurry of media attention. Over the following decades interest in the Sheppard case gradually abated, although authorities in Cleveland continued to receive reports from time to time of possible suspects. Then, in the fall of 1989, Sheppard's son, nicknamed Chip, announced that he was launching a new effort to solve his mother's murder and clear his father's name, motivated by new evidence linking a window washer at the Sheppard home to the crime. Interest in the case was again renewed in 1993, when a movie version of *The Fugitive* was released. After a decade of effort, including the exhumation of the bodies of both Sheppards, the securing of DNA evidence that some experts said absolved his father, and coauthoring a book about the case, Chip Sheppard succeeded in bringing suit against local authorities in Cleveland and Bay Village, alleging prejudicial mishandling of evidence. However, in April 2000 the jury declared that they could find no reason to declare Sam Sheppard innocent of his wife's murder. The Sheppard murder case remains officially unsolved.

• For biographical details of Sam Sheppard's life, see Cynthia L. Cooper and Sam Reese Sheppard, *Mockery of Justice: The True Story of the Sheppard Murder Case* (1995). Officials at Knollwood Cemetery in Cleveland, where Sheppard's ashes are now interred with those of his wife, provided Sheppard's birth date. See also Sheppard's memoir, *Endure and Conquer: My Twelve-Year Fight for Vindication* (1966). In addition, see Paul A. Holmes, *The Sheppard Murder Case* (1961), an account by a *Chicago Tribune* reporter that is credited with helping win a new trial for Sam Sheppard. For other accounts of the case, see Stephen Sheppard, *My Brother's Keeper* (1964), written by a brother of Sam Sheppard's with Paul Holmes; F. Lee Bailey, with Harvey Aronson, *The Defense Never Rests* (1971), which includes an extended account of Sheppard's successful retrial; and Jack Harrison Pollack, *Dr. Sam: An American Tragedy* (1972). See also "The Trial of Dr. Sam Sheppard" in Dorothy Kilgallen, *Murder One: Six On-the-Spot Murder Stories by America's Most Famous Crime Reporter* (1967). For an account of the lawsuit brought by Sam Reese Sheppard and its resolution, see Fox Butterfield, "Jury Rejects Innocence of Sheppard in '54 Murder," *New York Times*, 13 Apr. 2000. An obituary, together with a succinct summary of the Sheppard case, appears in the *New York Times*, 7 Apr. 1970.

ANN T. KEENE

SHERMAN, James S. (24 Oct. 1855–30 Oct. 1912), twenty-seventh vice president of the United States, was born James Schoolcraft Sherman in Utica, New York, the son of Richard Updike Schoolcraft Sherman, a newspaper editor and politician, and Mary Frances Sherman, whose maiden name was also Sherman. A distant relative of Union general William Tecumseh Sherman, he attended public schools in New Hartford (near Utica), the Utica Academy, and the Whitestone Seminary before entering Hamilton College. Although he was only an average student, Sherman excelled in public speaking and was popular among his peers. He won several class honors before receiving an A.B. in 1878 and an LL.B. in 1879. After gaining admittance to the bar, he entered the legal profession in the Utica firm of Cookinham, Gibson and Sherman, which was run by his brother-in-law Henry J. Cookinham. Long interested in political matters and intent on entering the political arena himself, he more or less restricted his legal activities to providing advice to clients in the business world. He married Carrie Babcock on 26 January 1881; they were to have three sons.

Acting against family tradition (his father had long been active in Democratic party circles), Sherman became a devoted Republican and, as such, became mayor of Utica—a normally Democratic town—in 1884. After declining to run for reelection, he won a seat in the U.S. House of Representatives in 1886 and served three terms. After a one-term hiatus, he was reelected to the House in 1892 and remained there for an additional sixteen years. As a congressman, Sherman (nicknamed "Sunny Jim" for his outgoing personality) gained a reputation as a parliamentarian without equal, which served him in good stead during his tenure on the Rules Committee. During his career in the House he also sat at various times on the Judiciary, Interstate and Foreign Commerce, and Civil Service committees, but he was perhaps best known for his work on the Committee on Indian Affairs, where he served for twelve years and was noted for his openly sympathetic attitude toward Native Americans. The Native American school at Riverside, California, was named Sherman Institute in his honor, and he became known within the Native American community as "Father Wau-be-ka-chuck" (Four Eyes—because of the glasses he wore).

Although respected by his colleagues as a hard worker in committee, Sherman took little initiative as a legislative leader. He made few speeches, and the list of legislation that he promoted during his twenty years on "the Hill" is remarkable for its brevity. Aside from his efforts on behalf of Native Americans, he was best known for presenting a committee report in 1896 that promoted federal financial assistance for a proposed canal across the Nicaraguan isthmus, for introducing a "false branding" bill that protected American cheese manufacturers, and for proposing the construction of a cable to the Philippines. Long aligned with the "regular Republican" faction and identified with such leaders as Thomas Reed and Joseph Cannon, Sherman remained content to follow their leadership.

During his time in Congress, Sherman pursued business interests at home, where he became president of the family-owned New Hartford Canning Company following his father's death in 1895; he also organized and presided over the Utica Trust and Deposit Company beginning in 1900. A mainstay in the organizational activities of the Republican party, he held the gavel at three New York state conventions (1895, 1900, and 1908) and was chairman of the national congressional campaign committee in 1906.

When the opportunity to claim the vice-presidential nomination presented itself in 1908, Sherman actively sought the post and gained the nomination with the assistance of "Uncle Joe" Cannon. Sherman and presidential nominee William Howard Taft swept to victory in the fall, but Sherman's joy was brief; he was diagnosed with Bright's disease shortly after he was inaugurated. Although Sherman had successfully controlled a previous kidney disorder four years earlier by careful attention to diet, his latest affliction proved harder to overcome. As vice president he generally received positive reviews for his performance of both professional and social duties, yet his health did cause him to relinquish the podium of the Senate on at least one occasion. In 1912 he wanted medical advice before seeking renomination. While his physician equivocated, Sherman overtaxed his strength when he met with a campaign committee at his home in late August and never fully recovered. He died in Utica during a campaign that saw a divided Republican party fall to the Democratic ticket of Woodrow Wilson and Thomas Marshall.

James S. Sherman's career illustrates how a professional politician can rise to high office without having a notable record of accomplishment. Sheer longevity and skill as a parliamentarian made him an important figure in the House of Representatives, and as a party loyalist he devoted his energies to committee work and convention management. Thus positioned to be nominated as vice president, he posed little threat of overshadowing the head of the Republican ticket in 1908, William Howard Taft. The disabling effects of chronic illness ensured that, like most vice presidents in American history, Sherman would play a minor role in the executive branch of government.

• Sherman's papers are held at the New York Public Library. Literature on Sherman is sparse, but he does receive mention in James E. Watson, *As I Knew Them* (1936), and Champ Clark, *My Quarter Century of American Politics* (2 vols., 1920). Additional information is in *James Schoolcraft Sherman: Memorial Addresses Delivered at a Joint Session of the Senate and the House* (1913), 62d Congress, 3d Session, Document no. 1134. Obituaries are in the *New York Herald* and the *New York Tribune*, both 31 Oct. 1912.

EDWARD L. LACH, JR.

SHOEMAKER, Gene (28 Apr. 1928–18 July 1997), geologist and planetary scientist, was born Eugene Merle Shoemaker in Los Angeles, California, to George Estel Shoemaker, teacher, farmer, trucker, and studio grip, and Muriel May Scott Shoemaker, schoolteacher. Gene spent his early years in Buffalo, New York, during the school year and in Wyoming during the summers. During his adolescence his family moved to Los Angeles, where he completed high school in two years to graduate at age sixteen. In 1944 he entered the California Institute of Technology in Pasadena in an accelerated wartime program. He graduated from Caltech with a B.S. in geology in 1947, after two and two-thirds years, and then stayed on to get a master's degree the following year.

Shoemaker became interested in rocks and minerals as an eight-year-old and followed this inclination all his life. He went to work for the U.S. Geological Survey in 1948 in the uranium exploration program in Grand Junction, Colorado, and in his spare time he worked on the geology of salt domes, planning to use this work for a thesis. Taking leave from the USGS to continue his education at Princeton University, he received another master's degree in 1954 and ultimately his Ph.D. in 1960 with a thesis on Meteor Crater, Arizona. He had been working on a variety of projects for the USGS during the intervening years and had begun studies of impact and nuclear craters, combining field mapping, cratering experiments, and theory. His early research on the structure and mechanics of craters was followed by the discovery at Meteor Crater, with E. C. T. Chao, of coesite as a diagnostic tool in distinguishing impact.

Field geology remained Shoemaker's primary enthusiasm throughout his life, but he developed an interest in the Moon while still at Caltech, where he watched the polishing of the mirror for the huge 200-

inch telescope. After graduation, he followed with increasing enthusiasm the development of rockets and realized at the age of twenty that space exploration of the planets, especially the Moon, would occur in his professional lifetime. He yearned to be the first man to set foot on the Moon, reasoning that a geologist would be the logical choice to do so. Shoemaker directed his career on a path to make himself qualified by the time astronauts were selected. When the Russians put up the first satellite, Sputnik, in 1957, the space age began—and Shoemaker was scrambling to be ready.

In August 1951, after his first year at Princeton, Shoemaker married Carolyn Spellmann, the sister of a Caltech roommate. Thus began a 46-year partnership and collaboration, as he shared his work and his dreams with her. Three children, a son and two daughters, were born, in 1953, 1955, and 1957.

When the National Aeronautics and Space Administration (NASA) was formed in 1958, Shoemaker set out to get a project of Moon-mapping started within the Geological Survey. By 1960 he had organized a new field of study called "astrogeology" and then established a branch for this study within the Survey in 1961. As he moved into space studies, he produced fundamental papers on the impact geology of the Moon and the nature of the craters found there. Shoemaker found that by knowing the flux of asteroids and comets impacting the Earth and counting the craters formed by them at different ages in the Earth's history, we can extrapolate a cratering rate to the Moon to provide a lunar time scale of the surfaces. This method measures the relationship between crater density and diameter and allows us to infer relative ages on surfaces not only of the Moon but of the other planets. In 1962 he also began a long-term association with Caltech, teaching one quarter a year; he gave the first course on astrogeology there.

With the goal of getting science into the national space program (and himself to the Moon), Shoemaker went from the Survey to NASA headquarters in Washington, D.C., in the fall of 1962 to set up the Manned Space Sciences Division at NASA and serve as its interim director. During this time, the first selection of scientist astronauts was made by a National Academy of Sciences committee chaired by Shoemaker. Unfortunately, he had been diagnosed with Addison's disease and could no longer be considered for space flight. He did succeed in starting a geology training program for the astronauts while in Washington. After nine months there, he returned to the Geological Survey, moving with his family to Flagstaff, Arizona, the new headquarters for the USGS Branch of Astrogeology.

Shoemaker became a co-investigator on the television experiment for Project Ranger (1961–1965) and principal investigator on the television experiment for Project Surveyor (1963–1968). Next, he became principal investigator of the geological field investigation in Apollo lunar landings (1965–1970).

At this point, ready for a change, he decided to leave astrogeology and go to Caltech as chairman of the Division of Earth and Planetary Sciences (1969–1972). He continued as a professor of geology there until 1985. Still, he could not forget his earlier interest when he was offered the opportunity to serve as a co-investigator on the television experiment of Project Voyager (1978–1990). His last formal contribution to the space program came as the science team leader on the Clementine Mission (1993–1995).

Interested in the objects that seemed responsible for most of the craters found on the solid bodies in our solar system, Shoemaker began a program at Palomar Observatory with Eleanor Helin in 1973 to search for Earth-crossing asteroids. In 1982 that program ended, but for twelve years starting in 1983, Gene and Carolyn Shoemaker conducted the Palomar Asteroid and Comet Search program on the eighteen-inch Schmidt telescope. They found many near-Earth and Mars-crossing asteroids and thirty-two comets, enabling Gene to estimate collision rates for small bodies impacting the Earth, Moon, and planets. Together with David Levy, they discovered Comet Shoemaker-Levy 9, which impacted Jupiter in 1994. Perhaps the most important result of this collision was mankind's realization that small bodies in space do, indeed, impact planets, and that Earth is not exempt from impact.

From 1984 until his death, Gene and Carolyn Shoemaker conducted a study in Australia of impact craters and ancient impact structures. They mapped them, studied the structural differences, made gravity and magnetic surveys, and searched for meteorites and impact glass in an effort to prove their impact origin. In 1997, shortly after arriving in Australia for more field work, Gene Shoemaker died in the outback from another kind of impact—a vehicle collision.

Over a long professional career, Shoemaker received many honors, including the National Medal of Science. His greatest honor came after his death, when a small portion of his ashes was sent by NASA to the Moon aboard *Lunar Prospector.*

A brilliant scientist, an inspiring teacher, an innovator, he is remembered as an articulate and enthusiastic proponent of field geology and space science, manned and unmanned. Above all, he is remembered by many as a warm human being with a deep belief in the capabilities of each of us.

• An interview with Eugene Shoemaker by Shirley Cohen in 1995, containing information about his early years until 1963, can be found in the Archives at the California Institute of Technology, Pasadena, Cal. *Science Year*, the World Book Science Annual, 1972, contains a profile by Joseph N. Bell on Shoemaker and his family with pictures. Richard Preston's book on the Palomar Observatory, *First Light*, has an amusing account of the Shoemakers' observing program. The National Geographic video *Asteroids: Deadly Impact*, which first appeared on NBC Television in 1997, is essentially the story of Gene Shoemaker. Obituaries appeared in many newspapers in July 1997, followed by memorial tributes in astronomical and geological journals. Among them were obituaries by Susan W. Kieffer, *Science*, 8 Aug. 1997,

p. 77, and Thomas Ahrens in *Nature*, 11 Sept. 1997, p. 132, and a memorial tribute by Bevan M. French in *Meteoritics and Planetary Science* 32 (1997): 985–86.

CAROLYN S. SHOEMAKER

SHUSTER, Joe. *See* Siegel, Jerry, and Joe Shuster.

SIDNEY, Sylvia (8 Aug. 1910–2 July 1999), actress, was born Sophia Kosow in the Bronx, New York, to Victor Kosow, a Jewish immigrant, and Rebecca Saperstein Kosow, who was of Romanian extraction. After her parents' divorce, Sophia Kosow was adopted by her mother's second husband, Dr. Sigmund Sidney, a dental surgeon. Sidney dropped out of New York's Washington Irving High School to attend the Theater Guild School in Manhattan.

Sidney's professional debut came in 1926 in a Washington, D.C., production of *The Challenge of Youth*. This was followed by *The Squall* (1926), a long-running Broadway play about Gypsies, seduction, and special effects, and by leading roles in *Crime* (1927), a gangland melodrama, and *Gods of the Lightning* (1928), a Maxwell Anderson–Harold Hickerson polemic on social injustice suggested by the Sacco and Vanzetti case. After a small role in a crime film for Fox (*Through Different Eyes*) and a season with George Cukor's stock company in Rochester, New York, Sidney returned to Broadway. Among her four plays in 1929–1930 was *Bad Girl*. Her role as a pregnant unmarried mother impressed Benjamin P. Schulberg, the production head of Paramount Pictures. Schulberg's novelist son Budd has written that it was his mother Adeline who brought Sidney to her husband's attention.

After replacing Clara Bow opposite Gary Cooper in Paramount's *City Streets* (1931), directed by Rouben Mamoulian, her mentor at the Theater Guild School, the dark, petite Sidney found herself a star at the age of twenty. By now the lover of Schulberg, she was cast in "prestige" films adapted from literary masterworks and guided by Paramount's best directors. According to Ephraim Katz, "There was an intense, vulnerable, waiflike quality about her that made her the perfect screen heroine of the Depression era . . ." (*Film Encyclopedia*, 2d ed., p. 1249).

Directed by Josef von Sternberg, Sidney played the doomed, pregnant factory worker Roberta Alden in the first screen version of Theodore Dreiser's *An American Tragedy* (1931). In playwright Elmer Rice's *Street Scene* (1931) she was a slum-trapped adulterous mother shot by her husband. She was a nonsinging Cio-Cio San in *Madame Butterfly* (1932), a film that apparently led to a brand of Japanese condoms being named "Sylvia Sidneys." Once more essaying a Dreiser adaptation, Sidney "suffered beautifully" as another fallen woman in the naturalistic *Jennie Gerhardt* (1933). During these years, she ranked at Paramount alongside Marlene Dietrich, Carole Lombard, Miriam Hopkins, and Claudette Colbert.

Sidney was freed from her Paramount contract in 1935 as well as from Schulberg; in that year she was married to publisher Bennett Cerf for eight months. Nevertheless, she continued to work with the best. Her only British film appearance was in Alfred Hitchcock's *Sabotage* (1936), based on Joseph Conrad's novel *The Secret Agent*. The expatriate German director Fritz Lang specifically requested Sidney for his first (and favorite) American film, *Fury* (1936), an expressionistic study of the self-destructive legacy of revenge in which she starred opposite Spencer Tracy. In Lang's *You Only Live Once* (1937), a nightmarish contemporary tale of doomed, flawed innocents on the run from injustice, Sidney portrayed the wife of a petty criminal (Henry Fonda). At Sidney's request, Lang directed *You and Me* (1938), a sardonic film interspersed with chanted "songs" by Kurt Weill, in which she was cast alongside George Raft in an odd tale of two paroled ex-convicts. Henry Hathaway's *The Trail of the Lonesome Pine* (1936) put Sidney in the middle of a mountain feud, and for William Wyler she was the long-suffering sister of a juvenile delinquent in the 1937 film version of Sidney Kingsley's play *Dead End*.

After quitting Hollywood—because she was unhappy with herself, she later said—Sidney gradually left behind her iconic status as Depression victim. Returning to the stage, she was rarely out of work. Her Broadway return as "the other woman" in the Theater Guild's production of Ben Hecht's *To Quito And Back* (1937) did not redeem an overwritten play. In 1938 she married the Group Theater actor Luther Adler. They had one child and were divorced in 1946. In 1939 Sidney performed with Franchot Tone and Elia Kazan in the Group Theater's production of Irwin Shaw's melodramatic *The Gentle People*. For many months in 1941–1942, as a replacement for Judith Evelyn of the original cast, she played a wife driven to the edge of madness in *Angel Street*, the popular Patrick Hamilton drama otherwise known as *Gaslight*. Briefly back in Hollywood, she appeared in another social drama, *The Wagons Roll at Night* (1941). After further touring, she played the Eurasian girlfriend of the James Cagney character in the anti-Japanese film *Blood on the Sun* (1945). In 1947 Sidney married publicist-producer Carleton Alsop; this childless marriage also ended in divorce.

In the 1950s and 1960s Sidney, no longer a waif, found a home in touring versions of classic plays, including *The Trojan Women*, *The Little Foxes*, *The Importance of Being Earnest* (as Lady Bracknell), *The Rivals* (as Mrs. Malaprop), *She Stoops to Conquer*, *The Dark at the Top of the Stairs*, and *Cabaret* (as Fräulein Schneider). A rare film role came as Fantine in *Les Misérables* (1953). The golden age of American television drama afforded a number of roles. These included "The Helen Morgan Story" for "Playhouse 90" and Paddy Chayefsky's "Catch My Boy on Sunday" for "The Philco Playhouse." In 1962 she was nominated for an Emmy for "Madman," an episode of the liberal law series "The Defenders." A humorous, witty person finally freed to be funny onstage, Sidney in 1963 portrayed Mrs. Kolowicz, mother of the stagestruck klutz played by Alan Arkin, in the Broadway adaptation of Carl Reiner's novel *Enter Laughing.*

During the early 1960s Sidney became interested in needlepoint and wrote *The Sylvia Sidney Needlepoint Book* (1968) and *Question and Answer Book on Needlepoint* (1974). She appeared in more television and in 1973 resumed her film career opposite Joanne Woodward as the mother (with a voice of "velvet sandpaper") in *Summer Wishes, Winter Dreams,* a tale of mid- and late-life truth telling. The role earned Sidney a National Board of Review award and an Oscar nomination for best supporting actress. In 1977 she had a supporting role in the film *I Never Promised You a Rose Garden* and returned to Broadway as the tenacious, vengeful landlady, Mrs. Wire, in Tennessee Williams's autobiographical *Vieux Carré.*

In 1978 Sidney received the Festival of Americas lifetime achievement award and in 1979 a special award (for a "long and distinguished career") from the Chicago Art Institute. In 1985 she won raves in a revival of Moss Hart's comedy of 1930s Hollywood, *Light Up the Sky.* Her supporting role in the television AIDS drama "An Early Frost" won a Golden Globe Award in 1986. After the death of her son from amyotrophic lateral sclerosis, Sidney served as an ALS volunteer.

In her later years Sidney demonstrated a gleeful, knowing talent for histrionics in such films as *Damien: Omen II* (1978), *Hammett* (1982), and two Tim Burton films, *Beetlejuice* (1988, as the guardian of the gates of Purgatory) and *Mars Attacks* (1997, as a crusty, wheelchair-bound social worker). In 1998 she signed a five-year contract to play Clia, a flaky travel agent, in a new version of the television series "Fantasy Island." An inveterate smoker, Sidney died of throat cancer in New York.

• Budd Schulberg, *Moving Pictures: Memories of a Hollywood Prince* (1981), gives a colorful and impressionistic account of Sidney's involvement with his father. Sidney's Broadway career is generally chronicled in Gerald Bordman, *American Theatre: A Chronicle of Comedy and Drama, 1914–1930* (1995) and *American Theater: A Chronicle of Comedy and Drama, 1930–1969* (1996). *The American Film Institute Catalog of Feature Films: 1931–1940* (1993) goes well beyond listing her films. Excellent discussions (by Fritz Lang and various critics) of *Fury* are in Don Whittemore and Philip Alan Cecchettini, *Passport to Hollywood: Film Immigrants Anthology* (1976). Among many obituaries of Sidney perhaps the most eloquent is Ronald Bergan's in the (London) *Guardian,* 6 July 1999.

JAMES ROSS MOORE

SIEGEL, Jerry (17 Oct. 1914–28 Jan. 1996), and **Joe Shuster** (10 July 1914–30 July 1992), a writer and an artist respectively, were born Jerome Siegel and Joseph Shuster in Cleveland, Ohio, and Toronto, Canada. (Their parents' names do not appear in readily available sources of information.) In 1924 Shus-

ter's family moved to Cleveland, and his love of American newspaper comic strips made him determined to become a cartoonist. His first work appeared in school publications as editorial cartoons and amateur comic strips drawn under the influence of popular adventure strips of the time.

In 1930 Shuster met Jerry Siegel, an aspiring writer, when they were working on the Glenville High School newspaper. Their first collaboration was a feature called "Goober the Mighty," which parodied superhuman fictional heroes. Their first formulation of a character called Superman was for a mimeographed fan magazine they produced starting in 1932 called *Science Fiction.* The issue for January 1933 contained a story called "The Reign of the Superman," about an evil figure, the product of a scientific experiment gone wrong, who tries to dominate the world.

The young creators decided to produce a comic strip for newspaper syndication in 1933, but their first efforts were turned down. During a sleepless summer night, Siegel dreamed up the idea of a man from another planet who could run faster and leap higher than ordinary human beings, perform extraordinary feats of strength, and bounce bullets off his chest. He related his concept to Shuster who, after several efforts, gave the character a handsome physical form and dressed him in a colorful red-and-blue costume consisting of tights and a cape with a large "S" shield across the chest.

While the concept was original, behind it was a wealth of cultural influences: the mythic figures Samson, Hercules, and Beowulf; romantic fictional characters such as the Three Musketeers and the costumed Scarlet Pimpernel; science fiction texts by Jules Verne, H. G. Wells—and especially Philip Wylie's novel *Gladiator,* which featured a superhuman protagonist; adventure characters from the comic strips, such as Tarzan, Buck Rogers, and the sailor with superstrength, Popeye; and the swashbuckling costume films of Douglas Fairbanks: *Robin Hood* and *The Mark of Zorro.* Although Shuster had some formal training at the Cleveland School of Art and the John Huntington Polytechnical Institute in Cleveland, he admitted that it was the movies that inspired the composition and design of his visual narratives based on Siegel's texts. Bold, full-bodied, and heavily outlined figures and fast-paced action characterized Shuster's style, which would influence an entire generation of comic book artists.

Superman was unlike previous superheroes, however, in that he was an alien from another planet, was devoted to truth and justice on earth, and assumed the appearance of a mild-mannered newspaper reporter named Clark Kent as a disguise. An extra ingredient that gave the story charm was a reporter named Lois Lane who shunned the advances of Clark Kent because she was enamored of Superman. This triangle of unrequited love provided many interesting plot situations. Partly a product of their own adolescent fantasies, as shy intellectuals unable to compete with male students who were successful with girls and sports, Siegel and Shuster imagined the kind of person they would like to be. Cartoonist Jules Feiffer has suggested too that Superman was the ultimate assimilationist fantasy in that both Siegel and Shuster found themselves in the Midwest at a time of widespread anti-Semitism and through the creation of Superman found a way to alleviate their own sense of being alien or "other." Either way, thousands of young male readers found it easy to identify with the plight of Clark Kent and enjoyed imagining that they too could set aside their insecure selves and become more like the "Man of Steel."

Originally intended as a newspaper comic strip, the feature found no takers among the syndicates, but it was finally purchased for publication in a new comic book series under development by Major Malcolm Wheeler-Nicholson called *Action Comics.* Earlier comic books had consisted entirely of reprinted comic strips, but Wheeler-Nicholson began to publish original material in such popular titles as *More Fun* and *Detective Comics.* It was the enormous popularity of the appearance of Superman in the first issue of *Action* (June 1938) that assured the continued success of the comic book, inspired thousands of titles and super-hero characters to come, and helped establish an industry.

Siegel and Shuster sold the rights to the first story and the character for $130 (thirteen pages at $10 per page) under the typical work-for-hire contract, not realizing that their creation would eventually be worth a fortune to the firm that became DC Comics under the ownership of Harry Donenfeld and Jack Liebowitz. In the beginning the creators themselves produced the stories for Superman and other features, but eventually they had to hire assistants and maintain a shop in Cleveland to keep up with the demand. A Superman comic strip began newspaper syndication in January 1939, a separate Superman comic book appeared that summer, a radio show debuted in February 1940, and a beautifully produced series of animated films from Fleischer Studios began release in 1941. Superman was earning Donenfeld and Liebowitz hundreds of thousands of dollars.

In 1945, the first of two widely distributed Superman serials starring Kirk Alyn appeared in movie theatres. A popular television series, *The Adventures of Superman,* with George Reeves began in 1951; a musical called *It's a Bird, It's a Plane, It's Superman* was produced on Broadway in 1966 but lasted for only 128 performances. The first of a highly successful series of films starring Christopher Reeve, *Superman: The Movie,* was released in 1978 to be followed by sequels in 1980, 1983, and 1987. Another television series in 1993, *Lois & Clark: The New Adventures of Superman,* proved to be a critical and popular success. In 1992 one issue of the *Superman* comic book devoted to what was reported as the death of Superman sold more than four million copies, one of the best-selling issues in comic book history. These and other merchandising efforts throughout the years would earn millions.

In 1947 Siegel and Shuster, then living in New York, filed a lawsuit there against the publisher to regain ownership of Superman. Unfortunately, they lost the case and were barred from further involvement with their creation. Although they developed other characters and titles during their careers—most notably a humorous costumed hero named Funnyman in a short-lived comic book series and newspaper feature in 1948—the kind of creative fulfillment that came with Superman was something they would never experience again. Except for odd jobs, they became almost destitute. A second lawsuit, which continued from 1963 to 1975, was also decided in favor of the publisher. By then a group of fellow cartoonists and creators, led by Neal Adams and Jerry Robinson, organized a public campaign on their behalf, and the publisher, under new management, had a change of heart. They were given in 1976 an annual stipend, benefits, and an agreement that all future products would carry their names as the creators of Superman.

Siegel was married twice, first to a woman named Bela, with whom he had a son. In 1948 they divorced and he married Joanne Carter, who was an artist's model for Shuster. They had one daughter.

In their final years, living near each other in Los Angeles, Siegel and Shuster had the pleasure of receiving tributes from many fans, former readers, and cultural historians, who celebrated the importance of their contribution to American mythology.

• In the absence of biographies of either Jerry Siegel or Joe Shuster, information can be gleaned from a variety of secondary sources, the most useful of which include Jerry Bails and Hames Ware, eds., *The Who's Who of American Comic Books* (1973–1976); Dennis Dooley and Gary Engle, eds., *Superman at Fifty: The Persistence of a Legend* (1987); Mike Benton, *Masters of Imagination: The Comic Book Artists' Hall of Fame* (1994); Les Daniels, *DC Comics: Sixty Years of the World's Favorite Comic Book Heroes* (1995); Robert C. Harvey, *The Art of the Comic Book: An Aesthetic History* (1996); and Daniels, *Superman: The Complete History* (1998). Jules Feiffer provided a personal memoir in "The Minsk Theory of Krypton," *New York Times Magazine,* 29 Dec. 1996. Obituaries are in the *New York Times,* for Shuster on 3 Aug. 1992 and for Siegel on 31 Jan. 1996.

M. THOMAS INGE

SIGMAN, Carl (24 Sept. 1909–28 Sept. 2000), songwriter, was born in Brooklyn, the elder son of Harry Sigman, a manufacturer of ladies' shoes, and Rae Bresson Sigman. After graduating from Thomas Jefferson High School in New York, Sigman received his bachelor of laws degree from New York University's law school and was admitted to the New York State bar. He was not happy in this kind of work, however, and gave up practicing law after a year. While teaching piano and working as a typist, he started writing songs. He later said that he had taken every opportunity to hang out at New York's Brill Building, "where all the songwriters were," adding that the great lyricist Johnny Mercer had told him, "A band has 15 musicians who can write a tune or one person who can write a lyric. You've got a flair for it; you'll get songs published." Although Sigman did not abandon composing, he made his living for the next six decades mainly from writing lyrics.

Sigman's songwriting career did not prosper until 1940, when Glenn Miller's orchestra turned "Pennsylvania 6-5000" into an international hit. The lyric was simplicity itself, being almost nothing but the repeated title—which was the telephone number of New York's Hotel Pennsylvania, where the great bands of the era regularly performed. Because Miller's popularity endured beyond his death in 1944, many of his recordings, including "Pennsylvania 6-5000," achieved the status of "standards." Sigman was not ordinarily a writer of standards. Always alert to trends or fads, he was more interested in finding something new and fresh that would catch a listener's ear, if only for a few weeks. Unlike some of his more flamboyant Tin Pan Alley contemporaries, however, he searched for simple "conversational" ways to express ideas and emotions, and because of those qualities many of his songs, frequently revived after decades of neglect, achieved a kind of permanence.

During World War II Sigman flew in the glider division of the 82nd Airborne, winning the Bronze Star. He wrote the division's official song, "The All American Soldier." Back in civilian life, he began to produce hit songs. In 1947 one of his lyrics written in collaboration with Bob Hilliard that had already become popular on radio and recordings was added to Sigman and Hilliard's Broadway revue for Paul and Grace Hartman, *Angel in the Wings*. Sung by Elaine Stritch it regularly stopped the show. The song, "Civilization," popularly known by its opening lines, "Bongo, Bongo, Bongo, I Don't Want to Leave the Congo," argued that the jungle was a better place to live than modern Manhattan; it received the honor of having inspired a number of parodies.

In 1948 Sigman married Terry Eleanor Berkowitz, who was working for Louis Prima when Sigman dropped by to watch Prima recording "Civilization." The couple would have three children and remain married until Sigman's death. Not long after "Civilization" came his melodramatic "Ballerina," which became a surprise hit for singing bandleader Vaughn Monroe and continued to be recorded for decades thereafter. The seriocomic "Enjoy Yourself, It's Later than You Think" (1950) illustrated Sigman's habit of picking up chunks of wisdom from everyday talk.

In 1951 Sigman was asked to turn the wistful "Melody in A Major," a 1912 "classical" composition by Charles Dawes, who later became Herbert Hoover's vice president, into a popular song. The result—Sigman said he had had to remove a few high notes—was "It's All in the Game," a hit in 1951 and again in 1958. Like many of Sigman's familiar songs, "It's All in the Game" continued to resurface in soundtracks for film and television dramas and comedies. Some popped up in advertising commercials—for example, "Enjoy Yourself" during the 2000 Olympic Games. A 1952 venture with Hilliard, writing the score for the

Hollywood musical *She's Back on Broadway*, proved unsuccessful, but in 1953 Sigman set words to "Ebb Tide," an evocative composition by Robert Maxwell that had become an instrumental hit for the sweeping strings of Briton Frank Chacksfield's orchestra. Sigman's version, beginning with "First the tide rushes in . . . ," was repeatedly recorded and proved even more popular than the original.

From 1955 through 1958 Sigman achieved a kind of cult immortality among television viewers with the galloping theme for the British "Robin Hood" series starring Richard Greene ("Robin Hood, Robin Hood, riding through the glen. . . ."). In 1955 Perry Como began his long-running television variety hour with Sigman's "Dream Along with Me"("I'm on My Way to a Star"), which became the singer's signature. Sigman's "A Marshmallow World" became another staple of Como's repertoire. For the next two decades Sigman's lyrical output continued along similar lines but with an increased number of foreign sources, such as the sentimental "Arrivederci Roma" and including "What Now, My Love?" (1966), whose challenging opening line—the title itself—perfectly matched the insistently driving melody. In 1970 he added a lyric to Francis Lai's theme for the notoriously sentimental film *Love Story*. Sigman later said that the melody had baffled him, that he had come home to talk it over with his wife and begun by saying, "Where do I begin?" This became the opening line of the lyric.

Often overlooked amid these highly popular concoctions were songs that were recorded by some of his era's best jazz vocalists, including "If You Could See Me Now" to the soaring melody of bebop-era composer Tadd Dameron, introduced by Sarah Vaughan in the 1950s and revived in 1997 by Natalie Cole, and "Crazy, He Calls Me," a late Billie Holiday classic. By 1972, when Sigman was inducted into the Songwriters Hall of Fame, popular music had come to be dominated by successive varieties of rock and roll. Sigman told a later interviewer that "with the advent of rap music [in the 1980s] I became totally out of it."

Sigman died in Manhasset, New York. It is not inflating the significance of popular songwriting to note that Sigman's art was harmonious with the poetic practice of his century—recognizing and highlighting the eloquence of the colloquial American idiom.

• Mrs. Terry Sigman of Delray Beach, Florida, who is the holder of Sigman's papers and manuscripts, as well as Sigmanson Music, his publisher, provided many family details that rounded out this entry. The files of the American Society of Composers, Authors and Publishers (ASCAP) contain full listings of Sigman's work. A particularly full and warm obituary is Myrna Oliver's in the *Los Angeles Times*, 4 Oct. 2000.

JAMES ROSS MOORE

SINATRA, Frank (12 Dec. 1915–14 May 1998), singer and actor, was born Francis Albert Sinatra in Hoboken, New Jersey, the son of Anthony Martin Sinatra, a captain with the Hoboken Fire Department, and Natalie Catherine "Dolly" Garavente Sinatra, a Democratic Party committeewoman. The child of Italian immigrants, Sinatra was born in a four-story tenement on Gordon Street in Hoboken's "Little Italy" section. The thirteen-and-a-half-pound baby almost died at birth, and the doctor's forceps used to extricate him from his diminutive mother scarred his ear and neck, wounds he bore for his entire life. The baby was baptized on 2 April 1916 at St. Francis Church in Hoboken. Because his working-class parents were busy trying to earn a living, Sinatra grew up a lonely boy who spent a great deal of time alone or with his grandparents and other relatives. He attended David E. Rue Junior High School and A. J. Demarest High School, from which he never graduated. Although his mother had hoped that he would be the first person in the family to attend college and was disappointed that he did not finish high school, she encouraged his ambition to be a singer. His father, on the other hand, was opposed and insisted that he should find a job. The young Sinatra worked briefly as a truck driver for a newspaper, a riveter in a Hoboken shipyard, and a fruit hauler. By 1932, he had decided that he wanted to be a professional singer, and, with $65 borrowed from his parents, he bought a portable sound system—consisting of a microphone and speaker—and some sheet-music arrangements.

Inspired by the success of his idol Bing Crosby, Sinatra wanted to become a crooner with a distinctive style. He began developing that style by singing evenings and weekends at nightclubs, roadhouses, social clubs, Democratic party meetings, and other venues, often for little or no money. In the summer of 1934, Sinatra, nineteen years old, met the young woman who would become his first wife, Nancy Rose Barbato, age seventeen, in Long Branch on the New Jersey Shore. As a condition for being allowed to continue seeing Nancy, Sinatra agreed to work for her father, Mike, a plastering contractor in Jersey City, but he soon left to pursue his ambition to be a singer. The couple was married on 4 February 1939 at Our Lady of Sorrows Church in Jersey City. They subsequently had three children—Nancy (born 8 June 1940), Franklin Wayne (born 10 Jan. 1944), and Christina (born 20 June 1948). The marriage ended in 1950 owing to Sinatra's love affair with actress Ava Gardner.

On 8 September 1935 Sinatra and a Hoboken singing group called the Three Flashes auditioned separately for a spot on "Major Bowes and His Original Amateur Hour," a popular NBC radio show. Each won, and Bowes decided to merge them into a single act called the Hoboken Four. When the group appeared on the show a week later, the audience's enthusiastic response prompted Bowes to bring them back for several weeks, to include them in two of his movie shorts, and finally to send them on a national tour with one of his amateur companies. After a short time on the road, however, Sinatra decided to leave the group. He was homesick, and he also began having conflicts with the other members of the quartet because audiences were paying much more attention to him than to the group as a whole. Most of all, though, he really wanted to be a solo act.

Back home in New Jersey in the spring of 1936, the young singer scraped around for singing jobs, doing mostly evening and weekend gigs at weddings, dances, and roadhouses. At the same time, he visited radio stations in Jersey City and New York, and he performed on the air, often being paid nothing or only carfare. Sinatra often spent time at clubs in New York City studying the singers who performed there; he also worked with a voice coach, John Quinlan, in an attempt to lose his New Jersey accent. A break came in 1938 when he auditioned for and won a spot as a singing waiter at the Rustic Cabin roadhouse in Englewood, New Jersey. He waited tables and sang with the house bands, earning little money but gaining experience and exposure. It was here, in 1939, that Harry James, who had left Benny Goodman's orchestra to form his own, discovered Sinatra and hired him to sing with his band for $75 a week. His first gig was on 30 June 1939 at the Hippodrome Theatre in Baltimore, and that summer was spent touring the East Coast. On 13 July 1939 Sinatra made his first professional recordings with James. In all, he made only ten recordings with the band during his six-month tenure, including one that would serve him in good stead a few years hence, "All or Nothing at All." When Sinatra approached James in late 1939 about leaving the orchestra to join Tommy Dorsey's popular band, replacing Jack Leonard as Dorsey's key vocalist, James tore up their contract and allowed the young man to pursue his ambitions. Sinatra would remain forever grateful to Harry James for giving him a chance to gain experience and then releasing him when a better opportunity presented itself.

The earliest radio aircheck (recorded rehearsal session) featuring Sinatra and the Dorsey band occurred on 25 January 1940 in Rockford, Illinois, though his first formal appearance with the band came at the Lyric Theatre in Indianapolis on 2 February. The day before the Indianapolis appearance, Sinatra was in Chicago making the first of his eighty-three RCA recordings with Dorsey. Almost immediately, Sinatra's career began to benefit from the national exposure that the Dorsey band afforded him, and only a few months later the band, with Sinatra and the Pied Pipers on vocals, had their first number-one hit with Ruth Lowe's touching tribute to her late husband, "I'll Never Smile Again." In many ways, Sinatra's two-year tenure with the Dorsey band was a veritable apprenticeship. Because of Dorsey's great popularity, Sinatra worked constantly, appearing in concerts, on the radio, on recordings, and in two Hollywood feature films: *Las Vegas Nights* (Paramount, 1941) and *Ship Ahoy* (MGM, 1942). Not only did these experiences give him exposure, but he also learned a great deal from Dorsey himself. One of the celebrated characteristics of Sinatra's singing is his breath control, the ability to sustain a long melodic line in ballads, and this was a technique that he learned by watching Tommy Dorsey play the trombone. Dorsey would blow up to sixteen musical bars by "sneaking" breaths out of the corner of his mouth, giving him a smooth, fluid sound. Sinatra imitated the trombonist and also worked to develop his lung capacity by swimming underwater in public pools for long periods, singing lyrics to himself. As a result, he could sustain lines much longer than most singers.

By the end of 1941, his unique soulful style of ballad singing was catching on from coast to coast, and Sinatra again began to entertain the idea of going solo, an ambition he had had since his days with the Hoboken Four. The United States had entered World War II in December 1941, and Sinatra was declared unfit for military service by the draft board because of a punctured eardrum, an injury sustained at birth. Instead of going off to war, therefore, he focused on his career. On 19 January 1942 he recorded four solo sides with Dorsey arranger Axel Stordahl, including, propitiously, two songs with which he would be associated for his entire career, "Night and Day" and "The Song Is You." Tommy Dorsey was displeased with Sinatra's ambition, and when the 26-year-old singer told him of his plans to go solo that year, Dorsey predicted that Sinatra would fail, as had been the case with many big-band singers once they detached themselves from the larger units that nurtured them. More significantly, Dorsey declared that he planned to hold Sinatra to the terms of their contract—more than a third of the singer's earnings for life. Eventually, attorneys from Music Corporation of America, Sinatra's new publicists, intervened, and the contract was bought out. The singer made his final appearance with Tommy Dorsey in a radio broadcast on 3 September 1942. Two ironies were evident in that broadcast. First, Sinatra introduced Dick Haymes, his successor as Dorsey's "boy singer," the very same singer who succeeded him when he left Harry James's band in late 1939. Then, as a farewell gesture, Sinatra sang not a Dorsey tune but "The Song Is You," one of the solo sides he had recorded earlier that year. Despite the apparent acrimony in their parting, Sinatra eventually made his peace with Dorsey, even recording a tribute album, *I Remember Tommy* (1961), some twenty years later.

In October 1942 Sinatra was heard on two CBS radio programs, one called "Reflections," and the other "Songs by Sinatra," but little else was happening in his career. It appeared that Tommy Dorsey's prediction of the singer's doom as a solo performer might be coming true. Everything, however, changed as the end of the year drew near. On 30 December 1942 Benny Goodman's orchestra was appearing at the Paramount Theatre in New York City, and Sinatra was booked as an "extra added attraction." No one could predict what would happen at that performance. When Sinatra was introduced, 5,000 screaming teenagers greeted him onstage. No singer had ever received such a reception, and the stunned Benny Goodman, hearing the squeals of the crowd, turned and asked, "What the hell was that?" Thus was born the first international entertainment "phenomenon"

of modern times. Beginning on that day and lasting through much of the decade, Sinatra's career soared to heights previously unseen. His concert appearances across the country became scenes of mass hysteria. The most notorious of such scenes came in New York on Columbus Day 1944. Students on school holiday packed the Paramount Theatre in Times Square, and the line to get into the theater stretched for blocks. When relatively few people left after the first show, the crowd became rowdy and began to riot, smashing store windows and causing traffic jams. The Columbus Day Riot, as it came to be called, drew the ire of parents and the conservative press. Sinatra was accused of encouraging truancy and promoting unseemly behavior in young people, particularly teenaged girls—much the same kinds of charges leveled against Elvis Presley and the Beatles in succeeding decades. Teenagers were not dissuaded by the censure of their elders, however, and fan clubs with names like "Slaves of Sinatra" sprang up across the country and abroad.

In addition to his work on the concert stage, Sinatra's influence was felt in other entertainment venues as well. In 1943 he signed a recording contract with Columbia Records, an association that would last until 1952 and produce some 285 recordings. A 1943 strike by the American Federation of Musicians prevented him from recording with an orchestra until November 1944, and his earliest recordings with the label were done a capella, with only the twelve-voice Bobby Tucker Singers as accompaniment. Ironically, his first big hit on Columbia was the recording of "All or Nothing at All" that he had made with Harry James in 1939. Although sales of the Columbia recording were poor at the time of its production, the four-year-old tune climbed to the top of the charts in 1943 and stayed there for twenty-one weeks. It was only the first in a string of hit recordings that decade. At the same time, Sinatra acted as a host of radio's most popular program, "Your Hit Parade" (1943–1945), as well as several other sponsored national radio programs. He also appeared in a number of feature films, most of them musicals, including three with dancer Gene Kelly—*Anchors Aweigh* (MGM, 1945), *On the Town* (MGM, 1949), and *Take Me Out to the Ball Game* (MGM, 1949). Perhaps most notably, Sinatra won a special Academy Award in 1945 for a film short about racial and religious harmony titled *The House I Live In.* This film reflected the singer's deeply held belief in civil rights, a cause for which he would work over the entire course of his long career. Finally, as the television era dawned, Sinatra also starred in his own television series, "The Frank Sinatra Show," which ran from 1950 through 1952.

Despite the dizzying heights to which his fame climbed in the years following his departure from Tommy Dorsey's band in 1942, Sinatra's career finally hit rock bottom by 1952. Many factors conspired to end his reign as entertainment's hottest property—the aging of the teenaged bobby-soxers and changes in the musical tastes of their teenaged successors, creative differences with the executives at Columbia Records, and a scandalous affair with actress Ava Gardner that led to the dissolution of his first marriage. (Sinatra married Gardner in 1951, and the couple divorced in 1954 owing to irreconcilable differences.) By 1952, the thirty-seven-year-old Sinatra was dropped by his publicist, lost his recording and movie contracts, and had his television program canceled. His phenomenal career appeared to have run its course.

Then, in 1953, Frank Sinatra did an extraordinary thing: he reinvented himself both as a singer and as a serious actor, rising to the top of both professions. When Sinatra learned that Columbia Studios was planning to make a film version of James Jones's novel *From Here to Eternity*, he arranged to do a screen test for the role of Angelo Maggio. Despite the initial reluctance of studio heads to cast a former singing idol in the film, Sinatra's screen test was impressive, and he won the part, for which he later won the Oscar for Best Supporting Actor (1953). His career as a serious actor, and not merely a song-and-dance personality, was assured at this point, and he was subsequently offered a variety of weighty roles, including the lead in Otto Preminger's disturbing study of drug addiction, *The Man with the Golden Arm* (UA, 1955), which would earn Sinatra yet another Oscar nomination, this time as Best Actor.

In the meantime, his career as a singer was revived, and, in keeping with his self-reinvention as a serious actor, his singing was also different from that of the sweet balladeer of the Columbia period—tough, mature, full bodied. In 1953 he signed with a relatively new recording label, Capitol Records, and began what would be a lifelong collaboration with arranger Nelson Riddle. Between 1953 and 1962 Sinatra recorded more than 300 songs on the Capitol label, and the sixteen albums he produced there are considered by many to be the finest work of his career and a veritable treasury of classic songs from the Great American Songbook, including works by Cole Porter, Richard Rodgers and Lorenz Hart, and Irving Berlin, to name only a few. Interestingly, these albums also gave Sinatra the opportunity to expand on an idea that he had initially explored during his Columbia days. Owing to the invention and growing popularity of the long-playing record, it became possible to group songs of a similar feeling, theme, and tempo, and Sinatra was the first artist to issue "concept albums" of this sort. Generally, these concept recordings fell into two broad types—heartbreaking ballads like those found on his classic albums *In the Wee Small Hours* (1955) and *Only the Lonely* (1958) and joyous swinging tunes like those recorded for his enormously popular album *Come Dance with Me!* (1959). By the beginning of the next decade, Sinatra was at the top of his form as a mature artist, and he decided that it was time to exercise the ultimate creative freedom.

In late 1960, while still under contract to Capitol, Sinatra formed Reprise Records; his first recording session took place on 19 December 1960, four days after his forty-fifth birthday. Over the next three days,

he recorded seventeen songs, a dozen of which constituted his first Reprise album, *Ring-a-Ding Ding!* In all, his Reprise output from 1960 through 1988 amounted to 452 songs, many of them remakes of tunes he had recorded in the past, others interesting assays at new sounds for the aging singer. In the middle 1960s, for instance, when rock and roll music dominated the charts and the culture, he scored three top-ten hits with "Strangers in the Night" (1966), "That's Life" (1966), and "Something Stupid" (1967), a duet with his daughter Nancy. "Strangers in the Night" won the Grammy Award for Record of the Year in 1966, another extraordinary feat in view of the fact that the fifty-year-old singer was in head-to-head competition with the teen idols of the time, a quarter century after he himself ushered in the era of the teen idol. In 1967 he recorded a beautiful bossa nova album with Brazilian musician Antonio Carlos Jobim, an album that is considered by many to be among the best recorded performances of his long career. Sinatra continued to appear in feature films throughout the 1960s, including a variety of so-called Rat Pack films such as *Ocean's Eleven* (WB, 1960), with his friends Sammy Davis, Jr., and Dean Martin, and what has come to be regarded as one of his best dramatic performances, that of Bennett Marco in John Frankenheimer's *The Manchurian Candidate* (UA, 1962). The middle 1960s brought other life and career milestones. Sinatra's fiftieth birthday in 1965 was marked by a Grammy Award for Album of the Year for his reflective *September of My Years*, a CBS documentary titled "Sinatra: An American Original," narrated by Walter Cronkite, an Emmy– and Peabody Award–winning television special called "Sinatra: A Man and His Music," a Grammy-winning album by the same title, and his first live album, *Sinatra at the Sands*, with Count Basie and Quincy Jones. Sinatra also made headlines during his fiftieth year for marrying nineteen-year-old actress Mia Farrow on 19 July 1966. The couple's wedded bliss was short-lived, and they divorced only two years later, in 1968.

Despite the success that the former teen heartthrob enjoyed at a time when he could have justifiably rested on past accomplishments, Sinatra gradually grew weary of the entire entertainment scene, and he shocked his fans when, in 1971, he announced his retirement from show business, taking his leave in a much publicized and emotional performance in Los Angeles in June of that year. The retirement lasted only until 1973, and in April of that year President Richard Nixon asked him to perform at the White House for visiting Italian prime minister Giulio Andreotti. In November 1973 the singer officially emerged from retirement with the release of an album titled *Ol' Blue Eyes Is Back* and the broadcast of an NBC television special by the same name. Although he continued to release albums and to appear in television specials and a few films, Sinatra's post-retirement career was centered primarily on the concert stage. To accommodate the thousands of fans who wanted to see him perform live, he began to play cavernous sporting stadiums and arenas, venues normally reserved for rock "royalty" like Paul McCartney, Bruce Springsteen, and Billy Joel. One such performance, titled "Sinatra: The Main Event," was telecast live around the world on 13 October 1974 from the stage of New York's Madison Square Garden. Much like a rock star, Sinatra maintained a grueling schedule of worldwide concert tours, and it was not until December of 1994—a year short of his eightieth birthday—that he finally ceased public performance.

At the same time, he also garnered a wide and impressive list of awards and honors for his lifelong humanitarian work and his prodigious career accomplishments. Among these awards were Philadelphia's Freedom Medal (1977), the Kennedy Center Honors for Lifetime Achievement (1983), the Medal of Freedom (1985), the Grammy Legend Award for Lifetime Achievement (1994), and the Congressional Gold Medal (1997), the nation's highest civilian honor. Perhaps the most extraordinary event in Sinatra's long and storied career came near its end. In 1993, the 77-year-old veteran performer returned to Capitol Records, the label he had left more than three decades earlier, and recorded some twenty-eight songs. Producer Phil Ramone then electronically matched Sinatra's vocals with those of other artists, most of them contemporary pop stars, including U2's Bono, Linda Ronstadt, and Luther Vandross. The result was two albums, *Duets* (1993) and *Duets II* (1994), which went on to become the highest-selling works of his entire recording career and to gain him an entirely new audience of younger fans. His last appearance in public came in Palm Springs, California, at the Frank Sinatra Desert Classic golf tournament on 25 February 1995, less than a year before his eightieth birthday. He spent his final years quietly with his wife, Barbara Marx Sinatra, whom he had married on 11 July 1976, and he died of a heart attack in Los Angeles in 1998.

Over the course of his sixty-year career, Frank Sinatra's influence over the field of contemporary entertainment was vast. He was the first mass musical teen idol of modern times, and some have argued that his unprecedented appeal to teenaged audiences helped to diminish the popularity of the big bands and to usher in the era of the solo musical "phenomenon." Moreover, Sinatra consistently exploited new technologies and expanded the horizons of recording and performance innovations, including the microphone in the 1940s, the long-playing record in the 1950s, and electronically programmed recordings in the 1990s. His music catalog, which includes more than 1,800 recordings, represents the very best in twentieth-century popular American music, and many of his recorded performances are regarded by music critics as the definitive interpretations of these songs. As an actor, he made more than sixty film appearances, earning two Oscars; as a radio and television personality, he appeared in scores of national broadcasts. His lifelong humanitarian works earned him hundreds of accolades, as did his work as a performer; his life,

however, was not without significant controversy, with continual allegations of his involvement with organized-crime figures dating back to the late 1940s and lurid media accounts of his sometimes violent encounters with news reporters and personal enemies. Curiously, however, these controversies also helped to sustain media interest in him and to ensure his fame for an unprecedented sixty years in the public eye.

• Frank Sinatra's most important legacy is his music, and virtually all of his recordings on RCA, Columbia, Capitol, and Reprise are available on compact disc. For a full discography, see Leonard Mustazza, *Ol' Blue Eyes: A Frank Sinatra Encyclopedia* (1998), and Luiz Carlos do Nascimento Silva, *Put Your Dreams Away: A Frank Sinatra Discography* (2000). Moreover, most of his films and many of his television specials are available on VHS and/or DVD. More than eighty-five books about Frank Sinatra's life and art have appeared since the late 1940s, though many of them are now out of print. There are also literally thousands of newspaper and magazine articles about him. For a comprehensive descriptive listing of printed materials, see Mustazza, *Sinatra: An Annotated Bibliography, 1939–1998* (1999). Some of the better assessments of his work are reprinted in Steven Petkov and Mustazza, *The Frank Sinatra Reader* (1995), and Ethlie Ann Vare, *Legend: Frank Sinatra and the American Dream* (1995). Sinatra did not leave behind an autobiography, though the two authorized biographies written by his daughter Nancy come close and are highly recommended: *Frank Sinatra: My Father* (1985) and *Frank Sinatra: An American Legend* (1995). The best books on Sinatra's music are Will Friedwald, *Sinatra! The Song Is You: A Singer's Art* (1995), and Charles Granata, *Sessions with Sinatra: Frank Sinatra and the Art of Recordings* (1999). Also noteworthy in terms of its analysis of the cultural significance of Sinatra's music is Donald Clarke, *All or Nothing at All: A Life of Frank Sinatra* (1997). For good book-length discussions of Sinatra's cultural importance, see John Lahr, *Sinatra: The Artist and the Man* (1997), Bill Zehme, *The Way You Wear Your Hat: Frank Sinatra and the Lost Art of Livin'* (1997), and Pete Hamill, *Why Sinatra Matters* (1998). Lengthy obituaries appeared in all of the major daily newspapers on 15 May 1998, including the *New York Times*, the *Los Angeles Times*, the *Philadelphia Inquirer*, and the *Chicago Tribune*.

LEONARD MUSTAZZA

SKAGGS, William H. (16 Sept. 1861–19 Jan. 1947), businessman, mayor, reformer, and commentator, was born in the North Alabama town of Talladega, the son of James M. Skaggs, a wagonmaker, and Mary Smith Skaggs. The brilliant child of an unpretentious family, Skaggs had the great ambition of making an impact on the world of public affairs. A voracious reader from childhood, he soon developed an interest in government and history. Yet his first career was in business, and for a time he was remarkably successful.

Skaggs's coming of age coincided with a wave of development in Alabama's mineral and timber industries. Talladega was growing (its population would reach 4,000 by the late 1880s) and local businessmen hoped to make it another Birmingham. Skaggs's drive and intelligence won their confidence. By his early twenties he was secretary and general manager of the

Talladega Real Estate and Loan Association and an agent for mortgage-loan companies; in 1886 he would found his own bank. Returns from investments in land, blast furnaces, and railroads gave him a sense of independence. In 1885, running as the self-proclaimed candidate of a new generation of southern Democrats, he won election as mayor of Talladega.

In the course of three two-year terms, Skaggs transformed the town. Working with a group of likeminded aldermen, he was responsible for paving city streets, launching a well-equipped public school, constructing a water and sewerage system, and improving city fire and police protection. Yet Skaggs had his shortcomings as a politician. He could be arrogant and dismissive of opponents, especially of those who viewed his improvements as hasty and too expensive. Before the civic elections of 1891 a group of prominent citizens, angry over the higher taxes and bonded debt that had accompanied the new regime, accused him of profiting from city construction projects. Defeated for reelection, Skaggs was cast upon his own resources at a pivotal moment in Alabama history.

The years of Talladega's prosperity had been a time of crisis for the state's yeomen farmers, many of whom were impoverished by declining cotton prices. Though as a moneylender he benefited from their need for credit, Skaggs was moved by the farmers' descent into debt and tenancy. For years he was a believer in the doctrine (associated with Henry W. Grady) that industrialization and diversification of agriculture would solve the south's economic problems. He resisted the inflationist solutions offered by the Farmer's Alliance, which by the late 1880s numbered thousands of Alabama farmers among its members. Nor was he inclined to make economic grievances the basis for political revolt, as some Alliance leaders urged. As late as 1892 Skaggs took the stump on behalf of Democratic gubernatorial candidate Thomas Goode Jones, who was opposed by former state commissioner of agriculture Reuben F. Kolb, the leader of a biracial coalition (or "fusion") of "Jeffersonian" Democrats, Populists, and Republicans.

Kolb was defeated in 1892, but Skaggs suffered pangs of conscience from the knowledge that Democrats in the state's Black Belt counties had resorted to ballot-box stuffing, bribery, and intimidation of black voters in order to retain power. An idealist with a strong sense of personal honor, Skaggs concluded that Democratic practices threatened basic American freedoms; by early 1894 he had joined the Jeffersonian Democratic party. In that year he rose rapidly among reformers, chairing a central committee that presided over Kolb's second fusionist campaign. After Kolb was again "counted out" by the Democrats, Skaggs worked with Joseph C. Manning and other Populists to effect a merger of the Jeffersonian Democrats with the People's Party. The Alabama reformers tried without success to interest Congress in an investigation of ballot fraud in Alabama; and after the defeat of Populism in the state and federal elections of 1896, Skaggs decided to return to private life.

While tending his neglected business interests, Skaggs was an observer of both Republican and Democratic politics. He watched Alabama Democrats debate the advisability of adopting a version of the "Mississippi Plan"—whereby black voters were to be disfranchised, supposedly in order to prevent the type of fraud that had marked Kolb's defeats in 1892 and 1894. Skaggs's racial views at this time were essentially conventional. He had no doubt that white men should dominate southern politics and life. He believed that, as a practical matter, few blacks voted freely; he had proposed in 1894 that blacks combat ballot-box stuffing by refusing to register and vote. By 1901 the disfranchisers were on the verge of triumphing; and Skaggs, who had recently moved to Chicago to expand his business opportunities, was able to return to Alabama to vote for the state's new constitution.

Whatever Skaggs had expected, the new laws did not purify Alabama politics. The 1901 constitution may have eliminated black voting, but it also disfranchised many poor white men, leaving the state utterly in the hands of the dominant Black Belt–New South coalition. Nor did the new regime solve the race question. Traveling in Alabama during the election year of 1904, Skaggs was distressed by the bitter racism he encountered among whites. As for the black victims of disfranchisement, Skaggs concluded that they were seeking to raise themselves through education. He admired their determination; and yet, given the high levels of poverty and illiteracy among whites, he viewed the prospect of a rising black race with alarm.

In a series of newspaper articles written in 1910, Skaggs implied that the South's educational backwardness was the product of a civic culture shaped by demagoguery (as practiced by Mississippi's James K. Vardaman and South Carolina's Benjamin Tillman), child labor, and the notorious sharecropping and convict lease systems. He developed these ideas more fully in his 1924 work *The Southern Oligarchy*, in which he argued that reactionary Democrats had maintained power at a huge cost to the region. Tracing by means of statistics and documentary extracts the economic, social, and political decline of white farmers, Skaggs noted that elite groups in Alabama and other states had suppressed the free exercise of the ballot and had opposed a variety of benefits offered by "outside" agencies, from educational funding to hookworm cures. In place of freedom and progress, leaders of the oligarchy had pressed upon poor whites a bigoted view of the world, a culture of lawlessness and violence, and had condoned Ku Klux Klan terrorism against opponents and nonconformists. Adopting the tones of an old-time Populist, Skaggs warned that southerners must shake off the influence of the oligarchy, or "we shall at last find, as we found in the slavery question, that there can be no peaceful settlement" (*Southern Oligarchy*, p. 444).

The Southern Oligarchy represents Skaggs at his best—controversial, emotionally engaged but well informed, open to new ideas. Before and after its publication he carried out projects of historical and public-affairs research; but his only other writings to reach a large audience were works of World War I propaganda, notably his 1915 volume *German Conspiracies in America, from an American Point of View, by an American.* Though Skaggs moved his business and journalistic enterprises to New York in the 1920s, he kept an eye on events in his old hometown. In 1928 at the request of Talladega historian E. Grace Jemison, he composed a long "Memorandum" of his years as mayor; in the late 1930s he contributed books to local libraries and schools. Incapacitated by poor health in the 1940s, he continued to write; according to Jemison, he had a book almost completed at the time of his death. There is some uncertainty about where Skaggs died, except that it was not in Talladega.

• There is no central collection of Skaggs papers; there are scattered letters in several collections, including the O. D. Street Papers, Hoole Special Collections Library, University of Alabama, Tuscaloosa, and the Robert McKee Papers and the John Witherspoon DuBose Papers, Alabama Department of Archives and History, Montgomery. A copy of Skaggs's 1928 "Memorandum" is also on file at the Alabama Department of Archives and History. In addition there is a file of Skaggs letters in the archives of the Talladega County Historical Society in Talladega. Skaggs's major extant work not cited by title is a pamphlet, *Some Newspaper Articles Regarding the Educational Situation and Other Civic Matters in the Southern States* (n.d.; 1910?). The most complete coverage of Skaggs's life is contained in Terence H. Nolan, "William Henry Skaggs: Alabama's Reform Prophet" (M.A. thesis, Florida State Univ., 1970); see also Nolan, "William Henry Skaggs and the Reform Challenge of 1894," *Alabama Historical Quarterly* 33 (Summer 1971): 117–34. E. Grace Jemison, *Historic Tales of Talladega* (1959), places Skaggs in his Talladega context and prints substantial portions of his "Memorandum." For Skaggs's crime-fighting career, see Paul M. Pruitt, Jr., "The Law Triumphs in Talladega: An Excerpt from William H. Skaggs's 'Memorandum,'" *Alabama Review*, 40 (Apr. 1987): 133–48. For the agrarian and political issues of late-nineteenth-century Alabama, see William Warren Rogers, *The One-Gallused Rebellion: Agrarianism in Alabama, 1865–1896* (1970).

PAUL M. PRUITT

SKELTON, Red (18 July 1913–17 Sept. 1997), actor and comedian, was born Richard Bernard Skelton in Vincennes, Indiana, the son of Joseph Skelton and Ida Mae Skelton (maiden name not known). Although 1913 is commonly cited as the year of his birth, some sources say he was born in either 1906 or 1910. The father, a clown and roustabout in a traveling circus, died of drink before Skelton was born. The boy and his three bullying brothers were raised in poverty by their overworked charwoman mother. At age seven, Red, as he was called, was a paperboy and sang for extra pennies on the street. He also held other menial jobs. At twelve, while performing in a medicine show he accidentally fell off the stage and broke some bottles, delighted the crowd, and was promptly hired to go on summer tour in Indiana, Arkansas, Illinois, and Missouri. His routine featured pratfalls, but he also sang in blackface. At fourteen, he quit school to work

on an Ohio and Missouri river showboat doing monologues and singing and joking in blackface, toured with an *Uncle Tom's Cabin* troupe, and clowned with a traveling circus. In 1930 he performed slapstick in a Kansas City burlesque show, then clowned at dance marathons called "walkathons." The feisty winner of one of the walkathons was Edna Marie Stilwell, whom Skelton married in 1931, when she turned sixteen. After walkathon gigs elsewhere, Skelton in 1934 acted in two-reel comic movies, auditioned in New York, and was assigned nightclub work in Montreal. Booed at first, he began heckling his hecklers and became a smash hit.

During the early 1930s Skelton had worked out his doughnut skit and performed it successsfully at the Paramount Theater in New York. Now, starring in Montreal and Toronto theaters—alternating weekly between the two cities—he perfected the skit: dunking and consuming doughnuts in twelve ways. Doing so thrice daily caused him to gain thirty-five pounds in three weeks, but the weekly $750 seemed excellent recompense until his agents took unfair cuts. A performance in early 1938 before President Franklin D. Roosevelt at the White House, with Mickey Rooney in attendance, led to Skelton's first movie appearance. Rooney, at the time a talent scout for Metro-Goldwyn-Mayer, recommended Skelton for a screen test, in which he ad-libbed death scenes of prominent film stars, evidently captivating those who saw it. MGM's *Having a Wonderful Time* (1938) turned out to be an unmemorable film, although it was improved by the doughnut skit.

Skelton and his wife, a talented writer, took their own musical revue on a money-losing tour and then did more vaudeville, but he was a success with patter, often ad-libbed, on weekly radio shows out of Cincinnati, Chicago, and New York (1938–1939). Highly paid vaudeville assignments followed (1939–1940) and featured Skelton's sidesplitting "Guzzler's Gin" routine—a gin salesman getting drunk advertising and sampling his product. Skelton returned to pleasing crowds at New York's Paramount Theater, for $4,000 weekly, with Frank Sinatra and Tommy Dorsey, and also Lupe Velez, rumored to be his lover briefly.

Through foresight or luck, Skelton required that his contract, which paid him $1,500 a week, include a clause permitting him to work in radio and on television, then only a fledgling medium. In the 1940s Skelton appeared in twenty-four movies. His success as the detective in the musical *Whistling in the Dark* (MGM, 1941) led to his radio program "Scrapbook of Satire" (Hollywood NBC, 1941–1944). It was a ratings giant in which he introduced the "Mean Widdle Kid," who keeps saying "I dood it," Clem Kadiddlehopper, and the singing cabbie, among other comic creations. The boring movie *I Dood It* followed (MGM, 1943), as did *Bathing Beauty* (MGM, 1944), adversely reviewed though featuring lovely Esther Williams. Divorced in 1943 because of his drinking and womanizing, Skelton was drafted as a private into the U.S. Army (1944), entertained troops in Italy with ten to twelve shows daily (1945), was hospitalized for a nervous breakdown, and received a medical discharge (Sept. 1945). Earlier in 1945 he had married Georgia Maureen Davis, a photographer's model; they had two children.

Back in Hollywood while resuming his radio show, Skelton made three poor MGM films (at $3,500 a week), then appeared in three hits: *The Fuller Brush Man* (Columbia, 1948), *A Southern Yankee* (MGM, 1948), and, with Esther Williams again, *Neptune's Daughter* (MGM, 1949). Meanwhile, he was introducing new comic characters on radio, such as drunk Willie Lump-Lump, boxer Cauliflower McPugg, and con-man San Fernando Red. Skelton entertained his live radio audiences not with warm-ups, which left them exhausted by laughter, but with aftershows complete with idiotic antics and sometimes raunchy lines. He continued on radio with NBC until 1949 and again from 1952 to 1953 and with CBS from 1949 to 1952.

The 1950s found Skelton, now in a 27-room Bel-Air mansion with seven Rolls Royces, less successful on the big screen than in television, where his greatest triumphs were to follow. He appeared in fifteen movies, many of them MGM flops but including *Three Little Words* (MGM, 1950), nicely presenting the careers of songwriters Bert Kalmar and Harry Ruby. Though fearing new material, Skelton was excellent playing Ruby in a straight role (opposite Fred Astaire's Kalmar). In *The Clown* (MGM, 1953), a maudlin remake of *The Champ* (1931), he was unimpressive as a washed-up, alcoholic funnyman. His cameo appearance in the prize-winning *Around the World in Eighty Days* (UA/Michael Todd, 1956) was laudable. During these years, the movie industry experienced budgetary and other difficulties competing with television, even as Skelton was achieving sensational success in that expanding medium. "The Red Skelton Show" began as a half-hour Sunday comedy-variety program (NBC, 1951–1953) then moved to Tuesdays (CBS, half-hour, 1953–1962; hour, 1962–1970). In 1953 alone, CBS paid him $12,000 a week for thirty-nine shows. His program won Emmy awards (1951, 1961) and made Nielsen Top Twenty lists seven consecutive years (1964–1970). Skelton was immensely popular reprising former monologues and creating new characters, including Deadeye the Mexican Bandit and a pair of seagulls, Gertrude and Heathcliff. After 1970 Skelton appeared irregularly on television variety shows and specials. His "Skelton Show" was second in longevity and audience size only to "Gunsmoke," and he earned a longer stay on television than anyone else except Ed Sullivan. Skelton took up painting, created thousands of clown faces, sold some for upward of $80,000 each, and made millions from lithographs alone.

Much in Skelton's life contributes to the Pagliacci myth—that of the laughing clown who secretly weeps. In 1957 his son Richard, then eight, was diagnosed with terminal leukemia. Skelton and his wife, Georgia, took him around the world, a trip tactlessly overpublicized. The boy died a year later in Los Angeles. Skelton immediately stopped drinking but began making poor investments. In 1960 the Skeltons left Bel-Air for Rancho Mirage, California. In 1969 Skelton began pursuing Lothian Toland, daughter of cinematographer Gregg Toland, and Georgia, ill, alcoholic, and mentally unbalanced, was no match for Lothian, twenty years Skelton's junior. Two years after Georgia divorced him in 1971, he married Lothian. Georgia shot herself to death in 1976.

Despite the emotional trials of the previous twenty years, Skelton performed superbly at Carnegie Hall in 1977 and over the following decade made three Home Box Office comedy specials. In 1986 he was inducted into the Academy of Television Arts and Sciences Hall of Fame. He died in a hospital in Rancho Mirage.

Groucho Marx, not only a superb comic but also a respected judge of his peers, regarded Skelton as the best clown in show business and the logical successor to Charlie Chaplin. Possessed of a unique talent, Skelton broke the comedians' rule book by laughing at his own jokes, which had an infectious effect on audiences. By combining clever if apparently graceless use of his tall, rubbery figure, his elastic face, and props as limited as a battered hat, he could create multiple, distinct personalities that brought joy to the millions who watched him.

• An informative biography, with excellent photographs, is Arthur Marx, *Red Skelton* (1979). Karin Adir, "Red Skelton," in *The Great Clowns of American Television* (1988), pp. 193–218, is biographical and analytical. Steve Allen, "Red Skelton," in *The Funny Men* (1956), pp. 265–75, explains Skelton's brilliance in vaudeville and radio but unnecessarily expresses fear of his failure in television (prior to his success in the Nielsen ratings during the 1960s). Bill Davidson, "I'm Nuts and I Know It," *Saturday Evening Post*, 17 June 1967, pp. 66–72, 74, 76, is a close-up biographical sketch with excellent color photographs. An obituary is in the *New York Times*, 18 Sept. 1997.

ROBERT L. GALE

SMITH, Bob. *See* Wilson, Bill, and Bob Smith.

SMITH, Jack (27 Aug. 1916–9 Jan. 1996), journalist, was born Jack Clifford Smith in Long Beach, California, to Charles Franklin Smith, a promoter of gold mines and real estate, and Anna Mary Hughes Smith. Smith was educated in Bakersfield, Whittier, and Long Beach schools before graduating from Belmont (Los Angeles) High School. After a stint in the Civilian Conservation Corps and a trip around the Pacific in the Merchant Marine, Smith returned to Bakersfield in 1938, resuming his sporadic attendance at Bakersfield Junior College while working as sports reporter for the *Californian*. In 1939 he married Denise Bresson; they were to have two children and remain married until Smith's death. He was working for the Honolulu *Advertiser* when Pearl Harbor was attacked. Joining the Marines as a combat correspondent, Smith was in the third wave ashore at Iwo Jima.

Before finding his niche at the *Los Angeles Times* in 1953, Smith had several other jobs, most notably as a city reporter and rewrite man at the *Los Angeles Daily News,* where he was generally credited with naming one of the most lurid of the era's murder cases: the Black Dahlia, derived from the sort of flower the murdered Elizabeth Short was fond of wearing. At the *Times* he was soon writing three columns weekly. In 1970 he started writing five and continued to do so for twenty-one years.

Smith was a gentler, more lyrical writer than his contemporaries in other big cities, such as Jimmy Breslin in New York, Mike Royko in Chicago, and Herb Caen in San Francisco. But Los Angeles was different from these urban centers. *Times* commentator Robert A. Jones noted, "L.A. . . . has an interior life that is private and hidden from view . . . [its] soul can be found behind the hedges, in its backyards and patios, around the barbecues. . . . Like all great columnists, Jack understood that crucial difference" (*Los Angeles Times,* 10 Jan. 1996).

Unlike the breathlessly newsy, gossipy "three dot" columns of Caen, his upstate friend and rival, Smith's were deceptively simple 830-word personal essays on a single topic, with significant digressions. Unlike other Los Angeles columnists before and since, he rarely paid much attention to bizarre or eccentric goings-on. He lived on a hillside near the city center (a pet peeve was writers who said Los Angeles had no hills), which was quieter than a suburb; his subjects were often his friends and neighbors, as well as the wildlife visible across the canyon. His insistence that he had seen a grackle led to a running debate (Smith sometimes implied that he made his "mistakes" in order to increase audience participation), which in turn resulted in an annual Jack Smith bird walk in a nearby nature reserve. Smith wrote often of his family but understood that "I am the joke in the family. About the only person you dare to make fun of is yourself."

Smith confessed that he had conducted his courtship in thrall to F. Scott Fitzgerald, but over the years he acquired a kinship with the graceful descriptive writing of Ernest Hemingway. He used his expertise on the famous writer by helping judge a Bad Hemingway contest run by a Los Angeles bar.

Smith is at his best in *God and Mr. Gomez* (1974). Arising from earlier columns, the book chronicles the building of the Smiths' vacation home (another icon of the "best years of our lives" postwar generation) in Baja, California. In contrast to others' all-for-laughs tales of woe—Eric Hodgins's *Mr. Blandings Builds His Dream House* (1946) is typical of the genre—*God and Mr. Gomez* is dryly philosophical ("What was the name of God? Random Chance"), full of wonder at natural things, and in its diffident way a tale of personal growth. Aside from the Smiths, the central character is Romulo Gomez, a man with a mysterious past and the builder of the house, whose "ownership" of the land, like so many other aspects of those years, Smith finally had to accept on faith. *God and Mr. Gomez* became a national bestseller and won for Smith

the wider audience he subsequently enjoyed, his column appearing eventually in 600 newspapers worldwide. The book's popularity suggested that a "laid-back" attitude was attractive beyond southern California.

Although frequently mentioned as a worthy recipient, Smith never won a Pulitzer Prize; one of his books, taking its title from a reader's mistake, was *How to Win a Pullet Surprise* (1982). He wrote increasingly about the art and craft of writing. Smith won the Joseph M. Quinn Memorial Award from the Los Angeles Press Club in 1991 and was an honorary member of Gamma Delta Upsilon, a journalism fraternity originating at Los Angeles City College. Awarded honorary doctorates by two Los Angeles institutions, Marymount Palos Verdes and Pepperdine University, he was also named an Alumnus of the Year by Bakersfield College, which caused him some anxiety, since he had never graduated.

Smith, who rarely wrote of Los Angeles's political and racial turmoil, was in his later years regarded by some as the voice of a sprawling, suburban Los Angeles that no longer existed. The dominant subject of the weekly columns of his last five years was his progressive illness. He chronicled heart attacks and recoveries, the onset of Parkinson's, encounters with doctors and nurses, and most of all the gradual failing of life. His rationale for continuing to write about these matters was that his readers "might be interested," but colleagues of his said that he had been covering his own death. In a late interview he mused, "In a sense, I've created myself by being a columnist—your column creates you. It gradually occurred to me that I had created a person that lived through the column, and that people expected certain things of me as a result." Smith's last column was published on Christmas Day in 1996, though by then he had been in the hospital for a week. He died of congestive heart failure and pneumonia at the University Hospital in Los Angeles. For his epitaph, he requested "Have a nice day."

One of the handful of columnists who defined and gave voice to the characteristics of a twentieth-century American metropolis during an important stage of its growth, Smith was a chronicler of a lifestyle and a climate of certain kinds of feelings. Typical of his wry loyalty to the place where he felt most at home was his riposte to the nickname of New York City: "The Big Orange."

• Much of this essay is written from personal acquaintance with its subject. Jack Smith's papers are held by family members in Los Angeles. In addition to the books cited above, Smith published *Three Coins in the Birdbath* (1965); *Smith on Wry or, the Art of Coming Through* (1970); *The Big Orange* (1976); *Spend All Your Kisses, Mr. Smith* (1978); *Jack Smith's LA* (1980), *Cats, Dogs and Other Strangers at my Door* (1984); and *Alive in La La Land* (1989). After Smith's death, his widow, Denise, and sons Curtis and Douglas edited *Eternally Yours* (1996), a compilation of columns mainly from the last ten years of Smith's life and often dealing with illness, death, and dying in his characteristically gentle and wry manner. An excellent article on Smith's life and approaching death is Mary Melton, "A Portrait of the Columnist as an Old Man," *LA Weekly*, 14 Sept. 1995. Obituaries and tributes filled the *Los Angeles Times* on 10 Jan. 1996 and several days thereafter, while tributes from fellow columnists were recorded in most of the nation's major newspapers.

JAMES ROSS MOORE

SMITH, James (17 Sept. 1719–11 July 1806), a signer of the Declaration of Independence, was born in northern Ireland, the second son of John Smith, a farmer. His mother's name is unknown. Although his family enjoyed prosperity in their native land, favorable reports by Smith's brothers, who had emigrated and settled in Chester County, Pennsylvania, induced Smith's father to join them in 1729. After settling his family in what is now York County, Smith's father sent him to Philadelphia, where he studied Greek, Latin, and surveying under the Reverend Francis Alison at the New London Academy. On completing his studies in Philadelphia, Smith read law under his older brother George's guidance in Lancaster and was admitted to the bar in 1745.

Perhaps sensing greater opportunities on the frontier, Smith soon relocated to Cumberland County (near Shippensburg). After a few years on the frontier—where he spent more time surveying land than practicing law—he returned to York, which became his residence for the rest of his life. Sometime around 1760 Smith married Eleanor Armor of New Castle, Delaware, with whom he was to have five children. Discouraged by the lack of legal business in his hometown (despite the fact that he was the only local attorney until 1769), Smith plunged into the ironmaking business and opened an operation on nearby Codorus Creek in 1771.

With tensions growing between Great Britain and the American colonies, Smith's attention was increasingly drawn away from business. An ardent Whig from the earliest days of the conflict, he attended in July 1774 a provincial conference at which he read an "Essay on the Constitutional Power of Great Britain over the Colonies in America" and urged both the formation of a general colonial congress and the boycott of British goods. Following the conference Smith returned to York and by December 1774 had raised a volunteer company of soldiers—by some reports the first such company in the Commonwealth of Pennsylvania—and was elected captain of the company. Although he eventually rose to the honorary rank of colonel after the company expanded into a battalion, he generally deferred to the leadership of younger men and concentrated his efforts on legislative matters. In January 1775 Smith served as a delegate to the provincial convention and between 18 and 25 June 1776 took an active role in the provincial conference, where he assisted in the drafting of resolutions urging independence from Great Britain, the formation of a new government, and the upgrading of provincial defenses. Smith also attended the Pennsylvania constitutional convention of 1776 where he served on a committee charged with planning a new government. Elected a member of the Continental Congress by the convention, he thereby took his place among the men who signed the Declaration of Independence.

Although Smith evidently did not serve with the first group of congressional delegates from Pennsylvania, he was reelected to that body in December 1777 and served the following year, during which time Congress—forced to abandon Philadelphia after the British occupation—sat in session in York. Smith donated the use of his office on South George Street to the Congress and served as the host for meetings of the Board of War as well as of the Committee of Foreign Affairs.

After declining reelection to Congress, Smith spent most of his remaining years in legal practice, having disposed of his iron works in 1778 after suffering a substantial financial loss. Although regarded by his contemporaries as somewhat eccentric, Smith possessed a sharp wit and and an expansive memory, and his law office provided training for a number of future attorneys. He did take time to serve one term in the state assembly (1779) and also held the position of judge of the Pennsylvania High Court of Errors and Appeals between November 1780 and May 1781. The state's Supreme Executive Council appointed him brigadier general of the state militia on 23 May 1782, and in early 1784 he acted as a counselor for Pennsylvania during the so-called Wyoming Controversy, a long-running land dispute with Connecticut. In 1785 Smith was again appointed to Congress—this time to replace Matthew Clarkson—but he declined to serve because of his age. After retiring from the law in 1801, he spent his remaining years in quiet retirement before dying in York.

Although less well known than many of the other men who signed the Declaration of Independence, James Smith's signature on that document secured his place in history. His career may have been somewhat colorless—perhaps made the more so by his choosing to advise rather than to lead—but men like him helped form the United States as a nation by repeatedly taking on civic responsibilities.

• Most of Smith's papers were destroyed in an office fire that occurred in the fall of 1805 just prior to his death. For information on his life and career, see W. C. Carter and A. J. Glossbrenner, *History of York County from its Erection to the Present Time, 1729–1834* (1834; new ed., with additions, ed. A. Monroe Aurand, 1975); W. H. Egle's "The Constitutional Convention of 1776," *Pennsylvania Magazine of History and Biography* 4 (1880): 362–64; and John C. Jordan's "York, Penna., in the Revolution," *Pennsylvania Magazine of History and Biography* 32 (Oct. 1908): 487–97.

EDWARD L. LACH, JR.

SNYDER, Jimmy "the Greek" (9 Sept. 1919?–21 Apr. 1996), gambler, newspaper columnist, and television sports broadcaster, was born Demetrios Georgios Synodinos in Steubenville, Ohio, the son of George Synodinos, owner of the White Star Meat Market, and Sultania Synodinos. In March 1928, when the boy was ten, his mother and his aunt, Theano Galanos, were murdered in front of the family home by Theano's estranged husband, a war hero suffering from "battle fatigue." After his mother's death, his father moved with the three children to Kios, a Greek island. It was in Kios that young Demetrios learned to gamble, tossing stones for drachmas with the local teenagers.

In 1932 George Synodinos remarried and the family returned to the United States. Growing up in Steubenville was apparently good training for a budding gamester. A mid-size steel town on the Ohio River that produced a number of gamblers, casino owners, and at least one nightclub entertainer (Dean Martin), Steubenville was, according to Snyder, "a farm club for Las Vegas" (*Jimmy the Greek* [JTG], p. 1). As a teenager, having changed his name to James George Snyder, he began his career at Money O'Brien's Academy Pool Room, where he ran the Big Six Wheel, a simple casino game also known as the Wheel of Fortune. By the time he dropped out of high school in the tenth grade he was dealing craps at the Blue Moon, a local casino. But he soon tired of casinos, because he didn't want to spend his time "in places where naked anxiety and naked greed go hand in hand" (JTG, p. 25), and traveled to Florida for the winter, where he concentrated on the horse track.

When he was nineteen Snyder decided to focus on sports betting, an area, he believed, where "a guy could research, form an opinion, then stake his judgment against another's" (JTG, p. 25). Calling himself the "B & F [baseball and football] Commissioner," he rented an office in Steubenville, where he operated a sports bookmaking operation. Kept out of World War II by a congenital medical condition (a hole in his stomach wall), Snyder continued to gamble and handle bets throughout the 1940s. He specialized in college football, especially games in the Southeastern Conference, using his friendships with coaches and players to gain information useful in determining the odds. In 1942 he married Pauline "Sunny" Miles after a three-day courtship; they divorced a little more than a year later, and he retained custody of their only child.

Concerned that he might lose custody of his daughter, Snyder in the late 1940s moved to Miami and curtailed his gambling and bookmaking activities, trying unsuccessfully to get rich in the oil business. His name was mentioned in the 1950–1951 hearings of the Special Committee on Organized Crime in Interstate Gambling, popularly called the Kefauver hearings. Throughout his life Snyder denied any involvement in the Mafia, but the hearings, which exposed ties between organized crime and gambling, led many states to enforce laws against betting. In 1952 he married Joan Specht; they had six children, two of whom died from cystic fibrosis in infancy or early childhood (a third child died of the disease in his twenties).

As a result of his failure in the oil business and the nationwide crackdown on gambling that followed the Kefauver hearings, Snyder in 1956 left his wife and children in Miami and moved to one of the few places in the country where he could legally practice his trade, Las Vegas, Nevada, which at the time was small but growing. By the early 1960s the desert city would become "a world of its own" (JTG, p. 102). He helped various casinos with public relations, work that would help to sustain him for the next thirty years.

In the early 1960s, his family having joined him in Nevada, Snyder started a successful bookmaking business, the Vegas Turf and Sports Club. A December 1961 article in *Sports Illustrated*, "The Greek Who Makes the Odds," helped to make him famous nationally. But his fame soon turned to notoriety when he was indicted in a Salt Lake City, Utah, federal court for violation of the newly passed laws against interstate transmission of gambling information, having given a local businessman the odds on a college football game over the telephone. He later pleaded *nolo contendere* and was fined $50,000. Snyder claimed that his indictment was retaliation by the John F. Kennedy administration. Financially devastated, he was forced to close his business but was soon hired by the *Las Vegas Sun* to write a weekly (later thrice weekly) column that featured his odds on sports and politics. The article, the first of its kind in the country, continued in publication until the 1990s.

After his indictment and the loss of his bookmaking operation, Snyder sought to shed his "shady gambler" image. He focused his energy on his column, through which he made his odds available to the public, and his newly formed public relations firm, Sports Unlimited, whose clients included Caesar's Palace and Howard Hughes. Snyder cultivated friendships with celebrities, athletes, and politicians, including President Richard Nixon. After Snyder picked the incumbent Republican over George McGovern in the 1972 campaign, he became known as "the President's favorite pollster" (JTG, p. 178). However, Snyder did not take the compliment personally; he compared politics to sports, saying, "You project them to win and they interpret this to mean you are on their side. And the reverse is equally true" (JTG, p. 178). But it was Gerald Ford, who took office after Nixon resigned over the Watergate scandal, that gave Snyder a pardon for the felony he had committed eleven years before.

In 1976, two years after he was pardoned, CBS Sports offered Snyder a $150,000-a-year position as a commentator on its Sunday football program "NFL Today," joining the host, Brent Musburger, and former Miss America Phyllis George. His two segments on the show, "The Greek's Grapevine," during which he revealed the latest gossip in the sports world, and "The Greek's Board," which featured game-day predictions, were popular with the fans and helped to rehabilitate his public image. (He even had a small part, playing himself, in the 1981 film *Cannonball Run*.) Later, relations between Snyder and Musburger soured, culminating in a well-publicized fistfight in a Manhattan bar. Snyder also barely escaped being fired when he told George, who at the time was married to the governor of Kentucky, John Y. Brown, that he hated her "[expletive] husband," on the air.

Snyder's television career ended, abruptly, on Martin Luther King, Jr., day in 1988, when in an interview with reporter Ed Hotaling of WRC-TV about the progress of African Americans in sports he ruminated on the reasons black people were superior athletes. He said that during the Civil War "the slave owner would breed his big black to his big woman so that he could have a big black kid . . . . That's where it all started." He also mentioned his fear that if blacks "take over coaching like everybody wants them to there's not going to be anything left for the whites" (Wadsworth, pp. 237–38). The four-minute exchange that aired nationally had been edited from a thirty-minute interview, prompting some, including Snyder himself, to charge that his comments were taken out of context. But his inflammatory words angered the network, and CBS, publicly calling the remarks "reprehensible," almost immediately fired him. After his dismissal, Snyder apologized, calling the comments "a foolish thing to say." He did, however, receive widespread support from the public, including many black athletes, who felt that the network was using him as a scapegoat.

Snyder became severely depressed and his health began to decline. In the early 1990s he filed a grievance against CBS for breach of contract, but in 1994 it was denied, primarily because of the time that had elapsed since he was fired. In his last years he divided his time between his home in Durham, North Carolina, and Las Vegas, where he died.

Snyder's ill-timed and foolish comments turned him into a pariah in broadcast sports, a casualty of the political correctness wars. His 1975 autobiography ended with a prediction that financier Bernard Baruch made to him when he was in his twenties: "Young man, you're going to be broke and rich seven times in your life. Be sure you watch the seventh." Snyder wrote that "it's possible that I have approached, even passed, the seventh cycle" (JTG, p. 247), but it seems that the eighth cycle didn't begin until 1988. Like most popular culture icons, Snyder had a gift for self-promotion, but his influence on the world of professional sports cannot be understated. Although he is remembered as a colorful figure who helped to popularize sports gambling in the United States, his legacy is overshadowed by the unfortunate comments that cost him his career.

• The best sources on Snyder's life are his autobiography, *Jimmy the Greek, by Himself* (written with the editorial assistance of Mickey Herskowitz and Steve Perkins, 1975), and Ginger Wadsworth with Jimmy Snyder, *Farewell Jimmy the Greek: Wizard of Odds* (1996), which basically is a reprint of the 1975 book with new material added, including an account of the CBS "conspiracy" to fire Snyder and details of his final years. Both are favorable treatments of his life. A video of Snyder making one of the comments that would end his television career is available at http://sportsillustrated.cnn.com/almanac/video/1988/#2. Obituaries are in the *Las Vegas Sun, New York Times, New York Daily News, Los Angeles Times*, and *Washington Post*, all 22 Apr. 1996.

STACEY HAMILTON

SOCKALEXIS, Louis M. (24 Oct. 1871–24 Dec. 1913), major league baseball player, was born in Old Town, Maine, a Penobscot Indian. A branch of the Algonquin family of tribes, the Penobscot constitute one of only two tribes now left in Maine, the other being the Passamaquoddy. Numbering only about 700 at the time of the American Revolution, the Penobscot sided with the colonists and were rewarded with a reservation in Old Town, where their numbers gradually increased to around 4,000 by the late twentieth century. Young Louis became famous as a baseball player in Maine, and Holy Cross College recruited him to play for them and get an education in the bargain. In 1894 Sockalexis hit .444 switching between pitcher and outfield, but a drinking problem got him expelled. He next went to Notre Dame, but again alcohol caused him to be kicked out of school. Patsy Tebeau, manager of the National League's Cleveland Spiders, bailed him out of jail and signed him to play major league ball.

His big league career was brief. In 1897 Sockalexis created a sensation, for he was the first full-blooded Indian to play in the majors. He was very fast and could throw a strike over the plate from deep center field. With his rifle arm, he compiled a remarkable 18 assists with the Spiders, but he was also erratic, committing 19 errors in his three campaigns. He hit a sterling .338 in his first season, but before it ended he had been suspended for drunkenness. Drink dogged him the next two years, and his 66 games in 1897 dwindled to 21 in 1898 and a mere 7 in 1899, while his average declined to .224 and .273. In essence, he drank himself out of the National League and became an object lesson for sportswriters about the evils of alcohol. He was reduced to playing for various state teams in places like Hartford, Meriden, and Bristol in Connecticut. Then his drinking undermined even that level of competitiveness, and he became a beggar, trying to get a little money for another drink. Finally, back in Maine, he died of a heart attack in Burlington, only forty-two years old.

The historical importance of Sockalexis lies not in his very brief career as a big league ballplayer but in his symbolism as an American Indian. When he first arrived in Cleveland, ill-informed stories portrayed him as a direct descendent of Sitting Bull, a rather obtuse suggestion concerning a Penobscot. Like almost every Indian to play in the early twentieth century, he was dubbed "Chief." Tragically, fans never let him forget that he was a Native American, greeting him with derisive war whoops wherever he played, including Cleveland. When the rowdy Spiders incited the wrath of opposing fans, they seemed to direct their most menacing threats at Sockalexis. Although some writers urged fans to lay off the "ki-yi's," many of the scribes began calling the team the Indians, particularly when the rookie was playing well. The hostility he evoked exacerbated his drinking problem, which, ultimately, drove him out of the game. His experience offers a poignant contrast to that of Jackie Robinson, the black pioneer a half-century later.

The Sockalexis legend began its ascent about a year after his death and is closely linked to the fact that in January 1915 Cleveland's American League team needed a new name. They had been known as the Naps since 1903 in honor of Napoleon Lajoie, their star second baseman and manager, but Lajoie had been traded to the Philadelphia Athletics. Team owner Charles W. Somers announced he would have a conference of local sportswriters select a new name. Between 9 and 15 January, four Cleveland newspapers printed suggestions from fans, with Grays and Hustlers drawing the most support. None of the names printed in the papers was the Indians. Nevertheless, on 17 January the press announced that the writers had chosen Indians as the new name, and it was an instant hit. The *Plain Dealer* cited two justifications for the choice. The Boston (later Milwaukee, then Atlanta) Braves had surged from last place in July to win the World Series the previous year, and there was hope that a miserable Cleveland team would emulate the "Miracle Braves." Second, the name Indians had some local history because sportswriters had applied the name to the Spiders back in 1897, even though the official name had never been changed. Though the papers made no mention of Louis Sockalexis on the day the team name was announced, the *Plain Dealer* made the connection the next day.

The 1968 Indians media guide was the first source to mention that the team name had been chosen in a fan contest back in 1915 and that the name Indians had been selected in honor of Louis Sockalexis. There seems not to have been a contest; although fans did send in their suggestions, the sportswriters clearly did the choosing, so that part of the legend is false. Still, the Sockalexis connection emerged very quickly after the announcement. In the political correctness debates of the 1990s, these facts mattered. Some Native American groups considered the team name and the mascot, Chief Wahoo, to be demeaning and demanded that the team abandon its long tradition. Other Native Americans pointed to the name as a sign of honor and respect and urged that it be maintained. Thus, long after his demise, Louis Sockalexis continued to have an impact on both Cleveland and Native Americans.

• Accounts of Louis Sockalexis's baseball career may be found in Connie Mack, *My 66 Years in the Big Leagues* (1950), and David Quentin Voigt, *American Baseball: From Gentleman's Sport to the Commissioner System* (1966). Donald Dewey and Nicholas Acocella's authoritative *The Ball Clubs* (1996) includes the legendary account of how the Indians got their name as the result of a poll of fans. In an article titled "Tale of Indians' Name Off Base," the *Cleveland Plain Dealer* of 17 May 1999 sums up the controversy to that date. Terry Pluto offers a thorough and skeptical appraisal of Sockalexis's career and legend in *Our Tribe* (1999).

JOHN R. M. WILSON

SOSENKO, Anna (13 June 1909–9 June 2000), producer, songwriter, manager, and archivist, was born in Camden, New Jersey, one of three children of Rebecca Sosenko (maiden name unknown) and Simon Sosenko. The family was not one of means; Anna's mother ran a restaurant and a sometime boarding house, occasionally renting out rooms in the family home. Sosenko's formal education came to an end when she graduated from Camden High School. Her life would change, however, in her early adulthood when the family let a room to a struggling girl-pianist who toiled in a "five-a-day" (five shows a day) vaudeville theater across the street. The struggling pianist was Hildegarde Sell, the Milwaukee-born daughter of German immigrants. The two girls struck up an instant friendship and eventually a partnership that would make both their fortunes.

The two young women were complete opposites: Hildegarde was attractive, willowy, glamorous; Sosenko was short and stocky, with intense, dark eyes gazing from a moon-shaped face, later adorned by heavy-framed round eyeglasses, and a cat-that-ate-the-cream mouth. Her manner was direct, forceful, and sometimes painfully honest. Sosenko moved to New York City, as did Hildegarde, who continued eking out a paycheck in the dying days of vaudeville, while Sosenko took a job sewing buckles on women's shoes. In her off-time Sosenko began writing songs for Hildegarde to perform, one of which, "Time Was," made a small success. From then on, they were formally business partners, and for the next twenty-three years Sosenko and Hildegarde shared a 50/50 split. Sosenko invented, managed, booked, and otherwise drove the performer's career, even choosing her songs, while Hildegarde ("*just* Hildegarde," as the performer once admonished a saleswoman who asked for her last name) became an international celebrity, perhaps the premier cabaret icon of the 1930s and 1940s.

In the earliest foray of their partnership, they sought to conquer Paris. But when they arrived, they found little work and much hardship, and they had to deal with a few hotel managers who locked them out when the bills could not be met. In the course of their stay they found a brief engagement at the Casanova Club, a tiny spot next to the cemetery where Alexandre Dumas's Lady of the Camelias is buried, and, although it paid practically nothing, it was here that Hildegarde began to learn the tricks of handling a noisy crowd, and Sosenko, the wiles of a business manager. After several months, they went to London, where in the festivity surrounding the duke of Kent's wedding after-dark spots were seeking new entertainers. Sosenko booked Hildegarde into some of the city's best hotels—the Ritz, the Carlton, and the Barclay—where the singer-pianist created a sensation. After that, they were given a first-class welcome back in Paris, and Sosenko subsequently secured bookings in cafes and nightclubs in Holland and Belgium and on the Riviera. Temporary expatriates, the two shuttled around this European circuit for several years, as Hildegarde's fame grew and with it Sosenko's reputation as a shrewd manager who demanded increasingly stiff fees for her star.

During her lifetime, Sosenko wrote some fifteen songs. By far the most famous, "Darling, Je Vous Aime Beaucoup (Je ne sais pas what to do)," had its inspiration when the two women were on a cycling tour in France; while stopping to ask for directions, they got their French and English mixed up. The idea for the song, words and music, popped into Sosenko's head, and when they got back to the hotel, she played it for Hildegarde, who took to it immediately. The 1936 song went on to become a hit—and Hildegarde's trademark. Sosenko would later comment, "Then Josephine Baker started singing it and believe me when I say I could have strangled her."

They caught the next boat back to the United States after Hildegarde received an offer from the National Broadcasting Company for a radio show at $500 an evening. Though the rage of Europe, the act took some time to catch on at home. Yet, with Sosenko's canny perseverance and Hildegarde's increasing skill at winning over an audience with her own brand of home-grown sophisticated glamour, Sosenko was soon booking the performer for lavish fees into the plushest hotel cabaret rooms in the country for ten months out of the year. At one engagement in 1946 Sosenko contracted for a fee of $17,500 a week, plus 50 percent of the gross over $80,000. *Life* magazine would call Sosenko (at thirty-three) ". . . just about the smartest manager in show business today." Dubbed by Walter Winchell "the Incomparable Hildegarde" and usually billed as such—though known to friends as "Hildy"—she was featured on the cover of *Life* in 1939, starred in her own Top Ten radio show ("Hildegarde's Radio Room"), and traveled around the country and abroad with Sosenko and her own orchestra. Along with "Darling, Je Vous Aime Beaucoup," her recordings of "The Last Time I Saw Paris" and "Lili Marlene" were worldwide hits. During World War II she was a favorite of servicemen, and she included among her fans King Gustav of Sweden and the Duke of Windsor. Through Sosenko's expertise in promoting her, she became so famous that Revlon marketed a Hildegarde shade of lipstick and nail polish; a nursery named a rose for her; and, reflecting the way she signed her autograph, a linen company came out with a "Bless you" handkerchief.

The two women shared a ten-room suite at New York's Plaza Hotel, where downstairs Hildegarde was the reigning queen of its Persian Room. Sosenko had for years been collecting art, which now included paintings by Renoir, Manet, Mary Cassatt, Fernand Léger, and Grant Wood. In the mid-1950s, however, Hildegarde and Sosenko split up their personal and professional partnership, though they never spoke publicly of the reason for doing so. The art collection was auctioned at what was then Madison Avenue's Parke-Bernet Galleries, and after twenty-three years together the women went their separate ways.

Sosenko by now had a circle of friends and associates that included some of the most celebrated figures of the time. Outspoken—sometimes impoliticly so, with a booming voice—she admired talent and was not known for her patience with those who irritated her. Beginning the post-Hildegarde phase of her life, Sosenko became a premier producer of star-studded gala benefits, often at Carnegie Hall, and usually for the Friends of the Theatre Collection of the Museum of the City of New York. These "Broadway" events included evenings devoted to Ethel Merman and Mary Martin, Alan Jay Lerner and Frederick Loewe, Dorothy Fields, Oscar Hammerstein II, Richard Rodgers, and others, and she was always able to seduce entertainment's biggest stars into appearing, including Ethel Merman and Mary Martin, Julie Andrews, Rex Harrison, Liza Minnelli, Natalia Makarova, Sid Caesar, and Douglas Fairbanks, Jr. Commenting on her ability to attract the cream, she said, "They know when I do a show, it's going to be a great show because I only do great things. If they're not great, I'm not interested."

Her decades-long habit of collecting both art and theater memorabilia gave her still another outlet. In 1976 she mounted an exhibition for the Museum of the City of New York of seventy-five years of great stars who had appeared on Broadway for the Shubert Brothers (including Lillian Russell, the Barrymores, Al Jolson, Josephine Baker, and the Marx Brothers). Moreover, for many years she housed her prodigious memorabilia collection in a basement shop on Manhattan's Upper West Side. Her clients, who shopped for items such as a Christmas card sent by Cary Grant (when he was still Archie Leach) and an 1893 program from the first American performance of Oscar Wilde's *Lady Windermere's Fan*, included the likes of Vivien Leigh and Barbra Streisand. Though she finally gave up the shop several years before her death, the late-eighty-something doyenne continued to deal privately from her Central Park West apartment.

Sosenko's extraordinary talents and striking personality won her a prominent place in New York theatrical, musical, and literary circles. On her death in New York City, participants in a special memorial service for her included such diverse personalities as bestselling romance novelist Barbara Taylor Bradford, Broadway producer Fran Weissler, fashion designer Pauline Trigère, and choreographer Donald Saddler, among others. She and Hildegarde had long since reconciled to amiability when Hildegarde celebrated her eighty-fifth birthday with a show at the Russian Tea Room's cabaret. Commencing "Darling Je Vous Aime Beaucoup" before the crowd, Hildegarde remarked that it was a song she never got tired of singing. Sosenko stole the show when she boomed from the dark, "But I'm tired of it."

• A valuable source on the life and career of Anna Sosenko is the clipping file held by the New York Public Library of the Performing Arts at Lincoln Center. Hildegarde is discussed in James Gavin, *Intimate Nights* (1991). An obituary is in the *New York Times*, 11 June 2000.

DEBORAH GRACE WINER

SPIRA, Henry (19 June 1927–12 Sept. 1998), animal rights activist, was born in Antwerp, Belgium, the son of Maurice Spira and Margit Spitzer Spira. In the late 1930s the family migrated to the United States, after making interim stops in Germany, England, and Panama, and settled in New York. Spira left home as a teenager and served in the merchant marine and the army before becoming an assembly-line worker at a General Motors factory in New Jersey.

During the 1940s Spira became active in left-wing political groups and the trade union movement and began writing for several militant publications; in the following decade he became an activist in the civil rights movement. In the mid-1950s Spira enrolled at Brooklyn College, earning an undergraduate degree in English in 1958. He then returned to service in the merchant marine and continued his activism in the maritime union. In 1966 he settled permanently in New York City and began teaching English at a Manhattan high school while continuing his political activities.

Spira first became interested in animals in the early 1970s, when he cared for a girlfriend's cat and became an instant ailurophile. About this time he also read *Animal Liberation* (1975), a plea by the Australian philosopher Peter Singer for humane treatment of animals. Convinced by Singer's arguments, and overcome by the absurdity, as he later put it, "of cuddling one animal while sticking a knife and fork into another," the longtime political activist launched himself on a new crusade that would become his life's work: improving the well-being of all animals.

The movement to treat animals humanely dated back more than a century, and there were several organizations, including the Humane Society and the Society for the Prevention of Cruelty to Animals (SPCA), that routinely promoted animal welfare. But the animal rights movement was reborn in the 1970s in the wake of the new environmental movement launched in the previous decade and aided by Singer's book and others like it. Many individuals were drawn to work with already established animal welfare organizations; others founded new, more radical groups like People for the Ethical Treatment of Animals (PETA). Spira chose to launch a crusade all by himself.

His first target was the common but not widely publicized practice of using animals as test subjects for everything from new cosmetics to behavioral research, a practice known as vivisection. He began close to home, organizing a campaign in 1976 against the American Museum of Natural History in New York City for its research on the sexual behavior of cats, which included castration and other mutilation. When Spira publicized the research, through demonstrations, advertising, and letter-writing campaigns,

there was a widespread public outcry, and within a year the museum, shaken by bad publicity and the possibility that this would adversely affect its funding, ended the program. Spira's victory was hailed by animal rights groups as the first successful antivivisection campaign in more than a century.

What would become Spira's characteristic approach as an animal rights activist was implicit in his initial campaign: publicizing a pointlessly abusive situation to prompt public indignation and thereby bring about its demise. In other words, his goals were finite, practical, and focused, and because of this, he more often than not succeeded in attaining them. Soon after his museum victory, he launched a second campaign, this time to force cosmetics companies to abolish the Draize test, whereby new products were applied to the eyes of rabbits before being declared safe for humans—despite the fact that safety tests that did not harm animals could be readily developed. Again organizing demonstrations and advertising as well as boycotts, he forced major companies to phase out such testing during the 1980s. "How many rabbits does Revlon blind for beauty's sake?" ran the headline in a full-page newspaper ad that was widely printed. A major factor in ending the use of the Draize test was the development of alternative methods at Rockefeller University—research that was initially paid for by a grant from the Revlon Corporation in response to Spira's campaign.

As the anti-Draize effort was gathering momentum, Spira began to strike another major blow against animal testing when he launched an effort to end Lethal Dose 50. LD50, as it was called, was the standard measure of chemical toxicity in consumer products. The test was commonly used to determine what percentage of a substance would kill 50 percent of the animals to whom it was administered. By the 1980s LD50 was widely held to have questionable practical value; when leading toxicologists came out in support of Spira, the use of LD50 declined dramatically.

Spira's campaigns against animal testing had broader repercussions as well. In 1981, with grants from Avon and other leading cosmetics companies, he brought together a coalition of scientists and industry leaders to found the Center for Alternatives to Animal Testing at Johns Hopkins University in Baltimore. And, thanks to his efforts, hospitals, government laboratories, and universities set up review boards to monitor the welfare of animals used in research and to use alternative methods whenever possible.

During the 1980s Spira began to focus on the treatment of farm animals and to find ways to reduce their suffering. He led a campaign to end face-branding of cattle, and he obtained agreements with McDonald's and other fast-food companies to more closely monitor the practices of their meat and poultry suppliers. He also promoted more humane methods of slaughter. He was somewhat less successful in a long campaign against Frank Perdue, whom he accused of using grossly inhumane methods in his chicken business.

Spira's work was supported mainly by mainstream animal welfare organizations, including the Humane Society and the SPCA, and by grants from private individuals. In 1982, after leaving his teaching job to devote himself full time to working for animal welfare, he founded Animal Rights International (ARI) as the umbrella organization for his efforts, but its only employees were Spira himself and a part-time aide, who worked together out of Spira's apartment on the Upper West Side of Manhattan.

Within the animal rights movement, Spira was classified—with disdain by more radical groups, such as PETA—as a moderate, but he steadfastly eschewed the extremism and violence of the militants. A dedicated vegetarian who used no animal products himself, he nevertheless maintained that only a gradualist approach would succeed in achieving his ultimate goal: a world in which animals are treated as fellow species and are not used as food, test subjects, or ingredients in consumer products. He exhibited great skill in bringing together scientists and business executives to advance his goals of relieving suffering and was quick to praise any progress he observed; because of this he was accused in later years by radical detractors of being too cozy with the establishment. The majority view, expressed by humane organizations, bioethicists, and scientists at the time of his death, was that Spira's efforts had saved the lives or at least eased the suffering of millions of animals.

Spira, who apparently never married, died at his New York apartment from cancer.

• Biographical information on Henry Spira is limited. See Barnaby J. Feder, "Pressuring Perdue," *New York Times Magazine*, 26 Nov. 1989, pp. 32ff. See also R. Davey, "Henry Spira: A Fighter Who Makes Things Happen for Animals," *Environmental Magazine*, Sept.–Oct. 1995, pp. 10–13. An obituary appears in the *New York Times*, 15 Sept. 1998.

ANN T. KEENE

SPOCK, Benjamin (2 May 1903–15 Mar. 1998), pediatrician and activist, was born Benjamin McLane Spock in New Haven, Connecticut, the son of Benjamin Ives Spock, an affluent railway lawyer, and Mildred Louise Stoughton Spock. Like his younger brother and four sisters, Spock obtained much of his early education at home under the supervision of his mother. At the age of sixteen, he entered Phillips Academy in Andover, Massachusetts, a boarding school for boys, where he placed among the top 5 percent of his class and set a school record in the high jump. He enrolled at Yale University in 1921 and obtained his bachelor's degree in English (with a minor in history) four years later. During his summer vacations, he worked at a home for crippled children in Newington, Connecticut; his experiences there led him to pursue a medical career. As an undergraduate, he rowed on Yale's crew team, nicknamed "Eli,"

which won a gold medal for the United States in the 1924 summer Olympics in Paris. He was also inducted as a member of the exclusive secret society Scroll and Key.

Spock met Jane Davenport Cheney, daughter of a wealthy silk manufacturer, during a Yale-Harvard regatta in 1923 and married in 1927; they had two sons. In the fall of 1927, they moved to New York City, where Spock finished his medical degree at Columbia University's College of Physicians and Surgeons, graduating first in his class in 1929.

Following his graduation from Columbia, Spock gained clinical experience through three prestigious internships. During the first, as a medical intern at Presbyterian Hospital in New York City (1929–1931), he studied the psychoanalytical theories of Sigmund Freud as he learned more about his wife's psychological work as a research assistant in the hospital's Constitutional Laboratory. He completed a pediatrics internship at the New York Nursery and Children's Hospital (1931–1932), formerly the New York Infant Asylum, where the preeminent pediatrician Luther Emmett Holt had influenced the hospital with his renowned "scientific" principles for child care. Spock questioned the rigidity of Holt's methods, such as standardized schedules for feeding and toilet training and harsh measures for preventing thumb-sucking. During a third internship in psychiatry at Cornell University's new Payne Whitney Clinic at the New York Hospital (1932–1933), Spock extended his practical experience in psychology.

By 1933, he began seeing his own patients—as assistant attending physician at the New York Hospital–Cornell Medical College (where he also taught courses in pediatrics), as a part-time physician at the Brearley School for girls, and in his private pediatrics practice on New York City's East Side. Discovering often that parents of his patients were concerned about the emotional as well as the physical welfare of their children, he decided to further his training in psychology. Also beginning in 1933, he attended weekly seminars at the New York Psychoanalytical Institute, an important American center for the study of Freudian theory, and explored psychoanalysis under Bertram Lewin and later Sandor Rado. His friendships with Lewin, Rado, and other Freudian-trained psychologists there—especially Erik Erikson and Caroline B. Zachry—proved critical to the maturation of his ideas on child rearing. At Zachry's invitation, Spock led discussions in weekly evening seminars of the Institute of Personality Development at New York University. He was certified by the American Board of Pediatrics in 1937 and served as a part-time pediatric consultant to the New York City Department of Health in the early 1940s.

By the late 1930s, with the encouragement of his wife and Zachry, Spock decided to publish his views on child care in a manual. This genre was growing in popularity because of the success of forerunners in expert pediatric advice such as Holt. Spock declined an offer from Doubleday in 1938; eight years later he signed a contract with Pocket Books. Because he wanted his views to be taken seriously by the medical profession, he also interested Charles Duell (whose three children were Spock's patients) of the Duell, Sloan, and Pearce firm in publishing a hardcover version. During the early years of World War II Spock took advantage of a lull in his practice and a medical exemption from military service to begin writing his book. By 1944 with improved health and imminent induction, Spock joined the U.S. Naval Reserve in New York; soon after he was transferred and served as lieutenant-commander at the Naval Air Station in Coronado, California. During his naval service he continued work on his manual, often reading additions and revisions over the telephone to his wife, who acted as typist, fact checker, and contributor throughout. In 1946, the hardcover edition appeared under the title *The Common Sense Book of Baby and Child Care*; the paperback edition (at a cost of twenty-five cents per copy) was titled *The Pocket Book of Baby and Child Care*.

Although stylistically following the structure of Holt's "catechism" manual, Spock's *Baby and Child Care* (the shorter title used in succeeding editions) decisively broke from its forerunner's "scientific" system. First, Spock advocated for feeding, sleeping, and toilet-training schedules that followed infants' needs and personal readiness rather than standardized intervals. Second, while he advised parents to consult with doctors, he emphasized how his readers' own "instincts" were as important as the experts' advice, a view captured by his introductory "Letter to the Mother and Father" and opening words, "Trust yourself. You know more than you think you do." Spock essentially advocated for a positive view of child rearing, guided by Freud's stages of development and the recent work of Arnold Gesell and Frances Ilg, *Infant and Child in the Culture of Today* (1943). The conversational tone of Spock's manual had public appeal; within the first year over 750,000 copies of the paperback version alone had been purchased.

Baby and Child Care was favorably reviewed by the *Journal of the American Medical Association* and well received among pediatric specialists. After reading the book, C. Anderson Aldrich, director of the new Child Health Project at the Mayo Clinic, Rochester, Minnesota, offered Spock positions—which he accepted in 1947—as consultant in child psychiatry at the clinic and associate professor in child psychiatry at the Mayo Foundation, University of Minnesota. The innovative project, in which Spock carried out an "Inborn Temperament Study," followed the development of a select group of children from infancy onward. Within a few years, he became codirector of the project, but his psychoanalytical emphasis received harsh criticism from conservatives on the clinic's staff, who succeeded in eliminating the project's funding in 1951. In that year, Spock accepted positions as professor of child development at the University of Pittsburgh and physician at the university's Arsenal Health Center. At Pittsburgh, Spock at-

tracted a talented staff and established both a prestigious child development program and a public health training center for medical professionals. He again, however, encountered resistance that prompted him in 1955 to take a visiting professorship of child development at Western Reserve University Medical School in Cleveland, Ohio. Western Reserve (later renamed Case Western Reserve) kept him on a permanent basis, and he launched his important Child Rearing Study, funded by the W. T. Grant Foundation and modeled on the Mayo Clinic project. The study allowed him to test the accuracy of Freudian explanations of child development and the efficacy of his pediatric advice. While the results proved generally inconclusive, as one outcome the study successfully pioneered reform among the medical community in support of breast-feeding, which most mothers in the study chose over bottle-feeding. Throughout these years and professional positions, he wrote, often in collaboration with his colleagues, numerous scholarly articles and books on child rearing. His books included a picture album focusing on the baby's first year, a nutritional guide for feeding babies, a child care manual concerned with disabled children, and a guide for teenagers. His professional work earned him renown—sometimes controversially—as a forerunner in the study of child behavior. In 1967, Spock retired from his academic post.

While *Baby and Child Care* brought Spock new professional opportunities, it also led to a highly public career. Updated editions of the manual followed in 1957, 1968, and 1976; in 1985 and 1992 (with Michael Rothenberg); and in 1998 (with Steven Parker). Spock expanded and updated each edition to acknowledge new medical findings and the diversity of American families. By 1998 the book had been published in over three dozen translations; it sold over 50 million copies, surpassing all other books except the Bible. Known popularly as "The Baby Bible" or simply "Dr. Spock," for most of the latter half of the twentieth century, *Baby and Child Care* was the single most influential child care manual in and beyond the United States. Spock's common-sense appeal, the U.S. postwar prosperity, and the baby boom together brought the book and its author household fame. In 1954 he began writing advice columns in popular magazines such as *Ladies' Home Journal* and *American Weekly*. Finding *Ladies' Home Journal* too conservative, in 1962 he began writing regularly for the more liberal *Redbook*. He handled these and other popularizing works under his own corporation, Spock Projects. "Dr. Spock" became a national paterfamilias and the unquestioned authority in childhood matters, cited in popular venues including the television series *I Love Lucy*.

By the 1960s, however, it was this very image that feminist activists targeted, and many singled out Spock's baby book as a prime example of sexism in advice manuals. Critics pointed out how he gave primary responsibility of parenting to mothers and consistently privileged male children in his language. As

Betty Friedan noted in her highly influential *The Feminine Mystique* (1963)—a touchstone of the twentieth-century women's liberation movement—Spock's book participated in the "Freudian mania" that unfairly blamed mothers for various social outcomes. From another quarter, in the 1970s conservative politicians—most notably Republican vice-president Spiro T. Agnew—charged Spock with fostering "permissiveness" in parenting and creating the generation of "hippie" protesters of the 1960s, a charge later reinvented to account for the "me decade" of "yuppies" in the 1980s. While the feminist critiques prompted him to overhaul his manual significantly for the 1976 edition, he continually defended himself against the "permissive" charge with little success, even when he cited passages in his book that showed a position strongly supportive of strict parental intervention in matters of behavioral discipline.

Spock's reputation as a permissivist owed much to his growing involvement in liberal politics and social activism. Despite a politically conservative upbringing, he gradually adopted democratic and even radically liberal views. He was first introduced to socialist ideas by his wife, who was a member of her college's undergraduate socialist club (at Bryn Mawr) in the late 1920s and an active organizer of the American Labor Party in New York City in the 1930s. By the 1960s, Spock saw how child care had as much to do with national security, health care, and education as it did with the right parenting. In a 1960 television campaign advertisement with Jacquelyn Kennedy, he endorsed John F. Kennedy for president; Spock believed that Kennedy's promising domestic reform programs would significantly improve health care and education. When the threat of nuclear warfare escalated during the early 1960s, Spock joined the National Committee for a Sane Nuclear Policy (SANE), becoming a cochairman of the national board in 1962. Under Spock, SANE (later subsumed under Peace Action) became the largest peace organization in the nation. As a public scientific figure, he increasingly felt a sense of political responsibility that compelled him to support the Medicare Bill on a committee appointed by Kennedy and later to testify before Congress in its favor during Lyndon B. Johnson's administration. Spock also served as a member of the National Advisory Committee of the Office of Economic Opportunity and as advisor to Johnson's Great Society domestic program.

The growing political unrest in Vietnam concerned Spock as early as 1962 when he wrote a letter to Kennedy to voice his opposition against U.S. threats of armed intervention. But with the large-scale introduction of U.S. ground forces in 1965, Spock objected both in letters to Johnson and through SANE demonstrations. He soon became one of the nation's most visible and outspoken protesters of the Vietnam conflict. When he encountered the resistance of other SANE members to engaging in more radical protests, Spock sought other alliances. He prodded Martin Luther King, Jr., leader of the civil rights movement and

cautiously neutral on the Vietnam conflict, to publicly denounce U.S. involvement in 1967. In spring of that year, Spock and King led a march called the "Spring Mobilization to End the Vietnam War" in New York City that gained wide public attention and prompted supporters to urge them to run on a third-party presidential ticket (as King-Spock) in the 1968 elections. By then Spock believed that a third-party candidate represented the only hope for ending the Vietnam conflict, and to realize this hope he joined the ineffective National Conference for New Politics. Despite the encouragement, the King-Spock ticket never materialized.

An antidraft protest at the army induction center on Whitehall Street, New York City, in December 1967 resulted in Spock's first arrest and attracted the attention of the media and the F.B.I. A month later the U.S. Department of Justice in Boston indicted him and four other draft protesters, all strangers to Spock—Rev. William Sloane Coffin, Jr., Marcus Raskin, Mitchell Goodman, and Michael Ferber—on charges of criminal conspiracy in aiding draft evaders. All but Raskin of the "Boston Five," as they became popularly known, were convicted in June, but a year later the U.S. Court of Appeals in Boston overturned the decision, acquitting Spock. The trials won Spock new popularity, especially among college campuses, where he delivered more than 500 speeches in the late 1960s and as public opinion became increasingly critical of the Vietnam conflict. After his acquittal, he became cochairman of the People's Party, which renewed his hope for a third-party solution. He was chosen as presidential candidate, with educator Julius Hobson as his running mate for the 1972 elections; but many considered Spock's ideas too progressive and he lost with a mere 78,000 votes. Despite the disappointment, he continued his involvement, serving as Margaret Wright's running mate in the 1976 elections. Even when his political participation waned, he remained a social activist, promoting causes such as public awareness of the health dangers of store-bought milk for infants.

Spock and Jane Cheney divorced in early 1976. In October of that year, Spock married Mary Morgan Councille, a conference organizer and social activist. Their marriage produced no children.

Throughout his career, Spock earned high recognition both professionally and popularly as one of the fathers of behavioral pediatrics. He received an honorary degree from the University of Durham, England, in 1962. Late in his life, he continued his popular advice writing (for example, in *Parenting Magazine*) and gave many public lectures and television appearances. *Ms. Magazine* declared Spock a hero of the feminist movement in their Tenth Anniversary edition in 1982; *Life* included him among its 100 Most Influential Americans of the 20th Century in 1990. SANE dedicated its building in New York City to him, renaming it the Ben Spock Center for Peace. In his leisure time throughout his life he enjoyed ballroom dancing and sailing. By the early

1990s, his health gradually weakened, but a macrobiotic diet and regular exercise managed by his wife Mary extended his life for several years. He died at his home in San Diego.

• The primary manuscript and oral interview collections relating to Spock's life and career are held in archives at Syracuse University, Yale University, the Mayo Clinic (Rochester), the University of Pittsburgh, Case Western Reserve University, Columbia University, the National Institutes of Health (National Library of Medicine), Swarthmore College (Peace Collection), the John Fitzgerald Kennedy Library in Boston, Massachusetts, and the Lyndon Baines Johnson Library and Museum in Austin, Texas. Private materials remain with surviving members of Spock's family. Most of Spock's academic publications were indexed in *Index Medicus*; many of his popular articles were collected in *Dr. Spock Talks with Mothers: Growth and Guidance* (1961); *Problems of Parents* (1962); and *Dr. Spock on Parenting* (1988). In addition to his famous child care manual, his other books on child rearing include *A Baby's First Year*, with John Reinhart and Wayne Miller (1950); *Feeding your Baby and Child*, with Miriam E. Lowenberg (1955); *Caring for Your Disabled Child*, with Marion O. Lerrigo (1965), and *A Teenager's Guide to Life and Love* (1970). Two essays in which Spock links behavioral development and politics are *Decent and Indecent: Our Personal and Political Behavior* (1969) and *Raising Children in a Difficult Time: A Philosophy of Parental Leadership and High Ideals* (1974). Posthumously, Mary Morgan founded The Dr. Spock Company, which launched an Internet advice site, DrSpock.com, based on her late husband's child care writings. In-depth studies of his life and work include biographies by Thomas Maier, *Dr. Spock: An American Life* (1998), and Lynn Z. Bloom, *Doctor Spock: Biography of a Conservative Radical* (1972); a historical essay by William Graebner, "The Unstable World of Benjamin Spock: Social Engineering in a Democratic Culture, 1917–1950," *Journal of American History* 67 (1980): 512–629; a dissertation by Mary Ellen Hubbard, "Benjamin Spock, M.D.: The Man and His Work in Historical Perspective," Claremont Graduate School (1981); and an autobiography conducted through interviews with Mary Morgan, *Spock on Spock: A Memoir of Growing Up with the Century* (1994). Maier's biographical account provides a good overview and introduction to the role of Freud in Spock's thought. On Spock's activism, the important sources include Jessica Mitford, *The Trial of Dr. Spock, the Rev. William Sloane Coffin, Jr., Michael Ferber, Mitchell Goodman, and Marcus Raskin* (1969); Spock with Mitchell Zimmerman, *Dr. Spock on Vietnam* (1968); and Maier's biography. Two historical works that situate Spock's work within a broader tradition of expert advice include Barbara Ehrenreich and Dierdre English, *For Her Own Good: One Hundred and Fifty Years of Experts' Advice to Women* (1978) and Kathleen W. Jones, *Taming the Troublesome Child: American Families, Child Guidance, and the Limits of Psychiatric Authority* (1999). Obituaries are in the *New York Times*, 17 May 1998, and the 30 March 1998 issues of *Maclean's*, *Newsweek*, *People Weekly*, *Time*, and *U.S. News and World Report*. A tribute appears in the *Journal of Developmental and Behavioral Pediatrics* 19, no. 3 (June 1998): 230–34.

DONALD L. OPITZ

STANKY, Eddie (3 Sept. 1917–6 June 1999), baseball player and manager, was born Edward Raymond Stankiewicz in Philadelphia, Pennsylvania, the son of Frank Stankiewicz, a leather glazer, and Anna Pokolska Stankiewicz, a clothing factory worker. He grew up there and graduated from Northeast High, more noted for his soccer than his baseball skills. Originally signed by the Philadelphia Athletics, he spent eight seasons in the minor leagues, including a year in Greenville (Miss.), three in Portsmouth (Va.), three in Macon, and a career-making 1942 season in Milwaukee. Despite hitting over .300 six of those years, he had to surmount the handicap of being typed as too small for the big leagues, although at five feet eight inches and 165 pounds he was not as slight of build as some of the early stars of the game. At Macon he played for Milt Stock, a manager who schooled him in the tricks of the baseball trade and trained him to become a future manager. In 1942 Stanky married Stock's daughter, Dickie, with whom he was to have two sons and four daughters. Purchased by Bill Veeck for his Milwaukee club in the American Association after the 1941 season, Stanky led the league in hitting (.342), runs (124), and doubles (56), thereby garnering the Most Valuable Player award. Having enhanced his promise of becoming a star, he was sold to the Chicago Cubs.

Following a .245 rookie season as the Cubs' second baseman, he was benched and then traded to Brooklyn after he begged to play. In 1945 he set a new National League record with 148 walks, frustrating pitchers by fouling off pitches until he coaxed a base on balls. Despite a modest lifetime batting average of .268, Stanky led the National League in walks three times, earning him the nickname "walking man." He was also a master of getting hit by pitches, even in the head, at a time when batting helmets were still not in use. This "win at any cost" style of play characterized his career and grew out of his father-in-law's recommendation that he work at being an effective lead-off hitter. Supporters and opponents alike characterized "the Brat" with terms like scrappy, brash, aggressive, and intelligent, a player who accomplished more than his skills would suggest. Dodger president Branch Rickey's famous comment on Stanky was, "He can't hit, he can't run, he can't field, and he can't throw, but when the chips are down he beats you." Or, as manager Leo Durocher completed the phrase, "but he is one hell of a ball player" (Jacobs, p. 118). Stanky himself said he would do anything possible to win a game.

With the Dodgers, Stanky began earning his reputation as a winner. In 1947 he helped lead the team to the pennant, playing alongside and supporting Jackie Robinson as he broke the color barrier. To his dismay, Stanky was sold to the Boston Braves after the season, allowing the Dodgers to move Robinson to second base. The Braves proceeded to win their first pennant since 1914, with Stanky hitting a career-high .320 before going down with a broken ankle. But Stanky and shortstop Alvin Dark were traded to the New York Giants after the 1949 season, and that combination helped lead New York to the pennant in 1951. Though owner Horace Stoneham assured Stanky of a position on the Giants team as a player or coach as long as he wanted, Stanky agreed to be traded to the Cardinals and fulfill his long-time ambition to manage. He became player-manager in St. Louis in 1952, playing sparingly in 1952 and 1953 before retiring as a player.

Moderately successful as a manager, he did not really meet the expectations expressed by Branch Rickey: "He was born to be a big league manager. . . . Baseball hasn't had such a dynamic little personality since John J. McGraw." In fact, McGraw's nickname, "Muggsy," was passed along to Stanky (Jacobs, p. 120). Bob Broeg, a St. Louis sportswriter, called Stanky the smartest baseball man he ever met. He led the Cards to a third-place finish in 1952 and again in 1953, but they slipped to sixth in 1954 and then to fifth when Stanky was sacked 36 games into the 1955 season (they wound up seventh). He came back to manage the Chicago White Sox in 1966 and piloted them to fourth-place finishes for two years before they fell to ninth midway through the 1968 season, at which point Stanky was fired. While in Chicago, George Will reports, he had continued to do whatever he could to win. Since the White Sox were a light-hitting team, Stanky would store game balls for a week in a room with a humidifier on full blast. When they were taken out for the game, though dry on the outside they would have two ounces of moisture inside, enough to knock twelve feet off opponents' fly balls (Will, p. 307). Stanky's itch to manage led him to a strange one-day stint as pilot of the Texas Rangers in June 1977. The Rangers won, but Stanky quit, citing homesickness, and returned to his home in Mobile, leaving behind a career record as manager of 467–435.

During his playing days, Stanky enjoyed something of a Jekyll and Hyde reputation. In contrast to his combative on-field demeanor, off the field the Brat was a gentleman, considerate, witty, and soft-spoken. He didn't drink, rarely smoked, and avoided profanity. Following his stint as White Sox manager, Stanky's soft side triumphed in his new job. He took over in 1969 as baseball coach at the University of South Alabama and built a powerhouse program there. His teams never had a losing season and compiled a 488–193 record by the time of his retirement in 1983. He achieved this success despite being one of few NCAA coaches with a no-cut rule: if a student came out for the team, he made it. As a firm believer in team participation, Stanky was proud of playing a record 38 players in one nine-inning game against Vanderbilt in 1971. Managing on the college level did not, from his point of view, call for winning at any cost; his thrills came from the thanks of mothers when his players graduated with his help. He died at his Fairhope, Alabama, home following a heart attack.

• Information on Eddie Stanky can be found in Bruce Jacobs, ed., *Baseball Stars of 1953* (1953), and George Will, *Men at Work* (1990). Obituaries are in the *New York Times*, 7 June 1999, the *Washington Post*, 8 June 1999, and the *St. Louis Post-Dispatch*, 13 June 1999.

JOHN R. M. WILSON

STARBUCK, George (15 June 1931–15 Aug. 1996), poet, was born George Edwin Beiswanger in Columbus, Ohio, the son of George W. Beiswanger, a college professor, and Margaret Starbuck Beiswanger. The family lived in Illinois and then in California during George's childhood as the elder Beiswanger accepted a series of academic appointments. After his parents divorced, their son's surname was legally changed to his mother's maiden name, Starbuck.

Excelling in mathematics and intending to make a career in a math-related discipline, Starbuck entered the California Institute of Technology at the age of sixteen. He was also drawn to literature, however, and after two years at Caltech he left to concentrate on writing poetry. From 1952 until 1954 Starbuck served in the U.S. Army, rising to the rank of corporal in the military police. He subsequently attended the University of California at Berkeley and the University of Chicago, where one of his classmates was the future novelist Philip Roth, who became a lifelong friend and whose first book, *Goodbye Columbus* (1959), he helped to edit. After moving from Chicago to Boston in 1957, Starbuck attended classes for several years at Harvard, where his teachers included the poets Archibald MacLeish and Robert Lowell, but he did not earn a college degree at any institution. In 1958, while enrolled at Harvard part time, Starbuck began working as a junior editor in the trade department at the Boston book publishing firm Houghton Mifflin. He now had a family to support: three years earlier he had married Janice King, and the couple eventually had three children.

Starbuck's fellow students in Robert Lowell's highly competitive seminar at Harvard in 1958–1959 included a number of soon-to-be-famous poets, among them Sylvia Plath and Anne Sexton. Casual romances among the participants were apparently commonplace, although Plath, still passionately involved with her husband, Ted Hughes, was by all accounts an exception. Sexton, who was also married, thrived, however, on extramarital attention and took Starbuck as a lover. Though only three years Starbuck's senior, Sexton, who like Plath had already attempted suicide and was fashionably "in therapy," seemed to the smitten Starbuck far older and wiser, sophisticated and possessed of a fierce talent that he suspected surpassed his own. The couple's relationship was intense, conducted openly—they often traveled together—and apparently nourishing to both, with each acting as muse for the other and helping their respective careers to flourish. Starbuck was instrumental in having Sexton's first book of poetry, *To Bedlam and Part Way Back*, accepted by his employer, Houghton Mifflin, and he edited the volume for publication in 1960. That same year, at the age of twenty-nine, Starbuck, too, became famous in literary circles virtually overnight when his first collection of poems, *Bone Thoughts*, dedicated to Sexton, won the Yale Younger Poets Prize. Over the next few years the couple's romantic involvement ceased, but they remained close friends and relied on each other for advice until Sexton's suicide in 1974.

Wryly written and offering personal observations on a variety of topics that ranged from the Bayeux tapestry to a summer course on Keats, *Bone Thoughts* was praised for its engaging and witty use of colloquial language. Starbuck was viewed by many critics as a promising youthful voice on the literary horizon, and some predicted that he would emerge as a major spokesman for his generation. After winning a Guggenheim fellowship to study at the American Academy in Rome, Starbuck left Houghton Mifflin in 1961 and spent two years in Italy. Having divorced his first wife in Boston, he married again in 1962; his second wife was Judith Luraschi, an Italian artist, with whom he had two more children. In 1963 Starbuck returned to the United States to become a lecturer at the State University of New York at Buffalo, where he remained for a single academic year then moved to Iowa City to become an associate professor at the University of Iowa's renowned Writers Workshop. During this period Starbuck published poetry from time to time in the *New Yorker, Harper's,* and other major periodicals; a second book-length collection, titled *White Paper,* appeared in 1966. Written in the same vein as *Bone Thoughts* and evoking favorable comments similar to those he received for his first book, the poetry in *White Paper* encompassed a variety of often intricate forms and included verses that aimed sardonic protests at the Vietnam War and its U.S. perpetrators. As the conflict continued, Starbuck became a major figure in the protest movement, reading his antiwar verse at teach-ins around the country that he helped organize. But his poetry, even at its ostensibly most serious, continued to exhibit a playful wit, buttressed by puns and other forms of wordplay, making it more a charming exercise than an emotionally engaging diatribe.

Starbuck became director of the Iowa Writers Workshop in 1967, and a year later, after divorcing his second wife, he married Kathryn Dermand; there were no children from this marriage. In 1970 he moved back to Boston to become director of the creative writing program at Boston University. He continued to write poetry, publishing four more slim volumes over the next twelve years. *Elegy in a Country Church Yard* appeared in 1975, followed by *Desperate Measures* (1978) and *Talkin' B.A. Blues: The Life and a Couple of Deaths of Ed Teashack, or How I Discovered B.U.* (1980). His last volume of verse, *The Argot Merchant Disaster: Poems New and Selected* (1982), included seventeen uncollected poems written during the previous two years; the remainder of the book reprinted verse selected from *Bone Thoughts, White Paper,* and *Desperate Measures.* The book was dedicated to his father, with whom he had apparently reconciled in adulthood.

Starbuck had been suffering from Parkinson's disease since the mid-1970s, and by 1989 he was forced to retire from his post at Boston University. In the early 1990s he moved to Tuscaloosa, Alabama, and he died at his home there of complications from Par-

kinson's. Significantly outshone by his contemporaries in both output and recognition, Starbuck remained a minor writer of verse, never becoming the major figure in American poetry that some hopeful critics prophesied following the publication of his first volume. Praised as a wry versifier, indeed often called "a thinking man's Ogden Nash," he entertained many readers but few considered him an important poet. In retrospect Starbuck was without question a master of intricate poetic forms, in particular double dactyls, but not in possession of a strikingly singular poetic message. One suspects that in trying to establish a unique personal voice for himself, he may have deliberately avoided the anguish and anger of confessional verse epitomized by his contemporaries Sexton, Plath, Adrienne Rich, and other American poets who came to prominence in the 1960s. But through their fame and even notoriety they created an audience for dramatic intensity in late-twentieth-century poetry that Starbuck's verse could not attract.

• Biographical information on George Starbuck is limited. See *Contemporary Authors,* vol. 21–22 (1969); *Contemporary Authors: New Revision Series,* vol. 23 (1987); and *Contemporary Authors,* vol. 153 (1997). Starbuck's relationship with Anne Sexton is discussed in Diane Wood Middlebrook, *Anne Sexton: A Biography* (1991). An obituary appears in the *New York Times,* 17 Aug. 1996.

ANN T. KEENE

STARGELL, Willie (6 Mar. 1940–9 Apr. 2001), major-league baseball player, was born Wilver Dornel Stargell in Earlsboro, Oklahoma, the son of William Stargell and Gladys Vernell Stargell, giving him an ancestry both African American and Seminole Indian. He faced challenges growing up in the projects in Alameda, California, with his mother and stepfather Percy Russell after his father abandoned the family, but his mother later recalled that he was always "Mr. Good Guy" (*Current Biography,* 1980). He played high school ball at Encinal High in Alameda; his teammates Tommy Harper and Curt Motton also became big leaguers. After a season at Santa Rosa Junior College, Willie was signed by Bob Zuk of the Pirates for $1,500 and pursued his dream of escaping from the projects through baseball. The low minors were intimidating, especially his first stop at Roswell, New Mexico, where he was threatened by drunk whites not sympathetic to integrated baseball. The conditions in which he played improved in Grand Forks, North Dakota, in 1960, Asheville, North Carolina, in 1961, and Columbus, Ohio, in the International League in 1962. His impressive power won him a call-up to the parent Pittsburgh Pirates in late 1962, and he remained a Pirate throughout his career.

Although his leadership skills were immediately evident, Stargell happily took a back seat to Pirate team leader Roberto Clemente for his first ten years with the club. Primarily a left fielder early in his career, he moved to first base in 1975 as his mobility declined and his size increased from 180 toward 240 pounds on a 6'3'' frame. He became famous for clouting prodigious home runs when he connected and for striking out frequently when he did not, exuding joy whatever the result. He hit two homers out of Dodger Stadium, the first in 1969 (no other player managed even one until 1999). At one point he had the longest homer on record in half the National League parks. Dodger pitcher Don Sutton said, "He doesn't just hit pitchers. He takes away their dignity" (*USA Today*). He led the league in 1971 with 48 home runs and in 1973 with 44 on his way to a career total of 475. On the other hand, his lifetime tally of 1,936 strikeouts trailed only Reggie Jackson's among the century's eminent whiffers. Stargell played on his first pennant winner in 1971, but it was Clemente's World Series as the Pirates beat the Baltimore Orioles and Stargell batted only .208 after going hitless in the league championship series. However, when Clemente died in a plane crash following the 1972 season, the mantle of team leadership fell to the now-veteran Stargell.

Stargell presided over the dominant team in the National League East in the seventies. The Pirates won six of ten divisional titles, and they did it with a decidedly multicultural lineup. On 1 September 1971 they became the first major league team to field an all-black lineup, the result of aggressive recruiting during the sixties among Latin and African American prospects. Stargell, with his own mixed-race background, provided a bridge among the various racial and ethnic players and managed to develop a harmonious atmosphere rare among big-league teams. "Pops," as the fatherly Stargell was dubbed, gave out "Stargell Stars" to players for outstanding contributions to the team, and his teammates were eager to get these symbols that seemed more geared to the rah-rah college level. The Pirates of the 1970s and Stargell himself reached a climax in 1979. He hit .281 with 32 home runs and 82 runs batted in only 126 games, and his natural leadership skills inspired the team to take the pennant. The team found its identity in the Sister Sledge song "We Are Family," a celebration of harmony that symbolized the distinctive quality of the 1979 Pirates. Then Willie had his post-season as Clemente had had his in 1971. He batted .455 with two homers and 6 RBI in leading a sweep of Cincinnati. Then he hit .400 with three more home runs in leading the Pirates to a world championship from a 3-games-to-1 deficit against the favored Baltimore Orioles. He collected an unmatched array of awards for the season: he was co-most valuable player for the season (with Keith Hernandez), MVP of the Championship Series, MVP of the World Series, *Sporting News* Player of the Year, and *Sports Illustrated* co-athlete of the year (with Pittsburgh quarterback Terry Bradshaw). Thereafter, injuries slowed him, and after three more abbreviated seasons, he retired in 1982 at age forty-two with a lifetime .282 batting average.

Stargell was an intelligent man, conversant on many subjects, and an active community leader. During the Vietnam War, he vocally opposed American intervention. In 1972 he participated in a Nixon White House

athletes-against-drugs effort. He founded and served as president of the Black Athletes Foundation, an organization set up to combat sickle-cell anemia. But above all, he was a truly beloved ballplayer. Joe Morgan, a fellow Hall of Famer, said, "When I played, there were 600 baseball players, and 599 of them loved Willie Stargell. He's the only guy I could have said that about. He never made anybody look bad and he never said anything bad about anybody" (*Pittsburgh Post-Gazette*). Other teammates saluted him as a teacher and an infectiously joyous person. Sportswriter Claire Smith said, "There are Hall of Fame people, as opposed to Hall of Fame players. The former grace the game as much as the latter. And if you combine in one body both ingredients, you have something truly special. Willie Stargell was truly special" (*Philadelphia Inquirer*).

Following his playing career, Stargell coached at the minor- and major-league levels, largely with the Atlanta Braves, before he returned to the Pirates in 1997 as a special assistant to general manager Cam Bonifay. He never did achieve his dream of managing in the major leagues.

Stargell had two daughters in a first marriage. His second and longest marriage, to Dolores Parker on 19 November 1966, ended in divorce after producing two daughters and one son. In 1993 he married a third time, this time to Margaret Weller of Wilmington, North Carolina, where they lived until his death. The very day Stargell succumbed to high blood pressure, kidney disorders, and a stroke, the Pirates opened their new PNC Stadium to inaugurate the 2001 season. Outside the new stadium stands a statue of the greatest of Pirate sluggers from their Forbes Field and Three Rivers Stadium days—Willie Stargell.

• Information about Stargell can be found in his autobiography, *Willie Stargell* (1984); Bill Libby, *Willie Stargell: Baseball Slugger* (1973); and Bob Adelman and Susan Hall, *Out of Left Field: Willie Stargell and the Pittsburgh Pirates* (1974). See also the 10 Apr. 2001 obituaries in the *Pittsburgh Post-Gazette*, the *Philadelphia Inquirer*, the *New York Times*, *USA Today*, and the *Los Angeles Times*, and the 16 April 2001 issue of *Sports Illustrated*.

JOHN R. M. WILSON

STEBBINS, G. Ledyard (6 Jan. 1906–19 Jan. 2000), botanist, geneticist, and evolutionist, was born in Lawrence, New York, the son of George Ledyard Stebbins, originally from Cazenovia in central New York, and Edith Alden Candler Stebbins, who was from Brooklyn, New York. His father was a wealthy New York financier and real estate developer who was responsible for developing the resort town of Seal Harbor, Maine, and for helping to create Acadia National Park, on Mount Desert Island, Maine. Ledyard Stebbins, named after his father, added until shortly after his father's death "junior" to his name. Stebbins was the third offspring in the family. His older brother Henry became a well-known doctor in Maine and his older sister Marcia became an artist.

Stebbins's interest in natural history and his fondness for plant life appeared early during the summers he spent with his family in Seal Harbor. Both of his parents encouraged the study of natural history and took their children out for frequent nature walks, canoe rides, and hikes. The resort life of Seal Harbor, which was popular with northeastern intellectuals, also brought the Stebbins children into contact with scientists like Edgar T. Wherry (1885–1982), an expert on ferns.

In 1914 the family was forced to move west when Edith Stebbins contracted tuberculosis. Stebbins was enrolled in the Cate School in Carpinteria, California, after the family settled in Santa Barbara. He appeared to be an average student and somewhat shy and awkward at social functions. In 1924 Stebbins followed his older brother to Harvard and planned to embark on a law career. He changed his mind after a summer of botanizing in his familiar Mount Desert Island environment. Despite initial parental disapproval, he was able to change his major to botany and to undertake research in taxonomy with Merritt Lyndon Fernald (1873–1950). He completed several taxonomic studies with Fernald but then switched to the more exciting area of cytology, working with Edward Charles Jeffrey (1866–1952). He completed a dissertation on the cytology of the genus *Antennaria* with the help of the new geneticist at the Arnold Arboretum, Karl Sax (1892–1973). Less than harmonious, his final dissertation committee had so many disagreements among themselves over the differing scientific approaches Stebbins had used that he was forced to edit the thesis several times before it was finally approved. The completed dissertation formed the backbone of his subsequent systematic and cytological studies. His Ph.D. was granted by Harvard in 1931.

In 1932 Stebbins took the offer of a position as teacher of biology at Colgate University. Though he did not have much time for research, he continued to refine his expertise in cytogenetics, the new science that concentrated on chromosomes and integrated cytology with genetics. He collaborated closely with Percy Saunders (1869–1953) at nearby Hamilton College. Saunders bred hybrid peonies in his backyard and subsequently studied the chromosomal behavior of the different varieties. In 1935 Stebbins was given the opportunity to pursue scientific research in genetics full time when he became junior geneticist to the University of California botanist E. B. Babcock (1877–1954). Babcock was working on an enormous project designed to identify and study the genetics of the evolutionary process in the genus *Crepis*. Together, Stebbins and Babcock published a series of important articles and a monograph titled *The American Species of Crepis* in 1938. They made a notable contribution in articulating the notion of "the polyploid complex," a complex of reproductive forms that centered on diploids fringed by apomictic or asexual forms.

In 1938 with Babcock's support, Stebbins was hired as full-time professor in the genetics department at the University of California at Berkeley. He was then required to teach the course in evolution. In preparation, Stebbins read widely in the literature on evolution and was quickly exposed to the exciting new research incorporating genetics and evolutionary studies. He became part of a small circle of biosystematists in the San Francisco Bay area that included leading botanists like Jens Clausen (1891–1969), visiting botanists such as Edgar Anderson (1897–1969), and the evolutionary geneticist Theodosius Dobzhansky (1900–1975). With their intellectual encouragement, Stebbins pursued evolutionary research closely and read so widely that he rapidly became one of the few botanists easily conversant with the disparate literature in genetics, ecology, systematics, cytology, and paleontology.

The opportunity to draw all the disparate branches together in a synthesis in understanding mechanisms and patterns of plant evolution came in 1946 when Stebbins was invited on the recommendation of Dobzhansky to deliver Columbia University's prestigious Jesup Lectures. In 1950 the lectures were published as *Variation and Evolution in Plants*, which proved to be one of the most important books published in twentieth-century American botany because of its synthetic breadth and because it brought botanical science into the new synthesis of evolutionary theory. It became part of the canon of biological works written between 1936 and 1950 that formed the backbone of the "modern synthesis of evolution," or the historical event known as the "evolutionary synthesis." From then onward, Stebbins became one of the few experts on modern evolutionary theory and the person generally credited with founding the science of evolutionary botany or plant evolutionary biology. Also in 1950 Stebbins moved to the University of California, Davis, where he began to build the department of genetics. His research interests shifted to areas associated with development and genetics. Through the 1950s and 1960s he trained over thirty graduate students, most of whom were in genetics, developmental biology, or agricultural science.

Throughout the course of his scientific career, Stebbins showed a remarkable ability to understand new problems and to apply new techniques. Unlike most botanists, Stebbins worked on an immense range of plant organisms from grasses to peonies to members of the daisy family. He published extensively in systematics, morphology, cytology, genetics, plant geography, and developmental biology. His publication list includes a staggering number of review articles that reflected his command of new literature and his ability to synthesize disparate information. Stebbins continued in this vein, although eventually in a diminished capacity, until the time of his death.

Stebbins's contributions extended far outside science, especially after the publication of his 1950 book of the Jesup Lectures. He became active in organizations such as the International Union of Biological Sciences. He served as president of the American Society of Naturalists, the Western Society of Naturalists, the Botanical Society of America, and the Society for the Study of Evolution. He was a member of the National Academy of Sciences.

Throughout the 1960s and the 1970s Stebbins actively defended evolution against the assaults of creationists. He worked closely with the Biological Sciences and Curriculum Study (BSCS) to develop curricula at the high school level that were built on the belief that evolution was the central unifying principle in biology. Stebbins contributed to the teaching of evolution even more heavily by writing textbooks and semipopular books of science and by giving many public lectures. Yet another of Stebbins's areas of interest was conservation. In the 1960s he helped create the California Native Plant Society, which he served as president in 1967. He organized field trips and fought tirelessly to protect ecologically sensitive areas, such as a well-known strip of raised beach on the Monterey Peninsula. For his work in conservation and in evolutionary science, the University of California, Davis, paid him the rare honor of naming a 227-acre tract near Lake Berryessa, California, the Stebbins Cold Canyon Reserve.

Stebbins was married twice. His first marriage produced three children, Edith (b. 1932), Robert (b. 1933), and George (1935), but ended in divorce. Stebbins remarried in the 1950s; his second wife, Barbara, had one son by a previous marriage.

Stebbins became emeritus professor in genetics in 1973. Stricken with cancer, he died at his home in Davis.

• In addition to the formal collection of Stebbins papers located in the Department of Special Collections, University of California, Davis, documents of his are scattered widely in U.S. archives. Correspondence and other papers are in the Bancroft Library at the University of California, the American Philosophical Society, and the archives of the Missouri Botanical Garden. Biographical accounts include Vassiliki Betty Smocovitis, "G. Ledyard Stebbins, Jr. and the Evolutionary Synthesis (1924–1950), " *American Journal of Botany* 84 (1997): 1625–37. Obituaries include ones by Carol Kaesuk Yoon in the *New York Times*, 21 Jan. 2000, and Elaine Woo in the *Los Angeles Times*, 22 Jan. 2000; see also Phyllis M. Faber, "G. Ledyard Stebbins, Jr. 1906–2000," *Fremontia* 27 (2000): 69–70.

VASSILIKI BETTY SMOCOVITIS

STEEL, Dawn (19 Aug. 1946–20 Dec. 1997), film producer and executive, was born in the Bronx, New York City, the daughter of Nat Steel, who worked in the textile industry, and Lillian Tarlo Steel. Dawn's father, born Nat Spielberg (he changed his surname in the hope of boosting his part-time career as a bodybuilder), suffered a nervous breakdown when she was nine, forcing her mother to take a position in an electronics firm to sustain the family. Within eight years Lillian Steel became general manager and the first female executive of the company; during that time the family moved to Great Neck, Long Island, where Dawn attended high school.

After graduation Dawn Steel entered Boston University, where she majored in marketing, paying tuition by working as a go-go dancer at a local bar. After her freshman year she transferred to the School of Commerce at New York University. In 1968, broke and exhausted from a hectic schedule of school and work, Steel left NYU to work full time as a receptionist for a sports book publisher. Despite opportunities to write and edit while employed by the Stadia Publishing Company, she left for an entry-level position at the new adult magazine *Penthouse*, telling her parents, however, that she was working instead for the more respectable women's magazine *Mademoiselle*.

The irony of taking a job with a publication meant to exploit male fantasies at the very time that Gloria Steinem was launching the feminist magazine *Ms.* was not lost on Steel. But she seized the opportunity, and *Penthouse* founder Bob Guccione promoted her to head of merchandising, charged with creating licensing and mail order operations for the magazine. One of her great marketing successes was the "Penis Plant" (a phallic-shaped amaryllis), which, according to the advertisement, could be had for "$6.98 and a lot of love."

In 1975, with Ronald Richard Rothstein, who on 31 December of that year would become her first husband, Steel began marketing designer toilet paper that parodied the Gucci company's logo. The product sold extremely well, but its success sparked a lawsuit from the Gucci family claiming trademark infringement. Although the case was eventually settled out of court, the story, with Steel portrayed as underdog, appeared in many of the New York papers, generating such headlines as "The Gucci Toilet Paper Caper." In late 1976 Steel and Rothstein were divorced, after a ten-month union that produced no children. But they remained business associates, forming in 1977 Oh Dawn! Inc. (a name inspired by friends' inevitable reaction when told of Steel's line of work), and expanded their enterprise to include toilet paper printed with everything from crossword puzzles to weight loss guides and novelty soaps.

In 1978 Steel moved to Los Angeles, where after several months of job searching she was hired as director of merchandising at Paramount Studios, then headed by entertainment tycoon Michael Eisner, who would become her lifelong friend and mentor. Within six months she was promoted to vice president of merchandising and licensing, earning a reputation for boldness and tenacity. Given *Star Trek: The Motion Picture* as her first assignment, Steel quickly impressed high-level Paramount executives by successfully marketing to retailers like McDonald's and K-Mart (whom she hoped would sell *Star Trek*–related products) a behind-schedule, over-budget movie based on a television show absent from the airwaves for several years. After finishing work on *Star Trek*, which was released in 1979, she was named vice president of production in features, her first job in movie production.

As a junior production executive, Steel was responsible for developing ideas for movies and for cultivating relationships with writers and directors, in the hope that they would bring new ideas to Paramount. She was a savvy businesswoman, learning her job "by doing and watching" and by making friends with powerful insiders of the movie industry—David Geffen, Jeffrey Katzenberg, Barry Diller, and Don Simpson (at the time Paramount's head of production). During these years Steel oversaw production of the unlikely hit *Flashdance* (1983), which portrays an ambitious woman who is a welder by day and a dancer by night; in her autobiography, Steel called it "*Rocky* with a female underdog" (p. 134). *Flashdance* made nearly $100 million in the United States. Her next hit, *Footloose*, was released the following year, earning $8.5 million in its first weekend.

In September 1984 Steel's mentors at Paramount—Diller, Katzenberg, and Eisner—resigned, Diller moving to Fox and Katzenberg and Eisner taking over Walt Disney Studios, leaving Steel as the senior ranking production executive. Just seven months later, in April 1985, Steel was named head of production at Paramount, only the third woman in history to assume the title. Under her control Paramount produced a string of commercially successful films that included *The Untouchables*, *Top Gun*, *Fatal Attraction*, and *The Accused*. Steel married Charles "Chuck" Roven, a film producer, in 1985.

In March 1987, literally while giving birth to her only child, Steel was fired from her position at Paramount. No reasons for her dismissal were given by Paramount, but in her autobiography she blames both Frank Mancuso, chair of Paramount, and Ned Tanen, chair of the company's motion picture division. Shortly thereafter, in October 1987, Steel became head of Columbia Studios, the first woman to hold such a position in Hollywood. At the time Columbia was nearly last in box office share and in need of very strong leadership.

During her tenure at Columbia, Steel oversaw production of many financially (if not all critically) successful films, including *Ghostbusters II* (1989); a restored version of *Lawrence of Arabia*; *When Harry Met Sally* (1990); *Awakenings* (1990); *Look Who's Talking* (1990); and *Flatliners* (1990). By 1990 Columbia, which had purchased Tri-Star Pictures, had moved to third place in box office share.

Steel left Columbia–Tri-Star in 1991, when Sony bought out the company. She then rejoined Katzenberg and Eisner at Disney, where as an independent producer she made *Cool Runnings* (1993), a popular movie about a Jamaican bobsledding team. Steel's *City of Angels*, starring Meg Ryan and Nicholas Cage, was released posthumously, in 1998, after she died in Los Angeles from a malignant brain tumor.

Steel not only was the first woman to head a major movie studio; according to writer Nora Ephron, "she was the first woman to understand that part of her responsibility was to make sure that eventually there were lots of other powerful women" (*New York Times*, 22 Dec. 1997), hiring numerous female executives, directors, and producers. Self-confident, determined,

and vibrant, Steel held her own in the often ruthless, male-dominated film production industry—but at a cost. Featured on the cover of *California* magazine's "Bosses from Hell" issue in 1988, Steel was accused of being mean, abrasive, and even profane toward her employees, labels commonly attributed to strong women in powerful positions. Steel used her talent and persistence to, in her words, "climb the male ladder of success" in Hollywood and in the process opened the field to a new generation of women.

• Dawn Steel's autobiography is *They Can Kill You . . . But They Can't Eat You: Lessons from the Front* (1993). Written in a very personal style and divided into sections titled "The Dawn of Dawn," "The Break of Dawn," and so on, the book intersperses details of her life with wisdom gained throughout her career in the film industry. The 30 Aug. 1993 issue of the *New York Times* has a long article on Steel in which she reflects on her career. Obituaries are in the *New York Times*, 22 Dec. 1997; *Entertainment Weekly*, 9 Jan. 1998; and *People*, 12 Jan. 1998.

STACEY HAMILTON

STEIN, Herbert (27 Aug. 1916–8 Sept. 1999), economist and policy advisor, was born in Detroit, Michigan, the son of David Stein, a Russian immigrant who was a mechanic at Ford Motor Company, and Jessie Segal Stein. When the Great Depression came, Stein's father spent some time working at General Electric in Schenectady, New York, and then was unemployed for a large part of the downturn. Stein graduated from high school at age fifteen and entered Williams College in Williamstown, Massachusetts, in the same year. He was a distinguished student and won the prestigious Wells Prize before he was twenty for scholarly work on Allied finances in World War I. As a scholarship student at Williams, Stein worked his way through, partly by washing dishes in the Sigma Phi fraternity house. Sigma Phi did not admit Jews as members; it was characteristic of Stein that he showed no resentment over this situation.

After graduating from college, he entered the graduate school of economics at the University of Chicago. He studied under some of the great names of economics in the twentieth century, including Jacob Viner, Frank Knight, and Henry C. Simons. In this milieu he came to appreciate the workings of the free market, and he also learned much from Knight about the role of wit in teaching and writing economics, and from Simons about the need for kindness and compassion in economics. He quoted from them frequently and often said they were the intellectual capital on which he drew for most of his life.

The main contribution of graduate school to his life, however, was that in a class on microeconomics taught by Viner, he met his future wife, Mildred Fishman, also a graduate student in economics. They married in 1937 and remained together until her death in April 1997; they had two children. Stein also formed long-lasting and important associations at Chicago with future Nobelist Milton Friedman, Aaron Director, George Stigler, and Lowell Harriss. To earn money to support his family, Stein left Chicago before finishing his Ph.D. studies. He taught briefly at Iowa, worked on a WPA project in Minneapolis, and then went to Washington, D.C., where he worked at the Federal Deposit Insurance Corporation, established only a few years earlier.

As war loomed, he joined the War Production Board until 1944, when he was inducted into the navy. He was sent back to the WPB in the fall of 1945.

In 1944, as a lieutenant in the navy, Stein won a nationwide contest sponsored by Pabst Brewing Company in which thousands of economists and others in the nation competed to design a plan for postwar economic reconstruction so as to avoid slipping back into another depression. Stein's 1944 plan called for a highly adaptive and supportive fiscal policy, limited government regulation, except in antitrust, and primary reliance upon the price system. Winning this prize at the age of twenty-eight put Stein into the national consciousness as an authoritative voice on macroeconomic policy, especially fiscal policy, and he remained a public figure until his death.

In 1945 Stein joined the fledgling Committee for Economic Development as associate research director and then research director. The CED was a group of moderately conservative, pro-free market but not radically antigovernment heads of large businesses. As research director, he guided the creation of highly regarded policy statements about fiscal policy, labor relations, international trade, and defense.

Stein's innovative approach to fiscal policy included the "full employment budget." This called for the federal government to use taxing and spending and borrowing powers to run a balanced budget at full employment, although he recognized the difficulties in determining what constituted "full employment" in various situations. As unemployment worsened, the government was to stimulate the economy by increasing the budget deficit. When the economy was growing too rapidly, the government was to generate a budgetary surplus to slow it down.

This prescription he later modified to call for tendencies in these directions and not necessarily an actual surplus or deficit of any particular size in boom or recessionary times. He also modified his prescription to call for balanced budgets at "high employment," which meant when the economy approached what was conceded by impartial observers to be full employment.

He was a free trader in terms of international trade and believed that all parties were better off when the doctrine of comparative advantage was called into play by free trade. He was skeptical of the ability of unions to raise wages for any but their members (and therefore suspected that they worsened conditions of work for those who were not in the unions). He believed that Milton Friedman and Anna Jacobson Schwartz had made historic contributions in monetary policy and did not attempt to improve on their work. He was for the strongest possible national defense in every situation and supported a high level of defense preparedness even if that meant higher taxes and larger deficits. He supported a progressive income tax and did not share in the belief that Keynesianism and the Democratic party were instruments of class warfare intended to carry America on a road to serfdom. Indeed, while he was skeptical of government efforts to help any but the very poorest, he was also dubious about the notion that government was itself always an enemy of freedom. (This was one of the few areas in which he disagreed with many of his colleagues from the University of Chicago.)

In 1965 Stein left the Committee for Economic Development and spent a year at the Stanford Center for Advanced Study in the Behavioral Sciences. There, in addition to making lasting friends and enjoying California, Stein began work on his magnum opus, *The Fiscal Revolution in America* (1968). It traced developments in fiscal policy from roughly the Herbert Hoover era to the Lyndon Johnson era. Stein's main thesis was that Hoover began the stimulative fiscal policies that were enlarged and increased by Franklin D. Roosevelt as the New Deal. He had high praise for the fiscal policies of FDR's wartime years and criticized John F. Kennedy and his advisors for shoddy, intellectually dishonest criticism of the Eisenhower years and for making false promises about economic growth.

In 1966, Stein joined the Brookings Institution as a senior fellow. In 1968 he was asked by Richard Nixon to join the Council of Economic Advisers under the chairmanship of Paul McCracken, an economist for whom Stein had the highest professional and personal regard. Stein's high and low points as adviser to Nixon came in the fall of 1971 when Nixon instituted wage and price controls to stifle the incipient but persistent inflation, along with closing the "gold window." Stein was put in charge of the wage price controls along with John Dunlop. Nixon later said that he put Stein in charge of the controls because he knew Stein disliked price controls and would not permit them to last for long. The controls became an unwieldy mess, but in the beginning they yielded a stunning combination of rapid growth and price stability (as might have been predicted on both counts).

In 1972, on the departure of Paul McCracken, Stein was made chairman of the Council. He served loyally and with great affection for Nixon until the president's resignation in August 1974. In that period, Stein fought against a resumption of wage price controls and attempted to figure out why inflation was so persistent when unemployment was high. Stein's tentative answer had to do with rigidities in the mechanisms that would allow prices to fall. He was so devoted to Nixon that his wife campaigned vigorously around the country for the president's reelection.

In 1974, Stein left government service to become the A. Willis Robertson Professor of Economics at the University of Virginia and was simultaneously made a senior fellow at the American Enterprise Institute. Stein's writing gradually shifted from strictly economics to public policy and then to human life in general.

He was a member of the board of contributors of the *Wall Street Journal,* briefly wrote a syndicated column, and appeared on the op-ed page in large daily newspapers around the nation for about twenty-five years. He served as a director of a number of corporations, including Reynolds Metals and United Virginia Bankshares (later Suntrust). Stein worked energetically in the Carter and early Reagan years on the Committee on the Present Danger for better military preparedness. He also wrote a monthly newsletter for the AEI entitled *The Washington Economist,* and helped to found the National Economists Club in Washington, D.C.

In the early 1980s, Stein was tapped by his longtime colleague and friend Secretary of State George P. Shultz to work with MIT professor Stanley Fischer (later deputy director of the International Monetary Fund) on stabilization of the Israeli shekel and salvation of the Israeli economy. Their plans for fiscal and monetary restraint and some freeing of markets worked well, although the proposals were originally highly controversial in Israel.

Stein's later works included *Governing the $5 Trillion Economy* (1989), which called for fiscal planning to help the economy achieve social and moral goals as well as grow soundly, and *Presidential Economics* (1984), about styles and means of fiscal governance in the period from the Great War to the Bush years, later updated through the Clinton years. Stein also published several books of his essays: *Washington Bedtime Stories* (1986), *On the Other Hand* (1995), and *What I Think* (1998), the latter including musings about life and love and the appreciation of being a free citizen in America in the twentieth century. At the time of his death, he had just finished a third revision of *An Illustrated Guide to the American Economy* with his close friend and colleague Murray Foss. He also collaborated on a novel, *On the Brink* (1977), about a hyperinflationary catastrophe, and a guide to surviving high inflation, *Moneypower* (1980), both with his son Benjamin.

Stein's importance as a commentator rests partly on his contributions regarding fiscal policy, but also largely on his lucidity and wit, as well as his calm, reasoned response to every situation, rising above partisan or doctrinal approaches to policy issues. He was also known for his aphorisms, especially "Stein's Law": "If something cannot go on forever, it will stop" (with reference to the U.S. trade deficit). He wrote often of how very little economists knew about the causes of even very large shifts in the economy; he called himself the leader of the "don't know" school of economics. His writings were deemed so clear and instructive to the general public that Nobelist Paul Samuelson called Stein "the Montaigne of our profession."

• Besides the works by Herbert Stein cited above, sources of information on Stein's life include articles in *Current Biography* (1973) and in *Who Was Who in America,* vol. 13

(1998–2000). Obituaries are in the *New York Times* and the *Washington Post,* both 9 Sept. 1999.

BEN STEIN

STEINBERG, Saul (15 June 1914–12 May 1999), graphic artist, was born in Râmincul-Sarat, Romania, the son of Moritz Steinberg, a printer and bookbinder, and Rosa Iacobson Steinberg. In later years, Steinberg recalled Romania as "a masquerade country." The work of Steinberg's life was largely concerned with masks of reality and the reality of masks. The only difference between Americans and others, he noted, was that they wore their masks more lightly.

After high school in Bucharest, in 1932 Steinberg enrolled in the local university to study philosophy and letters, moving a year later to the Reggio Politecnico Facoltà Architettura in Milan, Italy, where he (in 1940, by which time he had left the country) gained his doctorate in architecture. Steinberg never designed a building, preferring for the most part to make small, increasingly enigmatic line drawings.

By 1936 Steinberg was contributing cartoons—rather in the jangly manner of the *New Yorker*'s George Price—to the biweekly Milan magazine *Bertoldo.* The English translation of the caption to one cartoon—"Dammit! This isn't me! I got lost in the crowd!"—presaged the many variations on the search for identity that occupied Steinberg's next six decades. By 1940 his drawings had appeared in *Life* and *Harper's Bazaar.* As war enveloped Europe, Steinberg decided to flee westward. After once being rebuffed by Portugal and winding up in a detention camp, he was aided in 1941 by his New York agent and made it as far as Ellis Island before being sent to the Dominican Republic. Faked "official" documents, seals, and stamps emerged as motifs in his later work.

Traveling from the Dominican Republic, with the active sponsorship of the *New Yorker,* Steinberg was admitted into the United States in 1942. He was soon a naturalized citizen. In 1943, the year of his marriage to the painter Hedda Sterne (they had no children and separated in the late 1960s), Steinberg had his first one-man show at New York's Wakefield Gallery. When he was called up in the draft the same year, the *New Yorker* again intervened; on a single day he was granted citizenship and commissioned an ensign in the U.S. Navy. Such anomalies were the norm in Steinberg's life. Steinberg's wartime experiences, which apparently included flying the China-Burma "hump" to show Chinese how to blow up bridges, as well as serving in the Office of Strategic Services, produced for the *New Yorker* a series of nonhumorous drawings of China, India, North Africa, and Italy. Regularly describing himself as an observer-journalist, Steinberg saw the viewers of his art as his "readers." Discharged as a lieutenant in 1946, Steinberg returned to Manhattan. The wartime drawings formed the basis for Steinberg's first published collection, *All in Line* (1945), though the book also included a drawing of a man drawing himself, trying to finish off the chin.

In 1946 Steinberg was one of the "Fourteen Americans" showcased at the Museum of Modern Art, where he was called a "deft miniaturist." Steinberg's "war correspondence" resumed when he covered the Nuremberg trials for the *New Yorker*. He moved to Paris for a while before traveling to Mexico. Back in the United States, he took up mural-painting for the Terrace Plaza Hotel in Cincinnati. At one point he said he really wanted to exhibit his drawings in a Broadway shooting gallery.

The Art of Living (1949) saw Steinberg increasingly concerned with the nature of reality (or the questionable reality of nature.) The collection ("about: chairs, subways, . . . cats, horses, art and women") was also about perspectives on the reality of objects—the number four, for example. Steinberg called it an interesting number, "a shape [neither open nor closed] that would arouse the curiosity of a cat . . . The abstraction, number 4, became a reality, and the cat became an abstraction because it combined itself with this number."

In 1953 Steinberg had his first Paris show. The volume *Passport* (1954) offered the first of many illusionary studies of real and ersatz documents, disguised as photographs of collages and tabletops. In 1954 Steinberg, an inveterate traveler, whose destinations now included the Civil War battlefields and the wilder shores of California, went on the road for *Life* with the Milwaukee Braves baseball team. He found baseball "an allegorical play about America, a poetic, complex and subtle play of courage, fear, good luck, mistakes, patience about fate and sober self-esteem (batting average)."

In 1956 Steinberg was commissioned by the United Nations International Children's Educational Foundation (UNICEF) to create Christmas cards, which became highly popular. More travels followed—South America, Russia, Tashkent. In 1958 he created a mural for the American pavilion at the Brussels World's Fair. In 1960 came *The Labyrinth*, a series of enigmatic drawings that depict "frozen music" and the slippery nature of words, among other phenomena. In "Who Did It?" it is the word Who that does It—that is, plunges Did into the heart of the prone It. *The New World*, published in 1965, makes graphically clear how people try to communicate with each other even though they speak different languages. *Le Masque*, of a year later, includes a series of masks drawn on paper bags and photographed by Inge Morath. In 1967, the year he was artist in residence at the Smithsonian Institution, Steinberg and the novelist Saul Bellow traveled the Nile, worrying about being eaten by crocodiles—another favorite Steinberg image. His 1973 collection, *The Inspector*, is particularly concerned with "parades, biographies, . . . time and space, . . . rubber-stamp architecture, . . . words and letters"; one drawing simply shows "(1905–)" looming above all, an ambiguous and ominous message that we live our lives in the hyphen.

The single Steinberg illustration most recognizable to the general public is his Manhattanite's view of the world, published as a *New Yorker* cover in 1976. Looking westward, nothing past the Hudson really matters—mountains and cities and oceans are compressed into insignificance. The drawing has been regularly parodied, and in 1987 Steinberg won a lawsuit to stop a filmmaker from adapting it into a poster. Steinberg spent some time as official artist at Cape Canaveral trying to understand astronauts. His last collection, *The Discovery of America* (1992), shows his adopted countrymen in general as "blowsy characters amid tawdry settings." His latter-day *New Yorker* colleague Edward Koren said that Steinberg fixed on American life "without being too close to it."

Steinberg was called by one critic a veritable history of modern art. Obituarist Sarah Boxer credited him with having evoked Pablo Picasso, James Joyce, Paul Klee, Honoré Daumier, Eugène Ionesco, Marcel Duchamp, Samuel Beckett, Luigi Pirandello, and Charlie Chaplin. In the catalog accompanying the 1979 Steinberg retrospective at the Whitney Museum of American Art, the art critic Harold Rosenberg commended Steinberg for having kept the question "Is he an artist?" alive "for more than thirty-five years." Steinberg died at home in Manhattan.

• Brendan Gill, *Here at the New Yorker* (1975), clarifies Steinberg's entry into the United States. Harold Rosenberg's critical essay leads the Whitney Museum of American Art's catalog for the 1979 retrospective, *Saul Steinberg* (1978). The catalog includes a chronology of his life by Steinberg. Steinberg contributed illustrations to many books. Obituaries include Christopher Hawtree's in the (London) *Guardian*, 14 May 1999, and Sarah Boxer's in the *New York Times*, 13 May 1999.

JAMES ROSS MOORE

STEVENS, Brooks (7 June 1911–4 Jan. 1995), industrial designer, was born in Milwaukee, Wisconsin, the son of William C. Stevens, a vice president of the Cutler-Hammer Company, manufacturers of industrial equipment, and Sally Stevens, whose maiden name is unknown. Young Stevens showed an early aptitude for drawing, and while recovering from polio during childhood he spent many hours perfecting his skill. After attending local schools he enrolled at Cornell University in 1929 to study architecture; although he remained there for four years, he left before graduating, realizing that building construction was in abeyance thanks to the Great Depression. Returning home to Milwaukee, Stevens took his father's advice and set himself up in business as a design consultant for companies building machinery. Then Cutler-Hammer duly hired him to design a line of electrical controls as well as a corporate logo.

But soliciting work at other companies in the vicinity proved difficult. Industrial design in the United States was in its infancy, and the depression made it difficult to sell not only new products but new ideas for their manufacture as well. Nevertheless, Stevens kept at it, and word spread of his innovative and attractive designs that were helping companies succeed in garnering new business. One of his earliest clients was Evinrude, for whom in 1934 he designed the first streamlined shell to enclose an outboard motor; thirty years later he was still working for the company, designing sleek power boats. Another notable early achievement occurred in 1936, when he perfected the appearance of the first electrically powered clothes dryer. Although engineers at Hamilton Industries, based in Two Rivers, Wisconsin, had come up with a prototype for such a machine, their device was basically a sheet-metal box enclosing a rotating drum. With the keen eye for marketing that Stevens would exhibit throughout his career, he suggested that the engineers install a clear glass door on the front, so that users could see their clothes being dried; moreover, he advised the company to give department store demonstrations of the device using brightly colored boxer shorts. The dryer as designed by Stevens became a big success and inspired other companies to manufacture similar appliances modeled on his design.

As the depression economy began improving in the early 1940s, Stevens slowly prospered, guided always by a desire to make any product he worked on both easy to use and attractive for its users. In the middle of the decade, with the rapid growth of a postwar consumer-driven economy in the aftermath of World War II, Stevens was suddenly faced with a booming demand for his services in every area imaginable. Among his best-known designs were Briggs & Stratton and Lawn Boy lawn mowers, Harley-Davidson motorcycles, and a civilian adaptation of the army Jeep. For the Miller Brewing Company he not only designed the corporate logo but also advised the company to bottle its product, advertised as "the champagne of bottled beer," in clear rather than brown glass.

During his long career, Stevens and his company, Brooks Stevens Design Associates, by his own reckoning worked for 585 different clients. As much an inventor in his own right as a shaper and perfecter of others' ideas, he is credited with creating products as varied as the steam iron, the wide-mouthed peanut butter jar, the snowmobile, and the whimsical Oscar Mayer Wienermobile, a tiny car made of fiberglass with a logo-decorated hot dog mounted on top, which the processed meats company used for sales promotions. Products with a distinctive look were Stevens's specialty, and he firmly believed that attractive designs, not just functionality, sold products. Among his innovations was the use of bright colors in appliances—and the introduction of different colors on a regular basis. Indeed, he is credited with coining the term "planned obsolescence" to describe a company's design changes intended to encourage customers to replace their old products with new ones. Sales figures bore him out: a Stevens product was usually a guaranteed hit.

But often he had to persuade companies—in particular, their chief engineers—to adopt his ideas.

Working as a consultant to Allis-Chalmers, the farm machinery manufacturer, he offered them a more stylish design for their conventional tractors, complete with teardrop fenders. The engineers at the company were dubious, and scathing in their criticism: tractors are meant to plow, they said, not to be looked at. Nevertheless, Stevens's design prevailed, and the new tractors became a bestselling item. Farmers found them so attractive that they even reported driving them to church.

Occasionally Stevens's designs were accepted by companies but failed to win consumer approval. A collector of antique cars as a hobby, he had a weak spot—some critics called it a blind spot—for automotive design, but responses to his efforts in that area were mixed and sometimes failed altogether. In the late 1940s he designed a series of cars for Studebaker, including a station wagon with a sliding roof to accommodate large items, but the company went out of business and they were never produced. A Stevens two-seater sports car called the Excalibur, manufactured by the declining Kaiser-Frasier company in 1964, did go on the market, but it was not successful; neither was another car by that name, modeled on a 1930s Mercedes-Benz, that Stevens later designed and manufactured himself. The Studebaker prototypes, together with several versions of the Excalibur and the numerous antique cars in Stevens's collection, were later moved to a specially built facility, the Brooks Stevens Automotive Museum, in Mequon, Wisconsin.

As the demand for industrial design grew, other designers entered the field pioneered by Stevens and a handful of others, including the French expatriate Raymond Loewy, with whom Stevens had helped cofound the Industrial Designers Society of America in 1944. New York had become the design capital of the nation by the middle of the twentieth century, but Stevens remained in the Milwaukee area. He and his wife, Alice, whom he had married in the 1930s, had four children, and his eldest son, Kipp Stevens, took over the business, now known as Brooks Stevens Design, in 1979. In the early 1990s, in recognition of Stevens's pioneering efforts, the Brooks Stevens Gallery of Industrial Design, featuring prototypes of many Stevens products, opened at the Milwaukee Institute of Art and Design. Stevens taught design courses at the institute and also directed the Brooks Stevens Automotive Museum until his death, which occurred at his home in Milwaukee.

• Biographical information on Stevens was provided by Brooks Stevens Design in Grafton, Wisconsin. See also Isabel Wilkerson, "The Man Who Put Steam in Your Iron," *New York Times*, 11 July 1991. For a history of industrial design in the United States, which includes an assessment of contributions by Stevens, see especially Arthur J. Pulos, *The American Design Adventure: 1940–1975* (1988). See also Pulos, *American Design Ethic: A History of Industrial Design to 1940* (1983). An obituary appears in the *New York Times*, 7 Jan. 1995.

ANN T. KEENE

STEWART, James (20 May 1908–2 July 1997), actor, was born James Maitland Stewart in Indiana, Pennsylvania, the son of Alexander Stewart, a prosperous hardware store owner, and Elizabeth Jackson Stewart. Three generations of Stewart men had been employed in the family hardware business, which Stewart's great-granduncle founded in 1851. Stewart's father had attended Princeton University and then settled down in Indiana at the hardware store, and it was assumed that his son would follow a similar career path. In 1923 the younger Stewart was enrolled at Mercersburg Academy, a preparatory school with a reputation for sending graduates to Princeton. As a teenager his avocation was building model airplanes—as he later recalled, "airplanes were the last thing I thought about at night and the first thing I thought about in the morning" (quoted in Dewey, p. 62)—and his imagination was fired by Charles Lindbergh's solo flight across the Atlantic Ocean in 1927. He entered Princeton in the fall of 1928. A gifted architecture student, he received a scholarship during his senior year to pursue graduate work. He was also an adept accordionist, often playing in productions staged by the university's eating clubs. Because of this talent, he was invited upon his graduation in 1932 to join the University Players, a theatrical group composed primarily of Ivy League students that performed summer stock in Cape Cod. Faced with a decision that he did not yet want to make—between pursuing a career in architecture or returning to the hardware store—he accepted the offer.

Stewart spent the summer of 1932 playing his accordion and appearing in bit parts on the stage. In the fall he moved to New York City, where he shared an apartment with other former University Players, including Henry Fonda and Joshua Logan. In November he was cast as a chauffeur in the comedy *Goodbye Again*, written by Allan Scott and George Haight. He had only two lines: "Mrs. Belle Irving would sure appreciate it if she could have this book autographed," and, upon having this request rejected, "Mrs. Belle Irving is going to be sore as hell." But he made the most of his opportunity, as Burgess Meredith, who was acting in another play on Broadway, described:

> Here was this tall, lanky guy bringing down the house. . . . Jimmy stayed on that *sure* like a teletype machine that's stuck on typing out *r*. Then he's just standing there and looking awkward while the butler goes off. Then he gets the no, and we're back to another endless *r* with the word *sore*, followed by the always crowd-pleasing *hell*. He was really quite brilliant in bringing out those possibilities. (quoted in Dewey, p. 114)

Goodbye Again was a moderate hit, running for 212 performances, and Stewart was singled out for praise by newspaper critics. In 1934 he appeared in his first substantive role, as a soldier suffering from malaria in Sidney Howard's *Yellow Jack*. The experience of working with dedicated actors convinced him that he might make acting his career: "For the first time," he remarked, "I could see these men—good, mature men—out there working and concentrating, and this really meant something to them. . . . I think it's when I sort of got serious about it" (quoted in Dewey, p. 123). His continued good critical notices attracted the interest of MGM, which signed him to a film contract in April 1935.

Stewart presented a challenge to MGM casting directors. At almost six feet four inches, he weighed a mere 138 pounds when he arrived in Hollywood and spoke with a slow, nasal drawl. He looked and acted nothing like the studio's leading men, who included glamorously handsome Robert Taylor and two-fisted Clark Gable. Stewart's early roles reflected the fact that MGM did not know what to do with him. In 1936 he appeared in seven films for the studio: his parts ranged from a shy, crooning sailor in the musical *Born to Dance* to a psychotic killer in *After the Thin Man*. That year he was loaned out to Universal for the melodrama *Next Time We Love*, in which he costarred with Margaret Sullavan, another ex–University Player, who had threatened to go on strike unless he was given the role. Sullavan rehearsed with him extensively and carefully guided his performance; when he returned to MGM, casting director Bill Grady noted, his grasp of film technique was "startling" (quoted in Dewey, p. 147).

In 1938 Stewart was loaned out to Columbia to appear in Frank Capra's *You Can't Take It with You*, which won the Academy Award for Best Picture. The following year the director borrowed him again for *Mr. Smith Goes to Washington*, the film that defined his screen personality and made him a major star. Capra felt that Stewart as an actor combined "the character and rock-ribbed honesty of a Gary Cooper" with "the breeding and intelligence of an ivy-league idealist" (Capra, p. 242). Certainly he had ample opportunity to embody honesty and idealism in his role as Jefferson Smith, a scout leader–turned–U.S. senator. But he also brought raw emotion and vulnerability to the screen, particularly evident in the film's most famous sequence, when Smith confronts the corrupt Senate in an exhausting twenty-four-hour filibuster. Stewart realized the importance of the filibuster scenes, not only to the film but also to his career. During the three weeks that the scenes were shot, he had his throat coated with a mercury compound to make his hoarseness convincing. His costar Jean Arthur later recalled that he "was so serious when he was making that picture, he used to get up at five o'clock in the morning and drive five miles an hour to get himself to the studio. He was so terrified that something was going to happen to him, he wouldn't go any faster" (quoted in McBride, p. 416). Critics confirmed that the extra effort was worth it: the *New York Times* called his performance "a joy of the season, if not forever," and he was nominated for an Academy Award. Film scholars today suggest that his performance in *Mr. Smith* offered an alternative to Hollywood's traditional notion of screen masculinity. Whereas his male contemporaries were given to taciturn underplaying, Stewart's specialty became the no-holds-barred monologue. An anomaly in the 1930s, he was a precursor of later "emotional" male actors such as Montgomery Clift and Marlon Brando.

Between December 1939 and December 1940 Stewart demonstrated his versatility in three films, all now considered classics. In the comic western *Destry Rides Again* he played a sheriff who refuses to wear a gun, instead using his wit to tame the Wild West. The *New York Times* remarked on the contrast between Stewart's sardonic, deceptively folksy Tom Destry and his naive Jefferson Smith. In Ernst Lubitsch's *The Shop around the Corner* he again costarred with Sullavan. The romantic comedy involves two shop co-workers who are each involved in a pen-pal romance but do not realize that they have been writing to each other. The critic Andrew Sarris has described a scene in which Sullavan reads one of the pen-pal letters to Stewart, who must pretend that the letter is not from him: "It would have been very tempting for a flickering triumphant expression to have passed over Stewart's face, but instead an intensely sweet and compassionate and appreciative look transfigures the entire scene. . . . I could not think of any other actor who could have achieved an effect of such unobtrusive subtlety " (Sarris, p. 30). In George Cukor's *The Philadelphia Story*, he played opposite Katharine Hepburn and Cary Grant as a newspaper reporter who goes snooping into the lives of the very rich. Spending a good part of the movie with a champagne glass in his hand, Stewart delighted audiences with his comic drunk scenes; for his performance, he was awarded his only Academy Award as Best Actor.

In March 1941 Stewart enlisted in the U.S. Army Air Corps. He spent much of the next two years performing on patriotic radio broadcasts; as he later recalled, "I traded so many jokes with Edgar Bergen and Charlie McCarthy that I was beginning to feel that *I* had been carved out of wood, too" (quoted in Dewey, p. 238). Frustrated that he was being held back from combat because of his celebrity, he petitioned his superiors until he was finally assigned to the 445th Bombardment Group in August 1943. As a major, he commanded a squadron of Liberator bombers and flew in twenty raids over Germany. He received the Distinguished Flying Cross and the Croix de Guerre in 1944, and in 1945 he was promoted to chief of staff for the Second Combat Wing of the Eighth Air Force. Following the war, he continued in the reserves and eventually retired as a brigadier general.

On returning to Hollywood in the fall of 1945, Stewart chose not to renew his contract with MGM but instead signed with the MCA talent agency; for the rest of his career, he worked as an independent. He returned to the screen in Capra's *It's a Wonderful Life* (1946). Although the film is now widely embraced as a sentimental Christmas classic, there is nothing sentimental about his portrayal of George Bailey, a small-town family man, frustrated by his commonplace existence, who is driven to attempt suicide on Christmas Eve. Stewart later suggested that the film failed at the box office because its "dark side" did not appeal to postwar audiences, who were in the mood for escapism. In 1947 he returned to Broadway as a summer replacement for vacationing star Frank Fay in the comedy *Harvey*, written by Mary Chase. In the role of Elwood P. Dowd, a gentle eccentric whose best friend is an invisible rabbit, he received some of the worst reviews of his career. Determined to get the part right, he would return to *Harvey* in a 1950 film version and on New York and London stages in the 1970s, eventually making it one of his most beloved characterizations. In 1949 he ended years of being tagged by the press as "Hollywood's most eligible bachelor" by marrying Gloria Hatrick, a socialite divorcée; they had two children and enjoyed a devoted, stable marriage.

Critics consider the 1950s to be Stewart's "golden age" as an actor: during the decade he appeared in twenty-two films and, along with John Wayne, was Hollywood's biggest box office draw. In such films as *The Glenn Miller Story* (1953) and *The Spirit of St. Louis* (1957), he cemented his popularity with rather conventional performances as all-American heroes. But through his collaborations with the directors Anthony Mann and Alfred Hitchcock, he also provided some of his richest, most disturbing portrayals. In his five westerns with Mann, which include *Winchester '73* (1950), *The Naked Spur* (1953), and *The Man from Laramie* (1955), he played neurotic, bitter loners—men who have been wronged in the past and who cannot let go of their hatred. The screenwriter Borden Chase recalled a sneak preview for *Winchester '73* at which there were "some titters in the audience at seeing Stewart's name in the opening titles" of an action picture; then the audience watched his character grab an outlaw by the head and smash his face down onto a bar counter, and "there would be no more snickering" (quoted in Dewey, p. 346). In Hitchcock's *Rear Window* (1954), he played a "Peeping Tom" photographer who projects his fantasies onto the people he observes through his apartment window. In 1958 he gave perhaps his finest performance in *Vertigo*, Hitchcock's masterpiece, as a detective whose romantic obsession with a woman he is shadowing proves to be both horrifyingly destructive and undeniably touching.

Stewart continued to star regularly in films into the late 1960s. He won the Best Actor Award from the New York Film Critics for his role as a clever small-town lawyer in *Anatomy of a Murder* (1959) and appeared in several westerns for John Ford, including *The Man Who Shot Liberty Valance* (1962) and *Cheyenne Autumn* (1964). In 1969 he suffered a personal tragedy when his stepson Ronald, a marine, was killed leading a combat mission in Vietnam. In 1973 and 1974 Stewart's television series "Hawkins," in which he again played a small-town lawyer, enjoyed top ratings; however, his increasing problems with deafness led him to quit the show.

During his later years he was widely honored for his contributions to American cinema, by organizations as diverse as the Cannes Film Festival, the International Red Cross, and the Boy Scouts of America. At a tribute held by the Film Society of Lincoln Center, the critic Richard Corliss suggested that Stewart's achievement had been to reflect "the changing, aging, increasingly troubled face of America. . . . It takes an extraordinary actor to do this" (quoted in Molyneaux, p. 237). Following the death of his wife in 1994, he retreated from public view. He died in Beverly Hills, California.

• The James Stewart Collection, including correspondence and scrapbooks from Stewart's career and home movies of the Stewart family, is in the Arts and Communications Archives at the Harold B. Lee Library, Brigham Young University. Stewart published some of his doggerel verse, which he occasionally read on the television program "The Tonight Show," as *Jimmy Stewart and His Poems* (1989). An illuminating interview is "Jimmy Stewart as Told to Pete Martin," a five-part series that ran in the *Saturday Evening Post* in February and March 1961. Donald Dewey, *James Stewart: A Biography* (1996), is insightful and engagingly written. Other biographies are Allen Eyles, *James Stewart* (1984), and Gary Fishgall, *Pieces of Time: The Life of James Stewart* (1997). Gerard Molyneaux, *James Stewart: A Bio-bibliography* (1992), includes a complete filmography. For a critical appreciation of his career, see Andrew Sarris, "James Stewart," *Film Comment*, Mar. /Apr. 1990, pp. 29–30. For a discussion of his films with Frank Capra, see Joseph McBride, *Frank Capra: The Catastrophe of Success* (1992). For an analysis of his collaboration with Anthony Mann, see Robert Horton, "Mann and Stewart: Two Rode Together," *Film Comment*, Mar./Apr. 1990, pp. 40–46. The critical writings that comment on Stewart's performances in *Rear Window* and *Vertigo* are voluminous: two good places to start are Robin Wood, *Hitchcock's Films Revisited* (1989), and Donald Spoto, *The Art of Alfred Hitchcock* (1976). Dennis Bingham, *Acting Male: Masculinities in the Films of James Stewart, Jack Nicholson, and Clint Eastwood* (1994), is an excellent analysis of Stewart's acting style. For views of Stewart by his Hollywood peers, see Henry Fonda, *My Life* (1981); Burgess Meredith, *So Far, So Good* (1994); and Frank Capra, *The Name above the Title* (1971). An obituary is in the *New York Times*, 3 July 1997.

THOMAS W. COLLINS, JR.

STOKES, Carl (21 June 1927–4 Apr. 1996), mayor, was born Carl Burton Stokes in Cleveland, Ohio, the son of Charles Stokes, a laundry worker, and Louise Stone Stokes, a domestic. Stokes's father died when he was a toddler, and he grew up in poverty as his mother struggled to provide for him and his older brother Louis. He attended local public schools before dropping out of East Technical High School in 1944. After a year spent as a street hustler, Stokes joined the U.S. Army, serving in post-World War II occupied Germany and rising to the rank of corporal. Following his 1946 discharge, he returned to Cleveland and finished his high school education in 1947. He was briefly enrolled at West Virginia State College (now University) before he went back home to attend Western Reserve University (now Case Western Reserve).

Still unsure of his future, Stokes dropped out of college and became an agent with the Ohio State Department of Liquor Control. After three years of battling corrupt saloonkeepers, he decided on a career in law and entered the University of Minnesota. He graduated with a B.S. in law in 1954, but he realized that he needed additional training and returned yet again to Cleveland, where he attended Cleveland-Marshall Law School while working as a probation officer for the municipal court. Stokes received his LL.B degree in 1956, the year he ended his childless marriage to Edith Shirley Smith, whom he had married in December 1951.

After gaining admittance to the bar in 1957, Stokes practiced law with his brother in the firm Stokes & Stokes. His attention, however, soon focused on a career in politics, and he spent countless hours doing volunteer work with such groups as the NAACP and the local Community Council. In 1958 he was appointed assistant city prosecutor by Mayor Anthony Celebrezze and that same year married Shirley Edwards, with whom he was to have three children.

After two failed attempts in 1958 and 1960, Stokes became the first African-American Democrat to hold a seat in the Ohio State House of Representatives in 1962. Reelected twice, he served during his six years in office on the Public Welfare, Judiciary, and Industry and Labor committees and gained a reputation as a moderate who supported civil rights legislation while at the same time voting to empower the governor to employ National Guard troops in anti-riot activities. In 1965, after considering a run for Congress, Stokes entered the mayoral race in Cleveland as an independent and lost a narrow election to incumbent Ralph Locher. By 1967, Cleveland (which had suffered through years of decline, along with many other industrialized northern cities) was in political turmoil. A race riot had erupted in the Hough area of the city in July 1966, and under Locher Cleveland's urban renewal program had become so hopelessly befuddled that the Department of Housing and Urban Development (HUD) suspended the city's allotment of federal funds. Having defeated Locher in the Democratic primary, Stokes went on to win a narrow victory over Seth Taft, the grandson of President William Howard Taft, and in the process became the first African-American mayor of a major American city.

Stokes's election attracted national attention, and for a while Cleveland experienced a euphoric sense of uplift. Under his leadership, the city regained control of HUD monies (thanks in part to Stokes's friendly relationship with Vice President Hubert Humphrey), and Stokes also took justifiable pride in creating increased opportunities for the poor to obtain decent, affordable housing. African Americans and other minority groups that had long been excluded from city jobs and contracts also found increasing opportunities during his administration. Almost alone among major cities, Cleveland remained riot-free in the aftermath of the assassination of Dr. Martin Luther King, Jr., in April 1968. Shortly thereafter, Stokes helped engineer the creation of "Cleveland:NOW!" The program was meant to induce the business community and the general public to raise money to combat a variety of societal ills.

Despite his promising beginning, Stokes could not maintain the city's forward momentum in the face of nearly insurmountable urban problems and social upheaval. An ugly confrontation broke out in the Glenville section of the city in July 1968, leaving six citizens and three police officers dead. The riot ended Stokes's honeymoon with much of Cleveland's white community, many of whom apparently had felt that the election of an African-American mayor might prevent such disturbances. Worse still was the revelation that a local African-American militant leader, Fred Ahmad Evans, had used "Cleveland:NOW!" funds to purchase guns used during the disturbance. Although Evans was later sent to prison for his crimes, the damage had been done. Stokes had long sought to overhaul what he viewed as a corrupt, inefficient, and racist police department, but his exclusion of white officers from the Glenville riot scene and a series of disastrous appointments within the department left the city deeply discouraged.

Although Stokes was narrowly reelected in 1969, it was clear by the end of his second term that his effectiveness in office had dissipated. He moved to New York City and achieved another milestone by becoming the first African-American television news anchor in the city. After his second marriage ended in divorce, he married Raija Salmoniv, a former Miss Finland, in 1977; the couple had one daughter.

Stokes returned to Cleveland in the early 1980s and served as a municipal judge there from 1983 to 1994. In 1995 he was appointed ambassador to the Seychelles by President Bill Clinton, but he had to take a leave of absence after he was diagnosed with cancer of the esophagus. He died in Cleveland.

Colorful and charismatic, Carl Stokes could not during his relatively short tenure as mayor reverse the socioeconomic decline that had reduced his native city's identity from that of a thriving commercial and cultural center ("the Best Location in the Nation") to a byword for urban blight ("the Mistake by the Lake"). But as the first black mayor of a large American city, he succeeded in encouraging other African Americans to be competitive in electoral politics throughout the country.

• Stokes's papers are held at the Western Reserve Historical Society in Cleveland. His autobiography, *Promises of Power: A Political Autobiography* (1973), presents a reasonably balanced view of his career up until 1973. Kenneth G. Weinberg, *Black Victory: Carl Stokes and the Winning of Cleveland* (1968), is a largely celebratory account of his initial mayoral campaign, while Philip W. Porter, *Cleveland: Confused City on a Seesaw* (1976), presents a less-than-flattering view of his administration. An obituary is in the *New York Times*, 4 April 1996.

EDWARD L. LACH, JR.

STONE, Fred (19 Aug. 1873–6 Mar. 1959), actor, was born Val Stone on homesteaded land in Colorado to a jack-of-some-trades father, whose full name has not survived, and Clara Johnston Stone (the birthplace he cited, Valmont, which was also the source of his birth name, cannot be found on a map). After a younger brother, named Mont, was born, Stone's grandmother renamed the two boys, and Stone became Fred Andrew Stone. At first because of his principled but impulsive father's wanderlust and later because he was in show business, Stone was never educated beyond fourth grade.

The Stone family's traveling covered much western and midwestern ground, with Kansas at the nominal center. At age eight Stone won a contest for climbing a greased pole and by nine had taught himself to walk a tightrope. At thirteen he and his brother Ed joined their first circus, working their way up to the Great American Circus, a 47-wagon operation that toured the Wild West. By the time he was fourteen, Stone and his brother had added an acrobat act that played variety houses and carnivals.

For the next seven years, Stone essayed various entertainment genres, including a spell as Topsy in *Uncle Tom's Cabin*. It was during an abortive 1895 New Orleans engagement with Haverly's Great Mastodon Minstrels that he met Dave Montgomery, another youthful veteran of many genres. Stranded in New Orleans by the Minstrels' collapse, Stone and Montgomery formed a double act, got a job on a showboat, and headed for Chicago, where their careers quickly sprouted wings.

By 1900 Stone and Montgomery had worked with Joe Weber and Lew Fields in Boston and established enough of a foothold in New York to become two of the original eight White Rats, a "trade union-fraternal" organization formed in opposition to the Theatrical Trust's monopolization of the variety genre. Seeking relief from the Trust's harassment, the pair took their first British bookings. When they returned, they joined the cast of Charles Frohman's musical comedy *The Girl from Up There* (1901). Stone said it was the first musical comedy he had ever seen. Built around Frohman's star, Edna May, the show transferred to England with great success, and Montgomery and Stone were asked to stay on in Britain.

Back in the United States, however, the opportunity to star in L. Frank Baum's dramatization of his new book, *The Wizard of Oz,* had arisen. It opened at the Grand Opera House in Chicago in 1903 with Stone as the floppy, wisecracking Scarecrow and Montgomery (Stone had refused his part unless Montgomery got his) as the more laconic but jokey Tin Man. Counting its many tours, *The Wizard of Oz* surpassed even *The Merry Widow* as its era's most popular musical attraction and established Stone and Montgomery as stars of the musical stage. During the show's New York run, Stone's brother Ed (who played Imogene, the cow) suddenly died. A young actress, Allene Crater, joined the cast in 1903; she and Stone were married in 1906 and were to have three daughters. Allene Stone thereafter appeared in most of her husband's musical plays, followed eventually by two of their daughters.

The Wizard of Oz was followed by *The Red Mill*, the first of many Charles Dillingham productions built around Stone and—until his death in 1917—Montgomery. *The Red Mill*, with songs by Victor Herbert, was so profitable that it allowed Dillingham to build the vast Globe Theatre. Stone's entrance was of the sort that proved typical of his career: he fell backward eighteen feet down a two-story ladder, performance after performance.

Despite its popularity, *The Red Mill* was not of the type that the partners quickly made their own. It was too realistic. Stone's gift, which made him for twenty years the most consistently popular stage star in America, was for pantomime—not the mime show but the extravaganza composed of equal parts of fantasy (including well-known fairy tale characters), topical humor, interpolated song and dance, and whatever else the cast's capabilities allowed. The Dillingham-Stone productions carried immense appeal for youthful audiences—on tour there were often special morning performances for them--and throughout his career Stone remained committed to clean and simple entertainment.

In *The Old Town* (1910) Stone danced in and out of a twirling lariat as well as on a tightrope. In *The Lady of the Slipper* (1912) he did the "punch-bowl glide," which involved three trampolines, an apparent staggering fall downstairs onto a couch, and his finally being propelled through an oil painting; for this production Stone and Montgomery donned the familiar Oz makeup and helped Cinderella get to the ball on time. In the fantastic *Chin Chin* (1914), with superior music by Ivan Caryll and a book almost completely replicating the British pantomime *Aladdin*, the boys were slaves of the lamp; the play's long run defied that year's Broadway slump.

After Montgomery's unexpected death, Stone starred in the similarly fantastic *Jack O'Lantern* (1917) before trying out a film career. For Famous Players/Lasky, he starred in *The Goat* (1918), *Johnny Get Your Gun* (1919), and *Under the Top* (1919). His roles included a youthful stuntman who could run up the side of a building, a film cowboy who goes around shaping up other people's lives, and a circus acrobat. Stone performed all his own stunts.

Back on Broadway after World War I, Stone's brand of innocent merriment gradually faced more sophisticated competition. But his popularity was undiminished. In *Tip Top* (1920), a revue-like concoction in which he was supported by the Duncan Sisters and the precision-dancing Tiller Girls, Stone was propelled onstage by an explosion. He also fell off a horse and walked on his ear.

Stepping Stones (1923), a retelling of the Little Red Riding Hood tale, had music by Jerome Kern and introduced the Stoneses' daughter Dorothy as Rougette Hood. In *Criss Cross* (1926), Stone played a resourceful aviator marooned in Fable Land who tumbled and worked the flying trapeze.

Stone had more than a little of his father's recklessness, and, having learned a bit about flying from *Criss Cross*, he was determined to become a pilot. In 1927 he crashed at 100 mph in Connecticut, breaking an ankle, a shin, a thigh, some ribs, and his jaw. The crash left him with a progressive deterioration of vision, though he was not completely blind for another twenty-five years.

Unable to take up his projected starring role in *Three Cheers* (1928), Stone did not again take the stage until *Ripples* (1930), a show with four Stones, where, despite another characteristic entrance, flying onstage with hoofprints on his back and landing in a tulip bed, he suffered his first failure—a run of only seven weeks. The Wall Street crash had cast a gloom overshadowing genial, optimistic foolishness. (The departure of his most dependable star was one of the blows that sent Dillingham reeling into bankruptcy and humiliation.) After one more musical comedy, rather more realistic and less acrobatic, Fred Stone retired from the musical stage.

By 1935 he was back on the screen, winning good notices as Katharine Hepburn's semi-invalid father in *Alice Adams*, Hepburn's first Academy Award-winning film. In 1936 he closed his home in Forest Hills, New York, and moved to Hollywood. Between 1936 and 1940 Stone appeared in thirteen more films, including a series for RKO-Radio Films, in which he played such leading roles as a farmer who moves his family to Hollywood and becomes a movie star, the founder of a midwestern town who solves crimes although nearly being killed in the process, the laziest man in town who becomes a hero after helping to catch gangsters, and a mayor who saves his Kansas town from being taken over by crooks.

For other studios Stone appeared in more prestigious films, including in 1936 *The Trail of the Lonesome Pine* (as the feuding father of Sylvia Sidney) and *The Westerner* (1940), as a gritty homesteader trampled to death by the gang of Judge Roy Bean. He occasionally returned to Broadway in dramatic roles—as a lovable alcoholic liar in a revival of *Lightnin'* (1938) and as Grandpa Vanderhof in the screwball comedy *You Can't Take It with You* (1945), his last New York appearance. Back home, he appeared occasionally on Los Angeles area stages until 1950, when he once more played Grandpa Vanderhof in a small company's production. His wife of fifty-one years, Allene, died in 1957. Two years later, Stone died, blind, at his home in North Hollywood.

• Stone's autobiography, mainly notable for its rich picture of late-nineteenth-century circus and carnival life in the west, is *Rolling Stone* (1945). Stone's career on the musical stage is covered in Gerald Bordman, *American Musical Theatre: A Chronicle*, 2d ed. (1992), while Ethan Mordden, *Make Believe: The Broadway Musical in the 1920s* (1997), contains some helpful insights. Stone's film career is exhaustively detailed in the indexes published by the American Film Institute for 1911–1920 and 1931–1940. Obituaries appear in the *New York Times*, 7 Mar. 1959, and *Variety*, 11 Mar. 1959.

JAMES ROSS MOORE

STONE, Thomas (1743–5 Oct. 1787), patriot and signer of the Declaration of Independence, was born at Durham Parish in Charles County, Maryland, the son of David Stone, landowner, and Elizabeth Jenifer Stone. The scion of a prominent family (his great-great grandfather William Stone had served as the third proprietary governor of the province), Stone grew up on his father's estate, "Poynton Manor." After receiving his early education locally, he decided on a career in law and moved to the provincial capital of Annapolis. He studied under noted attorney Thomas Johnson, was admitted to the bar in 1764, and opened a practice in Frederick, Maryland. He married Margaret Brown, the daughter of a prominent Charles County doctor, in 1768. The couple had three children.

Stone returned to his native county in 1771 and settled near Port Tobacco, which was then the county seat. His home, "Habre-de-Venture," soon became one of the notable examples of prerevolutionary architecture in the state. With his legal practice thriving, he soon turned his attention to the world of politics. As was the case with so many of his contemporaries, he was soon serving the nascent revolutionary movement in a variety of roles. Despite his relative youth, Stone was appointed a member of the Continental Congress in 1774 and took his seat in that body on 13 May 1775. He served as a delegate from Maryland (except for a period in 1777 when he declined reelection) until October 1778. Stone also attended the Maryland Convention of 1775–1776 and was elected (but did not serve) on Maryland's First Committee of Safety in 1775. He even found time to serve his state as a senator and also as a member of the house of delegates.

Although Stone performed yeoman service on the committee that framed the Articles of Confederation, he is best remembered as a signer of the Declaration of Independence. Like so many of his contemporaries, Stone approached the idea of revolution with mixed feelings. As a member of a long-established Maryland family, he had supported the government's position in a controversy that had erupted in 1774 over the use of poll tax revenue to support the established Episcopal church and its clergy. His position on the issue placed him squarely against such men as William Paca, Samuel Chase, and Thomas Johnson; ironically, these same leaders would later join him in Congress. While serving as a member of the Maryland Convention, Stone made his feelings clear in a letter to his wife in April 1775: "We have this day received a confirmation of the unhappy contest between the king's troops and the people of New England. . . . This will reduce both England and America to a state which no friend of either ever wished to see; how it will terminate, God only knows . . . We have accounts . . . which I am apprehensive will preclude all hopes of a reconciliation between this and the mother country: a situation of affairs which all thinking men must shudder at" (Scharf, *History of Maryland*, vol. 2 [1879], p. 235). Nevertheless, when Maryland gave its delegates freedom to proceed as they saw fit, Stone voted to approve the Declaration and signed it.

Stone took an active role in matters closer to home as well. As a member of the state senate, he led (along with Charles Carroll of Carrollton) in articulating that body's position against the house of delegates in the controversy over confiscated British property. Late that same year, the state assembly, comprising the Maryland senate and house combined, appointed him as one of three commissioners to negotiate with the state of Virginia over respective rights to navigation and use of the Chesapeake Bay. Although this initial effort was unsuccessful, he served as a member of another commission that met at Mount Vernon in March 1785; with the aid of George Washington, an agreement was reached that remains largely in place to this day.

Elected to the Congress of the Confederation in November 1783, Stone took his seat on 26 March 1784. Although he served as chairman for a brief period near the end of his term, he decided against reelection and returned home. While his legal practice thrived, Stone had greater concerns. His wife, to whom he was devoted, had been in failing health since an ill-advised smallpox inoculation received in 1776 while she was visiting him in Philadelphia. Her health was of sufficient concern that Stone declined to serve as a member of the Constitutional Convention in 1787, and her death on 1 June 1787 devastated him. After sinking into a prolonged state of melancholy, he prepared (on the advice of his physicians) to undertake a voyage to England. While waiting to embark, he died in Alexandria, Virginia, and was buried at his home in Charles County.

Although relegated to relative obscurity because of his natural reticence, Stone has a secure place in history. As one of the four Maryland delegates who signed the Declaration of Independence, he was typical of any number of men who served the revolutionary cause in a supporting role.

• While few of Stone's letters have survived, material relating to his family can be found in the Raphael Semmes Collection at the Maryland Historical Society in Baltimore. The best secondary sources of information on his life and career are Henry C. Peden, Jr., *Revolutionary Patriots of Charles County, Maryland, 1775–1783* (1997); Edward C. Papenfuse et al., *A Biographical Dictionary of the Maryland Legislature, 1635–1789*, vol. 2 (1985); Margaret Brown Klapthor and Paul Dennis Brown, *History of Charles County, Maryland* (1958); and J. T. Scharf, *History of Maryland, from the Earliest Period to the Present Day*, vol. 2 (1879). Notice of his death appeared in the (Annapolis) *Maryland Gazette*, 10 Jan. 1788.

EDWARD L. LACH, JR.

STRIBLING, Young (26 Dec. 1904–3 Oct. 1933), heavyweight and light-heavyweight boxer, was born William Lawrence Stribling, Jr., in Bainbridge, Georgia, the son of William Lawrence Stribling and Lily Braswell Stribling. Together with his father, his mother, and his younger brother, Herbert, Young Stribling (as he was always known) toured the world in a vaudeville act called the Four Grahams from 1908 until 1917. The senior Stribling and his wife combined acrobatics and repartee on the stage, and the two children were clowns. As the boys grew, they engaged in a farcical boxing routine in which the climax had the smaller boy usually knocking out the larger and older one.

The family settled in Macon, Georgia, and W. L. Stribling, Sr., took a job as a bus driver. Their sons enrolled in elementary school, and the older son became a student at Lanier High School in 1918, playing on the basketball team and taking boxing lessons at the Macon YMCA. Young Stribling turned professional in Atlanta on 17 January 1921, fighting as a bantamweight (118 pounds) and made rapid progress in the ring. Within months he was boxing ten-round main events and defeating much more experienced opponents. Growing rapidly, he lost only three of his first 79 fights and then was matched with light-heavyweight champion Mike McTigue in Macon on 4 October 1923. The bout was billed by the promoter as a title fight, and McTigue's manager took the precaution of supplying his own referee. Stribling undoubtedly deserved the decision, but the referee called it a draw, then reversed himself and named Stribling the winner when the crowd became angry. Later, he reversed himself again and said that the official decision was a draw, and the publicity caused by the referee's shilly-shallying made Stribling famous.

Stribling was managed by his father, and his mother and brother usually accompanied them to fights. Sportswriters called the parents "Pa and Ma Stribling," and they were almost as famous as their son. As the years passed, Stribling's career was conducted mostly as a series of vaudeville-like tours. In 1925 a large bus was purchased to carry the family and a sparring partner (often the bus driver) from one fight venue to another; it was fitted out with bunks, a shower, a small kitchen, and even a boxing ring. Writer Damon Runyon bestowed the sobriquet "King of the Canebrakes" on Young Stribling as he defeated numerous southern and midwestern opponents during his campaigns.

Stribling's successes continued and included a sound beating of McTigue in a no-decision rematch in Newark, New Jersey, on 31 March 1924. Although allowed to fight only six-round bouts in New York because of his youth, he defeated one future light-heavyweight champion, Tommy Loughran, there, drew with another, Paul Berlenbach, and lost to a third, Jimmy Slattery. He defeated Loughran again in San Francisco and, in 1925, began to defeat good heavyweights, including Johnny Risko and Bud Gorman. In 1926 he earned another match for the light-heavyweight title by defeating Slattery in a ten-round rematch. On 10 June he met Berlenbach, now the champion, in Yankee Stadium in a fight that he was expected to win. Stribling failed to show his usual form, however, and was decisively defeated. Later it was revealed that he had been sick, but the Stribling family, in true show-business fashion, had decided that the fight must go on.

Stribling was a six-footer; strikingly handsome, witty, and gentlemanly in demeanor. His style in the ring was that of a fast-moving boxer, "awkwardly clever," with a tendency to avoid punishment by counterpunching and clinching frequently. He was a folk-hero in the South, where he usually knocked out his outclassed opponents easily, but in the North, where he fought tougher opposition, his safety-first and sometimes rough tactics earned him the unkind nickname of "Willie the Clutch" from sportswriters. Other reasons for Stribling's greater popularity in the South and Midwest were the attractiveness of his family and the perception that he was a family-oriented, clean-cut all-American boy, in contrast to the image of most boxers—crude in manner, lurking in seedy hotels and sweaty gymnasiums, and guided by managers who were crooks or at least of a shady reputation. In addition to his boxing, Stribling was a daredevil airplane pilot, belonged to the U.S. Army Air Corps reserve, and loved speedboats and motorcycles.

After the Berlenbach loss, Stribling had a long series of victories, interrupted only by a close loss to Loughran in Brooklyn. Although many of his victims were of little consequence, he did beat such good fighters as Lou Scozza and Chuck Wiggins, and he earned a fight with the heavyweight contender and future champion Jack Sharkey in Miami on 27 February 1929. In the early rounds it appeared that Stribling, who was a powerful right-hand puncher, would score a knockout. But he was suffering from neuritis in his left arm and fought mainly with one hand, without his effective left jab, and slowed down as the fight progressed, allowing Sharkey to win the decision.

During the next two years Stribling had many of his best victories, including knockouts of British heavyweight champion Phil Scott and Norwegian Otto von Porat. He fought future heavyweight champion Primo Carnera twice in Europe, winning and losing on fouls but outclassing the huge Italian both times. His victory over heavyweight contender Tuffy Griffiths in Chicago on 12 December 1930 earned him a heavyweight world title fight with the current champion, Max Schmeling, on 3 July 1931 in Cleveland, Ohio. Stribling won four of the first five rounds, and the fight was even after nine rounds, but Schmeling gave him a bad beating in the tenth. Although battered in each round thereafter, Stribling fought on until knocked down in the fifteenth and last round, and the referee stopped the fight with only fourteen seconds left. It was the only knockout defeat of Stribling's career.

Stribling continued to box, touring Australia in 1932; he then defeated the South African champion Don McCorkindale in Johannesburg. In his last fight, in September 1933, he outpointed light-heavyweight champion Maxie Rosenbloom. In October he was injured in a motorcycle accident when the driver of an oncoming automobile veered into his path and struck him. His left foot had to be amputated, his pelvis was broken, and he suffered internal injuries. Two days later he died in Macon. Thirty-five thousand people attended his funeral.

Stribling married Clara Kinney in December 1925, and they had two sons and a daughter. He earned over a million dollars in the ring and owned a large farm and was part-owner of a realty company in Miami when he died. He scored 126 knockouts in 287 fights, the most knockouts of any fighter until Archie Moore broke his record in 1958. He had more fights than any other heavyweight and was elected to the International Boxing Hall of Fame in 1996.

• Stribling's boxing record is available in *The 1978 Ring Boxing Encyclopedia and Record Book*, compiled by Nat Loubet and John Ort. Although containing some errors, *King of the Canebrakes* (1969) by Jimmy Jones is a useful biography. Articles in *The Ring* magazine include Francis Albertanti, "Ma and Pa Stribling Priming Their Boy for Dempsey's Crown," Oct. 1924, pp. 10–11; Milton R. Wallace, "Young Stribling: Enigma of the Prize Ring," Oct. 1930, pp. 30, 45; Wilbur Wood, "Hail and Farewell," Dec. 1933, pp. 3–5, 44; and Jersey Jones, "Remembering Young Stribling," Sept. 1963, pp. 26–27, 45. The 8 Oct. 1933 issue of the *New York Times* contains a tribute by Julian Harris, and details of his accident and death appear in preceding issues.

LUCKETT V. DAVIS

STRÖMGREN, Bengt (21 Jan. 1908–4 July 1987), astronomer and astrophysicist in Denmark and the United States, was born Bengt Georg Daniel Strömgren in Göteborg, Sweden, the son of Svante Elis Strömgren and his wife, Hedvig Lidforss Strömgren. Elis Strömgren, an old-school classical astronomer, had recently become director of Copenhagen Observatory, Denmark, and it was there that Bengt grew up, was educated, and worked for many years.

He was a brilliant boy, and his father delighted in teaching him calculus and numerical computing methods before he was twelve. Bengt began a regular astronomical observing program at age thirteen and published his first paper at fourteen. He had the run of Niels Bohr's Institute for Theoretical Physics, and he began helping in the reduction of laboratory spectroscopic data at sixteen. Strömgren graduated from high school at seventeen, from Copenhagen University at nineteen, and earned his Ph.D. at twenty-one with a thesis on the determination of near-parabolic cometary orbits.

Throughout his life Strömgren made important contributions to solving several of the most important astrophysical problems of his time, a number of which he had recognized himself. In all his research he drew on his deep knowledge of physics, the then-new quantum mechanics as well as classical theory, his solid experience with the older astronomy of stellar positions, dynamics, and kinematics, and his skill in numerical computing. At Copenhagen, analyzing the internal structure of stars using his own quantum mechanical calculations of the opacity of ions at high temperature, he demonstrated that hydrogen is an ex-

tremely abundant element. In 1935 he worked out the detailed theory of the optical aberrations of the recently invented Schmidt telescope, a mathematical project he could do alone in his office with his "computer," a glorified electromechanical adding machine.

Strömgren had married Sigrid Caja Hartz, a Dane, in 1931; they had two daughters and a son.

Then in 1936 Otto Struve brought Strömgren to the University of Chicago as one of the group of brilliant young astrophysicists who helped him rebuild its Yerkes Observatory in Williams Bay, Wisconsin, as an outstanding research center; the others were S. Chandrasekhar, G. P. Kuiper, and W. W. Morgan. There Strömgren analyzed and solved the nature of the large, irregular volumes of interstellar matter in the Milky Way that faintly radiate emission-line spectra. He showed that these "H II regions," often idealized later as "Strömgen spheres," are ionized by high-temperature, high-luminosity stars within them.

Strömgren had written Struve that he would accept the Chicago post only on a temporary basis, and in 1938 he returned to Denmark as a full professor, though the Yerkes director tried desperately to persuade him to stay. Strömgren could see that World War II was near and wanted to be in Denmark with his family, his father and mother, and his countrymen. There, unable to travel or to communicate with astronomers in England or America after the Germans invaded Denmark, he worked on stellar atmospheres, calculating "models" free of the simplifications used in earlier treatments, to match the observed spectra of stars. This involved varying systematically the assumed abundances of the elements, effective temperature, and gravity in the star's atmosphere. An important element in these calculations was the opacity of H−, the negative hydrogen ion, which Rupert Wildt had suggested would be important in the sun and stars like it. Strömgren and his group's calculations confirmed that it was. When Elis Strömgren retired in 1940, his son Bengt succeeded him as director of Copenhagen Observatory.

Soon after the end of World War II, Bengt Strömgren returned to Yerkes Observatory as a visiting professor for the academic year 1946–1947. He continued and extended his research on interstellar matter, analyzing and interpreting both the emission regions and interstellar absorption lines, which provided further quantitative information on its physical nature. After a few years back in Denmark, Strömgren returned to Yerkes Observatory as its director, succeeding Struve (who resigned to move on to Berkeley) on 1 January 1951. The University of Chicago operated McDonald Observatory, located in the mountains of west Texas, on behalf of the University of Texas, and Strömgren directed it, as Struve had before him. By then Strömgren was developing his plan of using narrow-band ("interference") filters and the methods of photoelectric photometry to do accurate, quantitative classification of stellar spectra. With these filters it was possible to measure parameters equivalent to effective temperature, surface gravity, heavy-element abundances ("metallicity"), and age (the last depending on further theory). He and his students did much of the observational work at McDonald Observatory. In 1957 he left Chicago and Yerkes Observatory to become the first professor of astrophysics at the Institute for Advanced Study in Princeton, "the man who got Einstein's office." There Strömgren continued the narrow-band filter or "stellar-population" research on the ages and elemental abundances in stars. Part of the goal was to trace back a star's orbit in the Galaxy (the Milky Way), from its current position and velocity, using its age, to its place of formation or "birth." Scientists at the NASA Institute of Space Sciences in New York collaborated with him in this work, using their powerful, advanced electronic numerical computers.

In 1967 Strömgren was elected extraordinary professor of astronomy by the Royal Danish Academy of Sciences and Letters, perhaps the highest honor a Danish scientist or scholar may attain. As part of this appointment, he and his family lived for the rest of his life in the Carlsberg Foundation's "Mansion of Honor," dedicated to the Danish people. Bohr had been the first person to hold this appointment, and Strömgren was the first scientist after him. During and after World War II, Strömgren had led the planning for a new astronomical observatory outside the lights, smoke, and exhaust fumes of Copenhagen, and by 1967 the new station was in operation at Brorfelde, in the Danish countryside. Students, postdoctoral fellows, and faculty members collaborated with him in pushing forward his research there as well as at a newer Danish telescope at La Palma in the Canary Islands and at the European Southern Observatory in Chile.

Throughout his career Strömgren took the widest possible view of science, kept up to date on research done everywhere, and was famous for his masterly reviews, published and oral, of all the fields in which he had worked, including stellar interiors and atmospheres, nebulae, interstellar matter, and their respective evolutionary histories. He was a true scientific leader. As a citizen of a small, traditionally neutral country poised near the border between East and West, he was also a superb diplomat. Trusted by nearly all, he was elected secretary-general of the International Astronomical Union in 1948 and its president in 1970, and he was chosen president of the American Astronomical Society in 1966 and of the Royal Danish Academy in 1968. He retired from his professorship in NORDITA, the Nordic countries' Institute of Astrophysics, located in Copenhagen, in 1978 and died there nine years later.

• There are many letters to, from, and concerning Strömgren in the Yerkes Observatory Archives, Williams Bay, Wisc. He published a short autobiographical account of his astronomical career, "Scientists I Have Known, and Some Astronomical Problems I Have Met," in *Annual Review of Astronomy and Astrophysics* 21 (1983): 1–11. The best published memorial biography of him in English is Russell Kulsrud, "Bengt Strömgen 1908–1987," in *American Philosoph-*

ical Society Yearbook (1987), pp. 216–22. Another good but shorter one, which emphasizes his Danish years, is by Mogens Rudkjübing , "Bengt Georg Daniel Strömgren," *Quarterly Journal of the Royal Astronomical Society* 29 (1987): 282–84. See also Adriaan Blaauw, *ESO's Early History: The European Southern Observatory from Concept to Reality* (1991), and Donald E. Osterbrock, *Yerkes Observatory 1892–1950: The Birth, Near Death, and Resurrection of a Scientific Research Institution* (1997).

DONALD E. OSTERBROCK

STRUNK, William, Jr. (1 July 1869–26 Sept. 1946), educator and grammarian, was born in Cincinnati, Ohio, the son of William Strunk, Sr., and Ella Garretson Strunk. He graduated from the University of Cincinnati in 1890 with an A.B. and was an instructor in mathematics at the Rose Polytechnical Institute in Terra Haute, Indiana (1890–1891). He then went to Cornell University in Ithaca, New York, where he was an instructor in English (1891–1898) while earning his Ph.D. there (1896). He spent the 1898–1899 academic year studying at the University of Paris.

Strunk returned to Cornell and remained there for the rest of his professional life; he was to die in Ithaca. Named an assistant professor of English in 1899, he was promoted to full professor in 1909 and retired in 1937. In 1900 Strunk married Olivia Emilie Locke; they had three children. During his early years at Cornell, Strunk produced editions of Thomas Babington Macaulay and Thomas Carlyle's *Essays on Samuel Johnson* (1895); John Dryden's *Essays on Drama* (1898), *All for Love* (1911), and *The Spanish Fryar* (1911); James Fenimore Cooper's *The Last of the Mohicans* (1900); Cynewulf's *Juliana* (1904); and Shakespeare's *Romeo and Juliet* (1911) and *The Tragedy of Julius Caesar* (1915). Through the Cornell Co-operative Society, Strunk published his *English Metres* (1922), a down-to-earth explanation of the subject. He also coedited a festschrift, *Studies in Language and Literature in Celebration of the Seventieth Birthday of James Morgan Hart, November 2, 1909* (1910).

By far the most challenging of Strunk's editorial tasks was his work on Cyenwulf's *Juliana*, written in Old English, which Strunk had meticulously studied. The most pleasant result of his editorial work was his being hired in 1935 as a consultant by Irving Thalberg for a Hollywood film production of *Romeo and Juliet* (1936). Strunk's function was to assure that the spirit of Shakespeare's play would not be violated. Although he expected to be in Hollywood for six weeks, Strunk was so genially accepted as "the Professor," and had such a good time, that he remained almost an entire year. In 1937 he reduced Shakespeare's *Antony and Cleopatra* to a two-act format. Excessive cutting, however, which included the omission of Enobarbus's suicide, caused the Broadway production to close quickly.

First and foremost, Strunk was a classroom teacher. His courses in English composition at Cornell, over a period exceeding four decades, made him a legend. To enable his students to write correct, concise, and vigorous prose, he put together *The Elements of Style*, a little textbook of forty-three pages. Privately printed in 1918, it succinctly spelled out rules of usage and principles of composition, discussed form, and offered a common-sense approach to punctuation and rhetoric. In parallel columns, Strunk gave examples of sloppy style and then correct style. A proponent of writing in the active voice, he encouraged the use of definite, concrete language, keeping to one tense, and other means of achieving a lucid, compact style. He also discussed such mechanical matters as margins and references and how to deal with colloquialisms.

The Elements of Style proved to be so popular, and so much in demand, that it was commercially published in 1920, and (with the assistance of Edward A. Tenney) Strunk revised and updated it in 1935. The little textbook was destined to become a classic, however, when in 1957 E. B. White, who had been one of Strunk's students at Cornell in 1919 and had gone on to fame as a writer, published an essay about his former teacher, "Will Strunk," which appeared in the *New Yorker* on 15 July 1957. The editors of the Macmillan Company located with some difficulty an old copy of *The Elements of Style* and persuaded White to reissue it with an introduction. He did so by modifying his *New Yorker* encomium in 1959. The book became a runaway success. In a second edition, published in 1972, White explained that in 1959 he had "tried . . . to preserve the flavor of [Strunk's] discontent, while slightly enlarging the scope of the discussion." He replaced outdated examples with fresher ones, making use of a few revisions Strunk himself had noted but never added. White did the same again for a third edition (1979). In going over Strunk's rules, White says he could visualize Strunk's "puckish face," short hair with middle part and bangs, blinking eyes, steel-rimmed glasses, nervously nibbled lips, and repeated adjurations to his students to be concise.

Strunk was a skillful scholar-educator but will be remembered almost exclusively as the author of *The Elements of Style*, which is now known as "Strunk and White" and which has improved the writing of countless thousands of grateful writers. In 1999 the editors of the Modern Library placed *The Elements of Style* by William Strunk and E. B. White number twenty-one on their "List of 100 Best Works of 20th Century Nonfiction," considerably below *The Education of Henry Adams* but just above *Principia Mathematica* by Alfred North Whitehead and Bertrand Russell, a work all but unreadable except to highly trained specialists. *The Elements of Style* will endure for precisely the opposite reasons.

• The Cornell University library lacks papers by Strunk but does have a small number of letters to him by William Dean Howells. A final revision of E. B. White's "Will Strunk" is in White's *The Points of My Compass* (1962). Essays by three scholars in *Cynewulf: Basic Readings*, ed. Robert E. Bjork (1996), make brief references to Strunk's edition of *Juliana*—one in indirect praise, two in disagreement. Bob Thomas, *Thalberg; Life and Legend* (1969), mentions Strunk's work in Hollywood. An obituary is in the *New York Times*, 27 Sept. 1946.

ROBERT L. GALE

SUESSE, Dana (3 Dec. 1909–16 Oct. 1987), composer, lyricist, pianist, and writer, was born Nadine Dana Suesse in Kansas City, Missouri, daughter of Julius Suess and Nina Quarrier Suess. The surname is pronounced "Sweese." A child prodigy, Dana Suesse won prizes—one, for composition, from the National Federation of Music—and scholarships when she was nine. As a child, she played the piano, danced and sang, wrote poetry that was published in newspapers, and designed clothes. Her earliest piano studies were in Kansas City with Gertrude Concannon, a student of Emil Paur. After her graduation from high school in 1926 she moved to New York, hoping to be discovered, and studied with Alexander Siloti, a pupil of Liszt.

By this time Suesse had already done some composing, primarily of "serious" music. When this proved difficult to sell to publishers, she turned her attention to the popular idiom and quickly gained some success with the instrumental "Syncopated Love Song" in 1930. In 1931 Suesse arranged its main theme to lyrics by Leo Robin to create "Have You Forgotten." She would go on to take other instrumental pieces she had written and draw from them to create songs, the most famous being "Jazz Nocturne" (1931), which became "My Silent Love" (1932) with Edward Heyman's lyrics.

Early in her career Suesse was nicknamed "Sally of Tin Pan Alley" by a music writer, and later the *New Yorker* in its issue of 16 December 1933 dubbed her the "Girl Gershwin." The latter appellation stayed with her and was not without justification; like George Gershwin, she was a superior pianist and wrote both concert works and successful popular songs.

In 1932 Paul Whiteman presented his second "Experiment in Modern Music," a sequel to the 1924 concert in which he had led the premiere of Gershwin's "Rhapsody in Blue." For this second event Suesse wrote a piano concerto called "Concerto in Three Rhythms." Concert music would continue to be an important part of her compositional work throughout her life alongside her more popular pieces; her compositions were featured on programs by the Boston Symphony Orchestra, the Philadelphia Orchestra, and the New York Philharmonic.

With "I Knew Him before He Was Spanish," inserted as additional material into Billy Rose's revue *Sweet and Low* in 1930, Suesse began a lengthy association with that great showman, often setting his lyrics in addition to providing songs for his shows. Later collaborations with Rose included the scores for *Casa Mañana*, produced in Fort Worth, Texas, in 1936 (with the hit song "The Night is Young and You're So Beautiful") and the *Aquacade* for the 1939 World's Fair in New York ("Yours for a Song" from the *Aquacade* served as the theme song for the fair), and she contributed songs to the *Diamond Horseshoe Revues* of the 1940s. In 1934 she wrote, with Edward Heyman, her best-known song, "You Oughta Be in Pictures." The song was used in a film short, *New York Town*, and later in another forgotten film, *Starlift* (1951).

Although little of her work was done for Hollywood, she provided songs and the score for the 1935 film *Sweet Surrender* (including "Love Makes the World Go Round").

One goal that eluded her was writing her own Broadway show, sexism being an undoubted factor. In a 1985 interview she spoke about it, saying that her publisher had suggested her for a show but had been told, "They don't want a female composer because backstage was kind of rough and the guys were using bad language." She met the disappointment with equanimity, saying, "I guess I had a reputation for being a rather nice girl."

Suesse married Broadway producer H. Courtney Burr on 26 July 1940; the marriage ended in divorce in 1954. She worked with Burr, often providing incidental music for plays he produced, among them *A Case of Youth* (1940), *Washington Slept Here* (1940), and *The Seven Year Itch* (1952).

Another of Suesse's aspirations was to write a play, and in 1947 she collaborated with Virginia Faulkner on a comedy, *Apartment 17-B*, which was produced and ran briefly in New York as *It Takes Two*. Later in 1947 Suesse followed the example of many American composers and went to Paris to study with Nadia Boulanger, staying for three years.

After returning to the United States, Suesse developed an interest in jazz piano, which culminated in 1955 with the *Jazz Concerto in D Major for Combo and Orchestra*. The composition was premiered in 1956 by the Rochester Civic Orchestra, under the baton of Frederick Fennell, with the composer at the piano.

As she grew older, Suesse's interest in writing plays became stronger, as did her desire to write lyrics. Her later songs have her own lyrics, and she credited Billy Rose with influencing her lyric-writing ability. She wrote a number of plays, which she submitted to leading producers, but none made it to Broadway.

In 1971, after moving to New London, Connecticut, Suesse married Edwin DeLinks. He convinced her to present a concert of her own music in New York, and on 11 December 1974 an all-Suesse concert was given at Carnegie Hall, which featured two of her piano concerti, *Concerto Romantico* and *Concerto in Rhythm*, performed by the American Symphony Orchestra with Frederick Fennell conducting and Cy Coleman on the piano. Suesse herself played a movement from her 1932 *Concerto in Three Rhythms*.

After their marriage, the couple moved from New London, Connecticut to St. Croix in the Virgin Islands. Following her husband's death in 1981, Suesse lived briefly in Shreveport, Louisiana, where she had family, before moving back to New York. Old age did not slow her down; at the time of her death in New York, she was working on a new play, *Nemesis*.

Suesse's music is always well crafted and at its best is the equal of work by her more celebrated contemporaries. Her piano accompaniments often feature a slow stride style, and a recognizable Suesse characteristic is her use of triplets (often in pairs) that drive the tune forward. Her concert music brings together jazz and traditional classical forms in a manner that does justice to both.

Because of her upbringing in Missouri, Suesse was more influenced by the piano styles of rag and honky tonk than the Tin Pan Alley sound that influenced native New York composers such as Gershwin and Richard Rodgers. Like many in her generation, Gershwin included, she was fascinated with French impressionism, in her case particularly by Debussy, as seen in the piano piece that draws both its name and musical style from the French composer, "Afternoon of a Black Faun." Her classical training makes her comparable to writers like Vernon Duke (also a respected classical composer under his original name, Vladimir Dukelsky) who brought a more sophisticated technique to their work than the seemingly improvisational styles of composition exemplified by Gershwin and Irving Berlin. Much like Duke's, her sophisticated style may have contributed to making her songs not as widely popular as those of Berlin.

Leading performers did sing and record Suesse's songs, however. Bing Crosby had one of his early hits with the song "Ho Hum" (1931) and recorded "The Night Is Young and You're So Beautiful"; Glenn Miller's band recorded the song "This Changing World" (1938); Billy Eckstine sang "My Silent Love"; and Jane Froman premiered "Moon about Town" (1934).

• An entry on Suesse appears in Virginia Grattan, *American Women Songwriters* (1993). Peter Mintun has provided informative liner notes for two Suesse recordings, *Keyboard Wizards of the Gershwin Era, Volume II* (1996) and *The Night Is Young: Concert Music of Dana Suesse* (a live recording of the 1974 Carnegie Hall concert, released in 1996). An interview with Suesse conducted by Brad Ross, Art Perlman, and Ernie Harburg on 1 May 1985 has been made available to the author of this article, who has also benefited from conversations with Peter Mintun, executor of Suesse's musical estate, and Professor Ann Sears of Wheaton College.

BENJAMIN SEARS

SULLAVAN, Margaret (16 May 1909–1 Jan. 1960), actress, was born Margaret Brooke Sullavan in Norfolk, Virginia, the daughter of Cornelius Sullavan, an affluent stockbroker, and Garland Council. She later recalled that during her childhood she "learned the surface manners and niceties that went with being a well-brought-up young lady of good stock, but inwardly I was an anarchist of the deepest dye" (quoted in Quirk, pp. 7–8). When she was fourteen, her parents pulled her out of the public school system after they discovered that she had been sneaking out at night to roam Norfolk, often on dates with boys. Thereafter, she attended at least three private high schools. She was removed from one school after she appeared in several plays because her parents regarded the stage as disreputable. In spite of her haphazard education, she was a successful and popular student, named the "most talented" girl in her class and elected student council president during her senior year. In 1927 she attended Sullins College in Bristol, Virginia. The following year her parents permitted her to enroll at a dance academy in Boston; but she surreptitiously dropped out after a few weeks to study acting at E. E. Clive's Copley Theatre.

In 1929 Sullavan joined the University Players, a theater group that performed summer stock in Cape Cod. Several members would go on to successful careers in Hollywood, including Henry Fonda, Joshua Logan, and James Stewart. She quickly gained a reputation for being the group's most argumentative and headstrong player. Stories abound about her tempestuous flirtations with Fonda, when she might suddenly slap him or dump a pitcher of ice water over his head. Nevertheless, her male cohorts found her irresistible, as Logan later described: "She had a pulsing and husky voice which could suddenly switch, in emotional moments, to a high choirboy soprano. Her beauty was not obvious or even standard. It showed as she tilted her head, as she walked, as she laughed. . . . One of my girlfriends complained that I talked too much about Sullavan, and she was right. We were all in love with her" (quoted in Logan, pp. 32–33). In 1931 she made her Broadway debut starring in Elmer Harris's *A Modern Virgin*. In December of that year she married Fonda; they had no children and divorced in 1933. While still married, she began a long-term affair with the powerful theater producer Jed Harris, a relationship that she apparently entered into more for career reasons than romantic ones. She starred in several plays on Broadway during the early 1930s, the most successful of which was George Kaufman's *Dinner at Eight* (1933). After seeing Sullavan in this play, the Hollywood director John Stahl persuaded her to star in his film *Only Yesterday* (1933), in which she gave a strong, restrained performance as an unwed mother. Universal Studios signed her to a nonexclusive three-year contract, which permitted her to continue her stage work. The following year she appeared in Frank Borzage's excellent *Little Man, What Now?*, a film about a young couple struggling financially in Germany's Weimar Republic, based on the novel by Hans Fallada.

Sullavan insisted to a publicity magazine in 1934 that she hated Hollywood, dismissing her profession as "making silly faces for that camera." She cultivated an image as an iconoclast, speaking frankly to interviewers about her sexuality, refusing to sign autographs for fans, and often going around the studio barefoot and in jeans. On the set of *The Good Fairy* (1935), she quarreled with director William Wyler. When their relationship had deteriorated to the point that filming was frequently halted, he asked her out to a conciliatory dinner; a few weeks later, after a whirlwind courtship, they married. However, they soon became notorious for their public fights; they had no

children and divorced in May 1936. While at Universal, she was instrumental in jump-starting James Stewart's screen career when she demanded that the studio borrow him from Metro-Goldwyn-Mayer to star with her in *Next Time We Love* (1936). Stewart, who had languished in small roles at MGM, was initially nervous and hesitant on the set, but she painstakingly worked with him on his performance. William Grady, a casting director at MGM, observed that "that boy came back from Universal so changed that I hardly recognized him. . . . Sullavan had taught him to march to his own drummer, to be himself, completely" (quoted in Dewey, p. 147).

For several months in 1936, Sullavan starred on Broadway in *Stage Door*, a play cowritten by George Kaufman and Edna Ferber. In November she married Leland Hayward, one of the most successful agents in show business; they had three children. He negotiated for her a lucrative contract with MGM. She received an Academy Award nomination for best actress for Borzage's *Three Comrades* (1938), with a screenplay by F. Scott Fitzgerald. The same year she reteamed with Stewart in *The Shopworn Angel*, a sentimental but deeply affecting drama about the relationship between a cynical actress and a naive soldier. Their screen partnership continued in 1940 with *The Shop around the Corner*, one of Ernst Lubitsch's most delightful romantic comedies, and *The Mortal Storm*, a drama about the rise of Nazism. In all of her roles, Sullavan displayed a gift for underplaying and a willingness to subordinate her own personality for the good of the picture, as described by Borzage: "She was one of the most generous and unselfish people I ever knew when it came to other actors. . . . She held the view that fine performances all around enhanced the star's contribution. [Her acting had] a quiet, effortless sincerity. There was no airy nonsense about her, no sham, no artificiality. . . . Stewart told me that even after four pictures with her he couldn't get over how *less* meant *more* in the way she got across her character" (quoted in Quirk, pp. 107–8). In 1941 she gave perhaps her best performance opposite Charles Boyer in the melodrama *Back Street*, as a "kept woman" who waits on the fringes of a married man's life for twenty-five years.

Contemptuous of most of the scripts that MGM offered her, Sullavan returned to Broadway in 1943 to star in John Van Druten's *The Voice of the Turtle*, for which she won the Donaldson Award from New York drama critics. At her insistence, Hayward gave up his Hollywood agency business and their family relocated to a farm in Brookfield, Connecticut; but the marriage quickly fell apart, and they divorced in 1948. During the late 1940s, she began to suffer from hearing problems in both her ears, a condition that worsened over the years until she was almost completely deaf. This affected her ability to recognize cues while acting; as a result, she retired from film making in 1950. That year she married Kenneth Wagg, an executive with a malted-milk company; they had no children. She continued to appear on stage in New York, starring in *The*

Deep Blue Sea (1952) and *Sabrina Fair* (1953). During this period, two of her teen-aged children were institutionalized for behavioral problems; in 1955, in an act of rebellion against their mother, they moved in permanently with Hayward in California. Thereafter, Sullavan became deeply depressed over her deafness and her difficulties with her children. She died from an overdose of barbiturates in New Haven, Connecticut, where she was rehearsing a play. Although she left no note, family and friends were certain that she had committed suicide.

• A revealing interview with Sullavan, given just weeks before her suicide, appears in *Theatre Arts*, Dec. 1959. Lawrence J. Quirk, *Margaret Sullavan: Child of Fate* (1986), is a useful, evenhanded biography. Sullavan's oldest daughter, Brooke Hayward, wrote a powerful memoir, *Haywire* (1977), that depicts her parents' divorce and the years preceding her mother's death; the book also discusses the suicide of her younger sister, Bridget, six months after their mother died. Joshua Logan, *Josh: My Up and Down, In and Out Life* (1976), is especially valuable for its portrait of the University Players. Henry Fonda's autobiography, *Fonda: My Life* (1981), as told to Howard Teichmann, describes in painful detail his failed marriage to Sullavan. Jan Herman, *A Talent for Trouble: The Life of Hollywood's Most Acclaimed Director, William Wyler* (1995), describes her failed second marriage. For her relationship with James Stewart, see Donald Dewey, *James Stewart: A Biography* (1996). An obituary appears in the *New York Times*, 2 Jan. 1960.

THOMAS W. COLLINS, JR.

SUZUKI, D. T. (18 Oct. 1870–12 July 1966), the foremost exponent of Zen Buddhism in the West, was born Teitarō Suzuki, the son of Ryojun Suzuki, a physician, and his wife, Masu (full name unknown), in what is now the city of Kanazawa in Ishikawa Prefecture, Japan. He was the youngest of five children. Suzuki's grandfather and great-grandfather were also physicians. The deaths of Suzuki's father, shortly after Suzuki's sixth birthday, and an older brother, the following year, influenced Suzuki's gravitation toward religious and philosophical study. As a teenager he sought out both Zen monks and Christian missionaries and engaged them in philosophical discussions. Suzuki's high school mathematics teacher, who had a strong interest in Zen and had studied with Kōsen Imagita, one of the great Zen masters of the time, intensified the youth's curiosity about Zen through discussion and distribution of literature on the subject.

After leaving high school because of family financial difficulties, Suzuki continued to pursue his interest in Zen while working as a teacher of English. In 1891, the year after his mother's death, one of Suzuki's brothers, who was working as a lawyer, sent him to Tokyo, where he enrolled in classes at what is now Waseda University and also at Tokyo Imperial University. But soon after arriving in Tokyo Suzuki began commuting to nearby Kamakura, the site of Engakuji, an important Zen temple, to study with Kōsen Imagita. Kōsen died in early 1892, and Suzuki continued his studies at the temple—eventually taking up residence there—with Kōsen's successor, Sōen Shaku. In 1893 Suzuki translated into English the address Sōen was to give at the World Parliament of Religions. (Sōseki Natsume, one of Japan's greatest modern novelists, checked Suzuki's translation.)

Held in Chicago that year as part of the World's Columbian Exposition, the World Parliament of Religions was a milestone in the introduction of Buddhism to the United States. At the conference, Sōen met Paul Carus, an author and editor with a strong interest in Eastern religions. Carus was editor of *Open Court*, a journal focusing on ethical and religious issues, and was instrumental in the founding of an eclectic philosophical publishing company of the same name. Sōen spent the week following the conference visiting Carus at his home in LaSalle, Illinois. As a result of this visit, Carus wrote *The Gospel of Buddha*, which Suzuki translated into Japanese at Engakuji while continuing to study Zen as a lay-disciple.

During his four years at Engakuji, Suzuki struggled fruitlessly with the kōan he had been given by Sōen—until it was resolved that in 1897 he would travel to the United States to assist Carus with his translation of the Taoist classic *Tao te ching*. The winter before his departure, Suzuki finally achieved enlightenment and became able to answer the monk's questions about the kōan. At this time Sōen gave him the name Daisetsu, meaning "Great Simplicity." Suzuki is known as Suzuki Daisetsu in Japan; Daisetsu is often spelled Daisetz in English.

After assisting Carus with the *Tao* translation, Suzuki remained at Open Court, studying Chinese and Sanskrit and working on a variety of projects, including translations of important early Buddhist texts. In 1905 he served as Sōen's interpreter during the latter's tour of the United States. His increasingly strong belief that westerners needed a lot of assistance in their attempts to understand Buddhism led Suzuki to publish his first original book in English, *Outlines of Mahayana Buddhism*, in 1907.

In 1908 Suzuki left LaSalle, traveling to New York and in Europe before his return to Japan in April of the following year. In Paris he spent time at the Bibliothèque Nationale copying, photographing, and studying ancient Chinese manuscript copies of sutras, and in London he translated Emanuel Swedenborg's *Heaven and Hell* into Japanese for the Swedenborg Society. (In 1912 the society would invite him back to London to translate several other works by Swedenborg.)

On his return to Japan in 1909, Suzuki became a lecturer at Gakushūin University and Tokyo Imperial University. The following year he was appointed professor at Gakushūin. Suzuki married Beatrice Lane, a Radcliffe graduate and Theosophist, in Japan in 1911; they had no children. The Suzukis lived at Engakuji until the death of Sōen in 1919. They then moved to Kyoto, where Suzuki became a lecturer, and later a professor, at Ōtani University. In 1921 the couple began publishing *The Eastern Buddhist*, an English-language quarterly largely intended for westerners. The first series of his *Essays in Zen Buddhism*, published in London in 1927, and the succeeding two series, published in 1933 and 1934, firmly established Suzuki's reputation in England; some of the essays first appeared in *The Eastern Buddhist*. In April 1936, Suzuki was invited to London to speak at the World Congress of Faiths. His encounter there with the twenty-year-old Alan Watts resulted in the publication, later the same year, of Watts's first book, *The Spirit of Zen*.

After the death in 1939 of his wife, who was his close collaborator throughout their marriage, Suzuki went into seclusion in Kamakura, remaining there for the duration of World War II. He emerged in 1949 to travel to Honolulu to attend the Second East-West Philosopher's Conference and taught at the University of Hawaii the following year. After spending the next year in California, he moved to New York in 1951, where he began teaching a series of seminars on Zen at Columbia University. Among his students at that time were the psychoanalysts Erich Fromm and Karen Horney and the composer John Cage. Cage, who attended Suzuki's seminars for two years in lieu of the psychoanalysis recommended by his friends, was profoundly influenced by them. Although Horney died shortly after a Suzuki-led tour of Zen monasteries in Japan in 1952, her final writings bear evidence of her association with him. Fromm in 1957 organized a groundbreaking workshop on Zen and psychoanalysis at his home in Cuernavaca, Mexico, at which Suzuki was the featured speaker. The long list of other Western intellectuals and artists on whom Suzuki is known to have had an influence includes Carl Jung, Thomas Merton, Gary Snyder, Allen Ginsberg, and potter Bernard Leach.

In 1953 Mihoko Okamura, a second-generation Japanese American student in his class at Columbia, became Suzuki's personal secretary and editor. At this time Suzuki took up residence at the home of Okamura, her parents, and her sister on West Ninety-fourth Street in Manhattan. Okamura remained his secretary, and he continued to live with her family—when not traveling—for the rest of his life.

After his retirement from Columbia in June 1957 and the subsequent summer in Cuernavaca, Suzuki traveled to Cambridge, Massachusetts, where he lectured and helped found the Cambridge Buddhist Society. Until his death in Tokyo at age ninety-five, Suzuki continued to travel widely, lecturing, attending conferences, and receiving a variety of honors.

In addition to playing a key role in the popularization of Buddhism in the Western world, Suzuki, who never formally graduated from any of the schools he attended, also made significant contributions to Buddhist scholarship, particularly to modern understanding of the Gandavyūha and Lankāvatāra sutras. In addition, his work resulted in a reawakening of interest in Buddhism in Japan after a period during which the study of Shinto had dominated Japanese religious scholarship.

Suzuki's collected complete works in Japanese occupy thirty-two volumes. The more than thirty titles he published in English include *An Introduction to Zen Buddhism* (first published in 1934) and *Zen and Japanese Culture* (1959).

Suzuki's last words were "Don't worry. Thank you! Thank you!"

• Masao Abe, ed., *A Zen Life: D. T. Suzuki Remembered* (1986), includes two autobiographical essays by Suzuki as well as personal recollections of him by many prominent individuals, among them Merton, Fromm, Watts, and Snyder. Mircea Eliade, ed., *The Encyclopedia of Religion* (1993), contains an informative article on Suzuki by William LaFleur. Rick Fields, *How the Swans Came to the Lake: A Narrative History of Buddhism in America* (1981), describes in detail Suzuki's role in Buddhism's spread to the West. A. Irwin Switzer, *D. T. Suzuki: A Biography* (1985), is a brief volume published by the Buddhist Society in London. A profile of Suzuki by Winthrop Sargeant in the *New Yorker*, 31 Aug. 1957, was reprinted in the Winter 1991 issue of *Tricycle: A Buddhist Review*.

DAWN LAWSON

SWAYZE, John Cameron (1906–15 Aug. 1995), television news anchor and product spokesman, was born in Wichita, Kansas, and grew up in nearby Atchison. After high school, Swayze, whose childhood dream was to become an actor, took a job with the *Kansas City Journal-Post*, where he worked as an editor and a writer. Realizing that radio was a more lucrative medium, he became a broadcaster in his home state.

Swayze achieved national recognition in 1948, when he provided television coverage of the presidential nominating conventions for NBC. The following year, in February, he became the host of the fifteen-minute nightly newscast known as the "Camel News Caravan." The show, sponsored by the makers of Camel cigarettes, broke fresh ground in television broadcasting by becoming the first news program to deviate from a straight news format. An early version of the evening news programs that became a staple of the national networks, it featured, on a limited scale, interviews with newsmakers, on-the-scene reporting, editorial commentary, and live film from current events. Swayze once said of the opportunity: "I think that in the pioneering days of anything, you can have more fun than when the money moves in and you get streamlined and you can't do this and you can't do that."

Throughout the early to mid-1950s Swayze, always wearing a carnation on his lapel (though viewers could not discern its red hue until 1954, when NBC began broadcasting in color), gained a large audience following, using to his advantage his genial personality, his distinctive voice, and his trademark signoff, "That's the story, glad we could get together." According to his son, John Cameron Swayze, Jr., the newscaster "managed to project a certain innocence, a feeling of promise, a genuine friendliness." His open and casual attitude carried over to his dress as well; his habit of wearing informal slacks with his suit jacket and tie led to rumors that, under his desk, he was wearing only underwear.

In 1956, after seven years of "hopscotching the world for headlines" (his opening line of each newscast), "Camel News Caravan" left the airwaves, replaced by "The Huntley-Brinkley Report," starring Chet Huntley and David Brinkley. Swayze had not limited himself to news broadcasting, however, making appearances during the 1950s on the popular NBC quiz show "Who Said That?" He also hosted a weekly show for children, "Watch the World."

Swayze's departure from television news did not mark the end of his career in the public eye. Capitalizing on the respect he had garnered as a television news anchor, Timex hired Swayze as its spokesman. For the next twenty years he put the shock-resistant Timex watch through every test imaginable and repeated one of the best-known catch phrases in the history of American advertising: "It takes a licking and keeps on ticking." And the watch did take a licking at the hands of Swayze, who secured the Timex to a motor propeller, a tackle line, and a plane pontoon, among other challenges. Although the commercials stopped running in the late 1970s, Timex began a new series of advertisements starring Swayze in the early 1990s.

Swayze died in Sarasota, Florida. His wife, Beulah Mae (maiden name unknown), survived him. Together they had a son and a daughter. His son became a radio news anchor in New York.

As one of the first genuine television "personalities," Swayze was in many ways the prototype of the modern television news broadcaster, suffering the same criticisms that many in that profession do today. Swayze believed his role was to leave people "feeling good." But critics said "Camel News Caravan" ignored hard news, focusing instead on people and pictures, an oft-repeated condemnation of modern television journalism. Swayze was a "true television pioneer," though not well remembered today. Upon his death, when television talk show host Tom Snyder requested film of Swayze from NBC to broadcast on his own late night program, the network could provide only eleven seconds' worth.

• Very little information is available on Swayze. Tom Snyder remembers him in the *New York Times*, 31 Dec. 1995. Obituaries are in *Newsday* and the *New York Times*, 17 Aug. 1995.

STACEY HAMILTON

SWIFT, Kay (19 Apr. 1897–28 Jan. 1993), composer, lyricist, and songwriter, was born Katharine Faulkner Swift in New York City, the daughter of Samuel Swift, a music critic, and Ellen Faulkner Swift, an interior decorator. She began her musical studies at the age of seven, later won a scholarship to the Institute of Musical Arts (now the Juilliard School), and in 1920–1921 attended the New England Conservatory, where she studied piano with Heinrich Gebhard and composition with Charles Martin Loeffler. Her

studies also included orchestration and counterpoint with Percy Goetschius, and she prided herself on writing a fugue a week as part of her "classical" training. Following graduation Swift was part of the touring Edith Rubel Trio and also toured as an accompanist for solo artists, in particular for her lifelong friend Louise Homer Stires, daughter of composer Sidney Homer and Metropolitan Opera contralto Louise Homer.

On 1 June 1918 Swift married banker James Paul Warburg, with whom she would have three daughters (her only children), April, Andrea, and Katharine. The marriage ended in divorce in 1934.

It was during her marriage to Warburg that Kay Swift met George Gershwin, who initially introduced her to the world of musical comedy and then became a serious romantic interest. Swift herself said that she "liked blues, spirituals, fast music, but not musical comedy." According to one version of the story, Gershwin reacted to her show-tune snobbery by playing Irving Berlin's and his own music for her, from which she gained a new respect and fascination for the genre. Swift was better versed in counterpoint and orchestration and was able to aid Gershwin in those areas.

Swift's association with George Gershwin proved beneficial to both. While she helped him in realizing performances of his concert works, he introduced her to the right people on Broadway, helping her to get a job as rehearsal pianist for Richard Rodgers and Lorenz Hart's *A Connecticut Yankee* (1927). In this position she was able to see at first hand a top Broadway team creating a show. With Gershwin's encouragement she began writing songs, her first hit being a song commissioned as additional material for Howard Dietz and Arthur Schwartz's *The Little Show*, titled "Can't We Be Friends?" A year later, in 1930, Swift's own show *Fine and Dandy* became the first Broadway show to have a score entirely by a woman. The title song was the big hit of the show, and it and "Can't We Be Friends?" remain Swift's best-known songs. Her lyricist for her early songs and *Fine and Dandy* was her husband James Warburg, writing as Paul James—a pseudonym used so as not to alarm his Wall Street colleagues with such a frivolous activity as writing light verse. In the 1930s Swift worked on commission for Radio City Music Hall, often writing with lyricist Al Stillman, producing a number of songs including "I Gotta Take Off My Hat to You" and "Sawing a Woman in Half."

As Swift's relationship with Gershwin developed, she worked closely with him on many of his compositions, and sections of the original score of *Porgy and Bess* are in her handwriting (as are parts of other Gershwin manuscripts), taken from Gershwin's dictation. She was a strong advocate for Gershwin's opera, even during times when it was not in favor. As the romantic side of this relationship grew more evident, many close to the couple felt that marriage was a likelihood, particularly after Kay's divorce. When Gershwin went to Hollywood in 1936, they chose not to have contact until his return to New York, at which time they would decide if they should marry. But Gershwin died in 1937 while still in Hollywood.

Swift's composing by no means remained confined to songs. In 1935 she wrote the score for a George Balanchine ballet, *Alma Mater*, a spoof on the annual Harvard-Yale football game. In 1939 she served as director of music at the New York World's Fair.

Swift's New York career was interrupted by her marriage to rancher Faye Hubbard in 1939. They moved to a horse ranch in Oregon, and she detailed their lives together in the 1943 book *Who Could Ask for Anything More!*, which later became an Irene Dunne film, *Never a Dull Moment*, for which Swift wrote the score and songs (both music and lyrics in this case), including "Once You Find Your Guy." She was divorced from Hubbard in 1947, and her career was centered in New York again. Her work there included a one-person Broadway show for Cornelia Otis Skinner, *Paris '90* (1952), for which Swift wrote the music and lyrics. In the 1950s she was briefly married to radio announcer Hunter Galloway, a marriage that also ended in divorce.

In her later years Swift composed many piano works and an ongoing song cycle, "Reaching for the Brass Ring," to which she added a new song upon the birth of each of her grandchildren and great-grandchildren; the songs in the cycle that were completed by 1953 received a performance by the Philadelphia Orchestra. For the 1962 World's Fair in Seattle, Washington, she wrote the orchestral work "Century 21."

Swift continued to compose into her ninetieth year. In 1986 she put together a program of her own works, featuring a number of performers, at Merkin Concert Hall in New York, and herself premiered two new piano pieces on the program, "Betsy" and "Keep On Keeping On." A song, "One Last Look," also had its premiere performance that evening.

Thanks to her thorough musical training, Swift's musical interests and compositional style were wide ranging. Her early songs are very much in the style of the late 1920s and early 1930s; the songs for *Paris '90* often reflect the French popular song of the later nineteenth century, although "The House Where I Was Born" is comparable to Schubert's lieder in its direct simplicity. Her brief interest in the harmonic advances of Arnold Schoenberg led to the tonally sophisticated song "Now and Always." A feeling of optimism runs through her output, even in the late piano work "Keep on Keeping On," written after the unfortunate death of her granddaughter Betsy. Stephen Holden of the *New York Times* called her two piano pieces at the Merkin Hall concert "quintessential Kay Swift compositions—terse, unembellished parlor songs that combine a pop simplicity with a classical sense of decorum," a critique that applies to her entire compositional output.

Perhaps the most enduring contribution Swift made to American song was her work with Ira Gershwin in organizing George Gershwin's manuscripts and making many ready for publication. In 1946 she worked closely with Ira Gershwin to create a "new" Gershwin score for the film *The Shocking Miss Pilgrim*, drawn both from Gershwin's manuscripts and from her remarkable powers of recollection—well into her seventies she could play the entire score of *Porgy and Bess* from memory. She would play tunes for Ira that she remembered George playing, and Ira would invariably affirm that he also had heard George play them, even though they may not have been written down. Swift insisted that she was doing nothing more than making these fragments playable, but there can be no doubt that many carry a certain Kay Swift quality, especially those where she needed to provide accompaniments because George had left only a melody line.

Swift suffered from Alzheimer's disease during the last three years of her life and died in Southington, Connecticut.

• Swift has not been the direct subject of any biographical writing. Some of the best information to be found on her is in a major historical account of a powerful family: Ron Chernow, *The Warburgs* (1993), in the chapters dealing with her first husband, James Warburg. There is an entry on Swift in Virginia Grattan, *American Women Songwriters* (1993). Most Gershwin biographies discuss her, including Robert Kimball and Alfred Simon, *The Gershwins* (1973); Edward Jablonski, *Gershwin* (1987); Joan Peyser, *The Memory of All That* (1993); and Lawrence Stewart and Edward Jablonski, *The Gershwin Years* (1958). The author of the present entry has also been helped by many conversations with Swift's granddaughter Katharine Weber and by Professor Vicki Ohl of Heidelberg College (Ohio). The *New York Times* of 29 Jan. 1993 has an obituary.

BENJAMIN SEARS

T

TABER, Norman (3 Sept. 1891–15 July 1952), track athlete and financial expert, was born Norman Stephen Taber, in Providence, Rhode Island, the son of Alfred Henry Taber and Mary Abbie Weeks Taber. He began his running career at age seventeen while a senior at Hope Street High School in Providence. After completing high school he entered Brown University and competed in track, specializing as a runner in the half-mile and mile distances and also in cross-country.

In the spring of 1912 Taber won the mile at the New England Collegiate Championship in a time of 4:23.6. He then ran a dead heat with John Paul Jones in the intercollegiate championship mile in Philadelphia with a time of exactly 4:20. Later that year the trials for American representation in the Olympic Games of 1912 were held at Harvard University, where Taber finished second to Abel Kiviat in the 1500 meters, the nearest metric equivalent of the mile, metric distances being the rule at the Olympics. Nevertheless, Taber made the U.S. team. In the 1912 Olympics, held in Stockholm, he finished third in the 1500 meters behind Arnold Jackson of Great Britain and Kiviat.

Resuming his intercollegiate career, Taber won the New England cross-country title in the fall of 1912 and was second to Jones in the collegiate championships for that sport. In the spring of 1913, he ran a 4:19 mile in a dual track meet between Brown University and Syracuse University, then two weeks later won the New England championship with a time of 4:18.6. He subsequently finished second to Jones in the collegiate championship mile race with a time of 4:16.4, a race in which Jones set a new world amateur record (4:14.4) and Taber also broke the old record.

Taber received his bachelor of arts degree from Brown in the spring of 1913 and was elected to Phi Beta Kappa; he then accepted a Rhodes Scholarship to Oxford University in England. While studying at Oxford he did not compete in athletics, but he continued to train with the intention of trying to break the world record in the mile when he returned to the United States. In the spring of 1915 he took part in the U.S. National Championship mile in San Francisco, finishing second to Joie Ray with a time of 4:15.2. Later, in the Millrose Athletic Association games at Celtic Park, Boston, he completed the mile in 4:17.4. These competitions were part of a six-month training program for the mile record attempt.

Taber's attempt to set a new world record in the mile occurred on 16 July 1915 at Harvard Stadium in Cambridge, Massachusetts. The Boston Athletic Association provided timing, expert advice, and pace-making runners. There were four pacemakers who started on marks up to 150 yards ahead of Taber. At a quarter-mile his time was 0:58 minutes, and at the half-mile mark his time was 2:05.75. Taber crossed the finish line in 4:12.6, well ahead of Jones's old amateur world record. This was the culmination of his athletic career.

Taber was extremely modest as an athlete, and reporters found it difficult to get him to talk about his career or the method by which he accomplished his world record. It was known that he did not believe in a special diet in an era when fads of that nature were common among athletes. The New York Times reported that many experts regarded him as a "manufactured miler," in that "he was apparently intended by nature for distances above a mile." He possessed a "peculiar plodding style," and "there was no intense natural speed in those sinewy limbs, but there was strength, and plenty of it." Taber's world record for the mile held until the great Finnish runner Paavo Nurmi broke it on 23 August 1923 in Stockholm, Sweden, with a time of 4:10.4. Taber continued to hold the American record until 17 March 1925, when Joie Ray ran the mile at an indoors meet in exactly 4:12. Taber's time for the American mile outdoors was finally surpassed by Lloyd Hahn, on 17 March 1927, setting the new record at 4:12.2.

Taber entered a career in financial management in 1915 and was a clerk for the Rhode Island Hospital Trust Company until 1919. From 1920 to 1930 he was a trustee or manager for estates and trusts affiliated with the John Nicholas Brown Estate, and from 1930 to 1933 he represented the Brookmire Economic Service. He moved to New York City and opened Norman S. Taber and Company, consultants on municipal finance, in 1933, and his best known accomplishment in that capacity was to reorganize the debt structure of the state of Tennessee in 1936. In 1948–1949 he was budget director for the Economic Cooperation Administration in Washington, D.C., and from 1949 until his death he was managing director of the U.S. Council of the International Chamber of Commerce, with an office on Wall Street in New York City.

Taber married Ottilie Rose Metzger on 2 December 1916, and they had one daughter. He served as a trustee for Brown University and also for Moses Brown School in Providence, Rhode Island. For several years he was chairman of the Brown University Athletic Council. He died in Orange, New Jersey, after an illness of several months.

• Taber's athletic career is described in detail in an unsigned article, "Norman S. Taber: Analysis of Running Style and Career," in the New York Times, 16 Jan. 1916. The details of mile records and record holders can be found in T. S.

Andrews's *World Sporting Annual Record Book*, a series published yearly from 1905 until 1934. Taber's biography appears in *Who Was Who in America: A Companion Biographical Reference Work to Who's Who in America*, vol. 3 (1960). An obituary is in the *New York Times*, 16 July 1952.

LUCKETT V. DAVIS

TARTIKOFF, Brandon (13 Jan. 1949–27 Aug. 1997), television and movie executive, was born in Freeport, Long Island, New York, the son of Jordan Tartikoff, a clothing manufacturer, and Enid Tartikoff (maiden name unknown), a marketing executive. He grew up in what he called a "perfectly symmetrical 1950s sitcom family" and, like many children of his era (and of later times), spent his evenings glued to the television set. When Tartikoff became an adolescent, his parents feared he was neglecting his schoolwork, so they sent him to preparatory school in Lawrenceville, New Jersey, where he excelled in sports and other extracurricular activities. After graduation in 1966, he attended Yale University, majoring first in economics but later switching to English. When Tartikoff told his writing seminar instructor, the novelist and poet Robert Penn Warren, that a particular D. H. Lawrence story would have worked better if it were plotted differently, Warren advised him, "You should probably think of a career in television."

After graduating with honors from Yale in 1970, Tartikoff worked first at an advertising agency but soon was hired for an advertising and promotional position at WTNH, a television station in New Haven, Connecticut. In 1973 he moved to Chicago, where he became director of advertising and promotion at station WLS-TV, an ABC affiliate. At twenty-five Tartikoff was diagnosed with Hodgkin's disease, and the young television executive began the first of three battles against the lymphatic cancer that would eventually take his life. A course of experimental chemotherapy restored his health, and in 1976 he moved to Hollywood and was hired by ABC programming chief Fred Silverman in the network's drama development department. The following year he was lured away by NBC to become head of their comedy division.

In 1980, at age thirty-one, Tartikoff was named president of the entertainment division of NBC, becoming the youngest person at that time to assume such a position. His first few years as president were a struggle, and at one point NBC chairman Grant Tinker had to defend him before the heads of local NBC affiliates, who—stung by consistently poor ratings—demanded his resignation. But the affiliates did not realize that Tartikoff was slowly turning the network around with such soon-to-be commercial successes as "Hill Street Blues," "St. Elsewhere," "Cheers," and "Family Ties."

In 1982 Tartikoff married Lilly Samuels; they had one daughter together and adopted a second. That same year his cancer returned. In the late summer of 1983, just as he was finishing his last chemotherapy treatment, he learned that NBC had received 133 Emmy Award nominations, the most for any network

that year. The following year, during a time when adult-oriented prime-time soap operas like CBS's "Dallas" and ABC's "Dynasty" garnered big ratings, NBC's fall lineup included a situation comedy about an upper-middle-class African-American family, starring veteran comedian Bill Cosby. "The Cosby Show," an immediate hit with baby boomers, who had just begun to raise families of their own, helped to move NBC's lineup from last to first in the Nielsen ratings, culminating in a record 68-week streak at the top of prime time in 1988–1989. Although some claim that Tartikoff took undue credit for inspiring the popular shows he developed at NBC (he reportedly slipped a writer a note during a meeting that said "MTV Cops," which resulted in the slick, popular drama "Miami Vice"), no one disputes that he was successful in convincing the network to stick with fledgling critical successes, despite their initial low ratings, allowing the shows to develop into the commercial hits they eventually became—a rarity in television by the end of the twentieth century.

In the late 1980s and early 1990s, Tartikoff's last years at NBC, critics charged that the quality of the programming at NBC was slipping, evidenced by, among other shows, the 1988 Geraldo Rivera special "Exposing Satan's Underground," which won huge ratings. That special, coupled with "Nightingales," a weekly drama that followed the lives of libidinous student nurses, convinced many that he was "selling out to sex and schlock." Ever the showman, Tartikoff called a news conference during which he swore in front of a "priest" to "never buy another special from Geraldo Rivera as long as I live."

On New Year's Day 1991 Tartikoff and his eight-year-old daughter were involved in an automobile accident near Lake Tahoe, Nevada. Both were seriously injured, with Tartikoff suffering mainly broken bones and his daughter sustaining head injuries. In July of that year, frustrated over Federal Communications Commission rulings that upheld prohibitions on networks earning profits from programming sold into syndication, Tartikoff left his position at NBC, reportedly with a $2 million annual salary, to become chair of Paramount Pictures. Surprised and dismayed by the studio's dependence on first-week box office receipts, he oversaw some hits (*Patriot Games*; *Wayne's World*) and some flops (*1492: Conquest of Paradise*; *The Butcher's Wife*). He stunned Hollywood when he resigned from Paramount in 1992 to move to New Orleans, where his daughter was receiving rehabilitative treatment at the Tulane University hospital. Though he insisted the sole reason for his departure was to be near his family full time, many believed his control of the studio was compromised by Paramount Communications president Stanley Jaffe.

After leaving Paramount, Tartikoff developed shows for New World Entertainment and fulfilled his lifelong dream of forming his own production company, which he named H. Beale (after Howard Beale, the character in the 1976 movie *Network* who famously declared, "I'm mad as hell and I'm not going to take it anymore"). In late 1996 he was again diagnosed with Hodgkin's disease. Tartikoff underwent more chemotherapy and a stem-cell transplant, but he died from complications, at the UCLA Medical Center in Los Angeles. Two days after his death, NBC ran a thirty-minute tribute to the former executive. It beat out ABC's ever popular newsmagazine "20/20" and won its time slot, which surely would have satisfied Tartikoff.

Tartikoff was a fierce competitor, who, for example, sheepishly admitted he could not watch NBC's football coverage on Sunday afternoons because of his tendency to root for player injuries, which would inevitably stop the game clock and cause people to forget that "60 Minutes" was starting on CBS. He reinvented television in the 1980s by promoting clever comedies and socially aware dramas whose success depended not only on Nielsen numbers but on critical acclaim as well. The hour-long drama with an ensemble cast and multiple story lines, made popular on such shows as "Hill Street Blues" and "St. Elsewhere," became the norm in network television at the turn of the twenty-first century with programs like "ER" and "Ally McBeal." The beleaguered situation comedy, deemed a dinosaur after popular 1970s comedies such as "M*A*S*H" and "All in the Family" left the air, was resurrected by Tartikoff in the form of the smart and sophisticated "Cheers," "Family Ties," and "The Cosby Show." As Internet and cable options increasingly promote audience-specific programming—and the market share of the original "big three" networks dwindles—a Brandon Tartikoff may not be seen again. The most successful television programmer of the twentieth century, he exhibited a genius for reaching a general audience without having to pander to it.

• Tartikoff's memoir of his years at NBC is *The Last Great Ride*, written with Charles Leerhsen (1992); the book, the cover of which features Tartikoff whispering to a peacock, is filled with humorous anecdotes detailing the day-to-day existence of an NBC television executive. His career is detailed in articles throughout the 1980s and 1990s in the *New York Times* and other publications; see especially "The Man Who Owns Prime Time," *New York Times*, 4 Mar. 1990. Obituaries and retrospectives of his life can be found in the *New York Times*, 28 Aug. 1997; *Entertainment Weekly*, 12 Sept. 1997; *Advertising Age* and *People*, both 15 Sept. 1997; *Esquire*, Nov. 1997; and *Newsweek*, 29 Dec. 1997.

STACEY HAMILTON

TAYLOR, George (1 Jan. 1716?–23 Feb. 1781), ironmaster and signer of the Declaration of Independence, was born into circumstances that remain obscure. Virtually nothing is known with certainty about his early life, but he may have been born in northern Ireland (although at least one source suggests a connection with the Taylor family of Derbyshire, England). The names and occupations of his parents are likewise unknown, although sources suggest that his father was either a clergyman or a well-established lawyer. In any event, he must have had some early education prior to his arrival in North America in 1736, when he settled in East Nantmeal Township, Bucks County, Pennsylvania, and took a job under Samuel Savage, Jr., at the Warwick Furnace. He evidently came to America through the use of his own resources; earlier reports that had him arriving in the colonies as a redemptioner appear to be without foundation. By 1739 Taylor held the position of bookkeeper at the Furnace and later became manager of another nearby iron mill, Coventry Forge.

Following the death of Samuel Savage, Jr., Taylor married his widow, Ann (Taylor) Savage, in 1742; the couple had two children. In 1752 Savage's son Samuel III came into majority and took over control of both iron operations. Sometime prior to 1755 Taylor relocated to Durham, Pennsylvania, and in the spring of that year entered into a partnership with Samuel Flower, a former comrade in the local militia, to operate an iron furnace owned by William Logan & Company under a five-year lease. Now well established in business, Taylor relocated his residence to Easton, Pennsylvania, in 1764 and quickly took a leading role in local public affairs. In addition to being active in the construction of the new courthouse in Easton, he was commissioned a justice of the peace in 1764; in October of that year he was elected to the provincial assembly. Returned to the assembly each of the next five years, Taylor soon drew attention to himself as a leading exponent of the minority (proprietary) faction within the legislative body.

As tensions between Great Britain and her American colonies worsened during the 1760s, Taylor assumed a leading Whig role. In 1765 the assembly charged him with authoring an address to the king on the subject of the hated Stamp Act, and he also served on the assembly committee that provided instruction to the delegates to the Stamp Act Congress. In the latter portion of the decade Taylor relocated to a large house in Catasauqua, Pennsylvania, and may have also engaged in agricultural pursuits. In 1768, after suffering the loss of his wife, he moved back to Durham, where he remained until 1779.

Following a period of political inactivity, Taylor was named to the Committee of Observation by the Northampton County Committee of Safety in September 1774. In January 1775 he represented the county at the Provincial convention in Philadelphia, and in July of that year Taylor became the colonel of the Third Battalion of the Bucks County Militia, although he took no active role in field exercises, leaving active command to Lieutenant Colonel Robert Robinson. In October 1775 Taylor was again elected to the assembly, where he served on a number of committees and assisted in drafting instructions to the delegates to the Continental Congress. He also served as a member of the second Committee of Safety between October 1775 and July 1776, when he was appointed to replace a fellow Pennsylvanian who had refused to sign the Declaration of Independence. Taylor signed the Declaration on 2 August 1776. On 20 January

1777 Taylor was named by Congress as its representative—along with George Wilson—at a conference with Native Americans in Easton.

Taylor's last public service was as a member of the Pennsylvania Supreme Executive Council, where he served with great vigor from March until mid-April 1777, when illness forced his extended absence. On regaining his health, Taylor spent the remainder of the war producing cannon balls for the Continental Army both at Greenwich Township, Warren County, New Jersey—to which he had moved in 1779—and at his iron works in Durham. In April 1780 he returned again to live in Easton, only to die there at his home a few months later. In addition to his children by his wife, he had five children out of wedlock with his housekeeper, Naomi Smith.

Although much of his life remains shrouded in obscurity, George Taylor has a secure—albeit small—niche in American history as a signer of the Declaration of Independence. An early and important supplier of ammunition to the Continental army during the American Revolution, he seems to have been a person always on the go, his mobility perhaps indicating a predisposition to living in a time of ferment.

• While no organized collection of Taylor's papers exists, some of his business records are held at the Bucks County Historical Society in Doylestown, Pennsylvania. The best secondary sources of information on Taylor's life and career are "George Taylor, Signer of the Declaration of Independence," by Warren S. Ely, and "The Homes of George Taylor, Signer of the Declaration of Independence," by B. F. Fackenthal, Jr., *Bucks County Historical Society Publications* 5 (1926): 100–133; see also James B. Laux, "The Lost Will of George Taylor, the Signer," *Pennsylvania Magazine of History and Biography*, Jan. 1920, pp. 82–87.

EDWARD L. LACH, JR.

TAYLOR, Margaret (21 Sept. 1788–14 Aug. 1852), first lady, was born Margaret Mackall Smith in Calvert County, Maryland, the daughter of Walter Smith, a well-to-do planter and former officer in the Continental army, and Ann Mackall. Details are few, but, like most girls in rural America at the end of the eighteenth century, Margaret—who was nicknamed Peggy—had only minimal education in reading, writing, and arithmetic. While Margaret was still a child, her mother died, and she helped her father at home. An anecdote suggests that when Margaret was about fourteen, Zachary Taylor, who was suffering from an old arrow wound in his leg, stopped at her farm home in Maryland. She dressed the injury, which had been aggravated by hard travel, and merited his appreciative attention. He was apparently on his way to Washington to apply for a commission in the U.S. Army. In any event, he became a first lieutenant in 1808. While visiting a married sister in Jefferson County, Kentucky, in 1809, Margaret again met Taylor, back from duty in Louisiana. The two were married in a Kentucky log house in June 1810 and began married life near Louisville. Taylor was promoted to captain later that year.

For decades, Margaret Taylor dutifully endured the life of a peripatetic infantry officer's wife. During the War of 1812, her husband was in combat against British forces and pro-British Indians, was promoted to brevet major, and eventually took command at St. Louis of American forces in the Missouri Territory. Reduced in rank to captain in 1815, Zachary Taylor resigned from the army; the family then returned to Kentucky and farmed there with the help of his slaves. Recommissioned a major in 1816, he served in the territory that became Wisconsin, did recruiting work in Louisville, and in 1819 was promoted to lieutenant colonel. In 1820–1824 he worked in and out of New Orleans and Cantonment Bay Saint Louis, Mississippi. In 1823 he purchased a cotton plantation in Feliciana (West Feliciana) Parish, and transported his slaves from Kentucky to the plantation. In 1824–1827 he supervised Western Department recruitment, headquartered in Cincinnati and Louisville.

As her husband moved about, Margaret Taylor was with him in Kentucky and Indiana; wanted to go to him in Wisconsin but did not; stayed at Bayou Sara, Louisiana, with her married sister, where she became seriously ill and then lived just outside Baton Rouge; and finally returned to Kentucky. During these troubled years, Margaret gave birth to five girls and a boy. Two of the daughters, Octavia and Margaret, died in Bayou Sara in 1820.

Margaret Taylor continued to have little in the way of a happy home life. From 1827 to 1837, Zachary Taylor was stationed in Louisiana and commanded at posts in Minnesota, Wisconsin, and Missouri. In 1829 the Taylors' daughter Ann married Dr. Robert C. Wood. Margaret Taylor was saddened when her husband's peacetime duty was punctuated by combat assignments. Promoted to colonel, he fought in the Black Hawk War in Wisconsin and Illinois and briefly in the protracted Second Seminole War in Florida. In 1835 daughter Sarah married Lieutenant Jefferson Davis but died of malaria three months after her wedding. In 1838 Zachary Taylor, breveted brigadier general, took command of all American troops in Florida and bought land in Mississippi adjacent to his Feliciana acreage. From 1840 to 1845 he held command positions at Baton Rouge and in Arkansas. In 1841 he sold his Louisiana-Mississippi property and a year later bought property in Jefferson County, Mississippi, including eighty-one slaves, for $95,000. Margaret Taylor continued her habit of occasionally leaving her home, whether in Louisiana or Mississippi, to be with her husband at post after post, on the frontier, or in Florida. In keeping with contemporary mores, she had little say in her husband's land purchases.

In 1845 began the events that propelled Zachary Taylor into the White House—to his wife's total and permanent disappointment. That year General Taylor commanded forces in Texas and during the Mexican War led them south to impressive victories. In the absence of regular mail, Margaret Taylor must always have wondered whether a long silence would be broken by news of his death. She reputedly vowed that if he returned safely she would never seek a life of fashion or high society. Late in 1847 he returned in triumph to New Orleans; reunited there, they went to their Baton Rouge cottage and their plantation in East Pascagoula, Mississippi. In 1848 their daughter Mary married Lieutenant Colonel Wallace Smith Bliss, Taylor's adjutant general. In 1848 Taylor was nominated for president at the Whigs' convention in Philadelphia. He was elected president in November, amid squabbles over California and New Mexico statehood, pro- and antiunion efforts at compromises, and the extension of slavery in the West. In 1850 Taylor bought a sugar plantation in Saint Charles Parish, Louisiana, with a complement of slaves. Later that year, with almost no warning, he died of gastroenteritis.

Margaret Taylor was privately critical of her husband's nomination and campaign for the presidency and after his inauguration resided unobtrusively in the White House. She pleaded ill health and participated in no ceremonies, whether pompous or simple. She remained in a pleasant upstairs room and delegated all official family functions to her daughter Mary and Mary's husband, William Bliss. After Taylor's death, President Millard Fillmore offered to delay his occupancy of the White House, but the night of her husband's funeral Margaret moved to a friend's home and nine days later left Washington permanently. She lived for three months with her daughter Sarah Wood in Baltimore, then returned to New Orleans to participate in settling Taylor's estate. Her final lonely years were spent in East Pascagoula, Mississippi, where she died.

Margaret Taylor probably shared her husband's vehemently expressed hope that none of their daughters would marry soldiers, because she well knew how deprived of happiness they too might be. What she did not live to see was that Mary's husband died of yellow fever in 1853, that Sarah's widowed husband became president of the Confederate States of America, that Ann's husband became acting surgeon general of the Union Army during the Civil War, and—most ironically—that her son Richard, who managed her Mississippi plantation until and after her death, became a lieutenant general in the Confederate Army. Even into the twentieth century, Margaret Taylor was viciously caricatured as a pipe-smoking illiterate. In truth, she was a devout Episcopalian and a decent and refined representative of the best virtues of frontier womanhood. No photograph, portrait, or sketch of her has ever been located.

• The following discuss, from various perspectives, Margaret Taylor's conduct as first lady in the White House: Paul F. Boller, Jr., *Presidential Wives*, rev. ed. (1998); Betty Boyd Caroli, *First Ladies*, exp. ed. (1995); Laura C. Holloway, *The Ladies of the White House; or, In the Home of the Presidents* (1871); and Mary Ormsbee Whitton, *First First Ladies 1789–1865* (1948). Holman Hamilton, *Zachary Taylor: Soldier of the Republic* (1941; repr. 1966) and *Zachary Taylor: Soldier in the White House* (1951; repr. 1966), and Brainerd Dyer, *Zachary Taylor* (1946), contain minimal information about Margaret Taylor and her relationship with her husband and their family. Varina Davis, *Jefferson Davis: Ex-President of the Confederate States of America* (2 vols., 1890), includes complimentary remarks by Davis's widow concerning her friend Margaret Taylor. Bessie White Smith, *The Romances of the Presidents* (1932), relates the anecdote of Zachary Taylor's stopping at the Maryland farm home of Margaret and her parents.

ROBERT L. GALE

TAYLOR, Telford (24 Feb. 1908–23 May 1998), attorney and prosecutor, was born in Schenectady, New York, to John Bellamy Taylor, an electrical engineer, and Marcia Estabrook Jones Taylor, both of whom were descendants of seventeenth-century New England colonists. Young Telford attended local public and private schools and received his undergraduate education at Williams College, receiving his B.A. degree in political science in 1928. He remained at Williams as an instructor for a year after graduation and then entered Harvard Law School in the fall of 1929. An outstanding student in law school, he was appointed to the staff of the *Harvard Law Review* and graduated in 1932.

After clerking for a year, Taylor decided to enter government service and became an assistant solicitor at the U.S. Department of the Interior. In 1934 he moved over to the Agricultural Adjustment Corporation as a senior attorney and a year later became associate counsel for the Senate Interstate Commerce Committee, which was then investigating the nation's railroads. One of the committee members was Senator Harry S. Truman, who would become president a decade later following the death of Franklin D. Roosevelt. In 1939 Taylor moved on to the claims division of the Justice Department, and in 1940 he became general counsel of the Federal Communications Commission, overseeing all telegraphic, telephonic, and radio communication in the United States and its territories and on its ships at sea.

In October 1942, with the United States heavily involved in World War II, Taylor left government service temporarily to join the army, where he was commissioned a major and despatched to the War Department. The following spring he was promoted to lieutenant colonel and soon thereafter sent to London to become head of the Special Branch of the War Department. There he served under the military attaché at the U.S. Embassy and was subsequently promoted to the rank of colonel in the fall of 1944. In the summer of 1945, following the end of the war in Europe, Taylor was transferred to the Office of the Chief Counsel of the International War Crimes Tribunal in Nuremberg, Germany. The chief counsel was former U.S. attorney general Robert H. Jackson, and Taylor became his assistant.

The War Crimes Tribunal had been established recently at the urging of the U.S. government for the purpose of trying major Nazi war criminals. Its chief prosecutor, Jackson, and his assistant, Taylor, were aided by prosecutors appointed by governments of the other victorious Allied governments—Great Britain, France, and the Soviet Union. The establishment of such a tribunal had initially been opposed as unnecessary by British prime minister Winston Churchill and Soviet premier Joseph Stalin, both of whom believed that major war criminals should be summarily executed and the rest tried in small courts throughout Germany. U.S. leaders, chief among them President Truman, strongly favored conducting a major international trial, believing that gradations of guilt should be fairly and reasonably determined, lest the Allies sink to the same level as the aggressors they had conquered. The American view prevailed.

It should be noted that at the inception of the trials in October 1945 the Allies were unaware of the horrifying extent of the Holocaust; had they been, then the United States might not have been as willing, or even able, to impose its demand for a tribunal. Nevertheless, Taylor himself said years later that when details of the Holocaust emerged after the trials were under way, he and Jackson still remained firmly committed to conducting a fair proceeding untainted by even a hint of vengeance. Undoubtedly bearing the consequences of Germany's treatment following World War I all too clearly in mind, both men believed that was the only way to bring about a final resolution to the war and to avoid paving the way for still another cataclysmic conflict.

In collaboration with Jackson, Taylor became a self-taught authority on the laws and history of warfare and established the guidelines for indicting and trying German war criminals. Under Jackson, the first indictments were handed down against twenty-two of the highest Nazi leaders; nineteen were convicted and twelve condemned to death by hanging. When Jackson stepped down in October 1946, Taylor, who had been promoted to brigadier general six months earlier, succeeded him as chief prosecutor. At that time the trials came under the sole jurisdiction of the U.S. Military Government in Germany. Within a month Taylor had won his first indictments—against twenty-three German doctors, scientists, and hospital officials for killing hundreds of thousands of people in brutal medical experiments. Over the next two years he also tried judges, government officials, and SS officers, ultimately obtaining more than a hundred convictions; thirty-seven of the defendants were sentenced to death and the remainder to prison terms of varying lengths. Taylor also tried major German industrialists and financiers, including munitions manufacturer Alfred Krupp and the directors of I. G. Farben, the major German chemical firm, on charges that included the use of slave labor, but he was unsuccessful this time due to lack of sufficient evidence.

Perhaps the most famous Nazi that Taylor convicted was Rudolf Hess, who outlived all the other Nazis consigned to Berlin's Spandau Prison and remained its sole inmate for many years, until his death by suicide in 1987 at the age of ninety-three. Taylor later termed Hess's lengthy solitary confinement "a crime against humanity." Overall, however, and de-

spite his disappointment at failing to win even more convictions, he pronounced himself pleased at the outcome of the trials, even as critics questioned their value. Taylor answered by pronouncing the Nuremberg Trials "a landmark in the development of international law," and they undoubtedly paved the way for subsequent United Nations–sanctioned war crimes tribunals in other parts of the world.

Taylor returned to the United States as a civilian in 1949 and briefly went into private legal practice. During the Korean War he served as head of the Small Defense Plants Administration in Washington, where he remained for more than a year before returning to private practice. In 1952 he published his first book, *Sword and Swastika: Generals and Nazis in the Third Reich*, an account of Germany under Hitler. Taylor was a much-sought-after public figure after his return to the States, and he became a frequent lecturer on the dangers of war as an instrument of national policy and on the importance of moral integrity in government. He also became an early and outspoken opponent of Joseph McCarthy, the rabble-rousing Wisconsin senator who created an atmosphere of fear with his frenzied claims that Communists had infiltrated the U.S. government. Taylor wrote his second book, *Grand Inquest: The Story of Congressional Investigations*, published in 1955, partly in response to the McCarthy phenomenon.

Taylor returned to the subject of World War II in other books that he wrote over the following decades, including *The March of Conquest* (1958); *The Breaking Wave: The German Defeat in the Summer of 1940* (1967); *Munich: The Price of Peace* (1979), which won a National Book Critics Circle Award; and *Anatomy of the Nuremberg Trials* (1992). He published additional books on international law, including *Perspectives on Justice* (1975) and *Courts of Terror: Soviet Criminal Justice and Jewish Emigration* (1976). During the Vietnam War he was openly critical of U.S. government policy, believing that the conflict was pointless and ultimately immoral. His book *Nuremberg and Vietnam: An American Tragedy* (1970) argued that principles of conduct in warfare established at the Nuremberg Trials were violated by the United States in Vietnam. He defended young men accused of evading the draft laws, called for the prosecution of military and civilian leaders who trained troops for the war, and even traveled to Hanoi in 1973 to visit prisoner-of-war camps.

In addition to his private practice, Taylor taught at Columbia University's law school for many years, becoming a full professor in 1962; he was named Nash Professor of Law there in 1974. From 1976 onward he also taught at Yeshiva University's Cardozo School of Law. During the Iran-Contra hearings in the mid-1980s he again spoke out against the abuses of military power, and in the wake of atrocities in Bosnia in the 1990s he voiced support for criminal indictments against perpetrators. He continued in private practice, developing sports law as a specialty during the 1980s; because of his expertise he was often called on to settle disputes within the National Basketball Association. As an avocation Taylor liked to compose music; he published a song and several military marches.

Taylor was married in 1937 to Mary Walker, also an attorney; the couple had three children before they divorced. Taylor's second wife was Toby Golick, whom he married in 1974 and with whom he had three more children. Taylor died at a hospital in New York City following a stroke.

• For biographical information, see entries for "Taylor, Telford," in *Current Biography Yearbook 1948*; *Current Biography Yearbook 1998*; *Contemporary Authors*, vols. 25–28 (1977); and *Contemporary Authors: New Revision Series*, vol. 16 (1986). An obituary appears in the *New York Times*, 24 May 1998.

ANN T. KEENE

TEBBETTS, Birdie (10 Nov. 1912–24 Mar. 1999), baseball player and manager, was born George Robert Tebbetts in Burlington, Vermont, the son of Charles Tebbetts, a meat delivery man, and Elizabeth Ryan Tebbetts. The family moved to Nashua, New Hampshire, when Birdie was one, and there an aunt gave him his lifelong nickname, saying that he chirped like a bird. His father died when he was four; his mother then supported the three children as a surgical garments distributor. Tebbetts began his long career in baseball as a batboy and mascot of the minor league Nashua Millionaires at age nine. He went on to star as a catcher at Nashua High School and in American Legion ball. Although the Detroit Tigers signed him, he insisted on getting a college education; the Tigers wound up paying his way through Providence College, from which he graduated in 1934 with a major in philosophy. In 1935 he started at Springfield (Ill.) in the Three I League, then moved up to Beaumont in the Texas League, where he managed only a .219 average. Returning to Texas in 1936, he raised his average to .292 and won a late-season call-up to Detroit, where player-manager Mickey Cochrane, a Hall of Fame catcher, began grooming Tebbetts as his successor.

Tebbetts played with the Tigers until 1947, developing into a solid defensive catcher who generally batted between .240 and .300. A right-handed hitter, he stood five feet eleven inches and weighed 190 pounds. Bright and articulate, he showed managerial promise as an inquisitive player and a natural leader who commanded respect from his teammates with his baseball savvy and hard work. He hit .296, his high as a Tiger, in 1940, the year that the Tigers won their first pennant since 1909; they then lost a tight seven-game World Series to the Cincinnati Reds. Tebbetts failed to contribute, going hitless in his 11 at-bats in the four games he played. Two years later he was selected to be on the American League all-star team, an honor he would receive three more times in his career. Tebbetts, like many of his contemporaries, lost potentially peak years to military service, serving from 1943 to 1945 in the Army Air Forces—mostly playing baseball but

developing ulcers nevertheless. He hit only .243 when he returned to Detroit in 1946. When he got off to a terrible .094 start the following season, the Tigers thought he was washed up and traded him to the Boston Red Sox for Hal Wagner, a catcher with a parallel but less distinguished career.

Tebbetts was far from through. He had his best seasons in Boston, batting .299 the rest of 1947 to move his average up to .267, then hitting .280 in 1948 as he helped Boston tie Cleveland for the American League pennant, only to lose the one-game playoff for a trip to the World Series. In 1949 he hit .270, then hit a career-high eight home runs in only 79 games in 1950 to go with his career-best .310 average. Nonetheless, he was 38 and old by baseball standards; his age and some caustic comments he vented about Red Sox teammates as "moronic malcontents" and "juvenile delinquents" made him expendable (*New York Times*, 26 Mar. 1999). After the season, he married Mary Hartnett, with whom he would have one son and three daughters in a marriage that lasted until her death in 1997. Then, in December, Boston sold him to the Cleveland Indians, where he spent 1951 and 1952 backing up Jim Hegan, the team's fine starting catcher. He wound up his playing career with a .270 batting average, an even 1,000 hits, and a modest 38 home runs in 1,162 games.

His managerial career began immediately. In 1953 he piloted the Indianapolis Indians of the American Association, then moved up to guide the Cincinnati Reds between 1954 and 1958. The Reds finished fifth his first two years, but in 1956, sparked by a then-record 221 home runs by the likes of Ted Kluszewski, Gus Bell, Wally Post, Frank Robinson, and Ed Bailey, the team won 91 games, placing third in the National League's final standings. As a result, Tebbetts earned the manager-of-the-year award. In the dugout, his high-pitched voice and quick wit made him one of the game's premier bench jockeys. The Reds slipped to fourth in 1957, and they were mired in seventh when Tebbetts was fired late in 1958. The Milwaukee Braves promptly hired him as an executive vice-president, but he preferred the excitement of being in the dugout and had himself named manager late in the 1961 season. He guided the team to an 86–76 record and fifth-place finish in 1962. Next he took the helm of the Cleveland Indians; in four seasons, though, he never got the team out of the second division. A heart attack in 1965 led to the end of his on-field career after 1966. His managerial record of 748–705, a .515 percentage, and his ability to get more out of his players than might be expected earned him, according to Bill James, a ranking as an above-average manager.

From 1968 until his retirement in 1992 Tebbetts scouted for the Reds, the New York Yankees, the New York Mets, and the Baltimore Orioles. His scouting reports could be right to the point. Once he told the Reds of a pitching prospect: "Major league stuff and a great arm. Screwy in the head. Eliminate head and I recommend him. Get good surgeon" (*New York Times*, 26 Mar. 1999). In all, Tebbetts spent more than half a century in the major leagues as a catcher, manager, and scout. He died of congestive heart failure in Bradenton, Florida.

• Bruce Jacobs, ed., *Baseball Stars of 1950* (1950), has a chapter on Tebbetts. His statistics as a major league player and manager appear in *Total Baseball*. Managerial rankings are in *The Bill James Guide to Baseball Managers from 1870 to Today* (1997). Obituaries appear in the *New York Times* and the *Boston Globe*, 26 Mar. 1999.

JOHN R. M. WILSON

THAXTER, Celia (29 June 1835–26 Aug. 1894), poet and essayist, was born Celia Laighton in Portsmouth, New Hampshire, the daughter of Thomas B. Laighton, a merchant, editor, and state legislator, and Eliza Rymes Laighton. Failing in his ambition to become governor of New Hampshire, Celia's father had himself appointed lighthouse keeper at the Isles of Shoals, a group of nine small, rugged islands about ten miles off the New Hampshire coast. In 1839, vowing never to return to the mainland, he took his wife, Celia, and her younger brother Oscar to tiny White Island, one of the shoals, to work as lighthouse keeper there. The parents tutored their children, soon three in number, with the help of occasional visitors, including a handsome, bright, but unstable Harvard graduate named Levi Lincoln Thaxter, who was eleven years Celia's senior. Thaxter soon noticed and fostered Celia's love of poetry.

Thomas Laighton resigned his post in 1845 and moved to the largest of the Isles of Shoals, Appledore Island, which he had purchased in 1834. In 1847 he began building a summer hotel there with the help of Thaxter's father. Perhaps the first of its kind along the Atlantic coast, the resort was enormous—with eighty sleeping rooms in the top three of its four stories. Opening in June 1848, it immediately attracted not only friends but also artists, musicians, preachers, scholars, and writers. From the outset, Celia was helpful and courteous to the guests. The structure was gradually added to: in 1860 it could accommodate 300 people; in 1866 its enlarged dining hall could seat 500. Over the years, the swarm of visitors included Thomas Bailey Aldrich, Ole Bull, Frances Hodgson Burnett, Caleb Cushing, Charlotte Cushman, Richard Henry Dana, Jr., Ralph Waldo Emerson, James T. Fields and his wife Annie Adams Fields, Childe Hassam (who gave Celia art lessons and painted pictures of her garden), Nathaniel Hawthorne, Thomas Wentworth Higginson, William Morris Hunt (who drowned, perhaps intentionally, in a pond at Appledore), Sarah Orne Jewett, James Russell Lowell, Herman Melville (whose aborted "Agatha story" was inspired by a sad woman living near the Isles of Shoals), Franklin Pierce, Harriet Prescott Spofford, Edmund Clarence Stedman, Harriet Beecher Stowe, Henry David Thoreau, Mark Twain, and John Greenleaf Whittier. In time, Celia met and favorably impressed most of this varied group of celebrities.

To keep Thaxter away from Celia, her parents sent her to the Mount Washington Female Seminary in Boston. But she soon returned, and in 1851 the two married and eventually had three children, one of whom, Roland Thaxter, became a prominent mycologist. For a while, Thaxter taught and preached on nearby Star Island. They lived in Newtonville, Massachusetts, for four years, during which Celia was always homesick for the islands. Part of that time, Thaxter deserted Celia to go on hunting trips. To support the family, she composed poems, the first of which, "Land-locked," James Russell Lowell published in 1861 without her permission in the *Atlantic Monthly*, which he edited. Its first line sounds a bitter tone, often struck in Celia's later works: "Black lie the hills; swiftly doth daylight flee." More of her verses appeared in the *Atlantic Monthly*, the *Century*, *Harper's*, the *Independent*, and other periodicals. She placed poems and stories for juvenile readers in *Our Young Folks*, *St. Nicholas*, *Youth's Companion*, and similar magazines.

In 1861 Celia Thaxter's brothers built their parents a large cottage near their resort hotel. In the 1860s, her professional success and her love of the shoals combined to help her establish a summer literary salon at Appledore. When her father died in 1866, Celia remained at the family cottage to care for her mother. She also took charge of her oldest son, who was mentally retarded. Though never divorced, she began to live in the cottage on Appledore apart from her husband, who resented her success as a writer and as a friend of the illustrious. After her mother's death in 1877, Celia conducted seances in an attempt to communicate with her spirit. In this venture she was aided by Sarah Jewett. In 1880 Celia moved to a house at Kittery Point, Maine, with a view of the shoals, and lived again with her husband. She and her brother Oscar enjoyed a six-month tour of England and the Continent (1880–1881). A decade after her husband's death in 1884, Celia died in her Appledore cottage.

Celia Thaxter assembled her periodically published pieces in book form, notably *Poems* (1872; enlarged ed., 1874), *Among the Isles of Shoals* (prose sketches, 1873), *Poems for Children* (1884), and *An Island Garden* (prose sketches, with illustrations by Childe Hassam, 1894). Her works sold well, and her delicate paintings on china also helped support her and her family. Her poetry is about the sea and weather, animals and birds, midsummer flowers, the stars, and a range of emotions including grim responses to the seeming indifference of forces—human, natural, and cosmic—beyond one's power to control. Her diction is uniformly old-fashioned, with standard but unforced rhyme schemes. Representative is her conclusion upon seeing the consequences of a shipwreck:

> Do purposeless thy children meet
> Such bitter death? How was it best
> These hearts should cease to beat?

Typical of her moralistic stories for children is "The Bear at Appledore," about a bear cub brought as a pet from Georgia to Appledore, but as it grew it escaped and rampaged until it had to be shot. Critics are usually in agreement that Celia's finest writing is in *An Island Garden*, a distillation of her abiding love affair with Appledore. There she planted, experimented with, and nurtured a spectrum of flowers, uncannily prevailing against inimical insects, fungi, and slugs, and fenced her blossoms against the adverse winds.

In 1914 Appledore House, together with seven nearby cottages, burned to the ground. In 1977 Celia Thaxter's unique island garden was reconstructed at its original location by the Shoals Marine Laboratory.

• The bulk of Celia Thaxter's widely scattered papers are at the Boston Public Library, in libraries at Colby College and Harvard University, and at the Henry E. Huntington Library, San Marino, Calif. Oscar Laighton, *Ninety Years at the Isles of Shoals* (1929), places his sister Celia in context in a quaint, lively, and observant memoir, which includes several of her poems and a few of his own. Celia Thaxter, *An Island Garden*, ed. John M. Kingsbury (1985), includes an informative introduction, color reprints of Childe Hassam's excellent illustrations, and a secondary bibliography. See also Julia Older's introduction to her edition of Celia Thaxter, *Selected Writings* (1997), which also has a brief bibliography. In *Literary Friends and Acquaintance* (1900), William Dean Howells praises Celia Thaxter's appearance as "fine, frank, finished," and calls her poetry "strangely full and bright." The most detailed of several comments by contemporaries concerning Celia Thaxter and the Isles of Shoals is in Nathaniel Hawthorne, *The American Notebooks*; see especially Claude M. Simpson's annotated edition (1972). Rosamond Thaxter, *Sandpiper: The Life and Letters of Celia Thaxter* (1962; rev. ed., 1963), is a loving biography by her granddaughter. An obituary is in the *New York Times*, 28 Aug. 1894.

ROBERT L. GALE

THOMPSON, Clara (3 Oct. 1893–20 Dec. 1958), psychiatrist, was born Clara Mabel Thompson in Providence, Rhode Island, the daughter of Thomas Franklin Thompson, a self-made businessman who eventually became president of a drug company, and Clara Medbury Thompson. The prosperous Thompson household, in a rural area outside Providence, also included both sets of grandparents as well as an assortment of aunts and uncles. By all accounts, the elder Clara Thompson was a strong-willed woman, and she decreed that her only daughter—the couple also had a younger son, named after his father—be called by her middle name. The younger Clara was therefore known as Mabel until she reached adulthood and could use her given name exclusively.

At the Classical High School in Providence Thompson was first in her class, led the girls' debating society, and excelled in sports. A surge of personal piety in her teens—the family were all churchgoing Baptists—led her to decide to become a medical missionary, and following graduation in 1912 she enrolled as a premed student in the women's division (later named Pembroke College) of Brown University. But during her sophomore year, Thompson apparently lost her religious faith, stopped going to church, which

led to a long estrangement from her mother, and gave up her plans to become a missionary. She remained determined to become a physician, however, and during one of her summers on holiday from Brown she worked as a volunteer at the Danvers State Hospital, a mental institution in Massachusetts—an experience that may have kindled her interest in psychiatry. Graduating from Brown in 1916 with distinction and election to Phi Beta Kappa as well as Sigma Xi, the science honorary society, she enrolled that fall at Johns Hopkins University in Baltimore to study medicine.

In her second year at Hopkins, Thompson was introduced to the relatively new field of psychoanalysis by Lucille Dooley, a classmate who had studied the subject under G. Stanley Hall at Clark University in Massachusetts. Thompson became fascinated by the psychoanalytic process, and during the summer of 1918 she joined Dooley as a volunteer at St. Elizabeth's Hospital, a prominent mental institution in Washington, D.C. St. Elizabeth's was then under the direction of William Alanson White, one of the nation's leading psychiatrists and an early American supporter of psychoanalysis. He urged his staff to employ its methods in dealing with patients, and his warm manner drew others, including Thompson, toward him for advice and counsel. Thompson's positive experience with White undoubtedly convinced her to specialize in psychiatry, and following her graduation from medical school in 1920 she spent a year as a psychiatric intern at Hopkins's Phipps Clinic. After interning for an additional year at the New York Infirmary for Women and Children, she became a resident at Phipps under the direction of Adolf Meyer, another prominent psychiatrist. She so impressed Meyer that during her second year he put her in charge of his private patients. About this time she presented her first scientific paper at a professional meeting at Phipps. Among the attendees was Harry Stack Sullivan, a pioneer in American psychoanalytic circles who had tempered and refined the traditional teachings of Freud, and he became a lifelong friend and mentor.

In her third and last year of residency at Phipps, Thompson became an instructor at the Hopkins medical school, and her career now seemed assured. However, despite her academic and professional success, she had by all accounts become an embittered and lonely young woman. Years earlier, at St. Elizabeth's, White had encouraged her to seek psychoanalytic help for herself, and in her final year as a resident she began psychoanalysis with Joseph C. Thompson (no relation), a member of the Hopkins medical faculty. The discipline was still controversial, however, and Adolf Meyer did not approve of her treatment. He may also have objected to the obviously warm relationship that existed between the two Thompsons. When Meyer asked her to stop psychoanalysis and she refused, he terminated their working relationship. This was a blow to Thompson but she completed her residency, and in 1925 she opened a private practice in psychiatry in Baltimore while continuing to undergo analysis with Joseph Thompson. Several years later she left Thompson to become a patient of the Hungarian psychiatrist Sándor Ferenczi, an early associate of Sigmund Freud who had been recommended by Harry Stack Sullivan, and she met with Ferenczi in Budapest throughout the summers of 1928 and 1929. During that period she also taught a class in mental hygiene at the Institute of Euthenics, directed by the psychiatrist Smiley Blanton at Vassar College, all the while continuing her private practice back in Baltimore. She lived alone, except for a maid and a cat, and had few social contacts apart from those engendered through professional meetings, but she was becoming an acknowledged leader in American psychoanalytic circles. In 1930 she was elected president of the Washington-Baltimore Psychoanalytic Society, newly organized by Sullivan and including among its members her former mentor William Alanson White, and during the following year she led a group of fellow practitioners in regular meetings to discuss their cases.

In June 1931 Thompson moved to Budapest to resume analysis full-time with Ferenczi. She quickly came to love the city, settling into a cozy apartment in the historic section of Buda, again with a maid and a cat for company. During her stay, which included daily sessions with Ferenczi, she also managed to find time for a romance with a fellow patient, a young American businessman. Her Budapest idyll soon came to an end, however, because of the unexpected death of Ferenczi in the spring of 1933. Ferenczi had come to believe, like Sullivan, that interpersonal relationships lay at the heart of psychiatry as a methodology for healing. He had spoken out in favor of a warm personal relationship between doctor and patient rather than the classic practice of detachment, and he had stressed as well the necessity for humility on the part of the analyst—concepts that had led him by the end of his life to a break with the dogmatic Freud. Ferenczi's approach made a profound impression on Thompson, whose own personality seemed to have been transformed by her years of analysis, and perhaps by her love affair as well. She returned to the United States in the summer of 1933 and settled in New York City, resuming her practice and becoming part of a professional and social group—whimsically named the Zodiacs, each of its members having a different astrological sign—that initially included Sullivan as well as the analysts Karen Horney and William Silverberg and was later joined by Erich Fromm. Through Horney she was introduced to the New York Psychoanalytic Institute, and she joined Horney as a faculty member and training analyst there.

By the late 1930s two opposing factions had emerged at the institute, loosely defined as doctrinaire Freudians, still wedded to the libido theory and rigidly dogmatic, versus the looser revisionists. Horney and Fromm were the most prominent among the latter, Sullivan having moved back to Washington, D.C., in 1937 to direct the Washington School of Psychiatry founded by William Alanson White. Thompson was firmly allied with Horney and Fromm, and

by 1938 tensions between the factions were rapidly escalating. During the spring of that year, Thompson met an émigré Hungarian painter named Henry Major at an art exhibition, and the two fell immediately in love. Although Major was married and apparently unable to get a divorce, this did not hinder their relationship. She bought a house for them in Provincetown, Massachusetts, on Cape Cod, and established a studio there for him. Their relationship lasted for ten years, until Major's death in 1948.

In early 1941 the traditionalists at the New York Institute succeeded in getting Karen Horney dismissed as a training analyst, and Clara Thompson, along with several other analysts, resigned in protest. The dissidents went on to found a new organization, the American Association for the Advancement of Psychoanalysis, with Thompson elected as vice president, and the association established a new training institute called the American Institute of Psychoanalysis. New tensions soon erupted, however, between Horney and Fromm, and in 1943 Fromm was ousted from the group. Though she was an ally of both, Thompson believed that Fromm's ouster was unfair, and she resigned. That same year, with the guidance of Harry Stack Sullivan, Thompson and Fromm went on to establish a New York branch of the Washington School of Psychiatry, with Thompson as executive director; it was renamed the William Alanson White Institute in 1946. The New York branch flourished under Thompson's direction, and Thompson now flourished as well, happily living in an apartment in Manhattan's East 80s, holding open houses every Sunday for her growing circle of friends and colleagues and having frequent trysts with Henry Major, with whom she spent summers in Provincetown.

Thompson's professional life comprised an ongoing assortment of responsibilities, including the training of analysts as well as seeing private patients. She also found time to contribute reviews and articles to professional journals, some of them on the sexuality of American women. Her stance in these essays is objective and commonsensical, taking note of how women had been wronged by prevailing cultural attitudes, in particular the so-called double standard for sexual behavior, but her writings betray no hint of ardent feminism. Among her best-known essays is "'Penis Envy' in Women" (1943), which acknowledges the trait but concludes that it is cultural rather than biological.

Thompson was devastated by the death of Major from lung cancer in 1948, and a year later she lost another important figure in her life with the passing of Harry Stack Sullivan. She also lost the continual company of another close friend in the late 1940s when Erich Fromm began spending most of each year in Mexico. Thompson assuaged her sorrow by working harder at the White Institute, which had been severed from the Washington School of Psychiatry following Sullivan's death, and in 1950 she published *Psychoanalysis: Its Evolution and Development*, a series of lectures she gave at the institute. Over the next few years Thompson devoted herself wholeheartedly to gaining accreditation of the White Institute by the American Psychoanalytic Association. In this she was unsuccessful, and she responded by helping to organize a rival parent group, the Academy of Psychoanalysis, in 1956. The following year she was diagnosed with colon cancer, and soon she was suffering as well from shingles and cirrhosis of the liver. She nevertheless remained professionally active until her death, which occurred at her home in New York City. At her request, she was buried alongside Henry Major in Provincetown.

Clara Thompson made no major contributions to psychoanalytic theory, published only one book during her lifetime, and receives only brief mention in histories of psychoanalysis. Yet she is arguably a significant figure by virtue of her work in perpetuating the development of the American school of interpersonal psychoanalysis formulated by her friends and mentors William Alanson White and Harry Stack Sullivan.

• The major source of biographical information on Thompson is Maurice R. Green's essay "Her Life," published as part 6 in *Interpersonal Psychoanalysis: The Selected Papers of Clara M. Thompson* (1964), edited by Green and with a foreword by Erich Fromm. *Interpersonal Psychoanalysis*, which includes a bibliography of all Thompson's work published during her lifetime, is a collection of her major essays, including "'Penis Envy' in Women." The essay also appears in a shorter collection, *On Women* (1971). See also the entry for "Thompson, Clara," in *Who Was Who in America*, vol. 3 (1951–1960). In addition, see Helen Swick Perry, "Thompson, Clara [Mabel]," *Notable American Women: The Modern Period* (1980); although based largely on Green's essay, it also includes personal observations by Perry, who knew Thompson. For an account of the psychoanalytic movement in the United States, see especially Nathan G. Hale, Jr., *The Rise and Crisis of Psychoanalysis in the United States* (1995), and Joseph Schwartz, *Cassandra's Daughter: A History of Psychoanalysis* (1999). A brief obituary appears in the *New York Times*, 21 Dec. 1958.

ANN T. KEENE

TINKER, Joe (27 July 1880–27 July 1948), baseball player, was born Joseph Bert Tinker in Muscotah, Kansas, the son of Samuel Tinker and Elizabeth Williams. Details of his early life are unknown. He attended public schools in Kansas City, Kansas, and thereafter worked as a paperhanger's apprentice. He began playing semiprofessional baseball for teams around Kansas City in 1896. In 1897 he helped the Bruce Lumbers win the city championship, after which he was traded for two uniforms and a bat to Kling's Schmeltzers. During an exhibition game against the Kansas City Blues in 1898, he caught the attention of Blues manager Bill Hulen, a former major leaguer, who recommended him to a minor league team in Denver. In 1901 he batted .290 and stole 37 bases for a Portland team in the Pacific Northwest League, although he also committed 61 fielding errors at third base. The following year he joined the Chi-

cago Cubs, where manager Frank Selee insisted that he was better suited to play shortstop.

Tinker batted .273 during his rookie season with the Cubs and .291 the following year, although he continued to experience defensive problems. By 1905, however, he had mastered his position. During his career, he led National League shortstops in fielding percentage four times, in total chances three times, and in putouts and assists twice each. He and second baseman Johnny Evers devised several plays that have since become commonplace defensive strategy. For example, they originated the rotation play used against the sacrifice bunt, whereby the shortstop covers second and the second baseman covers first, enabling the first baseman to charge toward home plate to better field the ball. Tinker was also the first shortstop to cover second base on a hit-and-run play with a left-handed batter—a situation where the second baseman had always covered previously. Because left-handers naturally hit toward right field, the ball would often be hit directly to Evers as he stood his ground, permitting him to make an easy double play. Tinker, Evers, and first baseman Frank Chance turned so many rally-killing double plays that they prompted writer (and New York Giants fan) Franklin P. Adams to pen "Baseball's Sad Lexicon" (1910), perhaps the most famous poem in American sports:

These are the saddest of possible words:
"Tinker to Evers to Chance."
Trio of bear cubs, and fleeter than birds,
"Tinker and Evers and Chance."
Ruthlessly pricking our gonfalon bubble,
Making a Giant hit into a double—
Words that are weighty with nothing but trouble:
"Tinker to Evers to Chance."

Although Tinker and Evers played side by side for the Cubs for eleven seasons, they despised each other. Following an incident in 1905 when Evers stole a cab from Tinker outside an Indiana hotel, they refused to speak to each other off the baseball diamond; their silence was finally broken thirty-three years later, when they met by chance at a World Series game and tearfully embraced.

Aggressive and hard-nosed, Tinker was an integral member of a Chicago club that dominated the National League between 1906 and 1910, winning four pennants (1906–1908, 1910) and two world championships (1907–1908). An accomplished base runner, he stole at least twenty bases for eleven consecutive seasons. In July 1910 he tied a major league record when he stole home twice in one game. Although he rarely batted higher than .280, he was regarded as a dangerous clutch hitter and particularly renowned for his success against the Cubs' arch rivals, the New York Giants, and their pitching ace, Christy Mathewson. Tinker batted .360 against Mathewson during his career, including posting a .400 mark against him in 1908 when their clubs were locked in a tight pennant race. After Chicago and New York ended the season in a tie, he hit a crucial triple off

Mathewson in a one-game playoff, which the Cubs won. He later recalled that his greatest game in baseball occurred on 7 August 1911 when he once again tormented the pitcher, rapping out four hits and stealing home.

In 1909 Tinker became the major leagues' first holdout when he demanded a $1,000 raise and then sat out part of the season; he eventually settled for $200. In late 1912 he was traded to the Cincinnati Reds, where he enjoyed his finest offensive season, batting .317. He also served as the team's manager, but the Reds finished in seventh place and he repeatedly quarreled with club president Garry Herrmann over personnel decisions and his salary. He was sold to the Brooklyn Dodgers in December 1913 for $25,000, but he refused to join the team unless he was given almost half of the sale price. When the money was not forthcoming, he became the first star to jump to the newly organized Federal League. He played and managed for the Chicago Whales for two seasons, leading them to a first-place finish in 1915. He was also actively involved in recruiting other stars to join the new league, including Washington Senators pitcher Walter Johnson, who was convinced to stay with his team only after being promised a sizeable salary increase. In 1916 the Federal League folded and Whales owner Charles Weeghman gained a controlling interest in the Cubs; the two teams were merged, and Tinker became the Cubs' player-manager. But he played in only seven games and the team posted a poor 67–86 record. At the end of the season he retired.

During his career, Tinker compiled a .263 batting average, made 1,695 hits, scored 773 runs, and stole 336 bases. He batted .235 in twenty-one World Series games. In 1946 he and his teammates Evers and Chance were elected to the National Baseball Hall of Fame.

Tinker was married twice—to Ruby Rose Menown, with whom he had four children, and to Suzanne Chabot in 1942. Following his retirement, he managed for Columbus in the American Association in 1917. That year he played a pivotal role in having the spitball banned from professional baseball. To draw attention to the fact that his batters were being thrown too many spitters, Tinker sent one of his pitchers to the mound with a metal file, with which he conspicuously began "doctoring" a baseball. The resulting controversy caused the American Association to outlaw spitters at the end of the season; the following year, the major leagues followed suit. Tinker bought a controlling interest in the Orlando Gulls in the Florida State League in 1921, and he also served for several years as a scout for the Cubs. During the 1920s he reportedly made more than a million dollars investing in Florida real estate, only to lose his fortune with the onset of the Great Depression. He later operated a billiard parlor and a bar in Orlando. During the early 1940s he developed diabetes, and in 1947 one of his legs had to be amputated. He died in Orlando.

• A clipping file on Tinker is at the National Baseball Library, Cooperstown, N.Y. Tinker describes his much-fabled success against Mathewson in John Carmichael, *My Greatest Day in Baseball* (1963). John Evers, *Touching Second* (1910), provides a vivid portrait of the Tinker-Evers-Chance infield. Peter Golenbock, *Wrigleyville* (1996), is an excellent history of the Chicago Cubs. Warren Brown, *The Chicago Cubs* (1946), is useful but somewhat dated. For brief overviews of his career, see Donald Dewey and Nicholas Acocella, *The Biographical History of Baseball* (1995); and Lowell Reidenbaugh, *Cooperstown: Where Baseball's Legends Live Forever* (1983).

THOMAS W. COLLINS, JR.

TOLER, Sidney (24 Apr. 1874–12 Feb. 1947), actor and author, was born in Warrensburg, Missouri, the son of Colonel H. G. Toler, a trotting-horse breeder. (His mother's name is not known.) At age seven Toler was in an amateur performance of *Tom Sawyer*. He became a professional actor in Kansas City, toured with a company from 1894 to 1898, and was a leading man at a Brooklyn theater. He joined the company led by Julia Marlowe and for two years appeared with her in Paul Kester and George Middleton's *The Cavalier* and Kester's *When Knighthood Was in Flower*. He owned theatrical companies in Bangor, Maine, and Halifax, Nova Scotia. Going briefly to Broadway, he appeared in *The Office Boy* (1903).

Once back in New York, Toler had a bit part in *Mrs. Bumpstead-Lee* (1911), a satirical comedy, and was thereafter in a series of plays, including the melodramatic comedy *Some One in the House* (1918), George S. Kaufman's first stage effort; *On the Hiring Line* (1919), a comedy; and *Poldekin* (1920), a feeble comedy by Booth Tarkington featuring George Arliss and Edward G. Robinson. In 1921 he coauthored a sugary comedy, *Golden Days*, which he also directed and which starred Helen Hayes. His fruitful association with the impressario David Belasco began with *Kiki* (1921), a popular, saucy comedy about a Parisian chorus girl, the lines of which Belasco laundered from the French original. Although Toler wrote and was to act in *The Exile* (1923), a costume drama, he missed its opening night because he was still appearing in the long-running *Kiki*. He also had a part in *Laugh, Clown, Laugh!* a Pagliacci story embellished by Belasco and starring John Barrymore. The following year he was coauthor of the libretto for *Bye, Bye, Barbara* (1924), a romantic musical that was adversely reviewed and soon closed. Other roles followed in steady succession: a counterfeiter turned murderer in *Canary Dutch* (1925); the wily uncle in *Tommy* (1927), Howard Lindsay's cute comedy about adolescents; a part in *Trigger* (1927), starring Katharine Hepburn; and with Humphrey Bogart in *It's a Wise Child* (1929), a comedy produced and directed by Belasco. Toler coauthored *Ritzy* (1930), a comedy about how money can corrupt marriage, which he also directed.

Toler broke into Hollywood playing an Englishman opposite Ruth Chatterton in *Madame X*, a 1929 remake of that theatrical warhorse. During the first half

of his screen career, he usually appeared in light, forgettable films with better-known stars, such as *Blonde
Venus* with Marlene Dietrich and *The Phantom President* with Claudette Colbert (both 1932); with Hepburn in *Spitfire* (1934), the movie version of *Trigger*;
and with Clark Gable and Loretta Young in *Call of the
Wild* (1935). His best role was as Daniel Webster in
The Gorgeous Hussy (1936), starring Lionel Barrymore and Joan Crawford in a story about Andrew
Jackson and his protégée, the notorious Peggy Eaton.
Toler also had bit parts in comedies featuring Fred
Allen, Joe E. Brown, Jimmy Durante, and Stan Laurel
and Oliver Hardy.

In 1938, however, Toler was to take a role that
would define his career. Twentieth Century–Fox executives encountered trouble with their Charlie Chan
series because Warner Oland, star of sixteen Chan
movies, became ill and had to withdraw from the ongoing production of *Charlie Chan at the Ringside*. Its
script was revised to become *Mr. Moto's Gamble*, with
Peter Lorre playing what would have been Chan's
part, as Japanese secret agent Kentaro Moto. The
movie was released in March, and a search was un-
dertaken to find a new Chan. Toler, the thirty-fifth
actor tested for the role, debuted as the detective in
Charlie Chan in Honolulu (1938), a fast-paced comedy of middling quality. His performance, however,
was an immediate success. He did not try to duplicate
Oland's usually gentle, polite, calm mien; instead he
was more acidic and sarcastic, his face more mobile,
especially with his trademark double-take. The movie
is enhanced by the introduction of Chan's "Number
Two Son," ably played by Sen Yung (later called Victor Sen Yung). Keye Luke, who had been "Number
One Son" for Oland's Chan, had left the series. Toler
continued Chan's pleasant Confucian maxims, such
as "Bait only good if fish bite on same." With success
assured, Toler starred in three Chan movies in 1939,
reputedly for $15,000 each: *Charlie Chan in Reno*,
Charlie Chan at Treasure Island, and *Charlie Chan in
City of Darkness*. Critics generally agree that Toler in
the *Treasure Island* movie was at the height of his powers, well supported by a fine cast including Cesar
Romero.

Of Toler's next eighteen Chan films, seven were
produced by Twentieth Century–Fox. In *Dead Men
Tell* (1941), called by some critics the last really splendid Chan movie, Toler shows exemplary range and is
supported by George Reeves, who was to star later as
Superman on television. In 1943 Toler interrupted his
Chan filming to appear with Jon Hall and Maria Montez in *White Savage*, a South Sea island romance. In
1944 Toler appeared in *Charlie Chan in the Secret Service*, which was the inauspicious first of eleven Chan
movies produced by Monogram. His role in it calls
for a turn toward a chillier personality. *Black Magic*
(1944), regarded as the most popular of Toler's
Monogram Chans, was followed by *Dark Alibi* and
Shadows over Chinatown (both 1946), after which, in
Dangerous Money (1947), Toler displayed alarming
fatigue on the set, a result of his declining health. In

mid-1946 he courageously finished *The Trap* (1947),
was soon bedridden with cancer, and died at his home
in Beverly Hills.

Little is publicly known about Toler's private life.
His first wife, Vivian, died in 1943, and later that year
he married Viva Tattersall, who in 1930 had appeared
with him in *Ritzy*. He enjoyed the friendship of many
Hollywood personalities. Although Toler was a multifaceted artist—a writer of dated plays and a musical,
and a skillful character actor on stage and screen—he
was at his best as a distinguished portrayer of Charlie
Chan in many fine movies. His Chan expertly combines puzzlement, shrewdness, and Oriental cunning
and humor.

• Edwin Bronner, *The Encyclopedia of the American Theatre,
1900–1975* (1980), and Samuel Leiter, ed., *The Encyclopedia
of the New York Stage, 1920–1930* (2 vols.; 1985), list some
thirteen plays in which Toler was involved—as author or director and/or actor—and the musical, the libretto of which
he coauthored. David Quinlan, *Quinlan's Illustrated Directory
of Film Stars* (1986), lists eighty-three of Toler's movies. Ken
Hanke, *Charlie Chan at the Movies: History, Filmography, and
Criticism* (1989), and Charles P. Mitchell, *A Guide to Charlie
Chan Films* (1999), sketch Toler's life briefly and discuss all
of his Charlie Chan movies and also the professionals associated with them. Ted Okuda, *The Monogram Checklist: The
Films of Monogram Pictures, 1931–1952* (1987), provides details of Monogram's Charlie Chan movies, with a one- or
two-sentence plot summary of each. An obituary is in the
New York Times, 13 Feb. 1947.

ROBERT L. GALE

TOMBAUGH, Clyde (3 Jan. 1906–17 Jan. 1997),
astronomer and discoverer of the planet Pluto, was
born Clyde William Tombaugh on a farm near Streator, Illinois, the son of Muron Tombaugh, a farmer,
and Adella Chritton Tombaugh. Clyde attended a
country grade school and then Streator High School,
where he became interested in science, especially astronomy. His first telescopic views of the stars were
with a small, inexpensive three-inch refractor that his
uncle Lee owned. Later Muron and Lee Tombaugh
bought a better two-and-a-half-inch refractor, which
Clyde used for many years. The sight of Mars through
this telescope in 1920, clearly showing its polar cap
and surface markings, inspired him to go on. He did
not consider college, because of the cost, but he hun-
gered for a career in astronomy; he did not want to
spend the rest of his life in farming.

In December 1928 Tombaugh sent some of his best
drawings of the planets to Lowell Observatory in
Flagstaff, Arizona, the center of planetary research in
the United States. His timing, though accidental, was
perfect. Lowell Observatory's director, V. M. Slipher,
was looking for a dedicated young astronomical observer who could point and operate a telescope all
night long. Slipher did not want a trained professional,
who he thought would be too independent. Tombaugh, with his high school education, was clearly an
industrious, dedicated farm boy who would work for
almost any salary that would enable him to do astron-

omy. He would follow directions eagerly and carefully. Thus in January 1929 Tombaugh paid his own way by train from Nebraska to Flagstaff to start work on the search for Planet X.

Planet X was the name that Percival Lowell had given the hypothetical planet he had predicted would be found beyond the orbit of Neptune. His prediction was based on calculations of where such a planet must be, in orbit about the sun, to cause the small deviations that had apparently been measured in the orbit of Uranus. Just such a prediction had led to the discovery of Neptune in 1846. Lowell had worked sporadically for years on where Planet X could be found and had launched three telescopic searches for it, in 1905, 1909, and 1914, all unsuccessful. He published his last prediction in 1914, two years before his death. Finally in 1928, during a burst of prosperity, Lowell Observatory obtained a new thirteen-inch, wide-field, photographic telescope optimized for this search.

On arriving at Flagstaff, Tombaugh was overjoyed to learn that his job would be to search for a "new" planet with this advanced telescope. The strategy was to take two long exposures of the same area of the sky, separated by several nights. Comparing these photographic plates carefully at a "blink microscope," which allowed the user to view them in rapid succession, all the stars would remain in exactly the same positions; but if there were a planet in the field, it would appear to jump back and forth between its positions on the two plates. Although Lowell's predicted position was the obvious place to look, no Planet X had been found near it in the three previous searches, so Tombaugh would take overlapping exposures all along the ecliptic, the great circle in the sky near which all the planets move.

Tombaugh began this program in April 1929. He was a careful observer, who honed and improved his techniques each night he worked. He developed the plates on the following day, after which V. M. Slipher and his brother E. C. Slipher, a Lowell Observatory staff member, were supposed to blink them. Both were busy men, with many other responsibilities, and after a first burst of enthusiasm they let the blinking slide, as Tombaugh industriously built up a backlog of developed plates awaiting their attention. Finally in June V. M. Slipher directed Tombaugh to take over the blinking himself, in addition to observing at the telescope. Tombaugh did so gladly, although it was a long tedious job and meant much more work. But blinking the plates let him see his results immediately, allowing him to modify and improve his techniques.

On 18 February 1930 Tombaugh found the object for which he had been searching, the image of a faint, apparently stellar object, jumping back and forth between its positions on the two plates he had taken on 23 and 29 January, six nights apart. It could only be a faint planet, and its motion, though easily detectable, was much too small for it to be an asteroid. He quickly measured the distance between the two images on the plates; the object's motion corresponded to that of a trans-Neptunian planet. Now Tombaugh knew he

had discovered Planet X. In fact, its position was only a few degrees away from Lowell's prediction. Tombaugh reported his discovery to Slipher immediately, and soon they and C. O. Lampland, another Lowell astronomer, were able to observe the "new" planet visually and photographically with larger telescopes. They held up announcement of the discovery until 13 March 1930, the anniversary of Lowell's birth.

Other observatories immediately began measuring positions of the "Lowell object," as it was first called; experts calculated preliminary orbits for it and with them several astronomers found prediscovery images on plates taken years earlier. The much better orbits calculated with these additional data showed that Pluto, as it was then named, was indeed a trans-Neptunian planet. It was much fainter than expected, and after the initial excitement died down Tombaugh continued the search to be sure that there was not another, possibly brighter planet out there. Ultimately he covered three-quarters of the sky, centered on the ecliptic, but neither he nor anyone else found one.

Ironically, since 1978 when Pluto's moon Charon was discovered, the mass of the planet (which could then be measured immediately) has been known to be much too small to perturb Uranus's orbit appreciably. Lowell's prediction had been based on what were later proved to be observational errors in the earliest positional measurements of Uranus. That Tombaugh found Pluto near the predicted position was a happy accident.

Now famous, Tombaugh was awarded a scholarship at the University of Kansas, where he enrolled as a twenty-six-year-old freshman in 1932, earning a bachelor's degree in 1936. While there he met Patricia Edson, who became his wife in 1934; they were to have two children. Each summer Tombaugh returned to his job at Lowell Observatory; after graduating from Kansas he spent two years full-time there then returned to Kansas for one year as a graduate student, earning an M.A. in 1939. During World War II he taught navigation to naval cadets at Arizona State Teachers' College in Flagstaff (now Northern Arizona University) for two years, then moved on to teach astronomy at UCLA for one more year.

In 1946 Tombaugh left Lowell Observatory to become an ordnance engineer at White Sands Proving Ground, New Mexico, working with telescopes and cameras in experiments with V2 rockets captured in Germany and brought to America after World War II ended. Then in 1955 he accepted a research position at New Mexico State University in Las Cruces and began teaching astronomy there. Tombaugh retired in 1973 but continued a very active career in research, lecturing, and fundraising for astronomy well into his nineties. He was the only person alive who had discovered one of the nine planets. He died in Las Cruces.

• Three good books contain copious material on Tombaugh and the search for Pluto: William G. Hoyt, *Planets X and Pluto* (1980); Clyde Tombaugh and Patrick Moore, *Out of the Darkness: The Planet Pluto* (1980); and David H. Levy,

Clyde Tombaugh: Discoverer of Planet Pluto. They all include many references to other books, articles, and letters. An informative scientific obituary article was published in *Physics Today* 50, no. 7 (July 1977): 77.

DONALD E. OSTERBROCK

TORMÉ, Mel (13 Sept. 1925–5 June 1999), popular singer and songwriter, was born Melvin Howard Tormé in Chicago, the son of William Tormé, a Russian immigrant who owned a dry goods store (the original family name, Torma, was changed by an immigration officer), and Betty Sopkin Tormé, who had changed her first name from Sabina. Tormé attended high schools in Chicago and Los Angeles. His father was an amateur dancing champion in New York; his mother played piano at a local music store; and his baby-sitter played "barrelhouse piano." Tormé made his singing debut at age four, singing Walter Donaldson's "You're Driving Me Crazy" on Monday nights at the Blackhawk Restaurant, where midwestern jazzman Ben Pollack's band held forth. The song remained a part of Tormé's repertoire for seventy years. Soon he began to sing occasionally in vaudeville. In 1934 he won a children's acting contest at the Chicago World's Fair and entered radio in the role of a newsboy on the soap opera "Song of the City."

Inspired by Duke Ellington, he started composing at thirteen. In 1940 the Harry James orchestra expressed an interest in hiring Tormé as a specialty drummer but ran afoul of child labor laws. In the same year, when he was still only fifteen years old, Tormé's "Lament to Love" reached number seven on the Hit Parade. Two years later he was hired as drummer, pianist, and singer by the Chico Marx band, and in 1943, when the band broke up, Tormé stayed in California. He made his film debut in *Higher and Higher*, a 1943 musical that also introduced Frank Sinatra.

While working in B movies, Tormé encountered The Schoolkids, a singing group of four Los Angeles City College students. When he joined them, the name was changed to the Mel-Tones, and as the group's new leader he created a sound patterned after a swing band's saxophone section: two altos, two tenors, and a baritone. The Mel-Tones survived Tormé's brief service with the Army Air Forces (from which he was discharged for flat feet). They recorded with Bing Crosby and with the Artie Shaw orchestra. With Shaw they made an album of Cole Porter songs including the bestselling "What Is This Thing Called Love?" The group, which eventually included composer-arranger Les Baxter, was a precursor of such jazz-influenced ensembles as the Hi-Los and the Manhattan Transfer.

When the Mel-Tones disbanded in 1946, Tormé embarked on a solo career as "the Velvet Fog." The nickname, invented by a local disc jockey, referred to Tormé's light, smooth, apparently effortless and seamless (some called it "soft shoe") delivery, but it ignored Tormé's exquisite sense of rhythm. After the Shaw album and well-received roles in the Metro-Goldwyn-Mayer musical films *Good News* (1947) and

Words and Music (1948), he was typed, however, as a whispery cabaret singer.

In 1946 Tormé and Bob Wells produced "The Christmas Song" (sometimes referred to as "Chestnuts Roasting on an Open Fire"). Recorded later by Nat "King" Cole (and nearly 1,500 others), its evocation of seasonal festivities on frosty winter evenings made it a permanent part of America's Christmas celebration, rivaled only by Irving Berlin's "White Christmas." Tormé was eventually credited with more than 300 compositions, including the tone poem *California Suite.*

Tormé's personal life was romantically chaotic and probably contributed to the emotional deepening of his singing. In 1949 he married a starlet, Candy Toxton, in Hollywood; they had two children and were divorced in 1955. In 1956 he married Arlene Miles in Las Vegas; they divorced in 1966. He then married the English actress Janelle Scott in Japan; they had three children and were divorced in 1977. In 1984 he married an attorney, Ali Severson, in St. Thomas, Virgin Islands.

From 1949 onward, the year of his surprise country-western hit "Careless Hands," Tormé was seen regularly on American television, often as a host of summer replacement variety shows. His dramatic supporting role in the "Playhouse 90" segment "The Comedian" (1956) earned an Emmy nomination. He had also begun to write scripts and apparently turned one into a Western novel, *Dollarhide* (1955), using the pseudonym Wesley Butler Wyatt. Although his scat-singing version of Richard Rodgers and Lorenz Hart's "Mountain Greenery" (1956) was a popular precursor of his later jazz style—Ronald Atkins commented that "few male singers could touch him when the tempo was really fast" (*Guardian*, 7 June 1999)—Tormé gradually faded from general popularity as a singer. His career revived, however, after lauded appearances and recordings in England. During 1963–1964, he became arranger and musical director for the Judy Garland television program; the wrenching experience of working with the singer led to his first book, *The Other Side of the Rainbow* (1971), a book that made few industry friends. In 1971 he hosted the nostalgic "It Was a Very Good Year," singing and talking to guests.

Tormé continued to record, making more than fifty albums, often with directors and arrangers focused on "cool" West Coast jazz. Ethel Waters proclaimed him the only white man who could sing with the soul of a black man. His repertoire was said to number more than 5,000 songs. In 1976 Tormé won the Edison Award as best male singer. He was nominated 13 times as best jazz singer by the National Academy of Recording Arts and Sciences, winning for the albums *An Evening with George Shearing and Mel Tormé* (1982) and *Top Drawer* (1983, also with the British-born Shearing). It was noted that his voice had changed remarkably little over the years: "if anything, the increased tonal depth added to its appeal" (Atkins, *Guardian*). A *New York Times* critic said, "There are those who have bigger vocal techniques, but no male singer of his generation, or since, has had the musical command that he does." In 1984 Tormé took on a recurring role (appearing as himself) in the television program "Night Court," continuing to 1992.

In 1974 Tormé's novel, *Wynner*, a tribute to jazz singers but according to *Variety* "a poison pen note to Hollywood and show business," was published. In 1988 came *It Wasn't All Velvet*, an autobiography. There followed *Traps, the Drum Wonder* (1991), his biographical study of jazz drummer Buddy Rich, and *My Singing Teachers* (1994). He provided the foreword to Burt Korall's *Drummin' Men: The Heartbeat of Jazz, the Swing Years* (1990). Tormé was still performing regularly when he suffered a stroke in 1996. In February 1999 the National Academy of Recording Arts and Sciences honored him with its Lifetime Achievement Award. He died in the UCLA medical center in Los Angeles, of the stroke's complications, with his wife, five children, and two stepchildren at his bedside.

Tormé's was a unique talent that gathered stature as the decades passed. A show business insider and musicologist, he wrote at least five books. Later it was said that he regarded his career as a work in progress, a "long learning curve." As a songwriter Tormé co-wrote one of the century's enduring songs; he felt that "the lyric is 95 per cent of what a song is. The lyric is the cake." As a singer he progressed from crooner to major exponent of jazz. He ranked alongside Frank Sinatra as an interpreter of the classic popular songs of the twentieth century.

• Tim Brooks, *The Complete Directory of Prime Time Network TV Shows 1946–Present* (1979), is useful, as is Stanley Green, *The Encyclopedia of the Musical Film* (1981). Obituaries of Tormé include those by Ronald Atkins in the (London) *Guardian*, 7 June 1999, Don Heckman and Myrna Oliver in the *Los Angeles Times*, 6 June 1999, and Richard Natale, *Variety*, 14 June 1999; see also the *New York Times* and the *Chicago Tribune*, both 6 June 1999.

JAMES ROSS MOORE

TREIGLE, Norman (6 Mar. 1927–16 Feb. 1975), opera singer, was born in New Orleans, Louisiana. (Information about his family and early education is not readily available.) He joined the U.S. Navy at the age of sixteen, and after his discharge two years later he enrolled in his home city at Loyola University, which he attended on a scholarship. There he studied singing with the noted contralto Elizabeth Wood and developed the distinctively dark-colored bass-baritone voice that became his trademark. During the late 1940s, he held local singing jobs, working variously as a synagogue cantor, as a singer in a touring religious revival group, and as a soloist for Protestant congregations, including the First Baptist Church, of which he was a lifelong member. He made his operatic debut in 1947 with the New Orleans Opera Company and joined the roster of the New York City Opera six years later, singing the role of Colline in Puccini's *La Boh-*

ème. According to reviews of his performance, he was well received by the audience, and critics noted a brilliance and resonance in his voice unusual for a bass-baritone.

Between 1953 and early 1956 Treigle sang minor parts at the New York City Opera in such roles as Angelotti (Puccini's *Tosca*), Sparafucile (Verdi's *Rigoletto*), Pistol (Verdi's *Falstaff*), and Banquo (Verdi's *Macbeth*). He first appeared in a major role in September 1956, creating the character of the hellfire preacher Olin Blitch in the premiere of Carlisle Floyd's opera *Susannah*. Treigle's dramatic interpretation of Blitch was based on his own experiences singing in the southern revival group years earlier, and he let it be known that he patterned his performances after the group's Bible-thumping leader, the Reverend Bob Harrington, who had been nicknamed "the chaplain of Bourbon Street." Treigle was hailed by the critics for his acting as well as his singing, and from then on he sought roles that called forth his dramatic talents.

One of Treigle's most memorable roles at the New York City Opera was that of the title character in Boito's opera *Mefistofele*, in which he debuted in September 1969. Costumed to appear nearly naked, the sinewy Treigle leapt and thrashed contemptuously about the stage, and his performance caused a sensation. Audiences loved his antics, and critics proclaimed him a natural for the part, praising his athleticism as well as his singing and acting. By this time, Treigle had become a much-beloved member of the New York City Opera company, whose roster included his friends Beverly Sills, the soprano, and conductor Julius Rudel, and he was agreeable to taking on a wide range of both standard and unconventional parts. His starring portrayals during his two decades with the company included Mozart's Don Giovanni, Don Escamillo in Bizet's *Carmen*, Puccini's Gianni Schicchi, Mussorgsky's Boris Godunov, and Figaro in Mozart's *The Marriage of Figaro*, as well as major roles in less frequently performed operas, among them Handel's *Julius Caesar*, Aaron Copland's *The Tender Land*, Orff's *The Moon*, and Walton's *Troilus and Cressida*.

Treigle, like most singers, had a lifelong ambition to appear at the Metropolitan Opera in New York City, but that opportunity never came, and in later years he acknowledged that he would not have been comfortable with the Met's prevailing star system; he much preferred being part of an ongoing ensemble, which is what he found at the New York City Opera. The family-like nature of that company changed somewhat after it moved in the mid-1960s from its longtime headquarters at the City Center to a new house, the State Theater, at Lincoln Center, across the plaza from the Met, and Treigle found himself gradually withdrawing from performances there. His last appearance at the State Theater occurred in October 1972, in Offenbach's *The Tales of Hoffmann*; he sang for the last time with the company in May 1973, performing his trademark title role in *Mefistofele*. By the time of his death he had severed all connections with the New York City Opera, although negotiations were reportedly under way to bring him back.

In the final decade of his life, Treigle gave occasional concert performances and recitals and also sang with several regional American opera companies. Up until then he had sung relatively little abroad, but he spent much of 1974 in London, where he had previously made several well-received recordings, including one of *Mefistofele*. In the spring he sang in a concert version of that opera, and that fall he debuted at Covent Garden as Mephisto in Gounod's *Faust*, singing what became the final performance of his life on 13 December 1974.

Treigle was known as a fun-loving man, and despite being a practicing Baptist he did not let church tenets restrict his enjoyment of life. He was known for his prodigious smoking and whiskey drinking and his affinity for racetracks; his customary attire—dark suit, dark shirt, light-colored tie—further suggested a character from *Guys and Dolls* rather than an opera star.

Treigle was married twice; little information is available about either marriage. With his first wife, Lorraine, he had a daughter. At the time of his death, he was separated from his second wife, Linda, whose daughter he adopted and with whom he had a son. Treigle died suddenly at his New Orleans apartment. Although suicide was suspected, the local coroner subsequently ruled that Treigle had succumbed to an accidental overdose of sleeping pills.

• Biographical information on Norman Treigle is limited. See "Treigle, Norman," in *The New Grove Dictionary of American Music* (1986), as well as obituaries in *Opera News*, May 1975, and the *New York Times*, 18 Feb. 1975. See also Alan Rich, "Happiest as a Villain," *New York Times*, 5 May 1963.

ANN T. KEENE

TRILLING, Diana (21 July 1905–23 Oct. 1996), critic and author, was born in New York City, the daughter of Joseph Rubin, a manufacturer of straw braid, and Sadie Helene Forbert Rubin. Both parents were Jewish immigrants from Poland. After graduating from Erasmus Hall High School in Brooklyn, Diana Rubin went to Radcliffe College, earning a B.A. in fine arts in 1925. She moved back to her parents' home in New York, then traveled widely with her widowed father, including to South America, and worked until 1929 for the National Broadcasting Company as an assistant to a writer for a children's radio serial. In 1927 she met Lionel Trilling in a Manhattan speakeasy. In 1929 they were married; much later the couple had one son.

In 1927 Lionel Trilling was a part-time teacher at Hunter College and an editor of the *Menorah Journal*, work with little income that presaged the couple's financial hardships during the Depression and later. In 1932 Lionel Trilling became the first ethnic Jew appointed as an instructor in the English Department at Columbia University. He was told not to think he was starting a trend—and anti-Semitism plagued the cou-

ple even after he had gained renown as a literary critic. By the late 1930s he was a leader of "The New York Intellectuals," a group of liberal thinkers and writers, many Jewish, some immigrants, and all knowledgeable about politics, art, and literature. Diana Trilling, who was active and vocal in the group, defined its members as intellectually avid while also being "ungenerous . . . and not always honest." They all wrote in a sociliterary tradition aiming to influence well-educated general readers. At this time, the Trillings supported at least one communist-front organization but later evolved into left-wing anti-Stalinists and then anti-communist, prodemocratic liberals.

Diana Trilling freely admitted that her husband, rather than any courses at Radcliffe, introduced her to great literature and that she was led by his example to become a critic. She often joked about standing in his shadow. At the same time she contended that her down-to-earth comments on his writings gave them, in her words, "a greater directness and greater fluidity." After a stint as fiction critic for the *Nation* (1941–1949), she became a freelance writer who appealed to a wide audience, publishing in a range of magazines from popular ones such as *Esquire*, *Glamour*, *Look*, and *Redbook* to more sophisticated journals like the *American Scholar*, and *Encounter*, but most frequently in the *Nation* and the *Partisan Review*. Her essays decrying McCarthyism and in support of civil liberties appeared in the *New Leader*. She also wrote on the movies, sexual promiscuity, the drug culture, student protests both civil and violent, contemporary novelists, and intellectual and political leaders, including President John F. Kennedy, whom she met once at the White House (though in her husband's shadow yet again). She often distressed readers and reviewers alike, because of positions she espoused on homosexuality, radical feminism, and many other topics. As an editor, she skillfully compiled and introduced two volumes: *The Portable D. H. Lawrence* (1947) and *The Selected Letters of D. H. Lawrence* (1958).

Lionel Trilling's death in 1975 ended a seemingly brilliant and enviable marriage, but one that in reality was marred by innumerable verbal tirades from Lionel and tears from Diana. The two had been beset from the start by deep-seated psychological phobias, which they related to their being Jewish, and by family pressures, financial worries, differing attitudes toward Marxism and Freudianism, excessive drinking, and, undoubtedly, professional jealousies. Over many years, both had been treated by psychoanalysts—she by a few malpractitioners.

Diana Trilling did not let being a widow keep her from continuing a vigorous intellectual life. She edited a uniform edition of her husband's works, including a few previously unpublished pieces (12 vols., 1977–1980). She assembled much of her earlier writing in *We Must March My Darlings* (1977) and *Reviewing the Forties* (1978); was fascinated by the trial of Jean Harris for the murder of Dr. Herman Tarnower and wrote *Mrs. Harris: The Death of the Scarsdale Diet Doctor* (1981) about the case; and while suffering from near-blindness dictated *The Beginning of the Journey: The Marriage of Diana and Lionel Trilling* (1993).

Trilling's *Claremont Essays* (1964) collects thirteen disparate, previously published pieces on a variety of subjects, especially culture, literature, and sex. Some of the essays focus on individuals—for example, Enrico Caruso, Alger Hiss, Alice James, Norman Mailer, Marilyn Monroe, Virginia Woolf, and J. Robert Oppenheimer (whose career she examined, in part, by wading through a thousand pages of hearings)—and another deals with the political scandal involving John Dennis Profumo and Christine Keeler in England. Characteristically, Trilling seeks to show how her subjects reflect their societies. Other essays are more objectively critical, as when she turns to Edward Albee's *Who's Afraid of Virginia Woolf*, which she views as "a document of contemporary society"; Mark Twain's character Tom Sawyer, often now seen, in her opinion, as "little less than certifiably disturbed"; and Edith Wharton's *The House of Mirth*, in which Trilling perceives a class awareness no Marxist could manage. Still other essays concern poetry by the Beat Generation and explicit writings about sex. All of these essays are notable for the research that went into them and their rhetorical force.

We Must March My Darlings contains fourteen widely different pieces, all opinionated and mostly concerned with the Women's Liberation Movement of 1954–1975 and various trends and themes on which it impinged. In her introduction, Trilling offers an implicit apology for being a literary intellectual wandering into wider cultural areas than would formerly have been tolerated. Thus she feels free to discuss the guru of altered consciousness, Dr. Timothy Leary, and the 1960s drug culture, John F. Kennedy's assassination, radical feminism, university disruptions, and protests against the war in Vietnam. Other intriguing pieces include a perceptive review of the 1970 movie *Easy Rider*; a robust exposure of dishonest comments about communism and about the Trillings themselves in Lillian Hellman's 1977 autobiography *Scoundrel Time*; a response to Mailer's macho posturings; and a prolific account of living for nine weeks in 1971 in a Radcliffe coed dormitory.

Reviewing the Forties contains selections of Trilling's many reviews of fiction dating from 1942 to 1949. Notable among the dozens of novelists discussed are Saul Bellow, Truman Capote, Vladimir Nabokov, George Orwell, Jean-Paul Sartre, Evelyn Waugh, and Edmund Wilson. Many of the pieces may strike later readers as important mainly for the light they shed on Trilling herself, concerning as they do Nazism, racism, radicalism, sex, and parenting.

Trilling's *Mrs. Harris*, a gripping but imperfect piece of journalistic reporting, was nominated for a Pulitzer prize. In 1980 Jean Harris fatally shot her lover, Dr. Herman Tarnower, famous at the time for a bestselling book on dieting; tried for the murder, she was convicted and sentenced to prison. Trilling, who attended the entire sensational trial, expected to be sympathetic toward Harris but became disenchanted

with her, while her dislike of Dr. Tarnower did not abate. Although Trilling's reporting of the trial is well done, her psychoanalysis of the motives of the killer and the victim is still better. Nevertheless, her distress at Tarnower's Jewish characteristics and her moralizing about money and social status are distracting.

The Beginning of the Journey is a valuable memoir of Diana Trilling's unhappy childhood, her husband's own upbringing, their often troubled marriage, and the first half of his career, ending in 1950. Sometimes she seems self-aggrandizing and petty, but she usually retains her dignity while exposing her faults and those of others. She is at her best when concentrating on the interplay—political, ethnic, personal, and cultural—between the Trillings and other intellectual leaders in New York culture in the 1940s. Diana Trilling was a keen observer-commentator both enjoying and troubled by her unique position. Because of her husband's enormous influence, she was often on the sidelines; all the same, she was frequently a keen, articulate observer of some of the most turbulent, creative, and dangerous decades of twentieth-century America. She died in New York at Columbia Presbyterian Hospital.

• Manuscripts of Diana Trilling's most important writings are in the Butler Library of Columbia University. Norman Podhoretz, *Ex-Friends: Falling Out with Allen Ginsberg, Lionel & Diana Trilling, Lillian Hellman, Hannah Arendt, and Norman Mailer* (1999), contains vicious criticism of Diana Trilling, mainly because of revelations in *The Beginning of the Journey* and her attitude toward "Jewishness." Two significant reviews of Diana Trilling's *The Beginning of the Journey* are by Robert Alter in the *New Republic*, 1 Nov. 1993, and by Midge Decter (Podhoretz's wife) in *Commentary*, Jan. 1994. Alter in great detail depicts Trilling as observant, revealing, and psychologically penetrating, whereas Decter emphasizes Trilling's fierce subjectivity, occasional pettiness, and puzzling memory lapses. Stephen L. Tanner, *Lionel Trilling* (1988), includes objective asides on Diana Trilling. Hilary Mills, *Mailer: A Biography* (1982), details Diana Trilling's part in the 31 Mar. 1971 debate in New York on women's rights that Mailer arranged. Peter Manso, *Norman Mailer: His Life and Times* (1985), is an anthology of long comments, by many observers, on Mailer and his associates, including Diana Trilling. An obituary is in the *New York Times*, 25 Oct. 1996.

ROBERT L. GALE

TROYANOS, Tatiana (12 Sept. 1938–21 Aug. 1993), opera singer, was born in New York City. Both of her parents were immigrants: her father, who was in the restaurant business, came from Greece and her mother from Germany. (Their names, however, do not appear in readily available sources of information.) She grew up in Forest Hills, Queens, and her obvious musical gifts were encouraged by her mother, who like her father was an amateur singer. Troyanos took piano lessons and sang in school and church choirs. Although she was as much German as she was Greek, she identified more closely with her father's family and always characterized herself as a Greek American. As a teenager she often attended performances at the Metropolitan Opera House as a standee and became a devotee of a fellow mezzo-soprano, Risë Stevens. She was also a fan of soprano Maria Callas, whose recordings she listened to frequently. Through the intervention of a teacher at Forest Hills High School, Troyanos auditioned at the Juilliard School in her senior year and was awarded a scholarship. During her years at Juilliard and for a time thereafter she worked as a secretary and waitress to help with expenses.

At Juilliard Troyanos avoided the opera department because it did not use students in its productions; instead she concentrated on oratorio and lieder singing. When the dean refused her request to study with the popular voice teacher Hans Heinz, she left the school and later studied with him privately. Troyanos made her professional debut in summer stock musicals in the New York area and appeared on Broadway as a singing nun in the original production of *The Sound of Music*. In 1963 she joined the roster of the New York City Opera, making her debut that April as Hippolyta in the New York premiere of Benjamin Britten's *A Midsummer Night's Dream*. She left the company abruptly a year and a half later, after she had first been promised and then denied the role of Carmen. Her idol, Risë Stevens, had heard her sing "The Gypsy Song" from Bizet's *Carmen* in a concert performance and arranged for Troyanos to audition with Rudolf Bing at the Metropolitan Opera, but she was offered only small roles, which she refused.

On an impulse Troyanos flew overseas to audition for European opera houses and returned with the promise of contracts from Frankfurt, Zurich, and Hamburg. At Hans Heinz's urging she accepted an offer from the Hamburg State Opera and began singing with the company during the 1965–1966 season. To her disappointment she was given only relatively minor parts at first—Lola in Mascagni's *Cavalleria Rusticana* (she would later make the lead, Santuzza, one of her most famous roles), Preziosilla in Verdi's *La Forza del Destino*, Suzuki in Puccini's *Madama Butterfly*—and did not sing them especially well. Bigger roles ultimately ensued—Carmen, Cherubino in Mozart's *The Marriage of Figaro*, Marina in Mussorgsky's *Boris Godunov*, Dorabella in Mozart's *Così Fan Tutte*—and these she sang with greater assurance. She was also given the part of Octavian in Richard Strauss's *Der Rosenkavalier*, which later became one of her best-known roles.

Another trouser role (besides Octavian) that came to be closely associated with Troyanos was the Composer in Richard Strauss's *Ariadne auf Naxos*, which she performed to great acclaim at the Aix-en-Provence Festival during the summer of 1966. The following year, on loan from Hamburg, she sang the role of Cherubino at the Paris Opera as a last-minute replacement, again to great acclaim. Among those present was Herbert von Karajan, who was so impressed that he hired her for a performance of Mozart's *Coronation Mass* in Rome with the Berlin Philharmonic. By the late 1960s she was singing in major opera houses and concert halls throughout Europe, though sometimes

with uneven results. By her own admission Troyanos was impatient and often impetuous, and in the early years of her career she often took on too many roles, resulting in less-than-satisfactory performances. Hard work, perseverance, and a determination to be the best carried her over the sometimes rocky path to eventual stardom.

While based in Hamburg Troyanos returned to New York on several occasions through the early 1970s, in part to study with her teacher Hans Heinz. She also performed from time to time in the United States during this period, singing with the Hamburg Opera in a New York performance of Igor Stravinsky's *The Rake's Progress*, doing a concert version of his *Oedipus Rex* with the New York Philharmonic, appearing as guest soloist with other orchestras, and singing leading roles with the Chicago Lyric Opera and companies in Los Angeles and Dallas. In September 1971, appearing in Handel's *Ariodante* opposite soprano Beverly Sills at the Kennedy Center in Washington, D.C., she upstaged Sills and created a sensation. Other notable successes followed in Boston, San Francisco, and other cities, in works by Bellini, Monteverdi, and Donizetti. Critics praised her for her dark, velvety voice, her great stage presence, and a manner that reflected an intuitive understanding of the characters she was portraying.

Troyanos finally debuted at the Metropolitan Opera in March 1976 in the role she had already made her own throughout Europe: Octavian in *Der Rosenkavalier*, under conductor James Levine. Her performances received rave reviews, as did her appearances in a second opera at the Met that season, *Ariadne auf Naxos*, in which she sang what had become another signature role, the Composer. Her appearance as Amneris in Verdi's *Aida* at the Met that same season received more qualified praise—she had only recently learned the role—but more accolades were forthcoming following her performances as Carmen with the Met on its spring tour. Another important debut for Troyanos occurred in January 1977, when she appeared for the first time at Milan's La Scala opera house, singing the role of Adalgisa opposite Montserrat Caballé in Bellini's *Norma*. That performance was the first opera to be broadcast live via satellite throughout the world.

Troyanos returned to New York in March 1977 to sing—again to great acclaim—the role of the Countess Geschwitz in the Met's production of Alban Berg's *Lulu*. Another milestone occurred in March 1978, when she gave her debut recital at New York's Carnegie Hall. By this time Troyanos was in great demand in opera houses and on concert stages in both the United States and Europe, and her appearance on opening night of the Met's 1978–1979 season—singing the role of Venus in Wagner's *Tannhäuser*—signaled her preeminence in the opera world.

The mastery of more roles followed over the next decade, including Countess Eboli in Verdi's *Don Carlo* and important parts in Wagnerian operas: Kundry in *Parsifal*, Fricka in *Das Rheingold*, Waltraute in *Götter-*

dämmerung. At the Met she also created the role of Queen Isabella in Philip Glass's opera *The Voyage.* In addition to singing opera, Troyanos continued to make numerous concert stage appearances in her final years as a performer; among the best known were duo-recitals with soprano Benita Valente, the last of which occurred in January 1992. Troyanos also had a major career as a recording artist, primarily of operas, beginning in the 1970s. Over the following years she became one of the most frequently recorded singers of the century, and her taped performances in such varied fare as *Carmen, Rosenkavalier,* Massenet's *Werther,* and the Leonard Bernstein–directed recording of his *West Side Story* are treasured by music lovers.

Troyanos returned permanently from Europe in the late 1970s and settled in New York City, where she had an apartment on the Upper West Side and remained single. She was fond of dogs and enjoyed walking, bike riding, swimming, and waterskiing as body-slimming pastimes. Diagnosed with cancer in the early 1990s, she nevertheless continued to perform as her condition warranted. Her last performance, as Clarion in Richard Strauss's *Capriccio* with the San Francisco Opera, occurred a month before her death. She died at a hospital in New York City.

• For biographical information, see entries for "Troyanos, Tatiana," in *Current Biography Yearbook 1979* and *The New Grove Dictionary of American Music* (1986). In addition, see Bernard Holland, "Tatiana Troyanos Sings the Praises of Handel," *New York Times,* 27 Jan. 1985; M. Mayer, "Tatiana Troyanos," *Opera News,* 20 Mar. 1976, pp. 20ff.; and K. Ames, "Mezzo Power," *Newsweek,* 22 Mar. 1976, p. 78. An obituary appears in the *New York Times,* 23 Aug. 1993.

ANN T. KEENE

TULANE, Paul (10 May 1801–27 Mar. 1887), merchant and philanthropist, was born in Cherry Valley, near Princeton, New Jersey, the son of Louis Tulane, a lumber merchant, and Marie Tulane (maiden name unknown), who died when Paul was fifteen. His father, a native of France, had relocated with his wife to New Jersey following a 1791 slave insurrection in Santo Domingo (now Haiti) that had claimed the life of several of his relatives. After attending a private school in Princeton and an academy in nearby Somerville, Tulane ended his formal education at age fifteen and became a clerk in the Princeton-based mercantile establishment of Thomas White. Two years later (1818), he set out on a three-year tour of the southern United States in the company of a French cousin. Family position gained him meetings with both Henry Clay and Andrew Jackson in the course of his journey, which eventually took him to New Orleans. Conditions in that city so impressed Tulane that, upon returning to Princeton, he resolved to return South and join in or take over the thriving fur trade with local Native Americans that his brother Louis had established.

Although Louis Tulane soon left New Orleans for Alabama, his brother's arrival in November 1822 came at an ideal time for commerce. A devastating yellow fever epidemic during the previous summer had resulted in scores of dry goods consignments being abandoned as residents fled the city. Paul Tulane shrewdly profited by purchasing merchandise at distressed prices and then reselling his wares at a generous markup as conditions in the city began to improve. With funds readily available, he took early advantage of the emerging trend toward factory-produced ready-made menswear. His lower costs enabled Tulane to undercut his competition, and the development of steamboat traffic on the Mississippi allowed him to expand his market with relative ease. By 1826 he had formed a partnership, Paul Tulane and Company, with a local tailor, and the firm underwent several relocations as its business grew.

In the late 1820s and early 1830s Tulane expanded into manufacturing, opening a factory in Plainfield, New Jersey, and headed Tulane, Baldwin & Company of New York. A tireless worker and a tenacious negotiator during business transactions, he eschewed both society and the numerous diversions offered by his adopted hometown and lived (despite his burgeoning wealth) in a modest apartment above his establishment. He took a rare vacation in 1840 and traveled with his father to France, where the elder Tulane made a point of singling out areas of that country that had been economically devastated following the abolition of the West Indian slave trade, warning his son that New Orleans faced a similar fate if slavery were to be overthrown in the American South. Tulane took his father's warnings to heart and began investing in real estate, as well as diversifying his holdings between New Orleans and New Jersey.

While Tulane had made some headway in his efforts by 1861, the outbreak of the Civil War still caught him off guard. On business in the North when hostilities erupted, he was able through family connections with New Jersey governor Charles Olden to cross battle lines and return to New Orleans. Despite his sympathy for the doctrine of states' rights, Tulane restricted his activities during the conflict to management of his affairs and wartime charitable relief. Despite his best efforts, he later estimated his losses from the resulting collapse of normal business conditions at $1 million.

Although Tulane had purchased a permanent residence near Princeton, known as Stockton Place, as early as 1857, the war and its aftermath disrupted his plans to withdraw from active participation in business, and it was not until 1873 that he was able to permanently return to Princeton. In his later years he lived a comfortable but somewhat reclusive existence and concentrated most of his efforts on philanthropy. Although he never formally joined the congregation, he gave generously to the First Presbyterian Church in Princeton. Long interested in education, he reported in his later years to a friend that he was spending $15,000 a year helping young people from various walks of life obtain an education.

It was in the field of higher education, however, that Tulane made his most notable contribution. Having observed during his initial visit to New Orleans that college students were migrating up the Mississippi River from Louisiana to Kentucky because of the lack of educational facilities in their home state, he was not unmindful of the deprivations resulting from the Civil War and Reconstruction. In the spring of 1881 he contacted Representative Randall L. Gibson of Louisiana (whose father had been a long-time friend of Tulane) and arranged to have his remaining Louisiana property—valued at $363,000—donated to a corporation known as the Tulane Educational Fund. In 1884 the state of Louisiana turned over control of the University of Louisiana to the fund, and, despite Tulane's initial protests, the school soon became known as Tulane University of Louisiana. All told, Tulane's gifts to his new endowment totaled $1,050,000 and yielded an annual income of $75,000.

Tulane, who never married, intended to make additional gifts to the school at a later time but unfortunately died intestate at his Princeton home before arrangements for further donations could be completed. His remaining wealth was spread among his relatives.

Like some other successful businessmen of the nineteenth century, Tulane was canny in exploiting opportunities for making money, yet enormously generous in disposing of his wealth. By his example, he helped to strengthen a growing American tradition of underwriting higher education through philanthropy.

• Tulane's papers have not survived. The best secondary sources of information on his life and career are John Smith Kendall, "Paul Tulane," *Louisiana Historical Quarterly*, vol. 20, no. 4, Oct. 1937, pp, 1016–66, and Edison B. Allen, "The Benevolent Recluse Paul Tulane," *The Tulanian*, vol. 40, no. 6, Sept. 1967, pp. 15–22. Obituaries are in the (New Orleans) *Times-Democrat*, 29 Mar. and 2 Apr. 1887, and the *Princeton Press*, 2 Apr. 1887.

EDWARD L. LACH, JR.

TUTTLE, Elbert P. (17 July 1897–23 June 1996), U.S. Court of Appeals judge, was born Elbert Parr Tuttle in Pasadena, California, the son of Guy Harmon Tuttle, a clerk for the Southern Pacific Railroad, and Marguerite Etta "Margie" Parr Tuttle. In 1900, the family moved to Washington, D.C., where Guy Tuttle worked in the Department of War until 1903, when he joined the Bureau of Immigration and was posted to Los Angeles and then to Nogales, Arizona (1904–1905). In 1907, through the intercession of friends of his wife who had gone to Hawaii as missionaries, he was offered a position as cashier for the Hawaiian Sugar Planters' Association. The family arrived in Honolulu on 23 September 1907.

Elbert and his older brother Malcolm attended the Punahou School, where their classmates included Chinese, Japanese, and native Hawaiian students. In 1910, they constructed a glider on which Malcolm took the first flight in the Hawaiian islands, and, along with Duke Kahanamoku, they regularly surfed at Waikiki. Elbert skipped sixth grade to catch up with Malcolm so that they would be able to return to the United States for college together. At their graduation in 1914 Elbert was awarded the Trustees' Cup. That fall, Malcolm and Elbert enrolled at Cornell University. Elbert entered a contest and won the lone seat awarded to a freshman on the *Cornell Daily Sun*; at the end of his junior year he was elected editor-in-chief. Unable to afford the trip home to Hawaii, he spent the summer of 1917 in Jacksonville, Florida, at the home of a classmate. On his first day there he met and fell in love with Sara Sutherland; they married on 22 October 1919; the couple had two children, a boy in 1921 and a girl in 1923. Over seventy-five years of marriage Sara and Elbert Tuttle's evident devotion to each other became legendary. Sara Tuttle died at home, her husband at her side, in 1994.

After graduating from Cornell in 1918, Tuttle enlisted in the U.S. Army. Within months the armistice was signed and he moved to New York, working briefly for the *New York Evening Sun* before moving to Washington, D.C., to join the staff of the *Army and Navy Journal*. In 1919 he returned to Cornell as publicity director of the endowment campaign and in 1920 entered the law school. Working and attending law school full time, Elbert Tuttle nonetheless found time for his family, as he would throughout his life. At the end of his second year, he won the Boardman Scholarship and was elected editor-in-chief of the *Cornell Law Quarterly*. When he graduated, in 1923, Tuttle turned down an offer from an established New York firm, Sullivan and Cromwell, to join his brother-in-law, Bill Sutherland, in Atlanta, Georgia, where they hoped to build a practice.

Tuttle and Bill Sutherland, a graduate of Harvard Law School and a law clerk to Justice Louis Brandeis, established their partnership in 1924. The firm of Sutherland and Tuttle, later known as Sutherland, Asbill, and Brennan, quickly became a nationally recognized firm. For two decades, Tuttle handled everything except the corporate tax cases that were the firm's hallmark. The demands of his law practice notwithstanding, he devoted substantial time to pro bono work. In the 1930s, as a national guard officer, Tuttle played a critical role in saving a black man, accused of raping a white woman, from being lynched and then spearheaded an unsuccessful effort to save him from the electric chair (*Downer v. Dunaway*; *Downer v. Georgia*). With his brother-in-law and Whitney North Seymour, he represented Alonzo Herndon, a young black labor activist convicted of insurrection for handing out Communist material. That litigation ended with the Supreme Court's landmark First Amendment opinion, *Herndon v. Lowry*. Before the decade ended, Tuttle represented a young marine who had been tried without counsel: *Johnson v. Zerbst*, the only case he argued before the U.S. Supreme Court, established the watershed rule that a waiver of federal constitutional rights must be knowing, intelligent, and voluntary.

In 1941 Tuttle, a lieutenant colonel in the Georgia National Guard, was called up to active duty; he then volunteered for overseas duty. As an artillery battalion commander, he fought in Guam, Leyte, and Okinawa and was wounded in hand-to-hand combat on the island of Ie Shima. He received the Bronze Star, the Legion of Merit, and the Purple Heart with Oak Leaf Cluster, and in 1948 he was awarded the rank of brigadier general (Res.). On his return from the war in 1945, Tuttle rejoined his law firm and again involved himself in civic affairs. As the decade ended, Tuttle was elected president of the Atlanta Chamber of Commerce and vice president of the State Bar of Georgia.

Convinced that a meaningful two-party system was critical to an effective democracy, and lacking all patience with the segregated White Democratic party, Tuttle and a scant handful of other community leaders banded together to create a viable Republican party in Georgia. Tuttle's work with the Republican party culminated in the seating of a Dwight Eisenhower delegation at the 1952 convention and proved critical to Eisenhower's ability to wrest the party's nomination from Senator Robert Taft. After the election, Tuttle was named general counsel to the Treasury, and on 7 July 1954 President Eisenhower nominated him to fill a newly created seat on the U.S. Court of Appeals for the Fifth Circuit, composed of six states in the Deep South. From 1960 to 1967 Tuttle served as chief judge. In difficult, even dangerous times, he was unfailingly polite to all attorneys who appeared before the court. He wrote spare, lucid opinions, and he wrote them quickly, a legacy of his training as a journalist. Determined to effectuate the constitutional rights of black Americans, Tuttle stripped the southern states of one of their most potent weapons—delay. As chief judge, he expedited hearings and decisions; moreover, relying in unprecedented ways on the All Writs Act, he introduced procedural remedies to ensure that justice was served. In a voter registration case, he wrote the first opinion in which the Fifth Circuit issued its own injunction pending appeal; that device became a staple of civil rights litigation (*United States v. Lynd*). When dealing with an obstructionist judge in a school desegregation case, writing for the panel Tuttle issued mandamus, drafted an order, and directed the trial court judge to enter it (*Hall v. West*).

Among Tuttle's most momentous opinions was a short order, circulated within an hour of oral argument. Sitting alone, he lifted a stay granted only that morning to the state of Georgia. The stay had barred Hamilton Holmes and Charlayne Hunter, both African Americans, from registering at the all-white University of Georgia until the state's appeal could be heard (*Holmes v. Danner*). After Tuttle's decisive intervention, their registration was accomplished quickly and without bloodshed. Two years later, after a federal judge in Mississippi ruled that James Meredith had not been denied admission to the University of Mississippi because of his race, Tuttle dissented

when the two other judges on the panel declined to order Meredith admitted until they had time to review the record. Meredith finally enrolled some six months later, only after a full-scale riot in which two people died. In 1963, when a federal district court judge upheld the expulsion or suspension of 1,081 high school and elementary students who had participated in civil rights demonstrations, Tuttle again agreed to hear the appeal on the same day the order had been entered. Sitting alone, he reversed, including in his ruling a direction to the state's attorney to notify every television and radio station in Birmingham so that parents would know that the students should attend school the next day (*Woods v. Wright*).

Tuttle was a member of the three-judge district court that struck down the county unit system, which gave disproportionate weight to rural voters in the Democratic party primaries in Georgia (*Sanders v. Gray*). He dissented from the ruling of another three-judge district court that declined to address the apportionment of a federal congressional district because it presented a "political question." On appeal, his dissenting opinion was adopted by the U.S. Supreme Court (*Wesberry v. Sanders*). He wrote the opinion for a third three-judge district court that held the method by which the Georgia legislature was apportioned unconstitutional (*Toombs v. Fortson*). Tuttle also dissented from the panel decision affirming the right of the Georgia legislature to decline to seat Julian Bond because of his public opposition to the war in Vietnam; again, the Supreme Court, agreeing with Tuttle, reversed (*Bond v. Floyd*).

Although Tuttle stepped down as chief judge and took senior status in 1967 at the age of 70, he continued to be a productive member of the Court for the next quarter century. In 1979 the Supreme Court appointed him Special Master in water rights litigation involving five Indian tribes, five states, and several federal agencies (*Arizona v. California*). When Tuttle had agreed to accept Eisenhower's nomination in 1954, he had done so only after his wife, Sara, assured him that she would travel with him; in nearly forty years, she missed only two sittings. They always went by car and she read to him as he drove, indulging their ageless intellectual curiosity and their shared love of good books. Besides sitting regularly with the Eleventh Circuit, he often filled in as a visiting judge in other circuits. Well into their eighties they drove annually to California, where he would sit with the Ninth Circuit.

Judge Tuttle was awarded honorary degrees from four universities: Emory (1958), Harvard (1965, "The mind and heart of this dauntless judge enhance the great tradition of the federal judiciary."), Georgetown (1978), and Tulane (1994). In 1981 he was awarded the Presidential Medal of Freedom by President Carter. He died in Piedmont Hospital in Atlanta. After his death, an editorial in the *New York Times* recalled, "He brought honor to his calling and justice to millions of Americans."

• Tuttle's professional papers are housed at Emory University in Atlanta. His career is discussed in two studies of the

United States Court of Appeals for the Fifth Circuit—Jack Bass, *Unlikely Heroes* (1981), and Frank T. Read and Lucy S. McGough, *Let Them Be Judged: The Judicial Integration of the Deep South* (1978)—and in a number of articles, including Arthur H. Dean, Judge John Minor Wisdom, and Jerome I. Chapman, "A Tribute to Chief Judge Tuttle," *Cornell Law Review* 53 (1967): 1; Anne S. Emanuel, "Lynching and the Law in Georgia Circa 1931: A Chapter in the Legal Career of Judge Elbert Tuttle," *William & Mary Bill of Rights Journal* 5 (1996): 215; and Anne S. Emanuel, "Turning the Tide in the Civil Rights Revolution: Elbert Tuttle and the Desegregation of the University of Georgia," *Michigan Journal of Race and Law* 5 (1999): 1. An obituary is in the *New York Times*, 25 June 1996.

ANNE S. EMANUEL

U

UDALL, Morris K. (15 June 1922–12 Dec. 1998), congressman, environmental leader, and presidential candidate, nicknamed "Mo," was born Morris King Udall in St. Johns, Arizona, the son of Levi S. Udall, a Mormon leader and later chief justice of the Arizona Supreme Court, and Louise Lee Udall. He was the fourth of six children. At age six, he lost his right eye while playing with a knife. His handicap proved to be hardly an obstacle as he became a star athlete, editor of the school paper, and student body president. Udall attended the University of Arizona in Tucson from 1941 to 1942 but left to enter the U.S. Army in World War II, rising to captain in the Army Air Forces. He commanded an all-black squadron while based in Lake Charles, Louisiana. Returning to the university in 1946, he pursued a law degree and earned honors as an all-Border Conference basketball player. He played professional basketball for the Denver Nuggets in the 1947–1948 season. In 1949 he married Patricia J. Emery; they would have six children and divorce in 1966.

He and his brother Stewart L. Udall formed a law partnership in Tucson. He became Pima County attorney in 1953 and lost a bid for superior court judge in 1954. In 1961 he was elected to the U.S. House of Representatives to replace his brother, who had been named secretary of the interior by President John F. Kennedy. Once when asked to reveal his golf handicap he replied, "Handicap? I'm a one-eyed Mormon Democrat from conservative Arizona. You can't find a higher handicap than that." Udall picked up where his brother left off in attacking the House's rigid seniority system, which he felt was impeding badly needed social legislation. In the 1950s he wrote *Arizona Law of Evidence*, a book still widely used by lawyers, and in 1966 he published a 446-page book, *Job of the Congressman*, which was designed to help new lawmakers learn the congressional system. He served on the Public Land Law Review Commission, a first step in his thirty years of congressional leadership in the environmental movement. He would later question technology that brought "growth and progress. . . . Modern man now carries Strontium 90 in his bones . . . DDT in his fat, asbestos in his lungs. A little more of this 'progress' and 'growth' and this man will be dead." Udall was one of the first members of Congress to speak out against the Vietnam War in the mid-1960s, and he helped force an investigation into the massacre of dozens of people in the South Vietnam village of My Lai.

In 1968 Udall married Ella Royston Ward, a secretary for the postal subcommittee on which Udall served. That year he and other members of the Arizona delegation gained passage of the multibillion-dollar Central Arizona Project that brought Colorado River water to Phoenix and Tucson. In 1969 he was defeated in his bid to topple House Speaker John W. McCormack, who soundly trounced him in a caucus voting. In 1971 he ran for House majority leader and again went down to defeat. In the late 1960s and early 1970s, Udall had introduced legislation to limit campaign costs, provide federal funds for campaigns, and require public disclosure of expenditures and contributions. Congress passed his campaign finance reform bills in 1971 and 1974, the first major changes in campaign financing since the Corrupt Practices act of 1925. He also sponsored the Postal Reorganization Act of 1971 which led to today's independent postal system. A remark of his about the U.S. mail was characteristic of his famous sense of humor: "Maybe we ought to turn [inflation] over to the post office. They may not stop it, but they'll damn well slow it down." In 1972 he published *Education of a Congressman: The Newsletters of Morris K. Udall.*

At the urging of House colleagues, Udall announced in 1974 that he would seek the Democratic nomination for president. He never came out ahead in a primary but was runner-up in seven that former Georgia governor Jimmy Carter won. He picked up 1.6 million primary votes and placed second to Carter in convention delegate votes. Former vice president Hubert H. Humphrey said after the campaign that Udall's reputation had been enhanced by his campaign. In 1977 Udall became chairman of the House Interior Committee, which he turned into a strong defender of the environment. He was instrumental in the passage of the Alaska Lands Act that doubled the size of the national park system, doubled the size of the national wildlife refuge system, and tripled the size of the national wilderness areas. He also led efforts to impose strip-mining cleanup laws, helped open Nuclear Regulatory Commission records to public scrutiny, and pushed through the National Wilderness Act that set aside eight million acres of wilderness in twenty states. He also was a strong advocate for improving the living conditions of Native Americans.

Udall was diagnosed with Parkinson's disease in 1979, effectively ending his prospects for future presidential bids. In 1980 he was rated the second most respected House member, the third most persuasive debater, and the most effective committee chairman for getting legislation through Congress. Eight years later his second wife committed suicide; a year later he married Norma Gilbert. He resigned from Congress on 4 May 1991. He had fallen backward down the stairs at his home in early January of that year, and he remained hospitalized until his death in 1998 from complications of Parkinson's disease. Udall's thirty years in Congress earned him a reputation as a reformer of a quirky liberal bent and as one of the giants of legislative environmentalism during the last half of the twentieth century.

• Udall's personal and professional papers and at least twenty oral histories are stored in the Special Collections Department of the University of Arizona Library and the University of Arizona College of Law. For a semi-autobiography, see Morris K. Udall, Randy Udall, and Bob Neuman, *Too Funny to Be President* (1988; repr., 2001). For his recollections of various events in his life, see the chapter concerning him in Abe and Mildred Chanin, *This Land, These Voices* (1977). A useful biography is Donald W. Carson and James W. Johnson, *Mo: The Life and Times of Morris K. Udall* (2001). The 14 Dec. 1998 issue of the *New York Times* has an obituary.

JAMES W. JOHNSON
DONALD W. CARSON

ULMANN, Doris (29 May 1882–28 Aug. 1934), photographer, was born in New York City to Bernhard Ulmann, a textile merchant who had immigrated to America from Germany as a young man in the late 1860s, and Gertrude Maas Ulmann, whose parents had also emigrated from Germany. Doris and an older sister grew up in an affluent and cultured Jewish household on the Upper West Side of Manhattan, where they attended public schools. An important influence on her early life was her uncle, Carl Ulmann, a business associate of her father's and a noted bibliophile who collected antiquarian books. Following her graduation from high school in 1900, Doris Ulmann completed a two-year teacher-training program at the Ethical Culture School and then studied at Teacher's College of Columbia University. Over the next decade she also took courses at other institutions in New York and attended law school briefly, all the while continuing to live at home; like most affluent young women of the period, she apparently remained unemployed. During this time she may have studied photography at Teacher's College. She was drawn to this relatively new art form because of her father's interest in the medium, and she began taking pictures of family and friends.

In 1914 Ulmann married Dr. Charles H. Jaeger, a prominent orthopedic surgeon who shared her upperclass, German-Jewish background. Jaeger was a skilled photographer, and with his encouragement she began taking classes with Clarence H. White, who had opened a school of photography in Manhattan and with whom Jaeger himself had studied. White, a former associate of Alfred Stieglitz, was also on the faculty at Columbia and the Brooklyn Institute of Arts and Sciences, and he was considered the leading teacher of the form in New York at the time. He went on to instruct some of the most prominent photographers of the twentieth century, including Margaret Bourke-White and Dorothea Lange. Indeed, many of White's pupils were female, for at a time when upper-class women were often limited in their choice of occupation, photography was considered a suitable pastime. It was then regarded as a handicraft, like pottery making and weaving, which the arts and crafts movement had helped to popularize, and articles in women's magazines extolled photography's appropriateness for the female sex. White's obvious respect for women, combined with his gentle manner and kindly encouragement, made him a popular teacher for aspiring female photographers.

Under White and his associates at the school, Max Weber and Paul L. Anderson, Ulmann studied artistic as well as technical aspects of photography, learning how to manipulate a camera and develop images while acquiring at the same time an eye for appropriate design and composition. An empathy for people and a desire to take their pictures had initially motivated Ulmann to become a photographer, and she was therefore drawn early on to specializing in portrait photography. Although several cameras were available for her use, including the popular Graflex, Ulmann was drawn early on to the so-called view camera, an older machine that she, along with her teachers, believed was the preferred medium for portraits. The view camera was bulky and presented a special technical difficulty to its users, casting an upside-down and reversed image on the viewing screen and thereby making composition a challenge. But that difficulty, as Ulmann later noted, forced her to work more closely with her sitters, developing an extended relationship with them as she enlisted their cooperation. The results were portrait studies that were more natural looking than the posed studio portraits that remained in vogue. To enhance this impressionistic look, she used a soft-focus lens and avoided the use of a shutter, preferring instead to provide exposure by removing the lens cap for a few seconds after deciding on a suitable composition.

Ulmann's husband, Charles Jaeger, had continued his studies with White and had become a noted portrait photographer himself. In early 1916 Ulmann, her husband, and a group of both amateur and professional photographers (including White) gathered in Jaeger's medical offices to form an association called the Pictorial Photographers of America. Its purpose was to advance the cause of photography as a fine art. At their first meeting, White was elected to head the association, and Jaeger, who had already helped underwrite several photographic exhibitions, became its treasurer. The following October photographs by both Ulmann and Jaeger were displayed at the association's first formally sponsored show, held at the National Arts Club on East Nineteenth Street. Ulmann's contribution was a portrait titled "The Blacksmith." Several months later, for an exhibition held in early 1917 at the Ehrich Gallery on Fifth Avenue and featuring photographs by Clarence White's students, Ulmann contributed an impressionistic scene titled "Substance and Shadow" along with a portrait, "The Coal Worker."

In the course of her relatively brief career, Ulmann would go on to specialize in portraits of ordinary, everyday people, although she also made celebrated photographs of the well-known and accomplished, including Albert Einstein, the Nobel Prize-winning Hindu poet Rabindranath Tagore, and Helen Keller, as well as notable studies of scenes and places like "Substance and Shadow." Though her subjects varied, her photographs had a consistently soft, painterly quality that was similar to, and probably influenced by, the work of mid-nineteenth-century British photographers, in particular that of David Octavius Hill and Robert Adamson (the noted Scottish team of portrait photographers), and the celebrated Julia Margaret Cameron.

Working under the name "Doris U. Jaeger," Ulmann began teaching at the White School in the fall of 1917, and over the next few years her participation, along with her husband, in various association-sponsored exhibitions increased. In 1920 the first collection of her photographs was published, *The College of Physicians and Surgeons*, which was a series of portraits of her husband's colleagues at Columbia University made over several years. This was followed two years later by another series, *A Book of Portraits of the Faculty of the Medical Department of the Johns Hopkins University, Baltimore*.

In late 1921 her marriage to Jaeger ended abruptly without public explanation, and she began using her maiden name in subsequent exhibitions and publications. By the early 1920s her work was being shown in cities throughout the country, and in 1925 she published her third collection, *A Portrait Gallery of American Editors*, consisting of photographs of prominent book and magazine editors.

Now living on Park Avenue, the cultured and always elegantly attired Ulmann still remained drawn to ordinary people, and by the mid 1920s she had become committed to documenting the lives of Americans who were still following the customs and traditions of a vanishing rural culture. She began photographing members of small religious sects— Shakers, Mennonites, Dunkards—in New York State, Pennsylvania, and Virginia, and then she traveled south to photograph Native Americans in the Carolinas. During her travels she met and became close friends with the novelist Julia Peterkin, who lived with her husband on a plantation in South Carolina, and Ulmann commemorated their friendship by posing with Peterkin for a series of photographs; this was one of the few instances in which Ulmann allowed herself to be photographed.

Ulmann's visits to the Carolinas, and particularly to Peterkin's plantation, introduced her to rural African Americans, and they and their way of life became the focus of her work for several years. Some of Ulmann's most memorable images were made of African Americans in the Carolinas during this period, including "The Chain Gang," "Footwashing, South Carolina," and "Baptism." A selection of these portraits was published in 1933 as *Roll, Jordan, Roll*, with a text by Julia Peterkin.

Some years earlier, Ulmann had become acquainted in New York with John Jacob Niles, then a young actor turned folk ballad singer, song collector, and composer. Niles, who would go on to prominence following Ulmann's death, became her close friend, nursing the increasingly frail Ulmann through a series of ailments, including an ulcer, that had begun to plague her. In the late 1920s he had begun accompanying her on trips to Kentucky and other areas of southern Appalachia, collecting traditional songs while she photographed mountaineers. In the early 1930s, as Ulmann turned her attention almost exclusively to photographing the denizens of Appalachia, Niles became her constant companion, looking after her welfare in the field (he followed her large chauffeured Lincoln in his own Chevrolet) and escorting her to plays and concerts back in New York. The relationship was apparently platonic. During this period, she made at least one side trip to New England, where she made portraits of Harvard professors and other luminaries, including ex-President Calvin Coolidge and his wife.

Ulmann's work had continued to be displayed at exhibitions sponsored by the Pictorial Photographers, and in 1929 she was featured in a one-woman show under their auspices, "Light and Shade." Her photographs also appeared in periodicals during the 1920s and early 1930s, often in art and literary journals but occasionally in popular magazines as well: a collection of her earliest photographs of Appalachia was published in *Scribner's* in 1928, under the title "The Mountaineers of Kentucky."

Ulmann made her last working trip in the summer of 1934, to the Appalachian regions of the western Carolinas, settling in a hotel in Asheville. She became increasingly fatigued until finally, on the verge of collapse, she was taken by Niles to Scranton, Pennsylvania, where her doctor was staying. At the doctor's urging, Niles took her back to New York for additional medical care but her condition worsened. She died at her apartment several weeks later.

Although a brief *New York Times* obituary on the day following her death called Ulmann "one of the foremost photographers in the United States," her work was gradually forgotten as the Great Depression took hold and a plethora of government-sponsored photographers began documenting the urban and rural poor alike across the nation. The images of Walker Evans, Dorothea Lange, and others supplanted Ulmann's earlier contributions, and she was not rediscovered until the mid-1960s, when a folklore scholar, Jonathan Williams, found a cache of her southern photographs in the basement of the library of Berea College in Kentucky. A selection made by Williams and others was published in 1971 as *The Appalachian Photographs of Doris Ulmann*, with a lengthy introductory essay by John Jacob Niles. In the ensuing years, as interest in women photographers grew in the wake of the feminist movement, other collections of her photographs were published and exhibited to great acclaim, and she is now widely recognized as a major pictorial chronicler of American life during the early twentieth century.

• For biographical information, see especially Philip Walker Jacobs, *The Life and Photography of Doris Ulmann* (2001), which includes a lengthy bibliography as well as a generous selection of her photographs. See also John Jacob Niles's essay, "Doris Ulmann: As I Remember Her," in *The Appalachian Photographs of Doris Ulmann* (1971). For other modern collections of Ulmann's photographs, together with commentary, see especially Robert Coles, *The Darkness and the Light* (1974), and Davis Featherstone, *Doris Ulmann: American Portraits* (1985). An obituary (which lists Ulmann's age incorrectly) appears in the *New York Times*, 29 Aug. 1934.

ANN T. KEENE

UNDERWOOD, John Thomas (12 Apr. 1857–2 July 1937), typewriter manufacturer, was born in London, England, to John Underwood, a chemist, and Elizabeth Grant Maire Underwood. The family was apparently prosperous enough to educate young John, the eldest son in the family, at boarding schools in London and France, though their means had apparently become reduced by the time John Thomas Underwood was in his mid-teens. The elder Underwood, who had studied under the noted British scientist Michael Faraday, specialized in the creation of printing inks and copying paper; in 1872, following the death of his wife and their sixth child, he immigrated to the United States, settling in New Durham, New Jersey, and opening a small business manufacturing paper and ink. John, along with a younger brother, joined him in New Jersey the following year and found work as a laborer in an iron foundry.

By the 1870s the large-scale manufacture of typewriters in the United States had begun, pioneered by the company of E. Remington & Sons in Ilion, New York. Believing the typewriter had a bright future, John Thomas Underwood and his father began a business in 1874 manufacturing carbon paper, ribbons, and other typing supplies. By the early 1880s John Underwood and Company, as it was known, was flourishing, and in 1883, following the death of his father, the younger Underwood moved the business to Brooklyn, New York. As it continued to prosper, he began investigating the possibility of manufacturing typewriters as well, and perhaps improving on their design. He was motivated in part by Remington's manufacture of its own typewriter ribbons, which meant that Underwood was losing an important share of the typewriter accessories market.

At that time, when the typewriter was still in its infancy, most American typewriters, and most importantly Remingtons, were constructed with bars of type hung in a circular basketlike formation underneath the platen. This was a serious design flaw, because it meant that the line being typed could be seen only if the carriage was lifted. Searching for a typewriter with a more practical design, Underwood found what he was looking for in a so-called front-stroke machine, built by a German-born mechanic, Franz Xavier Wagner, and initially patented in 1893. Buying the rights to this and Wagner's subsequent patents on improved machines, Underwood established the Wagner

Typewriting Company in 1895 and hired a factory in lower Manhattan to begin manufacturing the new typewriter. The first Underwood models, as they were called, appeared on the market in 1897.

Following his successful introduction of the new typewriter, Underwood incorporated the Underwood Typewriting Manufacturing Company in 1898, the same year that the factory expanded and moved to Bayonne, New Jersey. Two years later his business made a significant gain when the U.S. Navy ordered 250 Underwood machines. Underwood prominently featured this government affiliation in its advertising, and it undoubtedly aided the growth of the company. A still larger manufacturing facility soon became necessary, and over the next few years Underwood built a large factory in Hartford, Connecticut, moving his firm there in 1901. In its first year of operation, the Hartford factory turned out more than 12,000 typewriters.

In 1903 Underwood merged the Wagner and Underwood companies into a single entity, incorporating it as the Underwood Typewriter Company, and he became its president. Throughout this time Underwood had continued to maintain his sales of typewriting accessories, and with the rapid success of his new typewriter he was able to virtually corner the American market in both machines and supplies, successfully challenging his major rival, Remington. By 1915 the Underwood Typewriter Company employed 7,500 workers and produced close to 500 machines daily, making it the largest company of its kind then in existence. The Wagner design that Underwood had pioneered became the prototype for all modern typewriters.

Underwood continued to lead the company until 1927, following its merger with two other typewriter manufacturers, Elliott Fisher and Sundstrand. Underwood served for two years as chairman of the board of directors of the new Underwood Elliott Fisher Company. When the position was eliminated in 1929, Underwood remained with the company as a director. In 1936, a year before he died, the company established a new research facility in Hartford, called the General Research Laboratory, for the purpose of expanding its product line. The company that Underwood had founded continued to grow in the years following his death. During World War II the company turned its facilities over to the defense effort and it became a major manufacturer of M-1 carbine barrels. In 1945 it changed its name to the Underwood Corporation and returned to the peacetime manufacture of typewriters. An agreement in 1959 between the corporation and Olivetti, the prominent Italian typewriter manufacturer, led to the subsequent takeover of Underwood by that firm, ending the American company's sixty-odd-year reign as a pioneering typewriter company.

In 1901 Underwood had married Grace Brainard, and the couple had a daughter; the family lived together in Brooklyn, New York. Underwood enjoyed book collecting as a hobby, but much of his energy outside the office was devoted to civic and charitable work. As an active member of the Presbyterian Church and its Board of Foreign Missions, one of his major charities was the Chosen Christian College, founded in Seoul by his brother Harold, a noted missionary in Korea. Underwood also aided the poor of rural Kentucky as well as service projects closer to home, including the Brooklyn YMCA. In addition he was a patron of cultural associations, providing support to the Brooklyn Academy of Music and the Institute of Arts and Sciences, among other organizations. He was awarded the Cross of the Legion of Honor in 1926 for relief given to the soldiers and citizens of France during and after World War I. After suffering from heart disease for several years, he died at his summer home in Wianno, Massachusetts, on Cape Cod.

• Biographical information on Underwood is available in Lucien M. Underwood and Howard J. Banker, *The Underwood Families of America* (2 vols., 1913), a privately printed family history. Richard N. Current, *The Typewriter and the Men Who Made It* (1954), includes limited biographical data. For additional information on the history of the typewriter and the role of Underwood and his company, see especially Wilfred A. Beeching, *Century of the Typewriter* (1974). An obituary appears in the *New York Times*, 3 July 1937.

ANN T. KEENE

USHER, John Palmer (9 Jan. 1816–13 Apr. 1889), attorney and secretary of the interior, was born in Brookfield, Madison County, New York, the son of Nathaniel Usher, a physician, and Lucy Palmer Usher. After completing his education in local common schools, he studied law in New Berlin, New York, with Henry Bennett and John Hyde. Admitted to the state bar in 1837, he was by 1839 certified to argue before the supreme and chancery courts of New York State. Sensing greater opportunities to the west, he relocated to Terre Haute, Indiana, the following year and set up a practice with William D. Griswold. On 26 June 1844 he married Margaret Patterson, with whom he was to have four sons.

As his practice flourished in the 1840s and 1850s, Usher traveled across state lines to argue cases in Illinois. During a trial in Danville, Illinois, in the mid-1850s he was matched up against Abraham Lincoln, whom he befriended despite losing his case. Once he had formed a new legal partnership with his brother-in-law Chambers Patterson in the late 1840s, Usher's interests turned to politics. Initially a Whig, he served one undistinguished term in the Indiana state House of Representatives (1850–1851) before returning to his legal practice. After unsuccessfully running for the U.S. House as a Whig in 1856, he joined the newly emerging Republican party and spent the next several years quietly building up the party's local organization.

In November 1861 Indiana governor Oliver Morton appointed Usher to the post of state attorney general. But he resigned in March 1862 when he accepted the offer of the newly created position of assistant secretary of the interior; he moved to Washington, where he served under fellow Hoosier Caleb Smith. Distracted by outside matters and in declining health, Smith had limitations that provided Usher with ample opportunities to gain experience in office. With the Civil War now in full swing, most of Usher's time was initially spent trying to thwart efforts by the Confederacy to form alliances with disgruntled Native American tribes in the West. In October 1862 he personally traveled to Minnesota, where he investigated reports of alleged Native American misdeeds in the wake of the Sioux uprising and subsequent massacre at New Ulm. Based on his reports, (apparently exaggerated) claims by white settlers against Native Americans received by the Interior Department were mitigated, and Usher also supported Indian Commissioner William P. Dole's recommendation for pardoning Native American leaders previously sentenced to death for their role in the incidents.

Although Usher shared Lincoln's feeling that colonization might prove to be a solution to the problem of where newly freed slaves could live in peace, his support was insufficient to bring several proposed efforts to establish a colony to fruition. Long involved with litigation relating to railroad construction during his days in private legal practice, he supported the building of the transcontinental railroad; after the Union Pacific Railroad was organized in June 1862, his office (empowered to appoint commissioners responsible for oversight) was deluged with patronage requests. Secretary Smith's resignation in December 1862 to accept an Indiana judgeship prompted President Lincoln, then in the middle of the infamous Cabinet Imbroglio, to pass over several better-known candidates and name Usher as the new head of the Interior Department in January 1863.

Usher kept most of Smith's political appointees in place and generally enjoyed cordial relations with his staff. Continuing to work for the development of the transcontinental railroad, he payed special attention to the building of the eastern terminus in Kansas. Unfailingly loyal to the president, he was as a rule unassertive in cabinet meetings and thus was often overshadowed by men of greater ambition and more forceful personalities, such as William Seward and Salmon Chase. The so-called New Almaden affair proved to be the greatest challenge of his tenure. When the Supreme Court voided ownership of the New Almaden Quicksilver Mine in March 1863, the federal government temporarily assumed its title; operations at the California mine, which provided most of that state's production of mercury, were to be taken over by the Interior Department. Controversy ensued as Usher's hand-picked agent, Leonard Swett, badly mishandled the secretary's directives, and neighboring mine operators soon feared a government takeover of their operations. Although the situation calmed down after a number of months, the embarrassing clash provided additional ammunition to Usher's enemies, including Gideon Welles and Salmon Chase, who derided him as a "nobody."

Disgusted with cabinet politics and eager to rebuild his legal practice in Indiana, Usher resigned as secretary of the interior in March 1965 and left office in May. He was thwarted in his ambition to become the president of the Eastern Division of the Union Pacific and became, instead, general solicitor for the line. After spending a great deal of time traveling between his home in Terre Haute and points both east and west on railroad business, he relocated his family to Lawrence, Kansas, in 1872. In April 1879 he was elected mayor of Lawrence. Condemned by some as a lackey for the railroad interests and by others who resented his attempts to assert the authority of his office, he settled for a single two-year term that proved highly unpleasant for all concerned. He retired from the railroad in 1887; two years later, he died in a hospital in Philadelphia, Pennsylvania, after undergoing neck surgery.

A genial man who lacked the overweening ambition of some of his contemporaries, John Usher has become a footnote to one of the great periods of crisis in American history. While he was evidently an able administrator, he produced no lasting initiatives, and the Civil War diverted public attention away from the Interior Department. Usher made more of a mark in history as a result of the small but important role he played in the effort that eventually produced the transcontinental railroad.

• A collection of Usher's papers is held at the Kansas State Historical Society in Topeka. His reports as secretary of the interior were published as *Executive Document no. 1, vol. 3,* 38th Cong., 1st sess. (1863) and *House Executive Document no. 1, pt. 5,* 38th Cong., 2d sess. (1864). The most thorough secondary account of his life and career is Elmo R. Richardson and Alan W. Farley, *John Palmer Usher: Lincoln's Secretary of the Interior* (1960). *President Lincoln's Cabinet* (1925) is a 34-page publication containing an after-dinner speech by Usher delivered in 1887, with a foreword and biographical sketch of Usher by Nelson H. Loomis. Obituaries are in the *Lawrence Daily Journal,* 14 Apr. 1889; the *Lawrence Evening Tribune,* 15 Apr. 1889; and the *Topeka Capital-Commonwealth,* 16 April 1889.

EDWARD L. LACH, JR.

V

VANDERBILT, Cornelius, II (27 Nov. 1843–12 Sept. 1899), railroad executive and philanthropist, was born on his family's farm near New Dorp, Staten Island, New York, the son of William Henry Vanderbilt, a railroad magnate, and Maria Louisa Kissam Vanderbilt. He was the favorite grandson and namesake of the family patriarch, Cornelius Vanderbilt, known as "the Commodore," who from humble beginnings had built the family fortune in shipping and railway lines.

First educated at the country school near his family's home, Cornelius Vanderbilt II later attended a private school in New York City. This early independence from his family helped to foster in him the self-reliance and ingenuity he would need to manage the family fortunes. His grandfather especially favored young Cornelius but believed strongly that he should learn the family business from the bottom up.

Eager to gain experience, Vanderbilt clerked from 1859 to 1863 in the Shoe and Leather Bank, then joined the Kissam Brothers' Bank (which was owned by his mother's family), where he served as a clerk (1863–1864) and as assistant treasurer (1864–1867). When he was twenty-four, his grandfather appointed him assistant treasurer, then treasurer and director, and finally vice president (1880) of the New York & Harlem Railroad, which was owned by the Vanderbilt family. In 1886, shortly after his father's death, Cornelius became president of the railroad, a position he held until his own death thirteen years later.

William Henry Vanderbilt held high-ranking positions in the family enterprises and had greatly extended the Vanderbilt railway network, focusing capital resources on railroads rather than on ships or steamboats. By expanding the New York Central Railroad and purchasing the New York, Chicago & St. Louis railway, as well as railways in Cleveland, Columbus, Cincinnati, and Indianapolis, William Henry nearly doubled the $90 million he had inherited from his father. But because of poor health he had gradually begun in 1883 to turn his control of the railway lines over to his son. After his death, Cornelius Vanderbilt II inherited most of his father's executive positions within the family business. He also came to manage a family fortune valued at over $200 million, even though the wealth was shared with other family heirs.

The family trusted Vanderbilt's acumen, integrity, thrift, conservatism, and business sense. He was adept in his dealings with people, launched worthy projects, took little time off from his hectic schedule, and was often applauded publicly for his philanthropy. At a time when the influx of European immigrants was swelling New York's population, making improved health care an urgent necessity, the Vanderbilt family supported hospitals and their expansion and donated the resources to build the Vanderbilt Clinic for what would become Columbia University's College of Physicians and Surgeons, on whose board Cornelius Vanderbilt later served (as well as on the board of the university itself from 1891 to 1899). In addition, he was a trustee and board member of a number of New York hospitals and applied his managerial skills to ensure that duplication of services would not occur. Desiring to provide a safe and wholesome gathering place for the youth of New York City, he donated a clubhouse to the Railroad Branch of the Young Men's Christian Association.

Both Vanderbilt and his wife were extremely pious, and he was on the finance committee of the Domestic and Foreign Missionary Society of the Protestant Episcopal Church. Besides being a vestryman of St. Bartholomew's Church (where Stanford White was to design the bronze doors commemorating Cornelius Vanderbilt after his death), he sat on the board of St. John the Divine Cathedral in New York.

Vanderbilt had married Alice Claypoole Gwynne of Cincinnati in 1867. They had four sons and two daughters, one of whom, Gertrude Vanderbilt Whitney (married to Harry Payne Whitney), became known as a sculptor and an important patron of the arts. All of the sons attended Yale, and Vanderbilt donated a men's dormitory there in 1893 in memory of the eldest, William Henry, who had died while in his junior year at Yale. His cumulative donations to the school totaled over $1.5 million.

Vanderbilt and his family lived in the Fifth Avenue mansion in New York City that his father had built; it was a block long and housed one of the world's most valuable private art collections. In 1893 he began construction on "The Breakers," his summer estate in Newport, Rhode Island. Designed by Richard Morris Hunt and modeled on Italian palace-villas in sixteenth-century Genoa, the seventy-room house was elaborately decorated with plasterwork, gilt bronze, Italian marbles and frescoes, and mosaics by an international team of artists and artisans. Completed in 1895, only four years before Vanderbilt's death, "The Breakers" was designated a National Historic Landmark in 1995, and it remains one of the country's most magnificent mansions.

Vanderbilt was a devotee of the arts of the world and worked to bring them to the United States for Americans to enjoy. For the last twelve years of his life, he served on the Metropolitan Museum of Art's board as chairman of the executive committee, overseeing purchases and exhibits and donating numerous pieces of world-renowned artwork, including the 1887 gift of Rosa Bonheur's *The Horse Fair*. He was also a director of the American Museum of Natural History.

Working from an office at New York City's Grand Central Terminal that had been constructed by his grandfather, Vanderbilt often began his day before dawn, attending three to four philanthropic board meetings and supervising the family enterprises well into the early evening hours. He took little time off for social events. After suffering a mild stroke in 1896, Vanderbilt resigned most of his duties, which for a time were taken over mostly by his brother William Kissam Vanderbilt. He died in New York City following a cerebral hemorrhage.

Vanderbilt was a natural leader, for whom vast financial responsibility was second nature. He was a major figure in the management of the growing American railroad system and contributed greatly to railroad expansion in the eastern half of the United States during the industrial revolution.

• Book-length sources include Louis Auchincloss, *The Vanderbilt Era: Profiles of a Gilded Age* (1990); Robert B. King, with Charles O. McLean, *The Vanderbilt Homes* (1989); and Jerry E. Patterson, *The Vanderbilts* (1989). Still useful are Wayne Andrews, *The Vanderbilt Legend: The Story of the Vanderbilt Family, 1794–1940* (1941), and Edwin P. Hoyt, *Vanderbilts and Their Fortunes* (1962). Older sources that document the family empire include William A. Croffut, *The Vanderbilts and the Story of Their Fortune* (1886; repr., 1975), and B. J. Hendrick, "The Vanderbilt Fortune," *McClure's Magazine*, Nov. 1908. Well documented and supportive on industrial expansion are Gustavus Myers, *History of the Great American Fortunes* (1910), and John Moody, *The Railroad Builders* (1919; repr., 1974). A brief sketch appears in *Who's Who in America* (1899–1900). The family relationships and heirs are discussed in J. G. Wilson, *New York Genealogical and Biographical Record*, Oct. 1899, pp. 197–99. Obituaries are in the *New York Times* and *New York Tribune*, both 13 Sept. 1899.

BARBARA BENNETT PETERSON

VANDERBILT, George Washington (14 Nov. 1862–6 Mar. 1914), agriculturalist and philanthropist, was born at New Dorp, Staten Island, New York, the youngest of the eight children of William Henry Vanderbilt and Maria Louisa Kissam. His father, the son of "Commodore" Cornelius Vanderbilt, inherited most of the Commodore's fortune, including railroads, and became president of the New York Central Railroad. Upon his grandfather's death in 1877, George Washington Vanderbilt received a bequest of $1 million. When George turned twenty-one, his father gave him another million. When his father died in 1885, young Vanderbilt inherited $5 million more and controlled the income from a $5 million trust fund. While his three brothers—Cornelius Vanderbilt II, Frederick William Vanderbilt, and William Kissam Vanderbilt—were augmenting their fortunes, enjoying their positions in society, and building mansions, George Vanderbilt, shy and introverted, lived with his mother in their Fifth Avenue mansion in Manhattan, was privately tutored, and began to amass a large library. He read in philosophy and became a linguist fluent in eight languages, partly through worldwide travel. He collected art objects of various sorts—carpets, etchings and prints, ivory carvings, paintings, statues, tapestries, and vases—and also books, coins, jewelry, pottery, musical instruments, and weapons and armor.

In 1888 Vanderbilt and his mother wintered in the Great Smoky Mountains of North Carolina. Delighted with the climate, clear air, and scenic views, he decided to build his mansion there, instead of following his siblings to Fifth Avenue and Newport, Rhode Island. In 1889 he bought 5,000 acres south and southwest of Asheville and soon acquired 146,000 acres of forest land in Buncombe, Haywood, Henderson, and Transylvania counties, including 5,749-foot Mount Pisgah.

In 1890 Vanderbilt began construction of his mansion, which he called "Biltmore," and engaged specialists to help him. Frederick Law Olmsted, the premier landscape architect in the United States, advised him to create a European-style forest, for game and timber, with bottom land for livestock, and to build adjacent to his residence a park, pleasure grounds, and stables. With seemingly limitless funds and a large staff, Olmsted leveled the mountain top as a site for the mansion, surveyed and graded, built bridges and 200 miles of roads, and planned a twenty-acre lake, nurseries and fields, and a four-acre walled garden. A picturesque three-mile drive lined with trees would lead guests from gatehouse to main house. Vanderbilt engaged Gifford Pinchot to supervise 5,000 of his wooded acres as a forest-management demonstration. Pinchot, who described Vanderbilt in a diary entry as a "simple minded pleasant fellow," proceeded to initiate and expand the first systematic, scientific forestry in the United States. As his architect, Vanderbilt engaged Richard Morris Hunt, who had planned several Vanderbilt mansions and in addition a Romanesque family mausoleum on Staten Island. He patterned Biltmore House after three eighteenth-century French châteaus—at Blois, Chambord, and Chenonceaux. Hunt's neoclassical structure obliged Olmsted to adopt formal landscaping near it, mitigated by a more naturalistic feeling farther down the hills.

Biltmore House, which sits on five acres, is built of Indiana limestone, Bedford stone, and concealed iron girders. It has a commanding four-story, 780-foot front, with towers, mullioned windows, chimneys, loggias and arcades, and 250 rooms, including forty master bedrooms. The spectacular interior boasts a palm court and garden, a conservatory of sunken marble and many varieties of flowers, a 20,000-volume library lavishly decorated, a rich tapestry room ninety feet in length, an oak-paneled billiard room, and much else. Uniquely awesome is the tall, acoustically perfect, 3,000-square-foot banquet hall, with a triple marble fireplace and cathedral-style pipe organ. Next door to the banquet hall is an informal dining room, with marble wainscoting, leather-covered walls, and Wedgwood-tile fireplace. Individual rooms contain priceless paintings (including portraits of Hunt and Olmsted by John Singer Sargent), other artistic treasures, and carvings in limestone and oak. A bachelor's wing boasts a gun room, a smoking room, and rooms with single beds. For efficiency, Vanderbilt established his own tile, wood-carving, and brick factories nearby. At one point, 32,000 bricks came from his kilns daily. A large-scale arboretum, which Olmsted patterned after the arboretum at Kew Gardens in England, supplied daily bouquets to the mansion. The arboretum was supervised by Chauncey Beadle for sixty years, beginning soon after his arrival in 1890 as landscape director, and it ultimately housed 11 million specimens.

A thousand men worked six years to prepare the park, the 11,000 acres just outside the mansion, and the mansion, now the largest private residence in the United States. Its initial cost was $3 million, excluding furnishings, and $7 million for ground improvements. Vanderbilt invited family members and friends for an elaborate housewarming on Christmas Eve, 1895. They came by private railroad cars switched to his spur line off the Southern Railroad tracks in Asheville. During a week's stay, his guests were coddled by an army of servants and toured nearby Biltmore Village, where Vanderbilt had built homes patterned on cottages in Cheshire, England, for his eighty personal servants and three hundred permanent outdoor laborers. He ordered his tenants not to house dogs, hens, or servants because they would cause domestic disputes. The village had a school, post office, hospital, railroad station, shops, and All Souls Church, complete with parish house and rectory. Vanderbilt financed the church entirely, and all collections went to charity.

When his mother died in 1896, Vanderbilt, whose residence had been at her Fifth Avenue home, moved to Biltmore. In 1898 he and Edith Stuyvesant Dresser, a descendant of Peter Stuyvesant, were married in Paris. The couple had one child, Cornelia Stuyvesant Vanderbilt.

Vanderbilt founded the Biltmore School of Forestry on his estate and sold seedlings by the millions annually. Tens of thousands of mature trees were felled and processed by his saw- and planing-mills for commercial lumber. He sold firewood and also chestnut-oak bark to make tannic acid and chestnut extract. His gardens, greenhouses, barns, and dairies produced money-making vegetables, fruits, eggs and chickens, pedigreed livestock, and milk and ice cream. Vanderbilt avidly studied trees, flowers, other plants, animals, and birds, and the dialects of several Native American tribes. An oddity was his hobby of translating modern literature into classical Greek. A generous philanthropist, he built a branch circulating library in Jackson Square, New York, and gave it to the main library, which ultimately became the New York Public Library; he also built an exhibition gallery on Fifty-seventh Street in New York, adjacent to the American Fine Arts Society building, then donated it to the society. To Columbia University he presented the land on which its Teachers College was built.

By disbursing $250,000 annually for maintenance and improvements at Biltmore, Vanderbilt unwisely spent not merely income but part of his capital and was running out of cash. His offer to sell 120,000 acres to the U.S. Forest Preservation Commission was declined. When he died of a heart attack at his residence in Washington, D.C., he had personal assets of only $930,000. His widow inherited their three homes, including Biltmore, parcels of which she sold for living expenses until only 12,500 acres were left. Cornelia, who received the $5 million trust fund her father had inherited from his father, married John Francis Amherst Cecil, of British nobility, in 1924; they had two sons. Cornelia obtained a divorce in 1934, retired in England, and died there in 1976. Her sons inherited Biltmore, which has been open to delighted and astonished visitors since 1930.

• Arthur T. Vanderbilt II, *Fortune's Children: The Fall of the House of Vanderbilt* (1989), includes consideration of George Washington Vanderbilt and places him in the context of his illustrious family. Robert B. King and Charles O. McLean, *The Vanderbilt Homes* (1989), includes illustrated coverage of Biltmore. John Foreman and Robbe Pierce Stimson, *The Vanderbilts and the Gilded Age: Architectual Aspirations, 1879–1901* (1991), carries the history of Cornelia and John Cecil, their sons, and Biltmore to the year 1990 and has elaborate endpaper genealogical tables. For details on Vanderbilt and Pinchot, see M. Nelson McGeary, *Gifford Pinchot, Forester-Politician* (1960); on Vanderbilt and Hunt, see Paul R. Baker, *Richard Morris Hunt* (1980); and on Vanderbilt and Olmsted, see Melvin Kalfus, *Frederick Law Olmsted: The Passion of a Public Artist* (1990), and Charles E. Beveridge and Paul Rocheleau, *Frederick Law Olmsted: Designing the American Landscape* (1995). An obituary is in the *New York Times*, 7 Mar. 1914.

ROBERT L. GALE

VAN DER DONCK, Adriaen (7 May 1620–c. 1655), colonial officer and attorney, was born in Breda, Province of North Brabant, Holland, the son of Cornelis van der Donck, occupation unknown, and Agatha van Bergen van der Donck. After beginning his education in his hometown, he entered the University of Leyden in about 1638 and studied law. While searching for employment Van der Donck came to the attention of Kiliaen Van Rensselaer, an Amsterdam diamond merchant who also happened to be a director of the powerful Dutch West India Company. The company had sought to increase the number of permanent residents at its operations in New Netherland through the granting of patroonships, which entitled the patroon to near-feudal lord status over a large parcel of land within the territory in exchange for the establishment of settlers. While many such patroonships were contemplated, Van Rensselaer's manor, Rensselaerswyck (located in what is today Albany and Rensselaer counties in New York state), was the only one that was successfully established. Impressed by Van der Donck, Van Rensselaer commissioned him *schout*, or officer of justice, on 13

May 1641, and Van der Donck arrived at his new position in August of the same year.

Upon arriving in New Netherland, Van der Donck was granted the lease of a farm—"Welys Burg"—on Castle Island, just below Fort Orange (modern-day Albany, N.Y.) on the North River (now the Hudson River). His duties within the manor included law enforcement as well as the collection of debts and rents owed to the patroon. Van Rensselaer also apparently expected Van der Donck to provide guidance to his great-nephew Arent van Curler, who as *commis*, or business agent, of the manor had proved to be a source of exasperation to the elder patroon. Lax in business matters and more interested in commerce with the nearby Mohawks than in bookkeeping, van Curler also apparently traded in both alcohol and firearms with the Native Americans—despite his own edict forbidding such transactions—and had several sexual dalliances with Native American women as well. Despite Van der Donck's aristocratic background, he proved to be a fair-minded official and often displayed forbearance when his tenants had difficulty paying their bills. He also took a leading role in establishing a Dutch Reformed church on Castle Island in 1642, with a *dominie* (or minister) being sent from the Netherlands "for the edifying improvement of the inhabitants and Indians thereabouts."

Animosity that soon escalated into open conflict developed between Van Curler and Van der Donck, possibly fueled by their similarities in age as well as the demands of satisfying an absentee employer. After van Curler complained to Van Rensselaer about Van der Donck, his great uncle forbade Van der Donck from establishing a colony at Katskill; and in the chaotic conditions that followed Van Rensselaer's death in 1643, Van der Donck lost his position. He remained on Castle Island and continued to farm, and in the summer of 1645 he assisted New Netherland governor Willem Kieft in negotiating a peace treaty with the nearby Mohawks. That same year he married Mary Doughty, the daughter of an English clergyman who had been expelled from New England because of his unorthodox religious views; there is no record of any children resulting from the marriage.

After suffering fire damage to his property in 1646, Van der Donck sought to relocate. As a reward for services rendered on behalf of New Netherland, he was given permission to establish a colony on the east bank of the Hudson river in what is today Westchester County, New York. Originally known as "Colen Donck," the property soon came to be known by Van der Donck's nickname, "De Jonkheer" (meaning "esquire" or "young lord"). Its name, later corrupted to Yonkers, remains in place to this day.

Although Peter Stuyvesant's administration came to be known as the high-water mark of New York government during the Dutch colonial period, his arrogant and authoritarian ways soon antagonized the colonists following his arrival in 1647. Van der Donck became a member of the Board of Nine Men—a group that Stuyvesant had created ostensibly to assist

him in governing—and became its secretary in February 1649. After suffering contempt at the hands of Stuyvesant and later expulsion from the colony for his role in opposing the director general's leadership, Van der Donck composed the noted *Vertoogh van Nieu-Neder-Land* (*Remonstrance of New Netherland*) in which he accused Stuyvesant of being a "vulture [who] is destroying the prosperity of New Netherland" and which urged the States-General (the governing body of the Netherlands) to revoke the West India Company's charter and replace the colony's government with "godly, honorable and intelligent" men (*Gotham*, p. 62).

Van der Donck was one of three representatives from New Netherland who journeyed back to Europe and presented the *Remonstrance* at The Hague. While back in the Netherlands he completed work on his legal training and was awarded the degree "Supremus in jure" from the University of Leyden on 10 April 1653. He also took time to complete a narrative work, *Beschrijvinge van Nieuvv Nederlant* (*Description of New Netherland*), which was published in 1655 and which (despite his being denied the use of official records in its preparation by Stuyvesant) became an important source for scores of historians of early New York. Despite efforts by Stuyvesant and his secretary Cornelis van Tienhoven to discredit Van der Donck, the States-General took his accusations seriously. Stuyvesant did survive the controversy, but worried West India Company officials urged him to govern more circumspectly.

Van der Donck returned to New Netherland in late 1653 and died there of unrecorded causes before the end of 1655. Although a minor player in the drama that unfolded in the early days of New York history, he was a competent official who survived several political intrigues and in the name of Yonkers left a permanent trace.

• No collection of Van der Donck's papers appears to have survived. His life and career receive attention in Edwin G. Burrows and Mike Wallace's *Gotham: A History of New York City to 1898* (1999) and in Lloyd Ultan's *The Bronx in the Frontier Era: From the Beginning to 1696* (1993). Dated but still useful are J. R. Brodhead's *History of the State of New York* (2 vols, 1853), John T. Scharf's *History of Westchester County, New York* (1886), vol. 1, pp. 66–71, and A. J. F. van Laer's *Van Rensselaer Bowier Manuscripts: Being the Letters of Kiliaen van Rensselaer, 1630–1643, and Other Documents Relating to the Colony of Rensselaerswyck* (1908).

EDWARD L. LACH, JR.

VANDER MEER, Johnny (2 Nov. 1914–6 Oct. 1997), major league baseball player, was born John Samuel Vander Meer in Prospect Park, New Jersey, the son of Jacob Vander Meer, a Dutch-born stonemason, and Katie Vander Wall Vander Meer. He grew up in nearby Midland Park and spent his childhood eating, drinking, and sleeping baseball. Living about sixteen miles west of the Polo Grounds, home of the National League's New York Giants, he idolized Carl Hubbell, the team's superb left-handed pitcher; whenever he could afford it, he traveled to New York to see Hubbell pitch.

The Brooklyn Dodgers signed Vander Meer to his first professional contract and sent him to Dayton, Ohio, where in 1933 the eighteen-year-old left-hander won eleven and lost ten in his first professional season. After Dayton dealt him to Scranton, a jurisdictional dispute ensued over who controlled him. Major league commissioner Kenesaw Mountain Landis awarded him to Scranton, and there he compiled an 11–8 record with a 3.73 earned-run average in 1934. A rocky 1935 season at Scranton (7–10, 5.35) concluded with the Boston Braves purchasing his contract and assigning him to Nashville, who sent him on to Durham, where he blossomed. His 19–6 won-lost record and sparkling 2.65 earned-run average won for him the *Sporting News*'s Minor League Player of the Year Award for 1936. The Cincinnati Reds, who had a working agreement with Durham, bought him and took him to spring training with the big club in 1937.

As a rookie in 1937, Vander Meer had his dream come true: he made his first start against his idol, Carl Hubbell, at the Polo Grounds, pitching nine innings and getting no decision in an extra-inning game. His 3–5 record, with an earned-run average of 3.86, prompted Cincinnati to send him down to Syracuse to gain more experience. In 1938, his first full season in the big leagues, he pitched very well, finishing at 15–10 and an earned-run average of 3.12. More important, his brush with immortality occurred that season. On Saturday, 11 June, he pitched a fairly routine no-hitter in Cincinnati, a 3–0 blanking of the Boston Braves in which he walked three. Four days later he started the first night game in the history of Brooklyn's Ebbets Field, a special event that drew 38,748 fans, including around 700 fans from his hometown area. They got an unexpected treat. Though Vander Meer was characteristically wild, walking eight, he did not allow a hit through eight innings and took a 6–0 lead into the ninth. Then, with one out, he loaded the bases on walks before manager Bill McKechnie came out to the mound and settled him down. The next batter grounded to third base for a force-out at home, bringing up the pesky Leo Durocher. Vander Meer got ahead in the count, one ball and two strikes, then thought he had strike three on the outside corner of the plate, but umpire Bill Stewart called it a ball. Fortunately, Durocher hit the next pitch to center fielder Harry Craft, and Vander Meer had accomplished something that no major league pitcher had yet done: thrown consecutive no-hit games. Umpire Stewart, much relieved, was the first one to the mound, admitting he had blown the previous call. In his next start, Vander Meer hurled three and a third hitless innings before giving up a hit and finally breaking the string. Four other pitchers (Allie Reynolds, Virgil Trucks, Jim Maloney, and Nolan Ryan) have pitched two no-hitters in the same season, and Ryan accumulated an amazing seven no-hit games in his career, but no pitcher has matched Vander Meer's feat.

Even though Cincinnati won the National League pennant the next two seasons, Vander Meer contributed only minimally. A shoulder injury in 1939 led to his being sent back to the minors for rehabilitation in 1940, though he did come back to pitch twelve innings to win the pennant clincher, scoring the winning run himself. Following that season he married Lois Stewart, with whom he had two daughters. Over the next three seasons he compiled a 49–14 record and led the league in strikeouts all three years. He threw hard but was wild—he finished in the top four in walks each year as well, leading the league in 1943. After four All-Star Game appearances, he entered the U.S. Navy in 1944 and missed two seasons because of World War II.

Returning to the mound in 1946, Vander Meer went 10–12, with an earned-run average of 3.18, and in September pitched what he considered his greatest game: fifteen shutout innings against the Dodgers, who were fighting the Cardinals for the pennant, in a game that was called a scoreless tie after nineteen innings. That performance may have contributed to his arm trouble in 1947 and a disappointing record of 10–12, with an earned-run average of 4.40. He rebounded for his last fine season in 1948, winning seventeen and losing fourteen with a 3.41 earned-run average despite leading the league in walks for a second time, including twelve in one game. A 5–10 season finished his career in Cincinnati; he went 3–4 with the Chicago Cubs in 1950 and lost his one start for the Cleveland Indians in 1951 before being released.

Vander Meer pitched briefly in the minor leagues after that, with one memorable and appropriate flourish: he threw a no-hitter for Tulsa in the Texas League in 1952, beating a Beaumont team managed by Harry Craft, the man who caught Durocher's last out in the second 1938 no-hitter. He served as a coach and manager in the minor leagues for the Reds organization until 1963 and owned hardware stores in the Tampa area, where he died.

Despite four stellar seasons, Vander Meer's career statistics were mediocre. His lifetime major league record was 119 wins and 121 losses, and his earned-run average was 3.44. In 2,105 innings he struck out 1,294 and walked 1,132. But the "Dutch Master" earned lasting fame with his back-to-back no-hitters. Whenever a pitcher does manage to hurl a hitless game, the automatic question is, Can he match Johnny Vander Meer?

• The best treatment of Vander Meer is in Donald Honig's fine oral history, *Baseball between the Lines* (1976). Obituaries are in the *Cincinnati Post* and the *New York Times*, both 7 Oct. 1997.

JOHN R. M. WILSON

VAN DOREN, Dorothy (2 May 1896–21 Feb. 1993), author and editor, was born Dorothy Graffe in San Francisco, California, the daughter of George Graffe, a newsman, and Frances R. Lane. She grew up in New York City and went to college there, graduating from Barnard with an A.B. in 1918. The following year, she joined the staff of the *Nation* as an assistant editor and soon attained the position of associate editor (1925–1936). In 1922 she married Mark Van Doren, who in 1920 had completed his dissertation on John Dryden at Columbia University and soon began a distinguished career there as professor of English and as a poet, literary critic, and editor. His older brother, Carl Van Doren, also an author, educator, and editor, had been a member of Columbia's English department since 1911. Carl's wife, Irita Van Doren, was a literary critic, editor, and biographer.

In 1923 Dorothy and Mark Van Doren purchased a farm home in Cornwall Hollow, Connecticut, where they and their two sons regularly spent their summers. The Van Dorens were genial hosts and brilliant conversationalists. Over the years, their circle of professional and personal friends of various ages included many members of the literati of New York and elsewhere, notably Mortimer Adler, John Berryman, Clifton Fadiman, Robert Frost, Allen Ginsberg, Jack Kerouac, Joseph Wood Krutch, Archibald MacLeish, Thomas Merton, Carl Sandburg, and Allen Tate.

During World War II, Dorothy Van Doren was a news executive for the U.S. Office of War Information in New York City (1942–1945), after which she served briefly as a news executive for the Information Service of the U.S. State Department (1946).

Van Doren was the author of five novels, written during her stint at the *Nation* and later, up to the start of her wartime work. *Strangers* (1926) was her promising first novel, in which she narrates the loves and adulteries of two couples who inhabit the same literary, artistic milieu as the Van Dorens themselves. When Ann and Stephen grow intimate, the other two of the close quartet, Ann's husband, William, and Stephen's wife, Edith, seek what comfort they can manage together. A lesser subplot concerns Ann's sister Rachel's love of and tragic marriage to Paul. The title *Strangers* suggests that persons outwardly close are often not. *Flowering Quince* (1927) is a disappointing story of the unhappy relationship of Emily Ann, a sensitive girl, and her cold father, a minister whose wife directs her love not only to the girl but also to a quince bush. Emily Ann's warped upbringing contributes substantially to her adult struggles and unhappiness. *Brother and Brother* (1928) follows the lives of Ellery and John Downing, both of whom display their father's work ethic and their mother's wisdom even as they head for considerably different destinies. Ellery marries Laly, a mentally challenged girl, and John remains loyal to his sibling. As they did in regard to *Strangers*, some reviewers faulted Van Doren for mechanical plot patterning in *Brother and Brother*. *Those First Affections* (1938) portrays a Brooklyn family from the turn of the century to the year 1910. Dan Tower, an ex-newsman, and his wife fall from considerable affluence to dreadful poverty. The story is poignantly narrated by Sally, their little daughter, through whose sensitive consciousness the reader experiences a child's sadness and bafflement. *Dacey Hamilton*

(1942) concerns a beautiful young woman who marries Thatcher Hamilton, an egocentric American painter. Emotionally flattened when she is widowed in Hawaii, Dacey moves with her five children to New York, where she obtains work on a newspaper and finds solace in love with Urian Oakes, a crippled New Yorker rendered bitter by physical lameness. The symbiotic pair seek to mend each other's different paralyses. Van Doren sketches minor characters well, including Dacey's lovable kids, her mean mother, a Hawaiian nurse, and an uncle back from expatriation in France.

In the 1950s Van Doren wrote interesting nonfiction. In *The Country Wife* (1950) she presents semi-autobiographical sketches of the Van Doren family's life during their summers on the farm. The book is best when it tells about handling somewhat intrusive guests and how a city-bound family relishes the natural delights of their summer retreat. *Men, Women and Cats* (1960) is a collection of vignettes about television, little family squabbles, gardening fun, and even an occasional cat. Best is Van Doren's sparkling *The Professor and I* (1959), the professor of course being Mark Van Doren, and the time span being their happy first thirty-seven years of marriage. The author tells about their efforts at house selling, country pleasures, birdhouse building, family weddings and charming in-laws, and pride in their son Charles Van Doren's 1957 appearances on "Twenty-One," the television game show that won him $129,000. (Trouble came two years later, not long after the publication of *The Professor and I*, when widespread public suspicion forced Charles to admit that he had been provided answers to the questions.)

Van Doren was a skillful novelist and prose writer whose works were agreeably accepted by reviewers and general readers alike but have seemed dated to later audiences. Her nonfictional prose now seems semi-saccharine, even high-toned folksy. She was a loving wife, mother, and sister-in-law in a distinguished academic family. In her later years, she was active in such organizations as the board of trustees of Barnard College and the New York Barnard Club, the board of education of Cornwall, Connecticut, and the women's society of Cornwall. Widowed since 1972, she died of pneumonia in a hospital in the small town of Sharon, Connecticut, where she had made her final residence.

• Many of Mark Van Doren's personal letters, which reside in the Library of Congress and in libraries at Columbia University, the University of Minnesota, Princeton University, and elsewhere, make incidental reference to Dorothy Van Doren. Details of the extended Van Doren family are in Carl Van Doren, *Three Worlds* (1936), and in Mark Van Doren, *Autobiography* (1958). Harry R. Warfel, *American Novelists of Today* (1951), pp. 433–34, briefly analyzes Van Doren's novels. Clifton Fadiman in a review in the *New Yorker*, 5 Sept. 1942, pp. 49–50, praises *Dacey Hamilton* for displaying a rare combination of imagination and good sense that reminds him of Jane Austen's novels. In discussing the history of the *Nation*, Frank Luther Mott, in *A History of American Magazines: 1865–1885* (1967), mentions Van Doren's being its associate editor. An obituary is in the *New York Times*, 23 Feb. 1993.

ROBERT L. GALE

VAN DOREN, Irita (16 Mar. 1891–18 Dec. 1966), literary editor, was born Irita Bradford, in Birmingham, Alabama, the daughter of John Taylor Bradford, a lumberman and merchant, and Ida Henley Brooks, the daughter of William Brooks, a Confederate Army general. At age four, Irita moved with her family to Tallahassee, Florida, where her father was the owner of a sawmill. In 1900 he was shot to death by a discharged mill worker. His widow supported their four children by giving music lessons and selling preserves and jellies. The family loved literature and read many of the classics aloud.

Majoring in English, Irita Bradford graduated from Florida State College for Women at Tallahassee (now Florida State University) with a B.A. in 1908 and an M.A. in 1909. She then went to New York City to study English, Latin, and mathematics and to pursue a Ph.D. at Columbia University. She taught at Hunter College while working on her dissertation (never completed). While at Columbia she met Carl Van Doren, who in 1911 had joined the faculty of the English department and later became a distinguished critic and biographer. The two were married in 1912 and had three children. They purchased an old farm in Cornwall, Connecticut, and spent time there when they could get away from Manhattan.

In 1919 Irita Van Doren joined the editorial staff of the *Nation*, of which her husband had just been appointed literary editor. She was the advertising manager of the *Nation* in 1922–1923 and in the latter year was appointed its book editor. In 1922 Carl Van Doren's brother, Mark Van Doren, also an English professor at Columbia, married Dorothy Graffe, who was on the editorial staff of the *Nation* and soon became an author as well. The four Van Dorens, all brilliant conversationalists, made their city and country homes nothing less than informal literary salons.

In 1924 Irita Van Doren became assistant editor of *Books* (later called the *Book Review*), a Sunday supplement of the *New York Herald Tribune*. The two persons mainly responsible for this appointment were her friend Helen Rogers Reid, wife of Ogden Mills Reid, the *Tribune*'s editor-owner, and Stuart Pratt Sherman, editor of its *Books* section. Carl Van Doren had studied at the University of Illinois under Sherman before Sherman joined the English department at Columbia. He directed Mark Van Doren's master's thesis on Henry David Thoreau (published in 1916). When Sherman died in 1926, Irita Van Doren became editor of the *Book Review* and remained in that position until 1963. Her work was marked by an admirably eclectic taste, and her quick, fair, and judicious decisions won her international renown. She inaugurated a staff of "Visiting Critics" (1926–1931)—American, English, and European—to write leading articles weekly. They included Charles Beard, Thomas Beer, Mary Colum,

Ford Madox Ford, André Gide, Ellen Glasgow, Aldous Huxley, Philip Guadalla, André Maurois, Ezra Pound, H. M. Tomlinson, Paul Valéry, Rebecca West, Virginia Woolf, and Elinor Wylie. Her circle of friends ultimately included Stephen Vincent Benét and his wife Rosemary, John Erskine, Robert Frost, Edna Ferber, Lewis Gannett, John Gunther, Alfred Kazin, Joseph Wood Krutch, Harold J. Laski, Archibald MacLeish, Jan Struthers, Dorothy Thompson, Virgil Thomson, and Hugh Walpole.

In 1935 Irita and Carl Van Doren divorced and in 1937 Irita met Wendell Willkie, then chairman of the Commonwealth and Southern Corporation, a huge public utility holding company. Their friendship—augmented at first by their common interest in southern history, including Willkie's particular interest in her grandfather General William Brooks—soon developed into a love affair that was an open secret of the press corps. Though seriously thinking of marrying Van Doren, Willkie was aware that his political ambitions would be severely damaged by divorce. She introduced him to Ogden Reid, who in *Tribune* editorials sponsored his Republican presidential nomination in 1940. Van Doren also brought her literary expertise to bear on some of Willkie's magazine articles and speeches. While campaigning, he avoided personal contact with her, but they communicated daily by telephone. Once Franklin Delano Roosevelt was reelected president, Van Doren and Willkie resumed their friendship. She helped him write his influential *One World* (1943) and also edited his *An American Program* (1944). She was devastated by his death in 1944.

When she retired from the *Herald Tribune*, John Hay Whitney, its editor-in-chief and publisher, established the Irita Van Doren Award. A sum of $2,000 was to be given annually to the author of any book meriting unusual recognition. Beginning in 1963, Van Doren served the publishing house of William Morrow as an editorial consultant. She persistently declined requests by publishers for her memoirs, saying she was "the nonwriting Van Doren." During her last years she lived on West 77th Street in Manhattan. She died in a New York hospital.

• Irita Van Doren's papers are at the Library of Congress, Washington, D.C. Some of Carl Van Doren's voluminous correspondence, at the libraries of Columbia University, Cornell University, Harvard University, the University of Illinois, the University of Michigan, Vassar College, and Yale University, makes references to her. Her exemplary work as an editor is described in "'Books' Covers the World of Books," *Publishers Weekly*, 30 Sept. 1939, pp. 1338–47. Many authors honored her. For example, Vincent Sheean dedicated *This House against This House* (1946, about his wartime experiences) and *Dorothy and Red* (his 1963 biography of Dorothy Thompson and Sinclair Lewis) to her. In *And I Worked at the Writer's Trade: Chapters of Literary History, 1918–1978* (1978), Malcolm Cowley says that "[a]mong the kindhearted editors I have known, she [Irita Van Doren] was by far the kindest." In discussing the history of the *Nation*, Frank Luther Mott, in *A History of American Magazines*, vol. 5 (1968), notes that Irita Van Doren was its literary editor. For her association with the *Tribune*, see Richard Kluger, *The Paper: The Life and Death of the New York Herald Tribune* (1986). Van Doren's relationship with Wendell Willkie is discussed in Ellsworth Barnard, *Wendell Willkie: Fighter for Freedom* (1966), and Steve Neal, *Dark Horse: A Biography of Wendell Willkie* (1984). James H. Madison, ed., *Wendell Willkie: Hoosier Internationalist* (1992), says Willkie and Van Doren "became lovers, passionately devoted to each other, emotionally and intellectually." Obituaries are in the *New York Times*, 19 Dec. 1966, and *Publishers Weekly*, 26 Dec. 1966.

ROBERT L. GALE

VAN VOGT, A. E. (26 Apr. 1912–26 Jan. 2000), science fiction writer, was born Alfred Elton van Vogt in Neville, Manitoba, Canada, the son of Henry and Agnes van Vogt. His father was a lawyer but was not particularly well off, and much of van Vogt's childhood was spent in small towns before the family settled in Winnipeg. Van Vogt had a childhood interest in fairy tales and the supernatural, and at age fourteen he discovered science fiction by encountering Hugo Gernsback's newly created magazine *Amazing Stories*. He nevertheless did not consider a writing career until he had worked for a year as a census taker in the Bureau of Statistics in Ottawa. After completing high school, at age nineteen he took a course from the Palmer Institute of Authorship and wrote "I Lived in the Streets," selling it to *True Story*, a "confession" magazine, which in 1932 published it as "No One to Blame but Herself." In 1933 he won a $1,000 prize for "The Miracle in My Life," earning the equivalent of a year's salary as a census taker. Starting in 1934, he wrote a number of plays for Canadian radio, ultimately selling fifty plays but making only $600. In 1939 he married Edna Mayne Hull (1905–1975), a fellow Canadian writer; they collaborated on a revision of *Planets for Sale* (magazine, 1943–1946; book, 1954), *The Winged Man* (magazine, 1944; book, 1966), and *Out of the Unknown* (1948).

In 1939, inspired by John W. Campbell's "Who Goes There?" in the August 1938 issue of *Astounding Science Fiction* and by a pleasant response to a query letter written to Campbell, who was the editor of *Astounding*, van Vogt began to write science fiction. His first story was "Vault of the Beast" (*Astounding*, Aug. 1940), which shares with Campbell's story the idea of a shape-shifting alien; but while Campbell used his alien to create paranoia among an isolated group of humans and to elaborate on the problems of proving one is human, van Vogt's alien was a sentient robotic emissary of a supremely intelligent and unfriendly race requiring human help to open an imprisoning Martian vault.

Campbell held "Vault of the Beast," which became van Vogt's fourth science fiction story to be published. His first published science fiction work was "Black Destroyer" (*Astounding*, July 1939), which is about an intelligent catlike being named Coeurl taken on board a spaceship. Coeurl's craving for phosphorus and his ability to redirect energy result in a number of deaths before his ignorance of human inventions leads to his destruction. "Discord in Scarlet," a sequel utilizing the same crew and a different alien, appeared in the December 1939 issue of *Astounding*. These first two stories and two additional stories were later collected as *The Voyage of the Space Beagle* (1950). Because "Black Destroyer" is vaguely similar in conception to the 1979 motion picture *Alien*, van Vogt took legal action and in 1980 received a $50,000 settlement from Twentieth Century-Fox.

Van Vogt's first novel, *Slan* (*Astounding*, 1940; book, 1946; revised ed., 1951), combines a science fiction background with the traditional fairy-tale motif of an orphan's success. *Slan* is the story of a world in which human mutants—slans—can read minds and possess great endurance but are persecuted, for humanity cannot accept anything greater than itself. The narrative focuses on Jommy Cross, a slan boy whose mother is murdered by a mob as the novel starts. Cross comes of age, invents remarkable devices, and falls in love with a young slan woman, who turns out to be the daughter of the world dictator Kier Gray, himself a secret slan. Despite the weaknesses of its plot *Slan* contains serious subtexts questioning the nature of humans' acceptance of traits deemed abnormal and hinting at fascist persecution of minorities.

Van Vogt's second significant novel was the start of a three-novel cycle loosely known as the Null-A series. Inspired by the writings of Alfred Korzybski and by the General Semantics movement, which held that human problems tended to arise from muddled thinking and sloppy linguistics, van Vogt wrote "The World of Ā" (*Astounding*, 1945; in book form, 1948, as *The World of Null-A*). The story concentrates on Gilbert Gosseyn, who discovers that he is not what he believes himself to be but does not know what he is. Gosseyn (pronounced *go sane*) is chased across planets, killed, and resurrected with dizzying speed. The ultimate questions are of the nature of government, with van Vogt's conclusions being optimistic: that good humans make good machines and good governments. So popular was van Vogt that *The World of Null-A* became the first modern science fiction novel to be published by a major publisher. It was followed by *The Pawns of Null-A* (*Astounding*, 1948–1949 as "The Players of Ā"; book form, 1956) and finally by *Null-A Three* (1984).

In 1944, encouraged by Campbell, van Vogt moved to the United States and settled permanently in Los Angeles, becoming a naturalized American citizen in 1952. Additional notable works from this time include *The Weapon Shops of Isher* (*Astounding*, 1941–1942; book form, 1951) and *The Weapon Makers* (1946, revised ed., 1952), whose themes involve the search for balance between individuals and the state, *The Mixed Men* (*Astounding*, 1943–1945; book form, 1952), and *Empire of the Atom* (*Astounding*, 1946–1947; book form, 1957). The last is a retelling of Robert Graves's *I, Claudius* in a science fiction setting.

Slan, the Null-A series, and many of van Vogt's other works have the thematic idea that humans are latent or potential supermen in need of awakening and educating. Perhaps for that reason, in 1950 van Vogt retired from writing and embraced L. Ron Hubbard's Dianetics, becoming the head of the California Dianetics Foundation. He broke with Hubbard when Dianetics evolved into Scientology, but he remained connected with the California Dianetics movement until the 1980s.

Van Vogt returned to science fiction during the 1960s and in a 1970 letter to Campbell revealed that he was writing six novels exploring the nature of violence but was out of practice and unaware of modern scientific developments. Campbell rejected van Vogt's work—several pieces appeared in the second-tier publications If and Galaxy—and van Vogt's novels attracted ever decreasing audiences. He recycled early material, coining the term "fixup" to describe a book consisting of previously published stories fitted together, often with additional linking material, so they can be read as a novel. He had ceased to be a viable force in American science fiction, though he received a few genre honors and had significant French and Italian followings.

In 1975 E. Mayne Hull died and van Vogt married Lydia Brayman, a linguist and interpreter, in 1979. In 1980 he was awarded the first Caspar Award for his contributions to Canadian science fiction; in 1981 he received Italy's Premio Italiano di Fantascienza award and in 1983 France's Jules Verne Award. In 1996 the Science Fiction Writers of America named him a Grand Master. He developed Alzheimer's disease in the 1980s and died in Fountain View Convalescent Home in Hollywood, California, survived by his second wife, two stepchildren, and a sister. He had written sixty-five novels and collections, three books of nonfiction, and ninety-two short stories, the majority out of print at his death. So unfamiliar had his name become that a 500-copy signed edition of The Battle of Forever published in 1978 was not sold out until 1990.

The tributes from fans and writers were heartfelt yet muted, the majority of the praise coming from older writers who remembered the excitement of reading a new van Vogt story in the pulp magazines— writers who enjoyed his fiction as a quest for absolutes and forgave his inability to provide satisfactory answers to the difficult questions he raised.

From 1939 until the 1950s van Vogt dominated American science fiction, his best stories combining sophisticated ideas with breathtaking narrative drive. Although he is at present largely unread, his influence remains. The much greater science fiction writer Philip K. Dick (1928–1982) was directly inspired by van Vogt's ideas and plots, as was James Blish (1921–1975), who listed van Vogt as a primary influence and early in his career attempted to see if he could "out-van Vogt van Vogt: Write a story as complicated as any of van Vogt's but tie up all the ends." Others who were inspired by him include most of the science fiction writers who came of age from the 1940s through the 1960s.

• Some of van Vogt's papers are held at the University of Wyoming and in the manuscript collection at Syracuse University; a lengthy transcript of an interview is held by the University of California, Los Angeles. Lengthy autobiographical statements by van Vogt appear in Reflections of A. E. van Vogt: The Autobiography of a Science Fiction Giant, with a Complete Bibliography (1975) and in "On 'Black Destroyer'" in Astounding Science Fiction July 1939, as Edited by John W. Campbell, Jr., with memoirs edited by Martin H. Greenberg and a foreword by Stanley Schmidt (1981), a facsimile of the July 1939 issue of Astounding with commentary by the surviving writers.

The scholarly literature on van Vogt is relatively small, but he is accorded sympathetic biobibliographic discussion in Brian Aldiss and David Wingrove, Trillion Year Spree: The History of Science Fiction (1986); John Clute, "A. E. van Vogt," in The Encyclopedia of Science Fiction, ed. Clute and Peter Nicholls (1993); Sam Moskowitz, Seekers of Tomorrow: Masters of Modern Science Fiction (1966; repr. 1974); David Ketterer, Canadian Science Fiction and Fantasy (1992); Alexei and Cory Panshin, The World beyond the Hill: Science Fiction and the Quest for Transcendence (1989); Hazel Pierce, "A. E. van Vogt," in St. James Guide to Science Fiction Writers, 4th ed., ed. Jay P. Pederson (1996); and Colin Wilson, "A. E. van Vogt," in Science Fiction Writers: Critical Studies of the Major Authors from the Early Nineteenth Century to the Present Day, 2d ed., ed. Richard Bleiler (1999). Phil Stephensen-Payne and Ian Covell, A. E. van Vogt, Master of Null-A: A Working Bibliography (1997), is the most comprehensive primary bibliography extant.

Significant critical backlash first appears in 1945, with Damon Knight's "Cosmic Jerrybuilder: A. E. van Vogt," which mercilessly details van Vogt's deficient plots, inadequate characterizations, shoddy backgrounds, and poor prose. Knight, it may be argued, was strictly rational and recognized neither the irrational emotional power of van Vogt's work nor his grappling with ideas, but his essay achieved importance after it received book publication and is readily available in In Search of Wonder: Essays on Modern Science Fiction (1956; 2d ed., 1967). In 1947 van Vogt's essay "Complication in the Science Fiction Story" provided his critics with one of their recurrent arguments, for van Vogt revealed that one of his chief compositional principles was to write his stories in 800-word scenes, effectively introducing a new idea or new plot twist with every new scene. The essay first appeared in Of Worlds Beyond: The Science of Science Fiction Writing, a Symposium by Robert A. Heinlein, John Taine, Jack Williamson, A. E. van Vogt, L. Sprague de Camp, Edward E. Smith, Ph.D., John W. Campbell, Jr., ed. Lloyd Arthur Eshbach (1947).

Obituaries and appreciations of van Vogt appear in the New York Times, 4 Feb. 2000, and Locus, Mar. 2000.

RICHARD BLEILER

VELEZ, Lupe (18 July 1909–14 Dec. 1944), actress, was born Maria Guadalupe Vélez Villalobos in San Luis de Potosi, Mexico. Her father may have been a pharmacist named Jacob Villalobos or, as Velez claimed, a colonel in the Mexican Army nicknamed "El Gallo" (the Rooster) by his troops. Her mother, Josefina Velez, was an opera singer or a prostitute, or both.

Velez briefly attended the convent school of Our Lady of the Lake, run by the Sisters of Divine Providence in San Antonio, Texas, in 1923. Her father died when Velez was in her teens, so she returned to her family in Mexico, probably in order to help them financially. She was hired as a sales clerk in the Nacional Department Store in Mexico City. Possessed of enormous vitality and self-confidence, Velez resolved to make it big in show business and continued to take lessons in dancing and singing.

In 1924 Velez was hired to dance in *Ra-Ta-Plan*, a musical revue. She set out for Los Angeles in 1926 when she was offered a chance to audition for stage actor Richard Bennett's upcoming production of the Broadway hit *The Dove* by Willard Mack. The audition was disappointing and exposed her lack of experience. Nevertheless, she decided to stay in Los Angeles and was soon exhibiting her energy and high spirits as a dancer in Fanchon and Marco's *Music Box Revue*, starring Fannie Brice. Producer Hal Roach saw her and gave her a three-year contract. Roach's studio produced the popular Laurel and Hardy series of comic two-reelers and could always accommodate a beautiful actress with comedic ability who was willing to be hit in the face with a pie or two. Velez appeared in two of Roach's comic shorts, *What Women Did For Me* and *Sailors Beware*, both released in 1927. Swashbuckler Douglas Fairbanks, Sr. then cast her as the Mountain Girl in *The Gaucho* (1928). A silent film with the opening sequence shot in color, *The Gaucho* was a far-fetched tale of miracles, bandits, and cattle stampedes. In this part Velez "undertook the first in a string of fire-spitting vamps" (Hadley-Garcia, p. 45). Her performance earned lavish praise from critics for her comedic skills and acting abilities. *Variety* dubbed her "a feminine Fairbanks" (9 Nov. 1927).

Velez became a bona fide star in her next film, *Wolf Song* (1929). The *New York Times* characterized this mostly silent film as "a picture with periodical outbursts of melody" (25 Feb. 1929). It was directed by Victor Fleming and starred Gary Cooper. Velez and Cooper then embarked on what became a three-year affair with the cooperation and blessing of the Paramount Pictures publicity machine. Their relationship was marked by rages, tearful reunions, and epic brawls fueled by alcohol, in public and in private. Velez and Cooper might have married had Cooper's mother not disapproved of her so vehemently. A vengeful Velez once fired several shots at Cooper with a revolver as he boarded the Twentieth Century in Los Angeles.

Out of the upheaval sound technology had brought to Hollywood, one fact emerged—the film actor's voice became all-important. In the fantasy-fed world of 1930s Hollywood, an exotic accent was highly desirable, on screen or off, and Velez could match hers with Greta Garbo's or Marlene Dietrich's. She admittedly exaggerated her speech, and "Lupeisms" became a part of her act, as when she declared, "Sometimes I sound just like Donald *Duke*" (quoted in Hadley-Garcia, p. 53). *Tiger Rose* (1928 or 1929) was the first all-talking film in which she appeared, but in the part of Rose, a French-Canadian orphan, she was playing what "had become a stereotyped assignment

for her, that of a fiery half-caste" (Parish, p. 599). She was directed by D. W. Griffith in *Lady of the Pavements* (1929), by William Wyler in *The Storm* (1930), and by Cecil B. De Mille in *The Squaw Man* (1931). Gregory La Cava directed her in *The Half-Naked-Truth*, a comedy, in 1933.

In 1932 New York audiences saw Velez erupt on Broadway in *Ha-Cha!*, produced by Florenz Ziegfeld and also starring Bert Lahr, which ran for 119 performances (Parish, p. 603). She starred the following year with Jimmy Durante in the revue *Strike Me Pink*. New York Times critic Brooks Atkinson wrote approvingly of her "incendiary abandon" (*New York Times*, 6 Mar. 1933). Velez's last appearance on Broadway was in 1938 in Cole Porter's *You Never Know* with Clifton Webb. In it she sang, danced, and gave impressions of Shirley Temple and Katharine Hepburn.

Back in Hollywood Velez appeared in comedies and in lighter fare such as *Hot Pepper* (1933), *Hollywood Party* (1934), *Palooka* (1934), and *Gypsy Melody* (1936), which she filmed in England. Also in England, Velez charmed London audiences in the musical revue *Transatlantic Rhythm*. Velez married Olympic swimming champion–turned–actor Johnny Weissmuller in 1933. The couple had no children and were divorced in 1938.

Universal Pictures, to whom she was under contract at the time, exploited Velez's huge Latin and Central American following by remaking many of her films in Spanish. Velez herself went to Mexico in 1937 to shoot *La Zandunga*. It was a critical success in the United States and a huge box-office draw with Latino audiences everywhere.

Resigned by now to being labeled a "firecracker" and a "hot tamale," Velez agreed to make *The Girl from Mexico* (1939) for RKO Pictures. She played Carmelita Fuentes in what James Robert Parish called "[m]indless entertainment of high satisfaction for audiences of the day" (Parish, p. 616). This success led to the highly popular *Mexican Spitfire* series, which included *Mexican Spitfire at Sea* and *Mexican Spitfire Sees a Ghost* (both released in 1942), *Mexican Spitfire's Blessed Event* (1943), and several more. In an odd pairing, *Mexican Spitfire's Baby* was cofeatured along with *Citizen Kane* when it opened in New York (Parish, p. 619).

In 1943 Velez returned to Mexico to star in a new film version of Emile Zola's *Nana*, the story of the Parisian courtesan. Directed by Celestino Corostiza, *Nana* premiered in Mexico City in June, 1944. Reviews were mixed, but all agreed that Velez had given "the best performance of her career" (Parish, p. 622).

Over the years, Velez had liaisons with many men, including John Gilbert, Errol Flynn, Arturo de Cordova, and Gilbert Roland. In 1943 she met a drifter, sometimes described as an actor, named Harald Ramond. (According to the *Los Angeles Times*, 15 Dec. 1944, his name was Harald Ramond Maresch.) In November 1944 Velez announced their intention to marry. A few weeks later, in December, she suddenly stated that the relationship was over. Later it was learned that she was four months pregnant and in despair, in part because Ramond was proving to be unsupportive.

On the night of 13 December 1944, Velez donned her blue silk pajamas, climbed into her oversized white bed, and swallowed an overdose of Seconal, a potent sedative. She died in the hours before the housekeeper found her the following morning. Velez left behind two scribbled suicide notes: an accusatory one for the irresponsible Ramond and one to Mrs. Kinder, her secretary and friend, in which she begged everyone, including God, to forgive her. Years of failed relationships, alcohol, and an unwanted pregnancy in an unenlightened age had all taken their toll. Her final request was that her pets be cared for.

On 15 December 1944, the Los Angeles Times ran the story of Velez's death as a front-page news item. Before Velez's funeral, 4,000 of her fans filed past her casket at the Church of the Recessional at Forest Lawn Cemetery in Glendale, California (Parish, p. 624). In *Hispanic Hollywood*, George Hadley-Garcia called Velez one of the two "most successful Mexican actresses ever to work in Hollywood" (the other being Dolores Del Rio) (Hadley-Garcia, p. 27).

• Informative sources on Velez's life and career are James Robert Parish, *The RKO Gals* (1974); George Hadley-Garcia, *Hispanic Hollywood: The Latins in Motion Pictures* (1990); Jane Ellen Wayne, *Cooper's Women* (1988); and Alfonso Pinto, "Lupe Velez 1909–1944," *Films in Review*, Nov. 1977, pp. 513–25.

ANDREA WEEVER

VERDON, Gwen (13 Jan. 1925–18 Oct. 2000), dancer and actress, was born Gwyneth Evelyn Verdon in Culver City, California, the daughter of William Joseph Verdon, a film studio electrician, and Gertrude Lillian Standring Verdon, a Denishawn dance instructor. Verdon began studying dance when she was very young as therapy for a series of infantile ailments that left her knock-kneed and required her to wear high-topped, corrective boots during her childhood. She made her stage debut at the age of four and by age six was billed as the "Fastest Little Tapper in the World." Verdon trained in a variety of dance styles with notable instructors, including ballet teacher Ernest Belcher and, later, ethnic dancer La Meri. She danced in local civic opera productions and, as a teen-ager, was part of a ballroom team, Verdon and Del Velle.

When she was seventeen Verdon eloped with James Henaghan, a Hollywood reporter who drank excessively. During their marriage she gained journalism experience covering Hollywood gossip and writing nightclub and movie reviews, as she often had to finish putting together her freewheeling husband's column. The couple had a son in 1943 and divorced in 1947.

Verdon then resumed her dance career and began working for Jack Cole, the pioneering American jazz dance choreographer. She became one of the foremost interpreters of his challenging jazz style distinguished by its incorporation of East Indian, African-American and Latin-American dance influences. Verdon performed with Cole's troupe in nightclubs, danced for him in *Bonanza Bound* (a 1947 Broadway-bound musical that folded after its Philadelphia tryouts) and was his assistant choreographer for the 1948 Broadway musical *Magdalena*. In 1950 Verdon assisted Cole and danced with him in the Broadway revue *Alive and Kicking*.

Under contract to Twentieth Century-Fox, Verdon "danced-in" for stars on long shots, coached them in Cole's choreography, and dubbed in sounds of footsteps. She also appeared in specialty dance solos created by Cole in the films *David and Bathsheba* (1951), *Meet Me after the Show* (1951), *On the Riviera* (1951), *The Merry Widow* (MGM, 1952), *The I Don't Care Girl* (1953), and *The Farmer Takes a Wife* (1953), in which she also had an acting role. Verdon performed her own choreography in the films *Dreamboat* (1952) and *The Mississippi Gambler* (Universal, 1953).

In 1953 Verdon created a sensation on Broadway in the dance role, Claudine, in the musical *Can-Can*, choreographed by Michael Kidd. Her spellbinding dancing and effervescent humor eclipsed the show's leading lady, the French chanteuse Lilo, and elicited excited praise from the critics. For her performance, Verdon won the Tony Award for best supporting actress and Donaldson Awards for supporting actress and female dancer.

Following a brief return to Hollywood to dance for Cole in *Gentlemen Marry Brunettes* (United Artists, 1955), Verdon was cast in the 1955 Broadway musical hit *Damn Yankees*, in the role for which she is best known, the temptress Lola. A milestone in her career, and in the history of American musical theater dance, *Damn Yankees* paired, for the first time, the performing talents of Verdon and the choreographic imagination of Bob Fosse. Verdon's exquisitely trained body—from her years of rigorous work under Cole's tutelage—became the primary instrument and inspiration for the development of Fosse's distinctive Broadway jazz style.

Verdon followed her Tony Award-winning performance in *Damn Yankees* (which she repeated in the 1958 film version of the musical) with starring roles in the Broadway musicals *New Girl in Town* (1957) and *Redhead* (1958), both choreographed by Fosse. She garnered rave reviews and a Tony Award for each show. Fosse's work so keenly showcased her enchanting physical and comedic talents that Verdon soon emerged as the American musical theater's preeminent dancer-actress.

Verdon and Fosse married in 1960 and had a daughter in 1963. In 1966, Verdon returned to the Broadway stage in the title role of the musical *Sweet Charity*, directed and choreographed by Fosse. Even though Shirley MacLaine was cast in the 1969 film version of the show instead of her, Verdon traveled to Hollywood and taught Charity's dances to MacLaine, thus beginning her untiring commitment to reconstructing Fosse's work. Though the couple legally separated in 1971, Fosse gave Verdon the opportunity to create the role of the murderess Roxie Hart—a character she had longed to portray for years—in the Broadway musical *Chicago*, which Fosse directed and choreographed in 1975. Verdon assisted Fosse on his Broadway choreographic revue *Dancin'* (1978), his autobiographical film *All That Jazz* (1979), and a 1986 Broadway revival of *Sweet Charity*. In 1999 Verdon served as artistic adviser for the musical revue *Fosse*, Broadway's retrospective tribute to the choreographer.

During the last two decades of her life Verdon performed acting roles in movies and on television. She appeared in the films *Sgt. Pepper's Lonely Hearts Club Band* (1978), *The Cotton Club* (1984), *Cocoon* (1985), *Nadine* (1987), *Cocoon: The Return* (1988), *Alice* (1990), *Marvin's Room* (1996), *Bruno* (2000), and *Walking Across Egypt*, released in 2001. She was in the television movies *Legs* (1983), *The Jerk, Too* (1984), *Oldest Living Confederate Widow Tells All* (1994), *In Cold Blood* (1996), and *Best Friends for Life* (1998), and appeared on *M*A*S*H*, among other television series. Verdon died of a heart attack in Woodstock, Vermont.

A muse for the two choreographers most responsible for creating the dance style recognized as Broadway jazz, Verdon came to prominence during the Broadway musical's terpsichorean era—when choreographers were commandeering the role of director, and dance was usurping the dramatic responsibilities of song and speech. Furthering the achievements of performers such as Joan McCracken and Carol Haney, Verdon represented the pinnacle in the development of the Broadway musical's dancer-actress. She proved repeatedly that a dancing comedienne in a starring role could light up a musical with astonishing wattage. With her elfin smile, sassy red hair, perfectly proportioned figure, and raspy baby-doll voice, she tickled her way into the hearts of Broadway audiences and left an indelible mark on the American musical theater.

• The archival Bob Fosse/Gwen Verdon Collection at the Library of Congress contains video recordings of some of Verdon's film and television appearances and sound recordings from her stage performances. The Dance Division of the New York Public Library for the Performing Arts has a short film clip of Verdon in *Alive and Kicking* as well as video recordings of Verdon dancing and/or being interviewed for television documentary programs. The Library's Dance Division and its Billy Rose Theatre Collection have large clipping files for Verdon and photographs of her. Many of Verdon's films, including *Damn Yankees*, are commercially available for rent or purchase. The Museum of Television and Radio in New York has samples of Verdon's television appearances, including a 1962 "American Musical Theatre" program, in which she dances with Fosse, and a videotaped interview she granted the museum in 1999. Noteworthy journalistic profiles of Verdon include William Hawkin, "Something about Gwen Verdon," *Dance Magazine*, August 1956; Robert Wahls, "Gwen Verdon, the Eternal Gypsy," [New York] *Sunday News*, 1 June 1975; Hilton Als, "One of the Boys," *New York Times Magazine*, 7 Jan. 2001; and Margery Beddow, "Remembering Gwen Verdon," *Dance Teacher*, Apr. 2001. An informative analysis of Verdon's contributions to the Broadway musical can be found in Ethan Mordden, *Broadway Babies* (1983). An obituary is in the *New York Times*, 19 Oct. 2000.

LISA JO SAGOLLA

VESTEY, Evelyn (1 Aug. 1875–23 May 1941), business executive, known as Lady Vestey, was born Evelene Brodstone in Monroe, Wisconsin, the daughter of Hans Brodstone and Mathilde Brodstone (maiden name unknown), Norwegian immigrants. In 1878, the family moved to a farm near Superior, Nebraska. The following year her father died. As a youngster, one of her closest friends was Willa Cather. Cather lived in Red Cloud, about twenty-five miles from Superior. The girls often rode their bicycles to visit each other.

At age thirteen the precocious Evelene wrote an essay entitled "The Opinions, Tastes and Fancies of Evalina Brodstone." The change in her name signaled a mind that was very much her own. She declared that the place she most wanted to visit was London and, with a kind of eerie prescience, announced that she intended to marry a millionaire. At age fourteen, she was the youngest graduate ever from Superior High School. She then studied accounting and stenography at Elliott's Business College in Burlington, Iowa. Afterward, she returned to Superior where she worked for various businesses.

In 1895, ambitious to do more, Brodstone moved to Chicago, where she became a stenographer at the Vestey brothers' Union Cold Storage Company. This was a meat packing and refrigerating enterprise with home offices in Liverpool, England. In 1876, seventeen-year-old William Vestey had been sent to Chicago by his father to open a canning factory and obtain cheap cuts of beef for export to England. By 1882, his brother Edmund had become manager of the Chicago company, and William returned to England. One day when Edmund Vestey's private secretary was unavailable for dictation, Evalina Brodstone filled in. She was so efficient that he promoted her. Her new duties included taking notes and writing minutes. Her memory was remarkable; her opinions were invaluable. Eventually she became a board member and auditor of the Chicago office.

In 1896 the company's headquarters were relocated to London, and the Liverpool import business was expanded. Edmund Vestey returned to England leaving Brodstone in charge of the Chicago operation, but soon the Vesteys asked her to help set up the new offices in London. She arrived in England on 9 May 1897. At work she was general auditor and troubleshooter. At leisure, she visited historical places, studied art appreciation, went to the theater, and read. She took physical fitness classes and enjoyed canoeing. She dated several men and was romantically involved with one, Bernard Finch, for six years.

Often when William Vestey was in London, he treated Brodstone to dinner and the theater. Vestey was married, but there were signs that his wife was both mentally and physically ill. Although there were rumors about the nature of his relationship with Brodstone, she was circumspect in her dealings with him. Well liked and respected by the Vestey family, she knew that they relied on her both personally and professionally. Three years after she arrived in London, her mother joined her. In June 1901 she became head auditor and signed a five-year contract. In March 1902 Brodstone went to Riga, Russia (now Latvia) to set up a bookkeeping system at the Vestey's new plant there. Because her three-month stay was impeded by her inability to speak Russian fluently, she was determined never to suffer that indignity again. She subsequently learned twelve languages.

Brodstone's five-year contract expired on 30 April 1906. Later that year, she and her mother spent three months in Nebraska visiting friends. Then she signed a second five-year contract with the Vesteys and returned to London. By this time, she was a stockholder in the company and one of its most valued employees. A skilled troubleshooter, she traveled extensively on behalf of the company. When a South African manager embezzled a large sum of money and disappeared, she traveled around the world until she caught the culprit. When the company needed her to inspect the vast herds of cattle ranging in Venezuela, her trip included a thousand-mile trip on the Orinoco River and weeks of riding horseback with a pack train.

In the early 1900s steamships provided the main method of transporting goods across oceans, and long travel times were naturally a problem for exporters of meat and produce. In 1909 the Blue Star Shipping Line was born when the Vestey company was able to buy two steamships outfitted with refrigeration. The fleet grew to include forty ships, one of which was named *Brodstone*. By now powerful and wealthy, Evalina Brodstone remained a small-town Nebraska girl at heart. She and her mother wanted to share a home with her older brother, Lewis, in Superior. Between 1907 and 1914, the two women made several trips there. In Superior, she was a board member of a semiprofessional baseball association, shocking some townspeople who felt that baseball was only for men. When she traveled out of town with the team, a woman friend always accompanied her for propriety's sake. In 1914, when her second contract with the Vesteys expired, she returned to Superior intending to settle into small town life permanently.

If Brodstone had a major personality flaw, it was that she was somewhat inflexible. People said of her that when her mind was set, it stayed there. Yet one man was successful in changing it repeatedly. Each time she decided to retire, William Vestey talked her into just one more trip for the company. In August 1914, when England entered the First World War, the Vestey company was awarded contracts to feed both British and Allied troops. To accomplish this, the company needed to expand, and Brodstone's negotiating skills were requested. She went to Buenos Aires, Argentina, to buy into its meat industry. Then she

went on to Australia to buy six million acres of land and employ aborigines to raise cattle. As the first white woman to journey into the interior, she was accompanied by white male Vestey company employees and a large black man who served as a bodyguard. Controversy has arisen in modern times about the Vestey company's dealings with Australia's aboriginal people. Nevertheless, Brodstone accomplished what no other woman had done: she survived hazardous conditions and almost single-handedly set up an important food source for Allied troops.

When the war was over in 1918, Brodstone went back to Superior. She was forty-three years old and her salary was $250,000 a year, making her the highest-paid woman executive in the world. In Superior, she was asked to run for mayor but decided to accept a position on the Park Board instead. Because of a series of unfortunate circumstances, Superior's hospital was closed for a year and a half. With the arrival of the great flu epidemic of the time, centralized health care was imperative. In one of the town's fundraising efforts, Brodstone solicited donations door-to-door, and in May 1919 the hospital reopened.

In 1922 William Vestey traveled to Superior to convince Brodstone to handle some problems at the company's enterprises in Hankow, China. She completed her business, but revolution in the province caused her to travel downriver to Shanghai, spend a few weeks in Japan and return to Superior by way of Europe, Siberia, and Russia. In 1924 William Vestey was in Buenos Aires when he broke his leg. Now a widower, he asked Brodstone to join him there, finish their business, and accompany him back to England. When she arrived, he proposed and she accepted. They were married in New York City on her forty-ninth birthday, 1 August 1924. At William's request, she changed her name to Evelyn, which he felt better suited the wife of an English lord. So she was now Evelyn, Lady Vestey, wife of a multimillionaire residing in London, England, fulfilling her teenage prophecies.

Shortly after the wedding, the Vesteys learned that their plant in Rio de Janeiro, Brazil, was on fire. The new Lady Vestey left immediately for Rio and their honeymoon was canceled. Then her mother died. The Vesteys went to Superior to help Lewis Brodstone settle the estate. The siblings decided to build a new Brodstone Memorial Hospital dedicated to their mother's memory, and it opened on 1 January 1928. A poetic tribute to her mother written by Willa Cather was placed on a bronze plaque near the entrance.

Lord and Lady Vestey lived in London but kept their ties with Superior. In the 1930s, Lady Vestey anonymously sent Thanksgiving and Christmas dinners to the needy in Superior. She also set up a $3,000 rotating educational scholarship loan through the Federation of Women's Clubs. The scholarship money she provided was always in the form of loans rather than gifts because she felt it was important for people to learn self-reliance. (Today, Superior High School students are eligible for an annual scholarship administered through a fund derived from the interest on the original loan fund. This scholarship goes to an outstanding four-year student of history and the social sciences.) There was one exception to the loan rule. Each year Lady Vestey sent every first grader in Superior a Christmas gift so that every child, regardless of parental circumstances, could participate in the Christmas spirit. She also gave money to establish a bird sanctuary in the city's park and a new bridge over the creek. She and Lewis provided funds for a softball field. Lewis died in 1936.

Lord Vestey died on 10 December 1940 at the age of eighty-one. Lady Vestey died just five months later in Buckingham, England. She was sixty-five. Five years after her death, Lady Vestey's ashes were sent to Superior and placed on her mother's grave. The mayor issued a proclamation that all business should cease for the duration of the memorial services, a first in Superior's history. A collection of Lady Vestey's belongings is displayed in the Nuckolls County Museum in Superior. Each Memorial Day weekend she is commemorated by the Lady Vestey Victorian Festival, which attracts thousands of visitors.

• The only biography of Lady Vestey is Elizabeth J. Tremain, *Evelene: The Troubleshooter Was a Lady* (1985; repr., 1992). Also see the article "Leave it to Nebraska Woman; She Can Straighten Out Things," Omaha *Sunday World-Herald*, 3 Dec. 1911. Personal letters to her friends and articles about her have been published in the *Superior Express*. An obituary is in the *New York Times*, 24 May 1941.

JEAN SANDERS

VICKREY, William S. (21 June 1914–11 Oct. 1996), Nobel Prize–winning economist, was born William Spencer Vickrey in Victoria, British Columbia, Canada, the son of Charles Vernon Vickrey, an executive with the nonprofit organization Near East Relief, and Ada Eliza Spencer Vickrey. After his family relocated to the New York City area in 1914, he grew up surrounded by the victims of the Armenian massacres, an experience that left him with a profoundly developed social conscience. Between graduating from high school and enrolling at Yale, he attended prep school for a year. Interested in electrical engineering and sociology as well as a host of other subjects, he obtained his college degree in mathematics with high honors in 1935.

After deciding on economics as a career, Vickrey received his master's degree in that subject from Columbia University in 1937. He took a string of jobs within the profession. serving as a junior economist at the Natural Resources Committee in Washington (1937–1938), a predoctoral field fellow with the Social Science Research Council (1938–1939), a research assistant at the Twentieth Century Fund (1939–1940), an economist at the Office of Price Administration (1940–1941), and a senior economist in the U.S. Treasury Department's Division of Tax Research (1941–1943). A conscientious objector during World War II, he did a three-year stint of public ser-

vice and continued to study economics at the graduate level. In 1946 Vickrey joined the faculty at Columbia as a lecturer in economics and participated in an assignment that charged him with the design and installation of a new inheritance tax for the Commonwealth of Puerto Rico, the first of many such tax commissions, including the one responsible for designing the postwar Japanese tax system.

Vickrey's dissertation was published in 1947 under the title *Agenda for Progressive Taxation*, and the following year he received both his Ph.D. and an appointment to the Columbia faculty as an assistant professor. He remained at Columbia for the balance of his career, with promotions to associate professor in 1950 and full professor in 1958 and the honor of being named McVickar Professor of Political Economy in 1971. On 21 July 1951 he married Cecile Montez Thompson; the couple had no children.

During the course of his long career, Vickrey published several path-breaking theoretical and applied works on such topics as efficient auction markets, utility theory under risk, and most notably, the nature of marginal cost pricing in public and private transportation. As an undergraduate at Yale, he had noted the number of empty seats on railroad trains as he traveled to visit his parents' home in Scarsdale, New York, which prompted him to theorize that if the railroads were to cut their prices at non-peak hours, his classmates might be induced to travel more often, and that both parties would benefit from the transaction. While working at Twentieth Century Fund, he had analyzed the pricing practices of public utilities and came to the conclusion that the same principle might be usefully applied in this arena as well. In 1951, called on to study transit fares as part of New York City Mayor William O'Dwyer's Committee on Management Survey, Vickrey concluded that the field of mass transit also held promise for his theory. Long interested in solutions to practical problems, Vickrey was occasionally exasperated with his profession, leading him to remark, "Too many economists are basically astronomers, admiring our wonderful free-market systems, or weathermen, predicting what the economy is going to do."

Although his proposals made a great deal of sense (even if the technology of the day did not always exist to carry them out), Vickrey often found his ideas ignored. A 1959 proposal to equip motor vehicles with transponders that would monitor the number of times a particular vehicle entered a congested traffic zone—with the owner being billed accordingly—met with (in Vickrey's words) "discreet silence" when he testified before a Congressional committee investigating Washington, D.C., traffic conditions.

Despite the general indifference of policy-makers, Vickrey continued to develop and expand his ideas, publishing two volumes on economic theory in 1964, *Microstatics* and *Metastatics and Macroeconomics*. In the early 1960s he authored two highly regarded papers on the theory of bidding during auctions, concluding that the winners of a sealed bid auction should only have to pay the amount bid by the second highest bidder, a practice that Vickrey claimed would result in bidders offering the highest price that they could afford. He was also interested in the area of tax reform and during the 1960s advocated a proposal for the "cumulative assessment of income taxes" that would keep the progressive nature of American income taxes while eliminating many of the required forms. Vickrey claimed that his proposal would have "put the Internal Revenue Service out of business," but it was not seriously considered. Respected by his peers, he served as chairman of his department at Columbia between 1964 and 1967 and in 1976 was the subject of a festschrift, *Public and Urban Economists: Essays in Honor of William S. Vickrey*. In demand as a consultant within private industry, he also served the United Nations as an adviser on taxes in 1974–1975.

Although Vickrey officially retired in 1982, he remained active both on campus and as a policy advocate. He was (against the conventional wisdom) a strong advocate of full employment within the economy, and in his later years attacked what he considered to be an obsession on the part of governments with balancing budgets and eliminating fiscal deficits (see the essays in *Commitment to Full Employment: The Economics and Social Policy of Williams S. Vickrey*, ed. A. W. Warner et al. [2000]). Late in his career, ideas that he had long advocated began to gain credence, with Hong Kong and Singapore adopting variations of his proposals on traffic control. He served as president of the American Economic Association in 1992. In 1996 he shared the Nobel Prize for economics with James A. Mirrlees of the University of Cambridge, "for their fundamental contributions to the economic theory of incentives under asymmetric information." Vickrey's time in the limelight was tragically short. He died of a heart attack several days after learning of his award, in Harrison, New York, while en route to conference in Massachusetts.

Although denied the "bully pulpit" that he had so long sought, William Vickrey will be remembered both for the originality of his theories and for his influence on numerous students. Once dismissed as impractical, his ideas are now in evidence in such everyday phenomena as peakload pricing and E-ZPass technologies at highway tollbooths.

• Although Vickrey did not leave a collection of papers, one can find in the archives at Columbia University a small amount of his professional correspondence as well as a clippings file. In addition to the volumes already cited, he published in 1994 *Public Economics,* a collection of several of his papers. His career received coverage in *Challenge* magazine, Mar./Apr. 1993, and the *New York Times,* 4 Jan. 1992. Descriptions of the work for which Vickrey and Mirrlees won the Nobel Prize are in the *Scandinavian Journal of Economics* 99, no. 2 (1997): 173–77, and the *Journal of Economic Perspectives* 13, no. 1 (1999): 165–80. Obituaries are in the *Boston Globe* and the *New York Times,* both 12 Oct. 1996.

EDWARD L. LACH, JR.

W

WALD, George (18 Nov. 1906–12 Apr. 1997), biologist, was born on the Lower East Side of New York City to Isaac Wald, a Polish immigrant who worked as a tailor in a garment factory, and his wife, Ernestine Rosenmann Wald, originally from Bavaria. Raised in a poor Jewish household in Brooklyn, young George was encouraged by both parents to excel in school. He exhibited an early interest in science and developed a reputation in his working-class neighborhood for mechanical aptitude. In one notable instance Wald, not yet thirteen, rigged up a crystal radio so that he and his friends could listen to the 1919 World Series. During his years at the Brooklyn Manual Training High School, he improved upon an innate talent for building mechanical devices; he later noted that the skills he learned there subsequently helped him to build specialized equipment for his lab work. For recreation, Wald organized an amateur vaudeville ensemble of fellow students that performed stunts and musical comedy acts at Jewish community centers. Wald had intended to become an electrical engineer, but his success onstage suggested to him the possibility of becoming a lawyer, and following graduation in 1923 he enrolled as a prelaw student at New York University's Washington Square College, his tuition paid by family savings. He also supported himself during his college years by working summers as a crewman aboard a passenger ship sailing between New York and Argentina.

In college Wald was introduced to art history and classical music, and both became passions that remained with him for the rest of his life. He found his prelaw studies boring, however, and switched to a premedical program. He became especially drawn to biology, and his interest in that subject grew even as his desire to become a doctor waned. In his senior year Wald read Sinclair Lewis's novel *Arrowsmith*, whose title character is a microbiologist, and he decided to become a biological researcher. After graduating in 1927 with a B.S. degree, he began graduate work in the biology department at Columbia University, working as a graduate assistant to Selig Hecht, a prominent biophysicist. Hecht, whose specialty was eye physiology, treated Wald as a colleague in his research on vision in fruit flies and became his mentor. Wald in turn came to revere Hecht, and their close and productive relationship led Wald to specialize as well in the physiology of vision.

Wald earned a master's degree in 1928 and a Ph.D. four years later, although it was revealed after his death that the doctoral degree was never officially conferred because he had not fulfilled the requirement of having copies of his dissertation printed for distribution. Upon graduation Wald received a National

Research Council fellowship in biology, enabling him to do two years of postgraduate study. He spent the 1932–1933 academic year abroad, initially working with the prominent German biochemist Otto Warburg, a recent Nobel Prize winner, at his Berlin laboratory. There, in the course of Wald's ongoing research in the physiology of vision, he became the first person to locate vitamin A in the retina, a first step in understanding that vitamin's importance to eyesight and a discovery that would prove crucial to Wald's later research. Vitamin A had only recently been identified, its isolation achieved at the Zurich laboratory of another prominent scientist, Paul Karrer; at Warburg's instigation Wald traveled to Zurich to confirm his finding. After several months there he went on to Heidelberg to work with still another prominent scientist, Otto Myerhoff, a specialist in cell biology. Upon returning to the United States in the fall of 1933, Wald began the second year of his fellowship, working as a researcher in the physiology department at the University of Chicago during the 1933–1934 academic year.

Wald began his virtually lifelong association with Harvard University in the fall of 1934, when he joined the faculty as a tutor in biochemical science. The following year he became an instructor and tutor in biology and held that position until 1939, at which time he was promoted to faculty instructor. Wald became an associate professor in 1944, and four years later he was made a full professor. In addition to his Harvard affiliation, Wald spent most summers from the mid-1930s onward at the Marine Biological Laboratory in Woods Hole, Massachusetts, doing research and teaching a course in physiology. Wald remained at Harvard and Woods Hole for the remainder of his professional life, leaving only once to become a visiting professor of biochemistry at the University of California, Berkeley, in the summer of 1956.

From his first years at Harvard, Wald focused on vision research on a variety of animals, making pioneering discoveries about visual pigmentation and the ways in which the human eye responds to light, passing messages to the brain through the actions of receptors in the retina called rods and cones. Early on, Wald was able to demonstrate that yellow, the color of the eye's natural lens, enabled the eye to focus in the presence of a normal color spectrum; in the absence of yellow, the eye could see with precision in ultraviolet, or "black," light but was unable to distinguish objects clearly in ordinary illumination. In the 1940s, aided by his laboratory assistants Ruth Hubbard and Paul Brown, Wald turned his attention to the properties of rods, the eye's noncolor receptors that distinguish only shades of gray. He was subsequently able to identify the chemical agent in rods as a compound pigment called rhodopsin, or "visual purple," derived from a protein called opsin that existed in combination with a form of vitamin A; in 1950 Wald became the first person to successfully synthesize rhodopsin in the laboratory.

In the 1950s Wald turned his attention to cones, the eye's color receptors, and his research ultimately identified cone pigments sensitive to red, yellow, and green as other forms of vitamin A combined with opsin. The development of electronic microspectrometers by the early 1960s enabled Wald and his fellow researchers at Harvard to identify the heretofore elusive blue-sensitive pigment in still other cones; again, variants of vitamin A were components, along with protein. Coincidentally, an identical discovery was made at the same time by scientists at Johns Hopkins University.

Wald's determination that vitamin A played a critical role in eyesight had important implications beyond the laboratory. His work and the subsequent findings of other scientists demonstrated that adequate amounts of vitamin A in the human body were essential to visual health. Moreover, studies conducted by Wald in the 1960s demonstrated that color blindness resulted from a lack of one of the three pigments found in rods and cones. Over the years Wald received major recognition for his contributions to science, including election to membership in professional societies and honorary degrees, as well as an Eli Lilly Award for biochemical research in 1939, the Lasker Prize in 1953, and the Rumford Prize from the American Academy of Arts and Sciences in 1959. In 1967 Wald and Ruth Hubbard, to whom he was now married, jointly received the Paul Karrer Medal from the University of Zurich. That same year, Wald was named a winner of the Nobel Prize in medicine for his work on the biochemistry of photoreceptors; his two co-recipients were recognized for neurological research in eye function.

Wald continued to do research as well as teach at Harvard and Woods Hole for another decade. In 1968 he was named Higgins Professor of Biology at Harvard and held that chair until his retirement in 1977; at that time he was named professor emeritus. Although successful researchers are often not similarly gifted in the classroom, Wald was a notable exception, earning high praise from students for his teaching skills, and his classes were always oversubscribed. By the time he retired, however, Wald had become perhaps even better known in the United States for his political activities, which dated back more than a decade. In the 1960s he had become one of the first academics to openly protest the Vietnam War and was one of the signers of a letter to that effect which appeared in the *New York Times* in 1965. His antiwar activities, which included making speeches, participating in protest marches, and leading teach-ins, increased after he received the Nobel Prize. A speech he gave in 1969 at the Massachusetts Institute of Technology titled "A Generation in Search of a Future" attracted wide media attention and was reprinted in a number of newspapers, including the *New York Times*.

Wald's antiwar activities earned him a certain notoriety, and he later learned that he had been placed on President Richard M. Nixon's so-called enemies list. Undaunted, Wald also became a leading opponent of nuclear arms proliferation, as well as a critic of the cold war and a vocal supporter of various human rights movements, increasing these activities following the withdrawal of U.S. troops from Vietnam in 1974. On his retirement in 1977, he left the laboratory and the classroom behind to devote himself full-time to political causes, some of which took him on extensive travels around the world. He remained politically active until two years before his death.

Wald was married twice: to Frances Kingsley in 1931, and, following their divorce in 1958, to Ruth Hubbard that same year; he had two children from each marriage. In private life he amassed a significant art collection over the years, focusing on Rembrandt etchings as well as primitive art from Africa and Central and South America. He died at his home in Cambridge, Massachusetts.

• For biographical information, see especially John E. Dowling, "George Wald," in *Biographical Memoirs*, 78 (2000): 299–317, a publication of the National Academy of Sciences; Dowling's article also includes a selected bibliography of Wald's publications. See also "Wald, George," in *Current Biography Yearbook* for 1968 and 1997. For an account of Wald's antiwar activities, see especially Richard Todd, "George Wald: The Man, the Speech," *New York Times Magazine*, 17 Aug. 1969; the article includes excerpts from Wald's MIT speech as well as additional biographical information. For earlier accounts of Wald's antiwar activities, see "George Wald," *New Yorker*, 16 Apr. 1966, pp. 42–44, and "Professor with a Passion," *Time*, 6 May 1966, p. 84. Several articles on Wald's Nobel Prize and its significance, as well as a biographical essay, are in the *New York Times*, 19 Oct. 1967. An obituary appears in the *New York Times*, 14 Apr. 1997.

ANN T. KEENE

WALKER, Doak (1 Jan. 1927–27 Sept. 1998), football player, was born Ewell Doak Walker, Jr., in Dallas, Texas, the son of Ewell Walker, a high school teacher and football coach and later the superintendent of the Dallas Independent School District, and Emma (maiden name unknown) Walker, a teacher. Reared in a middle-class, blue-collar environment, Walker attended Highland Park High School, where he excelled at football. Doak later said that his father neither pressured nor discouraged him from pursuing football as a career, but once, when asked if he thought his son would one day be president, Ewell Walker replied, "No. He's going to be an All-American football player." Having grown up in the neighborhood surrounding Southern Methodist University, he decided to attend the school at the suggestion of his father, who felt that a degree from SMU would help him find work in Dallas after college.

After serving briefly in the U.S. Merchant Marine, in 1945 the five-foot-eleven, 170-pound Walker entered the university and joined the football team, but his college career was interrupted later that year when he was drafted into the army. His return to SMU in the fall of 1947 marked the beginning of an undefeated football season for the Mustangs. Walker, who wore number 37, played all positions, but he excelled as a running back. He saved SMU from a loss against Texas Christian when he returned a kickoff for 65 yards, setting up a touchdown pass that tied the game in the final seconds. Later, when asked about the game, Walker could only recall that he had missed the extra-point kick, denying the Mustangs the win. Since at the time football players competed on both offense and defense, Walker would often play the full sixty minutes of the contest. Once, in a game against his high school teammate and future Detroit Lions teammate Bobby Layne, who played for the University of Texas, Walker intercepted one of Layne's passes, and Layne reciprocated by intercepting one of Walker's.

By the 1948 season, during which the Mustangs lost only once, Walker's skills on the field and his wholesome image had made him a local celebrity, and fans from all over Texas began crowding into SMU's Ownby Stadium to see the handsome, blue-eyed football star. Soon school officials moved SMU games to the much larger Cotton Bowl, which by Walker's senior season was christened "The House That Doak Built." That year Walker easily won the Heisman Trophy, given to the best college player of the year; he was the first college junior to receive the award. On the flight back from the New York Downtown Athletic Club, where the Heisman is presented each year, his mother reportedly said, "All of this because one little blue-eyed boy could run with the football."

Walker's senior season was less spectacular because of injuries, but overall his college statistics are exceptional. During his four-year college career, he amassed more than 3,500 yards in total offense, scored 288 points in 30 regular season games, and broke school and conference records in rushing, scoring, interceptions, passing, punting, punt return yards, and kickoff return yards; many of his records still stand. Walker led the Mustangs to two Southwestern Conference championships and Cotton Bowl appearances in 1947 and 1948 and was a three-time All-American. In 1950 he married Norma Peterson; they had four children.

After graduation from SMU Walker played six seasons for the Detroit Lions of the National Football League (1950–1955), leading the league in scoring in his rookie season. Critics doubted that he would succeed in the NFL because of his small size, but he proved them wrong. In a relatively short pro career, Walker rushed or received for more than 4,000 yards, averaging 4.9 yards per carry and scoring 534 points. The halfback helped the Lions win the 1952 and 1953 NFL titles, in 1952 running 67 yards for the winning touchdown. He played in five Pro Bowls and was voted All NFL four times. He retired from football while still a young man, explaining that he wanted to leave the game "while I have all my teeth and both my knees." But his illustrious career did not fade from memory: he was inducted into the College Football Hall of Fame in 1959 and the Pro Football Hall of Fame in 1986.

Walker entered the business world as a sales executive for the general contracting firm George A. Fuller Co. in Denver, Colorado. He subsequently started his own company, Walker Chemical, which he later sold. In his early forties he moved to Steamboat Springs, Colorado, where he lived for the rest of his life. After taking up skiing, Walker, now divorced, married his instructor, Gladys "Skeeter" Werner, a former Olympian, in 1969; they had no children.

On 30 January 1998 Walker was paralyzed in a skiing accident on Steamboat Springs's Mount Werner, named for Skeeter Werner's brother Buddy, a U.S. Olympic skiing star killed in an avalanche in Italy in 1964. Over the next eight months Walker, a quadriplegic as a result of the accident, fought his injuries with characteristic determination and courage, struggling to speak and to move. He died in a hospital in Steamboat Springs from complications resulting from the accident.

The best player the Southwest Conference has ever produced, and some would say the greatest college football player in history, Walker was extremely versatile, acting as running back, quarterback, wide receiver, defensive back, punter, extra-point kicker, and kick and punt returner. At Walker's death, SMU president R. Gerald Turner remarked that he "represented the best of intercollegiate athletics—good sportsmanship, combined with good citizenship that was evident on and off the field." Indeed Walker was modest and unassuming to a fault, especially when compared to the vainglory and one-upmanship that characterize both professional and college athletics today. Walker is honored each year when the Doak Walker Award is given to the nation's best college running back.

• A biography is Dorothy Kendall Bracken, *Doak Walker, Three-time All-American* (1950). "Legends of the Fall," a long article in *Texas Monthly* 25, no. 11 (Nov. 1997), recounts an interview with four legends of college football in Texas: Walker, Darrell Royal, John David Crow, and Sammy Baugh. An obituary is in the *New York Times*, 28 Sept. 1998.

STACEY HAMILTON

WALKER, Harry (22 Oct. 1918–8 Aug. 1999), baseball player and manager, was born Harry William Walker in Pascagoula, Mississippi, the son of Ewert "Dixie" Walker, a former professional baseball player, and Flossie Vaughn Walker. He grew up in Birmingham, Alabama, in a family devoted to baseball. His father pitched for Washington from 1909 to 1912, roomed with Walter Johnson, and compiled a modest 25–31 won-lost record. His uncle Ernie played three seasons in the major leagues. The most famous player in Harry's family, his older brother Fred, also nicknamed "Dixie," starred for the Brooklyn Dodgers in the 1940s and won the National League batting title in 1944; but he undermined his reputation as "the peepul's cherce" in Brooklyn by his resistance to Jackie Robinson's breaking the color line in 1947. Harry, on the other hand, could never understand why the nation could not simply follow baseball's example of the relatively harmonious mingling of the races once Robinson was a star.

Walker, a six-foot-two, 185-pound left-handed batter, spent five years working his way up through the far-flung St. Louis Cardinals farm system. He appeared in a few games with the Cards in late 1940 and early 1941, with solid performances at Columbus those two years, which moved him to the big club to stay in 1942 at age 23. (Meanwhile, on 17 March 1941, he had married Dorothy "Dot" Fullmer; they had three daughters and a son, who died in 1947.) The Cards won the World Series his rookie year and the National League pennant in 1943. Drafted by the U.S. Army late in the 1943 season, he managed to get his induction deferred until the day after the World Series, which the Cards lost to the New York Yankees. Then he was off to Europe for two years of combat, earning a Bronze Star for his efforts as part of a reconnaissance unit and, when the fighting was over, organizing baseball teams to entertain the troops, pointedly including black players on them.

Walker had a poor season in 1946, but the Cards won the pennant again. The high point of his career came that year in the World Series against the Red Sox. With the score tied 3–3 in the bottom of the eighth of game seven, Enos Slaughter took off from first base on an attempted steal. Walker sliced the ball into left-center field and wound up on second base with a double, as Slaughter scooted around and scored the winning run when shortstop Johnny Pesky hesitated before throwing home, a play much analyzed by baseball fans for years afterward.

Walker was a gifted contact hitter, rarely striking out or showing much power. He believed in tomahawking the ball, swinging down on it to avoid pop flies and harmless fly balls. He would hit inside pitches late, dumping them into left field. He analyzed the game constantly and was a natural teacher, a proclivity he pursued to the end of his life. He was also a born talker who, if you only wanted to know the time, would tell you how to make a watch. His personal life was a model of clean living: he didn't smoke, drink, or use profanity. His fame was enhanced by his nickname, "the Hat." A Philadelphia sportswriter noted that Walker took off his uncomfortable hat between every pitch and smoothed back his hair. When Walker noticed that the delay irritated pitchers, he made it a routine that he continued throughout his eleven years in the big leagues.

Walker's second claim to fame occurred in 1947, the season following his World Series–winning hit. The Cardinals traded him to the Phillies after he got off to a slow start, and he caught fire in Philadelphia, leading the league in hitting at .363. This earned him two distinctions. He was half of the only brother combination to win major league batting titles, and he re-

mains the only National League player ever to win a batting crown playing on two different teams during the same season. Still, after he dropped off to .292 in 1948, the Phils sent him to the Chicago Cubs for Bill Nicholson. Midway through the 1949 season the Cubs passed him on to Cincinnati, and the Reds traded him back to the Cards. His major league playing days seemed over after 1951, when he became a player-manager in the St. Louis farm system.

In May 1955 he replaced Eddie Stanky as manager of the Cardinals, but despite Walker's close ties with owner Gussie Busch and a .357 average in 14 plate appearances, a seventh-place finish brought his release. A decade later he got another shot at managing in the big leagues when he piloted the Pittsburgh Pirates from 1965 through 1967, racking up two third-place finishes before slipping to sixth and getting fired midway through the 1967 season. When Houston dismissed its manager in mid-1968, the team tapped Walker to take over, but he was unable to improve their tenth-place position. He raised them to fifth in 1969 and fourth in 1970 and 1971 before he was fired with the team in third place. His career mark as a major league manager was 630–604, a .511 percentage. He wound up his baseball career coaching the team at the University of Alabama, Birmingham, from 1979 to 1986. His success in that position included a lively, friendly rivalry with Stanky, who coached the University of South Alabama.

During his career Walker batted .296. In 2,651 at bats, he hit only 10 home runs but also struck out only 175 times. Throughout his career he always returned to his beloved 35-acre home in Leeds, Alabama, just east of Birmingham. The Hat died in Birmingham of complications following a stroke.

• Sources on Harry Walker include obituaries in the St. Louis *Post-Dispatch*, 10 Aug.; the *New York Times*, 10 Aug.; the *Atlanta Constitution*, 13 Aug.; and *Sports Illustrated*, 23 Aug. 1999.

JOHN R. M. WILSON

WALKER, Margaret (7 July 1915–30 Nov. 1998), poet and novelist, was born Margaret Abigail Walker in Birmingham, Alabama, the daughter of Sigismund Walker, a Methodist minister and college professor, and Marion Dozier Walker, a music teacher. A studious and sensitive child, Walker was encouraged to write by her parents, who inspired in her a love of books and music. She was fascinated by her grandmother's stories of slave life in rural Georgia and began writing daily, both prose and poetry, at the age of eleven. Her parents moved to Louisiana to accept teaching positions at New Orleans College (later renamed Dillard University). Walker graduated from Gilbert Academy in 1930 and matriculated at New Orleans College, but, on the advice of poet Langston Hughes, her parents decided to send her north to study. In 1932 Walker transferred from New Orleans College to Northwestern University in Evanston, Illinois, from which she received an A.B. degree in

1935. During her time at Northwestern, she met the African-American activist and editor W. E. B. Du Bois, whose magazine *The Crisis* carried her first published poem in May 1934.

After graduating, Walker worked for the Federal Writers' Project in Chicago under the Works Progress Administration (WPA) and came to know such literary figures as Richard Wright, with whom she collaborated closely as a member of the South Side Writers Group. She returned to school at the University of Iowa, where in 1937 she wrote the poem "For My People," which earned her national acclaim and became the title piece in a collection of twenty-six poems that were accepted as her master's thesis in creative writing in 1940. The next year she returned to the South to become an English instructor at Livingstone College in Salisbury, North Carolina. That year her volume *For My People* appeared with an introduction by Stephen Vincent Benét. The collection won the Yale Series of Younger Poets Award, making her the first African American to be so honored. In 1942–1943 she taught English at West Virginia State College in Institute. In 1943 she married Firnist James Alexander, an interior decorator; they had four children.

For My People contains three sections written in different styles but bound together by the theme of the southern black experience and the directness of their diction. The title poem in the first part is written in long, flowing lines of free verse that suggests Walt Whitman or Carl Sandburg to many reviewers and prompted Benét to describe the poem as containing "a controlled intensity of emotion and a language that . . . has something of the surge of biblical poetry" (p. 5). A second section is devoted to rhyming dialect ballads celebrating such traditional black characters as John Henry and Stagolee. Like blues songs, they draw on folk tradition and earned the critical comment that they reflected the influence of Langston Hughes or were, as Louis Untermeyer wrote, "like Paul Laurence Dunbar turned sour" (p. 371). The six sonnets that constitute the third section were praised for their formal skill but dismissed by some critics as lacking the intensity of the title poem. Although the critical response to the volume was mixed, the poem "For My People" placed Walker firmly in the tradition of social protest as an activist of unusual emotional depth and passion.

Walker returned to Livingstone for two years as a professor in 1945, and in 1949 she moved to Jackson, Mississippi, where she served as professor of English at Jackson State College until her retirement in 1979. During her tenure there she created and directed the Institute for the Study of the History, Life, and Culture of Black People and originated the Phyllis Wheatly Poetry Festival. In 1965 she earned a Ph.D. from the University of Iowa, and the next year she published her only novel, *Jubilee*, which had been her doctoral dissertation. *Jubilee* is a realistic story of a slave family set before, during, and after the Civil War, based on the tales her grandmother had told her. It traces the life of the daughter of a white plantation owner and a slave, relating the oppression of her early life as a slave and the alienation of her postwar life cut off from the social structure she had known. Deeply researched over a period of 30 years, the novel was meticulous in its details of black folklore and culture and was generally well received, selling some three million copies in 11 languages during her lifetime. Some sources, however, criticized it for perpetuating the romantic myths of the nineteenth-century South from a black point of view and compared it to Margaret Mitchell's 1936 novel *Gone with the Wind*. In 1972 Walker defended her work vigorously, publishing *How I Wrote "Jubilee,"* a pamphlet describing its composition and the research that went into it. Alex Haley published his bestselling historical novel *Roots*, employing a similar oral style, in 1977; Walker in 1988 charged him with plagiarism. "There was nothing verbatim," she admitted, "but there were at least a hundred pages of outstanding similarities" (quoted in Milloy, p. 35). Although another writer did successfully charge Haley with plagiarism, Walker lost the case in court.

Three other collections of new poems—*Ballad of the Free* (1966), *Prophets for a New Day* (1970), and *October Journey* (1973)—appeared, all brief collections striking the same note of racial pride as her earlier volume, and in 1989 the University of Georgia Press published *This Is My Century: New and Collected Poems*. In 1974 she collaborated on *A Poetic Equation: Conversations between Nikki Giovanni and Margaret Walker*, discussing the experience of African-American woman poets. Her critical essays written between 1932 and 1992 were collected under the title *On Being Female, Black, and Free* in 1997. Her only effort at biography, *Richard Wright: Daemonic Genius*, appeared in 1987. Largely based on personal contact with her subject, it received a warm response in the literary community. Although long retired from teaching, Walker continued to be active as professor emerita, directing the Institute she had founded in the 1960s. She died of breast cancer at her daughter's home in Chicago.

Despite her modest output, Margaret Walker made a substantial contribution to the literature of African-American social protest, and the rolling cadences of "For My People" provide an enduring voice for her people.

• Among the best examinations of Walker's writing are Richard K. Barksdale, "Margaret Walker: Folk Orature and Historical Prophecy," in *Black American Poets between Worlds, 1940–1960* (1986), pp. 104–17; Eugenia Collier, "Fields Watered with Blood: Myth and Ritual in the Poetry of Margaret Walker," in Mari Evans, ed., *Black Women Writers (1950–1980): A Critical Evaluation* (1984), pp. 499–510; and R. Baxter Miller, "The 'Etched Flame' of Margaret Walker: Biblical and Literary Re-creation in Southern History," *Tennessee Studies in Literature* 26 (1981): 157–72. Valuable critiques of individual works are Stephen Vincent Benét, "Introduction," Margaret Walker, *For My People* (1942), and Louis Untermeyer, "Cream of the Verse," *Yale Review* 32 (1943): 370–91. Personal accounts are in Marilyn Milloy, "A Quiet Force in American Letters," *Newsday* (2 Mar.

1981), pp. 23–46, and in many published interviews. Among the best of these are Jerry W. Ward, "A Writer for Her People: An Interview with Dr. Margaret Walker Alexander," *Mississippi Quarterly* 41.4 (Fall 1988), and Maryemma Graham, "The Fusion of Ideas—An Interview with Margaret Walker," *African American Review* 27.2 (Summer 1993): 279–86.

DENNIS WEPMAN

WALLACE, George (25 Aug. 1919–13 Sept. 1998), politician, was born George Corley Wallace, in Clio, Alabama, the son of George C. Wallace, Sr., a struggling farmer, and Mozell Smith Wallace, a piano teacher. Both parents disliked using "Junior," so he was called "George C." to differentiate him from his father and his paternal grandfather. The oldest of four children, he became interested in politics at an early age, serving in 1935 as a page in the Alabama legislature. He quarterbacked for his high school football team and excelled at boxing, winning the state Golden Gloves bantamweight championships in 1936 and 1937. He also honed his salesmanship skills: summers he traveled around the East Coast and the Midwest with a group of young men selling magazine subscriptions door-to-door.

Wallace's father died in 1937, the year George C. graduated from high school and enrolled in law school at the University of Alabama in Tuscaloosa. Finances, previously tight, became more so. He worked odd jobs to remain in school. After obtaining his degree in 1942 but failing to secure a job in law, he drove a dump truck for the State Highway Department. In 1943 he married Lurleen Burns (Lurleen Burns Wallace), a dime store clerk. (They would have one son and three daughters.) That same year Wallace was inducted into the U.S. Army Air Forces, later flying several bombing raids over Japan as flight engineer of a B-29 bomber crew.

Medically discharged from the service in December 1945, Wallace returned to Alabama where Governor Chauncey Sparks hired him as an assistant attorney general. In 1946 Wallace was elected to the Alabama State Legislature. Wallace allied himself with Governor "Big Jim" Folsom, a populist and racial moderate, and successfully sponsored legislation to enhance industrial development and to create several trade schools. As an alternate delegate at the 1948 Democratic national convention, Wallace refused to join the southern walkout protesting a strong civil rights platform plank. He wished to serve as a trustee for all-black Tuskegee University and did so from 1950 to 1952. In 1952 he won election as a circuit judge, a position he held until 1959.

In 1958 Wallace ran for governor, losing decisively by a 12-percentage-point margin to Attorney General John Patterson in a racially charged campaign. Wallace, who received the NAACP's endorsement, disavowed Ku Klux Klan support, while Patterson accepted it. Brooding over his loss, Wallace explained in private to political activists that "John Patterson out-

nigguhed me" and "I'm not goin' to be out-nigguhed again" (quoted in Frady, p. 131).

Before his judgeship ended, Wallace underscored his shift to race-baiting, gaining notoriety as "the Fighting Little Judge." Wallace opposed a federal court order supporting an investigation by the U.S. Civil Rights Commission into voting rights in the South. Faced with the threat of a lengthy jail term for refusing to turn over voting records, Wallace publicly took a defiant stance, railing against federal intrusion into the southern way of life, but privately arranged for a grand jury to cooperate, thus avoiding the contempt of court charge. This would be the first of several clashes with his law school classmate and former close friend Frank M. Johnson, Jr., federal district judge for the Middle District of Alabama. Federal courts became a favorite target for Wallace's fiery rhetoric. (Johnson's decisions over the next couple of decades made him, in the eyes of some, the "real governor" of Alabama.)

Soon after his 1958 defeat, Wallace began laying the groundwork for another gubernatorial bid. In 1962 he won the Democratic nomination handily with 56 percent of the runoff vote, showing political acumen and a flair for connecting with voters. His inaugural address spoke to southern whites' fears of social upheaval, offering hard-core resistance to racial integration: "In the name of the greatest people that have ever trod this earth, I draw the line in the dust and toss the gauntlet before the feet of tyranny . . . and I say, Segregation now! Segregation tomorrow! Segregation forever!"

In June 1963 Wallace permanently linked himself to the issue of racial resistance with his "stand in the schoolhouse door" at the University of Alabama to block the enrollment of two African American students. Although he yielded to a federalized National Guard, Wallace's defiant stance catapulted him into national political prominence. By entering three Democratic presidential primaries in 1964, Wallace roiled national politics, winning surprisingly large vote totals in Indiana (30 percent), Wisconsin (34 percent), and Maryland (43 percent). His support revealed the intensity of white backlash to social unrest and the federal government's activism, particularly on behalf of civil rights. Ending his presidential bid, he claimed to have triumphed in alerting the nation to federal encroachment on states' rights.

Racial tension marked Alabama during Wallace's first administration as nonviolent protest met violent reaction. In 1963 civil rights demonstrators in Birmingham had faced fire hoses and police dogs. The bombing of a Birmingham church that same year killed four African-American children. The Selma March of early 1965 initially encountered tear gas and billy clubs from state and local lawmen. Critics accused Wallace of contributing to the atmosphere of intolerance in which such acts occurred.

Political campaigning absorbed Wallace, not the demands of governing, and his administration was often accused of cronyism. Wallace's popular appeal partly stemmed from a populist concern for the underdog. By promoting, for example, free school textbooks and a proliferation of junior colleges and technical schools, he could claim to have put education within the reach of many, both white and black.

Wallace's failure to rewrite state law so that a sitting governor could seek reelection led him to coax his wife, Lurleen Wallace, a reluctant politician, to run as his stand-in. When the strongest gubernatorial candidate, a Wallace foe, died in a plane crash while campaigning, the way was cleared for Wallace's wife, who easily won the 1966 election. The uterine cancer that had afflicted the new Governor Wallace before the race was to fell her in May 1968.

After a brief period of mourning, George Wallace returned to his 1968 campaign for president on the ticket of his newly formed American Independent Party. In what turned out to be a close contest between the Democratic candidate Hubert Humphrey and the Republican Richard Nixon, Wallace carried five southern states, polled 9.9 million popular votes (13.5 percent), and captured forty-six electoral votes. On the other hand, both Nixon's strategy of courting the white south and organized labor's efforts to keep union members Democratic in the end lowered Wallace's vote, which had reached 20 percent in some surveys. His running mate, General Curtis E. LeMay, hurt the ticket's chances by expressing an uninhibited willingness to use nuclear weapons to settle international conflicts.

In 1970 Wallace again ran for governor, against the incumbent, a former ally who had succeeded Lurleen Wallace at her death. Although he trailed in the primary, Wallace rebounded to win with a racially charged runoff campaign decrying the black "bloc vote" for his opponent. Watergate hearings later revealed that President Nixon and other Republicans had secretly funneled $400,000 into the push to defeat Wallace. In 1971, Wallace married Cornelia Ellis Snively, a photogenic, outgoing niece of Governor Folsom. (They would be divorced in 1978.)

Another run for the presidency in 1972 had Wallace vying for the Democratic nomination. "Send them a message" was his campaign slogan. He gave voice to the frustrated working- and middle-class voters who longed for a more stable world and felt overlooked by the major parties. Wallace hit hard on law and order, foreign aid giveaways and welfare handouts. His rhetoric mocked political elites, as when he railed against federal activism, referring to "briefcase-carrying bureaucrats . . . [who] can't even park their bicycles straight . . . trying to run your lives." But his central message attacked the federal courts and busing to promote school integration: "Busing is the most asinine cruel thing I've ever heard of"—ordered by "hypocrites who send your kids half-way across town while they have their chauffeur drop their children off at private schools" (quoted in Carter, pp. 425, 434). Wallace swept the Florida primary in March with 42 percent of the vote, carrying every county in the state. He also won Tennessee and North Carolina. Then in

May, while he was campaigning in Laurel, Maryland, an emotionally disturbed man named Arthur Herman Bremer shot Wallace, permanently paralyzing him from the waist down. Although this essentially ended his presidential hopes, he won Maryland and Michigan the next day.

For the rest of his life, Wallace lived in constant pain and precarious health, battling infections and complications. Even so, in 1974 he again ran for governor, winning handily. (State law had been changed in November 1968 to allow gubernatorial succession.) In 1976 Wallace made his final run for president, losing the Democratic primary in Florida to the eventual winner, Jimmy Carter, whom he ultimately endorsed.

Rather than pursue a U.S. Senate seat, as he had contemplated doing, Wallace became director for rehabilitation resources at the University of Alabama at Birmingham when his gubernatorial term ended in 1978. Out of office, he sought forgiveness for his segregationist past, contending that he had not been a hater of blacks, just against big government, and that the states' rights defense of segregation (which he now considered wrong but previously considered best for both races) was not racism. Detractors, noting the growing black vote, saw this as another indication of the master politician's shrewd opportunism. In 1981 he married Lisa Taylor, then thirty-two years old, who had sung at several of his presidential campaign stops in 1968; they would be divorced in 1987.

In 1982 Wallace ran for governor yet again, garnering some black voter support and endorsements—about one-quarter to one-third of the black vote in the Democratic primary and runoff, approximately 90 percent in the general election. Once elected, he found that his gubernatorial activities were seriously curtailed by his declining health. In early 1986, frail and suffering, Wallace retired from politics, saying, "I have climbed my last political mountain." He took a fundraising job for Troy State University's Montgomery campus. He died in Montgomery twelve years later.

The racial issues that catapulted Wallace onto the national political stage constrained his ability to reach beyond race. During the 1960s and 1970s, however, he tapped into a powerful undercurrent of American politics by expressing the fears of aggrieved working- and middle-class voters upset about the social upheavals that threatened traditional cultural values of work, family, patriotism, and religion. Ronald Reagan—smoother, sunnier, and unencumbered by Wallace's racist baggage—"sailed into the White House," as the *New York Times* put it, on the "tide George Wallace discovered" (4 Apr. 1986).

• The George C. Wallace official gubernatorial papers are held at the Alabama Department of Archives and History. His private papers are under the control of the Wallace Foundation, also in Montgomery. Dan T. Carter gives a detailed background picture of Wallace's rise and decline, focusing on his national impact, in *The Politics of Rage: George Wallace, the Origins of the New Conservatism, and the Transformation of American Politics* (2000). Assessments of his place in Alabama political history can be found in Jack Bass and Walter DeVries, *The Transformation of Southern Politics* (1995), and Anne Permaloff and Carl Grafton, *Political Power in Alabama* (1995). Marshall Frady's *Wallace* (1996) is entertaining, informative, and scathing. An obituary is in the *New York Times*, 15 Sept. 1998.

HAROLD W. STANLEY

WALLENDA, Helen (11 Dec. 1910–9 May 1996), trapeze artist, was born Helen Kreis in Germany to a family that operated amusement park rides (the names of her parents and her exact birthplace are unknown). At an early age she became fascinated by trapeze artists and began learning their moves and maneuvers. By the age of sixteen she had become skilled enough to join the Wallendas, a circus troupe recently formed by Karl Wallenda, five years her senior, and his brother, Herman. The Wallendas were themselves descended from many generations of circus and carnival performers.

The Wallendas had perfected many aerial stunts, but their unique specialty was an act called the high-wire pyramid. This called for two troupe members, Herman and another man, Joe Geiger, to walk a tightrope forty feet above the ground while they supported a crossbar. In the course of the act, a chair was tossed up onto the crossbar, and Karl Wallenda would then swing himself into the chair. The act would conclude with a fourth performer climbing onto Karl's shoulders and standing up triumphantly, forming the apex of the pyramid. Upon being hired by the troupe, Helen Kreis became the apex of the Wallendas' high-wire pyramid.

Kreis began touring with the Wallendas throughout Europe, and in the fall of 1927, while performing in Cuba, the troupe was hired by John Ringling, the American cofounder and leader of the famed Ringling Brothers Circus. The Wallendas first performed with the Ringling Brothers Circus in New York's Madison Square Garden in March 1928, and the high-wire pyramid, with Helen Kreis on top, created such a sensation that the crowd gave them a standing ovation reportedly lasting for over ten minutes. This was the beginning of the Wallenda troupe's long association with Ringling Brothers, which continued off and on for many years, though they also continued to perform on their own in Europe.

By the early 1930s Helen Kreis had become romantically involved with Karl Wallenda, who was married and had fathered several children both in and out of the marriage. In late 1934 he began divorce proceedings against his wife, and in June 1935 he and Helen were married. The couple had a daughter of their own, and also helped raise a son and a daughter of Karl's. Although the Wallenda troupe, now known as the Great Wallendas, performed other trapeze acts, the high-wire pyramid remained their specialty. In the years following their American debut Karl Wallenda devised ever more daring variations of the act, adding several more members and having the men who supported them ride bicycles along the wire. For years they performed without injury, and a miraculous aura

seemed to surround them. During the 1940s, while on tour with Ringling Brothers, they even survived several major circus fires, including the famous blaze in July 1944 in Hartford, Connecticut, that claimed 168 lives.

In 1947, now touring on their own, the Wallendas achieved a long-held dream of Karl's when members of the troupe joined together to perfect and successfully perform the first seven-person pyramid. "The seven," as it was known, became the highlight of their act, and Helen continued as its star for nine years. She also participated fully in the troupe's other aerialist acts, usually performed without safety nets, and by the early 1950s she had become celebrated as the "queen of the high-wire," notable for her charm and poise and a reserved demeanor that never betrayed fear.

Helen Wallenda retired from the troupe in 1956 and thereafter remained for much of the year in Sarasota, Florida, where the Wallendas had established a home in the off-season; they had been drawn initially to the city because it was the winter headquarters of Ringling Brothers. Having performed without serious accident throughout her career, she apparently had premonitions that the luck of the troupe, which now included her daughter and stepchildren, was running out, and she refused to be present during their public appearances. Her fears were realized in 1962, when she learned that the seven-person pyramid had collapsed during a performance in Detroit, killing two members outright and permanently paralyzing her stepson. Two years later she again experienced tragedy when one of her sisters, who had joined the troupe, was also killed in a fall.

In March 1978 Helen Wallenda agreed to accompany the troupe to Puerto Rico, where her husband was attempting to walk along a wire stretched between two ten-story buildings along the San Juan beachfront. A sudden gust of wind made him lose his footing, and he plunged to his death. In the face of this devastating loss, Helen remained stoical and supported the family's decision to continue the troupe. She spent the remainder of her life in Sarasota, presiding as the matriarch of a large family that grew to include six grandchildren and seventeen great-grandchildren, and died at her home there. Many of her descendants continued to perform with the troupe her husband founded, which became known as the Great Wallenda Circus.

• Biographical information on Helen Wallenda is limited. Scant details about her life are included in Delilah Wallenda and Nan DeVincentis-Hayes, *The Last of the Wallendas* (1993), which focuses on Karl Wallenda; Delilah is a granddaughter of Karl and his first wife. See also a posthumous tribute by Rebecca Chace, "Upstairs, Where It's Safe," *New York Times Magazine*, 29 Dec. 1996, p. 43. For additional information on the family, see the news article "Karl Wallenda, 73, Patriarch of the High-Wire Troupe, Dies in 100-Foot Fall," *New York Times*, 23 Mar. 1978. Charles Wilkins, *The Circus at the Edge of the Earth: Travels with the Great Wallenda Circus* (1998), is an account of an extended tour by the Great Wallendas in Canada during the 1990s. See also John Culhane, *The American Circus: An Illustrated His-*

tory (1990); and Rupert Croft-Cooke and Peter Cotes, *Circus: A World History* (1976). An obituary for Helen Wallenda appears in the *New York Times*, 11 May 1996.

ANN T. KEENE

WARBURG, Edward (5 June 1908–21 Sept. 1992), philanthropist and art collector, was born Edward Mortimer Morris Warburg in White Plains, New York, the son of Felix Warburg, a banker and philanthropist, and Frieda Schiff. Warburg's family connections and long-standing philanthropic activities, combined with his education in art history at Harvard University, contributed significantly to his success as a patron of culture and humanitarian causes throughout his life.

In 1928, along with Lincoln Kirstein and John Walker III (who later became director of the National Gallery in Washington, D.C.), Warburg, while still an undergraduate, helped found the Harvard Society for Contemporary Art, located on the second floor of the Harvard Coop Building. The society was dedicated to showing "the various manifestations of modern art and decoration"—art that the Boston Museum of Fine Arts and Harvard's Fogg Art Museum were hesitant to display at the time. The society's first exhibition opened in February 1929 and featured twelve contemporary artists, including painters Thomas Hart Benton, Charles Burchfield, Edward Hopper, and Georgia O'Keeffe and sculptors Gaston Lachaise and Alexander Archipenko. More than 2,500 people saw the exhibition, and many favorable reviews followed in the press.

In the following two years, the society organized groundbreaking exhibitions of works by American artists such as Stuart Davis and Charles Sheeler, European artists Henri Matisse and Pablo Picasso, and Mexican artists Diego Rivera, José Clemente Orozco, and David Siqueiros; exhibitions on Japanese and English pottery and weaving and American cartoon and caricature were also held. Another adventurous undertaking of the society was to host on 31 January 1930 the first public performance of Alexander Calder's *Circus*—wood and wire constructions that the sculptor set in motion. The gallery sustained itself with sales as well as with the membership of such generous patrons as Philip Johnson, Abby Aldrich Rockefeller, and Lillie P. Bliss. Loans of artwork came from prominent collectors including Duncan Phillips and John Quinn and contemporary art dealer Julien Levy.

On a trip to Europe in 1929 Warburg bought Picasso's 1905 gouache painting *Blue Boy*, despite his family's shock at the then outrageous price of $7,000. Following graduation from Harvard in 1930, he traveled for a year throughout Europe, where he bought art from the dealer Curt Valentin, including the work of Paul Gauguin, Paul Klee, whom he met at the Bauhaus in Dessau, Germany, and other artists. To house his early collection, in 1934 Warburg gave Philip Johnson, then a curator at the Museum of Modern Art, his first commission ever, to design an apartment in the International Style. During the mid-1930s Warburg became a patron for Lachaise. He collected the French artist's work, lectured on his art, and even occasionally paid his rent.

Following his European trip, Warburg returned to the United States to teach art history at Bryn Mawr in the 1931–1933 academic years. During the fall of 1932, he accompanied Arthur Upham Pope to an archeological dig in Isfahan, Iran. In 1933 he moved to New York and worked at the Museum of Modern Art, founded in 1929. Run by fellow Harvard alumnus Alfred H. Barr, Jr., the Museum of Modern Art followed the example of the Harvard Society in showing similar artists and sharing several generous patrons, including Abby Aldrich Rockefeller and Lillie P. Bliss. The museum invited Warburg, Kirstein, and Walker to be on its advisory committee in 1930, and Warburg served as a trustee from 1932 to 1958. Particularly interested in outreach and education, Warburg gave the museum's first public lecture (on Matisse), and he helped organize the museum's film library and programs. Warburg also assisted Barr in providing visas and positions for artists and architects fleeing Nazi Germany, including the Bauhaus artist Josef Albers who came to the United States to teach at Black Mountain College in North Carolina in 1933.

Also in 1933 Warburg and Kirstein brought Russian choreographer George Balanchine and manager Vladimir Dimitriev from France to the United States to form the American Ballet, a precursor of the New York City Ballet. Assisted by Warburg's extensive financial backing, the company's first public performance was *Alma Mater*, a parody of the Ivy League conceived by Warburg and performed at the Wadsworth Atheneum in 1934. After the ballet company became associated with the Metropolitan Opera House in New York, they presented an Igor Stravinsky festival in 1937 consisting of two extant ballets by Stravinsky and one new one, *Jeu de Cartes: Ballet en Trois Donnes* (Card game: ballet in three deals), commissioned by Warburg.

After his father's death in 1937, Warburg's philanthropic activities changed course as he took over some of Felix Warburg's responsibilities, in particular the American Jewish Joint Distribution Committee (JDC), an organization devoted to aiding Jews in distress overseas. Warburg cochaired the JDC from 1939 to 1966. Also in 1939 he married Mary Whelan Prue Currier, with whom he had two children. When the United States entered World War II, Warburg enlisted in the army; for his service aiding refugees during and after the war, he received the Bronze Star and decorations from the Belgian government. Through the JDC, Warburg continued his extensive refugee assistance efforts after the war and became a major supporter of the foundation of the state of Israel, giving speeches and serving in various organizations.

Continuously active in philanthropic and cultural causes, Warburg was involved in the United Jewish Appeal during the mid-1950s through the mid-1960s, served on the New York State Board of Regents from

1958 to 1975, and held the post of vice director of public affairs at the Metropolitan Museum of Art from 1971 to 1974. Warburg was a trustee of the Metropolitan from 1983 until his death of heart failure at the age of eighty-four in Norwalk, Connecticut.

Throughout his life, Warburg was an avid collector of modern art. In reference to his collecting Warburg said in a 1987 interview, "Somehow I felt that by owning these things and having had the courage to purchase them, I thereby established my credentials." He gave much of his collection, which included works by Toulouse-Lautrec, Cézanne, Degas, and Siqueiros, to the Museum of Modern Art, Smith College Art Museum, and museums at Harvard University.

Warburg's creativity, energy, and generosity benefited the lives of thousands of victims of World War II and Nazism as well as the modern art movement in America. In some cases, his two interests overlapped such as when, unbeknownst to himself, he helped the artist Marc Chagall travel to the United States during the war. By supporting the Harvard Society, the Museum of Modern Art, and the American Ballet during the Depression, Warburg helped nurture avant-garde movements in America during a particularly innovative time. Recalling the pioneering spirit of one of these early institutions, Warburg marveled in a 1971 interview, "My God, it is extraordinary to look back and see where we were on shoestrings trying to keep things together, trying to get patronage, or to get things going."

• Nicholas Fox Weber, *Patron Saints: Five Rebels Who Opened America to a New Art, 1928–1943* (1992), details this fertile period of contemporary art patronage with much information on Warburg, Kirstein, and Walker. Weber also wrote "Revolution on Beekman Place," an article on the apartment Philip Johnson designed for Warburg in *House & Garden* magazine (Aug. 1986, pp. 56–60). The Archives of American Art, Smithsonian Institution, in Washington, D.C., has unmicrofilmed information on Warburg's art collections as well as a transcript of a 1971 interview. The New York Times Oral History Program includes a 1967 interview with Warburg on the JDC, World War II, and his father, made for the Hebrew University Contemporary Jewry Oral History Collection. An interview with Warburg conducted in the early 1990s on his art activities can be found in the archives of the Museum of Modern Art. Sources for the history of the Warburg family include Ron Chernow, *The Warburgs: The Twentieth-Century Odyssey of a Remarkable Jewish Family* (1993); David Farrer, *The Warburgs* (1975); and Stephen Birmingham, *Our Crowd: The Great Jewish Families of New York* (1967). The *New York Times,* 22 Sept. 1992, has Warburg's obituary.

N. ELIZABETH SCHLATTER

WEIL, André (6 May 1906–6 Aug. 1998), mathematician, was born in Paris to Bernard Weil (the pronunciation is given variously as *Vay* and *Vayl*), a physician of Alsatian descent, and Selma Reinherz Weil, an accomplished amateur singer who was born in Russia to a wealthy Austrian merchant family. Her dowry had enabled her husband to establish a thriving medical practice in Paris, and their two children—André and his younger sister, Simone, who became a noted philosopher—were reared in a cultured and prosperous household. Although the Weils were Jewish, they did not practice their religion; André Weil later recalled in his memoirs that he did not become aware of his Jewish origins until he was about twelve. The fact of his Jewishness, once discovered, made little difference to him, he claimed.

André and Simone Weil grew up closely bound to each other, and until Simone's death in 1943 the two remained in continual contact, each spurring on the other's intellectual achievements. The major force in their upbringing was their mother, who closely supervised all aspects of her children's development. André was encouraged to play the violin as a small child, and he learned to read before he was five. When he was six, he was enrolled at the Lycée Montaigne, a local school of some distinction. There his teachers quickly noted his intuitive grasp of mathematics, without the need for instruction. At his mother's insistence, he skipped several forms (grades) in the early years of his attendance, and he was eventually placed under the tutelage of a Monsieur Mobeig (given name unknown), the first of several teachers whom Weil later recalled as playing an important role in his education. Mobeig soon recognized that his pupil had an exceptional intellect—a recognition apparently shared by the handful of other teachers whom Weil recalled with admiration.

Weil himself was without doubt aware of his gifts from earliest memory, in no small part because of his mother's continuous oversight. Forever on the lookout for the best teachers for her son, encouraging his wide-ranging curiosity not only in mathematics and the sciences but in literature and languages as well, she nonetheless cannot be charged with pushing her son into efforts that he was not willing to make on his own. In fact, Weil seemed a natural-born scholar, hungrily gulping down classical literature, math texts, and volumes of history. What his mother may stand accused of, however, is failing to temper her son's growing arrogance. Convinced of his invincible superiority from an early age, he proceeded through life with the assurance of one who believes himself never to be in error.

Following the outbreak of World War I in 1914, Bernard Weil became a physician to the French army, and during the course of the conflict his wife and children accompanied him to his various posts. André Weil continued his education through a series of correspondence courses prepared by his school in Paris and overseen by his mother; from time to time he also attended local schools, though not surprisingly they proved unsatisfactory. A seminal event in Weil's life occurred in early 1915, when he came across a secondary school algebra textbook by Carlo Bourlet, then a well-known mathematician and educator. Until then math had been just one of many absorbing subjects for the boy, but after reading Bourlet's text he announced that he, too, would become a mathematician.

Back in Paris Weil enrolled at the Lycée Saint-Louis, a prestigious school specializing in science and math instruction. There he came under the tutelage of another influential instructor, Monsieur Collin, the first of several teachers whom Weil later credited with "making a mathematician of me." On his own, he also began to learn Sanskrit, a pursuit that developed into a lifelong passion for Hindu literature. After completing his studies at the lycée in 1922, Weil enrolled at the celebrated École Normale in Paris, intent on specializing in mathematics. During his first year at the École he was allowed to participate in a seminar led by the renowned mathematician Jacques Hadamard at the Collège de France, another eminent institution in Paris. At the Sorbonne Weil continued his study of Sanskrit, reading the *Bhagavad Gita* and discovering therein "the only form of religious thought that could satisfy my mind."

After passing his examinations in 1925, Weil took time off from his studies to travel extensively in Italy for a year, attending concerts and church services and seeking out medieval and Renaissance art in churches and museums. In 1926, with a grant from the Rockefeller Foundation in New York City, Weil began a year of mathematical studies in Germany. Beginning at the University of Göttingen, he moved on to universities in Frankfurt, Berlin, and Hamburg; he also spent time in Stockholm, where he learned Swedish. Weil became especially interested in number theory during his stays in Germany and Sweden, and this topic, combined with tangential discussions of algebraic and Abelian functions, became the focus of his doctoral thesis, which he completed in 1928. During the following year he was allowed to perform his compulsory military service at a Paris garrison while living at home and preparing his thesis for publication.

Following the publication of his thesis, Weil should have assumed a teaching post at a major French institution, but apparently no such position was offered to him. In January 1930 he traveled to India, where he subsequently became head of the math department at Aligarh Muslim University, near Delhi. He remained there for two years, traveling extensively in the country when his teaching duties permitted and meeting a number of notables, including Rabindranath Tagore, Mahatma Gandhi, and Jawaharlal Nehru. But in 1931, the university, in Weil's words, "picked a quarrel" with him, and he was fired from his post. Weil returned to Paris in the spring of 1932, spending time in Rome en route.

During his two years in India Weil had remained focused on number theory. Now his mathematical interests centered on complex variable functions. In early 1932 he formulated a significant new theory of functions, the first in a series of important discoveries. A permanent teaching post back in France continued to elude him, however. After taking more time for travel in England, Switzerland, and Germany, Weil was hired for a brief time by the University of Marseilles in late 1932. He soon moved on to the University of Strasbourg, where, by his own account, he felt comfortable during the six years he spent on the faculty before war forced him to leave the country; in the wake of France's subsequent surrender to Germany, and as a consequence of his Jewish origins, he was fired from the staff in absentia.

Weil's years at Strasbourg were fruitful, though his accomplishments were made outside the university. He had for some time had the ambition of restoring preeminence to French mathematics, which had long since been eclipsed by the Germans. As a corollary he wanted to unify the field by reinstating a more philosophical and generalist approach to a subject that he and others felt had become, under German hegemony, increasingly specialized and even arid. In 1933 he joined with several like-minded École Normale math graduates, now teaching at various French universities, to found a series of seminars that met periodically at the Sorbonne to exchange ideas. These were unofficially named "the Julia seminars," after the École Polytechnique mathematician Gaston Julia, who was sympathetic to their interests.

Weil took a further step toward his goal in 1935, when he and several congenial young mathematicians, among them Henri Carton from Strasbourg and Jean Dieudonné at the Sorbonne, joined together over lunch at a Paris restaurant to form the group that eventually became known as Bourbaki. In a sly attempt to assure an outlet for their speculations Weil and his associates created a fictitious French mathematician, Nicolas Bourbaki, to become their collective mouthpiece. The origins of the name Bourbaki appear to lie in the town of Nancy, where Dieudonné had formerly taught and where a statue of a nineteenth-century general named Bourbaki stood in the town square. Weil's future wife, Eveline, who was married at the time to another member of the group, contributed Nicolas as a first name, and the group gave Bourbaki a fictitious nation of origin—Poldevia.

Beginning in 1939, under the authorship of "Nicolas Bourbaki," the group began publishing *Éléments de mathématique*, annual compilations of occasional papers on the structural components of mathematics. Volumes of the *Éléments*, as well as articles under Bourbaki's name, appeared until well into the 1960s, by which time the identities of the mathematicians who collectively published as Bourbaki had become known. The significance of Bourbaki and the *Éléments* was profound in the world of mathematics, for it had the practical effect of breaking down barriers that had been erected between algebra and geometry and creating the modern field of algebraic geometry. It had another consequence as well: the *Éléments* ultimately played a role in the development of the so-called new math in the schools, whereby children are taught to reason first rather than to perform rote calculations.

In the spring of 1937, while still on the faculty at Strasbourg, Weil spent a semester at the Institute for Advanced Study in Princeton, New Jersey, an appointment arranged for him by fellow mathematician John von Neumann. Despite the worsening political situation in Europe he returned to Strasbourg later that year, perhaps in part because no extension of his appointment at the institute had been offered but also because of his romantic relationship with Eveline, who was securing a divorce. The couple married in October 1937, and Weil adopted her son from her previous marriage. They eventually had two daughters of their own.

Weil had been seeking teaching offers from American universities for some time, but none were forthcoming. By the summer of 1939, unwilling to serve in an armed conflict, he moved to neutral Finland shortly before the outbreak of World War II in September. After several months he was sent back to France, where he was imprisoned for avoiding military service. His ensuing months of confinement were not unproductive, however: while in prison he formulated and proved a hypothesis about the behavior of algebraic curves that became a significant component of modern number theory. Following a trial in May 1940 Weil was convicted and sentenced to further imprisonment, but he avoided serving time by volunteering for combat. Assigned to a regiment in Normandy, Weil remained there for only a few weeks, until his unit was ordered to retreat in the wake of the German advance.

Weil soon found himself temporarily evacuated with his regiment to England, where they were detained at a series of military camps. After several unsuccessful attempts to become domiciled in England, he was repatriated to Vichy France, learned that he had been dismissed at Strasbourg, and began making efforts to emigrate to the United States in the summer of 1940. While residing temporarily in Clermont, he managed to convene a meeting of Bourbaki, giving the group an impetus to continue through the war years.

A teaching offer from the New School for Social Research in New York City finally enabled Weil to secure visas for his immediate family, and after a protracted journey via the Caribbean they arrived in New York in early March 1941. Weil soon discovered, however, that he was not going to be teaching at the New School per se; the offer had been fictitious, part of a program instituted by the Rockefeller Foundation to rescue scientists from German-occupied France. To his annoyance he was instead assigned to be an instructor—without pay—at Haverford College outside of Philadelphia, although the Rockefeller Foundation gave him a lump-sum stipend of $2,500. When his year at Haverford ended, Weil and his family moved to Bethlehem, Pennsylvania, where he taught mathematics at Lehigh University for several years as an instructor.

An embittered Weil, angry that no prominent American institution would hire him, moved to Brazil early in 1945 to accept a professorship at the University of São Paulo. That summer, with the war in Europe now ended, Bourbaki colleagues in France paid for Weil to return to Paris to meet with the group. In 1947, following the publication by the American Mathematical Society of his first book in English, *Foundations of Algebraic Geometry* (1946), Weil and his family left São Paulo and returned to the United States after his friend Marshall Stone, now head of the math department at the University of Chicago, invited him to teach there with the rank of full professor. Weil remained on the Chicago faculty until 1958, when he finally secured a permanent appointment at the Institute for Advanced Study in Princeton. Weil retired from the institute as professor emeritus in 1976, the year he published a second book in English, *Elliptic Functions According to Eisenstein and Kronecker*.

Apart from the fact that he traveled widely throughout the world, few details are known of Weil's personal life in the years following his return to the United States in 1947, the year in which his memoir, *The Apprenticeship of a Mathematician* (1992), ends. His professional accomplishments over the ensuing decades, however, are well documented and include important articles he published as both Weil and Bourbaki. Building upon his 1940 hypothesis about the behavior of algebraic curves, he advanced what became known as the Weil conjectures, a series of formulations on algebraic geometry and topology. The Weil conjectures became the basis for new developments in cryptology, computer modeling, data transmission, and elementary particle physics, and provided the theoretical groundwork for advanced study by successive generations of mathematicians. In 1994 the Weil conjectures, together with the contributions of Bourbaki, earned Weil the prestigious Kyoto Prize in Basic Science, awarded by the Inamori Foundation of Kyoto, Japan. The Kyoto Prize is considered equivalent to the Nobel Prize, which is not granted in mathematics.

Following his retirement in 1976, Weil continued to write articles on mathematics, and he edited works by the eminent mathematicians Jacques Bernoulli and Pierre de Fermat. Indeed, Weil is credited with paving the way for the proof of Fermat's last theorem, which had long remained a mystery, and for indirectly kindling a renewed interest in the field of mathematics. In 1994 a young British mathematician named Andrew Wiles announced a proof of the theorem based on work by Weil and two Japanese mathematicians. That proof, and the ensuing worldwide publicity, spawned a new public interest in mathematics and has led to a continuing sales boom for popular works on the subject.

Weil himself remained to the end a committed generalist, taking no interest in the practical consequences or applications of his life's work. He did, however, pay continuing attention to the posthumous rediscovery of his sister's life and work. Although as a lifelong agnostic he may have been somewhat bemused by Simone Weil's preoccupations with Christian mysticism, he remained a vigilant guardian of her memory, participating in conferences devoted to her and taking pains to correct her biographers and critics. Yet in spite of his scholarly rigor and crotchety demeanor, Weil could also be whimsical on occasion: in a brief autobiography he prepared for the Institute for Advanced Study, he indirectly acknowledged his alter ego Bourbaki by listing, as his single academic honor, membership in the Poldevian Academy of Science and Letters. At his death, which occurred at his home in Princeton, Weil was lauded as a peer of the twentieth century's most eminent thinkers, including Albert Einstein and the logician Kurt Gödel. Many scholars today consider him the leading mathematician of the century.

• For biographical information, see Weil's memoir, *The Apprenticeship of a Mathematician* (1992). Additional information is available at the website of the School of Mathematics and Statistics, University of St. Andrews, Scotland (www-history.mcs.st-andrews.ac.uk/history/Mathematicians/Weil.html). See also a posthumous tribute by Paul Hoffman, "Numbers Man," *New York Times Magazine*, 3 Jan. 1999, p. 39. For an explanation and discussion of Bourbaki, see Paul R. Halmos, "Nicolas Bourbaki," *Scientific American*, May 1957, pp. 88–99. A statement of Weil's approach to mathematics can be found in his article "The Future of Mathematics," *American Mathematical Monthly* 57 (1950): 295–306. For a nontechnical discussion of Weil's place in modern mathematics, see especially ch. 27, "Aspects of the 20th Century," in Carl B. Boyer, *A History of Mathematics* (1968). For Weil's role in the current popular interest in math, see Paul Lewis, "Math Emerges Blinking into the Glare of Popular Culture," *New York Times*, 13 Mar. 1999. An obituary is in the *New York Times*, 10 Aug. 1998; see also an important correction to this obituary in the *Times*, 21 Aug. 1998.

ANN T. KEENE

WESTON, Paul (12 Mar. 1912–20 Sept. 1996), musician, was born Paul Wetstein in Springfield, Massachusetts, the son of Paul Richard Wetstein, a teacher at Miss Hill's School for Girls, and Anna Grady Wetstein. Educated through high school in Pittsfield, Massachusetts, he was Phi Beta Kappa at Dartmouth College, majoring in economics and leading a jazz band, and graduating cum laude in 1933.

In 1933 or 1934, while a graduate student in economics at Columbia University, Paul Wetstein was injured in a train wreck; during his convalescence, he wrote some orchestral arrangements for the Joe Haymes orchestra. Then Rudy Vallee used some of his "charts" (arrangements) on the "Fleischmann Hour" radio program. When trombonist Tommy Dorsey took over the Haymes band in 1935, he hired Wetstein as arranger. Over the next five years of the Dorsey band's rise to fame, Wetstein wrote the charts for several hit records including "Who?" (notable for effective countermelodies), "Night and Day," and "Stardust" (the latter two characterized by using Dorsey's trombone as a clear leading "voice").

At the suggestion of a radio producer, Wetstein changed his surname to Weston after his arrival in Hollywood in 1940, where he scored Irving Berlin's songs for the film *Holiday Inn*. When songwriters Johnny Mercer and B. G. DeSylva joined record store owner Glenn Wallichs in creating Capitol Records in 1942, Mercer hired Weston as Capitol's music director.

Over the next eight years, Weston and Mercer were mainly responsible for the freshly swinging sound that characterized Capitol's classic years. Weston produced the early albums of the King Cole Trio (see Nat King Cole) and, with a studio orchestra, backed almost all Capitol's singers, including Mercer and the Pied Pipers singing group as well as its recent graduate, Jo Stafford, who became Weston's wife in 1952. (The couple had two children and remained married until Weston's death.) While at Capitol, Weston and Stafford showed a bent for musical humor, recording in hillbilly fashion "Tim-Tay-Shun" (a spoof of the melodramatic "Temptation") and "I'm My Own Grandmaw."

The distinctive Capitol sound needed only slight enhancement for the first *Music for Dreaming* album (1943), which helped create a controversial new direction in American popular music. The music writer Gene Lees later wrote that it was "[t]he dance band augmented with strings. . . . [Weston] toned down the brass and saxes to achieve a natural acoustical balance . . . the strings forming cushions for fine jazz soloists. . . . [The results] perfectly embody Paul's temperament, which is sunny, sensible, warm, generous, fair and very humorous."

Music for Dreaming and its sequels nurtured a genre sometimes labeled "mood music," related to what the British call Light Music, which became commercially popular after World War II with the advent of long-playing records and improved sound recording. Almost wholly instrumental, it partially filled the void created by the rapid disappearance of swing bands, but it was clearly intended for "easy" background listening, free of the excitement that innovation or improvisation could produce. Conscious of critics' adverse reactions, Weston contrasted his approach with that of others: "Robert Farnon [in Great Britain] would operate in the classic form of orchestra, not jazzy at all. Percy Faith [a Canadian characterized by his lulling vocal groups] was the same, and Kostelanetz [André Kostelanetz, a Russian émigré in the United States who popularized the classics] more so. I believe their reliance on strings without the jazz feel that I brought even to my ballads was the reason the term 'elevator music' came to symbolize most of . . . [these] attempts" (quoted at www.spaceagepop.com/weston.htm).

In 1950, when Weston and Stafford moved to Columbia Records, Stafford's career flowered, partly because of the songs Weston wrote for her. Among these were the ballads "Day by Day" and "I Should Care" as well as "Shrimp Boats," a kind of Cajun novelty. While at Columbia, Weston recorded his own light compositions *The Crescent City Suite* and *Gateway to the West*. Later came *The Mercy Partridge Suite*, *The Bells of Santa Ynez*, and *Memories of Ireland*. These were tone poems, often with choral passages.

In 1957 Weston began a five-year hitch as musical director for National Broadcasting Corporation Television. One of the founders of the National Academy of Recording Arts and Sciences, Weston was its first president in 1957. The same year, at a Columbia Records sales conference Weston casually imitated a dreadful cocktail lounge pianist, and "Jonathan Edwards" was born. Named, by Columbia executive George Avakian, after the eighteenth-century American Calvinist preacher Jonathan Edwards ("Sinners in the Hands of an Angry God"), "Edwards" made his recorded debut in *The Piano Artistry of Jonathan Edwards* (1957), a best-selling long-playing record. The identities of "Edwards" and subsequently Stafford as his vocal partner "Darlene" were barely disguised. In 1960 *Jonathan and Darlene Edwards in Paris* won a Grammy from the NARAS as best comedy album.

In a later comic interview with Richard J. Pietschmann, the Edwardses revealed some of their "strengths." Jonathan spoke of his penchant for "7/4 bars and sudden changes in tempo" and took pride in his arpeggios: ". . . they're not like other people's arpeggios. They contain a great many more notes." Darlene emphasized her savoir-faire: "I just love sophisticated types of songs, and when I find words that are really sophisticated, I just lay into them. I really give them their due. Rendezvous, for example, or nonchalant." Lees noted "what Jo calls 'crumbling thirds'" and "Darlene's eerily inaccurate intonation" (Stafford had perfect pitch). By 1982, when they claimed to have invented the "disco rest" amid their version of "Staying Alive" (from *Saturday Night Fever*), the Edwardses had produced six albums, including a sing-along blamed by recording executive Mitch Miller for ending the sing-along genre he had dominated for many years.

When the recording industry was altered by the development of compact discs, stimulating reissues, Weston created Corinthian Records in order to secure the masters of his and Stafford's earlier work. A highly competent, highly commercial, and subversively satirical musician, Weston also served as president of the Crippled Children's Society of Los Angeles for three years. He died in Santa Monica.

• Jo Stafford Weston aided in the research for this essay. An excellent portrait of both Westons is in Gene Lees, *Singers and the Song* (1987). Richard J. Pietschmann, "Jonathan and Darlene Edwards Talk!" originated in *Los Angeles* magazine, Dec. 1982. A sketchy obituary is in the *Los Angeles Times*, 23 Sept. 1996, while a substantial one appears in the *New York Times*, 24 Sept. 1996.

JAMES ROSS MOORE

WHITING, Richard (12 Nov. 1891–19 Feb. 1938), songwriter, was born Richard Armstrong Whiting in Peoria, Illinois, to Frank Whiting, a real estate broker, and Blossom Leach Whiting. After early childhood, he was sent west, where he acquired most of his formal education at the Harvard Military School in Los Angeles.

During his years at the military school, Whiting played piano at a Santa Monica café while pursuing a career in local vaudeville. Whiting and Marshall

Neilan, later a film director, created a songs-and-patter act; but when the act finally dissolved, Whiting returned to Peoria. At loose ends, he followed another friend's advice and moved to Detroit, where he got a job playing piano in a local Hawaiian orchestra. In 1913 he sold three songs to Jerome Remick, a Detroit music publisher, for $50. Taking a job with Remick, Whiting rose from copyboy to song plugger to office manager.

Working with lyricist Dave Radford, in 1915 Whiting produced his first hit, "It's Tulip Time in Holland," a tripping, not particularly original melody characteristic of its Tin Pan Alley era. Having sold the rights to the song for a new Steinway, Whiting watched as more than a million copies of sheet music were bought in the next six months. Thereafter he wrote for royalties. From this beginning, Whiting went on to compose some of the most engaging American popular melodies of the early twentieth century. "They Called It Dixieland" (1916, lyrics by Raymond Egan) was of the brassy faux-southern genre, made to order for Al Jolson. The evocative waltz "Till We Meet Again" (1918, lyrics by Egan), written for a "war-song" contest, became America's World War I favorite, with five million in sheet sales.

After contributing to Broadway shows in 1919, Whiting again teamed with Egan for "The Japanese Sandman" (1920). Selling two million copies in a year, the rhythmically tricky "Sandman" freshened the faux-Oriental genre and was to win from musicologist Alec Wilder praise for its wholly unexpected key shifts. Wilder, always amazed when a nontheatrical song showed innovation, called it "a phenomenon . . . and remember, it was only 1920!" "Ain't We Got Fun?" (1921, lyrics by Egan and Gus Kahn) was archetypical twenties pop. In 1921 Whiting joined the American Society of Composers, Authors and Publishers (ASCAP).

In 1923 Whiting married Eleanore Youngblood, a theatrical agent; they were to have two daughters and remain married until Whiting's death. Whiting's next major hit did not materialize until 1925. His collaborators for "Sleepy Time Gal" were composer Ange Lorenzo and lyricists Egan and Joseph Alden. The lilting "Gal," so evocative of feet quietly shuffling across a dance floor, was quickly recorded by many of the era's top dance bands and became a standard. In 1925, the high point of America's ukulele craze, Whiting wrote the faux-Hawaiian "Ukulele Lady," with lyrics by Kahn. "Breezin' Along with the Breeze" (1926, lyrics by Haven Gillespie), though a hit for Jolson, was written in a looser, nearly swinging style that prefigured the songs Whiting would write for Hollywood films.

In 1928 the Whitings moved to New York, where his only hit lyric emerged—the moody "She's Funny That Way," music by Charles Daniels (under the pseudonym Neil Moret). In the same year Whiting, urged by publisher-impresario Max Dreyfus, moved west to write for talking motion pictures and in his final decade wrote scores for forty films. In Hollywood, Whiting's range expanded. Collaborating with lyricist Leo Robin on the score for *Innocents of Paris* (1929), Whiting created the sunny "Louise," which quickly became a signature song for its first performer, Maurice Chevalier. Jointly composed with Newell Chase, the gently melancholy "My Ideal" (1930; lyrics by Robin) called for considerable vocal range and was later deemed by Wilder "one of the most respected songs of its era." For director Ernst Lubitsch's *Monte Carlo* (1930), Whiting's music provided the driving, liberating force behind one of the early talkies' most unforgettable fusings of image and music. To the strains of "Beyond the Blue Horizon," sung thrillingly by Jeanette MacDonald, the Blue Express surges through the south of France, waved exuberantly on its way by happy peasants.

During these years, Whiting made a single detour to Broadway in 1932, collaborating with Nacio Herb Brown and B. G. DeSylva on the score for *Take a Chance*. Whiting's songs included the low-down "Eadie Was a Lady" and the rippling "You're an Old Smoothie," which also became a swing-era standard. The only other non-Hollywood Whiting hit during the thirties was "Guilty" (1931, collaborators Harry Akst and Kahn). Back in Hollywood, "One Hour with You" (1932, lyrics by Oscar Straus), a dark ballad, was soon lightened and snatched away by Eddie Cantor for his theme song. In 1934 Whiting's "On the Good Ship Lollipop" (Sidney Clare) was among the earliest hits for moppet Shirley Temple. Whiting and Walter Bullock contributed the croonable ballad "When Did You Leave Heaven?" to *Sing, Baby, Sing* (1936). The song made twelve appearances on the radio program "Your Hit Parade." In the same year, Whiting and Robin's blithe, swinging "I Can't Escape from You" was the most popular of several songs from the film *Rhythm on the Range*.

In 1937 began perhaps the most rewarding collaboration of Whiting's career, when he was teamed by Warner Bros. with the jaunty young lyricist Johnny Mercer. The score of *Varsity Show* included the chatty "We're Working Our Way through College" and a song that eventually proved almost endlessly swingable, "Do You Have Any Castles That You Want to Have Built?" *Ready, Willing and Able* (also 1937) contained the last of the fabled Warner set-pieces—this one built around dozens of chorines, a gigantic typewriter and Whiting and Mercer's "Too Marvelous for Words." Wilder called the song "a model of pop song writing, musically and lyrically"; it has become a jazz classic. *Hollywood Hotel* (1938) included a piece of razzle-dazzle, "Hooray for Hollywood," which quickly became the unofficial anthem of the movies. "Ride, Tenderfoot, Ride" was the pair's sole contribution to *A Cowboy from Brooklyn* (1938).

A graduate of Tin Pan Alley, Whiting created effortless-sounding melodies. Anecdotalist Max Wilk quoted Whiting's singing daughter Margaret as having been told by the composer, "I hate to think of it as a craft, it's something that I love to do, but it is a job, it is work, and we work very hard to write a song

and make it work. You must sing this song with great affection and feeling. It takes the men who write the lyrics a long time. Just believe in their words, do them simply and honestly. That's how a singer should interpret a song." During twenty-five years that produced great changes in popular music and indeed in the expectations of American life, Richard Whiting exhibited a remarkable ability to adapt while staying fresh and innovative. His hit songs can be read as a corollary to social history. After a long struggle with heart disease, Whiting died in Los Angeles.

• The ASCAP archives were a great help in the preparation of this article. Mark White, *"You Must Remember This"* . . . *Popular Songwriters, 1900–1980* (1983), is a useful summary of Whiting's hit songs. Alec Wilder, *American Popular Song: The Great Innovators, 1900–1950* (1972), presents a composer's analysis. An obituary of Richard Whiting is in the *New York Times*, 20 Feb. 1938.

JAMES ROSS MOORE

WHITTAKER, Charles E. (22 Feb. 1901–26 Nov. 1973), U.S. Supreme Court justice, was born Charles Evans Whittaker in a farmhouse near Troy, Kansas, to Charles Evans Whittaker and Ida E. Miller. As a child he dreamed of one day becoming a lawyer, a goal inspired, he later said, by reading about court cases in local newspapers and by occasional visits to the county courthouse in Troy. He went to a one-room school until the age of fifteen when, after his mother's death, he started to work full-time as a plower and trapper. After three years, having saved $700, he enrolled in night law school at the University of Kansas City while he also received tutoring in high school subjects and worked part time as an office boy in a law firm. One of his fellow students in law school was a future president, Harry S. Truman. In 1923, a year before receiving his law degree, he was admitted to the bar and began practicing in Kansas City.

In 1930 Whittaker became a partner in the law firm of Watson, Gage, Ess, Groner & Barnett—the same firm where he had worked as an office boy a decade earlier. He specialized in corporate litigation and worked as a trial lawyer at Watson, Gage for more than a decade. In that role he established what became a lifelong reputation for diligence, hard work, and a masterly grasp of details. Much later in his career, he was characterized by both admirers and detractors as a "legal technician." In the early 1940s Whittaker became senior counselor at Watson, Gage and in that role began advising its major clients, which included the Union Pacific Railroad, Montgomery Ward, and the City National Bank and Trust Company. About this time he began taking a more active role in the state bar association, which he later served as president, and dabbled in Republican party politics.

Whittaker was named to his first judicial post in 1954 when President Dwight D. Eisenhower appointed him judge of the U.S. District Court, Western District of Missouri, in Kansas City. There he further enhanced his reputation for both hard work and inherent conservatism. In one noted case, *Davis v. University of Kansas City*, he denied the appeal of the plaintiff, a fired member of the university's faculty who at a Senate Internal Security Committee hearing would not answer questions about his possible ties with Communists. In 1956 Whittaker moved up the judicial ladder with his appointment to the U.S. Court of Appeals for the Eighth Circuit, which comprised seven midwestern states and was also in Kansas City.

The capstone of Whittaker's meteoric rise to judicial prominence occurred less than a year later when President Eisenhower, at the recommendation of Attorney General Herbert Brownell, named him an associate justice of the U.S. Supreme Court, succeeding retiring justice Stanley Reed. Whittaker seemed an appropriate choice as Eisenhower's fourth Court appointee (the first had been Chief Justice Earl Warren): his political affiliation gave the Court a fourth Republican justice, and his midwestern roots created geographical balance on the bench. Endorsed by the American Bar Association as well as by prominent Democrats, Whittaker sailed through his confirmation hearings and was approved unanimously by the Senate. He was sworn in on 25 March 1957 as the ninety-first justice of the Supreme Court.

Court observers assumed that Whittaker would be a conservative jurist, and they were ultimately proved correct. Initially, though, he took moderate and even liberal positions. In the fall of 1957 he cast the deciding vote in *Green v. United States*, which held that someone found guilty on a lesser charge after being tried for a more serious crime could not then be retried on the original charge. Again that fall, in *Moore v. Michigan*, he voted in favor of a new trial for a mentally disabled seventeen-year-old male whose supposed waiver of his right to counsel could not in fact be confirmed. In several cases he also voted to curb government power; in one instance he was part of a majority that ruled unconstitutional a law taking away the citizenship of an army deserter.

In subsequent votes during his five years on the Court, however, Whittaker generally sided with the conservatives to give them a five-man majority. He consistently voted to increase criminal penalties and to support a judge's right to declare individuals in contempt of court. Echoing his decision years earlier in *Davis v. University of Kansas City*, he also voted regularly in support of punishment for individuals who were either declared Communists or who refused to answer questions about possible Communist affiliations. In 1961 his vote in *Poe v. Ullman* supported the Court's refusal to decide whether a birth-control ban in Connecticut was unconstitutional.

The strain of work ultimately took its toll on the detail-consumed Whittaker, and in March 1962 he abruptly entered a Washington hospital suffering from fatigue. Realizing that a long recuperation would be necessary, and frustrated at his inability to participate in several important cases before the Court that spring, he resigned on 26 March. Returning to Kansas City, Whittaker spent several years in retirement. He

generally kept a low public profile, though at the height of civil disobedience demonstrations in the mid-1960s he wrote an article for the *FBI Law Enforcement Bulletin* urging that citizens take to the courts rather than the streets to rectify social ills. In 1965 he returned to work as a legal counsel for General Motors, relinquishing his retirement pay in order to do so.

Whittaker's wife was Winifred R. Pugh, whom he married in 1928; the couple had three sons. In private life Whittaker was a lifelong Methodist. He enjoyed fishing and baseball games, and as a hobby he raised cattle for many years on a small Missouri farm. Whittaker died of an abdominal aneurysm at a hospital in Kansas City.

• For biographical information, see the entries on Whittaker in *Current Biography Yearbook 1957* and in Leon Friedman and Fred L. Israel, eds., *The Justices of the United States Supreme Court, 1789–1978: Their Lives and Major Opinions*, vol. 4 (1978). In addition, see Daniel M. Berman, "Mr. Justice Whittaker: A Preliminary Appraisal," *Missouri Law Review* 24 (Jan. 1959): 1–15. An obituary appears in the *New York Times*, 27 Nov. 1973.

ANN T. KEENE

WHYTE, William H. (1 Oct. 1917–12 Jan. 1999), author and editor, was born William Hollingsworth Whyte, Jr., in West Chester, Pennsylvania, one of two sons of William Hollingsworth Whyte, a railroad man, and Louise Toth Whyte. He went to St. Andrews School in Middletown, Delaware, where he edited the school paper, before he enrolled in the college at Princeton University, where he won a playwriting contest and majored in English, receiving an A.B. cum laude in 1939.

After an apprenticeship at the Vick School of Applied Merchandising, Whyte worked for the Vick Chemical Company till 1941, when he joined the U.S. Marine Corps. In 1945 he left the corps as a captain, after serving as an intelligence officer and teaching at the command school in Quantico, Virginia.

When Whyte joined the staff of Henry Luce's *Fortune* in 1946, he was typical of the young "experts" Luce had recruited since in 1929 establishing his expensive glossy magazine dedicated to the romance of business. Whyte became an associate editor in 1948 and assistant managing editor in 1953.

During these years Whyte, heading *Fortune*s study of communications within business, wrote articles on corporations and executives based on firsthand research. These in turn became *Is Anybody Listening? How and Why U.S. Business Fumbles When It Talks with Human Beings* (1952), credited to Whyte "and the editors of *Fortune*." The book, described in a *New York Times* review as "an inquiry into the massive failure of American business to 'sell' free enterprise to the people," prefigured in some ways Whyte's *The Organization Man* (1956).

The Organization Man was published during a period of introspection about the pressures to conform that seemed to be forced on the post–World War II American citizen. Sociologist David Riesman detailed in *The Lonely Crowd* (1950) the alienation of the conformist; novelist J. D. Salinger portrayed adolescent rebellion sympathetically in *The Catcher in the Rye* (1951); popular novelist Sloan Wilson made of the faceless company man an antihero in *The Man in the Grey Flannel Suit* (1956); poet Allen Ginsberg in *Howl* (1956) made of the artist a tragic victim of conformity; sociologist C. Wright Mills outlined in *The Power Elite* (1956) the danger of trusting oligarchies; Vance Packard's *The Hidden Persuaders* (1957) warned of mind control via subliminal advertising; and in 1961 social psychologist Stanley Milgram would begin the experiments that led to his *Obedience to Authority* (1974).

The Organization Man was not an attack on mass society but a firsthand analysis of how contemporary corporate structures, stressing safety and security, wore away in its executives the very qualities of entrepreneurial dash and vigor that had made the corporations successful. According to Whyte, there were no romantics in contemporary business; rugged individualists were not to be found. Whyte went further in suggesting that the same bureaucratization—what C. Wright Mills termed the "organizational crawl"—was stifling individual innovation in education, medicine, and science. The book, a plea for principled individualism, won the first American Library Association Liberty and Justice Award (1957) in the category of contemporary affairs and problems.

The success of *The Organization Man* made Whyte financially independent. He left the staff of *Fortune*, but not before contributing to the magazine's 1957–1958 series "The Exploding Metropolis." Whyte's two articles, "Are Cities Un-American?" and "Urban Sprawl," initiated his second career as an empirical urbanologist. "Urban Sprawl," its title another example of Whyte's gift for coining resonant terms, galvanized the debate on an unattractive feature of postwar life. Whyte advised cities to preserve open spaces by buying the land on their perimeters—or at least the development rights. Whyte's paper "Conservation Easements," given at the Urban Land Institute in 1959, was helpful in gaining passage of open-space legislation in California, New York, Connecticut, and Massachusetts.

In 1964 Whyte married Jenny Bell, a designer. They had one daughter and remained married until Whyte's death. Firsthand research and analysis of urban problems dominated the rest of Whyte's professional life. His later books include *Cluster Development* (1964), *The Last Landscape* (1968), *The Social Life of Small Urban Spaces* (1980), and *City* (1988).

The Social Life of Small Urban Spaces originated in 1969 when Whyte was editing the text of New York City's master plan. He noticed that there was no provision for the evaluation of planning policies, past or present. In 1971, as a visiting professor at Hunter College of the City University of New York, Whyte ob-

tained an "expedition grant" of $35,000 to take students onto the streets, to film and observe—thus to understand, using the techniques of social anthropologists—what actually happened in sometimes underused public spaces, such as "plazas," that earlier planning had encouraged. In 1975 new zoning requirements, based on what Whyte's team had observed, were put into practice.

Among the notions explored in *Small Urban Spaces* is that people need cities, which always will be "something of a mess," and cities need people, a point reiterated in the 1980 paper, "Sitting," that Whyte gave at the "City as Dwelling" at the University of Dallas. The greatest public space could remain the street corner where "shmoozing" would occur; if people stood or sat (the best spaces would be eminently "sitable") sometimes, that would be the best possible sign. Improving a city area to discourage "undesirables" could be achieved by making it as attractive to as many other people as possible. Inner-city spaces could be as safe as suburban parking lots. Public spaces would benefit from the mix provided by retail activity; street peddlers would increase sales in local stores, especially if they peddled food. Shopping malls and other aspects of the "fortressing" of America—such as overhead walkways and underground passageways—are characterized as ". . . places designed with distrust [that] get what they were looking for."

Whyte's subsequent studies included sixteen years of watching and filming the behavior of New York City pedestrians, of whom he remarked, "[They] are the best. They walk fast and they walk adroitly. . . . With the subtlest of motions they signal their intentions to one another. They bully cars if they can." He derived from his own observations eleven rules of—not for—pedestrian behavior.

Whyte favored "honky-tonk"—anything that would invest sidewalks with hustle and bustle: "Up to seven people per foot of walkway a minute is a nice bustle." As early as 1980 he warned, "We have given a disproportionate amount of our street space to vehicles, and the time has come to start giving some of it back to the pedestrian from whom it was taken."

Another study concerned executives who had moved their companies "out of town" on the premise that business would be better away from an urban center. Whyte showed, however, that the relocations were usually within eight miles of the executives' suburban homes and that most of the businesses studied did not do as well in their new locations as those that remained in New York.

Whyte regularly served on various boards and commissions, including the Conservation Foundation and the Hudson River Valley Commission. He died in New York, the city he called home for many decades.

A persuasive liberal idealist, who was criticized for not really believing that people might leave cities for racist reasons, Whyte influenced generations of city planners. His ideas helped stem the tide of rampant suburbanization and helped lay the foundation for urban regeneration projects on a more human scale, such as those that revived many older American cities during the 1990s.

• Aside from Whyte's own books and articles, the following are of interest: Paul Leinberger and Bruce Tucker, *The New Individualists: The Generation after The Organization Man* (1991); and Steven S. Hall, "Standing on Those Corners, Watching All the Folks Go By," *Smithsonian* 19 (Feb. 1989): 119 ff. Albert LaFarge, ed., *The Essential William Whyte* (2000) includes selections from Whyte's books and many of his articles for *Fortune*. Whyte's "characteristics of a pedestrian" can be found at his website obituary (goodbye-mag.com/jan99/whyte.html). The obituary by Michael T. Kaufman in the *New York Times*, 13 Jan. 1999, is informative.

JAMES ROSS MOORE

WILLARD, Jess (29 Dec. 1881–15 Dec. 1968), world heavyweight boxing champion, the son of Myron Willard and Margaret Willard (maiden surname unknown), was born in St. Clere, Pottawatomie County, Kansas. His father, a Civil War veteran, died before he was born, and his mother was remarried in 1891 to Elisha Stalker. Willard grew up on Stalker's ranch and received only a few years of schooling. Developing to unusual size, approximately six feet six inches and 225 pounds, he was employed during his teenage and young adult years as a breaker and trainer of horses; he also worked in a livery stable and ran a wagon train. In 1908 he married Harriet "Hattie" Evans, whom he had known since childhood.

After Jack Johnson, the first black heavyweight champion, won the title in 1908 and defeated the former champion, James J. Jeffries, in 1910 a search began for a "white hope" who could defeat Johnson. Willard lived at this time in Oklahoma, where his large size and great strength attracted attention. Encouraged to try his hand at boxing, he sold his horses and began to train. He was already twenty-eight years old when he first put on boxing gloves and twenty-nine when he first saw a boxing match. His first fight of record occurred on 15 February 1911 in Sapulpa, Oklahoma, when he lost on a foul in ten rounds to Louis Fink.

Willard then won seven consecutive fights, including a knockout of Fink in a return match. His second loss occurred on 11 October 1911 in Springfield, Missouri, when he left the ring in the fifth round of a fight with a local man, Joe Cox. Afterward, he claimed that his life had been threatened, but he was labeled a "quitter." He then moved to the Chicago area, where he won three fights by knockout, and then to New York where he attracted serious attention by soundly defeating two other white hope heavyweights, Arthur Pelkey and Luther McCarty. After a few further successes, he was defeated in twenty rounds by Gunboat Smith in San Francisco. On 22 August 1913, in Vernon, California, Willard scored an eleven-round knockout of William "Bull" Young, and Young died soon afterward from injuries sustained in the fight.

Willard was not deterred by Young's death and soon defeated two other well-known white hope

heavyweights, Carl Morris and George Rodel. In 1914 he was surprisingly outpointed by Tom McMahon, but he then scored two more knockouts. By this time he was regarded as a serious challenger for the heavyweight title. A stock company of backers led by a prominent boxing figure, Jack Curley, was formed on 24 August 1914, the objective being to gain a heavyweight title fight for Willard with Johnson and, if Willard won the title, to profit from the lucrative personal appearances that he would make afterward.

Johnson, who had fled to Europe to escape prosecution for violation of the Mann Act, was persuaded to defend his title against Willard. On 5 April 1915, at Oriental Race Track, Havana, Cuba, the two fighters met in a "finish fight," scheduled to proceed indefinitely until one fighter was knocked out or could not continue. Johnson was much faster afoot and far more skillful, but he could not hurt the bigger Willard. By the twenty-third round it became apparent that Johnson was weakening, and in the twenty-sixth he was hurt badly by body punches and then knocked out by a powerful overhand right to the jaw. Years later, apparently to make money from a magazine article, he claimed to have lost intentionally to Willard, but the film of the fight was rediscovered in the 1960s, revealing that the knockout was genuine.

On 25 March 1916 Willard made the first defense of his title by outpointing Frank Moran in ten rounds at Madison Square Garden in New York City. This was his only fight in the interval from 1915 to 1919, most of his time being given to public appearances in vaudeville, with the Sells Floto Circus, Buffalo Bill's Wild West Show, and with his own 101 Ranch Circus. He also made a seven-reel feature film titled *The Challenge of Chance*.

During and immediately after World War I, Jack Dempsey came to prominence by scoring a long string of quick knockouts over other heavyweights. Inevitably, he was matched with Willard, and they met in Toledo, Ohio, on 4 July 1919, in a fight promoted by Tex Rickard. The twenty-four-year-old Dempsey was much younger than Willard, who was thirty-seven, but also smaller, weighing only 185 pounds to Willard's 250. He quickly attacked and knocked Willard down seven times in the first round, inflicting severe facial damage. Willard courageously continued and managed a rally in the second round, but he suffered another beating in the third, which so exhausted him that he told his seconds to stop the fight before the bell rang for the fourth round.

In 1922 Willard attempted a comeback and knocked out Floyd Johnson in eleven rounds in New York. He then fought a newcomer, Luis Firpo of Argentina, before 90,000 fans in Jersey City, New Jersey. Unable to hurt the crude Firpo with his own punches, and despite making the Argentinian miss many wild swings, Willard finally weakened and was knocked out in the eighth round, thus ending his boxing career. He had a total of thirty-five fights, losing six.

In the ring Willard depended on his great size and long arms to win. When he trained hard, as he did before the Jack Johnson fight, he was remarkably durable. When he trained less thoroughly, as was the case before the Dempsey match, he was more vulnerable. He was a reasonably good boxer but slower in his movements than almost any other heavyweight champion.

Willard made most of his money in the ring from the Dempsey and Firpo fights, for which he received $100,000 and $125,000, respectively. He fought Jack Johnson for nothing but his training experiences. Being frugal, he mostly managed himself and was secure financially when he left the ring. He and his wife raised five children. He owned ranches, first in Kansas and later in southern California, and obtained income from real estate holdings and from his jobs as a referee at wrestling matches. During World War II he did some overseas work with the United Service Organization (USO). He died of a cerebral hemorrhage following a heart attack in Los Angeles.

• An interview of Willard, "Then and Now," by Gladwin Hill, appeared in the *New York Times Magazine*, 27 Dec. 1953. Useful articles in *The Ring* magazine, both by Dan Daniel, are "Camera Shot Impugns Willard's Conquest," Nov. 1944, and "Toledo, Sixty Years Ago, and Dempsey Slaughters Willard," Aug. 1979. An obituary is in the *New York Times*, 16 Dec. 1968.

LUCKETT V. DAVIS

WILLIAMS, Frankwood E. (18 May 1883–24 Sept. 1936), psychiatrist, psychoanalyst, and contributor to mental health care policy, was born Frankwood Earl Williams in Cardington, Ohio, the son of James Leander Williams, a physician, and Amanda Elizabeth Wood Williams. Williams spent most of his childhood in Indianapolis, where he graduated from high school in 1903. He received his A.B. from the University of Wisconsin in 1907 and his M.D. from the University of Michigan at Ann Arbor in 1912. Here, he was resident physician at the recently established State Psychopathic Hospital under Albert M. Barrett the year following his graduation. In 1913–1915 he was executive officer and first assistant physician at the Boston Psychopathic Hospital; he was then appointed the executive secretary of the Massachusetts Society for Mental Hygiene, for which he developed extensive programs of public health education on matters related to mental illness. In 1917 he became associate medical director of the National Committee for Mental Hygiene, an organization that aimed to further psychiatric research and teaching as well as stimulate the development of preventive measures. From 1922 to 1931 he was the medical director of that organization. In 1917 he became the founding editor of the journal *Mental Hygiene*, a position he maintained until 1932.

Under Williams's guidance, the program of the National Committee for Mental Hygiene shifted away from a concern with mental illness and the improvement of mental hospitals toward a concern with prevention and the maintenance of the mental health of relatively well-adjusted individuals. Under his guidance, a program on the prevention of juvenile delinquency through Child Guidance Clinics was implemented. He also initiated research projects investigating the relationship between crime, dependency, and mental disorder and was instrumental in the establishment of programs at colleges and universities where students could receive counseling. In 1930 he was the program director of the First International Congress on Mental Hygiene, which attracted 3,000 psychiatrists from all over the world. Williams was involved with teaching social workers; at various points in time, he held teaching appointments at the Smith College School for Social Work, the New School for Social Research, and the New York School for Social Work.

In 1925 Williams, who had been a member of the New York Psychoanalytic Society since 1919, was psychoanalyzed by Otto Rank, who at that time was a leading figure in the psychoanalytic movement. Williams was an active participant in the affairs of the New York Psychoanalytic Society. He popularized psychoanalytic ideas through his teaching activities, articles, and public lectures. Partly because of his involvement in teaching social workers, Williams advocated lay analysis, which was at that time vigorously opposed by the American Psychoanalytic Association. In 1931 he was one of the founding editors of the *Psychoanalytic Quarterly*, entirely devoted to orthodox psychoanalysis. At that time, he began to devote himself full time to psychoanalysis.

After he resigned the directorship of the National Committee for Mental Hygiene, Williams visited the Soviet Union to investigate psychiatry in that country. He came to believe that, because of the superior organization of Soviet society, mental illness and all forms of maladjustment were on the decline there. For the last five years of his life, Williams promoted the achievements of the Soviet Union in the field of psychiatry and mental health. He joined a number of radical organizations, such as the Interprofessional Association for Social Insurance and the Social Economics Foundation, which advocated far-reaching measures of economic planning. In 1932 he was one of the founding editors of *Health & Hygiene*, a health magazine that was part of the Communist Party–USA's newspaper, the *Daily Worker*. He died on his way back from a long trip to the Soviet Union on board the ocean liner *Georgic* two days before it arrived in New York City.

As medical director of the National Committee for Mental Hygiene, Williams shaped the mental hygiene movement in the United States. Under his directorship, the activities of this committee focused less on mental illness. Believing that social factors significantly influence the mental health and well-being of individuals, he emphasized the prevention of maladjustment among school children, college students, and adults. He also favored interdisciplinary participation in mental hygiene work and taught social workers the principles of psychoanalysis. During the 1930s, he held a prominent position among radical professionals who wished to restructure American society along Soviet lines. In 1927 he received an honorary degree from Colgate University.

• In a widely quoted and circulated article, "Community Responsibility in Mental Hygiene," published in the *American Review* in 1923, Williams emphasized the importance of preventive measures in psychiatry. His views on raising children and the nature of adolescence are presented in *Adolescence: Studies in Mental Hygiene* (1930), which contained a number of previously published articles. Williams was convinced that mental and social conditions were closely related, a view that is expressed in a symposium he organized on the topic (see *Some Social Aspects of Mental Hygiene*, issued in 1930 as part 1, vol. 149 of the *Annals of the American Academy of Political and Social Science*). The papers presented at the Congress on Mental Hygiene he organized in 1930 were published as the *Proceedings of the First International Congress on Mental Hygiene, Held at Washington, D.C.* (1932). Williams's views on the successes of the Soviet Union in combating mental illness and disorder are presented in *Russia, Youth, and the Present-day World: Further Studies in Mental Hygiene* (1934). An obituary can be found in the *American Journal of Psychiatry* 93, 3 (1936): 750–54.

HANS POLS

WILSON, Bill (26 Nov. 1895–24 Jan. 1971), and **Bob Smith** (8 Aug. 1879–16 Nov. 1950), founders of Alcoholics Anonymous, were known publicly as "Bill W." and "Bob S.," in keeping with their organization's rule of anonymity for members.

Bill Wilson was born William Griffith Wilson in East Dorset, Vermont, to Gilman Wilson, a marble quarry foreman, and his wife, Emily Griffith Wilson. His parents divorced when Bill was about nine, ostensibly because of Gilman Wilson's heavy drinking, and Bill was thereafter warned repeatedly by his mother never to touch alcohol. Bill and his younger sister were sent to live with their maternal grandparents so that Emily Wilson could train as an osteopath in Boston. After five years in their well-to-do household, he was sent to a boarding school, Burr and Burton Seminary, in Manchester, Vermont, and then, upon graduation, to Norwich University, at that time a college-level military school.

Beginning in prep school and continuing in college, Wilson encountered a series of disappointments, from the sudden death of a girlfriend to failure in sports and a lack of popularity, and in response he apparently established a growing pattern of rationalization and fantasy as compensation. He also began to experience periods of depression, alternating with states of manic highs, though he apparently neither sought nor was offered treatment until he reached middle-age. This behavior did not, however, keep him out of the army, which he entered as a second lieutenant in 1917, shortly after the United States entered World War I; he served for a time in France but never directly engaged in combat. The only thing notable about his military service was the fact that he began consuming alcohol shortly after it commenced and soon gained a reputation as a heavy drinker.

During Wilson's teens he had met Lois Burnham, a New Yorker four years older than he, who vacationed in Vermont each year with her family. The couple married in 1918, while Wilson was on leave from the army; despite their attempts to have children they remained childless and perhaps partly for that reason the marriage was always troubled. Having never completed college and with no employable skills, Wilson was forced to take a variety of jobs following his discharge from the army in 1919. He worked at a variety of mostly menial tasks over the next few years and also studied law briefly, dreaming of success while his drinking escalated in the face of Prohibition. In the midst of the stock market boom of the 1920s, Wilson became convinced that he could make a fortune on Wall Street; with the help of a wealthy friend of his wife he set himself up as a securities analyst and consultant, selling tips on promising companies and investments along the Eastern Seaboard. After a year he became a moderately successful trader on Wall Street, but his heavy drinking continued, often causing rows with his wife.

When the stock market crashed in the fall of 1929, suddenly putting a halt to Wilson's career, he and his wife were forced to move in with Lois Wilson's parents in Brooklyn, and Lois became a saleswoman at Macy's. Wilson became a perpetual drunk, abusive to his wife and unable to hold any job. Finally, through the intervention of his sister and her husband, Wilson was admitted in late 1933 to the Charles B. Towns Hospital, a Manhattan institution that specialized in treating alcoholics by forcing withdrawal from drinking and administering belladonna. Alcoholism, considered a moral weakness by most authorities of the time, was regarded as a disease by the hospital director, and this new concept would eventually have a life-changing effect on Wilson. However, three separate stays at Towns between 1933 and 1934 did not cure him. He continued to go on binges in between until the fall of 1934, when he encountered an old prep-school classmate, known only as Ebby, who was newly cured of his own alcoholism, apparently for good. Ebby attributed his cure to the Oxford Group, then a popular spiritual movement that had been founded earlier in the century by Frank N. D. Buchman and that later became known as Moral Re-Armament. Members of the group practiced a simple regimen for spiritual renewal and health, consisting of self-surrender to God, prayer, and service without reward to others. Wilson was impressed and in December 1934, with Ebby's encouragement, he again entered Towns Hospital, vowing to overcome his dependence on alcohol. At the hospital, where Ebby visited and prayed with him every day, Wilson apparently experienced a spiritual conversion, and after seven days he was released, declaring he would never drink again.

The next few months were difficult, as Wilson tried unsuccessfully to find employment in what had become the Great Depression. He fought off the urge to drink by attending Oxford Group meetings with his wife and making bedside visits to alcoholics at Towns

Hospital. But in May 1935, finding himself alone in a hotel room in Akron, Ohio, following an unsuccessful attempt to mastermind a shareholders' takeover of a local rubber company, he felt himself in danger of a relapse. Seeking help, he called a local minister in an effort to locate a nearby Oxford Group. He was referred to Henrietta Seiberling, an Akron socialite who was active in the movement, and she introduced him to her friend and fellow member Bob Smith.

Robert Holbrook Smith had been born in St. Johnsbury, Vermont, to a prominent local family; his father, a probate judge, was a leading banker and had also served as superintendent of schools. (His parents' names, however, do not appear in readily available sources of information.) The Smiths were active in a local Protestant church, too much so for their son, who resented being forced to attend Sunday school and church youth group meetings. Good-looking and affable, Smith prepared for college at St. Johnsbury Academy and went on to Dartmouth, where he became by his own admission a serious drinker and spent much of his time playing cards while still managing to get reasonably good grades. Following graduation in 1902, Smith took a job as a traveling salesman of hardware in New England, eastern Canada, and as far west as Chicago, perhaps drawn there because it was near the Oak Park hometown of his college sweetheart, Anne Robinson Ripley, who had graduated from Wellesley. After three years on the road, Smith enrolled at the University of Michigan as a premedical student while continuing to drink heavily. Now having to deal with the serious physical side effects of alcoholism, including tremors and blackouts, Smith found it hard going, but he managed to be accepted at Rush Medical College in Chicago in 1907 and received his medical degree three years later.

After interning at City Hospital in Akron, Ohio, and completing a surgical residency, Smith settled there permanently, establishing a practice and marrying Anne Ripley in 1915. The couple had a son three years later, and in 1923 they adopted a daughter. Smith's drinking continued unabated, but he was not forced, like Bill Wilson and many other Prohibition drinkers, to rely on so-called bathtub gin. Pure grain alcohol was still available through a doctor's prescription, ostensibly for medical purposes, and Smith simply filled his own prescriptions at different drugstores around the city.

Paradoxically, the necessity to earn enough money to keep buying liquor kept Smith from succumbing completely: by carefully arranging his schedule and taking large doses of sedatives to calm his tremors, Smith managed to maintain his medical practice. He also hid his liquor and usually drank in private, keeping it, he thought, a secret from his wife. But as the years passed, Smith's alcoholism became apparent to his friends and family, and his physical conditioned worsened. Finally, in 1933, Anne Smith was able to get her husband to attend an Oxford Group meeting, having learned that participation had apparently helped several prominent Akron residents (among

them their friend Henrietta Seiberling) with their personal problems.

At first skeptical because of his longtime antipathy to religious practice, Smith became impressed with the group, began regularly attending meetings with his wife, and soon joined a local Presbyterian church. But he still drank, and his health was now so bad that he was losing patients and threatened with dismissal from the hospital staff. Finally, in the spring of 1935, he was induced by other Oxford Group members to acknowledge his problem publicly, at their weekly meeting; this public declaration, as well as being able to ask the other members to pray for him, apparently turned Smith around. Following the group's "divine guidance" that called for him never to drink alcohol again, Smith began to practice sobriety. Shortly afterward, Bill Wilson arrived in town and was put in touch with Smith. A born proselytizer, Wilson believed that he could help Smith remain sober, and he remained in Akron for that purpose, moving into the Smiths' house in June with the encouragement of Smith's wife and other Oxford Group members.

After a final binge during a trip to a medical convention in Atlantic City, Smith returned to Akron to dry out and make a permanent commitment to sobriety. He had his last drink, a bottle of beer, on 10 June 1935, the date that Alcoholics Anonymous claims as the day of its founding, although it was part of the Oxford Group during its early years. After Smith's recovery, he and Wilson began working with other patients hospitalized in Akron for chronic alcoholism, sobering them through medication prescribed by Smith and then reinforcing their sobriety through communal prayer combined with other precepts of the Oxford Group. From the outset, the guaranteed anonymity of participants was a watchword: members were known only by their first names, and if these were common, then the initials of surnames were appended. Wilson and Smith applied this rule to themselves as well, and were known henceforth as Bill W. and Bob S.

Wilson returned to his wife and home in Brooklyn at the end of the summer and continued to work with alcoholics through the Oxford Group while dabbling, usually unsuccessfully, in various business ventures. Smith meanwhile went on working with alcoholics in Akron while maintaining his surgical practice. Smith's and Wilson's "converts" grew steadily in number over the next four years in both Ohio and New York. They would meet in each others' homes, and they used as their texts for discussion the Bible, *The Varieties of Religious Experience*, by William James, and several bestselling books of the period that described personal conversions achieved through prayer.

By the late 1930s, however, Wilson had become convinced that a separate organization was needed to help alcoholics, who were often derelicts and felt out of place in the usually upper-class and increasingly clubby atmosphere of the Oxford Group. As word spread of the success of Wilson and Smith in treating alcoholics, John D. Rockefeller, Jr., a strong prohibitionist, became interested in their work. In 1938, with a small grant and legal help from some of Rockefeller's associates, Wilson and several New York group members established a tax-exempt organization to promote sobriety called the Alcoholic Foundation. To that end, Wilson began writing a textbook to be used as a guide in working with alcoholics. The textbook described his own experience as an alcoholic and his recovery, recounted his and Smith's work with other alcoholics, included a series of testimonials, and in a chapter titled "How It Works" laid out a progressive agenda, called the Twelve Steps, for an alcoholic's recovery. It began with an admission of the drinker's powerlessness, followed by his declaration of dependence on God and his subsequent progression toward spiritual enlightenment; it concluded with the recovered alcoholic promising to maintain his commitment to the principles he had accepted and to help others through the same process.

With the title *Alcoholics Anonymous*, Wilson's textbook was published in the spring of 1939. Manuscript versions had already been circulated among the New York and Ohio groups, but the bound text, nicknamed the Big Book, initially attracted few purchasers after receiving largely mixed reviews and outright hostility from the medical and scientific community. Nevertheless, the New York group, under Wilson's leadership, doggedly carried on, as did Smith's group in Akron. Through advertisements and magazine articles about the work of the two men, as well as organizing trips that Wilson made with his wife across the country, local groups in other cities began springing up. By 1944 Alcoholics Anonymous (AA), as the organization was now called, had some 10,000 members nationwide and had begun publishing a monthly magazine, *The Grapevine*. Although initially an all-male organization, AA now welcomed women, too, as members.

Even as AA gained success, Wilson's periodic depressions continued, and during the 1940s he sought the help of both psychiatrists and clergymen; he remained skeptical of organized religion, however, and did not join a church. Despite his personal problems, he continued to work vigorously for AA, which had spread to other countries. In response to an emerging need for organizational guidelines among the member groups he devised what became known as the Twelve Traditions, a series of bylaws that included the preservation of members' anonymity and a proscription against members profiting in any way from their work within the organization. The Twelve Traditions, which joined the Twelve Steps to form the philosophical framework of AA, were adopted at its first international convention, held in July 1950 in New York. By this time Bob Smith was ill with cancer; he died three months later, leaving Wilson to lead the organization with the assistance of a board of trustees. In the year following Smith's death, a group called Al-Anon was formed within AA to help families of alcoholics; Wilson's wife, Lois, was one of the cofounders.

During the 1950s AA and its claims to have rescued thousands from alcoholism began to be widely recognized. Wilson was offered honorary degrees and personal publicity, including a cover story in *Time*, all of which he refused in accordance with the Twelve Traditions. Though his marriage remained troubled, he continued to live with his wife in a house they had acquired some years earlier in rural Westchester County, outside New York. But he was on the road frequently on behalf of AA, and in the last decades of his life he became known as a womanizer. In the 1960s he also experimented with LSD, extolled vitamin therapy for mental problems, and became interested in spiritualism, organizing séances at his home. Despite his continuing personal problems, at AA conventions the man who had once ached for friends and prestige was now greeted with tears and adulation by grateful members, and his depression may have been relieved somewhat by the realization that his book now sold in the millions.

In addition to the so-called Big Book, Wilson was the author of *Twelve Steps and Twelve Traditions* (1953), a collection of essays about AA; *Alcoholics Anonymous Comes of Age* (1957), a history of the organization to 1955; and *As Bill Sees It* (1967), a collection of short pieces on a variety of topics. A heavy smoker for years, Wilson was diagnosed with emphysema in the last decade of his life. He died of that disease at his home and was buried in East Dorset, Vermont, his birthplace.

Though many continue to disagree with the philosophical underpinnings of Alcoholics Anonymous and argue that alcoholism is not a disease, the achievements of AA in turning millions away from addiction, as well as its sister organizations Al-Anon and Alateen (which helps children of alcoholics), cannot be denied. Wilson's, and to a lesser extent Smith's, legacy is not only the largest organization of its kind in the world but also the many other unrelated twelve step–based programs it inspired for the treatment of substance abuse and addiction.

• The most accessible and succinct source of biographical information on Wilson and Smith remains *Getting Better: Inside Alcoholics Anonymous* (1988), by Nan Robertson, a Pulitzer Prize–winning *New York Times* reporter. Robertson, herself an AA member, also offers a thorough history of the organization, toward which she is understandably sympathetic; her accounts of Wilson's and Smith's lives are, however, coolly objective. Among Robertson's sources is Robert Thomsen, *Bill W.* (1975), a biography of Wilson not authorized by AA. More recent and detailed unauthorized biographies of Wilson include Matthew J. Raphael, *Bill W. and Mr. Wilson: The Legend of A.A.'s Cofounder* (2000); and Francis Hartigan, *Bill W.: A Biography of Alcoholics Anonymous Cofounder Bill Wilson* (2000). The only known separate biography of Smith is *Dr. Bob and the Good Oldtimers* (1980), published anonymously by AA. For a history of alcoholism and various approaches that have been used to treat it, see especially George E. Vaillant, *The Natural History of Alcoholism Revisited* (1995), an updated edition of a now classic work first published in 1983. See also Mark E. Lender and James K. Martin, *Drinking in America: A History* (1982).

Obituaries for Bob Smith and Bill Wilson are in the *New York Times*, 17 Nov. 1950 and 26 Jan. 1971, respectively.

ANN T. KEENE

WILSON, Flip (8 Dec. 1933–25 Nov. 1998), comedian, actor, and writer, was born Clerow Wilson, Jr., in Jersey City, New Jersey, the son of Clerow Wilson and Cornelia Wilson, whose maiden name was also Wilson. His father, a handyman, was unable to support the large family of twelve children, and the boy was given up to foster care at an early age. Although his schooling was sporadic, he managed to appear in a number of school plays, including one in which he played the part of Clara Barton. Drag comedy would later become central to his success. He gained the nickname "Flip" as a teenager because of his inclination to break into sudden impromptu comic performances. Friends said he appeared to be "flippin' out." At age sixteen he left school and enlisted in the U.S. Air Force, serving from 1950 to 1954. It was here that he began to find his vocation as a comedian, delivering comic monologues and putting on skits for his fellow servicemen.

Following his discharge, Wilson settled in San Francisco hoping to begin a show business career in the city's nightclub scene, which was gaining a reputation as a hotbed of stand-up comedy. It was also one of the few places in the United States where black comedians could find work. While supporting himself as a bellhop at the Manor Plaza Hotel, he insinuated his way into the house nightclub by putting on an act, gratis, as a drunken bellhop during the breaks taken by featured acts.

Gaining notice this way, he was offered several gigs at local nightclubs and eventually made it onto the national circuit. Most of the clubs were cheap bars, known in the business as "toilets," and he often was forced to hitchhike from city to city during the late 1950s as he continued to write new material and develop a repertoire of original characters. By the end of the decade he was playing better venues, including the Fontainebleau Hotel in Miami Beach and the Apollo Theatre in New York.

A turning point came in 1965, when Johnny Carson invited Wilson to appear on "The Tonight Show" after hearing veteran comedian Redd Foxx's favorable comment about Wilson's nightclub act. This led to a string of guest appearances for Wilson on some of television's most popular programs, including "The Ed Sullivan Show" and "Rowan and Martin's Laugh-In." In 1969 he starred in his own prime-time comedy special on NBC. Its critical and commercial success led to the premiere of his weekly series, "The Flip Wilson Show," in 1970.

Following the classic comedy-variety format developed by such early television stars as Milton Berle and Jackie Gleason, Wilson typically began the hour with a monologue in front of a stage curtain and then presented himself and his guest stars in a series of short comic sketches and musical numbers. It was in these sketches that Wilson developed his signature characters. They included Geraldine, a sassy, outspoken woman who reveled in testing the limits of female propriety; the ultraspirited, if somewhat shifty, Reverend LeRoy of the Church of What's Happening Now; and Freddie the Playboy, a silver-tongued ladies' man.

Geraldine was by far the most popular. Drag humor was nothing new to prime-time television; Berle had made liberal use of it in the medium's earliest days. Wilson, however, reinvigorated the art by creating an enduring persona in Geraldine. He used the character's unabashed sexuality to push television content into areas that tested the limits of the still-vigilant network censorship codes of the 1970s. Geraldine was especially frank on the subject of her boyfriend, Killer, who Wilson also played on occasion. "The devil made me do it!"—her all-purpose excuse for misbehavior—achieved the status of a national catchphrase.

Wilson became a television star of the first magnitude, winning two Emmy Awards and a Golden Globe for the show. This was all the more remarkable in light of the commercial failure of earlier attempts to have such well-established African-American stars as Nat King Cole and Sammy Davis, Jr., serve as hosts of prime-time variety hours. During the peak of his stardom Wilson continued his live performances, becoming a frequent headliner in Las Vegas. He won a Grammy Award in 1970 for "Best Comedy Recording" with his album of stand-up monologues, *The Devil Made Me Buy This Dress*, which he produced for his own record company, Little David.

After the 1974 cancellation of "The Flip Wilson Show," the comedian's career took an unexpected—though not really unusual—turn for a television star. Professing a desire for the stable family life he had never known, he retreated from the national spotlight, only occasionally emerging from his Malibu home to perform. "I accomplished what I set out to do," he explained to an interviewer. "I wanted the whole cookie and I got it. Now I want to spend more time with my children—make sure they don't go through what I did" (article by Mel Watson, *New York Times*, 27 November 1998).

Over the next six years, his work was limited to minor roles in just three films: *Uptown Saturday Night* (1974), *Skatetown, U.S.A.* (1979), and *The Fish That Saved Pittsburgh* (1979). In 1980 he became corporate spokesperson for the soft drink maker 7-Up, but his contract was voided following his arrest on misdemeanor cocaine charges within a year's time. Two attempts at new television series during the 1980s both ended in early cancellations. In 1990 he surprised some critics with his dramatic performance as God in "Zora Is My Name," a play concerning the life of writer Zora Neale Hurston, on PBS's "American Playhouse." Though he would remain financially secure, Wilson never again would achieve anything like the fame he had known in the early 1970s.

Flip Wilson's personal life was complex. His 1957 marriage to dancer Peaches Wilson (her maiden name) ended in divorce that same year. Soon after, he entered into a long-term relationship with Blonell Pitman, eventually adopting Pitman's daughter, Michelle. Between 1960 and 1970 the couple had four children of their own; they never married, however. In 1979, Wilson wed Cookie Mackenzie, but this second marriage ended in a 1985 divorce.

Wilson told *Jet* magazine in a 1997 interview that he did not miss his acting career and that he had spent a good deal of the last two decades reading Eastern philosophy, especially the works of Kahlil Gibran. The comedian died of liver cancer at home in Malibu.

The first African American to host a successful prime-time variety show on television, Flip Wilson created several signature comic characters whose appeal transcended race. As Paul Brownfield of the *Los Angeles Times* wrote, "If Richard Pryor and Dick Gregory represented a school of black comics who translated their backgrounds into crackling, confrontational comedy routines, Wilson was from a different school—not as angry or political, and thus not as much of a threat to white audiences" (28 Nov. 1998).

• A sketch on Wilson's early career appears in the 1969 edition of *Current Biography Yearbook*. Obituaries can be found in most major American daily newspapers, including the *New York Times*, 27 Nov. 1998; see also the one in the 14 Dec. 1998 issue of *Jet* magazine.

DAVID MARC

WILSON, Orlandus (1917–30 Dec. 1998), gospel singer, was born in a rural area that is now Chesapeake, Virginia. Raised on a small farm along the James River, Wilson was one of seven children born to Maurice Wilson, a farmer, and Annie Cole Wilson, a teacher. His father initially operated a small farm, then later sharecropped; his mother, a graduate of Hampton Institute, taught school for three years before turning her full-time attention to their burgeoning family.

Growing up poor in Tidewater, Virginia, Wilson and all of his siblings attended public school. They walked more than two miles daily to the nearest school for African American children. Their neighbors and the other members of the Union Bethel Baptist Church provided their most important social network. Wilson's father had no musical talents, but his mother sang in the ladies' quartet and led their weekly practice sessions. In addition to his early exposure to music at church, Wilson received a harmonica for Christmas on which he performed imitations of barnyard animals, trains, and the sounds of a fox hunt.

Around 1930 Wilson, along with his brother James, formed a quartet—the Jollet Four—to sing at local churches. One of its members was William Langford, who would eventually sing with Wilson in the Golden Gate Quartet. The Jollet Four performed in local churches and participated in quartet contests, singing a repertoire of mostly older spirituals such as "Go Down, Moses," "I Wouldn't Take Nothing for My Journey Now," and "Sometimes I Feel Like a Moth-

erless Child." A few years later Langford moved to Portsmouth, Virginia, where he joined the Golden Crowns Quartette, while Wilson remained in the country attending school and working at a nearby Planters Peanuts processing plant. Needing talent for his new group, the Golden Gate Quartet, and recalling his old friend's skills, Langford asked Wilson's parents' permission for Wilson to try out for the group and come into the city twice weekly for rehearsals after work. The Golden Gate Quartet's members included Willie Johnson and William Langford (alto and lead), "Peg" Ford (an older man who sang bass), and Henry Owens (baritone).

Within several years the group had gained local fame singing nearly every weekend at churches, some of them many hours away. By 1936 their fame had grown to the point that they were on the road for several weeks at a stretch. Because of the travel Wilson could only "sub" into the group for local apperances but could not join them for extended engagements. When Ford was no longer able to travel with the group, the members, led by Langford, went to Wilson's parents asking if the nineteen-year-old might join the group on a full-time basis. Maurice and Annie Wilson reluctantly agreed, and Orlandus Wilson took his place in the Golden Gate Quartet, where he stayed for the next sixty-two years.

Buoyed by success on local radio and regular touring in Virginia and the Carolinas, the group easily supported itself for nearly a year before a recording deal with RCA's Bluebird division and several appearances on NBC's "Magic Key" radio program placed the group in the national spotlight. Langford had tremendous range and an emotional voice, Owens filled in the middle, and Wilson provided the group with a solid anchor. But it was Willie Johnson's innovative lead singing, in a narrative style that emphasized texts from the New Testament of the Bible, that distinguished the group from others.

From 1937 into the early 1950s, the Golden Gate Quartet was one of the most popular African-American gospel quartets in the United States, participating in John Hammond's ground-breaking 1938 Carnegie Hall Spirituals-to-Swing concert, landing a weekly radio program on CBS, and enjoying a long run at New York City's chic Cafe Society. President Franklin Delano Roosevelt invited them to entertain at his January 1941 inaugural gala. In the early 1940s the Golden Gate Quartet appeared in such Hollywood films as "Star-Spangled Rhythm" and "Hollywood Canteen." During this period they continued to record for RCA and Columbia before switching to Mercury in 1948. But the group began to change in the late 1940s. First William Langford left, followed by Johnson and Owens. By 1950 Orlandus Wilson was the only "original" member left in the Golden Gate Quartet, and he became its de facto leader.

The world of gospel quartet singing was changing, too: in the early 1950s rhythm and blues and rock and roll began to replace the a capella sound. In 1955 the Golden Gate Quartet toured Europe with immense success. This initial tour was quickly followed by two equally triumphant trips. Spurred by their success abroad and faced with an uncertain racial climate and a changing musical landscape at home, the group soon decided to relocate. Following a 1958 twenty-eight-country tour arranged by the U.S. State Department, Wilson and his group members decided to take up permanent residence in Paris. During this time they recorded several dozen albums and toured Europe regularly but did not perform in the United States until 1994. They returned to New York City in order to be inducted into the Hall of Fame of the United in Group Harmony, an organization devoted to preserving the history of vocal harmony. Wilson remained at the helm of the Golden Gate Quartet, managing, handling musical arrangements, and composing new material until two months before his death in Paris.

• Sources include an unpublished interview with Orlandus Wilson conducted by the playwright Dean Strober on 17 Mar. 1997 (Paris, France). See also Jon Pareles's obituary, "Orlandus Wilson," in the *New York Times*, 31 Dec. 1998.

KIP LORNELL

WINSOR, Justin (2 Jan. 1831–22 Oct. 1897), librarian and historian, was born in Boston, the son of Nathaniel Winsor, Jr., a prosperous merchant and ship broker, and Ann Thomas Howland. After attending a boarding school in Sandwich, Massachusetts, Winsor enrolled at the Boston Latin Grammar School. While there, he visited the New-England Historic Genealogical Society and became interested in studying the history of his father's ancestors, who had come from Duxbury, Massachusetts, and that of his mother's ancestors, one of whom had been a *Mayflower* Pilgrim. Winsor published *A History of the Town of Duxbury, Massachusetts, with Genealogical Registers* in 1849, having entered Harvard College earlier that year. Finding Harvard's classical curriculum dull, he turned to informal reading in literature and biography, frequented the theater, especially liked eighteenth-century British plays, and wrote at least three hasty and unsuccessful farces. He was suspended from school for a year, decided not to return to classes, and left, without a degree, for Europe in October 1852.

Deciding to become a man of letters, Winsor lived mainly in Paris and Heidelberg, mastered French and German, translated poetry, and read widely. He returned to Boston in September 1854, married Caroline Tufts Barker in 1855, and the couple took up permanent residence in his parents' home. They had one child. Winsor tried to develop a literary career, with no lasting success. He published twenty-six essays and thirty-six poems, some being translations of romantic German verse, in the *Crayon* (1855–1858); published book reviews and occasional verse in the *Round Table* (1863–1868); did some editorial work; and was a correspondent for the *New York World*. Weak eyesight kept him from military service during the Civil War. In 1866 he was named a trustee of the Boston Public

Library, wrote a brilliant statistically oriented examiner's report concerning the library in 1867, and became its director in February 1868. That same year Harvard granted him his B.A.

During the next nine years, Winsor expanded the Boston Library; he made it more useful to the public in countless ways and attracted great attention to it and to himself by beginning a nationwide professionalizing of librarians. He helped establish the American Library Association (1876), served as its first president (1876–1885), and became internationally known. In September 1877 he was appointed librarian of Harvard College and held that position for the rest of his life. To make the Harvard Library more an active facility and less a retreat, he supervised reclassifying its holdings, unifying campus libraries, opening the stacks to students, developing more substantial reserve collections, and expanding interlibrary functions.

Winsor wished to be a historian as well as a librarian. His *Historical Sketch of the Colony and County of Plymouth* (1879) grew out of his genealogical interest in his mother's forebears. He followed it with *The Reader's Handbook of the American Revolution* (1880), which is still valuable as a bibliographical resource. When Clarence Frederick Jewett, a Boston publisher interested in town histories, asked Winsor to edit a history of Boston, the energetic librarian-historian accepted the challenge. He decided on the topics to be covered, appealed successfully to some seventy writers, gathered and edited their submissions, and published *The Memorial History of Boston, Including Suffolk County, Massachusetts, 1630–1880*, with maps and other illustrative material (4 vols., 1880–1881). It was universally praised, and in 1880 Jewett asked Winsor to use the same method to create a history of the entire United States. Agreeing, Winsor developed a plan to combine narrative and critical chapters covering the history of South America as well as that of North America to the eighteenth century (vols. 1–5), the United States from 1763 to 1850 (vols. 6 and 7), and the later history of Spanish, Portuguese, and British America (vol. 8). Preparing individual chapters were thirty-nine men, for the most part scholars. The resulting *Narrative and Critical History of America* was published piecemeal (vols. 3–4, 1885; vols. 1, 2, 5–8, 1886–1889). Winsor provided numerous excellent maps and wrote roughly half of the entire publication himself, including most of the critical and bibliographical essays and even some of the narrative parts for which he gave contributors sole credit. Of special value are Winsor's extensive annotations and bibliographical lists and his coverage of early French explorers. Reviewers, though generally favorable, faulted Winsor for disproportionate emphasis on colonial America (British, French, Spanish, and Portuguese) and also for slighting the Civil War.

Winsor remained active and productive during his last eight years. His *Christopher Columbus and How He Received and Imparted the Spirit of Discovery* (1891) anticipates revisionist historians in its adverse opinions concerning his subject's personality and behavior. Winsor attempted to extend the monumental work of his friend Francis Parkman, a fellow Bostonian and historian of the French and Indian War in its broadest context, by writing *Cartier to Frontenac: Geographical Discovery in the Interior of North America in Its Historical Relations, 1534–1700* (1894), *The Mississippi Basin: The Struggle in America between England and France, 1697–1763* (1895), and *The Westward Movement: The Colonies and the Republic West of the Alleghanies* [sic], *1763–1798* (1897), his final book.

Winsor was an impatient writer. He would read in his library and pore over his map collection, take scraps of notes, hastily write page after page of text, paste on his annotations, and rush the results to the printer. He rationalized his work habits by claiming that history could most excitingly be conveyed to the reader by quick use of plain facts and terse statements. His disinclination to revise resulted not only in stylistic infelicities, making his prose at times wooden, but also in some factual errors, though usually minor. Scholars gratefully remembered him for astute footnotes leading them into unexplored terrain. Busy though he was, he was always willing to be interrupted, to reply genially to queries in person or by mail, and to share his knowledge and his library resources. Scholars also found useful his clever reinterpretations of received history on the basis of his legendary cartographical expertise. In 1896 the U.S. Arbitration Commission even called on him to define the exact boundary between British Guiana and Venezuela.

Winsor enjoyed considerable professional activity outside his study. As president of the American Library Association, 1876–1885, he headed a group of Americans attending the first International Conference of Librarians, held in London (1877). Long a member of the Massachusetts Historical Society in Boston, he served as its corresponding secretary (1881–1894) and as its vice president (1894–1897). In 1897 he was reelected president of the American Library Association, specifically so that he would lead another delegation to the second International Conference of Librarians in London. Shortly after his return to Boston he fell ill and died soon thereafter, in Cambridge, Massachusetts. Specialists in historiography point out that Winsor, by seeing history as both literary and scientific, provided an indispensable transition between the often amateurish historians of the late nineteenth century and the doggedly professional ones emerging at the outset of the twentieth century.

• Although some of Winsor's papers are widely scattered, the most significant ones are located in the American Library Association Archives at the University of Illinois, the Boston Public Library, the Melvil Dewey Papers at Columbia University, the Harvard University Library, and the Massachusetts Historical Society in Boston. Edward Channing, "Justin Winsor," *American Historical Review* 3 (Jan. 1898): 197–202, and Horace E. Scudder, "Memoir of Justin Winsor, LL.D.," *Proceedings of the Massachusetts Historical Society*, 2d ser., 12 (1899): 457–82, are contemporary, laudatory surveys of Winsor's life and professional accomplishments. Joseph Borome, "Winsor's History of America," *Boston Public Library Quarterly* 5 (July 1953): 119–39, discusses Winsor's *Narrative and Critical History of America*—his problems with contributors, the opinions of contemporary reviewers, and the favorable response to the work. Wayne Cutler and Michael H. Harris, eds., *Justin Winsor: Scholar-Librarian* (1980), provides a detailed biography of Winsor; reprints twenty-one of his reports, essays, and addresses concerning public and academic libraries, library professionalism, and "the scholar's craft"; and includes a bibliography of his fifty-four published and unpublished works, as well as an extensive secondary bibliography. An obituary is in the *New York Times*, 23 Oct. 1897.

ROBERT L. GALE

WISDOM, John Minor (17 May 1905–15 May 1999), judge, was born in New Orleans, Louisiana, the son of Mortimer N. Wisdom, an insurance broker, and Adelaide Labatt Wisdom. Wisdom was a youth when his father died, leaving three young children but sufficient resources for his widow to send them all through college. A high achiever as a boy, Wisdom ranked first in merit badges among Eagle Scouts in Louisiana and won the city doubles tennis championship for the public playgrounds (the top players, he would quickly point out later, belonged to private clubs). He played neighborhood football even though he weighed less than 100 pounds when he went to college, where he began to fill out physically.

Like his father before him, Wisdom attended college at Washington and Lee. (His father's diploma, signed by Robert E. Lee, hung in Wisdom's chambers after he became a judge.) After graduation from Washington and Lee in 1925, he entered Harvard as a graduate student in English, then found out that his lack of background in classical languages disqualified him from the degree program. But he remained at Harvard for a year, reading voraciously and developing a literary style that would give power to his judicial opinions. He returned to New Orleans to study law at Tulane Law School, where his grandfather had been a member of the first graduating class. The curriculum incorporated civil law, whose tradition had developed from the old Roman law that reflects Louisiana's early French and Spanish background and which became entwined with English common-law concepts in the state's legal codes. Before finishing first in his law school class—just ahead of Saul Stone, the son of Jewish immigrants—Wisdom registered as one of the handful of Republicans in Louisiana, a reaction to what he considered the dictatorial control of Governor Huey Long.

Stone had become a trusted friend of Wisdom's as they studied together, and they opened a partnership after their graduation in 1929. After discussing whether to draw up a legal agreement, they decided the partnership wasn't worth having if they needed a written contract. The law practice grew steadily, and Wisdom taught part time at Tulane Law School in such areas as trusts, estates, and the Louisiana Civil Code, in which he became recognized as a leading authority.

In 1931 Wisdom married a woman named Charles Stewart Mathews (she was named after her father), whom everyone knew as "Bonnie." They had three children.

During World War II, he served in the Office of Legal Procurement for the army, where he worked with top graduates of Ivy League law schools who would emerge as opinion shapers and academic leaders in the legal profession. Benjamin Kaplan, who after the war became a full professor at Harvard Law School and later a member of the highly regarded Supreme Judicial Court of Massachusetts, called the army unit "the best collection of lawyers I've ever seen." He remembered Wisdom then as a man "loaded with energy and love of life, extremely kindly, with marvelous compassion, enormous brilliance and heart" (quoted in Bass, *Unlikely Heroes*, pp. 48–49).

As a lawyer, no case stimulated Wisdom more than *Schwegmann v. Calvert Distillers* (1951), which he won in the U.S. Supreme Court. The decision struck down the so-called fair trade laws, the basis for retail price-fixing. The case led to the development of large-scale discount retailers. The path to a judgeship on the Fifth Circuit Court of Appeals began in 1951, when Wisdom became an early leader in the effort to draft Dwight Eisenhower as the 1952 Republican nominee for president. Wisdom worked closely with Herbert Brownell, who would become Eisenhower's campaign manager and then attorney general. In the closely contested nomination battle at the 1952 Republican national convention, Wisdom handled a successful challenge before the Credentials Committee to seat Eisenhower delegates from Louisiana against a competing slate committed to Ohio Senator Robert Taft.

While serving as Republican national committeeman from Louisiana, Wisdom was a member of the President's Committee on Government Contracts, which sought voluntary agreements against racial discrimination. He also had served on the board of the New Orleans Urban League and as president of the New Orleans Council of Social Agencies. That background created suspicion among segregationist southern senators when President Eisenhower nominated Wisdom in 1957 for a Louisiana vacancy on the Fifth Circuit, then a seven-member court that covered six states that had joined the Confederacy—Georgia, Florida, Alabama, Mississippi, Louisiana, and Texas. Wisdom was confirmed, however, and quickly emerged as a central figure in the legal battle over civil rights.

In much of the South a response of massive resistance followed the Supreme Court's landmark 1954 decision in *Brown v. Board of Education*, which struck down the "separate but equal" doctrine that almost six decades earlier had provided the legal basis for the South to develop a rigid system of racial segregation. The Supreme Court gave little direction to the lower courts except to apply equitable principles and to proceed with "all deliberate speed." Judge Wisdom's

Fifth Circuit Court soon became the legal battleground of the emerging civil rights movement.

Wisdom became the scholar and the driving intellectual force on the Fifth Circuit as it expanded the *Brown* decision in the following decade and a half into a broad mandate for racial justice. He viewed the Thirteenth, Fourteenth, and Fifteenth Amendments as a response to *Dred Scott*, the U.S. Supreme Court opinion in 1857 which held that even emancipated Negroes were "beings of an inferior order, and altogether unfit to associate with the white race, either in social or political Relations; and so far inferior that they had *no rights which the white man was bound to respect*." To Wisdom these amendments created "the right of Negroes to *national* citizenship, their right to share the privileges and immunities only white citizens had enjoyed as a class" (*United States v. Jefferson*, 1966).

Barely two months after his appointment, Wisdom in September 1957 granted a stay of execution for Edgar Labat, a black convicted of aggravated rape of a white woman in New Orleans. Nine years later, Wisdom wrote a landmark opinion in the case, upholding the contention that because of systematic exclusion of blacks from juries in Orleans Parish, Labat had been denied a fair trial. In *Labat v. Bennett*, he found discrimination in a jury selection system that excluded daily or hourly wage earners, ostensibly to spare them financial hardship. Wisdom wrote, "The system was neutral, principled, and—foolproof: No black ever sat on a grand jury or a trial jury panel in Orleans Parish."

One of his most frustrating cases involved the lengthy legal process before James Meredith entered the University of Mississippi in 1962 as that school's first known African-American student. When a Mississippi federal trial judge ruled that Meredith "was not denied admission because of his color or race," Wisdom replied caustically, referring in a judicial response to "the eerie atmosphere of never-never land." The segregation of Mississippi institutions of higher learning, he wrote, was a "plain fact known to everyone." In directing Judge Sidney Mize to hold a full hearing, Wisdom asserted that Meredith "should be afforded a fair, unfettered, and unharassed opportunity to prove his case." After the riot that accompanied Meredith's admission to the campus, violence that left two dead and dozens injured, Wisdom's was the strongest voice in what became for him a protracted losing battle to hold Mississippi Governor Ross Barnett in criminal contempt. Wisdom characterized it as the case of *The Man in High Office Who Defied the Nation*.

United States v. Louisiana was a landmark order in 1963 that struck down discrimination in voting rights. "A wall stands in Louisiana between registered voters and unregistered, eligible Negro voters," Wisdom noted. "The wall is the State constitutional requirement that an applicant for registration 'understand and give a reasonable interpretation of any section' of the Constitution of Louisiana or of the United States."

Wisdom's opinion concluded, "We hold: this wall, built to bar Negroes from access to the franchise, must come down." As lawyers in the Justice Department developed drafts of what became the landmark Voting Rights Act of 1965, John Doar, as head of the Civil Rights Division in the Justice Department, remembered their talking in the hallways about voting rights and referring constantly to "that wall that must come down" (Jack Bass, "Tribute to John Minor Wisdom," *Mississippi Law Journal*, Fall 1999, p. 32). The Voting Rights Act brought it down.

No opinion drew more fully on Wisdom's intellectual and imaginative force than *United States v. Jefferson*, which took almost a year to formulate before he issued it in 1966. This case effectively ended the concept of "all deliberate speed" contained in the Supreme Court's original school desegregation implementation order and placed an affirmative duty on school boards to develop plans that would result in "the organized undoing of past discrimination." The order spelled out that such plans meant integrating students, faculties, facilities, and activities.

Part of *Brown v. Board of Education*'s "important meaning," Wisdom asserted, was that it "wrote the Declaration of Independence into the Constitution. Freedmen are free men. They are created as equal as are all other American citizens and with the same unalienable rights to life, liberty, and the pursuit of happiness." With *Jefferson*, Wisdom contradicted and overcame the then tenacious holding of Chief Judge John J. Parker of the Fourth Circuit Court of Appeals in Richmond that the Constitution "does not require integration. It merely forbids discrimination." Wisdom's order included a model school desegregation order and declared that school boards had "the affirmative duty to bring about an integrated, unitary school system in which there are no Negro schools and no white schools—just schools."

In *Jefferson* he also developed the constitutional rationale to support the concept of affirmative action. "The Constitution is both color blind and color conscious," Wisdom wrote. "To avoid conflict with the equal protection clause, a classification that denies a benefit, causes harm, or imposes a burden must not be based on race. In that sense, the Constitution is color blind. But the Constitution is color conscious to prevent discrimination being perpetuated and to undo the effects of past discrimination. The criterion is the relevancy of color to a legitimate government purpose."

Wisdom's name came up as a possible Supreme Court nominee in 1969 after the Senate rejected President Richard Nixon's nomination of Chief Judge Clement F. Haynsworth of the Fourth Circuit Court of Appeals. The Baltimore Sun reported that a moderate Republican governor suggested Wisdom's name to Attorney General John Mitchell, who later served time in federal prison for Watergate-related crimes. "He's a damn left winger," the governor reported

Mitchell had snorted in reply. "He'd be as bad as Earl Warren" (*Baltimore Sun*, 14 Dec. 1969). Wisdom took the advice of a journalist friend and ignored Mitchell's remark. Also in 1969 Wisdom wrote the first of several landmark opinions in employment discrimination cases. In *United Papermakers & Paperworkers v. United States*, he established basic law for determining seniority rights for black workers who had been discriminated against. A decade later, the Supreme Court adopted the basic reasoning of his dissent in *Weber v. Kaiser Aluminum & Chemical Corp.* to uphold a hiring plan designed to overcome the effects of past discrimination.

Despite his liberal views on race and forceful opinions on civil rights, Wisdom retained his lifelong conservative friends and continued his associations in exclusive private clubs and Mardi Gras crewes that discriminated against blacks and Jews. "I think that my private life and people I go with is my own. . . . I certainly wouldn't change their views by getting out of the club" (Bass, *Unlikely Heroes*, p. 46). President Bill Clinton awarded Judge Wisdom the Presidential Medal of Freedom in 1993. Congress named the imposing Italian Renaissance structure across from Lafayette Square in New Orleans the John Minor Wisdom Fifth Circuit Court of Appeals Building. A memorial service there after his death ended with a New Orleans tradition, a marching band of black musicians softly playing, to a dirge-like beat, "When the Saints Go Marching In."

• Wisdom's papers are collected at Tulane Law School. Biographical information and evaluation of Wisdom's judicial record are found in Jack Bass, *Unlikely Heroes* (1981), and Frank T. Read and Lucy S. McGough, *Let Them Be Judged: The Judicial Integration of the Deep South* (1978). For a technical analysis of how the Fifth Circuit reshaped the use of the injunction as a legal remedy, see Owen Fiss, *The Civil Rights Injunction* (1978). For Wisdom's view in evaluating the Fifth Circuit's role, see his article, "The Friction-making, Exacerbating, Political Role of the Federal Courts," *Southwestern Law Journal*, 21 (1967): 411–28. For the John Minor Wisdom Lecture by Jack Bass at Tulane University School of Law in 1998, see "John Minor Wisdom and the Impact of Law," *Mississippi Law Journal* 69 (Fall 1999): 25–37. An obituary is in the *New York Times*, 16 May 1999.

JACK BASS

WOOD, Beatrice (3 Mar. 1893–12 Mar. 1998), artist, was born in San Francisco, to Benjamin Wood and Carrara Wood (maiden name not known). Beatrice then moved with her family to New York City, where she was raised. Her formal artistic training consisted mainly of drawing classes at the Académie Julien in Paris in 1910.

In 1916 Wood met French artist Marcel Duchamp, who, along with Man Ray and Francis Picabia, started the American branch of the modern art movement called Dada. Duchamp, a major influence on Wood's artistic career, loaned her his studio and arranged for her first abstract image (*Mariage d'une amie*, 1916) to be published in New York in the avant-garde magazine *Rogue*.

Duchamp introduced Wood to the Dada circle of artists, writers, and musicians. His studio was located above the apartment of modern art collectors Louise and Walter Arensberg, who hosted informal nightly salons attended by European and American modern artists and writers including Wood, Duchamp, Man Ray, Picabia, Charles Sheeler, Joseph Stella, and William Carlos Williams. Wood created many drawings based on evenings at the Arensbergs. Her moniker "The Mama of Dada" (a title she shared with Gertrude Stein) stems from one of her drawings titled *Béatrice et ses douzes enfants!* (1917), which depicts Wood as the mother of the Dada circle.

During this time Wood had what she called "un amour à trois" with both Duchamp and his friend Henri-Pierre Roché, a French diplomat and art collector. Roché's novel *Jules et Jim* (later turned into a film by François Truffaut in 1961) was rumored to have been based on their lives together. Dedicated to the Dada movement, Wood, Duchamp, and Roché collaborated in publishing and writing for the *Blind Man*, a short-lived Dada magazine. They were also instrumental in the Society of Independent Artists' first exhibition at the Grand Central Palace in 1917. Wood's painting *Un peu d'eau dans du savon* caused a sensation at the exhibition as it showed a naked woman resting in a bathtub. Wood originally drew a piece of soap over the subject's private parts, but, following Duchamp's suggestion, she attached a real, scallop-shaped bar of soap to the work. The painting incited derision by art critics and titillated several male viewers who left their calling cards under the bar of soap.

In 1918 Wood moved to Montreal to act in the French Theatre. She married the theater's manager, a Belgian named Paul (surname unknown), and returned to New York in 1920. They had no children and their marriage was annulled a few years later. Into the 1920s Wood supported herself with various acting jobs and writing assignments and continued drawing. In 1928 she moved to Los Angeles, reestablishing contact with the Arensbergs, who had settled there in 1921, and becoming associated with the Indian spiritual teacher Jiddu Krishnamurti.

The second phase of Wood's artistic career started with a trip to Europe in 1930. While in Holland, Wood purchased a set of plates with a luster glaze. Intending to create a matching teapot herself, she enrolled in ceramics classes in the adult programs at Hollywood High School. Between 1938 and 1940 Wood studied with ceramists Glen Lukens and Gertrud and Otto Natzler and then with Vivika and Otto Heino intermittently from 1954 to 1979. To the Natzlers, in particular, Wood credited her ability to use a potter's wheel (Gertrud was known for her throwing technique) and to experiment with glazes.

By the early 1940s Wood achieved modest commercial success as stores and galleries, including Neiman-Marcus and Gumps, bought her work wholesale.

The American House Gallery in New York hosted her first one-person exhibition in 1944. Also in the 1940s her work was included in exhibitions at the Metropolitan Museum of Art (1940) and the Los Angeles County Museum of Art (1947).

In 1948 Wood moved to Ojai, a town north of Los Angeles, and married her companion Steve Hoag that same year. Hoag died in 1960; they had no children. While in Ojai, Wood became involved with the Happy Valley Foundation, a school founded by Krishnamurti and Aldous Huxley among others, which provided students with a coeducational, noncompetitive learning environment.

By the 1950s Wood had gained acclaim for her luster glazes. Although she did not invent this form of glazing, which requires reduction firing (reducing the amount of oxygen in the kiln), her experimental glaze formulas applied directly to earthenware clay resulted in uniquely lush and durable surfaces. The iridescent colors ranged from pale pearly tones to intense violet hues. Of her famous glazes, writer Anaïs Nin wrote in 1965, "They have the rhythm and lustre both of jewels and of human eyes. Water poured from her jars would taste like wine."

In addition to her vessels and plates, Wood made figurative work that often portrayed humorous and sexual situations, with subjects such as prostitutes, bordellos, and pregnant brides. Her intentionally naive style was influenced by the figurative work she saw on trips to India between 1961 and 1972. Invited by the Indian government and the U.S. State Department, Wood lectured and exhibited her work on these trips and photographed the folk art of the local artisans as well.

Working almost consistently until her death at the age of 105 in Ojai, Wood had many solo exhibitions in her lifetime, including ones at the Honolulu Academy of Art (1951), the Pasadena Art Museum (1959), the Phoenix Art Museum and the Tucson Art Center (both 1973), the California State University in Fullerton (1983), and a traveling exhibition at the American Craft Museum in New York and the Santa Barbara Museum of Art (1997–1998). The Philadelphia Museum of Art held an exhibition of her two-dimensional work in 1978, and in 1989/1990 the Oakland Museum and the Craft and Folk Art Museum (Los Angeles) organized an exhibition of her two- and three-dimensional figurative work. The Smithsonian Institution designated her an Esteemed American Artist in 1994, and she was also honored as a "California Living Treasure" during the 1990s.

A self-confessed romantic, the sari-clad artist seemed to prefer discussing love affairs more than aesthetic theory, as evidenced in her autobiography *I Shock Myself* (1985). Her art and life inspired director James Cameron to use her as the model for the 101-year-old character "Rose" in his movie *Titanic*. Originally considered to be just a hanger-on of the Dada movement, Wood has more recently been credited by scholars as a Dadaist in her own right, both for her artwork and for her bohemian attitude and behavior.

After the demise of Dadaism, she retained the predilections of a free spirit, who nevertheless had the discipline needed to become a master ceramist.

• The Archives of American Art in Washington, D.C., has the most thorough source materials on Wood, including correspondence, drawings, and interviews. The archives also has a video of the one-hour documentary film "Mama of Dada," made in 1992 and coproduced by Diandra Douglas, Tom Neff, and Amie Knox. Exhibition catalogs include *Beatrice Wood Retrospective* (California State University, Fullerton, 1982) with essays by Francis M. Naumann and Garth Clark, and *Intimate Appeal: The Figurative Art of Beatrice Wood* (Oakland Museum, 1989), which also contains an essay by Naumann. The exhibition catalog for *Beatrice Wood: A Centennial Tribute* (American Craft Museum, 1997) includes twenty-eight prepublished magazine and newspaper articles by or about Wood. An essay by Wood on Duchamp is included in *Marcel Duchamp: Artist of the Century*, ed. Rudolf Kuenzli and Francis M. Naumann (1989), and she recounts a visit to artist Constantin Brancusi's studio in 1956 in the *Archives of American Art Journal* 32, no. 4 (1992): 19–24. A reassessment of Wood and the Dada movement is provided by Paul B. Franklin in his essay "Beatrice Wood, Her Dada . . . and Her Mama," in *Women in Dada*, ed. Naomi Sawelson-Gorse (1998). Informative obituaries are in the *New York Times*, 14 Mar. 1998, and the *Los Angeles Times*, 15 Mar. 1998.

N. ELIZABETH SCHLATTER

WRIGLEY, William, Jr. (30 Sept. 1861–26 Jan. 1932), businessman, was born in Philadelphia, one of nine children of William Wrigley, a soap maker, and Mary A. Ladley Wrigley. He had little formal education, having run away at age eleven in hopes of making his way in New York, but he returned to work for Wrigley's Scouring Soap, eventually as a salesman with horse and wagon. In a precursor of his later life, he set off westward, only to return to the factory, having lost his railroad ticket in Kansas City. In 1885 he married Ada E. Foote; they had two children and remained married until Wrigley's death.

Wrigley borrowed money from his uncle in 1891 and went into a business partnership with his cousin, starting out with soap and baking powder. After diversifying into chewing gum in 1892, he used employee incentives and large-purchase discounts to enlarge the business. At the time, there were more than a dozen other American companies manufacturing chewing gum. After marketing the brands Lotta and Vassar, Wrigley came up with the highly popular Juicy Fruit in 1893. In 1899 the company began to manufacture Spearmint, in 1907 spending $284,000—a huge sum at the time—in advertising the brand, the sales of which promptly leaped eightfold. (Litigation over the invention of Spearmint continued for seventeen years, concluding in 1928 when Wrigley paid L. P. Larson, Jr., $1.9 million.)

In 1911 Wrigley took complete control of the business, and soon the William Wrigley Jr. Company, headquartered in Chicago, was advertising in 30 languages and had factories in three American and five foreign cities. Often described as shy and retiring, he

nevertheless was quoted as remarking, "When two men in business always agree, one of them is unnecessary." A nominal Republican, Wrigley left the fold once, backing Teddy Roosevelt in 1912.

Wrigley's westering tendency resurfaced in 1914, when he began spending the winters in Pasadena, California, where he bought the Stimson House, a pseudo-Mediterranean mansion on posh Orange Grove Avenue. Called "The Shadows," the mansion was noted for its English rose gardens. (After Wrigley's widow's death in 1958, it was willed to the Tournament of Roses committee and continued life as the headquarters for that annual New Year's Day pageant.)

Wrigley's name was pervasive in Chicago, eventually becoming attached to the baseball park on the South Side as well as to the Wrigley Tower prominent on the skyline. The park had been built in 1914 as Weeghman Park, named for its owner, a local restaurateur. In 1916 Wrigley began buying into Chicago's National League baseball franchise, and in 1920 he completed his takeover, renaming the stadium Cubs' Park, for the team's nickname. By that time a transcontinental entrepreneur, Wrigley in 1921 purchased the Los Angeles baseball franchise in the Pacific Coast League. His Chicago enterprises continued to thrive; in 1924 he became the city's first employer to extend to all employees the privilege of Saturdays off.

Before long, with the purchase of another minor league franchise in Reading (Pa.), Wrigley was well on his way to founding the modern "farm system," whereby a major league club like Chicago could develop its players gradually, guaranteeing continuity by binding them to long-term contracts. In 1925 the most elegant minor league stadium in the land (seating 22,000) was opened in Los Angeles. Named Wrigley Field, the concrete-and-steel park was directly modeled on the larger Chicago stadium, with its characteristic ivy-covered outfield brick walls. In 1926 Cubs' Park in Chicago became Wrigley Field, too. Surviving various epochs of stadium architecture, Wrigley Field came to be revered as baseball's most beautiful venue—and the most conservative, being the last to install night lighting.

Wrigley's California enterprises multiplied. In 1919 he had purchased Santa Catalina Island from the heirs of Phineas Banning, founder of Los Angeles's seaside ports. Twenty-six miles out to sea, twenty-one miles long, and no more than eight miles wide, Catalina became Wrigley's main vacation home. There in 1920 he set about creating a holiday paradise and a wildlife sanctuary. Wrigley sought to build a "resort for everyman" featuring 2,500 "bungalettes," meant to accommodate two or three people apiece at the reasonable rate of $12.00 to $17.50 per week. There was golf and tennis, horseback riding, a large botanical garden and a remarkable aviary, stocked with birds from around the world. Wrigley purchased a Great Lakes steamer, which he renamed the *Avalon*, and later had its sister ship, the *Catalina*, built. Between them, the boats could transport 3,500 visitors to the island. Wrigley's baseball teams used the island for spring training, and by the late 1920s Catalina was visited by more than 400,000 people annually.

In Avalon, the resort's only town, Wrigley built for his wife (for whom he also named a Catalina mountain) a casino in Moorish-Venetian style, where, despite the name, gambling was not permitted. Boasting a 15,000-square-foot circular ballroom and a 1,250-seat motion picture theater, it opened in 1929 and became the focal point for the celebrities—usually from Hollywood—who gradually became Catalina's main clientele. The island became a favored location for the making of movies, and *The Vanishing American* (1925)—a notable silent film—left behind a legacy of imported buffalo, which proceeded to survive and multiply ever after. Decades later, the island became a center for environmental study for the University of Southern California.

Wrigley gradually left California for Arizona, where in 1929 he built yet another Wrigley mansion. He died in Phoenix, Arizona, and two years later was buried in a mausoleum in the center of a botanical garden on Santa Catalina Island. In 1996 California's authoritative historian, Kevin Starr, described it as remaining the most imposing funerary monument in the state. The Wrigley Company continued in family hands, though it gradually divested itself of its non–chewing gum interests, such as banking, mining, and the Chicago Cubs.

• William Zimmerman, Jr., *William Wrigley, Jr.: The Man and His Business* (1935), is a privately published biography. Three volumes of Kevin Starr's history of California are invaluable: *Material Dreams: Southern California through the 1920s* (1990), *Endangered Dreams: The Great Depression in California* (1996), and *The Dream Endures: California Enters the 1940s* (1997). An obituary is in the *Chicago Tribune*, 27 Jan. 1937.

JAMES ROSS MOORE

WYNETTE, Tammy (5 May 1942–6 Apr. 1998), country music singer and songwriter, was born Virginia Wynette Pugh on her grandparents' farm in Itawamba County, Mississippi, the daughter of William Hollice Pugh, a farmer and amateur musician, and Mildred Faye Russell Pugh. Her father died of a brain tumor when she was nine months old, leaving Mildred Pugh a young widow. Tammy—known to family and friends by the surname Wynette all of her life—was reared until age thirteen by her maternal grandparents, Chester and Floyd Russell. Later she went to live for brief periods in Alabama with her mother, who had remarried. Despite this somewhat unstable home environment, Wynette's childhood was happy, revolving around church and hard work in the cotton fields. She learned to play instruments by ear and mastered the guitar, piano, accordion, and flute. From an early age Wynette loved music and performing in front of an audience, and as a teenager she dreamed of singing with her favorite country music singer, George Jones, who was a little more than ten years her senior.

In 1959, at age seventeen, Wynette was expelled from high school after marrying Euple Byrd. According to her autobiography, she married Byrd to escape the cotton fields and conflicts with her mother. The couple was very poor, and Byrd had trouble keeping a steady job, forcing the family, which eventually included three daughters, to move from place to place, often living in shacks with no running water. During this time Wynette worked sporadically as a waitress and even sang for a time in a riverfront bar in Memphis. She finally found steady work when she obtained her cosmetology license, which she kept current even after becoming a country music star, reasoning that if her music career fell through, she would be able to support herself.

As a result of a nervous breakdown, Wynette was hospitalized in 1965 and underwent electroshock treatment. It was clear by this time that her marriage was falling apart, and she moved out with her daughters. Despite Euple Byrd's efforts to have her declared insane and unfit to raise their children, Wynette was granted a divorce. Soon after the couple's separation, she and the children relocated to Alabama, where she got her first break in the country music business, singing on the early morning "Country Boy Eddie" show on radio station WBRC. Her schedule was rigorous, however. She was raising three daughters, working full-time in a beauty shop, and rising early each morning to get to the radio station. But this taste of singing professionally fueled her career hopes, and Wynette began traveling to Nashville to visit record companies, seeking to secure a record contract. In 1966, the same year her divorce from Byrd became final, she moved to Nashville.

There, Wynette went to audition after audition, while her children, now aged five, four, and thirteen months, waited in the car. At last she met a record producer, Billy Sherrill, who liked her voice—saying she had a "real unique style"—and found her a song to record, "Apartment # 9." At Sherrill's suggestion, she recorded it under the name Tammy Wynette, and the song became a modest hit.

As Wynette's career took off, a string of top-ten hits followed: "Your Good Girl's Gonna Go Bad" (1967), "My Elusive Dreams" (duet with David Houston, 1967), "I Don't Wanna Play House" (1967), "Take Me to Your World" (1968), and "D-I-V-O-R-C-E" (1968). By becoming one of the first female country music superstars, Wynette broke new ground. She learned how to succeed in what was an exclusively male business, realizing that record companies held women to higher standards than their male counterparts and overcoming such sexist remarks as "we don't have good luck with girl singers." She demanded the respect accorded to men in the business, ushering in something of a "female liberation" movement in country music.

But the strides Wynette made on behalf of women in country music seemed to be overshadowed by the release of "Stand by Your Man" in 1968. Although the song won a Grammy Award in 1969 and crossed over the country charts to become a pop hit as well, many women criticized its message. Some believed the song encouraged "standing by your man" through infidelity or abuse, thereby promoting the kind of thinking that feminists had fought so hard against. But Wynette defended the song, explaining that the lyrics advise a woman to love and support her man and "be willing to forgive him if he doesn't always live up to your image of what he should be" (*Stand by Your Man*, p. 190). Wynette did not follow her own advice, as she was about to leave her second husband, songwriter Don Chapel. Their one-year marriage ended famously in 1968, when George Jones, whom Wynette had met and worked with on occasion, came to the couple's home and took Wynette and her kids away in his Cadillac Eldorado. Thus began the tumultuous six-year relationship that would become country music legend. Although Wynette and Jones announced their marriage in 1968, they did not wed until the following year.

The professional chemistry between the two made them a highly successful country duet, whose popularity was even greater than the adulation and acclaim that they had received individually. Wynette projected a naiveté on stage that seemed to bring out a more sensitive and mature Jones, who already was earning a reputation as a wild "honky-tonker." At least twelve of their songs (some of which were not released until after their divorce) became hits, including "We Can Make It" (1972), "We're Gonna Hold On" (1973), "Golden Ring" (1976), and "Two Story House" (1980). In 1969 they were asked to join the Grand Ole Opry.

But the success they found performing together did not carry over into their personal lives. Jones was a mean drunk who on occasion was violent toward Wynette; she, on the other hand, went out of her way not to do anything that would incite her husband. According to one widely publicized account, a drunken Jones chased Wynette around their Lakeland, Florida, home with a rifle (Jones denied the episode). Many times she left him, but they would reunite when he promised to quit drinking. The public saw a different relationship: a country music giant winning the heart of the "First Lady of Country Music" (as she was dubbed) and the two "living happily ever after in a glamorous, fairytale world" (*Stand by Your Man*, p. 212).

Jones and Wynette's troubled marriage ended in 1975; they had one daughter together. Wynette attributed the final separation to "my naggin' and his nippin'." The divorce hurt both of their careers because the public had come to know them as a couple. But Wynette bounced back, performing on her own again. She started to write more songs (she had co-written "Stand By Your Man" with Sherrill), enjoying success in the mid- to late 1970s with "'Til I Can Make It on My Own" (written with George Richey), "The Bottle," and "Slightly Used Woman." All of these songs were based on her personal experiences, which she began sharing with audiences.

After her divorce, Wynette's personal life turned into even more of a public soap opera, played out in the weekly tabloids. During a three-year period from 1975 to 1978 Wynette underwent at least three major surgeries, had an affair with actor Burt Reynolds, was abducted from a Nashville shopping mall (the case was never solved), and watched her Nashville home burn as a result of arson. In 1976 she married and divorced real estate executive Michael Tomlin (within forty-four days).

Wynette achieved a measure of stability in July 1978 when she married songwriter and producer George Richey, who also became her manager. They remained together until her death. In the 1980s her career suffered, mainly because of changing tastes in country music, but she did release the hit singles "Another Chance" (1982) and "Sometimes When We Touch" (duet with Mark Gray, 1985). In 1986 Wynette entered the Betty Ford Clinic for addiction to painkillers, a result of her lifelong abdominal ailments and other health problems, and in 1988 she and Richey filed for bankruptcy.

In 1993 Wynette joined with Loretta Lynn and Dolly Parton to record the album *Honky Tonk Angels*, which successfully brought together three of the most important female singers in the history of country music. The following year Wynette and a sober Jones were professionally reunited for an album, *One*, and a subsequent 35-city tour. The reunion album, which some characterized as bland, received mixed reviews but sold well, as fans seized the opportunity to hear the couple sing together again. At the time of her death, although her songs were no longer on the charts, she was still working steadily at fairs, festivals, and casinos.

Wynette died from a blood clot in her lung at her home in Nashville. A nationally televised memorial service was held at the Ryman Auditorium, the original home of the Grand Ole Opry. In 1999 Wynette's body was exhumed for an autopsy at the request of three of her daughters, who filed a $50 million wrongful death lawsuit against George Richey and their mother's doctor. Autopsy results failed to reveal any evidence of wrongful death, and the lawsuit against Wynette's widower was dropped.

During her career Tammy Wynette sold more than 30 million records, won two Grammy Awards and three Country Music Association Awards, and became the first female country music singer to sell a million copies of a record. Her influence has loomed large in Nashville, and her distinctive singing style has served as a model for performers who rose to stardom after her. According to a reviewer for *Q* magazine, in her recordings she "sings every word like she's coming to terms with the heartbreak of everyday life" (Feb. 1993). Her voice conveys the unmistakable sincerity of someone who felt what she sang, who lived the sad stories of divorce and lost love told in her music. Though it often portrays domestic unhappiness and infidelity, her music reflects a purity of heart. In the words of country music singer Rosanne Cash: "The world will never be innocent enough again to produce another Tammy Wynette."

• Tammy Wynette's life story until age thirty-seven is told in her autobiography, *Stand by Your Man*, written with Joan Dew (1979). Compact discs of both her solo work and her duets with George Jones are widely available. An especially good compilation is *Anniversary: Twenty Years of Hits* (Epic, 1987). A long article in *People* magazine, 20 Apr. 1998, tells her life story. Obituaries are in the *New York Times*, 7 Apr. 1998; *Entertainment Weekly*, 17 Apr. 1998; *Billboard*, 18 Apr. 1998; and *Newsweek*, 20 Apr. 1998. Articles that feature tributes by fans and fellow performers can be found in the *New York Times* on 8 and 10 Apr. 1998. *Newsweek*, 19 Apr. 1999, has a short article about the wrongful death lawsuit filed by Wynette's children.

STACEY HAMILTON

WYNN, Early (6 Jan. 1920–4 Apr. 1999), baseball player, was born in Hartford, Alabama, the son of Early Wynn, Sr., a mechanic, and Blanche Wynn (maiden name unknown), a waitress and fishing guide. He grew up there and worked after school hoisting 500-pound cotton bales for ten cents an hour. When the Washington Senators held a tryout camp, Wynn, a seventeen-year-old high school junior, jumped at the chance to escape. Once the scouts saw his fastball, they signed him and he was off to find his fortune, starting at $100 a month. He never did finish high school. At the end of 1939, after three years in the minor leagues, he was called up by the Senators, at which point the nineteen-year-old was clearly overmatched—and wild. His manager, Bucky Harris, ordered him to knock down any hitter he got two strikes on or be fined $25. Harris's strategy seemed to work: Wynn's speed, wildness, and reputation for throwing inside made hitters leery of facing him for most of his career. After two more seasons in the minors he was called up in late 1941, this time for good, at the age of twenty-one. He was 3–1 in that season-ending experiment and became a mainstay in the Senators' rotation through the 1948 season.

During his Washington years, the young Wynn was a thrower, not a pitcher, basically relying on his fastball and intimidating manner. His won-lost records reflected his pitching for a Washington team that was said to be "first in war, first in peace, and last in the American League." Actually, the Senators usually finished seventh in the eight-team league, though in 1943 they reached second because the war disrupted major league rosters. Wynn's records were 10–16, 18–12, and 8–17 in his first three full seasons. Meanwhile, his personal life had its ups and downs. In 1940 he married Mabel Allman, with whom he had a son before she died in an automobile crash in 1942. He remarried in 1944, and his union with Lorraine Follin lasted fifty years and produced a daughter. Wynn spent 1945 in the army while the team missed the pennant by just one game in his absence. Back on the mound in 1946, Wynn was 8–5, and he won 17 games in 1947. But in

1948 he slumped to a dismal 8–19 record and an earned run average that ballooned to 5.82. Not surprisingly, the Senators decided to trade him to the Cleveland Indians, along with first baseman Mickey Vernon, for Ed Robinson, Ed Klieman, and Joe Haynes.

In Cleveland, Wynn found pitching coach Mel Harder, who made a pitcher of him. Harder taught Wynn a curveball and a change-up (he later added a slider and knuckleball as well), and with the wider assortment of pitches and his continued penchant for knocking hitters down, the six-foot, 200-pound pitcher developed into an all-star famous for his mental toughness and determination. As part of one of the best pitching rotations in history during his nine years in Cleveland, he teamed up with Hall of Famers Bob Feller and Bob Lemon, as well as Mike Garcia and Herb Score. He had his first 20-win season in 1951 and repeated the feat in 1952, 1954, and 1956. In 1950 he led the American League in ERA, and in 1954 he and Lemon tied for the league lead in victories with 23. That year the Indians won 111 games, the American League record for a 154-game season, only to be swept by the Giants in a shocking World Series. The burly Wynn averaged 18 wins over his Cleveland years and developed a reputation as a workhorse. Three times in his career he led the league in innings pitched, and overall he pitched 290 complete games.

Wynn not only was a good pitcher; he could also hit well. Originally a right-handed hitter, he learned to switch-hit during his year in the army and went on to maintain a lifetime average of .214, with 17 career home runs. Over the years he was used as a pinchhitter 90 times and once hit a pinch-hit grand slam homer. And he could hit opposing batters. His reputation for brushback pitches led to inquiries from reporters about whether he would knock down his grandmother if necessary. "Only if she was digging in," he said (Will, p. 98).

When Wynn had a 14–17 mark in 1957 and his ERA climbed over 4.00, the Indians traded him to the Chicago White Sox with Al Smith for Fred Hatfield and Minnie Minoso. After a poor first season, he led the White Sox in 1959 to the American League pennant with a 22–10 record, for which he received the Cy Young award. He capped that achievement by winning the opening game of the World Series, which Chicago ultimately lost to the Dodgers. Thereafter, his pitching declined, and in 1962, at age 42, he fell to 7–15 and failed in several attempts to win his milestone 300th game. The next season Cleveland resigned him, and he finally got his 300th with a fiveinning effort on 13 July 1963.

Following his retirement in 1963, Wynn served as a pitching coach with the Indians and the Minnesota Twins, managed for the Twins in the minors, and worked as a broadcaster with the White Sox and the Toronto Blue Jays. He retired to Venice, Florida, where he succumbed to complications following a stroke.

In his long career Wynn won 300 games, lost 244, and had a career ERA of 3.54. He led the league in strikeouts and walks twice and had 2,334 strikeouts over his 23 seasons, at that time the longest anyone had ever pitched in the majors. In 1972 he was elected to the Baseball Hall of Fame; he said that being an all-star, pitching in a World Series, and that election were the three goals of his career. He achieved them all.

• Donald Honig, *Baseball between the Lines* (1976), includes information on Wynn in an interview with former roommate Mickey Vernon. George Will, *Men at Work* (1990), includes some insights about the pitcher. Obituaries are in the *Cleveland Plain Dealer*, 5 Apr. 1999; the *New York Times*, 6 Apr. 1999; and the *Washington Post*, 7 Apr. 1999.

JOHN R. M. WILSON

Y

YANKOVIC, Frank (11 Aug. 1915–14 Oct. 1998), musician, was born in Davis, West Virginia, the son of Andy Yankovic, a laborer, and Rose Mele Yankovic, a boardinghouse operator. Both parents were from Slovenia. When Frank was an infant, his father, who supplemented the family income by making untaxed liquor, fled from the West Virginia authorities to Cleveland. The family settled in the large Slovenian immigrant community of Collinwood on Cleveland's east side. There his father worked as a crane operator and later was a partner in a hardware store, while Rose ran a boardinghouse in their home, feeding, lodging, and laundering for half a dozen young Slovenian men.

From early childhood, Frank Yankovic's life was filled with Slovenian folk music. After meals his father and the boarders would lift their voices in Alpine-style harmonies, often accompanied by a small diatonic button accordion played by boarder Max Zelodec. Impressed by the esteem Max received, Frank persuaded the accordionist to give him a few lessons. Learning quickly, by the age of nine he was performing in the neighborhood with his own "button box."

By his teens, Yankovic felt frustrated by the limitations of the little squeeze box. During the 1920s radio and phonograph records were broadening the nation's musical horizons, and he was exposed to popular music and jazz. He yearned for a piano keyboard accordion, a modern instrument capable of playing tunes with jazzy chord progressions that were impossible to play on the button box. But Frank's father was a stern traditionalist who forbade his obtaining a piano accordion. In 1931, when Yankovic was 16, his mother acquired the instrument, hiding it at her daughter's house. Yankovic worked hard to learn to play it, and finally, on Christmas Eve, he strolled into the family holiday gathering, playing on the modern instrument "Maricka Pegla," one of his father's favorite Slovenian polkas. His father relented.

The incident is symbolic of the thrust of Yankovic's musical creativity. He was firmly grounded in Slovenian ethnic musical traditions, but as a first-generation American he wanted to reflect his own times and milieu. He thus successfully mediated between the musical aesthetics of his own generation and those of his parents,

During the 1930s Yankovic with dogged determination strove to establish his small polka band and developed his unique sound. He managed to secure a regular spot on local radio. When the major record companies rebuffed him, he cut four very successful self-produced 78-rpm discs.

Yankovic married June Erwith in 1940; they were married for twenty-eight years and had eight children.

In the early years Yankovich kept a day job, working as a milkman, a pattern maker, and an accordion teacher. In 1941 he purchased a tavern, arranging a grand opening party on 6 December—one day before Pearl Harbor! During the war the Yankovic Bar provided a steady income for his family and a venue for his band. It quickly became the hangout of Cleveland's finest polka musicians, such as Johnny Pecon, Kenny Bass, and Eddie Habat.

In 1943 Yankovic joined the army. During a two-week furlough before shipping out to Europe in 1944, he rounded up banjoist Joe Miklavic, bassist Johnny Hokavar, and pianist Al Naglitch for a recording session. They cut thirty-two sides, with no rehearsal and only one take per tune. They omitted the saxophone part and Yankovic never again used the instrument in his band.

During the Battle of the Bulge, Yankovic suffered severe frostbite. Because gangrene had set in, a doctor recommended that his hands and feet be amputated. Yankovic refused, and his extremities began to recover. An old accordion was rounded up; playing it was therapeutic, and before long he was providing entertainment at the hospital. On his release from the hospital he was assigned to special services to play for the troops with a five-piece band. His army experience, entertaining men of varied backgrounds from all parts of the country, gave him insights that helped advance his musical career as soon as he came home from the army in December 1945. Although he never ceased singing some vocals in Slovenian, he realized he needed to develop English lyrics in order to reach a broader audience.

Yankovic's definitive sound emerged when he brought in a second accordionist, Johnny Pecon, who added exciting improvised riffs. Yankovic began to employ the Solovox, an early portable electronic organ. Pecon taught him a country tune he had learned while serving in the Seabees, "Just Because." They reworked the number in polka style and it became the band's signature tune. When Columbia Records officials expressed misgivings about recording "Just Because" at a December 1947 recording session—the song had not been a hit as a country tune—Yankovic argued, kicked chairs, and threw sheet music around the room. When he offered to buy 10,000 copies of the record himself, they relented. The record was hugely popular, quickly sold a million copies, and launched the popular polka craze of the late 1940s and early 1950s. In 1948 Yankovic was declared "America's Polka King" at a "battle of the bands" event in the Milwaukee Auditorium.

Columbia wanted him to tour extensively, so he sold the tavern and devoted the rest of his career exclusively to the music business. His fame increased. In 1949 his recording of "Blue Skirt Waltz" was the year's second biggest seller. His sidemen from Cleveland's Slovenian community balked at 300 days a year of one-nighters (which would become Yankovic's way of life for decades to come), so he engaged professional musicians without previous polka experience. His definitive band during his peak period from 1949 to 1954 included Tops Cardone, accordion, Carl Paradiso, banjo, Buddy Griebel, piano, and Al Leslie, bass. In the early 1950s in Hollywood they played prestigious venues, made five short films for Universal Studios, and recorded with Doris Day as vocalist.

Over the years, the grueling touring schedule led to considerable turnover in the band. Thus the Yankovic band became an incubator for outstanding musicians, including accordionists such as Joe Sekardi, Frankie Kramer, Richie Vadnal, Roger Bright, Jim Maupin, and Joey Miskulin.

The touring took a toll on family life as well. His first marriage ended in divorce in the late 1960s. His second marriage, in the 1970s to Pat Soltesz, produced two children but also ended in divorce. He met his third wife, Ida Klanchesser, at his 70th birthday celebration in 1985. They married in 1986. Ida took an active role in his business, traveling with the band and taking responsibility for sales of his recordings.

In 1986 the National Academy of Recording Arts and Sciences initiated a polka category for the Grammy Awards, and Yankovic was its first recipient, for his album *70 Years of Hits*. In December 1994, an hour-long documentary on his life was shown on public television. He was an active musician virtually until his death in New Port Richey, Florida.

• It is surprising how little has been written about Frank Yankovic except for ephemeral music industry and polka fan publications. He produced a chatty autobiography with a Cleveland journalist: Frankie Yankovic as told to Robert Dolgan, *The Polka King: The Life of Frankie Yankovic* (1977). Frank J. Smodic, Jr., *The Legendary Frankie Yankovic "Through the Years": The Life and Times of America's Polka King* (1991) is a commemorative program booklet put together for Yankovic's seventy-fifth birthday. Victor Greene's scholarly book *A Passion for Polka: Old Time Ethnic Music in America* (1992) devotes several pages to Yankovic. He is discussed in Richard March, "Slovenian Polka Music: Tradition and Transition," *JEMF Quarterly* 21, no. 75/76 (Spring 1989): 47–50.

RICK MARCH

YERBY, Frank (5 Sept. 1916–29 Nov. 1991), writer, was born Frank Garvin Yerby in Augusta, Georgia, the son of Rufus Garvin Yerby, a postal worker, and Wilhelmina Smythe Yerby. As a child he was shy and bookish, and by the time he was a teenager he was writing verse, some of which he published locally. He became interested in pursuing writing as a career after his sister, a student at Fisk University in Nashville, Tennessee, showed some of his poems to James Weldon Johnson, who was then teaching at the university, and Johnson commented favorably on them. As an African American, Yerby attended segregated schools in Augusta, and after graduation from high school he enrolled at Paine College, a black institution in that city, and contributed poems and short stories to college publications and small magazines.

After receiving his undergraduate degree in 1937, Yerby did graduate work in English at Fisk, earning a master's degree a year later. He then moved to Chicago, where he did further graduate work at the University of Chicago while working for the Federal Writers' Project, a Depression-era program sponsored by the U.S. government. As part of the Writers' Project, a nationwide enterprise that extensively documented various aspects of American life, Yerby worked in the so-called Ethnics Unit and was assigned to write about a Muslim religious sect living in the city. He later described the experience, which included training in how to do detailed research, as the best preparation possible for an aspiring writer.

Yerby moved to Tallahassee, Florida, in 1939 to teach English at Florida A&M College, another all-black institution, and after a year there went on to teach at the all-black Southern University, in Scotlandville, Louisiana. It was at this time, in 1941, that he married Flora Williams, with whom he had four children. He moved north to Detroit in the summer of 1942 to work in a defense plant in Dearborn for several years, then moved east to spend another year working at an aircraft factory on Long Island in New York. During this period Yerby wrote short stories about racial tensions in contemporary America and submitted them to magazines, but most of them were rejected. He did score one success with "Health Card," which appeared in *Harper's* in May 1944. An account of a black couple mistreated by military police, it received an O. Henry Memorial Prize Award and was reprinted that year in the annual O. Henry collection of outstanding short stories.

Pleased to have recognition at last, Yerby nevertheless realized that little money would be made from short stories—he now had a family to support—and he shifted his focus to write a popular novel that he hoped would become a bestseller. The result was *The Foxes of Harrow*, a historical potboiler filled with melodrama, set in the antebellum South, and featuring the stock characters, predictable incidents, and steamy sex of a genre that came to be known as "costume fiction." Although black people appeared in the book, albeit as slaves, and were sympathetically depicted, the story focused on the rise to riches and power of a white protagonist—an unusual subject for a black novelist at that time. Critical opinion seemed to divide along racial lines. White critics writing in mainstream publications, while treating the novel respectfully and looking for political significance, found themselves struggling to find something to praise and usually focused on the authenticity of "period detail." Black critics, on the other hand, seemed somewhat defensive on Yerby's behalf; determined to take the book seriously—perhaps more so than the author had intended—they saw it as a breakthrough for the black novelist in America.

In one way it was: *The Foxes of Harrow* was no literary masterpiece, but it became a runaway bestseller. Within a year more than a million copies had been sold, excerpts from the book had been reprinted in both black and white periodicals, and Twentieth Century–Fox had bought the film rights; a movie version starring Rex Harrison and Maureen O'Hara was released in 1947. The book was reprinted many times and over the next forty years sold an estimated ten to twelve million copies. Yerby's astonishing success encouraged him to stay with a winning formula, and he never looked back. Thenceforth he turned out historical novels in a similar vein at the rate of nearly one a year, writing a total of thirty-three books that were translated into more than a dozen languages. Nearly all of them were bestsellers.

Most of Yerby's novels after *Harrow* were also set in the nineteenth-century South and featured the standard melodramatic panoply of the costume novel. They included such titles as *A Woman Called Fancy* (1951), *An Odor of Sanctity* (1965), *The Dahomean* (1971), and *A Darkness at Ingraham's Crest* (1979). But occasionally Yerby moved his locales: *Goat Song* (1967) is set in ancient Greece; *Judas, My Brother* (1969) in the early Christian era; and *Western* (1982) is subtitled *A Saga of the Great Plains*. Yerby defended these and several other works as "serious novels" rather than costume fiction, but most critics did not agree, concluding that his books indulged in two-dimensional characters and historical stereotypes. The public, seemingly oblivious to the conflict, kept on buying his books—close to sixty million copies to date. Though Yerby was obliquely accused of betraying his early promise by not writing novels of social protest, especially as the civil rights movement captured national attention during the 1950s and 1960s, he defended his work as popular entertainment, putting himself in the company of other bestselling novelists such as Thackeray and Dickens and declaring his refusal to write what he called "sociological tracts."

By this time Yerby had become an expatriate, having settled in Spain in 1952. There he continued to write bestselling fiction. Having divorced his first wife, he married his secretary and translator, Blanca Calle-Perez, in 1956. His last novel, *McKenzie's Hundred*, was published in 1985. Yerby died of heart failure in a hospital in Madrid.

• For biographical information, see entries for "Yerby, Frank," in *Contemporary Authors: New Revision Series*, vols. 16 (1986) and 52 (1996); *Current Biography Yearbook 1946*; and *Dictionary of Literary Biography*, vol. 76 (1988). For an assessment of his work see Robert A. Bone, *The Negro Novel in America* (1965), pp. 167–69; see also H. W. Fuller, "Famous Writer Faces a Challenge," *Ebony*, June 1966, pp. 188–90. An obituary is in the *New York Times*, 8 Jan. 1992.

ANN T. KEENE

YORTY, Sam (1 Oct. 1909–5 June 1998), mayor, was born Samuel William Yorty in Lincoln, Nebraska, the son of Frank Patrick Yorty, restaurant owner and handyman, and Johanna Egan Yorty. Yorty grew up in a home where money was scarce but political discussions were plentiful—William Jennings Bryan and Woodrow Wilson were family icons—and he became interested in politics at an early age. He worked at a variety of part-time jobs in order to assist family finances, and in high school he organized "Sam Yorty's Meloders," an orchestra that often performed at local functions.

Following graduation, Yorty moved to Los Angeles and began to study law at Southwestern University. Financial constraints soon forced him to alternate sales work with his studies. He also explored different political and social philosophies, becoming involved at various times with organizations such as the Parliament of Man, the Technocracy movement, and Dr. Frances E. Townsend's plan to provide universal pensions. After spending some time training to become a movie projectionist, he went to work for the Los Angeles Water and Power Department and helped to negotiate right-of-way agreements for power lines emanating from the then under construction Hoover Dam.

Yorty returned to his first love—politics—in 1933 when he worked for Frank Shaw's successful mayoral campaign. With assistance from his political mentor Dr. John R. Haynes, the president of the Los Angeles Water and Power Commission, he made his first bid for elective office in 1936 as a Democrat and won a seat in the California State Assembly. As a freshman legislator, Yorty championed a variety of liberal causes, including the establishment of state-run parimutuel betting, state-owned public utilities, and tighter usury regulations. Reelected in 1938, he dismayed many of his supporters by sponsoring legislation that created the first state-sponsored Un-American Activities committee, which he then chaired. Yorty's committee did find evidence of Communist influence within the Los Angeles office of the State Relief Administration, and he continued to drift to the right of the political spectrum for the balance of his career. He married Elizabeth "Betts" Hensel in 1938; they would have one child, a son.

After a failed attempt at the U.S. Senate in 1940, Yorty practiced law, having been admitted to the bar in the previous year. In 1942 he enlisted in the U.S. Army Air Corps, with which he served in the South Pacific theater; he rose to the rank of captain. On returning to civilian life in 1945, he ran for mayor of Los Angeles but finished sixth in a field of thirteen. In 1945, after practicing criminal and then corporate law for a few years, he won a special election that returned him to the California State Assembly. In 1950 he won election to the U.S. House of Representatives, and for four years he championed California oil and water rights in Washington. In 1954 he lost another U.S. Senate race; denied a rematch with incumbent Senator Thomas Kuchel by the state Democratic council in 1956, Yorty returned to his legal practice and seethed.

In 1960 Yorty astonished fellow Democrats by endorsing Richard Nixon over John F. Kennedy for the presidency. Determined to overcome what many thought had been his political suicide, Yorty ran for mayor of Los Angeles in 1961 against incumbent Norris Poulson. Despite the antagonism of many Democrats toward his candidacy, Yorty ran a flawless media campaign and capitalized on local resentment against what he called a "little ruling clique" as well as burdensome local ordinances. The result was an upset.

Yorty's administration won generally high marks for lowering property taxes, luring new industry to the city, and facilitating the construction of the Music Center. Although he had pledged, if elected, to remove the city's controversial police chief, William H. Parker, an avowed white supremacist, Yorty kept him on the job after publicly insisting on fair treatment for minorities. Within a short time of his reelection by a wide margin in 1965, Yorty was forced to deal with the aftermath of the Watts riots, a bloody disturbance in a predominantly black, impoverished area that left thirty-four people dead and over $40 million worth of property destroyed. Yorty was widely criticized for numerous incidents of police brutality as well as poorly coordinating with federal officials the handling of the crisis.

Yorty sought a third term in 1969 and was opposed by Thomas Bradley, an African-American city councilman and former police lieutenant. In a bitter campaign marked by open appeals to racism, Yorty won a runoff election despite the support of national political figures such as Hubert Humphrey and Edward Kennedy for his opponent. During his third term in office, while Yorty continued to seek other offices (running unsuccessfully for governor in 1970 and for the Democratic presidential nomination in 1972), his constituents grew increasingly frustrated with conditions in Los Angeles. Minority voters resented the unqualified support that Yorty gave police chief Ed Davis, and complaints of police brutality became commonplace. As the city's rampant development contributed to problems of congestion and pollution, many citizens viewed Yorty—now nicknamed "Travlin' Sam" for his frequent overseas excursions—as out of touch with their concerns.

In the mayoral election in 1973 Yorty again faced Bradley. The campaign was, if anything, even nastier than the previous one, and Yorty accused his opponent of seeking Black Panther party support and warned his white supporters of the perils of the "black block vote." When Bradley prevailed in the runoff, Yorty retired from public office. Having previously hosted his own local television program and made guest appearances on programs such as the "Tonight" show, Yorty became the host of a local radio call-in show. His final electoral bid came in 1981, when he was crushed by Bradley in an attempt to regain his former position as mayor. He died at his home in the Studio City section of Los Angeles following a brief illness.

Never easy to pigeonhole, Sam Yorty compiled in his early years as mayor a fairly notable record as a public servant, but his inability to adapt his policies and outlook to the changing demographics of Los Angeles eventually marginalized him. He came to represent a branch of Democratic politics that no longer had firm roots in the party either locally or nationally. His ouster from office by Tom Bradley was a watershed in the history of Los Angeles.

• Yorty's papers are held at the Los Angeles City Archives. He was the subject of Ed Ainsworth, *Maverick Mayor* (1966), and his career also received attention in Mike Davis, *City of Quartz: Excavating the Future in Los Angeles* (1990). His role in the Watts riots is examined in Gerald Thorne, *The Fire This Time: The Watts Uprising and the 1960s* (1995). Obituaries are in the *New York Times* and the *Los Angeles Times*, both 6 June 1998.

EDWARD L. LACH, JR.

YOUNG, Coleman (24 May 1918–29 Nov. 1997), mayor, was born in Tuscaloosa, Alabama, the son of William Coleman Young, a barber and a tailor, and Ida Reese Jones Young. After his family moved to Detroit in 1923, Young grew up in the Black Bottom section of town, where his father ran a dry-cleaning and tailoring operation and also worked as a night watchman at the post office. Although Young enjoyed his early years in the then–ethnically diverse neighborhood, his family did not altogether escape discrimination. A gifted student, he was rejected by a Catholic high school because of his race, and after graduating from public Eastern High he lost out on college financial aid for the same reason. Young became an electrical apprentice at Ford Motor Company, only to see a white man with lower test scores get the job. He then worked on Ford's assembly line but was fired for fighting a thug from Harry Bennett's Service Department who had identified Young as a union member.

After his dismissal from Ford, Young went to work for the National Negro Congress, a civil rights organization that focused on labor issues. While with the NNC, he worked at the post office and continued the fight to unionize Ford. When Henry Ford accepted a union contract, Young turned his attention to other issues such as open housing. Fired from his job in the post office for union activity, he was drafted into the army in February 1942. Young initially served in the infantry with the 92d Buffalo Division before transferring to the U.S. Army Air Forces, where he underwent pilot training with the famed Tuskegee airmen. Washed out of the pilot program—an action Young blamed on FBI interference based on his years of unionizing and associating with so-called radicals—he spent the rest of the war fighting for equal accommodations for African-American servicemen on a number of military bases.

Discharged from the air forces as a second lieutenant in December 1945, Young returned to Detroit, regained his position at the post office, and resumed his union organizing activities. In January 1947 he married Marion McClellan; the couple had no children before divorcing in 1954. Shortly thereafter, he married Nadine Drake; that childless marriage also ended in divorce a few years later. As a member of the United Public Workers, he soon ran afoul of Walter Reuther, whose conservative brand of anti-Communist leadership within the United Auto Workers extended to the Congress of Industrial Organizations. Although Young had been elected to an executive post with the Wayne County, Michigan, chapter of the CIO, he lost his position in 1948 on account of Reuther's political machinations. Following a disastrous run for the state senate as a candidate of Henry Wallace's Progressive party that same year, Young drifted through a series of jobs before becoming the executive secretary of the newly formed National Negro Labor Council, which achieved some successes nationwide in increasing the range and number of job opportunities for African Americans. Targeted by the federal government as a subversive group, however, the organization folded under pressure in the spring of 1956. After a few more years of drifting between jobs, Young lost a bid for Detroit's Common Council in 1960. Encouraged by the election results, he successfully gained a seat at Michigan's Constitutional Convention. Following the convention, Young spent several successful years as an insurance salesman for the Municipal Credit Union League before reentering politics for good in 1964, when he gained election to the Michigan State Senate.

Young remained in the senate until 1973, where he supported open housing and school busing legislation and eventually became Democratic floor leader. In 1973 he ran for mayor of Detroit and, with substantial union support, narrowly won a racially charged contest against former police commissioner John F. Nichols. After the election, Young pledged to work together with business and labor to help turn around the badly troubled city, which was then reeling from high unemployment, rampant crime, white flight, the effects of the gasoline embargo, and the loss of its industrial base. Young presided over the 1977 opening of Renaissance Center, a downtown office-retail complex designed to revitalize the city's riverfront, and was also instrumental in building new manufacturing plants for Chrysler and General Motors. Faced with the city's possible bankruptcy, he persuaded voters to approve an income tax increase and gained wage and benefit concessions from municipal workers. Having run on a campaign of reforming the Detroit police department (long viewed as a source of oppression among African-American residents), he increased the number of blacks and minorities on the force and also disbanded STRESS (Stop the Robberies, Enjoy Safe Streets), a special police decoy unit that was the focus of many complaints of brutality.

Reelected four times, Young enjoyed a particularly good relationship with President Jimmy Carter. Among the first to endorse Carter's presidential campaign in 1976, Young served as vice chairman of the Democratic National Committee between 1977 and 1981 and from 1981 until 1983 headed the United States Conference of Mayors. He fared less well under Carter's Republican successors, however, and also had to deal with long-running feuds with the local press as well as nearby suburban governments. Despite his long-held emphasis on racial cooperation, the blunt-spoken Young—who for years had a sign on his desk that read "Head Motherf**ker in Charge"—never gained the trust of many white voters, who deplored his confrontational style and his frequent overseas vacations. In addition to being the subject of federal criminal investigations, none of which resulted in any charges, Young was the target of a paternity suit by former city employee Annivory Calvert, with whom he had a son.

In declining health, Young chose not to run for reelection in 1993. He died in a Detroit hospital. Despite having to face a host of problems with resources that were limited at best, Young proved himself game in his efforts to preserve and revitalize one of America's major metropolitan centers.

• Young's papers are divided between the Walter Reuther Library at Wayne State University and the African-American Museum in Detroit. *Hard Stuff: The Autobiography of Coleman Young* (1994), written with Lonnie Wheeler, is a colorful and balanced view of his life and career. He is also the subject of Wilbur C. Rich, *Coleman Young and Detroit Politics: From Social Activist to Power Broker* (1989). An obituary is in the *New York Times*, 30 Nov. 1997.

EDWARD L. LACH, JR.

YOUNG, Robert (22 Feb. 1907–21 July 1998), actor, was born Robert George Young in Chicago, the fourth of five children of Thomas E. Young, a building contractor, and his wife, whose name cannot be ascertained. The family moved to Seattle in Young's infancy and then to Los Angeles when he was ten. He showed an interest in drama as a teenager and was encouraged by his older brother Joseph, a silent screen comedian. After graduating from Lincoln High School, he joined the Pasadena Community Players, a semiprofessional troupe, where he studied acting at night and appeared in some forty stage productions during the late 1920s. He supported himself at various jobs, including drugstore clerk, bill collector, and bank teller.

While appearing in a 1931 touring production of *The Ship*, the six-foot two-inch, 170-pound performer caught the attention of a Metro-Goldwyn-Mayer talent scout. The Hollywood studios, which had only recently gone over to sound-film production, were in particular need of male romantic leads whose voices matched their physical presence. Young was given a screen test and signed to a five-year contract. He quickly emerged as a familiar face in the American cinema, appearing in more than two dozen films between 1931 and 1936. Among them were some of MGM's most serious dramas, such as *Strange Inter-*

lude (1932), adapted from Eugene O'Neill's play, and *Hell Below* (1933), a war picture concerning a submarine crew. But he also appeared in several comedies, including the broadly played *Tugboat Annie* (1932) and the more sophisticated *Vagabond Lady* (1935). He told *Photoplay* magazine that he preferred comedy and that he had "never intended being a serious dramatic actor."

In 1933 the up-and-coming star married his high school sweetheart, Elizabeth Louise Henderson, and against all Hollywood odds the couple remained together for more than sixty years, until her death in 1994. They had four daughters and a number of grandchildren and great-grandchildren. Young became a licensed pilot and for many years owned a ranch in the San Fernando Valley.

Having built a reputation as a solid and dependable screen actor and a wholesome—if not particularly striking—leading man, Young found himself much in demand with both directors and the public. He made seven major motion pictures in 1936, including two that were produced in England: *It's Love Again*, a musical comedy in which he starred as a wise guy publicist for a nonexistent socialite, and *Secret Agent*, an Alfred Hitchcock spy thriller whose cast included John Gielgud, Lilli Palmer, and Peter Lorre.

The artistic fulcrum of the actor's career was arguably 1942, when he starred in three of the year's most celebrated pictures, revealing a wider spectrum of talents than many critics had given him credit for: *H. M. Pulham, Esq.*, an adaptation of John Marquand's novel about a socially introverted upper-crust Bostonian; *Journey for Margaret*, a topical drama set during the blitzkrieg of London; and *Joe Smith, American*, a patriotic World War II propaganda piece in which, quite out of character, he portrayed a blue-collar defense worker. *Newsweek* described his performance as a working-class hero as "unaffected and credible."

As Young approached his forties, he expressed a desire to moderate the breakneck pace of his schedule, and, after fourteen years, left MGM. A new contract, with RKO, committed him to no more than one picture per year and allowed him great leeway in choosing his projects. Young made several significant pictures at RKO, including *Crossfire* (1947), in which he played a detective investigating an anti-Semitic murder, and *Relentless* (1949), a Western that marked his first effort as a producer.

As the film industry tried to remake its image during the postwar years, it was becoming clear that there were only limited opportunities for an actor so thoroughly associated in the public's mind with the "old Hollywood." Moreover, Young had never become a truly top-rank star. Despite his remarkable ability and productivity, he had not starred in any notable blockbusters, nor had he been nominated for an Academy Award. The actor wisely redirected his efforts toward broadcasting.

Young had been a frequent guest on radio programs since the beginning of his film career, but in 1949 he signed on to play the title role in a new weekly NBC radio series, "Father Knows Best." The show became one of the major hits during the last years of the prime-time radio era, and in 1954 it was beckoned to the new medium of television. With his business partner, Eugene Rodney, Young bought the rights to the series and adapted it for the home screen. He remained in the lead role of Jim Anderson, while all the other parts were recast.

A lighthearted sitcom about an extraordinarily wholesome white, upper-middle-class midwestern family living in a spacious suburban home, "Father Knows Best" survives as a kind of McCarthy-era vision of a prosperous, homogeneous postwar America. Almost all the episodes concern the vicissitudes of child-rearing in the mythical town of Springfield. No problem arises that cannot be resolved in a well-articulated mini-sermon from Father. As was the case with several other displaced screen stars of Young's generation, including such notables as Fred MacMurray and Donna Reed, the actor made his peace with the artistic limitations of a leading role in a long-running sitcom, perhaps accepting the enormous wealth it brought him as adequate recompense. He received an Emmy Award for best actor in 1957.

Despite the popularity indicated by its number six finish in the Nielsen ratings for the 1959–1960 season, Young withdrew the show from production, apparently out of sheer boredom. Hoping to move on to new projects, he soon found himself in a kind of de facto retirement that would last for almost a decade. During the 1960s he would get only a few minor guest roles in films and TV shows. A 1961 attempt at a new sitcom was short-lived.

In 1969 Young's languishing career was suddenly resuscitated. Universal Television, then headed by Grant Tinker, was attempting to cast the lead role in a new medical series, "Marcus Welby, M.D." The studio was deadlocked in negotiations with another actor when, Tinker recalls, "Robert Young suddenly appeared and was sitting in my office. His opening words to me were, 'I want to be Marcus Welby.'" Tinker agreed on the spot. The series, about an extremely dedicated general practitioner in southern California, applied the patriarchal qualities that Young had cultivated in "Father Knows Best" to such issues as drug addiction and fatal diseases. It was an instant top ten hit for ABC, finishing number one in the ratings during the third of its seven seasons. In 1970 Young received his second Emmy Award for best actor.

In stark contrast to his screen persona, Young suffered frequently during his life from a complex of psychophysiological problems, including migraine headaches, alcoholism, and clinical depression. His stable family life allowed him to keep this from public knowledge. These problems, however, grew worse with age, culminating in a 1991 attempt at suicide by self-asphyxiation in a locked car. Following a long absence from the public eye, he had a role in a 1997 German TV miniseries, "Die Verlorene Tochter" ("The Lost

Daughter"). He died in his home in the San Fernando Valley at the age of ninety-one.

A prolific leading man in the movies during the 1930s and 1940s, Young appeared in more than 100 Hollywood features, as well as scores of television dramas and commercials. His chief legacy, however, rests with his portrayals of Jim Anderson and Marcus Welby, who embodied the ideals of middle-class America during the post–World War II era, although by the time "Marcus Welby, M.D." finished its run—following the end of the Vietnam War—some of those ideals were seriously in question. To millions of television viewers, Robert Young *was* the wise-father figure: a sage consoler and a benign authority.

• There is no known published autobiography or biography of Robert Young. A quite detailed account of Young's studio-era film career is available in *Current Biography 1950*. Virtually all major film reference works include entries on Young; see Ephraim Katz, *The Film Encyclopedia*, 2d ed. (1994). Detailed obituaries can be found in most major newspapers, including the 23 July 1998 editions of the *New York Times*, the *Los Angeles Times*, and the *Boston Globe*.

DAVID MARC

YOUNGMAN, Henny (16 Mar. 1906–24 Feb. 1998), stand-up comedian, was born Henry Youngman in London, the son of Yonkel Yungman and Olga Chetkin Yungman, Russian immigrants who had met in New York but had gone to England to live with relatives. (His date of birth has also been given as 12 Jan. 1906.) The family returned to New York in 1908, settling in an apartment in the Bay Ridge section of Brooklyn. Youngman's father, a sign painter, hoped that his son would become a professional musician and made sure he received violin lessons despite the family's poverty.

Considered a troublemaker at school for his compulsive wisecracking, Youngman was also a truant, frequently skipping classes in favor of vaudeville matinees and movies. At age sixteen, he was expelled from Manual Training High School and began earning money by playing the violin at silent-era movie theaters. In 1924 he enrolled in a program to prepare for a career in the printing trades at Brooklyn Vocational High School; but while still in school he formed a dance band, Hen Youngman and the Syncopators. The musicians dropped out of school the following year to pursue their music full time.

The Syncopators managed to play gigs at Coney Island dance halls and at the Borscht Belt hotels of the Catskill Mountains. It was at the latter that Henny Youngman learned the trade of stand-up comedy. A bandleader at a Borscht Belt resort was expected to double as a "toomler," a Yiddish term for an all-purpose emcee and joke-teller whose job it is to keep the patrons smiling. Toomlers were expected not only to perform on stage but also to give performances at poolside, in the hotel lounge, or any other place where they might encounter guests.

Unfortunately, most of the band's engagements were in the summer or during holidays, forcing the musicians to find "day jobs" much of the year. Youngman bought a small printing press and started up a service selling business cards to entertainers, eventually opening up a small shop in midtown Manhattan. In 1928 he married Sadie Cohen, a saleswoman at a Brooklyn department store; the couple had a daughter and a son and remained together until Sadie's death in 1987.

Youngman's band was never fully successful, and he spent much of the Great Depression barely eking out a living. "I'd wake up nights gasping for breath, strangling because I had no money," he recalled years later. "I couldn't breathe! So many disappointments. So many." At the urging of Milton Berle, a printing customer who had become a friend, Youngman gave up the band in 1936 and redirected his career toward stand-up comedy. With Berle's help, he was able to get several nightclub bookings in the New York area, and within a year he had gained a regular spot on "The Kate Smith Hour," a nationally broadcast NBC radio program. In his 1991 autobiography, *Take My Life, Please*, the comedian wrote that the "Kate Smith Hour" appearances made him a star "overnight."

Youngman's act changed little over the next sixty years, whether he was appearing at a Las Vegas hotel, on a network television show, or at a local bar mitzvah (a type of engagement he continued to accept well after he had become a nationally known personality). Armed with his violin, he would begin by playing, poorly, a few bars of "Smoke Gets in Your Eyes" and then abruptly stop to deliver a bombardment of jokes, none of them more than about twenty seconds long—and some considerably shorter. The most famous of these became the comedian's catchphrase and was entered into *Bartlett's Familiar Quotations* in 1988: "Take my wife—please."

Many of Youngman's signature jokes concern spouses and in-laws. This kind of subject matter was never considered very sophisticated, and by the end of the 1950s it was generally dismissed as utterly passé. Youngman, however, never abandoned it: "I miss my wife's cooking—as often as I can." "I've been married for 34 years, and I'm still in love with the same woman. If my wife ever finds out, she'll kill me." "I just got back from a pleasure trip; I took my mother-in-law to the airport." Self-deprecation also figured largely in the Youngman repertoire: "I was so ugly when I was born that the doctor slapped my mother." "A psychiatrist tells a patient he's crazy. The patient says, 'I want a second opinion.' The psychiatrist says, 'O.K., you're ugly, too.'" "At my age, I can't take yes for an answer." The comedian bought most of his jokes from professional gag writers. It is also worth noting that he steadfastly refused any joke he considered off-color, even after such material became standard fare.

Through his persistent dedication to the style and substance of the innocent and familiar comedy of a past age, he gained a position as a kind of iconic representative of that era to younger generations of comedians and audiences. Director Martin Scorsese made use of Youngman's mythic persona in his 1990 film *GoodFellas*, casting him as a stand-up comic ("Henny Youngman") at a nightclub frequented by gangsters. "I played in front of everybody," Youngman once commented. "I played in places where the check-out girl's name was Rocco and the owner would stab me good night." Although he worked mainly before live audiences in dance halls and nightclubs and on the radio, he appeared in more than a dozen Hollywood feature films, often playing himself, and was a frequent guest on popular network television programs, including "The Ed Sullivan Show," "The Tonight Show," "Batman," and "The Hollywood Squares."

By all accounts a lifelong workaholic, Youngman continued to perform into advanced age. Although he suffered a broken hip in 1995, he began to make public appearances within months of his discharge from the hospital. A new line, "Take my wheelchair—please," was incorporated into the act. In 1998, after returning to New York from an appearance in Las Vegas, he was admitted to Mount Sinai Hospital in New York with flu symptoms. He died in the hospital of pneumonia.

His encyclopedic knowledge and rapid-fire delivery of short jokes made Youngman the "King of the One-Liner," a title that earned him a place in the American show business pantheon.

• An autobiography, *Take My Life, Please* (written with Neal Karlen), was published in 1991. Youngman produced over a dozen compilations of jokes, including *Take My Jokes, Please* (1983) and *The Encyclopedia of One-Liners* (1989). Audio recordings include *The Primitive Sounds of Henny Youngman* (1968) and *The World's Worst Jokes* (1987). An obituary is in the *New York Times*, 25 February 1998.

DAVID MARC

Z

ZALE, Tony (29 May 1913–21 Mar. 1997), world middleweight boxing champion, was born Anthony Florian Zaleski in Gary, Indiana, the fourth son and the sixth of seven children of Joseph Zaleski, a steel mill worker, and Catherine Zaleski (maiden name unknown), both Polish immigrants. His father died in a traffic accident when he was two years old, but his mother and oldest brothers held the family together. Zale graduated from Froebel High School and then went to work in a Gary steel mill.

Zale, like all of his brothers, was an amateur boxer. He won 87 of 95 fights, losing in the finals of the welterweight division of the Chicago Golden Gloves tournament in 1932. He left his steel mill job to become a professional boxer in June 1934, winning 20 fights and losing 8, mostly in the Chicago area, in just over a year of activity. Torn muscles in his side forced him into temporary retirement, and he had only one fight in 1936, returning to the steel mills for employment. He resumed his career in July 1937, winning 11 of 14 fights; he suffered a one-round knockout by Jimmy Clark in February 1938 but avenged that loss four months later.

The turning point in Zale's boxing career came in June 1938. Managed previously by Harry Shall and then by his brother John, he was now under the direction of Sam Pian and Art Winch, who had managed welterweight champion Barney Ross. Zale's style was remade by Winch, a trainer and boxing teacher, who brought him down off his toes to a shuffling style of footwork that took more advantage of his punching power. Winch also taught him how to block punches and roll with them to diminish their effect.

Although drawing with Billy Celebron and then losing to him in his first two fights under Pian and Winch, Zale soon began to advance rapidly. He won 9 of his next 10 fights, gaining main event status. Then, on 29 January 1940, he fought National Boxing Association middleweight champion Al Hostak in Chicago. It was an exciting fight in which Hostak floored Zale seconds after the opening bell and later suffered a broken hand while giving Zale a severe beating in the fifth round. Zale then battered the injured Hostak in the last five rounds and won the decision, becoming the leading contender for the NBA title. Zale won his next three fights and then met Hostak for the title in Seattle, on 19 July 1940, leading throughout until referee Benny Leonard stopped the fight in the thirteenth round.

After being outboxed and defeated by Billy Soose in his next fight and then beating former middleweight title claimant Fred Apostoli, Zale defended his NBA title successfully twice in 1941, against Steve Mamakos and Hostak. On 28 November he met New York State titlist Georgie Abrams in New York, the winner to be proclaimed the undisputed middleweight champion. The result was a thrilling fight in which Zale was knocked down in the first round and badly hurt in the eighth, but he came back, using a devastating body attack to win decisively. Zale had only one fight in 1942, losing on points to light-heavyweight Billy Conn in New York on 13 February. He enlisted in the U.S. Navy on 9 April and married Adeline Richwalski of Gary the next day. The couple would have two children, both daughters.

The mild-mannered Zale was known for his gentlemanly behavior out of the ring, which was in sharp contrast to his aggressiveness and intensity when fighting. A fast puncher with both hands, he was neither quick afoot nor a clever boxer. He relied upon a relentless attack and hard body punching to win. Although often knocked down, he recovered rapidly and invariably took the offensive. Sportswriters, in deference to the city of his origin and to his ability to absorb punishment, called him "The Man of Steel."

Zale taught boxing to sailors from 1942 to 1945 at Great Lakes Training Station and later in Puerto Rico, but he refrained from boxing himself. He was rusty when he resumed his career in 1946, but he won a series of six nontitle fights before defending his title against Rocky Graziano in New York on 27 September 1946, thus initiating one of the most famous rivalries in the history of boxing. A terrific puncher, Graziano was supremely confident after a string of knockout victories and was the favorite to win. Although floored in the first round by Zale, Graziano scored a knockdown himself in the second and then launched a sustained attack that seemingly brought him to the edge of victory by the end of the fifth round. But in the sixth round Zale landed a terrific right to the midsection followed by a left to the cheek, putting Graziano down for the full count.

A rematch between Zale and Graziano was held on 16 July 1947 in Chicago. The result was another thrilling fight. Unlike the first match, Zale was ahead and appeared on his way to victory for the first five rounds, but in the sixth Graziano launched a devastating assault that finally brought Zale down. The referee stopped the fight and Zale lost the middleweight championship after having held it for over five years.

The third and last of the famous Zale-Graziano series occurred on 10 June 1948 in Newark, New Jersey. Graziano was knocked down in round one but recovered and waged a slam-bang attack in the second that had Zale worried. In the third round, Zale recaptured the middleweight title with a remarkably effective exhibition of two-handed punching to both jaw and body, sending Graziano down twice, the second time for the full count.

On 21 September 1948, Zale defended his title against Marcel Cerdan of France in Jersey City, New Jersey. Cerdan was a clever boxer and hard puncher, rugged enough to survive Zale's body punching, and able to land a glove frequently and effectively on his opponent. As the rounds passed, Cerdan's lead became more and more commanding, and he had the fight well in hand when Zale dropped from exhaustion near the end of the eleventh round. Unable to answer the bell for the twelfth round, he lost his championship again and ended his ring career.

Zale saved his money and lived comfortably after retirement. He was co-owner of a Chicago automobile dealership, and he taught boxing to boys at the Catholic Youth Organization in Chicago for many years. In 1970 he was married a second time, to Philomena Gianfrancisco, a former player in the All-American Girls Baseball League. Zale died in a nursing home from Parkinson's disease and lymph-node cancer. In 87 fights, he won 67, lost 18, and had 2 draws.

Zale received many honors. In 1990 he was awarded the Presidential Citizen's Medal by President George Bush. He was elected to the Indiana Hall of Fame, the Chicago Hall of Fame, the Polish Sports Hall of Fame, and the International Boxing Hall of Fame.

• Many of Zale's fights, especially those with Graziano, are described in *The Ring* magazine. For useful articles, see Gene Kessler, "This Zale's a Real Gale among Middles," *The Ring*, Apr. 1940, pp. 22, 42; Howard Roberts, "Hard-Luck Champion," *Saturday Evening Post*, 5 July 1947, pp. 26, 95–96; and Dan Daniel, "Hostak Toughest Foe, Says Zale," *The Ring*, Nov. 1966, pp. 19–21. Obituaries are in the *Chicago Tribune* and the *New York Times*, both 21 Mar. 1997.

LUCKETT V. DAVIS

ZINNEMANN, Fred (29 Apr. 1907–14 Mar. 1997), film director, was born in Vienna, Austria, the son of Oskar Zinnemann, a physician, and Anna Zinnemann (maiden name unknown). He later recalled that his well-to-do parents expected him to pursue a respectable professional career: "It was, of course, considered absolutely necessary to have an academic degree and to be called 'Herr Doktor,' no matter what one was a doctor of; in my case, the only practical answer seemed to be to study for a doctorate in law, which I duly tried and hated with a passion from the first moment" (Zinnemann, p. 8). While shirking his classes at the University of Vienna, he became an avid moviegoer. After taking a law degree in 1927 he announced to his parents that he wanted to pursue filmmaking instead. To their consternation, he enrolled at a fledgling film school, the École Technique de Photographie et de Cinématographie in Paris, where he studied optics and photochemistry. In 1928 he moved to Berlin, where he found work as an assistant cameraman on Eugen Schüfftan's influential semidocumentary *Menschen am Sonntag* (People on Sunday).

The movie, which depicted average working-class Germans on a Sunday outing, was shot entirely on location and utilized nonprofessional actors—realistic elements that Zinnemann would seek to incorporate in his own films. Intrigued by the advent of "talkies" in the United States, he left Europe in 1929 for Hollywood.

While working as a script clerk at Fox Studios, Zinnemann met the pioneering documentary filmmaker Robert Flaherty. As Zinnemann later remembered, "I was still green and impressionable and very much in search of a hero. . . . [Flaherty] didn't know the meaning of compromise and this quality attracted me to him above everything else" (Zinnemann, pp. 24–25). Flaherty, who wanted to make a picture about a remote nomadic tribe in Soviet Central Asia, hired him as an assistant. Although the two men spent much of 1930 planning the documentary, they aborted the project when the Soviet government insisted that they include communist propaganda. In 1933 Zinnemann codirected his first film, *Redes* (Nets), for the Mexican Federal Department of Fine Arts. The semidocumentary featured impoverished coastal fishermen as actors and depicted their efforts to form a union. In 1936 he married Renée Bartlett, who worked in the costume department at Paramount Pictures; they had one child. In 1937 he was hired to direct short subjects at Metro-Goldwyn-Mayer. The one-reel format forced him to learn economical storytelling; as he told an interviewer, "I remember doing the life of Dr. George Washington Carver, from the time he was kidnapped by slave traders as a baby until he was ninety-five, in ten minutes" (quoted in Phillips, p. 144). He directed several two-reelers in MGM's *Crime Does Not Pay* series, and in 1938 he won an Academy Award for *That Mothers Might Live*, a short film dealing with the life of Dr. Ignaz Semmelweis, who introduced the use of antiseptics in obstetrics.

In 1942 Zinnemann directed his first feature-length studio production, *Kid Glove Killer*, a low-budget film noir about a police criminologist. In 1944 he directed *The Seventh Cross*, starring Spencer Tracy, a taut, atmospheric chase melodrama about an escapee from a Nazi concentration camp. Although the film was a critical and commercial success, he subsequently found himself assigned to several "B" pictures featuring a child star, Jackie "Butch" Jenkins. Around this time, he learned that his parents, who were Jewish, had died in the Holocaust. He later recalled his frustration at directing MGM projects such as the racetrack comedy *My Brother Talks to Horses* (1946): while European filmmakers confronted the shattering upheavals caused by World War II, "in Hollywood studios there was a blissful ignorance; the average 'product' continued unchanged, full of bland escapism and a sticky, unreal sentimentality. It was sickening to think of working on that type of material" (Zinnemann, p. 55). In 1946, after refusing several assignments, he became the first director in studio history to be suspended for being uncooperative.

In 1947, with his Hollywood career at a standstill, Zinnemann was permitted to make a film for a Swiss producer about the war orphans who lived in United Nations refugee camps. *The Search* (released in 1948) was shot on location in bombed-out German cities and featured camp children in nonspeaking roles. Montgomery Clift, in his screen debut, gave an unaffected, largely improvised performance as an American soldier who befriends a Czech boy and helps him reunite with his mother. The film was well received by critics, and Zinnemann won a best director award from the Screen Directors Guild. After fulfilling his MGM contract in 1949 with *Act of Violence*, he began a partnership with independent producer Stanley Kramer and screenwriter Carl Foreman, both of whom were committed to socially conscious filmmaking. The following year they collaborated on *The Men*, Marlon Brando's first film, which dealt with the plight of paralyzed war veterans. In keeping with his penchant for authenticity, Zinnemann shot the picture in an army hospital and utilized paraplegic patients in supporting roles.

In 1952 the Zinnemann-Kramer-Foreman partnership continued with the western classic *High Noon*, starring Gary Cooper as an aging marshal who stands alone to fight a gang after his fellow citizens refuse to assist him. Zinnemann was fascinated by his protagonist's conflict of conscience—whether to place his personal convictions above those of his community—an issue that would recur in several of the director's subsequent films. *High Noon*'s visual design was groundbreaking: Zinnemann and cinematographer Floyd Crosby developed a grainy, burnt-out look, similar to Mathew Brady's Civil War photographs. "Up to that time, there was almost a religious ritual about the way that Westerns were made," the director commented. "There was always a lovely sky with pretty clouds in the background. . . . From the first day the front office complained about the poor photography [on *High Noon*]. . . . [But] subliminally the photography created the effect we wanted; it made the film look more real" (quoted in Philips, p. 153). The film's portrayal of a western hero as fearful and vacillating irritated genre purists such as John Wayne and director Howard Hawks, who made in response the two-fisted *Rio Bravo* (1959). Nevertheless, Cooper's marshal has become an American icon.

Zinnemann's *The Member of the Wedding* (1952), also produced by Kramer, was a poignant look at the relationship between a black woman and an awkward, tomboyish white twelve-year-old (played by Ethel Waters and Julie Harris, respectively); the film was an adaptation of Carson McCullers's novel and stage play. In 1952 the director won an Academy Award for best one-reel documentary for *Benjy*, a film about a handicapped child that he made to raise funds for a children's hospital in Los Angeles. The following year he won an Academy Award for best director for *From Here to Eternity*, a sharply critical examination of the prewar U.S. Army. Hollywood executives had considered James Jones's sprawling novel to be unfilmable,

but Zinnemann and screenwriter Daniel Taradash produced a tight, evocative narrative. For example, the picture's opening shot effectively encapsulates the first fifty pages of the novel—showing the protagonist, a "lone wolf" private (played by Montgomery Clift), as a tiny figure moving toward the camera, glimpsed through a marching platoon that dominates the foreground. Clift's soldier was the director's most complex protagonist, a nonconformist who remains stubbornly loyal to an institution that abuses him for his nonconformity.

In 1955 Zinnemann made the most conventional film of his career, a wide-screen version of the musical *Oklahoma!* In 1959 he directed *The Nun's Story*, one of the few American films to seriously address religious life. Audrey Hepburn starred as a nun, extremely skilled in medicine, who struggles with her sense of pride in her work as a nurse, unable to achieve the "emptying of self" required by her convent. Critics have cited the film as an example of the director's "compassionate distance" as a storyteller, his ability to be engaged with his characters without imposing a particular interpretation of their behavior: viewers are left to decide whether the nun's eventual return to the outside world is a triumph or a failure (Neve, p. 15). *The Sundowners* (1960), a good-natured story about migrant sheep-drovers in Australia, was ignored at the box office. During the 1960s, Zinnemann devoted a great deal of time and energy to projects that were never realized, including one about United Nations peacekeepers on the India-Pakistan border. In 1966 he directed *A Man for All Seasons*, an adaptation of Robert Bolt's stage play, with a powerful performance by Paul Scofield as Sir Thomas More. Zinnemann later recalled that Columbia Pictures had little interest in the film—because it had "very little action . . . no sex, no overt love story and, most importantly, *no stars*" (Zinnemann, p. 199)—and therefore gave him a minuscule budget and total artistic control; he was awarded a best director Academy Award for his efforts.

Zinnemann became increasingly frustrated with Hollywood during the late 1960s. He spent three years preparing an adaptation of André Malraux's novel *Man's Fate*, but studio politics at MGM caused the film to be canceled three days before shooting began. When the studio tried to hold him responsible for $1.7 million in unpaid bills, he filed a successful lawsuit. In 1971 he directed *The Day of the Jackal* (released in 1973), a superior thriller about a plot to assassinate Charles de Gaulle. *Julia* (1977) was one of his least satisfying works, a dreamy, soft-focus adaptation of a story by Lillian Hellman. He retired after completing *Five Days One Summer* (1982), a film inspired by his boyhood experiences climbing in the Austrian Alps. During his later years, he occasionally returned to the public eye to support artists' creative rights. He appeared at the Cannes Film Festival to encourage directors to band together to protect their work from tampering, and he testified before a congressional committee to demand that black-and-white films not be colorized for television. In 1993 the Directors' Guild of America honored him with the first John Huston Award for lifetime achievement in film. He died in London.

• The best source for information on Zinnemann's life is his autobiography, *A Life in the Movies* (1992), which includes discussions of the production of each of his films. Insightful interviews are Brian Neve, "A Past Master of His Craft: An Interview with Fred Zinnemann," *Cinéaste* 23, no. 1 (1997): 15–19; and Arthur Noletti, Jr., "Conversation with Fred Zinnemann," *Film Criticism* 18–19 (Spring–Fall 1994): 7–29. Zinnemann's realist aesthetic was attacked in the late 1960s by auteurist film critics, who preferred the flamboyant artistry of such directors as Orson Welles and Alfred Hitchcock; for an example of their opinions of Zinnemann, see Andrew Sarris, *The American Cinema: Directors and Directions, 1929–1968* (1968). For an excellent, balanced appraisal of the director's career, see Robert Horton, "Fred Zinnemann: Day of the Craftsman," *Film Comment* 33, no. 5 (Sept.–Oct. 1997): 60–67. For examples of academic scholarship on Zinnemann's films, see Gene D. Phillips, *Exiles in Hollywood: Major European Film Directors in America* (1998), and especially Arthur Noletti, Jr., ed., *The Films of Fred Zinnemann: Critical Perspectives* (1999). An obituary is in the *New York Times*, 15 Mar. 1997.

THOMAS W. COLLINS, JR.

AMERICAN NATIONAL BIOGRAPHY SUPPLEMENT 1
INDEX BY CONTRIBUTOR

AMERICAN NATIONAL BIOGRAPHY SUPPLEMENT 1
INDEX BY PLACE OF BIRTH IN THE UNITED STATES

For indexing purposes, places of birth have been indicated by names of the fifty states
and the District of Columbia rather than by historical names of colonies and territories.

ALABAMA
Allen, Mel
Durr, Virginia Foster
Elliott, Carl A.
Etting, Solomon
Finley, Charles O.
Gaston, A. G.
Johnson, Frank, Jr.
Maddox, Rose
Skaggs, William H.
Van Doren, Irita
Walker, Margaret
Wallace, George
Wynn, Early
Young, Coleman

ARIZONA
Bird, Rose
Frankovich, Mike
Goldwater, Barry
Jacobs, Helen Hull
Kleindienst, Richard G.
Udall, Morris K.

ARKANSAS
Cleaver, Eldridge

CALIFORNIA
Alioto, Joseph L.
Caen, Herb
Cowell, Henry
Desmond, Paul
DiMaggio, Joe
Drysdale, Don
Fujikawa, Gyo
Griffith-Joyner, Florence
Jarrico, Paul
Lemon, Bob
McCarey, Leo
Montgomery, Elizabeth
Moody, Helen Wills
Raymond, Arthur E.
Rigney, Bill
Shaw, Robert
Shoemaker, Gene
Smith, Jack
Tuttle, Elbert P.
Van Doren, Dorothy
Verdon, Gwen
Wood, Beatrice

COLORADO
Higman, Howard
Packard, David
Stone, Fred

CONNECTICUT
Alsop, Richard
Bowers, Fredson
Bristol, Sherlock
Hawkes, John
Mitchum, Robert
Ribicoff, Abraham
Spock, Benjamin

DELAWARE
Banning, Phineas

DISTRICT OF COLUMBIA
Brown, Ron
Bundy, William
Kennedy, John F., Jr.
Parks, Lillian Rogers

FLORIDA
Kessen, William

GEORGIA
Atwater, Lee
Crawford, George
Gordon
Jones, Thomas Goode
Stribling, Young
Yerby, Frank

HAWAII
Koopman, Karl

ILLINOIS
Bellamy, Ralph
Blackmun, Harry A.
Chancellor, John
Ellis, Edward Robb
Lewis, Janet
McNeill, Don
Miles, Josephine
Moore, Archie
Ness, Eliot
Nitschke, Ray
Norvo, Red

ILLINOIS *(cont.)*
Peattie, Donald Culross
Royko, Mike
Shambaugh, George E., Jr.
Sheean, Vincent
Shepherd, Jean
Tombaugh, Clyde
Tormé, Mel
Whiting, Richard
Young, Robert

INDIANA
Coleman, James S.
Graham, Shirley
Helms, Bobby
Johnson, J. J.
Johnston, Annie Fellows
McCoy, Kid
Reedy, George E.
Skelton, Red
Zale, Tony

IOWA
Hall, James Norman
Lee, Mabel

KANSAS
Arbuckle, Roscoe
"Fatty"
Clark, Georgia Neese
Hall, Wendall
Mack, Nila
Morgan, Barbara
Pratt, Wallace E.
Swayze, John Cameron
Tinker, Joe
Whittaker, Charles E.
Willard, Jess

KENTUCKY
Duncan, Todd
Flexner, Anne Crawford
Martin, George Madden
Mature, Victor
Monroe, Bill
Morgan, Garrett A.
Reese, Pee Wee

LOUISIANA
Kenner, Duncan Farrar
Lamour, Dorothy
Laveau, Marie
Rillieux, Norbert
Treigle, Norman
Wisdom, John Minor

MAINE
Muskie, Edmund S.
Povich, Shirley
Sepkoski, J. John, Jr.
Sockalexis, Louis M.

MARYLAND
Agnew, Spiro T.
Duvall, Gabriel
Hiss, Alger
Kempton, Murray
Lilly, Eli
Mudd, Samuel
Alexander
Newcomb, Josephine
Rouse, James
Shapiro, Karl
Stone, Thomas
Taylor, Margaret

MASSACHUSETTS
Amory, Cleveland
Bundy, McGeorge
Crockett, James
Underwood
Follett, Wilson
Holland, Josiah Gilbert
Leary, Timothy
Lord, Albert Bates
Macy, R. H.
Nolan, Thomas B.
Owens, Elisabeth
Parker, George S.
Peabody, Endicott
Perkins, Dexter
Richardson, Elliot
Weston, Paul
Winsor, Justin

MICHIGAN
Blackstone, Harry, Jr.
Bombeck, Erma

PENNSYLVANIA *(cont.)*
Stewart, James
Whyte, William H.
Wrigley, William, Jr.

RHODE ISLAND
Cantwell, Mary
Taber, Norman
Thompson, Clara

SOUTH CAROLINA
Bernardin, Joseph
Kirkland, Lane

SOUTH DAKOTA
Schultz, Theodore W.

TENNESSEE
Cheatham, Doc
Daniel, Jack

TENNESSEE *(cont.)*
Gore, Albert, Sr.
Morgan, William Wilson
Pearl, Minnie
Perkins, Carl
Polk, Sarah Childress

TEXAS
Autry, Gene
Corrigan, Douglas
 "Wrong Way"
Farmer, James
Flood, Curt
Hobby, Oveta Culp
Hogan, Ben
Howard, Robert E.
Jordan, Barbara
Landry, Tom
Mathews, Eddie

TEXAS *(cont.)*
Roddenberry, Gene
Walker, Doak

VERMONT
Tebbetts, Birdie
Wilson, Bill
Smith, Bob

VIRGINIA
Fitzgerald, Ella
Gosden, Freeman
Powell, Lewis F., Jr.
Scott, George C.
Sullavan, Margaret
Wilson, Orlandus

WASHINGTON
Ehrlichman, John D.
Greenfield, Meg
Kienholz, Edward

WEST VIRGINIA
Benedum, Michael L.
Johnston, Frances
 Benjamin
Randolph, Jennings
Yankovic, Frank

WISCONSIN
Cray, Seymour
Dickerson, Nancy
Dixon, Jeane
Luening, Otto
Stevens, Brooks
Vestey, Evelyn

UNKNOWN
Johnson, John

CUMULATIVE INDEX BY OCCUPATIONS
AND REALMS OF RENOWN:
Introduction and Synoptic Outline

This index includes all subjects found in the original edition of the *American National Biography* (*ANB*) as well as those found in *ANB Supplement 1*. The abbreviation "*Suppl. 1*" following a subject's name indicates that the subject is to be found in *ANB Supplement 1*. All other subjects will be found in the original edition of the *ANB*.

The Cumulative Index presents occupations and realms of renown in a different order than the alphabetical Index by Occupations printed in the original edition of the *ANB*. The Cumulative Index arranges the headings for occupations and realms of renown according to one or more broad topical areas so that related occupations can be viewed together. There are seventeen topics at the broadest level, as follows:

Archives, Collections, and Libraries
Art and Architecture
Business and Industry
Education
Exploration, Pioneering, and Native Peoples
Government and Politics
Health and Medicine
Humanities and Social Sciences
Law and Criminology
Military and Intelligence Operations
Miscellaneous Occupations and Realms of Renown
Performing Arts
Religion and Spirituality
Science and Technology
Society and Social Change
Sports and Games
Writing and Publishing

Many subjects of biographies pursued more than one occupation or achieved fame in several realms of renown. Their names will thus be found under multiple headings in this index. In addition, some of those headings are included in more than one broad topical area. For example, the heading Stage / Screen Actors appears under the broader topics of Film and also Theater and Live Entertainment, both of which are related to the broadest area of Performing Arts.

The best way to use this index is to start with the Synoptic Outline printed on pages 726–732, which will show the user where to look in the main body of the index for the occupational category of interest.

SYNOPTIC OUTLINE

ARCHIVES,
COLLECTIONS, AND
LIBRARIES

American Indian Artifacts
  Collectors
Antiquarian Book
  Collectors
Antiquarians
Antique Collectors
Archivists
Archivists of the United
  States
Arms and Armor
  Collectors
Art Collectors
Art Museum Curators /
  Administrators
Autograph Collectors
Automobile Collectors
Bibliographers
Book Collectors
Discographers
Encyclopedists
Genealogists
Indexers
Librarians
Librarians of Congress
Manuscript Collectors
Museum Curators /
  Administrators
Numismatists
Zoo Curators /
  Administrators

ART AND
ARCHITECTURE

Applied Arts
Blacksmiths
Book Designers
Bookbinders
Cabinetmakers
Calligraphers
Ceramists / Potters
Clockmakers
Engravers
Fashion Designers
Flatware Designers
Furniture Designers /
  Manufacturers
Glass Artists
Goldsmiths
Graphic Designers
Hatters
Industrial Designers
Interior Designers
Jewelers
Medal / Coin Designers

Musical Instrument
  Makers
Papermakers
Pewterers
Printers
Silversmiths
Tanners
Taxidermists
Textile Designers
Tilemakers
Type Designers
Typographers
Watchmakers
Weavers
Woodcarvers

Architecture
Architects
Golf Course Architects
Landscape Architects
Marine Architects

Art
Art Connoisseurs
Artist's Models
Cartoonists / Comic Strip
  Creators
Children's Book Writers /
  Illustrators
Folk Artists
Illustrators
Painters
Photographers
Printmakers
Scientific Illustrators
Sculptors

BUSINESS AND
INDUSTRY

Agriculture
Agriculturists
Apiarists
Cattle Raisers / Traders
Cowboys
Farmer Organization
  Leaders
Farmers
Foresters
Horticulturists
Plantation Managers /
  Overseers
Plantation Owners
Ranchers
Seedsmen
Soil Scientists
Winegrowers / Vintners

**Clothing, Fashion, and
Textiles**
Clothing Industry Leaders
Cosmetics Industry
  Leaders
Cotton Brokers /
  Merchants
Modeling Agency
  Executives
Seamstresses
Textile Industry Leaders
Wool Industry Leaders

Communication
Computer Industry
  Leaders
News Agency Owners /
  Managers
Telegraph Industry
  Leaders
Telephone Industry
  Leaders

Construction
Building Materials
  Industry Leaders
Carpenters
Construction Industry
  Leaders
Copper Industry Leaders
Lumber Industry Leaders

**Entertainment and
Recreation**
Amusement Park
  Owners / Managers
Brothelkeepers
Casino Owners /
  Managers
Circus Owners / Managers
Game and Toy
  Manufacturers
Greeting Card
  Manufacturers
Hotel Owners / Managers
Impresarios
Motion Picture
  Distributors
Motion Picture Studio
  Executives
Music Promoters
Nightclub Owners /
  Operators
Radio / Television
  Industry Leaders
Recording Industry
  Leaders
Resort Owners

Sporting Goods Industry
  Leaders
Sports Organization
  Executives
Sports Promoters
Tent Show Owners
Theater Owners /
  Managers
Theatrical Agents

**Finance, Management,
Insurance, and Real
Estate**
Accountants
Advertising Industry
  Leaders
Bankers / Financial
  Industry Leaders
Business Consultants
Business Machine
  Industry Leaders
Capitalists / Financiers
Computer Industry
  Leaders
Entrepreneurs
Financial Managers
Franchise Industry
  Leaders
Insurance Industry
  Leaders
Land Agents
Land Promoters
Real Estate Business
  Leaders
Speculators
Talent Scouts

Food and Beverage
Bakers
Bar Owners /
  Saloonkeepers
Brewers
Chefs
Chewing Gum Industry
  Leaders
Confectioners
Distillers
Fast-Food Business
  Leaders
Flour Milling Industry
  Leaders
Food Business Leaders
Grain Dealers
Grocery Store Owners
Meatpackers
Restaurateurs
Soft Drink Industry
  Leaders

GOVERNMENT AND POLITICS (cont.)

Commissioners of Education
Commissioners / Superintendents of Indian Affairs
Congressional Officers / Staff
Diplomats
Federal Government Officials
First Ladies of the United States
Foreign Advisers
National Park Officials
Postal Officials
Postmasters General
Presidential Advisers
Presidential Press Secretaries
Secret Service Agents
Secretaries of Agriculture
Secretaries of Commerce
Secretaries of Commerce and Labor
Secretaries of Defense
Secretaries of Health and Human Services
Secretaries of Health, Education, and Welfare
Secretaries of Housing and Urban Development
Secretaries of Labor
Secretaries of State
Secretaries of War
Secretaries of the Air Force
Secretaries of the Army
Secretaries of the Interior
Secretaries of the Navy
Secretaries of the Treasury
Solicitors General
Speakers of the U.S. House of Representatives
State Department Officials
Territorial Delegates
Treasurers of the United States
U.S. Presidents
U.S. Representatives
U.S. Senators
U.S. Supreme Court Chief Justices
U.S. Supreme Court Justices
U.S. Vice Presidents
White House Staff

Government (Non-Federal)

Attorneys General (State)
County Officials

Mayors
Military Governors
Municipal Government Officials
Resident Commissioners
State Government Officials
State Governors
State Legislators
Territorial Delegates
Territorial Governors

Government of the Confederacy

Confederate Agents
Confederate Legislators / Government Officials
First Lady of the Confederacy
President of the Confederacy
Vice President of the Confederacy

Politics

Abolitionists
Anticommunists
Antisuffragists
Black Nationalists
Civil Rights Activists
Communists
Environmentalists
Fenians
Lobbyists
Nationalists
Nazi Leaders
Political Consultants
Political Figures
Powerbrokers
Presidential Candidates
Socialists
Suffragists
Vice Presidential Candidates
Zionists

HEALTH AND MEDICINE

Abortionists
Allergists
Anesthesiologists
Artificial Heart Recipients
Cardiologists
Chiropractors
Dance Therapists
Dentists
Dermatologists
Eclectic Physicians
Gastroenterologists
Gynecologists

Homeopathic Physicians
Hydropathists
Hypnotherapists
Midwives
Music Therapists
Naturopaths
Neonatologists
Neurologists
Neurosurgeons
Nurses
Nutritionists
Obstetricians
Oncologists
Ophthalmologists
Orthopedic Surgeons
Osteopaths
Otolaryngologists
Parapsychologists
Pathologists
Pediatricians
Pharmacists
Phrenologists
Physicians
Psychiatrists
Psychoanalysts
Psychobiologists
Psychologists
Public Health Officials
Radiologists
Siamese Twins
Speech Therapists
Surgeons
Surgeons General
Syphilologists
Teratologists
Transsexuals
Urologists
Veterinarians
Veterinary Pathologists

HUMANITIES AND SOCIAL SCIENCES

Criticism

Architectural Critics
Art Critics
Dance Critics
Film Critics
Literary Critics
Music Critics
Television Critics
Theater Critics

History and Related Scholarship

Archaeologists
Architectural Historians
Art Historians
Buddhist Studies Scholars
Church Historians
Comparatists

Dance Historians
Documentary / Historical Editors
East Asian Studies Scholars
Ethnomusicologists
Film Historians
Historians
Historians of Science
History of Religions Scholars
Hymnologists
Legal Historians
Legal Scholars
Literary Scholars
Music Historians
Music Theorists
Musicologists
Mythologists
Natural Historians
Orientalists
Religious Studies Scholars
Social Historians &bsp;/n Commentators
Theater Historians
Theologians

Linguistics and Philology

Assyriologists
Classicists
Cryptanalysts
Egyptologists
Epigraphists
Grammarians
Hebraists
Interpreters
Language Theorists
Lexicographers
Linguists
Papyrologists
Philologists
Phoneticians
Phonographers
Sanskritists
Semitists
Slavists
Sumerologists
Translators

Philosophy

Ethicists
Logicians
Philosophers
Transcendentalists

Social Sciences

Anthropologists
Child Development Experts
Criminologists

Demographers
Economists
Epidemiologists
Ethnographers
Ethnologists
Ethnomusicologists
Folklorists
Home Economists
Industrial Relations
  Experts
Learning Theorists
Market Researchers
Organization and
  Management Theorists
Parliamentarians
Policy Analysts
Political Scientists
Pollsters
Sex Researchers
Sexual and Marital
  Counselors
Sociologists
Statisticians

LAW AND CRIMINOLOGY

Crime and Law Enforcement
Alleged Assassins
Alleged Murderers
Assassination Conspirators
Assassins
Bootleggers
Detectives
Forgers
Gangsters
Informants
Kidnappers
Law Enforcers
Murder Victims
Murderers
Outlaws
Perjurers
Pirates
Regicides
Smugglers
Swindlers
Thieves
Vigilantes

Legal Practice
Attorneys General
  (Federal)
Attorneys General (State)
Court Clerks
Court Reporters
Judge Advocates
Jurists / Judges
Justices of the Peace

Law Reporters
Lawyers
Litigants
Patent Experts
Public Prosecutors
Solicitors General
U.S. Supreme Court Chief
  Justices
U.S. Supreme Court
  Justices

MILITARY AND INTELLIGENCE OPERATIONS

American Revolution
Revolutionary Army
  Officers
Revolutionary Naval
  Officers

Civil War
Confederate Army Officers
Confederate Naval
  Officers
Union Army Officers
Union Naval Officers

Intelligence
Alleged Traitors
Informants
Intelligence Operatives /
  Officials
Spies
Traitors

Military (General U.S. and Foreign)
Blockade Runners
British Army / Navy
  Officers
Colonial Militiamen
Congressional Medal of
  Honor Recipients
Filibusters
French Army / Navy
  Officers
Guerrillas
Guides / Scouts
Inspectors General
Judge Advocates
Mercenaries
Military Chaplains
Military Deserters
Military Engineers
Military Governors
Privateers
Soldiers

Spanish Army / Navy
  Officers
War Heroes

U.S. Military Services
Air Force Chiefs of Staff
Air Force Officers
Army Air Corps / Army
  Air Forces Officers
Army Air Service Officers
Army Chiefs of Staff
Army Officers (1784–
  1860)
Army Officers (1866–
  1995)
Army Signal Corps
  Aviators
Chiefs of Naval
  Operations
Coast Guard Officers
Joint Chiefs of Staff
  Chairmen
Marine Corps Aviators
Marine Corps
  Commandants
Marine Corps Officers
Naval Aviators
Naval Officers (1784–
  1860)
Naval Officers (1866–
  1995)
Women's Airforce Service
  Pilots
Women's Army Corps
  Officers

MISCELLANEOUS OCCUPATIONS AND REALMS OF RENOWN

"Daughter of the
  Confederacy"
Confidantes
Duelists
Eccentrics
Eponyms
Family Members
Feudists
Folk Heroes
Gamblers
Holocaust Survivors
Legendary Figures
Lighthouse Keepers
Nobel Prize Winners
Press Agents
Psychics
Salon Hostesses
Slave Traders
Socialites
Travelers
Witchcraft Hysteria
  Victims

PERFORMING ARTS

Dance
Choreographers / Dance
  Directors
Dance Company Directors
Dance Therapists
Dancers

Film
Cinematographers
Costume Designers
Documentary Filmmakers
Film Animators
Motion Picture Censors
Motion Picture Editors
Motion Picture Producers /
  Directors
Screenwriters
Special Effects Experts
Stage / Screen Actors

Music
COMPOSING AND CONDUCTING
Bandleaders
Choral Directors
Composers / Arrangers
Librettists
Lyricists
Opera Company
  Managers
Orchestral Conductors
Songwriters

INSTRUMENTAL PERFORMANCE
Accordionists
Banjoists
Bassists
Calliope Players
Cellists
Clarinetists
Comb Players
Cornetists
Fiddlers
Flugelhorn Players
Flutists
Guitarists
Harmonica Players
Harpsichordists
Horn Players
Keyboard Players
Oboists
Organists
Percussionists
Pianists
Saxophonists
Sitar Players
Trombonists
Trumpeters

PERFORMING ARTS:
Music (cont.)
Vibraharpists
Violinists
Violists

TYPES OF MUSIC AND
SINGING
Blues Musicians / Singers
Cantors
Chanters
Concert Singers
Country Musicians /
Singers
Folk Musicians / Singers
Gospel Musicians /
Singers
Jazz Musicians
Jazz Singers
Opera Singers
Popular Singers
Ragtime Musicians
Reggae Musicians
Rhythm and Blues
Musicians / Singers
Rock Musicians / Singers
Soul Musicians / Singers
Western Swing Musicians

Radio and Television
Disc Jockeys
Radio / Television
Engineers
Radio / Television
Personalities
Radio / Television
Producers / Directors
Radio / Television Writers
Religious Broadcasters

Theater and Live
Entertainment
Acrobats
Burlesque Performers
Circus Performers
Clowns
Comedians
Costume Designers
Cowboys
Daredevils
Impersonators
Magicians
Midgets
Mimes
Minstrel Show Performers
Monologuists
Orators
Puppeteers
Rodeo Performers
Sharpshooters
Siamese Twins

Stage / Screen Actors
Theatrical Designers
Theatrical Producers /
Directors
Toastmasters
Vaudeville Performers
Ventriloquists

RELIGION AND
SPIRITUALITY

Denominations
Adventist Leaders
African Methodist
Episcopal Bishops
African Methodist
Episcopal Clergy
African Methodist
Episcopal Lay Leaders
African Methodist
Episcopal Zion Bishops
African Orthodox Bishops
Anglican Activists
Anglican Bishops
Anglican Clergy
Baptist Clergy
Baptist Lay Leaders
Christian Connection
Leaders
Christian Science Leaders
Colored Methodist
Episcopal Church
Bishops
Congregational Clergy
Disciples of Christ Clergy
Dutch Reformed Clergy
Episcopalian Bishops
Episcopalian Clergy
Episcopalian Lay Leaders
Evangelical Clergy
Evangelical and Reformed
Clergy
Free Methodist Clergy
German Reformed Clergy
Greek Orthodox Clergy
Islamic Leaders
Jehovah's Witnesses
Leaders
Jewish Clergy
Jewish Lay Leaders
Lutheran Clergy
Lutheran Lay Leaders
Mennonite Bishops
Methodist Episcopal
Bishops
Methodist Episcopal
Church, South, Bishops
Methodist Episcopal
Church, South, Clergy
Methodist Episcopal
Clergy

Methodist Episcopal Lay
Leaders
Methodist Pioneers / Lay
Leaders
Methodist Protestant
Clergy
Moravian Bishops
Moravian Clergy
Moravian Lay Leaders
Mormon Leaders
Polish National Catholic
Bishops
Presbyterian Clergy
Presbyterian Lay Leaders
Puritan Clergy
Puritans
Quaker Clergy
Quakers
Reformed Church in
America Clergy
Roman Catholic Bishops
Roman Catholic
Cardinals
Roman Catholic Clergy
Roman Catholic Lay
Leaders
Romanian Orthodox
Bishops
Russian Orthodox Clergy
Shakers
Southern Baptist Clergy
Southern Baptist Lay
Leaders
Swedenborgian Clergy
Swedenborgian Lay
Leaders
Unitarian Clergy
Unitarian Lay Leaders
Unitarian Universalist
Clergy
Universalist Clergy
Universalist Lay Leaders
Wesleyan Methodist
Clergy

Spiritual Communities
and Movements
Alleged Heretics
American Indian
Religious Leaders
Antinomian Leaders
Buddhist Leaders
Christian Converts
Christian Fellowship
Members
Cult Leaders
Ethical Culture Leaders
Evangelists
Freethinkers
Gurus
Humanists

Inspirationist Leaders
Military Chaplains
Millennialists
Missionaries
Monks
Mystics
Nuns
Occultists
Pentecostals
Religious Broadcasters
Religious Martyrs
Saints
Sectarian Leaders
Separatist Leaders
Spiritual Healers
Spiritualists
Theologians
Theosophists
Witchcraft Hysteria
Victims
Zionists

SCIENCE AND
TECHNOLOGY

Earth Sciences
Cartographers
Gemologists
Geochemists
Geodesists
Geographers
Geologists
Geomorphologists
Geophysicists
Hydrographers
Hydrologists
Limnologists
Meteorologists
Mineralogists
Oceanographers
Paleontologists
Petroleum Geologists
Petrologists
Seismologists
Soil Scientists
Volcanologists

Life Sciences
Anatomists
Bacteriologists
Biochemists
Biologists
Biometricians
Biophysicists
Botanists
Conchologists
Cytologists
Dendrochronologists
Ecologists
Embryologists
Endocrinologists

SPORTS AND GAMES
(cont.)
  Golfers
  Harness Racers
  Ice Hockey Players
  Jockeys
  Long-Distance Walkers
  Mountaineers
  Olympic Medalists
  Polo Players
  Race Car Drivers
  Racehorse Breeders /
    Trainers
  Rodeo Performers
  Rowers
  Speed Skaters
  Sports Inventors
  Sports Officials
  Sports Organization
    Executives
  Surfers
  Swimmers / Divers

  Tennis Players
  Track and Field Athletes
  Wrestlers
  Yachtsmen

**WRITING AND
PUBLISHING**

Editing and Publishing
  Anthologists
  Bible Editors
  Book Designers
  Book Editors / Publishers
  Bookbinders
  Crossword Puzzle Editors
  Documentary / Historical
    Editors
  Engravers
  Fashion Magazine Editors
  Literary Agents
  Literary Executors
  Magazine and Journal
    Editors / Publishers

  Music Editors / Publishers
  News Agency Owners /
    Managers
  Newspaper Editors /
    Publishers
  Printers
  Typographers

**Literature and
Journalism**
  Almanac Makers
  Autobiographers /
    Memoirists
  Biographers
  Broadcast Journalists
  Captivity Narrativists
  Cartoonists / Comic Strip
    Creators
  Children's Book Writers /
    Illustrators
  Cookbook / Food Writers
  Diarists

  Dramatists
  Essayists
  Etiquette Writers
  Fiction Writers
  Humorists
  Letter Writers
  Literary Inspirations
  Medical Writers
  Nature Writers
  Pamphleteers
  Photojournalists
  Poets
  Poets Laureate of the
    United States
  Print Journalists
  Radio / Television Writers
  Science Writers
  Screenwriters
  Slave Narrative Authors
  Speechwriters
  Sportswriters
  Tract Writers
  Travel Writers

Readers are encouraged to consult the Introduction and Synoptic Outline,
pp. 725–732, for guidance in using this index.

Draper, Lyman
Copeland
Duyckinck, Evert
Augustus
Fiske, Daniel Willard
Folger, Emily Jordan
Folger, Henry Clay
Gardiner, Leon
Hoe, Robert
Huntington, Henry
Edwards
Livermore, George
Logan, James
(1674–1751)
Mackenzie, William
Moorland, Jesse Edward
Nash, John Henry
Ray, Gordon Norton
Rollins, Philip Ashton
Rosenwald, Lessing
Julius
Schomburg, Arthur
Alfonso
Shaw, William Smith
Sprague, William Buell
Warden, David Bailie
Weeks, Stephen
Beauregard
Widener, Harry Elkins

Discographers
Allen, Walter Carl

Encyclopedists
Deane, Samuel
Deutsch, Gotthard
Duyckinck, George
Long
Heilprin, Michael
Neumark, David

Genealogists
Farmer, John
Whitmore, William
Henry

Indexers
Edmands, John
Griswold, William
McCrillis
Weeks, Stephen
Beauregard

Librarians
Ahern, Mary Eileen
Allibone, Samuel Austin
Anderson, Edwin
Hatfield
Bancroft, Frederic A.
Beach, Harlan Page
Beer, William

Bellini, Carlo
Billings, John Shaw
Bjerregaard, Carl Henrik
Andreas
Bogle, Sarah Comly
Norris
Bostwick, Arthur Elmore
Brett, William Howard
Burr, George Lincoln
Butler, Lee Pierce
Chadwick, James Read
Coggeshall, William
Turner
Cole, George Watson
Cutter, Charles Ammi
Dana, John Cotton
Davis, Raymond Cazallis
Dewey, Melvil
Dexter, Franklin
Bowditch
Durrie, Daniel Steele
Eames, Wilberforce
Eastman, William Reed
Edmands, John
Engel, Carl
Evans, Charles
Fairchild, Mary Salome
Cutler
Farrand, Max
Fiske, Daniel Willard
Flexner, Jennie Maas
Flint, Weston
Folsom, Charles
Foss, Sam Walter
Freedley, George
Galbreath, Charles
Burleigh
Garrison, Fielding
Hudson
Goff, Frederick
Richmond
Golder, Frank Alfred
Goldstein, Fanny
Green, Samuel Swett
Greene, Belle da Costa
Griffin, Appleton
Prentiss Clark
Griswold, William
McCrillis
Guild, Reuben Aldridge
Hamlin, Talbot Faulkner
Hanson, James Christian
Meinich
Harris, Thaddeus
William
Holden, Edward
Singleton
Homes, Henry Augustus
Hutchins, Margaret
Isom, Mary Frances

Jackson, William
Alexander
Jewett, Charles Coffin
Johnson, Theodore
Elliott
Klingelsmith, Margaret
Center
Kroeger, Alice Bertha
Larned, Josephus Nelson
Legler, Henry Eduard
Lydenberg, Harry Miller
Martel, Charles
Marvin, Cornelia
Marx, Alexander
Meigs, Return Jonathan
(1801–1891)
Miner, Dorothy Eugenia
Moore, Anne Carroll
Mudge, Isadore Gilbert
Oko, Adolph S.
Perkins, Frederic
Beecher
Plummer, Mary Wright
Root, Azariah Smith
Schomburg, Arthur
Alfonso
Sharp, Katharine
Lucinda
Shera, Jesse Hauk
Sibley, John Langdon
Smith, Lloyd Pearsall
Sonneck, Oscar George
Theodore
Spencer, Anne
Stearns, Lutie Eugenia
Steiner, Lewis Henry
Swem, Earl Gregg
Thwaites, Reuben Gold
Timothy, Lewis
Turner, William
Wadden
Tyler, Alice Sarah
Uhler, Philip Reese
Utley, George Burwell
Van Name, Addison
Vaughan, John
Ward, James Warner
Wheeler, William
Adolphus
Whitehill, Walter Muir,
Jr.
Whitney, James Lyman
Winser, Beatrice
Winship, George Parker
Winsor, Justin *Suppl. 1*
Wolfe, Linnie Marsh
Wood, Mary Elizabeth
Wroth, Lawrence
Counselman

Librarians of Congress
Beckley, John James
Evans, Luther Harris
MacLeish, Archibald
Mumford, Lawrence
Quincy
Putnam, Herbert
Spofford, Ainsworth
Rand
Watterston, George

Manuscript Collectors
Gardiner, Leon
Isham, Ralph Heyward
Quinn, John
Rollins, Philip Ashton
Schomburg, Arthur
Alfonso

Museum Curators /
Administrators
Allen, Joel Asaph
Angle, Paul McClelland
Anthony, Harold Elmer
Barbour, Thomas
Barnum, P. T.
Bickmore, Albert Smith
Chapman, Frank
Michler
Dana, John Cotton
Dow, George Francis
Du Simitière, Pierre
Eugène
Friedmann, Herbert
Goode, George Brown
Gordon, George Byron
Hodge, Frederick Webb
Hough, Walter
Kimball, Fiske
Lucas, Frederic
Augustus
Mason, Otis Tufton
Montgomery, Charles
Franklin
Otis, George Alexander
Putnam, Frederic Ward
Richmond, Charles
Wallace
Ridgway, Robert
Saint-Mémin, Charles
Balthazar Julien Févret
de
Savage, Edward
Stejneger, Leonhard
Hess
Stimpson, William
Stout, Gardner
Dominick
True, Frederick William
Vaillant, George Clapp
Wetmore, Alexander

Politics *(cont.)*
Vice Presidential Candidates
Bryan, Charles Wayland
English, William Hayden
Johnson, Herschel
  Vespasian
Miller, William Edward
Muskie, Edmund S.
  Suppl. 1
Thurman, Allen
  Granberry
Wright, Fielding Lewis

Zionists
Blackstone, William E.
Flexner, Bernard
Gottheil, Richard James
  Horatio
Greenberg, Hayim
Lewisohn, Ludwig
Lowenthal, Marvin
  Marx
Mack, Julian William
Magnes, Judah Leon
Mendes, Henry Pereira
Rosenblatt, Bernard
  Abraham
Sampter, Jessie Ethel
Silver, Abba Hillel
Sonneschein, Rosa
Syrkin, Marie
Szold, Henrietta
Weisgal, Meyer Wolfe
Wise, Stephen Samuel

HEALTH AND MEDICINE

Abortionists
Lohman, Ann Trow

Allergists
Schick, Béla

Anesthesiologists
Apgar, Virginia
Long, Crawford
  Williamson

Artificial Heart Recipients
Schroeder, William J.

Cardiologists
Herrick, James Bryan
Hirschfelder, Arthur
  Douglas

Chiropractors
Palmer, Bartlett Joshua
Palmer, Daniel David

Dance Therapists
Boas, Franziska Marie
Chace, Marian

Dentists
Barber, Jesse Max
Bayne, Thomas
Delany, Annie Elizabeth
  "Bessie". *See* Delany,
  Annie Elizabeth
  "Bessie", and Sarah
  Louise "Sadie" Delany
  Suppl. 1
Evans, Thomas
  Wiltberger
Flagg, Josiah Foster
Freeman, Robert Tanner
Garretson, James
  Edmund
Greenwood, John
Harris, Chapin Aaron
Howe, Percy Rogers
Keep, Nathan Cooley
Kingsley, Norman
  William
McQuillen, John Hugh
Miller, Willoughby
  Dayton
Morton, William
  Thomas Green
Parmly, Eleazar
Taylor, Lucy Beaman
  Hobbs
Wells, Horace

Dermatologists
Duhring, Louis
  Adolphus
Hyde, James Nevins
Morrow, Prince Albert
Pusey, William Allen
Schamberg, Jay Frank
White, James Clarke

Eclectic Physicians
Beach, Wooster
Foote, Edward Bliss
King, John
Newton, Robert Safford
Scudder, John Milton

Gastroenterologists
Ingelfinger, Franz Joseph
Jordan, Sara Claudia
  Murray

Gynecologists
Byford, William Heath
Chadwick, James Read
Dickinson, Robert Latou

Emmet, Thomas Addis
  (1828–1919)
Hurd-Mead, Kate
  Campbell
Hurdon, Elizabeth
Kelly, Howard Atwood
Levine, Lena
Martin, Franklin Henry
Meigs, Charles Delucena
Morris, John McLean
Parvin, Theophilus
Putnam, Helen Cordelia
Sims, J. Marion
Skene, Alexander
  Johnston Chalmers
Storer, Horatio
  Robinson
Taussig, Frederick
  Joseph
Van De Warker, Edward
  Ely

Homeopathic Physicians
Dunham, Carroll
Gram, Hans Burch
Guernsey, Egbert
Hale, Edwin Moses
Hempel, Charles Julius
Hering, Constantine
Kent, James Tyler
Leach, Robert Boyd
Merrick, Myra King
Talbot, Israel Tisdale
Wesselhoeft, Conrad

Hydropathists
Austin, Harriet N.
Baruch, Simon
Kellogg, John Harvey
Nichols, Mary Gove
Nichols, Thomas Low
Trall, Russell Thacher

Hypnotherapists
Erickson, Milton Hyland

Midwives
Ballard, Martha Moore
Van Blarcom, Carolyn
  Conant

Music Therapists
Nordoff, Paul

Naturopaths
Thomson, Samuel

Neonatologists
Dunham, Ethel Collins

Neurologists
Bailey, Pearce
Cobb, Stanley
Dana, Charles Loomis
Denny-Brown, Derek
  Ernest
Dercum, Francis Xavier
Geschwind, Norman
Goldstein, Kurt
Hammond, William
  Alexander
Jelliffe, Smith Ely
Myerson, Abraham
Putnam, James Jackson
Ranson, Stephen Walter
Sachs, Bernard
Seguin, Edward
  Constant
Spitzka, Edward Charles
Tilney, Frederick
Timme, Walter

Neurosurgeons
Cushing, Harvey
  Williams
Dandy, Walter Edward
Elsberg, Charles Albert
Frazier, Charles
  Harrison
Penfield, Wilder Graves

Nurses
Andrews, Ludie
Anthony, Sister
Arnstein, Margaret
Bacon, Georgeanna
  Muirson Woolsey
Beard, Mary
Bickerdyke, Mary Ann
  Ball
Blanchfield, Florence
  Aby
Bradley, Amy Morris
Buckel, C. Annette
Davis, Frances Elliott
Delano, Jane Arminda
Dock, Lavinia Lloyd
Fitzgerald, Alice
Franklin, Martha
  Minerva
Freeman, Elizabeth
Gardner, Mary Sewall
Goodrich, Annie
  Warburton
Haupt, Alma Cecilia
Hawes, Harriet Ann
  Boyd
Henderson, Virginia
  Suppl. 1
Hopkins, Juliet Ann
  Opie

Mumford, James
  Gregory
Murphy, John Benjamin
Mussey, Reuben
  Dimond
Ochsner, Alton
Otis, George Alexander
Otto, Bodo
Pancoast, Joseph
Park, Roswell
Parsons, Usher
Pattison, Granville Sharp
Prevost, François Marie
Price, Joseph
Randolph, Jacob
Ridgely, Frederick
Saugrain De Vigni,
  Antoine François
Seaman, Valentine
Senn, Nicholas
Sinkler, William H., Jr.
Smith, Alban Gilpin
Smith, Nathan
Smith, Stephen
Souchon, Edmond
Stitt, Edward Rhodes
Thompson, Mary Harris
Thorek, Max
Twitchell, Amos
Van Hoosen, Bertha
Warbasse, James Peter
Warren, Edward
Warren, John
Warren, John Collins
  (1778–1856)
Warren, John Collins
  (1842–1927)
Whipple, Allen
  Oldfather
Williams, Daniel Hale
Woodward, Theodore
Wright, Louis Tompkins
Yandell, David Wendel
Young, Hugh Hampton

Surgeons General
Barnes, Joseph K.
Benites, José María
Gorgas, William
  Crawford
Hamilton, John Brown
Lawson, Thomas
Lovell, Joseph
Parran, Thomas
Scheele, Leonard A.
Smith, Ashbel

Syphilologists
Hinton, William
  Augustus
Morrow, Prince Albert

Pusey, William Allen

Teratologists
Apgar, Virginia

Transsexuals
Jorgensen, Christine

Urologists
Flocks, Rubin Hyman
Lydston, G. Frank
Young, Hugh Hampton

Veterinarians
Kelser, Raymond
  Alexander
Law, James
Lyman, Charles Parker
Pearson, Leonard
Salmon, Daniel Elmer
Williams, Walter Long

Veterinary Pathologists
Moore, Veranus Alva

HUMANITIES AND SOCIAL SCIENCES

Criticism
Architectural Critics
Eidlitz, Leopold
Fowler, Orson Squire
Gilman, Arthur Delavan
Hamlin, Alfred Dwight
  Foster
Magonigle, Harold Van
  Buren
Mumford, Lewis
Sturgis, Russell
Van Brunt, Henry

Art Critics
Benson, Eugene
Caffin, Charles Henry
Chávez, Carlos
Coates, Robert Myron
Cook, Clarence
Cortissoz, Royal
Cox, Kenyon
de Kooning, Elaine
Gallatin, Albert Eugene
Greenberg, Clement
Hambidge, Jay
Hartmann, Sadakichi
Heap, Jane
McBride, Henry
Miller, Charles Henry
Pach, Walter
Partridge, William
  Ordway
Pepper, Stephen C.

Perkins, Charles
  Callahan
Porter, Fairfield
Porter, James Amos
Rosenberg, Harold
Ross, Denman Waldo
Saarinen, Aline
  Bernstein
Sargent, Irene Jesse
Shinn, Earl
Smithson, Robert Irving
Van Dyke, John Charles
Van Rensselaer, Mariana
  Griswold
Wright, Willard
  Huntington

Dance Critics
Amberg, George
Denby, Edwin Orr
Horst, Louis
Martin, John Joseph
Terry, Walter

Film Critics
Agee, James Rufus
Amberg, George
Crowther, Bosley
Macdonald, Dwight
Sherwood, Robert
  Emmet

Literary Critics
Aiken, Conrad
Arvin, Newton
Babbitt, Irving
Bacon, Leonard
Baker, Carlos Heard
Bate, Walter Jackson
  Suppl. 1
Beach, Joseph Warren
Blackmur, R. P.
Bodenheim, Maxwell
Bogan, Louise
Bourne, Randolph
  Silliman
Boyd, Ernest Augustus
Braithwaite, William
  Stanley Beaumont
Brooks, Cleanth
Brooks, Van Wyck
Brownell, William Crary
Burke, Kenneth
Clifford, James Lowry
Cournos, John
Cowley, Malcolm
Cuppy, William Jacob
Dabney, Richard
Dahlberg, Edward
Dell, Floyd James
Dennie, Joseph

Dupee, F. W.
Eckman, Frederick
  Suppl. 1
Eliot, T. S.
Ellmann, Richard David
Fadiman, Clifton
  Suppl. 1
Foerster, Norman
Freeman, Joseph
Fuller, Hoyt William
Geismar, Maxwell David
Gilder, Jeannette
  Leonard
Goodman, Paul
Greenslet, Ferris
Gregory, Horace Victor
Harby, Isaac
Harris, Corra
Hayne, Paul Hamilton
Hicks, Granville
Highet, Gilbert
Hillyer, Robert Silliman
Hoffman, Frederick John
Hofstadter, Richard
Howe, Irving
Howells, William Dean
Hyman, Stanley Edgar
Jacobs, Joseph
James, Henry
  (1843–1916)
Jarrell, Randall
Kazin, Alfred *Suppl. 1*
Kirkus, Virginia
Koch, Vivienne
Krutch, Joseph Wood
Lewisohn, Ludwig
Locke, Alain Leroy
Loveman, Amy
Lowell, Amy
Matthiessen, F. O.
McCarthy, Mary
McHenry, James
  (1785–1845)
Mencken, H. L.
Millett, Fred Benjamin
Moore, Marianne
Morley, Christopher
  Darlington
Newman, Frances
Noguchi, Yone
Otis, Brooks
Payne, William Morton
Poe, Edgar Allan
Pound, Ezra
Rahv, Philip
Ransom, John Crowe
Redding, J. Saunders
Richards, I. A.
Ripley, George
Rittenhouse, Jessie Belle
Schorer, Mark

History and Related Scholarship *(cont.)*
Tiedeman, Christopher Gustavus
Tucker, Beverley
Tucker, Henry St. George (1780–1848)
Tucker, John Randolph (1823–1897)
Von Moschzisker, Robert
Walker, Timothy (1802–1856)
Ward, Nathaniel
Wheaton, Henry
Wigmore, John Henry
Wright, Austin Tappan
Zeisel, Hans

Literary Scholars
Bowers, Fredson *Suppl. 1*
Boyesen, Hjalmar Hjorth
Brooks, Cleanth
Canby, Henry Seidel
Child, Francis James
Cross, Wilbur Lucius
De Leon, Thomas Cooper
Dupee, F. W.
Dykes, Eva Beatrice
Edel, Leon *Suppl. 1*
Folger, Emily Jordan
Follett, Wilson *Suppl. 1*
Furness, Horace Howard
Giamatti, Bart
Greenlaw, Edwin Almiron
Guiney, Louise Imogen
Hart, James D.
Hubbell, Jay Broadus
Isham, Ralph Heyward
Jakobson, Roman Osipovich
Lord, Albert Bates *Suppl. 1*
Lounsbury, Thomas Raynesford
Lowell, James Russell
Lowes, John Livingston
Matthiessen, F. O.
Miller, Perry
Norton, Charles Eliot
Parry, Milman
Pattee, Fred Lewis
Pottle, Frederick Albert
Preston, Harriet Waters
Reed, Henry Hope
Sanborn, Franklin Benjamin
Smith, Charles Alphonso

Smith, Logan Pearsall
Ticknor, George
Trilling, Lionel
Warren, Austin
Wellek, René
Wilde, Richard Henry
Wimsatt, W. K.
Wolfson, Harry Austryn
Woodberry, George Edward

Music Historians
Allen, Walter Carl
Feather, Leonard
Fillmore, John Comfort
Krehbiel, Henry Edward
Moore, John Weeks
Pratt, Waldo Selden
Stearns, Marshall Winslow
Thompson, Oscar

Music Theorists
Cowell, Henry *Suppl. 1*
Klauser, Julius
Schillinger, Joseph
Schoenberg, Arnold
Seeger, Charles
Ziehn, Bernhard

Musicologists
Crawford-Seeger, Ruth Porter
Gilman, Lawrence
Kirkpatrick, Ralph Leonard
Pratt, Waldo Selden
Seeger, Charles
Slonimsky, Nicolas

Mythologists
Bulfinch, Thomas
Campbell, Joseph

Natural Historians
Dall, William Healey
Dixon, Roland Burrage
Lapham, Increase Allen
Shepard, Charles
Upham

Orientalists
Davis, Charles Henry Stanley
Salisbury, Edward Elbridge

Religious Studies Scholars
Adams, Hannah
Ahlstrom, Sydney
Eckman

Alexander, Joseph Addison
Andrews, Edward Deming
Baron, Salo Wittmayer
Barton, George Aaron
Burrows, Millar
Cadbury, Henry Joel
Carus, Paul
Clebsch, William Anthony
Cohon, Samuel Solomon
Deutsch, Gotthard
Evans-Wentz, Walter Yeeling
Faruqi, Isma'il Raji al-
Feinstein, Moses
Fenn, William Wallace
Freehof, Solomon Bennett
Gavin, Frank Stanton Burns
Ginzberg, Louis
Glatzer, Nahum Norbert
Goddard, Dwight
Grayzel, Solomon
Harper, William Rainey
Haupt, Paul
Heschel, Abraham Joshua
Jacobs, Joseph
Kadushin, Max
Kaplan, Mordecai Menahem
Kent, Charles Foster
Knox, John
Kohut, Alexander
Kotler, Aaron
Leeser, Isaac
Lieberman, Saul
Lyman, Mary Redington Ely
Malter, Henry
Margolis, Max Leopold
Moore, George Foot
Morgan, Abel
Mudge, James
Norton, Andrews
Noyes, George Rapall
Perrin, Norman
Rahman, Fazlur
Rawidowicz, Simon
Riddle, Matthew Brown
Robinson, Edward
Salisbury, Edward Elbridge
Schaff, Philip
Schechter, Solomon
Smith, Henry Preserved
Stowe, Calvin Ellis
Stuart, Moses

Suzuki, D. T. *Suppl. 1*
Terry, Milton Spenser
Torrey, Charles Cutler
Watts, Alan Wilson
Wright, George Ernest
Zeitlin, Solomon
Zwemer, Samuel Marinus

Social Historians / Commentators
Adamic, Louis
Adams, Brooks
Adams, Henry
Adams, James Truslow
Allen, Frederick Lewis
Amory, Cleveland *Suppl. 1*
Asbury, Herbert
Austin, Mary Hunter
Barnes, Harry Elmer
Becker, Carl Lotus
Bontemps, Arna Wendell
Buley, Roscoe Carlyle
Bunche, Ralph Johnson
Calkins, Clinch
Calvert, George Henry
Cram, Ralph Adams
DeVoto, Bernard Augustine
Du Bois, W. E. B.
Eastman, Max
Ford, Henry Jones
Fox, Dixon Ryan
Frank, Waldo David
Galarza, Ernesto
Goodman, Paul
Gunther, John
Hayes, Carlton J. H.
Helper, Hinton Rowan
Herberg, Will
Hofstadter, Richard
Holbrook, Stewart Hall
Howe, Irving
Lasch, Christopher
Lerner, Max
Lindeman, Eduard Christian
Mayo, Katherine
Mencken, H. L.
Mitford, Jessica *Suppl. 1*
Moore, Clement Clarke
Morton, Thomas
Mumford, Lewis
Murat, Achille
Niebuhr, Reinhold
Norton, Charles Eliot
Packard, Vance *Suppl. 1*
Paul, Elliot
Potter, David Morris

Philosophy *(cont.)*
Ripley, George
Ripley, Sarah Alden
  Bradford
Ripley, Sophia Willard
  Dana
Thoreau, Henry David
Very, Jones

Social Sciences
Anthropologists
Angel, John Lawrence
Ardrey, Robert
Bartlett, John Russell
Bascom, William Russel
Bateson, Gregory
Benedict, Ruth Fulton
Boas, Franz
Castaneda, Carlos
  Suppl. 1
Chamberlain, Alexander
  Francis
Cobb, William
  Montague
Coon, Carleton Stevens
Cushing, Frank
  Hamilton
Day, Caroline Stewart
  Bond
Dixon, Roland Burrage
Dorsey, George Amos
Dozier, Edward Pasqual
Drake, St. Clair, Jr.
Eiseley, Loren Corey
Emory, Kenneth Pike
Fairbanks, Charles
  Herron
Farabee, William Curtis
Fewkes, Jesse Walter
Fishberg, Maurice
Fletcher, Alice
  Cunningham
Goldenweiser, Alexander
  Alexandrovich
Hallowell, A. Irving
Heizer, Robert Fleming
Herskovits, Melville Jean
Hewett, Edgar Lee
Hodge, Frederick Webb
Holmes, William Henry
  Suppl. 1
Hooton, Earnest Albert
Hrdlička, Aleš
Hurston, Zora Neale
Kluckhohn, Clyde Kay
  Maben
Kroeber, Alfred Louis
La Farge, Oliver Hazard
  Perry
La Flesche, Francis
Lewis, Oscar

Linton, Ralph
Lowie, Robert Harry
Malinowski, Bronislaw
  Kasper
McGee, William John
McNickle, D'Arcy
Mead, Margaret
Montagu, Ashley
  Suppl. 1
Mooney, James
Morgan, Lewis Henry
Morton, Samuel George
Murdock, George Peter
Parsons, Elsie Clews
Powdermaker, Hortense
Powell, John Wesley
Primus, Pearl
Putnam, Frederic Ward
Radin, Paul
Redfield, Robert
Reichard, Gladys
  Amanda
Roberts, Jack
Sapir, Edward
Sheldon, William
  Herbert
Spier, Leslie
Steward, Julian Haynes
Swanton, John Reed
Todd, Thomas Wingate
Turner, Victor Witter
Verrill, Alpheus Hyatt
Warner, W. Lloyd
Weltfish, Gene
White, Leslie Alvin
Wissler, Clark
Wyman, Jeffries

Child Development Experts
Arbuthnot, May Hill
Gruenberg, Sidonie
  Matsner

Criminologists
Bronner, Augusta Fox
Kirchwey, George
  Washington
Smith, Bruce

Demographers
Hagood, Margaret Loyd
  Jarman
Lotka, Alfred James
Spengler, Joseph John
Taeuber, Irene Barnes

Economists
Alexander, Sadie Tanner
  Mossell
Anderson, Benjamin
  McAlester

Ayres, Clarence Edwin
Ayres, Leonard Porter
Bissell, Richard Mervin,
  Jr.
Black, John Donald
Blodget, Samuel, Jr.
Bourneuf, Alice
  Elizabeth
Brown, Harry Gunnison
Burns, Arthur Frank
Callender, Guy Stevens
Campbell, Persia
  Crawford
Cardozo, Jacob Newton
Carey, Henry Charles
Carey, Mathew
Chase, Stuart
Clague, Ewan
Clark, John Bates
Clark, John Maurice
Commons, John Rogers
Coxe, Tench
Davenport, Herbert
  Joseph
Dew, Thomas Roderick
Dewing, Arthur Stone
Douglas, Paul Howard
Eckstein, Otto
Edwards, Corwin D.
Ely, Richard Theodore
Emery, Henry Crosby
Feis, Herbert
Fetter, Frank Albert
Fisher, Irving
Foster, William Trufant
George, Henry
Goldenweiser, Emanuel
  Alexander
Grady, Henry Francis
Hadley, Arthur Twining
Hamilton, Earl Jefferson
Hansen, Alvin Harvey
Harris, Abram Lincoln,
  Jr.
Harris, Seymour Edwin
Hauge, Gabriel Sylfest
Haynes, Williams
Heller, Walter Wolfgang
Henderson, Leon
Hollander, Jacob Harry
Hoover, Calvin Bryce
Hotelling, Harold
James, Edmund Janes
Jenks, Jeremiah Whipple
Johnson, Alvin Saunders
Katona, George
Keyserling, Leon
Knight, Frank Hyneman
Knight, M. M.
Koopmans, Tjalling
  Charles

Kuznets, Simon Smith
Ladejinsky, Wolf Isaac
Lerner, Abba
Lewis, W. Arthur
Loucks, Henry Langford
Lubin, Isador
Machlup, Fritz
Means, Gardiner Coit
Mitchell, Wesley Clair
Morgenstern, Oskar
Myrdal, Gunnar Karl
Nearing, Scott
Newcomb, Simon
Nutter, Gilbert Warren
Okun, Arthur Melvin
Rawle, Francis
Ripley, William Zebina
Rogers, James Harvey
Ruggles, Samuel Bulkley
Ruml, Beardsley
Schultz, Henry
Schultz, Theodore W.
  Suppl. 1
Schumpeter, Joseph
  Alois Julius
Seligman, Edwin Robert
  Anderson
Simons, Henry Calvert
Slichter, Sumner Huber
Spengler, Joseph John
Stein, Herbert *Suppl. 1*
Stigler, George J.
Sumner, Helen
Sumner, William
  Graham
Taussig, Frank William
Taylor, Fred Manville
Tolley, Howard Ross
Tucker, George
Veblen, Thorstein
  Bunde
Vickrey, William S.
  Suppl. 1
Viner, Jacob
von Neumann, John
  Louis
Walker, Amasa
Walker, Francis Amasa
Warne, Colston Estey
Wells, David Ames
Weyl, Walter Edward
White, Harry Dexter
Wolfson, Theresa
Wolman, Leo
Young, Allyn Abbott

Epidemiologists
Carter, Henry Rose
Chapin, Charles Value
Francis, Thomas, Jr.
Frost, Wade Hampton

Music: COMPOSING AND
CONDUCTING *(cont.)*
Holyoke, Samuel Adams
Hommann, Charles
Hope, Elmo
Hopekirk, Helen
Hopkinson, Francis
Horst, Louis
Hoschna, Karl L.
Howe, Mary
Humiston, William
Henry
Hupfeld, Charles
Frederick
Ives, Charles
Janssen, Werner
Alexander
Jenkins, Edmund
Thornton
Jenkins, Gordon
Johns, Clayton
Johnson, Budd
Johnson, Hall
Johnson, J. J. *Suppl. 1*
Johnson, James P.
Jones, Thad
Joplin, Scott
Kaiser, Alois
Kaper, Bronislaw
Kay, Hershy
Kelley, Edgar Stillman
Kenton, Stan
Kern, Jerome
Kieffer, Aldine Silliman
Kincaid, Bradley
Korngold, Erich
Wolfgang
Kreisler, Fritz
Kroeger, Ernest Richard
Kubik, Gail Thompson
Lamb, Joseph Francis
Lambert, Dave
Lane, Burton *Suppl. 1*
Lang, Margaret Ruthven
Lange, Arthur William
Larson, Jonathan
Suppl. 1
Lead Belly
Leginska, Ethel
Lennon, John
Levant, Oscar
Loeffler, Charles Martin
Loesser, Frank
Loewe, Frederick
Louvin, Ira
Luboff, Norman
Luening, Otto *Suppl. 1*
MacDowell, Edward
Mahler, Gustav *Suppl. 1*
Mana-Zucca
Mancini, Henry

Mannes, Leopold
Damrosch
Mantovani
Maretzek, Max
Marshall, Arthur
Martin, Roberta
Mason, Daniel Gregory
Mason, William
(1829–1908)
Matthews, Artie
McGhee, Howard B.
McMichen, Clayton
Mennin, Peter
Mercer, Johnny
Miley, Bubber
Millinder, Lucky
Mingus, Charles
Mitropoulos, Dimitri
Mobley, Hank
Monk, Thelonious
Moore, Douglas
Moore, Mary Carr
Moore, Undine
Morgan, Lee
Morrison, Jim
Morton, Jelly Roll
Moten, Bennie
Mulligan, Gerry *Suppl. 1*
Nabokov, Nicolas
Neuendorff, Adolph
Heinrich Anton
Magnus
Nevin, Ethelbert
Woodbridge
Newman, Alfred
Nichols, Herbie
Nikolais, Alwin
Niles, John Jacob
Noble, Ray *Suppl. 1*
Nordoff, Paul
Nyiregyházi, Ervin
O'Hara, Mary
Oldberg, Arne
Oliver, Sy
Ory, Kid
Paine, John Knowles
Parker, Charlie
Parker, Horatio William
Parker, J. C. D.
Parsons, Albert Ross
Partch, Harry
Pastorius, Jaco
Perez Prado, Damaso
Perry, Julia
Persichetti, Vincent
Ludwig
Peter, John Frederick
Pettiford, Oscar
Piatigorsky, Gregor
Piron, Armand John
Piston, Walter

Porter, Cole
Price, Florence B.
Pryor, Arthur Willard
Pullen, Don
Rachmaninoff, Sergei
Rapee, Erno
Read, Daniel
Redman, Don
Reeves, David Wallis
Reiff, Anthony, Jr.
Reinagle, Alexander
Revel, Harry
Riddle, Nelson
Riegger, Wallingford
Ritter, Frédéric Louis
Robinson, Earl Hawley
Robinson, J. Russel
Rodgers, Richard
Rogers, Clara Kathleen
Rogers, Shorty
Romberg, Sigmund
Rome, Harold
Ronell, Ann *Suppl. 1*
Root, George Frederick
Rosenblatt, Josef
Rózsa, Miklós *Suppl. 1*
Ruggles, Carl
Rushing, Jimmy
Russell, Luis Carl
Russell, Pee Wee
Rutherford, Leonard C.
Sauter, Eddie
Schelling, Ernest Henry
Schillinger, Joseph
Schnabel, Artur
Schoebel, Elmer
Schoenberg, Arnold
Schreiber, Frederick
Charles
Schuman, William
Howard
Scott, James
Selby, William
Sessions, Roger
Huntington
Shavers, Charlie
Shaw, Arnold
Shields, Larry
Slonimsky, Nicolas
Smith, Fiddlin' Arthur
Smith, Julia
Smith, Paul Joseph
Sobolewski, Edward
Sousa, John Philip
Stanley, Albert Augustus
Steiner, Max R.
Stevens, Leith
Still, William Grant
Stoessel, Albert Frederic
Stothart, Herbert Pope
Stravinsky, Igor

Strayhorn, Billy
Suesse, Dana *Suppl. 1*
Sun Ra
Swan, Timothy
Swift, Kay *Suppl. 1*
Szell, George
Taylor, Deems
Taylor, Rayner
Thayer, Eugene
Thompson, Randall
Thompson, Will
Lamartine
Thomson, Virgil
Thornhill, Claude
Timmons, Bobby
Tiomkin, Dimitri
Tobani, Theodore
Moses
Travis, Merle
Tuckey, William
Turpin, Tom
Ussachevsky, Vladimir
Varèse, Edgard
Vincent, Gene
Wakely, Jimmy
Walter, Bruno
Warren, Elinor Remick
Warren, Harry
Warren, Richard Henry
Warren, Samuel Prowse
Watters, Lu
Waxman, Franz
Webb, George James
Weill, Kurt
Weston, Paul *Suppl. 1*
White, Clarence
Cameron
Whiting, George
Elbridge
Wilder, Alec
Williams, Mary Lou
Willson, Meredith
Winding, Kai
Woodbury, Isaac Baker
Yon, Pietro Alessandro
Young, Victor
Zappa, Frank
Zeuner, Charles

Librettists
Atteridge, Harold
Richard
Blossom, Henry Martyn,
Jr.
Bolton, Guy Reginald
Caldwell, Anne
Cohan, George M.
Cook, Will Marion
Da Ponte, Lorenzo
Donnelly, Dorothy
Agnes

Music: COMPOSING AND
CONDUCTING *(cont.)*
  Green, Johnny
  Guthrie, Woody
  Hall, Wendall *Suppl. 1*
  Hanby, Benjamin Russel
  Handy, W. C.
  Harline, Leigh
  Harris, Charles Kassell
  Hays, Lee Elhardt
  Hays, Will S.
  Helms, Bobby *Suppl. 1*
  Henderson, Ray
  Hendrix, Jimi
  Hill, Joe
  Hoffman, Al *Suppl. 1*
  Holly, Buddy
  Howard, Joe
  Jenkins, Andrew
  Johnson, James P.
  Johnson, Robert
    (1911–1938)
  Kagen, Sergius
  Kern, Jerome
  Key, Francis Scott
  Kummer, Clare Rodman
    Beecher
  Lenoir, J. B.
  Lipscomb, Mance
  Maxwell, Elsa
  McDowell, Mississippi
    Fred
  Mercer, Johnny
  Miller, Roger
  Morgan, George
    Thomas
  Newley, Anthony
    Suppl. 1
  Niles, John Jacob
  Nyro, Laura *Suppl. 1*
  Ochs, Phil
  Olcott, Chauncey
  Orbison, Roy
  Pastor, Tony
  Perkins, Carl *Suppl. 1*
  Porter, Cole
  Ray, Johnnie
  Redding, Otis
  Robison, Carson Jay
  Romberg, Sigmund
  Ronell, Ann *Suppl. 1*
  Root, George Frederick
  Rose, Billy
  Rose, Fred
  Sankey, Ira David
  Schwartz, Arthur
  Shannon, Del
  Shaw, Oliver
  Shindler, Mary Dana
  Sigman, Carl *Suppl. 1*
  Sissle, Noble

  Smith, Chris
  Smith, Samuel Francis
  Sosenko, Anna *Suppl. 1*
  Speaks, Oley
  Spivey, Queen Victoria
  Stamps, V. O., and
    Frank Henry Stamps
  Styne, Jule
  Suesse, Dana *Suppl. 1*
  Swift, Kay *Suppl. 1*
  Thompson, Will
    Lamartine
  Tormé, Mel *Suppl. 1*
  Tubb, Ernest
  Van Heusen, Jimmy
  Vaughan, James David
  Von Tilzer, Harry, and
    Albert Von Tilzer
  Walker, James J.
  Waller, Fats
  Warren, Harry
  White, Anna
  Whiting, Richard
    Suppl. 1
  Whitley, Keith
  Wilder, Alec
  Williams, Hank
  Work, Henry Clay
  Wynette, Tammy
    Suppl. 1
  Youmans, Vincent
  Zunser, Eliakum

INSTRUMENTAL
PERFORMANCE
Accordionists
  Abshire, Nathan

Banjoists
  Akeman, Stringbean
  Ashley, Thomas
    Clarence
  Boggs, Dock
  Bumgarner, Samantha
  Cockerham, Fred
  Cousin Emmy
  Ford, Whitey
  Holcomb, Roscoe
  Jarrell, Tommy
  Johnson, Bill
  Kazee, Buell
  Macon, Uncle Dave
  Poole, Charlie
  Reno, Don
  Snowden, Elmer

Bassists
  Blanton, Jimmy
  Braud, Wellman
  Callahan, Walter
  Chambers, Paul

  Foster, Pops
  Hall, Al
  Holley, Major Quincy,
    Jr.
  Johnson, Bill
  Jones, Sam (1924–1981)
  Kirby, John
  Kirk, Andy
  Koussevitzky, Serge
  LaFaro, Scott
  Lindsay, John
  Mingus, Charles
  Page, Walter
  Pastorius, Jaco
  Pettiford, Oscar
  Stewart, Slam
  Ware, Wilbur

Calliope Players
  Marable, Fate

Cellists
  Bergmann, Carl
  Casals, Pablo
  Piatigorsky, Gregor
  Rose, Leonard
  Wallenstein, Alfred

Clarinetists
  Andrews, LaVerne
  Andrews, Maxene
  Bailey, Buster
  Baquet, Achille
  Baquet, George
  Bechet, Sidney
  Bigard, Barney
  Burbank, Albert
  Caceres, Ernie
  Dodds, Johnny
  Dorsey, Jimmy. *See*
    Dorsey, Jimmy, and
    Tommy Dorsey
  Fazola, Irving
  Goodman, Benny
  Hall, Edmond Blainey
  Herman, Woody
  Jenkins, Edmund
    Thornton
  Lewis, George
  Lewis, Ted
  Mezzrow, Mezz
  Nicholas, Albert
  Noone, Jimmie
  Parenti, Tony
  Picou, Alphonse
    Floristan
  Procope, Russell
  Robinson, Prince
  Scott, Cecil
  Sedric, Gene
  Shields, Larry

  Simeon, Omer Victor
  Tio, Lorenzo, Jr.

Comb Players
  McKenzie, Red

Cornetists
  Armstrong, Louis
  Beiderbecke, Bix
  Bolden, Buddy
  Celestin, Papa
  Davison, Wild Bill
  Hackett, Bobby
  Jones, Thad
  Keppard, Freddie
  LaRocca, Nick
  Mares, Paul Joseph
  McPartland, Jimmy
  Mitchell, George
  Morgan, Sam
  Nichols, Red
  Oliver, King
  Perez, Manuel
  Smith, Joe
  Spanier, Muggsy
  Stewart, Rex
  Wiggs, Johnny

Fiddlers
  Carson, John
  Choates, Harry
  Cockerham, Fred
  Cooley, Spade
  Cooper, Stoney
  Jarrell, Tommy
  McMichen, Clayton
  Robertson, Eck
  Rutherford, Leonard C.
  Smith, Fiddlin' Arthur
  Tanner, Gid
  Wills, Bob

Flugelhorn Players
  Jones, Thad
  Rogers, Shorty
  Sullivan, Maxine

Flutists
  Barrère, Georges
  Farrell, Joe
  Gryce, Gigi
  Lanier, Sidney
  Willson, Meredith

Guitarists
  Ashby, Irving C.
  Bond, Johnny
  Broonzy, Big Bill
  Callahan, Walter
  Carlisle, Cliff
  Carter, Maybelle

Theater and Live Entertainment *(cont.)*
Holtz, Lou
Howard, Willie
Irwin, May
Jessel, George
Kaye, Danny
Kelly, Walter C.
Kovacs, Ernie
Lahr, Bert
Langdon, Harry Philmore
Laurel, Stan, and Oliver Hardy
Levenson, Sam
Lillie, Beatrice *Suppl. 1*
Lloyd, Harold
Lynde, Paul
Mabley, Moms
Marx Brothers
Normand, Mabel
Olsen, Ole, and Chic Johnson
Pearl, Minnie *Suppl. 1*
Picon, Molly
Prinze, Freddie
Radner, Gilda *Suppl. 1*
Raye, Martha *Suppl. 1*
Raymond, John T.
Ritchard, Cyril
Ritz Brothers
Rowan, Dan
Sellers, Peter
Shean, Al
Silvers, Phil
Skelton, Red *Suppl. 1*
Smith, Stuff
Templeton, Fay
Three Stooges
Wilson, Flip *Suppl. 1*
Wynn, Ed
Youngman, Henny *Suppl. 1*

Costume Designers
Alexander, John White
Aronson, Boris
Bernstein, Aline Frankau
Head, Edith
Nikolais, Alwin
Orry-Kelly
Sharaff, Irene

Cowboys
Cortez Lira, Gregorio
Dart, Isom
Doolin, William
Glass, Charlie
James, Will Roderick
Love, Nat
Mix, Tom

Nigger Add
Rogers, Will
Russell, Charles Marion
Siringo, Charles Angelo

Daredevils
Houdini, Harry
Patch, Samuel
Zacchini, Hugo

Impersonators
Dooley, Ray
Eltinge, Julian
Hart, Tony
Janis, Elsie
Loftus, Cissie

Magicians
Blackstone, Harry
Blackstone, Harry, Jr. *Suppl. 1*
Davenport, Ira Erastus, and William Henry Harrison Davenport
Goldin, Horace
Houdini, Harry
Kellar, Harry
Thurston, Howard

Midgets
Tom Thumb

Mimes
Enters, Angna
Fox, George Washington Lafayette
Jackson, Joe

Minstrel Show Performers
Backus, Charles
Bland, James Allen
Bryant, Dan
Christy, Edwin Pearce
Christy, George N. Harrington
Dixon, George Washington
Dockstader, Lew
Emmett, Daniel Decatur
Hart, Tony
Haverly, Jack H.
Stratton, Eugene

Monologuists
Draper, Ruth
Howe, Helen

Orators
Ames, Fisher
Cockran, William Bourke

Curtis, George William
Darrow, Clarence
Depew, Chauncey Mitchell
Dickinson, Anna Elizabeth
Diggs, Annie LePorte
Everett, Edward
Gough, John Bartholomew
Grady, Henry Woodfin
Henry, Patrick
Hiawatha
Ingersoll, Robert Green
Jasper, John
Lease, Mary Elizabeth Clyens
Maffitt, John Newland (1794–1850)
Mazakutemani, Paul
Niebuhr, Reinhold
O'Hare, Kate Richards
Ostenaco
Phillips, Wendell
Randolph, John (1773–1833)
Remond, Charles Lenox
Simmons, Roscoe Conkling Murray
Simpson, Matthew
Smith, Gerald Lyman Kenneth
Taylor, Edward Thompson
Teedyuskung
Watson, Thomas Edward
Willett, Herbert Lockwood

Puppeteers
Baird, Bil *Suppl. 1*
Henson, Jim
Lewis, Shari *Suppl. 1*
Tillstrom, Burr

Rodeo Performers
Pickens, Slim
Pickett, Bill

Sharpshooters
Oakley, Annie

Siamese Twins
Chang and Eng

Stage / Screen Actors
Abbott, Bud, and Lou Costello
Adams, Edwin
Adams, Maude

Adler, Jacob Pavlovich
Adler, Luther
Adler, Sara
Adler, Stella
Aiken, George L.
Albertson, Jack
Alda, Robert
Aldrich, Louis
Aldridge, Ira Frederick
Allan, Maud
Allen, Gracie
Allen, Viola
Ameche, Don
Anders, Glenn
Anderson, Broncho Billy
Anderson, Eddie "Rochester"
Anderson, Mary (1859–1940)
Anglin, Margaret
Arbuckle, Roscoe "Fatty" *Suppl. 1*
Arden, Eve
Arlen, Richard
Arliss, George
Arnaz, Desi
Arthur, Jean *Suppl. 1*
Arthur, Julia
Astaire, Fred
Astor, Mary
Atwill, Lionel
Autry, Gene *Suppl. 1*
Ayres, Lew *Suppl. 1*
Backus, Charles
Backus, Jim
Bacon, Frank
Bailey, Pearl
Bainter, Fay
Ball, Lucille
Bangs, Frank C.
Bankhead, Tallulah
Bara, Theda
Barnabee, Henry Clay
Barnes, Binnie *Suppl. 1*
Barnes, Charlotte Mary Sanford
Barrett, George Horton
Barrett, Lawrence
Barry, Thomas
Barrymore, Ethel
Barrymore, Georgie Drew
Barrymore, John
Barrymore, Lionel
Barrymore, Maurice
Barton, James Edward
Bateman, Kate Josephine
Bates, Blanche
Baxter, Anne
Beavers, Louise
Beery, Wallace

Denominations *(cont.)*

Brown, Charles
  Reynolds
Bulkeley, Gershom
Burton, Asa
Bushnell, Horace
Byles, Mather
Cardozo, Francis Louis
Chauncy, Charles
  (1705–1787)
Cheever, George Barrell
Clark, Francis E.
Colman, Benjamin
Cook, Russell Salmon
Cooper, Samuel
  (1725–1783)
Croswell, Andrew
Cutler, Manasseh
Davenport, John
Davis, Jerome Dean
Deane, Samuel
DeBerry, William
  Nelson
Dewey, Chester
Douglass, Harlan Paul
Dow, Daniel
Dwight, Louis
Dwight, Sereno Edwards
Dwight, William
  Theodore
Eastman, Annis
Eastman, William Reed
Edwards, Bela Bates
Edwards, Jonathan
Edwards, Jonathan, Jr.
Eliot, Jared
Emerson, Joseph
Emmons, Nathanael
Everett, Robert
Faulkner, William John
Flint, Timothy
Foxcroft, Thomas
Gay, Ebenezer
Gladden, Washington
Goodrich, Charles
  Augustus
Goodrich, Chauncey
  Allen
Goodrich, Elizur
  (1734–1797)
Gordon, George Angier
Green, Beriah
Griffis, William Elliot
Grinnell, Josiah Bushnell
Gunsaulus, Frank
  Wakeley
Haynes, Lemuel
Hemmenway, Moses
Hillis, Newell Dwight
Horton, Douglas
Hume, Robert Allen

Humphrey, Heman
Hyde, William DeWitt
Kirk, Edward Norris
Langdon, Samuel
Lovejoy, Owen
Lyman, Mary Redington
  Ely
Magoun, George
  Frederic
Mather, Samuel
  (1706–1785)
Mayhew, Jonathan
McCulloch, Oscar
  Carleton
McKeen, Joseph
Moore, Zephaniah Swift
Morril, David Lawrence
Morse, Jedidiah
Moxom, Philip Stafford
Munger, Theodore
  Thornton
Nettleton, Asahel
Newcomb, Harvey
Ockenga, Harold John
Peet, Stephen Denison
Peloubet, Francis
  Nathan
Pennington, James
  William Charles
Phelps, Austin
Phillips, Channing E.
Pond, Enoch
Porter, Noah
Prince, Thomas
Proctor, Henry Hugh
Reed, Myron Winslow
Rogers, Daniel
Rogers, John Almanza
  Rowley
Saltonstall, Gurdon
Sanders, Daniel Clarke
Scofield, Cyrus Ingerson
Seccomb, John
Seccombe, Joseph
Sheldon, Charles
  Monroe
Smyth, Newman
Sperry, Willard Learoyd
Sprague, William Buell
Steiner, Edward Alfred
Stiles, Ezra
Stoddard, Solomon
Strong, Josiah
Sturtevant, Julian
  Monson
Taylor, Graham
Tennent, William, III
Thacher, Peter
Thacher, Thomas
Torrey, Reuben Archer
Tracy, Joseph Carter

Trumbull, Benjamin
Tufts, John
Tyler, Bennet
Walker, Timothy
  (1705–1782)
Ware, Henry
Washburn, George
Wheelock, Eleazar
Willard, Joseph
Williams, John
  (1664–1729)
Wise, John (1652–1725)
Woods, Leonard
Worcester, Noah
Wright, Henry Clarke

Disciples of Christ Clergy
Campbell, Alexander
Franklin, Benjamin
  (1812–1878)
McGarvey, John William
McLean, Archibald
Scott, Walter
Smith, Gerald Lyman
  Kenneth
Wharton, Greene
  Lawrence
Willett, Herbert
  Lockwood
Zollars, Ely Vaughn

Dutch Reformed Clergy
Berg, Joseph Frederic
Bertholf, Guiliam
Bogardus, Everardus
Corwin, Edward Tanjore
Freeman, Bernardus
Frelinghuysen,
  Theodorus Jacobus
Griffis, William Elliot
Hardenbergh, Jacob
  Rutsen
Krol, Bastiaen Janszen
Livingston, John Henry
Megapolensis, Johannes
Michaelius, Jonas
Milledoler, Philip
Seelye, Julius Hawley
Selijns, Henricus
Talmage, Thomas De
  Witt
Van Raalte, Albertus
  Christiaan
Van Rensselaer,
  Nicholas
Verbryck, Samuel

Episcopalian Bishops
Brent, Charles Henry
Brooks, Phillips

Brownell, Thomas
  Church
Chase, Philander
Cheney, Charles Edward
Clark, Thomas March
Cobbs, Nicholas
  Hamner
Coxe, Arthur Cleveland
Cummins, George
  David
Doane, George
  Washington
Doane, William Croswell
Gailor, Thomas Frank
Grafton, Charles
  Chapman
Greer, David Hummel
Griswold, Alexander
  Viets
Hale, Charles Reuben
Hare, William Hobart
Hobart, John Henry
Holly, James Theodore
Hopkins, John Henry
Huntington, Frederic
  Dan
Ives, Levi Silliman
Kemper, Jackson
Kip, William Ingraham
Lawrence, William
  (1850–1941)
Madison, James
  (1749–1812)
Manning, William
  Thomas
McIlvaine, Charles Pettit
McVickar, William
  Neilson
Meade, William
Moore, Richard
  Channing
Nash, Norman Burdett
Onderdonk, Benjamin
  Tredwell
Onderdonk, Henry
  Ustick
Otey, James Hervey
Perry, William Stevens
Polk, Leonidas
Potter, Henry Codman
Provoost, Samuel
Quintard, Charles Todd
Ravenscroft, John Stark
Rowe, Peter Trimble
Satterlee, Henry Yates
Schereschewsky, Samuel
  Isaac Joseph
Seabury, Samuel (1729–
  1796)
Slattery, Charles Lewis

Earth Sciences *(cont.)*
Davidson, George
Hassler, Ferdinand
Rudolph
Hayford, John Fillmore
Hilgard, Julius Erasmus

Geographers
Adams, Cyrus Cornelius
Atwood, Wallace Walter
Baker, Oliver Edwin
Bowman, Isaiah
Brown, Ralph Hall
Daly, Charles Patrick
Davis, William Morris
Gannett, Henry
Guyot, Arnold Henry
Hakluyt, Richard
Huntington, Ellsworth
Jefferson, Mark Sylvester
William
Morse, Jedidiah
Robinson, Edward
Sauer, Carl Ortwin
Semple, Ellen Churchill
Shaler, Nathaniel
Southgate
Tanner, Henry Schenck
Wheeler, George
Montague

Geologists
Agassiz, Louis
Ashburner, Charles
Albert
Barbour, George Brown
Barrell, Joseph
Bascom, Florence
Becker, George
Ferdinand
Blackwelder, Eliot
Boll, Jacob
Bowman, Isaiah
Boyé, Martin Hans
Branner, John Casper
Brooks, Alfred Hulse
Brush, George Jarvis
Bryan, Kirk
Buddington, Arthur
Francis
Chamberlin, Rollin
Thomas
Chamberlin, Thomas
Chrowder
Clapp, Asahel
Clapp, Charles Horace
Clark, William Bullock
Cook, George Hammell
Crosby, William Otis
Cross, Charles Whitman
Daly, Reginald Aldworth

Dana, James Dwight
Darton, Nelson Horatio
Davis, William Morris
Day, David Talbot
Dunbar, Carl Owen
Dutton, Clarence
Edward
Eaton, Amos
Emmons, Ebenezer
Emmons, Samuel
Franklin
Evans, Lewis
Featherstonhaugh,
George William
Fenneman, Nevin
Melancthon
Gardner, Julia Anna
Gibbs, George
(1815–1873)
Gilbert, Grove Karl
Gilluly, James
Gould, Laurence
McKinley
Grabau, Amadeus
William
Hague, Arnold
Hall, James (1811–1898)
Hayden, Ferdinand
Vandeveer
Hayes, Charles Willard
Hedberg, Hollis Dow
Heezen, Bruce
Heilprin, Angelo
Hess, Harry Hammond
Hilgard, Eugene
Woldemar
Hill, Robert Thomas
Hitchcock, Charles
Henry
Hitchcock, Edward
Hobbs, William Herbert
Holmes, William Henry
Suppl. 1
Houghton, Douglass
Hunt, Thomas Sterry
Irving, John Duer
Jackson, Charles
Thomas
Jaggar, Thomas
Augustus, Jr.
Keith, Arthur
Kennedy, Kathleen
Agnes
Keyes, Charles Rollin
King, Clarence Rivers
Knopf, Adolph
Knopf, Eleanora Frances
Bliss
Larsen, Esper Signius,
Jr.

Lawson, Andrew
Cowper
LeConte, Joseph
Leith, Charles Kenneth
Lesley, J. Peter
Lindgren, Waldemar
Lowdermilk, Walter
Clay *Suppl. 1*
Mackin, J. Hoover
Maclure, William
Marbut, Curtis Fletcher
Mather, William
Williams
McGee, William John
McKelvey, Vincent E.
Suppl. 1
Meinzer, Oscar Edward
Menard, Henry William
Mendenhall, Walter
Curran
Merrill, George Perkins
Mitchell, Elisha
Moore, Raymond Cecil
Newberry, John Strong
Nolan, Thomas B.
Suppl. 1
Orton, Edward Francis
Baxter
Owen, David Dale
Pecora, William Thomas
Percival, James Gates
Pirsson, Louis Valentine
Powell, John Wesley
Price, George McCready
Pumpelly, Raphael
Ransome, Frederick
Leslie
Riddell, John Leonard
Rogers, Henry Darwin
Rogers, William Barton
Rubey, William Walden
Ruffner, William Henry
Russell, Israel Cook
Safford, James Merrill
Salisbury, Rollin D.
Shaler, Nathaniel
Southgate
Shoemaker, Gene
Suppl. 1
Smith, George Otis
Spurr, Josiah Edward
Stevenson, Matilda Coxe
Evans
Swallow, George Clinton
Talmage, James Edward
Tarr, Ralph Stockman
Taylor, Frank Bursley
Taylor, Richard Cowling
Troost, Gerard
Ulrich, Edward Oscar

Van Hise, Charles
Richard
Vanuxem, Lardner
Vaughan, Thomas
Wayland
Veatch, Arthur Clifford
Walcott, Charles
Doolittle
Wanless, Harold Rollin
Ward, Lester Frank
White, Charles Abiathar
White, David
White, George Willard
White, Israel Charles
Whitney, Josiah Dwight
Willis, Bailey
Winchell, Horace
Vaughn
Winchell, Newton
Horace
Woodworth, Jay Backus
Worthen, Amos Henry
Wright, George
Frederick

Geomorphologists
Atwood, Wallace Walter
Johnson, Douglas Wilson

Geophysicists
Bauer, Louis Agricola
Benioff, Victor Hugo
Byerly, Perry
Chapman, Sydney
Day, Arthur Louis
Ewing, Maurice
Ferrel, William
Fleming, John Adam
Forbush, Scott Ellsworth
Griggs, David Tressel
Hubbert, M. King
Macelwane, James
Bernard
Reid, Harry Fielding
Schott, Charles Anthony
Vestine, Ernest Harry
Woodward, Robert
Simpson

Hydrographers
Davis, Arthur Powell
Davis, Charles Henry
McArthur, William Pope
Newell, Frederick
Haynes

Hydrologists
Darton, Nelson Horatio

Limnologists
Birge, Edward Asahel

Civics and Philanthropy
(cont.)
Winter, Alice Vivian
  Ames
Yates, Josephine A.

Foundation Officials
Barnard, Chester Irving
Buttrick, Wallace
Colcord, Joanna Carver
Gaither, Horace Rowan,
  Jr.
Harrar, Jacob George
Hiss, Alger *Suppl. 1*
Hutchins, Robert
  Maynard
Jessup, Walter Albert
Keppel, Frederick Paul
Knowles, John Hilton
Pritchett, Henry Smith
Ray, Gordon Norton
Trowbridge, Augustus
Weaver, Warren
Woodward, Robert
  Simpson
Young, Donald Ramsey

Freemasons
Bennett, John Cook
Etting, Solomon *Suppl. 1*
Hall, Prince
Hays, Moses Michael
  Suppl. 1
Morris, Robert
  (1818–1888)
Pike, Albert
Reason, Patrick Henry
Webb, Thomas Smith

Institutional Founders /
Benefactors
Baldwin, Abraham
Baldwin, John
Berry, Martha
  McChesney
Blair, James
Bliss, Daniel
Bliss, Lillie P.
Bolton, Frances Payne
Bradley, Amy Morris
Bradley, Lydia Moss
Burr, Aaron
  (1716–1757)
Burroughs, Nannie
  Helen
Butler, Mother Marie
  Joseph
Cataldo, Joseph Maria
Chafer, Lewis Sperry
Cornell, Ezra
Corson, Juliet

Crandall, Prudence
Damrosch, Frank Heino
Davidge, John Beale
Dickey, Sarah Ann
Dobbs, Ella Victoria
Drumgoole, John
  Christopher
Durant, Henry Fowle
Evans, William Thomas
Farmer, Fannie Merritt
Fee, John Gregg
Ferguson, Katy
Fitton, James
Flanagan, Edward
  Joseph
Folger, Emily Jordan
Freer, Charles Lang
Fuld, Caroline
  Bamberger Frank
Gallatin, Albert Eugene
Gardner, Isabella
  Stewart
Graham, Isabella
Gregory, Samuel
Guggenheim, Solomon
  Robert
Harvard, John
Huntington, Henry
  Edwards
Jolas, Maria
Jones, Bob
Kander, Lizzie Black
Kent, Aratus
L'Esperance, Elise
  Strang
Lange, Mary Elizabeth
Livermore, George
Lyon, Mary
Mannes, David
Mayo, William James,
  and Charles Horace
  Mayo
McGroarty, Sister Julia
Menninger, Charles
  Frederick
Merrick, Samuel
  Vaughan
Minor, Benjamin Blake
Morais, Sabato
Morrison, Nathan
  Jackson
Mossell, Nathan Francis
Newcomb, Josephine
  Suppl. 1
Palmer, Lizzie Pitts
  Merrill
Parkhurst, Helen
Parks, Oliver Lafayette
Passavant, William
  Alfred

Peabody, Endicott
  Suppl. 1
Peale, Charles Willson
Phillips, John
Phillips, Samuel, Jr.
Pierce, Sarah
Porter, Sarah
Rice, John Holt
Rice, William Marsh
Rogers, John Almanza
  Rowley
Sage, Henry Williams
Schofield, Martha
Scudder, Ida Sophia
Seelye, Laurenus Clark
Seymour, Mary Foot
Sill, Anna Peck
Smith, Sophia
Spreckels, Alma
Starr, Ellen Gates
Surette, Thomas
  Whitney
Thurston, Matilda
  Smyrell Calder
Tompkins, Sally Louisa
Tulane, Paul *Suppl. 1*
Van Rensselaer, Stephen
Vassar, Matthew
Vincent, George Edgar
Warren, Herbert
  Langford
Watteville, Henrietta
  Benigna von
Webb, Electra
  Havemeyer
Wheelock, Lucy
Whitney, Gertrude
  Vanderbilt
Wilbur, Earl Morse
Willard, Emma Hart
Willey, Samuel Hopkins
Williams, Walter
Yale, Elihu
Zimbalist, Mary Louise
  Curtis Bok

Organization Founders /
Officials
Abbott, Grace
Adler, Cyrus
Ainsworth, Dorothy
  Sears
Ames, Fanny Baker
Andrus, Ethel Percy
Baker, Ella Josephine
Bangs, Nathan
Barnard, John Gross
Barrett, Janie Porter
Barton, James Levi
Bauer, Harold Victor
Beebe, William

Bell, Luther V.
Bennett, Belle Harris
Benson, Oscar Herman
Bethune, Joanna
  Graham
Bethune, Mary Jane
  McLeod
Billikopf, Jacob
Blackwell, Randolph
  Talmadge
Boardman, Mabel Thorp
Booth, Maud Elizabeth
  Charlesworth
  Ballington
Booth-Tucker, Emma
  Moss
Bowles, Eva Del Vakia
Breen, Joseph Ignatius
Brown, Josephine
  Chapin
Browne, William
  Washington
Buchman, Frank Nathan
  Daniel
Burrell, Berkeley
  Graham
Capen, Samuel Paul
Caswell, Alexis
Clark, Francis E.
Cook, George Cram
Cratty, Mabel
Cunningham, Ann
  Pamela
Cuthbert, Marion Vera
Dahl, Theodor
  Halvorson
Dancy, John Campbell,
  Jr.
Darling, Flora Adams
Darrow, Karl Kelchner
Davison, Henry
  Pomeroy
Dearden, John F.
Delano, Jane Arminda
Dodge, Grace Hoadley
Dunn, Robert Williams
Dwight, James
Eichelberger, Clark Mell
Eliot, Samuel Atkins
Emery, Julia Chester
Empie, Paul Chauncey
Eustis, Dorothy Harrison
Evans, Luther Harris
Farmer, James *Suppl. 1*
Field, Jessie
Ford, Guy Stanton
Franklin, Martha
  Minerva
Gilder, Rosamond
Going, Jonathan
Gompers, Samuel

Political Activism and Reform Movements
(cont.)
Whitfield, James Monroe
Whittier, John Greenleaf
Williams, Peter, Jr.
Woolman, John
Wright, Elizur
Wright, Henry Clarke
Wright, Theodore Sedgwick

Agricultural Reformers
Aiken, D. Wyatt
Dickson, David
Hatch, William Henry
Murray, William Henry David

Alleged Slave Revolt Leaders
Jeremiah, Thomas

Alleged Traitors
Bayard, Nicholas
Billy
Hiss, Alger *Suppl. 1*

Anarchists
Berkman, Alexander
Bresci, Gaetano
Ciancabilla, Giuseppe
de Cleyre, Voltairine
Galleani, Luigi
Goldman, Emma
Most, Johann Joseph
Parsons, Albert Richard
Sacco, Nicola, and Bartolomeo Vanzetti

Animal Welfare Activists
Amory, Cleveland *Suppl. 1*
Bergh, Henry
Spira, Henry *Suppl. 1*

Antiabortion Rights Activists
Storer, Horatio Robinson

Anticommunists
Budenz, Louis
Chambers, Whittaker
Cohn, Roy
Cvetic, Matthew C.
Fischer, Ruth
Kohlberg, Alfred
Schine, G. David *Suppl. 1*
Welch, Robert

Antimasonic Movement Leaders
Morgan, William

Antinuclear Activists
Rabinowitch, Eugene
Sagan, Carl *Suppl. 1*

Antisuffragists
Conway, Katherine Eleanor
Dahlgren, Sarah Madeleine Vinton
Dodge, Josephine Marshall Jewell
Meyer, Annie Nathan
Parker, Jane Marsh
Putnam, Elizabeth Lowell
Wells, Kate Boott Gannett

Birth Control Advocates
Calderone, Mary S. *Suppl. 1*
Campbell, Loraine Leeson
Cannon, Cornelia James
Dennett, Mary Coffin Ware
Foote, Edward Bliss
Guttmacher, Alan
Levine, Lena
McKinnon, Edna Bertha Rankin
Morris, John McLean
Rock, John Charles
Sanger, Margaret
Stone, Abraham, and Hannah Mayer Stone
Yarros, Rachelle

Black Nationalists
Blyden, Edward Wilmot
Crummell, Alexander
Cuffe, Paul
Delany, Martin Robinson
Garvey, Amy Euphemia Jacques
Garvey, Marcus
Logan, Rayford Whittingham
Michaux, Lewis H.
Singleton, Benjamin
Whitfield, James Monroe

Civil Liberties Activists
Baldwin, Roger Nash
Bonnin, Gertrude Simmons

Chafee, Zechariah, Jr.
Chapman, Maria Weston
Coolidge, Albert Sprague
DeSilver, Albert
Flynn, Elizabeth Gurley
Foltz, Clara Shortridge
Hays, Arthur Garfield
McWilliams, Carey
Meiklejohn, Alexander
Milligan, Lambdin P.
Milner, Lucille Bernheimer
Ozawa, Takao
Porter, Benjamin Faneuil
Roe, Gilbert Ernstein
Rogge, O. John
Savio, Mario *Suppl. 1*
Schroeder, Theodore
Scopes, John Thomas

Civil Rights Activists
Abernathy, Ralph David
Adams, John Quincy (1848–1922)
Albert, Octavia Victoria Rogers
Albrier, Frances Mary
Alexander, Will Winton
Alston, Melvin Ovenus
Ames, Jessie Daniel
Andrew, John Albion
Apess, William
Baker, Ella Josephine
Baker, Josephine
Barber, Jesse Max
Bass, Charlotta Spears
Bayne, Thomas
Bethune, Mary Jane McLeod
Bird, Francis William
Blackwell, Randolph Talmadge
Boudinot, Elias Cornelius
Bowles, Eva Del Vakia
Braden, Carl James
Bright Eyes
Bruce, John Edward
Bunche, Ralph Johnson
Carmichael, Stokely *Suppl. 1*
Cass, Melnea Agnes Jones
Church, Robert Reed, Jr.
Clark, Peter Humphries
Clark, Septima Poinsette
Cleaver, Eldridge *Suppl. 1*
Cohen, Felix Solomon

Collier, John
Comstock, Elizabeth Leslie Rous Wright
Converse, Harriet Maxwell
Cook, George William
Cook, Vivian E. J.
Cooper, Anna Julia Haywood
Dancy, John Campbell, Jr.
De Baptiste, Richard
Deming, Barbara
Dillard, James Hardy
Douglass, Frederick
Downing, George Thomas
Drake, St. Clair, Jr.
Du Bois, W. E. B.
Durham, John Stephens
Durr, Virginia Foster *Suppl. 1*
Eastman, Charles Alexander
Evers, Medgar
Farmer, James *Suppl. 1*
Fauset, Crystal Bird
Fisher, Ada Lois Sipuel
Ford, Barney Launcelot
Fortune, Timothy Thomas
Green, Ely
Griffing, Josephine Sophia White
Grigsby, Snow Flake
Grimké, Archibald Henry
Grimké, Francis James
Groppi, James Edward
Hamer, Fannie Lou Townsend
Harrison, Hubert Henry
Hastie, William Henry
Hill, Charles Andrew
Holland, Annie Welthy Daughtry
Hope, Lugenia D. Burns
Houston, Charles Hamilton
Howe, Mark De Wolfe
Hundley, Mary Gibson Brewer
Hunter, Jane Edna Harris
Hunton, George Kenneth
Jackson, Helen Hunt
Jackson, Luther Porter
Jackson, Robert R.
Jemison, Alice Mae Lee
Johns, Vernon Napoleon

CUMULATIVE INDEX BY OCCUPATIONS AND REALMS OF RENOWN: Society and Social Change • 899

Social Welfare *(cont.)*
Trall, Russell Thacher
Trudeau, Edward
  Livingston
Valentine, Lila
  Hardaway Meade
Welsh, Lilian
Wiley, Harvey
  Washington
Wilson, Bill, and Bob
  Smith *Suppl. 1*
Winslow, Charles-
  Edward Amory
Wolman, Abel
Wood, Edith Elmer
Yarros, Rachelle

Housing Reformers
Bauer, Catherine Krouse
Dinwiddie, Emily
  Wayland
Flagg, Ernest
Levitt, Abraham
Stokes, Isaac Newton
  Phelps
Veiller, Lawrence
  Turnure
White, Alfred Tredway
Wood, Edith Elmer

Penologists
Bennett, James Van
  Benschoten
Brockway, Zebulon Reed
Van Waters, Miriam
Vaux, Roberts

Prison Officials
Duffy, Clinton T.
Harris, Mary Belle
McClaughry, Robert
  Wilson

Prison Reformers
Booth, Maud Elizabeth
  Charlesworth
  Ballington
Comstock, Elizabeth
  Leslie Rous Wright
Davis, Katharine
  Bement
Farnham, Eliza Wood
  Burhans
Gibbons, Abigail
  Hopper
Griffith, Goldsborough
  Sappington
Hodder, Jessie
  Donaldson
Hopper, Isaac Tatem

Little, Sophia Louisa
  Robbins
McClaughry, Robert
  Wilson
Nicholson, Timothy
Peter, Sarah
  Worthington King
Round, William M. F.
Tutwiler, Julia Strudwick
Wines, Frederick
  Howard
Wittpenn, Caroline
  Bayard Stevens

Public Health Officials
Abbott, Samuel Warren
Arnstein, Margaret
Baker, Sara Josephine
Beard, Mary
Bennett, Alice
Biggs, Hermann Michael
Boswell, Henry
Bradley, Charles Henry
Brigham, Amariah
Bryce, Peter
Calderone, Mary S.
  Suppl. 1
Caverly, Charles
  Solomon
Chapin, Charles Value
Cochran, John
Crandall, Ella Phillips
Crothers, Thomas
  Davison
Day, Albert
Dyer, Rolla Eugene
Earle, Pliny
Felix, Robert Hanna
Fitzgerald, Alice
Frost, Wade Hampton
Galt, John Minson, II
Gardner, Mary Sewall
Garrison, Charles Willis
Goldwater, Sigismund
  Schulz
Gray, John Purdue
Guiteras, Juan
Gunn, Selskar Michael
Heiser, Victor George
Hopkins, Juliet Ann
  Opie
Horsfall, Frank Lappin,
  Jr.
Hunt, Ezra Mundy
Hurd, Henry Mills
Kellogg, John Harvey
Knowles, John Hilton
Kolb, Lawrence
Lovejoy, Esther Pohl
Lumsden, Leslie Leon
Mahoney, John Friend

Manning, Isaac Hall
McCaw, James Brown
McCormack, Arthur
  Thomas
McCormack, Joseph
  Nathaniel
Mossell, Nathan Francis
Nichols, Charles Henry
Nyswander, Dorothy B.
  Suppl. 1
Pember, Phoebe Yates
  Levy
Pinn, Petra Fitzalieu
Poindexter, Hildrus
  Augustus
Potter, Ellen Culver
Rauch, John Henry
Rosenau, Milton Joseph
Sawyer, Wilbur
  Augustus
Snow, Edwin Miller
Snow, William Freeman
Soper, Fred Lowe
Stiles, Charles Wardell
Switzer, Mary Elizabeth
Terry, Charles Edward
Thompson, Mary Harris
Todd, Eli
Underwood, Felix Joel
Walcott, Henry
  Pickering
White, William Alanson
Williams, Daniel Hale
Winston, Ellen Black
Woodward, Samuel
  Bayard
Woodworth, John
  Maynard
Wright, Louis Tompkins

Relief Workers
Billikopf, Jacob
Empie, Paul Chauncey
Hoge, Jane Currie
  Blaikie
Porter, Eliza Emily
  Chappell
Reed, Esther De Berdt
Wood, Carolena
Wormeley, Katharine
  Prescott

Sanitarians
Agnew, Cornelius Rea
Bard, John
Baruch, Simon
Cabell, James Lawrence
Carter, Henry Rose
Chaillé, Stanford
  Emerson
Cochran, Jerome

Gorgas, William
  Crawford
Griscom, John Hoskins
Hunt, Ezra Mundy
Hurty, John Newell
Jones, Joseph
Livermore, Mary
Pearson, Leonard
Smith, Stephen

Social Reformers
Abbott, Edith
Abbott, Grace
Addams, Jane
Adler, Felix
Alcott, A. Bronson
Alinsky, Saul David
Allen, Nathan
Altgeld, John Peter
American, Sadie
Ames, Fanny Baker
Anderson, Matthew
Andrews, John Bertram
Andrews, Stephen Pearl
Anthony, Susan B.
Atkinson, Edward
Bacon, Leonard, Sr.
Bagley, Sarah George
Baker, Harvey
  Humphrey
Baldwin, Roger Nash
Barnard, Kate
Barnum, Gertrude
Barrett, Janie Porter
Barrows, Isabel
Barrows, Samuel June
Bates, Barnabas
Beecher, Catharine
  Esther
Beecher, Henry Ward
Belmont, Alva Erskine
  Smith Vanderbilt
Benezet, Anthony
Bethune, Joanna
  Graham
Bethune, Mary Jane
  McLeod
Birney, Alice Josephine
  McLellan
Blackwell, Antoinette
  Louisa Brown
Blackwell, Henry
  Browne
Blanchard, Jonathan
Bliss, William Dwight
  Porter
Bloss, William Clough
Bonney, Mary Lucinda
Booth, Maud Elizabeth
  Charlesworth
  Ballington

WRITING AND PUBLISHING

Editing and Publishing

Editing and Publishing
(cont.)
Paine, Albert Bigelow

*Magazine and Journal
Editors / Publishers*
Abbott, Lyman
Adams, Cyrus Cornelius
Adams, William Taylor
Ahern, Mary Eileen
Aiken, D. Wyatt
Aitken, Robert
Alden, Henry Mills
Aldrich, Thomas Bailey
Allen, Frederick Lewis
Allen, Paul
Anderson, Margaret
Angoff, Charles
Armstrong, Hamilton
  Fish
Arthur, Timothy Shay
Ascoli, Max
Auslander, Joseph
Ballou, Maturin Murray
Bangs, John Kendrick
Barber, Jesse Max
Barnard, Henry
Barrett, Benjamin Fiske
Baum, L. Frank
Beach, Alfred Ely
Benét, William Rose
Benjamin, Park
Bennett, Gwendolyn
Blackwell, Betsy Talbot
Bliven, Bruce
Bloomer, Amelia Jenks
Bok, Edward William
Booth, Mary Louise
Bostwick, Arthur Elmore
Bowker, R. R.
Bradford, Andrew
Bradwell, James
  Bolesworth
Brann, William Cowper
Brickman, William
  Wolfgang
Brown, Charles
  Brockden
Brownson, Henry
  Francis
Brownson, Orestes
  Augustus
Bruce, Archibald
Buckingham, Joseph
  Tinker
Bunner, Henry Cuyler
Burgess, Gelett
Burnett, Whit
Burnham, James
Burton, William Evans

Calverton, Victor
  Francis
Canby, Henry Seidel
Carpenter, Stephen
  Cullen
Carus, Paul
Cattell, James McKeen
Catton, Bruce
Chamberlin, Rollin
  Thomas
Chambers, Whittaker
Chase, Edna Woolman
Clark, Emily Tapscott
Clark, Lewis Gaylord
Clarke, Mary Bayard
  Devereux
Cobb, Cully Alton
Collier, Peter Fenelon
Como, William Michael
Conroy, Jack
Cousins, Norman
Cowles, Gardner, Jr.
Cowley, Malcolm
Crain, Gustavus
  Dedman, Jr.
Croly, Herbert David
Crothers, Thomas
  Davison
Crowninshield, Frank
Curry, Daniel
Curtis, Cyrus H. K.
Curtis, George William
Dannay, Frederic
Davis, Thurston Noble
De Bow, James
  Dunwoody Brownson
Demorest, Ellen Curtis
Dennie, Joseph
Dexter, Henry Martyn
Didier, Eugene Lemoine
Dodge, Mary Elizabeth
  Mapes
Donahoe, Patrick
Donovan, Hedley
  Williams
Dow, George Francis
Duffy, Francis Patrick
Durant, Thomas
  Jefferson
Duyckinck, Evert
  Augustus
Dymond, John
Eastman, Max
Eckman, Frederick
  Suppl. 1
Edwards, Bela Bates
Eliot, T. S.
Engel, Carl
Everett, Robert
Fairfield, Sumner
  Lincoln

Fauset, Jessie Redmon
Fenner, Erasmus Darwin
Fischer, John
Fishbein, Morris
Fixx, James Fuller
Fleischer, Nat
Flower, Benjamin
  Orange
Foley, Martha
Forbes, Malcolm
  Stevenson
Ford, Paul Leicester
Franklin, Benjamin
  (1812–1878)
Freeman, Joseph
French, Lucy Virginia
  Smith
Fuller, Hoyt William
Fuller, Margaret
Funk, Isaac Kauffman
Funk, Wilfred John
Gaillard, Edwin Samuel
Garreau, Armand
Gernsback, Hugo
Gibbs, Wolcott
  (1902–1958)
Gilder, Jeannette
  Leonard
Gilder, Richard Watson
Gildersleeve, Basil
  Lanneau
Gillis, James Martin
Gilman, Caroline
  Howard
Gingrich, Arnold
Gleason, Ralph Joseph
Godey, Louis Antoine
Godkin, Edwin
  Lawrence
Godwin, Parke
Gold, Michael
Goldwater, John L.
  Suppl. 1
Gould, George Milbry
Graebner, Theodore
  Conrad
Green, Abel
Griswold, Rufus Wilmot
Grosvenor, Gilbert
  Hovey
Hackett, Francis
Hadden, Briton
Hale, Sarah Josepha
  Buell
Hall, James (1793–1868)
Hall, John Elihu
Halsey, Frederick Arthur
Hamilton, Earl Jefferson
Hamilton, Thomas
Hapgood, Norman
Harbaugh, Henry

Harland, Henry
Harman, Moses
Harper, Fletcher
Harris, Frank
Harris, Seale
Hart, Joseph Kinmont
Harvey, George Brinton
  McClellan
Hasbrouck, Lydia Sayer
Haven, Emily Bradley
  Neal
Haynes, Williams
Heap, Jane
Heard, Dwight Bancroft
Hearst, William
  Randolph, Jr.
Hecht, George Joseph
Henry, Caleb Sprague
Herr, Daniel
Herrick, Clarence
  Luther, and Charles
  Judson Herrick
Herrick, Sophia
  McIlvaine Bledsoe
Hibbs, Ben
Hill, Daniel Harvey
Hoffman, Charles Fenno
Holbrook, James
Holt, Hamilton Bowen
Hopkins, Pauline
  Elizabeth
Hornblow, Arthur, Sr.
Horst, Louis
Howard, Blanche Willis
Howkins, Elizabeth
  Penrose
Hubbard, Elbert Green
Huberman, Leo
Hudson, Daniel Eldred
Ingelfinger, Franz Joseph
Isaacs, Edith Juliet Rich
Jameson, John Franklin
Jelliffe, Smith Ely
Jolas, Maria
Jones, Thomas P.
Jordan, Elizabeth Garver
Jordan, John Woolf
Josephson, Matthew
Kellogg, Paul
  Underwood
Kelly, Aloysius Oliver
  Joseph
Kendall, Willmoore
Kennedy, John F., Jr.
  Suppl. 1
Kerr, Sophie
Keyes, Charles Rollin
Keyes, Frances
  Parkinson
Kirkland, Caroline
  Matilda

Editing and Publishing
(cont.)

Green, Anne Catharine
Green, Bartholomew
Green, Duff
Green, Jonas
Greenfield, Meg *Suppl. 1*
Greenleaf, Thomas
Gresham, Newt
Griscom, Lloyd
  Carpenter
Guggenheim, Harry
  Frank
Hackett, Francis
Hale, David
Halstead, Murat
Hanson, Alexander
  Contee (1786–1819)
Harris, Benjamin
Harrison, Hubert Henry
Harvey, George Brinton
  McClellan
Hatcher, William
  Eldridge
Haven, Gilbert
Hawley, Joseph Roswell
Hayes, Max Sebastian
Hays, Will S.
Hearst, William
  Randolph
Hearst, William
  Randolph, Jr.
Heco, Joseph
Henni, John Martin
Hill, Daniel Harvey
Hill, Isaac
Hitchcock, Gilbert
  Monell
Ho, Chinn
Hobby, Oveta Culp
  Suppl. 1
Hobby, William Pettus
Holbrook, James
Holden, William Woods
Holland, Edwin Clifford
Holland, Josiah Gilbert
  Suppl. 1
Holt, John
Hotze, Henry
Hough, Henry Beetle
Howard, Roy Wilson
Howe, Edgar Watson
Howell, Clark
Howell, Evan Park
Howey, Walter
  Crawford
Howkins, Elizabeth
  Penrose
Hudson, Frederic
Hughes, Robert William
Humphreys, James

Isaacs, Samuel Myer
Jenkins, David
Jeter, Jeremiah Bell
Johnson, Albert
Johnson, Andrew N.
Johnson, John Albert
Jones, George
Jones, Hamilton C.
Jones, John Beauchamp
Kaufmann, Peter
Kendall, Amos
Kendall, George Wilkins
King, Charles
King, Henry
  (1842–1915)
King, Rufus
  (1814–1876)
Kirchwey, Freda
Kneeland, Samuel
Knight, John Shively
Knowland, William Fife
Knox, Frank
Kurtz, Benjamin
Laffan, William Mackay
Lawrence, David
Lawson, James
Lawson, Victor Fremont
Leavitt, Joshua
Leland, Charles Godfrey
Leslie, Frank
Leslie, Miriam Florence
  Follin
Litchman, Charles
  Henry
Locke, David Ross
Loeb, William, III
Lovejoy, Elijah Parish
Lundy, Benjamin
Lynch, James
Marble, Manton Malone
Markel, Lester
Martin, John Alexander
Maxwell, William
  (1766?–1809)
Maynard, Robert Clyve
McAnally, David Rice
McCarroll, Marion
  Clyde
McClatchy, Charles
  Kenny
McClure, Alexander
  Kelly
McCormick, Medill
McCormick, Robert
  Rutherford
McElroy, John
  (1846–1929)
McFerrin, John Berry
McGill, Ralph
McKelway, Alexander
  Jeffrey

McLean, William
  Lippard
McLemore, Jeff
McMaster, James
  Alphonsus
Medary, Samuel
Medill, Joseph
Mein, John
Mencken, H. L.
Meredith, Edna C.
  Elliott
Merz, Charles
Meyer, Eugene Isaac
Miller, Henry
  (1702–1782)
Mitchell, Edward Page
Mitchell, John, Jr.
Moore, Frederick
  Randolph
Moore, John Weeks
Mosessohn, David
  Nehemiah
Muñoz Rivera, Luis
Munsey, Frank Andrew
Murdock, Victor
Murphy, John Henry,
  Sr.
Murray, Orson S.
Nast, William
Nelson, William Rockhill
Newcomb, Harvey
Newhouse, Samuel
  Irving
Newsome, Joseph
  Thomas
Nicholson, Eliza Jane
  Poitevent Holbrook
Nicolay, John George
Noyes, Crosby Stuart
Oakes, George
  Washington Ochs
Ochs, Adolph Simon
Older, Fremont
O'Neill, Buckey
O'Reilly, John Boyle
Osborn, Chase Salmon
O'Sullivan, John Louis
Oswald, Eleazer
Otis, Harrison Gray
  (1837–1917)
Ottendorfer, Anna Behr
  Uhl
Ottendorfer, Oswald
Parker, James
Patterson, Alicia
Patterson, Cissy
Patterson, Joseph Medill
Patterson, Thomas
  McDonald
Peck, George Wilbur
Pelham, Benjamin B.

Pendleton, James
  Madison
Perry, Benjamin Franklin
Petersen, Hjalmar
Pinchback, P. B. S.
Pittock, Henry Lewis
Pleasants, John
  Hampden
Pledger, William
  Anderson
Polk, Leonidas
  LaFayette
Pope, Generoso
Porter, William Trotter
Post, Louis Freeland
Potter, Ray
Poynter, Nelson
Price, Thomas Frederick
Pulitzer, Joseph
Pulitzer, Joseph, Jr.
Pulitzer, Ralph
Pulliam, Eugene Collins
Rapp, Wilhelm
Raymond, Henry Jarvis
Regan, John
Reid, Helen
Reid, Ogden Mills
Reid, Whitelaw
Rind, Clementina
Ritchie, Thomas
Rives, John Cook
Rivington, James
Roberts, Ellis Henry
Robertson, James
  (1747–1816)
Rosewater, Edward
Ross, Charles Griffith
Ross, Edmund Gibson
Roudanez, Louis Charles
Rudd, Daniel
Russell, Benjamin
Russell, Charles Edward
Russwurm, John Brown
Schiff, Dorothy
Scott, James Wilmot
Scott, William
  Alexander, II
Screws, William Wallace
Scripps, E. W.
Scripps, Ellen Browning
Scripps, James Edmund
Scripps, Robert Paine
Scripps, William
  Edmund
Scull, John
Seabury, Samuel
  (1801–1872)
Seaton, William Winston
Seward, Theodore
  Frelinghuysen
Sherwood, Isaac Ruth

**Literature and
Journalism** *(cont.)*

Braithwaite, William
Stanley Beaumont
Branch, Anna
Hempstead
Bremer, Fredrika
Brodsky, Joseph *Suppl. 1*
Brooke, Henry
Brooks, Maria Gowen
Brooks, Walter
Henderson
Brown, Sterling Allen
Brown, William Hill
Brownell, Henry Howard
Bryant, William Cullen
Bukowski, Charles
Burgos, Julia de
Burt, Struthers
Bush-Banks, Olivia
Ward
Byles, Mather
Bynner, Witter
Calkins, Clinch
Calvert, George Henry
Campbell, James Edwin
Cane, Melville Henry
Cannon, Charles James
Carman, Bliss
Carmer, Carl Lamson
Carver, Raymond
Cary, Phoebe
Caulkins, Frances
Manwaring
Cawein, Madison Julius
Chandler, Elizabeth
Margaret
Channing, William
Ellery, II
Chapman, John Jay
Chivers, Thomas Holley
Church, Benjamin
(1734–1778?)
Ciardi, John
Clampitt, Amy Kathleen
Clarke, Joseph Ignatius
Constantine
Clarke, Mary Bayard
Devereux
Clarke, McDonald
Cliffton, William
Coffin, Robert Peter
Tristram
Conkling, Grace Walcott
Hazard
Cook, Ebenezer
Cooke, Philip Pendleton
Coolbrith, Ina
Corrington, John
William
Corrothers, James David

Cotter, Joseph Seamon,
Sr.
Crafts, William
Cranch, Christopher
Pearse
Crane, Hart
Crane, Stephen
Crapsey, Adelaide
Cromwell, Gladys
Crosby, Fanny
Cullen, Countée
Cummings, E. E.
Da Ponte, Lorenzo
Dabney, Richard
Daggett, Rollin Mallory
Dale, Thomas
(1700–1750)
Daly, Thomas Augustine
Dana, Richard Henry
Dargan, Olive Tilford
Davidson, Donald
Grady
Davidson, Lucretia
Maria, and Margaret
Miller Davidson
Davies, Samuel
Davis, Harold Lenoir
Dawson, William
De Casseres, Benjamin
Denby, Edwin Orr
Deutsch, Babette
Dickinson, Emily
Dinsmoor, Robert
Doolittle, Hilda
Dorr, Julia Caroline
Ripley
Drake, Joseph Rodman
Duganne, Augustine
Joseph Hickey
Dunbar, Paul Laurence
Dunbar-Nelson, Alice
Duncan, Robert Edward
Dwight, Theodore
(1764–1846)
Eckman, Frederick
Suppl. 1
Edwards, Harry Stillwell
Eliot, Charlotte Champe
Stearns
Eliot, T. S.
Ellet, Elizabeth F.
Elwyn, Alfred Langdon
Evans, Donald
Evans, Nathaniel
Fairfield, Sumner
Lincoln
Fauset, Jessie Redmon
Fearing, Kenneth
Flexner
Fenollosa, Ernest
Francisco

Ficke, Arthur Davison
Field, Eugene
Field, Sara Bard
Fitts, Dudley
Flagg, Edmund
Fletcher, Bridget
Richardson
Fletcher, John Gould
Foss, Sam Walter
Freneau, Philip Morin
Frost, Robert
Gallagher, William Davis
Garrigue, Jean
Gay, E. Jane
Gibran, Kahlil
Gilder, Richard Watson
Ginsberg, Allen *Suppl. 1*
Giovannitti, Arturo
Massimo
Godfrey, Thomas
(1736–1763)
Goodwin, Ruby Berkley
Gould, Hannah Flagg
Grant, Percy Stickney
Grayson, William John
Green, Joseph
Gregory, Horace Victor
Griffitts, Hannah
Grimké, Angelina Weld
Grosz, George
Guest, Edgar Albert
Guiney, Louise Imogen
Hagedorn, Hermann
Ludwig Gebhard
Halleck, Fitz-Greene
Hammon, Jupiter
Harper, Frances Ellen
Watkins
Harris, Thomas Lake
Hartley, Marsden
Hatton, Ann Julia
Kemble
Hayden, Robert Earl
Hayes, Alfred
Hayne, Paul Hamilton
Hays, Will S.
Henderson, Alice Corbin
Herford, Oliver
Heyward, DuBose
Hillyer, Robert Silliman
Hoffman, Charles Fenno
Holmes, Oliver Wendell
(1809–1894)
Homans, George Caspar
Home, Archibald
Hooper, Ellen Sturgis
Hope, James Barron
Hopkins, Lemuel
Hopkinson, Francis
Horton, George Moses

Hosmer, William Howe
Cuyler
Hovey, Richard
Howe, Julia Ward
Hubner, Charles William
Hughes, Langston
Hugo, Richard
Humphreys, David
Humphries, Rolfe
Imber, Naphtali Herz
Janvier, Margaret
Thomson
Jarrell, Randall
Jeffers, Robinson
Johnson, Georgia
Douglas
Johnson, James Weldon
Jones, Amanda
Theodosia
Jones, James Athearn
Kaufman, Bob
Kees, Weldon
Keimer, Samuel
Kemp, Harry Hibbard
Kennedy, William
Sloane
Kerouac, Jack
Killpatrick, James
Kilmer, Joyce
Knight, Etheridge
Krause, Herbert Arthur
Kreymborg, Alfred
Francis
Lanier, Sidney
Lanusse, Armand
Lathrop, George Parsons
Lathrop, Rose
Hawthorne
Latil, Alexandre
Lattimore, Richmond
Alexander
Laughlin, James *Suppl. 1*
Lawson, James
Lazarus, Emma
Le Gallienne, Richard
Lee, Muna
Leland, Charles Godfrey
Leonard, William Ellery
Levertov, Denise
Suppl. 1
Lewis, Estelle Anna
Blanche Robinson
Lewis, Janet *Suppl. 1*
Lewis, Richard
Lincoln, Joseph Crosby
Lindsay, Vachel
Linn, John Blair
Linton, William James
Lockridge, Ross
Franklin, Jr.
Lodge, George Cabot